DATE DUE

The

CHELSEA HOUSE LIBRARY *of* LITERARY CRITICISM

TWENTIETH-CENTURY AMERICAN LITERATURE

Volume 7

General Editor
HAROLD BLOOM

1988
CHELSEA HOUSE PUBLISHERS
NEW YORK
NEW HAVEN PHILADELPHIA

Printed and bound in the United States of America.

First Printing

1 3 5 7 9 8 6 4 2

Library of Congress Cataloging in Publication Data

Twentieth-century American literature.
(The Chelsea House Library of literary criticism)
Includes bibliographies and indexes.
1. American literature—20th century—History and criticism—Collected works. 2. Authors, American—20th century—Biography—Dictionaries. I. Bloom, Harold. II. Series.
PS221.T834 1985 810'.9'005 84-27430
ISBN 0-87754-801-3 (v. 1)
0-87754-807-2 (v. 7)

Acknowledgments for selections used in this volume commence on page 4548.

CONTENTS

The Index to this series, *Twentieth-Century American Literature*, appears in Volume 8.

ABBREVIATIONS

Bkm	Bookman (New York)
Com	Commonweal
Cmty	Commentary
F&SF	Fantasy and Science Fiction
HdR	Hudson Review
JCL	Journal of Commonwealth Literature
KR	Kenyon Review
LT	Listener
NR	New Republic
NS	New Statesman
NY	New Yorker
NYT	New York Times
NYTBR	New York Times Book Review
Parn	Parnassus: Poetry in Review
PoR	Poetry Review
PRev	Paris Review
Rep	Reporter
Scy	Scrutiny
Shen	Shenandoah
Spec	Spectator
SR	Saturday Review
SSF	Studies in Short Fiction
SwR	Sewanee Review
TA	Theatre Arts
TLS	Times Literary Supplement
TSLL	Texas Studies in Literature and Language
TZ	Twilight Zone
WPBW	Washington Post Book World
YR	Yale Review

ILLUSTRATIONS

Robert Stone

1937–

Robert Anthony Stone was born in Brooklyn, New York, on August 21, 1937. He studied at New York University between 1958 and 1959, and from 1958 to 1960 served as an editorial assistant with the *New York Daily News*. His first book, *A Hall of Mirrors*, was published in 1967 and was the recipient of the 1968 William Faulkner Foundation Award for a first novel. Stone was writer-in-residence at Princeton University in 1971–72, and has also taught at Amherst College (1972–75; 1977–78), Stanford University (1979), the University of Hawaii at Manoa (1979–80), Harvard University (1981), the University of California at Irvine (1982), and New York University (1983). His second novel, *Dog Soldiers* (1974), received the National Book Award in 1975. A third novel, *A Flag for Sunrise*, appeared in 1981, followed by *Children of Light* in 1986. As a screenwriter Stone has adapted *A Hall of Mirrors* as *WUSA* (1970; directed by Stuart Rosenberg), and *Dog Soldiers* as *Who'll Stop the Rain* (1978; directed by Karel Reisz). He is presently a member of the executive board of PEN.

This remarkable first novel ⟨*A Hall of Mirrors*⟩ was one of the best works of fiction published last year. It received a good deal of attention in the daily press, but there is more to be said about it, primarily because it confronts with unique directness the fearful and mindless violence in which America is presently immersed.

In bare outline *A Hall of Mirrors* resembles dozens of similar books whose estimate of our circumstances is bleak and even despairing, whose central characters are maimed victims and sufferers, whose modern urban setting, as the blurb (rather nicely!) puts it, "is that rootless one of the all-night tenth-run movie, the mission house lunch, the corner where everyone has to move on, buddy." But this novel is distinguished from the conventional *roman de malaise* as gold from dross.

Where in other superficially similar novels the despair seems forced or modish, in this one it is earned. Where other writers have been content with the abstract idea of the passive or suffering hero, Stone gives us characters whose weaknesses and deformities are projected with extraordinary and persuasive energy. Where in less successful novels the menace and violence and sordidness of the city are either indifferently rendered or are presented in descriptive set pieces—self-serving interludes really, which deflect our attention from the life of the characters or the thrust of the plot—in *A Hall of Mirrors* the urban setting is evoked with a brilliant sensory concreteness that is palpably true, and is also resonant of the psychic and moral anxieties which press upon the characters. ⟨. . .⟩

Unpretentiously, and without resort to fable, this novel tells us that we are drowning in the inhuman and the violent; it confronts us with precisely those visions which paralyze one of its characters: "If he looked back, he thought, there might appear against the awful clarity of that evening some dreadful procession of things as they are. . . ." It is not a perfect book. One feels in particular that its plot is somewhat contrived and that one of its central characters is less credible than the others. But these flaws barely affect the novel's power, its seriousness, its impressive authority as a kind of inspired *report*. It gives us things as they are, and with a lyrical evenness in which there is not a trace of surprise or even outrage.

This is what is most disturbing about the book. Stone's recognition of the violence and malignity which oppress his characters has about it something casual, something taken for granted. None of this is unusual or unexpected, the novel, in its pain, tells us; this is just the way things are.

And, more, unlike Mailer's heavy-handed allegory of brutality, *Why Are We in Vietnam?*, and unlike Styron's *The Confessions of Nat Turner* (where the violence is distanced as history), Stone's novel will not allow us to regard it as a metaphor; we are not protected from its insights by the comforts of analogy. In this book the people who feel compassion or human affection are pursued relentlessly. They are caught and destroyed. The places of power and authority are held by malignant and insane men. These men are the victors.

In its earned hopelessness, *A Hall of Mirrors* sees, and dramatizes with terrible conviction, a truth which has afflicted men at all times but which presses upon us in this moment with particular intensity: that we are all prisoners, our humanity imperiled, and in the grip of monsters.—David Thorburn, "A Fearful & Mindless Violence," *Nation*, April 1, 1968, pp. 452–53

Reviewing *In Our Time*, D. H. Lawrence had this to say: "Mr. Hemingway does it extremely well. Nothing matters. Everything happens. One wants to keep oneself loose. Avoid one thing only: getting connected up. Don't get connected up. . . . Just get away for the sake of getting away." Lawrence found Hemingway "really good, because he's perfectly straight about it. . . . He doesn't even *want* to love anybody." Robert Stone's second novel ⟨*Dog Soldiers*⟩ is also really good, reminded me frequently of Hemingway (the epigraph from *Heart of Darkness* extends the line further back) and has thus far met with universal praise. Good as the book is, it may be that its subject matter—Vietnam and drugs, the Great Confusion and various momentary stays against confusion—is partly responsible for the acclaim. That there is a "connection" between the phenomena is undeniable, and succinctly put in an early meditation by John Converse, American journalist in Vietnam who decides to make a pile by shipping some heroin back home. Converse's last "moral objection" to anything, he remembers, was in response to an event called "The Great Elephant Zap" when herds of elephants were slaughtered from the air so as to deprive The Enemy of their use: "And as for dope, Converse thought, and addicts—if the world is going to contain elephants pursued by flying men, people are just naturally going to want to get high." Thus events are set in motion.

The war-drugs connection is established not through analysis and profound meditation by Stone or his characters (of which Converse, his wife Marge—on the "habit" herself, and a murderous pal named Ray Hicks are featured) but through story: from Vietnam to S.F. to Mexico and the end of things.

This story is as elaborately twisty, as challenging to try and follow along without leaving something out, as a Raymond Chandler thriller, say *The Big Sleep;* the dialogue is ever-present, arresting and often very funny indeed—Lenny Bruce funny, that is. Here are Marge and Rowena, locked inside the ladies' room of the porno film house where they work, contemplating the patrons:

> "An awful lot of them are Chinese," she said to Marge. "You notice that?"
>
> The ethnic reference sounded a ghostly alarm from some dark place in the ruins of Marge's progressive conditioning.
>
> "Sure," she said. "Chinese are just as horny as anybody else."
>
> Rowena was thougtful as she handed Marge the joint.
>
> "I think the Chinese are into a different thing. I think they dig the beauty of the bodies in a kind of aesthetic way."
>
> "I think they're jerking off."
>
> "They could do both," Rowena insisted. "I mean why should beauty be platonic? That's a western hang-up. They don't have the Judeo-Christian thing. You know?"

No friendly author-narrator, winking at the reader, stands behind these assorted losers, these junkies, creeps and U.S. riff-raff circa 1970. Stone is really no more detached from Converse, or Marge, or even Hicks, than Hemingway was from Krebs in the remarkable story "Soldier's Home" which D. H. Lawrence singled out for special mention in his review. As a result of his war nausea Krebs tries, unsuccessfully, to keep his life from being complicated; there is a moment when John Converse moves beyond complication into somewhere else. In the midst of a fragmentation bombing by the South Vietnamese Air Force (our allies) Converse suddenly glimpses himself as, in memorable words, "a funny little fucker." He realizes that "the ordinary physical world through which one shuffled heedless and half-assed toward nonentity was capable of composing itself, at any time and without notice, into a massive instrument of agonizing death." Flat on his face on the earth, he is granted what I take to be the novelist's intuition also, that "Existence was a trap; the testy patience of things as they are might be exhausted at any moment." After that, moral objections to just about anything, including heroin, can be overcome.

Stone sees all his characters as funny little fuckers—dog soldiers who soldier on but just may be inclined, things being what they are, to speed up the trip towards death. As with the earlier *Hall of Mirrors,* it is a claustrophobic world; barely a moment of impulse allowed in the direction of a better life; no figure from his ill-assorted gallery likely to take time out to read, oh, say Wordsworth or Dickens, or make up a large corned beef sandwich on rye and watch the late show. Everybody is tainted, even the old people round the television in a cheap hotel where Converse's mother lives have "reptile faces." If it weren't for the razor's edge of comic brilliance, the rich lore about other modes of behavior (I speak as an East Coast Straight), the flick and spring of exchange—hardly conversation—this would be a dreary and deathly book. But no, the novel is the book of life said the dying Lawrence as through gritted teeth he saluted Hemingway and Huxley and would have *The Day of the Locust.* Reading Robert Stone's book you know more about how life was never worse than in 1974 and how art is still art, doing ruthlessly and strangely what it does.—WILLIAM H. PRITCHARD, "Novel Sex and Violence," *HdR,* Spring 1975, pp. 158–60

Probably the most talked-about novel of recent vintage, Robert Stone's *A Flag for Sunrise,* seems to me both an inevitable outgrowth of and an exciting step forward from his ferocious chronicle of post–Viet Nam drug-running—*Dog Soldiers* (1974).

Its principal setting is Tecan, a Central American slum of a country whose sadistic dictator is a puppet kept in power by a United States government fearful of communist influence there. A "copper grab" is ousting peasants from their land and has created a backlash of "insurgency"—in which the novel's major characters will become variously implicated. In alternating scenes we follow the gradually intertwining fates of four desperate outsiders. Frank Holliwell, an American anthropologist haunted by his experiences in Viet Nam, goes into Compostela, a country bordering Tecan, and becomes involved in an investigative junket as a favor for a CIA friend. Pablo Tabor, a Mexican-American drug addict aimlessly adrift near the Texas Gulf Coast, finds work with a thrill-seeking married couple, the Callahans, who are smuggling arms by boat to the Tecanian revolutionaries. Meanwhile the staff of an American Devotionist mission (soon to be closed down) struggle to cope with their moral natures. Sister Justin Feeney finds a purpose for her life by agreeing to offer the mission as a shelter for rebel activity. Her superior, Father Egan, loses himself in alcohol and the near-paralysis of "Christian witness": he is so incapable of acting that he merely *prays* for the conversion of a known child-murderer.

Some strained coincidences force these separate ordeals to converge in a grim climax and aftermath. A callously indifferent universe asserts itself: the only people "saved" are those who are indifferent to whether they live or die.

It is impossible not to admire the vigorous sweep and savage force of this novel. Though its reach repeatedly exceeds its grasp, it is filled with scenes which are sharply imagined and powerfully rendered. The opening scene—which establishes Father Egan's weakness and his complicity with Tecan's injustices—is stunning. So is our extended first view of Pablo's inflammatory self-loathing. Holliwell has a marvelous drunken speech before a Compostelan audience, in which he speaks with unplanned reckless candor about the real nature of U.S. "paternalism" in the Third World. In a later scene, during a snorkeling excursion, he is given a panicked vision of the predatory, death-haunted world in which he finds himself ("Something was happening down there. . . . He had no business down there"): it's a luminous moment.

The enormous flaw in this novel is the mindless restatement of its (perfectly self-evident) theme: the characters are permitted to belabor us with their realizations that Tecan is "a disaster of history," "a world far from God"—that "Satan is the way things are." The basic scene of despair is repeated over and over: the iteration of universal pessimism is unceasing (for example we glimpse a fishing net filled with shrimp, containing "the predators and the prey together, overthrown and blinded, scuttling after their lost accustomed world"—the kind of authorial heavy-handedness that you expect from Zola and Dreiser).

Its excesses never overshadow the very real sense of dread—and guilt—that the novel consistently communicates. *A Flag for Sunrise* is a moving portrayal of destroyed idealism, as well as a vision of the pit; in its bleak way, an honestly humanistic document. Beyond its obvious resemblances to *Nostromo* there are clear echoes of *For Whom the Bell Tolls,*

Man's Hope, and assorted novels by Graham Greene. In effect *A Flag for Sunrise* is a rewriting—as it is a reimagining—of the old idealistic novel of commitment. That commitment is now perceived as suicidal folly is a sign of the times. Another such sign is the likelihood that Robert Stone, a disturbingly accomplished younger novelist, may indeed have become one of the spirits of the age.—BRUCE ALLEN, "Three Masters," *SwR*, Summer 1982, pp. 494–95

Near the opening of *Children of Light*—Robert Stone's fourth novel, after *A Hall of Mirrors, Dog Soldiers* and *A Flag for Sunrise*—Gordon Walker, badly hung over, strung out on cocaine, sick, panicked and lonely for the wife who has just left him, catches sight of himself in the mirror and quotes from *King Lear*. "Thou art the thing itself," he declares. "Unaccommodated man is no more than such a poor bare forked animal as thou art."

Walker quotes from *Lear* because, as the actor he is when not writing screenplays, he has just completed a successful run as the lead in a Seattle production of the play. But we spot at once a second reason. Somewhere in this Hollywood novel—the children of light ironically referred to in the title also being the children of cinema's "magic lantern"—there is going to be some sort of replay of Lear's mad scene on the heath. And it better be good, a reader is inclined to mutter to himself.

Immediately, Mr. Stone begins to move the pieces into place. The singing of a bird reminds Walker of a game called Bats or Birdies he used to play with an actress named Lee Verger, the object of which was "making it through the night with your head intact to the moment when bird song announced the imminence of first light and day." Though apparently the game didn't always come out Birdies, Walker conceives a desire to be with Lee, who is now on location in Mexico (another source of light) starring in a film version of Kate Chopin's novel *The Awakening*, for which Walker has written the screenplay. Against the advice of his agent, who warns him that he can only cause trouble, Walker heads south, equipped with plenty of cocaine.

Switch now to Lee Verger's bungalow in Bahía Honda. In short order, we learn that Lee has recently stopped taking the pills that keep her mental condition stable, that her psychoanalyst husband is about to leave her with their two children and that Lee is beginning once again to have visits from the Long Friends who first came to her when one of her children by a previous marriage died. Liquor isn't good for her condition, we learn. Neither, we suppose, will be Walker's cocaine. We brace ourselves.

We are right to do so, because what follows is harrowing. The portraits of the film characters—from the famous director Walter Drogue (a windbag?) and his even more famous father (the son refers to himself as "Walter Drogue the Less") to the burned-out novelist working on a story for *New York Arts*—are tough and nasty enough to make the reader wince. The dialogue stings. The scenes of Lee Verger going mad make the scalp prickle. And the climax of Walker playing Lear to Lee's Fool—or is it Lee's Lear to Walker's Fool?—is very far from the embarrassment we sometimes anticipate.

Mr. Stone has taken some spectacular risks, particularly with his climax. His drama plays, and one's sense of dread builds up like a bank of storm clouds. Though *A Hall of Mirrors* won the Faulkner Award for a first novel in 1967, and *Dog Soldiers* won a National Book Award in 1975, *Children of Light* is the author's most dramatically coherent performance to date.

Yet underneath there is a mechanical quality about the way Mr. Stone manipulates his characters that keeps the reader's mind divided. Part of one's reaction is to be amazed at the effects he is pulling off, but another part is to wonder why his characters are so remorselessly condemned to their respective fates. Why is Gordon Walker a drunk and a coke addict? Why is Lee Verger schizophrenic? Why are all the film types so wiseacre, heartless and nasty? What do all the drugs and alcohol mean? Are they no more than God's way of telling Hollywood that it has too much money? Not that this reader was able to figure out.

The trouble is, finally, that *King Lear* mocks the world of Mr. Stone's novel. The comparisons he begs are overwhelming. Everything is diminished in his system—the cruelty of children, the ambiguity of nature, the wantonness of the gods, the sanity of madness, even the irony of these diminishments. At the center of *Children of Light*, one finds not love, knowledge, justice or religious ecstasy, but empty containers of liquor, pills and powder.

So Lee Verger goes crazy and does a walk into the sea better than Joan Crawford in *Humoresque*, Bruce Dern in *Coming Home*, James Mason in the second version of *A Star Is Born* and Fredric March in the original. So Gordon Walker gets hepatitis and has to give up booze. So, as an old friend points out to him, "You're no fun anymore now that you stopped drinking. Drunks aren't fun when you're not drunk."

Though the reader is deeply moved by *Children of Light*—though he laughs and laments, holds his breath and shakes his head in wonder—part of him is always asking, "So what?"—CHRISTOPHER LEHMANN-HAUPT, *NYT*, March 13, 1986, p. C21

L. HUGH MOORE

From "The Undersea World of Robert Stone"

Critique, Volume 11, Number 3 (1969), pp. 43–56

The choice of Robert Stone's *A Hall of Mirrors* for the 1968 Faulkner Award was appropriate, for no recent novel has more contemporary relevance nor more radical themes. The novel provides a profound and disquieting vision of contemporary American society and possible responses to that society. A measure of the artistic success of the novel is the fact that Stone's themes inhere in every aspect of the novel. Recurring images and metaphors, for example, develop the main themes and provide a convenient way to examine and classify the chief characters.

Many writers, Hawthorne and Camus among others, have warned of the dangers of detachment, the sin of isolation, of how it atrophies one's heart and destroys one's humanity. Stone, however, goes beyond this theme by undercutting the alternative. Detachment, or coolness, in his world, is the only way to survive. Involvement inevitably brings madness and a futile, usually violent, death. The moral values are the same as those of earlier writers, so that the theme becomes the immorality of survival, the wickedness of adaption. By images, metaphors, and direct references Stone connects his setting, modern New Orleans, a heightened vision of America, with the bloody, brutal, cold undersea world and his characters with the denizens of this icy environment. Further, he uses the metaphor of evolution to develop the comparison. Since the world is getting colder, the survivors are those who can withstand the moral chill and prey upon the less hardy creatures, those who maintain, anachronistically and non-adaptatively, the old values of pity, concern, mercy, responsibility, and love. The novel answers Yeats' question in "The

Second Coming"—the rough beast is he who, like the successful mutations on the ocean floor, can change to a different way of life. He and those like him are the cold ones.

The bearded, pot-smoking Bogandovich and his friend Marvin, who drop in and out of scenes, always observing, serve as the author's reliable explicators of what the world is coming to. They provide the overt explanation of the fish-sea floor-evolution metaphor. Bogandovich explains to Morgan Rainey, the sufferer who believes in a covenant of humanness and the accompanying values, that such beliefs are outmoded. "All that gift of life and humanness is a trip. Blood, man—blood was made warm to keep a scene circulating" (p. 250).[1] Marvin adds: "We know all about warm blood and gifts and humanness. But it don't apply now, you dig? They had that trip. Nobody could swing with it. It's over now" (p. 255). The gigantic right-wing rally, at which the millionaire Bingamon stages a riot as casually as he directs a movie star's oration on the virtues of the Old West or a red neck evangelist's ranting on Jesus and free enterprise, Bogandovich knows, inaugurates the "new epoch": "all flags and music and cold as frosted tit" (p. 323).

To Marvin what he sees on a walk through New Orleans can best be described by reference to the sea world. Garages, penny arcades, Walgreens convince him that: "It's all spine. It's like fish. And then I thought well how do the fish live in the sea, man, as men do on land" (pp. 251–52). After the Restoration Day Rally, in which nineteen people died senselessly, Bogandovich turns to his copy of *Living Fishes of the World*—"the wiggy fish"—rather than news commentary to understand the violence and absurdity of human affairs. The deep sea lantern fish, equipped with luminous limbs and rows of dagger teeth, seem especially meaningful: "It says these fish gotta be all teeth because at the bottom of the ocean it's like very competitive" (p. 391). Because it is logical and because he is a detached observer, Bogandovich finds such evolution "satisfactory."

Stone sets up the human side of his metaphor early in his novel. The story of Bruce, intended as an exemplum, indicates that the human world is no less cruel than the one undersea and its creatures nor more moral. Deciding on suicide, the despairing Bruce announced his intention to the customers of the Redcliff Hotel, where he was well known as a regular. No one took action or even tried to dissuade him—some out of boredom wanted something to happen, some did not want to get involved, while others simply did not want to have to listen to him. Outside in the snow Bruce tried to seek help by surrendering to the police. But just at that moment an angry and frustrated two hundred and fifty pound Mississippi cotton picker took his wallet and creased his skull with a mail-order blackjack, and a bus ran over his left foot. What finally happened to Bruce is obscure; there were rumors that he died of influenza, that he became a Trappist Monk of saintly renown, and that he joined the Federal Civil Service. But his eloquent suicide note, containing quotes from Oedipus' farewell speech, found on the mutilated body of the cotton picker, greatly puzzled the authorities. Bruce's history, thus, proves the relevance of the marine metaphor.

The human evolution that will produce the new man, the creatures of the cold who can cope with such an environment, requires an act of the will. The world, like the sea floor, does not necessitate adaptive behavior—in every case immoral. The world Stone portrays is a landscape of nightmare, but the nightmare is intensified rather than alleviated by men. He takes ample notice of tricks of fate, of what the gods cruelly do to men beyond their power to cope with. There are the grotesques—the derelict with a wart on his face so gigantic that he seems to have two noses, Philomene, twisted in braces, who offers five dollars to Tulane boys to make love to her. Babies die for no reason, and violent death comes to innocent bystanders. Events have no sense, logic, or pattern, except the pattern of cruelty; the real evil can be localized within man. The structure of *A Hall of Mirrors* offers four choices to the characters: adapt and survive, withdraw and observe, despair and die, or finally die in a futile but grand gesture of defiance directed against the world and creatures who run it. Only the last two are humanly and morally possible. An analysis of the novel in terms of the predominant "fish-sea floor-evolution" metaphors explains the characters, the way they relate to their environment, and provides a key to Stone's main themes.

Three of the main characters—Rheinhardt, Lester Clotho, and Farley the Sailor—choose to adapt and survive. Much of the novel is concerned with the attempts of Rheinhardt to survive in a world becoming increasingly cold. His name obviously suggests hollow hearted and just as obviously bring to mind the Rinehart, another master of change and adaptive behavior, of *Invisible Man*. Stone's character wills himself into becoming "the successful mutation." By resolutely putting aside the unhealthy and non-adaptive attitudes of the old epoch—pity, love, commitment—he loses his soul, which is as outmoded as a dinosaur in the cold new world. "Rheinhardt—not a soul" and "no soul" echo in every section in which he appears. The pitiful death of Geraldine, for which he is responsible, moves him to something like sadness but not enough to arrange for her burial or even to wreck a bar in defiant protest. He merely regards his emotion, which he calls weak nerves, as flaws in his mutation. Bogandovich is not fooled by Rheinhardt's belief that he is dying: "You look like a survivor to me. That's not a compliment, dig" (p. 398). The last comment that the author makes about Rheinhardt, as he boards a bus for the thinner atmosphere of the mile high city, is "He was a survivor" (p. 409). And, again, no compliment is intended.

What makes Rheinhardt so morally reprehensible is his complete grasp of the implications of his part in the survival of the fittest. Poor, weak Jack Noonan, Bingamon's whipping boy who accepts any indignity from the boss, at one point becomes disgruntled enough to ask who does Bingamon think he (Jack) is. Rheinhardt cooly replies, "That's a question you should spend some time with. Then you could arrange to be them" (p. 285). Rheinhardt, though, arranges a far more ambitious understanding that accommodating himself to one rich degenerate: he accommodates himself to the brute force of evolution. He realizes, too, the destructive consequences to others of his adaptive behavior. He terrifies a barmaid by telling her that he will invert for her and become nothing but ill-smelling blue (the color of cold) ectoplasm that feeds insatiably on love. Like a detached scientist he predicts the change in the weather and the awful consequences for the warm creatures. "One by one the warm weather creatures will topple dead with frosted eyelids. The creatures of the cold will proliferate. The air will become thin and difficult to breathe." But he knows the cold—significantly his tour of duty with the navy had been to Antartica—and is safe. "I'm Jack Frost, baby. I'm the original" (p. 253).

No change in the moral environment, no chill surpasses Rheinhardt's ability to adapt. Rheinhardt tells him that if she were chased she would run to water and drown. Rheinhardt answers with awful self-knowledge: "When they force me to the water I'll devolve, man. I'll unevolutionize. I'll turn back into an amphibian while you wait and disappear in a flurry of fins" (p. 150). Here he will be at home. "I'm not getting eaten by no fish," he says. He so admires change that he can take statements of the old values and relate them to his evolutionary attempts. While Geraldine admires the sacramental vision of *The Ancient Mariner*, Rheinhardt quotes another appropriately nautical poem, *The Wreck of the Deutschland*, on conversion and an altogether different kind of survival: "Let him be easter in us, be a dayspring to the dimness of us." The change he wants to affect into coldness and fins completely negates Hopkins' values. By working for Bingamon's radio station WUSA, he does become toothed and finned. At the rally for no apparent reason other than the logic of his evolutionary theory, he feeds the blood lust of the crowd by describing graphically a naked Negro with distended member lurking in a corn field to ravish the archetypal American fat lady. Going well beyond survival, he develops teeth rather than soul. ⟨. . .⟩

Survival in the undersea world of *A Hall of Mirrors* requires more than teeth and willingness to adapt. Most of the characters in Stone's world will their survival but lack the strength and nerve to become a predator on the scale of the lantern fish. These minnows survive until a larger fish consumes them. Calvin Minnow, small time state's attorney with large scale ambitions—he plans to make his political fortune by purging the welfare rolls—is completely engulfed by self-preservation. Like any minnow among lantern fish he lives in fear, gaining small relief by carrying a gun and surrounding himself with security guards. His environment is, of course, appropriately cold; he runs his office air conditioner on high, thus making the air chill and the surface of his desk like an icy sea, and his building reflects light like arctic ice. He shows his teeth when he threatens the weak Morgan Rainey but has no grand predations. He preys only on those, like half-starved welfare recipients, too weak or maimed to resist. Rainey says of him: "I believe that there's a kind of man among us who feeds on pain to keep himself alive. I believe it because I saw one man in one office who lives on blood. . . ." So Minnow travels in the wake of the mangling sharks for his meals of blood.

Many other scavengers patrol these icy depths. Stone consistently uses fish imagery to reveal their characters. In his soap factory Bingamon employs the derelicts and the wounded, those victims of the chilly waters of America. He exploits them outrageously, and their loyalty, which he gains by political indoctrination and military drills, gains him a powerful political base. Presiding over the relentless assembly line (three mistakes rate instant dismissal), two engineers in glass cages record errors with cold indifference. With a room full of scared men on one side of the window and the clean engineers on the other, Rheinhardt feels that he is looking at the microcosm. He wonders, "On which side of the glass does the aquarium begin?" (p. 88). Obviously, both workers and engineers exist in an aquarium run by Bingamon. His idea is to "stir up the bottom" to "bring up some big fish" (p. 376). One of his smaller ones is Reverend Orion Burn, who served the cause by amassing 24,000 signatures toward an initiative banning the teaching of the theories of "Evolution from fish, Quantumism, and those relative to relativity" from any institution of learning in Oklahoma (p. 287). His activity, again, serves as a reminder of the controlling metaphors. Representative Jimmy Snipe (named for a bird noted, at least in literature, for its stupidly non-adaptive behavior) thinks he can strike bargains with the predators. Bingamon calmly sells him out.

A strange and vicious aquarium of minnows is assembled by Bingamon within the dark green walls of the stadium for the rally. As the light reflects from their teeth Rheinhardt tries to believe that their "instinct to blood their palates [is] purely potential" (p. 334). But, owing to Bingamon's skillful stirring of the depths, the potential is realized—their "carnivore cry" rings out—and nineteen people are killed. Coldness and predation distinguish the crowd:

> Above the floodlights, in the darkness of the unseen crowd, throbbed a noise that carried to the field like waves of dark snow or the shadow of wings, the call of hunting birds on the wind. Rheinhardt looked into the lights and saw dead whitened eyes, the twitching of stalk necks, bloodied bone, pecking—a huge groaning aviary, beak and claw. (p. 328)

Other choices besides adaptation are available. Some choose to exist on the periphery merely observing the struggle for survival. Those who withdraw and observe constitute the second group of characters. A constant drug-induced comatose state makes their detachment possible. As self-absorbed as the adaptors, they lack the predatory killer instinct. When they occasionally awake from their contemplation of nothingness, Marvin and the girl tell the world "*Chingo su madre*"—an insult the world repays by driving them mad. Bogandovich, however, has his marijuana for comfort and his laundromat for therapy—the machines affirming the possibility of desirable changes and the dryers giving warmth. He observes only. "I'm always going places. Riots, the dog races, the hockey. Anything like that. I mean if I could go down to the bottom of the sea and see the funny fish, I'd go" (p. 393).

In the new epoch of rapid human evolutionary changes, adaptation and survival are not possible for all. Those who feel and love, those in the third group of characters who have chosen not to adapt, are, like pterodactyls, unfit for the ice of the new ecological system. The price of being unable to adapt is, of course, extinction. As Stone applies his evolutionary metaphor, both success and failure are acts of will, but only failure is morally and humanly appropriate. Because their values are no longer operable, they despair and die. Big and soft, warm and kind, scarred and battered, Geraldine comes to understand that only death is left for her. Stone connects her with water and aquatic creatures softer and less fierce than lantern fish. Her face was terribly scarred when Woody worked her over with an oyster opener, and to Rheinhardt she seems "some creature of lakes, of brack and still water" (p. 230). Unlike Rheinhardt, who, when he jumps into Lake Pontchartrain, sinks into the muck and walks to shore, Geraldine is a good swimmer and remains on the surface of the terrible aquatic world. She reads *The Ancient Mariner* and sings "Let Us All Gather by the River," but water and cold destroy her. She suffers terribly from frequent colds and her baby dies from one. When she arrives in New Orleans in the spring, she is greeted, not by tropical warmth, but cold, evil-smelling mist. Water and cold in her jail cell become unendurable: "Beside the deep sink was an uncovered toilet in which was a pool of deep black liquid" and the bars had "cold skin" (p. 387). Finally, she hangs herself with the "cold damp links" of the toilet chain" (p. 390).

The new environment is completely hostile to Geraldine and her warmth. Fate is hard on her: her mother and father die young, her husband and baby die. Society betrays her by failing to keep the promise of love and security implicit in her childhood memory of President Roosevelt, powerful and kind. She could not return to West Virginia because the mines had closed; she could find no work except prostitution in any of the cities to which she wandered, and the state employment office gives neither employment nor concern. The police exploit and taunt rather than protect her. They promise to go easy if she is cooperative, and the dyke of a police matron beats her up and denies her a Bible. Ironically, Geraldine reads detective magazines for the realism: "they had god-awful pictures and they left you feeling rotten but they did have things in them like the things that really happened" (p. 123).

Taunted by fate and betrayed by society, Geraldine turns to Rheinhardt, who offers no help. His desertion, prompted by his complete preoccupation with his own needs and survival, leads inexorably to her despair and suicide. She had turned to him for warmth because she failed completely to understand his detachment, his brutal adaptability, his utter selfishness. "Hey who are you goodbuddy?" she often asks (p. 138). Despite his efforts Rheinhardt comes to care for her, although this feeling is accompanied by no commitment. He tries to think of her as a salamander—"you walk through fire and you live on air" (p. 230)—to avoid any responsibility. But her needs are more complex, more human, than the amphibians who adapt without warmth.

The character of Philomene, however, defines the terms on which warm creatures can live in a cold world—a pitiful, crippled life of madness that most would find intolerable. Grotesque in braces and a man's T-shirt, suffering from fearful hallucinations brought on by the beer she drinks to escape the grimness of her life, Philomene is so desperate for love and warmth that even the tolerant Geraldine is shocked: "Philomene everybody's got to do the way they know how, but now what you do is you go up to people on the street and ask them to fuck and nobody is gonna tell me that ain't different from . . . from well, sociable polite mixin' between men and women like . . . even in bar, by God" (p. 136). In the cold this nightingale's song has become "Oh go back to the one that loves ye/Or the tides of life'll tear you apart" (p. 199), another reminder of the sea metaphor. Perhaps only her madness keeps her from being completely broken.

Geraldine's solution to the problems of the new environment—despair and die—appeals to Morgan Rainey also. But he is sustained by a hatred of the bloody creatures of the deep so intense that he yearns to destroy them. His deep love for humanity has now no outlet in positive action. His welfare survey, for example, which was, he thought, a way to serve, turns out to be fraudulent and a cruel hoax. In another, warmer world Rainey would have been an ancient mariner, blessing the creatures of the sea and spreading the gospel of love. Now such an attitude appears so strange and irrelevant that he seems mad and loathsome to those like Minnow and Rheinhardt. He cannot operate on Rheinhardt's dictum that extreme times demand extreme attitudes and conduct. He is, thus, marked for extinction, and his quest "to find about humanness" (p. 175) is doomed pitifully. His despair over the new coldness differs from Geraldine's in that he believes he can still accomplish something in the name of the old values by striking out at the predators. Even this weak action turns out to be futile. Rainey's physical appearance symbolizes his inability to adapt and survive. Tall and cadaverous, gaunt to emaciation, terribly uncoordinated, he predictably suffers from colds. His ill-fitting rain apparel does not keep out the cold. Even Muzak plays "Stormy Weather"—"don't know why there's no sun up in the sky"—at his approach.

Morgan Rainey behaves non-adaptively, for he refuses to grasp the logic of the new evolution. God, to him, is "the power that raised up the muck of the earth to walk and think" and without God people "tear like insects" (p. 214). So he tries to turn evolution away from the beautifully adaptive insect behavior, but all he accomplishes is to prove that he and those like him represent a moral dead end; they have not mutated successfully. None of the warm ones have surviving children; only those of Rheinhardt and Clotho live. Rainey rejects Clotho's Emersonian ideas that God is in the insect and hence directing evolution. Better a dead god, Rainey feels, than a deity who directs the changes that he has observed.

So when Rainey learns, belatedly, that he cannot work within the system, that he has been a pawn in "the Big Store Caper," he resolves to take more appropriate and violent action: "I'm going to strike this down. I'm going to break this" (p. 245). Violence in this undersea world is the only moral response—as Farley instinctively knew. All Rainey manages to do, however, is to threaten Minnow and at the rally save his life, an action that is not only inappropriate but immoral. He had wanted to defy "the rulers of the darkness of this world" (p. 349) by throwing his own flesh and blood, which sicken him because they remind him of his kinship with the predators, on the world's steel. In the crazy confusion he is shot in the head, a victim of the irrational creatures of the cold. He had willed himself out of the evolutionary process.

Of all the warm creatures S. B. Prothwaite, an old-fashioned Wobbly, makes the most magnificent and violent response to the new environment in which he is totally anachronistic. His slogan is lettered on the side of his truck for all the "creatures of the banks and railroads, lackeys of the vested interests, puppets, apes and hyenas" (p. 352), against whom he fights to see:

You Shall Not Crucify
S. B. Prothwaite Upon
A Cross of Cold

An old railroad man, he simply has no ecological niche in a heartless, plasticized world; his job no longer exists; even the rail yard where he had worked in dignity has been paved over. Self-destructive, non-adaptive violence is now the only appropriate response. Accordingly, he loads his truck with dynamite and would have blown up the entire collection of right-wing dignitaries if Morgan Rainey had not stopped him. So his mission fails; his gesture of defiance merely augments the fireworks. In the name of the old values, he futilely brings heat and light (dynamite) to the coldness of the rally. But, as in biological evolution, the new has little to fear from the old. The unsuccessful mutations only provide blood for the successful to fatten on. Stone's use of the prothwaite episode is appropriate in terms of the dominant metaphor of evolution. An old Wobby with his grand but outmoded values serves well to symbolize those who are as extinct as dinosaurs.

Stone's vision of the modern world and society is a profoundly pessimistic one. The implications of his main, related metaphors—the undersea world and evolution—are, indeed, disturbing. To see the world as an environment, an ecological system, that is as cold, hostile, and brutal as the sea floor is hardly new. Nor is his view of his characters as denizens of the deep profoundly original. What disturbs and what makes the novel contemporarily relevant is the fact that Stone offers no melioristic possibility. To survive in the new ice age is immoral; neither work, bitter humor, nor withdrawal is humanly possible. "Despair and die" is the final message of the novel.

Notes

1. Robert Stone, *A Hall of Mirrors* (New York, 1968). All page references are to this edition.

Rex Stout

1886–1975

Rex Todhunter Stout was born in Noblesville, Indiana, on December 1, 1886. He was educated in public schools in Topeka, Kansas, where his family settled when he was one year old; he then entered the University of Kansas, but left after only two weeks. After serving in the navy for two years, he traveled across the United States between 1908 and 1912, working at various odd jobs, including cook, salesman, bookkeeper, bellhop, hotel manager, architect, and cabinetmaker. Between 1912 and 1916 he worked as a freelance magazine writer in New York City, and then, in order to make enough money to be able to devote himself to more serious writing, he created and managed the Educational Thrift Service, a school banking system that eventually enrolled over two million children.

In 1927 Stout retired to Paris, where he remained for two years producing five psychological suspense novels, which were well received. Thereafter Stout devoted himself exclusively to detective stories. In 1934 he published *Fer-de-Lance*, the first of a long series of mystery novels centered on the exploits of his popular detective Nero Wolfe. The Nero Wolfe books, which have sold nearly sixty million copies in twenty-four languages, include *The League of Frightened Men* (1935), *The Hand in the Glove* (1937), *Too Many Cooks* (1938), *Some Buried Caesar* (1939), *Not Quite Dead Enough* (1944), *Murder by the Book* (1951), *If Death Ever Slept* (1957), *Death of a Doxy* (1966), *A Family Affair* (1975), and others.

Rex Stout died in Danbury, Connecticut, on October 27, 1975. At his death he had published more than seventy books.

Here ⟨in *Not Quite Dead Enough*⟩ was simply the old Sherlock Holmes formula reproduced with a fidelity even more complete than it had been by Jacques Futrelle almost forty years ago. Here was the incomparable private detective, ironic and ceremonious, with a superior mind and eccentric habits, addicted to overeating and orchid-raising, as Holmes had his enervated indulgence in his cocaine and his violin, yet always prepared to revive for prodigies of intellectual alertness; and here were the admiring stooge, adoring and slightly dense, and Inspector Lestrade of Scotland Yard, energetic but entirely at sea, under the new name of Inspector Cramer of Police Headquarters. Almost the only difference was that Nero Wolfe was fat and lethargic instead of lean and active like Holmes, and that he liked to make the villains commit suicide instead of handing them over to justice. But I rather enjoyed Wolfe himself, with his rich dinners and quiet evenings in his house in farthest West Thirty-fifth Street, where he savors an armchair sadism that is always accompanied by beer. The two stories that made up this new book—"Not Quite Dead Enough" and "Booby Trap"—I found rather disappointing; but, as they were both under the usual length and presented the great detective partly distracted from his regular profession by a rigorous course of training for the Army, I concluded that they might not be first-rate examples of what the author could do in this line and read also *The New Wolfe Omnibus*, which contains two earlier book-length stories: *The Red Box* and *The League of Frightened Men*. But neither did these supply the excitement I was hoping for. If the later stories were sketchy and skimpy, these seemed to have been somewhat padded, for they were full of long episodes that led nowhere and had no real business in the story. It was only when I looked up Sherlock Holmes that I realized how much Nero Wolfe was a dim and distant copy of an original. The old stories of Conan Doyle had a wit and a fairy-tale poetry of hansom cabs, gloomy London lodgings and lonely country estates that Rex Stout could hardly duplicate with his backgrounds of modern New York; and the surprises were much more entertaining: you at least got a room with a descending ceiling or a snake trained to climb down the bellrope, whereas with Nero Wolfe—though *The League of Frightened Men* makes use of a clever psychological idea—the solution of the mystery was not usually either fanciful or unexpected. I finally got to feel that I had to unpack large crates by swallowing the excelsior in order to find at the bottom a few bent and rusty nails, and I began to nurse a rankling conviction that detective stories in general are able to profit by an unfair advantage in the code which forbids the reviewer to give away the secret to the public—a custom which results in the concealment of the pointlessness of a good deal of this fiction and affords a protection to the authors which no other department of writing enjoys. It is not difficult to create suspense by making people await a revelation, but it does demand a certain talent to come through with a criminal device which is ingenious or picturesque or amusing enough to make the reader feel that the waiting has been worth while. I even began to mutter that the real secret that Author Rex Stout had been screening by his false scents and interminable divagations was a meagerness of imagination of which one only came to realize the full ghastliness when the last chapter had left one blank.—Edmund Wilson, "Why Do People Read Detective Stories?" (1944), *Classics and Commercials*, 1950, pp. 232–33

Nobody who claims to be a competent critic can say that Rex Stout does not write well. His narrative and dialogue could not be improved, and he passes the supreme test of being rereadable. I don't know how many times I have reread the Nero Wolfe stories, but plenty. I know exactly what is coming and how it is all going to end, but it doesn't matter. That's *writing*.

Does the ordinary reader realize how exactly right those Nero Wolfe stories are? There are no loose ends. One could wonder why Sherlock Holmes, fawned on by kings and prime ministers, was not able to afford rooms in Baker Street—price at the turn of the century thirty bob a week including breakfast—unless he got Doctor Watson to put up half the money, but in Nero Wolfe, a professional detective charging huge fees, you can believe. Those orchids, perfectly understandable. He liked orchids and was in a financial position to collect them. He liked food, too. Again perfectly understandable. He refused to leave his house on business, and very sensible of him if his wealth and reputation were such that he could get away with it. In other words, there was nothing contrived about his eccentricities, purely because Stout knew his job.

But Stout's supreme triumph was the creation of Archie Goodwin.

Telling a mystery story in the third person is seldom satisfactory. To play fair you have to let the reader see into the detective's thoughts, and that gives the game away. The alternative is to have him pick up small objects from the floor and put them carefully in an envelope without revealing their significance, which is the lowest form of literary skulduggery. A Watson of some sort to tell the story is unavoidable, and the hundreds of Watsons who have appeared in print since Holmes's simply won't do. I decline to believe that when the prime minister sends for the detective to cry on his shoulder about some bounder having swiped the naval treaty and finds that he has brought a friend along, he just accepts the detective's statement that "This is Augustus So-and-So, who has been associated with me in many of my cases." What he would really do would be to ring the bell for the secretary of state and tell him to throw Mr. So-and-So out on his ear. "And I want to hear him bounce," he would add. Stout has avoided this trap. Archie is a Watson in the sense that he tells the story, but in no other way is there anything Watsonian about him. And he brings excellent comedy into the type of narrative where comedy seldom bats better than .100.

Summing up, I would say that there is only one Rex Stout, and if you think I am going to say "That's plenty," you are wrong, witty though it would be. I could do with a dozen.—P. G. WODEHOUSE, "Foreword" to *Rex Stout: A Biography* by John McAleer, 1977, pp. xv–xvi

---

EDWARD L. GALLIGAN

"The Comic Art of Rex Stout"

Sewanee Review, Spring 1981, pp. 258–64

Clearly one is not expected to take Rex Stout seriously as a writer. Yet I and many other generally serious readers find that Stout's Nero Wolfe books are not only readable but rereadable. The pleasure and satisfaction that we gain from rereading them is, in substantial part, indistinguishable from the pleasure and satisfaction we gain from rereading books that are works of comic art. I would not argue that Rex Stout belongs in a class with Cervantes—I don't think *anybody* belongs in a class with Cervantes—but without worrying about class rankings, I would argue that the novels in his Nero Wolfe series embody some of the resonance that characterizes works of art in the comic mode.

To take seriously some books that are found in the mysteries section of bookstores and libraries is not bizarre. Witness the current interest in Dashiell Hammett's works. Witness, too, the high regard that John Williams and other black writers have for Chester Himes's Harlem crime stories, and the respect that a number of prominent European critics and writers have shown for Georges Simenon's Inspector Maigret stories.

Certainly Stout's work is highly admired by other mystery writers. Stout is a master of the craft: he can pose a classic problem such as murder in a closed room, give it fresh form, take it through an intricate series of complications without losing either clarity or narrative drive, and arrive at a credible yet surprising solution. Moreover, unlike many skillful plotters, he writes exact and graceful prose. (Unfortunately my use of the present tense is a literary convention; Stout died in October 1975 at the age of eighty-nine.)

Stout is also a master of the special problems involved in creating a coherent mystery series: his handling of the recurring characters and situations is distinctive. After the first few exploratory books in the Wolfe series, the cast of recurring characters remains substantially the same, and all of them stay fixed in age: Wolfe is always in his mid-fifties, Archie Goodwin always in his early thirties, and so forth. Yet the plots change with and often comment on the times. Thus *The Silent Speaker*, published in 1946, focuses on the conflicts generated by the government's control of prices in the immediate postwar period, and *A Right to Die* (1964) on the civil-rights movement in the early sixties. The plot of *The Doorbell Rang* (1965) is set in motion by the distribution of copies of Fred Cook's pioneering exposé, *The F.B.I. Nobody Knows*, which was published in 1964; and *A Family Affair* (1975) hinges, in part, on the scandal of the erasures in President Nixon's tape recordings. What is more important is that Stout devotes a relatively high proportion of space in any given book to portraying relationships among the recurrent characters, especially the complex relationship between Wolfe and Archie. It is impossible to express this in terms of percentages, but through most of the better Wolfes a reader's interest is likely to be focused as much on those timeless relationships as it is on the solutions of the puzzling mysteries which are located so carefully in time.

Nero Wolfe and Archie Goodwin are obviously variations of Sherlock Holmes and Dr. Watson, Wolfe being a Holmesian master of reason and Archie being a Watsonian assistant and reporter of the adventures in detection. These variations are wittily made. Wolfe is quite different from Holmes: he is fat, lazy, disrespectful of most constituted authority, and acutely aware of how much money it takes to support his tastes for orchids and for haute cuisine. And Archie is radically different from Watson: he is not the least bit dull and bumbling, he is strong and active, he is very fond of women, he is not deferential toward Wolfe, and—most important—he is an American with a Twainian delight in the American language and a Jeffersonian belief in equality. The two figures together enable Stout to have the best of both worlds of mystery stories. With Wolfe as master detective he can offer plots that are squarely in the English tradition of the mystery-as-deduction; with Archie as narrator he can offer books that have the linguistic raciness and some of the structural looseness of the American tradition of the hard-boiled detective story. It is no wonder that his series has been a resounding commercial success.

Stout read *Don Quixote* as well as the Sherlock Holmes stories; Wolfe and Archie are related to Quixote and Sancho, too, with similarly witty variations. Stout apparently did an unusually good job of reading *Don Quixote*, for he followed Cervantes' most brilliant and most demanding lead by gradually blurring the distinctions between his two figures. Just as Cervantes begins in book 1 with simple diametrically opposed characters and ends in book 2 with a Sanchoesque Quixote and a Quixotic Sancho, Stout begins in *Fer-de-Lance* (1934) with a Wolfe who is simply a master of ratiocination and an Archie who is not much more than a muscular boor and ends in *A Family Affair* (1975) with a Wolfe whose judgment is partially blinded by emotion and an Archie who is only a step behind Wolfe in solving the mystery and who actually takes charge of disposing of the problem that the solution creates for them.

In the later books Wolfe and Archie are equals. Admittedly, Wolfe continues to be the mastermind who solves most of the mysteries, and Archie continues to function as an assistant who carries out Wolfe's orders, but if metaphor is necessary it would be better to call them captain and executive officer of the enterprise operating out of the brownstone house on West 35th Street rather than master and servant. Each grants the other his special qualities, much as they might irritate him, and each trusts the other fully. Consequently the study of their relationship becomes a study of the ways of trust, or—to use a word that the characters avoid but that the books justify—the ways of love. Taking a hint from the title of Stout's last book, *A Family Affair,* I would call it familial love.

In Stout's vision a strong respect for diverse functions is basic to familial love. Wolfe and Archie, Fritz Brenner, the chef, Theodore Horstman, the gardener in charge of the orchids, the three free-lance detectives who are frequently called in to assist on cases, Saul Panzer, Fred Durkin, and Orrie Cather, Lon Cohen of the *Gazette,* and Inspector Cramer of Homicide West—each one has his own special function and gifts which entitle him to spaces, habits, and idiosyncrasies which the others must respect. (Cramer is a special case: normally Wolfe's foil, sometimes his antagonist, and occasionally his ally, he both is and is not a member of the family.) Courtesy, then, is very important within the family; even when Wolfe and Archie are so furious with each other they can hardly speak, they remain courteous. With courtesy comes ceremony or, at the very least, a remarkably elaborate set of rules for behavior.

In large ways and in small the ceremonious nature of life within the family is stressed throughout the series. Stout takes something like Homeric delight in developing little formulas for introducing a recurrent character whenever he finally appears in one of the books and in repeating little bits of action throughout the series. Most striking, though, is the way Stout manages almost all of his intricate plots so that they arrive at their dénouement in a gathering of all of the major characters in Wolfe's office at which Wolfe holds forth in high-handed style.

Certain modern critics have developed the theory that comedy is an essentially festive art, maintaining the rightness of festive attitudes and values over against worldly attitudes and values. In their terms the Nero Wolfe books can quite properly be described as a series of narratives in which a murderous melodramatic conflict is resolved by comic heroes who emerge from a festive life to deal with the conflict and who return triumphantly to it. Appropriately—and not the least bit accidentally—the last book in the series, *A Family Affair,* ends with Inspector Cramer, who as a policeman spends most of his life in a decidedly unfestive world, saying to Wolfe: "I'm going home and try to get some sleep. You probably have never had to try to get some sleep. You probably never will." When the sound comes of the front door closing, Wolfe says, "Will you bring brandy, Archie? And two glasses. If Fritz is up, bring him and three glasses. We'll try to get some sleep."

Stout may have started with the idea of making Wolfe a vehicle for Holmesian logic, but as Wolfe began to respond to and move toward Archie something curious and essential happened: Wolfe became much less a pure logician. As early as *Some Buried Caesar* (1939), in which the pivotal figure in a plot is a prize-winning Guernsey bull named Caesar, his sense of what people will do when they are immersed in competition is as crucial to the solution of the mystery as his observation and understanding of a "clue"—in this case the relative absence of blood on the face and horns of a bull that is supposed to have gored a man to death. Much later, in *The Doorbell Rang,* the crucial element in the plot is Wolfe's certainty that the head of the New York office of the FBI would expect his men to lie to him to cover up their involvement in a murder and would himself do everything he could to maintain the cover-up. And in *A Family Affair* the clue that reveals the shocking truth that a member of the family, Orrie Cather, is responsible for the murders they are investigating is Orrie's suggestion that he take a task that had been assigned to Saul Panzer—"It was unheard of for him to suggest that he would be better than Saul for anything whatever."

The Nero Wolfe series does give us an image of ideal intelligence, but it is not a Holmesian or even a simply Wolfean intelligence that is celebrated. Instead it is a shared or compound intelligence. The main components of it are supplied by Wolfe and Archie, but other members of the family make significant contributions to it. The central manifestation of this intelligence is an alert loving interest in words. Wolfe specializes in recondite terms and in a furious refusal to compromise with sloppy usage: he is likely to leave the room if someone uses *contact* as a verb, and he burns his copy of the Merriam-Webster Third because it condones such horrors. Archie is finely tuned to the meaning of slang and colloquialisms. Fritz Brenner contributes a European gift for polite indirection and occasionally a French term for which there is no exact American equivalent. And Saul is a master of exact terseness.

An intelligence which centers on words is humanistic rather than scientific or philosophical. It uses logic to serve its purposes but it does not let logic determine its purposes or control its behavior. This familial intelligence has a firm command of logical processes, yet it remains proudly unreasonable, if not downright irrational, in its major actions. *The Doorbell Rang,* in which Wolfe and Archie undertake the wildly unreasonable task of forcing the FBI to stop annoying their client, is a perfect example. Never mind sweet reason: they see a chance to earn a huge fee that will make months of loafing possible, and they share a Quixotic desire to demonstrate to J. Edgar Hoover that they have no need to bow and scrape to his arrogance, to prove that their resourcefulness and their vanity are more than equal to his.

Thus the intelligence which Stout celebrates in his series is emphatically a comic intelligence. All good comedians have a strong sense of logic and a fussy concern for language; they must, because they use the one to turn the other upside-down. A joke, according to Arthur Koestler, is the sudden discovery of a bisociation of two previously unrelated matrices of thought. To work skillfully with matrices of thought one must understand logic; to discover unsuspected bisociations of the matrices one must have an exacting curiosity about language. (Of course, it is body language which the slapstick comedian must know.) In general, as William Lynch has shown, comedy is hostile to anything like a rigidly logical intelligence on the grounds that it is ultimately deadly; comedy celebrates an impure compounded intelligence that is playful and life-enhancing.

If Stout is at one with great comic artists in his image of what intelligence should be like, he is also very much at one with them in his attitude toward justice. Comic artists have to say with Gerard Manley Hopkins "Glory be to God for dappled things," and the "dappling" that is hardest for them to accept is injustice in human affairs. There is no justice, not in this world, at least not most of the time, yet the comic artist must sing joyfully of this life in this world. Practically every major comic artist struggles with this painful necessity at some time.

In his less impassioned way Stout has used the Nero Wolfe series to express and accept fully the impossibility of justice. Justice is always done, in the sense that Wolfe always reveals the murderer. But Wolfe does not act out of a sense of justice—huge fees, not high ideals, motivate him; nor does Archie ever think of himself as a knight, or even a squire, on a white horse. Stout and his fictional heroes are well aware that most people most of the time get only as much justice as they can afford to buy. That's life. Since they love life, they must accept what they cannot change.

The Doorbell Rang nicely illustrates Stout's attitude toward justice. By trapping two FBI men attempting to do a bag job in their office, Wolfe and Archie are able to force the Bureau to stop harassing their client; and as a by-product of their entrapment scheme they expose a murderer. But when all is over, little has changed: government agents will continue to flout the law they are supposed to serve, murderers will continue to murder, and a pile of money will always be the best bulwark against injustice.

The closing paragraphs summarize Stout's position. Wolfe and Archie are arguing about listing among the expenses the client should pay the cost of a dinner at Rusterman's Restaurant for herself and Archie. Archie says yes because those free meals are actually payment for favors they have done for Rusterman's. The doorbell rings. It is "the big fish" himself, presumably come to beg for the credentials of the bag men which Wolfe is keeping in order to hold the Bureau to its bargain. Wolfe and Archie decide to let him wear his finger out on the doorbell while they go back to arguing over the expense sheet. Wolfe and Archie and Rex Stout will acknowledge the injustice of the way of the world without wasting time and energy bewailing it; but that is all the more reason for holding firmly to a prickly, even a preposterous, code of personal honor. The world may do as it wishes, but a man of honor will treat others justly and will tilt with whatever windmills or whatever government agencies challenge his pride and his courage.

In the *Saturday Review of Literature* (April 2, 1949) Stout published an article on detective stories entitled "Grim Fairy Tales." At first glance it seems to contradict what I have said about Stout's image of intelligence and of justice and to deny my claim of some artistic importance for the Wolfe books:

> [The detective story] gets its enormous audience . . . by outrageous and barefaced flattery. It tells over and over again, with what wit and ingenuity it can manage, two flagrant lies: that justice is always done and that man's reason orders his affairs. Men love it, desire it, and need it, and pay money for it. But they don't really believe it, and they can't be expected to take seriously something they don't really believe.

As Sir John Falstaff and Huckleberry Finn, not to mention William Shakespeare and Samuel Clemens, well know, lying is one of the great invaluable comic gifts. Rex Stout told the lies, skillfully and plausibly, in those parts of the Nero Wolfe books that are devoted to the detection of murderers. If mystery fans want to swallow those parts of the books like so many sleeping pills, fine—it beats tossing and turning half the night. But Rex Stout, who never had "to try to get to sleep" either, was a gifted, a comic liar; he was not silly enough to believe his own lies. In those parts of the Nero Wolfe books that are devoted to the timeless unchanging world of the house on West 35th Street, he told in classic comic ways comedy's perennial truths about intelligence and about injustice, and about many other matters I have not had space to discuss. Readers, insomniacs or not, are well advised to pay attention.

LEON EDEL

From "The Nature of Psychological Evidence"
Stuff of Sleep and Dreams: Experiments in Literary Psychology
1982, pp. 25–31

Some years ago I lectured in Boston on the writing of biography. Afterwards a young professor of English at one of the local colleges told me that he was about to become the Boswell of Rex Stout, the detective-story writer, then a very old man. How, asked my excited questioner, should he go about becoming a biographer? This was a large question. Yet, to my own surprise, an instant reply arose from my unconscious. I had, in my younger days, read a great many of Stout's Nero Wolfe mysteries, and I heard myself say, "You might inquire why Rex, being a king, chose to make his detective, Nero, an emperor. Also, why he chose a wicked emperor." Then I heard myself adding that I knew Rex Stout as a tall thin man. He made Nero Wolfe very stout indeed, 260 pounds, thereby reversing the saying that in every stout man a thin man struggles to be freed. In Rex Stout, apparently, a fat man resided somewhere within his fine spare athletic figure.

We had, I observed, an engaging mystery. A detective in fiction is nearly always some form of the creator's *persona*. Nero Wolfe is the opposite of all we superficially know about Rex Stout. Rex was a fighter for causes and a man with considerable bite to him; Nero Wolfe is quiet and retiring and stays home. Unlike the Nero of history, who was gross and fiddled while Rome burned, Nero Wolfe is a man of delicacy. Nero the emperor was violent. Nero the detective—whose surname Wolfe seems to contradict his fatness and outward passivity—dissociates violence from himself and hires a legman, named Archie Goodwin, to do the rough stuff of modern detective work, the spying and slugging and getting slugged. Archie often gets roughed up. Nero meanwhile fiddles with his orchids and gourmet recipes and puts his ratiocinative mind to work on the evil that must not go unpunished.

I told the young biographer that Rex Stout's nomenclature, personal and fictive, gave me the impression that the real-life author was converting certain powerful feelings, probably aggressive and violent, into his particularly clever art. In a highly creative and imaginative way, he was writing out little dramas of good and evil derived from his own problems. We notice that Archie Goodwin is a winner of the good. Nero Wolfe achieves the good by physical inertia and sheer force of intellect. I said that this probably pointed to ways in which Rex Stout was handling certain anxieties with which most humans have to cope. Stout dissociates violence from himself by choosing the name of violence; yet he makes the bearer of the name benign. Also, the lupine in Nero's name speaks for a ravenous ferocity, yet this is converted into the gourmet side of the fat detective.

Some weeks later, still intrigued by the name game I had begun to play in Boston, I told myself I had not accounted for the Wolfe in Nero Wolfe. The answer wasn't difficult to find. Rex Stout's middle name was Todhunter, his mother's family name. A *tod* is Scots for fox; so he came of a family of fox hunters on his mother's side. To summarize, the king was transformed into emperor, the Stout was literally turned into fatness, and the Todhunter was turned from fox into wolf. Good enough. These observations received a surprising validation: I came on the fact that Stout invented another detective before Nero Wolfe who proved to have little appeal. His name, however, was molded in the same pattern. He was called Tecumseh Fox. This shows how insistent fancy can be, how the unconscious imagination dictates choices which seem to most people simply accidental. Tecumseh was a Shawnee. He lived a great wishful dream of an Indian empire across North America. So *imperium* and the mother's fox family were united in Rex Stout's imagination long before he created Nero Wolfe.

Once one becomes involved in this kind of evidence, the inquiring imagination working on psychological signs and signals refuses to stop. I found myself pondering the relation between Archie Goodwin and Nero Wolfe, for Archie too is a creation of Stout's mind. Putting Archie and Stout side by side we can see, if we inform ourselves, that Archie, the winner of the good, is the pragmatic, compulsive, practical author himself; anyone who knew Rex Stout knew him as a man of goodwill, active, practical, and down-to-earth, agile both mentally and physically. He made a fortune in banking before he made his fortune in writing. His choice of names represented an interesting splitting apart of the man and his myth—Rex Stout as he appeared to the world, and the unconscious mythic Stout who emerged as stout Nero Wolfe. In my theorizing about biography, I have always argued that if a biographer can tap the unconscious myth of a subject, the battle is more than half won; we have a key to the material that is illustrative and relevant and can then know what is routine and irrelevant. The self myth is the truest part of an individual: by that myth we always seek to live; it is what gives us force, direction, and sustenance. The personality the world sees is usually much less interesting. Who does not remember Thurber's story of Walter Mitty? The hidden myth of Rex Stout was a dream of himself as a big man, a heavy man, an emperor. Indeed, for two decades and more he was king-emperor of the American Authors' Guild. He argued copyright with senators; he had access to the White House during the FDR era; he knew most of the public American figures of his time—in short, he acted out both the fox-self and the wolf-self, the king-self and the emperor-self. In his detective stories he embodied problems of crime and punishment, guilt, rivalry, competition, aggression—and his own large and on the whole benign and constructive drive to power.

Some time after I set down my observation of the curious use of opposites in the imagination of Rex Stout—passive-violent, fat-thin, good-evil—I learned that he himself used to say he invented Nero Wolfe by making him the opposite of Sherlock Holmes. The data were given me by someone who had talked with Stout. "He told us," this witness said, "that when he began to write detective stories he realized that Doyle was king." Notice Rex using kingship in this remark. "He, Stout, told us that Holmes was of the utmost importance, and so he decided that his detective would be the opposite of Holmes in appearance and personality and would perhaps arrive at a state of importance also. For example: Holmes was tall and thin, Wolfe would be short and fat. Holmes played the violin, Wolfe raised orchids. Holmes took dope, Wolfe drank beer. Holmes would go anywhere to solve a case, Wolfe would not leave the house." If we carry this further we also see that it applies to Archie Goodwin, bright as a penny, the opposite to the dull, stolid, Victorian Dr. Watson.

We now see that Stout was engaged in a double process: he not only created the opposite of himself in Nero Wolfe, but the opposite of a detective out of literature, with whom he seems to have identified himself—so much so that he wanted to make him over into his own mythic imperial image. On the surface Rex Stout and Conan Doyle seem dissimilar in all their externals. Conan Doyle was a doctor, a distinctive Victorian; Stout was an American. Conan Doyle had a strong romantic streak in him; he liked adventure, travel, sport, and romantic storytelling. He traveled on a whaling ship; he took a cargo steamer to Africa. He organized sports clubs. But if we look beyond the externals we see that in everything the two did, they resembled each other remarkably. Both had king complexes. They sought power, each in his own way. Their desire for rule, for eminence, for the heady feeling of domination—this was common to both, and both found their power in what they created. Given their personal myth, it is less of a coincidence that their creations are allied—that Stout should attach his *persona* to Doyle's and alter it as an outcome of his own psychic needs. They were born leaders—or, at the least, passionate would-be leaders. ⟨. . .⟩

While I was indulging in my name game about Rex Stout, his publishers sent me the proof copy of his newest Nero Wolfe mystery, written at the ripe age of eighty-five. I was interested to see how the old man was performing, with the sense I had that he could not live to write many more such books. The manifest evidence was there, as in all the other mysteries, although this work showed an inevitable slowing-down, a lack of the old force and rhythm. The latent content was surprising and saddening. For what Stout announced in this story—without, I am sure, realizing it—was that he was about to die. I made this assumption from the nature of his fantasy. For the first and only time in the more than forty Nero Wolfe mysteries, the murder occurs in Wolfe's own home, in his guest room. The plot revolves around his personal responsibility, since he himself is one of the suspects. In an earlier thriller, *The Red Box*, there are murders in Nero Wolfe's office; the significant statement of this novel is that death has finally entered Nero Wolfe's home. He solves the crime under a cloud; the fat orchid grower is in deep depression. Will he be able to solve the next crime? Or is he his own last case? It is interesting that quite independently Agatha Christie was concerned about her last case in a similar way. Stout died a few weeks after publishing *A Family Affair*.

MARK STRAND

1934–

Mark Strand was born on Prince Edward Island, Canada, on April 11, 1934. He did his undergraduate work at Antioch College, obtaining a B.A. in 1957, and then spent two years at Yale, where he received the Cook and Bergin prizes and, in 1959, his B.F.A. degree. Strand then continued his graduate work at the University of Florence (1960) and the University of Iowa (M.A., 1962). Since that time he has lectured and taught at many colleges and universities, including the University of Iowa, the University of Brazil, Mount Holyoke College, the University of Washington, Columbia, Yale, Brandeis, the University of Virginia, Wesleyan University, and Harvard.

Strand's poems, typically concerned with feelings of alienation and foreboding and written in a minimalist, somewhat surrealistic style, are collected in *Sleeping with One Eye Open* (1964), *Reasons for Moving* (1968), *Darker* (1970), *The Story of Our Lives* (1973), *The Sargeantville Notebook* (1973), *Elegy for My Father* (1973), *The Late Hour* (1978), *The Monument* (1978), *Selected Poems* (1980), and *The Planet of Lost Things* (1981).

HAROLD BLOOM
From "Dark and Radiant Peripheries: Mark Strand and A. R. Ammons"

Southern Review, January 1972, pp. 135–41

Reasons for Moving (1968) was preceded by Strand's first book, *Sleeping with One Eye Open* (1964), privately printed and largely apprentice work. The epigraph to *Reasons for Moving*, from Borges (and ultimately from the Chinese), establishes the irreality that never ceases to haunt Strand: "—while we sleep here, we are awake elsewhere and that in this way every man is two men." The title poem, which appeared in the first book under the title "A Reason for Moving," is now called "Keeping Things Whole":

In a field
I am the absence
of field.
This is
always the case.
Wherever I am
I am what is missing.

When I walk
I part the air
and always
the air moves in
to fill the spaces
where my body's been.

We all have reasons
for moving.
I move
to keep things whole.

Beneath the grace, this is desperate enough to be outrageous. This "I" might wish he were asleep elsewhere as well as here, and so be no man rather than two. His absence seems a void that his presence could not fill, or a wound that his presence could not heal. The poet of *Reasons for Moving* writes Borges-like parables in a limpid mode that sometimes has overtones of Elizabeth Bishop or Roethke or even Wilbur, but the pervasive reductiveness resembles the winter vision of the prime precursor, Stevens. This is the Stevens of "The Snow Man," "The Man Whose Pharynx Was Bad," "The Death of a Soldier," and the other small ecstasies of reduction to a basic slate or universal hue that mark *Harmonium*'s other music, the contrary to its Floridean excesses and gaudiness. The true epigraph to all of Strand is: "The poem refreshes life so that we share,/For a moment, the first idea. . . . " But the first idea in Stevens is quite deliberately unbearable, since to behold constantly nothing that is not there and the nothing that is would make us inhuman, or at least hopeless company for one another. Contemplating this aspect of Stevens, and its effect upon a younger poet of genius like Strand, I am reminded of Goethe's grim warning that anyone who destroys all illusion in himself and in others will be punished tyrannically by nature.

Some of the parables in *Reasons for Moving* read like scenarios by Beckett or Pinter, but the book's best poem, its last and longest, is harrowingly unlike its overt analogues and likely sources. "The Man in the Mirror" is at once phantasmagoria and simple narcist self-confrontation, an inescapable, daily, waking nightmare. First staring at his reflection, seeing an alien sleeper, the poet gasps: "How long will all this take?"—reminding me of Shelley's encounter with his double, before drowning, and the double's terrible "How long do you mean to be content?" Remembering the earlier Narcissus-delight ("how we used to stand/wishing the glass/would dissolve between us"), Strand is compelled to see the now-terrible reflection depart from him:

Your suit floating, your hair
moving like eel grass
in a shallow bay, you drifted
out of the mirror's room, through the hall
and into the open air.
You seemed to rise and fall
with the wind, the sway
taking you always farther away, farther away.

Alone ("The mirror was nothing without you") the poet waits, avidly, until the prodigal's return, as "a bruise coated with light." But the returned double is only a perpetual vision of loss, central emblem of the self unable to bear the self, ambivalence without resolution:

It will always be this way.
I stand here scared
that you will disappear,
scared that you will stay.

This is the last vision of *Reasons for Moving*, and is (consciously) no distance at all from the book's opening fantasy, the poet "eating poetry" in a library, romping like a dog "with joy in the bookish dark." The dark covers the honest terror of Narcissus, always at work composing more letters to himself, and always in the same vein: "You shall live/by inflicting pain./You shall forgive." The world outside this occluded self is almost formless, almost indeed without weather:

> There is no rain.
> It is impossible to say what form
> The weather will take.
> We blow on our hands,
> Trying to keep them warm,
> Hoping it will not snow.

"What the solipsist *means* is right," a gnomic Wittgensteinian truth, is in traditional American terms the Emersonian admonition "Build therefore your own world," which in turn is founded on the central Emersonian motto: "What we are, that only can we see." For Emerson knew he could only show (and not say) the truths, all eloquence (his own included) necessarily obscured. Pears, expounding early Wittgenstein, reads to me like an exegete of Emerson:

> But what is this unique self, of whose existence he feels assured? It is neither his body nor his soul nor anything else in his world. It is only the metaphysical subject, which is a kind of focal vanishing point behind the mirror of his language. There is really nothing except the mirror and what the mirror reflects. So the only thing that he can legitimately say is that what is reflected in the mirror is reflected in the mirror. But this is neither a factual thesis nor a substantial necessary truth about what is reflected in the mirror, but a tautology. It means only that whatever objects exist exist. So when solipsism is worked out, it becomes clear that there is no difference between it and realism. Moreover, since the unique self is nothing, it would be equally possible to take an impersonal view of the vanishing point behind the mirror of language. Language would then be any language, the metaphysical subject would be the world spirit, and idealism would lie on the route from solipsism to realism.

That route was Emerson's, from the solipsism of the early *Notebooks* through the idealism of *Nature* on to the realism of *The Conduct of Life.* Ammons is an Emersonian who has passed to idealism; Strand follows no route, and never departs from solipsism. The splendor of his poetry, only intimated by *Reasons for Moving*, emerges in *Darker* (1970), where nearly every poem *shows* what can be shown of the solipsist's predicament, while wisely eschewing the saying of what cannot be said. Pears, following Wittgenstein, speaks of "deep tautologies," and Strand, without metaphysical design, gives them to us. "There is what there is" might be the motto of *Darker.* Here is its characteristic kind of poem:

> I empty myself of the names of others. I empty my
> pockets.
> I empty my shoes and leave them beside the road.
> At night I turn back the clocks;
> I open the family album and look at myself as a boy.
>
> What good does it do? The hours have done their
> job.
> I say my own name. I say goodbye.
> The words follow each other downwind.
> I love my wife but send her away.
>
> My parents rise out of their thrones
> into the milky rooms of clouds. How can I sing?
> Time tells me what I am. I change and I am the
> same.
> I empty myself of my life and my life remains.

This poem's title, "The Remains," means everything about the self that ought to have only posthumous existence, when the poet will survive only in the regard of other selves. But his dread (which is one with the reality of him) is that already he survives only insofar as he has become an otherness capable of extending such regard. Dread born of spectral duality, dread identical with what Blake called the Spectre of Urthona, is peculiarly an anxiety that shadows poets, and is almost a distinguishing mark of Romantic tradition. "The Remains" is a poem written by Strand's *alastor* or Spirit of Solitude, his true voice of feeling. Its despairing wish—to be delivered from the self's prison without abandoning a self that can be embraced only when it in prison lies—is repeated throughout *Darker* in many superb modulations:

> that the lies I tell them are different
> from the lies I tell myself,
> that by being both here and beyond
> I am becoming a horizon . . .
>
> And there is the sleep that demands I lie down
> and be fitted to the dark that comes upon me
> like another skin in which I shall never be found,
> out of which I shall never appear. . . .
>
> Why do you never come? Must I have you by being
> somebody else? Must I write *My Life* by somebody
> else?
> *My Death* by somebody else? Are you listening?
> Somebody else has arrived. Somebody else is writing.

The mode is phantasmagoria, of which the American master will always be Whitman, the one supreme Emersonian bard. No poem by Strand (so far) is as dark and powerful as Whitman's *A Hand-Mirror* (*Looking-Glass* in its manuscript title) where the self has the strength of Satan to bear its outward and inward loss. Closer to Strand (and more approachable) is the Stevens who charted the "mythology of self,/Blotched out beyond unblotching." Strand's peculiar courage is to take up the quirky quest when "amours shrink/Into the compass and curriculum/Of introspective exiles, lecturing," concerning which Stevens warned: "It is a theme for Hyacinth alone." Throughout *Darker*, Strand's risk is enormous. He spares us the opaque vulgarity of "confessional" verse by daring to expose how immediate in him a more universal anguish rages:

> The huge doll of my body
> refuses to rise.
> I am the toy of women.
> My mother
>
> would prop me up for her friends.
> "Talk, talk," she would beg.
> I moved my mouth
> but words did not come.
>
> My wife took me down from the shelf.
> I lay in her arms. "We suffer
> the sickness of self," she would whisper.
> And I lay there dumb.
>
> Now my daughter
> gives me a plastic nurser
> filled with water.
> "You are my real baby," she says.

Strand's unique achievement is to raise this mode to an aesthetic dignity that astonishes me, for I would not have believed, before reading him, that it could be made to touch upon a sublimity. *Darker* moves upon the heights in its final poems, "Not Dying" and the longer "The Way It Is," the first work in which Strand ventures out from his eye's first circle, toward a larger art. "Not Dying" opens in narcist desperation, and reaches no resolution, but its passion for survival is prodigiously convincing. "I am driven by innocence," the poet protests, even as like a Beckett creature he crawls from bed to chair and back again, until he finds the obduracy to proclaim a grotesque version of natural supernaturalism:

> I shall not die.
> The grave result
> and token of birth, my body
> remembers and holds fast.

"The Way It Is" takes its tone from Stevens at his darkest ("The world is ugly/And the people are sad") and quietly edges out a private phantasmagoria until this merges with the public phantasmagoria we all of us now inhabit. The consequence is a poem more surprising and profound than Lowell's justly celebrated "For the Union Dead," a juxtaposition made unavoidable by Strand's audacity in appropriating the same visionary area:

> I see myself in the park
> on horseback, surrounded by dark,
> leading the armies of peace.
> The iron legs of the horse do not bend.
> I drop the reins. Where will the turmoil end?
> Fleets of taxis stall in the fog, passengers fall
> asleep. Gas pours
> from a tri-colored stack.
> Locking their doors,
> people from offices huddle together,
> telling the same story over and over.
> Everyone who has sold himself wants to buy himself
> back.
> Nothing is done. The night
> eats into their limbs
> like a blight.
> Everything dims.
> The future is not what it used to be.
> The graves are ready. The dead
> shall inherit the dead.

Self-trained to a private universe of irreality, where he has learned the gnomic wisdom of the deep tautology, Strand peers out into the anxieties of the public world, to show again what can be shown, the shallow tautologies of a universal hysteria, as much a hysteria of protest as of societal repression. Wherever his poetry will go after *Darker*, we can be confident it goes as a perfected instrument, able to render an image not of any created thing whatsoever, but of every nightmare we live these days, separately or together.

MARK STRAND

From "A Conversation with Mark Strand"

Ohio Review, Winter 1972, pp. 55–64

Interviewer: Let's just talk. I think what we're going to do is address your poems themselves. I wonder if you would comment on where you've come from. Where do you think you've come from, and where do you think you're going?

Strand: Well, I don't know where I'm going. If I knew where I was going I probably wouldn't go there. The idea is to—I wouldn't say surprise oneself . . . But I think you go, and then you discover where it is that you are, and writing is so . . .

Interviewer: It sounds like a line from one of your poems.

Strand: Maybe so. Where I started was—I started as a painter. I was a student of Joseph Albers at Yale, and somewhere early in my career there I discovered I wasn't destined to be a very good painter, so I became a poet. Now it didn't happen suddenly. I did read a lot, and I had been a reader of poetry before. In fact, I was much more given to reading poems than I was to fiction and the book that I read a lot, and frequently, was *The Collected Poems of Wallace Stevens*. And I think that a lot of American poets come from Stevens. The other book that had an influence on me was the *New Poets of England and America*, the Hall, Pack, Simpson anthology. I look back now and I read it, and I'm bored by a lot of the stuff, and some of it seems so forced and decorative. But I can still see why I was excited. There was an awful lot of 'technical authority' in many of those poems, and it's something that I, as a beginning poet, lacked. And I went directly to measured lines and rhyme as a way of, you know, nailing down poems. I felt secure with rhyme and meter—secure is the wrong word—but if I worked within definable bounds I was, I thought, destined to come up with something decent.

Interviewer: In that sense then, what is it you want to do in a poem?

Strand: Well, I could answer that in a roundabout way, saying what I want to do in a poem is discover what it is that I have to say.

Interviewer: It is an act of discovery?

Strand: Yes.

Interviewer: Having done it, what do you see that you have done?

Strand: Well, after the brief, and I think normal, period of exhilaration, there is a letdown. What I've done is written another poem. And what I have to do is write another one. Now I realize that . . . you see, what happens is, when I look back on my work I see my faults fairly clearly, and when I'm working on new poems, or the next poem, I try not to repeat myself, although I do, unconsciously. I don't have many things to say. I don't believe that many people do. I have a terrific sense of my limitations—because I'm one person, and I have, you know, one mind and one nervous system . . .

Interviewer: I think what I'm getting at is . . . Other people, in the reviews and the criticism, define what they perceive you as doing: I wanted to ask you what *you* perceived yourself as doing. I don't want to pose the question too naively, but I want to ask you what kind of poem it is you're making; the kind of poetry you are making is rather unique, I think, today.

Strand: Yeah, that may be, although I have a very unclear sense of the kind of poem it is that I make. I have a clearer sense of the kind of poem other people make. But if I tried to describe what it was that I did in a poem, I think I'd get in an awful mess, and I'd have a sick feeling that what I'd described wasn't in fact what I really am doing.

Interviewer: I think that's very good, and I think it's typical of the poem you're doing, as a matter of fact, the sense of withholding, the sense of silence, the sense of great transparency in the language—that you're not even dealing in language.

Strand: Well that's important. That's a good point. I think that one of the things I do try to do is call less attention to the verbal surface of the poem than I might have, had I been a poet of the 50's. There is a life in the poem that somehow comes through the language, or that the language points to, and it doesn't mean that it's not part of the language. It's just not part of the endless elaboration of language. It's a sort of direct language, suggestive and yet concrete. I deal with identifiable states of mind which are at the same time elusive. Does that make sense? I rely on dreams and on chance associations, as well.

Interviewer: A number of people of course have commented on the obvious fact of a severely plain vocabulary to your poetry, and . . .

Strand: It wasn't always that way.

Interviewer: Wasn't it? Well, actually I wanted to ask a kind of longwinded question, though I hope it's not just fatuous. Michael Hamburger, in his *The Truth of Poetry*, talks a good bit about what he calls the antipoetry movement of the decades after World War II. I mean the movement in poetry which was a reflection surely of a kind of distrust that a lot of people felt, a distrust of the surface of poetry and everything, and I wondered to what extent you see that continuing in contemporary poetry and even in your own, in this talk about the lack of concern for the verbal surface.

Strand: Well I'm not sure that I would characterize recent poetry or post-World War II poetry as anti-poetry. We had a terrific resurgence of formalist poetry in the 50's, and what we had combating that, I guess, was "beat poetry."

Interviewer: I meant to say World War I. If I said World War II, I didn't mean that.

Strand: Well, anti-poetry is really modern poetry. Contemporary poetry isn't modern poetry, and it isn't anti-poetry. I feel very much a part of a new international style that has a lot to do with plainness of diction, a certain reliance on surrealist techniques, a strong narrative element, etc. Now I realize this doesn't cover all of contemporary poetry, but there does seem to be a connection between, say, Parra and Zbigniew Herbert and Jaime Sabines and Vasco Popa and Charlie Simic, to pick a few scattered poets. Auden would say there can be no international style because there is no international language, but maybe that's my point—that poets are connected by a similarity of interests. With the amount of translation going on there is an enormous sharing of points of view. And I think we read other poets in translation, oddly enough, for content. You might even say that poetry is what is retained in translation, not what is lost (though I say this almost jokingly—because reading poets in translation is, at the same time, not quite like reading poetry written in English. It's more relaxing. A certain pressure is missing). But I'm talking—and perhaps mistakenly—about a certain sort of poetry being written—vaguely surreal, vaguely narrative—as I said.

Interviewer: You write very narrative poems, for example.

Strand: Yes, well there are other people who do too, and I think that a poem is less a moment that's endlessly elaborated on, or one sensation that's endlessly talked about (and I don't mean that in a bad sense). A poem really moves very quickly from point A to B to C to D; and you have a sense that you're moving through time, as well as that you're moving over the expanse of space that connects them.

Interviewer: One of the things that question was wanting to get at, was to what extent you think there is very firmly embedded in contemporary poetry now, the poetry of today, a distrust of what once on a time would have been called "poetic conventions," and now which we would probably put in quotation marks.

Strand: Are you speaking about rhyme and meter?

Interviewer: I don't mean only that.

Strand: Well, I don't know. I can say that we distrust rhyme because it sounds a little tinny, a little false, a little decorative, and a little unnatural. The point of writing a version of plain-style verse, it seems, is to affect as much as possible of the naturalness of conversation, or plain discourse, not overly-excited discourse. Rhymes would get in the way . . . I'm not talking about my own poetry when I say this. I'm sure Galway Kinnell and Robert Mezey, whom we mentioned at lunch, would not ever write in meters or rhyme.

Interviewer: Even though they have . . .

Strand: Even though they have, right. I still rhyme. I mean, I've rhymed fairly recently, and I find it useful. I don't mind that, and I don't mind meters either. It sometimes seems quite natural to me.

Interviewer: Sure. I was wondering if you thought there might be a distrust of a kind of conventionalized stance that poetry so often brought to a situation which we would, today, consider a kind of falsification of it. I mean that's the kind of thing that Mezey objects to in his past poetry, in a lot of his poetry of the years rejected.

Strand: But that's something he, of course, is in a much better position to talk about than anyone else. I mean, I don't feel the same way about my early rhymed poems. If I dislike them, it's not because they were in rhyme, it's because they just weren't as, as . . .

Interviewer: As authentic . . . ?

Strand: Well I'm not sure I would use the word "authentic." They just weren't in touch with the things that I now consider important. I mean I believe I was honest when I was writing those poems; it's just that I had an odd idea of what made me go. I don't have that idea now, and I think I perhaps was mistaken in those days. I had a very sentimental view of myself, which crops up now and again in my poems. I tend to dramatize certain weaknesses that I have, a certain incapacity, you know. And I am not an incapable person. I find that, perhaps, the most moving part of my work (if I sit down and think about myself, and we all do): the fact that I do have, do experience this strange kind of impotence in the contemporary world, and it makes me sad about myself and other people. . . .

Interviewer: There is this ongoing, if I may coin a phrase, ontological conversation with yourself. It seems to be underneath almost everything you're doing. And so many poets, who are 10 years, 15 years older than you, seem to have come to a point of near madness in their work. They seem to be almost fragmenting, falling apart right in front of their poems, so to speak.

Strand: Yes, it's true.

Interviewer: But your work still has this sense of great—great control, great form, as if you were containing it. You're still very much in control, and yet your poems are just as mad, it seems to me, in their own way.

Strand: Well I am really aware, too, that when I am writing a poem, I am writing a poem. I think that that makes certain demands. There are certain concessions made to that inner debate, artistic concessions, and they're important. You know, one of the horrifying things about many poets is that they lost, somewhere along the line, in the fervor of this inner debate, the idea of poetry.

Interviewer: That's really a very good point.

Strand: They become, in fact, "chroniclers" or "notators." They write notebooks or leaflets or what have you. As if to say, "I am connected to my times in this way, and I am connected to this debate in this way." But there's no sense of getting absorbed in the idea of the poem.

Interviewer: As if the poem is somehow in the way now; "I've got more truth to get at than that," they seem to be saying.

Strand: Poetry has always seemed to me the most truthful medium of all. To say that the poem gets in the way is to say that you don't trust what the poem can do. I mean I've always believed poems. Sir Thomas Wyatt's "They Flee from Me, That

Sometime Did Me Seek" strikes me as terribly honest, yet it's a poem and a very formal one, and I certainly don't say, "Gee, I wish he'd written that as a confession and not as a poem, because as a poem it lacks reality," or "I don't believe it because it rhymes." And the same goes for Shakespeare's sonnets—they're very sad, and some of them are heartbreaking, and just because they're sonnets, that doesn't mean you can't believe them. And so on and so forth, right up to the present.

Interviewer: Well, that makes me aware of a question I want to ask you. I was recently reading a thing by Alain Bosquet about poetry in which he says, basically, that he thinks the act of perfecting the poem (after the poem has been roughly indited, finally making it accessible as a thing that is meant to be enjoyed and experienced by other people, and which will re-create in them what he calls the sense of "magnificent disarray" which the poet felt) is an act which necessarily impoverishes somewhat the experience or the emotion that the poem was trying to embody. To what extent do you think that is true?

Strand: Well, I was going to say that it is not necessarily true. It depends on your habits, it would seem to me. You take that initial emotion, or whatever it is that you want to create in the poem when you first sit down to write the poem, and to say that that is the one thing that must be preserved, and what comes out first is going to be closest to that is one way of solving the problem of writing a poem, it seems to me. I myself feel that I'm never sure about what it is that I'm talking about at the beginning. I mean I have a rough idea and maybe a few images or a word, or just a mad desire to sit down and write; and in the process of writing, over an extended period of time—not only one sitting, but perhaps a couple of days or a few weeks—I suddenly get a clear sense of what it is that I'm headed toward . . . and maybe not such a clear sense, maybe just enough sense so that I can direct my, my procedure, you know. I have, when I sit, written very quickly, and found it impossible to improve on what I've done, and I consider myself, in those cases, very lucky. It certainly saves a lot of work.

Interviewer: Yes, but it's unusual.

Strand: I'm very—well, I think anyone who rewrites a poem or goes back and rearranges it, even if they do it a little, is saying that the poem can be improved. And what's the difference, once you give yourself that much leeway? (And jesus! I think anybody would. Anybody who's written a poem has something that they might change or improve.) Why quibble about, say, spending 10 more hours or 20 more hours improving?

Interviewer: Or, as in Yeats' case, years.

Strand: Years, yes. Then you're saying that if you can improve it at all the original thing wasn't that holy and maybe it wasn't as perfect an indication of the emotional life that went into it. It's very lucky that you get that one-to-one relationship between what's done and what was intended. ⟨. . .⟩

Interviewer: ⟨. . .⟩ Let me ask you about, since we're doing this, about your habits as a writer. Do you go at it everyday?

Strand: No. Oh, I used to. I used to be a compulsive worker. I couldn't sleep at night unless I put in my two or three hours of writing poetry. It's something I learned from my first teacher at Antioch College, Nolan Miller. He said you have to write two or three hours a day if you're going to be a writer. And I did, my first year at Antioch, when I thought I would be a writer. And then when I was told I would never be a writer (by other members of the Antioch English Department), I gave up. And later on when I went to Yale, I started putting in those hours again.

Interviewer: Do you now?

Strand: No. It's, it's—when I was writing when I lived in Iowa City and was teaching at the Workshop, I would write every day—maybe three hours, maybe one, but everyday, because I had a little study and it was quiet. I could get away and do that. But in the last few years, I only sit down and write when I feel like it. I write more quickly than I ever have, spend fewer hours on any poem, but I end up writing about as much.

Interviewer: Don't you have the sense, though, that you are doing the same work, now, walking around, as it were . . . a lot of it that you were doing sitting down? Do you think that a sense of the "profession of writing" being a compeller to turn out a certain amount of work is—leaving yourself out now for a minute—destructive of other poets, or of the quality of their work. Or that it is contributing to bad habits or a bad sense of objectivity?

Strand: You mean the need to get poems written?

Interviewer: Yes.

Strand: Well, what would be the conditions under which one would have to write? For publication? In other words, a University demands that their poet publish a certain amount, and he feels he has to?

Interviewer: I'm thinking even of a maybe subtler pressure than that. Maybe just the sense that a person, you know, has arrived middling young, ah, to some stature . . .

Strand: And he doesn't want to fall into obscurity?

Interviewer: Yes, and, well, people are saying, you know, "You write, and you have to get out this other book, this next book." One of the things I admire about your poetry very much, and I think that this is simply objectively true, is you have a higher proportion of successful, good poems among your published body of work than most poets.

Strand: Well, that's sweet of you to say. But, I'm very guarded. I mean, that's a very sensitive point. I publish more poems in magazines than eventually are included in my books. I do throw out a number because I think I've made mistakes in them, and I believe a book is important . . .

Interviewer: As a total entity?

Strand: Yeah. It's something that's going to be around for awhile, and it's something that other people have to live with, and it should represent the best that I can give them. If I just thought, "Well, whatever I do is good and they just have to take it or leave it . . . " There are a lot of young poets that publish, I think, far too much. But I don't know what the reasons are. I don't believe it's because they want to be "the most published poet in America." I wouldn't ascribe those motives. I think it's that some people are compulsive writers, and do a lot of it, and it's easy for them to publish. Everybody wants them to publish their poems so they become less discriminating. Now, I know that someone like Charlie Simic, who's a friend of mine, is very careful about what eventually comes out, and we both have poems that we sort of work on and work on and we like the fact that they remain private for a long time. And my feeling is that for me, in recent years, magazine publication's much less important. I mean, I've never written enough so that I would ever flood all the magazines in America at any one time, so I don't know what that feels like. But I do know that having a book is a distinctly different feeling. There's something about 2 years or 3 years or 4 years of work gathered together. And a book is also a way of putting a whole bunch of poems out of mind so that you have a sense you're beginning again. It's a bigger sense of beginning again than when you finish one poem and begin another. I, for one, work on several poems simultaneously—and I never have the sense that I'm finished, except when I have a book.

JESSE STUART

1907–1984

Jesse Hilton Stuart was born on August 8, 1907, in W-Hollow, near Riverton, Greenup County, Kentucky. The son of a tenant farmer, he was educated at Lincoln Memorial University (B.A., 1929), Vanderbilt University (1931–32), and Peabody College. After working with a circus, and as a farmer, newspaper editor, and steel mill laborer, Stuart taught school for twenty years, and for a time served as superintendent of schools in Greenup County. Under the auspices of the State Department's Bureau of Educational and Cultural Affairs and later the U.S. Information Service, Stuart traveled widely throughout the world as a lecturer on American literature beginning in the 1960s. Stuart married Naomi Dean Norris in 1939; they had one child.

Stuart's first published book, a collection of sonnets entitled *Man with a Bull-Tongue Plow*, appeared in 1934 and brought Stuart a reputation as a gifted regional writer. More than fifty volumes of poetry, novels, short stories, and children's works followed; the best-known are the novel *Taps for Private Tussie* (1943), the poetry collection *The World of Jesse Stuart* (1975), the short-story collections *Men of the Mountains* (1941), *Tales from the Plum Grove Hills* (1946), and *My Hand Has a Voice* (1966), and the autobiographical accounts *Beyond Dark Hills* (1938), *The Thread That Runs So True* (1949), and *The Year of My Rebirth* (1956).

Stuart, who has been called "the chronicler of Appalachia" and "the American Robert Burns," was named the poet laureate of Kentucky in 1954. He died after a long illness on February 17, 1984, in Ironton, Ohio.

EVERETTA LOVE BLAIR
From "Conclusion"
Jesse Stuart: His Life and Works
1967, pp. 246–65

What will be Jesse Stuart's place in literature? As Stuart himself reiterates from the lecture platform, "Time will be the great critic. Only Time can give the answer to the question of what will endure."[1] This writer predicts, however, that scholars and general readers in a future age will be searching for the writers of the movement forming a stubborn countertrend to the critical strictures, depersonalization, and the objective formalism of our time, much as the romanticists symbolized a rebellious force against neoclassicism in the eighteenth century.

In the vanguard of today's dynamic and individualistic writers who protest against the prevailing school of "new criticism," obscurantism, and objectivity is Jesse Stuart, yet he may not be placed with any group or cult. He is an "independent." He is *sui generis*.

"A marvelous phenomenon," Donald Davidson characterized Stuart, in his essay, "Still Rebels, Still Yankees."[2]

Editor and critic Frederic A. Birmingham, meeting the young author, soon after Stuart's first books had brought him fame, wrote enthusiastically: "Jesse Stuart, a queer sport (as biologists use the term, meaning a deviation from the species, a mutation), a natural-born writer, produced as by a miracle out of the illiterates of backwoods Kentucky, who will make his mark indelibly in the literature of the day—a volcano of energy, pouring out pages and pages of manuscript, as Thomas Wolfe did. . . . "[3]

Jesse Stuart's contribution to contemporary literature, and, if one may predict, his contribution to literature of the ages, is his strong individuality, which has made itself felt in defiance of the prevailing current of his era for aesthetic distance, for objectivity in writing. Stuart opposes these tenets with simplicity and the highly personal.

This determination to write in his own way, to be himself, took possession of Stuart when he first returned to his mountain home, after his adventures in the steel mills and his grueling days of work in obtaining a college education. Revisiting the pastures and woods where he had found time between chores and hunting to read the poetry of Robert Burns and dream of becoming a Burns of his Kentucky hills, he found his nostalgia overlaid with a new confidence in his own powers. As he expressed it in *Beyond Dark Hills*: "I didn't want to write like Burns now. I wanted to write like myself. I wanted to be myself. I didn't want to be a tree like another tree in the forest. I wanted to be a shoe-make with a little different color of leaves, a different kind of bark and different arrangement of limbs, so when the wind whipped through my body, I would sing a different song to my brother shoe-makes. I wanted to be different, not for the sake of being different but being different for something."[4]

Poetically, he defined his creed of independence in Sonnet 200 of *Man with a Bull-Tongue Plow*:

I cannot sing tunes that great men have sung.
I cannot follow roads great men have gone,
I am not here to sing the songs they've sung,
I think I'm here to make a road my own.
I shall go forth not knowing where I go.
I shall go forth and I shall go alone.
The road I'll travel on is mud, I know.
But it's a road I can call my own.
The stars and moon and sun will give me light.
The winds will whisper songs I love to hear;
Oak leaves will make for me a bed at night,
And dawn will break to find me lying here.
The winey sunlight of another day
Will find me plodding on my muddy way.

Through twenty-eight books, he has held with integrity to his guiding principle of individualism, and, in both poetry and prose, he has maintained, with equal fidelity, his twin principle of close communion with Nature.

Certainly, in looking back upon Jesse Stuart's full and dramatic life which has been reflected in his works, and upon considering Stuart's prodigious contribution in the fields of poetry, the short story, and the novel, as well as his contribution of an influential book and of innumerable articles in the field of education, it would seem clear that to confine him merely to the category of the regional writer of frontier-type humor is to be not only shortsighted, but dogmatic.

⟨. . .⟩ Jesse Stuart has made his Kentucky world believable, not only to his readers in other parts of America, but also to an ever-increasing number of readers in lands around the world. He has portrayed with deep faithfulness the life of his circumscribed region, his microcosm in the mountains, where the people live in close affinity with the land, governed by the cycle of the seasons and clinging to the simple pieties of their pioneer ancestors—superstitious religious faith, love of country, respect for the past, above all loyalty to family. In portraying his people, he has struck a deep understanding chord in many readers of other countries, and according to critics whose opinions have been cited in this work, has gone far beyond the realm of the regional to attain universality.

Jesse Stuart's conception of his role as a bardic poet, who would speak not only for the people of his region, but also for the common heart of mankind, is well stated in his concluding lines of Sonnet 3 in *Man with a Bull-Tongue Plow:*

> I speak of men that live in my lifetime,
> And I speak of the men of yesterday.
> I do not care to know if this is art—
> These common words born in a common heart.

Faults of construction, faults of diction, a tendency at times, in both poetry and prose, to overwork the vernacular, and the impression given by the author at times that, in his eagerness, he is overemphasizing, overstating, are weaknesses of Stuart's craftsmanship that have been pointed out by some critics noted in this work. But these critics have, as a rule, recognized the qualities of originality, of elemental strength and simplicity, and of an innate love of humanity, which give to Stuart's works a universal or cosmic meaning, and for which they have been willing to forgive weaknesses of execution.

Other critics noted have disputed the accusation of "carelessness," and have insisted that in Jesse Stuart's "rambling" and "loquacious" characterizations, there is "artful artlessness," a most careful attention to architectonics to portray a subject which will have archetypal meaning for his readers.

The Tussies and the Hammertights are archetypes of the lazy, shiftless people of the world. Jesse Stuart's father and mother are the opposing types, the hard workers, the God-fearing, and the ambitious. Mitch Stuart, Jesse's grandfather, is the archetype of the fighter. Uncle Jeff is the natural man harnessed to a machine, and finally beaten by the machine, the railroad, to which he has been a slave. Old Op, of *The Good Spirit of Laurel Ridge*, is natural man who refuses to be beaten by the Machine Age, who defies the threat of the atom bomb and clings to his hills and his life of peace. Alec, of "Alec's Cabin," one of Stuart's most poignant short stories, is man engulfed in primordial loneliness, seeking identity and a home in the place where he had once known happiness.

In the summation of Jesse Stuart, the point may be clearly made that he is both realist and romanticist in his depiction of and his interpretation of life, both in his poetry and in his prose. In the midst of his most lyrical descriptions of Nature and her beauties as a backdrop of action for a story, he may create a brutal caricature of a human being or set a scene of ugliness so powerful in its realism that it is shattering to the sensibilities of the readers.

This preoccupation with life as a paradox, with the juxtaposition of the cruel and the beautiful, the evil and the good, places Stuart in the tradition of such a writer as Thomas Wolfe and in the interpretations of the South held by Wolfe. In commenting upon Wolfe's "linguistic combination—the combination of concrete detail, accurate speech, and incantatory rhetorical extravagance," as associated with something in the tradition of Southern culture, critic C. Hugh Holman says: "Wolfe likewise shares the Southerner's willingness to accept and find delight in paradox . . . paradoxes bother Southerners less than they would bother their Northern neighbors, for while they hunger for order and are moved by a rage for tradition, they can at the same time accept instability as a permanent aspect of human existence, and the unresolved contradiction as a part of man's condition."[5]

Though this acceptance of the paradoxical in life may be inherent in Jesse Stuart as a Southern writer, it has a deep source, too, in the opinion of the writer, in the avid study which Stuart has made from his boyhood days of the life and works of his literary idol, Robert Burns. Along with Burns' love lyrics and Scottish songs, there were such bitter satirical poems as "Holy Willie's Prayer" and "Address to the Unco Guid," so that for Stuart, in his Kentucky hills, with inheritance from his Scottish ancestors of both *joie de vivre* and a stern Calvinistic conscience, it was natural to follow the example of Burns and mix the lyrical with searing social criticism and a moral doctrine.

The romantic realist, or realistic romanticist, George Crabbe, is another of Jesse Stuart's spiritual forebears, with his "Parish Register" and "The Village," revealing portrayals of the seamy side of life in contrast with the beauty of the pastoral.

Man with a Bull-Tongue Plow is a rivulet of poetry, containing, in the main, sonnets which are a paean to Nature. In the midst of the highest incantational verse, however, there appear such rugged denunciations in the vernacular as No. 380:

TO TOODLE WORMLAKE

> You are a belly-acher with a rope
> Tied round your neck where you can eat the grass;
> A belly-acher with a mental scope
> Of black-ants and your back is streaked with brass.
> Your heart is brass; your tongue is cankered brass.
> And round the radius of your pasture rope
> Your tongue lolls out—you eat and laze and mope.
> Do people fail to watch you when they pass?
> Lakewood: You are their politician boar.
> The stems of grass are dollars that you flank
> Down your intestinal channel with a roar;
> You are a liar, hypocrite and crank.
> When grass gets short they set and stake your chain;
> Gives you the chance to eat high grass again.

Equally striking contrasts in tone and diction may be noted throughout Jesse Stuart's autobiographical writing and his works of fiction. The most realistic passages may be followed by pure poetic prose, as in this passage (after a night service at the Plum Grove Church):

> On the outside of the house there would be a yellow moon up in the sky and a cold white glitter of thousands of summer stars. There would be moonlight on the hay fields and the tasseled corn. And there would be darkness in the little patches of oak trees. The air would be filled with the voices of frogs, katydids, whippoorwills and beetles. And there would be the white slabs gleaming in the moonlight

> where hundreds of dead lie buried on Plum Grove Hill.[6]

Here the prose is rhythmic, and the romanticist's preoccupation with the natural scene is evidenced—a scene which projects an atmosphere of remoteness, of death, in the midst of the animate voices of the poet's hill country churchyard. There is the romanticist's awareness of two time levels, the past and the present, which is found throughout Jesse Stuart's writing. Time past and time present, in dramatic continuity, constitute the theme of No. 484 in *Man with a Bull-Tongue Plow* as Tish Meadows speaks:

> I sleep beneath the earth-scarred battle ground;
> The English and the Indians were my foe.
> Now I have slept here many years below,
> Where wind and water and the trees make sound.
> America goes on because I sleep
> And others sleep—we died to make her go.
> Corn will grow over us and ripen brown;
> Wheat will grow over us year after year;
> Each year a coat of new leaves will drift down;
> Farmers will pass, not knowing who sleeps here.
> What does it matter who is sleeping here?
> For death is death just anyway we die;
> And when we died, we were fighting for
> The land you keep today—something to have;
> America, for you we took the grave!

Contrast these inspirational lines and their evocation of the romance of the past, with the sharp, primitive power of a paragraph from an early Stuart short story, "Kentucky Hill Dance":

> Outside in the yard one can hear the licks struck within the giant century-old log house. One can hear the cries and the curses of the men and the finer cries of the women. One can see the tall, strong and brown-skinnd mountain girls (skin made brown by working in the corn fields and the tobacco fields) come pouring out at the doors. And a voice among them is higher than the rest: "They got that old rot-gut down to Phil Conley's. I knowed what was going to happen all the time. This is the way of all our dances any more. We just can't have them for rot-gut whisky. We can't have church. We can't have anything."[7]

Rarely are the writings of Jesse Stuart didactic, it must be reiterated. His criticisms are implicit. They are expressed most vividly in his selection of material. Once he has selected his area for criticism, he will present his subjct in relentless documentation of detail to create reality. But he will not consciously point a moral, as a rule. He knows his region, and he loves and understands his characters, even the most reprehensible ones. He understands their human failings at the same time that he is exposing them.

Only in his novel *Foretaste of Glory*, with its dramatic plot of a false Doomsday alarm, does he lash out at hypocrites much in the manner of Burns in the "Unco Guid." In this work, he seems to depart from the subjectiveness that one feels in his other works, his deep affinity with his characters.

In *The Thread That Runs So True*, which, on the human level of *The Hoosier Schoolmaster*, has been hailed as a classic of American life, Jesse Stuart has direct and bitter criticism for the enemies of the welfare of schoolteachers and of their pupils, such enemies as the men in a Kentucky county who allowed four rural schools to remain closed because of lack of appropriations. "O hypocritical, shortsighted, ignorant politicians, living in the middle of this twentieth century. . . ." he flayed them.

It is the cause of the schoolteaching profession and the correction of inequities between urban and rural school systems which brings out the unequivocal and fearless crusader in Jesse Stuart. 〈. . .〉 *The Thread That Runs So True* is considered to be one of the most powerful American social documents of our time. Appearing as it does, in excerpts, in high school English textbooks, it may also be considered to be one of the most inspirational and best-known books by a contemporary author for the youth of America.

There is in Jesse Stuart a deep dichotomy, which has been reflected in his works and in his ambivalent view of life, embracing both the stern Calvinistic doctrine of hard work and the traditionally pious God-fearing attitude of his ancestors, along with the direct approach to God of the transcendentalist. God, man, and Nature in one understanding, all-embracing whole permeate the lyrical poetry and the subjective prose of Stuart. In his incantational poetry, Jesse Stuart seems akin to Wordsworth and Whitman, with their pantheistic worship of Nature, and is even akin to Hesiod.[8] Stuart is in sharp contrast to contemporary writers who affect a mystique of the soil. As an actual tiller of the soil, he is especially akin to Hesiod and Robert Burns, whose poetry of unrestrained joy in communion with Nature came from close, daily contact with earth.

"O Gods of Storm, best savage-white and cold!" Stuart intones in *Album of Destiny*, and, in the same sonnet sequence, "Give trees, you ancient Gods, new blood for veins"; "O Sun of gold, ride up with golden light"; "Sing out, you mighty organs of the wind!"

In the poem, "Impressions," in *Hold April*, Jesse Stuart concludes with the line, "Nature. You make; you make; Come often rain!" In the same volume, in "Back Where I Belong," written after recovery from his near-fatal heart attack, the poet writes, in the deep piety of his forefathers,

> I thank God that he granted my stay here
> To count the many songs in winds that blow.

The dichotomy which exists in Stuart is recognized by him in what he calls the "dreamer-doer" approach to life. Loving the solitude and communion with nature in his "ivory tower" in the hills, he has, at the same time, an intense love of people, a restless desire to be with them, for he gets material for his stories from life, and he has the profound feeling, too, that the writer has an obligation to society, to make his contribution toward solving the problems of the day. Stuart does not cling to his ivory tower, then, but comes to grips with the hard realities of our times, and, in his works of social criticism, reflects the vital and wholehearted attention he has given to his areas of interest, particularly the field of education.

This moral doctrine of hard work and of social awareness in the life and works of Jesse Stuart was predicted by one of Stuart's favorite professors at Vanderbilt University, Dr. Edwin Mims, in whose class in Victorian literature the young Kentuckian developed a great admiration for Carlyle. Dr. Mims reviewed Stuart's 1958 short-story collection *Ploughshare in Heaven* for the *Nashville Tennessean*, and maintained that the collection showed a "new maturity" in its author, "a broader scope, a new outlook for his powers." He concluded:

> One wonders just what course the writing of Jesse Stuart will take. He will still farm, he will still teach school, but will he, like so many of his predecessors, lose his creative power? Or will he sound the trumpet of a larger faith than he has expressed in his earlier volumes? Not in the mood of the 'Spoon River

Anthology' or of 'A Shropshire Lad,' which is so often expressed in his early poetry and prose, but in the mood of Carlyle when he wrote 'The Everlasting Yea,' he may lead us out of the confusion and chaos of the present time. Let the trumpet sound![9]

As Stuart continues to write poetry and prose imbued with the fundamental elements of strength and of optimism which were native to the American character of pioneer days, Dr. Mims might well say that Stuart has attained the peace of Carlyle's "Everlasting Yea" though recognizing and recording with realism the brutalities and weaknesses of life and meeting headlong the challenges of today. 〈. . .〉

It is interesting to note the following passage from Donald Davidson, in a letter to the writer, dated March 22, 1967, in relation to Stuart as a short-story writer, "I have been thinking recently that Jesse is the only American short story writer who could be said to be something of an American 'Chekhov'. There's much of the same spirit and range of subjects and characters that leap gustily right out of life, and a similar abundance, almost a profligacy, of creativeness. Jesse is perhaps less under literary influences than the Russian, and less melancholy—though Chekhov started his career with humorous skits and bits."[10]

One might well draw close parallels, too, between Sholokhov's *And Quiet Flows the Don* and some of Jesse Stuart's works, in the opinion of this writer, with the Nobel winner's deep affinity for his region, the land and the people, the strong poetic style, and the sharp, brutal, and tender characterizations. The Big Sandy and the Little Sandy, of the Kentucky hills, invoke a feeling of the timelessness of the Don, though in "the Stuart country" of America, a region most often compared with the Highlands of Scotland. This would seem to be a potent argument for the universality of Stuart, attained through strong regionalism. 〈. . .〉

Jesse Stuart's writing carries the flavor of authenticity because of his innate love for his region. He has believed his destiny to lie there with his own people, and he has spent the greater part of his life there, speaking with bardic fervor for his region. Tragedy, as well as the drama, which permeates the lives of the people who live close to the soil, in addition to the natural beauties of the hills, have been depicted vividly in Stuart's poetry and poetic prose. With piety and a lingering nostalgia for the past, he has, at the same time, exhibited a concern for the future of his region and has led his people in the ways of progress.

He has been the historian for the change in his region from an isolated pocket in the hills off the main road of civilization, where the people clung stubbornly to the eighteenth-century customs and beliefs of their ancestors, to an area now with good roads, scientific farming methods, consolidated schools, television, bookmobiles, and other symbols of modernization. Writing always with deep respect for the best of the past, Stuart has exhibited concern for the problems of the present, particularly in the equalization of educational opportunities in remote areas of America, such as his native region. This humanity expressed in the works of Stuart, which has formed a strong phase of his writing, along with his lyrical portrayals of the life lived close to the soil and the sincerity with which the author invests his words, is, perhaps, the most important reason for the feeling of kinship with the author which his empathic readers enjoy, whatever their nationalities.

Notes

1. Lecture at the University of South Carolina, March 23, 1960, and lecture at Vanderbilt University Literary Symposium, April 22, 1959.
2. Donald Davidson, *Still Rebels, Still Yankees and Other Essays* (Baton Rouge: Louisiana State University Press, 1957), 166.
3. Frederic A. Birmingham, *The Writer's Craft* (New York: Hawthorne Books, Inc., 1958), 174.
4. Jesse Stuart, *Beyond Dark Hills* (New York: E. P. Dutton, 1938), 229.
5. C. Hugh Holman, "Thomas Wolfe and the South," *South*, eds. Louis D. Rubin, Jr., and Robert D. Jacobs (Garden City, New York: Doubleday and Co., Inc., 1961), 189.
6. *Beyond Dark Hills*, 87.
7. "Kentucky Hill Dance," *The New Republic*, LXXIX (May 16, 1934), 15.
8. At the Award ceremony held by the Academy of American Poets in New York for Jesse Stuart in 1961, Mr. Stephen Xydos, of Columbia University's faculty, a native of Greece and member of the Academy's Advisory Board, remarked to the writer about the affinity between Stuart and the ancient Greek poets.
9. Sept. 28, 1958.
10. Quoted by permission.

H. EDWARD RICHARDSON

From "Stuart Country: The Man-Artist and the Myth"

Jesse Stuart: Essays on His Work

eds. J. R. LeMaster and Mary Washington Clarke

1977, pp. 5–10

That evening after dinner, we sat around the fireplace in the main room under the original low beams of the Stuart home, described in the author's *Thread That Runs So True*. "How old is this house?"

He quickly pointed beyond my shoulder as he said: "There was a man born over there in the corner behind you in 1840. This is the oldest part of the house. It was a cabin once." The flames flickered shadowy orange patterns around the room. I leaned closer to the fire, but I was not as close as Stuart. There were things I wanted to ask him.

We had corresponded while he was in Greece that summer of 1966. I had read *Taps for Private Tussie, Hie to the Hunters, Man with a Bull-Tongue Plow, Harvest of Youth, The Year of My Rebirth*, and many of the stories, some of them masterpieces of the genre like "Dawn of Remembered Spring," "Split Cherry Tree," "A Walk in the Moon Shadows," "The News Comes to Still Hollow," "Corbie," and "Here." During this period of reading and rereading, I had begun to reconsider Stuart's literary reputation as my colleagues had reflected it, often in vague terms declaring their lack of familiarity with his production. The remarks I heard in California had been kinder and more openly curious than they had been in mid-America.

Closer to home, it was to be understood that Stuart was a talented "primitivist" who, as the *Sewanee Review* people contended, "wrote too much." By mid-century, the fact that a long tradition of American writers—from Charles Brockden Brown, Cooper, and Melville to Whitman, Twain, Dreiser, and Sherwood Anderson—had a lot of skim milk in their cream separators was no longer relevant.

Stuart's dedication to his art was open to question: he had dissipated his energies as a public school superintendent and "wasted time meddling in politics." Where was his sense of métier? He was unquestionably talented, a colorful, voluble individualist who went his own way, but his writing unfortunately lacked the ironistic devices and intellectual subtleties so dear to the influential new critical voices. Although Stuart practiced what the Agrarians at Vanderbilt preached, one of their brightest young scholar-critics back in the 1930s had, with a snap of his fingers, dismissed Stuart's achievement and literary potential: "Why, he's just a big country boy."

The "big country boy" had worked his way nearly through his graduate program at Vanderbilt as a janitor, sweeping floors at night and sleeping in his spare time, only to see his hopes, already dashed by fatigue, poverty, and rigid academic requirements that threatened his grade-point standing, vanish in the flames of a dormitory fire that consumed his thesis on John Fox, Jr. Finding the intellectualized God-seeking among Agrarians as foolish as the theorizing on nature by academicians in the rarefied atmosphere of libraries and classrooms, the twenty-five-year-old genius heeded the advice of such professor-writers as Gordon Wilson, Harry Harrison Kroll, and Donald Davidson, and returned to his native ground. A young academic exile in rebellion, he was characteristically unsilent, articulate:

> I learned it did not take a Ph.D.
> To walk between the handles of a plow.
> . . .
> I found the Saintly Saints were very Devils
> Among whom were some graduated knaves,
> Living behind cord-wood stacks of lies
> And snooping round in search of paradise.[1]

My reading of *Beyond Dark Hills* confirmed my growing impression that Stuart was more than a local colorist. He was a contemporary writer of greater substance to my age than Hamlin Garland or Bret Harte had been to theirs. Here at last, under the charm of his regionalism and the uneven and sometimes impromptu quality of his work, were the deeps of archetypal and mythopoeic patterns: the earth as mother, father, provider; water images unfolding the evolution of primordial man; an abundance of folklore, myths, and tall tales; recurring allegories and symbols from the racial unconscious of mankind; fears and fantasies, mysticism and superstition emerging in nature images; and man in conflict with his own kind.

Now as we sat in the room that had heard an infant's birth cry in 1840, I was thinking of the chapter in *Beyond Dark Hills* called "Cool Memories of Steel." The very title echoes those consciously employed devices of synesthesia and oxymoron through which the French Symbolists sought to achieve a power of expression that the English Romantics had reached intuitively. The chapter records Stuart's work in the steel mills of Ohio, where the dirt is "black," made intimate through tactile and gustatory images of a thirty-minute lunch break when he rushed to eat at his boardinghouse: "Many times when I lifted a slice of white bread from the plate, my fingerprints were left on it. That did not matter. I ate my fingerprints with the bread." A hungry life force vibrates through these pages. I thought too about the force that drove Stuart to write so abundantly, that had driven him back to life after the nearly fatal heart attack in 1954, and I remembered his subsequent affirmation of life—"Because no man loves life so much as he who comes back from death." Again, he had written me one night after he had done three stories, "My mind is pregnant and I cannot sleep." Now he leaned forward, picked up a poker, and stirred the fire with it. He added an apple log and looked at me as he sat down.

"Tell me about *Beyond Dark Hills*," I asked. "Just when did you write it?"

"Let's see. It and the poems for *Man with a Bull-Tongue Plow* were written within twelve months of one another. In the summer of 1931 I raised a crop of tobacco on that round knoll we saw today, borrowed $300, and reached Vanderbilt with $130 in September" (he had lent his father the rest for the farm). "I handed the book in to Mims at the end of the spring semester in 1932—got a C in the course and couldn't get my degree, had to have a *B* average." The parataxis was typical of Stuart's conversation. "Then I came home in the summer and farmed. *Man with a Bull-Tongue Plow* was finished before March 1933." He looked around at something beyond the wall and nodded a direction. "The first poem was done up the hollow here on a sled by the old wash kettle where my mother did her clothes. The spring water was soft and sweet there. When I finished the poems I had 703 in a stack. I tied it up in a hand towel and put it in my room upstairs."

"But the poems didn't stay there."

"No, I sent some off to the *Virginia Quarterly Review*, bought the stamps with Mom's butter and egg money." He laughed now, thinking of it. "And *they sold!* They wanted *more*. Sent 'em to the old *American Mercury* and to *Poetry*. Then Dutton's editor wanted to know if I had any more poems like those in the *Virginia Quarterly*. I told him I had 703. They took the book in 1934."

The apple log hissed and popped. "You know, you treat many subjects in *Beyond Dark Hills*." Stuart nodded as I began to list them—"Love, revenge, remorse, pity, anger, friendship, family loyalty, craftiness, irony, superstition, nature, internal conflicts, the journey of a young man to find himself, religion including God and myth—but through it all runs the theme of the earth, this country you write so much about, the oaks and pines and what you call 'lonesome water'—and the love of your family."

Stuart's eyes were wide and round as he spoke into my face, "They're all in there."

"Tell me, how did you get the title for the book?"

"I got the title when I was coming up from Portsmouth, Ohio, back to Greenup. At the bend of the river just before you get to Greenup you can see all of Seaton Ridge here spread out before you. I looked up and saw the hills against the sky and they looked dark. I thought, 'Beyond those dark hills is my home.' *Beyond—Dark—Hills*. This is how I got that title."

"Could you put into words how you developed this love for the land, your country here?"

He looked at the fire, pursed his lips, and scratched his head. His hair is thick and iron-gray. Then, as he began to talk, he was up on the edge of his chair, and I wondered why the fire didn't burn his face. "You know, the land never fed you as it has fed me. When the land fed all these people long ago, it was different. We loved it and needed it. I always loved to rub the tree, touch its bark. My father loved the land; it is father to me."

"What is your earliest memory of the land?"

"The hills. It has always been the land—wild plums, poplar trees, redbirds, mules, geese. I hunted eggs down the creek; our chickens laid eggs away from the chicken house—they laid them under the ferns and rock-cliffs, in hollow logs and stumps and the pawpaw groves." He paused. "And the beauty of the land, the four seasons—autumn first, the brown hills of autumn—" and as if it were a sudden new realization, he said, "*I was born in August. . . .*"

When I asked him about the closeness of his family, he named off the seven Stuart brothers and sisters, both living and dead, including himself in the list: "Sophia, 1903; Jesse, 1907; Herbert, 1909–1918; Mary, 1912; James, 1915; Martin, 1918–1918; Glennis, 1921. The thing that made our family click was that closeness you said, how we would sit around the table at dinner and talk about the day's happenings; it was a pleasure." Stuart smiled like a boy with a Christmas box opening in front of him. "This family always met and decided what took place, usually around that table—I have it outside where I write in the warm weather now in the smokehouse. We were a strong unit and the older sister led us. If someone did something to us, he had the others to account to." His jaw tightened. "Someone said something about one of my sisters—I was standing in the yard waiting for him. It is a strong clannish family."

"Why did you write *Beyond Dark Hills?* Mims wanted only an 18-page paper, I believe, a short autobiography. You handed in about 300 pages."

Stuart nodded. "That's right, but I didn't think of it as a book. I thought writing was for the birds. I wanted to tell Mims two things: *one*, who I was; and *two*, how I got to Vanderbilt."

"Well, there are spiritual elements in *Beyond Dark Hills*, too. You call one chapter 'God and the Evening Sky,' associating God with nature. Would you mind telling me about your spiritual concepts?"

The tone of Stuart's voice was at once humble and direct: "I feel that I am *beyond* members in my own church. Maybe that isn't right, but that's the way I feel. I don't mean to downrate anybody. I think Martin Luther got beyond his church; I think people can rise *beyond* the church." He rubbed his shoe against the edge of the hearth. Self-chidingly, he spoke, "*I try my best to be dogmatic, but I can't be!* [John Sherman] Cooper is *beyond* politics; he can't follow the party. You don't think of Whitman as a Quaker." Now he mused aloud, "Look at Gandhi, Schweitzer, Emerson. They all got *beyond* their churches. Now, about nature, God created that, I believe that. I think of Jesse, stars, blue sky. It is God—I love the beauty in God."

"But not all of nature is beautiful, is it?"

"No, there is some ugliness, destructiveness, farmers know it." He straightened. "But man brings most of it on himself."

"Do you think that man is as much a part of nature as the plants and animals?"

"No," he asserted, "*higher* being," eliding words instead of syllables as he does in the fever of an idea. "The kingdom of God is within you, all men. Man can worship in nature, but he is *beyond* nature. Not all do. There are creators and destroyers in the world." He glanced sideways at the tops of the flames, then spoke the saddest words I had heard him say, "We have people who are not as good as a tree."

We talked on into the night, mostly about literature. He mentioned Thomas Wolfe and William Faulkner with admiration. He liked Hemingway's "novel on Spain, *For Whom the Bell Tolls*. There is flavor in the book." Fitzgerald was "a magnificent writer." He hitched up his chair, happily excited. "Good Lord, could that man write!" He expressed the belief that great fiction had to have "a sense of locale, people involved, a rounded sphere of the whole. Tolstoy. There is writing. Colossal! Thomas Hardy, John Steinbeck, Dickens. The sense of place, time, actual period. Aristotle said it, a great work has to lead out the soul, you've got to start *somewhere*. You've got to write from the stump or it's vagary. Good writing excites, entertains, may make people better." He paused and opened his hands, palms upward. "Good writing lifts you out to the stars."

I could not resist the question: "Is this why you write?"

"I have to write," he shot back. "*Writing chose me.*"

Notes

1. *Man with a Bull-Tongue Plow*, new rev. ed. (New York: E. P. Dutton, 1959), p. 314.

THEODORE STURGEON

1918–1985

Theodore Sturgeon was born Edward Hamilton Waldo on February 26, 1918, to Edward and Christine (née Hamilton) Waldo on Staten Island, New York. Sturgeon's parents were divorced in 1927. His mother remarried two years later, whereupon he was adopted by his stepfather and legally changed his name to Theodore Hamilton Sturgeon. He attended Overbrook High School in Philadelphia, where an early enthusiasm for gymnastics was cut short by a bout of rheumatic fever at the age of fifteen.

After spending three years on various jobs at sea, Sturgeon sold the first of more than forty stories to *McClure's* in 1937. He was persuaded by friends to try his hand writing science fiction in 1939. During the next two years Sturgeon sold more than a dozen short stories to the field's most influential editor, John W. Campbell, and quickly established himself as one of science fiction's most accomplished writers. His first collection, *Without Sorcery*, was published in 1948 to critical acclaim. Sturgeon's short stories continued to receive praise throughout his career; he published more than a dozen collections (among the more significant are *E Pluribus Unicorn*, 1953; *Caviar*, 1955; and *A Touch of Strange*, 1958), and won the Hugo and Nebula awards for his short story "Slow Sculpture" (1970).

Sturgeon's first novel, *The Dreaming Jewels*, was published in 1950 to mixed reviews. Its reputation has grown with time, however, because of its stylistic richness and its concern with themes that would become Sturgeon trademarks, particularly the creative imagination of children and the stifling of the individual by a stagnant and thoughtless society.

More Than Human (1953) was Sturgeon's breakthrough novel, and remains to the present day one of science fiction's most respected works. Its three connected novellas relate the growth to maturity of *homo gestalt*, humanity evolved to the state of integrated group consciousness. It was universally praised within the field, and was one of the first science fiction novels to receive significant critical notice outside the genre. Although none of Sturgeon's subsequent novels had the immediate impact of *More Than Human*, they all received more praise than criticism, and remain touchstones for the science fiction field. The most significant are *The Cosmic Rape* (1958), *Venus Plus X* (1960), and *Some of Your Blood* (1961).

During the 1960s Sturgeon wrote little, but in 1971 a collection of short stories, *Sturgeon Is Alive and Well . . .* , appeared. As one of the first writers of science fiction to place more emphasis on character development and stylistic concerns than on plot, and as one of the earliest to deal with controversial sexual themes, his permanent place in the field seems assured. After a long illness Sturgeon died on May 8, 1985, in Eugene, Oregon.

Theodore Sturgeon is a phenomenon out of Philadelphia, a yellow-eyed thing with a goatee, a mortician's voice, and Pan's original smile. He clashed with high school. He ran away to sea, took up nudism, ran a bulldozer, got married and unmarried, wrote music, advertising copy and fantasy, smoked cigarettes in a long holder, got married again, tinkered with gadgets. His biographical note in *More Than Human*, as wild as anything he's written, ends with this sentence:

> He lives with his wife and son, twelve-string guitar, and hot-rod panel truck in Rockland County, where he is at present working on an opera.

Now there you are; that's Sturgeon. *Damn* the man!

> The idiot lived in a black and gray world, punctuated by the white lightning of hunger and the flickering of fear. His clothes were old and many-windowed. Here peeped a shinbone, sharp as a cold chisel, and there in the torn coat were ribs like the fingers of a fist.

That's from the first paragraph of *More Than Human*, and it will do for a sample of the best Sturgeon yet. Or this from page 43, when a little girl named Janie has just walked out on her mother.

> Wima knew before she started that there wasn't any use looking, but something made her run to the hall closet and look in the top shelf. There wasn't anything up there but Christmas tree ornaments and they hadn't been touched in three years.

. . . My God, it's *all* like that, violins and stained glass and velvet and little needles in your throat. Even after the first reading, you can dip into this book anywhere and have to haul yourself out by the scruff. The *Galaxy* novella "Baby Is Three" is the middle section of it, and that's all it is; if you thought it was complete in itself when you read it, you'll never think so again after you've finished *More Than Human*. It's a single story that goes from here to there like a catenary arc, and hits one chord like the Last Trump when it gets there, and stops. There's nothing more to be said about it, except that it's the best and only book of its kind.

Sturgeon hasn't always had his big voice under the control he showed in *More Than Human* and "Saucer of Loneliness." He's been practicing, trying this and that, and along with the pure tones a lot of sad squawks have come out. (When a really good voice goes just a little off key, it's a hard thing to take.)

But Sturgeon's failures, some of them, are as triumphant as his successes; they made the successes. Sturgeon is the most accomplished technician this field has produced, bar nobody, not even Bradbury; and part of the reason is that he never stops working at it. He tried writing about each character in a story in a different meter once—iambs for one, trochees for another—a trick, not viable, but it taught him something about rhythm in prose. He has cold-bloodedly studied the things that make people angry, afraid, pitying, embarrassed, worshipful, and mortared them into his stories.

And for the last few years he has been earnestly taking love apart to see what makes it tick. Not what the word means on the cover of a pulp magazine, but love, all the different kinds there are or could be, working from the outside in. "It is fashionable to overlook the fact that the old-shoe lover *loves* loving old shoes." Some of the resulting stories have been as flat and unconvincing as others are triumphantly alive; but Sturgeon is learning, has learned more about the strongest theme in life or literature than anybody this side of Joyce Cary.

He writes about people first and other marvels second. More and more, the plots of his short stories are mere contrivances to let his characters expound themselves. "It Wasn't Syzygy," "The Sex Opposite" and "A Way of Thinking" are such stories: the people stand out from their background like Rubens figures that have strayed onto a Mondrian canvas: graphic evidence that Sturgeon, like Bradbury, long ago went as far as he could within the limitations of this field without breaking them.

For those who think they see an easy answer to the problem, here's a thought: Sturgeon *has* tried writing straight people-stories, without any fantasy in them at all. Two of them wound up in hard covers: but both were first published in science-fantasy magazines. "Hurricane Trio" evidently failed to sell in its original, stronger form; Sturgeon had to dilute it with space-opera to save it. "A Way Home" is not even remotely science fiction or fantasy: it saw print, undiluted, in *Amazing Stories*, but only God and Howard Browne know why.

This is laughable on the face of it, but it happens to be true: Cramped and constricted as it is, the science fiction field is one of the best of the very few paying markets for a serious short-story writer. The quality magazines publish a negligible quantity of fiction; slick short stories are as polished and as interchangeable as lukewarm-water faucets; the pulps are gone; the little magazines pay only in prestige. There are no easy answers.—DAMON KNIGHT, "The Vorpal Pen: Theodore Sturgeon," *In Search of Wonder*, 1967, pp. 114–16

JAMES BLISH (AS "WILLIAM ATHELING, JR.")
From "Caviar and Kisses: The Many Loves of Theodore Sturgeon" (1961)
More Issues at Hand

1970, pp. 68–78

One of the minor mysteries of Theodore Sturgeon's macrocosm is his hostility toward a popular and thoroughly competent story called "Microcosmic God." If you compliment the author on this yarn, he is likely to respond with the polite purr which is as close as he can usually come to a snarl. If you don't mention the subject, Sturgeon will probably bring it up himself.

It's a good story; why the antipathy? I don't propose to try to read the author's mind, which I regard as one of the major critical crimes; but looking back at "Microcosmic God" (1941) over the landscape of Sturgeon's long career, one can see that it is an atypical Sturgeon story in a number of ways. One of these differences lies in its central character, Kidder, who is—let us whisper it—a scientist maddened by power.

It's unlike any other story about a mad scientist you are ever likely to encounter, but its theme is about as close as Sturgeon has ever come to being conventional. It is characteristic of much of other writers' science fiction that its central figures tend to be great scientists, senators, galactic presidents, space-fleet admirals, interplanetary spies, and other wheelers-and-dealers, though very few of the authors involved have ever met so grand a man as their state assemblyman or even know his name. Sturgeon's work is not like this.

Sturgeon's characters, if assembled in one room, would make a marvelously motley crowd, but almost all of them would be people you would not look at twice in any crowd—not even if you knew who they were. A few bulldozer operators; a little girl disowned by her family (but how could you tell that?); a male clerk; a ragged outcast; a boarding-house peeping-Tom (but how would you know?); and so on. Ordinary, all of them—with the almost unique exceptions of Kidder, the mad scientist, and the anti-hero of "Mr. Costello, Hero," who bodies forth almost blindingly the author's positive and pure loathing for all wheelers-and-dealers.

This is not to say that any of these people is in the least ordinary in Sturgeon's hands. A good many of them are what most readers would regard as rather repellent characters, but Sturgeon almost always handles them with the love—not the forgiveness, which is another matter entirely—that is born of understanding.

This is, I repeat, a rare quality in science fiction, and of course a valuable one. And it leads us to another and even more important fact about Sturgeon's work: It is intensely personal.

Most writers who cling to some one form of specialized fiction—whether it be the detective story, the Western, or the slick story—do so, I have often suspected, because these more or less stereotyped forms do not require them to reveal themselves. As a good many other people have observed, any serious work of fiction is bound to be autobiographical at least in part. It was Thomas Wolfe who said that it would be hard to imagine a more autobiographical work than *Gulliver's Travels*—a startling choice of example at first encounter, but the more one mulls it over, the more just it seems. Category fiction requires no such tapping of the inner life. Science fiction in particular has often been criticized for its conventionality, and even more for the cold, cerebral atmosphere which its authors seem to prefer to breathe. Though these authors have as many idiosyncrasies of style as a porcupine has quills (unlike most reliable producers in other standard categories), the *emotional* tones of what they produce are virtually interchangeable.

Sturgeon's work is charged with highly personal emotion—so much so that it seems to embarrass his younger readers, who like science fiction precisely because it puts little stress on their own untried emotions. (And here it might be added that the emotional tone of "Microcosmic God" is pretty standard stuff for science fiction—which again makes it highly atypical Sturgeon.)

Kingsley Amis and others have also pointed to the undoubted fact that there is very little sex of any kind in most science fiction, and this fits nicely with my hypothesis that science-fiction authors cling to the genre because it doesn't require them to reveal themselves. For any author, writing about sex is at the beginning a hard hump (not "lump," please, printer) to get over, because it will reveal (or he thinks it will) a knowledge of matters previously supposed to be not proper, or perhaps even positively forbidden, depending upon his upbringing. That very first sex scene is almost impossible to write if what is really on your mind is, "Suppose Mom should read it?" I have the undocumentable suspicion that many science-fiction writers, including some of the major ones, have never gotten beyond this point in their development, and don't want to, either.

All of Sturgeon's major work is about love, sexual love emphatically included. He has so testified, but had he kept mum about the matter it would have been discovered anyhow; it is right there on the page. This, for Sturgeon, is far from a limited subject, for he has stretched the word to include nearly every imaginable form of human relationship. Here again I think he is probably always in danger of embarrassing a large part—the juveniles—of his audience; the rest of us are fortunate that, if he is aware of this danger, he evidently doesn't give a damn.

This is, as he himself has said, why he has written so much about complicated biological relationships involving three or more partners, most of which have technical names hard to find even in good unabridged dictionaries (e.g., syzygy, which doesn't appear even in Roland Wilbur Brown's magnificent *Composition of Scientific Words*). It is why, in recent years particularly, he has seemed so preoccupied with telepathy; it has nothing to do with the didactic madness on this subject which has dominated so much of the field (thanks mostly to John W. Campbell) since World War II, but instead reflects his larger preoccupation with all the possible forms of love relationships, even the most peculiar.[1] It is significantly different from the kind of telepathy one usually finds in such stories, too; in fact, what Sturgeon seems to be talking about is not telepathy at all, but something I am tempted to call telempathy—a barbarous word, but perhaps no worse a one than its model. Sturgeon's word for it is love, and a very good word it is.

Directly under this heading belongs Sturgeon's love affair with the English language, which has been as complicated, stormy and rewarding as any affair he has ever written about. He is a born experimenter, capable of the most outrageous excesses in search of precision and poetry; people who do not like puns, for example, are likely to find much Sturgeon text almost as offensive as late Joyce (and I am sorry for them). Nobody else in our microcosm could possibly have produced such a stylistic explosion as "To Here and the Easel," a novella based in language as well as in theme on Ariosto's 16th-century epic *Orlando Furioso*, because in fact nobody else would have seen that the subject couldn't have been handled any other way. (L. Sprague de Camp's and Fletcher Pratt's *The Castle of Iron* is also based on Ariosto, of course, but solely with comic intent and effect; the Sturgeon work, despite considerable lightness of touch and even some jokes, is primarily intensely serious.) And even Sturgeon's verbal excesses are his own; he does not call upon exotic or obsolete words for their own sakes, or otherwise the multitudinous seas incarnadine; he never says anything is ineffable or unspeakable, the very ideas embodied in those words being foreign to his artistic credo; he does not splash color on with a mop, or use the same colors for everything; and he does not say "partly rugose and partly squamose" when he means "partly rough and partly scaly."

This quality of freshness of language even when it is out of control—which is not often—is due primarily to the fact that Sturgeon is an intensely visual writer. His images come almost exclusively from what he sees, as Joyce's came almost exclusively from what he heard. (Sturgeon is a musician, as Joyce was, but his various attempts to *describe* music and its effects are all failures, reading at their worst like the kind of copy found on the jacket books of jazz LP's.) Readers who do not think in terms of visual images—a very large group, as the electroencephalographers have shown us; perhaps as many as half of us—are likely to be baffled by this, or at least put off. They will get along much better with a writer like Poul Anderson, who follows a deliberate policy of appealing to at least three senses in every scene. Sturgeon's extremes of visualization probably lie at the root of the rather common complaint that he is a "mannered" writer.

The charge as stated is untrue, for Sturgeon has many manners, adopted or cast off at the bidding of the subject-matter—in comparison, for instance, to a writer like Ray Bradbury, whose gestures and locutions seldom vary from work to work. But it is true that Sturgeon is often to be caught in visual similes that must seem wild indeed to that body of readers whose minds work most comfortably with abstractions. One of the commonest of such complaints in my experience homes on his comparison (in *More Than Human*, one of the very few authentic masterpieces science fiction can boast) of marmalade with a stained-glass window. Most of the complainers call this simile "strained" (in itself an un-visual word to apply to anything having to do with marmalade); yet to me it seems as just as it is startling, in particular when one observes that the man in the book to whom this breakfast is being served, and to whom the comparison occurs, is actually trembling on the verge of starvation.

It is possible—though I hope it is untrue—that Sturgeon's almost lifelong concentration upon the ramifications and implications of a single subject has reached the point of diminishing returns, like Heinlein's exploitation of the first person. Objectively it can at least be seen that his once considerable production has fallen off sharply; this is only emphasized by his 1964 Pyramid collection, *Sturgeon in Orbit*, which contains five stories the most recent of which first appeared in 1955 but is identified as "actually one of the first stories I ever wrote in my life"; the next most recent dates from 1953. Authors who have even one newer work to offer usually see to it that it finds its way into their most recent collection, and in fact most editors of such collections insist upon it.

As for novels, Sturgeon has published four since *More Than Human* (not counting a "novelization" of a movie by somebody else, from which it is only fair to look the other way); and of these only two are science fiction. The first of the four, *I, Libertine* by "Frederick R. Ewing" (Ballantine, 1956), was ostensibly written in collaboration with disc jockey-comedian Jean Shepherd, though his contribution is invisible to me. Surprisingly, the novel despite its publicity did not turn out to be a burlesque of a hairdryer or D-cup historical, but an authentic historical romance rather like those of Georgette Heyer, complexly plotted and researched up to the eyebrows. Set in 18th century England, it's ebulliently written, witty, and has for characters a fine gallery of ripe eccentrics in the best British tradition; my favorite is Lawyer Barrowbridge, the hero's mentor.

Despite some alchemical chitchat and one chapter in which a pharmaceutical miracle is blithely committed, it contains no traces of science fiction. Considering the circumstances under which it was conceived—a deliberate attempt to create a succès de scandale by radio publicity alone—the novel is much better than anyone could have dared to hope, but it is far from being a major work.

It was followed by *Venus Plus X* (1957), a boldly experimental science-fiction novel on Sturgeon's major theme which, sadly, failed to come off. Its text is interlarded by short sketches of contemporary life, mostly upper-middle class suburban, all intended to show how the roles of the sexes are mingling and blurring even now—and good enough to show, as did "Hurricane Trio," how expertly Sturgeon could write mainstream fiction given just one editor in that field with the wit to recognize the fact. The main story deals with a trip to a never-never land, ostensibly in the future, which is a utopia populated by a race of harmonious hermaphrodites. These, it turns out, have been surgically created, involving the author in the first of a series of scientific bloopers (his major proposal is immunologically impossible[2]); by the end of the novel, Sturgeon, usually a model of accuracy and responsibility toward technology, has two of his major characters *watching* fall-out come down, like a display of fireworks.

But such carelessness is only a minor sample of the dangers of becoming totally bound up in a Thesis. The worst outcome, visible here, is that there is no novel when you are through. As Theodore Cogswell once remarked to me, *Venus Plus X* bears a startling resemblance to one of those common and endless Victorian utopias in which most of the action consists of taking the marvelling visitor to inspect the great Long Island and New Jersey Bridge, the gas works, the balloon factory, the giant telegraph center, etc., etc. Furthermore, the author of a utopia always runs the risk of finding—or worse, failing even to suspect—that the parts of his dream-world he loves best will prove repellent to his readers. Revulsion certainly overcame *me* during the chapter of this novel describing a crèche, where the descriptions of dancing children and saccharine statues reminded me of nothing so much as the artsy-craftsy nostalgicks the Southern Agrarians were peddling thirty-five years ago. (The artistic taste of the future somehow always seems as depressing as its politics, which considering our own is a pretty chilling prospect.)

The next novel was *Some of Your Blood* (1961), a fictionalized case history of an authentic vampire, on which I can report no more than that I was unable to get beyond about the first twenty pages of introductions, diary extracts, psychiatrists' reports and other apparatus.

The other science-fiction novel is a multiple-viewpoint work, technically rather like an exploded diagram of *More Than Human*, published (1958) by Dell under the abominable retitling of *The Cosmic Rape* (Sturgeon's own title, which appeared over the magazine version, was "To Marry Medusa"). It expands his vision of shared consciousness, desire and sensation between a few individuals, this time to include—though only briefly—the entire human race. This is much like the vision which climaxed Clarke's *Childhood's End*, but Clarke had the auctorial caution to bring about the actual race-wide apotheosis off-stage, as essentially incomprehensible, like an author writing of a presumably great poet who has the good sense not to "quote" any of his poems. Yet so great is Sturgeon's gift for embracing—there is no better word—all kinds of people that he almost brings off the impossible, and perhaps would have, had he hewed to the line. Instead, his novel winds up with a brief travelogue of the universe, colorful in itself but conventional, and in this context something of an anticlimax. The work is in addition quite short, probably no more than 45,000 words.

I also ought to note here a rather unaccountably neglected novella about the problems of telempathy, "The Other Man" (1956), which carries on Sturgeon's subsidiary thesis that mind-to-mind contact will increase humanity's problems, not solve them. (Sturgeon is almost the only modern science-fiction author to take this tack, though it is solidly within the tradition of the Wellsian cautionary tale.) In *More Than Human*, the multiple-person New Man was completed only by a component whose contribution was responsibility, and in a fine short story, "When You're Smiling" (1955), Sturgeon explored the hell of a man whose gift it is to feel other people's pain. The apparent villain of "The Other Man" can sense directly when other people are in trouble, and in complete opposition to the rest of his nature—which longs to be indifferent to anyone but himself—is constantly driven to their rescue. It is in effect a minor portrait of that demon of whom Goethe said he eternally willed evil, and eternally worked good. As such, it is exceedingly well done—perhaps nobody else in our field could have done it all—but it is told from the outside, with the clue to the central character's apparent villainy saved as a surprise. The same construction was used in "When You're Smiling," and to good effect, but it cannot carry a longer story; and besides, in "When You're Smiling" we are given access to the telempath's feelings from the start, a more difficult trick to pull off but much more rewarding if it works, as in fact it does.

Sturgeon's output of new material for the magazines from 1951 through 1965—quantitatively a fair index of activity in a field where the magazines still serve as trial grounds for novels, and as a means of keeping one's name before the public—was greatest in the period 1951–1958 and then fell spectacularly, throwing his admirers into long and futile sessions of asking each other what the hell could be the matter. In the mid-Sixties he wrote two scripts for the television series *Star Trek*, but of the more than three dozen such scripts I have had the opportunity to study (as the show's adaptor, for Bantam Books), I thought them among the poorest—Sturgeon, like most masters, responds poorly to these make-work assignments, which involve the unrewarding task of being forbidden to re-think characters invented by other and lesser writers. His story in Harlan Ellison's 1967 Doubleday anthology *Dangerous Visions* (called "If All Men Were Brothers, Would You Let One Marry Your Sister?") was the first original Sturgeon in five years, an alarming gap for a man who used to exude striking and seminal stories with an apparent (if only apparent) effortlessness which was the envy of the prolific hacks in whose own dull output his work had to appear embedded.

Nevertheless, this long hiatus, or slump, or fallow period, may well be only one of those necessary explorations of blind alleys which seem to be part of the evolution of many major writers. There is still plenty of room for hope, and of the largest possible kind. The most recent previous piece of major Sturgeon to appear was the beginning of another novel, which was published in the September 1962 *F&SF* as "When You Care, When You Love," and it is totally remarkable, in theme, in characterization, in ingenuity, and in language. A quick description of its apparent subject—a young man doomed by a rare and peculiar form of cancer, who by virtue of that very disease becomes his own parents (both of them) and seems about both to relive his past in detail, and reclaim his future—no more than hints at the richness of the material, and of course cannot offer any idea of what the rest of the novel may prove to be like.

It is a fact that since the inception of modern science fiction in 1926, no single author has produced more than one masterpiece, though several have carried off more than one Hugo. From the existing text of "When You Care, When You Love," and some discussions of it with its author, I think it more than possible that Sturgeon may be the first man to make it.

But while we are waiting, it would be well to remember that no writer, not Dostoievski, not even Shakespeare, ever managed to be all things to all men; and Theodore Sturgeon has never bothered to try. He has concentrated a lifetime into being caviar for Theodore Sturgeon, and giving the rest of us the privilege of sharing the feast. In the process, he has made himself the finest conscious artist science fiction has yet had, which is purely and simply a bonus that we had no right to expect or even to ask. We are all more in his debt than we realize, no matter what future he may bring us.

Notes

1. Of sexual perversions, a subject most science-fiction writers stonily pretend doesn't exist, Sturgeon has remarked: "It is fashionable to overlook the fact that old-shoe lovers *love* loving old shoes." Dante would have understood this perfectly, only going on to add that *simultaneously* they also hate and fear it.
2. I am not going to specify further because the proposal is supposed to come as a surprise. I will add, however, that the subsequent apparent success of at least one human heart transplant operation in the real world shows Sturgeon's idea to be *not* immunologically impossible—just very damned unlikely, or in other words, entirely allowable in science fiction.

SAMUEL R. DELANY
From "Sturgeon" (1977)
Starboard Wine
1984, pp. 77–80

The Gregg Press edition of *The Cosmic Rape* presents both texts—the novel, followed by the earlier, shorter novelette—because, finally, there *are* no Sturgeon texts without interest.[1] The gentlest heightening of attention to any page yields its richness of insight into life and language, as well as into what makes language live.

Look at the initial Guido section in both versions (p. 20 [177]). The shorter is in the third person and is extremely distanced—almost like an overheard anecdote, in which details suddenly force themselves into patterns (cease to be data and become information). The longer version thrusts us directly into the demented Guido's mind with a first-person narrative: the boy is hiding on Massoni's roof. We listed to Massoni play a record, give a violin lesson, talk about Guido. For me, the shorter version works marginally better. For one thing, it is done presto. And in the longer version the verbal gestures Sturgeon has to make in one direction toward Pidgin English and in another toward madness, all the while straited by the present tense he has chosen for his narrative (at the same time getting in tremendous atmospheric information about postwar Rome, Guido's past life, his present situation, and his psychosis), just may define one of those fictive situations with defeat built-in. A lesser writer (unless a writer blind with the ambition often accompanying *complete* ineptitude) would probably not even have attempted it. Read the shorter version—as a sort of synopsis of the information that must be presented for the section to function in the novel's totality—and then reread the longer to see just how *close* to success Sturgeon came in an impossible self-imposed task.

But in the midst of all this music and discussion, Massoni makes himself a cup of coffee.

To my mind it is quite the most astonishing cup of coffee in all of science fiction. And it is this coffee that allows the scene to work as well as it does and lifts the scene above informational chaos. Nothing erupts from it, neither demon nor machine. No one hurls it at anyone; it is not spilled. It goes quite sedately from pot to cup, stays there till stirred, and is then, as sedately, drunk. It has no noticeable effect on anything that could even vaguely be called the plot. But what Sturgeon does with that coffee is *use* it—use its smell, the flames flickering under it, the bubbles at the cup's rim, the light shimmering off its surface—to initiate emotional transitions, to guide the reader's attention to one process occurring over here or distract that attention from another occurring over there that must be completed before it can be presented to the reader's view. This is the kind of thing we hear about in Chekhov—and read page after page of in Sturgeon. It is the kind of performance one writer watches another bring off, torn between jaw-hanging delight and jaw-clenching envy.

But comparing details between the two versions is endlessly fascinating: examine the modulation in tone effected by the paragraph extension of the Charlotte/Paul scene (p. 14 [155]). Or note how the interpolation of Danny's and Dimity's galactic romp (p. 157 [218]) reweights the concluding passage discussed earlier. Examine the effect of Henry's nightmare, used as a prologue to the waking dream of humanity's oneness (p. 11). The prospects should excite any lover of Sturgeon; indeed, it should excite any lover of fiction, i.e., any reader willing to do the work necessary to keep that love quick and vital. A comparison of the overall effects of the two versions may provide a matrix in which to organize one's subsequent exploration of details.

The shorter, earlier version develops a headlong narrative energy, the more impressive for the narrative's fragmentary structure. The later version, nearly double the length of the earlier, simply cannot sustain such a concerted thrust through such an innately episodic form. What Sturgeon chose to develop instead in the novel is that sense of *communitas*/communion we have already located as a primal Sturgeon theme. The novelette's narrative thrust arises mainly because all the subplots (and the tale really *has* only subplots) center on vanquishing the Medusa. The novel, primarily through the introduction of the Brevix family (and the expansion of the Guido and M'bala episodes), pictures the new communion as not only working to destroy an enemy, but also helping to benefit humanity itself (i.e., the rescue of Sharon), quite apart from the Medusa's threat. Certainly what the longer sacrifices in narrative drive it gains in overall intensity.

I think it only fair to warn the reader about to undertake such a detailed comparison that *The Cosmic Rape* does have its points of contradiction, in both longer and shorter versions. Faced with that incredibly precise and infinitely well-organized plan by which humanity destroys the Medusa's projectors and the spheres that transport them, we had best not inquire too closely *why* they must be destroyed . . . although all they seem to do, with their strange hootings ("part sound, part something else"), is accomplish the telepathic bond that allows humanity to form the plan in the first place. In the shorter version Guido's sacrifice of his newfound violin is presented as a sort of grace note to Henry's sacrifice of his life; but in the extended version we have time to reflect that, of *course*, someone will probably give him another one—and perhaps even the violin lessons he finally gets—if, indeed, humanity survives. And should we start to question Henry's death itself too closely . . . well, one of the troubles with plot on its grossest level is just how easily it can break down. Finally, in the first line of the novel's Chapter 12 (p. 80) we are told that the Brevix's have four children, but by the middle of the next page they have, out of nowhere, gained a fifth.

The reason for the first of these is no doubt that it was 1958; in 1958 aliens were—unless clearly spelled out otherwise—a menace; and they and their artifacts had to be gotten rid of as fast as possible. As for the last, well, not only does Homer nod and Flaubert count out 57 francs in two-franc pieces, but much science fiction of that decade *was* written first draft, very fast, with a burning, mystic vision drawing the author onward—and a bill collector giving a not-so-friendly nudge from behind.

Still, readers interested in the rhetoric of fiction—the various ways the writer of fiction weights what s/he is saying or produces in the reader an affect—have an extraordinarily rich laboratory to explore in the two versions of the tale. There is paragraphing and punctuation aplenty to compare for its modulation of scenic progress; there are scenic extensions, repositionings, and macrointerpolations. And what remains beautifully clear, whichever modulation we are considering, is that it is done by a master.

Notes

1. The novelette version, "To Marry Medusa," was first published in *Galaxy* in January 1958; the story's only American book publication, until 1978, was in Frederik Pohl, ed., *Time Waits for Winthrop and Four Other Short Novels from Galaxy* (Garden City, N.Y.: Doubleday & Company, 1962), pp. 149–219. Throughout this essay page references to the novelette are inserted in square brackets,[ ], after the page reference to *The Cosmic Rape* ⟨1958⟩ in the Gregg Press edition ⟨1977⟩, which contains both versions.

BRIAN ALDISS

"Sturgeon: Mercury Plus X"

Cheap Truth, "Special Unnumbered Edition" (1985), pp. 1–2

Sturgeon? The name was magnetic. There it was, perpetually cropping up attached to the stories I most admired. Sturgeon: quite an ordinary Anglo-American word among exotics like A. E. Van Vogt, Isaac Asimov, Heinlein, Simak, and Kuttner. Yet—spikey, finny, *odd*. And it was not his original name. Theodore Hamilton Sturgeon was born Edward Hamilton Waldo. To the usual boring undeserving parents. That was on Staten Island, the year the First World War ended.

So there were two of him, as there are of many a good writer. A bright side, a dark side—much like our old SF image of Mercury, remember, so much more interesting than banal reality. He had a mercurial temperament.

The bright side was the side everybody loved. There was something so damned nice, charming, open, empathic, and *elusive* about Ted that women flocked to him. Men too. Maybe he was at the mercy of his own fey sexuality. If so, he was quizzical about it, as about everything. One of his more cutesy titles put it admirably: "If All Men Were Brothers, Would You Let One Marry Your Sister?" Not if it was Sturgeon, said a too-witty friend.

He played his guitar. He sang. He shone. He spoke of his philosophy of love.

Ted honestly brought people happiness. If he was funny, it was a genuine humor which sprang from seeing the world aslant. A true SF talent. Everyone recognized his strange quality—"faunlike," some nut dubbed it; faunlike he certainly looked. Inexplicable, really.

Unsympathetic stepfather, unsatisfactory adolescence. Funny jobs, and "Ether Breather" out in *Astounding* in 1939. So to an even funnier job, science fiction writer. It's flirting with disaster.

I could not believe those early stories: curious subject

matter, bizarre resolutions, glowing style. And about sexuality. You could hardly believe your luck when one of Ted's stories went singing through your head.

"It," with Cartier illustrations, in *Unknown*. Terrifying. "Derm Fool". Madness. The magnificent "Microcosmic God," read and re-read. "Killdozer", appearing after a long silence. There were to be other silences. "Baby Is Three": again the sense of utter incredibility with complete conviction, zinging across a reader's synapses. By a miracle, the blown-up version, *More Than Human*, was no disappointment either. This was Sturgeon's caviar dish. Better even than *Venus Plus* X, with its outré sexuality in a hermaphrodite utopia.

As for those silences. Something sank Sturgeon. His amazing early success, his popularity with fans and stardom at conventions—they told against the writer. Success is a vampire. In the midst of life we are in definite trouble. They say Sturgeon was the first author in the field ever to sign a six-book contract. A six-book contract was a rare mark of distinction, like being crucified. A mark of extinction. Ted was no stakhanovite and the deal did for him; he was reduced to writing a novelization of a schlock TV series, "Voyage to the Bottom of the Sea," to fulfill his norms.

At one time, he was reduced further to writing TV pilot scripts for Hollywood. He lived in motels or trailers, between marriages, between lives. Those who read *The Dreaming Jewels* or *Venus Plus* X or the story collections forget that writing is secretly a heavy load, an endless battle against the disappointments which come from within as well as without—and reputation a heavier load. Ted was fighting his way back to the light when night came on.

About Ted's dark side.

Well, he wrote that memorable novel, *Some of Your Blood*, about this crazy psychotic who goes for drinking menstrual discharge. Actually, it does not taste as bad as Ted made out. That was his bid to escape the inescapable adulation.

One small human thing he did. He and I, with James Gunn, were conducting the writers' workshop at the Conference of the Fantastic at Boca Raton, Florida. This was perhaps three years ago.

Our would-be writers circulated their effusions around the table for everyone's comment. One would-be was a plump, pallid, unhappy lady. Her story was a fantasy about a guy who tried three times to commit suicide, only to be blocked each time by a green monster from Hell who wanted him to keep on suffering. Sounds promising, but the treatment was hopeless.

Dumb comments around the table. I grew impatient with their unreality. When the story reached me, I asked the lady right out, "Have you ever tried to commit suicide?"

Unexpected response. She stared at me in shock. Then she burst into a hailstorm of tears, collapsing onto the table . . . "Three times," she cried. Everyone looked fit to faint.

"It's nothing to be ashamed of," I said. "I've tried it too."

"So have I," said Sturgeon calmly.

He needn't have come in like that. He just did it bravely, unostentatiously, to support me, to support her, to support everyone. And I would guess there was a lot of misery and disappointment in Ted's life, for all the affection he generated. Yet he remained kind, loving, giving. (The lady is improving by the way. We're still in touch. That's another story.)

If that does not strike you as a positive story, I'm sorry. I'm not knocking suicide, either. Everyone should try it at least once.

Ted was a real guy, not an idol, an effigy, as some try to paint him. He was brilliant, so he suffered. I know beyond doubt that he would be pleased to see me set down some of the bad times he had. He was not one to edit things out. Otherwise he would have been a less powerful writer.

There are troves of lovely Sturgeon tales (as in the collection labelled *E Pluribus Unicorn*), like "Bianca's Hands," which a new generation would delight in. He wrote well, if sometimes over-lushly. In many ways, Ted was the direct opposite of the big technophile names of his generation, like Doc Smith, Poul Anderson, Robert Heinlein, et al. His gaze was more closely fixed on people. For that we honored him, and still honor him. Good for him that he never ended up in that prick's junkyard where they pay you a million dollars advance for some crud that no sane man wants to read.

Ted died early in May in Oregon, of pneumonia and other complications. Now he consorts with Sophocles, Dick, and the author of the *Kama Sutra*. He had returned from a holiday in Hawaii, taken in the hopes he might recover his health there. That holiday, incidentally, was paid for by another SF writer—one who often gets publicity for the wrong things. Thank God, there are still some good guys left. We are also duly grateful for the one just departed.

William Styron

1925–

William Styron was born on June 11, 1925, in Newport News, Virginia. He was educated at Davidson College and Duke University (B.A. 1947, Phi Beta Kappa). He served in the marines from 1944 to 1945 and in 1951, and achieved the rank of first lieutenant. In 1953 he married Rose Burgunder; they have four children. He was an editor at McGraw-Hill in 1947, and since 1952 has been an advisory editor for *Paris Review*. From 1970 to 1976 he was a member of the editorial board of *American Scholar*. Since 1964 he has been a Fellow at Silliman College, Yale University. He currently serves as an Honorary Consultant in American Letters for the Library of Congress.

Styron's novels have enjoyed both popular and critical success; though grounded in straightforward narrative, they deal thoughtfully with such universal themes as oppression and rebellion, heroism and victimization, and the betrayal of the individual by a cruel and heartless society. His works have also been attacked, and Styron's subject matter and popularity with a mass audience have made him among the most controversial of critically respected novelists. His first novel, *Lie Down in Darkness* (1951), was heavily indebted to Faulkner and the Southern literary tradition, but impressed critics with its sympathy and respect for the unfortunate and downtrodden. It was followed by a novella, *The Long March* (1956), concerning the struggle of an individual to maintain dignity amid the irrationality of war and the military. *Set This House on Fire* (1960), an existential study of the act of artistic creation, was praised for its thoughtfulness and studied despair but vilified for its overblown length and style. Styron's most recent novels have been both his most successful and most controversial. *The Confessions of Nat Turner* (1967) was lauded for its vivid portrayal of a slave rebellion; however, he was almost immediately attacked not only for his portrayal of the mind of a revolutionary black slave but for his presumption in making the attempt. Nonetheless, the book was extremely popular and won the Pulitzer Prize for fiction. The somewhat autobiographical *Sophie's Choice* (1979), another bestseller, was again both praised for its feeling for the human condition and criticized for its apparent lack of control in structure and style. It was awarded the American Book Award.

Controversy notwithstanding, Styron is a rarity in American letters: a critically respected artist who has achieved widespread popularity by his adept handling of powerful emotional themes. He has also published a play (*In the Clap Shack*, 1973), some criticism and social commentary, and several short stories.

JERRY H. BRYANT

"The Hopeful Stoicism of William Styron"

South Atlantic Quarterly, Autumn 1963, pp. 539–50

He who, oppressed by sorrows numberless
And driven from his realm, with unbent neck
Carries his burdens, not degenerate
Or conquered, who stands firm beneath the weight
Of all his burdens, he is great indeed.
(Seneca, *Thyestes*, V, ii, 5–12)

William Styron published his first novel, *Lie Down in Darkness*, in 1951. *The Long March*, a novella, followed the next year. In 1960 he came out with *Set This House on Fire*. Thus his work neatly spans the first full postwar decade, and to it we may go for what the new generation was thinking. Besides being representative, Styron has been well received. Alfred Kazin excepted him from a disparaging attack on contemporary writers.[1] Maxwell Geismar described *Lie Down in Darkness* as the best novel of 1951.[2] Granville Hicks gave *Set This House on Fire* an exceptionally good review.[3] And *Critique*, a quarterly edited by graduate students at the University of Minnesota but publishing articles by established critics, devoted half of the Summer, 1960, issue to Styron. Nor does this exhaust the list of attentions paid him. He continues, as his matter and manner deserve, to receive serious critical court.

As a southerner, Styron naturally owes a debt to Faulkner.[4] His connections, however, extend far beyond that fountainhead of southern writing. He shares with his countrymen of the twenties the conviction that our universe is, in the words of Joseph Wood Krutch, "one in which the human spirit cannot find a comfortable home."[5] The sentiments of Matthew Arnold's "Dover Beach" are not alien to him. And Samuel Johnson's proclamation in *Rasselas* that in this world there is much to be endured and little to be enjoyed applies with surprising accuracy to Styron's books. Johnson's choice of the word "endure" is crucial to all men who have discovered the rigor of existence. Oedipus endures the inescapable fate thrust upon him by the gods. Hamlet learns that "readiness is all." Faulkner writes that Dilsey and her progeny "endured." In this same tradition Styron believes that "one must end a credo on the word 'endure.'"[6] A reader fresh from John Webster can hear in Styron's work the echoes of "I am the Duchess of Malfi still."

The answer to What must man endure? is the thesis which informs all of Styron's novels. These undergo a development which I hope to demonstrate in the course of this discussion, but his basic thesis remains much the same. It is best expressed in an obscure treatise by Henri Estienne, translated in the early seventeenth century by Richard Carew under the title A *World of Wonders*. Estienne describes the "first Age of the world," that period when Adam and Eve lived in the Garden unspoiled by knowledge or civilization. But their idyll, as the all too familiar story goes, is destroyed by the eating of the forbidden fruit, and the children thereby are brought to "the knowledge of the mechanicall arts . . . wherby they had experimentall knowledge of good and euill."[7]

Styron's characters who are destroyed or who destroy have, like the children of the Garden, fallen away from the golden age. What Styron calls the "miseries of our century"[8] result from that "knowledge of the mechanicall arts," which is equated with civilized technology, urban areas like New York, the atom bomb and other instruments of war, and American materialism. We must endure these miseries of our time if our lives are to be anything more than meaningless vibrations lost in eternity. The children of modernity lack the strength necessary to endure because they have lost their simplicity. Endurance comes from a stoicism based upon innocence, faith, simplicity, which allows men, as the inscription from Seneca suggests, to bear their burdens. The paradox of the modern condition is apparent. The means whereby we might endure have disappeared during man's long flight into civilization, away from the bliss of the Garden of Eden or the reign of Saturn where innocent simplicity prevailed. The three novels which I shall discuss dramatize the despair of lost innocence and the hope which rises from the power to endure.

Styron's first novel, *Lie Down in Darkness*, shows the conflict between simplicity and complexity most clearly. Peyton Loftis, the doomed heroine, gazes out over the Rappahannock River on an early morning in the fall: "It was a beautiful river, broad and blue and serene, with no cities defacing its shore. There was something primeval about this river . . . undisturbed by the tools or weapons of man."[9] This is the landscape of innocence—the Garden before the serpent entered. But it is especially an escape to the simplicity of the countryside, a withdrawal from the fury of civilized endeavor. It recalls Hemingway's stories of Jake Barnes and Nick Adams, who take strength from the untrammeled purity of the wilderness, and Faulkner's *The Bear*, wherein civilization insidiously encroaches upon the primitive. Peyton sees in this landscape the childhood of humanity, unpolluted by man and his technology, what Estienne calls the "mechanicall arts." In *Lie Down in Darkness* this is the "good."

The opposite is technological complexity. With his mechanical knowledge man has built cities and created weapons and tools, but the price has been his innocence and those other two qualities which form his humanity, love and compassion. Although this rejection of civilized achievement is most pronounced in *Lie Down in Darkness*, it is an important ingredient in the other two works as well. Peyton hates the city-ness of New York and commits suicide in Harlem. The ironical opening of *The Long March* reveals eight young Marines lying dead against the pastoral background of a Carolina landscape, blown to bits by two mortar shells which fell short. And Mason Flagg, the villain of *Set This House on Fire*, has a "frenzied desire for speed" which is "an empty ritualistic coupling with a machine, self-possessed, craven, autoerotic, devoid of pleasure much less joy."[10] This last carries Styron's full indictment of the mechanical arts which have robbed mankind of their peace of mind.

There is no allegory in *Lie Down in Darkness*, but the picture is clear. The machine society contains its own destruction. Its children, like Mason Flagg, are neurotic and loveless, incapable of understanding or compassion. Helen and Milton Loftis, caught in an imbroglio of psychosis and self-obsession, destroy themselves and their children. Milton drinks and takes a mistress. Helen suffers from a paranoiac jealousy of her husband and daughter and alternates between passionate hatred and a desire to abase herself before them. When Milton finally leaves her for good, she expresses the utter negation of their lives in words very close to those of King Lear: "Nothing! Nothing! Nothing! Nothing!"

The significance of the Loftis family is most explicitly stated through Peyton. Having inherited the weaknesses of both her parents, she cries out that she is unable to love. She tortures herself and her husband by seeking adulterous sexual satisfaction in an effort to expiate a sense of guilt deriving from an unconscious incestuous desire for her father. In despair over the chaos of her life, she leaps from a Harlem building, symbolically returning to the innocence of her childhood by disrobing before she leaps. Her suicide coincides with radio broadcasts of the first atomic bomb dropped on Hiroshima. Her burial takes place as radios carry the news of Nagasaki. In her final minutes, Peyton throws the clock she has been carrying into the gutter, thinking, "I heard the last ticking, all my order and all my passion, globed from the atoms in the swooning, slumbrous, eternal light." Peyton has literally run out of time. Society, having created the instrument that could mean its own destruction, is also running out of time.

The story of the Loftises can be seen as a dramatic rendering of what Styron elsewhere calls "the miseries of our century." Helen, Milton, and Peyton repudiate the possibility of man's capacity to endure. Had Styron left his novel at that, the epithet "nihilism" might have applied. But he did not leave it at that and because he did not, *Lie Down in Darkness* must be seen as the first instalment in the diary of Styron's search for an ethic by which men might live.

In a letter to her father Peyton writes that perhaps "being sort of dumb" is the "key to happiness." This idea must not be disarmed by reducing it to the first cliché that comes to mind, that ignorance is bliss. Lawrence Durrell suggests the depths to which the sentiment might be carried when he puts into the mouth of Pursewarden, his novelist, these words: "One needs a tremendous ignorance to approach God."[11] For Styron the elements of this ignorance are simplicity and innocence, those qualities which define the value of the Garden of Eden and the Golden Age, the qualities which were part of Peyton's view that morning on the Rappahannock. Only the virgin mind contains the virtues of unquestioning faith and genuine love. Upon this foundation endurance is erected. Such endurance is characterized by stoicism, an unsophisticated acceptance of the sorrowful burden of living without surrendering to despair or ignominy.

The chief agents of this stoicism are the Negro and the Jew. Besides their survival in the face of centuries of persecution and suffering, the Negro and the Jew are appropriate symbols for more subtle reasons. Their roots, the commonplace goes, extend deep into the past. They are thus nourished by tradition, enriched by sameness. Because the past is constantly present to them through ethnical unity, they exist in a kind of timeless childhood, in which their innocence can never be lost. Thus they are not subject to the disintegration accompanying the knowledge of the "mechanicall arts."

Styron's Negroes, especially the Loftises' maid Ella Swan, possess this innocence, and it gives them a "transcendent understanding." Their part in the novel is minor in volume, but they are constantly present as a counterpoint to the Loftis despair. The "present" of the novel is the day of Peyton's funeral, her body having been brought back to Port Warwick, Virginia, for the interment. As the funeral procession moves toward the cemetery, toward the west, toward a storm, toward death, a caravan of Negroes celebrating the arrival of the evangelist Daddy Faith travels toward the east, the beach, baptism, rebirth, moving with a joy known only to the simple and the pure. On the evening of Peyton's funeral Daddy Faith preaches to his people about persecution and suffering, about the atom bomb and the wrath of God. "All flesh is grass," he says, and how quickly Peyton would have agreed with him. But his final sentence is not despair, like Peyton's and Helen's. It is the Judeo-Christian affirmation of the meaningfulness of life: "De grass withereth, de flower fadeth, but de word of your God shall stand forever."

This sermon transports Ella Swan, and she sees Jesus: "I seen him! Yeah! Yeah!" As she stands on the beach, after the sermon and after the baptismal waters of the ocean have cleansed and renewed her, the Richmond train, the machine which had brought Peyton's body to Port Warwick that morning, roars back toward the city, obscenely thrusting its death mission into the quiet of the night, scattering cinders and smoke over the placid landscape. Its noise almost drowns all sound. But Ella Swan does not admit defeat. Strengthened by her simplicity and her faith, she shouts above the tumult, striving with this final symbol of the Loftises' surrender, "Yeah! Yeah!" Her positive utterance, which ends the book, supersedes the final negation of Helen.

In *Lie Down in Darkness*, Styron uses the Jew to conceptualize what the Negro represents dramatically. On the day of her suicide Peyton visits her estranged husband, Harry Miller, a Jew and an artist. He is painting a picture—an old man, a rabbi or a monk, standing in front of "the ruins of a city, shattered, devastated . . . against it the old man's eyes looked proudly upward, toward God perhaps, or perhaps just the dying sun." "It's got belief," says Peyton, without belief herself. Harry rejoins that it is time for belief and speaks bitterly of the atom bomb's slaughter. Peyton goes faithless to her death, despair leading to self-destruction. But Harry, a Jew whose race's suffering equals that of Daddy Faith's people, paints faith into the upward gaze of his old man, whose tenacity, like Ella Swan's, is an example of man's ability to endure.

Lie Down in Darkness is weak in several ways. But the only way that concerns us is that the answer to "the miseries of our century" is too pat, too easy; the polarity between problem and solution is too pronounced. The forces that conflict do so because they are an effort of the artist's will and not because they are integral parts of a harmonious organism. *The Long March* is an artistic advance. The easy answer of the Negroes' simplicity is discarded for a deeper appreciation of the potentially tragic ambiguities in human experience. The action of the story is a conflict between the forces of endurance and the forces of destruction. Captain Mannix is a Jew from Brooklyn, called back into the Marines for the Korean war. From the beginning he rebels against the impersonally relentless system which has recalled him to face dangers he thought he had put behind him forever. His rebellion, "at once brave and somehow full of peril," is both admirable and foolish. In it is figured forth the paradoxical nature of the human condition, a condition which does not lend itself to easy answers.

There are many classical overtones in this short tale. Mannix struggles like a tragic hero against an inevitable fate, and in struggling, like Oedipus he calls forth our pity and admiration. As his specific antagonist Mannix selects the commanding officer of his battalion, Colonel Templeton, and in doing so he aspires to equality with the gods by presuming to struggle with them on equal terms. Templeton is above the conflict; he is the Olympian who coolly and disinterestedly ordains the fate of his underlings, singling out no favorites, admitting no peer. The difference between these antagonists is pointed up by the senseless slaughter of the eight young Marines with which the novella begins. Templeton reacts with cold, unfeeling, almost machine-like efficiency. But the absurd tragedy lays Mannix's compassionate heart open like a wound, emphasizing his helpless rebellion against that new war he can do nothing about.

Colonel Templeton calls for a forced march of thirty-six miles back to the camp as the climax of the battalion's field problem, regarding the hike impersonally as an exercise to train his men. Captain Mannix, however, sees it as a struggle between himself and Templeton. With the memory of the eight dead youths in his mind and his hatred of Templeton scorching his soul, he determines to outwalk the Colonel, who, he is sure, will ride most of the way. When Mannix develops a sore ankle, Templeton, quite unaware of the turmoil in Mannix's mind, orders him to finish the march in the trucks. But Mannix furiously accuses the Colonel of deceitfully riding alongside the suffering troops in a jeep. His error is all too obvious. When Templeton tries coldly to inform him of his mistake, Mannix interrupts and shouts obscenely, "*Fuck* you and your information."[12]

This is Mannix's *hubris*. The pride and resistance which draw our admiration and pity also determine his fall. He has dared to compete with the gods, now he must receive his judgment. Although his fate was virtually preordained, the obstinacy with which he greets the inevitability of his failure dignifies him; his defiance elevates his doom into the defeat of a tragic hero. His sentence, in keeping with the circumstances, is not death. Templeton orders him to complete the march on foot and informs him that court-martial proceedings will be started against him immediately.

Templeton is not a symbol of simple tyranny. He is almost an allegorical representation of that world from which Peyton fled. Cold and impersonal, Templeton is like a high priest of the civilized world of mortar shells, atom bombs, and iron discipline. But his nature, like that world, is ambiguous. His association with the senseless death of the eight youths marks him for our disfavor. But he is free of malice, for that is a human quality. At times, indeed, he expands with a god-like pity for his troops, though that pity finds no individual object. Templeton is neither good nor evil. This is the ambiguity against which Mannix hopelessly struggles. Its presence deepens the novel considerably. Less susceptible to diagramming than the similar forces in *Lie Down in Darkness*, the antagonists of *The Long March* are part of a more satisfying and organic whole.

But the essential patterns of the two books remain alike, and again Styron employs the Jew and the Negro as his modern stoics. Back at the base, Mannix creeps slowly and awkwardly on his swollen ankle to the showers, his nakedness mitigated only by a towel about his waist, his face showing "tortured and gigantic suffering." Lieutenant Culver, Mannix's friend, calls to Mannix in a gesture of sympathy and comfort. But Culver is a stranger to Mannix's suffering, for he lies outside that heritage which both strengthens Mannix and makes him a tragic figure. Succor must come from another quarter. At this moment a Negro maid appears, bucket and mop in hand. She stops and looks at the weird man approaching her. Jew and Negro regard one another and then, with a sympathy grown from her own suffering, she asks, "Do it hurt?" and answers it herself: "Deed it does." Watching one another, they communicate "across that chasm one unspoken moment of sympathy and understanding." And as Mannix stands transfixed in the Negro's gaze, his towel, already loose, slowly drops from his waist and he is naked. To the only other race that could understand, Mannix is as a child. Thus exposed and vulnerable as Adam, the defiant man speaks, not, as Culver tells us, "with self-pity but only with the tone of a man who, having endured and lasted, was too weary to tell her anything but what was true. 'Deed it does.'"

Peyton leaps into the Harlem night to escape pain and renders her existence meaningless. Mannix endures pain even after endurance has become, to all appearances, purposeless. His suffering purifies him, confronts him with truth. Through it he is able to admit a weakness to a compassionate Negro maid which he could never have acknowledged to the indifferent Colonel Templeton. In his struggle with his mortal condition Mannix imposes human meaning upon that which in surrender and despair would be meaningless. Nor is his suffering for its own sake; it is the token of his dignity as a human being.

Set This House on Fire has drawn conflicting opinions from reviewers. Some mocked it, some attacked it, some praised it. I happen to side with those who think it unsuccessful. Except for certain passages, the writing is verbose, the action is murky and melodramatic, the characters are stereotyped and wooden. For all this it is an important novel and although artistically disappointing, it demonstrates that Styron is that sort of novelist, like Hemingway or Faulkner or Cozzens, whose work is unified by an overriding idea which develops and deepens from novel to novel. That idea, of course, as I have tried to show, is that man must learn to endure the miseries of this century through a stoicism based upon innocence and simplicity.

Cass Kinsolving, the protagonist of *Set This House on Fire*, is faced with the same problems as the Loftises. He is self-obsessed, faithless, empty, bent on self-destruction. He thinks more than once of suicide. He dreams that God is dead. He drinks himself into numbness. And finally he endangers his integrity by allowing himself to fall under the sway of Mason Flagg, that machine-man whose "slick, arrogant, sensual, impenitently youthful, American and vainglorious face" marks him as the symbol of the empty materialism of a technological society. The dramatic conflict that was latent in *Lie Down in Darkness* and emergent in *The Long March* is clearly articulated here in these two opposites, Mason substituting for the city Peyton hated and the mortar shells that killed the young Marines. The link with the former books is even more explicit, for the destructiveness of the atom bomb as the context of Peyton's suicide is repeated in *Set This House on Fire*. At the very point in his relations with Mason when Cass's own destruction by the degradation to which Mason is subjecting him seems most imminent, Cass hears in a daze radio reports of a conference of nuclear physicists on the development of a new and more deadly bomb and he thinks, "*Madness! Madness!* . . . the gulf, the perishing deep." In the same moment Cass peers at Mason's face and sees his autoerotic coupling with the machine, thus relating Mason with the destruction of the bomb and the falling away of innocence with knowledge of the mechanical arts.

Simplicity comes with the Italian peasant girl Francesca. She teaches Cass about love and shows him that life has "some vestige of meaning." In a series of pastoral idylls in which Cass retires to the Italian countryside to paint Francesca, the two, who never join sexually, are returned to the innocence of the Garden. At the same time Francesca is part of a larger scheme of primitivism at whose center stands the Italian peasant. Above all it should be recognized that the peasant is linked in Cass's mind with the American Negro, for both share, as Cass says, the "bleeding stink of wretchedness." Thus the peasant assumes the role the Negro occupied in *Lie Down in Darkness* and *The Long March*. The peasants accept their suffering with the same quiet heroism that Styron gave to Ella Swan. Once, sitting in a café, Cass watches an old woman approach, bent under her load of faggots. Suddenly she loses balance and her bundle falls to the ground. She throws up her arms in "a noiseless gesture, touched not with anger or despair but only inevitability, acceptance of a world in which heavy loads fall and must forever be rehoisted." Later, dreaming of this incident, Cass realizes that God, through some capricious error, "had created suffering mortal flesh which refused to die, even in its own extremity."

This last statement comes as close as any single phrase to formulating Styron's view of man. Endurance consists of this profound undespairing stoicism, the refusal to surrender even when surrender means freedom from anguish. This is the quality which ennobles Mannix and which moves Ella Swan to utter "Yeah! Yeah!" And it is the quality implied in the title *Set This House on Fire*. In Christian tradition suffering expiates sin. Psychology might call it masochism. In either case it is what Styron's stoicism is made of. Cass is the man whose soul—or in the words of the Donne passage from which the title is taken, whose house—must be set on fire. Through suffering he must be born again, or at least find the way to a reconciliation between himself and the immutable conditions of existence.

The climax to Cass's suffering comes when Mason, the symbol of materialistic emptiness, rapes Francesca, the symbol of pastoral simplicity. When Francesca is later found dead, Cass retaliates by killing Mason, thinking that he was both rapist and murderer. The result of this painful holocaust does not effect a miraculous change in Cass, but he does arrive at a compromise approaching that of the old peasant woman. In the final lines he tells the narrator of the novel that he wishes he could report a discovery of grace, but he cannot. He can only say "that as for being and nothingness, the one thing I did know was that to choose between them was simply to choose being, not for the sake of being, or even the love of being, much less the desire to be forever—but in the hope of being what I could be for a time. This would be an ecstasy."

In addition to being uncomfortably vague, this statement is an unsatisfactory resolution to the problems advanced by the action. Nothing in what Cass does or says seems to have brought him to this conclusion. It is articulated but not dramatized. At the same time this conclusion suggests the rudiments of a workable solution to the human problem as Styron views it, a solution that goes beyond that of *Lie Down in Darkness* and *The Long March*. At the bottom of this solution is self-knowledge and personal responsibility. Mason Flagg, for all his despicable qualities, is not the only guilty party. Mason raped Francesca but did not kill her. He polluted an ideal but did not destroy it. Furthermore, Cass knew of Mason's innocence of murder at the time he threw him over the cliff. There was a brutal querulousness, a self-pity, in the action he took against Mason, and the revenge went beyond the actual crime committed. To allegorize, the technological society, represented by Mason, is not to blame for a sensitive soul's suffering. Cass himself corroborates this statement. At the same time we learn of Mason's freedom of the guilt of murder, at the Beginning of Part II, we also learn that Cass, after the act, has accepted his responsibility. He says, speaking of his own guilt and the weakness of his character, "It didn't *start* with Mason." Mason degraded him, it is true, but Cass had allowed himself to become especially vulnerable to that degradation.

The important point about the murder, however, is yet to be made. The real killer of Francesca was a kind of *deus ex machina*, a half-wit of the village who became frightened when the girl struggled against his harmless caresses and in his fear mutilated her. The half-wit's crime was irrational, just as fate or destiny or suffering is irrational. Discernible causes and related effects do not figure into the fabric of experience, and it is folly for men to think that they do. It is even greater folly for men to become angry when the relationship cannot be discovered, as Cass did when he cried that God is dead. Only man gives experience meaning, and he does so through his own powers of endurance, his capacity to survive the suffering that flesh is heir to. This, apparently, is what Cass learns, and his discovery moves him to *choose* (that is the critical word since it implies an effort of the will) being.

In *Set This House on Fire*, Styron has advanced in maturity beyond his two previous books. His new stoicism, no longer to be defined by the simple answers of primitive innocence, has deepened. The strength of Ella Swan and Captain Mannix, and even that of the Italian peasant, was a blind strength. Cass is fully aware of his actions and his problems, and because he is, his final choice is given more weight. Although he is unsuccessful as a character, Cass presents a new and stronger hope that the miseries of this world can be endured.

Notes

1. Alfred Kazin, "The Alone Generation," *Harper's*, CCIX (Oct., 1959), 131.
2. Maxwell Geismar, *American Moderns* (New York, 1958), p. 239.
3. Granville Hicks, "Literary Horizons," *Saturday Review*, XLIII (June 4, 1960), 13.
4. See Malcolm Cowley's review of *Lie Down in Darkness*, *New Republic*, CXXV (Oct. 8, 1951), 19.
5. Joseph Wood Krutch, *The Modern Temper* (New York, 1956), p. xi.
6. William Styron, "A Prevalence of Wonders," *Nation*, CLXXVI (May 2, 1953), 371.
7. Henri Estienne, *A World of Wonders*, trans. Richard Carew (London, 1607), p. 19.
8. Styron, "A Prevalence of Wonders," p. 371.
9. Compass Books (New York, 1957), p. 235.

10. Random House (New York, 1960), p. 411.
11. Lawrence Durrell, *Justine* (New York, 1960), p. 118.
12. *The Long March* (Vintage Books: New York, 1962), p. 112.

SHAUN O'CONNELL
"Styron's Nat Turner . . . "
Nation, October 16, 1967, pp. 373–74

Styron has run some risks with ⟨*The Confessions of Nat Turner*⟩. This is true despite its striking, contemporary relevance. Nat would have understood Stokely Carmichael's threat and gone him one better. When a honkie hits you, you indeed kill him, but first you *organize*, then you *plan* to kill them *all*. Still, this book is likely to raise some resentment. For Styron has presumed to *know* a Negro. A white ex-Southerner of the middle 20th century insists he knows enough to assume the guise of an early 19th-century black slave. Not only that but Styron admits—in an important essay, "This Quiet Dust" (*Harper's*, April, 1965) which explains his personal obsession with Nat—that "most Southern white people *cannot* know or touch black people," that the contemporary Negro "may feel that it is too late to be known, and that the desire to know him reeks of outrageous condescension." Yet, Styron insists on telling Nat's story in first-person narrative.

In a serious way he seems not to care *what* LeRoi Jones, say, might think of this presumption. This is something he had to do. In the desperately understated cliché, he is paying his dues, just as did Faulkner in *Intruder in the Dust* and Warren in *Who Speaks for the Negro?* For, Styron says, "to come to *know* the Negro has become the moral imperative of every white Southerner." To argue that this is arrogant and futile is to resign oneself to fragmentation, alienation, violence. Styron chances a daring, imaginative leap into a tormented black psyche to better understand himself and his country. He has taken to heart Baldwin's wisdom—hatred destroys the hater; the American white man must "find a way of living with the Negro in order to be able to live with himself."

For Styron this personal, social problem "resolved itself into an artistic one." How could he best understand, embody, *become* Nat? He could be circled from the outside with historical documents, the actual *Confessions* and the only book on the subject, *The Southampton Insurrection* (1900) by W. S. Drewry. These scant notes could be amplified by close readings in the history of slavery. Though these works provide Styron with a framework of the actual, reference points which had to be touched, and an abundance of specifics from which to draw, he had, finally, to confront Nat's single, isolated self. Who was he? Why did only he, in the long history of American slavery, lead an uprising? Why, when about sixty whites were slaughtered, did he personally kill only one? She was 18, her name was Margaret Whitehead, a belle, and, as Nat actually confessed, "after repeated blows with a sword, I killed her by a blow on the head with a fence rail." Why did the thrust of Nat's rebellion flinch after this murder? Styron asks, "Did he discover his humanity here or did he lose it?" History can help but, finally, Styron had to depend upon his novelist's first-rate sense of self to create situation and character which would convince us that these questions can be answered.

Nat's humanity is both Styron's and, as he sees it, Nat's problem. He was "favored" as perhaps no Virginia slave had been before. Son of the cook, he ate well. A cute pickaninny, he was pampered by whites. Further, he had the "luck" to be owned by a man of unusually enlightened convictions, Samuel Turner—"Turner" is, of course, his name, not truly Nat's—who felt "that the more religiously and intellectually enlightened a Negro is made, the better for himself, his master, and the commonwealth." At first Nat responds gratefully to this benevolent despotism. He develops a sense of his own significance that a field hand could never know. He feels the joy of becoming; "I shiver in the glory of self." Spurred by his heightened sensitivity to the promises of life he mimes the whites, their talk, their style, studies his Bible, learns his carpentry and, he says, becomes "a pet, the darling, the little black jewel of Turner's Mill." He pushes so successfully against the barrier of his "niggerness" that Turner promises emancipation. But Turner is weak, caught in a depression caused by the exhaustion of tobacco lands, and goes back on his word. When Nat is sold, when it is clear that he will never be free, that he can never more *become* in that way, he

> experienced a kind of disbelief which verged close upon madness, then a sense of betrayal, then fury such as I had never known before, then finally, to my dismay, hatred so bitter that I grew dizzy and thought I might get sick on the floor.

Having been promised more—through the white man's "wanton and arrogant kindness"—and seeing that promise denied, Nat had to kill. The need to slaughter those who are most compassionate is, Nat says, "the central madness of nigger existence." Their philanthropy, however patronizing, creates a sense of self in Nat, but their refusal to accept that self as fully human creates in him the capacity to deny their human reality, to make their blood flow "in a foaming sacrament." He *will* grow, if not one way, then another. If he cannot become white then he will be black with an unimagined power of blackness:

> I knew that . . . the whole world of white flesh would someday founder and split apart upon my retribution, would perish by my design and at my hands.

Given the alternative by two-faced whites of being Sambo or Black Daemon he chooses the latter so that he can forever wipe out the sight of those white faces.

But it is Nat's curse and his nobility that he cannot wholly do to the white man what they have done to him. Even though he is betrayed by one master, whipped by another, even when he sees his mother raped by an Irish overseer, his best friend sold down the river, Nat cannot fully reduce the white man to a caricature, the Oppressor, whose lack of human characteristics justifies any retributive horror. Nor, despite the uprising, can he successfully suppress his own humanity. Nat's burden of intelligence creates in him an ambivalence. He can hold two opposed ideas in mind at the same time—hatred and understanding—and not quite go mad. Understanding is not forgiveness—he has sixty killed. But it diminishes his ferociousness—he might have killed 600. He is almost successful in stifling his apprehension of the humanness in his enemy but, with Margaret Whitehead, comes to a kind of love which, though it does not save her, keeps him from more murder and insures his own defeat and death.

Styron's Margaret is the Southern belle seen with compassion and understanding. She is a charming thing, full of little lyric bursts of froth, sentimental about the darkies' lot and squashed turtles, but a first-rate sensibility, trapped in taffeta, who can only talk to Nat—this odd, brilliant slave—whom she performs for, respects, patronizes, flirts with, she hardly knows what. For she is as blocked and profoundly isolated as he. Nat can articulate his isolation:

> I thirsted to plunge myself into the earth, into a tree, a deer, a bear, a bird, a boy, a stump, a stone, to shoot milky warm spurts of myself into the cold and lonely blue heart of the sky.

He reaches for shimmering visions of God and bloody revenge. But Margaret is as lonely and knows it less. She is disgusted by her brother—a smug preacher who likes to hunt runaway slaves—distressed by the nonsense she hears about Negro inferiority at her girls' seminary, yet caught in the only world she knows. She and Nat cannot come together in life, in love, so they seek each other in death, in murder:

> Then when I raised the rail above her head she gazed at me, as if past the imponderable vista of her anguish, with a grave and drowsy tenderness such as I had never known, spoke some words too soft to hear and, saying no more, closed her eyes upon all madness, illusion, dream and strife. So I brought the timber down and she was swiftly gone, and I hurled the hateful, shattered club far up into the weeds.

"Such as I had never known." Can there be a greater isolation? Never until then had either seen his own humanity reflected in another's eyes. For this the houses of their bodies are on fire; for this lack they lie down in darkness.

In this novel, as well as intensifying his complex, compelling vision, Styron extends his craft, modulates his style. The soaring, personal rhetoric of his other books is here held back to better delineate a range of characters. T. R. Gray, who set down the original *Confessions*, speaks in legalistic, Latinate rhetoric which luxuriates in revealing, polysyllabic distinctions, as when he defines Nat as *"an-i-mate* chattel." Hark, Nat's right-hand man, has an earthy, sharp rhetoric—"Nigger life ain't worth pig shit!" Jeremiah Cobb, who passes death sentence on Nat, speaks in a style which is at once boozy, grand, self-pitying and perceptive—"God, God, my poor Virginia, blighted domain." Nat is up tight, masked, cool, so his rhetoric is controlled, fluctuating between "nigger gabble," when that will serve his ends, and formal, perfect English. Thus Styron's flexible style helps him portray a variety of characters, a range of experiences—a dramatized paradigm of "the peculiar institution" in its several aspects—and amplify the thin original *Confessions* into a full, plausible statement of a man's groping understanding of the significance in his own life.

Nat is believable, the gap between color and times can be bridged, because he is first and last a man, not a Negro slave. That is, as an imaginative, sensitive man concerned with ways to live a meaningful life, Nat is not so far apart from Styron as at first it seems. Styron has been able to detect and describe the man beneath the murderer. We accept the man and are thus implicated in his deeds. For example: Nat sits alone in his cell, in a "web of chains," watching flies buzz "in haphazard elastic loopings" through huge motes of dust. He wonders if the motes hinder the flies' flight, but then decides that they can be no more obstruction than the "harmless, dazzling, pelting flurry" of October leaves to a man. He fancies an envy for the flies' brainless state, "unacquainted with misery or grief." But then he turns this idea around to see the flies as "God's supreme outcasts, buzzing eternally between heaven and oblivion in a pure agony of mindless twitching." He thinks, then, of the infrequency of suicide among slaves, how he had mistakenly interpreted this as evidence of their Christian forbearance, but now, sitting in chains, musing upon a fly:

> It seemed rather that my black shit-eating people were surely like flies, God's mindless outcasts, lacking even that will to destroy by their own hand their unending anguish . . .

Here Styron dramatizes Nat's marvelous associations in terms which any man, any time, could understand. Who has not mulled the significance of flies? Then he dramatizes an extraordinary sensibility, one able to yoke seeming dissimilarities in a striking synthesis. Which of us has construed the mote/leaf, fly/man connection? Thus we are swayed into provisional acceptance of the fly-slave analogy because we have already agreed with the logic of his previous metaphors. So it goes throughout the novel. Nat impinges. His humanness cannot be denied.

Comfort, however, should not be taken from Nat's humanity. Styron's novel should be as disturbing to white liberals as to black militants. For, given character and conditions, Nat had to do what he did. Seeing it all from his point of view forces us into the paradoxical situation of urging his revenge even though we know it will also mean general horror and his own destruction. We flinch from the horror—women scalped, a baby smashed against a wall—but Nat, despite Margaret, does not.

> *I would have done it all again. I would have destroyed them all. Yet I would have spared one. I would have spared her that showed me Him whose presence I had not fathomed or maybe never even known.*

God is love and love is Margaret and, as she cites from John, "he that dwelleth in love dwelleth in God, and God is him. . . . " But love does not conquer justified hatred, nor should it. God is also righteous wrath and, Styron demonstrates, Nat is in every way sympathetic and right when he leads in vengeance "a majestic black army of the Lord." Styron has written an apologia for no political position, but a stunningly beautiful embodiment of a noble man, in a rotten time and place, who tried his best to save himself and transform his world.

CAROLYN A. DURHAM

"William Styron's *Sophie's Choice*: The Structure of Oppression"

Twentieth Century Literature, Winter 1984, pp. 448–64

In the face of repeated objections to the assertion in *What Is Literature* (1948) that a "good" anti-Semitic or racist novel would be a contradiction in terms, Jean-Paul Sartre maintained that whatever the theoretical value of his analysis, no one had yet taken up the practical challenge: "show me a single good novel whose deliberate intention was to serve oppression, a single one written against Jews, Blacks, workers, colonialized peoples."[1] If we judge by his most recent novel, William Styron seems to believe that his own work may represent for some readers an attempt to satisfy Sartre. *Sophie's Choice* incorporates frequent and barely disguised references to the negative critical reception of Styron's earlier novels, which frequently included charges of racism. Such reminders have served as strong evidence for the many reviewers of *Sophie's Choice* who are insistent on identifying its fictional narrator Stingo with William Styron himself.

Thus Nathan Landau notes signs of "ingrained" and "unregenerate" racism in Stingo's first novel,[2] highly reminiscent of Styron's own *Lie Down in Darkness;* and the mature Stingo comments on similar reactions to what is clearly a version of *The Confessions of Nat Turner*: "as accusations from black people became more cranky and insistent that as a writer—a lying writer at that—I had turned to my own profit and advantage the miseries of slavery, I succumbed to a kind of masochistic resignation . . . " (p. 37). Moreover, Stingo's and Styron's current *Sophie's Choice*, for Stingo is writing the novel we are reading, has aroused general critical acknowledgment that its treatment of Jewish experience invites charges of anti-Semitism, even if none has materialized to date.

The textual connections Styron chooses to establish in *Sophie's Choice* among his various fictions do have both aesthetic and ideological significance, not unrelated to Sartre's identification of bad literature with a politics of prejudice. The emphasis this structure places on Styron's literary output as oeuvre, as a body of work dealing with the concept and nature of oppression through the successive examination of particular oppressive systems, can point us toward a richer reading of Styron in general and, in the case at hand, of *Sophie's Choice*. For Styron's work serves of course as an illustration not of Sartre's ironic challenge to skeptics but rather of his original thesis. Styron's novels—and the distinction is important—are not oppressive but about oppression, not racist but about racism, not anti-Semitic but about anti-Semitism, and, I shall argue, not sexist although, in the instance of *Sophie's Choice* especially, are persistently about sexism.

Readers primarily interested in ideology have tended to dismiss formalism as an invalid critical method, choosing to value or to criticize commitment to a cause without concern for the literary means used to convey it. They thus ignore Sartre's fundamental hypothesis that an essential relationship exists between world view and form: "a novelistic technique always reflects the metaphysics of the novelist."[3] Ironically, in this case, early critics of *Sophie's Choice* may be paying both too much and not enough attention to form or, at least, to the nature of its connection to content in Styron's novel. For all of their insistence on equating Stingo and Styron, few reviewers appreciate the structural consequences they subsequently attribute to this intermingling of fiction and autobiography. *Sophie's Choice* has been criticized particularly severely for its organizational weakness: the supposedly chaotic combination of Stingo's sex life with Sophie and Nathan's destructive love; the unjustified comparison of anti-Semitic Poland to a racist American South; the confused linking of Stingo's experience as writer to Nathan's drug-induced madness; and, most importantly, the juxtaposition of all of the above themes to the horrors of the Nazi concentration camps.[4] Those reviewers most sensitive to Styron's novel do glimpse in the multiple riches of *Sophie's Choice* a common pattern, but these critics tend also to see the subject of the novel as too general—Evil—or too specific—the evils of Nazi Germany.[5] That *Sophie's Choice* should be criticized for a lack of structural coherence or for an excess of structural exuberance seems highly ironic; for it is in fact a novel whose very meaning lies embedded in its structure and, even more specifically, in the very concept of structure itself.

Styron attempts to alert us immediately to this important theme by opening the novel with the single chapter he himself has characterized in interviews as autobiographical, and which we may therefore expect to find potentially irrelevant or at least less relevant than others to the story of Sophie Zawistowska. But, in fact, the analysis of the McGraw-Hill publishing house where Stingo begins both his writing career and his narrative provides in its apparent thematic gratuity a paradigm of structure itself and therefore the very foundation of theme in Styron's *Sophie's Choice*. Mc-Graw Hill represents what Styron understands as *system:* the organized oppression of a given group of people in the name of their deviation from an established norm. Because this original form of systematic or organized evil remains free of any specific ideological content, it sets up a structural pattern that prepares us to comprehend the other systems which form the complex fabric of Styron's novel. Although no doubt pro-Wasp, pro-male, and certainly pro-conservative, McGraw-Hill is neither specifically racist, anti-Semitic, nor sexist; it is merely fundamentally pro-uniformity. Moreover, its function—the publication of good literature—and its fact—the publication of bad—serve from the very beginning of the novel to link Styron's concept of system to his conception of fiction.

Styron subsequently constructs *Sophie's Choice* upon a carefully woven network of parallels and repetitions in which all of the novel's characters gradually prove to share a single common characteristic: the same paradoxical form of prejudice. Only a few years after Auschwitz, the Jews Morris Fink declares his hate for "boogies" (p. 69). Stingo's father describes his friend Frank Hobbs as a "good solid man," although Hobbs is both an anti-Semite and a racist (p. 34). Only Stingo's obsession with Nat Turner and with the institution of slavery rivals his interest in the situation of Jews in prewar Poland and in Nazi Germany; yet even Stingo proves capable of brief lapses into both racism and anti-Semitism, and his experience with the Lapidus family amply illustrates the extent to which he harbors remarkably naive and stereotypical notions of Jewish domestic and religious life (pp. 196–98). Nathan deplores the historic suffering of his fellow Jews, but he does not hesitate to label all Southerners racist. Stingo's father proudly calls himself a liberal Democrat but considers Northerners an ignorant and vulgar caste. German hatred for Jews barely overshadows their horror of "Polacks," and Poles share the barracks of Nazi concentration camps with the Jews they despise. Wanda may best understand the endlessly replicable structure of prejudice and the need therefore to attack the form itself beyond any of its particular contents; she explains to the Jewish Feldshon: "once they finish you off they're going to come and get me" (p. 579).

Although Wanda speaks for herself and her "pretty blonde friend" Sophie only as unlikely victims, it is not insignificant that they are women. In much of his previous work, notably in *Set This House on Fire*, Styron has used the condition of women as a central metaphor for the general degradation of the self and others. In *Sophie's Choice*, sexism serves as a pervasive model of oppression, functioning as do the novel's formal analogies to invite us to see the structural equivalence of all systems of organized evil.[6] Thus sexism proves common not only to the apparently neutral structural shell of McGraw-Hill in which women serve as "mainly secretaries" (p. 19) but to racism and anti-Semitism as well. Stingo's carefully developed comparison between Poland and the American South includes the traditionally double-edged exploitation of females: "domination over women (along with a sulky-sly lechery)" (p. 301). In fact, virtually every chapter of *Sophie's Choice* contains the same consistent structural elements: a system of organized oppression, a particular example of sexism, and a commentary on language or literature, thus creating a structural paradigm in which *sexism* illuminates both the *systems* that oppress society and the *literature* that can lead toward an understanding of how they function.

Two episodes in particular of *Sophie's Choice* can quickly and effectively illustrate the structural and thematic importance that Styron attaches to sexism. Stingo's discomfort at inheriting money from his grandfather's sale of the slave

Artiste and his horror at the lynching of Bobby Weed are directly related to racism and, because of the parallels Nathan establishes, indirectly related to anti-Semitism. But more importantly, the two events also reveal a hostility to women which constitutes both their common element and an attitude shared by Stingo and Nathan. Artiste (by his very name an ally of Stingo) must be sold, because "in the first lusty flush of adolescence" (a situation painfully familiar to Stingo), he has made an "improper advance" toward a young white woman who turns out after the sale to be "an hysteric" prone to such false accusations (pp. 35–36). By the time Bobby Wood is castrated, branded, and lynched years later for the identical and equally nebulous offense, it has become a commonplace: "His reputed crime, very much resembling that of Artiste, had been so classic as to take on the outlines of a grotesque cliché: he had ogled, or molested, or otherwise interfered with (actual offense never made clear, though falling short of rape) the simpleton daughter . . . of a crossroads shopkeeper . . ." (p. 86).

Such stories impose an absolute double bind—one must necessarily choose to be either racist or sexist: either to condemn blacks for an attitude defined as normal in all other men or to condone the treatment of women as sexual objects. Moreover, whether the women in question tell the truth or lie, whether they are believed or not, they are directly responsible as females for both violence against men and for divisiveness among men. Stingo's attitude clearly implies that women are liars, hysterical, simpleminded, and either obsessed with sex and their own desirability or man-haters afraid of "normal" sexual advances. It is scarcely surprising that in Stingo's later resentment at his metaphorical castration he should invent for Leslie a comparable racist rape fantasy: "I finished my account with one or two Freudian furbelows, chief among them being one in which Leslie told me that she had been able to reach a climax only with large, muscular, coal-black Negroes with colossal penises" (p. 222).

Among critical objections to the structure of *Sophie's Choice*, or to its absence, distress at the inclusion of Stingo's sexual obsessions, fantasies, and adventures ranks particularly high. Robert Alter's comments reflect a typical discomfort with episodes perceived as tasteless and trivial when combined with the horrors of Nazi concentration camps: "it is hard to see how such concentration on a writhing priapic Stingo helps us to grasp the novel's subject of absolute evil."[7] Ironically, one consequence of a growing awareness of feminist concerns may be to provoke an almost instinctive reaction of hostility to every situation that even hints at the sexual exploitation of women. Yet, as is the case here, specific examples of prejudice, however offensive in themselves, may well function in a larger context to expose and consequently to undermine oppression. To focus our attention on the contextual importance of Stingo's sexual experiences, an issue first raised by his encounter with Leslie Lapidus, Styron has Stingo himself worry about the structural coherence of his novel:

> In itself this saga, or episode, or fantasia has little direct bearing on Sophie and Nathan, and so I have hesitated to set it down, thinking it perhaps extraneous stuff best suited to another tale and time. But it is so bound up into the fabric and mood of that summer that to deprive this story of its reality would be like divesting a body of some member—not an essential member, but as important, say, as one of one's more consequential fingers. Besides, even as I set these reservations down, I sense an urgency, an elusive meaning in this experience and its desperate eroticism by which at least there may be significant things to be said about that sexually bedeviled era. (p. 143)

In defining himself as one of the sexual "survivors" of the fifties (p. 145), Stingo by his vocabulary establishes a clear parallel between himself and Sophie. Although such a comparison may seem to undermine the importance of Sophie's fight for her sanity and for life itself, it in fact serves to emphasize the centrality of sexual experience in both of their lives, for Nazi Germany and prewar Poland prove no less sexually troubled than postwar America. Stingo's sexual fantasies thus relate directly to Styron's attack on the evil of sexism; those critics who denounce the former as gratuitous or trivial may well regard the latter in the same light.

For Stingo, "Little Miss Cock Tease" (p. 145) epitomizes the era of the fifties and, in general, he adheres to the standard male dualistic view of women. Yet, Stingo's division of the female sex into "cock teasers" or "cock suckers" differs sufficiently from the classic angel/whore dichotomy to reveal usefully the true hostility the latter conceals. The apparent idealization of women as pure and virginal reflects in fact a belief that such women are teases, frigid and inhuman. Thus Stingo's system corresponds to an absolute degradation of women; indeed, as he informs us, he has "not idealized 'femininity' in the silly fashion of the time" (p. 147).

Stingo illustrates this view of women through the repetition of a paradigmatic pattern into which his experience with Sophie eventually fits. The original model provided by Mavis Hunnicutt in the structurally rich opening chapter of *Sophie's Choice* makes it clear that nonsexual relationships with women are inconceivable for Stingo. The "loneliness" on which he insists throughout this period translates unambiguously as sexual frustration: "she could not know what she did to the loneliest junior editor in New York. My lust was incredible . . ." (p. 15). Through Mavis and her subsequent incarnations in Leslie and Mary Alice, Stingo fantasizes the women as cock sucker and cock teaser in turn, unfortunately in that inverted order. Stingo idealizes the female as sexual initiator or, in any case, as always responsive to male advances; thus, women are allowed volition to want what men do. Invariably, however, women who appear appropriately welcoming ultimately reject Stingo with increasingly dire consequences for him. Merely chagrined at Mavis' imaginary dismissal of him, Stingo falls ill after his failure with Leslie; and Mary Alice—"worse than a Cock Tease, a Whack-off artist" (p. 527)—drives him from his "lifelong efforts at good, wholesome, heterosexual screwing" (p. 534) toward homosexual relations.

Stingo claims a distinction between the women he desires and the women he loves for which, in fact, the novel provides no evidence. Stingo's expression of chaste adoration for Maria Hunt produces a "ferociously erotic" (p. 52) dream in which Maria behaves, to Stingo's delight, with "the abandon of a strumpet" (p. 53). Similarly, although Stingo professes a "poetic and idealistic" (p. 145) passion for Sophie, she too supports the fixed model of sexual identity already established. Stingo's initial encounter with Sophie occurs as Nathan defines her as "cunt" and "whore" (p. 55); Stingo's attention focuses immediately on her body and her sexuality; his desire "to win the affection" of Sophie marks at best a necessary step toward his real goal: "to share the bed" abandoned by Nathan (p. 63). Moreover, so that any lingering idealization of the female may be rigorously exorcised, Stingo finds Sophie most arousing when she is least erotic; her most tender, affectionate, and vulnerable moments become an invitation to seduction. When Sophie collapses, shattered by the loss of Nathan and her revelation just moments before of the existence of her son Jan, only Stingo's own fatigue persuades him to forgo a sexual pass: "Lying there, she seemed terribly vulnerable, but my outburst had tired me, leaving me somehow shaken and empty of desire" (p. 376). During the desperate and exhausting flight South to escape Nathan, the sight of Sophie asleep produces in Stingo a similar "seizure of pure lust" (p. 558). Thus, Stingo's synthetic dream in which he makes love to Leslie, transformed in quick succession into Maria and Sophie (pp. 363–64), has particular significance; it both confirms that love is inseparable from lust for Stingo and draws the inevitable conclusion: all women are equivalent and therefore interchangeable.

Yet Sophie does stand apart from other women as an ideal; she is the perfect women as defined and perceived in a male world. Originally a cock teaser—"a young woman brought up with puritanical repressions and sexual taboos as adamantine as those of any Alabama Baptist maiden" (p. 117)—Sophie has been transformed literally into a cock sucker, "the world's most elegant" (p. 602) according to Nathan, thereby proving the male maxim that women, however much they may initially resist, really welcome sexual advances.[8] Moreover, Sophie's behavior perpetuates the particularly vicious myth that women respond to physical and mental violence as pleasurable. In the midst of an orgy of abuse, Sophie blissfully sucks Nathan's cock (pp. 413–14); and after hours of torture involving physical beating, verbal abuse, and psychological assault, she welcomes immediately and without hesitation Nathan's invitation "to fuck" (p. 422).

Nathan misdirects his jealousy of Sophie, since its justification lies not in her attraction to other men but in their obsessive interest in her; for every man she encounters, however briefly or infrequently, Sophie becomes an object of desire, a seducible prize. But in the sexist world that Styron portrays, once Sophie has allowed herself to be seduced, she must be degraded as the whore she has become. Her very submission to Nathan confirms the justice and accuracy of his accusations, and marriage logically becomes the prize that Nathan proffers or withdraws on the basis of his current beliefs about Sophie's sexual fidelity. Stingo, tormented for months by his desire for Sophie, nonetheless characterizes her seduction of him on the beach as "forthrightly lewd" (p. 436), and the episode illustrates with particular clarity the incredible double standard to which women are subjected, the inescapable vicious circle in which they are trapped. When Sophie initiates lovemaking, immediately after her latest revelations about her past, Stingo implicitly condemns her for frivolity, capriciousness, an inability to feel deeply: "The shift in mood—the grisly chronicle of Warsaw, followed in a flash by this wanton playfulness. What in hell did it mean?" (p. 437). But when Sophie returns to her story after Stingo's premature ejaculation, his renewed horror is heightened. Sophie's failure to be appropriately affected by their recent intimacy, to live this sexual adventure as "cataclysmic" and "soul-stirring," offers evidence of an insensitivity far greater than any Stingo had yet imagined and leads him to one of the novel's relatively rare generalizations about "women": "Could women, then, so instantaneously turn off their lust like a light switch?" (p. 440).

Styron's careful construction of a globally sexist world provides a context in which the events of Sophie's arrival at Auschwitz cannot possibly be dismissed as an aberration. However great our shock and our horror, the "choice" that the Doctor Jemand von Niemand imposes on Sophie marks the logical extension of all male behavior toward women recorded in *Sophie's Choice* up to that point. Despite Stingo's elaborate attempts to "understand" the Doctor's action, to offer an explanation that inevitably becomes a defense, Jemand von Niemand fits into a clearly established pattern. He makes Sophie the same proposition that virtually every other man in the novel, implicitly or explicitly, had made her—"I'd like to get you into bed with me" (p. 586)—and when she fails to respond, he destroys her. For with tragic irony the perfectly pliant Sophie, who has always understood the necessity of female submission in a male world, fails to react quickly enough at the single moment when the metaphorical survival of the female becomes literal. Yet, the greatest horror recounted in *Sophie's Choice* may be less the cruelty of the Nazi doctor than its perpetuation in Stingo. For Stingo's reaction to the story of Eva's death is virtually indistinguishable from Jemand von Niemand's behavior during the actual event: Stingo too wants to go to bed with Sophie. The fact that she clearly initiates their night of inexhaustible sex changes nothing in a world in which women are required to be both prey and predator, except perhaps to confirm once and for all how well Sophie learned her lesson at Auschwitz.

The role of sexual oppressor that links all men and the use of sexism as paradigm to connect Nazi Germany to postwar America extend to the reader as well. One of the most remarkable successes of Styron's attack on sexism comes from his ability to implicate the reader himself in the system that victimizes Sophie; the male pronoun is for once authentically generic since all readers, male or female, will be forced to view Sophie from a masculine perspective. Our limited, popular, and generally sensationalist knowledge of history prepares us to suspect Sophie's involvement in sexual crimes or experiments at Auschwitz, and the mysterious secret announced in the novel's title encourages us to believe she participated more as collaborator than as victim. Moreover, Nathan serves as our representative in the text. He gradually plants the idea that Sophie's survival at Auschwitz is linked to her sexual behavior; this insidious process, reinforced by Sophie's evident obsession with her own guilt, culminates in his identification of Sophie with Irma Griese: "hey Irma how many SS pricks did you suck to get out of there, how much master race come swallowed for *Freiheit?*" (p. 411). Styron's technique effectively exposes the reader as participant in the same system of sexism the novel as a whole reflects; for at the moment we learn the true nature of Sophie's "choice" or "crime," we are forced to confront the discrepancy between the truth and our assumptions.

Women can ultimately be reduced to interchangeable sex objects, because sexist society denies them a personal identity, a sense of self. Styron's novel, consistent with much feminist theory, locates the origin and the model of female oppression in the father dominance of the traditional family. In general, Sophie's father reduces her to "virtually menial submission" (p. 293), but his most significant assault is aimed at Sophie's love of music, the representation throughout the novel of her identity, her individuality. As a significant prelude to her account of her arrival at Auschwitz, Sophie relates a dream in which she explicitly identifies her father's will to deny her access to music with the death of the self:

> "So in the dream that has returned to me over and over I see Princess Czartoryska in her handsome gown go to the phonograph and she turns and always says, as if she were talking to me, 'Would you like to hear the Brahms *Lieder?*' And I always try to say yes. But just before I can say anything my father interrupts. He is standing next to the Princess and he is looking directly at me, and he says, 'Please don't play that music for the child. She is much too stupid to understand.' And then I woke up with this pain. . . .

> Only this time it was even worse, Stingo. Because in the dream I had just now he seemed to be talking to the Princess not about the music but about . . . " Sophie hesitated, then murmured, "About my death. He wanted me to die, I think." (p. 566)

On at least three occasions in the novel, Sophie repeats the most fundamental of her lies and the one most puzzling to Stingo: she makes of her father a decent, brave, and loving man. Because Sophie has no sense of self—because her identity is entirely relational, alienated in that of the men who control and protect her—her only opportunity to experience self-esteem, however vicarious and reflected, is to belong to men of whom she and others can think well. Logically, when her hated father and the husband who is his mirror image are murdered, Sophie grieves not for their death but for her own: "Her entire sense of self—of her identity—was unfastened" (p. 306). Nathan offers Sophie an exact replica of her relationship with her father: she receives protection and identity at the price of "childlike dependence" (p. 388), a total self-alienation that Nathan correctly identifies: "My darling, I think you have absolutely no ego at all" (p. 416). In this context, the story of Blackstock and his wife Sylvia, structurally gratuitous if the unity of Styron's novel is situated elsewhere than in the institution of sexism, serves a central metaphorical function. Blackstock's adoration for Sylvia turns her into a pet, a doll, a pampered child whose total irresponsibility is not merely tolerated but encouraged; and Sylvia destroys herself in an automobile accident, the head she has never had occasion to use severed from her body and lost.

Styron continually places Sophie in impossible situations which have particular metaphoric significance for women: if they prove appropriately selfless, they participate in their own alienation and destruction, but any claim they make for the right to self instantly backfires by proclaiming them to be selfish. Not only does Stingo openly condemn Sophie; she traps herself in her own narrative. For example, Sophie justifies her attempt to seduce Höss as the disinterested and courageous effort of a mother to save her son, but until all hope is clearly lost, we hear Sophie ask Höss only for her *own* freedom; we are in fact still unaware that she has a child (pp. 330–45). Sophie demands what she desperately needs and deserves—the right to exist—but she does so in a morally ambivalent context in which we are led to condemn her for her egotism, for failing to live up to the ideal of female selflessness: motherhood. But Sophie cannot win, for when she acts as the good mother, she is also condemned for the same female sin of selfishness. Both Sophie's refusal to help the Home Army in Warsaw, out of fear for her children's safety, and her inability to steal Emmi's radio, lest she lose her last chance to save Jan, demonstrate the selfless other-orientation traditionally required of women. But through our identification with Wanda and the Resistance movement, we come to regard Sophie as not only morally weak and irresponsible but indeed as selfish for her inability to put the plight of the Jewish people before her own, suspecting as well that she uses her children as an excuse to hide her own cowardice. Condemned for her maternal role, whether she fulfills it adequately or not, Sophie ultimately must act as the quintessentially bad mother: she becomes a Medea, morally guilty of infanticide. Not only has she implicitly preferred one child to another in a society in which maternal love is by definition unconditional and all-encompassing, but she whose value as woman is based upon her ability to give life has sent one of her children to death.

Although Styron uses the concept of a slave world, common to the Nazi concentration camps and to the history of the American South, to examine the condition of women as well, slavery serves him as contrast as much as comparison. For Styron understands the limits of the analogy even if in his existential world it may in some terrible sense be preferable to remain an absolute slave. The ultimate horror of the situation of women rests precisely on the two factors that distinguish them from the Negro slaves and from the Jewish inmates of Auschwitz: *choice*, however limited, and *collaboration*, however enforced. Sophie may have been prepared to act in a particular way at Auschwitz because of her gender identity: "she had been a victim, yes, but both victim and accomplice, accessory" (p. 266). Certainly Sophie's understanding of her "complicity" (p. 296), not only in her own oppression but in a world in which systematic oppression is possible, long predates the war. The typing and distributing of her father's murderous tract force her to acknowledge her tragic responsibility: a volition too strong to allow her the comforting status of victim but too weak to permit her to revolt:

> "And this terrible emptiness came over me when I realized just then there was nothing I could do about it, no way of saying no, no way possible to say, 'Papa, I'm not going to help you spread this thing.' . . . And I was a grown woman and I wanted to play Bach, and at that moment I just thought I must die—I mean, to die not so much for what he was making me do but because I had no way of saying no." (p. 300)

Certainly Sophie's enforced choice between her children represents the ultimate tragic dilemma, for she is made to choose in a situation in which no meaningful choice is possible: any decision will produce morally and emotionally identical results. And yet Dr. Jemand von Niemand is not totally wrong to call Sophie's right to choose "a privilege" (p. 589); for as Sophie herself understands, without choice as possibility or concept, women would remain helpless victims, unable to institute change. Ultimately, Sophie can choose for herself only on choosing suicide, but the importance of that decision should not be underestimated. Not only, as Phyllis Chesler has pointed out, does physical action—including suicide—remain extraordinarily difficult for women,[9] but Sophie selects death over a new loss of identity in the marriage and motherhood that Stingo offers.

Throughout *Sophie's Choice*, all questions of sex and sexism are linked to language and literature: to Stingo's vocation as writer, to the construction of the novel we are reading, to the creation of the story of Sophie. For Stingo, writing and sex are inseparable, indeed indistinguishable. In the key first chapter of *Sophie's Choice*, Stingo professes "an affinity for the written word—almost any written word—that was so excitable that it verged on the erotic" (p. 12). The urge to masturbate invariably accompanies Stingo's one creative task of the moment, the composition of jacket blurbs (p. 14); and the fantasy garden parties he imagines from his window are not only dominated by his lust for Mavis but peopled with famous authors: "In these demented fantasies I was prevented from immediate copulation on the Abercrombie & Fitch hammock only by the sudden arrival in the garden of Thornton Wilder. Or e. e. cummings. Or Katherine Anne Porter. Or John Hersey. Or Malcolm Cowley. Or John P. Marquand" (pp. 15–16). To Stingo as hero, the equivalence of language and sex becomes a source of almost unbearable frustration. He consistently finds himself a sexual eavesdropper, a sort of oral voyeur, for whom knowledge of the act of love is limited to the words other people pronounce during sex (pp. 91, 362). With comic irony, the woman Stingo selects as his sexual initiator has a totally lingual sex life: Leslie only kisses and talks about sex, and the single concrete result Stingo gleans from the adventure is an inflamed tongue.

But to Stingo as writer, sex is language in the most positive of senses: both the source and the subject of art. Susan Gubar and Sandra Gilbert in *The Madwoman in the Attic* postulate that the pen acts as "a metaphorical penis";[10] and Stingo illustrates particularly well their thesis that male sexuality is the essence of literary power. The opening chapter of *Sophie's Choice* sets up a paradigmatic model of male bonding through art: an older male, denied a writing career, devotes himself instead to the support and encouragement of a younger and more gifted "son" or "brother." Farrell's intention to write is transformed into the nurturing of his talented son, subsequently replaced by Stingo: "Son, *write your guts out*" (p. 28). Nathan, a gifted mime and storyteller, has also wanted to write and becomes instead a "supportive brother-figure" (p. 510) for Stingo and the only reader and critic of his novel. Even the narrative technique of *Sophie's Choice* contributes. The dialogue between the old and the young Stingo provides an affectionate father/son tone which guarantees a constant framework of male bonding in the joint pursuit of the ultimate male task of artistic creation:

> "How I now cherish the image of myself in this earlier time . . . supremely content in the knowledge that the fruit of this happy labor, whatever its deficiencies, would be the most awesome and important of man's imaginative endeavors—the Novel. The blessed Novel. The sacred Novel. The Almighty Novel." (p. 133)

On the other hand, the relationship of women to language in *Sophie's Choice* reflects their negative status with equal accuracy. Women are not only degraded by the sexist language men use to reduce them to their sexual anatomy—for example, "a piece of ass" (p. 144)—but women are obliged to degrade themselves through their own use of language. Leslie's uninhibited sexual language is her greatest "turn-on," since "this concubine's speech" (p. 153) serves to assure Stingo that the Jewish princess is in reality only a whore. The degradation of Sophie, whose linguistic ability far surpasses that of any male in the novel, illustrates particularly well the obstinate determination of sexist society to deny women any authentic use of language. Fluent in German, Polish, French, and Russian, Sophie finds herself in a situation where she must speak English, the single language in which Stingo and Nathan retain total superiority. Indeed, at our first encounter with Sophie, Nathan is berating her for the parallel female sins of sexual and linguistic infidelity: "I *can't* be a cunt, you dumb fucking Polack. When are you going to learn to *speak* the *language?*" (p. 55). Stingo periodically quotes Sophie's speech verbatim so that we may observe for ourselves that it is indeed "fetchingly erratic" (p. 106), that is, riddled with lexical and syntactical errors. Moreover, Sophie essentially parrots Nathan: "All at once I became aware of the way in which Sophie echoed so much of Nathan's diction" (p. 78). The one linguistic skill for which we hear Sophie consistently praised is her perfect command of German, an ambivalent accomplishment at best given the historical setting of the novel; the writer Stingo, on the other hand, commands the "gorgeous" English tongue (p. 133).

If Nathan in his roles as knowledgeable reader, critic, and literary historian predicts the coming of Jewish Writing to replace Southern Writing, certainly neither he nor Stingo ever foresees a tradition of Women's Writing. By the time Sophie expresses the astonishing desire to write a novel about her own experiences, her linguistic incompetence has been sufficiently proven to make her project seem not only improbable but almost comic; should any doubt remain, we are treated immediately to the single sample of her writing included in the novel: "it was testimony indeed to the imperfect command of written English of which Sophie had so recently lamented to me . . . " (p. 606). Since Sophie nonetheless retains a terrible obsession with her personal history, she must delegate her story to a man.

Although Stingo apparently accepts the passive role of listener, comparable both to the religious confessor and to the analyst (p. 177), for Sophie there is ultimately neither redemption nor cure. The story she believes she is assigning to Stingo's pen is in the process stolen from her. As Gilbert and Gubar point out, not only does a writer "father" his text in Western literary tradition but "the chief creature man has generated is woman" (p. 12). Stingo, who places himself in the category of writers who exploit the tragedies of "others" (p. 132), that is, of women, continually generates the same female story of self-destruction: in every important sense, Maria Hunt is already Sophie Zawistowska. Moreover, the female story ultimately turns out to be in the service of and subservient to that of the male. Stingo sees in Sophie the experience of love and death he must have to mature into a writer (p. 28) as he reads *Sophie's Choice* as his own picaresque novel.

The peculiar interplay of the narrative voices in *Sophie's Choice* illustrates particularly well the respective roles of men and women in a sexist literature and society. Not only is Sophie's narrative punctuated with reminders of Stingo's presence, but in most cases Stingo and not Sophie actually recounts her past. As "herstory" becomes "History," a clear narrative pattern emerges to distinguish the female from the male narrator. Sophie tells her own story only when she is lying or confessing previous lies. Thus, Sophie's major interventions involve her creation of a false childhood in Cracow (pp. 93–104), a misleading portrait of Nathan as a supportive and loving "Prince Charming" (pp. 188–93), her malignant misrepresentation of Wanda (pp. 426–45), and so on. Not only is unreliability thus attributed to the female, but the male voice becomes in contrast the voice of Truth. Indeed, the male narrator is consistently obliged to identify the female as liar: "But now it again becomes necessary to mention that Sophie was not quite straightforward in her recital of past events . . ." (p. 176).

At other times, Stingo uses the opposite but functionally identical technique of the insistent assurance that Sophie tells the truth, or rather—and the distinction is important—that Stingo believes her (see pp. 294, 296, 306). Not only are Stingo's reassurances suspiciously overdone, not only do they imply that Stingo did not believe her at other times and thus remind us that Sophie lies, but they make it clear that truth is male-defined and that to merit belief, Sophie's story must receive male validation.

Moreover, Sophie's lack of credibility is directly and significantly linked to her alleged lack of fidelity: women are whores and liars. We should carefully note the context in which the issue of Sophie's credibility is first raised:

> Blackstock was a truly happy man. He adored Sylvia more than life itself. Only the fact that he was childless, he once told Sophie, kept him from being *absolutely* the happiest man on earth. . . .
>
> As will be seen in due course (and the fact is important to this narrative), Sophie told me a number of lies that summer. (p. 116)

By juxtaposing the first mention of Sophie's lying to the protestations of Blackstock that he is a truly happy man who adores his wife, Stingo at least suggests by association that Sophie's "lies" may include her denial of sexual involvement with Blackstock. In any case, Sophie's initial lie to Stingo falsely represents her sexual fidelity: "I note that Sophie told me a lie within moments after we first set eyes on each other. This was when, after the ghastly fight with Nathan, she leveled upon me her look of desperation and declared that Nathan was 'the only man I have ever made love to beside my husband'" (p. 116). The possibility that Sophie may be lying about her fidelity is further reinforced by Nathan's accusations, and this extraordinary promotion of Nathan to a figure of authority permits Styron to expose the irrational bias of systematic sexism. For insane or not, pathological liar or not, Nathan is established as credible, given the insistence elsewhere on his prescience, his insight, his power to predict correctly, and by his general association with the representation of the male as the possessor of knowledge.

While Sophie remains obsessed with her personal life and story, Stingo seeks to place the former in its historical and theoretical context. The female lies; the male provides statistics, information, facts. Styron portrays the male in general as the learned, objective, neutral scholar; for the liar Nathan, who inexhaustibly researches Nazi anti-Semitism and the Civil War, fulfills this vision as much as Stingo. Ironically, of course, Sophie's lies essentially concern men. She accepts her female role as their promoter and protector, perpetuating to the best of her ability one of the central myths of a world in which men dominate, namely, that men are *good:* Sophie's father risked his life to save Jews; Casimir was a generous, loving, intelligent husband; Nathan is a gentle and tender saviour, Stingo a devoted friend. And yet, or so a system founded on sexism would have it, Sophie is a liar, and Stingo and Nathan, who perpetuate harmful and degrading misrepresentations of women, are not only imaginative and creative but factual and reliable.

Although Styron has been repeatedly accused of exploiting the experience of others for his own personal and literary benefit, no one seems yet to have questioned his right as male to usurp a female life. Stingo himself expresses some concern that he may have "intruded" on Sophie's privacy, but his scruples involve Sophie not as woman but as the survivor of a concentration camp (p. 265). In fact, Styron demonstrates that the experience of women can be a particularly effective means of understanding an experience of oppression otherwise foreign. In part, Sophie's life attracts Stingo as the possibility for a story because of certain similarities between the two of them: both are non-Jews isolated in a Jewish community; the war leaves both to suffer from some degree of survival guilt; both feel shame for the racial or religious prejudice of their compatriots; and so on. Such parallels serve not to trivialize Sophie's experience, as many critics have suggested, but to insist on the important generic sense Styron means ultimately to attach to her life. Mary Daly has no doubt correctly identified the technique of "universalization" as one means used to deny the reality of the specific oppression of women. Styron uses the opposite method of particularization: the situation of women becomes the basic model through which a general concept of systematic oppression can be illustrated. In seeking a confrontation with the reality of twentieth-century dehumanization, Styron has understood the usefulness of women whose intermediate position between victim and collaborator permits him to illustrate the necessity of choice and responsibility for the liberation of the self. Thus does Stingo appropriately feel rage and sorrow at the end of *Sophie's Choice* not just for Sophie but for all "the beaten and butchered and betrayed and martyred children of the earth" (p. 625) who have peopled his fictional world.

Notes

1. Jean-Paul Sartre, *Qu'est-ce que la littérature* (Paris: Gallimard, 1948), p. 85, n. 3. My translation.
2. William Styron, *Sophie's Choice* (New York: Bantam Books, 1980), p. 253. Future references appear parenthetically in the text.
3. Sartre, *Situations I* (Paris: Gallimard, 1947), p. 86. My translation.
4. James Atlas (*N. Y. Times Book Review*, 27 May 1979, p. 18), for example, finds the canvas of the book "crowded with incidents that bear no relation to the novel's theme"; Robert Towers (*N. Y. Review of Books*, 9 July 1979, p. 12) notes the "tenuous" and "less than convincing" connection between Poland and the American South; John W. Aldridge (*Harper's Magazine*, Sept. 1979, p. 97) sees in Stingo "a character seemingly without thematic relevance to the main action"; and Julian Symons (*Times Literary Supplement*, 30 Nov. 1979, p. 77) discerns in *Sophie's Choice* two separate novels, one Jewish and one Southern, whose linking he perceives as arbitrary and artificial.
5. See, for example, Philip W. Leon, *Virginia Quarterly Review*, 55 (1979), 740–47; Jack Beatty, *New Republic*, 30 June 1979, pp. 38–40; Edith Milton, *The Yale Review*, Autumn 1979, pp. 89–103; and John Gardner, *N. Y. Times Book Review*, 27 May 1979, pp. 1, 16–17.
6. Styron potentially offers support for the position of Mary Daly and other contemporary feminists that sexism is "the basic model and source of oppression," that exploitation as concept can be eradicated only with the termination of the universal exploitation of women. See Daly, *Beyond God the Father* (Boston: Beacon Press, 1973), p. 190; Shulamith Firestone, *The Dialectic of Sex* (New York: Bantam Books, 1970), pp. 105–25; and Dorothy Dinnerstein, *The Mermaid and the Minotaur* (New York: Harper, 1976), p. 102.
7. Robert Alter, *Saturday Review*, 7 July 1979, p. 43; see also reviews by Beatty, Aldridge, and Towers.
8. Significantly, the first time Sophie appears in sexy clothes (selected and paid for by Nathan), she is made to confuse "seersucker" with "cocksucker" (p. 233).
9. Phyllis Chesler, *Women and Madness* (Garden City, N. Y.: Doubleday, 1972), p. 49.
10. Susan Gubar and Sandra Gilbert, *The Madwoman in the Attic* (New Haven: Yale Univ. Press, 1979), p. 3.

SAMUEL COALE
"Styron's Disguises: A Provisional Rebel in Christian Masquerade"
Critique, Winter 1985, pp. 57–66

Many of William Styron's strengths as a writer come from those that we associate with Southern fiction. Baroque rhetoric powers his narratives; Faulkner's ghost lingers in his language. He evokes the kind of doomed, guilt-ridden landscapes we associate with the Southern vision of the world. The problem of evil haunts him at all levels—social, psychological, metaphysical—and spawns the moral quest, the search for values of his heroes amid the stark realities of pain and suffering. Manichean conflicts ravage his prose, his outlook, his characters, as if an ultimate nihilism or irrevocable Greek fate savaged the vestiges of his own Christian faith or background. Such a war-torn spirit leads to certain death, to spiritual paralysis. He stalks the "riddles of personality" like the best romancers and sets up voices of "normalcy," moderate spokesmen, as clear-eyed witnesses to extraordinary events and persons: Culver to Mannix, Peter Leverett to Cass Kinsolving,

Stingo to Sophie Zawistowska and Nathan Landau. A kind of existential, finally unexorcized sense of guilt relentlessly hounds him.

Styron writes in the tradition of the Southern gothic romance, moving from revelation to revelation, surprise to surprise, pacing his fiction as a series of building climaxes, each more shattering than the preceding one. He has written in this manner from the very first, as in *Lie Down in Darkness:* "it finally occurred to me to use separate moments in time, four or five long dramatic scenes revolving around the daughter, Peyton, at different stages in her life. The business of the progression of time seems to me one of the most difficult problems a novelst has to cope with."[1] The secret remains "a sense of architecture—a symmetry, perhaps unobtrusive but always there, without which a novel sprawls, becomes a self-indulged octopus. It was a matter of form."[2]

Styron's gothic architecture comes complete with its aura of damnation and doom, a dusky cathedral filled with omens and auguries, nightmares and demonic shadows. And at the end of labyrinthine corridors appear the inevitable horrors: Peyton's suicide, Cass's murder of Mason Flagg, Nat's murder of Margaret Whitehead, Sophie's surrendering her daughter Eva to the gas ovens of Birkenau. Sambuco, "aloof upon its precipice, remote and beautifully difficult of access,"[3] the enclosed white temple of Nat Turner's dreams, "those days"[4] of the 1940s in *Sophie's Choice:* here are the removed, withdrawn settings for dark romances. Nathan Landau wonders, however, if such a structure for fiction could be "a worn-out tradition," (115) and John Gardner, reviewing *Sophie's Choice,* considered the ambiguous relationship between the evil of Auschwitz and "the helpless groaning and self-flagellation of the Southern Gothic novel."[5] The suggestion is raised by both Styron and Gardner whether or not this kind of romance has outlived its usefulness, however passionately and grippingly re-created.

The ambiguous nature of Styron's vision may serve to undermine his gothic structures. For one thing, he often relies too heavily upon psychological explanations, a kind of rational reductionism that reduces metaphysical speculations to Freudian solutions. In *Lie Down in Darkness,* Styron deals with what his character, Albert Berger, calls, "this South with its cancerous religiosity, its exhausting need to put manners before morals, to negate all ethos . . . a *husk* of culture,"[6] in the new suburban middle-class South, a world hung up on its own narcissistic corruptions. These may be the result of the Old South gone dead, but a stronger case can be made for Oedipal tensions and familial dislocations along a purely psychological grid: nostalgia and self-indulgence, however alcoholic, however wounding, seem almost disconnected from any Southern past, or for that matter any past at all.

The trouble with the elegantly rendered and moving *The Confessions of Nat Turner* is that the religious fanatic cum prophet tells his own tale. All explanations and suggestions—psychological, tragic, Christian, heroic—tend to look like mere self-justifications. Nat as both interpreter and actor may see himself moving from Old Testament vengeance to New Testament charity and contrition, but within his own psychological maneuverings and suggestions, even this broadly mythic and religious design dissolves. The tidy psychology of the case study threatens to undermine the realities of any political action, any historical commitment. Manichean conflict—black vs. white, good vs. evil, master vs. slave—produces a kind of paralysis, a deeply felt and exquisitely written blank like the smooth white sides of that dreamed windowless enclosure.

Styron once suggested "that all my work is predicated on revolt in one way or another. And of course there's something about Nat Turner that's the ultimate fulfillment of all this. It's a strange revelation."[7] As he once described himself, he remains a "provisional rebel"[8]: his sufferers are witnessed at a distance, Mannix's "revolt" by Culver, Cass's angst by Leverett, Sophie's choices by Stingo. It is as if he has his cake—the rebellion, the guilt—and eats it, too—the "resurrection" and increased awareness of his witnesses. If many of Styron's rebels participate in a kind of self-mutilation or self-flagellation, his witnesses experience this as well, but at a distance. As we shall see in both *Set This House on Fire* and *Sophie's Choice*—for me his most passionate and fierce romances—violence and revenge are just barely, if at all, transmuted into Christian symbols; at times, the Christian imagery seems itself "provisional," a literary laying on of uncertain hands. We get finally not tragedies but melodramas, exorcisms rendered "safe" by the remarkably unscathed witnesses.

The whole question of Styron's notion of evil remains ambiguous. In *Lie Down in Darkness* Styron writes: "Too powerful a consciousness of evil was often the result of infantile emotions. The cowardly Puritan . . . , unwilling to partake of free religious inquiry, uses the devil as a scapegoat to rid himself of the need for positive action" (113). Evil becomes a dodge, an excuse for inaction, paralysis, as if Manichean polarities produced only stalemate, fashioned in a fierce baroque prose style. And Styron adds: "Perhaps the miseries of our century will be recalled only as the work of a race of strange and troublous children, by the wise old men in the aeons which come after us."[9] Infantile emotions: troublous children: a hint of adolescent angst sounded in a void? Evil as howling self? Is there something to Mailer's indictment of *Set This House on Fire* as the "magnum opus of a fat spoiled rich boy who could write like an angel about landscape and like an adolescent about people"?[10] Does gothic doom become, then, rhetorical, a literary attitude, a Faulknerian mannerism laced with a fatal Fitzerald-like glamour, overwrought in a gothic style?

Jonathan Baumbach suggests that *Set This House on Fire* "attempts the improbable: the alchemical transformation of impotent rage into tragic experience. Styron's rage is the hell-fire heat of the idealist faced by an unredeemably corrupt world for which he as fallen man feels obsessively and hopelessly guilty."[11] This suggests also Gardner's assessment of Styron's writing as "a piece of anguished Protestant soul-searching, an attempt to seize all the evil in the world—in his own heart first—crush it, and create a planet fit for God and man."[12] The Manichean battles in this book reveal the passionate intensity of this alchemical urge.

The sacred and the profane, the prudish and the prurient, God and nothingness, being and nihilism, doom and nostalgia, Anglo-Saxon and Italian honesty battle it out in *Set This House on Fire.* Peter Leverett, the moderate realistic lawyer, confronts Cass Kinsolving, the guilt-ridden visionary artist. Each has been attracted and played sycophant to the "gorgeous silver fish . . . a creature so strange, so *new*" (454) that is Mason Flagg. Flagg represents a Manichean vision in his "dual role of daytime squire and nighttime nihilist" (161), a distinctively American Jekyll and Hyde, "able in a time of hideous surfeit, and Togetherness's lurid mist, to revolt from conventional values, to plunge into a chic vortex of sensation, dope, and fabricated sin, though all the while retaining a strong grip on his two million dollars" (161). Is this Styron's "provisional rebel?" He celebrates the new frontier of sexual adventure as a gnostic libertine, corrupt in his faith, and reveals "that slick, arrogant, sensual, impenitently youthful, American and vainglorious face" (194): the spoiled, self-indulgent American child, filled with unfulfilled desire, itself desirous of further increase. He suggests Styron's America in the Fifties, "a general wasting away of quality, a kind of sleazy common prostration of the human spirit" (118), in times "like these when men go whoring off after false gods" in a realm of "moral and spiritual anarchy" (13). Is there any wonder that Peter Leverett's father cries out for "something ferocious and tragic, like what happened to Jericho or the cities of the plain" (15), a promise to "bring back tragedy to the land of the Pespi-Cola" (121)?

The Manichean vision acquires metaphysical proportions in Cass's mind. He "dreamed wild Manichean dreams, dreams that told him that God . . . was weaker even than the evil He created and allowed to reside in the soul of man" (282). Dreams "of women with burdens, and dogs being beaten, and these somehow all seemed inextricably and mysteriously connected, and monstrously, intolerably so" (351) haunt him, the dog beaten to death but refusing to die, "which suffered all the more because even He in His mighty belated compassion could not deliver His creatures from their living pain" (365).

Peter Leverett suffers a recurring nightmare of a shadow beyond the window in the dark, a friend bent on betrayal and murder but for no apparent reason. It is Cass who suggests "that whatsoever it is that rises in a dream with a look on his face of eternal damnation is just one's own self, wearing a mask, and that's the fact of the matter" (371). Evil becomes the self trapped in itself, a spirit at war with itself, a narcissistic and ineradicable sense of guilt that despite Cass's explanations of exile, orphanhood, ignorance, the war, his wife's Catholicism, his own "puddle of self" (260) at the base of his artistic nature, his Anglo-Saxon background, his terror, his Americanness, his actions toward blacks, will not be overcome. "To triumph over self is to triumph over Death," Cass declares. "It is to triumph over that beast which one's self interposes between one's soul and one's God" (260). Between that soul and God lurks the beast of the self, the solipsistic psychological center around which Styron's metaphysical and socio-cultural explanations of Manicheism pale. At one point Cass discusses "the business about evil—what it is, where it is, whether it's a reality, or just a figment of the mind," a cancer in the body or something "to stomp on like you would a flea carrying bubonic plague" (130). He decides that "both of these theories are as evil as the evil they are intended to destroy and cure" (131). Evil thus remains either "the puddle of self," which Styron belabors in the book, or the mystery of endless pain that knows no justification, a cruel beating down of the human spirit that in the end, like that puddle, suggests a perpetual entrapment, an imprisonment both of mind and matter, a Manichean mystery that can know release only in the worship of a demonic God or the furtive celebration of sex and sensation.

Both Leverett and Kinsolving press on to make their personal nightmares make sense. "Passionately he tried to make the dream give up its meaning" (320), Styron writes of Cass. He might just as well be writing about his use of the gothic romance to surrender up the significance of his own dark dreams of perpetual conflict and combat. "Each detail was as clear in his mind as something which happened only yesterday, yet when he tried to put them all together he ended up with blank ambiguous chaos" (320). The details refuse to conjure up the overall design: we have reached a standstill, an impasse. "These various horrors and sweats you have when you're asleep add up to something," Cass maintains, "even if these horrors are masked and these sweats are symbols. What you've got to do is get behind the mask and the symbol" (375). Kinsolving suggests Melville's Ahab who, in penetrating the mask, reduces ambiguity to palpable design and submits willfully to the Manichean fire-worshippers at his side. He becomes his own devil. Cass cannot.

Set This House on Fire cries out for tragedy to alleviate its pain. Styron instead settles for melodrama, the *deus ex machina*, the Fascist-humanist Luigi who will not allow Cass to wallow in any more of his guilt. Luigi to Cass plays the wise father to the angst-ridden American adolescent: Cass is "relieved" of his guilt.

Kinsolving and Leverett meet years later to talk in a fishing boat on the Southern river of their childhoods. If at first both seem like opposites, they in fact blend into one Southern sensibility: bewitched and entranced by Flagg, they succumb to a rampant unanchored nostalgia that swallows everything before it, an omniverous sentimentality, "the sad nostalgic glamor" (268), the Southern mind's ravenous appetite for "a hundred gentle memories, purely summer, purely southern, which swarmed instantly through his mind, though one huge memory encompassed all" (378). Nostalgia begets narcissism or vice-versa: intensity of feeling replaces knowledge as the keystone to awareness. This nostalgia is not seen as tragic, as a flight from adulthood: it survives "pure" in its sweeping intensities, its rhetorical sweep—and is the ominous flip-side of Cass's dread, of Styron's gothic plot and structure. Catastrophe, doom, guilt, phantoms, and diabolical enchantment draw Leverett to Flagg, Cass to Flagg, Leverett to Cass, but a rampant childhood nostalgia surmounts and floods them all, feeding upon itself.

As Flannery O'Connor suggested, "When tenderness is detached from the source of tenderness, its logical outcome is terror."[13] That nostalgic tenderness cancels spiritual stalemate. As Joyce Carol Oates suggests in reference to Norman Mailer, "he has constructed an entire body of work around a Manichean existentialism [with] a firm belief in the absolute existence of Evil [and] a belief in a limited God, a God Who is a warring element in a divided universe. . . . his energetic Manichaeanism forbids a higher art. Initiation . . . brings the protagonist not to newer visions . . . but to a dead end, a full stop."[14] Melodrama deflates tragedy and for all its passion and power leaves a world split between suffering and sentimentality, a dark design of untransmuted spiritual impotence, mesmerized by a Manichean reality but unable or unwilling to succumb to its fatal power and terrifyingly realized inevitability. Perhaps "ultimate" rebellion would insist on such a vision. "Provisional" rebellion can only disguise it in Christian images and psychological explanations. The void which surrounds Cass's tirades, that outer world which dissolves in the wake of his internal cries, may reflect only his own narcissism, suggesting that Styron is intent upon withdrawing from the very Manichean vision he's so fiercely created into a safer hollow.

The Manichean vision of *Sophie's Choice* is announced in Styron's opening quotation from André Malraux's *Lazare*: "I seek that essential region of the soul where absolute evil confronts brotherhood." Nathan is both Sophie's savior and destroyer; love battles death; Calvanist Southerners are mesmerized by New York Jews; North and South fight over virtue or the lack of it; black and white, slave and master become both victims and accomplices of one another; out of the adversity Poland has suffered comes not compassion and charity but sustained anti-Semitic cruelty; sex in Stingo's 1940s at the age of twenty-two breeds both liberation and guilt; Sophie "could not bear the contrast between the abstract yet immeasurable beauty of music and the almost touchable dimensions of her own aching despair" (94); every choice is fraught with disaster; survival itself produces the ineradicable "toxin of guilt." Poland reflects a defeated South with "her indwelling ravaged and melancholy heart," the sense of inestimable loss, a legacy of "cruelty and compassion" (247). Opposites attract, become entangled, lead to suicide as ultimate paralysis. Steiner's "two orders of simultaneous experience are so different, so irreconcilable to any common norm of human values, their coexistence is so hideous a paradox" that they like "Gnostic speculation imply, different species of time in the same world" (216). Evil itself becomes the banality of duty and obedience, the belief in the "absolute *expendability* of human life" (235), the reality of Auschwitz that cannot be finally understood.

The most "common norm of human values," Styron undermines is Christianity, at the same time he uses Christian imagery, apparently without irony, to describe the scope and mythic archetypes of his material: "I mean it when I say that no chaste and famished grail-tormented Christian knight could have gazed with more slack-jawed admiration at the object of his quest than I did at my first glimpse of Sophie's bouncing behind" (358). A good line, but the Christian quest motif sticks to the entire form of Styron's use of the gothic romance: it is supposed to lead, however disastrously, to understanding, significance in ultimately religious terms. Stingo's own "Protestant moderation" (299) invests sex with guilt and his "residual Calvinism" (495) sparks his imagination with visions of doom and desecration. On the train, however, with the "dark priestess" toward the end of the book, the black woman, he "went into a bizarre religious convulsion, brief in duration but intense" and reads the Bible aloud with her, not the Sermon on the Mount, but "the grand old Hebrew woe seemed more cathartic, so we went back to Job" (506), the archetypal victim, but one of residual faith, a kind the agnostic Stingo does not share. He disguises himself as the Reverend Entwistle to get a room with Sophie and admits that "the Scriptures were always largely a literary convenience, supplying me with allusions and tag lines for the characters in my novel" (505), but what are we to make of Stingo's impression of Dr. Jemand von Niemand, the man who forces on Sophie her most chilling choice? He must have done so, Stingo speculates, because he thirsted for faith, and to restore God he first must commit a great sin: "All of his depravity had been enacted in a vacuum of sinless and businesslike godlessness, while his soul thirsted for beatitude" (486). The great sin will shadow forth a greater faith "to restore his belief in God" (486).

At the conclusion of the book, Stingo reads lines from Dickinson at the graves of Sophie and Nathan: "Ample make this bed. / Make this bed with awe; / In it wait till judgment break / Excellent and fair" (512). After a night on the beach of Poesque dreams, being buried alive and awaking to find himself buried in sand like "a living cadaver being prepared for burial in the sands of Egypt," he welcomes the morning, blesses "my resurrection," and explains: "This was not judgment day—only morning. Morning: excellent and fair" (515). The ironies are apparent, but so is the stab at symbolic resurrection, waking from the gothic nightmare, returned to the land of the living. It is as if Stingo/Styron wants it both ways again, provisionally damned, provisionally saved. Auschwitz disregarded "Christian constraint" (235); Stingo will not, despite the revelations of Sophie. He clings to his genteel moderation despite the "Sophiemania" (307) that engulfs him and "laid siege to my imagination" (59).

Gothic romance usually demands the waking from the nightmare, a return to normalcy after the exorcism. But Stingo, like Peter Leverett and Cass Kinsolving before him, will not surrender to being exorcized; he clings to the very fallacious and out-moded Christian doctrines the narrative of the romance undermines. Perhaps the gothic romance cannot embrace absolute evil; the term itself curdles the narrator's will to embrace it. Others will die; they will survive because of the very harried faith they have been "taught" during the romance to outgrow. Stingo's attraction to a certain morbidity is not the same thing as being "called the 'tragic sense'" (110). It is too guarded, too self-protected, too distanced from the real Manichean vision of things by splendid baroque rhetoric and vocabularies of doom and dark auguries. He loves the doom as he loves a nostalgic South; it is a feeling in his bones, shiveringly enjoyable, a *frisson* of the spirit. Within that emotional solipsism, absolute evil proves sheerest poppycock.

Yet *Sophie's Choice* works with its escalating confessions, its ominous rhetoric, its sheer dramatic scope and power, as we learn of the real nature of Sophie's father, the many lovers from the murderer Jozef to the lesbian Wanda, the incredible choice of surrendering her daughter to the ovens. Stingo's climax literally occurs in bed—at last—with the pale, radiant Sophie; hers occurs with her suicide pact with Nathan: sex and death, twin dark towers of Manichean castles: semen and cyanide brutally intermingled. "Everyone's a victim. The Jews are also the victims of victims, that's the main difference" (474). There is the frightening core of *Sophie's Choice*, evaded or at least displaced by Stingo's awakening from premature burial to the possibility of morning and of resurrection. Sophie weaves tale after tale before her "patient confessor" (355), each until the end "a fabrication, a wretched lie, another fantasy served up to provide a frail barrier, a hopeless and crumbly line of defense between those she cared for, like myself, and her smothering guilt" (237). But the Christian fabrications, the literary allusions, are themselves frail barriers and should crumble completely before the overwhelming presence of guilt, even as "small" in comparison to Sophie's as is Stingo's in relation to his mother's death, his native region, the money he inherited from the slave sold down river, Artiste (appropriately named). Gothic romance, aligned to Christian images of demonic nightmare, the dark night of the soul, and resurrection, itself crumbles as it did in Hawthorne's *The Marble Faun*, undone by the pit of Rome, or in Hawthorne's *The Blithedale Romance*, overwhelmed by the harsh reality of power, of masters and slaves beneath the veils. In Stingo's narrative, it does seem a "worn-out tradition."

Perhaps Styron writes at the end of Southern romance, or perhaps he has stretched the form to include a vision of the world that it cannot contain, that murky spurious mixture of Christian archetype and Manichean vision. Rational psychological explanations and Christian archetypes cannot encompass such a fierce conjuring up of guilt; they can only reduce and confine it. Styron's guilt will not be confined in any rational, religious scheme or design: it overwhelms every attempt to comprehend it, existing as some great Manichean "black hole" that can result only in ultimate withdrawal—the aesthetics of suicide—or in sexual revelry—the libertinism of Mason Flagg, of Stingo's starving lust. Rhetoric, however intense and poetic, cannot transmute it into anything finally significant other than its own dark irrevocable existence, men and women entombed for life. As Rilke suggests in Styron's opening quote, "death, the whole of earth,—even before life's begun . . . this is beyond description!"

In Styron's world, we are really in Poe country. Faulkner transcended it by his genius, the depth of his complexity of vision; Flannery O'Connor surmounted it through an ultimate religious faith garbed in grotesque disguises, in the grim visages of serious clowns. Carson McCullers and Styron seem trapped within it, McCullers more certain of the Manichean shadows of her vision, setting it up as dark fable, as inevitable as death itself. Styron cautiously moves around it, hanging on to Christian images, archetypes, symbols despite the splendid proofs that they do not apply. Perhaps this is where the Southern tradition in American fiction ends, grappling with absolute evil outside its borders, serving up horrors as it would serve up childhood fantasies. Styron excels at it. His fiction drives itself toward a revelation he cannot or will not accept. All the magnificent rhetoric in the world will not gloss over the provisional nature of his vision, not mere ambiguity but at last evasion. The line between paradox and paralysis is a thin one. Styron's marvelous conjurings up of the former leads finally to the latter, and perhaps this is the absolute evil in contemporary society that haunts him the most.

Notes

1. Interview with William Styron, in *Writers at Work: The Paris Review Interviews*, ed. by Malcolm Cowley (New York: Viking Press, 1958), p. 275.
2. William Styron, "Recollections of a Once Timid Novelist," *The Hartford Courant Magazine*, 3 January 1982, 8.
3. William Styron, *Set This House on Fire* (New York: Bantam Windstone Books, 1981), p. 3. Subsequent references are to this edition.
4. William Styron, *Sophie's Choice* (New York: Random House, 1979), p. 3. Subsequent references are to this edition.
5. John Gardner, "A Novel of Evil," *The New York Times Book Review*, 84, No. 21 (27 May 1979), 17.
6. William Styron, *Lie Down in Darkness* (New York: New American Library, 1951), p. 346. Subsequent references are to this edition.
7. Interview with William Styron by the author, 15 July 1969. Cited below as Interview.
8. Interview.
9. William Styron, "The Prevalence of Wonders," *Nation*, 176 (2 May 1953), 371.
10. Norman Mailer, "Norman Mailer vs. Nine Writers," *Esquire*, 60 (July 1963), 64.
11. Jonathan Baumbach, "Paradise Lost: The Novels of William Styron," *South Atlantic Quarterly*, 63 (Spring 1964), 215.
12. Gardner, 16.
13. Flannery O'Connor, "Introduction to *A Memoir of Mary Ann*," in *Mystery and Manners*, ed. Sally and Robert Fitzgerald (New York: Farrar Straus Giroux, 1962), p. 227.
14. Joyce Carol Oates, "Norman Mailer: The Teleology of the Unconscious," in *New Heaven, New Earth: The Visionary Experience in Literature* (New York: Vanguard Press, 1974), pp. 191–92, 200.

May Swenson

1919–

May Swenson was born in Logan, Utah, on May 28, 1919, of Swedish parents who were Mormons. She was raised in Utah and earned a B.S. at Utah State University in 1939. Between 1959 and 1966 she worked as an editor at New Directions Press, and in 1966–67 she was poet-in-residence at Purdue University. Since then she has been an instructor in poetry at the University of North Carolina at Greensboro (1968–69, 1975), Lethbridge University in Alberta, Canada (1970), and the University of California at Riverside (1973). Swenson has spent most of her adult life in or near New York City, and currently lives in Sea Cliff, New York. She was a co-winner of the Bollingen Prize in 1979–80.

Swenson's poems are marked by an experimentalism of technique, including the use of typography to form various "iconographic" shapes. Her collections include *Another Animal* (1954), *A Cage of Spines* (1958), *To Mix with Time* (1963), *Half Sun Half Sleep* (1967), *Iconographs* (1970), and *New and Selected Things Taking Place* (1978). *Poems to Solve* (1966) and *More Poems to Solve* (1971) are riddles for children, and *Windows and Stones* (1972) is a translation of the Swedish poet Tomas Tranströmer.

What is the experience of poetry? Choosing to analyze this experience for myself after an engrossment of many years, I see it based in a craving to get through the curtains of things as they *appear*, to things as they *are*, and then into the larger, wilder space of things as they *are becoming*. This ambition involves a paradox: an instinctive belief in the senses as exquisite tools for this investigation and, at the same time, a suspicion about their crudeness. They may furnish easy deceptions or partial distortions:

> Hold a dandelion and look at the sun.
> Two spheres are side by side.
> Each has a yellow ruff.
>
> Eye, you tell a lie,
> that Near is Large, that Far is Small.
> There must be other deceits. . . .

W. B. Yeats called poetry "the thinking of the body" and said: "It bids us touch and taste and hear and see the world, and shrinks from . . . every abstract thing, from all that is of the brain only—from all that is not a fountain jetting from the entire hopes, memories, and sensations of the body." But sometimes one gets the inkling that there are extrasenses as yet nameless, within the apperceptive system, if only one could differentiate them and identify their organs.

Not to be fully aroused to the potentialities of one's senses means to walk the flat ground of appearances, to take given designations for granted, to accept without a second look the name or category of a thing for the thing itself. On that ground all feelings and notions are borrowed, are secondhand. The poetic experience, by contrast, is one of constant curiosity, skepticism, and testing—astonishment, disillusionment, renewed discovery, re-illumination. It amounts to a virtual compulsion to probe with the senses into the complex actuality of all things, outside and inside the self, and to determine relationships between them.

Aroused to the potentialities and delights of the senses and the evaluating intellect and using them daily, the poet, however, comes eventually to their limits and notices that their findings are not enough—often fall short of yielding the total, all-comprehensive pattern that he seeks. A complete and *firm* apprehension of the Whole tantalizingly eludes him—although he receives mirages of it now and then which he projects into his work. He is not so separate from every man as not to be fooled by tricks of perspective, seduced by the obvious, or bogged down in old and comfortable myths.

The limitations of our minds and sensorial equipment partly stem from the brevity of our physical lives. Stendhal somewhere says that man is like a fly born in the summer morning and dead by afternoon. How can he understand the word "night"? If he were allowed five more hours he would see and understand what night is. But unlike the fly, man is sorely conscious of the vastness of the unknown beyond his consciousness. The poet, tracing the edge of a great shadow whose outline shifts and varies, proving there is an invisible moving source of light behind, hopes (naively, in view of his ephemerality) to reach and touch the foot of that solid whatever-it-is that casts the shadow. If sometimes it seems he does touch it, it is only to be faced with a more distant, even less accessible mystery. Because all is movement—expansion or contraction, rotation or revolution—all is breathing change.

The experience of poetry is to suppose that there is a moon of the psyche, let us say, whose illuminated half is familiar to our ordinary eye, but which has another hemisphere which is dark; and that poetry can discover this *other side*, that its thrust can take us toward it. Poetry is used to make maps of that globe, which to the "naked eye" appears disk-like and one-dimensional, seems to "rise" and "set" rather than to orbit; which remains distant and merely a "dead" object until, in the vehicle of poetry and with the speed of poetic light, we approach it. It then enlarges and reveals its surprising topography, becomes a world. And *passing around* it, our senses undergo dilation; there is a transformation of perception by means of this realization of *the round*.

Miniature as we are in the gigantic body of the cosmos, we have somehow an inbuilt craving to get our pincers of perception around the whole of it, to incorporate infinitude and set up comprehensible models of it within our little minds. Poetry tries to do this in its fashion. Science tries it more demonstrably. The impulses of the scientist and the poet, it seems to me, are parallel, although their instruments, methods, and effects are quite divergent. Contrasts between science and poetry are easily illustrated by such apparent opposites as: Objective/Subjective, Reason/Intuition, Fact/Essence—or let me boldly say: Material/Spiritual. However, a point of contiguity between them is that poet and scientist both use *language* to communicate their findings.—MAY SWENSON, "The Experience of Poetry in a Scientific Age," *Poets on Poetry*, ed. Howard Nemerov, 1966, pp. 147–49

No one today is more deft and lucky in discovering a poem than May Swenson. Her work often appears to be proceeding calmly, just descriptive and accurate; but then suddenly it opens into something that looms beyond the material, something that impends and implies. You get to feeling that if the world were different she would have to lie in order to make her point, but that fortunately the world is so various and fortuitous that she can be truthful and also marvelously effective.

So graceful is the progression in her poems that they launch confidently into any form, carrying through it to easy, apt variations. Often her way is to define things, but the definitions have a stealthy trend: what she chooses and the way she progresses heap upon the reader a consistent, incremental effect.

An example poem is "The Little Rapids" ⟨in *Half Sun Half Sleep*⟩. The words nimbly leap, at their best; they know what they are about. And the reader finds that they are about the heart, "its zest constant / even in sleep, / its padded roar / bounding in the grotto of the breast". The words, vivid and apt as they are, are not enough to account for their success; the reader finds himself encountering adventures that converge into the one steady vision of the whole poem.

In the continuing work of Miss Swenson the question becomes: will her luck provide worthy encounters? Will she become distracted by this poking so interestedly in a dilettantish way into stray things? Sometimes, as in "The Secret in the Cat," you think that she is just clever, apt with diction, able to maintain a chosen topic and to rev it up. But that same cleverness often leads into wilder and more interesting regions, as in "A Bird's Life." Some of the cleverest poems, just through their intense unity, succeed in becoming greater things, as in the heart poem mentioned earlier, or in "Sleeping Overnight on the Shore," or in a wonderful poem about "The Watch." Partly, the most successful poems succeed through the ambition, the scope of the curiosity, of the writer; she pursues remote things, how the universe started, what will happen when . . . if. . . .

The translations from six Swedish poets at the end of the book are also fascinating, particularly those from Ingemar Gustafson and Karin Boye. The whole book is impressive, memorable, exciting to read.—WILLIAM STAFFORD, *Poetry*, Dec. 1967, pp. 184–85

ANN STANFORD

From "May Swenson: The Art of Perceiving"

Southern Review, Winter 1969, pp. 58–75

May Swenson is the poet of the perceptible. No writer employs with greater care the organs of sense to apprehend and record the surfaces of the world. She is the exemplar of that first canon of the poet—*Behold!*

From the time her poetry began appearing in the early 1950s in such places as *New Directions in Prose and Poetry*, *Discovery*, the *New Yorker*, and *Poetry*, Miss Swenson's work in its concentration on the sensible has been very much her own. The preoccupation with perception dominates the poetry of her successive volumes—*Another Animal* (1954), *A Cage of Spines* (1958), *To Mix with Time: New and Selected Poems* (1963), *Poems to Solve* (1966), and *Half Sun Half Sleep* (1967). One can name, however, if not influences, at any rate some poets whose work runs parallel to hers. Her development of visual detail has some relationship to the accurate reporting of Marianne Moore. It is sometimes close to that other remarkable declarer of what is there, Elizabeth Bishop. Her interest in nature, its small creatures and their large implications, is reminiscent of Emily Dickinson. In form, her work may have had some relationship to the experiments of E. E. Cummings, though it has always been a distant one, her experiments having gone farther into the visual and less into the verbal than his.

In a recent essay in *Tri-Quarterly*, Richard Howard has traced through Miss Swenson's several books the thaumaturgical qualities of her work—her desire to cast spells and to escape into enchantment, her refusal to name lest this interfere with identifying. Certainly this is an essential aspect of Miss Swenson's poetry. But for all the casting of spells, there is another quality, noted also by Mr. Howard, without which the enchantment could not exist; that is the ground on which the enchantment is laid, the universe which is assumed—in Miss Swenson's case, the perceptible-to-the-senses.

It is as an observer that May Swenson has become best known. Such a comment as Robert Lowell's "Miss Swenson's quick-eyed poems should be hung with permanent fresh paint signs," represents a common reaction. Miss Swenson achieves this freshness by a good eye enlivened by imagination. But however imaginative, her poetry is continually tied to accuracy of sight, to truth to the literal and concrete. This is so even when the truth is conveyed by metaphor or in a spirit of aesthetic play. From the beginning, Miss Swenson has demonstrated an unusual ability to set down accurate and detailed observations. The opening lines of the early poem "Green Red Brown and White" furnish an example:

Bit an apple on its red
side   Smelled like snow
Between white halves broken open
brown winks slept in sockets of green
Stroked a birch white as a thigh
scar-flecked smooth as the neck
of a horse   On mossy pallets green
the pines dropped down
their perfect carvings brown

This kind of reproduction of the immediate view becomes the main burden of many poems. Sometimes what she sees astonishes by its inclusiveness—for instance, "Notes Made in the Piazza San Marco":

The wingèd lion on top of that column
(his paws have been patched, he appears to wear boots)
is bronze but has a white eye—
his tail sails out long . . . Could it help him fly?
On the other column St. Theodore
standing on an alligator,
he and it as white as salt,
wears an iron halo and an iron sword.
San Marco is crusty and curly with many crowns,
or is it a growth of golden thrones?
The five domes
covered, it looks like, with stiff crinkly parachute silk
have gold balls on twigs on turnip-tips,
sharp turrets in between with metal flags that cannot wave.

The poem is fourteen stanzas of such details.

The careful looking that we find in the "Notes" is often not rendered so directly. Instead of focusing on the easily apparent, Miss Swenson is apt to choose an unusual angle. For that matter, even the carvings of the Piazza San Marco seem caught in the enlarging lenses of binoculars. "Water Picture" is an exact description, but everything there is upside down, for it is seen in the water. In other poems, she takes other places for view—from low, "When You Lie Down, the Sea Stands Up"; from high, "Flying Home from Utah," "11th Floor, West 4th Street"; from close up to a small object, "The Surface"; through the lashes or with half-closed eyes, "While Sitting in the Tuileries and Facing the Slanting Sun."

Writing the poem from an unusual center point is one means by which May Swenson adds heretofore unseen qualities to objects. Sometimes the result is a new sense of the order of material in space or time. Miss Swenson admits the desire to restructure in a poem which reveals part of her poetic rationale:

Distance
and a certain light
makes anything artistic—
it doesn't matter what.
From an airplane, all
that rigid splatter of the Bronx
becomes organic, logical
as web or beehive. . . .
Rubbish becomes engaging shape—
you only have to get a bead on it,
the right light filling the corridor
of your view—a gob of spit
under a microscope, fastidious
in structure as a crystal. No contortion
without intention, and nothing ugly.
In any random, sprawling, decomposing thing
is the charming string
of its history—and what it will be next.

The same rationale—adding the unperceived to what is customarily seen—governs her many riddling poems. An early example is "Shadow-Maker":

After a season
apparently sterile he
displays his achievements
  Scale upon layered scale
  frieze upon frieze of animate
  pointed perfect spine-bright
    notes are they?
    gestures for a dance?
    glyphs of a daring alphabet?
      Innumerable intimations
      on one theme
      A primal color haunts the whole design

The refusal to name is part of the play of the poem, but it is also a response to the need to render the world in a new way. The above passage illustrates her use of direct, close observation which alternates with metaphor as means of revealing, not only in the riddling poems but in many of the others. Both ways of observing result in descriptions that are true to the perceptible state of the object before the eyes.

One recurring metaphor, the comparison of the human body to landscape, illustrates the kinds of tasks she lays upon analogy. An early poem, "Sketch for a Landscape," describes the human face in terms of landscape. The result is a surrealistic combination:

a clearing her forehead Brisk
wilderness of hair
retreats from the smooth dancing ground
now savage drums are silent In caves
of shade twin jaguars couch
flicking their tails in restless dream Awake
they leap in unison Asleep they sink
like embers Sloping swards her cheekbones
graduate to a natural throne Two lambs
her nostrils curled back to back Follow
the shallow hollow to her lip-points
stung blossoms or bruised fruits Her
lower lip an opulent orchard Her spiral smile
a sweet oasis both hot and cool
soft in center swollen a bole of moss
hiding white stones and a moist spring
where lives a snake so beautiful and shy His
undulant hole is kept a slippery secret A cleft
between the cliff-edge and her mouth we drop
to the shouldered foothills down the neck's
obelisk and rest In the valley's scoop
velvet meadowland

RANDOM HOUSE

William Styron

UPI/BETTMANN NEWSPHOTOS

Rex Stout

NEWSWEEK

Robert Stone

NEW YORK TIMES

Jesse Stuart

AP/WIDE WORLD PHOTOS

Sara Teasdale

THE BETTMANN ARCHIVE

Booth Tarkington

AP/WIDE WORLD PHOTOS

Peter Taylor

NEW YORK TIMES

Allen Tate

"A Lake Scene" includes the reverse metaphor, though not so developed:

I think of the smoothest thing:
the inside of a young thigh,
or the line of a torso when, supine,
the pectoral sheathe crosses the armpit
to the outflung arm;
at the juncture of lake and hills, that zone,
the lowest hill in weavings
of fainter others overlaid,
is a pelvis in shadow.

"Sketch for a Landscape" is a remarkable tour-de-force. "A Lake Scene" employs the body-landscape metaphor in a more casual way as an aid in the immediate rendering, just as one would employ simile. Metaphor plays a larger part in the riddling poems and others where mystery is created by description through analogy, and the likeness that the subject of the poem has to other entities becomes an essential part of its own definition.

"At First, at Last" moves through a succession of possibilities. It appears to be a description of passing over land described as sea, or vice-versa, before it lights upon its ultimate subject, the act of love or, as its original suggests, "A Diagram of Life."

At first the dips are shallow,
the peaks ever higher.
Until at last the peaks
are lower.
The valleys deepen.
It is a wave
that mounts and recoils.
Coming then to shadows
on the slopes,
rifts in the concaves,
what is there to do
but lie open-eyed and love
the wave? . . .

Similarly, "The Little Rapids" begins with what seems to be a description of a mountain stream:

Over its cliff
splashes the
little rapids,
a braid of glossy
motion in perpetual
flow and toss

But the second stanza reveals that the poet is speaking of the blood stream, and the poem ends:

Ravine of my body,
red, incredulous
with autumn,
from here curt death
will hurl me delirious
into the gorge.

In this poem and in "Sketch for a Landscape" the face or bloodstream and the landscape are jointly described in terms that will apply to either. A slightly different transformation, the physical joining of two distinct creatures, takes place in such poems as "The Centaur" and "Horse and Swan Feeding." In the latter, the horse's neck and head become those of a swan, and the swan too changes:

Her kingly neck on her male
imperturbable white steed-like body
rides stately away

In "The Centaur" the body of the child and the willow branch she rides merge into one.

Yet even where bodies merge—girl and willow branch, swan and horse, face and landscape—in Miss Swenson's poetry, they do not blend into each other in the way that they do in Wordsworth, where the "plots of cottage ground, the orchard-tufts" . . . "lose themselves mid groves and copses." Her merging of forms is the sleight-of-hand of the magician. Though for a moment two things appear to have the same qualities, the poem preserves the integrity of each of the objects:

My head and my neck were mine,
yet they were shaped like a horse.
My hair flopped to the side
like the mane of a horse in the wind.
My forelock swung in my eyes,
my neck arched and I snorted . . . .
I was the horse and the rider,
and the leather I slapped to his rump
spanked my own behind.
Doubled, my two hoofs beat
a gallop along the bank,
the wind twanged in my mane,
my mouth squared to the bit.
And yet I sat on my steed
quiet, negligent riding,
my toes standing the stirrups,
my thighs hugging his ribs.

In the Swenson poems, the poet is aware that the reader knows that things are separate and that it is only for the moment that they are one. There is a holding on to the demonstrably real in the most daring of Miss Swenson's flights:

If I could get
out of my
head and
into the
world . . .
O.K., let's say I'm
out and
in the
round free
word . . .
Back there's the tight aluminum sphere
I jumped
out of, slammed the door like an icebox.
A clean landscape
around me, an inch or two of "snow"—
rock-dust from those
peaks
in the distance. No colder here,
even if it is wider. Very few things
around —just the
peaks. It'll take weeks to reach them.
Of course I came here in my
head.
I'll be taking it
back.
The idea is to make a vehicle
out of it.

We have noted Miss Swenson's skillful use of observation and creation of fresh effects by her changes in the angle of vision and her holding back of the realization of what her poem is about until a new perception of it has been established.

One of her ways of doing this might be called "reversal." In "Water Picture," where everything is shown in reflection, nature has done the poet's work of turning things into a new perspective. In other poems, Miss Swenson herself turns something into its opposite. In "The Even Sea," waves are described as cattle, creatures of the land. In "To the Shore," the train for a few lines seems already on the sea:

We are seated
In a glass tube, that bullet-headed, cleaves
the scene, tossing a froth of fields and trees
and billowing land alongside.

In "Waiting for IT," the poet's cat is waiting for something he knows has already happened:

My cat jumps to the window sill
and sits there still as a jug.
He's waiting for me, but I cannot be
coming, for I am in the room.

His snout, a gloomy V of patience,
pokes out into the sun.
The funnels of his ears expect
to be poured full of my footsteps.

It, the electric moment, a sweet
mouse, will appear; at his gray
eye's edge I'll be coming home
if he sits on the window-ledge.

As in the cat poem, Miss Swenson often adds to a familiar scene relations not ordinarily thought of. A statue in the park ("Fountain Piece") takes on a new dimension with the addition of what has been there all the time, now set into a web of relationships heretofore unperceived.

A bird
is perched
upon a wing
The wing
is stone
The bird
is real
A drapery
falls about this form
The form is stone
The dress is rain
The pigeon preens his own
and does not know
he sits upon a wing
The angel does not feel
a relative among her large
feathers stretch
and take his span
in charge
and leave her there
with her cold
wings that cannot fold
while his fan
in air.
The fountain raining
wets the stone
but does not know it dresses
an angel in its tresses
Her stone cheek smiles
and does not care
that real tears
flow there

The relationships are drawn in the most directly realistic way, and the denial of the pathetic fallacy itself becomes part of the poem. Again, in "Sunday in the Country" the poet keeps the actual in mind even when she sets up an analogy. The poem develops the common Romantic concept of the outdoors as a place to worship. The effect is created by a series of comparison words, in which the metaphor is taken literally, rather than by an attempt to make the scene look like a church: "A cricket's creed intoned to the attentive wood . . . The sun's incessant blessing . . . Angels climb through my lashes . . . Long grass, silky as a monk's beard." As so often in the poems, the metaphoric play, having run its course, comes to rest again in the non-magical world from which it first sprang. The spell of sun and light—the Romantic fiction—is denied:

Until, at the tabernacle's back, a blurt
guffaw is heard. An atheistic stranger calls
a shocking word. That wakes the insurrection!
Wind starts in the wood, and strips the pompous
cassocks from the pines. A black and
impudent Voltairean crow has spoiled
the sacrament. And I can rise and go.

The wit and sense of play demonstrated here, together with accurate observation (we always know Miss Swenson has been there), give poem after poem the freshness of discovery. Sometimes the play, the making of metaphor for the fun of it, predominates. In "To the Statue," people embarking to visit the Statue of Liberty are so close together they are

stuck up tight as asparagus stalks
inside the red rails (ribbons tying the bunch.)

Returning

They've been to the Statue.
She has no face from here, but just a fist.
(The flame is carved like an asparagus tip.)

⟨. . .⟩ The territory that May Swenson has invaded and penetrated more deeply than other moderns is that of the perceptible. Except for an occasional flight into the abstract, she has remained at her essential task, that of showing us what we too might have perceived had we been gifted with such unusual sensibility and delight. The ultimate justification of the concentration on the exploration of this territory is best set forth by the poet herself:

any Object before the Eye
can fill the space can occupy
the supple frame of eternity

my Hand before me such
tangents teaches into Much
root and twig extremes can touch

any Hour can be the all
expanding like a cunning Ball
to a Vast from very small

skull and loin the twin-shaped Cup
store the glittering grainery up
for all the sandy stars to sup

any Single becomes the More
multiples sprout from alpha's core
from Vase of legend vessels of lore

to this pupil dark and wild
where lives the portrait of a Child
let me then be reconciled

germ of the first Intent to be
i am and must be seen to see
then every New descends from me

uncoiling into Motion i
start a massive panoply
the anamolecular atoms fly

and spread through ether like a foam
appropriating all the Dome
of absoluteness for my home

Given such a credo, the poem can go far. But it begins with the object before the eye. And in May Swenson's poetry, with that object as talisman, the world is recurrently made anew.

DAVE SMITH

"Perpetual Worlds Taking Place"

Poetry, February 1980, pp. 291–96

May Swenson's *New and Selected Things Taking Place* collects nearly thirty years of her remarkable poetry. At sixty, she may well be the fiercest, most inquisitive poet of her generation; certainly few are more brilliant or more independent of mien. Her poems, through six collections since 1954, are characterized by an extreme reticence of personality, an abundant energy, and an extraordinary intercourse between the natural and intellectual worlds. She has always been as formal as poets come, demonstrating early and late a skilled employment of traditional verse as well as a passion for invented patterns. There are two central obsessions in her work: the search for a proper perspective and the celebration of life's embattled rage to continue. Her poems ask teleological questions and answer them, insofar as answers are ever possible, in every conceivable poetic strategy: she writes narrative, catalog, image, concrete, interrogatory, and sequence poems (often mixing these in a single work). Her language is generally sonorous, remarkable for its Anglo-Saxon stress, alliteration, extensive word fusions, and a devotion (now declining, it appears) to rhyme. She has made language an instrument for pursuit of ideas, but always ideas discoverable only in things of the experiential world. She believes, apparently, that the world functions according to some hidden final purpose, and furthermore that a right apprehension ultimately reveals a Coleridgean interconnectedness of all parts. A section from "Order of Diet," an early poem, suggests her belief and her cadences, both essentially unchanged though refined:

Ashes find their way to green;
the worm is raised into the wing;
the sluggish fish to muscle slides;
eventual chemistry will bring
the lightning bug to the shrewd toad's eye.
It is true no thing of earth can die.

Nothing so excites Swenson's imagination or reveals her poetic investigation as that image of flight. In poems about airplanes, birds, insects, and especially space exploration, she celebrates the joy of flight. Motion is both her subject and her image, being life itself. Flight, however, rarely means escape; it is her means for exploration, penetration, for travel to and through the world; it is what humans cannot naturally do ("light pierces wings of jays in flight: / they shout my grief") but what becomes the passage toward and into vision. In this book's earliest poem, Swenson wrote "all that my Eye encircles I become" and risked an Emersonian cartoon. Vision, seeing, looking, recording are so pervasive in her poems that one almost forgets how active she makes all the senses in the service of penetrating surfaces. Flight is not only the revelation of human bondage, it is also the vehicle of imaginative and intellectual possibilities. As she writes in "Distance and a Certain Light," speaking of her poetics, "No contortion / without intention, and nothing ugly." Never a poet of ennui or cynicism, though often a poet of elegiac grief, she believes that all is beautiful if seen properly: "Rubbish becomes engaging shape— / you only have to get a bead on it . . . " And:

From an airplane, all
that rigid splatter of the Bronx
becomes organic, logical
as web or beehive. . . .

In her later poem, "Flying Home from Utah," her skied angle and distance produces what seems a purely descriptive record of geometric shades and shapes, but this macrocosmic vision ("it becomes the world") is partial, so long-distance is shifted to a microscopic look at a single leaf, and she concludes:

One leaf of a tree that's one tree of a forest,
that's the branch of the vein of a leaf
of a tree. Perpetual worlds
within, upon, above the world, the world
a leaf within a wilderness of worlds.

Swenson's emphasis on flight and perspective, always in the context that "earth will not let go our foot," extends from her conception of the primary tension of existence: "The tug of the void / the will of the world." By will she means the rage to survive and flourish which is continually contested by absence, death, and the void, hence "Though devious and shifty in detail, the whole expanse / reiterated constancy and purpose." Swenson's effort has been and is to make felt the nature of that purpose. In another early poem, "Snow in New York," she wrote:

. . . a magic notion
I, too, used to play with: from chosen words a potion
could be wrung; pickings of them, eaten, could make
you fly, walk
on water, be somebody else, do or undo anything, go
back
or forward on belts of time. . . .

"October," a new poem, shows she means to fly into the world, not out of it. Here she emphasizes the search for vision, not its verbal contrivance:

. . . Stand still, stare
hard into bramble and tangle,
past leaning broken trunks,
sprawled roots exposed. Will
something move?—some vision
come to outline? Yes, there—

Swenson, however, seems not to have come to any definitive identification of a teleological purpose. She has found or accepted no answer except her intuited conviction that all is interconnected and rooted in love. Her temperament, always religious and never orthodox, causes her to caution: "I do not mean to pray." Yet her newest poems seem prayerful, perhaps in the increased awareness of the void's tug, which makes her note, "Too vivid / the last pink / petunia's indrawn mouth." More acutely now she feels what age reveals, "the steep / edge of hopelessness," and writes more intimately of what's been loved: family, flowers, landscapes and seascapes, birds, and vibrant colors. Perhaps no poet since Wallace Stevens has so reveled in colors; they name poems, accrue into image patterns, are ingested as objects. For May Swenson, life is motion and *color.* Yet the colors of new poems are slightly less brilliant, are the colors of seasonal decline. Staring into the bramble thicket, she writes "Better here / in the familiar, to fade."

If Swenson's new poems are more attentive to the inevitable void, she remains at least as interested in chronicling what is happening as what has happened. Her sixty-two new poems evidence still a vigorous curiosity, a compulsive meticulousness, and a passionate sense of life which forces us toward poetry's accomplishment, renewed vision. She has plenty to write about, including Navaho rugs, bison, rodeos, western mountains, the sea, swamps, income tax, fashion, Georgia O'Keefe, baseball and football, an outhouse, parents, a junkyard dog, Mormonism, Nanook the Eskimo, and an aviary (there can hardly be a poet who has written more about birds or about more birds!). And writing of July 4th fireworks, she says:

> And we want more: we want red giant, white dwarf,
> black hole, extinct, orgasmic, all in one!

Dedicated as they are to angles of vision, avoiding autobiography and personality, Swenson's poems necessarily emphasize structure—sometimes to the point of mannerism. Often enough they possess a wonderful lyricism that celebrates; but primarily they nominate, and this occasionally leads to an annoyingly indiscriminate series of similes: a thing looks like this. Or this, or this. This mannerism reveals a kind of "scientific" attitude in her work, an attitude also marked by often esoteric and technical terminology—not in itself a problem though it helps create the impression of a dispassionate stance when there is passion present and the need to show it. Swenson's reticence may sometimes mean the difference between a powerful experience and no experience, as in riddles or dry humor. Indeed, one of Swenson's characteristics is a wry wit which sometimes trails off into whimsy, into the glib and clever. For me she has too strong a willingness to keep work marked by visual puns (particularly from *Iconographs*), work less felt and sustaining than contrived and biodegradable. Such work does disservice to her significant accomplishment, though some "readers" will doubtless applaud her gamesmanship and experimenting. For them, here is a stanza of "MAsterMANANiMAL":

> ANiMAte MANANiMAL MAtress of Nerves
> MANipulAtor Motor ANd Motive MAker
> MAMMAliAN MAtrix MAt of rivers red
> MortAL MANic Morsel Mover shAker

Swenson's interest in this sort of visual word-play extends to poems carved in zigzags, curves, a snail's shape (among others), and multiple, often opposed columns of print. Sometimes charming, sometimes bitingly effective as in "Women" and "Orbiter 5 Shows How Earth Looks from the Moon," the poems too often depend on a gimmickry that wears quickly thin. In "Look," for example, a poem about two people before a mirror, the right hand column of print uses a form of "look" twenty-two times, and one wants as much as anything not to look.

Neither are all of Swenson's more traditionally executed poems free from excess that may be attributed to her high and democratic spirit. She betrays a tendency to telegraph conclusions in some of the image poems. In "The Solar Corona" the sun's enormous ring becomes a pizza that "is 400 times / larger than the moon. / Don't burn your lips!" Here, we can only say Ouch! And we cringe when in a love poem, "Poet to Tiger," she writes, "You put your paws in your armpits / make a tiger-moo." Because there is a strain of the highly impressionistic in this eclectic poet, there is a scattering of poems of which the closest readings scarcely dislodge either subject or meaning or both so that poems such as "Written While Riding the Long Island Rail Road" and "O'Keefe Retrospective" remain interesting and baffling.

Any collection as rich and massive as this one must have, however, its weaknesses and I would hope they do not obscure the book's dominant strength. Swenson's voracious imagination makes her an extremely social and adventurous writer who turns poetry into a living, if idealized, human speech. From previous collections she has trimmed more than fifty poems and has reordered most of what remains, in effect creating not merely a Collected Poems but a freshly ordained and perpetual world of poetry. Among the new poems, I would cite for their excellence "Bison Crossing Near Mt. Rushmore," "Staying at Ed's Place," "The Willets," "That the Soul May Wax Plump," "Scroppo's Dog," "October," and "Dream after Nanook" in particular. Among the previous collections there is such an abundance of splendid, welcome old friends that it is impossible and nearly invidious to choose for citation, but to demonstrate Swenson's inventiveness, her power, her conviction in the right to be free and wild, I offer these stanzas from a favorite early poem:

> Watching you they remember their fathers
> the frightening hairs in their fathers' ears
>
> Young girls remember lovers too timid and white
> and I remember how I played lion with my brothers
> under the round yellow-grained table
> the shadow our cave in the lamplight
>
> Your beauty burns the brain
> though your paws slue on foul cement
> the fetor of captivity you do right to ignore
> the bars too an illusion
>
> Your heroic paranoia plants you in the African jungle
> pacing by the cool water-hole as dawn streaks the sky
> and the foretaste of the all-day hunt
> is sweet as yearling's blood
> in the corners of your lips
>
> LION

If Swenson sometimes generates consternation and dismay, that fault is born of a poetry urgently trying to tell us that everything matters, a poetry so affirmative that we cannot escape knowing we matter. Even random reading here produces surprise, delight, love, wisdom, joy, and grief. May Swenson transforms the ordinary little-scrutinized world to a teeming, flying first creation. Bother such words as *great* and *major*—she is a poet we want in this world for this world is in her as it is in few among us ever. I have been told she hasn't a great readership. Not in size or, perhaps, intensity. Too often we accuse poets of inattention when the fault is in ourselves. That she deserves readers as intense, as scrupulous, as intelligent, and as rewarding as May Swenson is seems to me as plainly true as the continually unfurling world of her *New and Selected Things Taking Place*. Twenty years ago she wrote of her relationship with the reader and called it "the lightning-string / between your eye and mine." The first poem in this eminent new collection, "A Navaho Blanket," re-engages that paradigmatic image and serves better than any reviewer's words to introduce what she does, who she is, why we are compelled to echo her and cry we want more!

> Eye-dazzlers the Indians weave. Three colors
> are paths that pull you in, and pin you
> to the maze. Brightness makes your eyes jump,
> surveying the geometric field. Alight, and enter
> any of the gates—of Blue, of Red, of Black.
> Be calmed and hooded, a hawk brought down,
> glad to fasten to the forearm of a chief.
>
> You can sleep at the center,
> attended by the Sun that never fades, by Moon
> that cools. Then, slipping free of zigzag and
> hypnotic diamond, find your way out
> by the spirit trail, a faint Green thread that
> secretly crosses the border, where your mind
> is rinsed and returned to you like a white cup.

BOOTH TARKINGTON

1869–1946

Newton Booth Tarkington was born on July 29, 1869, in Indianapolis, Indiana. The son of a lawyer, he was educated at Phillips Exeter Academy, Purdue University, and Princeton University, which he left in 1893 without obtaining a degree. Tarkington's first novel, *The Gentleman from Indiana*, was published in 1899, but it was with his next novel, *Monsieur Beaucaire* (1900), concerning the adventures of the Duke of Orleans in eighteenth-century England, that he first won popularity. In 1902 Tarkington ran for the Indiana legislature on the Republican ticket; he was elected and served one term, an experience later reflected in his novel *In the Arena* (1905). Also in 1902 Tarkington married Laurel Louisa Fletcher; their only daughter died in infancy, and they were divorced in 1911. In 1912 Tarkington married Susannah Robinson. Throughout the rest of his life Tarkington was a prolific novelist, writing in a popular, accessible style; his many books include *The Conquest of Canaan* (1905); *Alice Adams* (1921; Pulitzer Prize); the trilogy *Growth* (1927), consisting of *The Turmoil* (1915), *The Magnificent Ambersons* (1918; Pulitzer Prize), and *The Midlander* (1923); *The Plutocrat* (1927); *The Heritage of Hatcher Ide* (1941); *Kate Fennigate* (1943); and *The Image of Josephine* (1945). Tarkington is also remembered for his children's books; the best-known are *Penrod* (1914) and its sequels, *Penrod and Sam* (1916) and *Penrod Jashber* (1929). His many plays include dramatizations of *Monsieur Beaucaire* (1901) and *Clarence* (1919), and he also wrote short stories, essays, and *The World Does Move* (1928), a book of reminiscences. Tarkington died on May 19, 1946.

Personal

My father said once, "We have so much fun with Uncle Booth that we forget he's a famous man." And so we did. To me he was just Uncle Booth, and he was magic.

To understand even partially the aura that Uncle Booth projected to my generation, one needs some idea of the surroundings in which he lived and in which we knew him so well as we grew up in Indianapolis.

He, whose youthful devil-may-care antics in New York, Rome, Paris, and Capri were legend, had, by the time I knew him, settled into a serene and sheltered existence surrounded by the art objects he had collected in his wanderings. He went out only to see the family, visit the art museum, or hear the symphony. He told a reporter, "I began going to Maine forty-two years ago, but I always come back to Indiana. Your heart lies where home is." Nowadays many people are rootless, returning to their birthplaces only for weddings or funerals, but Uncle Booth's roots lay deep in Indiana. How else could he have written so compellingly of the midlands? He revealed the depth of his roots when he wrote his nephews, "Your two G'fathers came to Indianapolis when there were only a few acres of shanties and boardwalks and mud, and Fall Creek ran through the Columbia Club and the legislature met in a woodshed."

When did I first truly remember him and his magic? It was Christmas night, 1929. My parents, my little brother Johnny, and I went to the Tarkingtons for a visit. There are those who consider childish memories unreliable, but this visit has such clarity that many later events seem dim by comparison. The Tarkington house at 4270 North Meridian Street stood far from the smoky center of town, and it was a muted fairyland to me. Outside was cold and black, but inside the house was warm and lovely. It is not often that a pinpoint in time and space can later be realized as a turning point—for all our moments are fluid—a compound of echoes from the past, the present moment, and wonderings about the future. But that Christmas night over fifty years ago marked my first conscious and specific recollections of Uncle Booth.

Wearing dinner clothes, he was sitting in a brown velvet chair by the fire. One of his specially-made Turkish cigarettes burned between very long and slightly shaking fingers. How impressed I was when I eventually discovered that his initials were on each cigarette. (Years afterwards I sneaked one of those cigarettes home, and one puff nearly did me in.) Later memories of Uncle Booth have added dimension to that evening's memories of him, but what remains with me clearly are brown eyes twinkling behind heavy glasses and a haze of cigarette smoke.

His voice? At that tender age I could not have described it, but time has helped me articulate what I heard. It was resonant, had a deep timbre, and, though soft, carried when he spoke. I still do not know what makes a quiet voice more noticeable than a loud one. In his case, maybe it was a feeling that *this* voice had something special to say and that its owner had a more vivid presence than others in the room. At Princeton Uncle Booth had been a soloist in the glee club, and no evening of beer and singing was complete until Tark stood on a table and rendered "Danny Deever." He made this song famous at Princeton many years before I was born, but the baritone resonance lingered in his speaking voice throughout his life.

To me he seemed old. But then my parents seemed old, and they were no doubt in their early thirties. As a child of eight, I would not have used the word *electric*, but I recognized even then that he had a voltage that made the other people in the room seem dim. I remember feeling expectant. He was playing with a large pair of dice which he had received for Christmas, and I wondered why.

Before settling down beside him, Johnny and I made our tour, looking at our favorite treasures (so we must have been in the house before). We thought they were our *own* special treasures. Only much later did I realize that some of them were priceless, collected during Uncle Booth's visits to Europe—living evidence of his quintessential discrimination and taste. In the sunroom we trailed our fingers in the shallow water of the Greek white marble trough which always held long-stemmed pink roses, noticing casually in passing the marble

French Gothic madonnas who smiled eternally at their happy babies. We looked longingly at the golden Spanish desk, taller than a man, intricately carved, and containing, we were sure, many secret drawers; but parental nervousness had communicated itself, and we were loath to explore it. Much later, in 1944, this desk became an altar, banked by palms and candles; and my husband and I were married in front of it while Uncle Booth smiled at us, half hidden from us by the palms, and wholly hidden from the wedding guests.

That Christmas night I noticed, not his treasured portraits themselves—except for the pleasure in the glint of a sword hilt or a jewel—but the lights which illuminated them. Each painting had its own light with a shade attached to the top of the frame. How odd this seemed to me. In our house, lights were on tables or in the ceilings. Much later when we were more educable, Uncle Booth used to explain the portraits and the painters. He once said that most of them in his Indianapolis house were of fifteenth- or sixteenth-century men and women and added, "They were a hard people because they had to be. Most of them look capable of murder and that is because they were." This, of course, delighted us.

My own favorite treasure in the house was the carved wooden head of a young Greek boy with curly hair, his eyes gazing serenely into middle distance. I loved the feel of him. His ancient sculptor was asking that he be caressed, and I always did just that. My brother's favorite was what we always called "the poison ring." It was big enough for a giant and had probably been used to seal Renaissance correspondence; but since it opened at one end where one just might put poison in it, we chose, of course, to believe it had been used lethally. Uncle Booth never said anything to dissuade us.

He had his own favorite "treasure," which he loved to tell us about, and I think he did that evening. I believe that no purchase of an antique ever gave him more pleasure than the acquisition of his marble faun. Uncle Booth described him in *Your Amiable Uncle:*

> He stood six-feet-two on his pedestal of mottled green marble, cut from a column that Hadrian ravished from Egypt and that sank in the Tiber with a shipload which Alaric the Goth was bearing away after he sacked Rome. . . . He really belonged to me. . . . No antique comes near him to my mind and heart. . . . My fellow is so real . . . and so lazy and so understandful. How he must have laughed in his sleepy way at the girls who followed him and posed at him. He is not a gentleman at all . . . he is just a clever, idle, pure, winesipping, chestnut-eating, faun . . . dreamland humorist in marble.

Now the same faun stands, still smiling lazily, in a specially made niche at my brother's house. Depending on the season, his children have added autumn leaves or holly wreaths to his vine leaves. I have seen him bedecked with a wreath of chrysanthemums or, even, a fedora.

That evening I remember wondering why the Tarkingtons did not put their Christmas cards on the mantel as we did. They were in a decorated basket on the hearth. Much later I sensed that it would have been a desecration to put anything so trivial on that gorgeous piece of stone, carved after one that Francis I had at the Cluny Palace.

One of Uncle Booth's greatest traits was that he *never* disappointed children. Many parents must plead guilty to this charge, but not he. After our tour of treasures, we settled down beside him. He gave us the dice he had been holding, told us how to take turns, and said, "I'll give five dollars to the first child who throws a seven." I, at least, was struck dumb. (The most money I had ever had was an occasional dime from the tooth fairy.) And I won! Five whole dollars just for me. My little brother's disappointment meant absolutely nothing to me. Then, Uncle Booth said, "I'll give five dollars to the first boy who throws a seven." I was ecstatic. Maybe five more dollars just for me. In my avarice I had not even heard the word *boy*. Anyway, after the game—and I have never since played one like it—both Johnny and I went home with ten dollars apiece, and neither of us has ever forgotten how very rich we were. The feeble talk of parents about putting the money into our savings-and-loan accounts went unheeded. This money of ours was to be hoarded and gloated over. Magic, indeed. That is the only word for that Christmas night.—SUSANNAH MAYBERRY, *My Amiable Uncle: Recollections about Booth Tarkington*, 1983, pp. 46–51

General

Booth Tarkington is one of our literary assets whose value has not been subject to profound fluctuation, and that is the more remarkable since he has made a complete *volte-face* from pure romance to sheer realism. Apparently, ideas and beliefs which crowded his mind and obstructed his vision in early maturity have been modified or dislodged by life and experience. This metamorphosis may account for his steady ascent from the exclusively idealized picture of Helen Fisbee in *The Gentleman from Indiana* to the realistic revelation of the Beautiful Widow, or of Mrs. Dodge in *Women*. In his later novels, there is abundant evidence that he is determined to cast off every vestige of romanticism. Yet he never quite succeeds. He still allows his dreams to come true, though never with such violence or success as in his early books. ⟨. . .⟩

Mr. Tarkington does not let us watch life, with him, in his mirror. His method is not a direct one: he surveys his men and women and constantly interferes between them and us, telling us what to believe and what to see, what they do and what they like, but not what they think or what they feel. His views are purely objective, and because he does not mingle with the intimate life of his characters he deprives us of a fine feeling of complete harmony with them.

It is difficult to say whether the Tarkington heroes are idealized pictures of what he himself would like to be, or the expression of a valiant struggle to bring romance and ideals to an alien land. There can be little doubt that John Harkless, his first fullfledged westerner, is a self portrait. In that novel, reality was distorted in an effort to create a "type". It is the effort of a youth who takes life seriously, expecting to find a meaning to it. Harkless is pale, fascinating, lonesome and misunderstood, ambitious yet generous. His pattern is a simple one: a human image endowed with the virtues of greatness but with a void in the heart. Now and then imagination fills it with charming pictures. Only a goddess can satisfy his love longing. When Helen Fisbee comes, she runs true to form, the typical heroine of the late eighties: pure, beautiful, with melodious voice, sharp wit, coquettish grace, irresistible attraction, whose deeds were cloaked in virtue.

There may have been such people in the world, in Indiana even, when Mr. Tarkington wrote his first successful novel, but they have disappeared.

The refusal to admit that materialism has superseded ideals may be traced in all his novels. It may be camouflaged a bit, as in Bibbs Sheridan's efforts to get away from "big business" or in Harlan Oliphant's determination to turn a deaf ear to progress and development; in George Minafer's ambition to redeem himself from his moral crime against his mother, or in Alice Adams's purposeful blindness to the obvious, in search of false values she cannot reconcile to reality. But it is there none the less.

Mr. Tarkington has an eye for the particular, a talent for details which, in its great lines, rivets his attention to local interest, to the detriment of the universal scheme. With the exception of a few exotic tales which reveal him as a gifted cosmopolitan, Indiana is the beginning and the end of his world. In his most widely read novels, he is Indianian through and through. When his eye seeks repose and new interests, it lands on the virtues of his own people, on their gifts and the blessings that have been lavishly dispensed to them. ⟨. . .⟩

Much can be said, and has been said, in praise of Mr. Tarkington's novels. The reading world is indebted to him for much pleasure and some enlightenment. It regrets that he did not give equally of both: save in few instances we know very little about his men and women. All we know is what he tells us, for his is not the subtle gift which implies an idea with such power that it soon becomes our own. His bulk stands conspicuously between us and the inner light that would illumine the characters. We remain strangers to the fate of the men and women of his creation because we are not allowed a peep into their fundamental makeup. We are attentive listeners to their tales, never participants of their dreams.

His stories create pictures and situations, all in the impersonal, Tarkington manner; there is no effort at analysis, at critical understanding, at profound search into individual reactions, at semblance of logic in actions. We accept them as he gives them to us, and we are constantly confronted with Alice Adamses, Penrods, Mrs. Dodges and Sheridans. But none of the Tarkington heroes remain in our hearts and help us over the rough passages, as those of Howells or Maupassant do. It is all superficial and external, and it lacks, more than anything, the sacred fire of inspiration. Perfect background and an eye for incidental details make for greatness, but do not constitute it.

It is Tarkington's belief that primitive passions have no play in human characters. Lust and lustful desires, yielding to temptations that have been part and parcel of man's makeup since time immemorial, seem abhorrent to him. He will not admit that men and women have passions that may carry them away from the accepted code of morality. His heroes fall in love, but they seldom feel the call of the flesh; they dream about women, but they do not seem to mind much if their dreams never come true. They are as sexless as angels are reputed to be. There is never a time, in the lives of these men and women who breathe and suffer, when passions become so overwhelming in intensity as to make them lose sight of the way approved by convention.

The characters of Tarkington who are affected by love are generally sentimental and romantic, yet temptation never gets beyond their control. To deny passion its potency is to deny man and woman the greatest source of happiness and of inspiration that has been vouchsafed them. In none of Tarkington's novels is there one gallant surrender, one all powerful surge of emotion that sweeps convention to the winds and scatters its ashes on the way to a higher aim. We deal with the commonplace, the drab, the narrow side of realism, and we do not even have, as compensation, the beauty and the power of realism. The ideals with which Tarkington endows his men and women are of the sort that are not encountered in life, save in rare instances; whereas the struggle for beauty, the effort to rise from the daily drivel and drudge of life, are absent in his novels—such effort would require a code of morals not always in keeping with that of the "nice" people of the nineties who aimed at snuffing out self expression and self indulgence.

The Tarkington men work for an ideal, generally a woman, but they seldom have the courage to go after it as they do after success. They are in love with love, on an impractical and intangible basis; they love a picture of something their minds tell them is "ideal"; and they conform their conduct to the dictates of their heads, regardless of the claims of their hearts.

Heart, meaning emotion, is an unknown quantity in his world. For it he substitutes accuracy in details, a firm determination to remain within the narrow confines of western ideals. His books may be read without expense of innocence.
—JOSEPH COLLINS, "The New Mr. Tarkington," *Bkm*, March 1927, pp. 12–21

Works

Mr. Tarkington is by general consent our most skilful describer of the ordinary citizen as that citizen sees himself. Yet I, for one, should prefer to consider *The Midlander* a libel, for it does indeed speak for the millions, making articulate their aims and ideals, and if it does represent, as its author seems to intend that it shall, the best type that our American civilization has produced, then the "American spirit" is the shabbiest excuse for a national religion that any country ever had. Provided as he is with a novelist's privilege of choosing his incidents and of endowing his characters with whatever attributes he likes, Mr. Tarkington has deliberately chosen to tell a story in which nothing important is at stake and no central character is ever concerned about anything that cannot be seen and touched. Once, America was the home of the puritan, and however hard or narrow his heart may have been it at least burned with an intense flame, and his concern was with the soul more than with the goods of man. But, if we are to believe Mr. Tarkington, the extinction of that flame has left nothing except a tepid prudence and a business sense. The avowed defender of the average citizen calmly writes him down as incapable of a passion for anything less tangible than bank returns or of an ideal beyond that of a chamber-of-commerce man. Honest, energetic, kindly his Midlander is made, and these are excellent qualities. But they are no more than a groundwork and leave him as bare as our bitterest satirists say we are of those qualities of imagination and susceptibility to spiritual values which are necessary, not merely to cultivation, but to any dignity of character in peasant or professor. When Mr. Lowes Dickinson, for example, declares that we have no ideal beyond acceleration and that we are incapable of any disinterested intellectual operation he is accusing us of nothing that Mr. Tarkington does not glory in.

The nominal hero of the book is a young man who desires to serve his people and his nation by buying an outlying farm, persuading the street-car company to run a line to it, and then reselling it in small lots for a sufficient sum to make him one of those solid citizens to whom neighbors point as just the sort of man one would expect to come from his fine old pioneer stock. The whole story turns upon the failure or success of a commercial venture, and the real protagonist of the drama is a piece of real estate which is supposed to wring our hearts by its failure to blossom forth as soon as it should into suburban homes. It is, of course, nothing against Mr. Tarkington that his hero is dull and that after taking his B.A. at New Haven he never shows himself capable of an interest, enthusiasm, or valuation which would not be understood and shared by the boy who passed from primary school into a grocery store to weigh sugar or cut lard. That is merely sober realism. But it is something against Mr. Tarkington as an artist that he finds the mere belching forth of smoke in increasing volume and the spreading out of street-car tracks a sufficient proof of national greatness.

Many novelists, from Cooper to Willa Cather, have made pioneering the material of moving novels, but always they have shown what pioneering did to the pioneer, making him a great and heroic figure, whereas Mr. Tarkington attempts to write an epic around a central character who never rises above the level of the enthusiastic realtor. The building of a suburb to a midland city may possibly be as important in the history of the nation as the opening up of the West, but it cannot be made satisfactory material for heroic art unless it can be shown to have molded great men, and this Mr. Tarkington never attempts to show. Some great books (*Tom Jones*, for example) are books written about stupid people, but intended to be read by intelligent ones, whereas *The Midlander* would seem to be for as well as about the dull.

This is equivalent to saying that Mr. Tarkington has written a piece of typical magazine fiction, for the essential difference between such writing and literature lies not, as is sometimes supposed, in the moral timidity or imperfect execution of the latter—magazine stories are often revolutionary in tone and admirable in execution—but in the centering of all interest upon material things and the failure to suggest that either the characters or the author realize that other values exist or that what a man feels and is may be as important as what he has or does. Many a book both deserves and gets serious consideration from the critic which is not as well written or as skilfully observed as either *The Midlander* or a large portion of *Saturday Evening Post* fiction, but which soars above both by virtue of the fact that it does recognize that important things go on inside a man which have no relation to his business career or the growth of cities. From *The Midlander*, as from most magazine fiction, one gets the impression that man is a wealth-and-comfort-producing machine and that the function of fiction is the analysis of the efficiency of such a machine; hence to one sort of temperament such work will always seem merely vulgar. But it is not to be forgotten that the point of view has many supporters and that if ever the Boosters' Club should found an academy, *The Midlander* should be the first book crowned.—JOSEPH WOOD KRUTCH, "Crowned by the Boosters' Club," *Nation*, March 19, 1924, pp. 318–19

Opposite the title page in *The Heritage of Hatcher Ide* is a list of Mr. Tarkington's other works. The list contains two novels which have won the Pulitzer Prize, a distinction accorded to no other author. It contains nothing which is not a consistent performance, on a high level of technical achievement, and much which rises far higher. Our more ponderous critics must be bewildered, and those authors who must depend for their living on their literary output cannot but be cheered to discover that the greater part of Mr. Tarkington's work first saw light in the pages of the more popular periodicals which we are told have done so much to debauch literary talent.

Yet, Mr. Tarkington has been at this sort of thing for forty-two years and by his own unvarying standards and good taste has proved that literature can be produced outside of an ivory tower and sold in the market place. Further, he has proved that a man, if he is good enough, can keep up with the enormous variations of literary fashion. In all of his rather stupendous career he has never faltered; he has never been "dated." He has started with the horse-and-buggy age, but manners and eccentricities, even when they ride in stream-line motors, have never left him staring bewildered and defeated through the dust. He has been able through every decade to change his models and his tools.

Mr. Tarkington's latest novel, *The Heritage of Hatcher Ide*, necessarily assumes a peculiar significance in the light of what has gone before, but it does not need the bolstering of reputation. From the point of view of craftsmanship, very few novelists can match it, for Mr. Tarkington's experience has only added to his skill, without an aftermath of perfunctory weariness. His new book speaks as eloquently of today as *The Gentleman from Indiana* did of its own period. It has the wisdom of an older man, but also the zest for life and the good nature of a man who has never aged.

In spite of the deceptive ease and good temper of Mr. Tarkington's style, *The Heritage of Hatcher Ide* cuts deeply through the maladjustments and disillusions that obscure the stark outlines of our present financial depression. Actually it is a novel of social significance, although a socially-minded critic might not admit it, since Mr. Tarkington's characters all come from the neglected and harassed class of the "haves," as opposed to the "have-nots," these latter being lost almost completely in the soft coal smoke of the Ides' mid-Western city. Thus in its way the general tone and setting is reminiscent of *The Magnificent Ambersons*, except that the hero, Hatcher Ide, is indubitably a product of 1939, drawn with telling details quite characteristic of the period.

Up to his graduation from college young Hatcher lived in the security of that adolescent world, so carefully and unhappily designed for the children of "comfortably-off" parents. Until he was twenty-two he accepted, as his contemporaries did, the adult members of his family as genial symbols rather than human beings, completely ignorant of their problems and of their personalities. The opening of the story finds Hatcher Ide and the boys and girls he knew pathetically infantile, through no fault of their own. There is added pathos in the attitude of his parents and of his Uncle Victor, implied rather than definitely expressed, which prevents their accepting him as a member of a grownup circle. Yet Hatcher, pushed onto the side lines by a social compulsion, which breaks only toward the final pages, sees that things are very bad in this adult world.

The family real estate and investment business, which had grown with the almost magic waxing of the midland city where the Ides had lived for generations, was distinctly going to pot and Mr. and Mrs. Ide, though keeping up a serene facade, were sick with worry. The houses of all the best people around them were mortgaged to the hilt, although the best people were carrying on. His Uncle Victor, decorated and wounded in the last war, and once a successful architect, no longer lived at his club, because the club had disappeared. He dwelt instead in a second-rate boarding house. His father's partner was as jolly as ever, hysterically jolly, and was spending too much money. Their neighbor, Mrs. Sarah Florian, a rich grass-widow, had been forced to return from her continental stamping grounds because of the fall of France. This is the world which Fletcher Ide must face, a plausible environment in the light of the present. The reader is permitted to see it through the puzzled mind of Hatcher, through the patient and integrated eyes of his Uncle Victor, and through Mr. Tarkington's own. From Mr. Tarkington one gathers that things would have been better under a Republican administration, but Mr. Tarkington is too much of an artist for personal prejudices.

Half a man, half adolescent, young Hatcher bungles his way through the plot to a hopeful if not a happy ending. It is a comedy of manners, a field which is Mr. Tarkington's favorite, all of it skillfully and much of it beautifully told.

There are certain faults in this book which sometimes detract from its reality. Mrs. Florian, for instance, is frequently drawn with an emphasis on her brittle artificiality and selfishness that tends to make her unconvincing until the very end. Victor Linley may often be too much of a clear-eyed Galahad for his own good as a character, and Hatcher Ide's solution of his problem—the discovery that houses when painted and papered will rent more readily than dingy dwellings—smacks of a fictional contrivance that may be too simple to seem real. Yet faults like these do very little to destroy the final impression of the book, or the reader's consistent pleasure in Mr. Tarkington's deep knowledge of human beings and of the world as it moves today. There is the same vigor and the same unerring eye for detail that is present in all his other pages and, best of all, there is that spirit of optimism, that unconquerable glow of hope in Mr. Tarkington's young. Hatcher Ide and Dorcy and Hatcher's sister, Frances, and all their friends give *The Heritage of Hatcher Ide* an aura of gallantry and courage which raises it above its worldly plot and which lightens its shadows; and all this is done in a manner which is beyond the power of any other living novelist.—J. P. MARQUAND, "Tarkington and Social Significance," *SR*, March 1, 1941, p. 7

FREDERIC TABER COOPER
From "Newton Booth Tarkington"
Some American Story Tellers
1911, pp. 196–211, 222–24

Upon renewing acquaintance with *The Gentleman from Indiana*, from the vantage ground of a ten-year interval, one realizes by what a narrow margin Mr. Tarkington rescued the born story teller within him from the would-be maker of purposeful and serious fiction. This book in fact represents a parting of two ways, a battle-ground between two opposing impulses, two widely divergent views of the aims and ambitions of a novelist,—and for that reason it fails, in spite of occasional strength, to be a really good book, a piece of symmetrical and finished workmanship. Although it was his first published work, *The Gentleman from Indiana* was far from being Mr. Tarkington's first attempt at fiction. It has often been told that the germ of *The Two Vanrevels* was a short story of two thousand words written many years earlier; and that while *The Gentleman from Indiana* was not begun until 1898, *Monsieur Beaucaire* was written a year earlier and *Cherry* not only antedates them both but was accepted as a two-part serial at a time when its author was practically unknown. In a lengthy critical study of Mr. Tarkington's writings, Arthur Bartlett Maurice rather happily conjectures that "Perhaps it was of himself and of his own disillusionment that he was thinking when he described in *The Gentleman from Indiana* John Harkless occupied with a realization that 'there had been a man in his class whose ambition needed no restraint, his promise was so complete—in the strong belief of the University, a belief that he could not help knowing—and that seven years to a day from his Commencement this man was sitting on a fence rail in Indiana.'" And Mr. Maurice hereupon adds, "sitting on a rail-fence in Indiana was figuratively just what Tarkington was doing from 1893 to 1899."

Now, in order to understand how the author of *Monsieur Beaucaire* ever happened to write *The Gentleman from Indiana*, it is necessary to keep just a few facts in mind. In the first place, Mr. Tarkington had throughout these seven years been vainly trying to obtain a public hearing and had been persistently denied. Even after *Cherry* had been accepted for magazine publication, the editor seems to have had a sober second thought and the manuscript was side-tracked until the subsequent success of his other stories gave it an unforeseen and extrinsic value that hurried it into print. Secondly, in the closing years of the nineteenth century, there came a sudden demand for a rather serious type of political novel and of the novel that professed to study the social and economic problems of American life and especially of life in the West. The times were ripe for just such books as Brand Whitlock's *Thirteenth District*, Mr. Tarkington's *Gentleman from Indiana*, *The Virginian* of Owen Wister and, bigger and greater than these, *The Pit* and *The Octopus* of Frank Norris which were to come later. It was quite natural, quite pardonable, that a young man in Mr. Tarkington's position, sobered by discouragement, should have attempted for once to meet a specific popular demand,—especially when the attempt to meet it meant no greater effort than simply to open his eyes and set down faithfully what he could see from his viewpoint on the fence rail, and what he thought about the things that he saw.

Unfortunately, this method of work, which to many another writer is the simplest and most congenial, was one which Mr. Tarkington, with the best intentions in the world, found himself unable to sustain. He is of those whose worship of the God of Things-as-They-Are is at best an outward show. The mantle of realism is upon his shoulders a curious misfit; and he has done wisely in discarding it. *The Gentleman from Indiana* is a luminous object-lesson. There are in it two interwoven stories so radically different in their spirit, their outlook upon life and the key in which they are told that it is rather difficult to say with any assurance which of these two was Mr. Tarkington's starting-point, and just what important thought, if any, he undertook to develop. Apparently his theme was something of this nature: When a discouraged young man from the East,—discouraged because he knows that he has the ambition and the energy to succeed but lacks the opportunity,—finds himself at last in a somnolent Western town and by remorselessly driving himself day and night succeeds in instilling some sort of life into that town and at the same time making himself the most important and most respected of all its citizens: he is quite likely not to see that success is already holding out her hands to him; quite likely to feel that he is stagnating, wasting his strength and his years in a jumping-off place from which there is no escape,—and all the while he is building for himself unconsciously a big and splendid future. This is what I think that Mr. Tarkington was trying to say: that the surest way to play a big part before a large audience to-morrow, is to play your little part before your small audience to-day and to be sure that you play it with all your heart and all your soul and all your mind. The trouble with *The Gentleman from Indiana*, which might so easily have been made a really big book, is that in trying to say this Mr. Tarkington said it so very badly. The book makes one think of a long steel girder which has buckled and broken in the middle from sheer structural weakness.

⟨. . .⟩ *The Gentleman from Indiana* ⟨. . .⟩ is a book which one may quite sincerely like without being blind to its faults. It bristles with absurdities, yet in spite of them, one cannot help feeling the warm, lovable human nature in its characters. To create characters that seem thoroughly alive is part of the inborn gift of the true story teller, and no amount of farce or melodrama will quite hide it. But characters endowed with the breath of life are not the exclusive prerogative of either romance or realism. If on the one hand we have Major Pendennis and Colonel Newcome, on the other we have D'Artagnan and Chicot the Jester—equally alive, equally impossible to forget. It still remained to be seen which of the two methods was Mr. Tarkington's natural medium. The publication of *Monsieur Beaucaire* promptly solved the doubt. No one but a born romanticist could have written that dainty and consistent bit of fictional artistry. It had no more serious excuse for existence than a miniature on ivory or a finely-cut cameo,—and it needed none. Its best excuse was the blitheness of its mood, the symmetry of its form, the swiftness of its action, the tingling vitality of it, from start to finish. But it immediately, and once for all, defined Mr. Tarkington's proper sphere and limitations. It proved him one of those writers whose stories, whenever and wherever laid, should carry with them something of the "once-upon-a-time" atmosphere,—the fitting atmosphere of the story that aims frankly to entertain. It reduced at once to an absurdity the bare idea of Mr. Tarkington's ever again attempting to write a novel opening with such prosaic actuality as "There is a fertile stretch of flat lands in Indiana where unagrarian Eastern travelers, glancing from car-windows, shudder and return their eyes to interior upholstery." From the clumsy heaviness of *The Gentleman from Indiana* to the debonair self-mastery of *Monsieur Beaucaire* is indeed a rather far cry. 〈. . .〉

Cherry, written prior to either of the books already mentioned, followed next in order of publication. It is not one of Mr. Tarkington's significant books, but it attracts attention because of the whimsical nature of its theme and its still odder setting,—for it is a story of a college student in the days preceding the American Revolution. It is told in the first person by a certain Mr. Sudgeberry, intolerably priggish, incredibly self-satisfied, who at the age of nineteen is finishing his third year of study at Nassau Hall. Mr. Sudgeberry is, so far as his preoccupation with himself will permit, deeply enamored of a young woman, a certain Miss Sylvia Gray, who is addicted to cherry-colored ribbons and who is curiously tolerant of one of Sudgeberry's classmates, one William Fentriss, whose riotous and ungodly mode of life Sudgeberry sternly condemns. The exaggerated pedantry, the unbelievable thickheadedness of Sudgeberry, while cleverly sustained, become wearisome when prolonged throughout a hundred and seventy-four pages. The story of a girl who while accepting attentions from one man amuses herself by keeping another dangling upon the string and using him to keep her father engaged in conversation is too flimsy material from which to make a novel, even when eked out by a lovers' quarrel, a burlesque highway robbery and rescue and Christmas chimes presaging marriage bells.

No author can produce three volumes of such varying degrees of merit and of success, without learning a good deal about his readers and about himself. What Mr. Tarkington seems to have learned pretty thoroughly was that, whether the general public did or did not care for serious fiction,—problem novels with weighty lessons behind them,—from him at least they asked only entertainment,—and that entertainment was the commodity that he could most easily afford them. Accordingly he wrote *The Two Vanrevels*, a novel of the high-class comedy type, blithe, wholesome, optimistic, peopled with men of old-fashioned courtliness and women of gracious manners and soft-voiced charm. Technically, it was a better piece of work than *The Gentleman from Indiana*, which in date of composition immediately preceded it; the plot structure, although frail in substance, showed careful workmanship; the character drawing was done with a surer touch; and, best of all, Mr. Tarkington knew precisely in what key he was pitching his story, and he held to that key from first to last. There is nowhere in it the least suggestion of an attempt to pretend that it is anything else than sheer romanticism, which here and there trespasses across the border-line of melodrama. The setting is once more the Indiana which Mr. Tarkington knows so well; but he secures that rose-tinted mist of distance, so essential to romance of this type, by throwing back the time of action a couple of generations, to the days just preceding the outbreak of the Mexican war. As in all three of the earlier stories, the plot turns upon a prolonged misunderstanding; and, as in two out of the other three, the nature of the misunderstanding is a mistaken identity. And herein lies the inherent weakness of *The Two Vanrevels*, the lack of plausibility that no amount of verbal dexterity quite succeeds in disguising. Where a story hinges upon the chance confusion, in the mind of a young girl, of one man for another, in a town where every one knows every one else, and she is constantly meeting first one of the two men and then the other, at all sorts of social functions, talking with them, dancing with them, liable at any moment to hear them addressed by name: under such circumstances the difficulty of carrying conviction increases with each additional page of the story. In *Monsieur Beaucaire* the hero's identity is an easily kept secret because it is shared by no one but his loyal servants,—and *Monsieur Beaucaire* had the further advantage of being very short. In *The Gentleman from Indiana* the fact that the heroine is the substitute editor on the *Carlow County Herald* is easily kept from the hero because he is flat on his back in a hospital ward in another town many miles distant,—and there is the further advantage that the secret had to be kept throughout only a third of the volume. In *The Two Vanrevels* Miss Betty Carewe's blunder in taking Tom Vanrevel and Crailey Gray each for the other is the very essence of the whole book, its starting-point, its continued suspense, its culminating tragedy, its sole excuse for being. It would have served admirably as the sub-structure of a short story, in which form Mr. Tarkington is said originally to have conceived it; but as a full-length novel, in spite of a great deal of ingenuity, one feels that the situation is forced, artificial and perilously near a breakdown at almost any moment. Old Robert Carewe has the reputation of being not only the richest man but the best hater in the community; and at the time that his daughter Betty bids farewell to her convent school and comes home, his long-standing feud with the Vanrevels has blazed up with renewed heat. In his opinion, openly expressed, the law firm of Vanrevel and Gray is made up of a knave and a fool,—and in this opinion he is not in the slightest degree shaken by the fact that the public at large has never made up its mind which of the two it loves the more: steady, loyal, wholly dependable Tom Vanrevel or light-hearted, fickle, fascinating and utterly untrustworthy Crailey Gray. Betty Carewe, warned by her father that if young Vanrevel ever dares set foot inside his grounds he will shoot him on sight, finds a delicious and perilous joy in clandestine meetings with the man she thinks her father's enemy but who in reality is Crailey Gray: and all the while she is hearing disgraceful, scandalous tales of Crailey Gray and because of them doing her best to make herself hate and despise the man whom she fell in love with at first sight and who of course is the real Vanrevel. The story proceeds with clever artistry to its inevitable melodramatic tragedy and would deserve to rank rather high among Mr. Tarkington's productions excepting for the fact that we cannot escape from a sense of its being in a measure expert jugglery, a *tour de force* of a literary prestidigitateur.

〈. . .〉 In spite of much diversity in time and setting, his talent is not an instrument of many notes; his themes, as already suggested, are few and oft repeated. The basis of every story he has written is a misunderstanding of one kind or another, of identity, of purpose, of character. He sees life, even the prosaic, every-day life of his home environment, through rose-tinted lenses that both soften and magnify. He has an imperishable faith in the innate goodness of the human heart which, coupled with a wholesome scorn of sham and snobbery, gives to the people of his fantasy a certain whole-souled quality that makes them lovable even while we feel that they are a little bit too good to be true. All of these qualities offer in themselves as much promise of success in drama under existing conditions as in prose fiction; indeed one has only to glance at a play like *The Man from Home,*—in which his share in the collaboration with Mr. Wilson can be shrewdly guessed between the lines,—to see how every one of his favorite tricks in his novels is there reproduced with even more felicitous effect. There again, in that play, we have a situation depending on a whole series of misunderstandings and mistaken identities: a Russian prince masquerading as a simple German traveler, an escaped anarchist disguised as a chauffeur, a whole group of adventurers and tricksters, male and female, passing themselves off as shining lights of European aristocracy and the Man from Home himself voluntarily posing as a very simple homespun personality, but in reality the brightest, keenest, most indomitable personality in the whole group. And here, more than anywhere in his novels, Mr. Tarkington allows himself to fall back upon that favorite makeshift of the romanticist, Coincidence. Everything happens in the nick of time. A person's name is mentioned, and miraculously he appears upon the scene; a secret is whispered, and somewhere a window or door opens stealthily and the secret is overheard. A tangle of situations is tightly knotted up and the only people who can unravel it are supposedly scattered widely throughout Europe and Asia,—and presto, they are all discovered simultaneously beneath the roof of a Sicilian hotel. Here, indeed, we have the very essence of Booth Tarkington; from first to last, under various disguises, he has always been, as he is to-day, a successful exponent of glorified melodrama.

WINFIELD TOWNLEY SCOTT
From "Tarkington and the 1920's"
American Scholar, Spring 1957, pp. 181–86

In the 1920's Booth Tarkington's success and fame made him seem to a vast number of readers the literary ornament of the times. F. Scott Fitzgerald's friend Edmund Wilson, for one, knew better; nevertheless, Fitzgerald, right out of Princeton, became an immediate celebrity with *This Side of Paradise*, much of which is nothing but inferior emulation of Tarkington. Now, all the literary historians know better, so much better that they ignore Tarkington lock, stock and barrel. They are unaware that in his novel *Alice Adams* Tarkington made a far more significant contribution to American fiction in the 1920's than many an admired rover of the Riviera, Paris, Provincetown and Greenwich Village could possibly have made.

Alice Adams, much lauded in its day, is sometimes referred to, if at all, as "probably his best novel." In the past it has been in part misread by critics, and I cannot find that it has ever been read with any perception of its adumbration of American society in the decade that lay ahead. *Alice Adams* was written in 1920 and published in 1921. Commentators at the time could not have foreseen its prophetic accuracy; later they did not bother. And now, momentarily, *Alice* has gone down in the general collapse of Tarkington's reputation following his death. But think of the novelists more or less Tarkington's contemporaries whose names are a part of the brightness of his era: Edith Wharton, Ellen Glasgow, Joseph Hergesheimer, Carl Van Vechten, the somewhat younger Sinclair Lewis. Fade is on some of these, yet nobody judges it gauche to account for them; and yet, again, none of them wrote a better novel than *Alice Adams*. Tarkington's fellow Indianian Theodore Dreiser could not write as well as Tarkington or any of these others—he just wrote greater novels. The further exception is Willa Cather, who matched Dreiser in substance and surpassed them all in art.

Tarkington has paid the penalty of suiting his times and his huge audience too nicely; his books were charming, amusing and undisturbing. They minded their manners fatally. That *Alice Adams* escapes the mold is almost an accident, which can be analyzed in terms of its author's limitations as well as his great talents. Tarkington's biographer, James Woodress, reports that Sinclair Lewis wrote Tarkington a letter in which he said he was telling lecture audiences: "When you are considering the clever unknown youngsters, don't suppose that because he sells so enormously, Booth Tarkington can't write better than any of them." This was just after the publication of *Alice Adams*.

Years ago it was customary when anyone wrote about Booth Tarkington to make a good deal of his long, unpromising struggle as a writer; how, after Princeton, he returned to his parents' home in Indianapolis and wrote reams of rejected stories for seven years. Then, in 1899, *The Gentleman from Indiana* was published and Tarkington was made. He was thirty years old. He does not seem, after all, a major instance of delayed recognition. Furthermore, from the moment he was published he had a smashing success. *Monsieur Beaucaire* immediately followed *The Gentleman from Indiana*, and other stories and plays only increased his popularity. Throughout his long career (he died in 1946, nearing his seventy-seventh birthday) he was a famous and rich man.

Toward the end, *Life* magazine called him an old pro who could write rings around the rest of his class. And that was so. But Tarkington was not just a romancer; some of his books are less deeply meant than others, but he had always—in style, attack, material—the standards of an artist. He meant to tell the truth about such facets of American middle-class society as he knew most intimately, and he meant to tell it well. To a point his gifts were as brilliant as his outward success, and his having come so near to being a first-rate writer makes his general failure complexly interesting.

In Tarkington's heyday his busiest apologist, Robert Cortes Holliday, concluded with complete satisfaction that "his books are popular because of the same qualities that made their author popular as an undergraduate." At the same time, Grant Overton, conceding "most exceptional talent and even unmistakable genius," perceived that Tarkington was the victim of "largely comfortable circumstances." And now Mr. Woodress, an industrious, useful but uncritical biographer, has produced a theory of Tarkington success which is rather stunning in its simplicity. In effect, Woodress says Tarkington wrote as he pleased, and it just happened, most of the time, that what pleased Tarkington also pleased hundreds of thousands of readers. Translated, this signifies that Tarkington was a writer of complete integrity. Actually, in a way, this is true. It simply fails to examine the only question of importance: What were the values to which Tarkington's integrity adhered?

The graceful and lightly intended entertainments such as *Gentle Julia* and *Seventeen* and the three *Penrod* books are prominent on the Tarkington shelf because in them he did so skillfully what he set himself to do. They are comedies, here and there made wistful or untruthful by a point of view which is that of an older observer mostly amused and occasionally touched to nostalgic pity by the manners of youth. In every sense they are too easy. Granted that no other contemporary could do this sort of thing with Tarkington's flair, one has to note that his novels in general increasingly employed such an obsession with the child mind that a strong streak of infantilism ran through his work. He turned children and adolescents into clowns. And he did this so repeatedly that, except for *Kate Fennigate* with its solid title role, none of the many books of his last two decades adds anything to his reputation; they water it down.

I do not see why anyone should deny charm to *Monsieur Beaucaire*; a trifle, but there it is. But to determine what claims, if any, Tarkington has to a place among American novelists, all the fumbling early books and the thinly slick later ones may be forgotten; his best work falls between the time he was forty and fifty-five. I should mention one novel which comes beyond the later line, *The Plutocrat*, since both Tarkington's biographer and, before him, Van Wyck Brooks have made much of it. Brooks speaks as fairly for Tarkington as can be spoken, but he chose the wrong novel. *The Plutocrat* has in the Tarkington canon an air of importance for its conception of the successful American businessman as the modern Roman, its juxtaposition (denied by Tarkington but most unfortunately made by everybody else) as an answer to Lewis' best novel, *Babbitt*, and its summation, so to speak, of the Tarkington attitude (admiring and affectionate) toward capitalism. All this, as conception, is in the book, even its availability as a defense of George F. Babbitt; yet in substance it is childish—Earl Tinker is created on a vaudeville level and illustrates how the "eternal boy" was ruining Tarkington's adult characterizations; Mme. Momoro is as embarrassingly melodramatic as a movie notion of an international vamp, and such interpolations as the sneering attacks on modern art and poetry are utterly stale. The whole thing, one of the worst of his novels, amounts to a frightening exposure of what happens when an old pro advances the "unrelenting pressure of environment" in the guise of intellectual conviction.

Again setting aside *Alice Adams*, the three most important Tarkington novels are *The Turmoil*, *The Magnificent Ambersons* and *The Midlander*. Loosely, they form a trilogy. Indianapolis begets their common scene, and they portray the growth of a Midwestern city in various eras. One always remembers from them the very fine atmospherics, so typical of America, of the changing city: the fall and rise of particular families in the economic scale, the altering of neighborhoods—the old brownstone mansion descended to Board and Room signs, the thrust of dirty shops and glistening gas stations where, a generation before, comfortable householders played croquet in the evening dusk by the iron stag on the lawn, and the "new developments" pushing out beyond the ever-swelling business district. All three novels evoke that mutability of the American city, at once healthy and vulgar and saddening. No other novelist better recorded the pre-Depression, twentieth-century *feel* of the American city; no other, probably, as well.

Nevertheless, such passages in those three novels are minor and repetitious. Though the three have a dignity and substance absent from *The Plutocrat*, again their conception is thinned in the execution. Woodress' contention is indefensible, that "Tarkington pulled no punches in attacking the scramble for wealth and its attendant ugliness," if he applies it, as he does, to any book but *Alice Adams;* he applies it to *The Turmoil* and these others. It is true that Tarkington nostalgically mourned the changes which industrial growth created, but what he set alongside this attitude was not an anti-materialist satire or poetic passion—rather, the three novels lose all critical power by seeking the comfortable adjustments of the new materialism. Tragedy in the Tarkington view means loss of money and position; and from Georgie Amberson on down, Tarkington took care to "save" his characters by restoring them to the road toward prosperity. Dan Oliphant dies in *The Midlander*, but he dies in the high cause of materialistic progress; and in *The Turmoil* the sensitive Bibbs Sheridan is whipped into line in the same high cause. This easy acceptance of things as they are, coupled with Tarkington's evasion of writing anything you would not care to have your daughter read—as they used to say—leaves his most ambitious work disastrously vitiated. "One cannot be both a gentleman and an artist," said Bernard Shaw. This is what Booth Tarkington tried to be. The great laying-on of hands in his career had been the repeated blessing of William Dean Howells. A blessing from the author of *The Rise of Silas Lapham* need not be regrettable; however, it is the necessity of each new generation of writers to freshen and extend, if not to combat, the traditions of the elders. Tarkington was content to rest within the gentility congenial to Howells.

There is a well-established line of the American novel of mild social commentary. One way of isolating it is the observation that Frank Norris, Dreiser and their kind do not fit it. Mrs. Wharton almost belongs, and she suggests Henry James's kinship, made remote partly by a preoccupation with other facets of society but largely by greater intricacy of method. The line can be drawn unwaveringly from Howells through Tarkington and Lewis (so it seems, now Lewis' total view is examined) to John P. Marquand. The differences among the novels of these men are chiefly of fashion and generation; they are not fundamental differences. Satire, humor and evaluation all tend to be clever and compromised.

The youngsters in the line always recognize the elders, but not always vice versa. James Woodress says that Sinclair Lewis, some years after his generous praise of Tarkington, visited Indianapolis and expressed a desire to meet the great man of the town. "Tarkington made no effort to see him," and wrote Julian Street: "He had always classed Lewis 'among the people I don't want to sit down with.'" The remark is symbolic. There were too many people, things, subcutaneous truths, Tarkington did not want to sit down with. I don't know how one can avoid the charge of snobbery. An unimaginative thing in any human being, snobbery is crippling in an artist. Nevertheless, it is the underlying explanation of his one unqualified success, *Alice Adams*. There have been odder paradoxes.

ALLEN TATE

1899–1979

John Orley Allen Tate was born on November 19, 1899, in Clark County, Kentucky, to John Orley and Eleanor Varnell Tate. He was educated at Vanderbilt University (B.A. 1922). He was married three times: to the novelist Caroline Gordon in 1924, to the poet Isabella Stewart Gardner in 1959, and to Helen Heinz in 1966. He was a founding editor, with John Crowe Ransom, of the *Fugitive* from 1922 to 1925, and editor of the *Sewanee Review* from 1944 to 1946. He taught at various universities, including Southwestern College, Princeton University, New York University, the University of Minnesota, and the Woman's College at Greensboro, North Carolina; in addition, he served as a visiting professor or lecturer at more than a dozen other universities, including Oxford University, the University of Rome, and the Sorbonne. He served as Consultant in Poetry for the Library of Congress from 1943 to 1944.

Tate first came to public attention as a member of the Fugitive movement, a group of Southern writers who urged that the South adopt agrarian values and reject Northern industrialism. Other prominent Fugitives included John Crowe Ransom and Robert Penn Warren; they became Tate's lifelong friends and associates.

Tate's first commercially published book of poetry, *Mr. Pope and Other Poems*, appeared in 1928; it was praised for its depth of feeling tempered with formal structural discipline. Subsequent volumes furthered his reputation, and the publication of his *Selected Poems* in 1937, including the final version of his popular "Ode to the Confederate Dead," established him as an important American modernist poet and one of the most important of the South's writers. His later poetry is influenced by his growing Roman Catholic convictions—he was eventually converted to Catholicism in 1950—and much of it is satirical in tone. Many critics prefer his later verse, particularly such experientially based works as "Seasons of the Soul" (1944), "The Swimmers" (1953), and "The Buried Lake" (1953).

Tate was not only an accomplished poet but also a significant critic. He believed that art should be firmly embedded in experience of the world, and that the best art strives to clarify man's relationship to his culture. Though a modernist, Tate's influences were traditional and classical, and included Dante, Vergil, and the Greek classics. His most significant books of criticism include *Reason in Madness* (1941), *On the Limits of Poetry* (1948), *The Hovering Fly* (1949), and *The Forlorn Demon* (1953). He also wrote a novel (*The Fathers*, 1938), a play (*The Governess*, with Anne Goodwin Winslow, produced in 1962), and biographies of Stonewall Jackson and Jefferson Davis. His *Essays of Four Decades* was issued in 1968, and his *Memoirs and Opinions 1926–1974* was published in 1975. Tate received the Bollingen Prize in Poetry in 1956. He died on February 9, 1979, in Nashville, Tennessee.

CLEANTH BROOKS
"Allen Tate"

Poetry, September 1945, pp. 324–29

It is impossible to review these poems ⟨in *The Winter Sea*⟩ without taking into account the topical references which they make, for the references are many and obvious—to Henry Wallace, to Van Wyck Brooks, to Pearl Harbor, to the fall of France. They reflect a world scene with which the reader is thoroughly familiar; but they stem from a point of view with which he is quite unfamiliar. The average reader—if he is fortunate enough to come upon a copy of this handsome, highly limited edition—will therefore be inclined to take it as a bitter and puzzling book, though, even so, he will in his bewilderment hardly escape becoming aware of the power and authority which manifest themselves in poem after poem.

The work of a first-rate poet always constitutes a commentary on the age out of which it comes, and is, in turn, commented upon by the events of that age. Likewise, any poem by a serious poet becomes a commentary on the rest of his work and, perhaps, achieves its ultimate richness for the reader only in so far as it receives the commentary of the rest of his work. Both propositions are peculiarly true of Allen Tate's *The Winter Sea*. It is not a matter of the poems—the best ones, at least—lacking completeness. The title poem achieves, in my opinion, a perfection of formal organization beyond any other poem that Tate has ever written.

What is at stake is not the final detachment and formal independence of the poems as objects, but rather the accessibility of the poems to the reader of the present, who, lacking commentary, may feel that the poems are needlessly obscure, or may obfuscate them by applying to them the first rough-and-ready commentary that comes to hand—the commentary of the daily headlines. The point is not that the reader should wait until time allows him to see the poems "in proper perspective": it is rather that he should be prepared to see them in the perspective that the poetry itself provides and achieves. But this latter course will involve his reading the poems as wholes, as poems—not as mere tracts, or even as mere "satires."

The poems are political and topical, but in the deeper sense, as part of the total situation with which man attempts to come to terms in a time of violence—violence in which all are involved and to which we are all committed, though the violence imposes its effects in varying modes and to varying degrees. If this is war verse that will hardly please Van Wyck Brooks, neither will it afford any comfort to Burton K.

Wheeler. It cuts far below the special "political" interests of either of these gentlemen.

Actually, the best point of entry into these poems is that provided by the poet in the epigraph to *The Winter Sea*—the quotation from the twelfth canto of Dante's *Inferno*. Canto XII introduces the seventh ring of Hell where the violent are punished; and the reader will do well to reread not only this canto but all the rest that deal with the seventh circle. And it will also be well for the reader to recall the categories of the violent whom Dante assigns to the seventh circle: those who have committed violence against their neighbors, those who have done violence to themselves, those who have violently consumed their goods; and also, not to be forgotten, those who have committed violence against God, against Nature, or against Art.

The last-named category is worth remembering. It will indicate why the "satiric" poems of this collection, where the poet pays his respects to Van Wyck Brooks and the "new nationalists" who "give the yawp barbaric / Of piety and pelf," are not irrelevant to the main body of the poetry.

As satiric comments, some of the lines are brilliantly neat. (For the benefit of those who think that "Proust caused the fall of France," the poet remarks that at Oahu "Our Proustian retort / Was Kimmel and Short.") But effective as the satire is, the poems are not mere clever *ripostes*, retorts in a "literary" battle. The new attack on form—"(Who now reads Herrick?)"—the fashionable glorification of formless bigness—"Myself the old cock / With wind and water wild / (Hell with the privy lock)"—are part and parcel of the general violence of the time. It is at this level that the matter interests Tate, and, significantly enough, each of the "satires" ends quite unsatirically—ends with a seriously ironical image of our plight—an image of aimless, directionless movement.

For the violence of our time is interpreted in the fine central poems of this volume as ultimately self-violence. The branch which the poet plucks, like Dante's, drips its speaking blood, and drips it upon the poet,

> Their brother who, like them,
> Was maimed and did not bear
> The living wound of love.

But the self-violence, the blood-letting, points toward a final mechanization of impulse, a final exhaustion. The image of the emptied man recurs throughout the poems:

> Salt serum stays his arteries
> Sly tide threading the ribs of sand,
> Till his lost being dries and cries
> For that unspeakable salt land
> Beyond the Day of Jubilo
> . . .
> You will be Plato's kept philosopher,
> Albino man bleached from the mortal clay,
> Mild-mannered, gifted in your masters' ease
> While the sun squats upon the waveless seas
> . . .
> Regard us, while the eye
> Discerns by sight or guess
> Whether, as sheep foregather
> Upon their crooked knees,
> We have begun to die;
> Whether your kindness, mother,
> Is mother of silences.

The Winter Sea, for all that it is a tissue of Dante references, does not pretend to give Dante's vision. It could not and keep its full integrity. Dante's doctrine is not available to him except as reference. Moreover, he is not like Dante, the detached observer of the damned. He is one of the damned:

> We raise our tired eyes
> Into a sky of glass
> Blue empty and tall . . .

"We are the eyelids of defeated caves" of one of Tate's earlier poems becomes here:

> This earth—Platonic cave
> Of vertiginous chance!
> Come, tired Sisyphus,
> Cover the cave's egress
> Where light reveals the slave . . .

and, in *More Sonnets at Christmas:*

> Citizen, myself, or personal friend,
> Your ghosts are Plato's Christians in the cave.

The Winter Sea represents, then, no turning aside from the themes and methods of Tate's earlier work, but a development of them. I will not say that in this volume there is a completion of them, but certainly there is an increased richness and a further reduction of them to an overmastering "form."

As an aspect of this might be mentioned Tate's brilliant use of the Yeatsian refrain. It is used with special success in the title poem to set the basic character of the four "seasons of the soul" but the variations in the refrain develop and complicate the tone so that the refrain itself becomes an integral part of the poem. It is not an imitation or a borrowing from Yeats but a complete absorption of the device. And this is true of the refrain which recurs through the fine "Winter Mask to the Memory of W. B. Yeats."

It is interesting, by the bye, to speculate on what Yeats would have thought of these poems. They certainly would have interested him greatly. The bold dissonances he would probably have disapproved of, and I suppose that the poetry in general might have seemed to him somewhat angular and violent. But speculation about Yeats' opinion need not be wholly idle. There are passages in Yeats' prophecy for our time and the future of our civilization (a section which he omitted from the public edition of *A Vision* but which constitutes perhaps the most brilliant single passage in the 1925 privately printed edition) which apply beautifully to the present book.

> I discover [he writes] already the first phase . . . [of the closing period of our civilization] in certain friends of mine, and in writers, poets and sculptors, admired by those friends, who have a strong love and hate hitherto unknown in the arts. It is with them a matter of conscience to live in their own instant of time, and they defend their consciences like theologians. [It is here also, Yeats writes, that] there is a hatred of the abstract . . . [that] the intellect turns upon itself. . . .
>
> It is as though myth and fact, united until the exhaustion of the Renaissance, have now fallen so far apart that man understands for the first time the rigidity of fact, and calls up by that very recognition, myth—the *Mask*—which now gropes its way out of the mind's dark but will shortly pursue and terrify.

But more illuminating still are Yeats' notes on the nature of the world out of which the future art will come:

> In practical life one expects the same technical inspiration, the doing this or that *not because one would, or should, but because one can* [italics mine], consequent license, and with those 'out of phase' anarchic violence with no sanction in general prin-

> ciples. If there is violent revolution, and it is the last phase where political revolution is possible, the dish will be made from what is found in the pantry and the cook will not open her book. . . . Then with the last gyre must come a desire to rule or be ruled or rather, seeing that desire is all but dead, an adoration of force spiritual or physical [Tate's "Boys caress the machines they ride / On the day of Jubilo"], and society as mechanical force be complete at last. . . . A decadence will descend, by perpetual moral improvement [Tate's "Albino man bleached from the mortal clay"], upon a community which may seem like a woman of New York or Paris who has renounced her rouge pot to lose her figure and grow coarse of skin and dull of brain, feeding her calves and babies somewhere upon the edge of the wilderness.

I shall hardly expect the reader to take this seriously as political prophecy. I do not put it forward as such. Nor do I offer the passage as Tate's "source." (I cannot be sure that Tate has ever read it.) What I am sure of is that it offers brilliant insights into what must surely be counted a volume of some of the most powerful poetry of our time. As such *The Winter Sea* deserves to be read by every one seriously interested in modern poetry. And perhaps it should be required reading for some of our literary Pharisees who have been recently congratulating themselves on their failure to have a "failure of nerve."

VIVIENNE KOCH

"The Poetry of Allen Tate"

Kenyon Review, Summer 1949, pp. 355–78

I

I should like to propose two revisions of the customary valuation put upon the poetry of Allen Tate. First, it has become increasingly evident with each new work that Mr. Tate is a fugitive from the Fugitives. The Fugitives were that talented group of Southern writers who, finding the Northern poetic climate of the early twenties too exacerbatingly modern, reaffirmed their allegiances with "tradition," a term they took some care to define. While we commonly think of the Southerners as a group, and while in a loose personal sense this may be so, it is my belief that in a veiled but not altogether deceptive fashion Mr. Tate has been seeking to free himself from the claims of group loyalty, claims which at one time had threatened the temper of his own sensibility. For Tate, with an artistic humility strangely discordant with his critical arrogance, had publicly avowed his apprenticeship to his Southern master, John Crowe Ransom, and to his European one, T. S. Eliot. These poet-critics were the *maîtres* of the Southern group and a common devotion created additional pressures for orthodoxy.

Curiously enough, Tate's first symptomatic departure from his "tradition" came in what would seem, on the surface, to be the apotheosis of his conformance to it. It came in his translation of *Pervigilium Veneris* (1934), that neglected little classic never happily Englished, upon which he chose to exercise his powers, not so much as a Latinist, but as a poet of classical affiliations. Yet I think his choice of this delicately tinted but uninnocently erotic poem was perhaps motivated by the fact that, as Professor Mackail points out, it represents

> the first clear note of the new romanticism which transformed classical into mediaeval literature. . . . Nothing could be less like either a folk-song or an official ode. It touches the last refinement of simplicity. In the delicately running, softly swaying verses, that ring and glitter and return on themselves in interlacing patterns, there is germinally the essence and inner spirit of the whole romantic movement. All the motives of the old classical poetry survive, yet all have undergone a new birth.

The *Pervigilium Veneris* is Allen Tate's valedictory, from a safe distance, to the Fugitives, to the South, to the "classical" tradition, to his masters. The quickest way to get over the goodbyes is to say them in a strange language.

My second proposal flows from the historic process I have just described and is, at the same time and paradoxically, anterior to the whole development. I believe that Tate is a poet of romantic sensibility who has tried with varying success to compress his talents into a chastely classical form and that, in inverse degrees to his willingness or ability to do so, his best poetry has been written. Where his romanticism gets the better of him, or, to shift the metaphor, finds the classicist nodding, there we get the most enduring, vital and original poetry Tate is capable of writing. The *Pervigilium* was playing romanticism with the rules; with the publication of *The Winter Sea* it became clear that Tate was playing his own way.

In short, we have been assessing Tate too long in terms of his origins (the genetic fallacy) and his prose judgment (the doctrinal fallacy). It is time we began to follow the lead of the poems.

II

In Tate's *Selected Poems* (1937) it is possible to group together the work of the early 'twenties on several grounds. "Obituary," "Death of Little Boys," "Horatian Epode to the *Duchess of Malfi*," "The Subway," "Ditty," "Retroduction to American History," and "Mr. Pope," all bear the imprint of the Eliot of "Prufrock" in the characteristic quatrain (or aggregation of joined quatrains) with the typically anti-climactic, sometimes parenthetical usage of the fourth line. Similarly, the vocabulary is often derived from Eliot: "You have no more chance than an infusorian / Lodged in a hollow molar of an eohippus. / Come, now, no prattle of remergence with the *ontos on*." All, without a single exception, whether the subject be Webster, Pope, the death of little boys, or their sleeping, reveal a bitter, angry and passionate rejection of the present, of contemporaneity where "you, so crazy and inviolate" are "hurled religiously / Upon your business of humility / Into the iron forestries of hell; / . . . Dazed, while the worldless heavens bulge and reel/In the cold revery of an idiot."

It is a present in which even "little boys grown patient at last, weary / Surrender their eyes immeasurably to the night," and other "Little boys no longer sight the plover / Streaked in the sky," while "men, who fail . . . will plunge, mile after mile of men, to crush this lucent madness of the face, / Go home and put their heads upon the pillow. Turn whatever shift the darkness cleaves, / Tuck in their eyes, and cover / The flying dark with sleep like falling leaves." I hope it is excusable to resort to the kind of mosaic I have just composed in order to point a paradox: Allen Tate, at the start of his career in the early 'twenties, was affirming his allegiances with the classical past in the unsigned editorials of *The Fugitive* and, at the same time, betraying in every poem he was writing a frankly nihilistic temper which, in its alternating violence and absolution, was a romanticism of a somewhat more fiery brand than his criticism might have endorsed.

Perhaps the gauge of Tate's youthful romanticism may be best explored in his much-admired "Death of Little Boys" published in the *Nation* in 1925 when he was twenty-six years old:

> When little boys grown patient at last, weary,
> Surrender their eyes immeasurably to the night,
> The event will rage terrific as the sea;
> Their bodies fill a crumbling room with light.
>
> Then you will touch at the bedside, torn in two,
> Gold curls now intricate with gray
> As the windowpane extends a fear to you
> From one peeled aster drenched with the wind all day.
>
> And over his chest the covers in an ultimate dream
> Will mount to the teeth, ascend the eyes, press back
> The locks—while round his sturdy belly gleam
> The suspended breaths, white spars above the wreck:
>
> Till all the guests, come in to look, turn down
> Their palms, and delirium assails the cliff
> Of Norway where you ponder, and your little town
> Reels like a sailor in his rotten skiff.
>
> The bleak sunshine shrieks its chipped music then
> Out to the milkweed amid the fields of wheat.
> There is a calm for you where men and women
> Unroll the chill precision of moving feet.

The only "classical" element in this adventuresome poem is the plural in the title and the first line. The generalizing character of "boys" extends or is intended to extend an individual experience of death to a universal statement of it. But apart from this gesture (a successful one) there is no concession anywhere in the poem (unless it be in the rather diversified quatrains) to any poem I am familiar with in the "tradition" of English literature up to 1925. The poem is a consideration of the problem of identity or, more philosophically, the problem of permanence and change. The "you" of the second paragraph is not merely rhetorical address which seeks to involve the reader with the death of little boys, but it achieves exactly that. The bedside is "torn in two" by the "event" of death, which, let us note, does not destroy the little boys but rather the room which crumbles with light. (The room, of course, may be everything which is contained in it.) The "gold curls" are "now deftly intricate with gray" because of the blinding vision of death in which "you" (the onlooker, father, or little boy grown up) must participate because you too feel the fear extended by the windowpane (night or death to which the little boys have in Stanza One surrendered their eyes). The emotional affects throughout are persistently ascribed to the landscape.

In Stanza Three the death is individualized in the singular pronouns (abandoning the universal), in the magnificently concrete, yet symbolic detail of the "sturdy belly" round which "gleam the suspended breaths" of the dead boy, or rather boy-in-man, and "you" (like another Hamlet, a questioning, dubious intellect) pondering on your cliff feel delirium (death, shifting identity) assailing it (just as, in a similar transfer of affects, it was the *room* and not the body which crumbled in Stanza One), and your little town (something built, *made*, the ego, perhaps) "reels like a sailor in his rotten skiff." Here the image of the dead boy as a wreck and the little town (the ego) about-to-be-wrecked converge in the sea symbolism. It is at this point (the crisis of the poem) that the fusion of meanings is consummated and the question of permanence (identity) arises like a lonely phoenix from the wreck of little boys (your wreck, of course). The last stanza is an anticlimax, and is so intended. The "bleak sunshine," the discordant shriek of its "chipped music," reaches out to the level of external quotidian existence (milkweed, etc.) where there are no more "events terrific as the sea" but only an ironic calm whose inevitable "precision of moving feet" implies an ultimately similar dissolution of the almost-wrecked ego.

Perhaps this explication will have seemed forced. In that event, I suggest returning to the sea metaphor introduced in Stanza One, picked up and developed in Three and consummated in the harsh despair of "reels," "drunk," and "rotten," to say nothing of the flimsy, useless phonetic fluff of "skiff." By that route, it seems to me, almost the same reading may be developed as the one I have got by the long way. Little boys die in men before men die. Man is torn in two by his past (his little boyhood) and his present. The agency of childhood is mysterious and terrifying in the personality of the man (the aster is man "peeled"—revealed—by his youth). The certainty of identity (integration of personality) is seriously threatened in Stanza Four. In Five there is a sick rebound: the world and its dull, mechanic inevitability must be met again. The let-down in diction, the clarity of the last stanza as opposed to the complexity of the others, is Tate's cold and disdainful bow to the outer world, to the nowness he *will* not recognize. This, then, is the kind of poetry Tate was writing when he was raging with youthful hauteur against the *nouveaux-arrivés* "experimentalists." To recapitulate: "Death of Little Boys" is a very good poem; it is revelatory of Tate's "original" temperamental bent (if learning had not already disguised the interior man); it is certainly as "experimental" as any poem I know of written at that time, including the "romantic" experimentalism of Tate's friend, Hart Crane.

The following five years, 1925–30, are crucial to the direction of Tate's growth. Some residence in England and France during that time leave superficial traces in his work. If Tate ever thought of himself as an exile (and at least one poem, "Message from Abroad," bears witness that he did) it was certainly not the kind of willed exile represented by Joyce's categorical imperatives for the artist, "Silence, exile and cunning," nor by Henry James's ambassadorial *rapprochements*, nor by Eliot's British repatriation. Europe merely reinforces for Tate the feeling he started out with in Kentucky. He is exiled not from a place, but from a condition. The present (and Europe is just as contemporaneous as the South) exiles him from the past. He is cut off *through no fault of his own* from a more meaningful condition of living. He will begin to try in these years to find, focus, and define the character of that past and so, perhaps, to possess it. Like many young men of his time, but with greater tenacity and intellectual resourcefulness, he takes Eliot as his guide to the map of that dark country. It is now that Tate begins to deny the authority of his own sensibility as poet. It is his first misstep, but, happily, not a disastrous one.

In 1925 in "Retroduction to American History" Tate found it possible to arraign the present in these terms:

> Narcissus is vocabulary. Hermes decorates
> A cornice on the Third National Bank. Vocabulary
> Becomes confusion, decoration a blight;
> . . . scholarship pares
> The nails of Catullus, sniffs his sheets, restores
> His "passionate underwear"; morality disciplines the other
> Person; every son-of-a-bitch is Christ, at least Rousseau.

But there the cataloguing of deprivations and evils, wrought upon the poet by his environment, seems uncontrolled: there is a false and heavy-handed exaggeration in the view of historical scholarship (a method Tate despises) which is seen to restore Catullus' "passionate underwear"; there is an inchoate imprecision of epithet to "Every son-of-a-bitch is Christ, at least Rousseau." Yet an interesting premonition of the way in which Tate was later to define the past, a definition differing in subtle details from Eliot's, occurs in a Websterian passage later in this long poem: "A corpse is your bedfellow, your great-grandfather dines / With you this evening on / a cavalry horse. Intellect / Connives with heredity, creates fate as Euclid geometry / By definition." Nevertheless, the poem's end is more temperate than the violent castigations of the earlier sections might lead one to expect:

Heredity
Proposes love, love exacts language, and we lack
Language. When shall we speak again? When shall
The sparrow dusting the gutter sing? When shall
This drift with silence meet the sun? When shall I
wake?

Thus the past (heredity) begets love, love (containing the past) as an enduring, positive force demands to be communicated, but the means (language) is recalcitrant. Our past need not be sought; it is in the "sunlit bones" in our house. But how to establish this knowledge, this good, as an objective reality? Tate then, at the beginning, had a certain advantage over Eliot, an advantage deriving from the relative homogeneity of Southern culture as opposed to the crude mixture of frontier strains and Back Bay *manqué* which were, no doubt, the conditional and never-accepted "heredity" of the St. Louis of the latter's boyhood and adolescence.

But if such hope were possible in 1925, by 1927 the chances for solving the problem of communication, for removing the obstructive features of the material present, seem more slender. A delicate shadow of despair begins to invade the poems. In a nostalgic and deliberately archaic tone the poet asks his friend Edmund Wilson, the critic, "a Syracusan, domiciled at Rome" to "be still" lest he, "the city priest / Urging crab-like the busy quest" find suddenly that both East and West escape him and that he toils "more than the rest of us / For the idiot king of a savage court." The final quatrain, sustaining the intimate, epistolary Horatianism of the poem, describes somewhat sentimentally but with an effective hopelessness the character of the urban present:

Once we had marveled countrywise,
My friend. You know that light was brief.
Mile after mile the cities rise
Where brisk Adonis tied the sheaf.

"You know that light was brief." How just, how recriminatory, how resigned, in short, to the inevitable encroachment of the industrial Leviathan which modern economy symbolizes for Tate! The friendly address is merely the occasion for a wider generalization about the nature of American society, a society where the classical tradition (bound up as it was with the leisured way of life of gentlemen who could be philosophers and farmers at the same time) flared briefly, especially in New England (Wilson) and the South (Tate) only to be extinguished by "mile after mile" of an urban, unillumined industrial culture.

This poem, then, may be thought of as key to a period when Tate was trying to *think* out his dilemma, instead of merely *feeling* his way out of it, as in the powerful early poems. That these years initiated his most prolific critical activity is quite in line with the evidence of the poems themselves. "Fragment of a Meditation" (1928), as the title implies, continues this self-examination in an attempt to gather up "all the venom of the night—/ Th' equilibrium of the thirtieth age." The attempt is to abandon the vexation, the fury, the sense of loss of young manhood and to come to terms, somehow, with one's heritage heretofore seen as inoperative because of the problem of communication. The poet must *find* the language to *communicate* that past. And Tate does find it. He finds it in the forensic, yet casually idiomatic speech of his ancestors and of their own best survival in Southern cultural remains. (It was at about this time that Tate in an essay seeking to explain the curious aridity of the literary production of the great antebellum years of the South pointed out that its best energies and talents went into politics and the law, the latter the passport to the former.)

"It was a time of tributes." Tate pays them: to Calhoun "who divined / How the great western's star's last race will run / Unbridled round our personal defect / Grinding its ash with engines of its mind. / 'Too Southern and too simple'"; to Poe, "the poet against the world; he dreamed the soul / Of the wide world and prodigies to come; / Exemplar of dignity, a gentleman / Who raised the black flag of the nether mind; Hated in life, of all; in death praised." Still,

Perhaps at the age of thirty-one shall see
In the wide world the prodigies to come:
The long-gestating Christ, the Agnulus
Of time got in the belly of abstraction
By Ambition, a bull of pious use.

But the aftermath to this briefly sustained and ironic wish is an illusionless defeat powerfully articulated in the sonorous vowel-pattern of the massive, Dryden-like closing:

The Bull smoothly rolls his powerful tongue.

"Fragment of Meditation" breaks down precisely at the point where the moving loyalties to the past are exhausted and the satire against modern anti-miraculism takes over. Too many hypostatizations begin to do the work of the concrete particulars which are active in the early sections of the poem. We get instead "Agnulus," "Ambition," "Pasiphae," "Lamb," and "Holy Runt," in the space of a few lines. The irony is heavy, not cutting. One suspects that the split in the poem reflects a split in the poet's own spectrum of belief. He is positive, concrete and eloquent in his tribute to a past he believes in and lives; he is negative, allusive, literary in his view of the present which he distrusts and detemporizes. This is the obverse of the sin Tate in his criticism lays at the door of the scientific historians who seek to "detemporize" or neutralize the past which he prefers to view as a series of discrete particulars. Thus, Tate's satire on irreligion seems an act of fashionable piety, expressive of an outer malaise of spirit which was then becoming a stylish mood, one which the poet sought to incorporate into his own inner terror. It was as if an instructed but unbaptized cannibal child were seeking to eat his evangelized father who had given up the habit of dining on his relatives.

In different keys and with considerable invention and melody these years are devoted to a fuller exploration of the dilemma I have just outlined. Tate ponders in various settings the question he asks in "Message from Abroad," dated Paris, November, 1929:

What years of other times, what centuries
Broken, divided up and claimed? A few
Here and there to the taste . . .
to keep us
Fearless, not worried as the hare, scurrying
Without memory.

The sense of the past is here seen as a humanizing force. But it is "those others," ages "Not by poetry and statues timed," which he is bent on finding, for they are "lost" in the individual subconscious biography. Now an image is introduced which was to recur in various forms in Tate's poetry for the next fifteen years: it is a father-image, an ancestor-image, if you will, and it haunts the poet's imagination in concrete, visible shape:

> And the man red-faced and tall seen, leaning
> In the day of his strength
> Not as a pine, but the stiff form
> Against the west pillar,
> Hearing the ox-cart in the street—
> His shadow gliding, a long nigger
> Gliding at his feet.

This is an exact and personal diction. The last two lines with the encroaching shadow represented as a "long nigger" is appropriate to the physical context of the Southern man the poet is painting from memory and from love; the repetition of "gliding" in the last line completes the suggestion of time (a shadow) engulfing the individual, but with a tenderness which softens the impact of the last irrevocable line (shorter than any in the stanza).

But the image is "drowned deep," cannot be seen at all in exile, "Down Saint-Michel by the quays," and the failure to realize the individual image is extended to include the whole of that society which it represents:

> I cannot see you
> The incorruptibles,
> Yours was a secret fate . . .
> Your anger is out of date—

In the last three lines the symbol of a personal loss again dramatizes the elegiac theme of a lost past:

> The man red-faced and tall
> Will cast no shadow
> From the province of the drowned.

Perhaps the most ambitious poem of this period, one which summarizes Tate's intellectual situation in the early 'thirties is "Causerie" (1925–31). The tone is again forensic but the vigor of the indictment is sustained throughout. Unlike his practice in "Meditation" Tate here depends on a rugged, irregular blank verse manipulated with great flexibility in terms of caesura to effect a swelling and urgent rhetoric. The poet is the prosecutor; yet he is himself among the accused:

> I've done no rape, arson, incest, no murder,
> Yet cannot sleep . . .

Through another means he asks the question of "Message from Abroad":

> Where is your house, in which room stands your bed?

In ironic answer comes a swift, Elizabethan-in-texture arraignment of the fate suffered by the South:

> Have you a daughter,
> Daughters are the seed of occupations . . .
> Let her not read history lest knowledge
> Of her fathers instruct her to be a noted bawd.

The argument proceeds by a kind of rhetorical casuality (note the force of "For" in the passage connecting with the above):

> For miracles are faint
> And resurrection is our weakest point of religion.

Later, the moral confusion of modern life is attributed to a loss of absolutes:

> In an age of abstract experience, fornication
> Is self-expression, adjunct to Christian euphoria,
> And whores become delinquents; delinquents, patients;
> Patients, wards of society. Whores, by that rule,
> Are precious.

The result is "a race of politic pimps" without "The antique courtesy of your myths." What Tate regrets is the loss of the principle of evil, a loss of which Wallace Stevens was to say fifteen years later: "the death of Satan was a tragedy / For the imagination. . . ." But, and I think this is a distinction which illuminates Tate's special quality as a moralist, he does not, like Stevens, relate this loss to its effect on art, but rather to its effect on conduct. This is a didactic poetry of such high order that the didacticism is (as in Blake) through the purest rhetorical fusion indistinguishable from the poetry. The control is sure and adult. The entirety of the loss is acknowledged; there is no longer an effort to reclaim the lost from "the province of the drowned." The poet is operating on a higher level of social "reality," but there is no acceptance—yet.

III

In the long view, the years 1930–35 seem to have served as an intellectual and emotional marking-time for Tate. During this time he was active in prose composition. There is evidence of a good deal of reading especially in the metaphysical poets. There is much experiment in form—odes, elegies, pastorals, several fine metaphysical love poems (the only love poems composed up to this time). The titles reflect quite transparently some of the literary preoccupations: "The Mediterranean," for example, considered by some one of Tate's finest poems, is Coleridgean in form, and Arnoldian in symbolism. The Mediterranean is the sea of faith (as is another body of water in "Dover Beach"): "Atlantis howls but is no longer steep." The poem ends with a vision of the fecund and luxurious exhaustion of the South—the South conceived of as the inheritor of classical culture by a kind of mystical primogeniture, a notion Tate argues well in his essays: "the tired land where tasseling corn, / Fat beans, grapes sweeter than muscadine / Rot on the vine: in that land were we born."

"Aeneas at Washington" is another poem deriving from this nexus of speculation. The South is again conceived of as Europe, especially as it is the inheritor of Rome. Aeneas, of course, is the poet himself; like the antique poet, he is an exile. He sees "all things apart." The reference is to one of Tate's most abiding critical values: to see the past as a series of distinct concrete particulars. The poem closes on a note of frustration and perplexity:

> Stuck in the wet mire
> Four thousand leagues from the ninth buried city
> I thought of Troy, what we had built her for.

This poem as well as "The Mediterranean" and "To the Lacedemonians" betrays a weakness common to some poems of this period in that the poet's critical "ideas" or "philosophic metaphors" are visibly operative in the poems. The "ideas" are not sufficiently complicated by symbols of emotional opacity or sensuous richness to raise the language into that realm of verbal intensity where Tate's best poetry moves. Nevertheless, "To the Lacedemonians" is interesting in that it provides an independent exercise of one of Tate's favorite and, indeed, plausible hypotheses about the moral character of the antebellum South—the theory that it was a society destined to ruin by the very excess of its virtues: "Vain chivalry of the personal will!"—a theory he was later to crystallize with great poetic splendour in the "Ode to the Confederate Dead," a poem worked on concurrently with it.[1]

The stately language of "Aeneas" and "To the Lacedemonians" reflects the influence of St. J. Perse, perhaps assimilated through Eliot's translation of Perse's *Anabasis* in

1930. Indeed, Tate calls an elegy of this period "The Anabasis," the title serving as an equivalent for death. However, the poem's delicate archaism of language, largely got through inversion and metric distortions which affect customary pronunciation, is quite unrelated to Perse's epic tone.

"The Meaning of Life" (1934) described as a "monologue" and "The Meaning of Death" (1935) subtitled "An After-Dinner Speech" are discourses on time as it affects the security of personal values. Both poems are noteworthy for their reliance on cave symbolism, a type of symbol which Tate employs extensively and which stems from his deep consideration of Plato's parable of the cave. The closing line of "The Meaning of Death"—"We are the eyelids of defeated caves"—was to receive expanded statement in some of the later poems. (See for example, Sonnet IV or "More Sonnets at Christmas" which is centred in a cave metaphor.) It is a line which dramatizes the feeling of the poems of 1930–35 as one of a grave and bitter defeat in the search for absolutes.

IV

However, there is a certain strain in Tate's sensibility given sporadic but eloquent expression during these years which must be considered both for its own sake and for its foreshadowing by a decade the atmosphere of his very best work. It is the vein of introspective, subjective judgment, a mood which, in part, shares the content of the more purely ideological pieces I have just examined. But it is precisely the distinction between introspection and speculation which makes it possible to distinguish the poems of 1930–35 into two groups.

The "Sonnets at Christmas" (1934) illuminate the fact that Tate's earlier romantic agony had not been put down as thoroughly as the critic in him might have supposed. Sonnet I established the background for the poet's examination of conscience and memory. Sonnet II provides a particular instance of the past, an instance of personal guilt which, in a beautiful, concrete progress, relying for its imagery on the physical accoutrements of a Southern country house, builds up to a rebellion of the ego against the burdens pushed upon it by the id:

> Ah, Christ I love you, rings to the wild sky
> And I must think a little of the past:
> When I was ten I told a stinking lie
> That got a black boy whipped; but now at last
> The going years, with an accurate glow,
> Reverse like balls englished upon green baize—
> Let them return, let the round trumpets blow
> The ancient crackle of the Christ's deep gaze.
> Deafened and blind, with senses yet unfound,
> Am I, untutored of the after-wit
> Of knowledge, knowing a nightmare has no sound;
> Therefore with idle hands and head I sit
> In late December before the fire's daze
> Punished by crimes of which I would be quit.

Tate had accomplished this kind of interior dramatization as persuasively, although on the level of external drama, in "The Oath" (1931), a skillful Browning-via-Pound monologue with a similar context—a country house on a cold night with the trophies of ancestors on the walls. Where better to consider the metaphysics of "Who are the dead? Who are the living and the dead?"

But it is in the "Ode to the Confederate Dead," a poem whose final shape took a decade to solidify, that we have the best example in those years of the fruitful union of "philosophic metaphor" and personal, subjective experience. To make a detailed exegesis of the poem would be superfluous in view of the meticulous job of dissection the poet has performed in "Narcissus as Narcissus," a long essay in which every facet of the poem's genesis, intent and mechanics is considered with scrupulous objectivity.

The "Ode," Tate tells us, is about solipsism. But the attempt to connect solipsism (Narcissism) with the Confederate dead cannot be made "logically or even historically . . . the proof of the connection must lie, if anywhere, in the experienced conflict which is the poem itself." Still, one wonders whether the position Tate ascribes to Narcissus (the poet) is not remarkably like that he elsewhere ascribes to Thomas Hardy, the "philosophic" writer. Tate supposes that the keys to Hardy's poems are large abstractions or "philosophic metaphors" like "Necessity" and "Chance" or their Victorian equivalents "Mechanism" and Spencer's "Unknowable." These ideas, Tate argues, invade the poems' determining content but not structure. Hardy is at his best when "least philosophical" for "his 'philosophy' tends to be a little beyond the range of his feelings. . . ." Thus,

> Hardy's "advanced" position is only another way of saying that he had come very early to be both inside and outside his background which was to be the material of his art: an ambivalent point of view that in its infinite variations from any formula that we may state for it, is the center of the ironic consciousness.

But is not Narcissus both inside and outside his "background" (solipsism, the Confederate dead) as much as was Hardy with his advanced Darwinian teleology in relation to Wessex folkways and primitivism? A similar ambivalence, I think, generates in Tate the "ironic consciousness" signal to the mood of the "Ode."

It should be clear, then, that the components of the "Ode" as *idea* are not too remote from the concerns of Tate's poems and essays of the 'thirties, concerns which persist, indeed, as a major striation through all his work. I should like to add to Tate's discussion of the "Ode" some observations suggested by a comparison of the first published version (1927) with the final version of 1936.

First, there is, contrary to what we like to think of as axiomatic to creation, an expansion of material rather than a suppression of it. Apparently, there are other useful economies available to the poet beside cutting. Not only are many fine lines added to the body of the poem, but the subjective "wind-leaves" refrain, running through as a thread of opposition to the questions of the main theme, is entirely new. When there is suppression, it is of an entirely different order: the emendations so work as to suppress those *details* of a metaphor which tend to loosen its thrust. Compare, for example, ". . . the silence which/Engulfs you like a mummy in time, whose niche lacks aperture," with the final ". . . the silence which/Smothers you, a mummy in time."

Another large class of revisions is the substitution of concrete imagery for more allusive, literary abstraction. Consider, for example, the gain in decisiveness achieved by the substitution of "Here by the sagging gate, stopped by the wall" for the earlier Eliot-like wistfulness of "Here at this stile, once more, you know it all." In short, the aim is more consistently to render the experience rather than to make statements about it. Instead of "We have not sung; we shall not ever sing," we get "We shall say only the leaves whispering;" instead of "It has only a beginning and an end" we are given "Night is the beginning and the end." Perhaps the most valuable change of this sort is the magnificent substitution (about the serpent) of "Sentinel of the grave who counts us all," for the inconclusive "See what he knows—he knows us all."

If we add to these changes considerable simplification in punctuation (the over-punctuated first version hindered the flow of the soliloquy); devices like transposing the attributes of a simile from one term to the other; countless revisions in single words ("arrogant circumstance" for "immodest circumstance," "lurks" for "waits," "Shut gate" for "turnstile") all of which favor the stronger word; the change of tense from past to future ("You will curse the setting sun" from "You have cursed the setting sun") implying an oracular prescience in the revelations the poet is making; strengthening of an occasional key word (like "blood") by creating a new line to expand the emotion and to point it with an end rhyme ("flood")—it becomes clear that the version of 1936 represents a great fund of technical knowledge garnered during the decade of its making. Nevertheless, in spite of this consolidation of skill, it is not until almost ten years later that Tate comes into his proper functioning as a total rather than a split poetic personality.

V

We can measure the range of this progress by a study of *The Winter Sea* (1944). Although containing less than a dozen poems, it yet projects an almost complete break with Tate's earlier work in the forthright abandoning of the tendency to allow "philosophic metaphors" about tradition to determine the structure and content of the poems. It is possible that his fine historical novel of the antebellum South, *The Fathers* (1938), had served Tate as a sieve for draining off this long-nourished interest into the more flexible formal unit of experience of the story. *The Fathers*, like "The Ode," is about those who were destroyed through what Hart Crane in a letter to Tate calls "an excess of chivalry." The only echo of the past to be found in the diverse emphasis of the poems in *The Winter Sea* is the concern with childhood guilt noted in "Sonnets at Christmas." This theme now advances into a more elevated symbolic use in "More Sonnets at Christmas" and in "Seasons of the Soul."

It would not be over-emphasizing the personal situation revealed by this volume to say that it releases in Tate the full force of the romantic strain which had seemed successfully inhibited during the preceding years. Still, the didactic impulse and conscious moral aim is too habitual to suffer serious diminution and courses along, a parallel stream of intention, with the revitalized romanticism. Tate's own critical prescription for this mode of moral inquiry is certainly met by his achievement in "Jubilo," in "Ode to Our Young Proconsuls of the Air," and in "Eclogue of the Liberal and the Poet." "The moral intelligence," he had written in 1940, "gets into poetry . . . not as moral abstractions, but as form, coherence of image, and metaphor, control of tone and rhythm, the union of these features." Tate's essays in the satire are vigorous, witty and, as in classical satire, full of honest prejudices. A prejudice, let it be noted in passing, is different from a *willed* belief. "Jubilo," using as refrain a phrase from a Negro popular song, is a tongue-in-cheek celebration of boys who "caress the machines they ride." The mock-heroic epic, while not at all a model, makes itself felt in "Ode to Our Young Proconsuls" in the deliberately heightened mock-allegorical language which raises the invective to dramatic irony.

"False Nightmare," a telling although not altogether just indictment of Whitmanism, is sure to be quoted by Tate's enemies as evidence of his "reactionary" views. It is a bitter poem but, carefully read, as reactionary as Jeremiah.

We become aware, then, that in Tate's recent poetry the traditional influences (whether of structure, idea, or both) operate only as qualities, not as models. Thus, one is barely conscious of the Dante influence in the impressive "Seasons of the Soul," but it is there in the deeply religio-ethical purpose of the poem as well as in the implied descent of the poet into his own hell. In the same poem the influence of the *Pervigilium Veneris* is felt in the erotic elements as well as in the subtle use of refrain. "Seasons of the Soul" can, I think, be thought of as the summation of Tate's present position. It is an instructive guide to his technical practice; it is a map to his present values, even though it merely poses a problem. But it is by the way in which a problem is framed that the nature of its solution is implied. Let us examine the frame.

The scheme of the poem is simple: the four seasons correspond to the four elements of the ancients. Thus the chronicle is of the four ages of man in relation to the four aspects of the universe he inhabits. More specifically, however, it is modern man whose spiritual biography Mr. Tate records. Summer is the first season; the background is now:

It was a gentle sun
When, at the June solstice
Green France was overrun
With caterpillar feet.
No head knows where its rest is
Or may lie down with reason
When war's usurping claws
Shall take the heart escheat—

This suggests another summer (the summer of childhood which is identified with the summer of classical antiquity in its clarity and innocence) when "The summer had no reason; / Then, like a primal cause / It had its timeless day."

In Autumn, technically the most interesting section, the surrealist device of a dream is employed to enable the poet to prophesy, as it were, a vision of his own old age which is revealed to him as a trap. He is caught in a deep well, an empty house (the house of the past) peopled only by ghosts, his ancestors, who refuse to recognize him. The house of the past is not real, "The door was false—no key / Or lock . . . yet I could see / I had been born to it / For miles of running brought / Me back where I began." The failure of parents to recognize a son is another way of stating the problem of identity. We have seen how in his earliest writing this question engaged Tate. Now the dilemma is extended to the profoundest sort of personal epistemology: If your progenitors do not know you, if you are cut off from communication with your contemporaries ("I was down a well"), if, in short, there is no objective recognition of your identity, who are you? Along with this return to a study of his past, Tate also reverts to the more sensuous and concrete imagery of the early "romantic" poems, an imagery determined by inner, emotional connections and not by logical ones. I think especially of the father-mother imagery of Section II and the sea imagery of Section III.

From the frustration of this cyclical returning upon himself, the poet in "Winter," a strikingly beautiful section, pleads with Venus to return to her element. Christianity ("the drying God above / Hanged in his windy steeple") is dead and "No longer bears for us / The living wound of love." There is every reason to suppose that we must take this as Tate's mature view of the religious problem, a problem which he could not resolve with such brutal finality in the middle years. In "More

Sonnets at Christmas," composed a little before "Seasons of the Soul," he had implied the dismissal:

> Ten years is time enough to be dismayed
> By mummy Christ, head crammed between his
> knees.

The violence of this image, its quasi-obscenity, even, is the measure of the distance Tate traveled in the ten dismaying years from the time when the question of anti-miraculism disturbed him. It is clear enough now that, as Tate once flippantly remarked, the question of Mr. Eliot's submission to the Thirty-nine Articles was never to be a live option in his own poetry.

But the pagan values are dead, too ("All the sea-gods are dead"). There is sex: The pacing animal who turns "The venereal awl/In the livid wound of love." Again, a strange surrealist image connects the general with the poet's particular plight: In a grove under the sea the poet seizes the branch of a madrepore from which drips a "speaking blood/From the livid wound of love":

> We are the men who died
> Of self-inflicted woe,
> Lovers whose stratagem
> Led to their suicide
> I touched my sanguine hair
> And felt it drip above
> Their brother who, like them,
> Was maimed and did not bear
> The living wound of love.

The "living wound" of love would seem to be suggested by the famous Proem to *De Rerum Naturae* in which Lucretius, looking on a war-torn Italy, calls upon Venus (as a fertility-principle) to inflict upon Mars the eternal wound of love *(aeterno volnere amoris)* and thus win peace and increase for the Romans. For Tate the "eternal wound" becomes the "living wound" and I take the implication to be that Love, growing from a "livid" wound into the "living" wound is the only possible power which can rescue man from his otherwise maimed existence. The passionate and suppliant address to Venus makes clear that she is the complex erotic symbol around which cluster the poet's hopes for various kinds of regeneration:

> All the sea-gods are dead
> You, Venus, come home
> To your salt maidenhead.

This reading, I think, is confirmed by the next section "Spring," a liturgical chant (still within the frame of the ten-line iambic trimeter stanza) to the Mother of Silences, a figure who simultaneously suggests the principle of the Virgin (the Mother, Life) and the principle of Death (the Mystery); the figure, significantly, never speaks. The symbol has a certain obscurity not altogether relieved by the following passage:

> Come, mother, and lean
> At the window with your son
> And gaze through its light frame
> These fifteen centuries
> Upon the shirking scene
> Where men, blind, go lame:

Now the mother appears to be Saint Monica as she appears in Book IX of St. Augustine's *Confessions*. Mother and son stand alone "leaning in a certain window, from which the garden of the house we occupied at Ostia could be seen"; cataloguing a set of earthly conditions, which, could they be "silenced," would enable them to arrive at an apprehension of the "hereafter." Soon after, Monica dies and leaves Augustine with a living wound "from having that most sweet and dear habit of living together suddenly broken off." Thus the Mother of Silences is a particular mother (St. Monica), the Virgin, the Mystery, and through Augustine's unmentioned wound, she is identified further with the principle of Love. Love, then, is the luminous agency common to all the referents of the symbol. Yet, in the end, one feels that the hope of regeneration through Love is reluctantly abandoned and death is sought as the only certain "kindness" to which men can aspire.

"Seasons of the Soul" will stand as a major event in Tate's career as a poet. It is lyrical, sensuous and tragic. It is, for whatever meaning that chameleon term may still carry, romantic. In "Tension in Poetry," an interesting essay written some years ago, Tate distinguishes the metaphysical from the romantic poet in the following way:

> The metaphysical poet as a rationalist begins at or near the extensive or denotative end of the line. The romantic or Symbolist poet at the other, intensive end; and each by a straining feat of the imagination tries to push his meaning as far as he can toward the opposite end, so as to occupy the entire scale. . . .

But there is to be recommended a "poetry of the center," that is, a "poetry of tension in which the strategy is diffused into the unitary effect." I am not sure after several rereadings how this strategy is implemented. Indeed, the concept of "tension" has been used by some critics, although not by Mr. Tate, to get around critical problems more taxing to unravel than to designate as illustrative of "tension."

However, if there is a poetry of tension and if there is a living practitioner of this awesome and marvelous feat of poetic balance between the classic and the romantic, the metaphysical and the Symbolist among us, surely it is Tate himself. But it has become increasingly evident that the idea of the poet as the daring young man on the flying trapeze is giving way to a less perilous but more fruitful enterprise: the paradoxical roles of suppliant and teacher have lost their separate identities in a profound and humble appreciation of what de Unamuno calls "the tragic sense of life." In "Winter Mask to the Memory of W. B. Yeats" (1943) Tate writes:

> I asked the master Yeats
> Whose great style could not tell
> Why it is man hates
> His own salvation,
> Prefers the way to hell,
> And finds his last safety
> In the self-made curse that bore
> Him towards damnation:
> The drowned undrowned by the sea,
> The sea worth living for.

Notes

1. The "Ode" was begun in 1926 and not completed to Tate's satisfaction until 1936.

LILLIAN FEDER

From "Allen Tate's Use of Classical Literature"

Centennial Review, Winter 1960, pp. 109–14

Vivienne Koch[1] has attempted to show "that Tate is a poet of romantic sensibility who has tried with varying success to compress his talents into a chastely classical form and that, in inverse degrees to his willingness to do so, his best poetry has been written." She regards Tate's translation of the *Pervigilium*

Veneris as his "valedictory, from a safe distance, to the Fugitives, to the South, to the 'classical' tradition, to his masters. The quickest way to get over the goodbyes is to say them in a strange language." One may ask, what strange language? The language of Tate's translation of the *Pervigilium* is more "classical" than that of the original poem. It is cryptic and economical, as elegantly colloquial as Horace's, and full of incredibly graceful Latinisms. It is well known that the *Pervigilium Veneris* has many Romantic elements. However, that Tate chose to translate this poem proves nothing about his attitude toward classical literature except that his interest in it is broad and varied. It is illogical to assume, as Miss Koch does, that Tate's translation of a late Latin poem which is outside the strictly classical type is a sign that he has lost his feeling for and response to classical literature as a source and an influence. Moreover, the facts are against such a point of view.

Miss Koch says that "in Tate's recent poetry the traditional influences (whether of structure, idea, or both) operate as qualities not as models." This judgment is no doubt correct if one recognizes the importance of such "qualities" in Tate's poetry. In her analysis of *Seasons of the Soul*, which in some respects is excellent, Miss Koch seems to underestimate or to ignore certain qualities which depend upon classical literature and which express some of Tate's most subtle and most significant ideas.

She remarks that Tate's phrase the "living wound of love" seems to have been suggested by Lucretius' *aeterno volnere amoris*, and says: "I take the implication to be that Love, growing from a "livid" wound into the "living" wound is the only possible power which can rescue man from his otherwise maimed existence. The passionate and suppliant address to Venus makes clear that she is the complex erotic symbol around which cluster the poet's hopes for various kinds of regeneration." She then goes on to show the relationship between Venus and the Mother of Silences, who is "a particular mother (St. Monica), the Virgin, the Mystery, and through Augustine's unmentioned wound she is identified further with the principle of Love. Love, then, is the luminous agency common to all the referents of the symbol. Yet, in the end, one feels that the hope of regeneration through Love is reluctantly abandoned and death is sought as the only certain 'kindness' to which men can aspire."

This reading is a fine one, but Miss Koch seems to ignore the relationship between Tate's imagistic use of Venus and other references to classical literature in the poem. The first occurs in the second stanza, in which Tate says that the soul must "seize or deny its day." This is not merely a variation and extension of the phrase *carpe diem*, but a significant application of its meaning and associations in a new context. The soul, says Tate, must have vitality and courage despite man's mortality. All the associations of the *carpe diem* theme repeated and developed in poetry from Alcaeus to Marvell are evoked through Tate's use of the phrase. It suggests the intensity and tragedy of man's struggle not only in our time but throughout time to wrest from life satisfaction and meaning. Tate's unique adaptation of it reveals the plight of man's soul in our time: it must struggle for and seize the place that has been denied it or give up entirely.

The ancients, Tate says in the fifth stanza, lived in an eternal summer, a world of "timeless day," a period when to "seize the day" implied an easy pleasure as compared with the anguish of the soul struggling to live in a world without belief. We have lost this peace, but it is a part of our past. We recall its spirit as part of our history, our own childhood.

The invocation to Venus is a cry to the spirit of creation and love which we recall and inherit from the past. The image of Venus is contrasted with two images of futility and death which are taken from two ancient symbols: Plato's cave and Sisyphus' eternal frustration. Tate combines the two brilliantly:

It burns us each alone
Whose burning arrogance
Burns up the rolling stone
This earth—Platonic cave
Of vertiginous chance!
Come, tired Sisyphus,
Cover the cave's egress
Where light reveals the slave,
Who rests when sleeps with us
The mother of silences.

The earth is both the stone Sisyphus rolls without purpose and the cave in which the entrance of light reveals only human blindness and limitation. Death, for Tate, is not merely literal extinction, but life without goal or purpose. If man is to accept the role of Sisyphus, let him then complete his daily act of frustration by accepting death.

Though it is true that *Seasons of the Soul* is a tragic poem, it is not therefore a morbid one. Both Vivienne Koch and Richmond C. Beatty,[2] whose interpretation of the poem is similar to hers, emphasize the mood of despair. Yet *Seasons of the Soul*, while it deals with suffering and loss of faith, also portrays the heroic contest man has always fought against the despair which has seemed overpowering. He has even descended into hell to find knowledge of love, the source of life:

Wilfully as I stood
Within the thickest grove
I seized a branch, which broke;
I heard the speaking blood
(From the livid wound of love)
Drip down upon my toe:
"We are the men who died
Of self-inflicted woe,
Lovers whose stratagem
Led to their suicide."

Often in Tate's poetry his bitterest condemnations of man's conduct spring from his recognition of the contrast between man's heroic potentialities, his creative energies, and his "tragic fault,"[3] his misuse of these qualities. The ancient symbols of Venus and Sisyphus represent the two ways man may take. Tate implies at the end of the poem that man may accept death, but his invocation to Venus is a moving and powerful affirmation of the potentialities of life.

According to Miss Koch, classicism was an inhibiting influence on Tate. On the contrary, Tate is never held back by his sources and models, but instead uses them freely for his own purposes and transforms them to his own conception. He is not a neo-classicist in the sense that he decorates with a classical flourish or repeats the old formulas, such as nothing too much or the simple life is best. He knows the classics too well. His classicism exists not in external, imitative manners, but in his way of thought and of feeling in poetry. His nostalgia is associated with the Homeric longing for heroism; in expressing his distress at contemporary values he gains both proportion and depth through a Vergilian image. Like the poets of classical antiquity, Tate employs traditional material to suggest the universality and continuity of his themes.

Regarding man's limitations, as did the ancient classicists, from the tragic point of view, Tate often emphasizes the tragic contest, out of which man can emerge with "knowledge carried to the heart," a reward of the very struggle which may reveal his inevitable limitations. This knowledge is expressed in Tate's poetry to a large extent through classical myth transformed into symbol. He often employs an ancient story—that of Aeneas or Oedipus—as a dramatic and concrete representation of traditional values or perennial conflict. The mythical story is sometimes told cryptically, implied more than stated, for Tate's language is classical in its precision, suggesting the tension produced by controlled feeling. In adapting the ancient myth of eating the plates to a modern metaphor, "Eat dish and bowl to take that sweet land in," Tate reveals our overwhelming need of a heritage to guide us, by suggesting hunger and violent consumption in a hopeless attempt to appease it; yet the concreteness and simplicity of his image control the intense feelings and give them form. The result is not "dry hardness," but emotion eloquent through restraint. The leaf as a symbol of mortality in the "Ode to the Confederate Dead" is not romanticized or sentimentalized, but, through the Homeric associations it evokes, suggests tragic experience in the past and the present. Classical literature served Tate by broadening his view; if it imposed limits on him, they were only those resulting from the creative process of emulation, a discipline through which the "individual talent" can often flourish.

Notes

1. Vivienne Koch, "The Poetry of Allen Tate," in John Crowe Ransom, ed., *The Kenyon Critics* (Cleveland: World Publishing Co., 1951), pp. 169–181.
2. Richmond C. Beatty, "Allen Tate as Man of Letters," *South Atlantic Quarterly*, 47 (April, 1948), 233–234.
3. Allen Tate, "Four American Poets," *Reactionary Essays on Poetry and Ideas* (New York, 1936), p. 8.

DENIS DONOGHUE

Spectator, January 16, 1971, pp. 88–89

There is a moment in Allen Tate's novel, *The Fathers*, when the narrator, Lacy Buchan, says that people living in formal societies, 'lacking the historical imagination, can imagine for themselves only a timeless existence: they themselves never had any origin anywhere and they can have no end, but will go on forever.' This is one of many places in the novel where the narrator's voice, convincing in its own resonance, is joined by another voice, Mr Tate's, and the effect is a notable unison of feeling. The novel is not harmed. Novelist and narrator are two, not one, and they rarely sink their difference: when they do, the words on the page mark a sense of life which is simultaneously personal and historical. In the authority of the words the individual feeling, remaining human, has purged itself of eccentricity, of everything merely personal. Lacy Buchan testifies to his own experience, but he does not rest his case upon the quirks and turns of his personality. He respects idiosyncrasy, not least his own, but he lets it take its chance against the grand critique of history and eventually of life itself. If a quirk does not survive, well and good, it has had its day. The question is one of feeling; the relation between individual feeling, history, and form. It is my impression that Mr Tate's mind, like Lacy Buchan's, may be understood in this relation.

To begin with, Mr Tate was born in Kentucky and he is an American with that inflection. Wallace Stevens said, reading John Crowe Ransom's poems, that there were even more Ransoms in Tennessee than Tates in Kentucky, and that Ransom's poems were composed of Tennessee. The condition of being a Tate in Kentucky is the first theme of 'The Swimmers'; a theme as sturdy as, in *The Fathers*, the conditions of being a Buchan in Virginia. Mr Tate has always spoken the speech of his place, and he has been sharp with those Yankee critics who, not content to see the defeated South at Appomattox, determined to complete the spectacle by seeing it in Hell. He has not forgotten 'the immoderate past,' or the moral heritage of 'Shiloh, Antietam, Malvern Hill, Bull Run.' But he is a man of letters, a scholar, a Southern gentleman. So the rhetorical tradition of the South brings him back beyond Fugitives and Agrarians to the ancient poets and rhetoricians. 'The Mediterranean', the first and one of the finest poems in his collection ⟨*The Swimmers, and Other Selected Poems*⟩, sends the spirit back to Virgil, Cicero, Longinus, as later poems invoke Dante's Christendom. Mr Tate's history is 'knowledge carried to the heart,' and the civility of his style depends upon values brought from afar, tested by centuries of tribulation. Accustomed to historical defeat, he would scorn to win by virtuosity or personal stratagem. The Yankees won by such means, and look what happened. *The Fathers* was written, I believe, both to praise the Old South and to reveal that corruption in its source which made the New South inevitable. These are moral considerations, exacerbated by fact and history. So Mr Tate has a subject, a theme, and a culture rich enough to sustain the meditation. Largely as a result of these possessions, he is also gifted with an answerable style.

As for the presence of form, completing the triad with history and feeling: it is enough if we take form as comprising poetry, fiction, and religion, making no priority in the sequence. Poetry is syntax, an executive relation among the parts; and prosody, the music of that relation; and diction, often making an impression of density and weight, marking the significance of the past, so far as it is acknowledged in the words. Religion is belief, ritual, worship, each a form of humility, an escape from the self. Mr Tate has been a Catholic and, whatever his affiliation at this moment, he has Christendom in his veins. I think he has often envisaged a Rome greater than the pagan Rome or the Christian Rome, but compounded of both in their perfections. He would have his Christendom include much that the Christian Rome refuted or transcended: his translation of the *Pervigilium Veneris* speaks to me of such inclusions.

Such a great Rome would figure in Mr Tate's mind like the imagined Rome celebrated by Henry James in *William Wetmore Story and His Friends*; where James contrasts Rome with London, Paris, and New York, to their disadvantage, 'cities in which the spirit of the place has long since lost any advantage it may ever have practised over the spirit of the person.' Mr Tate has always wanted the spirit of the person, personal feeling, to live within the order of the greatest Romes one might conceive. Fiction speaks of that possibility, even while it shows disorder in the particular case; as in *The Fathers*, where George Posey is seen as 'heightened vitality possessed by a man who knew no bounds.'

The bounds which Mr Tate knows are indicated by his essay ⟨in *Essays of Four Decades*⟩ on 'the angelic imagination'. Briefly, what he has in view is a possible harmony among the three classical faculties: feeling, will, and intellect. He describes a hypertrophy of the first as 'the incapacity to represent the human condition in the central tradition of natural feeling.' The second hypertrophy is 'the thrust of the will beyond the human scale of action.' The third is 'the intellect moving in isolation from both love and the moral will, whereby it declares itself independent of the human situation in the quest of essential knowledge.' That last adjective explains why such an imagination is described as angelic: it represents a claim upon essence without the mediation of existence, flesh, or history. Mr Tate's text for all three forms of excess is Edgar Allan Poe, and it may be said that some of his most penetrating criticism arises from his engagement with 'our cousin, Mr Poe.' The other imagination Mr Tate calls 'symbolic', and his text is Dante: it is a dramatic imagination 'in the sense that its fullest image is an action in the shapes of this world: it does not reject, it includes: it sees not only with but through the natural world, to what may lie beyond it.' To the symbolic imagination the world is a place of good and evil, 'mandible world sharp as a broken tooth.' In 'Last Days of Alice' Mr Tate writes:

> O God of our flesh, return us to Your wrath,
> Let us be evil could we enter in
> Your grace, and falter on the stony path.

The angelic imagination is Manichean or, in another idiom, abstract: what it refuses is direct engagement with image, discourse, person.

Mr Tate's most sustained meditation on these matters is 'The Hovering Fly', a causerie on the imagination in its relation to the actual world. The fly appears out of nowhere in the last scene of Dostoievsky's *The Idiot*, settling upon the bed where Nastasya lies dead. I shall not humiliate Mr Tate's account of that great scene by paraphrasing it—it is included in *Essays of Four Decades*—besides, it is one of the grand occasions of modern criticism, and readers will want to have it intact. I admire particularly its tact, its extraordinary power of implication, its style at once lofty and specific. Every reader of Mr Tate's criticism carries in his head certain passages which are so gorgeously perceptive that they renew his faith in the relation between literature and criticism. My own short list favours 'Tension in Poetry', especially the pages in which Mr Tate comments on a detail in the Paolo and Francesca episode in the *Inferno*. These pages are included in *Essays of Four Decades*, too, the best selection of Mr Tate's criticism because it is the largest.

The poems and the essays ought to be held together in the mind. I came to the essays first, and for a long time I found the poems intractable. Mr Tate's sense of the relation between feeling, form, and history attends like a conscience upon the actual engagement with the words of his poems. There is the bearing of one word upon another, line by line, but there is also his response to the history of each word, what it has had to bear. It is probably impossible to write with nonchalance, given such a conscience. Mr Tate's verses are rarely prepared to move freely, mostly they are restrained by his respect for the awful history they inherit. Often the lines are so dense with history that to move at all they need a push. The best poems are those in which the push comes from a powerful feeling, and the words are not intimidated by the ancestral burden they carry. I think of 'The Mediterranean', 'Causerie', 'The Oath', 'Mother and Son', 'Ode to the Confederate Dead', 'Last Days of Alice', 'The Meaning of Life', and 'The Cross'.

There are some lovely moments in the *terza rima* of 'The Swimmers', a poem of middle length which was planned, I think, as something longer still. I assume that the idea of a long poem appealed to Mr Tate as 'conceit and motion to rehearse / Pastoral terrors of youth still in the man, / Torsions of sleep, in emblematic verse / Rattling like dice unless the verse shall scan / All chance away.'

An earlier collection of Mr Tate's essays was called *The Man of Letters in the Modern World*, and in two or three places the critic is willing to speak of his work under this phrase: there is also an essay on 'the profession of letters in the South'. It is clear that Mr Tate's favourite terms are deployed in that last essay, where he speaks of the relation between a writer and his society. In his own behalf Mr Tate speaks of a code of manners, and of form, religion, family, land, class, Europe, meaning especially England and France. The essay is perhaps the best introduction to a body of work which seems to me, in its concern for first and last things, heroic.

PETER TAYLOR

1917–

Peter Hillsman Taylor was born in Trenton, Tennessee, on January 8, 1917. He was educated at Vanderbilt University (1936–37), Southwestern College (1937–38), and Kenyon College (1938–40). While at Kenyon, where he received his B.A., Taylor formed close friendships with Randall Jarrell and Robert Lowell. Taylor then briefly studied with Cleanth Brooks and Robert Penn Warren as a graduate student at Louisiana State University (1940), but he soon left school in order to become a professional writer. Taylor served in the army from 1941 to 1945, and in 1943 married the poet Eleanor Lilly Ross. In 1946 he began teaching at the University of North Carolina, and since then he has taught at many other institutions, including Indiana State University (1948–49), the University of Chicago (1952), Kenyon College (1952–57), Ohio State University (1957–63), Harvard University (1964), and the University of Virginia (1967 to date).

Taylor's short stories, which typically concern contemporary upper middle-class life in the South, are collected in *A Long Fourth* (1948), *The Widows of Thornton* (1954), *Happy Families Are All Alike* (1959), *Miss Leonora When Last Seen* (1963), *Collected Stories* (1969), *In the Miro District* (1977), and *The Old Forest* (1985). *A Women of Means* (1950) is a short novel, and *Tennessee Day in St. Louis* (1956), *A Stand in the Mountains* (1968), and *Presences* (1973) are plays. Taylor's most recent book, *A Summons to Memphis* (1986), is his first full-length novel.

These stories ⟨*A Long Fourth and Other Stories*⟩ deal with the South, but not with the people and parts we know already from Faulkner and Caldwell or even from Porter and Welty. Taylor's people are more town than country, neither high nor low, the divided middle, Southerners all—some remembering, some forgetting—the way things were, but it's all trimmed down to the present. Even the military men: one is a Colonel, but from the Spanish American War. Another has become a Scoutmaster "to preserve those honorable things which were left from the golden days when a race of noble gentlemen and gracious ladies inhabited the land of the South." This is something new, at least to me, on the South.

For the good writer of fiction desiring to be widely read—poets necessarily know better—there is always the temptation to imagine things into a too-coherent mass, to make false currency of his private insights, his only fortune as an artist. By touching the common nerve with a timely or useful tract, he can trick his readers, even himself, into believing the truth about everybody is in him. And failing success, he can always settle for unpopularity as though it were voluntary—splendid unpopularity.

Peter Taylor has nothing to do with all this. He will not fit into any of the familiar categories of writers successfully tempted. If Taylor even remembers, he refuses to tell a story the way it was told before. He refuses, moreover, to exploit his material to the limit, to manufacture characters, drama, suspense—in short, he won't traffic in what is known as a "strong story line." He refuses to be electric. He knows that life itself has a very weak story line. To render it truly he distils it, though again not as you might think: his work is not remarkable for its form and conciseness. He likes to take a while to get a story underway. He has a feeling for naming his characters. He has the poet's gift for finding the clichés of a nation and getting his characters to say them so that they almost sound like something else (as when one uses them oneself).

In "The Fancy Woman" I saw the descendants of the settler-fundamentalists traveling light, womb to tomb, in cream convertibles—which is not the story. These Southerners are somehow more devastating than the New Californians who, on the conservative estimate of Evelyn Waugh, are a good ten years ahead of the rest of the country in their materialism.

In "Sky Line" Taylor explores a memory of boyhood—the kind of boyhood which still had something to do with Mark Twain and Booth Tarkington, though Taylor goes deeper than that. The neighborhood rather than the world was all, and the atomic swell guys and gals of the radio and movies were not yet coming through the doors and windows.

"A Spinster's Tale," which is the story of a little girl, struck me as absolutely unique. I thought the title strange, especially so as I began to read, but when it was all over, the title itself, I saw, continued the story and suggested in three words a lifetime and final end for the little girl.

The title story tells the most about the North and the South, the abiding concern of each for the sins of the other, and incidentally about Taylor as a writer. He lets the girl from New York (on a visit to Nashville) say some fine things about equality, economic and social, meaning the Negro's, but he also informs us that she edits a "birth-control magazine" and has legs like two fire-plugs. On the other side, the local belles deliver some gallant lines in behalf of the Confederacy, but they, like the New York girl, do not seem as good as their words. "Son," their brother, home from New York where he has been reading *The Decline of the West* and getting "advanced ideas" in the publishing business, is decent enough to keep his mind to himself in the presence of the home-folk. The mother, through whom, significantly, Taylor chooses to tell the story, is baffled by the new conversation: her daughters "told her that Son did not believe in marriage and that he certainly would not subject his family and the people of Nashville to the sort of thing he did believe in."

The characters do not speak as types in a problem novel. They do not take turns talking and the question, by sociological standards, doesn't get a very good airing. There are more people than there are theses to go around. It is a proof of Taylor's art, then, that the people don't fade and run together. Ultimately, they all quiet down and the question ends not as theory, where it began, but as a part of them they can't very well talk about. The honest ignorance, the pervading indifference, the righteousness on both sides all combine to defeat them. The awful weather of futility precipitated by the unnatural act of discussion sets in, and behind them stands the same servant Negro, at once strong and hollowed out from centuries of being looked after by these same Samaritans.

In his introduction to the collection, Robert Penn Warren says of Taylor's first stories which came to him in manuscript: "They were obviously the work of a very gifted young writer who had a flavor and a way of his own. . . . I have said that Peter Taylor has a disenchanted mind. In terms of his very disenchantment, however, he has succumbed to the last and most fatal enchantment: the enchantment of veracity. And that is what, in the end, makes the artist free."

Those who want the most fiction can give, who expect to read things they hardly knew they knew—to experience the shock of recognition—will enjoy Peter Taylor and remember these stories.—J. F. POWERS, *Com*, June 25, 1948, pp. 262–63

To complete Mr Taylor's quotation from *Anna Karenina*: '. . . every unhappy family is unhappy in its own way'. These stories ⟨*Happy Families Are All Alike*⟩ are so good that it would be hazardous to guess openly whether Mr Taylor imagines he is writing about happy families or unhappy ones. Certainly his families are not all alike, although they belong to the same level of the same kind of society, and tend to converse in the same tone of voice. Are they happy? Again, one cannot say. I believe in fact that Mr Taylor's title is ironical, for many of his stories seem to be telling us that at the heart of the most solid-seeming relationship there is a tiny blank area of misery, of no-communication, rarely apprehended even by those involved.

The setting is the American Middle-West or the borders of the South; the class, the affluent middle or decaying upper—if such terms have any meaning across the Atlantic. One is reminded at once, by the elaboration of social detail and the precise anatomising of the small smug towns in which Mr Taylor's creatures exist, of Sinclair Lewis; but this soon shows itself to be a false echo. Mr Taylor is after the reality that lies behind the seeming-reality of any situation; and because he is a true artist he makes no pretence of having once for all apprehended it. In each story the central situation or moment is approached from many oblique angles, and one knows that each complex statement is only an approximation to the truth, will certainly be qualified even further before the author feels that he has done his best to give us a glimpse of that elusive creature as it scuttles away again round the corner.—JEREMY BROOKS, *NS*, Aug. 6, 1960, p. 192

The collection of Peter Taylor's short stories ⟨*The Collected Stories of Peter Taylor*⟩, written over a period of some twenty years, is respectable, careful, craftsmanlike, but ultimately mind-deadening. They are a technical combination of Jamesian precision and symmetry, plus Faulknerian mood and atmosphere. The characters are reminiscent of Williams or Capote. We've had enough old-style, southern-fried realism, enough of eccentric or incestuous families tending their faded houses and lives, enough social events which the teen-aged children of "good" families attend in now-decadent mansions, enough about the humiliating behavior of not-so-nice relatives and "fancy ladies" who drink too much, of the premature deaths of beautiful young white girls with mysterious maladies, of the presumably restless young men who wonder if there is something more adventurous than their small town destinies, and of brave "old maid" ladies traveling by train back to Memphis to bury distant, dead relatives.

The majority of stories, and by far the poorest and most boring, are those exclusively concerned with mores and manners of the southern white ladies handling black servants, of economically or culturally impoverished "good families" trying to maintain life-styles that no longer (even romantically) seem worth preserving, of the bizarre behavior of the stagnating gentry who stayed behind to cling to a dead culture, of the endless contest between the old and the new, the black and the white, the north and the south, and the freeways built through "good ole sections of town." And we have definitely heard enough sympathetic accounts of southern white women whining about the difficulties of finding good servants nowadays.

The black folk who get top billing in several stories are handled tenderly by an author who seems oblivious to past or present realities. While Aunt Munsie, the ageless black maid who spent her life working for the Tollivers, is treated leniently by the white townsfolk, the only words she can mutter are "What You Hear from 'Em?" which is the title of her story and her basic theme of "why don't the nice white folk come back to our town and make things the way they used to be?" That Aunt Munsie might harbor such an illusion is legitimate, but the author too seems to believe that those really were the good ole days. Mr. Taylor projects neither compassion nor clarity about the circumstances which produced the creature he created.

"A Wife of Nashville" is a long chronicle of the maids Mrs. Lovell had over several decades and how they satisfied or failed to meet their human and domestic responsibilities. The surprise ending is that Mrs. Lovell finally conspires to free one black maid, Jess McGehee, who wants to leave slavery. The shock this inspires in the white family is enormous:

> [Mrs. Lovell] turned her eyes from the window to look at their faces around the table, and it was strange to see that they were still thinking in the most personal and particular terms of how they had been deceived by a servant, the ignorant granddaughter of an ignorant slave, a Negro woman from Brownsville who was crazy about the movies and who would soon be riding a bus, mile after mile, on her way to Hollywood, where she might find the friendly faces of the real Neil Hamilton and the real Irene Rich. It was with effort that Helen Ruth thought again of Jess McGehee's departure and the problem of offering an explanation to her family. At last, she said patiently, "My dears, don't you see how it was for Jess? How else can they tell us anything when there is such a gulf?" After a moment she said, "How can I make you understand this?"

There is another maid in another story entitled "Cookie" who lets on to her employers at the dinner table that she has discovered (through another maid in another household) that the white bossman has been philandering. The couple neglects to consider the accusation; instead the wife wonders, as the doctor-husband suspiciously departs after dinner for some unspecified destination, whether or not Cookie should be fired. "I can't have her talking that way to my husband," the wife said aloud, yet to herself, "But I won't fire her. . . . She's too much one of us—too much one of the family, and I know she'll be full of remorse for speaking out of turn like that."

The reader wonders whether these stories are really clever, underspoken put-downs of frivolous, unimportant, superficial, silly, Southern whites. But the length of the book and Taylor's return to the same insipid, if not insidious, situations, events, remembrances and nostalgia finally implicates and indicts the author as much as his work. He does take these people seriously. And worse, he created characters who never achieve any essentially human attributes or significance.

His best stories deal with younger people, for the most part ex-southerners, by geography or spirit, those who return home for annual visits and muse about academic existences or residencies in New York or Paris.

That the Miss Leonora Logans of Thomasville, still exist is undoubtedly true, but not necessarily interesting. That the Miss Patty Beans of Memphis still cling to past traditions might also be true, but they've already been pinned to the wall of American Literature. Surely there must be new complications, complexities, or configurations in the south that could be explored by a serious writer with an eye for the visual and vocal. But that is not for Mr. Taylor.—BARBARA RASKIN, "Southern-Fried," *NR*, Oct. 18, 1969, pp. 29–30

Taylor, arguably the best American short story writer of all time, writes about a society no longer contemporary. His fictional milieu, Nashville and Memphis during the Depression, is as remote from the world we now live in as, say, Shakespeare's England or Tolstoy's Russia. And yet he is far more successful than his younger colleagues in rendering characters recognizably human. Consider the situation Taylor presents in "The Old Forest," the title story of his most recent collection (*The Old Forest and Other Stories*). On the eve of his marriage to a Memphis debutante, a young man wrecks his automobile. His companion at the time, a woman from the city's "demimonde," flees the scene of the accident and goes into hiding. Following his narrator in search of the woman, Taylor must explain each nuance of Memphis society in excruciating detail, for its values are so alien to those of modern life that the story would otherwise be incomprehensible to modern readers. Despite the quantity and foreignness of the detail, the story manages to achieve a general meaning. It serves as a parable of the fecklessness of youth on the one hand, and on the other of the ultimate power of the weak and oppressed to assume control of their own lives. "The Old Forest" is an exemplary story in many ways, not least because the futures of its characters are shown to matter.

Taylor's achievement serves as a reminder that any general artistic purpose is best served by way of specificity. Like Kierkegaard's knight of faith, he approaches the universal through careful and loving attention to the particular. That movement is a task set to all writers, and it is a hopeful sign that some of them, both old and new, still perform it.—MADISON SMARTT BELL, "Less Is Less: The Dwindling American Short Story," *Harper's*, April 1986, p. 69

JOHN UPDIKE

"Summonses, Indictments, Extenuating Circumstances"

New Yorker, November 3, 1986, pp. 158–65

A *Summons to Memphis*, by Peter Taylor, is not quite the distinguished short-story writer's first novel; thirty-six years ago, he published *A Woman of Means*, which, little more than forty thousand words long, might be called a novella. The two books have much in common: a narrator who has been moved from a bucolic Tennessee childhood to a big house in a river city (Memphis, St. Louis), a handsome and strong-willed father recovering from a business setback, a witty but somehow incapacitated and mentally fragile mother figure (a mother, a stepmother), two older and wearingly vivacious sisters or stepsisters, a psychological core of ambivalent and ruminative passivity, and a lovingly detailed (architecturally, sociologically) portrait of life in the upper classes of the Upper South between the two world wars. This last is Mr. Taylor's terrain, and he rarely strays from it. The narrator of *A Summons to Memphis*, Phillip Carver, lives in Manhattan, on West Eighty-second Street ("one of the safer neighborhoods on the Upper West Side, but still we have to be very careful"), with a woman fifteen years younger, Holly Kaplan; New York, that bulging plenitude, is felt as a kind of blissfully blank limbo, and the principal charm of his mistress seems to be that she, from a prosperous Jewish family in Cleveland, shares with the forty-nine-year-old Southern refugee a rueful, guilty obsession with the tribal reality left behind. "She felt they had a real life out there in Cleveland that she didn't have, had never had, would never have now." Both Holly and Phillip are in publishing, and their principal activities seem to be reading galley proofs and discussing their families:

> Suddenly, with a sigh, Holly blew out a great billow of smoke and said irritably that I *was really* absolutely obsessed with my family!
>
> This was an accusation which Holly and I frequently hurled at each other. In the beginning our complaints about our families had been perhaps our deepest bond. We had long since, however, worn out the subject.

So worn out, indeed, that in the course of the novel they separate, only to be reunited on the firm basis of more family talk: "During the days and weeks that followed Holly and I talked of almost nothing but our two families . . . And we sat there in the twilight and sipped our drinks while we talked our own combined nonsense together, each his or her own brand of inconclusive nonsense about the reconciliation of fathers and children, talked on and on until total darkness fell . . ."

In the course of this meandering narrative, it is possible to feel like Holly when she blew out the impatient billow of smoke. After a lifetime of tracing teacup tempests among genteel Tennesseans, Mr. Taylor retains an unslaked appetite for the local nuance. The rather subtle (to Yankees, at least) differences between the styles of Memphis and Nashville are thoroughly and repeatedly gone into, with instructive side-glances at Knoxville and Chattanooga. "Nashville," an old social arbiter of that town explains, "is a city of schools and churches, whereas Memphis is—well, Memphis is something else again. Memphis is a place of steamboats and cotton gins, of card playing and hotel society." The narrator puts it, "Memphis was today. Nashville was yesterday." His own temperamental preference, as we could guess from his leisurely, laggard prose, is for yesterday: "As one walks or rides down any street in Nashville one can feel now and again that he has just glimpsed some pedestrian on the sidewalk who was not quite real somehow, who with a glance over his shoulder or with a look in his disenchanted eye has warned one not to believe too much in the plastic present and has given warning that the past is still real and present somehow and is demanding something of all men like me who happen to pass that way." When Phillip moves to Memphis, just turned thirteen, he reports to school "in knee britches and wearing a sort of Buster Brown, highly starched collar" and discovers that (this is 1931) not only is his costume retrograde but his hair is cut too long, and he even fails to carry his books the Memphis way—"alongside my hip or thigh, with my arm hanging straight down from shoulder to wrist" rather than (evidently Nashville-style) "like a girl, in the crook of my arm." The accents are different, and men play golf instead of riding to hounds and don't wear cutaways downtown to the office: "Unlike other Memphis businessmen [George Carver, Phillip's father] frequently went to his office wearing striped trousers and a cutaway jacket—a morning suit, no less—along with a starched wing collar and a gray four-in-hand silk tie." He comes to adopt the Memphis way of dressing: "In Manhattan or even in Nashville or Knoxville or Chattanooga people on the street might have turned and stared at Father and remarked on the peculiar cut of his jacket and the width of his hat brim." A hat alone will send Mr. Taylor into a rhapsody of Southern social history:

> It seems that when a local gentleman was on the courthouse square of Thornton or when he was walking his own land in that part of the world, a hat was a very important item of apparel. Father's father and his grandfather always ordered their hats from a manufacturer in St. Louis, and Father did so too, wherever he might be living. Even I can remember, as a small child, seeing my father and my paternal grandfather and great-grandfather, for that matter, in their hats walking the farm roads on the Town Farm, as we called it, or crossing the wide, wooden blocks in the streets on the courthouse square. In their law practice and even in their wide-ranging farm dealings (they also owned cotton farms in western Kentucky as well as in southern Illinois and southeastern Missouri) there were various occasions in the year when it was necessary for them to visit St. Louis and Chicago. Whether those visits related to their law practice or to their landowning I don't know. Anyhow, it was always in St. Louis that they bought their hats and in Chicago whatsoever sporting equipment they owned. They shopped there in person for those articles or they ordered them through the mail from "houses" where they were known. They spoke of St. Louis as their "hat place," and Father continued to do so always. I am sure it was in a St. Louis hat that he met me that near noonday when I arrived at the Memphis airport. On the other hand, his shoes would always be Nashville shoes.

Now, this is admirably circumstantial and, within the generous space demanded by the unhurried tone, elegantly turned; but it is talk, not action. Direct dialogue in *A Summons to Memphis* is sparse, and the plot feels skimped, even snubbed. Though Mr. Taylor tells us a great deal about costumes, furniture, and civic differences, there is a great deal he avoids showing. Indeed, he almost cruelly teases, with his melodious divagations and his practiced skill at foreshadowing and delaying climaxes, the reader of this novel. Its kernel of action—Phillip Carver's trip to Memphis at the summons of his sisters, in 1967—does not occur until well after midpoint. He at last boards the plane on page 132, arrives at the Memphis airport on page 135, and by page 153 is back on a plane, winging his way into more cloudy retrospect and having refused (implausibly, I think) to spend a single night with his father and sisters. And the events while he is briefly there seem oddly betranced; though his vital if elderly father has been frustrated in an attempt at marriage, the old man submits without a peep, and though his son has been summoned a thousand miles for a family conference, he says hardly a word. Concerning an earlier frustration, it is not made clear why or how the father covertly wrecks the romance between Phillip, who is a soldier and all of twenty-three, and Clara Price, who sounds lovely and, even if she does hail from far-off Chattanooga, would appear to be socially acceptable; she and her family live "in a splendid Tudor-style house atop Lookout Mountain"—presumably above bribery and bullying persuasion. Some nuance, no doubt, escaped me, just as, in trying to grasp the scarcely-to-be-forgiven trauma of being moved from Nashville to Memphis, I fastened on the tragic fact that the two girls thereby "came out" in the wrong city and wasted their débutante parties: "Young ladies in present-day Memphis and Nashville cannot possibly conceive the profound significance that the débutante season once held for their like or imagine the strict rules that it was death to disobey."

In any case, one might argue that the action of the novel is not so much the doings, past and present, of the Tennessee Carvers as the struggle by the self-exiled Phillip, staged in "these very irregular notebooks" of his which we are mysteriously reading, to come to terms with his past—the magnificent, crushing father, the "cluttered-up, bourgeois life," the tenacious, static idyll of the South. As the boy rode behind his father outside Nashville, "the foliage of the black gums and maples and oaks often met overhead on those lanes, and it seems to me that every morning somewhere on our ride there would be an old Negro man bent down beside one of the walls, making repairs. It was a timeless scene. I could not imagine a past time when it had not been just so or a future time when it would not be the same." From this South, with its omnipresent past, Mr. Taylor, like Faulkner, draws endless inspiration; he stirs and stirs the same waters, watching them darken and deepen, while abstaining from Faulkner's violent modernist gestures. He stirs instead with a Jamesian sort of spoon.

In praise of *A Woman of Means* thirty-six years ago, Robert Penn Warren claimed for it "the excitement of being constantly on the verge of deep perceptions and deep interpretations." We stay on the verge much of the time. *A Woman of Means* did plunge, with the empathy of a James Agee or William Maxwell, into the frightening dark of boyhood, when one is able to observe so much and do so little. Its evocation of a child's helpless, sensitive world seemed to close hastily, but not until our essential loneliness and the precariousness of even the best-appointed home were made painfully clear. In *A Summons to Memphis,* though the canvas is broader and adorned with fine comic splashes, some of the narrative churning brings up only what is already floating on the surface: "And I grasped at once that my not having other luggage meant to him that we would not be delayed by waiting at the baggage-claim window." Or, a perception still more hard-won:

> But as we turned between the boxwoods at the entrance to Father's two-acre plot, I at once became aware of a large rectangular object, somehow inimical to the scene, drawn up to the house and visible at the end of the two rows of old cedars that lined the driveway. The house was set back some three hundred feet from the road, and when we had traversed half that distance I recognized the unlikely object as a commercial moving van. I was able to identify it immediately then by the name of the local storage warehouse which was writ in large red letters on the side of the van.

James's heavily mirrored halls of mutual regard seem but feebly imitated by reflections like "I knew always that the affair referred to was pure fantasy but I do not know even now whether or not they knew I knew." The diction at times is so fastidious that a smile at the narrator's expense must be intended: "If slit skirts were the fashion, then my sisters' would be vented well above the knees, exposing fleshy thighs which by this time in my sisters' lives were indeed of no inconsiderable size." Some sentences can only be called portly: "But about Alex Mercer himself there was something that made him forever fascinated by and sympathetic to that which he perhaps yearned after in spirit but which practically speaking he did not wish himself to become." Such measured verbal groping among the shadows of morality and good intention has suffered a diminishment since James; he had no commerce with God but had retained the religious sense, and the ground beneath his characters authentically trembles when they—for example, Kate Croy and Merton Densher—commit what they feel is a sin. In Phillip Carver's world, no religion remains, just an old-fashioned code of behavior, and its defense is hard to distinguish from snobbery or, to use a word he uses of himself, "lethargy." He is so imbued with lethargy that he speaks of "debating the question of how many angels could sit on the head of a pin" when in the conventional image, of course, the angels dance. As a young man he registers for the draft as a conscientious objector (in peacetime, early in 1941), but when the draft-board clerk fails to understand and sends in his form with the others, "this was *so* like a certain type of Memphis mentality . . . I could not even bring myself to protest;" he indifferently puts on his uniform and goes off to Fort Oglethorpe. When, six years later, he flees Memphis for New York, "it was as though someone else were dressing me and packing for me or at least as though I had no will of my own"—his sisters are acting through him. And when, in 1967, he discovers himself in the same restaurant as his long-lost love, Clara Price, he doesn't trouble to get up from his chair and present himself; like those angels, he just sits. On his visits home, the dynamism of his ambitious father and animated, vengeful sisters oppresses him; it seems that "the whole and partly in protest at having been denied marriage and "frozen forever in their roles as injured adolescents." The father and sisters are old-fashioned characters, with costumes and settings and histories and psychologies; Phillip, by leaving the hinterland where clothes make a statement and the family "things" are worth inheriting, has become a non-character, a sensate shade dwelling in the low-affect regions of Don DeLillo and Donald Barthelme, a human being who assigns only a limited value, hedged about with irony, to himself. Someday, Phillip Carver fantasizes, he and Holly will simply fade away in their apartment—"when the sun shines in next morning there will be simply no trace of us." The lovers will not have been "alive enough to have the strength to die."

Peter Taylor's apparently cozy Tennessee world is bleaker than Henry James's transatlantic empyrean, for it is a century more drained of the blood of the sacred. The sacred, Mircea Eliade has written, "implies the notions of *being*, of *meaning*, and of *truth*. . . . It is difficult to imagine how the human mind could function without the conviction that there is something irreducibly *real* in the world." For James, the real constituted the human appetites, mostly for love and money, that flickered beneath and secretly shaped the heavily draped society of late-Victorian times. By Mr. Taylor's time, appetite has shrivelled to dread—dread of another's aroma, of being suffocated by one's father's appetites. For all the fussy good manners of his prose, the ugly war between parents and children has been his recurrent topic; one thinks of the short story "Porte Cochère" (the house in *A Summons to Memphis* also has a porte cochère), which ends with that old father, in the darkness of his room, while his adult children noisily besiege his door, taking out the walking stick "with his father's face carved on the head" and stumbling about "beating the upholstered chairs with the stick and calling the names of children under his breath." In *A Summons to Memphis*, Phillip Carver wins through to a real, non-trivial insight when he accepts "Holly's doctrine that our old people must be not merely forgiven all their injustices and unconscious cruelties in their roles as parents but that any selfishness on their parts had actually been required of them if they were to remain whole human beings and not become merely guardian robots of the young." The wrongs of the father are inevitably visited upon the son, as part of the jostle of "whole human beings" sharing the earth. Beneath his talky, creaking courtesies, Peter Taylor deals fascinatingly with the primal clauses of the social contract.

Sara Teasdale

1884–1933

Sara Teasdale was born on August 8, 1884, in St. Louis, Missouri, where she was privately educated. Upon marrying in 1914 she moved to New York City, where she remained, despite her divorce in 1929, for the rest of her life. Encouraged by her family, Teasdale had begun writing verse at a very early age, and in 1907 she published her first book, *Sonnets to Duse and Other Poems.* It was well received, and she soon became one of the most popular poets of the early twentieth century, winning the Pulitzer Prize in 1918. She wrote in simple, usually rhymed quatrains, with restrained use of image or metaphor, and her typical themes were love, beauty and, in later years, death. Other works include *Rivers to the Sea* (1915), *Love Songs* (1917; winner of a Poetry Society award), and *Dark of the Moon* (1926). In later years Teasdale became increasingly withdrawn and unhappy, a state that was intensified by her unsuccessful romance with John Hall Wheelock and by the death of her friend Vachel Lindsay in 1931. On January 29, 1933, she died in New York City of an overdose of sleeping medicine. *The Collected Poems of Sara Teasdale* was published posthumously in 1937.

Sara Teasdale stands high among the living poets of America. In an age of outpour, her constitution and her method combine to reaffirm the beneficence of limitation. Nature, rich in her gifts to Miss Teasdale, has been wisely severe in her refusals, and the poet's forbearing and chary art has enforced the continence of nature. She writes brief poems on few subjects; her diction is culled rather than copious; her imagery is unmarked by range or change. Even the verse-forms are few and obvious, though certain unrhymed poems offer to the caprice of the hour the distant courtesy of a passing salutation. I find in her no proof of that more than Gallic unreserve which a press notice sent me by her publishers is sharp enough to discover in her work; if it be there, I applaud the cunning with which Miss Teasdale has hidden her openness.

Still further, I am not sure that Miss Teasdale's second-best, which naturally exceeds her first-best in volume, is notably superior to the second-best of many other expert artists among her living compatriots. Her descriptions and monologues are forgettable; it is in her brief, passionate, unfalteringly modelled lyrics, at once flamelike and sculpturesque like fire in a Greek urn, that her true distinction becomes manifest.

The passion which these lyrics embody is a strong, but also an unhurried, unimpetuous, clear-sighted, and self-guiding passion. Most poets in our day utilize their transitory fervors hastily, anxiously, as they might consume their hot tea and waffles in alarm lest the life-giving heat should vanish. The stay of the feeling in their minds seems only long enough to insure its rebound to the page. With Sara Teasdale the case is different; her passions endure, and she can wait. Hence the rare combination of fervor with a high, serene discretion, a poised and steadfast art, which makes the expression of feeling in these compact poems "half-ardent, half-austere." Let me quote some of these lyrics, which might fitly lesson young poets in the truth that in verse as in explosives confinement is the spring of energy:

THE LOOK

Strephon kissed me in the spring,
Robin in the fall,
But Colin only looked at me
And never kissed at all.

Strephon's kiss was lost in jest,
Robin's lost in play,
But the kiss in Colin's eyes
Haunts me night and day.

Again:

Oh, I have sown my love so wide
That he will find it everywhere;
It will awake him in the night,
It will enfold him in the air.

I set my shadow in his sight
And I have winged it with desire,
That it may be a cloud by day
And in the night a shaft of fire.

Still again:

What do I owe to you
Who loved me deep and long?
You never gave my spirit wings
Nor gave my heart a song.

But oh, to him I loved
Who loved me not at all,
I owe the little open gate
That led thru heaven's wall.

It will be seen that Miss Teasdale scars her pages with the spelling "thru." I shall retaliate for the sufferings I have undergone from the practice only by calling my persecutor "up-to-date"—a revenge which is indistinguishable from homage in the ears of all lovers of that fashion of orthography. In other points, I should sum up Miss Teasdale as the inheritor rather than the copyist of the great English tradition, the tradition of refined vigor, vigor enclosed and ensheathed in comeliness, of feelings intensely personal yet delicately human, of a life whose springs are central and intimate, however great the variety of its individual outflowings.—O. W. FIRKINS, "Singers New and Old," *Nation*, Jan. 6, 1916, p. 12

"There is but one thing certain," says Pliny, with his curious mixture of matter-of-fact and melancholy, "that nothing is certain; and there is nothing more wretched or more proud than man." Human unhappiness and the pride that half causes it and half redeems—of the union of these two eternal contrasts *Flame and Shadow* is made. It is the utterance of a mood which all feel sometimes, some always; which all the generations have repeated, yet each of them yearns to hear expressed anew in the special accents of its own day—that particular kind of pessimism which feels the vanity, and yet the value, of life. And it needs to be re-stated still. For the present cannot live on the past, on dead men's words, alone; its own literature may be inferior, much of it must be, inevitably, minor; yet, as Homer had already learnt, men love the song which is new, and a living voice has in some ways an appeal that no dead eloquence can bring. This is the value of *Flame and Shadow*; not that it contains new ideas, but that a view of life which our age in part accepts, in part struggles to avoid, is here once more expressed with sincerity and skill—the feeling that for all the agony of transience, all the disillusion of hopes in vain fulfilled, there are no consolations, but the bitter beauty of the Universe, and the frail human pride that confronts it, for a moment, undismayed. "There is nothing more wretched or more proud than man." It is always strange that sorrow should possess this higher beauty than laughter, even children's or lovers' laughter, can possess; that Tragedy is so fundamentally a greater thing than Comedy. But for this, the sadness of the world would be unbearable; thanks to this, from sorrow itself there is wrung a kind of joy:

> Let it be forgotten, as a flower is forgotten,
> Forgotten as a fire that once was singing gold,
> Let it be forgotten for ever and ever,
> Time is a kind friend, he will make us old.
>
> If anyone asks, say it was forgotten
> Long and long ago,
> As a flower, as a fire, as a hushed footfall
> In a long forgotten snow.
>
> . . .
>
> Even love that I built my spirit's house for
> Comes as a brooding and a baffled guest,
> And music and men's praise and even laughter
> Are not so good as rest.
>
> . . .
>
> It is strange how often a heart must be broken
> Before the years will make it wise.

With a suspicion of insincerity the effect would be what Arnold called "a horrid falsetto"; some, perhaps, will suspect; but that is not the impression of the book as a whole. For the quietness with which the passion is controlled throughout is perfect, like the quiet of a small unruffled pool clasping a whole darkened heaven in stillness to its heart. And with this gentleness goes hand in hand another quality which makes the writer's attitude, though so familiar, new and individual—her deliberate restraint from bitterness. Bitterness has been the very salt of some of the intensest poetry from Archilochus and Juvenal to Hugo, from Wyatt and Webster to Hardy and Housman; it may be exaggerated or hideous or morbid—it is at least never insipid. And yet superb as scorn can be in its vibrant intensity, there is something a shade finer still in the ideal, though not, of course, therefore in the work, of a writer who rises above cursing the world for its cruelty to recognise its indifference, its lack of evil intent as well as good, and therefore to take alike its buffets and its beauty, in her own fine phrase—

> "with gay unembittered lips."

This indeed is one difference between Mrs. Teasdale and Edna St. Vincent Millay, whose general attitude and tone are so similar, though hers is an intenser and more brilliant gift. It is easy, for instance, to seize the contrast between the resilience and resonance of:

> White with daisies, and red with sorrel,
> And empty, empty under the sky!
> Life is a quest and love a quarrel.
> Here is the place for me to lie,

and the quieter resolution of *Flame and Shadow:*

> With earth hidden and heaven hidden,
> And only my own spirit's pride
> To keep me from the peace of those
> Who are not lonely, having died.

One other piece in this new volume stands out as being not only charming, but true and new as well:

> There never was a mood of mine,
> Gay or heart-broken, luminous or dull,
> But you could ease me of its fever,
> And give it back to me more beautiful.
>
> In many another spirit I broke the bread,
> And pledged the wine and played the happy guest,
> But I was lonely, I remembered you;
> The heart belongs to him who knew it best.

It is good that this kind of poetry should go on being written; it is not only good as poetry; it keeps alive an attitude to which the human mind is perhaps destined to be more and more driven back—the poetic philosophy of life. So, at least, Arnold thought, when he wrote: "In poetry the spirit of our race will find, as time goes on and other helps fail, its consolation and its stay." Theologian and philosopher have always tended to look at everything as means to some end; and it has been the poet and the artist who valued things, not for the uses they can be put to or the promises they hold, but for the interest and significance of what they are. In that mood we know we cannot possess; we do not desire to possess; the verb "to have" ceases to torture, and our pleasure is for once not a satisfaction that must be preceded and followed by the pain of craving. And if all is transient, this too must be endured:

> Denn aller schöner Dinge Schönheit ist
> Dass sie vergehen.

This is disinterestedness—loving life for its own sake. It is not a road for all, but for many; not an abiding place, but a refuge; it too is a blind alley in the end, but no mean or sordid one. —F. L. LUCAS, "Two Poetesses," *NS*, Nov. 29, 1924, p. 236

Lyric poetry, however deeply felt and felicitously contrived, nowadays falls dangerously near the line dividing the romantic nostalgia and mock heroics of the nineteenth century from more complicated and turbulent contemporary writing. The taste which cherished the simple lyric cry of grief, ecstasy or regret written into a sonnet or a series of quatrains has given way; modern ears demand a more complicated stimulus. It is practically impossible for a poet to express simply and without apology or *blaque* direct emotion concerning his own passions and his intimations of the universe at large. The human heart would seem to be outmoded; the eye of eternity has become an intellectual instead of a metaphysical concept. Yeats puts his later songs into the mouths of crazed maidens and fools.

Strange Victory, Sara Teasdale's last book, published posthumously, is the final expression of a purely lyrical talent and of a poetic career remarkable for its integrity throughout. An interval of more than twenty years separates Miss Teasdale's first book from her last. She correctly valued the quality of her talent from the start. Her matter—the record of a sensitive and gifted woman's emotions—was always rendered with clarity and justice definitely within the limits of her manner. Her range was far less wide than Emily Dickinson's: she never permitted herself any break with form or any flights into speculation; on the other hand, she added to a poetic equipment inherited in part from Emily Brontë and Christina Rossetti qualities peculiar to herself; a frankness of attack utterly lacking in her forerunners.

Miss Teasdale's sensibilities were completely sincere and therefore could function with freedom under the canons of her art. The pure lyric gift is notoriously narrow but notoriously strict as well. Its effects are based upon a true, subtle and naïve ear, and upon intensity rather than complexity of emotion. It is a medium that requires sincerity both in feeling and expression; inflation, cleverness and falsity show up only too plainly under its simple but inflexible demands. Sara Teasdale's poetry reflected, without distortion, every emotional change in her life from youth to late maturity. The two halves of her talent were delicately adjusted to one another to the end; her manner became clearer as her emotions became more calm. And because she had absolute faith in her own gift, she could eliminate from her work every effect of rhetoric. The twenty-two lyrics in her last book are poems reduced to the simplest terms. If a contemporary audience for lyric poetry may be postulated, the moving simplicity of these final poems must delight any responsive ear therein.—LOUISE BOGAN, "Sara Teasdale's Last Poems," *NR*, Nov. 15, 1933, p. 25

MARGUERITE WILKINSON

"Death as a Poet Sees It"

New York Times Book Review, October 31, 1920, p. 10

In the days when Sara Teasdale was writing of Colin and Pierrot and Helen of Troy I thought that her work was praised too much. The critics, it seemed to me, were giving gold for silver. That it was excellent silver I knew. Only ignorance could fail to perceive the felicity of her images and the fluency of her music. Only the moribund intellect could fail to acknowledge the charm of her moods. But was her gift unique? Was there much of universal importance in what she had to offer? I thought not.

Today, after reading *Flame and Shadow*, I ask myself these questions again, and I have another answer. Sara Teasdale has found a philosophy of life and death. In this latest book we may watch the conflict between the light that comes from the everlasting flame and the darkness that is the ever-present shadow. Here is another steel-strong, defiant intellect, answering the riddle of the universe with song!

Her philosophy is no dress parade of brilliant opinions showing the latest styles in thought. It is not new. But it is so costly that only the possessors of spiritual riches can make it their own. It is for the brave.

Cowards think of death euphemistically, accepting such assurances of immortality as are current without venturing to question their reasonableness, or else they put away the thought of death from their minds, with less and less power as time passes, until finally, in utter impotence, they meet what is grandly inevitable even for them. They cannot say, with Stevenson,

I lay me down with a will!

Children of sorrow think of death with equanimity because it brings peace. Children of nature, temperamentally optimistic, think as Walt Whitman thought. But the brave, who love life so well that death seems tragic to them, must find a way of facing the thought of it serenely. If the current assurances of immortality are satisfactory to their intellects after honest investigation, they have found their Elysium. If not, what then?

To this question Sara Teasdale offers a twofold answer. First, there is the answer of the strong ego refusing to take cognizance of a universe in which it cannot live and love eternally. Though worlds crumble and ages dissolve in mist, says the ego, for me there must be "some shining strange escape." This is a noble audacity. The stubborn will of man, powerless before the stark fact of mortality, would put on omnipotence like a garment. Says Sara Teasdale:

Since darkness waits for me, then all the more
Let me go down as waves sweep to the shore
  In pride; and let me sing with my last breath;
In these few hours of light I lift my head;
Life is my lover—I shall leave the dead
  If there is any way to baffle death.

But that is not all. If, in spite of this superb challenge, there is, indeed, no escape and no returning, even then, she says, the spirit of man can triumph through the love of beauty. This is the centre from which all the light of her thought radiates. This is the wisdom of "The Voice" that cries out of

Atoms as old as stars,
Mutation on mutation,

saying,

Forever
Seek for Beauty, she only
  Fights with man against Death!

This is the idea with which the book begins and the idea with which it ends. Sun, moon and stars, and even gardens, live longer than man if life is measured by lifetimes. But by the transcendent gift of consciousness man is enabled to realize beauty and to make of his brief lifetime a triumph instead of a defeat.

How many million Aprils came
  Before I ever knew
How white a cherry bough could be,
  A bed of squills, how blue!

And many a dancing April
  When life is done with me,
Will lift the blue flame of the flower
  And the white flame of the tree.

Oh! burn me with your beauty, then,
  Oh! hurt me, tree and flower,
Lest in the end death try to take
  Even this glistening hour!

O shaken flowers, O shimmering trees,
  O sunlit white and blue,
Wound me, that I, through endless sleep,
  May bear the scar of you.

That is the first lyric in the book. Her faith is even more

fully expressed in the last, "The Wind in the Hemlock." It is too long to quote in full. The first part of it expresses the longing of mankind to live forever—

With envious dark rage I bear,
Stars, your cold complacent stare;
Heart-broken in my hate look up,
Moon, at your clear, immortal cup,
Changing to gold from dusky red—
Age after age when I am dead
To be filled up with light, and then
Emptied, to be refilled again.

But the poem ends with these lines:

If I am peaceful, I shall see
Beauty's face continually;
Feeding on her wine and bread
I shall be wholly comforted,
For she can make one day for me
Rich as my lost eternity.

Since I have emphasized her philosophy of life and death, I ought not to pass on to a discussion of Sara Teasdale's technique as shown in this volume without saying that there are many poems in *Flame and Shadow* to delight those who cannot share her philosophy. There are songs of the faithful beauty of Aldebaran and Altair, and songs of the open sea and the mountains. Sara Teasdale does not write of nature as Robert Frost does, nor as William H. Davies does, with the purpose, or at least with the result, of giving to the reader a pleasure of the kind to be had from nature itself. She is invariably subjective, and what we care for in her poetry is her own reaction toward the fragile bit of beauty that she has detached from the rest of the universe to show to us. In "Water Lilies" we are not charmed by lilies, but by the mystery of the poet's mood. The lilies are there simply for suggestion.

It is necessary to mention, also, the songs of places, of St. Louis, of New York, and Santa Barbara, and the songs of people and of their secret thoughts, "rushing without sound" from the hidden places of their minds. But the best of Sara Teasdale's songs of people are her love songs, always. Deliciously passionate, limpid as a spring in a forest, their quality is too well known to need description. There are several in this book that are as good as any she has ever written. Among them is the following:

If I must go to heaven's end
  Climbing the ages like a stair,
Be near me and forever bend
  With the same eyes above me there;
Time will fly past us like leaves flying,
  We shall not heed, for we shall be
Beyond living, beyond dying,
  Knowing and known unchangeably.

There are in the book songs of wayward moods, glad and weary. In one the brave philosophy is momentarily forgotten and the poet says that the brave victories that seem so splendid are never really won and that rest is best of all. In another she has forgiveness for God. This might disturb some of her readers, but would not shock Him, I think. But when all is said, the richest gift that she gives us in *Flame and Shadow* is an upright and unflinching thought of death and eternity and a consolation that is never cowardly and evasive, but proud always, and courageous.

It is not enough to say that Sara Teasdale has grown intellectually since the publication of her earlier books and that in thought and feeling *Flame and Shadow* is the finest of them all. We must, perforce, acknowledge a growth in artistry. Her rhythms are much more subtle, more accurate psychologically, than they used to be. She has learned much of the great laws that lie under the rhythms of words as the bed of a stream lies under the waters, turning and troubling the course of their flowing. She has proved once more what all good poets have always proved, that these laws are not of the rhetorics, but of human bodies and minds. And so these lyrics have the lilt of absolute naturalness which is sincere and perfect music. Walter de la Mare, who is a master of melody, has never made a lyrical tune more enchanting than that of "Let It Be Forgotten." It is worthy of Yeats at his best. It is worthy of masters now dead.

Let it be forgotten, as a floker is forgotten,
  Forgotten as a fire that once was singing gold,
Let it be forgotten for ever and ever.
  Time is a kind friend, he will make us old.

If any one asks, say it was forgotten
  Long and long ago,
As a flower, as a fire, as a hushed footfall
  In long forgotten snow.

Almost as lovely and quite as irregular are the rhythmical tunes of "Water Lilies," "The Long Hill" and many other lyrics. They can be lovely and irregular at the same time only because the lapses from regularity are not lapses at all. If it were not for the fact that she loves beauty, Sara Teasdale could write as regularly as a high school student or a metronome's beating. But her transgressions of small rules are acts of obedience to great and profound laws.

Some reviewer, in commenting on the poetry of the Autumn season, was content to call this book "pleasantly lyrical." I was reminded of a stanza from "Greenland's Icy Mountains"—

In vain with lavish kindness
  The gifts of God are strown,
The heathen in his blindness
  Bows down to wood and stone.

There are, to be sure, two or three negligible lyrics in *Flame and Shadow*. "The Return" is one of them. "Eight o'Clock" is amusingly reminiscent of *A Child's Garden of Verses*. "In the End" disappoints us logically and emotionally by introducing an anti-climax. But most of the others are songs

As lovely and as full of light,
As hushed and brief as a falling star
On a Winter night.

This is a book to read with reverence of joy. Although I seldom prophesy I venture to say that it will have a long life.

BABETTE DEUTSCH

"The Solitary Ironist"

Poetry, December 1937, pp. 148–53

About the time that Masefield was trying to bring the Chaucerian plainness of speech back to English verse, and a bright-haired young man from Idaho was transposing Provençal music in a fashion startling to English ears, Sara Teasdale published the poems with which this book commences. They touched on recognized themes in the recognized way, they had nothing rough or foreign about them, and they possessed, beyond their pleasant familiarity, a fluent melodiousness.

The keynote (in *The Collected Poems of Sara Teasdale*) is struck in the opening sonnet to Eleanora Duse: "Oh beauty that is filled so full of tears." Beauty and sorrow; love, happy or crossed; death, shrunk from as the end of love and beauty, or desired as the peace they cannot give—these are the recurrent motifs. A girlish wistfulness is the distinguishing feature of the early lyrics. They have the charm of Heine's *Lieder*, without his sharpness, the poignancy of Housman's songs, without his bitterness. They are personal, without having the vice of privacy or the virtue of subtlety, honest but not profound. The properties are bread and wine, swords and viols; the settings are gardens, shrines and palaces; the characters: pilgrims, shepherds, knights, and kings and queens. Even where the poems bear titles that evoke common scenes—Union Square, Coney Island, Gramercy Park, the Metropolitan Museum—these are merely the background for a moment of sentimental drama or traditional romance. But always there is the subdued melody that redeems the easy imagery and the trite situation. Some have the Elizabethan grace of the lyric that ends

When thou art more cruel than he,
Then will Love be kind to thee.

Others strike the note that Edna Millay was to sound more vibrantly for a more deeply disillusioned generation:

I hoped that he would love me,
  And he has kissed my mouth,
But I am like a stricken bird
  That cannot reach the south.

For though I know he loves me,
  Tonight my heart is sad;
His kiss was not so wonderful
  As all the dreams I had.

Repeatedly there is the slight ironic touch at the close, which, though the irony is gentle and all too feminine, is an index to a discriminating sensibility.

The chief faults of Miss Teasdale's work are the monotony of her matter and the explicitness of her statements. Often vague where she should have been precise, as in the delineation of background, she was apt to be overly exact where she should have been reticent, as in defining the nature of the grief that troubled or the joy that exalted her. It is almost incredible that the poet who was to write the lyrics in *Flame and Shadow*, and more particularly those in *Dark of the Moon*, the woman who was to become "self-complete as a flower or a stone," should have been capable of the banality of lines like "I love, I am loved, he is mine" or "And when I am with you, I am at rest."

The fascination of this volume lies in the fact that it exhibits so clearly the poet's development. As the years went by, the themes did not alter much, but the cadences became more varied, the mood more reflective, the expression more sensitive. Gradually, the irony that pointed the best of the early lyrics deepened and strengthened the poetry of Miss Teasdale's maturity. She was moved by the same things, rejoiced by the same natural beauties, overcome by the same loneliness, haunted by the same recurrent terror. But the personal relation is realized with a keener sense of the nuances of human intercourse, the terror is measured by a fuller awareness of man's fate, even the landscapes are viewed with a more perceptive eye. With these sharpened responses to the world about and the world within, came also a better control of her instrument. The later poems do not require, as so many of the early ones seem to do, the accompaniment of voice and strings in order to give them a suggestiveness that they fail to achieve. The riper pieces are, as their author came to be, self-sufficient. It is no strange and bitter brew that Miss Teasdale offers—it is the wine that one expects with dinner in a civilized place. But with the years, one finds that the bouquet is finer and the flavor delightfully dry.

Aware, as every sensitive person must be, of the cruelties that beset mankind, Miss Teasdale scarcely ever touched upon the problems that are the subject of current poetry. This is brought home to the reader with sardonic force by the line, written, it is true, before the advent of fascism: "Oh when God made Italy He was gay and young." Her nearest approach to the Social Muse was in an early sentimental piece lamenting the lot of

the girls who ask for love
In the lights of Union Square,

and in a later sonnet where she speaks of standing at night before the window confronting the brilliant city, and being visited by a "stark

Sense of the lives behind each yellow light,
And not one wholly joyous, proud or free."

Even the poems written during the war show a signal ignorance of, if not quite aloofness from, the misery that eats the lives of the mass of humanity. Herself "not wholly joyous, proud or free," the circumstances of Sara Teasdale's life were yet sufficiently happy to enable her to savor the pleasures of travel and music, books and people, without too painful a realization of the disease infecting the society of which she was a part. It belongs, however, to a cultivated intelligence to appreciate the evils of existence as well as the gifts of fortune. But the later work, though it continues to be personal, harps upon a complaint so common to mankind as to raise the poetry to the level of the impersonal. There are still love poems that dwell upon the solace that perfect comradeship alone can give. The bulk of the later work, however, expresses an autumnal wisdom, or a craving for release from the burden of loneliness, the grief of lessening powers, the inevitable pain of living.

The poet of passion is the tender individualist, but when love's fulfillment is past, she can, if she is wise, find the sure refuge of the solitary in her own integrity. The recognition of her self-dependence finds contented expression in the lyric which opens her last and finest volume, where she confesses:

It was not you, though you were near,
  Though you were good to hear and see,
It was not earth, it was not heaven,
  It was myself that sang in me.

It is expressed with a sombre resonance in not a few other poems of the same collection, most forthrightly perhaps in "Day's Ending":

Aloof as aged kings,
Wearing like them the purple,
The mountains ring the mesa
Crowned with a dusky light;
Many a time I watched
That coming-on of darkness
Till stars burned through the heavens
Intolerably bright.

It was not long I lived there
But I became a woman
Under those vehement stars,
For it was there I heard
For the first time my spirit
Forging an iron rule for me,
As though with slow cold hammers
Beating out word by word:

"Only yourself can heal you,
Only yourself can lead you,
The road is heavy going
And ends where no man knows;
Take love when love is given,
But never think to find it

A sure escape from sorrow
Or a complete repose."

The sole complete repose is death. The one escape would seem to be in the occupations named in "Leisure":

The year will turn for me, I shall delight in
All animals, and some of my own kind,
Sharing with no one but myself the frosty
And half ironic musings of my mind.

Here, plainly, is no revolutionary, in any sense of the word. The technique is traditional. The prevailing temper is one of acceptance—joyous, mournful, or resigned. But though Sara Teasdale's scope was limited, it enlarged with the years, so that her mature work delights one with its deeper music and frosty beauty. Even the longed-for achievement of the good society will not appreciably lessen private griefs. While these remain, one can find some assuagement in the melody of such lyrics as these, and take courage from their quiet irony.

PAUL THEROUX

1941–

Paul Edward Theroux was born in Medford, Massachusetts, on April 10, 1941. After attending the University of Maine (1959–60), he transferred to the University of Massachusetts, where he received a B.A. in 1963; he then studied briefly at Syracuse University (1963). Between 1963 and 1972 Theroux lived abroad as a teacher of English in Italy, Malawi, Uganda, and Singapore. He began his prolific literary career with the novel *Waldo* (1967), which was followed by many other works, many of them reflecting his experiences abroad; these include the novels *Fong and the Indians* (1968), *Girls at Play* (1969), *Jungle Lovers* (1971), *Saint Jack* (1973), *The Black House* (1974), *The Family Arsenal* (1976), *Picture Palace* (1977), and *The Mosquito Coast* (1982), as well as the short-story collections *Sinning with Annie* (1972) and *World's End* (1980). Theroux has also written a biography of V. S. Naipaul (1972) and two accounts of train journeys, through Asia: *The Great Railway Bazaar* (1975) and through the Americas in *The Old Patagonian Express* (1979).

It takes courage for a writer to abandon a tone of voice which he has mastered and attempt something completely different; but it is the sort of courage a serious writer needs. Paul Theroux started publishing novels in 1967 and has produced a series of brilliant and much-praised books each of which, though more than funny, was without doubt very funny indeed. *The Black House* marks a departure from this series: any jokes lurking in the narrative are of a depressed and bitter kind, jokes involving disappointment, betrayal of friends, disgust with the way things are. This may be partly because the hero is neither a young man nor even—as Theroux's last hero, 'Saint Jack' was—a middle-aged man able to comfort himself with fantasy. Sickness, sourness and despair afflict Alfred Munday, an anthropologist forced into early retirement away from a sunny African location and 'his' people, the Bwamba, into the damp Dorset village his wife Emma has hankered after.

In part, then, it is a novel about the expatriate condition, a condition Theroux is in a good position to explicate; he has lived and set novels in Africa and Singapore since leaving his native America, and is now himself settled in England. He has to an unusual degree the qualities a travelling writer needs if he is to be more than a travel writer: he can soak up atmosphere as quickly and thoroughly as a sponge, and he does not intrude his own personality. His English village, its flora and fauna, topography and moods, indoor and out, are here as sharply outlined as any of his earlier exotic settings. Anyone who has been an interloper in an English village—and it's the commonest way of experiencing country life today—will recognise the accuracy of the descriptions. Pleasure has to be found in cold, rain and early darkness ('it never gets this dark in London', as one baffled visitor points out); there is a good deal of slyness, social unease, bonhomie that cracks quickly. Munday's views on Africa, delivered at the village hall, do not help him along any more than his bad temper when he is baited at the pub by the villagers or condescended to by the squire over sherry.

Two episodes touch in expatriate torments with particular acuteness. In one, Munday takes the umbilical train to London for the day and meets first with an old tea-planter friend who cannot disguise the misery of his present life, reduced to incompetent English whores, macaroni cheese in pubs, bus-catching and evenings of television in Ealing—he, who had once bossed hundreds. Later on in the same day Munday takes tea with an old flame whose only asset now is her pretty daughter; left alone over the fruitcake with this schoolgirl for a moment, Munday politely asks her how she likes London, and the child answers laconically, 'Mummy fucks my friends'. He is shocked, as we are. Mummy returns to assure him that marriages are broken by the strain of English life after the ease of post-colonial society.

Munday and Emma, however, have the innocent mutual dependence of certain childless couples. They don't feel that strain consciously. In parental mood, they invite down a Bwamba friend Munday had helped (and studied) from his boyhood; Emma is maternal, but Munday finds himself no longer able to like the younger man, aware of the villagers' suspicions of a black and unable to tolerate him outside his natural setting. One of the best things in the book is the cross-country walk on which Munday cruelly drags his friend in his thin shoes.

'I sometimes feel I could have discovered all I needed to know about isolation and perhaps even tribalism right here . . . and witchcraft of a sort,' says Munday at one point; the parallel between the African village community and the English one is never far from his mind. And in fact he is caught up in some English witchcraft, a haunting providing the other strand to the plot. Sinister and erotic, this is the most technically adventurous part of the narrative, and it put me in mind of a Henry

James ghost story; only there the sexual element is never allowed to surface, whereas here it is not only explicit but insistent.

There is perhaps a tremor of uncertainty at the end of the book. Munday reaches some resolution whose value is not quite made clear; and he himself grows shadowy at times, more possessed by his ghost (one feels) than in possession of himself. But then the book is about a man panicked by doubts about just where he and other creatures do belong. The degree of skill with which Theroux handles these various themes, and the level mastery of his writing, have produced a novel of unusual scope and promise still more for the future.—CLAIRE TOMALIN, "Out of Africa," *NS*, Oct. 4, 1974, p. 475

Paul Theroux is simply a wonder, and ⟨. . .⟩ his eighth novel a remarkable piece of work. In reviewing his last one, *The Family Arsenal*, two years ago I spoke of how it (and its very fine predecessor, *The Black House*) each featured a desperate man endowed with great sensitivity, irony, and visionary or novelistic powers of forecast and apprehension. I also noted that both novels were consistently entertaining—I had not been so entertained since discovering Anthony Burgess in the middle 1960's. *Picture Palace* is even bolder and more daring than the last two, partly because its narrator (a first-person narrative Theroux hasn't used since *Saint Jack*) is a tough seventy-year-old photographer named Maude Coffin Pratt who is both desperately wrong about things—as we see from the tale of her life she unfolds, and which provides the course of the novel—and righter about them than anybody else can be, the way artists are "right" about things. In other words, Theroux has worked the metaphor of "visionary powers"—all those nineteenth-century heroines who saw so much—into a shutter-snapping wise-cracking ugly duckling of a narrator whose (hopeless?) passion for her brother Orlando is the determining fact of her life, and the reason she becomes a photographer in the first place. The book undertakes a very complicated and satisfyingly dialectical exploration of blindness, sight, insight, vision and revision—which exploration is the equivalent to the moral and political argument of *The Family Arsenal*, or the anthropological and mystical one of *The Black House*.

An exploration, but not an argument, for one never feels after reading Theroux that one has learned something about the Nature of . . . of whatever. An even better word for it is "entertainment," and some of the most entertaining things about *Picture Palace* are the set-pieces in which Maude encounters famous modern artists—like D. H. Lawrence or T. S. Eliot or Frost or Raymond Chandler—and "does them" (play is made with the sexual force of this expression) into art, storing them in an old windmill on Cape Cod, but more truly in the picture palace of her mind put on display by this novel. (That song "The Windmills of your Mind" may also be kicking around someplace.) The first and best of these portraits is of Graham Greene, whom Maude at 70 goes to London to shoot for her final picture, but who reminds her of brother Orlando and who, after drinks at the Ritz and dinner at Bentley's, so moves her that she ends up not taking his picture after all. The description is masterful:

> Greene's face, made handsome by fatigue, had a sagging summer redness. He could have passed for a clergyman—he had that same assured carriage, the bored pitying lips, the gentle look of someone who has just stopped praying. And yet there was about his look of piety an aspect of raffishness; about his distinguished bearing an air of anonymity; and whether it was caution or breeding, a slight unease in his hands. Like someone out of uniform, I thought, a general without his medals, a bishop who's left his robes upstairs, a happy man not quite succeeding at a scowling disguise. His hair was white, suggesting baldness at a distance, and while none of his features was remarkable, together they created an extraordinary effect of unshakable dignity, the courtly ferocity you see in very old lions.

With prose like that Theroux convinces us that words are worth a thousand pictures.

The Family Arsenal was chock-full of London cockney tough-talk; *Picture Palace* is equally idiomatically alive, page by page, as Maude satirizes the new photographers with their highest priced equipment:

> These faddists of high contrast and golf-ball grain could shoot fly spit, the smell of an onion, sunspots, a virus picking its nose, bazooka shells bursting out of gun muzzles, indigestion, a fart in a mitten.

Or a new Japanese camera "so small you could swallow it at noon and photograph your breakfast." Or Arbus-inspired girl photographers who tell Maude that they're "into freaks, because it represents how I feel as a woman" and whom she (and surely Theroux) see as "like amateur assassins whose parents gave them a gun for Christmas: they brought me their victims." *Picture Palace* shares with Susan Sontag's recent *On Photography*, many moral and cultural reservations (to put it mildly) about taking pictures, but Theroux feels rather more inwards with the activity than does Sontag, and he is a lot more fun, as when Maude makes a scornful list of photographic clichés:

> Abandoned Playground, Rainy Street, Lady in Funny Hat, Torso with Tits, Shoeshine Boy, Honest Face, Drunken Bum, Prostitute in Slit Skirt Standing near *Rooms* Sign, Mr. and Mrs. Front Porch America . . . Haggard Peckerwoods, Every Hair of a Bush Beard, Spoiled Brat, Good-Humor Ice Cream Man, Country Road Leading to Bright Future, Muddy Field in Europe . . . Obviously Unemployed Man in his Undershirt, Dog Lover, Wrinkled Eskimo, Mother and Child, Jazzman with Shiny Instrument . . .

"You could see more exciting things . . . by sticking your head out the window," Maude snorts.

It's true that incest is the most heavily-used of literary themes, but it seems to me no more damaging here, with its theatrical heightening of experience, than in Faulkner or Ivy Compton-Burnett. It's all just a story, dazzlingly and intensely told, with the great modern fictional classics—James and Conrad and Ford and Faulkner, and Graham Greene too—giving Theroux ballast for the idea that the telling is enough. I think it is, because he never lets up, never writes a paragraph of filler or "transition" which has less than his full presence as a writer behind it. *Picture Palace* is another impressive testimony that as a steadily producing writer of long and short fiction, travel books, essays and reviews—of "letters" generally—no American writer matters more than this gifted and possessed word-man.—WILLIAM H. PRITCHARD, "Telling Stories," *HdR*, Autumn 1978, pp. 527–29

V. S. PRITCHETT
"On the Tracks"

New Statesman, October 17, 1975, pp. 474–76

Paul Theroux is a train-lover, though not one of those who dote only on puff-puffs on the branch line to Little Gidding. He wanted to suffer on those long bazaars or ramshackle supermarkets that snake along from one desperate frontier to another, eastward across Europe into the smells of Asia, hauling alleged sleeping cars and imaginary diners. He started off ⟨in *The Great Railway Bazaar*⟩ by the legendary Direct Orient—now run down: bring your own food, unless you are living on alcohol. He suffered the Van Gölü express in which Kurds make stews in couchettes and took down the dialogue of the rowdy, sex-starved oilmen of Teheran; skipped across the miseries of Afghanistan in a bus to catch the Khyber Pass Local, hoping it would meet the Khyber Mail to Lahore and the Frontier Mail to Peshawar on which he endured the company of a German heroin addict, argued about tickets and slipped bribes on the way with Tamils to Madras and Ceylon; watched the frantic dive through carriage windows in Rangoon; crawled up into sex-mad Thailand, descended to the rubber planters who have perfected the classic stance of the railway drinker as they raise a post-Maughamish glass to 'absent friends' on the way to Singapore. Then, by air, on to Japan, its odourless trains and bloody horror shows—until at last he turned homewards on the long day's night of the Trans-Siberian. His journey proves that round the world on a set of bogies is a thousand times more picturesque than 'round the world on a wheel', a coach or a plane.

For, in its dereliction, the railway offers what up-to-date forms of travel cut us off from: passengers. There is an instant meeting with the desperate, anxious, boasting, confessional, jabbering hopefuls and casualties of the modern world. We are not palmed off with national customs and crafts, public problems: we see private life as it screams at this very hour, sweating out the universal anxiety, the conglomerate Absurd. This is what Paul Theroux, with the eyes and ears of the novelist and the avidity of the responsive traveller, brings home to us, awaking us to horror, laughter, compassion at the sight of the shameless private will to live. His book is the most vigorous piece of travel among people I have read for years.

It is a good sign that when he wanted respite he stopped looking out of the window and read *Little Dorrit*: on long trains one needs long books. He has Dickens's gift for getting the character of a man or woman in a flash, of discovering the fantasies and language of the food-stained bores who settled upon him. We understand why poor old Mr Duffill, who treads on the cuffs of his trousers at Victoria, smells of bread crusts and travels with paper parcels, will get left behind at the Italian frontier—not so much from incompetence but because he is fated to have fits of sensibility when a train moves off as he gesticulates with his sandwiches.

The Victorian enemies of railway travel used to warn us that we would find ourselves close to the breath and bodies of people we had not met socially: Mr Theroux leaned eagerly and philosophically towards them. There were, east of Istanbul, the gaping hippies from the suburbs of Baltimore or California on their way to 'hang out' in Nepal or Ceylon 'if it's happening there', craving to go down the sink. Far better value were the dozens of purposeful fanatics, for trains bring out the crank in everybody: the man who is risking all in the sale of fluorescent tubes, or the cunning Mr Pensacola up to no good, perhaps in the opium traffic, a Thai with an eye—as he puts it—who knows what he's doing when he throws a police captain's suitcase off his berth: 'I bet he wasn't very happy,' suggested Mr Theroux.

> 'Was cross. "Who was You?" he said to me. "A traveller" I said. "What do you do?" "Travel". He got very annoyed and asked me for my ID card. I said "No ID card." Later on he went to bed—I made him take the upper berth. But he couldn't sleep. All night he was tossing back and forth. Holding his head and what and what'.
>
> 'I bet that upset him.'
>
> 'I don't know. Something like that. He was trying to think who I am.'
>
> 'I am trying to think the same thing.'

Or, for an instance of Mr Theroux's sardonic mastery of the conversation of official groups, there is a beautiful piece of circular exposition by the leader of a band of family planners. It is too long to quote, but the following lines show the planning brain, self-entranced:

> 'We must build a model—work with a model of aims and objectives. What are we trying to do? What do we aim to achieve? And why? And costings must be considered . . . Then, next important, is areas of information' . . . he spread his hands to suggest the size of the areas—'that is we must create areas of information. You can understand the importance of our work.'

The happy officials were unrepentant fathers of sizable families—or areas—themselves.

As for the changing scene: Mr Theroux is brief and vivid on the view from the window. He is especially fine on the mixture of magnificence and abandoned ironmongery in Laos. His generalised grasp of cities is always to the contemporary point. Take Bangkok, where there are not only bored inhabitants but the sexy hopes of the locusts of tourism: here indeed is the modern world:

> A hugely preposterous city of temples and brothels, it required visitors. The heat, the traffic, the noise, the cost in this flattened anthill make it intolerable to live in; but Bangkok, whose discomfort seems a calculated discouragement to residents, is a city of transients. It has managed to maintain its massage parlour economy without the soldiers, by advertising itself as a place where even the most diffident foreigner can get laid. So it prospers. After the early morning Market Tour and the afternoon Temple Tour, comes the evening Casanova Tour. Patient couples, many of them elderly, wearing badges saying *Orient Escapade*, are herded off to sex shows, blue movies and 'live shows' to put them in a mood for a visit later on in the same evening—if they're game—to a whorehouse. As Calcutta smells of death and Bombay of money, Bangkok smells of sex—but this sexual aroma is mingled with the sharper whiffs of money. Bangkok has an aspect of violation.

Only in Singapore—where Mr Theroux was once a teacher—does he sound depressed and catch the public worry and silenced indignation that grows nowadays when we are not on the move. The whole book is more than a rich and original entertainment. His people, places and asides will stay a long time jostling in the mind of the reader.

PAUL FUSSELL
"On the Go Again"

New York Times Book Review, August 26, 1979, pp. 1, 24–25

One of the casualties of travel by jet, together with civilized cuisine and the notion that people are not sardines, is the old-style travel book, the sort that used to be written by Norman Douglas and D. H. Lawrence and John Dos Passos and Graham Greene and Evelyn Waugh. The guide book, compiled by committees under the supervision of Eugene Fodor or Temple Fielding, has "replaced" the travel book. We now have books instructing us how to save money and time; but with rare exceptions, such as Herbert Kubly's *Stranger in Italy* (1956), we have few any more that satisfy the requirements laid down by Norman Douglas 50 years ago: "The reader of a good travel-book is entitled not only to an exterior voyage, to descriptions of scenery and so forth, but to an interior, a sentimental or temperamental voyage, which takes place side by side with that outer one; . . . the ideal book of this kind offers us, indeed, a triple opportunity of exploration—abroad, into the author's brain, and into our own. The writer should therefore possess a brain worth exploring; some philosophy of life—not necessarily, though by preference, of his own forging—and the courage to proclaim it and put it to the test; he must be naïf and profound, both child and sage." A book Douglas would have liked was Paul Theroux's *The Great Railway Bazaar* of four years ago, his account of a rail trip from London to Japan and back again, full of characters, scandals and disasters.

In this new book ⟨*The Old Patagonian Express*⟩ Theroux has attempted a replay, offering up a narrative of a masochistic two-month rail journey from his parents' house in Medford, Mass., all the way through Mexico and Central America to the southern tip of South America, the remote and barren Patagonia celebrated two years ago by Theroux's friend Bruce Chatwin in his excellent *In Patagonia*, another book Douglas would approve.

If this sequel—it must be called that—is not so delightful as *The Great Railway Bazaar*, the fault is as much geography's as Theroux's. Europe and Asia are a richer venue for this sort of thing than Latin America, which by contrast lacks character, deep literary and historical associations, and variety. For anyone experienced with Europe, it is desperately boring. Squalor in Mexico is identical to squalor in El Salvador; the ghastly Mexican town Papaloapán is too much like the horrible Costa Rican town Limón, 600 miles farther south. Illiteracy here is like illiteracy there. As Theroux proceeds, things do get worse, but not dramatically worse: "Since leaving the United States," he writes, "I had not seen a dog that wasn't lame, or a woman who wasn't carrying something. . . ." He seems aware that his sequel isn't quite up to the original, alluding to poor Jack Kerouac, fat and 50, trying to re-experience *On the Road* by hitchhiking West many years later. "Times had changed. The lugubrious man reached New Jersey; there he stood for hours in the rain, trying to thumb a ride, until at last he gave up and took a bus home."

Paul Theroux does not give up, although often he is brought close to despair. On a Mexican train he sees: "Two classes: both uncomfortable and dirty. No privacy, no relief. Constant stopping and starting, broken engine, howling passengers. On days like this I wonder why I bother: leaving order and friends for disorder and strangers. . . . Impossible to get comfortable in this seat. A jail atmosphere: the brown walls and dim light of the condemned cell." He is proud to be traveling alone, but now and then he miserably confronts his loneliness, as when he reads Donne and finds him saying, "The greatest misery of sickness is solitude. . . . Solitude is a torment which is not threatened in hell itself."

In addition, Theroux is crawled over by flies, roaches and rats; he cuts his hand and gets a diarrhea so violent that even his British "cement" won't arrest it; he suffers agonies from altitude-sickness crossing the Andes and relieves it only by squirting the contents of an oxygen-filled balloon (sold by a vendor on the train) into his mouth. By the time he's reached Ecuador he perceives that all decent people either drive or fly:

"I had been in Latin America long enough by now to know that there was a class stigma attached to the trains. Only the semidestitute, the limpers, the barefoot ones, the Indians, and the half-cracked yokels took the trains, or knew anything about them." In northern Argentina his train sits at a deserted platform. "There were orange peels and banana skins under every window . . . water poured from beneath the coaches, and there were heaps of [excrement] under each toilet pipe. The sun had grown stronger, and flies collected. . . ." A woman walking along the platform says to her nicely dressed friend: "This is the train to Tucumán—it came all the way from Bolivia. Aren't you glad we came by car?"

Like good conversation, a good travel book consists of two kinds of materials: narrative (including dialogue) and comment. Theroux's comments come in the form of little 300-word essays: on the Chisholm Trail, the ghastliness of Fort Worth, the wetback problem, the career of Juárez, the inferiority of Ambrose Bierce to Jonathan Swift (why the surprise?), and the inappropriateness of Latin American place names, such as Progreso in Guatemala and La Libertad in El Salvador. We are given essays (some of them a bit self-righteous and stiff) on the history of Guatemala, human sacrifice in 19th-century El Salvador, the curious secularism of Costa Rica, American colonial life in the "company town" of the Panama Canal Zone (it's like being in the army), the building of the Canal, Inca Culture and the drug traffic in Barranquilla, Colombia.

Interesting as these excursions are, Theroux's narrative is better—his rendering of a combined soccer game and riot in San Salvador is superb—and his dialogue is best of all. In Veracruz, he mees a middle-aged American divorcée who tells him about her terrible husbands, one "violent," the next "a bum" who has tried to squeeze alimony from her, because she has money. "*I'm* supposed to pay *him!*"

"What sort of business are you in?" Theroux asks.

"'I own slums,' she said. 'Fifty-seven of them—I mean, fifty-seven units. . . . God's been good to me.'"

In Costa Rica he meets a traveling American, Mr. Thornberry, who can't resist designating aloud everything seen through the train window: "Sawmill." "Pool of water." "Pipeline." "Poverty." "Bananas." "Pigs." "Pretty girl." "Kids playing." "Pipeline again."

But the finest dialogue of all is Theroux's conversation with Jorge Luis Borges. On his terrible trains Theroux has been solacing himself by reading Boswell's *Life of Johnson*, which, he says, "became my life line. There was no landscape in it. I had all the landscape I wanted out the window. What I lacked was talk, and this was a brilliant talk, sage advice, funny remarks. . . . I think if I had not had that book to read as I made my way through Colombia, the trip would have been unendurable." Looking out the window, he calls up such Johnsonian observations as this: "Where a great Proportion of the people are suffered to languish in helpless misery, that country must be ill-policed and wretchedly governed: a decent provision for the poor is the true test of civilization." Agonizing on the hard railway seats, hot, half-starved and wholly miserable, Theroux agrees with Johnson's finding that "there was more to be endured than enjoyed, in the general condition of human life." In Buenos Aires, Theroux is thoroughly primed to play Boswell to Borges's Johnson, and the resulting conversations constitute a delightful climax, a triumphant overflow of civility and intelligence after all the brutality and stupidity.

Borges is happy to meet Theroux because he admires an essay on Kipling that Theroux has just published. And Theroux realizes the magic of walking down a street in Buenos Aires with the blind Borges, "like being led through Alexandria by Cavafy, or through Lahore by Kipling. The city belonged to him, and he had had a hand in inventing it."

Theroux may Johnsonize Borges a bit, but he reports him saying some fine things: "People respect soldiers. That's why no one really thinks much of the Americans. If America were a military power instead of a commercial empire, people would look up to it. Who respects businessmen? No one. People look at America and all they see are traveling salesmen. So they laugh." On the Peróns: "He looted the country. His wife was a prostitute." "Evita?" Theroux asks. "A common prostitute." (Cf. Johnson: "The woman's a whore, and there's an end on't.") "As he fished out his door key," says Theroux, "I asked him about Patagonia."

"'I have been there,' he said. 'But I don't know it well. I'll tell you this, though. It's a dreary place. A very dreary place.'

"'I was planning to take the train tomorrow.'

"'Don't go tomorrow. Come and see me. . . .'

"'I suppose I can go to Patagonia next week.'

"'It's dreary,' said Borges. He had got the door open, and now he shuffled to the elevator and pulled open its metal gates. 'The gate of the hundred sorrows,' he said, and entered chuckling."

Theroux finds that Borges has been right about Patagonia when he comes to the end of his journey, the town of Esquel, Southern Argentina. He arrives there on the final "teeny-weeny steam train," the "Old Patagonian Express." He has arrived precisely at Nowhere, at "enormous empty spaces." "The nothingness itself," he concludes, "a beginning for some intrepid traveler, was an ending for me. I had arrived in Patagonia, and I laughed when I remembered I had come here from Boston, on the subway train that people took to work."

But except for the Borges episode, the reader gets little relief from the horrors and boredom. He misses the sheer joy of the anomalous, which surfaced frequently in *The Great Railway Bazaar*. Here Theroux is exhausted. Outraged by Latin America, he picks quarrels, depicts himself winning arguments, allows his liberal moral superiority to grow strident. He seems to think we have to be told that people should not starve or live in filth. Even though he knows he's doing these things ("I was sick of lecturing people on disorder"), he can't help himself, and sometimes the unpleasant effect threatens the reader's pleasure in Theroux's sharp eye, which is capable of such shrewd perceptions: he notices that an American on the train is wearing "the sort of woollen plaid forester's shirt that graduate students in state universities especially favor"; that in Peru "the Indians have a broad-based look, like chess pieces"; that the terrain outside the train window, at one low point, looks like a "world of kitty litter"; and that in the dark, "in one field, five white cows were as luminous as laundry."

In the former days of the travel book, Greene and Waugh would tour through horrors and make them something other than occasions for mere superior disgust. Their sympathy was wider than Theroux's, their involvement in history was deeper, and perhaps their knowledge of themselves was more profound. Theroux never says of the messes he observes: "That's me." And thus he fails to take us a sufficient distance (as Douglas would require) into our own brain. That's the ultimate weakness of this otherwise interesting performance: it's morally facile. But it has some wonderful things in it, and the encounter with Borges is alone worth the price of the book.

JONATHAN RABAN

"Theroux's Wonderful, Bottomless Novel"

Saturday Review, February 1982, pp. 55–56

One needs energy to keep up with the extraordinary, productive restlessness of Paul Theroux. He is alarmingly like the perpetual motion machine described in his new novel ("natural magnets . . . a thousand of them on a pair of wheels . . . you could light a city with something like that"), except that Theroux doesn't go in circles and has never moved in a predictable direction.

He is as busy as a jackdaw in the way he scavenges for forms and styles. In earlier novels he has taken conventional popular molds, like the ghost story *(The Black House)*, the thriller *(The Family Arsenal)*, the celebrity memoir *(Picture Palace)*, and made them over for his own thoroughly original purposes. The geographic locations of his tales now make an almost unbroken ring around the globe. His train journeys *(The Great Railway Bazaar, The Old Patagonian Express)* are best read as freewheeling, impromptu fictions—the adventures of a picaresque hero who happens to bear the same name as his author and who shares his author's chronic cabin fever.

Theroux is 40 now—the most gifted, most prodigal writer of his generation. That statement begs a significant question. When, say, Malamud, Mailer, Updike, or Roth were 40, one could have spotted a stray paragraph from any of their books as "typically" Malamud, Mailer, Updike, or Roth. Can one do the same with Theroux? I couldn't. He has moved in skips and bounds, never staying long enough in one place for the moss of a mannered style to grow on his writing. Even in the most trivial ways, he ducks classification. For his jacket photographs, he favors sunglasses that give him a rather nasty resemblance to one of the inscrutable henchmen of Papa Doc. He looks as if being unknowable is an essential part of his profession. In the United States, I have actually heard him spoken of as a "British" writer. In England, he is the rogue American on our doorstep. Disguised behind his shades, following an eccentric private route at dizzying speed, he is not a man who is easily nailed down.

Yet with *The Mosquito Coast* he has arrived at a temporary summation. This is not just his finest novel so far. It is—in a characteristically hooded way—a novelist's act of self-definition, a midterm appraisal of his own resources. It is a wonderful book, with so many levels to it that it feels bottomless.

In Allie Fox, Theroux has created his first epic hero. If one can imagine an American tradition that takes in Benjamin Franklin, Captain Ahab, Huey Long, and the Reverend Jim Jones, then Allie Fox is its latest, most complete incarnation. He is the King of Yankee know-how and know-all, an inventor of inspired gizmos—from a self-propelled, self-wringing mop to a machine that makes ice out of fire. He is a genius, clown, and monster, a commander of words, an angry demagogue. Listening to no one but himself, he leads his family out of the wilderness of modern America—its junk foods, imported plastics, and "hideola"—to create a new world in the bug-infested jungle of Honduras.

To his wife and children, and to a bedraggled cluster of starving sidekicks in both Americas, Allie Fox, devout atheist, is little short of God Himself. And *The Mosquito Coast* is the gospel according to his son, Charlie. The novel tells two perfectly interwoven stories. The first is of how Allie Fox leads his little flock up to the precipice of madness and beyond. The second is of how Charlie slowly emerges from the shadow of his father's divinity into the cold, frightening light of skepticism and sorrow. Out of the twin stories, Theroux has made a novel that has the richness, simplicity, and power of myth.

Even in the barest outline, *The Mosquito Coast* sets up a whole series of suggestive ripples. Jonestown is there, of course: the foul clearing, the loudspeakers in the trees, the piled cadavers, the spools of recording tape. Beyond that, there is *the* original American story: the stale Old World, the sea crossing, the Indians, the "first Thanksgiving" as Allie Fox himself names it. Then there is a universal fable about the nature of godhead and belief. Finally, and much the most important, there is a tale here about the limits and possibilities of the creative imagination. Allie Fox is very like a novelist. He is an inventor. He makes and populates a world with an artist's totalitarian joy in his creation, bending everything and everyone in it to the requirements of his aesthetic design. At the end, it turns on him and he is literally consumed by it, as vultures tear out the very brains that set the world in motion. Fox's great imaginative enterprise both mirrors and mocks the creations of Theroux the novelist: The overreaching hero and the writer are one and the same man.

I mustn't mislead here. These big themes (and one could hardly imagine bigger ones) are never proclaimed in the novel. They run deep, like subterranean rivers, nourishing the life of the book's surface. For, reading *The Mosquito Coast*, one is engrossed in a marvelously told realistic story. It is a measure of the obsessive exactitude of Theroux's writing that there is not a page in the book in which one doesn't know the particular color of the sky, the texture of the earth underfoot, the cast of a face, the rhythm of a voice. In simile after simile, these physical details spring from the print, exuberantly real. Here are "strips of glue-colored cloud" . . . "a tortoise-shell twilight"; pelicans go overhead "like a squadron of hedge-clippers"; a breaking sea looks "like whitewash hosed over black ice" . . . and so one could go on. This is an invented world that one can live in, smell, see, touch; and a style of writing so easy and precise that one reads through it like a transparent pane of glass.

The same loving particularity is what makes Allie Fox such an enthralling creation. Geniuses are notoriously hard to depict, but Fox—a cursed genius if ever there was one—is so solidly done that you can catch the stink of his armpits. Flaubert once boasted that he had gutted several hundred popular encyclopedias to write *Bouvard et Pécuchet*. Heaven knows what research Theroux has put into the construction of Allie Fox. For Fox knows *everything:* hydraulics . . . electronics . . . physics . . . navigation . . . chemistry . . . astronomy. Joking and hectoring by turns, he swaggers through the book, giving out what Hemingway called "the true gen" on every subject under the sun. One believes him, too. When he builds his ice machine, or rights a listing ship, his schemes always have the ring of authority and good sense. He is obstreperously plausible. He has a thing or two to teach every reader of this book. And so one finds oneself submitting, like Charlie Fox, to Allie's extraordinary capacity to spellbind and bludgeon.

That is part of Theroux's secret. He has rooted his story deep in the reasonable—in sense impressions that we can all share, in knowledge we can ascertain. All the nuts and bolts are secure. And from that stable platform, the novel is able to take off like a rocket into the empyrean. From the dingy familiarity of a hardware store in Northampton, Massachusetts, to a grotesque and tragic climax in the jungle, Theroux leads the reader cunningly on, step by reasonable step, reaching the exotic by means of the ordinary.

Here, too, the writer and his hero are in collusion. For that, of course, is just what Allie Fox does. Explaining his perpetual motion machine to the ship's captain, he says:

> Strictly speaking there is no such thing as invention. It's not creation, I mean. It's just magnifying what already exists. Making ends meet. They could teach it in school—Edison wanted to make invention a school subject, like civics or French. But the schools went for fingerpainting. . . .

Magnifying what already exists. Making ends meet. It is a prescription for making ice, or perpetual motion, or living nightmares. The Honduran hell that is Allie Fox's last act of invention is only a modest magnification of the commonplace social world he leaves behind in Massachusetts. Allie Fox himself is a magnification, no more, of the inventor who made him, Paul Theroux. If one bass-line runs consistently through *The Mosquito Coast*, it warns that to possess an imagination is to have a very dangerous faculty indeed. It brings one uncomfortably close to being both a god and a madman.

There is another deep satiric irony in the book. In the early days of his colonial venture, Allie Fox is a worker of famous wonders. He makes miracles for the tribesmen—ice, water, fire, explosions, giant vegetables. The locals come to gaze and marvel, much as readers do. Fox gets good reviews. In the argot of the swampland, a name is coined to describe Allie's fabulous inventions. His "experiments" are described as "spearmints"; and the word returns them straight back to the junk and "hideola" from which they were intended to be a triumphant escape. That is a fate that's known as well by novelists as by inventors. Never, though, mistake *The Mosquito Coast* for a gum wrapper. You could light a city with it, and make ice too.

HUNTER S. THOMPSON

1939–

Hunter S. Thompson was born on July 18, 1939, in Louisville, Kentucky, to Jack and Virginia Ray Thompson. He attended public schools in Louisville but did not attend college. From 1956 to 1958 he served in the Air Force. He married Sandra Dawn in 1963; they have one child. From 1959 to 1960 he worked as Caribbean correspondent for the *New York Herald-Tribune*, then as South American correspondent for the *National Observer* from 1961 to 1963. He was national affairs editor for *Rolling Stone* from 1969 to 1974, sometimes simultaneously appearing on the masthead of that publication under a pseudonym as sportswriter Raoul Duke.

Thompson has been a shaping force in the New Journalism; though not as prolific as journalist Tom Wolfe, he is the only writer of comparable stature and influence in that subgenre. His first book, *Hell's Angels: A Strange and Terrible Saga* (1966), examined the Hell's Angels motorcycle gang as a product and extension of modern American society. *Fear and Loathing in Las Vegas* (1972) is perhaps Thompson's best-known and most influential work. Beginning ostensibly as a sportswriter's report of a desert motorcycle race, it is the preeminent example of the writing style Thompson calls "gonzo journalism," in which events and personalities are hyperbolically exaggerated, distorted, fictionalized, and mythologized to the point of surreal caricature. The persona of the narrator undergoes similar transformations; within the narrative, which is written as if it were an ongoing dictation of immediate events, these dislocations are attributed to the influence of a wide variety of drugs. *Fear and Loathing: On the Campaign Trail '72* (1973) is an account of the 1972 presidential elections, written in a similar style. *The Great Shark Hunt* (1979) is a collection of Thompson's essays and shorter journalism, and *The Curse of Longo* (1985) is a short novel about Thompson's adventures in Hawaii with illustrator Ralph Steadman.

The change in journalism in the sixties showed itself more spectacularly on the fringes than at the center of established institutions. The so-called New Journalism, or "parajournalism," as its critics labeled it, developed parallel to the chief organs of information, influencing them only subtly and gradually, in tandem with the influence of the age. By New Journalism I don't simply mean Tom Wolfe and his crowd of imitators, or even the larger group canonized by Wolfe in his 1973 anthology *The New Journalism*, but a wider range of defections from the journalistic gospel—aberrations that were responsive to the cultural tone of the sixties and even helped set that tone. This work included a broad spectrum of underground writing—political, countercultural, feminist, pornographic, and so on—that dealt with cultural developments ignored, distorted, or merely exploited by the established media. ⟨. . .⟩

What these different strands of writing shared was the range of things traditional journalism left out: atmosphere, personal feeling, interpretation, advocacy and opinion, novelistic characterization and description, touches of obscenity, concern with fashion and cultural change, and political savvy. Sometimes these writers developed a new voice *simply* by including the forbidden, not only the forbidden subject but more often the device or approach forbidden by the older journalistic code. Thus Hunter Thompson learned to approximate the effect of mind-blasting drugs in his prose style, especially in his book on Las Vegas. More successfully in 1972 he affronted the taboos of political writing, and recorded the nuts and bolts of a presidential campaign with all the contempt and incredulity that other reporters must feel but censor out. The result was the kind of straightforward, uninhibited intelligence that showed up the timidities and clichés that dominated the field. But in high gear Thompson paraded one of the few original prose styles of recent years, a style dependent almost deliriously on insult, vituperation, and stream-of-invective to a degree unparalleled since Céline.—MORRIS DICKSTEIN, "The Working Press, the Literary Culture, and the New Journalism," *Gates of Eden: American Culture in the Sixties*, 1977, pp. 132–33

JEROME KLINKOWITZ
From "Hunter S. Thompson"
The Life of Fiction
1977, pp. 32–43

I. Hunter S. Thompson Is Not a Journalist

One problem with Hunter Thompson is simply, as the *Newsweek* slogan goes, that of separating fact from fiction.—*Columbia Journalism Review*

The President was not immediately available for comment on how he planned to spend his forty-five Big Ones, but Stans said he planned to safeguard the funds personally.

At that point, McGregor cracked Stans upside the head with a Gideon Bible and called him a "thieving little fart." McGregor then began shoving the rest of us out of the room, but when Stans tried to leave, McGregor grabbed him by the neck and jerked him back inside. Then he slammed the door and threw the bolt . . .

Jesus, why do I write things like that? I must be getting sick, or maybe just tired of writing about these greasy Rotarian bastards. I think it's time to move on to something else.—Hunter S. Thompson, *Fear and Loathing: On the Campaign Trail '72* (San Francisco: Straight Arrow Books, 1973)

In the context of journalism, here, we are dealing with a new kind of "lead"—the Symbiotic Trapezoid Quote. The *Columbia Journalism Review* will never sanction it; at least not until the current editor dies of brain syphilis, and probably not even then.

What?

Do we have a libel suit on our hands?

> THUMP! Against the door. Another goddam newspaper, another cruel accusation. THUMP! Day after day, it never ends. . . . Hiss at the alarm clock, suck up the headlines along with a beaker of warm Drano, then off to the morning class. . . . To teach Journalism: Circulation, Distribution, Headline Counting and the classical Pyramid Lead.—Hunter S. Thompson, "The Boys in the Bag," *Rolling Stone* #164 (7/4/74)

Some make the case that Hunter S. Thompson is a New Journalist, as Tom Wolfe uses the term. Thompson is so only to the extent that he employs some methods of traditional fiction to present his otherwise documentary material. In his critical anthology, *The New Journalism* (New York: Harper & Row, 1973), Wolfe argues that "Fiction writers, currently, are busy running backward, skipping and screaming, into a begonia patch that I call Neo-Fabulism." He adds that "the retrograde state of contemporary fiction" makes it easier to defend his own thesis: "that the most important literature being written in America today is non-fiction, in the form that has been tagged, however ungracefully, the New Journalism."

⟨. . .⟩ The American Sixties, Wolfe insists, "was one of the most extraordinary decades in American history in terms of manners and morals." Therefore the techniques of the mannerists and moralists, which were discarded by the new fictionists, would have to be resurrected by the New Journalists in order to craft the definitive literary work of our time. And among the New Journalists Wolfe includes Hunter S. Thompson. But Thompson's methods, as we shall see, go beyond traditional fiction into those of more innovative art—techniques and styles tasting more of Sukenick and Katz than of Fielding and Thackeray. Plus he identifies with (and even becomes a part of) the action more than does Tom Wolfe or most of the other New Journalists. Thompson calls his new style "Gonzo Journalism," and its effect discredits Wolfe's thesis that the techniques of recent fiction are inappropriate for the serious literature of our age.

Thompson began this style with *Hell's Angels: A Strange and Terrible Saga* (New York: Random House, 1967). As he describes it, "By the middle of summer I had become so involved in the outlaw scene that I was no longer sure whether I was doing research on the Hell's Angels or being slowly absorbed by them." Yet Thompson maintains an interesting tension: despite his sympathy and identification with the Hell's Angels outrages, he constantly views them from a middle-class perspective. The values and sensibilities of Southern California's solid citizens are the backdrop for everything that Thompson has the outlaws do. If there is a literary style involved here, it's not that of Balzac or Trollope, but of Fitzgerald having Nick Carraway reserve judgment all the way until his final absorption into Gatsby. But as a SuperFictionist Thompson plays a tougher game than a Modernist character.

For one, there is the baiting. Covering the Kentucky Derby for *Scanlan's*, Thompson recounts his barroom conversation with a visiting Texan:

> I shook my head and said nothing; just stared at him for a moment, trying to look grim. "There's going to be trouble," I said. "My assignment is to take pictures of the riot."
>
> "What riot?"
>
> I hesitated, twirling the ice in my drink. "At the track. On Derby Day. The Black Panthers." I stared at him again. "Don't you read the newspapers?"
>
> The grin on his face had collapsed. "What the *hell* are you talkin about?"
>
> "Well . . . maybe I shouldn't be telling you. . . ." I shrugged. "But hell, everybody else seems to know. The cops and the National Guard have been getting ready for six weeks. They have 20,000 troops on alert at Fort Knox. They've warned us—all the press and photographers—to wear helmets and special vests like flak jackets. We were told to expect shooting. . . ."

Another variation is Thompson's use of his British illustrator friend Ralph Steadman, to whom Thompson can play off his tales of rampage and paranoia against a chorus of "That's teddible, teddible." The Derby was Steadman's first visit to the U.S., allowing Thompson a conservative backdrop when the staid citizens themselves became more loony and depraved than the outlaw bikers of the Hell's Angels book. It all ends with Thompson driving his colleague to the airport:

> Huge Pontiac Ballbuster blowing through traffic on the expressway. The journalist is driving, ignoring his passenger who is now nearly naked after taking off most of his clothing, which he holds out the window, trying to wind-wash the Mace out of it. His eyes are bright red and his face and chest are soaked with the beer he's been using to rinse the awful chemical off his flesh. The front of his woolen trousers is soaked with vomit; his body is racked with fits of coughing and wild choking sobs. The journalist rams the big car through traffic and into a spot in front of the terminal, then he reaches over to open the door on the passenger's side and shoves the Englishman out, snarling: "Bug off, you worthless faggot! You twisted pigfucker! [Crazed laughter.] If I weren't sick I'd kick your ass all the way to Bowling Green—you scumsucking foreign geek. Mace is too good for you. . . . We can do without your kind in Kentucky."

Finally, Thompson stretches another Fitzgerald technique, that of simultaneously leading the parade and heckling oneself from the curb, to capture the spirit of the age in himself. He turns himself into a laboratory for the study of what's going on in contemporary America. *Fear and Loathing in Las Vegas* (New York: Random House, 1972) captures the essence of this in Thompson's favorite drug for the occasion, ether. "This is the main advantage of ether: it makes you behave like the village drunkard in some early Irish novel . . . total loss of all basic motor skills: blurred vision, no balance, numb tongue—severance of all connection between body and the brain. Which is interesting," Thompson stresses, "because the brain continues to function more or less normally . . . you can actually *watch* yourself behaving in this terrible way, but you can't control it." ⟨. . .⟩

III. Superfiction (Take One)

Thompson does more than his colleagues who adapt the literary conventions of the eighteenth century to modern life in order to produce the New Journalism. Beyond this, he uses techniques of contemporary innovative fiction, and gets results similar to Sukenick's *Out*, Katz's *Saw*, or Barthelme's *Snow White*. For one thing, he details the action with the speed and effect of a drug rush, with no surrender to credibility once the circus is underway. "Terrible things were happening all around us," he claims in *Fear and Loathing in Las Vegas* as he tries to settle down for a drink in the hotel lounge. "Right next to me a huge reptile was gnawing on a woman's neck, the carpet was a blood-soaked sponge—impossible to walk on, no footing at all. 'Order some golf shoes,' I whispered. 'Otherwise, we'll never get out of this place alive. You notice these lizards don't have any trouble moving around in this muck—that's because they have *claws* on their feet.'" Still more: "'We're right in the middle of a fucking reptile zoo! And somebody's giving *booze* to these goddam things! It won't be long before they tear us to shreds. Jesus, look at the floor! Have you ever *seen* so much blood? How many have they killed already?' I pointed across the room to a group that seemed to be staring at us. 'Holy shit, look at that bunch over there! They've spotted us!' 'That's the press table,' he said."

Another innovative technique is the collage method: in *Hell's Angels* Thompson incorporates verbatim, in their own form, quotes from *True Magazine*, the New York *Times*, personal comments from various observers, the Finch Report from the California attorney general's office, and so forth—all spatially organized as a graphic comment on the action. In his Superbowl coverage (*Rolling Stone* #155, 2/28/74) Thompson adds even more, with interpolations of tapes, letters, phone calls, news clippings, and fragments from the Old Testament prophets hurled in sermons from the twentieth-floor mezzanine of the Houston Hyatt Regency ("'Beware,' I shouted, 'for the Devils also believe, and tremble!'"). And occasionally an epigraph from Milton or Dr. Samuel Johnson. "He who makes a beast of himself gets rid of the pain of being a man" is a favorite, cited many times.

But the key method which makes Hunter S. Thompson a SuperFictionist on the order of Sukenick and Katz is the self-reflexive manner of his work. He never disguises the fact that he is a half-cranked geek journalist caught in the center of the action. Right in the middle of a story he will often break down, but the breakdown itself carries much of the "information" about the country of the writer's own imagination which he is, like Sukenick, reporting. "Television can best give us the news, fiction gives us *our response* to the news," Sukenick has said in a statement which describes Thompson's work as well as his own.

The method is first used in *Fear and Loathing in Las Vegas* (which was published in *Rolling Stone* under the name of Thompson's alternate persona, Raoul Duke). Chapter Nine begins, "At this point in the chronology, Dr. Duke appears to have broken down completely; the original manuscript is so splintered that we were forced to seek out the original tape recording and transcribe it verbatim. We made no attempt to edit this section, and Dr. Duke refused even to read it." Thompson uses the technique several times in his campaign book (originally a year's worth of articles printed month by month in *Rolling Stone*), where under the pressure of deadlines he would resort to "tearing my Ohio primary notebook apart and sending about fifty pages of scribbled shorthand notes straight to the typesetter." At times the manner is old-fashioned *cinéma vérité* ("Damn! Fuck! I can't believe those fuckin' helicopters! I'll leave it on the tape just to remind me how bad it was"), and elsewhere it is just comic—in "Rude Notes from a Decompression Chamber in Miami" (*Rolling Stone* #140, 8/2/73) Thompson sends his reports out by a nurse "who copied Dr. Thompson's notes as he held them up, page by page, through the pressure-sealed window of his Chamber" where he was recovering from the bends.

The best example is from his Watergate coverage (*Rolling Stone* #144, 9/27/73). Any possible tedium in Thompson's twenty-one-page piece is relieved when the author himself comes apart. "Due to circumstances beyond our control," reads an editor's note midway through, "the following section was lashed together at the last moment from a six-pound bundle of documents, notebooks, memos, recordings and secretly taped phone conversations with Dr. Thompson during a month of erratic behavior in Washington, New York, Colorado and Miami." This is a second-power use of Thompson's own collage and breakdown methods. The one reinforces the other, and along the way his personality-at-the-center-of-the-action is given further embellishment: "His 'long-range plan,' he says, is to 'refine' these nerve-wracking methods, somehow, and eventually 'create an entirely new form of journalism.' In the meantime, we have suspended his monthly retainer and cancelled his credit card. During one four-day period in Washington he destroyed two cars, cracked a wall in the Washington Hilton, purchased two French Horns at $1100 each and ran through a plate-glass door in a Turkish restaurant." ⟨. . .⟩

V. *Superfiction (Take Two)*

Like all of the SuperFictionists, Hunter S. Thompson favors an expressive (as opposed to descriptive) view of life. As we've quoted from Ronald Sukenick, the descriptions of television give us the news, but fictional techniques give us our response to the news; and the truth of things, these writers agree, lies in our response. The value of their work depends, in turn, on how well that response is expressed in writing. "Thucydides is the first New Journalist I know anything about," Kurt Vonnegut, Jr., writes in the preface to his own book of journalism, *Wampeters, Foma, & Granfalloons: Opinions* (New York: Delacorte, 1974). "He was a celebrity who put himself at the center of the truths he was trying to tell, and he guessed when he had to, and he thought it worthwhile to be charming and entertaining. He was a good teacher," Vonnegut emphasizes, and the way for a writer to accomplish this is to put the truth he tells into strikingly human terms—so that his students will remember, and not go to sleep. "I am crazy about Hunter Thompson on that account," Vonnegut confesses. When he reviewed Thompson's campaign book for *Harper's*, Vonnegut described the lapses into paranoia, insult, and frenzy as almost beautiful, as "the literary equivalent of Cubism: All rules are broken; we are shown pictures such as no mature, well-trained artist ever painted before, and in the crazy new pictures we somehow see luminous new aspects of beloved old truths." Sukenick has talked about how banal and insipid and dull we find reality, how the allegedly real world is unreal to us in our inability to relate to it. Vonnegut observes that for Thompson, "reality is killing him, because it is so ugly and cheap." Therefore the Gonzo Journalist/SuperFictionist writes like a person under torture, thrashing about and saying things not expressed in other circumstances. Writers like Thompson, Vonnegut concludes, "are Populists screaming in pain."

"He makes exciting, moving collages of carefully selected junk. They must be experienced. They can't be paraphrased." That's Vonnegut's justification for calling Hunter Thompson the rare sort of American writer who must be read. The same has been said about Donald Barthelme. Vonnegut's analogy with Cubism and Barthelme's analogy with the collage art of Max Ernst tell us what both Gonzo Journalists and SuperFictionists are doing. Like the Cubists, they rearrange our visual censors so that we see all planes—all sides of the story—at once. Like the masters of collage, they take our neatly self-imposed human order and mix in the exotically strange and terrible elements which just may be a crucial part of our lives. Moreover, Thompson amplifies his own work and extends its dimensions—even multiplies its perspectives—so that it may more properly express the "strange and terrible sagas" about which he writes. This technique is more SuperFictional than Journalistic; indeed, it is the very opposite of both conventional journalism and conventional fiction, since it admits that the omniscient and omnipotent writer (whether he be the author of *Tom Jones* or Tom Wolfe himself) holds only a single perspective, which may be inadequate to account for even the complexity of his own vision. Here's how Thompson multiplies himself:

—by making as much of the conditions under which he's writing as he does of the subject matter itself. This is the technique of the self-reflexive novel as written by Gilbert Sorrentino, Ronald Sukenick, Steve Katz, Kurt Vonnegut, Jr., and the other SuperFictionists. There is even a contemporary scientific analogy: that of Heisenberg's Principle of Indeterminacy, whereby the experimenter must include himself as an influence on the experiment. The net result of this candor is a gain in the writing's completeness, beyond the traditional conventions of fiction or journalism.

—by including references to his own mythology as a writer: his extravagant behavior, his experiences with drugs (which in his *Playboy* interview of November 1974 he admits are sometimes fabricated), and his self-created image as the Mad Doctor of Gonzo Journalism. Like Vonnegut with his Kilgore Trout stories, Thompson makes constant reference to tales of madness outside the subject at hand; in his *Rolling Stone* piece endorsing presidential candidate Jimmy Carter (#214, 6/3/76), he gets off the subject for a while by speculating on what would have happened if Nixon had actually lost his mind during the Final Days and ordered a Third World War—"But it is still worth wondering how long it would have taken Haig and Kissinger to convince all those SAC generals out in Omaha to disregard a Doomsday phone call from the president of the United States because a handful of civilians in the White House said he was crazy. Ah . . . but we are wandering off into wild speculation again, so let's chop it off right here." But of course the reader's speculation runs on, because Thompson's incremental fantasy breeds a life of its own, becoming a *Dr. Strangelove* story about the Fall of Richard Nixon which the SuperFictionist can write by only *threatening* to write about it.

The ultimate master of this technique, beyond Thompson and even Vonnegut, may be Jorge Luis Borges, who in the prologue to his *Ficciones* (New York: Grove Press, 1962; originally published in Buenos Aires in 1956) writes that "The composition of vast books is a laborious and impoverishing extravagance. To go on for five hundred pages developing an idea whose perfect oral exposition is possible in a few minutes! A better course is to pretend that these books already exist, and then to offer a résumé, a commentary." Borges cites as examples Carlyle's *Sartor Resartus* and Butler's *The Fair Haven*, peculiar nineteenth-century works which Tom Wolfe avoids, but which in a strange way Hunter Thompson seems to reflect. "I have preferred to write notes upon imaginary books," says Borges. But for Borges and Vonnegut and Thompson, those books and stories and fantasies are born of the writer's own imagination. Hence the system of allusions is fully organic, completely self-contained, and expressive of the fullest dimensions of the writer's mind.

—by dividing his own personality as a writer into mutually exclusive personae. In *Fear and Loathing in Las Vegas* Thompson travels as himself, but arrives under the credit-card pseudonym of Raoul Duke; much of the extravagant behavior is then attributed to Duke (Thompson's own nickname), whom Thompson can properly deplore. Acting and observing at the same time, Thompson also extends his persona to a third level: bringing along his attorney, identified on the dustjacket as Oscar Zeta Acosta, who in the book is made to perform the more outrageous acts which Thompson can amplify and extend by his own expressions of horror and disgust. Still, Acosta *represents* Thompson, giving life to the metaphor of "power of attorney." For the *Las Vegas* book, Acosta is fictionalized, representing more of Thompson's imagination than his own self. Likewise, in Chapters Twelve, Fourteen, and Fifteen of Acosta's *The Autobiography of a Brown Buffalo* (San Francisco: Straight Arrow Books, 1972), Thompson is fictionalized as "Karl King." Acosta uses the same technique of detached astonishment to describe King's/Duke's/Thompson's home in Woody Creek, Colorado, which he stumbles into after his own mad binge on the road:

> I walked into the living room . . . it was the front of the ranch house. One wall was a window. You could see a green meadow with horses and cows at the base of a mountain of green, red, yellow and brown. There were large, thick leather couches around a cartwheel that served as a burnt-oak coffee table. That was normal. Nothing to get excited about.
>
> But did you ever see dried bats with silver needles in their white guts up against the wall? A brown moosehead with blood dripping from its sockets? And how about a stuffed owl with a black rat in its beak and blue policemen's badges for eyes?

The plain facts of Acosta's work as a Chicano lawyer are presented in one of the earliest pieces Thompson wrote for *Rolling Stone*, "Strange Rumblings in Aztlan" (#81, 4/29/71), but the expressive truth of the relationship between these two renegade writers must be found in their *Las Vegas* and *Brown Buffalo* books, which detail their respective lives of fiction.

—by constantly downgrading his own paranoid fantasies in proportion to the raving madness of the so-called straight world. He takes his favorite Vegas casino, the Circus-Circus, and remarks on how it "is what the whole hep world would be doing on Saturday night if the Nazis had won the war." Above the gambling tables are any number of bizarre circus acts, "so you're down on the main floor playing blackjack, and the stakes are getting high when suddenly you chance to look up, and there, right smack about your head is a half-naked fourteen-year-old girl being chased through the air by a snarling wolverine, which is suddenly locked in a death battle with two silver-painted Polacks who come swinging down from opposite balconies and meet in midair on the wolverine's neck. . . ." The madness goes on, twenty-four hours a day of gambling and circus, "but nobody seems to notice. . . . Meanwhile, on all the upstairs balconies, the customers are being hustled by every conceivable kind of bizarre shuck." There is a video projection screen upon which for only ninety-nine cents you can send your image, two hundred feet tall, above downtown Las Vegas. For an extra ninety-nine cents the promoter will throw in your voice message:

> We will close the drapes tonight. A thing like that could send a drug person careening around the room like a ping-pong ball. Hallucinations are bad enough. But after a while you learn to cope with things like seeing your dead grandmother crawling up your leg with a knife in her teeth. Most acid fanciers can handle this sort of thing.
>
> But *nobody* can handle that other trip—the possibility that any freak with $1.98 can walk into the Circus-Circus and suddenly appear in the sky over downtown Las Vegas twelve times the size of God, howling anything that comes into his head. No, this is not a good town for psychedelic drugs. Reality itself is too twisted.

Thompson's career became successful as he developed from a journalist into a SuperFictionist. His days as a reporter for *Time* and then for the *National Observer* ended in a dispute over the Berkeley Free Speech Movement, to which he formed a personal allegiance (and which may have been what prompted him to ride with the Angels—to figure out why the bikers, with their socially radical lifestyle, could not join forces with the student radicals). A few years later it was the Chicago police riot at the 1968 Democratic National Convention which turned Thompson on to politics, but in a very personal way. His first *Rolling Stone* publication was "The Battle of Aspen" (#67, 10/1/70) which described his own campaign for sheriff in his adopted Colorado hometown, which he wanted to save from the big money developers. A major plank in his "Freak Power Party" platform was to rename Aspen "Fat City" as a way of deflating the real estate hype. His political tactic was "to spend his main energies on a series of terrifying, whiplash assaults on everything the voters hold dear. There are harsh echoes of the Magic Christian in this technique: The candidate first creates an impossible psychic maze, then he drags the voters into it and flails them constantly with gibberish and rude shocks." The technique is that of Thompson's writing, but in protesting the economic rape of Aspen he demonstrated its effectiveness as an approach to life as well as art. Thompson's party, which had candidates for mayor and coroner as well, lost by only six votes out of 1,200—by only one vote before five late-arriving absentee ballots were counted.

Living the life of fiction, writers like Thompson create fantasies which record the spirit—if not the misleading "actual" facts—of the life they've experienced. In *Playboy* (November 1974), Thompson tells interviewer Craig Vetter how he dealt with his own car in the context of riding heavy motorcycles with the Hell's Angels:

> I was always getting pulled over. Jesus, they cancelled my car insurance because of that goddamn bike. They almost took my driver's license away. I never had any trouble with my car. I drove it at full bore all over San Francisco all the time, just wide open. It was a good car, too, a little English Ford. When it finally developed a crack in one of the four cylinders, I took it down to a cliff in Big Sur and soaked the whole interior with ten gallons of gasoline, then executed the fucker with six shots from a .44 magnum in the engine block at point-blank range. After that, we rolled it off the cliff—the radio going, lights on, everything going—and at the last minute, we threw a burning towel in. The explosion was ungodly; it almost blew us into the ocean. I had no idea what ten gallons of gas in an English Ford could do. The car was a mass of twisted, flaming metal. It bounced about six times on the way down—pure movie-stunt shit, you know. A sight like that was worth the car; it was beautiful.

Plus more fantasies on Nixon's Final Days, the book which Thompson was unable to write because Resignation stole the drama from Impeachment:

> Thinking in football terms may be the best way to understand what finally happened with the whole Watergate thing: Coach Nixon's team is fourth and 32 on their own ten, and he finds out that his punter is a junkie. A sick junkie. He looks down the bench: "OK, big fella—we need you *now!*" And this guy is stark white and vomiting, can't even stand up, much less kick. When the game ends in disaster for the home team, then the fans rush onto the field and beat the players to death with rocks, beer bottles, pieces of wooden seats. The coach makes a desperate dash for the safety of the locker room, but three hit men hired by heavy gamblers nail him before he gets there.

Thompson was the only journalist to ride with both Richard Nixon and the Hell's Angels. These two poles of his experience influence each other, especially when they fuse in the person of the real subject of all these stories, Dr. Hunter S. Thompson. ⟨. . .⟩

VII. *Fear and Loathing*

For all of the charges against him, Hunter S. Thompson is an amazingly insightful writer. His "journalism" is not in the least irresponsible. On the contrary, in each of his books he's pointed out the lies and gross distortions of conventional journalism. As for "inventing" his material, his *Hell's Angels* documents just how the group was created by the conventional media and its "rape mania"—what Thompson calls "a publicity breakthrough, by means of rape, on the scale of the Beatles or Bob Dylan." Moreover, his books are richly intelligent. Against those who would fancy the Hell's Angels as heroic rebels and identify them with radical youth, Thompson argues that "there is more to their stance than a wistful yearning for acceptance in a world they never made. Their real motivation is an instinctive certainty as to what the score really is. They are out of the ballgame and they know it. Unlike the campus rebels, who with a minimum amount of effort will emerge from their struggle with a validated ticket to status, the outlaw motorcyclist views the future with the baleful eye of a man with no upward mobility at all. In a world increasingly geared to specialists, technicians and fantastically complicated machinery, the Hell's Angels are the obvious losers." Or in his Las Vegas book, where he charts the burning out of the Sixties: "What [Timothy] Leary took down with him was the central illusion of a whole life-style that he helped to create . . . a generation of permanent cripples, failed seekers, who never understood the essential old-mystic fallacy of the Acid Culture: the desperate assumption that somebody—or at least some *force*—is tending that Light at the end of the tunnel."

Thompson himself is capable of belief, and, like Vonnegut, hopes that there is a basic decency buried somewhere amid the junk-heap that contemporary life has become. Part of that very decency is Thompson's candid admission that he is a trash addict himself, that the conditions of our time have infected him even more than others. The reason is that he's placed himself at the center of the last decade's key events: the Berkeley Free Speech Movement and the subsequent nationwide college rebellions, the strange and terrible saga of the Hell's Angels motorcycle club, the 1968 Democratic National Convention in Chicago, the grassroots political reorganization of America, the violent reaction against the political organization of Chicanos and other minorities, the presidential campaign of 1972, the Watergate hearings, the House Judiciary Committee impeachment hearings, the fall of Saigon, and even America's very telling mania for brutal and oversized athletics—twenty years ago Thompson began his career as a sports reporter, and for the reporting of many of the events listed above he retained that designation on *Rolling Stone*'s masthead.

The June 3, 1976, issue of *Rolling Stone* featured Thompson's cover story; an endorsement, "with fear and loathing," of Jimmy Carter for the presidency. His attempt to explain Carter was made up mainly of explanations of himself, with the usual full run of self-reflexive and fabulative techniques. But Thompson uses this same style from his own life to spill over into his conversations with Carter, and the candidate's ability to pass Thompson's test establishes his credibility as needed material for the presidency. Thompson cites Adlai Stevenson to the effect that in a democracy people get exactly the kind of government they deserve; hence the ugly moods Thompson had been observing during the disruptions of the late Sixties and early Seventies yielded the inevitable results of Richard Nixon in 1968 and 1972. To Thompson, Carter reflects Thompson's own good intentions as voiced in Aspen, Aztlan, and the earlier stages of the McGovern campaign. To Thompson's relief, these intentions can be found in a viable candidate who hopes to reflect a true change in popular feelings.

Hunter Thompson has made his life and his writing style into a scourge for all that has gone bad in the world. That is the ultimate basis for his talent as a writer. In *Hell's Angels*, even with his constant middle-class perspective, Thompson was able to say of the bikers that "in this downhill half of our twentieth century they are not so different from the rest of us as they sometimes seem. They are only more obvious." Or at the end of his Kentucky Derby piece, after several days of drink and dope, looking for the ultimately depraved face from the crowd for Steadman to sketch:

> My eyes had finally opened enough for me to focus on the mirror across the room and I was stunned at the shock of recognition. For a confused instant I thought that Ralph had somebody with him—a model for that one special face we'd been looking for. There he was, by God—a puffy, drink-ravaged, disease-ridden caricature . . . like an awful cartoon version of an old snapshot in some once-proud mother's family photo album. It was the face we'd been looking for—and it was, of course, my own.

JOHN HELLMANN

From "Corporate Fiction, Private Fable, and Hunter S. Thompson's *Fear and Loathing: On the Campaign Trail '72*"

Critique, Volume 21, Number 1 (1979), pp. 16–21

New journalists, such as Thompson, and fabulators, such as Vonnegut, make opposing epistemological contracts with the reader for similar ends. While the one promises fact and the other fantasy, both seek a greater freedom for their fictive imaginations. Because they both assume that artifice is an essential element in all knowledge and communication, they even draw on similar techniques.[1] The results are in formal terms so close that a work like *On the Campaign Trail*, while certainly journalistic in its subject matter, is fabulist in its methods and purpose. Thompson has joined Mailer in using journalistic encounters with great media events as the ostensible subjects of reports that are actually self-consciously shaped studies of the engagement of consciousness and world. While Thompson is closely related to Mailer in his use of journalism as a form of experimental fiction, he is in his vision and fictive technique even closer to the parodistic world of Vonnegut.

Because tension results from the combination of factual claims and fictive form, a number of unique problems confront a critic of a work of new journalism. In discussing *On the Campaign Trail*, we must constantly make a crucial distinction between its narrator-protagonist and the author of the work. While the perception that the narrator and implied author of a work of fiction are two separate personae is a standard tenet of literary criticism, that distinction seems more difficult for readers confronting a work claiming to be journalism, particularly when the work's narrator-protagonist bears the author's name and even, in accompanying photographs, his visage. Just as Mailer transforms himself in a factual account into fictive "versions" of himself (characters called "Mailer," "the reporter," "Aquarius") through selective emphasis of the complex traits of his actual personality, Thompson has extended the principle to create a self-caricature. Using a comic, mock-psychotic persona as narrator-protagonist, Thompson has freed his fictive imagination to shape his journalistic works into inventive allegories—parodistic dramatizations of an individual mind experiencing, ordering, and interpreting national events. By clearly setting the account in the mind of his self-caricature, Thompson retains his journalistic contract while acquiring an extraordinary freedom to shape and flatten public facts into private meaning. In *On the Campaign Trail* and a number of other works Thompson calls this character "Dr. Hunter S. Thompson."[2]

The creation and use of this persona gives *On the Campaign Trail* the unique epistemological and ontological status, for a work of journalism, of being the comic, hyperbolic construct of a disordered consciousness. The clear status of the work as a parodistic version of the events which make up its subject matter enables Thompson to distort the surfaces of conventional journalistic accounts into symbols of fictive truth. *On the Campaign Trail* is thus journalism as experimental literature, a reporting of facts that is really concerned with providing a liberating experience of them. It provides the reader with an opportunity to explore the 1972 Presidential campaign through an individual consciousness which recreates the underlying anxieties it produced while also interpreting and controlling them through an aggressively inventive use of language. Thus the value and strength of the book lie not in the depth of its social insight or acuteness of its character analysis but—as with any work of fabulist shape and purpose—in its creation of a richly pleasurable and meaningful *form*. Thompson uses fabulist methods to penetrate the homogenized fiction within which the mass media shapes our national reality. Replacing commentary with rhetoric, stereotype with archetype, and formula with pattern, he frankly exploits the artifice of knowledge and communication to shape the facts of the campaign into a unique form and, therefore, a unique truth.

In brief outline, *On the Campaign Trail* is a collection of monthly and biweekly reports which form a public journal of Dr. Thompson's adventures during the 1972 Presidential campaign. Although the book includes an Introduction, Epitaph, footnotes, and a few passages interpolated in the interests of continuity, it is narrated from a perspective both temporally and physically close to its subject. Despite the supposed spontaneity of its composition (Thompson parodies the "deadline" aspect of reporting by having Dr. Thompson claim to compose at the last minute, sometimes even through a tape recorder) and the obvious problems of patterning a book dependent on events whose outcomes are unknown when the chapters were originally published, the work does have an overall form. Like *Tristram Shandy*, it is the highly contrived construct of an implied author who communicates experience as a perceived chaos—tenuously controlled by a personal assertion of meaning by an individual consciousness. The overall picaresque structure, subsuming a mixture of reporting, meditation, and digression, represents a mirror image of the disordered but determined consciousness of Dr. Thompson splicing together his imaginative experience.

Early in the narrative, Dr. Thompson explicitly rejects the illusory orderings of conventional journalism, pretending to forget one of its "Five W's"[3] and saying that the closest thing to "Objective Journalism" he has seen is a "closed-circuit TV setup that watched shoplifters in the General Store at Woody Creek," an observer generally ignored unless a known shoplifter appeared: "when that happened, everybody got so excited that the thief had to do something quick, like buy a green popsicle or a can of Coors and get out of the place immediately" (48). Through such parody, Thompson shows how Heisenberg's Indeterminacy Principle describes even the most objective of observations. Instead of such an illusory empiricism, his reporting attempts to order a reality imaginatively by overcoming various forces which he parodies as imminent apocalypse: the chaos of actual events, the pressures of his task, and even his own psychic disorientation. He introduces his report on the Ohio primary, for instance, with a portrait of himself, forced to sit at his desk in a maelstrom of confusion and pressure:

> The phone is ringing again and I can hear Crouse downstairs trying to put them off. . . . Only a lunatic would do this kind of work: twenty-three primaries in five months; stone drunk from dawn till dusk and huge speed-blisters all over my head. . . . Crouse is yelling again. They want more copy. He has sent them all of his stuff on the Wallace shooting, and now they want mine. Those halfwit sons of bitches should subscribe to a wire service; get one of those big AP tickers that spits out fifty words a minute, twenty-four hours a day. . . . So much for all that. The noise-level downstairs tells me Crouse will not be able to put them off much longer. So now we will start getting serious: First Columbus, Ohio, and then Omaha. But mainly Columbus, only because this thing began—in *my* head, at least—as a fairly straight and serious account of the Ohio primary. (186–87)

Such passages have been characterized as gratuitous entertainment that replaces a lack of substance: "far too much . . . consists of dodgy waffling precisely like the freshman essay every writing teacher receives at least once a year: 'Sitting in front of my blank page at 2:30 a.m. . . . I'll write about how it feels to be sitting in front of my blank page.'"[4] Such passages in Thompson's work function as sophisticated metafiction which emphasizes that the work is a personal construct which shifts its drama from the events reported to the experience of those events by an individual consciousness. By making Dr. Thompson's writing desk the central fact of his narrative, Thompson is able to present the Presidential campaign as an unfolding experience which lacks any apparent objective order and must instead be imaginatively ordered by the perceiving consciousness. Time in Dr. Thompson's narrative is thus not historical but spatial.

An historian or realistic novelist, looking at events from a perspective above and outside, perceives a certain cause-and-effect sequence, and then constructs a patterned narrative which creates a seemingly objective order. To bolster such a construct as an empirical representation of an actual pattern of events, he endeavors to focus the reader's attention on the events of the narrative and to make him forget about the artificer who imposes that pattern. Mailer, by drawing attention to his use of such narrative conventions, has sought in *The Armies of the Night* and his other journalism to make the reader aware of his artificial role while nevertheless carrying it out. In this way he confirms the conventional order of the novelist and historian without falsely suggesting that he is making an objective representation. Thompson, by focusing on his narrator's temporal and physical proximity to the events, makes those events far more formidable and his own ordering powers correspondingly weaker.

The page and deadline thus become the life and death of his narrative. The deadline makes the process of composition a meaningful act in itself; the page on the writing desk becomes the problematic reality that is the product of the meeting of consciousness and world, the place where Dr. Thompson must overcome the chaos of his subject and that of his mind in order to contrive something which will fill the blankness. By having Dr. Thompson constantly draw attention to himself in the act of pressured creation—as he seemingly composes through free association, digression, and fantasy, Thompson disappoints the reader's expectations for a narrative which will mirror an objective pattern of external events; instead, the report mirrors Dr. Thompson's struggle for meaning. The passage quoted above—far from being mere entertainment—affords a comically veiled critique of the journalistic "truth" offered by the corporate press under its business pressures, as well as a frank evaluation of the provincial vision of the American voter who will decide the election.

By further presenting such "reports" as the construct of a consciousness which is disordered and extreme in its perceptions, Thompson acquires the license to portray the campaign in the distancing and symbolic forms of parody. Although he has Dr. Thompson begin the chapter on the climactic California primary with a seemingly formless agitation, reporting his own bestial tendencies and use of the Black Vincent motorcycle, Thompson is preparing the reader for his view of the primary as "one of the brutal and degrading animal acts of our time" (220), a purpose that becomes clear at the moment Dr. Thompson berates himself for failing once again to write a conventionally coherent introduction: "Jesus! Another tangent, and right up front, this time—the whole *lead*, in fact, completely fucked. What can I say? Last week I blew the whole thing. Total failure. Missed the deadline, no article, no wisdom, no excuse . . . Except one: Yes, I was savagely and expertly duped by one of the oldest con trips in politics" (221). Further digressions create a self-extending chain: a fantasized revenge on McGovern's evasive campaign manager, Frank Mankiewicz, by severing his big toes; the attempt of a typewriter-rental service to bill him unfairly; his problems trying to ride an excessively powered motorcycle; his grudge against Democratic Chairman Larry O'Brien for supposedly breaking a promise made years before to award him the governorship of American Samoa. These entertaining but seemingly gratuitous tales lead not to irrelevancy but to a report on the acrimonious character of the political campaign in California.

Similarly, Thompson has Dr. Thompson begin his report on the last-minute maneuverings of the Old Guard of the Democratic party to prevent McGovern's nomination with a hilarious tall tale of the night a watchman at Random House, using a metal vacuum-cleaner tube, supposedly beat Dr. Thompson's harmless Blue Indigo snake to death. It had escaped from a cardboard box and caused the watchman to find himself suddenly "menaced by a hissing, six-foot serpent coming fast up the stairs at him from the general direction of Cardinal Spellman's quarters just across the courtyard" (253). The absurdist parable of "fear and loathing" suggests Thompson's interpretation of the forces behind the Stop-McGovern movement. Storytelling, then, is made to function as reporting, a reporting that is certainly fable but not falsehood.

Notes

1. A discussion of the similarity between new journalism and fabulation may be found in my "Fables of Fact: New Journalism Reconsidered," *The Centennial Review*, 21 (1977), 414–32.
2. In discussing *On the Campaign Trail* I will use "Thompson" when referring to the implied author and "Dr. Thompson" when referring to the self-caricature who appears as the narrator and protagonist. A more excessive and less engaging persona appears in *Fear and Loathing in Las Vegas* (1971) as "Raoul Duke." In *On the Campaign Trail* Dr. Thompson occasionally refers to Raoul Duke as though he were a different person. Thompson has extended his creation of separate personae into a parody of schizophrenia. To this day (Spring 1979) the masthead of *Rolling Stone* lists Hunter S. Thompson under "National Affairs Desk" and Raoul Duke as a Contributing Editor responsible for "Sports." Thompson has even written one article on Watergate in the form of separate memoranda from the two personae, one of which portrays their meeting; see Raoul Duke, "Memo from the Sports Desk and Rude Notes from a Decompression Chamber in Miami," *Rolling Stone*, 2 August 1973, pp. 8–10.
3. Hunter S. Thompson, *Fear and Loathing: On the Campaign Trail '72* (San Francisco: Straight Arrow Books, 1973), p. 92. Subsequent references are to this edition.
4. Wayne Booth, "Loathing and Ignorance on the Campaign Trail: 1972," *Columbia Journalism Review*, 12, No. 4 (1973), 12.

JAMES THURBER

1894–1961

James Grover Thurber was born on December 8, 1894, in Columbus, Ohio, to Mary Fisher Thurber and Charles L. Thurber. He was educated at Ohio State University. In 1922 he married Althea Adams, by whom he had one daughter. Soon after their divorce in 1935 he married Helen Wismer. Thurber worked as a code clerk at the American Embassy in Paris from 1918 to 1920, then for seven years was a reporter for various newspapers, including the *Columbus Dispatch*, the Paris edition of the *Chicago Tribune*, and the *New York Evening Post*. He was first an editor, then a staff writer, for the *New Yorker* from 1927 to 1938; he remained associated with the *New Yorker* as a freelance contributor for much of his career.

Thurber published his first book, *Is Sex Necessary? or, Why You Feel the Way You Do* in collaboration with fellow *New Yorker* staffer E. B. White in 1929. Dryly humorous and stylistically plain, it set the tone for his later work. Thurber never produced an entirely unified longer work of prose, but as a comic short story writer he had few rivals in the mid-twentieth century, and became a fixture at the *New Yorker* both as a writer and a cartoonist. More than twenty books of short stories and sketches have been published since his first, *The Owl in the Attic and Other Perplexities* (1931). Among the most significant are *My Life and Hard Times* (1933), *My World—and Welcome to It* (1942), and *The Thurber Carnival* (1945). Thurber was so adept at his type of humor that the "Thurber Man," bumbling yet lovable, has become a well-known figure on the American fictional landscape, and stories like "The Secret Life of Walter Mitty" are still cited as exemplars of the mid-century light humorous form. Thurber's reputation as a simple but effective stylist is not as great today as it was at his peak; some critics feel that both repetition and the general critical lack of respect for light humor as a serious art form have obscured his genuine craft and social sensitivity.

Thurber was also an effective and sympathetic children's writer; *The White Deer* (1945) and *The Thirteen Clocks* (1950) are considered by some to be among his finest work. *The Male Animal*, a play written in collaboration with Elliott Nugent, was produced in 1940 but received scant attention. *A Thurber Carnival*, an adaptation for the stage of his short stories, was produced in 1962 to critical and popular acclaim. *Vintage Thurber: A Collection of His Best Writings and Drawings* was published in 1963. Thurber died on November 4, 1961.

Here is Thurber again, with his vague and apologetic men, his two-dimensional *femme fatales*, his rudimentary landscapes and his raucous animals, in illustration of a set of modern beast fables ⟨*Fables for Our Time*⟩. Along with the fables goes a set of favorite English poems, richly embellished and commented upon by the Thurberian pencil. When I tell you that "Young Lochinvar" and "Ben Bolt" are among these, not to mention the masterpiece of them all, A. E. Housman's "Oh, When I Was in Love with You," nothing further is required by way of review. A critic who attempts to pontificate on the subject of humorous writers is sure to tread on too many toes. Men are jealous of their senses of humor. As in the case of Miss Beatrice Lillie, so with Mr. Thurber; either you like him or you don't.

The modern fables resemble in a superficial way the fables of George Ade. Both writers were attempting the same thing; to bring out the incongruous contrast of modern problems and contemporary slang diction with the conventional framework and accepted notion of the fable or fairy tale. Thurber's purpose is deeper and more sombre than Ade's preoccupation with college boys and turn-of-the-century flappers. There is nothing Andersonian about Thurber's fables, nor are they very hilarious. Their purpose is to provoke thought: about war, about injustice, about mankind. Their quality is bitterness without cheap cynicism, disillusion without hopelessness. As all of his predecessors in the great tradition of satire, Thurber hurls bolts against mankind because he loves men.—J. G. E. HOPKINS, *Com*, Oct. 11, 1940, pp. 514–15

The fairy tales that James Thurber has been doing are a phase in his rapid elimination of the last vestiges of the conventional humorist and his emergence as a comic artist of the top layer of our contemporary writing. It is as if these fairy tales had freed him from literary habits that he had long outgrown but that still sometimes lingered in his other pieces. Mr. Thurber, in these stories, is working in a new little fictional world, clear and bright and complete in itself, and a long way from, say, *My Life and Hard Times*, which was half self-burlesque of the old-fashioned routine kind that goes back to Bill Nye and half imaginative recreation of experience on a much higher humorous level. In *Many Moons* and *The Great Quillow*, he did two short and successful stories that had a fairy-tale purity of color and tone, and now, in *The White Deer* (Harcourt, Brace), he has tried one on a larger scale.

These fairy stories, so far as I know, are the best American things of their kind since Frank Stockton's, which, in certain respects, they resemble. Mr. Thurber, like Stockton, takes the characters and properties of the traditional fairy tale and, by introducing at moments, unobtrusively, a contemporary point of view, makes them produce unexpected results. Stockton performed these tricks with a matter-of-factness and solemn logic characteristic of the Howells era; Thurber is more poetic, wittier, and more unpredictable. By reversing, in *The White Deer*, a familiar fairy-tale situation, so that instead of having a princess transformed into an animal, you have (or the main characters think they have) a deer turned into a princess, and by ringing a few plausible changes on the three brothers that set out on three difficult quests, he makes a story which ought to please children and will certainly please grownups who like Thurber.

I thought, in fact, when I had read the first part of *The White Deer*, that it was perhaps one of the best things he had written and one of the best modern fairy tales, and if it seemed to me to fall short of this, it was not because the story did not hold up or continue to be amusing but because, in its later stretches, the line of the narrative gets a little cluttered and the style sometimes runs off the track. I suggest that the flashbacks to the castle when the king's sons are off on their quests are to some extent repetitious; that the transition, in the dialogue, to blank verse and rhyme is not always skillfully managed, and that the blank verse should not, as it occasionally is, be allowed to get into the prose narrative; that there is too much alliteration; and that the dénouement goes on too long. These blemishes are particularly noticeable because it is obvious that Mr. Thurber both plans and writes with care. The trouble is, I think, that he occasionally gets distracted by a conceit or a verbal trick which lets down the excitement of suspense or impairs the atmosphere of magic that he knows how to generate. But *The White Deer* has the essence of poetry, and it ought to be read in preference to almost any best-selling novel.—EDMUND WILSON, *NY*, Oct. 27, 1945, pp. 91–93

I would hesitate to say that ⟨Thurber's⟩ prose is the best now being written in this country. Other things being equal, the best prose would be that which was most effective in presenting the boldest subjects. Except in his fables, where he can touch them lightly, Thurber has always avoided bold subjects like war and revolution, love and death; he prefers to write about the domestic confusions of people whose sedentary lives are not too different from his own. It isn't a very complicated society that he presents, or one with a rich fabric of inherited values, or one in which men and women are destroyed by their splendid passions. His most ambitious hero is Walter Mitty, who has his visions of glory while buying puppy biscuits. His tragic lover (in "The Evening's at Seven") goes back to a *table d'hôte* dinner at his hotel and, in token of a shattered life, orders consommé instead of clam chowder.

Comedy is his chosen field, and his range of effects is deliberately limited, but within that range there is nobody who writes better than Thurber, that is, more clearly and flexibly, with a deeper feeling for the genius of the language and the value of words.

He tries never to intone or be solemn. "Humor," he once wrote in a letter to me, "cannot afford the ornaments and indulgences of fine writing, the extravagance of consciousness-streaming, or lower-case unpunctuation meanderings. There is a sound saying in the theater: 'You can't play comedy in the dark.' I saw Jed Harris and Billy Rose trying to disprove this one night in Philadelphia twenty-five years ago when they put on an eight-minute Don Marquis skit in absolute darkness: the sounds of voices, glasses, and the cash register of an old-time beer saloon. People fell asleep, or began coughing, or counting their change, or whispering to their neighbors, or reading their programs with pencil flashlights. Comedy has to be done *en clair*. You can't blunt the edge of wit or the point of satire with obscurity."

In his effort to be absolutely clear, he pays so much attention to the meaning and color of words that he speaks of them almost as if they had personalities to be cultivated or avoided. "What could be worse than 'eroticize'?" he asked in another letter. "It is one of those great big words, or tortured synonyms, with which psychiatry has infected the language, so that a page of type sometimes looks like a parade of Jack Johnsons wearing solid gold teeth and green carnations in the lapels of their electric-blue morning suits." He prefers the familiar words that would be used in conversation without a self-conscious pause. His art consists in arranging them so that they give the impression of standing cleanly and separately on the page, each in its place like stones in a well-built wall.

That impression is not an easy one to achieve, and Thurber takes endless pains with his stories. He spent fifty working days on "The Secret Life of Walter Mitty," which is four thousand words long. By contrast he did a whole book of fifty drawings, *The Last Flower*, in two hours of an otherwise idle evening. He has often explained to art critics that he draws for relaxation, as others doodle at the telephone. He never redraws, but he continually rewrites. Last year he told an interviewer that one of his stories—"The Train on Track Six," still unpublished—had been rewritten fifteen times from beginning to end. "There must have been close to 240,000 words in all the manuscripts put together," he said, "and I must have spent two thousand hours working at it. Yet the finished version can't be more than twenty thousand words."

His gradual loss of eyesight, now almost total, once threatened to put an end to his work. As early as 1941 he found that he could no longer distinguish the keys of a typewriter. When a series of painful operations failed to restore his vision, he took to writing with a black crayon on yellow copy paper. But his one eye kept growing weaker—the other had been lost in a boyhood accident—and his handwriting larger in compensation, until twenty words filled a page and a hundred used up the crayon. Nobody except his wife and his secretary could decipher what he had written.

Then slowly he trained himself to give dictation. It was harder for him than for most writers, because so much of his work depends on his finding exactly the right word and using it in exactly the right place, but at last he found a practical system that he follows most of the time. He spends the morning turning over the text in his mind, moving words around like a woman redecorating the living room, and then in the afternoon he calls in a secretary. The system would be impossible without his remarkable memory. Sometimes he remembers, word for word, three complete versions of the same story.

His loss of vision has had an effect on his style that will be noted by almost every reader of his new fables ⟨*Further Fables for Our Time*⟩. All the sound effects have been intensified, as if one sense had developed at the cost of another, and the language is full of onomatopoeia and alliteration. "The caves of ocean bear no gems," one studious lemming reflects as all the other plunge into the water, "but only soggy glub and great gobs of mucky gump." Man tells the dinosaur, in one of the best fables, "You are one of God's moderately amusing early experiments . . . an excellent example of Jehovah's jejune juvenilia." There are puns too, like "Monstrosity is the behemother of extinction," and there are rhymes not only in the morals but scattered through the text, so that whole passages could be printed as verse.

But this preoccupation with words, with their sound, sense, and arrangement into patterns, has affected more than the style of the fables. It is also transforming the imagination of the author, who seems to be presenting us with a completely verbalized universe. The only conceivable end for the inhabitants of such a universe would be mass suicide resulting from complete verbal confusion; and that is exactly how Thurber pictures them as ending, in the fable about lemmings which also ends the collection.

It seems that a single excited lemming started the exodus by crying "Fire!" when he saw the rising sun. Hundreds followed him toward the ocean, then thousands, each shouting a different message of fear or exultation. "It's a pleasure jaunt!" squeaked an elderly female lemming. "A treasure hunt!" echoed a male who had been up all night; "Full many a gem of purest ray serene the dark unfathomed caves of ocean bear." His daughter heard only the last word and shouted, "It's a bear! Go it!" Others among the fleeing thousands shouted "Goats!" and "Ghosts!" until there were almost as many different alarms as there were fugitives. Then they all plunged into the seas, and that was the end of the lemmings.

Symbolically it was also the end of mankind as only Thurber could have imagined it: not with a bang, not with a whimper, but in a universal confusion of voices and meanings.—MALCOLM COWLEY, "Lions and Lemmings, Toads and Tigers," *Rep*, Dec. 13, 1956, pp. 43–44

The appearance, in the yellow dust jacket that has become traditional, of one more collection of pieces ⟨*Credos and Curios*⟩ by the late James Thurber is a happy event, even for the reviewer obliged to report that the bulk of the pieces are from his last years and as such tend to be cranky, formless and lame. "The claw of the sea-puss," Thurber once wrote (quoting F. Hopkinson Smith), "gets us all in the end"; and toward the end Thurber's humor was overwhelmed by puns and dismay.

The puns are understandable. Blindness, in severing language from the seen world of designated things, gives words a tyrannical independence. Milton and Joyce wrung from verbal obsession a special magnificence, and Thurber's late pieces, at their best—for example, "The Tyranny of Trivia," collected in *Lanterns and Lances*—do lead the reader deep into the wonderland of the alphabet and the dictionary. But in such weak rambles as, in this collection, "The Lady from the Land" and "Carpe Noctem, If You Can," logomachic tricks are asked to pass for wit and implausible pun-swapping for human conversation.

As to the dismay: Mrs. Thurber, in her gracious and understated introduction to this posthumous collection, defends her husband against the charge of "bitterness and disillusion." But stories like "The Future, If Any, of Comedy Or, Where Do We Not-Go from Here?" and "Afternoon of a Playwright" do display, by way of monologue in the ungainly disguise of dialogue, an irritation with the present state of things so inclusive as to be pointless.

Television, psychoanalysis, the Bomb, the deterioration of grammar, the morbidity of contemporary literature—these were just a few of Thurber's terminal pet peeves. The writer who had produced *Fables for Our Time* and *The Last Flower* out of the thirties had become, by the end of the fifties, one more indignant senior citizen penning complaints about the universal decay of virtue.

The only oasis, in the dreadful world of post-midnight forebodings into which he had been plunged, is the Columbus, Ohio, of his boyhood, which he continued to remember "as fondly and sharply as a man on a sinking ship might remember his prairie home." In *Credos and Curios*, for a few pages entitled "Return of the Native," his prose regains the crisp lucidity and glistening bias of *The Thurber Album*. Then the dark tangled curtain falls again.

However, *Credos and Curios* should be cherished by every Thurberite for the seven random tributes he wrote, between 1938 and 1960, to seven artistic colleagues—Mary Petty, Elliott Nugent and five writers. His acute and sympathetic remarks on Scott Fitzgerald remind us that Thurber, too, was one of the curiously compact literary generation that came to birth in the twenties and whose passing has left the literary stage so strikingly empty. His affectionate memories of John McNulty and E. B. White, two friends who in their different ways achieved the literary tranquillity that eluded Thurber, better capture the spirit of *New Yorker* bonhomie than all *The Years with Ross*.

His generous appreciation of Robert Benchley is most welcome of all, especially when taken as an antidote to the oddly curt paragraph with which *The New Yorker* noted the death, in 1949, of this remarkable artist. For if Thurber, whose international celebrity made him seem to loom unduly over the other American humorists of his vintage, is to be measured against his peers, the first name we strike is Benchley's. The surprising thing about Benchley is that he remains rereadable. His writings were so ephemeral they seem to defy being outdated; their utterly casual and innocent surface airily resists corrosion. I wonder how much of Thurber will weather so well.

His cartoons, of course, are incomparable; they dive into the depths of the dilemma that he felt beneath everything. Of the humorists of this century, he and Don Marquis were the most complex, the most pessimistic and the most ambitious. Thurber, in comparison to Marquis and Benchley, was not especially sensitive to the surface currents of American life, and as a journalist, uncomfortable, and, as a writer of straight fiction, unconvincing.

His great subject, springing from his physical disability, was what might be called the enchantment of misapprehension. His masterpieces, I think, are *My Life and Hard Times* and *The White Deer*—two dissimilar books alike in their beautiful evocation of a fluid chaos where communication is limited to wild, flitting gestures and where humans revolve and collide like glowing planets, lit solely from within, against a cosmic backdrop of gathering dark. Thurber's genius was to make of our despair a humorous fable. It is not surprising that such a gallant feat of equilibrium was not maintained to the end of his life.—JOHN UPDIKE, "Indignations of a Senior Citizen," *NYTBR*, Nov. 25, 1962, p. 5

The old *New Yorker* slogan was 'not for the old lady in Dubuque', a private joke intended to amuse James Thurber's mother in Columbus, Ohio and any ancient aunts in Aspen, Colorado who still survived to recall the historic day on which that boy Harold Ross, the magazine's founder and shaper, took a fast freight east. Manhattan's urbanity is refashioned in every age by provincials from Baltimore, Brownsville, Texas or Walnut, Iowa. This is a truth universally acknowledged from Machias, Me. to Joplin, Mo. and only missed by people entitled to the name and sufferings of native-born New Yorkers.

When Ross began the magazine during the Thirties, Minnesota's Scott Fitzgerald was American prose laureate. His graceful, conservative style set the standard for good *New Yorker* writing. Ross's first star contributor, the gentle, silly and phobic Robert Benchley, was Fitzgerald's admirer and occasional bottle companion; Thurber had read *The Great Gatsby* three times over before his first and only meeting with Fitzgerald in 1934. If Thurber learned from *Gatsby* how to write a nervous and exact American prose, and from Benchley how to be funny about his own nervousness, it is evident that he was never merely the confluence of his influences. In a tribute to Mary Thurber written after her death in 1955 and reprinted in *Alarms and Diversions* Thurber testified to the life-long occupation of his mind by a sense of confusion apparently brought on by his formidable mother's addiction to practical jokes involving elaborate disguises and sudden shifts of identity. Images of this confusion—Mitty's autism, the 'chronic word garblings' of lady conversationalists in the party pieces, the famous drawings of the seal in the bedroom, the House-Woman and the enormous inscrutable rabbit blocking life's path to the Goal—proliferate in his work, suggesting that he wrote and drew with a firm professional hand to exorcize a deep uncertainty which was often dangerously close to sheer panic. And yet, because he was an authentic artist, Thurber's invention has given a shape and face to the unconfessed dreams and *angst* of all but the most robust men trying to hold their heads up and their gorges down in this century.

Thurber's attitude toward his favourite subjects was always complicated and sometimes ambiguous. In celebrating the modern sex war he regularly portrayed Woman as just a little bit taller, tougher, surer and faster on the draw than her opponent, and he agreed with 'those wiser men who spoke of the female with proper respect, and even fear.' At the same time he called himself a feminist and backed the feminine conspiracy on the cogent grounds that women sought to seize power in order to prevent the world from being blown to fragments. Another of his obsessions was language. An inveterate wordgamesman and a dictionary reader, he brooded and wrote a good deal about the 'disfigurations of sense and meaning' which accompany Cold War propaganda tactics and about the 'carcinomenclature of our time' fostered by the adulteration of common speech by professional and technological jargons. Withal, a demon of his imagination was unable to leave proper words alone, so that he sometimes found himself lying awake producing paraphrases like 'The Pie-eyed Peeper of Hamlin.' In certain moods he evidently regarded words with acute suspicion: unless kept under severe restraint a noun might turn into a creature that bit or a thing that went off like a grenade. Thus, in a drawing from his New Natural History the needle-beaked fowl rising in an aggressive manner from a clump of grass is actually 'a female Shriek rising out of the Verbiage to attack a female Swoon.' Thurber's whimsy is often more relevant to issues in the great world than first appears. Ever since 1945, when Einstein's bit of language about the conversion of mass to energy developed explosive connotations, the old saw about sticks and stones has not quite covered the case.

Alarms and Diversions, a reprint of his 1957 miscellany, is one of the richest gatherings of Thurber ever issued. There are dozens of drawings cleanly reproduced, and the prose selections range from *New Yorker* 'casuals' describing early days in Paris and old ladies in Columbus through examples of pure humour like 'The French Far West' to literary parodies, imaginary interviews, and pieces of straight reportage on such grisly subjects as the Hall-Mills murder case, the Loch Ness monster and *Punch* before 1900. *Credos and Curios* is a posthumous collection compiled by Helen Thurber, the writer's widow. Several essays in it were occasioned by his long visit to London in the spring of 1961. The volume closes with half a dozen short pieces on American writers he had known well or admired, among others the 'incomparable Benchley', John McNulty, and that haunted man Fitzgerald.

Mrs Thurber says in her foreword that her husband tried to avoid anger and fear and to aim at awareness. As Yeats once remarked, the peculiar heroism of modern artists is chiefly manifested in their unflinching attentiveness to the world's and the self's chaos as revealed to them by the contents of their own minds. Thurber had a good measure of this heroism, and that is why people will go on reading him long after certain bellowers and platitudinizers now active on the American literary scene have vanished without trace.—JULIAN MOYNAHAN, "No Nonsense," *NS*, Dec. 14, 1962, p. 872

CHARLES A. BRADY

"Our Man in the Moon: What Thurber Saw"

Commonweal, December 8, 1961, pp. 274–76

James Thurber wrote for the *New Yorker* for better than thirty-four years. Despite the contemporary critical *réclame* for the elusive Mr. Salinger, the never anything but palpable Mr. Thurber remains that magazine's first paladin in loyalty as well as genius. It was his affectionately iconoclastic hand that hymned the hero years with Ross; and he doubtless will be mourned most memorably in the columns of the famous periodical he helped build into its present pinnacle of lonely eminence among American magazines.

But though Thurber stayed throughout his life one of Eustace Tilley's boys, he was also, in a very real sense, sealed of the tribe of the celebrated Mr. Punch of 10 Bouverie Street, London, E.C.4. If possible, the English admired him even more than we did; and surely his proudest apotheosis took place across *Punch*'s mahogany one afternoon at the end of June, 1958, at which time he became the second American to grace that table of great jesters.

Punch's first American had been Mark Twain, fifty-one years before. When, at that time Twain was invited in accordance with the sacrosanct *Punch* ritual, to cut his initials on the board—it is something humorists do in symbol all their lives—he pointed to Thackeray's stylized W.M.T. and indicated that the latter two-thirds of that signature would do for him. Unable, for all his love of dancing letters, to duplicate Twain's gesture, Thurber cut a Th alongside the incised autograph of Shirley Brooks, and, for good measure, drew a Thurber dog in the visitors' book with this muttered incantation: "I can feel Mark Twain looking over my shoulder right now." It was not just Mark Twain, as the future's critics will one day record.

Punch continued to be James Thurber's great good friend. Within this present year it paid him another tribute, on the occasion of what turned out to be his final visit to London; and this time the compliment was delivered with pencil as well as pen.

In the *Punch* drawing, one of Her Britannic Majesty's most respectable desk-clerks is standing behind his reception-desk and speaking into a telephone: "Night clerk, yes? You thought you heard a seal bark . . . which room, please?" Just to the right of the clerk's Bond Street sleeve stands a board marked *Messages*. Letters are affixed to it. The only one visible bears, in flowing Spenserian script, the name of the addressee: *J. Thurber Esq.*

Now it seems to me that, in their two different ways, these *Punch* excursions into Thurberland have a great deal to tell us about the best American humorist since Mark Twain—the best one before him, too, for that matter. To take the cartoon first, with its complimentary reference to the best known of Thurber's many drawings, it is clear that he is one of the few artists of our day who have contributed to what may be described as the living folklore of the present. Who can forget, once he has seen them, the homely, domesticated surrealism of the Seal in the Bedroom or of the First Mrs. Harris crouched, reproachfully, atop her bookcase?

Much more significant is the emblematic nature of the *Punch* luncheon and the illustrious ghosts who sat with Thurber round the "mahogany tree"—Henry James alone is missing of the great congeners to whom he is sib. Without any of Twain's Mississippi flood of creative energy that broke through the levee of his day's professional humor and flowed into the moonlit delta of *Huckleberry Finn*, Thurber united, in his gangling person crowned by the dandelion mop of hair, the two main streams of American humor. He carries forward the folksy, homespun vernacular tradition that is attuned to the speaking rhythms of the human voice and expresses the wisdom both of heart and belly, the tradition one may trace throughout frontier anecdote and tall story to its mountain apex in Twain, and, after Twain, in the lesser foothills of Lardner and Salinger. He also continues the urbaner tradition that comes down to us, through Franklin's *bagatelles*, the miscellaneous squibs of the Connecticut wits and Irving's *Knickerbocker*, the essays of the first Holmes, into the work of Thurber's own fellow wits on the *New Yorker*, yesterday and today.

Nor is Thackeray's shade merely a fortuitous appearance. When totting up the Thurber canon, one should never forget the really peerless work he did in the neglected field of the original fairy story. If one seeks an American analogue for this charming side of Thurber, one may always pluck Frank Stockton from the critical hat. Actually *Many Moons, The Great Quillow, The White Deer*—to single out the best of these graceful fancies—are far closer to the literary Christmas pantomimes Thackeray initiated with his *Rose and the Ring*. (There are overtones of Lear and Carroll, too, but the form is surely Thackeray's.) Yet Thackeray never turned out anything quite so perfect as the tender foolery one finds in the tale of Princess Lenore and the Jester.

This vein, though it never ran out, began to harden in *The Thirteen Clocks*, for all the incidental felicities of the "gleeping" Todal and the Golux who gives us this dictum for the police states of our day: "Never trust a spy you cannot see." As is true everywhere in the later Thurber, the Snark has become a nightmarish Boojum, and the clocks have not so much run down as speeded up too frantically. The circle is complete with the too obsessive punning of "The Great O" whose super-Joycean word-play makes not only this book but the final short pieces almost too fatiguing in their dazzling verbal fence. For most of his writing life Thurber had stalked words. Now, frighteningly, words begin to stalk him.

Thurber's range was extraordinarily wide. He was an admirable parodist—remember "What Cocktail Party" and the wicked lampooning of the Raymond Chandler school of penny dreadful in "The White Rabbit Caper"? He was a perceptive, if oblique, critic of literature, refracting rainbow intimations through the prism of his many essays—yes, he was a first-rate familiar essayist, too, as good a one as we have yet produced. I give you, among many excellent examples, "The French Far West." He wrote an in-between kind of essay, too—half formal, half familiar—which permitted him to work out as social historian, amateur of American murder, and definitive analyst of that curious Anglo-American cultural phenomenon, the soap-opera. And all these different things got set down in a precisely elegant plain style, each clause as well-placed as a drop-shot at Wimbledon or a sneak-punch in Boyle's Thirty Acres, for Thurber carried on a life-long love affair with the English language.

In addition, he was a genuine fabulist—I give you, on this head, The Bear Who Could Take It Or Leave It and the house-broken Unicorn who protected henpecked husbands instead of harassed virgins. He was, from beginning to end, but more especially in his middle period, a short story writer of unusual distinction. He was also a unique biographer and a memoirist of considerable parts—his respective high points, in this latter category, are probably the rather late *Thurber Album* and the very early *My Life and Hard Times*, which may well turn out to have been his masterpieces.

As an artist James Thurber was something new under the sun. One may always cite Edward Lear, of course, but the resemblance is very, very distant. Thurber's wedding of picture and letterpress is as close as anyone can get to a new art form that is, at one and the same time, a primitivist doodle and an ultra-sophisticated pronunciamento delivered by a moralist, more resigned than angry, on our Age of Anxiety.

Lovers of *My Life and Hard Times* will recall the Thurber of World War I as a most indifferent soldier. On one front, however, the one where is fought out the perpetually drawn battle between the sexes, he was the premier male strategist of our generation.

The difference between man and woman remains one of the oldest and best jokes of nature's devising; and a tradition in English letters as old as *The Canterbury Tales*. Thurber's contribution to the logistics of this struggle is as immortal as Chaucer's. It is, moreover, aided and abetted by such important discoveries as Thurber's Law which has it that there is no safety in numbers or in anything else, and that the claw of the sea puss gets us all in the end.

This same jauntily pessimistic acceptance of the worst grew perceptibly darker toward the end. As is the way of merrymen everywhere, Jamie Thurber tended, year by year, toward a modulated kind of "moping mum." The moral darkness he saw spreading everywhere did not, however, impair his love of life any more than had the physical blindness which had struck so tragically early in his career. Nor did it chill his warm affection for his own past.

Besides London and New York, the cities Thurber loved best were Paris and Columbus, Ohio, where, sixty-six years ago Jamie Thurber was born to the mother he loved as well and immortalized as vividly as Barrie had Margaret Ogilvy. It is not the least of Thurber's achievements that Columbus, Ohio, is now, for readers in many languages, a thing of faerie, an enchanted wood wherein Bottom may not have loved Titania but where the youthful Thurber serving out his brief political career, once saw a ballot scrawled against Woodrow Wilson with the angry words: A *bas le professeur!*

Like the Henry James whom he admired and wrote about, and whose scrupulous artistry he emulated, there are really three James Thurbers: James I of *My Life and Hard Times* and the fine frenzy of the early pieces; James II of the famous drawings and the wonderful short stories; and James III—never, however, an Old Pretender—of the brittlely brilliant final pieces.

In his two latest published pieces—one for the *New Yorker*, the other for the *Times Literary Supplement*—Thurber expressed a somber conviction that the future of humor and comedy was at best a "cryptic" one, because they "require for existence, a brave spirit and a high heart, and where do you find these" in our "present era of Science and *Angst?*" Well, we found them in this valiant blind man whose mournful-eyed, huge-eared seeing-eye dogs of the mind will continue to guide us through today's ever-spreading Waste Land of no-humor for a good long time to come.

Thurber also pointed out that the "*Zeitgeist* is not crazy as a loon or mad as a March hare; it is manic as a man"—and now the manic is in the Moon! But there was another side of the Moon for Thurber. We see it, too, when, in his gentlest avatar as Court Jester, he tucks in Princess Lenore, content with the little golden moon on her necklace, and winks at the great silver orb, "for it seemed to the court Jester that the moon had winked at him."

Let our day's great panjandrums go on fretting us, if they insist: the Wizards, the Mathematicians, the Chamberlains, and the Kings, with their lunatic lunar trajectories. Our man in the moon, James Thurber, is worth the whole mad pack of them.

CARL M. LINDNER

"Thurber's Walter Mitty— The Underground American Hero"

Georgia Review, Summer 1974, pp. 283–89

James Thurber has long been recognized as one of America's leading modern humorists. His stories, sketches, and cartoons are engaging, often leading to chuckles of wry reminiscence. But when he created "The Secret Life of Walter Mitty," Thurber wrought better than he knew, for he had touched upon one of the major themes in American literature—the conflict between individual and society. Mitty's forerunners are readily observable in native folklore and fiction. On one side Mitty is a descendant of Rip Van Winkle and Tom Sawyer. On the other side he dream-wishes qualities customarily exhibited by the legendary frontier hero. Yet, while Thurber's story derives from American cultural tradition, it presents the quest for identity in an unmistakably modern context. In what may be the final scene in an unfolding tapestry of heroic situations, Mitty struggles to achieve a measure of self-respect, but finds himself restricted to the pathways of retreat and wish-fulfillment.

Mitty's closest literary forerunner is Rip Van Winkle, the "good-bad boy" of American fiction. Like Rip, Mitty has a wife who embodies the authority of a society in which the husband cannot function. Mitty's world is routine, trivial, and fraught with pigeon-holes; it persecutes the individual, strips his life of romance, and dictates what his actions (if not his thoughts) should be. The husband is often reduced to the status of a naughty child (as demonstrated by a prepubertal mentality); and he attempts to escape rather than confront a world symbolized by a wife who, more often than not, seems to be a mother-figure rather than a partner. Because of the threat which the wife-mother poses to the American male psyche, Rip must go hunting, Deerslayer cannot marry and dwell in the town, and Huck seeks the river rather than be *sivilized*.

Huck's boyhood companion, Tom Sawyer, is not only one of the most popular characters in American fiction, he is one of the most successful at circumventing authority-figures. He manages to do this in the real world, thus distinguishing himself from Rip and Mitty. But if he succeeds, it may be because the pressure is not as great; after all, he is only a boy, not subject to the strain of a day-to-day relationship with its attendant responsibilities. Society does not weigh heavily upon Tom's boyish shoulders, and his pranks and practical jokes permit him to squirm free from the little discomfort he experiences. Because Tom's freedom is never seriously threatened, his rebellion (a conventional one at that) remains on an adolescent level.

What Mitty and Tom do share, however, is an imagination based on book-adventures. Like Tom, Mitty romanticizes and inflates situations, and this goes far to explain why Mitty's mind will not (indeed, can not) grapple with the world about him. Because his imagination depends upon what he has read rather than what he has done, Mitty lives a vicarious existence. And, conversely, Mitty's misuse of words and concocted over-dramatizations betoken his unwillingness to dwell in a dimension which cannot feed his imaginative faculties. Given his routine external life, how could it be otherwise? Only in Mitty's world could an eight-engine hydroplane leave the water. The banker, Wellington McMillan (note the initials), falls prey to "coreopsis" during his operation—but "coreopsis" denotes a genus of plants. Captain Mitty, the courageous flier, mistakenly refers to the "Jerries" as the "Archies." And the Webley-Vickers 50-80, with which the one-armed defendant is so proficient (along with every other "known make of gun") is probably a Smith and Wesson. A dual purpose is evident here, for while Thurber deliberately places these wrong-way signposts to reveal Mitty's ignorance of the heroic experience Mitty remains oblivious of his blunders as he succeeds in fashioning his own reality. Simultaneously it is a sad and amusing show.

Mitty's visions, however, are more than mere adolescent fantasies with their theatricality and simplistic crises; they are surprisingly true to what Lawrence in *Studies in Classic American Literature* defined as the fundamental American male psyche: "The essential American soul is hard, isolate, stoic, and a killer." Lawrence went on to elaborate: "A man who keeps his moral integrity hard and intact. An isolate, almost selfless, stoic, enduring man, who lives by death, by killing, but who is pure white." (Mitty's "white" heroes are always officers and gentlemen—a "pure" aristocracy indeed.) It must be noted that nearly all of Mitty's visions deal with violence, and even the one exception dramatizes a matter of life and death. This kind of situation allows the ultimate in symbolic action in which the questions of self can be answered and personal values defined. One can speculate whether Mitty's visions of crises and correspondingly heroic responses are so familiar because they are inherent in the national unconscious or because they recur with such frequency in the national literature. The speculative game is one of chicken and egg; the undeniable fact suggests serious and alarming possibilities concerning the American male mentality in a time when football and military force provide over-simplified moral and physical confrontations.

This quality of self-reliance, so directly traceable to the American past, is manifested by Mitty's dream-self to a considerable degree. In both the frontier literature and that of the New England Romantic tradition, the hero always defined himself through actions which dramatically delineated his inner self and established his identity, as Daniel Hoffman points out in *Form and Fable in American Fiction*. A youthful culture naturally produced heroes with youthful qualities, most notably an unshaken self-confidence which framed their belief that they could always adapt to the world, no matter what the world might prove to be. This kind of unqualified optimism in one's ability (one side of the Romantic coin) reveals itself most clearly in Cooper's Natty Bumppo, Emerson's "Self-Reliance" and Thoreau's exploits in *Walden*. It is this swaggering self-assertion and a conviction regarding the control of one's destiny which characterize at once the American hero and Mitty's alter ego. (One need only recall how Mitty substitutes the fountain pen for the faulty piston in the failing anaesthetizer, how he strikes the villainous District Attorney from a sitting position with his one good arm in the chivalrous defense of a Byronic heroine, and how he prepares to fly, alone and weary, on a vital mission against the "Archies.") Like Davy Crockett, Mike Fink, and Natty Bumppo, the dream-Mitty can out-shoot, out-fight, and out-do any and all opposition. But the man who can surmount catastrophes, man-made or natural, exists today only in the mind of a bewildered and hen-pecked protagonist. Whether the potential for heroic action was greater in the past, or whether there were indeed giants in those days, Mitty, like Miniver Cheevy, can only *think* about it. "The greatest pistol shot in the world" is reduced to ordering puppy-biscuit, to fetching and carrying for his wife, and he has difficulty even recalling the name of the product.

The quality of self-reliance was a necessity for survival on the primitive battlegrounds in the American past—decisions were generally irrevocable in the crucible where masculinity was forged. But in the confusing complexity of the modern world this quality may understandably be reduced to a feeling of helplessness, of inability to cope. What had begun as a battle between man and natural world—a battle for physical survival—quickly became a struggle between man and his created world—a struggle for *self*-preservation. But the institution, like Norris' octopus, has grown monstrously large. In the world of Walter Mitty it becomes even more apparent how institutions dominate and frustrate that individual who possessed such freedom to act in the days of the frontier. The current world of industrialism and specialization severely restricts any potential for heroic action. With the frontier gone, and physical and psychological space limited, the typical male is reduced to fantasy-visions as outlets for that action which is now denied him. If it is depressing that Mitty cannot rise to traditionally heroic stature in today's world, it is also realistic. Today, Thurber seems to say, the combat is so unequal that the path to heroic action lies through the inner mind. The would-be hero must resort to the world of dream in order to inflate himself to that state where he can psychologically compete and win. Lacking the resources of the natural hero, the modern man acquires them by wish-fulfillment. Unfortunately, the victory, if and when it is attained, must occur in that same world of make-believe.

In the continuing battle with society, the individual resorts increasingly to escapism rather than to direct opposition. Rip sleeps away the time in order to avoid the wear and tear of prolonged and ineffectual confrontation. Mitty attempts a series of little sleeps, only to be awakened before each climax. Inevitably and ironically, the relentlessly real world determines both the origin and the premature conclusion of each fantasy. With the repeated stifling of each psychological orgasm, Mitty's predicament becomes more frustrated and with increasing desperation he returns to his dream-world to seek release. His triumphs, projected upon an internal terrain, are the more tantalizing because they are so fleeting and so abruptly terminated. There is no satisfaction at having beaten the system, for even his inward retreat provides no real haven.

What becomes more evident as the story progresses is the vision of the contemporary world as Hell for the Romantic individual. Mitty is recalled from his first vision when this word tolls, and the word is immediately followed by his wife's voice, admonishing him not to drive so fast. The dreamer is repeatedly forced to return to a world he neither desires nor understands. It is a world peopled with a host of authority-figures who plague the beleaguered Mitty like demons—doctors, bankers, district attorneys, mechanics, parking-lot attendants, and policemen—all of whom sound very much like Mrs. Mitty. (Notice how Mitty mistakes the voice and tone of the policeman for his wife's orders to keep his gloves on.) Mitty is the man who is constantly forced to backtrack by wife and/or society. Even a lowly parking-lot attendant assumes authority over him, telling him to "Back it up, Mac!" Mitty's spiritual and physical location are linked when the attendant informs him "Wrong lane, Mac." Our hero remembers how "once he had tried to take his chains off" but was forced to ask a grinning mechanic for help. And so, significantly, it is "an old copy of *Liberty*" that he peruses while awaiting his wife's return. When she rebukes him for hiding, Mitty can only resignedly muse to himself, "Things close in."

These three words circumscribe much of the contemporary American male's feelings toward adult responsibilities. Small wonder that he returns to boyhood methods of dealing with a world which confuses him—and small wonder that he conceives his wife as threat and stifler of his inner self. Thus Babbitt's infantile visions of a romance with a "fairy-child" as well as "he-man" experiences are matched by his physical appearance. "His large head was pink. . . . His face was babyish in slumber. . . ." In so many ways the American male resembles a child who has not yet awakened, or who prefers to pull the blanket over his drowsy head rather than confront and cope. Babbitt's conventional escapes—his luke-warm affair and fishing trip—are less disturbing than Paul Riesling's solution of shooting the wife. And just as serious is Harry "Rabbit" Angstrom's method of running away physically from adult relationships after he has committed himself to fatherhood. Mitty's internal flights are harmless by comparison, but the motivating factors are identical.

While it is unfortunate that the American male is bewildered and helpless, his inability to come to mature terms with his predicament is a sign of retarded personal and hence social development. The consequences of his failure become socially alarming. Whether one feels sympathy or revulsion for his personal state, it becomes apparent that here is a mentality which seeks an adolescent sense of freedom in response to an environment it perceives as overwhelmingly stultifying and complex. This search goes well beyond the bounds of nostalgic reminiscence as it augments a resentment which weakens the marital fabric. Naturally the wife comes to symbolize all external and confining pressures; and naturally the man seeks to discover freedom as he remembers it—in the heroic past where issues seemed much simpler and where men stood taller than their present-day counterparts.

The heroic mold has generally been cast by a juvenile imagination in America. Certainly the folk heroes were inflated to larger-than-life proportions. And the Romantic imagination would naturally have seized upon the frontier as a natural landscape whereon heroic deeds of a corresponding size and nature could be performed. But in Thurber's modern man only a dim memory of a heroic past remains, nurtured on puerile fantasies propagated by films and pulp fiction. With the frontier gone, and space and privacy at a premium, there is only one place where Mitty can hope to fulfill himself—in a world of self-projection. And even here he cannot totally escape, for the real world apprizes him of its presence by shattering each delusion before it can be climaxed.

As a result of being perpetually interrupted at crucial moments in these fantasies, it seems only proper that Mitty's final role should be that of the condemned man about to be executed by a faceless firing squad for reasons not explicitly given. This vision is a marvelously telling projection of Mitty's place in the world as he feels it. How fitting it is that the story ends, as it began, with a day-dream and that, to the external world (his wife, among others), Walter Mitty wears that "faint, fleeting smile" and remains "inscrutable to the last."

LOUIS HASLEY

"James Thurber: Artist in Humor"

South Atlantic Quarterly, Autumn 1974, pp. 504–15

Beyond question the foremost humorist of the twentieth century, James Thurber was a divided man. With minor exceptions he did not explore the century's large social and political problems. War, religion, crime, poverty, civil rights—these were not his subjects. Instead he struck at the immemorial stupidities, cruelties, and perversities of men that lie at the root of our ills. A disillusioned idealist, he satirized mean behavior to sound the clearest note of his discontent. Yet he considered himself an optimist or near kin to one. He insisted that the perceptive reader would detect in his work "a basic and indestructible thread of hope."

How valid, the reader may ask, are Thurber's strictures against our civilization when one finds scarcely a momentary glimpse of childhood, romantic love, the businessman, the scientist, the engineer, the clergyman, the factory worker, the lawyer, the physician? If none of these, who then are his subjects, his characters?

Aside from relatives and family servants, he gives us artists and intellectuals like himself, isolatoes in our time, self-exiled by a temperament alien to the world and at the same time treated contemptuously by that world. Validity might then be dismissed as an irrelevance because we are faced with two conflicting sets of ideas. It was the study of man, however, that absorbed Thurber, and the proof of his right to the title of artist lies in his ability to universalize his subjects.

The world of James Thurber is conjugal, social, artistic, and psychological, as it is in his favorite author, Henry James. It is, of course, less genteel, less sinister, less subtle, less refined, less elaborate than in James, but it fits the pace of life in today's journalistic offices and studios, as well as its upper-middle-class social gatherings that are viable only with plentiful alcoholic stimulation. Here the artist-intellectuals and their long-suffering spouses communicate among themselves, having only tangential contact with this or that "outsider" from the practical world of affairs. James Thurber found man a frightening subject, although a large part of his best work was in perceptive, affectionate, admiring tribute to such friends and *New Yorker* associates as Harold Ross, E. B. White, Robert Benchley, and John McNulty. Engaging tributes also deal with grandparents, parents, aunts, and other persons whom he knew in his youth and early manhood around Columbus, Ohio.

Thurber was born in Columbus in 1894 into the family of Charles L. and Mary Fisher Thurber. His father was an honest, idealistic small-time politician. In the household his mother, an irrepressible, intelligent woman with a bent toward practical jokes, was the dominant figure. At the age of seven, James was accidentally blinded in the left eye by an arrow while playing Indian with his brother William. This was the beginning of a lifelong trouble with his eyesight, culminating in total blindness some ten years before his death in 1961. In Columbus, Thurber attended Ohio State University, where he worked in undergraduate journalism, eventually becoming editor of the campus *Sun-Dial*. His poor eyesight was evidently responsible for his failure in biology and for his leaving the University in 1918 without a degree. For the next two years he served in Washington and Paris as a code clerk in the State Department. Returning to Columbus, he became a reporter on the *Dispatch*. His next stints were brief, first on the *Chicago Tribune* in France, and then on the *Evening Post* in New York. He joined the staff of the *New Yorker* in 1927 and eight years later resigned to take up free-lancing. In May 1935 he was divorced from Althea Adams, whom he had married in 1922 and by whom he had one child, a daughter, Rosemary. His marriage to Helen Wismer a month after his divorce was a happy union that endured till his death.

Aside from *The Male Animal*, the successful Broadway play which Thurber wrote with actor-playwright Elliott Nugent, and *The Years with Ross*, the book-length portrait of the founder-editor of the *New Yorker*, Thurber remained faithful to short pieces. "Pieces" is the term he customarily used, whether they were fiction, essays, articles, biography, autobiography, or fantasy. The *New Yorker* itself did not classify under the conventional genres what it printed, and by edict of editor Harold Ross it carefully avoided the plotted short story, as well as anything arty, literary, or learned.

Of the pieces that appear to be clearly fiction in the more or less currently realistic sense of the term, only a handful are outstanding. Triumphant among these is the incomparable story, "The Secret Life of Walter Mitty." In a civilization in which women were winning the battle of the sexes, Mitty the non-hero is among the defaulters by virtue of allowing his wife to dominate him. He achieves secretly a kind of compensatory victory by indulging in interludes of stream-of-consciousness fantasy, triggered whenever the immediate outside event threatens to run him down—fantasy in which he vividly and heroically figures as a man among men. The story is a masterpiece of associational psychology in its shuttling between the petty, humiliating details of his outer life and the flaming heroism of his self-glorifying reveries. He becomes the prime exemplification of the Thurber man, as critics have called him, a figure of the little man such as appears prominently in other Thurber stories to the end of World War II. This man is likewise brilliantly celebrated in many of Thurber's sophisticatedly primitive cartoons, which are necessary adjuncts to the full appreciation of the people whom Thurber envisioned. Similarly, Mrs. Mitty is the practical, no-nonsense, hard-headed wife ("the Thurber woman") who bosses her husband about as she might an irresponsible child.

"The Catbird Seat" presents a vigorous, blustery woman, Mrs. Ulgine Barrows (note that "Ulgine" suggests "ugly" and that "barrow" can mean a pig) and a mousy Erwin Martin, head file clerk, whose department is threatened by the efficiency ax of Mrs. Barrows. Martin first plans a quiet murder of his enemy, then changes to an extremely ingenious plan by which she is routed, and by which Martin becomes, so to speak, the canary that swallowed the cat.

If Mitty has only an escapist's psychological victory, Martin's triumph is complete and unalloyed; but both are widely considered exceptions in the female-dominated world of James Thurber. Still a third "exception" occurs in the fable, "The Unicorn in the Garden," wherein the man, whom the wife tries to have put in the booby-hatch, manages to have her put away instead. In the series of drawings called "The War Between Men and Women," it is the women who surrender to the men. Perhaps the number of such "exceptions" is sufficient to puncture the legend of the monolithic triumph of women over men in Thurber's world.

"The Catbird Seat" is a short story of traditional structure. So too is "The Greatest Man in the World," told in deadly earnest and with devastating effect. It presents a thoroughly detestable minor criminal, Jack "Pal" Smurch, who flies a flimsy airplane solo, nonstop, around the world. While the millions, including the President and other dignitaries, having been treated by the press to rose-tinted descriptions of Smurch's past life, make plans to honor him, Smurch arrogantly demands money and the parties which he expects as his due. His behavior is so egregious that the nation's leaders adopt a drastic expedient to dispose of him. In its contempt and grotesquerie, it is equaled only by Ring Lardner's story "Champion" (with its anti-hero, Midge Kelly), in depicting a blind and indiscriminate hero worship by the American public, with a secondary indictment of the press in pandering to the debased tastes of its masses of readers. The nation's political leaders likewise share guilt with the press for their time-serving part in the ignoble dispatch of Smurch.

In the realm of slangy satire, "The White Rabbit Caper" is a hilarious take-off on radio mystery stories as written for children. An animal story with clever dialogue that teems with puns and is touched with rare fantasy, it is one of the funniest pieces Thurber ever wrote. At another extreme is "A Call on Mrs. Forrester," a beautifully imagined and sensitive account of a visit by the narrator to the charming Marian Forrester, the central character in the novelette, *A Lost Lady*, done in the manner of its author, Willa Cather.

Among Thurber's half-dozen fantasy stories for children and childlike adults, his own favorite was properly *The White Deer*. It tells of an enchanted princess who at the outset inhabits the body of a white deer, but when she is changed back into a beautiful maiden she is unable to remember her name. The story's progress is the effort to identify her and to find her true love. Magic, mystery, and wizardry enter the story in a way that must surely appeal to children; adults will find the characterization often humorous and the style marked by intermittent nonsense, whimsy, and word play. Next to *The White Deer*, I feel (in adult favor), would be *The Last Flower*, which Thurber himself illustrated. It is a brief and fragile parable of a world of strife in which the survival of the race turns on the love between one last man and one last woman.

This century has seen the fable genre used distinctively by George Ade, Ambrose Bierce, Don Marquis, and James Thurber. The best of Ade's and of Thurber's vie for first honors, though they are very different. Ade's fables are realistic, the characters are people, and the application is principally to the life of the day. Thurber's fables are more nearly Aesopian, most of the characters are animals, and their extension is more widely philosophical.

Given Thurber's passion for brevity, clarity, and conciseness, and his satirist's desire to teach, it was reasonable that the fable as a form should exert a magnetic attraction upon him. That his didacticism was intentional many of the morals readily show:

> "Where most of us end up there is no knowing, but the hell-bent get where they are going."
>
> "It is wiser to be hendubious than cocksure."
>
> "A word to the wise is not sufficient if it doesn't make sense."
>
> "He who dies of a surfeit is as dead as he who starves."

Though most of the fables are universal in their cast, several are geared to political relevance in our day. The moral of "The Birds and the Foxes" is readily seen to have contemporary application: "Government of orioles, by the foxes, and for the foxes, must perish from the earth." The moral of "The Very Proper Gander" is ironic: "Anybody who you or your wife thinks is going to overthrow the government by violence must be driven out of the country." The most fully worked out and best realized symbolically is "The Rabbits Who Caused All the Trouble," an allegory of the operation of the Big Lie among nations and a satire of imperialistic, protective invasion. Ultimately the most charming and probably the most enduring of the fables is "The Unicorn in the Garden," a parable justifying the imagination and its sense for beauty, telling us that only those who can see a unicorn can truly see reality.

Dogs, mechanisms, language, women, marriage, and sex are the subjects about which Thurber wrote most of his delightful personal essays. One whole volume is a collection of his perceptive writings about dogs, of which the following paragraph may serve as a sample:

> Like the great Gammeyer of Tarkington's *Gentle Julia*, the poodle I knew seemed sometimes about to bridge the mysterious and conceivably narrow gap that separates instinct from reason. She could take part in your gaiety and your sorrow; she trembled to your uncertainties and lifted her head at your assurances. There were times when she seemed to come close to a pitying comprehension of the whole troubled scene and what lies behind it. If poodles, who walk so easily upon their hind legs, ever do learn the little tricks of speech and reason, I should not be surprised if they make a better job of it than Man, who would seem to be surely but not slowly slipping back to all fours.

The border warfare which Thurber so persistently waged with our machine civilization seems to have been a natural inheritance both from parents and from grandparents, including a grandfather who scolded and handled his electric runabout as he would a colt that had to be broken. Excellent incidents illustrative of Thurber's encounters with machines, along with suitable psychological, even Freudian, analysis, are found in "Sex ex Machina," "The Car We Had to Push," "Recollections of the Gas Buggy," and "A Ride with Olympy." His otherwise confident mother feared that their Victrola might blow up and considered it "dangerous" to drive an automobile without gasoline; his mother's mother "lived the latter years of her life in the horrible suspicion that electricity was dripping invisibly all over the house . . . out of empty sockets." A sense of mystery emerges as mechanical objects seem to try to speak. Thurber can tell of tires that "booped and whooshed" and fenders that "queeled and graked," while the machine in the operating room of Walter Mitty's mind goes on immortally with its "pocketa-pocketa-pocketa."

One of the passions of James Thurber was his devotion to language. He battled often and zealously against obfuscation, against "the carcinomenclature" of "an agglomerative phenomenon of accumulated concretations." What he insisted on was clarity, accuracy, and sense. He blamed the merchandisers and the "political terminologists of all parties" for the continuing debasement of our language, asking instead that it be used with dignity and grace. Some of this advocacy is straight, but much of it is woven lightly and wittily into a great variety of situations and contexts, including word games, of which he was inordinately fond and which cost him many night hours of sleepless tossing.

Something of his obsessive pleasure in toying with language comes out in his verbal encounters with a servant, Della, who constantly mispronounced and misused words. In discussing these words with her, he circles rather than attacks directly. He could have "simply come out in the beginning," he writes, "and corrected Della when she got words wrong. Coming at her obliquely with a dictionary only enriches the confusion; but I wouldn't have it any other way. I share with Della a form of escapism that is the most mystic and satisfying flight from actuality I have ever known. It may not always comfort me, but it never ceases to beguile me."

Women, marriage, and sex, being interrelated, come in for much collective attention. Beginning with his first book, *Is Sex Necessary?* (with fellow author E. B. White) Thurber was continuously preoccupied with relations between the sexes, bringing to the subject an extensive knowledge of modern psychology supported by a keen observation of what went on in the society around him. On a television program in 1959 the Irish actress Siobhan McKenna asserted that American women are spoiled. Thurber quickly agreed, saying that he had written twenty-two books to show it. The most characteristic of his women are business-like, matter-of-fact, dominating if not domineering, unintellectual, somewhat parasitical, and given to exasperating oversimplifications. Their husbands, feeling vaguely injured and resentful for having allowed the women to take command, must assume some small share of the responsibility with the wives for the quarrels—quarrels which are usually encouraged alcoholically during or after parties and which occur in such stories as "Am Not I Your Rosalind?" and "The Breaking Up of the Winships," as well as in *The Male Animal*. As to sexuality itself, Thurber temperamentally maintains (like Ade, Marquis, Lardner, and most literary humorists) a diffident distance and a decorously dressed posture.

A "sure grasp of confusion" is one of Thurber's hallmarks. Among college students (and probably all readers) two favorites are universal: "The Night the Ghost Got In" and "The Night the Bed Fell." In the second of these, Thurber's father decided one night to sleep in the attic. During the night an iron army cot on which "I" was sleeping tipped over with a "tremendous banging crash." In the arousal of the household and the resultant confusion, "I" was involved but didn't know it; Beall, an overnight guest, thought he was but wasn't; Herman feared Mother was, but she wasn't; the dog Rex thought Beall was, but he wasn't; and Mother thought Father was but he wasn't. A more orderly confusion is delineated in "File and Forget," an elaborate fictional exchange of letters involving a network of misunderstanding relating to a shipment of books to Thurber from his mythical publishers. The various "confusion pieces," demonstrating the often perverse irrationality in human endeavor, must be rated among the most humorous of all of Thurber's blends of the absurd and the commonplace.

During the last ten years of his life, Thurber turned more and more to serious treatments of literary subjects and people. His spirit followed a less creative, more critical turn, and while he never yielded wholly to despair, the note of gloom is unmistakable. Art, he declared, was "the one achievement of Man which has made the long trip up from all fours seem well advised."[1] But the present time, he said, meaning around 1960, "is one of formlessness in literature, in drama, and in comedy as well as in speech." Comedy, he asserted in a piece called "Magical Lady," "has ceased to be a challenge to the mental processes. It has become a therapy of relaxation, a kind of tranquillizing drug." As opposed to other expert opinion, he finds the time good for satire with its "organization, statistics, surveys, group action, program, platform, imperatives and the like." Both humor and comedy, he maintains, have declined in our time because of attacks by the intellectual left and the political right. Wise things are said in "The Case for Comedy." For instance: "As brevity is the soul of wit, form . . . is the heart of humor and the salvation of comedy." Also: "humor and pathos, tears and laughter are, in the highest expression of human character and achievement, inseparable." In "The Duchess and the Bugs" he asserts that "the nature of humor is anti-communistic, just as the nature of Communism is anti-humor," and "The only rules comedy can tolerate are those of taste, and the only limitations those of libel." In pointing up the decline of comedy, he calls attention to the prevalence of horror jokes and comics, sick comedians, and a *Zeitgeist* that is manic. In an entirely different vein, one of critical appreciation, "The Wings of Henry James" is a piece of which the master himself would undoubtedly have approved.

Turning to a final category, we cannot fail to recognize Thurber's eminence in the portrayal of actual people. There is, first of all, the volume that has the rightful claim to be considered his best, the somewhat burlesque autobiography, *My Life and Hard Times*. Despite its autobiographical basis, it is the most consistently creative and humorous of all his books. In *The Thurber Album* occur "Lavender with a Difference," a loving and unforgettably humorous tribute to his mother, and "Daguerreotype of a Lady," a tribute to a sturdy, courageous, lovable neighborhood nurse, Mrs. Albright, who delivered Thurber; these he declared to be the two best pieces he had done on women, and one finds it easy to agree. "E.B.W.," his brief profile of one of the *New Yorker's* most perdurable spirits, E. B. White, is perfect of its kind. And the book, *The Years with Ross*, is wholly charming, filled with fascinating incidents, anecdotes, and exchanges in a brilliant coterie of which Ross (who according to Charles MacArthur had "the charm of gaucherie") is the center.

Thurber's style is an enviable model of twentieth-century American—supple, witty, unmannered, sensitive to words, marked by humor that ranges from the quiet to the explosive, and by inspired metaphor. One of his women "whisked a cork out of a wine bottle as if it had been a maidenhair fern." In "The Day the Dam Broke" we were all "as safe as kittens under a cookstove." As a quarrel develops with her husband, Marcia Winship's "sentences were becoming long and wavy." In "The Catbird Seat," "the door to the office blew open with the suddenness of a gas-main explosion and Mrs. Barrows catapulted through it." About the only device of humor that crops up with regularity is some form of paronomasia—elaborate punning or word play, often done with song lyrics, as in "I want a ghoul just like the ghoul that buried dear dead Dad." Confusion is sometimes served by a snowballing technique or by exaggeration, as in "The Night the Ghost Got In." That night the police answered a burglar alarm from the Thurber residence by "a Ford sedan full of them, two on motorcycles, and a patrol wagon with about eight in it and a few reporters."

Thurber once declared in a letter to this writer, "I almost never plan the use of a literary device, but just take it when it comes along." Of course a number of them occasionally came along, several of which are the incongruous catalogue, the *reductio ad absurdum*, the comic neologism, understatement, altered clichés, nonsense, alliteration, slang, parody, literary allusion, and invective.

Thurber was, it must be conceded, a fastidious stylist with psychological depth, subtlety and complexity; with a keen sense of pace, tone, ease, and climax; and with imagination that often wandered into surrealism. He handled minor tragedy with unparalleled expertness. Revisions were frequent and painstaking, a given piece often being revised ten or (as with "Mitty") fifteen times. *The White Deer* underwent twenty-five revisions. The positive delight that the reader takes in his style, along with his often greater intellectual range and understanding, tells why he outdoes his contemporaries in his chosen métier.

Not that he has no limitations. The areas of contemporary life which he left unexplored are extensive, as indicated at the outset of this essay. There are no lengthy sustained, creatively structured works. He was a critic of manners only (as were James and Jane Austen!). Aside from the fantasy pieces, his writing was in one way or another confined to his experiences, which show an almost provincial concern with a narrow band of society. The essays in *The Thurber Album*, memorializing certain of his forebears and associates back in Columbus before 1925, are tinged with sentimentality. ("I haven't been in the house for more than a quarter of a century, because I want to remember it as it was when I was young.") And except for certain engaging eccentricities in his subjects, his nostalgia provides a *nil nisi bonum* principle of selection.

From what has been said earlier about his Mr. Mitty and Mr. Monroe, it is not to be inferred that James Thurber was personally meek and ineffectual. His longtime friend and *New Yorker* associate, the late Wolcott Gibbs, lays that chimera. "The idea that he would be helpless in the face of any known social situation seems very humorous to me. There have been times when I thought that he dealt a little more erratically with life than most of the men I know, but I have certainly never seen him defeated, or even perceptibly disconcerted, by it. . . . The essence of Thurber is such that in any real contest of personalities everybody else would be well advised to take to the hills."

On the score of attitudes to women he was ambivalent. Half-satirically he admitted that men had made a mess of things and that women would have to take over. In *Lanterns and Lances*, published the year of his death, he drops the satire and says flatly, "If I have sometimes seemed to make fun of Woman, I assure you it has only been for the purpose of egging her on." Throughout his work there is a distrust of science and reason, for which men are principally responsible; it would seem, therefore, that Thurber subscribes, though in no unmasculine way, to the more intuitive and human approaches to reality which characterize the feminine makeup.

He was chary of ultimates. His writings set this life in no perspective of religious or anti-religious conviction. Escapist that he admitted to being, one feels that he kept religious questionings and promptings closely in check. Theological comment like the following is rare: "Nature (I do not say God, because I think protective Providence washed Its hands of us long ago . . .)." In the posthumous volume, *Credos and Curios*, he states: "I do not happen to be a frenetically religious man myself, but I flatly refuse to accept [Russian cosmonaut] Gagarin as the Son of a new God." In the foreword to that volume, Thurber's widow refers to the contents as a varied collection of pieces, quite a few of which "express in some way his credos," but we are immediately disappointed to learn that the credos are confined to "his beliefs and feelings about humor and comedy."

A recent brilliant but uneven study by Jesse Bier entitled *The Rise and Fall of American Humor* (New York, 1968) reveals some fine insights but also some intemperate (not to say wrong) judgments about Thurber. For instance, "American misogyny receives absolute apotheosis in James Thurber, as everyone knows." "Thurber's work is a joyfully vengeful and tireless attack on womanhood." These are distortions and, as I have already pointed out, represent only one side of the coin. In his effort to simplify the discouraging aspects of modern life, Bier also oversimplifies Thurber's final stage as one of "complete misanthropy," in which his work is "replete with its accentuated and uncompromising pessimism," and characterized by "final hopelessness." Bier makes no reference to Morsberger's critical study of Thurber mentioned above. On the other hand, here is Morsberger's judgment: "Thurber did not belong in the ranks of futilitarians who see life as a hopeless blunder. . . . He also knew that people can be admirable and wonderful in many ways; and the fact that man is capable at all of love and aspiration indicates that he is not utterly damned. . . . his anger came not from misanthropy but from awareness of man's inhumanity to man."

Thurber's widow, Helen Thurber, in the already cited foreword to the posthumous *Credos and Curios*, is intent also on refuting any attribution of final hopelessness to her late husband. "It was not too long before his death that he wrote the lines: 'Let us not look back in anger, nor forward in fear, but around in awareness.' He showed all three at times—anger certainly, fear perhaps—but he always put awareness above the others. That, I think, is the real key to James Thurber as a person and as a writer."

And with that expert testimony, why not let the record stand until better comes along?

Notes

1. Quoted by Robert E. Morsberger, *James Thurber* (New York, 1964), p. 34.

JEAN TOOMER

1894–1967

Jean Toomer was born in Washington, D.C., on December 26, 1894. He attended the University of Wisconsin (1914) and the City College of New York (1917–18), and also studied at the Gurdjieff Institute in France. Toomer worked as a teacher in Georgia in 1920–21, and was associated with the Gurdjieff Institutes in Harlem (1925) and Chicago (1926–33). In 1934 he married Marjorie Content.

Toomer is best remembered for his first book, *Cane* (1923), a miscellany of stories, verses, and a drama concerned with the lives of blacks in America. His other books are *Essentials* (1931), a collection of aphorisms; *Portage Potential* (1932); and *The Flavor of Man* (1949). His novella "York Beach" is included in the anthology *The New American Caravan* (1929), and a selection from his writings has been published as *The Wayward and the Seeking* (1978). Toomer died on March 30, 1967.

PAUL ROSENFELD
"Jean Toomer"
Men Seen: Twenty-four Modern Authors
1972, pp. 227–33

Momentarily the prose of *Cane* is artificially exalted, hooked to the Frankian pitch as to a nail high up in the wall. And night is the soft belly of a pregnant negress, and "her mind" a pink mesh bag filled with baby toes. But quickly the inflations subside. The happy normal swing resumes, the easy rhythm of a strainless human frame.

Not all the narratives intend the quality of legendary song. Certain give the fragmentated moods of the contemporary psychic conflict, and throb with hysterical starts and tearing dissonance. Yet saving the few derailing exaltations, the swing and balance of the limber body walking a road is ever-present. The musical state of soul seems primary in Jean Toomer. The pattern generates the tale. He tunes his fiddle like a tavern minstrel, and out of the little rocking or running design there rises the protagonist, solidifying from rhythm as heroes once solidified from mist: crouched whitewoman Becky who had two negro sons; Carma in overalls and strong as any man; Kabnis with his jangling nerves and flooding nostalgic lyricism. The rhythm forms the figures most. The words are but flecks of light gleaming on the surface of bronze.

He has his hand lightly, relaxedly, upon substances. The words transmit the easy sensations. They come warm and fuzzy and rich not with the heat and density of bodies crowded in tenements, but with the level beat of a blood promenaded in resinous forests amid blotches of June sun on needles and cones. It is the "sawdust glow of night" and the "velvet pine-smoke air." "The sun which has been slanting over her shoulder, shoots primitive rockets into her mangrove-gloomed, yellow flower face." He assembles words as a painter negligently rubbing pastels; leaving where he touches warm singing blobs of brown and red.

There are no rings laming this imagination, most the time: and binding it in on his proper person. Toomer's protagonists, symbols and situations are not of the nature of prearrangements: objects glued together on a mental plane and revealing through wooden joints and inner dislocation the artificial synthesis. His creative power offers to bring this young poet-novelist high in the ranks of living American letters. Characters and narratives move, and move in unpremeditated, unpredictable curves. Yet in their sudden tangential departures and radical developments they remain logical with a logic profounder than the intellect's. Not all the personages and situations of the stories, it is true, are submitted to extended composition and developed. The majority remain exposed in a single scene and through a single view. Yet in the nouvelle "Kabnis" Toomer has produced an extended composition. The focal character is moved through several episodes, and with each episode the scope of the story deepens. Characters and situations are satisfying both as symbol and as fact; and toward the conclusion both are transposed without violence to a level of reality deeper than that upon which they were launched. Possibly the upper conscious level of mind alone could have produced the earlier scenes; they may be semi-autobiographical, and felt with the aid of Sherwood Anderson and *The Portrait of the Artist as a Young Man*. But not the fantastic scene in the cellar, with its opposition of the torn differentiating negroids and the figure of the ancient African slave mumbling in his corner. Some inner substance in the author moved while writing this tale. He was no longer the same man who began it, when writing the end. He had stepped on a level of pure invention.

Toomer's free gift has given him the vision of a parting soul, and lifted his voice in salutation to the folk-spirit of the negro South. He comes like a son returned in bare time to take a living full farewell of a dying parent; and all of him loves and wants to commemorate that perishing naïveté, only beautiful one America has had, before universal ugly sophistication cover it also. Those simple singing people who have joy and have pain, and voice them frankly, largely, utterly have come to hold for him a great earthly beauty and tragedy. Their sheer animal litheness and pathos have become savage and satisfying to his breast:

> A feast of moon and men and barking hounds
> An orgy for some genius of the South
> With blood-hot eyes and cane lipped scented
> mouth—

He follows the elasticity, resiliency of young rubber, into the brown belt of Washington: feels it in its conflict with the sophistication and mechanization of white America; watches it weakened and threatened and torn in the bodies of self-conscious, half-educated people, girls become self-centered and men playing the piano in vaudeville theatres and going dreaming of Walt Whitman under the lamps of Seventh Street. And here he perceives, like new strange harmonies sounding through the subtle dissonances of life, promises of an inner healing for these splintered souls, a new strength, swiftness and singleness of motive. A new soul calls. The negroid poet of the story pulled from his base by the wilfulness of a passionate white girl, half lets his amorous opportunity pass in a proud gesture of balladry. Through the woof of "Kabnis" there go the figures of Lewis and Carrie; and Lewis is a man who has become fearless and self-confident and fine; and Carrie is a girl in whom has persisted flowerlike a beauty of instinct.

But these figures are prophetic not only for men of negro blood. They throw forward much in America; for they are symbols of some future America of which Jean Toomer by virtue of the music in him is a portion. He looks two ways. Through this recognition of the beauty of a doomed simplicity some simplicity, sensuosity, passionateness not of the South or of the past asserts, cries out, comes conscious of itself: some America beyond the newspapers, regimented feelings, edgeless language—timid, uncertain, young—in streaming music nevertheless drawing more imminent.

Both Anderson and Frank have helped rouse the impulse of Toomer. Yet it was the imagists with their perfect precision of feeling that fevered him most for work. Some clarity in himself must have responded to the clearness of these poets. That his definiteness remains as yet less intense than theirs is plain. Perhaps because his gift is warmer and more turbulent, it is also less white and clear. Whatever the cause, the Frankian inflations, and the wobbling of the focus between Kabnis and Lewis in the finale of the novelette, leave the indecision a little plainer than we would have it. Large as is the heralding which comes through him, Toomer remains as yet much of the artist trying out his colors, the writer experimenting with a style. And still, these movements of prose are genuine and new. Again a creative power has arrived for American literature: for fiction, perhaps for criticism; in any case, for prose. Other writers have tried, with less happiness, to handle the material of the South. They have had axes to grind; sadisms to exhaust in whipping up passion for the whites; masochisms to release in waking resentment for the blacks. But Toomer comes to unlimber a soul, and give of its dance and music.

LARRY E. THOMPSON
"Jean Toomer: As Modern Man"
The Harlem Renaissance Remembered
ed. Arna Bontemps
1972, pp. 51–62

Jean Toomer was born on December 26, 1894, in Washington, D.C., of old New Orleans Creole stock. His maternal grandfather, P. B. S. Pinchback, had been acting governor of Louisiana during Reconstruction. Toomer attended Paul Laurence Dunbar High School in Washington, then studied law at the University of Wisconsin and later at City College of New York. There he abandoned law for literature and soon became an avante-garde poet and short-story writer, contributing to such magazines as *Broom*, *Secession*, *Double Dealer*, *Dial*, and *Little Review*.

In 1923 he published his only novel, *Cane*, a book that was lauded in reviews but received little attention from the general public. And in that same year, Toomer came under the influence of the mystic Georges Ivanovitch Gurdjieff, who advocated "a system . . . by which one sought to attain through instruction and discipline new levels of experience, beginning with the difficult first step to self-consciousness and progressing to world and possibly cosmic-consciousness." Gurdjieff had such an impact on Toomer that a year later he went to Fontainebleau, France, to study under the mystic. When he returned to the United States he set up schools in a number of cities, including New York and Chicago.

His fascination with this psychology of self and mankind led him to conduct an experiment with eight unmarried friends (male and female) in group living in Portage, Wisconsin, in 1931. This experiment led directly to his marriage a year later to one of the participants, Marjory Latimer. She died, a year later, bearing their only child. Soon afterward Toomer was married again, to Marjorie Content, and disappeared from the literary scene to Quaker Country in Bucks County, Pennsylvania. He died in 1967, a broken man, whose talents as a writer were never fully developed.

Why did a writer of Toomer's ability suddenly up and leave, tossing into the wind the possibility of a great writing career? Here is a man who was described by Langston Hughes as "one of the most talented of the Negro writers," during the early twenties and as "a poet" by Waldo Frank. Saunders Redding, speaking of *Cane*, said in his book, *To Make a Poet Black:*

> . . . his (Toomer's) moods are hot, colorful, primitive, but more akin to the naive hysteria of the spirituals than to the sophisticated savagery of jazz and the blues.

In *Men Seen*, Paul Rosenfeld, also referring to *Cane*, said:

> Toomer's free gift has given him the vision of a parting soul, and lifted his voice in salutation to the folk-spirit of the Negro South. He comes like a son returned in bare time to take a living farewell of a dying parent.

Clifford Mason tries to deal with this problem by speaking of Toomer's alleged duality: ". . . there was the Jean Toomer of legend who went around turbaned, bouncing from Russian mystic encampments to Quaker retreats, from one white wife to a second. And then there was the inner man who denounced in early youth his 'no darker than a paper bag,' Washington, D.C., high-yaller pedigree . . ." I disagree with this idea of duality in Toomer, and in his own words this idea of black and white clashing in his inner soul is laid to rest:

> My position in America has been a curious one. I have lived equally amid the two race groups. Now white, now colored. From my point of view I am naturally and inevitably an American.

No, the answer does not lie in Toomer's duality, it lies in his quest for singularity—in his concept of himself and man in the universe. In a book titled *Essentials*, published in a private edition in 1931, Toomer put forth his philosophy of life in a series of aphorisms and maxims that dealt with the whole spectrum of human relationships, from sex and education to religion and individualism. Toomer argues that we are beings of "actualities and potentialities" which make us one in a general sense but individual also since the "actualities and potentialities" are different for everyone. But he goes on to say that modern man is losing his perception of himself:

> Modern man is losing his sense of potentiality as regards himself. Hence he is losing his sense of himself and reality.

This loss of individuality has resulted in two things: 1) a loss in initiative and a desire to conform, and 2) the growth of material values. He says:

The desire to be has become the desire to belong we
can belong to things, not to ourselves.

and

We apply to machines what we do not apply to
ourselves.

I said earlier that Toomer's quest was for singularity in himself and in mankind—not conformity but individuality. He wanted to be free of all the restrictions of modern society, for according to Toomer "acceptance of prevailing standards often means we have no standards of our own." Therefore he rejected racial, regional, and sexual restrictions:

I am of no particular race. I am of the human race,
a man at large in the human world preparing for a
new race.

I am of no specific region. I am of earth.

I am of no special field. I am of the field of being.

To Toomer individuality meant freedom and the power to control one's destiny. In a poem published in *Dial* in 1929, titled "White Arrow," he expresses this belief:

Your force is greater than your use of it existing,
yet you dream that breath depends on bonds I once
contracted for. It is a false belief induced by sleep and
fear in faith and reason you were swift and free,
white arrow, as you were, awake and be.

This journey into self—this quest to find one's place in the cosmos—began to form early in Toomer. In an unpublished autobiography, *Earth-Being*, the title itself suggestive of his conception of himself, he speaks of how he first began to form opinions of himself in the universe. He says that because of his Uncle Bismarck he began to think about his position in the cosmos, "it was all wonderful. And, young though I was, I was growing a sense and forming an attitude towards my and our [all of humanity] position on earth in the universe." Toomer lucidly explains his position in that world and his function, which he claims is to be a soothsayer: "I see myself as one of countless millions of human beings. I also see some fraction of these others. I aim, then, to give a picture and critique of all life as I see it." When he talks about writing and how he perceives of himself as a writer, this image of prophet comes clearly through, "as for writing . . . I am an essentialist. Or, to put it in other words, I am a spiritualizer, a poetic realist."

This image of himself as "poet realist" or prophet helps to explain why his art is often proselytizing and why Toomer was to some degree a modern-ancient. Perhaps the best way to take a look at Toomer, the man, is to review his literature, beginning with his plays.

The fact that Jean Toomer wrote plays is a little known fact, but a very important one, for it points out a central problem in the man—the need to find different ways of communicating his ideas and beliefs to the general public. Therefore in his plays he was experimenting with forms long before anyone else. In 1922 when Toomer wrote his first play, the sound of the revolution that was to begin in the American theater was a faint whisper. O'Neill had written *The Emperor Jones* in 1920 and *The Hairy Ape* in 1922, but the plays of George Kaufman, Marc Connelly, E. E. Cummings, and John Dos Passos were still a few years in the future. Toomer was the first American playwright who was trying to do some experimentation with, as Darwin Turner says, "dramatic form and technique in order to blend social satire with lyric expression of modern man's quest for spiritual self-realization."

This can be seen clearly in Toomer's first play, *Natalie Mann*. In this play he argues passionately for the sexual and spiritual release of the middle-class black woman and by symbolic representation the sexual and spiritual freedom of all women. The core of the play is built around Nathan Merilh, a modern-day Jesus Christ, who to my mind turns out to be a voodoo priest, and his attempt to save the soul of Natalie from the confines of middle-class values. She lives with him in New York, defying convention. She finally reaches total self-realization when he sacrifices himself and does a ritual voodoo dance which separates "individual indentity from national or social origins," saving her soul.

Toomer's philosophy is built upon a feeling of the black man's natural closeness to the soil—nature (probably because he knows black folks have been prevented from entering the mainstream of society)—a theme we shall see again in the first half of *Cane*.

The black man is therefore spiritually freer and happier than the white man. In *The Sacred Factory*, he points out the mundane existence of the working class as well as the middle class with their assorted illnesses of emotional and sexual frustrations, all caused by their dependence on the machine. He again uses the ritual dance, this time having his characters dance around in circles with slow, sluggish movements, to bring home his theme—the spiritual death of a people.

There is no need to deal with Toomer's third play, "Kabnis," at this time, since it will be dealt with in the section on *Cane*. Suffice it to say, as Turner has, "Kabnis" is a spectacle of futility and impotence."

In all his plays Toomer uses dramatic techniques and experiments to better get across his theme. Darwin Turner, in his article "The Failure of a Playwright," speaks of Toomer's use of language, "there is an artificiality [in Toomer's use of language] that is used to reflect the dullness of superficiality of the guardians of middle-class morals." Each character in Toomer's work is representative of a human type rather than a unique individual; this shows his concern with mankind—the society rather than the person. He uses dance as "the rhythmic means by which characters release themselves from inhibiting forces," as well as to show their enslavement to society's morals.

His career as a playwright was unsuccessful probably because society was not ready for his themes and experimentations.

Cane
Oracular.
Redolent of fermenting syrup,
Purple of the dusk
Deep-rooted Cane

Her skin is like dusk on the eastern horizon
O cant you see it, O cant you see it,
Her skin is like dusk on the eastern horizon
. . . When the sun goes down.

This is the beautiful Karintha. Doomed to a fate she cannot control, she becomes pregnant because of the impatience of young and old men. "God grant us youth, secretly prayed the old men. The young fellows counted the time to pass before she would be old enough to mate with them." Bearing her fatherless child, she buries it in a sawdust pile and takes out her hate of men by selling her body: ". . . men do not know that the soul of her was a growing thing ripened too soon. They will bring their money; they will die not having found it out . . ." Karintha is doomed to a tyranny of body.

Becky was the white woman who had two Negro
sons. She's dead; they've gone away. The pines

whisper to Jesus. The Bible flaps its leaves with an aimless rustle on her mound.

"Becky" is the story of a conspiracy to hide what took place under pine trees on moonless nights: miscegenation. The townspeople, black and white, try to deny Becky's existence. "When the first was born, the white folks said they'd have no more to do with her. And black folks . . ." When the second is born, Becky is regarded as dead: "Becky has another son . . . but nothing was said . . . if there was a Becky . . . Becky now was dead." Becky is symbolically killed by the chimney on the house that the town built for her, thus easing their guilt.

"Fern," born of a Jewish father and black mother, is again a study of miscegenation. Fern is a picture of sterility and pain: ". . . if you have heard a Jewish Cantor sing, if he has touched you and made your sorrow seem trivial when compared with his, you will know my feeling when I followed the curves of her profile, like mobile rivers, to their common delta." Fern, like Karintha, is destroyed by the greatest tyrant of all—sex. "Men were everlastingly bringing her their bodies." And like Karintha, her soul perished under the onslaught of human pleasures.

Red Nigger Moon. Sinner!
Blood-burning moon. Sinner!
Come out of that fact'ry door.

In "Blood-Burning Moon," Toomer shows another form of oppression of black people. Like the preceding stories, its driving force is sex. Louisa, the heroine, has two lovers, one black, one white, whose sexual rivalry is built upon a foundation of racial antagonism. The issue of who has the right to the black woman is not solved by the two men fighting, but by the white lynch mob. Toomer, in this story, successfully captures the essential injustice of a society which claims to be civilized, yet denies those humanistic values which make a society civilized to certain of its members.

The second part of *Cane* shifts from the rural South to the urban North, and in particular, to Washington, D.C.

Money burns the pocket, pocket hurts,
Bootleggers in silken shirts,
Ballooned, zooming Cadillacs
Whizzing, whizzing down the street-car tracks.

"Seventh Street" is the place where black people from the Southland, straight out of the cotton fields, put life into the dull life of Washington, "a crude-boned, soft-skinned wedge of nigger life breathing its leafer air, jazz songs and love, thrusting unconscious rhythms, black reddish blood into white and whitewashed wood of Washington." In Toomer's world, black folks, people used to working with their hands, people close to the soil—the cane—represent not only the "full life" but the only life. And white folks, people living in an urban environment, people out of communication with the soil, represent a monstrous farce of that life. Therefore civilization, by imposing upon us a number of meaningless bourgeois values, denies to the human soul the only thing which makes us human, the ability to empathize with one another.

"Rhobert" is therefore an attack on the value of private ownership of property—an essential Western value. The central metaphor of the story is Rhobert trying to carry a house on his head. Of course it is a losing struggle and the harder he tries the deeper he sinks into the mud of civilization:

Brother, Rhobert is sinking
Lets open our throats, brother,
Lets sing Deep River when he goes down.

"Box Seat" is the one story in which the central theme of *Cane*—the essential goodness of man being buried by houses, machines, nightclubs, newspapers, and anything else which represents modern society, that goodness being man's sense of brotherhood born out of toil with the soil and constant battle with nature—is best presented. The hero is a Christ-like figure named Dan Moore: "I am Dan Moore. I was born in a canefield. The hands of Jesus touched me. I am come to a sick world to heal it." Dan doesn't walk on water but he is from the underground, the soil, and he (the soil-canefield) will be the only saving grace for this world.

The central metaphor is the Box Seat, symbolic of the bourgeois values Muriel, the heroine of the story, carries within her soul. The seat Muriel occupies is at a vaudeville show where the main event is two dwarfs fighting for the "heavy-weight championship," again symbolic of the kind of farce of life that is called living in American civilization. The two dwarfs viciously beat each other, and at the end of the fight, the winner presents a blood-covered rose to Muriel, who recoils in horror. The dwarf pleads with her to take it, through his eyes.

Do not shrink. Do not be afraid of me
Jesus
See how my eyes look at you
the Son of God
I too was made in His image
Was once
I give you the rose.

As Muriel finally accepts the rose from the dwarf, Dan shouts: JESUS WAS ONCE A LEPER! And runs out of the theater, finally understanding the hypocrisy of civilization and the futility of trying to save it.

In "Kabnis" our journey is completed; we return again to the red soil of Georgia. Kabnis, the hero of the story, a Georgia schoolteacher from the North, is deathly afraid to confront his black Georgia tradition, preferring to hide behind his books. But like most men who try to hide, his tradition—his past—confronts him:

> Night winds in Georgia are vagrant poets whispering. Kabnis, against his will, lets his book slip down, and listens to them. The warm whiteness of his bed, the lamp-light, do not protect him from the weird chill of their song:
>
> White-man's land.
> Niggers, sing.
> Burn, bear black children
> Till poor rivers bring
> Rest, and sweet glory
> In Camp Ground.

Kabnis is full of self-hatred, not only for the South but for himself as well. Moreover, he is consumed by an overwhelming fear of the land, "whose touch would resurrect him." He is contrasted with Lewis, another Christ figure, whose only function in the story is to make other characters aware of their moral deficiency. Lewis is the one who confronts Kabnis on his fear of the land: "Can't hold them, can you? Master; slave. Soil; and the overarching heavens."

Halsey, unlike Kabnis, whose manhood has been taken from him in his fear of the South, and Lewis, who has grown in his confrontation with it, has grown into Southern life and has also been destroyed by it. He belongs to the society, Kabnis doesn't, but in order to survive he has denied his manhood by not fighting the insults and indignities of black Southern life.

Father John is the symbolic connection with the ancestral past. A former slave, he lives in a basement that looks like the hole in a slave ship. Through him, Lewis and Halsey's little sister, Carrie Kate, become one with their past. But Father John cannot be the guide for Carrie Kate and the rest. Toomer himself says, "It is well to remember that the past, having meaning, cannot serve as an objective for contemporary man." Therefore, when he finally does speak, his words mean nothing. However, Kabnis in his total denial of the old man can only sink into the quicksand of self-hate.

Jean Toomer in this small book has captured the beauty and the ugliness, the power and the weakness, the "triumph and the tragedy" of life in the United States. *Cane* is a masterpiece in modern literature. It is a chronicle of Toomer's search as writer, as man, as modern man trying to find himself and consequently, peace. "I am what I am and what I may become I am trying to find out." Therefore he experimented with literary form, mixing poetry, prose, and dramatic form in his work. He used techniques such as ritualization, repetition, and understatement to give his work a poetic quality and a honey-sweet tone that pulls us into this small book to glimpse the world through the eyes of Jean Toomer.

ROBERT BONE
From "Jean Toomer"
Down Home
1975, pp. 204–8, 235–38

A vast body of Toomer criticism has appeared since the Harper and Row paperbound edition of *Cane* was published in 1969. Most of it has been restricted to the book itself, which no one will deny is still in need of explication. [1] But there is a great danger of distortion in isolating this enigmatic masterpiece from the full body of Toomer manuscripts now available in the Fisk University Library. While an exclusively exegetical approach may have been justifiable prior to 1967, when the Toomer papers were deposited at Fisk, now no one who has not made his pilgrimage to Nashville can expect to be taken seriously as a Toomer critic. That is known, in the world of scholarship, as paying your dues.

A prime example of critical myopia is a recent essay by Clifford Mason called "Jean Toomer's Black Authenticity." After assuring us that "Toomer, unlike almost any other writer, really talks to Black people about themselves, giving white reality very little play indeed," Mason concludes his essay by praising Toomer for "creating a Black world of reality that lived for itself, by itself, . . . strictly of itself, and that treated whiteness with the indifference or the hate or the tolerance that it may or may not have deserved. . . ."[2]

Doubtless an accurate enough rendition of Mason's personal philosophy, such a statement simply has no bearing on the historical personage of Jean Toomer. It is Mason, and not Toomer, who desires to partition the social world, and even the realm of metaphysics, into black and white compartments. While Mason strives to harden these racial categories, it was Toomer's lifelong aim to decrystallize them. At no point in his career was Toomer's concept of reality racially exclusive. On the contrary, he insisted repeatedly and emphatically on a noumenal reality that existed beyond the phenomenal world, and specifically beyond the categories of race.

But let Toomer speak for himself in this regard. In *The Crock of Problems*, one of the unending versions of his autobiography preserved at Fisk, Toomer writes: "Damn labels if they enslave human beings. Enough of race and nationality and labels. Above race and nationality there is Mankind. Beyond labels there is reality."[3] Toomer was concerned in everything he ever wrote, including *Cane*, with this transcendent reality. This fact will be readily apparent to anyone who cares to peruse "Bona and Paul," one of the more finely crafted stories to be found in *Cane*.

Unless we grasp Toomer's neo-Platonism, with its basic commitment to noumenal reality, we cannot comprehend his attitude toward race. As early as 1914, on the eve of his departure for the university, Toomer formulated a racial stance that would remain essentially unchanged throughout his life:

> Going to Wisconsin, I would again be entering a white world; and, though I personally had experienced no prejudice or exclusion either from the whites or the colored people, I had seen enough to know that America viewed life as if it were divided into white and black. Having lived with colored people for the past five years, at Wisconsin the question might come up. What was I? I thought about it independently, and, on the basis of fact, concluded that I was neither white nor black, but simply an American. [4]

In the 1930's, Toomer elaborated his racial views at considerable length, both in poetry and prose. [5] He wrote, for example, in *A Fiction and Some Facts*, an autobiography published privately in 1931, "As for being a Negro, this of course I am not—neither biologically nor socially. . . . In biological fact I am, as are all Americans, a member of a new people that is forming in this country. If we call this people the Americans, then biologically and racially I am an American. . . . As long as I have been conscious of the issues involved, I have never identified myself with any single racial or social group."[6]

The crucial point concerning Toomer's racial stance is, in Darwin Turner's pithy phrase, that "he is not merely denying that he is black; he is also denying that he is white."[7] In other words, Toomer is challenging the philosophical validity of these racial categories. He maintains that in America the older races—Indian, African, and European—have fused and blended so as to produce a new race that transcends its historic origins. Any man is free to agree or disagree with this position (personally I find it quixotic, and of disastrous consequence for Toomer's art). But no critic, in the light of his repeated and unequivocal assertions to the contrary, can write responsibly of Toomer's "black authenticity."

Anyone who reads the many versions of Toomer's autobiography will readily acknowledge that his blackness, far from being a pillar of psychological stability, was a source of unending agony and consternation. As for his resolution of this bitter conflict, the facts speak for themselves. In the course of a lifetime, Toomer was deeply in love with three women, all of whom were white. For most of his life he lived exclusively among white people. The overwhelming bulk of his writing was not concerned with blacks in any way. There was no black writer, in short, with a lower ethnicity quotient. The norm and standard of his life and work, from which *Cane* constitutes a momentary deviation, was emphatically non-ethnic.

If this be so, and if Toomer maintained his transcendent view of race consistently throughout his life, how can we account for *Cane*, which is, or seems to be, a celebration of ethnicity? The apparent contradiction is readily resolved by sundering the future from the past, or in other words, by stressing the vatic nature of Toomer's art. He is essentially a poet, and a poet in the prophetic tradition of Blake and Whitman. His characteristic stance is that of an Old Testament prophet. And a prophet is by definition one who lives more intensely in the future than the past.

Cane is Toomer's tribute to the past; his reconciliation to the painful history of the black man in America. It is a celebration of the Negro folk-spirit, which Toomer sees as being rapidly obliterated by the forces of modern industrialism. To lament that loss is the aim of his magnificent lyric, "Song of the Son," which stands at the spiritual center of *Cane*. When Toomer writes of "a song-lit race of slaves," whose plaintive soul is "leaving, soon gone," he employs the language and the form of pastoral elegy. For *Cane* is in essence a pastoral interlude, like Thoreau's trip to the woods, through which the author seeks to achieve a consolidation of the self, in order to move forward to the fundamental task of prophecy.

Cane was Jean Toomer's hail-and-farewell to his blackness. Springing from a sojourn of several months in Sparta, Georgia, the impulse that gave birth to *Cane* was soon exhausted. Toomer was never to touch on these materials again. "The folk-spirit," as he explains in the *Outline of an Autobiography*, "was walking in to die on the modern desert. That spirit was so beautiful. Its death was so tragic. Just this seemed to sum up life for me. And this was the feeling I put into *Cane*. *Cane* was a swan song. It was a song of an end. And why no one has seen and felt that, why people have expected me to write a second and a third and a fourth book like 'Cane' is one of the queer misunderstandings of my life."[8] ⟨. . .⟩

The Angelic Imagination

In an essay on Edgar Allan Poe entitled "The Angelic Imagination," Allen Tate accuses Poe of seeking to evade the human condition. He finds in Poe a tendency, deriving from his neo-Platonism, to deny the reality of the physical world. Lacking a commitment to the order of nature, Poe's imagination soars off into the Beyond, where it tries to create a transcendental order of its own. This thrust of the imagination beyond the human scale Tate denominates "the angelic fallacy." For it leads to a grandiose presumption on the part of man: "When neither intellect nor will is bound to the human scale, their projection becomes godlike, and man becomes an angel."[9]

The angelic tendency of Toomer's imagination is everywhere apparent in the fiction of his Gurdjieff phase. Several of his stories, including "Love on a Train," "Mr. Costyve Duditch," and "Winter on Earth"; his two novellas, "York Beach" and "The Angel Begori"; and his novel, *The Gallonwerps*, are based on the concept of angelic visitation. The White Island fable which comprises the core of "Winter on Earth" is perhaps the most explicit statement of the theme.[10] Here he depicts a band of angels "commissioned to teach and aid the men of Earth to improve their way of living." The truth is that Jean Toomer, under the influence of Gurdjieff and Ouspensky, cast himself in the angelic role, and displayed in his writing a sense of mission whose grandiose pretensions stem from the angelic fallacy.

It is in his sketch of Alfred Stieglitz, however, that the metaphor is most revealingly employed. Ostensibly describing Stieglitz, Toomer might be speaking of himself:

> He will sometimes tell you that he feels uprooted. From one point of view this is true. He has not had a fixed establishment. What is more to the point, he is not a tree. The human nostalgia to revert to the vegetable may occasionally move him, but with him, as with so many of us, it has come to nothing. Yet I do not feel he is suspended or unplaced. Always I feel he is rooted *in himself* and to the *spirit* of the place. Not rooted to things; rooted to spirit. Not rooted to earth; rooted to air."[11]

"Rooted to air." There in his own phrase is the essential tragedy of Jean Toomer. His urge to transcendence leads him to project a world above the body, above the solid earth, in the element of air: thin, etherial, appropriate to birds or angels. But the task of the imagination, as a master-craftsman has instructed us, is to "give to airy nothing / A local habitation and a name." What, in Toomer's case, does such a dwelling place for the imagination mean? What if not the Southern soil? But under the spell of Gurdjieff, his sense of soil has eroded. He prefers Utopia (literally, no place) to a Georgia canefield. As for the name, let it remain unspoken: he would rather be etherial than black.

No one familiar with Toomer's life history will fail to grasp the connection between that history and his neo-Platonism. To question the reality of matter was natural enough for a man whose very existence challenged the reality of race. To such a man the world of nature was only skin-deep. Toomer's Platonism was at bottom a projection of his impulse to escape his fate. He resented being earth-bound as much as being race-bound. In rebelling against the artificial boundaries of race, however, he tried to overleap the immutable boundaries of human existence. He denied, in short, the limitations of the flesh. The result was a disembodied art.

Throughout his Gurdjieff phase, Toomer's style becomes increasingly abstract. The vivid images that were its crowning glory give way to windy generalities. The pungency of *Cane* is nowhere to be found. We are served a drab and tasteless gruel and told that it is rich in vitamins. Toomer's later fiction, which suffers from his grandiose intentions, is at once overwrought and underimagined. Dramatization is thin, and incessant sermonizing takes the place of narrative. As imagination falters, the dry rot of abstraction sets in. The rich concreteness of experience is sacrificed to the pursuit of philosophic Absolutes.

"I call that imagination angelic," writes Allen Tate, "which tries to disintegrate or circumvent the image in the illusory pursuit of essence." That is the crux of Toomer's failure as an artist. He abandons the image for precept and idea. Concreteness and transformation, the primary laws of the imagination, are violated by abstraction and exposition. Toomer's first allegiance in the Gurdjieff years is to some other than the esemplastic power. But Imagination is a jealous god, and will not be supplanted without exacting a terrible revenge.

There is something heroic in Jean Toomer's lifelong effort to transcend the arbitrary bounds of race and establish his existence as an individual. His stubborn insistence that social reality is not the ultimate reality will not fail to touch a responsive chord in thoughtful men. Nonetheless, the fiction of his Gurdjieff phase must be counted for the most part as a devastating failure. It is primarily a failure of imagination, but behind that lies a moral failure, whose essence is that pride has conquered love. For it is pride that tempts man to usurp the role of angels, and love, as Richard Wilbur has observed, that recalls us to the things of this world.

Notes

1. A notable exception is Darwin Turner's essay on Toomer in his book, *In a Minor Chord* (Carbondale: Southern Illinois University Press, 1971). Turner has absorbed the huge mass of unpublished materials at Fisk and brought them, in convenient summary form, into the public domain.
2. For these quotations see Clifford Mason, "Jean Toomer's Black Authenticity," *Black World*, November 1970, pp. 75–76.

3. *The Crock of Problems*, p. 28. Toomer Collection.
4. *Outline of an Autobiography*, pp. 15–16. Toomer Collection.
5. See especially the long, Whitmanesque poem called "Blue Meridian," in Kreymborg, et al., eds., *The New Caravan* (New York: Macaulay, 1936).
6. Quoted in Darwin Turner, *In a Minor Chord*, p. 34.
7. Darwin Turner, *In a Minor Chord*, p. 35.
8. *Outline of an Autobiography*, pp. 58–59. Toomer Collection.
9. Allen Tate, *The Man of Letters in the Modern World* (Cleveland and New York: Meridian Books, 1955), p. 122.
10. See Alfred Kreymborg, et al., *The Second American Caravan* (New York: Macaulay, 1928), pp. 694–715.
11. See "The Hill," in Waldo Frank, Paul Rosenfeld, and Lewis Mumford, editors, *American and Alfred Stieglitz: A Collective Portrait* (New York: The Literary Guild, 1934), p. 297. Italics in the original.

CHARLES R. LARSON

From "*Cane* by Jean Toomer"

New Republic, June 19, 1976, pp. 31–32

Certainly, *Cane* is not a typical novel. It is, in fact, *sui generis*—a unique piece of writing in American literature as well as in the entire scope of Third World writing. I suggest that *Cane* should be regarded as a lyrical novel—a narrative structured by images instead of the traditional unities. Its tripartite structure is developed from a series of thematic tensions: North/South; city/country (with the almost ubiquitous image of the land); past/present; black/white; male/female. Structured by these counterparts or tensions, *Cane* achieves a lyrical beauty and power which make it, for me, the most compelling novel ever written by a black American writer.

The first part of *Cane* is composed of six prose sections and ten poems. The time is shortly after World War I, the setting is the South, and the concentration is, for the most part, upon a number of women: Karintha, Becky, Carma, Fern, Esther and Louisa. Except for the last of these, the women's names are used as titles for the individual sections. Almost all of them have led frustrated lives. All of the male/female relations recorded here leave something to be desired, two of them ending tragically for the men involved. Although these women are usually stronger than the men in their lives, they achieve little satisfaction from their roles. Furthermore, all of these stories take place in the dead of night, in darkness or at dusk—the implication being that black people are free to act and be themselves only after the sun goes down. The darkness liberates them, but it can also destroy them. These images of darkness and dusk (also developed in many of the poems in this section of the novel) establish a major tension, creating a nightmarish world of frustration and violence. They are important because they depict a race of people living on the fringes of reality, repressing the horrors of the past and the realities of the present. The future, Toomer implies, will be a continuation of these frustrations unless the black man comes to grips with the realities of his past, rooted as it is so horrendously in slavery and its tragic aftermath.

The aftermath of slavery is presented even more chaotically in the second part of Toomer's novel (seven prose sections, interspersed with five poems), in which we see the results of the Great Migration. Here the emphasis shifts from the South to the North, to Washington, DC, and Chicago, during and after World War I. As a counterpoint to the first part, the focus is mostly upon black men and the crippled lives they lead in industrialized Northern cities. While most of the stories in the earlier part take place in the natural world of cane fields and pine forests, most of the stories of the second take place inside of buildings which confine man's natural yearnings. Toomer appears to believe that the black man is better off in the South than in the North. The poems, again, reiterate these common themes.

The setting shifts back to the South in "Kabnis," the third part of *Cane*. Some readers have referred to "Kabnis" as a novella, others have called it a play. My own feeling is that it was intended to be a movie scenario. Whatever, there are stage directions, occasional lines of poetry, and movement in and out of the main character's mind. Characteristically, much of Kabnis' story is set in the darkness of night. At the beginning, we see him alone in his cabin, frightened by the noises from the darkness outside. He longs for his home in the North, from where he feels estranged. The scenario ends several days later, at daybreak, after Kabnis and two of his friends, Halsey and Lewis, have spent a night with two women in the basement (known as the "hole") of Halsey's shop. During the night, Kabnis renounces his color, identifying with his white-skinned ancestors. Hidden away in the "hole" Halsey keeps an old man, an ex-slave, whom Lewis refers to as Father John. Kabnis and Halsey both ignore the old man's preachings, thus renouncing their history and their color; Lewis identifies the man as his source.

The most fascinating aspect of Toomer's novel for me is not the correspondences that one can draw between Kabnis and Toomer himself but the narrator-observer who wanders throughout the book. This is the author's emotional center, for the fact is that *Cane* does have a central character—a figure who resembles Toomer himself, though cleverly disguised. In the course of the narrative he undergoes a number of metamorphoses, sometimes appearing as a first-person narrator (in 12 of the 28 sections of the first two parts), that is, as a participant in the activities described; or as an observer in a third-person narrative, like Conrad's Marlow. In two other main sections ("Bona and Paul" and "Kabnis") Toomer has disguised himself as the mulatto who cannot decide whether he should be black or white, thus introducing the theme of passing. *Cane*, then, may be regarded as the story of Jean Toomer's own vacillation between races—a rather common theme of American fiction during the 1920s.

In "Song of the Son" (one of the early poems in the novel), Toomer sets forth his symbolic position as that of the recording consciousness of a race of people before its past is forgotten. He speaks of the poet's duty to his people, before their history is forgotten. Before the sun sets on the aftermath of slavery, he will record this heritage on paper; that is, he will write *Cane*. He emphasizes that even though the sun is setting "on / A song-lit race of slaves, it has not set." One seed from the past has survived and that seed will become

> An everlasting song, a singing tree,
> Caroling softly souls of slavery,
> What they were, and what they are to me,
> Caroling softly souls of slavery.

It is, of course, one of the great ironies of Toomer's life that his book fulfilled his artistic intentions though Toomer himself was unable to accept this heritage. One suspects that the publication of *Cane* must have acted as a kind of exorcism, bringing Toomer's own identity problems to a climax. Like his alter ego, Ralph Kabnis, Toomer's personal vacillation between black and white damaged his own psyche beyond repair. Darwin T. Turner is correct when he says that in the end Toomer did not identify himself as a Caucasian any more than he did as an Afro-American, that he was "self-exiled from all races." *Cane* was his swan song, yet if Toomer in the long run was unable to accept his mixed heritage, there is little doubt that *Cane* has made it possible for others to find theirs. (The last scene in the novel—a symbolic sunburst surrounding Father John and Halsey's younger sister, Carrie Kate—is, in fact, a resounding affirmation of blackness.)

The novel, however, remains. Its influence on subsequent black writing cannot be denied—especially on the writers who wrote during the last years of the Harlem Renaissance, in the '20s and '30s. Yet its significance is much more than this, for *Cane* is one of the most innovative works of 20th-century American fiction—a landmark in American literature, foreshadowing the soon-to-follow experimental works of John Dos Passos and William Faulkner. The experimental novel in America begins not with those writers but with Jean Toomer's *Cane*.

One final note. In the first printing of *Cane*, there were three different circular markings or arcs—one at the beginning of each section of the novel. By some string of accidents, the first of these has been inadvertently omitted from all subsequent printings of the novel—including the new Liveright edition. Toomer considered these designs integral to his novel, and they have variously been interpreted as male and female symbols (ying and yang) and as signs representing the sun and the moon. When they are superimposed on top of one another, they do not form a complete circle as some readers have suggested, but, rather, a circle not quite whole, which relates, once again, to the novel's central theme: the instability of black lives, the unfulfilled nature of their existence because of the inability to understand the past. Whatever their intention, one cannot help but feeling that these designs also hold the secret of Toomer's own enigmatic life.

Dalton Trumbo

1905–1976

Dalton Trumbo was born in Montrose, Colorado, on December 9, 1905. He was educated at the University of Colorado (1924–25), the University of California at Los Angeles (1926), and the University of Southern California (1928–30). Trumbo began a long and prolific career as a Hollywood screenwriter with his screenplay for the 1934 film *Jealousy*. In 1939 he married Cleo Beth Fincher, a photographer, with whom he had three children.

Trumbo's many screenplays written during the 1930s and 1940s include *A Man to Remember* (1938), *Kitty Foyle* (1940), *The Remarkable Andrew* (1942; based on his novel of the same title), *Tender Comrade* (1943), *A Guy Named Joe* (1943), *Thirty Seconds over Tokyo* (1944), and *Our Vines Have Tender Grapes* (1945). In the late 1940s Trumbo was called before the House Un-American Activities Committee to explain his relationship to the Communist Party, which he had joined in 1943. As one of the so-called Hollywood Ten, a group of writers and actors who refused to testify, he was sentenced to a year's imprisonment at the Federal Correctional Institution in Ashland, Kentucky. After leaving prison the blacklisted Trumbo was unable to work in Hollywood and went into self-exile in Mexico, where he continued, under various pseudonyms, to write screenplays, notably for *The Prowler* (1950; as "Hugo Butler"), *The Brave Bulls* (1951; as "John Bright") and *The Brave One* (1957; as "Robert Rich"). This last-named screenplay won an Academy Award, but it was not until 1960, when Otto Preminger publicly announced that he had hired Trumbo to write the screenplay for *Exodus*, that Trumbo's name was removed from the blacklist and he was able to work openly in Hollywood. Among his films from this later period are *Spartacus* (1960), *The Last Sunset* (1961), *Lonely Are the Brave* (1962), *The Sandpiper* (1965), *Hawaii* (1966), *The Fixer* (1968), and *Johnny Got His Gun* (1971; based on his novel of the same title).

Trumbo was the author of four novels. His first, *Eclipse* (1935), was followed by his best-known one, *Johnny Got His Gun* (1939), which was banned during World War II because of its anti-war message. His other novels are *The Remarkable Andrew* (1941) and *Night of the Aurochs* (1979), edited and completed by Robert Kirsch. Trumbo died of a heart attack in Los Angeles on September 19, 1976.

⟨*Johnny Got His Gun*⟩ is one of the most horrifying books ever written. Reading it on The Chief, between Chicago and the Coast, I found myself putting it down time and again to look out for comfort over the rich fields of Missouri, the high mesas of New Mexico, and the inhuman waste of the Mojave; putting it down, not because I was bored, but because the tale was more than mind and stomach could endure without occasional respite and refreshment.

You have heard of the "basket cases" that are a byproduct of war. Perhaps you have seen one, and if you have you have almost certainly asked youself, as you looked at the armless, legless object: What is it thinking and feeling? How can it go on living? The obvious answer to the second question is that a basket case has no power of self-destruction. The answer to the first question is the story of *Johnny Got His Gun*.

Joe Bonham, who went from Shale City, Colorado, by way of Los Angeles, to a war that he did not understand to fight men with whom he had no quarrel, came out of the war not only armless and legless but deaf and dumb and blind, and there was only a hole where his eyes and nose and mouth had been; a gaping hole covered by a mask. But he was alive. He could think and he could feel. He could remember the days when he had been complete, he could still feel movement in the limbs that he had lost, could still respond to the keen messages of the senses that were no longer his. He was more helpless than any slave had ever been; as helpless as a man in a coffin with the lid screwed down, as helpless as a child in the womb. But he was alive. He was a living dead man—a triumph of the surgeon's art.

The remnant of the man that had been Joe Bonham rose gradually, as through a dark pool, to the surface of consciousness. His first realization was that he was alive, the second that he was deaf. Then he knew that his left arm was gone; then he missed his right. A little later he discovered that he had no legs, and almost immediately afterward that he had no face.

> He threw back his head and started to yell from fright. But he only started because he had no mouth to yell with. He was so surprised at not yelling when he tried that he began to work his jaws like a man who has found something interesting and wants to test it. He was so sure the idea of no mouth was a dream that he could investigate it calmly. He tried to work his jaws and he had no jaws. He tried to run his tongue around the inside of his teeth and over the roof of his mouth as if he were chasing a raspberry seed. But he didn't have any tongue and he hadn't any teeth. There was no roof to his mouth and there was no mouth. He tried to swallow but he couldn't because he had no palate and there weren't any muscles left to swallow with.

Interwoven with his realization of his present condition was his memory of the past—the night with Karen before he went to war; fishing trips with his father; the pleasant, modest home in Shale City; his first calf-love and the agony of boyish disillusionment; his father's death; the Los Angeles bakery where he worked as a night bread wrapper—and, as Dalton Trumbo writes the tale, the poignancy of the one matches and complements the poignancy of the other.

Joe Bonham awoke to a timeless world, and his first need was to recapture time. "If you can keep track of time you can get a hold on yourself and keep yourself in the world but if you lose it why then you are lost too. The last thing that ties in with other people is gone and you are all alone." The description of how this man carried out his "idea of trapping time and getting himself back into the world" is one of the most moving chapters of his history; no reader can fail to share in the urgency and agony of his quest. But still more moving is the account of his frantic but persistent efforts to establish communication with the outside world. And when he was at last successful—but such things are not told well at second-hand.

To say that this book is a terrific indictment of war is to employ a phrase that has been robbed of its proper weight of meaning by careless and promiscuous use. Yet the phrase must serve. To insist that this book should be required reading for all men big and little, for those who are capable of making wars and for those likely to be herded into them, is to betray an innocent and mistaken faith in the power of the printed word. Yet one must insist, even though one knows that there are some indictments that simply will not stick, and that war has survived them, and doubtless will survive them, beyond numbering. It is possible to insist conscientiously, too, on more grounds than one, for *Johnny Got His Gun* is not merely a powerful anti-war document; it is also a powerful and brilliant work of the imagination. In giving voice to a human experience that has hitherto been voiceless, Mr. Trumbo has written a book that can never be forgotten by anyone who ever reads it.—BEN RAY REDMAN, "In the Midst of Death," *SR*, Sept. 9, 1939, p. 5

LEONARD KRIEGEL
"Dalton Trumbo's *Johnny Got His Gun*"
Proletarian Writers of the Thirties
ed. David Madden
1968, pp. 106–13

Whatever else can be said about the literature of the Thirties, it should be apparent by now that it was both far more complex and far more varied than has generally been assumed. The decade's complexity cannot be excessively stressed, which is one of the things that make such books as Alfred Kazin's *Starting Out in the Thirties* so peculiarly discouraging; such memoirs succeed only in making of the decade a kind of never-never land to be approached with whispers of celebration. And if the Thirties seems to be on the verge of becoming literarily fashionable once again, this, too, seems to be for the wrong reasons. The fact is that we continue to be embarrassed by the literature of the Thirties, treating it as an unwanted legacy discovered in some unlamented aunt's attic, some poor relative for whom we apologize with all sorts of gestures about her good intentions. Even those books which have survived the general critical condemnation of the generation—much of it a *mea culpa* breastbeating—have frequently been praised for the wrong reasons. The recent revival of James Agee's *Let Us Now Praise Famous Men*, for instance, focussed far too much on Agee himself as a kind of American *Wunderkind*, tragically dead before his time, tragically unfulfilled as an artist, a kind of natural cousin to Fitzgerald and Hemingway. The focus should have been on the book itself, on the fact that *Let Us Now Praise Famous Men* is probably the single most painful documentary in our literature, and that even to read it today from cover to cover demands an act of will that goes beyond what art may legitimately demand of us. In the same way, Henry Roth's *Call It Sleep*, now evidently selling in the hundreds of thousands as a paperback, seems to be slated to serve as the official precursor of the Jewish canonical revelations that have played so significant a role in recent American fiction, a glimpse into the childhood of Moses Herzog rather than what it is, a nakedly sensitive portrayal of the immigrant child's terror in the face of all that this America, this *goldena medina*, actually represents.

Dalton Trumbo's *Johnny Got His Gun* has suffered a similar fate. It was reissued in 1959, but after reading Trumbo's flippant introduction to the new edition one is not quite sure why. There is a myth about the novel which such flippancy does little to dispel. According to the myth, the novel was put together as a kind of contemporary *exemplum* to be used by the American Communist Party in the days of the Hitler-Stalin Pact—one envisions old men who smell of garlic and wear horn-rimmed glasses secretly plotting the overthrow of god, mother, apple pie, and J. Edgar, and all by insidiously trying to get the public to read a book which portrayed the mutilation produced by war. This is, of course, to ignore the history of the Thirties, when revulsion over the First World War swept not only the campuses but the country at large. Still, if one subscribes to the myth instead of to the reality, all that prevented our blood from turning to water was Hitler's invasion of the Soviet Union, an act which made American Communists even more ferocious than John Wayne.

It is, one sees, a rather ironic fate for a novel whose very

NEWSWEEK

ANNE TYLER

UPI/BETTMANN NEWSPHOTOS

DALTON TRUMBO

TIME MAGAZINE

JAMES THURBER

WNET

PAUL THEROUX

AP/WIDE WORLD PHOTOS

Mark Van Doren

AP/WIDE WORLD PHOTOS

Carl Van Vechten

TIME MAGAZINE

John Updike

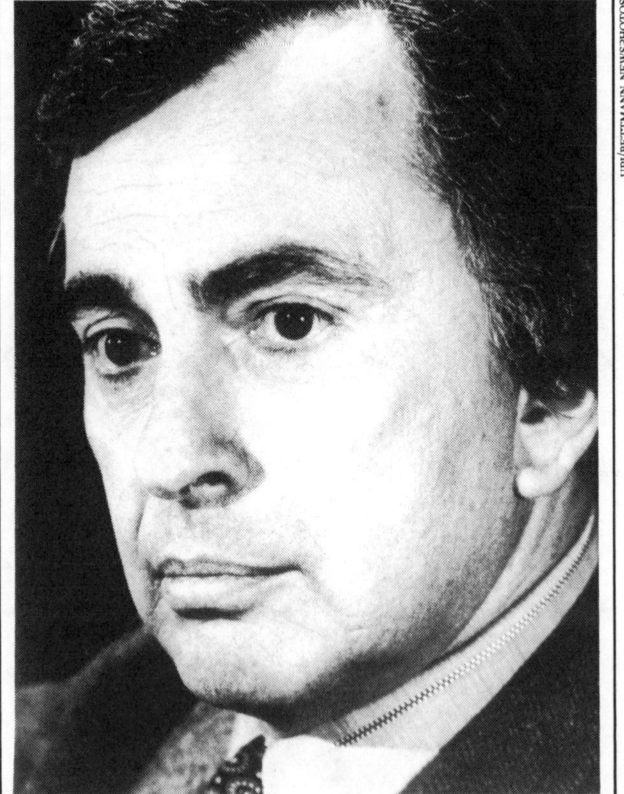

UPI/BETTMANN NEWSPHOTOS

Gore Vidal

ugliness possesses power as excruciating as Zola's. Simply as a *tour de force, Johnny Got His Gun* is remarkable. In its successful use of the mind of a basket case as its point of view, it can stand comparison to Faulkner's use of the mind of the idiot Benjy as the point of view for the opening section of *The Sound and the Fury*. No novel, however, can exist as a mere *tour de force*, and if this were all that could be said of *Johnny Got His Gun* it would probably be better forgotten. After all, a television newscast on which we see an American marine applying a cigarette lighter to a jungle hut in Vietnam offers a far more graphic portrayal of the horror of war than Mr. Trumbo ever could have. We watch such newsreels every evening, while the professionally reportorial tones of Huntley and Brinkley assure us that even if this is not the best of all possible worlds it certainly is the most natural.

Mr. Trumbo is an American novelist and American novelists have rarely been particularly squeamish about death, at least not in our century. But other than Hemingway, for whom death and the prospect of death remained from the first some sort of mystical apotheosis, our novelists tend to avoid the more mundane realities death demands that we admit to our daily lives. Our novelists are fascinated by death, but only our newspapermen, those men of brick-and-straw talents, have understood that its possibilities are more than biological. And for all the vaunted gothicism of our literature, physically and mentally deformed characters are usually meant merely to shock the reader rather than to increase his awareness of life's possibilities and dimensions. Let the reader compare the world of a Carson McCullers to that of a Genet. And so Trumbo's ability to make a Joe Bonham human seems even more remarkable. To create him so that the revulsion we feel is, at least in part, the same kind of mixture of fascination and disgust that we feel when Proust's Charlus parades before us like some homosexual peacock, to force the reader merely to admit to himself Joe Bonham's awareness of his existence—to do this is a substantial achievement for any novelist.

This is not to deny that by any critical standards, even those incorporated in such Marxist semantics as "socialist realism," *Johnny Got His Gun* is a novel which contains a multitude of sins. Even worse, so many of the sins are boring: much of the novel is sentimental; the stream-of-consciousness is often faked; the simplistic good guys–bad guys view of the world is apparent from the very first page; and the Rousseauistic nobility of the much-heralded "common man" has become an increasing liability as that creature spits in Martin Luther King's face when he doesn't burn down huts in Vietnam. But the power is there. And the novel still lives, both as a pacifist plea, perhaps as relevant today as when it was written (although for entirely different reasons), and, even more important, as a work created around a thing, a consciousness endowed with a humanness which we see as being so revolting that it tests our humanity. As contemporary readers, we recognize life's complexity; we are even victims of that recognition. Our sophistication, our refusal to be taken in by the myths of a previous generation—each forces us to respond cautiously to Dalton Trumbo's novel. *Johnny* is certainly not a difficult book to read; its trouble is that it remains so personally embarrassing.

What remains most significant about modern fiction is its intensely personal vision. Tolstoy spoke for the world; Joyce spoke for Joyce. And Joyce's *Portrait* remains the artistic *modus vivendi* for our century's fiction; we see the world through Stephen's eyes and what is most significant about Stephen is that he is himself. Not that Stephen is not also a number of other things; his is, after all, a portrait of *the artist*. But his world is created in one man's brain, his own. And so is Joe Bonham's. But the brain of Joe Bonham is unlike any other brain in all of literature, for it is a brain without a body. *Cogito ergo sum*, wrote Descartes, thus changing the nature of western reality. How vicious a parody *Johnny Got His Gun* offers on that famous syllogism. For Joe Bonham's is the reality of caricature, the kind of reality which so distorts the world that we see it as a hall of mirrors until truth is thrust upon us by the very insanity of the angles. It is caricature, but so is the reality with which it deals. The brilliant English critic, Raymond Williams, in distinguishing between types of realism speaks of how in contemporary literature realism can be seen as "a principled organized selection" of "observed reality." A basket case is the *sine qua non* of war as an action engaged in by men. In Williams' words, Joe Bonham is, as he lies on a hospital bed trying to make contact with the world around him, our "principled organized selection" (minus eyes, legs, arms, face, etc.); the "observed reality" is the war, the First World War—and all wars—which produce the Joe Bonhams. The dead who are living are an embarrassment to all of us. Who wants to be reminded of Hiroshima or Buchenwald, especially of their survivors? How nauseated we are when, after years in darkness and isolation, Joe finally does manage to communicate, and the finger that taps against his chest asks him, "WHAT DO YOU WANT?" What an absurd question!

To attempt a critical analysis of *Johnny Got His Gun* seems just as absurd. One can speak only of his reaction to the continued existence of Joe Bonham. Now this is a reaction we can better imagine if we think of ourselves as sitting in a darkened theatre watching the first newsreels which depicted the heaped bodies and parts of bodies which greeted the Allied armies when they entered the German death camps near the end of the Second World War. Suddenly, a voice from a part of a body, say some stray leg or arm, begins to address us in matter-of-fact tones to tell us what it is all like. In the face of this kind of thing, literary criticism, like history or political science or sociology or even physics, is simply inadequate. It is even useless, for it cannot even conceive of a reaction to such a horror. Read, say, any essay by T. S. Eliot, and then read this novel. It is certainly not Eliot's fault that Joe Bonham exists or that what caused Joe Bonham to be what he is exists. But Joe Bonham is that voice; he is that voice despite the overblown rhetoric, despite the sentimental nonsense of his remembering how his mother "read the story of the little Christ-child of the baby Jesus," despite the overly propagandistic ending (not that the ending is a total failure, for one of the questions we must learn to ask of novels accused of being propagandistic is how accurate their propaganda is). Joe Bonham simply *is*, and, in creating him, Trumbo succeeded in creating our nightmare.

The power of the nightmare is especially evident in Book I, "The Dead," where Trumbo carefully works the mind of a basket case becoming aware of exactly what his situation is into the life he has come out of, a life that seems typical enough. In fact, it is this very typicality, Joe's apple-pie and mother origins, which is one of the aspects of the novel which justify the charge of sentimentality. But Joe has to be typical because the very atypicality of the horror he is to become must emerge from the everyday world itself. Trumbo's sense of detail is unusually skillful here. It is one of the better lessons that the novelists of the Thirties learned from Hemingway. As he awakes to the ringing of a telephone, Joe's first memory is of a night he was working in a factory in Los Angeles when another ringing telephone brought him the news of the death of his father. He leaves the factory and heads for "the place." (Even before the First World War, Americans did not have homes.) "The place was on the alley above a garage behind a two story house. To get to it he walked down a narrow driveway which was between two houses close together. It was black between the two houses. Rain from the two roofs met there and spattered down into wide puddles with a queer wet echo like water being poured into a cistern. His feet squished in the water as he went." This is the way death is meant to be. Joe feels the pain of remembrance, the pain of a young man's sense of loss, of fragmentation, of the passing of a father who was loved and needed and who failed, as all fathers inevitably must, to provide for his son a buffer against the knowledge of death.

Trumbo learned his other lessons from Joyce and Dos Passos. The modified stream-of-consciousness of Book I seems natural enough; in Book II, "The Living," it frequently seems forced, perhaps because Trumbo is beating us over the head with his message. Dos Passos' weaving of American history and contemporary events into the narrative is also quietly made part of Joe's memory before the shell that made him into what he has become exploded. "Lincoln Beechy came to town. It was the first airplane Shale City ever saw. They had it in a tent in the middle of the race track over in the fair grounds. Day in and day out people filed through the tent looking at it. It seemed to be all wire and cloth. People couldn't understand how a man would risk his life just on the strength of a wire. One little wire gone wrong and it meant the end of Lincoln Beechy. Away up in front of the plane ahead of the propellers was a little seat with a stick in front of it. That was where the great aviator sat." In the jingoistic patriotism of "the people who are willing to sacrifice somebody else's life," Lincoln Beechy is the American ideal. But it is an ideal of heroism without the true recognition of death, with neither questions asked nor emotions permitted. The growing consciousness of Joe Bonham is to become revolted by that same kind of super-patriotism which Dos Passos scathingly envisions for us in the concluding line to the section of *Nineteen-Nineteen* entitled "The Body of an American": "Woodrow Wilson brought a bouquet of flowers." Of course, both Trumbo and Dos Passos are guilty of oversimplification. Novelists generally are. There undoubtedly was a purpose to the war. Not all generals, as Hemingway writes, die in bed. And not all politicians are soulless automatons eager to send thousands of men to their deaths for the sake of mere abstractions. So what? All Joe Bonham knows is, "You're dead, mister. Dead."

Political rhetoric is a denial of death's reality, just as it is a denial of war's reality. Ultimately, it is an extension of the child's view of the world. Joe Bonham, a living consciousness, is physically dead. In a country which pretends to as much religious faith as ours does, such a reversal of traditional Christian immortality seems deeply ironic.

Book II is definitely something of a falling off as far as the novel's power is concerned. It is here, I suppose, that Trumbo lays himself open to the charge of writing propaganda. Book II is devoted to Joe's attempts to communicate the consciousness within him to the world around him; at times, it is done with a kind of grueling humor. Joe Bonham's tapping with his neck comes to seem, even to him, a kind of insanity. And yet, like so much "black humor," it is the insanity of life. "There were times when he knew he was stark raving crazy only from the outside he realized he must seem as he always had seemed. Anyone looking down at him would have no way of suspecting that beneath the mask and the mucus there lay insanity as naked and cruel and desperate as insanity could ever be."

And then, as Joe finally manages to make himself understood, that terrible question comes: "WHAT DO YOU WANT?" The furious rhetoric of the last two chapters of *Johnny Got His Gun* are an attempt at an answer. Joe wants himself seen, recognized, perhaps exhibited as the end result of Woodrow Wilson's Fourteen Points. Let us admit that this is propaganda of a rather elementary sort. Meant to be an impassioned plea against war, the rhetoric falls short of the mark. Trumbo is too conscious of what his objectives are, too much in control, to create the kind of surrealistic explosion that is needed. It would have been better if Joe had wanted simply to die, really to die, to end his suffering and his isolation. It is rhetoric; it is propaganda; it is, one reminds oneself, not very different from that other simplification, the patriotism of such groups as the American Legion. All of this is true. But as I write this, entire villages in Vietnam are being sacrificed to the expediency of accidents. Like the shell destined to make Joe Bonham a basket case, napalm is its own logic. It needs no defense. One begins to suspect that it is the logic of existence itself. All we can do is to react to the rhetoric, just as all we can do is to react to Joe Bonham's existence. But if one must think in choosing between such rhetoric, admittedly futile, and the rhetoric of a Lyndon Johnson as he, too, saves the world for democracy, then the failure is far more than a failure of art.

ROBERT KIRSCH

From "Introduction"

Night of the Aurochs by Dalton Trumbo

1979, pp. xiii–xx

> The thing I am after here, the devil I am trying to catch, is that dark yearning for power that lurks in all of us, the perversion of love that is the inevitable consequence of power, the exquisite pleasures of perversion when power becomes absolute, and the dread realization that in a time when science has become the servant of politics-as-theology, it can happen again. (Dalton Trumbo, afternote to *Night of the Aurochs*)

More than once Dalton Trumbo compared the writing of his troubling and troublesome novel, *Night of the Aurochs*, to wrestling with the devil. He knew the story would not be an easy one to write when he began it in 1960 though its premise was daring and sensational: to tell the life of an unrepentant, unregenerate Nazi, Ludwig Richard Johann Grieben, through Grieben's own words. In the end, Grieben both fascinated and repelled him, "a hero of a Satanic rather than a godly morality," yet, Trumbo went on, "by definition a hero." In a letter to Michael Wilson, he reveals his suspicions of "the idea of morality as a fact or cause." He adds, in a tone which is almost always present when he refers to the book: "Anyhow, so it goes, and so do I blunder toward the heart of this goddamned book I never should have started."

Trumbo did not complete the book by his death on September 10, 1976, though he had worked on it on and off for sixteen years. "No matter what I am working on, not a week passes that I don't get *something* written on *Aurochs* or *Grieben*, or whatever the hell it will end up being called," he wrote Wilson. To his agent Shirley Burke, in a letter written in 1976, he revealed another aspect of the work: "This is my first uninterrupted prose work in years and I am enjoying it immensely. I will, of course, enjoy it much more if it turns out to be any good."

The two views are not necessarily contradictory. Trumbo was divided about the book, aware almost from the beginning that it was the most disturbing and challenging work he had ever attempted. This in itself did not bother the author of *Johnny Got His Gun*. More upsetting was that the longer he wrote from the point of view of Grieben the more his idea of Grieben changed. The German who had started out as a representative Nazi became over the years a character Trumbo could not easily dismiss in stereotyped terms. He found it necessary to remind himself and the reader often of the horrors committed in the Nazi persecution of the Jews and in the death camps. He wanted to get to the human center of such acts.

Trumbo, the professional writer, the prolific writer, made a decision: tell the story in the first person. He had to shift that approach somewhat as you will see in these pages but he could not escape the empathy and role reversal this method demanded. Inside Grieben, he found what he also knew as a writer: that no person can be the villain of his own life. "Characters change as they are written and take on lives of their own," he writes in his afternote.

Grieben both fascinated and repelled Trumbo. A writer must energize his characters with his own experiences and emotions. It is no accident that he has given Grieben the very same operation and heart condition which he experienced, the illness which would ulitmately take both his life and Grieben's. There is more than a hint that experiences in Trumbo's early life, his witness of the vindictive treatment of German-Americans in World War I, his radical hopes for a more just and equitable system in America, gave him a certain understanding of Grieben's idealistic youth.

Trumbo himself was a child of war and depression. Born in Colorado in 1905 (he thought for a time to give Grieben the same year of birth, decided to make him a veteran of World War I and moved his birth back), Trumbo came from an old American family, grandson of a frontier sheriff, son of a veteran of the Spanish-American war. Although his father had worked hard, he had little to show for his efforts and was discharged from his job as a shoe clerk because his health failed. The family moved to Southern California and Trumbo watched his father die as his family struggled for a living.

Witty, acerbic, unpredictable, Trumbo became a multimedia writer, producing four novels between 1935 and 1941, the best known of which was *Johnny Got His Gun*, and nearly forty screenplays including *Kitty Foyle*, *Our Vines Have Tender Grapes*, *Thirty Seconds over Tokyo*, *Exodus*, *Spartacus*, *Lonely Are the Brave*, *The Fixer*, and *Papillon*. He tried playwriting, pamphleteering, and took his responsibilities as a principled citizen seriously. The contrast with Grieben is important. Trumbo was a radical of the Western Populist tradition, fought social and economic injustice, sought to help average people to fight those who sought to use, abuse, or dictate to them.

Trumbo was far from the true believer Grieben epitomized. He joined the Communist Party in the early forties, seeking the social justice it appeared to offer. But dogma and discipline went against his nature and though he became a central figure in the Hollywood Ten, the group of screenwriters imprisoned for contempt of Congress for refusing to cooperate in the hearings of the House Un-American Activities Committee, he did not consider that this was an act of heroism. He thought it nothing less than the minimum of principled action against repression and thought control.

His view was not a softening or blurring of the experience. He had paid his dues along with hundreds of blacklisted writers, actors and actresses, producers, and others in Hollywood's crafts. Trumbo was blacklisted for thirteen years, from 1947 to 1960, but managed to earn a living and to win an Oscar under the pseudonym Robert Rich for the screenplay of *The Brave One*. He was the first of the prominent blacklisted Hollywood people to win an open credit, for the film *Exodus*, and that was a turning point of the exclusionary policy. Trumbo wanted no credit for doing what he felt was his obligation as a man devoted to freedom and justice.

In *Night of the Aurochs*, Trumbo is not concerned with forgiveness or rationalization of the horrors committed by the Nazis. What he is after in this powerful and unremitting story is the notion that history, society, and ideas can victimize us and what we do to resist the victimization is the measure of our worth. The notion of *hubris* in ancient Greek tragedy is reversed. Grieben's total commitment to Nazism and German destiny is his acceptance of becoming the creature of that doctrine, which permits him to see every act as justified by the ends. His cleverness and certainty, his arrogance and affected superiority, his consistency are all evidence of his self-delusion. By making himself the total instrument of Nazi policy, Grieben believes that he has elevated himself from "a mild-looking man of no importance who shows in face and body the ravages of struggle" to a man who has lived "colossally," who has found power. What he has lost is his humanity.

Grieben's average qualities, his sense of being the mean, median, and mode of Germany, his roots implanted in aristocracy and peasantry, in contrasting regions of the country, in Protestant and Catholic religions, in the poetry, philosophy, and intellectual pursuits of German culture, in the mean and mischievous and cruel aspects of it, were intended to allow Trumbo to examine a whole range of questions about the unimaginable crimes committed by the Nazis. Trumbo wants to remind us that human beings committed those horrors, not supermen, not subhumans.

Cleo Trumbo, who knew her husband's intent, writes in her eloquent foreword: "To become Grieben meant to confront the darkest corners of his soul." She goes on to say, "he meant to transcend the inhumanity of Grieben." If necessary, Trumbo was prepared to transcend "the limits of his own personality."

Bruce Cook, Trumbo's biographer, who had read more than one hundred pages of *Night of the Aurochs*, concluded the fragment was "more than an impressive act of literary impersonation; it is in some private sense a kind of spiritual autobiography of Trumbo, a mighty effort to understand not just a Nazi, but part of himself as well, and thus to master his own demon."

Certainly, *Night of the Aurochs* even in its imperfect state, even with its contradictions and shock, is the most important novel Trumbo ever attempted and will remain, I believe, a brave attempt to confront in fiction the human center of tyranny and unspeakable cruelty. *Johnny Got His Gun*, perhaps the most effective anti-war novel ever written in America, is a much simpler book. Trumbo's masterly techniques of ridicule and irony, his sarcasm and satire, although present in *Aurochs*, were not sufficient to encompass the horror of the holocaust. He needed to surpass his own strengths as a writer and in many respects he did.

To develop empathy with Grieben was part of this challenge. The German stood in opposition to most of what Trumbo believed in and fought for. In his life and work, Trumbo resisted victimization and dehumanization. *Aurochs* was a further expression of that impulse, the last bequest of his art and skill.

In any case, Trumbo's words speak best for himself. He completed enough of *Night of the Aurochs* (his original title, though later he toyed with the idea of calling it *Grieben*) to make the short novel, which is the main text of this book. The work consists of ten chapters, which relate the present circumstances of Grieben and the years of his early life in some detail, some bridging notes, a "diary" Grieben kept during his service with the SS extermination groups in Russia and later as commandant of Auschwitz-Birkenau, and finally, a long section which begins as a synopsis but quickly becomes a third-person narrative relating Grieben's experiences. Here we find the most shocking part of the story, his relationship with Liesel, the half-Jewish woman whom Grieben "loved," whom he had arrested and sent to the concentration camp he runs, and over whom he exercised that complete power which Trumbo began to think is at the heart of the authoritarian impulse. Finally, *Night of the Aurochs* is about the eroticism of power and the power of eroticism. 〈. . .〉

In a certain way, *Night of the Aurochs*, as it stands, represents not only Dalton Trumbo's dilemma in the face of this monstrous problem but a continuing one. Each generation must find its own answers to Grieben and the crimes he committed in the name of idealism and national destiny. There are hints throughout of the way human beliefs and indeed human ways can be distorted into unimaginable cruelty and violence.

Perhaps Trumbo could never have finished the *Night of the Aurochs* to his own satisfaction, perhaps it is the wrestling match rather than the verdict we must consider. He gave it his best, his considerable talents as a writer. The text is an anthology of his styles from the wry, satiric, ironic tones of his earlier work, through the screen treatment and synopses he did so well, to the lyrical and philosophical notes he lent to Grieben's narration to give him life and human dimension. Trumbo's notes are haunted by the Jekyll-and-Hyde nature of the process. Which one speaks when he says, "Dig beneath the surface of human character and you will come up with something ugly, be sure of it"? Or when Chekhov is quoted: "Man will become better when you show him what he is like." Many times it is hard to determine. Grieben explains: "With me the problem has always been one of belief. By that I mean that I cannot live without believing in something more important than myself. God is too remote for my need. My whole life has been lived in present time. From the day I was born I have watched present time become past and God, who lives in time future, has shown no interest. I reciprocate."

At the end, Trumbo and his fictional character, whom he can neither accept nor purge, seem to merge, share the same illness. In the hundreds of notes Trumbo left, one gives us the heartfelt cry: "Oh dear God, don't drabble it out like this. Let me have it in one big lump." It is not clear whether the dying Trumbo is speaking of his condition or of Grieben's.

Yet, Trumbo's voice is unmistakable when he asks himself, as the writer, the oracular question: "Is this the story of man's return to humanity?" The work itself may hold the answer.

ANNE TYLER

1941–

Anne Tyler was born in Minneapolis, Minnesota, on October 25, 1941. She attended Duke University, receiving her B.A. in 1961, and then did graduate work at Columbia University (1961–62). After leaving school Tyler worked as a Russian bibliographer for the Duke University Library (1962–63), and as an assistant to the librarian of the McGill University Law Library in Montreal (1964–65). She now lives in Baltimore, the scene of most of her fiction. She married Taghi Modarressi, a psychiatrist, in 1963, and has two children.

Tyler's novels, many of them bestsellers, deal with family life and the pain of separation through death or isolation. They include: *If Morning Ever Comes* (1964), *The Tin Can Tree* (1965), *A Slipping-Down Life* (1970), *The Clock Winder* (1972), *Celestial Navigation* (1974), *Searching for Caleb* (1976), *Earthly Possessions* (1977), *Morgan's Passing* (1980), *Dinner at the Homesick Restaurant* (1982), and *The Accidental Tourist* (1985). She has contributed short stories to the *Saturday Evening Post*, the *New Yorker*, *Seventeen*, the *Critic*, the *Antioch Review*, and the *Southern Review*. With Shannon Ravenel, Tyler edited *Best American Short Stories 1983*, for which she also wrote the introduction.

The fact that 24-year-old Anne Tyler, who was born in Minneapolis and now lives in Toronto, grew up in Raleigh, N.C., must seem to her significant enough to make her publishers note on the jacket of this book 〈*The Tin Can Tree*〉 that she "considers herself a Southerner." And this novel, in so far as it goes in for regional subject matter, does report upon life in still another rural Southern pocket. Her characters are the eight inhabitants of a three-family house on the edge of backwater tobacco fields—two bachelor brothers, two spinster sisters and the Pike family, whose small daughter has just been killed in a tractor accident when the book opens.

There are, indeed, some fine scenes and sounds of a regional sort, especially in one chapter in which a group of women talk over the Pike tragedy while tying tobacco. Here, as elsewhere in the book, she makes use of a nice specificity of local detail and neatly captures the casual and yet complex movement of Southern rural speech with its indirections and interruptions, its reticences and awkwardnesses which manage to express emotion.

Yet rurality and Southernism are not really Miss Tyler's chief interest. Despite some obvious debts to the tradition of the Southern novel, she has none of the Faulknerian anguish over a present rooted in past wrongs. Nor does she share the late Flannery O'Connor's sense of a religious soil out of which characters are thrust forth into the withering present, taking grotesque and tragic shape—though Miss O'Connor's style with its austere notation of scene and dialogue, may have taught her to make an eloquence of spareness. If she reminds me of anyone, it may be the Carson MacCullers of 25 years ago—who then as young as Miss Tyler, also wrote of human disconnection and the need for love in a stagnant community.

Carson MacCullers herself, of course, was only in part a regional writer. Her gothic tales of loneliness and inchoate longing carried on the mood and themes of Sherwood Anderson among the older generation of American writers. Thinking back that far we discover the significant precursor for Miss Tyler's story. More a vignette than a novel, it glances at lives twisted by inhibition and loneliness, gnarled like frostbitten apples (Anderson's metaphor) because the sap of community has grown thin.

Miss Tyler sets before us James and Ansel Green who have each, in his own way, rejected home and family in a distant town. They now live together, Ansel a hypochondriac, who has willed himself to a sickbed; James, more obscurely crippled, unable to move over the threshold of inaction towards a marriage with Joan, a young cousin of the Pikes. Joan herself is a fugitive who has never been loved by her parents and lives like a boarder among the Pikes, despite her love for their children, the dead Janie Rose and 10-year-old Simon. It is Simon's discovery of the fact of human separation—first by death, but more profoundly in the alienation, albeit temporary, of his mother—that is the real crisis of the book. Finally, the old Faye sisters who live amidst a maze of screens and tight-sealed windows in the mid-section of the house provide a half-comic parody of these instances of isolation.

Like the Winesburg stories, *The Tin Can Tree* shows us human beings frozen into fixed postures. And James, it happens, is a photographer whose snapshots have a way of capturing people in characteristic single attitudes—Ansel reclining on a couch, his hand idly playing with the window shade, Jane in a dust storm which makes her look like a ghost. At the end of the book they pose for a group picture:

> In the finder of the camera Joan could see them moving, each person making his own set of motions. But the glass of the finder seemed to hold them there, like figures in a snow-flurry paperweight who would still be in their set positions when the snow settled down again. Whole years could pass, they could be born and die . . . They were going to stay this way, she and all the rest of them, not because of anyone else but because it was what they had chosen, what they would keep a strong hold of.

Life, this young writer seems to be saying, achieves its once-and-for-all shape and then the camera clicks. This view, which brings her characters back on the last page to where they started, does not make for that sense of development which is the true novel's motive force. Because of it, I think, her book remains a sketch, a description, a snapshot. But as such, it still has a certain dry clarity. And the hand that has clicked its shutter has selected a moment of truth.—MILLICENT BELL, "Tobacco Road Updated," *NYTBR*, Nov. 21, 1965, p. 77

It's hard to classify Anne Tyler's novels. They are Southern in their sure sense of family and place but lack the taste for violence and the Gothic that often characterizes self-consciously Southern literature. They are modern in their fictional techniques, yet utterly unconcerned with the contemporary moment as a subject, so that, with only minor dislocations, her stories could just as well have taken place in the twenties or thirties. The current school of feminist-influenced novels seems to have passed her by completely: her women are strong, often stronger than the men in their lives, but solidly grounded in traditional roles. Among our better contemporary novelists, Tyler occupies a somewhat lonely place, polishing brighter and brighter a craft many novelists no longer deem essential to their purpose: the unfolding of character through brilliantly imagined and absolutely accurate detail.

In *Searching for Caleb* she has invented a family whose very conventionality borders on the eccentric. The Pecks of Baltimore are wealthy, standoffish, stolidly self-satisfied. In their suburban enclave of wide lawns and spacious houses, four generations have lived quietly together, tactfully ignoring a world they consider loud and frivolous and full of rude people with outlandish surnames. To be a true Peck is to sink into a kind of lukewarm bath that is comforting but enervating, a perpetual childhood presided over by the brisk, formal, aging grandfather, Daniel. Only two have rebelled: Caleb, Daniel's dreamy, cello-playing brother, who disappeared without a trace 60 years ago, and Duncan, Daniel's grandson, a wild boy in love with scrapes and danger who grows into a strange, private, restless adult.

When Duncan marries his cousin Justine, hitherto an ardent Peck, she begins to discover her own thirst for adventure. For years the two careen through the small towns of Maryland and Virginia as Duncan quits one makeshift job for another. He refuses to acknowledge the past that propels them both into an even bleaker and dingier future. Justine is pulled both forward and back: an amateur teller of fortunes who advises her clients always to go along with change, she remains in thrall to her own childhood. And so, when Daniel decides to find his lost brother, Justine is the one who joins him. For the old man the quest is a way of recapturing the past, but for Justine it becomes a search for the self she has mislaid. The outcome is marvelously ironic, since the answers to her questions are themselves enigmatic. Yet she emerges triumphant, her own woman at last.

Less perfectly realized than *Celestial Navigation*, her extraordinarily moving and beautiful last novel, *Searching for Caleb* is Tyler's sunniest, most expansive book. While etching with a fine, sharp wit the narrow-mindedness and pettishness of the Pecks, she lavishes on them a tenderness that lifts them above satire. Consider Daniel Peck. A cold and unoriginal man, aging gracefully but without wisdom, he is yet allowed moments in which we glimpse his bewilderment at a life that has been in the end disappointing: "In my childhood I was trained to hold things in, you see. But I thought I was holding them in until a certain *time*. I assumed that someday, somewhere, I would again be given the opportunity to spend all that saved-up feeling. When will that be?"

Reading *Searching for Caleb*, one is constantly being startled by such moments: gestures, words, wrinkles of thought and feeling that are at once revelatory and exactly right. But at the center of Tyler's characters is a private, mysterious core which is left, wisely, inviolate. Ultimately, this wisdom is what makes Tyler more than a fine craftsman of realistic novels. Her complex, crotchety inventions surprise us, but one senses they surprise her too.—KATHA POLLITT, *NYTBR*, Jan. 18, 1976, p. 22

New work by a young writer who's both greatly gifted and prolific often points readers' minds toward the future. You finish the book and immediately begin speculating about works to come—achievements down the road that will cross the borders defined by the work at hand. Anne Tyler's books have been having this effect on me for nearly a decade. Repeatedly they've been brilliant—"wickedly good," as John Updike recently described one of them. *Dinner at the Homesick*

Restaurant is Anne Tyler's ninth novel; her career began in 1964 with a fully realized first novel (the title was *If Morning Ever Comes*, and there are piquant links between it and her latest book); everything I've read of hers since then—stories, novels and criticism (Anne Tyler is a first-rate critic, shrewd and self-effacing)—has been, at a minimum, interesting and well made. But in recent years her narratives have grown bolder and her characters more striking, and that's increased the temptation to brood about her direction and destination, her probable ultimate achievement.

The time for such brooding is over now, though—at least for a while. *Dinner at the Homesick Restaurant* is a book to be settled into fully, tomorrow be damned. Funny, heart-hammering, wise, it edges deep into truth that's simultaneously (and interdependently) psychological, moral and formal—deeper than many living novelists of serious reputation have penetrated, deeper than Miss Tyler herself has gone before. It is a border crossing. ⟨. . .⟩

On its face *Dinner at the Homesick Restaurant* is a book about the costs of parental truancy (a subject that surfaces in Miss Tyler's first novel and elsewhere frequently in her *oeuvre*). None of the three Tull children manages to cut loose from the family past; each is, to a degree, stunted; each turns for help to Pearl Tull in an hour of desperate adult need; and Pearl's conviction that something's wrong with each of them never recedes from the reader's consciousness. But no small measure of the book's subtlety derives from its exceptional—and exceptionally *wise*, the word bears repeating—clarity about the uselessness of cost accounting in human areas such as these. Cody Tull suffers from obscure guilt (was it something I said, something I did that made my father go away?). Ezra Tull suffers from want of desire. Jenny Tull suffers from fear of connection. And the behavior and feelings of all three are linked somehow with the terrible, never-explained rupture: their father's disappearance.

But it's also the case that what is best in each of these people, as in their mother, has its roots in the experience of deprivation that they jointly despise. Jenny's outward exuberance flows from instinctive knowledge of how overwhelming the need for cheer can be among young or old. Ezra's movingly unconsidered kindness and generosity have a similar source. Even Cody, who for much of the story is perceived as an enemy of light, emerges at the end as a man elevated by what he's obliquely learned from his father's irresponsibility.

Adversity teaches? We advance well beyond that truism in *Dinner at the Homesick Restaurant*. We arrive at an understanding that the important lessons taught by adversity never quite make themselves known to the consciousness of the learners—remain hidden, inexpressible. Outsiders stumble on them sometimes and behave in their innocence as though the lessons couldn't be missed—but oh yes they can.

There's a nearly throwaway moment late in this book that exquisitely underlines the point. A child sees a grim-faced photograph of Jenny Tull at age 13 and insists to her that it's like a "concentration camp person, a victim," and that it can't be her. "It isn't! Look at it! . . . It's somebody else," he told [Jenny]. "Not you; you're always laughing and having fun. It's not you." Jenny glances at the picture showing "a dark little girl with a thin watchful face," an image of the mirthless youth she shared with her brothers—and then says dismissively: "Oh, fine, it's not me, then." It is Jenny Tull, of course; the wisdom of the moment resides in the perception of our impatience with the sight of our own discontinuity. If we pause too long in contemplation of a former self, we run the risk of forgetting how to take our present selves for granted. And down that road there's a risk of starting to treat life as a mystery instead of the way smart people treat it—as a set of done and undone errands. No way, says Jenny, clearly one of us.

Will so much talk of wisdom hide the truth that *Dinner at the Homesick Restaurant* is, from start to finish, superb entertainment? I hope not. Much as I've admired Miss Tyler's earlier books, I've found flaws in a few—something excessively static in the situation developed in *Morgan's Passing*, for instance, something arbitrary in the plotting of *Earthly Possessions*. But in the work at hand Miss Tyler is a genius plotter, effortlessly redefining her story questions from page to page, never slackening the lines of suspense. There are, furthermore, numberless explosions of hilarity, not one of which (I discover) can be sliced out of its context for quotation—so tightly fashioned is this tale—without giving away, as they say, a narrative climax. There are scenes that strike me as likely to prove unforgettable: Pearl Tull attempting, after years of silence on the matter, to explain to her adamantly inattentive children that their father isn't coming back; Jenny Tull revising and revising, as though aiming at a masterpiece in the mode of the laconic-sublime, a letter accepting a marriage proposal; Cody Tull declaring his suspicion to his wife that his brother is the father of their son; and many more.

And everywhere there's a marvelous delicacy of finish, witness Pearl Tull's drifting remembrance as she falls off into her long sleep: "She remembered the feel of wind on summer nights—how it billows through the house and wafts the curtains and smells of tar and roses. How a sleeping baby weighs so heavily on your shoulder, like ripe fruit. What privacy it is to walk in the rain beneath the drip and crackle of your own umbrella."

Seriousness does insist, in the end, that explicit note be taken of the facts of this career. Anne Tyler turned 40 just last year. She's worked with a variety of materials, established her mastery of grave as well as comic tones. Her command of her art is sure, and her right to trust her feeling for the complications both of our nature and of our nurturing arrangements stands beyond question. Speculating about this artist's future is, in short, a perfectly natural movement of mind. But, as I said before, I'm reluctant to speculate, and I expect other readers, in quantity, will share my reluctance. What one wants to do on finishing such a work as *Dinner at the Homesick Restaurant* is maintain balance, keep things intact for a stretch, stay under the spell as long as feasible. The before and after are immaterial; nothing counts except the knowledge, solid and serene, that's all at once breathing in the room. We're speaking, obviously, about an extremely beautiful book. —Benjamin DeMott, "Funny, Wise and True," *NYTBR*, March 14, 1982, pp. 1, 14

JOHN UPDIKE
"Loosened Roots"

New Yorker, June 6, 1977, pp. 130–34

Anne Tyler, in her seventh novel, *Earthly Possessions*, continues to demonstrate a remarkable talent and, for a writer of her acuity, an unusual temperament. She is soft, if not bullish, on America: its fluorescent-lit banks and gas stations, its high schools and low life, its motels and billboards and boring backwaters and stifling homes and staggering churches and scant, innocent depravities and deprivations are all to her the stuff of a tender magic, a kind of Midsummer Night's Dream scenery where poetry and adventure form as easily as dew. Small towns and pinched minds hold room enough for her; she is at peace in the semi-countrified, semi-plasticized, northern-Southern America where she and her characters live. Out of this peace flow her unmistakable strengths—her serene, firm tone; her smoothly spun plots; her apparently inexhaustible access to the personalities of her imagining; her infectious delight in "the smell of beautiful, everyday life;" her lack of any trace of intellectual or political condescension—and her one possible weakness: a tendency to leave the reader just where she found him. Acceptance, in her fiction, is the sum of the marvellous—or, as *Earthly Possessions* would have it, the end of travelling is to return. This is not untrue. Nothing Anne Tyler sets down is untrue. But the impending moral encloses the excitements of her story in a circle of safety that gives them the coziness of entertainment. It may be that in this Protestant land, with its reverence for sweat and constipation, we distrust artificers, peaceable cultivators of the imaginary. Miss Tyler tends her human flora for each book's season of bloom and then latches the garden gate with a smile. So, one could say, did Shakespeare; but in the tragedies, at least, the enclosure of final order is drawn around a group of chastened survivors, while Miss Tyler here gathers in to safety the very characters she has convincingly shown us to be sunk in "a rich, black, underground world . . . where everyone was in some deep and dramatic trouble." The depths that her lucid vision perceives through the weave of the mundane are banished, as it were, by a mere movement of the author's eyes. *Earthly Possessions* contains, for instance, a chilling portrait of a habitual criminal, Jake Simms, Jr., who blames every destructive and chaotic act of his own on someone else. He kidnaps our heroine, the surpassingly amiable Charlotte Emory, because while he was robbing a bank a bystander happened to produce a gun. "I could be clean free," he tells his victim, "and you safe home with your kids by now if it wasn't for him. Guy like that ought to be locked up." As the chase continues, the kidnapping lengthens into a kind of marriage, he persuades himself, "It ain't *me* keeping you, it's them. If they would quit hounding me then we could go our separate ways . . ." This is perfect loser psychology, the mental technology for digging a bottomless pit; but Anne Tyler would have us believe that Jake is saved from falling in by the doll-like apparition of a wee seventeen-year-old girl he has impregnated, Mindy Callender:

> She really was a tiny girl. The biggest thing about her was that stomach, which Jake carefully wasn't looking at. . . . She raised a thin, knobby wrist, with a bracelet dangling heart-shaped charms in all different colors and sizes. The pink stone in her ring was heart-shaped too, and so was the print of her dress. "Hearts are my *sign*," Mindy said. "What's yours?"

With such a figure, the Shakespearean ambience of dark comedy turns Spenserian; we are travelling in an allegory, and Love (Mindy) points to the Grail with one of those bursts of articulate insight that overtake even the dim-witted in Anne Tyler's sensitive world.

The excitements of *Earthly Possessions* include both headlong suspense and the surprises of retrospective revelation. Charlotte, the narrator and heroine, tells in her wry, patient voice two stories: she describes, hour by hour, the few days of her southward flight with Jake Simms and, synopsized in alternating chapters, the thirty-five years of her life. The two accounts flow parallel, to the same estuary of uneasy repose. As in the author's previous novels *Celestial Navigation* and *Searching for Caleb*, a fundamental American tension is felt between stasis and movement, between home and escape. Home is what we are mired in; Miss Tyler in her darker mode compulsively celebrates domestic claustrophobia and private stagnation. Charlotte is the late and only fruit of a very fat first-grade teacher and a faded, fussy "travelling photographer named Murray Ames." Ames stops travelling, and sets up a studio in his wife's "dead father's house," where a child is born with grotesque inadvertence. The mother's obesity and innocence have hidden the pregnancy. "One night she woke up with abdominal spasms . . . All around her the bed was hot and wet. She woke her husband, who stumbled into his trousers and drove her to the hospital. Half an hour later, she gave birth to a six-pound baby girl." The little girl grows up lonely. The common American escape from home into the "whole new world" of public school is feelingly evoked:

> I hadn't had any idea that people could be so light-hearted. I stood on the edge of the playground watching how the girls would gather in clumps, how they giggled over nothing at all and told colorful stories of family life: visits to circuses, fights with brothers. They didn't like me. They said I smelled. I knew they were right because now when I walked into my house I could smell the smell too: stale, dark, ancient air, in which nothing had moved for a very long time. I began to see how strange my mother was. I noticed that her dresses were like enormous flowered undershirts. I wondered why she didn't go out more; then once, from a distance, I watched her slow progress toward the corner grocery and I wished she wouldn't go out at all.

From embarrassing parents Charlotte moves to an embarrassing husband. Saul Emory, a boy who had lived next door, returns from the Army, courts her, weds her, and abruptly announces that he has been called to preach, in the local fundamentalist Holy Basis Church. Charlotte is a non-believer; while her husband preaches she sits deafly in church scheming how to get him into bed. "He was against making love on a Sunday. I was in favor of it. Sometimes I won, sometimes he won. I wouldn't have missed Sunday for the world." They live in what has become *her* dead father's house; she diffidently runs the studio that she has inherited, and the house fills up with charity cases and Saul's brothers. Charlotte says, "I felt like something dragged on a string behind a forgetful child. . . . I gave up hope. Then in order not to mind too much I loosened my roots, floated a few feet off, and grew to look at things with a faint, pleasant humorousness that spiced my nose like the beginnings of a sneeze." Childhood fantasies of flight recur; she keeps giving away the furniture; she finally decides to leave, goes to the bank "to get cash for the trip," and is seized by Jake Simms. Her adventure begins.

Writing a self-description for the Washington *Post*, Anne Tyler said, "Mostly it's lies, writing novels. You set out to tell an untrue story and you try to make it believable, even to yourself. Which calls for details; any good lie does." Her details are superb, tucked in with quick little loops of metaphor:

> When she was angry, her face bunched in now as if gathered at the center by a drawstring.
>
> When he lifted me up in his arms I felt I had left all my troubles on the floor beneath me like gigantic concrete shoes.

Without pushing at it, she establishes her characters in authentic occupations. Murray Ames's photography and his daughter's continuation of it become very real, and a paradigm for art:

> "Move that lamp off somewhat," he would tell me from his bed. "You don't want such a glare. Now get yourself more of an angle. I never did like a head-on photograph."
>
> What he liked was a sideways look—eyes lowered, face slanted downward. The bay window displaying my father's portraits resembled a field full of flowers, all being blown by the same strong breeze.

The author's attention to American incidentals is so unblinking that we are rather relieved when she seems to nod, as when Charlotte observes the "snuff adds" ("ads," surely) in Georgia or a "pair of giant fur dominoes" (dice, more likely) hung from a rearview mirror. Every bit of junk food the fugitives nibble as they drive their stolen car south is affectionately noted, and the subtle changes in scenery and climate are continental in their cumulative effect. When, having at last arrived in Florida, Charlotte says, "It was one of those lukewarm, breezy evenings that make you feel you're expecting something," we have arrived, too, and feel exactly what she means.

What else do we feel, after our two hundred (no more or less) pages with Charlotte Emory? She belongs to what is becoming a familiar class of Anne Tyler heroines: women admirably active in the details of living yet alarmingly passive in the large curve of their lives—riders on male-generated events, who nevertheless give those events a certain blessing, a certain feasibility. Jake comes to need his victim: "Charlotte, it ain't so bad if you're *with* us, you see. You act like you take it all in stride, like this is the way life really does tend to turn out. You mostly wear this little smile." Amos, a brother of Emory's who turns amorous, exclaims in admiration, "Now I see everyone grabbing for pieces of you, and still you're never diminished. . . . You sail through this house like a moon, you're strong enough for all of them." These intelligent, bustling, maternal, helpless moon-women trouble us with the something complacent in their little smiles, their "faint, pleasant humorousness." Their detachment has been achieved through a delicate inner abdication, a multiplication and devaluation of realities. Anne Tyler stated in the *Post*, "I write because I want more than one life." Charlotte Emory as a photographer poses her subjects in odd bits of costume, "absent-mindedly" holding feathers and toys, antique swords and pistols; she has come to believe that such elaborations "may tell more truths than they hide." In the crisis of her mother's dying, Charlotte says, "My life grew to be all dreams; there was no reality whatsoever." Her life, from lonely childhood to lonely marriage, spent in an old house between two gas stations, photographing workaday people with dream baubles, has a terror and a sorrow of which the outlines are acknowledged but not the mass, the terrible heft. She seems less a character than a creator, who among the many lives that her fantasizing, empathizing mind arrays before her almost casually chooses to live her own.

DIANE JOHNSON

From "Southern Comfort"

New York Review of Books, November 7, 1985, pp. 15–17

In Anne Tyler's *The Accidental Tourist*, Sarah asks her husband Macon (an author of guidebooks for people who hate to travel) for a divorce. Since the death of their only child, murdered during a holdup at a burger stand, there has seemed little point to their life together. When Sarah leaves, the reserved and methodical Macon falls strangely apart, breaks his leg, and has to go home to live with his unmarried sister and two divorced brothers who have also come home. Brothers and sister relapse into their withdrawn, eccentric, childhood world, bound by the self-indulgent little rituals and protective patterns that have, perhaps, made their marriages fail. But when his dog, Edward, begins to bite and be unruly, Macon becomes involved with Muriel, the dog trainer, an ebullient and endearing young woman from a lower-middle-class milieu unfamiliar and rather fascinating to him. She sets her cap for him, before we know it they are living together, eventually Sarah wants to come back . . . the issue is what Macon, who has until now simply passed through life with things happening to him, will do, or will allow to happen to him now.

As with ⟨Bobbie Ann⟩ Mason's book ⟨*In Country*⟩, a summary scarcely conveys the richness of descriptive detail, the apt but unaffected diction, the assurance and charm, the engaging characters, high comic tone, and wonderful ear for small-town language: "Rose laid a king on Porter's queen, and Porter said, 'Stinker'"—which is probably what Amos Grundy and Sam Spangler say too. Tyler's version of Baltimore, like Mason's small town, suggests all of small, middle, rural America.

Everyone has remarked the popularity of such settings in recent fiction, though with some difference of opinion about what such popularity means. Is it a reaction against the artistic domination of New York, as some have suggested? Or Tobacco Road-style realism, where "sweat, usually in the background of arcadia, now glistens in the foreground," in Ann Hulbert's apt phrase?[1] In this view, the city as the locus of adventure, despair, boredom, terror, and anomie, has exhausted its traditional metaphoric possibilities, and writers have had to move to small towns, finding there, instead of the sweetness and charm we like to remember, the tedium and despair of anywhere else.

But it's hard to generalize because different writers are at work here, and there are matters of fashion, politics, and temperament to consider. *In Country* seems less a work of fearless realism than one of romantic pastoral charm in a long tradition which includes, among other books, *Little Women*, while recent novels like Douglas Unger's *Leaving the Land* follow Steinbeck or Erskine Caldwell. After all, two views of rural life have always existed in literature as in painting, formal opposites, like Boucher and Breughel.

But what does strike one as new has to do with their method, in particular, of narrative distance. Most familiar is the sort of traditional novel as practiced by James or Bellow, in which you see through the eyes of the characters. For the past several decades we've also had a sort of fiction of the self, where the character is identified with the real life of the author, who seems to go on to lead the character's life (Erica Jong, Philip Roth). Now we could say that this is fiction of the "other," in which the authors, very detached, describe mostly what can be seen, and the clarity of visual detail strangely objectifies the characters. The process that describes the surface also makes that surface relatively impenetrable: "Her skin is flawless. Her frosted curls resemble pencil trimmings." As when looking through the wrong end of a telescope, the detail seems fine and bright but the object seems far away and small. Because you cannot at a distance identify with the characters, you are cut off from them and feel their "otherness."

In the traditional novel, the hero or heroine, though foolish and luckless, and however related to the actual author, was also the reader, a more articulate, differently placed, or cleverer you, whose perceptions widen your own. Mr. Sammler or Maggie Tulliver know more than you do, however much you may worry about their fates. In these new books, the "other" knows less about himself than you know about him. You experience a poignant realization that the hero or heroine is never going to find out the things that you and the author know about his or her situation, while the character just experiences a mute feeling, usually of disappointment. ⟨. . .⟩

If the characters are somehow thinner, they are also wider, like run-over cartoon cats. In Forster's example, Mrs. Micawber is a flat character because, not wanting to focus the book on her, Dickens concentrated her qualities (foolishness, loyalty) into a tag phrase ("I never will desert Mr. Micawber") and allowed the repetition of that phrase to do the work of presenting her. The more widely flattened characters in the books of Tyler and Mason are the sum of a number of observed qualities of dress, speech, action, observed the way a painter might see them, carefully, in full color, in a keen-eyed way (in the way of Norman Rockwell), exaggerating to the brink, but not over the brink, of caricature.

Anne Tyler's Muriel wears "a V-necked black dress splashed with big pink flowers, its shoulders padded and its skirt too skimpy; and preposterously high-heeled sandals." We also know that she has dark-red painted fingernails, nearly black lipstick, frizzy hair—all signifying her poor taste, lower social class, and so on. It will emerge that these sluttish costumes conceal a heart of gold. Although throughout the book Muriel's vulgarity, brashness, and lack of "good taste" are constantly detailed, the effect is not of derision but of a celebration of eccentricity, communicated by visual signals, as on a TV screen. Any quality of satire must be in the mind of the beholder, with the author maintaining an even tone of exemplary charity, neutrality, and geniality. In these and in other works by these two writers, males in particular are seen as frail, domestic, and helpless, presented with an indulgence that borders on sympathy, while the women, creations of female authors who understand the sturdiness of women, are presented as pluckier and left to fend for themselves.

"The pictures focus not on the rich or mighty, but on everyday Americans and the pleasures of home, outdoors, and family that all of us can enjoy," writes Ronald Reagan in his foreword to *Norman Rockwell's Patriotic Times.*[2] Art critics used to warn us not to admire Rockwell's works. Back then we were told that however amusing we might find them, they were infected with easy sentimentality, and that while they might seem by exaggerating the length of an adolescent's neck or detailing an older person's wrinkles not to be flinching from the awkwardness of youth or age, they were in fact trivializing these tormenting life phases the way a funny birthday card is meant to ameliorate the fleeting of time, but in doing so conceals "reality," which, in the fashion of the times, it was seen as our duty to confront.

Whether or not one is entitled to evade or obliged to confront unpleasant details of the human condition, and whether this choice is a matter of fashion, it is true that people have long been imprinted with a view of seriousness heavily biased toward confrontation, having at the same time a strong inner impulse to have things put in a comforting way. It may be that writers now are turning from confrontation. Certainly this new mode of combining an almost photorealistic surface with a strongly ameliorative point of view meets with warm approval, and after all, amelioration has always been one province of literature, though we usually call it myth.

The Accidental Tourist is irresistible and, in its way, gripping. On one level you are terrified that Macon will stay with his dull wife. But on a deeper level you know you are in the mode or in the hands of an author who will not permit terrible disappointment, although either resolution (Sarah or Muriel) could be "real." The larger strategy is to urge a whole agenda of comforting, consoling ideas, among them that spunkiness and *joie de vivre* win over dullness; that social class doesn't count; that affection can cure allergies; that when you are traveling in France, a likable personality will get you invited to dinner by French people; that you are likely to find real bargains in the flea market; that you can return to childhood and invite others back with you; that legs mend, mean dogs can be trained, and, above all, that the dead do not suffer. When Macon is called to identify the dead body of his murdered child, the boy looks peaceful, and he does not look like himself. The pain of bereavement passes, and like Macon you will get another little boy anyway.

All of these ideas are powerfully attractive. It's just that they are not true. *In Country*, with its apparently more serious political concerns, equally proposes a reassuring resolution in which people who have suffered from Vietnam can sense if not articulate peace and reconciliation—can come to terms. The war, like the death of Macon's child, lies in the past of the book; as in a fairy tale, in the present of either book nothing bad can happen. In *The Accidental Tourist*, only the discarded wife, Sarah, who hasn't succeeded in her attempts at liberation, seems to have strayed in from someone else's novel, a realistic novel about woman's lot, and can't quite make it in this one—she hasn't enough personality or oddness. (She has the only bit of bleak realism, when she confides to Macon after her return that she hasn't slept with anyone else during the separation.) The imagery of the final pages of *In Country* is of love and nurture. As they touch the names on the war memorial, Sam finds her own name. "Mamaw says, 'Coming up on this wall of a sudden and seeing how black it was, it was so awful, but then I came down in it and saw that white carnation blooming out of the crack and it gave me hope. It made me know he's watching over us.'"

When Macon wakes up in the middle of the night in Muriel's shabby house to the sound of merriment, we are shown a similar view of a benign and reassuring social order:

> Who would be playing a game at this hour? And on this street—this worn, sad street where nothing went right for anyone, where the men had dead-end jobs or none at all and the women were running to fat and the children were turning out badly. But another cheer went up, and someone sang a line from a song. Macon found himself smiling. He turned toward Muriel and closed his eyes; he slept dreamlessly the rest of the night.

Our wishes are equally fulfilled by Anne Tyler's account of a holdup:

> He went grocery shopping with her unusually late one evening, and just as they were crossing a shadowed area a boy stepped forth from a doorway. "Give over all what you have in your purse," he told Muriel. Macon was caught off guard; the boy was hardly more than a child. He froze, hugging the sack of groceries. But Muriel said, "The hell I will!" and swung her purse around by its strap and clipped the boy in the jaw. He lifted a hand to his face. "You get on home this instant or you'll be sorry you were ever born," Muriel told him. He slunk away, looking back at her with a puzzled expression.

These are in a sense Reaganesque dream novels, where the poor are deserving and spunkiness will win. In the real world of the newspapers people are brutalized, and killed in holdups. But perhaps it is tiresome in the reader to insist upon reality. After all we don't require it in our president. Is Muriel's version of life more satisfying? Or in the long run does this kind of folksy escapism fail to satisfy? The great works of the past by their form console us for the harshness of human reality that they confront. But perhaps confrontation is not the national mood, and these are books of our times.

Notes

1. *The New Republic* (September 2, 1985), p. 30.
2. Written with George Mendoza (Viking, 1985).

JOHN UPDIKE

1932–

John Hoyer Updike was born on March 18, 1932, in Shillington, Pennsylvania, to Wesley Russell and Linda Grace (née Hoyer) Updike. He was educated at Harvard University (A.B. *summa cum laude*, 1954) and the Ruskin School of Drawing and Fine Arts, Oxford (1954–55). In 1953 he married Mary Pennington, with whom he had four children. After their divorce in 1977, he married Martha Bernhard. He worked as a staff reporter for the *New Yorker* from 1955 to 1957. While at Harvard he edited the *Harvard Lampoon*, for which he also wrote and drew.

Updike published his first book of poetry, *The Carpentered Hen and Other Tame Creatures*, in 1958; the following year he published his first collection of stories, *The Same Door*, and his first novel, *The Poorhouse Fair*. His second novel, *Rabbit, Run* (1960), thrust him into popular and critical acclaim. In its concern with the middle-class experience and in Updike's treatment of his confused, somewhat drab yet sympathetic Everyman character Harry "Rabbit" Angstrom, *Rabbit, Run* set the pattern for much of Updike's subsequent fiction. Novels such as *The Centaur* (1963), *Couples* (1968), and especially the second and third "Rabbit books," *Rabbit Redux* (1971) and *Rabbit Is Rich* (1981), detail in intricately crafted prose the problems of ordinary, middle-class existence in contemporary America. Critics have attacked Updike for wasting his talent on inconsequential subjects, at the same time acknowledging the craft and metaphoric power of his prose. An admirer of the theologian Karl Barth, Updike has often explored matters of religious faith in his novels, most overtly in *A Month of Sundays* (1975) and *Roger's Version* (1986).

Unusually for a successful novelist, Updike has consistently excelled in a number of other literary forms as well. Among his more than two dozen books are a play, *Buchanan Dying* (1974), seven short-story collections, six volumes of poetry, and three collections of criticism, including the massive *Hugging the Shore* (1983). Updike won the National Book Award in 1964 for *The Centaur* and the American Book Award and Pulitzer Prize in 1982 for *Rabbit Is Rich*. He lives in Beverly Farms, Massachusetts.

Personal

Interviewer: I'd like to ask a bit about your work habits if I may. What sort of schedule do you follow?

Updike: I write every weekday morning. I try to vary what I am doing, and my verse, or poetry, is a help here. Embarked on a long project, I try to stay with it even on dull days. For every novel, however, that I have published, there has been one unfinished or scrapped. Some short stories—I think offhand of "Lifeguard," "The Taste of Metal," "My Grandmother's Thimble"—are fragments salvaged and reshaped. Most came right the first time—rode on their own melting, as Frost said of his poems. If there is no melting, if the story keeps sticking, better stop and look around. In the execution there has to be a "happiness" that can't be willed or foreordained. It has to sing, click, something. I try instantly to set in motion a certain forward tilt of suspense or curiosity, and at the end of the story or novel to rectify the tilt, to complete the motion.

Interviewer: When your workday is through are you able to leave it behind or does your writing haunt your afternoons and echo your experience?

Updike: Well, I think the subconscious picks at it and occasionally a worrisome sentence or image will straighten itself out and then you make a note of it. If I'm stuck, I try to get myself unstuck before I sit down again, because moving through the day surrounded by people and music and air it is easier to make major motions in your mind than it is sitting at the typewriter in a slightly claustrophobic room. It's hard to hold a manuscript in your mind, of course. You get down to the desk and discover that the solution you had arrived at while having insomnia doesn't really fit. I guess I'm never unconscious of myself as a writer and of my present project. A few places are specially conducive to inspiration—automobiles, church—private places. I plotted *Couples* almost entirely in church—little shivers and urgencies I would note down on the program, and carry down to the office Monday.

Interviewer: Well, you're not only a writer but a famous one. Are you experiencing any disadvantages in being famous?

Updike: I'm interviewed too much. I fight them off, but even one is too many. However hard you try to be honest or full, they are intrinsically phony. There is something terribly wrong about committing myself to this machine and to your version of what you get out of the machine—you may be deaf for all I know and the machine may be faulty. All the stuff comes out attached to my name and it's not really me at all.

My relationship to you and my linear way of coping out loud are distortive. In any interview, you do say more or less than you mean. You leave the proper ground of your strength and become one more gassy monologist. Unlike Mailer and Bellow, I don't have much itch to pronounce on great matters, to reform the country, to get elected Mayor of New York, or minister to the world with laughter like the hero of "The Last Analysis." My life is, in a sense, trash, my life is only that of which the residue is my writing. The person who appears on the cover of *Time* or whose monologue will be printed in *The Paris Review* is neither the me who exists physically and socially or the me who signs the fiction and poetry. That is, everything is infinitely fine and any opinion is somehow coarser than the texture of the real thing.

I find it hard to have opinions. Theologically, I favor Karl Barth; politically I favor the Democrats. But I treasure a remark John Cage made, that not judgingness but openness and curiosity are our proper business. To speak on matters where you're ignorant dulls the voice for speaking on matters where you do know something. 〈. . .〉

Interviewer: 〈. . .〉 Are you conscious of belonging to a definable American literary tradition? Would you describe yourself as part of an American tradition?

Updike: I must be. I've hardly ever been out of the country.

Interviewer: Specifically, do you feel that you've learned important things or felt spiritual affinities with classic American writers such as Hawthorne, Melville, James, people of this sort?

Updike: I love Melville and like James but I tend to learn more from Europeans, because I think they have strengths that reach back past Puritanism, that don't equate truth with intuition—

Interviewer: In other words, you want to be nourished by the thing that you don't feel is inherently your tradition.

Updike: Right. I'm not saying I can write like Melville or James, but that the kind of passion and bias that they show is already in my bones. I don't think you need to keep rehearsing your instincts. Far better to seek out models of what you *can't* do. American fiction is notoriously thin on women, and I *have* attempted a number of portraits of women, and we may have reached that point of civilization, or decadence, where we *can* look at women. I'm not sure Mark Twain *was* able to.

Interviewer: Let's get into your work now. In an interview you gave *Life* you expressed some regret at the "yes, but" attitude critics have taken toward it. Did the common complaint that you had ducked large subjects lead to the writing of *Couples?*

Updike: No, I meant my *work* says "yes, but." Yes, in *Rabbit, Run,* to our inner urgent whispers, but—the social fabric collapses murderously. Yes, in *The Centaur,* to self-sacrifice and duty, but—what of a man's private agony and dwindling? No, in *The Poorhouse Fair,* to social homogenization and loss of faith, but—listen to the voices, the joy of persistent existence. No, in *Couples,* to a religious community founded on physical and psychical interpenetration, but—what else shall we do, as God destroys our churches? I cannot greatly care what critics say of my work; if it is good, it will come to the surface in a generation or two and float, and if not, it will sink, having in the meantime provided me with a living, the opportunities of leisure, and a craftsman's intimate satisfactions. I wrote *Couples* because the rhythm of my life and my oeuvre demanded it, not to placate hallucinatory critical voices.—JOHN UPDIKE, Interview by Charles Thomas Samuels, *PRev,* Winter 1968, pp. 96–101

General

Updike's versatility is as obvious as his mastery of the language. But, some people ask, isn't he spreading himself too thin? Has he written anything that is worthy of his talents? Isn't it time he wrote a Great Book?

Updike himself has something to say on this general theme in his review of Salinger's *Franny and Zooey:* "When all reservations have been entered, in the correctly unctuous and apprehensive tone, about the direction he has taken, it remains to acknowledge that it is a direction and that the refusal to rest content, the willingness to risk excess on behalf of one's obsessions, is what distinguishes artists from entertainers, and what makes some artists adventurers on behalf of us all."

But, the opposition inquires, what risks has Updike taken, and is he driven by obsessions of any sort? So far as the use of language is concerned, he is extremely bold and extremely effective, but how often does one feel a sense of urgency in his fiction?

These are reasonable questions, but I should be sorry if Updike were to pay much attention to them. Certainly we want him to write a great book, but we don't want him to feel that he must do something great or be a failure. In a wise comment on James Agee, Updike says: "A fever of self-importance is upon American writing. Popular expectations of what literature should provide have risen so high that failure is the only possible success, and pained incapacity the only acceptable proof of sincerity." If, he goes on, Agee had justly estimated what he had done, instead of weeping over what he had wanted to do, he would not have taken so unhappy a view of his career. In the same way, it might be a good thing for critics to contemplate what Updike has accomplished in a decade—two excellent novels and many first-rate stories—and not to spend so much time worrying about the books he hasn't yet even attempted.—GRANVILLE HICKS, "John Updike" (1965), *Literary Horizons: A Quarter Century of American Fiction,* 1970, pp. 122–23

Updike's characters represent many things to him; he glosses all his own novels. And because Updike fancies them as many-sided and intellectual designs, they are unusually distinct and memorable among characters in contemporary fiction. They always *mean.* Updike's fiction is distinguished by an unusually close interest in every character he writes about. But these characters who represent so much never struggle with anything except the reflections in their minds of a circumscribing reality that seems unalterable. Updike is a novelist of society who sees society entirely as a fable. It stands still for him to paint its picture; *it* never starts anything. On the other hand, it is always there to say "American," now and in the future—Updike's first novel, *The Poorhouse Fair,* started with the future as tyranny, institutions that are there to say that institutions always take over.

The older American novelists of society were not this much used to it. Scott Fitzgerald, who loved its color, its prodigality, profoundly distrusted it and thought it would revenge itself on its critics. Updike, who persistently recalls Fitzgerald's ability to show society as a dream, has accommodated himself to its dominating possessiveness. Where there are no alternatives, even in one's memory, the proliferating surfaces encourage myths, transferable symbols—a sense of situation, not opposition. Updike is in the best sense of the word an intellectual novelist, a novelist of paradox, tension and complexity who as a college wit in the Fifties learned that we are all symbols and inhabit symbols. His easy mastery of social detail never includes any sense of American society as itself a peculiar institution, itself the dynamo, the aggressor, the maker of other people's lives. Society is just a set of characteristics. Society—our present fate!—shows itself in marvelously shifting mental colors and shapes. Brightness falls from the air, thanks to the God on whose absence we sharpen our minds. But Updike's own bright images of human perception fall along a horizontal line, metaphors of observation that connect only with each other. The world is all metaphor. We are not sure *who* is thinking these brilliant images in *Rabbit, Run*. Need Updike's fine mind be so much in evidence?

> His day had been bothered by God: Ruth mocking, Eccles blinking—why did they teach you such things if no one believed them? It seems plain, standing here, that if there is this floor there is a ceiling, that the true space in which we live is upward space. Someone is dying. In this great stretch of bridge someone is dying. The thought comes from nowhere: simple percentages. Someone in some house along these streets, if not this minute then the next, dies; and in that suddenly stone chest the heart of this flat prostrate rose seems to him to be. He moves his eyes to find the spot; perhaps he can see a cancer-blackened soul of an old man mount through the blue like a monkey on a spring. . . .

Updike is indeed a great mental traveler through the many lands of American possibility. Though *The Poorhouse Fair*, *The Olinger Stories*, *The Centaur* and others of his best works deal with the southeasternmost corner of Pennsylvania he comes from, he no more judges the rest of America by it than puts America into it—as O'Hara put everything he knew into his corner of Pennsylvania. Updike has nothing of the primitive attachment to early beginnings that made a whole generation of American realists once describe the big city as a total dislodgement. As a believer in tradition rediscovered, he can weave a surpassingly tender novel about his father, *The Centaur*, into a set of mythological associations and identifications that in other hands would have academicized the novel to death. *The Centaur* is one of his best books. In *Rabbit, Run* he wrote the marriage novel of a period marked by an increasing disbelief in marriage as the foundation of everything. At the end of *Rabbit, Run* the oversize Harry Angstrom ran away from his mopey wife Janice, who while drunk had accidentally drowned their baby, and from the unfathomable insatiable domesticity of the "tranquilized fifties," as Robert Lowell calls them.

Rabbit Redux of course opens on the day in 1969 that saw the first manned American flight to the moon, "leaving the rest of us here." Harry was once too young and is now mysteriously too old. He is now a decaying man in an American city typically running down, is proud to support the Vietnam War when everybody else has seen though it, and in order to provide the reader with a glibly topical symposium, suddenly finds himself sharing his house with Jill, a wild young hippie runaway from her family, and her sometime lover and drug supply Skeeter, a young Black Vietnam veteran who has jumped bail. Yet even an inferior novel, *Couples*, the book of suburban marriage and its now conventional adulteries that shows Updike exercising his gifts and putting up his usual intellectual-religious scaffolding with somewhat too bountiful ease, is *not* a document, for Updike is happily a novelist excited by his characters. And in *Bech* Updike not only takes on the Jew, the Jewish novelist, a subject that has long fascinated and provoked him because "the Jewish novelist" is so much a fact of our times, so important a social category and rival, the most striking sudden success in a society of sudden successes—he even manages to show the comedy in Bech, a failure.

Everything seems possible to Updike; everything *has* been possible. He knows his way around, in every sense, without being superficial about it. His real subject—the dead hand of "society," the fixity of institutions—has gone hand in hand with the only vision of freedom as the *individual's* recognition of God. This is a period when, as Updike says, "God has killed the churches." There is no nemesis: just an empty space between those untouching circles, society and the individual. Updike has managed to be an intellectual without becoming abstract; in an era of boundless personal confusion, he has been a moralist without rejecting the mores. If poise is a gift, Updike is a genius. If to be "cool" is not just a social grace but awareness unlimited, Updike is the best of this cool world. All he lacks is that capacity for making you identify, for summoning up affection in the reader, which Salinger (now "poor Salinger") expressed when in *The Catcher in the Rye* he had Holden Caulfield reserve his praise for authors who make you want to call them up.—ALFRED KAZIN, "Professional Observers: Cozzens to Updike," *Bright Book of Life*, 1973, pp. 121–24

Works

On record are the opinions of a partisan. So it is necessary to admit that John Updike's novel ⟨*Rabbit, Run*⟩ was approached with animus. His reputation has traveled in convoy up the Avenue of the Establishment, *The New York Times Book Review* blowing sirens like a motorcycle caravan, the professional muse of *The New Yorker* sitting in the Cadillac, membership cards to the right Fellowships in his pocket. The sort of critics who are rarely right about a book—Arthur Mizener and Granville Hicks, for example—ride on his flanks, literary bodyguards. *Life* magazine blew its kiss of death into the confetti. To my surprise, *Rabbit, Run* was therefore a better book than I thought it would be. The Literary Establishment was improving its taste. Updike was not simply a junior edition of James Gould Cozzens. But of course the Establishment cannot nominate a candidate coherently. Updike's merits and vices were turned inside out. The good girlish gentlemen of letters were shocked by the explicitness of the sex in *Rabbit, Run*, and slapped him gently for that with their fan, but his style they applauded. It is Updike's misfortune that he is invariably honored for his style (which is atrocious—and smells like stale garlic) and is insufficiently recognized for his gifts. He could become the best of our literary novelists if he could forget about style and go deeper into the literature of sex. *Rabbit, Run* moves in well-modulated spurts at precisely those places where the style subsides to a ladylike murmur and the characters take over. The trouble is that young John, like many a good young writer before him, does not know exactly what to do when action lapses, and so he cultivates his private vice, he *writes*. And there are long overfingered descriptions in exacerbated syntax, airless crypts of four or five pages, huge inner exertion reminiscent of weight lifters, a stale sweet sweat clings to his phrases.

> Example: *Redbook, Cosmopolitan, McCall's*.
>
> Boys are playing basketball around a telephone pole with a backboard bolted to it. Legs, shouts. The scrape and snap of Keds on loose alley pebbles seems to catapult their voices high into the moist March air blue above the wires. Rabbit Angstom, coming up the alley in a business suit, stops and watches, though he's twenty-six and six-three. So tall, he

> seems an unlikely rabbit, but the breadth of white face, the pallor of his blue irises, and a nervous flutter under his brief nose as he stabs a cigarette into his mouth partially explain the nickname.
>
> Example: *True Confessions*.
>
> Outside in the air his fears condense. Globes of ether, pure nervousness, slide down his legs. The sense of outside space scoops at his chest.
>
> Example: *Elements of Grammar*.
>
> His hands lift of their own and he feels the wind on his ears even before, his heels hitting heavily on the pavement at first but with an effortless gathering out of a kind of sweet panic growing lighter and quicker and quieter, he runs. Ah: runs. Runs.

It's the rare writer who cannot have sentences lifted from his work, but the first quotation is taken from the first five sentences of the book, the second is on the next-to-last page, and the third is nothing less than the last three sentences of the novel. The beginning and end of a novel are usually worked over. They are the index to taste in the writer. Besides, trust your local gangster. In the run of Updike's pages are one thousand other imprecise, flatulent, wry-necked, precious, overpreened, self-indulgent, tortured sentences. It is the sort of prose which would be admired in a writing course overseen by a fussy old nance. And in Updike's new book, *The Centaur*, which was only sampled, the style has gotten worse. Pietisms are congregating, affirmations à la Archibald MacLeish.

The pity is that Updike has instincts for finding the heart of the conventional novel, that still-open no man's land between the surface and the deep, the soft machinery of the world and the subterranean rigors of the dream. His hero, Rabbit Angstrom, is sawed in two by the clear anguish of watching his private vision go at a gallop away from the dread real weight of his responsibility. A routine story of a man divided between a dull wife he cannot bear to live with and a blowsy tough tender whore he cannot make it with, the merit of the book is not in the simplicity of its problem, but in the dread Updike manages to convey, despite the literary commercials in the style, of a young man who is beginning to lose nothing less than his good American soul, and yet it is not quite his fault. The power of the novel comes from a sense, not absolutely unworthy of Thomas Hardy, that the universe hangs over our fates like a great sullen hopeless sky. There is real pain in the book, and a touch of awe. It is a novel which could have been important, it could have had a chance to stay alive despite its mud pies in prose, but at the very end the book drowns in slime. Updike does not know how to finish. Faced with the critical choice of picking one woman or another (and by the end, both women are in fearful need), his character bolts over a literal hill and runs away. Maybe he'll be back tomorrow, maybe he'll never be back, but a decision was necessary. The book ends as minor, a pop-out. One is left with the expectation that Updike will never be great; there is something too fatally calculated about his inspiration. But very good he can be, a good writer of the first rank with occasional echoes from the profound. First he must make an enemy or two of the commissioners on the Literary Mafia. Of course a man spends his life trying to get up his guts for such a caper.—NORMAN MAILER, "The Argument Reinvigorated" (1963), *Cannibals and Christians*, 1966, pp. 120–22

Judging from a number of evasive explications, John Updike's latest novel, *The Centaur*, is not going to be widely understood. Judging from the book's central ambiguity, it may be that Updike does not understand it himself. Like most post-Joycean short story writers, Updike has learned to shape his material—character and situation—around a modified version of epiphany. *The Centaur* is built upon a series of epiphanies, and although each in itself is effectively realized, together they are not finally resolved into a clear and artistically logical pattern. The effect is an odd one—a novel that is structurally unified and yet thematically incoherent. At its various levels—realistic and mythical—*The Centaur* is brilliantly written, alternately moving and funny, exasperating and inconclusive.

On its realistic level the novel is characterized by the same intimate conception of structure that distinguished *Rabbit, Run*. One of Updike's traits as a novelist is that he is reluctant to foreshorten. He fixes upon small time areas and then details virtually every experience within that unostentatious frame. Hence forty pages in one novel may cover no more than an hour of his protagonist's experience, and the apparent pattern is no more contrived than that of life itself. This is partly the strict discipline of the short story imposed upon another form, the acquired habit of a specialist whose gift for precise imagery is especially suited to sharply concentrated narrative areas. In this novel, however, Updike's conception of structure, his minutely inclusive development, has a specific thematic function; for *The Centaur* is essentially about Time, Time for one man in its most agonizing, subjective form.

The centaur of the title is an improbable modern Chiron, a Pennsylvania high school teacher, George Caldwell, whose students regard him with a mixture of admiration and contempt. In the beginning one of them shoots Caldwell in the foot with an arrow, and this proves to be a symbolic wound. For Caldwell, existence itself is a wound that he is determined to tolerate, and his time is measured chiefly in waves of pain. The novel is not foreshortened because Caldwell's experience is not: his day to day life is spun out in a continuum of anxieties and belittling defeats. (In his lecture on the origins of life and the dimensions of the universe he strings out zeroes across the blackboard—years, light years, eons. "Do these figures mean anything to you?" he asks. "They don't to me either. They remind me of death.") His career is all the more nightmarish and dispiriting for its having no objective, no clearing that he can struggle towards. At fifty Caldwell has achieved all that he is going to achieve. Now he can only fight to keep his wife, his son, and his father-in-law healthy and alive. Unlike Rabbit, he has not run because he is anchored by his sense of responsibility—somehow both noble and quixotic—and by his anguished, self-deprecating love for his son. Because of his conditioned economic fear he cannot escape his absurd commitment, and yet because of his latently romantic temperament he cannot fully compromise with his situation and make a bearable existence of it; as Peter says, there was always in their household a sense that they would someday be moving on. Caldwell is tortured, too, by the thought that he is incompetent as a father, incapable of becoming the kind of symbol that Peter needs.

The son, Peter, is our point of view throughout most of the novel, and his role is crucial, for in his love for his father, mingled with vexation and adolescent despair, he endows Caldwell with a dignity and a kind of strength that Caldwell cannot see in himself. For three days we follow the pair through a variety of commonplace misadventures. On the way to school they pick up a moronic and obscene tramp before whom Caldwell compulsively bares his soul ("You *cook!* That's a wonderful accomplishment, and I know you're not lying to me. . . . You're a man I admire. You've had the guts to do what I always wanted to do: move around, see the cities.") At school Caldwell continues to abase himself, before his students, before the principal of the school. He has been ridiculed and exploited by people, mocked by nature and machines, for so long that he is incapable of personal dignity. A knot of paradoxes and conflicts, his real wisdom is shrunken by the stunted minds he has to contend with and by the overpowering trivialities that defeat his spirit. In the classic pattern, he both fears and hopes for death. Convinced that he has an intestinal cancer, he has himself examined by his friend Doc Appleton and learns that he is suffering only from nervous exhaustion; life has had another snicker at his expense.

Peter, meanwhile, is carrying an ironic theme of regeneration. As his father despairs of existence, Peter rejoices in his, drifting through the innocently erotic pastoral of first love. He does not know it, but the kind of love that he feels for Penny Fogleman (and later for one of his father's friends, Vera Hummel) will one day free him from his father; now, however, in his confusion, his love for his father and his love for Penny have somehow become the same. Ultimately, after contending with a series of maddening frustrations—including a broken drive-shaft, a snow-storm, and tire-chains that will not go on—Peter and his father spend two nights and three days together in Olinger. When they finally return home neither knows much more about the other than he had before, but each is somehow more sharply conscious of what the other means.

The mythic parallel is there to redeem Caldwell in art from the sad anonymity he is doomed to in life. Chiron was the wisest and gentlest of the centaurs, afflicted by an incurable wound and yet immortal. Tormented with pain, he offered to give his immortality in atonement for Prometheus. The gods heard his prayer and he was allowed to die like any other man. Prometheus was set free. During those frequent intervals when Caldwell is both himself and Chiron, he becomes something more symbolically than he is allowed to be in actuality.

At the end, however, Caldwell gives up—apparently—and takes his own life. That event is difficult to decipher because, for one thing, it is shrouded in the myth ("Chiron accepted death"), and for another we are unprepared to see Caldwell, suddenly, as a suicide. (It is possible, even, to argue that there is no actual death at all, but merely Caldwell's acceptance of a metaphorical death in life.) Moreover, in having Caldwell take his own life, Updike unavoidably robs him of most of the lonely heroic stature he has so effectively conveyed up to this point. Whatever the effect of his death, by intention Caldwell dies selfishly. When he thinks in his last hour of the joy he is able to bring by giving his life for others, "A white width of days stretched ahead. The time left him possessed a skyey breadth in which he swam like a true grandchild of Oceanus. . . ." (Much earlier he had told his students of the coming of inevitable death into the structure of life: "while each cell is potentially immortal, by volunteering for a specialized function within an organized society of cells, it enters a compromised environment. The strain eventually wears it out and kills it. It dies sacrificially, for the good of the whole.") And yet when he thinks of the fearsome actualities of his sacrifice, that skyey breadth of time constricts sharply. "The invisible expanse the centaur had in an instant grasped retreated from him with a pang" and "a steep weariness mounted before him." He then dies "like any wearied man."

Caldwell's lifetime has been sacrificed to his son; perhaps Updike means for his death to be—accidentally—a sacrifice as well. Perhaps we are meant to see here that, in spite of his motivations, in dying Caldwell dramatizes for Peter the hollowness and the mockery of an altruistic existence—the life that is idealized as noble and good but is in reality tedious, humiliating, and grotesquely absurd. Peter (Prometheus) is freed of this vaguely tyrranic authority (he is unchained), and begins his own rebellious existence in Greenwich Village—a second-rate abstract-impressionist painter living with a Negro mistress. And yet Peter himself wonders, "Was it for this that my father gave up his life?"

If it is true that Caldwell literally dies at the end, then most of the novel's moving eulogy is meaningless. If it is meant that Caldwell simply resigns himself to his living death, that decision is rendered so ambiguously that it becomes meaningless too. Updike cannot have it both ways, and it is annoying to have to choose for him. With all of that ammunition (including the elaborate but largely arbitrary and irrelevant mythic parallels) one somehow expects a greater explosion. The novel succeeds brilliantly in small ways, but as a whole it seems at once meaningful and perversely obscure. Ultimately *The Centaur* fails of its purpose simply because its purpose is not clearly conceived.—VEREEN BELL, "A Study in Frustration," *Shen*, Summer 1963, pp. 69–72

John Updike is one of those writers around whom we have generated a flamboyance of celebrity quite out of keeping with the value of anything they have so far written. In any reasonably discriminating age a young man of Mr. Updike's charming but limited gifts might expect to make his way in time to a position of some security in the second or just possibly the third rank of serious American novelists. But this is not a discriminating age. Hence, Mr. Updike has been able to arrive with ease at the very gates of first-rank status, and considering the size and fervor of his following, he should have no trouble at all getting in.

Just why this should be so it is extremely difficult to say, and the appearance of his new novel, *Of the Farm*, does not make it any easier. Mr. Updike has none of the attributes we conventionally associate with major literary talent. He does not have an interesting mind. He does not possess remarkable narrative gifts or a distinguished style. He does not create dynamic or colorful or deeply meaningful characters. He does not confront the reader with dramatic situations that bear the mark of an original or unique manner of seeing and responding to experience. He does not challenge the imagination or stimulate, shock, or educate it. In fact, one of the problems he poses for the critic is that he engages the imagination so little that one has real difficulty remembering his work long enough to think clearly about it. It has an annoying way of slipping out of the mind before one has had time to take hold of it, and of blending back into the commonplace and banal surfaces of reality, which are so monotonous a part of our daily awareness that the mind instinctively rejects them as not worth remembering.

Yet there can be no doubt that Mr. Updike does on occasion write well, although often with a kind of fussiness that makes one feel that the mere act of finding words that look attractive together on the page occupies entirely too much of his time and energy. There are, nonetheless, passages here and there in his novels of excellent description, mostly of landscapes, such as the long account in *The Centaur* of Peter Caldwell's early morning drive with his father into town, and Rabbit Angstrom's abortive flight down the highways in *Rabbit, Run*. There are also moments when Mr. Updike seems on the verge of becoming profound on the subject of the larger issues of life, love, death, and God. But then as a rule one senses that he does not, after all, know quite what he means to say and is hoping that sheer style will carry him over the difficulty. It is true, as Norman Mailer once remarked, that Mr. Updike tends to become confused when the action lapses, and so he cultivates his private vice: he *writes*. And the conviction grows on one that he *writes* a great deal too much of the time, and is too frequently ridden by the necessity to distract the reader's attention from the lapse by planting in his path yet another exquisitely described tree, shack, or billboard.

In his first three novels Mr. Updike should have been able to avoid these problems because he appeared to take great pains never to treat a subject for which a safe and secure precedent in literature did not exist. This, in fact, may well account for the high esteem in which he is currently held by so many people. For what he essentially accomplished in those novels was a skilled adaptation of the standard mannerisms and styles that have come over the years to be identified as belonging to the official serious modern mode of treating experience in fiction, and with which, therefore, many people felt comfortable, since they were relieved of the obligation to accommodate themselves to the new and unfamiliar and could sit back and enjoy being informed once again of what they already knew. Mr. Updike, in turn, was relieved of the obligation to think creatively and free to indulge his considerable talent for mimicking to perfection the best effects of other writers' originality.

It became apparent, however, that Mr. Updike shared with his admirers the handicap of being a good many years behind the times in his literary tastes. For example, his first novel, *The Poorhouse Fair*, was exactly the sort of book that back in the twenties and thirties would have represented an honest and rather radical confrontation of reality, but which by the middle fifties had become so respectably and fashionably "modern" that schools of writing were proudly turning it out by the dozens. It was a book essentially of style and terribly oblique and opaque and tinily inward observations of people, in which nothing discernible *happened*, but everything went on with dark throttled meaningfulness just beneath the surfaces, and faint ectoplasmic wisps of sensibility floated spookily about the page. In it Mr. Updike proved not only that he could work well in an outmoded convention, but that he could, if the need arose, *write* to cover a lapse of book-length duration.

Rabbit, Run, although brilliant in many of its superficial effects, was a botched attempt to explore certain important disorders of the modern will and spirit. It raised vital questions of freedom and responsibility that it answered vapidly. At just the point where it should have crystallized into meaning, it collapsed into a shambles of platitudes and stereotypes of alternative—rebellion versus conformity, the loving, passionate prostitute versus the dull, drunken, respectable wife—which nicely dramatized Mr. Updike's failure to come to fresh imaginative grips with his materials. *Rabbit, Run* might have been a deeply subversive book. Instead, it merely recapitulated subversive elements that had ceased with time and repeated literary usage to be subversive. It was spiced with a stale, High-Camp brand of *Angst* and a sexuality that had become merely a form of *writing* done with a different instrument, and, perhaps appropriately, the most viable possibility it appeared to hold out was that Rabbit probably ought to try very hard to make his peace with society, family, and God.

At the time he wrote *The Centaur*, Mr. Updike must have been alone among living writers in supposing that there could still be anything interesting or original to be done with the device of juxtaposing ancient myth and contemporary fact in fiction. Although T. S. Eliot did say after *Ulysses* was published that "Mr. Joyce is pursuing a method which others must pursue after him," one had assumed that the serious imitators of Joyce had all by now died of old age. But Mr. Updike, with his infallible instinct for the dated, apparently decided that there might be some kind of intellectual chic or status value to be found in carrying on the pursuit. He seems accordingly to have set out equipped only with the idea that all one needed to do was bring together some mythological figures and some contemporary characters and say that they were parallels, without troubling to create a dramatic situation in which they actually *became* parallels and therefore meaningful. Thus, he indicated in a thoughtfully provided epigraph and index that his story was a moderndress reenactment of the legend of Chiron and Prometheus. But there was no reason to suppose that his protagonist, George Caldwell, was Chiron or anybody else but George Caldwell. His actions did not relate significantly or even coherently to those of the noblest of centaurs, and Chiron's shadow behind him contributed none of the comic irony that Odysseus contributed to Joyce's Bloom. It only served to muddle more completely a story that had no structure or point, and that Mr. Updike was clearly attempting to trick out in a bogus and antiquated literariness.

Of the Farm, although physically a small book, affords Mr. Updike a large opportunity to exercise his considerable powers of description. Never before has his private vice been so eloquently publicized. In fact, since he now has no rabbits or centaurs running for him, Mr. Updike is forced to describe pretty much all the time. There are descriptions of houses, barns, fields, flowers, trees, farm equipment, garden produce, and dogs. There is also a very good description of a tractor mowing a hay field.

The story itself is slight enough to have served as the basis for one of Mr. Updike's *New Yorker* stories, but even in the *New Yorker* it probably would have had to crescendo just a little, and this it does not do. It simply stops. It concerns the tensions that develop between a son and his ailing mother and the son's second wife when they all come together during a weekend down on the mother's farm. The mother, it seems, really preferred the first wife, although she appears not to care very much for either wife, and she certainly does not care for her son, who is full of bitterness toward her. At any rate, this drama, which develops at about the speed of creeping crab grass, is interrupted at intervals to give Mr. Updike an opportunity to make sure that the reader has the scene firmly in mind. And just to make doubly sure, he inserts some further descriptions of details he failed to mention earlier, such as the appearance of a church where the mother and son attend service, a supermarket where they go to buy groceries, and the new wife's excellent thighs in a bikini.

But these digressions come to seem more and more pleasant and necessary as the novel proceeds. Indeed, one begins to feel almost grateful to the action for lapsing, for at least the interludes of scenic commercials introduce subjects about whose reality there can be no question. They have what Henry James would have called "density of specification," and finally they justify their existence in the novel by creating a happy heterogeneity of clutter into which the domestic tensions sink and finally disappear. It seems after a while that all the difficulties we have watched developing among the characters become assimilated into the bucolic setting, that a satisfactory mediation has been achieved between the petty troubles of men and women and the eternal harmonies of nature, so that what at first promised to be a disturbing book turns out to be an essentially placid and contented book.

The effect of the book is finally so agreeable and reassuring that one feels that it would be almost offensive to speak of its possible meaning. Yet meaning it most assuredly has. In fact, one can even say that it has a message, although as is the case with all Mr. Updike's books, it does not yield up this message easily. Every effort is made to keep it subtle, and the reader is constantly being put off its track by various cagey covering movements of Mr. Updike's. But one can, after some searching, ferret it out from its hiding place behind the rich, beautiful scenery of the descriptive prose. I suppose there is no harm in revealing it, since it is bound to become common knowledge very soon. Mr. Updike has nothing to say.—JOHN W. ALDRIDGE, "The Private Vice of John Updike" (1965), *Time to Murder and Create*, 1966, pp. 164–70

In a memoir written in 1962, entitled "The Dogwood Tree: A Boyhood," John Updike told how his three great boyhood fascinations were sex, religion, and art. They have not radically altered in the past twenty-two years, through twenty-eight books. Like ingredients in a witches' brew, they have been mixed again and again and then poured into different molds: small-town Pennsylvania, small-town Massachusetts, middle-class marriage, the roving life of an author, Africa. They are the trinity of his dubious faith, the elusive grail of his erudite and merciless detailed quests.

His new novel ⟨*The Witches of Eastwick*⟩, about three witches and the intrusion of a mysterious, wealthy stranger from New York City into their small Rhode Island town, maintains Updike's three perennial concerns. In fact, the sexually active trio of witches are all artists of a sort: Alexandra is a sculptress, Jane is a musician, and Sukie is a writer. Moreover, their supernatural powers call into question, in a playful way, the role of spiritual energy in the modern world.

Alexandra, for her part, whose former husband rests "on a high kitchen shelf in a jar, reduced to multi-colored dust, the cap screwed on tight," can create thunderstorms. Jane, a cellist, can fly through the air; her former husband hangs in the cellar of her ranch house "among the dried herbs and simples and was occasionally sprinkled, a pinch at a time, into a philtre, for piquancy." Sukie, who can turn milk into cream, has "permanized" her ex-husband in plastic and uses him as a place mat.

Enter Darryl Van Horne, a pushy Manhattanite who sets up an alchemist's lab in an old mansion, and promises to refurbish it in a way that may prove an environmental threat both to the marshes and mentality of Eastwick. The time is the 1960s during the Vietnam war and the rising American drug culture. Predictably, Darryl and the three witches become involved, and then disinvolved. As a preeminent novelist of manners, Updike makes meaningful every nuance of behavior that occurs in Eastwick, and like Jane, sprinkles every happening for pungency.

In essence, this novel is yet another charming, clever, deft spell conjured up by an incredibly prolific imagination in Updike's continuous battle against the demons of the Enlightenment. For there is in Updike's work, and in this novel as well, invariably a war between rationalism and mysticism, between what is known, felt, and sensuously apprehended on the one hand, and what is beyond reason on the other.

In an early Updike story, "The Astronomer," the narrator relates a visit to him and his young wife by a learned astronomer. The narrator has been reading Kierkegaard. After the astronomer leaves, the narrator says: "The mingle on the table was the only part of the greater confusion as in the heat of rapport our unrelated spirits and pasts scrambled together, bringing everything in the room with them, including the rubble of footnotes bound into Kierkegaard."

The confusion, the scrambling pasts and spirits, and the rubble of footnotes (which turn into literature) are all central for Updike. The problem with that brief story, however, is also the problem with Updike's new novel. Alas, it is the conception, the interspersed commentary, that is multi-dimensional; the characters themselves, and their situations, lack transcendence.

Perhaps no major writer in English since Yeats has been able to create literature out of personal experience to the extent Updike has. Perhaps no major American writer since Faulkner, or Hawthorne, has been able to find such richness in regionalism and parochial superstition. Yet Updike's achievement seems to be more one of artistic virtuosity than of coming to terms with a great theme, and often he dazzles with a superficiality that reminds one of a Fourth of July sparkler—sparks but no heat, light but no illumination; a treasured amusement, but no treasure.

Again and again John Updike has told us the particulars of white, middle-class social life in the rural Northeast. He has done it each time with shimmering, learned bursts of words, wit, and in this case, witchery. But at the end, one is hard pressed to take seriously the spirits and parts and rubble of Kierkegaardean implications. At the end one wonders, in the words of one of Updike's coven, which witch is which. Or, if it matters.—PHILIP CORWIN, "Oh, What the Hex," *Com*, June 1, 1984, pp. 340–41

The language of fiction is a medley. The novelist, unlike the lyric poet or essayist, must command many styles and speak to us through a plurality of borrowed or imitated discourses as well as in what passes for his or her own voice. There are at least five distinct discursive strands interwoven in the texture of John Updike's *Roger's Version*. Four of them will be familiar to readers of his previous novels, but the fifth is, I believe, a new development, or acquisition, and a remarkably interesting one.

To start with the familiar: there is the discourse of theology. The central character and narrator, pipe-smoking, 52-year-old Roger Lambert is a professor of divinity, a former Methodist minister who adopted an academic career after the scandalous breakup of his first marriage and his union with Esther, 14 years his junior. He teaches the history of the early Christian heresies at a large university in an unnamed Northeastern city that might be Boston. He is a somewhat dilettantish disciple of Karl Barth, the austere Swiss theologian who fiercely insisted on the utter separateness of the divine and the human, and the utter dependence of the latter on the former. Roger admits to insulating this "hot Barthian nugget" in "layers of worldly cynicism and situation ethics." Mr. Updike is well able to evoke the ethos of an academic theology department, and to have sly fun with its professional rivalries, pretensions and jargon (this one has specialists in "'Ethics and Moral Logistics" and "holocaustics"). He has manifested an interest in religion and theology in previous books. If there was ever such a species as the Protestant novelist, comparable to that much discussed animal, the Catholic novelist, Mr. Updike may be its last surviving example.

There is the discourse of eroticism, or pornography—the distinction is not always easy to draw, and Mr. Updike has taken a leading part in the tendency of contemporary art to blur it, incorporating previously taboo matter and diction into serious fiction. His *Couples* was something of a landmark in this respect. Roger Lambert never tires of reading theology, but confides, "Lest you take me for a goody-goody, I find kindred comfort and inspiration in pornography, the much-deplored detailed depiction of impossibly long and deep, rigid and stretchable human parts interlocking, pumping, oozing." His own descriptions of such acts certainly have the sharp focus, the closeup detail, the glossy sheen and vivid color of pornographic photography—with the added perversity, or poignancy, that they are mostly imagined rather than reported, mental projections of his conviction that he is being cuckolded by a young graduate student, Dale Kohler. ⟨. . .⟩

The fifth, and unfamiliar, discourse in *Roger's Version* is that of science—mathematics, physics, biology and, above all, computing. Dale Kohler is a graduate in computer studies and a fundamentalist Christian. At the beginning of the story he visits Roger not just to tell him about Verna but to ask his assistance in obtaining a grant from the theology department. He is convinced that the more science discovers about the mathematical equations underlying the universe, the more unavoidable becomes the conclusion that they are not the result of chance. "God is showing through," he assures Roger, though the scientific establishment is desperately trying to conceal the fact.

"Everywhere you look," Dale says, "there are these terrifically finely adjusted constants that have to be just what they are, or there wouldn't be a world we could recognize, and there's no intrinsic reason for those constants to be what they are except to say *God made them that way*." His ambition is to prove this assertion by calculations and model manipulations on the university's giant computer. The project is as repugnant to Roger as its tall, gawky, virile proponent. It offends his Barthian theological principles, but it also threatens his cynicism and "situation ethics." "Your God sounds like a nice safe unfindable God," Dale shrewdly observes. Much is at stake.

The pair debate the issue in a series of set pieces that cover cosmology, evolution and the relation of body to mind. These are fascinating and important issues—topical too, given the rising tide of Christian fundamentalism in America today—and it is heartening to see a literary novelist taking them on board. A note on the copyright page gives some indication of the research that all this entailed, and one can only salute Mr. Updike's energy, boldness and sheer brainpower in undertaking it. He is not content to give us a mere impressionistic whiff of physics, math and biology. He makes Dale Kohler speak with the passion and particularity of the true enthusiast:

> Take the strong force, which binds the atomic nuclei together. Make it five percent weaker, and the deuteron couldn't form and there would be no deuterium, which means the main nuclear reaction chain used by the sun couldn't function; if it were two percent *stronger*, two protons could stick together and the existence of the di-protons would make hydrogen so explosive the present universe would consist entirely of helium.

There is quite a lot of this sort of talk, and the scientifically illiterate reader (like myself) may find that much of it goes over his head, at least on first reading. The book seems initially to be shaping up as a rather static novel of ideas, but as it proceeds the different discourses within it begin to interact excitingly. There is, for instance, a remarkable chapter in which Roger's wrestling with Tertullian's arguments for the resurrection of the body elides into a startlingly explicit account of Esther and Dale making love, which in turn gives way to a debate between two men about the body-mind problem. Each strand illuminates the others.

Admittedly the plot (never Mr. Updike's strong point) ticks on rather slowly. The cracks in the Lambert marriage begin to show. Verna gets carelessly pregnant again, and Roger shoulders both the financial and the moral responsibility of arranging an abortion. Will he overcome his fear of catching some "state-of-the-art venereal diseases" and sleep with her? Is Esther really sleeping with Dale?

Since all the discourses in the novel are uttered or mediated by Roger, as narrator, the question of his reliability becomes crucial. The title of the novel suggests that there might be other, very different versions of the story, and a number of clues seem planted in the text warning us not to trust him. Early on he begins to put himself in Dale's place, and see the world through his eyes with what he himself calls "an odd and sinister empathy." His detailed narratives of Esther's infidelity appear to be based on pure suspicion, and could well be the voyeuristic fantasies, at once compensatory and self-punishing, of middle-aged impotence. As the novel moves toward its narrative climax (Verna, with Roger's collusion, narrowly escapes a charge of child abuse and gratefully invites him into her bed; Dale's faith and mental equilibrium begin to crack under the stress of his impossible project), the novel seems poised for a reversal that will reveal Roger's suspicions as delusory. But at the very end they are casually confirmed by Verna: Dale's "been having an affair with some older woman, somebody married who I guess is a pretty hot ticket. . . . Somewhere in your neighborhood, I got the impression."

The absence of an expected reversal is itself a reversal. This twist is effective in narrative terms, but does not entirely solve the problem of authority in the novel. Where did all the detail of Roger's erotic imaginings come from? How does he know what Dale's room looks like, down to the Korean crucifix, of ambiguous substance, that hangs over the bed? How is Roger, in a tour de force chapter, able to give a minutely circumstantial account of the Cube, the building that houses the university's computer services, where Dale works all night in a supreme effort to conjure the hand or face of God on his computer terminal, when he (Roger) states at the outset of his narrative that, "I have never entered it, nor do I hope to"? First-person narrators are allowed, by poetic license, to borrow some of the author's eloquence, but not his omniscience.

One is tempted to seek a clue in Roger's comment on the inconsistencies and circularities of early Christian documents: "First-century people just didn't have the same sense of factuality that we do, or of writing either. Writing was sympathetic magic . . . writing something down was to an extent making it so."

So, of course, is writing fiction. If Mr. Updike were a novelist given to metafictional tricks, we might suspect him of holding up a mirror to the reader's credulity, by making his character claim the same freedom to invent that we grant the novelist. But everything we know about Mr. Updike suggests that he shares the modern sense of factuality and believes that fiction should create the illusion of it. Otherwise, why take all that trouble to get the scientific discourse right?

There is, then, an unresolved enigma or contradiction at the heart of *Roger's Version*, blurring the exact nature and degree of the narrator's "bad faith." For all its richness and virtuosity, the novel makes its effect by a somewhat arbitrary suppression of the discourse of objective report. Nevertheless, one finishes it with gratitude—for it is challenging and educative—and with renewed respect for one of the most intelligent and resourceful of contemporary novelists.—DAVID LODGE, "Chasing After God and Sex," *NYTBR*, Aug. 31, 1986, pp. 1, 15

I haven't actually read John Updike's latest novel, *Roger's Version*. But I have just read David Lodge's review of it (Aug. 31), and that's probably enough to offer a suggestion.

Let's see. There's a fellow named Roger. He's married to a woman named Hester. Sorry, *Esther*. And he's being cuckolded by a chap named Dale, who's a fundamentalist Christian. Takes place in New England. Roger spends the novel talking to Dale and wondering whether his wife has slept with Dale; in the end he discovers that she has.

Having that much information, I suspect that John Updike was aware of the parallel. And I suspect that if it had occurred to your reviewer, he would have found answers, or other answers, to certain problems. Example: "How does [Roger] know what Dale's room looks like?" Believe me, he knew. Example: Ought we to infer from the title that there are other versions, and that Roger's might not be sound? Perhaps; but I suspect that we are to see this novel as *Roger's* version, as opposed to its ancestor, Hawthorne's *Scarlet Letter*, which was, really, Hester and the Reverend Dimmesdale's version. —DAVID PETERSON, "Updike and Hawthorne," *NYTBR*, Sept. 28, 1986, p. 45

EUGENE LYONS

"John Updike: The Beginning and the End"

Critique, Volume 14, Number 2 (1972), pp. 44–59

John Updike's *Rabbit Redux*, touted by *The New York Times* as perhaps the best American novel of 1971, [1] is hardly that, and one does not need to have read very much of the competition to speak with assurance. It is a novel so jarring and offensive to both mind and taste that it is very likely to send many readers back to its predecessor *Rabbit, Run*, published in 1960, to see how they could have been so wrong. They were not. Like Roth's unjustifiably snubbed *Letting Go*, Bellow's *Seize the Day* and *Augie March*, and Sylvia Plath's late entry *The Bell Jar*, to mention only a few at random, it was a real fictional document of the Fifties, that period in American life which lasted from roughly 1948 to 1966 or so. Considering the real virtues of that early novel, and even granting Updike's somewhat disappointing work since then, the breathtaking ineptitude of the recent one is surprising. Less remarkable is the favorable reception it has gotten, considering the nature of its badness, since the literary climate in which it was written seems at least partly to blame for its failure. As if to atone for the triviality his detractors have accused him of, Updike has returned to the subject matter of his first success, the inhabitants of that vast hinterland between the Hudson and San Francisco Bay, and has confirmed what he was supposed to have known then: that they are contemptible slobs not worthy of our attention. Or let us say such would be the effect, were one not already convinced and able to take *Rabbit Redux* seriously on any level. For Updike himself it is a sad story re-told: yet another of our novelists has followed his thoroughly American urge to self-destruct as a serious writer by trying, in a phrase brought to mind by the book itself, to "shoot the moon," to have both critical and financial success, to be famous, socially significant, and an artist as well. Sadly, there simply is not enough of him to go around.

To appreciate fully the kind of dogged compulsiveness and inability to see which plagues Updike's latest novel, one might review the real qualities of *Rabbit, Run*[2] in a backward light. Harry "Rabbit" Angstrom, a high school basketball star turned twenty-six, found his life had come to nothing. Arriving home from a day demonstrating the "Magi-Peel Peeler," he found his wife Janice drunk and pregnant, watching the Mickey Mouse Club on television, their apartment a wreck, and their three-year-old son Nelson farmed out to his grandparents for the day. Taking his cue from the mouse-eared MC, plucking a guitar and urging the kiddies to "Know Thyself," Rabbit was off on a circular journey of self-discovery: fleeing wife, child, and job in an abortive one-night drive South; returning to hole up with Ruth, a semi-professional good-time girl; heading back to Janice when their second child is born; taking leave again in the middle of the night when she, only a few days out of the hospital, will not accommodate herself to his desires; showing up at the funeral of the infant, whom Janice accidentally drowned in sorrow-induced drunkeness; then going back to Ruth, who turned up pregnant herself, and by demanding either a commitment or a permanent break, drove Rabbit, at novel's end, over the horizon, running.

What did Rabbit want?

> What held him back all day was the feeling that somewhere there was something better for him than listening to babies cry and cheating people in used car lots and it's this feeling he tries to kill. (270)

As a summary of the compulsions of many characters in American fiction of the period, that is hard to beat. Although sometimes difficult to determine, because Updike did not permit himself the editorial voice, Rabbit wanted success, elegance, a sense of congruence in his life, and most of all grace, both the kind he had on the basketball court (his coach tells us he never fouled) and the other kind, which shines intermittently, or seems to, from the church window he can see from his mistress's bed. "Is it these people I'm outside or all America?" (33). Updike's hero is prone to wonder, constantly measuring himself against the seedy limits of Brewer, a middle-sized industrial city in eastern Pennsylvania that in real life we suspect to be Reading or Bethlehem.

Besides scrubbing Ruth's face of makeup on their first night together (it will not wash clean), and his overnight drive into West Virginia, Rabbit's most decisive attempt to make something better of his life is to climb to Mt. Judge's peak, which at least gives him a different perspective. From there it is "Brewer, the mother of 100,000, shelter of love, ingenious and luminous artifact" (113).

To the Rev. Eccles, an ineffectual clergyman who plays beagle to Angstrom's rabbit, the man is an enigma. Does his wish to transcend make him a saint, or is he merely unable to grow up? The reader too is likely to wonder. At one moment he sympathizes with Rabbit, and at the next is prone to agree with an angry Eccles:

> the truth is . . . you're monstrously selfish. You're a coward. You don't care about right or wrong; you worship nothing but your own worst instincts. (133)

And if the reader is unable to make up his own mind, Updike himself did not seem to know and kept out of it. The novel, like *Rabbit Redux*, is written in the third-person historical present and from a narrative angle in which Updike allows himself to describe but not to comment upon the thoughts of his characters. For people who like their fiction to come neatly packaged with moral conclusions, this can be annoying, but it does have the virtue of honesty. For the record, the evidence weighs clearly against sainthood, particularly at the end when Ruth tells Rabbit that through his indulgence (in that other thing rabbits are famous for besides circular flight) he now has two families and has to make a choice; but the point is arguable. *All* of the characters have their weaknesses, their blind spots, their own inabilities to cope. Janice *is* a whiner and a drunk, and Ruth *has* shacked up a little too often in a pre-pill world to be overly self-righteous about her pregnancy. In short, they are fully human; one of the principal flaws of *Rabbit Redux* is that none of the characters is: the question of their humanity seems to be the only real question the novel poses.

Whatever its shortcomings *Rabbit, Run* is very good on the simultaneous mystery and banality of self and place, on the characters' fear of loneliness and their inability to reach out. The problem of grace, the dilemma of responsibility versus freedom, all rise out of specific events, observed detail, compassion, and real emotion. At pivotal moments the novel is very convincing: Rabbit's visit to the hospital at the child's birth where his former coach is partly paralyzed by a stroke, the past collapsing and future emerging; Rabbit's terrible fear as he takes care of Nelson while Janice is in the hospital, feeling the robin's egg fragility of the child's skull, the tentative beating of his heart; the mordantly precise description of Janice, drunk, slopping around the apartment leaving wet diapers on the TV set and drawing the baby's last bath; her perception through an alcoholic fog as her mother knocks on the door and she fishes the body out of the water "that the worst thing that has ever happened to any woman in the world has just happened to her" (264). There is much to praise here; it works.

Rabbit Redux[3] is exactly opposite. Partly the problem is a technical one, perhaps because Updike wanted to remain consistent, perhaps because he was kidding himself. The angle of narration is maintained, but the suspension of judgment which made the narration effective is gone. Updike no longer wonders; he knows. Here is a *message*, a message which rises out of stiff, unyielding abstractions, out of pop-psychology, and out of fashionable attitudes one must apparently share if one is to remain long in favor along the Hudson where they beat the drums. Having denied himself the privilege of telling us what his story "means," Updike aims to "show" us. Is not that how it is supposed to be done? Ten years have passed. Rabbit is back with Janice. Nelson is now thirteen. There have been no more children. Traumatized by the death of the baby, he no longer makes love to his wife. Or does he? He thinks he does, she thinks not. Given Updike's penchant for oral endearments, except for one bout on the floor after he finds out about her lover, we do not really know. But no matter. Rabbit is a responsible man. He is, if not a hard-hat exactly, what used to be known as a "working stiff" in the romantic pre-labor-union days. He runs a linotype machine for an outfit known as "Verity Press," publishers of "The Brewer *Vat*," which gives Updike a chance to comment on the news of the day even before it hits the presses. The *Vat* is a weekly which specializes in boosterism, "crime in the streets," and racial innuendo. Rabbit owns a cheap "ranch" in a bulldozed subdivision outside the city. Beginning to catch on? What happens, see, is that his wife runs out on him this time, partly because she isn't getting enough (isn't everyone entitled?) and partly, apparently, because he is *for* the war in Vietnam. And Rabbit starts hanging around with these blacks at work, just for a little adventure, you understand, and they sort of give him this white hippie chick who takes dope; she moves in with him and Nelson and they (she and Rabbit, we never do find out about Nelson) start doing what is natural for any two consenting adults to do, but she has this black militant boy friend and he arrives and has a fight with Rabbit and loses, but sort of moves in too, and they all live together, and then . . . But save the rest for later, anything can be parodied, although the novel lends itself more readily than most. There is a point to be made.

One thing that has happened since *Rabbit, Run* is that Updike has developed a social conscience, something hostile critics were always saying he did not have. One is tempted to say, in fact, that he has nothing else. In the earlier novel our hero had a temporary job working in the garden of Mrs. Smith, a widow so wealthy that she could afford to pay $200.00 to import a rhododendron from England. Nor did we sense a particle of disapproval. Mrs. Smith simply *was*. Rabbit, among the flowers, could tell her "This must be what heaven is like" (141). And if there were blacks in Brewer, they kept pretty much in their place. At least Rabbit never noticed them. True, there was "a singing negress" on the radio, and at one point "a colored boy" brought Rabbit a drink, but by 1969 things had changed. Either a large in-migration or Rabbit sees with different eyes. On the bus home from work, or whenever he is in the city, he hardly ever thinks of anything else:

> They are a strange race. Not only their skins but the way they're put together, loose jointed like lions, strange about the head, as if their thoughts are a different shape and come out twisted even when they mean no menace. It's as if, all these Afro hair bushes and gold earrings and hoopy noise on busses . . . were taking over the garden. His garden. Rabbit knows it's his garden and that's why he's put a flag decal on the back window of the Falcon even though Janice says its corny and fascist. (13)

Somewhat hackneyed and mannered perhaps, but not objectionable in itself. If you missed that flag decal the first time around, it comes back every time the car pulls in sight. That is the point. Updike's social perceptions, hardly in evidence until this novel, have already stiffened into attitudes, para-political positions which so limit and define his imaginative response to his subject that to read the novel is to be taken on a guided tour of virtually every negative cliche that can be applied to America today. The principal touchstones are race and Vietnam, which seem to Updike to divide human beings from the lesser animals, with the result that the narrative tension which keeps the novel going is something like: "Can one live in America"; or, "is this not hell on earth"; or even, "are these people human?" So starkly obstrusive is the selection of detail that one would think that to live in America is to live in the inner circles of Dante's hell. Whatever observed particulate reality is reflected in his language (and there is a lot of it, Updike has always been strong in that), it is selected and presented so didactically that the novel takes on the texture of allegory, only without allegory's responsibility to be consistent. Rabbit cannot visit the "Burger Bliss" for a quick dinner without being treated to

> a Lunar Special (double cheeseburger with an American flag stuck in the bun) and a vanilla milkshake, that tastes toward the bottom of chemical sludge. (113)

Whether we sneak out for an occasional McDonald's "double cheese" or not, we have been trained how to respond. The bus cannot take him by a shopping center without our being told of the acres of "fins" marring the landscape (which may tell us something in itself, the Detroit product having been "finless" since about 1960).

It is not that Updike's implied attitudes are *wrong*. Most of his readers will agree with many or all of them. It is that taken in the aggregate, presented with such consistently humorless solemnity, they are oppressive, and finally, we sense, a lie. Things are simply not that bad. Image follows predictable image of ugliness, sterility, decay, hostility, and betrayal. As Rabbit's life falls apart with Janice's leaving, his father watches the first moon landing in the next room, commenting with the heavy pedantry of a stupid but patriotic parrot. Technology, we deduce, is not the answer. Aw shucks, we all thought it was. The security Rabbit has bought on time, his quarter-acre spread in the suburbs, does not satisfy. Brewer is crime-ridden, full of desperately violent blacks. The suburbs are barren, lifeless oases of loneliness, houses set against one another. Think about this: although Rabbit was a star athlete in his town and has never really left it, no one on the street knows or recognizes him, ever. While he has lived in his home for several years, he does not know a single one of his neighbors by name, not one. And at the age of 36, he does not play ball at all anymore, nor does he hunt, fish, bowl, play cards, drink with friends, tinker with his car, have a small boat or snowmobile, or even watch sports on television. He lives for the evening news, which he comprehends with the sullen idiocy of a lobotomized Archie Bunker. (All this gives Updike further opportunity to solemnize. Once seeing a funeral on the screen with the sound turned off, Rabbit is unable to tell whether it is Ho Chi Minh's or Everett Dirksen's. Anyone for cheap ironies? Or would eyeglasses be more in order? When Rabbit defends the war to his wife and her lover it is by saying "all we want to do [is] make a happy rich country full of highways and gas stations. Poor old LBJ, Jesus with tears in his eyes on television . . . just about offered to make North Vietnam the fifty-first fucking state of the Goddam Union if they'd just stop throwing bombs" (45). The stagy condescension of this last makes "All in the Family," whch is played for laughs, subtle by comparison.) Although he has lived in the immediate area all his life and even works in the same plant as his father, Rabbit belongs to no organizations we hear of: not Moose, Masons, Eagles, Elks, Lions, Odd Fellows, American Legion, VFW, Brewer Athletic Club, nothing. He has no friends. He does not go on excursions with his neighborhood tavern. In fact, and perhaps most astonishing of all, he is apparently unknown to the bartender and all the other patrons of the Phoenix Tavern, to which he and his father repair "almost every afternoon" for a beer and a dacquiri. Why, the dacquiri alone would make him a minor local celebrity, and ordering it would involve a whole formulaic ritual, had Updike been in a working man's bar recently and long enough to know. More seriously, both Updike and his early reviewers seem to have opted for what Whitehead called the "Fallacy of Misplaced Concreteness," mistaking a trite list of all the things wrong with America for the real thing.

Jill, the hip counter-culturalist who moves in with Rabbit, at first gives the impression of having been seen before. She is a runaway from a wealthy family in Connecticut, having rejected their "plastic" way of life. She is eighteen, very pale, has straight dark hair, and the hips and breasts of a boy. She has done lots of dope and acid, and reports having seen God on a recent trip. She really digs spade dudes and misses her family, especially her brothers, whom she loved. In one exquisitely contrived exchange with Nelson, whose father cannot afford to buy him a mini-bike and who is envious of her stories about sailing the ocean in her family's yawl, she even lets us know how fundamentally good she really is: "In the spring we all used to have to scrape it and caulk it and paint it. I like that almost the best, we all used to work at it together, my parents and me and my brothers" (152). She talks about love a lot, even advising Rabbit that "people've run on fear long enough . . . let's try love for a change" (170). Since Nelson is thirteen and lost his sister, and her favorite brother is also thirteen, we can see what happens with them. "*Love is here to stay*", Daddy reads Nelson's face to say, and it sure is.

Daddy finds her quite lovable, although on the first night he is forced to confine himself to masturbation, even though she has tried to help. Not long after, Rabbit is getting it up regularly; we, in turn, are getting dialogue like this:

> "Fuck me," she says cooly . . . and when under him and striving, continues, "I want you to fuck all the shit out of me, all the shit and dreariness of this shit dreary world, hurt me, clean me out, I want you to be all of my insides, right up to my throat, yes, oh yes, bigger, more, shoot it all out of me . . ." (201)

To Rabbit's credit, this unmans him; at least he has some taste. Or maybe he has heard it all before, too. A few pages later she is talking like the abstraction she is once again: "Your life has no reflective content, it's all instinct. Cynicism, it has been said, is tired pragmatism" (228).

Dialogue, in fact, is often as didactic as the selection of detail, the major difference being that unlike the description, it lacks consistency. One sometimes has the feeling that Updike has a certain number of set pieces in his notebooks and is determined that they be delivered, regardless of who delivers them or how much characterization has to be wrenched in order to do it. Take, for example, the meeting between Rabbit and Charlie Stavros, his wife's lover, whom he has just called a "slick-talking kinky-haired peacenik-type Japanese-car salesman" (180). After the we-have-met-through-the-body-of-the-same-woman homosexual implications are out of the way, Rabbit challenges his man:

> "Listen Stavros. You're the one in the wrong. You're the one screwing another man's wife. If you want to pull out, pull out. Don't try to commit me to one of your coalition governments."
>
> "Back to that", Stavros says.
>
> "Right. You intervened, not me."
>
> "I didn't intervene, I performed a rescue."
>
> "That's what all us hawks say." *He is eager to argue about Vietnam, but Stavros keeps to the less passionate subject* [my italics]. (181)

Really now. "Coalition governments" has wit, but what are we to do with that last sentence? Hawk and patriot or not, hear Rabbit some pages later on the Commander-in-Chief:

> "Nixon, who's Nixon? He's just a typical flatfooted Chamber of Commerce type who lucked his way into the hot seat and is so dumb he thinks it's good luck. Let the poor bastard alone, he's trying to bore us to death so we won't commit suicide." (225)

A quick change of hats and our ignoramus is a snide Assistant Professor accounting for the fact that the dummies run the world while brilliant articles like himself babysit freshmen. One could compile endless examples, but the most striking has to be Skeeter, Jill's militant black and the agent of apocalypse. His arrival provokes Rabbit into "So he is evil" (208). Skeeter's speech, like his place in the novel, is strikingly anomalous. After the above-mentioned fistfight, which Rabbit wins easily because he is 6'3" and Skeeter is 5'6", Rabbit remains terrified of him. We all know what this fear is because we have read Leslie Fiedler and Norman Mailer; in case we have not, Skeeter, weeping, tells us: "We fascinate you, white man. We are in your dreams. We are technology's nightmare" (234). Later, as the happy family smokes grass together after watching "Laugh-In" (it gives Rabbit a hangover), our putative angry black waxes philosophical over Jill's generation:

> "Now the Romans had technology, right? And the barbarians saved them from it. The barbarians were their saviors. Since we cannot induce the Eskimos to invade us, we have raised a generation of barbarians ourselves, pardon me, you have raised them, Whitey has raised them, the white American middle-class and its imitators the world over have found within themselves the divine strength to generate millions of subhuman idiots that in less be-

> nighted ages only the aristocracies could produce. The last Merovingian princes were dragged about in ox carts gibbering and we are now blessed with motorized gibberers. (276)

Passing over the correctness or incorrectness of this opinion, where did Skeeter get it? Or more properly where did he learn his elocution? Pompous enough in a bad Richard Burton movie, where it could have been followed by a belt of neat whiskey and a coughing fit, or from a less colloquial Mr. Sammler, but here?

Later, Skeeter begs Rabbit to read to him from *The Life and Times of Frederick Douglass* in the following words: "It's not the same, right? Doin' it to yourself. Every school kid knows that, it's not the same" (282). As Rabbit reads aloud a passage describing Douglass' violent resistance to a harsh master, we find out what is not the same. Skeeter begins masturbating. Naturally, Rabbit and Jill, terrified by black sexuality, flee to the whiteness of their bedroom and cling to one another shuddering, in spite of the fact that Jill, as we suspect already and soon have cause to know, has been seeing a good deal of that particular black. Before starting, Skeeter had removed his shirt to give us some idea of what was to come:

> His skinny chest, naked, is stunning in its articulation: every muscle sharp in its attachment to the bone, the whole torso carved in a jungle wood darker than shadow and more dense than ivory. Rabbit has never seen such a chest except on a crucifix. (279)

This kind of gratuitous symbol mongering marks the novel's most serious failure. However much we may disagree with a novelist's implied values and judgments of the reality we perceive, we ought to leave him free to use language as he sees fit, so long as he remains consistent. Through most of this novel, when he is talking about Rabbit and the world he inhabits, Updike's use of language is "realistic." He pretends, and we grant him his pretense, that words have concrete specific referents, and that therefore the word picture he is drawing is objectively true. We may quarrel with his selection of words and conclude that the picture is not representative and not true—which up to this point I have been doing—but we allow him his point of view. After all, we can argue with it.

In the novel, however, whenever certain characters and subjects intrude, Updike suddenly shifts gears and becomes another kind of writer, superimposing a second point of view on top of the first, another whole layer of reality with an implied morality often directly contradictory to the first, with which it is impossible to argue. If Rabbit has a chest and a fat belly, he is overweight. Skeeter, on the other hand, is thin; and we are led to infer that he is Christlike. We may think that Rabbit looks like Saint Peter, Moses, or the Count of Monte Cristo, but we find no textual support for our hypothesis, although on the basis of plot and character each would be logical. Skeeter is associated in this coy manner with Christ not once but again and again. I am reminded of the creative writing student of a friend's, who having been praised for a short story of hers rather simply and realistically describing some adolescent crisis or other was urged to submit it to the campus literary magazine. She promised to, only after taking it home for a week end and "putting in the symbols." This is exactly what Updike has done, intentionally creating a wholly specious "second meaning," placing his "symbolic" characters Skeeter and Jill simultaneously within and outside the moral logic of the rest of the novel and creating a false dichotomy between them and the other characters, who have to muddle along on the literal level alone. To put it simply as it works itself out in the novel, some characters are morally accountable for what they do and others are not. As an extended example, consider the following scenes.

When, some nights after this masturbation, we see Skeeter naked again, he is in front of the picture window with the lights on, and Jill is on her knees in front of him. Not sure of the symbology, I think at this point it makes her Mary Magdelene,

> the white lily of a hand floating beside his balls as if to receive from the air a baton. An inch or two of Skeeter is unenclosed by her face, a purple inch bleached to lilac, below his metallic pubic explosion, the shape and texture of a goatee. Keeping his protective crouch, Skeeter turns his face sheepishly toward the light; his eyeglasses glare opaquely and his upper lip lifts in imitation of pain. "Hey man, what's with that, cut the lights."
>
> "You're beautiful," Rabbit says. [Read: "black is"]
>
> "O.K., strip and get into it, she full of holes, right?"
>
> "I'm scared to . . ." (298)

Surely an odd crucifiction, lilies and the lamb of God notwithstanding ("sheepishly toward the light"). Excessive reading you say? But one is pushed in the direction in so many ways. Moments later, after they have realized that the neighbors were watching from the garden, Rabbit takes pity on the girl:

> A string of milkweed spittle is on her chin; Rabbit wipes her chin and mouth with his handkerchief, and for weeks afterward, when all is lost, will take out his handkerchief and bury his nose in it, in its imperceptible spicy smell. (299)

Holy relics? In this sentence, students, the only use of a tense other than the past or the historical present in the novel, we see an example of the technique of foreshadowing. In other words, ladies and gents, keep your eye on the handkerchief.

The next evening, after Jill has portentously told Rabbit that "It's too late for you to try to love me" (301), and while Rabbit, for a change of pace, is in Janice's best friend's bed, his neighbors burn his house down with a gasoline bomb. Naturally. Had enough? Skeeter escapes, Nelson is with Rabbit, but Jill, unconscious from a shot of heroin her savior has given her, is burned to death. Now that is a new twist on an old story, isn't it? I bet you thought Skeeter was going to get it.

Jill is dead. The innocent-corrupt, virgin-whore, freak-child is gone. The reader feels nothing. Who can feel when a symbol is burnt? Nor do the other characters, but must Skeeter tell Rabbit to console Nelson because "there's a ton of cunt in the world" (336). Or Rabbit tell his sister Mim, now a call-girl on leave from Las Vegas, that what he learned from the whole thing (noticing up her dress that she wears no panties under her transparent panty hose) is that "I'd rather fuck than be blown" (358).

But we are not finished with Skeeter. When an uncomprehending cop at the scene asks Rabbit, "Did he terrorize you?" the answer is prompt: "No, he entertained us" (327). Ironies continue to multiply as Skeeter's given name, according to the authorities, turns out to be "Hubert Johnson." If you have missed the point, the police radio call clears everything up:

> "All cars . . . be on the lookout. Negro, male, height approx five-six, weight approx one-twenty-five medium dark skinned, hair Afro, name Skeeter, that is Sally, Katherine, double Easter—" (329)

Second Coming anyone? But which aspect of the Christian myth is Skeeter being compared to? Is he a victim? a savior? Is it his masturbation or his heroin dispensing we are asked to admire? Perhaps he is the Anti-Christ. It is almost as difficult to know as it is to care. Skeeter, of course, has been hiding in the briar patch all along, asleep in Rabbit's car, which gives our hero a chance to reject the idea of a "Judas kiss" and convey him to safety. Still "waiting for the word" Rabbit leaves Skeeter "hanging empty handed" in a cornfield next to a sign reading (honest) "Galilee 2" (336–7). Seldom, if ever, has any white writer been paralyzed into sentimental and self-contradictory blather quite so foolishly in attempting to deal with a black character. Its example is almost enough to convince one that perhaps it is best not to try. If you want more: when Rabbit visits the Furnace Twp. police station for questioning, it turns out to be in the basement of a former madhouse.

Little more needs to be said. Amazingly, once Jill and Skeeter are out of the novel, it actually begins to cohere for the last sixty-odd pages. But it is far too late: only one matter needs to be resolved. Can one live in America? Can one be human in so degraded a world? Of course one can, for Updike is a liberal, and it is incumbent on him at this point to affirm. Since the question, as I have tried to show earlier, is based on ludicrously overdrawn dichotomies, it can be settled in only one way, having nothing to do with the logic of the plot or with any other kind of logic. It has to do with words, pretty words, the kind of free-floating language Updike employed so often in *Couples*. Rabbit loses his job, but Janice comes back to him. At novel's end they take a room together in the "Safe Haven Motel," but do not make love. Sensing the end, Updike's prose develops wings of its own and lumbers toward the runway, lifting off heavily as the happy couple, having survived, fall asleep.

> He lets her breasts go, lets them float away, radiant debris. The space they are in, the motel room long and secret as a burrow, becomes all interior space. He slides down an inch on the cool sheets and fits his microcosmic self limp into the curved crevice between the polleny offered nestling orbs of her ass; he would stiffen but his hand having let her breasts go comes upon the familiar dip of her waist, ribs to hip bone, where no bones are, soft as flight, fat's inward curve, slack, his babies from her belly. He finds this inward curve and slips along it, sleeps. He. She. Sleeps. O.K.? (406–7)

Get it? Rabbit, burrow. Radiant debris, space, flight, free fall, maybe free to fall? Everyman has arrived. Mr. Bloom is home. But the handkerchief, dear reader? Not having been told differently, we must assume that like Poldy's potato, *it is still in his pocket.*

Notes

1. See both Anatole Broyard, "Updike Goes All Out at Last," *New York Times* (6 Nov. 1971), p. 40; and Richard Locke, "*Rabbit Redux*," NYTBR (14 Nov. 1971), pp. 1 ff. The latter says, for example, "*Rabbit Redux* is a great achievement, by far the most audacious and successful book Updike has written" (p. 24).
2. John Updike, *Rabbit, Run* (New York: Alfred A. Knopf, 1960). All quotations are from this edition.
3. John Updike, *Rabbit Redux* (New York: Alfred A. Knopf, 1971). All quotations are from this edition.

ROBERT S. GINGHER

"Has John Updike Anything to Say?"

Modern Fiction Studies, Spring 1974, pp. 97–105

Much of the critical controversy over John Updike's writing seems to stem from the critic's frequent inability to differentiate between what the author has to say and the method in which he imparts his ideas. In other words, particularly in Updike's case, an implicit confusion of style and content makes assessment of actual literary contribution the more difficult. The confusion derives from the unconventionality of Updike's baroque and microscopic style which appears itself to be a kind of subliminal end. Indeed, upon first examination the *raison d'etre* of Updike's prose seems to be his quaint stylistic preciosity—what the author himself refers to as his "little congruencies and arabesques."[1] More than anything else, it is this unique, carefully refined style which compels certain critics to admit the extent of his talent and others to slight him for the lack of it. A few examples of critics who recognize his stylistic talent are Mary McCarthy, who praises and defends his style; Arthur Mizener, who considers him to be today's "dazzlingly talented young man" in prose fiction; and Richard H. Rupp, who remarks that Updike "probably has more sheer talent than any other writer of our time."[2]

But Updike's distinguished talent—his exquisite, photographic ability to capture and preserve the small details, the quotidian minutiae which fills the spaces of his characters' lives—is often viewed disparagingly or at least an insufficient claim to significant literary stature. His style is seen as no more than a kind of phony effulgence which charms less discerning critics into admiration. A case in point is D. J. Enright's seemingly paradoxial observation:

> John Updike is a remarkably skilled writer, but to me he seems hardly an author at all. He is less a maker than a dismantler, though the magic of his style has won the admiration of a number of critics (including Mary McCarthy) with whom I tremble to disagree.[3]

In this assessment, then, Updike is a "remarkably skilled writer," yet "hardly an author," a careful artificer or craftsman, but not a creative artist. According to Enright, Updike, at least in most of his works, does not create, "doesn't seem to have found something to write about" (p. 136). In agreement with such an evaluation is John W. Aldridge, who simply concludes that Updike "has nothing to say."[4] For Aldridge, Updike's style is merely a parlour trick ineffectually disguising the fact that he hasn't anything to say; Updike hopes that "sheer style will carry him over the difficulty" "of becoming profound on the subject of the larger issues of life, love, death, and God" (p. 165).

How valid is such a point-blank adverse criticism of Updike's fiction? It strikes me that Updike, a remarkably astute and erudite author, *pace* Aldridge and Podhoretz, would hardly be so naive or hopeful as to assume that exquisite style would obviate the necessity of dealing with universal truths. Furthermore, I am not at all certain that we have an either-or proposition working here anyway, i.e., Updike's linguistically recherché style need not, I think, vitiate his treatment of what Faulkner called "the problems of the human heart in conflict with itself."[5] Nevertheless, Updike is at times guilty not so much of camouflaging his content as of being diverted by his forte as a stylist from the "larger issues of life, love, death, and God." Updike feels that his meticulous stylistic ornamentation deserves more careful evaluation than it generally receives: "All the little congruencies and arabesques prepared with such delicate anticipatory pleasure are gobbled up [by insensate critics] as if by pigs at a pastry cart."[6] But if Updike's critics befoul his stylistic lacework, oftentimes they feel that they have to dig too deeply for his contentual truffles, the "larger issues." The question of whether Updike's characterizations elicit our compassion and sympathy is pertinent here. Much of his fiction does, in fact, seem to be emotionally vapid; one senses successful pathos or poignancy in characterization only infrequently. In regard to the handling of "larger issues," Faulkner stated his conviction that the writer's task is to render the "old universal truths" compassionately and transparently. He must treat only

> the old verities and truths of the heart, the old universal truths lacking which any story is ephemeral and doomed—love and honor and pity and pride and compassion and sacrifice. Until he does so he labors under a curse. He writes not of love but of lust, of defeats in which nobody loses anything of value, of victories without hope and, worst of all, without pity or compassion. His griefs grieve on no universal bones, leaving no scars. He writes not of the heart but of the glands. (p. 723)

Without attempting to use Faulkner as a yardstick or inviting an invidious, fallacious comparison, there is a sense in which Updike—writing in his secluded hovel on Labor in Vain Road outside Ipswich, Massachusetts—is felt to be laboring "under a curse." Richard Gilman contends that Updike skillfully dodges entering into "the problems of the human heart in conflict with itself," thereby indulging an

> avoidance, accomplished with a scrupulous cunning and high-wire grace that resembles a brilliant neurotic maneuver, of the supreme task and burden of literature: the appropriation and transfiguration, in one way or another, of suffering, struggle, conflict, disaster and death . . . he *shuns* the major sorrows and calamities while pretending to deal with them . . . he glosses them, coats them with "fine" writing and disarms them by turning them into nostalgia and soft wisdom.[7]

Notwithstanding the accuracy of his critical archery in detecting the emotional vapidity in Updike's prose, Gilman is, nonetheless, busy at the pastry cart, overlooking the sentience and nuances of Updike's language and failing to perceive the universal truths which, though rendered more intellectually than feelingly, are, nevertheless, revealed. The fact is—finally and tentatively answering this paper's query—that Updike does have a great deal to say. His fiction is indeed surcharged with hidden meaning and so "highbrow" as to be intimidating. To a greater degree than most of his contemporaries, Updike treats the larger issues in the subsurface architechtonics of his fiction.

Several current studies of Updike's fiction confirm the author's artistic merit and conviction of purpose. Larry E. Taylor has undertaken the task of examining the pastoral theme in Updike's works. Very much an autobiographical author, and remembering his teenage days on the family farm near Plowville, Pennsylvania, Updike invokes the rural scene of Firetown (Plowville) just outside Olinger (Shillington) in many of his short stories and in *The Centaur* and *Of the Farm*. He describes the fictional towns as being essentially symbolic rather than serving any geographical function: "The difference being Olinger and Tarbox is much more the difference between childhood and adulthood than the difference between two geographical locations. They are stages on my pilgrim's progress, not spots on the map."[8] Taylor's study establishes the symbolic significance of place—of bucolic and anti-bucolic structures in Updike's fiction—and is a fine study for what it attempts. But it is basically a kind of slot-filling venture having a strong dissertational odor. *Pastoral and Anti-Pastoral Patterns* describes only a fraction of Updike's larger issues, i.e., the ones which are tangential to the pastoral investigation.

A study in larger scope is Rachael Burchard's *Yea Sayings.*[9] Besides managing, sometimes rather unsuccessfully, the thesis that Updike is a writer of affirmation with melioristic tendencies, Burchard bares a much more ample package in her discussions of Updike's dualisms—life vs. death, the individual vs. society, love vs. hate, matter vs. spirit, and intuition vs. Christian instruction, for example.

The most complete study of Updike available, however, is Alice and Kenneth Hamilton's *The Elements of John Updike*. This work is painstakingly thoroughgoing in its efforts to defend Updike as a serious writer. *Elements* deals with most of Updike's fiction and all of his major themes including nostalgia, sex, death, religion, and the married state. In their preface the Hamiltons state:

> This study has been undertaken because of our conviction that John Updike is one of the most elegant and most serious authors of our age. The artistry of his style is widely recognized, but the seriousness of what he has to say is not so generally admitted.[10]

The Hamiltons make the best effort of anyone, to date, to illustrate just how much Updike does have to say in his fiction. Analytically, they are superelemental, yet for all their subsymbolic, overly ingenious dissections, they do suggest the extent of Updike's artistic seriousness. But the Christian perspective of their analysis is often forced; sometimes one has the feeling that motif-indices to the Scriptures were used paragraph by paragraph. To be fair, the authors admit that they "have said no more about Updike's literary technique than was [considered] necessary for explaining how he represents his ideas." But such a caveat cannot, I think, disarm the charge that many elements of John Updike have been stripped and squeezed through the eye of a theological needle. But, more importantly for our purposes, the Hamiltons leave no doubt as to the vacuity of the assertion that Updike has nothing to say.

Updike has described some of the themes with which he attempts to concern himself:

> Domestic fierceness within the middle class, sex and death as riddles for the thinking animal, social existence as a sacrifice, unexpected pleasures and rewards, corruption as a kind of evolution—these are some of the themes.[11]

The implications here are that Updike is concerned with human needs vs. society's demands. There is an inherent tension in man, much of which derives from the pressures of civilized society, the codes of conduct that would legislate the human condition. Updike feels that "to be a person is to be in a situation of tension, is to be in a dialectical situation. A truly adjusted person is not a person at all—just an animal with clothes on or a statistic" (p. 101). For Updike, "unfallen Adam is an ape." Man is a *naked* ape who attempts "to lead on this terrestrial ball,/With grasping hand and saucy wife,/The upright life,"[12] but who inevitably vacillates between individual wants and social dictates. Unlike all other animals, he is a "thinking animal" with a "grasping hand," which is both responsible for a highly technological society and symbolic of his acquisitive nature. His "saucy wife" signals the less attractive aspects of monogamy; the "upright life" of a faithful marriage and righteousness *per se* are threatened by instinctual desires.

It seems to me that Updike has more to say concerning "sex and death as riddles for the thinking animal" than concerning any other thematic strain in his fiction. Morality in his fiction becomes more and more exclusively a system of socio-sexual ethics instead of the more direct, God-seeking morality of the earlier nostalgic stories—especially those stories in *The Same Door*—which seek to find some glint of knowledge of our origin, the soul, and heaven. In Wolfean language, Updike's adolescent protagonists often "seek the great forgotten language, the lost lane-end into heaven, a stone, a leaf, an unfound door."[13] The door to eternity being ultimately undiscoverable, his characters find instead temporal doors of pleasure and self-indulgence. In despair of finding "the same door" through which they entered mutable, sublunary time, Updike's couples attempt to defy time by entering other doors through which the body is sated but the soul is abandoned. But amidst the self-indulgence, there are still moments—as in his earlier fiction—when, as Updike writes, the "muddled and inconsequent surface of things now and then parts to yield us a gift."[14] There are still intimations of immortality in the midst of our profligacy.[15]

Much of Updike's treatment of the problems of married life seems to follow certain ideas suggested by Denis de Rougement's *Love in the Western World*. In a review of de Rougement's *Love Declared*, Updike indicates that the author's purpose is " 'to describe the inescapable conflict in the West between passion and marriage.' "[16] The conflict between passion and marriage is perhaps the central concern of *Rabbit, Run* and *Rabbit Redux* and certainly of *Couples*. Updike's seriousness of purpose, the fact that he has much to say on this score, should be manifestly evident, but additional insights into the passion vs. marriage theme are gained by focusing upon de Rougement's tenets. De Rougement describes Tristan and Iseult as prototypal Western lovers whose unhappiness "'originates in a false reciprocity, which disguises a twin narcissism.'"[17] Such a self-centered, narcissistic love is the source of the Applesmith games and other adulterous affairs in *Couples*. The self-aggrandizement of Harry Angstrom, who is "just *wild* about Harrr-ree—" (*RR*, p. 97) and who cannot "look outside [his] own pretty skin" (*RR*, p. 250), is indicative of Updike's interest in unreciprocated love. Piet Hanema's show-off acrobatic stunts and self-indulgence again suggest the narcissist.

Updike has remarked that, according to de Rougement, "each man aspires toward a female Form of Light who is *his own true spirit*, resident in Heaven, aloof from the Hell of matter."[18] Several of Updike's protagonists—especially Rabbit Angstrom, Piet Hanema, and Richard Maple—endeavor to seek their impossible female counterparts, their "Unattainable Ladies," at the jeopardy of their family and neighbors. Updike has this impossible quest in mind when he asserts, "Yes, in *Rabbit, Run*, to our inner urgent whispers, but—the social fabric collapses murderously."[19] He seems to be saying that, paradoxically, we must reckon some social restrictions among our freedoms. Rabbit Angstrom functions like his animal counterpart, "Br'er Rabbit, [who] demonstrated: freedom is made of brambles."[20] Though "social existence as a sacrifice" cannot be denied, within certain limits such a sacrifice is a necessary one.

Man must not seek to find "*his own true spirit*" on earth; he can make neither his attainable wife or neighbor an unattainable spirit. If he insists upon such a narcissistic venture, he poisons with impossible dreams the possibility of a viable relationship.[21] The self-centered lover is destined to be self-defeated. As Updike tells us in his "Erotic Epigrams," "Hoping to fashion a mirror, the lover/doth polish the face of his beloved/until he produces a skull."[22] Death and futility are planted where life and the possibility of love had been.

The "riddles of sex and death" are interrelated in Updike's fiction. In his review of de Rougement, Updike remarks "Eros is allied with Thanatos rather than Agape; love becomes not a way of accepting and entering the world but a way of defying and escaping it."[23] Accordingly, seeking to defy his monotonous existence though active, concupiscent love, Piet—a kind of lost Pietas (the Roman personification of familial affection)—is haunted by dread and death:

> "Jesus, I hate not seeing you. I find myself—"
> "Say it." Perhaps she thought he was going to confess another woman.
> "Terrified of death lately."
> "Oh, Piet. Why? Are you sick?"
> "It's not practical death I'm worried about, it's death anytime, at all, ever."
> She asked, "Does it have to do with me?"
> He had not thought so, but now he said, "Maybe." (C, p. 284)

In the satisfaction of passion, Piet is not troubled by thoughts of death. When with Foxy, as indicated above, or when engaging in adultery with Bea Guerin, he thinks "Death no longer seemed dreadful"[24] (C, p. 352). It is only when he cannot defy time by satisfying his lust that he is haunted by a dread not of a "practical death," but of a realization of mortality. Updike tells us that "our fundamental anxiety is that we do not exist—or will cease to exist. Only in being loved do we find external corroboration of the supremely high valuation each ego secretly assigns itself" (p. 299). But having chosen the life of pleasure to verify his existence, Piet, consequently, senses the "sickness unto death" and despairs of finding the "lost lane-end into heaven." Rabbit, too, has moments when he feels that "his body has betrayed his soul" (*RR*, p. 230), and Richard Maple (in "Sublimating") feels himself detached from the organic and living, coasting toward death. Richard's death wish derives from his defunct marriage and his own unstable, adulterous passion. Like the passion of Tristan and Iseult, his passion "secretly wills its own frustrations and irresistibly seeks the bodily death that forever removes it from the qualifications of life, the disappointments and diminishments of actual possession" (p. 284).

The human need for self-assertion through love is defiant of social restrictions. In fact, the "heart *prefers* to move against the grain of circumstance; perversity is the soul's very life. Therefore, the enforced and approved bonds of marriage, restricting freedom, weaken love" (p. 299). But man's paradox is this: though he is free to choose and can deny the very restrictions which impose upon his pursuit of pleasure, since he is a rational creature, a "thinking animal," his conscience punishes him by bringing dread to bear. Thus, as Kierkegaard proclaims in *Either/Or*, the choice of worldly values against spiritual ones may be made, but not without a consequent fear, a "sickness unto death."

Other than his concern with religious elements and the treatment of nostalgia, Updike's treatment of "sex and death as riddles for the thinking animal" remains the most important focal point for examining his fiction. Indeed, especially in his later fiction, a good case can be made for the sex-and-death themes being his chief concerns. With such a focus in mind one cannot fail to discern the meaningfulness and richness of texture in Updike's fiction. What is often mistaken as a pretentious style is merely Updike's "noncommittal luminosity of fact," his objective amplification of surface detail and his particular and express refusal to preach to the reader.[25] Updike, as we have seen, is very much concerned with "the problems of the human heart in conflict with itself." But he deals not so much with individual psychologies as with an aggregate portrayal of the human condition. If his characters are often on the psychological level emotionally jejune, as focal points for the human paradox they are ample. Not only the "little congruencies and arabesques" of his prose but his social commentary, too, places him squarely within the first rank of contemporary writers. A hasty perusal of his fiction will invariably result in disparagement and esthetic "indigestion."

Notes

1. Quoted by John Updike in "Henry Bech Redux," *The New York Times Book Review*, 14 November 1971, p. 3.
2. Mary McCarthy's remarks are paraphrased by Norman Podhoretz in his *Doings and Undoings: The Fifties and After in American Writing* (New York: Farrar, Straus and Co., 1964), p. 251. See also Arthur Mizener, *The Sense of Life in the Modern Novel* (Boston: Houghton Mifflin Co., 1964), p. 249 and Richard H. Rupp, *Celebration in Postwar American Fiction, 1945–1967* (Coral Gables, Fla.: University of Miami Press, 1970), p. 100.
3. D. J. Enright, *Conspirators and Poets* (Chester Springs, Pa.: Dufour Editions, Inc., 1966), p. 135.
4. John W. Aldridge, *Time to Murder and Create: The Contemporary Novel in Crisis* (New York: David McKay Co., Inc., 1964), p. 170. In his *Doings and Undoings*, Norma Podhoretz, too, offers an extravagant attack of Updike's prose style. He finds Updike's prose "overly lyrical, bloated like a child who had eaten too much candy" (p. 251) and even "mandarin [?] and exhibitionistic" (p. 257). Most vehement, though, is his *ad hominem* remark to Mary McCarthy that Updike has "no mind at all" (p. 251).
5. William Faulkner, "Address upon Receiving the Nobel Prize for Literature," Malcolm Cowley, ed., *The Portable Faulkner* (New York: Viking Press, 1967), p. 723.
6. John Updike, "Henry Bech Redux," p. 3.
7. Richard Gilman, *The Confusion of Realms* (New York: Random House, 1969), pp. 63–64.
8. "The Art of Fiction, XLIII: John Updike," *Paris Review*, 45 (Winter 1968), 90–91.
9. As valuable a study as Burchard has provided, it must be said that there are moments in her investigative process when the title seems misplaced—when the affirmation or "yea sayings" are stretched to the outer limits of credibility. For example, Burchard stresses Harry Angstrom's "quest" in *Rabbit, Run* as a "yea saying," an affirmation of people's instinctive ability to sense the presence of God, when in fact, an equally valid case can be made for the quest being Harry's safari for self-indulgence. See Rachael C. Burchard, *John Updike: Yea Sayings* (Carbondale: Southern Illinois University Press, 1971), pp. 52–53. Updike better describes the nature of Rabbit's quest, I think, when he says, "I think we all would like to be 'nice,' but there is in us an animal or an angelic something that wants infinitely, has infinite demands in a way and isn't really 'nice' at all" ("Interview with John Updike," National Public Radio telecast, Nov. 1971: *Bookbeat*, Interviewer: Robert Cromie).
10. Alice and Kenneth Hamilton, *The Elements of John Updike* (Grand Rapids: Wm. B. Eerdmans Co., 1970), p. 7.
11. "The Art of Fiction," p. 117.
12. John Updike, "The Naked Ape," *Midpoint and Other Poems* (New York: Fawcett Crest Books, 1963), p. 99.
13. Thomas Wolfe, *Look Homeward, Angel* (New York: Scribner's 1929), p. I.
14. This part of the preface to Updike's *Olinger Stories* is quoted in "*Rabbit Redux*," *The New York Times Book Review*, 14 November 1971, p. 2.
15. Piet Hanema senses Foxy's teeth in fellatio like "glints of light": he "seeks the light" (John Updike, *Couples* [Greenwich, Conn.: Fawcett Publications, 1968], p. 235). Harry Angstrom feels that "somewhere behind all this . . . there's something that wants me to find it" (John Updike, *Rabbit, Run* [Greenwich, Conn.: Fawcett Publications, 1960], p. 107). The Hamiltons, though mentioning Wordsworth's now hackneyed "Getting and spending," neglect more pervasive Wordsworthian notions in Updike's fiction, *i.e.*, nostalgia and intimations of immortality in the concrete.
16. Quoted in Updike's "More Love in the Western World," *Assorted Prose* (New York: Alfred A. Knopf, 1965), p. 284.
17. "More Love in the Western World," p. 284. Iseult is, too, a "prototype of the Unattainable Lady to whom the love-myth directs our adoration, diverting it from the attainable lady (in legal terms, our 'wife'; in Christian terms, our 'neighbor') who is at our side" (p. 285).
18. Ibid. Cf. Piet trying to "seek the light" through Foxy (above).
19. "The Art of Fiction," p. 100.
20. John Updike, "Minority Report," *Midpoint*, p. 76.
21. The possibility of at least approaching one's "*own true spirit*" seems, however, to be suggested by Updike here: "The images we hoard in wait for the woman who will seem to body them forth include the inhuman—a certain slant of sunshine, a delicate flavor of dust, a kind of rasping tune that is reborn in her voice; they are nameless, these elusive glints of original goodness that a man's memory stores toward an erotic commitment. Perhaps it is to the degree that the beloved crystallizes the lover's past that she presents herself to him, alpha and omega, as his Fate" ("More Love in the Western World," p. 280).
22. John Updike, *Verse* (Greenwich, Conn.: Fawcett Publications, 1968), p. 170.
23. "More Love in the Western World," p. 285.
24. "A woman, loved, momentarily eases the pain of time by localizing nostalgia; the vague and irrecoverable objects of nostalgic longing are assimilated, under the pressure of libidinous desire, into the details of her person" ("More Love in the Western World," p. 287).
25. "The Art of Fiction," p. 116. The Hamiltons provide an excellent beginning for a stylistic inquiry of Updike. Their investigation validates the conclusion that Updike's style, rather than being superficial elegance, attempts to stretch art to the furthest bounds as a mirror of nature and reality.

MARY ALLEN

From "John Updike's Love of 'Dull Bovine Beauty'"
The Necessary Blankness: Women in Major American Fiction of the Sixties
1976, pp. 114–21

Waiting at home ⟨in *Rabbit, Run*⟩ is the archetypal Updike wife, Janice Springer Angstrom—vulnerable, sexual, good-natured, and stupid. She makes a striking image, this housewife of 1960, mesmerized in front of the T.V., drinking an old-fashioned and watching the Mouseketeers. Her pregnancy hardly suggests the great gift of life as she sags inertly into her chair. Both Janice and the prostitute Ruth, as Gerry Brenner points out, represent the ultimate "natural" state. They do nothing and are reduced to mere vegetables.[1] Janice's physical vegetation reflects a thorough mental vegetation. In contrast to graceful Rabbit, who has just come from shooting a perfect basket as he was able to do in high school, she is noticeably clumsy. Arriving at home, Rabbit is confronted by the absence of all grace and the presence of mere clutter, of which Janice is a part. The only light in the room comes from the T.V., which she once nearly smashed by getting tangled in the cord. His means of response to this mess is to carefully unfold his own coat and neatly hangs it up.

The Angstrom marriage is far from a success, but there are no dramatic, bitter battles. The couple simply drag along through years of tedious irritations. In appearance Janice is neither beautiful nor downright ugly, just small, a woman "with a tight dark skin, as if something swelling inside is straining against her littleness. . . . Her eyes dwindle in their frowning sockets and her little mouth hangs open in a dumb slot."[2] Her passivity is overwhelming. She cannot even care for her child, who has been taken, appropriately, to the more capable Mother Angstrom. Janice relies heavily on her own mother (whom she dislikes) as well, one more sign of weakness. Rabbit is in no way fond of her mother either, but a mother-in-law can never be in the class of a mother. Rabbit sees Mrs. Springer as something comic. His own mother is the one person in life whom he fears, despite others who have reason to consider him an enemy.

Rabbit's world consists of a pattern of nets and other constrictions to be escaped. When he comes home the door is locked on his domestic trap. But at the moment, at least, he is on the *outside* of that trap, enlightened enough to understand its ugliness and to attempt a retreat. Viewed from the inside, which Updike is not inclined to do, the locked door suggests much more of a trap for Janice than it does for Rabbit. She has no idea how the door got locked; it "just locked itself" (10). Only after Rabbit runs away is Janice forced to consider altering her life, and then the only possibilities are pitifully based on the simplest absolutes: she will get a divorce and be like a nun, or her husband will come back and love her. She may be too pitiful to elicit much compassion, and if she is only a caricature created to illustrate Updike's concern with the banal, she is not worth serious discussion. But Janice may be all too representative of a great many housewives sitting dully behind closed doors.

Janice first met Harry Angstrom when they both held dreary jobs in Kroll's department store, work which they and the other employees hated. Years later Rabbit's work has not improved much as he demonstrates MagiPeel Peelers in five-and-dime stores, a trifling occupation for a man, so close to the trivia of housework. We are made very aware that he must have talents for something better. Even tending Mrs. Smith's garden is an improvement. But what about Janice? Our author never allows us to *expect* her to do anything important or interesting. On the Mouseketeer show Janice is watching when Rabbit comes home, Jimmy, the big Mouseketeer, delivers this message: " 'God wants some of us to become scientists, some of us to become artists, some of us to become firemen and doctors and trapeze artists. And He gives to each of us the special talents to become these things, *provided we work to develop them*. We must *work*, boys and girls. So: Know Thyself. Learn to understand your talents, and then work to develop them. That's the way to be happy' " (12). Trite as the message sounds, the idea is not far from Updike's own stated feelings about the importance of significant work. The T.V. program presents the message effectively to children, and the Mouseketeer intrigues Rabbit, who is interested in his sales pitch. The subject of using one's talents, too, is particularly timely to Rabbit in his current struggle with his unchallenging life.

But what impact does the message have for Janice, who is the person at home watching the show? As far as we can see she has no talents (even the hot dogs she prepares are split and twisted). The vocations mentioned by the Mouseketeer are obviously those traditionally followed by men. And if she were to know herself as he suggests, what would she find? What encouragement is there for her to emerge from her stupor? Rabbit is aware of the image his company tries to present of the housewife, and he kiddingly reminds his wife of it. She is *supposed* to look tired, because she *is* a housewife. She does look tired, but not from a day's work—just from doing nothing. Rabbit seems sympathetic, but neither he nor Janice can imagine other possibilities for her. It is never suggested that *she* run away.

Janice epitomizes the trait most prominent in the Updike wife: stupidity. "There seems no escaping it: she is dumb" (14). Updike uses the word *dumb* consistently in reference to young women, although few are as dumb as poor Janice. One way of defining such stupidity is if a woman is unable to grasp the meaning of a man's jokes. Rabbit tries to tease Janice into seeing what he does with the image of the housewife by relating his work to her. When she does not laugh he considers her to be stupid. His humor, of course, is not funny to her. She vaguely senses but does not truly comprehend the unfortunate parallels between her husband's work and her own life. Neither women nor men are expected to be highly intelligent in Updike's world, but his women lack even the merest awareness of complexity, seeing things in simplistic absolutes as both Janice and Ruth do. Rabbit's skill has been primarily athletic (in contrast to women's physical awkwardness), but beyond that he does imagine that there is some better "thing" out there, a perception none of the women have.

In their stupidity the women become alike. When Ruth tells Rabbit that Tothero's girl friend is "dumber than you can know" (60), he says that he does know because he is married to her twin. A wife may be unique in her association with a particular man, but there is little else to distinguish her. The male wishes to impress his identity on the female's blankness, but she is often so blank that little impression can be made. Rabbit dreams that Janice is weeping for something his mother did, and "to his horror her face begins to slide, the skin to slip slowly from the bone, but there is no bone, just more melting stuff underneath" (76). There is no identity to hold Janice together. He tries futilely to catch the melting stuff in his hands and form it into something complete.

Janice, like nearly every Updike woman, is a sexual creature. Rabbit fondly recalls how they first made love in a friend's apartment after work. They were married when she was pregnant, an instigating factor in many Updike marriages but one having little to do with their ultimate mediocrity. When Janice comes home from the hospital with their second child, Rabbit is again obsessed with making love to her. When she refuses him because it is too soon after giving birth, he runs from her a second time. Janice, who is not frigid, would not ordinarily have abstained from lovemaking. But this one refusal turns out to be a fatal mistake.

Like most Updike women, Janice is good-natured in her sexuality, combining qualities we rarely find linked in female characters in American literature. The undramatic virtue of geniality can be easily passed over in light of Janice's more obvious limitations. But certainly good-naturedness such as hers is one reason why many marriages survive as well as they do. Janice is affectionately forgiving when Rabbit comes to her in the hospital during the period when he is living with Ruth. In her limited way she loves him, and he always answers back, "I love *you*," somehow making it sound convincing at the moment. For her loyalty and affection Janice merits affection in return, but her meagerness of soul is incapable of inspiring great love (which is probably not possible for any of Updike's people). Rabbit, who at least envisions some kind of grandeur, laments to Tothero that the " 'little thing Janice and I had going, boy, it was really second-rate' " (90).

After Rabbit runs from Janice, the only person she can look to for help is her mother, an unfortunate choice, for the contact is always demeaning. "There was always that with Mother the feeling she was dull and plain and a disappointment, and she thought when she got a husband it would be all over, all that" (208). (Rabbit's mother also belabors Janice's incompetence, attributing her only with the skill necessary to trap a husband.) Rabbit and Janice are made primarily responsible for their baby's death, but Mrs. Springer is also partially responsible. It is immediately after she phones Janice, discovering that Rabbit has gone again and insisting on coming over immediately, that her daughter is panicked into cleaning up her house and her baby and the accident in the bathtub occurs. Mrs. Springer does not visit her daughter to help but to make fun of her because she cannot keep her husband. And Janice, already self-consciously aware of her inadequacy, tragically demonstrates it by accidentally drowning her child.

Updike rarely considers a woman's point of view. But both Janice and Ruth are shown on occasion through interior monologues, Ruth's being reminiscent of Molly Bloom's as she recalls in detail her many sexual experiences. Janice's simple mind dwells with little new insight on the crisis in her life, but there is pathos in her lonely confusion. We now begin to see the effects on her of continually being considered stupid. In her own mind she makes a sensible defense for herself which she would probably never have the confidence to announce to her husband effectively: "Here he called her dumb when he was too dumb to have any idea of how she felt" (209). Rabbit admittedly is not interested in how she feels, for the important thing, he says, is how *he* feels. Surely one reason for Janice's ineptness is the image of her that is set by others. Her consciousness is not being understood, which is shown no place outside of this one interior monologue, is as poignant as it is unexpected: "That was what made her panicky ever since she was little this thing of nobody knowing how you felt and whether nobody could know or nobody cared she had no idea" (209). Only with this rare insight into Janice do we begin to imagine the lonely horror she must feel—to be clumsy, slow, and "dumb," to be referred to constantly in such a way; and then, in a drunken daze, to bring about the death of her own child.

Rabbit, however, does have valid motivation to run from Janice. She *is* disgusting, and he is all too aware that there is something better than his limited life with her. Thus, we would expect him, in turning to another woman as he naturally does, to look for superior qualities not found in Janice. But again he opts for inferiority. Some readers see his affair with Ruth as a love match. But it is merely another sexual adventure for Rabbit, and when the involvement demands that he consider her welfare, he runs from her as he runs from everything else. Ruth is somehow sexually appealing to Rabbit, but not outstanding in any other way. She is far from beautiful, and yet her coarseness rather attracts him; she may be overweight, but he says she is "not *that* fat. Chunky, more . . . her thighs fill the front of her dress so that even standing up she has a lap. Her hair, kind of a dirty ginger color, is bundled in a roll at the back of her head" (49). From her plumpness Rabbit deduces that she is good-natured (a thought process Updike frequently employs, just as he concludes that sexual women must be stupid). The morning after his first night with Ruth he finds her homeliness pitiful, something he had not noticed the evening before. The lack of beauty never daunts the Updike lover, however. Rabbit comes back for more, drawn on by Ruth's limitations and her need for him, running toward the very things he claimed were unbearable in his marriage.

For Rabbit to prove that his is a winner he needs women like Janice and Ruth. Only their incapacity can confirm his superiority. To explain his mediocre golf game he replaces thoughts of his own inadequacy with the concept of women's stupidity: "In his head he talks to the clubs as if they're women. The irons, light and thin yet somehow treacherous in his hands, are Janice. *Come on, you dope, be calm. . . . Oh, dumb, really dumb*" (110). Like Janice, Ruth is "dumb," which is just the quality to appeal to Rabbit. When he finds her reading a book he taunts her by saying there is no need for her to read when she has him. A woman immobile is a delight to such a man; Ruth is a "perfect statue, unadorned woman, beauty's home image" (70) (the image developed in "Museums and Women"). When she speaks, however, the image is spoiled as her crude expressions spill forth. When Tothero, Rabbit's former coach, claims that he develops his athlete's three tools—head, body, and heart—she quickly adds, "the crotch" (54). When Ruth is not immobile, like Janice she is uncoordinated—an awkward bowler, a bloated and a lazy swimmer—while Rabbit continues to regard himself as the graceful athlete. His concepts are lyrical and ideal in contrast to the practical, dull thoughts that enter the heads of his women. Life for them holds no quest of higher things, no sense of the meaningful ambiguities which make Rabbit a more interesting character than they have the possibility of being.

For Updike to consider the "dreams" of his women characters is something of a parody, although he claims that he never satirizes. When Rabbit reminisces about his glory as a basketball star, which he frequently refers to in his conversation with Ruth, she admits to her dream of wanting to be a great cook. This accomplishment would presumably distinguish her from the inadequate Janice, whose lamb chops are greasy. But in fact Ruth has become a good eater, not a good cook. Her culinary skill is given a test only in the preparation of hot dogs, which she can indeed cook without splitting them open as Janice does. When Rabbit first asks Ruth, "What do you do?," that question terrible to so many women, she answers the familiar "Nothing." She can hardly reply that she is a prostitute, although the lowly state of whore, as Ruth later points out, is not really unlike that of other women. Rabbit is aware of this and declines to use the word *prostitute* in reference to Ruth unless it is used for every woman who is not married. Categorizing all unmarried women this way, however, which is meant to elevate Ruth, only results in denigrating all unmarried women. Married women, if not referred to as prostitutes, are often treated as such. When Rabbit attempts to make love to his wife after she has had her baby, demanding that she "roll over," she points out to him that he treats her like a prostitute.

Notes

1. "*Rabbit, Run:* John Updike's Criticism of 'The Return to Nature,'" *Twentieth Century Literature*, 12 (Apr. 1966), 9.
2. *Rabbit, Run* (Greenwich, Conn.: Fawcett Publications, 1960), pp. 10, 13. Further page references to this edition are included in the text.

JANE BARNES

From "John Updike: A Literary Spider"

Virginia Quarterly Review, Winter 1981, pp. 79–98

I

In 1979, two collections of John Updike's stories appeared, *Too Far to Go*, published in February by Fawcett, and *Problems*, published by Knopf in October. Rather than review these books by themselves, I want to discuss the stories in the new collections that round out one distinct phase of Updike's involvement with themes of family life. It is a phase which began with the Olinger stories and which follows a single narrator through his adolescence, marriage, and divorce. From story to story, this narrator appears in slightly different guises—his name changes, he lives in different towns or cities. Of course, not all the narrators of all the stories are this narrator; but from the Olinger fictions to the most recent ones, certain traits of character and key repetitions from a particular life story identify several heroes as one man.

To a great extent, the tension in these stories derives from the conflict between the illusions fueling the adult from the past and the demands made on him as a parent and husband in the present. His childhood hopes, desires, dreams are frustrated by family life, and Updike's narrator is constantly turning back—less and less, however, to rediscover his childhood's glory. As he passes through his cycle of hope, discouragement, and liberation, his childhood becomes the text which he earnestly studies for clues to who he is and what he should do and how he got into his situation in the first place. Over the 20 or so years during which Updike has published stories, much of the drama has been generated by the narrator's changing view of his relation to his mother and father, as well as the changing way he regards their marriage. In fact, his first marriage seems largely undertaken in imitation of his parents'. The narrator's slow coming to terms with his unhappiness in the marriage, his falling in love, and gradual accumulation of the nerve to act (to divorce and remarry)—all these occur because of revisions in his understanding of the past. 〈. . .〉

III

As the narrator comes to view himself as the author of his parents' marriage, so the author of the narrator seems increasingly to write out of a simple, coherent core. Both books of short stories published in 1979, *Too Far to Go* and *Problems,* demonstrate how fully fledged the author's understanding is of his narrator's place in his domestic world. *Too Far to Go* collects all the Maple stories, the first of which was written in 1956. None of them suffers from the stylistic excesses that mark other stories—as if the Maple series were the best stories from any given stage of Updike's developing perception. At each stage, Updike has written many stories about the insight of that stage, but the Maple stories represent his most polished statement. An exception to this is "Domestic Life in America" in which the narrator is named Fraser, though everything else about his life—his divorce, his wife, children, mistress—are straight out of Richard Maple's résumé, including the clarity of the story's style.

Because of the purity and sureness of the writing, the Maple stories are a clear medium for the narrator's moral dilemmas. The medium is rendered clearer still by the fact that the Maples' experience is considered all by itself, in terms of Richard and Joan and their children. The stories about the narrator's most romantic passion are not written through or for Richard Maple; yet it is known throughout the series that he has had love affairs, and he ultimately leaves Joan for another woman. Tonally, the stories are dominated by the itchy, loving irritation of Mr. and Mrs. which can't include the wilder reaches of emotion. That life swells in secret, and I make the assumption that the unhappily married narrator in the stories about a raging love affair is actually Richard Maple stepping outside his marriage. This is an assumption based on the differences and limitations of tone. The tone of the Maples' domestic affection outlaws lyricism in a literary as well as an emotional sense. Yet Richard seems to benefit from the experience of other narrators, which is why I imagine they are all one man.

But there are other links between the Maple series and the wider exploration of all of Updike's stories about marriage, family, and adulterous love. In *Too Far to Go,* the central problem between man and wife is sex. He wants it more than she does (sometimes it seems she doesn't want any). His sexual frustration, in its most profound implications as "unlived life" (Lawrence's phrase), reminds us of the unhappiness which allied the younger narrator with his mother. In *Too Far to Go,* Richard Maple's frustrated longing meets Joan Maple's cool reserve much as in the Olinger stories the mother's restlessness collided with the father's more temperate nature. Like that father, Joan is both "better and less" than Richard; his slow advances toward freedom and love identify his journey with the narrator, who realizes his mother's dream against his father's restrictions.

In the first story in *Too Far to Go,* "Snowing in Greenwich Village," that dream exists as the young husband's niggling lust for a woman dinner guest. In "Here Come the Maples," the last story in the collection, the couple gets divorced. Richard has fought for his desires and won, though it means failing his father even as he sheds him. Richard says to his eldest son, after he has told the boy about the separation, "I hate this. *Hate* this. My father would have died before doing it to me." In the course of the collection, what starts as weakness, slyly acknowledged, becomes a transforming force. The Maple's disagreement about sex is, in the end, a debate between the claims of society and the claims of the self. For a long time, Joan's side—the former—has more power in the marriage because she has rules to go by and Richard has not.

There are times when this makes her less appealing than her husband. In *Too Far to Go,* two stories specifically contrast her virtue with his irresponsiblity—"Giving Blood" and "Marching through Boston." Both are about her insistence on doing something for people they have no real personal connection with and his sense of being deprived of her most important affections. "Marching through Boston" is a comic masterpiece about Joan's involvement with the 1960's Civil Rights Movement. Despite a bad cold, Richard goes with her to a march in Boston, gets a worse cold, and comes home wildly raving, "Ah kin heeah de singin' an' de banjos an' de cotton balls a burstin' . . . an' mebbe even de what folks up in de Big House kin shed a homely tear or two. . . .' He was almost crying; a weird tenderness had crept over him in bed, as if indeed he had given birth, birth to his voice, a voice crying for attention from the depths of oppression." His charm carries the day; he wins the story hands down. Joan gets no points in the reader's heart, despite the fact that she is out saving the world.

In other stories, Richard's attunement to the "life that flows within" makes him quite awful. For one thing, in the earlier stories, he is hopelessly ambivalent. This compares badly with Joan's prim, but unswerving commitment to duty. In "Twin Beds in Rome," Richard's move toward and retreat from divorce are emotionally exhausting to no avail. The lust which troubled him at the start of the marriage has graduated to love, but the fact that he addresses it to his mistress *as well* as his wife seems self-indulgent. Joan's dutifulness is clear, constructive, restful. In "Waiting Up," Richard's dependence on his wife's virtue is actually disgusting. The story describes him waiting for Joan's return from an encounter with Richard's mistress and *her* husband. It's not exactly clear what the encounter was supposed to accomplish, but it was deliberately planned and executed in a thoroughly grown-up way. Possibly its purpose is for Joan to smooth over the social awkwardness of the affair having been discovered. In any case, the meeting doesn't change the situation. At the end, Richard persists in wanting both women, and the fact that he does makes us prefer the claims of society in the form of Joan over the claims of the self in the form of this selfish vascillator.

About halfway through *Too Far to Go,* it has become obvious that both of them have lovers. We have to assume that Joan's adultery is at least partially retaliatory, but regardless of what drives her to it, the fact that they are both having affairs and both know it brings them equally low. At first, in "Your Lover Just Called," there is a little spurt of intimacy and rediscovery which comes with Richard's first realizing that Joan is attractive to other men. This accelerates in "Eros Rampant" when he learns that she has also been involved in complete love affairs. Finally, however, in "Red-Herring Theory," they seem more petty than racy. They bicker about whom the other is really sleeping with. Joan's red-herring theory is that he pretends to be interested in one woman as a way of drawing attention from his real mistress of the moment. Set after a party, the story is as gritty as the overflowing ashtrays the Maples are cleaning up. The reader longs for one of these characters to make some sweeping, noble gesture, to renounce something, anything—even if it's just to give up smoking. In this story, they seem to have been endlessly treading the same dirty water, both of them, getting nowhere, stirring the same pain round and round and round.

Just as we lose patience with their problems, a new spiritual strength appears in their relationship. They pass beyond sexual discontent and competition. In "Sublimating," they actually decide to give sex up between themselves (and thus to stop arguing about it). Other lovers are still in the background, but there is new clarity to Richard and Joan's characters—like windows which have just been washed. This sharpness does not bring them closer together. In fact, in "Nakedness," the last story before the Maples tell their children they are separating, various bodies are stripped, but all that's exposed is Richard's and Joan's individual loneliness within the marriage. We don't know about Joan, but Richard's thoughts about his mistress have a loving, solid—one might say husbandly—ring. His encounters with his wife are hollow. He nurses his insults about her in the privacy of his thoughts. "'My God,' Joan said, 'It's like Masaccio's *Expulsion from the Garden.*' And Richard felt her heart in the fatty casing of her body plump up, pleased with this link, satisfied to have demonstrated once again to herself the relevance of a humanistic education to modern experience." If he once loved her for her erudition, he now no longer does.

"Separating," another excellent story, does not surprise us with its news about the end of the Maple's marriage. It is remarkable as a relevation of Richard's changed character. He has altered slowly through the stories, but here he emerges, speaking with real authority. He has mixed feelings of love and guilt, hope and regret, but he no longer slides back and forth between the two poles of his ambivalence. He has made a decision in favor of the woman he really wants. As cruel irony would have it, his self-assertion robs his wife of the support of everything she's stood for. When he leaves her, Joan's virtue does not keep her warm. In "Divorcing: A Fragment," she has lost her control; she is miserable; she begs him to come back after a year and a half of separation. There is the horrible suggestion that without a self to suppress, duty hasn't got a leg to stand on. It turns out that her virtue was just her form of selfishness, her method of keeping her husband. It was also her way of denying him, as his self-assertion is his way of denying her.

At the end of the collection, their roles are reversed. "Here Come the Maples" is the story of the couple's moment before the judge. Richard's values are triumphant. He knows what he wants and insists that his wife play by his rules. Joan is as fragile and accommodating as her young husband had once been when she was the keeper of the social order. If only because the author takes sides, lavishing his gifts on Richard's subtleties, we do, too. In the course of time, Joan will probably make a comeback as the world's most wonderful person, but at the end of *Too Far to Go,* we feel that Richard's upper hand is more than just a win. It seems like a step in the right direction of freedom, truth, and love.

IV

Updike seems to write the way spiders spin: weaving his webs to catch life as it passes, spinning, spinning as much to survive as to astonish. He is probably the most prolific gifted writer of his generation, though the quality of his outpouring is uneven. The problem of picking and choosing between what is good and what is less good is related, I think, to his subject. As a rule, the stories about the particular narrator I have described seem to be better than Updike's other stories. These others fall into several categories: experimental ("Under the Microscope," "During the Jurassic"), descriptive ("The Indian," "Son"), and—for lack of a better word—journalistic ("When Everyone Was Pregnant," "One of My Generation," "How to Love America"). All of these stories have in common the absence of such literary conventions as character, plot, or dialogue. They seem to serve the purpose of unburdening the author's receptive mind of all the different kinds of information that he breathes in from his environment.

What distinguishes the stories about the narrator is the emotion irradiating the finely spun structures. They are more truly felt than the experimental or journalistic stories which seem too much like demonstrations of the author's facility with language and data. At the same time, the stories about the narrator also vary; between the earliest stories and the most recent ones, while the narrator is struggling to come to terms with sex and love, the style is often puffy, sometimes it seems downright anxious—as though the author were really not sure of the material. In the course of Updike's development, the problem of meaning has been complicated by and interlocked with the problem of handling his talent. At moments, he seems to have been swept away by sheer youthful delight, as though his gift were a marvelous toy; other times, a terrible piety seems to have possessed him, as though he could only live up to his promise by taking his Style seriously. And then his intelligence, along with his remarkable observing powers, presented real problems by crowding his attention with an embarrassment of impressions, details, facts.

These distractions get the upperhand when the author's moral grasp of his material is weakest. In "Packed Dirt, Churchgoing, a Dying Cat, a Traded Car," for instance, the overwriting goes hand in hand with the falsely ancient tone of the young man. He comes home to see his sick father in the hospital, his thoughts coated by a world weariness worthy of a very old person who'd seen nothing but war, torture, and death. In fact, the narrator is a young, suburban husband who's seen nothing but peace and domesticity, whose real problem (as he confesses to a hitchhiker) is that he doesn't see the point of his virtuous life. This is not quite the same thing as confronting the void, though there is a tendency in Updike's stories to inflate American boredom into French existentialist despair. At his worst, there is more sneakiness than evil in Updike, more opportunism than moral questing in his restless, curious narrator.

Then, too, though the narrator is clearly a self-centered person, it is not clear that his suffering is more than the pinch we all feel trying to live decently with others. His suffering sometimes seems like pure whining—his philosophizing nothing more than a complaint that spouses can cramp a person's sexual style. It is generally assumed that Updike's stories about domestic life are autobiographical. This assumption seems to be made out of a worldly wisdom which allows all sophisticated people to connect what is known about the author through articles (i.e., that Updike has been married, divorced, and recently remarried) and what happens in the fictional life of his central hero (who has been married, divorced, and recently remarried). It *is* hard not to wonder if the narrator hasn't benefited from Updike's possible experience. At the start, the narrator is a timid, even a cowardly man. That he slowly, but surely has his way with women probably has less to do with a change in his personal charm and more with the unadmitted fact that the author's fame made him desirable and gave him unexpected opportunities, ones which Updike passed on to his narrator. There are times when the narrator's cheerlessness about his adulteries seems just insupportable, only explicable by something having been left out—such as the fact that this is not the typical experience of a lusty suburban male, but rather the typical experience of a celebrity who suddenly finds himself in sexual demand. The narrator's depression would be more believable if it *were* openly identified as the cynicism a famous author might feel towards a rise in his desirability that had nothing to do with his true human self.

Yet having made these criticisms, I want to disassociate myself from the knowing, wordly assumption that Updike's work must be autobiographical. I want to consider the role of autobiography in these stories, but I want to do it from the inside out. Instead of talking about them as reflections of the author's life, I want to discuss their importance in his development as a writer.

Updike himself makes the connection between the human content and the author's art. He speaks of his hero's sense of being the "creator" of both his parents and his mistress. From the start, we know the narrator tends to regard women and art as equally mysterious, if not equivalents. We know that women have dominated his experience, that they are the media through which he comes to terms with the past, learns to love and begins to act for himself. When the author refers to the narrator's sense of himself as the artist of his private life, the association of women with art naturally teams up with Updike's identification with his hero. We can take this as the primary, the *essential* starting point of any discussion of the role of autobiography.

Having begun, there are several paths open to us, all leading to "Domestic Life in America" as a culmination of the art the author has evolved through his hero's quest. Through time, the resonance in these stories has deepened, the authorial voice has become true, simpler, wiser. As a collection, *Problems* is marked by the author's growth as a writer, but the best stories in the book are best because they are about the subject which is most crucial to Updike. In those, form and feeling are one; the problem raised and the problem solved matter because the human heart is at stake; the drama is literally tied to it like a creature punished in the flames.

The narrator is not that complicated a character, but he seeks complexity out. As he has explored the varieties of erotic experience and conflict, Updike's style has reflected the alteration in values and depths and types of feeling. The best Olinger stories provide us with a model of what Updike's recent stories have returned to. In "Flight," "Pigeon Feathers," "A Sense of Shelter," there is more fancy writing than there is in *Too Far to Go* or *Problems*, but in both groups of stories the writing all serves a purpose. In the long run, the unruly impulses in his style seem to have been brought under control by the same principle that liberates the narrator from the past.

"His life must flow from within." As the narrator clarifies his values, as he becomes his own man, free of his ties to the past, Updike's style becomes simpler again. In "Domestic Life in America," there are few unnecessary words, almost no irrelevant descriptions. There is a very clean-cut relationship between content and art, between the narrator's inner state and the story's language and design. In fact, it is a photograph of the narrator's feelings at this moment in his life, yet the story has more power than this description of stasis might imply. It has the power of Updike's best writing—his quick insight, wit, and catlike tread. I associate this purity of style with another source of power in the story: it reveals a new resolution of conflicts which the narrator has been wrestling with from the start.

"Domestic Life in America" describes Fraser's visit to his estranged wife and two of their children, followed by a trip to his mistress's household. The parts mirror each other like two halves of an inkblot. Though there are different people in each place, they present the same degree of difficulty. Fraser's guilty relationship to his own children is no better than his problematic relationship to his mistress's offspring. The reminders of death he finds at his first wife's do not go away when he goes to his next wife's. At the first, he is involved in the burial and emotion attending the death of their dog, a yellow Labrador. As he arrives at his mistress's house, he sees her pinching mealybugs off her plants and killing them. It is almost a tie between the trade-offs each woman involves. The wife, of course, has claim to his guilt; but in her intelligence, her nonchalance under pressure, her decisiveness, Jean also seems personally more attractive than Fraser's mistress. Gerta is rather vulgar, though humorous, and much more selfish than the woman he has left for her.

The sexual pleasure Fraser finds with his mistress is compared to the pleasure he always got coming home from work and diving into the channel beside his land. "It was as when, tired and dirty from work, Fraser had stripped and given himself to that sustaining element, the water in the center of the channel, which answered every movement of his with a silken resistance and buoyed him above its own black depth." While this comparison shows yet another similarity between the two households, it also contains the essence of their difference. There is pleasure for him in both places; and that pleasure has something to do with the unconscious (underwater) life of the senses. But his first wife contributes to this satisfaction only insofar as she is an aspect of his property. If she were all he had, he would have lost what made him happy as her husband. Though he owns nothing with his mistress, though he is actually a trespasser on her property (the gift of her husband), still Fraser is happy with her.

The equations between one household and the other mount as the story progresses, culminating in Fraser's glimpse of the time and temperature as he returns to Boston: 10:01 and 10°. The perfection of this image sets the drama in final clarity before us, recalling the whole history of the narrator's problem even while it casts this dilemma in a new form. The series of numbers demonstrate the similarity between the narrator's choices, but as the witness he is also another actor—one who can and does tip the balance.

Originally, the narrator was paralyzed because every action involved a life-and-death struggle. He could not move without moving against someone else. For the young narrator, identification with one parent meant attacking the other. For Richard Maple, giving his wife her way meant giving up his own. Finally, however, the narrator is compelled to act because not acting hurts himself. No one else is going to act on his behalf; he has to. But for him to reach this point the problem has had to change. The extreme either/or that characterized the important people in his life has subsided. The narrator slowly but surely has incorporated into himself the parts of his parents which, at first, he served alternately as absolutes. He takes his own shape, and as he does, the opposing principles in the universe around him cease to clash so violently. The sense of futility so often present in the early stories is transformed, not because the problem goes away, but because the narrator has become engaged in it. "Domestic Life in America" is there as proof. The narrator is alive and well by virtue of his willingness to pursue what he wants. He has accepted the fact that this will hurt others, and does what he can to take responsibility for his part in the dog-eat-dog reality. He cannot change his feelings, but he does not hide or suppress them. While he also fulfills his obligations at the level of finances and work, the most important form his responsibility takes is acting on what he perceives to be "the real relation between things."

This last is from Marx, who also said that people would only know what these real relations were once they had rid themselves of their illusion. Through time, the narrator's illusions have worn away, allowing the difficult, tiring, moving human truth to emerge. The relationships which have had various kinds of power over the narrator turn out to be commanding for the simplest reason. These people, after all, are not the symbols he once envisioned. They are just the people he happened to know in life. He probably would have known them anyway, even if they had not fit into his sense of how the world was divided.

Division has haunted the narrator and informed the writer's art. It grew out of the boy's understanding of the differences between his parents and grew into his conflict between marriage and wife, on the one hand, and love and mistress, on the other. For some time, the division between parents and women was also between duty and self, morality and pleasure. In "Domestic Life in America," the element of compulsion, of one thing versus another, has fallen away. There is still strife and conflict, but it is between characters who are both good and bad, who are as mixed as the blessings they enjoy and the penalties they pay. The arguments which the narrator worked out through them were always only partially true about the human beings. And the real debate was always one the narrator was having with them about his own nature.

DAVID GALLOWAY

From "The Absurd Man as Saint"

The Absurd Hero in American Fiction (1966)

1981, pp. 50–61

I have more than once suggested the degree to which John Updike's increasing artistry and philosophical complexity anticipate his best-selling, sensational novel *Couples*, which either baffled or angered many reviewers, and more than a decade later is still wont to animate the critic's latent Calvinism. More generous detractors accused Updike of picking up the windfall in an orchard formerly tended by Henry Miller, Peter De Vries, John O'Hara, and Mary McCarthy; those more acerb suggested his indebtedness to Grace Metalious and Jacqueline Susann. The novel's sexual explicitness is a prominent and essential aspect of the complex socio-political texture Updike creates, the dense web of manners and mores against which his characters act and react. As he himself has argued, the book, "in part, is about the change in sexual deportment that has occurred since the publication of *Rabbit, Run.*"[1] As in the earlier work, the hero's priapic vigor is one measure of the life-drive with which he seeks to thwart death. Furthermore, sexual groupings and re-groupings are integral to the novel's examination of mythical and religious metaphor; but so, too, are Updike's recurrent allusions to contemporary events (the Cuban missile crisis, the space program, Kennedy's assassination); to concentrate on one activity to the exclusion of the others falsifies the novel's sumptuously baroque structure—elaborate, intricately textured, mythically resonant, and full of finely calibrated effects.

The omnipotence, the omnipresence, the insidiousness of death forms the dark undertow of the work, explicitly linking it to Updike's earlier fiction, though the motif has never before been so amply orchestrated. The sacrificial fall of the everyman Piet Hanema—"*me, a man, amen ah*"[2]—can only be fully appraised in terms of the compulsive death anxiety that permeates *Couples*. The actual deaths of pets and other animals, of invented characters and of public personalities are threaded through the novel; sequentially, they include the crew of the *Thresher*, Ruth's hampster, the gutted mice in Ken Whitman's lab that lay "like burst grapes on a tray" (97), the trapped mouse "like a discarded swab in a doctor's office" (114) in the house where Frank and Marcia make love, Jackie Kennedy's premature baby, George Braque and Robert Frost, "a Pakistani mother bewailing the death of her child by earthquake" (283) in a photograph Piet discovers in his daughter's room, Jack Kennedy and Lee Harvey Oswald, a frozen bird Nancy seeks to restore to life, the fetus Foxy has aborted, and the Korean physicist John Ong. Punctuating this litany are Piet's recurrent memories of the deaths of his parents and, on one occasion, of his grandmother. In addition to these literal deaths, one repeatedly encounters—in what at first seem throw-away colloquialisms—phrases like "dead tired," "tired to death," "scared half to death," and "deadly serious."

The seasonal and religious motifs of the novel, whose time span stretches from early morning on Palm Sunday, 1963, to Easter, 1964, further stresses this dominant pattern. Images of the rank decay of nature recur in every season, and Whitmanesque lilacs that grow in the Whitmans' own dooryard stab Piet beneath one eye (402). At the first of the two dinner parties in the novel, on the Saturday preceding Easter Sunday, underdone "sacrificial" lamb is served; and at the second, on the evening of Kennedy's assassination, a mock *missa sollemnis* is performed. Ken Whitman, a biochemist who specializes in photosynthesis, comments that the specimens he uses all die: " 'That's the trouble with my field. Life hates being analyzed' " (33). Bored with the "dead experiments" he supervises, Ken yearns to study the transformation of chlorophyll—"the lone reaction that counterbalances the vast expenditures of respiration, that reverses decomposition and death . . ." (95).

Freddy Thorne, Tarbox's Tiresias, its Lord of Misrule, cynical conscience, spoiled priest and anti-Christ, repeatedly points the group's attention to death. At the Easter dinner he describes meeting the Jew Ben Saltz as " 'a fate worse than death' " (29), and Frank Appleby clumsily changes the subject to suggest that Tarbox's oldest inhabitant will soon be crushed to death by the accumulated back issues of *National Geographic*. Proposing a toast to the lost crew of the *Thresher*, Freddy remarks, " 'We're all survivors. A dwindling band of survivors' " (32). When his sprained finger is splinted with a green plastic spoon, Freddy makes it into a death ray that he points at Eddie Constantine, Piet, and Foxy, saying, " '*Zizz*. Die. *Zizz*. You're dead' " (71). Freddy's longest diatribe on death occurs at midpoint in the novel, in one of its most densely symbolic episodes, when he lectures a group of weary partygoers:

> "Losing a tooth means death to people; it's a classic castration symbol. They'd rather have a prick that hurts than no prick at all. They're scared to death of me because I might tell the truth. When they get their dentures, I tell 'em it looks better than ever, and they fall all over me believing it. It's horseshit. You never get your smile back when you lose your teeth. Imagine the horseshit a doctor handling cancer has to hand out. Jesus, the year I was in med school, I saw skeletons talking about getting better. I saw women without faces putting their hair up in curlers. The funny fact is, you don't get better, and nobody gives a cruddy crap in hell. You're born to get laid and die, and the sooner the better." (241–242)

While Piet protests that " 'Things grow as well as rot' " (242), he secretly admires Freddy for having learned to live with "the antiseptic truth" (242). Here, as elsewhere in the novel, Freddy articulates in crude form Piet's most secret fears, acting as his comic-grotesque *Doppelgänger*, as anti-Christ to his Christ. Significantly, it is Freddy who arranges for Foxie Whitman's backstreet abortion, while an anguished Piet waits outside in the spring rain; for him, the unwanted pregnancy had been "a disaster identical with death" (345).

In exchange for arranging the abortion, Freddy claims a night with Piet's angelic wife Angela. Nervous and impotent, he seeks to distract her with further lessons derived from his dentistry:

> "We die. We don't die for one second out there in the future, we die all the time, in every direction. Every meal we eat breaks down the enamel."
>
> "Hey. You've gotten bigger."
>
> "Death excites me. Death is being screwed by God. It'll be delicious."
>
> "You don't believe in God."
>
> "I believe in that one, Big Man Death. I smell Him between people's teeth every day . . ."
>
> "Piet's terrified of death," she said, snuggling.
>
> Freddy told her, "It's become his style. He uses it now as self-justification. He's mad at the world for killing his parents."
>
> "Men are so romantic," Angela said, after waiting for him to tell her more. "Piet spends all his energy defying death, and you spend all yours accepting it." (370)

In a moment of genuine comic brilliance, Updike has the mismatched pair discuss Freud's *Beyond the Pleasure Principle* while Angela tries to coax Freddy into an erection. " 'He says we, all animals, carry our deaths in us—that the organic wants to be returned to the inorganic state. It wants to rest'," Angela adds (367).

The writings of Shakespeare are frequently invoked in *Couples*, in part as a comic device suggesting Frank Appleby's intellectual pretentiousness; but the clustering and patterning of images—of death, light, dreams, carpentry, vegetation, the eucharist—also achieve a cumulative effect reminiscent of Shakespeare's technique. A mere summary of recurrent images fails to convey their intricate structure, the reinforcement they contribute to the elaborate narrative armature that supports this highly episodic work. Two ski weekends, for example, contrast and define shifting allegiances among the couples; two ritual dinners show their hunger for ceremonies that will bring wholeness into a desacralized world—and hence the embarrassed "bump of silence" (25) that takes the place of grace at the Guerins' dinner. The death of the Kennedy baby, " 'born too tiny' " (212), is echod in Foxy's abortion, and the aborted fetus is foreshadowed in the coughball Angela holds in her hand as she sits beside Foxy—"smaller than a golf ball, a tidy dry accretion visibly holding small curved bones" (63). For Ruth's new hamster, Piet constructs a minimal, parabolic cage, to protect the animal from death, but later complains to Angela that he feels himself to be in a cage. The sacrificial fall of the Jew Ben Saltz (presumably the result of sexual license) is a prelude to that of the symbolic Jew, Piet Hanema; seeing the man's archaic profile, with its patriarchal beard, Piet thinks of Ben as someone who "had touched bottom and found himself at rest, safe" (255).

The first of the two epigraphs with which Updike precedes his novel is from Paul Tillich's essay "The Effects of Space Exploration on Man's Condition," in which the theologian stresses space travel as the logical extension of Renaissance man's concentration on horizontal exploration of the physical world as opposed to the vertical/spiritual understanding of the cosmos.[3] In Tarbox the space program is a frequent topic of party talk; furthermore, Eddie Constantine is a jet pilot, and Ben Saltz has, supposedly, contributed to the Mariner Venus probe. Angela Hanema, the "remote" and heavenly female, is repeatedly associated with the stars, with Venus, and, occasionally, with the moon; when the couples play a new game called "Wonderful," she picks stars as the most wonderful thing she knows, and in fact was once taught the names of all the first-magnitude stars by an astronomer uncle. On the night of Kennedy's assassination, while the television set flickers with images of the President's coffin arriving in Washington, Angela and Piet dance to "Stars Fell on Alabama," "Soft as the Starlight," and then "It Must Have Been Moonglow." Later during the Thornes' "wake" for Kennedy, Piet is trapped in the upstairs bathroom with Foxy, and escapes through the window only to land beside Bea Guerin and Ben Saltz, who are hidden in the shadow of an elm. Bea explains, " 'Ben brought me out here to watch a satellite . . .' " (*Cs*, 314), but all they have seen is a falling star. As they return to the house, Doris Day is singing "Stardust." In the opening scene of the novel, staring at his wife's nakedness, Piet had thought of the April night as "a blackness charged with the ache of first growth and the suspended skeletons of Virgo and Leo and Gemini" (10); as summer wanes and he sees the star patterns shifted toward winter, he thinks again of his own small mortality: "Vertigo affected him. Amid these impervious shining multitudes he felt a gigantic slipping . . ." (286). When, after separating from Angela, he takes their two children to a planetarium, his daughter Nancy—also obsessed by death—feels a similar vertigo: " 'Mommy'," she cries hysterically, " 'the stars went round and round and round' " (425).

Just as all the couples enjoy playing games, usually ones employing puns or "secret" identities, it is clear that John Updike, a brilliant wordsmith, thoroughly enjoys laying down the novel's ingenious verbal marquetry. If, at times, the entire performance borders on preciosity or archness (as when, during the showdown between the Whitmans and the Hanemas, Angela sips five-star Cognac), it more typically rewards the careful reader with a sense of the profoundly religious vision that characteristically illuminates Updike's craft. The clusterings of astrological images described in the preceding paragraph complement the Tristan and Iseult theme of the search for the pure white maiden, and parallel the allusions to Dante's Beatrice in the luminously pale and childless Bea Guerin, who is caught looking at the stars. Updike's quotation from Tillich's *The Future of Religions*, which incidentally anticipates the metaphor of the moon launch in *Rabbit Redux*, ties the theme of space exploration to the novel's central concern with the death of the church and man's hunger for eucharistic ritual. That hunger is parodied in both of the "last suppers" referred to above. In the latter Freddy and Georgene and Angela enter ceremoniously with salads and a ham; Freddy sharpens the carving knife "With a cruciform clashing of silver," intoning all the while, "'Take, eat'," and "'This is his body, given for thee'" (319). (The Eucharist is more tenderly parodied in the pregnant Foxy's gorging herself with cheap chemical bread in the early hours of Easter Sunday.) Tillich's argument about the exploration of horizontal rather than vertical space points us once more toward Updike's persistent concern with contemporary morality, whether reflected in jerry-built houses, wife-swapping, or athletic events. Each can have, frequently *does* have, in Updike's cosmology, its spiritual emanation. Even the sharp tabs on pop-top beer cans produce, according to Harold Little-Smith, "'the new stigmata'" (71).

In the world of Tarbox, loudly reiterant of death, to hear even the faintest intimations of immortality is extraordinary; to devote one's existence to a denial of death's supremacy is clearly absurd—in the fullest and noblest sense of the concept as Camus developed it. One should, perhaps, stress again Camus's concern with the very problems that have traditionally fallen within the province of theology:

> the absence of God, the relationship of a God who is all powerful and all-knowing to the evil and the suffering that exist on earth, the contrast between the routine of life and the crisis of being lost and alone and doomed that the Existentialist hero experiences, the disruption of familiar, human reality by the knowledge of the inevitability and imminence of death, the search for the authentic life on this journey to the end of night.[4]

Piet's dogged desire, in an age of shoddy and planned obsolescence, to build houses of fine, enduring craftsmanship is already an indication of the essential conflict between intention and reality—the same conflict which prompts Angela's observation that "'Piet spends all his energy defying death . . .'" (Cs, 370). He is Sisyphus and Everyman, Christ, Noah, and a randy Don Quixote; by Updike's own interpretation, he is also Tristan and Don Juan, "Hanema / anima / Life," and "Lot, the man with two virgin daughters, who flees Sodom and leaves his wife behind."[5] He is, one might easily add, Peter, the rock on which a new church will be raised; and he is Piet—piety, *pietà*, *pietas*. In the structure and imagery of the novel, the Christian allusions are perhaps the most obvious; at the beginning of the novel, Piet leaves church with a palm frond in his hand, and gazes down the hill to see Foxy, dressed in white; only these two characters are regular churchgoers, and at the end of the novel—when their commitment to each other is sealed—the physical church is destroyed by fire and the earth purified by torrential rains. Freddy Thorne speaks of the couples themselves as a "communion," a church, a magic circle to keep out the night. Piet, with the "cruciform blazon of amber hair" on his chest (*Cs*, 7), dreams of himself as "an old minister making calls" (10), and is mocked with signs of his mission—as by Bernadette's "crucifix hopping in the shallow space between her breasts . . ." (12). A carpenter in his early thirties, Piet is most at home "amid the holy odor of shavings" (197). It is he who laments that "'*We've fallen from grace*'" (200), and his own fate will leave the other couples "haunted and chastened, as if his fall had been sacrificial" (456). Foxy, whose first affair was with a Jewish artist, comes to think of Piet in terms of "a Jew she has refound in him" (204); the Saltzes remark after his separation from Angela that "'it's a pity you're not a Jew,'" and Ben sends him away with the words "'*ain ben David ba elle bador shekulo zakkai oh kulo chayyav*. The son of David will not come except to a generation that's wholly good or all bad'" (420). The austere office in which Piet spends the first three days of his separation from Angela, shortly before Easter, is described as a "tomb" (416); and he even develops physical hints of stigmata: "His side hurt; his left palm tingled" (432). Risen from the tomb, Piet finds himself a social outcast, ostracized by the couples who fear his failure will somehow prove contagious. Nonetheless, old friends stop him on the streets and begin to confess to him their secret hopes and fears—much as his frustrated and estranged tenants begin to open their troubled hearts to the Christ-like rent-collector in Edward Lewis Wallant's *The Tenants of Moonbloom*.

The Christ imagery of *Couples* is repeatedly fused with images of Eden, with allusions to Adam's sexuality and to the naming of the beasts,[6] to the sin of sexual knowledge and banishment from the garden. In a further parallel analogy, Foxy refers to Piet as her "*flying Dutchman*" (263), reminding us of Piet's curious aversion to the ocean, and of how the legendary Dutchman was condemned to sail the sea against the wind until Judgment Day, unless an innocent maiden should agree to share his exile. He is also the handsome prince who kisses Snow White back to life after her seven-year sleep.[7] Piet, furthermore, has indicated in playing "Wonderful" that for him the most wonderful thing on earth is a sleeping woman—that is, both the bewitched Snow White and the voluptuous female figure in William Blake's drawing of "Adam and Eve Sleeping," reproduced on the dust-jacket of *Couples*. Through the concatenation of figures—mythical, Biblical, operatic, fairytale—with whom Piet is associated in the novel, two dominant types emerge: the spiritual redeemer and the passionate lover. In fusing those dualistic roles, Piet emerges as one of the most intriguing, real, and "heroic" characters we have had in American literature for a great many years.

Above all, it is the recurrent image of the greenhouse which gives a three-dimensional embodiment to Piet's tangled, visceral plight. Recurrent memories of his gardener parents and their greenhouse evoke strains of innocence and Edenic simplicity. Yet when he is told of his parents' sudden death in an automobile accident, Piet has just returned from a vigorous sexual encounter—"his fingertips alive with the low-tide smell of cunt . . ." (318). Thereafter, the generative aspects of sexuality will be confused in his own mind with images of death, and he will be abnormally stunned and grieved by such commonplace events as the family cat's killing Ruth's hamster (in orange color and protuberant masculinity, another burlesque *Doppelgänger* for Piet himself); the cat's pouncing thus becomes "a thunderclap of death" (76–77). Piet digs a grave for the animal along the edge of the woods, where the children's pets have over the years composed a cemetery. Seeing the trees beginning to leaf, he feels "spring's terror" washing over him, and can only think, in echo of Eliot's *Waste Land*, of this "slow thronging of growth as a tangled hurrying toward death" (78). His thoughts shift ineluctably to his father's "green fond touch" (78), just as, later in the day, the sight of the local funeral home prompts a cluster of images that relate parents, sexuality, and death: "Growing up in odor of embalming oil instead of flowers, corpses in the refrigerator, a greenhouse better, learn to love beauty, yet might make some fears seem silly. Death. Hamster. Shattered glass. He eased up on the accelerator" (81). Sexual embrace is the gesture with which Piet seeks to ward off death, but sexuality also represents his imagined guilt for the death of his parents: had he been tending the garden instead of trying to slake his own sexual hunger, his parents might somehow have been spared. Hence, he has chosen an "angelic" wife who rarely experiences orgasm and maintains a certain virginal innocence—through her origins in Nun's Bay, her associations with Venus, Diana, and Eve, and her refusal to bear another child.

Angela Hanema is also Updike's most fully realized contemporary version of the legendary Iseult; indeed, in her fusion of passion and aloofness she is both Iseult the Fair and Iseult of the White Hands. Updike's interest in the story of Tristan and Iseult was first acknowledged in print in 1963, when his long, profound review of Denis de Rougemont's *Love Declared* appeared in the *New Yorker*, together with introductory comments on *Love in the Western World* which suggest he had for some time been familiar with the Swiss author's theories. Two years later, Updike included the review in his collection *Assorted Prose*, and at the same time published in the *New Yorker* a rather stilted quasi-modernization of the Tristan-Iseult legend entitled "Four Sides of One Story." The announced intention of *Love in the Western World* was to explore "the inescapable conflict in the West between passion and marriage" (*AP*, 284), and it provoked Updike to elaborate his own theories of passion, marriage, and death. De Rougemont concludes that Tristan and Iseult are, essentially, not in love with each other but with love itself; hence, as Updike paraphrases the argument, "their passion secretly wills its own frustrations and irresistibly seeks the bodily death that forever removes it from the qualifications of life . . ." (284). Passionate love, according to the Venus myth disseminated by the wandering troubadours, feeds upon denial, and both de Rougemont and Updike consequently stress the legendary episode in which Tristan and Iseult lay together in the wood of Morois with the "sword of chastity" between them—an image that perhaps accounts for the moment in *Of the Farm* when Joey Robinson, thinking of his pale first wife, remembers how "repeatedly she had taken me into her bed and her body as she might have taken an unavoidable sword . . ." (*OF*, 88).

The contrasts between chaste courtly love and the indulgence of physical passion, between pre-lapsarian innocence and the guilty, death-rendering knowledge of man after the fall, between images of light and of darkness, repeatedly thread their way through the fabric of the novel. Unlike the myth of Chiron in *The Centaur*, the legend of Tristan and Iseult is never rigorously applied to the plot; indeed, in a rigorous parallel, Angela should be Piet's mistress and Foxy his wife (though Foxy is also endowed with something of Iseult's luminosity, and as a married woman she is "unattainable"). Yet the legend is repeatedly evoked in imagery, theme, and individual incident; Piet's dangerous plunge from the bathroom window is the comic equivalent of the wounded Tristan's death-defying leap across the flour-strewn floor that protects his Queen's chastity. It is, however, in the recurrent intermingling of Eros and Thanatos that the novel shows its most profound indebtedness to Updike's readings of Denis de Rougemont. The twin narcissism of the lovers may disguise a death wish, but "A man in love," Updike argues, "ceases to fear death" (*AP*, 286); in the complementary myth of Don Juan, which de Rougemont and Updike acknowledge as an inversion of the Tristan story, "Don Juan loves Woman under the guise of many women, exhaustingly" (298). The two statements, taken together, help to focus the significance of Piet Hanema's seemingly inexhaustible sexual appetite. And hence, when Piet makes love to Bea Guerin, he experiences a "crisisless osmosis" in which "Death no longer seemed dreadful" (*Cs*, 336). As Robert Detweiler has argued in an extensive analysis of the role of the Tristan theme in *Couples*,

> Tristan seeks to avoid death by losing himself in the passionate love of a woman, and yet that effort, precisely because it has the flight from death as its object and not the true encounter with another being, only betrays the continuing intensity of the death wish. Don Juan attempts to outdo and overcome death by the conquest of many women, and yet the variety and exhausting athleticism of his seductions are in themselves death-dealing. Piet acts out both these roles, although he is a more thoroughgoing Tristan than a Don Juan, and embodies the different attitudes toward love and death.[8]

Central to Detweiler's thesis—and borne out by Updike's choice of a second epigraph from Alexander Blok's "The Scythians"—is the notion that pursuit of the Unattainable Lady is concomitant with the pursuit of death, though Piet's energies have allegedly been directed at defiance of death's dominion. This central and essential paradox of his stance becomes clear when he actively collaborates with death by helping to arrange Foxy's abortion; not only must he conspire with the priest of death, Freddy Thorne, but he must also sacrifice his own "virginal" wife in order to gain Freddy's compliance.

Standing in the Boston Common while Foxy is being aborted, Piet moves through meaningless mock-gestures of fasting, of charity and communion, yet he knows all along that he has "set a death in motion" (*Cs*, 375), and it is precisely this complicity which results in his redemptive fall. His suffering and entombment are balanced by three days of marathon love-making with Foxy, the sensuous and uninhibited woman of the earth, as opposed to the unattainable Venus-Virgin-Iseult who has, for centuries, dominated conceptions of romantic love in the West. A measure of Piet's progress is found in comparing the catalogue of death he draws up on an insomniac night and the reaction he feels, after his separation from Angela, when he reads of the death of John Ong. The earlier fantasies are almost all violent, from "The Chinese knife across the eye" and "The knotted silk cord" to "The splintered windshield. The drunken doctor's blunder shrugged away. The shadow of fragility on the ice, *beneath the implacably frozen stars* . . ." (259–260).[9] In dramatic contrast, Piet sees through John Ong "how plausible it was to die, how death, far from invading earth like a meteor, occurs on the same plane as birth and marriage and the arrival of the daily mail" (428).

Until the concluding pages of *Couples*, Piet Hanema's struggle beneath the stars is highlighted and enriched by allusion to an entire galaxy of striving, quixotic, and absurd heroes. If *The Centaur* at moments seems constrictingly explicit in its mythological allusions, *Couples* may well strike many readers as too prodigal, even profligate, though here the allusions to myth, legend, fairy tale, and the Bible are considerably less intrusive. What is most remarkable about the performance is that, having carefully erected so many metaphorical waystations in the novel, Updike abandons them all in the concluding pages. In effect, he moves beyond myth, in a kind of leap of faith, a robust embrace of the quotidian that had been prefigured in *Of the Farm*. The stylistic equivalent of this existential choice is to be found in the sheer wonder with which Updike's prose can infuse the most banal objects, glorying in their mundane existence. If, as Sartre has argued, the ultimate evil consists in making abstractions of concrete things, Updike must be praised for attempting the opposite. That quality of "thingness," in which a jelly glass or a window sash is rendered with patient, radiant detail, links him to a tradition of realism that includes such great American poets as Walt Whitman and Robert Frost, as well as the Pennsylvania painter Andrew Wyeth. Indeed, in an article on Whitman, Updike cited the following declaration as a "thrilling" metaphysics of American realism:

> "Whatever may have been the case in years gone by, the true use for the imaginative faculty of modern times is to give ultimate vivification to facts, to science, and to common lives, endowing them with the glows and glories and final illustriousness which belongs to every real thing, and to real things only."[10]

Through such a technique, Updike concludes, real things are assigned "the sacred status that in former times was granted mysteries,"[11] and one cannot resist the sense that he is speaking as much of his own art as of Whitman's.

So long as Piet Hanema is aware of the choice he makes at the end of his vigil—so long as he, like Joey, acknowledges the radical protest involved in opting for the earthy, the commonplace, he maintains the stance of an absurd hero; in this case the necessary "disproportion" is contained in the inevitable dialectical tension between what he desires and what the forces of myth and society esteem. But when the protest is succeeded by contentment, the tension slackens: Piet is then no longer a carpenter but a building inspector, no longer the Flying Dutchman but another landlocked husband. Or, one might suggest, he is a Sisyphus without a rock to push—hardly a figure to inspire wonder, except at the novelistic courage Updike shows in his creation. That Piet's hard-won knowledge should lead him to embrace the conventional was foreshadowed in *Of the Farm;* in turn, it anticipates the peace Harry Angstrom makes with his wife, Janice, at the end of *Rabbit Redux*, which ends in the equanimity of a husband and wife peacefully asleep together.

Notes

1. Charles T. Samuels, "The Art of Fiction: John Updike," interview originally published in *Paris Review* (Winter 1968); reprinted in *Writers at Work: The Paris Review Interviews*, ed. George Plimpton, p. 441. References here are to the collected edition.
2. John Updike, *Couples* (New York: Knopf), 1968, p. 13. Further page references to this edition are included in the text.
3. Paul Tillich, "The Effects of Space Exploration on Man's Condition," in *The Future of Religions*, ed. Jerald C. Brauer (New York: Harper & Row), 1966, p. 50. The epigraph plays a more intricate role in the novel's thematic structure than it is possible to discuss in these pages. However, the reader should note Tillich's stress on "a mood favorable for the resurgence of religion but unfavorable for the preservation of a living democracy." Allusions to national and international politics form an important leitmotif in the novel, and the couples are generally disgruntled with the effectiveness of the annual town meeting in Tarbox. Tillich also stresses, in this chapter of *The Future of Religions*, that a society overly concerned with horizontal exploration must inevitably lay such a stress on science and technology that an elite will be created of specialists who cannot share their knowledge with others. Note that the couples are repeatedly confused about what the scientists Ken Whitman and Ben Salz actually "do," and that the brilliant mathematician John Ong speaks a garbled Korean-English that only his wife can translate.
4. Charles A. Glicksberg, "Camus's Quest for God," *Southwest Review* 44 (Summer 1959): 250.
5. Samuels, "The Art of Fiction: John Updike," p. 443.
6. See, for example, Angela's remark on Michelangelo's drawings of male genitalia: "'Michelangelo's, the ones on Adam, are terribly darling and limp, with long foreskins . . ." (389).
7. See "Foxy was Snow White" (288) and *"You have woken me from my seven years' sleep"* (265).
8. Robert Detweiler, "Updike's *Couples:* Eros Demythologized," *Twentieth Century Literature* 17 (October 1971): 242.
9. The italics are my own.
10. Quoted in John Updike, "Walt Whitman: Ego and Art," *New York Review of Books*, February 9, 1978, p. 36.
11. Ibid.

MARK VAN DOREN

1894–1972

Mark Van Doren was born on June 13, 1894, in Hope, Illinois, to Charles Lucius and Dora (née Butz) Van Doren. He was educated at the University of Illinois (A.B. 1914, A.M. 1915) and Columbia University (Ph.D. 1920). He served in the army during World War I. In 1922 he married Dorothy Graffe; they had two children. He taught at Columbia University from 1920 to 1959, and lectured at St. John's College in Annapolis, Maryland, from 1937 to 1957. In addition, he was a visiting professor at Harvard University in 1963. From 1924 to 1928 he was literary editor of the *Nation*, where he also served as a film critic from 1935 to 1938.

Although Van Doren published a great deal of criticism and social commentary, some plays, and several books of fiction, he is known primarily as a poet. His first book of verse was *Spring Thunder and Other Poems* (1924); over the next five decades he published more than a thousand poems, most of which were collected in *Collected and New Poems 1924–1963* (1963). While he was rarely called dazzling or brilliant, and was not a technical or thematic innovator, Van Doren was celebrated as a solid, skilled wordsmith in the American mode of Robert Frost. His primary poetic concerns were not with himself but with such universal themes as love, existence, and knowledge; his confident and often powerful handling of such traditional subjects earned him a reputation as a careful craftsman. Van Doren was also an influential teacher and critic; among his students at Columbia were Louis Zukofsky, Thomas Merton, Jack Kerouac, and Allen Ginsberg. Mark Van Doren died in Torrington, Connecticut, on December 10, 1972.

Mr. Van Doren's latest book ⟨*The Last Look and Other Poems*⟩ represents no new development of his talent. On the other hand, all the virtues familiar to his readers are present here: the suavity, the whimsicality, the gift for occasional telling phrases, the neat jointure of rhyme. Mr. Van Doren is an elegant poet, one who does not presume to shake the world, who finds it sad but not terrible. He has no furies; rather a few fireside ghosts.

Poetry written in English has for some years been undergoing a change. It has tended to become tighter in its structure, more forceful in its language and psychologically more searching. Poets have become increasingly distrustful of the vague effusions of sensibility which are still vulgarly termed "poetic." The trend has been toward a greater precision both of thought and feeling (the two, of course, are concomitant).

Now Mr. Van Doren is aware of these changes and has defended and expounded them frequently. But as they express an essential change in the attitude of the poet toward his material, he seems to have remained outside them. There is a softness and looseness of mind apparent in his work. This is illustrated both in the way he apprehends a subject and in the blurred quality of his descriptive language. His imagery is vague; no pictures remain. Compare, for example, the following lines from a poem in the present volume,

> Upon a summer Sunday: wide the song
> Of strengthless wings that bore the sky along;
>
> Upon a summer Sunday: strange the power,
> Inaudible that opened every flower;
>
> On Sunday, in the summer, through the white
> Mid-world they wandered, meditating flight.

with these lines from Marianne Moore's poem "New York":

> The center of the wholesale fur trade,
> starred with tepees of ermine and peopled with foxes,
> the long guard hairs waving two inches beyond the
> body of the pelt;
> the ground dotted with deer-skins—white with white
> spots
> "as satin needle-work in a single colour may carry a
> varied pattern."

The difference between the hazy impression in one case and the extraordinarily sharp focus in the other is more than a mere difference in subject matter or poetic "style." It is a difference in mind inherent in the creative processes of the two poets. Thus it is not surprising to find that the imprecision with which Mr. Van Doren interprets the sensuous world is paralleled by the vagueness of the mental states he describes. His character sketches, so reminiscent of Robinson, are, unlike the latter's, almost always seen in a sentimental perspective.

In Mr. Van Doren's love poetry the result of this unresolved mixture of thought and feeling is to weigh almost every line with an intimation of things which lie beyond the power of saying. This is annoying when it appears to result not from an inherent complexity in the situation but from a sentimental ambiguity in the author's mind. This is not to say that the experiences which produce poetry can be analyzed like chemical compounds. But it is to say that poetry becomes cheap when the poet too easily assumes his reaction to be rare and mysterious.

> This is the bare beginning; she was endless.
> There is no number named that would enclose
> Each of her dear particulars; abstraction
> Dies in the deed, as language in the rose.

Or,

> Intelligent her waist was,
> As though both heart and brain
> Lived there along with silence,
> And with them love had lain.

When one compares these lines with the passionate, direct, physical awareness of the beloved person in Donne or Marvell, one sees how thoroughly Mr. Van Doren belongs to the sentimental tradition. By comparison, the love poetry of Donne seems almost brutal!—WILLIAM GILMORE, "A Few Ghosts," *Poetry*, Dec. 1937, pp. 164–67

The abundant promise of better things, which, more than ten years ago, caused Mr. Allen Tate to regard Mr. Mark Van Doren as "if not the most brilliant stylist of our time, one of the most accomplished craftsmen" (*The Nation*, Dec. 19, 1928), has not been fulfilled. In the work written since that time there is little of brilliance, and the craftsmanship seems to have become more of a hindrance than a help. The 369 pages of these *Collected Poems* do not make a very readable book. The freshness and grace of the earlier lyrics peter out after the first hundred or so pages, and from there on it takes a great deal of patience to last out to the end.

Mr. Van Doren has at his command a quite sharply individual, useful set of poetic devices, and a diction perfected by hard work and sensitive reading. Unfortunately, however, he has mastered his devices (or they have mastered him) so well that he has fallen into the fatal trap of being able to continue writing extremely plausible verses even after his subject-matter has been used up—sometimes, indeed, even when he hasn't got a subject at all. In addition, his habit of saying things in oblique fashion, after the admirable manner of many of his contemporaries, has become so ingrained that he does it whether it contributes anything to his statement or not:

> All he can hope for is that hills and children
> In a sky-eyed conspiracy will say:
> "There he goes now, the old one . . ."

There are hundreds of unjustifiable personifications:

> The dominoes that once amused us well
> Lie in their box and envy bagatelle . . .
>
> The hub caps foundered, and a number plate
> Rose out of mire to recognize the spate . . .
>
> To him the fall said nothing of spent sap . . .

as well as other affectations:

> And yet he started;
> And the black sky became a listening shell,
> Contracted in an instant to the size
> Of a thin voice beseeching . . .
>
> The beaver is only credulous of meadows
> A rising river enters . . .

Since there is nothing in their contexts to make such locutions inevitable (and if they are not inevitable, they cannot help sounding affected), the reader is constantly irritated by them, in spite of sympathy with the poet's intentions.

Mr. Van Doren, that is to say, proceeds in a kind of sentimental automatism of obscure evocations and poetical turns of thought and phrase. This semi-automatic writing sounds so much like poetry that, apparently, even the author is deceived. He is particularly prone to being deceived by his endings, such as the following:

So he stands
Exploring silence with his hands;
Wonders, waits; and leans to hear
That valvèd sound of yesteryear

This habit also leads him into stretching conceits which have barely enough substance for an epigram (for example, "The Bundle," "Exaggerator," etc.) into thirty and forty line poems.

The tragedy of Mr. Van Doren's verse is that it doesn't need to be as muzzy as it is. He has sharp eyes. His range of poetic sensitivity is narrow, but within it he always knows what he is talking about. His talents, which are descriptive rather than dramatic, objective rather than psychological, enable him to record with remarkable felicity those aspects of day-to-day rural existence which come to have, through long habituation and loving reminiscence, an almost ritual significance:

Clear jellies that will soothe us when we dine:
Crab-apple, quince, and hardly ripened grape,
With jam from every berry, and the shape
Of cherries showing pressed against the jar;
Whole pears; and where the tall half-gallons are,
Tomatoes with their golden seeds; and blunt
Cucumbers that the early ground-worms hunt . . .

We barely could hear their shouting as the saw
Paused, and the great trunk trembled, and a raw
Circle of odorous wood gaped suddenly there.
Now maple and oak and cherry, and a rare
Hard chestnut piece, with hickory and birch
Piled here in shortened lengths, await my search:
Coming with lantern and with leather gloves . . .

His *Winter Diary* (1935), from which these passages are quoted, is excellent, imparting a magic to common things by sheer fidelity of observation. However, his *Jonathan Gentry* (1931), the long narrative poem, in style and in subject-matter more typical of his later manner, is a disaster from beginning to end. Was it ambition or the bad advice of friendly critics that made him stray so far and in vain from the kind of work he did best—the kind represented in *Winter Diary* and in his earlier volumes up to 1928?—S. I. HAYAKAWA, "The Allusive *Trap*," *Poetry*, June 1939, pp. 157–60

Mr. Van Doren, hemmed round by the American world of business and technology, chooses what is perhaps the most difficult strategy of all: to write poetry that employs rhyme and metre but keeps mainly within the rhetorical limits of informal prose. In this he follows Robinson and Frost, but relies less than Robinson on a strong rhythmic movement, less than Frost on colloquial effects (using no contractions, for instance, except in dialogue). He has so perfected his method that he is able to develop a highly subjective train of thought, sometimes at length, sustaining elusive figures and conceits, while keeping the alert tone and perfectly even temper of conversation. He can also be very compact, as in the remarkable poem on faith, "Most Difficult", where every phrase has both dramatic and logical force. In a poem comparing language and music, he is skeptical of the sensory effect of words, calling them "scrannel gongs":

In them another music, half of sound
And half of something taciturn between;
In them another ringing, not for ears,
Not loud; but in the chambers of the brain
Are bells that clap an answer when the words
Move orderly, with truth among the train.

Short of inquiring into what constitutes the truth of poetry, this is as good a definition of his poetic as one could ask. Like other poets, Mr. Van Doren succeeds when he is writing on themes that engage his affections as much as they appeal to his fancy. Like others, he consistently fails, though sometimes in a bold and interesting way, when he neglects them. Fortunately he has not lacked such themes; and they have much variety, as any short list of his really effective poems will show: for example, "The Monument"; "Axle Song"; "Humanity Unlimited?"; "He Loves Me"; "Schooltime"; "This Is the Boy"; "Sleep, Grandmother"; "Here Then He Lay"; "Homer, Sidney, Philo"; "The Bird Desire"; "The Liquid Heart"; "The Uncle I Was Named For"; "No Word, No Wind"; "The Merry Trainman"; "If They Spoke." In these poems, which seem to me as durable as any contemporary work, he is concerned with the objects of emotion, or with scenes and incidents that arouse it, or with symbols that comprehend it; not, primarily, with analyzing it or with deriving an abstract philosophic connotation. When feeling is steadily engaged, not flinching away from the crude devices of language, only the simplest argument may be needed:

And he has terrors that he can release.
But when he looks he loves me; which is why
I wonder; and my wonder must increase
Till more of it shall slay me. Yet I live,
I live; and he has never ceased to give
This look at me that sweetens the whole sky.

It seems to me that Mr. Van Doren sometimes yields to the audience by trying, perhaps in fear of monotony, to make a line or a phrase more casual or more emphatic than it is or should be; this results in a few mannerisms, including the now popular device of beheaded sentences formed of conjunction and predicate. But these effects have tended to disappear. The recent poems are, generally, the best; since the new book (*Selected Poems*) is weighted in their favor, and contains also A *Winter Diary*, it has an especially triumphant air.—GEORGE DILLON, "Style and the Many-Headed Beast," *Poetry*, August 1955, pp. 289–90

Sometimes the requirements of the fully human—the demands of an emotionally saturated life—are arduous; sometimes the poet falters: "I think I'll sit / till the stones turn empty. / They don't mind." But to become no more than immortal is too easy, the trance which sustains the flesh beyond centuries omits too much for Van Doren, and his poetry murmurs and rustles on, *past* the stones, though it notes that "the spirit best remembers being mute"—passes on to the life which includes but does not oppose death:

Death is our outline, and a stillness seals
Even the living heart that loudest feels.
I am in love with joy, but find it wrapped
In a queer earth, at languages unapt;
With shadows sprinkled over, and no mind
To speak for them and prove they are designed.
I sing of men and shadows, and the light
That none the less shines under them by night.

As long ago as 1939, such couplets, their ease and sanity, made it clear that Van Doren was the appropriate heir of Dryden—a relationship to which I shall return; but what most caught the attention of Van Doren's (generally admiring) critics was his accommodation of extremes in the general tenor—one recalls Edmund Wilson and then John Peale Bishop, especially, who marveled at the poet's apparently out-of-the-way concern with such old-fashioned fidelities as family, region, and the enduring of mortality rather than the striving against it. Since the romantic movement, we have been so accustomed to the imagination as a borderer, dwelling in risk and self-loathing upon the contours and verges of experience, that the impulse toward centrality, toward integrity and accommodation rather than alienation and exclusion ("that's me in the middle," Van Doren exclaims, as anyone might on glimpsing himself in a group photograph, and again, apostrophizing the doleful Don and his lumpy Squire, "halfway between them, that will do"—though who else has the choice,

Who else could be serene at truth's circumference
When only the known center of it sings?),

the undertaking to unite seems to us an alien, an inadequate account of our situation, unpromising in drama when it is the dramatic conflict which promises to redeem. A life so firmly natural, so happily given over to the leagues and affections of family, of filiation and paternity, of marriage and companionship, of fraternity most of all, and so proudly committed to its own failing body as well—a life unalienated by the kind of demonic aspirations which have created an entire literature of fragmentation and partiality among us—is an exotic indeed, and what is more, a *mild* exotic, the hardest kind to entertain, to appraise, to answer!—RICHARD HOWARD, "To Be, While Still Becoming," Foreword to *Last Poems*, 1973, pp. xix–xxi

JOHN PEALE BISHOP
"The Poetry of Mark Van Doren" (1939)
The Collected Essays of John Peale Bishop
ed. Edmund Wilson
1948, pp. 296–300

The *Collected Poems* of Mark Van Doren show that the poet's manner was formed as soon as he had found his material. The manner is remarkable in that, almost alone among his contemporaries in this country, Mr. Van Doren shows no trace of French influence. He is in the English tradition; his master, we can hardly doubt it, is Dryden. He has the ease of Dryden, as he has the sanity; though he has always clarity, he does not have a comparable radiance. He has his own grace, but does not give that sense of inexhaustible strength which, more than anything else in Dryden, contributes to the impression of manly nobility. Mr. Van Doren is more easily resigned. He has come late to the English tradition, as he is rather belated in coming to his particular New English material. The style he has made for it is properly autumnal and dry. But if we should by any chance be about to complain that it has the dryness of an October cornstalk, it is then we discover, under the dry rustle of the long leaves, the authentic golden grain. Mark Van Doren is extremely prolific; and yet his poetry is presented, amid his verse, with a sparse hand. Nevertheless, it is always there.

The enormous influence of the French poets of the nineteenth century on contemporary American poetry is easily accounted for if we remember that these poets were the first to explore the effects on the sensibility of a civilization in which, with each decade, industry played more and more the predominant part. It cannot be too often said that what the symbolist poets sought was not an escape from the life of their times. What they sought was life; they could only report where it failed. The poetic means which they created to that end corresponded to the exasperation of nerves which accompanied the hunt, the distraction of the mind, the extremity of the heart that came with its failure. There was not one of the great symbolist poets who might not have declared, as the last of them did, that his aim was to write of his race and of reality. That, it is true, is also Mr. Van Doren's intention. It is significant that in adhering to the English tradition, which he has adapted to the use of a modern sensibility with no small skill, he has been constrained to take as his peculiar province a place where industrialism has not apparently penetrated. It has, of course; only in that portion of Connecticut that is Mr. Van Doren's poetic property, it does not look like industrialism. It looks like death.

And yet, having made his choice, how honestly Mark Van Doren has held by it! He is a completely integrated person in an age when all we have known disintegrates. He seems while young to have become accustomed to the fact that his own particular world was already lost. And these things make him not altogether of our time. He is not solitary but remote. The region into which he takes us is one where "Time smiles at us and rests his heels."

His poetry proceeds from the New England air and, like it, is both harsh and delicate. And, like that atmosphere, it lends itself continually to fine perceptions; it has its own clarity, which may perhaps conceal, as the district it celebrates, how intricate its thought really is. Mr. Van Doren's corner of Connecticut may now appear old, harmless, and mad. It was not always so.

For New England is more than a section of the country; it is a peculiar spiritual climate. And it may well be that they will weather it best who, like Mr. Van Doren, were born and nurtured in the Middle West. The native New Englander, if he happens to be a poet, will probably revolt like Cummings against Concord, Cambridge, and all their works. He will escape as rapidly as possible and yet continue to breathe, with full lungs, upon its furthest confines of air. The Middle West was settled by New Englanders who sought less inclement elements and hoped to find an earth not so frugal with her children. Across country they carried a spiritual culture, and the Middle West has no other. It is a soulless region. The Middle Westerner must either be content to get along without a soul and record, as Hemingway has done, all the circumstance of living without an inner life, or he must look elsewhere. It may be that he will return, as Mark Van Doren has done, to New England. The old landscape is still there. Much in Connecticut is permanent. And yet it is a land that men have abandoned. The poet looks at what was once a farm to see a fallen barn whose timbers the rain will soon sink into sod.

Nothing remains
Of what it was that made these beams a barn.

This country around West Cornwall was where a man once could say:

I can go home. I can be my own master.
I've got a house now, a little patch of corn,
A plow, and a shed, and a one-eyed mule;
As ignorant and poor as I was when I was born;
But I'm my own pauper and I'm my own fool.

That was the self-reliance of the 'sixties. But that was long ago. Now, where there were such men, is

No corn upon an aged trembling hand.

To look for the genius of the place is to find, in a poem appropriately called *Spirit*,

A straight old woman, tall and very pale,
Moving from room to room of a musty house
No voice is ever heard in.

It is a land, not only abandoned by its men, but of men abandoned by their gods. (Mr. Van Doren's *American Mythology* is not about gods, but about folkways, which he calls by the names of gods.) It is a land of death and resignation to the approach of death by way of a dragged-out living, which is no longer desperate and scarcely tragic, which is, in fact, no longer much of anything.

That Mr. Van Doren loves this land almost every page of his bears witness. Though he is without romantic illusions about it, he finds in these hills somehow his proper surroundings. He makes them the landscape of his spirit. It is the land of his poetry. Out of it he has made much, for it is his by choice. He comes there to write his *Winter Diary*, and it is a charming account, in most skilful couplets, of a cold season spent there with his family, playing at being snowbound. For it is play. The snow that falls is real. But the Van Dorens, not being farmers, not being cut off whenever they like from escape, only pretend to be confined by the long cold. Yet it is for them, as for the reader, a pleasant pretense.

When so much has been given of New England, it seems ungrateful to ask for more. But what is lacking here is something that went out of the region long ago and whose loss was set down with incomparable intensity by another poet who was completely aware of what had gone.

> The missing All prevented me
> From missing minor things.
> If nothing larger than a World's
> Departure from a hinge,
> Or Sun's extinction be observed,
> 'Twas not so large that I
> Could lift my forehead from my work
> For curiosity.

That is the authentic New England note, not self-reliance, which before and after Emerson could be carried away, but the soul sufficient to itself. That is the note. But we can scarcely blame Mr. Van Doren that he has come too late into the country to hear it. For none since Emily Dickinson has heard it. It is no longer there.

The capacity for tragic action, which is continually present in Emily Dickinson's verse, is gone. And the strain of loss is over. What is left has assured Mark Van Doren a singular tranquillity and enabled him to write his elegies of New England.

Carl Van Vechten

1880–1964

Carl Van Vechten was born in Cedar Rapids, Iowa, on June 17, 1880. He was educated at the University of Chicago, where he received a Ph.B. in 1903, and then became assistant musical critic for the *New York Times* (1906–07; 1910–13) and drama critic for the *New York Press* (1913–14). His critical articles are collected in several books, including *Music after the Great War* (1915), *Music and Bad Manners* (1916), *Interpreters and Interpretations* (1917), *The Music of Spain* (1918), *Red* (1925), and *Excavations* (1926). Van Vechten married Anna Elizabeth Snyder in 1907, but divorced her in 1912, and in 1914 married Fania Marinoff, a Russian actress.

At the age of forty Van Vechten turned from criticism to novel writing and produced a series of books beginning with the pseudo-biography *Peter Whiffle* (1922). This was followed by other novels written mostly in a witty and satirical style: *The Blind Bow-Boy* (1923), *The Tattooed Countess* (1924), *Firecrackers* (1925), *Nigger Heaven* (1926), *Spider Boy* (1928), and *Parties* (1930). His other works include *The Tiger in the House* (1920), about cats, and the autobiographical *Sacred and Profane Memories* (1932). Van Vechten was active as a photographer between 1932 and 1964, and was also the editor of Gertrude Stein's posthumously published works. He died on December 21, 1964.

Personal

At dinner a funny-looking man sat opposite me. He was about thirty-five years old and his evening clothes looked a little queer to me, maybe because of his shirt, which was frilly, full of little tucks. He had nice brown eyes, full of twinkling, good-natured malice, and there was a squareness in his face, for his brow seemed square and his jowls were square. He had finely textured, red skin, and though the lower part of his face was heavy and unmodeled, he had a very delicate, small nose. His mouth was his most difficult feature, because of the large teeth with slits showing between them that jutted out and made him look like a wild boar, though the rest of him looked quite domesticated.

His name was Carl Van Vechten and he came of Dutch parentage; this, perhaps, explained the porcine texture of his skin and the suggestion of the wild boar in him, for many Hollanders have that quality.

He seemed amused at everything; there wasn't a hint of boredom in him. "A young soul," I thought of myself in my superior way, as I smiled across at him.

After dinner he sought me out and made gay, affectionate fun of the Armstrongs in an undertone, standing there, his long body bent in two places, at the waist and at the neck. This threw his stomach and his jaw forward, while his knees wobbled. He was really queer-looking, I thought, his neck never seeming able to hold up his head, or his knees his body. When he laughed, little shrieks flew out between the slits in his big teeth.

"Really, those teeth," I thought. "They seem to have a life of their own apart from the rest of him. They are always trying to get on to the outside of his face. If they weren't there he'd be quite a different man, but his body has to struggle against them all the time!"

He amused me because he had such a sense of humor and was so full of life. When we were leaving he left with us and we took him along and dropped him at the Metropolitan Opera House, "Where," he said, "I have to meet some fellows in the lobby in the last act and see what we're going to say about it tomorrow." He was the musical reporter on the *Times* and took his sacred trust, apparently, rather casually.

"And if Mary fainted or anything," he went on, "or if the Opera House caught fire, or if the President was there," he embroidered; "after all, one takes one's job seriously, I hope," he concluded, looking at me sententiously, trying to screw his lips over his teeth, and shut them inside his smile.

I asked him to come and see me and soon he did and so began a long, drawn-out friendship with ups and downs in it and a good deal of sympathy and anger alternating on my part.

He was the first person who animated my lifeless rooms. He entered the exquisitely ordered and prepared apartment and he enjoyed it so much that he seemed to give it a gently vibrating awareness of itself. He never realized that the lovely objects all gathered together in a perfect pattern had no life of their own nor even any borrowed life from me, and he gave them such an appreciation of the cozy living world they made, soft in firelight and sunshine, drenched with the smell of tea roses and heliotrope, and fine cigarette smoke, that there was an instant response from all those inanimate things and the place became alive for us and for all others who ever afterwards entered there. He set it going on its changing round of appearances.

But it is never enough to say somebody made a place live. One must somehow tell of the tone and quality of its life, for each one makes it differently. Carl's soft silk shirt had turned-back cuffs that were comfortably buttoned with gold links that had some dull, half-precious stones embedded sleepily there in the shining metal, and they surrounded his small wrists with a considerate look of well-laundered old texture, and the gentle, continuous friction of unperilous employment.

He wore a merry intaglio depicting Leda and the swan, set in a gold ring, an emblem of his attachment to *scabreux* subjects rather than to an ancient, half-forgotten truth, and his neckties came from Fifth Avenue shops.

That kind of life emanated from him to the rooms and set them instantly into a background for amusement.

With him "amusing" things were essential things; whimsicality was the note they must sound to have significance. Life was perceived to be a fastidious circus, and strange conjunctions were more prized than the ordinary relationships rooted in eternity. It was no more than fair then that life answered to this taste of his by fixing his unanticipated encounter with Fania into one of the few inalterable and permanent relationships in his set! That was a strange conjunction that was rooted in eternity, odd and everlasting.—MABEL DODGE LUHAN, "At 23 Fifth Avenue," *Intimate Memories*, Vol. 3 *(Movers and Shakers)*, 1936, pp. 14–16

General

To Carl Van Vechten was granted a less distinguished but more functional role in what threatened, as the twenties ran out, to become a movement. For beginning as its playboy, Van Vechten ended as its historian. He had been a music critic and he had a flamboyant knowledge of the world. It was he who brought the Charleston to literature, took the esthetes on slumming parties through Harlem, retailed the gossip, memorialized the fads, and—a sardonic Punch to the last—brought one dream of the twenties to a close by writing its obituary in *Parties* before he gave up writing for photography. As a stylist he proved so dexterous that he came uncomfortably close to ridiculing himself. From at least one of his novels, *The Tattooed Countess*, one culls such interesting examples as "The Countess replied, in a conciliatory manner, apparently with morigeration"; "She caught sight of her passerine sister"; "A sciapodous Bohemian girl in a shirtwaist and skirt"; "They had, in a sense, been responsible for his oppugnancy towards his environment." What saved him and gave him his signal importance at the moment, however, was the range of his facile cynicism. As the novelist of the speakeasy intelligentsia, he carried sophistication to its last possible extremity by refusing steadfastly to admit the significance of anything west of Manhattan Island. He represented the Jimmy Walker era in literature as Mr. Walker represented its politics, Texas Guinan its pleasures, and George Gershwin its music. In a series of novels that proceeded with becoming regularity from *Peter Whiffle* (1922) to *Parties* (1930) he meticulously detailed the perversions, the domestic eccentricities, the alcoholism, the esthetic dicta, and the social manners of ladies and gentlemen who did nothing, nothing at all. The world he so amiably described was careless, violently erotic, and cheerfully insane. Written up in Van Vechten's snakelike prose, it boasted an extraordinary appetite for evil; if there was no evil his characters played at being evil. It was a satanism grown weary of being dissolute, a lechery so sated with sex that it took to snake-charmers and hysterical visits to Coney Island.

Like most of the Exquisites, Van Vechten thrived on his own affectations. He began and ended his career as a novelist on a good, heartily satiric note, but there were times—notably in *The Blind Bow-Boy*—when he took such pleasure in his freaks that they seemed to climb all over him. A nudging good sense, of course, never deserted him; he giggled steadily at his own pretensions for eight years. But at last the eroticism became more perverse, the alcoholism more opulent, the lechery for nonsense uncontrolled. It was but a step from the buffoonery of *Peter Whiffle*, in which Van Vechten demolished a whole school of poseurs, to the carnival of idiocy represented in *The Blind Bow-Boy*. There, superintended by the gorgeous Campaspe ("You have such romantic ideas about America. Is there such a thing as a tired business man in America?"), Van Vechten's aristocratic perverts and idlers enjoyed their last triumph. The Duke of Middlebottom lived by the Julian calendar, since the herd lived by the Gregorian; Campaspe pronounced Van Vechten's own convictions on literature when she mused: "The tragedies of life were either ridiculous or sordid. The only way to get the sense of this absurd, contradictory and perverse existence into a book was to withdraw entirely from reality." Ineffably bored with their own pursuits, his characters then turned to Harlem, which, as Van Vechten described it in the torrid pages of *Nigger Heaven*, was a place where colored folk slashed each other merrily and had fun.

The final word came in *Parties*. At Donald Bliss's last party "there was Simone Fly, a slim creature in silver sequins from which protruded, at one end, turquoise blue legs and from the other, extremely slender arms and a chalk-white (almost green) face, with a depraved and formless mouth, intelligent eyes, and a rage of cropped hair. Simone Fly resembled a gay death." Unhappily, it was amidst the detonations of a falling stock market and an expiring culture that Van Vechten had gathered his creatures for the last party and the last exquisite sensation of extravagance and futility.

"It's just like the opening chorus of an opera-bouffe," one character laughs. "Somehow it's more like the closing chorus" replies another. "I think we're all a little tired." *Da capo.*

—ALFRED KAZIN, "The Exquisites," *On Native Grounds*, 1942, pp. 244–46

JOSEPH WARREN BEACH
From "The Peacock's Tail" (1925)
The Outlook for American Prose
1926, pp. 141–61

Mr. Van Vechten is the Baedeker of the intelligentsia. His novels are veritable guidebooks to Paris and New York, with the stars on everything that Baedeker leaves undistinguished and E. V. Lucas ignores. In *Peter Whiffle* he devotes many solid pages to a list of the things he did in Paris during his visit there in his twenties. He concludes with the modest declaration: "In short, you will observe that I did everything that young Americans do when they go to Paris." It is a very modest declaration. What he means is that he did very much more than other young Americans do, having inside information, and that other young Americans will do well to profit by his suggestions. "I dined with Olive Fremstad at the Mercedes and Olive Fremstad dined with me at the Café d'Harcourt." Not all young Americans will be in a position to invite distinguished opera-singers to dinner, let alone being invited to dine with them. But they can look up the Mercedes or the Café d'Harcourt and invite to dinner whatever most distinguished friend they find in Paris. They can follow Mr. Van Vechten to lunch at the Deux Magots in the company of unidentified artists presided over by the two bland grotesques. They can learn from him where to get their perfumery and dresses, if they are women; what bars and music halls to frequent, if they are men; where, in either case, to find Brittany china-ware and impressionist paintings. They can learn to speak easily of Dranem and Max Dearly, André Gide and Jeanne Bloch.

In the later chapters of *Peter Whiffle*, Mr. Van Vechten does much the same things for New York, and in *The Blind Bow-Boy* again, the scene is New York. It is true that the leading character is an English duke who talks French, and whose talk is "of Capri, from whence the Duke had recently emerged, the new English plays, Poiret's inventions for the grues at Auteuil, Cocteau's café, and kindred subjects." The cultural specialty of the book is perhaps the many detailed descriptions of interiors anything but banal in decoration; the reader has but to turn the leaves to learn what pictures and bibelots are the last word for the salon of a lady, the bedroom of a duke, or the boudoir of a kept (a very well-kept!) woman.

Unfortunately, *The Tattooed Countess* does not share in this kind of interest. We hardly need a Baedeker for Maple Valley, Iowa, and if we did, the need has been amply supplied by Mr. Floyd Dell. The Countess Nattatorrini arrived in Maple Valley in the now uninteresting year of 1897, and if she brought with her remembrances of Italy and Paris and London, they referred to matters which are now but ancient history, like the New York of Mrs. Wharton's archaizing novels or Mr. Hergesheimer's Philadelphia and Salem. The novelty of *The Tattooed Countess* lies solely in the words—a subject to which I shall come in due course, after a little further consideration of Mr. Van Vechten's discoveries in the world of art.

The reader who likes to be "in the know"—and who of us is exempt from this pardonable, nay, this intellectual aspiration?—must perforce be grateful to Mr. Van Vechten for his useful hints. It may seem ungracious to suggest that the thing is overdone. But indeed it does smack a bit of ostentation. Our author seems in such a hurry to pluck his flowers, to bring in his armful of novelties, as if he feared that someone might get ahead of him. He is so much concerned to avoid the commonplace, to deal solely in the caviare. He loses no opportunity to present a list of things—of pictures, music, books. He catalogues the libraries of his friends. He reminds us of the hostess who gives to the newspapers a complete list of her guests.

There is a passion for things of the mind, and there is another passion for being in the know. Most widespread of all ambitions of young men is the ambition to order the right drinks. One is reminded in some of Mr. Van Vechten's cultural flights of the passage—itself, for that matter, a cultural flight—in which he tells us of his exploits at the Café de la Paix.

> It had become my custom to pass two hours of every afternoon on this busy corner, first ordering tea with two brioches, and later a succession of absinthes, which I drank with sugar and water. In time I learned to do without the sugar, just as eventually I might have learned to do without the water, had I not learned to do without the absinthe. I was enjoying my third pernod while my companions were dallying with whisky and soda.

It is comforting to think that it was not the alcohol that attracted Peter Whiffle's friend so much as the sense of being right in a matter of taste.

In literary theory and in his own practice Mr. Van Vechten displays the same passion for the last word of modernity. The word which he finds is the word "sophistication," and the evidence of sophistication is, in his view, a light, ironic manner. In *The Blind Bow-Boy* the mouthpiece of his ideals is a New York society women who for all feeling and for all sentiment seems to have substituted a lively set of opinions on aesthetics. She has, for one thing, no patience with the heavy manner of Waldo Frank and Theodore Dreiser.

> Why, she wondered, did authors write in this uncivilized and unsophisticated manner? How was it possible to read an author who never laughed? For it was only behind laughter that true tragedy could lie concealed, only the ironic author who could awaken the deeper emotions. The tragedies of life, she reflected, were either ridiculous or sordid. The only way to get the sense of this absurd, contradictory, and perverse existence into a book was to withdraw entirely from the reality. The artist who feels most poignantly the bitterness of life wears a persistent and sardonic smile. She remembered the salubrious remark of a character in André Salmon's *La Négresse du Sacré Cœur:* There is only one truth, steadfast, healing, salutary, and that is the absurd.

What, indeed, could be more up to the minute than such sophistication, such disillusion, such a sense of the tragic futility of life? It is particularly prevailing, particularly natural, in war-disordered Europe. One cannot read such books as *La Négresse du Sacré-Cœur* or Paul Morand's *Fermé la nuit* without receiving a dismal impression of a world bewildered, in which not merely destiny but even man is without aim, without hope, without values. One receives the same impression from a show of paintings in which the artists have deliberately renounced all charm of line, all splendor of color and light, from a concert of music made up of nervous jerks and snarls and ending forever off key in a whimpering question. There is a certain character to much of this work, a deal of ingenuity and erudition, and it seems indeed the sincere expression of a characteristic view of life. It is the art of our time in Europe, and as such must be respected.

The trouble is that it has, at the same time, a sort of market value as being the last word. And thousands of artists who have no color of their own make it their pride to take the color, the latest color, of the time. Particularly in America, where the sort of thing is not at home, it has often a factitious and apelike bearing. It seems to say, "Behold me! have I not divested myself completely of the old sweetness and the old simplicity? Can you not sense the heartbreak and disillusion behind my mask of gaiety?" And we cannot always give the answer demanded. Sophistication, if that be something to be desired, is a state of mind implying a process of thought and initiation; it is a philosophical makeshift, a *pis-aller*. Disillusion is a *modus vivendi* of idealists whose ideals have suffered damage; it implies a depth of feeling, a seriousness of aspiration.

Mr. Van Vechten admires *La Négresse du Sacré-Cœur*, from which he has taken, one suspects, some suggestions for drawing the nude, and he quotes, somewhat inaccurately, certain remarks of the writer of Montmartre. He has not given us anywhere the equivalent of the actual tragedy which inspired the remarks of Florimond Daubelle. Nor of the German, suspected of being a spy, who brought up the body of little Léontine from the pit where she had thrown herself. "He looked not on the crowd nor on the sky but on something that is not of these lands nor of the country yonder, something which is between earth and sky and which a very few men begin to perceive, if they are very brave and persevering." Mr. Van Vechten admires Aldous Huxley, ironic and sophisticated, but he has not given us tragedy like that of the painter Phillotson in *Mortal Coils* who outlived his own fame, nor that of the dwarfs in *Crome Yellow* who were put to shame by their giant offspring. He admires Mr. Cabell, amusing and ironic, but he does not realize perhaps that *Jurgen* and *Figures of Earth* are the history of souls aspiring, and sophisticated in their own despite, flames "wind-driven but aspiring," as Meredith says of Diana. He admires the witty master of all ironists, Anatole France. But does he realize the gravity of the *Isle of Penguins*, of *Thaïs?* The characters of Anatole France, by the way, are never sophisticated, like Campaspe Lorillard. Terribly earnest is Thaïs, the apostle of love, and Paphnuce, apostle of asceticism, and all the philosophers of that amazing Egyptian banquet. If there is any sophistication in Anatole France, it is the net result of his long dealings with matters the most serious to the human heart and head.

"How could anything serious be hidden more successfully," thinks Campaspe Lorillard, "than in a book which pretended to be light and gay?" In Mr. Van Vechten's books the serious things are certainly well hidden. An amusing creation is Peter Whiffle, this runaway from Toledo, who has exhausted all the force of his will in escaping from the mediocrity of his father's bank and espousing vaguely the life of art; this irresolute artist who can never make up his mind on any question, and who drifts from one absurd theory of writing to another without ever putting any into practice. But he does not seem to stand for anything more significant than futility in the abstract. It might be supposed at times that it is all intended for a satire on the type of writing represented by Mr. Van Vechten, only it is too evident that his creator shares with him his enthusiasm for literary ideals out of the common road, no matter what, so long as they are surprising and not shared by the vulgar.

The Blind Bow-Boy appears to be intended for a study in disillusion. But disillusion implies the loss of ideals, and Harold Prewett is not known to have had any ideals to lose. The story serves actually as an occasion for the author to parade such figures as Campaspe and the Duke of Middlebottom—people whose aim in life is to seek out new gratifications for their aesthetic vanity. One remembers the words of Flaubert: "I seek new perfumes, larger flowers, pleasures untried." But there is none of the holy passion of Flaubert in these lives; there is little but the complacency of Flaubert's contemporaries whose aim in life was to shock their neighbors, *épater les bourgeois*. And they and their discovery, the child of nature, Zimbule O'Grady, give the author his opportunity to shock the bourgeois a little on his own account—an exercise which, for the rest, has now at last its market value in America.

It is clear from many indications that the great models of Mr. Van Vechten are George Moore (of the *Confessions of a Young Man*) and Huysmans (of *À Rebours*)—men who so loved to swim against the current of their time. It is a bit ironic, indeed, to consider that, of this author so proud of bringing us ever the last word in the arts, they should say now on the rue de l'Odéon that, compared with Waldo Frank, he is old style, still walking in the track of *À Rebours*. *À Rebours* is verily the Bible of those who follow the cult of the rare, of the *au delà de l'art*. But we find in Van Vechten none of the heat and depth of feeling of the hero Des Esseintes, who, when he had to return to vulgar Paris from his aristocratic seclusion, addressed his fervent prayer to a god in whom he did not believe. "Lord, take pity on the Christian who doubts, on the unbeliever who longs to believe, on the convict of life who embarks alone, in the night, under a firmament no longer lighted by the consoling lanterns of the old hope!" We know that, beneath the crust of vanity, of snobbishness, there was in Huysmans the profound love of a cultivated man for whatever is rare, the patience and tenacity of a scholar, and the desperation of a man bent on saving his soul, who in the end did save it in the one way he could conceive.

In his American disciple we tap the crust of vanity in anxious and uncertain hopes of finding something solid underneath.

As for the disciple of George Moore, we should acclaim him with enthusiasm if he gave promise of some day presenting us with an *Esther Waters* or an *Evelyn Innes*. We should even give him a high place as an English stylist if he would show us pages written like any page in the *Confessions*. Already in those early days Mr. Moore had achieved a style strong, supple, and above all simple. He was already an English purist of the school of Oscar Wilde—another of Mr. Van Vechten's admirations. It was from the best French models that these men learned to write such impeccable English, in a classic manner worthy of Congreve and Addison. Very different is the ideal of Mr. Van Vechten as set forth in the Preface to *Peter Whiffle*. In this testamentary letter to his friend Van Vechten, Peter Whiffle explained how difficult it was to recover the lucid moments of vision when he was potentially an author. "To recapture them I should have been compelled to invent a new style, *a style capricious and vibratory* as the moments themselves. In this, however, as you know, I have failed, while you have succeeded." It is perhaps a pardonable vanity on the part of the author to claim for himself a success which has been so generally accorded him by the critics. London and New York unite to grant him, as his dominant quality, glitter, and New York has added the revealing judgment that "he has some very happy hits in verbal virtuosity."

The phrase is most appropriate, reproducing so well in its alliterative and slightly facetious turn some of the means by which Mr. Van Vechten produces his effect of glitter. He is, for one thing, a diligent collector of rare words from the most out-of-the-way places, and his pages sparkle with outlandish terms as the diadem of an actress sparkles with apocryphal gems: "koprologniac tastes," "adscititious qualities," "fragrant acervation," "dehiscent jaw," "pimpant and steatopygous figures," "pinguid and amblyoptic gentlemen." There is, to be sure, nothing new in this. It has long been a recognized device of humorous writing in English—not the humor of Swift or of Max Beerbohm—to provoke the reader's smile by saying simple things in elephantine periphrasis. And Mr. Van Vechten is fond of the sort of wit which consists in saying "paronomasia" where he means a play on words, "vocatively adjured" where he means severely prohibited, "impinging on her consciousness" where he means coming into her mind, and "a feline death scene" where he means the death of a cat.

But such individual flowers of rhetoric give but an inadequate idea of the quality of his style when he is most conscious of the call for verbal virtuosity. This can best be suggested by more extended passages of lively writing.

> *Completely confident* by now that his father was *certainly* more terrified than he had been at any *stage* of *this strange game*, Harold *grew steadily* cooler. He *stared* at the rows of books in *shelves*. . . . and then he ventured *to look back* at this eccentric figure who seemed *to be ostentatiously pretending to be unaware of his presence*.

If I have failed to italicize any words it is not that any of them fail to illustrate one trick or another of this capricious and vibratory style. A captious reader might complain of such an intemperate use of alliteration as passing the bounds of discreet humor and verging on the burlesque. He will open the book at random and come upon phrases like this, "moodily occupied with such morbid meditation," and sentences like this, "These wasters, apparently, incessantly staggered about seeking sensation." And a reader versed in the virtuosity of Meredith or Lamb is inclined to wonder whether he should not attribute to the awkwardness rather than the cleverness of the author these jaw-breaking series of adverbs, "apparently incessantly staggered," "a particularly ornately constructed sofa"; these staggering series of infinitive phrases, "to look back at this figure who seemed to be pretending to be unaware," "to get on sufficiently well to enable him to support his wife."

A writer less enamored of the capricious style would have asked himself whether there was no way to avoid these awkward combinations. And he would have seen at once that, in avoiding the awkwardness he might at the same time contribute to the lucidity and forcefulness of his writing. George Moore would never have said, "to get on sufficiently well to enable him to support his wife." He would have said simply, "to get on sufficiently well to support his wife." Oscar Wilde would never have said, "completely confident that his father was certainly more terrified," but simply "confident that his father was more terrified." It would be to say everything that Mr. Van Vechten says and to spare us both of the offending adverbs.

It is not fashionable in our day, and it may be thought pedantic, to point out the habitual misuse of English in popular writers. But when it is a question of an author who has a reputation for style, it might be a consideration of real value in determining whether his reputation is deserved. The unit of musical excellence is the musical phrase. The unit of excellence in English style is the English word. When I find myself bewildered by a new painter or a new composer—he has a certain vogue among lovers of the up to date; he interests me by the novelty of his formula; but his formula is certainly not that of Degas or that of Haydn—I find it natural, first of all, to consult those who have a technical knowledge of the art in question. This painter, whatever his formula, does he know how to paint? This composer, does he know music? And when I receive an affirmative answer, I am prepared to look again, to listen once more, and to give the benefit of the doubt to a Darius Milhaud or a Severini. But when the answer is negative, I am more inclined to question the formula, to doubt whether the pretensions of this artist are not bogus ones. How can his novelties be worth while if he does not know how to paint, or to put together the elements of music?

And so when I find myself inclined to question the formula of Mr. Van Vechten, when I am in doubt how much to allow for certain amusing inventions in an author who strikes me as rather flashy, I say it may be helpful to take into consideration the elementary features of style. And it seems to me not without significance that he is constantly misusing English words; that he uses "betray" when he means "discover" ("Only once did Harold *betray* what he thought was a trace of affectation in the Duke"); that he uses "withal" when he means "although" ("*withal* this taste was somewhat bizarre"); "communication" where he means "communion" ("He held daily *communication* with himself"); "aggrandize" where he means "increase" ("a suspicion which seemed to *aggrandize* with every new opportunity"); and "scantily" where he means "hardly" or "slightly" (a man "*scantily* past thirty," i.e., insufficiently past thirty—when was ever man insufficiently past thirty?); and that all this he does in one of the latest of his many published works, and one that represents presumably the maturity of his style. And it seems not without significance, too, that these slips are generally made in the use of words a bit archaic, or rare, or otherwise showy, as where, again, he says of the duke that he "seemed free from a mania for exhibitionism." He means simply "exhibitionism," or a mania for making a show of himself. But "exhibitionism" is a somewhat technical word, and the author betrays himself a little in his mania for verbal virtuosity.

But there is always, one says, the glitter. And one thinks of Meredith; one thinks of Anatole France. One is prepared for the pointed phrase, the flashing figure of speech, sharp as a sword, the amusing paradox, the intellectual illumination. Here at least, one says, there will be no truce with *cliché*, no compromise with the banal, no drab and drossy figures, no flavor of the bromide. And one opens the book on such gems as these: "Friendship, indeed, is as perilous a relationship as marriage; it, too, entails responsibility, that great god whose existence burdens our lives"; where the precious stone of thought is so innocent of the cutter's tool, so little disengaged from its native ore. Or such an epigram as this: "I think it is Oscar Wilde who has written, only mediocre minds are consistent. There is something very profound in this aphorism." I find it hard to believe that Oscar Wilde should ever have let go so flat and unfashioned a saying. Perhaps Mr. Van Vechten is thinking of Emerson's more pointed version: "With consistency great souls have nothing to do."

Mr. Van Vechten devotes more than one chapter of his history of Peter Whiffle to an account of his own travels in France. It is perhaps to give us sentences like this:

> The trip across England—I had landed at Liverpool—and the horrid channel, I will not describe, although both made sufficient impression on me, but the French houses at Dieppe awakened my first deep emotion and then, and so many times since,

> the Normandy cider, quaffed in a little café, conterminous to the railroad, and the journey through France, alive in the sunlight, for it was May, the fields dancing with the green grain spattered with vermilion poppies and cerulean cornflowers, the white roads, flying like ribbons between the stately poplars, leading away over the charming hills past the red-brick villas, completed the siege of my not too easily given heart.

It is a long sentence, with much in it to provoke thought. And, first of all, one is surprised to think of the number of times it was necessary for the cider and the journey to complete the siege of this difficult heart. And then one thinks of certain pages of Stevenson, of Pater, of George Moore, and of the French landscape as it appears in them. Then one thinks of the patient search for the *mot juste* by the great masters of prose in French and English. One scans again these "white roads, flying like ribbons between the stately poplars," these "fields dancing with the green grain spattered with vermilion poppies and cerulean cornflowers." And one wonders whether, if this be not actually the last word of modern style, it may not be perhaps the "limit" of the banal.

No, Mr. Van Vechten does not reach the limit of the banal until in *The Tattooed Countess* he essays a subject in itself without distinction, and applies to it, not the vocabulary of George Moore writing the history of Esther Waters, but, literally, the vocabulary of Maple Valley. The gala entertainment given in Hall's Opera House in honor of the returned countess is described in just the vein of sophomoric burlesque which might have been employed by a young man of Maple Valley recently back from college. And throughout the book the diction and syntax are indistinguishable from that prevailing among educated midwesterners, except for the frequent intrusion of big words familiar to those only who have made a special study of the dictionary. Generally speaking, there is no suggestion of a humorous intention, but since there is almost invariably some more familiar word available in the context, the effect is to show the author himself in a somewhat humorous light. In the following passage of my own invention I have collected some of the more striking words and locutions, in order to give in essence the general effect of this style of writing. Whatever attracts attention by its strangeness is taken direct from the pages of *The Tattooed Countess;* I have done nothing but weave together these bizarreries into a connected pattern of discourse.

> The pinguid countess was sitting on her porch, vainly endeavoring to overcome her egrimony by watching the procession of inhabitants of Maple Valley passing down Main Street. Suddenly she noticed a carious and otiose carriage—a buggy, in fact—which so nearly resembled the vehicle in which she drove from Sorrento to Amalfi with her dear Cecco that it only increased the epithumetic, not to say emetic, quality of her mood. Quite as suddenly it passed out of sight, drawn by its scrawny and sciapodous horse, and there was nothing left but the procacious sparrows, hopping about on the grass, and causing the dry twigs to crepitate in a way that filled her with a sense of impending doom. She remembered that the sparrow is Venus's bird, and not wishing to be a mere sciolist, she decided to call them precocious. That was evidently no more than the truth when you considered the enormous number of them in this one family; and this only emphasized her own inappetency in so far as regarded sexual emotion or any enjoyment that she might have profited by in her home town. They were of that species that show a striated wing, being strongly imbued with the protective coloration of the town, and she saw no excuse for God having created any creature as helpless as herself. Suddenly she remembered that cyanide of potassium is a painless method of taking one's own life. She discarded the cigarette which she had been subconsciously smoking, and started to enter the house. But just at that moment her sister Dinah came out the front door, and the countess quite suddenly made up her mind that here if ever was a chance for morigeration. With a fastuous, considering all the elements of the situation, air of finality, she said to her sister, "Why don't you stay in the house and mind your own business?"

And so I went to take counsel of the Deux Magots where they sit enthroned in the café opposite the church of Saint-Germain-des-Prés. It was New Year's Eve, and all the world had come to read the countenance of our new master as he made his entry in the rain. The Wise Men from the East sat with ordered skirts and with grave, calm faces, untroubled by the tragedy or the absurdity of life. Slowly they spoke, deliberately, and with long intervals of meditative silence. And first he of the turban and the rosary made himself heard, his face seeming to brighten as he spoke: "What then is new and what is old?" he said. "The truth is a phoenix, and newborn every day."

And the other Wise Man spoke, he with his hands spread open toward the boulevard. "The Temple," he said, "was not built in a night."

And the first Wise Man spoke again. "Vanity," he said, "is not the shadow of pride. Without the substance there can be no shadow. Where is no pride," he said, "vanity takes its place in the heart."

And the other Wise Man spoke again, and it was the last of the words of wisdom, "Each new year a new peacock spreads his tail on the steps of the Temple."

And the New Year made his entry in the rain.

DONALD PIZER

From "The Novels of Carl Van Vechten and the Spirit of the Age"

Toward a New American Literary History: Essays in Honor of Arlin Turner

eds. Louis D. Budd, Edwin H. Cady, and Carl D. Anderson

1980, pp. 221–29

Of Van Vechten's seven novels, three are too weak or slight to warrant more than brief discussion as independent works. *Peter Whiffle* is too closely related to the form of the familiar essay as successfully cultivated by Van Vechten in the early portion of his career. Its hoax device, its first person narrator, its leisurely told anecdotes and set pieces (such as the account of a young American's first visit to Paris), all suggest the source of the novel in an idea which was then translated uneasily into fiction. And the idea itself, once we realize that it revolves around the demonstration that Peter's artistic impotence stems from his search for the avant garde, becomes repetitious and eventually cloying. *Peter Whiffle* contains some delicious literary parody, but this is not enough to make the novel work as fiction.

Whereas *Peter Whiffle* is insubstantial beneath its froth, *Nigger Heaven* is too "heavy" in theme and manner. The principal weakness of the novel is not that Van Vechten attempts to depict the full range of Harlem life, from pimps and racketeers to lawyers and artists. The novel could survive this sociological effort if all else were well. But in seeking to present a major tragedy of modern black life, Van Vechten adopts a dull and hackneyed love plot as his vehicle. Stripped of its Harlem setting, the love story of Mary and Byron is sentimental and lugubrious. High-minded starving young writer and equally noble and self-sacrificing young girl fall in love. She tries to help him with money and advice, but he is too proud to accept her aid. Wounded by his failures and by what he believes to be her pity and condescension, he takes up with a lascivious siren. Misunderstandings and complications follow and all ends in tragedy. The novel does not rise above this plot. As in a popular historical romance, only the local color and some of the minor characters have life.

Spider Boy, like *Peter Whiffle*, is limited by the obviousness of its principal theme—in this instance, a demonstration of the bad taste and elephantine egoes of Hollywood. Van Vechten's satire is one dimensional and his Gulliver-like central character too shallow. Despite some high-spirited burlesque incidents, *Spider Boy* is his least successful novel.

The Tattooed Countess, the first of Van Vechten's major novels which I will discuss at some length, is not only conventional in form but also, by 1924, in subject matter and theme. *Winesburg, Ohio* and *Babbitt* had by then appeared and the "revolt from the village" was an acknowledged and widely publicized literary movement. Indeed, Van Vechten's contribution to the movement is less radical than either Anderson's or Lewis's, since *The Tattooed Countess* lacks both the experimental form of *Winesburg* and the almost surrealistic caricature of *Babbitt*. The novel opens with the Countess surreptitiously smoking a cigarette in the women's lavatory of the Overland Limited on her way to Maple Valley; it ends with the report of her departure several months later. In the interval she has been lionized by the town because of her "successes" abroad and has scandalized it because of her Bohemian ways. Most of all, she has assuaged, by means of the youthful Gareth Johns, the ache in her heart caused by the loss of her French lover.

The Tattooed Countess lacks the high style, the exotic characters, and the wit and naughtiness of Van Vechten's New York novels. Indeed, his tone is occasionally that of a nostalgic local colorist. Village types, occupations, pastimes, and tastes are characterized in detail and often with affection. Of course, this detail has a satiric center; like Mark Twain's Hadleyburg, the town is inordinately proud of itself. As one resident tells the countess, Maple Valley is "not as big as Paris yet, but it's newer." Nevertheless, the effect of much of this satire, as in the running joke of every resident describing at length to the countess the town's new waterworks, is more humorous than biting.

The sharp edge of Van Vechten's satire is felt more in the action and characterization of the novel than in its style and tone. All that is most vital in human nature, and particularly man's sexual nature, is hidden and suppressed by the residents of Maple Valley. Women sublimate sex into a hysterical religiosity, men secretly visit the immigrant girls of the town or the whores of nearby cities, and family life is a battlefield because of disguised or unacknowledged emotions. Lou, Ella's sister, is a warm, responsive woman who has been beaten into timid conformity by the town; the Colmans have an alcoholic father; the Johnses are bitterly divided because Gareth wishes to live his own life; and so on. The Countess is an anomaly in this setting of emotional repression because she has made her emotions her life and wears openly the scars of a life of feeling. In particular, she bears on her wrist a light tattoo commemorating her lost love, a "scar" which represents as well the commingled joy and pain of her many loves. Her values increasingly clash with those of the town as she realizes that what to her is "life—love and sex and beauty—is to the town sin and idleness and thus must be hidden or disguised. "I am tattooed on my arm," she reflects bitterly, "while they are tattooed on their hearts."

The Tattooed Countess is most successful in Van Vechten's depiction of the relationship between Ella and Gareth. Theirs is no simple story of the seduction of a young man by an older woman but rather a subtly rendered account of a complex relationship. Initially, the Countess is drawn to Gareth because she needs a replacement for her French lover and because he is one of the few people in the town to show an interest in her and not merely to use her as a sounding board to enlarge upon the glories of the town. Gareth is drawn to the Countess because she can tell him about the world of art, ideas, and famous personalities that he wishes to enter. But gradually the relationship deepens and begins to reveal the essential nature of each character as well as the paradox at the center of the novel. Although the Countess appears to be a hardened woman of the world who is preying upon an innocent provincial youth, in fact it is Gareth who is hard and selfish and who is exploiting the Countess. He has already discovered in his experience with others in the town "that his interest in people depended entirely on what they had to give him," and the Countess is of great value because she can help him escape "this dull, sordid village." He is not drawn to her as a lover but he quickly senses that she wishes him to play this role. And so he muses:

> The Countess could do everything, everything, that is, that he wanted. She had it in her power to reveal to him all that his imagination had taught him about art, life, and the world in general. In the beginning, she could perform the initial service of freeing him from the environment which until now had stifled him, take him away from this cursed town for ever, to set him down in a milieu where he might expand and grow. To this end he was willing to make primary sacrifices in the matter of taste.

But Gareth realizes that much of his appeal to the Countess lies in his supposed innocence and that she thus does not wish him to play an active role in their relationship, that "by far the greater part of her present feeling for him was created by her hope of conquering his imagined reluctance." With a calculated self-interest he permits himself to be seduced, all the while storing up a contempt for the Countess which will permit him to discard her (as we learn in *Firecrackers*) once he has finished using her; indeed, which will permit him to exploit their relationship still further by later writing a novel about it.

The response of the Countess to Gareth also is more than it appears to be. Gareth's beloved mother becomes ill and then dies during the summer the Countess is in Maple Valley. Gareth is both crushed and hardened by this blow. His mother is the only being he had ever loved, and his spirit now assumes a permanent coldness and bitterness. Yet he also needs warmth and comfort at this moment, and the Countess—who has no children—responds to his need with these emotions as well as with desire. "I will be everything to you," she tells him, "mother, mistress, wife. Tu es mon bébé!"

Although the Countess and Gareth are using each other, there is no degradation in this use. For each is also expressing a deep emotional need, and each is gaining emotionally from the relationship. It will all end in bitterness, but so do other kinds of relationship, kinds in which freedom is not gained and pain not relieved, even if only temporarily, by love. Thus, at the heart of what appears in style, form, and subject matter to be an anomalous work among Van Vechten's novels, there lies his central theme of the seemingly contradictory yet fertile ways in which the desire for freedom and the expression of need and temperament express themselves.

Whereas *The Tattooed Countess* rests on the conventionally rendered but deeply paradoxical relationship beween the Countess and Gareth, *The Blind Bow-Boy* has a much more immediate ironic theme and form. From first to last the novel is a burlesque *Bildungsroman*. Harold's father tells him early in the novel: "You must see more of life and learn to live; you must learn to discount what you have been taught. In other words, you must learn to think for yourself, and become capable of *choosing* an occupation which will do you credit, which will be a reflection of your own personality and not of mine." But in fact the elder Prewett has so ordered the circumstances of the naive and inexperienced Harold's entrance into life that Harold will be forced to choose a way of life that is indeed a reflection of his father's personality. His plan is to throw Harold into a world of immoral licentiousness and thereby shock him into gladly accepting a safe marriage and career in the family cloak and suit business.

Initially Harold responds as his father anticipated. He is affronted and dismayed by the idleness, drinking, and casual sex of Paul Moody, Campaspe, and others of their set and turns in relief to the pursuit of the pure and ultrarespectable Alice. But gradually he comes to see that he has been deceived by others and deluded about himself—that his father and Alice have tricked him; that Alice's tastes are stuffy and colorless; and that he misses Campaspe and Paul when apart from them. He deserts Alice and after a brief period of indecision begins a new life of freedom and choice, of discovering who he is and what he wishes to do, first in a deliciously sensual affair with the beautiful and amoral Zimbule O'Grady and then in a trip to Europe with the Duke of Middlebottom.

This outline of *The Blind Bow-Boy* reveals little of the important role of Campaspe as guide and confidante of Harold and as "moral" center of the novel. Her elegant but independent taste in books, art, and interior decoration are the external signs of a temperament devoted to freedom. Hers is no flashy and noisy rebelliousness but rather an almost languid and obliquely expressed independence of mind and spirit. "Give me an intelligent hypocrite every time," she remarks at one point. In her relations with her friends, her children, and her husband (the ludicrously sentimental and insipid "Cupid"), she believes that she must not vigorously express her personality and "philosophy" and thereby perhaps shape their values. Rather, she seeks to be "different . . . with each of them" and thus, by reflecting "their respective temperaments," to play "the part of mirror" in their self-discovery.

Another major figure in *The Blind Bow-Boy* is Zimbule O'Grady, the novice snake charmer whom Campaspe and Paul rescue from a Coney Island sideshow at the beginning of the novel. Like Harold she is young and inexperienced and like him she is absorbed into Campaspe's set for "instruction." But unlike Harold she has an animal freshness and openness and a simple delight in her own feelings and pleasure. She is similar in this respect to Campaspe, who "took quite as much pleasure in her body as she did in her mind. Was not her body, indeed, her chief mental pleasure?" And she differs from Alice, whose dreams rest upon "a little gray home in the east." Thus, the principal characters in *The Blind Bow-Boy*, as in *The Sun Also Rises*, fall into two distinct groups. Campaspe, Paul, and Zimbule live dissolute lives but are true to themselves, while Alice, Harold's father, and Campaspe's husband are respectable but disguise their true feelings and seek to impose their conventionality upon others.

The language and incidents of *The Blind Bow-Boy* sparkle with Van Vechten's inventiveness at its boldest and most ingratiating. Perhaps something of this quality can be suggested by the character of Roland, Duke of Middlebottom, the genial homosexual who is recalled early in the novel by his former servant, Oliver Drains, who appears initially disguised as a sailor, who helps Campaspe organize a summer opera season in New York which consists of a single performance of a Stravinsky-like spectacle, whose family motto is "a thing of beauty is a boy for ever" and who is last seen with Harold strolling the deck of an ocean liner.

Toward the end of *The Tattooed Countess*, Van Vechten introduces a newspaper report of a meeting between the Kaiser and Tsar at which they pledge eternal friendship and peace. His implied point is that the moral hypocrisy of the age is not limited to middle America but is worldwide and that it will eventually lead to conflict and war. Political allusiveness of this kind is rare in Van Vechten's fiction, but even its occasional presence suggests a quality of mind which could seek, in *Firecrackers*, to write a novel of ideas with an almost allegorical symmetry.

Firecrackers opens with several characters suffering from ennui and nerves. The principal victims of this malaise are Paul, who has married an older woman for her money, and Consuelo, the precociously sophisticated ten-year-old daughter of Campaspe's sister. Into their lives comes Gunnar O'Grady, a mysterious young man who works at a series of jobs—furnace repairman, flower salesman, window dresser—with ease, grace, and intensity. His major vocation and avocation is acrobatics, and the perfect "balance" he achieves in this activity through his effort, skill, and absorption has the beauty and spirit of religious devotion. Paul and Consuelo are converted by the example and character of Gunnar—Paul to seek work for the first time in his life, Consuelo to herself become an acrobat. There is something ludicrously inept in these efforts: the light-minded and improvident Paul working as a stockbroker and advising others on their investments, the frail and ethereal Consuelo on the parallel bars. But Paul and Consuelo are nevertheless initially happy in their new faith. Campaspe, however, is troubled both by Gunnar and by the conversions of Paul and Consuelo, and the novel soon becomes a conflict between her and Gunnar—that is, between two opposing philosophies of life—for the "souls" of Paul and Consuelo.

Gunnar, we soon realize, represents the contemporary reemergence, in somewhat different form, of a Victorian ethic of perfection through effort. "Each of us is God," he tells Campaspe. "Each can be what he desires to make himself." Thus man must seek through intensity of commitment to achieve perfection in whatever he undertakes. Campaspe has been confident enough in her own vision of life to contemptuously reject such mental health and self-improvement programs as those purveyed by "Swamis, Coués, or Freuds." She now perceives as well that though Gunnar's ideal has an appealing nobility and grandeur, it is "unnatural" and potentially harmful. Although she is attracted by Gunnar because "she had never before seen such great beauty in a face, physical, spiritual, and mental beauty, . . . yet she observed something else there, too, dimming the glory, a suggestion of hideous pain and incessant struggle."

The weaknesses in the ideal of work arise from its absolutism and its exploitability. The first is illustrated principally through Paul, the second through Consuelo. It is "unnatural" for Paul to work as a stockbroker because he cares neither for money nor business. He plays at this occupation, as he does with all life, and thus parodies rather than fulfills Gunnar's ideal. And Consuelo's governess senses the commercial possibilities of a regimen of acrobatics designed for those seeking relief from the anxieties of the modern world. Her chain of "clinics" is immediately and immensely successful. The most significant weakness in Gunnar's ideal, however, is revealed by Campaspe herself in her relations with Gunnar. He has left love and sex out of his "religion," and when he falls victim to these in the person of Campaspe, he feels himself burdened and defiled and runs away. In short, his high idealism is untrue to human nature, a quality which explains both its initial attraction and its inevitable pain and failure. And so again a Van Vechten novel turns on the belief that man must be true to his temperament—that the noble ideal of a Gunnar can imprison as fully as the conventional respectability of an Alice.

Firecrackers is more thematically explicit and tightly structured than Van Vechten's other major novels but this is not to suggest that its tone is gray or sombre. Although Gunnar himself is humorless, the remainder of Van Vechten's New York world—Campaspe, Paul, Consuelo, etc.—is rendered with his usual wit and panache. The novel is almost a repository of Van Vechten's most successful characters from earlier works, since not only do Paul and Campaspe reappear from *The Blind Bow-Boy* but also Gareth and the Countess from *The Tattooed Countess* and even (briefly) Edith Dale from *Peter Whiffle*. And some of the extended burlesque scenes reveal Van Vechten at his best—a vacuous New York cocktail party, for example, or the attempted seduction by Paul of Wintergreen Waterbury, a "simple child of Michigan" and a professional virgin of great fortitude. And as always in Van Vechten the novel gathers strength from its central paradox, in this instance that of the battle between the devil and an angel for human souls in which the "devil" is a latter-day amalgam of Emerson and Carlyle and the "angel" is a cosmopolitan New York libertine.

Parties is probably Van Vechten's most significant and permanent work of fiction. Subtitled "Scenes from Contemporary New York Life," the novel consists of a series of parties at which a more or less integral "set" intermingle and interact to produce not a plot but rather an impression of a particular phase of contemporary life. The artistic method of *Parties* resembles that of atonal music and surrealistic art in that Van Vechten does not seek to impose order upon experience but rather to heighten an impression of the disharmony and disjunctiveness of experience, with the loud and discordant conversation of a party one of the principal means toward this effect.

Parties are the subject matter and theme of the novel. They occur in London, Paris, and New York for a full "season" of fall to spring and with a wide variety of participants. But basically there are three reappearing New York settings and a coherent group of celebrants. The places are the Wishbone speakeasy, Rosalie Keith's house, and the living room bar of the Westlakes' apartment. The principal participants are Rilda and David Westlake, their friend Hamish, the Gräfin and her protégé Roy Fern, the bootlegger Donald Bliss (who owns the Wishbone), Rosalie, Simone Fly, and the actress Midnight Blue.

The alcoholic party as a symbol of contemporary life has several meanings in the novel. It suggests on one hand the potential violence and physical debilitation of drinking to excess, and on the other the "exhilaration" and "pleasant glow" of drinking to precisely the right point where, for a moment, "every value is enhanced." To the Gräfin the party is indeed life enhancing and she finds in it friendship and gaiety and sparkle and openness. To David and Rilda the party is a narcotic addition, since they find in its drunkenness and enforced gregariousness an escape from their all-possessive love.

Parties contains almost all of the Jazz Age activities and preoccupations of Van Vechten's other novels—sexual promiscuity, homosexuality, alcoholism, Harlem, and Hollywood (through Midnight Blue)—but all appear with a sharper satiric edge than before. The Gräfin is now the sole remnant of a Campaspe-like ethic and power, while the Westlakes represent more fully than in any other Van Vechten novel the neurotic underside of a life of seeming pleasure and indulgence. Sex in particular in *Parties* is exploitative and self-aggrandizing, more a vengeance than a fulfillment. The darker tone of the novel is fully evident at one of Rosalie Keith's parties when a clairvoyant shatters the fragile self-protective masks of the guests by revealing the emptiness and shallowness of their essential natures. The structure of the novel also enforces through its circularity this theme of vacuity. The farcical "dream murder" of Roy Fern which opens the novel (David wakes up believing he has killed Roy at a drunken party the night before) is confirmed at its close in Roy's death, largely because of David, during a drunken party. And "partying" itself has a life-deadening, repetitious circularity, as David remarks at the party which closes the novel:

> Hamish and I will get drunk as usual this afternoon, and . . . we shall somehow manage to arrive at Rosalie's in time for dinner where, of course, we shall meet Rilda and . . . despite the fact we have purchased tickets to see Zimbule O'Grady in Buttered Toast, we shall spend most of the evening at Donald's and probably end up in Harlem. That is the life of our times in words of two syllables. I am not bitter about it. I accept it as the best we can do.

Parties maintains the high level of verbal wit, sexual farce, and satiric characterization of Van Vechten's other New York novels. But it goes beyond them in the brilliance of his evocation of the cacophony of New York—riveters hammering outside, loud drunken conversation within—and in the power of his use of the symbol of the party to suggest that gaiety is often not what it appears to be, that for many it is only a prison or a mask. *Parties* thus suggests that Van Vechten had come to accept fully a major corollary of his belief that self-discovery was the principal quality of the spirit of the age which he wished to communicate. For he now stressed that the superficially glamorous "scenes from contemporary . . . life" which were the context of self-discovery often disguised the "true tragedies" of mind and spirit which were inseparable from the pursuit of that ideal.

GORE VIDAL

1925–

Gore Vidal was born Eugene Luther Vidal, Jr., on October 3, 1925, in West Point, New York, to Eugene Luther and Nina Gore Vidal. His parents were divorced in 1935, and he thereafter lived intermittently with his grandfather, Senator Thomas Pryor Gore, whom Vidal has acknowledged as an influence upon his life. He was educated at Phillips Exeter Academy, then served in the army for three years. He worked as an editor at E. P. Dutton in 1946. Since then he has made his living as a full-time writer.

Vidal published his first novel, *Williwaw*, in 1946. Although atypical of Vidal's novels, it was praised at the time and was considered unusually restrained and mature for the work of a nineteen-year-old. His third novel, *The City and the Pillar* (1948), brought him national attention for its sympathetic portrayal of homosexuality. Because of the controversy surrounding the book Vidal found it difficult to get more than perfunctory attention from reviewers over the next several years, and his next five novels were neither bought by the public nor praised by critics, though in retrospect *The Judgment of Paris* (1952) and the SF novel *Messiah* (1954) show clear signs of artistic maturity. By the early 1950s, however, Vidal was forced to turn to pseudonymous mystery novels (writing as "Edgar Box") and television and movie scripting in order to support himself.

Vidal came once more to public attention with the production of his play *Visit to a Small Planet* (televised in 1955). Like most of his subsequent plays, it is bitingly satirical. Other significant plays include *The Best Man* (1960), *Romulus* (1962), and *An Evening with Richard Nixon* (1972). After a ten-year hiatus, Vidal returned to prose fiction with the novel *Julian* (1964). A fictional treatment of the life of the Roman emperor Julian the Apostate, it was a critical and commercial success, and since then Vidal has published a number of highly praised historical novels, including a trilogy about the growth of the American republic (*Washington, D.C.*, 1967; *Burr*, 1973; and *1876*, 1976); other historical novels are *Creation* (1981) and *Lincoln* (1984). Since the revival of his career in the early 1960s he has also published comic novels such as *Myra Breckinridge* (1968), *Myron* (1974), and *Duluth* (1983); this last is also a work of science fiction, as is the relatively more straightforward *Kalki*, an apocalyptic tale with some of the same elements as his earlier *Messiah*. A frequent critic of post-modernist and metafictive techniques in modern fiction, Vidal nonetheless makes use of them for both straight and satirical purposes, particularly in the partially autobiographical *Two Sisters* (1970). With all his novels since *Julian*, Vidal has received praise as a careful artist and craftsman, despite his considerable commercial success.

Vidal also has a notable reputation as an essayist; many critics feel his witty, acerbic, and polemical style is at its best in nonfictional forms. Significant collections of his essays include *Homage to Daniel Shays: Collected Essays 1952–1972* (1972), *Matters of Fact and of Fiction: Essays 1972–1976* (1977), and *The Second American Revolution* (1982). He has also published one collection of short stories, *A Thirsty Evil* (1956).

Unlike most serious writers, Vidal has moved easily throughout his life in the circles of wealth and power. Descended from a political family, Vidal also has familial connections with Jacqueline Bouvier Kennedy. In 1960 he ran as a Democrat for Congress from his home district in upstate New York; although he lost, he polled more votes than any Democrat in the district had done for decades. In the early years of the Kennedy administration he was often identified as a writer in favor at the White House; later, in 1968 and 1972, he served as a high official in various liberal third-party campaigns, notably as the "shadow Secretary of State" for Dr. Benjamin Spock's People's Party. In 1982 he ran in the Democratic Party primary for senator from California, again losing but again finishing better than expected. Throughout, despite his radicalism and his iconoclastic social views, Vidal has retained his standing as a member of America's aristocratic class—an unusual member, but an accepted one nonetheless.

Gore Vidal occupies an unusual position in American letters. He is simultaneously a popular artist, a political maverick, and an entertaining public performer, frequently seen on television and quoted in the popular press. It is doubtful that there exists in the United States a social and aesthetic thinker more persistently in the public view.

Personal

Gore came. We slide easily into a sincere, warm talk. He dropped his armor, his defenses. "I don't like women. They are either silly, giggly, like the girls in my set I'm expected to marry, or they are harsh and strident masculine intellectuals. You are neither."

Intellectually he knows everything. Psychologically he knows the meaning of his mother abandoning him when he was ten, to remarry and have other children. The insecurity which followed the second break he made, at nineteen, after a quarrel with his mother. His admiration, attachment, hatred, and criticalness. Nor is it pity, he says. He is proud that she is beautiful and loved, yet he condemns her possessiveness, her chaos, her willfulness, and revolts against it. He knows this. But he does not know why he cannot love.

His face, as the afternoon light changed, became clearer. The frown between his eyes disappeared. He was a child thrust out too soon, into a world of very famous, assertive, successful, power personalities. His mother confesses her life to him. He moves among men and women of achievement. He was cheated of a carefree childhood, of a happy adolescence. He was rushed into sophistication and into experience with the surface of himself, but the deeper self was secret and lonely.

"My demon is pride and arrogance," he said. "One you will never see."

I receive from him gentleness and trust. He first asked me not to write down what he would say. He carries his father's diplomatic brief case with his own poems and novel in it. He carries his responsibilities seriously, is careful not to let his one-night encounters know his name, his family. As future president of the United States, he protects his reputation, entrusts me with state secrets to lighten his solitude. Later he wants to write it all down, as we want to explore his secret labyrinth together, to find the secret of his ambivalence. To explore. Yet life has taken charge to alter the situation again. He, the lonely one, has trusted woman for the first time, and we start the journey of our friendship, as badly loved children who raised themselves, both stronger and weaker by it.

He suffers the consequences of his wartime frostbite, great malaises and neuritis. He suffers from black depressions. He is nearsighted. A boy without age, who talks like an old man. My other children do not accept him, understand him.

While all the society mothers are looking for him for their cocktails, dances, we may be talking quietly somewhere in a restaurant, a night club. A debutante wrote him: "Why are you so detached?" Gore attends the functions, bows, dances, leaves. Dear mothers and debutantes, can you give this boy back his childhood, his mother, his security, the warmth and understanding he needed then? Can you answer his thoughts, dialogue with his brightness, keep pace with his intelligence?

He came at four and left at midnight. He made me laugh with the most amazingly well acted pastiches of Roosevelt, Churchill, a southern senator, a petition at the House of Commons. He has a sense of satire.

He is very much concerned with establishing a contrast between Pablo, Marshall, and Charles, as adolescents not yet successful, not yet matured, and himself, already mature in his roles as writer, editor, etc.

"I give you the true Gore."

And then: "I'm coming Wednesday. Send the children away."

Wednesday I met Gore at a restaurant. He had news for me. Dutton had had an editorial conference, was offering an advance of one thousand dollars, and a contract for all the novels. We celebrated. He tells me I must finish the new book, *Ladders to Fire*, in two months. I am not sure I can do it, with the work at the press, the visitors.

Gore thinks I live a fantasy, that I see things that are not there, that I am inventing a world.

Gore's visits on Sunday now a habit. He brings his dreams written out, his early novel to show me: the one he wrote at seventeen, *Williwaw*.

I enjoy his quick responses. He never eludes. He holds his ground, answers, responds. He is firm and quick-witted. He has an intelligent awareness, is attentive and alert, and observant.

Part of the great fascination of Gore's age, and the children's, is the mystery of what they will become. One is watching growth. Unlike Wilson, who sits determined and formed, with opinions, judgments.

Already set, in these young men one sees the ambivalences and conflicts. Is the illumination which surrounds them that of hope? They are still tender, still vulnerable, still struggling.

Gore said: "I belong nowhere. I do not feel American. I do not feel at home in any world. I pass casually through all of them. I take no sides."

The writing I do has created a world which draws into it the people I want to live with, who want to live in my world. One can make a world out of paper and ink and words. They make good constructions, habitable refuges, with overdoses of oxygen.

"I think, dear Gore, that you choose to write about ordinary people in an ordinary world to mask the extraordinary you and the out-of-the-ordinary world in which you live, which is like mine. I feel in you imagination, poetry, intuition of worlds you do not trust because they are linked with your emotions and sensibilities. And you have to work far removed from that territory of feeling where danger lies."

To find the poet in Gore was more difficult. Leonard looked like a poet and a dreamer. Gore looks warm, near and realistic. But there it is, another inarticulate poet, a secret dreamer.

The direction of Gore's writing distresses me. But at twenty did I know my direction? At twenty I imitated D. H. Lawrence.

My never glorifying the famous, the achieved, powerful figures restores to Gore a sense of his individual value. I am not awed by success.

I do respond when he tells me about his worship of Amelia Earhart, and how shocked he was by her death. She was a friend of the family. Gore's father financed her fatal trip.

Gore has a feeling of power. He feels he can accomplish whatever he wishes. He has clarity and decisiveness. He is capable of leadership. This on the conscious, willful level. In the emotional realm, imagination and intuition are there, but not trusted. It may be that he associates them with softer and more feminine qualities he does not wish to develop in himself.

Gore's three evenings. One with a writer: a drinking bout. One escorting a debutante to the Victory Ball, and feeling stifled and bored. The third evening with me. He brings me a poem, two pages of childhood recollections, the fourth chapter of his novel, his physical troubles from the war, talks about his mother, his father, his childhood. Complains of a feeling of split, of unreality. Talks of death. Reveals the mystic. Obsessed, as Leonard was, by the circles.

Sunday. Midnight. Gore is sitting at the foot of the couch writing his play on the werewolf.

He said: "We met just at the right moment."

He reads my new book and likes it. He tells me his father read *This Hunger* and saw himself in Jay.

"But I won't let you meet him. He would like you too well, and you might like him too well. You might get along too well."

"Not better than you and I."

"It is so good to be oneself without poses," he said. ⟨. . .⟩

Gore says about my continuation of *This Hunger* into *Ladders to Fire*: "You have expanded in depth, now expand in width."

He finished his play and brought it as a Christmas present. It was intense and strong. "I've never written this way, impulsively, directly, and without plan." He was pale. Worn. I let him read my pages on adolescence and snow and the timidities of adolescent love.

Gore wanted to know when I would make his portrait. "I made it in the diary when you gave me permission."

"I gave you permission because I knew you would do it anyway."

He asked if he could read it.

I let him.

I was uneasy, anxious about unmasking him.

"I didn't mind being unmasked by you," said Gore.

The end of *Ladders to Fire* brings two worlds into opposition: nature and neurosis. The external world, the salon, the garden, the mirrors, and the reflections of them in the mirror. The sense of unreality in the neurotic comes when he is looking at the reflections of his life, when he is not at one with it.

Gore says his feeling about writing is changing. He wants color, magic. He is aware of the conventional mask of his first novel.

His hidden self is emerging. His imagination is manifesting itself in the play. He is no longer dying. There is a warm flush on his cheeks, and warmth in his voice. The frown has vanished.

He mocks his world, but draws strength from being in the *Social Register*, from his friends' high positions, from the power of his father and mother. He needs his class privileges. I was saddened by his vanity, his display of position. He was partly dependent on wordly attributes. Terribly in need of glorification. I saw his persona in the world. It was another Gore.—Anaïs Nin, *The Diary of Anaïs Nin: 1944–1947* (entry for Dec. 1945), ed. Gunther Stuhlmann, 1971, pp. 112–17

There is less dissimulation in the brilliant mind of Gore Vidal than almost any other writer-friend I have known. He seems to have none of most writers' apprehensions and timidities in their relation to "The Great Society," he doesn't care what he says or to whom he says it, and he sails along more valiantly all the time with his good looks, his social charm and poise, his wise but tolerant adjustment to "things as they are" in and out of "The G. S." And yet, marvelously, his lighthearted way of going along with the world does not at all make him a conventional artist. His world is never the world of a self-limiting and often self-pitying sensibility. It is the world of a modern Voltaire, and I have heard him publicly declare that he will live to be quite old, and I believe that, if he avoids a plane crash, he will travel very far indeed, knowing more and more as he goes and saying all that he knows, and saying it wittily, coolly and memorably.—Tennessee Williams, "Gore Vidal," *McCall's*, Oct. 1966, p. 107

Works

NOVELS

In the six years of his literary life Gore Vidal has had one of the strangest careers ever endured by a young writer of talent. As the 26-year-old author of seven serious novels dealing with a remarkable variety of subjects, he is easily the most precocious, versatile and prolific member of the newest generation of novelists now under 30. Yet I believe it is perfectly fair and accurate to say that Vidal has the least secure reputation of any of the contemporaries with whom he may legitimately be compared.

To understand the reason for this, one must first understand a peculiar and unfortunate fact about Vidal. Up to now in each of his novels he has shown himself to be the relatively rare sort of young writer in whom precocious creative energy is largely unaccompanied by precocious creative brilliance. His versatility has never been that of a restless and highly endowed talent testing out its abundant powers first on one subject and then another. It has been the versatility of a dedicated but somewhat average talent searching anxiously for the materials of a theme.

In sharp contrast to Truman Capote, who arrived on the literary scene fully equipped with a subject and a manner distinctly his own, Vidal has never been certain what his subject and his manner were. As a result, his novels have been like badly balanced darts thrown at a moving target. They have never been entirely successful because they have never known precisely where they were supposed to go. Too many of them appear to have been written not out of a deep urge in Vidal to get something said, but out of a disturbing suspicion that, having missed the target the first time, he had better throw another dart.

This compulsion to hurl his books at a theme rather than find a theme for his books has driven Vidal to undertake one of the most frenzied and wasteful apprenticeships in recent literary history. It has caused him to publish novels which he never should have published and others which he should have taken time to revise and complete. It has made him impatient before the job of learning his craft, with the result that not one of his novels since *Williwaw*, his first, has had unity of structure or style, not one of his characters has been adequately conceived or motivated, not one of his frequently excellent insights has been completely embodied in action.

The appearance of this new novel ⟨*The Judgment of Paris*⟩ is, therefore, a crucial event for Vidal; and I am glad to be able to say that, in most respects, it is a salutary one. To be sure, some of the old weaknesses still show through. The story lacks form, some of the incidents merely take up space, the characters harangue one another rather than converse, and many of them have no dramatic substance whatever. There are also some new weaknesses, such as Vidal's disturbing tendency to comment on the action in his own person and his rather sly use of characters out of the earlier novels. But *The Judgment of Paris* is the best and most ambitious of his novels, the richest in texture and the most carefully executed. In it, with the help of classical myth and a cosmopolitan setting, Vidal has found the way to a dramatic statement of his theme.

The story of the novel is a modern version of the ancient Greek legend of Paris and the Golden Apple of Eris or Discord. Vidal's Paris, a limp young man named Philip Warren whose problem is that he can feel nothing and love no one, wanders across Europe and Africa in vague search of romantic distraction. In the course of his travels he meets three temptresses, each of whom attempts to seduce him into positive action. Regina Durham, a contemporary Juno, offers him power and dominion in politics. Sophia Oliver, an archeological Minerva, offers him skill and knowledge in scholarship; while Anna Morris, a Venus become Helen of Troy, offers him a life of love.

But the legend of Paris is only a symbolic framework for the far more significant story which Vidal wishes to tell—the story, in the largest sense, of the modern conscience searching for truth in a world bereft of the ancient wisdom of the gods. Each of the three women in Philip Warren's life holds out to him the promise of a plausible faith; but for two of them, Regina and Sophia, the promise can be fulfilled only at the expense of Philip's humanity. Their way leads not to truth but to dogma; and dogma leads finally to the kind of self-deceiving mysticism indulged in by the mad monarchists and homosexual fanatics who try to entice Philip into their ranks. His decision to follow Anna's way is, therefore, a decision to affirm life in the only way it is possible to affirm it in an anti-human age, through an acceptance of one's self and, through one's self, of the love of another.

The necessity for self-discovery in love has been the buried theme of all of Vidal's work up to now. The fact that it has at last been brought to the surface and dramatized in a novel of genuine force and substance is the best of possible assurances that the long apprenticeship is finally coming to an end.—JOHN W. ALDRIDGE, "Three Tempted Him," *NYTBR*, March 9, 1952, pp. 4, 29

"To bring the dead to life," Robert Graves wrote, in one of his more memorable lyrics, "is no great magic": and there stands *I, Claudius*, that stunning pastiche of the fubsy, senescent Emperor's *ipsissima verba*, to demonstrate beyond cavil that Graves the novelist could fulfil Graves the poet's claim. This remarkable *tour de force* set something of a fashion. Since it appeared, a number of other Imperial ghost-raisers have been at work, conjuring the laurel-wreathed statues down from their plinths and turning them into dignified, indiscreet ventriloquists' dummies. Rex Warner gave us a prosy but professional Caesar, and Marguerite Yourcenar a stupendously solemn-aesthetic Hadrian. Now, jumping forward over two centuries, Gore Vidal has resurrected that unacknowledged humanists' culture-hero, Julian the Apostate—though perhaps "resurrected" is an unfortunate word to use in connection with the Emperor who called Christians "Galileans" and their churches "charnel-houses."

It was ungrateful of Mr. Vidal to make a mildly patronizing reference to Mr. Graves in his foreword, since of all the novels I have mentioned, *Julian* owes by far the biggest debt to that idiosyncratic style—relaxed, worldly-wise, full of neat in-group allusions and sub-Latinate sentence-endings—which Graves hammered out in the *Claudius* memoirs and *Count Belisarius*. On the other hand, Vidal has one rather ambiguous advantage which Graves did not: unlike most Emperors, Julian wrote a great deal that was not only sedulously applauded during his lifetime, but actually survived for posterity. We have his letters and orations (including a tongue-in-cheek encomium on the Emperor Constantius, his father's murderer), we have a satirical *Symposium* on earlier Caesars, which Gibbon, unaccountably, describes as "one of the most agreeable and instructive productions of ancient wit." We have a weird squib composed, in a fit of pique, at Antioch, and entitled *The Beard-Hater*, which suggests that Julian was not only puritanical but more than a little dotty. We do not, alas, have what would have been far more interesting—his private journal, his treatises on the Gallic and German wars, or his full-scale polemical assault on Christianity.

No reader can get very far into Julian's platitudinous, mock-classical prose without realizing that as a Hellenistic man of letters (which he liked to consider himself) the Apostate was a dead flop. Any intelligent novelist who sets out to impersonate him has my sincere sympathy, and Mr. Vidal is as bright as they come. He solves the problem, quite simply, by making Julian a far more witty and astrigent writer than in fact he was, and by interspersing his memoirs with acidulous comments from two ancient and bitchy rhetoricians, who are planning to edit the Emperor's *obiter dicta* for posterity. These marginal glosses are by far the most amusing part of the book, since in them Julian's weaknesses are exposed with uncommon vigor: his bogus mysticism ("that craving for the vague and incomprehensible which is essentially Asiatic"), his superstitious dabbling in arcane hocus-pocus, his priggishness, his prejudices, his inflated sense of grandeur.

On the whole, Mr. Vidal succeeds far beyond reasonable expectations, and when he fails it is generally because he refuses to fudge or distort intractable history. A surprisingly large part of Julian's life—he died at thirty-two, his liver transfixed by a Persian (or perhaps a Roman) javelin—was spent either in quasi-imprisonment or on the field of battle, neither of them situations offering much scope for the imaginative novelist. I wish Mr. Vidal had been more free with one enchanting device, hitherto unknown to me, for dodging round military set-pieces: "*Note to secretary* [Julian writes]: At this point insert relevant chapter from my book *The Gallic Wars*." We do, in the latter half of the book at any rate, get far too much hacking and slashing—but then the odd thing about Julian is that, against all expectation, he turned out a brilliant and imaginative field-commander, who beat hell out of the Gauls and Germans in a way that had not been seen since Julius Caesar's expeditions.

Mr. Vidal chronicles Julian's early days with immense relish and a wealth of convincing detail: the constant nagging fear of execution at his cousin's hands, the uneasy relationship with his sadistic half-brother Gallus, the insane theological disputes, the ubiquitous secret agents, and, above all, Constantius' court, with its monstrous regiment of eunuchs and labyrinthine protocol. The narrative suffers a little for lack of what the tabloids call a sex-angle: Julian was never much one for the girls, and became celibate after his wife's death—not surprisingly, perhaps, since she was a middle-aged horror dumped on him for dynastic reasons. Mr. Vidal provides the young Athens student with some semi-wild oats in the shape of an inky-fingered philosopher's niece, who nags him briskly into bed and talks a blue streak up to and during orgasm. Otherwise we have to make do with a little sadism and (something for the connoisseurs) a eunuch's palace orgy.

Long stretches of *Julian* are good, competent Graves-and-gravy, well researched, graphically presented, but not telling us much more, really, than we could get from leafing through Ammianus Marcellinus or Gibbon. Where Mr. Vidal scores is in his vigorous grasp of Fourth-Century *ideas:* he plots the moral and spiritual climate much more clearly than Graves bothered, or indeed needed to do. Behind the embattled Arians and Athanasians we glimpse the bumbling *clochardisme* of the New (new?) Cynicism; and beyond them both move the mystery-mongers and the thaumaturgists, for whom Julian had so regrettable a partiality. Delphi sends its dusty answer, Eleusis offers no salvation. Julian's fate—Mr. Vidal sees this very clearly—was to be a Christian mystic *manqué* in an era of bad Christians, a great pagan Emperor struggling in vain to resuscitate the rotten corpse of paganism, a man, if ever there was one, born out of his age, slandered by Christians, praised for the wrong reasons by his friends. (Even his alleged dying words, *Vicisti Galilaee!*, which are all that many people connect with his name, were fabricated a century after his death by Theodoret.) Mr. Vidal's ambitious novel is a more balanced appraisal than any which Julian received in antiquity, and arguably, the best thing of its kind since *Count Belisarius:* a book to buy rather than borrow.—PETER GREEN, "Resuscitated Emperor," *NR*, June 13, 1964, pp. 23–24

Any panoramic novel, like any technicolor epic, is likely to seem trashy these days. The necessary elisions of scene and character have been given a bad name by fifty years or more of junk: historical novels, news magazines, digests, the lot. If the panoramic novel deals with U.S. politics it carries a double burden. For, as every small child knows, our public life has long since been processed, inflated, and simplified to the point of incredibility: so that a book about such gross unrealities as the outbreak of war or the rise of Senator McCarthy is already halfway to a Bible movie.

And then, there is that impossible setting. Washington, D.C. must be the dullest capital city in the world to write about outside of Canberra, Australia. Its social life comes through as a brackish blend of Northern hospitality and Southern vitality, which, combined with the bleached man-of-distinction sets and the notoriously poor quality of the acting, is more than enough to explain the absence of good political novels in this country. Gore Vidal has been accused of creating cardboard characters in ⟨*Washington, D.C.*⟩, but if they were not cardboard, they would be truly unbelievable.

Thus, Vidal has set himself a brutal task: to play Trollope in the land of Alan Drury. He takes us into the stage politician's boudoir—and finds him performing just like a stage politician; he digs below the surface of a typical senator and comes upon nothing but more senator. Unless the whole thing is a terrible mistake, it would seem that the author is in the same bind as the Hollywood novelist: the more he tells the truth, the more artificial and journalistic he sounds.

For the first couple of hundred pages, the going is just as sticky as you would imagine. Prior to his last book, *Julian*, Vidal had been away from the novel for quite a while, and his style shows it. He seems to have forgotten what you do with the spaces in between the dialogue, and has crammed them with he-looked-at-him-sourly's and she-grinned-at-him-crookedly's plus a catty, worldly-wise commentary which is clearly coming from some place outside the story and punctures any illusion that any of this is really happening.

To make matters slightly worse, he jumps in and out of his characters' heads pretty much *ad lib*: and what he finds there turns out to be remarkably similar. This may be the truth about official Washington, but it only serves to make a flat situation flatter. The good guys and the bad all draw from the same fund of stoic wisdom, Vidal's private stock. It heightens the pulp fiction effect to hear the same point of view expressed four different ways, or rather one way under four different sponsors. It is like three roommates staying in bed while the fourth one wears the suit.

These are serious defects: and yet, if you have the patience to stay with Vidal (several reviewers, I suspect, didn't) you will observe that he turns them in the end to something like advantage. For it seems that pop fiction with all its superficiality and melodrama is not a bad medium for discussing our government. It is part of Vidal's message about Washington that personality does indeed not matter, that situation is everything; government people are ultimately not people at all, but points in space, clustering and separating like atomic particles. Their existence might be defined as pure relationship.

Thus our puzzle at finding so many people motivated by the same brand of cynicism is at least partly cleared up—cynicism is not a motive at all, but a reaction. It is what a rational man feels at the end of the day. The motive is much simpler: you play the game simply because you are on the field. You find the ball in your hands and you run like hell. If you are reflective, you sometimes wonder afterward why you did: but it doesn't matter what you decide about that. The philosophizing is done on your own time.

Whether or not this proposition stands up historically, Vidal has written a very plausible story about it. The heart of it, leaving out side orders of adultery, buggery, and incest, goes like this. An elderly senator named Burden Day is prettily conned out of his Presidential ambitions by President Roosevelt, and then methodically chopped down by a young man in his own office, one Clay Overbury: a heartless streamlined new-thing politician zooming down the middle of the road past the old buggies on the right. Abetting Overbury is an evilminded presslord named Blaise Sanford who helps to concoct a wonderful war record for him and to stomp on any loose enemies. (Vidal's feelings about the Kennedy family are all too well known by now, and one looks for parallels here, but the author has been deft: Overbury is not nor has he ever been, altogether, a Kennedy.)

This version squares almost too well with an outsider's paranoid nightmares about our leaders. Wars, depressions, Communist scares are almost as unreal to these men as they are to us. Their only reality is as opportunities for self-advancement. World War II was image-making time. The McCarthy foolishness was a time to settle scores—with a hand over one's own groin of course. And so on. Even dear old Senator Day, the courtly old patsy from another era, has only one serious conviction, and this is more on the lines of a hobby: he believes that the Japanese-Americans got a raw deal during the war. Characteristically, this nearly destroys him politically.

No doubt the history of our times can be explained in these terms, as in so many other terms. Vidal gives us a neat parallel to this when he observes that the professional politicians could not tolerate the idea that Eleanor Roosevelt acted out of altruism and only accepted her after they had convinced themselves that she was acting cynically. There may be a touch of this in Mr. Vidal. (After all, it was *possible* to explain Eleanor in those terms.)

But as might be expected, this philosophy of politics by Drew Pearson out of Ayn Rand is harder to establish psychologically. For instance, Clay Overbury is presented as a completely empty man, moved only by a simple power mechanism. But his emptiness is demonstrated simply by leaving things out. In the end, we don't know enough about him to know whether he is really empty or not. It is inconceivable that any man of ability has ever gone around thinking, "I want power"; what he thinks is, "I want this and I want that," and from this we deduce that what he wants is power. Vidal has omitted the concrete symbols of emptiness. To put it another way, a man may be empty in effect, without being so to himself.

Overbury wants nothing at all. He hasn't even a phony dream of the Presidency to keep him going, only a dull upward reflex. All right, one grants the possibility—you about this politician, I about that one—but we must allow *something* in his head besides these Max Lerner abstractions. Overbury is not even permitted to like girls—he only likes his power over girls. If Vidal were writing about a real character, I would call this a vindictive refusal of imagination. Even Kennedys are not that cool. At that, Clay Overbury might be barely acceptable if he were the only frostbitten robot in the book. But his patron Blaise Sanford turns out to be another one. It seems he is backing Clay because of a *fascination with power*. Even the official nice guy, Blaise's son Peter, is frozen solid, although attractively so: he starts a left-wing magazine with neither faith nor enthusiasm. So it goes, down to the sexual arrangements of the minorest characters.

The trouble is built into the author's method. You can't tell where his melancholy aphorisms are coming from half the time, and it really makes no difference. Everyone has arrived at the same plateau of intelligence and inner detachment as the author. Even the men of action speak with a literary man's sense of futility. Not only is their game meaningless, but they are condemned to know it, like so many saints and philosophers. This somehow does not sound right for Washington.

The book would improve enormously if the characters' interiors were removed altogether. Their actions are convincing and so is their dialogue. If the author wants to play Marcus Aurelius to them, he should play it by himself. The characters should be allowed to think that they are accomplishing something, even if Vidal knows better. The game is not interesting if nobody believes in it. And the game as played in this book requires a more specific dedication than his characters seem capable of.

It could be that Vidal's various talents have worked against each other here. He is a playwright, and *Washington, D.C.* would probably make a truthful play. He is also an essayist, and *Washington, D.C.* might even, who knows, make a truthful essay. But a play and an essay put together do not make a novel: the urbane overview of the essayist rings false when foisted onto people-in-action, and the playwright's flower arrangements are bunched too closely for a longish novel. Yet the story is good, the wit is medium-to-good, and there is a nice air of gossipy bustle. And this does sound right for Washington.—Wilfrid Sheed, "Affairs of State," *Cmty*, Sept. 1967, pp. 93–94

The high baroque comedy of bad taste is a rare genre. *Myra Breckinridge* belongs to it and is a masterpiece: the funniest event since *Some Like It Hot* (and some can't recommend more hotly than that).

By plausible grace of 'the operation', the old transvestite fantasy-joke has been emotionally stepped-up into transsexualism. Myra is in fact Myron as was—a piece of information the narrative withholds conceivably just a touch too long, but forgivably, since Myra as first-person narrator is splendidly adept at, so to speak, keeping her balls in the air.

The getting-under-way mechanics of the plot form a shaft rigid and driving enough to pin the book's exuberance together: how (pointed question indeed) is Myra, posing as the widow of a Myron supposedly defunct in New York, to possess herself of Myron's inheritance which she has come to California to claim? It consists of a share in an academy of (cine)dramatic art run by Myron's uncle, an ex-singing cowboy of radio and movies, whose unpunctuated, formless recorded discourses intersperse Myra's own narrative, providing a view of her in the round and, by the contrast, in the fully literate.

What, however, makes the work an air-borne imaginative vehicle is the personality of Myra and the language Mr Vidal has fashioned for its self-expression. Vertical take-off happens at the very start, when Myra strikes one of the wide-screen-heroic poses from her fantasy life against a naturalistic background of pedantically pressed and dried snippets of anthropology: 'I am Myra Breckinridge whom no man will ever possess. Clad only in garter belt and one dress shield, I held off the entire élite of the Trobriand Islanders, a race who possess no words for "why" or "because".'

From then on, Myra is in bold, controlled, mastermistressly flight. The book's artistic toughness is hers personally. Her camp draperies, such as her erudition about old films, are no wisps but precise cutting edges. She swishes them in majestic scythe-strokes of scorn, meanwhile hissing in near-Nabokovian vituperative pedantry, against the stupidity, philistinism, intellectual pretentiousness-and-superficiality and conformism of our society. (I'd love to read her on the subject of the jacket of the English edition, which is no transvestment but sheer travesty.) Myra isn't bitchy. She's pardic.

It is from this personality itself that Mr Vidal spins the later development of the plot, which is an intricate, decorative, steel-hard trap. Myra is pursuing Myron's revenge against the college boys who excited him to sexual desire but intellectual contempt. Myra picks the most college-boy college boy at her dramatic academy and imposes on him her bizarre and brilliant triumph. By the tragic inevitability that forms the iron, ironic skeleton of all great comedy, it is her own hubris that brings on her the accident whereby her transformation is undone. Myron is re-virilised and, by the same stroke, intellectually castrated. The end is nightmare, and by an inspired reversal of the sci-fi conventions the nightmare consists in the triumph not of fantasy but of conformism. Myron marries the college boy's girl and lives suburbanly ever after. The way we actually live now is horror enough.

The trans-sex fantasy explodes, I suspect, at a level even deeper than the one from which it liberates the homosexual imprisoned in every heterosexual—and also, of course, the heterosexual in every homosexual (for what, after all, was a respectable, presumed-exclusive queer like Myron *doing* taking such an erotically detailed interest in lady film stars?). Conceivably it carries us right back to the good old pre-, even bi-, sexual days, when we were in genuine intellectual doubt about which sex *was* which, let alone whether we wanted to have or be mama. (And if they opt for *be*, little girls as well as little boys have to go into drag and have recourse to padding.) It is because of the area of interchangeability between *have* and *be* that a superficial observer might have misconstrued Myron's interest in those big-and-glittering hypnotic images of mama as one first remembers her—film actresses. And Myra, of course, is fully intelligent and self-aware enough to know that what she has made herself is a maternal deity.

Possibly the splendid odour of bad taste (bad taste is a far more useful gift for an artist than good taste) which attends the trans-sex joke represents the actual intellectual uncertainty infants feel about the anatomy of the sexes. Classicising, classifying intellectual activity is very likely the psychological successor of the first great intellectual feat of getting the sexes correctly sorted out. In that case, it must be a baroque work which re-confuses them and brings back that tang of infantile uncertainty. For baroque is the art of wreaking an explosion deep inside the classical structure and re-assorting the classical elements into an incongruity grotesque, ironic, comic, barbarically majestic or all at once, but always—by virtue of the discipline which creates a new form to hold the lurching elements together—beautiful. The baroque incongruity of pediment and dome juxtaposed on the same structure is equivalent to finding Myra's (artificial, plastic-surgeon-made) breasts on Myron's torso.

Because the baroque is so analytically formal, the baroque mode and his baroque subject-matter are a perfect metaphor for Mr Vidal's satirical purpose. He finds intellectual sloppiness destructive. He destroys it by an explosive, centrifugal force far more inherently destructive than its enemy, but which he controls and creatively deploys into an artistic form. Myra's intelligence and the intelligence of the book's design are alike unremitting. Her fake breasts soar and bounce, but the book whale-bones them into a beautifully architectural bodice.

After Myra's, which are 'reminiscent of those sported by Jean Harlow in *Hell's Angels* and seen at their best four minutes after the start of the second reel', Candy's 'pert, inquisitive young breasts' have all the fushionlessness of the natural.—BRIGID BROPHY, "The Tang of Uncertainty," *LT*, Sept. 26, 1968, p. 412

It seems to me that *Burr* is Mr. Vidal's witty revenge on an America he doesn't like very much. It gives him an opportunity to snap at the ankles of the Founding Fathers, and some of them did have fat ankles. The portraits in *Burr* of Washington and Jefferson might have been done by Diane Arbus. Nobody is going to tear down the monument to one or the memorial to the other as a result of these pages—graffiti on marble—but it is useful to be reminded that the heads on our coins and our paper currency were, in their day, full of mean schemes, colossal vanities, low cunning, even a libidinal twitch or two. It is the pseudo-Greek solemnity of post-Jeffersonian America that especially annoys Mr. Vidal; he has his own Greece, and it is a lighter thing by far. Rather surprisingly like D. H. Lawrence, Mr. Vidal seems to feel that democracy is based on envy; it is interesting only inasmuch as it releases certain energies from unsuspected sources. Energy, of course, is very interesting. When, however, the lawyers put on wigs and send out press releases announcing that they are philosopher-kings, Mr. Vidal unfastens the safety-catch on his quill-pen.

Moreover, when Jefferson as President refuses to turn over Government documents to the court trying Aaron Burr for treason—a court presided over by John Marshall, Jefferson's cousin and enemy—we have a nice parallel with the Watergate tapes. It is not an exploitative parallel of the Lance Zeitgeist sort (instant-fiction-just-add-bile-and-mix-with-headlines); clearly Vidal had finished *Burr* before any of us knew that Nixon was bugging himself. But certainly the Supreme Court will soon be looking at the way John Marshall resolved his predicament; and just as certainly, what Vidal has to say about civil liberties cuts close to our current boneheadedness.

Why pick on Aaron Burr to be your hero, aside from the exercise of making a plausible case for his patriotism and a marvelous guess at what actually drove him to challenge Hamilton to a duel? Julian the Apostate tried to reinstitute paganism in the 4th century; Vidal was understandably sympathetic to this endeavor. But Burr? He was an adventurer. There was a lot of pirate in him, and of this, too, Vidal apparently approves: if one is to deal with something as rude as an American, let him be a pirate, without rhetorical wiggery, a swashbuckler who wants to invade Mexico because he is bored with New York; a gambler. The other week in the 10th anniversary issue of *The New York Review of Books*, Mr. Vidal was explaining that he is descended from Roman legionnaires, that the men in his family had been professional soldiers for several centuries, that his father went to West Point. Ah, there is a little bit of atavism in us all.

Anyway, there aren't many writers around today who can put together sentences as craftily as Gore Vidal, who promise a story and deliver it as well, for whom wit is not a mechanical toy that explodes in the face of the reader but a feather that tickles the bare feet of the imagination. Not to read *Burr* is to cheat yourself of considerable charm, intelligence and provocation.—JOHN LEONARD, "Vidal—Another Opinion," *NYTBR*, Oct. 28, 1973, p. 55

It is rare for a sequel to be an improvement on the original, but *Myron* takes over where *Myra Breckinridge* left off in more than the literal sense. Gore Vidal is clearly at the height of his literary powers: just as *Burr* consolidated the qualities of his earlier historical novels and made a considerable advance on them, so the basic joke established by *Myra Breckinridge* is used in *Myron* as a launching-pad for increasingly dazzling and outrageous elaborations. These twin exercises in cerebral fantasy are unlike anything else in literature, except perhaps the two *Alices*. It is often said, I think unjustly, that Vidal the brilliant essayist succeeds while Vidal the competent novelist never quite makes it. *Myron* may not measure up to some purists' ideal of a novel, but its originality is undeniable. So too is the hermetic shapeliness of its construction, which is elegant without being precious. It is also very funny.

Myron Breckinridge, trying to forget his embarrassing past, has settled down as a cosily married supporter of Nixon in the middle of Middle America. One evening his alter ego, the unpredictable Myra, who has all this time been dormant rather than dead, pushes him through the television set and back twenty-five years into the back lot of MGM where Maria Montez, Bruce Cabot and Louis Calhern are starring in a movie called *Siren of Babylon*. Myra then schemes to regain ascendancy over Myron, whose person she needs for some ambitious plans of her own. Exquisitely ingenious tricks are played with the temporal and sexual dualities resulting from this complex situation; and the narrative is shared between Myra and Myron, who engage in a running verbal battle of insult and innuendo reminiscent of such comedy duos (a bit before your time, Myra) as Marie Dressler and Polly Moran in *Politics*, *Reducing* and *Caught Short*.

Like most moviegoers in the 1940s, Myra ignores the contribution to the medium made by directors and is only concerned with the star system. By adding some subliminal shots of nudity to *Siren of Babylon* that were not in the script, she hopes to turn the vehicle from a floperoo into an all-time box-office grosser. This, she reasons, will "put Metro out of the red" in 1948 and thus preserve the future not only from the bogus literary pretensions of Bertolucci and Peckinpah but also from the tatty squalor of the Watergate scandal. In her perverse way, Myra is a culture-snob; her apparent philistinism is an assault on artiness, not on art.

This is dimly recognized by her arch-enemy, Mr Williams, an Uncle Tom figure who has been over-educated into a sinister parody of Henry James. Mr Williams is dedicated to destroying the cinema, that "most depressing and demoralising of all pseudo-art forms", and restoring the primacy of The Word. His hint that "the golden bowel has begun ever so slightly to most beautifully crack" is lost on Myron, but he openly crows to Myra about "the young people of the seventies who laugh at Lana Turner as they read Holkein and Tesse and Vonchon and Pynegutt". Myra replies with dignity: "I see your grand design, Mr Williams, and I am happy to be able to shatter it. You are my creation." "No! No, Breckinridge," says Mr Williams, "You are my aberration."

The "uppity dinge from Albany, New York" has a point here: Myra is herself the creation of a highly sophisticated literary imagination and, if her aberrant logic acquires the destructive power of a comic myth (for Myra is satisfied with nothing less than mythic status), it is because of the purely verbal ingenuity that gives it expression. Mr Vidal's device of substituting the names of seven American "warriors in the battle against smut" for the words which might have offended them seems at first an amusingly insolent, if rather obvious, prank. It is exploited, however, with consummate invention and wit: Mr Vidal has as much linguistic fun with burger, rehnquist, powell, whizzer white, blackmun, keating and father hills as Raymond Queneau does with his refinements on Parisian slang.

One of the key movies in Myra's pantheon is (naturally) *Four Jills in a Jeep*, which put Kay Francis, Carole Landis,

Martha Raye and Aline MacMahon into uniform and sent them to Europe to entertain the troops (with guest appearances by Alice Faye and Betty Grable). When Myra wants to be warm and gracious like Kay Francis, she "jills" in a throaty lisp; when she needs to be tough and sexy like Carole Landis, she aggressively "jeeps". By their nature silly, such obsessions may also be semantically fruitful; Mr Vidal has added two useful new verbs to the language. His scurrilous satires on Truman Capote (a gossipy hairdresser) and Norman Mailer (a cook from Philly with a fat blackmun) are perhaps nearer to *Private Eye* than to *Finnegans Wake;* but only Max Beerbohm could have equalled the creative pastiche of Myron's "amusing" monograph, "Penny Singleton and Sally Eilers: The Orality of Florality" and his "masterpiece", "The Banality of Anality or *Thirty Seconds over Tokyo*: The Gunner's View".

The book's funniest effects come from the exalted lunacy of Myra's *Weltanschauung* and the prosaic briskness with which she translates it into action. Her great moment arrives when she actually *becomes* Maria Montez. Needless to say, she rises beautifully to the challenge (and so does Mr Vidal) in spite of a few minor disappointments stemming from Maria's marriage to "Gallic heartthrob Jean-Pierre Aumont"—"Not only does he keep talking French to me but the only people we ever see in this town are *not* Lana, Judy, Bette and Dolores Moran, who are at their zenith, but all the goddamned French actors like Charles Boyer. . . ." (She does, on one unforgettable occasion, meet Judy, and offers her some sisterly advice. "What the burger business is it of yours?" asks the bewildered star.)

As a sideline to her rescue operation on MGM, Myra also proposes to save the world from overpopulation and its attendant horrors of famine, war and plague by the radical solution of emasculating the prototype of the all-American stud. In her Book of Revelations, the Four Horsemen of the Apocalypse (Alice Terry, 1921) would be replaced by the Four Jills in a Jeep (see above). Hence the famous buggery setpiece in *Myra Breckinridge* and the sly variation on it in *Myron*—nearly a rescue operation in all too literal fact. Anticipating the "deschooled society" of Ivan Illich, her Master Plan would de-sex the Universe and people it with "sterile, fun-loving Amazons". Myra thinks big.

Yet, in her way, she is even more conservative than Myron, who signs off in 1973 "by saying that the highly articulate silent majority to which I am darned proud to belong are happy with things as they are and that we are not going to let anybody, repeat *anbody*, change things from what they are". Myra's aesthetic revolution would only turn the clock back to the Golden Age of Hollywood—and then stop it for ever. Lana Turner for President! It—or something like it—might still happen. I would appreciate Myra's thinking on the mythic qualities of that potential superstar Margaret Thatcher (no relation to Heather Thatcher, who never really got going in Hollywood in spite of her monocle, but made a distinct impression in *Fools for Scandal, But the Flesh Is Weak* and *Mama Steps Out*).—FRANCIS WYNDHAM, "Hooray for Hollywood," *TLS*, April 11, 1975, p. 389

"Son of Burr" has propitiously arrived this Bicentennial year in the craftily appropriate form of *1876*. For Gore Vidal is above all a master craftsman with the ability to interweave grand historical warp with fictional woof in a manner which is—like Vidal himself—both plausible and preposterous.

Drawing on the controversial political election of 1876 as well as his own literary history for this most recent dramatization of American politics, Vidal again speaks in the cynically detached voice of the hypothetical Charles Schermerhorn Schuyler, illegitimate son of Aaron Burr and ostensible biographer of that shrewd adventurer who sought to topple Jefferson and conquer Mexico—as chronicled by Schuyler/Vidal in *Burr*, his best-seller of 1973.

Schuyler, returning to America in late 1875 with his daughter Emma (the widowed Princess d'Agrigente) after a thirty-seven-year absence, plunges into the political and social intrigue of New York and Washington City in order to restore his fortune and literary reputation—and to marry off his lovely, worldly daughter. Through Schuyler's explorations of the changed city, Vidal enables us to imbibe the flavor of high society among the Astors, Belmonts, et al., in their uptown brownstones—as well as that of the low downtown society of such social sewers as Five Points (where Schuyler had spent time as a young man in *Burr*), and the more recently shady areas beneath the elevated railway along Sixth Avenue.

The point in time is felicitously chosen, benefiting not only Vidal but readers for whom the political issues and ambience of a century ago are only rather vague, although they are represented here as not so dissimilar to those of our own times. Gen. Ulysses S. Grant is the incumbent President, seen as increasingly unlikely to succeed himself after the financial panic of 1873 and a series of scandals during his administration. Gov. Samuel Tilden of New York is the favored Democratic candidate, supported by Schuyler—who hopes to be appointed his envoy to France and live out his remaining days in the country where he and his daughter have spent most of their years abroad.

Schuyler's daughter Emma, born in Europe and speaking French more fluently than English, looks on the social and political shenanigans of New York and Washington as the antics of a theatre of the absurd. When she goes to Washington with Schuyler, who will write about the elections for the New York *Herald*, Emma delightedly qualifies as "African" the subtropical, predominantly black city with its savage white politicians. The brass spittoons, the smoke-filled rooms, the Capitol cloakrooms crowded with lobbyists, the beards and other facial festoonery, and above all the cynical and self-serving manipulations of the primitive politicians—the "Africans"—are so palpably described that one is loath to doubt the authenticity of any detail.

Certainly passing through these segments of American history with Vidal as cicerone is more entertaining—and possibly more enlightening, if more disillusioning—than reading the dry record. It is tempting to remark that in the way of history Vidal writes plausible literature, and in the way of literature he writes lively history; but I think this does injustice to his skill at combining the two. Given the facts (as he has assiduously pursued them), his characterizations of the people who perpetrated the memorable events of our history are astute and credible. As the Baron Jacobi says, "We *cannot* know any history, truly. I suppose somewhere, in Heaven perhaps, there is a Platonic history of the world, a precise true record. But what we think to be history is nothing but fiction. Isn't that so, Mr. Schuyler? I appeal to you, perversely, since you are an historian."

"And therefore a novelist?" Schuyler replies.

"*Malgré vous*," says the Baron.

Reading *1876* is a pleasure that satisfies the curiosity and intellect but requires little else of the reader—except occasional pushing. I could almost have written this review without having read the book, so predictable have Vidal's political novels become. Not, of course, in their intriguing particulars but in their dry, witty revelations of roguery in high places, their elegantly portrayed personae driven by not so varying degrees of greed for money, sex, power—especially power, for which the first two are usually vehicles. While these may be elemental forces in us all, there is a human dimension lacking in these brightly brittle characters, limited—except for Schuyler's brief, touching reflections on his own mortality—to their pyrotechnical verbal displays and power plays. One would like to believe more in their possible nobility, and less in their pervading knavery.

1876, as Vidal points out in his Afterword, forms the midpoint of a trilogy (a literary form he claims to deplore). With *Burr* starting off in Revolutionary times and *Washington, D. C.* taking us to "the beginning of Camelot," these two historical novels form a kind of matrix in which *1876* is embedded. 1976 is an auspicious time for this parturition, in the wake of Vietnam and Watergate, for the era is not unlike the aftermath of the Civil War and the Whiskey Ring and the railroad scandals of a century ago. The Republican Presidency too, under U.S. Grant, bears some resemblance to that of our Ford, as do the continuing exposés of wrongdoing and the unseemly scrambling among the candidates.

If Vidal cannot become President himself, a dream he once nurtured, he can at least write about Presidents and those who intrigue with and around them, cutting them all down to size with his rapier pen. (Not an entirely anachronistic image, for Vidal says that he drafts his writings in pen rather than by typewriter—that newfangled machine just introduced in Schuyler's time—and would no doubt prefer to use quail's quill if it were available.) He cannot resist, too, taking slashes at Mark Twain, along with other popular writers and with pompous publications like *The New York Times* (*The Nation*, almost uniquely, comes off well—even in its infancy virtuous and underpaying). Vidal is suspicious of his own popularity with the reading masses, and has often commented that he "must be doing something wrong." As long as he does not risk moving readers—and himself—to any degree of emotion or action that may be considered "revolutionary" (not just titillatingly "rocking the boat," the title of one of his essay collections), he will no doubt safely continue "doing something wrong," selling well and moving many to admiration of his elegantly elaborated political gossip.

Vidal's competent craft has carried him well these thirty years—"like little wanton boys that swim on bladders / this many summers in a sea of glory"—bearing us provocative pleasures. As for Charles Schuyler, his pen is stilled, in his 64th year, by high living and low politics—or perhaps just by having fulfilled his mission: seeing his daughter's future secure and recording this scurrilously entertaining piece of the past. But history stumbles on and Vidal is still with us to illuminate the recesses of power with his prismatic perceptions, inevitably distorting but ever bedazzling.—ANN MORRISSETT DAVIDON, "Doing Well by Doing Wrong," *Nation*, April 17, 1976, pp. 474–75

Until now, Gore Vidal's fiction has mostly been wickedly clever. With his latest novel, *Kalki*, Vidal ascends into a new category: diabolically clever. I say "diabolically" rather than the more innocuous "devilishly" because what has increased is not the cleverness but the nastiness. *Kalki* is a hybrid: part social satire; part slick entertainment (in the Graham Greeneian sense); and part doomsday comedy in the manner of, say, Stanley Kubrick's cinematic black comedy, *Dr. Strangelove*.

Some of Vidal's diabolism manifests itself right away, in the plot's construction. For *Kalki* is a thriller, and by an ancient and honored custom, reviewers are not allowed to give away the main twist in a thriller's plot. What comes to their aid, however, is that the twist tends to be a single fact near the end of the book, one that the critique can easily sidestep. Here, however, the presumably unbetrayable twist comes much earlier and permeates and affects everything before and after it, just about tying a reviewer's hands before he can properly begin.

Still, if I tell you that in *Kalki* the world does come to an end, I am not committing an unpardonable crime. For such is Vidal's cleverness that the suspense continues beyond Armageddon and hinges on such fascinating posers as "Will anyone survive?" and "If so, who?" and, above all, "Can a new race arise, and if so, what will it be like?" With such tricks still up his sleeve, Vidal can go on flaunting his mastery of suspense within suspense. And about his eschatology—or is it dysteleology?—I shall keep strictly mum.

The heroine and narrator of *Kalki* is Teddy Ottinger, divorced and self-sterilized mother of two, champion aviatrix and Amelia Earhart idolater, and perpetual student of engineering and the humanities, with a dominant interest in French literature—particularly Pascal. Teddy is also the nominal author of *Beyond Motherhood*, ghostwritten by one Herman V. Weiss, hack. Furthermore, she is a practicing bisexual with a preference for lesbianism, living with Arlene Wagstaff, aged forty-two plus, who is a sort of combination Arlene Francis and Barbara Walters, plus, of course, Vidal's vivid fantasy. Teddy has at least a working knowledge of a great many other things, and herein lies the novel's first problem: She is too multi-farious to be a fully believable character. At the very least, she is distressingly twofold: the bright, enterprising, but also eminently fallible thirty-four-year-old female dilettante and the omniscient author of *Kalki*—well, at least as omniscient as Vidal is capable of being: say, somewhere far beyond your standard entertainment writer but still this side of Pico della Mirandola.

Not only is Teddy at least two people, she also is at least two styles—perhaps rightly so for a bisexual, about whom one of her presumably favorite authors might have said, "The styles are the man-woman." Though much of what she sets down is sharp, pertinent, and virilely concise, she will also resort to the kind of sneaky shortcut appropriate to what used to be referred to with the now justly obsolete term "the weaker sex." At such times, Teddy (or Vidal) merely invokes a phrase like "as H. V. Weiss would have put it" and blithely plunges into blatant platitude. And even when she is not Weissianizing, Teddy fluctuates disturbingly between an enlightened best seller style (better, to be sure, than an unenlightened one) and an intermittent finer thing. Exactly what that is is hard to define; call it an American approximation of Evelyn Waugh—just as deadly, but a shade less funny.

Here enters the second problem. Vidal conceives of the novel as a receptacle for all of his personal gripes. Settling a personal score by dragging in a real person from left field seems needlessly bitchy. And not only bitchy but also something worse: essayistic rather than novelistic. There was, of course, a style of novel writing in the eighteenth century that could accommodate the odd essayistic excursus, but amid Vidal's fast, nervous forward movement even a clever disquisition on Jewish princes and princesses in fact and fiction feels inappropriate—to say nothing of a less skillful harangue against politicians. Moreover, Vidal often makes things too easy for himself, as when he describes Weiss as a "cliché master and structuralist" and demonstrates only the former sin. I happen to dislike structuralism every bit as much as Vidal does, but guilt by association is not an honorable procedure even in fiction.

A word or two about the plot now seems indicated. A new incarnation of the god Vishnu appears to have materialized in Nepal. This Kalki, as he calls himself, whose cult is rapidly encircling the globe, preaches the proximate end of the world and the chance for his converts to be in line for eventual reincarnation rather than face the irredeemable destruction that awaits everyone else. For some reason, Kalki—who turns out to be ex-sergeant Jim Kelly from New Orleans, who was assigned to a chemical warfare unit in Vietnam and who may be using this religious revival as a front for his international dope racket—wants no one but Teddy Ottinger to write the series of articles with which *The National Sun* hopes to scoop Mike Wallace. And so Teddy goes off to Katmandu.

That may be enough of the basic plot, though mention should be made of a few other major characters. There is the beautiful and blonde goddess, Lakshmi, the consort of Vishnu-Kalki-Kelly, whom Jim met in Chicago's Drake Hotel when she was Doris Pannicker and engaged to another chap. There is the pretty and smart redhead, Geraldine O'Connor, who forsook a professorship in biochemistry at MIT to become one of Kalki's five Perfect Masters. And there is that mysterious Indian, Dr. Ashok, whose card reads "Professor of Comparative Religion at Fairleigh Dickinson University" (how cunningly Vidal picks the aptest title and spot for a potential phony), who may or may not be Dr. Giles Lowell, Jim Kelly's former professor of medicine, and who may also be a narc, a member of the CIA, and a hit man for a rival Chinese dope ring out to get Kalki.

All this would be fine if *everyone* in the novel were not a double agent of Vidal's—a pawn of his whimsy rather than a character real enough to dictate his own terms to the author, as truly successful fictional creations seem to be able to do. Here, however, a narc (a triple agent, but still a narc) will openly declare, "The single, nay, unique objective of the Bureau [of Narcotics] is the *increased* sale of every kind of drug all over the world," to which a demagogic senator running for the presidency will add that without international drug rings his richly funded Committee on Narcotics Abuse and Control "would wither away." Equally implausibly, a fellow from Internal Revenue will proclaim, "We at the IRS never assume that anyone is innocent until he is proved guilty. That is the American way."

Satirist's privilege? Not so; in high gear, satire has its own crazy plausibility, as Vidal well knows. Thus when a television director for *60 Minutes* says about the interview in which Kalki announces the date on which he will end the world, "This segment will run ten, ten and a half, maybe eleven minutes, you know, an in-depth study," this is barely, if at all, tampering with the preposterousness of things as they are. Or take a doctor's urging Arlene "to give up tequila in the morning. He begged her to switch to a good, light, refreshing breakfast wine from the Napa Valley. He himself owned a share in a vineyard. He would sell her his own brand." Vintage satire, that. Equally crushing is a seemingly casual remark like, "Over the years what Arlene had not had lifted could never have fallen"—which might have been even better with the addition of two commas.

A man who can so easefully carry off such sardonic effects ought not to settle for less. Yet Vidal will stoop to the heavy and obvious. He writes: "Dr. Ashok looked so crazed that, for the first time, I thought him not only sane but possibly serious despite the essential frivolity of his alleged employer the CIA." Here both the facile paradox and the unduly propaedeutic tone of "the essential frivolity of his alleged employer" seem to me miscarriages of satirical justice. Yet Vidal can do worse. He will become pontifical and leave a good piece of satirical raw material uncooked: "This was a commonplace in that era: events were only real if experienced at second hand, preferably through the medium of the camera." Moreover, he will mix metaphors (and not deliberately—the speaker is his alter ego, Teddy): "the dark caravans of words that cross the pages of newspapers to invade and ravish the delicate house of memory like killer ants." It is unnerving to have camels shrink in mid-metaphor to ants, however deadly. Or take, "Miscegenation was in the air; it hovered like a mushroom cloud between us." This is not mixed, merely clumsy: Even in an ironic context, a mushroom cloud is too much to invoke apropos a black man's stare at a white bosom, and the image bombs out. And any schoolboy of Vidal's acquaintance could have written "the effect . . . was ghostly, ghastly," which is only ghastly.

But then, for a fastidious, indeed finicky, writer, Vidal can become remarkably sloppy. Thus the Hindu phallus is the *lingam*, not the *linga*; the Latin for duplicity is *duplicitas*, not *duplicitatem;* Chomsky's first name is Noam, not Noah; "imposter" is a vulgar error for impostor; "Myna birds" is a redundancy for mynas; "forthcoming" is not acceptable in the sense of communicative or outspoken; no Frenchmen would write "de Vigny" for Vigny; "could not help but" is tautological; and so on.

But—and it is, as it is so often with Vidal, "but" time once more—there are also wonderful things in *Kalki*. There is at times a lightness of touch that nevertheless reduces the satire's butt to mincemeat: "I was able to read the odd page by Joan Didion, the even page by Renata Adler," which with the greatest gentleness makes both writers out to be unreadable. Or take: "Since talking to taxicab drivers was the hallmark of the higher journalism, I asked the driver what he thought of Kalki." Again: "I affected an even deeper sincerity. I sounded to myself like a Malibu surfer discussing ways of getting together his/her inner space." Or, a TV commentator lapsing into TV grammar: "I think all of we Americans. . . ." And what about this splendid *reductio ad absurdum:* "The Australian press was unusually aggressive. Apparently, they had once been able to drive Frank Sinatra out of Australia. This feat had made them overconfident," And, most devastating of all in its lethal concision: "Ms. Brownmiller's book on men, and rape," where putting the declared subject last and what Vidal takes to be the real one (sour grapes rather than bitter rape) first is a masterstroke of ingenious—or insidious—ridicule.

But—again but—this meticulous writer is capable of such lapses as having a singular child on page 245 turn into plural children on the next page. Such things are disturbing. But more disturbing still is the ultimate question this novel raises: Can one really pardon the feeling one gets in reading *Kalki* that Vidal would welcome the end of the world? This slips out time and again: "But then [if I were God] I would not have gone to the trouble of inventing the human race"; or "I did not believe that Kalki would switch off the human race . . . as desirable a happening as that might be." Not even Swift, in all his *saeva indignatio*, went that far.

And yet, and yet—one cannot help savoring a master satirist able to put down a whole subcontinent with a mere description of arrival at New Delhi airport: "The moon was still bright in the western sky. The dawn was pale pink. The air smelled of wood smoke, curry, shit." And who is able to dismiss the end of the entire world with, "You cannot mourn everyone. Only someone."—JOHN SIMON, "Vishnu as Double Agent," *SR*, April 29, 1978, pp. 31–33

What God did in six days and a few verses of Genesis, Gore Vidal ⟨in *Creation*⟩ has redone in a few years and more than 500 pages. The revised Creation also cheats a bit: it begins on 20 December 445 B.C. Our on-the-scene reporter is Cyrus Spitama, grandson of Zoroaster, uncle of Democritus of Abdera, friend of Xerxes, world traveler and ambassador from the court of Persia to Periclean Athens. As we begin, Cyrus has just heard indignantly Herodotus' account of the Persian wars. He is beginning to dictate to Democritus his version of what for him are the Greek wars. Later he adds the topic of his life and wanderings. The philosopher Anaxagoras adds another topic: "more important than trade routes are the notions about creation that you've encountered." Cyrus is 74, blind, garrulous and willing: "I shall begin at the beginning and tell you what I know of the creation of this world, and of all other worlds too. I shall also explain why evil is—and is not."

"At the beginning there was fire," while the god Ahura Mazdah spoke from the altar to Zoroaster and Cyrus. Zoroaster died; Cyrus went to the court of Darius the Great and was raised with Xerxes. We hear much about the courtiers, the politics, the history and the great cities of Susa, Babylon and Ecbatana. Cyrus grows up and is sent by Darius to open a trade route to his Indian kingdoms. There Cyrus meets the reigning kings, princes and courtiers, as well as an influential Chinese merchant. And he engages in theological discussions with Brahmans, with the Jain holy men Gosala and Mahavira and with Tathagata a.k.a. Siddhartha a.k.a. the Buddha. He also marries and fathers two sons. And then, four years older, he returns to Persia to catch up on the news and be billeted to China.

Trouble with the Greeks and Darius' death slow him down, but then Xerxes, now King of Kings, sends him off with 2,000 men. They take a shortcut, possibly through the Takla Makam desert. Two hundred survive, are enslaved and disappear into China. Cyrus hangs on, makes a fortuitous connection with his Chinese merchant, and rises in esteem at the most powerful court. He teaches the science of smelting (offstage), arranges for a caravan back to Persia and learns some local ideas about life. Li Tzu explains wu wei and the Tao to him, and he goes fishing with Confucius. Then he sets out for India, shedding his caravan to visit his wife and kids and to hear about the latest wars and massacres.

Not much interested, he pushes on and settles down in Persia. His old buddy Xerxes has become a drunken romantic (that is, he keeps falling in love) and neglects his empire. But Cyrus has a happy dozen years until Xerxes is killed and Artaxerxes takes over and sends him off to Athens—where, after much dictation and a meeting with Pericles and Aspasia, Cyrus dies. Forty years later, Democritus adds a page to his transcriptions, in order to tell us the Real Truth for which we've been panting:

> As Cyrus Spitama was beginning to suspect, if not believe, there is neither a beginning nor an end to a creation which exists in a state of flux in a time that is truly infinite. Although I have nowhere observed the slightest trace of Zoroaster's Wise Lord, he might well be a concept which can be translated into that circle which stands for the cosmos, for the primal unity, for creation.

Creation: 528 pages of small type. As I picked up the heavy book, I knew terror, for I am that rarest of reviewers who actually reads every word, and rather slowly. What I saw on the first page was disquieting. With an obviously bogus protagonist, Vidal must depend upon the cunning of his narrative gift to propel these characters through great events, and not only must he describe the sweep of military and political action but also give us close-ups of Darius, Xerxes, Zoroaster, the Buddha, Confucius and many more. The detail is painstaking and generally authentic. The naïve portraits of the great men convince rather more than subtler work might have done. This is not at all bad, except as prose. His reconstruction of history is painless and, I should think, most useful to simple readers. Yet there is a good deal of Pop-writing silliness, though Vidal's prose is generally correct, if uninspired, and though I suspect he is a writer best read swiftly by the page in order to get the sweep of his narrative while overlooking the infelicities of style and the shallowness of mind. I realize my sort of slow reading does a disservice to this kind of book. But then I hope the author will be pleased to know that at least one person has actually read his very long novel. Few people will.

In "The Top Ten Best Sellers," an essay written in 1973, Vidal reviews some bad Pop lit. The paragraph above, with some obvious changes, is cobbled together from sentences in his dissection of Herman Wouk's *The Winds of War.* The same article contains an admiring description of Mary Renault's *The Persian Boy,* mentioning Darius, Alexander, "marvelous cities, strange landscapes, colliding cultures"; "the device of observing the conqueror entirely through the eyes of an Oriental is excellent and rather novel." If we choose we may see here the genesis of *Creation.* From Solzhenitsyn's *August 1914* Vidal selects some "Wisdom Phrases," and after quoting a deeply meaningful encounter between a young man and Tolstoy he exclaims, "This is best-seller writing with a vengeance." He describes Frederick Forsyth's *The Odessa File* as "the sort of storytelling that propels the hero from one person to the next person, asking questions." And finally he generalizes: "The authors prefer fact or its appearance to actual invention. . . . As Christianity and Judaism sink into decadence, religioso fictions still exert a certain appeal." It is disturbing, the appropriateness of these passages to *Creation.*

Creation, says Cyrus, is "the only important subject that there is." The novel spends about twenty-five pages on the subject, total. Usually it is given a mere mention in passing, but most of the Wisdom Figures speak about it. Unfortunately, Cyrus "cannot follow any of this," as he says about Democritus' observations. "It is hard to take seriously another world's wise man, particularly at second hand," Cyrus remarks. And to Democritus he says, without heeding his own advice,

> even your teacher Protagoras would agree with Confucius' strictures on how necessary it is to examine what you've learned. Confucius also thought that a teacher must always be able to reinterpret the old in terms of the new. . . . Unfortunately, it is also obvious that few teachers are able to do anything but repeat, without interpretation, old saws.

Setting out to propel his hero from interview to interview, Vidal has contrived a questioner with so anemic a private life and character that he is always free to memorize answers and to notice the scenery. Such a figure can be contrived out of research and used to communicate oodles of facts. But in effect, we go to marriages with a fashion editor and to burials with a geologist; in place of imaginative involvement we get reports. Back from six years in the Orient, Cyrus arrives at his first personal meeting with Xerxes. Between the sentences "Later that evening he sent for me to join him in his bedroom" and "Xerxes lay upon the bed," we are given 150 words, beginning, "Despite all my years at court, I had never before seen the fabled bedroom furniture of the Great Kings." And we see it.

In 1961, Vidal said that the highest points of the novel "were always reached by those who set their characters free from making a living and were then able to carry forward the debate, the interplay of character." But Cyrus hits and runs, leading a solitary and unruminative existence, and all these great figures and their wisdom flow past us like an overloaded introduction-to-philosophy course based on Xeroxed handouts. Even the politics is presented in Pop-lit terms: "Years later I discovered that every word that was spoken in the grotto beneath the mountain was carefully taken down by an agent of the Magadhan secret service"; "every word that is said at a royal drinking party is taken down by a scribe." One finds even that old mystery of the missing sibilants: "'Do not interrupt,' hissed Atossa."

The writing has other problems, and "that" is one of them. Cyrus describes Herodotus' history as "nonsense of a sort that were I less old and more privileged, I would have risen in my seat at the Odeon and scandalized all Athens by answering him." He says, "What little influence that I still exert derives from an accident of birth." Also:

> Under full sail our lives were always at risk, since we were never so far from the spiky coral shore that a sudden gust of wind might have wrecked us.
>
> Not a day passes here in Athens but that I am not told how two or three thousand . . . Greeks defeated a Persian army and navy of two or three million men.
>
> At the time, I wondered that if there should be a sixty-fifth art, would it be diplomacy or conspiracy?

Yet in 1975 Vidal, asked how he'd like to be remembered, said, "I suppose as the person who wrote the best sentences in his time."—J. D. O'Hara, "The Winds of Vidal," *Nation*, March 21, 1981, pp. 343–45

In an afterword to his novel *1876*, Gore Vidal confesses to a "deep mistrust of writers who produce trilogies", having just completed one himself, but, not yet presumably having contemplated a novel on Lincoln, regards tetralogists as being "beyond the pale". He does not say why, but I suspect that he considers the spreading of a single theme—American history, for example—over a long fictional sequence as an indication of creative impotence, an inability to invent. In an essay in *Matters of Fact and of Fiction* he upbraids certain best-selling authors for preferring "fact or its appearance to actual invention. This suggests that contemporary historians are not doing their job if to Wouk and Solzhenitsyn falls the task of telling today's reader about two world wars and to Forsyth and Trevanian current tales of the cold war." And if to Vidal falls the task of an earlier war and its hero, one ought to be making a smiliar assumption about the failure of the professional recordist, when no period in history is better documented than that of the American Civil War, and no hero better served than Abraham Lincoln—from the twelve-volume biography of Hay and Nicolay to Carl Sandburg and beyond. Why write the book at all?

There's a good commercial reason. As I write, *Lincoln* heads the *New York Times* best-seller list. It is not what Mr Vidal calls "quality lit", being as plainly written as anything by Mr Wouk, eschewing—except for a couple of paragraphs in the final chapter—anything like a consideration of the complexities and ambiguities inherent in the character of either Lincoln or his times. As Vidal says of Wouk's *The Winds of War*, "his reconstruction of history is painless and, I should think, most useful to simple readers". What skill there is in the novel resides precisely in the reduction of a tangle of complexities to a not over-long narrative in which the simple reader will learn the basic facts about Lincoln and the Civil War—namely, that Lincoln was no more against slavery than Washington and Jefferson had been, and that the Civil War, which was wasteful and inefficiently fought, was waged for an abstract idea—the conservation of the Union.

The novel of the period which raged effectively against slavery is not even mentioned, probably because Uncle Tom has taken on the wrong resonance among progressives, and in spite of the fact that Lincoln greeted its author with the words "So this is the little woman who made this great war." Readers who expect Simon Legree and large battle scenes out of *Gone with the Wind* will be disappointed. There is no sensationalism and, despite the multiplicity of brothels in Washington, no explicit sex—though we do learn the etymology of *hooker* (General Hooker's girls). Vidal is mainly concerned with a metaphysical question—the Union and the sustention of the Union—and it is this obsession with the Union which makes Lincoln bizarrely impressive and even, in his quiet way, manic. But it does not make him much of a figure for fiction.

Vidal, to his credit as a fiction-writer, does his best with the long, lean, ascetic figure unblessed by self-doubt, cursed with constipation, a born politician but totally incorrupt, unless his blazing faith in the Union be a form of corruption. The corruption is discussed belatedly in the last chapter, where, at a reception at the Tuileries, John Hay, formerly Lincoln's secretary and prospective co-author of his biography, meets a character from *1876*—the wholly fictional Charles Schermerhorn Schuyler. Hay, placing Lincoln above Washington, says that he had a far more difficult task than the first president:

> 'You see, the Southern states had every Constitutional right to go out of the Union. But Lincoln said, no. Lincoln said, this Union can never be broken. Now this was a terrible responsibility for one man to take. But he took it, knowing he would be obliged to fight the greatest war in human history, which he did, and which he won.'

And then Schuyler speaks of Bismark:

> 'Curiously enough, he has now done the same thing to Germany that you tell us Mr Lincoln did to our country. Bismarck has made a single, centralized nation out of all the other German states.'

We, with the gift of hindsight, are thus made to wonder whether Lincoln did the right thing.

And yet, in the body of the book, this mystique of the Union is not fully explicated. There are hints that it may be a geographical concept, finding a logical conclusion in the annexation of Canada as well as Mexico, servant or master of a new technology of railroads and telegraphs which makes devolution obsolete, history working through the apparently insentient Lincoln to bring about the modern American whose fat rump is ready for the taws of Mr Vidal. We need a poet somewhere in the book who can display prophetic insight, but all we have is a rather humble Walt Whitman looking for a job and the transcendentalist authoress of "The Battle Hymn of the Republic". It seems to be part of Vidal's brief to depoeticize to the limit. This is, of course, essential for a commercial enterprise.

The setting is Washington and environs. Vidal leaves the log cabin and rail splitting to legend and begins his story with Lincoln's arrival in the capital for his inauguration. The author's affection for a city which he has described as having the charm of the north and the efficiency of the south is as evident here as elsewhere. It is very well rendered, with its canal described twice as "odiferous" (an obsolete term which Vidal likes, since he uses it also in *1876*), its fried oysters and spittoons, mosquitoes and fever which everybody catches—even Lincoln, though only once. The presidential home which Mrs Lincoln inherits is a mess of dirt and dried tobacco-spit, but she soon puts it right. She spends too much, gets into debt, cooks the books, eventually goes mad. She also has Confederate connections. The suspicions which attach to Caesar's wife never touch Caesar: Lincoln's heroic stoicism is matched by total integrity. Inevitably, supporting characters such as Chase, the State Treasurer but always in money trouble, have more of the interest proper to fiction. Sprague, the "boy governor" of Rhode Island, is of exceptional interest. Through his marriage to Chase's daughter, Chase's own fortunes improve, but Sprague's fortune depends on the illegal, indeed treasonous, importation of cotton. This is the real stuff of fiction, though it is also fact.

Vidal takes the character of the young David Herold, whom history hears of only in connection with the Booth conspiracy, and builds him up, though to little purpose. He works as a dispenser and delivery boy in Thompson's drugstore, which, in the interests of dramatic compression, is placed closer to the White House than it actually was. David is a supporter of the Confederacy who acts as a spy, crossing the Potomac with impunity to make his deliveries and passing on coded messages. Both Mr and Mrs Lincoln need laudanum, and Lincoln also needs a massive weekly purgative: the opportunity to poison the President seems always to be there and yet not there. Booth shoots him, without crying "Sic semper tyrannis" (we are in the wrong market for a quote from *Cato*), and David fails to kill Secretary of State Seward. There is too much of David: he is not interesting enough to justify the space alloted. He is really there to feed Vidal's hunger to invent.

He, one of the most inventive novelists modern America has produced, must have felt damnably oppressed by the need to follow history. It must have been especially oppressive when the moment approached for the re-enactment of a scene that is so historic that it seems already to have been invented. When Gettysburg is first mentioned, we settle in our seats and prepare not only for the Address many of us have by heart but for a chance to judge the author's ingenuity in washing it clean of its sentimental accretions. Vidal comes through remarkably. He does not give us what we know—"Lincoln's final tinkered-with draft"—but what Charles Hale of the *Boston Daily Advertiser* wrote down. And he breaks it up with clever dramatic insertions:

> 'We are met on a great battle-field of that war. We are met to dedicate a portion of it as the final resting place of those who have given their lives that the nation might live.' Seward nodded, inadvertently. Yes, that was the issue, the only issue. The preservation of this unique nation of states. Meanwhile, the photographer was trying to get the President in camera-frame.

As for the assassination, this is flat and even perfunctory—something that happened and had best not be brooded upon. Vidal spends a good deal of care on the background and character of the assassin, but the more we learn of him as an extrovert actor the less we are able to accept him as an avenger of the stricken South. The final words of the book are,

> 'It will be interesting to see how Herr Bismarck ends *his* career,' said Hay, who was now more than ever convinced that Lincoln, in some mysterious fashion, had willed his own murder as a form of atonement for the great and terrible thing he had done by giving so bloody and absolute a rebirth to his nation.

This turns Booth into a mere shadowy device of expiation and the final scene in the theatre into a yawning attendance at mass rather than a catastrophe of world-shattering proportions. "Rebirth to his nation" is probably, given Vidal's cinematic background, a deliberate device to evoke the fourteenth Amendment, the carpetbaggers and the Ku Klux Klan. The interesting, or Vidalian, things are often on the margin in this novel, and all the rest is history sedulously followed and minimally dramatized. It is a novel not of great battles but of telegrams about them arriving at the White House.

So that the novel itself seems only to be a device for awakening wonder at the historical actuality; it points at history without heightening it through art. In this respect, *Lincoln* belongs to that popular and very American pseudo-fictional genre which Mr Vidal, concentrating particularly on Mr Wouk, condescendingly accepts as wholesome if simplistic teaching but condemns for pretending to be a kind of literature. Irving Stone has written on Michelangelo, Freud and Darwin in much the same way ("sighing, he lighted a fresh cigar, and wrote his title: *The Interpretation of Dreams*"). James A. Michener has made a vast fortune out of blockbusting history tomes, well-researched and indifferently written, which are presented as novels. There is something in the puritanical American mind which is scared of the imaginative writer but not of the pedantic one who seems to humanize facts without committing himself to the inventions which are really lies.

In putting himself beyond the pale as a tetralogist, Gore Vidal is in danger of making the wrong sort of reputation for himself—the popular recorder of American political history, and not the brilliant scabrous fantasist of *Myra Breckinridge* or the revivifier of the remote past as in *Julian* and *Creation*. His recent *Duluth* remade the geography of the United States, created a new kind of eschatology (when you die in Duluth you go into a television series called *Duluth*), and smote American *mores* hard through every technique available to modern fiction. *Creation* was a remarkable attempt to depict the age of Darius, Xerxes, Buddha, Confucius, Herodotus and Socrates. Both highly-sexed satire and imaginative penetration of ancient history should be enough for him. But he cannot leave American politics alone. I am not altogether sorry that he has written *Lincoln*, since this ghost has sent me back to the flesh and blood reality, but its writing could have been left to any best-selling American who, short of a subject, found Honest Abe as good as any.—ANTHONY BURGESS, "Honest Abe's Obsession," *TLS*, Sept. 28, 1984, p. 1082

DRAMA

Mr. Gore Vidal has declared himself to be, as playwright, "a sport, whose only serious interest is the subversion of a society which bores and appalls" him. However true this may be, it can be reported that *The Best Man*, his markedly successful *comédie à clef* of contemporary politics, is, like his earlier *Visit to a Small Planet*, the work of an intellectual dandy, resourceful and suavely insolent, notably void of any distinguished impulse or effect. In an election year, Mr Vidal has stewed up a *bouillabaisse* of some rather raunchy fish heads—full of saffron and spice and nothing quite nice—which will decidedly nourish the buffet crowd. His pepper is never less than hot, and a good thing too, for it stimulates his players to that sanguine volatility the American actor will always call up when he is summoned to the demonstration of *real life. The Best Man* is a credit then, very much, to this lamentable theatrical moment, and one would be niggardly to deny its arrowing and supple wit.

Yet I am not at all certain how much it contributes to the subversion of nations, much less their enlightenment, and I was moved to reflect on the curious esteem writers such as Mr. Gore Vidal enjoy among us. Is it a tribute to their audacity? But surely the heresies of Mr. Vidal, say, or his coeval Miss Marya Mannes, are hardly as autonomously convulsive as the *Schadenfreude* of—to choose at random—the Europeans Gênet and Beckett; rarely so obsessive as those of Mr. John Osborne; not so exhilarating, even, as Miss Mary McCarthy's authentic intellectual sharpshooting. Are they not, rather, those social "gestures of complaint" that Mr. Harry Golden called Miss Mannes' strictures: "indices for what class we belong to, and where we come from, and what we do, and whether or not we want to be invited again"? And is not their relation to intelligence, as such, peripheral? Indeed, might not intelligence be said to begin directly such polite and unexceptionable lamentations are recognized, assessed for their general truth, and disposed in the order of their relevance? The wonder is that the middle-class American community persists in thinking so elementary a posture of the intellectual life singular, rewards it with attention, sponsors and endures its insistent iteration of the obvious with pathological relish.

I have sometimes thought of these figures who live by such energies as the traditional Ministers Without Portfolio—councillors and hostages to a world they never made (though this rarely gives them pause) and—which of us would deny it?—too often wanting in awe before its complex manifestations. But I must no longer invoke the paranoic *they:* the moment has come to employ the ambivalent *we*. For am I not now, and have I not always been, myself a card-carrying Minister without Portfolio: does not the security with which I call upon those honorific terms *culture* and *society*—preferably entwined with *our*—testify amply to my good standing in Our masonic hierarchy? And what a hierarchy it is!—with Pontifex Maximus himself, Our Liberal Imagination, presiding over the Capitoline on Morningside Heights; with our London branch safely under the august paws of Old Possum; with our Permanent Executive Committees permanently executive in all the funds, foundations and faculties: all of us with all our O.K. opinions at all the O.K. times—who's in, who's out—vigilantly preparing the consummation of that celebrated Minister-without-Portfolio-Rallying-Cry: *Everybody in his place*—AND ME ON TOP!

It is, again, one of the winning idiosyncrasies of the Minister without Portfolio that he so often, with headstrong and unswerving dedication, uniquely misses the point. Consider Mr. Vidal, whose free-wheeling ironies on the political theme in *The Best Man* deny him an ultimate glimpse of that last irony and sobering intuition of all power: that it *will* be exercised, and must, and that the humanism of imperfection is a fragile shield before an assault. Or what, more dangerously, of that other possibility which has always tantalized the imagination, and upon which all of us act, practically—Mr. Vidal, who has just declared for Congress, not least—that power might be, in some undreamed-of way, a good? It is these lacunae, partially, that deny *The Best Man*'s most arresting figure—the Nixon prototype—more than a circumstantial reality, neglect his singularity as a phenomenon—one unique response to a moment of stasis in social evolution—and propose him only, though ironically, as a moral whipping-boy. Irony may be a defense, as Mr. Marvin Mudrick subtly observed in his study of Jane Austen, but it must also be a discovery.

Or take Mr. Vidal on the signficant relation of public to private: he professes indifference to Miss Y's laments about her analyst, or to whether Mrs. X is resolving her marital disputes with Mr. Z, and so on: rather, he asserts, it is "society"—ministerial word again!—that involves *him*. But surely the state of "society" is the sum of individual states, and surely the genuine horror of history is that it turns so often on a bad digestion, a childhood snub, a sexual obsession: "the course of self-interest," as Mrs. Sybille Bedford wrote in *A Legacy*, "seen as a beeline only at the moment." How brilliantly Schiller marked this in *Mary Stuart*, when Elizabeth, wavering, was recalled to venomous purpose by her remembrance of the insolent "Bastard!" flung at her by Mary. And what are the Shakespearean Historical Plays but a monument to the discovery of that point at which personal destiny intersects with history, time and the state. The private dossiers of the figures in *The Best Man* are rife with local color—birth control, promiscuity, Lolita-ism, homosexuality in the Aleutians: literally something for *everybody*—but how little of it comes into anything like conviction.

I have perhaps driven a literate entertainment into pretensions quite beyond its scope, and no one should fail of gratitude to Mr. Vidal for much of his engaging buckshot, as well as for a clever lively production, softened by Miss Leora Dana's patrician coolness. But one last cavil, and I shall minister along, with or without portfolio. How are we to account for the savage righteousness, the almost indecent glee, exhibited by New York audiences whenever a mildly liberal sentiment is trotted out for approbation? At several of the more water-logged passages in *The Best Man*, I indicated unconsciously—by occasional perhaps rather too generous sighs—my moral impatience, and directly, as if by radar, vigilant A.D.A. eyes were riveted on me: *get that man*, was in the air, *get him!* and indeed, I felt quite like the victim of Miss Shirley Jackson's *The Lottery*. Then I remembered how, earlier this season, at that grade-school political reader *The Gang's All Here*, only the preemptory rise of the curtain had prevented my being compelled to accept an invitation to brawl in the alley. How "liberal" are we Ministers without Portfolio, anyhow? I shall have to take this up with old Pontifex Maximus, who will doubtless make an honorific pronouncement.—RICHARD HAYES, "The Ministers without Portfolio," *Com*, April 29, 1960, pp. 128–29

Gore Vidal is a reliable farceur. His writing is sophisticated, amoral, reasonably witty, almost as urbane as it thinks itself to be, and should make for an enjoyable evening in the theater. Why does *Weekend* turn out to be only bearable? (Mind you, bearable is not bad by current standards.) I suspect it has something to do with a basic coldness in the author. Like his characters in *Weekend*, he seems to care only in a narrow way about achieving his aims—in this case, to write a successful Broadway play—and there is no sense of feelings, intellectual passion, human concern beyond the basic requirements. Yet the spoils belong to the play with spilth.

It may be thought captious to ask of a farce more than a funny situation and bright lines. Or it might be claimed, especially by Mr. Vidal, that *Weekend* is, in fact, a comedy. Well, comedy must take human beings seriously, get at their very essence, in order to laugh at them; whereas Vidal's senator angling for the Republican presidential nomination is no more sharply examined or richly conceived than any of the pleasant or unpleasant human façades gravitating around him. This leaves farce, which I see as the acceleration and escalation of comedy into something demonic. But Mr. Vidal's play is neither deep nor devilish, only dapper.

Senator MacGruder is a debonair liberal Republican living in an easygoing *ménage à trois* with his wife and secretary. He is also a lucky Pierre in between conservatism and radicalism, jovially dallying with both. His erratic anthropologist son comes back from Paris with the girl he is about to marry: a Negro. This may cost Dad his political future, but—here comes switcheroo No. 1—Sonny knows this, and the threat of wedding bells tolls only for Dad, who is to be blackmailed (no pun intended) into underwriting Junior's unorthodox Lévi-Straussianizing ("Had he been like everybody else, the Ford Foundation would have supported him"). From here on in, the switcheroos rain thick and fast; the trouble is that when the unexpected comes like clockwork, it becomes very hard to distinguish it from the expected.

The play turns, really, into a literary-political platform for Vidal, from which to air his airy views on everything from Eisenhower to Vietnam, via love, marriage, swingerdom (if that is the right suffix) and what have you. There is, if I may speak Aristoteleanly, absolutely nothing wrong with Vidal's politics, or even his posterior analytics; it is his poetics that are deficient. Lines like "Next to the Vatican, the Kremlin is the last stronghold of romantic conservatism," or "Father, you're good, and that's why Lyndon Johnson will defeat you: because he represents the bloodymindedness of the people," or "No political career is every finished in the United States—look at Richard Nixon!" may have their modicum of insight; but though straw is required for the making of bricks, you cannot build your play from straws, skipping the intermediate step. —JOHN SIMON, "Dapper Gore," *Com*, April 5, 1968, pp. 74–75

CRITICISM

On the jacket of *Homage to Daniel Shays*, the *New Statesman* is quoted as saying that Gore Vidal is America's finest essayist. This is hardly true, but one knows why someone who thinks writing essays is a matter of keeping cool and writing well might think so. There are 45 occasional pieces in Vidal's volume, and there isn't a clinker in the bunch. If that doesn't make one America's finest essayist, it sets one well apart from the run of the mill. Furthermore, it seems that Vidal is getting better. The early essays—on the postwar novel, on television and writing for television, on the Great Golfer called Eisenhower—all now seem brittle, monochromatic. The *New York Review* pieces of recent years, on the other hand, range from truly Olympian views of David Reuben and the battle of the sexes to an engaged, nostalgic and lovely picture of Eleanor Roosevelt. But the appearance may well be deceiving.

The trouble is that Vidal is always timely. Twenty years ago it was customary to wonder who were the best, the two or three best and half dozen best, American writers or novelists or whatever. So here is Vidal announcing that the best writers of the 1940's are Carson McCullers, Paul Bowles and Tennessee Williams. It's not that Vidal backed the wrong horses, but that he thought of judging writers as a matter of backing horses. So, too, in the fifties people were seriously interested in television, preposterous though that may now seem, and here then is Vidal writing for and about television because the action was there, and Vidal never asks if he should always go where the action is.

Here is the first blush and later disenchantment with Kennedy, accompanied by a "what you can do for your country" piece on police brutality. Here is an interview with Goldwater and a touristic rundown on Nasser, both done at a time when interviews and touristic rundowns were our accepted means of keeping up to date. In more recent years, when Vidal worries about the novel it is not to decide who is in or out on the American scene but to grapple with the French theorists and Susan Sontag, and if he flatters these subjects by taking them as seriously as others did five years ago, he also says all the right things about them. Again, more recently, when he writes about politics he writes about the Establishment and the country, not about people, apparently not realizing that in our era one always does that when the Republicans are in power.

In other words, when confronted with today Vidal will write about today, and in today's modes. Ten years ago he explained himself this way: "I should have thought that that was why one wrote—to make something useful for the survivors, to say: I was and now you are, and I leave as good a map as I could make of my own traveling." Well, though that does smack of the Kennedy period, it is a decent enough motive for writing. The trouble is that it makes one's audience into the subject, and makes one's surroundings into a kind of foreign country for which a map is needed. If one were a possessed spirit, driven powerfully from the inside, such a sense of audience and surroundings might be a useful counterweight. But Vidal is no Mailer, but a detached, decent and witty man. For Vidal to want to "make something useful for the survivors" is, it turns out, to lock himself into the present. Significantly, the best things in the book are an elegy on John Horne Burns and reviews of Suetonius and of Steven Runciman's history of the fall of Constantinople, none written with an attitude of "I was and now you are."

For as long as Gore Vidal has been writing essays it has been a commonplace that the center of American writing is not the novel but the occasional piece. What is really meant by this is that right now more people take the essay seriously than read novels. Vidal knows his novels are not much read and that his essays are, and that this is true not only of him but of others like Mailer and Baldwin and Mary McCarthy and Paul Goodman. But when this is true—when, like Vidal, one is more ambitious of acceptance than of fame, when there is always a danger that what seems most appropriate is really only the most fashionable—one's guard must always be up. Perhaps it is precisely when novels don't seem to count that they should be written and read, when a more abrasive and insistent tone is needed in writing occasional essays. At one point Vidal wisely observes that the more money an American accumulates the less interesting he becomes. It might also be true that the more an American can claim to be truly in tune with the moment, the greater will be his immediate success and the sooner will his writings date.

In Vidal's case the point is not that he should be abjuring essays for the serious business of writing fiction. In fact, his essays are almost always good and his novels are not so good. The point is that Vidal is a writer without a center, without a passion or a prose that can make mistakes seem irrelevant or timeliness something beside the point. Almost every specific detail of Paul Goodman's *Growing Up Absurd* has dated, and in most respects Gore Vidal writes better on his worst days than Goodman did on his best. But still, Goodman counts in a way that Vidal does not, because he knew that no matter how strong the hold of the present seems to be, the subject is still the human condition.

This means that except for a very few essays that drop out of time, Vidal is best when we share his present concerns and his present tastes. Give Vidal subjects like David Reuben or Kate Millett or Richard Gilman, or even Mailer, and he can always be good enough to make it worth buying the magazine he's writing for just to read him. But of the four targets just named, the first three have already ceased to count as news, which means perhaps they weren't ever worth more than fleeting attention. The news just doesn't stay news long enough to make reading Vidal's collected essays a rewarding experience.

It may be, of course, that being timely is enough for Vidal and should be enough for our consideration of him. For every Ruskin, for every Bagehot even, there are 20 or 30 Victorian writers who may seem dull now but who commanded a decent prose and a decent view of their own time. No one who writes, especially no one who writes essays and reviews, can think that scorn is the only reward such men deserve. But I think that we should think of Vidal as such a writer—as one who, in his own eloquent words, seeks to make "the gossip of his day our day's gospel." It seems to me a not very lofty aim, but if one is convinced that the time is truly artless and that literature is a declining kingdom, then it may seem aim enough. It is certainly true that for those who can find the gospel of their days in their gossip, Vidal has rightfully secured an important place.—ROGER SALE, *NYTBR*, Dec. 31, 1972, p. 7

Nobody dissents from marking Gore Vidal high as an essayist, not even those—especially not those—who would like to mark him low as a novelist. His *Collected Essays 1952–1972* was rightly greeted with all the superlatives going. Since one doesn't have to read far in this new volume ⟨*Matters of Fact and of Fiction: Essays 1973–1976*⟩ before realising that the old volume has been fully lived up to and in some respects even surpassed, it becomes necessary either to wheel out the previous superlatives all over again or else to think up some new ones. Rejecting both courses, this reviewer intends to pick nits and make gratuitous observations on the author's character, in the hope of maintaining some measure of critical independence. Gore Vidal is so dauntingly good at the literary essay that he is likely to arouse in other practitioners an inclination to take up a different line of work. That, however, would be an excessive reaction. He isn't omniscient, infallible or effortlessly stylish—he just knows a lot, possesses an unusual amount of common sense and writes scrupulously lucid prose. There is no need to deify the man just because he can string a few thoughts together. As I shall now reveal, he has toenails of clay.

Always courageous about unfolding himself, Vidal sometimes overcooks it. He is without false modesty but not beyond poor-mouthing himself to improve a point. 'The bad movies we made 20 years ago are now regarded in altogether too many circles as important aspects of . . . ' But wait a minute. It might remain a necessary task to point out that the nuttier film-buffs are no more than licensed illiterates: the ability to carry out a semiotic analysis of a Nicholas Ray movie is undoubtedly no compensation for being incapable of parsing a simple sentence. But some of those bad movies were, after all, quite good. Vidal himself had his name writ large on both *The Left-Handed Gun* and *The Best Man*, neither of which is likely to be forgotten. It suits his purposes, however, to pretend that he was a dedicated candy-butcher. He wants to be thought of as part of the hard-bitten Hollywood that produced the adage: 'Shit has its own integrity.'

As a Matter of Fact, Vidal rarely set out to write rubbish: he just got mixed up with a few pretentious projects that went sour. Summarising, in the first of these essays, the Top Ten Best Sellers, Vidal makes trash hilarious. But there is no need for him to pretend that he knows trash from the inside. He was always an outsider in that regard: the point he ought to make about himself is that he never had what it took to be a Hollywood hack. It was belief, not cynicism, that lured him to write screenplays. Even quite recently he was enthusiastically involved in a mammoth project called *Gore Vidal's Caligula*, once again delivering himself into the hands of those commercial forces which would ensure that the script ended up being written by Caligula's Gore Vidal.

Yet you can see what he is getting at. Invention, however fumbling, must always be preferred over aridity, however high-flown. In all the essays dealing with Matters of Fiction, Vidal is constantly to be seen paying unfeigned attention to the stories second-rate writers are trying to tell. His contempt is reserved for the would-be first-raters obsessed with technique. For the less exalted scribes honestly setting about their grinding chores, his sympathy is deep even if his wit is irrepressible. Quoting a passage from Herman Wouk, he adds: 'This is not at all bad, except as prose.' Taken out of context, this might seem a destructive crack, but when you read it in its proper place there is no reason to think that the first half of the sentence has been written for the sole purpose of making the second half funny.

If this were not a nit-picking exercise we would be bound to take notice of Vidal's exemplary industry. He has actually sat down and read, from front to back, the gigantic novels by John Barth and Thomas Pynchon for which the young professors make such claims. Having done so, he is in a position to give a specific voice to the general suspicion which the academic neo-theologians have aroused in the common reader's mind. Against their religious belief in The Novel, Vidal insists that there is no such thing—there are only novels. In this department, as in several others, Vidal is the natural heir of Edmund Wilson, whose *The Fruits of the MLA* was the opening salvo in the long campaign, which we will probably never see the end of, to rescue literature from its institutionalised interpreters.

But Wilson is not Vidal's only ancestor. Several cutting references to Dwight Macdonald are a poor reward for the man whose devastating essay 'By Cozzens Possessed' (collected in *Against the American Grain*) was the immediate forerunner of everything Vidal has done in this particular field. It would be a good thing if Vidal, normally so forthcoming about his personal history, could be frank about where he considers himself to stand in relation to other American critical writers. In his introductory note to this book there is mention of Sainte-Beuve; in a recent interview given to the *New York Times* there was talk about Montaigne; but among recent essayists, now that Wilson is gone, Vidal seems to find the true critical temperament only among 'a few elderly Englishmen'. Yet you have only to think of people like Macdonald or Mary McCarthy or Elizabeth Hardwick to see that if Vidal is *primus* it is only *inter pares:* there is an American critical tradition, going back to Mencken and beyond, which he is foolish to imagine can be disowned. This is the only respect in which Vidal seems shy of being an American, and by no coincidence it is the only respect in which he ever sounds provincial.

Otherwise his faults, like his virtues, are on a world scale. In the Matters of Fact, which occupy the second part of the book, the emphasis is on the corrupting influence of power and money. Born into the American ruling class, Vidal is as well placed as Louis Auchincloss (about whom he writes appreciatively) to criticise its behaviour. He is angrily amusing about West Point, Robert Moses, ITT, the Adams dynasty and the grand families in general. Indeed it is only about Tennessee

Williams and Lord Longford that he is *un*angrily funny—for the most part his humour about Matters of Fact is sulphuric. There is no question of Vidal's sincerity in loathing what he calls the Property Party. On the other hand he is a trifle disingenuous in allowing us to suppose that all connections have been severed between himself and the ruling class. Certainly he remains on good terms with the ruling class of Britain—unless Princess Margaret has become as much of an intellectual exile from the British aristocracy as he has from the American.

As a Matter of Fact, Gore Vidal is a Beautiful Person who chooses his drawing-rooms with care. He hobnobs with the rich and powerful. He hobnobs also with the talented, but they tend to be those among the talented who hobnob with the rich and powerful. He likes the rich and powerful as a class. He hates some of them as individuals and attacks them with an invective made all the more lacerating by inside knowledge. For that we can be grateful. But we can also wish that his honesty about his own interior workings might extend to his thirst for glamour. Speaking about Hollywood, he is an outsider who delights to pose as an insider. Speaking about the ruling class, he is an insider who delights to pose as an outsider. In reality he is just as active a social butterfly as his arch-enemy Truman Capote. But in Vidal's case the sin is venial, not mortal, since his writings remain comparatively unruffled by the social whirl, whereas Capote has become a sort of court dwarf, peddling a brand of thinly fictionalised tittle-tattle which is really sycophancy in disguise. Vidal reserves that sort of thing for after hours.

Yet even with these nits picked, it must still be said that Vidal is an outstanding writer on political issues. 'The State of the Union', the last essay in the book, is so clear an account of what has been happening in America that it sounds commonplace, until you realise that every judgment in it has been hard won from personal experience. Only one of its assumptions rings false, and even there you can see his reasons. Vidal still assumes that any heterosexual man is a culturally repressed bisexual. This idea makes a good basis for polemical assault on sexual intolerance, but as a Matter of Fact it is Fiction. As it happens, I have met Gore Vidal in the flesh. The flesh looked immaculately preserved. In a room well supplied with beautiful and brilliant women, he was as beautiful as most and more brilliant than any. I was not impervious to his charm. But I examined myself in vain for any sign of physical excitement. He might say that I was repressing my true nature but the real reason was simpler. It was just that he was not a female.

Not even Gore Vidal is entirely without self-delusion. On the whole, though, he is among the most acute truth-tellers we possess. Certainly he is the most entertaining. The entertainment arises naturally from his style—that perfectly disciplined, perfectly liberated English which constitutes all by itself a decisive answer to the Hacks of Academe. Calling them 'the unlearned learned teachers of English' and 'the new barbarians, serenely restoring the Dark Ages', he has only to quote their prose against his and the case is proved. A pity, then, that on page 260 there is a flagrant (well, all right: barely noticeable) grammatical error. 'Journalists who know quite as much or more than I about American politics . . .' is not good grammar. There is an 'as' missing. But the other 281 scintillating pages of error-free text go some way towards making up for its loss.—CLIVE JAMES, "The Left-Handed Gun," *NS*, Aug. 19, 1977, pp. 245–46

SEYMOUR KRIM
"Reflections on a Ship That's Not Sinking at All"

London Magazine, May 1970, pp. 26–43

> 'Seymour who do you think you are? You're a little, resentful failure, going around judging everyone else's life and abilities and you have none of either.' (Jimmy Breslin)

I ask again: Does creative literature have any meaning in America now, real power to affect, hell, even to NICK the soul of a people who have left behind an earth they never really knew for the moon with no regrets? Or is it a cultural glamour stock yes sir Shakespeare, Dostywhatsky, Hemingway riding on the values of the past that gets a conscience salute from hard-drinking, sex-nutted, status-kissing norteamericanos who know what the image is worth on the market but certainly don't want their busy lives interrupted by its schoolgirl peepants pining?

The question applies to Gore Vidal and even Vidal, Gore; for twenty years he wrote novels with no loud success until *Myra Breckinridge* (1968)—yet all of a sudden he seems to have walked into a spotlight glittering with a million bucks, 'national prestige', intellectual respect, multiplying projects and also the very tangible power denied to most pathetic dollar-begging literary lives in our disunited states. The interesting thing is that while the practice of literature or at least the common novel gave Vidal the opportunity to be a Somebody, it is not on the basis of letters pure and simple (even complex) that he has created a stir about himself. No, what he has done takes other qualities, equally fascinating for what they can tell you about America and the demything of the Great American Novelist and even the entire communications shadow government today, but literature is only a training-ground for this kind of success.

The success itself is in close-combat American life, that daily suspense show, and by extension the international scene which copies our own; sweetly superior muscle in the here-and-now is its effect although this was probably not its conscious intention at the beginning, and no matter how this force might be minimized by long-distance thinkers since we live in a time beginning to show an excess of star-personalities and a quicker rate of sudden eclipse, it can't very well be dismissed by myself because in basic issues like fame (degree), fascination, wealth, conspicuous brightness and the capacity to have your own way in power areas that run from publishing to moviemaking to politics the Vidals have more leverage than you and I. The world today, of course, is a fantastic crapgame with no established favourites and you or I might steal the entire insane pot in a year or two; but right now on the basis of performance it is Vidal who is the hot roller and inasmuch as that winning form conceals a unique self-made figure whom one is foolish to underestimate, I want to fade him as they say with the currency we both trade in: words.

The years of comparative obscurity (Vidal claims with enough modesty to make it seem valid that he was singled out on the publication of his first novel *Williwaw* in 1946, but I was on the verge of reviewing books then and recall no shooting stars) when he was pounding out his novels, most of them having a small audience and revolving around comparatively exotic themes, made him a professional writer in a tough-hided sense that most of us were unaware of until he started becoming a 'spokesman' at the beginning of the 'sixties. The eight novels that he wrote before *Julian* (1964), which was the first of his bestsellers, did not make much money nor did they reach beyond a coterie in the main; what audience they did have seemed to be mostly a dilettantish gay boy or female one, I don't think it's unfair to say, removed from what was then the centre of events; but these books did constitute a long and remarkably singleminded apprenticeship for Vidal, so that when he moved or was moved into a wider circle he was unusually ready to capitalize on it.

Since *Julian*, the historical novel about a late Roman emperor who tried to stop the advance of Christianity, which came out five years ago and which he is now producing as a film (with his left hand?), Vidal has been enormously productive. *Washington, D.C.* (1967) and the—it's goddamned difficult to find the right word—'notorious' *Myra Breckinridge* have been added to the fiction that Vidal calls 'probably . . . the largest oeuvre of any contemporary American writer' (again somewhat misleading for all its casual tone since at least the late Jack Kerouac and probably Evan Hunter in his dual role of Ed McBain have equalled him in 'plain bulk') and there have been innumerable appearances on television, in magazines, the press, of a personal and nonfictional kind culminating in his latest book, *Reflections upon a Sinking Ship* (1969). Although Vidal has never stopped writing fiction, and include in that plays for TV and live theatre as well, his position as a man to cope with on the present American playing field only really got under way when he stepped out of the many quick-change costumes of his fictions and used the imagination that so easily invented different characters to finally invent, or let's say consolidate, his own for the public. Novelists of my generation have been doing this increasingly in a country where the compulsive interest in another player ('What's the prick got? See, he's not that goodlooking. Brains? I could've said what he just said in my SLEEP, baby, but that Carson didn't invite me on his lousy show did he?'), the man behind the name, the stuff that the 'I' in everyone can measure itself against, has made irrelevant the superstructure of their books and sucked the naked ego out of its hiding place to face the nation. Telling and for a moment BEING their story over the instant wire of the media, they as individuals usually command greater interest today than the calculated works of their imaginations, an initially warming and then confusing mixup in what one thought was one's original purpose in life which I'll return to. Other formerly shy novelists of the same generation got there ahead of Vidal in responding to the siren hum of the electric age for direct projection of the writer's personality: James Baldwin, friend Mailer, Truman Capote, Jack Kerouac, most recently Eldridge Cleaver before he fled the States (and who doesn't have to write novels as long as he keeps on living them), but it is to Vidal's credit that he has added a definitely new twist to the novelist-as-personality and one that we haven't seen before.

When his first collection of critical and smartly cut state of the nation pieces came out in 1962—*Rocking the Boat*, predecessor to the new *Ship* one—a number of people with very overactive intellectual glands were surprised that Vidal, a fellow they had overlooked if not actually patronized, proved himself to be a literate and serious-sounding contender. 'Where has the momser come from?' was a question that didn't remain unasked on the New York abstract thinking scene, accompanied by a sort of wry Jewish smile at having been caught unprepared again, but with a certain amount of genuine surprise. The reason for the surprise was that any midwestern (everything west of the Hudson) boy can write novels in a time that can take them or leave them, but criticism and 'deep' thought in New York produce an immediate stiffening of the spine and a whiff of fear—'Is so-and-so possibly smarter than I am?' Vidal, to everyone's bafflement including my own, was quite obviously no intellectual greenhorn in spite of the fact that he diddled around with hothouse-smelling fiction that none of us in the elite hornrimmed book corps, and the majority of you reading this, either, could be bothered with up to then. At any rate the essays were a revelation to some and they rubbed off sufficiently on his novels so that those who had never read them felt obliged to either pick them up or pay close attention when the new ones like *Julian*, *Washington, D.C.*, and *Myra B.* came out after *Rocking the Boat* had paved the way. And if Vidal's first book of nonfiction had this kind of reinforcing, and slightly intimidating, effect on both his fiction and his status, the latest one, *Reflections upon a Sinking Ship*, probably helps even more.

But before holding it up to the light let me give a rundown on these three recent novels, all published in the mid to late 'sixties, which have received the benefit of Vidal's increased prestige as a dangerously keen blade about town and country, too. They are all readable (*Julian* gets slightly tedious toward the end, perhaps) as you might guess with the knowledge that Vidal got on top of the craft part of his art very early, his first novel was published when he was 20, and that his sense of manipulating or controlling an audience has since been refined by hardboiled five and six figure works for Broadway, television and film—'hack work' he tells us in the latest collection without any trace of apology, all of which adds to his image of selfconfidence and charm. (More than that, many of us who spent lost years in the little or literary-magazine league wouldn't have turned up our noses at this glamorous hackwork ourselves had it been offered; you can only stand so much of being degraded with begging for pennies and living on paper dreams based on inverted snobbery. Vidal HAS been a hack in his life but his present attitude of so what? is the correct one judged by my experience—who is in a position to throw platitudes when the so-called literary life is crawling with so many punctured illusions and indignities that you could write a book?)

Writer for hire at one time or not, Vidal knows how to tell a story and he tells it well, skilfully, enjoyably, but without any great originality or deep point; the most pointed of the three books is *Myra Breckinridge*, a veritable mouthpiece for the author's peeves and horselaughs at various kinds of current buncombe, and a weird enough story about a homosexual who becomes a career girl through an operation and then ends up a straight man although lacking a penis to be fodder for any crafty analyst to sink theories into, but still not a profound satire (*Catch-22*, *Naked Lunch*) in any sense. More about *Myra* in a minute. Probably the best writing in these three books is in *Washington, D.C.*, where there are lightning strokes of fine electrical prose all done with that dispatch and imaginativeness which seems to characterize Vidal at his best: no lingering, getting on with his story and punctuating it with laconic descriptive passages that illuminate in a flash what heavier writers would slop around in. But the book as a whole suffers from a leak that runs throughout all of Vidal's fiction, the failure to be entirely convincing. It becomes a conventional novel, finally, or at least a novel novel, because of its old-fashioned plot machinery, you just can't swallow its more lurid moments—the convenient complicity of Hitchcock-sinister psychiatrists in putting a sane if alcoholic lady away in the good old nuthouse, the too-neat suicide of a hitherto incorruptible senator because he was involved in one unsavory deal (suspicious echoes here as well of Judge Irwin's end in Robert Penn Warren's *All the King's Men*), etc. Yet it does have a very comfortable familiarity with the Washington scene and its power-people that I found convincing and also illuminating to Vidal's preoccupations with actual power and strength as opposed to talk.

Washington, D.C. also seems to owe less to other writers than the other two novels, even including the probable swipe from Warren. *Julian*, although told in its own nicely artful and workable way, can't escape coming under the shadow of Robert Graves, whose historical fiction, especially *Count Belisarius*, covers roughly the same period; more important, Graves's uncanny documentary recreation of the times of the Eastern Roman Empire almost by necessity makes Vidal's tale seem a bit cute and predesigned in comparison. Learned about this era as Vidal has made himself—and he is something of a fanatic at self-education, which comes out in the essays in a more revealing way—he can't hope to match Graves's prodigious knowledge of the period and his book seems thin in texture as a result, Made in Detroit more than in ancient Constantinople. It is for the most part readable and often charming (lousy word but in my judgement true here as elsewhere for Vidal) when you make allowances for a slight artificiality in the technique, but its central theme, that the Emperor Julian was conscious of what would later become—Vidal's view—the worldwide evil of Christianity and valiantly tried to stop it in its childhood because of greater insight than his contemporaries, is again not really convincing. Julian seems more of a nostalgic worshipper of pagan mumbo jumbo than a prophetic anti-Christ, a premature Friedrich Nietzsche with a crown, and in spite of Vidal's serious efforts to get us to believe in his unique importance and heroic failure in altering history that has implications up to the present, we are entertained by the detail in the book but very sceptical about the moral.

As for swinging *Myra Breckinridge*, which according to a recent interview with Vidal in a celebrity-pimping men's magazine I am not at liberty to name in this one (motto: 'We Joyfully Kiss Their Asses When They're Our Kind Of Names And Pay For The Privilege To Insure Our Crusade For Tit Heaven On Earth Among Gun-Controlled Consenting Adults') has sold something like 41 million copies, this is not meant to be taken in any realistic way and so Vidal can't be called on his usual credulity-stretching. As a matter of fact, as I've mentioned, the book is less of a novel than a device for letting Vidal get off a series of sharp shots about dozens of irritations that exercise his pearl, including the death of the novel, over-obeisance to film as High Art, ponderous jargon of psychiatry (old hat), fraudulence of California-type commercialism (old hat but very well done), lustful lady actor's agents, the temptation for homosexuals to now become actual women with the co-operation of a medical science that promises more than it gives—fat targets of this kind, and he lays into his subject with obvious fun and a kind of cruel wildness. The book is imaginative but also, unexpectedly, aimless and flat in places where he runs out of ideas; and even when he recovers his pace and practically rapes the reader with outlandish sexual inventiveness you keep getting the dim memory that the groundwork for this has been set before, that it is a pastiche cooked up by a very nimble exploiter of ideas first developed by others, in this case probably by Terry Southern in *Candy* and Evelyn Waugh in *The Loved One*, perhaps Nabokov is also involved with *Lolita*.

Whatever the precise books that set the author's mind to rolling, we know instinctively that even though Vidal's targets are his own perverse property and belong to no one else, the frame in which he works is not quite his own invention and has been borrowed without a thank-you note for the occasion. But putting that aside right now, for it is the main thought here that Vidal's fascination for today rests not on what he has done in literature but what literature has done for him as a powerful presence in a new personality-orientated climate of culture, what is most interesting about the book is its closeness to Vidal's nonfiction. The novelist turned public prosecutor in the 'sixties, both in essays and in the flesh by campaigning unsuccessfully for Congress (1960) and appearing on the box as an aggressive progressive well-groomed human lance, has here hit on a form that is the perfect dark counterpart to his journalism. Where the articles are astringent, neat, practical and cleanly aimed, *Myra* spreads out into all the suppressed weirdo directions that Vidal keeps under control in his first-person prose; she compliments his new nonfiction reputation for being 'the most . . . devastating . . . of iconoclasts' (Mayor John V. Lindsay of NY, new white hope lit. critic) by being equally slashing on a wilder, squashier less standard turf and she also testifies to Vidal's new selfconfidence as an arbiter of American immorals who no longer needs to conceal his true grit behind the cushion of the conventional novel he had been writing before.

So much for the background. Vidal is now totally out in the open as a nervy corrector and satirist of the present, all the forms he works in having finally coalesced to make one man and one image—'a new model Bernard Shaw' (the English critic Normon Shrapnel, which recalls the American Ivan Gold's remark in *Sick Friends* of GBS as 'that brittle, dead, not-even-faggot')—and it is in this most recent vein of integration among the several Vidals that we meet him in *Reflections upon a Sinking Ship*. Apart from its contents although very much related to their 'feel' in my view, it is eye-opening to see the number of fashionable publications, whether of the Establishment Left or the Center, all chic, where Vidal's first published the prose for this book. They make up a veritable transatlantic *Who's Who* of periodicals: *Times Literary Supplement*, *Encounter*, *New York Review of Books*, *New York Times Book Review*, *Esquire*, *Partisan Review*, *New Statesman*, *The Reporter* (now defunct), etc., all the most proper places to appear on both sides of the ocean.

Also very interesting and pertinent, I believe, is the number of English magazines on the list, rare for an American writer, but indicative once you get into the quality of Vidal's first-person writing. It is succinct, witty, intelligent without being labored, and above all an example of chiselled good manners at work even when he is being nasty and occasionally bitchy to people like Mary McCarthy, Paddy Chayevsky, Susan Sandbag (er, Sontag), John Hersey, Henry Miller, the Kennedy family and others. These good manners, which show themselves in literary courtesy and a style and polish which almost never becomes obtrusive, in general a truly cultivated tone of talking in print not unlike the best chat at what Nancy Randolph in the *Daily News* would call the best gatherings, have by tradition come more to be associated with upperclass British journalism than the coarser-grained American article. Vidal can pull a blunt verbal weapon out of his pocket when he has to, he can even be a 'clerk' when the demands of annotating a piece force it—'clerk' is his contemptuous word for drudges in the US literary business and Normie Podhoretz gets conveniently gored—but he is obviously most at home when he is being a trim aristocratic type speaking candidly but always with a kind of thinlipped selfdiscipline.

This style of expression, the bitten phrase, the patrician cool, has been rare in recent American criticism and opinion-delivering to my knowledge and would once have put off a large audience instead of winning its respect, which Vidal's first-person manner(s) usually does; there have been exceptions like Clare Booth Luce, perhaps, and the guiltlessly snobbish journalist Lucius Beebe, but neither of them combined their uncompromising Tiffany tone with that larger arc of a literary man's concern for the entire world as Vidal wants to. The dead Eleanor Roosevelt, of all people, is not dissimilar to Vidal (judged by her journalism) in having had a wellbred sense of social responsibility along with a very alert awareness of the feelings of others, although she was altogether too good unfortunately in the lollipop sense to match Vidal's outspokenness and mod worldliness. Edith Wharton, just as spirited and at least as gifted a writer as Vidal, is probably a closer example of the blueblood manner at work in American prose, always implicitly censuring cruder personalities by mere stance as well as that straight-thinking braveness which the sons and daughters of Wasp families who have built commercial/political empires sometimes display when they don't go completely sour.

Whether in fact Vidal comes out of such a background, or whether in his case it was much more ambiguous—his divorced mother was apparently very Washington Social, married for a time to the multi-millionaire stepfather of Jackie Kennedy Onassis and young Vidal was silverspooned from 10 to 16, but his father seems to have been of US-Italian blood and something of an outsider to this way of life—the evidence is clear from the newest book that this is the natural environment of his mind, his ideal persona, and it is a new kind of suavity he is showing us. Since the death of Wharton I (at least) would be hard put to find an American writer with a voice who came from that class and stance; Louis Auchincloss, Vidal's contemporary, apparently qualifies on the basis of background but so far not in imposing style or manner—the same might be said for Cleveland Amory; from what I have heard Maude Hutchins also has all the necessary peerage papers but her voice is secretive and almost unheard in our national uproar; as for Robert Lowell, he has the genealogy and more, but is wrapped up in moral and ethical concerns that put him somewhat above the dirty everyday part of writing and certainly not someone who had to navigate through dead commercial seas with a different swirl to his sail.

Vidal then, in his very posh nonfiction style, brings a cleancut, goodlooking, expensive air to serious problems that is as attractive on the surface as the Kennedys' style was in serious politics. And even though Vidal rails at this 'holy family' from within—he and Jackie are or are not technically related, but it's close, as he never tires of reminding us—the same well-mannered, breezy and even liberal patricianism that swept the Kennedys into power has also brought along Vidal as a literary-theatrical equivalent of the same general cut, a little younger (now 44) but dusted by the identical imported talc. He has much the same easy authority in dealing with books, ideas and what he calls 'moral values' that the murdered president had in seeming to handle the issues of the day; as well as a quick-witted, slightly imperial bearing held erect by an insistently elevated sense of civic responsibility, just like the 'good' politicians he writes about in *Washington, D.C.*, and this air of being without sin gives Vidal an effective headstart from which to move, in his criticisms, in practically any direction he cares to swivel.

But our boy Gore is not content with merely impressing the ordinary 'voters', or reader-viewers, who find his dash and air of public dedication refreshing and also worthy of respect. Based on what he says in *Reflections*, he is also in very hairy competition with almost every prominent novelist alive in his own time, from John O'Hara to Nathalie Sarraute, from the recent Ernest Hemingway to William Burroughs, in fact from Ian Fleming to Samuel Beckett, and the amazing thing is the amount of cool snotty shots he is able to hit them with. (Vidal by the way has a steady hand for the kill in case anyone cares to fuck with HIM in print; I assume I'll get mine at some later date but what must be said must be said, and so forth.) Almost the only writers who escape unharmed and with praise are those venerably dead like the Marquis de Sade or those who offer no threat like Edgar Rice Burroughs, the creator of Tarzan. All writers, particularly Americans, are psychotically competitive in the middle of the (lonely) journey so there is nothing that outrageous in itself about Vidal's jabs and back-handed knocks at his colleagues. What is different is the ease and conviction with which he can make himself sound superior to novelists who until now, anyway, have been his leaders in impressing their contemporaries by the depth or richness or uniqueness of their work.

For example, William Burroughs' writing should appeal to 'anal eroticists who like science fiction'; it is odd that not once in the course of *Sexus* does anyone say to Henry Miller, 'Henry, you're full of shit'; Saul Bellow (whom Vidal actually respects but can't help criticizing out of habit) 'overstates the case' against academic literary-intellectuals; Robbe-Grillet's theory of fiction is 'naive'; Susan Sontag's 'well-known difficulties in writing English continue to make things hard for her'; John O'Hara's stuff, 'finally, cannot be taken seriously as literature'; Chester Himes 'has a sense of humor that sinks his work like a stone'; 'unlike Mary McCarthy' that 'intelligent . . . literary critic', Vidal doesn't extend confidences to nosy biographers; 'Beckett's *Watt*, Donleavy's *The Ginger Man* are incapable of summoning up so much as the ghost of a rose . . .'

That's Vidal on some of his pen-pals; but at the same time that he belts them with such pleasure, all phrased very objectively and lucidly as if it were the law, any charge that he might be the least bit prejudiced is set off by his vigorous public concerns which are all delivered in the same tone of voice as the literary judgements. His by now well-known scourges of overpopulation, the uses of unjust wealth in American politics, commercial TV, repressive and reactionary sex laws in the fifty states, the mordant description of the US as the 'American Empire', etc., all make him a public good guy of the first water, fearless, witty, plain spoken, concerned with the fate of the nation before himself and very much a newstyle patriot. The net result is that Vidal can be transparently petty to my mind where his selfinterest is threatened, such as his own position as a writer overshadowed (so far) by more original or grander talents, and generous in the extreme when he gets into the pure air of standing up to ignorance, stupidity, bigotry, vulgarity—not dirty words—, impersonal factors that don't make him selfconscious and permit him to use every bit of his cleverness and, in fact, his literary gift itself for positive purposes.

This gift, or part of it, as opposed to that of writers whom Vidal makes seem less intelligent or astute than himself, seems to lie chiefly in the ability to convert private reactions into what is publicly effective, to simplify and even eviscerate the complexity of an experience ('. . . Jean Genet, always lyric and vague when celebrating cock . . .') down to its neat outlines in order to score debater's points; to use the skills of a lawyer, in other words, to convince you of the justice of his position rather than bending all of his being into the work itself (as in the obsessional possessiveness of a Beckett, Miller or Burroughs) with indifference to audience approval. In coming on this way, if my assessment is correct, Vidal is drawing heavily on two major sources that have shaped his public personality as both writer-arbiter and, more to the point, the new kind of force figure in the culture who uses a literary cachet to enter the 'national mind' through the bullying reach of the media.

1. The first of these sources is political: Vidal wears the very name of American politics in 'Gore', inherited from his mother's father, Sen. Thomas Gore (R.) of Oklahoma, and his early immersion via family into the vote-getting political process, with its dependence on popularity, wooing the majority, cutting a figure on the hustings, all the necessary and often cynical artifacts of the professional representative of the people, is decisively different from the experience of any American writers his age whom I am aware of. It certainly might be expected to have played a PERMANENT part in conditioning Vidal's hard-headed sense of the public and exactly what works before it and what does not if one is to stay on 'top'.

2. The second chief source is what the writer himself calls 'homosexual-ist', since, to quote him, 'there is of course no such thing as a homosexual'. Despite current usage, Vidal writes, 'the word is an adjective describing a sexual action, not a noun describing a recognizable type'. This is a fine point, apparently important to Vidal as an individual, but for the majority of readers who know very well that there is a rough grouping of American Jewish writers and one of American Negro/Black writers, the fact that there is another undercover minority of American Homosexual-ist writers—no more of a type than the Jewish-Blacks, probably, but still a loose unit with certain things in common—must be commented upon, especially since I believe it is indispensably important to understanding Vidal's particular kind of public strategy.

First, it should be said that within a decade or two with everyone becoming more of a sexual Independant, going his or her own way and even several ways at once in the search for an erotic home and even what John Updike has called erotic 'religion', such simple-minded distinctions as homosexual and heterosexual will hopefully seem irrelevant or at least very dated. Perhaps, as Vidal says, 'All human beings are bisexual' and all discussion will start at that point. But at this present time the American writers whose work and thematic preoccupations put them in the homosexualist group are a specific cultural influence in the US and abroad (although less than ten years ago I think), and their criticism of majority values comes as much from their watchful minority position as do similar insights from Blacks, white hippie-revolutionaries, Jews in all-goy suburbia, everyone on the fringe who has lived with danger real or imagined. What has been evident throughout the 'sixties, however, is the increasing outspokenness and even militancy of writers whose subjects legitimately connect them to a homosexualist group—not unlike the Blacks, although less raw; James Baldwin (double status), Allen Ginsberg, Paul Goodman, Parker Tyler, Randolfe Wicker and Taylor Mead are some who have cut through the mists as straight talkers or diagnosticians while in the more purely imaginative zone Tennessee Williams, William Burroughs, Edward Albee, Alfred Chester, and even that one-time flower songster Truman Capote have pulled no punches and spared no particular feelings.

Vidal might be said to have begun with the second group, as a solely imaginative writer, but one whose industriousness (nuts, genuinely fierce application to work!) didn't compensate for the lack of a truly bold signature in the eye of the public; then to have discovered himself by greater participation in the media as a polemicist and personality, and brought that new extra-literary tingle back to his fiction with much greater reader impact than before. His work now as a fighting dandy, a deft crusader, in both fiction and essay makes very open use of values that are not hard to associate with the homosexual school—and the lifestyle in which it is grounded—in almost a classic sense: elegance, narcissism, sex as power, wit and ridicule as lethal verbal poisons, superior coolness in the face of bourgeois fire, a very pragmatic concern with money and appearance ('fat' is a horrible word in the Vidal lexicon), an identification with the Greek and Roman civilisations which can't be conceived of without their homosexual traditions, a very punctilious regard for what is correct behaviour and what isn't. In sum, a deerlike alertness to unpleasant worldly realities, how to cope with them, how to defend yourself, and how to attack those slower of mind and more complacent than experience has permitted you to be.

Among the American writers of my generation associated with homosexualist themes Vidal has developed his thrust and parry more highly than almost any of them, and because of this essentially defensive skill—coupled with the inherited political cunning that makes turning any given opportunity your way that gut-principle of public survival—he has been able to advance his ideas and personality before a sizeable mass of potentially mean bastards Out There with much less hesitation than his buddies in the same vulnerable bag have had the courage, chutzpah or quick IQ resources to do. For this alone he deserves considerable respect, in my opinion, but the price could be something else again. In this sense: If it is true that Vidal has only come into his own as a 'sixties celebrity due to the inflamed needs of the media (as I believe) and the demand they make upon literary talent to project itself in person, directly, theatrically, like a movie star, where does this leave him in letters, is it still his main concern in the midst of all the ego-bonbons, and if it is where does he actually stand under a hard but honest light?

There seems to me little doubt (and keep in mind that I'm also involved, Jewish-Black School, 1922–, and my analysis may not be entirely snow-white either) that the vigour with which Vidal has pursued his career on the big board was a genuinely novelistic one at the start. His great energy, inventiveness, natural ear, sense of scene, plot-masterminding—did you ever read *Plotto* for kicks as I did, Vidal, back in the days when *Writer's Digest* was our *Partisan Review?*—were all staples of the conventionally made novel that first attracted him and which he did his best to recreate in his own books with slightly bizarre subject-matter. But the aesthetics of fiction, or what's left of it, changed radically under his proud nose and Vidal's kind of novel was beginning to seem antique until he syphoned off its more aggressive intellectual qualities and put them into 'journalism' (not meant disparagingly in any sense) in all of its present new forms, including *Myra Breckinridge.* Where he stands now, therefore, is in the shadow of at least half a dozen unacknowledged living writers who taught him the method of savage contemporary satire; he himself is not the author of any genuinely original or sizeable literary accomplishment unless you're impressed by 'plain bulk', certainly not of a major vision of reality which could only have been put into a book. His biggest accomplishment has been the refinement of a very point-scoring manner of asserting himself in a variety of interchangeable outlets that require spit and polish with words. And without detracting in the least from the stylish bravery (and bravado) of the assertion, I believe it could not have won the audience it apparently has on the basis of the written word alone. The needed push was supplied by TV, which valued his attractive male model qualities—looks, wit, forcefulness of delivery, 'challenging' point of view, etc.—and encouraged Vidal's reliance upon his own personality and on-camera style to make his future way, even in 'literature', instead of using the indirect horse-and-buggy route of the pre-*Myra* books.

I would call this, then, a personal triumph in that new blurred no-man's land that lies slightly west of showbusiness although selfelection to being a Serious Writer provided the platform and the veneer. As Vidal himself says in a sharp little piece in *Ship* that examines his own situation in a camouflaged way, the 'talking writers' are much more on display now than ever before. But he doesn't probe the implications of this display (the handicap by definition of a novelist appearing mentally nude before a live audience, without his usual cast of characters, and then the compensatory clutching at one's popularity-rating like Zsa Zsa Gabor instead of chuckling at it) except to say that the 'obvious danger for the writer is the matter of time' lost for his work. But suppose, in fact, that THIS HAS BECOME HIS WORK, as I believe has happened with Vidal in the broadest sense and not necessarily a pejorative one? Without his most vivid creation, a crisp public personality commenting in a stylishly nasty way on the nasty world we live in, would Vidal's books have the inherent power to distinguish themselves on their own? I strongly question it. (The best of them, likely, is the very slender *Dark Green, Bright Red* published when he was 24, a veritable world ago, and doomed to die of anaemia until Vidal raised a rumpus in other areas and got it reprinted in 1968 by NAL.) With this personality, however, interest in the older ones is whetted and in the last two—*Myra* and *Ship*—the content is practically indistinguishable from the new image Vidal has carved for himself, the schizophrenia separating public performance and private expression has been healed, they are one and the same. So that while it is all very highminded for Vidal to brush aside the significance of the 'talking writer' in relation to the 'writing writer', even to amplify his own would-be purity with a set of serious abstract values which I'm sure he believes he believes in, his actual professional behaviour tells a much more candid story.

It shows the worldly heights that a certain kind of novelist in America can attain in our day when he acts out his idea of fiction instead of confining it to the writing table. The opportunities have never been greater for putting a nineteenth century novelistic imagination (think of the variety in Balzac and Dickens, the 'masters' whom Vidal would identify with the very idea of the novel) into twentieth century life itself—TV hero, politician, movie producer, public scold, Broadway success, indeed bestselling novelist, the entire range of gossip-column fantasy—especially when the kind of fiction Vidal basically feels closest to is a pale substitute today for its realization in actuality. It is impossible to read Vidal consecutively, as I have just done, without seeing that he is a very ambitious man, not unlike those worthy supermen he is drawn to in Greek and Roman times, but in spite of his towering and often foolish pride as shown toward his writing competitors it is finally not literary ambition that is his driving concern, but rather a broad variety of ACHIEVEMENTS copious enough to go down in the pages of some history—preferably one (and I don't say this sarcastically) written by himself.

If his view of the modern novel itself were more profound, even more modern, as an investigation of reality in the sense that it is used by contemporaries of his and mine like John Barth and Marguerite Young his ambition would probably be taken care of by the fulltime detective work of his art. But the essentially boyish love of an outward story that has always been buried underneath his more acquired tastes—'that rare thing, the narrative gift', he tells us with a bit of solemn pretension at this late date when the golden age of story-telling as such has probably been usurped by film and is no longer the first excitement of adult prose—has led him to the world where events are made and prizes given rather than the less visible one where they are remade and justice given. (And let it also be made clear that the present writer doesn't claim this final dedication and immunity from the world's tempting tit for himself; I am contrasting Vidal to other novelists who have shown other alternatives and keep the idea of serious literature alive in our society whether you care for their work or not.)

But by imposing himself on that more obvious scene, the one that includes us all as greedy people and not only as readers or writers, in being concerned with personal success as a means (I believe) of protecting himself in a period that no longer offers its sweetest laurels to art as a thing apart from money and prestige, Vidal is really not that different from other amibitious literary personalities of my generation who have learned to DISTRUST the power of literature compared to the compensatory powers of life that can flow from it. What separates him, as I've said, is that he has reached this sophisticated bigtime nihilism from a formerly shadowed literary trail which has traditionally skirted the brawling centre and he has done it with a new rakish style. Vidal's courage and agility in making his way in the cruel environment of Success City has been rare and even pioneering, but these virtues must finally be applied to the hustling of a gutsy personality in our time with splendid materialistic results, not to the creation of original gold. Vidal has yet to do this and so far, in spite of his invoking grand names like Henry James, Kafka, Proust, Joyce et al. when he talks about writing—and he is a compulsive literary namedropper, almost as if to prove that even if he didn't go to college 'because of the war' he's read you into hopeless inferiority (which might even conceivably be true but should go unflaunted, Nancy Randolph would probably say)— I'm afraid he has really been more of a go-getting entertainer than anything else, the act getting slicker all the time.

The most successful go-getters have always taken themselves very earnestly, so it is no paradox that Vidal does the same; the only important thing is the performance and here—once he's on—G. V. is frightened of no man, certainly not his literary betters. He is turning it on right now in front of a larger public than his dear Kafkas and Prousts and even [sic!] Evelyn Waughs ever dreamed of, and I admire him for his sass, and for all the sober midnight rehearsal-time it took him to get there, but the answer to my opening question is obviously: No, apart from its noble associations literature is only a means to climb the American beanstalk today, you'd be a fool to take it seriously on its own terms because the way things are you'd never be heard from again.

STEPHEN SPENDER
"Private Eye"

New York Review of Books, March 22, 1973, pp. 6–8

I first met Gore Vidal in 1947 (or was it '49?). He was very young and looked spruce and golden. He had tawny hair and eyes that made me think of bees' abdomens drenched in pollen. The center of each eye, perhaps its iris, held a sting. He wore a bow tie and a well-tailored light-brown English country-style suit. He discussed his success (had he just published *The City and the Pillar?*) like a joke which we shared. He showed me an envelope on the inside cover of which an ardent fan had glued an ecstatic self-photograph. He could not have been more enviable.

Perhaps it was on this occasion that I made the priggish remark he quotes in his essay on Norman Mailer's *Advertisements for Myself.* The conversation had shifted for a moment from his success to some other young writer who had "unexpectedly failed, not gone on, blown up." Apparently I said, "The difference in England is that they want us to be distinguished, to be good." I should have added, of course, that in England success is supposed to be kept within the bounds of decency: that is to say, to bring to your friends credit for knowing you but not pushed to that extreme where they might become envious. I have always suspected that the real reason why E. M. Forster gave up writing novels was in order not to provoke his English friends.

Just about this time there was an even younger American writer who, when we met, looked at me coolly and said: "When I meet older writers I can just *smell* failure!" Fortunately I was able to get back my own some minutes later when he asked me, as one infinitely acquainted with the sordid ways of the literary world, whether I considered that he should follow his publisher's advice and have himself photographed entering a brothel. I saw my chance and answered: "I assure you there isn't a brothel in the world that could do you more harm than your publishers are already doing by promoting you." The remark went unheard.

The difference between Gore Vidal and the second writer was the sense in which Gore Vidal wasn't serious. Or perhaps I should have written "was serious." For he is one of those who had learned "to care and not to care," and to discriminate between things that are worth and things that are not worth caring about. For all he talked about it, I do not think he really cared about success. Certainly someone mad about success would not achieve his most genuine effects in a form so modest as the essay; and this is what Gore Vidal does in ⟨*Homage to Daniel Shays: Collected Essays 1952–1972*⟩. Not only are the individual essays excellent, the whole volume is more than the sum of its parts. For taken together these essays compose the features of the writer, complex and a bit mysterious, like a face mirrored in the darkened waters of a well.

There are at least two or three Gore Vidals. One is the earnest and attentive student of literature, doggedly informative about subjects such as the *nouveau roman*. The second is the tipster of the authors' stakes: a great expert on the running form of Norman Mailer, and with much inside knowledge of the fixers and the rackets. And the third is the President-watcher, standing at a respectful distance while inspecting Presidential candidates, but with a glint in an eye that is altogether too observant.

The essays about literature are probably the most studied and the least at ease with themselves, for Gore Vidal, superbly self-assured at his best, can be painfully painstaking, as he is in "French Letters: Theories of the New Novel." He is much happier when he moves from the written to the writer, as is shown in the first essay in the volume. "Novelists and Critics of the 1940's." This essay hardly counts as literary criticism, but that does not matter, for there is justification for an attack on the extraordinary pretensions of modern critics to make absolute judgments.

It is difficult, on the internal evidence provided by the essays, to measure his learning, but in this first essay he already shows that he has access to an arsenal of random information about the ancient Romans and the church fathers (it may well have come out of Gibbon) which he draws on to make swift thrusts at an opponent. The arguments of new critics remind him of

> the semantic and doctrinal quarrels of the church fathers in the fourth century, when a diphthong was able to break the civilized world in half and spin civilization into nearly a milennium of darkness. One could invent a most agreeable game of drawing analogies between the fourth century and today. F. R. Leavis and Saint Jerome are perfectly matched, while John Chrysostom and John Crowe Ransom suggest a possibility. The analogy works amusingly on all levels save one: the church fathers had a Christ to provide them with a primary source of revelation, while our own dogmatists must depend either upon private systems or else upon those proposed by such slender reeds as Matthew Arnold and T. S. Eliot, each, despite his genius, a ritual victim as well as a hero of literary fashion.

This is delightful and gives one a ringside feeling like that which the Israelites must have had watching their youthful David go out to meet Goliath. One wonders, a bit anxiously, how many of these learned pebbles Vidal has in his sling. (He has mentioned earlier on that doubt is cast on Matthew Arnold's enthusiasm for Dante on account of Arnold's inadequate Italian.)

The pleasure conveyed by the passage I have just quoted is not as elementary as it may seem. This is partly on account of its style, which is worth considering, for Gore Vidal is an elated stylist. He carries weights of packed allusion with a buoyant air. In so far as he has an argument he is well on top of it. What is most characteristic of him in this passage is a kind of mock pomposity. The learning or the pseudo learning verges on the hectoring or lecturing manner. But just as he seems about to cross the line which divides riding high from pomposity, he wheels his charger around and turns the whole thing into a joke, just as he turned the talk about his success into a joke when we first met.

As Gore Vidal several times reminds us, his grandfather was a senator and he himself electioneered to become a congressman, as though to turn into his grandfather. That he should ever have wished to be in Congress is utterly absurd. His strength and his deepest seriousness are that he himself sees the absurdity. He has turned pomposity *manqué* into a life style. The charm of his essays when he describes important people in public life is that the description seems constantly to inflate little balloons of importance—and then to stick pins into them.

The underlying activity which he sees to be common to the academic, the literary, and the political life is the success game. He does not forget, of course, that games can be serious, especially in politics; the fascination of his President-watching essays is that he sees in Washington the interlocking games of high seriousness and low comedy.

A game which he rather enjoys playing himself is that which he calls, in an essay of that name, "Literary Gangsters." Stung by opening a number of *Playbill* and reading some remarks by Mr. Richard Gilman in which Gore Vidal is referred to as "a culture hero of the Fifties," he launches forth into a wonderful attack on certain theatrical and literary journalists. It is written with such relish that sometimes it reads like Advice to a Graduate Student about to Embark on a Literary Career. He lists the rules for this hectic infighting, and concludes:

> Finally, the gangster can never go wrong if, while appearing to uphold the highest standards (but never define those standards or say just when it was that the theater, for instance, was "relevant"), he attacks

> indiscriminately the artists of the day, the popular on the ground that to give pleasure to the many is a sign of corruption and the much-admired on the ground that since all values now held by the society are false (for obvious reasons don't present alternative values), any culture hero must reflect perfectly the folly of those who worship him.

His account of some of those he labels gangsters is so boisterous that I can hardly believe they could be offended. In a swift summation, he relates one writer's career: how Mr. John W. Aldridge, Jr., set up in 1947 "as a legitimate literary businessman, opening shop with a piece describing the writers of the postwar generation in which he warmly praised John Horne Burns and myself. The praise made us think he was not a hood, his shop a legitimate business not a front." Alas, though, it was all a monstrous plot, even including the move to Connecticut "in order to be close to certain of his victims." It turned out that

> . . . he was thoroughly casing the territory. Then he struck. In a blaze of publicity, Mr. Aldridge bit one by one those very asses he had with such cunning kissed, earning himself an editorial in *Life* magazine congratulating him for having shown up the decadence and immorality of the postwar writers. He has long since faded from the literary scene . . . as have, fortunately, those scars on which we sit.

Gore Vidal is brash, but in a passage such as this, he elevates brashness to satire through the style. Satire is unfair, simplifies those attitudes it attacks, and then expresses the simplification with an elegance and elaboration pleasing in themselves. What he does with the literary gangsters is cut through the gordian knots of their style and show that it often conceals a brashness less justified than his own (he is very good at playing his opponent's game better than he does himself).

Memories of having been the young lion who shook out his mane before ten thousand glowing sophomores, who leaped from the circus floor to jump through the same hoops as Norman Mailer, and who scorned to be thought whelped of the same litter as Truman Capote—these are aspects of Vidal's self-mockery, which does not call his whole personality into play. It is when he is writing about politicians that he becomes like one of those "opposites" in a Yeatsian world of antinomies, the perfect negation of its own hugged secret self-image. The negative of his positive Senator Vidal, but also deep down the projection of him, he looks with the glare of an unthinkably powerful searchlight at Ronald Reagan, illuminates every pore and wrinkle exposed under the grease paint, and writes the description down with the diamond pen of hell's least kind recording angel:

> Ronald Reagan is a well-preserved not young man. Close-to, the painted face is webbed with delicate lines while the dyed hair, eyebrows, and eyelashes contrast oddly with the sagging muscle beneath the as yet unlifted chin, soft earnest of wattle-to-be. The effect, in repose, suggests the work of a skillful embalmer. Animated, the face is quite attractive and at a distance youthful; particularly engaging is the crooked smile full of large porcelain-capped teeth. The eyes are interesting: small, narrow, apparently dark, they glitter in the hot light, alert to every move, for this is enemy country—the liberal Eastern press who are so notoriously immune to that warm and folksy performance which Reagan quite deliberately projects over their heads to some legendary constituency at the far end of the tube, some shining Carverville where good Lewis Stone forever lectures Andy Hardy on the virtues of thrift and the wisdom of the contract system at Metro-Goldwyn-Mayer.

It is description of this kind, done with the fervor of a scientist exploring a strange land and making a description of its fauna of such accuracy that the language itself acquires the clarity of cells magnified under a microscope, that Gore Vidal does best. The language becomes an apparatus designed to capture very rare specimens observed in highly characteristic but not often reported situations, like that of camels in heat—

> Ordinarily Rockefeller's face is veal-white, as though no blood courses beneath that thick skin. But now, responding to the lowering day, he has turned a delicate conch pink. What is he saying? "Well, let's face it, there's been some disagreement among the pollsters."

Just as Vidal is even better on writers than on writing, so he is better on politicians than on politics, about which he is always interesting. But as President-watcher he ceases to be either frolicsome or satiric, he is contributing to knowledge in describing with great attention a new American species: the public man seen as a fusion of all the external forces of publicity, presentation, and advertising media concentrated upon him and the extraordinary transformation of the inner man into mechanical will and perpetual guardedness which is the result of exposure to these conditions.

Joseph Alsop, also a President-watcher, once explained to me that men like Johnson and Nixon are not at all like the rest of us. They think of power unceasingly, and they tap resources of will and duplicity which by ordinary standards are unthinkable. Obviously, politicians like Adlai Stevenson (to whom, humanly, Hugh Gaitskell was a close equivalent) are too nice and cultivated for such a task. Occasionally they think of something other than power, and this is debilitating to a system which ought to be fueled on nothing but high-octane publicity. Some men have energy that is human and some have energy that is inhuman, but they rarely have both at once. Increasingly presidents tend to conscript the inhuman or superhuman qualities in themselves (perhaps Nietzsche's Superman is really a mid-twentieth-century American president).

Descriptions such as those of Governors Reagan and Rockefeller are cruel not because they are satiric or malicious, but because they are true. As President-watcher, Gore Vidal is personally often quite sympathetic to the objects of his attention. Of course, failure, like absence, lends enchantment to the view, and his portrait of Barry Goldwater renders him positively charming.

In his famous essay on the Kennedys, "The Holy Family," he combines satire with observation. The satiric idea that the Kennedys have projected onto the American public their sense of family which derives from Ireland, "priest-ridden, superstitious, clannish," is worked out to the point where the satire is superseded by the tragedy:

> Meanwhile, the source of the holy family's power is the legend of the dead brother. . . . Yet the myth that JFK was a philosopher-king will continue as long as the Kennedys remain in politics. And much of the power they exert over the national imagination is a direct result of the ghastliness of what happened at Dallas. But though the world's grief and shock were genuine, they were not entirely for JFK himself. The death of a young leader necessarily strikes an atavistic chord. For thousands of years the man-god was sacrificed to ensure with blood the harvest, and there is always an element of ecstasy as well as awe in our

> collective grief. Also, Jack Kennedy was a television star, more seen by most people than their friends or relatives.

The modern world absorbs the atavism and legends of the past and transforms the Fisher King into its own terms—hence Jesus Christ Superstar. Gore Vidal, President-watching, expresses this process with exceptional vigor, but where he is most original is in his insight into the qualities of personality (or lack of it) required today of the holders of highest office. The public does not require the President to be, as a person, trustworthy. What they do require is that they can trust him never to stop thinking about the presidency:

> Hypocrisy and self-deception are the traditional characteristics of the middle class in any place and time, and the United States today is the paradigmatic middle-class society. Therefore we can hardly blame our political gamesmen for being, literally, representative. Any public man has every right to try and trick us, not only for his good but, if he is honorable, for ours as well.

Trust in this context means not trusting the President to refrain from trickery during elections, but trusting him to be wired into, *powered* by his own ambition unceasingly, like a dynamo.

When he writes about power, one is impressed by something authoritative in Gore Vidal's manner. The features reflected on the surface of the well have muscles compressed to seriousness, yet they do not lose the self-awareness which includes a trace of self-mockery. The writer who can quote to such effect in parenthesis, "("It all began in the cold": Arthur M. Schlesinger, Jr., A *Thousand Days*)," is not likely to fall into the trap of solemnity.

Gore Vidal is by now obviously irremediably saved from his public persona. His essays celebrate the triumph of private values over the public ones of power. They represent the drama of the private face perpetually laughing at, and through, the public one. At the same time, their seriousness lies very largely in his grasp of the conditions and characteristics which make up the public world. What makes an essayist? It is curious to reflect that the greatest English essayist, Francis Bacon, was also a man with the strongest sense of public values consistently questioned in his essays by those of the private human condition; and that Montaigne was a magistrate who retired from public life to his country estate and thought much about the world, and about power, and about friendship.

PETER CONRAD

"Re-inventing America"

Times Literary Supplement, March 26, 1976, pp. 347–48

Although the array of Gore Vidal's personae is bemusing, they tend to come in pairs: the American and the Roman, the historian and the formalist, the candidate for political office and the propagandist for bisexuality. Even his name bifurcates—Gore is the caption attached to him by populist America (he inherits it from his maternal grandfather, the Oklahoma senator Thomas Pryor Gore); Vidal has become the badge of his elegant Italian exile. He has had faces to fit each name: he recalls that as a child he looked like a Gore, "blond and pig-nosed but growing older, I've grown more Vidal". Photographs confirm his account of the dandy's pilgrimage: the child is eager and porcine; the young man is spry; the fifty-year-old of today has composed his face into the likeness, as he himself admits, "of one of the later, briefer Roman Emperors", even down to the sculptural details of a few dignified seismic cracks for wrinkles.

As a writer, too, he has made the journey from Gore to Vidal. The early novels, in accordance with his juvenile heroism—piloting a plane at the age of ten, later the youngest warrant officer in the army—are stoutly Gore-ish. *Williwaw* has the blunt, laconic manner of American naturalism which Hemingway had made the style of hearty masculinity. Even the homosexual novel *The City and the Pillar* derives its originality from this tight-lipped, muscular manner: the hero is not an empurpled aesthete but a tennis champion whose sexual preference is determined by the conviviality of the locker-room. This novel, written in sanctimonious earnest by Gore, can now be read as an adroit parody by Vidal, treating a love which defies nature in the bluff, nonchalant style of naturalism, bending Hemingway to a defence of sexual subversion. The more recent fictions have been the impudent inventions of Vidal, who is represented by the lavishly fecund Aaron Burr and the cellulose phantom of Myra Breckinridge—though she has lately had to fight down a reincarnation of Gore, the repressively conventional Myron, proprietor of a Chinese laundry in the San Fernando Valley.

But the more extreme the enmity between these different roles, the closer together they draw. The quarrelsome personages are secretly identical, as they are for Gore Vidal's dandified forbears—the misanthropy of Childe Harold has relaxed into the promiscuous indifference of Don Juan; the moral outrage of Jokanaan has been prissily inverted and epigrammatized by Jack Worthing; the political heritage and military distinctions of Gore (born at that granite shrine of callow masculinity, West Point) unfold into the witty perversities of Vidal, who has retired from the American world of power, but in order to write its history. He has renounced the collaborative power of the legislator (he was a congressional candidate in 1960) so as to enjoy the omnipotence of the satirist. Rather than making history, he writes it—or invents it. The distinction is crucial. Gore conscientiously writes history; Vidal unscrupulously invents it—although he has said that Truman Capote has made lying into an art form ("a minor one"), Vidal himself has made the falsification of historical record into a major art.

The trilogy of political novels now completed—*Burr*, *1876* and *Washington, D.C.*—is the result of a precarious, dazzling partnership between Gore the researcher and Vidal the frivolous meddler with history. The latter disparages the former in the afterword to *1876*: "Although I have always had a deep distrust of writers who produce trilogies (tetralogists are beyond the pale), I have done exactly that." The polyphiloprogenitive fiction, spawning sequels, is the work of Gore, disowned by Vidal who is suspicious not only of trilogies but of novels, since they offend his notions of compulsory population control. The novel is a reproduction of life and thus a danger to an already wrecked and overcrowded world; Vidal has a seditious habit of tampering with the novels of Gore, formalistically sterilizing them, converting the products of re-creative research into demonstrations of technique delighting in its own skill. His agent in *1876* as in *Burr* is the narrator, Charles Schermerhorn Schuyler, who unmakes history in writing it down, treating the nation's revered past as a chaos of mismanagement and incompleteness which is as shoddy and disreputable as the present.

As a surrogate for Vidal, Schuyler writes a historical novel which is an insult to history. *1876* is Vidal's offering to the bicentennial, his reminder, in a year when the United States is anxiously fabricating a history for itself, that the past is as sullied as the present. Equally it is a denial of history. Since history is a labour of justification, assembling the evidence backwards so as to plead a self-interested case, *1876* disperses history into hectic, improvisatory journalism; Schuyler scribbles down notes for articles on the Philadelphia centennial exhibition or the presidential election. Journalism records things in the random order of their happening; history arranges them in explanatory retrospect. Vidal both ridicules the past and comically actualizes it by treating it as if it were the present. Gore, however, with his familial piety, has his own revenge: Schuyler finds himself written into the history he derides when Aaron Burr is revealed to be his father. And from Gore's point of view Vidal's escape to Rome has given him the authority of a universal historical conscience, brooding over the mischances of time between Julian and Nixon, noting the likeness between the transformation of the Roman and American republics into bellicose world-states and foreseeing their collapse; he resembles his own sibylline Clarissa in *Messiah*, who has survived two thousand years and is at liberty to correct history, restoring, in her inventions, a "forgotten reality".

Schuyler's disconcertedness at being enveloped in history, and his resentment at its imposition (in *1876* he keeps his parentage a secret from his daughter), are qualified by Vidal in a recent review of Tennessee Williams's memoirs, which concentrates on fastidious correction and loving expansion of every reference to himself in the book: those whom history preserves pay for their immortality by becoming victims of its errors and arbitrary combinations. This attitude of vain irritability is beautifully evinced by the Gore-ish annoyance of Eugene Luther in *Messiah*, who finds himself written out of history as alarmingly as Schuyler or Vidal are written into it by Burr or Tennessee Williams: a dangerous revisionist, his name is obliterated from all accounts of the religious cult he personally created. Conversely, Vidal interpolates himself into history in the chivalric romance *A Search for the King*, where Blondel the troubadour compliments his colleague Peire Vidal, a singer whose diction is fashionably (and Gore-ishly) "rough".

The good faith of Gore and the irresponsibility of Vidal have different motives for doing the same thing. Vidal's booby-trapped contribution to a bicentennial which is primarily a festival of industrial consumption, marketing patriotic beer cans and historical (but disposable) paper towels, is also Gore's earnest attempt to equip Americans with a past which will arm them against the present. America abolished history, which in practice has left history free to repeat itself rapaciously: Nixon could rig up a replica of the corrupt administration of Grant, which is described in *1876*, because Grant had been forgotten. In *An Evening with Richard Nixon*, Gore Vidal argues that Nixon was made possible by this American amnesia: because the voters collectively ignore a man's record, the politician "can reinvent himself every morning. Edward Kennedy's Presidential campaign will doubtless feature him as the Hero of Chappaquiddick—the man who swam 20 miles with a wounded secretary under one arm." Fidelity to historical sources in this case—the victims convict themselves by exact, annotated self-quotation, Nixon, for instance, amiably likening his invasion of Cambodia to the Soviet assault on Czechoslovakia—serves the same purpose as the interferences with history in *Burr* and *1876*, because both methods reveal the past to be a sorry, shaming caricature. Since the function of official history is to conceal the truth, the more scandalous one's fantasy about the past, the more chance it has of coinciding with what happened: hence the validity of Clarissa's gossip about Julian or Gibbon, or of the indiscretions in *Washington, D.C.* about the sexual activities of Presidents Roosevelt and (by innuendo) Kennedy. History thus becomes what has never been recorded, but can be recovered by malicious conjecture; and even the bumbling semi-literate Eisenhower of *An Evening with Richard Nixon* has the wit to protest, when traduced, that "what I did *not* do is history". From Gore's point of view, all fiction is history, and must justify itself by cautionary attachment to fact; from Vidal's point of view all history is fiction, a tissue of mendacity and evasion. In the present trilogy Gore is following Mailer and Capote in writing nonfiction novels; but simultaneously Vidal is inverting the form and writing anti-historical novels.

Mailer's pretension, in attending presidential conventions or commenting on the moonshot, has been to promote journalism to history by force of ego: happenings become events because they have the good fortune to be observed by the sovereign intelligence of the reporter. Vidal's method is the opposite. He discomposes history, passing off his laboured reconstruction of America in *1876* as the erratic and hasty impressionism of a journalist. Because the past does not know itself to be the past, and is as messily inchoate as the present, history is nothing more than gossip about our grandfathers. The ideal historian would be the undying Clarissa, who has known everyone and has a limitless repertory of embarrassing disclosures to make. Schuyler complains about the research he has been required to do—"my magpie brain retains from the thousands of lines of newspaper print I feed it with each day all sorts of odd useful facts"—and wherever possible exults in his disqualifications as a historian, proudly noting that he has no notion of the purpose of the Corliss engine exhibited in Philadelphia: "mercifully, the directors of the Fair are providing us journalists with elaborate descriptions of the various exhibits".

The historian turns into the enemy of history. As *Washington, D.C.* develops, the political ambition of Clay Overbury is controverted by the irony of Peter Sanford the journalist, who recoils from the exertions of politics into listless pampering of his body, overeating and lying in bed. Peter is the historian, whose vocation is to observe Clay and learn to hate him. In his renunciation he has the ironist's sour consolation of knowing that the dishonest men will win, but knowing as well how to use slander, subterfuge and caricature to see that they do not win easily. The writing of history becomes the revenge of the weak against those who make history. Schuyler, rejoicing in having irritated Grant, remarks to Garfield that it is the privilege of the historian to get a politician on the defensive.

There is a further subtle perversity to Vidal's form: his historical novel is not only anti-historical; it is also anti-novelistic. Peter Sanford in *Washington, D.C.* considers the unfolding and inter-implication of social acquaintance as "a vast novel-in-progress with numerous chapters one had to skim or guess at since only a few pages at a time could ever be carefully studied"; but Schuyler vigilantly maintains the difference between his record and the novel. When Baron Jacobi proposes making a bonfire of all historians, and learning about the past instead from Dante, Shakespeare and Scott, Schuyler agrees that there can be no absolute record but protests, "thinking of those dreadful novels by Dumas", that he still wants to know the truth. Peter thinks the present is like a novel, but specifies that it is a novel only patchily read: the novelist's work of substantiation must be overtaken by the reader's impatient guesses. Schuyler denies that the past can be a novel, because the novelist is an apologist for his subject, tenderly filling in and protectively covering up, rather than its antagonist. On several occasions he indignantly prides himself on never having written a novel. Nor does he read novels, except for those of Turgenev, which he admires for their very lack of imagination:

> With uncommon passion he writes only of politics and so is able to create living men and women on the page, unlike all the other novelists who are so intent on rendering in words the people they think they know or have read about that they end up with a kind of chatter not so good as the sort we hear every day of our lives.

The deadly irony of *1876* is that the scribbled journal Schuyler keeps during the campaign is published, after his death, as a fiction. He dies, indeed, at a point where history and fiction change places. Attending the unveiling of a statue in Central Park, he sees the fraudulent new President Hayes: "I stared at him with some fascination for he is, after all, my creation, a major character in the book that I am writing. It is not often that writers are actually able to see their fictional creatures made flesh." He dies after he has written this sentence: his fiction has materialized as unprepossessing fact in the person of Hayes; his factual record is now transformed into fiction as *1876*. Where a novelist would be gratified to awake and find his dream a truth, to meet a character he believes himself to have created, Schuyler is alarmed—and does not, perhaps, recover from the shock. In the afterword, which follows a mock-obituary of Schuyler by William Cullen Bryant, and is itself a devious fictional construction, Vidal adopts Schuyler's attitude towards Hayes to describe his own attitude towards Schuyler; listing the characters he has had the temerity actually to invent, he says: "Charles Schermerhorn Schuyler and his daughter Emma are invented (though by now Charlie seems very real to me)." A novelist would be pleased to have created a character; Vidal, with ironic grace, begs to be forgiven for having done so, and pleads in extenuation that his invention has become almost indistinguishable from a real person. Schuyler's efflorescence as a character is used to slight history: rather than conducting a diagnosis of the pestilential body politic, he is preoccupied by the malfunctions of his own ailing body, his cardiac arrests, toothache, cramps, fainting-fits and hay fever, his halting sexual performance, double vision and racing pulse. Gluttony is Peter Sanford's alternative to politics; hypochondria is Schuyler's. The one attends to his body's greedy cravings, the other to its maladies. Schuyler's certainty of the closeness of his own extinction is another denial of history—anxious for the completion of his own life, he is indifferent to the continuing life of the adolescent republic. Though Vidal takes advantage of Schuyler's self-pity, he slyly punishes him for the offence of becoming a character by having Bryant, at the end of his obituary, again mistake the title of Schuyler's study *Paris under the Commune*, which is rechristened throughout the novel by everyone who refers to it. Schuyler may have sneaked into immortality as a character, but Vidal sees to it that his works do not share the privilege.

Vidal refuses to allow the past to become a novel because that form justifies the past by envisioning its characters enclosed in time, summed up and redeemed by it. For him, history is not a novel but a play. His people are not characters but actors, and history for them is not action but performance; they are not generous puritans, endeavouring and accomplishing, but cynical hedonists who aspire to high office because it provides them with a stage for the exhibition of themselves. Senator Burden in *Washington, D.C.* retires "because he felt that the time had come for him to cease to be an actor and to join the audience". In *1876* Conkling gestures towards a committee room "like Edwin Forrest as Othello confronting Iago"; Abram S. Hewit collapses and is carried from the Congress chamber like Hamlet in the last act; the horsewhipped Jamie goes into exile like Coriolanus. Observers treat politics not as government in process but as theatre, as Emma applauds the procession of justices, generals, admirals and congressional leaders at the Philadelphia exhibition. The participants may mimic the gestures of tragedy, but they belong in a different genre: Schuyler regards American politics as "an ongoing comedy" which is liable to veer "into wildest farce". Marx's epigram about the double plot of history has been amended, for in America at least it happens first as comedy, then again as farce. This perception gives shape to Vidal's notion of Nixon's career: the convenient forgetfulness of the electorate allowed him to repeat the comedy of the 1950s—baiting Reds and taking tearful inventory of his wife's wardrobe—as bungling technological farce in the 1970s.

The vicissitudes of Burr in the course of the trilogy follow a similar pattern. His jovial libertinism undergoes a first comic metamorphosis in *1876*, turning into the sleek aptitude for intrigue which Schuyler senses in his daughter, and which he attributes to the "curious blood" of Burr. Emma has Burr's eyes, "absolutely intense and entirely resolute—the eyes of a world conqueror", but now, as a Jamesian princess, she conquers not politically or even amorously but by the astute manipulation of social nuance. By the time of *Washington, D.C.*, Burr has withered into a sad ghost, the victim of successive farcical indignities: a graduate thesis is written about him (Peter Sanford considers making him the excuse for doing a master's degree), his portrait suffers physical violence (an eye is put out by a bullet during a domestic quarrel), and he is at last consigned to redundancy by fashion (the new tenants of Laurel House replace the portrait with "an elaborate collage of old newspapers").

The language of politics is also theatrical, a high diction of resonant inanity, innocent of content. As Nixon's obfuscations show, the politician despises language and needs it only for purposes of display or camouflage: "the thing not spoken in politics", as Burden perceives in *Washington, D.C.*, "is invariably the essential", and Schuyler, too, notices that political deals are atmospheric rather than crassly verbal. This is one of the junctions between politics and sex, an alliance which fascinates Vidal: seduction and political persuasion are both arranged by gesture and intimation, winks, glances, overtones, silent signals, since a relationship between people is, in both cases, being altered in a way too fugitive and dangerous to survive translation into verbal propositioning. When a politician condescends to the use of language, the ephemeral spoken word is more to be trusted than anything he writes down: Schuyler remarks of Tilden that so serpentine a lawyer "can never make a written agreement without arranging for himself, amongst the qualifying clauses, an escape hatch", whereas in speech he can permit himself a hint (in this case, promising Schuyler a job in payment for his campaign biography) which acquires the firmness of a contract.

The model for Vidal's political theatre is Shakespeare—perhaps because, as Garfield says in *1876*, his "history is always wrong". In *Washington, D.C.*, the corpulent Peter plays a sceptical, pusillanimous Falstaff to Clay's thrusting, energetic Hal; similarly, Schuyler takes "the part of foolish elder sage, of Falstaff" to the Hal of Jamie, his "exquisite athlete, yachtsman, equestrian, millionaire publisher", a princeling who leads Schuyler on tours of dissipation through the brothels of New York. Vidal's two Falstaffs confront not only glacial Lancastrians like Clay but the noble, marmoreal

Romans of Shakespeare's classical history plays. Burden, who "at crucial moments . . . saw life as a Shakespeare play", stops to consult with "several citizens of the Republic" at the door of the Senate, and in his office salutes a bust of Cicero. Like Shakespeare's actors, who are always complaining of the disparity between their unheroic selves and the roles allotted to them, Vidal's politicians know they are travestying history while they play at making it. When Roosevelt dies, Burden repairs directly to the Senate from the barber's shop, "still wearing the barber's white cloth about his neck" and resembling "some toga-ed Senator, arrived too late at the Theatre of Pompey". In *1876* the Congressmen deport themselves "like the very worst sort of actors trying to look like Roman Senators while sounding like country Jonathans".

The neoclassical fiction so incompetently acted out by Vidal's provincials is one of those untruths which, Schuyler and Baron Jacobi agree, constitute history, for Washington is based, constitutionally and architecturally, on the same absurd Roman metaphor. Bumpkins and venal fat cats play at being Brutus and Cicero; steel masquerades as marble, and domes and obelisks cast improbable shadows over the African jungle of tenements in which the pullulating and unclassical life of the city is actually proceeding. Americans adhere to the Roman style because it is so implausible, so nonsensically unsuited to the rude, anarchic, gothic liveliness of their society. The most extravagant of their stylistic misconceptions is their fondness for neoclassical railway stations: buildings which demand gothic, being temples of motion and aspiring restlessness, are made to resemble the Baths of Caracalla and to conform to an architectural ethic of stasis and repose. But although the Roman style is burlesqued by this brawling demotic republic, it is a fiction in which Vidal perceives a truth. To him, America is Rome reborn: the decadent comedy of ancient history happens a second time as coarse, uncultivated farce.

The analogy between the two elephantine world-states connects the separate parts of Gore Vidal's literary existence as the biographer of Julian and Caligula and as the biographer of Burr, as the explorer of apostasy, inversion and the thirsty evils of a corrupt, dying world and as the political campaigner and satirist. Shakespeare's Roman plays demonstrate the fatal expansion of republic into empire, with the tribal rivalries of *Coriolanus* giving way to the urban politics of *Julius Caesar*, which in turn deliquesce into the oriental indolence and satiety of *Antony and Cleopatra*. Austere republicans ripen into the sensual profiteers of empire. Vidal takes these plays as his model because he finds the same demoralizing calamity in American history. Washington catches Kennedy using the word "empire" in *An Evening with Richard Nixon*, and warns that "no democracy, no republic, can survive once it aspires to dominion over other people in other lands against their will". *1876* and *Washington, D.C.* conspire to snub history and discount any possibilities it might contain for education and improvement by revealing the same fatal choices being obtusely made in both periods: the betrayal of Tilden and Grant's armed imposition of a Republican victory recalls, for Schuyler, Caesar's heedless dismissal of the old republic; Peter Sanford charges Roosevelt with the same crime, of rousing an isolationist republic into war-mongering commercial expansion, making it into "what would no doubt be the last empire on earth".

The righteous Gore may regret the transformation of an agrarian republic into an empire ruled by militaristic industrial magnates, but Vidal, who after all has the face of a terminal emperor, can only welcome it. For he is an imperial novelist. He luxuriates, imaginatively, in the spoils of empire, impudent, opulent, stylistically and formally profligate, confidently international. His fictions are expensive and elaborate, ornamental products of a culture in which form is devouring content.

A hundred years ago Henry James described the social empire in *The Portrait of a Lady*, in which the refinement of manners, purchased by wealth, enabled errant Americans in Europe to transform themselves into works of art, glossy, gelid and perfect. Vidal's empire, in which Schuyler courts Napoleonic dowagers in Paris and the gilded vulgarians of the Astorocracy in New York, is that of James, who has a walk-on part in *1876*. Making himself agreeable to Schuyler at the Astor mansion, James confides that he is leaving "to live in Paris, the sort of life *you* have led, Mr Schuyler"; but it is Vidal himself who has gone to Rome to live the sort of life, and to write the sort of novels, that James did.

HAROLD BLOOM

"The Central Man"

New York Review of Books, July 19, 1984, pp. 5–8

I

Walt Whitman elegized Lincoln as "the sweetest, wisest soul of all my days and lands." "The actual Lincoln was cold and deliberate, reflective and brilliant," according to Gore Vidal's brief meditation on the martyr president in *The Second American Revolution and Other Essays: 1976–1982*. That somber "Note" by Vidal gave us a Lincoln "at heart . . . a fatalist, a materialist" who "knew when to wait; when to act." This is the Lincoln of Vidal's superb novel, celebrated by the author as the master politician who invented what is now in crisis, the American nation-state.

If I could count accurately, this is Vidal's nineteenth novel and thirtieth book, and he is (or is going on) fifty-nine. I have read thirteen of the novels, and two books of essays, which may be enough to yield some reasonable estimate of at least the relative nature of his achievement, if only to see how his work might be placed, so far. Though Vidal has a substantial audience, which certainly will be augmented by *Lincoln*, he has had rather mixed esteem among the most serious readers whom I know. I myself found his fiction very readable but not greatly memorable until the appearance of his ninth novel, *Julian*, which seems to me still a beautifully persuasive historical tale, a poignant; portrait of the Emperor Julian, known forever as the Apostate by the Christian tradition that be rejected and abandoned.

Of the earlier novels, I had read only the first, *Williwaw*, and the third, *The City and the Pillar*, both refreshing, but then I was disappointed by the book just before *Julian*, an ambitious yet sketchy work that courageously was entitled *Messiah*. What the far more powerful *Julian* showed, I thought, was that Vidal lacked invention, and so was most gifted at reimagining history. The political and historical *Washington, D.C.*, which followed *Julian*, seemed to confirm this intimation, since everything and everyone weakest in it was of Vidal's own creation. But I underestimated Vidal badly. *Myra Breckinridge* followed, an apocalyptic farce that rivals Nathanael West's *A Cool Million* and Evelyn Waugh's *Scoop*, three outrageous travesties that will outlive many of the more celebrated visions of our century. After many readings, *Myra Breckinridge* continues to give wicked pleasure, and still seems to have fixed the limit beyond which the most advanced aesthetic neopornography ever can go.

Myra compelled a revisionary estimate of Vidal, who had

powerfully demonstrated that superb invention was his strength, provided that the modes were farce and fantasy. The polemic of *Myra* remains the best embodiment of Vidal's most useful insistence as a moralist, which is that we ought to cease speaking of homosexuals and heterosexuals. There are only women and men, some of whom prefer their own sex, some the other, and some both. This is the burden of *Myra Breckingridge*, but a burden borne with lightness, wildness, abandon, joy, skill. It was a little difficult to see just how the author of *Julian* was one with the creator of *Myra*, but that increased a sense of expectation for what was to come.

I have never encountered a copy of *Two Sisters*, which followed *Myra*, but I have read the half-dozen intervening novels before *Lincoln*, with some appreciation and much puzzlement, until now *Myron* and the recent *Duluth* seem to me failures in the exuberant mode of *Myra Breckinridge*, though I was stimulated by the references in *Duluth* to the egregious Thornton Bloom, author of *The Kabbalah*. The fictions of political history, *Burr* and *1876*, were far better, and indeed *Burr* stands with *Julian* and *Myra Breckinridge* as Vidal's truest contributions before *Lincoln*. But *Kalki* was another *Messiah*, contrived and perfunctory, in the religious mode that Vidal should perhaps handle only historically, while *Creation*, a civilized and learned narrative, showed that Vidal, even working historically, is simply not a philosophical novelist. *Creation*, unlike *Julian*, reduces to a series of essays, which are always provocative, but almost never very consequential. Vidal, reimagining our cultural origins, is no Burckhardt and no Nietzsche, but then why should he be?

What he is, in *Lincoln* is a masterly American historical novelist, now wholly matured, who has found his truest subject, which is our national political history during precisely those years when our political and military histories were as one, one thing and one thing only: the unwavering will of Abraham Lincoln to keep the states united. Vidal's imagination of American politics, then and now, is so powerful as to compel awe. Lincoln is to our national political mythology what Whitman is to our literary mythology: the figure that Emerson prophesied as the Central Man. No biographer has been able to give us a complete and convincing account of the evasive and enigmatic Whitman. No biographer, and until now no novelist, has had the precision of imagination to show us a plausible and human Lincoln, of us and yet beyond us. Vidal, with this book, does just that, and more: he gives us the tragedy of American political history, with its most authentic tragic hero at the center, which is to say, at our center.

II

Lincoln: A Novel begins in the early, frozen morning of February 23, 1861, as Lincoln, flanked by the detective Pinkerton and by his presidential bodyguard, Lamon, slips into Washington so as to avoid being murdered before his inauguration. A minority president, elected with less than 40 percent of the total vote, he confronts a crisis that no predecessor, and no American head of state since, could even envision. Though his election committed him only to barring the extension of slavery to the new states, and though he was a moderate Republican and not an Abolitionist, Lincoln was violently feared by most of the South. Vidal's opening irony, never stated but effectively implied, is that the South beheld the true Lincoln long before Lincoln's own cabinet had begun to regard the will and power of the political genius who so evasively manipulated them. Vidal's Lincoln is the most ambitious of all American presidents. The South feared an American Cromwell, and in Vidal's vision the South actually helped produce an American Bismarck.

But there is no Southern perspective in Vidal's novel, nor should there be. Lincoln, the first Westerner to be elected president since Andrew Jackson, is presented as the heir of Jackson and Polk, a believer in the strong executive tradition and a respecter of neither the states, nor the Congress, nor the courts, nor the parties, nor even the Constitution itself. This Lincoln, rather enigmatically, is transcendental and idealist only in the mode of the later Emerson, author of the grim essay "Power" in his superb *The Conduct of Life*. "Power" works by the dialectic of Emerson's Lear-like revision of Coleridge's compensatory imagination. Coleridge thought (or hoped) that experiential loss could be transformed into imaginative gain. Emerson rephrased this formula as "Nothing is got for nothing," which seems the sacred motto of Vidal's Lincoln, who follows another great essay, "Fate," in *The Conduct of Life*, by worshipping, not Jehovah nor Jesus, but only what Emerson called the Beautiful Necessity, the American tragedy of the struggle between freedom and fate, in which the heroic agonist secretly loves neither freedom nor fate, but only power. Vidal's strong Lincoln, triumphant at last over both the South and his own cabinet and party, is such an agonist, a dialectician of power, and finally a kind of self-willed Orphic sacrifice who, in the closing words of Vidal's book, "had willed his own murder as a form of atonement for the great and terrible thing that he had done by giving so bloody and absolute a rebirth to his nation."

It is Vidal's skill as a narrator, and his art as a reimaginer of historical personages, that makes plausible this curiously nihilistic rebirth. The book's narrative principle is a highly traditional one: deferred revelation, enacted throughout by Lincoln's brilliant alternation of an endless, almost passive waiting with sudden, overwhelming acts of decision. What is perpetually deferred is a full awareness of Lincoln's preternatural ability to prophesy the moves of every other politician, as well as his uncanny sense of his own greatness, his own central place in national and world history. That this savage greatness paradoxically has been revised by American mythology into Whitman's "sweetest, wisest soul" and later debased into Carl Sandburg's homespun sentimentalist may be the provocation for Vidal's novel, yet one senses that Vidal's motives are more immediate. With the likely, impending reelection of Reagan, the nation confronts what might become the final crisis of Lincoln's presidential creation. If our system is, as Vidal contends, Lincoln's invention, then the American age of Lincoln finally approaches its apocalypse. Should Vidal prove correct, his tragic vision of Lincoln as Orphic dictator may serve also as an elegy for the one hundred and twenty years of Lincoln's invented America.

III

On its surface, Vidal's novel is a grand entertainment, maintaining a tonal intensity that might be called humorously somber. Lincoln himself is presented as the master of evasions, strongest when he strives to appear weakest, and a purposive self-mythologizer. Vidal cunningly contributes to the mythologizing by adding "the Tycoon" and "the Ancient" to "Old Abe" and "Father Abraham" as presidential nicknames. The crucial game probably is "the Ancient," who indeed is what Emerson called "Spontaneity or Instinct" in the crucial essay, "Self-Reliance." Lincoln falls back continually upon what is best and oldest in his own self, an ancient spark that seems to have originated not only before the creation of the Union, but before the Creation itself. More than Whitman, this Lincoln is Emerson's American Adam, post-Christian and self-begotten, who knows no time when he was not as now. If this is Vidal's ontological Lincoln, the empirical Lincoln, archetypal politician yet tragic sufferer, nevertheless more winningly dominates the novel.

Vidal demystifies Lincoln to the rather frightening degree of suggesting that he had transferred unknowingly a venereal infection, contracted in youth and supposedly cured, to his wife, Mary Todd, and through her to his sons. The gradually developing madness of Mrs. Lincoln, and the related early deaths of two of the boys, form one of the dark undersongs of this novel, plausibly suggesting a more than temperamental basis for Lincoln's profound melancholia. Counterpointed against this sadness is Lincoln's celebrated humor, conveyed by Vidal with authentic verve, but always with a Freudian sense of wit, in which the laughter carries the burden of double or antithetical meanings:

> "Sometimes I say those things and don't even know I've said them. When there is so much you *cannot* say, it's always a good idea to have a story ready. I do it now from habit." Lincoln sighed. "In my predicament, it is a good thing to know all sort of stories because the truth of the whole matter is now almost unsayable; and so cruel."

The "predicament" here overtly refers to the Southern Rebellion and the "truth of the whole matter" perhaps to the endless catastrophe of the sequence of incompetent Northern generals, but the underlying references are to Lincoln's inner despairs. Vidal seems to be suggesting, quite subtly, throughout the novel, that Lincoln's obsessive drive to preserve and restore the Union of the states was a grand restitution or compensation for what never could be healed in his own personal and familial life. Combined with a metaphysical will to power, this results in the gradual emergence of Lincoln as the first and most forceful dictator-president, forerunner of the Roosevelt and of Lyndon Johnson.

It seems to me an astonishing achievement that Vidal makes us love his Lincoln, "cold and deliberate, reflective and brilliant," qualities that do not often engender affection whether in fact or fiction—particularly because we have to struggle also against our mystified sense of the Sandburgian or Hollywood saintly Lincoln. I suspect that Vidal succeeds because his Lincoln is an authentic image of authority. Freud taught us that love reduces to love of authority, love of the father image that seems not to love us in return. Vidal's Lincoln is Shakespearean, not just in his recurrent quotations from the plays, but in his lonely and heroic fatalism. He inspires love partly because he seems to be beyond needing it.

IV

Surrounding Vidal's Lincoln swarms an almost Dickensian roster of fabulistic caricatures: politicians, generals, White House aides, Washington ladies, newspapermen, Northern and Southern conspirators, and amiably evil bankers, including Jay Cooke himself. These are Vidal's America, then and now, and they are rendered with an almost invariable and unfailing gusto. The most memorable and entertaining is the sanctimonious Salmon P. Chase: archetypal Republican, pious Abolitionist, hero of bankers, endless plotter to seize power from Lincoln, and forever ungrateful to the president for his appointments as secretary of the treasury and chief justice. Vidal's Chase is the comic foil to Vidal's tragic Lincoln, for Chase has every quality except aesthetic dignity. Inwardly humble, but in the Dickensian mode, Chase pursues greatness, to the parodistic extent of obsessively yielding to a ruling passion for collecting the autographs of famous writers.

In a finely rendered scene of comic pathos, Chase confronts the job-seeking and highly disreputable Walt Whitman, who is devoting himself to the care of sick and wounded soldiers. Since Whitman bears with him a letter of recommendation from Emerson, Chase's sole concern is to extract the desired letter while rejecting the obscene bard. Whitman splendidly starts off wrong by comparing the inside of the Capitol to "the interiors of Taylor's saloon in the Broadway, which you doubtless know." Chase shudders at thus encountering a populist beast, and proceeds to his triumph:

> "In Mr. Emerson's letter, does he mention *what* you might do in the government's service?" Chase thought this approach subtle in the extreme.
>
> "Well, here it is," said Whitman. He gave Chase the letter. On the envelope was written "The Honorable S. P. Chase." Inside was a letter dated January 10, endorsing Walt Whitman highly for any sort of government post; and signed, Chase excitedly saw, with the longed-for-but-never-owned autograph "R. W. Emerson."
>
> "I shall give Mr. Emerson, and yourself, sir, every sort of consideration," said Chase, putting the letter in his pocket where it seemed to him to irradiate his whole being as if it were some holy relic.
>
> "I shall be truly grateful. As will Mr. Emerson, of course." Chase shook Whitman's hand at the door and let him out. Then Chase placed the letter square in the middle of his desk, and pondered what sort of frame would set it off best.

As the novel progresses, Vidal's exuberance in depicting Chase increases, and the reader begins to share the author's dialectical sympathy for this comic monster who nevertheless is the clear ancestor of all sanctimonious Republicans since, down to the menagerie currently staffing the White House. Though a paragon of selfishness, Chase nevertheless is sincere in behalf of the slaves, while Lincoln frees them only reluctantly, and then idly dreams of shipping them off to the West Indies or back to Africa. Chase seeks power, but for presumably idealistic purposes; Lincoln, with the single purpose of keeping his nation unified, stalks power with no concern whatsoever for human rights.

Vidal does not celebrate Lincoln's destruction of civil liberties, but shows a certain admiration for the skill with which the President subverts the constitution he is sworn to defend. There is a split in Vidal between the man of letters who has a friendly contempt for politicians and the born political man who would make a remarkable senator, if only even California was quite ready for him. The audacity that distinguishes Vidal as visionary politician, amiably and sensibly urging us to withdraw tax-exempt status from churches, synagogues, foundations, and universities, is matched by his audacity as political novelist, urging us to see Lincoln plain while giving us a Lincoln that our mythological needs cannot quite accept.

V

I return to the still ambiguous question of Vidal's strength or perhaps competing strengths as a novelist. *Lincoln*, together with the curiously assorted trio of *Julian*, *Myra Breckinridge*, and *Burr*, demonstrates that his narrative achievement is vastly underestimated by American academic criticism, an injustice he has repaid amply in his essayistic attacks upon the academy, and in the sordid intensities of *Duluth*. But even *Lincoln* (unlike the slighter but flawless *Myra Breckinridge*) has its disappointments. Booth's conspiracy against Lincoln's life was melodramatic enough in mere actuality, but that does not justify Vidal's rendering of it as a quite perfunctory melodrama. The difficulty appears again to be Vidal's relative weakness, except in farce, for inventing characters, as opposed to his immense gifts for revisualizing historical personae. David Herold, upon whom the Booth conspiracy is made to center, remains a name upon these pages; he simply does not stimulate Vidal's imagination, unlike Lincoln, Chase, and other personages of our common past. Lincoln's striking Epicurean fatalism is asserted rather than dramatized; the ideological and religious vigor that portrayed Julian the Apostate so memorably is simply absent here. And though Vidal's humor is a pleasure throughout, he restrains himself too strictly from relying upon his genius for farce. This may be just as well, since the author of *Myra Breckinridge* is also the author of *Duluth*. But it does prompt the critical question: will it ever be possible for Vidal to reconcile all of his talents within the dimensions of a single novel?

The question would be unjust or misleading if *Lincoln* did not testify so persuasively that Vidal, in his late fifties, remains a developing rather than an unfolding novelist, to borrow a useful distinction from Northrop Frye. There are several extant American novelists, more highly regarded by critics than Vidal, who nevertheless will never surprise us. Vidal, like the very different Norman Mailer, has the capacity to confound out expectations. Such a capacity, in so bad a time for the republic, both of letters and of politics, scarcely can be overpraised.

KURT VONNEGUT

1922–

Kurt Vonnegut, Jr., was born on November 11, 1922, in Indianapolis, Indiana, to Kurt and Edith Leiber Vonnegut. He was educated at Cornell University, Carnegie Institute, and the University of Chicago. He served in the army during World War II, and was awarded the Purple Heart. In 1945 he married Jane Marie Cox; they had three children and adopted three others. After their divorce in 1979 he married Jill Krementz. He was a reporter for the Chicago City News Bureau in 1946, and worked for the General Electric Company from 1947 to 1950; since 1950 he has supported himself as a freelance writer. He teaches at Hopefield School in Sandwich, Massachusetts, and has been a visiting lecturer or professor at a number of colleges, including the University of Iowa, Harvard University, and the City University of New York.

Vonnegut published his first story, "Report on the Barnhouse Effect," in *Collier's* in 1950. During the next fifteen years he published most of his short stories and his first five novels—the bulk categorized as science fiction and published as such. Though at first none of his novels was widely appreciated outside the genre, *Player Piano* (1952), *The Sirens of Titan* (1959), and *Cat's Cradle* (1963) have since been recognized as biting social satires and early examples of the Black Humor movement Vonnegut helped to spearhead in the sixties. In 1965 Vonnegut, finding himself with only one novel in print, felt forced to take a job at the University of Iowa. Unhappy with the marketing restrictions associated with science fiction and the attendant critical stigma, Vonnegut insisted that his future books be marketed as mainstream novels. Continuing to employ the tropes of science fiction, he achieved a popular and critical breakthrough with *Slaughterhouse-Five* (1969). The story of a man who is "unstuck in time" and has difficulty making sense of reality, it was in part inspired by Vonnegut's experiences as a prisoner of war during the firebombing of Dresden. Vonnegut's play *Happy Birthday, Wanda June* (1971) enjoyed similar success, and critics began to reassess Vonnegut's earlier work.

During the late sixties and early seventies Vonnegut became a popular counterculture guru of sorts. While his novels have consistently been bestsellers, they have come under severe critical fire. Charging that his imagination has flagged, critics have viewed such later novels as *Breakfast of Champions* (1973), *Slapstick* (1976), and *Jailbird* (1979) as empty exercises in absurdity and cynicism without the depth of human feeling that characterizes his earlier work. Some critics, however, saw a return to his earlier form with *Galapagos* (1985). Vonnegut has received serious critical attention relatively recently, and his reputation is likely to remain a subject of dispute. His short stories have been collected in *Canary in a Cat House* (1961) and *Welcome to the Monkey House* (1968).

C. D. B. BRYAN
"Kurt Vonnegut, Head Bokonist"

New York Times Book Review, April 6, 1969, pp. 2, 25

Kurt Vonnegut Jr., the author of six novels and two short-story collections, lives and writes in an old house in West Barnstable on Cape Cod with his wife, six children, a sheep dog, and a tidal wave of house guests. Vonnegut is over 6 feet tall, a rumpled and shaggy 46-year-old fourth generation German-American with a drooping mustache, a brow chevroned like a sergeant-major's sleeve, and the eyes of a sacrificial altar-bound virgin caught in mid-shrug.

Seated, Vonnegut disappears so deeply into cushions that he resembles a corduroy covered bat-wing chair that has been dropped 2,000 feet from a passing airplane. He is the impatient humanitarian, the disappointed-but-constant optimist, an ex-P.R. man for General Electric, ex-Volunteer Fireman (Badge 155, Alpaus, N. Y.), ex-visiting lecturer, Iowa Writers' Workshop, and ex-Cornell chemistry major turned amiable Cassandra whose short stories and novels since 1951 have reflected an admirable—if not sinister—blending of H. G. Wells and Mark Twain.

Among Vonnegut's earliest fans were Conrad Aiken, Nelson Algren, Marc Connelly, Jules Feiffer, Graham Greene and Terry Southern. But today whether because of, or in spite of, the fact that Vonnegut's novels are now being taught at universities, the under-30's are beginning to grant him a cultish attention which Vonnegut finds "very gratifying, it really is. It's charming," an attention that has long been overdue. And, happily, an increasing number of general readers are finding in Vonnegut's quiet, humorous, well-mannered and rational protests against man's inhumanity to man an articulate bridge across the generation chasm. For a distressingly long period Vonnegut's novels have been ignored by just exactly the broad readership he has most hoped to reach simply because critics, uncertain quite how to categorize him, either dismissed him as a "science fiction" writer—

(*Vonnegut:* "I objected finally to this label because I thought it was narrowing my readership. People regard science-fiction writers as interchangeable with comic-strip writers.")

Or called him a "Black Humorist"—

(*Vonnegut:* "One day I was sitting on the beach at Cape Cod and this enormous bell jar was lowered over me and I managed to read the label. It said, 'Black Humor by Bruce Jay Friedman.' I find the label mystifying.")

Or, with nothing but the best intentions, critics judged Vonnegut a "satirist" and thereby all but doomed him to a life of abject poverty.

(*Vonnegut:* "I speak a lot at universities now, and people ask me to define 'satire' and, you know? I've never even bothered to look it up. I wouldn't know whether I'm a satirist or not. One thing about being a chemistry major at Cornell, I've never worried about questions like that. It was never important for me to know whether I was one or not.")

Still other critics, unwilling to forgive Vonnegut for having written patently commercial short stories, ignore his work entirely.

(*Vonnegut:* "When I was supporting myself as a freelance writer doing stories for the *Saturday Evening Post* and *Colliers*, I was *scorned!* I mean, there was a time when to be a slick writer was a disgusting thing to be, as though it were prostitution. The people who did not write for the slicks obviously did not need the money. I would have liked very much to have been that sort of person, but I wasn't. I was the head of a family, supporting the damn thing in what seemed—to me, at least—an honorable way. During most of my freelancing I made what I would have made in charge of the cafeteria at a pretty good junior-high school.")

In the hopes of avoiding similar pitfalls I telephoned Vonnegut and asked him, if he had his choice, what he would most like to be known as. He answered, "George Orwell."

In *God Bless You, Mr. Rosewater: Or, Pearls Before Swine*, published in 1965, Eliot P. Rosewater, heir to the Rosewater fortune, crashes a science-fiction writers convention being held in a Milford, Pa., motel and interrupts their meeting to say, "I love you sons of bitches. You're all I read any more. You're the only ones who'll talk about the *really* terrific changes going on, the only ones crazy enough to know that life in a space voyage, and not a short one either, but one that will last for billions of years. You're the only ones with guts enough to *really* care about the future, who *really* know what machines do to us, what cities do to us, what big, simple ideas do to us, what tremendous mistakes, accidents, and catastrophes do to us. You're the only ones zany enough to agonize over time and distance without limit, over mysteries that will never die, over the fact that we are right now determining whether the space voyage for the next billion years or so is going to Heaven or Hell." The speaker may have been Rosewater, but the voice was Vonnegut's own.

"All writers are going to have to learn more about science," says Vonnegut, "simply because the scientific method is such an important part of their environment. To reflect their times accurately, to respond to their times reasonably, writers will have to understand that part of their environment . . . C. P. Snow and I are both very smug on this subject because we both have two cultures—H. L. Mencken, by the way, started as a chemist. H. G. Wells, too."

Vonnegut has stated that he deliberately keeps his books short because he wants to be read by men in power and he knows politicians have neither the time nor the inclination to read thick books. "I've worried some about why write books when Presidents and Senators and generals do not read them," he says, "and the university experience taught me a very good reason: you catch people before they become generals and Senators and Presidents, and you *poison their minds with humanity*. Encourage them to make a better world."

One can judge Vonnegut's success with the young by measuring the expanding cult of Vonnegut fans which a few years ago was concentrated in the Village in the East and San Francisco in the West and which today spans the country. The golden spike that links them is *Cat's Cradle*, Vonnegut's best known book, published in 1963, which created a religion and a language that have now been incorporated into our national vocabulary. The religion is "Bokonism" and the gist of it is found in its "Genesis":

"In the beginning, God created the earth and He looked upon it in His cosmic loneliness.

"And God said, 'Let Us make living creatures out of mud, so the mud can see what We have done.' And God created every living creature that now moveth, and one was man. Mud as man alone could speak. God leaned close as mud as man sat up, looked around, and spoke. Man blinked, 'What is the purpose of all this?' he asked politely.

"'Everything must have a purpose?' asked God.

"'Certainly,' said man.

"'Then I leave it to you to think of one for all this,' said God. And he went away."

The Books of Bokonon urge us to, "Live by the *foma* that makes you brave and kind and healthy and happy." Harmless untruths are "foma." Another invented word is "karass." "If you find your life tangled up with somebody else's life for no very logical reasons," writes Bokonon, "that person may be a member of your *karass*."

"Karass" is the name of one of Vonnegut's Cape Cod neighbors. "All I know about him," said Vonnegut, "is his mailbox." And, as any Bokononist knows, any attempt to put Vonnegut in a *karass* with Karass would result in a *granfalloon*.

Two messages recur through all of Vonnegut's writing. The first is Be Kind; the second is God doesn't care whether you are or not. In his introduction to *Mother Night*, a novel (published initially in paperback in 1961, republished in hardcover in 1965) about an American intelligence agent whose cover was as an anti-Semitic radio broadcaster for the Nazis, Vonnegut introduced a third message: "We are what we pretend to be, so we must be careful what we pretend to be."

Vonnegut's message in *Slaughterhouse-Five, Or the Children's Crusade* is:

"I have told my sons that they are not under any circumstances to take part in massacres, and that the news of massacres of enemies is not to fill them with satisfaction or glee."

Is he a pacifist? "I've got four boys of military age and none of them are going," he told me. "It's a decision they reached on their own, I've certainly not brought any leverage—one thing I've said to them, too, is that if I were them I *would* go. Out of morbid curiosity. This exasperates a lot of people. But, knowing myself, I think I probably would go, although I'd be sick about it the minute I got over there and realized I'd been had."

Should Vonnegut go, Bokonon's epigraph at the end of *Cat's Cradle*, seems appropriate:

"If I were a younger man, I would write a history of human stupidity; and I would climb to the top of Mount McCabe and lie down on my back with my history for a pillow; and I would take from the ground some of the blue-white poison that makes statues of men; and I would make a statue of myself, lying on my back, grinning horribly, and thumbing my nose at You Know Who."

JACK RICHARDSON
"Easy Writer"

New York Review of Books, July 2, 1970, pp. 7–8

There are many types of social fantasts in literature, but the quality common to them all is a suspicion that the accepted customs of human society, if carried to their logical conclusions, would prove to be grotesquely absurd. Thus Swift, who, next to David Hume, had the best analytic imagination of his century, laid out a micro- and macroscopic demonstration of man and his society as no more than a Brobdingnagian piece of vanity and something less than a fraternity of honest beasts.

Samuel Butler was somewhat less savage, deducing the cool ironies of *Erewhon* with a delightful rigor from the values of an age from which we are still trying to liberate ourselves. Shaw, a disciple of Butler's, but not quite his equal at subtle deductions, settled for polemical rhetoric and dramatic paradox to make the citizen question the first principles of his social being. If he gave us no Erewhon or Lilliput, he was every bit as much a fantast as Swift or Butler, and only a very poor critic would try to make Shaw's plays examples of social observation rather than acts of fantastic projection.

Finally, there is Orwell, a writer who, of all those who have given us a glimpse of the dark utopias our society is capable of engendering, made perhaps the shortest leap from actuality to fantasy. Swift, Butler, and even Shaw had to get beneath an apparent social order to uncover the hidden absurdities of their ages; Orwell, however, lived in a time of such mad political designs that only the smallest literary inference was needed to project them into the pattern of *1984*.

On my way to talking about the work of Kurt Vonnegut, Jr., I have started with these four writers because they provide a neat descending scale of fantast ability which anticipates the arrival and style of a writer like Vonnegut. Now it is no disgrace to be anticipated, but in Vonnegut's case he so badly abuses the tradition of deft argument and intelligence which his predecessors have established that one wonders whether they didn't anticipate him as a character rather than as a fellow writer, whether somewhere in their imagined worlds they didn't foresee that an age like ours would get and deserve a soft, sentimental satirist like Vonnegut, a popularizer of naughty whimsy, a compiler of easy-to-read truisms about society who allows everyone's heart to be in the right place.

For if there is one hard irony issuing out of all the novels and stories of Kurt Vonnegut, it is that should those drab, mindless worlds he conjures up so easily should ever come to pass, his work would fit in perfectly with their values. After reading *Player Piano*, for example, that novel of what life will be like when man lives in a society based totally on technological efficiency, one can imagine those infantile executives of the state reading and enjoying the very work that created them. After all, what else could their minds grasp but a book which deals with the broadest simplicities of a technocratic world, which is written in a prose that appears to have been designed by a computer programmed for slang and a "natural style," and which ends with the incendiary insight that the common man should take preference over the most intricate of his tools?

Even the most despotic, semiliterate government could tolerate the banalities of *Player Piano* simply because they contribute to the very process such states wish to encourage: the destruction of fine distinctions and the substitution of blurred, flaccid fault-finding for critical rage. A novelist who, like Vonnegut in ⟨*Slaughterhouse-Five*⟩, puts his good guys in rumpled suits and infuses them with alcohol and a desire for human values *must* be writing for a simpler time somewhere in the future where the Parthenon of heroes will include the good prostitute, the crippled teen-ager with visions, the murderer who is kind to animals, and similar effusions of a mind that does not speculate about life but merely softens it for general consumption.

While we are on the subject of the future, we can look at another Vonnegut prophecy, the title story of the volume *Welcome to the Monkey House*. Like *Player Piano*, this tale picks out a contemporary social problem—in this case the population increase—and imagines a solution that might be proposed by a depersonalized government which places its notion of progress over humbler human pleasures. The hero is a small, unprepossessing man called Billy the Poet who is waging a campaign against the use of ethical birth-control pills, government-issued tablets that remove all sexual desire from those who use them.

In a world of moribund abdominal nerves, Billy goes about upending honest ladies of the state, trying to revive in them the near forgotten instincts for love and passion. His victim in the story is hostess from an Ethical Suicide Parlour whom he reluctantly rapes when his argument extolling old-fashioned values fails. Billy is, of course, more humanitarian than libertine—he doesn't enjoy the rape and he leaves the lady with his good wishes and a copy of Elizabeth Browning's *Sonnets from the Portuguese*.

Now there are a number of things that can be said about the imagination that devises such a story, the first being that it is fond of gimmicks. Vonnegut may be in the fantast tradition, but he is also what in show business idiom is called an idea man. And like most ideas issuing from that creative area, his ideas are facile and flashy. The worlds that he gives us are not surprising contradictions and indictments of what we consider best about ourselves and our laws. They are, instead, quick, patched-together constructions of what we already know to be wrong about our social preferences. The way he seizes upon fashionable issues makes it seem as though Vonnegut were running for office rather than trying to write a novel, and one can't help feeling, as a constituent, that some very black dilemmas indeed are being put to meretricious use by a politician awkwardly pretending to a sense of humor.

Another noticeable aspect of Vonnegut's imagination is that it takes no pains to disguise how pleased it is with itself. One can almost hear the self-congratulations each time it comes up with a cute, futuristic notion like Suicide Parlours and then rests on this achievement, certain that it has done enough to justify our attention and now need not be too generous and give us anything like an intricate world, a compelling narrative, or an astounding person or two. Indeed, many of Vonnegut's stories seem made up merely of bright notions and metaphors surrounded by wastelands of writing so flat and graceless that, should it ever be judged as having anything to do with ordinary life on this planet, it would be considered grimly sentimental. For an example, let us take the last page of "Welcome to the Monkey House." Billy is trying to explain to the erstwhile frigid hostess just why he abducted and raped her:

> "So you see, Nancy," said Billy, "I have spent this night, and many others like it, attempting to restore a certain amount of innocent pleasure to the world, which is poorer in pleasure than it needs to be." Nancy sat down quietly and bowed her head.
>
> "I'll tell you what my grandfather did on the dawn of his wedding night," said Billy.
>
> "I don't think I want to hear it."
>
> "It isn't violent—it's meant to be tender."
>
> "Maybe that's why I don't want to hear it."
>
> "He read his bride a poem." Billy took the book from the table, opened it. "His diary tells which poem it was. While we aren't bride and groom, and while we may not meet again for many years, I'd like to read this poem to you, to have you know I've loved you."
>
> "Please—no. I couldn't stand it."
>
> "All right, I'll leave the book here, with the place marked, in case you want to read it later. It's the poem beginning:
>
> How do I love thee?
> Let me count the ways.
> I love thee to the depth
> and the breadth and height
> My soul can reach,
> when feeling out of sight
> For the ends of Being
> and the ideal Grace."

Now if one were to take the above peroration out of the story's anaphrodisiac world of the future and place it, say, in present-day Cleveland, one would have a good example of that emotionally blowzy style that infested ladies' magazines before Women's Lib called for harder hearts and tougher minds. Not unfairly one feels that Vonnegut skips off into the future so often because the present is less sympathetic to his literary weaknesses.

Vonnegut's partisans, however, will claim that his real strength is very much tied to the world around us. There is a string of quotes festooning the jackets of all his books that proclaim his "dark humor" and "savage satire," qualities which, it is stated, he turns with numbing accuracy upon our present world of wars and political lunacy. Literary publicists may believe this but, in fact, just as he is an unsubtle fantast when he narrates the future, Vonnegut is also a too easily understood parabolist of the present.

Slaughterhouse-Five, with its time jumps, trips to other planets, the firebombing of Dresden, and the casual mingling of the current history of the author with that of his fictional world, remains, when all of its wearisome inventiveness is done, one of the most unsurprising, self-indulgent little books ever to work so hard at being selfless and memorable. Not one character emerges from it with anything like the grotesque clarity which, say, Malaparte gave to a briefly encountered soul caught in the inferno of World War II; not one attitude in all of Vonnegut's darkly humorous anecdotes of life and death stays in the mind except the infantile stoicism exemplified by the recurrent and infuriatingly Olympian phrase "and so it goes." There is no intimation in this book of a sensibility which understands what is relevant to the conjunction of history and personal imagination, understands, finally, how carefully balanced a book must be that wishes to encompass the annihilation of millions and the mental caprices of one dull hero.

Billy Pilgrim—like most other Vonnegut characters, he drags around a portentous, morality play name—is a gentle heart driven to madness by the experience of war. (A good number of Vonnegut's heroes are given to us in a lunatic state. Examples, I suppose, of what society does to the sensitive mind.) Billy's madness, however, is of an amiable sort, turning him into a passive, observing voyager through human holocausts, time, and even through galactic boundaries to another planet where he is taught a larger view of life and an insufferable tolerance for the pains that nettle the majority of unenlightened earthlings. Billy's loadstone in all this roaming through space and time is, of course, Dresden, before, during, and after its destruction. His experience of being mated while caged for display by the inhabitants of the planet Tralfamadore and his difficulties in being a good citizen of suburbia are interrupted by stark little chunks of actual martial horror laid out in an affectedly offhand way so that the author can be credited with having digested the experience he is writing about to the point of breath-taking casualness.

What is made of all these structural shenanigans? Well, one conclusion could be that, as a species, human beings should be caged, studied, and advised by a higher order of life before being set loose in the universe again. Or, perhaps, another would be that they must stop driving themselves mad with wars. And then, again, it could be best simply to hold onto some second-rate resignation, sigh, and affect the attitude of one who has seen too much history, who knows too much of the future, and who counts tragedy an odd notion of the inhabitants of the water planet. And so it goes.

It would be unjust to harp on the conclusions of Vonnegut's mental odyssey through *Slaughterhouse-Five* if the voyage itself had had some interest. After all, a book is under no obligation to come to any conclusion at all about itself. *Slaughterhouse-Five*, however, seems to be nothing else but conclusions. The tone of judgment surrounds all the events of the book, jostling the reader again and again into an atmosphere of self-pity, into moments thick with unearned, lyrical agonies. Along the way, Vonnegut tries to come up with a moment or two to justify his reputation as a black satirist. But his imagination is not so much antic as it is willful, an imagination which does not disguise the fact that, however swaggering and adventurous in tone, it is in the service of a moralist too easily satisfied that the world confirms his point of view. This might be artistically excusable if the point of view were at all complex or idiosyncratic, but it is, rather, much too obvious and commonplace to need so much baroque substantiation. For all his notoriety, Vonnegut never really goes further than the poor estimate society has about itself even in its most official pronouncements. He therefore stops where an intelligent imagination ought to begin.

Still, with all his apparent faults, Vonnegut undeniably is in high favor today with a large variety of readers. While it is always possible to mutter something about untutored taste whenever an author in whom one sees little merit attracts a large public, Vonnegut, I believe, is reaping the benefit of the desire for a social fundamentalism on the part of individuals who should know better. As more and more minds take on the primitive political notion of a vague "us" and a blurred "them," Vonnegut will have a better and better chance of becoming the official novelist of one side or the other, of becoming a simple, unthought-out piece of literary propaganda. That is a fate that even Vonnegut is writer enough not to deserve.

JEROME KLINKOWITZ

"The Literary Career of Kurt Vonnegut, Jr."

Modern Fiction Studies, Spring 1973, pp. 57–67

The poster appears in practically every bookstore window: "Kurt Vonnegut, Jr.," with a picture of the man himself, looking (as an early reviewer put it) like a corduroy-covered bat-wing chair, peering across the list of books he has written. *Cat's Cradle, Slaughterhouse-Five,* and his eight other titles are stacked inside, for another million readers to buy this year and almost certainly for many years to come.[1] There is no other living American novelist one could imagine on such a poster—not Saul Bellow, nor at the other extreme Harold Robbins. Yet the posters remain, and can be found in head shops, pizzarias, and college bars, stamping those places as the dusty portraits of William Butler Yeats define an Irish pub.

College sales have undoubtedly been the factor which pushed Vonnegut over the top, making him not only one of the largest sellers, but probably the most talked-about American novelist since Ernest Hemingway.[2] But Kurt Vonnegut, Jr., marked like a painted bird with his self-proclaimed attention-getting name, has been around for two decades, doing stories for *The Saturday Evening Post* and letting three of his books see first light as shoddy drugstore paperbacks,[3] while waiting for America to discover him as its great public writer. The country is having its field day now, as the resurrected *Post* digs up Vonnegut's 1950 nostalgia pieces for each quarterly issue, and old paperback bins are riffled for copies of those queer editions: *Utopia-14,*[4] *Canary in a Cat House,* and the totally disreputable first edition of *Sirens of Titan* with its garish advertisements and sexy come-on cover. Vonnegut served a twenty-year apprenticeship, from 1949 when he left his job as public relations man for General Electric's Research Laboratory to support his growing family by writing stories for the slicks instead, up to 1969 when *Slaughterhouse-Five* became his first best-seller. Within those years lies the work of a lifetime: six novels, two story collections, and the roots for his plays on Broadway and TV. For an America grappling with some fast, confusing changes, Kurt Vonnegut's newly discovered career was the missing link, spanning the years from today's issues back to the simpler times when the television adaptation he helped write, "Auf Wiedersehen," was the vehicle for Ronald Reagan to introduce Sammy Davis, Jr., in his first dramatic role.[5] General Electric Theatre, *Colliers Magazine, The Saturday Evening Post*—these were the markets Vonnegut worked, spinning tales of Buick Roadmasters and All Electric Homes that seem, in their almost grandfatherly tone, to have been written for us today.

For twenty years, while Vonnegut wrote his simple stories of the American middle class, his publishers tried frantically to build him a novelist's reputation as exotic as his name. His first novel, *Player Piano* (1952), was given a large book club printing, and a quarter of a million copies were prepared in paperback. But it was a science fiction book club, and a retitled and luridly dressed paperback pitched to the s-f audience, and neither succeeded as well as the several hundred copies of the first edition which sold in Schenectady, New York—home of the General Electric Corporation and of the people who recognized some very down-to-earth things of which their former p.r. man was making fun. *The Sirens of Titan* followed in 1959: 177,550 paperback copies. Even at 35¢, if each one had sold Vonnegut could have rested from the *Post* for half a year. But the page one blurb proclaimed, "Malachi Constant was the richest man in America . . . Since attaining manhood, there was no woman he desired who had not succumbed," hardly suggesting that within was a technically challenging and very serious novel. To complicate matters, Vonnegut picked the same time to hit the catastrophe of all serial writers, a slack year when absolutely nothing sold. "In those days," says Vonnegut, "if you had published something you could go to a paperback house and give them one chapter and an outline and they would give you money which would pay your grocery bill, anyway."[6] And so his third novel, *Mother Night* (1962), which many critics today call his best, was sacrificed as a pulp paperback. Encountered in this edition, it is often mistaken for what it fictionally purports to be, "an American traitor's astonishing confession" of his hideous acts as a Nazi in World War II. *Canary in a Cat House,* a curiously uneven collection of Vonnegut's stories from every which place, died a similar death with the same publisher. In 1963 an editor from one of the paperback houses which printed Vonnegut got a job with Holt, Rinehart and Winston, taking the manuscript of *Cat's Cradle* with him. *God Bless You, Mr. Rosewater* followed in 1965, and for the first time in a decade Vonnegut could boast of original hardbound publication. But only 6,000 copies of each were printed, not many sold, and reviewers and librarians alike followed habit in classifying the books as "science fiction," even though in the presidential election of 1964 seventy million Americans had voted on issues—the reconstitution of society, the possible military destruction of the world—very close to the themes of Vonnegut's two novels. In fifteen years of writing Vonnegut had won success only in the topically familiar but auctorially anonymous field of popular magazine fiction. His career seemed schizophrenic: scores of stories read by a mass popular audience and a group of curious novels acknowledged by only the smallest of intellectual elites, neither of which appeared to admit the other's existence.

Yet for an ever-increasing paperback market, Kurt Vonnegut, Jr., provided fodder. By 1966 all his novels were available in low-priced but quality editions, widely distributed to drugstores and paperback bookstalls. His full canon was for once at hand, and when personal details about the man started coming out, readers could finally put things in place. His reviews for the *New York Times Book Review,* beginning in late 1965, showed him not a raving sci-fi lunatic nor an anonymous hack writer, but rather as the guy next door who, faced with the evaluation of a dictionary, could only shrug, "Prescriptive, as nearly as I could tell, was like an honest cop, and descriptive was like a boozed-up war buddy from Mobile, Ala."[7] Other pieces, crafted in the new style of personal journalism which placed the writer himself at the imaginative center of experience, followed in the Sunday magazine sections of the *Times* and other papers, and in such popular journals as *Esquire* and *McCall's*.[8] A reprint of *Mother Night*,[9] where Vonnegut added a preface clarifying his role as author, revealed something which was in fact true: as a 22-year-old prisoner of war he had survived the Allied firebombing of Dresden, Germany, an atrocity killing more people than the atomic bomb at Hiroshima. Readers now knew something about this man, a solidly middle-class kid from Indianapolis who went to Cornell to study chemistry and who witnessed scientific truth when America and British warplanes dropped it on an open city. And those same readers could now buy all his books in paperback to discover that the tangled world of middle-class homes, Nazi perversity, and unimaginable machines of destruction was in its cumulative effect their world, too, only glimpsed a few years earlier by this son of an Indiana architect.

When Seymour Lawrence, the independent Boston publisher who had spotted Vonnegut this very way through the *Times* reviews and paperback reprints, published *Slaughterhouse-Five* in 1969, it was almost inevitable that Vonnegut's careful and complete preparation would make the book a best-seller. Swelled by a college underground where the science fiction paperbacks had their best market, people had been "hearing" of Vonnegut for some time. Now he was presentable in a widely distributed hardbound edition, promptly picked up by the Literary Guild and serialized as well. Moreover, the book was a coming-to-terms with the matter of Dresden, beginning with a first-person chapter locating Vonnegut securely within this book and explaining his work for the past twenty years. "What do you say about a massacre" had been the unsaid premise of his five previous novels. From *Player Piano* through *God Bless You, Mr. Rosewater,* Vonnegut had dealt with an unending series of catastrophes, from social revolutions and a world war through a Martian invasion to the ultimate destruction of the world itself. The short stories, written "to finance the writing of the novels,"[10] spoke more directly of Vonnegut's day-to-day life, as a solid ex-Midwesterner trying to support his wife and six children by writing stories of people in similar predicaments, spinning fantasies to take himself and his readers beyond their quotidian lives for a better perspective on them. *Slaughterhouse-Five* traced the two streams back to where they join in a meat locker five stories beneath the city of Dresden, where on February 13, 1945, the young soldier from Indianapolis witnessed the greatest single military destruction of human life in modern time.

Expressing what he saw took Vonnegut five books of trying. To clarify what was really going on, he kept rearranging what we take to be our world. First to be transformed was society, the wrong way in *Player Piano,* where indeed social change could take us if technology were to overrule human value, and later the right way in *God Bless You, Mr. Rosewater,* where our whole social ethic is stood on its head so that there might be some worth for man. Why not change everything? It is all convention anyway, Vonnegut demonstrates, since a science fiction writer's vision of interstellar travel is not a bit more fantastic than a millionaire's ability to scribble his name on a piece of paper and have it be worth just so much money. "Think about the silly ways money gets passed around now," Eliot Rosewater tells a group of science fictionists, "and then think up better ways."[11] Better Living Through Chemistry, Progress Is Our Most Important Product—Kurt Vonnegut, the public relations man who could easily have written those slogans, took his own advice and wrote novels which effectively created whole new worlds. "Americans have long been taught to hate all people who will not or cannot work, to hate themselves for that,"[12] observes Kilgore Trout, the s-f writer *manqué* who often suggests Vonnegut himself. So what can one do when automation denies a job for everybody? Change the social ethic and treasure people for something other than what they can produce.

The second note of Vonnegut's new world symphony is sounded in his novels which reach beyond the immediately social toward the larger forces which determine man. How far is man responsible, where does he stand in the Universe, and what does that Universe think of him? *The Sirens of Titan, Mother Night,* and *Cat's Cradle,* novels written at the center of Vonnegut's career, try to answer these overwhelming questions. For man's responsibility, the author rewrites the history of World War II, showing how an American spy, trapped in the pose of broadcasting anti-Semitic propaganda for the Nazis, seeks refuge by being simply ludicrous. "But this is a hard world to be ludicrous in," he learns, "with so many human beings so reluctant to laugh, so incapable of thought, so eager to believe and snarl and hate."[13] And so his efforts as the best American spy are countered by his success as the best German propagandist, and the war ends not in 1943 but in 1945 with a top Nazi telling him, "You alone kept me from concluding that Germany had gone insane."[14] If that is responsibility, our whole system of causes and effects is absurd, and Vonnegut would strongly agree. In fact, *Cat's Cradle,* with its religion of obvious yet comforting lies, argues against a Universe where man is directly invested with responsibility for what the world is. Its final word, when the world is destroyed by a military scientist's *ice-nine,* is simply this advice: "If I were a younger man, I would write a history of human stupidity; and I would climb to the top of Mount McCabe and lie down on my back with my history for a pillow; and I would take from the ground some of the blue-white poison that makes statues of men; and I would make a statue of myself, lying on my back, grinning horribly, and thumbing my nose at You Know Who."[15] The Renaissance was one thing; but the consummate horrors of the twentieth century have made it an unbearable trial for man to identify himself with the center of the Universe, especially when at that center resides so much apparent evil. Claiming responsibility, claiming God's purpose, only bring that evil more quickly down to earth. Man's salvation can only be like the Bokononism of *Cat's Cradle,* or the religion established in Vonnegut's second novel, *The Sirens of Titan:* The Church of God the Utterly Indifferent.

Or so the novels suggest. But they are novels, not tracts, and Vonnegut is only doing what any artist does, creating imaginative solutions to the very real problems of our lives. Vonnegut's great youth following may seem to have run off after a prophet, but there has been precious little guru-making of the man, certainly less than for Salinger and his Zen wisdom a decade ago, and nothing resembling the cult surrounding Tolkein. Rather there is a great correspondence between what Vonnegut says when he appears at colleges and what he wrote for the same students' parents in the days of *The Saturday Evening Post*. "We're not too young for love," a teenage runaway admits to her boyfriend in an early story.[16] "Just too young for about everything else there is that goes with love." Vonnegut was saying the same thing a decade later, in his Bennington commencement speech (which made the lead item in *Time*),[17] that young people should not accept responsibility for reforming the world. In practical terms, that is an impossible duty to bear, for any human being. The answer lies rather in our attitudes, our philosophies—in short, what comes from our imagination. Vonnegut's beliefs in human decency are perhaps the most consistent thing about his writing, whether it be the occasional stories in the *Post*, where basically good and simple people—storm-window salesmen, small town businessmen—triumph over far more imposing people and ideas,[18] or in the novels, where with much more artistic apparatus he sets about redefining our Universe, which is, as he establishes, nothing more than a dominant state of mind.

Slaughterhouse-Five is the triumph of imagination, a product of twenty years of prototypes where at last the author has found a way to emphasize the good times and forget about the bad. Science fiction time-travel is his metaphor, but behind this device stands man's greatest power, what separates him from other living creatures—the ability to imagine that anything, even he himself, is different from what is. Turn things around, make them different. Overcome the trouble, in one's mind to start with, but, when you have the technology, that way too. The horrors of war, our complex machines of destruction: why not reinvent them as they would be reinvented when we take a war movie and run it backwards:

> American planes, full of holes and wounded men and corpses, took off backwards from an airfield in England. Over France, a few German fighter planes flew at them backwards, sucked bullets and shell fragments from some of the planes and crewmen. They did the same for wrecked American bombers on the ground, and those planes flew up backwards to join the formation.
>
> The formation flew backwards over a German city that was in flames. The bombers opened their bomb bay doors, exerted a miraculous magnetism which shrunk the fires, gathered them into cylindrical steel containers, and lifted the containers into the bellies of the planes. The containers were stored neatly in racks. The German below had miraculous devices of their own, which were long steel tubes. They used them to suck more fragments from the crewmen and planes. But there were still a few wounded Americans, though, and some of the bombers were in bad repair. Over France, though, German fighters came up again, made everything and everybody as good as new.
>
> When the bombers got back to their base, the steel cylinders were taken from the racks and shipped back to the United States of America, where factories were operating night and day, dismantling the cylinders, separating the dangerous contents into minerals. Touchingly, it was mainly women who did this work. The minerals were then shipped to specialists in remote areas. It was their business to put them into the ground, to hide them cleverly, so they would never hurt anybody ever again.[19]

With such a theme, and the innovative techniques to express it, Vonnegut took his place with the other American fictionists come to prominence during the late 1960's: Donald Barthelme, Richard Brautigan, Ronald Sukenick, and Jerzy Kosinski, to name just a few, who in each of their novels[20] carefully examined conventional reality to show how appallingly unreal it is before offering a personal fantasy closer to the truth of experience, more relevant to our needs and hence more real.

In the four years between his sudden fame and the publication of his most recent novel, *Breakfast of Champions* (1973), Vonnegut was as a man without a genre. In the first chapter of *Slaughterhouse-Five,* he declared that after twenty years and six novels, he had come to terms with (and apparently exhausted) the substance of his fiction. "I've finished my war book now," he proclaimed. "The next one I write is going to be fun."[21] But the new novel was soon abandoned—publicly recalled and suppressed in fact—[22] while he scripted the Broadway production of *Happy Birthday, Wanda June,*[23] an entirely new vision wherein society favorably transformed itself and left its reactionary central character behind, quite the opposite of Vonnegut's mode in fiction. Following that were ambitious plans for more plays, musicals, and films, but the only concrete issue of the years 1971–1972 turned out to be his redrafting of a committee-written script, *Between Time and Timbuktu,* broadcast as a ninety minute special on National Educational Television.[24] As if in celebration of the feat of *Slaughterhouse Five,* the N.E.T. production gathered the bits and pieces of Vonnegut's twenty-year world and presented them as a cosmic Yoknapatawpha: the "chronosynclastic infundibulum" of pure imaginative freedom when a poet is launched into space and his responses measured back on earth. "What does the show mean?" Vonnegut considered, having the record of his literary career placed so handily before him. "Well—it means, for one thing, that we will never get very far from this planet, no matter how much money we spend. So we had better stop treating the planet as though it were a disposable item to be used up and thrown away. It means, too, that, no matter how far we may travel, we can never get out of our heads."[25]

Breakfast of Champions[26] brought Vonnegut back to fiction, building on the years of self-imposed retrospective study since *Slaughterhouse-Five.* "I have become an enthusiast for the printed word again," he announced in 1972. "I have to be that, I now understand, because I want to be a character in all of my works. I can do that in print. In a movie, somehow, the author always vanishes. Everything of mine which has been filmed so far has been one character short, and the character is me."[27] The subsequent novel deals with something before and beyond Dresden: the "great depression," which can be a reference to what happened in America during the 1930's, what is happening to the ecology and survival-potential of our planet now, and to the very personal effect both these events (and the years inbetween) have had upon the psyche of a literary artist. Vonnegut remembers the 1930's as a time when jocular impoliteness got one through the day, when his own childhood models (cited elsewhere as Jack Benny, Fred Allen, and Henry Morgan, and incorporated into *Breakfast of Champions* as a wildly irreverent columnist for the Indianapolis *Times*) survived the decade-long "Blue Monday" by their black humor, a term some contemporary critics use to define such works as Terry Southern's *The Magic Christian,* Bruce Jay Friedman's *Stern,* John Barth's earlier work, and Vonnegut's novels. But our own times of curruption, pollution, overpopulation, and decay are a far different matter, for no one can hope, as forty years ago, "that the nation would be happy and just and rational when prosperity came."

To write a novel adequate to our present reality, Vonnegut synthesizes not just the themes, but also the techniques of his literary career which spans America's change. Kilgore Trout, the prolific science fiction hack from Vonnegut's two previous novels who seems the epitome of the wildest flights of fantasy, is brought to meet the most thoroughly middle-class character Vonnegut ever created: Dwayne Hoover, proprietor of "Dwayne Hoover's Exit Eleven Pontiac Village" and owner of a share in the Holiday Inn and a string of Burger Chef's in Midland City, Indiana. Like Vonnegut, Trout creates fantasies of impossibly hospitable worlds, which, as in *God Bless You, Mr. Rosewater,* are marketed as pornography. At the same time

Hoover has been learning the relative and totally conventional nature of reality, since by amassing economic power he can increasingly effect changes in the world around him. The state of our planet, however, has by the time of *Breakfast of Champions* outstripped the limits of conventional middle class control. Ice-cream, aluminum siding, and even the martini, euphemised in the book's title, pale before the new synthesis needed to keep our dying world in order. Trout, arguing the transformative power of ideas, of the imagination, writes a book explaining to any reader why things are so bad: every person, place, and thing in the Universe is a robot, existing simply for the test of one human being as a free-will prototype. That prototype, of course, is Dwayne Hoover, the reader.

That Dwayne cracks beneath such pressure and runs through an orgy of destruction does not discredit Trout's synthesis. "Of course it is exhausting," his novel admits, "having to reason all the time in a universe which wasn't meant to be reasonable." What Trout, with Vonnegut behind him, never denies is that his synthesis is simply a fiction. Kurt Vonnegut, Jr., the public writer and reluctant guru of the American 1960's and 1970's, has created religions in his books; but each time, with Bokononism in *Cat's Cradle* and the Church of God the Utterly Indifferent in *The Sirens of Titan*, he has warned against construing external divine purpose for anything. *Breakfast of Champions* has its keys to knowledge too: "leaks," described as "holes in the Universe," but which in practice become nothing other than mirrors or reflecting sun-glasses. For organizing the other, one invariably comes back to self, to one's own imagination, of which we and no one else are the creator. The ultimate reality then rests with the work itself, for Vonnegut in his novel (where he appears as the final creator, retracting his imaginative apparatus and releasing his characters at the end) and for life at large in the ideas by which it chooses to see itself.

The structural and even closely stylistic techniques of *Breakfast of Champions* vindicate Vonnegut's artistic development and place him with the most respected innovators of the decade. His "pastiche" or "collage" method, which has been praised in *Cat's Cradle* and *God Bless You, Mr. Rosewater* as an especially apt method of epistemology,[28] continues in *Breakfast of Champions* as a key device. Approximately one hundred felt-tip pen sketches by Vonnegut dot the book. Instead of the palliative "so it goes," Vonnegut here resolves the problematic by fixing it in its primal objectivity, where—much like pop art—common objects are seen more revealingly, even magically, outside the light of common day. Ideas are not logically presented, but rather are strung along in loose association as the reader follows a hopscotch pattern to the truth. And Vonnegut remains firmly present as the imaginative center of his work, a structural pose of so much fiction come to prominence since the time Vonnegut himself was becoming famous.

The literary career of Kurt Vonnegut, Jr., is one exceedingly rich. He is at once common and exotic, quotidian, and elite, and by his ability to comprehend and express such extremes, has become our great public writer. Spanning the length of America's mid-century development and reaching the far limits of audiences, forms, and topics, Vonnegut has melded the disparate elements of what we have been into a coherent picture of what we are now.

Notes

1. There are more than fifty distinct American editions of Vonnegut's novels, story collections, and plays, plus scores of foreign issues. His Dell paperback editions are each reprinted six to eight times per year, in press runs of 25,000 to 50,000 copies each, as they have been since January, 1970.
2. Since 1969 over three dozen interviews with Vonnegut have appeared in major magazines and newspapers, and in that same brief time twice that many critical books and articles (and of course hundreds of reviews) have been published. For a complete list, see Klinkowitz *et al.*, "The Vonnegut Bibliography," in *The Vonnegut Statement*, ed. Jerome Klinkowitz and John Somer (New York: Delacorte/Seymour Lawrence, 1973), pp. 255–277.
3. *The Sirens of Titan* (New York: Dell, 1959); *Canary in a Cat House* (Greenwich, Conn.: Fawcett/Gold Medal, 1961); *Mother Night* (Greenwich, Conn.: Fawcett/Gold Medal, 1962).
4. The retitled paperback edition of *Player Piano* (New York: Scribners, 1952) prepared by Bantam Books (New York) in 1954.
5. A television drama by Kurt Vonnegut, Jr., and Valentine Davies, adapted from the story "D. P.," *Ladies Home Journal*, 70 (August 1953), 42–43, 80–81, 84, by Kurt Vonnegut, Jr., produced by William Frye, directed by John Brahm, and transmitted nationally on "General Electric Theatre" by the Columbia Broadcasting System, October 5, 1958.
6. Interviewed by Robert Scholes on the University of Iowa campus and broadcast locally October 4, 1966.
7. "The Latest Word" [rev. of *The Random House Dictionary*], *New York Times Book Review*, October 30, 1966, p. 1.
8. See especially "Excelsior! We're Going to the Moon! Excelsior," *New York Times Magazine*, July 13, 1969, pp. 9–11; "Physicist, Purge Thyself," *Chicago Tribune Magazine*, June 22, 1969, pp. 44, 48–50, 52, 56; "Yes, We Have No Nirvanas," *Esquire*, 69 (June 1968), 78–79, 176, 178–179, 182; "Biafra," *McCall's*, 97 (April 1970), 68–69, 134–138. A complete bibliography of Mr. Vonnegut's uncollected works may be found in Klinkowitz and Somer, *The Vonnegut Statement*.
9. (New York: Harper & Row, 1966); also included in second paperback edition of *Mother Night* (New York: Avon, 1967) and all subsequent editions.
10. "Preface," *Welcome to the Monkey House* (New York: Delacorte/Seymour Lawrence, 1968), p. xiv.
11. *God Bless You, Mr. Rosewater* (New York: Holt, Rinehart and Winston, 1965), p. 31.
12. *God Bless You, Mr. Rosewater*, p. 210.
13. *Mother Night*, pp. 106–107.
14. *Mother Night*, p. 71.
15. *Cat's Cradle* (New York: Holt, Rinehart and Winston, 1963), p. 231.
16. "Runaways," *Saturday Evening Post*, 234 (April 15, 1961), 26–27, 52, 54, 56.
17. "Vonnegut's Gospel," *Time*, June 29, 1970, p. 8. The text of Vonnegut's speech is reprinted as "Up Is Better Than Down," *Vogue* (August 1, 1970), pp. 54, 144–145.
18. See especially the uncollected stories "Poor Little Rich Town," *Collier's*, 130 (October 25, 1952), 90–95; "Bagombo Snuff Box," *Cosmopolitan*, 137 (October, 1954), 34–39; "A Present for Big Nick," *Argosy* (December 1954), pp. 42–45, 72–73.
19. *Slaughterhouse-Five* (New York: Delacorte/Seymour Lawrence, 1969), p. 63.
20. Key novels, and respective critical studies, are Barthelme, *Snow White* (New York: Atheneum, 1967), and Jerome Klinkowitz, "Literary Disruptions; Or, What's Become of American Fiction," in *Surfiction*, ed. Raymond Federman (Chicago: Swallow, 1973); Brautigan, *Trout Fishing in America* (San Francisco: Four Seasons, 1967), and John Clayton, "Richard Brautigan: The Politics of Woodstock," *New American Review*, #11 (1971), pp. 56–68; Sukenick, *Up* (New York: Dial, 1968), and Jerome Klinkowitz, "Getting Real: Making It (Up) with Ronald Sukenick," *Chicago Review*, 23 (Winter 1972), 73–82; Kosinski, *Steps* (New York: Random House, 1968), and Daniel J. Cahill, "Jerzy Kosinski: Retreat from Violence," *Twentieth Century Literature*, 18 (April 1972), 121–132.
21. *Slaughterhouse-Five*, p. 19.
22. Bruce Cook, "When Kurt Vonnegut Talks—And He Does—The Young All Tune In," *National Observer*, October 12, 1970, p. 21; Carol Kramer, "Kurt's College Cult Adopts Him as Literary Guru

at 48," *Chicago Tribune*, November 15, 1970, sec. 5, p. 1; Richard Todd, "The Masks of Kurt Vonnegut, Jr.," *New York Times Magazine*, January 24, 1971, p. 19.
23. *Happy Birthday, Wanda June* (New York: Delacorte/Seymour Lawrence, 1971).
24. March 13, 1972. Published in book form as *Between Time and Timbuktu* (New York: Delacorte/Seymour Lawrence, 1972).
25. Ms. comments on production, Kurt Vonnegut, Jr. Quoted with the permission of Mr. Vonnegut. [Original draft of a preface for *Between Time and Timbuktu* which was dropped in favor of final preface cited below.]
26. (New York: Delacorte/Seymour Lawrence, 1973). All subsequent quotations from this work, to be published in April of 1973, are taken from the book's advance galleys which were distributed to reviewers in November, 1972.
27. "Preface," *Between Time and Timbuktu* (New York: Delacorte/Seymour Lawrence, 1972), p. xv.
28. David H. Goldsmith, *Kurt Vonnegut/Fantasist of Fire and Ice* (Bowling Green, Ohio: Bowling Green University Popular Press, 1972), pp. 35–40. Other favorable commentators on Vonnegut's method include Robert Scholes, *The Fabulators* (New York: Oxford University Press, 1967); Raymond Olderman, *Beyond the Waste Land/The American Novel in the Nineteen-Sixties* (New Haven: Yale University Press, 1972); Peter J. Reed, *Kurt Vonnegut, Jr.* (New York: Warner Paperback Library, 1972).

EDWARD GROSSMAN
"Vonnegut & His Audience"
Commentary, July 1974, pp. 40–46

Wampeters, Foma & Granfalloons is the name of Kurt Vonnegut, Jr.'s new book, a collection of essays, reviews, speeches, etc. Only a writer with Vonnegut's power base could get a book of occasional writings published today, let alone get away with giving it such a title. Simply the sound of the apparently nonsensical words is enough to kindle recognition in those who have been initiated into Vonnegut's universe, and by the most cautious estimate the number of reader-initiates must be in the hundreds of thousands. The very definite *meaning* of these not-so-secret words is stored in the memories of probably almost as many people, and is fairly often retrievable and can be recited in paraphrase—the novel *(Cat's Cradle)* in which Vonnegut invented the words and originally set forth their meanings in 1963 has gone through thirty-two printings in the last four years. But *Cat's Cradle* is not the only book in which Vonnegut has made up words; in this practice, as in other ways, his work is of a piece, and once the reason is understood why any of his writing should have become immensely popular, it is understandable why all of his books—almost impossible to find in bookstores when first published—are now continuously in print. The prevalence of Vonnegut cannot be overstated. Another of his novels *(Slaughterhouse-Five)* has been translated into fifteen languages, and another *(Breakfast of Champions)* recently spent a year on the best-seller list, at the top of it much of that time.

If Vonnegut's work is widely known, his face and voice are not unfamiliar. He can fill the largest auditorium on any American campus or in any city with a public appearance. In the acoustically perfect Heinz Hall in Pittsburgh, which accommodates three thousand sitting down, and where the Pittsburgh Symphony occasionally draws a capacity audience, Vonnegut has spoken to more than three thousand, including standees. The Heinz Hall scene was strongly reminiscent of those that used to occur some years ago around the persons of Timothy Leary or Marshall McLuhan. A crowd of the knowledgeable and curious waited patiently for Vonnegut to be introduced. Many in the audience were obviously college students, but people were also there who could have been their parents, and it was not exclusively the young who had brought along paperback copies of one or another of Vonnegut's novels. Perhaps they hoped to have them autographed. To see the bright-colored covers flashing up and down the rows and aisles, however, was to fancy that these were book-talismans, like Mao's *Thoughts*, or the Bible. In fact, the evening did have an air of the mass audience with an oracle or prophet, of the kind Vonnegut himself treats satirically and somewhat ambiguously in several of his novels. This atmosphere was heightened, if anything, with Vonnegut's shuffling entrance onstage. A skinny, awkward figure in a rumpled suit, Vonnegut bears a resemblance to pictures of Mark Twain that will grow more striking as his hair and mustache turn white. He began by mumbling that he had no speech prepared. Having confessed this, he proceeded to ramble for something like an hour, in casual, homely, haphazard yet self-confident fashion over such topics as the legroom in Volkswagens and genocide. The overwhelming majority of his listeners were extremely attentive, sympathetic, and grateful, and ready to laugh at his jokes. Later, leaving, they seemed happy to have been there, and satisfied that they had got their money's worth (the price of admission was five dollars).

To be an American writer, and to be paid this kind of attention, especially by Americans born since World War II, is unusual and remarkable. Of course, collegians and college graduates and dropouts are said to like the work of other writers, too, and they can be seen voluntarily buying and reading these other books in paperback: the productions of Donald Barthelme, Ken Kesey, Joseph Heller, perhaps Thomas Pynchon and Joyce Carol Oates among the native novelists; Hermann Hesse and J. R. R. Tolkien from the Old World; and of the New Journalists, Tom Wolfe and Hunter Thompson and sometimes Norman Mailer. But Vonnegut is the champion—actually in a class by himself. The sale of his books and the love accorded them and their creator are such as are ordinarily reserved for the reading matter that caters best to a larger public's appetite for violence, inside dope, and sentimentality, and those who produce it (examples are unnecessary). It is therefore not only in strict terms of the economics of publishing that Vonnegut may be said to have gained what amounts to power after years of feeling misunderstood and neglected, if not powerless.

Considering the ability of his books to hold the attention of large numbers of people in a society supplied with many distractions more vivid than books, it is not surprising that Vonnegut's standing with literary critics should be unsettled. Some seem to think he is suspect because his work enjoys a success that is anomalous for "serious" writing; others, having skimmed or read his books, say more or less that they are not worth a critic's time. Vonnegut is a "sententious old salt in ontological drag," the late Charles Thomas Samuels wrote in the *New Republic*, and his is "a bogus talent. . . . [He] can tell us nothing worth knowing except what his rise itself indicates: ours is an age in which adolescent ridicule can become a mode of upward mobility." According to Jack Richardson, Vonnegut is a "compiler of easy-to-read truisms." But as Benjamin DeMott sees it, the kids' lighting on Kurt Vonnegut is an undeservedly good break for the age," and, in Leslie Fiedler's opinion, the Vonnegut novels do belong "to what we know again to be the mainstream of fiction," by which Fiedler does not mean what he calls "High Art," but rather "American Pop . . . the quest of the absolute wilderness." Graham Greene is less sly, more explicit: Vonnegut is "one of the best living American writers."

Vonnegut's novels are full of stories—no plotless novels in the hyper-modern manner could have become so popular. They are also full of characters, surprises, episodes, suicides, apocalypses, science-fiction fantasies, morals drawn and underlined. And certain persistent motifs run through all of them. The Vonnegut hero is typically an American who has either been born or worked his way into what society considers a privileged position. But he is more than dissatisfied—he is ashamed, and tries to redeem himself by dropping out and associating with those believed less privileged, by helping the unwashed, the insulted, or merely exploited, the little people worn down by industrial and scientific consequences. Sometimes this saintly program is an obsession, an end in itself *(God Bless You, Mr. Rosewater)*, sometimes a nagging temptation along the way of a quest or odyssey *(Player Piano; The Sirens of Titan; Cat's Cradle)*. One way or another, it continually seems that it might be the right thing if the main character devoted what energy and ingenuity he had to it, in spite of the fact that he realizes such a program cannot change anything for the better, that the unfortunate are no more lovable or deserving than the intelligent, the high, and the mighty, and that in any event fate has an absurd and painful end in store for all.

To note this recurring theme is misleading, if it suggests that Vonnegut creates failed saints to study and dissect them, like a psychologist. With several exceptions, the characters, even the presumptive heroes, who appear and reappear in his novels are not deep enough and they do not stay in one place long enough to be studied as in a psychological novel. Mostly, Vonnegut's figures are mechanical contrivances bathed in a stroboscopic glare—fleshless robots galvanized by his will, moving jerkily toward the next joke, moral, or plot-advancing surprise.

Another thread: In all his novels, and even when he uses the whole universe for scenery, Vonnegut has originated this repertory of characters in upstate New York, Rhode Island-Cape Cod, and Indiana. In *The Vonnegut Statement*, a *Festschrift* compiled by some of his academic admirers in the Middle West, these locales are compared to Faulkner's Yoknapatawpha County. As Vonnegut sketches them, the places are meant to seem sadly comic, haunted by American ghosts: of the coastal Indians and whalers, the Iroquois tribes and Erie canalmen, the pioneers. Technology and salesmanship have stripped and raped the land and divested the people of pride, leaving them ridiculous—mechanical men and women whom it is a duty to love. In his speeches, Vonnegut has explicitly blamed all this degeneration and suffering on American scientists and technologists, the inspired tinkerers, the sons of Edison in the employ of the Rockefellers and Rosewaters and the government. In his fiction, from the automated lathes in *Player Piano* to the incendiary bombs in *Slaughterhouse-Five*, the products of American know-how are nothing but unlovable—only late, in *Breakfast of Champions*, is a good word said for any product of modern technology and it turns out to be tranquilizers, which the narrator swallows to restore his chemical balance.

It is risking nothing to take a quick guess that some of these ideas about America—let them be called political instead of philosophical, though they are connected to no party or program— eventually helped Vonnegut's books win an appreciative audience among college-age readers and, later, their elders: it was a matter of waiting for the *Zeitgeist* to catch up. His politics—implied, inferred—are a factor in his appeal, and need to be examined. But while they may have become agreeable to an ever larger audience, it is probably the style that they, and the story line, are presented in which first pleased, delighted, seduced. Vonnegut's is a brief, repetitious style, rhetorically mock-naive, relying for effect on the regular delivery of a quantity of some kind of satisfaction every page or so. It arrives in the shape of a surprise, a moral, a giggle, a laugh. After what now looks like a false start in *Player Piano*, Vonnegut fastened on the form that works best with such a style: a series of self-contained, sometimes arbitrarily divided, "chapters" of no more than five hundred words, often as few as fifty. "My books are essentially mosaics made up of a whole bunch of tiny little chips," he says in a *Playboy* interview reprinted in his new book, "and each chip is a joke." Whether he is speaking here in all honesty, or out of false modesty (he evidently thinks of himself as more than a comedian, and harbors exalted ideas of the role of writers), as a description of his method it is not bad.

Vonnegut's novels are constructed in a way that can also be likened to the structure of an old-fashioned cartoon booklet with figures painted in primary colors which is flipped with the thumb. *Cat's Cradle*, for example, has 121 "chapters," headed with ironical inscriptions like title-cards, contained in a grand total of 191 pages. The divisions between each "chapter" function like the frames between cartoons, so that read over quickly (as Vonnegut's novels are meant to be read on first encountering them, before going back to search out, talmudically, allegories, symbols, and designs), they blur into a semblance of motion. The effect is cinematic, as if a basic pattern, and resource, of the movies had been appropriated to a book without pictures.

The affinity of Vonnegut's work to comic books and the movies is suggestive regarding his popularity with a generation that was raised on these media and has its own ideas or feelings about what literacy is and what it is good for. Not only are Vonnegut's "chapters" short—so are his books; each one of them can be consumed in a sitting. His first, *Player Piano* (1952), which is about an engineer living some time in a totally technologized American future who joins in an abortive revolt against the machine, is the exception. It runs to 321 pages, with 35 chapters, divided along traditional lines of change of scene and passage of time. Vonnegut's pay-offs here are cumulative rather than instant and the style is generally more dense:

> Paul had thought often of the peculiar combination of Kroner and Baer, and wondered if, when they were gone, higher management could possibly duplicate it. Baer embodied the knowledge and technique of industry; Kroner personified the faith, the near-holiness, the spirit of the complicated venture. Kroner, in fact, had a poor record as an engineer and had surprised Paul from time to time with his ignorance or misunderstanding of technical matters: but he had the priceless quality of believing in the system, and of making others believe in it, too, and do as they were told.

It is a recognizable literary project in the approved manner, down to the basic device of casting a misfit in the anti-utopia. "I cheerfully ripped off the plot of *Brave New World*," Vonnegut told *Playboy*. Although the perfectly bad society that irks the hero is not coercive or totalitarian, but rather a benevolent welfare state where corporations look out for what they consider the public interest and bright young men in crewcuts do not get too drunk, *Player Piano* is another cautionary fantasy extrapolating from what is actual, in the tradition of Zamyatin, Huxley, and Orwell. Sometimes it also reads like *Babbitt*. It partakes in a gently pessimistic way of anger at what the boosters of mass production and the assembly line are doing to bodies and souls, and fear of what they may do still worse.

Player Piano, being a first novel, was not ignored, but it made no real dent on critics or the public. Some reviewers called it "science fiction," dismissively. "I have been a soreheaded occupant of a file drawer labeled 'science fiction' ever since," Vonnegut says in *Wampeters, Foma & Granfalloons.* "I would like out, particularly since so many serious critics regularly mistake the drawer for a tall white fixture in a comfort station." The circumstances of Vonnegut's early rejection are behind the portraits of writers and the ideas about the publishing business that he elaborates in all his books, and the legend that is cherished by his counter-cultural constituency.

To write *Player Piano,* Vonnegut had quit his job as public-relations man for the GE research laboratory in Schenectady. He now moved to Cape Cod and sold short stories to *Cosmopolitan, Saturday Evening Post,* and *Ladies' Home Journal,* as well as to the science-fiction pulps. These stories, which Vonnegut says he wrote to buy time, and which have been collected in *Welcome to the Monkey House,* adhere to formula while mildly worrying the strain of disaffection evident in *Player Piano.* Their heroes are eccentric villagers, precocious dropouts, average U.S. citizens taking advantage of a windfall to improve their model train sets or HAM radio apparatus. In the meantime, *Player Piano* was issued in paperback, renamed *Utopia 14.* It took Vonnegut seven years to write the first of a couple of books *(The Sirens of Titan* and *Cat's Cradle)* that, with the help of the bosomy covers their publishers wrapped them in, assured his consignment to the demeaning science-fiction drawer. These novels made Vonnegut's underground reputation; in them he found his form and oracular voice.

The Sirens of Titan (1959) and *Cat's Cradle* (1963), unlike *Player Piano,* are fairly original in conception, quite consistent in tone. They are also highly contrived and as didactic as sermons. Here, in its entirety, is the first page of *Sirens,* which is about a war between Martians and Earthlings:

> Everyone now knows how to find the meaning of life within himself.
>
> But mankind wasn't always so lucky. Less than a century ago men and women did not have easy access to the puzzle boxes within them.
>
> They could not name even one of the fifty-three portals to the soul.
>
> Gimcrack religions were big business.
>
> Mankind, ignorant of the truths that lie within every human being, looked outward—pushed ever outward. What mankind hoped to learn in its outward push was who was actually in charge of all creation, and what all creation was all about.
>
> Mankind flung its advance agents ever outward, ever outward. Eventually it flung them out into space, into the colorless, tasteless, weightless sea of outwardness without end.
>
> It flung them like stones.

This was one of Vonnegut's achievements, that he could make a certain audience read what are essentially books of ideas, using multiple plots, self-consciously intricate designs, and flashy characters, and intruding himself continually, without breaking the spell. A load of moralistic message is what puts *Sirens* and *Cat's Cradle* into the category of science fiction—more precisely, into that subcategory of science fiction, fantasy, that depends, for credibility, not on detailed descriptions of possible machines or experiments with nature, but on a seamless web of dreaming about a universe that can never be, populated by impossible beings, humanoids embodying urges and ideas.

It is more the stuff of teleology than ontology; paperback readers who do not know the meanings of these words can appreciate that the dreamlike quests of Vonnegut's heroes in fantastic worlds and universes are about finding purpose here, in this world. And purpose there is, finally. The mocking voice, seemingly parodying itself, denying any aim in life, demands not to be believed, yet always taken seriously—this is the unspoken understanding between writer and reader in Vonnegut's books.

Preachy as it is, the voice never talks down, nor does it depress. It is breezy, charming, confidential, fully clued in to the popularity of sticking gun turrets on model aircraft carriers with Duco cement, and other pre-pubescent American joys; it shares rather than imparts dark-sounding truths, funny jokes. An American "kid" who had bought *Sirens* or *Cat's Cradle* in a bus station (both novels were published only in paperback, went unreviewed) could wish when done reading that the author was a terrific friend of his, whom he could call up on the phone whenever he felt like it. In fact, during the years when rare copies of *Sirens* were being sold for up to fifty dollars, many of Vonnegut's young enthusiastic readers did that, and turned his house into a place of pilgrimage. Vonnegut, unlike Salinger, was no recluse; the difference between the two writers' unofficial popularity will tell something about cultural changes between the 50's and today.

An anti-scientific bias is also less unusual, more popular now than fifteen years ago. "You scientists *think* too much," a Miss Pefko says in *Cat's Cradle,* which ends with the end of the world. A marked animus against scientists, and thinking, and a propensity to toy with apocalypse, characterize all of Vonnegut's books. He has another preoccupation. Except in two books, it is never more than continually alluded to. The Martian soldiers in *The Sirens of Titan* "wore knee spikes, and glossy black uniforms. . . . Their insignia was a skull and crossbones." Von Koenigswald, saintly jungle doctor of *Cat's Cradle,* has "the terrible deficit of Auschwitz in his kindliness account."

World War II, the Nazis, the war's long-lasting effect on individual Americans and America, are themes that loom large for Vonnegut for autobiographical and other reasons. He gets around to facing them directly in *Mother Night* (1961) and *Slaughterhouse-Five* (1969).

At first, it seems that *Mother Night* is intended as the study of an insane man, in the form of that well-known fictional conceit, the self-portrait or confession. "I've always been able to live with what I did," writes Howard W. Campbell, an American double agent awaiting trial in Israel as a Nazi war criminal. "How? Through that simple and widespread boon to modern mankind—schizophrenia." To try and create a character who will bear scrutiny would seem to be a departure for Vonnegut, albeit he uses here the same episodic style dotted with jokes and epigrams. The reader of *Mother Night* is asked to believe that he has before him the testament of a 20th-century lunatic of medium notoriety, trying to come to terms, under the shadow of death, with the ambiguities of his life story. In and out of this story move personalities he has been acquainted with named "Goebbels," "Eichmann," "Hess." This is a very ambitious project—locating a publicly harmful madman within modern history, undercutting revulsion for him by showing his all-too-human, even sympathetic sides, never losing sight of his diseased soul under the welter of well-known documentary facts that needn't be mentioned but are, as always, "in his own words."

The prime prerequisite in a confessional novel has always been that the novelist get inside his creature, becoming invisible. Nabokov did this with Humbert Humbert, also a disturbed man in jail, Salinger with Holden Caulfield, Roth (almost) with Alexander Portnoy. However, Howard Campbell's words are not all his own; many of them, and his ideas and sentiments as well, are Vonnegut's. Instead of strategically subsuming his intentions in Campbell's craziness, Vonnegut mainly uses him as a mouthpiece, so that *Mother Night* quickly turns into an exercise in ventriloquism. Often the voice does not even trouble to disguise itself, and sounds just like the one in Vonnegut's speeches, saying the same things—for example, that infantrymen are morally superior to their officers or the air force. It is no more possible to believe Campbell when he says he was "a loathsome anti-Semite" than it would be if Vonnegut said this of himself. Rather than a "split personality," Campbell seems to be a harmless fellow who became a Nazi in a fit of absent-mindedness, and an American agent in the same way. The motivation that Vonnegut suggests in his preface to *Mother Night*—that Campbell, a playwright by profession, played roles in real life—is not borne out by the characterization.

If *Mother Night* were intended as a psychological novel, the flat characterization of Campbell could be blamed for the book's failure to move beyond the level of a slapstick, melodramatic spy story. But the main intention is, again, moralistic, and the book is a vehicle for messages, attached this time to events and personalities in the unimagined world, in a contemporary history that is already legendary for younger readers. The message is to the effect that reality and men are such masses of contradiction, that, among other things, it is useless saying who is finally villainous or heroic, though villainy and evil are obvious. As for what looks like unmitigated villainy, the best one can do, looking back, is provoke laughter at it. Eichmann was more laughable than sinister—even in 1941, when Campbell met him in Berlin.

Günter Grass wrote raucously in *The Tin Drum* without in the least depriving Nazism of an aura of important, brutal force, or getting smeared by nearness with sentimentality. Vonnegut makes the Nazis, and by implication, evil itself, seem absurd, ridiculous, and inevitable. To counter it, he enlists laughter, but not only that.

Campbell in conversation with a New York cop:

> "I guess there were good people killed on both sides," he said.
> "I think that's true," I said.
> "You think there'll be another one?" he said.
> "Another what?" I said.
> "Another war," he said.
> "Yes," I said.
> "Me too," he said. "Isn't that hell?"
> "You chose the right word," I said.
> "What can any one person do?" he said.
> "Each person does a little something," I said, "and there you are."

This throwaway presages the famous refrain in *Slaughterhouse-Five*, "So it goes," a counterpoint to facts that are stranger than fantasy, recitations of stupidity or moral obtuseness in high places, the hideous suffering of ordinary people. While *Mother Night* is grotesque, like mummery on a stage, *Slaughterhouse-Five*, Vonnegut's first hardback best-seller, has a maudlin feel about it. Both books present the spectacle of a writer facing the world, trying to write saving myths about it using documentary material.

That this is what Vonnegut was about in *Slaughterhouse-Five* can easily be inferred. The story—told by a narrator who is a writer established on Cape Cod—concerns a harmless optometrist, Billy Pilgrim who, as a prisoner of the Germans in World War II, lived through the American bombing of Dresden and is obsessed to the point of madness with the memory. Coming "unstuck," Billy lives simultaneously on earth and on the planet Tralfamadore where he learns a new religion of stoicism. The kinship of Billy Pilgrim with his namesake in Bunyan, not to mention Christ and Everyman, is obvious. The style, "in the telegraphic schizophrenic manner of the planet Tralfamadore," attempts to get at something by accretion of extremely unconnected bits in time and space, and the bombing of Dresden actually disappears in the shadows thrown by placard-like announcements from the narrator: "I have told my sons that they are not under any circumstances to take part in massacres, and that the news of massacres of enemies is not to fill them with satisfaction or glee."

More than once in *Slaughterhouse-Five*, the narrator pronounces the book he is writing a failure, though this will not keep him from letting it be published. He makes himself a promise that his next book will be only "fun." That turned out to be *Breakfast of Champions*, last year's best-selling favorite about a fifty-year-old writer who resolves to clear his head by setting free the creatures of his imagination who have served him in numerous novels. *Breakfast of Champions*, as seemingly miscellaneous as *Slaughterhouse-Five*, is the summation of the discoveries Vonnegut has made in writing, the whole held together by the crude drawings he supplies to illustrate it. It is like a children's encyclopedic picture album with detours and definitions, naming the animals, presuming to treat as if for the first time of pornography, suicide, racism, and madness in Middle America, without neglecting the plot, or despairing of methods of salvation proposed in earlier novels. The drawings are the logical goal of Vonnegut's writing over the years. They supplement the words, and begin substituting for them. They are meant, in their crude friskiness, to increase the horror by playing against it, as a comedian in silent films might deadpan against a hilarious or hazardous situation. The effect is not necessarily the one intended. They also mean to charm, to draw forth love and mercy, and there can be no doubt that for some reader-viewers they succeed.

One may give Vonnegut credit for fixing on a prose and picture style that fits his purposes and his powers, without implying that he discovered it in unexplored territory or that he has had no precursors. The stories of George Ade—an Indiana humorist and ironist almost completely forgotten now—are characterized by a blackout style as in burlesque-house sketches. Nathanael West's books are parables about failed Christians made of neon tubing instead of flesh and blood. In his anti-intellectualism and depiction of scientists, too, Vonnegut is in a tradition—that of science fiction, and especially science-fiction movies. "Disinterested intellectual curiosity," Susan Sontag has commented about this tradition, "rarely appears in any form other than caricature, as a maniacal dementia that cuts one off from normal human relations." But it is not enough to say that Hoenikker, the atomic scientist in *Cat's Cradle*, was a cliché ten years ago. It is necessary to add that this cliché speaks with increasing force to a generation of students, and their parents who take after them, because of what they read in the papers and breathe in the air. "I was in Dresden," Vonnegut says, "when America dropped scientific truth on it."

It seems particularly unlikely that novels and speeches so popular with young Americans as Vonnegut's are should keep coming back to deal with World War II; that war is distant, legendary, boring. It is the war of the fathers and grandfathers, not the sons—whose war has been Vietnam, even if they have not fought in it, even if they have not dodged the draft or demonstrated against it. Before taking a guess as to how Vonnegut gets them to listen to tales of his generation's war, three pieces of biographical information might be introduced; Vonnegut often harps on two of the three himself, in prefaces to his novels, in the novels themselves, in his speeches. First, his parents—atheists, pacifists, believers in the Constitution—though Americans long established in the Middle West, remembered not without pride that the family came from Germany; second, Vonnegut, a POW, happened to be in Dresden (like Billy Pilgrim in *Slaughterhouse-Five*) when the Allies bombed it; the third fact, which Vonnegut never mentions, is that some of his earliest writings, published in the Cornell student newspaper in 1941, were editorials lampooning preparedness and Lend Lease and propagandizing against American intervention in the war against Hitler.

Vonnegut's German extraction, which made him briefly feel like an outsider in America, though white and Protestant, and especially his presence in Dresden as an American under American bombs, are autobiographical facts transmuted continually and none too subtly into his fiction, putting a new and more topical slant on ancient history. His editorials in the Cornell *Sun* (reprinted in *The Vonnegut Statement*), also display a tone and push ideas about warmaking which have not changed since Vonnegut was a sophomore. They could still appeal to college students today. The editorials, in fact, were run as humor or joke columns under Vonnegut's by-line, and though some of them were earnest appreciations of Charles Lindbergh, most strove to make their point in much the same way that Vonnegut still tries to—by provoking laughter, for instance, at ROTC bayonet drill.

Vonnegut anticipated a succeeding generation of students in their suspicions of, if not contempt for, official institutions. Having been in Dresden, and then finding no reliable report of the raid in official Air Force histories, taught him, he says, that the American government lied. The lesson is not lost on those who know about the Pentagon Papers and Watergate. Perhaps more significant still, Vonnegut's recurring reference to having been firebombed by his own countrymen lends him cachet, though he denies (in both *Slaughterhouse-Five* and *Wampeters, Foma & Granfalloons*) that Dresden changed him much. He was present at a fiery massacre—a holocaust—planned and carried out by "our side." This gives him, his work, and his opinions, additional importance and validity in the eyes of his audience.

Although the pacifism Vonnegut preaches is couched in absolute terms, and his imaginary ideal American hero is a man who absolutely refuses to kill or be a party to killing, Vonnegut does not fail to say in speeches now that during his war the enemy deserved to be crushed by any means—so long as innocent, defenseless people (for example, the Dresdeners) were not incinerated. Vonnegut is not unaware of the tortured relation of guilt and innocence, and of the practical difficulty, probably the impossibility once the logic of total war is rolling, of sparing civilians. Indeed, he is ever ready to indicate moral dilemmas and paradoxes, in the best manner of innocence lost, while never really altering or complicating the thrust of his simple, absolute preachment.

The preacher is a sinner, too, of course; he does not deny it. In denying his own virtue Vonnegut can go to such extremes of language and hypothetical example that one can either be disarmed by his honesty, or begin suspecting that this writer not only has the power to do harm, but actually does it—by the crude, unreal, and actually soothing pictures of human behavior that he draws. "If I'd been born in Germany," he says in the preface to *Mother Night*, "I suppose I would have been a Nazi, bopping Jews and Gypsies and Poles around, leaving boots sticking out of snowbanks, warming myself with my secretly virtuous insides. So it goes."

Cartoon characters "bop" each other, painlessly. Vonnegut's choice of words is his own. His purblindness, perhaps willed, to the difference between being a murderous member of a murder organization, and being so human as to refrain from joining the Resistance, is also typical, though this vision is not his exclusively; in a recent French movie about the Occupation, a boy joins the *Milice* rather than the *Maquis*, and he does it by chance. On the face of it, when these revisions are not simply the defected side's getting its own back after letting things settle for a generation, they look like truth-telling, because they seem to complicate by describing reality as random. History has come to this, that only what leaves us bereft can pass for the truth. Villains and heroes do not exist in such accounts, needless to say, but neither do any humans, if humans think, decide, act, regret. Yet Vonnegut's fictions, with their flat characters who are put through their paces to make the author's humanistic point ("only humans are sacred"), most probably do not leave Vonnegut's devotees feeling empty or sad.

Vonnegut is not an apologist for evil, nor does he mean to sound neutral; he is sure it exists, and that he knows what it is—he could not be so popular if he did not. Of World War II he says in *Wampeters, Foma & Granfalloons*, "We had fought something which was totally obscene." That is only the beginning, however, for "this was very bad for us." The war against Hitler gave Americans a long-lasting sense of righteousness and of a global mission finally expressing itself, he says, in what Lieutenant Calley did at Mylai. If the after-effects of Vonnegut's generation's war were bad for America, they were and continue to be worse for people in the rest of the world, because of the power America acquired to harm with its good intentions. In Vonnegut's books, greed and narrowmindedness go with self-righteousness and power. The world is on the road of war, pollution, and starvation, of final extinction around the corner, and so far as humans can be, his generation of Americans is responsible for this.

During the last decade or so such ideas have become common currency in this country, and surely would have even if Vonnegut had not contributed his share. Obviously it takes more to attract the young than to blame the world's troubles on their parents. In fact, it would be bizarre if reading or listening to Vonnegut set a young person against his elders, or reinforced a previous hatred or contempt. Vonnegut's anger at his generation is mild, as his pessimism concerning the human prospect is gentle, and presumably all-inclusive: though he sympathizes with the young founders of backwoods communes, who try to adapt Bokononism (the religion of fatalism practiced in Tralfamadore) to their separate realities, he has little or no hope of their success. It is either too late for that, or it is written somewhere, in the book of Fate, that these experiments, too, are doomed.

"Everything is going to become unimaginably worse, and never get any better again," Vonnegut told the graduating class at Bennington, when the shootings at Kent State were fresh news in 1970. "If you want to become a friend of civilization," he said to the girls, "then become an enemy of truth and a fanatic for harmless balderdash." He told the crowd at Heinz Hall in Pittsburgh some of the same things, to its evident pleasure, and without a doubt to the dismay of a few in the audience, who on that occasion held their tongues. They do not always. Vonnegut says in his new book that one of the reasons he no longer gives so many speeches is that "a recent refugee from Middle Europe" interrupted him once with the question, "You are a leader of American young people—What right do you have to teach them to be so cynical and pessimistic?"

But one can only understand the anger of Vonnegut's Czech or Polish questioner if one is convinced of many things—that the Vonnegut phenomenon is a cultural-political test case, that books really are bisected into "High Art" and "Pop," that taste is debased, that books are important. Most of all, one would have to believe, as Vonnegut says he does, that good or bad ideas in books have the power to do good or to harm.

JOHN UPDIKE
"All's Well in Skyscraper National Park" (1976)
Hugging the Shore
1983, pp. 263–73

Kurt Vonnegut abjures the appellation "Junior" in signing his new novel, and, indeed, after his furious performance in the preceding work, *Breakfast of Champions*, does seem relatively at peace with himself, his times, and the fact of his writing a novel at all. He introduces this one with the customary noises of exasperation over his "disagreeable profession" ("He asked me politely how my work was going. . . . I said that I was sick of it, but that I had always been sick of it"), but, once launched, the tale floats along without interruption, and is something of an idyll. A hundred-year-old man, Dr. Wilbur Daffodil-11 Swain, who has been President of the United States ("the final President, the tallest President, and the only one ever to have been divorced while occupying the White House"), lives with his granddaughter, Melody Oriole-2 von Peterswald, and her lover, Isadore Raspberry-19 Cohen, in the otherwise empty Empire State Building, on the almost deserted island of Manhattan, which has been decimated by plague and is variously known as "The Island of Death" and "Skyscraper National Park." The awkward middle names of the inhabitants, we might as well explain now, have been assigned them in the last and only reform of the Swain Presidency, a measure to combat "American loneliness" (the root of all our evil: "all the damaging excesses of Americans in the past were motivated by loneliness rather than a fondness for sin") through the division of the population into huge (ten thousand siblings, one hundred ninety thousand cousins) artificial families by means of computer-bestowed middle names, "the name of a flower or fruit or nut or vegetable or legume, or a bird or a reptile or a fish, or a mollusk, or a gem or a mineral or a chemical element." This scheme, the basis of President Swain's successful campaign (slogan: "Lonesome No More!") for the highest office in the land, was concocted years before, when Wilbur and his twin sister, Eliza, like himself a monstrous "neanderthaloid" two meters high, enjoyed in a secluded Vermont mansion an emotional and intellectual symbiosis that amounted to sheer genius, though separately the two were dullards named Bobby and Betty Brown.

Lost already? *Slapstick*, whose sole present action consists of the narrator's hundred-and-first birthday party, which kills him, is a reminiscence about the future, a future braided of a half-dozen or so scientific and sociological fancies. The lonesome-no-more-thanks-to-new-middle-names notion is about the silliest of them, the least charming and provocative, however dear to the author's heart. The others, roughly in descending order of charm and provocativeness, are:

1. That gravity on Earth has become variable, like the weather. "Well—the gravity . . . is light again today," Wilbur writes in his memoir. On days of light gravity, all males have erections, and lovers build a pyramid of large rubble at the intersection of Broadway and Forty-second Street. When the gravity is heavy, men crawl about on all fours, and the insides of horses fall out. Heavy gravity first struck when Wilbur Swain was fifty, and had just learned that his sister had died in an avalanche on Mars:

> An extraordinary feeling came over me, which I first thought to be psychological in origin, the first rush of grief. I seemed to have taken root on the porch. I could not pick up my feet. My features, moreover, were being dragged downward like melting wax.
>
> The truth was that the force of gravity had increased tremendously.
>
> There was a great crash in the church. The steeple had dropped its bell.
>
> Then I went right through the porch, and was slammed to the earth beneath it.
>
> In other parts of the world, of course, elevator cables were snapping, airplanes were crashing, ships were sinking, motor vehicles were breaking their axles, bridges were collapsing, and on and on.
>
> It was terrible.

In this superbly simple fancy (and why not? what do we know about gravity, except that it is always there, and has not yet broken its own "law"?) Vonnegut gives enormous body to his own moodiness, and springs a giddy menace upon the city he inhabits.

2. That the Chinese, on the other side of the world from the lonely, destructive Americans, have succeeded in miniaturizing themselves, to the size first of dwarfs, then of dolls and elves, and finally of germs; the plague, called the Green Death, it turns out "was caused by microscopic Chinese, who were peace-loving and meant no one any harm. They were nonetheless invariably fatal to normal-sized human beings when inhaled or ingested." This last *reductio* is a bit much, but a radical divergence of the Chinese from our own brand of *Homo sapiens* sounds right; we laugh in recognition when the Chinese Ambassador, sixty centimeters tall, severs diplomatic relations "simply because there was no longer anything going on in the United States which was of any interest to the Chinese at all." China is another planet, Vonnegut has discovered.

3. That a brother and a sister might "give birth to a single genius, which died as quickly as we were parted, which was reborn the moment we got together again." In childhood, Wilbur, who does the reading and writing, and Eliza, who makes the intuitive leaps and juxtapositions, concoct theories and manuscripts that a half-century later are of interest even to the Chinese. In adulthood, after a long separation, the siblings reunite in a kind of psycho-sexual explosion that produces, besides a houseful of wreckage, a manual on child-rearing which becomes the third most popular book of all time.

Vonnegut in his prologue claims this novel to be "the closest I will ever come to writing an autobiography" and movingly writes of the Indianapolis Vonneguts and of his sister Alice—her importance to him as "an audience of one," her death at the age of forty-one of cancer, her final days in the hospital, her hunched posture, her description of her own death as "slapstick." In *Slapstick* these memories become:

> She was so bent over that her face was on level with Mushari's—and Mushari was about the size of Napoleon Bonaparte. She was chain smoking. She was coughing her head off. . . .
>
> "Oh, Wilbur, Wilbur, Wilbur—" said my mother as we watched, "is that really your sister?"
>
> I made a bitter joke—without smiling. "Either your only daughter, Mother, or the sort of anteater known as an *aardvark*," I said.

The image shocks us, offends us, twists us inside, and successfully asks to be recognized as somber and tender. It is a moment peculiarly Vonnegutian, tapping the undercurrents of pure melancholy which nurture the aggressively casual surface growths of his style. These moments arise unexpectedly, and seem to take the author unawares as well—the pathetic valedictory conversation, for instance, between Salo and Rumfoord near the end of *The Sirens of Titan* (1959), or the odd interlude, amid the "impolite" "junk" of *Breakfast of Champions* (1973), wherein the homeless, jobless black ex-convict Wayne Hoobler, hanging out in a used-car lot, in his extreme of lonesomeness begins to talk to the highway traffic:

> He established a sort of relationship with the traffic on the Interstate, too, appreciating its changing moods. "Everybody goin' home," he said during the rush hour jam. "Everybody home now," he said later on, when the traffic thinned out. Now the sun was going down.
>
> "Sun goin' down," said Wayne Hoobler.

It will vary, where Vonnegut's abashed and constant sorrow breaks through to touch the reader; here, though, in this fantasy, as it pays tribute not to the extended family he hopes for but to the nuclear family he has known, he places his rather mistrustful art in frank proximity to the incubator of his passion for—to quote his prologue—"common decency."

4. That the United States, as the world's energy resources have dried up, has pleasantly settled back into a rural society, powered by slaves and horses as before; that the old Inca capital of Machu Picchu, in Peru, has become "a haven for rich people and their parasites, people fleeing social reforms and economic declines"; and that when the White House, containing President Wilbur Swain, who is stoned on tribenzo-Deportamil, quite ceases to rule, the nation falls into a feudal anarchy dominated by such guerrilla chieftains as the King of Michigan and the Duke of Oklahoma.

5. That a religion has arisen called the Church of Jesus Christ the Kidnapped, which holds that Jesus has come again but has been kidnapped by the Forces of Evil and is being held captive somewhere. The members of this cult, the most popular ever in America, distinguish themselves by an incessant jerking of the head, as if to discover the Kidnapped Jesus peering out "from behind a potted palm tree or an easy chair."

6. That a scientist named Dr. Felix Bauxite-13 von Peterswald has discovered a way to talk to the dead, who irritably and disconsolately inhabit a dreary hereafter known as the Turkey Farm. The late Eliza reports to her living brother, "We are being bored stiff."

This saucy spaghetti of ideas, strange to report, seems in the consumption as clear as consommé, and goes down like ice cream. *Slapstick* has more science fiction in it than any other novel by Vonnegut since *The Sirens of Titan* and lays to rest, in an atmosphere of comic exhaustion and serene self-parody, the obsessive Prospero figure who first came to life there. The Prospero in *Sirens* is Winston Niles Rumfoord, a Rhode Island aristocrat who acquires superhuman powers by steering his spaceship straight into a "chrono-synclastic infundibulum" and who thenceforth arranges an interplanetary war so that its guilt-engendered slaughters may form the basis for a new religion, the worship of God the Utterly Indifferent. With a demonic elaborateness that argues a certain demon of overplotting in the author, Rumfoord furthermore manipulates Malachi Constant (one of Vonnegut's long line of boob heroes) and his little family through a ramshackle series of space flights and changes of identity toward an ultimate goal that turns out to be the delivery, in Constant's son's pocket, of a replacement part for a spaceship from the planet Tralfamadore. The unseen Tralfamadorians are manipulating not just Rumfoord but much of the planet Earth; Stonehenge, the Great Wall of China, and other terrestrial wonders of human enterprise are in truth messages ("Replacement part being rushed with all possible speed"; "Be patient. We haven't forgotten about you") in the Tralfamadorian language to the messenger Salo, who in the course of delivering from "One Rim of the Universe to the Other" a message consisting of a single dot ("Greetings" in Tralfamadorian) has become stranded on Saturn's biggest moon, Titan, for hundreds of thousands of years. Well, it's some book, full of laughs yet operatically flaunting Vonnegut's concern with the fundamental issues of pain, purpose, and Providence. Though raised in a family of atheists, Vonnegut quarrels with God like a parochial-school dropout. In *Mother Night* (1961), Prospero has shrunk to the dimensions of a Second World War master-spy: Colonel Frank Wirtanen, the Blue Fairy Godmother, controls the hero's life by appearing to him only three times, and his final act of magical intervention is rejected.

In *Cat's Cradle* (1963), the idea of a religion devoted to an indifferent God is codified as Bokononism, and Prospero retreats to still lower visibility; Bokonon, the black founder of the cult, emerges from the underbrush of the Caribbean island of San Lorenzo only at the novel's end, to direct the hero (called John, and rather less of a boob) to commit suicide, while thumbing his nose skyward, at You Know Who. But Bokonon, who like Rumfoord has the gifts of foresight and cynicism, oversees the events on this island of survivors—a most *Tempest*-like setting. There is even a Miranda, called Mona.

In *God Bless You, Mr. Rosewater* (1965), Prospero and the boob have merged; the very prosperous Eliot Rosewater, after exercising the powers of the rich rather inchoately in the isolation of Rosewater County, Indiana, stands to full stature when threatened by a usurper, whom he smites down with a surprising disposition, both regal and cunning, of his fortune. In *Slaughterhouse-Five* (1969), Billy Pilgrim, like Winston Rumfoord, communicates with the Tralfamadorians and sees future and past as parts of a single panorama—"All moments, past, present, and future, always have existed, always will exist." But his prescience is impotent to change the sad course of Earthly events; planes crash, bombs fall, though he knows they will. His access to Tralfamadore merely gives him the wonderful accessory bubble of the second life he lives there, more Ferdinand than Prospero, mated with the gorgeous Montana Wildhack in a transparent dome in a Tralfamadorian zoo. *Breakfast of Champions* reveals the author himself as Prospero, "on a par with the Creator of the Universe," sitting in the cocktail lounge of a Holiday Inn wearing mirroring sunglasses, surrounded by characters of his own creation, whom he frees in the end: "I am going to set at liberty all the literary characters who have served me so loyally during my writing career." (Nevertheless, *Slapstick* revives the obnoxious lawyer Norman Mushari from *God Bless You, Mr. Rosewater;* Vonnegut's ongoing puppet show is irrepressibly self-cherishing.)

> Now my charms are all o'erthrown,
> And what strength I have's mine own,
> Which is most faint. . . .

Slapstick gives us the Prospero of Shakespeare's epilogue, his powers surrendered, his island Manhattan, his Miranda his granddaughter Melody. Vonnegut dreamed the book, he tells us, while flying to a funeral. "It is about desolated cities and spiritual cannibalism and incest and loneliness and lovelessness and death, and so on." It is about what happens after the end of the world. The end of the world is not an idea to Vonnegut, it is a reality he experienced, in Dresden, as a prisoner of war, during the holocaustal air raid of February 13, 1945. He has described this repeatedly, most directly in the introduction to *Mother Night* added in 1966:

> We didn't get to see the fire storm. We were in a cool meat-locker under a slaughterhouse with our six guards and ranks and ranks of dressed cadavers of cattle, pigs, horses and sheep. We heard the bombs walking around up there. Now and then there would be a gentle shower of calcimine. If we had gone above to take a look, we would have been turned into artifacts characteristic of fire storms: seeming pieces of charred firewood two or three feet long—ridiculously small human beings, or jumbo fried grasshoppers, if you will.

Vonnegut's come-as-you-are prose always dons a terrible beauty when he pictures vast destruction.

> Eliot, rising from his seat in the bus, beheld the fire storm of Indianapolis. He was awed by the majesty of the column of fire, which was at least eight miles in diameter and fifty miles high. The boundaries of the column seemed absolutely sharp and unwavering, as though made of glass. Within the boundaries, helixes of dull red embers turned in stately harmony about an inner core of white. The white seemed holy.

The end of the world can be by fire, as in the quotation above, from *God Bless You, Mr. Rosewater*, or by ice, as in *Cat's Cradle:*

> There was a sound like that of the gentle closing of a portal as big as the sky, the great door of heaven being closed softly. It was a grand AH-WHOOM.
> I opened my eyes—and all the sea was *ice-nine*.
> The moist green earth was a blue-white pearl.

The New York of *Slapstick* has been destroyed several times over. Gravity has pulled down its elevators and its bridges, plague has devoured its population. An ailanthus forest has grown up, and a rooster crowing in Turtle Bay can be heard on West Thirty-fourth Street. Amid collapse, the barbarous fabulous is reborn. Wilbur Swain's nearest neighbor, Vera Chipmunk-5 Zappa, arrives at his hundred-and-first birthday party encrusted with diamonds, in a sedan chair. "She had a collection of precious stones which would have been worth millions of dollars in olden times. People gave her all the jewels they found, just as they gave me all the candlesticks." Swain has become the King of Candlesticks, the possessor of a thousand. For a birthday present Vera Zappa gives him a thousand candles she and her slaves have made from a colonial mold. They set them about on the floor of the Empire State Building lobby and light them. Swain's last written words are "Standing among all those tiny, wavering lights, I felt as though I were God, up to my knees in the Milky Way." He dies, happy, but the narrative carries on, relating how Melody arrives in New York, fleeing the seraglio of the King of Michigan, helped along the way by her fellow-Orioles.

> One would give her a raincoat. . . .
> Another would give her a needle and thread, and a gold thimble, too.
> Another would row her across the Harlem River to the Island of Death, at the risk of his own life.

The novel ends "*Das Ende*," reminding us of German fairy tales and of Vonnegut's pride in his German ancestry; in *Mother Night* he even dared to be a poet in the German language. In *Slapstick* he transmutes science fiction into something like medieval myth, and suggests the halo of process, of metamorphosis and recycling, that to an extent redeems the destructiveness in human history to which he is so sensitive. The end of the world is just a Dark Age. Through a succession of diminishingly potent Prosperos, the malevolent complexities of *The Sirens of Titan* have yielded to a more amiable conclusion.

Slapstick enjoys a first printing of a cool one hundred thousand copies, and Vonnegut's popularity, which has grown even as his literary manner becomes more truculent and whimsical, has attracted comment from many reviewers, who usually find it discreditable to author and audience alike. But there need be no scandal in Vonnegut's wide appeal, based, as I believe it is, on the generosity of his imagination and the honesty of his pain. Who of his writing contemporaries strikes us as an imaginer, as distinguished from a reporter or a self-dramatizer? There is in Vonnegut a fine disdain of the merely personal. His prologue to *Slapstick* says, "I find it natural to discuss life without ever mentioning love," and his fiction, stoic in an epicurean time, does have a pre-sexual, pre-social freshness; he worries about the sort of things—the future, injustice, science, destiny—that twelve-year-old boys worry about, and if most boys move on, it is not necessarily into more significant worries. Vonnegut began as a published writer with the so-called slick magazines—the credits for the stories in *Welcome to the Monkey House* feature *Colliers, The Saturday Evening Post*, and the *Ladies' Home Journal*. Rereading such exercises as "D.P.," "Deer in the Works," and "The Kid Nobody Could Handle" is a lesson in what slickness, Fifties vintage, was: it was a verbal mechanism that raised the spectre of pain and then too easily delivered us from it. Yet the pain in Vonnegut was always real. Through the transpositions of science fiction, he found a way, instead of turning pain aside, to vaporize it, to scatter it on the planes of the cosmic and the comic. His terse flat sentences, jumpy chapters, interleaved placards, collages of stray texts and messages, and nervous grim refrains like "So it goes" and (in *Slapstick*) "Hi ho" are a new way of stacking pain, as his fictional ice-nine is a new way of stacking the molecules of water. Such an invention looks easy only in retrospect.

If any slickness lingers, it is as a certain intellectual haste. Introducing his collected non-fiction, Vonnegut says he is impressed by the "insights which shower down on me when my job is to imagine, as contrasted with the woodenly familiar ideas which clutter my desk when my job is to tell the truth." His fiction itches to seize the human truth by its large handles—by its wars, its religions, its fortunes, its kings and prophets. Ordinary people in Vonnegut's novels live hapless in

Rosewater County or its equivalents; a middle-class Midwestern car salesman like Dwayne Hoover goes insane from sheer mediocrity, it would seem. So, too, the little circumstantial nuances of history are rather condescended to; Thomas Jefferson, for instance, rates an automatic sneer for being "a slave owner who was also one of the world's great theoreticians on the subject of human liberty"—as if Jefferson were hypocritical in helping advance those concepts by whose light slavery, an institution deemed respectable and even humane for millennia, would eventually be condemned. And a patient reading of Vonnegut's pronouncements leaves me uncertain as to whether he thinks the United States was evil, foolish, or right in waging war against Nazi Germany. Of course, no need to decide is laid upon the fiction writer; indeed, the interestingness and fertility of the puzzle derives from its unsolvability: our pain deserves dramatization only where it is paradoxical. I, too, prefer his ideas as they come twisted into his imaginings, and *Slapstick* abounds in those. War is being waged in *Slapstick*, and slavery has reconstituted itself, and "the history of nations," President Wilbur Daffodil-11 Swain concludes, "seemed to consist of nothing but powerless old poops like myself, heavily medicated and vaguely beloved in the long ago, coming to kiss the boots of young psychopaths." Such is the world, Vonnegut seems to be saying, but it is the one we have, and beats the Turkey Farm, if not Tralfamadore.

ROBERT MERRILL

"Vonnegut's *Breakfast of Champions*: The Conversion of Heliogabalus"

Critique, Volume 18, Number 3 (1977), pp. 99–109

The reviews of Kurt Vonnegut's *Breakfast of Champions* (1973) seem remarkably misleading. Where one reviewer speaks of the book's "gratuitous digressions,"[1] another refers to the "banality, the nearly Kiwanian subtlety of [its] social criticisms."[2] Yet another describes it as "a deliberate curiosity, an earnest attempt to play after getting Dresden out of the way."[3] The reviews talk much about Vonnegut's "stick figures"[4] and "facile fatalism."[5] Anyone who reads the reviews must conclude that *Breakfast of Champions* is an act of sheer audacity, that Vonnegut has apparently exploited his enormous popularity by throwing between covers nothing but "textural irrelevancies."[6] Yet to speak of *Breakfast of Champions* as "play" suggests an almost absolute misunderstanding of Vonnegut's intentions. Whatever else it might be, Vonnegut's novel is hardly a literary rip-off.

Breakfast of Champions can only be understood as a novel *about* "facile fatalism." Like *Slaughterhouse-Five* (1969), it is a novel in which Kurt Vonnegut is his own protagonist, but the "Vonnegut" of this book is rather less appealing than in the earlier novel—so much so that his facile fatalism and banal social criticisms have tended to alienate his readers altogether. The effect is largely deliberate: *Breakfast of Champions* is "a moving, tortured, and honest book,"[7] because in it Vonnegut turns an extremely cold eye on his own artistic practices and philosophical assumptions. In a rather zany way, it is a *Bildungsroman* about a fifty-year-old artless artist and facile philosopher. It is also a novel about the regeneration of this sorry figure. Far from being the dispirited effort its reviewers have taken it to be, *Breakfast of Champions* is an artistic act of faith.

Such assertions must be fleshed out, but one should perhaps also insist on what the novel is *not*. Most crucially, *Breakfast of Champions* is not a traditional novel of character. Vonnegut remarks in *Slaughterhouse-Five* that "There are almost no characters in this story, and almost no dramatic confrontations, because most of the people in it are so sick and so much the listless playthings of enormous forces."[8] The characters in *Breakfast of Champions* are "stick figures" for much the same reason, since the novel also examined the apparent "sickness" and "listlessness" of contemporary man. The novel's thematic structure requires that Vonnegut's characters seem wooden or mechanical, for they are exemplary figures in a moral fable. As a number of critics have suggested, all of Vonnegut's novels are fables.[9] One might doubt that Vonnegut is capable of writing more traditional fiction in which "rounded" characters are of the essence. Strictly speaking, however, he has never tried to write so.

Still, the novelist of ideas must somehow interest us in the fictional debate which informs the work. In *Slaughterhouse-Five* and *Breakfast of Champions*, Vonnegut focuses on his own attempt to comprehend the problems of his characters. Vonnegut has said that these two novels were once "one book,"[10] and nothing points up the family resemblance so well as Vonnegut's use of himself as a persona in each novel. His self-portrait is essential to the meaning of each fiction, though the two personae are crucially different.

The "Kurt Vonnegut" of *Slaughterhouse-Five* is an attractive figure. Above all he is honest. In the first chapter, Vonnegut charts the decline of his youthful idealism. Once he and his wife were World Federalists, but now, as they near fifty, he is not sure what they are. He supposes they are Telephoners (S 11). *He* is a Telephoner, at any rate, for he admits that he is in the habit of calling up old friends after getting drunk and driving his wife away "with a breath like mustard gas and roses" (S 4). But if Vonnegut is "an old fart with his memories and his Pall Malls, with his sons full grown" (S 2), he is an engaging old fart—one who speaks fondly of Guggenheim money ("God love it") and likes to quote dirty limericks (S 1,2–3). Surely, we are made to feel that his idealism has not really evaporated; rather, it has been challenged by the most fearful of realities: his memories of the firebombing of Dresden. We strongly identify with Vonnegut's predicament, for the first chapter traces his successful attempt to throw off an understandable depression and somehow deal with those terrible memories. Vonnegut may tell his publisher that *Slaughterhouse-Five* is "short and jumbled and jangled . . . because there is nothing intelligent to say about a massacre" (S 19), but the book still represents one man's attempt to exorcise the numbing sense of helplessness we all must feel in an age of cataclysmic horrors. We love Vonnegut for becoming "a pillar of salt," like Lot's wife (S 22), for in doing so Vonnegut has looked back. He has asserted, implicitly, that even the worst of modern disasters can be dealt with from a human point of view. Finally, we do not remember Vonnegut's depression so much as his transcendence of this melancholy, reflected in his promise to Mary O'Hare that when he finishes his war novel it will not have any parts for Frank Sinatra or John Wayne (S 15) and in the advice he offers to his sons: "I have told my sons that they are not under any circumstances to take part in massacres, and that the news of massacres of enemies is not to fill them with satisfaction or glee" (S 19).

The "Kurt Vonnegut" we encounter in *Breakfast of Champions* is a good deal less heroic. He is still self-deprecating, telling us that he feels "lousy" about his book,[11] suggesting that he is "programmed at fifty to perform childishly" (5), but his depression seems rather more serious. We get no stirring speeches to his sons; the man we meet is not so much depressed by man's inhumane practices as by his very nature. He suspects "that human beings are robots, are machines" (3); he is tempted to say, when he creates a fictional character, "that he is what he is because of faulty wiring, or because of microscopic amounts of chemicals which he ate or failed to eat on that particular day" (4). Nothing is very amusing about this Kurt Vonnegut; instead of witty limericks he offers us pictures of assholes (5). He does not seem to love anything, not even Guggenheim money.

Of course, both "Kurt Vonneguts" are literary constructs. When he tells us that his mother committed suicide, we are sure he is telling the truth, but he has assimilated such facts into a fictional context, so the question of their "truthfulness" is irrelevant. Vonnegut was probably a slightly happier man while writing *Slaughterhouse-Five,* but his fictional strategy demanded that he so represent himself. Vonnegut's tactic in that novel is to establish a vital contrast between himself and his protagonist, Billy Pilgrim. In writing his novel "Vonnegut" faces much the same problem as his hero—how does one make sense of such hopelessly irrational events as Dresden? Pilgrim's answer is escapist, involving his space-travel to Trafamadore and his adoption of the deterministic philosophy he encounters there. Vonnegut suggests the inadequacy of that "solution" by depicting his own inability to rest content in the quietistic assumptions of Tralfamadore. The very meaning of his novel requires Vonnegut to present himself as a sympathetic figure, one who can make speeches to his sons that are anything but quietistic in nature.

The "Kurt Vonnegut" of *Breakfast of Champions* is a different character because the novel treats a different problem. Here Vonnegut does not protest the social attitudes which lead to wars and ultimately to Dresden; instead, he explores the possibility that our attitudes are irrelevant to such events. To do so, he creates a persona who fears that men are machines, utterly without free will. Notice that the persona does not tell us that men *are* machines, but he refers to his "suspicion" that they may be (3). Moreover, he remarks that he is tempted to say that his characters are controlled by chemicals, so implying an element of doubt. In the course of *Breakfast of Champions,* these suspicions are tested and finally exorcised. In a real sense, the novel *dramatizes* its author's intellectual dilemma.

One value of seeing the book in this way is that we can explain its much-lamented "digressions." The novel is filled with social commentary of every conceivable variety, especially a series of rather crude reflections on American hypocrisy. Vonnegut devotes much of his book to insulting the national anthem (8–9), the idea that Columbus discovered America (10), the nobility of the founding fathers (11–12), the justice of our cause in Vietnam (11–12), and other American myths. These remarks are invariably expressed in the baldest manner possible, as when we are told that "the demolition of West Virginia had taken place with the approval of the executive, legislative, and judicial branches of the State Government" (123), or when West Point is defined as "a military academy which turned young men into homicidal maniacs for use in war" (157). Given Vonnegut's reputation as a comic novelist, he is oddly humorless. Even when he provokes a smile, as when he records the size of each character's penis, the humor is soon dissipated through an almost manic repetition. One can understand why a reviewer would speak of the nearly Kiwanian subtlety of the novel's social criticisms, for Vonnegut's attack would seem to have no subtlety at all—and roughly half of the book is given over to it.

Vonnegut's social and philosophical reflections must be seen in the dramatic context suggested above. In his preface, Vonnegut[12] explains that he has dedicated his book to an old friend, Phoebe Hurty, who lives in his memory as a child of the Great Depression: "She believed what so many Americans believed then: that the nation would be happy and just and rational when prosperity came" (2). Phoebe Hurty believed in the very myths Vonnegut debunks so gracelessly throughout the novel. As his discussion of Phoebe makes clear, however, Vonnegut attacks the myths from the point of view of a disillusioned "believer": "nobody believes anymore in a new American paradise. I sure miss Phoebe Hurty" (3). To have the faith of a Phoebe Hurty would be wonderful, but we know too much for that. After such knowledge, what forgiveness? Vonnegut turns on the idealistic myths of America with the passion of a betrayed lover. When he tells us that he is "trying to clear my head of all the junk in there" (5), he means to include all those patriotic ideals which have come to seem the soiled heritage of a past forever lost. Vonnegut wants to believe in this heritage; he says that he "can't live without a culture anymore." But the reality of both past and present America is such that he must also say, "I have no culture, no humane harmony in my brains" (6). Vonnegut's social comments reflect his anger and frustration, as if he would cultivate a cynical pose in order to cast out such "junk" once and for all. We see much the same process when Vonnegut speaks of his "suspicion" that men are machines. If men are not the noble beings of myth, they must be robots.

Such dubious logic is also seen in the "story" Vonnegut creates to illustrate his new cynicism. The story involves two characters who embody different aspects of his own personality. Dwayne Hoover represents his Midwestern, middle-class background, while Kilgore Trout is a somewhat comic embodiment of his artistic and philosophical career. Like his creator, Trout has become a devout pessimist in his old age: "But his head no longer sheltered ideas of how things could be and should be on the planet, as opposed to how things really were. There was only one way for the Earth to be, he thought: the way it was" (106). Indeed, Trout thinks that "humanity deserved to die horribly, since it had behaved so cruelly and wastefully on a planet so sweet" (18). Why humans "deserve" to die horribly is not clear if they are merely machines and "there was only one way for the Earth to be"—but Vonnegut contrives to bring Trout to Midland City, Hoover's home town, to confront the folk with this bracing "truth" and contrives to have Dwayne Hoover suffer the experience of receiving his "truth." Vonnegut seems to want to rub middle America's nose in the sheer ugliness of life.

Trout's resemblance to Vonnegut is, in many ways, quite playful; for example, Trout's remarkable anonymity is surely meant to remind us of Vonnegut's early problems in securing hardcover publication, not to mention a significant audience. *Breakfast of Champions* presents a more serious link between the author and his creation: both are frustrated idealists. We know from the nature of his innumerable publications that Trout, as a young man, sheltered ideas of how things could be and should be on this planet, as opposed to how things really are. (Trout will die in the harness, at work on his 209th novel.) In *God Bless You, Mr. Rosewater* (1965), we learn that "Trout's favorite formula was to describe a perfectly hideous society, not unlike his own, and then, toward the end, to suggest ways in which it could be improved."[13] As summarized in *Breakfast of Champions,* Trout's tales teach such lessons as our tragic failure to communicate (58), the tendency of government to deal with secondary rather than primary causes (74), our disastrous inattention to ecological problems (88–9), our contempt for art (132–3), and our ridiculous obsession with national averages (173). Of course, Trout is an unappreciated prophet, almost literally unread, and he has gradually lost faith in the possibilities of reform, finally becoming a rather frightening misanthrope. Early in *Breakfast of Champions* he tells his pet parakeet that "We're all Heliogabalus, Bill" (18), alluding to the Roman Emperor best known for entertaining friends by placing a human inside a hollow, life-sized iron bull and lighting dry firewood under the bull (18–9). No wonder each of Trout's three wives has been "shriveled" by his pessimism (113).

The most interesting of Trout's fables, *Plague on Wheels*, radically qualifies his despair. While the moral of the tale is gloomy enough—"There was no immunity to cuckoo ideas on Earth" (27), the book suggests Trout's unwavering belief in the importance of ideas. As Trout says elsewhere, "Ideas or the lack of them can cause disease!" (15). His very epitaph, taken from his last, unfinished novel, suggests that "We are healthy only to the extent that our ideas are humane" (16). Nothing connects Trout and Vonnegut so securely as the "faith" in the power of ideas.[14] The Kurt Vonnegut we meet early in *Breakfast of Champions* may be a pessimist, but even he must concede that it will take more than chemicals to unhinge his "hero," Dwayne Hoover: "Dwayne, like all novice lunatics, needed some bad ideas, too, so that his craziness could have shape and direction" (14). Kilgore Trout, of course, will provide the bad ideas through one of his own books. Trout's attitude toward ideas is contradicted by his misanthropy. As a young man Trout has understood that if bad ideas can destroy us, humane ideas can give us health. He has known that "the purpose of life" is to be "the eyes and ears and conscience of the Creator of the Universe" (68). Implicit here is the notion that we *can* exercise conscience. At the time of the novel, Trout has turned away from such implications, yet he will return to them, for in 1981 he will say that we are healthy only to the extent that our ideas are humane. What happens to cure Trout of his misanthropy?

What happens is that both Trout and Vonnegut encounter a *wrang-wrang*. According to Bokonon, the prophet of *Cat's Cradle* (1963), a *wrang-wrang* is "a person who steers people away from a line of speculation by reducing that line, with the example of the *wrang-wrang's* own life, to an absurdity."[15] The narrator of *Cat's Cradle* meets such a figure in Sherman Krebbs, a nihilistic poet. The narrator lends his apartment to Krebbs for a brief period of time. He returns to find the apartment "wrecked by a nihilistic debauch" (C 58). Krebbs has set fire to his couch in five places, killed his cat and avocado tree, and torn the door from his medicine cabinet. He has hung a sign around the dead cat's neck with reads: "Meow." The narrator comments: "Somebody or something did not wish me to be a nihilist. It was Krebb's mission, whether he knew it or not, to disenchant me with that philosophy" (C 59). In *Breakfast of Champions*, Dwayne Hoover is Trout's and Vonnegut's *wrang-wrang*.

Hoover is a slightly revised version of Billy Pilgrim. Like Pilgrim, he is a successful entrepreneur: besides his Pontiac auto lot, he owns part of the local Holiday Inn (41), "three Burger Chefs, five coin-operated car washes, and pieces of the Sugar Creek Drive-In Theatre, Radio Station WMCY, the Three Maples Par-Three Golf Course, and seventeen hundred shares of common stock in Barrytron Limited, a local electronics firm" (65–6). He lives "in a dream house in Fairchild Heights, which was the most desirable residential area in the city" (17). But Hoover is also like Pilgrim in that he suffers terribly despite his apparent prosperity. While Pilgrim is haunted by memories of World War II, Hoover is burdened with the suicide of his wife, the homosexuality of his son, and a growing sense that his life is meaningless. At one point he even compares himself to Job: "I couldn't help wondering if that was what God put me on Earth for—to find out how much a man could take without breaking" (170). As he first appears in the novel, he is a man in search of "new truths"; he wants to meet artists at the Midland City Festival of the Arts "to discover whether they had truths about life which he had never heard before." He hopes these truths might "enable him to laugh at his troubles, to go on living, and to keep out of the North Wing of the Midland County General Hospital, which was for lunatics" (200). Hoover is in the same position as Billy Pilgrim and Eliot Rosewater in *Slaughterhouse-Five*. In the aftermath of Dresden, Pilgrim and Rosewater find themselves dealing with "similar crises in similar ways. They had both found life meaningless. . . . So they were trying to re-invent themselves" (S 101). Pilgrim finds his "answer" in the Tralfamadorian theory of time, which assures him that "everybody has to do exactly what he does" (S 198), and reassures him because it means that no one is responsible for anything. Dwayne Hoover comes to believe the same thing, but the consequences are something less than reassuring for Trout and Vonnegut.

Hoover discovers his comforting "truth" in *Now It Can Be Told*, a book Trout has carried with him to Midland City. The book is in the form of a long letter from the Creator of the Universe to his experimental creature, a man with free will. In his letter the Creator tells the man, "You are the only creature in the entire Universe who has free will. You are the only one who has to figure out what to do next—and *why*. Everybody else is a robot, a machine" (259). Billy Pilgrim learns something similar on Tralfamadore, though the Tralfamadorians allow for no exceptions: "Tralfamadorians, of course, say that every creature and plant in the Universe is a machine" (S 154). Billy Pilgrim is pleased by the message, but Dwayne Hoover's response suggests another side to the coin. Hoover reasons that if all other men are "unfeeling machines" (266), he can do whatever he wants to them. At the end of the novel he acts on his belief, beating up everyone around him until he has sent eleven people to the hospital, Trout among them. He acts with no sense of shame, for he has been "liberated" from such feelings: "I used to think the electric chair was a shame, . . . I used to think war was a shame—and automobile accidents and cancer." But now he does not think *anything* is a shame: "Why should I care what happens to machines?" (270). Why indeed? If men are machines, why should we be horrified by Heliogabalus himself?

Dwayne Hoover's thematic function is to point up the disastrous consequences of adopting a deterministic view of man. Dramatically, his function is to reveal these consequences to Trout and Vonnegut. Following his trip to Midland City, Trout rejects his belief that "there was only one way for the Earth to be." He returns to his former task of alerting mankind to its inhumane practices[16] in the belief that man's capacity to believe anything can be his salvation as well as his cross. As he finally says in 1979 as he accepts the Nobel Prize for Medicine, "now we can build an unselfish society by devoting to unselfishness the frenzy we once devoted to gold and to underpants" (25). Vonnegut's playfulness is not without meaning, for by 1979 Trout has become a true "doctor"—one who would restore us to health through good ideas.

Vonnegut is "rescued" from his own despondency by the example of Dwayne Hoover and also through a speech by one of his other characters, Rabo Karebakian, who has contributed a painting to the Midland City Festival of the Arts called *The Temptation of Saint Anthony*. The huge picture consists of a green field painted in Hawaiian Avocado and a vertical orange stripe. The people of Midland City are outraged that Karebakian has received $50,000 for the picture, but the artist is eloquent in his own defense. He gives his word of honor that the painting shows everything about life which truly matters, with nothing left out:

> It is a picture of the awareness of every animal. It is the immaterial core of every animal—the "I am" to which all messages are sent. . . . It is unwavering and pure, no matter what preposterous adventure may befall us. A sacred picture of Saint Anthony alone is one vertical, unwavering band of light. . . . Our awareness is all that is alive and maybe sacred in any of us. Everything else about us is dead machinery. (226)

The speech marks a dramatic reversal in *Breakfast of Champions*. We had been led to anticipate a climax where Trout would teach Hoover everything he did not want to know about the vanity of human wishes. But before the encounter takes place, their creator stumbles upon a "spiritual climax" of his own. Vonnegut tells us that he is "transformed" by Karebakian's speech (223); he had feared that he might kill himself as his mother did (198); he had come to believe that "there was nothing sacred about myself or about any human being, that we were all machines, doomed to collide and collide and collide" (224–5). Karebakian's speech saves him because it suggests how we might "adapt ourselves to the requirements of chaos": by asserting our sacred awareness in the face of chaos itself. As Vonnegut says, "It is hard to adapt to chaos, but it can be done. I am living proof of that: It can be done" (215). By this point Vonnegut's dark "suspicion" about man's nature, expressed at the beginning of the novel, must be identified with the "bad ideas" Dwayne Hoover learns from Kilgore Trout. At the end of *Breakfast of Champions*, Vonnegut rejects both the suspicion and the ideas, just as Trout will do in the last years of his life.

In the novel's final pages, the newly-rescued Vonnegut bestows a final gift upon his most famous creation. Vonnegut arranges a final meeting where he tells Trout that he is going to follow Jefferson's and Tolstoi's example and set all his literary characters at liberty. From now on, Trout is *free* (301–2). His gesture seems to have been misunderstood, for one reviewer has said that Vonnegut "seems to conclude on an even grander destructive note, namely the destruction of his own fictional universe."[17] Surely, a distorted view. Just before he releases Trout from literary bondage, Vonnegut offers a second gift, an apple. As he tells Trout, "We Americans require symbols which are richly colored and three-dimensional and juicy. Most of all, we hunger for symbols which have not been poisoned by great sins our nation has committed, such as slavery and genocide and criminal neglect" (301). So he first offers Trout an apple, a superior symbol, then his freedom. Such an ending is hardly "destructive"; it might even seem sentimental, but to forestall such a reading, Vonnegut has Trout call after him, "*Make me young, make me young, make me young!*" (303). Freedom is not enough. Indeed, freedom can be frightening. Earlier, Trout has offered freedom to his parakeet, but the bird has flown back into his cage (35). That man will reject the possibilities inherent in his freedom is always a danger. What Vonnegut is telling us on every page is that man has been doing just that from the beginning of time. He is also telling us, in the fable he contrives, that only by asserting our freedom can we possibly adapt to the requirements of chaos. We cannot make ourselves young again, but we can make ourselves more humane.

Vonnegut *contrives* this fable because throughout *Breakfast of Champions* he insists on his role as master puppeteer. As another critic has said, discussing Vonnegut's earlier novels, where the appearance of fleshless robots may be something less than artistically ideal, "Vonnegut's figures are mechanical contrivances bathed in a stroboscopic glare—fleshless robots galvanized by his will, moving jerkily toward the next joke, moral, or plot-advancing surprise."[18] Here, however, Vonnegut allows no pretense about the status of his fictional creations; toward the end, Vonnegut even seats himself at the same bar with his characters. While sipping his favorite drink, he proceeds to explain why he has decided to have these characters act as they do—such a Nabokovian device is, of course, anticipated in *Slaughterhouse-Five*. The insistence on the artificiality of his dramatis personae emphasizes that *Breakfast of Champions* really has only one "character." That Karebakian's painting is named after Saint Anthony is no accident, for *Breakfast of Champions* is about its author's triumph over a great temptation. Saint Anthony's temptation was of the flesh, and Vonnegut's is of the spirit; we should know by now that the spirit both kills and dies. At the end of the novel, Vonnegut's spirit refuses to die: "I am better now. Word of honor: I am better now" (199). His hope is that we might all become "better"; his message is that to become so we must resist the seductions of fatalism.

Notes

1. Peter S. Prescott, "Nothing Sacred," *Newsweek*, 14 May 1973, p. 114.
2. Richard Todd, review of *Breakfast of Champions, The Atlantic*, 231 (May 1973), 106.
3. J. D. O'Hara, "Instantly Digestible," *New Republic*, 12 May 1973, p. 26.
4. O'Hara.
5. Prescott.
6. Peter B. Messent, "*Breakfast of Champions:* The Direction of Kurt Vonnegut's Fiction," *Journal of American Studies*, 8 (April 1974), 111.
7. Robert W. Uphaus, "Expected Meaning in Vonnegut's Dead-End Fiction," *Novel*, 8 (Winter 1975), 173.
8. Kurt Vonnegut, Jr., *Slaughterhouse-Five* (New York: Dell, 1971), p. 164. Subsequent references to this edition are indicated by the abbreviation S.
9. See, for example, Robert Scholes, *The Fabulators* (New York: Oxford Univ. Press, 1967), pp. 35–55; Raymond M. Olderman, *Beyond the Waste Land* (New Haven: Yale Univ. Press, 1972), pp. 189–219; Karen and Charles Wood, "The Vonnegut Effect: Science Fiction and Beyond," in *The Vonnegut Statement*, Jerome Klinkowitz and John Somer, eds. (New York: Delta, 1973), pp. 133–57.
10. Kurt Vonnegut, Jr., *Wampeters, Foma & Granfalloons* (New York: Delacorte Press, 1974), p. 281.
11. Kurt Vonnegut, Jr., *Breakfast of Champions* (New York: Delacorte Press, 1973), p. 4. Subsequent references are to this edition.
12. Rather than continue to use quotation marks, I would simply have it understood that the Vonnegut I refer to is the persona who appears in *Breakfast of Champions*.
13. Kurt Vonnegut, Jr., *God Bless You, Mr. Rosewater* (New York: Dell, 1970), p. 20.
14. Cf. Vonnegut's personal remarks: "Writers are specialized cells in the social organism. They are evolutionary cells. Mankind is trying to become something else; it's experimenting with new ideas all the time. And writers are a means of introducing new ideas into the society." *Wampeters, Foma & Granfalloons*, p. 237.
15. Kurt Vonnegut, Jr., *Cat's Cradle* (New York: Dell, 1965), p. 59. Subsequent references to this edition are indicated by the abbreviation C.

16. Cf. Vonnegut's comment in an interview: "But I continue to think that artists—all artists—should be treasured as alarm systems." *Wampeters, Foma & Granfalloons*, p. 238.
17. Otto Friedrich, "Ultra-Vonnegut," *Time*, 7 May 1973, p. 66.
18. Edward Grossman, "Vonnegut & His Audience," *Commentary*, 58 (July 1974), 41.

CHARLES BERRYMAN
"After the Fall: Kurt Vonnegut"
Critique, Winter 1985, pp. 96–102

Kurt Vonnegut has continued after *Slaughterhouse-Five* to explore the images of a haunted memory, but he has produced a very uneven series of novels. One scene near the end of *Deadeye Dick* is perfectly emblematic of Vonnegut's fiction of the past fifteen years. A minor character suddenly amazes the narrator of the novel by successfully raising a spirit from the grave. The scene is comic, the supernatural feat is inexplicable, but the ghostly reminder of crime and death is genuine Vonnegut.

Billy Pilgrim in *Slaughterhouse-Five* (1968) survives the bombing of Dresden, a plane crash in Vermont, and the accidental death of his wife. The narrative is a series of traumatic events, and the psychological interest of the novel is the attempt of Pilgrim to cope with the shadows of horror. Neither the dull routine of optometry, nor the fantasy escape to the planet of Tralfamadore, can prevent the ghosts of the past from surfacing in his mind.

Vonnegut introduces himself in *Breakfast of Champions* (1973) as a comic figure who is injured by one of his own creations. The persona of the author is hurt during the mad and violent rampage of Dwayne Hoover. Violence and suicide are both explained in the novel as the result of chemical imbalance. The mind is still troubled by ghosts and demons, but the explanation now is a parody of science.

The setting of *Slapstick* (1976) is the island of Manhattan after it has been largely depopulated by a mysterious plague. The destruction caused by random gravity has also turned the city into a wasteland reminiscent of the ruins of Dresden. The novel is presented as a memoir of an old man who cannot escape the shadows of guilt and fear that remain from his grotesque childhood. After the death of his twin sister, the narrator also feels doomed. Vonnegut reports in the prologue that *Slapstick* is "the closest I will ever come to writing an autobiography." The recent death of his own sister may be projected in the novel. Vonnegut admits that "she was the person I had always written for," and her early death adds another ghost to the haunted landscape of Vonnegut's fiction.[1]

The story of *Jailbird* (1979) is told against a background of the Cuyahoga Massacre and the deaths of Sacco and Vanzetti. Vonnegut agrees with several of his critics who feel that *Jailbird* is a better book than its predecessor. (What other contemporary writer has given himself a report card? There is a passage in *Palm Sunday* which includes grades for all of his books.[2] Vonnegut gives *Slapstick* a "D" and *Jailbird* an "A.") Perhaps the difference has to do with the power of history in fiction. The detailed accounts of massacre and execution in *Jailbird* raise questions of public guilt and morality that cannot be invoked by the bizarre events of the earlier novel. The narrator of *Jailbird* is in prison for a time because of his connection with the crimes of the Nixon administration, but the guilt he feels goes back to his role during the McCarthy hearings. His mind is haunted by the victims of injustice.

The narrator of *Deadeye Dick* (1982) spends less time in jail despite the fact that his crime is more destructive. As a twelve-year-old boy, he is initiated into manhood with the single firing of his father's rifle. The bullet happens to kill a pregnant woman, and from that moment forward, his life is haunted by guilt and shame. He only spends one night in jail because of his age, but his mind is imprisoned forever in the tragic past.

Vonnegut himself admits to a version of the nightmare which appears in all five of his novels from *Slaughterhouse-Five* to *Deadeye Dick*. An autobiographical passage in *Palm Sunday* describes the "bad dream I have dreamed for as long as I can remember."[3] The nightmare of crime and guilt—"I know that I have murdered an old woman a long time ago"—resembles the plot of *Crime and Punishment*. Vonnegut even acknowledges that he and Dostoyevsky have the same birthday. Puzzled by the recurring dream, Vonnegut asked a psychiatrist if the dead woman could be his mother. The ambivalent response—"the woman might not even be a woman"—is typical of the uncertain truth Vonnegut expects from any oracle. He also consulted "a Hindu with occult powers" who told him that in a previous life he "had in fact killed a child accidentally." Vonnegut's account in *Palm Sunday* of his efforts to find the meaning of his dream is typically ironic and bemused, but the subject is important enough to inform all five of his recent novels.

Vonnegut's fiction has always included a measure of autobiography, but in his recent work this trend has become more explicit. The first chapter of *Slaughterhouse-Five* depicts a persona of the author attempting to come to terms with the idea of writing about the bombing of Dresden. The autobiographical basis for the fiction is explored more fully in the introduction Vonnegut added in 1976 for a new edition of the novel.

Breakfast of Champions not only begins with an autobiographical preface, Vonnegut also introduces himself as a character in the narrative. The novelist pretends to offer freedom to the other characters, but his gift turns out to be an image of the forbidden fruit. The freedom his characters will be granted amounts to the crime and guilt of the fallen world. The same is true in the preface to the novel. Vonnegut announces that *Breakfast of Champions* is "my fiftieth birthday present to myself," and "I am trying to make my head as empty as it was when I was born onto this damaged planet fifty years ago."[4] The attempt of course is in vain. The ghosts in the mind cannot be exorcised. Many of the characters, even Midland City itself, will reappear in *Deadeye Dick* where Vonnegut will try killing them again with a neutron bomb.

Slapstick has a prologue in which a persona of the author explains his relationship with his brother and sister. The narrator of the novel then proceeds to tell about his childhood with his twin sister. In this way, Vonnegut uses autobiography as an envelope for his fiction. The twins in the novel are a typical gothic device for dramatizing a mind on the verge of schizophrenia. Wilbur and Eliza Swain are a contemporary version of Roderick and Madeline Usher. The brothers are both haunted by the loss of their twin sisters because each represents a state of mind that is incomplete by itself. The gothic fantasy of Poe becomes the black humor and science fiction of Vonnegut, but the psychological meaning is consistent.

The prologue to *Jailbird* is also autobiographical. Vonnegut talks about his father as a failed architect and his mother as a probable suicide, but the family relationships are set against the background of the Cuyahoga Massacre and the references to Sacco and Vanzetti. In this way, Vonnegut uses history to support the personal narrative which in turn reinforces the fiction. In all three, the theme is unjustifiable violence and death. The narrator of *Jailbird* feels guilty for crimes which history and circumstance have forced him to inherit. His life has been a nightmare for longer than he can remember.

The subtitle for *Palm Sunday* (1981) is "An Autobiographical Collage." In this book, Vonnegut gathers together several of his occasional pieces from recent years, and then adds a framework of personal narrative. He even includes a history of his family for several generations. The book invites the public to join Vonnegut in his attempt to find the roots of fear and guilt. The story of his family, like the record of the Compsons in *The Sound and the Fury*, is the rise and fall of a family dynasty. Each family inherits a memory of better times, but the present is marked by separation and suicide. Vonnegut's mother could recall her visits to relatives in German castles, but the prospect of her son taking part in the war against Germany may have prompted her to take her own life. Seven months later her son became a prisoner in Dresden.

Vonnegut speculates in *Breakfast of Champions* about the semblance of his mother's death and the suicide of Celia Hoover. The fictional character is presented as a pathetic copy of the lost parent. After her beauty has disappeared and her ambitions have all been frustrated, Celia takes her life by swallowing Drano. Vonnegut explains that his mother and Celia "both boiled over with chaotic talk about love and peace and wars and evil and desperation."[5]

Vonnegut describes the suicide of his mother again in *Palm Sunday*, and then reintroduces Celia Hoover as a character in *Deadeye Dick*. The retelling of the same story becomes an almost ritualized attempt to exorcise the ghost. Vonnegut not only retells the story of Celia Hoover with new details which parallel the fate of his own mother, he also gives the narrative of *Deadeye Dick* a parent who dies of radiation poisoning. The images of death and guilt multiply, but the ghosts cannot be put to rest.

Vonnegut dreams repeatedly about the murder of a woman, and all of his recent novels have important female characters who come to tragic ends. Billy Pilgrim's wife is killed by carbon monoxide in *Slaughterhouse-Five*. Dwayne Hoover's wife swallows the detergent in *Breakfast of Champions*. Wilbur Swain's sister is killed by an avalanche in *Slapstick*. Walter Starbuck's former love and present benefactor dies after being hit by a car in *Jailbird*. And the women in *Deadeye Dick* are either shot to death, poisoned by radiation, or commit suicide. This record does not have its equal in American literature since Poe first advocated the subject of the death of a beautiful woman in his "Philosophy of Composition."

The single deaths in Vonnegut's recent fiction are often overshadowed by the vision of a massacre. The bombing of Dresden in *Slaughterhouse-Five* is the most famous example, but the vision is recreated for different novels. A tide of industrial waste is threatening to bury Midland City in *Breakfast of Champions*. The island of Manhattan has been devastated by changing gravity and a mysterious plague in *Slapstick*. The story of the Cuyahoga Massacre is retold in the prologue to *Jailbird*, and the familiar Midland City is recreated in *Deadeye Dick* so that Vonnegut can depopulate it with a neutron bomb. Is there another contemporary novelist more concerned with visions of destruction and mortality?

If the images of a massacre haunt the characters in Vonnegut's fiction, it is not surprising that so many of his narrators behave as passive victims of a hostile fate. One of the many ironies of *Slaughterhouse-Five* is that Billy Pilgrim, who merely wants to die at the beginning of the novel, should be the survivor of the bombing of Dresden, not to mention his wife's death and a plane crash. The price for his survival is a memory haunted by fear and death. He moves from one disaster to another unable to either banish or accept the experience of Dresden. The images of the massacre are so deeply repressed that the full memory does not surface until near the end of the novel.

No matter how comic and forlorn the character of Billy Pilgrim may appear as he enters Dresden in his Cinderella boots, the enormity of what is about to happen is enough to insure the sympathy of Vonnegut's audience. In the novels which follow, however, the weight of history is often lacking, and the narrators who suffer a private trauma are apt to appear more absurd than tragic. Wilbur Swain, for example, may suffer as long as he wants from his grotesque childhood or the loss of his sister, but he will always seem more or less ridiculous. There is no credible reference point in *Slapstick* for his state of mind. How can a reader possibly respond to an avalanche on Mars?

Vonnegut has a similar problem with the narrator of *Jailbird*. Walter Starbuck is more sympathetic than the absurd Wilbur Swain, but his connection with history is still rather tenuous and often unconvincing. The massacre at the Cuyahoga Bridge and Iron Company took place before he was born, and his knowledge of Sacco and Vanzetti is merely hearsay. Left in the shadows of history, it is not surprising that Walter Starbuck has such a low opinion of his own character. He thinks of himself as "the demented son of a Cleveland chauffeur," and he admits that others view him as an "inconceivable twerp."[6] The self-criticism may at times be disarming, but for the most part it leaves the reader feeling indifferent to the fate of the character. Who cares whether the narrator of *Jailbird* is sentenced to another term in prison or to be a vice president of the RAMJAC Corporation?

It is typical of the narrator of *Jailbird* to feel so inhibited by guilt and fear that he is incapable of any genuine passion. When the first woman he ever cared for is dying at the end of the novel, she forgives him for his inability to love: "You couldn't help it that you were born without a heart." The same is characteristic of all the Vonnegut narrators who are haunted by images of crime and death. The latest example is the narrator of *Deadeye Dick*. He describes himself as a "neutered pharmacist" who is "so sexless and shy that he might as well be made out of canned tuna fish."[7] How does Vonnegut expect his audience to respond to a main character who has all of the passion and courage of tuna fish? The emotional growth of the narrator has been arrested at the age of twelve when the killing of a pregnant woman filled his life with guilt and shame. For decades thereafter, he denies himself almost all freedom in a vain attempt to make amends to his own parents. No peace of mind, not to mention love or happiness, is available to the repressed and tormented narrator. His only chance for self-expression comes in the form of writing a pathetic play about the search for Shangri-La.

The narrator's attempt to be a playwright may stand as a parody of Vonnegut's own efforts to turn the ghosts of the mind into literature. "I have this trick for dealing with all of my worst memories," he says, "I insist that they are plays."[8] The narrator of course is not the only frustrated writer in Vonnegut's work. The best known example is Kilgore Trout. Neither the science fiction of Kilgore Trout nor the fantasy drama of "Deadeye Dick" will compensate for their abiding sense of loss.

The drama about the search for Shangri-La also reflects another of Vonnegut's favorite devices for coping with the ghosts of failure. The narrator of *Deadeye Dick* attempts to compensate for his impoverished life by imagining a promised land: "There's room for everybody in Shangri-La." In a similar fashion, the narrator of *Jailbird* indulges in wish fulfillment when he describes how all of his friends have been rewarded with high positions in the RAMJAC Corporation. It is the old mistake of Eliot Rosewater who tried to banish his guilt by giving away his fortune. Vonnegut's characters know that the fallen world cannot suddenly be converted back into the lost paradise, but that does not stop them from trying.

All of the narrators who try to escape from the fear and guilt of a fallen world are attempting to regain an innocence which they feel was lost in childhood. The subtitle for *Slaughterhouse-Five* is "The Children's Crusade," and Vonnegut describes himself in the preface to *Breakfast of Champions* as "programmed at fifty to perform childishly." The style of the novel with its drawings of a light switch, a cow, and a hamburger is so apparently childish that perhaps Vonnegut should be taken at his word. "I've often thought," he once declared, "there ought to be a manual to hand to little kids, telling them what kind of planet they're on, why the don't fall off it, how much time they've probably got here."[9] *Breakfast of Champions* unfortunately reads like such a manual, and its mixed critical reception is therefore no surprise.

Slapstick is presented as the memoir of a very old man, but the focus of the novel is primarily the grotesque childhood of the narrator. The subject of extended families is also important in *Slapstick* because that is another way of trying to retain the security of childhood. The narrators of *Jailbird* and *Deadeye Dick* both lose the sense of being children when the news of death and guilt breaks into their lives. The novels are told by adults who are tormented by a sense of paradise lost.

"The museums in children's minds," Vonnegut suggests, "automatically empty themselves in times of utmost horror—to protect the children from eternal grief."[10] But in novel after novel, he has dramatized just the opposite. The children are exposed to horror, and the experience is then repressed to a level of the mind where it continues to haunt their conscious behavior. The mind is never empty, and the children cannot be protected.

The uneven quality of Vonnegut's recent fiction may be the difference between feeling "programmed at fifty to perform childishly" and the vital expression of "the museums of children's minds." Vonnegut is true to the latter when he allows the memory of the "children's crusade" to break through the limits of repression in *Slaughterhouse-Five*. The prevalence of this psychological drama may also contribute to the success of *Jailbird* and *Deadeye Dick*, while its absence may help to explain the weakness of *Breakfast of Champions* and *Slapstick*.

Vonnegut identifies his own fiction with the voice of a child, and in *Palm Sunday* he cites Henry David Thoreau as his literary ancestor: "Thoreau, I now feel, wrote in the voice of a child, as do I."[11] In so far as Thoreau can be viewed as the "American Adam" attempting to live at Walden Pond as if it were paradise regained, he foreshadows the efforts made by Vonnegut's narrators to regain the innocence of their lost childhoods. The reference book for children which Vonnegut wanted to call "Welcome to Earth" may be a contemporary version of Thoreau's *Walden*. Just as *Walden* often reads like a parody of a how-to-do-it book, Vonnegut's *Breakfast of Champions* with its absurd pen and ink drawings is a parody of an illustrated manual. Thoreau and Vonnegut typically assume the voice of a child for purposes of satire.

When it comes to writing in the voice of a child, however, Vonnegut's most important literary ancestor is not Henry David Thoreau but Mark Twain. It was Twain who "wrote childishly" when he created a world seen through the eyes of Tom Sawyer. Such a world is often viewed with satire, but it is very limited in psychological depth. Tom Sawyer would be good at writing a fantasy play for Midland City, about a treasure hunt perhaps or a search for Shangri-La, but there is no convincing fear and guilt in his soul. It was also Twain, however, who at times could truly enter "the museums in children's minds," and then he created the haunted and wonderful imagination of Huckleberry Finn. Here is the prototype for many of Vonnegut's narrators: a child marked by the loss of parents, not ready yet for marriage, love, or responsibility, but lighting out for the territory with a mind haunted by images of death and destruction. The territory ahead, of course, is not Tralfamadore or Shangri-La—it is the great river of life with fugitives and charlatans. The territory ahead includes *Slaughterhouse-Five*, *Jailbird*, and *Deadeye Dick*.

Notes

1. Kurt Vonnegut, *Slapstick* (New York: Delacorte, 1976), p. 15.
2. Kurt Vonnegut, *Palm Sunday* (New York: Delacorte, 1981), pp. 311–12.
3. *Palm Sunday*, pp. 189–90.
4. Kurt Vonnegut, *Breakfast of Champions* (New York: Delacorte, 1973), p. 5.
5. *Breakfast of Champions*, p. 186.
6. Kurt Vonnegut, *Jailbird* (New York: Delacorte, 1979), p. 110.
7. Kurt Vonnegut, *Deadeye Dick* (New York: Delacorte, 1982), p. 136.
8. *Deadeye Dick*, p. 83.
9. Kurt Vonnegut, *Wampeters, Foma & Granfalloons* (New York: Delta, 1975), p. 276.
10. *Slapstick*, p. 15.
11. *Palm Sunday*, p. 58.

MIRIAM WADDINGTON

1917–

Miriam Dworkin was born in Winnipeg, Manitoba, Canada, on December 23, 1917. She was educated at the University of Toronto (B.A. 1939; Diploma in Social Work, 1942; M.A. 1968) and the University of Pennsylvania (M.S.W. 1945). In 1939 Dworkin married Patrick Donald Waddington, but they were divorced in 1965. She has two sons, Marcus and Jonathan. Since 1945 she has been the assistant director of the Jewish Child Welfare Bureau in Montreal (1945–46), a field instructor at McGill University's School of Social Work (1946–49), a staff member at Montreal Children's Hospital (1952–54), a staff member at the John Howard Society in Montreal (1955–57), a caseworker for the Jewish Family Bureau in Montreal (1957–60), and a casework supervisor for the North York Family Service in Toronto (1960–62). She has been associated with York University in Toronto since 1964, first as an assistant professor and now as a professor of English and Canadian literature, and she has also been writer-in-residence at the University of Ottawa (1974) and the Windsor Public Library (1983). In 1980 she was chosen as the Canada Council exchange poet to Wales, and in that same year she also toured Yugoslavia, lecturing and giving poetry readings.

Miriam Waddington's books include *Green World* (1945), *The Second Silence* (1955), *The Season's Lovers* (1958), *The Glass Trumpet* (1966), *Say Yes* (1969), *Driving Home: Poems New and Selected* (1972), *The Dream Telescope* (1973), *The Price of Gold* (1976), *Mister Never* (1978), *The Visitants* (1981), and *Summer at Lonely Beach and Other Stories* (1982).

In a poem entitled "Losing Merrygorounds," Miriam Waddington regrets that loss as well as ". . . the careful prose / of growing up". Indeed, throughout *The Glass Trumpet*, one feels that Miss Waddington is willing to abandon care entirely to avoid writing "prose". The battle against prose is exhausting, finding its expression in run-on syntax and sentimental attitudes. It includes lots of crying, wishing, dreaming, and singing. Half of everything seems to be blinded or blinding.

None of this would be quite as bothersome if Miss Waddington would exploit the best of the metaphors she so casually picks up, instead of dropping each for abstractions in those places where she is led to significant thought by her materials. The language is not without a talented urgency—quite deserving of care, even at the cost of the infiltration of "prose". As it is, all that this technique allows to be clear is the most general of feelings.

The best of Miss Waddington's poems seem to me those which arise from her harshest attitudes; the best of these is "Pleasures from Children," of which I quote the beginning and end:

> *Er ist gewesen*, I tell you,
> absolutely on top of the world,
> then he went whoring and
> she got him, the little snake.
> *Das ist ein Maedchen?*
> . . .
> I know I know,
> I know what she intends
> with her low love tricks;
> a boy needs to go to a woman
> now and then, but to that slut
> that serpent? Oh why don't you
> see that my father's heart
> is in a sackcloth why don't you
> absolutely from the top of the world
> help me?

—MARVIN BELL, *Poetry*, Feb. 1968, pp. 326–27

Professor Waddington has wit, invention, and a powerful *copia verborum*. Her talents match the photographs in *Call Them Canadians* well. The tone is set by the poem—if it is a poem—which matches a photograph of a child in a pram looking at the photographer while behind are the crowded backs of adults looking at—what?—Cole's Toy Fair, perhaps? The child has a curious yet sceptical air and on the opposite page, occupying about as much space as the child (about a twentieth of the area) is this:

> What is a Canadian
> anyway? A mountain, a maple
> leaf, a prairie, a Niagara Fall,
> a trail beside the Atlantic, a
> bilingualism, a scarred mosaic,
> a yes-no somehow-or-other may be
> might-be should-be could-be
> glacial shield, grain elevator,
> empire daughter imperial order of
> man woman child or what?

The fifty-five poems in *The Glass Trumpet* deal with 'man woman child' and the reader must ask what is the 'what' of them? They are headed 'Things of the World', 'Carnival', and 'The Field of Night'. They are printed in a small type down the centre of the page. Gaps are often used instead of punctuation and may be a guide to the reader-aloud who has not been taught punctuation in an advanced school. The more orthodoxly written and set poems are more attractive to eye and mind. The content consists of personal experience—the apparently autobiographic content of, say, 'saints and others'—of random reflections, as in 'Summer Letters', of family, as in the Judith Wright–like poem 'The Gardeners'. There are more consciously literary poems in the 'Carnival' section (reflections of Yeats, Eliot); while in 'The Field of Night' there are Biblical echoes, and a sense of an inarticulate poetic cry moving into the deliberation of words.

What is the achievement? The reflection, certainly, of an intense, imaginative, intellectual woman's responses to the world of natural phenomena, ideas, and human beings. This is poetry which is based on wide reading and on a sensitive capacity to match emotions with words, disciplined in most cases, into a cohesive form. From these poems some Canadian flavour emanates: but not obtrusively. It is there as background to poetry—which might have been written by this poet anywhere in the world where her thoughts and feeling were engaged. It is written out of experiences many of which will be accepted as part and parcel of modern life, with its movement, strain, self-awareness, intensity and complexity.—A. NORMAN JEFFARES, "Poetic Deliberation," *JCL*, June 1971, pp. 135–36

In ⟨. . .⟩ a way that avoids the tight, intellectual challenge of the expertly managed *haiku* and relies on a fade-out *con innuendo* (as if that were a musical term), Mrs. Waddington's poems in her fifth book of verse ⟨*Say Yes*⟩ give us pictures of love, small joys, and the grand disillusions of our urban landscape. Some of the poems build neither to climax nor to complaint but to a finale that seems halfway between a bad imitation of Gertrude Stein and a bad imitation of A. A. Milne:

> but who wants to get to sleep
> with a cup of ovaltine what
> kind of sleep is that for some-
> one who used to have someone
> to ask do you love me and
> be sure that the answer
> would always be yes?

Others head for the heart of what she feels she feels. They chase after those images for whose sake she writes, whom we might say she propitiates in verse. Neither classically pure nor modernistically precise, the images which she has "begun to worship" have a biographical immediacy and vitality, and they are, for her, firm enough to be treated like old photographs. She can "prop them up on bureau tops in hotel rooms."

> there is
> no such thing
> as love left in
> the world but
> there is still
> the image of it

Mrs. Waddington sees and is fond of the "little fringes" of the frayed, everyday world. She responds to drabness with sprightly charm and a little girl's imaginativeness. The more personal she is, the more engaging is her work, able to

> dictate when the
> tigerlilies should
> stop blooming and
> when the redgrass
> should ripen to hay,
> a comic laurel wreath
> for a serious
> apprentice

—F. D. REEVE, "Faces at the Bottom," *Poetry*, July 1971, pp. 236–37

IAN SOWTON

"The Lyric Craft of Miriam Waddington"

Dalhousie Review, Summer 1959, pp. 237–42

The Season's Lovers is Miss Waddington's third volume of poems. In it she makes metaphysical lyrics that are governed by venerable images like the city as a macrocosmic being, the paradox of intermingled selves that remain ultimately strangers, the word as creator, and the dream that outreals reality. These images are exciting ones that have long been the matter of good poetry, and precisely because of this they are very difficult to manipulate well. Their very richness is embarrassing; in using them it is difficult to avoid using, for instance, the seventeenth-century manner. While there is no particular virtue or merit in "being original" (tables of degrees in originality are a device of lazy reviewers), there is great virtue in putting things meaningfully for one's contemporaries. In *The Season's Lovers* it seems to me that the meaningful poetic statement, or the modern manipulation of old images, has been on the whole successfully brought off.

The organizing, dominant image of the first three sections of this volume is the City. In the first section, "Poets and Statues" (one poem), the City is projected as miraculously instinct with tragedy in innumerable forms and also with excruciating wonder. It can be a desert kingdom, but the poet-queen can also summon up the water to plant an oasis with a magic garden. Section Two is called "The City's Life". Here we move from the loss of a kind of urban Eden in "When World Was Wheelbarrow" to an ironic vision of the New Jerusalem—in this case the New Montreal—in "The Through Way". The urban Eden of the first of the poems is imaged in the simple juxtaposition of the crocus, the brash first-comer in city gardens, with the youthful, enthusiastic performance of the city's multiple activities. The Fall is imaged in a fall of snow: mobility falls into immobility; speed into lethargy; sensitivity into deafness; innocence into ignorance. The central irony of the poem is that the urbanites know enough to fall off from an innocent enthusiasm but not enough to understand their own fallen condition. In "The Through Way", the New City is ironically set forth in a climactic fusion of the garden and the city:

> I sit and drive, hands sleepy at the wheel,
> My eyes continual messengers
> For the strangeness of love; though no one asks them
> to,
> They do a workman's duty,
> And over the broken city, the dynamited stairs,
> They plant the asphalt field.

Part Three, "To Be a Healer", gives a vision of the City as prison in which prisoner, gaoler, and healer are almost identified—are equally trapped and equally guilty. "In a Corridor at Court" contrasts the dark weight of imprisonment with the bright buoyancy of freedom while bringing in overtones of the trapped beast: the court, like the zoo, is powerfully haunted by the ghost of freedom:

> . . . only my brow is weighed by iron bars
> Which criss-cross window like a bloodied rope,
> or press like law with all its heavy books
> against lost freedom's lovely antelope,
> whose leap has left a mark upon the air,
> and stirred the stillness in the corridor.

In Part Four, which is headed "No Earthly Lover", the large society of the City is brought down to its lowest common denominator, the society of two. In the first three parts a number of selves are expressed in their being as diverse parts of a city; in this last part whatever is cosmic is expressed in its being as the tensile, paradoxical union of two selves. To reduce these poems even further into prose, one might say that they read like a dialogue between the agonizing beatitude of oneness and the blessed curse of twoness. The trinitarian who likes his three terms might prefer to read these poems as a threefold movement between the loving self, the beloved self, and the union between the two which is cosmic in import but totalitarian and mercurial in practice. In celebrating the union, these poems fix it; in fixing it, they deny it. This is the eternal lyric predicament and whatever else they are, these poems are a moving imitation of that predicament. Hence the cry to unfix at the end of "Song", which is a poem about lovers (as poet and painter) asserting themselves in and through each other:

Draw me falcon, paint me bird,
Erase my poem, love my word.

"You Are My Never" is a piece of very high metaphysical jinks in which affirmation equals the fusion of two negations; nowhere does Miss Waddington put more strongly the paradox that twoness is the condition of oneness.

Although some self or other is not necessarily the dominant image in any given lyric, surely one of the chief characteristics of the lyric mode is that its final subject is always the self. In submitting this I do not propose to commit the personal heresy. I have no suggestions or gratuitous illuminations whatsoever about Miss Waddington's personal life as a result of reading her poetry. The self of a successful lyric is a fully projected, poetic self. It should exist in an uncluttered situation that is evoked, implied, or realized well enough for the reader not to have to play an elaborate game of hide-and-seek with the poet's "real" personality. There are many degrees to drama, and even the lyric is dramatic to the extent that it achieves the poetic self in rapport with some object. This object may be vague, concrete, ambiguous, personal, in potency rather than in act, and so on—it makes no difference. Within this lyric situation there are two main directions of movement: initiative and responsive; that is to say, the lyric imitates the self either initiating a situation or responding to one, either establishing a rapport or answering from within one. The self's intenser modes of operation or awareness are essentially spasmodic and discontinuous, and the lyricist imitates these modes in celebrating his poetic self in motion. For the finished poem the structural corollary of this is brevity; the stylistic corollary is the metaphor—small in space but large in connotation—or, in any case, the heavily freighted image.

Miss Waddington is a passive lyricist. The movement of her poetic self is almost invariably responsive. The situations she projects are of the sensitive and intelligent self in the various attitudes of response from ecstatic to revulsive. The ultimate theme of *The Season's Lovers* is in fact the horrific glory of responsive self. Hence there is in Miss Waddington's work a peculiarly direct relation between the lyric form and its content; her content is almost lyricism itself. This proposition is neither meliorative nor pejorative: her way, though striking, is just one way of doing things.

How well does Miss Waddington do things in her own way? My own opinion would be, very well. But for literary criticism the question simply raises another, more important one: what is the technique of these poems? in what consists their lyric artistry? If the imitation of the self in its brief, heightened movements is the essence of lyricism, then the lyric of all forms can least afford moments of thematic and verbal leisure. Of all forms it is the one in which tense self-containment and self-consistency are at a premium, the one which can least afford to settle into the prosaic logic of discursiveness. The secret of that first requirement lies in the taut manipulation of images and rhythms; the secret of the second in the inviolable poetic self: the reader must be free of having to postulate the artist's everyday self. In lyrics the commonest form of the lapse into discursiveness is the confusion of the everyday with the poetic self; the two other lyric diseases are slackness of rhythm and inaccuracy of image. Let me go afield to—or rather, aboard, Miss Macpherson's work *(The Boatman)* to illustrate. In no volume of Canadian lyrics would the personality hunt be more irrelevant, and nowhere are images and rhythms, in their own may, more taut and trim. Although *The Boatman* has a system, it is not discursive; although it bears an obvious self, this is a purely poetic self. These qualities fuse with the precision of the imagery and rhythm to give as it were a perfectly firm, crystalline surface which guarantees, or constitutes, Miss Macpherson's particular, exact lyricism. Some readers no doubt consider this surface hard and cold and wish the Boatman nothing so much as a good icebreaker. But it is precisely because of this still, fast surface that we can see with perfect clarity beneath us a poetic self going freely about its lyric business in a highly self-contained and self-consistent universe. Not Freudian, not Jungian critics—only God Himself could cut through this ice and fish for the poet's real self. Granted that Miss Waddington and Miss Macpherson are doing different things in different ways; granted that their respective lyric dramaturgies are quite dissimilar; granted that critical metaphors of a surface do not apply at all to *The Season's Lovers*: granted all these things, this digression will have been useful if it gives meaning to the assertion that, occasionally, Miss Waddington's muse dips to be discursive and that, very occasionally, her image slips off target. Take, for instance, the last stanza of "The City's Life": she—the "woman possessed by cities"—

. . . does not own the burglar's forcing tools
Or have his abstract grasp of puzzling parts,
All she has are her own human channels,
Eyes that observe, a pulse that beats,
A heart that moves to other troubled hearts;
Somewhere she keeps her mind's prepared collation—
Numerous theories, projects, and some orphan facts,
But she is impatient and values them much less
Than all the discontinuous evidence,
Which haunts her every step and holds her powerless
Against the city's life, its poignant annals.

This poet responds to nothing more vividly than to the single, discontinuous member within the multiple, flowing body, but here the response strikes me as too much of a prosaic statement, too much of a commentary. There is about those lines something too clinically analytic for a poem that is not about clinical analysis; they seem more of a mnemonic evocation of a private impression than the imaginative projection of a dramatically self-sustaining situation. But there are not many moments like this in *The Season's Lovers*. Miss Waddington is a social worker, and when one considers what a harrowing and dominating business it must be for a sensitive self continually to be encountering other, troubled selves, it is a considerable measure of success that so few of her lines are merely discursive. The difficulty of her tune and her skill in playing it are most apparent in Part Three, especially in "The Drug Addict", "The Non Supporter", "My Lessons in the Jail", and "The Women's Jail",—all of which are potent, well-realized lyrics.

The only important image in Miss Waddington's poetry that seems a bit imprecise and lax to me is that of the drowned (or drowning) person. In "Poets and Statues" the early phrase "she drowns in heat" sets vibrating connotations that merely clutter up the impact of the latter image of the magic oasis. In "You Are My Never" the notion of being united in division, of being something as nothing, is expressed in geographic imagery that manages to remain strikingly suspended, or mediumless:

And though we're polar and must lie apart,
We have our tropic where we fuse within.

> We cross no fields, no cities and no miles,
> For nothing needs no medium to sin,
> Here never loves his no one with denials
> And arbitrates against himself to win.
>
> So be my never and long may nothing live,
> Bless all distance and intensity
> Which strain our kisses through a starry sieve,
> And drowning you have also here drowned me.

The paradox of a placeless geography and of locales that are a medium for nothing gives great power to the poem. Everything's going nowhere very satisfactorily until, with talk of drowning in the last line, we enter a specific medium with a vengeance, and a cold and clammy one at that. I am aware that this last line completes the cosmic geography of the poem. I am also aware that the juxtaposition of stars with the sea reinforces the notion of proximity simultaneous with infinite distance. Even so, on suddenly landing in the water like this the reader gets into what seems to be the wrong swim of things, and he has to flounder pretty hard before perceiving that there is a kind of rightness to them. I don't mind floundering hard as long as the labour doesn't dissipate the poetic force of what has gone before. Drowning, after all, is drowning: its primary state is of being good and dead, suffocated, picked clean, well lost at sea. Water baptizes into everlasting life only a few of the famous literary drownees; but it thoroughly drowns them all. Unless a poem's whole element is water, drownings should be very carefully arranged. Miss Waddington does have a poem whose whole element is water: "An Elegy for John Sutherland", in which Sutherland's death is quite appropriately imaged as a drowning. But here, too, the image is a bit lax, though for a different reason. Death by drowning (or death as drowning) is easily one of the oldest and richest poetic images. It can be used as a standard, mass-produced piece of poetic furniture or rediscovered as an infinite reservoir of genuine variety. In this elegy I do not think that that infinitude has been plundered of any compelling new variety. Perhaps I should conclude this strain on dry land. "People Who Watch Trains" is a poem that is really excellently conceived, but even here I am not quite sure: are the people watching the trains go by genuine symbols of the loss of enthusiasm or are they only argumentative evidence of it?

Rhythm is the other secret of lyric artistry, and Miss Waddington has solved completely the rhythms appropriate to her work. There are three rhythmical idioms in the lyric mode: that in which the rhythm precedes the content and its impact; that in which the rhythm follows the content; and that in which the two coincide. Think of a ship riding waves and let ship be poetic content and waves the rhythm. Sometimes the waves move faster than the ship and so overtake and go before it; sometimes the ship outstrips the waves; and sometimes, their forward speed being equal, the ship appears to ride a single, continuous wave. Many of Donne's poems are in the first rhythmical idiom; you must catch his rhythm to perceive his content; the rhythms are prior—not in import but in impact. Wallace Stevens' poems are often in the third idiom where the content, not the rhythm, has the prior impact. His rhythms are corroborative; they confirm the passage of his content like the waves that fall away from a ship's wake. Miss Waddington is a poet of the second idiom where content and rhythm tend to coincide. One of her favourite rhythms is based upon a run of ten-syllable lines, caesuraed into 4/6 cadences, which is briefly held up, or rested, in an unbroken, decasyllabic cadence. This ground rhythm coincides with the poet's ultimate content, namely, a very powerful, attractive drive of the self toward other selves together with an equally powerful, repulsive drive away from them. This paradoxical movement is rhythmically conveyed, or cradled, in the double to single, dividing to uniting, pattern of the cadences. It is a bad poem in which content and rhythm coincide merely to cancel each other out. In *The Season's Lovers* this happens only in "An Elegy for John Sutherland", which seems to me to be quite the weakest poem in the collection. Otherwise, the strongly tensive motions of the poet's theme are well rhythmed in her cadences.

In this essay I have written, perhaps *ad nauseam*, of poetic and everyday selves as they figure in a definition of the lyric art. Translated into the terminology of public utility, Miss Waddington's imitations of the self-in-motion are yet another assertion of the value and the cost of individuality. They are also another assertion of the individual's entity, if not his primacy, in the so infinitely complicated social dance. What is there more useful than making such assertions? The faithful will have heard this umpteen times before, but here we are again: the lyric craft (as practised well by Miss Waddington or anybody else) is no parlour game; it has absolutely to do with matters of life and death.

TOM WAYMAN

"Miriam Waddington's New Talent"

Canadian Literature, Spring 1973, pp. 85–89

I think most of Miriam Waddington's poems in her recent collection of new and selected poems, *Driving Home*, are boring. But as this collection spans thirty years of work, boredom here is perhaps not entirely her fault: the worst poems reflect the fashions of times they were written in. It is difficult not to be bored with intricate little home-made myths and texts designed to fill up with sentiment the empty prairies or an empty life. And it is difficult now not to be bored with the careful encapsulating into *rhyme* of the passions and anguish of a social worker in the 40's and 50's, and of the lives of those she was in contact with.

But I wonder if Waddington doesn't share these views. The best of the poems in *Driving Home* are mostly in the section of new poems (since 1969). Here she is able sometimes to get inside her present life and show it to the reader in a convincing way. In "Eavesdropping" she imagines all the wonderful things she hopes for at the sound of the telephone: literary fame, academic recognition, and long-distance love. Yet the reality of her life reasserts itself:

> . . . the telephone
> keeps on ringing and
> I know if I answer it
> it will only be the
> insurance adjuster
> saying: your car is
> a total wreck madam
> but not a complete
> write-off so what
> do you want us to do
> about it?

In the same direct style, another poem shows a fence post in her back yard becoming a signpost in the passage of the seasons and the poet's life:

> . . . then
> autumn went south and
> all of a sudden the boys
> I used to go around with
> were sixty years old and

telling me money
isn't everything.

Not that wistfulness is the only tone Waddington uses in these newer poems. She satirizes effectively a lot of the silliness of recent Canadian poetry in "Sad Winter in the Land of Can. Lit."

There are many
things I must learn
in order to write
better in Canada.
I must learn . . .
to spell everything
my own swt way just
to prve my indep
endens of all thr
shtty authrty.

Waddington's appeal in this poem is to the world's standard of writing:

Dear Nelly Sachs,
dear Nathalie Sarraute,
isn't there anything
you can teach me
about how to write
better in Canada?

In "Polemics" she charts a course of affirmation for her writing and life. She wants monuments to the future that make it clear that

There were heroes, wars
were halted, men were
healed, children were
born, people sang,
worlds were changed . . .

And as a contribution towards these monuments, she offers two looks backward at where she has come from. In these poems, the reader duly sees the changes she mentions, and can feel something of Waddington's dissatisfaction at being what she is today. From "The Nineteen Thirties Are Over":

. . . I am not really
this middle-aged professor
but someone from
Winnipeg whose bones ache
with the broken revolutions
of Europe, and even now
I am standing on the heaving
ploughed-up field
of my father's old war.

Some hint of the powerful poems Waddington might have written out of her social work in clinics, jails and as a welfare official can be seen in "Investigator" (1942) where she captures for a moment something of the inside of the homes and lives of the poor:

I could tell you, and no exaggeration,
of the in and out of houses twenty times a day
of the lace antimacassars, the pictures of kings and queens
the pious mottoes, the printed blessings, the dust piling up on bureaus,
the velour interiors, the Niagara souvenirs
the faded needlepoint, the hair pulled tight
and the blinds drawn against day and the feel of sun.

But too often the emotion is lost in the prison of rhyme, as in her attempt to tell of her reaction to interviewing a thief (1957):

Armand Perault, petty thief
what do I know of your belief?

This poem clunks along to the stunning insight of:

I haven't heard much that was new to me
or brought any word that was new to you;
it seems our separate selves must curve
wide from the central pulsing nerve
which ought to unite us, you and me . . .

Waddington's poems such as this one fail to let any particular emotion break out, to transcend the confines of rhyme in any way so that the poem is more than reporting in verse. Or maybe there *was* no further emotion? In "The Women's Jail" (1956), an unrhymed poem, Waddington tells of how she secretly admires the beautiful young girls in jail for cheque-forging.

Being especially human
I am no judge of evil
but hear how it has
a singing life in them
how it speaks out
with an endowed voice.

She ends this poem by comparing herself unfavourably to the women prisoners.

my blood is free from alcohol
I am law-abiding, I am completely
resistible—is there anything
praiseworthy in that?

It is the tag of "evil" applied to these girls or their crime, plus the self-doubt expressed as the easy comparison of the social worker to the inmates, that bother me. As someone raised with the left-wing background that Waddington mentions, plus having experienced her work among the poor, could she really believe that cheque-forging is "evil"? I can't help feeling that there is something awfully genteel about this poem and its neat final comparison—as though the poem is a careful, conventional mask for a more jagged and powerful response to this situation. And so with a number of her other social poems.

My lack of complete belief in what Waddington is saying appears even in the new poems of this collection. Something is missing, for me, in a poem like "Transformations" when she says she wants to spend her life in Gimli listening to the silence and that

. . . I will compose
my songs of gold-eye tunes
send them across the land
in smoke-spaces, ice-signals
and concentrate all winter
on Henry Hudson adrift
in a boat . . .

Granted, this poem is doubtless meant to be a bit of *joie de vivre*, but even so I'm not convinced there is much *joie* in concentrating all winter on Henry Hudson adrift in a boat. Henry Hudson strains the credibility even in the midst of a willing suspension of disbelief. Similarly, in "Dead Lakes":

I look down
in the dead waters
of Sudbury and
I think of Flaubert . . .

I lose the poem entirely when leaps like this are too large for me. Something else must be going on in the poet's mind, I keep thinking, to make these images mean more to her than she has conveyed to me.

And I find this strain throughout the older poems. In "Summer Letters" (1965) Waddington is attempting to compare a young Canadian postman at work to various academic and artistic problems, specifically those having to do with Old

English scholarship. The leap between the two subjects loses me: that there is no connection seems pretty obvious. The postman is also unrelated to the price of eggs, although there is no poem pointing this out.

And disconnectedness appears in more of the early poems. In some sort of try to give Canada a veneer of European mythical and traditional history, Waddington has lines like (from "Lullaby" (1945)):

> and night's sweet gypsy now
> fiddles you to sleep
> far from snows of winnipeg
> and seven sisters lakes.

Images of gypsies, or Elizabethan rhetoric in poems like "Thou Didst Say Me" (1945), "Sea Bells" (1964) or "The Mile Runner" (1958), appear slightly incongruous in the Canadian reality, to say the least—like the pseudo-gothic Houses of Parliament rising over the sawmills of Hull.

Just how Waddington herself fits into the Canadian reality is the question dealt with in some of the better poems of this collection. In "Fortunes" (1960), Waddington considers how luck and chance finally don't alter her own specific historical being:

> I went out into the autumn night
> to cry my anger to the stone-blind fields
> just as I was, untraditional, North American
> Jewish, Russian, and rootless in all four,
> religious, unaffiliated, and held
> in a larger-than-life seize of hate.

In a poem about her travels (1966) she describes how around the world she finds both beautiful things and hatred of Jews. Her response here is to suddenly feel that there is nowhere she can be at home. But in "Driving Home" (1968) she seems to find home where she *is*, under the huge signs of the corporations:

> the traffic roars
>   in the mirror
> tells me
>   I am on my way home;
>   home?
> Fool
>   you *are* home
>   you were home
> in the first place
>   and
> if you don't look out
>   it's going to be
> now this minute
>   classic ESSO
>   bloodlit SHELL
> forever

The finest of the older poems in *Driving Home* to me are the poems about love. In "Interval" (1943) Waddington shows a man who has idealized women being forced at last to recognize their humanity.

> Then he knew there is no golden key
> no one has hidden it, there is no joyous room
> where man completes his marriage in a moment,
> there are no easy signposts, only a lonely road
> that each one travels with his suffering.

In "In the Sun" (1958), Waddington tells of an incident where her reason knew

> The world was not more or less
> because we looked at it . . .

But when she is with the man she chooses, then: "in me the world was more". There are also poems that speak of the men that fail her, however: the poignant "Remembering You" (1965):

> When you kissed you
> kissed like a young man
> filled with greeting and gaiety;
>
> when you loved you
> loved like an old man
> filled with slowness and ceremony;
>
> when you left you
> left like a man of no age
> filled with fear that ceremony
>
> had given me something
> to keep more lasting than ritual
> richer and brighter than darkness.

Despite such betrayals, Waddington can celebrate another relationship in "The Lonely Love of Middle Age" (1966). And in "Icons" (1969), she says she carries with her the idea and memory of love, to hold out against the darkness of her age and our age.

> . . . there is
> no such thing
> as love left in
> the world but
> there is still
> the image of it
> which doesn't let
> me wither into
> blindness which
> doesn't let me
> bury myself
> underground which
> doesn't let me
> say yes to the
> black leather police . . .
>
> The world is getting
> dark, but I carry
> icons, I remember
> the summer
> I will never forget
> the light.

Celebrations like this of the dilemmas of Waddington's recent existence seem to me the best and most interesting work she has ever done. These poems speak more directly and openly of her predicament than her earlier work does, and thus the recent poems give me the impression of greater accuracy. I like Waddington's work of the last seven years or so so much better than her previous poems that I find it difficult in my mind not to think of her as a new talent: emerging strong and mature in middle age with a lot to say about that time of life in her social position in modern Canada.

Diane Wakoski

1937–

Diane Wakoski was born on August 3, 1937, in Whittier, California, to John Joseph and Marie (née Mengel) Wakoski. In 1965 she married magazine editor Shepard Sherbell, from whom she was later divorced. She married Michael Watterlord in 1973, but that marriage also ended in divorce in 1975. Since 1982 she has been married to Robert J. Turney. She has taught and lectured at a number of institutions, including the New School for Social Research, and has been a poet-in-residence at the University of Virginia, Michigan State University, the University of Wisconsin, and the University of Washington.

Diane Wakoski has been labeled a Beat Poet, a Confessional Poet, and a Woman Poet, among others; but she resists labels and generalizations, preferring to develop her own aesthetic. Her first book of verse was *Coins and Coffins* (1962); as early as *The George Washington Poems* (1967) Wakoski began to attract attention with her vivid imagery and her development of an intriguing and intricate personal mythology featuring such diverse elements as George Washington, the King of Spain, Beethoven, the woodsman/motorcycle mechanic, and herself, frequently personified as the moon. *Inside the Blood Factory* (1968), *The Motorcycle Betrayal Poems* (1971), *Virtuoso Literature for Two and Four Hands* (1975), and the Greed sequence (collected as *The Collected Greed: Parts 1–13*, 1984) continued to develop her primary themes of love sought and betrayed. She has been praised for her depth of feeling and ear for a well-turned phrase; she has also been criticized for her self-obsession and occasional lack of discipline.

Wakoski has earned a reputation as one of the more individualistic modern poets; while her vision is personal, its intensity speaks powerfully to many readers. Her most recent book of poems is *The Rings of Saturn* (1986).

If Denise Levertov's poems are in danger of being taken too solemnly, ⟨Wakoski's⟩ *The Motorcycle Betrayal Poems* may not be taken seriously enough. Again, the measures are conventional post-Williams and -Lowell, but the range of images and wit is wider and the presentation of self more humorous, ironic, desperate to resist pathos and self-pity, and make the language into a weapon equivalent to the power of men who will not accept the poet as totally equipped lover. Diane Wakoski is expansive—her poems need space to conquer, and she is certainly out to conquer. These are part of an endless autobiography to establish character in a largely male-dominated world, instanced as the bike scene—not so much speed as engineering made into the central male fascination. Warhol's *Bike Boy* is turned inside out. The core is in the final poem:

> That pink dress betrayed my one favorite image
> —the motorcyclist riding along the highway
> independent
> alone
> exhilarated with movement
> a blackbird
> more beautiful than any white ones.
> And the irony
> of my images.
> That you are the motorcycle rider.
> Not I. . . .

The book is a set of variations on these materials—and in fact most of the poems have the form of variations in themselves. Her work has a baroque effect; it is not a book to be read too much at a time, since there is little variety of voice or theme ("Conversations with Jan" contains more invention, especially the sixth). Her poems are letters never sent: "this letter writer, / this passionate piece of paper / you will all / someday / read." The threatening tone here and in the murderous epigraph continues throughout, and fools no one, let alone Diane Wakoski; but the desperation is substantial. She operates in a world of women as adjuncts to men and the erotics of bikes; the poems are survival gestures, but with none of Denise Levertov's political strain. They are dense with information used as defensive attack: a passionately alert sense of the uselessness of self-regard, ⟨. . .⟩ : "Life lived as object lesson / and not as life / fills you with terror / about the continual / juxtaposition of absurdity and / significance." This poem—"The Moon Has a Complicated Geography"—challenges the abstractions of the other poets: "for those of us who never live / except through / the people we love / life is never lived. It is always / somehow / an exercise for living it." Diane Wakoski's love poems care for facts rather than psychological convention and those orgasmic obsessions brandished by the mob who discovered Reich last month. Tradition appears in how she is haunted by the moon, Diana the huntress: "Poets have speculated about me over long. / At last I am circled, / photographed, / and soon to be explored." So her poems stand firmly where Female Liberation movements, moon shots, and mythical tradition meet: a rare intersection, thoroughly projected in "I Lay Next to You All Night," which seems to cover more of American culture than whole books of sociology. Her dry appraisals have the whole culture under observation because she stands to lose if all she has is self-consciousness, stoicism, and pathos: "Love me / if you can. / I will not make it easy for you." So equality, in "The Equinox," is the book's pivot: "something which none of us has." She takes over the trite masculine imagery of guns, bullets, bikes, the Angels, mustaches, and male Beethoven-playing maestros, for her own usage and dumps them for the man who relaxes as a man with his own kind of body and life, exercising his ability to live as the necessary other coupling of sexual love. The rest is, broadly, perversion and its main image, games and women as adjuncts to sport.

Too much consecutive reading in *The Motorcycle Betrayal Poems* begins to bore with the sameness of materials, which arises partly from the poet not penetrating, as for instance Burroughs does in *The Wild Boys*, to the evil of what he calls "total need"—whether of bikes or men or sexual fulfillment or anything else. But at least the need is open—the poet's assumption of the role of sexual haven for "straight men," the seduction of the "small and soft and elegant," and the undermining of such male dominants as con men, gangsters, robbers, and embezzlers. On the other hand, she wants one aspect of them to win, mustaches and all—she is in love with "wanted men." So that, if one considers the book politically, the center is conquest in "The Ten-Dollar Cab Ride," a Poem exercising a finely various ease with women and the moon, and the moonshot as an attack on Diana the White. But the moon is lit by the sun: the plight is sidestepped in the poem but the suicidal potential remains and links the book with Denise Levertov's and much else in our time. The danger is the seventeenth-century pile-up of analogies, milking an image-potential till it withers into coy rhetoric ("Black Leather Because Bumblebees Look Like It"). But she can also speak out without image—most movingly in "To the Wives."

If betrayal seems inevitable from the book, it is because the poems demonstrate the locked possibilities of the body, the recalcitrance in the poet who has become armored in toughness and over-demand, and the terror of "the failure / on such a simple level / of human responsiveness." Diane Wakoski has a radically metaphorical imagination, rare in contemporary American poetry, and nearly old-fashioned. Her conception of female vulnerability in the male-dominated world, with all its nagging obsessiveness, maps its region conclusively.—ERIC MOTTRAM, "The Limits of Self-Regard," *Parn*, Fall–Winter 1972, pp. 160–62

ROSELLEN BROWN
From "Plenitude and Dearth"

Parnassus: Poetry in Review, Spring–Summer 1973, pp. 51–58

Twice in the last year I've encountered poems by college girls that refer in obvious fascination to Diane Wakoski's face; one, naming its source, referred readers to her poem, "I Have Had to Learn to Live with My Face." Referred to the poet, that is, through her poem, curious about what she "really" looks like, uncertain whether this admission of homeliness ("no one could love it . . . a desert mountain, a killer . . .") is an artful exaggeration or a hard, mean fact with which they will be able to go on identifying even after they've checked her out. Wakoski is a superstar of poetry in this sense, transcending the poems in which she stars, compelling people to think of *her*. When they do, they see themselves, not idealized but—in this day of real girl-next-door movie stars with Barbra Streisand noses, men on the Alka Seltzer ads who look like the awful Joneses, or, worse, like the face in the mirror—as themselves.

Her poems ⟨in *Smudging*⟩ create a persona who is not heroic but who is demanding nonetheless; the apotheosis of all our own plainness to a level where its other, presumably more basic, virtues *must* begin, mercifully, to be searched for. Because she lacks beauty, the man who lives with her, she says, "must see something beautiful

> Like a dark snake coming out of my mouth,
> or love the tapestry of my actions, my life.

That is the best hope of all adolescents, certainly, except (or many especially?) the beautiful ones whom everyone is happy enough never to bother to get to know. Before one is confirmed in believing in his value (or has it confirmed by love and work) one does a lot of worrying about one's face: as metaphor and as actuality. And at the risk of having this sound like the Eureka! in that Alka Seltzer advertising campaign, still I can see it's true; Wakoski has had the good sense to make her whole style out of this ordinariness, which she expresses in plain talk, no shit, an unadorned, "straight," anti-poetic voice[1]—in skillful alternation with its opposite. For all her unfeigned simplicity and the accommodation to reality her lack of conventional, hence easy, beauty demands (as metaphor for all the other good reasons for being open and honest), it is hard to think of a poet who writes more lyrically: invoking jewels and flowing hair, exotic animals, landscapes as stylized and exaggerated as fairy tales—in these she is Diana of the moon. So, she has hit her readers, especially the young ones on the college circuits, twice: first precisely where they live and then where they go to dream. In this her poetry is more like Brautigan's prose than even his own poetry: cool, syntactically innocent, damn hard sometimes, fresh with the insights given only to the undeceived—while underneath beats a heart as sentimental as old gold.

(I should add, parenthetically, that her ideal in men, vigorously and endlessly and attractively detailed, is similarly double: much conventional machismo—motorcycles and mustaches, a Clyde to her Bonnie—crossed with the truest sweetness and patience; the warrior-prince, virile, a little menacing, but gentle up close, a tender lover of poets and plain women. There must be three men like him in America, and two probably have the wrong kind of mustache.)

Here are parts of a poem called "The Duchess Potatoes" that illustrates every one of these polarities of diction (and desire):

> my people grew potatoes,
> my hair is lanky and split edged and dishwater blonde.
> My teeth are strong but yellowish
> I am fleshy without muscles
> my energy is thin and sharp like gravy
> but I crawl into bed as if I were pulling a counter of rubies over me,
> dream past all my lower class barbed wire
> walk down the street in a silk glove
> try to scrub myself to an aristocratic bone,
> and always come back to the faded colors,
> lumpy shape
> . . .
> And I,
> peasant,
> have no compassion for the lumps,
> the lumpy mashed potatoes
> that weren't beaten with enough butter and milk.
> and made so fine
> so fine
> they were called "Duchess"

The same dichotomy is beautifully realized in the title poem which begins, ambiguously, "I come out of a California orange grove / the way a meteor might be / plucked out of an Arizona desert." Struggling beyond the disastrous memories of a childhood in which warmth was uncertain, she, like the delicate orange trees that need smudging, sees her life undefended, in constant danger of a killing frost—so she ends by asserting herself in the face of the men who have constantly deserted her:

> There is part of me that trembles,
> and part of me that reaches for warmth,
> and part of me that breaks open

UPI/BETTMANN NEWSPHOTOS

KURT VONNEGUT

UPI/BETTMANN NEWSPHOTOS

ROBERT PENN WARREN

UPI/BETTMANN NEWSPHOTOS

ALICE WALKER

NEW YORK TIMES

DIANE WAKOSKI

UPI/BETTMANN NEWSPHOTOS

EUDORA WELTY

AP/WIDE WORLD PHOTOS

GLENWAY WESCOTT

FARRAR, STRAUS & GIROUX

NATHANAEL WEST

like mythic fruit,
the golden orange every prince will fight
to own.

In this book as in much of Wakoski's previous work, I find myself fascinated and puzzled by what I think are lapses of a sort, but which in the end may pull with the general strategy of her writing; may be, in fact, part of what prods readers like the college girls I mentioned to look outside the poems at the poet as if *she* were an artifact, or as if the poems were not. In the midst of this tautly-constructed poem (half her poems are—seem—to work by causal accretion, the other half are "composed" and often more abstract), there will come a conjunction of voices like this:

and I who grew up in a little house
frightened of soot and angry
at the voices of men in the night,
long for you
with all the mystery of my childhood.
You threw me out once
for a whole year,
and I felt that all the masculinity I knew about was
gone:
saw blades humming through stiff wood,
the hand that threaded wire into place and made
light
the soaking parts of motorcycles and cars which
were sloshed free of old dirt and put meticulously
back
into now running
machines,
the hands and mind which could fix the shower
or the furnace if either
didn't work.
("Smudging")

Or:

You are
that new snow covering our late-night street.
You are so different from me,
a strong man who builds, thinks designs,
a mechanic and architect,
an important freeway in my life.
("A Winter Poem for Tony Weinberger Written on the Occasion of Feeling Very Happy")

In one of the *Motorcycle Betrayal Poems,* during a fanciful (which is not to say un-serious) shooting, she imagines herself toppling her lover, "you big loud symphony who fell asleep drunk," and says:

I shoot you each time in that wide dumb back,
insensitive to me,
glad for the mild recoil of the gun
that relieves a little of my repressed anger
each time I discharge a bullet into you;
. . .
You too, betrayer,
you who will not give me your name as even a
token of affection;
("Love Letter Postmarked Van Beethoven")

Two long poems, "Greed," Parts 3 and 4, are in fact a solid mass of just such extraordinarily laborious and awkward prose. (I haven't seen Parts 1 and 2, published a few years ago by Black Sparrow.) The first is an ironically self-excused raking over the coals of various of her poet friends for the assorted violences they have done her, their wives, themselves—naming the names, just as in the past she has enjoyed the bold naming of the men she's liked or wanted, with all the reasons why. (And later, in a parody of Anne Waldman's style, she apologizes, or at least has a laugh at herself for it.) But she doesn't manage to bring it off in "Greed," though not because she has indulged meanness in herself or the voyeur in us: rather because the friend, not the poet, nags in her most abstract voice, a bloody bore. Her perceptions here are occasionally interesting:

Rarely do I express my hostilities
without also defending the person
I feel anger towards.
Sometimes defending him more than
he would himself.

But:

Desire
for the purpose of control or
excluding others
or of total ownership
is greed
whether motivated out of extreme need
or sheer petulance.
The effect can only debase the spirit.

The *Communist Manifesto* is a lot more riveting than that. When her list of disappointing friends is finished, she goes on to complicate the role of "landlord of the emotions" mightily and often subtly, dragging along every metaphor she mentions, for later elaboration. Perhaps her intention is to seem not to be able to let go of anything: greed exemplified. In any event, there is a great deal of slackness to be got through; but there are few poets whose styles have so much amplitude—like pockets and folds in a huge garment into which all manner of encumbrance can be stuffed. Add to this regrettably spontaneous (i.e., unworked-sounding) style which occasionally takes over, Wakoski's other primitive quality—in content, not diction—and once again it appears that all of it, flaws and all, works toward a larger picture of incredibly naive open-ness. But past a certain point it begins to resemble simple-mindedness, and I begin to lose patience with it:

You are going to ask me about my life now.
Why it is such a failure,
why I have never found a husband,
a man to love me,
why I have no family,
why no one wants me
very much.
And I am going to tell you
the story of a woman who collects wishbones.
She is hard to talk to.
She feels like a failure.
She sometimes is very beautiful
with long hair and a soft voice
but she is often alone and
she writes poems to keep from breaking her heart all
the time
because she falls in love with men
who don't take her seriously.
("Wishbones")

With Wakoski's long wordy books, one can reach in anywhere for an illustration of flaccid writing. In "The Mariachis—A Glimpse"—is the qualification meant to excuse a fragment, an unfinished poem?—there is a line that galled me out of all proportion to its significance: "I see another party of local people—about twenty." Again, it's a failure of ear, or sloppiness where her natural ear wasn't working, by a poet who, granted, does not work for delicacy and subtle refinements (except in certain short, gem-like poems which seem to announce themselves on the page before you've read them:

swimming in white margin, they have been whipped into frugal form). Granted she achieves her effects by building somewhat crudely with big blocky statements. If one were to see Wakoski's poems as whole languages, they would be synthetic, rather than analytic—structures that heap up and join words rather than build long and complex and precise single words which enclose meaning. This may seem irrelevant carping about that kind of poet, but I've just been re-reading one of my touchstones in useful criticism, the chapter of Hugh Kenner's *The Pound Era* in which he looks closely at a very spare William Carlos Williams poem and traces the syntactic dependencies in the poem: how each "as" or "then" pulls with it certain weights of expectation, sets whole systems of necessity in taut motion. And though this poem (about a cat walking, setting his feet in a flowerpot) seems just about the single most unlikely poem to cite in a discussion of Wakoski, who chats and ambles and declaims in full voice, unashamed, raunchy, idealizing, nonetheless I find myself, ungratefully, looking at this her twelfth book (153 pages; less of a solid structure than her last, also long, *Motorcycle Betrayal Poems*, which was like variations on a theme) and wondering, if there were less, would more of it be strong and shapely? She is a marvelously abundant woman who sounds, in her non-goddess moments (which predominate), like some friend of yours who's flung herself down in your kitchen to tell you something urgent and makes you laugh and respect her good old-fashioned guts at the same time ("So then I told him . . ."). Would that flow itself be curtailed if less of it were to see the light of print?

She can write poems with extreme and immaculate care. See the disciplined tone, no less "realistic" and conversational than in the lesser poems, of "Steely Silence," of "Sour Milk." See the tour de force "Screw, A Technical Love Poem," which manages in spite of its ostensible subject, to be a poem about love, with all the other implications of its title held quite miraculously at bay. See "The Joyful Black Demon of Sister Clara Flies Through the Midnight Woods on Her Snowmobile," whose title is a joyous catalog of the remarkable contents of Wakoski's mind when it is really engaged; whose lines are a richly orchestrated music which feels like a vastly extended sestina because of the tolling recurrence of words and images.

Smudging contains so much that is good that I resent being worn into satiety and inattention by its length, and by all that is easy and disheveled and nagging in it. What she is trying to do is well-served by her two kinds of voices, the broad and profane and the more precise and intellectualizing, and she deserves a lot of latitude in return for that versatility. ("Building up / in any way / a structure that will permit you to say / no, / a structure that will permit you to say / yes.") There is little this poet says that is uninteresting per se; but she can and should be more than interesting.

Notes

1. Her publishers even caught the *look* of that voice in *The Motorcycle Betrayal Poems* (Simon & Schuster 1971). The print is large, black, sanserif: blunt, right on.

ALAN WILLIAMSON

From "The Future of Personal Poetry"
Introspection and Personal Poetry
1985, pp. 149–65

It would be surprising if the sense of the impossibility of knowing the self, or of the elusiveness of what is "deep" and valuable in it, that preoccupies the range of poets from Ashbery to Strand to Wright had not affected the writing of explicitly autobiographical poetry in America. Moreover, the very success of "confessional" modes posed a threat to younger personal poets, since the idea of authenticity ⟨. . .⟩ virtually demanded a reinvention of the tactics of autobiography to correspond to what was unique in the self under examination. In the early 1970s, there was a sense of diminishing returns. As more and more young confessors began their sentences and stanzas in the same way, combining a blurting factual candor with an uneasy complacency at assuming the rhetorical mantle of Lowell, Plath, or Berryman, what had begun as a method of investigating sensibilities became, itself, a sensibility. And there was a revulsion of taste against the whole enterprise ⟨. . .⟩

For later poets, I think it was easy to feel not only that this convention was artificial and confining (as all conventions eventually become), but that it assumed too easy a presentational mastery over the mysteries of the self. More recent poetry has tended to take a more petitionary attitude toward those mysteries, going deeper or else going shallower. Going deeper, one finds a poetry that has absorbed many of the ideals of the middle generation, emphasizing dream-like images, symbols of identity at once more central and more enigmatic than the flux of daily feeling. Going shallower, one finds a poetry that confines itself to the drama, the bafflement, the abstraction of a person explaining himself to others, risking the prosaic and even the banal in a new version of the perennial Wordsworthian return to actual speech. In this poetry one finds a reaction against the cult of the image, a defense of the "discursive" (as it is called in Robert Pinsky's *The Situation of Poetry*, in many ways the manifesto of this current of taste) which might have troubled even the poets of Lowell's generation, committed as they were to Eliot's ideal of unified sensibility, and with it to a fairly continuous presence of sense impressions in poetry.

But the most important distinction to be made is the relative humility of both modes toward the self, in comparison with the typical confessional mode. The first mode, by restricting itself to a kind of dream narration, concedes or pretends to concede that the inner language is not reducible to paraphrase past a certain point. At the other extreme, the plain style poet, by insisting on the need for paraphrase, for explanation, implicitly sides with the puzzlement of others—even admits that the conscious self shares in that puzzlement—thus abandoning the Rimbaldian project of finding an equivalent for the narcissistic taste, or atmosphere, of his own psyche. ⟨. . .⟩

II

⟨. . .⟩ I should like to pause over a poet who has, at different periods, fitted both categories, but whose particular distinction is inventiveness of structure, a new variation on what I have called the reflexive mode. Diane Wakoski has been one of the sadder casualties of the shift in taste in the last decade; she is so fixed in many readers' minds as an artless instance of heart-on-the-sleeve confessionalism that a serious, discriminating discussion of her work from the formal point of view is almost impossible to find. Wakoski has partly invited this reputation, by overproduction, self-repetition, and a peculiarly unfortunate habit of arguing with her critics in her own poems. Still, I don't think the reputation will survive even a cursory reading of her early poems, or a careful reading of the best of her later ones.

All of Wakoski's best poems do essentially the same thing: they use a governing image or group of images to look at the same situation from a number of perspectives, rather as a cubist painting (to use one of Wakoski's favorite points of comparison) might look at a chair from three sides at once. The images tend, especially in the early poems, to be splendid, scary, even over-romantic (gold scorpions, green horses, a girl joining hands with the wind). One feels that the legacy of Spanish surrealism came almost too ready to hand to a lonely young woman already inclined to prefer fantasy to reality. And yet the design of the poems works to correct this, from the very beginning. The cumulative effect of the repetition of images is claustrophobia, not escape. "There are so many ways / of telling the story," a very inventive poem concludes: but the feeling—in context—is clearly one of gloom and entrapment. The poems insistently speak of emotions as static things, "structures": "The structure of anger / is repetition"; "the structure of dream, / like a harness / lowered over my head." The macabre ending of the early poem "Tour"—

> I hope you will not be alarmed to learn
> that you may not leave this place again;
> because you have seen the black fox
> mate the white,
> and to satisfy your curiosity
> let me say,
> both animals are now
> dead

—is paradigmatic both in its dry crispness, and in its sense of what it means to close a symbolic circuit, to purify and mate the mind's internal opposites. And one remembers that Wakoski's other early love, besides Lorca, was Stevens—the Stevens of *Harmonium*, whose rather chilly factorings of aesthetic impressions (think of "Domination of Black") convey the same sense of the mind's inability to escape from itself, in epistemological terms, that Wakoski's poems do in emotional terms.[1]

Given these preoccupations, Wakoski would be a born writer of rather tight formal poems, and one can't help being ambivalent about the early identification with the idea of the avant-garde that steered her in other directions. A sestina, for instance, seems the perfect vehicle for her sense of proliferation and sameness, the mind trapped by its images; and when she in fact writes one, "Sestina from the Home Gardener," it is at once one of her best poems and a strong contender for the best contemporary example of the form.

The choice of end-words tends to be the *pons asinorum* of sestina-writers. If the words are too emotionally laden, too wide in their applications, the poem gets easy and dull. If they are too narrow, it becomes gimmicky. Wakoski chooses with discrimination. Three of her words, "sections," "precise," and "pointed," are narrow enough to be a challenge, yet resonant: they can suggest the pleasant crispness of work with tools; they can also turn into images of self-division, dismemberment, aggression. ("Pointed" also carries a phallic suggestion, and a suggestion of direction or distance.) The other words run an ascending scale from the ambiguously mechanical to the unequivocally emotional: "removed," "unfamiliar," "losses."

The title suggests the poem's rather wistful, charming premise: a woman turns to fixing up house and garden (or a woman artist to art) to fill the empty time, and the emotional emptiness, after a marriage ends. But the tasks quickly become a language for her emotions and bodily sensations. There is a touch, here, of Plath's sense of being victimized to the point of being turned into a thing by one's relations to others; but with a difference:

> These dried-out paint brushes which fell from my
> lips have been removed
> with your departure; they are such minute losses
> compared with the light bulb gone from my brain,
> the sections
> of chicken wire from my liver, the precise
> silver hammers in my ankles which delicately banged
> and pointed
> magnetically to you. Love has become unfamiliar

We feel at once how much more various in tone, and gently witty, Wakoski's images are than Plath's: from the gritty feel of the inner scratchiness, raggedness of lust (associated with the liver in Elizabethan physiology), to the wonderful image for a delicate, sexually self-aware woman walking. Wakoski's poems from this early period are full of similarly arresting, original uses of mechanistic imagery to convey the helpless indwelling force of erotic feeling: "Blue of the heaps of beads poured into her breasts," or the "delicate / displacement of / love" that "has / pulled all my muscles / diagonal." These images surely enhance, at least as much as they diminish, the humanity and feminity of the speaker. Yet they have disturbing implications, which grow stronger as the sestina advances: that emotions, like tools, have an existence separate from the will and consciousness; that, like objects, they can be "removed"; that the poem's sense of the self is a fragmented one, allowing the possibility of integration through love, but not of self-integration.

The poem proves this, in a sense, by exploring all the avenues of autonomous integration. For a while, art seems stronger, more powerful, in the absence of the lover ("each day my paint brushes get softer and cleaner—better tools, and losses / cease to mean loss"). Yet there is an uneasy awareness that parts of the self are becoming "unfamiliar," and so given over to nightmare or paranoiac projection: "the unfamiliar / corridors of my heart with strangers running in them, shouting"; the "sections / of my brain growing teeth" while "unfamiliar / hands tie strings through my eyes." The mind sinks, wittily and honestly, from art to money as a source both of power and of connection:

> and I explain autobiographically that George Washington is sympathetic to my losses;
> His face or name is everywhere. No one is unfamiliar
> with the American dollar, and since you've been
> removed
> from my life I can think of nothing else. A precise
> replacement for love can't be found. But art and
> money are precise
> ly for distraction. The stars popping out of my blood
> are pointed
> nowhere.

Not the least graceful aspect of the poem is the way in which this rather outrageously relaxed conversational voice—which points up the speaker's search for autonomy, and not incidentally breaks up the potentially drab unity of the form—plays off against the entrapping returns of surrealistic imagery. At last the speaker bursts out:

> But there are losses
> Of the spirit like vanished bicycle tires and losses
> of the body, like the whole bike, every precise
> bearing, spoke, gear, even the unfamiliar
> handbrakes vanished.

Only through the body does the self cease to be fragmented; and "the real body has been removed."

> Removed by the ice tongs. If a puddle remains what
> losses
> can those sections of glacier be? Perhaps a precise

count of drops will substitute the pointed mountain,
far away, unfamiliar?

The concluding metaphor drives home the terrible central insight: how the emotional equipment of the self in isolation is precisely the same as, yet utterly different from, that of the self integrated in the body, through love; and how nothing can be done about it. But the "precise count of drops" is also, of course, the sestina form itself—its exhaustive monotony, the sum of parts that will never be a whole.

This poem is a perfect instance of the reflexive mode, in its tightly drawn net of images, its unity-in-diversity, and above all in the way in which the self is driven, fighting all the way, to a recognition of the limits of its mastery over itself. Other poems may use the method with a more "cubist" clash of contradictory perspectives; they may also lead it toward a happy ending, but with the same sense of the mind's confusions and misdirections. Consider, for instance, the lighter and happier "Rescue Poem." It is another poem about tools: "the tools to chop down an invisible telephone booth." The telephone booth is, fairly clearly, the solipsistic sensibility, the "shadow foot between the real foot and the ground." The "tools" are the body made vivid to itself, in the metaphorical extensions of sexuality ("diamond breasts and a silver penis"), in an almost frightening imagery of perception as incorporation ("an apple inside the ear"), and in a vision of passive desires become active faculties ("teeth chipped out of the navel," a "saw made of all the soft parts of / a cheek"). But if the images can proliferate endlessly, the event is single, simple, and unexpected: "Need I say the obvious? / That you found the door?" And yet, the sealed consciousness is not, finally, left behind; rather, it becomes one with the resurrected body—in what is at once a sexual image and an image of the brain's electrical intricacy—as the poet says

Join me
on the silver
wirey
inside.

It is a charming, rather Zen-like strategy: two incompatible endings which are in reality the same ending. And again it enforces a sense of the mind's limitations, its tendency to look in the wrong or the half-right place, its need of the body, and of others, for its fulfillment.

Some readers, I suspect, will recognize the merit of these early poems but still feel that the discursive turn Wakoski has taken in the last ten years has been an unmitigated disaster, given her lack of critical distance on feelings of self-pity and defensive anger—so obviously unpromising in a poet of wisdom. Four-fifths of the time, perhaps, these readers would be right. Yet Wakoski continues to insist that she is just as much interested in questions of form in these later poems as in her early ones. And every once in a while a poem comes along that is so ingenious in its structural play with its bare and prosaic terms, that it triumphantly vindicates her.

One such poem is "The Story of Richard Maxfield" in *Virtuoso Literature for Two and Four Hands*. The poem deals with the suicide of a homosexual electronic composer, who once made a composition out of tapes of people coughing at concerts, called "Cough Music." More centrally, the poem is a meditation on the mystery of psychic strength: why it is available to some people and not to others of equal intelligence and talent. From the beginning, Maxfield's death is at once an enigma and a banality:

He jumped out of a window.
Or did he shoot himself?
Was there a gun,
or was it pills?
Did anyone see blood?

Banality continues to be the poem's chosen method. It drives home our ignorance concerning psychic strength by its merciless, deliberate overuse of two conventional question-begging expressions: a person who has such strength is "well organized"; one who loses it "falls apart."

He was brilliant and well organized.
And then he fell apart.
He was homosexual and took drugs.
He was brilliant and well organized.
I loved "Cough Music" and could not see how such
a fine
composer could fall apart as Richard fell apart.

But as the words are rubbed clean of what little explanatory value they ever had, the concepts are subtly, unexplicitly given new metaphorical bodies: music for organization—

a piano piece by
Debussy, delicate and sparse,
like a dress you can see through

—and the sensation of coughing for falling apart. And so Maxfield's own subject becomes a way of refiguring and elucidating his fate. The question, why do people cough more during a piece like the Debussy, suggests rich if unexhaustive answers to the question, why do people fall apart? Is it a wish to draw attention to oneself; a wish, on the contrary, "just to join the whole crowd"; or a kind of panic in the face of the sexual and existential nakedness of the clarified life? And the poet, restraining herself from coughing during the Debussy though she feels the mysterious temptation to do so, arrives at a small illustration and assurance of why "I would never fall apart." There is a kind of structural genius in this poem, deliberately choosing the most unpromising materials in order to redeem from within our commonplace, confused ways of "telling our troubles." Most of Wakoski's more controlled later poems aim at something like this, though only a few succeed so completely ("Searching for the Canto Fermo" is one that comes to mind). But at this level of accomplishment in extending the range of poetry, a few are enough; they deserve the envy of many writers who have gotten into the habit of dismissing Wakoski without reading her.

Notes

1. Wakoski's undergraduate thesis at Berkeley was on *Harmonium*, considered as the American equivalent of Surrealism.

ALICE WALKER

1944–

Alice Walker was born on February 9, 1944, in Eatonton, Georgia, to Willie Lee and Minnie Tallulah (née Grant) Walker. She was educated at Spelman College and Sarah Lawrence College (B.A. 1965). She married civil rights lawyer Melvyn Rosenman Leventhal in 1967; they had one child before their divorce in 1976. She has taught at Jackson State College and Tougaloo College, and lectured at Wellesley College and the University of Massachusetts. Since 1977 she has taught at Yale University.

Alice Walker has written five books of poetry, including *Once* (1968) and, most recently, *Horses Make a Landscape More Beautiful* (1984). They have received considerable praise, particularly from the black and feminist communities. However, Walker is primarily known as a novelist. Her first novel, *The Third Life of Grange Copeland* (1970), presents a straightforward narrative of three generations in the life of a poor farm family. It was praised for the sensitivity with which the characters were drawn, but it received little attention from either popular or academic circles. *Meridian* (1976) caused considerably more stir, and is considered by many to be the best novel of the civil rights era. *The Color Purple* (1982), an epistolary novel concerning the growth to maturity of a poor black woman in an oppressive, brutish society, launched Walker to mainstream critical success and bestseller popularity. It received the 1983 Pulitzer Prize and the American Book Award, and was made into an Academy Award–nominated film.

In addition to poetry and novels, Walker has written two volumes of short stories, *In Love and Trouble: Stories of Black Women* (1973) and *You Can't Keep a Good Woman Down* (1981); a biography of Langston Hughes for children; and a book of criticism and social commentary, *In Search of Our Mothers' Gardens: Womanist Prose* (1983), that has been widely praised.

In this arresting and touching novel ⟨*The Color Purple*⟩, Alice Walker creates a woman so believable, so lovable, that Celie, the downtrodden, semi-literate, rural black woman joins a select company of fictional women whom it is impossible to forget.

Raped at fourteen by the man she believes to be her father and to whom she eventually bears two children who are taken from her, Celie is married off to Albert, Mr. _____, as she calls him. Taking along her pretty little sister Nettie, Celie becomes a household slave. Albert beats her, forces himself upon her, refuses even to buy her a decent dress. When he begins to look appreciatively at Nettie, Celie panics and persuades the younger girl to run away. Nettie disappears and is lost to Celie.

In the absence of human warmth, Celie turns to God, pouring out her heart in one letter after another, the difficult form in which the book is written. Everything that happens to her is recorded and commented on, Albert's cruelty, the hopelessness of Celie's life. Then Shug Avery turns up, the only woman Albert had ever wanted to marry, blues singer of some presence and a warm heart. With her arrival, Celie begins to thaw and to know what it is like to love another person. Shug is wild and wicked and delightful. She stands up to Albert and tells him what's what. She persuades him to buy Celie a new dress and to let Celie come and hear her sing. Shug takes the place of Celie's mother, sister, lover, and she gets the onus of Albert's presence off Celie, opening her own bed to him once again. Because of Shug, Celie begins to take tentative steps toward self-realization, and even discovers a talent for making pants, fancy pants, that enables her to start her own business.

Alice Walker is, of course, a feminist and she understands well the circumstances that force a woman into an anti-man stance. Her gallery of women are living examples of man's inhumanity to women: Sophia, wife of Harpo, Albert's eldest son, who only wanting to be herself and not the fantasy woman Harpo thinks she ought to be, changes from a warm, happy woman to a bitter paranoiac who only wants to get through her life without killing anyone. Mary Alice, "Squeak," who takes Sophia's place with Harpo when the latter is jailed for sassing the mayor's wife (white), and who allows her uncle, the warden to rape her in exchange for Sophia's freedom. Even Shug, the indomitable, has her share of suffering at men's hands. Only Nettie (who turns up first in letters that Albert has hidden from Celie; then in person with her missionary husband and Celie's lost children) seems to have escaped the general mayhem, and she is a curiously colorless character. Her letters, by comparison with Celie's, are pedantic, her nature prim. The other women leap out of the book, Nettie stays safely within its confines, as does her husband, Samuel.

But Alice Walker is too much of an artist to write a purely political novel, and so her feminist impulse does not prevent her from allowing her characters, women and men, to grow and change. The men in her story lead miserable lives, too, but like their women they begin to come to terms with what life doles out to them, and accept it. And the women turn from rage to acceptance as well. One of the best scenes in the book occurs as Mr. _____ and Celie sit sewing on the front porch, old now and calm together, and talking about the lessons life has taught them. Albert tells her he has learned to wonder, to wonder about all the things that happen and "the more I wonder, he say, the more I love.

"And people start to love you back, I bet, I say.

"They do, he say, surprise. Harpo seem to love me. Sophia and the children . . ."

They go on sewing and talking and waiting for Shug to come home, and Celie says to herself, "If she come, I be happy. If she don't, I be content.

"And then I figure this the lesson I was supposed to learn."

And so bitterness leaches out into a hard-won wisdom, and the lively characters of Alice Walker's invention become human beings with a life of their own. She is a remarkable novelist, sometimes compared to Toni Morrison, but with a strong, individual voice and vision of her own, and a delicious humor that pervades the book and tempers the harshness of the lives of its people.

Opening with a dedication to the Spirit, the novel ends with a postscript: "I thank everybody in this book for coming. A. W., author and medium." This reader's thanks to the medium; may she call up hosts in the future.—ELIZABETH BARTELME, "Victory over Bitterness," *Com*, Feb. 11, 1983, pp. 93–94

TRUDIER HARRIS
"Violence in *The Third Life of Grange Copeland*"

CLA Journal, December 1975, pp. 238–47

Unlike black writers in whose works the object of violence on the part of blacks is usually the white oppressor, Alice Walker, in *The Third Life of Grange Copeland*, turns for a look at violent acts blacks commit against each other and themselves. The novel is the story of the Copelands, Grange and Margaret, and their son Brownfield, who live under a rural Georgia sharecropping system. As a result of Grange's desertion of his family, Margaret kills her infant son and commits suicide, leaving the fifteen-year-old Brownfield to fend for himself. Grange migrates to New York, stopping on the way for a short visit in a neighboring town with Josie, his fat yellow girlfriend. Grange proceeds from his immoral adventures in Georgia to illegal ones in New York. Convinced that freedom for blacks on northern soil is a myth, he returns south and marries Josie. Meanwhile, Brownfield has married Josie's "adopted" schoolteacher daughter Mem and is following in his father's footsteps of sharecropping, immorality (he takes up with Josie in his father's absence), and brutality to his family. When Brownfield kills Mem, Grange takes in Ruth, his youngest granddaughter, and settles down to the tranquility of a rural Georgia farm. But this tranquility is shattered by the violent climax of the novel.

Brownfield's and Grange's experiences are similar, in that they both become trapped in a Georgia sharecropping system which has the potential to destroy both body and spirit; but the way in which each responds reflects the different extent to which each allows circumstances to triumph over him. Grange escapes the situation physically and to some extent emotionally; Brownfield never does. From his unenthusiastic reception at birth to his violent death, Brownfield is destroying and self-destructive, a personality Walker suggests is only partially accounted for by his involvement in the sharecropping system.

Grange responds to the circumstances controlling his life in a way that evokes understanding from the reader if not condoning of his actions. In the 1920's and 30's, options were few for the black sharecropper who tried to rise above the state predetermined for him by whites. As a representative of this era in black history, Grange's condition is portrayed purely naturalistically. His life is controlled by Mr. Shipley, who literally owns him in the new system of slavery euphemistically called "sharecropping." He has no choices in determining his family's future. Each year, at the end of harvest, he will find that his bill adds up to more than the price of his bales of cotton. He is trapped and he shows his entrapment by "stalking" his tiny cabin like a caged animal and swinging from the rafters to set loose his tensions. Because he is powerless against his oppressor, he turns to exert power in the one place he is presumably dominant, that is, in his home. He threatens his wife with shooting and his son with drowning. When the oppression intensifies, when Brownfield has to go to work instead of school, when the family begins to dissolve, Grange walks away and heads "up Norse." He simply takes himself out of a situation he is impotent to change.

All of this is familiar sociological material (though certainly not nonsense). However, Walker consistently pushes beyond what some might term the typical "bleeding heart" explanations for various black conditions in the United States. Hers is a more demanding idealism. While the reader might be led to understand Grange's problems, Walker does not condone his neglect of family and responsibility. It is not morally right that Grange walks away from his family; but by so doing, he does not directly destroy them physically as Brownfield does under similar circumstances. In fact, it would have been better for Mem and her children if Brownfield had left them. They would not have had to suffer the insults, beatings and death that he calculatedly plans for them. Whereas Grange has only threatened his family, Brownfield continually extends these threats to their physical manifestations. We as readers are not led to understand, condone, or in any way tolerate Brownfield's actions. They are inexcusable considering the time period in which they occur and the various choices he has if he would but exercise them.

Brownfield becomes a completely irresponsible man, forever blaming his station in life on the white folks. Through the forties and fifties and on into the sixties, Brownfield uses sharecropping as the scapegoat upon which to heap all his sins. When Martin Luther King is marching all over America for civil rights, Brownfield is still blaming whites for his not doing anything in life. Such blame might have been justified in the twenties, Walker seems to say, but Brownfield's degeneracy cannot be blamed on sharecropping. He had more options about determining his life; his situation is not at all the naturalistic counterpart to Grange's. Upon his mother's suicide, Brownfield starts for the North. He is *free* at this point. He does not owe Shipley or anyone else in the world one brown cent. Instead of continuing north, he stops at Josie's Dew Drop Inn and becomes resident stud for Josie and her daughter Lorene; when one puts him out of her bed in the middle of the night, he simply goes next door and climbs into bed with the other one. On the way to the Dew Drop Inn, when Brownfield is smothered with attention by a group of "menless" women, Walker comments that he "liked commanding their uninhibited attention."[1] He concludes he's gone far enough when he reaches Josie's and *consciously decides* to wallow in filth and immorality for *two years* before Mem comes home from school and he sees her. Thus, his basic character of irresponsibility and immorality is already set; his tendency to violent and evil doings soon follows.

In order to get Mem as quickly as possible and prevent her from marrying a fellow schoolteacher, Brownfield runs out and contracts work with a nearby farmer. This move becomes a logical extension of his irresponsibility, of his not carefully planning or thinking of the future for himself and his wife, but simply of what he can get for the pleasure of the moment. Initially, he thinks he has done well to marry a schoolteacher. However, when he realizes three years later that he is hopelessly enmeshed in the snare of sharecropping (when he didn't need to be and when he has foolishly, unthinkingly made a wrong choice), he takes it out on Mem. Not content with degrading her by forcing her to quit schoolteaching, Brownfield beats his once plump wife into a skinny ugliness. "Brownfield beat his once lovely wife now, regularly, because it made him feel, briefly, good. Every Saturday night he beat her, trying to pin the blame for his failure on her by imprinting it on her face; and she, inevitably, repaid him by becoming a haggard automatous witch, beside whom even Josie looked well-preserved" (p. 63). Mem becomes a toothless hag before she is thirty.

Because he cannot or will not improve his family's lot, Brownfield does not want Mem to do anything that will outshine him. He steals money she has saved to invest in a house and buys a diseased pig. The second time she saves money for a house, he steals it and buys a car. Finally, Mem gets a job "in town" and signs a lease for a house. When she complains that she is sick of the mess in which they live and sick of Brownfield, he reacts in a typical bestial fashion.

> No sooner had the words fallen out in a little explosive heap than Brownfield's big elephant-hide fist hit her square in the mouth. . . . The one blow had reduced her to nothing; she just hung there from his hands until he finished giving her half-a-dozen slaps, then she just fell down limp like she always did. "You going to move where I says move, you *hear* me?" Brownfield yelled at her, giving her a kick in the side with his foot. . . . "You say one more word, just one more little goddam *peep* and I'll cut your goddam throat!" He fumbled in his pocket for his knife and reached down and grabbed Mem in a loose drunken hug. Mem closed her eyes as he dropped her abruptly against the bedpost and gave her a resounding kick in the side of the head. She saw a number of blurred pale stars, then nothing else. (pp. 98–99)

These scenes are a major contrast to Grange's treatment of his family. Although he threatened Margaret and Brownfield, not once did he carry out a threat, not once did he actually hit either one of them. Instead, he would usually break down in tears and on Sunday morning repentantly go to church. Grange has the potential for feelings of pity, remorse and guilt that Brownfield never has. His children get no show of love from him and Mem is always a handy cushion for his foot. Between bouts of familiar destruction, Walker says, "for fun he poured oil into streams to kill the fish and tickled his vanity by drowning cats" (p. 67).

Mem fights for her children in the matter of the house and exacts submission from Brownfield at gunpoint. They do move to town. Unfortunately, Mem is not violent by nature; she is fighting for the future of her children. Brownfield simply waits to take vengeance until she is persuaded that he has changed and drops her guard. Two miscarriages cause the long-awaited "come down" Brownfield has planned for Mem. While she is ill, he allows the heat to be turned off and the rent to fall two months in arrears. Politely he hands her an eviction notice and announces that they are moving to Mr. J. L.'s place, as he had planned before the move to town. "They arrived at the house he had reserved for her 'come down' in the middle of the night, and even his skin prickled at the sight of it. Mr. J. L. had promised that someone would clean it out, but it was still half full of wet hay. There were no panes in the windows, only wooden shutters. Rain poured into all three of the small rooms, and there was no real floor, only tin, like old roofing, spread out to keep the bottom of the hay bales from getting soggy." (pp. 113–14). Brownfield wants ugliness around him to reflect the ugliness he has within so that he might feel justified in his squalor. The methodicalness with which he calculates injuries to his family are inconceivable with Grange.

Years after his family dissolves, Brownfield relates to Josie, his "bosom buddy," that he killed his own son a few days after its birth because it was albino and ugly. This occurred at Mr. J. L.'s place.

> "An' one night when that baby was 'bout three months old, and it was in January and there was ice on the ground, I takes 'im up by the arm when he was sleeping, and like putting out the cat I jest set 'im outdoors on the do'steps. Then I turned in and went to sleep. 'Fore I dropped off, Mem set up and said she thought she heard the baby but I told her I had done looked at him and for her to go back to sleep. I kept her so wore out them days that she couldn't even argue; she was so tired she didn't fall asleep like folks—she just fell into a coma.
>
> "I never slept so soundly before in my life—
>
> "Now, 'cording to you I done that 'cause I thought that baby was by a white man. But I knowed the whole time that he wasn't. For one thing, although it were white, it looked jest like me—" (p. 233)

Grange's wife Margaret also had an albino son, yet the most violent action Grange ever heaped upon it was a pinch. The calculated act of destruction on Brownfield's part provides again the sharp contrast with his father and shows the extent to which Brownfield likes evil for evil's sake. He is consciously a murderer even when he knows he has no reason to be. Yet, he will not make the choice which will deny a white influence upon him; he never fails to become the violent monster the whites have molded (or at least what he credits them with molding).

Brownfield's ultimate violent act is against his own wife. In a drunken rage on Christmas Eve, while two of his three children shudder in a hen house in fear of him, he empties both barrels of a shotgun into Mem's face. It is significant to point out here that Mr. J. L. had fired Brownfield several weeks or months earlier, presumably because of incompetence as a result of drink. Thus, again, at the specific moment of his greatest violence, he is *free* of any direct influence of whites. Sent to jail for murdering his wife, Brownfield refuses to repent. In jail he cries; but, says Walker, "his tears did not soften him, did not make him analyze his life or his crime. . . . Introspection came hard to Brownfield and was therefore given up before he became interested in it" (p. 174). There is not an element of remorse to compare with Grange's feelings toward his desertion of his family and his indirect responsibility for Margaret's poisoning of her infant son and committing suicide. Grange even accepts his share of what he has indirectly caused his son to become; Brownfield is unforgiving and unrepentant.

As we follow Brownfield's actions of unrelenting cruelty, we are prepared for the final scene of Grange's destruction of his own son. Upon his release from jail, Brownfield with Josie, who has lost Grange's affections to Ruth, his granddaughter, conspire to take Ruth away from Grange. Brownfield does not *want* Ruth; he wants to spite Grange. A white judge friendly to Brownfield is enlisted in the scheme and, in a courtroom pronouncement, turns the daughter's custody over to a father whom she finds thoroughly repulsive. As the judge, "a man who was allowed to play God," dismisses the group and prepares to go fishing, Grange takes his concealed "blue steel Colt .45" and shoots his son to death. He retreats to the seclusion of his farm and meets his own violent death at the hands of pursuing lawmen. Although he dies violently, Grange can die in peace. He has made plans for Ruth's welfare and he knows Brownfield will not be around to threaten that welfare. His act is a necessary evil to destroy evil. It is appropriate that he, as creator or progenitor of Brownfield, should destroy the monster of his loins.

This destruction is necessary because Brownfield has failed to evolve, as his father had started to evolve. He remains responsive to forces that have twisted and destroyed black families for centuries, forces Grange had begun to deny. He has the potential to destroy future black generations that can grow, represented by Ruth; and Walker, through Grange, says no to such a racial suicide. Ruth is the last of the Copeland line. Of his other two surviving children, Brownfield has driven one to prostitution and the other to insanity. Therefore, Grange goes to extreme lengths to prevent a similar fate for Ruth.

Throughout the courses of their actions with sharecropping, we observe Grange's and Brownfield's responses and consistently conclude that they are to be viewed differently. Brownfield's choices reject any application of naturalism to his actions. While Grange's situation is naturalistic at first, even he is able eventually to move beyond that. Even more so, suggests Walker, should Brownfield transcend and move beyond the circumstances that *he allows* to control his life. Because he does not, his father, in an effort to preserve the racial family, must destroy him.

We see with Grange's action at the end of the novel that premeditation is a major element of the violence that results in murder. Unlike Bigger Thomas' accidental killing of Mary Dalton, Grange plans for days in advance the violence he will commit against his son. Margaret kills her son and herself after a similar manner of planning. Even Brownfield is not without strategy as he waits, as if in ambush, for Mem to return home from work in order that he might execute her. For a man to sleep "soundly" while his infant son freezes to death is perhaps the height of planned execution in the novel.

The lack of incidental or accidental occurrence of violence in the novel has interesting implications. Many sociologists have suggested that blacks are more prone to plan violence against other blacks than against the whites who control them. A black man would suffer a hundred times more for committing a crime against a white person than he would for committing the same crime against a black person. (Brownfield spends only seven years in jail for his violent dispatch of Mem.) Also, blacks generally feel that white laws do not protect them to the same degree as whites. Commenting on this phenomenon in the 1930's, Arthur F. Raper writes: "Not infrequently Negroes reported that they, feeling that the authorities would not protect them, had provided for their own protection, oftentimes resulting in a ready use of firearms in trivial matters."[2] Ruth's welfare is far more than a trivial matter to Grange, and such an idea might account for his action in killing Brownfield, because he does not believe (and rightly so) that the judge will protect Ruth's interests. Also, as Raper points out, white laws and courts were seldom lenient to black offenders when they affronted whites in some way. Grange's action in the courtroom is the epitome of saying, "White rule be hanged!" Thus he has sealed his own death warrant.

This theory of black violence may explain Grange's murder, but what of Margaret as suicide and murderess? Few suicides occur in black literature. Four that come to mind under similar circumstances of external control of the characters' lives are William Wells Brown's Clotel in the novel of the same title, the Pattons in Arna Bontemps' "A Summer Tragedy," and Rosa in "The Final Supper." All four of these characters kill themselves when they judge that they cannot escape the outside forces that control their lives. Jess and Jennie Patton can never get out of debt in the sharecropping system and decide to cheat their master of further services by driving their car into a river at the edge of the plantation.[3] Clotel is about to be captured and re-sold into slavery and, thus, cheats her master of the highly valued quadroon sale by jumping off a bridge into the Potomac.[4] Their actions, though sentimentalized, are forms of defiance to those forces that shape their lives. Rosa's actions are an even more overt form of defiance. Before dispatching herself, she poisons the food which has been served at an elaborate dinner for her master's guests and fatally stabs him when he stalks into her bedroom after dinner.[5] However, Margaret's murder and suicide are not defiance; they are a bow of defeat, a resignation to the forces outside. She is *destroyed by* the forces that have dissolved her family; she does not, like the other characters, *destroy herself.*

Margaret becomes a tool of the white power structure; she does a better job of killing herself emotionally and physically than it ever could have. The same theory applies to Brownfield. By extending the mental cruelty that has been heaped upon him to its physical manifestation, Brownfield continues what the whites started and destroys his family and himself in a way that, perhaps, the whites would never have effected. But one's becoming the right hand of the monster who would cut off one's head, Walker seems to suggest, is neither sympathetic nor forgivable. While the reader understands Grange's violent actions, Brownfield's are condemned. Margaret's actions are tossed off in a sentence and the reader is not inclined to dwell on her tragedy.

The key to survival, Walker suggests through her spokesman Grange, is to keep some corner of one's soul sacred from the corrupting abuses of any external, destructive forces. Something within should have kept Brownfield sane and loving. Powerlessness against whites is no excuse to destroy one's family or one's self. In speaking on this subject, Grange comments about Dr. Martin Luther King: "'The thing about him that stands in my mind is that even with them crackers spitting all over him, he gentle with his wife and childrens'" (p. 240). Specifically about Brownfield, he says:

> "And with your [Ruth's] pa, . . . the white folks could have forced him to live in shacks; they might have even forced him to beat his wife and children like they was dogs, so he could keep on feeling something less than shit. But where was the *man* in him that let Brownfield *kill* his wife? What cracker pulled the trigger? And if a cracker did cause him to kill his wife, Brownfield should have turned the gun on himself, for he wasn't no man. He *let* the cracker hold the gun, because he was too weak to distinguish that cracker's will from his! The same was true of me. We both of us jumped our responsibility, and without facing up to at least *some* of his wrong a man loses his muscle." (pp. 215–16)

The difference between Brownfield and Grange is that Grange ultimately does accept responsibility for deserting his family and seeks to make amends through assistance to Brownfield's family ("Grange felt guilty about his son's condition and assuaged his guilt by giving food and money to Brownfield's family"—p. 78) and through his loving protection of Ruth. Brownfield never looks beyond Grange "and the white folks to get to the root of *all* his problems" (p. 214). Grange not only accepts responsibility for his neglect of his family, but also for his own inevitable death. ". . . if one kills he must not shun death in his turn" (p. 162).

Brownfield never grows up; on one occasion when Grange takes food to the family, he notices that Brownfield's face "was as sulky as a child's" (p. 81). People change, Grange continually asserts, in their perceptions and evaluations of the world around them. Brownfield becomes an anachronism in a world that passes him by. This is not to suggest that sharecropping was not cancerous. What is important for Walker is that, where the body is confined, the mind or soul or spirit does not necessarily have to deteriorate along parallel lines. The soul can soar above that which would destroy the body, as Frederick Douglas so long ago discovered in his bondage. Such an idea is not presented as a religious concept (in fact Grange can be said to be blasphemous); it is simply a practical expedient for survival.

Notes

1. Alice Walker, *The Third Life of Grange Copeland* (New York: Avon Publishers, 1970), p. 40. Subsequent references will be taken from this edition with pages indicated in parentheses following the quotations.
2. *Mass Violence in America: The Tragedy of Lynching* (New York: Arno, 1969), p. 35.
3. Langston Hughes, ed., *The Best Short Stories by Negro Writers* (Boston: Little, Brown and Company, 1967), pp. 60–69.
4. *Clotel, or the President's Daughter* (New York: Collier, 1970), p. 177.
5. Barbara Woods, "The Final Supper," in *Ten Times Black*, ed. by Julian Mayfield (New York: Bantam, 1972), pp. 100–111.

MARY HELEN WASHINGTON
"An Essay on Alice Walker"
Sturdy Black Bridges: Visions of Black Women in Literature
eds. Roseann P. Bell, Bettye J. Parker, and Beverly Guy-Sheftall
1979, pp. 133–49

From whatever vantage point one investigates the work of Alice Walker—poet, novelist, short story writer, critic, essayist, and apologist for black women—it is clear that the special identifying mark of her writing is her concern for the lives of black women. In the two books of poetry, two novels, one short story collection, and many essays and reviews she has produced since she began publishing in 1966, her main preoccupation has been the souls of black women. Walker herself, writing about herself as writer, has declared herself committed to "exploring the oppressions, the insanities, the loyalties, and the triumphs of black women."[1] In her first four published works—*Once*,[2] her earliest book of poetry; *Revolutionary Petunias*,[3] also poetry; *The Third Life of Grange Copeland*,[4] her first novel; *In Love and Trouble*,[5] a collection of thirteen stories—and her latest novel, *Meridian*,[6] there are more than twenty-five characters from the slave woman to a revolutionary woman of the sixties. Within each of these roles Walker has examined the external realities facing these women as well as the internal world of each woman.

We might begin to understand Alice Walker, the apologist and spokeswoman for black women, by understanding the motivation for Walker's preoccupation with her subject. Obviously there is simply a personal identification. She says in her interview with John O'Brien, "I believe in listening—to a person, the sea, the wind, the trees, but especially to young black women whose rocky road I am still traveling."[7] Moreover her sense of personal identification with black women includes a sense of sharing in their peculiar oppression. In some length she describes her own attempts at suicide when she discovered herself pregnant in her last year of college and at the mercy of everything, especially her own body. Throughout the interview with this writer in 1973,[8] Ms. Walker spoke of her own awareness of and experiences with brutality and violence in the lives of black women, many of whom she had known as a girl growing up in Eatonton, Georgia, some in her own family. The recurrent theme running throughout that interview and in much of her other pieces on women is her belief that "Black women . . . are the most oppressed people in the world."[9]

In one of her earliest essays, "The Civil Rights Movement: What Good Was It?"[10] she herself recalls "being young and well-hidden among the slums,"[11] knowing that her dreams of being an author or scientist were unattainable for a black child growing up in the poorest section of rural Georgia, that no one would encourage a black girl from the backwoods to become an artist or writer. In the same essay she recounts an episode in her mother's life that underscores her sensitivity to the peculiar oppression of black women. She saw her mother, a woman of heavy body and swollen feet, a maid in the houses of white women for forty years, having raised eight children in Eatonton, Georgia, turn to the stories of white men and women on television soap operas to satisfy her yearnings for a better life:

> My mother, a truly great woman who raised eight children of her own and half a dozen of the neighbors' without a single complaint—was convinced that she did not exist compared to "them." She subordinated her soul to theirs and became a faithful and timid supporter of the "Beautiful White People." Once she asked me in a moment of vicarious pride and despair, if I didn't think that "they" were "jest naturally smarter, prettier, better."[12]

Walker understands that what W. E. B. Du Bois called double consciousness, "this sense of always looking at one's self through the eyes of others, of measuring one's soul by the tape of a world that looks on in amused contempt and pity,"[13] creates its own particular kind of disfigurement in the lives of black women, and that, far more than the external facts and figures of oppression, the true terror is within; the mutilation of the spirit *and* the body. Though Walker does not neglect to deal with the external *realities* of poverty, exploitation, and discrimination, her stories, novels, and poems most often focus on the intimate reaches of the inner lives of her characters; the landscape of her stories is the spiritual realm where the soul yearns for what it does not have.[14]

In the O'Brien interview Ms. Walker makes a statement about Elechi Amadi's *The Concubine*, a Nigerian novel, and in that statement there is an important revelation about Walker's own writings. She sees Amadi as unique among black writers because through his book he exposes the subconscious of a people; that is, he has written about the dreams, rituals, legends, and imaginings which contain the "accumulated collective reality of the people themselves."[15] It would be possible to apply that same description to Walker's writings about black women, particularly the stories in *In Love and Trouble*, through which we can see a conscious effort by Walker to explore the imaginings, dreams, and rituals of the subconscious of black women which contains their accumulated collective reality. We begin this analysis of Walker's writings with a discussion of her personal identification with the lives of black women because it is that internal personal sharing that has put Walker in touch with this selective reality. Speaking of her short story "The Revenge of Hannah Kemhuff," Walker says:

> In that story I gathered up the historical and psychological threads of the life some of my ancestors lived, and in the writing of it I felt joy and strength and my own continuity. I had that wonderful feeling writers get sometimes, not very often, of being *with* a great many people, ancient spirits, all very happy to see me consulting and acknowledging them, and eager to let me know, through the joy of their presence that indeed I am not alone.[16]

One vital link to those "historical and psychological threads" of her ancestors' lives is the stories passed on to her by her mother, stories which Walker absorbed through years of listening to her mother tell them. The oral stories are often the basis for her own stories, as are the lives and stories of people she grew up with in Eatonton, Georgia. Once when questioned about the violence and pain in the lives of so many of her women, she recounted an incident from her childhood which was the basis for the story of Mem in Walker's novel *The Third Life of Grange Copeland.* When she was thirteen, a friend's father killed his wife, and Walker, a curious child, saw the mother's body laid out on a slab in the funeral home:

> . . . there she was, hard working, large, overweight, Black, somebody's cook, lying on the slab with half her head shot off, and on her feet were those shoes that I describe—hole in the bottom, and she had stuffed paper in them . . . we used to have, every week, just such a murder as these (in my home town), and it was almost always the wife and sometimes the children.[17]

The true empathy Alice Walker has for the oppressed woman comes through in all her writings—stories, essays, poems, novels. Even in a very brief review of a book of poetry by a woman who calls herself "Ai," Ms. Walker exhibits, almost with conscious design, her instinctive concern for the experiences of women. The choice of *Ai* as a pen name appeals to Ms. Walker because of the images of women it suggests:

> And one is glad she chose "Ai" as her name because it is like a cry. If I close my eyes and say the word (the sound) to myself, it is to see a woman raising an ax, to see a woman crying out in childbirth or abortion, to see a woman surrendering to a man who is oblivious to the sound of her true—as opposed to given—name.

Raising an ax, crying out in childbirth or abortion, surrendering to a man who is oblivious to her real name—these are the kinds of images which most often appear in Ms. Walker's own writing and have prompted critic Carolyn Fowler to say that Walker has the true gift of revealing the authentic "Heart of Woman" in her stories.

What particularly distinguishes Alice Walker in her role as apologist[18] and chronicler for black women is her evolutionary treatment of black women; that is, she sees the experiences of black women as a series of movements from women totally victimized by society and by the men in their lives to the growing developing women whose consciousness allows them to have control over their lives.

In historical terms the women of the first cycle belong to the eighteenth and nineteenth centuries and the early decades of the twentieth century. Although only one of Walker's characters is a slave, the institution of slavery set up the conditions and environment for the period immediately following, extending from the end of the Reconstruction Era to the first two decades of the twentieth century. Borrowing the term first used by novelist Zora Neale Hurston, the black women of this period are "the mules of the world," carrying the burdens heaped upon them by society and by the family, the victims of both racial and sexual oppression. Walker calls them her "suspended" women: a concept she develops in an important historical essay entitled "In Search of Our Mothers' Gardens: The Creativity of the Black Woman in the South," published in *Ms.* magazine in May 1974. Walker explains this state of suspension as caused by pressures in society which made it impossible for the black women of this era to move forward:

> They were suspended in a time in history where the options for Black women were severely limited. . . . And they either kill themselves or they are used up by the man, or by the children, or by . . . whatever the pressures against them. And they cannot go anywhere. I mean, you can't, you just can't move, until there is room for you to move *into.* And that's the way I see many of the women I have created in fiction. They are closer to my mother's generation than to mine. They had few choices.[19]

Suspended in time and place by a century, an era that only acknowledged them as laborers, these women were simply defeated in one way or another by the external circumstances of their lives. For such women—the great-grandmothers of the black women of contemporary times—pain, violence, poverty, and oppression were the essential content of their lives. Writer June Jordan calls them "black-eyed Susans—flowers of the blood-soaked American soil."

If these were the pressures and obstacles against the ordinary black woman who existed in the eighteenth and nineteenth centuries, what, then, did it mean for a black woman to be an artist, or want to be an artist in such times? Walker poses the question: "How was the creativity of the Black woman kept alive, year after year, century after century, when for the most of the years Black people have been in America, it was a punishable crime for a Black person to read or write?"[20] If the freedom to read and write, to paint, to sculpt, to experience one's creativity in any way did not exist, what became of the black woman artist? Walker says it is a question with an answer "cruel enough to stop the blood."

> For these grandmothers and mothers of ours were not "Saints," but Artists; driven to a numb and bleeding madness by the springs of creativity in them for which there was no release. They were Creators, who lived lives of spiritual waste, because they were so rich in spirituality—which is the basis of art—that the strain of enduring their unused and unwanted talent drove them insane. Throwing away this spirituality was their pathetic attempt to lighten the soul to a weight their work-worn, sexually abused bodies could bear.[21]

Of course, in spite of these many circumstances in which the art of the black woman was denied or stifled, some evidences of the creative genius of the black women of that age still remain. Walker cities the poetry of Phillis Wheatley, the quilt making of so many anonymous black women of the South, the wise woman selling herbs and roots, as well as the brilliant and original gardens designed and cultivated by her own mother, as evidence that the creative spirit was nourished somehow and showed itself in wild and unlikely places. Though Ms. Walker is the first writer to define and develop the concept of the black women of the post-Reconstruction period as "suspended," as artists "hindered and thwarted by contrary instincts," the suspended black woman is a recurrent theme in the writers who deal with black women. Many of the black women characters in women writers from Frances Harper to Toni Morrison, as well as the women of Jean Toomer's *Cane*, are suspended women, artists without an outlet for their art or simply women of deep spirituality who "stumble blindly through their lives . . . abused and mutilated in body . . . dimmed and confused by pain, unaware of the richness of their gifts but nonetheless suffering as their gifts are denied."[22]

So we have part one of Walker's personal construct of the black woman's history—the woman suspended, artist thwarted and hindered in her desires to create, living through two centuries when her main role was to be a cheap source of cheap labor in the American society. This is the construct developed mainly in Walker's interviews and essays: How, then, does this construct fit in the fiction of Alice Walker?

Most of Walker's women characters belong to the first part of the cycle—the suspended woman. Three women from her first novel, *The Third Life of Grange Copeland*, and seven of the thirteen women from her short story collection, *In Love and Trouble*, are women who are cruelly exploited, spirits and bodies mutilated, relegated to the most narrow and confining lives, sometimes driven to madness. They are the contemporary counterparts of the crazy, pitiful women Jean Toomer saw in the South in the early 1920s.

In "Roselily," the opening story of *In Love and Trouble*, the main character, Roselily—young, black, poor, trapped in the southern backwoods, unmarried, the mother of three children, each by a different man—is about to give herself in marriage to a Muslim man. His religion requires a set of customs and beliefs that control women and subordinate them to men. She will have to wear her hair covered, sit apart from the men in church; her required place will be in the home. There will be more babies regardless of her wishes. She also senses another kind of oppression, dictated not by his religion, but by his condescension. He is annoyed by country black folk, their way of doing things, the country wedding. Roselily knows that in his eyes her three illegitimate children, not all by the same man, add to her lowliness. He makes her feel "ignorant, wrong, backward." But he offers her a chance that she must take. A chance for her children. A chance for her to be "respectable," "reclaimed," "renewed." And it is a chance she cannot afford to miss because marriage is perhaps her only way out of brutal poverty.

The excerpt from Elechi Amadi's *The Concubine*, a prefatory piece to *In Love and Trouble*, is a particularly interesting one for the light it throws on Roselily's situation. This excerpt depicts a woman named Ahurole who is given to unprovoked sobbing and fits of melancholia. An intelligent woman, Ahurole is generally cheerful and normal, so her parents blame her fits on the influence of an unlucky and troublesome personal spirit. At the end of the excerpt, it is revealed that "Ahurole was engaged to Ekwueme when she was *eight days old*." Walker sees Roselily, like Ahurole, as a woman trapped and cut down by archaic conventions, by superstition, by traditions that in every way cut women off from the right to life. Their personal and inner rebellion against the restrictions of their lives is reduced to the level of an unlucky spirit.

Roselily, too, has no way to explain her troubled and rebellious spirit. She has married off well, she will give her children a better life; but she is disturbed by what she senses will be an iron shackle around her life and her self. All of the fleeting images that inadvertently break through her consciousness are premonitions of what is to come: *quicksand, flowers choked to death, cotton being weighed, ropes, chains, handcuffs, cemeteries, a cornered rat*. The very robe and veil she is wearing are emblems of servitude that she yearns to be free of.

Mrs. Jerome Franklin Washington III, a beautician, another of Walker's suspended women, not unlike Roselily, is caught in a marriage that destroys her little by little. When she discovers how very little she means to her husband, she burns herself up.

Ms. Washington (we know her in this story only through her husband's name) is an unlovely, unloved woman: big, awkward, with rough skin, greasy, hard pressed hair. She is married because of a small inheritance, to a quiet, "cute," dapper young schoolteacher whom she adores. She buys him clothes and cars, lavishly spending money on him, money she has earned in her beauty shop by standing many hours on her feet. It is not long before he is beating her and ridiculing her coarseness; for he considers himself one of the elite, the "black bourgeoisie," and his wife is so obviously, in spite of her hard-earned money, a woman of no learning, no elegance. In short, she is devoid of any black middle-class pretensions. Even her pretensions are clearly indicative of her lower class. She tells her customers as she does hair behind dark glasses, "'One thing my husband does not do, he don't beat me.'" She discovers Jerome's infidelity is his dedication to some sort of revolutionary cadre. He has hidden it from her no doubt because she is ignorant, but it is a revolution financed by her money and her devotion to him. She sets fire to their marriage bed, and she herself is caught in the blaze.

The physical and psychic brutality that are part of the lives of several other women in Walker's *In Love and Trouble* are almost always associated with poverty. Rannie Toomer, in "Strong Horse Tea," for example, struggling to get a doctor for her dying child, is handicapped by poverty and ignorance as well as by the racism of the southern rural area she lives in. No "real" doctor will come to see about her child, so she gives in to the "witche's" medicine of Aunt Sarah and goes out in the rain to catch horse urine, which is the "strong horse tea" the old rootworker has requested. Her child dies while she is out filling up her shoes with the tea. In his death, all of the elements seem to have conspired—the earth, the "nigger" magic of Aunt Sarah, the public and private racism of the South. One wonders what desperate hysteria allowed Rannie Toomer to stomach the taste and smell of horse urine.

In "The Child Who Favored Daughter," the father presides over the destruction of three women in his family: his own wife, whom he drives to suicide after beating and crippling her; his sister, named Daughter, whose suicide is the result of the punishment her family exacts after she has an affair with a white man; and his own daughter, whom he mutilates because she will not renounce her white lover. To understand the violence of this man toward these three women in his family, author Walker makes us know that it is the result of an immense chaos within—the components of which are his impotent rage against the white world which abuses him, his vulnerable love for his child and his sister, both of whom chose white lovers. He is so threatened by that inner chaos that the very act of violence is a form of control, a way of imposing order on his own world. By killing his daughter, he has at once shut out the image of Daughter which haunts him, he has murdered his own incest, and he has eliminated the last woman who has the power to hurt him. His brutality toward women foreshadows other Walker characters—Grange and Brownfield in *The Third Life of Grange Copeland*, the farmer who cripples his wife in "Really Doesn't Crime Pay?," Hannah Kemhuff's husband ("The Revenge of Hannah Kemhuff"), and Ruth's father in "A Sudden Trip Home in the Spring."

It is Walker's own documentation and analysis of the historical struggles of the black women that authenticates the terrible and chilling violence of these stories. These are stories about several generations of black women whose lives were severely limited by sexual and racial oppression. First slaves, then sharecroppers, then part of the vast army of the urban poor, their lives were lived out in slow motion, going nowhere, a future not yet within their grasp.[23]

Such were the women Jean Toomer discovered in *Cane*, and the similarity between Toomer's women and the women of Walker's first cycle (the suspended woman) is striking:

> To Toomer they lay vacant and fallow as Autumn fields, with harvest time never in sight: and he saw them enter loveless marriages, without joy; and become prostitutes without resistance; and become mothers of children, without fulfillment.[24]

Both Toomer and Walker have explored the tragedies in the lives of Black women—the tragedy of poverty, abuse from men who are themselves abused, the physical deterioration—but there is greater depth in Walker's exploration because not only does she comprehend the past lives of these women but she has also questioned their fates and dared to see through to a time when black women would no longer live in suspension, when there would be a place for them to move into.

In the second cycle of Walker's personal construct of the history of black women are the women who belong to the decades of the forties and fifties, those decades when black people (then "Negroes") wanted most to be part of the mainstream of American life even though assimilation required total denial of one's ethnicity. Several literary critics have labeled this period in black literature a period of "mainstreaming" because of the indications in literature that writers such as Willard Motley and Frank Yerby and even one novel of Zora Neale Hurston were "raceless." And what of the black women during this period, particularly the woman who had some chance at education? Walker writes of her as a woman pushed and pulled by the larger world outside of her, urged to assimilate (to be "raceless") in order to overcome her background. In Walker's historical construct, these black women were, ironically, victims of what were ostensibly greater opportunities:

> I have this theory that Black women in the '50's, in the 40's—the late 40's and early 50's—got away from their roots much more than they will probably ever do again, because that was the time of greatest striving to get into White Society, and to erase all of the backgrounds of poverty. It was a time when you could be the Exception, could be the One, and my sister was The One. But I think she's not unique—so many, many, many Black families have a daughter or sister who was the one who escaped because, you see, that was what was set up for her; she was going to be the one who escaped, and the rest of us weren't supposed to escape, because we had given our One.[25]

The women in this cycle are also victims, not of physical violence, but of a kind of psychic violence that alienates them from their roots, cutting them off from real contact.

The woman named Molly from Walker's poem "For My Sister Molly Who in the Fifties" is the eldest sister in a poor rural family in Eatonton; she is, in fact, Alice Walker's sister and Walker is the child narrator of the poem mourning the loss of her talented and devoted "Molly." When Molly first comes home on vacation from college, she is very close to her brothers and sisters, teaching them what she has learned, reading to them about faraway places like Africa. The young narrator is enraptured by Molly, spellbound by the bright colorful sister who changes her drab life into beauty:

WHO IN THE FIFTIES

Knew all the written things that made
Us laugh and stories by
The hour. Waking up the story buds
Like Fruit. Who walked among the flowers
And brought them inside the house
And smelled as good as they
And smelled as good as they
And looked as bright.
Who made dresses, braided
Hair. Moved chairs about
Hung things from walls
Ordered baths
Frowned on wasp bites
And seemed to know the endings
Of all the tales
I had forgot.[26]

As a writer especially concerned with the need for black people to acknowledge and respect their roots, Walker is sensitive to these women who are divorced from their heritage. As she describes them, the Chosen Ones were always the bright and talented ones in the family. They were the ones selected to go to college if the family could afford to send only one; they were meant to have the better life, the chance at success. And they learned early the important lesson that to be chosen required them to feel shame for their background, and to strive to be as different and removed as possible from those not chosen. But being a child, the narrator does not realize or suspect the growing signs of Molly's remoteness. Molly goes off to the university, travels abroad, becoming distant and cold and frowning upon the lives of the simple folks she comes from:

Who Found Another World
Another life With gentlefolk
Far less trusting
And moved and moved and changed
Her name
And sounded precise
When she spoke And frowned away
Our sloppishness[27]

From her superior position she can only see the negatives—the silent, fearful, barefoot, tongue-tied, ignorant brothers and sisters. She finds the past, her backward family, unbearable, and though she may have sensed their groping after life, she finally leaves the family for good. She has, of course, been leaving all along with her disapproval of their ways, her precise speech, her preference for another world. The tone of the last two lines suggest the finality about her leaving, as though Molly has become too alienated from her family to ever return:

For My Sister Molly Who in the Fifties
Left us.

The women of the second cycle are destroyed spiritually rather than physically, and yet there is still some movement forward, some hope that did not exist for the earlier generation of American black women. The women in this cycle are more aware of their condition and they have greater potential for shaping their lives, although they are still thwarted because they feel themselves coming to life before the necessary changes have been made in the political environment—before there is space for them to move into. The sense of "twoness" that Du Bois spoke of in *The Souls of Black Folk* is perhaps most evident in the lives of these women; they are the most aware of and burdened by the "double consciousness" that makes one measure one's soul by the tape of the other world.

In June of 1973 in an interview with this writer, Ms. Walker made one of the first statements about the direction and development of her black women characters into a third cycle:

> My women, in the future, will not burn themselves up—that's what I mean by coming to the end of a cycle, and understanding something to the end . . . now I am ready to look at women who have made the room larger for others to move in. . . . I think one reason I never stay away from the Southern Movement is because I realize how deeply political changes affect the choices and life-styles of people. The Movement of the Sixties, Black Power, the Muslims, the Panthers . . . have changed the options of Black people generally and of Black women in particular. So that my women characters won't all end the way they have been, because Black women now offer varied, live models of how it is possible to live. We have made a new place to move. . . . [28]

The women of the third cycle are, for the most part, women of the late sixties, although there are some older women in Walker's fiction who exhibit the qualities of the developing, emergent model. Greatly influenced by the political events of the sixties and the changes resulting from the freedom movement, they are women coming just to the edge of a new awareness and making the first tentative steps into an uncharted region. And although they are more fully conscious of their political and psychological oppression and more capable of creating new options for themselves, they must undergo a harsh initiation before they are ready to occupy and claim any new territory. Alice Walker, herself a real-life prototype of the emergent black woman, speaks of having been called to life by the civil rights movement of the sixties, as being called from the shadows of a world in which black people existed as statistics, problems, beasts of burden, a life that resembled death; for one was not aware of possibilities within one's self or of possibilities in the larger world outside of the narrow restraints of the world black people inhabited before the struggles of the sixties. When Walker and other civil rights activists like Fannie Lou Hamer[29] began the fight for their lives, they were beaten, jailed, and, in Fannie Lou Hamer's case, widowed and made homeless, but they never lost the energy and courage for revolt. In the same way Walker's own characters, through suffering and struggle, lay the groundwork for a new type of woman to emerge.

The process of cyclical movement in the lives of Walker's black women is first evident in her first novel, *The Third Life of Grange Copeland*. The girl, Ruth, is the daughter of Mem Copeland and the granddaughter of Margaret Copeland—two women whose lives were lived out under the most extreme forms of oppression. Under the pressure of poverty and alienation from her husband, Margaret kills herself and her child; and Mem, wife of Brownfield Copeland, is brutally murdered by her husband in one of his drunken rages. Ruth is brought up by her grandfather, Grange, who in his "third life" attempts to salvage some of his own wasted life by protecting Ruth. Ruth emerges into a young woman at the same time as the civil rights movement, and there is just a glimpse at the end of the novel of how that movement will affect Ruth's life. We see her becoming aware, by watching the civil rights activists—both women and men—that it is possible to struggle against the abuses of oppression. Raised in the sixties, Ruth is the natural inheritor of the changes in a new order, struggling to be, this marking the transition of the women in her family from death to life.

Besides political activism, a fundamental activity the women in the third cycle engage in is the search for meaning in their roots and traditions. As they struggle to reclaim their past and to re-examine their relationship to the black community, there is a consequent reconciliation between themselves and black men.

In Sarah Davis, the main character of Walker's short story, "A Sudden Trip Home in the Spring,"[30] we have another witness to the end of the old cycles of confusion and despair. Her search begins when she returns home to the South from a northern white college to bury her father. She is an artist, but because of her alienation from her father, whom she blames for her mother's death, she is unable to paint the faces of black men, seeing in them only defeat. It is important for her, therefore, to answer the questions she is pondering: What is the duty of the child toward the parents after they are dead? What is the necessity of keeping alive in herself a sense of continuity with the past and a sense of community with her family? Through a series of events surrounding her father's funeral, Sarah rediscovers the courage and grace of her grandfather and re-establishes the vital link between her and her brother. Her resolve at the end of the story to do a sculpture of her grandfather ("I shall soon know how to make my grandpa up in stone") signifies the return to her roots and her own personal sense of liberation. This story, more than any other, indicates the contrast between the women of the second cycle who were determined to escape their roots in order to make it in a white world and the emergent women of the third cycle who demonstrate a sense of freedom by the drive to re-establish those vital links to their past.

In Walker's second novel, *Meridian*, the cyclical process is clearly defined in the life of the main character, Meridian Hill, who evolves from a woman trapped by racial and sexual oppression to a revolutionary figure, effecting action and strategy to bring freedom to herself and other poor disenfranchised blacks in the South. Again, as with other third-cycle women who are depicted in the short story collection, the characters in the two novels—*Grange Copeland* and *Meridian*—follow certain patterns: They begin existence in a numb state, deadened, insensible to a life beyond poverty and degradation; they are awakened to life by a powerful political force; in discovering and expanding their creativity, there is a consequent effort to reintegrate themselves into their culture in order to rediscover its value. Historically, the second novel, dealing with a woman who came of age during the sixties, brings Walker's women characters into the first few years of the seventies.

Notes

1. John O'Brien, ed., *Interviews with Black Writers* (New York: Liverwright, 1973), p. 192.
2. New York: Harcourt, Brace & World, 1968.
3. New York: Harcourt Brace Jovanovich, 1973.
4. New York: Harcourt Brace Jovanovich, 1970.
5. New York: Harcourt Brace Jovanovich, 1973.
6. New York: Harcourt Brace Jovanovich, 1976.
7. O'Brien, p. 211.
8. Interview with Mary Helen Washington, Jackson, Mississippi, June 17, 1973. I traveled to Jackson in June of 1973 in order to meet, talk with, and interview Ms. Walker.
9. "Interview with Mary Helen Washington," Part 1, p. 7.
10. *American Scholar*, Winter 1970–71.
11. Ibid., p. 551.
12. Ibid., p. 552.

13. W. E. B. Du Bois, *Souls of Black Folk* (New York: Blue Heron Press, 1953), pp. 16–17.
14. Carolyn Fowler, "Solid at the Core," *Freedomways*, 14 (First Quarter, 1974), p. 60.
15. Alice Walker, "Interview," in O'Brien, p. 202.
16. Reid Lecture at Barnard College, November 11, 1975.
17. "Interview with Mary Helen Washington," p. 6.
18. *Apologist* is used here to mean one who speaks or writes in defense of a cause or a position.
19. "Interview with Mary Helen Washington," p. 6.
20. "In Search of Our Mothers' Gardens," *Ms.*, May 1974, p. 66.
21. Ibid.
22. Ibid., p. 69.
23. Ibid., p. 66.
24. Ibid.
25. "Interview with Mary Helen Washington," Part 1, p. 1.
26. *Revolutionary Petunias* (New York: Harcourt Brace Jovanovich, 1973), p. 17.
27. Ibid., p. 18.
28. "Interview with Mary Helen Washington," Part 2, p. 2.
29. The identification of Hamer as a model for the emergent woman is developed in Walker's review of a biography of Hamer by June Jordan. The review appeared in *The New York Times Book Review*, April 29, 1973.
30. In Mary Helen Washington, ed., *Black-eyed Susans: Classic Stories by and about Black Women* (Garden City, N.Y.: Doubleday & Company, 1975).

DEBORAH E. McDOWELL

"The Self in Bloom: Alice Walker's *Meridian*"

CLA Journal, March 1981, pp. 262–75

> And she had nothing to fall back on: not maleness, not whiteness, not ladyhood, not anything. And out of the profound desolation of her reality, she may very well have invented herself.—TONI MORRISON[1]

> What are we talking about when we speak of revolution if not a free society made up of whole individuals? I'm not arguing the denial of manhood or womanhood, but rather a shifting of priorities, a call for Self-hood. . . . —TONI CADE[2]

Central to any consideration of Alice Walker's fiction is her preoccupation with black womanhood and its myriad shadings.[3] Both *The Third Life of Grange Copeland* (1970) and *In Love and Trouble: Stories of Black Women* (1973) explore, to varying degrees, the dynamics of being a black woman. But in *Meridian* (1976), Walker's latest and probably most artistically mature work, she transcends the boundaries of the female gender to embrace more universal concerns about individual autonomy, self-reliance,[4] and self-realization. In the tradition of the *Bildungsroman*, or apprenticeship novel, the book chronicles the series of initiatory experiences which Meridian, the title character, undergoes in an effort to find her identity, or her own moral center, and develop a completeness of being. Jerome Buckley lists the principal elements of the *Bildungsroman:* "childhood, the conflict of generations, provinciality, the larger society, self-education, alienation, ordeal by love, the search for a vocation and a working philosophy. . . . "[5] Meridian's struggle for identity embraces most of these elements, not all of which can be addressed here. Hers is a formidable struggle, for she lives in a society that domesticates conformity, that censures individual expression, especially for women; but she flourishes notwithstanding and evolves into a prototype for psychic wholeness and individual autonomy.

There is much in the novel to recommend such a reading, particularly the motif of death and rebirth that runs throughout and that recalls the force in nature which transforms decay into growth, loss into gain. When the novel opens, Meridian is seemingly in a state of decay. She is suffering from fainting spells and her hair has fallen out. Her face is "wasted and rough, the skin a sallow, unhealthy brown, with pimples across her forehead and on her chin. Her eyes were glassy and yellow and did not seem to focus at once. Her breath, like her clothes, was sour."[6] At the end of the novel, however, she has reflourished. Her hair has grown back; she is strengthened and renewed.

Similarly, the flashback of events between the opening and closing chapters sustain the death/rebirth motif and are congruent with this evolutionary theme which I am suggesting. Meridian's most significant, most insightful experiences occur in the spring—archetypically a time of both death and rebirth. For example, her husband deserts her in the spring, an experience which triggers a period of "death-like" introspection, culminating in her decision to offer her child up for adoption. Replacing the "old skin" of marriage is the new one of social activism. Likewise, just before her graduation from Saxon College, she falls into a death-like coma only to emerge renewed in a fashion which borders on the mystical.

It is important to note that this idea of Meridian's "New Birth," her cyclical self-transmutation is psychological rather than theological, for Meridian exemplifies the Emersonian notion that true growth and change can occur only when the individual discovers the "god" or divinity in himself or herself.[7] Meridian makes this discovery gradually[8] and develops a reliance on the "sacredness and integrity" of her own mind, even though the gods of social authority would provide her with a "ready-made" set of female role patterns.

One of the most perpetually looming obstacles to Meridian's struggle for self-discovery is the god of American tradition.[9] But rather than cower and defer to its menacing force, she confronts it. Whether represented by people, institutions, established "truths," or time-worn abstractions, Meridian examines tradition with a critical eye and rejects those aspects which impinge upon her self-discovery.

That much of Meridian's growth process will entail a confrontation with the god of tradition, or the "dead hand" of the past, is established in the richly symbolic, tightly compressed opening chapter in which two of America's most cherished institutions—racism and sexism—meet head-on in a skillful, simultaneous dramatization. The chapter recounts the circus show, conducted Jim Crow style, featuring the mummy woman, Marilene O'Shay, "one of the Twelve Wonders of the World: Preserved in Life-Like Condition." At the most fundamental level, Walker is satirizing the tenacious but untenable belief in tradition, which is at the bowels of American culture, for the preservation of the mummy woman is a metaphor for the preservation of dead, no longer viable traditions and institutions. Thus Meridian challenges this Southern town's "separate-but-equal" racial tradition by leading a group of black school children to the circus wagon on a day not authorized by the local government.

While defying the tradition of separate-but-equal race relations, Meridian, in her active social role, concurrently challenges traditional and synthetic images of women. She is in sharp contradistinction to the images presented of the mummy woman (which are, Walker suggests, images of all women). The marquee of the circus wagon flashes the captions "Obedient Daughter," "Devoted Wife" and "Adoring Mother," the traditional stages of a woman's life. The circus bill (significantly written by the mummy woman's husband) explains that she had been "an ideal woman" a "goddess," who had been given "everythin," that is, "a washing machine, furs, her own car and a full-time housekeeper cook." Her only duty was to "lay back and be pleasured" (p. 20). But the mummy woman loses her fringe benefits and her life in the process. Her husband kills her because she "had gone outside the home to seek her 'pleasuring,' while still expecting him to foot the bills" (p. 20). This image of woman as passivist, as "a mindless body, a sex creature, something to hang false hair and nails on" (p. 71), is actively challenged by Meridian in her role as a human rights crusader.[10] It is not incidental that her physical features in this chapter most resemble a male's. Most of her hair has fallen out and she wears an old railroad cap and dungarees which have masculine suggestions. But the fact that she is physically unattractive does not concern Meridian, an unconcern contrary to conventional notions of womanhood. Not only does Meridian look like a male, but she also acts like one. She is decidedly out of her "place" as a woman in her demonstration of unwavering leadership qualities, those generally associated with the male. Although there are armed policemen stationed in a "red-white-and-blue" army tank to prevent Meridian from fulfilling her mission, she bravely marches on, facing the tank aimed at her chest. "The silence as Meridian kicked open the door, exploded in a mass exhalation of breaths, and the men who were in the tank crawled sheepishly out again to stare" (pp. 21–22). Thus a symbolic inversion of roles occurs in this scene and Meridian can be said to triumph over tradition and authority. Her achievement in this series of attacks on tradition is a pointed commentary on America's role-dependency. She exemplifies Toni Cade's assertion that

> You find your Self in destroying illusions, smashing myths . . . being responsible to some truth, to the struggle. That entails . . . cracking through the veneer of this sick society's definition of 'masculine' and 'feminine.'[11]

and striving towards creating an androgynous, fluid self.

Such fluidity of personality is necessary because rigid role definitions are static; by their very nature, they deny human complexity and thereby stifle growth, completeness of being.

This critical chapter, then, as it explores the tension between Stasis (Tradition) and change (Meridian), sets the stage for the flashback of events which form the story of Meridian's development, which give rise to her self-discovery, to her obsession with finding her own distinctive "step" amid a composite of imitative marchers.

Like the mummy woman, Meridian is, at various stages in the novel, a daughter, though not obedient; a wife, though not devoted; and a mother, though not adoring, for the demands of these roles are circumscriptive and stifling. It is in her role as daughter, particularly in her stormy relationship with her mother, that Meridian's insurgent self-awareness and independence first surface. This conflict between the generations is a motif peculiar to the apprenticeship novel. It is imperative that the initiate come to terms with a parental figure to free himself or herself from that parent's possessive hold before personal development can proceed.[12] Although her mother's domination is powerful, Meridian is intent upon freeing herself from its strangling clutches. She regards her mother as a "willing know-nothing, a woman of ignorance" (p. 30), who blindly adheres to tradition in its most sacrosanct forms. The Christian religion is one such form. The mother has been critically victimized by the European's gift of Christianity as an opiate to the black slave, a comforting myth which dimmed the horrors and brutalities of oppression. The mother has relinquished all responsibility for her own welfare to God and, in turn, wants Meridian to do so as well. But even at age thirteen, in the "mourner's bench" ritual, suffered and misunderstood by many a black child, Meridian questions the rationality of her mother's Christian beliefs and refuses to submit to them. Her adamant refusal costs her her mother's love; it "was gone, withdrawn and there were conditions to be met before it would be returned. Conditions Meridian was never able to meet" (p. 30).

Not only does Meridian challenge her mother's blind devotion to an escapist religion, but she also challenges her equally blind and passive acceptance of the overlapping constraints of marriage and motherhood. She sees her mother as "Black Motherhood personified" (pp. 96–97) in her self-sacrifice. Although once a school teacher, her mother had been brainwashed into believing that she was missing something as a single person, and that that "something" was marriage and motherhood. She buys this myth wholesale, and while she later discovers that her twin roles of wife and mother are stymying, she accepts them, albeit with consuming resentment. Meridian believes that by surrendering to the demands of these roles, her mother has collaborated in her own suffocation:

> Her mother was not a woman who should have had children. She was capable of thought and growth and action only if unfettered by the needs of dependents, or the demands, requirements of a husband. (p. 49)

Finally, Meridian challenges her mother's unquestioning acceptance of her secondary citizenship. Of Meridian's involvement in the civil rights movement, her mother responds:

> "As far I'm concerned . . . you've wasted a year of your life fooling around with those people [civil rights activists]. The papers say they're crazy. God separated the sheeps from the goats and the black folks from the white. And me from anybody that acts as foolish as they do. It never bothered me to sit in the back of the bus, you get just as good a view and you don't have all those nasty white asses passing you." (p. 85)

And later, on the subject of no restroom facilities downtown for blacks, her mother states, "If somebody thinks he'll have to pee when he gets to town, let him use his own toilet before he leaves home! That's what we did when I was coming up!" (p. 85).

In her mother's "blind, enduring, stumbling through life," then, Meridian sees an example of thwarted potential resulting from a capitulation to the demands of tradition. Her mother's only release from the frustrations which these traditions impose is making artificial flowers and prayer pillows "too small for kneeling. They would only fit one knee" (p. 30). The sterility and essential uselessness of these two activities markedly contrasts with Meridian's now flourishing sense of purpose and independence.

> It seemed to Meridian that her legacy from her mother's endurance, her unerring knowledge of rightness and her pursuit of it through all distractions, was one she would never be able to match. It never occurred to her that her mother's and her grandmother's extreme purity of life was compelled by necessity. They had not lived in an age of choice. (p. 124)

Because she *does* live in an age of choice, Meridian opts for the twin "ills" of ending her marriage and offering her child up for adoption, thus willfully abdicating her roles as Devoted

Wife and Loving Mother. Likening her life as wife and mother to being "buried alive, walled away from . . . life, brick by brick" (p. 51), Meridian escapes and commits herself to the civil rights struggle, a commitment that earns her a scholarship to Saxon College (Anglo-Saxon?), which represents tradition in another guise, and thus, still another deterrent to her growing individuality. "The emphasis at Saxon was on form, and the preferred 'form' was that of the finishing school girl . . . [who] knew and practiced all the proper social rules" (p. 95) and was, thereby, "ushered nearer to Ladyhood every day" (p. 39). The school song at Saxon began:

> We are as chaste and pure as the
> driven snow.
> We watch our manners, speech
> and dress just so.
> (p. 93)

But the twin concepts of Ladyhood and chastity form another set of growth-retarding mythical abstractions which Meridian must reject. And she must reject them, among other reasons, because they are inherently contradictory. Nowhere is this made more explicit than in her sexual relationship with Truman Held, the young black French-speaking, dashiki-wearing "revolutionary." Truman is a student at a men's school across the street from Saxon, and he and Meridian are romantically and sexually drawn together because of their common involvement in the voters' rights crusade. But their relationship and their sexual encounters are soon baffling for Meridian, their conversations about them even more so, for Truman represents the traditional male in his hypocritical separation between "good" girls and "bad" girls. Truman "had wanted a virgin, had been raised to expect and demand a virgin; and never once had he questioned this. He had been as predatory as the other young men he ran with, as eager to seduce and de-virginize as they. Where had he expected his virgin to come from? Heaven?" (p. 142). In Truman's failure to recognize the contradictions and inequities in his sexual ideology, he condemns himself to a spiritually tragic divisiveness.

Despite her disappointing affair with Truman, Meridian stays at Saxon, but she defies its "Zoo restrictions and keeper taboos" and distinguishes herself as a "willful, sinful girl" (p. 94).

The extent to which Saxon upholds tradition in its emphasis on form is pointedly dramatized in the account of the Wild Child, an uncivilized, pregnant, orphan girl whom Meridian brings to the honors dorm of Saxon to care for. Shortly afterwards, the Wild Child runs to her death and Meridian arranges a funeral to be held in the school's chapel. By order of the president, however, the chapel guards refuse to let the coffin in. Meridian, who knows the president well, imagines him

> coming up to the Wild Child's casket and saying, as if addressing a congregation: "We are sorry, young woman, but it is against the rules and regulations of this institution to allow you to conduct your funeral inside this chapel, which, as you may know, was donated to us by one of the finest robber baron families of New York. Besides, it is nearly time for Vespers, and you should have arranged for this affair *through the proper channels* much earlier." (p. 46)

The bureaucratic mentality epitomized by the president pervades the Saxon community, and Meridian becomes increasingly aware that her growing individuality cannot be nourished in such a convention-bound climate. Therefore, she intensified her search for an opposing set of values which would provide relief from the strictures of the Anglo-Saxon value system, a search which takes her into the realm of the mystical. This notion of mysticism is congruent with the evolutionary motif, for the idea of a New Birth, a remaking or transmutation of the self, inheres in mysticism.[13]

While still at Saxon, Meridian begins to neglect her body; "she hated its obstruction" (p. 97). She begins to bald. Continually forgetting to eat, she begins to suffer fainting spells and blurred vision, which result in a coma. This coma and its aftermath resemble mystical ecstasy,[14] described by Evelyn Underhill as a death-like trance lasting for hours or several days, during which "breathing and circulation are depressed. The body is more or less cold and rigid. . . ."[15] Underhill adds that the mystic emerges from ecstasy "marvellously strengthened," ready for "the struggles and hardships," for "the deliberate pain and sacrifice of Love."[16]

Meridian's experience strikingly parallels Underhill's description. She emerges from the coma after two days:

> As the days passed . . . and she attempted to nibble at the dishes Anne-Marion brought—she discovered herself becoming more and more full, with no appetite whatsoever. And, to her complete surprise and astonished joy, she began to experience ecstasy.
>
> Sometimes, lying on her bed, not hungry, not cold, not worried . . . she felt as if a warm, strong light bore her up and that she was a beloved part of the universe; that she was innocent even as the first waters. And when Anne-Marion sat beside the bed and scolded her for not eating, she was amazed that Anne-Marion could not see how happy she was. (pp. 119–20)

What is described in this passages is a mystical "dying-into-life" which involves a repudiation of the body's claims for those of the spirit. This accounts for Meridian's stolid indifference to food and other physical concerns, and her phenomenal spiritedness and strength following the coma. More significantly, however, is the light which Anne-Marion notices around Meridian's head; "the spikes of her natural had learned to glow" (p. 120). It is suggested here that Meridian has emerged from the trance-like state a saint. She explains to Truman that she has volunteered to suffer until her people are delivered from oppression. Her suffering takes an extremely ascetic form congruent with her nascent sainthood. She restricts herself to the "gross necessaries" of life, to borrow from Thoreau.

> Each time Truman visited Meridian he found her with less and less furniture, fewer and fewer pieces of clothing, less of a social position in the community—wherever it was—where she lived. (pp. 31–32)

To Meridian, such concerns are negligible, alien to all that she has cultivated up to this point. Her cultivation of self has necessitated her weeding out many of the most cherished values and institutions of the Western tradition, and she is left, despite her deepened commitment to the racial struggle, with the existential alienation that is the mark of the twentieth-century individual. She is the archetypal "outsider." The last stage in her development, then, requires the formation of an alternate value system, a system outside the sterility and meaninglessness of the Western orbit. She finds this alternative system in psychically repatriating to the most viable aspects of the black cultural heritage. In other words, the continued progress of her search for identity requires that she go backward in order to move forward, and backward is the South. It is significant that much of the novel is set in coastal Georgia, where the survival of Africanisms—particularly of the oral, religious, and musical traditions—is said to be most salient. Echoing Jean Toomer, Walker sees the South, despite its history of racism and oppression, as regenerative, for it is the South that is the cradle of the black man's experience in the New World, and the South that has continued to shape his experience in this country.

It is in the South, then, that Meridian rediscovers the power of the black past, accepts it and draws strength from its vital traditions, most notably the symbiotic musical and religious traditions. While crusading among older black people, she "was constantly wanting to know about the songs. 'Where did such and such a one come from?' or 'How many years do you think black people have been singing this?'" (p. 38).

Concomitant with the rediscovery of the black musical tradition is her rediscovery of its counterpart—the black church, which is, according to E. Franklin Frazier, "the most important cultural institution created by Negroes."[17] It is important to note, however, that the church which Meridian finally accepts is not her mother's church, not the church of the white Christian tradition with its futuristic eschatology, not the church which severed the black man's attention from the exigencies of the "here and now" and riveted it to the putative rewards of the hereafter. It is rather the *restored* church of her slave ancestors that Meridian ultimately embraces, the Church of Nat Turner, of Denmark Vesey, the church rooted in the soil of protest against oppression, the church of "communal spirit, togetherness, righteous convergence" (p. 199).

The musical and religious traditions converge in the critical chapter entitled "Camera." Falling strategically near the end of the novel, the chapter renders a certain completion to Meridian's characterization, for it is in this chapter that she resolves some of the most besetting quandaries of her life. The chapter begins by likening Meridian to a camera (an image suggesting distance and detachment) as she watches a group of churchgoers assemble for Sunday service, but it ends with her reunion with kindred black souls in a communal purpose. Wandering into a church shortly after Martin Luther King's assassination, she notices a number of changes which trigger her reexamination of the function of the black church in the social and political struggle. What strike her at first are the church's physical changes. It was

> not like the ones of her childhood; it was not shabby or small. It was large, of brick, with stained-glass windows . . . an imposing structure; and yet *it did not reach for the sky*, as cathedrals did, *but settled firmly on the ground*. (p. 93; my italics)

That the church is settled firmly on the ground suggests its temporal rather than compensatory concerns. Its outer transformations mirror its internal changes. A man is called on to pray, but his is a short prayer and, significantly, he doesn't kneel. "He said he would not pray any longer because there was a lot of work for the community to do" (p. 195).

Similarly, Meridian observes a change in the music. It now has a tone which urges her to quote Margaret Walker's lines, "Let the martial songs be written. . . . let the dirges disappear" (p. 195).

The sermon has even changed from those unintelligible ones she knew as a child. The minister, boldly reminiscent of Martin Luther King, has a decidedly political thrust to his sermon, which is punctuated by references to President Nixon, "whom he called 'Tricky Dick.'" He admonishes the young men in the audience not to participate in the Vietnam War and challenges the young women "to stop looking for husbands and try to get something useful in their heads. . . . God was not mentioned except as a reference" (pp. 195–96).

But the most telling transformation in the church is the picture in the stained-glass window, not of the traditional pale Christ with stray lamb, but rather of "B. B. with a Sword," a picture of a tall, broad-shouldered black man with a guitar in one hand and a blood-dripping sword in the other. The reference to blues singer B. B. King is obvious. Here, Alice Walker, like a number of other black writers,[18] is using the black musician as a symbol of an enduring cultural tradition and as an exemplification of unity and community.[19]

It is this same sense of unity and community evoked by "B. B. with a Sword" that Meridian experiences as she contemplates the meaning of the picture. In an epiphany of sorts, she discovers that her identity is inextricably tied to her black people, that she is a mere particle of a much larger, more complex composite, and that "[her] existence extended beyond herself to those around her because, in fact, the years in America had created [black people into] one life" (p. 200).

Upon perceiving her essential Oneness with black humanity, Meridian reassesses her commitment to the racial struggle once again. This time she feels duty-bound to make a commitment that extends beyond registering black voters and integrating rest room facilities. She begins to contemplate the power of the sword; the sword of the pictures begins to have meaning for her. Thus, while throughout the novel Meridian could not contemplate killing for the struggle, she now sees the necessity for it. Even though she vacillates in the belief that she herself can kill, she thinks,

> ". . . perhaps it will be my part to walk behind the real revolutionaries—those who know they must spill blood in order to help the poor and the black and therefore go right ahead—and when they stop to wash off the blood and find their throats too choked with the smell of murdered flesh to sing, I will come forward and sing from memory songs they will need once more to hear. For it is the song of the people, transformed by the experiences of each generation, that holds them together, and if any part of it is lost the people suffer and are without soul. If I can do that, my role will not have been a useless one after all." (p. 201)

Thus, the self has bloomed; Meridian has found her identity, an identity fashioned not from the Western tradition, but rather from the artifacts of her own heritage. Moreover, she, like Claude McKay's Bita Plant of *Banana Bottom*, has found a connecting link to that heritage which enables her to prevail in comparison to all of the other characters in the novel. At the end of the book, she receives from Anne-Marion a sheet of paper, in the center of which is a gigantic tree stump from which a tiny branch is growing. Anne-Marion has written: "Who would be happier than you that the Sojourner did not die?" (p. 217). The Sojourner was the tree, a symbol of both the black oral and musical traditions, planted during slavery on a plantation which later became Saxon College, the tree destroyed by a group of rioting students. Metaphorically speaking, Meridian is that branch from The Sojourner and the clarion testimony that although systematic attempts have been made at its destruction as the nucleus of black life, it is not dead. Anne-Marion's "grotesquely small" handwriting on the note parallels her stunted and puny existence, pale in significance to Meridian's, pale because she has suffered a self-authored separation from the trunk, from her root source.

Truman, unlike Anne-Marion, gradually realizes the

source of Meridian's vitality and the ultimate value of her life. When the novel ends, Meridian is leaving the town of Chickokema for still other crusades. She leaves behind her cap and sleeping bag, the articles that have identified her throughout the novel. More importantly, however, she leaves Truman behind struggling to experience self-discovery and rebirth. After Meridian leaves, Truman climbs into her sleeping bag and then dons her cap, almost in an effort to "become" Meridian, to experience, through osmosis, her vitality. But like Meridian, Truman and Anne-Marion must individually sift through the shards of their cultural past to heal and re-create themselves.

Notes

1. Epigraph used by Mary Helen Washington, ed., *Black-Eyed Susans* (Garden City, New York: Anchor Books, 1975).
2. Toni Cade, "On the Issue of Roles," in *The Black Woman: An Anthology*, ed. Toni Cade (New York: The New American Library, Inc., 1970), p. 105.
3. Walker has stated that her fictional preoccupation is "exploring the oppressions, the insanities, the loyalities, and the triumphs of black women" (John O'Brien, ed., *Interviews with Black Writers* [New York: Liveright, 1973], p. 192).
4. There are very clear echoes of Emersonian idealism in the novel. *Meridian* embodies many of the underlying assumptions of transcendentalism.
5. *Season of Youth: The Bildungsroman from Dickens to Golding* (Cambridge, Mass.: Harvard University Press, 1974), p. 18. For a more detailed statement of the *Bildungsroman*, see Susanne Howe, *Wilhelm Meister and His English Kinsmen* (New York: Columbia Univ. Press, 1930).
6. Alice Walker, *Meridian* (New York: Pocket Books, 1977), p. 25. All further page references are to this edition and will be cited parenthetically in the text.
7. For a discussion of this notion of the divinity within the individual, see Emerson's "The Divinity School Address," where he states that a "true conversion" takes place only when all individuals "[come] again to themselves, to the God in themselves . . ." (Ralph Waldo Emerson, *Nature Addresses and Lectures* [New York: Houghton Mifflin and Company, 1903], p. 132).
8. It is significant that the old sweeper in the opening chapter says that Meridian "thinks she's God . . ." (p. 22).
9. American tradition assumes many forms in the novel, one such being the symbolic presence of guards. The frequency with which guards appear in the novel is not incidental, for their appearance suggests protection, preservation, in this case protection and preservation of tradition. The guards also appear at the circus wagon and at the door of the Saxon chapel.
10. See also Walker's short story, "Really, Doesn't Crime Pay?" in *In Love and Trouble* (New York: Harcourt, Brace, Jovanovich, 1973). Myrna, the protagonist, wants to prove to her husband that she is not "a womb without a brain that can be bought with Japanese bathtubs and shopping sprees," (p. 18).
11. "On the Issue of Roles," p. 108.
12. Buckley, *Season of Youth*, pp. 65–66.
13. See Evelyn Underhill, *Mysticism* (New York: E. P. Dutton and Company, Inc., 1930), pp. 140–41.
14. The word "ecstasy" is used several times in the novel to describe Meridian's experience, and thus, it is fairly accurate to assume its connections with mysticism.
15. Underhill, *Mysticism*, pp. 359–60.
16. Ibid., p. 379.
17. *The Negro Church in America*. (New York: Schocken Books, 1969), p. 70.
18. See especially James Baldwin's short story "Sonny's Blues."
19. For similar discussions see Shirley Williams, *Give Birth to Brightness* (New York: The Dial Press, 1972), pp. 140–41. See also Ralph Ellison's "Blues People," in *Shadow and Act* (New York: Vintage Books, 1972).

GERALD EARLY

From "*The Color Purple* as Everybody's Protest Art"

Antioch Review, Summer 1986, pp. 270–75

II. And Reflections in the Light

O Mary, don't you weep
And tell Martha not to moan.
(Black gospel queen Inez Andrews's "O, Mary, Don't You Weep")

A good friend and colleague, Elizabeth Schulz, pointed out in passing not very long ago that Alice Walker's *The Color Purple* has a certain similarity to Harriet Beecher Stowe's *Uncle Tom's Cabin*—something to the effect that both novels have suffered from the popularity they have had to endure. I think she meant that both novels have been burdened by their pop-culture status and, as a result, both mass audiences and the critical elite have tended to misinterpret these works. The misinterpretations have arisen partly because these have been extremely popular works of social protest, indictments about the ways we live, written by women who, many believe, cannot really write, and so they have been subject to the most intense and awkward forms of admiration and suspicion. The popularity of the works has tended to blunt and distort the response of some critics by antagonizing their snobbish sensibilities, convinced as they are that these works could be popular only by pandering to certain mass expectations. For these reasons, among others, I suppose it is not surprising that my colleague should begin to think of these novels along the same lines. It may be the judgment of literary and cultural history that these books will be condemned to be yoked together and exist in that limbo of literary reputation between hack work and greatness.

I have said that *The Color Purple* is not a good novel, but it does articulate one useful observation that I can dispense with quickly. The book utterly condemns the black male's glorification of his pimp mentality, and for this we should be thankful. For an insufferably long time, the black American male has been convinced, both by himself and by white males, that he is the monstrous stud on our cultural block. It is one of the few contemptible misrepresentations dreamed up by the white male that the black male has taken to heart, has clutched feverishly. Perhaps he has taken an unseemly pride in this perversion because it has titillated some white women (which in turn has titillated him) or because it has endowed him with the power of the slave master and permitted him to turn his community into a kind of brothel filled with "bitches" and "'ho'es." Whatever the case, Walker was quite right in linking that attempt to the oppressive attitude of the slave master, to the attitude of a rapist. It is appropriate that the lazy Mr. Albert should run something akin to a plantation with a big house as he remained a pimp in his soul.

Despite this, *The Color Purple* remains an inferior novel not because it seems so self-consciously a "woman's novel" and not because it may be playing down to its mass audience, guilty of being nothing more than a blatant "feel-good" novel, just the sort of book that is promoted among the nonliterary. *The Color Purple* is a poor novel because it ultimately fails the ideology that it purports to serve. It fails to be subversive enough in substance; it only *appears* to be subversive. Indeed, far from being a radically feminist novel, it is not even, in the end, as good a bourgeois feminist novel as *Uncle Tom's Cabin*, written 130 years earlier. Its largest failure lies in the novel's inability to use (ironically, subversively, or even interestingly) the elements that constitute it. Take, for instance, these various Victorianisms that abound in the work: the ultimate aim of the restoration of a gynocentric, not patriarchal family; the reunion of lost sisters; the reunion of mother and children; the glorification of cottage industry in the establishment of the pants business; bequests of money and land to the heroine at novel's end; Celie's discovery that her father/rapist is really a cruel stepfather; the change of heart or moral conversion of Mr. Albert, who becomes a feminized man by the end; the friendship between Shug Avery and Celie, which, despite its overlay of lesbianism (a tribute to James Baldwin's untenable thesis that nonstandard sex is the indication of a free, holy, thoroughly unsquare heterosexual heart), is nothing more than the typical relationship between a shy ugly duckling and her more aggressive, beautiful counterpart, a relationship not unlike that between Topsy and Little Eva. Shug convinces Celie that she is not black and ugly, that somebody loves her, which is precisely what Eva does for Topsy. For Walker, these clichés are not simply those of the Victorian novel but of the *woman's* Victorian novel. This indicates recognition of and paying homage to a tradition; but the use of these clichés in *The Color Purple* is a great deal more sterile and undemanding than their use in, say, *Uncle Tom's Cabin*. Together, for Walker, these clichés take on a greater attractiveness and power than for the female Victorian, since they are meant to represent a series of values that free the individual from the power of the environment, the whim of the state, and the orthodoxy of the institution. The individual still has the power to change, and that power supersedes all others, means more than any other. Human virtue is a reality that is not only distinct from all collective arrangements except family; in the end, it can be understood only as being opposed to all collective arrangements. But all of this is only the bourgeois fascination with individualism and with the ambiguity of Western family life, in which bliss is togetherness while having a room of one's own.

The heart of *The Color Purple* is this rhetoric of virtue from which its theological propositions spring. The novel is not representing Celie as a powerless victim simply to establish a critique to Calvinist or Conservative Christianity, but to create an outright revolt against such inhuman orthodoxy. For Walker, conservative theology endorses weakness, is enthralled by it because the existence of a superior power demands a corresponding submission; an elect is nothing more than a collective of power, an unnatural sovereignty symbolized first and finally by the Calvinist male God. Two separate concepts become fused at some point in this book: the subversion of Calvinist Christianity by its replacement, which is something like liberal religion, and the absolute elimination of evil. Thus the resulting necessities of two conversions in the book: Celie's transformation to self-assertion and human dignity denies a Calvinist world, and Mr. Albert's feminization transforms the power of evil. Walker insists on a theology without victims; this must, to be sure, be a theology in which victims can never be possible, dependent on a world where all are equally strong and where all are equally humbled. This is finally expressed in the novel through a fairly dim-witted pantheistic acknowledgment of the wonders of human potential that begins to sound quite suspiciously like a cross between the New Age movement and Dale Carnegie. Nothing symbolizes the overthrow of this male-centered Calvinism more than Celie's refusal, about two-thirds of the way through the book, to write letters to God any more. She writes to her sister instead. These quotations from various characters toward the end of the novel signify the coming of the winds of theological change:

> I think it pisses God off if you walk by the color purple in a field somewhere and don't notice it. (Shug)
>
> God is different to us now, after all these years in Africa. More spirit than ever before, and more internal. Most people think he has to look like something or someone—a roofleaf or Christ—but we don't. And not being tied to what God looks like frees us. (Nettie)
>
> I think us here to wonder, myself. To wonder. To ast. And that in wondering bout the big things and asting bout the big things, you learn about the little ones, almost by accident. But you never know nothing more about the big things than you start with. The more I wonder . . . the more I love. (Mr. Albert)

As we can see, the transformation of values among the book's characters has been completed by the end. God has been reduced, though made invisible and nonhuman in a way, and thoroughly accountable to creation. And everyone has, through conversion, been able to become his or her own minister, a community without leaders, all equally endowed with the light: from an oppressive ghetto of political and social unequals to a black Little Gidding.

What Walker does in her novel is allow its social protest to become the foundation for its utopia. Not surprisingly, the book lacks any real intellectual or theological rigor or coherence, and the fusing of social protest and utopia is really nothing more than confounding and blundering, each seeming to subvert the reader's attention from the other. One is left thinking that Walker wishes to thwart her own ideological ends or that she simply does not know how to write novels. In essence, the book attempts to be revisionist salvation history and fails because of its inability to use or really understand history.

There is certainly no lack of history associated with the novel: its title and elliptically rendered episodes harken back to Jean Toomer's *Cane* (and Faulkner's *As I Lay Dying*); its speech patterns and love of anthropological folklore bring to mind Zora Neale Hurston (its specific imagery of swollen male bellies is a direct reference to *Their Eyes Were Watching God*); and the epistolary style, which may have emanated from the feminist's realization, as Barbara Christian points out, that "letters were the dominant mode of expression allowed women in the West," is more likely the result of the influence of Samuel Richardson's novels of innocent women in distress. And there is also a great deal of history within the novel itself, references to Harlem, Bessie Smith, African emigration, J. A. Rodgers, and European imperialism. The problem with the novel's historicity is that it seems false and unconvincing, a kind of obvious scaffolding. The bits of history seem undigested and set in the text like lumps. Like the film, Walker's novel, despite its historical references, really wishes to deny history by refusing to show what change and passage of time mean in a society. This is why the social-protest aspects of the novel, some nicely worked up bits of grim naturalism, are inchoate and why the utopian ending must exist. Walker decided that her heroine has no real way to work out her problems within the context of history. And salvation history becomes the utter supersession of oppression-history through the assertion of an unoppressed self. The problem this presents for the reader is that Celie does not find a convincing way to reclaim her humanity and to reassemble the values of her world.

It is equally difficult for Stowe to find a convincing way

for Tom to reclaim his humanity and reassemble the values of his world. The difference between the two novels is that Stowe does not believe in the necessity of a world without evil in order for Tom to be a hero or in order for his virtue to mean something. Nor does she believe that salvation history is the supersession of the history of the world as we know it or the history of oppression; rather, she believes that we live now in salvation history. On the surface, one might say that the difference is that Tom (and Eva and St. Clair) are sacrificed for the *atonement* of the sin of slavery while Celie is allowed to survive and triumph (and so are the other major characters of the book) for the *supersession* of a male-dominated, oppressive world. Tom dies without changing the worst evil with which he is confronted: Simon Legree. In fact, because he dies resisting Legree's will, he is really protesting against that evil. Celie lives as the victor, ultimately being the source of change for the evil Mr. Albert. Stowe knows from her experience with the abolitionist movement in Ohio and from suffering the death of one of her children that to rid this world of evil will not simply be the act of good asserting itself, of saying simply that evil is impossible, but the act of the shedding of the blood of virtue. Walker is unwilling to accept anything less than the conversion of evil and this is because certain pointed theological questions never occur to Walker that are extremely important to Stowe: Is this world worth saving? Should it be saved if the price must be so high? Stowe does not question the nature of a price, as a good Calvinist-tinged Christian would not. A refusal to grant the price its proper respect born of its necessity and its nature would simply be Manichaeanism. Walker refuses to see the necessity of the price itself and certainly does not appreciate its nature as any sort of heroism. Thus she will not have her characters pay it. It seems to me that no matter how much as modern readers we prefer this revised rhetoric of virtue, the Calvinist imagination has a greater grasp of the political and social cost of virtue, a greater sense of the drama of the existence of virtue in a fallen world. Stowe pleads just as strenuously and far more effectively for the humanity and protection of women and children and for the assertion of the values of the home against the values of the marketplace that have dehumanized and debased all human relationships. But her sense of history is greater, knowing that events like the Revolution of 1848, the abolitionist movement, the Fugitive Slave Act, and African emigration are the result of large social and political trends that affect *all* citizens. Small but significant changes, such as the son of Shelby freeing all of his father's slaves, come hard; utopias do not come at all. Stowe knows that conversions like the one experienced by St. Clair are rare; most people who participate in a comfortable social order will not change until they are forced to. *The Color Purple*, book and movie, has become everybody's protest art: an indication of our need to have a bloodless eschatology where there are no devils in the end, no evil that cannot be repented and, indeed, no final rendering up of things because there will be no sin, only all of us simply going, quietly and softly, into that good light.

Robert Penn Warren

1905–

Robert Penn Warren was born on April 24, 1905, in Guthrie, Kentucky, to Robert Franklin and Anna Ruth Penn Warren. He was educated at Vanderbilt University (B.A. 1925, *summa cum laude*), the University of California at Berkeley (M.A. 1927), Yale University, and Oxford University (Rhodes Scholar, B.Litt. 1930). In 1930 he married Emma Brescia; they were divorced in 1950. He married writer Eleanor Clark in 1952; they have two children. He has taught at Louisiana State University, the University of Minnesota, and Yale University. From 1923 to 1925 he edited the *Fugitive*, which he founded with Allen Tate. He founded the *Southern Review* in 1935 with Charles W. Pipkin and Cleanth Brooks, and edited it until 1942. From 1942 to 1963 he was an advisory editor for *Kenyon Review*, and he served as Consultant in Poetry for the Library of Congress in 1944 and 1945.

As a prominent poet, novelist, and critic, Warren ranks as one of the most versatile American writers of his time. Warren was initially attracted to writing at Vanderbilt University, where he was a student under John Crowe Ransom and a member of the influential Fugitive Movement. His first published book was *John Brown: The Making of a Martyr* (1929). Though he has continued to publish social comment and literary criticism throughout his career, particularly as an influential proponent of the theories of New Criticism, it is as a novelist and poet that he is primarily known. Warren published his first book of poetry, *Thirty-six Poems*, in 1936, but his early verse attracted little attention, and his early reputation rested primarily upon his novels. His first published novel was *Night Rider* (1939). It was his third novel, *All the King's Men* (1946), that brought Warren widespread popular and critical attention. A fictionalized portrait of the notorious Louisiana governor Huey Long, it has continued to hold critical interest for its treatment of such themes as corruption, self-examination, and determinism. Subsequent novels have upheld Warren's high reputation, though none has had the initial impact of *All the King's Men;* among the most important are *World Enough and Time* (1950), *Band of Angels* (1955), and *A Place to Come To* (1977).

Warren regards himself as primarily a poet, and while he tends to examine similar themes in both his fiction and poetry, it is in his poetry that his growth as a stylist and technician can be charted. His early work is strictly formalist, but by the time of *Eleven Poems on the Same Theme*

(1942) he had begun to experiment with loose metrical structures and alternating narrative voices. *Brother to Dragons* (1953), a book-length "Tale in Verse and Voices" about a murder committed by Thomas Jefferson's nephews, firmly established Warren as one of America's most versatile and ambitious poets. Subsequent volumes, including most notably *Audubon* (1969) and *Chief Joseph of the Nez Perce* (1983), have continued to demonstrate Warren's skill at a variety of poetic forms and styles, and have also broadened his subject matter to include an impressive breadth of human experience, self-examination, and self-definition. He received the National Book Award for Poetry in 1958 for *Promises: Poems 1954–1956* (1957) and the Bollingen Prize in Poetry for *Selected Poems: New and Old, 1923–1966* (1966) in 1967. In addition, he is the only person to win the Pulitzer Prize in both fiction and poetry, for *All the King's Men* in 1947 and *Promises* in 1958. His appointment in 1986 as the first Poet laureate of the United States is a tribute to his stature in modern American letters.

In spite of its Plutarchan decor, *Brother to Dragons* is a brutal, perverse melodrama that makes the flesh crawl. On a chopping block in a meat house in West Kentucky, "on the night of December 15, 1811—the night when the New Madrid earthquake first struck the Mississippi Valley—" Lilburn and Isham Lewis, nephews of Thomas Jefferson, in the presence of their Negroes, "butchered a slave named George, whose offense had been to break a pitcher prized by their dead mother, Lucy Lewis." Coming upon this preface, the reader is warned that he will not find Monticello and Jefferson with his letters from John Adams, his barometers and portable music stands, but Lizzie Borden braining the family portraits with her axe. This incongruity, which dislocates nearly everyone's sense of Jeffersonian possibility, was fully appreciated by Thomas Jefferson himself, who, so far as we know, never permitted his nephews' accomplishment to be mentioned in conversation. Yet the Lewis brothers are as much in the Southern tradition as their Uncle, rather more in the literary tradition which has developed, and so it is workaday that their furies should pursue them with homicidal chivalry, the pomp of Vestal Virgins—and the murk of Warren's four novels. Indeed these monstrous heroes are so extremely *literary* that their actual lives seem to have been imagined by anti-Romantic Southern moderns, and we are tempted to suppose that only gratuitous caprice caused Warren to blame their bestiality on the Deist idealism of their detached relative, Thomas, the first Democratic president. Portentous in their living characters, when Lilburn and Isham Lewis reach in 1953 their first artistic existence, they draw upon a long line of conventions established by their imaginary counterparts: it is as true inheritors that they speak a mixture of Faulkner's iron courtesies, country dialect, and Booth's *sic semper*. Like their ancestor Cain, these late-comers were prior to their poetic fulfillment. The disharmony between the brothers' high connections and their low conduct, however, is less astonishing than Warren's ability to make all his characters speak in unfaltering, unstilted blank verse. (I trust it is this Jeffersonian and noble technical feat, and not the lurid prose melodrama, which has three times caused me to read *Brother to Dragons* from cover to cover without stopping.) ⟨. . .⟩

Brother to Dragons is the fourth remarkable long poem to have been published in the last ten or twelve years. *Four Quartets*, *Paterson*, and *The Pisan Cantos* are originals and probably the masterpieces of their authors. Warren's poem is slighter, lighter and less in earnest. This judgment, however, is ungrateful and misleading. *Brother to Dragons* is a model and an opportunity. It can be imitated without plagiarism, and one hopes its matter and its method will become common property. In a sense they are already, and anyone who has read Elizabethan drama and Browning will quickly have opinions on what he likes and dislikes in this new work.

There *are* faults in this work. Warren writes in his preface, "I have tried to make my poem make, in a thematic way, historical sense along with whatever other kind of sense it may be happy enough to make." And more emphatically, " . . . a poem dealing with history is no more at liberty to violate what the writer takes to be the spirit of his history than it is at liberty to violate what the writer takes to be the nature of the human heart." Obviously the kind of historical sense claimed here is something more serious and subtle than the mere documentary accuracy required for a tableau of Waterloo or a romance set in 1812. The incidents in *Brother to Dragons* are so ferocious and subnormal they make *Macbeth* or Racine's *Britannicus* seem informal interludes in Castiglione's *Courtier*. Warren's tale is fact, but it is too good melodramatically to be true. To make sense out of such material he uses an arrangement of actors and commentators, a method he perhaps derived from Delmore Schwartz's *Coriolanus* in which Freud, Aristotle, and I believe Marx, sit and discuss a performance of Shakespeare's play. Warren's spirit of history has a rough time: occasionally it maunders in a void, sometimes it sounds like the spirit of Seneca's rhetoric, again it just enjoys the show. The difficulties are great, yet the commentary often increases one's feelings of pathetic sympathy.

As for the characters, nothing limits the length of their speeches except the not very importunate necessity of eventually completing the story. Warren improves immensely upon that grotesque inspiration which compels Browning to tell the plot of the *Ring* twelve times and each time in sections longer than *Macbeth*. Structurally, however, Browning's characters have the queer compositional advantage of *knowing* they are outrageously called to sustain set-pieces of a given length.

A few small points: Warren's bawdy lines—I sometimes think these are pious gestures, a sort of fraternity initiation, demanded, given, to establish the writer firmly outside the genteel tradition. Secondly, the word "definition" is used some fifty times. This appears to be a neo-Calvinist pun, meaning defined, finite and perhaps definitive and final, or "know thyself for thou art but dust." Warren used this word in his short poems and fiction and in an obsessive way I'm not quite able to follow. Time and History: the poet addresses these ogres with ritualistic regularity, reminding us a bit of a Roman pro-consul imposing the Greek gods on the provinces, those gods which have already renounced the world in Eliot's *Four Quartets*. ⟨. . .⟩

Finally there is R.P.W., the author, who speaks at greater length than any of the other characters and with greater imagination, power and intelligence. He is Pilgrim, Everyman, Chorus and Warren, the real person, who like everyone has his own birthplace, parents, personal memories, taste, etc. It is his problem to face, understand, and even to justify a world which includes moronic violence. As with Hugo at the beginning of *Le Fin de Satan*, the crucial catastrophic act is not the eating of the apple but the murder of Abel. Warren suggests that the pursuit of knowledge leads to a split in body and spirit, and consequently to "idealism," and consequently to an inability to face or control the whole of life, and consequently to murder. He is concerned with evil and with the finiteness of man. I'm not sure of Warren's position but it is often close to neo-Humanism and neo-Thomism, and so deliberately close that he frequently suffers from hardness. Yet sometimes you feel he is taking the opposite position and is merely a commonsense, secular observer. The character R.P.W., as we see him in the poem, is himself split between a love for abstractions and an insatiable appetite for sordid detail, as though Allen Tate were rewriting Stavrogin's "Confession." R.P.W. has his own troubles with "definition." The two halves embarrass each other: the character is at once unreal and again irresistibly energetic.—ROBERT LOWELL, "Prose Genius in Verse," *KR*, Autumn 1953, pp. 619–24

A good many reviewers of *Promises* have been taken aback by the violent distortions of language. But one reviewer is Mr. James Dickey, in the *Sewanee Review*, who describes and clarifies my own response to the book.

The first point concerns the distortions of language, and the critic felt that most of them were flaws: "Warren has his failings: his are a liking for the over-inflated, or 'bombast' as Longinus defines it; he indulges in examples of pathetic fallacy so outrageous that they should, certainly, become classic instances of the misuse of this device. Phrases like 'the irrelevant anguish of air,' and 'the malfeasance of nature or the filth of fate' come only as embarrassments to the reader already entirely committed to Warren's dark and toiling spell." I think this is a pretty fair description of the kinds of awkwardness that frequently appear in *Promises*. However, the really curious and exciting quality of the book is the way in which so many of the poems can almost drag the reader, by the scruff of the neck, into the experiences which they are trying to shape and understand.

But this very triumph of imaginative force over awkward language is Mr. Dickey's second point, and the critic states it eloquently: "Warren's verse is so deeply and compellingly linked to man's ageless, age-old drive toward self-discovery, self-determination, that it makes all discussion of line-endings, metrical variants, and the rest of poetry's paraphernalia appear hopelessly beside the point."

Yet, so very often in this new book, Mr. Warren simply will not allow the reader to consider the rhetorical devices of language "hopelessly beside the point." That he is capable of a smoothly formal versification in some poems, and of a delicate musical variation in others, he has shown many times in the past. We are not dealing with a raw, genuine, and untrained talent, but with a skilled and highly sophisticated student of traditional prosody. In effect, a major writer at the height of his fame has chosen, not to write his good poems over again, but to break his own rules, to shatter his words and try to recreate them, to fight through and beyond his own craftsmanship in order to revitalize his language at the sources of tenderness and horror. One of the innumerable ironies which hound writers, I suppose, is the fact that the very competence which a man may struggle for years to master can suddenly and treacherously stiffen into a mere *armor against experience* instead of an instrument for contending with that experience. No wonder so many poets quit while they're still behind. What makes Mr. Warren excitingly important is his refusal to quit even while he's ahead. In *Promises*, it seems to me, he has deliberately shed the armor of competence—a finely meshed and expensive armor, forged at heaven knows how many bitter intellectual fires—and his gone out to fight with the ungovernable tide. I mean no disrespect—on the contrary—when I say that few of the poems in this book can match several of his previous single poems. Yet I think there is every reason to believe that his willingness to do violence to one stage in the development of his craftsmanship is not the least of the promises which his book contains. I do not wish to argue about any of the poems in *Promises* which I consider at the moment to be failures, though I shall mention one of them. But I think that a book such as this—a book whose main importance, I believe, is the further evidence it provides for the unceasing and furious growth of a considerable artist—deserves an attention quite as close as that which we conventionally accord to the same author's more frequently accomplished poems of the past.

The distortion of language in the new book is almost always demonstrably deliberate. When it is successful, it appears not as an accidental coarseness, but rather as an extreme exaggeration of a very formal style. The poetic function of the distortion is to mediate between the two distinct moods of tenderness and horror. This strategy—in which formality is driven, as it were, to distraction—does not always succeed. It is dishonest critical damnation, and not critical praise, to tell a gifted imaginative writer that he has already scaled Olympus when, as a matter of frequent fact, he has taken a nose-dive into the ditch. The truest praise, in my opinion, is in the critic's effort to keep his eye on the poet's imaginative strategy, especially if the poet is still alive and still growing. I think that the failure of Mr. Warren's strategy is most glaring when the material which he dares to explore will somehow not allow him to establish one of the two essentially dramatic moods—the tenderness and the horror of which I spoke above. An example of this failure is the poem "School Lesson Based on Word of Tragic Death of Entire Gillum Family." The horror is stated, and the reality of horror is a lesson which everyone must learn, as the poet implies in the last line. But there is no tenderness against which the horror can be dramatically drawn, and there is no dramatic reason that I can discern for presenting the ice-pick murder of the Gillum family. Now, I am sure the reader will allow me to claim a human concern for the Gillum family, wherever and whoever they were. All I am saying is that they are *not here*: that is, their death seems to me a capricious horror; and the distorted language, in spite of its magnificent attempt to achieve a folk-like barrenness and force, remains a capricious awkwardness.

My speaking of "failure" in a poet of so much stature is of course tempered by my statement of a conviction which constantly grows on me: that a failure like the "School Lesson" is worth more than the ten thousand safe and competent versifyings produced by our current crop of punks in America. I am spared the usual but boring critical courtesy of mentioning names by the fact that we all know who we are. But I am not comparing Mr. Warren's performance in *Promises* with the performance of us safe boys. I am trying to compare it with his capacities.—JAMES WRIGHT, "The Stiff Smile of Mr. Warren," *KR*, Autumn 1958, pp. 645–48

When I am asked how much *All the King's Men* owes to the actual politics of Louisiana in the '30's, I can only be sure that if I had never gone to live in Louisiana and if Huey Long had not existed, the novel would never have been written. But this is far from saying that my "state" in *All the King's Men* is Louisiana (or any of the other forty-nine stars in our flag), or that my Willie Stark is the late Senator. What Louisiana and Senator Long gave me was a line of thinking and feeling that did eventuate in the novel.

In the summer of 1934 I was offered a job—a much-needed job—as assistant professor at the Louisiana State University, in Baton Rouge. It was "Huey Long's University," and definitely on the make—with a sensational football team and with money to spend even for assistant professors at a time when assistant professors were being fired, not hired—as I knew all too well. It was Huey's University, but he, I was assured, would never mess with my classroom. That was to prove true; he was far too adept in the arts of power to care what an assistant professor might have to say. The only time that his presence was ever felt in my classroom was when, in my Shakespeare course, I gave my little annual lecture on the political background of *Julius Caesar;* and then, for the two weeks we spent on the play, backs grew straighter, eyes grew brighter, notes were taken, and the girls stopped knitting in class, or repairing their faces. ⟨. . .⟩

Conversation in Louisiana always came back to the tales, to the myth, to politics; and to talk politics is to talk about power. So conversation turned, by implication at least, on the question of power and ethics, of power and justification, of means and ends, of "historical costs." The big words were not often used, certainly not by the tellers of tales, but the concepts lurked even behind the most ungrammatical folktale. The tales were shot through with philosophy.

The tales were shot through, too, with folk humor, and the ethical ambiguity of folk humor. And the tales, like the political conversations, were shot through, too, with violence—or rather, with hints of the possibility of violence. There was a hint of revolutionary desperation—often synthetically induced. In Louisiana, in '34 and '35, it took nothing to start a rumor of violence. There had been, you might hear, a "battle" at the airport of Baton Rouge. A young filling station operator would proudly display his sawed-off automatic shotgun—I forget which "side" he was on, but I remember his fingers caressing the polished walnut of the stock. Or you might hear that there was going to be a "march" on the Capitol—but not hear by whom or for what.

Melodrama was the breath of life. There had been melodrama in the life I had known in Tennessee, but with a difference: in Tennessee the melodrama seemed to be different from the stuff of life, something superimposed upon life, but in Louisiana people lived melodrama, seemed to live, in fact, for it, for this strange combination of philosophy, humor, and violence. Life was a tale that you happened to be living—and that "Huey" happened to be living before your eyes. And all the while I was reading Elizabethan tragedy, Machiavelli, William James, and American history—and all that I was reading seemed to come alive, in shadowy distortions and sudden clarities, in what I saw around me.

How directly did I try to transpose into fiction Huey P. Long and the tone of that world? The question answers itself in a single fact. The first version of my story was a verse drama; and the actual writing began, in 1938, in the shade of an olive tree by a wheat field near Perugia. In other words, if you are sitting under an olive tree in Umbria and are writing a verse drama, the chances are that you are concerned more with the myth than with the fact, more with the symbolic than with the actual. And so it was. It could not, after all, have been otherwise, for in the strict, literal sense, I had no idea what the now deceased Huey P. Long had been. What I knew was the "Huey" of the myth, and that was what I had taken with me to Mussolini's Italy, where the bully boys wore black shirts and gave a funny salute.

⟨. . .⟩ However important for my novel was the protracted dialectic between "Huey" on the one side, and me on the other, it was far less important, in the end, than that deeper and darker dialectic for which the images and actions of a novel are the only language. And however important was my acquaintance with Louisiana, that was far less important than my acquaintance with another country: for any novel, good or bad, must report, willy-nilly, the history, sociology, and politics of a country even more fantastic than was Louisiana under the consulship of Huey.—ROBERT PENN WARREN, "*All the King's Men:* The Matrix of Experience," *YR*, Winter 1964, pp. 161–67

Robert Penn Warren's virtuoso piece of criticism, his analysis of *The Rime of the Ancient Mariner*, is well known. That poem, Warren says, posits as its primary theme man's necessity for repentance and reconciliation after crime and punishment:

> The Mariner shoots the bird; suffers various pains, the greatest of which is loneliness and spiritual anguish; upon recognizing the beauty of the foul sea snakes, experiences a gush of love for them and is able to pray; is returned miraculously to his home port, where he discovers the joy of human communion in God, . . . [and the meaning of] the notion of a universal charity, . . . the sense of the "One Life" in which all creation participates.

Warren further claims that the "unmotivated" killing of the albatross is "exactly the significant thing about the Mariner's act" because it "reenacts the Fall . . . ." Warren stresses the Mariner's willing perversity—his individual, not inherited, responsibility for the act—and the crew's willing complicity. Having then submitted himself to "the great discipline of sympathy," the Mariner can walk again, in Coleridge's words, "with a goodly company." In Warren's interpretation, the terms which the Mariner accepts for his reintroduction into human society are resonant of the traditional, mythic punishment of Cain or the Wandering Jew and the dark verbal gift of the *poète maudit*.

Whether or not Coleridge's Mariner encompasses those typal figures is probably academic, since the part of the story to which most readers have always responded dramatically is the Mariner's need to communicate his experience to as many wedding guests as he can find. In our own time we have come to regard that need as a psychological—and even moral—commonplace. Warren's view of Coleridge's Mariner has been questioned, and it may or may not satisfy students of *The Rime of the Ancient Mariner*, but there is no doubt that Warren's interpretation of that famous figure in his critical essay is anticipated and corroborated in his fiction.

Warren's Mariner is characterized by a need, sometimes compulsive, to recite his story. But Warren's Mariner is not Coleridge's. In novel after novel, Warren rings his own changes on Coleridge's pattern. In the episodes involving this recurring character, who invariably proclaims his guilt for the past acts, his storytelling itself is usually an attempt to justify the teller to others *and* to himself. In such novels as *Night Rider* and *Band of Angels*, Warren's Mariner can more often define his crime and punishment than he can his repentance and reconciliation. In some instances even part of his punishment, the self-flagellating need to tell someone about it, suffers from lack of focus; he is unable to see his true role in his own act, and often the very recital of his story is halting, convoluted, imprecise, even incorrect.

When minor characters act out the Mariner role, their stories become the interpolated tales which readers have come to expect in many of Warren's novels. Sometimes the protagonist, who impatiently or reluctantly listens to the story, becomes in turn another Mariner, a wedding guest who comes to acknowledge the truth of what he has been told and acts upon it. The recurrence of this figure and his checkered fortunes in the Warren universe, in a variety of refinements and developments, indicates two aspects of the author's concern in his fiction.

Morally, that concern is the burden of man's salvation and the adequate verbalizing of it, which is to say, the resolution of guilt and responsibility requires confession (Coleridge's Mariner must explain, cajole, and persuade others of both his sin and his salvation). Aesthetically, that concern is providing statement with a necessary and appropriate vehicle (Coleridge's Mariner can begin his return journey after he composes a poem of blessing). These two related interests Warren writes of elsewhere in various ways—

Morally:

> [Conrad's work] is about the cost of awareness and the difficulty of virtue, and his characteristic story is the story of struggle and, sometimes, of redemption.
>
> Man must make his life somehow in the dialectical process . . . , and in so far as he is to achieve redemption he must do so through an awareness of his condition that identifies him with the general human communion, not in abstraction, not in mere doctrine, but immediately. The victory is never won, the redemption must be continually re-earned.

Aesthetically:

> We must sometimes force ourselves to remember that the act of creation is not simply a projection of temperament, but a criticism and purging of temperament.
>
> [W]hat good fiction gives us is the stimulation of a powerful image of human nature trying to fulfill itself.
>
> The poet [creates] . . . a self as well as a poem—but neither except in so far as he creates a structure, a form. . . . The poem is, then, a little myth of man's capacity for making life meaningful. And in the end, the poem is not a thing we see—it is, rather, a light by which we may see—and what we see is life.

In this respect certainly Warren's criticism and his fiction are of a piece. Warren's Mariners morally relive the ceremony of confession and aesthetically re-enact the process of the artist.
—JAMES H. JUSTUS, "The Mariner and Robert Penn Warren," *TSLL*, Spring 1966, pp. 117–19

UNSIGNED
"Fables for Our Time"

Times Literary Supplement, November 27, 1959, p. 269

When some painstaking official literary analyst of the twenty-first century worms a way through the fiction of our time, separating the artificially tough from the oversensitive and carefully categorizing Angry, Humorous and Sentimental Young Men, he will surely cry out in bewilderment at some point: "Why didn't they write about the things that were not merely under their noses but quite obviously directed their actions? The problems of power and corruption, of idealism disastrously exercised, and of those who, more unhappily still, identified history's course with some sort of romantic Nihilism?" If it was too difficult, too indiscreet, too crude, to write directly about Stalin and Hitler, or even about the effects of Communism and Fascism on individual lives, surely these subjects could have been dealt with indirectly, fabulously even? But here the official literary analyst's voice might die away as he discovered, among the piled literary litter of a century, the novels of Robert Penn Warren, for these are almost precisely the subjects with which Mr. Warren deals in his three major books, *Night Rider* (1940), *All the King's Men* (1948), and *World Enough and Time* (1951)—the dates are those of first English publication. All of these books are set in the past, distant or near; all take as their starting-points actual characters or situations; each exists in its own right as a work of art, yet has an obvious relevance to our own time.

At the time that his first novel, *Night Rider*, was published Mr. Warren was already well known in America as one of the most gifted in a highly talented group of Southern poets and critics. The book's setting was Kentucky, and some of the strength and colour in Mr. Warren's work comes from the fact that he deals always with a primitive, violent and materially backward society. *Night Rider* was "suggested by certain events which took place in Kentucky in the early years of this century," although, here and elsewhere, great freedom is used in dealing with actual people and situations. The book's theme is the moral, and at last the physical, destruction of a lawyer named Percy Munn, a destruction accomplished through his determination to fight for what he believes to be right.

At a meeting of the Kentucky tobacco growers, called to protest against the way in which the buyers' ring has forced down the price of tobacco, Munn is unexpectedly called on to speak. He discovers in himself a capacity for moving the crowd by oratory, and is elected to the committee of the Association of Growers of Dark Fired Tobacco. The association's objective, as one farmer puts it, "is to make those son-of-a-bitching buyers pay me what my tobacco's worth." Members are recruited who agree to withhold their tobacco from sale until a fair offer is made for it. But when a higher offer is received the association splits, deciding by the chairman's vote not to accept it. The senator who has been the association's chief public figure resigns, and the remaining members turn to violence. Munn has voted for acceptance, but he joins the terrorist group who warn anti-Association men to join, and if the warning is neglected make night raids to destroy their tobacco by scraping the plant beds. Before long they take farmers out at night and force them to scrape their own beds. Then they visit a town where tobacco is stored, and blow up the warehouses with dynamite. Munn, who has given instructions that no townspeople shall be attacked, finds himself committed to violence when one of his own band is killed. Troops are called in, a counter-terror begins, the Association is defeated. Munn ends his life like a hunted animal, shot down by the soldiers.

Munn's character is developed with great subtlety. One key to it is given in the opening paragraphs when, in the close-packed train to Bardsville, he is plunged hard against the man next to him, smells the sweat of his body and the lye soap in which his shirt has been washed, and feels "a momentary irritation and disgust with that dead, hot weight of flesh which would plunge against him and press him, with the shouting and talking, with the smell of sweat and whisky, and with the heat of the day and of the crowded bodies." At the heart of Munn's abstract desire for justice is coldness and frustration, exemplified in his relations with women. But it is suggested that Munn's desire for justice is in any case part of an historical process leading towards its opposite. It was inevitable, Mr. Warren seems to be saying, that the growth of the Association, which was founded to fight extortion, should lead to terrorism and extortion in its turn, and in this context Munn's motives are comparatively unimportant. Yet there is one more twist to be noticed, in the fact that to Mr. Warren as a novelist the workings of the individual will are the spring of the story and what he is showing us, here and in later books, is a tragic conflict between individual will and individual pattern.

In *All the King's Men*, as in *Night Rider*, Mr. Warren's prose is fluent, powerful, and by modern English standards almost indigestibly rich. The triumphant justification of such prose is seen in the first pages of the book, which with their description of the great highway's approach to Mason City, that unimportant outpost of civilization "where, no doubt, the hogs scratched themselves against the underpinnings of the post office," evoke with wonderful skill the kind of world and the kind of people from which a demagogic dictator can come. The fictional career of Willie Stark, as is well known, follows closely that of Huey Long, the Louisiana Kingfish. Like Huey Long, Stark came from a poor and backward part of the state, was a remarkable orator, and rested for power upon the semi-literate hill-billies who worshipped him. Like Long, Stark ruled by popular consent yet also through bribery and threats, like Long was assassinated by a young doctor. But Willie Stark is shown to us consistently as an idealist who went wrong, whereas Long's political career, in spite of the social and economic revolution that he prompted in Louisiana, was corrupt and vicious from the start. In his innocence Stark allows himself to be used as an electoral puppet, a hill-billy whose candidature may siphon off a few votes, and his discovery of the way in which he has been tricked signals the change from the solemn young man copying out quotations from Emerson, Macaulay and Benjamin Franklin to the power-hungry Boss whose contempt for individuals is complete, but who still carries out his intention to build a magnificent free hospital:

> I'm going to build me the God-damnedest, biggest, chromium-platedest, formaldehyde-stinkingest free hospital and health centre the All-Father ever let live. Boy, I tell you, I'm going to have a cage of canaries in every room that can sing Italian grand opera and there ain't going to be a nurse hasn't won a beauty contest at Atlantic City and every bedpan will be eighteen-carat gold and by God, every bedpan will have a Swiss music-box attachment to play "Turkey in the Straw" or "The Sextet from Lucia," take your choice.

It is absurd, however, to accuse Mr. Warren of partiality towards Willie Stark. What he has done is to transform and complicate the character of Huey Long for his own artistic purposes. By the side of Stark is placed his henchman Jack Burden, whose Oblomovish compulsion towards inaction draws him to Stark's natural force, whose emotional blankness is filled by Stark's furious enthusiasm, who tries to protect himself from the pressures of life by Berkeleyan metaphysics:

> I heard someone open and shut the gate to the barn lot, but I didn't look around. If I didn't look around it would not be true that somebody had opened the gate with the creaky hinges, and that is a wonderful principle for a man to get hold of. I had got hold of the principle out of a book when I was in college, and I had hung on to it for grim death. I owed my success in life to that principle. It had put me where I was. What you don't know don't hurt you, for it ain't real. They called that Idealism in my book I had when I was in college, and after I got hold of that principle I became an Idealist.

The joke is, as Burden very well knows, that Idealism can never protect you enough, that the world will always wash over the Idealist's walls of sand and come flooding in; and it is even true that in a sense the Idealist positively welcomes the incursion of a rough character like Willie Stark upon his world of imaginary Ideal childhood and Ideal love. Mr. Warren's concern in this book with the corruption induced by power is given much additional complexity by the device of showing Stark's career always through the eyes of Jack Burden, since Stark's conduct appears almost admirable by the side of Burden's readiness to do any sort of dirty action for his employer, while consoling himself by the idea that in the eye of history these things are unimportant. In the end Burden decides that his friend, the incorruptible doctor Adam Stanton who killed Stark, and Stark himself "were doomed to destroy each other, just as each was doomed to try to use the other and to yearn toward and try to become the other, because each was incomplete with the terrible division of their age." He adds a significant rider: although they were doomed, they did not know it, "they lived in the agony of will."

In discussing the ideas in Mr. Warren's novels one pays, inevitably, insufficient attention to the effect of his luxurious, and in its way undoubtedly magnificent, romantic style upon his material. This style is seen at its full reach in *World Enough and Time*, a book in which the invented quotations from early nineteenth-century histories, autobiographies, newspapers and pamphlets, are done with such skill and at such leisurely length that they have an air of absolute fidelity. In spite of all its rhetorical glitter the style is used here positively to enhance the force with which Mr. Warren puts forward his ideas about man's place in history. The book is placed again in Kentucky, and is founded on an actual trial for murder in which both sex and politics were involved. Jeremiah Beaumont, Warren's hero, is an idealist but, unlike Burden, an idealist whose belief in purity of conduct finds an outlet in action. Beaumont kills from the most virtuous motives, to preserve a woman's honour. He discovers during the story that he has been deceived in everything, betrayed by friends, tricked by enemies, emotionally deceived by the woman he loves. In his final despair, Beaumont writes at the end of his autobiography:

> I had longed for some nobility, but did not know its name. I had longed to do justice in the world, and what was worthy of praise. Even if my longing was born in vanity and nursed in pride, is that longing to be wholly damned? For we do not damn the poor infant dropped by a drab in a ditch, but despite the mother's fault and tarnishment we know its innocence and human worth. And in my crime and vainglory of self is there no worth lost? Oh, was I worth nothing, and my agony? Was all for naught?

The book's last words echo Beaumont's cry: "Was all for naught?"

It is disconcerting to turn from these books to *The Cave*: disconcerting not simply because *The Cave* is, like the novel that preceded it, *Band of Angels*, much inferior to Warren's best work but because the book's defects are implicit even in his earlier novels. One of the most important sections in *All the King's Men* is that in which Jack Burden, on Stark's instructions, delves into the past of a man he has known and respected all his life, Judge Irwin. Burden finds the single discreditable passage in Irwin's past and, again in obedience to Stark, threatens him with exposure. It is only after Irwin's suicide that Burden discovers he has been threatening his own unacknowledged father.

This element of Lyceum melodrama, for the most part kept under control in Warren's writing, is right at the centre of *The Cave*. A young man named Jasper Harrick who has gone, as we should say, pot-holing, is found to be trapped, and stuck in one of a series of caves. That, at least, is the tale told by his friend Isaac Sumpter, who crawls in after him, takes food and drink to the trapped boy, and brings out a number of inspiring messages which he records on tape:

> A man is in the ground. He is a young man. He is a brave man. He has been decorated for valour, in the Korean War. Wounded, he rallied a platoon, and hung on to a shell-swept, hell-swept hillside. This afternoon, he looked into my face, deep underground, trapped in the crawlway of a cave, a stone on his leg, and said. "This is tougher than Korea. But I'm going to make it."

Isaac says that Jasper cannot be dug out. The rescuers must drill in to the cave round the back of him. While this lengthy drilling process goes on the fate of Jasper Harrick becomes a matter of national concern, so that the whole resources of television, radio and Press are concerted not to help him but to get the utmost publicity from the story. In fact Jasper Harrick is dead, and Isaac Sumpter has lied deliberately to make his own name known in the world of Big Media, which in due time he enters.

It is possible to imagine ways in which the theme might have been treated to make it a significant fable, but Warren's customary subtlety has deserted him here. The satire is crude, the characters are conventional, and there is only perfunctory probing into the dense thicket of motive: the power that moves all of these people is sex. Isaac Sumpter (who is not a Jew and does not like being called Ikey) is frustrated because, although he truly loves a Jewish girl named Goldie Goldstein, his puritan background has impelled him to be unfaithful. Nick Papadoupalous, the Greek restaurant proprietor who falls in with Isaac's scheme, is frustrated because even when he closes his eyes tightly he cannot quite believe that his blonde wife is Jean Harlow. Jasper Harrick's young brother Monty is frustrated because his girl, Jo-Lea, won't sleep with him often enough, and their father, old Jack Harrick, is frustrated because he has cancer and the days when he used to "tear off drawers like a high wind in October stripping a sycamore to bare-ass white" have gone for ever. The single clue we are given to the life of such a minor character as the bank manager, Mr. Bingham, is a sexual one. "Mr. Bingham . . . wore pince-nez glasses rather than plain steel rims, which he would have preferred, because his wife, between whose legs he had not managed to get in five years, thought pince-nez more refined and suited to his position."

There is (need one say?) nowadays no moral objection to the description of sex in novels. The objection here is that sexual "explanation" on this level is superficial, a most inadequate substitute for analyses properly rooted in social life and habit. Mr. Warren has done enough for remembrance as a novelist in his three major books: and he is a writer so intelligent, so inquiring and so gifted that one looks on *The Cave* as an occasion on which his instinct for melodrama has unhappily run wild, rather than as any evidence of declining power.

EVERETT CARTER

"The 'Little Myth' of Robert Penn Warren"

Modern Fiction Studies, Spring 1960, pp. 3–12

Art is the little myth we make, Robert Penn Warren suggested, and history is the big myth we live. "Myth," that tricky and difficult word, has been abused, but Warren has used it consistently, since his review in 1935 of Ransom's *God Without Thunder*, to mean a pattern of belief involving emotion, imagination, and intellect, which provides the uncriticized assumptions by which men conduct their moral lives: "The myth, then, defines the myth-maker's world, his position in it, his destiny, and his appropriate attitude."[1] The little myth of the artist is the personal pattern which the individual sensitivity imposes on its world, the big myth the pattern by which a society makes sense of its universe. When the relation between the artist and society is stated in this way, it becomes clear that the relation between the private myth of the artist and the public myth of his culture is a crucial one. In what ways does the little pattern emerge from, or react against, the public myth? The answer to this question, one may deduce from Warren's formulation, will lead to an understanding of both the materials an artist uses, and the forms by which he organizes that material; and if this be a possible hypothesis about art in general, then it should specifically serve as a touchstone for Warren's fiction, his "little myths," in particular.

Such an approach must begin with the most dangerous of all attempts at generalization—an attempt to fix a central body of "American" belief. We can avoid trying to answer this impossible question by restating it; by asking *not* "What is this belief?" but rather "What, in general, have Americans believed this belief to be?" We are then no longer concerned with a search for a probably undiscoverable objective unity, but with an identification of what has commonly been accepted as an unofficial "faith" which America has been supposed to embody. And this faith has been almost universally identified by native and foreign observers as the American variation upon the Enlightenment of eighteenth century England and France: the concept of worldly salvation, of progress, and those faiths associated with it— a belief in the essential goodness of nature and of man, and the possibilities of those societies which men agree to organize. This body of belief sustained Jefferson and Franklin and has come down to be the core of modern popular pragmatic acquiescence: witness the words of that most typical of modern Americans, Harry Truman, who writes in his memoirs: "What kept me going in 1945 was my belief that there is far more good than evil in man, and that it is the business of government to make the good prevail."

Now our American fiction—the little myths we have made—have often accepted this great myth: for example the works of Howells, the earlier and greater Mark Twain, Sinclair Lewis, James T. Farrell, and John Dos Passos. But this central core of American belief has often run into violent and brilliant opposition in the stories of Hawthorne, Melville, Henry James, and at no time has the opposition been more violent or brilliant than in the works of Hemingway and Faulkner. Warren's fiction, on the other hand, although generally taken to be an expression of this same mood of rejection, neither accepts nor rejects the great myth. All his fiction deals with the struggle, the dialectic between the little myths men make and the great myth that Americans live, with the tragedies that ensue when these are kept separate, and with the comedy that is possible when a synthesis is reached. His fiction takes as its major theme the conflict between the acceptance of this "world" of American assumptions and a rejection of this "world" and a consequent devotion to a code or an "idea"; it almost always points out the fatal consequences of this conflict for both American man and American artist, and demonstrates the need for a synthesis of the two opposing elements. The depiction of this conflict and the need for fusion and synthesis is seen, in his works, on multiple levels: on the level of history as the conflict between northern pragmatism and Southern absolute traditions and codes; on the level of art as the conflict between romanticism and realism; and on the level of the personality as the conflict between the individual and society or the child and the parent.

In Warren's view, the American thesis, the American "world" against which his protagonists of the "idea" react, is no simple belief in man's inevitable perfectibility; rather it is itself a synthesis of this "pure" and naive conception with the dark facts of fallen human nature and the stubborn realities of the material universe, a synthesis which the late nineteenth century termed "pragmatism." The birth of this thesis in the prototypical American consciousness—that of Thomas Jefferson—was the subject of Warren's long verse narrative *Brother to Dragons*, a poem which both describes the genesis of the modern American myth, and projects Warren's private view of the meaning of American experience. The poet describes his leaving his old father slumbering in the seat of a car while he clambers into an old Southern field, in the midst of which stand the fragments of a Southern plantation house. He relives the revolting story that was enacted here: two brothers had butchered a slave on a chopping block before the terrified eyes of the other plantation workers. They had been captured and tried and convicted; but in the meantime a more significant figure had been drawn into the tragedy. This was Thomas Jefferson, author of the Declaration of Independence, soon to be one of the early Presidents of the United States, who was kin to the murderers. He who had proclaimed the essential virtue of man comes up against the truth of the human condition. But Jefferson, as a recent commentator has observed, ". . . is then able to effect a fruitful reconciliation between aspiration and reality," achieving, as a result, a "wholeness of spirit."[2] The sense of reconciliation, of the bringing together of tradition and modernity, of parent and child, or real and ideal, is embodied in the poem's conclusion when the poet turns his back on the scene of the old tragedy, walks to the modern road which winds its asphalt way through Kentucky, climbs into the seat of his car, and rejoins his old father. *Brother to Dragons* is the description of the birth of the American pragmatic "myth."

The entire body of Warren's fiction, before and after *Brother to Dragons*, is concerned with an analysis of the history of America and Americans in terms of the struggle between this "world" of pragmatic, optimistic, chastened secular faith and the succession of pure "ideas" by which individual Americans have tried to live when the world of their cultural assumptions has seemed inadequate. The thesis which Jefferson had reached at the end of *Brother to Dragons* is embodied in the Cassius Fort and the James Madison of *World Enough and Time*; it becomes the final happy position of Tobias Sears in *Band of Angels*; corrupted by a century of excessive materialism, it becomes the warped pragmatism of Senator Tolliver in *Night Rider*, of Bogan Murdock in *At Heaven's Gate* and, most conclusively and brutally, of Willie Stark in *All the King's Men*. In each work, an essentially romantic idealist opposes the embodiment of pragmatism; there ensues (in all but *Band of Angels*, whose happy ending sets it apart from the others) a catastrophe which cancels out the absolute claims of the pure idea, and affirms the need for a reconciliation, a "saving union of the idealist and pragmatist impulses of modern man."[3]

This pattern of conflict and implied synthesis appears very early in his fiction. In *Night Rider*, Mr. Munn is the first of Warren's Southern idealists who destroy themselves and others in their rejection of the world of pragmatic fact. Munn has never outgrown his childhood dream of a perfection untainted by realities. He remembers the stereopticon picture of his youth. "It was a little world. . . . he had felt that if he could just break through to that little world where everything was living, it seemed, but at the same time frozen in its tiny perfection, he would know the most unutterable bliss." Allied with him at first in his formation of an association of tobacco farmers, but breaking with him when the ideal of the association meets the hard political and economic realities, is Senator Tolliver, for whom "all life is a compromise." An older man, who is satisfied with saying that "we did the best we could," Tolliver is the first in a long line of imperfect fathers or father surrogates, whom the protagonists reject. He is described as laying his hand on Munn's shoulder, as "leaning confidentially toward him." Munn, rejecting all compromise, along with rejecting Tolliver, becomes inhuman: he ruins an old friend's tobacco bed because "the idea of the Association was more important to him than Mr. Goodwood."

Mr. Munn, Warren suggests, has been overtaken by the fatal tendency of the liberal to erect his humanism into an abstract ideal which ends by crushing the claims of humanity. In his next novel, *At Heaven's Gate*, he explores the similar fatal attachment of men to absolutes. He depicts the ruthless "purity" of the aesthete, Slim Sarrett, who sacrifices humanity to art; he shows the devotion of Sweetie Sweetwater to economic justice, a devotion which sacrifices Sue Murdock to its religion of liberalism. Above all, he shows how expediency, cut adrift from the idealism of Jefferson, creates a monster like Bogan Murdock, whose life is devoted to the absolute idea of power. And then, in his two major novels, *All the King's Men* and *World Enough and Time*, Warren embodies most fully and effectively the complexities of what he conceives to be the recurrent drama of American moral and imaginative history.

World Enough and Time is the story of Jerry Beaumont, a tormented young Southerner born in Kentucky at the turn of the nineteenth century. Fatherless, his heritage tainted by guilt, he searches for some idea to give meaning to his life. The world about him is not enough; he must try to impose some pattern upon it, to create some drama in which he can become an actor. At first he believes that the drama can be one of a return to innocence—an escape to the woods and to savagery, where a man would never grow old and know the "burden of time and things." He yearns for the truth beyond the "bustle of an hour." He momentarily turns to religion, only to find that it turns into a snaggle-toothed hag with whom he couples in the woods after a revivalist orgy. At this point he meets Cassius Fort, a brilliant frontier politician who gives him a new, more worldly hope. Cassius becomes "like a father" to him, and Jerry is about to re-enter the world and involve himself in the flow of American life. Then Wilkie Barron, the mask, the false face of the "world," tells him of the dishonor of a lovely girl, Rachel Jordan, at the hands of Cassius Fort.

Immediately Jerry returns to the old despair and can see but one solution: he can play his part in a tragedy, and plan toward the moment when, with "all dross and meanness of life consumed, he could live in the pure idea." He searches out and finds Rachel; she lives in a dream world, like a princess in her enchanted castle; she embodies the essence of the plantation ideal: the beautiful woman of chivalry who gives her lover a favor to wear as he goes out to do battle for her. Their favorite reading together is classic idealism, and they lose themselves in the world of Plato's pure perfection; at the end Jerry turns from Plato to Locke, and under his influence writes in his diary:

> It is the first and last temptation, to name the idea as all, which I did, and in that error was my arrogance,

> and the beginning of my undoing and cold exile from mankind. And now I remember a passage I once read by the ingenious Mr. John Locke in his book on our Understanding, in which he says that we are wont to regard any substance we meet as being a thing entirely by itself, and having all of its qualities independent of all other things, and that in doing so we neglect the operation of those invisible fluids which compass the substance about and spring from all other substances. Take a piece of gold, Mr. Locke says, which is of a tawny color, and is heavy and malleable, and has great worth, and put it aside in some place beyond the world, and the influence of all other substances. Then it may lose that color, and the weight become nothing that it may float as a feather, and the malleableness be changed into a perfect friability, and that worth we put upon it—ah, what becomes of that worth in the cold and silent dark beyond the stars?

(Melville had written of this dilemma of Western thought: the vision of the ship balanced precariously between the enormous heads of two whales one of which is Kant, and the other Locke.) But Jerry's disillusion with Plato comes too late; the force which leads him to disaster is the force of a pure idealism, shunning the taint and corruption of the world of contingency. He marries Rachel, after unconsciously forcing her to make him vow to "kill Fort" in a perfect act of justice, outside the world, pure and untarnished. Jerry kills him, is captured, and is brought to trial. He has covered his tracks carefully, and tells truth after truth about his movements—all except the final lie of his innocence; other witnesses tell lie after lie, but they add up to the final truth—that he is the murderer. Jerry learns "that life tells no lies in the end, for all the lies, single and particular, will at last speak together in a great chorus of truth in many voices."

The meaning of the novel on the level of history seems clear: to the American, the Southerner, comes the vision of an idea; in terms of the novel, to Jerry Beaumont comes Rachel Jordan. The idea is one which Jerry has forced into being through his need for a certainty, for an ideal, for something to live for beyond the "bustle of an hour." Cassius Fort, on the other hand, is the face of the world—imperfect, heir to the animal within, working in terms of compromise, process, and adjustment. Cassius Fort ("the world") violates Rachel Jordan ("the idea"), and Jerry must destroy the world, must kill Fort. When he does so, Jerry discovers his deep, unpardonable sin—the sin of Ethan Brand and of Ahab: the sin of rejection of the world for the idea. "What becomes of the idea," he finally asks himself, "if we place it apart from our warm world and its invisible fluids by which we live?" He had thought that the idea in and of itself might redeem the world, and in that thought had scorned the world." He had sought to justify himself, "not by the world, which he would deny, but by the idea."

World Enough and Time is about the South's and about America's past; *All the King's Men* is about its present, and perhaps it is this contemporaneity which makes it seem a more impressive presentation of this conflict, and a more compelling attempt at fusion and synthesis. Accepting, as always, the hints of history, Warren wrote what appears to be the story of a man like Huey Long, a red-necked representative of democracy who rises to power through his concern for social justice, and is corrupted by the power he has achieved. But it is not, as Warren has said repeatedly, the story of Willie Stark. It is the tale of Jack Burden, a young reporter who bears the weight of the modern intellectual's rejection of his country's great myth and who watches while his Southern friends spurn the modern world and attempt to impose an idea upon it—the idea of a feudal chivalric responsibility. Like Jerry Beaumont, Jack Burden is both spectator of and participant in the conflict between "world" and "idea" that rages about him. For Willie Stark is the modern man of pragmatic action. (In his Introduction to the Modern Library edition, Warren says that "in the shadows of imagination behind Willie Stark" is the "scholarly and benign figure of William James.") Willie is the political realist for whom the law is "like the pants you bought last year for a growing boy; but it is always this year and the seams are popped and the shankbones to the breeze. The best you can do is do something and then make up some law to fit." When there are complaints about his methods, he answers: "Dirt's a funny thing. . . . Come to think of it, there ain't a thing but dirt on this green God's globe except what's under water, and that's dirt too. It's dirt makes the grass grow. A diamond ain't a thing in the world but a piece of dirt that got awful hot. And God-a-Mighty picked up a handful of dirt and blew on it and made you and me and George Washington and mankind blessed in faculty and apprehension." And then he adds, "It all depends on what you do with the dirt."

The characters in the novel who represent the other side of the dialectic are Judge Irwin and Adam Stanton. Irwin is an old gentleman, full of the grace, dignity, and honor of the idealized old South, Adam Stanton a young doctor who in a youthful way represents the same absolute codes. Willie Stark, the modern world of pragmatism, runs headlong into these men of the ideal. At the beginning of the story, Stark hears that Irwin is about to oppose him; he drives down on a modern concrete highway to the little corner of the unchanged Old South where, in the mansion attended by his Negro servant, the aged Judge sits in "an old-fashioned velvet smoking jacket and tuxedo pants and a boiled shirt." Willie's Palm Beach coat is "all crumpled" where it had crawled on his shoulders, with the "sweat-stains of the afternoon showing dark at the armpits." Suit of synthetic fabric stained by sweat against smoking jacket and boiled shirt; modern activity and pragmatism against older codes and traditional standards. Adam Stanton, like Judge Irwin, represents these latter absolute ideas; Jack Burden says of him:

> "He has lived all his life in the idea that there was a time a long time back when everything was run by high-minded, handsome men wearing knee breeches and silver buckles or continental blue or frock coats, or even buckskin and coonskin caps, as the case may be . . . who sat around a table and candidly debated the good of a public thing. It is because he is a romantic, and he has a picture of the world in his head, and when the world doesn't conform in any respect to the picture, he wants to throw the world away."

In the turmoil of this conflict Jack Burden abandons himself to despair, to the dream that "all life is but the dark heave of the blood and twitch of the nerve." It is, Burden declares, the nightmare, the "dream of our age." But as he watches, the patterns begin to form: Willie Stark ruins Judge Irwin and possesses Anne Stanton, Adam's sister; Adam destroys Willie, and in turn is destroyed by Willie's follower. Burden realizes that he has been watching a Hegelian tragedy where two opposing forces, each partly good but each incomplete, have been reconciled by catastrophe:

> "He had seen his two friends, Willie Stark and Adam Stanton, live and die. Each had killed the other.

> Each had been the doom of the other. As a student of history, Jack Burden could see that Adam Stanton, whom he came to call the man of idea, and Willie Stark, whom he came to call the man of fact, were doomed to destroy each other, just as each was doomed to try to use the other and to yearn toward and try to become the other, because each was incomplete with the terrible division of their age."

The pattern of conflict and synthesis is not only presented on the level of history in Warren's fiction; it is also presented on the level of art and the artist. On the title page of *World Enough and Time* there is the hint of this pattern and this purpose in the announcement that it is "A Romantic Novel," and with a sophisticated writer like Warren, this classification is significant. It announces an attempted fusion between two forms of prose fiction, one that has been associated with the idea and the ideal—the romance, and the other which has been associated with the world of social appearances—the novel. From the Spanish picaresque tales and the English rogue stories of the sixteenth and seventeenth centuries, through Fielding and Smollett, Austen and Trollope, the novel has been the medium of the fiction which is deeply involved with the world of physical perceptions and social involvements. And through these same centuries, from the romances of Sidney and Lyly, through the *romans à clef* of the seventeenth century, and the Gothic romances of the late eighteenth and early nineteenth centuries, the term "romance" has been reserved for these fictions which dealt, on the surface, with other than the natural and the normal. In America Hawthorne, Melville, and Poe consciously adopted the romance as their form, and Hawthorne defined the two types and distinguished between them in his prefaces.

Henry James began to fuse the forms, and Warren's fiction continues to try to end this division. It attempts to fulfill all the usual requirements of the novel: an allegiance to the natural and probable, a concern with social and historical realities. He wishes it to be a "highly documented" picture of the world, but at the same time he wishes it to be much more than "straight" naturalism. He hopes to succeed where the essentially artistic protagonists of his novels have failed. His major characters are almost all men of essentially artistic disposition, filled with a desire to find order, form, and meaning. When the world about them appears to be emptied of form and meaning, they either strive to impose a pattern upon that world, as does Jerry Beaumont, or they flee from the world and despair of writing about its essential meanings, as does Jack Burden in *All the King's Men* who, as we remember, gives up the possibility of writing the story of his ancestor, Cass Mastern. And in each case the artist discovers that to alienate himself from that world is to court disaster. The act of aesthetic pride is no less fatal in Warren's works than the act of scientific pride was in the works of Hawthorne.

These patterns of conflict and synthesis on the historical and aesthetic levels of Warren's fiction are everywhere reinforced by persistent allusions to the corresponding divisions within the human personality. The surface stories of the novels are projections of what one dominant school of psychoanalysis has insisted is the basic division in the psyche of man: the conscious need for the parent, and the subconscious desire to destroy the parent who threatens the maturity of the child. We note the ubiquity of this pattern in all of Warren's works. The protagonists are almost all fatherless children who search for their father, then reject and destroy their father, and then, in some way, find they must come to terms with the parent or what he represents. Jack Burden, we remember, rejects three parent images—Judge Irwin, the Scholarly Attorney, and Willie Stark; then, having understood himself as well as the forces of history, he goes to live in his father's house, and, having lived in it, is only then prepared to go out "into the convulsion of the world, out of history into history, and the awful responsibility of time."

More explicit than in the earlier novels is this pattern of search for, rejection of, and the final acceptance of the parent in *Band of Angels*, a revelatory, if minor romance. "Oh, who am I," cries Amantha Starr, the divided, torn personality of this fiction. She rejects her white father, who has allowed her to be sold into slavery, and finds peace only when she can say that she knew "my father loved me." She reaches this awareness at the moment when her husband and a young Negro from Chicago have ritualistically become "somehow suddenly gay and free and young again" by accepting and washing Old Slop, the ancient Negro garbage man: "the bottle passing gravely from hand to hand, mouth to mouth, the application of suds, the scrubbing of the scaly, smelly old black hide, the dousing with Eau de Cologne, the honoring of Father. . . ." As in the rest of his fiction, so too in this vivid novel is the pattern of conflict and reconciliation with the parent made identical with the design of conflict between the world of pragmatic complexity and the pure idea, and the reconciliation of the two. Before the final ritual of the washing of Old Slop, Tobias Sears, the Emersonian, the transcendentalist devoted to the idea of total human whiteness and goodness, "had not been involved in the commonality of weakness" but "had merely leaned down from his height, had inclined his white hieratic head that glimmered like a statue." This allegiance to an ideal of pure goodness alienates him from humanity, and only at the end, when he is willing to reconcile the idea with the actuality of human frailty, is he capable of partaking of the final happy ending with Amantha in his arms, the "old shadows" of their lives "cancelled in joy."

This view of Warren's fiction, of course, neglects the ambiguities and paradoxes with which his works are rife; these point to a "mysterious depth" which he feels is "one of the chief beauties of art," but which we have not time to explore here, if, indeed, these depths are possible to communicate in any way other than by the exact symbolic structures in which they are embodied. On the levels about which we can communicate, however, the fiction of Robert Penn Warren seems a dramatic realization of the "terrible divisions" of our age, and an attempt to suggest the need for the healing of those divisions. As such, they take a peculiarly significant place in the history of modern fiction. The earlier and most representative stories of Hemingway and Faulkner, those two giants of postwar fiction, essentially rejected the world of American pragmatic thought, the Great Myth of Worldly Salvation, of Progress, of the Enlightenment; in their rejection they were forced to face a vision of the modern world as meaningless, a world which is all "dark heave of the blood and twitch of the nerve," where man can at best suffer in dignity. Their evolution has been away from this vision, and Robert Penn Warren, in many ways their heir, has profited by their brilliant rejections and has tried to make them a part of another larger conception. If Warren's fiction is prophetic, man must and will accept the mixture of good and evil which is his past and his present, American writers will struggle to fuse romanticism and realism, symbolism and naturalism, and Americans in general must come to terms with themselves as neither exclusively a band of angels nor brothers to dragons. These syntheses in turn will become new myths against which the little myths of the artist will continue to measure themselves; this tragic, but necessary and beneficent, conflict constitutes the little myth which Warren has used as the controlling pattern of his fiction.

Notes

1. Robert Penn Warren, "John Crowe Ransom: A Study in Irony," *Virginia Quarterly Review*, XI (January 1935), 97.
2. Frederick P. W. McDowell, "Psychology and Theme in *Brother to Dragons*," *PMLA*, LXX (September 1955), 566.
3. Robert Heilman, "Melpomene as Wallflower; or, The Reading of Tragedy," *Sewanee Review*, LV (Winter 1947), 166.

LEONARD CASPER

From "The Running Gamble"

Robert Penn Warren: The Dark and Bloody Ground

1960, pp. 165–82

American literature in his time has profited from Warren's independence, the relentless claim of his work to the right of self-determination and his refusal to be subject to the professional whims of chronic uncritics beyond their depths in supposed main currents. This is not to say that Warren has remained aloof from his times. Rather, he has avoided ready-made images, formulas for liberals. His dialectic, for example, has always been essentially more Socratic than Marxian. When the thirties required "proletarian novels" Warren was writing of the Ku Klux tactics employed by farmers' unions in the South's tobacco wars, as well as the damage done a whole society by the venality of finance capitalism. When public depravity, spurred by depression, brought statism to the outlying parishes, Warren rang brazen bell warnings in *All the King's Men*. When Guernica and the Guaderramas, Buchenwald and Anzio flashed in the headlines, Warren was not immune. To the proving grounds of the world he dedicated "Letter from a Coward to a Hero," "Terror," and *Circus in the Attic*, not with the "sense of urgency" used by propagandists to justify those galvanic reflexes that pass for first thoughts, but with consideration for the abiding truth which alone, however unflattering, sanctifies the journey into man's interior. During the days of roaring employment in the fifties he wrote *Promises* to the future—a caveat, not a canticle. For he had also written:

> May we not, however, in some chill hour between dark and dawn, have the thought that our own age may—just possibly—have its own frauds and deceits, deeper and more ambiguous than those anatomized in *The Great Gatsby*, that though this is not the age of provincial self-satisfaction, it may be the age of national self-righteousness and require a sharper scalpel than even *Main Street*, and that Divine Providence has given no written guarantee that It will not rebuke the smuggery of the Great Boom?[1]

His whole effort as author has been to deny the existence of any "literature to specification."

Private scruple—nourished by the understanding that sometimes comes to Southerners after a century of acting the official accused, as well as by the New Critics' propensity for keeping literature in reserve as a mode of meditation—has prevented Warren's dependence on the axioms of society. As a result even anti-Marxist critics have chastised him for not being more useful to their causes. Regardless, Warren continued to respect individual natures more than those cared to permit who followed the allegedly fixed course of social forces.

The dialectical configuration in Warren's works does not derive from undiscerning adherence to the romantic Hegelian formula for irresistible progress, peculiar forms of which survive in the supposedly realistic twentieth century. As he explained in his American Academy in Rome interview, when he was a child he was impressed by Buckle's *History of Civilization*, which offered

> . . . the one big answer to everything: *geography*. History is all explained by geography. I read Buckle and then I could explain everything. It gave me quite a hold over the other kids, they hadn't read Buckle. . . . Buckle was my Marx. . . . After I had had my session with Buckle and the one-answer system at the age of 13, or whatever it was, I was inoculated against Marx and his one-answer system when he and the depression hit me when I was about twenty-five.[2]

Warren finds the dialectic valuable as a dramatic device because it suggests that any movement upward, toward a superior realization and state of being, is possible only as struggling evolution, fetal uncoiling, emergence not despite but through the rub of outer and inner circumstance. Sudden mutations, like unprepared intuitions, are rare. Nor is ascent inevitable. The dialectic is also valuable, therefore, as an equivalent to the implacable sifting and winnowing of the self, inasmuch as progress toward the apocalypse has to be earned by the individual rather than by throngs and masses. Or its erratic motion is comparable to multiple vision in painting, to Picasso's only apparent distortions in time and volumetric displacement, composed with insight rather than the oversight of mirror realism. It is a predication of experience, a technique for elaborating the complex exertions of any man to be both human and himself.

However externally motivated certain of Warren's characters may seem to be, the clearly moral center of his work argues that their author is not himself victim of a deterministic philosophy. He has made clear time after time that the darkest compulsions are subconscious, and public motives mere rationalization of these private desires. His interpretation of Coleridge, with whose views he is in sympathy—that "original sin is not hereditary sin; it is original with the sinner and is of his will"—coincides with the admission that Hamish Bond finally makes, after previously absolving himself because he did not make the world. Although the diseased dictates of every character are not exposed to the sunlight on the forum steps, the consensus is that man is a condition in his own conditioning. The cause of any action, therefore, has to be sought in the self as well as in society or in transcendent doom.

If there is no simple division of classes in *Night Rider* or *At Heaven's Gate*; if no ready-made judgment of the "American dictator" in *All the King's Men* can satisfy the novel's purpose; if "Terror" questions the pointless enthusiasm of the "liberal" soldier scurrying after death around the compass; if *Brother to Dragons* questions even Jefferson, compadre with John Taylor of American agrarian theory; if *Band of Angels* is in all honesty critical of the average plantation holder (Bond is exceptional) as well as of Yankee slave traders and fumbling "do-gooders," the critic restricted to the expected and to epigrammatic expression objects. Neither "proletarian" nor "liberal" in his work, Warren slips through the major categories of such a mind, nor is he sufficiently obscure to be treated with half envious scorn. Consequently, *World Enough and Time* is simply demoted to the rank of "costume novel," romanticized historical fiction. In other works, violence and yeoman farmer settings are dismissed as "typically Southern, typically naturalistic."

Warren's choice of formidable structures (his willingness,

for example, to risk an anticlimax by refusing Beaumont his historic execution) and of thorny textures (his habit of total recall even of seemingly insignificant details, because all life interlocks) has not catered to popularity. The canon itself has been too unorthodox to win quick admiration or even agreement. Furthermore, his critical essays have from the start admonished facile prejudgment of intent and achievement in literature. He has long admired not only Tudor and Jacobean drama, but also the "kitchen criticism" of the period, its connoisseur interest in "how to make the cake,"[3] as he has called it. Not finding ready at hand the judicious kind of readers required by his work, he has had to help train them.

Even if Warren had used crude experience classifiable as "proletarian" or "liberal," he would not have felt that subject alone, without art and craft, had already decided the issue of values. The priority assigned a writer's concerns was confirmed by Warren during the Vanderbilt reunion in 1956. Throughout two sessions he had hardly spoken while other ex-Fugitives lamented their failure to write a culture epic or at least poems resonant with political pronouncements. Finally he interrupted, saying that

> . . . it seems to me greatness is not a criterion—a profitable criterion—of poetry; that what you are concerned with is a sense of contact with reality. And it's maybe a pinpoint touch or a whole palm of a hand laid . . . but the important thing is the shock of this contact. . . . And when you get around to talking about the scale, it's not the most important topic . . . it's something that comes in very late in the game. . . . It's that stab of some kind, early; that's the important thing for me in the sense of an image that makes that thing available to you indefinitely, so you can go back to it, can always find that peephole on the other world. . . .

Later he quoted with approval Wordsworth's reply to a clergyman who had admired his poems "for their fine morality." Wordsworth had answered, "I don't value them for that. I value them for the new view they gave of the world." That is, meaning is never pre-experiential but processive.[4]

The writer has to accept responsibility for his work just as certainly as his characters must be made responsible for their actions. His signature is his risk, and sometimes his glory. Because Warren has respected his characters, refined in the fires of dramatic irony, whatever they wear or say or touch becomes a memorable part and projection of them, and they live with an authentic intensity far beyond the anesthetic average. Life is true to *them*.

However, if Warren's works have refused to snuggle up cozily in the day's categories, if they have voted themselves the right to self-determination, have they also achieved in any sense self-sufficiency? There is much in his textbooks to suggest that such a condition is possible and desirable. Repelled by the abuse of literature as a means to paltry ends, the New Critics at first spoke of literature as an end in itself (just as the Agrarians argued that labor, through fulfillment of the worker, could be its own best reward). Fortunately, Warren has been enabled to enjoy the undeniable advantages of the New Critics' procedures for literary investigation, while still avoiding their earliest confusion of self-possession with self-indulgence, through the sacramental vision of life which he has uncovered in others and, in turn, verified in his own poetry and fiction.

In "Causerie," Allen Tate has discountenanced Warren and others for reluctance to be doctrinaire ("Warren thirsty in Kentucky, his hair in the rain, asleep . . ."). Yet Warren's example has encouraged the survival in American letters of the thinking and moral man, as well as the economic and political man. His characters struggle to appropriate their own unconscious will, to know themselves completed—a more exhausting and perplexing task than even that set by the true courtier, the Elizabethan "complete man," a model Warren has admired only less than the seventeenth-century metaphysical visionary. Why does man feel that he inhabits an alien world? Because birth is separation; because identity is division as well as classification; because some compulsion, half-comprehended, drives him to repudiate his past, makes him want to rinse his mouth of the taste of his father's failures and, instead, fulfill to its farthest corner his own sense of self and his importance, in new circumstances.

This is the first stage in the life of Willie Stark, Jerry Calhoun, Dr. Charles Lewis, and the young boys in "Eidolon" and "Blackberry Winter." A wind comes out of the West, and the young man yearns for more flesh, just as anyone might wonder if he is man yet or still a bobbing plug in a booming tiderace, or might long to play renegade from old wounds in a newfound land. From God or the fathers, those founts of generic traditions, he leaves so abruptly that he crystallizes his incompletion. There is temporary buoyancy in the motionless waters of the moment. There is trial innocence, the attempt to be untouchable, the sanitary silence of the hospital. But selfhood is more than being; it involves hazards of engagement. There can be no secession from grandeur. Although each man may distinguish himself from unaspiring nature, once begun to emerge, self asks for justification to prevent itself and its actions from appearing gratuitous. There is admission of a continuum of selves. Anything short of that would be mutilation, denial of cycles of dreams and seasons of memories. But the momentum of these same mechanisms for self-assurance reaches back, acknowledging the past; reaches out, covering human multitudes under the beatitude of one common skin; reaches up, for assumption into the Mystical Body and the higher innocence that more than compensates for the confession of sin, price of belief in God. Thus analogies are cantilevered outward from the literary concept of indivisible form and the unified sensibility.

Warren once said that John Milton's writings have a single continuous theme, developed through a variety of subjects.[5] This has become true of his own world of fiction, with its exploration of unbroken years of homesickness.[6] Some men feel satisfactorily cured in the world, finding secular salvation through human community and living undisturbed in nature, like the grackles in *Night Rider*. Others are convinced that present agony is meant to be a rehearsal of future glory, that to avoid assimilation by matter they must finally accede to divine absorption. For these, violence can become the pangs of birth rather than death spasms; there can be a splendor of wounds, changed to stigmata by religious discipline. Stoicism, the Hemingway acceptance of disability without self-pity, is not enough: even the mountains erode. Because ignorance is not true innocence, endurance in darkness is also not enough, for the darkness festers and after a little time flesh rots. In the canon of Robert Penn Warren, people live with the knowledge of abortion and miscarriage as well as with assassinations and fatal duels, symbols of death and the end of man, but also directives for mortification.

Ashby Wyndham lives by a vision. So do Cass Mastern, the Scholarly Attorney, Munn Short, Jerry Beaumont in his last moments, and others. Each fashions his myth, that body of symbols which stimulates awareness of human possibility (through trial self-images) not in response to wish-fulfillment but through immersion in the destructive element itself. Jerry

Beaumont's hope is in immortality, his faith as strong as foreknowledge; he is content to die because life is contamination. For others the fact of guilt and the desire for innocence are never stilled but between them attenuate the human form like the figures of El Greco, living currents of worried light.

Such characters, suffering from the daily failure of their dream, not because it is false but because it is too demandingly true, act as a corrective to the easy optimism that science occasionally adopts as a result of small successes. Warren is not alone in objecting to the extreme tendency of scientism to predict the growing adequacy of man in his universe only by reducing the dimensions of both man and that universe. The doctors in *Proud Flesh* and *All the King's Men* belong to the society of surgeons who, confronted by the soul, cry first for amputation. Warren's characters discover that self-assertion, in its elementary stages an act of pride, matures paradoxically through the humbling effect of understanding (Perse Munn, who does not quite understand, is only humiliated and baffled), through comprehension of one's station in the gossamer cosmic web. Like Amantha Starr they earn their right to themselves by accepting the necessity of pain and error as natural elements in their definition. They try to meet life on their own terms, but these are terms informed by life itself. There is a mutual roil of verification between introspective man and the tumble of events. It requires consummate imagination to measure accurately the motion of a system in which the calculator himself is moving. This, too, is cause for humility and caution though not for the indulgence of despair.

In Warren, the artist's instinct for amplification has checked the critic's tendency to circumscribe. Attempting to place judgment of literary value beyond the reach of clinical pragmatism, which accepts only what it can test and therefore rejects metaphysical problems, Warren helped promote the New Critical concern for assessing inner relationships of literature considered as literature-in-itself (in the jargon of the early days: intransitive, autotelic, autonomous). At times his views have seemed indistinguishable from John Crowe Ransom's (literature affords a means of realizing the world, not of improving it) and from Cleanth Brooks's or early Allen Tate's (the work of fiction is its own best scholar and lover). Permission for fiction to live in the world has been granted reluctantly, lest it be corrupted again. But if love is not lust, mere possession and use, neither need it be the mutual contemplation of navels. It should be consummated. 〈. . .〉

It would be difficult to determine how much the static view of literature has tampered with the fiction and poetry of Robert Penn Warren. (*Band of Angels*, however, affords sufficient duration for its disclosures to mature, so that the climax is no antidramatic summing up of the issues or mere program for the future; and *Promises* is a motion made toward the future, an act of testament offering the past for ratification by the next generation. These are reassuring signs.) Perhaps the early New Critics' assumption that belief without action is possible, like the doctrine of the efficacy of faith without works, accounts in part for the fact that so many of Warren's major characters have died at the moment of revelation or disappeared with their intention to change not yet put to the test of action. Perse Munn dies still a stranger to his life processes; Jerry Calhoun lies abed, accusing himself of contributing to the death of his fiancée, but no act of amendment proves his contrition; Jack Burden sits down to write a book before re-entering time; penitent Jerry Beaumont is overtaken and slain, a welcome end to the misery he has caused in his confusion.

Rather, it is the minor characters from the *exempla*—Willie Proudfit, Ashby Wyndham, Cass Mastern, and Munn Short—who, having survived their spiritual crises, painstakingly tend their own gardens. However, with the possible exception of Cass Mastern, none of these men has suffered the nagging agony of the tormented, self-flagellating mind of the major characters. In terms of the canon they are too extraordinary to serve adequately as models of conduct. Furthermore, the *exempla* are short and are narrated by the subjects themselves. The stories of the central characters are long, compiled in detail, not in summary, and are generally related by an additional narrator whose analysis adds to their complexity. Before Amantha Starr, there was never quite space enough and ripening time to demonstrate convincingly an idea in action.

Still, if the hermetic view of literature can threaten art, so too can the web philosophy of multiple relations. The cry "nothing is lost, ever lost" properly magnifies the implication of "Crime" that conscience is a stern judge and constant warden. But, when total recall is practiced as a technique in the novels to such an extent that the texture of things weighs down and muffles the introspective parts (even when this is intended to represent man's struggle to throw off the saddle of Thingism), any advance of the characters toward enlightenment may seem to arrive suddenly, preparations meanwhile having become indistinct. Total recall jeopardizes *All the King's Men* on several occasions: Cass Mastern's unjustifiably itemized search for Mrs. Trice's slave is one. It is a recurrent distraction throughout *World Enough and Time*. The physical particulars do not demonstrably bear constant witness to each other, as the philosophy might suggest, and it is well that they do not, or officious fate would seem to be managing each character each agitated instant. Even such friendly critics as William Van O'Connor and John Crowe Ransom have at one time or another overemphasized the naturalistic elements in Robert Penn Warren, as a result of this reproduction of minutiae.

Fortunately, these tendencies resist each other. The ascetic recluse and the lover with the world-wide embrace are counter-forces. The problem of their reconciliation, the fumbling for mutual respect of self and society, ego and superego is not the artist's alone. A risk more personally Warren's is his concept of the gropings of history as magnification of the individual's dark grasp of his own life span. If the past is part of every man's identity, but history is obscure, how can he ever know himself? How can he ever be sure of his motives? And, without such certainty, what confidence can he have in his moral standards? Although Warren has cautioned against rash judgment of others, he has never advised suspension of the conscience. But which inner voice shall a man trust?

Such inarticulateness is descriptive of a common flaw in the characters, not of deliberate perversity in their author. The struggle for self-knowledge *is* the act of definition and therefore *is* the line of resistance in Warren's novels, the pattern for figurative elaboration. *Exempla* have been relied on because, the vision of each major character being afflicted in some degree, clarification has to come in part from outside. For the character trying to understand himself, language and action are useless, worn thin through too much handling as the currency for self-delusion. "The Mango on the Mango Tree" and "End of Season" imply the need for communion but do not specify any path for the pilgrim. If each has his own path, his own truth, is this not a return to the nominalism and personal relativism of romanticism? God's eye watches; but what is his will? Warren's canon justifies the existence of evil, but the questions asked incidentally in *All the King's Men*—What is good? Where does value come from?—go unanswered. If evil helps define man, what defines evil? Does a thin line, or only thin air, separate Willie Stark's definition of good from pragmatism? Is the darkened judgment of the individual satisfactorily differentiated from the descriptive morality of science? Colonel Cassius Fort, who has a plan to resolve the questions, What is law? Is it absolute or man-made? is killed before it can be announced.

Spiritual truth in Warren is never given into the custody of the ministry, as a whole cast of characters prove: hypocritical Seth Parton in *Band of Angels*, the saturnalian revivalist in *World Enough and Time*, the perjured preacher of "The Confession of Brother Grimes" or *At Heaven's Gate* (Sweetwater's father), the slothful shepherd from "The Circus in the Attic." It is the dogmatic and the doctrinaire whom Warren has satirized most.[7] Rejection of formal authority places the problem back in the world where it must be solved in perilous, and therefore more meritorious, fashion.

Because the preliminary stages of man's way are confused and misdirected, any clarity at the culmination of his journey may seem to come with the suddenness of grace bestowed gratuitously, a providential act, like the sorting out of damned and elect by the Puritan God. Warren, however, is suspicious of gifts since they weaken the beneficiary's self-reliance and self-respect. But a reward is different, a reward is honorable. Salvation can be earned by subscribing to responsibility. It must be earned in the world and in time. This requirement is one of the few human constants: to define oneself in motion, under reversible circumstances; to know some unity in the varieties of change; to treasure that knowledge more than peace.

From his early poems through *World Enough and Time* and *Brother to Dragons*, Warren's imagery has recognized an autumnal time, given a legend of meaning in "Knowledge and the Image of Man":

> Man can return to his lost unity, and if that return is fitful and precarious, if the foliage and flower of the innocent garden are now somewhat browned by a late season, all is the more precious for the fact, for what is now achieved has been achieved by a growth of moral awareness. . . . Man eats of the Tree of Knowledge, and falls. But if he takes another bite, he may get at least a sort of redemption.[8]

In the same address Warren speaks of literary form as a "vision of experience, but of experience fulfilled and redeemed in knowledge. It is not a thing detached from the world but a thing springing from the deep engagement of spirit with the world." Literature is a mode of knowledge, the "evocation, confrontation, and definition of our deepest life," but not a program for inducing a trance: "No, that gazing prepares for the moment of action, of creation, in our world of contingency." Therefore literature is not tidy or genteel, prissy or impotent. It is a living gamble, an act of faith meant to redeem the demand of those finally born: *Was all for naught?* But the terms of the gamble turn with the game and change again with the player. A man who has written as he willed and who has respected the individual voice of his characters would not be consistent if he failed to regard the experience of others, and to trust it.

Notes

1. "A Lesson Read in American Books," *New York Times Book Review*, December 11, 1955, p. 1.
2. Ralph Ellison and Eugene Walter, "The Art of Fiction, XVIII: Robert Penn Warren," *Paris Review*, IV (Spring-Summer, 1957), 115–16.
3. Ellison and Walter, "Robert Penn Warren," p. 130.
4. *Fugitives' Reunion: Conversations at Vanderbilt*, ed. Rob Roy Purdy (Nashville: Vanderbilt University Press, 1959), pp. 142–43, 162.
5. "Some Recent Novels," *Southern Review*, I (Winter, 1936), 627–28.
6. Warren has suggested that "Blackberry Winter," *All the King's Men*, and his reading of Coleridge's *The Ancient Mariner* share a common realization, discoverable elsewhere in his work as well, that "out of change and loss a human recognition may be redeemed, more precious for being no longer innocent." "Writer at Work: How a Story Was Born and How, Bit by Bit, It Grew," *New York Times Book Review*, March 1, 1959, p. 5.
7. Logically, therefore, even Warren's firmest conviction and vision must be free to develop and to be verified by subtler, broader experience. When Ralph Ellison in Rome asked him if a sense of righteousness in an author was not fatal to the seriousness of his work, Warren agreed: "Once you start illustrating virtue as such you had better stop writing fiction. Do something else, like Y-work. Or join a committee. Your business as a writer is not to illustrate virtue but to show how a fellow may move toward it—or away from it." Ellison and Walter, "Robert Penn Warren," p. 138. What fiction communicates is fundamentally the experience of a discovery.
8. "Knowledge and the Image of Man," *Sewanee Review*, LXIII (Winter, 1955), 187.

PAUL WEST

From *Robert Penn Warren*

1964, pp. 5–18, 34–38

Reviewing Robert Penn Warren's *The Legacy of the Civil War* (1961) Alfred Kazin suggested that the same title defines the whole of Warren's output, by now some twenty books in thirty-five years. It is a just suggestion, deceptive only in making Warren, who shares the existential preoccupations of such writers as Camus, Sartre, and Malraux, a more narrowly American, a more exclusively historical writer than he in fact is. Born a southerner, he has remained one spiritually, but his allegiance has been complex and tormented. His knowledge of and profound concern for the American South have taught him about the penalties and advantages of being not only American but also human. And this double lesson has flowered in extraordinary, widely differing ways in part at least because he has spent his life in intimate touch with the leaders of intellectual movements of various kinds, from the Vanderbilt Fugitives to the Agrarians and New Critics. He is very much a man of his time, and of history too.

Born in 1905 in Guthrie, Kentucky, Warren graduated in 1925 from Vanderbilt University and two years later took his M.A. at Berkeley, going on to Yale and, as a Rhodes scholar, to Oxford. At Vanderbilt he met Allen Tate (another Kentuckian), John Crowe Ransom, and Donald Davidson, and joined them in editing *The Fugitive* (1922–25), a magazine dedicated to the idea of the poet as an outcast soothsayer. In 1929, a year before receiving the Oxford B.Litt. degree, Warren published his first book, *John Brown: The Making of a Martyr*. After returning to the United States he held various teaching posts in the South until in 1934 he went to Louisiana State University. A year later *Thirty-six Poems* appeared and was well received. Warren the poet, like Warren the teacher, had arrived.

At Louisiana he again met Cleanth Brooks, whom he had been with at Vanderbilt and Oxford. Together they founded the *Southern Review* (1935–42) and then collaborated on a "New

Critical" textbook, *Understanding Poetry* (1938), which in demanding minute and disciplined analysis revolutionized the teaching of poetry in American universities and colleges. In 1942 Warren took up a post at the University of Minnesota, leaving for Yale in 1950. He retired in 1956 to devote himself to writing, but subsequently resumed his connection with Yale.

Warren's early intellectual associations have determined many of his abiding concepts and might even be said to have formed the pattern of his career. His essays witness to his belief that a work of art creates its own terms and must be taken on them: its fullness, its mercuriality and complexity, its inclusion of "impure" figures such as irony and paradox, are its own form of power; and this power has nothing to do with the unequivocal, generally serviceable propositions and facts on which everyday life has to be based to work at all.

Yet Warren, a founding and surviving Fugitive, has always shared Ransom's anti-aestheticism. "I subordinate always Art to the aesthetic of life," Ransom wrote to Tate in 1927, "its function is to initiate us into the aesthetic life, it is not for us the final end." Warren's distaste for the remoteness of aestheticism extended into distaste for the man with the blueprint: the megalomaniac idealist such as John Brown. But Warren the empiricist held fast to the actualities of Tate's True Southern Spirit ("*Nous retardons*") only to find the reformer in him objecting to that spirit and then denouncing, as the epitome of modern secularism and soulless stereotyping, its replacement, the "New" South.

Such are the conflicts and paradoxes of Warren's encounter with the "deep, twisting strain of life." In him the equilibrium for which the New Critics extoll the Middle Ages has occurred only rarely and unstably. He has within him, but disordered, all the elements of an immaculate balance; and a nervously alert mind has done the rest, keeping those elements in constant disturbance. He belongs within his own defense of Proust, Eliot, Dreiser, and Faulkner who all, he says, "tried . . . to remain faithful to the complexities of the problems with which they were dealing," against "the mind which is hot for certainties." Always arguing for "the arduous obligation of the intellect in the face of conflicting dogmas," he is not the man to provide slogans or catchphrases—or not to provide them either. It all depends on the exigencies of his sense of irony and his respect for the grain of life. To him irony is not static but a tug-of-war.

Not surprisingly, then, his "aesthetic of life" is almost impossible to codify but fascinating in evolution. One of the four Fugitives who became Agrarians, he was also one of the three contributors to *I'll Take My Stand* (1930) who wanted that manifesto against mechanization called "A Tract against Communism." His own contribution, "The Briar Patch," subjects theory to an onslaught of data—a favorite procedure of his ever since. Unless, he argued, rural life in the South rearranged itself around agricultural nuclei, Negroes would keep on defecting to an illusory better life in northern industrial cities. In *Segregation* (1956), however, he was less Procrustean, conceding a less rigid image of the Negro and expressing more openly his belief in man's capacity to assess and announce his own potential.

This respect for individual dignity underlies all Warren's incursions into the privilege, responsibility, and pain of self-knowledge. Identity, for him, is a religious condition: one of the rites of passage through life. This is why in "Literature as a Symptom" contributed to the volume *Who Owns America?* (1936) he opts for regionalism, not socialism, as the galleon to which the modern artist should attach his canoe. Regionalism permits individuality; socialism, dealing in a class abstraction, cannot. Warren's is a simplifying view, of course, just as rigid in its stereotyping of socialism as some socialism is in its public propaganda. All the same, his devotion to the South, the region whose most cherished virtues ensured its defeat, embodies his common sense. That part of the land has known subjugation, acknowledges history, would define a charmed life as a life where charm and elegance count, whereas the North fancies itself and its industrial ingenuity as invulnerable. This is not just to work the Dixie past against an untested present; it is to set in focus what Warren in *Segregation* calls "the philosophy of the ad-man, the morality of the Kinsey report, and the gospel of the bitch-goddess."

Like the other Agrarians, Warren finally relinquished social reform for the arena where he had some power and say: literature and criticism. Necessarily, then, the secluded critic impeded the experience-hungry novelist; but no writer has worked harder than Warren to substantiate narrative through close, doting observation of the physical, emotional world. He sees it, captures it, makes the page tremble with it. His homework is always done, and not by his mind alone: there is little of his writing that will not pass the test of empirical exactness, and few of his intellectual characters reach a conclusion without being sidetracked by a clamant sense of something rich in the memory or miraculously at hand. The writer in him has always welcomed the routine and discipline of teaching as a means of producing "truly profound and humanistic people." And what Warren the ex-Fugitive from southern penury has disseminated through northern colleges has its physical equivalent in the hectic counterpoint of his writings: no endeavor but he tries to work the opposite against it, searching always for wholeness and completeness.

On the one hand, he makes a special case for the South, speaking of a change of heart as even now a possible "treachery . . . to that City of the Soul which the historical Confederacy became," and specifying the Civil War as the South's "Great Alibi" by means of which "the Southerner makes his Big Medicine. He turns defeat into victory, defects into virtues." The war gave the South a mandate for incessant obsolescence and made nostalgia seem a forward-looking mood.

On the other hand, while noting how the South remains more obsessed about its identity than the North, he cuts through to wider perceptions. All men, not southerners only, are "trapped in history"; southerners, like Jews, *happen* to feel it more acutely than most and have at hand all the apparatus of paranoia. This is one of the incidents of history; things might have been otherwise, but were not. Civil war, Warren argues, is "the prototype of all war" and the most grievous proof of all war's pain. So too the studiedly severe argument which intelligent southerners conduct within themselves emerges as both futile and honorable: an earnest of compassionate, bewitched patriotism. Such a mind as Warren's is indeed trapped in history, is full of "bitter paradoxes," just as loyal to a defeated past and a convicted geography as to the tasks of conscience in the present and in the congenially liberal North.

No wonder Warren seems torn apart, dramatizing in his own head the thesis that "it's human to be split up" and, like the guilty lovers in his novels, risking discovery. No wonder he himself deals in the sad science of abstractions until human nature and his own identity disappear into a fog consisting of "the Great Twitch," "the Great Sleep," "Higher-Law Men" (Abolitionists), original sin, pragmatism, and "charismatic arithmetic." Against vast forces of nature he works his own vast-sounding concepts. But the quarrel with himself remains, a process of self-study conducted in public; and his paradoxes, large or small, sometimes stifle one another. Not finding answers, Warren proves the value of keeping alive a needed attitude and the discomfort of being a resolute participant rather than the spectator an ex-Fugitive and powerless Agrarian might have become. His "texture of relations"—to his past, to his work, to familiars and strangers—is something he fingers endlessly; and in the long run it is the feel, not the feel's meaning, that he communicates, although many meanings are tried on for size on the way.

His early poems in *The Fugitive* introduce his interest in the melodrama of history, in "The agony of gasping endless / columns, / Skulls glaring white on red deserts at noon." But only one of these poems appeared in his first book, *Thirty-six Poems* (1935), and this, "To a Face in the Crowd," characteristically probes the immensity and blankness of the past, memorializing nameless progenitors in a racial elegiac: "We are the children of an ancient band / Broken between the mountains and the sea." Such a vision, anticipating the ground bass of the novels, is that of human involvement: we are all, through blood and time, connected, even to those we cannot know about.

Many of the poems in this first collection are little cascades of worry: Warren muses on vicissitude and the seasons, deciding the only peace is to be as stone, but gaining no pleasure or comfort from his stylish affirmation. The question "Why live?" recurs, but the copperheads, rocks, harvests, cardinals, jays, and the dead from the Civil War, have no answer. Mute life-forces compel man onward according to no ascertainable syllabus. In "Watershed" the poet yearns for the hawk's high, synoptic view: life on the hard surface of this planet is too fragmented, too teeming, and the variety of created things in all their phases defeats attempts at résumé. *Tout passe* is the leitmotiv, and Warren senses terrors in the earth's very familiarity. One choice—that between being someone and being at peace—is unavoidable: to be someone demands sacrifice and should instill responsibility; to try to efface oneself for the sake of peace is to ape the rocks vainly.

Already Warren is the master of literate paradox, the split man willing himself into unity. In "The Return: An Elegy" the son anticipates finding his mother dying like a fox in the hills and, in a startling identification of himself and her with the early pioneers, submits to remorse that varies from the portentous to the austere. Another poem, "Eidolon," sketches the insomnia of a runaway boy miserably returned. He lies "in the black room" with his father and grandfather, dreaming of the white eidolon that reveals how to meet a future he did not will upon himself.

It is not surprising that Warren incorporates a great deal of landscape into these poems: the land holds all ancestors; it is the compost that lies down whereas the society of men, ever changing, is the compost that moves about. What grows is the sense of an ancestrally determined obligation to be a definite someone: "The act / Alone is pure," so a completed act is no longer pure. All that is pure is the instant of movement. Man has a choice, especially a young man; the seasons have not. Man can, if he wishes, identify with his environment ("I am as the tree and with it have like season") but he remains distinct from it. Life twists and turns, coiling like the copperhead, and men express their bewilderment in lazy, self-deceiving metaphors: "The stiff trees rear not up in strength and pride / But lift unto the gradual dark in prayer." But who knows *what* the trees are doing? This is a poetry of conundrums, hard-edged in phrase but sometimes flatulent ("arrogant chastity of our desire"). Warren would write just as vividly without being as melodramatic, just as poignantly without the verbal diluteness, but the antitheses—idea and fact, word and flesh, inorganic and human, process and identity—survived to be the polarities of all his work to come.

In *Eleven Poems on the Same Theme* (1942) he no longer vacillates but states his problems in a manner compressed and impersonal. The poems say more and replace distraught obsession with a reconciled stare. The result is a fugue on the most fundamental problem of all: human fraternity versus, but also sustaining, sin.

The tone and manner of "End of Season," one of the most striking and spectacular poems, are something new. The poem opens with a bland imperative: "Leave now the beach, and even that perfect friendship" and the almost blasé attitude extends to include a mannered iteration: "Leave beach, *spiagga*, *playa*, *plage*, or *spa*." But such sallies are only fool's gold to attract the reader into cruder, less idyllic territory: "The Springs where your grandpa went in Arkansas / To purge the rheumatic guilt of beef and bourbon." The speaker is bemused by effects and his idea only just straggles through. Purity, desiderated, is "wordless," so the only way to salvation of any kind is through a submarine solitude: "the glaucous glimmer where no voice can visit." But, in the mailbox at home, letters wait; there is no escape, terrestrial or spiritual. All that is left is "Hope, whose eye is round and does not wink."

In another poem, "Bearded Oaks," the lovers lie together, "Twin atolls on a shelf of shade," hoping in vain for exemption from identity. Their hope, being futile, is hopeless, like the innocence and purity evoked in "Picnic Remembered" and again bathed in the amber marine light that connotes illusory safety.

There is no way back; and resolute attempts to forget ensure only that we remember. *Eleven Poems* describes a progress toward self-knowledge. First there is a fall from some blithe, cushioned state; then a traumatic first taste of separateness; and finally a resolve to trust vaguely in the larger hope of "love's grace" in a world that sees American volunteers killing now on one side, in Spain, now on another, in Finland. Aspiring man (Alexis Carrel with his test-tube heart) only discovers his limitations and is then tempted to abandon hope. Warren's principal method in these poems itself reflects his theme. He sets sharp, Auden-like vignettes of individuals against or amid a vague malaise that recalls the romantic discontent of all times ("What has availed / Or failed? / *Or will avail?* / Hawk's poise, / The boxer's stance, / The sail"). As if proving the shock of separateness, certain images leap out from their context: "And seek that face which, greasy, frost-breathed, in furs, / Bends to the bomb-sight over bitter Helsingfors." So too, certain facile injunctions ("Go to the clinic") bark vainly against the pull of spiritual desolation. There are no bright and brisk correctives to the growing sense of guilt.

These poems reconnoiter until they bump against life where it will not yield. But not all the collisions determine, as they well might, the structure of the poems. Warren, always fond of long lines and willing to let adjectives crowd nouns, works regularly into transitional passages in which, under the appearance of motivic accumulation, he marks time while shuffling ideas, one of which eventually gains purpose and urges the poem to its next goal. Most of Warren's poems oscillate in this way at some point or other, and only his over-all strength of purpose brings them to a conclusion rather than merely stopping them. As a result, litter lies by the way, colorful but otiose:

> The peacock screamed, and his feathered fury made
> Legend shake, all day, while the sky ran pale as milk;

That night, all night, the buck rabbit stamped in the
moonlit glade,
And the owl's brain glowed like a coal in the grove's
combustible dark.

This fondness for minor pageantry sometimes impedes the novels too while the idea behind it all, like a snubbed survivor, waits at a distance. Hence Warren's strength and weakness: he never neglects the surfaces of life and he sometimes fails to retrieve his interpretation or his point before it vanishes beneath a clutter of instances.

Thirty-six Poems presents man's share in the world's evil through images of decay, sequestered animals, and the division of son from parents. The vision is not profound, but ecological and domestic. *Eleven Poems*, a subtler collection by far, registers evil in ways more massive, more sustained. The advance is from desultory studies to a polyptych of man bearing darkness within him wherever he goes. An inclusive certainty of grasp succeeds the previous grasshopper techniques, and a gathering sense of mystery informs and unites the eleven poems included. Gravid, slow-moving, and enameled, they introduce religious terms only to clinch an argument or, more often, to transfigure retrospectively a succession of images.

Selected Poems, 1923–1943 (1944) gathers together most of the poems from these preceding volumes and includes some new pieces too. "Variation: Ode to Fear" with its refrain, "*Timor mortis conturbat me*," and its list of cumulative banal occasions ("When Focke-Wulf mounts, or Zero, / And my knees say I'm no hero") is a mock-ode intendedly brittle and grotesquely poignant. The speaker, nauseated by cant, routine, slogans, hypocrisy minor and major, skimped or flip comments on Jesus, Saint Joan, and Milton, by silly discord and jejune pursuits—in short by the ephemera that engross diurnal man—relates all to the fear of death. This underestimated poem exposes a world too complex for any romantic, homogeneous mood or any sublime posture.

So too "Mexico Is a Foreign Country: Five Studies in Naturalism" includes a much wider array of emotions than the earlier poems. Gritty, facetious, sly, and willfully vulgar, the five parts introduce a Warren less resolutely grandiloquent, who now imports undignified objects and unprofound views into his lines:

If only Ernest now were here
To praise the bull, deride the steer,
And anatomize for chillier chumps
The local beauties' grinds and bumps . . .

It is not satire but a pert way of documenting the near-Dadaistic side of intelligent distress: " . . . here even the bladder achieves Nirvana, / And so I sit and think, 'mañana.'"

If such verse is destructive it also instructs. The poet's jaundiced review of the trivialities that survive all great ideas and noble motives attends a deeper, unshifting perception. All passes: "Viene galopando," says the old Mexican, "el mundo." This time round, the poet is willing to notice anything; nothing is excluded or lost, and the gain is a more complex view, all antinomies and incongruity:

I do not know the mango's crime
In its far place and different time,
Nor does it know mine committed in a frostier
clime . . .

It is God, the archetypal parent, who has now to be forgiven; and not only for the guilt man feels but also for making the world as harsh in meaningless contrasts as it is, and for conferring such delusive ideas as those of peace and innocence. Man and mango have to work out their respective salvations alone: "In separateness only does love learn definition." And the disquiet that pervades Warren's poems must finally, to any sensitive reader, seem a form of anger at causation. It is one thing to note that "Because he had spoken harshly to his mother, / The day became astonishingly bright," but quite another thing to confront the guilt consequent on having been born at all. Warren often degrades intermediate causes, relegating love ("Fellow, you tupped her years ago / That tonight my boots might crunch the snow") to animal level, man's nature to happenstance, and human intimacy to frantic parasitism.

These themes and motifs reappear full-scale in "The Ballad of Billie Potts." The prodigal son returns home and is murdered by parents who fail to recognize him. Warren handles this folktale from western Kentucky through alternating narrative and commentary, the one rich and awkward with doggerel sounds and Kentucky speech mannerisms, the other lofty, meditative, and often diffuse. A bizarre poem, it approaches caricature and cartoon, yet the moral—the wasted chance of trust—comes through unspoiled and, if anything, sharpened and straitened through contrast. Such a moral could hardly be exaggerated; it gains strength through being given such a hard time technically. Billie's father is an innkeeper who ambushes solitary travelers, each time doing violence to the recurring possibility of man's being a brother to man. Each time he attacks he destroys a chance of human community which, merely by doing nothing, he could preserve. He has free choice in this, but interferes with an established and maintainable peace until he causes the death of his own son. The point is that when Billie returns, rich and looking it, Billie too is a stranger who fits a stereotype, innocently counting on the absence of ill-will as all men must if they are not to become either paralyzed with fear or brutish through distrust. But his father "set the hatchet in his head," wrecking both the occasion for charity and the paternal-filial bond.

The father works by a defective ethic, regretting not the act of murder but his choice of victim. He regrets for immoral reasons, and Warren thus proves that an impersonal reflex of charity is superior to emotions that are merely partial. The world is full of strangers; therefore man must devise and uphold a code that gives each new relationship a chance to flourish. Whatever Billie's delusions about himself, he is entitled to human rights; but he loses more as a human than he could gain as a known son. And life's grand design is poorer far for his death than his parents are in bereavement. Special criteria, such as Billie's birthmark which the parents find when they dig up his body, are beside the point; it is the commonplace that counts in the arithmetic of goodwill.

If "Billie Potts" is blasphemous, it blasphemes as only the poem of a believer can. If Billie's father is God, striking categorically down irrespective of identity or age, then Warren has fixed on the harshness of mortality to make one point: trust in the long run is inevitable, whether it amounts to ignorance or fatalism. The only virtue in learning from experience is that life goes on, perpetually offering new chances against the old, depressing background:

(There is always another country and always another
place.
There is always another name and another face.
And the name and the face are you, and you
The name and the face . . .)

Innocence cannot be retrieved, but it can be created out of evil: a man's children always start clean, and all the father can do is be humble before life's incessant renewals and seek to know himself, and his kind, better. For knowledge can sometimes improve man or help him to adjust, even if it can never perfect or redeem the defective, coiling human heritage: ". . . water is water and it flows, / Under the image on the water the water coils and goes / And its own beginning and its end only the water knows."

It is this concern that shapes Warren's outlook: the effort toward self-knowledge and responsible identity amidst the inscrutable flux. This is why, for ten years, away in a sense like Billie Potts, he deserted poetry for fiction. He could best express his main obsessions in narrative. He required space, sheer length, and mere succession to demonstrate his views on time's "brumal deeps" and "the great unsolsticed coil" of human destiny. Poems, distilling and compressing, present conclusions but not the dullness, the tedium, the *longueurs* of life. Proof sooner or later has to be made through accumulation, through a mass of "circumstantial texture" presented in full. The poems are points of light above the hubbub of the novels, but always related to that hubbub—its violence and eventfulness—through deploying the same view of history and guilt. ⟨. . .⟩

A single volume, *The Circus in the Attic* (1948), contains all of Warren's short stories, of which *Blackberry Winter*, published separately in 1946, is outstanding in the history of the genre as well as the most compact epitome of Warren's output. A man in his early forties recalls his initiation into manhood and the ways of nature. When a city-clad stranger comes to work on the farm during a time of storm and flood (like December 1811 in *Brother to Dragons*) the boy, little apprehending the devastation and stoicism evident everywhere, fastens to him and thus vicariously "goes away." This symbolic infidelity the adult narrator has come to regret; like the speaker in several of Warren's early poems he is saddened that as a boy he responded poorly to the beleaguered devotion of his parents. Guilt, ever-present in Warren's writings, dogs him until like old Jebb in the story he realizes the past is as unalterable as a ruined crop. Moreover, as if perfidy were not enough, it was perfidy at the wrong time: "blackberry winter" is when the genial spring unnaturally regresses and turns its back, reneging, just like the boy.

Once again Warren explores man and his relationship to the land. Neither is wholly predictable: the Negro maid uncharacteristically strikes her child; the river floods. There are no absolutes, but only risky combinations of transient circumstances. And the boy responds to the disorder of the time by holding to what is newest. "I did follow him, all the years," the narrator says remorsefully, stressing "did" to evoke the ghost of a foregone alternative.

Nothing of Warren's more convincingly demonstrates how complex his traditionalism is. The inevitability of change is a southern fact too, even though, as he is always saying, the supposed and usually mythical stability of the past is succeeded only by the instability of an unknown future. Man makes uneasy truces with nature which is reliable only because, in the mass, it never dies.

Predictably, then, Warren's favorite images express both an entranced horror with nature and horrified relief at man's power to control. Submerged in nature, man can know a vegetable peace; against it he can achieve a sterile safety. But he cannot safely ally himself with it, for it is inscrutable. Images of flood depict the odds. In "History among the Rocks" it is "a creek in flood" which will tumble and turn "a body, naked and lean." In *Brother to Dragons* R. P. W. speaks of "that deep flood that is our history," exemplifying "the drowned cow, swollen," while *Blackberry Winter* presents another cow "rolling and roiling down the creek." A poem in *Promises* tells how "A drowned cow bobbled down the creek" and Warren's most recent novel is itself called *Flood*. Man cannot flood out the flood of history and time. On the other hand he can create roads, imaging the direct-mindedness of efficient modernity and facilitating the hectic placelessness to which the nation turns in escape. Only history has unlimited accommodations, and Warren's vision of America, a land cut cleanly across by numbered highways, is ironical: man applies Mercator to things fluid, aiding navigators but dominating nothing. *All the King's Men* opens with Jack Burden going on Highway 58 "northeast out of the city"; it is a straight, white-shimmering highway with a water-mirage forever ahead—"that bright, flooded place." *Flood* opens with a highway and stays on it for several pages; and nothing could be clearer than this from *Brother to Dragons:*

> Up Highway 109 from Hopkinsville,
> To Dawson Springs, then west on 62,
> Across Kentucky at the narrow neck,
> Two hours now, not more, for the road's fair.
> We ripped the July dazzle on the slab . . .

"Mexico Is a Foreign Country" makes its point with sinister levity: "The highways are scenic, like destiny marked in red"; and *Segregation* commemorates Highway 61 cutting south from Memphis, "straight as a knife edge through the sad and baleful beauty of the Delta country." *Flood* ends with "the chrome and safety glass of cars passing on the new highway, yonder across the lake." New mastodons for old.

Such images, recurring, evoke one another and crystallize Warren's feeling that man can best nature only by cutting across, by disregarding and dividing, never by eliciting secrets from within. The highway, symbol of initiative, speed, and control, is sterile, plagued by fatigue, mirages, boredom, advertising, and death. The flood, symbol of revenge, impersonality, and accident, is the element that contains the highways. And, just as no road ever conquers what it cuts through, so no neat network of ideas can open up history; such is the gist of Warren's treatment of his intellectual characters. But men who live close to nature achieve understanding, inchoate as it is. They accept earth as their element and source, privilege and torment.

Most of Warren's best stories are painful, guilt-ridden commemorations of some young person's rites of passage. Grandfather Barden in "When the Light Gets Green" waits four years for death and love. But his grandson, prey to familiar Warren incapacities, cannot love: he lies, feels guilty, and, grown adult, feels even guiltier for still being unable to comprehend his deficiency. It is, probably, an unexpressed resolve to submit as little as necessary to the processes of mortality. Another boy, in "Christmas Gift," is similarly confounded by premature difficulties; but he copes by exchanging tokens with the doctor: candy for the chance to roll a cigarette. The boy in "Testament of Flood" does all his growing up in one instant of recognition. And, just as the young take their stand, gropingly or with unpracticed severity, so do those who have no future at all. Like Grandfather Barden, Viola the Negro cook in "Her Own People" lies in bed; discharged, she has nowhere to go, only death to look forward to. So she creates guilt all around her, exposing the spiritual debility of those who, like her employers, dare not love or live.

These are the problems of home, of growth within the tribe: having home, leaving it, aching to return, and being unable to dismiss intervening years. Home is also to be defined unsentimentally as any available intimate basis. For young and old alike, there must be a rock to build on even if it is only being unloved or unloving. The professor in "The Unvexed Isles" discovers how much of an unsophisticated, homesick midwesterner he is, but in re-establishing his marriage on this admitted truth cannot be wrong. Home is where candor sites it. So too the gelid marriage in "The Love of Elsie Barton: A Chronicle" stabilizes itself on bleak habit. Warren presents a choice: return to the source of one's being, like Billie Potts, or found a new home in maturity. All men crave the place where they are not naked or totally vulnerable. Bolton, the muted hero of "Circus in the Attic," is a case in point. He has repudiated his ancestors and must therefore find something to cleave to: his soft-pine circuses carved in secret, his draftee stepson, or writing his desultory, halfhearted history of the county.

Yet the longed-for world of home remains a terra incognita, less welcoming than present adversity. The reason is that childhood identity begins with the search for freely chosen, as distinct from inherited, attachments—and the guilt of cutting free. Warren's best stories prove the search a new imprisonment; his least successful posit odd, fey ironies on situations not evaluated by characters who are themselves inscrutable.

Warren, like Bolton's father, has become increasingly "aware of the powerful, vibrating, multitudinous web of life which binds the woman and child together, victor and victim." The search for new complicities returns man to old paradoxes. Life's patterns vary little; only private, poetic truth is abundantly various; historical and cosmic truth is infinitely monotonous—something to hold to but also something aloof.

FRANK GRAZIANO

"The Matter Itself: Warren's *Audubon: A Vision*"

Homage to Robert Penn Warren, ed. Frank Graziano

1981, pp. 17–32

> One is an artist at the cost of regarding that which all non-artists call 'form' as content, as 'the matter itself.' (Nietzsche)

"If the law of thought is that it should search out profundity," Mishima wrote not long before his public *harakiri*, ". . . then it seemed excessively illogical to me that men should not discover depth of a kind in the 'surface,' that vital borderline that endorses our separateness and our form, dividing our exterior from our interior."[1] Mishima, of course, later found his way of permeating the division between the exterior and the interior, of pushing this endorsement beyond the extreme: disembowelment.

Warren has found another way.

If *Audubon: A Vision* is a great poem, it is a great poem not because our hero was, "In the end, himself and not what / He had known he ought to be," nor because he ran "'the gantlet throu this World'" and died in his bed a good man;[2] it has nothing to do with the poem's thematic grandeur, with the fact that *Audubon* is "about," as Warren tells us, "man and his fate."[3] The "meaning" of *Audubon*, of any poem, has little to do with its theme ("man and his fate," after all, is at the very threshold where grandeur yields to cliché), but has everything to do with its theme-in-motion, its theme inter-woven with and inseparable from the fabric the surface is, the fabric-in-motion, a palimpsest-like fusion of linguistic qualities. The surface or form, the "matter itself," must simultaneously address the reader on a number of levels, it must be genuinely polysemous and complex. "One might say the former depth," as Deleuze wrote in a separate context, "has spread itself out, has become breadth."[4] But this is not to imply that the poem in question is in some sense "shallow," or that it rectifies a lack of content with verbosity. I rather wish to suggest that we reorient our approach and look elsewhere for the qualities—the criteria—by which we assess the excellence of a poem like *Audubon:* in the depth and texture of the surface.[5] Warren's language is a "language lined with flesh,"[6] a language lined with the haunt of the flesh passing; here moribundity generates the passion. If one were in search of a label for this passionate and human speech he would find none better, I believe, than Nietzsche's "intelligent sensuality."[7] Thought mingles with image, sound with mood, trope with concept, and thus the poem triangles ahead in its dialectics, with meaning yielding the foreground to motion. It is "an interplay of signs arranged less according to its signified content than according to the very nature of the signifier."[8] There is no lesson worth hearing regarding "man and his fate"; it is the telling that teaches. The Warren poem tests reality not against reason but rather—at bottom—against sound, against the ear. "The tune is the mood groping for its logic."[9] *Audubon* is a vision *heard.*

II

The composition of *Audubon* has a history. In the late 1940's, while immersed in early nineteenth-century Americana in preparation for the writing of *World Enough and Time*, Warren became interested in "the man and his life," and thus turned to Audubon's journals. The poem which would eventually become *Audubon: A Vision* was begun at that time, but abandoned because "it was a trap," because Warren "couldn't find the frame for it, the narrative line." So the poem sat in twenty years of gestation until the 1960's, when Warren again had occasion to return to Audubon's work while preparing an anthology of American literature with R. W. B. Lewis and Cleanth Brooks.

One morning, as the story goes, while Warren was making his bed ("something I don't usually do, because I'm not housebroken very well"), a line from the abandoned version popped into his head: "Was not the lost Dauphin."

> That's when I started composing, by writing at night, going to sleep, and waking up in the morning early—revising by shouting it all out loud in a Land Rover going to Yale. Each element in the poem would be a 'shot' on Audubon rather than a narrative.[10]

The "trap," the narrative proper would be avoided by structuring the piece in these "shots," or, elsewhere, "snapshots"; the narrativity would be essentially dismantled, and yet the still-shots or flashes, like those in the hand-cranked, nickel-fed picture show of the past, would fall on and into one another to deliver a unified and smooth-flowing story line.

One such "shot," which is well read—as Hopkins would say—with one's ear, is in Part B of the poem's first section, which is titled after the 1940's line remembered. The concluding couplets read as follows:

> The bear feels his own fat
> Sweeten, like a drowse, deep to the bone.
>
> Bemused, above the fume of ruined blueberries,
> The last bee hums.
>
> The wings, like mica, glint
> In the sunlight.
>
> He leans on his gun. Thinks
> How thin is the membrane between himself and the
> world.
>
> (86)

To say that this passage is a showplace for sonics would be, of course, a hardy understatement. The assonantal series of long *e* throughout (f*ee*ls, Sw*ee*ten, d*ee*p, B*e*mused, berr*ie*s, b*ee*, H*e*, l*ea*ns, betw*ee*n); the overdone but forgivable long *u* in the second-quoted stanza balanced subtlely by short *u* in *hums* and *gun;* the *own* / *bone* balance; the third-quoted stanza with its long and short *i*'s, the former in *like, sunlight* and *mica*, and the latter beginning in *wings glint* and *in*, then spilling into the fourth stanza with *his, thinks, thin* and *himself;* all of this delicate and melodious orchestration spins the early threads of the thematic web the poem will tangle with later, and does so via imagery that astounds. We have a bear whose fat sweetens him to sleep, a drunkish bee humming in the air above fermenting blueberries; we move from bee-wing ("like mica") to membrane, to the film between the name of the world and what we would name it, to the borderline Mishima thought he put his knife in.

But Mishima's knife, in the present context, is the gun Audubon leans on. The gun—Audubon's shot—brings its target through the membrane between man and world, it reconciles discrepancies:

> Thought: 'On that sky it is black.'
> Thought: 'In my mind it is white.'
> Thinking: '*Ardea occidentalis*, heron, the great one.'
> (85)

The gun is an instrument of knowledge, it makes a place in the subject for unknown objects, it mingles man with world: "He put them where they are, and there we see them: / In our imagination" (99). Audubon, in Wordsworth's dictum, murders to dissect, he kills what he loves because, as we learn in the poem's penultimate section, one name for love is knowledge.

Whether or not these acts of love/knowledge are honorable is another issue, but one thing is certain: Audubon's gun, like Warren's pen, makes its shots in order to transform fact into art, to alchemize empiricism, to put a derivative of matter in the mind. It is almost as though both men—indeed, all men of artistic temperament—unwittingly reinforce the membrane between man and world (via their art), then struggle, via their art, to find a way to break through it. Imagination, Warren reports in *Now & Then*, "is only / The lie we must learn to live by, if ever / We mean to live at all."[11] We move from reality or fact (bird) to painting, and from fact (autobiographical vignette) to poem. Liberties, therefore, must be taken; Audubon's being the obvious, murder-to-dissect one, and Warren's stemming from a primary responsibility to verse rather than to history (fact). Warren must rid himself of "compunction about tampering with non-essential facts," as long as "the spirit of history" is not violated by whatever modifications the poem makes.[12] *Audubon: A Vision* thus adopts both narrative and spirit from the naturalist's journals, but maintains a willingness to make necessary alterations.

Of the many "shots," or series of "shots," that piece *Audubon* together, the most prevalent and elaborate is the second section, "The Dream He Never Knew the End Of." This section is perhaps doubly appropriate for the present discussion because we see in it an Audubon somewhat puzzled by his own behavior: he cannot bring himself to shoot. Although his life is endangered by the hag and her two sons, Audubon remains in a dreamy state of inertia, longing to know the nightmare's ending (death), while Reason nags a periodic *Now, Now!* in an attempt to jar him into action. "He cannot think what guilt unmans him, or / Why he should find the punishment so precious" (90).[13] He cannot bring himself to fire an artless shot, a shot that would save both himself and his pocketwatch, his Time, but that would, in doing so, deprive him of the dream's ending. The deprivation, of course, is then provided for despite Audubon's inertia, by the three travellers (two in the journal account), who by chance enter the cabin and thus prevent the crime.

"The Dream He Never Knew the End Of" is largely derived from an Audubon *Episode*, "The Prairie," which recounts this incident as it occurred during a return trip to St. Geneviève in the early spring of 1812.[14] Audubon's account is charming and descriptive, but lacks the music and reverence for precision of detail that give Warren's fiction-from-fact, Warren's poem, its life. A first and fundamental distinction between the two texts is a technical one; Audubon tells an engaging tale employing a simple but well-calculated device to pull the reader more deeply into the mounting suspense, while Warren, after he adopts this method, goes beyond it to heighten the drama by revealing in advance, via exacting descriptions, the nature of the nightmare that Audubon is about to enter.

> There
> Is the cabin, a huddle of logs with no calculation or
> craft:
> The human filth, the human hope.
> (86)

The passage then bridges the stanza break on the *o*-sound from *hope* for a subtle perception—Warren's own but attributed to Audubon—which gives further indication of the folk we might find at home here:

> Smoke,
> From the mud-and-stick chimney, in that air,
> greasily
> Brims, cannot lift, bellies the ridgepole, ravels
> White, thin, down the shakes, like sputum.
> He stands,
> Leans on his gun, stares at the smoke, thinks:
> 'Punk-wood.'
> Thinks: 'Dead-fall half-rotten.' Too sloven,
> That is, to even set axe to clean wood.
> (86)

The Audubon of the poem will, from signs like the creosote-heavy, belly-dragging smoke of punk-wood burning, begin to deduce the qualities of—at least—the air he is about to enter, the ambience. "Once one entered into the full smell of it," as Rilke's Brigge wrote, "most things were already decided."[15]

> In imagination, his nostrils already
> Know the stench of that lair beyond
> The door-puncheons.
> (87)

And indeed, as we learn, the cabin stinks, the Indian (with one eye blood and mucus caked from an arrow that split on the bow-string and jounced back to blind him) stinks, the not-well-cured bear skins stink, and we may well guess that our hostess, "Large, / Raw-hewn, strong-beaked" and hair-moled, stinks as well, as will her sons.

Once inside the cabin-stench the focus shifts, as it does endlessly in the Warren canon, to the notion of Time. Our guess would be an educated one if we supposed that Warren's original attraction to "The Prairie" was magnified by the pocketwatch at the episode's center. "The Prairie," that is to say, has the potential to align well thematically with much of the Warren canon. In the naturalist's version the incident is relayed as follows:

> I drew a fine time-piece from my breast, and told the woman that it was late, and that I was fatigued. She

had espied my watch, the richness of which seemed to operate upon her feelings with electric quickness. She told me there was plenty of venison and jerked buffalo meat, and that on removing the ashes I should find a cake. But my watch had struck her fancy, and her curiosity had to be gratified by an immediate sight of it. I took off the gold chain that secured it, from around my neck, and presented it to her; she was all ecstacy, spoke of its beauty, asked me its value, and put the chain round her brawny neck, saying how happy the possession of such a watch would make her. Thoughtless, and as I fancied myself in so retired a spot secure, I paid little attention to her talk or her movements.[16]

Warren's account remains essentially faithful in content to the original, but transcends it by virtue of an odd, almost-magical tension or aura, generated, it seems, primarily through carefully calculated rhythm, and through the images of the hag's girlish, stomach-curling gestures:

It is gold, it lives in his hand in the firelight, and the woman's
Hand reaches out. She wants it. She hangs it about her neck.
And near it the great hands hover delicately
As though it might fall, they quiver like moth-wings, her eyes
Are fixed downward, as though in shyness, on that gleam, and her face
Is sweet in an outrage of sweetness, so that
His gut twists cold. He cannot bear what he sees.
Her body sways like a willow in spring wind. Like a girl.

(88)

And then "The time comes to take back the watch," a pun that will initiate the crank into a brief but continual elevation of tension, before concluding on a line (perhaps difficult to appreciate fully out of context) unexcelled in *Audubon*:

The woman hulks by the fire. He hears the jug slosh.

(88)

The jug will slosh again as Audubon and the Indian feign sleep and the woman calls the foreheads of her sons close together in firelight to suggest to them the theft and murder. Warren then reels into another song-like and vivid passage describing the woman wetting a sharpening stone with her saliva and running a blade thereon, in preparation for the deed she and her sons have conspired.

He hears the jug slosh.
Then hears,
Like the whisper and whish of silk, that other
Sound, like a sound of sleep, but he does not
Know what it is. Then knows, for,
Against firelight, he sees the face of the woman
Lean over, and the lips purse sweet as to bestow a kiss, but
This is not true, and the great glob of spit
Hangs there, glittering, before she lets it fall.

The spit is what softens like silk the passage of steel
On the fine-grained stone. It whispers.

(89)[17]

Judge of my astonishment, reader, when I saw this incarnate fiend take a large carving-knife, and go to the grindstone to whet its edge; I saw her pour the water on the turning machine, and watched her working away with the dangerous instrument, until the cold sweat covered every part of my body, in despite of my determination to defend myself to the last. Her task finished, she walked to her reeling sons, and said: 'There, that'll soon settle him! Boys, kill yon ——, and then for the watch.'

I turned, cocked my gun locks silently, touched my faithful companion, and lay ready to start up and shoot the first who might attempt my life. The moment was fast approaching, and that night might have been my last in this world, had not Providence made preparations for my rescue. All was ready. The infernal hag was advancing slowly, probably contemplating the best way of dispatching me, whilst her sons should be engaged with the Indian. I was several times on the eve of rising and shooting her on the spot; but she was not to be punished thus. The door was suddenly opened, and there entered two stout travellers, each with a long rifle on his shoulder. I bounced up on my feet, and making them most heartily welcome, told them how well it was for me that they should have arrived at that moment. The tale was told in a minute.[18]

In comparing the original with Warren's version we learn that the "great glob of spit" is an invention, a human one, adding not only color but a further indication of this hag's crudity. Beyond that, however, we learn something more thematically important: in Audubon's account the inaction is simply a matter of time, he was prepared to defend himself to the last had the armed hag finished her approach, whereas in Warren's account Audubon is crippled by an inexplicable inertia, a longing—almost—to know the end of the dream, to *live* the death the dream's ending is, to get beyond "the dregs of all nightmare" we call life.

If we accept *Audubon*'s logic, truth cannot be spoken, but can only be enacted in dream, or in dream become action. Why is it then that Audubon, in a context where "necessity / Blooms like a rose," is on the brink of experiencing the climax of the dream-become-action when he is obliged, in effect, to resort to making a testimony to the rescuers, thus talking himself out of the dream's ending? Why is the dream (which is truth) necessarily interrupted, why must Audubon—who is feigning sleep—be "woken"?

One answer is in Warren's "Virtue is rewarded, that / Is the nightmare";[19] whatever virtue Audubon is accredited for being what he must—rather than what he "ought"—is rewarded with the nightmare's (life's) continuation. The Audubon of "The Prairie" thinks he speaks the truth to the travellers about what has happened, or, more accurately, what was about to happen, but in the logical framework *of the poem* truth cannot be spoken, only enacted,[20] only experienced: the dream's ending cannot be imagined ("the lie we live by"), it can only be suffered.

The travellers provide for the nightmare's continuation, and Audubon feels in a strange sense cheated of the ending. But this same provision dictates that she who was without virtue would be given the end of her nightmare. Unlike her sons, "long jerking and farting as they hanged," and unlike the blackman lynched by Mr. Dutcher and the boys, the blackman who let his feet hold onto the bread truck thus opting for strangle instead of snap,[21] the hag approached her death open-eyed and stoically, she crossed the borderline with a willful step, she *lived* the end of her nightmare "In a rage of will, an ecstacy of iron, as though / This was the dream that, lifelong, she had dreamed toward" (92).

In a cast of hangees who pitifully aggravate their dreams' endings, who move from gloom to gloomier, we have here an ugly one who achieves a clean snap, then dangles in "a new dimension of beauty," who achieves a certain transformation. The hag did nothing to resist her death—as Audubon had wallowed in inertia when his death was pending—and thus she exits in the *enactment* of the dream's ending, the truth, rather than "waking" to the impossibility of truth spoken: the scream (see 90).

It is in this light that we can understand why Warren opts for a punishment distinct from and more severe than the actual one inflicted on the hag and her sons.[22] Audubon and the men who rescue him, in the autobiographical account, are content with burning down the cabin and giving the skins and implements to the one-eyed Indian. In the above-quoted passage Audubon even suggests that the hag, due to some shadowy notion of fate, was not ripe for death: " . . . she was not to be punished thus." In the Warren account, however, we witness an exchange: the hag dies the death, or, one might say, lives the dream's ending, which Audubon longed for. After the hanging, with tears in his eyes, with a hand on the gold watch in realization that he denied the hag who dangles there a right to it, "He thinks: 'What has been denied me?'" Had she acquired the watch, Audubon would have known the dream's ending. He took from the hag a pocketwatch (*his* Time), and she took from him the dream's ending he longed to know the meaning of.

> Continue to walk in the world, Yes, love it!
> He continued to walk in the world.
>
> (93)

III

And then he who loved "'indepenn and piece more / than humbug and money,'" who was "only / Himself, Jean Jacques, and his passion," who, Pan-like, once played his flute in the forest, "He died, and was mourned, who had loved the world," and he entered "the dream / Of a season past all seasons." Warren "cannot hear the sound of that wind" blowing in what he names a dream beyond the nightmare's ending, but he can hear "the great geese hoot northward," he can make the sounds of *this* world, which is "'*perhaps* as good / as worlds unknown,'" come alive on the page and be heard.

Most of the time. If Warren is at his best when enraptured in a passion that permits sonics to prevail in the generation of the content of a poem, that permits him, by virtue of adherence to form—"the matter itself"—to *discover*, that shifts the focus from *What can I say* to *What can I be told* as the overseer of a dialectic between sound and meaning, then he is at his worst when the balance between the rational and the poetic becomes lopsided, when one overexerts itself and forces out the other, when he "defends the letter while the spirit flees." *Audubon* the poem, like Audubon the man, must synthesize passion and intellect. The possibilities for failure, thus, are two: on the one hand passion becomes carried away in a Dionysian overjoy of sound: an intelligent man's word-salad made song; and on the other hand the poet abandons an architectonic compromise, a fusion of linguistic qualities, to allow for an in-cramming of information necessary to advance plot or theme. Reason, in other words, muscles in for this second flaw; the poet ceases to listen and begins to Write. We see this most clearly—"we" meaning "I" since Helen Vendler, to cite a second opinion, has referred to the below-quoted lines as "stunning"—in an easy mini-conceit established in the poem's fourth section:

> To wake at dawn and see,
> As though down a rifle barrel, lined up
> Like sights, the self that was, the self that is, and
> there,
> Far off but in range, completing the alignment, your
> fate.
> Hold your breath, let the trigger-squeeze be slow and
> steady.
> The quarry lifts, in the halo of fold leaves, its noble
> head.
> This is not a dimension of Time.
>
> (94)

We see this second pitfall, in addition, in a handful of other weak, easy and/or flat passages: the snow-thatched heads "like wisdom," the Daniel Webster couplet, the line "He dreamed of hunting with Boone, from imagination painted his portrait," Section C of "The Sound of That Wind" (which Warren wrote "just like that!"), and one or two other moments, but these disappointments—insofar as they are harbingers of no more than themselves—are easily absorbed in a monument like *Audubon*.

It is mortal flesh that suffers the "human filth, the human hope" of enshrining itself in language. We write because we grope, because we are lost in a dream without our names or a name for the world, because we know nothing for certain but the inevitability of the dream's ending. Audubon's *Who am I?* is Warren's *I am* giving way to *I was*. It is: In *was*, who am I going to be? It is: How will the sound I have made be heard?

A poet who lives and writes to Warren's age makes us painfully aware of the fact that "what matters in art is precisely the unique, unrepeatable, unresurrectible mixture of flesh and spirit, and what makes the achievement of the latter all the more precious is the very moribundity of the former."[23] If America is short on trumpeteers hailing appreciation and debt to Robert Penn Warren, it is because we live among readers who lack what I. A. Richards dubbed "sensuous apprehension," readers who cannot *hear* the Warren poem, who do not know what to do with the mind's senses, who do not, as it is vogue to say, understand the poem's grammar. "Poetry requires that one institute and maintain an indefinable harmony between what pleases the ear and what stimulates the mind";[24] poetry is born of the indefinability. If one overlooks what pleases the ear, one has overlooked the pulse of what stimulates the mind, and in doing so has overlooked Warren.

"My genius," Nietzsche once wrote, "is in my nostrils." Warren's genius, one must realize, is in his ear.

Notes

1. Yukio Mishima, *Sun & Steel*, tr. John Bester (New York: Grove Press, 1970), p. 23.
2. Robert Penn Warren, *Selected Poems: 1923–1975* (New York: Random House, 1976), pp. 94 and 97. Further references to *Audubon: A Vision* in this collection will appear in the text.
3. Robert Penn Warren, *Talking: Interviews 1950–1970*, ed. Floyd C. Watkins and John T. Hiers (New York: Random House, 1980), p. 235 (see also p. 110).
4. Josué V. Harari, ed., *Textual Strategies: Perspectives in Post-Structuralist Criticism* (Ithaca: Cornell Univ. Press, 1979), p. 280.
5. This should not, of course, be a reorientation, but rather the premise a critic begins with in his analysis of any given poem. The state of contemporary poetry has helped us forget what exactly it is we are reading for, it has numbed our expectations and sensibility to the point where we are quite content to abandon any hope for a fusional reading. If one were to approach the bulk of recent poetry rigorously and with full expectations, with the belief that he would have his senses, emotions and intellect simultaneously stimulated and pleased, he would find this endeavor to be as dismal as holding a sieve—in Kant's famous simile—while someone milks a he-goat.

6. Roland Barthes, *The Pleasure of the Text*, tr. Richard Miller (New York: Hill and Wang, 1975), p. 66.
7. Friedrich Nietzsche, *The Will to Power*, ed. Walter Kaufmann (New York: Vintage, 1968), p. 421.
8. Michael Foucault in Harari, p. 142.
9. R. P. W. in Elaine Barry, ed., *Robert Frost on Writing* (New Brunswick: Rutgers Univ. Press, 1973), p. 160.
10. *Talking*, p. 276 (see also 235).
11. Robert Penn Warren, *Now and Then* (New York: Random House, 1978), p. 4. Cf. "Antinomy: Time and Identity," Sec. 1; Warren seems to have modified his position.
12. Robert Penn Warren, *Brother to Dragons (A New Version)* (New York: Random House, 1979), p. xiii.
13. Cf. "A Way to Love God": "Theirs [the mountains] is the perfected pain of conscience, that / Of forgetting the crime, and I hope you have not suffered it. I have."
14. The editors of Audubon's journals suggest that the naturalist was returning *to* St. Geneviève; if we can trust Audubon's autobiographical account in "Myself," however, then the incident occurred while returning *to* Henderson *from* St. Geneviève: "On my return trip to Henderson I was obliged to stop at a humble cabin, where I so nearly ran the chance of losing my life, at the hands of a woman and her two desperate sons. . . . "
15. Rainer Maria Rilke, *The Notebooks of Malte Laurids Brigge*, tr. M. D. Herter Norton (New York: W. W. Norton, 1964), p. 211.
16. John James Audubon, *Audubon and His Journals*, ed. Maria Audubon, Vol. II (New York: Dover, 1960), p. 227.
17. An interesting observation to note in passing is the onomatopoeic alliteration of *s* in imitation of the knife's sound on the whetting stone.
18. Audubon, p. 229.
19. Warren, *Selected Poems*, p. 21.
20. This is why in the poem no word is spoken when the travellers enter (the Indian points and gestures, he *enacts*), whereas in the original version "The tale was told in a minute" of speedy talking on Audubon's part.
21. See "Ballad of Mister Dutcher and the Last Lynching in Gupton" in Warren, *Selected Poems*, p. 35.
22. A second reason may be found in the following statement of Nietzsche's: "This, indeed this alone, is what *revenge* is: the will's ill will against time and its 'it was.'"
23. Joseph Brodsky in Bernard Meares, ed., *Osip Mandelstam: 50 Poems* (New York: Persea, 1977), p. 7.
24. Paul Valéry quoted by Gérard Genette in Harari, p. 367.

W. J. STUCKEY

From "The Fortunes of War"
The Pulitzer Prize Novels: A Critical Backward Look
1981, pp. 132–37

After having awarded the prize to Hersey's supersentimental short story, "A Bell for Adano," in 1945, and having given no prize in 1946, the Pulitzer judges made in 1947 what has since proved to be one of their best decisions. They bypassed two big best sellers, *The Hucksters*, by Frederick Wakeman, and *B. F.'s Daughter*, by J. P. Marquand, to give the prize to Robert Penn Warren's *All the King's Men*, an unusually complex and only moderately popular novel. The main plot of Warren's novel deals with the rise of Willie Stark from a struggling country lawyer to governor of a Southern state, and of his fall from idealism to opportunism. *All the King's Men* is also the story of Jack Burden, Warren's narrator, for whom the struggle of Willie Stark and Adam Stanton is a projection of his own internal conflict and a symbolic enactment of a serious modern dilemma:

> As a student of history, Jack Burden could see that Adam Stanton, whom he came to call the man of idea, and Willie Stark, whom he came to call the man of fact, were doomed to destroy each other just as each was doomed to try to use the other and to yearn toward and try to become the other, because each was incomplete with the terrible division of their age.[1]

For a time, Jack attempts to live out his role as historian, to observe and record disinterestedly the career of "the boss," Willie Stark, but Willie's evil finally impinges upon Jack's life in a very personal way: Willie becomes the lover of Anne Stanton, Jack's childhood sweetheart. And Jack plunges into the "real life" equivalent for historical neutrality—unconsciousness, or as he calls it, the "Great Sleep." For a time he subscribes to the theory of the "Great Twitch," a mechanistic view of life in which man is regarded as an autonomous nervous system. At first he finds it "rather bracing and tonic" because when you believed that, then

> . . . nothing was your fault or anybody's fault, for things are always as they are. And you can go back in good spirits, for you will have learned two very great truths. First, that you cannot lose what you have never had. Second, that you are never guilty of a crime which you did not commit.[2]

Jack's cynicism, however, dissolves in the love and pity he learns to feel for his mother and for his natural father, Judge Irwin. When Willie Stark dies at the hands of Dr. Stanton, Jack is able to see the historical implications of their lives, but at the same time he sees "that though doomed they have nothing to do with any doom under the godhead of the Great Twitch. They were doomed, but they lived in the agony of the will." Willie Stark is the proponent and the embodiment of what Jack calls "the theory of the moral neutrality of history":

> All change costs something. You have to write off the costs against the gain. . . . Process as process is neither morally good nor morally bad. We may judge results not process. The morally bad agent may perform the deed which is good. The morally good agent may perform the deed which is bad. Maybe a man has to sell his soul to get the power to do good.

Jack reasons, however, that:

> The theory of historical costs. The theory of the moral neutrality of history. All that was a high historical view from a chilly pinnacle. Maybe it took a genius to see it. To really see it. Maybe you had to get chained to the high pinnacle with the buzzards pecking at your liver and lights before you could see it.[3]

Jack Burden at last rejects the theory of the moral neutrality of history and comes to believe that though "History is blind . . . man is not."

In an attempt to explain why so many novelists who are better than Robert Penn Warren have been ignored by the Pulitzer authorities, Arthur Mizener has suggested that Warren has been honored because he shares the conservative views of other Pulitzer novelists.[4] It is true that Warren is conservative, but his conservatism is of a far different stripe. Whereas his predecessors' outlook is primarily social and economic, Warren's is primarily philosophical and moral. Tarkington, Ferber, Bromfield, Barnes, Stribling, Mitchell, Flavin, and the others are concerned mainly with the individual's allegiance to certain rules of conduct having to do with money, work, and sexual behavior; Warren is concerned with the total problem of individual responsibility and the individual conscience. Ironically, the "moral" force in most of the Pulitzer novels is not the individual conscience at all, but the very "historical force" which Warren condemns in *All the King's Men*. ⟨. . .⟩

Since *All the King's Men* is an attack on the theory of the moral neutrality of history, to which so many Pulitzer novels are committed, and considering the demonstrated taste of the jurors, it might well be wondered why the authorities voted to give *All the King's Men* a prize. The answer is, doubtless, that the Pulitzer jurors did not recognize the full implications of the novel. For them, as for many of the daily reviewers, *All the King's Men* was probably another historical novel, an account of the "violent regime of Huey Long" for whom Willie Stark seemed but a fictional counterpart.[5] Further, *All the King's Men*, although not a best seller, was a fairly popular novel, and though tightly structured and bristling with un-Pulitzer moral, political, and philosophical implications, it employs many of the techniques of popular dramatic forms.

Eric Bentley observed, and Wallace Douglas has since pointed out in detail, Warren's indebtedness to the techniques and stereotypes of the movies.[6] He uses the "close-up," and the "fade-out," the melodramatic gesture, and the external tags by which movie makers indicate "character" on the screen. Jack Burden at times even functions as a kind of neutral camera who merely photographs the scene, as in the following description of Willie Stark's early home:

> It looked like those farmhouses you ride by in the country in the middle of the afternoon, with the chickens under the trees and the dog asleep, and you know the only person in the house is the woman who has finished washing up the dishes and has swept the kitchen and has gone upstairs to lie down for half an hour and has pulled off her dress and kicked off her shoes and is lying there on her back on the bed in the shadowy room with her eyes closed and a strand of her hair still matted down on her forehead with perspiration. She listens to the flies cruising around the room, then she listens to your motor getting big out on the road, then it shrinks off into the distance and she listens to the flies. That was the kind of house it was. . . .[7]

Jack Burden also functions as commentator and interpreter, pointing out philosophical implications and explaining the book's meaning. The last sixteen or so pages constitute, in fact, an explication of the novel, and in this we see an indication of Warren's limitations as a novelist. For although he is an intelligent critic and a writer who is very much in control of his ideas, Warren's characters are sometimes puppets, and his story is an intellectual maze through which the narrator and his author lead the reader in order to reveal what naïve undergraduates call "the hidden meaning." As Eric Bentley puts it, the theme of the novel and its vehicle separate, at last—the vehicle becoming merely an illustration of the theme. Consequently, the implications of Warren's novel rest somewhat less upon his art than upon the explanations provided by Jack Burden's explicit remarks—upon bare statement rather than fictional rendering. Thus, the "narrative voice" of *All the King's Men*, which is handed over to Jack Burden, is the book's chief weakness. Whereas the style of Faulkner, for instance, extends and enriches the meaning of his narrative at almost every point, the style in which *All the King's Men* is written turns back upon the narrator and seems to say, "See how smart, how clever I am?" And although the style may create Jack Burden, "we cannot forgive all the fancy writing, as some critics do, merely on the grounds that the writer is supposed to be Burden and not Warren. Burden was chosen and created by Warren."[8]

In spite of this failure, however, *All the King's Men* is a serious literary work that attempts to view life, not as a simple matter of obeying or breaking rules about money and sex, but as a highly complex tangle of intellectual, moral, emotional, and also very practical considerations. The novel's successes outweigh its failures, however, and *All the King's Men* remains one of the best novels to be awarded a Pulitzer prize, second only to *The Age of Innocence* by Edith Wharton.

Notes

1. Warren, *All the King's Men* (New York, Harcourt, Brace & Co., 1946), 462. (All quotations are from this edition.)
2. Ibid., 329–30.
3. Ibid., 417–18.
4. Arthur Mizener suggests that Warren belongs on the same side of the moral fence as other Pulitzer novelists: "The Pulitzer Prizes," *Atlantic Monthly*, Vol. CC (July, 1957), 44.
5. *Book Review Digest* (1946), pp. 858–59.
6. Eric Bentley, "The Meaning of Robert Penn Warren's Novels," *Forms of Modern Fiction*, ed. by William Van O'Connor (Minneapolis, 1948), 269–86; Wallace W. Douglas, "Drug Store Gothic: The Style of Robert Penn Warren," *College Engl.*, Vol. XV (Feb., 1954), 265–72.
7. Pages 25–26.
8. Bentley, "The Meaning of Robert Penn Warren's Novels," *Forms of Modern Fiction*, ed. by William Van O'Connor, 285.

C. HUGH HOLMAN

"Original Sin on the Dark and Bloody Ground"[1]

Robert Penn Warren's A Brother to Dragons: *A Discussion*, ed. James A. Grimshaw, Jr.

1983, pp. 193–99

Few novelists and poets have made more explicit comments about history than Robert Penn Warren. At the Fugitive's reunion in 1956, he said: "your simpler world is . . . always necessary—not a golden age, but the past imaginatively conceived and historically conceived in the strictest readings of the researchers."[2] In *All the King's Men*, Jack Burden tells Anne Stanton, ". . . if you could not accept the past and its burden there was no future," and then they are ready to go "out of history into history and the awful responsibility of Time."[3] In both the published versions of *Brother to Dragons: A Tale in Verse and Voices*, Warren says in the foreword: "I have tried to make my poem make, in a thematic way, historical sense. . . . Historical sense and poetic sense should not, in the end, be contradictory."[4] Such remarks, and there are many of them in Warren's work, would lead us to see him as a practitioner of historical fiction, as one subscribing fully to the author's comment in *World Enough and Time* that "we are like the scientist fumbling with a tooth and a thigh bone to reconstruct for a museum some great, stupid beast extinct from the ice age. Or we are like the louse-bit nomad who finds, in a fold of land between his desert and the mountains, the ruin of parapets and courts, and marvels what kind of men had held the world before him. But at least we have the record: the tooth and thigh bone, or the kingly ruins."[5]

When we examine Warren's use of history in *Brother to Dragons*, however, a substantial doubt about how he is using it arises. In the foreword to both versions, he recounts briefly the events of the slaughter of the slave George by his master Lilburne Lewis in Kentucky in 1811. This account, although brief in each case, is persuasively circumstantial. Then Warren adds to the disingenuous statement, "I have stayed within the general outline of the available record, but have altered certain details" (p. xi), [6] a seemingly frank acknowledgment of some of the changes he has made. In the notes at the end of each published version, he quotes from documentary sources to explain, or substantiate, material in the text. The unwary reader, looking at these Scott-like acknowledgments of conscious historical inaccuracy and at this parade of documents, in the absence of historical accounts of the actual occurrences, may be led to declare, as I did in 1976, that "this long poem . . . deals with the past with great accuracy." [7]

There is no longer any excuse for such a judgment, for late in 1976 Boynton Merrill, Jr., published his detailed, thoroughly documented account of Lilburne Lewis's crime, *Jefferson's Nephews: A Frontier Tragedy*, [8] and the historical data is now clearly before us. Those who wish to examine the historicity of the poem may do so. Merrill, with a recognizable and understandable touch of asperity, says, in his "Discussion of Sources," "In regard to the historicity of *Brother to Dragons*, Warren states in the preface: 'I am trying to write a poem and not a history, and therefore have no compunction about tampering with facts.' Warren succeeded admirably, both in his poem and in tampering with the facts. However, it might be ventured that facts usually do stand in the way of poetic expression and artistic triumph, such as Warren has achieved." [9] Warren has twice responded to Merrill's account, which differs from his in the poem in many respects, even indeed in its "outline of historical fact." In a footnote to the dramatization, *Brother to Dragons, A Play in Two Acts*, he acknowledges several of the discrepancies, but asserts, about his mislocation of Lucy's burial place, "This discrepancy no more than the others affects the meaning of the play." [10] In the foreword in the 1979 version, he declares the Merrill book to be "a conscientious and scholarly account" (p. xi) but denies its relevance to the poem, repeating a statement made in the 1953 foreword: "Any discussion of the relation of this poem to its historical materials is, in one perspective, irrelevant to its values" (p. xiii).

I shall not attempt the task of demonstrating that *Brother to Dragons* is not historically accurate in detail or even in broad outline. I shall simply mention a few basic situations in the poem that are false to the facts. Letitia was Lilburne's second wife; his first, whom he dearly loved and over whose grave the suicide pact was to have been carried out, had borne him five children. Letitia did not leave on the night of the murder; she stayed on at Rocky Hill and in January bore him a son. She was taken away by her father and brothers after Isham's indictment as an accessory. The murdered slave was not dismembered in the meat-house on a butcher's block, but in the kitchen-cabin on the floor. Warren seems to follow the account of the abolitionist the Reverend William Dickey, but not very accurately. Lilburne did not trick Isham into killing him, but rather killed himself, probably accidentally, before the double suicide pact could be put in motion. There are many other discrepancies than these. Indeed, one is forced to the conclusion that the suggestions of deranged motives for Lilburne—the Oedipal struggle, Letitia's sexual frigidity, the suggestions of class hatred between her family and the Lewises, and Lilburne's dominance of Isham—all have little or no support in historical fact.

One interpretation of the great discrepancy of *Brother to Dragons* with history might rest on the Warren poem which most clearly adumbrates the verse play, "The Ballad of Billie Potts" (1935), which is laid in Kentucky about the same time and rests on oral legend heard from a kinswoman when Warren was a child, and which tried—most successfully it seems to me—to combine that traditional ballad quality: "Big Billie Potts was big and stout / In the land between the rivers / His shoulders were wide and his gut stuck out"—with rhetorical, philosophical discourse—"Weary of innocence and the husks of Time, / You come, back to the homeland of no-Time, / To ask forgiveness and the patrimony of your crime." [11] In 1950 he had turned to documents as the source for an historical romance, *World Enough and Time*, using the documents of the Beauchamp-Sharp murder case, as he would use the Lewis court records, but also relying heavily on tradition yet changing names, inventing characters, and giving a new and highly melodramatic ending.

Brother to Dragons had a similar origin. Warren says in the foreword to the New Version: "My poem, in fact, had its earliest suggestion in bits of folk tale, garbled accounts heard in my boyhood. Then came a reference or two, years later, in print. Then . . . I . . . sought out . . . the little bundles of court records . . ." (p. xii). Thus, in the beginning it was not formal history but legend with which he was dealing, and not with fact—aside from the few court records—but the meaning those data could embody or express. So, "when Truth broke in / With all her matter-of-fact," [12] Warren could hardly be expected to greet her with open arms. Indeed, the change of the victim's name from the historical George to John is a quiet but emphatic declaration to Clio, in the guise of Boynton Merrill, of "non serviam."

But the true and basic issue is really the purpose to which material—whether from folk tradition or from the unquestioned annals of history—is put. On this issue Warren embraces a purpose and a method older by far than that of historical fiction as it was practiced by Sir Walter Scott. Historical fiction, in what Georg Lukacs, its most important critic, calls "the classical form" is a social and essentially—despite the frequent extravagance of its plots—realistic form. [13] It explores man in society, the individual caught in the inexorable trap of social and economic forces. Its protagonists are average citizens, helplessly in the middle, caught, in Hegelian terms, in the struggle of antithesis against thesis. It reconstructs the social texture of an age and dramatizes the tensions that tore average citizens in that time. It speaks with the authority of demonstrable fact of the pressures unique to one age upon a person whose essential nature is common to all ages. It is to these aspects of the tragedy of Lilburne Lewis that Boynton Merrill quite properly addresses himself. He explains and defines the issues, as an historian should, in such terms as the nature of the frontier, the inherent violence of Kentucky, the financial depression of the early 1800's, the sense of class and caste, the practice of slavery. The historical novel, like the scientific history whose development made it possible, whether Hegelian in doctrine or not, sees history as process, and it seeks to displace myth with fact.

On the other hand, myth exists when what is unique about periods is dissolved away, when time becomes meaningless and space replaces time as the dominant ingredient in fiction. Myth tries to tell us what is eternal not temporal. The order of its meaning is ultimately cosmic not terrestial, and what it means it means independent of time and place. It speaks not of social forces but of philosophical propositions.

It is no accident and in no sense whimsical that Warren locates *Brother to Dragons* in "no place" and at "no time," and then adds, "This is but a way of saying that the issues that the characters here discuss are, in my view at least a human constant" (p. [xv]). It may be argued that he is really talking about the scene wherein Jefferson and R. P. W. reconstruct and interpret events and not about the actions or the motives of Lilburne, Isham, Letitia, or Lucy. But such an objection is not valid, for these characters, like Jefferson and Meriwether Lewis, who had, in fact, been dead two years when the murder occurred, exist not in time or space but in memory. They all function as counters in a structure of meaning rather than as persons in time and space.

In all of Warren's fictions, he seems to feel the need to express the meaning that is, he feels, inherent in his materials. In *All the King's Men* not only does the witness—narrator Jack Burden—have the ability to explain and discuss meaning with dramatic propriety, but the interpolated story of Cass Mastern constitutes a commentary on the main action. In "The Ballad of Billie Potts," the mediating voice of the poet, as opposed to the balladeer, explores meaning intensely, as in:

> The answer is in the back of the book but the page is gone.
> And Grandma told you to tell the truth but she is dead.
> And heedless, their hairy faces fixed
> Beyond your call or question now,
> . . .
> Sainted and sad and sage as the hairy ass, these who bear
> History like bound faggots.[14]

In *World Enough and Time* Warren as discursive author can and does discuss the significance of the actions. In *Band of Angels* a first person narrator can and does express the meaning.

In *Brother to Dragons* he makes his strongest and most concerted effort to force the reader to see the fiction in terms of meanings and values by making the entire work an inquiring meditation not on history but on the permanent meaning of history. In order to do this, he frames the action with Thomas Jefferson, in a role not unlike that of Hawthorne's Young Goodman Brown, this time contemplating his Faith put to the crucial test in Kentucky. Like Hawthorne's Brown, who after seeing Faith in Satan's embrace in the wilderness, became "a stern, a sad, a darkly-meditative, a distrustful, if not a desperate man,"[15] Jefferson, after the Lewis atrocity, says:

> But I could not accept it. I tried
> To buckle the heart past fondness or failure.
> But the pain persisted, and the encroachment of horror.
> I saw the smile of friendship as a grimace of calculation.
>
> (85)

This Jefferson, his faith in man's essential goodness and perfectibility shattered by the depravity of his nephews, is totally unhistorical. As Merrill says, "No evidence has been discovered to date indicating that Jefferson ever wrote or spoke a word directly concerning this crime, or that it changed his life or attitudes."[16] Warren's intention is clearly not to describe an historical Jefferson but to criticize the view of man and human possibility which Jefferson is generally considered to embody, and which the Lewis atrocity teaches him in the dialogue with R. P. W. to call "a lie." To the ghost of Meriwether Lewis, who followed this optimistic dream of the West to his suicidal fate, Jefferson says:

> If what you call my lie undid you,
> It has undone me too. For I, too,
> Was unprepared for the nature of the world,
> And I confess, for my own nature.
>
> (117)

For ultimately *Brother to Dragons* is an extended and dramatized gloss on Warren's poem, "Original Sin: A Short Story," in which he says:

> Not there when you exclaimed: "Hope is betrayed by
> Disastrous glory of sea-capes, sun-torment of white-caps
> —There must be a new innocence for us to be stayed by."
> But there it stood, after all the timetables, all the maps,
> In the crepuscular clutter of *always, always,* or *perhaps.*[17]

In fact, *Brother to Dragons* might be aptly subtitled *Original Sin on the Dark and Bloody Ground.*

Jefferson is another of Warren's absolutist protagonists who pursues an impossible ideal until he is destroyed by the reality of evil, darkness, sin, depravity, and suffering—from which, at the last, his ideal cannot shield him. And the poem in which his disillusionment is recorded takes people and events from history and uses them to a most unhistorical, very mythic purpose, to state a universal truth about the nature of man and his world and not a local or temporal truth about a crime in Kentucky in 1811. Such a use of history is very old. Shakespeare uses it in *Hamlet* and *Lear,* in *Julius Caesar* and *Richard the Second.* Homer has used it in the *Iliad.* And, dear probably to the hearts of Warren's feminine ancestors, Jane Porter has used it in her very unhistorical celebration of Scotch virtue in *Scottish Chiefs.* Questions of accuracy pale to nothingness before such a purpose, for the author intends his readers to grieve on universal bones.

Notes

1. A modified version of this paper was presented at the MLA convention's special session, "Robert Penn Warren's *Brother to Dragons* (New Version): A Discussion and a Tribute on the Occasion of His 75th Birthday," December 29, 1979, San Francisco, Calif.
2. Rob Roy Purdy (ed.), *Fugitives' Reunion* (Nashville, Tenn.: Vanderbilt University Press, 1959), 210.
3. Robert Penn Warren, *All the King's Men* (New York: Harcourt, Brace, 1946), 461 and 464.
4. Robert Penn Warren, *Brother to Dragons: A Tale in Verse and Voices* (New York: Random House, 1953), xii; *Brother to Dragons, A New Version* (New York: Random House, 1979), xiii. All quotations from and citations to the text will be to the 1979 New Version, unless otherwise noted, and will be given parenthetically in the text.
5. Robert Penn Warren, *World Enough and Time* (New York: Random House, 1950), 4.
6. In the 1953 version he writes, "have modified details in two respects" (p. x).
7. C. Hugh Holman, *The Immoderate Past* (Athens, Ga.: University of Georgia Press, 1977), 83.
8. Boynton Merrill, Jr., *Jefferson's Nephews: A Frontier Tragedy* (Princeton, N.J.: Princeton University Press, 1976).
9. Ibid., 426–27.
10. Robert Penn Warren, *Brother to Dragons, A Play in Two Acts, Georgia Review,* XXX (Spring, 1976), 67 [q.v., p. 297]. The play is on pp. 65–138.
11. Robert Penn Warren, *Selected Poems, 1923–1975* (New York: Random House, 1976), 271 and 281.
12. Robert Frost, "Birches," *The Poetry of Robert Frost* (New York: Holt, Rinehart and Winston, 1967), 152.
13. Georg Lukacs, *The Historical Novel,* trans. Hannah and Stanley Mitchell (Boston: Houghton Mifflin Company, 1963).
14. Warren, *Selected Poems,* 273.
15. Nathaniel Hawthorne, "Young Goodman Brown," *Mosses from*

an Old Manse (New York: American Publishers Corporation, n.d.), 86.
16. Merrill, *Jefferson's Nephews*, 327.
17. Warren, *Selected Poems*, 289.

LOUIS D. RUBIN, JR.
"Robert Penn Warren: Critic"
A Southern Renascence Man: Views of Robert Penn Warren, ed. Walter B. Edgar
1984, pp. 19–37

Literary criticism, despite recent efforts to elevate it into equality with the literature it is criticizing, is essentially an ancillary activity. To the extent that it calls attention to itself rather than to the work of art, it fails in what it is meant to do.

So much, admittedly, is an assumption, based on premises that no right-thinking structuralist critic would grant, and today structuralists, post-structuralists and deconstructionists are riding high. It is, however, my assumption, and I assume it is also Robert Penn Warren's, as when he declares in his essay on *The Rime of the Ancient Mariner* that "a poem works immediately upon us when we are ready for it. And it may require the mediation of a great deal of critical activity by ourselves and by others before we are ready. And for the greater works we are never fully ready. That is why criticism is a never-ending process."[1] In other words, the purpose of literary criticism is to enable us to experience the work of literature with greater richness and depth than might otherwise be possible.

As I understand it, the theory of structuralism would have it that the poem or the story, having no identity beyond that of a system of signs, can have no existence except insofar as the signs are decoded by the reader. What the reader does, therefore, is to give existence to the work by making it his own work: he breaks down the system of signs and reconstructs it in order to display its functions. To the verbal object that is the work, he adds intellect; the result is a simulacrum, in which the functions are made intelligible.

Everyman is therefore his own poet, his own novelist; and since there is no check upon the activity of the reader doing the structuring, in the form of a text that must be deferred to, the structuralist critic is the virtuoso, playing word games, after the manner of the juggler keeping as many balls as possible in motion simultaneously: "Look, ma, no hands!" The critic is thus equally the creator; the only restraint upon his virtuosity is his own imagination.

If certain premises about the nature of language are granted, there is some logic to this way of looking at what the act of criticism involves. But it has its dangers. It can tempt the critic into a display of pride. Since the critic no longer explicates the poem or story, but rather thinks in terms of creating it for himself, he is encouraged to downgrade the poet's or the novelist's imagination in favor of his own. Pride, as we know, goeth before a fall; and the prideful critic, inflated with the brilliance of his own virtuosity, may find himself taking on a good poet or novelist on a one-on-one basis, and end up executing a pratfall in full public view.

We find this nowhere more perfectly illustrated than in the late Roland Barthes' *S/Z*, in which that performing Frenchman set out to develop his own simulacrum around and alongside the text of a story by Balzac. Dazzling and provocative though Barthes' verbal pyrotechnics were, it was a strategic error of crippling proportions, because he was up against a first-rate storyteller telling a tale. It was not very long, therefore, before I found myself skimming through Barthes' speculations in order to get to the next paragraphs of Balzac's text, so that I could find out what happened next. The "writerly" experience of Barthes at work on Balzac engaged my imagination so much less compellingly and vividly than the formal "readerly" experience of Balzac's story that it was only after I had finished the story that I was willing to go back to what Barthes was saying with sufficient patience to follow his commentary. Moreover, when I did I was both disappointed and annoyed, because the specificity of Balzac's text was so firmly in my mind that what I wanted from the critic was more help with understanding the reality of the literary experience I had just enjoyed, and not self-conscious demonstrations of his virtuosity. What I wanted, in short, was explication: a close reading of Balzac's text by someone skilled in literary analysis.

So much, then, for Geoffrey Hartman's assertion that literary exegesis is the "whore of Babylon," impoverishing our experience of the work of literature; what I needed at that moment was just such whoring.[2] I wanted a good critic to help me recognize the implications of what had been the powerful, intuitive immediacy of an engagement with a work of literature. A good literary critic could do that for me, because however much we might differ in our personalities and thus our personal responses to the story, it was Balzac's text that would dictate the terms on which both our responses took place.

I go into all this because Robert Penn Warren's kind of literary criticism is supposedly passé nowadays, and the textbook he edited with Cleanth Brooks, *Understanding Poetry*, occupies approximately the same place in the structuralist canon as the economic theories of John Maynard Keynes do in the Reagan administration. And this is as it should be, for the fundamental premise of the New Criticism, whatever its wide variety of approaches to literature, is that the essential job of the critic is to prepare us to read the poem, whereas that of structuralism is that this not only shouldn't but can't be done, and that what the critic perforce does is to recreate the poem in his own image. It is an important difference, because your working New Critic willingly and by conviction subordinates his personality to the authority of the poem he is reading, preferring to let the text of the poem itself authenticate the terms of his response, while the structuralist views that as an unwarranted limitation on his own experience, and he grants no such authority—or author - ity as he might put it—to those verbal signs on the printed page. The choice is between humility and arrogance. Needless to say, I prefer the former.

It is scarcely an accident that not only Mr. Warren but many of the other leading figures among the New Critics of the 1930s and 1940s and 1950s were and are themselves poets and sometimes novelists as well as critics, while to my knowledge none of the leading proponents of structuralism is thus inclined. If one writes poetry or fiction oneself, there is relatively little incentive to want to claim for criticism a priority with the work of art it criticizes, and every inclination to let it remain an activity designed to help make the poem or story available to the reader. With the structuralists no such inhibition exists. The literary work, they declare, enjoys no privileged status as discourse; it is *écriture*, and so are critical essays, letters, political manifestos, and whatever. Presumably the difference between, say, "The Rime of the Ancient Mariner" and the *Biographia Literaria* is in degree of resonance only.

Without going very far into the semiotics and, I think, politics that lie behind this approach, I am constrained to note that if it opens up the supposedly closed system of the unitary poem to the freedom of intertextuality, self-reference, and participation in function, it also serves to elevate the critic into a position of creative status coexistent with that of the poet or novelist. Especially if you are an English professor, this is rather nice.

It is also very democratic and free from any tendency toward class snobbery, in which instance—I quote Mr. Terence Hawkes—it is most unlike the New Criticism, which prizes such things as "sophistication, wit, poise," the stances "of a decaying aristocracy characteristically revered by a sycophantic middle class" and emblematic of "a bourgeois mistrust of single-mindedness and commitment."[3] If you are a dominie at an effete institution patronized largely by the children of the rich, this too is very nice.

Because Mr. Warren has published a great deal of poetry and fiction, he need have no fears for his creative status; that much at least is assured him. As for his chances of avoiding the imputation of being a bourgeois, however, he would appear to be in deep trouble. For to repeat what Mr. Terence Hawkes has pointed out to us, the values of the New Criticism are based on "a bourgeois mistrust of singlemindedness and commitment," and if there is a single characteristic that Mr. Warren as critic tends to most admire in a work of literature, it is precisely its recognition of human complexity, its refusal to settle for single-mindedness, its awareness of mixed motives, modes, and responses.

Let me convict him with his own words. In his essay on "Pure and Impure Poetry," for example, we discover him praising certain writers—Proust, Eliot, Dreiser, and Faulkner—"because they have tried, within the limits of their gifts, to remain faithful to the complexities of the problems with which they are dealing, because they have refused to take the easy statement as solution, because they have tried to define the context in which, and the terms by which, faith and ideals must be earned."[4] Of Conrad's *Nostromo* we are informed that "nothing, however, is easy or certain. Man is precariously balanced in his humanity between the black inward abyss of himself and the black outward abyss of nature. What Conrad meant by and felt about man's perilous balance must already be clear, if I can make it clear at all."[5]

Mr. Warren commends Faulkner because that novelist "holds out no easy solutions for man's 'struggle toward the stars in the stepping-stones of his expiations,'" and for "giving a sense of the future, though as a future of struggle in working out that truth referred to in 'The Bear.'"[6] He admires Hemingway but is compelled to point out the narrowness of that writer's range: "We never see a story in which the issue involves the problem of definition of the scruple [of honor], nor do we ever see a story in which honor calls for a slow, grinding, day-to-day conquest of nagging difficulties. In other words, the idea is submitted to the test of a relatively small area of experience, to experience of a handpicked sort, and to characters of a limited range."[7] Katherine Anne Porter's irony is declared to imply "a refusal to accept the formula, the ready-made solution, the hand-me-down morality, the word for the spirit. It affirms, rather, the constant need for exercising discrimination, the arduous obligation of the intellect in the face of conflicting dogmas, the need for a dialectical approach to matters of definition, the need for exercising as much of the human faculty as possible."[8]

What such attitudes represent, we now know, is a barely covert elitism on the part of Mr. Warren. His belief in the complexity of experience and the difficulty of moral judgment is thoroughly middle class. I again cite Mr. Hawkes in mostly approving exposition of Barthes and others: "Thus, New Criticism's admiration of complexity, balance, poise and tension could be said to sustain the characteristic bourgeois concern for a 'fixed' and established, unchanging reality, because it disparages forceful, consistent and direct action."[9] He goes on to point out the insidiousness of all this, how the New Criticism corrupts the young: "The attitudes implicit in New Criticism itself may, in turn, be said to have been influential on the 'real foundations.' How many, one wonders, of the civil servants, the teachers, the journalists who generate the climate of opinion that ultimately shapes the actions of politicians and generals, derive at least some element in their total view of life from experiences whose essence is literary?"[10] Well might Mr. Hawkes declare, therefore, that from a Marxist perspective the New Criticism is "one of the ideological outgrowths of capitalism; dependent upon the 'real foundations' of its economic ordering of the world, and covertly reflecting and reinforcing these, while overtly it appears to address itself to quite other matters."[11]

Now if all this sounds familiar, there is a reason for it. It is the literary Marxism of the 1930s dressed up in semiotics, and what it is engaged in doing is not very different from what the comrades were doing back in the days of Christopher Caudwell, Mike Gold, Granville Hicks, and the Party line. That is, the assertion is that any work of literature, or way of reading works of literature, that doesn't contribute singlemindedly *to* the class struggle is *per se* lined up against the class struggle. Though the new code word is elitism rather than escapism, the premises—and the objectives—are similar. The New Critics are accused of having infected the young with their literary values of acquiescence in the capitalistic order. Their bland blunting of a single-minded commitment to social action, their belief in tolerance, their refusal to pass instant moral judgments, produced the war in Vietnam and other such civic delights, in exactly the same way that Marcel Proust caused the fall of France in 1940. In short, literature is at the barricades again, or at least criticism is, and what Winston Churchill once described as the "bloody-minded professors" are striving to show their militancy, for fear of being branded as lily-handed, superfluous intellectuals.

I do not know what Mr. Warren can do about this accusation. He may claim, as he does, that there is no such thing as a concerted critical movement known as the New Criticism: "Let's name some of them—Richards, Eliot, Tate, Blackmur, Winters, Brooks, Leavis (I guess). How in God's name can you get that gang into the same bed? There's no bed big enough and no blanket would stay tucked."[12] But then he turns around and declares that "one thing that a lot of so-called New Critics had in common was a willingness to look long and hard at the literary object."[13] But to admit that is to imply the existence of the literary work, and that what a critic ought to do is to look at it long and hard, as if it were important *because* it is literary. It is to suggest that there is such a thing as a fixed text, the existence of which ought to control or at any rate guide our response to the story or poem, over and above what personal political, social, psychological, or economic assumptions we might bring to it. Mr. Warren's willingness to look long and hard at the poem even sounds like he favors that dread bourgeois activity known as explication. He appears to believe that we ought to use our intelligence, to the extent that we can, to develop a reading of the poem in terms of its own words, phrases, images, syntax, both single and as a totality, before going on to submit what it says to the test of its relevance to the "real life" experience about which it purports to comment. If so, then he is ignorant of the fact that, to quote Susan Sontag, "to interpret is to impoverish, to deplete the world—in order to set up a shadow world of 'meanings'. . . . Interpretation, based on the highly dubious theory that a work of art is composed of items of content, violates art."[14]

So there is no help for it: to the extent that Mr. Warren is a critic, he is a New Critic. The importance that he places on rendering the complexity of human experience, his belief that there is little in this world that is easy or certain, his assertion of the constant need for exercising discrimination, and his unwillingness to jump at conclusions about one part of a poem without first testing them against other parts of the poem, make the identification inescapable. Anyone who, in the course of discussing a poem by Robert Frost, could propose that "with our knowledge of the total poem, we can look back, too, at the next several lines and reread them" clearly deserves everything that he gets in the way of being accused of (in Ms. Sontag's formulation) depleting and impoverishing his experience through attempting to think about what it means.[15]

I exaggerate, perhaps—but only a little. One senses, behind so much of the convolutions of structuralist theory, the same impatience with "mere literature" that in the early 1930s sent the intellectuals fleeing toward the Finland Station. It turns up in strange ways. Geoffrey Hartman, for example, is no parlor Marxist and nobody's fool, but observe him in action, discussing I. A. Richards' notion of literary form as serving to reconcile tensions and helping to unify discordant experience. "This theory is open," he says, "except for the very insistence upon unity or reconciliation, which has become a great shibboleth developed by the New Critics on the basis of Eliot and Richards. . . . It is important not to be deceived by the sophisticated vagueness of such terms as 'unity,' 'complexity,' 'maturity,' and 'coherence,' which enter criticism at this point. They are code words shored up against the ruins. They express a highly neo-classical and acculturated attitude, a quiet nostalgia for the ordered life, and a secret recoil from aggressive ideologies, substitute religions, and dogmatic concepts of order."[16] In other words, to say that one admires a poem because it has both complexity and unity, to praise it because even in its variety it is coherent and because the sensibility it exhibits is not that of an adolescent, signalizes a wish to avoid the discomforts and uncertainties of social change in favor of the *status quo ante* Sarajevo.

Thus when Mr. Warren declares of the *Rime of the Ancient Mariner* that it is a poem "in which the vital integration is of a high order, not one of the 'great, formless poems' which the Romantics are accused of writing," and asserts that his intention as a critic is "to demonstrate that the poem taken as a whole is meaningful," and says of Coleridge's poem, in terms of approval, that it is "in general, about the unity of mind and the final unity of values," what he is engaged in doing is exhibiting a quiet nostalgia for the ordered life.[17] Ripeness, in short, is not only *not* all; it is an elitist shibboleth.

It may be so, but I doubt it. The whole political analogy seems pretty sleazy to me. If we could take all the leading New Critics past and present and arrange them along the political spectrum, from left to right, I suspect, from the politics of those that I know, that the distribution would be fairly even all the way across. The history of American and English literature defies any such easy equation of attitudes toward openness of literary form with political allegiances. Whose notion of what a poem should be was more revolutionary in its time, that of the high church Tories Wordsworth and Coleridge, or the atheist-anarchist Shelley? Could there be any poet-critic whose literary views were more subversive of the fashionable middle-class notions of literary form in his day than the royalist T. S. Eliot? Wasn't it the Fascist Ezra Pound whose motto was "Make it New"? And when did either Eliot or Pound, as poets, show much concern for "balance" or "poise"? Allen Tate was politically a conservative; was he therefore, during his heyday in the 1920s and 1930s, a radical or a conservative force in his attitude toward the form and language of the poem? And so on; there is simply no reliable way to develop any meaningful correlation between a writer's or a critic's politics and his attitude toward the preservation of the literary *status quo*, for the reason that the latter is customarily the product not of political but of literary history.

It is far more probable that the widespread discomfort with the New Criticism that has surfaced in recent years on the part of the structuralists and others, however ascribed to political and social outrage, is in actuality the inevitable manifestation of a change in literary generations. From the standpoint of the insurgents, what is really wrong with the New Criticism is not what Mr. Hawkes describes as its "bourgeois concern for a 'fixed' and established, unchanging reality," so much as the fact that it was developed and practiced by the academic literary generation immediately antecedent to that which is now engaged in attempting to run the show. In such a transaction the mere accession to power through orderly inheritance is never enough; what is demanded is repudiation. In any event, my own hunch is that when the smoke of critical battle subsides and Harkness Tower is securely occupied, it will turn out that what the structuralist critics on this side of the ocean do with a poem—as opposed to what they *say* they do with it—is remarkably similar to what the New Critics did. With the French, of course, it is another matter.

So much for the structuralist versus New Criticism dispute. What kind of a literary critic *is* Robert Penn Warren? He tells us that he is not a "professional critic," that a "real critic, like Cleanth Brooks or I. A. Richards, has a system—they develop a system," where he wishes to understand only this particular work or writer, and his criticism is a social activity in which he finds himself talking about books more or less as an extension of his teaching activities.[18] There is no reason to doubt this. I would only add that for a part-time activity pursued mainly for enjoyment and spare cash, his work has managed to be extremely influential insofar as the reading and teaching of poetry is concerned. *Understanding Poetry* completely revolutionized the way that poetry is taught in English and American colleges and secondary schools. Nor do I see any sign that its influence is receding; the structuralist controversy has not affected the basic way that a poem is now read and taught. The reason for this is that, structuralist polemics to the contrary notwithstanding, the abiding importance of the New Criticism is not as a theory but as a method, and it is Mr. Warren and Mr. Brooks who have developed that method.

It is a common assertion that the method of the New Criticism, as exemplified in *Understanding Poetry*, strips the poem of its history, ignores the personality of its author, and converts it into a meretricious verbal exercise. (I have seen Mr. Warren's colleague Cleanth Brooks criticised, in the course of a single polemic, both for being uninterested in the historical dimensions of literature and for conducting a covert apologia for the Old South, which is a pretty neat trick if you can bring it off.) Now anyone who possesses an acquaintance with Mr. Warren's work ought to know that, whatever else may be said of him, a lack of interest in history is not among his personal shortcomings. From the publication of his biography of John Brown in 1929 onward, he has been steeped in historical consciousness. To conceive of Robert Penn Warren without an abiding concern for the historical past is like trying to imagine a James Joyce who is unconcerned with Roman Catholicism, or a Laurence Sterne devoid of an interest in smutty stories.

What Mr. Warren and Mr. Brooks did do in *Understanding Poetry*, and did it very well indeed, was to establish the methodological principle that when you approach a poem the first thing you do is to read the poem. You look at the particular words and images the poet chose to use, and you do not jump to conclusions about what the poem means until after you have read it through and checked your response to any part of it against the rest of it. After that, whatever you do, in terms of history, biography, politics, psychology, theology, or whatever, is up to you. You can extend the poem's relationships to the world outside the poem just as far as you wish, subject only to the proviso that the ultimate place to look for corroboration of whatever you say about it is the language of the poem itself.

If this way of proceeding now seems very obvious, it wasn't when Mr. Warren and Mr. Brooks first published their anthology in 1938. Anyone who attended college during the 1920s, 1930s, 1940s, and even into the 1950s can remember courses in English or American literature in which the instructor talked about everything under the sun and moon except the actual words, images, and lines of the poem itself. When I studied Wordsworth in English Romantic poetry in 1942, I learned all about Annette Vallon, the French Revolution, Nature, the Lake Country, Neoplatonism and preexistence, Grasmere, Dorothy Wordsworth and Mary Hutchinson, and about emotion recollected in tranquillity, but when it came to the actual poems themselves, all that the teacher did was to read passages aloud in a husky voice and comment on the biographical or philosophical significance. Nowadays, thanks to Brooks and Warren, the equivalent of the same teacher will almost certainly begin, however mechanically or without imagination it may be, with the words and images themselves, so that whatever kind of pedantry or nonsense he or she might then proceed to pronounce, the students will at least have been exposed to what Wordsworth himself did in fact write. More than that, the fact that the teacher has been made to begin with the poem itself may serve as a checkrein on any impulse to stray too extravagantly far away from the poem under study, though this can by no means be guaranteed.

It has been charged that the method of the New Criticism, with its emphasis on close reading, places far too high a value on elements such as paradox, intricacy of image patterns, verbal wit, intellectual as opposed to emotional rigor, and so on, so that while it serves to show off the virtues of English Metaphysical poems and those of Eliot and his followers to good advantage, it is inherently biased against the Romantics and Victorians, and cannot properly uncover the strengths of poets such as Shelley or Walt Whitman. This seems dubious to me. It is quite true that Brooks and Warren, particularly in the early years of their collaboration, tended to admire the Metaphysicals and not to care for the Romantics, but there is little or nothing in the method itself that would establish any such favoritism. It is not in the close reading of the text, but in what is done once the text has been read, that Mr. Warren's—or anyone's—personal predilections come into play. The method itself, it seems to me, has no built-in bias at all, unless it is a bias in favor of reading what the poet actually wrote and taking it seriously. Mr. Warren himself has managed through close reading of texts to write sympathetically on Coleridge, Melville, Frost, and even John Greenleaf Whittier.

If we want to understand what Mr. Warren as a critic looks for in a poem or a story, we might examine the section of his introduction to Melville's poems in which he compares that poet's war poetry with Walt Whitman's. Though he begins with the flat assertion that "to my mind it is clear that Whitman is the bigger poet," it is obvious that Melville's poems interest him far more than Whitman's, for the reason, as he says, that Whitman's gift is for intensity and purity of feeling, while Melville's is for "complexity and painful richness of feeling."[19] Whitman, he says, is ritualistic in his war poems, while Melville is "dramatic, ultimately tragic."[20] He remarks of Melville that "his own yearning for absolutes—including, we shall assume, the absolute of Unionism—was modified by an agonizing awareness of the relativism of experience. The streak of mysticism in Melville was at war with his ferocious appetite to know. He was a mystic who hated mysticism."[21]

It is precisely there, in that recognition of the potentially dramatic conflict between a desire for intellectual clarity and absolute consistency and a need to acknowledge the claims of the irrational, the material, the carnal, the contingent aspects of one's humanity, that Warren's engagement with works of literature customarily takes place, and it is to literary works that in one way or another focus on such a division that as critic he is drawn. Such words as "*yearning* for absolutes" and "*ferocious appetite* to know" are quite characteristic. It is no simple division of head and heart, intellect and emotion that is involved; the lure of the intellect, the desire for absolute knowledge, is perceived in terms of passionate emotional appeal. As critic he is quick to spot the presence of this opposition, and to develop its ramifications through close examination of the text. The conflicting demands cannot be left alone and ignored; an accommodation must be sought. The poem, the story therefore become arenas in which the rival claims strive to be reconciled in time, through action. Thus he says of Melville that what the Civil War "specifically did for him was to lead him to see that the fate of man is to affirm his manhood by action, even in the face of the difficulty of defining truth."[22]

Much of Warren's talent as a critic lies in his ability to search out and identify the lineaments of this dialectical conflict in terms of how they manifest themselves in and through literary technique: language, theme, form become dynamic elements rather than static entities. As critic what he does is to explore the workings of the division he has identified, extending his search throughout the texture of language and image and the structural development in time and action, tracing out the consistency of the development, and when encountering apparent contradiction attempting if possible to reconcile it. If it is impossible to do so, then he wants to know why. Thus of Thomas Wolfe's *Of Time and the River* he remarks of the characterization of Francis Starwick that it "is more artificial, because he is at the same time a social symbol and a symbol for a purely private confusion of which the roots are never clear."[23] What he demands of a work of literature is internal consistency: its implications must be fully worked out.

By no means need this internal consistency be articulated on the level of conscious abstraction, however; where Mr. Warren looks for it most of all is in the imagery, the plot, the dramatic action. "The degree of consciousness in the creation of a poem," he says in connection with Coleridge, "is not necessarily relevant to its import: the real question is how fully, deeply—and veraciously because deeply—the poem renders the soul and the soul's experience, and thus enables us to understand it by living into its structure as projected in the structure of the poem. The only test of what . . . is 'latent' in a poem is the test of coherence."[24]

In Mr. Warren's instance, at least, nothing could be further off target than the claim, cited earlier, that what characterizes the New Criticism is its admiration for "complexity, balance, poise and tension" as devices for inhibiting change through disparagement of "forceful, consistent and direct action."[25] The recognition of complexity, the identification of difficulty are by no means sufficient; on the contrary, Mr. Warren again and again stresses, in his reading of a poem or a story, the absolute necessity for action. Knowledge must be put to the pragmatic test of being made to function in time. "But to live in any full sense," he says of Melville's war poetry, "demands the effort to comprehend this complexity of texture, this density and equivocalness of experience, and yet not forfeit the ability to act."[26] Discussing Frost's poem "Come In," he concludes that "so here we have again the man-nature contrast (but we must remember that nature is in man, too), the contrast between the two kinds of beauty, and the idea that the reward, the dream, the ideal, stems from action and not from surrender of action."[27] And so on.

What he does insist upon, however, is that the action be undertaken with a full realization of its consequences. If, as Mr. Terence Hawkes claims, "singlemindedness" is an object of "bourgeois distrust," then Mr. Warren is thoroughly bourgeois.[28] He is highly suspicious of self-proclaimed virtue; the literary work that simply asserts and does not examine is not for him. As critic he most assuredly does not value the poem that makes easy, self-serving moral judgments, that does not question its own premises or seek to avoid oversimplification. He declares that "a poem, to be good, must earn itself. It is a motion toward a point of rest, but if it is not a resisted action, it is motion of no consequence."[29] Facile critical assumptions and pat formulas are viewed with suspicion; "every new work," he writes in the course of a discussion of Eudora Welty's early fiction, "is in some degree, however modest, wrenching our definition, straining its seams, driving us back from the formalistic definition to the principles on which the definition was based."[30] A critic who can admire, and say why he admires, such divergent kinds of poetry as Whittier's "Snow-Bound," the *Rime of the Ancient Mariner*, and Melville's "On the Slain Collegians," and fiction ranging from Conrad to Faulkner to Theodore Dreiser, obviously operates from no critical straitjacket. In James Justus' apt summation, "Warren's criticism finally reveals less the rigidities of formalism, including the doctrine of autotelic art, than an older notion of art as a complex function involving biography, history, other art forms, religion, and psychology. Respect for the text is not lessened thereby, but appreciates insofar as it is regarded as the product of a maker who is not aesthetic man only."[31] What being a New Critic means, so far as Warren is concerned, is that one starts with the text, and not that one is locked into it.

I hope it is obvious that in describing what Mr. Warren does as a critic, and what he looks for in the poem or story, I have also been describing what happens in his own poetry and fiction as well. The same sort of metaphysical dialectic between the lure of the idea and the exigencies of proud flesh that he discovers in the work he examines provides him with the dramatic situations that become stories and the occasions for often-anguished first-person meditation that lie at the basis of so much of his best poetry. It is his strength, and occasionally his weakness; when he goes wrong it is usually because he has attempted to force the kind of dialectic I have described upon a situation that will not sustain it throughout, so that he is led to try to get his point across by emotive rhetoric. But at its best, his work is made compellingly alive because of the way it breathes with the ardor of an urgent quest for human truth.

In an often-cited pronouncement made in the course of a critical analysis of Conrad's *Nostromo*, Mr. Warren declares that "the philosophical novelist, or poet, is one for whom the documentation of the world is constantly striving to rise to the level of generalization about values, for whom the image strives to rise to symbol, for whom images always fall into a dialectical configuration, for whom the urgency of experience, no matter how vividly and strongly experience may enchant, is the urgency to know the meaning of experience."[32] The passage has been frequently singled out as a description of his own poetry and fiction. What I would note now is the emotive quality of the words he ascribes to the effort to discover truth: "striving to rise," "strives to rise," "the urgency of experience," "enchant," "urgency to know." The imagery is that of struggle, of compulsion. There is no room for complacency, no indulgence for efforts to take an easy way out. As critic of literature the work he customarily values is that which tests assumptions, uses language for purposes of exploration, seeks to leave nothing unexamined. In his essay on "Pure and Impure Poetry" he remarks characteristically that "nothing that is available in human experience is to be legislated out of poetry," and that "other things being equal, the greatness of a poet depends upon the extent of the area of experience which he can master poetically."[33] Again, the imagery is that of struggle. How anyone can describe the New Criticism, insofar as the work of the coauthor of *Understanding Poetry* is typical of it, as a conspiracy to propagate the notion of a fixed, unchanging reality is difficult to see.

It has been said of Mr. Warren's most recent verse that he has extended the range of his poetic experience to a remarkable degree, and this is quite true. The dialectic is still at work, however, whether in poetry, fiction, or crtiicism. Those who yearn for easy solutions, literary or otherwise, at whatever cost to intellectual integrity and moral honesty, had best look elsewhere than at Mr. Warren's writings for comfort. What he has to say as critic of literature is what he declared early on, in his essay on "Pure and Impure Poetry": "This method, however, will scarcely satisfy the mind which is hot for certainties; to that mind it will seem merely an index to lukewarmness, indecision, disunity, treason. The new theory of purity would purge out all complexities and all ironies and all self-criticism. And this theory will forget that the hand-me-down faith, the hand-me-down ideals, no matter what the professed content, is in the end not only meaningless but vicious. It is vicious because, as parody, it is the enemy of all faith."[34]

Notes

1. Robert Penn Warren, "A Poem of Pure Imagination: An Experiment in Reading," in *Selected Essays* (New York, 1958), 271.
2. Geoffrey H. Hartman, "Beyond Formalism," in *Beyond Formalism: Literary Essays, 1958–1970* (New Haven, 1970), 56.
3. Terence Hawkes, *Structuralism and Semiotics* (Berkeley, 1977), 155.
4. Warren, "Pure and Impure Poetry," in *Selected Essays*, 30–31.
5. Warren, "'The Great Mirage': Conrad and *Nostromo*," in *Selected Essays*, 55.
6. Warren, "William Faulkner," in *Selected Essays*, 79.
7. Warren, "Ernest Hemingway," in *Selected Essays*, 117.
8. Warren, "Irony with a Center: Katherine Anne Porter," in *Selected Essays*, 155.
9. Hawkes, *Structuralism and Semiotics*, 155.
10. Ibid., 155–56.
11. Ibid., 154–55.
12. "Warren on the Art of Fiction," interview with Ralph Ellison, in Floyd C. Watkins and John T. Hiers (eds.), *Robert Penn Warren Talking: Interviews, 1950–1978* (New York, 1980), 34.
13. Ibid., 34.
14. Susan Sontag, "Against Interpretation," in *Against Interpretation and Other Essays* (New York, 1966), 7, 10.
15. Warren, "The Themes of Robert Frost," in *Selected Essays*, 130.

16. Hartman, "Toward Literary History," in *Beyond Formalism: Literary Essays, 1958–1970*, 365.
17. Warren, "A Poem of Pure Imagination," in *Selected Essays*, 266, 302, 253.
18. "A Conversation with Robert Penn Warren," interview with John Baker, in *Robert Penn Warren Talking*, 257; "Dick Cavett: An Interview with Robert Penn Warren," in *Robert Penn Warren Talking*, 287.
19. Robert Penn Warren, "Introduction," in Warren (ed.), *Selected Poems of Herman Melville: A Reader's Edition* (New York, 1970), 26.
20. Ibid., 27.
21. Ibid., 31.
22. Ibid., 25.
23. Warren, "A Note on the Hamlet of Thomas Wolfe," in *Selected Essays*, 174.
24. Warren, "A Poem of Pure Imagination," in *Selected Essays*, 281–82.
25. Hawkes, *Structuralism and Semiotics*, 155.
26. Warren, "Introduction," *Selected Poems of Herman Melville*, 22.
27. Warren, "The Themes of Robert Frost," in *Selected Essays*, 127.
28. Hawkes, *Structuralism and Semiotics*, 155.
29. Warren, "Pure and Impure Poetry," in *Selected Essays*, 27.
30. Warren, "Love and Separateness in Eudora Welty," in *Selected Essays*, 159.
31. James H. Justus, *The Achievement of Robert Penn Warren* (Baton Rouge, 1981), 119.
32. Warren, "'The Great Mirage': Conrad and *Nostromo*," in *Selected Essays*, 58.
33. Warren, "Pure and Impure Poetry," in *Selected Essays*, 26–27.
34. Ibid., 31.

THEODORE WEISS

1916–

Theodore Weiss was born in Reading, Pennsylvania, on December 16, 1916. His childhood was spent in various small Pennsylvania towns, and he was educated at Muhlenberg College in Allentown (B.A. 1938), and Columbia University (M.A. 1940). In 1941 he married Renée Karol, a violinist and author of children's books. Since 1941 he has served on the faculties of the University of Maryland (1941), the University of North Carolina at Chapel Hill (1942–44), Yale University (1944–46), Bard College (1947–66), and Princeton University, where he was first a poet-in-residence (1966–67) and then a professor of English and creative writing. Weiss has also been a lecturer at the New School for Social Research in New York, a visiting professor of poetry at the Massachusetts Institute of Technology, a lecturer at the New York City Young Men's Hebrew Association, the Visiting Hurst Professor of Creative Literature at Washington University, and poet-in-residence at Monash University in Melbourne, Australia. Since 1943 he and his wife have edited and published the *Quarterly Review of Literature*, and between 1974 and 1977 he acted as poetry editor for the Princeton University Press series, Contemporary Poets. He lives in Princeton, New Jersey.

Weiss's own poems are collected in *The Catch* (1951), *Outlanders* (1960), *Gunsight* (1962), *The Medium* (1965), *The Last Day and the First* (1968), *The World before Us: Poems 1950–70* (1970), *Fireweeds* (1976), *Views and Spectacles: Selected Poems* (1979), *Recoveries* (1982), and *A Slow Fuse* (1984). He has also published *The Breath of Clowns and Kings: Shakespeare's Early Comedies and Histories* (1971) and *The Man from Porlock: Selected Essays* (1982).

Theodore Weiss's new book ⟨*Outlanders*⟩, for which we have waited far too long, is well worth waiting for. Weiss is a writer who works his language hard, and he knows exactly how to cultivate it for what it can give him. The opposite of poets like Lee Anderson and Charles Olson, who build for years a kind of complicated and contrived deadness into their poems, Weiss arrives at a clear, intense, vivid verbal life through the most laborious analytical processes, and it is apparent that he could not have achieved the extraordinary intensity of these poems by any other means than this approach. One has the feeling that Mr. Weiss has lived with each phrase for a long time, testing it in all sorts of ways, like a man edging cautiously out over thin ice, trying each footstep carefully before putting his full weight on it, until, in the center of the lake (for this simile must pertain to poetry rather than to fact), he can not only dance on the ice but on the water itself when the ice melts. Many of his passages seem to me to be nothing more or less than visionary, with the vision-seeing that only the poet's truest and most personal language can attain, with "the world/lit up as by a golden school." And yet you never lose the sense of Weiss's presence, either: the poems never seem to be the products of anything but a knowable and very human mind. The mind is an exceedingly complex one which operates by building small, deeply observed details ("the wood/in its own dark/middle lost") into difficult and rewarding structures: poems which never give all they have to give on any one reading but withhold, withold, always retaining something essential of themselves, something to bring the reader back and reward him again. The poems have both the immediacy one wishes for and the power of engaging the remoter, more abstract regions of thought; they have both the concreteness of things, objects, and whole ranges of meaning which the things inform, until the world does, indeed, turn into a "golden school." It is in the vicinity of such a school, after hours, that I like to think of Weiss and his censor sitting down together to have a beer, and of the censor idly throwing onto the tabletop the great keys to Mr. Weiss's splendid imagination which together they have designed and made over the last twenty years. Weiss has worked for a long time, and in a way right for him, to understand his means and to employ them as they were intended to be employed. This labor has paid off fully, and with interest, in the present book, and what must certainly be

Mr. Weiss's very great pride in looking back and seeing how the thing was done is my pleasure to try to imagine. Readers who want to connect first with the poems *I* like best should begin with "The Fire at Alexandria," "A Canticle," and "To Forget Me." From there they should go in any direction, knowing that it is the right one. After all, Mr. Weiss is on every page; *Outlanders* is in all senses his book.—JAMES DICKEY, "The Death and Keys of the Censor," *SwR*, Spring 1961, pp. 329–30

Most poets attempt one or two long poems which don't often get anthologized because editors automatically lean on the prejudice for short lyrics, and also because most modern long poems, like Eliot's *Quartets*, Pound's *Cantos* or Williams' *Paterson*, are collections of short lyrics embedded in connective tissue, or else, like some of Stevens' very long lyrics of varying intensity. Frost is the only major American exception since Robinson. What Poe wrote on the subject still has a terrible logic. People may not bore more easily today than in Poe's time, but they look for their boredom elsewhere. They think poetry should at least *look* intense, like a high bred show-dog, as it sits on the page.

Theodore Weiss, the experienced editor of *The Quarterly Review of Literature* and author of two earlier books of verse, *The Catch* (1951) and *Outlanders* (1960), was clearly well aware of all this when he wrote *Gunsight*, the most ingenious and, to my mind, the best long American poem since *Paterson*. In his earlier work, Mr. Weiss showed an opulence of sensibility and language straining, still more or less plotlessly, at fairly conventional forms. "Still it is brute magnificence/we desire, that drowsy girl, a bait/to hook the rutting heavens."

On the page, *Gunsight* looks like a uniform series of beat-Poundian ejaculations in the Charles Olson manner, without obvious clues. Different voices in matching type-faces sing in various keys, shout, or offer brief visionary flashes, some in italics, some in parentheses. Bits of jazz rhythm, snatches of childlore, blocks of elegant formal versification. A canny reader soon realizes that no true beat would leave himself as defenseless as this. There must be, as indeed there is, a new principle of cohesion here well outside the best philosophy of composition. The most highbrow of the beats, Robert Duncan, writes chiefly about the act of writing; his poetry is a set of florid gestures affirming the poetic stance. *Gunsight* is another story entirely. The speaker is a soldier who has fought in Italy, been wounded and sent home in a troopship to have his leg amputated. As the poem opens, he is going under ether and beginning to relive the crucial moments of his life from early boyhood through love to marriage and war. Voices return contrapuntally, the fabric of association is as rich and thick as the poet can make it, some help is provided by the typography, but essentially the poem must be read at least twice before its outlines grow clear. Event is linked to event by an emblematic tissue of natural imagery—birds, roses, a boyhood hill where raspberries grew, snow, the sea—in a subtle adaptation of Whitman's technique in "When Lilacs Last."

In other words, the poem aims to be as generic and "classical" as *The Red Badge of Courage*, as clearly drawn a poetic action as the Crane is a moral action. It adapts the "beat" idiom descended from Pound and Williams to a classicizing monumentality much as Seurat and Puvis de Chavannes adapted Impressionist techniques. The *tesserae* of this handsome mosaic are indeed colorful for the most part. The grand outline encourages a pungency, candor, and, sometimes, a compression lacking in earlier Weiss. But it would be wrong to praise the poem chiefly for this, as if it were merely a stage on the way to eventual beathood and the "crazy" freedoms of a Corso. Its strongest movement is toward the center rather than the edges of experience; it revives the pure pleasures of composition. The last few pages, where the speaker encounters the ghosts of his parents, are a shade too rhetorical; perhaps a concession to the conventional strong ending. The poem's intricate circularity doesn't really need it.

I recommend *Gunsight* to anyone still looking for the long breath and the full-blooded particularity that only a good long poem can provide.—R. W. FLINT, "Something New," *NR*, Nov. 16, 1963, pp. 25–26

The miniaturist in ⟨Richard⟩ Wilbur—when his grace is reduced to delicacy, and his perceptions stiffen with lacquer—finds its counterpart in Theodore Weiss, or at least in an attitude echoed throughout *Fireweeds*, his seventh collection and the first since his major statement, *The World before Us: Poems 1950–70*. His St. Atomy is its spokesman, in a poem called "A Slow Burn":

> Although I am a very little
> known and even less respected saint,
> I have my uses. Unlike those who pant
> for the instant bliss, consummate
> glory, of an all-consuming blaze, I am
> content with less, a steady smolder.
> Let the godly say who lasts longer,
> who's the one grows soonest cold.

Elsewhere Weiss celebrates the poetry tuned to the minor scale: "not a mad beeline / to the honey but laying out the slow, / pedestrian cobbles block by block, / then footing it uphill." Such insistent modesty risks turning coy or, worse, pharisaical. But more to the point, in Weiss's case the caution is unnecessary—and therefore annoying—since he is a fine, substantial poet. The reader familiar with Weiss's previous work will find nothing unexpected here. The tone is familiar, with its slightly professorial, gently self-deprecating accents of a man who meets "the monster deep / inside with a paper shield, a vision / that's bifocal, and a year's supply / of ballpoint ink." Weiss composes these poems as if they were letters to acquaintances who share his values and culture, but whom he does not know well enough to write with any urgent intimacy. Poems like "The Library Revisited," "News from Avignon," or "A Charm against the Toothache" are warmly humorous and intelligent, but do tend to grow discursive. Even as several poems could have been pruned from this long book, so too any single poem could have been sharpened or braced—say, by Hollander's flair for wit and paradox, or Wilbur's elegant schemes and grids.

In his critical study of Shakespeare, *The Breath of Clowns and Kings* (1971), Weiss admires that poet's prodigious learning and canny economy. Not surprisingly, these are prominent qualities of Weiss's own nostalgic and domestic poems, which ring changes on a few themes and situations, especially the ways in which marriage completes its couple, and the relationship memory establishes with the past:

> You carefully unfold your memory.
> Its views develop, horses
> whinny, rain spreads out its wares.
> All of it happening
> as easily as pebbles, jewels
> wrapped in a handkerchief, jewels
> lit up in an extended palm.

And this book's jewel and its touchstone is its longest poem,

"The Storeroom," a sixteen-part lyric retelling of *The Odyssey's* last books. The figure of Odysseus, with his frank curiosity and ironic heroism, has always attracted Weiss, but the speaker in this poem is Penelope, at the moment she visits the cool, dark room in which her absent husband's gear is stored. And that storeroom is, of course, memory's own. The poem employs a kind of stylized archaism, not of diction (as Pound might have done it) but of a syntax which diffuses its accounts and suspends its resolutions, resulting in a language half-dream, half-chant, appropriate to the woman's projective invocation of her husband:

And when he takes light—light!—
hold of her, under those extended talons
dove most godly, no, most human, tender,
to embrace her into flying clouds
cannot compete with, their high room a riot
shadows conjure.
And in a half-drowse—
O that it would come to that again!—
side by side, after the wine she has set
out for him, the bread, bread of her body,
they have shared, in the firelight watching,
like a drama nearly forgotten, fitful
snatches from their lives.
There catching
on the flames' far side a glimpse of those
not yet, and of that one straining, as he
used to in her tapestry, to overhear,
to weave into, their story.

But the poem is no conventional romance; or else it is precisely that. In its generic perspective, the poem poses time as a story in which we read our parts, accomplish our plots. The final section is an eloquent summary of that confidence:

But still she takes her time as he knows how
to do, for time is what they have together,
have apart, proved most accomplished in.
Both understand like stars tales of such deeds—
the lightning and its thunder, laggarding—
require time, time to be heard, be felt.
Had they not learned it at the first
from one another, earth's own seasoned dance,
the measured pace of things completing
themselves,
from their good time together,
the great tide washing over them, yet lovely-
slow, as honey, pouring from a vase?

—J. D. McClatchy, *Poetry*, April 1977, pp. 45–47

HAYDEN CARRUTH

"The Cycle of Sensibility"

Nation, January 4, 1971, pp. 25–26

When I opened this new book (*The World before Us*) by my friend Ted Weiss, a handsome volume containing a selection of poems already published, together with twenty-three new ones, I found myself on the first page, as it were, eating Proust's madeleine: I was cast back on waves of sensuous language to the exact feeling of literature in our youth a quarter-century ago. In Weiss's early poems I seemed to hear at once every bell of a distant peal. Not just Valéry or Pound or Joyce or Rilke or Ford or Stevens but the entire tintinnabulation, our epoch's first literary renaissance, jumbled timbres both great and obscure, the linguistic intoxication of an age. Not that we young ones merely imitated our seniors, though imitation in some sense was important to us. We were poor scholars, by and large, lazy readers, and half the time didn't know what our predecessors had been talking about; besides, we wanted to be ourselves. But how we reveled in their reputations, their power won through words! It was the triumph of language, or so we thought. We set out to equal them, and what we wrote, the good or the bad, could not have been in greater contrast to the studiously plain, careless, unambitious writing of young poets today. It had its dangers, that old wild dream of style, as I have pointed out elsewhere. But it had its pleasures too; *raptures, ecstasies*, as we kept calling them, only half in irony; and I can think of no better poet than Weiss with whom to celebrate our nostalgia.

Amid ocean of wish—
and the dolphins of whim
with slippery fins flick up
the playful swishing spray
in my comber-briny face—
amid ocean of wish,
shaped no doubt like pine-
apple, bristling and resolute
on its dish, carapaced
as any crab, crabbed
as any apple can be,
amid swirl-
ing and so certain sea (palms
to the right no doubt
as the stalk, saw-toothed,
tusked worthy of a snout, roots
out night-borne chough
chattering as the sea, bruited
from the daysprings of a voice
beyond appeal) with me
the root
I suddenly see
her rising a reasonant, a serene,
the dolphins flipt around her,
pips of spray punctual in eyes
seagreen . . .

So (among other matters) Venus mounting from the waves—billows of irony!—which was an almost obligatory theme with us, and no wonder. War-battered, we needed love. Denatured, we needed ways to restore a pre-Freudian mystery to sex. Don't think we did not write in urgency simply because we chose set themes. But notice the language. Imitative, of course; we know that the "night-borne chough" is Yeats's, and that no one says "bruited" in verse who has not read Ransom; the whole poem, of which I have quoted a third, has a flavor of the derivative. But there is plenty of Weiss in it too, especially the way he uses language, uses it with purpose and for all it is worth, every craftsmanly element, every device, vocabulary, grammar, rhythm, tone, all the nuances of association and echo, with the result that his poem has a quality of tension which rises through its imitativeness and nearly through its substantial meaning. And this quality of language, this tension and tensility, is to my mind what characterizes the best poetry by young poets of that period, whatever our writing may have lacked in perceptual directness and experiential relevance, just as it is the quality I find so evidently and regrettably absent from the poetry of today's young writers, who may have ample other merits and whose unfortunate disdain for the craft of poetic articulation has a certain historical justice.

I hope I will be forgiven for having dwelt so long on

Weiss's early poems. His book, *The World before Us*, naturally places the emphasis the other way around, not on origins but on destinations, and is a splendid selection for this purpose, though Weiss's longest poem, *Gunsight*, which is one of his best, is not included. Other shorter narrative and dramatic poems, like "Wunschzettel" and "Caliban Remembers," show his storytelling skills equally well perhaps, and the rest of the poems, lyrical, reflective, erotic, show a remarkable diversity of themes within a remarkable consistency of texture. The inner part of this consistency comes from the poet's characteristic turn of mind, which is dialectical, the simplest questions being posed in terms of conflict, so that often quotation marks are used to distinguish abstract points of view even where no speaking persons are present. The outer part of the consistency comes, of course, from language. Weiss has evolved in a straight line from his early poems, which is my excuse for writing about them at length. He soon sloughed off the imitative elements, which I have exaggerated anyway, and turned from set themes to more personal frames of reference and firmer concepts of expressiveness; yet still with the same winding syntax, precise diction and rhythmic tension. A poem by Weiss is indelibly his own. Indeed I often cannot understand the separate components of his idiosyncratic prosody, such as his hyphenated line endings or absolutely capricious interior line breaks; yet where I question such matters in the work of other poets, here I cannot, because they are so firmly and unalterably fixed in their totally individualized parent structures. They are the essential parts of a poem by Weiss, whose prosodic reasoning, even intuition, may be obscure, but whose end product, the poem in its wholeness, is not.

The shape of Weiss's poetry on the page, its coiling, spiraling movement up and down, corresponds to the way his language winds ever back on itself in the search for more precise discriminations of feeling, moral and aesthetic judgment and descriptive rightness. It is civilized poetry, in both the ordinary meaning of polish and refinement and in the higher meaning of eagerness to discover, reaffirm, and transfigure its own primitivism. It does not appeal to everyone. Impatient readers, who are willing to overlook the moral consequence of the moment when a feeling passes from one state to another, find it finicky or pedantic. But it is nothing of the kind, and I am sure its appeal is not limited to the poet's contemporaries. On the contrary, young people will prize this work, perhaps more than we do, because like all poetry which is both intrinsically sound and somewhat at variance with the immediate cultural and social needs of the day, this poetry is prophetic. It cannot help being prophetic. It bears one required phase of the cycle of human sensibility, from whose turning civilization is generated. If it is on the downturn now, it will come up again, as long as the generator keeps going, and the young people who see this are those upon whom we bestow what faith we have in the continuance of the generator, i.e., in the eventual restoration, when the other phases of sensibility have done their work, of civilized value. Thus a fine and modest book may have a role greater than its appearance implies, the transmission of excellence across a cultural gap. I am not being sententious; I know these same things may be said of other books. The point is to overcome one's fear of anomaly and say them, and to say them at the time and place of greatest advantage when one has a chance to be heard by the people to whom the books in question must be commended. Have I such a chance? Is the time too late, the place too remote? I don't know. Someone has remarked that "literature is what will be rediscovered after the revolution." This makes our present belief in the importance—not the supreme importance, not at all, but still the great importance—of literary values seem anomalous indeed. One does one's best, as Ted Weiss has done and is doing. And with that, one rests.

EDWARD HIRSCH

"To Hell with Holy Relics"

American Poetry Review, May–June 1976, pp. 35–36

Theodore Weiss is a poet of enthusiasms: for the world, for the word, and for the renewals of sensibility which unite the two. Nothing excites his imagination so much as decay, the thrill of fear, the mind at play with the forces that destroy it, the individual confronting ruins. Words like "astonished," "astounded," "marvelous," and "amazed," run through twenty years of his poems like an adjectival wind carrying the fragrance of metal; not as personal clichés but as the marks of an intellect continually surprised by reality. "The Hook" which is the first poem in *The Catch* (1951) contains the lines,

> Eagerness seizes us
> like love that leaves its best sailors
> in the mighty waves, love the word
> for hook whose catching, and the struggle
> there, is our deep pleasure.

Or,

> We strain forward
> as to some fabulous story.

As indeed we do. Or should. Or must.

Theodore Weiss' selected poems, aptly entitled *The World before Us*, contains fifty-five old poems and twenty-three new poems dating from 1950–1970. Except for Weiss' long poem *Gunsight* (1962) which is excluded, *The World before Us* is a representative collection of a vastly underrated body of work. Weiss has been a continual presence, but never a fashionable figure in American poetry; an impasse which has left his work in a peculiar limbo between notice and neglect. The key to the relative nature of that neglect and to the displacement of Weiss' work within the contemporary poetry world lies, I believe, in the romantic grandeur and determined breadth of his most characteristic gestures (which are simultaneously appealing *and* unfashionable) as well as in the fabric of his individual poems. In fact, reading and rereading through twenty years of his work one is drawn to, but nearly inundated by a confrontation with so much energy, so much beginning and re-beginning on such grand scales, and in poems with a rich and clotted verbal texture. There is a tremendous sense of abundance in Weiss' poetry, a great welling up of images and phrases, almost a generosity of words heaped on words heaped on words. His poems have a deep alliterative resonance, a sensuous intellection that constantly totters on the brink of verbal excess. Weiss' style has a vitality that is refreshing and contagious, though the technical price of that vitality is a syntax that sometimes seems slightly out of control like a car going too fast down a wet road at night. At those times the poems grow overloaded, ponderous, even as a cake can be too heavy or a cup of chocolate too thick. In one breath he can take in "a Bach of a beetle" or "that very Shelley of a nightingale" and in the next speak of "a million million people . . . /turning like a million/million leaves on a mammoth tree/like one strong wind." He is prone to large, extravagant statements like "the greatest hurt of grandeur" or "New York's a Troy burning." Furthermore his poems are decidedly not colloquial;

they are neither spare nor elegant. If anything, to use one of Weiss' own metaphors, they can be characterized as "luscious weeds." But if this makes them vulnerable and out of tune with the predominant tones of American poetry, it also accounts for their originality and magnitude. No other living poet has a livelier sense of the English language. In "Studying French" Weiss writes,

> I, who love our English words
> and loll in them against
> the several terror and the cold
> like any little furry animal
> grown cocky in his hole . . .

And later,

> I who debonarily strolled
> (I rallied them, I twitted them
> with double talk) among my words
> like one among his animals . . .

If Weiss's sensuousness is sometimes annoying because too "poetic" or florid, even as Stevens can be too glittering and Latinate, his poems are usually redeemed by their sheer wit and visual accuracy. Copious and digressive by nature, his enthusiasm continually strays from and redirects itself back toward the object in front of him. Stevens might have been speaking for Weiss when he wrote, "The greatest poverty is not to live in a physical world." The opulence of the physical world continually inspires Weiss' verbal scrutiny, even as the crated masterpieces and individual texts in his well known poem, "The Fire at Alexandria" inspire each other to burn. Yet for all of their sensuousness Weiss' poems are infused with an uncertainty that is often both painful and engaging, even as his more comic and rueful admissions are disarming. Hence a poem like "Clothes Maketh the Man" ("to be read aloud awkwardly") is a healthy antidote to what the poet recognizes as his own more sentimental tendencies. The poem is in fact reminiscent of and may even have been spurred by a famous, misogynous, and cranky remark of Joyce's that he was no longer interested in women's bodies, only in their clothes. In "The Last Day and the First," the title poem of Weiss' fourth and finest volume of poetry, published seventeen years after *The Catch*, the poet asks,

> am I at least
> not a little old now (like the world)
> to be trembling on the edge
> of nakedness, a love, as Stendhal
> knew it, "as people love for the first
> time at nineteen and in Italy"?

But foolish and absurd as he may feel, trembling he still is, feeling "this world/(is) in what may be its last days," finding it "hard not to believe that we are/teetering on creation's brink all over/again." Thus after his disclaimer about growing old (which is, after all, exhausting), Weiss closes the poem with a statement characteristic in its unraveling of syntax and the symbolic resonances of its final affirmation:

> Ah well, until I have to crawl
> on hands and knees and then can crawl
> no more, so may it every Italian—
> returning season be, ever the last
> day of this world about to burst
> and ever for blossoming the first.

"Ah well" is like a conversational signature. The crawling on hands and knees is the kind of half comic, half earnest, self-deprecating gesture that recurs often in his poems. The suspension of the verb in the fourth line and the repetition of "every" and "ever" in the third, fourth, and last lines give the stanza a dense, almost awkward quality. The words loll on the tongue. But most fundamental of all is the depiction of every returning season as Italian. The poem sensually confirms Stevens' "Italy of the mind." This is indeed the last day and the first, as is every day, and the poem affirms the continuity of a world always about to burst, always destroying itself and reblossoming, always emerging. Thus under the plentiful and attractive surface, the only kind of surface that could feasibly bring off a statement of this kind, Weiss returns to his most powerful and compelling theme—his preoccupation with ruins, his need to confront and, in the end, to praise those ruins, thus acknowledging his attachment to the decaying physical world. This is the world "which seems to lie before us like a land of dreams" and it is Weiss' intention to capture that world, those luscious weeds, in the secondary world of his poems, to "slither/under the skin of things," and to "see each thing, free/at last to its own nature."

To revise a statement of Henry James: show me an artist and I will show you not what he is conscious of, but what he is obsessed by. Weiss is obsessed by ruins, by any place where destruction is apparent, be it a spot of blood on the sidewalk or a library burning at Alexandria. The title itself, *The World before Us*, (the phrase is modified from Arnold), suggests the close of *Paradise Lost* when Adam and Eve, having lost their innocence, are banished from Eden and forced to make a new beginning. The hard, frightening necessity of making that beginning, and of beginning again and again, fascinates Weiss and it is a subject which he has returned to, in different guises, for twenty years. Moreover, there is always the sense that these ruins may be the last ruins: the last day does not guarantee the first. What hurts most about the fire at Alexandria

> are those
> magnificent authors, kept in scholarly rows,
> whose names we have no passing record of:
> scrolls unrolling Aphrodite like Cleopatra
> bundled in a rug, the spoils of love.

The sense of obliteration, often impending, creates intensity. Even more important, throughout Weiss' work there is the suggestions, usually tentative, that the facing of death may provide a window to the truth. "The Last Letters" makes this quite clear.

> The Last Letters,
> whether they be followed
> by what we call a natural death
> or suicide, tend to be the most engrossing.
> A certain amount of excitement,
> sensationalism even, attaches to them.
> But that's real enough and not to be denied,
> a kind of undressing
> so complete nothing else can possibly compare.
> Beyond that, as we lean closer,
> squinting at the lines,
> we have the sense of drawing near
> not only the most, but the ultimate of living;
> for here, whatever the strength
> of the occasion and the affectations,
> not to say disingenuousness, death may induce,
> a man, precisely
> as he turns his back on what
> he has been thirty years or seventy, is bound
> as much as he ever can,
> to tell the truth.

Weiss continues: no matter how apparently empty or mundane

something must crackle
even that last broken line,
something, we cannot help feeling,
from the other side, of that life even as it
is being consumed,
even as it consumes itself forever
in its own private flame, now breaking loose,
like some great moth
throwing itself into the fire
that is itself to enlarge it, but lost to it
in the very moment of having.

What is left for the survivors is the sense of mystery, of life quickened, almost but not quite forgotten. The past exists in fragments—a torn papyrus, a dull suicide note—and what those of us who are left can do, and must do, is attempt to reconstruct it. But what is perhaps most frightening of all Weiss suggests (the idea is almost Borgesian), is that in doing so we jostle against the lines of our own "destiny unbudgeable." "The Fire at Alexandria" concludes:

Now whenever I look into a flame,
I try to catch a single countenance:
Cleopatra, winking out from every joint;
Tiresias eye to eye; a magnitude, long lost,
restored to the sky and the stars he once
struck unsuspected parts of into words.
Fire, and I see them resurrected,
madly crackling perfect birds, the world
lit up as by a golden school, the flashings
of the fathoms of set eyes.

And yet for Weiss the real miracle remains the physical world. Arnold's phrase, in "Dover Beach," "so various, so beautiful, so new" might almost serve as an epigraph for the passionate assumption of the unstable world he starts from. For those who can crawl and continue to crawl, the ruin does, in fact, presuppose the reblossoming, the destruction yields to rebirth. In "Lines for an Ending" Weiss states

What troubles
most is forgetting, the poignancy
of passions once everlasting.

This is not a naive assertion, but a determined vision, for Weiss insists upon the necessity, and the essential grandeur, of beginning after the expulsion from Eden. Yet in his unfashionable, almost nineteenth century determination to reconstruct "a magnitude, long lost," he is haunted by inadequacy, the loss of innocence, the general and overwhelming deterioration. In "Ruins for These Times" he sketches out his proximate aesthetic,

To hell with holy relics,
sniffing like some mangy dog
after old, dead scents (saints?),
those who went this way before
and went. More shambling about
in abandoned, clammy churches
and I abjure all religion,
even my own!
It's much too late
to heft a Yorick skull and, ear
to it as a surf-mad shell,
hold forth foul breath to breath
on man's estate.

And yet he does, and must, attempt to speak, pottering about in his own memory, trying not to seem too personal, to stumble into loveliness. He is aware now of the cost, the heavy ruins we carry within us. The past is not only there to be guessed at and reconstructed, but to be escaped from. "To hell with holy relics" is a long way (five years), from "Fire, and I see them resurrected." It is an even longer way (fourteen years), from "Eagerness (that) seizes us like love." The expulsion is beginning to weigh heavy.

There too
I poke out bits, still standing,
from my wrecks, begun in fervor,
aspiration, joy:
those passages
through which the morning strode,
enlightened in its retinue,
choke on the plaster falling,
raspy stenches, refuse of lives
trapped in them.
Is the building
lust for ruin so strong in those gone
before that I and mine are nothing
but a story added, foundation
for new ruins?
The prospect
that seemed the way to heaven
glimmers mainly with the promise
of a final storm, a monument
of glittering bones to gratify
most dogged fates.
Our own.

And yet, after this powerful and existential ending, the next poem "An Opening Field" begins

To mind and not to mind,
to be exposed . . .

This generosity and willingness to put himself under fire, to make himself vulnerable, is one of the most appealing aspects of Weiss' work. To begin again and again is to be exposed, to luxuriate in the senses, to shun respectability, to challenge the last day, and to remain like Williams "always open, always desperate." It is to acknowledge doubt, to be personal in a way that is neither snippety nor confessional, to speak out of a terrible need and to attempt to speak spontaneously. Perhaps most important of all, Weiss' poetry is a struggle to see clearly, to always approach the world with fresh eyes. He keeps that world distinctly in front of him.

After such a day, too cluttered
for clearing and no way out, no way
to grasp this nameless yet pervasive woe,
after such a day turn to *Genesis:*
("Working Day")

For Weiss poetry is a way of perceiving and knowing the world, of discovering the way which "the yearning that is love still blunders/into loveliness." The poet attempts

To see the divine matters, the stars that,
foiled by some events and fouled by others—
wars and trials and deaths—serenely shine . . .
("Two For Heinrich Bleucher")

This visionary quest begins in "a place of blood" where the poet must bear witness, which is probably the reason that Weiss returns again and again to the idea of ruins; a quarry, an Acropolis, a burnt library, or an eighth day. The destruction is the precipice at which he measures the integrity of his perception.

Weiss' most heart-rending poem, "Caliban Remembers," is a long dramatic monologue spoken by Caliban after he has been abandoned by Prospero on the island of *The Tempest.* The poem progresses by a series of half sentences, alliterative fragments that move quickly and capture with uncanny fidelity the strangely inarticulate, strangely articulate movements of

Caliban's mind. In a language as crumpled as his own body Caliban attempts to deal with his most human emotions: his attraction to Miranda whom he wanted to rape, his physical repulsiveness, his foolish, drunken betrayal of Prospero, and most of all his loneliness, his perplexing memories, even his longing for enslavement again. He must bear

> Times I'd welcome the old, heavy
> chores, his orders at roughest irk
> echoed in cramps, nips, pinches,
> hedgehogs packed and inchmeal wedging
> through me

who had once heard himself say

> All the infections that the sun sucks up
> From bogs, fens, flats, on Prosper fall, and make him
> By inch-meal a disease!
>
> (*The Tempest*, II, ii)

Wearing Prospero's tattered gown, lurking about in Prospero's abandoned books, baffled by his own needs, Weiss' Caliban is a deeply moving figure. The language he has learned, but never mastered, gnaws at him like the aches he suffered from his master, a symptom of the world he cannot forget. Finding Prospero's magic book he presses his ear to the page and dreams of a magician's power, fashioning himself a prince!

> Ah the sweet tasks
> I'd conjure up for them as—standing,
> upright, rigid, by, they glare
> their envy's deadly looks—I lie
> in my flower-soft bed, she, flower
> among flowers by me, mistress
> to my least worded, far-fetched whim,
> breath mixed with, winging, lilac, thyme.
>
> And him I bid bring turtle eggs,
> struggle through fanged briers for berries,
> prickles too of bees he must snatch
> choicest honeysucks from.

Later he dreams of switching places with Ferdinand. And why not?

> Our names with their three syllables,
> two mountains humping a crouched "i"—
> Cal-i-ban and Ferd-i-nand,
> Ferdinand and Caliban—
> are surely like enough so that
> the mouth which shaped out his with loving
> breath, trill birds would stop to hear,
> to mine could be as kissing-kind?

As indeed they are. A fine logic, that. But the names also signify the men and the men are different; perhaps not as different as they may initially appear, but different nonetheless. And so Caliban must return to his own reality. It is a hard moment when he once again confesses

> if only he came back how gladly
> I would give this book, myself,
> and all the isle to him once more—

And yet even that is not possible. Caliban is left to himself, to his own nostalgia, to the dark thought of the thing he was.

Because of the intensity of "Caliban Remembers" Weiss bears comparison to the other twentieth century poet who has chosen *The Tempest* for her theme: Sylvia Plath. But whereas Plath chose Ariel, whom Robert Lowell has called that "lovely, though slightly chilling and androgenous spirit," for her symbolic guise, as her racehorse. Weiss has chosen Caliban, "a freckled whelp," a sluggish and deformed creature whom Prospero calls

> A devil, a born devil, on whose nature
> Nurture can never stick; on whom my pains,
> Humanely taken, are all lost, quite lost;
>
> (*The Tempest*, IV, i)

The difference is telling. Sylvia Plath was an hysterical and brilliant young woman involved in a frantic and high pitched game of Russian roulette; the result was not only some of the most intense Gothic poetry of our time, but the death of its creator. Weiss' imagination is slower, quieter, both more bounding and more plodding, but it too is haunted, plundered and plundering, paging in a clotted, clipped speech through the emotions of inadequacy. What is finally most striking about "Caliban Remembers" is the ruthless and incisive honesty of Caliban himself. The strength of the creation is that Prospero is surely wrong; Weiss' Caliban is supremely human. Moreover, Caliban is human because he acknowledges his own loneliness, because of his integrity and openness, his difficult attempt at clarity. These are all characteristics that could be identified with Weiss' work itself. Like the half savage character he has reinvented, Weiss' poetry speaks out of a terrible honesty, a fine self questioning intensity. If less spectacular a poet than Sylvia Plath, he is no less exacting in his scrutiny. In his slow, arduous way Theodore Weiss has compiled a book of poems with haunting resonance, a solid achievement in American poetry.

Eudora Welty

1909–

Eudora Welty was born on April 13, 1909, in Jackson, Mississippi, to Mary Chestina Andrews and Christian Webb Welty. She was educated at Mississippi State College for Women, the University of Wisconsin (B.A. 1929), and the Columbia University School for Advertising. During the 1930s she worked in broadcasting and journalism. She was also active as a photographer, and had a one-women gallery show in New York City in 1936. Welty was on the staff of the *New York Times Book Review* for six months in 1944, and in 1958 served as an Honorary Consultant in Letters for the Library of Congress.

Welty published her first short stories, "Death of a Traveling Salesman" and "Magic," in 1936. The former attracted immediate attention, and soon her short stories were being praised by such critics as Robert Penn Warren, Ford Madox Ford, and Katherine Anne Porter. "Worn Path" (1941) won Welty the first of five O. Henry prizes. The publication of her first short-story collection, *A Curtain of Green* (1941), and her first novel, *The Robber Bridegroom* (1942), helped secure Welty's reputation for intricate, imagistic prose and moving characterization. Her second and third novels, *Delta Wedding* (1946) and *The Ponder Heart* (1954), were widely praised, as was her short-story cycle *The Golden Apples* (1949), which some critics consider her masterpiece. After more than a decade of publishing short stories and nonfiction, Welty returned to the novel with her two most ambitious efforts to date, *Losing Battles* (1970) and the Pulitzer Prize-winning *The Optimist's Daughter* (1972). In addition to gaining critical acclaim, both novels made the bestseller lists, as did *The Collected Stories of Eudora Welty* (1980).

Welty has also written a book of verse (*A Flock of Guinea Hens Seen from a Car*, 1970) and a substantial body of criticism and nonfiction, including the highly praised, autobiographical *One Writer's Beginnings* (1984). Eudora Welty is among the most honored of living American writers; in addition to the Pulitzer Prize she has received the American Book Award for the *Collected Stories*, and in 1980 she was awarded both the National Medal of Literature and the Presidential Medal of Freedom.

The Ponder Heart is in its presentation one long unbroken monologue issuing from the lips of Edna Earle Ponder, the proprietress of the Beulah Hotel, the main hostelry of Clay, Mississippi. Let no one object that Edna Earle isn't really one of the folk since she has deserted the countryside and become a townie, subject to some of the corruptions of a citified existence. In the first place, Clay is evidently not very much of a town. It merges easily into the country. The inhabitants of Clay are, to all intents and purposes, as Edna Earle would say, still country people. I admit that she is capable of amiably putting someone down by advising him not to be "so small town." But that is part of the joke. If Clay isn't small town, what town is?

In any case, Edna Earle is uncommonly good company. In her exuberance and in her earthy complacency, she reminds me of Chaucer's Wife of Bath. Like the Wife, Edna Earle is perceptive, on occasion even witty, and always the complete mistress of her own little domain. And like the Wife of Bath, how Edna Earle can talk! It is interesting to note what she says to her auditor as the narrative opens.

> "*You're* here [that is, here at the Beulah Hotel, she tells him] because your car broke down, and I'm afraid you're allowing a Bodkin to fix it." [The Bodkin family is obviously in Edna Earle's black book.]

Is this remark a warning or a bit of commiseration? In any case, the man with the disabled car seems willing to let the subject drop; he has evidently picked up a magazine or a book, for Edna Earle immediately says: "And listen: if you read, you'll just put your eyes out. Let's just talk."

Edna Earle compels a hearing even as Coleridge's Ancient Mariner did, and like the Ancient Mariner she evidently does all the talking. Whether her victim eventually leaves her as a wiser and a sadder man, we do not learn. But one fact becomes plain: Edna Earle is clearly not a devotee of Yeats's written tradition. Reading just puts your eyes out. She is a high priestess of the oral tradition.

Someone has said that the many clichés and trite expressions that Miss Welty's characters, including Edna Earle, employ "reflect unimaginative thinking and [a] distrust of the new. . . ." To give an example, Edna Earle rattles off glib comparisons such as "she was shallow as they come," she was as "pretty as a doll," "he ate me out of house and home," "good as gold," could "cut your hair to a fare-ye-well," "didn't bother her one whit," and so on. These are well-worn phrases, but all oral art makes use of such formulas and couldn't proceed without them. The English and Scottish folk ballads are filled with such conventional phrases, and even Homer in his *Iliad* uses over and over again such formulas as "the rosy-fingered dawn" and "the fleet-footed Achilles."

Another critic may ask: "Don't her people often use literary words that are quite out of character with their usual vocabulary?" For example, Edna Earle Ponder conjectures that "Maybe anybody's heart would *quail*, trying to keep up with Uncle Daniel's." Jack Renfro asks his father, "What brought you forth?" and tells Judge and Mrs. Judge Moody that "Banner is still my realm." How did these bookish terms, "quail" and "realm," not to mention "brought forth," get into the folk speech? Easy as pie, as Edna Earle would say. Right out of the King James Version of the Bible, or out of the hymns sung every Sunday morning in the Methodist and Baptist churches. If we need a reminder of the latter source, Miss Welty makes verses from the popular evangelical hymns resound again and again through the pages of *Losing Battles*.

A moment ago I mentioned the use of the word *whit* to mean a particle, a tiny bit. I remember my own mother's frequent use of the term. But just to be sure of the status of this word, I took the precaution of looking it up in the *Oxford English Dictionary*. It is a good English term going back as early as the fifteenth century, but the *OED* characterizes it as "now archaic or literary"; and this designation, it appears to me, is an excellent description of much of the vocabulary of the Southern folk speech such as one finds in the pages of Eudora Welty. The words are pleasantly out of date and may in fact sound "literary" just because they are not the ordinary speech of everyday as we hear it typically on national television or read it in *Time* magazine.

So much for what I trust may be my last digression. It's high time to get back to Edna Earle. Eudora Welty is an artist, and she has permitted Edna Earle to be a kind of artist too. In proof, listen to Edna Earle's summary account of her addle-pated Uncle Daniel's marriage to Miss Teacake Magee.

> At any rate, Uncle Daniel and Miss Teacake got married. I just asked her for recipes enough times, and told her the real secret of cheese straws—beat it three hundred strokes—and took back a few unimportant things I've said about the Baptists. The wedding was at the Sistrunks', in the music room, and Miss Teacake insisted on singing at her own wedding—sang "The Sweetest Story Ever Told."

This is masterly.—CLEANTH BROOKS, "Eudora Welty and the Southern Idiom," *Eudora Welty: A Form of Thanks*, eds. Louis Dollarhide, Ann J. Abadie, 1979, pp. 14–17

Ever since I was first read to, then started reading to myself, there has never been a line read that I didn't *hear*. As my eyes followed the sentence, a voice was saying it silently to me. It isn't my mother's voice, or the voice of any person I can identify, certainly not my own. It is human, but inward, and it is inwardly that I listen to it. It is to me the voice of the story or the poem itself. The cadence, whatever it is that asks you to believe, the feeling that resides in the printed word, reaches me through the reader-voice. I have supposed, but never found out, that this is the case with all readers—to read as listeners—and with all writers, to write as listeners. It may be part of the desire to write. The sound of what falls on the page begins the process of testing it for truth, for me. Whether I am right to trust so far I don't know. By now I don't know whether I could do either one, reading or writing, without the other.

My own words, when I am at work on a story, I hear too as they go, in the same voice that I hear when I read in books. When I write and the sound of it comes back to my ears, then I act to make my changes. I have always trusted this voice. ⟨. . .⟩

When we at length bought our first automobile, one of our neighbors was often invited to go with us on the family Sunday afternoon ride. In Jackson it was counted an affront to the neighbors to start out for anywhere with an empty seat in the car. My mother sat in the back with her friend, and I'm told that as a small child I would ask to sit in the middle, and say as we started off, "Now *talk*."

There was dialogue throughout the lady's accounts to my mother. "I said" . . . "He said" . . . "And I'm told she very plainly said" . . . "It was midnight before they finally heard, and what do you think it *was*?"

What I loved about her stories was that everything happened in *scenes*. I might not catch on to what the root of the trouble was in all that happened, but my ear told me it was dramatic. Often she said, "The crisis had come!"

This same lady was one of Mother's callers on the telephone who always talked a long time. I knew who it was when my mother would only reply, now and then, "Well, I declare," or "You don't say so," or "Surely not." She'd be standing at the wall telephone, listening against her will, and I'd sit on the stairs close by her. Our telephone had a little bar set into the handle which had to be pressed and held down to keep the connection open, and when her friend had said goodbye, my mother needed me to prize her fingers loose from the little bar; her grip had become paralyzed. "What did she say?" I asked.

"She wasn't *saying* a thing in this world," sighed my mother. "She was just ready to talk, that's all."

My mother was right. Years later, beginning with my story "Why I Live at the P.O.," I wrote reasonably often in the form of a monologue that takes possession of the speaker. How much gets told besides!

This lady told everything in her sweet, marveling voice, and meant every word of it kindly. She enjoyed my company perhaps even more than my mother's. She invited me to catch her doodlebugs; under the trees in her backyard were dozens of their holes. When you stuck a broom straw down one and called, "Doodlebug, doodlebug, your house is on fire and all your children are burning up," she believed this is why the doodlebug came running out of the hole. This was why I loved to call up her doodlebugs instead of ours.

My mother could never have told me her stories, and I think I knew why even then: my mother didn't believe them. But I could listen to this murmuring lady all day. She believed everything she heard, like the doodlebug. And so did I.

This was a day when ladies' and children's clothes were very often made at home. My mother cut out all the dresses and her little boys' rompers, and a sewing woman would come and spend the day upstairs in the sewing room fitting and stitching them all. This was Fannie. This old black sewing woman, along with her speed and dexterity, brought along a great provision of up-to-the-minute news. She spent her life going from family to family in town and worked right in its bosom, and nothing could stop her. My mother would try, while I stood being pinned up. "Fannie, I'd rather Eudora didn't hear that." "That" would be just what I was longing to hear, whatever it was. "I don't want her exposed to gossip"—as if gossip were measles and I could catch it. I did catch some of it but not enough. "Mrs. O'Neil's oldest daughter she had her wedding dress *tried on*, and all her fine underclothes featherstitched and ribbon run in and then—" "I think that will do, Fannie," said my mother. It was tantalizing never to be exposed long enough to hear the end.

Fannie was the worldliest old woman to be imagined. She could do whatever her hands were doing without having to stop talking; and she could speak in a wonderfully derogatory way with any number of pins stuck in her mouth. Her hands steadied me like claws as she stumped on her knees around me, tacking me together. The gist of her tale would be lost on me, but Fannie didn't bother about the ear she was telling it to; she just liked telling. She was like an author. In fact, for a good deal of what she said, I daresay she *was* the author.

Long before I wrote stories, I listened for stories. Listening *for* them is something more acute than listening *to* them. I suppose it's an early form of participation in what goes on. Listening children know stories are *there*. When their elders sit and begin, children are just waiting and hoping for one to come out, like a mouse from its hole.—EUDORA WELTY, "Listening," *One Writer's Beginnings*, 1984, pp. 12–16

Welty stories are almost entirely filled with Southerners, Mississippi Southerners, as authentically Southern as they come in their idiom, their gestures, their moods, their madnesses, everything to the finest detail. Black and white both, though mostly white. There are no Compsons or Sartorises, no hero with a tragic flaw, no doomed families with ancestral ghosts. With few exceptions—one thinks of *The Optimist's Daughter*—they are unsophisticated and very plain people. Some are as objectionable as the Snopses, but they are never types, only individuals. They never speak for the author, only for themselves or the community. Miss Welty writes with detachment and sympathy but without identification. She has no fictional spokesman. "I don't write out of anger," she says, for "simply as a fiction writer, I am minus an adversary." It could be said that she is apolitical, nonideological, perhaps even ahistorical.

It is not that she is indifferent to history. The Natchez Trace runs right through her world. She even introduces historical figures—an imaginary encounter of Audubon, Lorenzo Dow, the evangelist, and John Murrell, the outlaw, in "A Still Moment," for example. Aaron Burr turns up in Natchez. But they appear from a legendary past, not as regional symbols or as "the past in the present." She passes over the Civil War with only one short story, and that as seen through the eyes of a totally uncomprehending slave girl. If the distinguishing "historical consciousness" were going to appear, it would in *Delta Wedding*, but it doesn't. Whole families pass in review, several generations of them, trailing no clouds of destiny, no hereditary curse, no brooding guilt or racial complications or torments of pride and honor. They are located in time and place but are never seen as the pawns of historical or social forces. That is not the Welty way. As much as she may admire that way in works of her contemporaries, she has left it to them.

She has her own way, and it would be a mistake to push her into any traditional category. Her fiction is often enigmatic, elusive, elliptical, difficult. Much is said between the lines or in the *way* it is said. Distinctions between love and hate, joy and sorrow, innocence and guilt, success and failure, victory and defeat are often left vague. So are the lines between dream and reality, fantasy and fact. One critic was brought up sharp by the suspicion that the whole story in "The Death of a Traveling Salesman" was hallucination on the part of the main character. The same sort of suspicion arises in that gem of a story "A Worn Path" or in "Powerhouse" or in "The Purple Hat." The author keeps her counsel. She records but never judges and often leaves enigmas enigmatic and mysteries mysterious.—C. VANN WOODWARD, "Southerner with Her Own Accent," *NYTBR*, Feb. 19, 1984, p. 1

ROBERT PENN WARREN

"The Love and the Separateness in Miss Welty"

Kenyon Review, Spring 1944, pp. 246–59

> He could understand God's giving Separateness first and then giving Love to follow and heal in its wonder; but God had reversed this, and given Love first and then Separateness, as though it did not matter to Him which came first. ("A Still Moment")

If we put *The Wide Net*, Eudora Welty's present collection of stories, up against her first collection, *A Curtain of Green*, we can immediately observe a difference: the stories of *The Wide Net* represent a specializing, an intensifying, of one of the many strains which were present in *A Curtain of Green*. All of the stories in *A Curtain of Green* bear the impress of Miss Welty's individual talent, but there is a great variety among them in subject matter and method and, more particularly, mood. It is almost as if the author had gone at each story as a fresh start in the business of writing fiction, as if she had had to take a new angle each time out of a joy in the pure novelty of the perspective. There is the vindictive farce of "The Petrified Man," the nightmarish "Clytie," the fantastic and witty "Old Mr. Marblehall," the ironic self-revelation of "Why I Live at the P.O.," the nearly straight realism of "The Hitch-Hikers," the macabre comedy and pathos of "Keela, the Outcast Indian Maid." The material of many of the stories was sad, or violent, or warped, and even the comedy and wit were not straight, but if read from one point of view, if read as a perforamnce, the book was exhilarating, even gay, as though the author were innocently delighted not only with the variety of the world but with the variety of ways in which one could look at the world and the variety of things which stories could be and still be stories. Behind the innocent delight of the craftsman, and of the admirer of the world, there was also a seriousness, a philosophical cast of mind, which gave coherence to the book, but on the surface there was the variety, the succession of surprises. In *The Wide Net* we do not find the surprises. The stories are more nearly cut to one pattern.

We do not find the surprises. Instead, on the first page, with the first sentence, we enter a special world: "Whatever happened, it happened in extraordinary times, in a season of dreams . . ." And that is the world in which we are going to live until we reach the last sentence of the last story. "Whatever happened," the first sentence begins, as though the author cannot be quite sure what did happen, cannot quite undertake to resolve the meaning of the recorded event, cannot, in fact, be too sure of recording all of the event. This is coyness, of course; or a way of warning the reader that he cannot expect quite the ordinary direct lighting of the actual event. For it is "a season of dreams"—and the faces and gestures and events often have something of the grave retardation, the gnomic intensity, the portentous suggestiveness of dreams. The logic of things here is not quite the logic by which we live, or think we live, our ordinary daylight lives. In "The Wide Net," for example, the young husband, who thinks his wife has jumped into the river, goes out with a party of friends to dredge for the body, but the sad occasion turns into a saturnalian fish-fry which is interrupted when the great King of the Snakes raises his hoary head from the surface of the river. But usually, in the present stories, the wrenching of logic is not in terms of events themselves, though "The Purple Hat" is a fantasy, and "Asphodel" moves in the direction of fantasy. Usually the events as events might be given a perfectly realistic treatment (Dreiser could take the events of "The Landing" for a story). But in these cases where the events and their ordering are "natural" and not supernatural or fantastic, the stories themselves finally belong to the "season of dreams" because of the special tone and mood, the special perspective, the special sensibility with which they are rendered.

Some readers, in fact, who are quite aware of Miss Welty's gifts, have recently reported that they are disturbed by the recent development of her work. Diana Trilling, in her valuable and sobering comments on current fiction, which appear regularly in the *Nation*, says the author "has developed her technical virtuosity to the point where it outweighs the uses to which it is put, and her vision of horror to the point of nightmare." There are two ideas in this indictment, and let us take the first one first and come to the second much later. The indictment of the technique is developed along these lines: Miss Welty has made her style too fancy—decorative, "falsely poetic" and "untrue," "insincere." ("When an author says 'look at me' instead of 'Look at it,' there is insincerity . . .") This insincerity springs from "the extreme infusion of subjectivism and private sensibility." But the subjectivism leads not only to insincerity and fine writing but to a betrayal of the story's obligation to narrative and rationality. Miss Welty's stories take off from a situation, but "the stories themselves stay with their narrative no more than a dance, say, stays with its argument." That is the summary of the argument.

The argument is, no doubt, well worth the close attention of Miss Welty's admirers. There is, in fact, a good deal of the falsely poetic in Miss Welty's present style, metaphors that simply pretend to an underlying logic, and metaphors (and descriptions) that, though good themselves, are irrelevant to the business in hand. And sometimes Miss Welty's refusal to play up the objective action—her attempt to define and refine the response rather than to present the stimulus—does result in a blurred effect. But the indictment does not treat primarily of such failures to fulfill the object the artist has set herself but of the nature of that object. The critic denies, in effect, that Miss Welty's present kind of fiction is fiction at all: "It is a book of ballets, not of stories."

Now it is possible that the critic is arguing from some abstract definition of "story," some formalistic conception which does not accomodate the present exhibit, and is not concerning herself with the question of whether or not the present exhibit is doing the special job which it proposes for itself, and, finally, the job which we demand of all literature? Perhaps we should look at a new work first in terms of its effect and not in terms of a definition of type, because every new work is in some degree, however modest, wrenching our definition, straining its seams, driving us back from the formalistic definition to the principles on which the definition was based. Can we say this, therefore, of our expectation concerning a piece of literature, new or old: that it should intensify our awareness of the world (and of ourselves in relation to the world) in terms of an idea, a "view." This leads us to what is perhaps the key statement by Diana Trilling concerning *The Wide Net*: she grants that the volume "has tremendous emotional impact, despite its obscurity." In other words, she says, unless I misinterpret her, that the book does intensify the reader's awareness—but *not* in terms of a presiding idea.

This has led me to reread Miss Welty's two volumes of stories in the attempt to discover the issues which are involved in the "season of dreams."[1] To begin with, almost all of the stories deal with people who, in one way or another, are cut off, alienated, isolated from the world. There is the girl in "Why I Live at the P. O."—isolated from her family by her arrogance, meanness, and sense of persecution; the half-witted Lily Daw, who, despite the efforts of "good" ladies, wants to live like other people; the deaf-mutes of "The Key," and the deaf-mute of "First Love"; the people of "The Whistle" and "A Piece of News," who are physically isolated from the world and who make their pathetic efforts to reestablish something lost; the travelling-salesman and the hitch-hikers of "The Hitch-Hikers" who, for their different reasons, are alone, and the travelling-salesman of "Death of a Traveling Salesman" who, in the physically and socially isolated backwoods cabin, discovers that he is the one who is truly isolated; Clytie, isolated in family pride and madness and sexual frustration, and Jennie of "At the Landing," and Mrs. Larkin of "A Curtain of Green," the old women of "A Visit of Charity" and the old Negro woman of "A Worn Path"; the murderer of "Flowers for Marjorie" who is cut off by an economic situation and the pressure of that great city; Mr. Marbelhall in his secret life; Livvie, who, married to an old man and trapped in his respectable house, is cut off from the life appropriate to her years; Lorenzo, Murrell, and Audubon in "A Still Moment," each alone in his dream, his obsession; the old maids of "Asphodel," who tell the story of Miss Sabina and then are confronted by the naked man and pursued by the flock of goats. In some of the cases, the matter is more indirectly presented. For instance, in "Keela, the Outcast Indian Maid," we find, as in *The Ancient Mariner*, the story of a man who, having committed a crime, must try to reestablish his connection with humanity; or in the title-story of *The Wide Net*, William Wallace, because he thinks his wife has drowned herself, is at the start of the story cut off from the world of natural joy in which he had lived. "The Petrified Man" and "A Memory" present even more indirect cases, cases which we shall come to a little farther in the discussion.

We can observe that the nature of the isolation may be different from case to case, but the fact of isolation, whatever its nature, provides the basic situation of Miss Welty's fiction. The drama which develops from this basic situation is of either of two kinds: first, the attempt of the isolated person to escape into the world; or second, the discovery by the isolated person, or by the reader, of the nature of the predicament. As an example of the first type, we can remember Clytie's obsessed inspection of faces ("Was it possible to comprehend the eyes and the mouth of other people, which concealed she knew not what, and secretly asked for still another unknown thing?") and her attempt to escape, and to solve the mystery, when she lays her finger on the face of the terrified barber who has come to the ruinous old house to shave her father. Or there is Jennie, of "At the Landing," or Livvie, or the man of "Keela." As an example of the second type, there is the new awareness on the part of the salesman in "The Hitch-Hikers," or the new awareness on the part of the other salesman in the back-country cabin. Even in "A Still Moment" we have this pattern, though in triplicate. The evangelist Lorenzo, the outlaw Murrell, and the naturalist and artist Audubon stand for a still moment and watch a white heron feeding. Lorenzo having seen a beauty greater than he could account for (he had earlier "accounted for" the beauty by thinking, "Praise God, His love has come visible"), and with the sweat of rapture pouring down from his forehead, shouts into the marshes, "Tempter!" He has not been able to escape from his own obsession, in other words, to make his definition of the world accommodate the white heron and the "natural" rapture which takes him. Murrell, looking at the bird, sees "only whiteness ensconced in darkness," and thinks that "if it would look at him a dream penetration would fill and gratify his heart"—the heart which Audubon has already defined as belonging to the flinty darkness of a cave. Neither Lorenzo nor Murrell can "love" the bird, and so escape from their own curse as did, again, the Ancient Mariner. But there remains the case of Audubon himself, who does "love" the bird, who can innocently accept nature. There is, however, an irony here. To paint the bird he must "know" the bird as well as "love" it, he must know it feather by feather, he must have it in his hand. And so he must kill it. But having killed the bird, he knows that the best he can make of it now in a painting would be a dead thing, "never the essence, only a sum of parts," and that "it would always meet with a stranger's sight, and never be one with the beauty in any other man's head in the world." Here, too, the fact of the isolation is realized: as artist and lover of nature he had aspired to a communication, a communion, with other men in terms of the bird, but now "he saw his long labor most revealingly at the point where it met its limit" and he is forced back upon himself.

"A Still Moment," however, may lead us beyond the discussion of the characteristic situation, drama, and realization in Miss Welty's stories. It may lead us to a theme which seems to underlie the stories. For convenience, though at the risk of incompleteness, or even distortion, we may call it "Innocence and Experience." Let us take the case of Audubon in relation to the heron. He loves the bird, and innocently, in its fullness of being. But he must subject this love to knowledge; he must kill the bird if he is to commemorate its beauty, if he is to establish his communion with other men in terms of the bird's beauty. There is in the situation an irony of limit and contamination.

Let us look at this theme in relation to other stories. "A Memory," in *A Curtain of Green*, gives a simple example. Here we have a young girl lying on a beach and looking out at the scene through a frame made by her fingers, for the girl can say of herself, "To watch everything about me I regarded grimly and possessively as a need." (As does Audubon, in "A Still Moment.") And further: "It did not matter to me what I looked at; from any observation I would conclude that a secret of life had been nearly revealed to me. . . ." Now the girl is cherishing a secret love, a love for a boy at school about whom she knows nothing, to whom she has never even spoken, but whose wrist her hand had once accidentally brushed. The secret love had made her watching of the world more austere, had sharpened her demand that the world conform to her own ideas and had created a sense of fear. This fear had seemed to be realized one day when, in the middle of a class, the boy had a fit of nose-bleed. But that is in the past. This morning she suddenly sees between the frame of her fingers a group of coarse, fat, stupid, and brutal people disporting themselves on the sand with a maniacal, aimless vigor which comes to climax when the fat woman, into the front of whose bathing suit the man had poured sand, bends over and pulls down the cloth so that the lumps of mashed and folded sand empty out. "I felt a peak of horror, as though her breasts themselves had turned to sand, as though they were of no importance at all and she did not care." Over against this defilement (a defilement which implies that the body, the breasts which turn to sand, had no meaning), there is the refuge of the dream, "the undefined austerity of my love."

"A Memory" presents the moment of the discovery of the two poles—the dream and the world, the idea and nature, innocence and experience, individuality and the anonymous, devouring life-flux, meaning and force, love and knowledge. It presents the contrast in terms of horror (as do "The Petrified Man" and "Why I Live at the P. O." when taken in the context of Miss Welty's work), and with the issue left in suspension, but other stories present it with different emphases and tonalities. For instance, when William Wallace, in "The Wide Net," goes out to dredge the river, he is acting in terms of the meaning of the loss of his wife, but he is gradually drawn into the world of the river, the saturnalian revel, and prances about with a great cat-fish hung on his belt, like a river-god laughing and leaping. But he had also dived deep down into the water: "Had he suspected down there, like some secret, the real true trouble that Hazel had fallen into, about which word in a letter could not speak . . . how (who knew?) she had been filled to the brim with that elation that they all remembered, like their own secret, the elation that comes of great hopes and changes, sometimes simply of the harvest time, that comes with a little course of its own like a tune to run in the head, and there was nothing she could do about it, they knew—and so it had turned into this? It could be nothing but the old trouble that William Wallace was finding out, reaching and turning in the gloom of such depths." This passage comes clear when we recall that Hazel, the wife who is supposed to have committed suicide by drowning, is pregnant: she had sunk herself in the devouring life-flux, has lost her individuality there, just as the men hunting for the body have lost the meaning of their mission. For the river is simply force, which does not have its own definition; in it are the lost string of beads to wind around the little negro boy's head, the cat fish for the feast, the baby alligator that looks "like the oldest and worst lizard," and the great King of the Snakes. As Doc, the wise old man who owns the net, says: "The outside world is full of endurance." And he also says: "The excursion is the same when you go looking for your sorrow as when you go looking for your joy." Man has the definition, the dream, but when he plunges into the river he runs the risk of having it washed away. But it is important to notice that in this story, there is not horror at the basic contrast, but a kind of gay acceptance of the issue: when William Wallace gets home he finds that his wife had fooled him, and spanks her, and then she lies smiling in the crook of his arm. "It was the same as any other chase in the end."

As "The Wide Net," unlike "A Memory," does more than merely present the terms of contrast, so do such stories as "Livvie" and "At the Landing." Livvie, who lives in the house of wisdom (her infirm husband's name is Solomon) and respectability (the dream, the idea, which has withered) and Time (there is the gift of the silver watch), finally crosses into the other world, the world of the black buck, the field-hand, in his Easter clothes—another god, not a river god but a field god. Just after Solomon's death, the field-hand in his gorgeous Easter clothes takes Livvie in arms, and she drops the watch which Solomon had given her, while "outside the redbirds were flying and criss-crossing, the sun was in all the bottles on the prisoned trees, and the young peach was shining in the middle of them with the bursting light of spring."

If Livvie's crossing into the world of the field god is joyous, the escape of Jennie, in "At the Landing," is rendered in a different tonality. This story assimilates into a new pattern many of the elements found in "A Memory," "The Wide Net," "Livvie," and "Clytie." As in the case of Clytie, Jennie is caught in the house of pride, tradition, history, and as in the case of Livvie, in a house of death. The horror which appears in "A Memory," in "Clytie," re-appears here. The basic symbolisms of "Livvie" and especially of "The Wide Net" are again called into play. The river, as in "The Wide Net," is the symbol of that world from which Jennie is cut off. The grandfather's dream at the very beginning sets up the symbolism which is developed in the action:

> The river has come back. That Floyd came to tell me. The sun was shining full on the face of the church, and that Floyd came around it with his wrist hung with a great long catfish. . . . That Floyd's catfish has gone loose and free. . . . All of a sudden, my dears—my dears, it took its river life back, and shining so brightly swam through the belfry of the church, and downstream.

Floyd, the untamed creature of uncertain origin, is William Wallace dancing with the great catfish at his belt, the river god. But he is also, like the buck in "Livvie," a field god, riding the red horse in a pasture full of butterflies. He is free and beautiful, and Jennie is drawn after him, for "she knew that he lived apart in delight." But she also sees him scuffling playfully with the hideous old Mag: the god does not make nice distinctions. When the flood comes over the Landing (upsetting the ordered lives, leaving slime in the houses), Floyd takes her in his boat to a hill (significantly the cemetery hill where her people are buried), violates her, feeds her wild meat and fish (field and river), and when the flood is down, leaves her. She has not been able to talk to him, and when she does say, "I wish you and I could be far away. I wish for a little house," he only stares into the fire as though he hadn't heard a word. But after he has gone she cannot live longer in the Landing; she must set out to find him. Her quest leads her into the woods (which are like an underwater depth) and to the camp of the wild river people, where the men are throwing knives at a tree. She asks for Floyd, but he is not there. The men put her in a grounded houseboat and come in to her. "A rude laugh covered her cry, and somehow both the harsh human sounds could easily have been heard as rejoicing, going out over the river in the dark night." Jennie has crossed into the other world to find violence and contamination, but there is not merely the horror as in "Clytie" and "A Memory." Jennie has acted out a necessary rôle, she has moved from the house of death, like Livvie, and there is "gain" as well as "loss." We must not forget the old woman who looked into the dark houseboat, at the very end of the story, and understands when she is told that the strange girl is "waiting for Billy Floyd." The old woman nods, "and nodded out to the flowing river, with the firelight following her face and showing its dignity."

If this general line of interpretation is correct, we find that the stories represent variations on the same basic theme, on the contrasts already enumerated. It is not that there is a standard resolution for the contrasts which is repeated from story to story; rather, the contrasts, being basic, are not susceptible to a single standard resolution, and there is an implicit irony in Miss Welty's work. But if we once realize this, we can recognize that the contrasts are understood not in mechanical but in vital terms: the contrasts provide the terms of human effort, for the dream must be carried to, submitted to, the world, innocence to experience, love to knowledge, knowledge to the fact, individuality to communion. What resolution is possible is, if I read the stories with understanding, in terms of the vital effort. The effort is a "mystery," because it is in terms of the effort, doomed to failure but essential, that the human manifests itself as human. Again and again, in different forms, we find what we find in Joel of "First Love": "Joel would never know now the true course, or the true outcome of any dream: this was all he felt. But he walked on, in the frozen path into the wilderness, on and on. He did not see how he could ever go back and still be the boot-boy at the Inn."

It is possible that, in my effort to define the basic issue and theme of Miss Welty's stories, I have made them appear too systematic, too mechanical. I do not mean to imply that her stories should be read as allegories, with a neat point-to-point equating of image and idea. It is true that a few of the stories, especially some of those in the present volume, such as "The Wide Net," do approach the limit of allegory, but even in such cases we find rather than the system of allegory a tissue of symbols which emerge from, and disappear into, a world of scene and action which, once we discount the author's special perspective, is recognizable in realistic terms. The method is similar to the method of much modern poetry, and to that of much modern fiction and drama (Proust, James, Kafka, Mann, Isak Dinesen, Katherine Anne Porter, Pirandello, Kaiser, Andreyev, O'Neill, for example); but at the same time it is a method as old as fable, myth, and parable. It is a method by which the items of fiction (scene, action, character, etc.) are presented not as document but as comment, not as a report but as a thing made, not as history but as idea. Even in the most realistic and reportorial fiction, the social picture, the psychological analysis, and the pattern of action do not rest at the level of mere report; they finally operate as expressive symbols as well.

Fiction may be said to have two poles, history and idea, and the emphasis may be shifted very far in either direction. In the present collection the emphasis has been shifted very far in the direction of idea, but at the same time there remains a sense of the vividness of the actual world: the picnic of "The Wide Net" is a real picnic as well as a "journey," Cash of "Livvie" is a real field-hand in his Easter clothes as well as a field god. In fact, it may be said that when the vividness of the actual world is best maintained, when we get the sense of one picture superimposed upon another, different and yet somehow the same, the stories are most successful. The stories which fail are stories like "The Purple Hat" and "Asphodel" in which the material seems to be manipulated in terms of an idea, in which the relation between the image and the vision has become mechanical, in which there is a strain for atmosphere, in which we do find the kind of hocus-pocus deplored by Diana Trilling.

And this brings us back to the criticism that the volume "has tremendous emotional impact, despite its obscurity," that the "fear" it engenders is "in inverse ratio to its rational content." Now it seems to me that this description does violence to my own experience of literature, that we do not get any considerable emotional impact unless we sense, at the same time, some principle of organization, some view, some meaning. This does not go to say that we have to give an abstract formulation to that principle or view or meaning before we can experience the impact of the work, but it does go to say that it is implicit in the work and is having its effect upon us in immediate aesthetic terms. Furthermore, in regard to the particular work in question, I do not feel that it is obscure. If anything, the dream-like effect in many of the stories seems to result from the author's undertaking to squeeze meaning from the item which, in ordinary realistic fiction, would be passed over with a casual glance. Hence the portentousness, the retardation, the otherworldliness. For Miss Welty is like the girl in "A Memory":

> . . . from any observation I would conclude that a secret of life had been nearly revealed to me, and from the smallest gesture of a stranger I would wrest what was to me a communication or a presentiment.

In many cases, as a matter of fact, Miss Welty has heavily editorialized her fiction. She wants us to get that smallest gesture, to participate in her vision of things as intensely meaningful. And so there is almost always a gloss to the fable.

One more word: It is quite possible that Miss Welty has pushed her method to its most extreme limit. It is also possible that the method, if pursued much farther, would lead to monotony and self-imitation and merely decorative elaboration. Certainly, the tendency to decorate elaboration is sometimes present. Perhaps we shall get a fuller drama when her vision is submitted more daringly to the fact, when the definition is plunged into the devouring river. But meanwhile *The Wide Net* gives us several stories of brilliance and intensity; and as for the future, Miss Welty is a writer of great resourcefulness, sensitivity, and intelligence, and can probably fend for herself.

Notes

1. Limitation of space has prohibited any discussion of the novelette, *The Robber Bridegroom*, but I do not feel that it breaks the basic pattern of Miss Welty's work.

JOYCE CAROL OATES
"The Art of Eudora Welty"
Shenandoah, Spring 1969, pp. 54–57

What shocks us about this art is its delicate blending of the casual and the tragic, the essential femininity of the narration and the subject, the reality, which is narrated. How can the conversational and slightly arch tone of her fiction give way to such amazing revelations? That horror may evolve out of gentility—and, even in stories dealing with the very poor or the very unenlightened, Miss Welty is always "genteel"—is something we are not prepared to accept. Our natural instinct is to insist that horror be emphasized, underlined, somehow exaggerated so that we may absorb it in a way satisfying to our sensibilities. Fiction about crime and criminals suggests always the supreme importance of crime and criminals; it is a statement of moral value. The kind of black comic-naturalism that has descended from Celine also insists, heavily, upon a moral point, about the crazy depravity of the world and the endless combinations and permutations in which it may be located . . . and this too, though it is constructed as a kind of joke or a series of jokes, may be related to a sense of proportion, a feeling that outrages certainly deserve more attention than normal events.

Eudora Welty baffles our expectations. Like Kafka, with whom she shares a number of traits, she presents the distortions of life in the context of ordinary, even chatty life; she frightens us. I have no doubt that her intentions are not to frighten anyone, or to make particular judgments on life, but the effect of her fiction is indeed frightening. It is the bizarre combination of a seemingly boundless admiration for feminine nonsense—family life, food, relatives, conversations, eccentric old people—and a sharp, penetrating eye for the seams of this world, through which a murderous light shines. Flannery O'Conner, who was certainly indebted to Miss Welty's stories, abandons entirely the apparatus of "realism"; she has no patience for, no interest in, real people. Amazing as some of Flannery O'Connor's stories are, they are ultimately powerless to move us seriously—like the beautiful plays of Yeats, they are populated with beings not quite human. Eudora Welty's people are always human.

The most impatient and unsympathetic of readers will find himself drawn in gradually, even charmed, by the Fairchild clan of *Delta Wedding*. They are indeed a "capricious and charming Southern family" (quote from paperback edition cover). That the foundation of their charm, the leisure in which to develop their charm, is something wholly ugly and unacceptable—the obvious exploitation of Negroes, inside an accidental economic structure in which the Fairchilds are, certainly, American nobility in spite of their lack of real wealth—is something one comes to accept, just the same as one comes to accept the utter worthlessness of certain characters of James and Proust, in social and human terms, but maintains an interest in their affairs. And then it is stunning to realize, as one nears the conclusion of *Delta Wedding*, that in spite of the lovingly detailed story, in spite of her seemingly insatiable generosity toward these unexceptional people, Miss Welty understands clearly their relationship with the rest of the world. So much cute nonsense about a wedding!—and then the photographer announces, making conversation, that he has also taken a picture of a girl recently hit by a train. "Ladies, she was flung off in the blackberry bushes," he says; and Aunt Tempe says what every aunt will say, "Change the subject." The dead girl may have been as pretty and flighty and exasperating as the young bride, but her human value is considerably less. She is on the outside; she is excluded from society. Her existence is of no particular concern to anyone. So, a member of this claustrophobic and settled world may well venture into hers, make love to her, leave her, and her death is a kind of natural consequence of her being excluded from the "delta wedding" and all its bustling excitement. It is more disturbing for the mother of all those children to be told, by her Negro servant, that he quite seriously wishes all the roses were out of the world—"If I had my way, wouldn't be a rose in de world. Catch your shirt and stick you and prick you and grab you. Got thorns." Ellen trembles at this remark "as at some imprudence." Protected by her social position, her family, her condition of being loved, protected by the very existence of the Negro servant who must brave the thorns for her, it is only imprudence of one kind or another that she must tremble at.

In "The Demonstrators"—the O. Henry First Prize story of 1968—the lonely consciousness of an ordinary, good man is seen in a context of greater, more violent loneliness, the terrible general failure of mankind. The demonstrators themselves, the civil rights agitators, do not appear in the story and need not appear; their intrusion into the supposedly placid racist society of this small Southern town is only symbolic. They too are not to be trusted, idealistic as they sound. Another set of demonstrators—demonstrating our human powerlessness as we disintegrate into violence—are the Negroes of the town, a choral and anonymous group with a victim at their theatrical center, one of themselves and yet a curious distance from them, in her death agony.

The story begins with the semi-colloquial "Near eleven o'clock" and concerns itself at first with the forceful, colorful personality of an aged woman, Miss Marcia Pope. Subject to seizures as she is, crotchety and wise in the stereotyped manner of such old dying ladies, she is nevertheless the only person in town "quite able to take care of herself," as the doctor thinks at the conclusion of the story; a great deal has happened between the first and last paragraphs. The doctor's mission is to save a young Negro woman, who has been stabbed by her lover with an ice pick; his attempt is hopeless, the woman is bleeding internally, too much time has been wasted. And so she dies. The doctor goes home and we learn that he himself is living a kind of death, since his wife has left him; his wife left him because their thirteen-year-old daughter, an idiot, had died . . . everything is linked to everything else, one person to another, one failure to another, earlier, equally irremediable failure. The doctor is "so increasingly tired, so sick and even bored with the bitterness, intractability that divided everybody and everything." The tragedy of life is our permanence of self, of Ego: but this is also our hope, in Miss Welty's phrase our "assault of hope," throwing us back into life.

The next morning he reads of the deaths of the Negro lovers, who managed to kill each other. The homespun newspaper article concludes, "No cause was cited for the fracas." The doctor had not failed to save the Negro woman and man because there was never the possibility of their being saved. There was never the possibility of his daughter growing up. Of the strange failure of his marriage nothing much is said, yet it too seems irreparable. But, as he looks into the garden, he distinguishes between those flowers which are "done for" and those which are still "bright as toys." And two birds pick in the devastation of leaves, apparently permanent residents of the garden, "probing and feeding."

"The Demonstrators" resist analysis. It is a small masterpiece of subtlety, of gentleness—a real gentleness of tone, a reluctance to exaggerate or even to highlight drama, as if sensing such gestures alien to life. We are left with an unforgettable sense of the permanence and the impermanence of life, and especially of the confused web of human relationships that constitute most of our lives. The mother of the dying Negro girl warns her, "*I* ain't going to raise him," speaking of the girl's baby. Of course she is going to raise him. There is no question about it. But the warning itself, spoken in that room of unfocussed horror, is horrible; the grotesque has been assimilated deftly into the ordinary, the natural.

It is an outstanding characteristic of Miss Welty's genius that she can write a story that seems to me, in a way, about "nothing"—Flaubert's ideal, a masterpiece of style—and make it mean very nearly everything.

RUTH M. VANDE KIEFT

From "The Vision of Eudora Welty"

Mississippi Quarterly, Fall 1973, pp. 530–36

The short-story cycle, *The Golden Apples*, exhibits sheer virtuosity in its use of point of view, most of all in "June Recital," which seems to me also the greatest story in that collection. Loch Morrison, a young boy supposedly confined to bed with malaria, enjoys a full view of the old abandoned MacLain house and its temporary occupants. Loch's head is stuffed with fantasies about wild men, giants, his big fig tree like "a magic tree with golden fruit . . . a tree twinkling all over."[1] On this particular day, however, he watches closely the activities of Virgie Rainey and her sailor boyfriend, chasing each other in an upstairs bedroom, eating pickles and making love on a bare mattress; Miss Eckhart, the music teacher, setting fire to the parlor where the piano is; Booney Holifield, night watchman at the gin, sleeping in another bedroom through most of the excitement. Loch looks out, "all the eyes like Argus, on guard everywhere" (p. 25), with and without his father's telescope, but his youth and ignorance of the histories and relationships of the persons involved prevent him from understanding what he sees: he takes Miss Eckhart for the sailor's mother, King MacLain for Mr. Voight, the ticking metronome for a time-bomb. Shortly before a peak moment when several of the "wanderers" in the cycle converge, Loch hangs on a tree branch upside down. He sees Old Man Moody and Mr. Fatty Bowles—the town marshal and his friend, cronies of Mr. Holifield come to wake him—and it seems in Loch's "special vision . . . that they could easily be lying on their backs in the blue sky and waving their legs pleasantly around, having nothing to do with law and order" (p. 69). They haven't, particularly; Loch's generally "upside down" view of things, his delight in freedom and lawlessness, forms a comic parallel and contrast to the "right side up" vision of his more conservative sister Cassie.

She has been dyeing scarfs in her room, preparing for a hayride, daydreaming. Her literal position prevents her from seeing what goes on in the MacLain house; yet her knowledge of and relationships to Virgie and Miss Eckhart give her the perspective through which the reader may interpret the events in the house. "Für Elise," the theme Miss Eckhart begins on the piano, sets off in Cassie's mind the chain of associations and memories unfolding the tragic history of the German-speaking music teacher so improbably placed in Morgana, Mississippi. Miss Eckhart's story is one of continual frustration, of passions and dedications apparently wasted and thwarted, the love and hope she was for Virgie, as her sole musically gifted student, rejected by the girl along with Miss Eckhart's hated metronome. At the climax of the story, when the fire is discovered and everybody in the house is routed, Virgie and Miss Eckhart come together on the sidewalk. This particular moment exactly coincides with the most hilarious sequence of comical if not farcical action leading to the convergence of Virgie with the "wall" of ladies spilling out from a Rook party, her half-naked sailor boyfriend, Old Man Moody's party, King MacLain, Loch in his nightie, and Cassie in her petticoat. It is one of the most striking juxtapositions of the comic and tragic in all of Miss Welty's fiction. Strangely, however, because of the time perspective of both narrator and characters, the moment or period of tragedy has passed. Late that night in her "moonlit bed" Cassie thinks about the "meeting" of Virgie and Miss Eckhart on the sidewalk, after Virgie had "clicked" nonchalantly through the Rook party:

> What she was certain of was the distance those two had gone, as if all along they had been making a trip. . . . It had changed them. They were deliberately terrible. They looked at each other and neither wished to speak. They did not even horrify each other. No one could touch them now, either.
>
> *Danke schoen*. . . . That much was out in the open. Gratitude—like rescue—was simply no more. It was not only past; it was outworn and cast away. Both Miss Eckhart and Virgie Rainey were human beings terribly at large, roaming on the face of the earth. And there were others of them—human beings, roaming, like lost beasts. (p. 85)

That strikes me as clear-eyed, "unblinking" vision. It recognizes both the love and cruelty of which human beings are capable, and what time may do to both—deadening them by distance. It sees the anguished search for fulfillment of human beings as part of a vast natural panorama in which lost beasts also roam. But the vision isn't left on that broad, nonhuman plane, for the thoughts which push Cassie over into the literal dreamworld are of the Wandering Aengus in the Yeats poem which has been weaving in and out of her consciousness. "She slept, but sat up in bed once and said aloud, '*Because a fire was in my head*.' Then she fell back unresisting. She did not see except in dreams that a face looked in; that it was the grave, unappeased, and radiant face, once more and always, the face that was in the poem" (p. 85). Always, in Eudora Welty's fiction, the appetite, the quest for life reasserts itself, the radiant face of that expectant wanderer.

Nor is Cassie's vision about the distance between Virgie and Miss Eckhart at the stage of their last meeting the final one in the story cycle. The time comes, in the last story (titled "The Wanderers"), when Virgie, past forty, has learned the lessons of dedication and discipline—not as Miss Eckhart had planned them for her, by developing her musical gifts, but by staying on with her old mother, setting her supple fingers and strong hands to typing and such farm chores as milking cows. Kate Rainey, her mother, has just died; Virgie has endured all the rituals of the last rites, festive and sometimes funny as well as lugubrious in smalltown Mississippi. Virgie goes through stages of feeling numbed, dissociated, cleansed and liberated after a solitary swim in the Big Black River. Returning from the cemetery she remembers another return when she had come back home after running away at seventeen, and the fields had seemed to her bathed "in a kind of glory" (p. 234), all of nature meeting in herself a rebirth of joy and hope. "Virgie never saw it differently, never doubted that all the opposites on earth were close together, love close to hate, living to dying; but of them all, hope and despair were the closest blood—unrecognizable one from the other sometimes, making moments double upon themselves, and in the doubling double again, amending but never taking back" (p. 234).

Out of her mature view of life, Virgie conceives, perhaps for the first time, a full appreciation of Miss Eckhart, long since dead. Virgie remembers a picture Miss Eckhart had on her wall of Perseus holding up the head of Medusa—the uplifted arm of the hero, vaunting; she thinks of the roles of heroes and their victims, of the sequence of time in its moments, creating separateness. And beyond that, "only the secret, unhurting because not caring in itself—beyond the beauty and the sword's stroke and the terror lay their existence in time—far out and endless, a constellation which the heart could read over many a night" (p. 243). She sees how Miss Eckhart had given her own love and hate, absorbed and transmitted through her Beethoven. "She offered, offered, offered—and when Virgie was young, in the strange wisdom of youth that is accepting of more than is given, she had accepted *the* Beethoven, as with the dragon's blood" (p. 243).

And so, belatedly, Miss Eckhart's gift has been recognized and gratefully received; a cycle has passed, and Virgie, from her now deeply distanced perspective, understands more than she can articulate, only what she can share with an old black woman who sits with her in the rain under a big tree, "listening to the magical percussion, the world beating in their ears. . . . the running of the horse and bear, the stroke of the leopard, the dragon's crusty slither, and the glimmer and trumpet of the swan" (p. 244). The world has become as it was when the wanderers on the face of the earth were beasts: so have the human wanderers slipped back into nature, actual and mythical.

The story of Virgie Rainey and Miss Eckhart is only one of many which illustrate several of the paradoxes of Miss Welty's vision—the use of concrete detail and impressionism (the latter coming together most effectively in "Moon Lake"), the convergence of tragedy and comedy, despair and "primal joy," nearness and distance of perspective. She makes free use of myth as well as the symbolism of nature, and even these are used visually. One onlooker, Cassie, sees the wanderers "to be by their own nature rising—and so alike—and crossing the sky and setting, the way the planets did. Or they were more like whole constellations, turning at their very centers maybe, like Perseus and Orion and Cassiopeia in her Chair and the Big Bear and Little Bear, maybe often upside down, but terribly recognizable. It was not just the sun and moon that traveled" (p. 51). So do all those who search, like the wandering Aengus, for the golden apples of the sun. Extraordinary events turn them "upside down" (as Loch's inverted vision also upends them) in some slow propulsion of their own deepest motives and the mysterious workings of fate (in contrast with furious and frenzied terrestrial drives). But they are always "terribly recognizable," nothing but themselves, each revelatory gesture a personal mark or talisman, as much as a Panama hat or a swivel chair where the road goes by; yet ancient as the heroes and heroines of Greek mythology. For virtuosity as well as power of vision, I believe *The Golden Apples* to be one of Miss Welty's strongest works, and am pleased to note that in a recent interview she named it as being "in a way closest to my heart of all my books."[2]

Losing Battles[3] is a joyful noise made to life itself, a celebration: an extended psalm of praise, though interspersed with laments, and sung between silences. But even the silences are filled: they are those of the briefest and brightest heralding of dawn, a longer night of a boy's inward journey and a thunderstorm, a few moments of people closed in to all but themselves or one other, the silences of the eloquent dead and the unborn, and above all, of the narrator, who everywhere binds together with her own lyric voice. She keeps it stilled as author and interpreter of thoughts and feelings, but her inward vision goes out to meet and embrace this family with delight, amusement, and a large tribute to their courage in the teeth of several losing battles.

Despite the preponderance of dialogue, scenes and action are all clearly visualized. The day opens hotly on a bright new tin roof, there is a great domestic flurry, and the family begins to arrive in a clatter of burgeoning old cars, trucks and wagons, raising clouds of red dust that never get a chance to settle until nightfall. Judge Oscar Moody's Buick must be twice rescued, the second time when it is poised toward destruction on the brink of Lover's Leap. There is horseplay with an old school-bus, a rickety and overused bridge about to collapse, endless activity to match the tales told, the family history spread out in a rambling and contrapuntal manner by various members of the clan. Endurance and zest, staying power to match that of the narrator and her characters, openness to common people, their amusements, concerns, pains, are required for this long auditory and visual feast of folk-talk and activity; and a wicked little thought may invade the mind of somebody who feels he's had enough of baby Lady May Renfro or yet another wave of barking dogs—W. C. Fields's notion that anybody who hates children and animals can't be *all* bad.

The novel, though comic in every important sense, is more than a series of hilarious sequences, providing further evidence of the paradoxical quality of its author's vision. Miss Julia Mortimer, a teacher whose history and purposes are tied in with the history of the Vaughn-Beecham-Renfro clan as well as the whole Banner community, seems to have fought a losing battle with ignorance; her rare victories, in the persons of receptive and successful students, have all scattered to other parts of the country, except for Judge Moody, who stays, at her urging but unwillingly, to work with his own people. She had chosen Gloria Short to be her successor. But Gloria betrayed her calling, in Miss Julia's eyes, by loving and marrying Jack Renfro. Gloria resists all claims and ties except those binding her to the intimate family group of her husband and child, and asks Jack wistfully during one of the few moments when she is alone with him in that crowded day of the reunion, "When will we move to ourselves?" (p. 111). That too seems a losing battle, for the family are "piled all over" (p. 163) Jack, and threaten to inundate her completely by putting together a fairly credible story of her origins which would make of her as much a Beecham as Jack. The war on dedication to aspirations and ideals alien to the community, the persistent battering down of personal doors marked "Private Keep Out," are serious matters in the novel, bordering on the tragic. And yet without compromise to any streak of cruelty or intolerance in these people, how the author sees love thriving, even the give and take of individuality! "Forgiving seems the besetting sin of this house" (p. 319), remarks Judge Moody in his melancholy voice; he might as well have called it loving.

Notes

1. *The Golden Apples* (New York: Harcourt, Brace and Company, 1949), pp. 22–23.
2. *Southern Review*, 8 (Autumn 1972), 714.
3. *Losing Battles* (New York: Random House, 1970).

CLEANTH BROOKS

"The Past Reexamined: *The Optimist's Daughter*"

Mississippi Quarterly, Fall 1973, pp. 576–87

Eudora Welty's *The Optimist's Daughter*[1] has the power and authority of a small masterpiece. Line by line, her writing has never been better. This short novel is filled with descriptive passages such as these: (of an old man's arm) "its skin soft and gathered, like a woman's sleeve" (p. 33); (of Judge McKelva's aging secretary) "She came in with her nonchalant, twenties stalk on her high heels" (p. 64); (of a gull over Lake Pontchartrain seen through a train window) "a seagull was hanging with wings fixed, like a stopped clock on a wall" (p. 45). The conversation is just as memorable: (a country woman reminiscing about how badly patients are treated in hospitals) "'He shot hisself or somebody shot him, one. He begged for water. The hospital wouldn't give him none. Honey, he died wanting water'" (p. 39); (of Mrs. Verna Longmeier who sewed for a living) "If even a crooked piece of stitching were pointed out to her, she was apt to return: 'Let him who is without sin cast the first stone'" (p. 72); (of old Mrs. Pease on the unexpected arrival of the Chisom family at Judge McKelva's funeral): "'You can't curb a Baptist,' Mrs. Pease said, 'Let them in and you can't keep 'em down, when somebody dies'" (pp. 108–9).

Yet *The Optimist's Daughter* is much more than a tapestry

of brilliantly evoked scenes from small-town life and dialogue in the Southern idiom; it is a novel with a very definite shape. As a fictional structure it shows a surprising complication of development and a rich exfoliation of themes.

Laurel McKelva Hand, a widow in her early forties, has been summoned from Chicago, where she now lives, because of the illness of her father, Judge McKelva. Laurel's mother had died some ten years earlier. Her father, now in his early seventies, had, a year and a half before, married a woman much younger than he, Wanda Fay Chisom, a shallow little vulgarian. As the story begins, we obviously do not know very much about Laurel, but we can sense her feelings as she listens to the conversation and witnesses the conduct of her father's second wife. Wanda Fay comes of the plain people; some would use a harsher phrase: common white trash. She is cheap, self-centered, aggressive, and completely unmannerly. Her tactlessness all too clearly manifests her lack of understanding and concern for other people.

Fay's conduct at the hospital before and after Judge McKelva's death is so outrageous that a reader not well acquainted with Miss Welty's work might be tempted to attribute her treatment of Wanda Fay to a contemptuous dislike for the Southern poor white, but he would be badly mistaken. Eudora Welty knows the poor white inside out—knows his faults and his lacks, but his virtues too. In her stories and novels she has treated him in all sorts of modes: with considerate understanding as in that beautiful story, "A Piece of News"; with gusto and good humor in *The Ponder Heart;* with a loving admiration for the heroic dignity of the characters whom she depicts in *Losing Battles*. Her intimate knowledge of the way in which the Southern countryman (whether sturdy yeoman or down-at-heels subsistence farmer) thinks and talks—indeed of the very cadences of his speech—bespeaks a fascination with, and a loving attention to, the rural whites of the South. She never degrades and dehumanizes them by reducing them to a stereotype: in Eudora Welty's fiction they are always individuals. Her depiction of the conduct of Fay McKelva—and Fay's conduct is perfectly awful—is not to be taken as a snobbish slap at the Southern poor white. Miss Welty has intimated this point quietly but effectively by bringing into the hospital scene the Dalzells, a sizable clan of poor whites, who have come to wait out the operation of old Mr. Dalzell. The Dalzells are primitive, unlettered, and earthy in their thought and speech, but they are not sleazily cheap; they are not on the make; they have not cut their connections with the land; they are family-minded. Mrs. Dalzell has nothing of the utter self-absorption of Fay.

When the Judge's young widow and his daughter return from the hospital in New Orleans to Mount Salus, Mississippi, with his corpse, we move into—on one level at least—social comedy. We are aware of Laurel's feelings at the funeral, which takes place in the McKelva house, but Miss Welty does not subdue the scene to the tone of Laurel's grief. She expects her reader to attend to the social types and personalities, and there is a considerable human variety among Laurel's own friends.

Major Bullock, the father of one of the bridesmaids at Laurel's wedding, is not very bright, indeed something of a numbskull. Later it becomes plain enough that the Major has been making a number of trips to the sideboard to solace his grief. Mrs. Bullock ("Miss Tennyson") is no numbskull, but she has her eccentricities. So it goes, through a series that includes the Judge's secretary, the Presbyterian minister who is to preach the funeral sermon, his wife, crotchety old Mrs. Pease, and many another friend and, not to be left out of account, the very efficient undertaker with his "Baptist face" (p. 62). To complete the range of social types, there come into the house, at the last minute, and to Laurel's shocked surprise, Fay's family—she had earlier denied having any family left at all—including her mother, brother, sister, her grandfather, old Mr. Chisom, and several children. Fay's nephew, little Wendell, wearing a cowboy suit, is not too much overawed by his first funeral; Wendell can't wait to peer into the face of the corpse lying in the open casket.

Laurel had tried to prevent her father's body being put on display, but her objections are overborne, not merely by Wanda Fay and her unmannerly clan, but, rather disconcertingly, by some of Laurel's own friends. Miss Tennyson protests: "'But honey, your father's a Mount Salus man. He is a McKelva. A public figure. You can't deprive the public, can you? Oh, he's lovely'" (p. 63).

The scene is a set piece of the sort that Miss Welty always does so well, but she has not created the scene simply because she does this sort of thing well, or to exploit regional folk ways; it has its function in the story to be told. The funeral is in the most profound sense a social occasion. A closely knit community is here gathered around the bier of one of its more prominent members, not so much to mourn him as to celebrate—and with genuine affection—his achievements. The community means to do him honor, but as the Judge's friends, talking together before the funeral begins, exchange reminiscences about him, Laurel is shocked to find how many things about her father they have got quite wrong. They have described—apparently in good faith—virtues that she knows he simply never had, and they have failed to mention what she regards as his truly admirable qualities. In spite of the presence of life-long friends and the company of her six bridesmaids, she feels that she is now really alone—driven back upon herself. She even tells herself that the community hadn't deserved her father any more than Fay had deserved him (p. 120).

If Laurel is critical of the community's lack of any deep understanding of her father, this does not mean that she is completely comfortable at dismissing the community's implied censure of her. Though that censure is implied rather than stated, and given jokingly rather than seriously, some of Laurel's friends make it plain that if she had come home after her husband's death and stayed with her father, he would not have fallen a victim to Wanda Fay. Why, old Mrs. Pease asks, did she, in the first place, have to go away to Chicago and marry a boy from the great world outside? (p. 115). Why, now that her father is dead and her inheritance leaves her well off, does she want to return to her job in Chicago? Why not stay here with her friends? (p. 112).

Yet, though Laurel cannot accept the notion that she was personally responsible for what happened to her father, the question as to why he married Fay obviously troubles her. Fay violates—in her cheapness, her lack of feeling, her hard aggressiveness—every concept of womanly behavior that the Judge reverenced. We, as readers, witnessing Fay's violent behavior—attempting to pull her dying husband out of his hospital bed, and later, hysterically embracing him as he lies in his coffin—are made thoroughly sympathetic with Laurel's bepuzzlement. How could Judge McKelva have chosen this creature for his second wife? Neither the usual explanation offered—a lonely, old man, flattered by youth and what he takes to be beauty—nor the reason given by the Judge's servant: "'He mightily enjoyed having him somebody to spoil'" (p. 59), satisfies the daughter. Not even the more charitable remark by Miss Adele, Laurel's first-grade teacher: "'She gave a lonely old man something to live for'" (p. 116), really explains his choice.

Laurel has been more than shocked and puzzled by her father's strange second marriage: all her feelings about her father and mother and what their married life was have been terribly disturbed. She will not allow herself to ask: Did my father truly love my mother. Instead she says out loud to her friends: "'He loved my mother,'" But in the context of the story, her assertion before the world protests almost too much. We gradually come to understand that Laurel is a far more troubled woman than the opening pages had revealed. The novel thus moves from fairly broad satire and social comedy into Laurel's reexamination of the past. Bereft and alone, her review of her early life becomes urgent and almost compulsive: "In her need . . . Laurel would have been willing to wish her mother and father dragged back to any torment of living. . . . She wanted them with her to share her grief . . ." (p. 150).

Laurel's dark night of the soul is literally that. Miss Welty has very skilfully cleared the stage for her retreat into the past and into herself. The pickup truck from Texas which had brought Fay's family to the funeral is returning to Texas that same evening, and Fay, on impulse, decides to ride back with her family for a short visit, planning to return on the day on which Laurel will leave for Chicago.

With Fay's departure, Laurel has the family house (which now belongs legally to Fay) to herself for the last time. As she wanders through it, she cannot help noticing the little changes in decoration, the tell-tale rearrangements of furniture and objects, that speak of the new wife and of the Judge's closing years. His desk is empty—emptied not only of his legal papers but of all the letters that her mother had written to him. But Laurel soon recalls that the destruction of the letters is not to be attributed to Fay. Her father never had kept her mother's letters; it was his habit to answer *any* letter promptly and drop it into the waste basket. There was nothing in his desk of her mother for Laurel to "retrieve." But her father's letters to her mother have been preserved: Laurel finds them in her mother's little secretary which had been shunted away into the sewing room.

Laurel makes the discovery on the last evening that she is to be in her old home. She has had dinner with friends, and Major Bullock has escorted her home on this rainy night of early spring. Closing the door on the night, she enters the house and finds that a chimney swift—Laurel had acquired an irrational horror of swifts in her childhood—has got down the chimney and is now frantically flying about in the darkened house. She is terrified by the swoops and dartings of the bird, and finally, in desperation, shuts herself away from it in the little sewing room where she had sometimes slept as a child. Here she finds her mother's secretary and the letters that her mother had preserved—presumably all the letters she had received from her husband and from her own mother. Laurel spends the night reading those letters and at last falls asleep in a chair. Next day, with the return of morning light and of the old family servant, Missouri, who had known and loved her mother and father, Laurel manages to capture the bird and release it into the sunshine.

Does the bird merely represent the vague terrors of the night that beset Laurel? Or does the sooty bird, soiling with its meaningless lunges the curtains that Missouri had washed so carefully the day before, betoken the alien presence of Wanda Fay in the house, troubling its old inhabitants, putting a smudge on everything? Or is the bird, so eager to get out of this strange labyrinth into which it has fallen, Laurel herself, trapped in the past that has suddenly become to her strange and problematical? Perhaps all of these suggestions apply, yet the author has wisely not directly hinted at any of them. Whatever we want to make of the bird episode, or even if we dismiss from it any symbolic import, we will almost certainly feel that the incident is beautifully placed and answers perfectly to Laurel's emotional situation: her sense of a disturbing element in the house on this gusty night of spring, one that creates in her mind anxieties and vague fears—for what troubles her, of course, is not the literal darkness, but the darkness of her past, which she now realizes she does not understand.

One of the most brilliant aspects of this novel is the way in which Laurel's mother, Becky, is made to rise up as a vivid presence out of her notebooks, school books, recipes, the letters her own mother had written to her from West Virginia, and the letters written to her by her husband. Becky was evidently a tremendously intense person. She was brave, as Laurel believes her father, for all his other virtues, was not. Becky was demanding—perhaps she demanded too much of her loved ones. She was hard on the Judge—in her own special way, as hard on him as Fay. Laurel remembers the last months of her mother's life, her failing eyesight, her pain in her last illness, and her reproaches to her husband. Becky actually called him a coward, presumably because he would not face the tragic possibilities of life, the tragic "irremediable things," as George Santayana has termed them. Judge McKelva, in his more "optimistic" view of the world, could not grant that anything was truly irremediable.

Laurel's commiserative understanding almost extends to Fay herself. At the funeral, Laurel, looking at Wendell as he begins to cry, thinks: "He was like a young, undriven, unfalsifying, unvindictive Fay. So Fay might have appeared, just at the beginning, to her aging father, with his slipping eyesight" (p. 76). And now on this night of self-examination and casting up of accounts, Laurel realizes that "Both times [her father] chose [a wife], he had suffered. . . . He died worn out with both wives . . ." (p. 151). Laurel realizes further that whatever rivalry there was between her mother and Fay, it was not "between the living and the dead, between the old wife and the new; [it was] between too much love and too little" (p. 152).

Laurel is not trying here to justify Fay, but to understand her father and to realize that though her father did love her mother, the relation between them had never been an easy one. How could it have been in view of their polar opposition in outlook? Her mother, for example, had always been passionately attached to her mountain home in West Virginia, and in her last illness, when she mentioned the wild strawberries that she used to gather there, her husband had cried out: "'I'll take you back to your mountains, Becky.'" To which Becky replied: "'Lucifer! Liar!" (pp. 149–50). And Laurel remembers that in her last illness her mother had irrationally reproached her too: "'You could have saved your mother's life. But you stood by and wouldn't intervene. I despair for you'" (p. 151). After her father's death, Laurel had thought: "I [do] not any longer believe that anyone [can] be saved, anyone at all. Not from others" (p. 144).

Yet in the deeper understanding achieved on this night—even in gaining some comprehension of why her father might have turned to Wanda Fay—Laurel never for a moment comes to doubt the significance and the importance of the relationship that existed between her mother and her father. If there was any element of torment in that relationship, and it is now plain to Laurel that there was, "that torment was something they had known together, through each other" (p. 150). Even when her mother "despaired" of her father and demanded of him "'Why is it necessary to punish me like this and not tell me why?'" she "still . . . held fast to [his hand and] to Laurel's too. Her cry was not complaint: it was anger at wanting to know and being denied knowledge; it was love's deep anger" (p. 148). Such a relation, if full of pain, is nevertheless profoundly human, and therefore infinitely valuable. Laurel has at last come to recognize and accept the relationship between her father and mother, and her numbed heart at last comes to life. "A flood of feeling descended on Laurel. . . . [She] wept in grief for love and for the dead. She lay there with all that was adamant in her yielding to this night, yielding at last. Now all she had found had found her. The deepest spring in her heart had uncovered itself, and it began to flow again" (p. 154). Throughout the first third of the book the reader could scarcely have guessed how badly hurt Laurel had been and how frozen had been her heart. Now, looking back from the vantage point of this crucial moment, all becomes apparent, and many of the earlier events in the novel fall into proper perspective.

This summoning back into vivid life of her parents and their long and, at the very end, difficult relationship, serves to recall Laurel's own brief and, as she remembers it, perfect love affair with her own husband. (He had been killed aboard a naval vessel in the Pacific in the Second World War.) "[Laurel] had gone on living with the old perfection undisturbed and undisturbing. Now, by her own hands, the past had been raised up, and *he* looked at her, Phil himself—here waiting, all the time, Lazarus. He looked at her out of eyes wild with the craving for his unlived life, with mouth open like a funnel's" (p. 154). The revivification of her parents' fulfilled, though somtimes tormented life, makes her realize with new poignance the fact that her own life with Phil was not, and never can be, fulfilled.

> What [she asked herself] would have been their end, then? Suppose their marriage had ended like her father and mother's? Or like her mother's father and mother's? Like—
>
> "Laurel! Laurel! Laurel!" Phil's voice cried.
>
> She wept for what happened to life. (pp. 154–55)

Yet even if Laurel's night of memories and explorations of the inner self ends with the "deepest spring in her heart [having begun] to flow again," Laurel has not yet resolved all her problems, for she is not yet quite done with Fay. Fay returns a little earlier than she had been expected, and there is a final encounter between Judge McKelva's daughter and his second wife. Earlier on that morning, before Fay had turned up, Laurel had burnt every scrap of her mother's papers—the recipes, including one for "My Best Bread," the school notebooks, the letters written to her by her husband and those written to her by her own mother, Laurel's grandmother—everything, so that the slate is now wiped clean—or almost clean. She can now turn the house over to its legal owner without regret: "There was nothing she was leaving in the whole shining and quiet house now to show for her mother's life and her mother's happiness and suffering, and nothing to show for Fay's harm; her father's turning between them, holding on to them both, then letting them go, was without any sign" (p. 170). But when, looking into a kitchen pantry, she finds the breadboard so lovingly made by Phil for her mother and always kept clean and polished by Becky for her breadmaking—when she finds that board scarred and gouged (Fay had used it to crack black walnuts on)—it is almost too much. She bursts out to Fay, '"You desecrated this house'" (p. 173).

At last she puts a question about the scene in the hospital room on the night of her father's death, the question that hitherto she had suppressed. She asks, "'What were you trying to scare Father into—when you struck him?'" Fay's answer is simple and, according to her lights, sufficient: "'I was trying to scare him into living! . . . I wanted him to get up out of there, and start him paying a little attention to *me*, for a change'" (p. 175). Then Laurel tries to tell Fay about the breadboard—why it matters—but none of her explanations can make any impression on this woman. All bread "'tastes alike, don't it?'" Fay asks. And as for Phil's labor of love in making the board for Becky, Fay asks in perfect good conscience: "'What has *he* got to do with it? He's dead, isn't he?'" (p. 177). Fay goes on to tell Laurel that the "'past isn't a thing to me. I belong to the future, didn't you know that?'" (p. 179). Fay's estimate of herself is profoundly true and this, of course, is why she is not fully human. People to whom the past means nothing cannot be fully human. In this matter Fay resembles Faulkner's Flem Snopes and Jason Compson. They all lack the pieties that bind one generation back to another, the loyalties and the imaginative sympathies which affirm that all men are of one race and, further, that the living and the dead are of one race too.[2]

After her experience of the night before, however, Laurel is at no loss to handle the situation. She is aware that the past is nothing to Fay, but what she says to Fay is: "'I know you aren't anything to the past. . . . You can't do anything to it now'" (p. 179). Nor can Laurel, as she now well knows, do anything to the past either. She does not speak this aloud to Fay, but she does say to herself: "The past is no more open to help or hurt than was Father in his coffin. The past is like him, impervious, and can never be awakened. It is memory that is the somnambulist. It will come back in its wounds from across the world, like Phil, calling us by our names and demanding its rightful tears. It will never be impervious. The memory can be hurt, time and again—but in that may lie its final mercy. As long as it's vulnerable to the living moment, it lives for us, and while it lives, and while we are able, we can give it up its due" (p. 179).

Other writers, of course, have come to this insight. Wordsworth, for example, wrote:

> Thanks to the human heart by which we live,
> Thanks to its tenderness, its joys, and fears,
> To me the meanest flower that blows can give
> Thoughts that do often lie too deep for tears.

The discovery is made over and over again, and is dramatized—through flower or breadboard—by each successive writer in his own appropriate fashion.

So Laurel can now put her mother's scarred breadboard "down on the table where it belonged," forgoing the quixotic gesture of taking it along with her. All that she leaves behind—family home, furnishings and all—is impervious to Fay and the future. What for her is precious in it is past any harm that can be done to it by anyone.

Notes

1. New York: Random House, 1972.
2. Fay's statement that she belongs to the future has a further significance. Though *The Optimist's Daughter* is not designed to be a tract for the times, it is, nevertheless, a document of our times. Fay represents a human type to which the future may indeed belong: the rootless, finally amoral, individual whose insistence on self-aggrandizement is not countered by any claim of family or clan or country. The true significance of Fay's ethos is not a reflection of a particular class or section; she might just as well have been born in the Bronx or the Bay region of San Francisco.

PEGGY W. PRENSHAW

From "Woman's World, Man's Place: The Fiction of Eudora Welty"
Eudora Welty: A Form of Thanks
eds. Louis Dollarhide and Ann J. Abadie
1979, pp. 46–56

When I was a little girl growing up in a little Mississippi town in the 1940s, my days were spent mostly in a pleasurable routine of family, school, and play, which was almost always "p'like." What my friends and I played like, of course, was being grown up, being alluring, beautiful women, brides, mothers with husbands and children to command. In our imagined households, desires were swiftly answered with simple will—dreams of love came true with a pretended lover or baby.

As I grew into adolescence, I lived the life of the imagination less and less with dolls and playmates, more with the books in the one-room library that offered a world, as Eudora Welty has said, for a sweet devouring. When I was nine or ten, I remember the librarian's urging on me a new book by a Mississippi writer. It had all the things I liked best, she said—a motherless girl who found a new family, young lovers, a wedding, and a haunted house. And so I took it along with the one other I was allowed at the twice weekly opening of the library.

Delta Wedding was not at all what I expected, or wanted. Though I don't remember the other book, I am sure I read it first and only grudgingly went on with the strange, unexciting book that lacked so much of what I favored. The bridegroom wasn't handsome, the ceremony wasn't romantic, and the haunted house wasn't scary. It was not a girl's book. Not until later, after I had married and returned to college, did I come again to read Eudora Welty's fiction. But the stories had waited for me, and, reading them with some knowledge of the heart as well as desire, I found a world I vaguely recognized. It lacked the simple romance of a girl's dreams, but it shone forth in a reflection of mystery and everydayness, love and uncertainty that I had begun to see as my world—and to think about.

Through the years I have come to comprehend my terrain more surely, to a considerable degree because Miss Welty has shown me how to open my eyes to see. But focusing now on her fictional world, I feel somewhat uncertain of the boundary between my perceiving and the stories' showing. Teacher that I am, ordinarily I duck the old ontological problem and proclaim myself the ideal reader Cleanth Brooks has tried to teach us how to be. Now, however, an admission of wariness seems in order, for I am anxious about the topography I have mapped here, about the announcement that Miss Welty's fiction reveals a woman's world. It sounds distinctly like the report of a new feminist critic, but perhaps that is what I am.

Eudora Welty reveals a world brimming with life—natural, sensual, rational, moral—and she invests in her characters, male and female, a boundless capacity for bodying forth the rich diversity. They bid for attention and praise when, wisely, like old Phoenix Jackson, they shape their lives in obedience to the ancient laws of birth and death or when, heroically, like Julia Mortimer, they pursue a private vision.

As Simone de Beauvoir has shown, we are accustomed to thinking of these two human destinies as characteristically sexual.[1] Traditionally, the woman's place is in the home. She is the mother who gives us life and with it our mortality. Transcendence of death comes from her in nature's promise of natural renewal, a sexual immortality. By contrast, man justifies his being in vaunting, death-defying acts of courage. He redeems the natural life by winning significance for the separate person and the single moment. Throughout most of Western civilization, his daring in the face of death has led to a tragic grandeur more admirable and uplifting than comedies of renewal. But such conventions are not the way of Welty's world, in which heroes are more often female than male and, regardless of sex, possess a grandeur that ultimately pales in the cycles of nature's, and the family's, renewing life. Take *Delta Wedding*, which presents a grandly matriarchal order, the ancient order of powerful mothers. Nine-year-old Laura McRaven leaves Jackson and her widowed father to attend the wedding of cousin Dabney Fairchild. The return to Shellmound Plantation in many ways represents for Laura a recovery of her mother, for the Fairchilds are her mother's clan and the plantation is the place of Laura's birth. Despite her longing to join the family circle, to be a member of the wedding, she is at times nearly overwhelmed by the thriving, heedless life of the eight cousins, and the ordered, measured control of the aunts and great-aunts. It occurs to her that "when people were at Shellmound it was as if they had never been anywhere else." In fact, Laura thinks of the plantation as the center of life:

> . . . it was as if they considered her mother all the time as belonging, in her life and in her death (for they took Laura and *let* her see the grave), as belonging here; they considered Shellmound the important part of life and death too. All they remembered and told her about was likely to be before Laura was born, and they could say so easily, "Before—or after—Annie Laurie died . . . ," to count the time of a dress being made or a fruit tree planted.

Death at Shellmound contains few horrors, so easily does it yield to the assurance of nature's repeating cycles. In the scene in which Laura in the cemetery struggles against the memory of her mother, she and the cousins run into Dr. Murdoch, the family physician. The exchange illustrates clearly the source of Fairchild power. "He tipped his hat to Shelley, and then puckering his handsome, pale lips, looked down at the Fairchild graves. 'How many more of you are there?' he said suddenly." Shelley, the oldest, answers quickly, but then, clearly caught off guard, admits she has forgot the old people and even the little Jackson cousin standing beside her. No matter, Dr. Murdoch obviously is calculating numbers loosely anyway. What engages him is the broad solid line of the family stretching from its graves into its future. "Dabney and that fellow she's marrying will have three or four at the least. That will give them room, over against the Hunters. . . . Primrose and Jim Allen naturally go here, in line with Rowena and What's-his-name that was killed, and his wife. An easy two here. George and the Reid girl probably won't have children—he doesn't strike me as a family man." The *memento mori* loses its traditional somberness not just through the doctor's teasing, good-natured brusqueness, but from the incontrovertible fact that the graveyard will hardly contain the present generations, much less the boundless Fairchild families of the future. When he begins to consider their progeny—Shelley will probably have a houseful like her mother, he says—he finally gives up his assignment of grave sites: "How many more of you are there? I've lost track."

Not only does the matriarchal order express itself in the human and natural fertility of Shellmound, but in the busy activity of the plantation. Everywhere one encounters the work and ceremonies of women in an agrarian society. Cooking and feeding occupy much of their time. Ellen draws Laura into the comfort of the family by letting her help bake a "Mashula Hines" cake. Jim Allen and Primrose are distinguished by their complementary talents—one the cake maker, the other a specialist in preserving and candy making. Typically the loving, nurturing side of the Fairchilds shows up in their gifts of food. Laden plates go out and return magically laden with different foods. As the children know well, for they are the errand-runners, one never sends back an empty plate. Even the prestige of the family is gauged by the quantity and quality of the table it sets. Ellen worries not only about Dabney's future happiness but about the wedding food: "Now I'm thinking about the chicken salad—we've made two or three tubs and got it covered in ice—and do you think frozen tomato salad turned in the freezer would be a reproach on us for the rehearsal supper?"

The cooking, sewing, gardening—the nurturing—are not trivial activities, or, if they are, the way of life is trivial, for its ways and values are formed in these rhythms of work. Beautiful handmade quilts of treasured patterns—like Delectable Mountains—go out to newlyweds to help in the making of the new home. A handmade stocking doll holds Laura's most vivid memory of her mother's love. The account of the dollmaking, in fact, embodies the significance of the Shellmound culture. One hot, humid summer afternoon, having just returned to Jackson from a visit to the plantation, Laura's mother offers to make a doll. While her father stands in the hallway winding the clock—he always likes to know what time it is—Laura and her mother go to the sewing baskets, finding the scraps and pieces that lead irresistibly to the new creation. The heightened tone of the prose suggests the drama of childbirth. Wearing a blue dress, her hair disheveled from the car ride, Laura's mother is "excited, smiling, young—as the cousins were always, but as she was not always—for the air at Shellmound was pleasure and excitement, pleasure that did not need to be explained, tears that could go a nice long time unsilenced, and the air of Jackson was different." While under the spell of the Delta, racing to finish the doll before a threatening storm breaks outside, she makes Laura a baby named Marmion, named for one of the Fairchild plantation houses near Shellmound. The great empty house is Anne Laurie's inheritance and will one day perhaps be Laura's. As her Uncle Battle says, "Someday you'll live there like your Aunt Ellen here, with all your children." The gesture of Annie Laurie's handing the doll to her daughter, an act of a loving mother, prideful of her skills, is the generational correlative of "passing the torch" in Julia Mortimer's realm in *Losing Battles*. The mother's link forms the human chain, and in *Delta Wedding* the connections lead ultimately, even mystically, back to the earth.

In a passage reflecting the consciousness of the outsider Robbie Reid, the connection between the women and the land is bluntly stated: "It was notoriously the women of the Fairchilds who since the Civil War, or—who knew?—since the Indian times, ran the household and had everything at their fingertips—not the men. The women it was who inherited the place—or their brothers, guiltily, handed it over." Robbie sees that "in the Delta the land belonged to the women—they only let the men have it, and sometimes they tried to take it back and give it to someone else." Poor landless girl in love with Memphis, Robbie is at a loss to understand either the land transactions or the Fairchild women's oblique command of power. But she recognizes it as the power Elizabeth Janeway describes in *Man's World, Woman's Place* as the dominance of the givers, whose riches and substance are needed and thus bestowed upon children and men. Robbie thinks, "It was as if the women had exacted the place, the land, for something—for something they had had to give. Then, so as to be all gracious and noble, they had let it out of their hands—with a play of the reins—to the men. . . ." ⟨. . .⟩

Delta Wedding, set in 1923, gives us a world rooted in this ancient past. Miss Welty said once in an interview that in planning the novel she made "a careful investigation to find the year in which nothing very terrible had happened in the Delta by way of floods or fires or wars which would have taken the men away."[2] Battle and George Fairchild and bridegroom Troy Flavin are, to be sure, present throughout the action of the novel, but their role—their place—is chiefly defined by their relationship to the women. Let me be clear about what I find distinctive here. The Fairchild women are neither more nor less *domineering* than the women one finds typically in a nineteenth-century plantation novel, or a Faulkner novel, or in actual experience. But their functions and rituals *dominate* the action of the novel and signify its vital impulse—the joyous celebration of the green and dying life that is the earthly province of women.

In *Delta Wedding* the cycle of ever-renewing natural life attaches to the fertile land and to the female Fairchilds. Ellen is pregnant with her ninth child; cousin Mary Denis Summers Buchanan has just given birth; daughter Bluet is the rosy-cheeked baby of the clan. The nine-year-olds—Maureen, Lady Clare, India, and especially Laura—all stand on the child's side of puberty, intrigued by the grownup world and caught up by the excitement of Dabney's wedding, a ritual that awes older sister Shelley. Like Cassie Morrison of "June Recital," Shelley desires and fears the passionate sacrifice of the self that the wedding signifies. By contrast, Dabney pursues marriage with the same relish and sense of celebration that Roxie, Vi'let and Little Uncle show in announcing young Pinchy's entry into the ranks of womanhood. The aunts, Primrose and Jim Allen, for all their maidenhood, are not so much sterile as virginal keepers of the family's stories and patterns and recipes—the revered ways of the past, which like the land are passed on to succeeding generations of Fairchilds. Childless, they are nevertheless mothers like Great-Aunts Mac and Shannon, who reared the seven Fairchild nieces and nephews. They serve to teach the human bond, particularly the obligation of the men to nurture the women and children. In her book *Male and Female*, Margaret Mead discusses human fatherhood as a "social invention," noting that the basic biological unit is mother and child while the basic unit of human society is the family, which rests upon the learned nurturing behavior of men. Such behavior, she writes, is tenuous and fragile and can disappear rather easily under social conditions that do not teach it effectively.[3] That Battle and George are well taught offers testimony of the success of their aunts' and sisters' mothering.

To a degree sister Tempe stands outside the steady, timeless life of the plantation. Like Annie Laurie she married and moved to the town, and she regards Shellmound as shamefully permissive and old fashioned. She resembles Lizzie Stark in *The Golden Apples* or Becky McKelva in *The Optimist's Daughter*, who resist an easy asquiescence to life's disorderly ways. But drawn into the circle of Shellmound life, Tempe can no more hold out against it than she can resist red-haired Mr. Buchanan's claim of her daughter—or red-haired Troy Flavin's claim of Dabney. Resigned, she too acquiesces to Fairchild life. At the wedding rehearsal, young Ranny weaves through the group shouting, "I'm the wedding!" Herald of the renewing life of the clan, green peach limb in hand, he at last runs to Aunt Tempe, shouting still as he twirls her about, and "in that moment Tempe, laughing, experienced not a thought exactly but a truer thing, a suspicion, that what she loved was not gone with Denis [the dead brother], but was, perhaps, perennial. . . . Indeed the Fairchilds took you in circles, whirring delightedly about, she thought, stirring up confusions, hopefully working themselves up."

Notes

1. *The Second Sex*, trans. H. M. Parshley (1953; rpt. New York: Vintage-Random House, 1974), pp. 71–74.
2. Linda Kuehle, "The Art of Fiction XLVII: Eudora Welty," *Paris Review*, 55 (Fall 1972), 85.
3. *Male and Female* (1949; rpt. New York: Mentor, 1962), pp. 146–48.

PATRICK AND TERESA NIELSEN HAYDEN

From *A Study Guide for* One Writer's Beginnings

1986, pp. 2–5

I. Listening

In "Listening," the first section of *One Writer's Beginnings*, ⟨. . .⟩ Welty says, "Ever since I was first read to, then started reading myself, there has never been a line read that I didn't *hear*. As my eyes followed the sentence, a voice was saying it silently to me . . . It is to me the voice of the story or poem itself. The cadence, whatever it is that asks you to believe, the feeling that resides in the printed word, reaches me through the reader-voice. I have supposed, but never found out, that this is the case with all readers—to read as listeners—and with all writers, to write as listeners."

That more complex possibilities existed within the narrative voice was revealed to her through the offices of a sociable neighbor lady, and by Fannie, a black sewing woman who sometimes came to their home to make clothing; both were great talkers. On Sundays the neighbor would accompany the Weltys for an afternoon drive, and Eudora, sitting next to her, listened in fascination to her endless gossipy monologues. "What I loved about her stories," she recalls, "was that everything happened in *scenes*. I might not catch on what the root of the trouble was in all that happened, but my ear told me it was dramatic. Often she said, 'The crisis had come!'"

Listening to Fannie's racy gossip on sewing days produced the same effect; while Welty might not catch the gist of it, she recognized that there was a story being told all the same: "Long before I wrote stories, I listened for stories. Listening *for* them is something more acute than listening *to* them. I suppose it's an early form of participation in what goes on. Listening children know stories are *there*." And eventually, she learned to listen for something else besides. In her own family it was taken for granted that no one lied, and Welty was well into adolescence before she realized that in other families this wasn't the case. It finally dawned on her that "children lied to their parents and parents lied to their children and to each other . . . these very same everyday lies, and the strategems and jokes and tricks and dares that went with them, were in fact the basis of the *scenes* I so well loved to hear about and hoped for and treasured in the conversation of adults." The right track for a storyteller, she found, is knowing that a scene is full of hints, things to find out and know about people. She says, "I had to grow up and learn to listen for the unspoken as well as the spoken—and to know the truth, I also had to recognize a lie."

Eudora Welty is not a deliberately difficult writer; what she has to say, she says very clearly. However, it should be noted that at no time does she underline what is already on the page, flagging the reader with announcements that 'I am now going to talk about such-and-such topic', nor does she provide tidy summaries of the points she makes as she goes along. To briefly give an example of this technique, the passage starting on page 13, wherein she describes herself as a child listening for the presence of stories in the conversations of the adults around her, does not introduce anything that could be identified as a formal topic sentence until the third paragraph from its end, on page 16. Instead she begins by sketching the sociable habits of the ladies of Jackson, only gradually showing the reader her intended direction. ⟨. . .⟩ she lets her material speak for itself, all the while never losing control of its direction and linkage, and introduces substantially all of the themes she thereafter develops. ⟨. . .⟩

III. "Finding a Voice": From Particularity to Confluence

The opening scene is a journey with her father by train; the contrast given is between her father's experience of such a trip as well-clocked routine, and her own experience of it as ever-surprising, always fundamentally mysterious. "The dream was what lay beyond, where the path wandered off through the pasture, the red clay road climbed and went over a hill or made a turn and was hidden in trees, or toward a river whose bridge I could see but whose name I'd never know." But it was as she grew older that she came to understand that, rather than being the acted-upon subject of the journey, instead it was "*I* who was passing" over those rails; with that realization, her "self-centered childhood was over." "*Memory* had become attached to seeing"; the imagination had to learn to act upon and live with the outer world.

She went off to college; she acquiesced to dorm life in the small women's school she first attended, wrote humor pieces in the style of *Judge* magazine for the college newspaper, and after two years went farther away, to the University of Wisconsin at Madison. There she had an epiphany of the immediacy of poetry, reading Yeats in the stacks of the library—all standard events in the development of a sensitive young intellect, but more. She learned the meaning of artistic intensity, the possibilities of creative passion.

Her mother supported her desire to write; her father was mistrustful of fiction in that it said things which were not "true"; his life had never had any use for such things. But he remained positive toward his daughter; if it was good enough for her, it was good enough for him. In 1931, though, he suddenly died; her mother's attempt to save his life via blood transfusion, as he had saved hers years previously, came to nothing; he was struck down in middle age by a disease he'd never heard of mere months before, a peculiar indignity for such an exacting man. Her mother never quite forgave herself this failure. Eudora returned to Jackson, unable to find work in the fabled advertising agencies of New York, and took small jobs for the local newspapers and for the radio station housed in the modern office building that had been her father's crowning achievement as president of the Lamar Life. A couple of years later she took the famous job with the WPA which was to lead to her well-known hundreds of photographs of Mississippi life; within a few years, she was selling stories regularly and becoming a nationally-known literary figure. Here the "personal" begins to fade out of the narrative; instead signposts of her public life alternate with observations drawn from her deep interior. Between those extremes we can only assume a middle life of personal friends, living arrangements, small accomplishments of the day, week, month, year. But it doesn't matter. What she tells us about instead is more important: about the images she finds herself compelled by, and how they grow into stories like crystals forming in a glass of water. About how "the author writes at his own emergency"—a typically subtle wordplay, both the literal *emergency* and the implied *emergence-y*—"and needs to remain at his private remove." (So much for comprehensive autobiography. We forgive her, nonetheless.) She quotes from her own early stories, from "A Memory" and "Death of a Traveling Salesman," winding her way around points with all the time in the world, and the effect is never prideful or ostentatious, but illuminating. She reiterates and concretizes points about her parents from earlier in the book, points about her father's conscientiousness regarding time and the importance of sequence in narrative, about her mother's associative patterns of thought and her own version, in writing, of the same. She returns to the train journey, steadily pulling further and further away from Jackson, and meditates on the large continuities of motion through space and time; on the roads not taken, on her recent (as of the writing) discovery that her parents very nearly chose the Thousand Islands area of the St. Lawrence River valley as a place to raise a family before choosing Jackson instead. A small difference, a small particularity, and from it a vast difference; from this she smoothly slides into discussing the importance of particularity, of telling detail and individualization of character in the building of fiction. The small details may not seem to matter in the overall pattern, but they do; they are its very stuff, they must be authentic, possessed, known. Finally, spiralling down through this multiplicity of points, she settles softly in the last pages of the book on a single concept summing up the journey in which each of us "is moving, changing, with the respect to others. As we discover, we remember; remembering, we discover; and most intensely do we discover this when our separate journeys converge." That concept—a single word—is *confluence*, "the only kind of symbol that for me as a writer has any weight . . . Of course the greatest confluence of all is that which makes up the human memory." Her memory is a "treasure", as a person and as a writer; a "living thing—it too is in transit. But during its moment all that is remembered joins, and lives—the old and the young, the past and the present, the living and the dead." And here at this Mississippi Delta of the mind, where all the rivers flow together at last, she ends her book.

Glenway Wescott

1901–1987

Glenway Wescott was born in Kewashkum, Wisconsin, on April 11, 1901. In 1914 he left home to live with relatives because of difficulties with his father. Wescott entered the University of Chicago in 1917, but he left a year and a half later without taking a degree. His first book, *The Bitterns: A Book of Twelve Poems*, appeared in 1920, and in 1923 he began writing reviews for the *Dial* and the *New Republic* and became involved with a number of little magazines. Wescott's first novel, *The Apple of the Eye*, set in the American western frontier, appeared in 1924. In the following year he moved to Paris; for the next eight years, except for brief visits, he remained in Europe, where he continued to write books about life in the American Midwest, including *The Grandmothers* (1927), a novel published in England as *A Family Portrait*; *Goodbye, Wisconsin* (1928), a collection of short stories; and *The Babe's Bed* (1930), a novel. *Fear and Trembling* (1932) is a nonfiction work, based on personal experience, on the political and social problems of central Europe, and *A Calendar of Saints for Unbelievers* (1932) is a retelling of some of the saints' lives from an agnostic point of view.

Wescott returned to the United States in 1933 and settled permanently on the East Coast, first in New York City, then on his brother's estate in New Jersey. His next two novels were set in Europe; they are *The Pilgrim Hawk* (1940), which takes place in a Paris suburb, and *Apartment in Athens* (1945), about a Nazi officer living with a Greek family. *Images of Truth* (1962) is a collection of literary reminiscences. Wescott died on February 2, 1987, in Rosemont, New Jersey.

C. E. SCHORER
"The Maturing of Glenway Wescott"
College English, March 1957, pp. 320–26

From a résumé of local materials in the writings of Glenway Wescott one may glean more than a catalogue of regional data having merely parochial interest. One discovers that the changing emphasis on Wisconsin bears a close correlation with the artistic development. By taking a wider view still, one sees that his work is a revelation in several of the senses outlined by him in *Fear and Trembling* (1932), where he gives the five functions of an author: to preach, teach, and govern, to reflect the age, to reflect himself, to emphasize the tendencies of the coming times, and to pander to popular taste. In addition to himself, he reveals the course of the expatriate group of which he was a member and which included our recent Nobel prize winner, Ernest Hemingway. Because of the peculiar relationship of his life and writings to events in the social sphere, he foreshadows the future of our nation in the world.

In a few words, Wescott's work reflects his maturation insofar as he moved from the land of his birth and boyhood to a different world of his own. In his first published fiction, *The Apple of the Eye* (1924; begun, according to one account, when he was seventeen), the scenes and characters are exclusively of eastern Wisconsin, near Fond du Lac, where he was brought up. The peculiarities of this region, moreover, play essential and emphatic parts. In fact, the heart of the story resides in the liaison between the characters and the "fecund but useless" marsh—a typical feature of the kettle moraine country of Wescott's birth—as opposed to the laborious farm life and bleak society of the hamlets and towns. Furthermore, the local economics, morals, and manners become the essential conditions in which the characters move; the time corresponds mainly to that of Wescott's boyhood; and one of the chief characters, a farm youth, goes through a family conflict and separation from home which must have been similar in many ways to that which Wescott himself experienced.

This first novel suggests by its title that to break the commandments may after all be a permissible part of the good life. Fornication, prostitution, the rejection of parents' demands and of the local code of righteousness seem to receive the author's approval; certainly much disapproval is registered for the confining, spiritless, and often cruel local mores. This recurring idea shares with characterization (rather than with plot) the task of unifying a book which consists otherwise of three essentially separate parts. The characters are connected, perhaps not as completely as they might be, with a single aspect of the land, that is, the marsh, against which as a unifying standard they can be measured. The marsh, its "wide fecundity unused and unbeloved" is Han's companion, to Rosalia "it was like her life at the end," and to Dan it was first an enormous grave, and later a peaceful place which had given him all it had to give.

In Wescott's second "novel," *The Grandmothers* (1927), he widened the focus a bit to portray life outside of Wisconsin. He gave a little attention to the ancestral background in the East; he followed a few characters to other situations in the Middle West, in the Far West, and even in Europe; and he further enlarged the perspective of his book by introducing contrasts between Europe and Wisconsin, chiefly through the viewpoint of a central character who, like Wescott, had gone abroad to live. This character serves to investigate and spiritually animate the past, even though such activity defies local morality, and to emerge with the prediction that the younger generation can be expected to "betray their West to the East . . . to betray their native land as a whole for love of some characteristically native land of their imagination"; the growth of intellectual independence takes on the forbidden tinge of sexual deviation.

Really a series of more or less separate family portraits without plot, *The Grandmothers* yields on analysis two possible schemes of organization by ending (a) with the death of the grandmothers (the chief repositories of family lore) and (b) with the ripening of an impression made on the narrator by the various characters he portrays. These are more numerous but less intense and individual than the characters in *The Apple of the Eye*, and the monotony of characterization appears to be part of a plan wherein the reader is told omnisciently how the various figures of the narrator's family—grandparents, aunts, uncles, parents, and the like—responded as they found grievances in their lives. It is this impression upon the narrator which cumulatively produces his final opinion that his heritage is a grievance, and that Wisconsin is yet a promised land because it had not kept its promise.

The Grandmothers is concerned with human striving and disappointment prevailing in "Hope's Corners"—a specifically eastern Wisconsin town. The next book, *Good-bye Wisconsin* (1928) brings in more of the outside world by making the contrast of Wisconsin and Europe a dominant concern. The introductory essay, in fact, is organized by the impressions made upon the expatriate as he re-enters at Milwaukee, travels to his home, surveys the way of life, and moves out again to southern France in an admittedly autobiographical manner. Kewaskum, Wescott's birthplace, is named from the Indian word for "his tracks are homeward," and the title therefore not only reflects the wider view of books like *A Farewell to Arms*, but also plays ironically on a local term. A conflict, arising as the protagonists readjust to Wisconsin after living in France, forms the crux of two of the stories, and enriches the characterization by giving a new, timely, and widely appealing issue in terms of which the characters become known to the reader.

Discontent plays a large part both as a product of local dreams, for example, the slaying by a teacher of her lover, or a bridegroom's memory of his first adulterous affair as he awaits his bride—or as a result of the comparison with other cultures, as a returned sailor recalling his infatuation with a French prostitute who became enamored of another prostitute. Here the sexual deviation is presented not as an unqualified, necessary part of joy but appears to have double values, causing sorrow and suffering even though leading to growth and wisdom. The Middle West is defined as "a state of mind of people born where they do not like to live," and the rejection of home includes the specific leavetaking from Wisconsin by the author.

Although the ten stories are independent, they have a few interrelating elements, such as the display of characters successively ranging from innocent to sophisticated, the common Wisconsin background, and the pattern of passive characters finding disappointment in Wisconsin circumstances and then coming to a decision or a new realization of themselves in the world. Thus the numerous characters actually cover a narrow range after accidents of occupation and situation are eliminated; or, as Wescott writes, the "strangely limited moral order. Drunkenness; old or young initiations into love; homesickness in one's father's home for one's own, wherever it may be, or the more usual sort with its attendant disappointment; the fear of God; more drunkenness." Unfortunately the stresses and strains through which the personages must live seldom seem soul-shaking; an adolescent at a birthday party is troubled by sexual inferiority, or farm misfits run away to work for a carnival. As a result the characters are not so memorable as those in Wescott's first novel.

Wescott had not yet said goodbye to Wisconsin in fiction, however, for in *The Babe's Bed*, a little book appearing in 1930, the scenes and characters are again of the state, with once more the unhappy return and leavetaking of a prodigal. This book and the three preceding books have a common train of events—the culmination of sinful deeds in the removal of a central character by death or emigation. Here the childhood love of brother and sister is awakened, and the sister offers her baby to be the brother's. The incestuous relationship, leading to conflict between man and wife and between father and son, appears to point out the truism that immorality, while part of growth, must be outgrown. Just so parental guidance, which inflicts the discontent of frustrated adults upon a "weeping, ungratified" infant for its own good must be rejected, and one's homeland must be abandoned with the realization that some frustration is inescapable. The author widens the significance of Wisconsin to a symbol of youth's everlasting problem—to grow away from its discontented ancestors into its own world.

Of equal importance with this maturing viewpoint is a new strategy of characterization that might be called the characterizing symbol, by which Wescott chiefly shows his progress as an artist. He employs a living creature, the baby in its bed, which functions to symbolize certain human traits, to illuminate the characters by their reaction to it, and obviously to unify the story in another sphere in addition to plot. The device had been used, woodenly and occasionally in *The Apple of the Eye*, where characters were revealed by their relation to the marsh; and in "The Whistling Swan" of *Good-bye Wisconsin*, in an exotic and ephemeral manner, by relating the protagonist to the bird. Here the device is used as a crucial center of interest throughout the novella.

Thereafter, Wisconsin and even America appeared only incidentally and almost by way of footnote in Wescott's books. *Fear and Trembling* (1932) takes the reader on a polemical trip into militarizing Germany, with the observation that Europe is Christendom, the civilizing center of the world, and America a part of Europe—"the hope of the world, and the despair of us all." Wisconsin enters in the marginal comment that it "is as German as it ever was—and more permanently, the change having been brought about in peace." The following year, *A Calendar of Saints for Unbelievers* contained no references whatsoever to Wisconsin and merely a few passing comments on contemporary world affairs amid the trenchant biographical notes: "this Italian bishop had a vision of the end of the world, much like that of the present European and American prospect: all battles, invasions, breakage and burning." The only glimpse we get into Wescott's own life is the remark that when St. Maurelius returned to his native lands, the ruler, "his brother, regarded it as none of an expatriate's business, and put him to death."

Certain ideas which one associates with earlier, Wisconsin-bound books by Wescott appear in this pair of nonfictional works. In *A Calendar of Saints* Wescott appears to endorse immorality obliquely by casting doubt on the virtue of self-sacrificing saints who would endure death rather than marry a profligate or who would throw purses to street walkers to spare them their shame. It is obviously a wicked book presented in disarming simplicity. In *Fear and Trembling*, the theme is the abandonment of nationalism, which should give way to common endeavor before the great threat of another war. Unlike the thematic change to relative dignity, Wescott's language becomes less effective. The imagist manner of earlier books deteriorates into cryptic exposition often lacking clarity in the smaller structural components.

With *The Pilgrim Hawk* (1940) Wescott's writing enters a new, international phase. The scene becomes a town in France, where two expatriate Americans, a Cockney, two Irish, and two French characters dramatically interact. "That was in May of 1928 or 1929, before we all returned to America [Wescott returned in 1934]. . . . In the twenties it was not unusual to meet foreigners in some country as foreign to them as to you, your peregrination just crossing theirs." The narrator is the same Alwyn Tower as in *The Grandmothers*, and we are told that he "had been a poor boy, on a Wisconsin farm, and in a slum in Chicago and in Germany in 1922." This reverses the relative importance, quantitatively and qualitatively, of Wisconsin and Europe obtaining in *The Grandmothers*.

At this stage of his career Wescott had so learned restraint that the mere suggestion of infidelity rather than its gross appearance sufficed, and such violence as occurs—the feeding of a hawk, a drunken husband's threat to kill the hawk, or himself—has the limitations of civilized married life. The assuagement of marital insecurity and jealousy by the warmth of love among English, Irish, French, and American characters, rather than the resolution of problems facing a prostitute, an unwed mother, or a boy who finds the decomposing body of his cousin, betrayed by his best friend, shows the trend of Wescott's thinking. He seems very nearly to have reached the aim professed in *Good-bye Wisconsin*, to write on "only the inavertible troubles, all in the spirit."

What makes *The Pilgrim Hawk* a favorite example of good modern writing is its tight and economical organization: for one day, in one house, from the single point of view of the narrator, seven characters carry forward the revelation of marital tension to crisis and resolution. This unity is enhanced by the characterizing symbol which, by its appearance in the avocations of *The Sun Also Rises*, *Across the River and into the Trees*, and *The Old Man and the Sea*, marks Wescott's affinity to Hemingway, and receives its most masterful treatment in *The Pilgrim Hawk*, where it serves in a more complex and extensive manner than elsewhere in his fiction. Here all seven individuals are symbolized in some degree by the hawk which is the focal point of the novel, and all are characterized mainly by their behavior in relation to the hawk. The characterization is almost altogether dramatic: this is closet drama in which words and gestures rather than reflection requiring an omniscient author tell us about the talents and tastes of the personages. And since these reactions are all given to the reader from the point of view of a narrator, characterization here performs the function of unification both through the symbolizing hawk and the narrator. Moreover the grouping of the figures—three couples, Irish, American, and French, plus real or suggested third parties—unifies the book in still another way while giving depth through an echo-like recurrence of a single theme among different strata of society and different national pairs.

To this formal integrity *The Pilgrim Hawk* does not add the earlier difficulty of obscure phraseology, for the reading problem which it presents is of an intellectually tantalizing, not to say satisfying kind, and is due to the dramatic form and the characterizing symbol. One's difficulty lies in deciding how much of the hawk's apparent significance applies to the humans clustered animatedly about it. The difficulty with meaning here, that is, is not in simple grammatical matters but in the deeper and overall significance.

In *Apartment in Athens* (1945), Wescott's latest book, Wisconsin is not mentioned at all, just as the world outside Wisconsin does not appear in his first novel. The characters are all European and the scene is Greece during the last world war. Here, then, Wescott has reached the extreme in his travel from West to East. At least as regards literal fictional material, his last work totally abandons the region from which he sprang. It completes a trend of his writing with all the regularity of a linear mathematical equation. Here, too, the respect accorded family and country are quite different from that shown in earlier works. The plot is a thorough fulfillment of the promise that character may be proved under duress, that the stress of invasion may turn marital life into rich understanding and produce both a true family spirit and a proper realization of national humanist ideas. As the father of the family becomes more actively devoted to the tradition of heroic Greek individualism, the man and wife are drawn more closely together, and the children grow more steady and secure. The plot of this novel is the most conventional one Wescott has constructed. At the same time the point of view tends to shift, unfortunately, from one character to another, and the time span now is six months. Still, the unity of place and idea, and the climatic arrangement are again notable, and are achieved at greater length than in any previous book.

Although nationalism is supposed to mean something to the characters of *Apartment in Athens*, it is hard to see any importance in the nationality beyond an occasional rather haphazard reference to Greek history and ideals, to Athenian society and architecture. It is hard, also, to see what the characterizing symbol might be in this book; the nearest one can guess is the boarder himself, for certainly the reaction to the Nazi is an important test of character. No narrator appears, however to unify the impressions, and the author puts more reliance on his explicit statement of the events in his characters' minds than on dynamic interaction. A balance of characters, at least, is preserved in the structure of the Helianos family: man and wife, son and daughter. This characterization, then, is less thorough, less craftsmanlike, and more conventional than Wescott's career would lead us to expect. It has given up the solidity and individuality of characters in his early work—virtues resulting from his establishing a connection between the characters and the Wisconsin land or the Wisconsin life-situation—without a proportionate gain of wide and stirring appeal. Likewise the language lacks any troublesome obscurity and conforms to conventional novels of this century without gaining great force thereby.

In summing up the relation between Wescott's localism and his artistic growth one notes first that his proliferation in prose concerning Wisconsin certainly exceeded in a merely quantitative way the productions in which Wisconsin played no part. In the six years from 1924 to 1930, four books about his home state appeared. In the quarter-century since, four books (two non-fictional) also have appeared. One need not be so simple-minded as to assume that the geographical focus was the sole cause of productivity. Other factors—waning talents, changed health, difficulties of publicaton—may well have played their parts. One can simply conclude that Wescott's fictional pen was most prolific while he was dealing with Wisconsin.

The recurrence of certain ideas, modified in succeeding publications, shows them to be the counterpart of the local detail in his fiction. A dominant idea is sexual deviation and its associated theme of a child in the tense relation to its home. At first Wescott dealt with the more gross aberrations and violent attitudes; later he turned to civilized and traditional problem-solving. And whereas Wescott's ideas seem to have lost shocking power as he grew older, his books have generally showed increasingly adept organization. The first three books are rather collections than novels (and so are the two non-fictional works, the structure of which can not be easily correlated with the structure of the novels and stories); on the other hand, the last two books are related masterfully to a single plot.

Wescott's characterization has varied with the novelty of his ideas, the localization of his scenes, and the economy of overall organization. In a way this is to say that the characters are appropriate; yet fitness is only one standard by which to judge an author's skill. Most readers will prefer such bold and original figures as Han and Mike, with their local connections, to the Greek merchant Helianos, with his dimly realized family and city relations.

The obscurity of Wescott's early and middle-phase books, and especially *Fear and Trembling*, becomes at worst annoying; in *The Pilgrim Hawk* it stimulates the mind. The style of *Apartment in Athens* neither annoys nor stimulates. It is as adequate as tea. In short his use of language has progressed from relative obscurity, imagistic and impressionistic, to a relative clarity, dramatic and dialectic. This strikes one as a fulfillment of his early prediction that "for another book I should like to learn to write in a style . . . without slang, with precise equivalents instead of idioms, a style of rapid grace for the eye rather than sonority for the ear, in accordance with the ebb and flow of sensation rather than with intellectual habits, and out of which myself, with my origins and my prejudices and my Wisconsin, will seem to have disappeared."

Skepticism, at least of one kind, Wescott may have learned by living through a cycle of critical reception. He has experienced the beginning of recognition, the climb to a position of promising to become the "top American novelist," the award of the Harper Prize, with which he attained the summit of his reputation, having produced in *The Grandmothers* what Clifton Fadiman called "the first artistically satisfying rendition of the soul of an American pioneering community and its descendants"; the decline, thereafter, into the non-fictional works of the thirties, generally condemned for superficiality; and the grudgingly granted esteem of an entirely different kind with his two recent novels to gain, by the last volume, the acclaim of "the finest book whose roots were in the second world war."

This pattern of achievement, decline, and recovery of critical favor can be related easily but too facilely to the use of Wisconsin in Wescott's writing; clearly he was most highly esteemed when he wrote of Wisconsin. With this simplified view, however, must be combined (for the sake of a more complicated and yet more sound orientation) the awareness that concomitantly with Wescott's changing productions occurred shifts of national and world affairs and altered emphases in American literary taste. One need only suggest points of harmony and dissonance between his progress and the world of affairs: the pre-depression years, isolationism, Roosevelt, Freud, Henry James, the second world war. To say that in the end he adapted himself to the times is another way of saying that he reveals the times.

The development of Glenway Wescott clearly produced mixed merits: a gain of technical virtuousity, a loss of reality. In some ways like other American expatriates—and one thinks, often, of James, Garland, Hemingway—his late work shows improved economy and centralization, drama and clarity, with a loss of local connections, memorable ideas, and vigorous characters. His last phase showed the clarification and cumulative enrichment of his artistry. Of the three expatriates just mentioned, however, he most resembles Garland, for his early work remains the most noteworthy and the best remembered. Like Garland in 1914, too, his Wisconsin having given him all it could, he moved on with less success of realization to treat of other regions.

This pattern reminds one distinctly of the dilemma facing the expatriates in the 1930's, as portrayed by Malcolm Cowley:

> they could go . . . back to Wisconsin, but only to say goodbye. They had been uprooted from something more than a birthplace, a county or a town. Their real exile was from society itself, from any society with purposes they could share, toward which they could honestly contribute and from which they could draw new strength.

It reminds one, too of the new role America is playing: having outlived the days of self-reflective provincialism, with whatever minor notes of self-criticism, it now finds itself having to consider how to apply local American methods and viewpoints to the situation of a major industry in Europe or a farmer in Asia. With the abandonment of isolated bucolic American life for international guidance, haphazard individualism gives way to more systematically planned enterprise directed toward socially constructive goals. The change may involve some loss of the glamorous American freedom and prosperity. It may well be reflected in a literature of similarly modified characteristics. Wescott's literary career, a very model of such changes, has consciously or unconsciously wrought out this moral for a student of our life. If he in 1934 seemed a prototype of Cowley's socially alienated exile, he now stands as a suggestive indicator of our future.

SY KAHN
From "Glenway Wescott's Variations on the Waste Land Image"
The Twenties: Fiction, Poetry, Drama
ed. Warren French
1975, pp 173–79

We look to the work of Eliot, Fitzgerald and Hemingway as among the major literary achievements of the ⟨1920s⟩—for compelling image in Eliot and for rich variations in the novelists. I wish now to turn to a writer who, like Fitzgerald and Hemingway, was an expatriate Midwesterner writing in France, and who provided an additional and special amplification of the wasteland image. Glenway Wescott during the 1920s enjoyed a reputation that rivalled Fitzgerald's and Hemingway's, and he seemed then a writer of equal promise. Born in Wisconsin in 1901, now living in New Jersey, Wescott mainly lived and wrote in France during the 1920s, not returning to live again in the United States until 1933. During the 1920s he produced two novels, *The Apple of the Eye* (1924) and *The Grandmothers* (Harper's Prize novel for 1927), an essay and ten short stories under the title *Goodbye Wisconsin* (1928) and a privately printed small edition of a short work *The Babe's Bed* (1930). All of these works, though not to the same degree, explore the past in an attempt to understand, define and exorcise it. Among Wescott's complex motives was his desire to account for the cultural wasteland he felt Wisconsin, and by implication the Midwest and the United States in general, to be. Troubled, even haunted by the past, Wescott sought self-definition through an imaginative rendering of family history in his major work of the 1920s, *The Grandmothers*. He also wanted to understand the sadness and sullenness of failed pioneers, their narrow Protestantism, their repressed lives, their suspicion of, even hostility toward a child of esthetic and creative impulse. To Alwyn Tower, his protagonist of the novel, as well as of *The Babe's Bed*, the return to the past is necessary to gain knowledge and to go forward. In the last chapter of *The Grandmothers*, Wescott wrote:

> So some of these feverish, reactionary ones (he himself, for example) went back, in imagination, to what had produced them; their hope, anxiety, and interest went back. Against the law. The weak stayed; the strong returned once more to the place from which they had gone back, from which they would have to go forward. Backward and forward, two continual motions of the imagination making up that of their lives. Forward finally . . .

In Wescott's work of the 1920s fictive narrator and author are never far removed from each other—persona is almost person, fiction almost biography, or discovered biography. One has the impression that the past is not simply recalled for its record of things past but imaginatively evoked for the purpose of exploration and definition, that the work itself is the definition. The setting for all of Wescott's work of this period is Wisconsin, but that is simply the stage, not the substance, of these works. Indeed, the region is richly evoked in a highly distinctive lyrical and imagistic prose, and through the strategies of this style, Wisconsin becomes the microcosm by which the American experience and *mythos*, as Wescott understood them, is rendered.

In the essay, "Good-bye Wisconsin," which gives the book its title, Wescott speaks to us, as it were, in his own voice and makes explicit those loves, concerns and rejections fictionalized and symbolized in the stories and novels he wrote in the 1920s. For Wescott, Wisconsin is the place you cannot go back to after such knowledge and experience Europe offers. The Wisconsin towns, bleak in winter, but with a new material prosperity that might have dazzled the pioneers of a previous century, suggest to Wescott that materialism has displaced imagination, that dowry has replaced dream. The rural landscapes still invite the imagination, stimulate it to speculate upon the older ideas of exploration, virgin territory, human restlessness and courage that propelled people toward the west, toward the beckoning rather than the rising sun. But now, in the 1920s, Wisconsin seems to him an enervated cultural wasteland, a barren ground for artists, and its human native crop "seedless." Surely many of Wisconsin's characteristics that urge Wescott's departures during the 1920s are the same ones that prompted other artists to abandon the Middle West: its melancholy atmosphere, its materialism, its moral taboos and drab religion, and its depressing towns. Now even more alienated from home because of his expatriate life, Wescott concludes that life in 1927 has outdistanced to a greater degree than in his youth the "poetry" of pioneer times.

The essay opens with Wescott on a train going home, north from Milwaukee, with a blizzard coming south. In contrast to the bleak landscape he recalls that "stiff carnations of the Mediterranean are in bloom." He is his own symbol of exotic change and the estranged with his Basque beret, his gloves, cigarette lighter and foreign cigarettes, and with Thomas Mann's *Hochstapler Krull* in his hands. If he has changed, so has Wisconsin. The house in town where his family lives is not like the old "fruitful and severe" farmhouse of his youth that "seemed to have an immortal soul . . ." Now there are a bathroom and waxed floors; carpets like everyone else's have replaced the rag rugs of his grandmothers. "Progress," he thinks. "Deprivation is dead . . . I rejoice, but regret some of his poetry." The town too is without "poetry." There can be no idylls, no pastorals in the "lamentably impressive" town. The essay strikes the notes here of dirge and lament for a way of life regrettably and permanently lost. The old "rustics" had become "provincials." Urbanization has unsettled the youth, keeping them uneasy and discontent, but at the same time they are not strong enough to break away. Movies, "imagination's chapel in the town," keep them stimulated and nervous—but the final effect is narcotic. Impulse and imagination are indulged in vicariously.

Since the morality of the town recognizes no sexual liberty, there is either early marriage or bad reputation. The former means "Wisconsin forever, with never any wholesome dissipation of a thousand chimeras—travels, ambitions, curiosities." For some there is fever. Erotic songs, "syncopated bewilderment on the dance floor" and "the disastrous and vacillating ease in Miss Garbo's face" create vibrant, anxious nights. Nevertheless, the young people are disturbingly herdlike. Group-consciousness rather than self-awareness motivates their actions; there is a lack of courage and candor. He concludes that the chief work of the fraternity he visits is "to beat out of each other all conceit and incivility."

In 1927 Wescott found Wisconsin more comfortable but less conforting than was the former rustic life. What was ardent feeling and compelling dream is now nervous indecision; what was a kind of pagan pleasure, because of, or in spite of, hardship is now sterile luxury. With a book of Gide's in his hand this time, he takes his leave and returns to Europe. For him the road back, as for Alwyn Tower, is the road ahead.

However, the land outside the towns, outside the train windows, has not changed. Its natural beauty endures, yet unspoiled by the towns, and the old enchantment of the land, evoked in the lyrical manner of the earlier novels, takes hold of him again as he rides away through the cold, Wisconsin night. The land still enchants, and glimpses of people working their farms, or remembered glimpses in other seasons, stimulate Wescott to render them in classic, statuesque images of dignity and endurance. It is the land, stretching out and gigantic, that makes for the seemingly heroic stance and gesture of its workers, in contrast to the urbanized lives that seem to him cramped, dessicated, and repressed, and whose horizons, physical as well as emotional, are short and limited.

Both Wescott and Hemingway have used the land as a purgative against the glutted human scene, as a corrective for urbanized Wisconsin, or, as in *The Sun Also Rises*, for the dissipations of the Left Bank in Paris. Certainly the differences between the work of the two men, not to mention the men themselves, are profound and numerous, but there is parallel purpose here. In the fishing interlude that takes Jake Barnes and his friend Bill Gorton to the Burguete, the honest simplicity of action and pleasure gives their activities a ritual purity, much as the actions and emotions of Wescott's remembered "rustics." The unsullied land in both works inspires purified action. Indeed, Hemingway has remarked that the true hero of his novel is the land, as the title of his novel taken from Ecclesiastes suggests. It is interesting to note that Hemingway ridiculed Wescott in *The Sun Also Rises*, a *roman à clef*, by casting Wescott as Robert Prentiss, an unlikeable rising young novelist Jake meets in Paris. (In an early draft of the novel Wescott was less masked as Robert Prescott.) Nevertheless, in works of great dissimilarity in style and technique, both Wescott and Hemingway make the land prevail as counterbalance to scenes of human emotional wastelands. At this point, one may recall Hemingway's earlier stories of his boyhood in Michigan which celebrate the land. Michigan and Wisconsin, parallel states with similar landscapes, are recalled by both writers for a similar purpose—and in Hemingway's novel, Michigan is translated to Burguete as well. Not so in Fitzgerald's *The Great Gatsby*. ⟨. . .⟩ the land itself is wasteland, as if feverish human corruption has incinerated it.

The ten stories in *Good-bye Wisconsin* that follow the essay were written during 1921 to 1927 and in one sense are a record of various disillusionments. Wescott has remarkable capacity for variations on this theme. He expresses the disappointments of expatriation, maturity, labor, faith, art and love. In consequence, there are sorrow, tears, drunkenness, terror and murder, in a crescendo of reactions. In commenting on his work, Mary Butts, a writer and critic of the 1920s, said of *Good-bye Wisconsin* that it was "The book of a man fallen out of love, and in his embarrassment likely to overscore his subject than show the least ingratitude or brutality." She concludes, "So much for the adieus of a young man supremely sensitive to 'sacra' and 'rite,' whose childhood was passed without them, among a people with taboo for ritual, prosperity for imagination."

Wescott's disillusionment with the Middle West reflected his feeling of a general cultural failure in America. To him there were so few memorable Americans—Lincoln, Lindbergh, the "gloriously bizarre" Isadora Duncan—so few genuinely artistic acccomplishments. He missed the "wholeheartedness" and the "desire for immortality" that he felt marked and animated ancient Greek culture. In the essay he compares the "dead-leaf complexion" of American youths to the "marble-headed Greeks." Americans seemed intense only about wealth. Its youth are corrupted; their potential comes to nothing. Sex replaces or defeats intellectual activity and creativity, and a nation only physically creative Wescott thought was beneath contempt.

Catching the sense of malaise, the failed tradition, the empty social rituals, the creative and spiritual aridity above all, of Eliot's poem, Wescott, as Fitzgerald and Hemingway, responded in ways suitable to his experience and talent. In the 1920s it was the Midwest that Wescott best understood, and making the region a metaphor for America in general, he, along with many other American writers of the period, found it culturally wanting. The pervasive and persuasive image of the wasteland that Eliot objectified in his adroit poem, that caught so well the mood of an age, was amplified by Wescott, a writer who, as Marjorie Brace has noted ("Thematic Problems of the American Novelist," *Accent*, Autumn, 1945), marks in his entire work "a progressive exploration of every American theme in a kind of aesthetic pilgrimage. . . ."

As Eliot's poems and Hemingway's novels of the period make clear, the sense of cultural and moral wasteland was not peculiar to America and Americans; Europe and Europeans are equally indicted. Eliot was writing of a condition and an age, not a location or a particular people. Like Shelley's "traveller" in the poem "Ozymandias," the speaker in *The Waste Land* has a tale of deserts to tell. Shelley's traveller "from an antique land" tells us of his seeing "two vast and trunkless legs of stone," and nearby a half sunk, shattered visage. From these remnants, and an inscription on the pedestal, the traveller can surmise that these are the relics of a once powerful and prideful dynasty and culture. Nothing remains except "colossal wreck," and "boundless and bare / The lone and level sands stretch far away." Shelley's poem mocked pride and power, and the stretching sands make the ironic comment that a civilization may be reduced to a wasteland. Eliot turns the image. In his poem we are located in the wasteland, figurative rather than literal, and travellers stumbling upon relics would only know them as "withered stumps of time," since those travellers would have no historical, cultural or religious contexts by which to understand either the artifact or its symbolic meaning. Those stretching sands, whether they mock or magnify a cultural condition, touched many shores. Certainly there is nothing new in depicting spiritual "dryness," in making images of failed hope and the loss of tradition and its vital roots. That story is old and repetitive; but Eliot gave it a fresh imprint in the 1920s, and under his seal each writer unrolled his own scroll.

Wescott's testimony during the decade, unique by virtue of his special style and sensibility, made an important, sometimes brilliant, contribution to the literature of disillusionment. That disillusionment was redeemed, if by nothing else, by the variations that gave it complex shape and meaning.

NATHANAEL WEST

1903–1940

Nathanael West was born Nathan Wallenstein Weinstein on October 17, 1903, in New York City, to Max and Anna Wallenstein Weinstein. He was educated at Brown University (Ph.B. 1924). In 1940 he married Eileen McKenney, the sister of Ruth McKenney, author of *My Sister Eileen*. From 1930 to his death he made his living primarily as a writer; in addition, he managed a hotel in the early 1930s, assisted William Carlos Williams in editing *Contact* in 1932, and wrote for various Hollywood studios, including Columbia, RKO, and Universal.

West wrote four novels: *The Dream Life of Balso Snell* (1931), *Miss Lonelyhearts* (1933), *A Cool Million: The Dismantling of Lemuel Pitkin* (1934), and *The Day of the Locust* (1939). His fiction received little attention during his lifetime. Since his death, however, his cinematic, fragmentary style and bleak yet sardonically comic view of life as an incessant string of dashed hopes and broken promises have earned him recognition as a leading chronicler of the Depression and a forerunner to the post–World War II black humorists. *Miss Lonelyhearts* and *The Day of the Locust* in particular have been praised in retrospect for their vivid, almost surreal depiction of psychic deterioration and decay. West also wrote a play with Joseph Shrank (*Good Hunting: A Satire*, produced in 1938). West and his wife died in an automobile accident on December 22, 1940.

West's four novels were republished together under the somewhat misleading title of *Collected Works* in 1957. Miscellaneous stories, articles, and poems were included as an appendix to William White's bibliography of West, published in 1975.

General

If Nathanael West appears to us from our present vantage point the chief neglected talent of the age, this is largely because he was immune to the self-deceit which afflicted his contemporaries; he knew what he was doing. Despite his own left-wing political sympathies and the pressures of friends more committed than he, he refused to subscribe to the program for proletarian fiction laid down by the official theoreticians and critics of the Communist movement. And he turned unashamedly to the business of rendering the naked anguish he felt, rather than projecting the commitment to action and faith it was assumed he should feel. Even more importantly he rejected the concept of realism-naturalism, refused to play the game (variously connived at by Dos Passos and Steinbeck and Farrell) of pretending to create documents rather than poetry. He returned, despite the immediate example of three decades of falsely "scientific" writing, which sought to replace imagination with sociology, the symbol with the case report, to the instinctive realization of the classic American fictionists that literary truth is not synonymous with fact. West's novels are a deliberate assault on the common man's notion of reality; for violence is not only his subject matter, but also his technique.

His apprenticeship was served in Europe, in the world of the Left Bank, where from the Surrealists he learned (his finger-exercises are to be found in his first book, *The Dream Life of Balso Snell*) a kind of humor expressed almost entirely in terms of the grotesque, that is to say, on a perilous border-line between jest and horror. Yet his Surrealist-inspired techniques—the violent conjunctions; the discords at the sensitive places where squeamishness demands harmony; the atrocious belly-laughs that shade off into hysteria—are not very different, after all, from the devices of *Pudd'nhead Wilson* or *Gordon Pym*. Surrealism is only a late European development of the same gothic themes, the same commitment to atrocity, the same dedication to mocking the bourgeoisie which helped form the work of Poe; and, indeed, it is through Poe that the tradition descends to the Surrealists themselves. West is, in a sense, then, only reclaiming our own; yet, in another, he is introducing into the main line of American fiction a kind of sophistication, a view of the nature of art, of which our literature was badly in need.

It is possible for an American, of course, to find in his native sources, his native scene and his American self cues for the special kind of horror-comedy which characterizes West's novels. The uneducated Twain once did precisely that, and the half-educated Faulkner has pretended at least to follow his example. Yet in Twain everywhere, and in Faulkner more and more as the years go by, there is evident a presumptuous, home-made quality, which mars their work whenever they pass from the realm of myth to that of ideas. Nothing is more bald and thin than the back-porch atheism of Twain's *The Mysterious Stranger*, except perhaps the red-neck Protestantism of Faulkner's *A Fable*. For a contemporary reader, both Faulkner and Twain seem to betray the anguish and absurdity of the culturally insecure whenever they are tempted from narrative to discourse. Both are driven compulsively toward religious themes, but dissolve them into easy rationalism or sentimental piety.

The religious dimension to which they aspire, West attains in part because he is aware of a European tradition in thought and art, out of which Kafka, so like him in certain ways, had earlier emerged. It is not accidental that both these anguish-ridden comedians, as uncompromisingly secular as they are profoundly religious, should be Jews; for Jews seem not only peculiarly apt at projecting images of numinous power for the unchurched, but are skillful, too, at creating myths of urban alienation and terror. The '30's, not only in America (where Daniel Fuchs and Henry Roth—the latter in a single astonishing book, *Call It Sleep*—are outstanding figures) but everywhere, is a period especially favorable for the Jewish writer bent on universalizing his own experience into a symbol of life in the Western world. More and more it has seemed to such writers that what they in their exile and urbanization have long been, Western man in general is becoming. This is, presumably, the claim implicit in West's name (he was originally called Nathan Wallenstein Weinstein), his boast that he is an American Everyman; though surely to none does the epigram of C. M. Doughty apply more tellingly than to West, who quotes it in *Balso Snell:* "The Semites are like to a man sitting in a cloaca to the eyes, and whose brows touch heaven."

Yet West is a peculiarly American case, too. In one of his few published critical notes he declares: "In America violence is idiomatic, in America violence is daily." And it is possible to see him as just another of our professional tough guys, one of the "boys in the backroom" (the phrase is applied by Edmund Wilson, in a little study of our fiction, to West along with John O'Hara). This is not to deny, though West himself tried to, that West is, in some meaningful sense, a Jew. He is enough the child of a long tradition of nonviolence to be racked by guilt in the face of violence, shocked and tormented every day in a world where violence is, of course, daily and most men are not at all disturbed. In *Miss Lonelyhearts*, he creates the portrait of a character, all nerves and no skin, the fool of pity, whom the quite ordinary horror of ordinary life lacerates to the point of madness. His protagonist is given the job of answering "letters to the lovelorn" on a daily newspaper; and he finds in this job, a joke to others (he must pretend in his column to be a woman, for only women presumably suffer and sympathize), a revelation of human misery too acute for him to hear. It is the final modern turn of the gothic screw: the realization that not the supernatural, the extraordinary, but the ordinary, the everyday are the terrors that constrict the heart.

> Dear Miss Lonelyhearts—
>
> . . . I would like to have boy friends like other girls and go out on Saturday nites, but no boy will take me because I was born without a nose—although I am a good dancer and have a nice shape and my father buys me pretty clothes.
>
> I sit and look at myself all day and cry. I have a big hole in the middle of my face that scares people even myself so I can't blame the boys for not wanting to take me out . . .
>
> What did I do to deserve such a terrible bad fate? I asked Papa and he says he doesnt know, but that maybe I did something in the other world before I was born or that maybe I was being punished for his sins. I dont believe that because he is a very nice man. Ought I commit suicide?
>
> Sincerely yours,
> Desperate

Miss Lonelyhearts is, finally, the comic butt who takes upon himself the sins of the world: the *schlemiel* as Everyman, the skeptical and unbelieved-in Christ of a faithless age. But such a role of absurd Christ is West's analogue for the function of the writer, whom he considers obliged unremittingly to regard a suffering he is too sensitive to abide; and in no writer is there so absolute a sense of the misery of being human, though he also believes that such misery is a more proper occasion for laughter than tears. He is child enough of his time to envision an apocalypse; but his apocalypse is a defeat for everyone. The protagonist of *Miss Lonelyhearts* is shot reaching out in love toward a man he has unwillingly offended; while the hero-*schlemiel* of the more deliberately farcical *A Cool Million: or The Dismantling of Lemuel Pitkin* (in theme and style a parody of Horatio Alger) staggers from one ridiculous, anti-heroic disaster to another, becoming after his death the idol of an American fascist movement. But the true horror-climax of his life and the book comes when, utterly maimed, he stands on the stage between two corny comedians, who wallop him with rolled-up newspapers in time to their jokes, until his wig comes off (he has been at one point scalped), his glass eye pops out, and his wooden leg falls away; after which, they provide him with new artificial aids and begin again.

It is not until *The Day of the Locust*, however, which is West's last book, and the only novel on Hollywood not somehow trivialized by its subject, that one gets the final version of the Apocalypse according to Nathanael West. At the end of the book, a painter, caught in a rioting mob of fans at a Hollywood première, dreams, as he is being crushed by the rioters, the phantasmagoric masterpiece he has never finished painting, "The Burning of Los Angeles." West does not seem finally a really achieved writer; certainly, no one of his books is thoroughly satisfactory, though there are astonishing local successes in all of them. His greatness lies like a promise just beyond his last novel, and is frustrated by his early death; but he is the inventor of a peculiar kind of book, in which the most fruitful strain of American fiction is joined to the European tradition of avant-garde, anti-bourgeois art, native symbolism to imported *symbolisme*. The Westian or neo-gothic novel has opened up possibilities, unavailable to both the naturalistic semi-documentary and the over-refined novel of sensibility, possibilities of capturing the quality of experience in a mass society—rather than retreating to the meaningless retailing of fact or the pointless elaboration of private responses to irrelevant sensations. Putting down a book by West, a reader is not sure whether he has been presented with a nightmare endowed with the conviction of actuality or with actuality distorted into the semblance of a nightmare; but in either case, he has the sense that he has been presented with a view of a world in which, incredibly, he lives!

In West, there emerges, side by side with an intent to move American literature back into the mainstream of European modernism, a willingness to reinterpret the formulae of gothicism in the light of Freudian psychology. The first gothic novelists had written at a time when the sole name for the unconscious was "hell"; and only their intuition had served them as a guide in their infernal descent. By the twentieth century, however, psychoanalysis had begun to work out a science of the irrational, a lexicon of the dream symbols, which the earlier tale of terror had exploited without a real sense of their ultimate meanings. The Freudian world-view suggested, in addition, new grounds upon which to base the artist's attack on the moral codes and taboos of the bourgeoisie; and along with Marxism, it helped define the contemporary intellectual's view of himself as an enemy of society. Such a view was generally associated in the '30's, however, with an espousal of realistic modes in fiction; and it is the special contribution of Nathanael West to have demonstrated the superiority of gothicism for projecting a denial of middle-class values and the analysis of the secret soul of the bourgeoisie.—LESLIE A. FIEDLER, "The Power of Blackness: Faustian Man and the Cult of Violence," *Love and Death in the American Novel*, 1960, pp. 461–66

It begins to be a cliché in the critical discussion of West's work to speak of his "narrowness," and, indeed, there is no gainsaying the highly specialized character of his vision. But to remark this fact is not, as a certain kind of humorless don supposes, to have pushed him down a peg. For the literary imagination—except in the great, rare, monumental instances of a Dante and a Shakespeare and a Tolstoi—is normally governed by what Dr. Johnson spoke of as its "ruling passion." And those writers whose work becomes in some irresistible way a part of the permanent furniture of one's mind are never artists—as Camus reminds us at a certain point in *Le Mythe de Sisyphe*—whose work consists only of "a series of isolated testimonies." They are, on the contrary, writers *all* of whose work is distinguished by a markedly consistent kind of singular resonance and by a certain slant of vision that takes us in one direction rather than in a dozen possible others. So the moot question for literary judgment is not so much the narrowness of the artist's perspective as the degree of cogency with which he manages to organize and interpret the particular range of issues embraced by his field of view. And we will not be inclined to cavil at his basic standpoint, however much idiosyncrasy may be involved in a given case, if his work presents us with a statement which has (in a phrase of Lionel Trilling's) "the authority, the cogency, the completeness, the brilliance, the *hardness* of systematic thought." For, when this is what we meet, we can take pleasure, as Mr. Trilling reminds us (in his essay on "The Meaning of a Literary Idea" in *The Liberal Imagination*), in the power and grace of the mind with which we are dealing, without needing to make any "final judgment on the correctness or adaptability of what it says." And it is precisely this sort of satisfaction that belongs most especially to the order of *aesthetic* pleasure.

So perhaps our most appropriate response to those who insist upon the narrowness of vision represented by West's fiction will be to say that, yes, but, for all of that narrowness, it is a marvelously *cogent* body of writing. The imaginative space of his fiction is, to be sure, extremely limited—by its fixation on the anguish which is a consequence of our forgetfulness and phantasizing, and by its pervasive desolateness and pessimism. And we find it difficult to credit the assurance that he gave his publisher Bennett Cerf after the appearance of *The Day of the Locust*, that his future books would be "simple and full of the milk of human kindness," for it was of the essence of his particular genius to say "beware" and (as I have elsewhere remarked of other modern writers) "to use violence and melodrama as instruments for awakening his age out of its lethargies, for destroying its specious securities and revealing its underlying nightmare and tragedy." Yet it was not in spite of but, indeed, just by virtue of his very immoderateness and extremism that he was able to throw some light on the chaos of our time. For he knew, with a fierce kind of clarity, that, amidst the "other-directed" world of the *Masse-Mensch*, things (as Saul Bellow said a few years ago) have "gotten all mixed up somewhere between laughter and insanity," in so far as the modern multitudes have been persuaded by the *Kitsch* industries of what Faye Greener believes, that "any dream [is] . . . better than no dream, and beggars [can't] . . . be choosers." And nowhere in the literature of our period is there to be found a more stringent or illuminating account of the disintegration that consequently threatens than that which West presents. Indeed, he did so master a particular malaise of the modern spirit that W. H. Auden, "in honor of the man who devoted his life to studying it," facetiously names it "West's Disease."

His Cautionary Tales, as Mr. Auden calls them, do not, of course, offer the pleasures of the kind of realistic illusion in which "the plain reader" finds what he takes to be the norm of prose fiction, and we cannot somnambulate our way through *Balso Snell* or *Miss Lonelyhearts* in the way we do through the fictions of the great mesmerizers, of writers like Trollope and Hardy and Galsworthy and Snow. His characters, as Mr. Auden says, "need real food, drink and money, and live in recognizable places like New York or Hollywood, but, taken as feigned history, they are absurd." For they belong to a fabric of metafiction whose "anti-literariness" was a consequence of West's belief that, when you are dealing with what he called (in *The Day of the Locust*) "the truly monstrous," you cannot permit your readers to relax: you must keep them awake and take such a tack as was chosen by one of the most gifted American writers in the line of West's succession, the late Flannery O'Connor, who said: ". . . to the hard of hearing you shout, and for the almost blind you draw large and startling figures"—in order that they shall not fail to discern in the narrative design "objective correlatives" of their own distress. And, following such a stratagem, in the two superlative triumphs of his career—*Miss Lonelyhearts* and *The Day of the Locust*—West, through the remarkably taut coherences of these books, achieved a kind of beautiful transparency that makes them, quite simply, masterpieces of twentieth-century fiction which require that we judge him in the terms we use for judging the Kafka of *Amerika*, the Borges of the *ficciones*, the Djuna Barnes of *Nightwood*, the Nabokov of *Lolita*, and the Ellison of *Invisible Man*.—NATHAN A. SCOTT, JR., *Nathanael West: A Critical Essay*, 1971, pp. 41–43

Works

Whatever other issues *Balso Snell* may raise, 〈. . .〉 its dominant theme is literature itself. Literary considerations pervade its every aspect. Balso enters the Trojan Horse, itself a literary creation, because, "A poet, he remembered Homer's ancient song," and later we are told, "The wooden horse, Balso realized as he walked on, was inhabited solely by writers in search of an audience." Almost every character and even some of the characters' characters are writers, and they explore the act of composition from a number of points of view. The numerous allusions, borrowings, literary burlesques, and references to a wide range of writers and artists further establish its literary and artistic frame of reference. Clearly, West intends *Balso Snell* to be a searching extended commentary on literary art.

It is true that West seems to satirize, debase, and undercut the value of literature. He succeeds in representing an extraordinary number of literary genres in this short work: poetry, drama, the short story, the diary, biography, letters, a saint's life, and literary criticism; and he subjects each to satire and ridicule. He reduces even literature to scatological and sexual terms, suggesting repeatedly that all literary creation is sexually motivated. And finally, he seems to assert that literature and art are hypocritical, that is, idealized falsifications of reality.

However, in view of West's technique of inversion, it behooves us to look more closely at precisely what he criticizes and rejects. When we do so, we find that *Balso Snell* is not a dismissal of literature, but rather a scathing critique of its misuses, abuses, and perversions. First and foremost, West rejects all attempts to use literature as a defense against, or escape from, life. He demonstrates within the work the manner in which an excessive dependence on literature can depersonalize the individual. Virtually all the characters have assumed literary roles. As a result, when they think, express themselves, or act, they can do so only in terms of the conventions and categories they have learned from literature. West depicts them as literary beings who have no existence beyond their literary responses; they lack emotions, personal feelings and individual identities. He has Saniette's lover admit this explicitly: ". . . a series of literary associations . . . remove me still further from genuine feeling. The very act of recognizing Death, Love, Beauty—all the major subjects—has become, from literature and exercise, impossible."

John Raskolnikov complains briefly about this situation: "I am an honest man and feel badly about masks, cardboard noses, diaries, memoirs, letters from a Sabine farm, the theatre," but Beagle Darwin reveals the actual motive behind the characters' retreat into literature: "You once said to me that I talk like a man in a book. I not only talk, but think and feel like one. I have spent my life in books; literature has deeply dyed my brain its own color. This literary coloring is a protective one—like the brown of the rabbit or the checks of the quail—making it impossible for me to tell where literature ends and I begin." The characters in *Balso*, including Balso himself, have retreated into literature in order not to become involved, to escape their own feelings, to avoid being hurt. Beagle Darwin composes the two letters to Janey as a means to keep her away from him. Saniette, Janey Davenport, and Miss McGeeney turn to art or literature to escape life: in listening to her lover's pessimistic tirade, Saniette fastens on his literary phrasing, and in this way evades his meaning; when they first meet, Miss McGeeney rejects Balso's kiss to "discuss something"; and the girl cripples gather in Carnegie Hall "because Art is their only solace"—they cannot accept the grotesqueness of life. West will not permit literature to deny reality, or even to romanticize and idealize it; he demands that literature depict things as they are in all their fullness and complexity.

West has also constructed *Balso Snell* so as to expose misuses of literary conventions. A writer can also retreat into established techniques in order to avoid having to create his own modes of communication. To too great an extent, perhaps, *Balso* illustrates what it criticizes: for example, West carries certain conventions such as the use of multiple refractors and shifting centers of perception and the dream within a dream or literary work within a work, to such extremes that they become absurd. Yet West makes the point that too much borrowing, the use of relatively untransmuted conventions (as in the seduction speech), and excessive dependence on mechanical formal devices can render any fiction artificial, stiff, and impersonal. In view of his extensive burlesque of *Ulysses*, it is difficult not to conclude that West felt such artificiality in Joyce's great work. West saw that any imitation of Joyce, or of a narrative technique such as Conrad's in *Lord Jim*, would run the risk of having the reader respond as much to Joyce or Conrad as to West. By implication, West demands that each writer create his own distinctive, individual fictional style and techniques.

Finally, West also analyzes the relationship between the performer and his audience, or between the artist and society, to explain abuses of art and literature. In *Balso Snell*, there is no audience that understands or appreciates the artist. This is one of the primary causes of the perversions of art that West depicts. Saniette's lover describes the process by which this comes about. His "relations with Saniette were," he tells us, "exactly those of performer and audience." Furthermore, "Saniette represents a distinct type of audience," the one that we would expect to be most sensitive. But instead, "Saniette accepted my most desperate feats in somewhat the manner one watches the marvelous stunts of acrobats. Her casualness excited me so that I became more and more desperate in my performances." He makes them, "by straining my imagination, spectacular": "Because of women like Saniette, I acquired the habit of extravagant thought. I now convert everything into fantastic entertainment and the extraordinary has become an obsession. . . ." He grows to hate this audience: he speaks of the "natural antipathy felt by the performer for his audience," and at the end he wishes to cover it with "tons of loose excrement."

The indifference of this audience drives the artist to perversions and excesses. We may well wonder whether the picture of the artist in *Balso Snell* is West's or the picture society accepts. John Gilson is a case in point. Although Balso himself is a poet, he is also completely lacking in understanding and appreciation when he acts as the audience. After reading the rich, complex story of John Raskolnikov Gilson, the most fully executed artistic achievement in *Balso*, he concludes: "Interesting psychologically, but is it art?" His failure to recognize its artistry is representative of society's failure to identify and support true art. It is this Balso who sees John as a twelve-year-old boy in short pants, and Balso's description may well be West's portrait of the artist as society sees him: as an immature, disabled being who is cut off from the "real" business of life and who therefore could not possibly say anything worth-while, and whose motives are always hidden but probably suspect, degraded, and gross anyway. In commenting on his two years in Paris, West describes clearly the concept of the artist he is trying to exorcise in *Balso Snell:*

> "In order to be an artist one has to live like one." We know now that this is nonsense, but in Paris in '25 and '26 we didn't know it. "Artists are crazy" is another statement from the same credo. Of course all these ideas were foisted on us by the non-artists, but we didn't realize it then. We came to the business of being an artist with the definitions of the non-artists and took libels for the truth. In order to be recognized as artists, we were everything our enemies said we were.

The artists in *Balso* are also the creations of their society, and this society is in part responsible for the weaknesses of the art they produce.

Finally, however, the most effective answer to the charge that *Balso Snell* is a dismissal of literature is the short fiction itself. In spite of its deeply critical orientation, as a whole it possesses a vitality and strength that are ultimately positive. It is certainly the work of an active, creative imagination; and even taking into account its weaknesses, it is a skillfully constructed and well-made work of fiction. Perhaps the decisive consideration is that it depends exclusively on literary techniques to make its criticisms of literature. If West had truly rejected the value of literature, he would have written no more books. But when asked what he had done when he finished *Balso Snell*, he replied with considerable surprise that he had begun another book.—THOMAS M. LORCH, "The Inverted Structure of *Balso Snell*," *SSF*, Fall 1966, pp. 37–40

I can't do a review of *Miss Lonelyhearts*, but here, at random, are some of the things I thought when writing it:

As subtitle: "A novel in the form of a comic strip." The chapters to be squares in which many things happen through one action. The speeches contained in the conventional balloons. I abandoned this idea, but retained some of the comic strip technique: Each chapter instead of going forward in time, also goes backward, forward, up and down in space like a picture. Violent images are used to illustrate commonplace events. Violent acts are left almost bald.

Lyric novels can be written according to Poe's definition of a lyric poem. The short novel is a distinct form especially fitted for use in this country. France, Spain, Italy have a literature as well as the Scandinavian countries. For a hasty people we are too patient with the Bucks, Dreisers and Lewises. Thank God we are not all Scandinavians.

Forget the epic, the master work. In America fortunes do not accumulate, the soil does not grow, families have no history. Leave slow growth to the book reviewers, you only have time to explode. Remember William Carlos Williams' description of the pioneer women who shot their children against the wilderness like cannonballs. Do the same with your novels.

Psychology has nothing to do with reality nor should it be used as motivation. The novelist is no longer a psychologist. Psychology can become something much more important. The great body of case histories can be used in the way the ancient writers used their myths. Freud is your Bullfinch; you can not learn from him.

With this last idea in mind, Miss Lonelyhearts became the portrait of a priest of our time who has a religious experience. His case is classical and is built on all the cases in James' *Varieties of Religious Experience* and Starbuck's *Psychology of Religion*. The psychology is theirs not mine. The imagery is mine. Chapt. I—maladjustment. Chapt. III—the need for taking symbols literally is described through a dream in which a symbol is actually fleshed. Chapt. IV—deadness and disorder; see Lives of Bunyan and Tolstoy. Chapt. VI—self-torture by conscious sinning; see life of any saint. And so on.

I was serious therefore I could not be obscene.

I was honest therefore I could not be sordid.

A novelist can afford to be everything but dull. —NATHANAEL WEST, "Some Notes on Miss L.," *Contempo*, May 15, 1933, pp. 1–2

⟨*A Cool Million*⟩ has been criticised, and probably underrated, because it adopts a parody of a mock-melodramatic woman's magazine style. This paragraph, from near the beginning, is sufficiently representative of both the advantages and the disadvantages of the method:

> Our hero's way home led through a path that ran along the Rat River. As he passed a wooded stretch he cut a stout stick with a thick gnarled top. He was twirling this, as a bandmaster does his baton, when he was startled by a young girl's shriek. Turning his head, he saw a terrified figure pursued by a fierce dog. A moment's glance showed him that it was Betty Prail, a girl with whom he was in love in a boyish way.

As a *tour de force*, *A Cool Million* comes off. No one had ever dared to try such a thing before. It remains exquisitely readable, even when the posturing melodrama of its prose becomes too much of a good thing; and there are nuances, cruelly aware nuances, in its parody that go well beyond mere criticism of bad, superficial narrative. Consider, for example, the significance of the 'stout' stick in the passage quoted above: it is only a slight reminiscence of the kind of prose that boys are told to admire at school, but the effect of these subtle touches is cumulative.

A Cool Million is entirely successful as satire. There is still no more devastatingly contemptuous exposure of naïve 'Americanism' and capitalist optimism than this story of the honourable, trusting and parodically innocent Lemuel Pitkin, who loses an eye, his teeth, his scalp and his leg, and after being jailed and used as a tool for both communist and fascist conspiracies, is killed and becomes a martyr in the fascist cause. It disappoints only because it fails to transcend its immediate object and become a major work of imagination. The precedent for this is, of course, *Gulliver's Travels*, of which West was clearly acutely aware, since his hero's Christian name is Lemuel.

For Pitkin, besides serving as a butt, very nearly comes to life, and serves to represent something much more than just the idiotic Horatio Alger–American. Has anyone noticed the resemblance between West's satire and John Crowe Ransom's famous poem, 'Captain Carpenter'? Carpenter, as will be remembered, is just such an honourable innocent as Pitkin: he rides out, and is systematically shorn of his eyes, ears, limbs and life. But whereas Ransom's poem is deliberately archaic and unmodern, West's novel is as slickly sick as his fundamentally poetic imagination would allow it to be. Nevertheless, there is enough promise in *A Cool Million* to suggest that had West lived he might have produced books that would have made such admirably ambitious but literary-egg-bound fowls as *Giles Goat-Boy* look contrived and even silly.—MARTIN SEYMOUR-SMITH, "Prophet of Black Humour," *Spec*, July 19, 1968, pp. 94–95

Nathanael West, the author of *Miss Lonelyhearts*, went to Hollywood a few years ago, and his silence had been causing his readers alarm lest he might have faded out on the Coast as so many of his fellows have done. But Mr. West, as this new book happily proves, is still alive beyond the mountains, and quite able to set down what he feels and sees—has still, in short, remained an artist. His new novel, *The Day of the Locust*, deals with the nondescript characters on the edges of the Hollywood studios: an old comic who sells shoe polish and his film-struck daughter; a quarrelsome dwarf; a cock-fighting Mexican; a Hollywood cowboy and a Hollywood Indian; and an undeveloped hotel clerk from Iowa, who has come to the Coast to enjoy his savings—together with a sophisticated screen-writer, who lives in a big house that is "an exact reproduction of the old Dupuy mansion near Biloxi, Mississippi." And these people have been painted as distinctly and polished up as brightly as the figures in Persian miniatures. Their speech has been distilled with a sense of the flavorsome and the characteristic which makes John O'Hara seem pedestrian. Mr. West has footed a precarious way and has not slipped at any point into relying on the Hollywood values in describing the Hollywood people. The landscapes, the architecture and the interior decoration of Beverly Hills and vicinity have been handled with equal distinction. Everyone who has ever been in Los Angeles knows how the mere aspect of things is likely to paralyze the aesthetic faculty by providing no *point d'appui* from which to exercise its discrimination, if it does not actually stun the sensory apparatus itself, so that accurate reporting becomes impossible. But Nathanael West has stalked and caught some fine specimens of these Hollywood lepidoptera and impaled them on fastidious pins. Here are Hollywood restaurants, apartment houses, funeral churches, brothels, evangelical temples and movie sets—in this latter connection, an extremely amusing episode of a man getting nightmarishly lost in the Battle of Waterloo. Mr. West's surrealist beginnings have stood him in good stead on the Coast.

The doings of these people are bizarre, but they are also sordid and senseless. Mr. West has caught the emptiness of Hollywood; and he is, as far as I know, the first writer to make this emptiness horrible. The most impressive thing in the book is his picture of the people from the Middle West who, retiring to sunlit leisure, are trying to leave behind them the meagerness of their working lives; who desire something different from what they have had but do not know what they desire, and have no other resources for amusement than gaping at movie stars and listening to Aimee McPherson's sermons. In the last episode, a crowd of these people, who have come out to see the celebrities at an opening, is set off by an insane act of violence on the part of the cretinous hotel clerk, and gives way to an outburst of mob mania. The America of the murders and rapes which fill the Los Angeles papers is only the obverse side of the

America of the inanities of the movies. Such people—Mr. West seems to say—dissatisfied, yet with no ideas, no objectives and no interest in anything vital, may in the mass be capable of anything. The daydreams purveyed by Hollywood, the romances that in movie stories can be counted on to have whisked around all obstacles and adroitly knocked out all "menaces" by the time they have run off their reels, romances which their fascinated audiences have never been able to live themselves—only cheat them and embitter their frustration. Of such mobs are the followers of fascism made.

I think that the book itself suffers a little from the lack of a center in the community with which it deals. It has less concentration than *Miss Lonelyhearts*. Mr. West has introduced a young Yale man who, as an educated and healthy human being, is supposed to provide a normal point of view from which the deformities of Hollywood may be criticized; but it is also essential to the story that this young man should find himself swirling around in the same aimless eddies as the others. I am not sure that it is really possible to do anything substantial with Hollywood except by making it, as John Dos Passos did in *The Big Money*, a part of a larger picture which has its center in a larger world. But in the meantime Nathanael West has survived to write another distinguished book—in its peculiar combination of amenity of surface and felicity of form and style with ugly subject matter and somber feeling, quite unlike—as *Miss Lonelyhearts* was—the books of anyone else.—EDMUND WILSON, "The Boys in the Back Room: Postscript" (1939), *Classics and Commercials*, 1950, pp. 52–55

EDWARD GREENFIELD SCHWARTZ
From "The Novels of Nathanael West"

Accent, Autumn 1957, pp. 252–62

One of the most profane, bawdy, humorous novels in American literature, *Balso Snell* records West's Rabelaisian probing of his own agitated mind for answers to the eternal riddles: What is man? What is reality? What is truth, beauty, love? I read the novel as a strangely detached self-study: it's as though West were two persons, one acting inside the dream, the other observing himself from the outside. West demands of himself that he look at reality as it is, not as convention would have him see it. With savage humor and irony, he despoils the frustrated artist of his self-deluding poses and, like a Karl Marx of the human emotions, exposes the "real" motive of the artist—the desire for sexual satisfaction. His most important discovery during his dream journey is that man's pretensions, his romantic conception of himself, lead to the abnegation of basic human needs and to tragic frustrations. Since our pretensions stem from the false gods of religion, art, and civilization, the novel may be considered "as a protest against writing books." (Actually, West's protest is different from the Dadaists'; they were reacting against the meaningless world of reason, the inhuman world of science and the machine.)

Because *Balso Snell* has puzzled so many of its few readers and because West's temperament so clearly emerges in it, an attempt at a detailed analysis of this episodic, disjointed fantasy may be worth while. Balso begins his dream journey by entering the Trojan Horse (that is, himself, his own self-betraying mind, the receptacle of the cunning, deceitful culture symbolized by the Horse) through the "Anus Mirabilis," for what he will find within is the disgusting animalistic soul of man. On the threshold of his grand quest, Balso (like the hero-poets of the past) prays to the Gods: "O Beer! O Meyerbeer! O Bach! O Offenbach! Stand me now as ever in good stead." West's irreverent burlesque of James Joyce's dedicated hero-artist, Stephen Dedalus (*A Portrait of the Artist as a Young Man*), stridently announces his refusal to take seriously the artist's priestly functions. Later, when we realize that Balso's journey is nothing more than a wet dream, we understand that West's mockery of the artist is just one aspect of his misanthropy.

Entering "the gloom of the foyer-like intestine," Balso begins to feel depressed by its silence and emptiness. He sings to keep his spirits high. His song has to do with "roundness," an obvious sexual image, for what he seeks is the wholeness that is to be achieved by sexual union. The song's progression from the roundness of "the Anus of a Bronze Horse" to higher forms, the roundness of the wheels of the Lord's chariot or the roundness of art ("Giotto Painter of Perfect Circles") or the roundness of "the Dew-Loaded Navel" of the Virgin Mary, blasphemously and humorously suggests that Balso may be seeking philosophical wholeness, too, some kind of mystical idealism to resolve the conflicts and confusions of his daily living. (I don't think Balso's search for spiritual unity can be taken too seriously. A recent graduate in philosophy at Brown University, West parades his learning a little too gaudily and sophomorically in this novel for my taste.)

But Balso's skepticism is indicated by the names he gives his song: "Anywhere Out of the World, or a Voyage Through the Hole in the Mundane Millstone . . ., or Toe Holes for a Flight of Fancy." Unsettled by his own self-consuming wit, he thinks of "the Phoenix Excrementi, a race of men he had invented one Sunday afternoon while in bed," a race that "eat themselves, digest themselves, and give birth to themselves by evacuating their bowels." Within his own bowels—West's way of identifying man's unconscious as well as what we like to call the collective unconscious of mankind—Balso's adventure for sexual fulfillment and philosophic certainty are equated with ironic effect.

Dream logic at this point requires a splitting up because Balso's desire for the wholeness, the oneness of idealism has been shattered. His mind conjures up a guide to the marvels of the Trojan Horse. Personifying the impulse within Balso's mind toward idealism, the guide tells Balso a marvelous story about how a "traveler in Tyana, who was looking for the sage Apollonius, saw a snake enter the lower part" of the sage's body. This peculiarity of "the philosopher-saint" appeals to Balso, who admires the sexual-spiritual perfection symbolized. But the guide's idealism soon bores Balso.

Coming suddenly upon "a place where the intestine had burst through the stomach wall," Balso cries out, "'What a hernia! What a hernia!'" This enrages the idealistic guide, who sees not a hernia but a beautiful art object. (Earlier what the guide had seen as a "beautiful Doric prostate gland" the realistic Balso had called "simply an atrophied pile.") Trying to pacify the guide, Balso blunders further: "'Hernia! What a beautiful name for a girl! Hernia Hornstein! Paresis Pearlberg! Paranoia Puntz!'" Unexpectedly pained, the guide cries "in an enormous voice, 'I am a Jew! and whenever anything Jewish is mentioned, I find it necessary to say that I am a Jew. I'm a Jew! A Jew!'" The guide's Jewishness is like the hernia and the atrophied pile, a disgusting reality he would shun, so that his fanatic idealism seems to be little more than an escape.

Such an interpretation suggests to me that the unflattering gallery of Jews in West's novels may have been his peculiar way of facing with scrupulous honesty what he saw as an unpleasant reality. Perhaps he had the sophistication to consider the Jewish obsession with its historical guilt a romantic falsification. At any rate, I am inclined to the view that his Jewishness contributes to his self-mocking temperament.

Realizing that he and the guide represent opposite views of human life, Balso humors the guide by contemplating Picasso's idealistic proposition, "there are no feet in nature." This return to the contemplation of the ideal connects the search for roundness in art with Balso's sexual and philosophical quests. Fleeing from the fetid idealism of art, Balso's next encounter is with himself in the guise of a flagellating mystic, Maloney the Areopagite, who appears "naked except for a derby in which thorns were sticking." Tortured by guilt and fear, Maloney is "attempting to crucify himself with thumb tacks." When he isn't abusing himself, he works on a biography of St. Puce, "a flea who was born, lived, and died, beneath the arm of our Lord." Reduced to this absurd physical image (a favorite device of West), the religious myth has no appeal to Balso, who finds it slightly morbid.

Having rejected the idealism of art and religion, cornerstones of western civilization, Balso now seeks a new view of mankind. He finds it, comically, in the English composition of a twelve-year-old prodigy named John Gilson. Like Balso, Gilson is searching for "the Real," but, though he willingly smells his own excrement, he cannot discover his true self. Sexually frustrated, Gilson assumes a mask before the world. Sometimes he assumes the role of the guilt-haunted murderer Raskolnikov, sometimes of the calculating deceiver Iago; he never could be "plain John Gilson—honest, honest Iago, yes, but never honest John." Gilson's pretense, like Iago's, is to a simple, honest nature, while actually he is constantly scheming. (I am reminded of West's tale of how he made "a lucky hit" among the expatriates in Paris.)

Wearing his Raskolnikov mask, Gilson keeps a crime journal which he calls "The Making of a Fiend." In it he tells a grotesque tale of murder committed for "literary reasons," to discover "the horrors" of such an act. Symbolically, his action is a repudiation of reason—the reason of society (the policeman) and of science (Darwin). His "reason" is that of the unconscious; it has to do with his sexual drives. Consequently, the culmination of the murder (itself a sexual act) leads to his discovery of his homosexual self and to a sexual climax. Reality, then, includes this nasty mixture of irrational guilt and desire, discovered in Balso's own consciousness, though protectively removed from his sense of responsibility by being attributed to Gilson.

That Balso's search for reality takes him through the disgusting mire of man's animality is inevitable because West believed that man is a comic victim of his own flesh, a subservient clown performing at the whim of an unseen master named Instinct. West has Gilson admit: "I need women and because I can't buy them or force them, I have to make poems for them." "All my acting has but one purpose, the attraction of the female." These confessions would seem to be West's as well as Gilson's. Humorously stated, the confessions are nevertheless at the root of West's bitterness. Not endowed with physical beauty, West (like Gilson) had to prove himself worthy of his love by revealing his innermost beauty (i.e., he wore "his heart and genitals" around his neck).

What Gilson resents is the burden of responsibility. After all, he can't help himself; his personality is split by his fleshly needs and his idealizing soul. Even worse, he isn't really a free agent, but is controlled like a machine ("an automobile") by an unrelenting force within him:

> "When you think of me, Saniette," [Gilson tells his mistress in a scene that burlesques Marcel Proust] "think of two men—myself and the chauffeur within me. This chauffeur is very large and dressed in ugly ready-made clothing. His shoes, soiled from walking about the streets of a great city, are covered with animal ordure and chewing gum . . .
>
> "The name of this chauffeur is The Desire to Procreate.
>
> "He sits within me like a man in an automobile. His heels are in my bowels, his knees on my heart, his face in my brain . . .
>
> "From within, he governs the sensations I receive through my fingers, eyes, tongue, and ears."

Like all other men, the artist is governed by "the chauffeur within"; the artist's pose is like the pose of other men, motivated by similar desires. His artistic creations and intellectual accomplishments are thus seen as emanating not from his spiritualism or altruism but from his id.

Deprived of the illusions of art and culture, Balso seeks beauty. Stimulated, his mind brings forth a naked, slim young girl "busily washing her hidden charms in a public fountain." The impassioned Balso throws his arms around her only to discover that his search for roundness is not yet to be consummated, even on the sexual level. In the middle of a kiss, he suddenly feels himself "embracing tweed," discovers in his arms another potential writer, "a middle-aged woman dressed in a mannish suit and wearing horn-rimmed glasses." Disillusioned, Balso comes to realize that the inhabitants of the Trojan Horse are "writers in search of an audience," i.e., merely aspects of himself in search of a woman, his favorite audience.

The remainder of the novel, a brilliant *tour de force*, provides confirmation of Balso's discovery of man's real nature, his backside personality. The dream logic takes him in waves toward the final climax, the release his body craves, even at the expense of spiritual confusion. West creates a dream-within-a-dream, two hypothetical versions of a bathetic modern love affair, an amusing parody of Joyce, and, as a final ironic twist, a long seduction speech in which Balso, just as he is about to take his pleasure, tries to rationalize the justness of the act. Balso's speech is a grotesquely realistic parody of the familiar language of the smart set West knew so well in New York and Paris. Balso recites all the time-worn justifications for illicit pleasure—the Time-argument, the political, philosophical, and aesthetic reasons.

Although West's style and ideas are refined in his later novels, his outlook and method do not, in my opinion, undergo any fundamental changes. For West, the old gods are dead; no miraculous loves or births occur among men any more: at our slightly ridiculous births, "instead of the Three Kings, the Dove, the Star of Bethlehem, there was only old Doctor Haasenschweitz who wore rubber gloves and carried a towel over his arm like a waiter." Yet we destroy ourselves by holding up an idealized image of mankind that can never be. We indulge in a "terrible competition" that demands our "being more than animals." Our idealized notion of ourselves derives from our worshiping false gods, cultural as well as religious. West's antidote for this corrupting poison would seem to be his scoffing, humorous vernacular style and his hard, derisive, realistic look at the world without the illusive veil of religion, culture, or art.

Other visions than cynical hedonism are tried out in West's second novel, *Miss Lonelyhearts* (1933), a story about a young newspaperman who writes a lonely hearts column. A modern Everyman, the anonymous reporter who writes under the Miss Lonelyhearts by-line becomes obsessed by the impossibility of alleviating the terrifying misery and suffering of the grotesques who seek his advice: Sick-of-it-all, a Catholic woman who has had seven children and can't stand the pain and the fear of her eighth pregnancy; Desperate, a girl who was born without a nose and who out of loneliness and despair contemplates suicide; Harold S., a fifteen-year-old boy whose deaf-mute sister has been raped; Faye Doyle, a lusty woman married to an inadequate cripple; Broad Shoulders, a deserted wife who wants a home for herself and her children. Sickened by his heightened awareness of the griefs of mortality, Miss Lonelyhearts (like the cripple Peter Doyle) becomes desperate to know "what is the whole stinking business for."

This is essentially the same question raised in *Balso Snell*. Because it cannot be answered, Shrike, Miss Lonelyhearts' cynical boss and foil, ironically suggests various escapes. But Shrike knows that "neither the soil, nor the South Seas, nor Hedonism, nor art, nor suicide, nor drugs, can mean anything to us . . . God alone is our escape. The church is our only hope, the First Church of Christ Dentist, where He is worshiped as Preventer of Decay." Parodying the unhappy letters of the lovelorn, Shrike humorously dictates a letter to the "Miss Lonelyhearts of Miss Lonelyhearts" (i.e., to Christ):

> I am twenty-six years old and in the newspaper game. Life for me is a desert empty of comfort. I cannot find pleasure in food, drink, or women—nor do the arts give me joy any longer. The Leopard of Discontent walks the streets of my city; the Lion of Discouragement crouches outside the walls of my citadel. All is desolation and a vexation of the spirit. I feel like hell. How can I believe, how can I have faith in this day and age? Is it true that the greatest scientists believe again in you?
>
> I read your column and like it very much. There you once wrote: 'When the salt has lost its savour, who shall savour it again?' Is the answer: 'None but the Saviour?'
>
> Thanking you very much for a quick reply, I remain yours truly,
>
> A Regular Subscriber

Obviously, Shrike doesn't have much hope for "a quick reply." Nor does West. The failure of religion as an acceptable answer is painfully (though almost humorously) illustrated by Miss Lonelyhearts' violent death, which occurs just when he fancies himself bringing Christ's love into the life of a lovelorn cripple, his murderer Peter Doyle.

The theme of man in search of salvation, of a way of life, the flat, oversimplified characterizations, the uncanny, nightmarish atmosphere, and the allegorical style of *Miss Lonelyhearts* remind me of *The Pilgrim's Progress*. But what a difference there is between West's world and Bunyan's. Miss Lonelyhearts' progress toward an acceptance of Christ parallels Christian's, but with one tragic difference. Unlike Christian, who awakens from his dream refreshed, Miss Lonelyhearts never emerges from his dream. Deeply engrossed by his Christ-dream, he goes to a monstrously ironic death that is described with complete objectivity. His self-deception is exposed by the event, and his dream, shattered.

I don't think West's pessimism underwent any change in *Miss Lonelyhearts*. If anything, it deepened. Evidently, West had come to believe that man's dreams couldn't work in the modern world even as opiates: "Men have always fought their misery with dreams. Although dreams were once powerful, they have been made puerile by the movies, radio, and newspapers. Among many betrayals, this one is the worst." Bad enough that our dreams can't come true, but to have our false dreams reduced to childishness is even worse. West laments this betrayal not because it deprives man of an essential dignity, nobility, and idealism, nor because it attenuates his tragic strivings, but because it deprives man of a comfortable escape that can withstand the assaults of the rationalist. This is the essence of his temperament; this is what makes the quality of his pessimism so different from that of Conrad or Hemingway or K. A. Porter or Faulkner.

In his last two novels, *A Cool Million* (1934) and *The Day of the Locust* (1939), West considers the political, social, and psychological significance of "the worst betrayal," the reduction of man's dreams to immature banalities. Although *A Cool Million* is a rather funny burlesque of the Horatio Alger theme, it isn't up to West's best work. Subtitled "The Dismantling of Lemuel Pitkin," it is a picaresque tale about a strong, spirited, red-blooded American boy who loses his teeth, one eye, one leg, his scalp, and eventually his life in pursuit of the American success dream. Evidently, West intended to show how banal myths, supported by emotional jargon and clichés, could make unthinking simpletons like Lemuel a tool of fascistic demagogues. Written hurriedly to meet a publisher's deadline, *A Cool Million* reads like a very good outline for what might have been an excellent American version of Voltaire's *Candide*.

Four years after publication of *A Cool Million*, West completed his last and finest novel, *The Day of the Locust*. Luck—the purchase of *Miss Lonelyhearts* by 20th Century Fox, which so altered the story that when it appeared as *Advice to the Lovelorn* it was unrecognizable, merely a silly cops-and-robbers movie—luck had taken West to Hollywood, the fabled land of dreamers and dream-makers. To one already deeply affected by how the frustration of man's impossible dreams led to emotional starvation, bitterness, and readiness for vengeful violence, Horace Greeley's dictum must have seemed sound; Hollywood was the golden land. It provided West with material for the most complete statement of his major theme. Unchanged is his abiding pessimism, but his pictorial method has undergone development and clarification. That method had been labeled "surrealistic" by Clifton Fadiman. And, though West protested that Fadiman "knows enough about Surrealism, I am sure, to know that I am not a Surrealist at all," later critics, following Fadiman's lead, have vaguely identified West with the surrealist movement.

While certain aspects of West's novels resemble surrealistic paintings, his attitude toward the materials of his art differs considerably, in my opinion, from the surrealists'. Like the surrealists, West was aware of the violence, dissonance, and pain of life; like some of the surrealists, he was a Freudian who sought reality in man's irrational dream world. But, unlike the surrealists (and the dadaists), West had no program. His pessimism didn't lead to nihilism or to an intense hatred of the rational world. On the contrary, his pose is that of the objective observer who merely records the horror.

He seems more akin to Albert Camus than to the surrealists. Part of Camus' *Le Mythe de Sisyphe* could easily be applied to *The Day of the Locust*:

> Ce divorce entre l'homme et sa vie, l'acteur et son décor, c'est proprement le sentiment de l'absurdeté. . . .
>
> . . . l'homme se trouve devant l'irrationnel. Il sent en lui son désir de bonheur et de raison. L'absurde nait de cette confrontation entre l'appel humain et le silence déraisonnable du monde.

Like Camus, West seems to doubt the possibility of philosophical explanations in a world of "the absurd," the incoherent, the senseless. The job of the writer is to achieve a lucid portrayal of the anguished human consciousness journeying to the end of night without meaning or hope.

That is the task Tod Hackett, the artist-hero of *The Day of the Locust*, sets for himself in his projected painting "The Burning of Los Angeles." Tod's maturing conception of his painting provides the ideational pattern of the novel, which may be read as West's version of man's fate as well as his view of the function of art. (Through Tod's development, we can see just how unlike the surrealists West is in his attitude toward the subjects of his art.)

Our first glimpse of Tod in the opening scene of the novel is one of West's most brilliant scenes. "Around quitting time, Tod Hackett heard a great din on the road outside his office. The groan of leather mingled with the jangle of iron and over all beat the tattoo of a thousand hooves." Tod hurries to the window and sees "an army of cavalry and foot" passing, hears above the clamor of horses and men "a little fat man" pursuing the retreating army and screaming through a megaphone, "Stage Nine—you bastards—Stage Nine!" Without much ado, West provides us with the ironic situation that is at the very core of his novel: the flat reality ("around quitting time"), the unglamorous act ("Stage Nine—you bastards—Stage Nine") juxtaposed against the marvelous scene of human action on the grand scale as created in a Hollywood film.

Against this strange backdrop of romantic man-made shows, visions of the ideal, Tod observes the everyday life of Hollywood where two kinds of people, "the masqueraders" and "the spectators," enact their roles in an environment that seems almost to parody the romantic movies.

> . . . As he walked along, he examined the evening crowd. A great many of the people wore sports clothes which were not really sports clothes. Their sweaters, knickers, slacks, blue flannel jackets with brass buttons were fancy dress. The fat lady in the yachting cap was going shopping, not boating; the man in the Norfolk jacket and Tyrolean hat was returning, not from a mountain, but an insurance office; and the girl in slacks and sneaks with a bandanna around her head had just left a switchboard, not a tennis court.
>
> Scattered among these masquerades were people of a different type. Their clothing was somber and badly cut, bought from mail-order houses. While the others moved rapidly, darting into stores and cocktail bars, they loitered on the corners or stood with their backs to the shop windows and stared at everyone who passed. When their stare was returned, their eyes filled with hatred. . . .
>
> He reached the end of Vine Street and began the climb into Pinyon Canyon. Night had started to fall.
>
> The edges of the trees burned with a pale violet light and their centers gradually turned from deep purple to black. The same violet piping, like a Neon tube, outlined the tops of the ugly, hump-backed hills and they were almost beautiful.
>
> But not even the soft wash of dusk could help the houses. Only dynamite would be of any use against the Mexican ranch houses, Samoan huts, Mediterranean villas, Egyptian and Japanese temples, Swiss chalets, Tudor cottages, and every possible combination of these styles that lined the slopes of the canyon. . . .
>
> On the corner of La Huerta Road was a miniature Rhine castle with tarpaper turrets pierced for archers. Next to it was a little highly colored shack with domes and minarets out of the *Arabian Nights*. Again he was charitable. Both houses were comic, but he didn't laugh. Their desire to startle was so eager and guileless.
>
> It is hard to laugh at the need for beauty and romance, no matter how tasteless, even horrible, the results of that need are. But it is easy to sigh. Few things are sadder than the truly monstrous.

What Tod feels is essentially the same as what the Easterners feel in Stephen Crane's "The Blue Hotel," when, travelling through the great Nebraska prairies, they are "overcome at the sight" of the garish blue hotel and express "shame, pity, and horror, in a laugh." Shame for man's vermin-like pollution of the natural world; pity for feeble mankind entrapped on "a whirling, fire-smitten, ice-locked, disease-stricken, space-lost bulb"; horror for man's dreadful fate. Embarrassed by the grotesque and the outlandish, the Easterners express their feelings "in a laugh." West's Easterner, Tod, feels shame, pity, and horror, too, but, because he is an artist, he feels no embarrassment, just a desire to understand, to capture the essence of the scene in a great work of art.

One purpose of this digression is to suggest that West is not an isolated figure in American literary history. Although in "Some Notes on *Miss Lonelyhearts*" he expressed his dislike for the naturalistic, documentary novels of Sinclair Lewis and Theodore Dreiser, he shares some of the attitudes of the naturalists, particularly Stephen Crane's horror and sadness at the sight of "the truly monstrous."

About the gaping loiterers, Tod Hackett later discovers that "All their lives they had slaved at some kind of dull, heavy labor, behind desks and counters, on the fields, and at tedious machines of all sorts, saving their pennies and dreaming of the leisure that would be theirs when they had enough." When their dreams become a reality, they go to California, "the land of sunshine and oranges." But, once there, "they discover sunshine isn't enough." They don't know what to do with their leisure. "Their boredom becomes more and more terrible. They realize that they've been tricked and burn with resentment . . . Nothing can ever be violent enough to make taut their slack minds and bodies. They have been cheated and betrayed."

Disillusioned with their dreams, the loiterers become the audience of the masqueraders, whose clothing symbolizes their self-deception, their present participation and enactment of the romantic dreams that, ironically, give them life. Among these masqueraders are a special group whom Tod thinks of as "The Dancers": Abe Kusich, a contentious dwarf who wants all the pleasures of the tough, masculine world; Faye Greener, an ambitious, incredibly inept actress whose beauty the infatuated, pursuing Tod thinks of as "structural like a tree's, not a quality of her mind or heart"; her father, Harry, an old vaudeville ham who has been reduced to peddling "Miracle Solvent, the modern polish par excellence, . . . used by all the movie stars"; Earle Shoop, an ignorant small-town Arizona cowboy who stiffly plays the role of the strong, silent type he's seen at the movies; Claude Estee, a successful screen writer who lives "in a big house that was the exact reproduction of the old Dupuy Mansion near Biloxi, Mississippi," and tries to do an "impersonation that went with the Southern Colonial mansion"; Adore Loomis, an obnoxious child prodigy who is being primed by his mother for a movie career.

In a series of Tod's lithographs, these dancers are driven by the stares of their audience "to spin crazily and leap into the air with twisted backs like hooked trout." And this is how they appear in the novel: "hooked" by their separate dreams, they become capering manikins indulging in extraordinary antics. West's idea reminds me of Sherwood Anderson's conception of "the grotesque." In *Winesburg, Ohio*, Anderson tells how

> . . . when the world was young there were a great many thoughts but no such thing as a truth. Man made the truths himself . . . All about in the world were the truths and they were all beautiful . . . And then the people came along. Each as he appeared snatched up one of the truths . . . It was the truths that made the people grotesques . . . The moment one of the people took one of the truths to himself, called it his truth, and tried to live his life by it, he became a grotesque and the truth he embraced became a falsehood.

What Anderson calls "truths" West calls "dreams." Like Anderson's grotesques, West's characters come alive when they give themselves up to a "truth."

The characters in *The Day of the Locust* are either lifeless onlookers no longer capable of dreaming, spectators waiting for the moment when they can wreak their vengeance, or dancers who are animated by an impossible desire to live a dream-role, to achieve the beauty of an ideal. Only by accepting a dream can one become a participant in the dance of life. So it had been, ironically, for Homer Simpson, a quiet midwesterner who looked "like one of Picasso's great sterile athletes [brooding] hopelessly on pink sand, staring at veined marble waves." After meeting Faye, he is hooked by the dream of love. Ironically, by coming alive Homer is "destroying himself." His dream of love makes him susceptible to Faye's sadism and infidelity, and culminates in the insane attack upon the annoying child prodigy which leads to his own violent end. Life, for West, is destructive: when a man begins to enact a dream, he inevitably destroys himself; when the cheated spectators merge in a mob and for a brief moment "come alive," they achieve their aliveness through violence.

To illuminate this bizarre, sordid Hollywood dream world in his painting, Tod had studied the methods "not only of Goya and Daumier but also of certain Italian artists of the seventeenth and eighteenth centuries, . . . the painters of Decay and Mystery." After watching the worshippers

> . . . writhe on the hard seats of their churches, he thought of how well Alessandro Magnasco would dramatize the contrast between their drained-out feeble bodies and their wild, disordered minds. He would not satirize them as Hogarth or Daumier might, nor would he pity them. He would paint their fury with respect, appreciating its awful, anarchic power and aware that they had it in them to destroy civilization.

And this is the attitude and method of West in *The Day of the Locust*, for Magnasco, not surrealism, was the decisive influence on West's style. Like his artist-hero Tod Hackett, West evidently was impressed by Magnasco's baroque scenes of desolation. Shrouded in unearthly twilight, Magnasco's canvases are peopled by spectre-haunted, gaunt monks, self-tortured inquisitors, spastic punchinellos, and convulsive gypsies. The forms of his grotesques are distorted, at times even shattered, heightening the effect of the occasional bursts of light that illuminate the pervasive gloom. Even in his most morbid scenes of human anguish, Magnasco has the remarkable ability to perceive the farcical aspects of the scene. So, too, does West have this comic insight, and, though his morbidity and fantasy derive from a world slightly altered since Magnasco's time, West's sparseness and poetic intensity can be considered linguistic equivalents of Magnasco's style.

Magnasco's attitude toward his subject is important to West: no mockery of the human "need for beauty and romance, no matter how tasteless, even horrible, the results of that need are"; and no pity, since that would be self-pity. I can't agree with Edmund Wilson's opinion (in *Classics and Commercials*) that *The Day of the Locust* "suffers a little from the lack of a center in the community with which it deals." Mr. Wilson's criticism stems from his dissatisfaction with West's conception of Tod Hackett, "a young Yale man who, as an educated and healthy human being, is supposed to provide a normal point of view from which the deformities of Hollywood may be criticized." To West all men are involved in the fantasy; we all of us strive for the fulfillment of impossible dreams. West no more than Tod can control "the chauffeur within." Even more than Homer Simpson, Tod understands what an infatuation with Faye can mean, but he can't help himself; reason moves us less than need, and need is a hungry, roving hyena, often gorged but never sated.

West's acceptance of his own involvement is not in the least self-pity, as W. H. Auden contends (*Griffin*, May, 1957). Like Camus, West sought to illuminate the absurdity of human life for man's enlightenment; he has a touch, however slight, of the meliorist in him. At one point in *The Day of the Locust*, he has Tod question the validity of his artistic conception: maybe he was "exaggerating the importance of the people who come to California to die. Maybe they weren't really desperate enough to set a single city on fire, let alone the whole country." While it doesn't make any difference "because he was an artist, not a prophet" and his work "would not be judged by the accuracy with which it foretold a future event but by its merit as painting," Tod "refused to give up the role of Jeremiah." Not a do-gooder, not given to social or political dogmas, West evidently believed that his work had some social value, some special insight not to be found in proletarian novels or religious tracts. West thought it important for man to know his own nature; within us the real dangers lurk. His probing of the human heart and mind is as compassionate as the Christian compassion of Mr. Auden, even though it is more anxious and anguished.

The real virtue of West is his absolute clear-sightedness, his complete rejection of the conventional, the dogmatic, and the hackneyed. Those unmentionable trivia of daily living that have so much to do with making our lives, as well as the profanity, the vulgarity, the meanness, the perversity, the violence that is an important (if dreadful) part of human living, West describes in his novels. Disgusted or disdainful, we nevertheless must admit the concreteness, the reality of his vision.

Yet, while we may admire West's substantial accomplishments, we need not find him congenial. While reading his novels, I have often been struck by the resemblance between his notion that man's sustaining dream is delusive and destructive and Conrad's concept of dreams as "the destructive element." To me, Conrad's pessimism is deeper, more philosophical, more humane than West's. Although Conrad recognized the terrible incongruity of life—that man's dreams may not be realized, that man's instincts, his nature, impinge upon his dreams, his ambitions, his hopes—he saw that by following the dream man could at least maintain the ideals, the disciplines that make us human. The pursuit of the dream, though futile, could be tragic and beautiful to Conrad. But not to West, whose personal involvement prevented him from achieving the objectivity, the larger view, of Conrad.

Still, West's novels have value in a world as close to George Orwell's *1984* as ours, where expediency, the pragmatist's truth, has come to be accepted sincerely as reality. West's comic insight is a good antidote to our complacency and cant. At the center of his interest in popular culture, violence, the grotesque, and the search for authoritarian faith is his perception that the inability of a prosperous people to avoid boredom, sterility, and frustration can lead to fascism. The recent decline in the United States of the avant-garde has quieted the protest against the press, radio, and movies, which reduce man's dreams to banalities. The few who have attempted to combat our self-flattery and self-delusion we have derisively called egg-heads, ivory-tower-dwellers, bohemians, decadents. Yet as this democracy "settles in the mould of its vulgarity, heavily thickening to empire" (to quote Robinson Jeffers), perhaps we shall need to be reminded of our pretensions and our failures by satirists like Nathanael West.

ALVIN B. KERNAN

From "The Mob Tendency: *The Day of the Locust*" *The Plot of Satire*

1965, pp. 69–80

As a moralist Nathanael West would seem to be about as far from Pope as it is possible to get. The neoclassical values of tradition, culture, common sense, and Nature are so diminished for West that he could once write, wryly but accurately, that "there is nothing to root for in my work and what is even worse, no rooters."[1] But the particular form of dullness which is the disintegrating force in *The Day of the Locust* still seeks out and expresses itself in those jumbles and mobs which it finds so "naturally" in *The Dunciad*, or which new wealth and lack of taste create in Petronius' *Satyricon*, or which pedantry, ignorance, and the burning desire for fame discover so regularly in that greatest image of confusion, Swift's *Tale of a Tub*. A poet like Pope will often dramatize the mob tendency of dullness in a single line, using, or purposely misusing, some rhetorical device such as zeugma or antithesis: "Or lose her heart, or necklace, at a ball"—"Puffs, Powders, Patches, Bibles, Billet-doux." In a novelist like West the crowding effect is not so obviously rhetorical or so concentrated; it is built up in blocks of semirealistic description of scenes, characters, and actions. But the effect is still to show dullness' disorganization of all the fundamental patterns of sense.

The dynamics of *The Day of the Locust* are focused in Tod's painting, "The Burning of Los Angeles." In the background is the mob which exerts a downward and outward pressure on the people below and on the picture as a whole. The mob is made up of "the people who come to California to die." These are the retired farmers from the midwest, the "senior citizens" tired of ice and snow, the housewives and clerks and small merchants dissatisfied with their dull, dreary lives in some small town, who come to California for sunshine, orange juice, and excitement. But these people are already sophisticates in violence.

> Every day of their lives they read the newspapers and went to the movies. Both fed them on lynchings, murder, sex crimes, explosions, wrecks, love nests, fires, miracles, revolutions, war. (Ch. 27)

Only disappointment can follow, and they quickly discover that you can get enough orange juice and sunshine, that one wave in the ocean looks much like another, and that airplanes almost never crash and consume their passengers in a "holocaust of flame." As simpler entertainments fail, these people, dressed in their dark, mail-order suits, begin to loiter on street corners staring with hard, bold gazes at the brighter passersby. Themselves empty of talent; lacking beauty, vitality, and intelligence; and completely without compassion, the people who come to California to die search more and more wildly for the life that is not in themselves. They attend funerals waiting for the collapse of a mourner or some other show of strong emotion, they follow movie stars hoping that their personalities will magically be changed by proximity to beauty and dynamism, they take up fad diets which promise health and vigor if they avoid meat and cooked vegetables, they learn "Brain-Breathing, The Secret of the Aztecs" in a search for contact with mysterious powers which will bring them to life. But nothing works, for "Nothing can ever be violent enough to make taut their slack minds and bodies. They have been cheated and betrayed. They have slaved and saved for nothing." As this realization comes home to them, their expressions change to "vicious, acrid boredom" that trembles on the "edge of violence," and their fury at being cheated becomes "an awful, anarchic power" that can "destroy civilization."

Before the destroying mob in "The Burning of Los Angeles" runs a group of fugitives made up of the principal characters of the novel. These men and women are imperfect, but each has some one virtue which the mob lacks. Faye Greener is completely emptyheaded, but she has a breathtaking beauty, "structural like a tree's, not a quality of her mind or heart"; her father Harry Greener is a clever vaudeville actor, a master of the art of staying alive in a world fraught with dangers; Claude Estee is a writer and a talented wit; Tod Hackett a painter; and Homer Simpson a simple man capable of and needing love and kindness. But they are not complete people. It seems as if some god with a wry sense of humor had decided to give them only one virtue apiece while withholding the auxiliary virtues needed to make the gift meaningful.

The relationship of these people to the mob in the background is not simple. They are in one way, as the picture suggests, the victims of the mob, pursued and destroyed because they are different and talented. In another sense they are the purveyors of excitement to the mob, the representatives of all those people in the "entertainment industries" who make a living manufacturing the fake "amour and glamor" needed by the tired barber in Purdue who has spent his day cutting hair. But these people with their single talents, while contemptuous of the mob which follows them, "run before" in another sense, for they too are people who have come to California to die. They too seek vicarious pleasure or strange experiences to compensate for lives which, despite their gifts, are still inadequate. Because they have money or are cleverer and more attractive, their escapes into fantasy are more expensive and glossed over with a show of indifference and sophistication. But they are still escapes. Claude Estee puts a dead horse made of inflated rubber at the bottom of his swimming pool, and he and his friends visit a fancy bawdy house to see pornographic films with such titles as "Le Prédicament de Marie, ou La Bonne Distraite." He lives in an exact reproduction of an old southern mansion where he stands on the porch trying to look like a Civil War colonel and calling "Here, you black rascal! A mint julep," to a Chinese servant who comes up with a scotch and soda. Faye Greener's beauty is so overwhelming that she can be described only as a Botticelli Venus, "smiling a subtle half smile uncontaminated by thought . . . just born, everything moist and fresh, volatile and perfumed." Yet because her beauty is joined with no other virtue, she cannot find her life in the world and seeks it instead in daydreams built on

Hollywood plots. In her dream world she becomes a rich-young-girl cruising on her father's yacht in the South Seas. Engaged to a Russian count, she falls in love with a young sailor, and they alone are saved in the inevitable shipwreck. They swim to a desert island where she is attacked by a huge snake while bathing, etc., etc.

The major portion of *The Day of the Locust* is made up of a panorama in which each of these talented people "dies" in some fashion. Harry Greener literally dies of a bad heart, exhausted and feeling cheated because he never became the great actor he thought he was. Homer Simpson's dreams of love sour into hate. He ends by killing a most unpleasant small boy and is in turn torn apart by an excitement-seeking mob. Claude and Faye survive physically, but their abilities, thwarted, lead only to sterility and emptiness. Tod Hackett ends as a wailing madman after being caught in the maelstrom of the mob.

This is West's image of Hollywood, but, as Richard Gehman says, "West used Hollywood as a microcosm . . . because . . . everything that is wrong with life in the United States is to be found there in rare purity, and because the unreality of the business of making pictures seemed a most proper setting for his 'half world'."[2] The same point is made in *The Day of the Locust* where the people who come to California to die are described as the "cream of America's madmen" which is skimmed from a milk "just as rich as violence." West is not condemning all of American life but isolating and exposing in grotesque forms a peculiar danger or brand of dullness within it. This is, specifically, the peculiar emptiness of many people and lives, and the search for compensation in vicarious excitement and glamor. This appetite is always fed and sharpened by sensational newspapers, lurid writing, impossibly romantic movies, enthusiastic religions, health fads, and quackery of all kinds which trade on dullness, fear, and hatred. These substitutes for life, West shows, are necessarily illusions, and because they are such, they—like Jonson's alchemy or the contemporary half-world created by television and Madison Avenue—cannot but fail in the end to satisfy the impossible desires they have fed and fanned. When the inevitable drop to reality comes and it is discovered that sunshine, orange juice, and waves are not really very exciting, the cheated fools will turn to mobs and destroy civilizations to revenge themselves and "get a little fun out of life."

West offers no specific cure for these empty lives. In fact, like many satirists, he deliberately leaves any positive, reforming element out of his work in order to intensify the shrillness of the siren announcing disaster.

> If I put into *The Day of the Locust* any of the sincere, honest people who work . . . [in Hollywood] and are making such a great, progressive fight, those chapters couldn't be written satirically and the whole fabric of the peculiar half-world which I attempted to create would be badly torn by them . . . I believe there is a place for the fellow who yells fire and indicates where some of the smoke is coming from without actually dragging the hose to the spot.[3]

I doubt if West really had any cure, except the dynamite blast of satire, for the deep-seated ills which he isolates, but he did diagnose the disease and predict its course with remarkable accuracy. Because he believed in no traditional value systems, he could only denote the disease in pragmatic and symbolic terms. He could not say, for example, that men were wrong to try to escape from unsatisfactory lives because each man is created by God as a part of a great plan; nor could he argue that every man has his allotted work in society which, properly done, will be richly rewarding and serve the best interests of the society and the individual. But he could show again and again that while the phony may momentarily satisfy some desire for the impossible, that it can only disappoint more painfully, and dangerously, in the end. Eggs bathed in a rich cream-colored light in the supermarket can only turn out to be plain eggs when you get them home, and romantic dreams of passion and adventure lived in the darkness of the Bijou can only make more unsatisfactory the ordinary lives which inevitably begin again at the sidewalk.

The particular horror of West's satiric world is that in their search for romance the people who have come to California to die, and those who pander to their appetites, create such a grotesquely phony and pitifully illusionary world. Whatever they put their hand to is unreal, and unreality begins to build on unreality—furniture "painted to look like unpainted pine," or movie indians cracking jokes in fake German accents, "Vas you dere Sharley?" As the fake encrusts itself on the fake, obeying no law except the need for the novel, the result can only be fantastic disorder, combinations of things unrelated, great jumbles, and the division of those things which properly belong together. The search for glamor creates the strange dress of the Angelenos:

> Their sweaters, knickers, slacks, blue flannel jackets with brass buttons were fancy dress. The fat lady in the yachting cap was going shopping, not boating; the man in the Norfolk jacket and Tyrolean hat was returning, not from a mountain, but an insurance office; and the girl in slacks and sneaks with a bandanna around her head had just left a switchboard, not a tennis court. (Ch. I)

A dwarf in a high green Tyrolean hat, black shirt, and yellow tie may be an amusing, harmless kind of disorder, but the disintegration of architecture and a city into a dream world sounds a more serious note:

> Only dynamite would be of any use against the Mexican ranch houses, Samoan huts, Mediterranean villas, Egyptian and Japanese temples, Swiss chalets, Tudor cottages, and every possible combination of these styles that lined the slopes of the canyon.
>
> When he noticed that they were all of plaster, lath and paper, he was charitable and blamed their shape on the materials used. Steel, stone and brick curb a builder's fancy a little, forcing him to distribute his stresses and weights and to keep his corners plumb, but plaster and paper know no law, not even that of gravity.
>
> On the corner of La Huerta Road was a miniature Rhine castle with tarpaper turrets pierced for archers. Next to it was a little highly colored shack with domes and minarets out of the *Arabian Nights*. (Ch. I)

The dreams that know no law, not even such impersonal laws as gravity and complementary colors, also ignore the simple laws of chronology and distance. The movies which feed this hunger for romance make cheap pretenses and a jumbled heap—"a Sargasso of the imagination"—out of the long history of human efforts to achieve a civilization. Tod Hackett wanders through the "dream dump" of a studio lot, moving from a giant *papier mâché* sphinx across a manmade desert to the front of the Last Chance Saloon, from where he can see a conical grass hut in a jungle compound, a charging Arab on a white stallion, a truck loaded with snow and sled dogs, a Paris street, a Romanesque courtyard, and a group of people in riding costume eating cardboard food on a fiber lawn in front of a cellophane waterfall. Crossing a bridge, he comes to a "Greek temple dedicated to Eros. The god himself lay face downward in a pile of old newspapers and bottles." Tod moves on through a

> tangle of briars, old flats and iron junk, skirting the skeleton of a Zeppelin, a bamboo stockade, an adobe fort, the wooden horse of Troy, a flight of baroque palace stairs that started in a bed of weeds and ended against the branches of an oak, part of the Fourteenth Street elevated station, a Dutch windmill, the bones of a dinosaur, the upper half of the Merrimac, a corner of a Mayan temple, until he finally reached the road. (Ch. 18)

After this we can only ask, "What road?"

Not only does the search for dreams mangle history, making it impossible to believe in it or see in it such simple patterns even as enduring human courage or ingenuity; it fragments and jumbles the human character as well. *The Day of the Locust* is populated with strange inhuman mixtures and the broken wholes of men. A small child brought to Hollywood to win fame and fortune combines a childish innocence with phony adult manners, learned from the movies, such as bowing low and clicking his heels together when introduced. He moves his small body in a suggestive manner while dancing and singing sexy songs, which he does not understand. Men yearn to be women and croon lullabies to imaginary babies they pretend are real, and then they pretend to be men again. An incredibly beautiful young woman speaks always in the most vulgar tones and voices the most trivial of clichés. A "dried-up little man with the rubbed features and stooped shoulders of a postal clerk" pretends that he is a southern colonel and at the same time dresses in ivory shirts, black ties, red-checked trousers, and enormous rust-colored shoes.

This division of human nature becomes most apparent in Homer Simpson, the quiet hotel clerk who has wandered to Hollywood looking for health and for the love of which he is capable but can never find. He is described as large and muscular yet not looking strong or fertile. "He was like one of Picasso's great sterile athletes, who brood hopelessly on pink sand, staring at veined marble waves." He sleeps whenever he can, seeking in unconsciousness the peace he cannot find in the world. The disintegration of self which he has suffered is clearest in the disjunctive, awkward movements of his body, and particularly in his hands, which have become separated from the rest of his being:

> He got out of bed in sections, like a poorly made automaton, and carried his hands into the bathroom. He turned on the cold water. When the basin was full, he plunged his hands in up to the wrists. They lay quietly on the bottom like a pair of strange aquatic animals. When they were thoroughly chilled and began to crawl about, he lifted them out and hid them in a towel. (Ch. 8)

Beaten by a world where he cannot find or take what he needs, he retreats in on himself and coils back into the position of Uterine Flight. Then, in the final scene of the book, this kindly but ineffective man, frenzied by finding nothing but hatred and violence in people where he hoped for love and gentleness, turns into a savage murderer who stamps to death the small boy who throws a stone at him. Homer's simple dream of love and peace is more acceptable than the dreams of most of the people who come to California to die, but West's point would seem to be that Homer's is still a dream which, because it is not realistic and is therefore hopeless, leads to the same fragmentation and violence that grows from the more grotesque dreams of fame, passion, and adventure. The retreat into sleep to find peace is finally as fatal a dream as the visit to the movies to find love.

In *The Day of the Locust*, as in most satires, there is no consistent story and, therefore, by the usual standards, no plot. The narration does come back frequently to the life of a few major characters, and we are most often led on our tour of Hollywood by Tod Hackett. But the total effect is of phantasmagoria now thrusting forward a vaudeville act filled with brawny acrobats tossing a helpless clown about; then a shift to the charge of an army of extras up a plaster Mont St. Jean at Waterloo for the glory of Grotenstein Productions. We stop to watch a lizard emerge from a tin can and trap flies, pass on to a funeral, a scene on Hollywood Boulevard, and move in to look at the furnishings of a house. We attend the showing of a blue film in which all the members of a household attempt to seduce the maid, who is attempting to seduce the young daughter, and then move on to the Church of Christ Physical "where holiness was attained through the constant use of chestweights and spring grips." As disjunct as these scenes may seem to be, each shows the dream seekers searching for satisfaction and achieving only the flimsiest illusion, which in turn creates what is at first an amusing and then a terrifying disorder. This recurring movement from dream through illusion to disorder is the basic action of the novel. As these madmen search more and more feverishly for what is missing in their lives they turn all they touch to a mob. Clothing, furniture, architecture, history, the human personality are jumbled into monstrous collages, and under the pressure of the need for excitement and dreams every relationship, every ritual occasion, every social meeting turns to bedlam, babel, riot. A funeral becomes a sideshow as an Eskimo family, the Four Gingos, grunts in time to a record of Bach's chorale, "Come Redeemer, Our Savior," and the sensation-seekers pour in from the street to look at the corpse. A church service turns to a scene in a madhouse as a man "from one of the colonies in the desert near Soboba Hot Springs where he had been conning over his soul on a diet of raw fruit and nuts" explodes in anger against the wicked world:

> The message he had brought to the city was one that an illiterate anchorite might have given decadent Rome. It was a crazy jumble of dietary rules, economics, and Biblical threats. He claimed to have seen the Tiger of Wrath stalking the walls of the citadel and the Jackal of Lust skulking in the shrubbery, and he connected these omens with "thirty dollars every Thursday" and meat eating. (Ch. 19)

The search for amusement creates cock-fights in which one bird cuts another to pieces and then eats its eyes. A typical "party" ends with a dwarf, frantic with lust for the cold Venus, Faye Greener, being kicked in the stomach when he tries to break in between two dancers.

> The dwarf struggled to his feet and stood with his head lowered like a tiny ram. . . . He charged between Earle's legs and dug upward with both hands. Earle screamed with pain . . . then groaned and started to sink to the floor, tearing Faye's silk pajamas on his way down.
>
> Miguel grabbed . . . [the dwarf] by the throat. . . . Lifting the little man free, Miguel shifted his grip to his ankles and dashed him against the wall, like a man killing a rabbit against a tree. He swung the dwarf back to slam him again. (Ch. 23)

The pressure toward disorder evident in each of these

scenes is embodied in the episodic form of the novel, and it takes its final form in the great mob scene with which the book ends. Here, as in the scene of chaos and uncreation with which *The Dunciad* closes, all forms of dullness are gathered together to express their ultimate nature and to achieve the final shapelessness toward which they have been constantly moving. The crowd begins to gather to see the moving-picture stars arrive at a premiere at Khan's Persian Palace—"Mr. Khan a Pleasure Dome Decreed." As the people who came to California to die come up to the crowd they look "diffident, almost furtive," but once they enter it all their inhibitions are released and they become arrogant and pugnacious. The inevitable panders are present to stir the mixture more violently and amuse the folks at home who couldn't make it this year. Colored lights flash madly about, and a radio announcer stands above the crowd asking, in a high, hysterical voice broadcast over a national network and amplified for the benefit of those present, "can the police hold them? Can they? It doesn't look so, folks." The mob grows every moment, shoving, bulging, pushing, breaking out of any lines authority attempts to impose on it. Within, it mills about, stumbling and swirling and releasing the most primitive powers, hatred, lust, dislike for anyone different, and the desire to break and kill to avenge a life of emptiness.

Only a spark is needed to touch the mob off and release its full destructive power, and this comes when Homer Simpson, who has wandered into the crowd in a state of shock resulting from the loss of his own dream, kills the small boy who is tormenting him. One form of riot releases another: the rumor sweeps through the crowd that a pervert has attacked a child, and it explodes, surging and churning over all barriers. Homer is torn apart, Tod's leg is broken, an old man attacks a young girl pinned helpless by other bodies, men and women are crushed and trampled down. Here is "The Burning of Los Angeles," the great Vortex of Dulness sucking all down into nothingness, the final expression of the mob tendency.

Broken by the mob's awesome power, the satirist Tod Hackett goes mad. Taken to a police car, he begins to imitate the siren as loudly as he can. In the end the only style which the satirist can turn to is the wail sounding all the fires, bombings, accidents, and violences of a world which has tried to cure emptiness with illusion. [4]

Notes

1. Unpublished letter written in 1939 to George Milburn, quoted by Richard B. Gehman in his introduction to *The Day of the Locust* (New York, 1957), p. xx.
2. Gehman, p. xviii.
3. Letter to Jack Conroy, quoted by Gehman, pp. ix–x.
4. The progress in *The Day of the Locust* of the painter-satirist from realist, to painter of grotesques, to the loud wail of disaster is but one instance of the classic pattern which most satirists picture themselves as following. They usually begin as young idealists of some variety, who usually write love poetry or pastorals, but because the world is so gross and corrupt they are forced, if they wish to write truthfully, to abandon their pleasant verses and gentle ways for the writing of harsh, crabbed satire. Pope, for example, presents himself in this manner in the *Epistle to Dr. Arbuthnot* and in the *Epilogue to the Satires*. In the Renaissance the satirist was conventionally pictured as a disappointed scholar; see my *The Cankered Muse* (New Haven, 1959), pp. 17–18, 148.

R. W. B. LEWIS

From "Days of Wrath and Laughter"
Trials of the Word
1965, pp. 213–18

The world of *Miss Lonelyhearts* is an airlessly tight little island—Manhattan Island, in fact, plus a short stretch of countryside; a world so narrowed, in a novella so compressed, that its rhythms and tensions (which themselves are eschatological in nature and have to do with the last things) are well-nigh uncontainable. The novella moves unfalteringly between nightmare and actuality, its tone between horror and jesting; which is West's exemplary way of apprehending *our* world as under the dominion of a contemporary Antichrist. The human condition thus apprehended is characterized by a sort of absolute dis-order, by a dislocation observable pre-eminently in the relations of love, in almost every heterosexual and homosexual variety; but also a dislocation in man's other crucial relations—his relation to things, to words, to the rituals of life, to his own perennial aspirations. Human life, as depicted in *Miss Lonelyhearts*, has become a grotesque parody of itself; and the name of the book's Antichrist, Shrike, has the merit not only of meaning a toothbeaked bird of prey, but also of being as it were a parody of the name Christ, or Christ almost spelled backward. It is Shrike who rules over and preys upon an urban scene composed of the heartless, the violent, and the wretched. And it is Shrike who pits himself against the would-be imitator of Christ, the hapless columnist we know only by his pen name Miss Lonelyhearts, and whom Shrike torments in particular by spoken parodies of the Eucharist—that holy *communion* after which Miss Lonelyhearts so yearns. The central image of the novella, indeed, is a parody of the Gospel encounter between Christ and the Devil—in this case between a man, on the one hand, whose soul is sickened by a human misery he cannot assuage; and, on the other, the spokesman of an ice-cold and yet witty and intellectually brilliant inhumanity. In speech after speech, Shrike tempts and taunts Miss Lonelyhearts with vistas of grandeur, channels of escape, resources of compensation; until he drives the columnist to attempting the final absurd miracle. In a ludicrously ill-timed and feverish effort to embrace and hence to redeem by love at least one individual human victim—a crippled homosexual named Pete Doyle—Miss Lonelyhearts is accidentally shot and killed; and in the abrasively ironic eschatology of this novella, the field is left to the further machinations of the Antichrist. But Shrike, consummate satirist though he be, is at the same time an object of satire—that is, of West's satire—and the field of his triumph is no more than a frozen chaos.

The enlargement of setting in *A Cool Million* is suggested by this: that Miss Lonelyhearts is shot (in an obscure rooming house) not even by a man but, as though in its supreme revolt, by a thing, by the freakish explosion of a gun wrapped in a newspaper; while Lemuel Pitkin, whose gradual "dismantling" is half of the theme of *A Cool Million*, is shot by a hired assassin, "Operative 6348XM," during a huge political rally staged in New York by the National Revolutionary Party. The satire in *A Cool Million* is cruder and broader than in *Miss Lonelyhearts;* and West is not himself implicated in that which he satirizes, as he had been earlier. Still, while *A Cool Million* plays comical havoc with the Horatio Alger tradition and the American daydream of the easy surge upward to fame and fortune, it is also this country's most vigorous narrative vision of the political apocalypse—far more penetrating, for example, than the rather hastily contrived image which appeared the following year in Sinclair Lewis' *It Can't Happen Here.* The devil as the editor Shrike is succeeded in *A Cool Million* by the devil as national political Fuehrer: by Shagpoke Whipple, a more ambitious and amiable and even more completely fraudulent figure than his predecessor. The "mantling" of Shagpoke, former President and future dictator of the United States, is the other half of the book's theme; his loudmouthed and evidently interminable reign is just beginning as the story ends. On the national holiday commemorating young Lemuel's assassination, Whipple spells out his triumphant program to shouting thousands at a Fifth Avenue parade:

> The National Revolutionary Party [has] triumphed, and by that triumph this country was delivered from sophistication, Marxism and International Capitalism. Through the National Revolution its people were purged of alien diseases and America became again America.

This is a fine example of what Richard Hofstadter has defined as the paranoid style in American politics: a style historically based, as Mr. Hofstadter points out, on a most intensive apocalyptic outlook—a belief in some evil worldwide conspiracy, and identification of a wild conglomeration of elements as agencies of the Antichrist (communism, eastern capitalism, intellectual sophistication, and so on), a conviction of approaching disaster unless counteraction is swiftly taken.[1] West's complex achievement in *A Cool Million* is to satirize this apocalyptic temper in such a way as to show that it is itself the source of the potential catastrophe. But Mr. Hofstadter was talking primarily not about the political debaucheries of the 1930s, the actual scene of *A Cool Million*, but about the presidential campaign of 1964; and it is because that phenomenon is still so close to us that one finds it harder to laugh at Shagpoke's speech or at Shagpoke than it used to be. Yet, even as we are once again astonished at the capacity of life to follow slavishly in the wake of art, and as our admiration for West's prophetic power deepens into downright awe, we also become aware that the perspective in *A Cool Million* is exactly right. For in West's perspective of rough-hewn satire, the squalid reality of American fascism—the absurdities that pervade its spurious nostalgia and its venomous racism, its radical ignorance and contradictory assortment of fears—gets utterly exposed. What passes among the brutalized citizenry as the New Jerusalem is revealed to be a catastrophic vulgarity. And the very real menace, even as it is uncovered and defined, is in part overcome (insofar as a work of art can overcome anything) through the restoration of sanity by laughter.

But *The Day of the Locust* ⟨. . .⟩ is West's supreme Book of Revelations. This beautifully composed novel makes dreadfully and hilariously evident in the superb dance of its elements a threat beyond that of *A Cool Million:* a threat to the very roots of life in America, a threat as it were to the human nature of American humanity. It is a threat incarnate in a certain mass of people—bored, frustrated, vindictive, and moribund—who have come to California impelled by a dream of their own obscene millennium, by a sterile lust for some experience of violence that might exhilarate and revivify. They are disappointed—"nothing [could] ever be violent enough to make taut their slack minds and bodies"—and with a devouring sense of having been betrayed, they await the summons to provide out of themselves the violence denied. The summons begins to be audible in the animal roaring of a mob rioting outside a Hollywood theater as the novel ends.

Against that tremendous force of hatred—and for West, since love is the sign of spiritual grace, hatred, its polar opposite, is the defining quality of apostasy and damnation—West poses the allied powers of art and comedy. His hero is a young painter named Tod Hackett, presently employed as a set designer in Hollywood; a tougher-spirited Miss Lonelyhearts and a more self-protective Lemuel Pitkin. It is Tod who takes to studying the dead ferocity of the invaders, seeking them out in odd nooks and corners of the city, driven by a profound fascination with their "awful anarchic power" and determined to represent them on canvas. He finds them gathered, more than anywhere else, in the temples and churches, the lunatic-fringe cults of California; for one of the most terrible of the truths and prophecies disclosed in *The Day of the Locust* is the organic connection in America between radical religiosity, an extreme Protestantism gone finally insane, and the organized impulse of hatred and destruction.

> As [Tod] watched these people writhe on the hard seats of their churches, he thought of how well Alessandro Magnasco would dramatize the contrast between their drained-out feeble bodies and their wild disordered minds. He would not satirize them as Hogarth and Daumier might, nor would he pity them. He would paint their fury with respect, appreciating its awful, anarchic power, and aware that they had it in them to destroy civilization.

Nathanael West does not precisely satirize them either; despite its carefully wrought poetic intensity, *The Day of the Locust* stays closer to a palpable historical reality than his other fictions. The tone and movement of the novel are comic, nonetheless, and both are suited to a world in which, due to the utter instability of its outward forms, everything is on the verge of giving way.

The scene upon which the locusts descend is a scene made up of masqueraders and impostors; of movie actors dressed up as French and British generals and of ordinary citizens dressed up as Tyrolean hunters. Even plants and natural phenomena are fictitious: cactus plants are made of rubber and cork; a hill on a movie set, as it collapses, spills the nails and rips the canvas of which it is composed. A world so grotesquely insubstantial is ripe for conquest; and yet within its atmosphere, the wrath to come can be contemplated with just that drunken and hazily amused equanimity that Tod Hackett expresses when, lying on his back in a clump of wild mustard, he thinks about the invasion of California by "the cream of America's madmen" and feels certain that "the milk from which it had been skimmed was just as rich in violence. The Angelenos would be first, but their comrades all over the country would follow. There would be civil war." That antic Armageddon, however, takes place not quite in the actual rioting and lynching and sexual assaults of the final scene; but, rather, in an interpretive work of art, in the painting (and it is to be a great painting, West clearly wants us to believe) Tod Hackett is meticulously projecting on the last page, even as he is being mauled and half-crushed by the frenzied mob.

Thus superimposed in thought above the actual disorders, the painting—it will be called "The Burning of Los Angeles"—will eventually explain and comment upon the apocalypse it describes by the patterned juxtaposition of its elements. It will show a "mob carrying baseball bats and torches" down a long hill street, a mob that includes "the cultists of all sorts" whom Tod had been observing—"all those poor devils who can only be stirred by the promise of miracles, and then only to violence." Now, "no longer bored, they sang and danced joyously in the red light of the flames," following the leader who "had made the necessary promise"; "they were marching behind his banner in a great united front of screwballs and screwboxes to purify the land." Elsewhere on the canvas, various postures suggest various responses to that savage absurd Puritanism: a girl running naked in smiling mindless panic; a man named Claude turning to thumb his nose; Tod himself pausing to throw stones at the mob like a small boy. Nose thumbing and stone throwing are commendable acts of derision; but Tod's major response is of course his painting, just as West's major response is the novel that contains it. And both painting and novel fulfill their purpose by portraying these maddened humans, whirling forward in their orgiastic dance, as devils who are yet poor devils, seized by a fury of hatred which is as silly as it is explosive.

Notes

1. *Harper's Magazine*, November, 1964.

JONATHAN RABAN
"A Surfeit of Commodities: The Novels of Nathanael West"
The American Novel and the Nineteen Twenties
eds. Malcolm Bradbury and David Palmer
1971, pp. 215–31

If Nathanael West did not exist, then Leslie Fiedler would probably have had to invent him. For West, after a couple of decades of critical *purdah*, has become a necessary figment of American literary mythology. Indeed, flicking over the pages of the *PMLA* bibliographies of the last ten years, one might reasonably assume that West's bones had long ago been picked clean by the assistant professors and their assiduous graduate students. The arrival, in the mid fifties, of what is now confidently termed 'the comic apocalyptic novel', occasioned an evangelical wave of ancestor baptism. In the search to legitimize recent writers like Joseph Heller, Terry Southern, Thomas Pynchon, Thomas Berger and the young novelist Edward Stewart (whose *Heads* strikes me as a very clever pastiche of the Westian style), West has been posthumously credited with a wonderfully virile and promiscuous talent for parenthood. Like most mythical figures, his powers have been variously, and exaggeratedly labelled: First American Surrealist, Sick Comedian, Dreamdumper, Nightmarist, Social Critic (of all things), Laughing Mortician. And for the mythmakers, West had an almost embarrassing abundance of convenient attributes: he was a Jew who renounced his religion; he was briefly expatriated during the twenties; he went the right distance out to the political left in the thirties; he worked in, and wrote about, Hollywood; he died young in a violent accident at the end of the decade. His four short, wildly uneven novels are a beachcomber's paradise; a junkshop of part-worn, part-used symbols and literary references. He is the indispensable minor modern novelist: once neglected, but now fully restored; use him anywhere, handy for your book or thesis. Especially suitable for Despair, Comedy and Violence.

Leslie Fiedler, who, along with Alan Ross in Britain, was among the first to open a West stall in the literary bazaar, puts the basic ingredients of the myth beautifully in *Waiting for the End:*

> He is the inventor for America of a peculiarly modern kind of book, whose claims are perfectly ambiguous. Reading his fiction, we do not know whether we are being presented with a nightmare endowed with the lineaments of reality, or with reality blurred to the uncertainty of nightmare. In either case, he must be read as a comic novelist, and his anti-heroes understood as comic characters, still as much *shlemiels* as any imagined by Fuchs, though they are presented as sacrificial victims, the only Christs possible in our skeptical world. In West, however, humor is expressed almost entirely in terms of the grotesque, which is to say, on the borderline between jest and horror; for violence is to him technique as well as subject matter, tone as well as theme.

Reading Fiedler, like reading most recent critics of West who tend slavishly to echo him, we hardly know whether we are being presented with a novelist and his actual work, or with a plausible diagram of a certain kind of writer, and a certain kind of literary technique, which arguably *ought* to exist somewhere in the labyrinth of recent American fiction. In the literary histories and the books on the modern novel, West most frequently exists as a cipher for a style which is far more readily identifiable with, say, Thomas Pynchon's *V.* than with his own *Miss Lonelyhearts*. And in the earnest exegetical articles, symbolist explication of West's novels has gone into a wonderland of its own, full of failed Christs, illusions masquerading as realities, phallic guns and hatchets, ritual deaths and *shlemiels* galore. But all that is a long way away from the spikey, spoiled surface of the novels, themselves, with their short sentences facetiously pursuing their own metaphors into absurdity; their desperate patter of gags working their way through the prose like a nervous tic; characters like cartoons in livid crayon; everywhere an atmosphere of the kind of surrealism which might have been rigged up by an enterprising handyman in his back garden. Nowhere can the jitterbugging craze have worked itself into the texture of literature so successfully as in the frantic phrasing of West's style.

It's a profoundly maimed style; as unambiguous as a shriek. West's work is pathetically incomplete: re-reading his novels one watches again and again as the shrill personality of the author extrudes from behind the papery mask of his assumed style. With most novelists of a comparable public stature, the work is larger, more rounded, than the biography which produced it; with West, one needs biography in order to understand the peculiar hiatuses, the grammatical breaks, the awkwardnesses and the often uncontrolled hysteria of a fictional *œuvre* that has been fractured, even ruined, by its own history.

West seemed destined to miss every available boat. He was six years younger than Hemingway, eight years younger than Fitzgerald; and by the time he graduated from college and joined the colony of expatriates in Paris, his near-contemporaries were already established writers. He was an awkward, gangling figure with an acned face, who aspired to Brooks Brothers suits and the latest dance steps. He had neither the glamour of Hemingway's war service and apprenticeship as a newspaperman, nor the polish of Fitzgerald's Ivy Leaguery. Brown University in the early twenties sounds like a dull, coltishly provincial establishment, where the sons of the small-professional and commercial middle class acted out a hammed pastiche of the Harvard-and-Princeton style. Worst, West was a Jew; he was born Nathan Wallenstein Weinstein, and grew up in a period when to be Jewish was to be stigmatized as a Robert Cohn, or one of Pound's Usurers, or Eliot's 'The jew squats on the windowsill, the owner, / Spawned in some estaminet of Antwerp . . .' No Weinstein could join any of the fraternity clubs at Brown, or participate easily in the confident protestantism of the literary tone of the twenties. And West had an agonising sense of social propriety. He seems to have spent his time at Brown developing an edgy, imitative style that would hide his Jewishness under his Coca-Cola nickname of 'Pep'. John Sanford, who knew West in New York, wrote of him:

> More than anyone I ever knew Pep writhed under the accidental curse of his religion. . . . He changed his name, he changed his clothes, he changed his manners (we all did), in short he did everything possible to create the impression in his own mind—remember that, in his own mind—that he was just like Al Vanderbilt. It never quite came off. [1]

Part of the Al Vanderbilt act consisted of West playing the country squire, surrounded by gun-dogs and toting a twelve-bore with which he was a spectacularly careless and inaccurate shot. He was an urban Jew who tried to storm WASP America with endless frantic mimicry; it's hard to miss the obsessive, yearning inadequacy which characterized his life style—a desperation channelled into the relentless acquisition of social masks. Dance floor lizard, home-town Raskolnikov, Paris bohemian (on a parental allowance), hotel clerk, hunter, movie writer . . . Whatever West did seemed to take on the characteristics of a theatrical role; a part to be learned and played out with slightly over-large gestures. Deeply embedded in his novels is the notion of life as a kind of vulgar, snobbish vaudeville show. Certainly West himself was adept at the painful clowning in which the touring performer gets up in rouge and worn white slicker suit, to go through a travesty of the high-life style.

He was, prototypically, a marginal man, perched uneasily on the edge of his society. His acute sense of social conformity led him into an infatuation with the values of the twenties which was so overdone that it turned insidiously into conscious parody. At the same time he inflected his own contortions with shrill, self-destructive irony; he was simultaneously inside and out, passionately involved in his own activity, yet able to mock it with a ribald series of Bronx cheers. In West's early work, the social style that one recognizes from the anecdotes of his classmates at Brown is readily turned into a literary trick—indeed becomes, at first, his sole piece of literary equipment.

In an unpublished, semi-autobiographical story called 'L'Affaire Beano', he treated the experience of expatriation in a tone of such bland condescension that the writing itself becomes merely a crude mode of exorcism:

> 'In order to be an artist one has to live like one.' We know now that this is nonsense, but in Paris in '25 and '26 we didn't know it. 'Artists are crazy' is another statement from the same credo. Of course all these ideas were foisted on us by the non-artists, but we didn't realize it then. We came to the business of being an artist with the definitions of the non-artists and took libels for the truth. In order to be recognized as artists, we were everything our enemies said we were.
>
> By the time I got to Paris, the business of being an artist had grown quite difficult. . . . When I got to Montparnasse, all the obvious roles had either been dropped or were being played by experts. But I made a lucky hit. Instead of trying for strangeness, I formalized and exaggerated the costume of a bond salesman. I wore carefully pressed Brooks Brothers clothing, sober but rich ties, and carried gloves and a tightly rolled umbrella. My manners were elaborate and I professed great horror at the slightest breach of the conventional. It was a success. I was asked to all the parties. [2]

The confident air is too exaggerated; the inclusive use of 'we' too strident. West adopts a strategy of unearned absurdity: by reducing everything to short, slangy sentences, phrased in glib generalities, he achieves a thin horse-laugh at the expense of the narrator, of Paris, of the whole generation embodied in that sweeping 'we'. The passage exhibits a barely-veiled hysteria; it is *about* authorial distance; one feels West frantically disengaging himself from his subject, reaching for a language that is cool, urbane, above all, knowing. But West doesn't know when to stop, and the effect is blatantly unconvincing.

When West stepped off the boat from France, he had the manuscript of *The Dream Life of Balso Snell* in his valise. Talking to A. J. Liebling, he said that he had written his first novel as 'a protest against writing books'. Both the remark and the book itself are of a piece with West's nervously brash social style. *The Dream Life of Balso Snell* filters the figureheads of modernism—Dostievsky, Huysmans, Dada, Joyce—through the vulgarity of undergraduate revue. It is an impertinent satire, remarkably devoid of cunning, and maintains a consistent, irritating air of cocking a snook at the teachers, as West flails inaccurately around his pond of fashionable names. The core material of the novel was apparently in existence by 1924, when West lent an *ur-Balso* manuscript to Quentin Reynolds, to use as a crib for a Spring Day speech. The surprise is that West could continue living with his skittish ephemerid until 1931, when the book was finally published.

Its optimistic target was to demolish western culture with a snigger; its effect is to set in motion the lineaments of a style of contrived bogusness—a style which, in *Miss Lonelyhearts* and *The Day of the Locust*, was to be sharpened into a literary weapon of considerable force and subtlety. For the intestines of the wooden horse, where *Balso Snell* takes place, contain the remains of a stew of partially digested rhetorics. The characters—John Raskolnikov Gilson, Miss McGeeney, Maloney the Areopagite—are ciphers enclosed by the platitudes of their own languages. Together they compose a kind of Bartholomew Fair of social and cultural clichés.

It is quite clear that West had little intention of satirizing his modern humours in any detail. The parodies of *Balso Snell* are parodies of parodies; they work on schoolboy notions of 'literary English', 'avant garde writing', 'religious rhetoric' and so on. When West turns on specific authors, he assimilates them into a childish convention; as in the garbled pastiche of Molly Bloom's soliloquy at the book's end:

> Hard-bitten. Casual. Smart. Been there before. I've had policemen. No trace of a feminine whimper. Decidedly revisiting well-known, well-ploughed ground. No new trees, wells, or even fences.
>
> Desperate for life. Live! Experience! Live one's own. Your body is an instrument, an organ or a drum. Harmony. Order. Breasts. The apple of my eye, the pear of my abdomen. What is life without love? I burn! I ache! Hurrah!
>
> Moooompitcher yaaaah. Oh I never hoped to know the passion, the sensuality hidden within you—yes, yes. Drag me down into the mire, drag. Yes! And with your hair the lust from my eyes brush. Yes . . . Yes . . . Ooh! Ah!

Its badness is at least partially deliberate. For West's writing, by its very lack of satiric specificity, forces us to attend, not to the thing parodied (in this case *Ulysses*), but to the chaotic detritus of a consciousness brutally assaulted by this mess of styles, names, lists of objects. The random breaks, the structurelessness, the noisy nonsense, the constant posing of *Balso Snell* go to make up the actual subject of the book. And West is very good at recreating the stimuli of physical nausea as he lets his language cascade into a trough of absurdities. Again and again we are deluged by a style of gratuitous enumeration, as sentences reduplicate themselves in a runaway rhetoric, as repetitive as the flow of identical articles off an assembly line:

> 'And Death?—bah! What, then, is there still detaining you in this vale of tears?' Can it be that the only thing that bothers me in a statement of this sort is the wording? Or is it because there is something arty about Suicide? Suicide: Werther, the Cosmic Urge, the Soul, the Quest, and Otto Greenbaum, Phi Beta Kappa, Age seventeen—Life is unworthy of him; and Haldington Knape, Oxford, author, man-about-town, big game hunter—Life is too tiresome; and Terry Kornflower, poet, no hat, shirt open to the navel—Life is too crude; and Janey Davenport, pregnant, unmarried, jumps from a studio window in Paris—Life is too difficult . . .

Here is a style of writing which sets out to prove its own sogginess, its own inadequacy under the pressure of the objects which it is forced to catalogue platitudinously. The failed surface of *Balso Snell* represents West's attempt to exhibit language and a sensibility which have been raped to a point of retching exhaustion.

As a satire, *Balso Snell* is a pretentious flop. But as the inauguration of a style, it is an auspicious technical essay, marred by grandiose overreaching and by the intrusive uncertainty of the author. For West himself shows up anxiously every few pages, nudging the reader in the ribs, all too ready to explain just what he's trying to do. The book is full of passages with the ring of deadly earnestness about them:

> An intelligent man finds it easy to laugh at himself, but his laughter is not sincere if it is not thorough. If I could be Hamlet, or even a clown with a breaking heart 'neath his jester's motley, the role would be tolerable. But I always find it necessary to burlesque the mystery of feeling at its source; I must laugh at myself, and if the laugh is 'bitter', I must laugh at the laugh. The ritual of feeling demands burlesque and, whether the burlesque is successful or not, a laugh. . . .

This poses real problems. On the one hand, West cursorily tries to incorporate the passage itself with the other exhausted rhetorics of the book, by quotating 'bitter' and slipping in the phrase about the broken hearted clown (then overdoing it with the archaism "neath'); on the other, he allows it to stand as a *propria persona* statement. For a book as bland in its general approach as *Balso Snell*, such lapses act as remarkable confessions of insecurity. They work like distress signals, shouts for help from the centre of a muddle he clearly doesn't fully understand. He becomes the victim of his own lucidity; his language runs away with him, as if the mask had commandeered the face behind.

For West's novels, though they aspire to burlesque and laughter, rarely manage to climb out of that state of anxious self-scrutiny. His second book, *Miss Lonelyhearts* (1933), is frequently credited with being West's most assured and controlled piece of fiction; if that is true, it is only because he had learned to incorporate his uncertainty into the design and texture of his writing. Originally he was going to subtitle *Miss Lonelyhearts: A novel in the form of a comic strip*—and the tautness of that initial idea has stayed with the book, in its use of short illustrative chapters, stylized language and primary-coloured locations. The comic strip gives the novel its extraordinarily rapid tempo; working on West like a harness, so that his tendencies towards diversive extravaganza are kept firmly in check. But the apparent single-mindedness of *Miss Lonelyhearts* is deceptive: an uneasy tension throbs away in the novel, just under its carefully polished surface. (It is indicative of West's painstaking care with the book that he rewrote it more than six times: and, when working on it full-time, produced only 700–1,000 words a week.)

Like *Balso Snell*, *Miss Lonelyhearts* presents us with a menagerie of rhetorics; between them they make up a splintered portrait of a society that has become consumed by its own clichés. At the same time it is a novel which explores the possibility that the conventions of the Novel—its machinery of 'plot' and 'character' and psychological tensions and development—have been made unworkable by the urban industrial world of pulp media and cheapjack commodities. West does not merely create 'two-dimensional' characters; he attempts to obliterate the notion of character altogether. For the people in *Miss Lonelyhearts*—Desperate, Broken-hearted, Sick-of-it-all, Mr. and Mrs. Doyle, Shrike, Betty and the rest—act simply as labels on which to stick a jaded, received language of sickening platitudes. The book basically belongs to them; it is their confusing and contradictory *noise* which assaults both the reader and Miss Lonelyhearts.

What then of Miss Lonelyhearts himself? The first phrase of the novel is 'The Miss Lonelyhearts of the New York *Post-Dispatch* . . .' and West never fully allows him to disambiguate himself from that definite, but inanimate, article. He is a function; a vibrating diaphragm set in the centre of the communications business, as stereotyped in his available roles as the voices which beset him. He is described once in the book, and the description is made in such generic terms that it almost becomes a parodic satire on the convention of bodying-out the central 'character' in all his particularities:

> Although his cheap clothes had too much style, he still looked like the son of a Baptist minister. A beard would become him, would accent his Old-Testament look. But even without a beard no one could fail to recognize the New England puritan. His forehead was high and narrow. His nose was long and fleshless. His bony chin was shaped and cleft like a hoof.

Compare this with the other descriptions in the book: of Shrike, 'Under the shining white globe of his brow, his features huddled together in a dead, gray triangle'; of Mr. Doyle, 'He looked like one of those composite photographs used by screen magazines in guessing contests'; of Mrs. Doyle, 'Legs like Indian clubs, breasts like balloons and a brow like a pigeon.' In all cases, the similes are there, not to illuminate, but to deaden the character. West robs each of them of any recognizably human attributes, and turns them into things. The language they speak is the mass-produced grammar and vocabulary of the newspaper, the magazine, the movie. Not only are they likened to objects, but on occasions become confused with objects. Thus in the chapter, 'Miss Lonelyhearts and the Party Dress', Miss Lonelyhearts begins by encountering Betty (a splendid talking doll out of a woman's weekly) person-to-person, then slides rapidly, through a dialogue of resounding banality, into an object-to-object relationship:

> He begged the party dress to marry him, saying all the things it expected to hear, all the things that went with strawberry sodas and farms in Connecticut. He

> was just what the party dress expected him to be: simple and sweet, whimsical and poetic, a trifle collegiate yet very masculine.

This technique of synecdoche turns Shrike into a talking newspaperman's eyeshade, with his glibly cynical spiels; Doyle becomes merely an extension of his enormous cripple's shoe; and Miss Lonelyhearts himself grows into a walking evangelist's soapbox. By reducing his characters to these formulae West deadens our expectations of human sympathy or change: deeply rooted in the novel is the suggestion that the only way in which we can be surprised or moved is by the introduction of things so shocking or grotesque that they transcend all normal social categories. And this is the function of the letters—

> *I sit and look at myself all day and cry. I have a big hole in the middle of my face that scares people even myself so I cant blame the boys for not wanting to take me out. My mother loves me, but she crys terrible when she looks at me.*

The only alternative to cliché is illiteracy; the only alternative to the conditioned social responses of the Shrikes and the Mrs. Doyles is gross deformity. But we should, I think, be honest enough to admit that the letters rise to such a level of crude extremity that they are merely funny. The predicaments to which they refer are so unimaginably awful that one takes refuge in the comic-proletarian humour of bad spelling and impossible grammar. If we are shocked by, say, the first or second letter in the book, they soon become a convention as predictable as Betty's homely flutings. The girl with the hole in the middle of her face turns, along with all the other characters in the book, into just another cliché. What is truly shocking is our own incapacity to respond to, or to make sense of, the human confusion which the novel appears to enact.

I say 'appears to' because *Miss Lonelyhearts* works like a baited trap; it assaults the reader with extremities, then leaves him wondering, embarrassedly, about his own emotional inadequacy in the face of this battering. But West effectively prevents us from responding by deliberately deadening his characters and by turning even the most bizarre rhetorics in the book into cliché. What is real in the novel is the procession of images which focus, not on any fictional predicament inhabited by the characters, but on the dilemma of West the writer, the unwilling creator of this perverse menagerie.

For the central tone of the narrative is one of jokey circumspection; it pries, investigates, works in beautifully sharp visual flashes, constantly counterpointing the violent hysteria of the novel's social world. In the second chapter, for instance, Miss Lonelyhearts crosses a park on his way to the speakeasy:

> He entered the park at the North Gate and swallowed mouthfuls of the heavy shade that curtained its arch. He walked into the shadow of a lamp-post that lay on the path like a spear. It pierced him like a spear.

One is brought up sharp by that last sentence; it looks like a facetious indulgence, a piece of verbal by-play for which there shouldn't be room in a passage supposedly centring on Miss Lonelyhearts' agony over the desperation of his correspondents' lives. But in *Miss Lonelyhearts* there always is room; the narrative continually steps back and films in sardonic slow motion. In the middle of a violent row with Betty—

> He began to shout at her, accompanying his shouts with gestures that were too appropriate, like those of an old-fashioned actor.

The narrative is positively garrulous in its readiness to stop by the way and chat, throwing in eloquent, but static, similes. Its effect is to make the social situation both trivial and unreal; it offers an alternative world of objects and exact descriptions—a world of concretes: bottles ranged above a bar, the colour of tobacco smoke, a flapping newspaper, flagstones, clothes, domestic implements. Throughout the novel, West constantly shifts from his object-like people to objects themselves, which he treats with relish. His imagery is invariably more alive than the characters who occasion it, as if the ordering process of writing were of far greater importance than the people and events out of which novels are usually, if unfortunately, made.

The reader of *Miss Lonelyhearts* becomes its proto-author; his central problem is to shape the hectic and confused voices of the book into the stylized patterns offered him by West. The subject of the novel becomes the desperate play of sensibility as it attempts to reconcile the noisy, heterogeneous fragments of a mass-media world. The images become more contorted, to the point of growing surreal; the noises get louder; the paper characters dance frenziedly on the spot. But our attention remains fixed on the jugglery of West, the most psychologically convincing character in the novel, as he tries to keep all those multiple, crude voices and objects in balance. The trouble is that West seems to be in love with his own failure. The grotesquerie of the letters, of Miss Lonelyhearts' eventual death at the hands of Doyle, of the snatched sex and casual speakeasy brutality in the book, is carried out with a kind of sadistic delight. West's tone, as he transforms his people into mechanical devices or exhibits their pathetically stereotyped rhetorics, is never less than gay. He, not Miss Lonelyhearts, is the failed hero of the novel; he subsides under its pressures like an old-style tragedian, waving his arms and bellowing with obvious enjoyment.

As a novelist, West establishes himself by destroying his own creations with the easily-won indifference of a god. He grossly indulged himself in *A Cool Million* (1934), accurately subtitled, 'The Dismantling of Lemuel Pitkin'; an extended act of writer's vengeance on the notions of 'character' and 'society'. By reducing his hero to an innocent who is even flatter and more simple-minded than Alger's Ragged Dick, and by turning American fascism into a society more lurid than that of most horror comics, West gives himself the opportunity to write in a vein of extraordinary nastiness:

> He also made an unsuccessful attempt to find Mr. Whipple. At the Salvation Army post they told him that they had observed Mr. Whipple lying quietly in the gutter after the meeting of the 'Leather Shirts', but that when they looked the next day to see if he were still there they found only a large blood stain. Lem looked himself but failed even to find this stain, there being many cats in the neighbourhood.

One would surely have to be very insensitive indeed to find this humorous; it goes considerably further than the letters in *Miss Lonelyhearts* in its direct exploitation of a literary trick, enabled only by the complete unreality of the fictional characters and situations involved. There is a totalitarian streak in West's writing; a tendency to turn his novels into Charentons, where he can victimize his witless characters at his pleasure. For a novelist, it seems an odd revenge.

And West appears to have realized this in the five years that followed before the publication of *The Day of the Locust* (1939). In Tod Hackett, the Tiresias-like artist through whose eyes we see the waste land of Hollywood, West partially embodied his own predicament as a writer. When he first encounters Homer Simpson, the retired hotel clerk from Iowa, on the landing of the San Bernardino Arms, he behaves remarkably like West's authorial persona:

> Tod examined him eagerly. He didn't mean to be rude but at first glance this man seemed an exact model for the kind of person who comes to California to die, perfect in every detail down to fever eyes and unruly hands.

Through Tod, West is able to inflect his own aesthetic sadism with a degree of irony. But West and Tod jockey for position in the novel, and it's often difficult to determine who is in control where. So, after the marvellous description of Hollywood as a landscape of pure artifice and simulation, the last paragraph of chapter one reads:

> It is hard to laugh at the need for beauty and romance, no matter how tasteless, even horrible, the results of that need are. But it is easy to sigh. Few things are sadder than the truly monstrous.

Its tone is both apologetic and sententious. Does it belong to Tod or West? It reads like most professions of sentiment in West's fiction, as if it ought to go into quotation marks, yet its positioning in the chapter suggests that it is an authentic narrative voice which we must accept if we are to continue to collaborate with the novel. In combination with the passage describing Tod's specimen-hunting approach to Homer Simpson, it is a strong indicator of West's unease. In *The Day of the Locust,* he covers himself both ways by creating a promiscuous irony with which to ambiguate almost everything in the book.

The structure of *The Day of the Locust* is that of an exactly timed series of improvizations. It is built round its set-pieces: two celluloid battles, a Hollywood party, a cheap rooming house inhabited by the dreamers, a funeral, a cockfight and a gala première. Each of these major scenes are 'long shots'; they display the characters at a distance and treat them through a filter of imagery that rubs out their individual details and emphasizes their generic characteristics. They are balanced by interlinking flashback-biographies and close-ups which continually test the individual characters against the large thematic patterns proposed by Tod as he assembles the material for his painting, 'The Burning of Los Angeles', and tacitly underwritten by West. This dialectical structure works smoothly and eloquently; for the first time, West is able to use the Novel as mode of exploration rather than flat statement.

More powerfully than ever before, the destruction of character grows organically out of the texture of the fiction. The magnificently realized location of Hollywood—the lurid illusions of the studio lot and the Cape Cod colonial house in paper and plaster, the antiseptic smelling corridors of the San Bernardino Arms, the sickly, pervasive heat in which Harry Greener peddles his cans of home-made polish, the mawkish kitsch of the Californian way of love and death—provides a backdrop of epic dimensions, against which the characters scuttle pitifully, reduced to twitching puppets by the overpowering articulacy of their environment. And West manages his structural devices with a new cunning. In the fourth chapter, for instance, he alternates between brief, cruel portraits of the guests at Claude Estee's party and their tinny dialogues; then, just when the rhythm of the section demands a new portrait of a partygoer, West introduces the black mass at the bottom of the darkened swimming pool:

> A row of submerged floodlights illuminated the green water. The thing was a dead horse, or, rather, a life-size, realistic reproduction of one. Its legs stuck up stiff and straight and it had an enormous distended belly. Its hammerhead lay twisted to one side and from its mouth, which was set in an agonized grin, hung a heavy, black tongue.

It is perfectly timed, and the party never recovers from the insidious suggestion of that passage: the twisted penis and the hanging tongue carry, like sustained bass notes, into the next chapter, where the party migrates to a brothel to watch blue movies.

In *The Day of the Locust,* the shifts of tone are rapid and unexpected; West darts in and out of his characters like a skilled saboteur. Describing Homer Simpson's move into his cottage, he spends four paragraphs of neutral narrative, in which the reader is allowed temporarily to inhabit Homer as a character, before shifting, through an intermediary paragraph, into a passage of brilliantly managed detachment:

> He got out of bed in sections, like a poorly made automaton, and carried his hands in to the bathroom. He turned on the cold water. When the basin was full, he plunged his hands in up to the wrists. They lay quietly on the bottom like a pair of strange aquatic animals. When they were thoroughly chilled and began to crawl about, he lifted them out and hid them in a towel.

This is far more fully developed, and less flashy, than the comparable images of *Miss Lonelyhearts.* Almost every character in the novel—Abe Kusich, the dwarf who is initially mistaken for a pile of soiled laundry; the cowboy, Earle Shoop, who has 'a two-dimensional face that a talented child might have drawn with a ruler and compass'; Harry Greener who behaves like an overwound mechanical toy when he has his first heart attack—is transmuted into the kind of object that can be found on the garbage dumps of an industrial society. But West does not simply leave it at that; he gathers the threads of his images together to project them into a large and complete metaphor of estrangement. In Hollywood, the dreams are faked in the studios; the houses are faked on the hillsides; emotions are faked (consciously and with style) in Harry Greener's music hall routines; religion, and even death, are faked by the funeral industry (where Harry's shaved and rouged corpse is made to look 'like the interlocutor in a minstrel show'); and people are faked in a relentless process of image-making. The novel itself works like a production line; it takes the scattered ingredients of a recognizably real Hollywood and turns them into the hard, bright patterns of cheap industrial design.

For West never allows us to lose sight of the artifice of his own novel; his carefully managed structure is often deliberately obtrusive. One watches the novelist keep Harry Greener alive until the time is ripe for the funeral; then West, without warning, snuffs him out. And Tod's insistent interior monologues, as he collects characters and bits and pieces for his painting, are a way of reminding us that it is the process of the novel that is at stake; the characters and their situations are merely the bundles of hair and leaves and mud out of which the glittering structure may be composed. The final effect is of a lunatic baroque edifice which stuns the onlooker with its sheer brazenness, its air of suffocating overpopulation. *The Day of the Locust* obsessively accumulates its details; characters are switched into objects and added to the pile; objects themselves take on a bizarrely vivid life of their own; the landscape of Los Angeles is broken down into a heap of brightly painted junk. The apocalyptic finale, when the rioting mob lynch Homer Simpson, is both a description and an encapsulation of the process of the novel: the heat, stench, frustration and noise of a packed crowd is expanded to breaking point.

Then one is left only with a quietened shuffle of people round an ambulance, while the artist goes into an hysterical imitation of the sound of its klaxon.

West never got beyond that point. His unease is taken to the edge of hysteria and left there. On the one hand there is the shrill confidence of his imagery, the harshly didactic rhythm of his sentences. He strains all the time for a literary voice that will carry the ring of the stern authoritarian, and rules his novels like a dictator. On the other, there is a strain of excruciatingly evident insecurity. His irony teeters between the gross (as in *A Cool Million*) and the nervously diffuse. His style of masquerade slips frequently into lapses of embarrassing earnestness. He is, pre-eminently, the novelist as victim.

West's fictional world is essentially one of objects, of commodities. When people enter it they become transfixed and assimilated into the dime-store jumble of parti-coloured rubbish. On this account, West is often called a surrealist (a title which he himself vehemently rejected). And, clearly, there are deliberate echoes of Huysmans's *A Rebours* in all of West's novels; the glutted consciousness, fed to the point of nausea with sensations, images, people, things, which forms the centre of each narrative often seems exactly like a coarsened and vulgarized version of Des Esseintes. It is almost as if Huysmans's hero had lived into the post-war boom of industrial manufacturing, and found his dreams on sale at every Woolworths'. But this is why West's work is a far cry from European surrealism; his wildly juxtaposed objects always belong to an explicitly commercial context. The passage most frequently quoted as evidence for his 'surrealism' is that section from *Miss Lonelyhearts* in which Betty and Shrike compete for the fevered columnist's soul. Lying ill in bed—

> He found himself in the window of a pawnshop full of fur coats, diamond rings, watches, shotguns, fishing tackle, mandolins. All these things were the paraphernalia of suffering. A tortured high light twisted on the blade of a gift knife, a battered horn grunted with pain . . .
>
> A trumpet, marked to sell for $2.49, gave the call to battle and Miss Lonelyhearts plunged into the fray. First he formed a phallus of old watches and rubber boots, then a heart of umbrellas and trout flies, then a diamond of musical instruments and derby hats, after these a circle, triangle, square, swastika. But nothing proved definitive and he began to make a gigantic cross. When the cross became too large for the pawnshop, he moved it to the shore of the ocean. There every wave added to his stock faster than he could lengthen its arms. His labours were enormous. He staggered from the last wave line to his work, loaded down with marine refuse—bottles, shells, chunks of cork, fish heads, pieces of net.

It is too easy merely to see that here are the lineaments of a painting by Ernst or Dali. We shouldn't miss the fact that the vision starts in a pawnshop; that the objects over which Miss Lonelyhearts exercises his sickened imagination are either pieces of rubbish or things in hock. West turns his hero into a crazed consumer, haphazardly patterning the goods on display; his revulsion is focussed on a peculiarly American style of mass commercial wastage. If it is surrealism, it is the home-town surrealism of the neighbourhood supermarket. One can echo this with passages from any of West's books; for instance, when Homer Simpson goes shopping in *The Day of the Locust:*

> The SunGold Market into which he turned was a large, brilliantly lit place. All the fixtures were chromium and the floors and walls were lined with white tile. Coloured spotlights played on the showcases and counters, heightening the natural hues of the different foods. The oranges were bathed in red, the lemons in yellow, the fish in pale green, the steaks in rose and the eggs in ivory . . .

Behind West's chilling, cartoonlike treatment of people and objects (and people-as-objects) there always lies the chink of money and the grinding of the industrial machine. He is a surfeited realist. The surface strangeness and 'violence' of his novels never rises far above the simple level of being sickened by the excess of an overstocked refrigerator or a sweaty crowd on a Christmas-shopping spree.

It seems helpful to remember Fitzgerald's thorny transition from the twenties to the thirties. In *The Great Gatsby* he was able to allow Daisy to weep over the beauty of Gatsby's opulent shirts; to catalogue with open-eyed wonder the magnificence of that machine for gutting oranges and the brilliant yellow of Gatsby's car. But in *Tender Is the Night*, his tone hardens. Nicole, the child of American success, is discovered in a psychiatric clinic which is explicitly described by Fitzgerald as a kind of spunging-house for a society that is going sour on its own affluence. Nicole, the consumer heroine—for whose sake

> trains began their run at Chicago and traversed the round belly of the continent to California; chicle factories fumed and link belts grew link by link in factories; men mixed toothpaste in vats and drew mouthwash out of copper hogsheads; girls canned tomatoes quickly in August or worked rudely at the Five-and-Tens on Christmas Eve; half-breed Indians toiled on Brazilian coffee plantations and dreamers were muscled out of patent rights on new tractors—these were some of the people who gave a tithe to Nicole and, as the whole system swayed and thundered onward, it lent a feverish bloom to such processes of hers as wholesale buying, like the flush of a fireman's face holding his post before a spreading blaze. She illustrated very simple principles, containing in herself her own doom, but illustrated them so accurately that there was grace in the procedure, and presently Rosemary would try to imitate it.

—shakes hysterically in the bathroom, immersed in some obscure schizophrenic fit. Surrounded by the *embarras de richesse* which he acquires with Nicole (and which prominently includes another pneumatic rubber horse), Dick subsides into broken alcoholism. The wealth of possibilities which seemed once to extend, like the green light over Daisy's dock, has narrowed down to the rank aftertaste of used commodities. Fitzgerald accommodates these opposites in his fiction with a wonderful doubleness of vision; West works obsessively around only the seamy underside of that flawed dream.

For West had a more parochial, mean and hysterical talent than the best of his contemporaries. Like Nicole, he vividly expressed the ruin that came in the wake of the spree; but unlike her, and unlike Fitzgerald too, he never participated in the style which the spree temporarily enabled. Perhaps his novels have been overvalued because American literary history has needed a scapegoat—a novelist so violated that he stands as a symbol for the violent estrangement with which the thirties looked back on the hopes and excesses of the previous decade. He created a voice of shrill, high-pitched nausea; and his mutilated novels are as much symptoms as they are diagnoses of the disease.

Notes

1. Quoted in James F. Light, *Nathanael West: An Interpretative Study* (Evanston, 1971), p. 132.
2. Quoted by Richard B. Gehman, introduction to *The Day of the Locust* (New York, 1953), pp. xiii–xiv.

GERALD B. NELSON
"Lonelyhearts"
Ten Versions of America
1972, pp. 79–90

> Although his cheap clothes had too much style, he still looked like the son of a Baptist minister. A beard would become him, would accent his Old-Testament look. But even without a beard no one could fail to recognize the New England puritan. His forehead was high and narrow. His nose was long and fleshless. His bony chin was shaped and cleft like a hoof. On seeing him for the first time, Shrike had smiled and said, "The Susan Chesters, the Beatrice Fairfaxes and the Miss Lonelyhearts are the priests of twentieth-century America."

Diver was full, red, and open in his American looks. Lonelyhearts is sparse and gaunt. While Diver suggests Cape Cod summers, Lonelyhearts means harsh Vermont winters. If, in the angularity of his face, he suggests the stern self-righteousness of his father, there is also in him the warped thirst for love of his mother. Shrike is frighteningly correct when he lumps Lonelyhearts, Susan Chester, and Beatrice Fairfax together as "the priests of twentieth-century America." The Puritan conscience got confused and mixed mother-love and discipline, and Lonelyhearts wants to love the people who write him letters, but can't because they are naughty children. A real priest is trained not to love in the personal sense, but to feign a love from a distance for his "flock." A mother loves by instinct, and in a very personal sense. When you mix the roles, you end up with a creature compelled, driven by a desire to love everyone in a personal sense, yet inadequate, if not repelled, whenever anyone gets too close.

What Lonelyhearts wants to achieve in his "Imitation of Christ" is a sacrifice of himself for the principle of love, by which he means he wants to die because he hates other people, that the touch of another human being is repugnant to him. His messianic impulse is not the urge for self-sacrifice for the mankind he loves better than they will ever know; it is the urge for self-destruction of the mother who feels herself unnatural because she can't bring herself to love her deformed child.

Lonelyhearts is mad. He looks at himself and finds himself inadequate. Not guilty but inadequate. He cannot do what he wants to do and feels that there must be a way to overcome his problem. The more Shrike mocks him, the more Lonelyhearts turns to his notion of Christ. He even recrucifies his own Christ, taking it off its small wooden cross and nailing it with spikes to his wall, but "Instead of writhing, the Christ remained calmly decorative."

> He knew now what this thing was—hysteria, a snake whose scales are tiny mirrors in which the dead world takes on a semblance of life. And how dead the world is . . . a world of doorknobs. He wondered if hysteria were really too steep a price to pay for bringing it to life.

"This thing" is Lonelyhearts' Christ fixation. He knows that Shrike's reasoned badgering has rendered any sane approach to Christ impossible, and at this early point in his deterioration, he still has the ability to wonder if madness is too great a price to pay for Christianity. Lonelyhearts is a truly "mad Puritan." His insanity comes from the desperate urge to be good, not from the recognition that being good is impossible of a Dick Diver. His lust for Christ is precisely that. He can experience Him only in an evocation of dark pre-Christian mysteries. He chants "Christ, Christ, Jesus Christ. Christ, Christ, Jesus Christ," relishing the words, believing that his ivory Christ has the ability to bleed. It is the blood of "the mystery" that Lonelyhearts wants and it is the blood that terrifies him. He remembers a drunken attempt at the sacrifice of a lamb that happened in college. Despite his incantation of Christ's name, the rite turned out a disaster. The knife broke and the lamb crawled off into the bushes, where Lonelyhearts later crushed its head with a stone. There was blood, but it was untransformed. No mystery, just a slow, ugly dying.

With his cynical, rational eyes, this is what Shrike sees in life. He is not satanic. He simply knows that there is no help for the world. When man faces man, most knives break, and, if there are no bushes to wait in, it is still the stone that crushes us. Things die, not beautifully, but gradually gagging on their own blood. The process of living is the process of dying and nothing brings a mysterious beauty into it. The fact that Shrike is mean, ugly, and totally self-interested has nothing to do with the fact that he is able to survive. That he does is West's comment on the nature of the world in which we live. A world where the Lonelyhearts are driven mad and the Shrikes prosper. A world where the word "love" is no more meaningful or joyful than the consumptive's final cough.

America's Puritanism made it possible for the country to become the most powerful nation in the world. But as its power increased, its individuals disappeared. In our frontier society, one built forts because of the fear of enemies waiting beyond the next hill. The people banded together for safety and convinced themselves that they were necessary one to the other. It makes no difference whether this society was the church of the seventeenth century, where the enemy was man's increasing knowledge of the universe, or the American West of the nineteenth century, where the enemy was the very visible Indian; the problem is the same: there is something dangerous out there and we can only protect ourselves against it by standing strong and shoulder to shoulder. But as the power of either church or nation increases, defense against the enemy must decrease, because once the enemy is either dead or harmlessly absorbed, the weapons of defense have an ugly propensity of turning inward, wreaking more havoc on the hands that hold them than any external enemy could ever have done.

Unfortunately the attitude of the frontier brings to the minds of the power-hungry the irresistible illusion of permanence, the feeling that "I" can run the world. And so it is. From the simple and obvious stance of frightened people, we develop a principle of power and control, where the leaders, instead of trying to assuage fear, promulgate it, withholding knowledge in order to maintain control.

The key is training. The people must be given enough of either bread or facts to sustain them, but not enough to corrupt them. They must be trained to believe certain things about the reality and the possibility of their world and then held in certain specific postures, frozen, believing that they are moving forward. But the only movement is time, the rest static.

In his father's church, Lonelyhearts encountered Christianity. But it had no effect of control. On the contrary, he faced the blood and the dying of the Crucifixion with the wild passion of the first martyrs. He genuinely wanted Christ's death to be meaningful; he wanted to see the fact of death transformed into something spiritual and not remain the blunt end of existence. He wanted meaning. Lonelyhearts plunged into the faith of his fathers trying to find the substance he was so desperately sure must be there.

Shrike speaks for West: Lonelyhearts is a pathetic fool, sick in his head because he can't accept the world for the piece of shit that it is and himself as an effeminate, sickly adolescent.

Shrike is the real world, but that doesn't mean it's good.

West is after the world that Shrike represents, a world where cynical acceptance is the only sane approach, a world where a love-haunted man like Lonelyhearts is driven to an insane suicide because he cannot accept his inability to love, a world which has systematically driven the humanity out of man. It is this vision of the world that marks the difference between a Fitzgerald and a West. Fitzgerald saw the world as bearable to the sane—in fact, good, if one could approach it properly. His Barbans function beautifully, and his Divers at least survive, richer for their knowledge. To West the world is unendurable: being sane means being Shrike; being sensitive means being Lonelyhearts. These are the only two approaches to the world left for the intelligent being; the others are all variations on the Doyles, stupid and groping. If Diver sounds like Dostoevski's Grand Inquisitor in declining to tell Mary North that she is not "nice people," Lonelyhearts wants so much to be Aloysha that it kills him.

With Jake Barnes we encounter cynicism, but it is a malleable type of cynicism. Barnes is, after all, basically a nice guy. If he knows the world is hopeless, he at least has the manners and consideration to keep his knowledge to himself. Shrike won't keep his mouth shut. He has a messianic mission: "This is the truth, foul as it is, accept it!" And there is ministerial glee in him. Lonelyhearts goes through "dark night of the soul" after "dark night of the soul" trying to escape the truth and grasp for what he wants to be true. Shrike seems all sunshine and poisonous flowers when he preaches his gospel. Barnes knows truths and wants to keep them to himself, work for peace, be a "steer among bulls." Shrike knows and wants everyone to accept the knowledge whether they can understand it or not. Shrike is not a black priest; there is no perversion in him. He merely speaks of the world as he sees and believes it. He does not try to cover up or delude his parishioners. He preaches, with a beautifully pristine, deliberate Calvinistic ruthlessness. It is not his fault if he drives his flock mad.

The central conflict of *Miss Lonelyhearts* is in the battle between Shrike's knowledge and Lonelyhearts's hope, and Shrike's knowledge coupled with Lonelyhearts's intelligence has, as Lonelyhearts knows only too well, "made a sane view of this Christ business impossible." Lonelyhearts comes to this conclusion after reading the words of Father Zossima in *The Brothers Karamazov*, praising love for all living creatures, a pure, all-embracing love which would free the lover for the purest of happiness. Yet what Lonelyhearts thinks about Zossima's idea of love is that it would make him "a big success. His column would be syndicated and the whole world would learn to love." And through his success the Kingdom of Heaven would arrive as the commercial and the religious mixed together, one dependent on the other, the fulfillment of the Puritan American Dream. All Shrike asks is that the religious hypocrisy be tossed out, that Lonelyhearts not try to say that there is any justification for his dream in the sense of bringing good to mankind. Shrike knows full well that the only reason for doing anything is self-aggrandizement, that the hope that he will be a success with a syndicated column is the believable part of Lonelyhearts's dream, but that it will never come to pass so long as he believes that the whole world could actually learn to love. He wants Lonelyhearts to believe in the possibility of the evolution of ideas as well as species, that it is possible to take the proven economic values of Puritanism and use them without feeling guilty for not enriching the spiritual life of the people one must use. Make money and forget that altruistic nonsense; realize that suckers are suckers, and that if you don't use them someone else will.

Lonelyhearts would be good. He would also be successful. "Put your hand on the radio." "Pay me." "Listen." But don't "take a healing." Suffer, sons of bitches, because you're worse than you ever dreamed you were. Jonathan Edwards with mass media in his bitter, shaking fists.

Shrike is "right reason" and he has no hope. He does not offer a way out, unless scorn is a solution. He simply describes the futility of hope, of any answer. Anywhere else, it is as bad as, if not worse than, it is here, and there is no way of changing anything. In fact, if one questions his motives carefully enough one will discover that he really doesn't want to change anything; he just thinks that it might be good if he did. This is what Lonelyhearts recognizes in Shrike's words. He realizes that his yearning for Christian altruism is a fraud; that his own vocation is really of a much different sort. He recognizes that his concern with his Christ is a fascination with the very real physical fact of bleeding and death; that he likes not so much the idea of transcendence as the preceding gore of the dying; that he would rather hurt than heal.

Lonelyhearts is a man who loves the suffering of others. Shrike is not the Antichrist of *Miss Lonelyhearts;* Lonelyhearts himself is. His Christianity is voyeurism. He wants his little ivory Christ to writhe and bleed on the wall. It won't, so he imagines it does. Shrike would offer cynical, offhanded pap to Lonelyhearts's pathetic, beseeching letter writers; he would tell them anything tongue-in-cheek to stop them from writing, but, in a strange paradox, the things that he suggests would also help them in their suffering, because he would treat them as the helpless fools that they are. And, desperate to believe anything, they would bless him with their haltness, lameness, and blindness. "Don't worry, you're not as ugly as you know you are." What Lonelyhearts would do is ask them to add a spiritual dimension to their physical suffering: instead of merely moaning, he wants them to really face the agony of emptiness, and die. So that he can watch.

In a sane, beneficent world, Lonelyhearts would be able to recognize and understand his nature. Lonelyhearts looks out at his world of cripples and criminals and feels that since he was raised to be a good Christian, he should do something for them. He should open their eyes to the reality of their suffering. This is the core of his madness. He thinks he wants to immerse himself in the groaning world around him, but the slightest touch of that world sends him into paroxysms of disgust.

Lonelyhearts is a hater corrupted. He should have been allowed the privilege of living his disgust privately. But he wanted to "make it," to accept the world and be accepted by it. He wanted to go to bed with Shrike's wife; he wanted to enjoy going to bed with Betty; he wanted to be able to stomach going to bed with Mrs. Doyle. "Wanted": that one, simple, plaintive word echoes throughout *Miss Lonelyhearts:* If only *I could.*

If Shrike appears to be evil, it is because he says "YOU CAN'T" with such reasoned authority. He is a hysterical hypocrite, but the world is run by hysterical hypocrites. They are the ones who survive and triumph. This is what Shrike tries to tell Lonelyhearts, when, in much more than a "Temptation of Christ," he tries to explain to him and demonstrate by example exactly how the world works:

> "You spiritual lovers think that you alone suffer. But you are mistaken. Although my love is of the flesh flashy, I too suffer. It's suffering that drives me into the arms of the Miss Farkises of this world. Yes, I suffer."

Shrike knows who he is and, in a sense, revels in his lack of grace. Lonelyhearts knows only who he would be.

It is Lonelyhearts' final desperate immersion in Shrike's world, without Shrike's sight, that brings about his downfall.

Shrike, when talking to Doyle, asks him to tell them about humanity from his vantage point as a gas-meter inspector. Doyle, whom West describes as a "little cripple—a partially destroyed insect," responds with:

> "Everybody's got a frigidaire nowadays, and they say that we meter inspectors take the place of the iceman in the stories."

Shrike:

> "I can see, sir, that you are not the man for us. You know nothing about humanity: you are humanity. I leave you to Miss Lonelyhearts."

Shrike is right. It is only fitting and proper that an impotent "partially destroyed insect" should make a feeble, leering attempt at a joke about sexual prowess. Doyle is humanity—the crippled, in mind as well as body, humanity of the twentieth century; desperate, hopefully writing letters under the veil of anonymity and yet forced to break through that veil in a dim hope of such human contact. Destroyed, not ennobled by the world.

The American Dream come true, bringing with it madness and shame for the unfortunate, to whom the world is a bitterly critical mirror. Making them aware at all times of their ugliness and inadequacy. Even before television brought the miracle of perfectly formed bodies into every living room, where potbellied men, sweating in sleeveless undershirts, and their unattractive, gone-to-seed, pin-curled wives could watch, each disdaining the other, the lithe and the brilliant tell them that they, too, could be beautiful—even before this, the ugly of our always-expanding economy *knew* that they were ugly, and, even more appalling, they knew that it was their own fault, and here the madness of Lonelyhearts becomes the most abhorrently manifest. He tells the Doyles that if they love Christ—and, through Christ, each other—they will become beautiful. The Puritan minister has become an insane TV pitchman, Cotton Mather reincarnate in Bert Parks, and the Doyles know it. To Mrs. Doyle, Lonelyhearts' chatter about Christ and love means only that she wants to go to bed with him, and to Mr. Doyle that he has a friend who will play a little bit of faggy hanky-pank with him without daring to show his disgust. When Lonelyhearts screams his "Christ Is Love" message, Fay Doyle only says, "You were a scream with your fly open."

To the Doyles, and not only the Doyles of the crippled, poverty-stricken nineteen-thirties but the Doyles of any time and any place, "Christ Is Love" is nonsense. Christ is one thing, love is another, without a capital "L."

Lonelyhearts, in his last attempt to write his column:

> Christ died for you.
>
> He died nailed to a tree for you. His gift to you is suffering and it is only through suffering that you can know Him. Cherish this gift, for . . .

This is his love. To Lonelyhearts, the Crucifixion is not only a justification for suffering, it is a demand for it. Christ becomes not the Saviour but "the black fruit that hangs on the crosstree," and Lonelyhearts, in his desperation to purify his Christ lust, joins hands with Satan in a beautifully executed Black Mass, urging man to accept the darkness of Christ so that he may suffer his way to a grisly death. "Suffer, damn you," he is saying, "because you don't deserve to live."

But the Doyles don't want to suffer; they don't want to die. They want to grab whatever tacky pleasures they can before life ends. They want to believe that they are "all right" so that they can pluck more forbidden fruits. Where Lonelyhearts fails most grievously as a priest is in the fact that he offers only negation, not salvation; he is talking about dying, not about being resurrected; he is talking about dead-end death for its own sake to people who only want life, who turn to him because they want answers for their pain, a way out, not a demand to bleed. They don't want a priest; they want a healer. So when Shrike tells Lonelyhearts to feed their illusions, offer them foolishness, like art, that they can believe in, he is much more right than wrong. The girl with no nose wants to be told where she can find one, not told to pray and relish her suffering. And Doyle, when he comes up the stairs to Lonelyhearts' apartment with a gun wrapped in newspaper, wants to bluff and then be let off the hook, not driven by Lonelyhearts' madness into killing him.

JEFFREY L. DUNCAN

"The Problem of Language in *Miss Lonelyhearts*"

Iowa Review, Winter 1977, pp. 116–28

Almost halfway through his story Miss Lonelyhearts gets sick. His sickness is essentially spiritual—he is, the chapter title says, "in the Dismal Swamp"—and it has been brought on by his job. His girl friend, Betty, brings him some hot soup and advice: quit, try another line of work. He tells her that quitting would not help much because he would still remember the letters. She does not understand, so he offers her an explanation of unusual length and formality:

> Perhaps I can make you understand. Let's start from the beginning. A man is hired to give advice to the readers of a newspaper. The job is a circulation stunt and the whole staff considers it a joke. He welcomes the job, for it might lead to a gossip column, and anyway he's tired of being a leg man. He too considers the job a joke, but after several months at it, the joke begins to escape him. He sees that the majority of the letters are profoundly humble pleas for moral and spiritual advice, that they are inarticulate expressions of genuine suffering. He also discovers that his correspondents take him seriously. For the first time in his life, he is forced to examine the values by which he lives. This examination shows him that he is the victim of the joke and not its perpetrator. [1]

Here he stops, satisfied it seems that there is no more to say. Betty still does not understand, to no one's surprise, but we do: Miss Lonelyhearts cannot answer the letters because he has found that his values do not, cannot, justify genuine suffering, including his own. (For he is suffering too, languishing in the dismal swamp.) Hence he is the victim of the joke: the advice-giver is himself sick-of-it-all, in desperate need of advice.

He does not say what his values are (or were), but he does not really need to. He has found them, he implies, not just wanting, but false. His crisis then is intensely personal, because *he* has been false, and still is. He no longer claims a proper name, and he wears at all times his workaday non de plume, a women's at that. But not only is he no lady, he cannot fulfill the requirements, as he construes them, that his pseudonym entails. He has become a misnomer. In one sense, though, the name suits him: he is as lonely a heart as any of his correspondents. Accordingly, the only identity he feels entitled to is the same one they assume, the victim. Better any identity than none, we might say, but not so. For he has come to doubt all values and therefore the value of suffering itself. If it has no value, neither does the role of victim. One simply suffers, that's all, without upshot or significance, the butt of a joke.

What makes the joke *bad* is the fact, as Miss Lonelyhearts sees it, that the suffering his correspondents express is genuine. Others have agreed. In his review of the novel, for instance, William Carlos Williams protested, "The letters which West uses freely and at length must be authentic. I can't believe anything else. The unsuspected world they reveal is beyond ordinary thought." Thirty some years later Randall Reid said the same thing: "They [the letters] have the vividness of the unarguable reality of revelation."[2] Both statements, cueing off Miss Lonelyhearts, couple authenticity and revelation. The letters reveal a reality that is unarguable. They are, like revelation, their own evidence. Upon seeing them one believes them, if not instantaneously, like Williams, then slowly, gradually like Miss Lonelyhearts. Their truth, in other words, is not a matter of fact, but an article of faith, and no one has questioned it. I think we should, just as I think that, deep down, Miss Lonelyhearts himself does. At issue is a central concern, the nature of language, both as a theme and as the medium of West's novel.

Miss Lonelyhearts deals primarily not with people, but with letters, with various orders and disorders of words. In his personal relations he is not engaged in dialogue, the language of spontaneous give and take, nearly so much as he is confronted with speeches, with words as deliberately composed as those of the letters, if not more so.[3] Notably, in the two days (and chapters) before he beds himself in the dismal swamp, he hears two speeches, one by Mary Shrike, then one by Fay Doyle, that amount to letters in the flesh. "People like Mary were unable to do without such tales. They told them because they wanted to talk about something besides clothing or business or the movies, because they wanted to talk about something poetic" (p. 199). Like Mary like Fay: they simply have different poetics. Understandably Miss Lonelyhearts listens to neither. They reveal a reality, unarguably, but it is hardly one of genuine suffering, much less of profound humility. Instead they betray mere attitudes struck, postures assumed, poses wantonly displayed, a comic pornography of suffering and trouble. If they express anything authentic—though it is doubtful that these women give a fig about authenticity—it is a desire for suffering, for indisputable reality, personal significance. And if they are to be pitied, it is because they do not, perhaps cannot, suffer.

That is, they have nothing really to speak of, Mary and Fay. Their words merely fill in their blanks. And what is true of them may also—since West's characters are consistently thin—be true of the others, of Betty, of Desperate, of Broad Shoulders, of Shrike, of Miss Lonelyhearts himself.[4] For that reason, if no other, Shrike can burlesque the letters, the expressions of undeserved, unmitigated suffering, just as effectively as he can parody the conventional formulae of value, of the life worth living:

> This one is a jim-dandy. A young boy wants a violin. It looks simple; all you have to do is get the kid one. But then you discover that he has dictated the letter to his little sister. He is paralyzed and can't even feed himself. He has a toy violin and hugs it to his chest, imitating the sound of playing with his mouth. How pathetic! However, one can learn much from this parable. Label the boy Labor, the violin Capital, and so on . . . (p. 240)
>
> So you buy a farm and walk behind your horse's moist behind, no collar or tie, plowing your broad swift acres. As you turn up the rich black soil, the wind carries the smell of pine and dung across the fields and the rhythm of an old, old work enters your soul. To this rhythm, you sow and weep and chivy your kine, not kin or kind, between the pregnant rows of corn and taters. (p. 212)

Shrike can handle them with equal facility because he insists that they bear the same message, and that it is their only message: the human race is a poet that writes the eccentric propositions of its fate, and propositions, fate, the race itself amount only to so much noisy breath, hot air, flatulence.

Miss Lonelyhearts reluctantly suspects as much. That is why he can find no sincere answers, why he can take nothing he says or thinks seriously, why he lacks the courage of his clichés, why he converts even an original formulation immediately into a cliché.[5] "Man has a tropism for order," he thinks to himself; "The physical world has a tropism for disorder, entropy. Man against Nature . . . the battle of the centuries." A capital "N" no less. Four sentences later he dismisses it for good: "All order is doomed, yet the battle is worthwhile" (p. 209). No wonder then that only a little while later he casts his explanation to Betty in the third person—it accommodates exactly his ironic self-consciousness, the distance between what he wants to believe and what he suspects. No wonder as well that his explanation sounds like another speech, one that he has often rehearsed to himself; it is so pat, so articulate, the cool, collected rhetoric of desperation, of futile resolves, private last-stands. For if he can only bring himself to believe what he says, that the suffering is genuine, he may yet hope to believe that it can be justified. That is, faith, once succumbed to, may wax and multiply like irony succumbed to. But the "if" is difficult; it requires breaking the force of irony, which is considerable. Not only can it move mountains, it can annihilate them. And people, too.

Irony is not always humorous, but humor is always ironic. And the letters in the book are humorous.

> I am in such pain I dont know what to do sometimes I think I will kill myself my kidneys hurt so much. . . . I was operatored on twice and my husband promised no more children on the doctors advice as he said I might die but when I got back from the hospital he broke his promise and now I am going to have a baby and I don't think I can stand it my kidneys hurt so much. (p. 170)

The writers have had nothing to do with the terrible turns their fates have taken—they are innocent—and neither they nor anyone else can do a thing about their difficulties. Their problems are, by their own terms, insoluble; they themselves are, by their own accounts, schlmiels with Weltschmerz; "I don't know what to do," concludes Sick-of-it-all (p. 170). "Ought I commit suicide?" queries Desperate (p. 171). "What is the whole stinking business for?" muses Peter Doyle (p. 232). They are actually seeking confirmation, not advice; they want someone else to see them as they see themselves. Also, the letters are all graced by the common touch, illiteracy. The writers seem sublimely unaware that their words, like double agents, constantly betray them. "But he [Broad Shoulders' boarder] tries to make me bad and as there is nobody in the house when he comes home drunk on Saturday night I dont know what to do but so far I didnt let him" (p. 226). Betrayal is revelation, but of a fundamentally ambiguous sort: we cannot say whether the words of the letters misrepresent or faithfully execute their authors as they really are. Either way, though, they are funny. The slip of the tongue, Freudian or otherwise, reliably gets a laugh.

Miss Lonelyhearts, however, no longer finds the letters funny because he assumes they are authentic. Genuine suffering, he tells Betty, is no joke. This difference between his response and ours gets us at last into the troubled heart of the novel. Suffering is not funny, certainly, but it has been since Eden, no less than vanity and folly, the very stuff of humor. Pathos, too, of course, and tragedy, but we pay for the loss of Paradise with laughter as well as tears, and comedy is one of the more common forms of man's inhumanity to man. But nothing is more human, for we are considering one application of our capacity for abstraction, our ability to translate instances of suffering and pain into symbol systems that go absurdly awry. Humor is a function of symbolic consciousness. It involves the displacement if not the annihilation of persons, their particular reality, by words, a particular scheme of concepts. The unnamed perpetrator of the joke is language, like West's, for example, when he describes the letters as all alike, "stamped from the dough of suffering with a heart-shaped cookie knife" (p. 169). Just as West's words undercut the letters, so the letters' words displace their writers: "it dont pay to be inocent and is only a big disapointment" (p. 170). Miss Lonelyhearts no longer finds the letters funny because he refuses to consent to this displacement, to bless this annihilation with a laugh. He looks over or through their words to their writers, as he imagines them: profoundly humble, genuinely suffering, terribly real.

But Shrike recognizes a laugh when he sees one, and Miss Lonelyhearts knows it. That is why he has to insist that the letters are not funny: they are not because in truth they are, and that, in his opinion, is wrong, all wrong. For it is not just the letters—he doesn't find anything funny. He will not be a party to humor per se, and therefore, consistently enough, he tries to leave the premises of language altogether, in violence, in women's flesh, in a rural retreat, and in a hand-holding soul-session in a speakeasy.

His expeditions fail, hardly to his surprise, because in them he only finds himself engaged face-to-face with more words on the loose. Sometimes they are spoken, sometimes they are enacted, but they are always there, inescapable.[6] "With the return of self-consciousness, he knew that only violence could make him supple" (p. 183). Spiritually, speaking, I take it. His violence serves a metaphysical cause self-consciously conceived.[7] Instead of delivering him from language into whatever—say reality—it necessarily forces him into obeisance to language. For language is its maker. He works over the clean, old man for his story, the dubious words of his life—"Yes, I know, your tale is a sad one. Tell it, damn you, tell it" (p. 191)—and sees him at last as the embodiment of his correspondents, his letters. Mary gives him a little of her body to tell him all of her tale; Fay uses her story as a pretext for sex, but she also uses sex as a pretext for her story. Betty believes in a *Sunset* version of *Walden*, and for a while Miss Lonelyhearts is able to relax in her belief, but when they get back to the city he realizes that "he had begun to think himself a faker and a fool" (p. 220). So he is back in language again, and not at all sure that he ever really left it. Like violence, his session of silence with Doyle serves a metaphysical purpose self-consciously forced to its crisis: "He . . . drove his hand back and forced it to clasp the cripple's . . . pressed it firmly with all the love he could manage" (p. 232). This may be a flight of the alone to the alone, but the wings are words, words like "love" and "communion," like "together" and "alone." His only real hope, then, as he has seen it along, is Christ, appropriately enough.

Let us go back to the dismal swamp. "He was thinking of how Shrike had accelerated his sickness by teaching him to handle his one escape, Christ, with a thick glove of words" (p. 212). Shrike does not get his entire due: he has taught Miss Lonelyhearts to handle everything with a thick glove of words, to suspect that there may be nothing really for the glove to handle, nothing for it to do but make figures of itself, or that the glove, like a magician's white one, renders whatever reality it handles null and void. Genuine magic, though, not legerdemain. Destructive force. The word "escape," in this context, usually means a flight from reality to some more tenable opposite. In Miss Lonelyhearts' case, however, it seems to mean a flight from words in and of themselves to that only (as he sees it) which can redeem them, put them in their proper place—a flight from the terrible logic of Shrike to the Logos itself, Christ, the Word made flesh. The Word informs flesh, flesh substantiates the Word: reality then carries a life-time guarantee, its value insured by language. Then tropes can become unironic Truth, victims can become martyrs, and Paradise, that place of complete integration, can be regained.[8]

Or so a Christian might have it: not an escape, like Tahiti, the soil, hedonism, or art, but a redemption. West's script, however, follows the Christian's with a thumb on its nose and its fingers sadly crossed.[9] Peter Doyle's letter moves Miss Lonelyhearts to holding hands. Later, though, Doyle's hearthside demeanor bankrupts the credibility of his prose, so much that Miss Lonelyhearts takes himself to bed. This time, however, instead of languishing in despair, he becomes the rock. In that metaphor of the Church he has finally, he solipsistically thinks, found himself. "The rock was a solidification of his feeling, his conscience, his sense of reality, his self-knowledge" (p. 245). Thus solidified, though, he feels nothing, and nothing (except the rock) seems real. Betty is a party dress to whom he can say anything without deliberately lying because there is no one to lie to and nothing to lie about. "He could have planned anything. A castle in Spain and love on a balcony or a pirate trip and love on a tropical island" (p. 245). He has changed the game from show-and-tell to play-pretend. As a preliminary to his union with Christ he seems to have gained himself by renouncing words and the world, as he had apparently hoped. But he has actually done nothing of the sort: Miss Lonelyhearts, a pseudonym, has merely become a metaphor, the rock, in a world that was never his.

Up to this point he has always been afraid of Christ. "As a boy in his father's church, he had discovered that something stirred in him when he shouted the name of Christ, something secret and enormously powerful" (p. 179). Later he construes this thing in clinical terms, as hysteria, though he wishes he could believe that it is more than that, that it is actual divinity. Whatever it actually is, his fear is the traditional one of self-relinquishment, of letting go. But now that he has such a definitive sense of self—a rock is definite, if nothing else—he is ironically no longer afraid, and silently shouting the name Christ to himself, he gives himself up and over and has his union. "Christ is life and light" (p. 245). He is also love and Miss Lonelyhearts' new feature editor (p. 246).

He is, in other words, yet another metaphor, a whole string of them—not the Word, but a word, signifying neither more nor less than any other. Nothing is redeemed, least of all language. Doyle arrives, bad poetry on a field rampant. He has come in the name of secular romantic love to avenge Miss Lonelyhearts' alleged insult to his wife's honor. The allegation is hers, of course, and it is as false as her honor, as her husband's love, as his mission's motive. Miss Lonelyhearts sees him as a sign and, mistaking his warning for a humble plea, goes in the name of divine love to perform a literal miracle, to save Doyle, to save all his correspondents in Doyle's figure, just as he had sought to hurt them all in the figure of the clean old man. Doyle loses heart, so to speak, and tries to flee. Betty, the idle figure of Miss Lonelyhearts' secular fancy, blunders in. Doyle's gun accidentally goes off, and Miss Lonelyhearts meets his end at last, not as martyr, but as unwitting victim, and not as victim of "reality" but of a symbol system gone absurdly awry—of a joke, if you will—because there is no other way for it to go. There is no truth for Miss Lonelyhearts, only words.[10]

It may seem then that Shrike has the last word. All we really have, all we really are, says Shrike, is words, but he does not stop there. There is no cause for grief, he consistently implies, only occasion for jokes. Jokes are his form of prophecy, and they are self-fulfilling. Their form is their content, for their only point is the perfect pointlessness of it all. Nothing is wrong because nothing ever was or could be right. Nothing really matters, not even the fact that nothing really matters. This second step, though, Shrike follows by choice, not of logical necessity. He pronounces "truth" only in order to evade it, to protect himself from pain. Between nothing and grief he will take nothing, not because it is true, finally, but because it is easier.

But while Shrike may take this second step for the sake of comfort, one could argue that the novel takes it of necessity. In open concord with Shrike, it depicts language as radically false, a fundamentally misleading order of being, or nonbeing, as the case may be. Yet the novel is itself a form of language. It would seem then that either the theme must render the form futile, a design of dumb noise, or the form must render the theme gratuitous. But if the theme is gratuitous, the form is perforce futile: it is predicated on counterfeit, a phony issue. Either way (or both ways?) the novel would amount to a display in negation, like the self-dismantling sculpture of Tinguely, like the jokes of Shrike. But Shrike is good only for a laugh, whereas the last elaborate joke of the novel occasions dismay. That is, we respond as if both the statement and the structure were ontologically sound. Now it could be that West has misled us to the very end, that we, to the extent that we care about the outcome, are the unwitting butts of his joke and he is snickering up his sleeve. If so, then West's novel would seem to give us the void as a stripper, taking it all off. On the other hand, our response may be warranted. Curiously enough, we have the same problem with the book that Miss Lonelyhearts has with the letters: whatever we finally deem it, we are necessarily engaged in an act of faith. But we need not, as a consequence, simply toss the book up for grabs.

For the sake of his faith, Miss Lonelyhearts must ignore the bad language of the letters. We enjoy the same language because it is so good: "I bought a new sowing machine as I do some sowing for other people to make both ends meet . . ." (p. 225). The paradox is simple yet profound. All of the demonstrations of bad language—the letters, Miss Lonelyhearts' awful answers, Shrike's parodies—all involve not only an exhibition of West's skill, but of the adequacy of language to his skill. In order to make humorous "nonsense" (as in the quote just cited), language must be able to make common sense. Further, it must make both kinds at once, since it is precisely the play of the one off the other that is funny. A joke reveals the meaningfulness of language. And like revelation, it constitutes its own evidence: the simple fact that it is funny, that *we* laugh, makes the case.

Now we can understand why Shrike is such a desperate character, insistent, shrill. He cannot make his point—the meaninglessness of it *all*—without contradicting himself. Jokes are his form of prophecy, and they betray him every time. He is the victim of his own success. He grieves, in his fashion, that he cannot have nothing.

But the fact that language is meaningful does not necessarily mean that it is significant, any more than a correct sentence is necessarily true. A philosophical idealist might disagree, of course, but West's characters are not idealists, They want some words that signify something beyond their own sound and sense, something, preferably a redemptive Absolute, that can be empirically ascertained. Miss Lonelyhearts, for example, has no quarrel with the coherence of Betty's "world view," but with its significance. Her order, as far as he is concerned, does not match reality—they are an odd pair—whereas his own disorder does (p. 183). His experience tells him so, or so he thinks. However, we cannot say whether his confusion results from or produces the confusion he perceives, nor whether the world he perceives is in fact a disorder. For it is not the relation between words and reality that West depicts, it is the disjunction: his characters cannot find out what, if anything, lies on the other side of their words. As a bridge, language breaks; as a window, it shuts out, like stained glass, and keeps his characters in. But it does not become genuinely false, actually misleading, until West's characters believe the bridge is sound, the window perfectly transparent, their words reliably significant, true. As, for instance, when Shrike insists there is nought beyond, and when Miss Lonelyhearts insists there is confusion, or Christ, the Word intact. They do not know, literally, what they are talking about.

Words in the novel fail to do the job West's characters assign them—to reveal a reality beyond themselves. But at the same time the words of the novel, West's words, manage quite successfully to do their job, to reveal all they need to, the patterns their sound and sense make: "the gray sky looked as if it had been rubbed with a soiled eraser. It held no angels, flaming crosses, olive-bearing doves, wheels within wheels. Only a newspaper struggled in the air like a kite with a broken spine" (pp. 174–75). These words do not match reality, fit any empirical facts. Neither do they distort any facts or displace reality. They are not *about* something beyond themselves, an actual person's experience, a historical event. They constitute, rather, their own reality, and their only job is to be true to the structure of which they are a part, that is, to be right, self-consistent, aesthetically correct. Were it some other character than Miss Lonelyhearts sitting there, the sky might very properly contain angels, crosses, doves, wheels, a cloud that speaks, a breeze that inspires, a pulse that beats. In art, language is free of obligation to referents; it is free to be strictly itself, and it stands or falls entirely on its own. And when it stands, it satisfies the idealist and the empiricist alike, for it is simultaneously as conceptual as any law and as phenomenal as an apple falling. It is completely sensible. The poet, as Emerson happily put it, "adorns nature with a new thing."[11]

Our relationship with the novel, then, is not exactly

analogous to Miss Lonelyhearts' with the letters. The language of each (even when it is the same) draws different duty. For that reason, the demonstrable error of his and his companions' ways does not necessarily compromise the validity of ours. We place our bets on a different thing, and we have demonstrably good grounds for our wager, namely, the novel's coherence. Being or nonbeing, it is an *order* of experience. Thus the novel's theme does not necessarily undermine its form. Still, we must recognize that the center of the analogy holds: the novel's coherence depends upon our faith. The world seems able to survive capricious gods, but a work of fiction cannot survive an unreliable third-person narrator. (First-person narrators are a different story, of course, but their implied third-person narrators are not.) Try to imagine, for instance, the last passage I quoted as misleading, false, the sky as actually blue, bearing crosses, wheels, and so forth. The whole show stops: all bets are off. But we in fact read on because we trust the narrator. In order to read on, we must. And in reading on we find constant justification of our faith: the novel elaborates its problem without sentimental dodges or cheap solutions. True to itself, it is true to us. As for those novels that self-consciously make even their third-person reliability suspect, our willing suspension of belief amounts to a working agreement based on the same trust, that they will prove to be meaningful orders of experience. But by meaningful I do not want to suggest comfortable or reassuring. On the contrary, almost all art worth the name repays our faith by raising hell within us, with our cherished assumptions and secret illusions, with our workaday values and beliefs. For it takes us as far as words can go, and thus brings us face-to-face, finally, with silence, mystery. "Emotion" comes from *emovere*, "to move out of," "disturb." Let us momentarily suppose that West has conned us at the end. Now that we are on to it, we can easily dismiss the book, for he has given us the void *merely* as a stripper, a tease, not a real threat but a pretence of one. "Ah," we can say in relief, "he didn't mean it after all."

But West's novel does disturb us, threaten, because its form makes its theme intensely meaningful, utterly real. Here we witness words falling short of reality, and here, and here, and we watch their continual shortcomings compose an actual pattern of doom. We are unsettled because most of us are, like Dr. Johnson, rock-kickers—we ordinarily assume that our words signify something beyond themselves—and reading this story forces us to face the possibility that they do not. The story defines the issue that has become major in certain circles, "the problem of language." But West simultaneously solves the problem *in* the form, every word of the way. For unlike his characters, malpracticing empiricists all, and unlike most of us, West was, as an artist, a practicing idealist. We know that he got the idea for his novel from seeing actual letters to an advice columnist. Had he been concerned with historical-empirical fidelity, he could have used them more-or-less intact. But we also know that he changed them radically, that he in truth wrote his own letters, to make them right, aesthetically correct.[12] All artists, of course, change things to suit their purposes, but their purposes have a single premise, that the work of art must be absolutely true to itself, self-integral, one. Then it can stand and unfold itself, an articulated body of ideas, an avatar of Being.

The novel is an order of being, finally, because in it West shows us that words realize our possibilities as well as define our limits. Miss Lonelyhearts looks at a gray sky and, empiricist that he is, sees only a dirty *tabula rasa*. Against that he sees the most referential and hence ephemeral of all literature, a newspaper, failing (naturally) to soar. But West's words lift nicely, bearing for the space of our imagination all the significance Miss Lonelyhearts misses in his, not in the form of crosses and doves, to be sure, but in the form of figures, of ideas, of words touched with life and touching us with the same.[13]

West's other three stories suffer to varying degrees in comparison with *Miss Lonelyhearts*. They demonstrate a precise but simplistic satire, a sentimental obsession with easy pickings: in *The Dream Life of Balso Snell*, the contrived labyrinths of literary journeys, in *A Cool Million*, the Horatio Alger myth, in *The Day of the Locust*, the Hollywood motif.[14] The unreality of West's marks is patent, their exposure therefore, funny or not, perfunctory: "The fat lady in the yachting cap was going shopping, not boating; the man in the Norfolk jacket and Tyrolean hat was returning, not from a mountain, but an insurance office . . . " (p. 2). They expose bills of fraudulent goods that we, his readers, declined to buy in the first place; hence they do not disturb, they merely confirm our glib assumptions. *Miss Lonelyhearts*, on the other hand, makes us reconsider.

Here is the difference I mean:

> It is hard to laugh at the need for beauty and romance, no matter how tasteless, even horrible, the results of that need are. But it is easy to sigh. Few things are sadder than the truly monstrous. (*The Day of the Locust*, p. 4)
>
> . . . I would like to have boy friends like other girls and go out on Saturday nites, but no boy will take me because I was born without a nose—although I am a good dancer and have a nice shape and my father buys me pretty clothes. (*Miss Lonelyhearts*, p. 171)

A girl without a nose is monstrous, truly, yet it is hard not to laugh, particularly when she expresses her need for beauty and romance. A nice shape does not compensate for a noseless face. Perhaps it should, but it does not. Perhaps we should not laugh, either, but we do. Perhaps words should not take precedence over persons, but here (pretending for the moment the girl is real) they do. On the other hand, West does not permit us to indulge in cant. The letter's words spell out a troublesome truth, that this girl, however unfortunate, has tacky values. She would give a great deal to be Homecoming Queen. Victims can be insufferably vain, no less than Presidents, and pity can be primarily self-gratifying. My point is that in the first passage West is keeping certain suppositions intact—the value, for instance, of pity—while in the second he orders his words so that we have to recognize ourselves as we truly are, not as we might prefer to suppose we are. It is recognizing this difference that makes us laugh, and our laughter implies a major admission: that the idealist's absolute may finally be more significant, more real, than we mere mortals are.

We regard West loosely as a writer ahead of his time. I would say that it is specifically *Miss Lonelyhearts* that warrants this reputation, and that it anticipates in particular the work of Barth, Barthelme, Coover, Elkin, Gardner, Pynchon, of all those writers loosely bunched as comic whose humor, by trying its own limits, examines how language does and undoes us, what it gives and what it takes, what it may mean and what it may not, and if we are at last full of fear and wonder, we should be: Being is finally awful, no matter how we look at it.

Notes

1. *Miss Lonelyhearts* and *The Day of the Locust* (1933, rpt. New York: New Directions, 1962), p. 211. Hereafter cited in parentheses within the text.
2. *The Fiction of Nathanael West: No Redeemer, No Promised Land*

(Chicago and London: The University of Chicago Press, 1967), p. 49. Reid quotes Williams on the same page.
3. Jay Martin makes the same point. *Nathanael West: The Art of His Life* (New York: Farrar, Straus, & Giroux, 1970), p. 179.
4. On this point see also Thomas H. Jackson, *Twentieth Century Interpretations of* Miss Lonelyhearts: *A Collection of Critical Essays* (Englewood Cliffs, N.J.: Prentice-Hall, Inc., 1971), p. 7. The best account of the shape of West's characters is W. H. Auden's "West's Disease" in *Nathanael West: A Collection of Critical Essays*, ed. Jay Martin (Englewood Cliffs, N.J.: Prentice-Hall, Inc., 1971), pp. 147–53.
5. For a different interpretation of this point, see Irving Malin, *Nathanael West's Novels* (Carbondale and Edwardsville, Ill.: Southern Illinois University Press, 1972), pp. 32–3.
6. See also Reid, pp. 9–10.
7. For a good psychological account of the significance of violence in West, see James W. Hickey's, "Freudian Criticism and *Miss Lonelyhearts*" in *Nathanael West: The Cheaters and the Cheated; A Collection of Critical Essays*, ed. David Madden (Deland, Fla.: Everett/Edwards, Inc., 1973), p. 142.
8. See also James F. Light, *Nathanael West: An Interpretative Study*, 2nd ed. (Evanston, Ill.: Northwestern University Press, 1971), p. 57.
9. A point also made by Martin, pp. 189–90.
10. The best account of the religious theme is Reid's—see especially p. 84. Robert J. Andreach has dealt admirably with the mythic patterns in the novel; see "Nathanael West's Miss Lonelyhearts: Between the Dead Pan and the Unborn Christ," in *Twentieth Century Interpretations of* Miss Lonelyhearts, ed. Jackson, pp. 49–60. For a different interpretation of the ending, see Arthur Cohen's "Nathanael West's Holy Fool," *Commonweal*, 64 (1956), pp. 277–78.
11. "The Poet," in *Selected Writings of Ralph Waldo Emerson*, ed. William H. Gilman (New York: New American Library, 1965), p. 310. The most important spokesman for this position is William H. Gass, *Fiction and the Figures of Life* (New York: Random House, 1971); see especially "The Medium of Fiction," pp. 27–33.
12. See, for example, Martin, pp. 186–87.
13. A point made by Josephine Herbst: "Nathanael West," in *Nathanael West*, ed. Martin, p. 14.
14. For interpretations of these three works I particularly recommend three essays in Madden's *The Cheaters and the Cheated:* on *Balso Snell*, John M. Brand's "A Word Is a Word Is a Word," pp. 57–75; on *Cool Million*, T. R. Steiner's "West's Lemuel and the American Dream," pp. 157–70; and on *Day of the Locust*, Kingsley Widmer's "The Last Masquerade: *The Day of the Locust*," pp. 179–93.

Philip Whalen

1923–

Philip Glenn Whalen was born on October 20, 1923, in Portland, Oregon, to Glenn Henry and Phyllis (née Bush) Whalen. He was educated at Reed College (B.A. 1951). From 1943 to 1946 he served in the air force. He was ordained a Zen Buddhist priest in 1973, and in 1975 became Shuso (acting head monk) at the Zen Mountain Center. He has also lectured at the San Francisco Zen Center.

Whalen is a poet in the line running from Walt Whitman to William Carlos Williams and Allen Ginsberg. His poetry is also considerably influenced by Asian culture, particularly Zen Buddhism, but he uses colloquial American language and writes largely of quotidian details.

Whalen's first commercially published book of poetry was *Self-Portrait, from Another Direction* (1959). He has since published more than a dozen books of poetry, loosely structured and heavily reliant upon bare sound and stark imagery; he is frequently associated with such post-modern American poets as Frank O'Hara, Gary Snyder, and Ted Berrigan. Books like *Memoirs of an Interglacial Age* (1960), *Three Mornings* (1964), *Decompressions* (1977), and *Heavy Breathing* (1983) have also received favorable notice from mainstream academic critics, who cite his acute ear and perceptive treatment of the everyday. He has also written criticism and two novels (*You Didn't Even Try*, 1967; *Imaginary Speeches for a Brazen Head*, 1972).

Personal

123 Beaver Street is the downstairs apartment of an old oblong Victorian house in the Mission District of San Francisco. Philip Whalen has been living here since 1963. House-guests and quarter-sharers have come and gone; e.g., Richard Brautigan, Allen Ginsberg, and Lew Welch. The downstairs apartment is divided into two one-room apartments and one two-room apartment; the kitchen and bathroom being shared. Rumor has it that Philip Whalen began his sojourn in the front room and gradually worked his way to the room in back, where he now lives, as it is the closest room to the kitchen. Food, it would seem, is his sustenance, his security, his pastime, his faith in the future.

His many friends are fond of feeding him, for "although he is appreciative of good food he can enjoy anything set before him." The center of his universe seems to be his expanding stomach, and he regards its growing girth as a victory he has earned. His blue workmen's shirts concede and defer to its size by exposing the man between buttons.

What little money comes his way seems to be spent in only two other ways: books and toys; and, like Joe in *The Time of Your Life*, he believes he can do no further harm to the already sorry state of man's affairs on earth if only he refuses to leave his chair.

Poised and self-assured he sits like Joe, in The Chair of His Life, in scorn of the world out there—flapping his arms at the doors and windows, beyond which lies the "reality" he is forever railing against. His friends, who he insists are a source of irritation and displeasure to him

> The minute I'm out of town
> My friends get sick, go back on the sauce
> Engage in unhappy love affairs

are in truth, the great protectors of his inner world, not only by accepting him without equivocation, but by acting as buffers against the reality-world he chooses to avoid. They bring him the food of love (and often sustenance) and he, his paternal instincts long mellowed to avuncular good cheer and subtle and fanciful wit, returns their thoughtfulness with his own gentle understanding.

Many poets today look on themselves as the saviors and martyrs of their time. Whalen, on the contrary, is not concerned with revolutions and social panaceas. If he sees the big man at all he sees him in the small situation: tripping over a pebble on his journey to deliver a rose. Out of themes that are often seemingly mundane and prosaic he creates poetry of significance because his vision is peculiarily his own and because the clarity of his intelligence is capable of grasping and arresting meaning in seemingly ephemeral and unimportant subjects. He has an ear for conversational language that reveals those absurd convictions which render him immune to any belief in sweeping changes. For Whalen, social responsibility means friendship in a field of limited reaction. The power of action is nonexistent. There is no decision or choice, only "discovery," as he puts it. The "I" that speaks is the occasional "I" behind the particular impression; hence, his world is directionless, without beginning or end. The questions he poses himself do not arise from moral considerations. Its

Not I love or hate:

but

WHAT IS IT I'M SEEING?
&
WHO'S LOOKING?

This "seeing" involves an assimilation of trivia that mounts from poem to poem. Conversation picked up at parties serves a purpose, centered as it is around a personal mystique that has to do with the clichés and dogma of his youth and a Pantheon which includes Victorian aunts and uncles. His act of propitiation before these ancestral divinities consists of perfecting their inane speech patterns in a slightly altered context. The voices, usually anonymous, recall the echoes of that earlier period. When not actually speaking himself his persona becomes diluted. He *is* the conversation that passes around him. One suddenly feels there is no choice to be made, no real situation to alter. It's always been like this. The poet cannot indicate the possibility of change when there is nothing to compare by. Hence, his time-feeling is unalterable. This petty talk, heard as if on a phonograph record, is the world. There are no moral crises, no wars, etc., only this vague eternal sing-song. The poet, adamant in his passivity, becomes his situation. His watery journey precludes no shore. This is his immortality.—DAVID KHERDIAN, "Philip Whalen," *Six Poets of the San Francisco Renaissance*, 1967, pp. 73–74

Works

Whalen's *You Didn't Even Try* is amiable, rambling, intensely self-involved. Tired. Nothing very much happens and no one seems to mind, which is pleasant, but wearing—especially since the writing has so little to do with the liveliness of mind that forever mocks its own activities including those of the setting-down of words. The book alludes to varying, recognizable tensions, actions (anxiety, affection, anger), yet Mr. Whalen seems preoccupied, at some tonal distance from the thing he is saying. What can one make of writing out of touch with the very feelings it is intending to convey? What is best in the book are those points where Kenneth, the protagonist, goes off on some distracted flight, an imaginative sidestepping where there is clear tonal accuracy.

"She was talking. He thought about nasturtiums,
he'd seen a great field on a sloping hillside in the park
just for a moment on Saturday. It had been foggy the
ground was dry the nasturtiums glowed. . . ."

Yet even here there is some evasion in that the writing remains tentative, fails even after an entire scene to follow through. One is continually struck, in Whalen's poems, by the mind's speed, the tonal and rhythmic rightness (as in "Delights of Winter at the Shore"). Why in the fiction is there a need for discursive qualification, thoughts and afterthoughts, talk-talk-talk, an author's bland intrusion?—ROBERT SWARD, "Poets at Novels," *Poetry*, Aug. 1968, pp. 355–56

Philip Whalen is the Old Faithful of contemporary American poetry. For twenty years he has averaged a poem a week—some three hundred of which are collected here ⟨in *On Bear's Head*⟩ on 406 pages—and since 1958 he's published on the average of one volume every two years. In one of his best poems—"For My Father"—he describes himself as a poem-producing phenomenon in a figure in which he appears as a Rube Goldberg contraption which manufactures countless poems: a "Cross between a TV camera and a rotary press / Busy turning itself into many printed pages . . ."

. . . the flywheel horizontal
Spinning two directions at once
A walking-beam connected to a gear train turning
camshafts—
Which produces material like this
Sometimes worth money to folks in New York
Or not, nobody knows why.

A handful of Mr. Whalen's poems are excellent, the kind of poem one reads again. Many, many other poems are merely average—good line here, a flicker of insight there; sometimes the title itself may be worth one's attention—Mr. Whalen writes the best titles since Wallace Stevens. A lot are simply boring: the poem to be read as penance during Lent. Still, I suggest that an interesting way to read Mr. Whalen is to read everything—the warts-and-all method of Appreciation of Poetry 101. Read *On Bear's Head* straight through as you might read Whitman if you loved him because he wants to give the reader a poem big as the whole world. Don't restrict yourself to finding only the moments of high poetry.

The reason I suggest this is that Mr. Whalen is the laureate of the day after the Seven Days of Creation, the prosaic everyday, the world of Monday at 10 a.m.: the poet of the drawing room to which Alice returns after her adventures behind the looking-glass. Dinah and her kittens become cats once again, the ball of worsted safely tucked in a corner of the great arm chair, the fire cheery in the fireplace, sister as exacting and unimaginative as ever, the chessmen in their proper positions on the chessboard on the table. What *On Bear's Head* offers us is, in short, the everyday world as poem. And the interesting possibility is, it seems to me, that the more one reads Mr. Whalen—even the punk and Lenten poems—the more one can participate in his special vision that the routines and newspaper and streets and books of Monday are as poetical as the glory of the creation that began one week before when the spirit of God moved over the waters.

What Mr. Whalen accomplishes by means of such inclusiveness is, of course, good news. It is a condition of grace for which many poets have longed, I would bet: the freedom to include any reality from one's daily life into the poem one happens to be writing at the moment. This is the core of his *ars poetica* and it accounts, I suspect, for the veneration he arouses in some of the younger poets.

One sees this freedom in action at its most attractive and successful in "Twin Peaks," for example, where in the midst of what is probably the description and exploration of a nightmare we read how the poet sneezes five or six times; or in the merry confession of cupidity which begins at line 70 in the long *My Songs Induce Prophetic Dreams*: "69 lines / \$.50 per line / \$34.50, if Mr. Rago were to find the poem 'convincing'" or in his decision to include cold-turkey reflections on what the delicate, poignant haikus of "Japanese Tea Garden Golden Gate Park in Spring" might mean in both the philosophical and literary sense: an inclusion which creates both a new poem and a fresh image of the poet writing a poem.

What emerges from *On Bear's Head* is, finally, a portrait of the artist seen in a new, revolutionary role: the poet as the fellow in the apartment next door: an affectionate, lonely, extremely witty, good-humored, intelligent, still dutiful, often deprived, quite well-read, occasionally whining man named Philip Whalen who likes to spend most of his time writing poems about what he's thinking or eating or the scene in which he's living at the moment or about the art and act of poetry. Other features in the portrait, however, aren't so compelling, as far as earning the reader's sustained attention is concerned: his sensibility is, at best, no more than a cut above the average; his world pretty parochial; his attitudes at times sophomoric as in the god-awful poem "Dear Mr. President"; and his ear wooden as the alleged acting of Mr. Mel Ferrer.

With these reservations, I suspect that Mr. Whalen's primary distinction is that he's a poet's poet. Now, this may seem an eccentric opinion: he lacks all of the traditional attributes. He doesn't live in or east of the Writers' Workshop at the University of Iowa; he has always lived out in Joaquin Miller country, usually in or near the San Francisco Bay area. Translations or imitations of his or the latest Russian or Transylvanian poet never appear in *The New York Review of Books* nor does one come across his work in *The New Yorker*; he publishes in *Coyote's Journal* and *Desert Review* (edited and published "somewhere in New Mexico"). Nor is he a familiar, beloved figure on stage at the 92nd Street Poetry Center or in the small lecture hall at the Guggenheim Museum in which the rituals of the Academy of American Poets are celebrated; on the contrary, Mr. Whalen has been seen reading with Beat poets in sweaty, endless poetry orgies held whenever possible in locations such as the Longshoreman's Hall on the docks of San Francisco. But I call him a poet's poet because no other poet has duplicated, as far as I know, the *exemplum* he offers his fellows; namely, poetry can be found anywhere in one's immediate, daily life and thoughts, and it can be found there day after day, week after week, month after month, year after year, decade after decade.—PAUL CARROLL, "Laureate of the Day after the Seven Days of Creation," *Poetry*, Feb. 1971, pp. 338–40

Self-indulgence is Whalen's nemesis, the puerile belief that whatever he puts on paper assumes significance, bird-droppings raised to the curb heights of avant-garde sculpture: "Everybody downtown / Miserable today / Bought the wrong size / Overdrawn at the bank". This is the initial stanza of a poem intent upon relating the author's parochial hipster milieu to the larger inequities of a flawed American scene. Like so many of his fellow free spirits', Whalen's verses are readily identifiable by their persistent diatribes against national materialism and other of society's hideous crimes, which presumably grants automatic relevance to automatic droppings, and their more persistent, incestuous cross-references and dedications to comrades-in-arms, Kenneth Rexroth, Tom Clark, and that most minimal of minimalists, Aram Saroyan. Another poem, "Mozambique," which has the benefit of brevity, can serve as totem for the unearned arrogance that governs ⟨*The Kindness of Strangers: Poems 1969–1974*⟩:

Out of gas. Here is flaked ice
Here is the bottle of Pernod
Here is the garden to sit in
Gassing up.
I must really try to like it.

The only things missing are truth, beauty, discipline, and the backbreaking labor required to transform raw experience into poetry. If this sounds harsh, it is the consequence of frustration, because Whalen is not without potential. From time to time, he is capable of witty perceptions, does push language to the tension point where a metaphysical shift appears imminent, as in a "Message" about winter: "Uninvited lily / (what bulb so dim / what Dora so dumb / Not to see sun's heat / snow white) / howling flower in my skull". When he learns to distinguish between mirror and self, Whalen might yet conduct electricity between word and idea.—EDWARD BUTSCHER, "Fathers and Sons," *Poetry*, June 1977, p. 171

Those who buy this book ⟨*Enough Said: Poems 1974–1979*⟩ will know what to expect. Philip Whalen has been around for a while, at least in San Francisco, and the kind of poetry he writes—light-headed rococo graffiti—has passed from cult to corporation. Through the shredder of what he calls his "blissed out" sensibility he feeds the "incunabula tightrope novel of blank mind," so that a "neutrotic smoke alarm gribbers in the zendo." As Dr. Johnson said of Macpherson's Ossian, "a man might write such stuff forever, if he would *abandon* his mind to it." Whalen's book is mindful of its abandonments, its "aimless luxury." There is little conceptual shape, no argument of vision or from experience. Still, there is a certain charm. Some of its may be the *misérable miracle* (in Michaux's phrase) of drugs; certainly it is the "trill and marble hallelujah" of language and free association. Is it self-indulgent? Very. Hans Memling and Sonny Rollins are thrown together in the same poem, while Thomas Mann boogies with "'a lady who comes in' daily." His method is the pan-shot or zoom-in, "not to claim or be claimed." Latin tags, paranoia flashes, lunch leftovers, ex-lovers, radio spots, and reading scraps—all drift through the poems. Whalen's is, if not a wise passivity, then a mellow one.—J. D. MCCLATCHY, *Poetry*, Sept. 1982, p. 353

WILLIAM DICKEY

From "A Time of Common Speech"

Hudson Review, Summer 1970, pp. 344–48

The most recent time I met Philip Whalen was on Powell Street, a block down from Geary, in San Francisco. We agreed to have lunch together, and as we walked up the block, we talked about confrontations that had just been taking place at San Francisco State College. One of us—I can't remember who—used the word "revolution," at which a tiny lady walking beside us suddenly turned and shouted at us: "Do you know what comes after the revolution?" "Certainly, Madam," Philip said, bowing formally toward her, "the repression." And toward a Japanese restaurant (where his expertise with chopsticks depressed me) he walked composedly on.

Now I have *On Bear's Head*,[1] the collected (though not the complete) body of poems, or single long continuous poem, that Philip must have been working on for longer than the twenty years that I have known him. And in these 400 pages, with their exceptional wealth and range, I find both the unexpectedness and the formality of that encounter on Powell Street. That those two particular elements should come together strikes me as a curious and an instructive marriage, and one whose nature may, I think, extend beyond Philip's work into that of a number of other contemporary American poets.

For it seems to me that both here and elsewhere the pattern on much current American poetry depends not upon the long-continued possibility of the Romantic isolation of self and voice—the deliberately cultivated independence and even idiosyncrasy of style—but upon the acceptance of a poetic language that is shared and general. Of the changes that have taken place in recent American poetry I think this is the most serious and distinguishable, and I think it results in a poetry that is much closer in character to the work of the major English poets of the early eighteenth century than it is to either English or European models of the nineteenth century.

The question of voice is the first of the several elements that lead me to this conclusion. I doubt that it would be easy, or even possible, to smuggle a passage of Arnold into a poem of Browning's, and have the substitution escape detection. Independence and differentiation of voice is seen as a central part of the poetic. The point becomes more acute as we move forward in time. What, if anything, could be interchanged in the work of Marianne Moore, Wallace Stevens, Dylan Thomas, Edith Sitwell? Our real sense of these people as poets depends (to the extent that parody and even self-parody is possible) on the existence of a uniquely distinguishable voice.

But of course it wasn't always that way. The poetry of Pope—that most exultant edifice of light and air in the English language—depends not upon idiosyncrasy, but upon making the most successful and entire statement of a poetic diction and understanding that poets of the period generally share. Poetry of the Augustan period is very frequently communal. *The Dunciad* depends in part on the "hints" Pope solicited and received from his friends; *The Beggar's Opera* has its genesis in a "hint" from Swift; *Gulliver's Travels* is prefixed by a number of ingenious dedicatory poems by Pope; Addison directs the re-writing of Swift's *Baucis and Philemon*, and Swift is prepared, though perhaps a little sullen about it, to accept the compliment of the criticism. This agreement on a common poetic language, which any man who presumes himself a poet will try to speak, reaches very far; even when Stephen Duck, "The Thresher Poet," became a popular figure in literary circles, he did not try to write in an absolute thresher's language. He saw a normative language of poetry and followed it, and it does not appear that he thought there was anything else to do.

I think that many of the qualities of this normative and common poetic language can also be seen in *On Bear's Head*. First of all, the language is personal and occasional, and sensitive to its exact location:

> Hot sunny morning, Allen and Gary, here they come, we are ready.
> Sutras in creek-bed, chants and lustrations, bed of Redwood Creek
> John Muir's Woods.

Let us compare this to Thomas Sheridan, in a poem written to Swift:

> I've sent to the ladies this morning, to warn 'em
> To order their chaise, and repair to Rathfarnham;
> Where you shall be welcome to dine, if your Deanship
> Can take up with me, and my friend Stella's leanship.

The tone is different, but the similarities are greater than the differences. Both poems respect certain assumptions: that a poet should name (rather than making abstract or divine or symbolic) the people he is with, the place he is at, the time of day and the time of year it is, and what exactly it is that is happening. Philip respects this exactitude to the extent that each poem is dated, and when it has been revised or completed later, the revision is also dated. There is a central consideration here: to be real, poetry must derive its authority from a real life.

To effect that end, it follows that the poetry must be various in the experiences it discusses, and must vary its tone widely to respond to the differing nature of those experiences. Philip assumes, as I don't think Arnold did, that a poem can be funny:

PARANOIA REVISITED

> I see in the mirror, these mornings
> That I'm now completely mad:
> Ambition, fear and rage look back at me . . .
>
> I suppose that noise was only the man next door
> Feeding his rabbit.

Let me compare that tone with the tone of Swift, in a passage from "Verses on the Death of Dr. Swift":

> AND, then their Tenderness appears,
> By adding largely to my Years:
> "He's older than he would be reckon'd,
> "And well remembers *Charles* the Second.
>
> "HE hardly drinks a Pint of Wine;
> "And that, I doubt, is no good Sign.
> "His Stomach too begins to fail:
> "Last Year we thought him strong and hale;
> "But now, he's quite another Thing;
> "I wish he may hold out till Spring."

In each instance the poetry is colloquial and occasional, and it is also dependent on the presence of domestic objects: the rabbit, the pint of wine. Such a poetic assumes not only the occasion, but that the occasion is continuous. The poetry of Prior and Gay, for example, supposes that virtually any experience is accessible to it: poetry does not begin or end when a man goes either to bed or to the bathroom. Sexual, scatalogical, lyric, moral—there is a continuous spectrum of experience and a continuous spectrum of poetic language prepared to greet it:

FRAGMENT OF GREAT BEAUTY & STILLNESS

> I thought that if I read Homer a little
> while before going to sleep, I could lie in
> the dark hearing the sound of waves breaking
> on the shore and the cry of seagulls and
> feel hot sun on my back and wind blow
> in my ear. I might see my shadow flat on
> the sand beside me among the shallow
> ripples and rills, thin smooth heavy
> edge of the sea, light in varying densities
> make the wrinkled waters look thick as honey.

This poem interests me particularly because it so clearly suggests what the range is of a poetic that—like the Augustan—is based on common speech. I would think of English poetry as having a rough but radical division: a poetry of speech and a poetry of song. Romantic poetry should finally be sung. It really *does* try to approximate to the condition of music, and thus its effect will often be narcotic, denying the possibilities of definition and distinction. Think of *The Lotos Eaters;* think (if thought has still any meaning or activity in those circumstances) of Swinburne. Objects and definitions melt; Keats's immortal bird may not have been born for death (a melting statement in itself) but it surely was not born for syllogism.

I find "Fragment of Great Beauty & Stillness" particularly helpful, then, in defining the lyrical possibilities of a poetic that does not start with a detachable lyric assumption. "I thought that if I read Homer a little" is the necessary occasion of the poem; its anchor. From that occasion it is possible to reach as far as "light in varying densities / make the wrinkled waters look thick as honey." The feel of these last lines is to me lyric, but because their origin is in common speech and common observation, they are not *transcendentally* lyric: it is their intention to celebrate an object, rather than to subsume it by an absolute either of emotion or sound. The term "lyric" is dependent always on some musical analogy. I am myself prepared to find formal talk musical, epigrams musical; but of course that music is of Campion or of Purcell; it is not Wagner or Mahler, not music of the totally dissolving, totally symphonic sort.

There is another important way in which Philip's poetry can be compared to that of the Augustans: it is learned, and the kind of learning it has extends principally in history and in time. When I think of the work of a poet like Wallace Stevens, the time extension does not seem to be a central one to me: he is not much to Hecuba nor Hecuba much to him. But Philip has the Augustans' capacity to be haunted by time, and the additional problem of being haunted not only by Lucretius, but also by the T'ang Dynasty. In considering the contrast between personal and social poetry, I think it is worthwhile to note that Pope, revising two of Donne's *Satires*, changes every image that extends in space, that is large geographically, to an image that extends in time. Space exists for him as a moment along a line in time. For all of Philip's geographical motion and location, and even in view of the fact that his most successful recent work has been written in Japan, I think he shares Pope's sense of the necessity of a place limitation, a grotto, a small room in which to write. Against this solidity and limitation of place the time line can be released, and argue for the interdependence of ideas, responses, civilizations:

To the Moon

O Moon!
Gradually
        Milo of Croton
Lifting all the seas
        indifferently
Leaf shadows & bright reflections
        simultaneously

The last comparison I would like to make here is between a passage from "The Rape of the Lock" and a poem of Philip's, which I choose not because it is framed on my study wall and signed in Philip's formal calligraphy, but because I think it suggests as Pope suggests the reach and syntactical complexity of a poetic that can be founded on common speech. From Pope:

He summons strait his Denizens of Air;
The lucid Squadrons round the Sails repair:
Soft o'er the Shrouds Aerial Whispers breathe,
That seem'd but *Zephyrs* to the Train beneath.
Some to the Sun their Insect-Wings unfold,
Waft on the Breeze, or sink in Clouds of Gold.
Transparent Forms, too fine for mortal Sight,
Their fluid Bodies half dissolv'd in Light.

And from *On Bear's Head*, this poem, which seems to me to share a number of the essential qualities of Pope:

Goddess

Where I walk is with her
In fire between the ocean waves
Towards that Lady I stand beside
Center of the earth in the center of the air
Stand moving star cloud
Roar music silence
Waves break over our muddy heads
Dash against our sunny feet

I don't have space here, and I don't really have knowledge enough to explore this poetry of common speech as completely as I would like to. Some of its derivations are clear: its colloquial subjects might come easily from Gay or from William Carlos Williams; the abrupt logic of its relationships, the omission of middle terms, from Eastern verse or through transmitters and energizers like Pound. Excellently or indifferently, it is the poetry students I encounter in writing classes write now; it is where their tongues are, though they are not often able to make their speech as spare and as exactly recorded as Philip can.

Notes

1. *On Bear's Head*, by Philip Whalen. Harcourt, Brace & World and Coyote. Paperback (Harvest Books). The unusual conjunction of publishers seems to support my argument.

Edith Wharton

1862–1937

Edith Wharton was born Edith Newbold Jones on January 24, 1862, in New York City. She was educated privately, and traveled widely as a child. In 1885 she married Edward Wharton; they were divorced in 1913. During World War I she helped organize the American Hostel for Refugees and the Children of Flanders Rescue Committee. She lived in Newport, Rhode Island, during most of the years of her marriage, then in Europe (mostly France) from 1907 until her death.

Wharton published a number of short stories in the 1890s that were collected in her first book of fiction, *The Greater Inclination* (1899). During the early years of her writing career she met Henry James; they became close friends, visiting and corresponding regularly. Wharton was to write to a friend during James's last illness in 1915 that "his friendship has been the pride and honour of my life." While they looked to each other for comment and criticism, and James had some influence on the younger writer, their letters suggest that neither truly appreciated the other's best work.

Wharton's first published novel was *The Touchstone* (1900), but her first novel to receive significant attention was *The House of Mirth* (1905). The story centers on the moral dilemma of Lily Bart, a young woman from an aristocratic, old New York family who hopes to repair the family fortunes with an advantageous marriage. She requires luxury and comfort but refuses to marry a man she does not love to obtain them. Unfortunately, she cannot bring herself to marry the man she loves when it would involve living in relative squalor. Ultimately, she preserves her values and dies in poverty, morally (but ambiguously) triumphant.

The concerns of the rich and of characters in conflict with their society continued to be themes in Wharton's work during most of her career. Other significant novels include *The Reef* (1912), *Ethan Frome* (1911), *Summer* (1917), *The Custom of the Country* (1913; the first of a series of novels satirizing American society), and *The Age of Innocence* (1920). Her later novels are heavily satiric in tone, and some critics consider them overly broad and unconvincing, with the possible exceptions of *The Mother's Recompense* (1925) and *The Buccaneers* (1938), which was unfinished at the time of her death. Despite her later lack of success, Wharton is praised for both her solid prose style and her social commentary, including her deft handling of social nuance. She also published three books of verse (*Verses*, 1878; *Artemis to Actaeon*, 1909; *Twelve Poems*, 1926) and several books of nonfiction. Her autobiography, *A Backward Glance*, appeared in 1934, and *The Collected Short Stories*, edited by R. W. B. Lewis, was published in 1968. She was awarded the Pulitzer Prize in 1921 for *The Age of Innocence*. Wharton died on August 11, 1937.

I had to break off the other day, my dear Edith, through simple extremity of woe, and the woe has continued unbroken ever since—I have been in bed and in too great suffering, too unrelieved and too continual, for me to attempt any decent form of expression. I have just got up, for one of the first times, even now, and I sit in command of this poor little situation, ostensibly, instead of simply being bossed by it though I don't at all know what it will bring. To attempt in this state to rise to any worthy reference to *The Reef* seems to me a vain thing; yet there remains with me so strongly the impression of its quality and of the unspeakably *fouillée* nature of the situation between the two principals (more gone into and with more undeviating truth than anything you have done) that I can't but babble of it a little to you even with these weak lips. It all shows, partly, what strength of subject is, and how it carries and inspires, inasmuch as I think your subject in its essence, [is] very fine and take in no end of beautiful things to do. Each of these two figures is admirable for truth and *justesse;* the woman an exquisite thing, and with her characteristic finest, scarce differentiated notes (that is some of them) sounded with a wonder of delicacy. I'm not sure her oscillations are not beyond our notation, yet they are so held in your hand, so felt and known and shown, and everything seems so to come of itself. I suffer or worry a little from the fact that in the Prologue, as it were, we are admitted so much into the consciousness of the man, and that after the introduction of Anna (Anna so perfectly named), we see him almost only as she sees him—which gives our attention a different sort of work to do; yet this is really I think but a triumph of your method, for he remains of an absolute consistent verity, showing himself in that way better perhaps than in any other, and without a false note imputable, not a shadow of one, to his manner of so projecting himself. The beauty of it is that it is, for all it is worth, a Drama and almost, as it seems to me, of the psychologic Racinian unity, intensity and gracility. Anna is really of Racine, and one presently begins to feel her throughout as an Eriphyle or a Bérénice: which, by the way, helps to account a little for something *qui me chiffonne* throughout; which is why the whole thing, unrelated and unreferred save in the most superficial way to its milieu and background, and to any determining or qualifying *entourage* takes place *comme cela*, and in a specified, localised way, in France—these non-French people "electing," as it were, to have their story out there. This particularly makes all sorts of unanswered questions come up about Owen; and the notorious wickedness of Paris isn't at all required to bring about the conditions of the Prologue. Oh, if you knew how plentifully we could supply them in London and, I should suppose, in New York or in Boston. But the point was, as I see it, that you couldn't really give us the sense of a Boston Eriphyle or Boston Givré, and that an exquisit instinct, "back of" your Racinian inpiration and settling the whole thing for you, whether consciously or not, absolutely prescribed a vague and elegant French colonnade or gallery, with a French river dimly gleaming through, as the harmonious *fond* you required. In the key of this, with all your reality, you have yet kept the whole thing, and to deepen the harmony and accentuate the literary pitch, have never surpassed yourself for certain exquisite *moments*, certain images, analogies, metaphors, certain silver correspondences in your *façon de dire:* examples of which I could pluck out and numerically almost confound you with, were I not stammering this in so handicapped a way. There used to be little notes in you that were like fine benevolent fingermarks of the good George Eliot—the echo of much reading of that excellent woman, here and there, that is, sounding through. But now you are like a lost and recovered "ancient" whom *she* might have got a reading of (especially were he a Greek) and of whom in *her* texture some weaker reflection were to show. For, dearest Edith, you are stronger and firmer and finer than all of them put together; you go further and you say *mieux*, and your only drawback is not having the homeliness and the inevitability and the happy limitation and the affluent poverty, of a Country of your Own (*comme moi pour exemple!*) It makes you, this does, as you exquisitely say of somebody or something at some moment, elegiac (what penetration, what delicacy in your use there of the term!)—makes you so that, that is, for the Racinian-*sérieux;* but leaves you more in the desert (for everything else) that surrounds Apex City. But you will say that you're content with your lot; that the desert surrounding Apex City is quite enough of a dense crush for you, and that with the *colonnade* and the gallery and the dim river you will always otherwise pull through. To which I can only assent—after such an example of pulling through as *The Reef.* Clearly you have only to pull, and everything will come.—HENRY JAMES, Letter to Edith Wharton (Dec. 9, 1912), *Henry James Letters*, Vol. 4, ed. Leon Edel, 1984, pp. 644–46

In *The Age of Innocence*, a novel of the early seventies in New York, we receive the same impression that here is the element in which the author delights to breathe. The time and the scene together suit Mrs. Wharton's talent to a nicety. To evoke the seventies is to evoke irony and romance at once, and to keep these two balanced by all manner of delicate adjustments is so much a matter for her skilful hand that it seems more like play than work. Like Mr. Galsworthy's novel ⟨*In Chancery*⟩ it is a family piece, but in *The Age of Innocence* the family comprises the whole of New York society. This remote, exclusive small world in itself is disturbed one day by the return of one of its prodigal daughters who begs to be taken back as though nothing had happened. What has happened is never quite clear, but it includes a fabulously rich villain of a Polish Count who is her husband and his secretary, who, rumour whispers, was all too ready to aid her escape. But the real problem which the family has to face is that Ellen Olenska has become that mysterious creature—a European. She is dangerous, fascinating, foreign; Europe clings to her like a troubling perfume; her very fan beats 'Venice! Venice!' every diamond is a drop of Paris. Dare they accept her? The question is answered by a dignified compromise, and Ellen's farewell dinner-party before she leaves for Paris is as distinguished as she or the family could wish. These are what one might call the outer leaves of the story. Part them, and there is within another flower, warmer, deeper, and more delicate. It is the love-story of Newland Archer, a young man who belongs deeply to the family tradition, and yet at the same time finds himself wishing to rebel. The charm of Ellen is his temptation, and hard indeed he finds it not to yield. But that very quality in her which so allures him—what one might call her highly civilized appreciation of the exquisite difficulty of her position—saves them from themselves. Not a feather of dignity is ruffled; their parting is positively stately.

But what about us? What about her readers? Does Mrs. Wharton expect us to grow warm in a gallery where the temperature is so sparklingly cool? We are looking at portraits—are we not? These are human beings, arranged for exhibition purposes, framed, glazed, and hung in the perfect light. They pale, they grow paler, they flush, they raise their 'clearest eyes,' they hold out their arms to each other 'extended, but not rigid,' and the voice is the voice of the portrait:

> 'What's the use—when will you go back?' he broke out, a great hopeless *How on earth can I keep you?* crying out to her beneath his words.

Is it—in this world—vulgar to ask for more? To ask that the feeling shall be greater than the cause that excites it, to beg to be allowed to share the moment of exposition (is not that the very moment that all our writing leads to?), to entreat a little wildness, a dark place or two in the soul?

We appreciate fully Mrs. Wharton's skill and delicate workmanship; she has the situation in hand from the first page to the last; we realize how savage must sound our cry of protest, and yet we cannot help but make it; that after all we are not above suspicion—even the 'finest' of us!—KATHERINE MANSFIELD, Review of *The Age of Innocence* (1920), *Novels and Novelists*, ed. J. Middleton Murry, 1930, pp. 319–20

Edith Wharton's value seems to me ⟨. . .⟩ not merely, as Mr. Edmund Wilson said in a recent article ('Justice to Edith Wharton.' *The New Republic*, June 29th, 1938) that she wrote 'in a period (1905–1917) when there were few American writers worth reading.' I am convinced that anyone interested in the cultural basis of society, and anyone sensitive to quality in the novel, will find this selection of her writings I have made of permanent worth and unique in character. The final question then is, what order of novelist is she?—i.e., not how permanent but how good? She was, until her decay, a tough-minded, robust artist, not the shrinking minor writer or the ladylike talent. It is characteristic that she should refer to 'that dispassionate and ironic critic who dwells within the breast' of authors, and equally so that she should have considered the unencouraging atmosphere (indifference to her literary success and disapproval of her choosing to write) of her family and social circle, and the adverse reviews she received from outside, stimulating to talent, just as she accepted the severest professional criticism as valuable. This, she said, was better for fostering literary ability than 'premature flattery and local celebrity' and having one's path smoothed; one contrasts this with Mrs. Woolf's claims for the creative temperament. She was a born artist; of the work of her prime she could justly say 'My last page is latent in my first.' Of how many novels in the English language before hers can that be said? She had the advantage of being a solidly-educated lady frequenting the most cultivated society of England and France. As an artist she had Henry James behind her work, whereas Sinclair Lewis, when he later attempted similarly to epitomize his environment in fiction, had only H. G. Wells behind his. She was remarkably intelligent; it is easy as well as more popular to be wise after the event (like Sinclair Lewis) but it takes a kind of genius to see your culture from the outside to diagnose what is happening and plot its curves, contemporaneously as she did. Jane Austen never got outside (of course she could never have imagined doing so): her social criticism is all from the inside and remains indoors without so much as a glance out of the window. It is not only that in Jane Austen social forces never come up for comment or that she accepts the theory of the rich man in his castle and the poor man at his gate, but that she can mention the enclosure of the commons as the natural subject of conversation for the gentlemen at dinner—just that and no more. Yet there can be no question that Jane Austen was a great novelist while Edith Wharton's greatest admirer would not claim that title for her. What makes a great novelist? Apparently not intelligence or scope or a highly-developed technique, though, other things being equal, they often give an advantage. But what then are the other things?

Again, compare Edith Wharton with George Eliot. George Eliot was a simple-minded woman except where great sensitiveness of feeling gave her a subtle insight—even her learning was deployed with solemn simplicity. Undeniably Mrs. Wharton had a more flexible mind, she was both socially and morally more experienced than George Eliot and therefore better able to enter into uncongenial states of feeling and to depict as an artist instead of a preacher distasteful kinds of behaviour. Her Undine Spragg is better sustained and handled than the other's Rosamund Vincy. Undine's sphere of action is dazzling and she always has a fresh surprise for us up her sleeve in the way of moral obtuseness; it was cleverer to make Undine end up at the top of the tree with her only disappointment that her last husband couldn't get made Ambassador (on account of having a divorced wife) than to involve herself in disasters like Rosamund: the manifold irony of worldly success is more profitable than any simple moral lesson and artistically how much richer! Mrs. Wharton writes better than George Eliot, who besides lacking grace rarely achieves the economy of language that Mrs. Wharton commands habitually. Her technique is absolutely right and from the works I have instanced it would be difficult to alter or omit without harm, for like Henry James she was the type of conscious artist writing to satisfy only her own inflexible literary conscience. Now George Eliot in general moves like a cart-horse and too often takes the longest way round. But again it is George Eliot who is the great novelist.

I think it eventually becomes a question of what the novelist has to offer us, either directly or by implication, in the way of positives. In *Bunner Sisters*, *Summer*, and some other places Mrs. Wharton rests upon the simple goodness of the decent poor, as indeed George Eliot and Wordsworth both do in part, that is, the most wide-spread common factor of moral worth. But beyond that Mrs. Wharton has only negatives, her values emerging I suppose as something other than what she exposes as worthless. This is not very nourishing, and it is on similar grounds that Flaubert, so long admired as the ideal artist of the novel, has begun to lose esteem. It seems to be the fault of the disintegrating and spiritually impoverished society she analyses. Her value is that she does analyse and is not content to reflect. We may contrast Jane Austen, who does not even analyse, but, having the good fortune to have been born into a flourishing culture, can take for granted its foundations and accept its standards, working within them on a basis of internal relations entirely. The common code of her society is a valuable one and she benefits from it as an artist. Mr. Knightley's speech to Emma, reproving her for snubbing Miss Bates, is a useful instance: manners there are seen to be based on moral values. Mrs. Wharton's worthy people are all primitives or archaic survivals. This inability to find any significance in the society that she spent her prime in, or to find 'significance only through what its frivolty destroys,' explains the absence of poetry in her disposition and of many kinds of valuable experience in her books. She has none of that natural piety, that richness of feeling and sense of a moral order, of experience as a process of growth, in which George Eliot's local criticisms are embedded and which give the latter her large stature. Between her conviction that the new society she grew up into was vicious and insecurely based on an ill-used working class and her conviction that her inherited mode of living represented a dead-end, she could find no foundation to build on. We may see where her real strength lay in the critical phrases she uses—'Her moral muscles had become atrophied' ['by buying off suffering with money, or denying its existence with words']; 'the superficial contradictions and accommodations of a conscience grown elastic from too much use'—and in the short story 'Autres Temps . . .' a study of the change in moral codes she had witnessed since her youth. Here the divorced mother, who had for many years hidden her disgrace in Florence, returns to America to succour, as she thinks, her divorced and newly remarried daughter. At first, finding the absence of any prejudice against divorce in the new America, she is exalted, then she feels in her bewilderment '"I didn't take up much room before, but now where is there a corner for me?"' 'Where indeed in this crowded, topsy-turvey world, with its headlong changes and helter-skelter readjustments, its new tolerances and indifferences and accommodations, was there room for a character fashioned by slower sterner processes and a life broken under their inexorable pressure?' And finally, depressed by what she feels to be the lack of any kind of moral taste, she loses her illusions about the real benefits of such a change, she finds it to be merely a change in social fashions and not a revolution bringing genuine enlightenment based on good feeling. She explains to an old friend: '"Traditions that have lost their meaning are the hardest of all to destroy . . . We're shut up in a little tight round of habit and association, just as we're shut up in this room . . . We're all imprisoned; of course—all of us middling people, who don't carry freedom in our brains. But we've accommodated ourselves to our different cells, and if we're moved suddenly into new ones we're likely to find a stone wall where we thought there was air, and to knock ourselves senseless against it."' She chooses to return to Florence, 'moving again among the grim edges of reality.'

Mrs. Wharton, if unfortunate in her environment, had a strength of character that made her superior to it. She was a remarkable novelist if not a large-sized one, and while there are few great novelists there are not even so many remarkable ones that we can afford to let her be overlooked.—Q. D. Leavis, "Henry James's Heiress: The Importance of Edith Wharton," *Scy*, Dec. 1938, pp. 273–76

For 60 years the 1905 best-seller ⟨*The House of Mirth*⟩ by Edith Wharton has continued to appear on reading lists for college students. Now with the great surge of interest in women writers and women characters, Lily Bart has become a heroine of the "Movement," a character whose tragic life shows the coruscating effect of patriarchal society upon women. *The House of Mirth* has become a textbook of feminism. One goes back to it to discover why.

In the first 100 pages of the first edition we learn almost everything about Lily Bart that we will need to know during the remaining months of her life. She is just under 30, beautiful and stately, "calculating" about the necessity to marry soon, living by "design" and "plan" because she has no parental sponsorship to help her "campaign," very little money, and only her looks as weapon. (The words I have quoted appear in this way in the first pages, suggesting, inevitably, the clearly laid-out strategies of Julien Sorel, his Napoleonic logistics against women.) She is conscious that she's "been about too long—people are getting tired of me; they are beginning to say I ought to marry," unlike her friend, Lawrence Selden, who is tired of the practice of law but not tired enough to marry well "to get out of it." Lily has no choice about marrying or not: "A girl must, a man may if he chooses." For a possible husband, Percy Gryce, whom she thinks about as her "prey," she organizes "a method of attack."

Lily's vulnerable position in society is accented by what she realizes all too well, that she has been spoiled by the need for luxuries she cannot afford on her own: "She was not meant for mean and shabby surroundings, for the squalid compromise of poverty. Her whole being dilated in an atmosphere of luxury; it was the background she required, the only climate she could breathe in." After losing heavily at bridge, she comes back to her bedroom in a great house in which she is a weekend guest, and sees in her mirror the trace of lines in her face, the face which her mother had assured her, after they had lost their money, would henceforth constitute her fortune: "You'll get it back."

Lily never lacks the power to criticize the surroundings so essential to her existence. The other houseguests are dull but still "lords of the only world she cared for." She is heartened by the thought that, with the possibility of Percy as husband, "there was room for her, after all, in this crowded selfish world of pleasure whence, so short a time since, her poverty had seemed to exclude her." She finds herself, nonetheless, admiring Selden's "certain social detachment" from it all. She listens with interest to his declaration that for him success is personal freedom, the ability "to keep a kind of republic of the spirit." Engaged in "the business" of and "the design" for attracting a wealthy husband, Lily cannot afford the indulgence of Selden's freedom. She cannot join him in his democracy for, from her cradle, she tells her impoverished cousin, Gerty Farish, she was taught that she must be "comfortable." It is all to be blamed on "the way I was brought up," and "the things I was taught to care for" that have determined her destiny.

At the turn of the century money and society were

synonymous. The first faint cracks of the amalgam were appearing (a Jew named Rosedale figures prominently in this novel as the beginning of the separation), but for Lily, extraordinary care must be taken to achieve either one or both. While she sometimes yearns "for anything different, remote and untried," she is quickly brought back by the recognition that to be excluded from this world would be fatal; nowhere "but in a drawing room diffusing elegance as a flower sheds perfume" can she bear to live. She loves to smoke (in 1905 smoking is the sign, for women, of extreme freedom), but she tells Selden she has given it up as a *jeune fille à marier*. Her acquiescence parallels her earlier critical sense: it is not so much that she agrees with society in its dictates as she knows its utility. She understands that money and society are opportunities "which may be used either stupidly or intelligently, according to the capacity of the user."

From this early view of Lily one feels her charm, her intelligence, her rare beauty. In these characteristics she has a strong alliance with Anna Karenina, in the same way as in her emotional and physical reliance on the world of luxury she resembles Emma Bovary and, in still another respect, when a woman friend later observes that "she despises the things she's trying for," she reminds us of Hester Prynne. She is a clear-eyed anti-romantic, a rueful realist whose cold insight cannot do more than make her situation appear hopeless to her. For she lacks "continuity of moral strength" and "purpose" to avoid the pitfalls of the strict social code, and the character to resist its seductions. Unlike Hester, for whom the scarlet letter had not done its office of punishment, Lily is defeated, sinking down through successively lower levels of New York life until she accidentally takes an overdose of sleeping drops.

Although it was inevitable that Lily should not succeed, small accidents help the predetermined defeat along. A careless social slip frightens Percy Gryce away; a more major accident which appears as an indiscretion used by a jealous wife unsettles Lily from her precarious social perch in the house of mirth. But these are incidental to the larger fatalism of the novel. In what Blake Nevius calls "the spectacle of a lonely struggle with the hostile forces of the environment," classic fates are at work on Edith Wharton's doomed Lily, making her a victim of her time, almost a Sophoclean heroine. This may be hyperbole, but it is my feeling that Blake Nevius, the most perspicacious of Wharton's critics, underestimates Lily when he characterizes her as an essentially "lightweight and static protagonist." Static she often is, sometimes by design: there is one scene where she appears in a society entertainment, a *tableau*, in which she poses as Reynolds' "Mrs. Lloyd," pedestaled and bigger than life, like Hester on the scaffold.

But I think he misses the full force of this situation. There is no lightweightedness in her posture. Her immobility is tragically fated and prophetic. Edith Wharton leaves us in no doubt of that when she tells us, early in the book, that "she had a fatalistic sense of being drawn from one wrong turning to another." And then, having committed a crucial social *faux pas*, she flees to the mirthless apartment of Gerty Farish. Lying in Gerty's arms, in her bed, in one of those rare feminine scenes of sexual tenderness in the fiction of this time, she cries out against ". . . the furies . . . you know the noise of their wings—alone, at night, in the dark." Again: moved now to the second and lower level of society where she struggles for financial survival as social secretary to a woman of dubious reputation, the fear of "the mounting tide of dinginess" haunts her in the person of the vengeful Bertha Dorset, the "pursuing fury."

There can be no doubt. To Edith Wharton, Lily Bart is a woman in the classic and aristocratic mold. Her name alone (the abbreviation for baronet) tells us this, and her elevation dooms her to fall. Noble and heroic, her struggle is futile, and in this lies a genuine, early criticism of the society into which Edith Wharton was born, and in which she spent a long and seemingly comfortable existence. Lily's is what has been called "the trapped sensibility." She is the woman whose beauty and whose poverty together are her destiny in an implacable American society.

As I have said, Lily herself knows the true nature of this society, and this makes her situation harder to bear. She sees that divorcées are excluded from polite society, "except those who had showed signs of penitence by being re-married to the very wealthy." She understands her aunt's hospitality to her "because she had the kind of moral *mauvaise honte* which makes the public display of selfishness difficult, though it does not interfere with its private indulgence." At the last, she has moved through these awarenesses to a self-knowledge which speaks for all dependence and lonely women, in her time and, after almost 70 years in ours:

> . . . it was the clutch of solitude at her heart, the sense of being swept like a stray uprooted growth down the heedless current of the years . . . as she looked back she saw that there had never been a time when she had any real relation to life. . . . She had grown up without any one spot on earth being dearer to her than another; there was no centre of early pieties, of grave endearing traditions to which her heart could revert and from which it could draw strength for itself and tenderness for others.

It is significant that this epiphany comes when she is admitted to the kitchen of a former object of her charity, Nettie Struther, and she witnesses the warmth and security of Nettie's family life. Here she has "her first glimpse of the continuity of life." It comes on the last day of hers.

Lily Bart, "fashioned to adorn and delight," "an organism as helpless out of its narrow range as the sea-anemone torn from the rock," dies of her impotence in the face of social hostility, and her own over-reliance on the warm comforts of the great houses of mirth. She dies because she is an unmarketable product in the only arena open to her, the marriage mart. "*A girl must, a man may if he chooses.*" In those poignant words is the tragedy of the unfree woman since "civilization" and "society" assigned her to bondage.—Doris Grumbach, "Edith Wharton," *NR*, April 21, 1973, pp. 29–30

ALFRED KAZIN

From "Two Educations: Edith Wharton and Theodore Dreiser" *On Native Grounds*

1942, pp. 73–82

II

The society into which Edith Wharton was born was still, in the eighteen-sixties, the predominant American aristocracy. Established in New York behind its plaster cast of Washington, its Gibbon and its Hoppner, its Stuart and its Washington Irving, it was a snug and gracious world of gentlewomen and lawyers who stemmed in a direct line from the colonial aristocracy. Though it was republican by habit where its eighteenth-century grandfathers had been revolutionary by necessity, it was still a colonial society, a society superbly indifferent to the tumultuous life of the frontier, supercilious in its breeding, complacent in its inherited wealth. It was a society so eminently contented with itself that it had long since become nerveless, for with its pictures, its "gentlemen's libraries," its possession of Fifth Avenue and Beacon Hill, its elaborate manners, its fine contempt for trade, it found authority in its own history and the meaning of life in its own conventions.

To a writer's mind it was a museum world, delicately laid out on exhibition and impeccable in its sanctuary. To Edith Wharton that society gave a culture compounded equally of purity and snobbery. If no one soared above the conventions, only bounders sought to degrade them. Its gentility boasted no eagles of the spirit and suffered no fanatics. The young Edith Newbold Jones accepted it from the first and admired its chivalry to the end. Its kindliness, its precision of taste, its amenability, were stamped on her. She was educated to a world where leisure ruled and good conversation was considered fundamental. Even in New York, a city already committed to a commercial destiny, ladies and gentlemen of the ancien régime gathered for elaborate luncheon parties. "Never talk about money," her mother taught her, "and think about it as little as possible." The acquisition of wealth had ceased to interest her class. They looked down not in fear, but with an amusement touched by repulsion, upon the bustling new world of frontiersmen who were grabbing the West, building its railroads, and bellowing down the stock exchange. The revolution in Edith Wharton's world, characteristically a revolution of manners, came when the vulgarians of the new capitalism moved in upon Fifth Avenue. For to the aristocracy of New York, still occupying the seats of splendor in the sixties and seventies, the quiet and shaded region just above Washington Square was the citadel of power. There one lived soundlessly and in impeccable taste, the years filtering through a thousand ceremonial dinners, whispering conspiracies, and mandarin gossip. One visited in one's circle; one left one's card; one read the works of Mr. Hawthorne, Mr. Irving, Mr. Edward Bulwer-Lytton. Even as an old woman Edith Wharton was to fill her autobiography with the fondled memory of the great dishes eaten in her childhood, the exquisite tattle, the elaborate service, the births and marriages and deaths of slim patrician uncles and aunts and cousins bestriding time.

It was the way of a people, as its not too rebellious daughter described it in *The Age of Innocence*, "who dreaded scandal more than disease, who placed decency above courage, and who considered that nothing was more ill-bred than 'scenes,' except the behavior of those who gave rise to them." There were standards: the word "standard," she confessed later, gave her the clue her writer's mind needed to the world in which she was bred. Bad manners were the supreme offense; it would have been bad manners to speak bad English, to nag servants. Edith Wharton's first literary effort, the work of her eleventh year, was a novel which began: "'Oh, how do you do, Mrs. Brown?' said Mrs. Tompkins. 'If only I had known you were going to call I should have tidied up the drawing-room.'" Her mother returned it coldly, saying, "Drawing-rooms are always tidy."

Edith Wharton became a writer not because she revolted against her native society, but because she was bored with it; and that restlessness of the spirit was a primary achievement in such a world as hers. Whatever its graciousness, its almost classic sense of the past, its mildewed chivalry, the gentility which a colonial culture must always impose with exaggerated fervor and weight excluded women from every function save the cultivation of the home. Its distrust of the creative intelligence was as profound and significant as its devotion to the appurtenances of culture and the domestic elevation of library sets and vellum manuscripts. It worshiped literature as it worshiped ancestors, for the politeness of society; and if it distrusted the passions of literature, this was not because its taste was conscious and superior. It had not even that generous contempt for literature so marked in the boorish patronage of the arts by the industrial tycoons of the Gilded Age; it rejected what it could not understand because the creative élan affronted its chill, thin soul. It had already become a lifeless class, rigidly and bitterly conservative, filling its days with the desire to keep hold, to sit tight, to say nothing bold, to keep away from innovation and scandal and restless minds. There was no air in it, nothing to elevate an intellectual spirit; even its pleasures had become entirely ceremonial. To judge it in the light of the new world of industrial capitalism was to discriminate against it, for it offered no possibilities of growth.

By becoming a writer Edith Wharton did discriminate against it; but in the effort she liberated only her judgment, never her desire. She became a writer because she wanted to live; it was her liberation. But what it was she wanted to live for as a writer, she did not know. Unlike her master, Henry James, she did not begin with the conviction of a métier, the sense of craftsmanship and art; she did not even begin with that artist's curiosity which mediates between cultures, that passionate interest in ideas and the world's experiences which stimulates and nourishes the energy of art. She asked only to be a Writer, to adopt a career and enjoy a freedom; she offered nothing in exchange.

Even Edith Wharton's marriage, which might in other circumstances have liberated and matured her, repressed her. Her husband, as she confessed with remarkable candor in her autobiography—and the intensity and poignance of that confession was itself significant in so reticent and essentially trivial a record—was a conventional banker and sportsman of her own class, without the slightest interest in ideas and humiliatingly indifferent to her aspirations. Her greatest desire in youth had been to meet writers, not some particular master, but Writers; her marriage forced her into a life of impossible frivolity and dullness. It was a period in the middle eighties when the younger generation of American aristocracy challenged the vulgar nouveaux riches by emulating their pleasures but soon came to admire them; the aspirant young novelist who had been married off at twenty-three in peremptory aristocratic fashion now found herself dreaming of literary conquests amidst a distracting and exasperating round of luncheons, parties, yachting trips, and ballroom dinners. "The people about me were so indifferent to everything I really cared for," she wrote in later life, "that complying with the tastes of others had become a habit, and it was only some years later, when I had written several books, that I finally rebelled and pleaded for the right to something better." In her earliest years her family had discouraged her; her husband and his friends now ridiculed her. They evidently spoke to her of her work only to disparage it; the young society woman had now to endure the crowning humiliation of pursuing even spasmodically a career which her immediate circle thought disgraceful and ridiculous. Then her husband became ill and remained so for a good many years. It was not a pleasant illness, and it diverted her from literature. Significantly enough, it was not until she was able to arrange for his care by others that she moved to Paris—her true home, as she always thought of it—where she lived until her death.

III

It is easy to say now that Edith Wharton's great subject should have been the biography of her own class, for her education and training had given her alone in her literary generation the best access to it. But the very significance of that education was her inability to transcend and use it. Since she could do no other, she chose instead to write, in various forms and with unequal success, the one story she knew best, the story that constituted her basic experience—her own. Her great theme, like that of her friend Henry James, became the plight of the young and innocent in a world of greater intricacy than they were accustomed to. But where James was obsessed by the moral complexity of that theme and devoted his career to the evaluation and dramatization of opposing cultures, Edith Wharton specialized in tales of victimization. To James the emotional problems of his characters were the representative expression of a larger world of speech, manners, and instinct—whose significance was psychological and universal. He saw his work as a body of problems that tested the novelist's capacity for difficulty and responsibility. To Edith Wharton, whose very career as a novelist was the tenuous product of so many personal maladjustments, the novel became an involuted expression of self.

She was too cultivated, too much the patrician all her days, to vulgarize or even to simplify the obvious relations between her life and her work; she was too fastidious an artist even in her constricted sphere to yield to that obvious romanticism which fulfills itself to explicit confession. But fundamentally she had to fall back upon herself, since she was never, as she well knew, to rise above the personal difficulties that attended her career. She escaped the tedium and medocrity to which her class had condemned her, but the very motivation of that escape was to become a great artist, to attain by the extension of her powers the liberation she needed as a woman; and a great artist, even a completely devoted artist, she never became. James, who gave her friendship, could encourage but not instruct her. Actually, it was not to become such a writer as he, but to become a writer, that she struggled; what he had to give her—precision of motive, cultivation of taste, the sense of style—she possessed by disposition and training. James's need of art was urgent, but its urgency was of the life of the spirit; Edith Wharton's was desperate, and by a curious irony she escaped that excessive refinement and almost abstract mathematical passion for art that encumbered James. She could speak out plainly with a force he could never muster; her own alienation and loneliness gave her a sympathy for erratic spirits and "illicit" emotions that was unique in its time. It has been forgotten how much Edith Wharton contributed to the plain-speaking traditions of American realism. Women wrote to her indignantly asking if she had known respectable women; Charles Eliot Norton once even warned her that "no great work of the imagination has ever been based on illicit passion."

The greater consequence of Edith Wharton's failure to fulfill herself in art was its deepening of her innate disposition to tragedy. She was conscious of that failure even when she was most successful, and in the gap between her resolution and her achievement she had recourse to a classical myth, the pursuing Eumenides who will not let Lily Bart—or Edith Wharton—rest. She was among the few in her generation to attain the sense of tragedy, even the sense of the world as pure evil, and it found expression in the biting edge of her novels and the superficially genial fatalism of their drama. "Life is the saddest thing," she wrote once, "next to death," and the very simplicity and purity of that knowledge set her off in a literary generation to whom morality signified the fervor of the muckrakers and for whom death as a philosophical issue had no meaning. Spiritually, indeed, Edith Wharton was possessed of resources so much finer than any contemporary American novelist could muster that even the few superior novelists of her time seem gross by comparison. It was a service, even though, like so many artistic services, it was an unconscious one, to talk the language of the soul at a time when the best energies in American prose were devoted to the complex new world of industrial capitalism.

Yet what a subject lay before Edith Wharton in that world, if only she had been able, or willing, to use it! Her class was dying slowly but not painfully, and it was passing on into another existence. To write that story she would have had to tell bluntly how her class had yielded to the *novi homines* of the Gilded Age, how it had sold itself joyfully, given over its houses, married off its acquiescent daughters, and in the end—like all bourgeois aristocracies—asserted itself in the new dominion of power under the old standard of family and caste. It would have been the immemorial tale of aristocrat and merchant in a capitalist society, their mating, their mutual accommodation, their reconciliation. Edith Wharton knew that story well enough; its significance had sundered the only world she knew, and its victims were to crowd her novels. The fastidious college lawyers who had scorned the methods of a Daniel Drew in the seventies would do the work of a Carnegie in the nineties; the Newport settled first by the Whartons and their friends was now to become the great summer resort of the frontier-bred plutocracy; the New York that had crystallized around the houses and reputations of the Livingstons, the Crugers, the Schuylers, the Waltons, now gave room to the Vanderbilts, whose family crest might properly have been the prow of a ferryboat on a field gilded with Erie Railroad bonds, with the imperishable boast of its Commodore founder for a motto: "Law! What do I care about law? Hain't I got the power?" So had the eighteenth-century Dukes of Nottingham developed the mines on their hereditary estates; so would the seedy marquises of France under the Third Republic marry American sewing-machine heiresses. Howells had said it perfectly: the archetype of the new era was "the man who has risen." To tell that story as Edith Wharton might have told it would have involved the creation of a monumental tragicomedy, for was not the aristocracy from which she stemmed as fundamentally middle-class as the rising tide of capitalists out of the West it was prepared to resist?

Edith Wharton knew well enough that one dynasty had succeeded another in American life; the consequences of that succession became the great subject of her best novels. But she was not so much interested in the accession of the new class as she was in the destruction of her own, in the eclipse of its finest spirits. Like Lily Bart, Ellen Olenska, Ralph Marvell, she too was one of its fine spirits; and she translated effortlessly and pointedly the difficulties of her own career into the difficulties of young aristocrats amidst a hostile and alien culture. It is the aristocrat yielding, the aristocrat suffering, who bestrides her best novels: the sensitive cultivated castaways who are either destroyed by their own class or tied by marriage or need to the vulgar nouveaux riches. Henry James could write of revolutionaries and nobility, painters and politicians, albeit all talked the Jamesian language with the same aerial remoteness from plain speech; Edith Wharton's imagination was obsessed by the fellow spirits of her youth. Though she had been hurt by her class and had made her career by escaping its fundamental obligations, she could not, despite all her fertile powers of invention, conceive of any character who was not either descended from that class or placed in some obvious and dramatic relation to it. At bottom she could love only those who, like herself, had undergone a profound alienation but were inextricably bound to native loyalties and taste. Indeed, their very weakness endeared them to her: to rise in the industrial-capitalist order was to succumb to its degradations. "Why do we call our generous ideas illusions, and the mean ones truths?" cries Lawrence Selden in *The House of Mirth*. It was Edith Wharton's stricken cry. She had accepted all the conditions of servitude to the vulgar new order save the obligation to respect its values. Yet it was in the very nature of things that she should rebel not by adopting a new set of values or by interesting herself in a new society, but by resigning herself to soundless heroism. Thus she could read in the defeat of her characters the last proud affirmation of the caste quality. If failure was the destiny of superior men and women in the modern world, failure was the mark of spiritual victory. For that is what Edith Wharton's sense of tragedy came to in the end; she could conceive of no society but her own, she could not live with what she had. Doom waited for the pure in heart; and it was better so.

Is not that the theme of *Ethan Frome* as well as of *The House of Mirth?* Ethan, like Lily Bart or Ralph Marvell, fails because he is spiritually superior and materially useless; he has been loyal to one set of values, one conception of happiness, but powerless before the obligations of his society. It was not a New England story and certainly not the granite "folk tale" of New England in esse its admirers have claimed it to be. She knew little of the New England common world, and perhaps cared even less; the story was begun as an exercise in French while she was living in Lenox, Massachusetts, and she wanted a simple frame and "simple" characters. The world of the Frome tragedy is abstract. She never knew how the poor lived in Paris or London; she knew even less of how they lived in the New England villages where she spent an occasional summer. There is indeed nothing in any of her work, save perhaps the one notable story she wrote of people who work for a living, *The Bunner Sisters*, to indicate that she had any conception of the tensions and responsibilities of even the most genteel middle-class poverty. Sympathy she possessed by the very impulse of her imagination, but it was a curious sympathy which assumed that if life in her own class was often dreary, the world "below" must be even more so. Whenever she wrote of that world, darkness and revulsion entered her work mechanically. She thought of the poor not as a class but as a condition; the qualities she automatically ascribed to the poor—drabness, meanness, anguish—became another manifestation of the futility of human effort.

Edith Wharton was not confined to that darkness; she could hate, and hate hard, but the object of her hatred was the emerging new class of brokers and industrialists, the makers and promoters of the industrial era who were beginning to expropriate and supplant her own class. She disliked them no less fiercely than did the rebellious novelists of the muckrake era—the Robert Herricks, the David Graham Phillipses, the Upton Sinclairs; but where these novelists saw in the brokers and industrialists a new and supreme condition in American society, Edith Whaton seemed to be personally affronted by them. It is the grande dame, not the objective novelist, who speaks out in her caricatures of Rosedale and Undine Spragg. To the women of the new class she gave names like Looty Arlington and Indiana Frusk; to their native habitats, names like Pruneville, Nebraska, and Hallelujah, Missouri. She had no conception of America as a unified and dynamic economy, or even as a single culture. There was old New York, the great house in Lenox (from which she gazed down upon Ethan Frome), and the sprawling wilderness that called itself the Middle West, a land of graceless manners, hoary jests, businessmen, and ridiculous provincial speech. It was a condescending resignation that evoked in her the crackling irony that smarted in her prose; it was the biting old dowager of American letters who snapped at her lower-class characters and insulted them so roundly that her very disgust was comic. As the world about her changed beyond all recognition, she ignored the parvenu altogether and sought refuge in nostalgia. Her social views, never too liberal or expansive, now solidified themselves into the traditional views of reaction. After 1920, when she had fulfilled her debt to the past with *The Age of Innocence*, she lost even that interest in the craft of fiction which had singled her out over the years, and with mechanical energy poured out a series of cheap novels which, with their tired and forlorn courtesy, their smooth rendering of the smooth problems of women's magazine fiction, suggest that Edith Wharton exhausted herself periodically, and then finally, because she had so quickly exhausted the need that drove her to literature.

If it is curious to remember that she always suggested more distinction than she possessed, it is even more curious to see how the interests of the American novel have since passed her by. James has the recurrent power to excite the literary mind. Edith Wharton, who believed so passionately in the life of art that she staked her life upon it, remains not a great artist but an unusual American, one who brought the weight of her personal experience to bear upon a modern American literature to which she was spiritually alien.

EDMUND WILSON

"Justice to Edith Wharton" (1938/1947)

The Wound and the Bow

1947, pp. 195–213

Before Edith Wharton died, the more commonplace work of her later years had had the effect of dulling the reputation of her earlier and more serious work. It seemed to me that the notices elicited by her death did her, in general, something less than justice; and I want to try to throw into relief the achievements which did make her important during a period—say, 1905–1917—when there were few American writers worth reading. This essay is therefore no very complete study, but rather in the nature of an impression by a reader who was growing up at that time.

Mrs. Wharton's earliest fiction I never found particularly attractive. The influences of Paul Bourget and Henry James seem to have presided at the birth of her talent; and I remember these books as dealing with the artificial moral problems of Bourget and developing them with the tenuity of analysis which is what is least satisfactory in James. The stories tended to take place either in a social void or against a background of Italy or France which had somewhat the character of expensive upholstery. It was only with *The House of Mirth*, published in 1905, that Edith Wharton emerged as an historian of the American society of her time. For a period of fifteen years or more, she produced work of considerable interest both for its realism and its intensity.

One has heard various accounts of her literary beginnings. She tells us in her autobiography that a novel which she had composed at eleven and which began, 'Oh, how do you do, Mrs. Brown? . . . If only I had known you were going to call,

I should have tidied up the drawing room'—had been returned by her mother with the chilling comment, 'Drawing-rooms are always tidy.' And it is said that a book of verse which she had written and had had secretly printed was discovered and destroyed by her parents, well-to-do New Yorkers of merchant stock, who thought it unladylike for a young woman to write. It seems to be an authentic fact, though Mrs. Wharton does not mention it in her memoirs, that she first seriously began to write fiction after her marriage during the period of a nervous breakdown, at the suggestion of Dr. S. Weir Mitchell, who himself combined the practice of literature with his pioneer work in the field of female neuroses. Thereafter she seems to have depended on her writing to get her through some difficult years, a situation that became more and more painful. Her husband, as she tells us, had some mental disease which was steadily growing worse from the very first years of their marriage, and he inhabited a social world of the rich which was sealed tight to intellectual interests. Through her writing, she came gradually into relation with the international literary world and made herself a partially independent career.

Her work was, then, the desperate product of a pressure of maladjustments; and it very soon took a direction totally different from that of Henry James, as a lesser disciple of whom she is sometimes pointlessly listed. James's interests were predominantly esthetic: he is never a passionate social prophet; and only rarely—as in *The Ivory Tower,* which seems in turn to have derived from Mrs. Wharton—does he satirize plutocratic America. But a passionate social prophet is precisely what Edith Wharton became. At her strongest and most characteristic, she is a brilliant example of the writer who relieves an emotional strain by denouncing his generation.

It is true that she combines with indignation against a specific phase of American society a general sense of inexorable doom for human beings. She was much haunted by the myth of the Eumenides; and she had developed her own deadly version of the working of the Aeschylean necessity—a version as automatic and rapid, as decisive and as undimmed by sentiment, as the mechanical and financial processes which during her lifetime were transforming New York. In these books, she was as pessimistic as Hardy or Maupassant. You find the pure expression of her hopelessness in her volume of poems, *Artemis to Actaeon,* published in 1909, which, for all its hard accent and its ponderous tone, its 'impenetrables' and 'incommunicables' and 'incommensurables,' its 'immemorial altitudes august,' was not entirely without interest or merit. 'Death, can it be the years shall naught avail?' she asks in one of the sonnets called "Experience": '"Not so," Death answered. "They shall purchase sleep."' But in the poem called "Moonrise over Tyringham," she seems to be emerging from a period of strain into a relatively tranquil stoicism. She is apostrophizing the first hour of night:

> Be thou the image of a thought that fares
> Forth from itself, and flings its ray ahead,
> Leaping the barriers of ephemeral cares,
> To where our lives are but the ages' tread,
>
> And let this year be, not the last of youth,
> But first—like thee!—of some new train of hours,
> If more remote from hope, yet nearer truth,
> And kin to the unpetitionable powers.

But the catastrophe in Edith Wharton's novels is almost invariably the upshot of a conflict between the individual and the social group. Her tragic heroines and heroes are the victims of the group pressure of convention; they are passionate or imaginative spirits, hungry for emotional and intellectual experience, who find themselves locked into a small closed system, and either destroy themselves by beating their heads against their prison or suffer a living death in resigning themselves to it. Out of these themes she got a sharp pathos all her own. The language and some of the machinery of *The House of Mirth* seem old-fashioned and rather melodramatic today; but the book had some originality and power, with its chronicle of a social parasite on the fringes of the very rich, dragging out a stupefying routine of week-ends, yachting trips and dinners, and finding a window open only twice, at the beginning and at the end of the book, on a world where all the values are not money values.

The Fruit of the Tree, which followed it in 1907, although its characters are concerned with larger issues, is less successful than *The House of Mirth,* because it is confused between two different kinds of themes. There is a more or less trumped-up moral problem *à la* Bourget about a 'mercy killing' by a high-minded trained nurse, who happened to have an 'affinity,' as they used to say at that period, with the husband of the patient. But there is also the story of an industrial reformer, which is on the whole quite ably handled—especially in the opening scenes, in which the hero, assistant manager of a textile mill, is aroused by an industrial accident to try to remove the conditions which have caused it and finds himself up against one of those tight family groups that often dominate American factory towns, sitting ensconced in their red-satin drawing-rooms on massively upholstered sofas, amid heavy bronze chandeliers and mantels surmounted by obelisk clocks; and in its picture of his marriage with the mill-owning widow and the gradual drugging of his purpose under the influence of a house on Long Island of a quality more gracious and engaging but on an equally overpowering scale.

Edith Wharton had come to have a great hand with all kinds of American furnishings and with their concomitant landscape-gardening. Her first book had been a work on interior decorating; and now in her novels she adopts the practice of inventorying the contents of her characters' homes. Only Clyde Fitch, I think, in those early nineteen-hundreds made play to the same degree with the miscellaneous material objects with which Americans were surrounding themselves, articles which had just been manufactured and which people were being induced to buy. I suppose that no other writer of comedies of any other place or time has depended so much on stage sets and, especially, on stage properties: the radiators that bang in *Girls,* the artificial orange in *The Truth,* the things that are dropped under the table by the ladies in the second act of *The Climbers.* But in the case of Edith Wharton, the *décors* become the agents of tragedy. The characters of Clyde Fitch are embarrassed or tripped up by these articles; but the people of Edith Wharton are pursued by them as by spirits of doom and ultimately crushed by their accumulation. These pieces have not been always made newly: sometimes they are *objets d'art,* which have been expensively imported from Europe. But the effect is very much the same: they are something extraneous to the people and, no matter how old they may be, they seem to glitter and clank with the coin that has gone to buy them. A great many of Mrs. Wharton's descriptions are, of course, satiric or caustic; but when she wants to produce an impression of real magnificence, and even when she is writing about Europe, the thing still seems rather inorganic. She was not only one of the great pioneers, but also the poet, of interior decoration.

In *The Custom of the Country* (1913), Mrs. Wharton's next novel about the rich—*The Reef* is a relapse into 'psychological problems'—she piles up the new luxury of the era to an altitude of ironic grandeur, like the glass mountain in the *Arabian Nights*, which the current of her imagination manages to make incandescent. The first scene sets the key for the whole book: 'Mrs. Spragg and her visitor were enthroned in two heavy gilt armchairs in one of the private drawing-rooms of the Hotel Stentorian. The Spragg rooms were known as one of the Looey suites, and the drawing-room walls, above their wainscoting of highly varnished mahogany, were hung with salmon-pink damask and adorned with oval portraits of Marie Antoinette and the Princess de Lamballe. In the center of the florid carpet a gilt table with a top of Mexican onyx sustained a palm in a gilt basket tied with a pink bow. But for this ornament, and a copy of *The Hound of the Baskervilles* which lay beside it, the room showed no traces of human use, and Mrs. Spragg herself wore as complete an air of detachment as if she had been a wax figure in a show-window.' In the last pages—it is an admirable passage—Undine Spragg's little boy is seen wandering alone amid the splendors of the Paris *hôtel* which has crowned his mother's progress from the Stentorian: 'the white fur rugs and brocade chairs' which 'seemed maliciously on the watch for smears and ink-spots,' 'his mother's wonderful lacy bedroom, all pale silks and velvets, artful mirrors and veiled lamps, and the boudoir as big as a drawing-room, with pictures he would have liked to know about, and tables and cabinets holding things he was afraid to touch,' the library, with its 'rows and rows of books, bound in dim browns and golds, and old faded reds as rich as velvet: they all looked as if they might have had stories in them as splendid as their bindings. But the bookcases were closed with gilt trellising, and when Paul reached up to open one, a servant told him that Mr. Moffatt's secretary kept them locked because the books were too valuable to be taken down.'

It is a vein which Sinclair Lewis has worked since—as in the opening pages of *Babbitt*, where Babbitt is shown entangled with his gadgets; and in other respects *The Custom of the Country* opens up the way for Lewis, who dedicated *Main Street* to Edith Wharton. Mrs. Wharton has already arrived at a method of doing crude and harsh people with a draftsmanship crude and harsh. Undine Spragg, the social-climbing divorcée, though a good deal less humanly credible than Lily Bart of *The House of Mirth*, is quite a successful caricature of a type who was to go even farther. She is the prototype in fiction of the 'gold-digger,' of the international cocktail bitch. Here the pathos has been largely subordinated to an implacable animosity toward the heroine; but there is one episode both bitter and poignant, in which a discarded husband of Undine's, who has been driven by her demands to work in Wall Street and left by her up to his neck in debt, goes home to Washington Square through 'the heat, the noise, the smells of disheveled midsummer' New York, climbs to the room at the top of the house where he has kept his books and other things from college, and shoots himself there.

The other side of this world of wealth, which annihilates every impulse toward excellence, is a poverty which also annihilates. The writer of one of the notices on Mrs. Wharton's death was mistaken in assuming that *Ethan Frome* was a single uncharacteristic excursion outside the top social strata. It is true that she knew the top strata better than she knew anything else; but both in *The House of Mirth* and *The Fruit of the Tree*, she is always aware of the pit of misery which is implied by the wastefulness of the plutocracy, and the horror or the fear of this pit is one of the forces that determine the action. There is a Puritan in Edith Wharton, and this Puritan is always insisting that we must face the unpleasant and the ugly. Not to do so is one of the worst sins in her morality; sybarites like Mr. Langhope in *The Fruit of the Tree*, amusing himself with a dilettante archaeology on his income from a badly-managed factory, like the fatuous mother of *Twilight Sleep*, who feels so safe with her facial massage and her Yogi, while her family goes to pieces under her nose, are among the characters whom she treats with most scorn. And the three novels I have touched on above were paralleled by another series—*Ethan Frome*, *Bunner Sisters* and *Summer*—which dealt with *milieux* of a different kind.

Ethan Frome is still much read and well-known; but *Bunner Sisters* has been undeservedly neglected. It is the last piece in the volume called *Xingu* (1916), a short novel about the length of *Ethan Frome*. This story of two small shopkeepers on Stuyvesant Square and a drug-addict clockmaker from Hoboken, involved in a relationship like a triple noose which will gradually choke them all, is one of the most terrible things that Edith Wharton ever wrote; and the last page, in which the surviving sister, her lifelong companion gone and her poor little business lost, sets out to look for a job, seems to mark the grimmest moment of Edith Wharton's darkest years. Here is not even the grandeur of the heroic New England hills: '"Ain't you going to leave the *ad*-dress?" the young woman called out after her. Ann Eliza went out into the thronged street. The great city, under the fair spring sky, seemed to throb with the stir of innumerable beginnings. She walked on, looking for another shop window with a sign in it.'

Summer (1917), however, returns to the Massachusetts of *Ethan Frome*, and, though neither so harrowing nor so vivid, is by no means an inferior work. Making hats in a millinery shop was the abyss from which Lily Bart recoiled; the heroine of *Summer* recoils from the nethermost American social stratum, the degenerate 'mountain people.' Let down by the refined young man who works in the public library and wants to become an architect, in a way that anticipates the situation in Dreiser's *American Tragedy*, she finds that she cannot go back to her own people and allows herself to be made an honest woman by the rather admirable old failure of a lawyer who had brought her down from the mountain in her childhood. It is the first sign on Mrs. Wharton's part of a relenting in the cruelty of her endings. 'Come to my age,' says Charity Royall's protector, 'a man knows the things that matter and the things that don't; that's about the only good turn life does us.' Her blinding bitterness is already subsiding.

But in the meantime, before *Summer* was written, she had escaped from the hopeless situation created by her husband's insanity. The doctors had told her he was hopeless; but she had had difficulty in inducing his family to allow her to leave him with an attendant. The tragedy of *Bunner Sisters* is probably a transposition of this; and the relief of the tension in *Summer* is evidently the result of her new freedom. She was at last finally detached from her marriage; and she took up her permanent residence in France. The war came, and she threw herself into its activities.

And now the intensity dies from her work as the American background fades. One can see this already in *Summer*, and *The Age of Innocence* (1920) is really Edith Wharton's valedictory. The theme is closely related to those of *The House of Mirth* and *Ethan Frome*: the frustration of a potential pair of lovers by social or domestic obstructions. But setting it back in the generation of her parents, she is able to contemplate it now without quite the same rancor, to soften it with a poetic mist of distance. And yet even here the old impulse of protest still makes itself felt as the main motive. If we compare *The Age of Innocence* with Henry James's *Europeans*, whose central situation it reproduces, the pupil's divergence from the master is seen in the most striking way. In both cases, a Europeanized American woman—Baroness Münster, Countess Olenska—returns to the United States to intrude upon and disturb the existence of a conservative provincial society; in both cases, she attracts and almost captivates an intelligent man of the community who turns out, in the long run, to be unable to muster the courage to take her, and who allows her to go back to Europe. Henry James makes of this a balanced comedy of the conflict between the Bostonian and the cosmopolitan points of view (so he reproached her with not having developed the theme of Undine Spragg's marriage with a French nobleman in terms of French and American manners, as he had done with a similar one in *The Reverberator*); but in Edith Wharton's version one still feels an active resentment against the pusillanimity of the provincial group and also, as in other of her books, a special complaint against the timid American male who has let the lady down.

Up through *The Age of Innocence*, and recurring at all points of her range from *The House of Mirth* to *Ethan Frome*, the typical masculine figure in Edith Wharton's fiction is a man set apart from his neighbors by education, intellect and feeling, but lacking the force or the courage either to impose himself or to get away. She generalizes about this type in the form in which she knew it best in her autobiographical volume: 'They combined a cultivated taste with marked social gifts,' she says; but 'their weakness was that, save in a few cases, they made so little use of their ability': they were content to 'live in dilettantish leisure,' rendering none of 'the public services that a more enlightened social system would have exacted of them.' But she had described a very common phenomenon of the America of after the Civil War. Lawrence Selden, the city lawyer, who sits comfortably in his bachelor apartment with his flowerbox of mignonette and his first edition of La Bruyère and allows Lily Bart to drown, is the same person as Lawyer Royall of *Summer*, with his lofty orations and his drunken lapses. One could have found him during the big-business era in almost any American city or town: the man of superior abilities who had the impulse toward self-improvement and independence, but who had been more or less rendered helpless by the surf of headlong money-making and spending which carried him along with its breakers or left him stranded on the New England hills—in either case thwarted and stunted by the mediocre level of the community. In Edith Wharton's novels these men are usually captured and dominated by women of conventional morals and middle-class ideals; when an exceptional woman comes along who is thirsting for something different and better, the man is unable to give it to her. This special situation Mrs. Wharton, with some conscious historical criticism but chiefly impelled by a feminine animus, has dramatized with much vividness and intelligence. There are no first-rate men in these novels.

The Age of Innocence is already rather faded. But now a surprising lapse occurs. (It is true that she is nearly sixty.)

When we look back on Mrs. Wharton's career, it seems that everything that is valuable in her work lies within a quite sharply delimited area—between *The House of Mirth* and *The Age of Innocence*. It is sometimes true of women writers—less often, I believe, of men—that a manifestation of something like genius may be stimulated by some exceptional emotional strain, but will disappear when the stimulus has passed. With a man, his professional, his artisan's life is likely to persist and evolve as a partially independent organism through the vicissitudes of his emotional experience. Henry James in a virtual vacuum continued to possess and develop his *métier* up to his very last years. But Mrs. Wharton had no *métier* in this sense. With her emergence from her life in the United States, her settling down in the congenial society of Paris, she seems at last to become comfortably adjusted; and with her adjustment, the real intellectual force which she has exerted through a decade and a half evaporates almost completely. She no longer maims or massacres her characters. Her grimness melts rapidly into benignity. She takes an interest in young people's problems, in the solicitude of parents for children; she smooths over the misunderstandings of lovers; she sees how things may work out very well. She even loses the style she has mastered. Beginning with a language rather ponderous and stiff, the worst features of the style of Henry James and a stream of clichés from old novels and plays, she finally—about the time of *Ethan Frome*—worked out a prose of flexible steel, bright as electric light and striking out sparks of wit and color, which has the quality and pace of New York and is one of its distinctive artistic products. But now not merely does she cease to be brilliant, she becomes almost commonplace.

The Glimpses of the Moon, which followed *The Age of Innocence*, is, as someone has said, scarcely distinguishable from the ordinary serial in a women's magazine; and indeed it is in the women's magazines that Mrs. Wharton's novels now begin first to appear. *A Son at the Front* is a little better, because it had been begun in 1918 and had her war experience in it, with some of her characteristic cutting satire at the expense of the belligerents behind the lines. It is not bad as a picture of the emotions of a middle-aged civilian during the war—though not so good as Arnold Bennett's *The Pretty Lady*.

Old New York was a much feebler second boiling from the tea-leaves of *The Age of Innocence*. I have read only one of Mrs. Wharton's novels written since *Old New York*: *Twilight Sleep* is not so bad as her worst, but suffers seriously as a picture of New York during the middle nineteen-twenties from the author's long absence abroad. Mrs. Wharton is no longer up on her American interior-decorating—though there are some characteristic passages of landscape-gardening: '"Seventy-five thousand bulbs this year!" she thought as the motor swept by the sculptured gateway, just giving and withdrawing a flash of turf sheeted with amber and lilac, in a setting of twisted and scalloped evergreens.'

The two other books that I have read since then—*The Writing of Fiction* (which does, however, contain an excellent essay on Proust) and the volume of memoirs called *A Backward Glance*—I found rather disappointing. The backward glance is an exceedingly fleeting one which dwells very little on anything except the figure of Henry James, of whom Mrs. Wharton has left a portrait entertaining but slightly catty and curiously superficial. About herself she tells us nothing much of interest; and she makes amends to her New York antecedents for her satire of *The Age of Innocence* by presenting them in tinted miniatures, prettily remote and unreal. It is the last irony of *The Age of Innocence* that Newland Archer should become reconciled to 'old New York.' 'After all,' he eventually came to tell himself, 'there was good in the old ways.' Something like this seems to have happened to Edith Wharton. Even in *A Backward Glance*, she confesses that 'the weakness of the social structure' of her parents' generation had been 'a blind dread of innovation'; but her later works show a dismay and a shrinking before what seemed to her the social and moral chaos of an age which was battering down the old edifice that she herself had once depicted as a prison. Perhaps, after all, the old mismated couples who had stayed married in deference to the decencies were better than the new divorced who were not aware of any duties at all.

The only thing that does survive in *A Backward Glance* is some trace of the tremendous blue-stocking that Mrs. Wharton was in her prime. The deep reverence for the heroes of art and thought—though she always believed that Paul Bourget was one of them—of the woman who in earlier days had written a long blank-verse poem about Vesalius, still makes itself felt in these memoirs. Her culture was rather heavy and grand—a preponderance of Goethe and Schiller, Racine and La Bruyère—but it was remarkably solid for an American woman and intimately related to her life. And she was one of the few Americans of her day who cared enough about serious literature to take the risks of trying to make some contribution to it. Professor Charles Eliot Norton—who had, as she dryly remarks, so admirably translated Dante—once warned her that 'no great work of the imagination' had 'ever been based on illicit passion.' Though she herself in her later years was reduced to contemptuous complaints that the writers of the new generations had 'abandoned creative art for pathology,' she did have the right to insist that she had 'fought hard' in her earlier days 'to turn the wooden dolls' of conventional fiction 'into struggling, suffering human beings.' She had been one of the few such human beings in the America of the early nineteen hundreds who found an articulate voice and set down a durable record.

The above was written in 1937. An unfinished novel by Edith Wharton was published in 1938. This story, *The Buccaneers*, deserves a word of postscript. The latter part of it, even allowing for the fact that it was never carried beyond a first draft, seems banal and a little trashy. Here as elsewhere the mellowness of Mrs. Wharton's last years has dulled the sharp outlines of her fiction: there are passages in *The Buccaneers* which read like an old-fashioned story for girls. But the first section has certain brilliance. The figures of the children of the *nouveaux riches* at Saratoga during the seventies, when the post-Civil-War fortunes were rolling up, come back rather diminished in memory but in lively and charming colors, like the slides of those old magic lanterns that are mentioned as one of their forms of entertainment. And we learn from Mrs. Wharton's scenario for the unfinished part of the tale that it was to have had rather an interesting development. She has here more or less reversed the values of the embittered *Custom of the Country:* instead of playing off the culture and tradition of Europe against the vulgar Americans who are insensible to them, she dramatizes the climbing young ladies as an air-clearing and revivifying force. In the last pages she lived to write she made it plain that the hardboiled commercial elements on the rise in both civilizations were to come to understand one another perfectly. But there is also an Anglo-Italian woman, the child of Italian revolutionaries and a cousin of Dante Gabriel Rossetti, who has been reduced to working as a governess and who has helped to engineer the success of the American girls in London. The best of these girls has been married to a dreary English duke, who represents everything least human in the English aristocratic system. Laura Testvalley was to forfeit her own hopes of capturing an amateur esthete of the older generation of the nobility in order to allow the young American to elope with an enterprising young Englishman; and thus to have let herself in for the fate of spending the rest of her days in the poverty and dulness of her home, where the old revolution had died. As the light of Edith Wharton's art grows dim and at last goes out, she leaves us, to linger on our retina, the large dark eyes of the clever spinster, the serious and attentive governess, who trades in worldly values but manages to rebuff these values; who, in following a destiny of solitude and discipline, contends for the rights of the heart; and who, child of a political movement played out, yet passes on something of its impetus to the emergence of the society of the future.

BLAKE NEVIUS

From "Toward the Novel of Manners"

Edith Wharton: A Study of Her Fiction

1953, pp. 53–77

If we can take seriously one of Mrs. Wharton's earliest recollections, she was destined from the beginning to be a realist. As a child in Paris, she used to sit in a chair, holding in her lap a book she could not read (frequently it was upside down), and make up stories about the only people who were real to her imagination—the grownups with whom she was surrounded almost to the exclusion of company of her own age. Mother Goose and Hans Christian Andersen bored her, but the very mundane domestic crises of the Greek gods roused the future novelist's imagination to a creative boil. Then, as later, she evidently was prolific, but none of her stories was taken down: "All I remember is that my tales were about what I still thought of as 'real people' (that is, grown-up people, resembling in appearance and habits my family and their friends, and caught in the same daily coil of 'things that might have happened')." It is no great descent, after all, from Olympus to the House of Mirth.

Edith Wharton's account of the problems she met and overcame in the writing of her second novel may be found in *A Backward Glance*. Edward Burlingame, to whom the unwritten story was promised, had cut into her leisurely program with the request that she deliver the novel ahead of schedule so that its serial publication in *Scribner's Magazine* could begin immediately. Faced with the task of writing the book in six months, she tied herself for the first time to the professional routine of daily composition. With *The Valley of Decision* the only major work to her credit, she still regarded herself as an apprentice and *The House of Mirth* as the first real test of her powers. "It was not until I wrote *Ethan Frome*," she recalled in her memoirs, "that I suddenly felt the artisan's full control of his implements."

She had long since settled on her subject: the pleasure-seeking society of fashionable New York at the turn of the century. But although it was the material she knew best, the question of its "typical human significance" defied her. "In what aspect," she asked herself, "could a society of irresponsible pleasure-seekers be said to have, on the 'old woe of the world,' any deeper bearing than the people composing such a society could guess?" Almost at the same moment, Henry James was recording his renewed impressions of the United States for *The American Scene*. Confronted, in Newport, by "the ivory idol, whose name is leisure," he decided he would hardly choose that idle and luxurious little world, where the social elements, "even in their own kind, are as yet too light and thin," for the materials of a tragedy. "People love and hate and aspire with the greatest intensity when they have to make their time and opportunity."[1] If this was true of Newport, it was no less true of the fashionable New York world of *The House of Mirth*.

It is to Edith Wharton's credit that she recognized the perilous transparency of the human nature she had to deal with—a human nature subject to no stresses that money could not alleviate, and therefore incapable of expressing itself with the greatest intensity. The characterization of Lily Bart was central to the problem; and since Lily, in order to satisfy her function in the novel, had to take her cue from the more wordly of her associates, she remains, so far as the moral significance of her actions is concerned, until almost the end of the novel an essentially lightweight and static protagonist. Nevertheless, she has, if only in embryo, certain qualities which raise her above her associates and make her distinctly worth saving, so that her fate, if not tragic according to any satisfactory definition of the term, at least impresses us with the sense of infinite and avoidable waste. Edith Wharton's own answer to her question was "that a frivolous society can acquire dramatic significance only through what its frivolity destroys. Its tragic implication lies in its power of debasing people and ideals." Change the word "frivolous" to "materialistic," and the story of Lily Bart assumes a larger significance. Edith Wharton was one of the first American novelists to develop the possibilities of a theme which since the turn of the century has permeated our fiction: the waste of human and spiritual resources which in America went hand in hand with the exploitation of the land and forests. *The House of Mirth* belongs in the same category with *Windy McPherson's Son, The Professor's House*, Robert Herrick's *Clark's Field*, and countless other novels which tried to calculate the expense of spirit that a program of material self-conquest entailed.

There is some indication that Mrs. Wharton conceived of her action, perhaps unconsciously, in terms of naturalistic tragedy. In *A Backward Glance* she recalls her introduction to "the wonder-world of nineteenth century science" and the excitement of reading for the first time the works of Darwin, Huxley, Spencer, Haeckel, and other evolutionists. It is impossible, perhaps, to calculate their influence, but it has never been considered. She was perfectly acquainted, moreover, with the French naturalistic tradition beginning with Flaubert, and it is not impossible that Emma Bovary is the spiritual godmother of Lily Bart. But this is at best circumstantial evidence, whereas the novel itself adequately conveys the suggestion. Its theme is the victimizing effect of a particular environment on one of its more helplessly characteristic products. It was the discovery of the nineteenth century, as someone has said, that Society, rather than God or Satan, is the tyrant of the universe; and the society into whose narrow ideal Lily Bart is inducted at birth conspires with her mother's example and training to defeat from the start any chance of effective rebellion. In the naturalistic tradition, the action of *The House of Mirth* is in a sense all denouement, for Lily's conflict with her environment—no more than the feeble and intermittent beating of her wings against the bars of "the great gilt cage"—is mortgaged to defeat. Her vacillation between the claims of the spirit represented by Selden and the prospect of a wealthy marriage is never quite convincing. Beyond Selden's tentative solicitations there is nothing in her life to encourage rebellion. And undermining his influence is the symbolic figure of Gerty Farish, Lily's cousin, embodying the "dinginess" which above everything else Lily dreads.

Lily, in short, is as completely and typically the product of her heredity, environment, and the historical moment which found American materialism in the ascendant as the protagonist of any recognized naturalistic novel. Like any weak individual—like Clyde Griffiths or Carrie Meeber—she is at the mercy of every suggestion of her immediate environment; she responds to those influences which are most palpably present at a given moment. Although we are asked to believe that two sides of her personality are struggling for possession, there is no possibility of a genuine moral conflict until near the end of the action when as a result of suffering she experiences the self-realization which is the condition of any moral growth. Through no fault of her own, she has—*can* have—only the loosest theoretical grasp of the principles which enable Selden to preserve his weak idealism from the corroding atmosphere in which they are both immersed.

> Inherited tendencies had combined with early training to make her the highly specialized product that she was: an organism as helpless out of its narrow range as the sea-anemone torn from the rock. She had been fashioned to adorn and delight; to what other end does nature round the rose-leaf and paint the humming-bird's breast? And was it her fault that the purely decorative mission is less easily and harmoniously fulfilled among social beings than in the world of nature? That it is apt to be hampered by material necessities or complicated by moral scruples?

The idea, much less happily expressed, might have been taken from Dreiser. It is all there: the deterministic view reinforced by analogies drawn from nature, even the rhetorical form of address. True to the logic imposed by her subject and theme, Mrs. Wharton seems to imply what Dreiser everywhere affirms: that in the struggle for survival the morally scrupulous individual has in effect disarmed himself. Lily's vagrant impulses of generosity and disinterestedness and her antique sense of honor are the weak but fatal grafts on her nature.

I do not want to press the point too far. The impact of the passage is after all still very different from what it would be in Dreiser, for Edith Wharton never rode determinism as a thesis. Her view was conditioned by a faith in moral values that collided head on with the implications of determinism, and it was impossible for her to present a situation without regard to its moral significance. But the day is past when we necessarily see a contradiction if the two views are embraced simultaneously. Naturalism allies itself conveniently—and, if need be, temporarily—with a personal mood of despair, and I think it likely that this is what happened in Mrs. Wharton's case. The mood renews itself periodically, but except in *Summer* (1917) it is never so strong again as in *The House of Mirth*. There is added support for this view, I believe, in the fact that both verbal and dramatic irony are usually active in this novel, helping to establish an unmistakably pessimistic tone.

It should be clear, at any rate, that we are deceiving ourselves if we try to account for the compelling interest of *The House of Mirth* by the nature or intensity of the moral conflict. Besides the reasons I have suggested, the alternatives proposed to Lily Bart in the persons of Selden and Gerty Farish are not at all attractively urged. It was beyond Edith Wharton's powers of sympathy and imagination, and at odds with her distrust of philanthropy, to make Gerty Farish, with her social work, her one-room flat, and the unrelieved dinginess of her life in general, an engaging figure. And what can we say of Selden, who maintains his integrity at the cost of any nourishing human relationship? Like Winterbourne in *Daisy Miller*, he is betrayed by his aloofness, his hesitations, his careful discriminations. He is the least attractive ambassador of his "republic of the spirit," and Mrs. Wharton knows this as well as her readers. In fact, the tragic effect of Lily Bart's fate is jeopardized by an irony directed principally at Selden, for she accidentally takes an overdose of sleeping pills while he is trying to make up his mind to marry her.

The quality in the novel that seizes and holds the reader, and that accounts more than any other for its persistent vitality, is the same which we find in the novels of Dreiser. In the spectacle of a lonely struggle with the hostile forces of environment, there is a particular kind of fascination which is not at all diminished by the certainty of defeat. The individual episodes in Lily Bart's story are moves in a game played against heavy odds, and the fact that the game is conducted according to an elaborate set of rules which are unfamiliar to the general reader gives it an added interest. After her initial success and unexpected reverses, the advantage moves back and forth, but always inclining toward the opponent's side, until Lily is maneuvering frantically to retrieve her position. On the whole, she plays like an amateur, but luck combined with flashes of skill keeps the game from going constantly against her. The episodic structure of the novel, which Mrs. Wharton labored vainly to control,[2] reinforces this impression: the individual moves and countermoves stand out prominently from the action as a whole. In contrast to *The Valley of Decision*, the author treats her subject for the most part scenically, letting the episodes speak for themselves. Moreover, if the interest were centered in the moral conflict instead of the external drama, it would be reasonable to expect a narrower aesthetic distance, as in *The Reef* or *The Fruit of the Tree*. Either that or we must agree with Mrs. Wharton's implication in A *Backward Glance* that she has learned very little from the later Henry James and is still inclined, as the master himself complained, to survey the psychological terrain from too great a height. But the fact seems to be that our attention is directed to a scene of life presented in its broader aspects rather than to a complicated moral dilemma.

For its contemporary interest, the novel relies less heavily than is sometimes assumed on the portrait of a particular society and on the value to the social historian of Mrs. Wharton's authentic delineation of manners. Lily Bart as a type has survived and multiplied, and the society in which she figured is still recognizable, although it has democratized itself to the point where it has lost some of the dramatic possibilities with which a complex gradation of manners once endowed it. Lily is what Justine Brent, in *The Fruit of the Tree*, lives in dread of becoming and what Sophy Viner, in *The Reef*, becomes—"one of those nomadic damsels who form the camp-followers of the great army of pleasure." In return for their hospitality, she serves her wealthy friends—or, rather, is used by them—as social secretary, chauffeur, auxiliary hostess, and, less agreeably, as go-between and scapegoat in their extramarital adventures. The personal freedom of Selden or Gerty Farish seems to her to be purchased at too great a cost. Her compromise is a familiar one in our society; her successors are legion. She is still around, in the person of Susy Lansing of *The Glimpses of the Moon* (1922), when Edith Wharton makes her first survey of postwar manners. Today, every community that can boast the equivalent of a four hundred has its quota of Lily Barts.

If there is a single dominant emphasis in the fiction of the decade and a half preceding the First World War, it is on the drama of social aspiration—a drama managed, I should add, almost entirely by women. *The House of Mirth* joins a trend that had become noticeable in such pioneer treatments of the theme as Henry Blake Fuller's *With the Procession* (1895), Robert Herrick's *The Gospel of Freedom* (1898), and Robert Grant's *Unleavened Bread* (1900). According to these novelists, the moral landscape was being altered by middle-class wives oppressed by two much leisure and by the fact of their husbands' increasing devotion to business. Bored, restless, and conscious as never before of their individuality and their right to a freedom not yet adequately defined, they had begun to exert their powers in the social arena. Although Lily Bart was single and moved in a more inaccessible sphere than the emancipated heroines of Fuller, Herrick, Grant, and David Graham Phillips, her motives were none the less familiar to the public that established *The House of Mirth* among the year's best sellers. Nevertheless, it was in *The Custom of the Country* that Edith Wharton most nearly approximated the type of novel established by her predecessors, and for that reason we will have occasion to look more closely at the "new woman" novel in relation to the career of Undine Spragg.

For present purposes, it is only necessary to remind ourselves that it is the novelist of manners who is able to dramatize most effectively the social-climbing adventure. When Lily Bart, following the debacle on the French Riviera, finds herself reduced to the hospitality of the Gormer set, she is able to measure the extent of her fall by certain unmistakable signs: "The people about her were doing the same things as the Trenors, the Van Osburghs, and the Dorsets: the difference lay in a hundred shades of aspect and manner, from the pattern of the men's waistcoats to the inflexion of the women's voices." In the total context of Mrs. Wharton's fiction, the passage is of the utmost significance, for it emphasizes the importance of manners—the "hundred shades of aspect and manner"—in conditioning the view of reality we get through her novels. Never for a moment was she unaware of the conflict of appearances by means of which the individual and his values, as well as the constant changes within the social structure, are defined. In novel after novel she uses the data resulting from her careful observation and differentiation of manners at various levels of American society not merely to enhance the illusion, but to plot the real undertaking in which most of her characters are engaged: that of determining, fixing, or altering their status in society. In the fulfillment of this purpose, no data is too trivial—not even the pattern of waistcoats. Writing on Balzac, Henry James betrayed his envy of the great French novelist because for him "the old world in which costume had . . . a social meaning" had happily lingered on.

> The most personal shell of all, the significant dress of the individual, whether man or woman, is subject to as sharp and as deep a notation—it being no small part of [Balzac's] wealth of luck that the age of dress differentiated and specialized from class to class and character to character, not least moreover among men, could still give him opportunities of choice, still help him to define and intensify, or peculiarly to *place* his apparitions.[3]

The same assumption underlies everything Edith Wharton wrote. When Halo Tarrant, in *Hudson River Bracketed*, is coaching Vance Weston in the writing of his elegiac novel *Instead*, her advice echoes the passage from James: "Don't forget that Alida would always have had her handkerchief in her hand: with a wide lace edge. . . . It's important, because it made them use their hands differently. . . . And their minds, too, perhaps." Edith Wharton's absorption in the minutiae of appearance has such a direct bearing on her intent that we can forgive her the comparatively few occasions when details of dress and decor are elaborated for their own sake.

In his important and suggestive essay "Manner, Morals, and the Novel," Lionel Trilling has defined the novel as "a perpetual quest for reality, the field of its research being always the social world, the material of its analysis being always manners as the indication of the direction of man's soul."[4] He insists that the definition requires the broadest interpretation of the term "manners." To limit it to the forms, gestures, and ceremonies which relieve the friction of social intercourse would be absurd, and to extend it to include the larger notion of "customs" would make the definition only slightly more valid. The term is all but undefinable because it must be used to suggest so much: customs and polite usages, surely—but also language, names, dress, cuisine, the various expressions of religious, moral, political, and aesthetic values—all the signs, tangible and vague, by which a group either comprising or functioning within a culture emphasizes its separateness.

In a long-established, traditionally rich culture the signs will be abundant and generally reliable. Manners will be more or less stabilized and thus provide a surer guide to the novelist. But in a new, amorphous, self-consciously democratic culture the signs will be fewer and more uncertain. Henry James, recognizing this, complained to his friend William Dean Howells that there was little material for the novelist in a rudimentary social order. Howells' reply was characteristic and rather smug: "There is the whole of human nature!" *But*, comments Edith Wharton in relating the exchange, "what does 'human nature' thus denuded consist in, and how much of it is left when it is separated from the web of customs, manners, culture it has elaborately spun about itself?"[5] Howells' remark starts from an assumption that most American novelists have tacitly shared, that a preoccupation with manners is antidemocratic because it admits the existence of class; and the fact that it is addressed to James implies a gentle rebuke. But as Mr. Trilling has observed in another essay: "In fiction, as perhaps in life, the conscious realization of social class produces intention, passion, thought, and what I have called substantiality."[6] Human nature, however we define it, can accommodate itself to a myriad of forms, and these forms in turn provide the data from which we generalize about "human nature." The novelist of manners is above all aware of the importance of these forms as the only reliable index to the passions and ideals of his characters. For Henry James, as for Edith Wharton, human nature could not express itself with any concreteness or dramatic significance except through the medium of manners, and a society that offered a complex field for this kind of scrutiny was more valuable for the novelist's purpose than one that did not. "It is on manners, customs, usages, habits, forms," he wrote to Howells, "upon all these things matured and established, that the novelist lives—they are the very stuff his work is made of."[7] George Frenside, the elderly critic of *Hudson River Bracketed*, speaks with the wisdom of Edith Wharton's three decades as a novelist when he urges Vance Weston to mingle in society: "A novelist ought to, at one time or another. . . . Manners are your true material, after all."

The elegiac tone in Edith Wharton's writing became more pronounced as the opportunities for exercising her particular talent seemed to her to diminish—as manners within her main sphere of observation lost their distinctness and were merged at a dead level of culture. In large part, her fiction is a record of the deterioration of Old World ideals under the impact of industrial democracy. In 1927 she complained that modern America, "inheriting an old social organization which provided for nicely shaded degrees of culture and conduct, . . . has simplified and Taylorized it out of existence." In European fiction, on the other hand, even the novel of provincial life had a "depth of soil" to work in: "This indeed is still true of the dense old European order, all compounded of differences and nuances, all interwoven with intensities and reticences, with passions and privacies, inconceivable to the millions brought up in a safe, shallow, and shadowless world."[8]

There must always have been a great temptation for Edith Wharton to follow James's example and locate her subject in the richer territory of European culture, or, as in *Madame de Treymes*, *The Age of Innocence*, *The Buccaneers*, and to some extent in *The Custom of the Country*, to fasten on the conflict between foreign and domestic manners as at once more easily understood and dramatically more distinct. Her values were European, and she found it impossible to conceive of an "American" culture which, in striving toward some sort of integration, would not sacrifice those values and, along with them, the interest which manners imparted to the social scene. Nevertheless, even during the thirty years of her residence abroad, she kept her eye constantly on America, and practically all of her best fiction, including *The House of Mirth*, *The Custom of the Country*, *The Age of Innocence*, and even *The Reef*, whose setting for no absolute reason is France, demonstrates that the novel of manners can be domesticated. It was the fault mainly of her experience (certainly not of her reading) that she had such a limited conception of its possibilities. As a whole, the America of her last two decades offered a sharper challenge to the novelist of manners than did the America of her youth; but although she admitted that "the tendency of all growth, animal, human, social, is towards an ever-increasing complexity,"[9] she failed to see that tendency confirmed in the development of American society. Even if she had, she probably would have been unable to shift her field of analysis, for she was mainly interested in examining the crisis faced by her own class beginning in the 'eighties and continuing through the opening years of the new century. Her awareness of social change was confined to its impact on the little society to which she belonged. Although she bewailed the increasing standardization of manners in America, it would have been more accurate to admit that they were undergoing a change beyond the range of her notation. She demanded a fixed point of reference, which was provided by the manners of her class but which in the end proved a handicap since it limited her vision. As the manners which defined her world lost their reality and with it their moral significance, the understanding which she brought to bear on her subject, in every novel after *The Age of Innocence*, became more superficial. It was an unfortunate day for the novelist as well as for the daughter of old New York when, as she had foreseen, the Undine Spraggs inherited the earth. In contrast to her subtle differentiation and skillful dramatic use of the manners she knew at first hand, her treatment of the manners of Apex was crude and uncertain.

That she was successful, ultimately, only when diagnosing a partial segment of society seems to me less important than the fact that she made the attempt, unusual at any period in the history of the American novel, to adopt the characteristic interest and method of her great English and continental predecessors—Balzac, Flaubert, Jane Austen, and Thackeray—so far as the resistant nature of her material would permit. Once we have defined her, as she did Henry James, as preëminently a novelist of manners, we are able to estimate her importance in American fiction. It was not by accident that both Sinclair Lewis and Scott Fitzgerald admired her work and that she returned their admiration.

"Manners," wrote Alexis de Tocqueville, "are generally the product of the very basis of character, but they are also sometimes the result of an arbitrary convention between certain men." It seems necessary to make some distinction between manners as an expression of individual character, or what Tocqueville called "natural" manners, and manners as an expression of a particular social ideal, or "acquired" manners. The former are more prominent in any group which is in process of breaking away from one class and forming another, as in the frontier society described by Crèvecoeur or—to bring the example nearer home—in the fast-rising but still indistinct society of *nouveaux riches* who invaded Edith Wharton's New York following the Civil War. Henry James, contemplating the showy mansions, the eternal quest for publicity, and the evanescent values of this group, defined the problem it presented to the restless analyst as one of "manners undiscourageably seeking the superior stable equilibrium." What one noted most of all was the vagueness of its "acquired" manners and, at the same time, the spectacle of its "trying, trying its very hardest, to grow, not yet knowing . . . what to grow *on*." (James merely had a finer sense of the problem's complexity than did E. L. Godkin, whose blunt query in *The Nation*—"Who knows how to be rich in America?"—was prompted by the same observations.)[10] On the other hand, the settled predominance of acquired manners among the mercantile aristocracy of New York was its very hallmark as a class; and since Edith Wharton belonged so wholeheartedly to this class, it is not strange that character in her novels is conceived primarily in terms of acquired manners, the manners which distinguish one class from another, and that she frequently gives us the type only slightly modified by individual traits.

There is another point to be derived from Tocqueville's classification. The conservative individual, whether his name be Newland Archer or George Babbitt—or Edith Wharton—takes refuge, as it were, in the acquired manners of his class. They are a badge of status; they provide evidence of "belonging." The record of Edith Wharton's "motor-flight," some forty years ago, from Rouen to Fontainebleau, contains this pertinent digression:

> Never more vividly than in this Seine country does one feel the amenity of French manners, the long process of social adaptation which has produced *so profound and general an intelligence of life*. [Italics mine.] Everyone we passed on our way, from the canal-boatman to the white-capped baker's lad, from the *marchande des quatre saisons* to the white dog curled philosophically under her cart, from the pastry-cook putting a fresh plate of *brioches* in his appetising window to the curé's *bonne* who had just come out to drain the lettuce on the curé's doorstep . . . each had their established niche in life, the frankly avowed interests and preoccupations of their order, their pride in the smartness of the canal-boat, the seductions of the show-window, the glaze of the *brioches*, the crispness of the lettuce. And this admirable *fitting into the pattern*, which seems almost as if it were the moral outcome of the universal French sense of form, has led the race to the happy, the momentous discovery that good manners are a short cut to one's goal, that they lubricate the wheels of life instead of obstructing them.

Not even in the final chapter of *The Valley of Decision* is the conservative viewpoint more complacently expressed. But notice also that the passage proceeds from a consideration of manners in the larger sense to a conclusion about manners in the narrow sense of "good manners," from manners as revealing a "profound and general intelligence of life" to manners as administering to the ease of social intercourse. Even in the novels, one is never quite sure when Mrs. Wharton is going to make the transition. Although she apparently means "good" in the sense of "appropriate," it is clear elsewhere that merely polite manners had for her a personal value which led her to exaggerate their importance. Inwardly a shy person, she used them as a buffer against the impact of other personalities. According to her friend Mrs. Winthrop Chanler, the formality of French manners was "comfortable to her,"[11] and the accuracy of the observation is implied in Mrs. Wharton's own statement that the French have a "safeguard against excess in their almost Chinese reverence for the ritual of manners."[12] Few people have written about their friendship with Edith Wharton without commenting on the imposing front she erected to the world. Most were frankly terrified at their first encounter with her. "She was one of the few people I have ever known," recalls Percy Lubbock, "who did what severe ladies used to do so readily in novels: she 'drew herself up.'" There is little doubt that before she could confront a large group of people she needed the assurance that formal manners provided. In the shifting social panorama, they enabled her to "place" herself—not necessarily in an invidious sense—in relation to the people around her.

For the novelist's characters, manners have a similar value. By defining their relationship to the other characters, they become a means of penetrating to the reality of the situation. Waythorn, the perplexed husband in one of Mrs. Wharton's best short stories, "The Other Two" (1904), is involuntarily thrust into a situation involving his wife's two former husbands, the outcome of which may be expected to shed some desirable light on Alice Waythorn's character. Varick, the second husband, he understands immediately; they "had the same social habits, spoke the same language, understood the same allusions." But the first husband, Haskett, is a shabby, deferential creature, who wears a "made-up tie attached with an elastic." For Waythorn, the tie becomes the clue to his wife's remoter past.

> He realised suddenly that he knew very little of Haskett's past or present situation; but from the man's appearance and manner of speech he could reconstruct with curious precision the surroundings of Alice's first marriage. . . . He could see her, as Mrs. Haskett, sitting in a "front parlour" furnished in plush, with a pianola, and a copy of *Ben Hur* on the centre-table. He could see her going to the theatre with Haskett—or perhaps even to a "Church Sociable"—she in a "picture hat" and Haskett in a black frock coat, a little creased, with the made-up tie on an elastic. . . . On Sunday afternoons Haskett would take her for a walk, pushing Lily ahead of them in a white-enamelled perambulator, and Waythorn had a vision of the people they would stop and talk to.

Waythorn reviews the illusions which surrounded the first days of his married life: "It was a pity for his peace of mind that Haskett's very inoffensiveness shed a new light on the nature of those illusions." To give him his due, he is ashamed of his snobbery in fastening on the symbolic detail of the ready-made tie. Nevertheless, the revelation which it affords him, taken together with the known fact of Alice Waythorn's callous treatment of her first two husbands, indicates not only the temporal progress she has made but the boundless extent of her ambitions, and in the concluding episode of the story it helps explain the vulgar ease with which she accommodates herself to the normally embarrassing situation of having to play hostess simultaneously to her present husband and two ex-husbands.

There is no better capsule demonstration than in "The Other Two" of the imaginative use to which Edith Wharton put her interest in manners. By and large, manners are to the social scene what form is to the physical: both regulate our sense of the landscape. Absence of manners in the social scene is likely to be accompanied by absence of form in the physical. It is significant that Edith Wharton felt most at home in France and Italy, where centuries of civilized living have conferred a recognizable form on the landscape and architecture as well as on the manners of the people. In *Fighting France* (1915) she speaks of "the sober disciplined landscape which the traveller's memory is apt to invoke as distinctively French." In *A Motor-Flight through France* she remarks that the French villages, as opposed to the English, have "more, perhaps, of outline—certainly of line." The French discovery, alluded to earlier, that good manners are a lubricant, "seems to have illuminated not only the social relation but its outward, concrete expression, producing a finish in the material setting of life, a kind of conformity in inanimate things."

> Here in northern France, where agriculture has mated with poetry instead of banishing it, one understands the higher beauty of land developed, humanized, brought into relation to life and history, as compared with the raw material in which the greater part of our own hemisphere is still clothed.

In such countries as Germany and Switzerland, but particularly in the America west of the Hudson, Edith Wharton missed this particular amenity in both the physical scene and the manners of the inhabitants. I have spoken of the "absence" of manners in the social scene and of form in the physical. As a matter of fact, this is hardly permissible, since what is really implied is a lack of distinction—the failure of landscape, architecture, and manners to impress upon the observer any notion of their civilizing value. What accounts for that distinction where it exists? The answer has already been hinted at in an earlier quotation from Mrs. Wharton: it is the "intelligence of life" which landscape, artchitecture, and manners may, as they do in France, eloquently suggest.

A "profound and general intelligence of life"—it is, after all, the key phrase to an understanding of Edith Wharton's interest in manners. I would refer back for a moment to Mr. Trilling's definition of the novel as a "perpetual quest for reality, the field of its research being always the social world, the material of its analysis being always manners as the indication of the direction of man's soul." Edith Wharton was a realist in the most literal sense of that unreliable term. To her way of thinking, reality was to be sought for in the present and visible, not in the realm of the ideal, in a romantic primitivism, or in the findings of modern psychology. Freud became available to her too late, and then only to be rejected; and the importance of the subconscious she acknowledged only indirectly in her ghost stories and such psychological horror stories as "The Eyes." In the quest for reality, manners were necessarily almost her only guide. She would talk by the hour, Percy Lubbock recalls, "about people, their manners and customs, their scrapes and scandals, so long as these [threw] light upon the human chase." When she testified, as she did repeatedly, to the true "intelligence of life" which prevailed in France, she was in effect announcing her view of reality as shadowed forth by a particular system of manners. That view is comprehensively developed in her little book *French Ways and Their Meaning* (1919), but it may be summarized briefly. Throughout the ranks of French society the diffusion of certain traits is apparent: a reverence for tradition, a sense of continuity with the past, taste, intellectual honesty, absolute probity in business, a love of privacy, and a respect for the practical and intellectual abilities of women. And all of these traits are embodied equally in the manners which are apparent at various levels within this rich culture. It was obvious to Edith Wharton that the French had solved the art of living in a way which vindicated the notion of reality fostered by her own background and training. She found in them a respect for the same traits that were venerated in the society of her youth, although she was grateful at the same time that they did not share her parents' intellectual timidity or their generally low estimate of women's capabilities.

At any rate, it is in the light of a reality conveniently implied by French manners that we may view the world of Edith Wharton's fiction. The manners of the "sham" society which figures in *The House of Mirth* helped to generate illusion because they were based largely on considerations of wealth. "Wages, in the country at large," commented James in *The American Scene*, "are largely manners—the only manners, I think it is fair to say, one mostly encounters,"[13] and he stressed the necessity, for those uninterested in making money merely, of breaking the tie with America. The same objection applied to the manners of Apex and Euphoria, that mythical hinterland of Edith Wharton's ungenerous imagination: they revealed no "profound and general intelligence of life." Fanny de Malrive, in *Madame de Treymes*, an expatriate who is occasionally nostalgic for America, professes to be enchanted with the idea of John Durham's married sister "spending her summers at—where is it?—the Kittawittany House on Lake Pohunk." But the picture has less appeal for Durham: "A vision of earnest women in Shetland shawls, with spectacles and thin knobs of hair, eating blueberry pie at unwholesome hours in a shingled dining-room on a bare New England hilltop, rose pallidly between Durham and the verdant brightness of the Champs Elysées. . . ." Mrs. Wharton's treatment of provincial America broadens as the geographical distance between herself and her subject increases. By the time she comes to write *Hudson River Bracketed*, she is content with a caricature of Midwestern life so gross that we can take it only as a literary expression of the aversion toward America which came out in the intimate conversation of her later years. Perhaps she was encouraged by younger writers such as Sinclair Lewis and Sherwood Anderson to give free rein to her prejudice, and undoubtedly the tasteful decor of the Pavillon Colombe must have made the living rooms of Euphoria seem more hideous. At any rate, the Midwest of her later novels, with its narrow religion, its go-getting philosophy, and its paramount bad taste to architecture, cookery, and speech, has only the most limited authenticity, and consequently it plays havoc with any serious attention which as a novelist of manners she may have had.

Much earlier in her career, of course, the tendency toward exaggeration and oversimplification had been noticeable—not when she was viewing provincial life and provincial types in isolation, as in *Ethan Frome* and *Summer*, but when she was forcing them into a contrast with the world she admired, as in *The Custom of the Country*. At such times, the children of darkness make an all out attack on the canons of taste. As Alfred Kazin has pointed out, they appear with such names as Mabel Blitch, Ora Prance Chettle, Elmer Moffatt, Indiana Frusk, and Undine Spragg, and their everyday conversation betrays the same degenerative influences at work. "Do you mean to say," Undine asks Mrs. Heeny, her mother's masseuse and confidante, "Mr. Marvell's as swell as Mr. Popple?" "As swell?" replies the other. "Why, Claud Walsingham Popple ain't in the same class with him." Somewhat later, Undine has difficulty keeping her oar in the conversation at a formal dinner party:

> . . . She had read no new book but *When the Kissing Had to Stop*, of which Mrs. Fairford seemed not to have heard. On the theatre they were equally at odds, for while Undine had seen *Oolaloo* fourteen times, and was "wild" about Ned Norris in *The Soda-Water Fountain*, she had not heard of the famous Berlin comedians who were performing Shakespeare at the German Theatre. . . . The conversation was revived for a moment by her recalling that she had seen Sarah Burnhard in a play she called *Leg-long*. . . .

Fortunately, it is not often that Edith Wharton overreaches to this extent in the earlier novels. At the same time, she loses no opportunity to enforce the contrast of manners latent in the names, speech, dress, and cultural interests of her characters. In general, it is by such signs, rather than by the explicit commentary, that we establish the tone of her treatment. The names of the men and women in her novels whom we can trust have a certain aristocratic distinction—Lawrence Selden, Ralph Marvell, John Amherst, Justine Brent, Anna Leath—and not only do they speak pure English but they read Montaigne and Shakespeare rather than *Quo Vadis* and *Ben Hur,* and admire Italian primitives rather than "The Light of the World" and the "Mona Lisa." It is not, of course, so simple a matter as these extremes imply, for Edith Wharton has utilized the intervening gradations of taste to differentiate more subtly. If this were not so, her method would be limited always, as in the passages I have just reproduced, to the crudest sort of social satire.

Notes

1. *The American Scene*, ed. with introduction by W. H. Auden (New York: Scribner's, 1946), p. 485.
2. Letter to W. C. Brownell, Aug. 5, 1905 (before publication, Brownell evidently had praised the novel highly): "I was pleased with bits, myself; but as I go over the proofs the whole thing strikes me as so loosely built, with so many dangling threads, and cul-de-sacs, and long dusty stretches, that I had reached the point of wondering how I had ever dared to try my hand at a long thing— So your seeing a certain amount of architecture in it rejoiced me above everything."
3. *Notes on Novelists, with Some Other Notes* (New York: Scribner's, 1914), p. 155. The society of Balzac's day had, for James, "the inestimable benefit of the accumulated, of strong marks and fine shades, contrasts and complications" (p. 136).
4. *Forms of Modern Fiction*, ed. by William Van O'Connor (Minneapolis: University of Minnesota Press, 1948), p. 150.
5. "The Great American Novel" (*Yale Review* n.s. XVI, July 1927) p. 652.
6. "Art and Fortune," *Partisan Review*, XV (Dec., 1948), 1277.
7. *The Letters of Henry James*, ed. by Percy Lubbock (New York: Scribner's, 1920), I, 72. The remark is quoted by Mrs. Wharton in her article "Henry James in His Letters" (*Quarterly Review* CCXXXIV, July 1920) p. 198.
8. "The Great American Novel," p. 652.
9. Ibid., p. 651.
10. *The American Scene*, p. 162.
11. *Autumn in the Valley* (Boston: Little, Brown, 1936), p. 111.
12. *French Ways and Their Meaning* (New York: Appleton, 1919), p. 137.
13. *The American Scene*, p. 197.

GARY LINDBERG

From "The Emergence of Society: Manners in Narrative"

Edith Wharton and the Novel of Manners

1975, pp. 100–108

In her most complex and successful study of manners (*The Age of Innocence*), Wharton analyzes the weaknesses in the amenable social traditions of old New York that caused them to fail sensitive characters like Ralph Marvell and Newland Archer and finally to collapse themselves. But she also presents here a peculiar communal strength. Although old New York was far from her ideal society, its manners were still connected with real human activities. The details in *The Age of Innocence* are more immediate than those in *The House of Mirth* and more substantial than those in *The Custom of the Country* because the manners of old New York represent for her a coherent attitude toward life. By the time she wrote this novel, however, old New York had disappeared, and her historical distance also contributes to the change in her handling of manners. When she writes of the contemporaneous, she presents manners through controlling abstractions if she does not entirely disapprove of them; specificity of detail serves satiric purposes. Here her distance allows her to criticize and to admire at the same time, and the immediacy arises from nostalgia. She is evoking a lost way of life.

To see how her criticism blends with her nearly archaeological zeal, one could look at almost any descriptive passage early in the book, such as the section of chapter 3 devoted to the Beaufort house on the night of the annual ball. One is struck by the analytical cast of the observations, the constant comparison and evaluation. The Beauforts are "among the first" in New York to own the awning and carpet for the ball instead of renting them, and they "inaugurate" the custom of having the ladies remove their cloaks in the hall. In the first instance, such analysis places the scene historically and emphasizes the immersion of old New York in social change. Wharton does not simply describe the Beauforts' house and their way of giving a ball; she stresses the changes they are making. Manners here tend to indicate historical development more than social position. They are not being imitated by outsiders so much as they are undergoing innovation, prodded along by semioutsiders like Beaufort and eccentric insiders like Mrs. Mingott. Beaufort boldly plans his house in such a way that old New Yorkers can get to the ballroom more comfortably and impressively than at other houses, "seeing from afar the many-candled lustres reflected in the polished parquetry, and beyond that the depths of a conservatory where camellias and tree ferns arched their costly foliage over seats of black and gold bamboo." As they begin to feel the effects of new money, they are even proud of Beaufort. That he can give a better ball than they are accustomed to, obscurely makes up for his "audacity" in hanging Bouguereau's nude in his drawing room. His scandalous bank failure later in the book will profoundly shock old New York because his entertainments have implicated traditional society in the world of financial manipulation.

But the historical analysis underlying the very conception of the scene emerges indirectly, for Wharton has incorporated the angle of vision within the perceptions of what might be described as a communal intelligence. Specifically, we see over Newland Archer's shoulder, but his attitudes in these early chapters so entirely reflect old New York that we view the ball, in effect, as New Yorkers do. This accounts, in part, for the immediate, vivid, and inviting details: "the light of the wax candles fell on revolving tulle skirts, on girlish heads wreathed with modest blossoms, on the dashing aigrettes and ornaments of the young married women's *coiffures*, and on the glitter of highly glazed shirt-fronts and fresh glacé gloves." The scene is accessible to the senses, and it is animated by the darting movement of a participant's eye. But the communal point of view also represents a cast of thought. It is the immediate source of the analytic tendencies in the passage. It is not Wharton but old New York that compares this ball to the Chiverses' and notes Beaufort's "audacity" and "fatuities" (his footmen wear silk stockings). The profound relation of manners to perceptions appears in the communal reaction to subtle changes in behavior.

We are confronted with a society that concentrates on the foreground of experience, that is alive to particular manners as evidence, not of acceptance or exclusion, but of propriety or disintegration. The informing quality of old New York is the complex system of interpretation accompanying its manners, and the subtle, discriminating cast of mind shared by old New Yorkers indicates both the strength and the weakness of this system. The refined interpretation of behavior is based on an acute sense of "good form." Throughout the novel particular observations are filtered through a screen of custom; we are constantly reminded of the way things have always been done. Archer arrives at the ball late, "as became a young man of his position," and we learn in a characteristic parenthesis that the "young bloods" usually go to the club after the opera. The rigidity of these customs suggests a rough equivalence in the various ways of "going too far"—there seems to be no way of distinguishing the bad form of a young man coming on time to a ball and that of the Mingotts bringing a "disgraced" countess. The system thus encourages disproportionate responses—Archer cannot simply defend the Countess Olenska, he must "champion" her. His phrasing of his determination during the ball to "see the thing through" reveals a standardized response in which lapses from good manners appear in moral formulas.

The weaknesses of this system are most evident when the New Yorker encounters new ways of behaving, as Archer does in chapter 9 when he first visits Ellen Olenska's house in the "Bohemian" quarter. By having Ellen herself out when Archer arrives, Wharton contrives a scene in which the young man can respond to the setting while he waits; she then illustrates the effects of that setting on his personal relationship with Ellen. The curious thing about Archer's view of her room is that he cannot see much. He spots a few details—some slender tables, a Greek bronze, a stretch of red damask—and his mind darts away. Most of the particularities of interior decoration in his mind do not involve Ellen's house at all but a projection of the house in East Thirty-ninth Street where he and May will live. He cannot come to terms with the unforeseen style of Ellen Olenska except by referring back to the interiors he has learned to see. As in the description of the Beaufort ball, the analysis here sets the scene historically and emphasizes signs of change. Young architects are striking out from the uniformity of New York's brownstone, and the freer spirits who have read Charles Eastlake's *Hints on Household Taste* (first published in America in 1872) have learned how to rebel against the ornamental excrescences of the Victorian interior. Thus Archer assumes that May will simply carry on her parents' style—"purple satin and yellow tuftings . . . sham Buhl tables and gilt vitrines"—whereas he will break away from the conventional by arranging his library as he pleases, "which would be, of course, with 'sincere' Eastlake furniture, and the plain new bookcases without glass doors." His smug sense of originality blinds him to the fact that the lines of his rebellion have already been laid down. The conventions themselves are changing, and, like New Yorkers attending Beaufort's ball, Archer is simply moving with the times.

But how does his mental excursion into New York's interior decorating help him place Ellen's house? Her style does not fit, and Archer's perceptions are so bound up in the conventional that he cannot see her drawing room specifically. Instead he feels "the sense of adventure"; he confronts the scene abstractly ("the way the chairs and tables were grouped") and stylizes its effect—"something intimate, 'foreign,' subtly suggestive of old romantic scenes and sentiments." The New Yorker's intense concentration on the surface of life makes him acute in recognizing deviations from the customary—"only two Jacqueminot roses (of which nobody ever bought less than a dozen)," "perfume that was not what one put on handkerchiefs"—but such scrutiny also places undue emphasis on the mere fact of deviation. The unusual becomes the "foreign," and because of New York's blending of manners and morals, the foreign is associated with the suggestive and the romantic. Instead of assessing the arrangement of a room, Archer finds himself confronting something alien, immoral, and extraordinarily enticing.

With such a cast of thought, more is at stake than aesthetic simplification or imprecision. Archer is virtually seduced by a room, and once Ellen herself returns, his behavior is confused by his previous excitement. He means to warn her about being seen with Beaufort, "but he was being too deeply drawn into the atmosphere of the room, which was her atmosphere, and to give advice of that sort would have been like telling some one who was bargaining for attar-of-roses in Samarkand that one should always be provided with arctics for a New York winter." In this bewildering milieu, his conventional moralizing can find no hold. Moreover, once the New Yorker has noted a divergence from accepted forms, he has no way to measure degrees of foreignness. If perfume is not like what one puts on a handkerchief, it suggests "a far-off bazaar." The unusual quickly extends into the most exotic, and Archer finally feels as far from New York as Samarkand. This vulnerability to the unforeseen is the most obvious weakness of old New York's manners. Having stepped outside his conventions, Archer can no more assess his personal ties with Ellen than he can account for the decoration of her room. It seems as if he must either disregard what his system cannot explain or discard the system itself as irrelevant to his experience.

But if Archer's social habits schematize Ellen's nature, the complexities of his own system are also obscured in the disorienting context of his experience with the "foreign." It is on its home ground that Wharton can indicate the subtler expense and the finer compensation of old New York's system, as she does during chapter 30 in a scene between Archer and May. They dine alone and spend the evening in the library, a characteristic context in which to observe the domestic side of New York's manners. But this is also a special evening, for Ellen has returned to New York, and Archer, delegated to meet her at the station that afternoon, found himself so agitated by his feelings for her that he walked home, forgetting his promise to meet May at Mrs. Mingott's house. There is thus considerable strain between husband and wife in the scene, however much it may be concealed.

The strain is most apparent as Archer feels it, for we see from his perspective. The imagery, theme, and selection of detail here emphasize monotony and oppressiveness, and one does not need Archer's experience with the "foreign" to suffer from such entrapment. All one needs is inward cravings; that old New York cannot acknowledge these represents one of its major failings. While the heaviness of the detail reflects Archer's immediate feelings—May's workbasket under his green-shaded student lamp, her wedding ring moving painstakingly above her embroidery—the effect of the details also arises from accumulation. Throughout the novel Wharton has been circumstantially describing the interiors of old New York, the enclosures of its domestic life. It is not surprising in such a context that Archer needs to open the library window, to get "the sense of other lives outside his own" and clear his head. But even so simple and symbolic a gesture is enmeshed in more decorative detail: "He had insisted that the library curtains should draw backward and forward on a rod, so that they might be closed in the evening, instead of remaining nailed to a gilt cornice, and immovably looped up over layers of lace, as in the drawing-room."

Wharton has been accumulating more than details, however. By this point she has presented so many interpretations of the customary that old New York's manners appear as a complete system, the full weight of which can be felt in each detail. May has on the tightly laced dinner dress exacted by "the Mingott ceremonial"; her hair has its "usual accumulated coils"; her face, "its usual tenderness"; and the dinner talk, "its usual limited circle." While Archer reads after dinner, she embroiders a cushion for him because wives embroider cushions for their husbands, and "this last link of her devotion" completes a chain binding Archer to her and both of them to the entire social order. Thus Archer feels her presence not simply as May but as the incarnation of a system. She is, for Archer, so overwhelmingly *there*, in his library, at his table, under his student lamp, "laboriously stabbing the canvas," that he focuses his discontent on her and momentarily wishes her dead.

Although Archer's feelings are comprehensible under the circumstances, his behavior and motives in the scene are not attractive, and it is in revealing his cruelty to May that Wharton explores the other potentialities of old New York. Archer's own interpretations of May's conduct here suggest the immense significance of silences; that she makes no allusion to Ellen during dinner strikes him as "vaguely ominous." This mode of communication is rooted in communal manners. Throughout the novel New Yorkers talk by glances and "faint implications." "In reality they all lived in a kind of hieroglyphic world, where the real thing was never said or done or even thought, but only represented by a set of arbitrary signs." These hieroglyphics make the social surface dense and significant, and the complex system of interpretation necessitated by them defines the peculiar strength of old New York. It demands astute perception, subtle analysis, and careful attention to a social code and to another person. Such habits obviously discourage outright selfishness and insensibility. No matter how limited the range of moral content may be in New York, at least its forms enrich the moral life. And Wharton elucidates these forms so thoroughly that one is drawn into the same system of interpretation; from this perspective one judges Archer in the scene.

Ironically, the personal cost of Archer's rebellion is estimated within the potentialities of the very system he finds so stifling. He is so absorbed with his own feelings that he ignores the set of signs between himself and May. He forgets that he can send as well as receive hieroglyphic messages, that his own silence about Ellen tells more disturbing things than May's. When they go to the library he takes down a volume of Michelet: "He had taken to history in the evenings since May had shown a tendency to ask him to read aloud whenever she saw him with a volume of poetry." Again May seems to discern his meaning here, for only after "seeing that he had chosen history," does she fetch that oppressive embroidery. And his sense of her as a responsibility, as the embodiment of the oppressive system, blinds him as well to the personal messages she is sending. He assumes with dismay as he glances at her in the library, that he will always know what goes on behind her "clear brow," that she will never surprise him "by an unexpected mood, by a new idea, a weakness, a cruelty, or an emotion." But this is to deny his own astuteness within the system, for only a week earlier he constructed a whole paragraph in "code" from one of May's statements, attributing to her an awareness of his feelings about Ellen. May's "wan and almost faded face" at dinner, her "strained laugh" at his condescending pity in the library, her hestitation before changing the artificially light tone and telling him "I shall never worry if you're happy"—all these ought, against such a background, to be telling signs, but for Archer they are mere appearances. The subjects of Ellen's arrival, his trip back from the station with her, and his neglect of his promise to meet May would no doubt have been as painful to her at dinner as to himself.

Her "clear brow," then, is not the appalling sign of innocence that Archer reads, but the indication of her self-control. And such control illustrates the other major strength of old New York's manners: they sustain personal dignity while providing a delicate measure of one's feelings and sacrifices. May's ceremonial appearance at dinner, despite her suffering and suspicion, combines with her resolute effort to do her domestic duty even though "she was not a clever needlewoman," to elevate and to enlarge her character. Near the end of the novel Archer reflects on his marriage to May: "Their long years together had shown him that it did not so much matter if marriage was a dull duty, as long as it kept the dignity of a duty: lapsing from that, it became a mere battle of ugly appetites." The scene in the library is far from a battle of ugly appetites.

Thus, while Wharton clearly and firmly indicts old New York for its evasiveness, its vulnerability, and its narrowness, she indicates the complexity of the social order by showing how its virtues arise from its very defects. If the New Yorker is overly excited by the "foreign," he also finds in it more joy and subtle possibility than would be perceptible from a less provincial perspective. The richness of Ellen Olenska emerges largely from the way in which she is seen. If the "hieroglyphic world" encourages misunderstanding and evasion, it also enforces delicacy of perception. The complex interlocking of manners and their interpretation makes daily life oppressive; yet at the same time it habituates the mind to careful, serious analysis. And the very narrowness and rigidity of the system sustain at least one kind of personal dignity; no one in *The Age of Innocence* is quite so pathetic, foolish, or bewildered as most of the characters Wharton presents as the products of New York's later days.

The qualities Edith Wharton saw in old New York provided her with the materials not only to write one of the purest novels of manners in American fiction but to probe the very possibilities of human experience as predicated on manners. She shows in *The Age of Innocence* how a social order can create a meaningful area of human life. In her earlier novels she demonstrates the importance of manners primarily in a negative fashion, by their powers of impairing the individual life or by their inadequacy to human needs; the significance of manners lies in their capacity to impinge on values determined within another framework entirely, on personal development, for instance, or honesty or coherence. Old New York, on the other hand, generates meaning and value positively: it creates serious issues of conduct; it encourages subtle modes of understanding; and it develops in its products qualities of character that cannot be laughed away, stuffy as they may seem. When its values are wrong or arbitrarily narrow, at least they are intelligibly so; and the coherence of its habits and its means of interpreting them provides a stable configuration of values against which an individual's divergence and growth can be estimated with fine clarity. Old New York is obviously not a satisfactory social order, but it *is* a social order.

GORE VIDAL
"Introduction"
The Edith Wharton Omnibus
1978, pp. vii–xiii

A few years ago I was asked by the publisher of a biography of Edith Wharton to provide him with what is known, elegantly, in the trade as a "blurb." Now the writing of blurbs is an art form as difficult as that of the haiku; and far less appreciated. I sometimes think that a good blurb may be harder to write than a good book. Too often perfectly reputable writers will come up with the "not since General Eisenhower's *Crusade in Europe* have I laughed so much" sort of thing. Dutifully, I read the biography of Mrs. Wharton. There was new material about her private life (after twenty-three years of marriage, she had her first sexual experience at forty-six). There was a good account of the ups and downs of the reputation of a writer who . . . well, herewith, the blurb that eventually decorated the dust jacket of R. W. B. Lewis's *Edith Wharton*. "At best, there are only three or four American novelists who can be thought of as 'major' and Edith Wharton is one. Due to her sex, class (in every sense), and place of residence, she has been denied her proper place in the near-empty pantheon of American literature. Happily, Mr. Lewis's biography ought to convince the solemn of her seriousness; with much new material, he has illuminated a marvelous figure and her age." When, eventually, I collect in a single slender volume the various blurbs that I have produced over the years, I shall give, I hope not too immodestly, pride of place to this small but subtly cut zircon of the blurb-maker's tiny art (flawed only, I notice now, by the repetition of the word "place" in the second sentence).

Edith Wharton's publishers have had the good sense to make available in one volume some of her best writing. I can only say that I envy anyone reading for the first time *The Age of Innocence* or *New Year's Day*. Why? Well, let us examine the points I raised in that blurb.

"At best, there are only three or four American novelists who can be thought of as 'major' and Edith Wharton is one." Who are the other two or three? I don't think I will go into that beyond noting that, to my mind, Henry James and Edith Wharton are the two great American masters of the novel. Most of our celebrated writers have not been, properly speaking, novelists at all. Hawthorne and Melville wrote romances. Hemingway and Crane and Fitzgerald were essentially short story writers (a literary form that Americans have always excelled at). Mark Twain was a memoirist. William Dean Howells was indeed a true novelist but as Edith Wharton remarked (they were friendly acquaintances), Howells's "incurable moral timidity . . . again and again checked him on the verge of a masterpiece." She herself was never timid. Somehow in recent years a notion has got about that she was a stuffy grand old lady who wrote primly decorous novels about upper-class people of a sort that are no longer supposed to exist. She was indeed a grand lady, but she was not at all stuffy. Quite the contrary. She was witty. She was tough as nails. As for those upper-class people, they are still very much with us. But as their age ceased to be gilded and became discreetly chrome, they have decided wisely to stay out of sight. Nevertheless, they run the United States just as they did when Edith Wharton and her friend Henry James wrote about them.

"Due to her sex . . . she has been denied her proper place" as a great American writer. This seems to me to be altogether true, and sad. For a very long time it was an article of faith among American schoolteachers and writers of book-chat for newspapers that no woman could be a major writer. Predictably, it was Norman Mailer who put the conservative case: "I have nothing to say about any of the talented women who write today. . . . Indeed I doubt if there will be a really exciting woman writer until the first whore becomes a call girl and tells her tale." If anyone can figure out what that last sentence means, drop me a line. For Mailer, women writers are "fey, old-hat, Quaintsy Goysy, tiny, too dykily psychotic, crippled, creepish, fashionable, frigid, outer-Baroque, *maquillé* mannequin's whimsy, or else bright and stillborn." He then adds a nervous footnote to the effect that, well, there are *three* contemporary women writers who are not too bad. But the point that he has made not only reflects the positively Old Testament hatred that so many American men have for women (particularly notable in the fifties when the gabble that I've just quoted was written) but also the looney conviction that only men can do anything of major importance in literature, quite forgetting that the best novelist in the English language was a lady who was forced (partly by the Mailers of her day) to take the name George Eliot. Edith Wharton was quite aware that her sex was held against her. There are hundreds of Mailers in every literary generation and they write most of the book reviews. But I suspect that she was far more disturbed by the attitudes toward women of the class she was born into where a woman . . . no, that word was not used . . . where a lady was expected to be supremely ornamental, and nothing else. From the beginning, Edith Jones (later Wharton) was far too clever. Or as she ruefully noted, Boston thought her too fashionable to be clever while New York thought her too clever to be fashionable.

"Due to her . . . class" Edith Wharton was denied her proper place. Class is a delicate subject in the United States. We are not supposed to know anything about class because everyone is exactly like everyone else except, naturally, for those who are rich—and for those who are poor—and of course for the rest of us. Edith Newbold Jones was born in 1862. The Joneses were a large proud New York family (it is said that the expression "keeping up with the Joneses" referred to them). Edith was related to almost everyone. And kinship is what society with a capital "S" is all about. For that matter, society with a small "s" (at least in small communities) tends to be pretty much the same thing. One of the reasons that the American South produced so many good writers was that until recently each small town included a number of families who had become so involved with one another over the centuries that the often quite lurid stories of kin that were passed on from generation to generation on slow, hot afternoons were the very stuff of literature for any attentive child with a liking for stories, writing. One needs a well-defined society to make good novels. On the other hand, although the New York of Edith Jones's day was a splendid subject for a novelist, it was an article of faith that no one *in* Society could ever be a writer. Writers were "not like us." Of course they were brainy. But then so were chemists, and you did not have a chemist to dinner . . . or a writer.

Edith Jones's New York was still that of *The Age of Innocence*. There were dinner parties, appearances at the opera, Assembly balls; there was Newport in the summer, with the afternoon *passegiatta* along Ocean Drive; there was, best of all for her, Europe where she spent much of her childhood because her father was suddenly obliged to economize and it was cheaper to live in Paris than New York. When, finally, nervously, tentatively, she began to publish, her friends and family were deeply puzzled, and only one relative (a bedridden lady) ever admitted to having read her books. The making of literature in that world was like some wasting, sad disease which, luckily, was not thought to be contagious. Otherwise, she would have been locked up; kept permanently in quarantine.

In Edith Wharton's memoir *A Backward Glance*, she contemplated her long life (she died in 1937). Of her education: "I used to say that I had been taught only two things in my childhood: the modern languages and good manners. Now that I have lived to see both those branches of culture dispensed with, I perceive that there are worse systems of education." She also regarded with a sharp eye the New York gentry of her youth. They had bored her a good deal at the time. A girl who liked to read and think did not have many people to talk to in Old New York. But, later, looking back, she was surprised at her own nostalgia. "Social life with us as in the rest of the world, went on with hardly perceptible changes till the war (1917) abruptly tore down the old frame-work, and what had seemed unalterable rules of conduct became of a sudden observances as quaintly arbitrary as the domestic rites of the Pharaohs." Finally, "the compact world of my youth has receded into a past from which it can only be dug up in bits by the assiduous relic-hunter. . . ."

By and large, American writers belong to the middle class. In Edith Wharton's day they were the sons and daughters of small-town lawyers, doctors, realtors. The ruling class (which does not exist of course) is supposed to rule not write. There was—and is—a good deal of resentment on the part of the middle-middlers that a bona fide aristocrat (American style) should be not only a bestselling novelist but also a genius. The sales of her books could not be falsified. But her genius could be denied, as it so often was, and for years she has been categorized, in Mailer's phrase, as "Quaintsy Goysy."

Although Edith Wharton professed a certain nostalgia for the customs of a class that after 1917 changed its style (but kept its money), she saw to it that she herself was delivered, as soon as possible, into a happier world where she was not only admired as a writer but where she could move among intellectual equals. Needless to say, such a world was not to be found in the United States of that day but in Europe. In Paris a woman could be taken seriously as an intellectual, and it was in Paris that she finally settled.

Due to her place of residence, she was much criticized by those America Firsters who never seemed to mind the fact that writers like Ernest Hemingway seldom lived in the United States. Some sort of double standard is obviously at work.

"With much new material, [Mr. Lewis] has illuminated a marvelous figure and her age." What was the new material? Well, some of it was fairly shocking even in these candid days. In 1885 Edith Jones married the charming but dim Edward Wharton. As was the custom in that far-off time, Edith went to the bridal bed a virgin. Whether or not she was still a virgin the next day is moot. We do know that whatever happened so traumatized her that that was that: no more sex. The marriage itself was not too bad (they both liked animals). Eventually Teddy Wharton found friends elsewhere while Edith wrote, gardened, lived a full if not fulfilled life. Then, at forty-six, she had her first love affair with a clever, not entirely trustworthy bisexualist. But the lover's shortcomings made no real difference. After all, it is not who or what one loves but the emotion itself that matters. In middle life, she was rejuvenated. More to the point, the honesty with which she had always treated intimate relations between her characters now possessed a new authority. Despite her reputation as being a stuffy *grande dame*, she had always been the most direct and masculine (old sense of the word, naturally) of writers; far more so than her somewhat fussy and hesitant friend Henry James. Spades got called spades in Edith Wharton's novels. As a result, she was always at war with "editorial timidity." Early on, she was told by one of the few good editors of the day that no American magazine would publish anything that might offend "a non-existent clergyman in the Mississippi valley; . . . [I] made up my mind from the first that I would never sacrifice my literary conscience to this ghostly censor." But she lived long enough to find disquieting the explicitness of writers like D. H. Lawrence and James Joyce. With a certain dryness, she speaks of the difficulties that writers of her epoch had, turning "the wooden dolls of that literary generation into struggling suffering human beings; but we have been avenged, and more than avenged, not only by life but by the novelists, and I hope the latter will see before long that it is as hard to get dramatic interest out of a mob of irresponsible criminals as out of the Puritan marionettes who formed our stock in trade. Authentic human nature lies somewhere between the two. . . . " When the drunk Scott Fitzgerald tried to shock her by saying that he had just come from a bordello, old Mrs. Wharton silkily asked, "But what, Mr. Fitzgerald, did you *do* there?" Later, she complained of Fitzgerald's "insufficient data."

The four stories that made up the volume *Old New York* together with *The Age of Innocence* can be read as a history of New York Society from the 1840s to the 1870s, all told from the vantage point of a brilliant middle-aged woman, looking back on a world that had already become as strange to her as that of the Pharaohs. *The Age of Innocence* was published in 1920 when Wharton was fifty-eight. *False Dawn, The Old Maid, The Spark* and *New Year's Day* were published four years later.

Ethan Frome (a long short story first published in 1911) stands somewhat outside the canon of her work. For one thing, she herself is plainly outside the world that she is describing. Yet she is able to describe in a most convincing way a New England village filled with people of a sort that she could never have known well. The story is both readable and oddly remote. It could have been written by Daudet but not by her master Flaubert. Although she was very much under the influence of the French realists at the time, she does pay sly homage to Nathaniel Hawthorne, who had worked the same New England territory: a principal character in *Ethan Frome* is called Zenobia after the heroine of Hawthorne's *The Blithedale Romance*.

With the four New York stories and *The Age of Innocence* we are back in a world that she knew as intimately as Proust knew the Paris of much the same era. The stories begin. . . . But I am not going to say anything about them other than to note that they are precise and lucid, witty and passionate (there is no woman in American literature as fascinating as the doomed Madame Olenska). Not only does one live again in that lost world through Edith Wharton's art (and rather better to live in a far-off time through the medium of a great arist than to experience the real and probably awful age itself), but one is struck by the marvelous golden light that illuminates the world she reveals to us. How is this done? Through a total mastery of English. Now that our language is in trouble (reread that quotation from Mailer, read the New York *Times*), one can if not mourn the narrow world that she grew up in, at least respond with some sympathy when she observes that: "My parents' ears were wounded by an unsuitable word as those of the musical are hurt by a false note." But then "This feeling for good English was more than reverence, and nearer: it was love."

In *The Age of Innocence* the language is unusually beautiful. That is to say, the prose is simple, straightforward, loved. When it comes to rounding off her great scene where Madame Olenska is decorously destroyed by the Old New Yorkers at a dinner, Edith Wharton writes with the graceful directness of the Recording Angel: "It was the old New York way of taking life 'without effusion of blood': the way of people who dreaded scandal more than disease, who placed decency above courage, and who considered that nothing was more ill-bred than 'scenes,' except the behavior of those who gave rise to them."

Great writers are seldom great in everyday life. Edith Wharton seems to have been an exception. In the First World War she remained in Paris. She worked hard for the refugees; visited the Front; was decorated by the French government. She was a loyal if tiring friend, as Henry James noted with awe: "Her powers of devastation are ineffable, her repudiation of repose absolutely tragic and she was never more brilliant and able and interesting." Traditionally, Henry James has always been placed slightly higher up the slope of Parnassus than Edith Wharton. But now that the prejudice against the female writer is on the wane, they look to be exactly what they are: giants, equals, the tutelary and benign gods of our American literature.

DAVID EGGENSCHWILER

"The Ordered Disorder of *Ethan Frome*"

Studies in the Novel, Fall 1977, pp. 237–46

In his brilliant essay, "The Morality of Inertia," Lionel Trilling claims that Wharton's Ethan Frome lives in the incomprehensible universe of Job, that he acts out of habit and necessity, and that "between the moral life of Ethan and Mattie and their terrible fate we cannot make any reasonable connection." In a useful reply to this interpretation Kenneth Bernard argues that Ethan causes his tragedy through his weakness and negation of life.[1] This is an important and complex disagreement: important because most commentators on the novel have upheld one or the other of these interpretations, and complex because neither interpretation is entirely convincing or entirely implausible. Ethan does seem more responsible for his suffering than Trilling allows, but he does not seem the precisely flawed hero of Bernard's Aristotelian tragedy. The moral universe of the novel does not seem, either to the reader or to the characters, as incomprehensible as does Job's, but neither does it seem as tidy as Bernard suggests with his schematic patterns of moral imagery: light (good) versus darkness (bad), warmth (good) versus coldness (bad), pickles (good) versus dead cucumber vines (bad), and so on. Perhaps, however, we have created this dilemma ourselves by trying to see the novel through either extreme of Job or Aristotle, by trying to organize it too simply through one or another traditional view. If we return to the novel without assuming that Ethan is either the pathetic victim of necessity or the morally flawed tragic hero, if we are attentive to the various responses that the character demands of us and the various responses that he makes to his circumstances, then we might find more flexible ways to describe the moral and emotional experiences that the tale offers, and we might avoid the dangers of trying to find the right point of view, the key, the interpretation.[2]

The narrative frame story that opens the novel provides us, if we are so inclined, with the makings of an allegory. The winter storms are pitiless armies that besiege the remote village of Starkfield, and through this symbolically frozen wasteland Ethan Frome limps like a bound Samson: "it was the careless powerful look he had, in spite of a lameness checking each step like the jerk of a chain."[3] And when a villager says that Ethan is one of the few smart ones who did not "get away," the pattern quickly becomes clear: Ethan is a strong, intelligent man who would have escaped this "negation" of life (the term is the narrator's) had he not been pathetically destroyed by circumstances (later identifiable as fate, accident, or the moral inertia of his society) or tragically destroyed by his own flaws (weakness of will, sexual impotence, habit). But even within the frame story the novel requires much trimming to fit such a pattern. The predominant militance of winter is lightened by glittering snow, blazing blue sky, and crystal clearness—images that will recur throughout the novel to complicate the chill of sleet storms and the entrapping snow drifts.[4] And when we recognize that Ethan's grave dignity is inseparable from the harsh weather and granite outcroppings of this countryside, we should also suspect that the forces, both from within and without, that have lamed him have also helped to give him "the bronze image of a hero." When Ethan surpasses his agreement and drives the narrator ten miles in a snowstorm and when, returning, he struggles through a blizzard, he shows that such elemental strength to endure requires adversity, as it does with Wordsworth's old shepherds and soldiers or with Oedipus, blind at Colonus rather than full of bread at Thebes. So, as we go into the past to find, as the narrator says, "the clue to Ethan Frome," we should already suspect that the clue will not be as simple as a literary, ethical, or psychological detective might wish.

In the first chapter on Ethan's past the narrator mentions the scientific studies that Ethan had followed before his father's death forced him to return home, and the narrator does not make those studies as solemnly ideal as an allegorist would like. He says that Ethan "dabbled in the laboratory" and that the courses had "fed his fancy and made him aware of huge cloudy meanings behind the daily face of things" (p. 28). The tone here is ambivalent: while it suggests the touching stirrings in a mute, inglorious Milton, it also condescendingly suggests the fuzzy longings of a Jude Fawley or a James Gatz. Throughout the novel Ethan's dreams of escape call for such ambivalent responses because they mix admirable desires for knowledge, beauty, and freedom with such triteness and sentimentality, and the narrator repeatedly points out this mixture by his ironic tone.[5] So, for example, he describes the response to natural beauty that distinguishes Ethan and Mattie from the more practical people around them: "And there were other sensations, less definable but more exquisite, which drew them together with a shock of silent joy: the cold red of sunset behind winter hills, the flight of cloud-flocks over slopes of golden stubble, or the intensely blue shadows of hemlocks on sunlit snow. When she said to him once: 'It looks just as if it was painted!' it seemed to Ethan that the art of definition could go no further, and that words had at last been found to utter his secret soul . . ." (pp. 34–35). Surely we are to accept these sensations as exquisite and to be touched that a secret soul has at last found expression and understanding, but are we not also to smile at the naive, dated remnant of the picturesque tradition in which the characters find that expression? Wharton points out in her introduction that "the looker-on is sophisticated, and the people he interprets are simple"; this perspective encourages the mixture of admiration and condescension that is often provoked by pastoral literature (at least as Empson defines it) from the comedy of *As You Like It* to the tragedy of *The Return of the Native*.

Mattie Silver herself is a perfectly imagined object for Ethan's confused desires. She dances gaily in the church basement, wears red scarves, flirts coyly with the village gallant, walks with a light step, admires sunsets, and is becomingly modest when Ethan makes his embarrassed gestures of affection; as a silver girl, she is the "bit of hopeful young life" that has come to the Fromes' cold hearth. But Mattie is not solid silver; she has less glittering qualities that also appeal to Ethan. After her bankrupt parents died, she was left alone to make her way in the world: "For this purpose her equipment, though varied, was inadequate. She could trim a hat, make molasses candy, recite 'Curfew shall not ring tonight,' and play 'The Lost Chord' and a pot-pourri from *Carmen*. When she tried to extend the field of her activities in the direction of stenography and bookkeeping her health broke down, and six months on her feet behind the counter of a department store did not tend to restore it" (p. 60). This description makes the orphan seem not only pathetic but also a bit silly. The narrator is obviously amused at the "equipment" of this spoiled daughter of a nouveau-bourgeois father, and his ironic account of her venture into the world seems less appropriate to a bit of hopeful young life than it does to some of the anemic heroines of Tennessee Williams. Accordingly, Mattie is too weak to do all of her work at the farm, so that, to protect her from criticism, Ethan must secretly scrub floors and churn butter like an emasculated Hercules among the handmaidens of Omphale. And Ethan is attracted by her deficiencies, for her weakness makes him feel strong, her ignorance makes him proud of his knowledge, and her dependence makes him feel authoritative in small matters. Repeatedly, he boasts and swaggers, enjoying moments of male vanity when a slight gesture—eavesdropping at the dance, talking of steering a sled, reassuring her about the broken dish—has overcome his usual shyness with her. Obviously in both her strengths and weaknesses the girl is the opposite of Zeena, the ugly old woman who scornfully dominates her husband,[6] and just as obviously we sympathize with Ethan in his attraction to that opposite. Yet the characters and motives are too complex to produce the clear patterns of life versus death, freedom versus imprisonment, that would make the novel more easily explainable. How could such patterns render fully enough our mixed impressions of Ethan's feelings as he stands outside the dance, treasuring the sensibilities that unite him with Mattie and distinguish him from other villagers, envying and scorning the brash son of a successful grocer, feeling as loutish as he used to when, a country-bred student, he tried to jolly city girls? Here are rudimentary touches of one of Joyce's favorite character types as seen in Little Chandler or Gabriel Conroy; and the similarity should remind us that, even if we do not find Joyce's sharp, detached irony in this novel, we should be careful not to sentimentalize Ethan's longings for beauty, love, and knowledge any more than Wharton does.

If Mattie is complex, Ethan's fancies about her are even more so, as an early passage amusingly imples. Mattie has been described as lively, sensitive, forgetful, and dreamy, as a girl having no natural turn for housekeeping: all of these qualities appeal to Ethan's romantic side because—like science, sunsets, and Florida—they suggest the opposite of his tedious farm life. But "Ethan had an idea that if she were to marry a man she was fond of the dormant instinct would wake, and her pies and biscuits become the pride of the country" (p. 36). You cannot take the country out of the boy; as he dreams of his silver girl, he can still imagine her at the oven and perhaps with blue ribbons at the county fair. Throughout the novel his fancies about Mattie vacillate between romantic adventure and domestic stability; sometimes amusing, sometimes touching, sometimes chilling, these pointed contrasts reveal and evaluate Ethan's opposing needs.

As the potential lovers walk home through the "irresponsible night," Ethan presses the girl against him, steals his arm about her, and feels so excited by her touch that he can think afterwards that he should have kissed her. But he feels subtly different as they pass the Fromes' graveyard. In the past the graves had mocked his restlessness, warning him that he would not escape, yet as he walks by with Mattie they seem comforting:

> But now all desire for change had vanished, and the sight of the little enclosure gave him a warm sense of continuance and stability.
>
> "I guess we'll never let you go, Matt," he whispered, as though even the dead, lovers once, must conspire with him to keep her; and brushing by the graves, he thought: "We'll always go on living here together, and some day she'll lie there beside me" (p. 51).

The overt point of Ethan's meditation is obvious and traditional: love can transform a prison, even the grave, into paradise. But one is tempted to reply that none can there embrace, for Ethan has shifted disturbingly from exhilaration to a sense of continuance and stability, from a potentially illicit relationship to an image of domestic peace, from the warm pressure of the girl at his side to the chaste twin beds of the graveyard. We would distort the scene to talk of morbidity and the negation of life here, for we must not ignore the moving sense of fulfillment that this restless man feels; we must not ignore major effects to exaggerate minor ones. But we should still feel troubled that, as with the imagined pies and biscuits, Ethan has again confused his adventurous conception of Mattie.

We might feel less troubled when, finding that he will have a night alone with the girl, Ethan looks forward to their spending a quiet evening "like a married couple"; a comfortable kitchen, although not a bedroom, is not a grave either, and only an unkind Lawrentian would scorn Ethan's substituting a warm stove for the dark fires of the blood. As Ethan imagines them together, "he in his stocking feet and smoking his pipe, she laughing and talking in that funny way she had," we are prepared to indulge sentimentally in that domestic idyll. Whatever we recognize of Ethan's psychological evasions (and Wharton will make us recognize some), we must still remember that the warm, shy, gentle relationship between the lovers that evening suggests the kind of life that Ethan ought to have. But he cannot have such a life because seven years earlier he had married Zeena, trying blindly to fulfill some of the same desires that still torment him. And the narrator reminds us of this when, in the midst of Ethan's quiet joy, he says, "he set his imagination adrift on the fiction that they had always spent their evenings thus and would always go on doing so" (p. 90).

The narrator also disrupts this idyll with momentary surges of passion and conscience to remind us what motives are precariously balanced in this scene, which is not, after all, the innocent evening of a newly married couple. No sooner has Ethan set himself adrift on the "illusion of long-established intimacy which no outburst of emotion could have given," than he says, "this is the night we were to have gone coasting," (p. 90). Coasting with Mattie, which Ethan mentions on each of the four evenings of the main story, suggests to him excitement, danger, a night "as dark as Egypt" (which outdoes Florida for pat associations), and masculine domination (again he swaggers and swells with authority). To prolong his feeling of authority he adds, "'I guess we're well enough here,'" and so he reabsorbs the excitement into the "warm lamplit room, with all its ancient implications of conformity and order" (pp. 91, 93). Yet even in this room he refers roguishly (and, he immediately fears, vulgarly) to having seen a friend of Mattie being kissed, and he makes shy, guilty gestures of love with the material she is sewing. But she remains modest and he tactful; the next morning he can be glad "he had done nothing to trouble the sweetness of the picture" of what life with her might be.

Ethan's moral scruples in the scene are even more troubling than his shifts from passion to propriety. There is some value in his conventional, even habitual, fidelity and in his possible sense of Mattie's morally delicate position in the household. But there is also neurotic violence in his guilt, which tortures him more histrionically than the facts warrant. Twice during the evening he sees Zeena's image replace Mattie's as the girl performs simple acts that the wife had done. If one were fond of psychological case studies one could make much of the fact that Zeena has replaced Ethan's mother as the invalid who keeps him on the farm, but it seems enough to note that Ethan's fidelity and duty are tainted with an unmanly fear of his shrewish, self-righteous wife. Perhaps we are to understand that the sensitive, honorable nature is easily victimized by the insensitive, dishonorable one and that Ethan's weakness is a defect of his virtue, but the weakness is not entirely excusable, for all that.

In following scenes between the climax of the novel (Mattie's banishment) and the catastrophe (the abortive suicide attempt) Ethan continues to vacillate emotionally; and Wharton shows precisely that his impulses to escape and to stay are both caused by good and bad motives. Again Wharton shows that Ethan's circumstances make conflicting demands on him, that Ethan has conflicting desires, and that each of these desires has noble and ignoble forms. She is not being morally vague or ambiguous by avoiding a simple pattern of guilt or victimization; she is exactly manipulating the reader to produce the complex moral and emotional responses that most good fiction requires.

When Ethan confronts his wife over Mattie's dismissal, his ineffectualness is vexing and sometimes embarrassing, but in part it results from admirable traits. When, for the first time in their seven-year marriage, they fight openly, the narrator sympathizes with Ethan's squeamishness: "Through the obscurity which hid their faces their thoughts seemed to dart at each other like serpents shooting venom. Ethan was seized with horror of the scene and shame at his own share in it. It was as senseless and savage as a physical fight between two enemies in the darkness" (p. 111). The narrator's imagery and the characters' dialogue do present a horrible scene, and we can appreciate Ethan's shame at fighting with this coarse, vindictive woman: "Ethan felt as if he had lost an irretrievable advantage in descending to the level of recrimination. But the practical problem was there and had to be dealt with" (p. 112). What telling irony! If one ignores practical consequences, Ethan's sensibilities *are* a moral and psychological advantage; they exist because he is an intelligent, gentle man. Also his pride in them has helped to protect him for years against Zeena's attacks and has probably served as a weapon, vexing her as she repeatedly has failed to provoke his anger. But at what cost this advantage! Never refusing her, never asserting his needs, Ethan has allowed Zeena's bitter willfulness and domination to grow, while he has found comfort in a moral superiority. We should be reminded of Ethan's standing in the shadows outside the dance two evenings before, treasuring his sensitivity and scorning the gregarious grocer's son who dances with Mattie.

Defeated by his wife, Ethan retreats to his makeshift study to thrash about. For a while he thinks of going west with Mattie to make his fortune. (The West has become the enchanted land of his conventional fancy, replacing the City, which has become the unholy place where a million bread-seekers would crush the exiled girl.) But as moral and financial problems occur to him, he vacillates with half-pathetic, half-ludicrous abruptness between hope and despair. The next day, realizing that he must act, he decides to lie to his neighbor. Andrew Hale, secure an advance on the lumber he supplies, and run away with Mattie, leaving Zeena to her relatives and eventual alimony payments. Although the scheme is desperate and poorly planned, Ethan is acting and making a choice that circumstances have required. He has been scrupulous in considering the moral issues of running away—Zeena's financial state, his inability to help her emotionally, Mattie's dependence—and his decision seems right in a situation in which no decision can be guiltless. But on the way to the contractor's he meets Mrs. Hale, who pities him for his misfortunes (an uncommon act in Starkfield), and he is unable to deceive the two kind people who have pitied him. Again the scene calls for a complex response. Ethan's sudden reversal, his extreme feelings ("with a sudden perception of the point to which his madness had carried him"), and his readiness to despair—all suggest that he is hypersensitive and unable to assume the burden and consequences of acting. Yet we should not scorn Ethan, because his reason for not deceiving the Hales is both honorable and emotionally understandable. Earlier, when he had thought of asking Hale for an advance, although with no thought then of cheating him, Ethan soon backed down because of a habitual pride. The later scene is different. There he shows not pride but humility, not a habitual, conventual sense of honor but gratitude and affection. Appreciating Ethan's reaction to unusual kindness, we cannot say confidently than his refusal to lie is wrong.

Ethan's refusal to cheat Andrew Hale is his last decisive act in the novel; from now on, he abandons himself to circumstances, acting weakly to postpone and avoid. He insists on driving Mattie to the railroad but only to prolong their last hours together; he stops by Shadow Pond to reminisce about their summer picnic; and when he suggests that they go coasting, he does so merely to postpone the last part of their drive to the railroad. Up to the moment of the collision he continues to vacillate, from proudly exulting in his ability to steer on the dangerous slope to childishly clinging in his despair at losing Mattie, from recoiling in horror at her plea for suicide to finally acquiescing in it. Even the time of day reflects his ambivalence: "it was the most confusing hour of the evening, the hour when the last clearness from the upper sky is merged with the rising night in a blur that disguises landmarks and falsifies distances" (p. 161). In such confusion Mattie must control Ethan and force the last actions of despair. Even as he sits in the sled he almost springs out again; even as they coast toward the tree he again imagines Zeena's face and momentarily swerves from the path. And even the attempt at suicide is not a decisive choice but another evasion, an admission that no course of action seems tolerable among the complicated circumstances and contradictory desires.

The immediate aftermath of the collision, as experienced through Ethan's semiconsciousness, is painfully pathetic; and the consequent twenty-four years of suffering are so grim that no one could reasonably consider Ethan's and Mattie's fate to be deserved. We have sympathized too much with these characters and understood too well their difficulties and confusions to speak righteously about moral flaws and deserved tragedy. But Trilling was wrong when he said that "only a moral judgment cruel to the point of insanity could speak of [their fate] as anything but accidental" (Trilling, p. 46). Fate, as Oedipus or Michael Henchard could testify, often scorns proportion, and this fate is excessive; but it is not accidental. In fact, it is mercilessly, ironically precise in giving the three characters appropriately metaphorical sufferings. Ethan, whose moral and emotional conflicts kept him from acting decisively, is chained with lameness. Mattie, whose birdlike frailty made her dependent on others, is made a complete invalid. Zeena, who secured Ethan in marriage by nursing his mother and playing on his sense of obligation, must dutifully nurse the girl whom she had once scornfully evicted and who is now a permanent guest. Throughout the concluding pages of the frame story there are ironic, and sometimes grotesquely comic, variations on past themes. Remembering Zeena's continuous search for healing, we are amused at Ruth Hale's comment that Zeena rose up as if by a miracle when the call came to her after the injuries. Remembering the times when Ethan guiltily imagined Zeena's face in place of Mattie's, we see how appropriate, if cruel, it is that Mattie has become so much like Zeena in her shrill complaining. And if we are especially shrewd in our humor, we might find irony in Ruth Hale's references to the Fromes' "troubles." Nearly half a novel earlier the narrator explained the difference between troubles and complications: "People struggled on for years with 'troubles,' but they almost always succumbed to 'complications'" (p. 108); so we can assume that if Ethan and Mattie had had complications they would have died in the crash, but with mere troubles they must struggle on for years. Whether or not Wharton intended this grim joke, she obviously intended the irony with which Mrs. Hale's comments end the novel. Remembering Ethan's wishes that he and Mattie could go on living in their farmhouse and then lie together in the Fromes' graveyard, we hear of his wishes symbolically fulfilled and telescoped: "'and the way they are now, I don't see there's much difference between the Fromes up at the farm and the Fromes down in the graveyard; 'cept that down there they're all quiet, and the women have got to hold their tongues'" (p. 180).

These punishments and ironically fulfilled wishes in the concluding frame story can give contradictory impressions, as shown by Trilling's opinion that Ethan's universe is cruelly incomprehensible and by Bernard's opinion that it is just. If one ignored the symbolic precision of the punishments and the partial responsibility of the characters, one could see the characters' fate as perverse and the novel as excessively cruel. If one ignored the extreme pathos and the sympathy that Ethan and Mattie stimulate throughout the book, one could see the conclusion as symbolically appropriate like the punishments in Dante's *Inferno* or Ovid's *Metamorphoses*, in which outward form and action horribly express mind and soul. But Wharton will have it both ways, showing that man does determine his life in a universe that is not chaotic, but also showing that his lot is hard, his choices difficult, his sacrifices many, his strengths inseparable from his weaknesses, and the consequences of his actions often different from what he had expected. And this is not a perversely ambiguous position, but a strictly classical one. Nor is it a moral demonstrated in a pat conclusion; it is essential to Wharton's method throughout the novel. When she shows that suffering both sours and ennobles, that longings for knowledge and beauty can be both admirable and silly, that a strong sense of duty can be honorable and neurotic, that man can long for both freedom and stability and try confusedly to combine the two, when she shows characters suffering in situations over which they have only partial control and creating painful situations out of conflicting motives, and when she makes the reader appreciate these complexities by manipulating his sympathy and detachment, making him feel compassionate, amused, and vexed, then she does the hard work of making a coherent and complex novel. We must be careful to respect both the coherence and complexity and not obscure them in our rage for another, simpler kind of order.

Notes

1. Lionel Trilling, "The Morality of Inertia," in *Great Moral Dilemmas in Literature, Past and Present*, ed. R. M. MacIver (New York: The Institute for Religious and Social Studies, 1956), p. 46; Kenneth Bernard, "Imagery and Symbolism in *Ethan Frome*," *College English*, 23 (1961), 179–84.
2. Trilling was reacting against a request to discuss the moral issues of *Ethan Frome*, and Bernard was reacting against the kind of reading that Trilling had made popular. Thus, as with the works of much greater debate like *The Turn of the Screw* and *The Good Soldier*, we proceed from reaction to reaction without recognizing enough that the general questions we debate restrict our responses to the work itself. Walter Slatoff has made the point precisely: "The strength of our desire to see closure is indicated by the fact that every time a critic discovers a countercurrent he tries to insist that it is the main stream" (*With Respect to Readers* [Ithaca: Cornell Univ. Press, 1970], p. 159).
3. Edith Wharton, *Ethan Frome* (New York: Charles Scribner's Sons, 1922), pp. 3–4. This edition, the first to be published with Wharton's Introduction, is cited throughout this essay with page references included parenthetically in the text.
4. None of the image patterns have the consistency that Bernard claims. If winter can freeze the possible tenderness and sociability in Ethan, it can bring the children out for joyful sledding or young sparks out for reckless sleigh rides. Warmth is associated with the "volcanic fires" of the forbidden gaiety that Ethan sees at the dance and with the safe domesticity of his kitchen as he sits comfortably with Mattie. Darkness oppresses the bedroom in which Ethan lies with Zeena but exhilarates the "irresponsible night" through which he walks with Mattie. The imagery is often metaphorical, but it is not schematic.
5. Wharton may not be ironic when she reveals that during his short period of escape Ethan worked for awhile in Florida, but one is tempted to imagine Ethan walking Wallace Stevens's palmy beaches with the bottoms of his trousers rolled.
6. Lest we assume that Zeena is just plain nasty, the narrator briefly speculates on various causes of her cold silence, including the isolated farm life that has made many women "queer," the taciturnity with which Ethan defends himself in his ineffectual way of dealing with her, and Zeena's social insecurity, which finds relief in the distinctions of the invalid (pp. 72–73).

ELIZABETH AMMONS

"The Business of Marriage"

Edith Wharton's Argument with America

1980, pp. 97–124

Emily Putnam observed in 1910, three years before *The Custom of the Country* was published: "In defiance of the axiom that he who works, eats, the lady who works has less to eat than the lady who does not. There is no profession open to her that is nearly as lucrative as marriage, and the more lucrative the marriage the less work it involves."[1] By the time *The Custom of the Country* appeared in 1913, Putnam's principle, given theorists such as ⟨Charlotte Perkins⟩ Gilman and ⟨Thorstein⟩ Veblen before her, was a commonplace of feminist criticism; Wharton herself had given the idea qualified dramatic rendering as early as 1905 in *The House of Mirth* with its contrast between the marriages, for example, of Judy Trenor and Nettie Struther. No doubt, Wharton would ⟨. . .⟩ have argued with Putnam that the lady who is married *does* have work to do; the work, as Veblen explains, of conspicuously consuming for her wealthy husband as living testimony to his pecuniary prowess. But at the same time Wharton would not have disagreed with the characterization of marriage as a profession, and the most lucrative one available, for a woman seeking status and power in American society. Her brash, ambitious heroine Undine Spragg successfully plots her whole life on that principle in *The Custom of the Country*.

The novel is Wharton's tour de force on the marriage question (and perhaps, the best novel she ever wrote): it throws a brilliant, satiric light on the institution of marriage, stripping it of all sentiment and sentimentality. The key is Undine herself. Unlike Lily Bart, she does not fear marriage as a threat to her autonomy. Unlike Justine Brent or Anna Leath, she has no illusions about the marriage union as a bond of love which will perfect her personal happiness or complete her personality. And she would never, like poor romantic Mattie Silver, choose death over separation from a man she wants to marry. Instead, like Sophy Viner but entirely without her scruples. Undine approaches marriage as a simple economic contract in which both parties have well-defined, mutually aggrandizing, agreed-upon roles; and because she accepts the commercial nature of matrimony and is willing to negotiate herself on the marriage market (which she manages to do not just once, but four times), Undine is unique among Wharton's early heroines. She controls her own life. First she marries a loyal son of old New York, Ralph Marvell; then she marries an elegant French nobleman, the Marquis Raymond de Chelles; then she remarries her first husband, Elmer Moffatt, who always showed spunk but who now, as a newly rich multimillionaire capitalist, also shows a fabulous cheque book.

Wharton's own feelings about her heroine clearly were intense yet divided. As both R. W. B. Lewis and Cynthia Griffin Wolff point out, and they are surely correct, Wharton cast Undine as her opposite—ignorant, intrepid, unintrospective—yet also as her twin: Undine's energy, her anger and pride, her love of travel and gorgeous clothing and her impatience with failure and shabbiness—these, although exaggerated and simplified in the fictional character, do bring to mind the author herself.

The buried affinity probably explains why Edith Wharton had a difficult time writing *The Custom of the Country*. She started it in 1908 after completing *The Fruit of the Tree*, which was published in 1907. But she put it aside, not coming back to her devastating heroine until after she had finished *Ethan Frome* and *The Reef*. Originally *Scribner's* had wanted to begin serializing the novel in January 1909; but the love affair with Morton Fullerton followed by the last ugly stages of her breakup with Teddy, fights and bitter misunderstandings that climaxed in her decision in 1911 to sell her Massachusetts home, "The Mount," kept her from successfully resuming work on the novel. Then her long stagnation on the book broke, not surprisingly, at about the same time that her marriage collapsed completely. She signed the final sale papers on "The Mount" in June 1912, finished *The Reef* in August, picked the story about Undine back up in the autumn and had enough done for serialization to begin in January 1913. On April 16, 1913 her divorce from Teddy was formally decreed by a Parisian court; by August she had completed the novel.

If there is an undeniable ferocity about the book it is probably because *The Custom of the Country* was freed—let loose—from Edith Wharton's imagination by her final break with her own husband. In biographical terms, if *Ethan Frome* and *The Reef* served to help get the romance with Fullerton out of her system, *The Custom of the Country* seems to have done the same for her unfortunate marriage. After years of smothered resentments and then terrible quarrels, which settled on money as the issue to wound each other with (rather than focus on their far deeper problems of sexual and intellectual incompatibility), Edith Wharton must have felt enormous relief to be able to pile divorce upon divorce in *The Custom of the Country*. It makes sense that, until her own freedom from marriage was secured and official, she would be unable to complete Undine's story: personally, divorce was repugnant to Wharton; but so was marriage in many respects, and *The Custom of the Country* gave her the opportunity to attack both with vehemence.

The novel also allowed her to enter Undine, a compelling but in some ways vicious character, in the lists of American heroines, which by 1913 overbrimmed with attractive, blithe New Women whose authors led them through remarkable adventures that typically stopped at the altar. In terms of plot, Wharton drew most obviously on a story written by her friend Robert Grant, *Unleavened Bread* (1900), a best-seller that was unusual, though hardly unique, in *not* holding the New Woman up for admiration and *not* stopping with marriage. Grant's heroine, Selma Babcock, then Selma Babcock Littleton, then Selma Babcock Littleton Lyons, uses marriage, much as Undine does, as her means of moving up the social ladder. Along the way to becoming the wife of a United States senator she discards two husbands who fail to keep up with her notions of status and social prominence. Divorce has no more sting or stigma for Selma than it does for Undine, or Undine's girlhood friend Indiana Frusk, whose career even more closely follows Selma's in scaling, by means of divorce, to the heights of being a famous senator's wife.

Wharton enjoyed Grant's book and was definitely influenced by it: her heroine and his both come from small towns, are ambitious, have no qualms about divorce, and remain supremely confident throughout of their moral rectitude. Nevertheless there is a major difference in the authors' attitudes toward their subject matter. Grant has absolutely no sympathy for Selma, or interest in her beyond capturing her as a "type," the laughable modern clubwoman who bounds from cause to cause (and in this case husband to husband as well) in restless quest of something entertaining yet also morally righteous to do with her otherwise pointless life. In *The Custom of the Country* it is almost as if Wharton, inspired by Grant's book, went on to answer his shallow portrait of the female opportunist with her own tough economic analysis of the basic issue involved, which she, unlike Grant, knows is quite serious: marriage as woman's business in life. As Charlotte Perkins Gilman phrased the truism in *Women and Economics* at the turn of the century: "To the young woman confronting life there is the same world beyond [as there is to the young man], there are the same human energies and human desires and ambitions within. But all that she may wish to have, all that she may wish to do, must come through a single channel and a single choice. Wealth, power, social distinction, fame—not only these, but home and happiness, reputation, ease and pleasure, her bread and butter—all, must come to her through a small gold ring."[2] We may not admire Undine's avaricious approach to marriage, but neither can we fault it as illogical or perverse; it is simply realistic.

Indeed, Undine has seemed so real that Edmund Wilson has called her, in rather ugly language, "the prototype in fiction of the 'gold-digger,' of the international cocktail bitch" and many critics have followed his lead by arguing that the novel is flawed by Wharton's animosity toward her heroine, an uncouth bounder whose greed and ignorance she finds repellent.[3] It is true that Undine Spragg has little to recommend her. She forgets her five-year-old son's birthday. She has the Marvell heirloom jewels reset. She ignores a cable about her husband's illness while she vacations in Europe and then, while he is close to death, takes up with another man. She proposes that her next husband sell the family château in order to have ready cash to lavish on her. Undine shares her water sprite namesake's ability to attract men—Millard Binch, Elmer Moffatt, Aaronson, Popple, Ralph Marvell, Peter Van Degen, Raymond de Chelles—and also appears sirenlike in her heartless exploitation of them. After all, it is "the feeling of power that came with the sense of being loved"[4] that appeals to her. This heroine, in short, does seem a modern Circe: cruel, destructive, misandrous; and *The Custom of the Country* can be read as a conservative satire on the nouveaux-riches invaders who threatened the leisure-class values Edith Wharton grew up with.

Such a view, however, mistakes the superficial for the real object of attack in the novel. Not Undine Spragg, self-centered and insensitive as she is, but the institution of marriage in the leisure class is the main target of Wharton's satire in *The Custom of the Country*. The point about Undine is that, as something of an outsider and therefore a "naïf," she does not bother with the hypocritical rhetoric that rationalizes marriage—she sees what marriage is rather than what people say it is and she acts on what she sees. Consequently, her behavior and her assimilated values reflect Wharton's criticism less of the parvenu than of the established American upper class, which in her view, as in Veblen's, is looked to as the ideal by all of American culture and thus epitomizes pervasive American attitudes (even if not practices) toward women. That is, Edith Wharton *uses* Undine to reveal her criticism of the attitudes implicit in leisure-class marriage, an institution that has long, and unfortunately, been the envy of women dreaming of freedom but that in fact encourages the husband to assert his autonomy as an international playboy like Peter Van Degen or as a manager in the business world (a financier on Wall Street or a lawyer in a prestigious legal firm) while the wife, expected to be supportive and dependent, must channel her desires for self-assertion into the role of conspicuous consumer for him. Her life, in contrast to her husband's, is by definition parasitic and vicarious.

Although the solution offered by Charles Bowen, a wise older man in *The Custom of the Country*, is paternalistic, his analysis of the problem is sound. Taking "a general view of the whole problem of American marriages," he concludes that the weak point is "the fact that the average American looks down on his wife" (p. 205). He charges: "Where does the real life of most American men lie? In some woman's drawing-room or in their offices? The answer's obvious, isn't it? The emotional centre of gravity's not the same in the two hemispheres [Europe and America]. In the effete societies it's love, in our new one it's business. In America the real *crime passionnel* is a 'big steal'—there's more excitement in wrecking railways than homes" (p. 207). "And what's the result—how do the women avenge themselves?" Bowen asks and then remarks: "All my sympathy's with them, poor deluded dears, when I see their fallacious little attempts to trick out the leavings tossed them by the preoccupied male—the money and the motors and the clothes—and pretend to themselves and each other that *that's* what really constitutes life!" (p. 208). Bowen goes on to identify the main point of *The Custom of the Country* when he dubs Undine "a monstrously perfect result of the system: the completest proof of its triumph" (p. 208). For Wharton dramatizes her criticism of marriage ironically in this novel. She focuses on the marriage market not as it victimizes one of Bowen's "poor deluded dears" but as it is successfully played by one fiercely ambitious and highly imitative young woman. Ever since she was a little girl out in the midwest, where she used to "'play lady' before the wardrobe mirror" (p. 22), Undine Spragg has longed for status among the fashionably rich. *The Custom of the Country* simply shows how she goes through three marriages, two divorces, one annulment, several engagements, and one lover to achieve that goal.

When the novel opens, the Spraggs have been installed in New York for two years hoping that Undine, on the strength of her good looks and her father's money, will be admitted to the ranks of the socially elite. Though that hope has not yet been fulfilled, the whole family perseveres. Mr. Spragg continues to accumulate wealth to keep his daughter well-furbished and properly displayed. Mrs. Spragg stoically endures impersonal hotel-life and fancies she contributes to the cause because her masseuse, Mrs. Heeny, enters the portals of New York's rich and famous as familiarly as Mrs. Spragg might have stepped next door back home in Apex. Undine keeps herself beautiful, studies "Boudoir Chat" in the newspaper, and vows "to trust less to her impulses—especially in the matter of giving away rings" to imposters like the supposedly aristocratic Aaronson, an Austrian riding-master she met in Central Park (p. 26). Her social career begins, in other words, as a group enterprise, a family investment in the leisure class. Although her parents do not aspire to membership themselves, they agree that her social ambitions are worthy and sensible. For Undine is no libertine. She may appear *"diverse et ondoyante"* (p. 83), but her underlying values and motives are as uncomplicated as her small-town background. "She wanted, passionately and persistently, two things which she believed should subsist together in any well-ordered life: amusement and respectability; and despite her surface-sophistication her notion of amusement was hardly less innocent than when she hung on the plumber's fence with Indiana Frusk" in Apex (p. 354).

Even conservative, upper-class Ralph Marvell, though he disapproves of his wife's desires when he finally understands them, recognizes their innocence. Midway through the novel he realizes "it was admiration, not love, that she wanted. She wanted to enjoy herself, and her conception of enjoyment was publicity, promiscuity—the band, the banners, the crowd, the close contact of covetous impulses, and the sense of walking among them in cool security" (pp. 223–24). Ralph is correct. Undine invades the leisure class primarily to show herself off: she just wants the best possible mirror to reflect her belief that she is extraordinary.

In a deeper sense, though, Undine desires the publicity she associates with status in the leisure class because "public triumph . . . was necessary to her personal enjoyment" (p. 549). The important word is triumph. Undine is fiercely competitive and determined to win. Of the Fairfords and Marvells, old New York families, she says to Mrs. Heeny: "I want the best. Are they as swell as the Driscolls and Van Degens?" Assured they are even better, she exalts (again in front of the mirror): "There were to be no more mistakes and no more follies now! She was going to know the right people at last—she was going to get what she wanted!" (pp. 24, 29).

Undine wants power—the kind of power over people and circumstances which will enable her to be a social "triumph," one of the leisure-class potentates who personify her concept of success.

Nowhere is this love of power more significantly expressed than in the image Wharton associates with Undine when she appears at the opera, engaged to marry a brahmin. "Now at last she was having what she wanted—she was in conscious possession of the 'real thing'; and through her other, more diffused, sensations Ralph's adoration gave her such a last refinement of pleasure as might have come to some warrior Queen borne in triumph by captive princes, and reading in the eyes of one the passion he dared not to speak" (pp. 98–99). The image of a warrior queen borne in triumph by captive princes not only describes the structure of *The Custom of the Country*, which Wharton called a "chronicle-novel"[5] and which, in place of a conventional plot, recounts a series of campaigns, each followed by its brief "progress" in the regal sense of the term. The image also describes Undine's character: her capacity to wield and embody power. By nature aggressive, assertive, confident, and ambitious, Undine is at the same time manipulative, theatrical, and adaptable. Reared as the family princess, she has all the requisites of a warrior queen, and the book chronicles the fierce social campaigns she wages in order to capture the right princes.

There is a primitivism about Wharton's image, and Undine's character in general, that roots this novel not only in Veblenesque socioeconomics but also in feminist anthropological assumptions popular at the turn of the century. Hildegarde Hawthorne in 1908 exclaimed in disgust: "Whence that absurd term 'New Woman'?" Strong women were not new in her opinion,[6] any more than they were, for example, in Anna Garlin Spencer's or Charlotte Perkins Gilman's or Olive Schreiner's. All of these theorists, and they are typical, argue that the contemporary woman's female ancestor was man's complete equal—if not his superior—with respect to vigor, economic production, and inventiveness. Spencer, for instance, begins her study *Woman's Share in Social Culture* (1912) with a chapter on "The Primitive Working-Woman" (it is the groundwork for her next chapter, "The Ancient and Modern Lady"), and her anthropological claims for woman as the race's first inventor and manufacturer were by no means new in 1912. Many years earlier it was decided that woman was in fact the race's original industrial genius. Indeed, part of the purpose of the Woman's Building in 1893 (and it had to be a conservative venture, of course, to be included in the Chicago Exposition) was to impress that idea upon the public. As the all-female Board of Managers announced in 1892: "It will be shown that women, among all the primitive peoples, were the originators of most of the industrial arts, and that it was not until these became lucrative that they were appropriated by men, and women pushed aside. . . . Woman constructed the rude semblance of a home. She dressed and cooked the game. . . . She cured and dressed the skins. . . . She invented the needle. . . . She invented the shuttle. . . . She was the first potter. . . . She originated basket-making. . . . She learned to ornament these articles."[7]

This pride in woman's ancestry permeates Olive Schreiner's *Woman and Labour*, a best-seller in America in 1912 (one year before *The Custom of the Country* was completed). Schreiner takes the argument out of the home and gives it military dimension:

> The truth is, we are not new. . . .
> We have in us the blood of a womanhood that was never bought and never sold; that wore no veil, and had no foot bound. . . . We are women of a breed whose racial ideal was no Helen of Troy, passed passively from male hand to male hand, as men pass gold or lead; but that of Brynhild whom Segurd found, clad in helm and byrne, the warrior maid. . . .
> We are of a race of women that of old knew no fear, and feared no death. . . . If you would understand us, go back two thousand years, and study our descent. . . . We are the daughters of our fathers as well as of our mothers.[8]

Undine Spragg, fresh out of the raw midwestern regions of America that both alarmed and fascinated Edith Wharton for their sheer vigor and crudity, is Wharton's first contribution to popular anthropology (next would be Charity Royall in *Summer* and then the tribal sexual politics of *The Age of Innocence*); and Wharton's thoughts on the subject, although they are expressed with great sophistication, concur with contemporary notions. She makes Undine, who we are told can stare down her opponent (even her father) like an "Amazon" (p. 124), both a warrior and an entrepreneur.

Kingdoms, in Wharton's twentieth-century America, are won on the stock exchange. Wall Street is the field of battle for the modern robber baron, and although his female counterpart, the modern "warrior Queen," is denied that battleground, she is given her own stock exchange: the institution of marriage in which she herself is the stock exchanged. To create her empire, she invests herself in the right marriage—an enterprise Undine understands and embraces. In fact, she is so highly motivated by a "business shrewdness which was never quite dormant in her" (p. 354) and so confident of her objective, that her ambitiousness puzzles Ralph Marvell. "He wondered from what source Undine's voracious ambitions had been drawn: all she cared for, and attached importance to, was as remote from her parents' conception of life as her impatient greed from their passive stoicism" (pp. 317–18). Ralph cannot see the familial connection because he sees Mr. Spragg in the drawing room, rather than the counting room. As Wharton explains

> the student of inheritance might have wondered whence Undine derived her overflowing activity. The answer would have been obtained by observing her father's business life. From the moment he set foot in Wall Street Mr. Spragg became another man. Physically the change revealed itself only by the subtlest signs. As he steered his way to his office through the jostling crowd of William Street his relaxed muscles did not grow more taut or his lounging gait less desultory. . . . It was only in his face that the difference was perceptible . . . showing itself now and then in the cautious glint of half-closed eyes, the forward thrust of black brows, or a tightening of the lax lines of the mouth. (p. 119)

Undine is her father's daughter. They have the same "scowl" (p. 59), the same kind of "resolute will" (p. 43), and the same business cunning and enthusiasm. When "resolutely bent on a definite object," Undine is "too sternly animated by her father's business instinct to turn aside in quest of casual distractions" (p. 236). Wharton compares her manipulation of Peter Van Degen with her father's financial maneuvering—"So Mr. Spragg might have felt at the tensest hour of the Pure Water move" (p. 294)—while her decision to live with Peter Van Degen is "as carefully calculated as the happiest Wall

Street 'stroke'" (p. 364). Ralph Marvell's wry speculation that modern leisure-class marriages ought to be "transacted on the Stock Exchange" (p. 78) is an idea Undine would no doubt consider very sensible. Wharton's "warrior Queen" has a passion for the business of negotiating herself on the marriage market.

Unlike Lily Bart in *The House of Mirth*, this heroine does not fear marriage as a threat to her independence. To Popple's jocular "I can paint you! He [Ralph] can't forbid that, can he? Not before marriage, anyhow!" Undine responds with "joyous defiance": "I guess he isn't going to treat me any different afterward" (p. 100). And if she does not believe that the proprietorship of marriage will affect her, neither does Undine share with Justine Brent in *The Fruit of the Tree* a vision of husband and wife as partners mutually engaged in meaningful social work. The only social work that interests Undine Spragg is the leisure-class wife's business of publicly displaying her husband's wealth, and therefore power, by consuming for him in ostentatious splendor.

In fact, *The Custom of the Country* is one of America's great business novels. It belongs in the tradition of Howells's *The Rise of Silas Lapham* (1885), *A Hazard of New Fortunes* (1890), and *The Landlord at Lion's Head* (1897), from the first two of which (if not from all three) Edith Wharton borrowed for her novel. The way Silas Lapham carried himself in his office, propping his feet up on his scrap basket while he talks with Bartley Hubbard in the opening scene of Howells's book, echoes in Wharton's description of Abner Spragg at the end of book 1 in *The Custom of the Country* when Elmer Moffatt talks money with him at his office. Likewise, the literary device of the disastrous formal dinner at which the nouveaux riches horrify their genteel old-money-hosts, Wharton surely took from Howells. Silas's drunken bragging at the Coreys' quiet dinner for him produces the same effect on his hosts as Undine's offhand chatter about divorce—"He isn't in the right set, and I think Mabel realizes she'll never really get anywhere till she gets rid of him" (p. 94)—does on her blueblooded hosts, the Marvells, at their elegant small engagement dinner for her. Probably Wharton even took the name for her successful capitalist in *The Custom of the Country*, Elmer Moffatt, from Howells's Moffitt, Indiana, the birthplace of his aging capitalist, Dryfoos, in *A Hazard of New Fortunes*. In any event, her novel, like Howells's, and then some of Norris's and Dreiser's, takes the ambitious capitalist for its subject and arrives, by means of that focus, at a critique of large areas of American life.

That the capitalist of most importance in *The Custom of the Country* is a woman is unusual, but not without precedent. Three years earlier, in *The Iron Woman* (a best-seller in 1911, the year after it was published) Margaret Deland surprised readers with an awesome woman industrialist, an owner/manager of an iron-works, who possesses a genius for making money which is the equal of any man's in American fiction. Deland tries to be firm in her condemnation of Sarah Maitland, who neglects her children in her passion for work, but the book succeeds instead in giving its title-character mythic stature. Against a midnight backdrop of flames, smoke, and molten ore, Sarah, in heavy boots and wide-hemmed skirts, strides majestically through her iron-yards with each of her children in two of the book's crucial scenes; and she dies the death of a hero, holding on to life for days after being wounded while supervising rescue work in the yards in the wake of a horrible accident. If her life is finally repudiated by Deland because of her failure as a mother, her success as a capitalist is still impressive.

Less literal and therefore even closer to what Wharton does in *The Custom of the Country* is Frances Hodgson Burnett's 1906 best-seller about capital, *The Shuttle*. As a matter of fact, Burnett's novel has all the appearance of having been written to attract the audience Wharton landed with *The House of Mirth*, a big best-seller the year before Burnett's book came out, and it is very possible that Wharton knew the novel and made *The Custom of the Country* in some ways a response to it. Burnett's title refers to the first steamers used by the very rich at the turn of the century to make rapid transatlantic crossings—jetting, so to speak, with great frequency from New York to fashionable European watering holes and then back again. But even if her title is realistic, her heroine, Betty Vanderpoel (the last name needs no gloss), in contrast to the heroine in Wharton's best-seller, Lily Bart, is pure fantasy—a flawless New Woman who possesses limitless wealth, beauty, courage, and freedom.

Setting out alone to rescue her sister from a tyrannical British nobleman she made the mistake of marrying, Betty Vanderpoel knows no fear. She explains to one of her amazed shipmates, "Women have found out so much. Perhaps it is because the heroines of novels have informed them. . . . I believe it is years since a heroine 'burst into a flood of tears.' It has been discovered, really, that nothing is to be gained by it." She adds: "Whatsoever I find at Stornham Court, I shall neither weep nor be helpless. There is the Atlantic cable, you know."[9] Betty hardly needs it. Single-handed, she finds her sister, restores her to health and hope, and uses her vast Vanderpoel wealth to completely do over the shabby baronial manor that has been timid Rosalie's prison (the project makes one think of Undine, who is always wanting to re-do heirlooms, while the image of imprisonment that the book is built on brings to mind Anna Leath's entombment at Givré as well as Undine's at Saint-Désert, the ancestral home of her third husband, Raymond de Chelles).

From start to finish *The Shuttle* is an entertaining escapist novel, an adventure fantasy for women with gothic trimmings. But it is also an accolade to American capitalism. Burnett's heroine declares of herself: "I am of the fighting commercial stock, and, when I see a business problem, I cannot leave it alone, even when it is no affair of mine."[10] Betty Vanderpoel, who we are told closely resembles her father, embodies in a woman the American myth of high morality, fearless individualism, and unlimited monetary success.

Wharton's capitalist heroine, in contrast, is no such fantasy creature. Undine is selfish and shrewd, the only one of Wharton's early heroines to deal successfully (that is, to her advantage) with economic and social reality; and she does so precisely because she is not virtuous. She is beautiful, she is clever, she is eager to be prominent within the structure of American society, and the way she achieves her goal is by playing—and playing to the hilt—a very old feminine game: snaring men as husbands. She is closer in type to Chaucer's Wife of Bath than she is to Burnett's romanticized capitalist do-gooder Betty Vanderpoel. As Wharton makes clear through her spokesman Charles Bowen, the world has not really changed. For all the excitement about the New Woman in America at the turn of the century, for all the anxiety expressed in a character like Margaret Deland's Sarah Maitland, and for all the optimism fantastically caught up in a character like brave Betty Vanderpoel, what—this novel asks—has really changed? Divorce has made it easier to switch alliances, that is true. But women—even dashing young New Women like Undine and her friend Indiana—still live through men. In Wharton's view the woman who wants to make it to the very top of the American pyramid still has only one route: confederate with a man already up there, or one on the way. There is nothing "new" about this. Undine is an utterly modern American woman, and her story is ancient.

She decides to marry Ralph Marvell because, she thinks, as a member of the most elite stratum of the leisure class, he represents the apex of her social ambitions. Given their different temperaments and backgrounds, however, his attraction to Undine seems less understandable. Of course she is beautiful and vital. But why are even "her crudity and her limitations . . . a part of her grace and her persuasion" (p. 83)? The answer lies in the challenge Undine poses for Ralph, another in the growing ranks of Pygmalion figures in Wharton's fiction. A would-be artist who has never been able to finish a single work, he sees Undine as raw material for his creative impulse. He worries that her "virgin innocence" (ironically, she has already been married and divorced) will be corrupted by another and less idealistic artist. Popple, whose "vulgar hands were on it already—Popple's and the unspeakable Van Degen's! Once they and theirs had begun the process of initiating Undine, there was no knowing—or rather there was too easy knowing—how it would end!" (p. 82). Ralph wants to initiate her himself. "To save her from Van Degen and Van Degenism" therefore becomes the mission he romantically envisions for himself: "he seemed to see her like a lovely rock-bound Andromeda, with the devouring monster Society careering up to make a mouthful of her; and himself whirling down on his winged horse—just Pegasus turned Rosinante for the nonce—to cut her bonds, snatch her up, and whirl her back into the blue . . ." (pp. 82, 84; Wharton's ellipsis).

Even after four unhappy years of marriage, Ralph, still considering it his task to shape and improve Undine's character, is full of rationalizations: "After all, she was still in the toy age; and perhaps the very extravagance of his love had retarded her growth, helped to imprison her in a little circle of frivolous illusions. But the last months had made a man of him, and when she came back [from Europe] he would know how to lift her to the height of his experience" (p. 309). Accustomed to women who "yielded as a matter of course to masculine judgments" (p. 178), Ralph assumes that Undine wants to be lifted and will adopt his unostentatious way of life, his taste for reserved people, and his educated aestheticism. He assumes, in other words, that she wants to become a supportive, emotionally and intellectually dependent wife—both the object and the nurture of his creativity. Undine, however, wants to serve neither as his impressionable pupil nor his muse, and Ralph must eventually abandon the project. His wife simply will not adopt his values, especially his belief in the innate passivity of female human nature.

Undine's idea of marriage Thorstein Veblen captures perfectly when he describes the function of the rich man's wife, who should be "supported in idleness by her owner. She is useless and expensive, and she is consequently valuable as evidence of pecuniary strength." He explains that "the reason for the more extreme insistence on a futile life for this class of women than for the men of the same pecuniary and social grade lies in their not only being upper-grade leisure class but also at the same time a vicarious leisure class. There is in her case a double ground for consistent withdrawal from useful effort." In short: "In the ideal scheme, as it tends to realize itself in the life of the higher pecuniary classes . . . attention to conspicuous waste of substance and effort should normally be the sole economic function of the woman."[11] Mrs. Ralph Marvell would have no quarrel whatsoever with Veblen's description of the "ideal scheme." Her problem is that Ralph does not have the kind of money or attitudes that will allow her to realize that ideal.

As important as the relative poverty that limits her opportunities for conspicuous consumption, Undine also resents Ralph's Pygmalion attitude toward her, his subtle attempts to mold and upgrade her values. Before they marry, when he intimates that Popple's portraits are vulgar, she begins to resist Ralph's mentorship; and when he implies that he should choose her friends for her on their honeymoon, she is astonished, and then defiant. Alone in Europe a few years later, Undine thinks about that honeymoon summer when

> there had been no child to hamper their movements, their money anxieties had hardly begun, the face of life had been fresh and radiant, and she had been doomed to waste such opportunities on a succession of ill-smelling Italian towns. She still felt it to be her deepest grievance against her husband; and now that, after four years of petty household worries, another chance of escape had come, he already wanted to drag her back to bondage! (pp. 282–83)

Undine's taste may need educating, but that is beside the point. She married in order to be displayed, not educated and hidden away in elegant seclusion like Ralph's mother or his cousin, Clare Van Degen. Consequently marriage with Ralph seems like "bondage" to her; she feels "imprisoned" (p. 245); she wants to "escape" from him.

Divorced from Ralph and deserted by Peter Van Degen, with whom she has had a brief miscalculated affair (it did not produce the marriage she had counted on), Undine experiences an obscurity far worse than the attention she resented from Ralph. She tries to create a life for herself as a single woman living abroad but fails because, without her married name, she has no identity of value to society. "Her new visiting-card, bearing her Christian name in place of her husband's, was like the coin of a debased currency testifying to her diminished trading capacity" (p. 361). Unmarried, she has no social status and nothing to do. Worse yet, when she returns to New York to live with her parents and attends the opera, society so obviously "cuts" her as a divorcée and Van Degen's former mistress that her first reaction upon return to the hotel is "immediate submission to her father's will" (p. 378); she agrees to send back the pearls Van Degen gave her. Normally defiant, Undine is so humiliated that, thinking in terms of the "pathetic allusions to woman's frailty" she has picked up from her novel-reading (evidently she has not read the same novels Betty Vanderpoel has), she considers her father "heroic" and depends for the moment on his rather than her own judgment (p. 376). Wharton's point is important. As a single woman, Undine is unrecognized, even ostracized; and she consequently grows spiritless and insecure. She must marry again in order to have identity itself, much less power.[12]

At first Undine thrives as the wife of Raymond de Chelles, Ralph's successor. "Her husband was really charming (it was odd how he reminded her of Ralph!), and after her bitter two years of loneliness and humiliation it was delicious to find herself once more adored and protected. The very fact that Raymond was more jealous of her than Ralph had ever been—or at any rate less reluctant to show it—gave her a keener sense of recovered power" (p. 480). This happiness is very short-lived. Even on their honeymoon Raymond dictates where she may go and with whom she may associate, and he expects her "to give a circumstantial report of every hour she spent away from him" (p. 481). His lovely jealousy, as Undine comes to realize too late, is not a sign of affection but of power. As Charlotte Perkins Gilman says in *The Man-Made World* of the limitations traditionally set on women (and Raymond is, if nothing else, a traditionalist), "the dominant male, holding his women as property, and fiercely jealous of them, considering them always as *his*, not belonging to themselves, their children, or the world, has hedged them in with restrictions of a thousand sorts."[13] It is not surprising that Wharton devotes little space to Raymond de Chelles; it takes little space to show that the "charming" Raymond is simply a nightmarish exaggeration of Undine's previous husband.

He has such a strong sense of proprietorship and cherishes such a suffocating ideal of passive femininity that Undine finds herself virtually entombed in his château, appropriately named Saint-Désert. There her "enforced seclusion" (p. 492) is relieved only by rare visits from dull relatives; Raymond lacks both the cash and the philosophy that would allow her to occupy herself with conspicuous consumption. Instead, the sole activity permitted her in this extremely conservative but nevertheless completely conventional environment is needlework. As Anna Garlin Spencer, following Veblen's lead, emphasizes in *Woman's Share in Social Culture*: "the lady must not earn money; she must not be a producer of any values not included in domestic and social occupations as outlined in the 'theory of the leisure class.' . . . Fine needlework; decorative weaving; 'arts and crafts' in reminiscent play-work; illuminating or binding books that only wealth can own or preserve"—these activities, plus a few more that recall the social arts in which Lily Bart was so well-trained, define the lady's realm.[14] Missing the point of Wharton's satire, one critic cites Undine's contempt for needlework as evidence of her moral poverty: "Next [after Ralph] is Raymond de Chelles, a French nobleman of 'simplicity and intelligence' who mistakes Undine for a beautiful candid American girl. But of course she hasn't inherited the dream of all the ages [woman as man's elevating moral force: especially the symbol for him of American idealism], merely the materials—energy and ambition and limitless egoism. This marriage bores her because she cannot adapt herself to the role required of 'the ladies of the line of Chelles,' who sit 'at their needlework on the terrace.'"[15] Certainly Undine *should* be bored with her restricted life at Saint-Désert. The fact that she is a highly flawed character does not make Raymond or his concept of a wife's role admirable; and we should no more wish that Undine could adapt to such a dreary life than we should lament her not having "inherited the dream of all the ages"—a male fantasy that casts woman in the impossible role of nymph/nun cultural messiah. (Not surprisingly, there is no such idealized, redemptive American girl in Wharton's fiction.)

In her marriage to Ralph, and in this one to Raymond, Undine entered the relationship expecting to be placed on triumphant public display—modelling fabulous gowns, being seen dining leisurely at the finest restaurants, shuttling back and forth across the Atlantic, sporting jewels that would be written up on society pages from New York to Apex—only to find that her third husband, like her second (but with none of his tolerance) abhors publicity: he belongs to a very special subclass that prides itself on its *in*visibility. As if that weren't bad enough, compounding Undine's misery is Raymond's loss of interest in her because she will not acquiesce in his will. Although she resolves to "cultivate all the arts of patience and compliance" to win him back (p. 496), she cannot carry off the role of submissive wife—for which she is ingeniously punished by Raymond's refusing to sleep with her. Childless, she steadily loses status within the French family structure, the basis of power in French society. For a while she fights back—tormenting her mother-in-law, buying extravagant clothing, arguing with Raymond. But she develops "the baffled feeling of not being able to count on any of her old weapons of aggression. . . . A blind desire to wound and destroy replaced her usual business-like intentness on gaining her end" (pp. 527–28). This is Undine's nadir. The almost literal imprisonment she suffers at Saint-Désert erodes her confidence in her own power and rectitude, and it brings out in her a conscious viciousness, a desire to wound. She reacts to entrapment as would any healthy, active creature: she becomes demoralized, mean, and desperate. The wonder is not that she contemplates selling the Chelles's ancestral tapestries, but that she does not do so.

In 1907, six years before *The Custom of the Country* appeared (but only one year before the novel was begun), Wharton published a finely chiseled novella very much in the Jamesian mode, *Madame de Treymes*, which shows how powerful an opponent Undine overcomes in freeing herself from Raymond de Chelles and his family. In this earlier story Madame de Malrive, formerly Fannie Frisbee of New York City, manages to obtain a separation from a similarly repulsive French husband but never from his despotic family. They agree to the divorce that will enable her to remarry, but they do so only because, unbeknownst to her or her future husband, remarriage would automatically prohibit her from keeping her son by Malrive. In fact, the family secretly connives for divorce so that they can appropriate the son. (Separated from Malrive, Fannie is entitled to legal custody of the boy; remarried, she would have no rights.) To show how indomitable the solidarity of the French family is, Wharton makes Malrive's sister, Madame de Treymes, who is Fannie's one friend and defender, the family's instrument in the deception. To her credit, though she does the family's bidding by encouraging Fannie to divorce, Madame de Treymes betrays their motive—theft of the boy—before it is too late; and Fannie does not divorce Malrive and remarry. It is a sad victory, however. To keep her child she must sacrifice her own happiness and all dreams of immediate independence from the Malrives. Undine would probably not make the same choice, but then that is conjecture. Faced with the same type of ruthless domestic tyranny but with no child at stake, she defies French custom and leaves Raymond de Chelles without one regret.

Undine is not admirable, of course. But neither is any other character in *The Custom of the Country*, Raymond de Chelles and Ralph Marvell included. To attribute Ralph's suicide to Undine's Circe-like destructiveness is to ignore the self-pity and fatuous self-sacrifice that motivate it. "He said to himself: 'My wife . . . this will make it all right for her . . .' and a last flash of irony twitched through him" as he pulled the trigger (p. 474; Wharton's ellipsis). Both Ralph and Undine have been playing the same game of trying to change the other person; put crudely, Ralph is an exceptionally poor loser. Similarly, to deplore Undine's abuse of her son as either an irrelevance or an "acquisition" (p. 478)—the book plainly encourages sympathy for the boy—should not obscure the fact that she treats him as his beloved stepfather, Raymond, treated her. That by no means excuses her behavior, but it does place it in context. And within the commercial context of this novel Undine's failure as a mother emphasizes Wharton's contention that the social system, much like Wall Street, is designed to promote the success of precisely the most callous, rapacious people. Concern for others and tenderness are weaknesses in the "jungle" of social, no less than economic, competition. (Given Wharton's fondness for mythology, it is likely that she plays with the idea here that the undine, according to myth, can acquire a soul only by marrying a mortal and bearing a child. Wharton's Undine remains soulless even in maternity, suggesting perhaps that the mortal world that inseminates her has no soul to bestow. If so, her lack of maternal concern, figuratively as well as sociologically, accentuates the culture's as much as her own inhumanity.) Moreover, even as we recognize that Undine is a terrible mother, we should ask: in this book who, in her own way at the over-solicitous other end of the spectrum, is not? Mrs. Spragg, Mrs. Marvell, and the Marquise de Chelles dote on their children (and look at them: Undine, Ralph, Raymond) with a vested devotion only somewhat less selfish than Undine's neglect of her child. No mother in *The Custom of the Country* would win any awards.

Even Undine's two most reprehensible actions Wharton takes care to place in context. Undine ignores the cable about Ralph's illness because she believes, as is plausible, that his mother and sister, who spend their lives protecting him and are always manufacturing sentimental terrors, would think nothing of alarming her as a device to bring her back from Europe. Equally significant, Moffatt conceives and suggests Undine's scheme to extort annulment money out of Ralph by threatening to take their son away from him. I do not point these things out to exonerate Undine, but to emphasize how carefully Wharton implicates most of the characters in the central theme of human usury, especially as manifest in the business of marriage.

Undine's story stands in much the same relation to Lily Bart's, a saddening treatment of the marriage question, as one of Edith Wharton's own shining Panhard-Lavassors (the "motor" that swept trembling Henry James off with her on their whirlwind excursions of sightseeing) did to the horse-drawn barouche of quieter times. By 1913, with *Ethan Frome* and *The Reef* immediately behind her, and a few years before them *The House of Mirth* and *The Fruit of the Tree*, Edith Wharton knew exactly what she had to say about the business of marriage, and she was not at all timid on the subject. Whereas in *The House of Mirth* she delicately expresses her criticism of leisure-class marriage by dramatizing a sensitive, but only vaguely self-aware young woman's fear of becoming some man's property within marriage, in *The Custom of the Country* Wharton adopts a bolder strategy. She creates in her protagonist an ambitious young woman who not only accepts the commercial nature of marriage but is also eager, as the image of a warrior queen emphasizes, to triumph by means of it—in the vernacular, eager to make a "killing." The stock market parallels are more than decoration. Endowed with a cunning business sense, Undine makes marriage her business in life. She speculates in husbands just as husbands speculate in stocks, and she is skillful at it. True, she makes a couple of investments that turn out badly: she did not understand that both Ralph and Raymond belong to the stable, aboriginal leisure class of their native countries and therefore desire a wife who, in Veblen's terms, will display conspicuous leisure for a small, exclusive group of people rather than conspicuous consumption for the benefit of the masses.[16] But she is smart enough to "unload" in each case. Consequently she is able to make a profitable deal in the end by remarrying Elmer Moffatt, her first husband, who, as a nouveau-riche multimillionaire, shares her belief that she should devote her life to conspicuously spending his money as vivid, public proof of his wealth and power.

Undine Spragg is no more exploitive than the culture that produced her. Instead of rejecting marriage because it is a usurious arrangement or enduring a restrictive marriage and thereby accepting failure, Undine—like an ambitious man changing jobs until he finds the "right" one—regards marriage as a commercial enterprise and, in fact, goes the system one better by viewing men as *her* possessions: she coolly gives "a smile of possessorship to Ralph" at the opera and, in Paris with Raymond, she "enjoyed going about with her husband, whose presence at her side was distinctly ornamental" (pp. 97, 507). There is a genius to Wharton's ironic strategy. What better way to expose how exploitive and demeaning leisure-class marriage is for wives than by placing men in the belittling role usually reserved for women? The book implicitly asks why, if it is distasteful to see a woman regard a man as an acquisition, is the reverse not equally true?

A character like Undine is rooted in two worlds. When Wharton's friend Bernard Berenson suggested that the names she gave Undine Spragg and her friend Indiana Frusk were unbelievable, Wharton laughed: "*Naïf enfant*. And how about Lurline Spreckels . . . and Florida Yurlee, two 'actualities' who occur to me instantly? As for similar instances, the 'Herald' register will give you a dozen any morning."[17] However, Undine not only brings to mind America's Lurline Spreckelses and Florida Yurlees; she also, because of her third marriage, calls up Consuelo Vanderbilts and Anna Goulds, envied American princesses whose glamorous marriages to titled Europeans—the Duke of Marlborough and Count Boniface de Castellane—seemed perfect fairy tales until their alliances, like Undine's equally bad match, ended (in 1912 and 1906) in ugly separations and divorce. First in Anna Leath's marriage to Fraser Leath in *The Reef* and then one year later in Undine's marriage to Raymond de Chelles in *The Custom of the Country* (and, as we will see, once again a few years later in Ellen Olenska's awful marriage to Count Olenski in *The Age of Innocence*), Wharton argues that bad as American marriages may be, tradition-bound aristocratic European ones can be worse. The higher up the social scale in Europe, the more historically dictated the marriage is likely to be, and hence the more restrictive for women. Wharton sympathizes with some of Undine's discoveries. Despite seductive press given the subject at the turn of the century, marrying into an old European house and title was not, in Wharton's view, an enlightened thing to do.

As a young American woman whose goal is to reach the very top of the American social ladder, Undine must climb through marriage: attachment to the right man is her only means of ascent; there is no independent route. She must agree to trade herself in marriage. (The option taken by the Princess Estradina—being married in name but not in practice—is clearly European not American.) Undine has two alternatives. Like Clare Van Degen, Laura Fairford, and Ralph's mother, she can conform to an old-fashioned ideal of acquiescent femininity and thus perpetuate the aboriginal leisure-class ideal of feminine self-effacement and conspicuous leisure displayed within a narrow circle. Or she can emulate the aggressive opportunism of her girlhood friends, Indiana Frusk and Mabel Blitch: she can marry new money and express her ambitious nature vicariously but publicly as the ostentatious spender of her husband's millions. By any standard, neither wifely role is attractive, for both designate the woman her husband's property, his chattel. As Elmer Moffatt, not yet totally financially successful, puts it when asked if he plans to marry: "Why, I shouldn't wonder—one of these days. Millionaires always collect something; but I've got to collect my millions first" (p. 419). Undine is not an admirable character because, within marriage as it is defined in this novel, there is for women no admirable way to accept or escape the collected state. To submit to it is to become a masochistic, self-effaced Clare Van Degen. To escape it one must apparently be a callous, profiteering Undine Spragg

Moffatt Marvell de Chelles Moffatt—a woman as ruthless and exploitive as the culture she mirrors.

In her memoir, *A Backward Glance* (1934), Wharton recalled how Henry James "often bewailed to me his total inability to use the 'material,' financial and industrial, of modern American life. Wall Street, and everything connected with the big business world, remained an impenetrable mystery to him." Wharton had to admit that her old friend was right about himself: "The attempt to portray the retired financier in Mr. Verver, and to relate either him or his native 'American City' to any sort of concrete reality, is perhaps proof enough of the difficulties James would have found in trying to depict the American money-maker in action."[18] Wharton, in contrast, perfectly understood the modern American money-making scene, including the woman's stock market of marriage and divorce. The incidence of divorce was rising sharply in America, of course, when *The Custom of the Country* appeared;[19] and among the culprits commonly cited was the ambitious modern woman supposedly produced by the Woman Movement. Anna B. Rogers's *Why American Marriages Fail* (1909), for instance, attacks feminism and its self-centered New Woman for the alarming increase in divorce, which promised in her view, as in many others, to destroy the family in America. A little more than a decade later Edith Wharton would be agreeing; but not when she wrote *The Custom of the Country*. When she told Undine's story, it was still marriage, not divorce, that roused her cynicism.

Notes

1. Emily James Putnam, *The Lady: Studies in Certain Significant Phases in Her History* (New York: Putnam, 1910), p. 69.
2. Charlotte Perkins Gilman, *Women and Economics: A Study of the Economic Relations between Men and Women as a Factor in Social Evolution* (Boston: Small, Maynard and Co., 1898), p. 71.
3. Edmund Wilson, *The Wound and the Bow: Seven Studies in Literature* (Boston: Houghton Mifflin, 1929), p. 202.
4. Edith Wharton, *The Custom of the Country* (New York: Scribner's, 1913), p. 89. Further references are to this edition.
5. Millicent Bell, *Edith Wharton and Henry James: The Story of Their Friendship* (New York: George Braziller, 1965), p. 242.
6. Hildegarde Hawthorne, *Women and Other Women: Essays in Wisdom* (New York: Duffield & Co., 1908), p. 35.
7. Hubert Howe Bancroft, *The Book of the Fair: An Historical and Descriptive Presentation of the World's Science, Art, and Industry as Viewed through the Columbian Exposition at Chicago in 1893*, 2 vols. (New York: Crown, 1894), 1: 267, 269.
8. Olive Schreiner, *Woman and Labour* (London: T. Fisher Unwin, 1911), pp. 144–45, 147.
9. Frances Hodgson Burnett, *The Shuttle*, (New York: Frederick A. Stokes, 1906), pp. 74–75.
10. Ibid., p. 294.
11. Thorstein Veblen, *The Theory of the Leisure Class: An Economic Study of Institutions* (New York: Macmillan, 1899), p. 63.
12. As Eva Figes puts it for a modern audience (repeating of course the argument made by Gilman and others), "it is important to remember that, although we may regard marriage with dependence as a form of slavery, for the woman of the past it was regarded as the only possible form of freedom—it was only through marriage that she could become a woman in her own right in the eyes of the world, and much depended on finding a tolerable and reasonably tolerant mate" (*Patriarchal Attitudes* [Greenwich, Conn.: Fawcett, 1970], p. 74).
13. Charlotte Perkins Gilman, *The Man-Made World, or Our Androcentric Culture* (New York: Charlton Co., 1911), p. 38.
14. Anna Garlin Spence, *Woman's Share in Social Culture* (Philadelphia: Lippincott, 1912), p. 28.
15. See William Wasserstrom, *Heiress of All the Ages: Sex and Sentiment in the Genteel Tradition* (Minneapolis: University of Minnesota Press, 1959), p. 56.
16. For the distinction between these two methods of displaying upperclass status, conspicuous leisure or conspicuous consumption, see Veblen, *The Theory of the Leisure Class*, pp. 85–86.
17. R. W. B. Lewis, *Edith Wharton: A Biography* (New York: Harper & Row, 1975), p. 349.
18. Edith Wharton, *A Backward Glance* (New York: D. Appleton-Century, 1934), p. 176.
19. The divorce issue during the Progressive Era, an issue that inevitably reflected conflicting attitudes toward the institutions of marriage and the family and often split down feminist and antifeminist lines, is the subject of an excellent study by William L. O'Neill, *Divorce in the Progressive Era* (New Haven: Yale University Press, 1967).

MARILYN FRENCH

From "The Emergence of Edith Wharton"

New Republic, June 13, 1981, pp. 29–31

Edith Wharton is one of America's finest novelists; during her lifetime she was highly respected, well known, and successful. But since her death 40 years ago her work has been largely neglected: only a few of her books remain in print. Few writers of quality have suffered such an eclipse. There have been intermittent efforts, by critics like Edmund Wilson and Irving Howe, to resuscitate her reputation, and indeed there has been increasing interest in Wharton's work recently. But some of the very people who have attempted to revive such interest are responsible for impeding that process, by writing essays tainted with undisguised patronization for this "lady writer," and by approaching her work negatively. That is, critics frequently direct more attention to what Wharton did not do than to what she did do. They have skirted the task of focusing and elucidation which is surely the first business of criticism.

But part of the reason for our long neglect of Edith Wharton may also be that, without a change in certain attitudes, it was difficult to recognize her central concerns. One of her more perceptive critics, Blake Nevius, writing in 1953, accused Wharton of a "lurking feminism." Feminist concerns do appear in her work, although she did not associate herself with the feminist movement of her time. She wrote frequently of the way in which women were educated to become ornaments, mindless and self-regarding, not people but products. The double sexual standard chafes some of her female characters. And one of her major themes—constriction—appears most powerfully when it is linked with the rules governing the lives of women. Whether she writes about lives lived narrowly inside social constrictions, or in isolation outside of them, Wharton is subtle, delicate, and precise. The seeming innocence of male critics about the difference between a woman's life and a man's, about the profound effects of learning to adapt the self to a small anteroom in life, has led to an impercipience about Wharton's work. She does not shout: therefore she is not heard. (Had she shouted, she would not have been published.) ⟨. . .⟩

Most criticism of Edith Wharton declares her central concern to be the manners and mores of the old New York society as they gave way before the onslaught of the nouveau riche, the Vanderbilts, Astors, and Whitneys—vulgar, flamboyant, and obscenely rich. She is often described as exalting the past and condemning the present.

In fact, she never exalted the old ways, although, as she grew older, she came to believe there were some fine things in them. But she was never blinded to the stifling quality of the old life; she never forgot being unable to breathe. In any case, the manners and mores of society never provided more than the backgrounds of her novels. They seem emphasized because she describes them so brilliantly.

Wharton had an intense visual awareness, especially of nature—a sensitivity she shares with many of her characters. She had an intense visual awareness of interiors as well. (Edmund Wilson called her—in what spirit is not clear—the "poet of interior decoration.") She was able to conjure an entire way of life with a few concrete details. And she could do this not only with the muted, proper, good but shabby interiors of the old rich, but with the surroundings of the new rich, the very poor, and with landscape, cultivated or wilderness:

> He could see her, as Mrs. Haskett, sitting in a 'front parlour' furnished in plush, with a pianola, and a copy of *Ben Hur* on the centre table. *(Roman Fever and Other Stories)*
>
> It was the beginning of a June afternoon. The springlike transparent sky shed a rain of silver sunshine on the roofs of the village, and on the pastures and larchwoods surrounding it. A little wind moved among the round white clouds on the shoulders of the hills, driving their shadows across the fields and down the grassy road. *(Summer)*

Wharton's visual apprehension included people as well as things. She noted vividly postures, gestures, manners of speech, manners of walk, the tilt of a head, the way someone held a handkerchief. She paid attention to clothes, but also to the way they were worn. She knew that surfaces reveal values, that the depiction of significant details creates the texture of a life, and that the deepest beliefs of a person or a culture are perceptible in that texture.

> He gave a little bow, like the bend of a jointed doll, and with infinite precaution let himself down in the chair. *(Roman Fever and Other Stories)*
>
> She had just time to take her seat before the train started: but having arranged herself in her corner with the instinctive feeling for effect which never forsook her, she glanced about in the hope of seeing some other member of the Trenors' party. *(The House of Mirth)*

In addition to her observant eye for detail, Wharton had deep empathetic currents. Very early in her writing career she wrote a story called *Bunner Sisters*. It was not published until 1916, but it demonstrates that right from the outset she was able to extend her sympathies and imagination beyond her own class. The story concerns a pair of very poor women, shopkeepers, both unmarried when the tale begins. Wharton was able to describe their surface life—what they wore, ate, how they worked or rested—but she was also able to enter their imaginative horizon believably. In *Ethan Frome* and *Summer*, she entered fully into the dreams and fears, the senusous texture and moral underpinnings, of people who were deprived culturally, economically, and socially. In *The Children*, she created a set of youngsters who are ill matched, ill trained, and thoroughly delightful, without being sentimental idealizations. She wrote a novel set in *settecento* Italy; she dealt with the war in *The Marne* and *A Son at the Front;* she dealt with working conditions in a factory in *The Fruit of the Tree*. About half her novels and stories are written from the perspective of a male, and of these, at least three are among her finest work—*The Age of Innocence, The Children*, and *Ethan Frome*. There are also the strong Ralph Marvell sections of *The Custom of the Country*, and the George Darrow section of *The Reef*.

The things I have been discussing are talents, abilities. They allow Wharton to provide a brilliant surface for her work, a surface which has sometimes been taken for the theme of that work. It is not. Wharton's main theme, her deepest concern, was the emotional and moral life, especially in the area of sexuality.

This large theme is tied to other themes. Female experience is often central in her work. This is true sometimes even when the focus of the story is a male. *The Touchstone*, for instance, depicts a man suffering from guilt as he gradually shifts his contempt for himself onto his wife because he cannot bear "the necessity of defending himself against the perpetual criticism of his wife's belief in him." This early long story (1900) is not one of Wharton's best works, but it is acute in tracing subtly what men do to women in their minds. Since sexual regulation was a major factor in the lives of young women, many of the tales and novels deal with sexual constriction and the social restrictions that arose from it.

The critic Percy Lubbock claimed that Wharton did not have a philosophy. But she did, insofar as any novelist can be said to have a coherent philosophy. Writing continually of constriction and paralysis, emphasizing the bleakness of lives based upon them, she pointed out another direction. "Alas, I should like to get up on the house-tops and cry to all who come after us: 'Take your own life, every one of you!'" she wrote to her friend Sara Norton, who sacrificed her life to her aging famous father, Charles Eliot Norton. Wharton meant take hold of, grasp, live in accord with desire and need. Years later, she wrote to another friend, Mary Berenson, that the "real unpardonable sin" was the denial of life. And by life, she meant largely sexual experience, but also an existence created by the self rather than by society.

Wharton's strongest and most sympathetically rendered characters are women who risk: Justine Brent *(The Fruit of the Tree)*, Anna Leath *(The Reef)*, Charity Royall *(Summer)*, and Kate Clephane *(The Mother's Recompense)*. These women have moral courage, something even Wharton's most sympathetic men lack. They are not passive victims of their lives, although there is no question of their triumphing over circumstances. What they do is live their lives out fully, by feeling and thinking through whatever occurs, by refusing to blind themselves. They risk discovering their own dark sides, their sexuality, their guilt, their jealousy. Wharton's term for this process in one novel is "facing it out," confronting and dealing with troublesome emotions—their own and others'—instead of locking them away. Since all these women are confronted with serious, even insoluble difficulties, their behavior makes them large-sized, even heroic. Although all of them end with diminished expectations, with lost dreams, the subtlety, delicacy, strength, and courage of their approaches to life make them admirable. Their lives are rich not because of what they are able to take from life but because of what they are. Thus, in a sense, all Wharton's work aims toward a definition of what constitutes full humanity; it is not victory over circumstance, but knowledge of the deepest sort, the full living of life.

Wharton is usually assumed to be a lesser Henry James, to be attempting to do precisely what James did. It is true that they were personally close and perhaps had similar sensibilities, and that they were looking at the same world. But James, a man, emphasized the individual within society; he had a strong sense of legitimacy that strengthened and colored what he created. Wharton was far more aware of the power of the environment over the individual, of the sapping of energy caused by a sense of illegitimacy, and of the impossibility of getting beyond the bodily and social consequences of sex. James's genius was linguistic and psychological. Wharton's was sociological and psychological. Without seeming to diminish James—who cannot be diminished—one must separate the two authors and focus on Wharton's excellences. She has a wider scope; she is more interested in the particular experience of women; and she had a profounder sense of constriction.

But this, precisely, is what most dismays some of her critics. Her vision is bleak; for her, life is a prison, they moan. She has been damned as immoral for her vision. Yet the very critics who do not like her insistence on constriction do not hesitate to castigate female characters for whom Wharton has obvious sympathy—or even Wharton herself—for having abandoned a husband, or a child, or for trying to envision fulfilled happy lives for themselves. They thereby prove the accuracy of her vision. Critics also complain that Wharton's men are either ineffectual—morally or emotionally stunted—or boors. The range of her male characters is far greater than this, and many of them are sympathetic. But there are no knights on white horses in her work, as there are none in life. There are no idealizations, female or male.

Many readers may prefer novels that concentrate on the individual as author or strong co-author of his or her fate, and that diminish the overwhelming pressure of environment and inheritance. Such an attitude is certainly more pleasant and probably healthier to live with than its opposite. But the reverse is also true, a fact we are aware of at least in certain moments of life. And it is morally healthier to remember that we are small units in a large world we cannot control than to delude ourselves. There is room for both kinds of books. To condemn those which refuse to compromise, which refuse to admit that things are for the best in this best of all possible worlds, is to demand that literature be fairy tale.

Wharton had a tougher mind. She would have agreed with Aquinas's statement that "matter is never lacking privation: inasmuch as it is under one form, it is deprived of another." If Wharton concentrated on the privations attendant on a form, rather than on its fulfillment, perhaps that is because she was a woman and more aware of that side of things. It is not an accident that the most vapid and fantastic literature—romance—is written for women, who use it to escape from lives they cannot change. Henry James wrote of Wharton's work: "We move in an air purged at a stroke of the old sentimental and romantic values." Wharton forces her readers to acknowledge the fact that form is imprisonment, that any course has particular consequences, that everything costs something, that actuality is always a diminishment of the ideal, and that the richness of life lies in one's moral and emotional response to one's situation. That is not a small accomplishment.

John Hall Wheelock

1886–1978

John Hall Wheelock was born on September 9, 1886, in Far Rockaway, New York, to William Efner and Emily Charlotte Hall Wheelock. He was educated at Harvard University, where he contributed to the *Harvard Advocate* and was named official poet of his graduating class of 1908. While at Harvard Wheelock collaborated with Van Wyck Brooks on his first book, a privately printed volume of poems called *Verses by Two Undergraduates* (1905). He later studied in Germany at the universities of Göttingen and Berlin. In 1940 he married Phyllis de Kay.

Wheelock's first commercially published book of poetry, *The Human Fantasy* (1911), attracted considerable favorable attention from critics, including the poet Sara Teasdale, who subsequently met and fell in love with him. Though they were companions for a time, Wheelock was not able to committ himself to her because of other romantic entanglements, and her sudden death a short time later had a profound effect upon him.

Wheelock's next book, *The Beloved Adventure* (1912), was also praised, though the admiration was more muted; his third volume, *Love and Liberation: The Songs of Adsched to Meru, and Other Poems* (1913), was not well received, critics finding it repetitious and banal. While his next several books, particularly *Dust and Light* (1919), *The Black Panther* (1922), and *The Bright Doom* (1927), restored his reputation somewhat, some critics continued to find his poetry too abstract and self-conscious. He was also criticized for his strict adherence to traditional rhyming and metrical structures.

Late in his career Wheelock wrote less and less poetry as he rose in the editorial hierarchy at Scribner's, eventually succeeding Maxwell Perkins as senior editor. The retrospective collection *By Daylight and in Dream: New and Collected Poems 1904–1970* appeared in 1971, and *This Blessed Earth: New and Selected Poems 1927–1977* in 1978. Though he was very much a romantic and a traditionalist, his poetry continued to be read and valued. He was an Honorary Consultant in Poetry for the Library of Congress from 1967 to 1973, and was awarded the Gold Medal of the Poetry Society of America in 1972. He died on March 22, 1978.

Mr. John Hall Wheelock discourses thus of "The New Love":

> Before the morning I arose and went
> Over the snowy meadows clear and cold,
> And with the dawn a deep and new content
> Awoke in me. Farewell, dear love of old.
> Now that I love you, what is there to say!
> Who would have harmed you, what shall now be said!

AP/WIDE WORLD PHOTOS

John Hall Wheelock

UPI/BETTMANN NEWSPHOTOS

Edith Wharton

HARCOURT BRACE JOVANOVICH

Richard Wilbur

UPI/BETTMANN NEWSPHOTOS

E. B. White

UPI/BETTMANN NEWSPHOTOS

TENNESSEE WILLIAMS

THE BETTMANN ARCHIVE

WILLIAM CARLOS WILLIAMS

THORNTON WILDER

UPI/BETTMANN NEWSPHOTOS

EDMUND WILSON

The morning wind has purged it all away.
  Before this love all the old lusts lie dead.
The holier love more deep than all desire
  Into my spirit from the morning came,
Out of the sacred and the whitening Fire
  It rose within me like a silent flame;
And the winds blew it to me from the west,
  Over the sad fields of unbroken snow,
Patient and pure as your own naked breast
  And hopeless as our love of long ago.

The verses *sound* as if they meant something, but close scrutiny discloses little more than inarticulate emotion tricked out with imagery. We quote this poem, and make this comment upon it, because most of the contents of Mr. Wheelock's volume, *The Belovèd Adventure*, invite similar observations. Gauzy fancies and nebulous ideas abound in his collection, but we rarely find in it either clear-cut thought or lyric rapture. Moreover, Mr. Wheelock's verses are somewhat freer in form than is permissible to anyone not an approved master. It is only at great risk that a minor poet may attempt what a Verlaine or a Whitman is free to do without censure.—WILLIAM MORTON PAYNE, *Dial*, March 16, 1913, p. 245

Mr. Wheelock ⟨. . .⟩ has failed, during the six years since the publication of his last volume, to learn, what is the most important thing for an American poet to know, that vagueness is fatal. ⟨In *Dust and Light*⟩ Mr. Wheelock is handy with his meters, and is something of an expert when it comes to distributing emphasis; but when it comes to speaking the things that educated people read poetry for, he is only the husk and shadow of a poet. He goes through the approved motions, but he cuts no figure, he makes no impact. As incorrigibly minor poets will, he talks proprietarily of Poetry and God. Like many who have no message to convey, he is glib with wonder at the message-bearing powers of verse. Of course he is a pantheist, and worships Earth; he is a diluted Emerson, without aromatic fire, and a diluted Meredith, without tangled, wooded passion. He pretends to intimacy with the immensities, including among these all "shimmering cries and stars and dreams," not to mention "the sacred spaces of the vast and virgin sea." He is often found near the ocean, leaning against mighty gales and harkening to the philosophic gulls that fly and cry. He dreams with eyes that cannot blink, and he hungers on a comfortably full stomach. Because he lacks a single stray wisp of humor, his ardors are never convincing; one sees they are hardly his own.—M.V.D., "Vacancies and Vagaries," *Nation*, Jan. 17, 1920, p. 76

At the age of 75, John Hall Wheelock has published his best book of poems ⟨*The Gardener and Other Poems*⟩. As a practitioner in the field, I cannot think of any success so enviable and, as a common reader, of any that should make his readers feel quite so warm and happy. For of course the triumphs of such older poets are rare. But they happen, and when they do, they tend to produce a spare, keen-edged, wise, sometimes rough-textured verse (it is now the truth, the truth that most matters), which makes younger poetry, no matter how ecstatic or brilliant or beautiful, certainly seem less mature.

In the case of Wheelock, who prolifically flourished a lyric talent in his youth, all the signs indicated he was through some quarter of a century ago. His rhetoric, which had tended to be pretty windy, had evidently faltered and failed; apparently he was yet one more of the throng of young poets who couldn't carry the impulse into the Forties and Fifties.

But no—not at all. After a long stretch of silence, Wheelock in recent years has begun to publish again and to be, as I say, a finer poet than in his early decades.

The actual props—the furnishings—of his poems have altered little if at all. Those well acquainted with his work know that he has repeatedly used a house in a gardened landscape by the sea. And he has always employed the impedimenta of Romantic poetry—the sea predominantly, and stars and thrushes and love and death and weathers and time and the individual human in the stress of joy and grief. He even dares to say "bright star." All these in the present volume as in the far earlier collections.

What then is the difference? Unarguably, I think, the cutting away of rhetoric, the aged and sparer tone. Passion understated, passion stated at arm's length, informs poetry, somehow, with a tenser passion than ever youthful outburst can do. In such longer poems as "Complaint of the Indifference of Things" and "Anima" and others there is a conversational style, easy-going but never wordy, which is most effective—even, as in "Anima," achieving haunting effects. Yet, by the way, it is "the beautiful indifference" of things of which he writes—in despair, in sorrow and in ultimate joy. One thinks sometimes of Jeffers, sometimes of Yeats. But Wheelock's way is his own.—WINFIELD TOWNLEY SCOTT, *NYTBR*, Oct. 22, 1961, p. 38

John Hall Wheelock has learned nothing from Pound or Williams, is not out to influence younger poets, and titles his latest book, unembarrassedly, *Dear Men and Women*. Without becoming J. Donald Adams and using him as a stick to beat other contemporaries, it should be said that Mr. Wheelock, at age 80, has looked back on his life and written some wholly affecting, totally genuine songs of experience. Two stanzas from the longer poem "Question and Answer" serve to indicate the tenor of the best of these poems. The question:

And can *this* be the room where, oh, such eons ago,
A young man grieved and exalted, can *this* have been me?
I need wonder no more what it's like to have died, who now stand here and know.
  All shall be taken.

and the answer:

Like swallows when summer is over, like the clear light
Of morning that fades into dusk, they vanish away,
And our autumn is on us, a gradual darkening, the first chill of night.
  All shall be taken.

With fine dignity, but a wondering reluctance to admit that this should be so, the poet sings of how the Eden we dream of in our youths is equally the dream of old age, except that it now lies behind us, in the past:

And there they dwell, those ineffable presences,
Safe beyond time, rescued from death and change.
Though all shall be taken, they only shall not be taken—
Immortal, unaging, unaltered, faithful yet
To that lost dream world they inhabit.
("Dear Men and Women")

This is all these poems have to say, and unexpectedly, it is enough.—WILLIAM H. PRITCHARD, *HdR*, Summer 1967, pp. 312–13

HENRY TAYLOR

"The Collected Poems of John Hall Wheelock"

Sewanee Review, Summer 1971, pp. 460–63

John Hall Wheelock's career spans all that has elapsed of this century. That this approaches some sort of endurance record may, for a while, arouse greater interest than the more genuine triumphs which go along with it. Wheelock's development has been slow and sometimes painful; in his determination not to succumb to the whims of fashion, he has sometimes seemed to move backward instead of forward. But in his later years he finally wrote a number of poems which are worth all the trouble, and which are not diminished by the lesser poems in this volume ⟨*By Daylight and in Dream: New and Collected Poems, 1904–1970*⟩.

By Daylight and in Dream contains, in roughly chronological order, all the poems which Wheelock wishes to preserve. The collection is weighted in favor of relatively recent work; though eight of Wheelock's twelve books of poems had appeared by 1936, almost half of this book is devoted to poems published since then.

But even though vast numbers of early poems have been left behind, those which remain are enough to suggest the difficulties which plagued the young poet. He wrote, for one thing, with incredible haste—he published sizeable collections in 1911, 1912, 1913, 1919, 1922, 1927, and 1936—and so must often have failed to see how little of this verse was his own, and how much of it was a pastiche of early favorites such as Henley, Whitman, and Wordsworth. There are whole poems here which seem to have been written by the ghost of an anonymous nineteenth-century voice, as in these lines from "Epilogue":

> Ah, then I listen, and hear as in a dream,
> Amid the chords of the travail and pain and joy
> Of all things human, a young, an undaunted voice—
> With wanton exuberance and immortal lust,
> The music of life welling up strong and clear.

But even as Wheelock continued to pour out volumes of this kind of work, he gradually increased his command over formal and structural elements, so that even bad poems began to reveal arresting musical and rhythmical details, as in this final stanza from "Translation":

> Now, as you read these verses—from afar,
> This very moment, from this printed rhyme,
> I cry to you out of the wheels of Time,
> I call to you across the morning-star.

The arrangement of stresses and vowel-sounds is more artfully controlled here, and arouses some pleasure, still too slight to overcome the sentimental and derivative phrases; but the control and the pleasure are there, and are the foundation for the good poems Wheelock came to write in his late sixties.

Between *Poems, 1911–1936*, his eighth collection, and *Poems Old and New*, his ninth, Wheelock went through twenty years of relative silence. One reason for this decreased poetic activity was that his responsibilities as an editor at Scribner's became more demanding; but I believe this editorial work had a favorable effect on his later poetry. During his late sixties and early seventies, he was editor of Scribner's "Poets of Today" series, which published the first book-length collections by poets such as Louis Simpson, James Dickey, and George Garrett; Wheelock's recognition of their virtues must have helped him to see his own poetry in a clearer light.

Whatever the reasons, there is no doubt that Wheelock's later work is a great improvement over the earlier; the improvement is especially remarkable when we realize that no radical shift occurred in thematic or formal preoccupations. The later poems grow naturally out of the earlier ones, pursuing the same themes of love, death, and the tragic nature of life; they move in the same traditional forms. But their voice is distinctively Wheelock's own.

I have suggested in another essay[1] that "Scherzo", the section of humorous poems which precedes the later poems in this collection, contains some work in which Wheelock gave himself freer rein than he had in more serious poems. For example, "The Plumber as the Missing Letter", which first appeared in this journal, and subsequently in *Dear Men and Women* (1966), is a parody of Wallace Stevens in which even the passages of broadest burlesque contain attractive elements:

> His dream shall be of these, of frogs at sunset,
> Moonlight upon bald heads, and something more,
> Worthier than these, more plausible; but no,
> He dreams of oddities, air-conditioned graves,
> Serpents that totter, mice that sing soprano . . .

I can think of a dozen young poets, myself included, who might wish to have dreamt of air-conditioned graves; but I wonder which of us would have had the sense not to elaborate on the image, even in a parody. The writing of this poem seems to have been a liberating experience for Wheelock; other poems in *Dear Men and Women* display similar qualities of energy and inventiveness, and are more inclusive in tone than his earlier poems. In a sequence of "Eight Sonnets", for example, Wheelock explores the nature of love between two aged people; his comprehensive attitude allows him to move swiftly and gracefully between humor and seriousness, as he does in "The Sea's Voice":

> Our talk has been all banter, to-and-fro
> Of raillery, the bland mischief of your smile
> Still leads me on, with nonsense we beguile
> An empty hour: we speak of So-and-So,
> Of Eliot and Michelangelo,
> And of James Jones, his high, pedantic style—
> And touch, by chance, after a little while,
> Upon some sadness suffered years ago.
>
> Now your eyes darken, turning serious,
> As thoughts of the long past, by memory stirred,
> Waken—life's venture, tragic and absurd,
> How strange it is, how brief, how hazardous.
> Far-off, the sea's voice says it all for us.
> Saying one thing forever, barely heard.

The profound change in Wheelock's poetry has been wrought by comparatively slight adjustments in the earlier style. Some phrases here still border on triteness, but they have been absorbed into a distinctive, controlled, and dateless voice. Old ideas restated with a minimum of idiosyncrasy are hard to work into poems, but Wheelock manages to do so regularly and memorably.

One source of Wheelock's new strength is his house in Easthampton, Long Island, where he has spent some part of almost every summer for the past eighty years. It is a place Wheelock knows better than any other; and as his familiarity with it has deepened, so has his ability to use it as a focal point in a number of long meditative poems, whose structures are partly determined by the shape of the house and its landscape.

Among the best of these "Bonac poems" is the most recent: the title poem of this collection, which opens the section of new poems. In three long sections of blank verse, the speaker confronts his impending death, made more poignant by the remnants of his past, which lie all around him. Wheelock has wisely avoided trying to resolve the vast questions which suggest themselves in the course of his meditation. At certain moments, he looks toward the possibility of eternal life, and at other moments he accepts the finality of death, celebrating the holiness of earth, "the graveyard of the self-effacing dead". The poem concludes with a dream in which various voices offer various answers to the question of what follows death; but the speaker is still living at the end of the poem, and there is a strong suggestion that the importance of the future still lies this side of the grave. A small formal detail underscores this notion; the blank-verse line is broken between the end of one section and the beginning of another, and the third section ends with a short line. It has not been filled out, which hints that there is more to come, not of this poem, but of the stuff of which it is made.

Wheelock has at last written his share of fine poems, and they are all here; and there is extra pleasure to be gained from respect for the perseverance I mentioned at the beginning, and from the realization that Wheelock, at eighty-five, continues to contemplate his future work.

Notes

1. "Letting the Darkness In: The Poetic Achievement of John Hall Wheelock", *The Hollins Critic*, VII, No. 5 (December 1970), 1-15.

JOHN HALL WHEELOCK

From an Interview

by William Cahill and Molly McKaughan

Paris Review, Fall 1976, pp. 161–72

When we called on ⟨John Hall Wheelock⟩ in his New York apartment, the front door was ajar, as he had told us it would be. He was waiting in the dark in a straight-back chair at the end of the hall, silhouetted in gray afternoon light from the living-room beyond; he was dressed formally in a vested suit and tie. He is somewhat stooped and walks slowly using a cane, but he rose immediately to greet us, and insisted on helping us hang up our coats. He ushered us into the living-room and without further ado began to talk about his long life and poetry. ⟨. . .⟩

Interviewer: May I ask why you are a poet?

Wheelock: I can't think of myself as not wanting very much to be a poet. Of course, "poet" is rather a sacred word, isn't it? Wasn't it Robert Frost who said that no one has a right to say, "I'm a poet" because "poet" is a word of acclaim.

Interviewer: Do you feel that your poetry has an available audience? Is this an important consideration?

Wheelock: I'll be ninety this September and it's obvious that a man reaching ninety is not likely to be in full accord with the taste of this period. My poetry is primarily a poetry of feeling. Feeling has been rather played down by modern poets, partly as a result of what the world has been through with its depressions and wars. The nerve of feeling has been exhausted. The modern reader will not tolerate a direct attack on his emotions. It seems that even the driest expression of emotion in poetry presents obstacles to readers in key with the mood of these times. So that time, a good deal of time, will have to pass, before my work comes into more general recognition again.

Interviewer: Which writers have influenced you most?

Wheelock: Well, I've been fortunate enough, in the course of a long life, to have accumulated memories of writers that go back quite far. I even saw Walt Whitman . . . though being a baby I was not aware of it. My father held me up on a ferry boat—I don't know whether it was going to New Jersey or coming to New York—and said: "Do you see that man?" He turned my head—my mother was with him—toward Whitman, who was standing in the bow of the boat, and he said, "That is the great poet, Walt Whitman." Apparently—as my father described it—I refused to look at him, and kept turning my head the other way. I have no memory of this great occasion, not being then equipped to receive the spirit of Walt Whitman, although I suppose for a moment his image was in my eyes.

The sight of Whitman must have made a great impression on my mother. She was a passionate lover of poetry, and saw to it that my brother and I learned poems by heart, every week a new poem. I took a dislike to poetry at the beginning, when as a six-year-old I was supposed to memorize poems by Longfellow with such lines as "All are architects of fate, working in these walls of time." But the practice gradually infected me with a feeling for poetry which increased as time went on. When I was at Harvard in 1906, I was so influenced by Swinburne that I kept after my father, saying that I wanted to go over to England to see him. My father wasn't very well-off that year—it was a recession year—but he said, "Well, since you're so persistent you can go, but you'll have to go steerage; I can't afford to send you even cabin class." I said, "Well, that's fine with me," and I went over in the steerage and it wasn't bad at all. But I made the pilgrimage stupidly; I didn't get a letter of introduction. All I knew was that Swinburne was living with Theodore Watts-Dunton—a much lesser poet but quite well known as a critic—in "The Pines" in London, in a part of the city called Putney.

So I just went over and hung around "The Pines" for several days. I waited for I forget how many days, and then one August afternoon Swinburne appeared—this very short man wearing a turban—an odd idea, it was very hot—and I was disappointed because he was so short, almost giving the effect of being a dwarf—and he was talking to himself. At that time he must have been about seventy, and, of course, to me, as a youth, he seemed very old. As he came near me I thought I was going to faint, because my heart began palpitating so rapidly that I didn't know whether I'd be able to make it, I mean walk the rest of the distance without fainting. But I did, and as he passed me I touched his coat with my hand, and I hardly dared look at him. You must remember that I'd been reading Swinburne devoutly and knew many of his poems by heart. He had a very powerful influence on any poet, particularly a young poet, because he has such a marked style; I think after Pope probably the most marked style of any English poet. So, seeing the source of all this verbal magic and music, the poetry that so intoxicated me, was almost like, well, seeing God. I survived it, however, and passed him, and I went back to my room in a small, inexpensive hotel and lay down on the bed and just thought about it all the rest of the day. I went back for several days in the hope of seeing Swinburne again, thinking that I might even have the courage to say a word to him. I'd written him many letters, and also I'd written poems and an essay about him, which came out in *The Harvard Advocate*, and I had sent these to him. But, of course, I added in all my letters, "I would never forgive you if you answered this. Do not answer it, please." The *thought* of his being bothered to answer it—it was real hero-worship.

There are one or two other writers I can think of who were a strong influence. Several years after graduating from college, when I was living in New York, Edwin Arlington Robinson, to whom I had sent a copy of my first book, *The Human Fantasy*, invited me to come to his apartment. I say *his* apartment—he was very hard up all his life but he had warm friends, and during the summers he was usually living in the empty apartment of some friend who was out of town. Actually, it was in the apartment of another contemporary, a poet, Louis Ledoux, that I went to see Robinson that evening. A lean, introverted, shy, aloof man. It was very flattering that he had asked me. He sat down at one end of the room and offered me a seat at the other. Everything was swathed in these sheets put over furniture in apartments in summer. The first remark he made was, "I can't offer you a drink or a cigarette because I have none." But, we had an interesting talk that influenced me, excited me, because here was a man who by that time had published two remarkable books. Theodore Roosevelt, then president, had taken notice of the second book—*The Town Down the River,* I believe—and had written an article about it in the magazine that he was connected with, *The Outlook.* ⟨. . .⟩

Interviewer: Did you write at night after you worked your day as an editor ⟨at Scribner's⟩?

Wheelock: Yes. I had to, or felt that I had to. I couldn't resist the desire to make poems, so I made them at night, I made them on weekends. But as an editor, there's no limit to the work. So after I became senior editor, for many years I didn't publish a book and I hardly ever wrote a poem. Yet, those twenty years of editing stand as a divide between my lesser work and my best.

Before I became an editor, I just wrote whenever I got a chance, at night and on vacations. I learned early to do my work in my head. For many years I had a vacation of only two weeks; I would work during that time, walking along the beaches of Bonac and composing poems in my head and all the time revising them, too, in my head. I wouldn't write down any of them. When I got back to the city, I would write them down when I had the chance.

I know my poems by heart. All the various revisions of them. You work so hard over them, you know, that you never can forget them. I used to give readings from time to time—I can't do this now—but while I would always have the book there in case I lost my way through nervousness, I rarely had to use it. At night, when I can't sleep, I can say poems over endlessly. Not mine, necessarily, but any poems that come to mind. It's a great resource. Yet most poets today are visual. Marianne Moore told me that she didn't know any of her poems by heart. Robert Frost knew most of his. But some of the best poets couldn't recite any one of their poems.

Interviewer: Do you try to write every day now?

Wheelock: Oh heavens, no. I never did try to do that. Certain things will start a poem in you. It could be something no more important than the sound a broken radiator makes in a room, the knocking of water against pipes, or a murmuring sound, a steady sound . . . the sound of grasshoppers and cicadas in the autumn in the countryside . . . these things will start the feeling of a poem, though the poet doesn't know what's coming or what it's going to be. Or an incident. I was in the street the other day. I walk with some difficulty now, with a stick. A boy rushed into me by mistake shouting, his head back this way . . . rushed right into me so that his arms came around me like this. Almost knocked me over. I thought about that random momentary encounter between two strangers, and in it the possibility of a poem? I didn't know what kind of poem it would be, but I made a note of it in my notebook.

Interviewer: I gather music has been an influence, a source of inspiration.

Wheelock: Oh, music is to me the supreme art . . . a revelation of reality. In music you get glimpses of something that you can't put into words, not even in poetry. In fact, music is a bad influence on a poet because listening to music lulls your critical sense. In the euphoria and exaltation of listening to music you are apt to start a poem, which sounds fine until the music stops, and then it is nothing; your critical sense comes back. Music, perhaps, comes nearest to reality . . . the mathematical relationships within the universe made audible. All the arts tend to that, but in music it seems to succeed, at least for me . . . I don't see how anyone could listen to a Bach fugue without feeling that he's coming as close to reality as possible.

Interviewer: Does the poet have any advantage over the musician?

Wheelock: If a poet is really good he can give you a moment of reconcilement to the tragic nature of things. Poetry, as with all the arts, enables us to re-experience. Most of us pass through life in a state of semi-anaesthesia, with life itself blotted out by the business of living. We shut out life itself in order to carry on and survive, and the function of the arts is to pierce that shield and make us suddenly re-experience something that we've always known but haven't been experiencing anymore. Shelley said it when he described poetry as stripping the veil of familiarity from things. It can only be done obliquely or by implication. A certain musical phrase, or combination of sounds by Beethoven, will arouse feelings of intense sadness which would not have been aroused if Beethoven had just put his head down and cried.

Interviewer: Have you been aware of a change in your themes as you have grown older?

Wheelock: Yes. I've written a great many poems about age, and about the experience of growing old, and being old. That is natural in going through the experience. I didn't write poems about it until "Song on Reaching Seventy," which seemed to me at the time a vast age. One has no conception, in youth, of what it will be like to be very old—no conception whatever.

Interviewer: It doesn't affect your wanting to write . . .

Wheelock: No, it doesn't. Of course, as you get older, the urge to write is less because making poems is tied up with what you experience. As you get old and can't go out very often, being confined to one or two rooms, and all your friends are dead . . . or most of them . . . you see few people . . . you see less of the world . . . there's less experience; and consequently less of what you do with experience.

Interviewer: What's your reaction to today's school of the absurd, to the prevalent cynicism . . .

Wheelock: This age is a little bit like the age of Queen Anne or the time of Dryden, when the same state of mind prevailed. Cynicism, disillusionment, and wit take the place of feeling. But I, myself, don't feel cynical or disillusioned about life. It has been a tremendous experience. To be conscious is a great privilege, and it's only maintained by the most enormous effort . . . think of the work that the heart does, and all the other organs, coordinated like an orchestra to maintain this little thin film of consciousness; the cessation of any of these activities or any of them getting seriously out of order, and consciousness is gone. I think about growing old a great deal. In one of my longer poems, "Night Thoughts in Age," I record the thoughts of an aged man sleeping in a room which he had occupied as a child and then later as a boy, and as a youth and as a grown man, and feeling the beauty of the place and the presence of all the beloved people, no longer alive, who had lived there.

Everything is in flux. Our places are taken by others. The generations can't be poured into one lifespan. It almost seems as if time was an invention to make it possible to provide space for more to come, and with them their poetry.

E. B. White

1899–1985

Elwyn Brooks White was born on July 11, 1899, in Mt. Vernon, New York, to Jessie Hart White and Samuel T. White. He was educated at Cornell University (A.B. 1921). In 1918 he served as a private in the army. He married Katharine Sergeant Angell in 1929; they had one child before her death in 1977. He worked as a reporter for the Seattle *Times* and as an advertising copywriter before joining the *New Yorker* as a contributing editor in 1927; he remained associated with the *New Yorker* throughout his life. From 1937 to 1943 he also wrote a column for *Harper's*. Among his many awards were the Presidential Medal of Freedom (1963) and the National Medal for Literature (1971).

His first published books were *Is Sex Necessary? or, Why You Feel the Way You Do*, with James Thurber, and a book of light verse called *The Lady Is Cold* (both 1929). White was, along with Thurber, the quintessential *New Yorker* humorist, and his essays and sketches are among the most popular of his time. While his early work is lightly humorous, his later work, particularly *One Man's Meat* (1942), *The Second Tree from the Corner* (1954), and *The Points of My Compass* (1962), examines everyday life, human relationships, and mortality, often with profound depth. *A White Reader* (1966) and *Essays* (1977) offer retrospective selections from his work. He helped prepare *Letters of E. B. White* (1976), edited by Dorothy Lobrano Guth.

In addition to his essays, White is also noted for his children's novels. All three (*Stuart Little*, 1945; *Charlotte's Web*, 1952; and *The Trumpet of the Swan*, 1970) reveal a humane sympathy for the problems of loss and maturity combined with a keen understanding of children. They are undisputed classics of their field.

E. B. White died on October 1, 1985.

WARREN BECK
"E. B. White"

College English, April 1946, pp. 367–73

Discussing the American blend of humor, Max Eastman once speculated "about what might be done by a mind trained in fact and true to it, equipped as such a mind must be with humor, and yet not ill-at-ease in deeps of feeling and among fervent adventures of imagination, not ill-at-ease among revolutionary ideas, not condemned to make a final resting place of fact and laughter." If such a writer has not yet appeared full-fledged, at least America has his prototype in E. B. White. Some will think White is it, the man himself. Some may think he is better than that, is more than anyone would have known how to specify, a truly original writer, with the unique fusion of basic traits and idiosyncrasies which makes an artist's work freshly representative.

A who's-who glance at E. B. White shows a middle-aged man, migratory between New York City and Maine, a graduate of Cornell University, husband of one wife and father of one son, an editor, a magazine contributor, and the author of a few volumes of prose pieces and verse, together with a story for children. Gradually emergent as a journalist in the tradition of Addison and Hazlitt, White has always been a writing man, having done time in reporting and advertising. He has reaped from his Maine farm, besides its indigenous produce, a number of fresh experiences and well-ripened opinions, regularly brought to market in *Harper's* under the gracious label "One Man's Meat." In the decade preceding his *Harper's* engagement he supplied the *New Yorker* with the "Notes and Comments" which contributed so greatly to that magazine's brilliance. For a professional nearing fifty, his output is comparatively slim and casual, but there are good and honorable reasons for this. White has never allowed himself the commercial advantages of being slick, obvious, and grossly prolific. He is an intellectually fastidious man, who has practiced letters as a vocation, not a racket; and his laconic, critically humorous writing is an honest product. It is to the credit of not altogether creditable times that such a writer has not lacked appreciation.

Editors of pedagogical anthologies have increasingly exhibited White's work. Well they might, for he aids teachers in marking out a continuing stream of literature, a present momentum aware of historic culture and expressive, in modern terms, of those immortal longings, large and small, which beget art. Here is a plain contemporary who has brought back substance as well as polish to the journalistic paragraph, and who can also stand consideration along with the Augustan and Romantic essayists, in such pieces as "Sabbath Morn," "The World of Tomorrow," "Walden," "Camp Meeting," "Freedom," "On a Florida Key," "Once More to the Lake," "Aunt Poo," and "Morningtime and Eveningtime"; and for younger students there is easier access in essays like "Movies" and "Motor Cars." Two qualities above all earn E. B. White high academic regard. One is his prose style, which for a combined ease, scope, and incisiveness is perhaps the best American expository writing in a personal vein since Thoreau. Another of White's achievements is the rehabilitation of the informal essay, which in recent times has often ailed, either of a hectic preciosity or a boisterous madness. White is never precious, never boisterous; and he is always sane, though most characteristically it is with the poet's transcendent sanity, an imaginative bent, paralleling sublime relativities.

Since the haunting dictum that the style is the man himself is often superstitiously interpreted by students to mean a fine frenzy of untrammeled effusion, teachers have special use for any successful contemporary whose style demonstrates the broad, stern meaning inherent in that apparently inescapable definition. White's prose not only shows facets of the matter, it embodies the whole truth. It has a nice diction ranging from the naturally colloquial to an intellectual aptness as juicily tart as a plum. He hears "The Indian Love Call" over loudspeakers at a fair "bathing heaven and earth in jumbo tenderness." He sees a retriever come into the house "full of greetings on a grand scale." When he learns that San Quentin's inmates deluge their prison paper with verse, his leaning toward similitudes identifies all poetry as "the hopeful wing-sprouting of the incarcerated spirit." With that sharp perception of the grotesque which humorists so often reveal by incongruous juxtaposition, White notes that "last week the Forhan toothpaste people put Evangeline Adams on the air . . . Miss Adams being the famous astrologer, versed in the signs of Cancer, Sagittarius, Virgo, and, more recently, Pyorrhea." His is the quick, pinioning phrase, as in naming Hitler's crowd "opportunists in bullet-proof vests." When he characterizes Thoreau's "tale of individual simplicity" as "the best written and the cockiest," he shows a twofold familiarity, doubly pleasing. In the firm context there is no unpleasant jar, but only a rich dissonance, between the word "cockiest" and such phrases as "a document of increasing pertinence." This easy range is seen in the fused allusions of an April item that "the frogs have begun their song of songs, deep in the heart of wetness."

White's prose nears the ideal style defined by Hazlitt, except that White makes freer use of words which have not taken out their final papers with the lexicographer. His colloquialism, an aspect of his independence and informality, can give students of English a model, too, in that it is always a precise diction, and never trite. Actually he is a purist in the best sense, and not least in that he is helping to fix meanings of words that will appear in future editions of dictionaries. Moreover, it is all done without flourish or groaning; White has the true artisan's unaffected dexterity. His sentences are as sure-footed and lightly vigorous as an athletic youth in sneakers. However, if style is the man himself, it is more than a matter of diction and construction, it inheres in the largest possible sense of the thing said, and must be discerned in the whole body of a writer's work, as it projects his temperament and outlook. Such a concept of style is especially important in judging White, whose pieces often have a deceptively cursory look.

The integration of his essays is both subtle and tough. Unimaginative reading would miss, for instance, the reflective sinuosity of such a composition as "On a Florida Key," and might even call it inconsequentially rambling. Nothing could be more erroneous; it is vibrant with thematic tensions. In the rainy weather the Florida Chamber of Commerce writes publicity behind drawn blinds. There is the vacationer's choice concerning the gas heater, whether "to congeal in a well-ventilated room or suffocate in comfort." White's struggle to catch up with the fresh milk contrasts with a news-story centenarian's coming out just right on half a gallon of whiskey a day. The Flag and the motto "Liberty for all" are applauded at the theater from which Negroes are excluded, in a South which seeks to enhance the orange by "Color added." The woman next door tracks in sand bringing pamphlets to prove that America (at least) should mind its own business. (White decides against removing the sand, since "this is the way keys form, apparently," and he has "no particular reason to interfere.") He archeologizes the grass-grown paving of Florida's "unfinished cities . . . conceived in haste and greed" in "real estate's purple hour" with "orchestras playing gently to prepare the soul of the wanderer for the mysteries of subdivision"; now on the adjacent beaches he hears the sea's eternal murmur, "So soon?" The essay itself is like a series of breaking waves, repeatedly propounding a skepticism confronting human folly. Yet, it also implies White's belief, which he seems to find applicable not only to gas stoves, that "after a little practice a nice balance can be established—enough oxygen left to sustain life, yet enough heat generated to prevent death from exposure."

Out of his work emerges a spare but striking profile. It is that of the ironic spectator, the minority report personified, the man with eyebrows raised but never harshly supercilious, the uncompromising individualist who would as lief split a hair with himself as with anybody else, and a still, small, humane voice through two troublesome decades, when to be at the same time a sensitive, serene, incorruptible, polite, rugged, and charitable person has been the rarest of achievements. White's geniality and fancy, detectable in his briefest jottings, are more generally recognized than his penetration and virility. The worst mistake to make about him is to assume, as the hyper-solemn may, that he is a lightweight, a trifler and escapist. Intellectually and morally he is hard as nails, and he is as unpretentiously functional as a snow fence. His informal and whimsical manner is no theatric quaintness; he is above egoistic or self-promotional airs. He is a proud realist, too, and soberly conscious of the intellectual's obligations. His integrity makes it possible for him to speak of serious matters quietly and conversationally, with frequent quips and smiles, and yet with no deviation from good sense. Thus he describes shingling a barn roof while the Munich conference proceeded: "In my trance-like condition, waiting for the negotiations to end, I added a cupola to the roof," he says implicatively, "to hold a vane which would show which way the wind blew." He defends this "sitting out a dance with a prime minister and a demigod," inquiring, "Who has the longer view of things, anyway, a prime minister in a closet or a man on a barn roof?" Calling it England's "ugliest peace," he winds up with a judgment emphasized by its handy blending of figure, frolic, and irony. Chamberlain's sacrifice to preserve peace reminded White of "the strange case of Ada Leonard, the strip artist of superb proportion," who, rather than have her appendix out, "risked her life in order to preserve, in unbroken loveliness, the smooth white groin the men of Chicago loved so well." "But," he goes on, "there comes a point beyond which you can't push Beauty, on account of the lines it leaves in the face."

White's basic seriousness is the more remarkable in that it outran the tendency of its time, the inclination to rest cynically in fact and laughter. He came to his work when the pantaloon humorists of the twenties were at their height, peddling the anodyne of nonsense as raw as the era's gin, or busy at what Lamb called "wringing out coy sprightliness." White never joined that sad assembly line, despite its bonuses, or got his bread by literary preening. No man has written more wittily of our time than he, but he has had no truck with inanity. Neither can his excursion into the pastoral life be judged escapist. Indeed, in 1938, the critical year of his retirement to Maine, he at once began to express in *Harper's* a realistic internationalism well ahead of the *New Yorker* and of lagging public opinion generally. (It seems likely that White is responsible, too, for recent *New Yorker* "Notes and Comments" which have argued, with such logical and ethical force, the cause of a genuinely dedicated and empowered world order.)

Even more revealing than White's prompt, right stand on the war and world peace is his earlier position as the deftly humorous but never merely playful satirist of the incredible twenties, which could not wring either acquiescence or cynicism from him. Hearing a businessman's boast of how an entire clerical department was moved, desks and all, from one building to another so expeditiously that the hundred employees sat down to work again in about an hour, he asked, "And didn't any of the clerks escape?" "But," White concludes, "it was the wrong question." Apparently the inquirer remained unabashed; he went on asking just the right wrong questions. White's probings have gone a long way beyond Sinclair Lewis's crude satires of crudity and puerile escapist reactions against conventionality, just as they rose above such typical sophistications as Benchley's short-winded jesting or Woollcott's capsuled sentiment and morbid fascination with the decadence of his own age and kind. At times such a fascination has seemed to sway the *New Yorker*, crazing its polish, as if it really navigated under its jibing slogan, "Not for the old lady from Dubuque," and meant to take up where Lewis and Mencken might well have left off. The acquisition of White's services and influence probably has been the fortunate *New Yorker's* greatest single piece of luck with personnel, in helping it transcend the snobberies and seasonal enervation of a locale and a period. Certainly White never evinced the twenties' faddish hatreds of the sticks and everything therein. He has not conceived of culture or felicity bounded by fences geographical, economic, or formally intellectual. He escaped the lure of the Left Bank and the addictions of the Village. When asked, on his removal to Maine, whether he was not afraid of becoming provincial, he retorted with another question: "Aren't you afraid of becoming metropolitan?" Neither does White belong to that stylishly nauseated group of demi-metropolitans who escaped to Connecticut cottages, wherein to deplore the city, whence cometh their sports clothing. White often writes of Manhattan with a zest as keen as Morley's, though with a more detached humor and without any laureate arpeggios. Whether at the typewriter or in the henhouse, White is ingenuously himself, cool but appreciative, at once fanciful and sensible. When he lives on the land, he is no ruddy country gentleman posed in riding boots, nor does he try to enact the flinty rustic. His neighbors expectantly ask, "You goin' to get your deer?" but, says he, "I can't seem to work up a decent feeling of enmity toward a deer. Toward *my* deer, I mean." And of his appearance on his own acres he writes, "I have fitted myself out with standard equipment, dungarees and a cap; but I should think twice before I dared stand still in a field of new corn." (It must be remembered, though, that Farmer White—phone Waterlot 40 Ring 3—brought a lot of hens' eggs to market during the war years.)

Neither is White's history one of discreet abstention from sticking his neck out. In courageous and consistent assertion he has surpassed both the cynical humorists who aped the mode of a Neronian frivolity and a whole decade of angry ideologists marching in cadence with a prescribed social consciousness. And White has not only spoken out, he has made it stick. He has never been caught napping intellectually; he has not had to beat his breast publicly and read himself out of a previous folly, or still more shamefully, to sneak down from a flat-tired band wagon; he is not yet dated. Many of his winded and backtracking contemporaries must ruefully envy his record, which in a generation's lengthening perspectives is seen to have resulted not from temporizing or cautious aloofness, but from force of judgment, faith, and conscience. Humorously White has blamed his hay fever for a "tendency toward the spineless middle ground . . . in time of political strain," charging himself with "the compromising nature of a man who from early childhood has found himself without a pocket handkerchief in a moment of defluxion," but here he is only elaborating a wry essay on Webster's summer catarrh. There is nothing spineless about White's serious comment on a litterateur who in the same days of political strain pledged himself never to write anything that wasn't socially significant. "A writer must believe in something, obviously," says White, "but he shouldn't join a club. . . . Even in evil times, a writer should cultivate only what naturally absorbs his fancy, whether it be freedom or cinch bugs. . . . Only under a dictatorship is literature expected to exhibit an harmonious design or an inspirational tone." To write that in the late thirties required wisdom; to publish it then required pluck. White has achieved his place by moving across professional currents, not drifting with them. The abnormal thing about him has been that he has quietly maintained a humanistic norm in a period of noisy aberrations, naturalistic or dogmatic. In a double sense, he has stood up well.

Politically White seems to be a sweat-of-brow, easy-does-it, lower-case democrat. While condemning the system of free enterprise for having been "predatory and unfair," he thinks that "in essence it was a good thing, which might have fitted people like a glove" had it chosen to recognize that "what the common man wanted really was a sense of participation," had the bonus at Christmas, "season of generosity and remorse," been "given a ring and a name and made into an honest woman." White thus differs not only from the rival zealots of laissez faire or Marxism, but from intermediate pessimists, for he evidently believes that there is in men a cultivable and rightful human quality (neglected by extremists, denied by cynics), a potentiality of independent conduct both provident and reciprocally considerate. To this ideal, slowly emergent in men's most generous experience, and basic to the theory of democracy, White seems firmly committed. It is this faith which enabled him to refute Mrs. Lindbergh's *Wave of the Future* so devastatingly. "Is my own intellectual resistance," he asks, ". . . any less promising than the force of nazism itself, merely because mine does not spring from human misery but from human sympathy? I don't see why. And I do not regard it as a sin to hang fast to principles which I approve of and believe are still applicable." Here, as in many similar passages, White seems to voice something comparatively inarticulate but fundamental and staunch in American life. It is his special honor to have kept this value in sight during a time when the writers with the simpler answers, or despairing of answers, were clouding the air with slung mud, custard pies, and good red brick.

The gold medal of the Limited Editions Club has gone to *One Man's Meat* as "the book which is considered most nearly to attain the stature of a classic." Though enthusiasts are prone to count classics still unhatched, it is not impossible to pick a winner in his own time. Landor gave the essayist Elia a verbal gold medal and a passkey to immortality; a century has approved the judgment. Lamb, too, was an informal, ironic, fanciful, and humane writer whose quietly conversational remarks got heard in an era of big bow-wowing. How do they do it, Elia and E. B. White and the other rare writers of quiet-voiced, casual, classic paragraphs? Certainly not by being mousy or childish or inconsequential. Those who see them in any such light are describing shadows cast by their own stuffy postures. Hearing Lamb blandly tell off Southey for religious hypocrisy, hearing White politely put down Mrs. Lindbergh for impercipience, one recognizes a firmness that quite suffices without any pulpit-thumping, a conviction resting not on a prefabricated ideology but on the writer's own humanity, that constant which he verifies in his fellow-men, and in the whole pitiable and joyful history of man.

Thus, in his classic discussion of freedom, White can report his awareness that he "traveled with secret papers pertaining to a divine conspiracy," which had begun in childhood with "the haunting intimation . . . of nature publishing herself through the 'I.'" This, he says, is the feel of freedom in a planetary sense; "to be free, in a social sense, is to feel at home in a democratic framework." In Hitler, White pointed out, "we do not detect either type of sensibility," for he has "no sense of communion but rather an urge to prevail," and "his feeling for men is not that they co-exist, but that they are capable of being arranged and standardized." White holds his nose at the "adaptable natures" who compromise such a fundamental distinction. Resenting "the patronizing air" of such persons, he declares that "if it is boyish to believe that a human being should live free, then I'll gladly arrest my development." White's position is boyish only in the Wordsworthian sense that "the Child is father of the Man." The basing of democratic sympathies in his personal-planetary sense of freedom interestingly parallels the Hartleyan element in Wordsworth, as White's fanciful confusion of himself with his own son in "Once More to the Lake" resembles Wordsworth's sense of life's resounding cycle, with its potent recollections.

Such a deep-flowing, intense existence, romantic in the fundamental and best sense of the word, is what gives White's writing not only its humane integrity but its great charm. That charm involves the sincerity and gusto of a capable writer genuinely concerned with his subject. It employs the understatement by which an independent and civil personality would allow others also the inalienable right of taking or leaving it. It plays gracefully with the heterogeneous and discrepant, in that most disarming and endearing judiciousness which is humor. Aesthetically it adds to an intellectual comprehensiveness the candor, lively allusion, tactful implication, and the cordial pauses of sympathetic conversation. White is an eudaemonist, whose mind is his kingdom, in which he is a benevolent monarch, blessed with good genius, diligent in the regulation of internal affairs and the conduct of free trade and genial diplomacy with the world. He has gone beyond sad fact and cynical laughter to prove the humane value he once defined as "gaiety, or truth in sheep's clothing."

In art as well as in conduct, individualism needs the regulative ingredient of common kindness. On this score White surpasses Thoreau, whom he admires, and with whom he is often admiringly compared. Thoreau's independence sometimes stooped to spiritual parsimony; his transcending was often a deliberate skipping, so that he failed to read the whole text of life. Conversely, White's expense account on a visit to Walden includes a baseball bat and glove, "gifts to take back to a boy"; and he remarks that Thoreau "never had to cope with a shortstop." White has had to, and apparently the compulsion is not just of circumstance but of temperament. Empathy has moved him to cope with much that a self-centered individualist would overlook, or that a Levite would pass by. Egoistic preoccupation sometimes makes the informal essay inhuman; but White's writings, however personal, abound in that wide-ranging awareness and response essential to an achievement of literature's fullest dimensions.

MARION GLASTONBURY

"E. B. White's Unexpected Items of Enchantment"

Children's Literature in Education, May 1973, pp. 3–12

Shortly before Christmas 1938, E. B. White wrote an article for *Harper's Magazine* complaining that his Maine farmhouse was overrun with children's books sent to his wife to review. 'Throw open the door of our kitchen cabinet, out will fall the Story of Tea.' This contact with children's literature inspired thoughts which have themselves a random haphazard look, as if ideas fell out of cupboards onto a man who was not expecting them.

He reflects that one should keep abreast of what the children of the country are reading because it is a mirror of the age. He notes the paradox that old familiar literary paths lead to new destinations and laughs hollowly at the irony of books on domestic safety in 'this year of infinite terror when the desire of everyone is for a safe hole to hide in'. He concludes that 'it must be a lot of fun to write for children—reasonably easy work, perhaps even important work'. Particularly exciting would be the search for 'a place, a period or a thing that hasn't already been written about'.

Around this time White started his first children's book in the hope of amusing a six year old niece; by the time he finished it, she had grown old enough to read Hemingway. A prolific journalist and a professional meeter of deadlines, White has produced only three books for children in the course of a long life: *Stuart Little* published in 1946, *Charlotte's Web* 1952, and *The Trumpet of the Swan* 1970. I believe the reason for the long intervals between the books is that the subject he hit upon, so far from being easy, involved the distillation of much experience and the synthesis of problems which exercised him, in theory and in practice, throughout his life.

White was born in 1899 in a suburb of New York and was educated at Cornell University where he edited the *Cornell Daily Sun*. Before he joined the staff of the *New Yorker* in 1926 he wrote automobile ads for a Madison Avenue agency, a job he hung onto longer than his friends expected because he had 'no confidence in my ability in the world of letters'. His editorials had a certain influence in the city—he got the lights on the tower of the Empire State Building changed from coloured to white, and freed the passengers in Grand Central Station from broadcast commercials. His main ambition was to be esteemed as a poet but he collaborated with James Thurber in producing cartoon captions and satirical sketches. The book they wrote together *Is Sex Necessary?* was illustrated by the first Thurber drawings to appear in print. Both writers moved out of the city in the thirties—a colleague remarked that the *New Yorker* was run by two country bumpkins—and while White admits that the animals got into his stories, there is evidence that Talk of the Town got into the animals. The books encompass the elements of the earth and what man has made of them, politics and privacy, innocence and experience, confrontation and retreat.

Thurber's definition of humour, 'a kind of emotional chaos told about calmly and quietly in retrospect', applies in some measure to White who described himself as celebrating 'trivial peaceable pursuits knowing all the time that the world hadn't arranged any true peace or granted anyone the privilege of indulging himself for long in trivialities'. As a youth in the First World War he had written a poem strongly advising himself to get killed in action; in the Second World War, his liberal ideals and his observation of racialism in America convinced him that the times needed heroism which a writer could preach but not practice.

The rueful comedy of Stuart Little emerges from these preoccupations. Stuart is a model hero, cool in a crisis, dauntless in a quest, unflinching in the defence of principle—but he is a mouse. Endlessly resourceful, Stuart is the converse of White's Mittyesque depiction of himself 'at the mercy of inanimate objects which deliberately plot to destroy a man'. The son of Mr and Mrs Little of New York masters the intricacies and hazards of the apartment and the city by pioneering zeal and technical ingenuity, adjusting piano keys from inside and boarding trams in trouser turn-ups. His triumphs of self-help are contrasted with the unproductive brainwaves of his brother George, who litters the bathroom floor with tools. White is particularly good at rendering boisterous boys and sorely-tried parents, and this realism sets off the paragon of American family life which Stuart embodies, with his adventurous spirit, courtesy, early rising and well-exercised stomach muscles. Virtue is exposed to discomfort and indignities. When he retrieves his mother's ring from the drain he needs to be deodorized. He gets caught up in the window shade and remains there, despaired of, until George pulls down the shade to show his respect for the dead. When he is carted off with the garbage by mistake, he is the envy of his father whose business prevents him from travelling far from home.

Stuart combines many heroic traditions and the eloquence of literary pastiche enriches the comedy of his exploits. A clubland dandy with his hat and cane, he requests a 'nip of brandy' after being shut accidentally in the fridge. A crack shot with bow and arrow, he quotes speeches from the movies as he chivalrously rescues his bird friend Margalo from the cat. In the epic boat race on the pond in Central Park, he is a swashbuckling champion and, returning home, is too sophisticated to boast. 'George asked him where he had been all day. "Oh knocking around town," replied Stuart.' When danger at home puts Margalo to flight, Stuart takes to the road in a car powered by five drops of gasoline, and, a picaresque wayfarer, comes to the aid of a pensive stranger.

'"You see, I'm the Superintendent of Schools in this town." "That's not an impossible situation," said Stuart, "It's bad but it's not impossible."' Stuart's moral courage matches his physical daring. While deputizing for an absent teacher Stuart dismisses the conventional curriculum as trivial and irrelevant—'Who knows what is really important?'—and leads a discussion of universal ethics. An autocrat within a democratic procedure, he discovers that being Chairman of the World takes more running and leaping and sliding than he had imagined, and leaves the class with a benediction: 'Never forget your summertimes, my dears'.

Significantly the only setback in Stuart's career occurs with the failure of his romantic overtures to a girl of his own size—a well-rehearsed evening on the river which turns into a muddy fiasco. It has an inauspicious start since the paddles for the birch-bark canoe are cardboard spoons for eating ice-cream, disquietingly inauthentic. 'I would hate to meet an American Indian while I had one of these things in my hand.' Rejecting comfort and compromise, the solace of a dance at the Country Club with wealthy Harriet, Stuart resumes the challenge of his original task, the search for Margalo in which nothing is certain or guaranteed. He journeys northward (White's own route home from the city) encouraged by a telephone repairman:

> 'I have sat at peace on the freight platforms of railroad junctions in the north, in the warm hours and with the warm smells. I know fresh lakes in the north, undisturbed except by fish and hawk and, of course, the Telephone Company, which has to follow its nose. I know all these places well. They are a long way from here—don't forget that. And a person who is looking for something doesn't travel very fast.'

Some readers find this conclusion inconclusive; my six-year-old son was moved to write a sequel in which Stuart and Margalo reached home 'and never went away again without coming back.' This book reads you.

I think the intensity of the tale comes from White's own predicament: his frustration as a teacher who knew 'what is really important' and was not hopeful of getting it across; as a modest writer with topics on his mind too big to express; as an idealist whose aspirations for humanity exceeded his powers and position. 'Law is extremely solemn,' Stuart tells the class.

Yet this solemnity does not detract from the entertainment of the book. For the young, Stuart provides a chance to identify simultaneously with underdog and topdog. His mastery of the world is achieved through the universal paraphernalia of miniature boats and cars with which children rehearse their own adult performances; his feats complement their fantasy. There are scatological jokes: 'Phew Stuart, you do smell awful'—and wordplay with a touch of Schadenfreude—the strangulated talk of the patient in the dentist's chair—which in my experience children find side-splitting.

Stuart's infancy is unusually short—less than a week. White's second book, *Charlotte's Web*, dwells on babies—piglets, goslings, lambs, children. Stuart is a detached self-sufficient character, soon independent of his family and pitting his wits against the domestic sub-culture of cats and dogs, a wise guy making his own way in a predominantly public world—street, park, store. The narrative is linear, a solo with a supporting cast. The farm by contrast is densely populated with intimate relationships; the characters live in and through each other; the strand of each individual destiny is enmeshed in the collective fabric. Stuart's deepest feeling, his commitment to Margalo, is unfulfilled, a goal in the distance; in *Charlotte's Web* emotions are reciprocal, realized and followed through. The dynamic of feeling within a complex community *is* the movement of the book—nurture and maturation, attachment and loss. The mock heroics of Stuart Little depend on your consciousness of incongruity; the difference between the hero's picture of the figure he is cutting and our own. In the second book, the satirical core is the interdependence and mutual influence of the public image and the true self, social valuation and its effect on personality. Within the web of the title, Charlotte the spider contrives a publicity stunt to ensure the survival of her friend the pig. By advertising his noble qualities she turns him into a celebrity and Wilbur and the farm flourish in the ensuing fame which culminates at the County Fair, the great occasion which brings to each character his heart's desire.

E. M. Forster remarked on the rarity in fiction of 'the facts of birth'. Characters usually 'come into the world more like parcels than human beings'. But birth is White's special province. Nests abound—White says he spent the war years 'publishing my belief in the egg'. Wilbur, the runt of the litter, owes his life to the intervention of Fern, the farmer's eight-year-old daughter—'If I had been very small at birth, would you have killed *me?*'—and is passionately cherished with bottle and doll's pram. When he is weaned and transferred to the barn, Fern's tender vigilance continues and more lives begin—the miracle of creation, the slog of parenthood. Birth has a social dimension: when seven goslings hatch out, Charlotte formally congratulates their mother on the lucky number. 'Luck had nothing to do with this,' said the goose, 'it was good management and hard work.'

Waiting and working are in some forms familiar to children but the rarity of birth in their literature is related to a deeper omission which corresponds to a limitation in their lives—the dimension of time. Just because children's temporal span is so short and their experience of relationships necessarily one sided, it is difficult to convey gradual transition; the pattern of changes which make up the full compass of a life. Since the child is conscious of so few years, so few seasons, he lacks—and needs—an imaginative grasp of the facts of growth and generation. In the absence of time as the element in which lives are lived, people in fiction are incomplete and their acts lack significance. Hence the static, eventless quality of many novels for children. Scenes tend to be 'stills' with dramatic devices sandwiched between. If the plot requires a character to grow up, the parts are played, as it were, by two actors, one small and one large.

White transcends these limitations. His solid evocation of shifting seasons, the perpetually changing landscape, the ceaseless mobility of 'here and now' is the foundation of his achievement in making us believe in his characters and care about the events which affect them. Risk and pleasure combine in the unifying imagery of height and flight which symbolizes the launching of new life—the children swinging from the barn roof, the spider-balloonists sailing off into the unknown, Henry and Fern on the Ferris wheel. 'They've got to grow up some time,' said Mr Arable, 'and a fair is a good place to start, I guess.'

The child reader's own history is charted in Wilbur's archetypal journey from private bliss with Fern to public exposure and hard-won friendships in the wider community, amid the rumours, rivalries, business meetings and formal procedures of the barn. Having been Fern's nursling and Charlotte's protégé, he becomes in his turn a protector entrusted with an egg sac containing five hundred and fourteen unborn children just before the spider dies.

> When the first light comes into the sky and the sparrows stir and the cows rattle their chains, when the rooster crows and the stars fade, when early cars whisper along the highway, you look up here and I'll show you something. I will show you my masterpiece.

Animals mature quickly, their successive roles have a short term and can be readily perceived. Human development is slower, more obscure. In anxious phases parents seek reassurance from the longer perspective of experts; Mrs Arable consults the doctor about Fern's obsession: '"I would say off-hand that spiders and pigs were fully as interesting as Henry Fussy. Yet I predict that the day will come when even Henry will drop some chance remark that catches Fern's attention. It's amazing how children change from year to year."' The doctor is right; Fern turns from her pets to the love of her contemporary and is soon 'careful to avoid childish things like sitting on a milk stool near a pigpen'.

White's depiction of the natural order includes conflict as well as cooperation and mutual support, destruction as well as survival. Charlotte herself is a predator:

> 'I'm not entirely happy about my diet of flies and bugs, but it's the way I'm made. And furthermore, do you realize that if I didn't catch bugs and eat them, bugs would increase and multiply and get so numerous that they'd destroy the earth?'

Stuart Little's cat suffers psychologically from his repression of his hunting instincts; the collecting urge of small boys is a natural threat to the spider, a danger which the hoarding mania of the rat happens in this case to avert. White has given much thought to rats and their place in the scheme of things. They are the outcast species which Stuart insists should be granted full citizenship in the reformed world system. They exemplify the least likeable aspects of our society—acquisitiveness, alienation, self-seeking. Templeton is recognizable as one of us with his profiteering 'I handle this stuff all the time', his contempt for play and his lust for high living. Yet within the fictional world he has created, White is 'fair to rats' for Templeton's actions are better than his motives. Cynicism and callousness notwithstanding—'Let him die. I should worry.'—he is an agent of salvation for Charlotte, Wilbur and the eggs, since self-interest lies in Wilbur's feeding trough. Destinies are chronologically linked; no animal is an island.

Walter Benjamin wrote 'An orientation towards practical interests is characteristic of many born storytellers'. White's books are rich in skills and strategems, solid with feasts, tools, gear. You could stock your farm from his inventory and go away on holiday with the bags he packs. You could also choose your car from his traffic jam: 'Fords and Chevvies and Buick roadmasters and GMC pickups and Plymouths and Studebakers and Packards and De Sotos with gyromatic transmissions and Oldsmobiles with rocket engines and Jeep station wagons and Pontiacs.' Actuality is a brand name; even *things* have a history, a past and a future. There is a lot of twentieth century junk around the garbage that entraps Stuart on the East River, the stormblown newspapers and candy wrappers in the Philadelphia Zoo. But the trash dump raided by Templeton is the repository of the media, food for fantasy, and speaks the twentieth century message. 'Bring me back a word,' Charlotte called after him. The rat tears out ads and labels—'Crunchy' 'Pre-shrunk' 'With New Radiant Action'. 'Actually,' said Wilbur, 'I *feel* radiant.'

Commercials are satirized with affection: 'People will believe almost anything they see in print'. Everyone but the farmer's wife assumes that it is the subject of the slogan and not the creator who is remarkable and this delusion saves Wilbur from slaughter. Yet it is precisely his ordinariness that makes Wilbur lovable and his rise to fame a source of joy. Appreciation is a self-fulfilling prophecy: 'But I'm not terrific, Charlotte. I'm just about average for a pig.' 'You're terrific as far as I'm concerned,' replied Charlotte sweetly, 'and that's what counts.' The unreality of competition and status is exposed by the uniqueness of love.

Charlotte's Web ends with a tribute to 'a true friend and a good writer', perhaps referring to the author's wife who was literary editor of *The New Yorker* for many years. (*The New Yorker*, like the web, is influential and renewed at regular intervals.) White's latest book celebrates music, the universal language that transcends even the power of words. The Trumpeter Swan of the title is called Louis; the book pays homage to Armstrong and the men who composed his tunes.

Once again the traditional formula of a meteoric career is parodied and the story describes the struggles of an animal hero to overcome an initial handicap within a relationship with a maturing child. This time the human hero, Sam, is adolescent, concerned with what he is going to be when he grows up, while in the life cycle of the swans, attention is focused on courtship and marriage. The sanctuaries of the wild and the centres of society are further apart than ever; the flight of the swan is paralleled by Sam's air travel, and the ventures of each into the territory of the other have the quality of 'firstness' which John Berger has characterized as the essence of sexual experience. Sam meets the swans' brood while camping by a remote lake in Canada. One cygnet turns out to be voiceless. The cob's distress at this discovery: 'Fatherhood is quite a burden at best. I do not want the added strain of having a defective child,' becomes determination to provide for Louis's future since a voice is vital for courtship. Louis attends school with Sam but, though literacy enables him to communicate with humans, he can make no headway with the swan he loves. The impotence of muteness is finally mastered by art when Louis learns to play the trumpet which his father has stolen for him, earns money to pay for it and successfully woos Serena. The fulfilment of Louis's love has a more than personal importance since we learn from the game warden that Trumpeter Swans were once almost extinct, 'But now they are making a comeback,' *'I'll* say they are making a comeback!' says the storekeeper and donates Louis's money to the Audubon Society.

White's technique uses time honoured literary conventions as a sort of ambush for originality. Psychological insights lurk behind clichés of the genre. Louis's rise to stardom, fame and fortune reveals the grind of making a living in show business. The standard adventure story rescue occurs when Louis saves from drowning a boy who doesn't like birds, but without the standard conversion of the rescued—'I still don't like birds'. 'Really?' said Mr Brickle. 'That's quite remarkable.' Sam hopes Serena won't marry Louis for his money (which hangs in a bag round his neck) and when at last the deus ex machina of a storm blows Serena into the Philadelphia Zoo and the conventional happy ending is in sight, she is too 'mussed' and 'pooped' to be approached. It is a measure of White's success in creating the romance that he can afford to tell this kind of unglamorous truth. The more exalted the theme, the more down-to-earth the treatment. Sentimentality is a sin of omission, White's completedness is the converse of this. He shows us priceless things and tells us honestly what they cost. When the mother is incubating her eggs, her husband asks, 'Don't you ever feel the pangs of hunger or suffer the tortures of thirst?' 'Yes I do,' said his mate, 'as a matter of fact I could use a drink right now.' The parent swans epitomize the enduring intensity of what survives satire, what can be laughed at and still loved. (Thus humanizing the modern American reversal of the patriarchal tradition which treats fathers as buffoons.) Sources of emotional strength can also be sources of comedy just as true poetry can withstand parody. When Louis plays Brahms' Cradle Song it's interrupted by the ping of pellets from an airgun—only good tunes make jokes. The points of the compass are a recurring symbol in White's work and this book is remarkable for its impression of space and flight, distances travelled and contrasting landscapes. The secret life of wild places—frog, chipmunk, jay, fox—is matched by the panorama of metropolitan fauna—lobby clerks, bellboys, people drinking cocktails, chambermaids in bedrooms who pause to listen to the trumpet. White's comic scenes are played on a wide screen, often with choral effects, as in the cob's invasion of the vibrating music store. Melodrama serves to illumine the reaction of bystanders to momentous events. Most observers are as unmoved as the horse in Auden's poem who 'scratches its innocent behind on a tree.' Alfred Gore, deadpan, sees a swan laden with money shot by a storekeeper and covered with blood; then, still thirsty, he continues his journey to the candy store. Others leap joyfully onto bandwagons: the boatman sees a chance to 'sextoople' his business; the teacher wants to get her picture in *Life* magazine. The wise are neither blasé nor opportunist. Miracles give them food for thought; they are left pondering the mysteries of life. And their meditations bring these old men of authority, the telephone engineer, the headman of the zoo, into relationships with the young, earnest, questing, eager for knowledge. The result is a sort of fusion of seriousness and frivolity, rather as if *The Leechgatherer* and *The Aged Aged Man A-Sitting on a Gate* had both been composed by the same author.

The reader is left with an impression of charm and wisdom, two qualities which may appear somewhat antithetical. Charm involves a self-effacing responsiveness, an awareness of one's audience; wisdom responds only to truth and tells it, welcome or not. Charm is compliant; wisdom is uncompromising. Charm implies ease; wisdom urgency. I suspect that White's dissatisfaction with himself as a writer in troubled times stemmed from the fact that he knew that he was charming and yet wanted to be wise. His touch was too light to take the weight of what needed to be said. Yet in stories for children the contradiction resolves itself; there is no tension between the demands of style and content. In the witty handling of serious themes, a modest undertaking with immense potential influence, White found the exact mode of expression for his gifts; more appropriate than either advertising with its overtly seductive aim or journalism which would change the world if it could.

Thurber repeatedly used the word 'perfection' of White's work. White himself is fascinated by images of natural perfection. The artifacts of instinctive skill, the spider's web, the swan's nest—'Nobody ever taught her'—are set beside the processes of teaching and learning, the effort and frustration involved in mastering human skills, writing and making music. White has said that he finds writing 'difficult and bad for one's disposition', but seems driven to it by the need to acknowledge particular blessings and to pay particular debts of gratitude. His readers have reason to be grateful to one who wrote in 1962:

> As a writing man, I have always felt charged with the safekeeping of all unexpected items of worldly or unworldly enchantment, as though I might be held personally responsible if even a small one were lost.

JOHN UPDIKE
"The Shining Note" (1976)
Hugging the Shore
1983, pp. 187–95

A rare thing it is for the living to collect and publish their letters; as E. B. White says, with his unfailing crispness, in a prefatory note to *Letters of E. B. White*, "ideally, a book of letters should be published posthumously. The advantages are obvious: the editor enjoys a free hand, and the author enjoys a perfect hiding place—the grave, where he is impervious to embarrassments and beyond the reach of libel." The advantages of pre-posthumous publication are obvious also: the living epistolist can supply his editor, in this case Dorothy Lobrano Guth, with leads and clarifications; he can write, as White has done, delightful introductory and interstitial paragraphs; he can help shape the collection of letters toward its ideal condition, of involuntary autobiography. White's refining touch is felt throughout this well-designed, considerately annotated volume—six hundred and sixty-two pages' and sixty-eight years' worth of prose treasure strewn along the wayside by a diffident-appearing but at heart highly determined literary pilgrim.

Mrs. Guth's introduction states that when a collection of his letters was suggested to White by one of his editors at Harper & Row, he "wrote back that he didn't really consider himself much of a letter writer." In a letter to his brother Stanley in 1968, White said, "I avoid writing letters—it resembles too closely writing itself, and gives me a headache." Yet, once settled to the typewriter, he is a generous communicant—devoting, for example, nearly a thousand exquisitely chosen words to a librarian who petulantly mailed back a letter White had written to a little girl explaining how overwhelmed by mail he was and suggesting that the child form a movement called "Don't write to E. B. White until he produces another book." White's mail, indeed, swollen by all those adults and children who feel that in his work he has addressed them personally, must be as voluminous as a movie star's, and only an extravagantly decent man would answer as much as he seems to. In this collection one can find, recovered from their recipients by heaven knows what miracles of retrieval, perfect examples of the types of letter an author is called upon to write: to the term-paper writer ("Dear Mr. Cole: I don't know how to 'reveal any aspect' of myself deliberately. Everything a person does or says is, of course, revealing. But *you're* going to write that term paper, not me"); to the random inquirer ("Dear Miss Gravely: I don't know where to begin. I am five feet eight inches tall—but that's an odd place to begin. I am fifty years old—but that's a dreadful place to begin. I ate too much for lunch—but nobody would want to begin *there*. As for my work, the only thing I can tell you about it is that a lot of it has been published, all of it was hard, and some of it was fun"); to the proposer of a deal ("Dear Miss Strauss: . . . Your proposal is certainly challenging enough for anybody. It had never occurred to me that the life of Christ could be a subject for a comic book—probably because it doesn't seem funny. Now that I have adjusted to the idea, I still don't want to undertake it, as it is primarily a labor of adaptation, rather than of creation, and I'm not a very adaptable man"). White's letter of January 14, 1948, to E. J. McDonald is a consummate specimen of the Apology to a Friend Who May Have Been Offended by a Story (here the ungratefully received narrative was a masterpiece, "Death of a Pig"), and his communication of June 6, 1950, to James Thurber a model of the Letter to a Friend Who Has Sent His Book (*The Thirteen Clocks*, and White manages to disguise as pleasantries a number of shrewd criticisms). Refusals to lecture, to comment on galleys, to name three favorite books of the year—there is no piece of professional fending so mechanical that White begrudges its phrasing a pinch of grace and fun. His responses to children who are baffled by the ending of *Stuart Little* or the meaning of *Charlotte's Web* are marvels of affectionate patience. At guileless length he defends himself against the charge, by "some students of children's literature," that there was too much money and violence in *The Trumpet of the Swan*. His gingerly relationships, fond yet sometimes fiercely firm, with publishers and editors weave a pretty pattern as White steers one book after another around his own doubts and the helpful interferences of others. His correspondence, in 1971 and 1972, with the makers of the unfortunate film of *Charlotte's Web* constitutes a heartbreaking outpour of justified anxieties and ignored advice. His letter to Katharine White, his wife, in June of 1948 describes drolly and harrowingly another authorial peril, the honorary degree—even the hood proves a menace: "I guess it must have been when I reached over to pick the program off the chair that my hood got hung up on Ben Ames Williams. Anyway, when I got seated the thing was up over my face, as in falconry." His letter to William Maxwell of November 16 that same year, worrying about the foreign translations of *Stuart Little*—"I'm not enough of a linguist to know whether a Dutch Stuart Little should be called Stuart Little or Tom Trikkelbout. But it is beginning to dawn on me that I damn well better find out"—stands as a rebuke to those authors who imagine that their responsibilities are confined to the language they write in. White has taken his citizenship in the community of letters seriously; whenever he has felt freedom of expression threatened, whether by McCarthyism in the Fifties or by the Xerox Corporation's sponsorship of an *Esquire* article in 1976, he has spoken up, and his public letters, written gratuitously to newspapers, are among the more impressive extensions of his vocation. Even in indignation he twinkles: "I can only assume that your editorial writer, in a hurry to get home for Thanksgiving, tripped over the First Amendment and thought it was the office cat."

A trio of letters from December of 1936 shows White's ethical sense, and his generous epistolary nature, thrice activated by the same affront: Alexander Woollcott had lent himself to a Christmas promotion of Seagram's whiskey. Woollcott's bulk-mailed solicitation for Seagram's as a Christmas present was reprinted in *The New Yorker*'s Open-Letters Department, with a mordant response, signed "Eustace Tilley" but composed by White, which concluded, ". . . this Christmas of 1936, thanks to your thoughtful note, has been given an unforgettable flavor, has become a season pervaded with the faint, exquisite perfume of well-rotted holly berries." In a personal Christmas card to Woollcott, White continues in the same saucy style, referring quite uncontritely to his published jape at "your open affair with La Seagram. After all, a man's personal excesses are his own business. Privately, I may wish you joy of the lady, but publicly I must give so lewd an alliance a jab, mustn't I?" The third letter, at great length, and with a courtesy as total as its frankness, carefully explains the abuse of trust that White sees in the older writer's commercial involvement:

> My other reason is the one that everything really hangs on: the importance of a writer's maintaining his amateur standing. . . . I still cling (by my teeth these days) to the notion that writing is a trust. . . . The next time I come across you, in the mail, in print, I feel I must be on my guard, must see what the catch is, may have to read half way through before I can determine whether this is an affiliated utterance or an unaffiliated utterance.

White's own determination to remain amateur and unaffiliated is reflected in his affectionate, respectful, yet edgy correspondence with Harold Ross. White's value to the young *New Yorker* was estimated by James Thurber for *The Saturday Review* in 1938: "Harold Ross and Katharine Angell, his literary editor, were not slow to perceive that here were the perfect eye and ear, the authentic voice and accent for their struggling magazine . . . His contributions to the Talk of the Town, particularly his Notes and Comment on the first page, struck the shining note that Ross had dreamed of striking." Yet the shining-note producer's early notes to the persistent dreamer are gruff and wary and often mailed from afar, like this one from Ontario in 1929:

> On account of the fact that *The New Yorker* has a tendency to make me morose and surly, the farther I stay away the better. I appreciate very much your extraordinary capacity to endure, and in fact cope with, my somewhat vengeful attitude about *The New Yorker* and my crafty habit of slipping away for long intervals . . . Next to yourself and maybe one or two others, I probably have as tender a feeling for your magazine as anybody. For me it isn't a complete life, though.

The search for the complete life took him out of New York City entirely from 1938 to 1942 and from 1957 to the present, and to Maine every summer from 1930 on: "I would really rather feel bad in Maine than good anywhere else." While remaining a supremely prized contributor, visible and invisible, to *The New Yorker*, and identified in the public mind with what is best and blithest about it, White has often asserted his unaffiliated talent elsewhere; his fame in large part rests upon his three best-selling novels for children, the essays of the "One Man's Meat" column he wrote for five years in *Harper's*, his surprising revival and revision of his old Cornell professor's handbook of English grammer and usage (*The Elements of Style*, by William Strunk, Jr.), and an essay done at *Holiday's* behest, "Here Is New York." "If I had no responsibilities or obligations of a domestic sort, I would most certainly arrange my life so that I was not obliged to write anything at any specified time for anybody," White wrote Ross in 1939, after he had taken on the *Harper's* commitment; though he has felt editorial pressure and constraints (and quit "One Man's Meat" when its writing seemed only "to fulfill a promise, or continuing obligation") he has not passed this feeling on to his readers. His readers, instead, feel flattered by the directness of his prose and caught up in its playfulness as his apparently unconstrained utterances gracefully poke toward the light. His quintessentially American style aspires to the very texture of freedom, the unfussy smoothness of something growing. "Many of the things he writes seem to me as lovely as a tree," Thurber wrote in 1938. This quality, of arboreal self-shaping, was not unearned; White struggled to keep it, to keep his distance from whatever would claim him and crowd him, even his beloved and hard-working wife, to whom he wrote in 1937, in explanation of a year's holiday he proposed to take from magazine work,

> A person afflicted with poetic longings of one sort or another searches for a kind of intellectual and spiritual privacy in which to indulge his strange excesses. To achieve this sort of privacy—this aerial suspension of the lyrical spirit—he does not necessarily have to wrench himself away, physically, from everybody and everything in his life . . . but he *does* have to forswear certain easy rituals, such as earning a living and running the world's errands.

Most of these letters scarcely touch on literary matters. He mentions reading Santayana and Thoreau, and writes John Kieran a fan letter for his *Natural History of New York City*. He several times casts a skeptical sibling eye in the direction of Hemingway, a fellow-lover of the outdoors and clean prose, and with easier fraternity confides some of his professional acumen and ambition to Thurber, Frank Sullivan, and Howard Cushman. Cushman, a Cornell friend who drove with White across the country in 1922, lived to act as his Philadelphia legman in the research for *The Trumpet of the Swan*, and never quite dropped from correspondence in between. "Sweet Hum," White addresses him, and signs himself "Ho." Thurber, in those years before (in White's obituary phrase) "blindness hit him, before fame hit him," offered himself as a partner to White's sensibility, and received letters unique, among these many, in their tone of frank, urbane, wised-up ennui:

> Sunday afternoons are about the same as when you left, people walking their dog out, and the dog not doing anything, the sky grey and terrible, and the L making the noise that you hear when you are under ether. . . . Even when an artist has the ability and the strength to assemble something of the beauty and the consternation which he feels, he is usually so jealous of other artists that he has no time for pure expression. Today with the radio yammering at you and the movies turning all human emotions into cup custard, the going is tough. Or I find it tough.

This letter also holds one of the few glimpses through White's eyes of the New York literary scene: "Joe Sayre is back from the Vineyard with third act trouble. . . . Walter Lippmann and Mrs. Lippmann are getting a divorce." White deliberately snubbed the cosmopolitan he could have become, and his later letters tend to confirm his diagnosis of himself as "not a bookish fellow."

But what a busy fellow! The launching ground of these missives is crammed with poultry and livestock, with goslings White has helped to hatch ("as green as grass, and they immediately begin playing their flutes, an enchanting sound") and with trout he is helping to spawn, with hurricanes and early risings, sailing and shingling, orphaned robins and willful dogs, and chores, chores, chores. Any impression that his retreat to rural life had an evasive or ironical side should be dispelled by these letters. White is a doer, a maker.

> Practically the most satisfying thing on earth (specially after fifteen years of trying to put English sentences together against time) is to be able to square off a board of dry white pine, saw to the line (allowing for the thickness of the pencil point) and have the thing fit perfectly.

In 1943, he "produced 14 lambs, 5 pigs, and 272 chicks and 5 goslings in spite of the weather" and expressed willingness to take on Louis Bromfield in a farming duel, "he to choose the weapons—anything from dung forks to post-hole diggers or 2-ounce syringes for worming sheep." Nor is this willingness to tackle anything a late offshoot; in his trip West with Cushman, White repaired their Model T, sold pocket calculators, picked pears, sandpapered a dance floor in Cody, Wyoming, played the piano in Hardin, Montana, and, in Louisville, Kentucky, wrote a sonnet on a race horse and sold it on the spot. White is so handy, so faithfully amused by his transactions with the material world, that his writing comes to us as largesse. The fine words have been trickled through a sieve of natural busyness. Another screen on the sieve has been his physical frailty, an unsteadiness in the head and a queasiness in the stomach that seem always there, or around the corner of the next ominous hour (though, airily, he shows no nervousness in high places; at Cornell he tried to walk across the Fall Creek gorge on the handrail of a bridge, and as a Talk of the Town reporter he ascended the unfinished Chrysler Building by ladder and scaffold). In 1936, he wrote Christopher Morley, "My health is always whimsical, and I turn out shockingly little work in the course of a week."

His attitude toward his own writing is volatile. Against the discouragement he expressed to Thurber may be set the happiness of his statement to Stanley White in 1929 that "to write a piece and sell it to a magazine is as near a simple life as shining up a pushcart of apples and vending them to passersby." To Ross, who found in White's shined apples the shining note he was looking for, White wrote in 1945, "I am not as sure of myself as I used to be, and write rather timidly, staring at each word as it comes out, and wondering what is wrong with *it*." To a college student he wrote in 1936, "I was a writing fool when I was eleven years old and have been tapering off ever since." For all his protests of fragile gifts progressively enfeebled, the sustained energy and charm of these letters, dashed off from odd corners of crowded days, confirm our impression of a writing fool still, irrepressibly felicitous and fluent. As early as his Western trip of 1922 he could with impish lyricism say that a small town "consists mainly of four stores and an excellent view of the mountains."

His letters to his brother Stanley, who taught him to read

before first grade, trace the longest curve in the book, and make the most deliberate accounting. Stanley, a landscape architect, lived in Illinois and has retired to Colorado, and White's periodic letters record the writer's life with the caringness of a family album, and a sepia touch of "the literary":

> The lake hangs clear and still at dawn, and the sound of a cowbell comes softly from a faraway woodlot. In the shallows along shore the pebbles and driftwood show clear and smooth on bottom, and black water bugs dart, spreading a wake and a shadow. A fish rises quickly in the lily pads with a little plop, and a broad ring widens to eternity.

In praise of a cane, White writes, "It gives dignity, direction, restraint, and a general sense of owning whatever you set the point of the cane down on," and, in memory of Robert Coates, "Bob shining like a great red lantern over everybody and everything, with his mind darting about like a swallow in air."

Well, one expects to find gems in Tiffany's. This collection, addressed to many people, will speak to many more. The index is excellent, and the photographs, of snowy, grassy yesteryears, are haunting. White was born in a Mount Vernon castle and works in a Maine boathouse, and both are shown. Young or old, he has parted his hair next to the middle. This is his biggest book—the only one, indeed, hard to hold with one hand—and, as he says, his most naked. "A man who publishes his letters becomes a nudist—nothing shields him from the world's gaze except his bare skin." In 1964, he described an essayist as one "who must take his trousers off without showing his genitals. (I got my training in the upper berths of Pullman cars long ago.)" His drawers here are not altogether off, as we can see by the polka dots of ellipsis that intervene sometimes; nevertheless White has allowed some tart thoughts to slip into print: "The firm of Harper, I have discovered over a period of years which might roughly be described as too long, is feeble-minded, but it is the sort of feeble-mindedness which holds a man in thrall." We laugh, and even his publisher must be disarmed by the aptness of expression. White's style, in the manner of the eighteenth-century journalist-philosophers and of Thoreau, strikes a colloquial pose but seeks the finality of aphorism:

> A writer is like a beanplant—he has his little day, and then gets stringy.
>
> There is some slight advantage in living as a recluse, in that one makes one's own crises, instead of getting them out of the newspaper.
>
> I don't know which is more discouraging, literature or chickens.
>
> Medals should be edible, so you could get it over with and have a moment of enjoyment.
>
> It is always sobering to encounter the intellectual idealists at work, for they seem to live in a realm of their own, making their plans for the world in much the same way that any common tyrant does.
>
> When I get sick of what men do, I have only to walk a few steps in another direction to see what spiders do.
>
> I always write a thing first and think about it afterwards, which is not a bad procedure, because the easiest way to have consecutive thoughts is to start putting them down.

SPENCER BROWN

From "The Odor of Durability"

Sewanee Review, Winter 1978, pp. 146–50

White's position in the essay ⟨. . .⟩ is that of the schooner *America* off the Isle of Wight. "Who is second?" asks Queen Victoria. "Madam, there is no second." White has been our preeminent essayist so long that many would say there is no other. If you want to know what the modern informal essay is, you must read *One Man's Meat* or *The Second Tree from the Corner* or *The Points of My Compass.* Here you find both the best and the only true exemplar—a precise definition of a classic, as, for example, Milton *is* the English epic. When White tells us that he has chosen a few of his pieces that seem "to have the odor of durability clinging to them," we feel confident that here, as always, his nose knows. Yet I am a bit disappointed that he didn't wish to be remembered also by "The Door"—if it is an essay—surely one of his most remarkable achievements. Perhaps he considers it already anthologized enough, or bravura and therefore too easy.

Elsewhere I have tried to make a case for White as poet. He is so in part but not altogether. The poet writes with his ear cocked for sounds: for him, in the beginning was the Word. White writes more with his eye on the object. He seeks and often attains a precision so deft that it does soar off the ground into poetry. He is also so enchanted by the very words that he often adopts the other, the poet's, direct way—especially in his reminiscence "Years of Wonder," which recounts his journey to Alaska in 1923, drawing heavily and amusedly from his journal kept on the voyage. "Alaskan towns," wrote White of 1923, "are just murmurings at the foot of mountains." White of 1961 writes: "Sandburg had me by the throat in those days." Later: "A lookout had been posted on the forecastlehead and Tony, the giant Negro watchman, was heaving the lead. Although I was busy getting squared away in my new job, my journal for that date contains a long, fancy description of the heaving of the lead. I was tired, but not too tired for a burst of showy prose." Self-mockery, the lightest fluff of romantic irony, makes the best of both past and present.

Like White's letters this essay suggests the extraordinary unity of his career. He portrays himself as socially gawky, financially feckless, vocationally indecisive; also single-minded in his ambition for literary success, into which, over the years, he continually sidles, each time as astonished as Dumbo to find himself up so high and yet gratified that dedicated skill has won superiority over a slovenly and illiterate world.

"The essayist," says White in his foreword, "is a self-liberated man, sustained by the childish belief that everything he things about, everything that happens to him, is of general interest." It is, if you can write like White. One such thing, for him, is birds, from city pigeons to the Harris's sparrow he saw in Maine, "at least a thousand miles from where he belonged"; and one of the pleasantest of the essays is "Mr. Forbush's Friends," concerning a three-volume work on the birds of Massachusetts. White's professional conscience only moderates his admiration: "If Edward Howe Forbush's prose is occasionally overblown, this results from a genuine ecstasy in the man, rather than from a lack of discipline. Reading the essays, one shares his ecstasy." So too is White's ecstasy genuine, though the prose is scarcely overblown.

Even casual readers of the *New Yorker* have long been aware of White's style and observing eye. The author has generously included in his selection a number of such long-esteemed or even famous pieces as "Coon Tree," "Death of a Pig," "Bedfellows," and "Once More to the Lake." These and others like them, about his farm and life in Maine, give the characteristic flavor to the book—a flavor compounded of shrewd insight, hindsight, and artfully rambling structure. "Bedfellows," ostensibly a memorial for White's disreputable and mendacious dog Fred, actually ruminates on politics, democracy, the nurture of heterodoxy, and the shadow of death—not Fred's death, but, one might say,

> It is the blight man was born for,
> It is E. B. White you mourn for.

The structure of a White essay resembles the configurations of a *corps de ballet,* in its confusing and harmonious and interlacing whirls of snowy tutus, gliding long-legged on point (in what Noel Coward once called a *pas de tout*) into the predestined arrangement. White's genius is in expatiation, in byways. He is not a thinker; he is a wry observer; but he achieves peripheral vision.

Yet his elegantly controlled digressions are less remarkable than the sentences they ride on. And since we are more familiar with his notes on Maine than with his Florida pieces, it is in the latter that we can best admire his quality. In "The Ring of Time," after a tenderly ironic picture of a girl training as a rider in the circus winter quarters, he writes:

> It has been ambitious and plucky of me to attempt to describe what is indescribable, and I have failed, as I knew I would. But I have discharged my duty to society; and besides, a writer, like an acrobat, must occasionally try a stunt that is too much for him. At any rate, it is worth reporting that long before the circus comes to town, its most notable performances have already been given. Under the bright lights of the finished show, a performer need only reflect the candle power that is directed upon him; but in the dark and dirty old training rings and in the makeshift cages, whatever light is generated, whatever excitement, whatever beauty, must come from original sources—from internal fires of professional hunger and delight, from the exuberance and gravity of youth. It is the difference between planetary light and the combustion of stars.

Like the two greatest American poets, Dickinson and Frost, White can become exasperatingly cute; but normally he is saved from cuteness by humor that they achieve only irregularly. Though he may pose as much as they, his poses are more natural and less noticeable. Wilbur, the hero of *Charlotte's Web,* is SOME PIG, but at the last triumphs by being HUMBLE.

White's sentences can be sharp and memorable. His first view of Siberia: "On shore we could see dogs curled up asleep among patches of tired snow." On the USSR: "The West has a real genius for doing approximately what the East wants it to do." "The side that enjoys numerical superiority stands to gain by disarmament, the side that does not have any intention of remaining unarmed for more than a few minutes stands to gain, and the side that uses the lie as an instrument of national policy stands to gain. If disarmament carried no chance of advantage, Mr. Khrushchev would not be wasting his breath on it." On Thoreau: "It is probably no harder to eat a woodchuck than to construct a sentence that lasts a hundred years."

The essay on Thoreau, "A Slight Sound at Evening," deliberately points up the differences between White and Thoreau. Thoreau's humor—what there is of it—is savage. White's is tolerant—with teeth. Thoreau's finest sentences are those of an angry man. Says White: "Henry went forth to battle when he took to the woods, and *Walden* is the report of a man torn by two powerful and opposing drives—the desire to enjoy the world (and not be derailed by a mosquito wing) and the urge to set the world straight. One cannot join these two successfully, but sometimes, in rare cases, something good or even great results from the attempt of the tormented spirit to reconcile them."

White loves the past. His is true nostalgia, full of detailed knowledge, avoiding stock responses. He is too humorous to be overtly sentimental, and usually too accurate. The Model-T Ford, which he eulogizes as mechanically uncanny in "Farewell, My Lovely!", was really not better than its successor. "Here Is New York" shows the city in 1948 as safer and kinder than it is now. White considers this essay a period piece, written about New York emerging from the depression. He loved it, though its face even then was pockmarked.

He is at his best when nostalgia merges with current observation and when the drift toward sentimentality turns to genuine emotion:

> Here in New England, each season carries a hundred foreshadowings of the season that is to follow—which is one of the things I love about it. Winter is rough and long, but spring lies all round about. Yesterday, a small white keel feather escaped from my goose and lodged in the bank boughs near the kitchen porch, where I spied it as I came home in the cold twilight. The minute I saw the feather, I was projected into May, knowing that a barn swallow would be along to claim the prize and use it to decorate the front edge of its nest. Immediately, the December air seemed full of wings of swallows and the warmth of barns. Swallows, I have noticed, never use any feather but a white one in their nest-building, and they always leave a lot of it showing, which makes me believe that they are interested not in the feather's insulating power but in its reflecting power, so that when they skim into the dark barn from the bright outdoors they will have a beacon to steer by.

REED WHITTEMORE

1919–

Edward Reed Whittemore II was born on September 11, 1919, in New Haven, Connecticut, to Edward Reed and Margaret (née Carr) Whittemore. He was educated at Yale University (A.B. 1941) and Princeton University. From 1941 to 1945 he served in the air force, achieving the rank of major. In 1952 he married Helen Lundeen; they have four children. He taught at Carleton College from 1947 to 1966, and edited the literary quarterly *Carleton Miscellany* from 1960 to 1964; since 1967 he has been a Professor of English at the University of Maryland. From 1939 to 1953 he edited *Furioso*, and was literary editor for the *New Republic* from 1969 to 1973. He served as a Consultant in Poetry for the Library of Congress from 1964 to 1965, and as an Interim Consultant from 1984 to 1985.

Whittemore published his first book of verse, *Heroes and Heroines*, in 1946; though it attracted some attention for his extension of the methods of William Carlos Williams, his next book was not published for another ten years (*An American Takes a Walk and Other Poems*, 1956). Since then he has been recognized as an important new poet in the American idiom, utilizing rhythms of speech and loose metrical structures, colloquial and open. Whittemore is both praised and criticized for his lightness of tone and subject and his sense of humor. Particularly important in his canon are the long poem "The Self-Made Man," included in *The Self-Made Man and Other Poems* (1959), and the collections *The Boy From Iowa: Poems and Essays* (1962), *Fifty Poems Fifty* (1970), and *The Mother's Breast and the Father's House* (1974). He has also written a biography of William Carlos Williams and several books of criticism, notably *Ways of Misunderstanding Poetry* (1965) and *From Zero to the Absolute* (1975). A retrospective entitled *The Feel of Rock: Poems of Three Decades* was published in 1982.

Works

POETRY

As a poet with certain very obvious and amusing gifts, Reed Whittemore is almost everyone's favorite. Certainly he is one of mine. Yet there are dangerous favorites and inconsequential favorites, and favorites like pleasant diseases. What of Whittemore? He is as wittily cultural as they come, he has read more than any young man anybody knows, has been all kinds of places, yet shuffles along in an old pair of tennis shoes and khaki pants, with his hands in his pockets, saying to every head-down, hustling graduate student he meets, "Shucks, fellow, don't take all this so seriously. Learn, as I was born to know, that all literature, all life, is secretly funny." How does this attitude get into the poems Whittemore writes? The mechanics of the transition, Whittemore tells us in "A Week of Doodle," are effected something like this:

> It [doodling] does, in my case, for my work, what others expect
> Of courses in writing—how to express and impress;
> And improves my condition no end in a different respect
> Since, in a pinch, I can sell it for (minor) verse.

That is modest enough, though fortunately Whittemore is a great deal better.

> I prefer to sit very still on the couch, watching
> All the inanimate things of my daytime life—
> The furniture and the curtains, the pictures and books—
> Come alive,
> Not as in some childish fantasy, the chairs dancing
> And Disney prancing backstage, but with dignity . . .

There is a good soberness here, despite the whack at Disney. The passage is never very far from treating the whole mood as a joke, but it is never too near it, either. The felt and unspoken imminence of cutting humor gives the lines the characteristic tone, the good compression present in the best Whittemore poems, and from this balance of an almost fundamental distrust of appearances and a calculating good humor something else emerges: a sense that humor is used in these poems as the most adequate of defenses, or perhaps as the only defense, against things that no ordinary satirist would let in: serious commitment to the subjects he writes about (instead of commitment to their opposites), or total chaos, or poetry. You feel that you shouldn't insist on this too strenuously, however, for Whittemore is wickedly delightful, deft as Willie Hoppe, as good in spots as Auden himself, and a great deal more fun. Yet, as I have been suggesting, something else keeps grazing these poems, and the mind that reads them: something more valuable, more difficult than the poems themselves would have you believe anything is.

As he stands, Whittemore has plenty of whatever it takes to get you to "reassess the world around you," and is not much interested in the other thing, that makes you *like*, or hate in any significant way, anything you know, or think you know. The Subjects of the world stand around you, during your reading of Whittemore's poems, revealed in their inconsequentially ridiculous, very recognizable, and humorously contemptible attitudes, and never in their most deeply characteristic and unknown gestures, in unmanageable love. I suppose this is to say that Whittemore is essentially a satirist—yet even as I write I am not sure of that "essentially." But it *is* true that almost all the poems here ⟨*An American Takes a Walk*⟩ are full of very telling satiric invention and observation, Americanized Auden, and "wonderful fun" (as in "Paul Revere's Ride," which is just that). For Whittemore is himself the perfect *Furioso* poet. Certainly I never saw anything published in that genuinely-lamented magazine half so good of its kind as the best of these poems. Yet . . . what *is* it, exactly, in terms of the immovable values of real poetry, to be or to have been "the perfect *Furioso* poet"? To have been wittily uncommitted to anything save a few vague humanistic principles that have no issue except to mock, condescendingly and as from a great distance, inhumanly cool with the scintillant remove of knowledgeable superiority, a few of the things we are all against: War, the City, the Army, Science Divorced from Man? To have said to one's eager Cerberus, before the beginnings of dozens of poems, "Keep those three heads grinning. Not laughing. Not growling. Just keep the same expression that's always served us as the very Face and Image of Wit. Nothing living can get past that look." Strength of feeling, it is true, uncritical and breathless with unsanction, comes in a few times, but, save in one or two wonderful exceptions, the effect is that of a jar, and we tend to look up guiltily, saying, "What is *wrong* with Whittemore here, anyway?" Yet we are saying this of the poet who wrote, "And the laced-in hazards of the covert hills," and, for anybody's terror and helpless acquiescence, "Caught in an offshore breeze / A butterfly will turn / Too late to fight the air . . ." Truly hearing the way that "fight" works, no one could argue the effectiveness of this passage. Yet it is more than *effective*. If the theory of the "objective correlative" takes any value from examples, it ought to stand deep in the theorist's mind through this one, bearing with it all the latent terror of the natural world. The image realized here is part of that world, and finally that of man, gained, in an unforeseen and indispensable way, through Whittemore's words. Of the two (or more) poets in Whittemore, I should like most to see the one who wrote those lines emerge. Yet this is not really to posit a choice. May we not have cutting and transitory delight, and the unabashed lyric world, too?—JAMES DICKEY, "Five Poets," *Poetry*, Nov. 1956, pp.115–17

Two mock epics contain the unifying theme in this selection of Reed Whittemore's 1957–1962 writings ⟨*The Boy from Iowa*⟩, which seems at first glance a book of poems and a book of essays arbitrarily bound together. For like the hero of his title poem, Whittemore throughout his work keeps demanding, "How has (gol darn it) it come to pass / That I am . . . *so* middle class?" In an essay, Whittemore calls one of his own poems "a middle class business" and suggests that no writer can be honest unless he is in some sense a revolutionary. No hurler of sizzle-fused cannonballs but an associate professor of English who didn't take a graduate degree, Whittemore seeks honesty for his own revolutionary principle.

All nine beautiful essays set out in one way or another to do just this. They blast whatever institutions of our play-it-safe society prevent us from saying and doing what we believe: the gift shoppe with its sickly cute greeting cards, the hard-sell campaigns of organized charity. Why Whittemore's concerns are so broad is apparent from his essay "A Brief History of a Little Magazine," which concludes that a literary periodical can't confine itself to the "merely literary life". (He realized he was editing *Furioso* not for people who wanted to read it, but for those with manuscripts of their own to sell and for publishers' talent-scouts.) Written in what may be at the moment one of the lithest prose styles going, the essays are bitter-witted harangues by an engaging egoist.

But Whittemore doesn't eschew speaking now and then of the literary life, about which he has much more worth saying than most of us. One of his concerns is the role of the writer as teacher; and in another essay he argues that courses in creative writing ought not to be for creative writers. It is the mock epics, however, that really sum up his sense of the absurdity of being a writer in a world wherein fewer and fewer people want to read. Besides "The Boy from Iowa," there is "The Odyssey of a B**t." Each is ambitious to the extent of several cantos. It is too bad they aren't more painstakingly written, more consistently funny. They should be, for Whittemore lacks neither skill nor wit, and as the essays plainly show, possesses the chief requisite of a great mock epic: a clear-cut principle (honesty) by which to assail the ridiculous. Yet he seems unsure whether to take for his model Byron's *Don Juan* or the work of Ogden Nash. The poems too obviously keep digging us in the ribs, advertising their own deliberate comic ineptitudes: the forced rimes (*readah* with *he'd a-/ chieved*), the wrenched inversions. Moments are funny indeed: the invocation to the reader as Muse, and a remark about how hard it is to write a Homeric simile:

I know a fellow who started one ages ago;
At eighty he drowned, still paddling toward his "So".

But Whittemore's goofy heroes (the Iowan weary of suburbia who simply plunks himself into the Atlantic, the ex-coffeeshop bard who switches to addressing Lions' clubs) seem shadowy bit-players. The poet himself keeps stealing their scenes from them. And it's a good thing he does, too, for the funniest, most penetrating thrusts occur in his own interpolations.

Like the mock epics, nine shorter poems written since Whittemore's last gathering, *The Self-Made Man* (1959), exemplify the tenets of his criticism. An essay on "The 'Modern Idiom' of Poetry" makes these tenets clear or easily inferable: shun rhetoric, don't be symbolic or metaphysical, seek your own honest and colloquial voice. By these principles Whittemore's non-narrative poems succeed well, but occasionally they have the admirable flaw of sounding (as the mock epics also do) as if the speaker just can't take himself very long in earnest. (For a wonderful soliloquy slightly loused by levity, see "Three Poems to Jackson," with its dragged-in hipster talk.) He is afraid that his agonies are only "Mild, middle-class agonies from which drink / Or publication / Or the purchase of something expensive, maybe a car" will relieve him.

And yet I can't think of anyone else writing poetry today who is actually getting these fears down on paper. In Whittemore, we are up against a mind that nourishes itself in the actual world, that doesn't depend entirely on itself, or on other people's literature. This book won't take the place of the full collection of best Whittemore articles, reviews, and editorials that there ought to be. But these essays must be read side by side with the poems to be seen for what they are: one of the most devastating and compassionate attacks on two-car owning America yet written by a poet on the inside.—X. J. KENNEDY, "Reed Whittemore's Mock Epics," *Poetry*, Feb. 1963, pp. 356–57

In so many of Reed Whittemore's poems ⟨in *Poems: New and Selected*⟩, the ear is flawless. His voice is perfectly pitched, immaculate, suave, urbane. There are no slips, no mistakes—if he trips, it is always accidentally-on-purpose, he comes up smiling, and we smile with him, not at him. He is one of our dwindling few tasteful and intelligent satirists, and we don't dare risk putting him off on some other track; but we do wish he would surprise us a bit more.

When the good poem starts to unwind, to uncoil, it serpentines cunningly, and as the poem rises to a perfect little loop at the finish, and sticks its little forked tongue out at me, I am genuinely tickled and stung. But there is always a moment just before the finish when I want to slash through the poem's sleek hide and expose the rough second skin, and this devilishness of mine lingers with me as an aftertaste when I finish reading the poem. With ample selections from all his previous books before me, I am reminded that Whittemore's style, tone, manner, and range of targets had become too predictable. He has stuck to the same mode for so long, I had begun to associate only one type of poetry with him—the low guttural chuckle of a highbrow Ogden Nash. Perhaps the comparison is unfair; his sensibility is sophisticated, closer to Jules Feiffer's cartoons.

In general, I think we enjoy reading Whittemore to the extent that he is in a pleasurable mood when he writes. When he seems hampered from within by a nondescript small poison that he can't rout out of his system, the tone becomes quizzical, self-chiding, and poetry loses its charm, as in "The Philadelphia Vireo":

> It's a bad day and I feel like a fool out here with the
> birds,
> And now I'm writing these lines, dissonant things,
> and thinking bird things,
> Because I'm a bloody professional bird and must
> damn well sing.
> So I sing: chirk, chirk.

Now and then, particularly in the recent poems, there is a nihilistic tendency to turn the eye of his wit back on itself, shaming him into a state of jaded withdrawal.

Among my favorites in the section of new work are the vivifying family poems, ranging from the explicit tenderness and father-son chumminess of "clamming" to the throwing of sardonic poison-pen-darts in "The Bad Daddy":

> And anyway you should know that your mother and
> I
> Really think you're a frightful bitch. Love, Dad.
> So now the bad Daddy feels much much more like
> himself.
> His typewriter pants pleasantly in its shed; the beast is
> fed.
> Down the long waste of his year he sees, suddenly,
> violets.
> He picks them and crushes them gently, and is at
> peace.
> Gettem all, bad Daddy, and sleep now.

The most memorable single poem is the caustic and wildly funny "Dear God," a mock-heroic lampoon against foundation-supported American artists, exposing their moral grandiosity, as well as their leaning to opportunism and grantsmanship. But I am most taken with "Six Shaggy," a sequence of poems in which a new manner seems to be emerging. Halting rhythms, inverted syntax, a roughing around the edges of the line, more verbal texture and compression of effects—all add up to a significant redirection in Whittemore's art:

> Once upon a time, a long time not ago, in Flint,
> Mish.,
> Lived a man who was very affluent and well-to-do
> and rish
> With six sweet children lovely and long shiny motor
> cars three
> And a wife *charmante* and a home *charmante* and a
> thoroughly life happy,
> When in the midst mist leafy of a Flint-gorgeous
> warful Fall
> Pronto this man popped out with symptoms several
> of withdrawal.

At times, there are knotty, gymnastic rhythms in these poems that seem difficult for the sheer sake of exercising the reader's ear to unravel them—devices that seem to be derived from the art of Berryman's *Dream Songs*—nevertheless, it is a fresh and promising tone frequency that could lead to a strangely alive new scale in Whittemore's art.—LAURENCE LIEBERMAN, "The Expansional Poet: A Return to Reality," *YR*, Winter 1968, pp. 267–69

If, like Holden Caulfield, one's criterion for a good writer is that he be someone "you want to call up," Reed Whittemore qualifies. In his work, there is a highly attractive blend of wit, warmth and fury that could send a like-minded reader straight to the phone. In spite of the fact that it is for the most part a sad and occasionally horrifying vision of the contemporary scene, there is great satisfaction—a rare commodity—in reading Whittemore's work.

The new poems, and selected earlier poems, of this volume (*The Mother's Breast and the Father's House*) give a clear picture of what Whittemore intends to do and how he goes about it. He is, to begin with, one of those rare-as-the-whooping-crane poets who are sincerely, by temperament, conviction and ability, political poets. If he has narrowed his possible range—and he has—it seems to be because, moving as well and strongly as he does within this territory, he regards it as his proper field. Being a poet of intellect and self-questioning, he is acutely aware of the limits he has set. In "Jackson in Winter" he ironically forecasts his forthcoming book:

> . . . making few affirmations, avoiding inversions,
> Using iambics distrustfully, favoring lines
> of odd lengths and irony.

But the problem goes a lot deeper than that. There is a healthy terror of the era's most pompously and slickly exploited word: *love*. There is a beautiful dignity in the lines:

> If there is love
> and I think there is
> It survives the saying only with difficulty
> It needs prayer rather
> I will not play with it

The trouble is that the last line promises only the negative half of a good thing. In the slush of hyprocrisy, self-righteousness and self-delusion in which all aspects of love often seem mired, it is perhaps the more important half. But the fact is that Whittemore is so repelled by the prospect, or even the possibility of the superficial, the maudlin, the fake, that he tightens up at the approach of any emotion other than that of fury, disdain or dismay, and takes refuge in irony, wit, advertizeese mocking itself.

There are few things more annoying in a critic than persistence in telling the poet what he should be doing instead of considering what he has done. But it is impossible to read Whittemore thoroughly, and to sense the emotional capability in his work, without regretting that he has decided that the cliffs above bathos and easy emotion are too slippery to climb, even in search of the rarest game. In doing so, he has settled for a tone of somber wit and music-hall bitterness, which makes his work tough, viable, rewarding, but more limited, and dryer in its sources, that it need be, given its intuition and force. It seems a shame.

This choice is increasingly in evidence in the new poems. And to stop considering what Whittemore might do if he chose, and consider what he has done in this collection, is to realize that these poems are more important now than they would have been two months ago, when their message would have been more facilely accepted; because their anger and disgust, their outrage about the state of the national soul, spring from causes deeper than one man, more difficult of solution than a dozen political scandals.

For 40 years there have been American poetic voices crying "Usura!" "Moloch!" But Whittemore is more fiercely rational, and his poems are very frightening indeed. No Utopian, he accepts the odds that

> . . . our love is the kingdom of the 10% joy the 15%
> satisfaction the 20% love
> That exists and will continue to exist beyond all
> misery. . . .

However what he cannot consider without rage is a ravening greed that he sees as tearing his land apart: the power of money, the money of power; money as a discrete cause.

> It is robbery it is stealing it is theft
> It is taking away the earnings of labor
> And giving to those who do not labor. . .

And he is equally tough on the prophets who "have prattled about revolution and pocketed the proceeds."

> They have built the hysteria of constant and drastic
> social change into each breakfast
> They have taught our children how to stop war on
> Monday poverty on
> Tuesday racism on Wednesday sexism on Thursday
> and final exams on Friday . . .

He is so perfectly accurate that one might forget how somber his conclusion is:

> We are on the edge
> . . . Get wise
> Get the crooks where they are see!
> they are in
> MONEY

Though there are better poems here than the poems of denunciation ("Lines," the gentle, fey and terrifying "Abominable Snowman," the uncharacteristically tender "Mrs. Benedict"), the denunciation is articulate, intelligent and right on target. And if we tend to say, on reading

> For make no mistake the money game
> as now played smells
> In the private sector
> In the public sector
> In the Congress and in the White House
> In the state capitals the city halls
> And the smells beyond smelling where the cartoon
> capitalists
> Hang out fat as ever taking their cut . . .

"ah, yes, that was awful," as we bask—with good reason—in the candor of a smile and the good breeze of openness, we would do well to dig for those roots, postulated in these poems, that nourished the "money game." Whether because of its salutary warnings, or of its strong and straightforward poetry, it's a book to value, and to keep at hand.—JOSEPHINE JACOBSEN, "Political Poet," *NR*, Oct. 12, 1974, pp. 28–29

PROSE

In the last few years, the poetry ⟨of William Carlos Williams⟩, at least, has come increasingly to be acknowledged for what it surely is: among the work of American poets in this century, singularly powerful and alive. Behind this judgment stands a revaluation of the myth of a rootless modernism. As critics so diverse as Richard Ellmann, Hugh Kenner, and Harold Bloom endeavor to establish the importance to modernism of homeland, tradition, and "influence," it is no wonder that not only Williams's art, but also his life, with its complex but unequivocal commitment to what Whittemore calls the "normalcies"—paying the bills, serving on committees—has come to seem significant and brave.

In its attitude toward Williams's modernism, Whittemore's *William Carlos Williams: Poet from Jersey* partakes in its own way of the current revisionary impulse. The chapter he calls "Moment of the Twenties" is a good example. Williams spent most of that decade in his attic, producing, among other things, the book of historical-biographical sketches called *In the American Grain*. It is an extraordinarily difficult text, with an odd mixture of inwardness and historical narrative, and neither the conditions of its writing nor the nature of its project seem typical of its particular literary "moment." But Whittemore's acute reading shows not only the close relation between Williams's personal tensions and fears and the "anti-puritan obsession" of the text, but also the extent to which, as a consequence of that relation, the book is indeed a "20's" artifact: anti-puritanism is after all the animating impulse of, say, *Tender Is the Night*, though Williams's treatment is both more heated and more thoughtful than the novel's—closer, as Whittemore chooses to say, to Lawrence than to Fitzgerald.

It is not, precisely, a critical biography that Whittemore has written. Few individual works are studied in detail. Rather, the strength of this biography lies in its illuminating account of Williams in relation to the literary movements with which he had more or less to do at various points in his development, beginning with Imagism and Cubism in the early 1900's, through Objectivism and Social Realism, to the Black Mountain and San Francisco schools of the 50's. Whittemore is at his most skillful in demonstrating the poet's participation in, and detachment from, the long parade of such "isms." The drama of any writer's career is the emergence of his individual voice from the competition of attachments, tastes, models. In Williams's case it is the drama of his near-approach to poetic ideologies, his unfailing openness to their value, and his ultimate reassertion, after each encounter, of a unique poetic identity. ⟨. . .⟩

Whittemore's book is interesting and valuable; the main objections are to its style. Its plainspokenness, for example, reflecting Williams's own famous anti-academicism, is laudable in itself, but occasionally results in oversimplification and pointless flippancy. As for the facts of Williams's life, they have nowhere else been so completely gathered and arranged. Whittemore clears up for the first time the story of how Williams's appointment as Poetry Consultant to the Library of Congress was delayed and finally made impossible by the political climate of 1952. On the whole, however, there is a curious sparseness of anecdote, and Whittemore does seem at times to be writing with an air of secrecy, as though entrusted with confidences he cannot betray. He has apparently had access to a great deal of material not available before now, but seems to feel that the moment for complete openness about Williams's personal life has not yet come. Until it does, the present biography is certainly the most intelligent and thorough account we have of the poet's life.—JOHN ROMANO, "A Poet's Life," *Cmty*, May 1976, pp. 81–82

For a hundred years certain avant-garde writers urged a separation between art and life. The modernists, whose gods were Flaubert and Baudelaire, decreed that the work of art was answerable only to itself, its own internal laws of style and structure. The poet does not serve the world.

Reed Whittemore will have none of this: he wants writers to respond to the needs of society. He calls for "critical realism," writing that fixes its attention on "people and their plight." He wants a literature of social and historical awareness, subordinating the writer's private life to the general welfare.

Accordingly, in 1969 Whittemore made himself a guinea pig. A poet and teacher of English, he went to work as a journalist. For four years on *The New Republic* he reviewed books about many things: race relations, the New Left, Lindbergh, the Lone Eagle and Senator Eagleton, who seemed even loner. He wrote essays on the Gallup Poll and the Teapot Dome scandal. He wrote articles on TV. The only subject he seems not to have discussed with any real bite is poetry. This is odd, for no doubt the editors of *The New Republic* thought that when they hired a poet to do reviewing they would have secured that flank, if anyone cared.

I have searched *The Poet as Journalist* in vain for an explanation of poetry that could not have been made by someone who stopped liking it 30 years ago. There is a low bow to Ezra Pound, with no judgment, however, concerning his fascism and anti-Semitism—a remarkable omission in view of Whittemore's insistence on writers' being socially responsible. There are brief discussions of Eliot, Cummings, Macleish, Ogden Nash and other "name" poets. Ginsberg and his *Howl* are mentioned as significant—of something that Whittemore doesn't want to touch with a 10-foot pole. Newsworthy people such as Kenneth Koch and the Beatles are duly noted. But in general Whittemore thinks that the current scene in poetry is "sick," and he accuses poets of not talking about and to the life that surrounds them. The writing he would like to see would involve writers' "thinking of the writing act as a service to society rather than, or over and above, service to self—and nobody who deems of being a writer in this unhappy country ever has such a thought."

William Blake, in his notes scribbled in the margin of Joshua Reynolds' writings on painting, has this remark: "This man was hired to depress art." When I see Whittemore's explanations of modern poetry I have the same feeling. There are, in fact, several American poets who believe that they are performing a service to society. Denise Levertov was outspoken against the war in Vietnam; Gary Snyder has written about ecology; Adrienne Rich is writing on behalf of women. I could name a dozen others who are just as "engaged." Whittemore's criticism strikes me as a rationalization of his distaste for the kind of single-minded absorption that serious writers have. It is not what they write about or don't write about that he dislikes, but their pretensions. It is significant that he doesn't blame lightweight, civilized poets such as Ogden Nash and the later W. H. Auden for not being responsible. He has great tolerance for writers of light verse.

Whittemore is more reliable when he is dealing with culture. One of the longer pieces describes a journey he made to Russia. He asked some questions about "forbidden" writers, Solzhenitsyn, Mandelstam, Brodsky, and was given to understand that the questions were out of place. His account of a Sunday morning in Moscow is one of the memorable passages in his book. When he is not venting his opinions Whittemore can evoke a situation:

"The crowds were so large—and mixed in with the civilians were so many platoons of the Red army, tough young farm boys careening along in brown phalanxes—that the sidewalk seemed a great river with the current always against us, and we did not want to go to the Kremlin at all and look at those churches but go back to the hotel and shut the door. We were fragile; we might not last there." Whittemore gave a few talks to the Russians about American writing. I can imagine the impression he gave of our poetry.

The writing about TV is accurate and amusing. Whittemore deplores the brainwash of advertising, which is obviously what killed the medium, right at the start, as any kind of serious entertainment. I am glad to see that he doesn't praise the programs that are touted as "culture"—mere eyewash to placate the viewers. He prefers Lucy, and I prefer old movies.

Whittemore attacks the "commodity system" in book publishing as well as TV. Publishers are governed by what will sell, and so are big-name writers!

> I see us slowly being *not* asphyxiated by car fumes, and *not* drowned in oil, and *not* submerged by old tin cans, but buried intellectually, spiritually and physically by Mickey Spillane, Norman Mailer, Simenon . . . by Doubleday, Random House . . . and by a whole fleet of journalists and the like who make their living by words.

"Journalists and the like" would include Whittemore himself. There is a tone of self-denigration in this writing—denigration not only of the author but what he does. This may be why I find Whittemore unsympathetic, though I agree in theory with some of his opinions. Obviously America is being polluted, the air waves as well as the beaches, and Whittemore has sensible ideas for cleaning up the mess. At times he even comes on as a kind of socialist. But I feel that while he may be moved against things, he isn't really moved on behalf of people. He writes with acerbity, rarely with affection. The message I get is that even if our present social ills were cured, Americans still wouldn't like one another.—LOUIS SIMPSON, *NYTBR*, July 25, 1976, pp. 6–7

MICHAEL BENEDIKT

"Listening and Not Listening"

Poetry, June 1968, pp. 194–98

Appearances and his own reputation aside (bolstered by such extra-poetic activities as his editing of the jolly old *Furioso*, and its successor-magazine, *The Carleton Miscellany*), there is nothing particularly hilarious about the poetry of Reed Whittemore. One might have grown suspicious about the critical truism about Whittemore's funniness from the phenomenon that though most of those who have written about him think Whittemore is best characterized by mirthfulness, almost nobody accuses him of writing light verse. Somewhere an overlap lurks, needing accounting for. Whittemore is, in fact, a poet of spiritual misery. The particular kind of spiritual misery engaged in his work has to do with the utter emptiness of all the realities—but especially the American reality—around him. And, as other conscientious Americans can readily testify, there is not much room for joking here. The idea in Whittemore's work, particularly his earliest work, is, moreover, an idea which many American thinkers have put forth: that America is a kind of *tabula rasa*, but one whose inordinate beauty has become inordinately spoiled in proportion. "How in that Eden could Adam / Be lost," the poet wondered in the title poem of his second volume, *An American Takes a Walk* (1956). As that title suggests, Whittemore sees all things, even walking, as being somehow conditioned by the peculiar realities of the U.S. He even feels that his own existence, as a poet, is not free from it. "The Self-Made Man," the title poem of his third volume (1959), goes so far as to see in the American poet a certain breed of representative American. Whittemore's archetypal "self-made man", here and throughout the work, is one, who, after

> Making a pile in the market . . . put his old mother
> To pasture and started to buy things—
> Planes, wives, ranches—until he could look
> For miles in any direction and see only
> His own, very own creations, and thus was led
> Into philosophy, where he bred

A phoenix as mascot and climbed onto rostrums. . . .

Philosophically, it seems to me that there are some startling problems here. This idea of America as an Eden, for example, is appealing as a kind of "conceit", worthy of a modern metaphysical (which Whittemore, one of the first post-war poets to emerge, *is* in a sense); but is it a concept solid enough from which to project a contemporary, somewhat sociologically oriented poetry? Surely present wisdom tells us that the Adamic American is simply a European Methuselah, transplanted. As a poet, one perhaps needs to be a kind of visionary, like Whitman or Crane, to erect a considered philosophy on a belief both so odd and so weary: already we are apt to value the nineteenth century American prose theorists of this belief as interesting more for their appealing quirkiness than for their accuracy. Whittemore's omnipresent wish to analyze is thus in part undermined by a feyness in the basic stuff of his assumptions.

A further difficulty: why should the key figure around whom his philosophy revolves—the indigenous man of affairs and the indigenous poet, whom he pictures as identical—stand indeed? Whittemore is certainly right to find such a connection between the materialistic and the spiritual piquant ("With considerable bother / He had shown his father / You can never tell / What will sell" ends his verse biography of—of all people—Tennyson); but it is wrong, I think, to expand the dossier of odds and ends into a casebook about the character of an entire country, much less its poets. The problem is that the American who takes a walk, the self-made man around whom, in a recent poem, "The Seven Days," Whittemore sees all creation turning is too particularized; he is, in truth, identical with Whittemore himself. Whittemore's work with the *Miscellany*, his present labors as a kind of advisor to Washington on little-magazine matters, and his various capacities in between—that of teacher, most prominently, but also his appearances as a valued member of a wide spectrum of cultural conclaves—have resulted in his wielding an unusual amount of power, as poets go. Indeed, about a third of the pieces in the *Poems: New and Selected* were clearly written in connection with if not actually *at* these public festivals of intellect: we can commit no biographical fallacy here! These poems are unnecessarily long, bitterly ironical, and on every level unnecessarily self-lacerating, it seems to me (from "The Cultural Conference": "The author, critic and cultural messenger (me) / Comes to the cultural conference with snap-on tie, . . ."). It makes no difference that whether the connection is modest, as in the early "The Teacher," or grander, as in the recent "Return, Alpheus: A Poem for the Literary Elders of Phi Beta Kappa," the poet's responses are negative. Even discontentment does not permit these poems to transcend their category. Like Tennyson, Whittemore is more successful in his role of man of affairs than in his poems of affairs.

Whittemore's best poems have the habit of dealing not with the folkways of art, but with the processes of art. There is an exhilarating lack of consideration of art as the burden of some kind of cultural colonist; and a concentration on its actually sustaining pleasures. Among his poems are many in which he attends to the positive and real task of examining the things that he has really been up to (and insistently so, for all his "doubts", since 1946, when his first book, *Heroes and Heroines*, was published). There are some beautiful, unembarrassed poems in this section, poems which, even better than being thematically "serious", are tough. Such a piece as "The Philadelphia Vireo" has a justness which none of the lamentations in the longer poems about the burdensomeness of public intellectual life, can touch:

> It's a bad day and I feel like a fool out here with the birds,
> And now I'm writing these lines, dissonant things, and thinking bird things,
> Because I'm a bloody professional bird and must damn well sing.
> So I sing: chrrk. chrrk.
> But why should I run down the birds? They have energy; they are strange.
> There is wonder in energy, strangeness. Art needs that; man needs that;
> And I seem to be in these woods for that, . . .

Perhaps because here the artist concentrates on the things he knows best—almost all of them having to do with the mysterious compulsions of art—these poems tend to be more compact than the other class of work. They tend to revolve around a single symbol, like the Vireo, instead of partaking of the structure of tract, or of diffuse public speech. Here are some startlingly lyrical, though truly tough, unyielding poems. As at the close of "A Porch Chair," in which a simple rocking-chair is presented as a symbol of art and wildness (the poem closes: "Now . . . he is not playing. / He sits on the porch holding tight, with his eyes closed, / As the wind freshens."). There is a grudgingly rueful joy even in "The Radio under the Bed," in which art, even vulgar popular art (though a more thoroughly modern meditator might consider this judgment itself vulgar; are the American poets of the 1930s really better artists than Cole Porter or Gershwin?) is pictured as somehow sustaining: ". . . the songs still remain, the old vulgar songs, and will play me, / Tum-te-tum, tum-te-tum, into my grave." This pleasure is sharply reflected in two poems from the old and new part of the book which might almost be sequels. "In September / A great many high school bands beat a great many drums, / And the silences after their partings are very deep," ends a poem called "The High School Band." The silences echo not only in the parental heads but, we learn in "Summer Concert," the silences echo in the halls of art. "We could get the whole town out on a Tuesday night," Whittemore notes, but upon awakening the morning after the concert "It was dead, dead, dead under the shingles, . . ." This genre of delicate poem about a (guarded) love of art is, happily, only slightly less frequent, despite the increasing number of roles the author has chosen to assume. Poems of the excellent genre from the *Old Poems* include: "Travel," "Still Life," "On a Summer Sunday," "The Girl Friend," "After Some Day of Decision," "The Kaylavasi," "The Farmhouse," "A Storm from the East," "The Radio under the Bed," "An Early Call," "The Party," "A Floridian Museum of Art," "A Porch Chair I," and "The High School Band"; from the *Selected* part: "Summer Concert," "The Philadelphia Vireo," "The Fourth of July," "The Citizens Haven't Been Able," "The Genie," "The Departure," "The Bad Daddy," "The Bad Knight," and "Clamming." The last two are particularly strong poems and particularly strong as advice. "Knight" speaks admiringly of "a vinegar soul . . . entered . . . against the siropy souls of romance . . . But the ladies, the ladies, despise him. He does his work." In "Clamming" the poet wisely advises his son to leave off dramatizing his deeds when he hunts the bivalve, lest he "inhibit [his own] children and sicken / At last into opera on somebody's sandbar. Son, when you clam / Clam." Would that Whittemore would exclusively clam while clamming! Would that he would more economically "do his work"! "On a Summer Sunday," one of his very finest poems, has not only the zest of Whittemore's best art—the elegantly formed free-verse periods, the bright and often delicate use of rhymes—but it is a distillation of the excellence of his best moments as a man. It is, it would seem, precisely a praise of the paradise of art:

On that midsummer Sunday
Of naps, birds, children and slamming doors,
The mind withdrew to its den in a green wood
And listened and did not listen to the desultory
Sunday anarchy of neighbors.
Into the den
Shakespeare and Dante and soft furry poets slipped
And lay down; out of it sauntered
Miscellaneous nonsense in stocking feet.

And that day,
That somnolent summer Sunday day,
Crept away, crept away
To deep and delicate distances, as the den
And the wood and the mind unobtrusively darkened,
And the birds and the children slept, and the doors
were still.

RUDY WIEBE

1934–

Rudy Henry Wiebe was born on October 4, 1934, in Fairholme, Saskatchewan, to Abraham J. and Tena (née Knelsen) Wiebe. He was educated at the University of Alberta (B.A. 1956, M.A. 1960), the University of Tübingen, Germany, the University of Manitoba, and the University of Iowa. In 1958 he married Tena F. Isaak; they have three children. He was a research officer for the Glenbow Foundation in Calgary in 1956 and a foreign service officer in Ottawa in 1960; in addition, he has taught in high schools and universities, including Goshen College in Indiana and the University of Alberta. He edited the Mennonite Brethren *Herald* from 1962 to 1963.

Wiebe is a prolific novelist, anthologist, and short-story writer. His first novel, *Peace Shall Destroy Many*, was published in 1962; eighteen novels and collections of stories have followed. His work is suffused with the Mennonite faith in which he was reared, and probes the nature of faith, commitment, and the importance of individual action. *The Blue Mountains of China* (1970), an ambitious novel about a people on a quest for paradise, was his first book to receive a significant amount of attention; it was followed by his most successful novel to date, *The Temptations of Big Bear* (1973), in which he attempts to view history and modern culture through the eyes of the American Indians. It is heavily reliant upon oral tradition and the rhythms of speech for its effects, and amounts to an incisive indictment of the standard methods of viewing history and culture through the perceptions of the ruling class. Though some critics feel Wiebe occasionally allows his moral concerns to overwhelm his prose, his work is consistently praised for its heartfelt approach and ability to make the reader reconsider his preconceptions. Recent novels, particularly *The Scorched-Wood People* (1977), *The Mad Trapper* (1980), and *My Lovely Enemy* (1983), have continued to add to Wiebe's reputation as one of Canada's most distinctive voices. Most of his short fiction is collected in *Where Is the Voice Coming From?* (1974) and *The Angel of the Tar Sands and Other Stories* (1982). He has also written a play, some criticism, and cultural essays; in addition, Wiebe has edited a number of anthologies of Canadian literature and folklore. He lives in Edmonton, Alberta.

PATRICIA A. MORLEY
"From One Blood Created"
The Comedians: Hugh Hood and Rudy Wiebe
1977, pp. 97–107

Wiebe's fourth novel is a tragedy of order, a stark portrait of a conflict between two cultures in which one culture is doomed to defeat. It is at the same time the individual tragedy of a man who embodies the best of the Indian culture and whose death signifies its fate. *The Temptations of Big Bear* is a spiritual history of one man's love for a land and a people, of his hopes for peace and universal brotherhood, and his reverence for the Only One or Great Spirit, the life-giver. The brooding presence of Big Bear dominates the long and involved narrative.

The novel is a piece of Canadian history, the story of the nineteenth-century land grab told primarily from the Indians' point of view. It is also an allegory of many of the might-is-right actions going on today, including the James Bay power project. Its six parts cover events between September, 1876, and January, 1888. Big Bear, head of a loose confederacy of Cree Indians called The People, is the last chief to resist the treaty offers of Her Majesty's government. For some years the whites have been offering to the various chiefs small reserves, money, and food in times of famine, in exchange for the hundreds of thousands of square miles we call Canada. Who could imagine so much land, thinks Lt. Governor Morris: "Thank God others would have to concern themselves with the continuing justice of it, thank God." Who would sign away such a land, Morris wonders. *As if they had a choice.*

The Indians have no choice. This becomes increasingly obvious as Wiebe's tale unrolls with tragic inevitability, building towards the Indian attack on the settlers at Frog Lake in 1885, the Indian defeat, and Big Bear's trial and imprisonment. The Indians are trapped by superior numbers, superior weapons and, worst of all, by the prospect of famine through the extinction of the buffalo herds upon which they depend.

Every single character in the novel, as Wiebe told Donald Cameron, is an historical person, and many of the facts and dates are absolutely accurate. Cameron called Wiebe's short story, entitled "Where Is the Voice Coming From?" a kind of dry run for the novel. Wiebe pointed out the difference in narrators while acknowledging that both story and novel assemble historical material in artistic form.[1] The short story tells of an Indian shoot-out with the RCMP in 1896; of the historical relics of the event and the wanted Indian as preserved in museums, and of the discrepancy between two descriptions of the Indian leader Almighty Voice and the photograph of him: "any face of history, any believed face that the world acknowledges as *man*—Socrates, Jesus, Attila, Genghis Khan, Mahatma Ghandi, Joseph Stalin—no believed face is more *man* than this face. . . . A steady look into those eyes cannot be endured. It is a face like an axe."[2] The entire Indian war with the whites is termed a war already lost the day the Cree watched Cartier hoist his gun ashore at Hochelaga and began the retreat west. White hypocrisy, a motif in the novel, is suggested in the short story by a derogatory, italicized refrain beginning *"hey injun"* which contrasts ironically with the language of official reports. Finally the voice, a death chant rising from among the dead, "so unbelievably high and strong in its unending wordless cry . . . no less incredible in its beauty than in its incomprehensible happiness." Big Bear is also famous for his voice. The short story brings an evocative power to the driest and barest of facts. It brings the bones to life, as in Ezekiel's vision. Perhaps both short story and novel should be described as christologies.

Wiebe told Cameron that he was writing the novel from the Indians' point of view, trying to catch their alienation and "totally different viewpoint." He admitted that this posed formal problems, but not *human* ones:

> They are human beings who have exactly the same kinds of longings and aspirations as we do. They want to be loved, they want to take care of their families—they have a much stronger sense of community than most white people do, mind you. But if you write about the basic human being, you've got an Indian, you've got an Eskimo, you've got a Mennonite, you've got a Scot. You can't whitewash them; they do some ugly things, sometimes because we don't understand the context in which they're doing them.[3]

It is Big Bear's *yearning* for brotherhood with all men which links the two worlds in the novel. The alien cultures are also linked through formal devices such as the whites who are sympathetic to the Indian point of view. Wiebe's primary sympathy lies with the Indians, yet he described the situation as a "hellish dilemma" for the white administrators and even for the missionaries. There are seldom easily rejected villains in tragedy, as there are in melodrama.

To the whites, land is something to be bought, owned, tamed, cultivated. The white concept of private property is alien to the communal and nomadic Indians. "Not quite $53,000 for a bit more than 50,000 square miles of grass and hills," gloats David Laird in his Annual Report for 1877. The dying Big Bear has a demonic vision of the world under white domination squared into right angles and divided by unending straight lines composed of bleached bones:

> . . . between the strange trees gleamed straight lines of, he comprehended it suddenly, white buildings. Square inedible mushrooms burst up under poplars overnight; but square . . . . He was seeing; the apprehension which the settler-clustered land of Manitoba and Winnipeg's square walls and gutted streets had begun drove like nails into the sockets of himself and his place was gone, he knew Earth and Sun which had been his gifts to accept and love and leave to others were gone, all gone.[4]

Despite the fact that the whites talk constantly about order, Big Bear sees their world as a greedy and chaotic one, a kind of inevitable devouring by "an insatiable gigantic beast wanting without bottom" (*BB* 62). He is further puzzled by their frantic restlessness, their habit of ripping up land and knocking down trees, their "desperate placelessness" (*BB* 101).

The *un*meeting of the two minds is revealed as the Indians parley with the whites to consider the proffered treaties. Wiebe catches the contrasts in a word-painting: stiff, scarlet rows of policemen at the foot of a flagpole, against a tent surrounded by hundreds of Indians, their warriors on horseback outlined against the sky. Colours are stark, not shaded, suggesting the inevitabilities of a situation where nothing can protect the Indians against the flow of surveyors, settlers, sickness, whisky traders, all destructive to the Indian way of life. Sweetgrass offers brotherhood while the whites *endure* Indian embraces and talk of the Grandmother's love for her Red Children. The Governor fears that the courtliness in the Indian Chiefs can never be conveyed to Ottawa or Britain.

Big Bear welcomes friendship, but says he is fed from Mother Earth by the Only One, not by the Grandmother. And Mother Earth belongs to all alike. The sudden flight of a horse suggests the Indians' wild freedom. Big Bear's fear of a rope around his neck is an image of white law and culture. Years before, he had had a demonic vision of Indians hanging from broken necks (a prophecy fulfilled in the novel). The Governor says the law is the same for white and red alike, a statement which is developed ironically and culminates in the trial of Big Bear. By this point, the reader is likely to find that the Governor's cliché has considerably less validity than it might have had at the beginning of the novel. White hypocrisy becomes one of the main motifs of the novel.

Big Bear's fate as tragic hero illustrates the rise and fall of the wheel of fortune commonly found in Shakespearean tragedy. His personal fortunes are in the ascendancy in the first half of the novel, including the sacred Thirst Dance in Part Three; they decline from this mid-point and the erosion of his power is finally evident in Part Four, when the Indians refuse to obey him at the Frog Lake Easter massacre of white settlers. It is Big Bear's integrity and greatness that make compromise impossible for him.[5] His tragedy follows inevitably from the collision of his being with his time and place.

The trial scene in Part Six provides a brilliant contrast of the two cultures. The legal rhetoric, which expresses hundreds of years of British mores, is farcical when one hears it (as we do at this point in the novel) with a sympathetic understanding of Big Bear's position. It is, of course, untranslatable into Indian, just as Zogliu's artificial rhetoric in *You Cant Get There from Here* cannot be expressed in the Ugeti language. Uncomprehending, and conscious of the many layers of wood between him and the earth, Big Bear listens to the "long snore" of the legal language and the few words of translation. The hypocrisy in white rhetoric is apparent in the chasm that looms between realities and the theoretical assumptions behind the law. The blatant distortions of Stanley Simpson are apparent to the reader, if not to the jury, and the stereotypes of white thought are exposed in the magistrate's "Was he a good Indian, or a bad

Indian?" William McLean testifies that Big Bear could not have pillaged, since there was no one in the Indian camp so wretchedly poor looking as him; Halpin adds that Big Bear had no horse but walked all the way to Fort Pitt, and was treated with contempt by the leading men of his band.[6] Big Bear's poverty is apparent at the trial. We see him through the sympathetic eyes of the young Kitty McLean: grey, unbuttoned prison shirt, cheap blanket of matted cotton exposing his dark chest, "hammered" face and eyes "tight as slits" (*BB* 383). Kitty's ironic view of liar Stanley "Pointnose" Simpson, pouring himself out like water pouches slit by a knife, provides comic relief. The verdict of *guilty* comes as no surprise.

The title of the novel suggests a medieval saint's tale, except for the curious incongruity of the Indian name. The author told Donald Cameron that his fourth novel is "totally non-religious in a formal sense," but "fantastically religious" in another way because of the religious attitude of Indian people. I find the first half of the statement surprising. The novel *is* religious in a formal sense, since the religious quality depends upon the way Wiebe has structured Big Bear's perceptions, and upon other formal elements such as imagery and narrative which support characterization.

Big Bear's temptations are to despair, to hate, to kill; to cheat, like his white opponents who ask to be trusted but whose written treaties take out half the "sweet things" promised earlier. With Sitting Bull, Big Bear considers killing, but knows this is not the answer. At the trial Big Bear looks around at chained Indians and rigid white faces, and thinks of his people hiding in the woods, fearful and starving. His heart staggers as he remembers the lost goodness of their past life. His thundering voice lifts in the small courtroom to say that it pleases the Great Spirit for men to do good. He pleads, not for himself, but for help for his people: "Is there nothing but punishment in the Grandmother's law?" Earlier, over a small campfire near Fort Pitt, Big Bear prayed to the Only One to "have pity on every human being who is poor like we are" (*BB* 335).

The strength and beauty of the portrait of the Indian chieftain lies in Wiebe's success in making Big Bear's spiritual depths absolutely congruous with a warrior, a hunter of great personal courage, a forceful leader of his people. Big Bear's incredible voice is linked to his religious vision and spiritual joy. At times the author guides the reader's reaction to Big Bear through the perspective of the young English girl, Kitty McLean. Kitty both loves and reveres the chieftain. His voice makes her legs turn to water; on one occasion she thinks of that voice as the sun, "all golden." Kitty aspires to be, like Big Bear, "a Person." She speaks Cree, and Big Bear talks with her while she is a prisoner of the band after the Frog Lake massacre. He serves her, doing the woman's work of spreading her wet clothes to dry over the rushes. Kitty's coldness (Wiebe employs a pattern of death imagery: blackness, cold, worms) turns to warmth as Big Bear dances and chants in the sun. The two are specks on the sand, surrounded by light. The scene ends with an ironic juxtaposition: "A month later she saw him again; in Prince Albert when he was led out for his daily exercise" (*BB* 315).

Wiebe's skill in revealing the spiritual affinity between the Indian and the land is most effective in the buffalo-hunting scene. Big Bear is still in his prime at the time. Wiebe catches the Indians' feeling for the hunt, for the wild buffalo whose freedom images their own, and for the Only One from whom they all come. The iron thong of the railway has split the land and is driving away the game, while in the south American soldiers are reputedly preventing some herds from moving north. The band is hungry and excitement runs high when Kingbird sights a small herd of buffalo. Big Bear prays, giving thanks and asking for a good running. He lies on the ground, open to its warmth and smells, "empty except of the hunt, the total consuming unconscious joy of one more run merging with *mus-too-wuk* given once more . . . ." He thinks of the crawling iron road and the innumerable soldiers. But the sixteen buffalo are everything that could be asked for life at this moment.

Wiebe's language is generally simpler, less involuted in this novel than in earlier work. But the long rhythmic sentences in the description of the buffalo hunt[7] catch the rhythm of the pounding hooves and suggest the mystic oneness of creation:

> He was the curl of a giant wave breaking down upon and racing up the good beach of earth . . . . the buffalo effortlessly fanned out before him in the lovely grace of tumbleweed lifting to the western wind. The gashed wounds left in the cows' shoulders and flanks by hunters they had once and then again outrun dripped brilliant red in the rhythmic bunch and release of their muscles, simply beautiful black crusted roses in the green and blue paradise of their running . . . . Then there was only the cow, floating strong, floating nearer wave by wave . . . and he felt life surging like sweet water within her, her heart in that violent, happy thunder as she ran true the great curve of earth . . . . (*BB* 128–9)

The novel is linked with two major motifs, *sun* and *rock*. These patterns converge in the ending and help to create the final mood of peace, acceptance, even joy, which surrounds Big Bear's death. *Rock* is the eternal grandfather, the unchanging certainty, as Big Bear tells Kitty McLean, "the first of all beings as well as the last" (*BB* 315). *Sun* is the life-giver. Kitty thinks of the Chieftain's voice as golden, sun-filled.

Circle images occur frequently in relation to the land, human love and co-operation, and belief in the Only One. Kitty feels the curve of the earth beneath her as Big Bear dances. Indian co-operation in the face of the common danger posed by the whites is termed a "life circle." The buffalo cow runs on the curve of the earth, and after the kill Big Bear feels complete "in the circle of sun and sky and earth and death." His demonic vision of the land divided by the whites with straight lines of bones follows a description of the land as an "endless circle" around him. Many of his prayers are made in the midst of a circle of Indians.

The demonic form of the image occurs too, although far less frequently. Big Bear's last speech to the Indian council issues from a "black hole" in his face and the gun brandished at the whites in their chapel at Frog Lake moves in a "blue slow circle in the sunlight" (*BB* 287, 252). The circle, then, is a metaphor for earth and the life and death lived out upon it.

The novel concludes with Big Bear's release after three years in prison. He is an old man now, physically broken by age and prison conditions and accompanied by his youngest son.[8] As they trudge through a blinding winter storm, Big Bear has a vision of spring and the thunder of *mus-too-wuk* bellowing in happiness. He roars like his giant namesake. The prison bell and prison memories sound intermittently. The circling land gives way to a vision of a square, bleached bones land under white domination. Big Bear sees that his place, his gifts, have gone. He sees an empty sky, a dead land, a wolfish wind. In his agony he beats the mare on over the bones of buffalo and people down the hill of the South Saskatchewan

Forks and out onto the river ice. The horror of his vision of the squared land is in his hammering fists. The mare drowns. There are two more horrors to be endured: first, the vision of hangman Hodson, and the six River men whom Big Bear has seen hanged, their faces horribly disfigured. Horsechild tells his father what has happened to the remaining Indian leaders. Kingbird and others of the band are in Montana, surviving on the garbage of white towns.

After this horror, the mood changes. Big Bear knows that it is time to finish "the long prayer to the Only One that was his life." He walks up the sand hills (Indian name for the place of death) and gives thanks for his life. He was born near this place. Happiness breaks in him as he contemplates the circle of his life and of the earth. He lies down. His last sight is of the sun over the rim of the earth; his last sound, the whispering of sand grains closing over him in delicate streams. The earth provides a burial for this chieftain. The novel's final image, of the sand and the body it encloses becoming "everlasting, unchanging, rock," comes through the point of view of an omniscient narrator whose perceptions telescope time.

The novel employs a multiplicity of narrators and techniques. We see through many eyes, including missionary John McDougall, Indian Affairs official Edgar Dewdney, various white settlers, Indians other than Big Bear, an RCMP inspector, white newspaper reporters, magistrates and lawyers. One chapter may be in the form of a journal, the next a letter to the Prime Minister, while the next reverts to third-person narration. Shifts in point of view are smooth and sophisticated, while continuity is maintained throughout. Young Kitty McLean's admiration for Big Bear helps to align the sympathies of the reader with the plight of the Indians. The multiple points of view highlight the differences between the two cultures and the tragic ironies involved in their confrontation in the new land.

Big Bear's sojourn in prison is told through pastiche, by juxtaposing three newspaper clippings from *The Globe* (December 9, 1885), *The Saskatchewan Herald* (January ll, 1886), and *The Toronto Mail* (February 27, 1886). The writer of the first article appears to be impartial. He informs his reader that Big Bear is learning to be a carpenter and that the half-breeds are docile and contrite. The writer allows himself a few conjectures such as the longing for the Plains that must lurk in Big Bear's eyes. The second clipping states that Robert Hodson has been appointed public hangman for the Dominion. Hodson was cook to the McLean family and suffered the two months Indian captivity with them. (Hodson appears in Big Bear's nightmarish visions after the latter's release from prison.) The third newspaper article is obviously by someone who thinks, with Stanley "Pointnose" Simpson, that good Indians are dead ones. He describes Big Bear as a small, "weazen-faced chap, with a cunning, restless look." The reporter's prejudices shape up some beautiful ironies, not the least of which is Poundmaker's comment that it was sometimes hard to say what the truth was. Wiebe has described the division between history and fiction as "an impossible line." A fiction writer, he adds, "doesn't have to pretend that he has *the* authentic account of what happened."[9] Wiebe's reader is likely to be aware of the truth of Poundmaker's remark.

The Temptations of Big Bear is Wiebe's finest work to date,[10] and its fictional techniques deserve a great more comment than is possible in this brief study. Although it is his first full-scale tragedy, it is by no means devoid of humour. Some sections are very funny indeed. The novel includes various kinds of humour which reflect the personalities of the different characters. There is Kitty McLean's refreshing wit, linked to a shrewd intelligence and a sympathetic understanding of Indian ways. There is the Indian sense of humour which expresses their courage and will to survive.[11]

The most hilarious chapter is told by an unnamed Canadian volunteer in the fifth section of Part Five. The butt of the fun is Major-General Bland T. Strange, a stout British general whose service in the Hindu Mutiny some thirty years earlier befits him, in Ottawa's sublime wisdom, for Canadian conditions. The volunteer calls him "our elephantine eminence," "our peerless leader" and "our terrifying Mogul of the Mustaches." The general travels with a spring mattress and the comforts of marmalade and jam. The Canadian has nothing but scorn for the "imported old women" who lead them, men who hold up their pants with red tape and who cannot distinguish between dignity and pomposity. He envies the freedom of Major Steele's Scouts. When the general sinks to his stirrups in a swamp, Steele's boys relish the prospect of hauling him out. The pragmatism, common sense and wry humour of the Canadian troops contrast comically with the General's grandiose schemes and incredible delays. The volunteer parodies British ideas and turns of speech in phrases like "the degraded and undisciplined savage, you know" or "this blawsted, howling wilderness," and with interjections such as "by jove." Evening campfires occasion some good-natured one-upmanship in the telling of tales, and an apostrophe to tea, the sublime infusion which makes life bearable: "Who givest zest to the unfailing pork and beans of our native land, gladly for thee do we suffer and swear in inpenetrable forests." The commissariat is manned by idiots, but with tea they are prepared to suffer, as they "bloody well will."

Humorous scenes connected with the Indian mind include the adolescent Kingbird's sexual caressing of the mare (*BB* 53–5); and the black comedy of parts of the trial. At one point Big Bear misinterprets a reference to "her crown and her dignity" and denies that he has tried to steal the Grandmother's hat. In the fighting near Fort Pitt, Little Poplar defies the Canadians by dancing on the skyline wearing nothing but a beaver hat and black velveteen waistcoat: "He bent over, slapped his naked twitching rear to them and so danced gracefully out of sight as bullets snickered longingly around him" (*BB* 299). One thinks of Pratt's definition of poetry (read *art*) as a grand binge which shows the world backside up, making for healthy physiological releases.[12]

Comedy, then, *and* tragedy. This is a story of brotherhood betrayed. It is a story of two ways of seeing man's relationships to the land.[13] A passage in a fictional letter to Sir John A. Macdonald sums up the challenge posed by the land and the tragic clash of the two cultures:

> Believe me, Sir John, it can drive a small man to madness, this incomprehensible unending at any point seemly unresisting and unchecked space. To control, to humanize, to structure and package such a continent under two steel lines would bring any engineer headier joy than the lyric prospects of heaven. The man you find who can do it will be a man indeed and I envy him, as certainly every engineer will ever after, but old Big Bear has lived into his own understanding of that land and sometimes while I was out there his seemed the more beguiling prospect; it may, in the end, last much longer than steel. (*BB* 114–5)

Notes

1. Donald Cameron, "Ruby Wiebe: The Moving Stream Is Perfectly at Rest," *Conversations with Canadian Novelists*, Part Two (Toronto: Macmillan, 1973), p. 151.

Both Hood and Cameron testify to the remarkable effect made by this particular short story on its original audience, at a conference of prose writers in Fredericton, 1970. Hood writes that the story "caused entranced silence in his audience." Cameron introduces his interview with Wiebe with a reference to the same occasion.

2. John Metcalf, ed., *The Narrative Voice* (Toronto: McGraw-Hill Ryerson, 1972), p. 254.

   See also Barry Broadfoot, *Ten Lost Years 1929–1939. Memories of Canadians Who Survived the Depression* (Toronto: Doubleday, 1973), p. 262: "naturally we were all in sympathy with Almighty Voice. Just a youngster, and fighting for what he felt was justice. Yes, he killed several men but it was white man's stupidity that caused it all."
3. Cameron, *Conversations with Canadian Novelists*, p. 151.
4. *The Temptations of Big Bear* (Toronto: McClelland & Stewart, 1973), p. 409. Hereafter cited as *BB*.
5. See Northrop Frye, *Anatomy of Criticism* (New York: Atheneum, 1967), p. 207. "The tragic hero is typically on top of the wheel of fortune, half-way between human society on the ground and the something greater in the sky . . . . Tragic heroes are so much the highest points in their human landscape that they seem the inevitable conductors of the power about them, great trees more likely to be struck by lightning than a clump of grass."
6. This passage, and Big Bear's journey from prison to his place of death at the Forks of the South Saskatchewan River, may be compared with Shakespeare's King Lear on the heath, and on the road to Dover. Like Lear, Big Bear moves from having outer authority and prestige to poverty and humiliation. The Indian chieftain, however, has none of Lear's initial arrogance.
7. One sentence is seventeen lines long (*BB* 128–9).
8. Northrop Frye describes the two components of the tragic vision as "the ironic sense of being in time and the heroic effort that struggles against it." See *Fools of Time: Studies in Shakespearean Tragedy* (Toronto: University of Toronto Press, 1967), p. 70.
9. Cameron, *Conversations with Canadian Novelists*, p. 152.
10. The novel received the 1973 Governor General's Award for Fiction.
11. See pp. 50, 54, 55, 67, 76, 90, 199, 355, 356.
12. See Earle Birney, "E. J. Pratt and his Critics," in Carl F. Klinck and Reginald Watters, eds., *Canadian Anthology*, rev. ed. (Toronto: Gage, 1966), p. 529.
13. For examples of white rhetoric and attitudes with regard to the land, see Forrest E. La Violette, *The Struggle for Survival: Indian Cultures and the Protestant Ethic in B.C.* (Toronto: University of Toronto Press, 1973). The following is from a report of a Royal Commission on Indian Affairs: "In the case of the Indians of Vancouver Island and British Columbia, Her Majesty's Government earnestly wish that when the advancing requirements of colonization press upon lands occupied by members of that race, measures of liberality and justice may be adopted for compensating them for the surrender of the territory which they have been taught to regard as their own" (p. 10).

WAYNE A. TEFS

"Rudy Wiebe: Mystery and Reality"

Mosaic, Summer 1978, pp. 155–58

Rudy Wiebe clearly believes that the business of writing and the role of the writer are profoundly important. In a recent interview he asserted "writing is a very serious business . . . I want to be better than Nabokov, I want to write the greatest novel in North America." Coming from a writer whose tortured convolutions recall Faulkner's worst rather than Nabokov's best, this comparison might seem presumptuous or at least premature. But there is still something to Wiebe's claim. It lies, I think, in the fact that the best in his fiction, as in all great fiction, is a striving after meaning. Wiebe continually haunts the trail of the big twentieth century issues—passion, guilt, repression, commitment. And like Faulkner, to whom he is akin in this respect as well, the power of his work emerges from his dramatic representation of the hold that these emotions and responses exercise over the minds and lives of his people. In a very important respect he wrestles with "ghosts"—the past in both its personal and historical manifestations.

In Wiebe's first novels those ghosts were of a people without a place, the Mennonites of Wiebe's personal past. With increasing subtlety of metaphor and breadth of tone *Peace Shall Destroy Many*, *The First and Vital Candle* and *The Blue Mountains of China* uniquely dramatize the Mennonite experience. In the first Wiebe analyzes the effects of repression and guilt upon devout believers. His story of a Church Deacon's failure to make an ethical choice—a failure which eventually ruins his family—demonstrates Wiebe's profound belief that men must act according to the visions informing their lives. This chronicle of guilt is balanced by one of sacrifice in *The Blue Mountains of China*. Here Wiebe illustrates the other side of the Mennonite coin. His Mennonites in flight from Stalinism towards the ever-receding paradise symbolized by the blue mountains, depict the triumph of faith, hope and humility over oppression and exploitation. Despite doubts about the successes they achieve in their new homeland, Paraguay, they nevertheless take great pride in having triumphed over adversity:

> We can thank. Our Lord has been good, here in the Chaco. Maybe they won't ask you, maybe they'll just blame us like—like some for moving here and who knew to what land we were going or dragging our children, not even the Elder or the delegation. But you don't bother yourself with that. We were the parents. Maybe we were wrong, maybe we were right, but we thought we couldn't raise our children when they took the German and the Bible lessons away in school. Maybe we were wrong, maybe we were right, but we believed it. Here we have land, we have had quiet here: peace and quiet. [1]

Both novels, then, capture the agony of good men in ethical trials. And they reveal Wiebe to be a profoundly Christian thinker, wrestling with the ghosts of his heritage and achieving meaning within its spiritual values.

In his two most recent novels Wiebe dramatizes the "ghosts" of a people who, unlike the Mennonites, once possessed a place. *The Temptations of Big Bear* and *The Scorched-Wood People* show how the plains Indians and Metis were violently stripped of their lands. Here the issues are more profoundly political than spiritual. *The Temptations of Big Bear* documents the betrayal and destruction of the plains Indians by the financial powers of Canada. Wiebe focuses on the human suffering and anguish of Big Bear, depicting through him the agony of a man torn between commitments to a way of life and the temptations of self-aggrandizement. In the end Big Bear has only a vision of the destruction that accompanies the white man:

> I saw everything grey. I saw the valley of the Great River empty, with very few trees; and then I saw Fort Carlton as anyone can see it right now if he stands on the coulee hill above the valley; all the buildings and high wall, and I could see nothing there at all but black scattered around, wide, with a little smoke going straight up as a wood resting after burning too fast. I don't know when that will be. I tried to see better and I think there were places where snow lay

> on the ground. But it was all grey, there weren't any leaves, and smoke was all I could see where there should have been Fort Carlton. I saw that, and I am telling you. These are my words.[2]

Wiebe's latest novel, *The Scorched-Wood People*, goes a step further, demonstrating that the more "civilized" Metis of Manitoba and Saskatchewan were exploited and finally destroyed by the imperialist policies of Eastern Canada. With unflinching honesty Wiebe traces the crushing of the North-West peoples by the agents of "Canadian" finance capitalism—The Hudson's Bay Company and the CPR. Dumont and Riel, betrayed by MacDonald and his corporate henchmen on the issue of parliamentary representation, suffer the ultimate humiliations of exile and execution. They, too, are just men who suffer agony for their peoples. And Wiebe lays the blame for the ruin of those peoples squarely on the shoulders of MacDonald:

> The Right Honourable John A. Macdonald lied in his teeth like a trooper. When people naïvely presume that their country at least is run by honesty, what happens when leaders lie to save their necks. No one has ever accused me of being a cynic, but the story of our people versus Ottawa tells one that if a leader seems forthright, definite, and very lucky his lie may work long enough to break his opponent's neck and then, of course, his own is safe until the next election.[3]

No more pointed condemnation of "progress" in Canada has ever been written.

Writing of Canada's literary history Earle Birney once said, "by our lack of ghosts we're haunted." *The Temptations of Big Bear* and *The Scorched-Wood People* demonstrate that Rudy Wiebe would not agree: he might rather say, "by our ignorance of our ghosts we're haunted."[4] These novels, which capture the emotional and psychological quality of what happens to individuals, liberally re-create the events that constitute the centres of Canadian prairie history. They depict the suffering of those caught in the advance of capitalism from "Canada" to the North-West. And, like the earlier "Mennonite" novels, they illustrate the agony of good men faced with ethical choices.

Wiebe develops those ethical choices in a striking metaphor throughout his work. Time and again he creates the image of a man inside a diminishing circle who escapes that circle only to return to it and confront his fate. In *The Blue Mountains of China* his protagonist, David Epp, eludes the threatening Russian authorities and actually reaches China. But just when he is free he returns inexplicably to Russia's oppression. In *The Scorched-Wood People* Louis Riel finds peace and serenity in exile from the Canadian authorities. But he too goes back to the conflicts he knows will be his undoing. Wiebe seems to be suggesting that ethical choices can only be made in freedom: that moral decisions cannot be made in the stresses of life-death circumstances, but only when one chooses volitionally, not necessarily. Ethically this is sound thinking.

But Wiebe takes this ethical commitment one step further. His characters return to the scenes of their "temptations" by surrendering themselves into the hands of God, whose divine plan they trust to unravel the contradictions of their lives. However opaque that divine plan may be it nevertheless becomes the sole source of meaning to Wiebe's troubled protagonists. They simply have faith that "God will show us the way."

Thus *The Scorched-Wood People*, a work which toys with social and political reality, actually treats the Metis "rebellion" as a spiritual dilemma. For as this work unfolds the Metis struggle to accept the divine plan overshadows their resistance to economic and political oppression. The issue is dramatized in Riel. Wiebe's concern about Batoche focuses on Riel's conviction that "God will fight for us all here and break our enemies and it will not be men alone fighting" (264). Riel's subsequent attempts to reconcile himself to God's betrayal of his "vision" becomes the centre of the novel:

> He was sitting with his head in his hands, staring at the floor, when he began to understand. The infinity of God in relation to the set formulas of the priests was like sunlight on the open prairie in relation to the patterns of barred light on the floor at his feet. To burst out, into the infinity of God! He cried aloud for sheer joy, the incredible knowledge broke from him like a spring flood. To die and explore the infinity, was freedom of that measureless wisdom! The way of the cross was humiliation; the prophet must die to reveal his ultimate vision, and this conviction transfigured Riel's understanding of himself even as he heard workmen at the end of the guard-house begin to hammer together what he knew must be his scaffold. (330–1)

And, as a result, Riel's resistance to the imperial design of MacDonald, The Hudson's Bay Company and the CPR diminishes in importance. Riel is transformed into a Christian mystic whose most profound confrontation occurred on inward terrain as he struggled to reconcile himself to the divine plan.

Wiebe's reconciliation of social and political dilemmas in these spiritual terms reveals that at times his profound Christianity defies political and social realities. The betrayals and exploitation which occurred in the Canadian North-West reflect an essential feature of Canada's history—the deliberate economic and cultural colonialization of the outlying constituencies by the financial powers of central "Canada." While Wiebe nicely captures the anguish of key figures in the indigenous culture who resisted the imperialist advances, casting their plight in spiritual terms blurs the origins of their dilemmas: reconciling their agony through mystery avoids the social realities behind their personal suffering. At issue here is not the sincerity of Wiebe's conception: the issue is the adequacy of his visionary Christianity to adequately account for the lives and deaths of Big Bear, Riel and Dumont. Fully appropriate to the struggles of twentieth century Mennonites to come to term with secular societies in Russia and Canada, Wiebe's mystical framework somehow falls short when applied to the "ghosts" of prairie history. Any assessment of such experience cannot adequately be constructed without scrupulous attention to the social determinants underlying personal agonies.

Notes

1. *The Blue Mountains of China* (Toronto, 1970), p. 148.
2. *The Temptations of Big Bear* (Toronto, 1973), p. 206.
3. *The Scorched-Wood People* (Toronto, 1977), p. 217. Subsequent citations from this work are noted in parentheses following the quotation.
4. "Can. Lit." in *Collected Poems of Earle Birney*, Vol. I (Toronto: McClelland & Stewart, 1975), p. 138.

RICHARD WILBUR

1921–

Richard Purdy Wilbur was born on March 1, 1921, in New York City, to Lawrence Lazear and Helen Ruth (née Purdy) Wilbur. He was educated at Amherst College (B.A. 1942) and Harvard University (M.A. 1947). From 1943 to 1945 he served in the army, achieving the rank of staff sergeant. He married Mary Charlotte Hayes Ward in 1942; they have four children. He has taught at Harvard University and Wellesley College, and is currently a writer-in-residence at Smith College.

Wilbur published his first book of poems, *The Beautiful Changes and Other Poems*, in 1947. Formal in structure and dealing sensitively with the details of everyday living, it set the tone for his subsequent works. His third book, *Things of This World* (1956), was the first to receive extensive attention; critics admired his strict formal control tempered by an ebullient sense of wonder at the world. It won the Pulitzer Prize and the National Book Award. Later volumes such as *Walking to Sleep* (1969), *The Mind-Reader* (1976), and *Advice from the Muse* (1981) have continued to attract praise, though Wilbur has been criticized in recent years for playing it safe, both in his failure to address social and political issues and in his continued reliance on traditional forms. However, even those critics who question the worth of his endeavor acknowledge that he handles his chosen material well.

In addition to his poetry, Wilbur has written essays, criticism, books for children, and several highly regarded translations and adaptations of plays by Molière and Racine. His translation of Molière's *Tartuffe* (1963) won a Bollingen Prize. He also won the Bollingen Prize for verse in 1971 with *Walking to Sleep*.

A. K. WEATHERHEAD

From "Richard Wilbur: The Poetry of Things"

ELH, December 1968, pp. 606–17

> I think it a great vice to convey everything by imagery, particularly if the imagery is not interrelated. There ought to be areas of statement. . . . The statement should have obliquity, and congruence to the imagery, as Marianne Moore's does—not vitiating the objects, but rather finding in them another and ideal dimension. (Richard Wilbur: "The Genie in the Bottle")

The question that has most engaged poetry in this century concerns the image. To what extent, to what end, and with what success may the image stand alone, unorganized, unencumbered, or unassisted by connective rhetoric? In the beginning there was T. E. Hulme, and Imagism, and Pound going in fear of abstractions; later there was the qualitative progression of the *Cantos*; there was Eliot, whose use of the image was designed to restore poetry to the health it had enjoyed before the Revolution when, very curiously, "something" had "happened to the mind of England." A little later there was Williams, the arch-priest of *things*—not necessarily images in the usual poetic sense, but items from history and newspapers, advertisements and shreds of overheard patois, a list of groceries or other miscellaneous details; and now there are the sons and devotees of Williams, whose poems are thronged with items like a Goodwill store and to whom words themselves are things. And whereas the images in Eliot, though they were details of private experience, had he claimed a public meaning, these items, not having been submitted to the poet's interpretation, are as secure from that of the reader as their makers would wish.

The broad scattering of autonomous things throughout much recent poetry carries, I believe, the implication that there is intrinsic virtue in them. Allen Ginsberg tells us flatly that a number of things are holy—parts of his own anatomy not excluded—that we had not formerly thought to be so; and Robert Duncan wants to bring us as naive, intuitive children to a fair field full of fresh things. Elsewhere though, even when it is not made explicit, we receive the sense that, for the poet himself, the things that proliferate in the poems have the iridescent dew of Eden upon them and that not only valley, rock, and stream but red wheelbarrows, dixie cups, lemons, and bird droppings are appareled in celestial light all the time.

Then, on the other hand, there is the broad stream of traditional poetry which does not assume that since the daily businesses of life are transacted among facts and things, unarranged and conglomerate, the truth about life thereby inheres in the mere amassing and reproduction of them. That it should be thought to do so, W. H. Auden suggests in a recent review, is a symptom of a "grave cultural disease." In his own poetry, for eminent example of the traditional kind, the imagery, though brilliantly selected, has never been vivid; and it has never been unaccompanied by interpretation or unsubordinated to idea. His increased acceptance of an imperfect world and the consequent celebration in his poetry of the fifties and sixties of the things of this world have not signally modified his treatment of them: they don't run amok, claiming autonomy like Berkeley undergraduates; they don't just occur, bald and uncontexted, haphazard and self-justifying.

These things may be usefully mentioned in introducing a discussion of the poetry of Richard Wilbur: judged by his use of imagery he is clearly to be assigned to the traditional rather than the other of the two main streams of contemporary poetry; but furthermore the argument of his poetry is often similar to parts of the long and continuing debate about imagery. Frequently a poem of his is concerned with the rejection of abstraction and the defining of a commitment to things of this world; for while his use of imagery implies a belief that facts and images do not autonomously bear meaning, his subject matter nevertheless works with the premise that ideas must exist in familiar things. The commitment he is anxious to define is one which is delicately balanced between the attraction of a non-physical world on the one hand and a too crass luxuriance in objectivity on the other.

There is, first, a plenitude of things in the poetry, since it is in things that realities profounder than they themselves are revealed. Thus, in "'A World without Objects Is a Sensible Emptiness,'" he bids the tall camels of the spirit to turn from the abstraction of "pure mirage" for which they are thirsting to "light incarnate," such as "Lampshine blurred in the stream of beasts"; for, as Ralph Mills has pointed out, spiritual things are not to be sought by a denial of the physical. There is no gnostic contempt for the concrete world in Wilbur; on the other hand, he doesn't want to indulge in it, and he tends to dispossess himself of things that are cloying. In "Grasse: The Olive Tress," for example, the olive, with features and associations of movement, hunger, aridity, and doubt, provides relief from the wet, static satiety of the landscape of Southern France, where

> . . . luxury's the common lot. The light
> Lies on the rain-pocked rocks like yellow wool
> And around the rocks the soil is rusty bright
> From too much wealth of water, so that the grass
> Mashes under the foot, and all is full
> Of heat and juice and a heavy jammed excess.
> Whatever moves moves with the slow complete
> Gestures of statuary. [1]

Wilbur withdraws from before what is too solid and static rather as Wallace Stevens does, and like him he occasionally uses the metaphor of the statue to designate it. In Stevens, in one moment of his chronic avoidance of a fixed unplastic world, the statues are blown by the wind; in Wilbur also the statue appears now and then, as it does in "Grasse," as a symbol for the world of solid fixed things. It is to be assaulted, for example, by blown newspapers or by crows in "After the Last Bulletins" and "Beasts" respectively, when in both poems our dreams parole us from the responsible city of waking life. The poem "Statues" celebrates a scene in which children are playing at being statues, but theirs is a fluid world not a fixed one; and they assume attitudes, "gargoyle attitudes," only to "melt in giggles and begin again." Over their heads, maples shimmering in the wind reflect the children's metamorphoses with their own. In their game, the children mock the defined postures that they imitate, "as if / All definition were outrageous." Countering this scene and surveying it are those who have in *fact* assumed defined statuesque roles: two nuns, a soldier, and "linked lovers"; and for a moment "every role / Relents." But Wilbur isn't giving everything to the pretty fluctuation and evasions of the protean children: the poem concludes with the image of "one aging bum" who also stares at the scene and sees in it "the image of his kingdom come." We admire the brilliant mobility of children and trees and record how the rigidity of the nuns, soldiers, and lovers momentarily deliquesces under its influence. But we do not admire the ultimate shiftlessness of the bum; for his is a paradoxically "adamantine shapelessness"—shapelessness so far gone as to be itself defined. As the connotations of the olive trees in "Grasse" restore a balance, so here between the complete "definition" and utter shapelessness a balance is adumbrated.

Wilbur, then, by no means wishing to dispense with his world of sensible, solid objects, counters the fixed, defined, and immobile with their opposites. In so doing, however, he does not go so far as to espouse abstractions or ideals, such as the "sheer horizon" that the camels yearned for in the poem cited above. The olive tree with its "hue of far away" balances the vegetation of Southern France; but elsewhere the far-away itself must be balanced by the near at hand and immediate. These opposing values are juggled in "Castles and Distances," a poem which clearly confirms that the good life—the spiritual life, we may say even—flourishes in commitment to defined and immediate things of this world, while the result of dwelling on the far away is evil. 〈. . .〉

Richard Wilbur, 〈. . .〉 though he tends to shun the immediacy of crowded fact, maintains a duty to the things of the world that are near at hand and concrete; and in such things he finds a vocabulary for speaking of the unfamiliar or for articulating ideas. To some extent the process can be seen at the level of diction, as for example when he attempts to image the original geologic process in the unfamiliar juxtaposition of familiar verbal elements:

> . . . crannies flooding with a sweat of quartz,
> And lathered magmas out of deep retorts
> Welled up, as here, to fill
> With tumbled rockmeal, stone-fume, lithic spray,
> The dike's brief chasm . . . [2]

More regular, however, than diction so constructed is the practice of using known things to define what is not known, which may be observed in various forms throughout the poems. It occurs most often, perhaps, in the rendering of the mysteries of humans in terms of nature; it is most clear in "Advice to a Prophet," where the right procedure for the prophet is manifestly the right one for the poet. The prophet of doom is instructed not to try to capture our imaginations with talk of the force and range of weapons or of the death of the race; these are abstractions we cannot conceive. He is to speak to us rather in terms of what we know, the injury or destruction of things in nature; for there we can be touched:

> What should we be without
> The dolphin's arc, the dove's return,
> These things in which we have seen ourselves and spoken?

We remember the pronouncement of Pound about the inability of the mind to grasp an abstraction that it has not itself made; and we note the radical difference between the kind of poetry in which that notion results in him and the kind in which it results in Wilbur: in Pound, the concrete images range free and may be interpreted as we will; in Wilbur, they are corralled, harnessed and put to perform specific labor. And, so the orderliness, form, and neatness of the poem suggest, they are put to perform their work as if they cannot fail to do it well. Wilbur's neatness is not obtained without cost: rhymes are sometimes dearly bought and occasionally lines are manifestly padded to make them match. It is on account of the neatness, moreover, that the method incurs the danger of facility: do not the problems posed lend themselves all too easily to resolution by repetitions of the same strategy? Wilbur is perhaps aware of this danger. At least he has an ironic poem in which the facility is held up to ridicule, and it draws our attention to how limited a space is held by irony throughout the poems in general. In "We," the unknown "we" find definition by means of the old hawkish clichés of the cold war: responding to such ingenuous remarks as "We ought to drop the bomb at once before / Those Russians do" or "We mustn't shilly shally any more," the speaker ruminates,

> How good to have the Russians to abhor:
> It lets us dance the nation on our knee
> Who haven't been quite certain since the war
> Precisely what we meant by saying *we*. [3]

The conceit of dancing the nation on one's knee suggests that the poet may recognize the danger of facility in his process.

II

Although Nature may be fallen in many of Wilbur's poems, it enjoys occasionally the advent of grace, and this changes things. The eyes of the stag bearing the cross, in "Castles and Distances," are "clear with grace"; grace has brought about and presides over this supernatural phenomenon. It may also, on the other hand, bring about a less unusual result and simply irradiate a common daily experience. The leaves, for example, in "October Maples, Portland," though about to fall were "never so unfallen as today," and they yield the "very light from which time fell away." There is nothing supernatural here; the sight is a credible miracle, like the hedgerow that "blossoms" in midwinter in "Little Gidding." And like this again, it is associated with grace: "Where friends meet," it goes on, "They parley in the tongues of Pentecost." An early poem entitled "Grace," however, defines it in a special sense, a less miraculous one, which leads us to the idea that Wilbur conceives of a poem itself as an act of grace. "Grace" develops from an observation of Gerard Manley Hopkins', quoted as epigraph, that the bounding lambs give the appearance of being flung by the earth not by their own motor activity. They please, says the poet in his Marianne Moorish tone of voice, "and Nijinsky's out-the-window leap / And marvelous midair pause please too." What pleases is not merely the *sprezzatura*, which can "tickle" one even in a dining car waiter's agility; it is that "flesh made word / Is grace's revenue." The poem celebrates the speaking power of action and, as a part of the action, the pause, a "graceful still reserve"; "'I merely leap and pause,'" said Nijinsky.

Here is a formula by which we may come, fancifully enough perhaps, upon the characteristic art of Richard Wilbur. A poem of his typically manifests what he here defines as grace. It shows the speaking power of action, of poetic action, by which the form that presents the things of this world simultaneously reflects upon them; his strategy is to work with facts and images subjected to interpretation, not presented bold and bald like a broken bottle in Williams. A poem may be simply one such interpreted image—a single simile, such as "Piazza di Spagna, Early Morning," "Mind," "A Simile for Her Smile," or "A Glance from the Bridge." But the same strategy is at work in longer poems where one image or a series is exploited for its moral meaning, as it is, for examples of poems already mentioned here or about to be, in "October Maples," "Statues," "Castles and Distances," "Junk," or "A Hole in the Floor." These poems result not only from the pure perception of objects but from the imaginative leap that accompanies that perception and, without being explicit, finds the meaning. Wilbur might have said of himself, "I merely leap and pause."

The means by which objects and facts are interpreted in Wilbur's poems varies endlessly, formal and rhetorical devices supporting each other reciprocally. A rhetorical comment which invests an image with meaning may succeed immediately upon the presentation of the image, as in "Junk," which begins:

> An axe angles
> from my neighbor's ashcan;
> It is hell's handiwork . . . .

Or the comment may be delayed: in "A Hole in the Floor," the central fact of the poem, the hole and the speaker looking into it, is only gradually given meaning; meaning infiltrates the imagery stanza by stanza. In the first there is the image literally presented and then, virtually separate, there is the comment, which orchestrates the foregoing commonplace with vague undertones of the discovery of mystery and glory:

> The carpenter's made a hole
> In the parlor floor, and I'm standing
> Staring down into it now
> At four o'clock in the evening,
> As Schliemann stood when his shovel
> Knocked on the crowns of Troy.

In the second stanza the reflection is similarly reserved to the last two lines: the old wood shavings are "silvery gold, the color/ Of Hesperian apple-parings." As the poem progresses, however, the reflection creeps up the stanza into the hitherto bare imagery. In Stanza 3 the joists make a "pure street" which "enters the long darkness," and one observes incidentally that the exotic of Greek legend is dropped in favor of what is less "far-away." In the penultimate stanza the imagery is almost wholly withdrawn, as the poet asks, "What am I after?" and when it returns in the last it is thoroughly saturated with meaning: what the poet is searching for in the solid details, is, he says

> the buried strangeness
> Which nourishes the known:
> That spring from which the floor-lamp
> Drinks now a wilder bloom,
> Inflaming the damask love-seat
> And the whole dangerous room.

The imagery is impregnated: *now* we may say, so much depends upon a hole in the floor, cut by the carpenter, beside the gold shavings!

A similar strategy informs "Museum Piece," in which philistinism and art, separated in the first two stanzas when embodied respectively in the custodians of the museum and the pictures, are brought together in the last when Degas the painter becomes Edgar Degas the man who hangs his pants upon his El Greco. The separation here in the opening stanzas between the image and meaning is not quite so acute as that in "A Hole in the Floor," and the union is adumbrated by a good rhyme:

> The good gray guardians of art
> Patrol the halls on spongy shoes,
> Impartially protective, though
> Perhaps suspicious of Toulouse.

The above discussion of "A Hole in the Floor" speaks as though form by itself made no commentary upon the presented things. And this is not so; although, after one has observed a minor act of linkage performed by imperfect rhymes between the image and the reflection upon it, the commentary of the form is not especially demonstrable. The operation of the form is more apparent in "Love Calls Us to the Things of This World"; and a consideration of this operation will also serve, finally, to demonstrate in summary Wilbur's precarious balance among these things. The dramatic situation of the poem shows a man half asleep seeing in the swinging laundry a vision of angels and then, fully awake, repudiating the vision and the irresponsibility to the world it had fostered in him. The contribution of form is mostly clearly manifest in the sounds and the syntax: the description of the laundry as angels is dominated by liquids and nasals, and the sentences are made up of parallel clauses and an accumulation of phrases introduced by present participles.

> Some are in bed-sheets, some are in blouses,
> Some are in smocks: but truly there they are.
> Now they are rising together in calm swells

Of halcyon feeling, filling whatever they wear
With the deep joy of their impersonal breathing;
   Now they are flying in place, conveying
The terrible speed of their omnipresence, moving
And staying like white water. . . .

The commitment of the man awake, on the other hand, is expressed in short clauses, in which the sound is dominated by stops. The triple rhythms evident in the above passage give way somewhat to the iambic in the one that follows. Triple rhythms are still present, however, and so are the participles, the liquids and nasals; for the waking attitude of duty does not exactly replace that of the dreamer, but rather there is a compromise, the balance.

   Bring them down from their ruddy gallows;
Let there be clean linen for the backs of thieves;
Let lovers go fresh and sweet to be undone,
And the heaviest nuns walk in a pure floating
Of dark habits,
                    keeping their difficult balance.

So the sounds of the poem become in part its statement; action becomes word; and this, in the terms of the poem so titled, is grace.

Wilbur then is conscientiously committed to immediate things, despite the allurements of abstractions and the far-away. But things are imperfect; and if by their means a reality beyond themselves may be grasped, unaided they do not bear meanings. Submitted to the interpretive action of poetic technique, on the other hand, they speak.

Notes

1. Unless otherwise indicated, poems quoted appear in *The Poems of Richard Wilbur* (New York, Harcourt, Brace & World, 1963).
2. "On the Marginal Way," *The New Yorker*, XLI (Sept. 25, 1965), 48.
3. "We," *Poetry*, LXXIII (Dec., 1948), 127–8.

CHARLES R. WOODARD

"Richard Wilbur's Critical Condition"

Contemporary Poetry, Autumn 1977, pp. 16–24

Critical commentaries on Wilbur's poetry have come to seem rather highly stylized and predictable, like bullfighting. First there is the ritual praise of his technical virtuosity (music, diction, imagery, metrics), to show that the critic is not devoid of the appreciation of beauty, followed quickly by the disclaimers which establish his awareness of its irrelevance to contemporary life. Objections to Wilbur's poetry, to phrase them in the simplest terms, take the following forms: (1) He thinks too much. (2) He does not suffer enough.

Strictly speaking, it is not Wilbur's thought so much as his imagination that is derogated. Clearly we cannot condemn him for his epistemological interests if we are to permit them to Wallace Stevens. It is Wilbur's use of the things of this world, his chosen poetic province, which gets him into trouble; he is not tough enough with them, not sufficiently insistent upon their thinginess, but persists in allowing them to pass through his mind, where his recalcitrant imagination may act upon them. Back of such criticism there hover the dicta and practice of William Carlos Williams, whose followers put their faith in an objective "rendering" of reality or experience as little tampered with by mind as possible. The chief emphasis is on outwitting the mind's insidious attempts to impose its own patterns on reality or to substitute them *for* reality—an end accomplished by limiting its reported activities to acts of perception or "prereflective cognition." It is as if the poet were arrested in his linguistic development on the verge of the invention of language, striving for an arrangement of shells on the shore from which we as readers are to deduce an idea, rather as Deism could deduce God's existence from an inspection of the natural world. Perhaps it is not quite so primitive as this; a better comparison would be the still-life tableau of such objects as apples, pears, and a freshly killed hare, except that the seemingly arbitrary grouping must "mean" something, without saying it. With a red wheelbarrow, glazed with rain, and white chickens, Williams takes us back to an approximation of pictographic writing. Thus the snares and delusions of discursive thought and emotive language are avoided, but only until we read an analysis of such symbols by one of Williams' exegetes. The reader is permitted to use his mind, we are tempted to say, but not the poet, except in the most rigorous "demonstrative" sense. It was Williams' insistence that there be no new wine in old bottles, and thus Wilbur is condemned for using older forms and conventions. Paradoxically, it is acceptable for Williams' imitators to put their wine in his old bottles, but Wilbur may not put his in Eliot's and certainly not in those of Pope and Donne. If wit and cleverness were not generally outside the laws governing the works of the Williams school, one of its members might write a satire on Wilbur, similar to that written by Dryden on Shadwell—no doubt it would be entitled "MacDonne."

The second complaint, which appears to have its origin in the vogue for "confessional" poetry, may at times be viewed as a result of the first; if Wilbur did not take refuge so habitually in his own mind, he would see the world for the pit of horror that everyone else knows it to be. Lowell and his followers, with their categories of "cooked" and "raw" poetry, take it as a priori that the good poet will suffer and, further, that good poetry consists precisely in the reporting of this suffering. Emotional Jacksonians, the critics who take this position, want no one whistling within hearing of their misery. They appear to view poetry as having some therapeutic function, but if poets are their physicians how can it profit them to be prescribed continuing doses of their own sickness? The answer must be that misery continues to love company; they want the assurance that the poet is not sunny or happy—that he is, in fact, exactly like themselves. They want it reaffirmed that man is beastly, the "human condition" hopeless. Thus assured, they may turn out the light and fall into dreamless sleep. In such a critical environment, Wilbur is a kind of Mauberley, born out of his due time in "a half-savage country, out of date"—a country with a taste, where a taste can be discerned, for meat not merely rare but raw.

The effect of such criticism is to confine poetry to immediate sensation and emotion. We appear to have reared a race of critics who go about with their tongues probing their aching teeth, hungering to see lepers, monstrosities, freaks, wounds, blood, madness. We require to be told that we are mad, or have at least the rich potential for going mad. We still, in some strange perversion of Victorianism, require our poets to be sages, but sages of a very rare and specialized breed, sages of suffering. Their hands display their stigmata, their wrists their slashes. The lurid path cut through our skies by the Welsh comet Dylan Thomas, Eliot's resigned nerveless suffering, Auden's frequent reminders of "the suffering to which we are fairly accustomed," Yeats even, with his cyclic cataclysms, our own grim expectations of life in the twentieth century, the dreadful tragedies of our younger poets—all these have led us to believe that the poet's role requires that he put the stamp of sincerity upon his work by stepping in front of an automobile or leaping off a bridge.

We seem, in fact, to have arrived, in recent years, at a kind of unwritten contract with our poets. Were it formalized, it might read more or less as follows: "You may be a poet, and we will reward you with grants and fellowships and readings if you are fashionable, and publish your doings in the papers, like those of football players and television performers, but never forget that it is your suffering for which you are being paid. We will begin to take most interest in your work precisely when it shows clearest symptoms of your breaking down. We want to know of every visit to a sanitarium, every cut, cuddled, and sucked thumb, your bouts with alcohol and depression, your flirtations with suicide. And then to prove your seriousness, you must write a final poem, in the form of a leap from a bridge or a pulled trigger. Then we will believe. Then we will establish a cult and proclaim you unreservedly a poet."

Confessional poetry may be quite as much a result of this attitude as its cause. The wounds! we cry, all the wounds, licked by so many bloody tongues. Knowledge is sorrow, but must art be pain? Must we now have suffering only, without catharsis? Unused to hearing confessionals, knowing only our own local pain, we are overwhelmed. This is what life is, we say, like the blind man laying hold of some part of the elephant. Granted that life is grim, that this may be, as Elizabeth Bishop said, "our worst century yet," must our poetry continue compulsively to rehearse this one obsessive fact? The mind's indwelling powers are capable of more; the vulture reminds the alert of Noah; another world opens through a hole in the floor. Even a man on the way to a madhouse may smile at a girl in the street.

Arnold criticized the Romantics for not knowing enough; another generation of critics condemns Wilbur for not suffering enough. He comes and sets up shop before us, dazzling us with displays of virtuosity such as to make him seem a creature from another world—or from another age, at the very least. His technical skill is immense. His poems stand apart from him in the independent world of art; both he and they are like cats, licking their fur in total self-sufficiency, self-possession. It is almost as if he were too blessed with talent. We may be tempted to see him as a kind of happy fool, a "natural," into whose pockets apples fall as he dawdles cheerfully across the verdancy of an outmoded romantic landscape. "How graceful," we say, "but does he go through life without pain?" His poetry is a reminder that the tragic vision which we prize so highly in our poets need not rule out the "wit and wakefulness," the free play of the mind delighting in itself, which Wilbur proclaims as his own. "It's pretty," say Kipling's Philistines doubtfully, "but is it art?" "It's art," we say of Wilbur's poetry, shaking our heads with equal doubt, "but is it life? Does he not suffer?" He does not say, overtly, and thus we conclude that he *has* nothing to say. We might pay him the compliment, however, of thinking that he is perhaps not trying to say so much as to make, and with materials subtler than oyster-shells. The play of his mind, as shimmering and translucent as the spray of his fountains, may be a delight to the reader; if it is an equal delight to Wilbur, so much the better. It was once considered a virtue to suffer in silence; if Wilbur suffers, it is thus he does. Socialized suffering can only be ruinous; shared property dwindles; shared pain multiplies until every emotional reservoir is overflowing. The giver retains a full store, no matter how fully he burdens his recipients. It would be tragic indeed if we forced Wilbur, as the price of our adulation, to take to drink and end a suicide in some peaceful New England summer, and thus to become overnight another of our cult-heroes.

In lamenting man's tragic circumstance, however, and supposing that Wilbur is unaware of it, we do him a very real injustice. Apart from man's mortality, with its attendant suffering, there is perhaps no more tragic situation in his life than the discrepancy between the world he perceives and the world which he knows intellectually to exist. A study of Wilbur's poetry—we may confine ourselves to the collection *The Poems of Richard Wilbur* (New York: Harcourt, Brace and World, 1963)—shows how often the things of this world which he celebrates are shadowed by an awareness of this discrepancy. His little poem "Epistemology" states a theme implicit in much of his writing:

I

Kick at the rock, Sam Johnson, break your bones:
But cloudy, cloudy is the stuff of stones.

II

We milk the cow of the world, and as we do
We whisper in her ear, "You are not true."

This is not merely the cow of Berkeley's idealism but the cow of current science, without milking machines. Nothing can bridge the gap between appearance and the reality which we know to exist but cannot perceive. Wilbur for his poetry chooses the cow he can see and milk rather than some molecular cow which cloudily fails to abide our question. Nevertheless, he is far removed in his epistemology from Williams and his followers. Though he knows, as the title of one of his poems tells us, that "a world without objects is a sensible emptiness," his poetry is ironically informed with the further knowledge that a red wheelbarrow possesses no quality of redness and that the chickens in a barnyard are cloudy stuff indeed, as is his cow. His poetry itself, the milk from that cow, must thus partake of the general untruth of those things whose fragile beauty it celebrates; and that fragility is more moving than the traditional theme of mutability. The Williams school accepts without question the world as our senses give it to us, while rejecting the validity of any Wordsworthian recollection in tranquillity. It is as if Margaret Fuller had said, "I accept the universe, but I will not allow my mind to contaminate it." Wilbur permits the entry of mind into the reality-equation, and not without logic. If the world which the Williams school uses as the materials of poetry is "unreal," as scientifically viewed, then it is difficult to see that the senses are more reliable than the intellect for poetry or more valid than the imagination. How can the mind contaminate in any significant way a world which the mind knows already not to exist except as invisible particles awhirl in infinite immensities of space? Poets, after all, are not philosophers or scientists; their observations are neither methodologically nor logically immaculate. If on the other hand the world is "unreal" in philosophic terms, with no existence outside mind, then intellection is not only the order of the day—it *is* the day, and the night.

We may, if we please, insist upon the validity of sensations and the "reality" of sensible objects; but such an assumption, in the context of modern scientific knowledge, is in itself a denial of the validity of the mind's operations; and thus we are returned to a primitive state of existence—a pre-cortical state, we are tempted to say—scratching or painting our visual perceptions on the wall of the cave. Such a state is not Wilbur's. In a world eternally in motion, where nothing is stable, where even atomic particles are beset with an uncertainty principle, the play of the individual mind, itself reducible to the activity of chemically generated electrical impulses, may be as good a model of reality as we have. If it imposes its own patterns on the outer world, perhaps that is not a calamitous event after all, since those patterns are a part of that world. Beneath the sensible surface of Wilbur's world another threatens, like the crack in Auden's teacup, to open into unspeakable voids—"the buried strangeness / Which nourishes the known" ("A Hole in the Floor"). His is a landscape of ephemera, of "opulent bric-a-brac," mined country, touched with the fatal "seeming" of the Edenic pear in "June Light," which constantly erodes the "truth and new delight" of the visible world. Each poem is a temporary victory over our knowledge of the nature of things; in each, like his juggler, he "has won for once over the world's weight," even as his prophet is being rehearsed to preach the "worldless rose" of an atomized earth ("Advice to a Prophet"). In this connection, Wilbur's tendency to concentrate on things rather than on dramatic situations (people), is perhaps not without its own sinister implications, as much a commentary by omission as Housman's excluding the fully adult and the aged from *A Shropshire Lad.*

Wilbur's concern is not mutability alone (although this too is a central theme) but the precariousness of a physical world which is known to be different from what our physical senses tell us it is, as we know that sand may be a component of glass, without being able to see it ("Junk"). A tension is set up between eye and mind. Wilbur must praise appearance even as he is being hoodwinked by it, because a molecular world is not a workable stuff for poetry, though it is always there, an undeniable adjunct to the assertions made by the poetry. His is not the too-solid flesh of Hamlet; things of summer growth "raise / Plainly their seeming into seamless air" ("June Light"); the erratic flight of birds suggests a world "dreamt" by "cross purposes" ("An Event"), and misty weather brings a fear of the loss of the physical world ("A Chronic Condition").

If Wilbur is to be criticized for being "too happy," for employing his mind too much, it might be well for those who do so to consider the poised fragility of his world as set against the "bloody loam," apparently eternal, which is the basis of Williams'. Both Williams and the confessional school appear to accept the sensible world at face value; in his later work Williams' world is poised between the mythic primal slime on the one hand and the momentary display of spirit on the other. The uneasy ground of Wilbur's poetry is the irreconcilable oppositions of appearance and knowledge. It is not immediately apparent that Williams' world is more "real," and thus more unhappy, than Wilbur's, or that it deals more rigorously with its facts and artifacts, since it does not show any inclination to question the evidence of the senses as the basis of its epistemology.

Between the two poles of sensation and knowledge, Wilbur's mind functions as mediator. Its graceful error may "correct the cave" of reality ("Mind"); it milks the cow of the world which it knows to be untrue. The perceived world, with its fine gauzy shimmer of fountains and its colored juggling balls, is equally a world of the fine shimmer and juggling of mind. His poetry constitutes a realm of its own, with its own truth, constantly reiterating that the mind's reflections are hardly less substantial or valid than the objects of its perceptions. If a critic, standing at the edge of one of Wilbur's displays, cries, "Unreal!" Wilbur need only allow a wider spin of the lariat to rope him into the scene whose existence he is denying. After all, Wilbur has denied it from the beginning.

BRUCE F. MICHELSON

"Richard Wilbur: The Quarrel with Poe"

Southern Review, April 1978, pp. 245–61

All that we do
Is touched with ocean, yet we remain
On the shore of what we know.
("For Dudley")

Now in his fifties, Richard Wilbur has perhaps the best reputation any working poet can reasonably hope for: he is widely admired, sometimes read, and generally misunderstood. Even the best of recent comment on his verse[1] seems, in large part, to acquiesce to the notion that Wilbur stays well clear of those "darker" visions—those hair-raising insights, or inklings of insights—for which so many of us congratulate ourselves as genuine "moderns." And the interest Wilbur has shown for the art and the grand designs of Edgar Allan Poe does not seem to have helped matters. Certainly, Wilbur's 1959 essay "The House of Poe" is now recognized as one of the very best studies of symbolic values in both the tales and the verse, and since then, in other writings, Wilbur has more than maintained his stance as a leading Poe scholar and critic. But little indeed has been done to relate Wilbur the scholar and critic to Wilbur the poet. As general editor of the Laurel Poetry Series, Wilbur personally edited the Poe volume, fitting it with an extensive, lucid, and revealing introduction—which had a similar lack of impact upon the reading of his own verse. To readers of Wilbur the poet, most remarkable, one would think, should be the fact that his poetry reverberates with allusions to Poe's work and adaptations of Poe motifs. But again, very little has been said on the subject. In fact, all of Wilbur's longstanding concern with Poe (including his sadly-misunderstood or ignored remark a few years ago that much of his own poetry can be read as a "quarrel" with Poe's aesthetics[2]) seems now merely to reinforce a misconception: if Wilbur would "quarrel" with Poe at such length and on so many fronts, and if Poe is the great poet of dark and dangerous imaginative voyages and extravagant visionary flights, then Wilbur must be a poet of surface interests, of "things of this world" and all that, steering well clear of any self-test, as an imaginative artist, in or near the ultimate abyss of vision and dream.

I hope to begin here to correct such notions about Wilbur, using precisely his self-avowed "quarrel" with Poe for that purpose. Surely an extended quarrel between artists, especially one that a living man picks with a dead one, can never be assumed a clash of opposites; if such were the case, who with any sense would bother to quarrel at all? But one need not do much assuming here: how very *un*opposite these poets are can be demonstrated. I shall look at the important and pervasive presence of Poe in Wilbur's poetry, his impact on Wilbur's symbolism, his language, and his understanding of imagination. And I shall indicate how Wilbur's improvisations upon Poe contribute to our understanding of his honest and courageous vision, as well as to his stunning impact. A "modern" poet in the true sense, Wilbur can offer us our fill of suitably harrowing and hopeful possibility, and yet remain ever aware of himself and his readers *not* as one-way travelers on a careening excursion into dream but as beings who must ultimately forsake dream for a return to the temporal, or rather, to that so-difficult imaginative course *between* the temporal and the dream—that course which offers the mind the greatest intensity and the highest of sane hopes. No doubt Poe can take us on wilder, more fanciful, more abandoned dream-voyages, but certainly not more audacious ones.

Here are the closing lines of Wilbur's introduction to his edition of *Poe: Complete Poems;* the italics are mine:

> By the refusal of human emotion and moral concern, by the obscuration of logical and allegorical meaning, *by the symbolic destruction of material fact, by negating all that he could of world and worldly self,* Poe strove for a poetry of spiritual effect which should seem "the handiwork of the angels that hover between man and God," and move the reader to a moment of that sort of harmonious intuition which is to be the purifying fire of Earth and the music of the regathering spheres. *There has never been a grander conception of poetry, nor a more impoverished one.*[3]

The grandest, and the most impoverished conception: in this paradox is an important critical clue to what Wilbur respects so thoroughly in Poe as to wish to quarrel with it. Poe's classic symbol for "the destruction of material fact" is, certainly, the whirlpool or the abyss in the sea of experience: any use of the abyss in literature since Poe has owed him a substantial debt. And the process of self- and world-negation, the movement toward the abyss, generates (according to Wilbur) the essential allegory behind many of the tales. In "The House of Poe," we learn to read "MS. Found in a Bottle," for example, as:

> . . . an allegory of the mind's voyage from the waking world into the world of dreams, with each main step of the narrative symbolizing the passage of the mind from one state to another—from wakefulness to reverie, from reverie to the hypnagogic state, from the hypnagogic state to the deep dream.[4]

For Wilbur, the symbol of the abyss or the whirlpool, and the problem of the unrestrained, Supernal-seeking imagination, are essential to Poe. Both, I believe, are essential to Wilbur's art as well, and when considered in detail, the symbol and the problem as they present themselves in his work reveal much about his divergence from and "quarrel" with Poe. Accordingly, I shall consider first the vortex symbol; once its implications are clear, the meaning of "imagination" for Wilbur and the price that he, like Poe, finds must be paid in exchange for it, can be more readily understood.

Poe's cherished motif of world-escape has, as Wilbur explains it, at least two very opposite effects on the poetic sensibility: a flight back toward whatever unity was lost at birth must be at the same time a terrifying adventure into the unknown. And, in Poe as in so much Romantic and Symbolist verse, the dream is the great self-surrender (that is, short of death itself) to the imaginative powers for the voyage beyond the temporal. Accordingly, the release of the imagination is both the most frightful and the most wished-for of consummations. More precisely, it is the *process* of escape which, like dying, holds the terror; it is the *end* of that process, shrouded like death in obscurity, that excites the hopes of the voyager.

A longed-for transcendence and a terrible doom; a flight into unity with the still essence behind nightmarish reality, and nightmare itself: these opposing fates and contending emotions are all drawn together for Poe in the symbol of the whirlpool, the abyss, the "vertiginous plunge" as Wilbur sometimes calls it; in these varied forms, the symbol pervades the tales as both the ultimate fulfillment of dream and the end of life itself. Here is Wilbur once more in his Introduction:

> . . . the end of Poe's journey tales is always, more or less obviously, a plunge. The canoe dives dizzily into the valley, the ship enters the whirlpool or the polar gulf on the way to Tartarus or the Earth's womb. Where the scenery and properties of the tale do not permit a giddy and plunging close, Poe *alludes* to the idea. At the end of "King Pest," to give but one of many possible examples, the intoxicated Hugh Tarpaulin is cast into a hogshead of ale and disappears "amid a whirlpool of foam."

Convincing as Wilbur may be here, he can be at the same time remarkably blunt in his disclaimers: "Poe's aesthetic, Poe's theory of the nature of art, seems to me insane. To say that art should repudiate everything human and earthly, and find its subject in the flickering end of dreams, is hopelessly to narrow the scope and function of art" ("The House of Poe").

Skilled as he is at tracking the flight of Poe's imagination over the edge of the most awesome abyss, Wilbur has little indeed of Poe's obsession with irretrievably dropping to the ambiguous bottom. How, therefore, can a symbol such as the whirlpool, so central to the "mechanism of destructive transcendence"[5] that Wilbur has called Poe's art, serve such a poet as Wilbur himself, much less prove a central symbol in some of his finest poetry?

For answers, let us turn first to "Marginalia," a poem which has caused some interpretive trouble: knowing of Wilbur's special taste and distaste for Poe helps to explicate the poem's obscurities and to clarify the particularly difficult closing lines. In fact, the title of the poem seems a Poe-like clue that one should have Poe in mind. Certainly Poe's use of the word "Marginalia" is the most famous in American literature, and the title of Wilbur's poem seems to suggest, like a clue from one of Poe's detective stories, that Poe has something to do with this poem as well.

In any case, Wilbur's "Marginalia" surely treats qualities of consciousness with which Poe himself is preoccupied. We are to look again to the borderlands between states of awareness, between being and non-being, between temporality and existence of some timeless, unworldly kind. "Things concentrate at the edges," the poem begins; we learn that these "things" include the experiences of the hypnagogic state. For Wilbur, a sane man can perceive a "sublime decor"—illusion, perhaps, or perhaps something more than illusion—only when the mind is near some strange edge between the retrained, waking sensibility and the self-loss of deep dream. What recollection should make of such peripheral experience is a mystery. We cannot know, Wilbur asserts, just how closely our "centrifugal" reveries, there on the rim of the vortex that draws all beyond time and life, resemble any truth independent of both imagination and worldly experience.

But given all this, and given the familiar, modern skepticism which seems implicit in it, the "good drowning" and the "hope" of the poem's closing line can both confuse and trouble a reader. Indeed, how is Wilbur's conception that all imaginative experience projects from the self (as the final stanza seems to claim) to be resolved with any hope at all, save as some last-minute failure of existential nerve? There are important ambiguities in the word "drowning" as well: after all, it can be either a final, most-visionary instant before oblivion, or the opening of some altered condition of being. We shall have better luck with the sense, the implications, and the coherence of this last stanza if we look to the situation and symbol that Wilbur is adapting here, as well as to the sensibilities of Poe's own voyagers. Of the many journeys and plunges in Poe, two seem most strongly suggested by "Marginalia": aboard a phantom derelict rushing toward its doom, the narrator of "MS. Found in a Bottle" finds that his terror of the whirlpool before him is turning to something else:

> . . . a curiosity to penetrate the mysteries of these awful regions, predominates even over my despair, and will reconcile me to the most hideous aspect of death. It is evident that we are hurrying onwards to some exciting knowledge—some never-to-be-imparted secret, whose attainment is destruction.

The phantom sailors show a similar mood:

> The crew pace the deck with unquiet and tremulous step, but there is upon their countenances and expression more of the eagerness of hope than of the apathy of despair.

The lone survivor of "A Descent into the Maelstrom" undergoes a like change of heart, even as he begins his drop into the destroying swirl:

> It may look like boasting—but what I tell you is truth—I began to reflect how magnificent a thing it was to die in such a manner, and how foolish it was in me to think of so paltry a consideration as my own individual life, in view of so wonderful a manifestation of God's power.

In Wilbur's view, Poe's voyagers are nearly all embodiments of the visionary mind, the mind that would give itself utterly to the dream experience regardless of the personal cost. And an enormous cost that can be! His hair, and his mind, for that matter, blanched by the terror and hope of his excursion, only the fisherman of "A Descent" returns to us from the whirlpool. But as we see Wilbur's closing image now in the context of its literary heritage, it seems clear that he shows here, albeit in a limited shape befitting a skeptical age, a visionary faith of his own. It sometimes confuses readers that Wilbur will not ignore one lasting restraint: that one should not, *must* not give over one's self entirely to a dreaming pursuit of the absolute, if he would not lose himself in the dream-world trap of madness and self-deceit. To take such an awareness as any failure of nerve does Wilbur no justice at all, for to reject madness is by no means to reject the power and promise of *vigilant* dreaming. Close reading suggests that if we take the repeated "which" of line 19 to refer either to the voices on the rim of the abyss or to the rim itself, rather than, as some have suggested,[6] to refer to the plunge itself, then we are yet some distance from the precipice. After all, we know from "MS." and "A Descent" that the real fall does not begin with the crossing of the rim, but rather nearer to the heart of the swirl. But we are not so very far away: we have our doom and its ambiguous promise, although no one alive can give us a trustworthy preview of either. Like the silent, anxious phantoms of "MS." we are still about our business, not frozen with fright and extravagant hope. And we must found our faith on those "centrifugal" and fleeting intuitions—or fictions—that we have found or contrived to explain the mystery and give provisional sense to life.

The poem's strong implications that dream and imagination are so far from being one and the same give added meaning to the common observation that Wilbur prefers mutable to static and unsullied beauty. To follow a difficult, ultimately doomed but yet prevailing course on the bounds between the waking and the hypnagogic state is, in fact, to choose a maculate and a changing world over timeless and inhuman perfection: at the heart of both the world and the imagination itself are that subtle melding and constant change which yield the most stunning intensity and the greatest hope.

To clarify this optimism, we need to look at one more abyss: "The Beacon," in the same volume, *Things of This World*, again shows a Wilbur far less sure than Poe of the deep dream as a bridge to an absolute reality, but it is, I think, noticeably more optimistic than "Marginalia" and thus deserving of our attention. The creative, projective powers of "our human visions"—that is, those of the sane and wakeful mind—seem to strike vague but telling reverberations in an autonomous order beneath or beyond all the apparent chaos. Here it seems that an imagination that can resist Poe's manic and mystical extremes might indeed experience moments of real insight.

The whirling abyss and the sea that are for Wilbur an always-changing mergence of the eternal and the temporal have, in "The Beacon," much the same paradoxical promise that they have in Poe. The great paradox is stressed here by several clever ambiguities in Wilbur's diction, among them the clearest reference to the whirlpool itself. The "pitchy whirl / At the mind's end," as it is called here, we may understand in any or all of several ways: "pitchy" is the tumultuous motion of the water, or, as in "Marginalia," the chorus of voices with which it calls and warns, or its ultimate blackness on this black night—Wilbur is widely known for his skill at causing words to reverberate in so many telling directions. Likewise, "the mind's end" can be, as in Wallace Stevens' famous phrase, either the end of the mind in dreamless unconsciousness, or the limits of the mind (as in Land's End), or the "end" of the mind with the end of existence.

All this may remind one very much of "Marginalia", but what "sense of the sea" we are to make through this darkness, what hopes for ultimate order we can console ourselves with at this harrowing vista seem not entirely out of our own fictions. Wilbur's diction is quite precise, and what he says is this: that the absolute is not absent but merely "veiled" beneath a disordered surface, and that the beacon of imagination (which is at once our projective power and our insight) will finally come round again, "one grand chop" of its light giving our hopes and visions new "clearance"—not the final ambiguity of the poem but certainly among the most significant. What sort of "clearance" is this? A moment of clear, deeper insight which accordingly "clears" (or supports and welcomes) further imaginative life? Or is it "clearance" in the sense of *adequate* depth of insight, like the clearance under a low bridge, allowing us to persist for a while in feeling our way along with cautious and vigilant assurance? Unanswerable as these questions are, the overall tone of the poem is, I think, surprisingly affirmative—and indicates even greater faith in an imagination which holds to its hard course along the edges of waking and dream.

One cannot long consider the imaginations of two poets without at least some search for the impact of their ideas on their art, and so far these abyss poems, each something of a metaphysical statement, have been of limited use in that direction. If Poe's poetry is, as Wilbur has it, "an account of the process of aspiration, and a rationale of the soul's struggle to free itself of earth and move toward the supernal,"[7] and if such aspirations and movement are precisely what Wilbur rejects, then wherein lie the power and reason for his own poetry? Again the answer has very much to do with Poe. Let us turn to one of Wilbur's observations on "the essential poetic act":

> People feel a real unease and separation when confronted by the nameless, and it is perfectly understandable that the first man set down in the centre of the first landscape, applied himself at once to redeeming it from anonymity. *What had been*

> *spoken into being he spoke again, re-creating the creation*, giving each creature a relation to himself, and gaining a kind of symbolic control over what lay around him.[8] (italics mine)

The emphasized phrases strikingly echo a familiar conception of Poe's, perhaps most memorably expressed at the climax of his curious allegory "The Power of Words." Here we meet the exquisitely anguished Agathos (some kind of immortal spirit of The Good) as he surveys the fair "wild star" which he himself "spoke—in a few passionate sentences—into birth" ages before. This echo suggests an answer to our question: in Poe's universe, where the immortal may mingle so freely and devastatingly with mortal experience, the word is the potent and perilous *creative* force which the dreamer-poet shares with the Supernal Powers. For Wilbur, the word is the supreme *re*creative force; "the essential poetic act" is not one with the creative powers of reality. It is rather the symbolic creation or rediscovery of temporal order and beauty, and, possibly, a momentary perception of something beyond temporality. For Poe, the "power of words" is enormous, very real, and bewilderingly free of restraint. For Wilbur it is symbolic, dependent upon the imagination's constant interaction with a difficult temporal world, but absolutely essential nonetheless. That is, perhaps, the most fundamental distinction to be recognized between the aesthetics of Wilbur and Poe.

Once we have seen how important Poe can be, as both teacher and adversary, in some of Wilbur's most significant poems, one may, if he wishes, begin turning up allusions to Poe, and echoes of Poe, and hints of echoes of Poe, nearly anywhere he looks in Wilbur, although both the surety and the usefulness of such finds is likely to vary. Certainly Poe does show up clearly and significantly on occasion. Wilbur's "Bell Speech," for example, is as forthright a response as we are likely to find in modern verse to Poe's "The Bells," and knowing that is of use in reading Wilbur's poem. No longer, it says, do our bells speak with the varied rhetoric of old, matching their voices to each human event; their new "sameness of sound" suggests to the poet some sublime "language without flaw," an ambiguous but perhaps powerful language, able (as for Wilbur, a real language must be) to reshape turmoil into something coherent. And quite as surely, Wilbur's surprisingly contentious and vigorously celebratory lines "For the New Railway Station in Rome" have as their foil the passion for ruins that Poe so eloquently indulges in "The Coliseum":

> Rich reliquary
> Of lofty contemplation left to Time
> By buried centuries of pomp and power!
> At length—at length—after so many days
> Of weary pilgrimage and burning thirst
> (Thirst for the springs of lore that in thee lie,)
> I kneel, an altered and an humble man,
> Amid thy shadows, and so drink within
> My very soul thy grandeur, gloom, and glory!

It seems implausible that, from the evidence of his language and of his abiding aesthetic concerns, Wilbur does not have Poe and "The Coliseum" in mind when he proclaims:

> Those who with short shadows
> Poked through the stubbled forum pondering on decline,
> And would not take the sun standing at noon
> For a good sign;
> Those pilgrims of defeat
> Who brought their injured wills as to a soldiers' home;
> Dig them all up now, tell them there's something new
> To see in Rome.

But what of "The Beautiful Changes" and "Conjuration" and "The Juggler" and "Still Citizen Sparrow" and so many of the others? Are they not, each in its own way, quarreling with Poe's excessive taste for an unearthly and pristine Supernal? Do they not all contend somehow that the only true discovery of the wonder is through the worldly and the maculate? No doubt each of these poems could be reexamined with Poe in mind; what we would gain from doing so, however, is highly variable, and in this limited space it seems best to look at a very few poems in which the gain is important indeed. I shall confine myself to three more, three with which our understanding of the *quarrel* reveals something truly significant about the poetry and the man.

Just as Poe, for Wilbur, is a teller of tales that are in fact symbolist poetry, Wilbur is now and then a maker of verse tales about the pitfalls of the dream. Among these, "The Undead" is ostensibly a poem about vampires—surely that suggests something of Poe and his fellow gothics. These are very creditable vampires, possessing quite a few of their proper characteristics: "Mirrors fail to perceive them"; they take to the air as great bats and flap off into the night in search of blood. But how these poor creatures have reached such perverse and pathetic "grandeur" is not precisely in the vampire tradition:

> Even as children they were late sleepers,
> Preferring their dreams, even when quick with monsters,
> To the world with all its breakable toys,
> Its compacts with the dying;
> From the stretched arms of withered trees
> They turned, fearing contagion of the mortal,
> And even under the plums of summer
> Drifted like winter moons.

No infection has taken their souls but their own bad judgment. They have dreamed too much, pursued the Supernal too hotly, refused reconciliation with a natural world. All of this is, of course, not so much in the usual manner of vampires as in the usual manner of Poe. Wilbur's lines seem to reverberate with the fervent wish at the opening of the young Poe's "Dreams":

> Oh! that my young life were a lasting dream!
> My spirit not awak'ning till the beam
> Of an Eternity should bring the morrow.
> Yes! tho' that long dream were of hopeless sorrow,
> 'T were better than the cold reality
> Of waking life, to him whose heart must be,
> And hath been still, upon the lovely earth,
> A chaos of deep passion, from his birth.

That urge for "destructive transcendence" so familiar in Poe is, in "The Undead," the "negative frenzy" of the vampire: a hopeless frenzy, that is, for the negation of worldly reality, of the self, of all genuine possibilities of existence and the understanding. And such a denial leads only into pathetic paradox:

> Think how sad it must be
> To thirst always for a scorned elixir,
> The salt quotidian blood.
> Which, if mistrusted, has no savor;
> To prey on life forever and not possess it,
> As rock-hollows, tide after tide,
> Glassily strand the sea.

As well as this closing captures the irony Wilbur finds at the heart of Poe's great ambition, that to seek so fervently transcendence and imaginative escape from worldly life is, finally, to deny the self both transcendence and life, Wilbur's culminating metaphor is itself indebted to Poe. The poetic spirit's disaster, its search for just such immortality and its end in an appalling stasis and eventual annihilation constitute, Wilbur claims, the real subject of "The City in the Sea." According to his reading, such stasis and doom are for Poe still preferable to both the mutable world and to an awareness of what Wilbur calls that "knowledge of His Truth which God confers on the angels";[9] here are lines from "The City in the Sea" which the close of "The Undead" may recall:

Not the gaily-jewelled dead
Tempt the waters from their bed;
For no ripples curl, alas!
Along that wilderness of glass—
No swellings tell what winds may be
Upon some far-off happier sea—
No heavings hint that winds have been
On seas less hideously serene.

It is true that Wilbur's "Merlin Enthralled" once again uses the motif of "hideously serene" waters to signify the price of surrender to deep dream; but the poem needs here at least a little further discussion. For not merely does "Merlin Enthralled" portray the end of a great artist and the fate of his art in the triumph of dream and oblivious sleep; it seems to celebrate the magnificence that dream can achieve so long as the dreamer-artist maintains his grip against the utter erosion of the waking, controlling, none-too-trusting side of his mind. And the poem is something of an explanation, in fact, of how the art of one like Poe can be for Wilbur so "grand" and "impoverished" at the same time. In "Merlin Enthralled," the great art is Camelot itself, entirely the product of Merlin's wakeful dream, wonderful and alive because that imagination seeks no self-loss in the Supernal. But as the poem opens, Merlin has succumbed to the lure of Niniane (a nymph, born herself of his dreaming imagination and embodying its greatest perils) beyond the hypnagogic state, beyond even the "deep transparent dream"—the temptation to ultimate and immortal oblivion.[10] So much seems familiar. But what is to become of the living art? Vital and meaningful so long as Merlin neither sought nor found his destructive transcendence, Camelot can no longer be the continuing celebration of growth and change and life. It must become now like some quaint relic, the static leavings of a mind which has foregone it and the kind of imagination upon which it has subsisted. Surely the art has its magnificence, but there shall be no more of it from a mind which has moved so far. As the dreaming, creating consciousness passes through the real world on its way into deeper reverie, it may both triumph and defeat itself in the creation of the sublime, as the astonishing conclusion to the poem would have us understand of Camelot and Merlin:

Arthur upon the road began to weep
And said to Gawen *Remember when this hand*
Once haled a sword from stone; now no less strong
It cannot dream of such a thing to do.
Their mail grew quainter as they clopped along.
The sky became a still and woven blue.
(emphasis Wilbur's)

But enough, now, of the perils and pains Wilbur warns against in the doctrine of self-loss that he associates with Poe. Does Wilbur see no price to be paid for the aesthetic and visionary stance that he himself takes? Or should one agree, after all, with his detractors that Wilbur has opted for a suspiciously safe and comfortable place of resistance to aesthetic and visionary excesses? To provide a brief response, I shall close this study with a look at "Beowulf," which seems to me a terribly important as well as a marvelously atmospheric poem, a retelling of the epic story with remarkable brevity, dignity, and power, and at the same time, I think, a portrayal of the enforced loneliness of precisely the sensibility that Wilbur himself upholds, against the prevailing taste of the world for one destructive spiritual excess after another.

A case that one should read "Beowulf" as a poem of Wilbur's own condition, or rather of his plight and the plight of anyone who would follow the changing, subtle edges between waking and dream, is founded in the strongly symbolic shape and look of the poem, a shape and a look comprehensible in light of the rest of his poetry, his opinions on Poe, and the simple fact that the poem will not make much sense any other way. Let us look, for example, at the Denmark we are landed upon in the opening stanza:

The land was overmuch like scenery,
The flowers attentive, the grass too garrulous green;
In the lake like a dropped kerchief could be seen
The lark's reflection after the lark was gone;
The Roman road lay paved too shiningly
For a road so many men had travelled on.

How are we to understand this place, no quality of which we recognize from the text of the original epic, except as a world of excessive and perverse dream, a world where imagination trusted too blindly has led the inhabitants into dreams which have turned toward nightmare? Indeed, in these "garrulous green," all-too-scenic landscapes Wilbur finds particularly alarming evidence that the rampant dream is ready to betray the dreamer. He inveighs against such mind-landscapes very clearly in "Walking to Sleep," a long poem which is, in many ways, an extensive guide to survival in the hypnagogic state:

Let them not be too velvet green, the fields
Which the deft needle of your eye appoints,
Nor the old farm past which you make your way
Too shady-linteled, too instinct with home.
It is precisely from Potemkin barns
With their fresh-painted hex signs on the gables,
Their sparkling gloom within, their stanchion-rattle
And sweet breath of silage, that there comes
The trotting cat whose head is but a skull.

To this perverse and haunted world, this land "childish" not merely in its obsessions with dream and nightmare but also in that the monster which besets them is a "child" of those too-free fantasies, comes Beowulf, a champion fit to do battle with a nightmare. Beowulf, as we come to know him here, has sailed long upon the changing seas of mind and experience. His greatest power is his caution and his self-possession as a visionary, allowing him at once to enter a dream and combat its own allurement and power. In short, Beowulf is himself a dreamer. The difference is that he is wise and wakeful enough not to dream overmuch. Unlike the Danes, therefore, who "wander" to sleep helplessly and leave their champion to fight alone, Beowulf finds no master in the hypnagogic state, but may pass through its nightmares to a "rest so deep" as to be open to only he who is both visionary and self-possessed man.

All seems to be well with Beowulf. He has freed a world of its vexing dreams, maintained his strong but vigilantly-reined imagination. But the poem soon takes a painfully ironic turn, revealing the condition which Beowulf, and by implication Wilbur, must share with Poe in their very quarrel with his purposes: that is, isolation. The Danes now find that they have had too much of visions, and so, like true men, they take up the opposite excess. The world now puts on an aesthetic coldness which suspects all imagining; a soulless, passionless, hopeless stance in which the hero himself embodies the threat of the imagination, as alone as one of Poe's wandering, solitary, visionary knights:

> The lake gave up the lark, but now its song
> Fell to no ear, the flowers too were wrong,
> The day was fresh and pale and swiftly old,
> The night put out no smiles upon the sea;
> And the people were strange; the people strangely
> cold.

For his victory, Beowulf receives his "hard reward," the play upon words working in every possible way. It is a hard-won reward, of a hard material nature, itself soulless and bestowed by a hardened, cold folk who now wish very soon to be rid of him. Beowulf's sensibility is and shall ever be such that few around him shall understand, and fewer still attempt to emulate. And so the life and death of this hero are touched with great pathos as well as victorious joy, with isolation as well as with the sublime. The poem closes with such stateliness and compassion that, knowing what we do of Wilbur's struggles to maintain himself a hard place amid a world which does not well understand his task, we cannot but be more convinced than ever that Wilbur's Beowulf is one in whom Wilbur sees much of himself:

> He died in his own country a kinless king,
> A name heavy with deeds, and mourned as one
> Will mourn for the frozen year when it is done.
> They buried him next the sea on a thrust of land:
> Twelve men rode round his barrow all in a ring,
> Singing of him what they could understand.

All that Beowulf has done is touched with ocean, yet, in his death as in his life, he remains on the lonely shore of what he knows. And so we have begun to know something of the Wilbur-Poe quarrel as it continues now and of its usefulness in reading the living poet as well as the dead one. In an age which ever clamors for honesty and suspects it if it be not utterly bleak, an age which clamors for visions and suspects them if they be not tinged with madness, Wilbur strives to be an artist of both intense imagination and wakeful skepticism. He is a poet struggling to speak to men, to speak to a world which has either despaired of the power of imaginative flight or given itself excessively to hopeless and solipsistic fantasy. On the difficult edges and margins, Wilbur seeks a way to recover the primal freshness of things, to stun and stretch our awareness without enslaving or blinding it, just as the first language-maker felt himself awed and exhorted in Wilbur's myth of the first poem. In his quest for such moments of "symbolic control," and in his recognition of ourselves as both largely sane and largely unsatisfied men, Wilbur's fleeting dream-glimpses of underlying order and the ambiguity of his surface world create together a harmony and a vision which can seem true even to the troubled modern spirit, and stun and excite even the modern imagination.

Notes

1. Three critical studies of particular use to readers of Wilbur: Donald Hill, *Richard Wilbur* (New York, 1967); J. P. Farrell, "The Beautiful Changes in Richard Wilbur's Poetry," *Contemporary Literature*, 12 (Winter, 1971), pp. 74–87; A. K. Weatherhead, "Richard Wilbur: Poetry of Things," *ELH*, XXXV (1968), pp. 606–17.
2. Richard Wilbur, "On My Own Work," *Shenandoah*, XVII, No. 1 (1966), p. 66.
3. Wilbur, "Introduction," in *Poe: Complete Poems*, The Laurel Poetry Series (New York, 1959), pp. 38–39.
4. Wilbur, "The House of Poe," in *Anniversary Lectures: 1959* (Washington, 1959), pp. 24–25.
5. Wilbur, *Poe: Complete Poems*, p. 17.
6. See, e.g., Hill, p. 107.
7. Wilbur, *Poe: Complete Poems*, p. 11.
8. Wilbur, "Poetry and the Landscape," in *The New Landscape in Art and Science*, ed. Gyorgy Kepes (Chicago, 1956), p. 86.
9. Wilbur, *Poe: Complete Poems*, p. 30.
10. It is interesting to note that Merlin himself passes out of reality through a version of the vortex: lured by a voice like "dark diving water," he enters a "deep unsoundable swell" which spells the end of his imagination and his magical art. But it seems to the reader a smooth and unharrowing journey: those whirlpools and abysses into which Wilbur drops himself, and us with him, are likewise plunges which we can manage without terror and reconcile with our continued imaginative existence: holes drilled in a living room floor ("A Hole in the Floor"), a pit dug by an eager child in a New Jersey farmyard ("Digging for China"), the drop of a leaf into the "falls of a pool" ("Piazza di Spagna, Early Morning").

MICHAEL HULSE
"The Poetry of Richard Wilbur"

Quadrant, October 1981, pp. 49–52

It was too much to expect, I suppose, that a reading public that has been systematically neglecting Richard Wilbur's work ever since it began to fall from favour at the beginning of the sixties should remember to honour him on his sixtieth birthday. On March 1 this year Richard Wilbur turned sixty. Not one magazine and certainly no newspaper that I have seen in the last few months, British or American or Australian, has troubled to mention this fact; the movement which Alvarez set in motion nearly twenty years ago, when he allowed Wilbur's name to disappear entirely from his account (in the introduction to his famous and influential Penguin anthology, *The New Poetry*) of the recent poetry scene, has been gaining momentum for two decades, and Wilbur's work in the seventies, mannerist, tired and flat if measured against the poetry he wrote in the fifties and before, has not helped matters. Wilbur wasn't even mentioned in Michael Hamburger's *The Truth of Poetry* (1969) or in Ian Hamilton's collection of essays from *the Review, The Modern Poet* (1968); he disappeared from the Boyers anthology of *Salmagundi* essays, *Contemporary Poetry in America* (1974) and from Denis Donoghue's *Seven American Poets* (1975); on both sides of the Atlantic, and, it goes without saying, further afield, readers could search volume after volume on poetry in America since the War, but if those volumes were published in the last twenty years the likelihood that Wilbur would be mentioned in them diminished in direct relation to the lateness of the date. Very sad.

And sad not only as a comment on Wilbur but also as a comment on the reading public. Granted, the reading public has been under fire for a long time; Q. D. Leavis wasn't the first (in her impressive *Fiction and the Reading Public*, 1932) to notice that the ability of the average reader to meet a direct challenge to his capacity for earnest wrestling with the dilemmas that thought brings with it has diminished alarmingly in this, our literate twentieth century. Randall Jarrell and many more have eloquently attested the post-War era's unprecedented flunking of any demand on the mind; it would be tedious to go into the familiar arguments about the television age of Instant Literature and entertainment for idiots. Nevertheless, every time one comes across an example of a living writer who has suffered at the hands of the New Age's shift of interests, the terrible consequences for our future ability to comprehend *any* of the great but difficult writing of our past become apparent. Wilbur *is* difficult. Even at his worst he can be difficult; at his best he unites the neo-Augustan severity of a Donald Davie or (at times) an A. D. Hope with the elegance of an Anthony Hecht or a John Glassco, he assimilates the various directions of a Donne, a Hopkins, or a Dylan Thomas, and he produces out of it all something uniquely his own and uniquely pleasing and complex. To forget Wilbur is to ignore the rich satisfactions which can be afforded the mind.

The secret of Wilbur's satisfactions when the poet is at his most successful lies in the impeccable matching of subject to language. Consider, for instance, these lines from 'A Firetruck' (in *Advice to a Prophet*, 1961):

> Right down the shocked street with a siren-blast
> That sends all else skittering to the curb,
> Redness, brass, ladders and hats hurl past,
> Blurring to sheer verb,
>
> Shift at the corner into uproarious gear
> And make it around the turn in a squall of traction,
> The headlong bell maintaining sure and clear,
> *Thought is degraded action!*

Of course the street isn't shocked, of course the bell can't be described as headlong: but the transferred epithets are just one contributive part of the complex mechanics of kinetic recreation. Wilbur's note tells us that this eighth line was derived from Henry Adams, but we do not need to know the provenance of the idea to find it implicit in the effortless presentation of action in these two stanzas. "Right down", we read; and immediately the rush of action is there in the push and thrust of the words. How that skidding *s* hisses and squeals through the first stanza! And how well it is knit to other hectic sounds: the clattering *k* and the brash *a* of "blast", "brass", "ladders" and "hats" and "past" . . . The "hats hurl past": watch those aspirates, heaving with energy as the stress cluster power-packs its way past the cowed onlooker on imagination's pavement. In passing (how the language mimics the idea!) the fire engine is already becoming less a thing, more an idea: it is "Blurring", and that eighth line simply lifts out explicitly a statement that is already implicit in this word in the fourth. And it blurs "to sheer verb": the terminology of language itself takes over with an energetic punch, and if we have seen the kinetic weight that Wilbur can assign to verbs in poems like 'Juggler' or 'A Baroque Wall-Fountain in the Villa Sciarra' we know the energy that is loaded into that word "verb". But not just "verb"—"sheer verb". The stress goes on the pure essence of action, just as in the moment presented in these two stanzas the fire engine asserts its existence so fully and vehemently that it seems well-nigh to obliterate "all else"; as we might say, "nothing else is" . . . But the word "sheer" performs not only this function; it also links the two stanzas through the alliterative pattern of "shocked", "sheer" and "Shift", and at the word "Shift" we meet another of those humped punches of effort that the syllabic stanza is so eminently equipped to deliver, as the stress pattern echoes that of the opening "Right down". As the fire engine moves on, the verse becomes more open and less dense, and as the momentary vision recedes and blurs the idea replaces the fact: "*Thought is degraded action!*" The passing of the vehicle is followed in all its squalling, skidding clamour, and when it is gone its meaning (a word which I ought perhaps to place between inverted commas) clicks into place: there has been a (brief) confrontation between cognitive (contingent) and necessary reality, and the true fact of being comes out way ahead of the secondary condition of thinking ("degraded") . . .

This interpenetration of language and subject is Wilbur's most characteristic triumph, and his most characteristic failure, conversely, is made inevitable the moment he grabs over-hastily at such an effect, without the patience to set it up as carefully as he does in 'A Fire-truck'. And "set it up" is the right term: those who accuse Wilbur of being artificial are of course perfectly correct in saying this, and it remains only to decide whether we are to see such artifice as a positive or a negative quality. For those who would insist on the impulsive, spontaneous nature of poetic expression, such artifice as Wilbur's, such elaborately-conceived artistry, must of necessity seem sterile, and its failure to connect *obviously* and *completely*, at *every* point, with human values, must seem a damnation; yet others who, while agreeing eagerly that Lowell and Berryman and Plath are quite likely the most important poets we've had since the War, would nonetheless insist on a plurality of taste in poetry, might (rightly, I feel) prefer to accept Wilbur alongside the great confessionals. No one disputes that they're as different as chalk and cheese. The secret of a successfully liberal understanding of literature, though, is surely to remain equally open to many and various *different* types of writing. Our reading public shows itself to be anti-pluralist in rejecting the elegant art of a Wilbur.

Wilbur himself has commented amply on the nature of art and artistry in his poems; in the much-anthologized early success 'Juggler' (in *Ceremony*) Wilbur explores the role of the artist with an uncanny tact and cunning.

> A ball will bounce, but less and less. It's not
> A light-hearted thing, resents its own resilience.
> Falling is what it loves, and the earth falls
> So in our hearts from brilliance,
> Settles and is forgot.
> It takes a sky-blue juggler with five red balls
> To shake our gravity up. Whee, in the air
> The balls roll round, wheel on his wheeling hands,
> Learning the ways of lightness, alter to spheres
> Grazing his finger ends,
> Cling to their courses there,
> Swinging a small heaven about his ears.
>
> But a heaven is easier made of nothing at all
> Than the earth regained, and still and sole within
> The spin of worlds, with a gesture sure and noble
> He reels that heaven in,
> Landing it ball by ball,
> And trades it all for a broom, a plate, a table.
>
> Oh, on his toe the table is turning, the broom's
> Balancing up on his nose, and the plate whirls
> On the tip of the broom! Damn, what a show, we cry:
> The boys stamp, and the girls
> Shriek, and the drum booms
> And all comes down, and he bows and says good-bye.
>
> If the juggler is tired now, if the broom stands
> In the dust again, if the table starts to drop
> Through the daily dark again, and though the plate
> Lies flat on the table top,
> For him we batter our hands
> Who has won for once over the world's weight.

Wilbur is actually *doing* with words what the juggler is doing with his balls and broom and plate and table. Damn, what a show!

This is so accomplished it almost begins to look easy, and it would be tempting to underrate Wilbur's achievement in a poem like this. It isn't simply alliteration, it isn't simply stress clusters, it isn't simply mimetic patterns of metre and syntax: it is all these things *with* an ironic sense of the poet himself behind them. Look at that final line: "Who has *w*on for *o*nce over the *w*orld's *w*eight." What effort goes into those *w* sounds! But also, what a sense of accomplishment at the end of the line—yes, we think, Wilbur too has won over the world's weight. What satisfaction. What repose in the knowledge that it *is* possible for the trickster or artist to beat the lot down under his own mastery now and then. And yet: "for once" . . . How very frail an achievement it is, how very temporary a triumph.

Three examples of Wilbur's mimetic use of language in this poem will prove a number of points amply. The first example: in the first line, how patly the ball bounces on each regular beat of the iambic line—and sets up a pattern of falling, linked in sense and sound. This falling pattern then persists in lines 3 to 5, where the foot at the beginning of each line is reversed, and, like the slower and lower bouncing of the ball, the descent settles through falling until . . . the door is closed on what has been lost: "forgot". What a wealth of meaning that "forgot" carries here! The sense of failing and falling, of losing and forgetting, is open-ended to that loss of innocence and original perception, that loss of prime in the heart, which expanded the dimensions of 'My Father Paints the Summer' (in *The Beautiful Changes*). We are back with the Fall, but a Fall seen not only in terms of a loss of innocence imposed by virtue of the human condition, but also in terms of growing up out of childhood and into . . . "gravity" (Wilbur's love of puns serves him well here). It is the virtue of the juggler—of the artist—that he can (however temporarily) restore that pristine condition to our vision of the world.

The second example: underpinning the densely alliterative patterns of the second stanza we have a remarkable use of verbs, even more sophisticated than in 'My Father Paints the Summer' (the poem with which 'Juggler' invites comparison). The exuberant, childlike exclamation in "Whee" is taken up in "wheel" and "wheeling" (where the *l* looks back to "balls roll" and forward to "Learning . . . lightness"), and in the next four lines we have no fewer than three verbs in present participle form, conveying a vivid sense of action really *happening;* and to give special stress to his verbs as the bearers of meaning, Wilbur has contrived to place them all at the beginnings of the lines. What this means is not only that the lines have an unparalleled vigour which mimics the juggler's number, but also parallel those lines in the first stanza where the underlying iambic pattern was meddled with to place verbs ("Falling", "Settles") in initial positions. The dying fall is echoed from stanza to stanza, and through the metrical pattern an ironic echo is set up too, so that "light-hearted" at the beginning becomes ironically present behind the phrase "Learning the ways of lightness"—ironically, because we feel that, lightness having been lost, it cannot, within the terms of the poem, be regained. The irony enters the second stanza obliquely, but once we see it we realise that in the word "Learning" Wilbur is compounding his point about the *temporary* nature of art's transcendence of the world's limitations. Nothing actually *is* learnt; the word is at best a paradox, at worst an illusion, and as such reflects copiously upon the nature of artistic sleight-of-hand.

Our third example:

> Damn, what a show, we cry:
> The boys stamp, and the girls
> Shriek, and the drums boom
> And all comes down, and he bows and says good-
> bye.

First, we are given four words that may as well be in inverted commas; and what is their function, with that colon following? They are there to pinpoint a climax. And sure enough: every subject is a monosyllable, every verb is a monosyllable, and they are linked simply by conjunction plus article in a breathless dash from one stress cluster to the next. How the stresses slam and squash and jostle! And all so noisy! And then: "all comes down", where the verb preserves the thump of the booming drum and the *d* alliterates with the drum as well, and we know it's finished . . . and then there are all those breathless, skipping conjunctions again as the juggler bows quickly and hurries off the stage. We can almost see him do it.

Babette Deutsch wrote of this poem: "As Hopkins wished to be read with the ears, so too, Richard Wilbur composes in a fashion that demands aural sensitivity if the poem is to be fully comprehended. His braiding of rhyme, cross-rhyme, assonance and alliteration is one of the finest features—when too rich, one of the defects—of his melodious verse."

As in 'A Fire-truck', so in 'Juggler', Wilbur's craftsmanship is quite staggering. And this is true of the juggler too: what the performer in the poem clearly possesses is a wealth of training, a mastery of a method, and a perfect sense of timing. And what he possesses too is a gift for entrancing an audience; we may well suspect that his audience does not consist only of the boys and girls that are mentioned, but it is important that it is the instinct of the child that reacts in the audience response. How closely the position of the juggler resembles that of Wilbur himself, as he writes the poem—writing from a wealth of craftsmanship and labour, judging every last point of phrasing to the nicest of niceties, and keeping the reader on the very edge of his seat. And how like any artist the juggler is, for that matter, who learns his trade in order to transport us . . . Transport us? Where to? And here, as so often with Wilbur, we notice that the poet's trip-wire irony is really very subtly stretched across our response to his poem. If we are tempted, with the father in 'My Father Paints the Summer', to seek escape in dimensions of fantasy—if we are tempted to suppose that Wilbur is speaking here of the ability of the artist, or of artistry, or of the artefact, to transport us into "the dreamt world" (the phrase is from 'A Baroque Wall-Fountain in the Villa Sciarra')—if we think this, Wilbur can reply: yes, in a sense I do mean that, but I also want to insist on the peripheral, temporary nature of any such suspension of reality. Because art *isn't* real. My poem is my artefact, you admire it, you're outside reality . . . for a few minutes. That's all. And what you've been given is "a heaven", which it is so terribly easy to contrive; what is impossible to recapture is reality, to regain the earth.

So in the very fabric of this superlative piece of writing there is a final irony at the expense of the poet himself, who sees that the crafted artefact may have a supposed existence but cannot in fact ever make any meaningful connection—the artist is always out there on the fringe of existence, wheeling his balls, writing his poems. That "for once" has an almost tragic weight for the practising artist.

Ceremony, the collection which included 'Juggler', was published in 1950; it was preceded by *The Beautiful Changes* (1947), and it is arguable that these two first books contain the finest of Wilbur's work. Certainly the adoption of rhetorical positions was already stiffening into a pose in the Pulitzer

Prize-winning *Things of This World* (1956), and *Advice to a Prophet*, which appeared two years after Lowell's *Life Studies*, was the last thoroughly enjoyable book of poems from Wilbur's hand. In *Advice to a Prophet*, indeed, the very fine poems—'A Hole in the Floor', 'A Fire-truck' (the first two stanzas), 'Junk', 'Advice to a Prophet', and the comic lyric 'Pangloss's Song', a cast-off from the *Candide* opera on which Wilbur collaborated—are outnumbered by many more which have an air of going through motions which have become arthritic; if it was possible to say, with Jarrell, that his early poems "compose themselves into a little too regular a beauty", the later work, in *The Mind Reader* and *Walking to Sleep* and to some extent in *Advice to a Prophet* already, too often creaks with an overstiff selfconsciousness. And to go with this stiffening of linguistic pose went a smoothing out of the subject matter, an elimination of complexity, of that quasi-metaphysical difficulty which made the early Wilbur so rich a pleasure. I think Clive James, in an essay of 1971, was the first to point this out, when he wrote: "what *guaranteed* failure was when the disturbing force, the element of awkwardness, was smoothly denatured before being introduced as a component."

Nevertheless, we judge poets, like other writers, by their best work written in their best period; and Wilbur's best is very fine and encourages us to pass over the later failures with regret rather than condemnation.

I have tried briefly to indicate one or two of the sources of strength which make Wilbur's language so potent a poetic energy; I could of course have written a lot more. Perhaps for now it will be enough to say that he should be read, and that the richness in the subject matter which in turn justifies the richness of the language will be pleasingly apparent in the reading.

THORNTON WILDER

1897–1975

Thornton Niven Wilder was born on April 17, 1897, in Madison, Wisconsin, to Amos Parker Wilder and Isabella (née Niven) Wilder. He was educated at Oberlin College, Yale University (A.B. 1920), the American Academy in Rome, and Princeton University (A.M. 1926). From 1918 to 1919 he served in the Coast Artillery Corps, and during World War II in the army air intelligence, achieving the rank of lieutenant colonel and earning decorations from the governments of the United States and Great Britain. He taught at a number of universities, including Chicago, Hawaii, and Harvard.

Wilder published his first novel, *The Cabala*, in 1926, but it was his second novel, *The Bridge of San Luis Rey* (1927), that brought him literary fame; it won the Pulitzer Prize and was a surprise bestseller as well. Wilder published five more novels in his lifetime, all of which received mixed critical reaction upon initial publication. *The Ides of March* (1948), an intricate Gertrude Stein–influenced novel about Julius Caesar and the society surrounding him, was particularly damned, but the critical consensus has since largely shifted to admiration. Many consider *The Eighth Day* (1967) his masterpiece, although *The Bridge of San Luis Rey* remains the most popular.

Wilder was perhaps best known as a playwright. After several years of writing short plays (many of which are collected in *The Angel That Troubled the Waters and Other Plays*, 1928, and *The Long Christmas Dinner and Other Plays*, 1931) he produced the classic *Our Town* (1938). A great popular success, it won Wilder another Pulitzer Prize, making him the first writer to be granted that award in both fiction and drama. The controversial *Finnegans Wake*–influenced *The Skin of Our Teeth* (1942) also received the Pulitzer Prize. Wilder's *The Merchant of Yonkers* (1939), revised as *The Matchmaker* (1955), was the basis for the hit musical *Hello, Dolly!*

Wilder's reputation declined somewhat during the fifties and sixties, but during his peak period he was probably the most successful American playwright-novelist. Publication of *The Eighth Day* in 1967—almost twenty years after *The Ides of March*, his most recent previous novel—helped to renew interest in Wilder. He died in his sleep on December 7, 1975.

JOSEPH J. FIREBAUGH
"The Humanism of Thornton Wilder"

Pacific Spectator, Autumn 1950, pp. 426–38

Ever since the success of *The Bridge of San Luis Rey*, critics have been disturbed about Thornton Wilder. He is so candidly didactic, so forthrightly a schoolmaster; and one of the first laws of the modern critic is that great art is not didactic. There are, to be sure, Dante, Milton, and Goethe to be dealt with; but they managed to get themselves established before this law was passed; it wouldn't be fair to make it retroactive.

The public, on the other hand, shows a preference for didactic art. As Sabina puts it in *The Skin of Our Teeth*: "Oh—why can't we have plays like we used to have—*Peg O' My Heart*, and *Smilin' Thru*, and *The Bat*, good entertainment with a message you can take home with you?" The satire here is two-edged: for all its shoddiness, Mr. Wilder might be commenting, popular melodrama does give "a message you can take home with you." He himself never hesitates to give a message—or rather, as many messages as he can compact into a single fable. He accepts, that is, the responsibility of the artist.

Against the didactic, though, Mr. Wilder is on record. "Didacticism," he once wrote, "is an attempt at the coercion of another's free mind." But he followed this immediately with the remark that "beauty is the only persuasion," which shows rather clearly that he does want to persuade. In a symposium on *The Intent of the Artist*, published in 1941, he has more to say on this matter. Storytelling ability, he thinks,

> springs, not, as some have said, from an aversion to general ideas, but from an instinctive coupling of idea and illustration; the idea, for a born storyteller, can only be expressed embedded in its circumstantial illustration. The myth, the parable, the fable are the fountain-head of all fiction and in them is seen most clearly the didactic, moralizing employment of a story. Modern taste shrinks from emphasizing the central idea that hides behind the fiction, but it exists there nevertheless, supplying the unity to fantasizing, and offering a justification to what otherwise we would repudiate as mere arbitrary contrivance, pretentious lying, or individualistic association-spinning . . . .
>
> It is the task of the dramatist so to co-ordinate his play, through the selection of episodes and speeches, that though he is himself not visible, his point of view and his governing intention will impose themselves on the spectator's attention, not as dogmatic assertion or motto, but as self-evident truth and inevitable deduction.

Mr. Wilder's real objection, one sees, is to *inartistic* didacticism. One is almost ready to abandon that word, however, and to substitute *philosophical*. But he forestalls us there, by saying: "Imaginative narration—the invention of souls and destinies—is to the philosopher an all but indefensible activity." Despite such disavowals, he is certainly both didactic and philosophical, yet both because of and in spite of these facts, he is an artist too.

To an extent Mr. Wilder has never quite succeeded as a novelist, in that ideas are often more important to him than the fiction he is writing. Parable is the device, after all, of the moralist. His ideas are too often embedded—it is his own word—rather than integrated. Yet his artistry has frequently triumphed over his didacticism.

At least in part, his didacticism seems to have been responsible for his popularity. And, in view of the fact that the 1920's were accompanied by a breakdown in conventional moral standards, this popularity may appear inexplicable. But even during the 'twenties there was more headshaking over lost values than there was actual loss. A glance at the magazines and newspapers suggests as much. If flapper and cake-eater drank their bathtub gin with modern bravado, their hang-overs must certainly have been in an earlier tradition. For the early-morning moods of the late 1920's Mr. Wilder's books were at hand. Both those who needed to confess, and those who did not, found solace in his novels; he had found his audience, and it was larger than historians of the day would lead us to think existed. It was perhaps not drawn primarily from the intellectual world, whose members were inclined to string along with the Menckenist 'twenties until they reached the Marxist 'thirties. But an audience there was, and it was an audience which wanted to be taught, not one which already knew.

Then, too, Mr. Wilder's treatment was sophisticated. Seduction and incest and extramarital establishments are all depicted without the admonitory shake of the head. His taste was impeccable, his motives were soundly ethical and religious; but he knew his way around and, for the privilege of teaching, was willing to show others around.

Although his ideas merge to form a unified philosophical position, we shall separate them here, and discuss in orderly fashion his treatment of the following themes: love; the Platonic idea; intuition and revelation; the otherworldly; human worth; freedom and responsibility; and poetry and scholarship. From first to last, Mr. Wilder combines these themes to achieve his characteristic attitude of civilized otherworldliness.

1. *Love.*—In *The Bridge of San Luis Rey* (1927), the Marquesa de Montemayor writes from Peru long letters to her daughter in Spain, letters expressive of her love for her daughter and her malice for most other human beings. Mr. Wilder remarks that the Marquesa's son-in-law, too, read and

> delighted in her letters, but he thought that when he had enjoyed the style he had extracted all their richness and intention, missing (as most readers do) the whole purport of literature, which is the notation of the heart.

This was a bold statement for 1927; the new jargon of drives, inhibitions, frustrations, and repressions found no place for such old-fashioned words as "heart." Yet Mr. Wilder not only used the word in its old-fashioned sense; he made of it a literary credo. The main purport of his books has been the notation of the heart.

Love is his most persistent theme. He turns the subject over in his mind, as a sculptor might his work in progress, examining it from all sides, seeing now this gleam of light, now that shadow, now this line, now that plane. He finds there an inexhaustibly bewildering and revealing subject. Of its worth he is convinced; but as to the reasons for its worth, he cannot make absolute commitments. His method, therefore, is often one of irony. But it is a tender irony, for Mr. Wilder always respects the human beings who are struggling with this most difficult of life's problems.

In *The Bridge of San Luis Rey* he tells the story of five Peruvians of varying ages and stations in life who are plunged to their death when an old bridge collapses into a deep chasm. The eldest and noblest of the little group loves deeply but possessively her daughter, who, to gain her independence, has married and gone to Spain. The Marquesa writes a series of brilliant and witty letters to her daughter; but they are exacting letters, as well—letters which reveal that, vast as it was, her love "was not without a shade of tyranny." There is Pepita, a twelve-year-old servant girl, who, in her devotion to the competent Abbess who has reared her, gives the Marquesa her first glimpse of courage in love; reading a letter the child has written to the Abbess, the Marquesa "longed to command another's soul as completely as this nun was able to do. Most of all she longed to be back in this simplicity of love, to throw off the burden of pride and vanity that hers had always carried." Then, learning that the child is not sending the letter because it lacks courage, she writes her last and greatest letter to her daughter. She and Pepita die two days later when the bridge falls. Also killed in the accident are Esteban, who is mourning the death of his twin brother; Uncle Pio, an adventurer whose love of the theater—that world of the human passions—has led him to sponsor and train the great actress, Perichole; and Perichole's young son. Uncle Pio's theory of love has been that it is "a sort of cruel malady through which the elect are required to pass in their late youth, and from which they emerge, pale and wrung, but ready for the business of living." It is a sort of school for life—and for the theater. On the day of his death he is taking the son of his former protégée to his home, to tutor him for a year. As in his labors to make the Perichole a great actress, he dies devoted to something beyond himself.

In one way or another, the love experienced by these persons was disinterested. Their life was fulfilled when they had experienced it. As the Abbess reflects, in the closing pages of the novel: "It seemed to be sufficient for Heaven that for a while in Peru a disinterested love had flowered and faded."

Love is the subject also of *The Woman of Andros* (1930), a brief novel set on an Aegean isle in the century before Christ. It is the story of a famous hetaera, Chrysis, and of the love affair of her younger sister, Glycerium, with a young man, Pamphilus. One day Chrysis tells her guests a fable of the dead hero who receives Zeus's permission to return to this earth to relive the least eventful day of his life, on condition that he see it both as onlooker and participant. (Mr. Wilder tells the same story with variations eight years later, when in *Our Town* Emily returns from the graveyard to relive her twelfth birthday.)

> Suddenly the hero saw that the living too are dead and that we can only be said to be alive in those moments when our hearts are conscious of our treasure; for our hearts are not strong enough to love every moment.

He quickly asks to be released from this experience. It is the opinion of Chrysis that

> all human beings—save a few mysterious exceptions who seemed to be in possession of some secret from the gods—merely endured the slow misery of existence, hiding as best they could their consternation that life had no wonderful surprises after all and that its most difficult burden was the incommunicability of love.

Pamphilus, the hero of the novel, fears that he will not be able "to save these others and himself from the creeping gray, from the too easily accepted frustration." He asks desperately: "How does one live?" He falls in love with Glycerium; she dies in childbirth. Pamphilus reassures himself with the words of Chrysis:

> I have known the worst that the world can do to me, and . . . nevertheless I praise the world and all living. All that is, is well. Remember some day, remember me as one who loved all things and accepted from the gods all things, the bright and the dark. And do you likewise.

Pamphilus, too,

> praised the whole texture of life, for he saw how strangely life's richest gift flowered from frustration and cruelty and separation.

Mr. Wilder was reminding his generation that pure sensation, pure release, could not produce the value of love.

2. *The Platonic idea.*—Mr. Wilder's early novels are filled with Platonism: with the world of realities underlying the world of appearances. In *The Woman of Andros,*

> It seemed to [Pamphilus] that the whole world did not consist of rocks and trees and water nor were human beings garments and flesh, but all burned, like the hillside of olive trees, with the perpetual flame of love.

Platonism was just as apparent in *The Bridge of San Luis Rey,* and Platonic love, love as an eternal idea underlying reality, is expressed again in *The Ides of March* (1948). Catullus, the poet, writes to Clodia, the courtesan who has enslaved him:

> Never, never can I conceive of a love which is able to see its own termination. Love *is* its own eternity. Love is in every moment of its being: all time. It is the only glimpse we are permitted of what eternity is. . . .
>
> All, all that Plato said was true.
>
> It was not I, I in myself who loved you. When I looked at you, the God Eros descended upon me. I was more than myself. . . . and when your soul was aware that the God was in me, gazing at you, for a time you too were filled with the God.

3. *Intuition and revelation.*—This Platonic notion is an expression of a belief in intuition, in revelation, a belief which Mr. Wilder explores especially in the first novels. In *The Cabala* (1926), the hero, an American student spending a year in Rome, is working on a play about the life of St. Augustine. He is thrown with a group, called locally the Cabala, who, as he learns in the penultimate chapter of the novel, believe that the ancient gods still live and occasionally take possession of the life of a man—enter his being and inspire his thoughts and deeds.

Religious faith is beyond human reason. As Mr. Wilder says in *The Bridge of San Luis Rey,* "The discrepancy between faith and the facts is greater than is generally assumed." Nor does that discrepancy matter. Intelligence is not necessary to faith. In *The Cabala,* a brilliant Cardinal who has lost his faith is juxtaposed with a wealthy but stupid lady whose faith is childlike. Mlle Astrée-Luce de Morfontaine is a sort of "fool in Christ," a prototype of George Brush, the religious traveling salesman of *Heaven's My Destination* (1935). Despite her lack of intelligence, "she was able to let fall remarkably penetrating judgments, judgments that proceeded from the intuition without passing through the confused corridors of our reason." When the Cardinal puts doubts into her mind she very simply attempts to shoot him. He has become for her a devil.

One of Mr. Wilder's devils is the scientific spirit. In *The Bridge of San Luis Rey,* Brother Juniper, a monk who seeks a scientific proof of God's plan, sees in the episode of the collapse of the bridge a perfect laboratory experiment. He assembles all the data of the dead persons' lives, in the hope that the accumulation of data will provide the proof. His book is condemned as heretical by the church and he is burned at the stake:

> [He] thought there was no one in the world who believed him. But the next morning in all that crowd and sunlight there were many who believed, for he was much loved.

Love had accomplished what reason could not. It was his life, not the inductive method, that recommended his beliefs: intuition, not proof.

In one of the early playlets by Mr. Wilder, the donkey who is carrying Mary and Jesus to Egypt is made to say:

> Lord, what a donkey I was to be arguing about reason while my Lord was in danger. . . . Well, well, it's a queer world where the survival of the Lord is dependent on donkeys, but so it is.

Such "fools in Christ" as Astrée-Luce have as antitheses such thinkers as the Cardinal, of *The Cabala,* Burkin in *Heaven's My Destination,* and, in the main, Julius Caesar in *The Ides of March.* Caesar, at one point, draws up an edict abolishing all religions, but he destroys it. He cannot be certain, though he would like to be:

> Am I sure that there is no mind behind our existence and no mystery anywhere in the universe? I think I am. What joy, what relief there would be, if we could declare so with complete conviction. If that were so I could wish to live forever. How

> terrifying and glorious the role of man if, indeed, without guidance and without consolation he must create from his own vitals the meaning for his existence and the rules whereby he lives.

Caesar has three reasons for doubting that his disbelief is sound: love, poetry—which he profoundly respects—and his own epilepsy or falling sickness, which has brought him indescribable insights. As a ruler, he believes that to his people he must seem "not only wise but supernatural"; that is, he is capable of employing as a ruler a force which he scorns as a thinker.

"Life," Caesar believes, "has no meaning save that which we confer upon it." Clodia, the courtesan whom Caesar has known in his youth, accuses him of teaching her that life has no meaning: "You said that *the universe did not know that men were living in it.*" Yet she does not think he believes that, for he acts as though something "holds meaning, holds reason." Clodia's ugly career, she hints, is due to Caesar's destruction of her faith. She, like all ordinary people, lacks the power to impose meaning on a universe that seems hostile or indifferent. For these, faith is necessary. As one observer puts it, "The essence of what [Caesar] has to teach is moral, is responsibility." To another it seems that "Caesar does not love, nor does he inspire love." That this is not true we know from other witnesses. But that intellect without love, responsibility without emotion, are not enough—that is the point.

4. *The otherworldly.*—In one way or another, all Mr. Wilder's work deals with love and religion. The solution to the problem of life is a Christian solution reached through emotion, not through reason. In *The Woman of Andros*, love is a "sad love that was half hope, often rebuked and waiting to be reassured of its truth." But eventually "a sun [Christianity] would rise and before that sun the timidity and the hesitation would disappear."

To the religious man, the temporal is always less important than the eternal. In the last scene of *The Cabala* the poet Vergil appears to the author, and assures him that he would regret being alive again; in the last scene of *Our Town* the dead scorn the living as "not understanding." From first to last Mr. Wilder prefers the otherworldly to the worldly. Two of his heroes—Pamphilus and George Brush—practice occasional fasting and prayer.

George Brush, in *Heaven's My Destination*, sees that "the world's in such a bad way that we've got to start thinking all over again." He decides that our system of credit and banking is all wrong, and withdraws his savings:

> No one who has money saved up in a bank can really be happy. . . . To save up money is a sign that you're afraid, and one fear makes another fear, and that fear makes another fear. No one who has money in banks can really be happy.

In *The Merchant of Yonkers* (1938), Mrs. Levi expresses her opinion of money, which is not dissimilar to George Brush's: "Money's like manure, which isn't worth anything until it's spread about encouraging young things to grow." The businessman, in this farce, is presented as the gull, with little to recommend him but his money. In *The Ides of March*, Caesar expresses a similar attitude toward the businessman, whose chief concern, Caesar thinks, is what to be afraid of next. Money as a sign of fear is one of Mr. Wilder's favorite themes.

5. *Human worth.*—That the human race has enduring value is a conviction that has remained with Mr. Wilder throughout his career. It is more fully emphasized in the later plays, such as *Our Town* (1938) and *The Skin of Our Teeth* (1942), but it is to be found in both *The Bridge of San Luis Rey* and *The Woman of Andros*. Uncle Pio thinks that those who had suffered in love "never mistook a protracted amiability for the whole conduct of life, they never again regarded any human being, from a prince to a servant, as a mechanical object." In the same novel, an archbishop—another of Mr. Wilder's worldly clergymen—has as one of his favorite notions the idea

> that the injustice and unhappiness of the world is a constant; that the poor, never having known happiness, are insensible to misfortune. Like all the rich he could not bring himself to believe that the poor (look at their houses, look at their clothes) could really suffer. Like all the cultivated he believed that only the widely-read could be said to *know* that they were unhappy.

In *The Skin of Our Teeth*, Lily Sabina is urging George Antrobus to desert his wife for her. She argues:

> . . . other people haven't got feelings. Not in the same way that we have—we who are presidents like you and prizewinners like me. . . .
>
> Listen, dear: everybody in the world except a few people like you and me are just people of straw. Most people have no insides at all.

As Caesar writes in *The Ides of March*, "There is no rapacity equal to that of the privileged who feel that their advantages have been conferred upon them by some intelligence."

But Caesar immediately adds: and there is "no bitterness equal to that of the ill-conditioned who feel that they have been specifically passed over." In *Our Town*, Mr. Wilder permits a small-town editor named Webb to express a more generous conservative position. Webb would welcome a state of things in which the "diligent and sensible," at least, would have no cause for bitterness:

> Well, we're ready to listen to anybody's suggestion as to how you can see that the diligent and sensible'll rise to the top and the lazy and quarrelsome sink to the bottom. We'll listen to anybody. Meantime until that's settled, we try to take care of those that can't help themselves, and those that can we leave alone.

Even if there is an inequality of man, Mr. Wilder would seem to say, there is no excuse for ignoring suffering. Chrysis, the woman of Andros, being pre-Christian, prays to the gods for her beloved:

> Let him rest some day, O ye Olympians, from pitying those who suffer. Let him learn to look the other way. This is something new in the world, this concern for the unfit and the broken. Once he begins that, there's no end to it, only madness. It leads nowhere. That is some God's business.

The God has now come. Men are worth saving.

But men are terribly imperfect. Mrs. Levi says in *The Merchant of Yonkers*, "Inside of all of us nice people are the seeds of quarrels, lawsuits, and wars, too. It's nice people, also, who tear their fellow man to pieces." In *Our Town*, the Stage Manager says: "Christianity strictly forbade killing, but you were allowed to kill human beings in war and government punishings," and the Fortune Teller in *The Skin of Our Teeth* says:

> Some of you will be saying: "Let him drown. He's not worth saving. Give the whole thing up." I can see it in your faces. But you're wrong. Keep your doubts and despairs to yourselves. Again there'll be the

> narrow escape. The survival of a handful. From destruction—total destruction.

Mrs. Antrobus, the type of Eternal Mother in the same play, says, "Just to have known this house—is to have seen the idea of what this world can do some day—can do some day, if we keep our wits about us."

It would not be fair to Mr. Wilder, then, to say that he ignores the world and the suffering of mankind. Even the early books satirize those who deny it. And in a later play, *The Merchant of Yonkers*, Mrs. Levi tells us:

> Yes, we're all fools and we're all in danger of destroying the world with our folly; but the one way to keep us from harm is to fill our lives with the six or seven human pleasures which are our right in the world; and that takes a little money, not much, but a little; and a little freedom, not much, but a little.

Mr. Wilder, then, fits into no neat pattern of liberalism or conservatism. He neither worships nor scorns the common man. He wishes neither to deprive him of freedom, nor to lavish it upon him. He distrusts people who think—as Caesar sometimes does—that they know what is best for men, and he detests the greedy businessman who would exploit others. Mrs. Levi perhaps sums it up best:

> The first sign that a person's refused the human race is that he makes plans to improve and restrict the human race according to patterns of his own.
>
> It looks like love of the human race, but believe me, it's the refusal of the human race—those blue-print worlds where everyone is happy, and no one is allowed to be free.
>
> If you accept human beings and are willing to live among them, you acknowledge that every man has a right to his own mistakes.

6. *Freedom and responsibility.*—Mr. Wilder's concern with the problems of freedom and choice is to be seen in *The Skin of Our Teeth* and *The Ides of March*. There must be order within the individual before there can be order for the world. Mr. Antrobus tells his son Henry, who represents the evil in all of us, the Cain in mankind:

> How can you make a world for people to live in, unless you've first put order in yourself. Mark my words: I shall continue fighting you until my last breath as long as you mix up your idea of liberty with your idea of hogging everything for yourself.

Caesar, who in many respects appears to stand for the modern "liberal," believes that "the crown of life is the exercise of choice." One learns to live by living:

> The first and last schoolmaster of life is living and committing oneself unreservedly and dangerously to living; to men who know this an Aristotle and a Plato have much to say; but those who have imposed cautions on themselves and petrified themselves in a system of ideas, them the masters themselves will lead to error. Brutus and Cato repeat liberty, liberty, and live to impose on others a liberty they have not accorded to themselves—stern, joyless men, crying to neighbors: be joyful as we are joyful; be free as we are free.

In the view of Cytheris, a great actress of the time, we need limits:

> Wickedness may be the exploration of one's liberty . . ., the search for a limit that one can respect. . . . Can't we say that a great deal of what we call "wickedness" is the very principle of virtue exploring the laws of its own nature? . . . Only the Gods have put a veto on the adventure of our minds. If They do not choose to intervene, we are *condemned* [my italics] to fashion our laws or to wander in fright through the pathless wastes of our terrifying liberty, seeking even the reassurance of a barred gate, of a forbidding wall. . . . Caesar is a tyrant . . . It is not that, like other tyrants, he is chary of according liberty to others; it is that, loftily free himself, he has lost all touch with the way freedom operates and is developed in others; always mistaken, he accords too little or he accords too much.

Mr. Wilder's method here as elsewhere is to present several views persuasively. But it is Cytheris, the artist, who sees the value of traditional restraints, with whom he seems most in sympathy.

7. *The praise of poetry and scholarship.*—Mr. Wilder's respect for the poet and scholar constitutes one part of his respect for the eternal. Yet he balances his regard for pure learning with an awareness of its limitations. *The Cabala* introduces a young man who spends his life in scholarship which to the rest of the world appears futile. There is some suggestion in the story that such devotion to abstract knowledge is inhumane. In *The Skin of Our Teeth*, Mr. Antrobus is made to dismiss contemptuously the suggestion of a useful employment for the wheel, which he has just invented. His son says to him: "You could put a chair on that." Mr. Antrobus replies: "Yes, any booby can fool with it now; but I thought of it first." The practical but evil Henry does "fool with it," and modern war is one disastrous result. Mr. Antrobus' love of pure knowledge, of the abstract idea, has kept him from seeing that the idea can be violated in the application if the thinker irresponsibly surrenders it to the "practical" man, interested only in immediate advantage. Such practical natures as that of Mrs. Antrobus, for instance, can see little use in poetry. When the Ice Age threatens, Mr. Antrobus tells her to use everything for fuel, but to save the Shakespeare. "He knows," she remarks, "I'd burn ten Shakespeares to prevent a child of mine from having a cold in the head." And later, when Antrobus wants to save Homer and the Muses from frost and starvation, his wife is most reluctant to take them into her house.

The very form of *The Ides of March*, ostensibly a collection of documents, shows Mr. Wilder's respect for scholarship. In that novel, Caesar is shown as admiring poets greatly. "At a very early age," he writes, "I was convinced that the true poets and historians are the highest ornaments of a country . . . They alone use all of themselves in every moment of their work."

In *The Ides of March* occurs the great debate between Clodia and Catullus on the value of poetry. Poetry, Clodia thinks, is "the most seductive of lies and the most treacherous of counselors." Catullus' answer is couched in a fable, which he does not complete, for Caesar is taken with a spell of the "falling sickness." But the fable would seem to reject alike complete unconcern with human suffering, and pure poetry—"tricks that had no relation to anything outside themselves." If this reading is correct, Mr. Wilder holds, in his latest book, the same theory of literature that he held in a volume published twenty years earlier. In the Preface to his little volume of playlets, he expressed his desire to assert, without offensive didacticism, the truths of his religious faith. There seems to have been little alteration in point of view throughout Mr. Wilder's career. It is true that the later work pays more attention to humanity, and less to religion per se. But the faith is present by implication. Love of God, love of Man, and love of the Art which expresses and synthesizes both—these have been from beginning to end Mr. Wilder's articles of faith.

That Mr. Wilder is a religious person, a person concerned with the moral problems of man, is important for him and for those of his readers who find his teaching of value. If he were only a teacher of morals, he would not interest us as a literary man. But he is much more.

He is, in the first place, a humorist—one of the brightly comic literary men of his generation. This fact appears less in the early novels than in the later novels and in all the plays. But even in *The Cabala* and *The Bridge of San Luis Rey*, it is there, chiefly as an urbane sort of irony, or in pungently phrased aphorisms. Beginning with the playlets of *The Angel That Troubled the Waters* (1928), the one-act plays such as *The Long Christmas Dinner* (1931), and proceeding through *Heaven's My Destination* and the later plays, a heartier humor appears. In the one-act plays it is based on a sheer joy in human life—in experience itself, as in the marvelously uneventful circumstances of *A Happy Journey from Trenton to Camden* (1931). Joy in little things is the basis of this humor—the humor almost of a delighted newcomer to the human scene.

The loving smile of these plays becomes a mirthful roar in *Heaven's My Destination*, the novel in which Mr. Wilder manages to discuss eternal subjects even while recounting the affair of a traveling salesman and a farmer's daughter. Yet the loving-kindness is still there. George Brush, outrageously tricked into having Sunday dinner with some Kansas City prostitutes, retains his dignity throughout. One laughs at him, and then realizes that one should be laughing at oneself. The joke is, after all, on us, who laugh at a naïveté which has resulted only in thoroughly Christian behavior. The joke suddenly becomes different from the one we had expected—a joke as deep as human tragedy. One might call this effect the humor of human compassion. It has artistic purpose. In *Our Town*, for example, the humor prevents the pity from becoming sentimentalism.

The Skin of Our Teeth, with the usual serious emphasis on human values, is the funniest of Mr. Wilder's plays. Our more venial sins—those of appetite—are embodied in Sabina, a character whose blend of selfishness and good-heartedness creates sheer mirth. The technique, which Mr. Wilder here perfects, of treating time as relative, and jumping back and forth in it with gay abandon, is used for both serious and comic purposes. He used it in his earliest book, *The Cabala*, where, under another name, the dying poet Keats is introduced briefly into the story. *The Long Christmas Dinner* takes a family through several generations. But nowhere is Mr. Wilder so successful with the device as in *The Skin of Our Teeth*, where it becomes an integral part of the play, and no mere trick caught from the expressionists. It suggests the eternity of Mr. Wilder's themes, and it startles us to laughter; this dual effect of the serious and the comic is a most valuable asset to the theater. The technique of breaking down the barriers between actors and audience, between the play and reality, has a similar dual function: it provokes laughter, and it supplies that actual integration of art with life which John Dewey might theoretically approve. At the same time it emphasizes Mr. Wilder's constant theme: the eternity of human values.

In style there is more development than in thought. The early style is rather on the precious side, and includes such sentences as "Triumph had passed from Greece and wisdom from Egypt, but with the coming on of night they seemed to regain their lost honor, and the land that was soon to be called Holy prepared in the dark its wonderful burden." True, his early style does not cloy; but it is mannered and it does call attention to itself. Not until *The Long Christmas Dinner* and *The Happy Journey from Trenton to Camden* did Mr. Wilder's excellent grasp of colloquial speech become fully apparent, and with it his respect for ordinary people—mothers and wives, boys and girls, husbands and sons, living ordinary lives. It is present in all his plays, as well as in *Heaven's My Destination*. Ma Kirby, in *The Happy Journey*, scolds her young daughter Caroline in a classic American maternal manner:

> Mind yourself, Missy. I don't want to hear anybody talking about rich or not rich when I'm around. If people aren't nice I don't care how rich they are.

Mrs. McCoy, quite another type, tells George Brush:

> Sit down. Don't you smoke, either? No wonder you feel like a fool, just sitting and talking. Remus, give'm some ginger ale, anyway. That way he can at least hold something in his hand, my-God.

Another quality which has developed as his career has continued is the ability to adjust speech and tone to the character of the speaker. The individualization of persons is not great in the early books. It becomes better in the plays, but it is best of all, I think, in *The Ides of March*, where each document is written in the manner, almost unmistakable, of its writer rather than of Mr. Wilder. Cicero's dry description of Clodia's bosom as "a much-travelled thoroughfare, only occasionally available to birds"; or his classicist's resentment of the new poetry:

> If we are to be condemned to a poetry based on buried trains of thought . . ., we shall soon be at the mercy of the unintelligible parading about us as a superior mode of sensibility.

Pompeia's silliness: "What I have to say is very *very* confidential"; and Clodia's duplicity in a letter to Pompeia:

> May I make one small suggestion, however, and one which I would only make to you because only you *could* put it into effect?

—these will serve as specimens.

As a novelist, Mr. Wilder's gravest fault is a lack of narrative movement. His books and plays often end where they began. We are told in the first paragraph of *The Bridge of San Luis Rey* what its outcome will be. Caesar, we know all along, will be stabbed to death. Sabina repeats her opening speech and tells us, "This is where you came in." So, although it is not correct to say that there is no action and no interest in fable, for there is both, it is true that four of Mr. Wilder's five novels—the exception is *Heaven's My Destination*—move very slowly. No doubt this is a defect to many readers. But those who seek insight rather than excitement, thought rather than event, will not find the slow pace unattractive.

Mr. Wilder, then, as I see it, has been unfairly ignored by serious literary critics. As much as any writer of our day, he needs to be studied and evaluated. He is a humorist who knows the underlying seriousness of comic events, a satirist who loves the human race. True, his style has sometimes been pretentious, and his stories slow-paced; but he deserves our respect as an artist. The bold attempt of his whole career has been nothing less than the reestablishment of human values in a world which, he believes, desperately needs them. Consistently he has attempted to write literature which, having a value of its own, would still not be an end in itself. He deserves our admiration for accepting as his task the difficult artistic problem of suiting fable to idea and sound to sense, producing thus an integrated whole.

EDMUND FULLER

From "Thornton Wilder: The Notation of the Heart"

American Scholar, Spring 1959, pp. 210–12

Thornton Wilder has to his credit one of the greatest novels *(The Bridge of San Luis Rey)* and one of the greatest plays *(Our Town)* in this century's American writing. The rest of his body of work is consistent in quality. Success has visited him: he is a Pulitzer Prize winner in both fiction and drama; his plays have had packed houses; one of the novels was a best-seller. Yet, proportionate to his achievement, this man's stature is singularly overlooked or taken for granted. Until quite recently three of his five novels, all of them among the best American writing, had been out of print for years, and even *The Bridge* was not in hard covers.

He has had his due more among the drama critics than among those who study the art of prose fiction. In the books that talk of the contemporary American novel, where a fixed set of names is bandied about among a fixed set of critics, Wilder seldom is discussed. Malcolm Cowley is a notable exception, having written an excellent essay as Introduction to *A Thornton Wilder Trio* (1956), which brought back into print the first three novels.

This curious general neglect is partly because literary critics tend to inherit their subjects, passed along from one group to their successors. Within the contemporary field, one echelon seldom has the imagination to study someone whom the preceding echelon has ignored. Due to a socioeconomic accident, Wilder was slighted by most critics practicing in the thirties and, accordingly, has not received attention since that time to any extent commensurate with his importance as a novelist.

The strange public history of *The Bridge of San Luis Rey*, its abrupt drop from acclaim to neglect, is worth pausing to examine. The book became a best-seller and a Pulitzer Prize winner. Malcolm Cowley remarks, wrongly I believe, that this success is "still a little hard to understand, for the best qualities of *The Bridge* are not those usually regarded as being popular." It "exactly fitted the mood of the moment, and nobody knows exactly why."

Public response often is surprising and hard to explain. The stylistic excellences and subtleties of thought and observation in this novel are not mass commodities. Yet greatness, which this book possesses, is never in itself a bar to popularity, given other viable elements. Shakespeare was a mass artist, and a substantial number of fine books make the best-seller list.

The Bridge is short and wonderfully lucid reading, with a simplicity hardly suggesting its extensive substrata. The question that the fall of the bridge thrust upon humble Brother Juniper: "Either we live by accident and die by accident, or we live by plan and die by plan"—in short, whether the events of life are chance or design—presents itself intensely, even agonizingly, at some time in almost every life. Thus it is that the Marquesa de Montemayor sometimes would be "dizzy with despair, and . . . would long to be taken from a world that had no plan in it." Consciously or unconsciously, from the French existentialists to the beat generation, this is a major psychic problem of the hydrogen age. The unlettered and the educated alike ponder the question in their own terms. It is a problem that presents itself as much amidst plenty as at any other time, which is why the book spoke to the anxieties beneath the boom of the flush twenties.

Another basis of the book's appeal is that its characters are sufficiently strange, colorful and remote to be fascinating, yet they are so universally human in their qualities that we can identify ourselves with them. Its original success and its re-emergence are gratifying, but not mysterious.

The book's abrupt eclipse (which engulfed all of Wilder's early novels) is a peculiar story. When the depression struck, the dreary wave of "social" novels, "protest" novels, "proletarian" or Marxist novels was ushered in and caused a corresponding literary depression, both in creation and criticism. What was possibly the best single book of that genre, *The Grapes of Wrath*, does not survive the passing of its topicality as well as *The Bridge* survives its temporary, circumstantial eclipse. I am one of many who came of age in the early thirties, heard *The Bridge* spat upon as bourgeois, escapist, popular pap, and had to find it for myself after depression and war had passed and writers had again discovered that the problems of man are not narrowly topical, or uniquely and exclusively centered on the masses, on workers or even on soldiers.

Wilder is unique among modern American novelists for possessing in the highest degree certain qualities currently undervalued and hence desperately needed among us. No one of his countrymen rests his work upon such an understructure of broad scholarship, cultivation and passion for the beauty and integrity of the English language. This equipment, rare in our time, gives tone to his work, especially the novels, and yet brings with it no taint of pedantry. To find work equally rich in allusion and grounded in humane learning, we must turn to English-born Aldous Huxley, although Wilder employs these attributes even more gracefully and unobtrusively than he. In a period when literary honors are bestowed often upon the craftless, the semiliterate and uncultivated, and in which the Yahoo has become hero, we need to recall that we have Wilder working among us. He helps to redeem the time.

He is notable for his versatility. Although he is not the only man writing both the novel and the play, no one else has written both at such a level of excellence, in such a marked diversity of modes, or in such form-renewing and form-extending ways as mark his work in the two media.

Wilder is a conspicuous exception to the common generalization that American writers tend to be youthful, writing of and from youth and immaturity, failing to mature in art as they age in years. He juxtaposes his always mature vision of life and character to our predominantly adolescent literature, while his range is greater than that of those established men who are most nearly his peers. There is an immense spread between the sophistication of *The Cabala* and the homely simplicity of *Our Town*, and Wilder is comfortably at home in both.

He is neither compulsive in his choice of material and method nor conditioned by some warped piping from a private clinical world. His view of life and behavior is broadly encompassing and humanely compassionate in the only true compassion, which is blended of sympathetic perception and clearly defined values.

He has the highest development and conscious control of style—having no close rival among Americans in this respect—yet he spelled out the limits of style in *The Bridge*, in a passage about the Conde's relish for the famous letters of the Marquesa de Montemayor (which are like those of Mme. de Sévigné):

> . . . he thought that when he had enjoyed the style he had extracted all their richness and intention, missing (as most readers do) the whole purport of literature, which is the notation of the heart. Style is but the faintly contemptible vessel in which the

> bitter liquid is recommended to the world. The Marquesa would even have been astonished to learn that her letters were very good, for such authors live always in the noble weather of their own minds and those productions which seem remarkable to us are little better than a day's routine to them.

It is in this "whole purport of literature . . . the notation of the heart" that Wilder's genius is felt, and the flexible grace and individuality that attend his work in both his chosen media proceed from that "noble weather" of his own mind.

The novels are dazzlingly epigrammatic—a word that often carries with it a suggestion of glibness that does not fit this work. The epigram is a stylistic device, a perfectly shaped single thought, calculated to arrest attention and then, at its best, to start thought moving in a fresh direction. Such ability to shape and state things is sometimes given to shallow minds who waste it on minor witticism. In Wilder this gift is coupled with penetrating perception and wisdom. It helps him to communicate the depth and sharpness in which he sees character, motivation and impulse, and the significance that he discerns in things.

Wilder's work is permeated by a profound mystical and religious sensibility—too mature to war upon or sneer at orthodoxy, too creative to fit snugly in its confines. His vision and celebration of man is harmonious with Christian humanism. He gives us a *creature*, touched with the divine image, but scarred and maimed somewhat in his human state, perishable in his flesh and eternal in his soul; a creature variously perverse and responsible, despicable and indomitable, vulgar and rarefied. The separateness of these attributes remains blurred in Wilder's work as it is blurred in the creature and in the creature's self-understanding. Applying here some words from the foreword to his first volume of short plays, *The Angel That Troubled the Waters*, "there has seldom been an age in literature when such a vein was less welcome and less understood."

He has been publishing and producing intermittently since 1926, and there is no reason to suppose that we have heard the last from him. His productive years, to date, span the time from his twenties to his late fifties, so he has been walking in step with his century. The reference of his work is always universal, regardless of its period identification. In times of depression and war he has not occupied himself with the obviously topical that commands attention sometimes to the temporary exclusion of all else. His nearest approach to the topical—the perennial topicality of the catastrophic—was in *The Skin of Our Teeth*, cast in such imaginative terms as to baffle literal minds.

ROBERT W. CORRIGAN

"Thornton Wilder and the Tragic Sense of Life"

Educational Theatre Journal, October 1961, pp. 167–73

Of all modern American dramatists, none is more difficult to pin down than Thornton Wilder. He is thought of, together with O'Neill, Miller, and Williams, as one of our "Big Four," and yet his reputation is based on only three full-length plays and was made on one. And whereas reams of criticism have been written on the other three playwrights, only an occasional article on Wilder is published. This is all the more surprising since no one seems to agree about his work. For some he is the great American satirist; for others he is a soft-hearted sentimentalist; and for still others he is our only "religious" dramatist. Furthermore, no American playwright is more respected by contemporary European dramatists than is Wilder; Brecht, Ionesco, and Duerrenmatt have all acknowledged their debt to this "great and fanatical experimentor." Therefore, it is about time that we reëvaluate his work.

From his earliest volumes of one-acts, *The Angel That Troubled the Waters* and *The Long Christmas Dinner*, to his last play, *The Matchmaker*, Wilder has dealt boldly and affirmatively with the themes of Life, Love, and Earth. Each of his plays is a hymn in dramatic form affirming life. But the important question is: What is the nature of this affirmation? It is not, as some would have it, Christian. To begin with, Wilder has no belief—at least in his plays—in a religion that is revealed or historical. These are basic premises of Christianity. To be sure Wilder is deistic, but as almost all of his critics have pointed out, he is essentially a religious Platonist; and this position must ultimately reject the historic dimension as meaningful. Francis Fergusson ties these two ideas together when he writes:

> The plays are perfectly in accord with the Platonic kind of philosophy which they are designed to teach. The great Ideas are timeless, above the history of the race and the history of actual individuals. Any bit of individual or racial history will do, therefore, to "illustrate" them; but history and individual lives lack all real being; they are only shadows on the cave wall.

Mary McCarthy approaches this another way when she writes of *The Skin of Our Teeth:*

> In other words, if George misses the five-fifteen, Chaos is come again. This is the moral of the piece. Man, says Mr. Wilder, from time to time gets puffed up with pride and prosperity, he grows envious, covetous, lecherous, forgets his conjugal duties, goes whoring after women; portents of disaster appear, but he is too blind to see them; in the end, with the help of the little woman, who has never taken any stock in either pleasure or wisdom, he escapes by the skin of his teeth. *Sicut erat in principio*. . . .
>
> It is a curious view of life. It displays elements of Christian morality. Christ, however, was never so simple, but on the contrary allowed always for paradox (the woman taken in adultery, the story of Martha and Mary, "Consider the lilies of the field") . . . No, it is not the Christian view, but a kind of bowdlerized version of it, such as might have been imparted to a class of taxpayer's children by a New England Sunday School teacher forty years ago.

Now, I happen to believe that both Fergusson and Miss McCarthy (even in their admiration for Wilder) overstate their arguments, because Wilder, except in his preface to *The Angel That Troubled the Waters*, has never thought of himself as a Christian or a religious playwright. He best states his position when he writes: "*Our Town* is not offered as a picture of life in a New Hampshire village; or speculation about the conditions of life after death. . . . It is an attempt to find a value above all price for the smallest events of daily life." Wilder is talking about *Our Town*, but what he says applies to all of his work. In short, Wilder is a humanist, an affirming humanist—a "yea-sayer to life" as Barnard Hewitt calls him—but nonetheless a humanist.

When we examine the nature of Wilder's humanistic

affirmation, what do we discover? His plays celebrate human love, the worth and dignity of man, the values of the ordinary, and the eternity of human values. From the little boy in Wilder's first play who says: "I am not afraid of life. I will astonish it!" to Dolly Levi and her cohorts in adventure in *The Matchmaker*, Wilder has always been on the side of life and life is seen to be most directly affirmed through love. Love, then, is his most persistent theme and it has been for him an inexhaustible subject. Of its worth he is convinced, but it is interesting to note that Wilder has never been able to make any commitments as to the reasons for its worth. Wilder can deal with life and love directly and concretely; but when he moves to the edges of life, the focus becomes less sharp. Certainly, Wilder deals with death—he is not afraid of it, but death in his plays is terminal. When Mrs. Soames says in Act Three of *Our Town*: "My, wasn't life awful—and wonderful," Wilder is reminding us that beauty is recognizable because of change and life is meaningful because of death. But as both John Mason Brown and Winfield Townley Scott have pointed out, Wilder never deals adequately with Death's own meaning. And as for what's beyond death? The Stage Manager in *Our Town* tells us:

> You know as well as I do that the dead don't stay interested in us living people for very long. Gradually, gradually, they let go of the earth. . . . They get weaned away from the earth—that's the way I put it,—weaned away. Yes, they stay here while the earth-part of 'em burns away, burns out, and all that time they slowly get indifferent to what's going on in Grover's Corners. They're waitin'! They're waitin' for something that they feel is comin'. Something important and great. Aren't they waitin' for the eternal part in them to come out clear?

But what is this eternal part, this Platonic essence, which in our imperfect awareness of living is only a shadow on the wall of the cave? What is death's meaning? The Stage Manager has just told us:

> everybody knows that *something* is eternal. And it ain't houses and it ain't names, and it ain't earth, and it ain't even the stars . . . everybody knows in their bones that *something* is eternal, and that something has to do with human beings. All the greatest people ever lived have been telling us that for five thousand years and yet you'd be surprised how people are always losing hold of it. There's something way down deep that's eternal about every human being.

So, we are right back where we started: Life is reality and eternity is the perfected essence of that reality to which we are too often blind and of which we can't stand too much.

It is this tendency—a tendency consistent with his Platonism—to reduce the dimension of eternity so that it can be encompassed by life itself, that has led me to believe—although he has written no tragedies—that Wilder has essentially a tragic rather than a Christian or even religious view of life. Why his plays are not tragedies I shall come to, but first I should like to describe briefly what I mean by the tragic view of life. Scott Fitzgerald described it in a letter to his daughter as "the sense that life is essentially a cheat and its conditions are those of defeat." It seems to me that the awareness of the tragic nature of things informs every serious outlook. You can escape it in play or other forms of illusion; you can transcend it in religion; or you can celebrate it in exaltation; but it is always there! It is the backdrop of fate which insists that part, if not all, of life's glory is in its doom.

The tragic view of life is derived from that form of Greek mysticism known as gnosticism. The simplest statement of the gnostic attitude that I know of—and Wilder is very pertinent here—is Hegel's "the truth is in the whole!" What this means is that any adequate philosophy of life must not only include everything, but affirm everything. It must not suppress any aspect of reality because some moral code finds it offensive or ignoble; or because some human emotion or action is unpleasant or shocking; nor can it prefer some aspect of life because it is beautiful, noble, or good. In short, if the truth is in the whole, then reality is neutral, not partisan—it is beyond good and evil. But life as it is lived is fragmentary and denies the possibility of neutrality: flesh-and-blood men are always partisan. Living is taking sides; and neutrality in life is always the taking of sides by default. Thus, if "the truth is in the whole," it is mocked by life as it destroys it. Life depends on the interplay of polar opposites, and this fact is the lowest common denominator of the tragic view of life. The differences in tragedy are the differences in the way the clash is conceived. But finally, the very existence of separate, discrete individuals is itself sufficient to set up a tragic conflict. Tragedy is the inevitable result of our ontological solitude. As long as, to use Rilke's phrase, "I am I and you are you and we are separated by a void," the possibility of tragedy exists. For Thomas Wolfe was right when he saw: "Naked and alone we came into exile. In her dark womb we did not know our mother's face; from the prison of her flesh have we come into the unspeakable and uncommunicable prison of this earth. Which of us has known his brother? Which of us has looked into his father's heart? Which of us is not forever a stranger and alone?"

For this reason the stage of tragic drama consists of two ever-shifting backdrops or perspectives: the ultimate perspective which is neutral and beyond good and evil, and in which all experience is equally valid and real; and the finite perspective of men in action; the perspective of life's strife, tensions, and contradictions. And man, being finite, will of necessity always challenge the ultimate perspective, and tragedy is the dramatization of that conflict. It is for this reason that man's pride, whether it be in the form of an inordinate pursuit of a finite goal or the suicidal aspiration toward the infinite, should not be viewed as a character defect of egotism, or as a tragic flaw. Rather it is a part of human nature, the necessary counterpart of man's creative capacity as a rational being.

Tragedy, then, sees man as the questioner—naked and alone—facing the mysterious forces of life, and particularly those irreducible forces of suffering and death. We must understand that tragedy does not attempt to abolish the suffering of pain, fear, and sadness, rather it embraces that suffering as the fulfillment of maturity and self-understanding. The tragic vision impels man to fight against his destiny. It impels the hero, the playwright, and finally the audience into "boundary situations." Those situations where man is at the limits of his sovereignty: Job on the ash-heap; Prometheus on the crag; Oedipus discovered; Lear on the heath; Ahab on the quarter-deck. Here, with all the protective coverings stripped off, the hero faces—as if no man had ever faced it before—the existential question: Job's "What is man?"; Lear's "Is man no more than this?" The tragic writer always presses these boundary situations to their fullest yield, and this is the discovery of tragedy. The hero discovers through this suffering not God, or Nature, but himself. In tragedy, action is carried to the uttermost limits, in order that the farthest reaches of human possibility may be explored. And in so doing the hero's defeat is vindicated by his capacity to impose meaning on the void, even while in the act of falling.

Now, Wilder has not created any Ahabs or Lears, but this

is not because he hasn't a tragic view of life. He happens to believe—as did Maeterlinck—that the tragedy of life can best be seen in the drama of the everyday—in life's smallest events. For this reason he does not dramatize great conflicts in order to capture the quintessence of tragedy, for there are times in each of our lives when we are conscious of moving into boundary situations. I think it is important to see the validity of this, although we must point out that this is tragic but not always dramatic. And this, I think, accounts for the fact that Wilder's plays are usually called "hymns," "odes," "songs," and so on, and most critics feel that there isn't much conflict in their plots. It might be helpful to take a specific example to illustrate Wilder's position on this matter.

Over and over again in Wilder's work, the belief is stated directly and indirectly that "life is what you make of it." The fullest discussion of the idea is in *The Ides of March*, where Caesar says: "Life has no meaning save that which we confer upon it." Later he says:

> Am I sure that there is no mind behind our existence and no mystery anywhere in the universe? I think I am. . . . How terrifying and glorious the role of man if, indeed, without guidance and without consolation he must create from his own vitals the meaning for his existence and the rules whereby he lives.

Many of us believe this idea when stated in its simpler form: "Life is what we make of it." But we are unaware that this is really an existential position and that Wilder is very close to Sartre's "Man is condemned to be free."

In fact, upon reflection, we discover that in starting from "Life is what we make of it," Wilder is really in the mainstream of the modern drama beginning with Ibsen and Strindberg. And this is a dangerous position and usually in the drama has led to despair. The image of man in this drama is an image of collapse. Certainly, Kierkegaard saw this when he wrote in *Fear and Trembling:*

> If there were no eternal consciousness in a man, if at the foundation of all there lay only a wildly seething power which writhing with obscure passions produced everything that is great and everything that is insignificant, if a bottomless void never satiated lay hidden beneath all—what then would life be but despair.

Most modern dramatists have answered with "that's all!" But Wilder hasn't, even though he holds a position that should lead this way. I think he averts despair—and also tragedy, even though his view of life is essentially tragic—with a kind of Santayana-like belief in life. In fact, Wilder's Platonism can make sense only if it is seen as coming through Santayana. Wilder is—as probably most of us are—saved from despair and its paralyzing effects by what Santayana calls "animal faith." We admit that life may be only an irrational nightmare and there is no reality except that which we imagine, but the animal faith which bids us believe in the external world is much stronger than all the logical arguments which would make life absurd. As Joseph Wood Krutch put it: "Everybody acts as though he believed that the external world exists; nearly everybody acts as though he believed that his version of it is a dependable one; and the majority act as though they could also make valid value judgments about it." It is this belief, this animal faith, that permits Wilder to say "Life is what you make of it," and still come up in affirmation on this side of despair. All his plays might be described by that verse of Theodore Spencer's (and I think Wilder and Spencer have great affinities):

> Oh how to praise that No,
> When all longing would press
> After the lost Yes!
> Oh how redress
> That disaster of No?

But although Wilder can assert meaning to life, the meaning is almost in the assertion itself and this is not a very comfortable position to be in. One gets the feeling that Wilder has to keep saying it to make sure that it is true. The danger of this position is that it lacks the necessary polarity and tension for full meaning; the tension between an ultimate perspective and a finite one. This in itself keeps Wilder from being a religious dramatist. In all great religious drama: the works of Sophocles, Calderón, *Everyman*, and in more recent times the later plays of Hofmannsthal, Eliot and even Fry, there is the backdrop of religious belief which gives meaning to and informs the hero's "life is what you make of it." There is the greater stage. The medieval theatre and the Spanish theatre of Calderón exhibit this, and this is what Hofmannsthal tried to achieve at the Salzburg festivals with his productions of *Everyman*, *The Great World Theatre*, and *The Tower*. In all of these plays the actors—man—are faced with a moral choice under the very eyes of God and his angels upstage. The scaffold of these multiple stage structures not only serves as a magic mirror for the visible world and its invisible order, but the invisible order is made visible. For in these plays the idea of man as a player on the world's stage becomes the very principle of the *mise-en-scène*. For God, the master, speaking from the top of the scaffold, actually orders the world to produce a play under his eyes, featuring man who is to act out his part on earth.

More important than the absence of a religious dimension to Wilder's work, however, are the many experiments he has made in theatrical technique to compensate for this lack of an ultimate perspective. It is a commonplace in talking about modern literature to comment on the loss of a community of values and the disappearance of public truths in our time. It is equally well known that writers tend to compensate for the lack of a community of belief with new techniques of expression. The problem for the dramatist is how to make a highly individual standard of values appear to the audience to be a natural objective standard. Most of the modern dramatists have attempted to meet this problem by focussing on the psychology of their characters. In so doing they leave begged the question of value by confining the world of the play to the limits of an individual character's mind and then assessing value solely in terms of the consciousness of that mind. Thus, an incident in *Hedda Gabler* may not be important by any communicable standard of human significance, but if the universe is confined to her mind and Ibsen makes us look deeply enough into it, we can at least see it as important in that tiny context. In this way psychology makes possible such a drastic limitation of context that a private world can be the subject of a tragedy. Furthermore, by new techniques of presentation that private world and its values can be made, at least for the duration of the performance, convincing.

Wilder has not been interested in psychology and has never used psychological techniques to solve the "modernists'" problems in the theatre. This accounts, I think, for his great influence on the continental avant-garde dramatists who are rebelling against our psychologically oriented theatre. Wilder sought to achieve the sense of an ultimate perspective by immaterializing the sense of dramatic place on stage. The bare stage of *Our Town* with its chairs, tables, and ladders, together with the Stage Manager's bald exposition, are all that he uses to create the town. The same is true of *The Skin of Our Teeth;* you never really know where the Antrobuses live—nor when. This is his second dominant technique; by destroying the illusion of time, Wilder achieves the effect of any time, all time, each time. But this is risky business, for without the backdrop of an ultimate perspective to inform a play's action, it can very easily become sentimental or satirical, or even pretentious. Wilder at his best keeps this from happening, but his only weapons are wit and irony. And a production which does not succeed in capturing these qualities (as alas most college and school productions do not) is bound to turn out bathetic and sentimental; when technique is used as a compensation for the ultimate perspective, the resultant work of art always lies precariously under a Damoclean sword.

It is important that we see the dangers in Wilder's methods, but that a tragic sense of life informs his plays is best illustrated by his sense of destiny. In Wilder's novel, *The Woman of Andros,* Chrysis tells her guests a fable of the dead hero who receives Zeus' permission to return to earth to relive the least eventful day of his life, on the condition that he see it both as onlooker and participant.

> Suddenly the hero saw that the living too are dead and that we can only be said to be alive in those moments when our hearts are conscious of our treasure; for our hearts are not strong enough to love every moment.

He quickly asks to be released from this experience, and it is the opinion of Chrysis that

> All human beings—save a few mysterious exceptions who seemed to be in possession of some secret from the gods—merely endured the slow misery of existence, hiding as best they could their consternation that life had no wonderful surprises after all and that its most difficult burden was the incommunicability of love.

Eight years later Wilder incorporated this into the last scene of *Our Town.* When Emily comes back on her twelfth birthday, she discovers that "we don't have time to look at one another. I didn't realize. So all that was going on and we never noticed . . . Oh, earth you're too wonderful for anybody to realize you. Do any human beings ever realize life while they live it?—every, every minute?" The answer, of course, is "no," and Emily must conclude with "That's all human beings are!—Just blind people."

What Wilder is saying here is that human beings cannot stand to have a sense of destiny—the awareness that there is a continuity in all our acts, the awareness that every present moment comes from a past and is directed to a future. Only at moments—usually of emotional crisis—do we have this sense of destiny, this sense of awareness of the future. It is this sense of destiny that is the great human reality and the tragedy of life lies in our fragmentary and imperfect awareness of it. Wilder is aware, like Eliot, that "human kind cannot bear very much reality," but his plays fall short of tragedy because he takes the Platonic escape, he moves into a world that denies the reality and the nemesis of destiny. Nor does he have the solution of an Eliot. For in denying, finally, the reality of destiny he shuts out the possibility of ever providing the means to perfect our fragmentary and imperfect vision. He fails, to use Karl Jaspers' phrase, to go "Beyond Tragedy." That Wilder lacks this dimension, is not to discredit him, however, for no other American dramatist more fully affirms that miracle of life which so much modern drama would deny.

ALEXANDER COWIE

From "The Bridge of Thornton Wilder"
Essays on American Literature in Honor of Jay B. Hubbell, ed. Clarence Gohdes
1967, pp. 307–28

Thornton Wilder enjoys life: this is the testimony of all who know him personally. He seems to have remained unscathed by potentially traumatic phenomena to which the first half of the twentieth century has exposed him: two world wars, one depression, the advent of Freud, the invention of the hydrogen bomb, the escalation of race conflict, the birth of existentialism, the disclosures of space exploration, etc. He seems an imperturbably cheerful person. Life, he says—and his books say—is eminently worth living. It may present troubling questions; but Wilder is a man who can entertain doubts without being destroyed by them. He does not resolve the doubts; he lives with them—equably. He seems to have his own version of Keats's "negative capability." He is not tormented or rendered schizophrenic by being unable to decide which of two opposing theories is the "correct" one. He manages to subsist in between them. If he does not achieve certainty, he has established for himself a kind of balance or equilibrium which serves him well both as a lay philosopher and as an artist.

In his own life, too, Wilder has been a sort of in-between person. He was born on April 17, 1897, at Madison, Wisconsin, but he did not stay put in the Middle West. As a youngster he was whisked off to China, where his father was Consul General and where he spent two intervals, one of a few months and one of two years. His early schooling was in China; in California (a school in Berkeley: Wilder was to spend many years first and last in academic communities); and, for the first two years of college, at Oberlin. After a period of military service in World War I he completed his work for the A.B. degree at Yale University; his Master's degree was from Princeton (1935). Meantime he had studied archaeology at the American Academy at Rome, taught French at Lawrenceville, and had begun his career as a writer. From 1930 to 1935 he was on the faculty of the University of Chicago. Later he taught at Harvard. During World War II he served as intelligence officer with the Air Force in northern Africa and in Italy. In recent years he has lived in his own house (he has remained unmarried) in Hamden, Connecticut.

In some ways the career of Wilder has been an anomaly. It seems a bit odd that a writer of his apparent stature, a writer who has been before the public forty years, should have received so little formal criticism. Granted that he is apparently not destined to be ranked ultimately as one of the giants of our literature—the peer, say, of Faulkner or Mark Twain or Melville—he has at least been a serious, highly talented professional writer devoted to his art: the author of best sellers, the recipient of three Pulitzer prizes, the author of a play *(Our Town)* that has been performed probably more frequently than any other recent American play, and a box-office success with movie versions of his works. Yet until recently there was only one book-length study of him published in this country (now there are three) besides one medium-length German monograph. There has been a moderate number of articles about him, but often these have amounted to little more than personalia. In a number of books on American literary history of the twentieth century his name is not mentioned. Moreover, the tone of those writers who do discuss his works is often curiously reluctant or embarrassed. No one has fully explained this anomaly. His latest biographer, Malcolm Goldstein, hazards the thought that Wilder has been the victim of chronology: he came to his artistic maturity under the influence of the New Humanists (Paul Elmer More, Irving Babbitt, and others) at the very time, in the late teens and the early twenties, when naturalism was beginning to steal the show, later to be followed by the existential era—schools of literature with which Wilder has had little affinity. To critics bred in the naturalist-existentialist atmosphere Wilder seemed to show very little of life as it is actually lived. His books were too tame, too pretty, too little involved with "the fury and the mire of human veins." Perhaps there are other reasons for the anomaly that may appear if one surveys his production.

Wilder's first book, *The Cabala* (1926), created little critical stir, but it revealed characteristic elements that in later books would earn the author more flattering attention. It is a youthful book, a comedy flecked with farce and fantasy as well as invested with darker tones that do not comport well with comedy. Set in almost contemporary Rome, it deals with a group of decaying aristocrats whom the reader is asked to think of as reincarnations of ancient gods. There is an interview with dying John Keats near the beginning, and near the end the young American narrator (and protagonist) conjures up Virgil in quest of his advice. The body of the novel is concerned particularly with the problems of three of the elegant, learned, sophisticated members of the somewhat mysterious Cabala, which is beginning to lose some of its long-held political and social sovereignty in the Eternal City. In each case the aid of the narrator, Samuele, is sought. When Marcantonio, scion of a distinguished line, seems about to destroy himself in a sexual marathon with a series of girls of less than patrician provenance (and thus, his mother fears, deal a mortal blow to family pride), the mother prevails on Samuele to try to cope with the lad's condition. But the effect of the narrowly Puritanical Samuele's well-meant "lecture" only accentuates the young man's perversity (he takes to incest with his sister), and the result is tragedy. A second sufferer is a neurotic princess Alix d'Espoli, who conceives a vain passion for Samuele's American friend Blair, a young man who seems as little available for love and sex as Samuele himself. Blair seeks safety in a flight from Rome, and Samuele can do nothing to help the princess. The third person to solicit aid is Mlle Astrée Luce de Morfontaine, a sensitive older woman who is pathetically obsessed with the idea that the way to secure Church authority is to have the Divine Right of Kings established as part of Church dogma: will Samuele try to get Cardinal Vaini to help? The Cardinal, however, a veteran cleric who has drifted into skepticism anyway, politely declines the gambit. At the end Samuele gets a hint from Virgil that since Rome is on the way out, the hero had best go home and concern himself with building a new city in the new world. It is an assignment pretty heavy, one thinks, for the frail shoulders of the attractive, graceful, innocent scholar-dilettante Samuele, who has little aptitude for the practical, no apparent capacity for love, and only a surface knowledge of the messier problems of mankind. Frequently the author-narrator adopts a tone of self-mockery which cues the reader not to take his role too seriously. After all Samuele is but a youngster, and he seems best qualified to render the external scene: the streets and alleys of Rome, the mansions and acres of the aristocrats, the play of fountains on the terrace, the contours of the distant hills seen from a parapet in the lingering twilight. This he does with charm and skill. He loves the country: "It was Virgil's country and there was a wind that seemed to rise from the fields and descend upon us in a long Virgilian sigh, for the land that has inspired sentiment in the poet ultimately receives its sentiment from him."[1] Even if the phrasing (influenced, thinks Edmund Wilson, by Proust) is occasionally a bit precious, it is also phrasing that is to the last degree disciplined in accordance with Wilder's ideals at that stage in his career. If not the philosopher, Wilder is at least the artist in this, his first book.

The Bridge of San Luis Rey (1927), Wilder's next novel, was a brilliant popular success, and it has retained its place in the affections of many people. It is again a book of no great philosophical weight. Its action is spectacular and in a sense tragic, but it creates no unbearable emotions in the reader. The deaths of five people who went down when the bridge gave way are rendered tolerable by their remoteness in time (1712) and place (Peru). One remembers them sadly but without acute distress: the old Marchesa whose daughter has cut herself off in cold disdain from a mother she could not endure; the little servant Pepita whom the Abbess sends to aid the old woman; Esteban, the lonely young public scribe, stricken by the death of a twin orphan brother to whom he had been profoundly, perhaps homosexually, devoted; Uncle Pio, who had made a great actress out of the wilful, sensual Camila Perichole; and young Don Jaime, Camila's illegitimate son. What does it all mean—the summary snuffing out of the lives of these five? The reader never knows; this book is open-ended. Brother Juniper, who witnessed the fall of the bridge, thought he could prove that the event did not represent an accident but the will of God; these lives, he believed, could be shown to be "perfect wholes." This presumptuousness in explaining God's ways earned Brother Juniper the stigma of heretic and the doom of being burned at the stake. Wilder himself does not resolve the problem: his first chapter is entitled "Perhaps an Accident"; his last, "Perhaps an Intention." Apparently he believed man's condition to be governed by a mixture of partly unknowable factors. He once wrote, in phrasing reminiscent of Melville, "It is the magic unity of purpose and chance, of destiny and accident, that I have tried to describe in my books."[2] That "magic unity" is never elucidated. Throughout most of his writings, whether through an awareness of the limitations of his own intelligence or a natural propensity to leave things in suspension—on a bridge—Wilder refrains from dogmatizing regarding religion. A kind of stoic acquiescence in the inevitable—what must be—seemed to help him to harmonize such intuitions as he had regarding the mystery of life. And this without any descent into despair or pessimism. He knew (and demonstrated in *The Bridge*) the pain of immediate circumstance, but, as he was to suggest in *The Woman of Andros*, he deprecated prolonged emphasis on grief and suffering. Ultimately, he seems to say, the sadness that inheres in the human condition will be easily borne. At the end of *Our Town* the dead speak gently and equably to each other; and throughout "The Long Christmas Dinner," during which no less than eight persons silently move into the realms of the hereafter, the audience participates in the drama without suffering acute pain. Lucia in the latter play suggests one clue to the tone of Wilder when she says: "But sad things aren't the same as depressing things."[3] And so with the ending of *The Bridge of San Luis Rey:* it is sad but not depressing. Not even the assurance of life after death seems to be requisite; at the end of the book, indeed, Wilder appears to deny it. The sole indubitable comfort he offers is the high premium he appears to place on human love as an end in and of itself. This emerges in the thoughts assigned to the kindly Abbess at the very end of the book.

> Even now [she thought] almost no one remembers Esteban and Pepita, but myself. Camila alone remembers her uncle Pio and her son; the woman Donna Clara her mother. But soon we shall die and all memory of those five will have left the earth, and we ourselves shall be loved for a while and then forgotten. But the love will have been enough; all those impulses of love return to the love that made them. Even memory is not necessary for love. There is a land of the living and a land of the dead and the bridge is love, the only survival, the only meaning.[4]

Skipping for the moment the plays Wilder published in the 1920's, one comes to his next novel, *The Woman of Andros* (1935). Although based on a comedy, Terence's *Andria*, Wilder's novel is, characteristically, neither comedy nor tragedy. Often its tone is pastoral. Its setting is in pre-Christian Greece: the obscure beautiful Aegean island of Brynos. Here the courtesan Chrysis, a disciple of the teachings of Socrates, holds symposia during which there are readings and discussions in part designed to serve as therapy for many young men who come to her with their problems, their anxiety about a life they can neither understand nor master. One of her visitors is Pamphilus, a youth of aristocratic lineage, for whom she has a passion but who falls in love with Glycerium, her sister. When Pamphilus announces to his family that he proposes to marry this charming suffering peasant girl (by now pregnant), his parents are shocked by this threat to their dignity and affront to society. Ultimately the patrician father begins to relent. In the end both Glycerium and her baby die. This is the simple external action of the book, but it is featured much less than the meanings with which Wilder aims to invest his story, chiefly meanings related to Greek humanism, through the agency of Chrysis the prostitute. She emphasizes love for one's fellow-men; the wisdom of trying to realize and savor life moment by moment (a theme which Wilder also stressed in *Our Town*); and the acceptance of this world in its every guise, whether apparently beneficent or baneful and whether or not there is an afterlife:

> "I want to say to someone . . . that I have known the worst that the world can do to me, and that nevertheless I praise the world and all living. All that is, is well. Remember . . . me as one who loved all things and accepted from the gods all things, the bright and the dark."[5]

She also insists that one must not pay too much attention to suffering as such:

> "Why cannot someone tell him [Pamphilus] that it is not necessary to suffer so about living. . . . Let him rest some day, O ye Olympians, from pitying those who suffer. Let him learn to look the other way. This is something new in the world, this concern for the unfit and the broken. . . . That is some god's business."[6]

The pagan acceptance of what must be is a characteristic Wilder response, but he chooses to fix his novel in time partly by two allusions to the Christian religion. Christ's birth is adumbrated at the beginning, and at the end Glycerium's role is seen to symbolize that of Mary: "And in the East the stars shone tranquilly down upon the land that was soon to be called Holy and that even then was preparing its precious burden."[7] This, the last sentence in the novel, provides an example of Wilder's mastery of a stylistic mode which has been denigrated by some critics as "sentimental" or "precious" but applauded by others as "classical" in its clarity, poise, and grace.

Wilder's public response to adverse criticism has been the wise one: absolute silence. There have been two major periods of attack on his work, one of them occurring in the early 1930's. At that time, when the United States was in the midst of the Great Depression, it was natural to evaluate a play or a novel partly on the basis of its economic and/or sociological stance. By this time even Wilder's friends found it a bit curious that a man of such talents as he, the author of three books, should have paid so little attention to his own country. Why, outspoken critics asked, did he expend his talents on remote places, flimsy fables about fake gods, the corrupt idle rich, neurasthenic young men lolling around when they might have been better employed digging potatoes? Why so much toying with fine and fancy images: viola d'amore, ivory, terra cotta, spices, silks, alabaster figurines, paintings on fans, etc.? Critics seemed now to be retroactively angry that a Pulitzer prize had been given to a writer who apparently regarded himself as too elegant to address himself to the reek and racket of contemporary America. The most notable outburst was that of Michael Gold, who found in Wilder's books only "a pastel, pastiche, dilettante religion . . . a day-dream of homosexual figures in graceful gowns moving archaically among lilies. . . ." He called for a treatment of "the blood, horror, and hope of the world's new empire." "Where," he asked, "are the modern streets of New York, Chicago and New Orleans in these little novels? Where are the cotton mills . . . the child slaves of the beet fields . . . the stockbroker suicides, the labor racketeers . . .?"[8] A number of Wilder's friends rushed to his defense, but he himself made no answer to the charges.

Or did he? Was his next novel, *Heaven's My Destination* (1935), a tacit attempt at confession and restitution? Geographically it seemed to be, in the amount of American soil it embraces in some twelve states of the Union. There were changes in personnel and in subject matter too. Here are many characters obviously not top-drawer society, not Ariadne-like Greek girls mourning their dejected state, not scented young men of debatable masculinity. Here are village bums; here is a whorehouse; here are roadside adventures in Kansas, Michigan, Oklahoma; here is some discussion of commerce and finance; here are American businessmen in convention; here is a traveling salesman; here is a good deal of American dialogue that rings true in accent and syntax; and here are many other notations of contemporary American life.

The central character, George Marvin Brush, is an incurably idealistic young man chock-full of benevolent impulses and a strong will to reform society, which he thinks rotten in its basic structure. He is a pacifist, a believer in racial equality, and a perfectionist. Armed with texts from the Sermon on the Mount and other scriptural counsel, imbued with the ideas of Gandhi, he sets out to crusade for his conception of the true life. His constant campaigning against tobacco and alcohol creates only minor irritation among people on whom he foists himself, but his theories of voluntary poverty and non-violence finally evoke anger, even rage, against him. A little like a latter-day Thoreau, who ridiculed the rationale of insurance, Brush has decided that the theory of banks is wrong; and when he comes to take his savings out, he refuses to accept the interest accrued: he says it doesn't really belong to him. "To save up money," he tells the president of the bank, "is a sign that you're afraid, and one fear makes another fear. . . . No one who has money in banks can really be happy."[9] Imprisonment for crime and capital punishment are also wrong, he tells a judge:

> "It's a crime to kill, and the government does that, and it's a crime to lock somebody up in a room for years on end, and the government does that by the

thousands. The government commits thousands of crimes in a year. And every crime makes more crimes. The only way out of this mess of crimes is to try this other way."[10]

The other way is to freely give the potential criminal what he wants—yes, even if he is raping your sister: this good act (of forbearance) will "make an impression" on the man. Indeed Brush had got arrested for giving a robber forty dollars that did not belong to him—though he was going to pay it back. If he were in a war, he said, he would refuse to kill a man who was trying to kill him. This seems a bit extreme to the judge: "Suppose," says the judge, "that man in the shell-hole shot you. What becomes of your lesson to him then?" "Well, Judge," replied Brush, "*ahimsa* would have been in my mind. That's Gandhi's word for it, Your Honor. And if somebody has *ahimsa* in his mind, I believe it has a chance of jumping from mind to mind."[11] Brush is allowed by Wilder to present his arraignment of society with considerable skill and persuasiveness. Even Mrs. Efrim, whose money he lifted without permission (in her presence) to give to the robber, is half won over. Brush himself is a handsome, strong, essentially likable person with a marvelous tenor voice which enchants listeners. His very presence sometimes has a healing effect on people—they feel as if they had somehow been blessed—a little like the effect that Rabbit Angstrom has on people in John Updike's *Rabbit, Run.* Of course the trouble is that besides having the odor of divinity about him he is a man lacking in ordinary good sense—a specimen of the holy fool. He pesters people and tries to prevail by sheer logic, making little or no allowance for the fallibility and weakness of ordinary human nature. Says Lottie plaintively near the end of the book: "Nobody's strong enough to live up to the rules."[12] Inevitably people finally think that he is really crazy. The stout oak of rooted purpose and enduring wisdom which sustained Thoreau and Gandhi is but feebly parodied by this tumbleweed of the prairie. Brush's behavior becomes farcical. Sooner or later he violates, under extenuating circumstances perhaps, a great many of his own principles: he gets drunk, he slugs a man, he smokes a pipe, and (no one knows how) he gets a girl with child. He later spends months trying to find the girl in order to make up for his sin by marrying her. Of course the girl, a simple farmer's daughter, does not want to marry him, but she finally gives in to his magnetic ways—with dire results, chiefly because Brush is really incapable of love. Brush has his moments of discouragement, and he is intelligent enough to diagnose part of his trouble: "I made the mistake all my life of thinking that you could get better and better until you were perfect." Like Holden Caulfield in *The Catcher in the Rye,* he has been quixotically tilting against "phony" elements in society. And like Holden he eventually has a severe breakdown, suffering utter physical and psychological prostration; but he recovers and resumes his former ways.

What is Wilder's attitude toward his monstrous creation? He has avowed that his portrait of Brush is heavily autobiographical. One wonders. In any case critics remonstrated with the author for his ambivalence—again his remaining on the bridge—regarding Brush's behavior. One gets the impression that Wilder is glad of the chance to ventilate social theories, to force society to examine the assumptions on which it lives—no doubt taking some sly pleasure in the process, for, as Judge Carberry says, "Most people don't like ideas."[13] Yet Wilder stays far short of committing himself to Brush's idealistic program; indeed he undercuts his protagonist to the point of making him absurd. Moreover, he seems to have no love for his own literary progeny. He permits one of the other characters, Burkin, to destroy much of what has been built up, by showing what a half-baked person Brush essentially is—even to the point of letting Brush know that the woman-evangelist originally responsible for his conversion had been under the influence of drugs at the time. If Wilder began by modeling his hero on himself as a Calvinistically bred, pinched, censorious Puritan young man, he escalated him into a full-blown blunder-boy such as Wilder has surely never been. By a process of canceling out values, then, Wilder almost completely destroys the philosophical validity of the protagonist's position. Possibly the reader is expected to take some comfort in the thought of the indestructibility of a moral idea and in the presence of disinterested human love symbolized by a silver spoon sent to the ailing Brush by a Catholic priest who had never met him. But Wilder did not destroy the story interest of *Heaven's My Destination:* it remains a critically ambiguous but very readable book. Although Brush is humorless, the jams he gets into are often productive of real comedy and some farce. A trifling example may suffice; it highlights the character of Brush. In a jail-yard Brush walks up to a fellow-violator of the law who is lying on a bench. Emitting bonhomie at every pore, Brush shakes hands and says in his best, brisk American manner:

> "My name is George M. Brush. I come from Michigan and I sell textbooks for Caulkins and Company."
>
> "Any birth marks?"
>
> "What?"
>
> The man lay down again. "My name is Zoroaster Eels. I lie on benches for a living."[14]

One fears that the lesson was lost on George M. Brush. ⟨. . .⟩

Thornton Wilder is one of the most difficult American writers to evaluate and interpret under a few rubrics. He tends to fall between categories. This is apparent when one considers him in terms of (1) his choice of material, (2) his philosophical outlook, and (3) his technique.

First for his materials. It is obvious that he exhibits great diversity in both his novels and his plays with respect to scene and dramatis personae. No such homogeneity characterizes him as exists, for example, in John O'Hara, in whom one discerns a large degree of sameness as year after year he adds another unit to his sociological, sexual saga of his beloved Gibbsville. Or in Faulkner, who tends one domain. Or in Marquand, whose cup of tea is Boston and environs. Wilder has no favored plot of ground: no Yoknapatawpha, no Poictesme, no Wessex, or Gibbsville, or Combray, or Winesburg. He gets around. He has a certain attraction to classical soil, setting two novels in Rome and one on a Greek island—not to mention shorter pieces. *The Bridge of San Luis Rey* took him to Peru. The clamor for him to pay attention to his native land resulted (indirectly) in stories and plays set in a variety of verifiable American regions: New Jersey, New England, the Middle West. Inevitably his characters constitute a variegated personnel, ranging from Roman aristocrat to Manhattan busboy; from devoted, learned eighteenth-century South American priest to quasi-illiterate twentieth-century Kansas farm girl; from shy, naïve soda-sipping New Hampshire high-school girl to Cleopatra. The characters tend to be lightly delineated, in crayon rather than oils, but they are representative of many strata—social, professional, cultural, economic—in many milieux. Diversity also characterizes Wilder's narrative and dramatic actions. He does not confine himself to one or all of the traditional matters for novel or play, namely, making money, making war, and making love. Instead it is a matter of interpreting a complex, sophisticated in-group *(The Cabala)*; the philosophical causes and human effects of a major catastrophe *(The Bridge of San Luis Rey)*; the psychology of characters trying to cope with the problem of suffering *(The Woman of Andros)*; the adventures of an idealist embattled against the proponents of a rotten society *(Heaven's My Destination)*; the average daily behavior of small-town people who realize too late the value of life *(Our Town)*; the deeply implanted instinct of mankind to survive and rebuild after no matter what or how many disasters *(The Skin of Our Teeth)*. The nearest to "standard" material appears in *The Matchmaker*, in which a wealthy sixty-year-old man decides to get married—with hilariously farcical consequences.

In the second place, philosophically Wilder—to judge by his writings—is neither an affirmer nor a nay-sayer. He arrives at no camp of dogma but remains on a bridge of reflection. In him one finds no basis for a strong Christian faith or for bleak existential despair, still less nihilism. He seems to imply that one must take the long view. Nor is he an adherent of the cult of the absurd. About the "government" of the universe he makes no final statement. Like his Caesar, he just doesn't know; like Caesar he seems to have a pagan poise, ready to accept what the gods decree. Even about whether there is an after-life he appears to have no settled convictions. Yet in *Our Town* we see characters in a cemetery, between life and death, apparently taking off on some strange spiritual voyage or evolutionary sequence which may argue on off-beat version of immortality.

For a writer who proffers so little overt religious or philosophical assurance, Wilder has been remarkably acceptable to average readers. At the very least they know that he has no paralyzing fears and that, unlike some of his juniors, he has no self-pity. Perhaps they sense, too, that he has intuitions, only in part given expression, which proceed beyond the area of demonstrable proof. They like his emphasis, in *The Bridge of San Luis Rey* and *The Woman of Andros*, on the necessity and the good effects of the love of human beings for one another. There is vague comfort also in the Stage Manager's insistence that there is "*something*" eternal about man. At times, too, he seems to believe in the existence of some good principle operating among men which, if indefinable and unprovable, is perhaps indestructible. No sentiment of goodness or love is ever lost—as with Gandhi's *ahimsa*, it may "jump from mind to mind." Wilder, then, is often ambivalent philosophically, but he is not tormented and torn to pieces: he is not schizophrenic, and he is not "lost." In fact he comes close to harmonizing such opposing views as he harbors. If life exists in halves, he seems to say, try to join the halves—make a unity as well as you can. Such counsel comports with a kind of overall classical balance and repose that characterizes Wilder in general.

Thirdly, Wilder's technique evinces the same tendency to move freely between alternative modes. He uses the concrete well but he veers toward abstraction. He is capable of clear, straightforward characterization of individuals: Samuele in *The Cabala* in an example of this; and there are patches of very effective small realism in most of his books. Yet in general he is not attracted to the slice-of-life school of the late-nineteenth-century realists or the endless factual Dreiser-like documentation of the naturalists of the twentieth century. Wilder clearly does not think that 20-20 vision is an asset to the artist. He is less interested in transcription than in representation. The "busy little world of door-bell and telephone," he once said, was a bore to him. The single fact, he thought, has little significance unless its relationship to a general law is felt. Accordingly, he used abstraction, sought the universal. For this reason he resorts much to emblems, symbols, allegory, myth—the instruments of universality. For this reason many of his characters, though tagged with small tokens of "reality," are not quite real in the usual sense of the word—not the girl-next-door type of person—but, rather, pallid figures slightly misted over and blurred. They are finally figures in a parable or pageant, who have their exits and their entrances at the will of a master of ceremonies or puppeteer. Ultimately they are absorbed into the universal.

In this quest for universality through abstraction Wilder used his three handmaids: distance, time, and recurrence or repetition. Distance enabled him to see mankind as a group, as community, even, in *The Skin of Our Teeth*, as race. Depth in time also helped him to understand the dimensions of mankind. Individuals as such are often allowed only scant rights as separate identities—only a tenuous momentary validity in the colossal reaches of time that extend back behind their immediate movements in the fast-ebbing present and forward into endless future ages. Birth, procreation, death; something built, something lost, something aspired toward: the patterns of man repeat themselves endlessly. In this enormous perspective the importance of the individual's agenda shrinks. Death is not clinical but symbolic. One soon finds it hard to remember the five persons on the bridge at San Luis Rey who were dashed to their deaths in a rocky gorge or boiling torrent; for the reader they are dropped into eternity, their legacy a philosophical problem. Brother Juniper died the agonizing death of one burned at the stake; but in his account of the burning Wilder all but annuls reality: "he [Brother Juniper] called twice upon St. Francis and leaning upon a flame he smiled and died."[15] The eight people in "The Long Christmas Dinnner" who one by one pass off the stage, silently, without protest, without religious consolation, are being absorbed, as noiselessly as Ahab, into universality. "I am interested," said Wilder, "in those things that repeat and repeat and repeat in the lives of the millions."[16] Even the characters in *Our Town*, which provides so many winning details of New England village and domestic behavior, are being translated into the universal language of eternity, fractions being converted into an integer whose size no one can conceive of. George and Emily relinquish their tiny identities to become emblems of innocent young love anywhere, any time. And even Emily's death (which we never see) only ranges her in an uncountable sisterhood, among the billions of mankind "dreaming through the twilight that doth not rise nor set." George Brush has a million kinfolk, in history past and to come, who pit their strength if not always their common sense against apparent evils in our lives. The Antrobus family in *The Skin of Our Teeth* carries the process even further: Mr. and Mrs. Antrobus, symbols of the survival quotient of mankind, have been married five thousand years—surely a record for steady employment in the theater. Son Henry (for Henry read Cain) had been around wandering almost equally long, before Wilder drafted him for a tiny exposure in twentieth-century New Jersey. He will soon be at large again. He will finally belong nowhere—and everywhere. So what becomes of the importance of the town of Excelsior, New Jersey, in 1942?

Thus Wilder, vendor of abstractions. What is the effect of this technique on his works in the large? It is mixed. For some readers and audiences it is disquieting to see characters in whom they have staked an interest dissolving into symbols. For people who like cash on the narrative line, Wilder's proffered long-term investments are somehow unsatisfactory. He himself recognized this problem when he wrote that although *Our Town* is "an attempt to find a value above all price for the smallest events in our daily life," he "made the claim as preposterous as possible" for he has "set the village against the largest dimensions of time and place."[17] He notes that "buried [back] in the text . . . is a constant repetition of the words 'hundreds,' 'thousands,' 'millions.' It's as though the audience . . . is looking at that town at ever greater distances through a telescope."[18] Yet most audiences and readers appear to bear with him in his quest for generalized truth. On a bare stage or amid exploding scenery, on a remote myth-enshrouded island, on a bridge that has its existence more in allegory than in veritable space, Wilder has cast humanity itself in age-old roles destined to be re-enacted ceaselessly as the future replaces the present.

For the rest, Wilder's technique in detail is often superb. Making no pretensions to Olympian stature as a writer, he is yet one of the most finished craftsmen in American fiction and drama of the past generation, one of the most devoted disciples of art. In this respect his books *are* homogeneous. His thinking may be open-ended but his art is fixed and finished. His most serious limitations are a certain thinness in invention (most of his works have been primed by sources) and some ineptitude in handling larger structures. His architectonics are sometimes shaky as in *The Bridge* and *The Cabala*. He himself said he had a "passion for compression," and he admitted that this was an offset to his "inability to sustain a long flight."[19] He approaches perfection in many small units, within which he makes the most of his skill in image, in line and mass, in tone, in cadence and resonance. His dialogue tends to be superior, whether of the formal sort suited to allegorical sequences or the modified colloquial speech of average citizens in a village square. All is controlled, all is finished. Every paragraph executes its author's will; no sentence or phrase escapes him without knowing its assignment. Within his own realm—a principality, perhaps, rather than a kingdom—he rules with unquestioned authority.

Thornton Wilder has had a successful career. Yet as a writer he has a curious relationship with his public. Some of his books have been best-sellers, and he has been greatly admired, but readers do not seem to feel that they know *him* or that he belongs to them. He is gregarious as a man, one hears, but somehow he seems to forbid intimacy: a distance exists between author and reader. He does not confide his hopes and fears, his private life, to the reader; his books are not (what is the mode at present) "confessional." He does not woo or exhort or frighten the reader. He has no program to gun for, no point of view to sell. He is less the debater than the moderator. This is no doubt partly because he is not too sure of conclusions himself.

Thornton Wilder is a spectator, an observer of life. In a sense he is himself a man on a bridge. A bridge enables you to see much but commits you to nothing. Beneath you, at uncertain depths, are the arteries of communication and transport: railroad, river, or motor highway. Freight of all kinds is moving, some of it marked fragile. Yonder, perhaps, is the teeming city. Far away are the hills, purpled with distance and the invitation to reflection. Overhead is the sky, a route, not well marked, to eternity. So you may linger, bemused, immobilized for the time being—yourself for the moment frozen into a fragment of parable or pageant. The bridge is open at either end, but you are under no immediate compulsion to choose a way. You are in balance. For a while your thoughts may be in suspension between alternative ways of doing. Wilder is often an in-between sort of person, unable or unwilling to commit himself to one mode. He is between comedy and sadness; between realism and parable; between a dimly apprehended mystical faith and cool skepticism; between the conviction that man can order his own existence and the acceptance of a distant cosmic determinism; between the will to reform and the awareness that man must not strive fanatically for perfection—a bridge must not be too rigid, must allow for expansion and contraction; between the pulsing present and a nobody-knows-how-old past. Thornton Wilder is there, listening to the old earth sigh and beginning to order his own thoughts.

Readers sometimes wish Wilder would get off the bridge, be an actor in life rather than observer and recorder of it. They wish he would be more involved personally. They wish he would get more excited, make more downright decisions, really lose himself, and go all out for *some*thing. He is too exasperatingly cool, has too steady a pulse, never runs a fever. At times he seems a man wearing gloves, surgically safe from life's infection. Why doesn't he ever portray passion or pain, his own or his characters', at close range? Why is he so prim and prissy about sex? And does he really have love for his characters? Does Wilder love George Brush in the way Salinger loves Holden Caulfield? And why doesn't he deliberately run more risks? Why doesn't he take off on some titanic Melvillean voyage in quest of the deeper wisdom, or with Walt Whitman on a "passage to India," risking self, ship, and all? Why does he never get out of sight of shore?

How foolish to ask. How unreasonable of his readers. Aren't they in effect asking him to jeopardize the very qualities which subtend his greatest asset, the principal benefit he may confer on the reader, namely, his balance, his classical repose and poise, his fine sense for order and harmony, his long-range vision of things? If he shows passion, ecstasy, agony, tragedy only obliquely, doesn't he serve his readers by helping to put *their* troubles, big and small, their sorrows and griefs, even their fun (all the dark and the light of life) into a perspective that may help them to experience life with fullness and equanimity as well as help to prepare them for a time when they too will be gathered into the artifice of eternity? If he doesn't seem to be capable of the love of individuals, he at least has a broad-gauge human tenderness, and he does love mankind in general. He is in a way a comforter and a healer. Yet as a humanist he is less concerned finally with worrying about or preparing for the next world than he is in celebrating things of this world. He is acquainted with suffering and doubt, but (like Chrysis in *The Woman of Andros*) he counts upon man's ability to transcend suffering and to live with his doubts. He insists not only upon the dignity of man but also upon his capacity for the enjoyment of life. He thinks of man as a fun-having animal; and he knows the uses of humor. To him this world is not necessarily the best of all possible worlds, but he thinks of it as mainly a good place.

Notes

1. Thornton Wilder, *The Cabala* (New York, 1926), p. 7. There is no uniform edition of Wilder's writings. A useful bibliography is J. M. Edelstein's *A Bibliographical Checklist of the Writings of Thornton Wilder* (New Haven, 1959). Biography and criticism may be found in Rex Burbank, *Thornton Wilder* (New York, 1961); Helmut Papajewski, *Thornton Wilder* (Frankfurt am Main, 1961); Malcolm Goldstein, *The Art of Thornton Wilder* (Lincoln, Neb., 1965).
2. Walter Tritsch, "Thornton Wilder in Berlin," *Living Age*, CCCXLI, 4380, 44–47 (Sept., 1931). This is a translation of a report that first appeared in *Die Literarische Welt* for June 12, 1931. See Edelstein, op. cit., p. 43.

3. Thornton Wilder, *The Long Christmas Dinner & Other Plays in One Act* (New York and New Haven, 1931), p. 10.
4. Thornton Wilder, *The Bridge of San Luis Rey* (New York, 1928), pp. 234–235.
5. Thornton Wilder, *The Woman of Andros* (New York, 1930), p. 107.
6. Ibid., pp. 77–78.
7. Ibid., p. 162.
8. Michael Gold, "Wilder: Prophet of the Genteel Christ," *New Republic*, LXIV, 267 (Oct. 22, 1930).
9. Thornton Wilder, *Heaven's My Destination* (New York, 1935), pp. 22–23.
10. Ibid., pp. 242–243.
11. Ibid., p. 241.
12. Ibid., p. 290.
13. Ibid., p. 247.
14. Ibid., p. 214.
15. *The Bridge of San Luis Rey*, p. 220.
16. Quoted in Goldstein, *The Art of Thornton Wilder*, p. 152.
17. *Three Plays by Thornton Wilder* (New York, 1961), Preface, p. xi.
18. *Writers at Work*, p. 113.
19. Thornton Wilder, *The Angel That Troubled the Waters and Other Plays* (New York, 1928), Foreword, p. xiii.

TENNESSEE WILLIAMS

1911–1983

Tennessee Williams was born Thomas Lanier Williams on March 26, 1911, in Columbus, Mississippi. He was educated at the University of Missouri, Washington University, and the University of Iowa (A.B. 1938). He worked various odd jobs, including screenwriting for MGM, before becoming a full-time writer in 1944.

Tennessee Williams was one of the most popularly successful and critically lauded (and vilified) dramatists of the twentieth century. His plays are noted for their moving portrayal of people living in deteriorating circumstances, often surrounded by madness and violence. He has been criticized for overindulging in sexuality and violence, and his later, rather disjointed and stylized plays have been subjected to particularly harsh criticism. Nonetheless, among Williams's more than seventy produced plays are some of the most significant of modern times. His first play to reach the stage was *Cairo! Shanghai! Bombay!* in 1936; his first to be published was *At Liberty* (published in *American Scenes*, edited by William Kozlenko, 1941). *The Glass Menagerie* (1945), whose family of lonely, slowly disintegrating people mirrors Williams's own childhood, was his first major success. It won the first of four New York Drama Critics' Circle Awards given to Williams during his lifetime. *A Streetcar Named Desire* (1947) solidified his status as a major American playwright, and won Williams the first of two Pulitzer Prizes. Other significant plays by Williams include *Summer and Smoke* (1948), *The Rose Tattoo* (1951), *Cat on a Hot Tin Roof* (1955, in a somewhat bowdlerized version Williams's most popular play and his second Pulitzer Prize winner), and *The Night of the Iguana* (1961).

Though all his work is controversial, and much of it is considered insignificant, few would question Williams's immense influence and position as one of the twentieth century's preeminent dramatists. He also wrote two novels (*The Roman Spring of Mrs. Stone*, 1950; *Moise and the World of Reason*, 1975), three books of poetry, and several collections of short stories, many of which served as the kernels for later plays. His *Memoirs* were published in 1975, and *Where I Live: Selected Essays* in 1978. He died on February 24, 1983, in New York City.

Making allowance for those aberrant periods when the stage has been cluttered with realistic details, the theatre has always been a platform for poets, a showplace for symbols, a puppetry where dreams define. I refer, of course, to the ideational use of the theatre in the study of human relationships, and not to its incidental function as entertainment, though the two are frequently confused. No argument bars comedy from drama as an application of humor to the disclosure of character, but the general rule dictates that the serious poetic purpose is better served without comedy, or with small and intermittent appeals to the laughter stimulant. That is why most of the masterpieces of drama are tragic, or narrowly escape catastrophe.

Among our contemporary playwrights, Tennessee Williams has aligned himself with the experimentalists, who are flouting the old conventions of structure and mounting. Without going to such extremes as the masks, or the soliloquies and asides of Eugene O'Neill, he has dispensed with the formal pattern of acts and relied upon a loose concatenation of scenes projected against a single stage set so arranged as to shift the attention of the audience from one crux of action to another by the use of the color switchboard. His dependence upon this optical trick he has rather naively expressed as an article in his artistic code: "A free, imaginative use of light can be of enormous value in giving a mobile, plastic quality to plays of a more or less static nature."

However true the statement may be, it obviously stands in this case as an argument in self-defence, for the plays of Mr. Williams are static, more than less, and desperately in need of a movement uncompensated by the drive of the dialogue. The strongest in action and the most naturalistic in atmosphere is *A Streetcar Named Desire*, but it is also the least poetic, and the poet in Mr. Williams is what the theatre needs. Hearsay reports that *Summer and Smoke* is an early play recovered from the hope chest to take advantage of the vogue that two Broadway successes brought him. If this is true, one hopes that he will work that vein deeper and strike a richer ore. He has the high courage of a seeker after beauty and that courage should not fail him when stubborn problems of stagecraft confront him.

He will need courage also to acknowledge his own limitations and to enlarge them; to study human nature more penetratingly; to heighten his own esteem for the average sensual man, and to increase his respect for the dignity inherent in all human beings. Whether or not *Summer and Smoke* is an early play, it is motivated by a fervor more adolescent than mature; it ridicules the pretensions of small-town culture; it fumbles amateurishly with the task of converting personages into characters, and it employs symbolism in the most elementary manner. Its title is provocative, but the interest it provokes remains unfulfilled; it does not even convey the fundamental thesis of the drama, which is the immemorial conflict between the flesh and the spirit, or, if you wish to put it that way, between evil and good.

Let us consider the plot which concerns the plight of two young people who have grown up as next-door neighbors in a Mississippi town that the playwright contemptuously nicknames Glorious Hill. Alma Winemiller is the daughter of an Episcopal clergyman whose mentally defective and kleptomaniacal wife is a "cross" he has to bear. John Buchanan is the son of a physician, and has studied medicine for the purpose of succeeding to his father's practice. Alma, dowered with a soprano voice good enough to dominate the church choir and to sing such popular pieces as *La Golondrina* with the town "orchestra" at public fêtes, is a teacher of music as well as the practical head of household and social affairs in the rectory.

Alma, who has the annoying habit of reminding you with a self-conscious snatch of laughter that her name means "soul" in Spanish, has fallen in love with John, who sees nothing sexually attractive in such a pious *precieuse.* While a student at Johns Hopkins, he acquired wine-bibbing and lechery as side-lines, and pays more attention to them than to helping with his father's patients. He picks up Rosa Gonzales, daughter of the proprietor of dubious Moon Lake Casino, and on the eve of running away with her to South America, throws a party in his father's house. Alma, perturbed by the roistering and wishing to save John from his folly, telephones to Dr. Buchanan, who is fighting an epidemic in a neighboring town. The physician returns post haste, and in a quarrel with Rosa's father is mortally wounded by a pistol shot.

Sobered by this shock, John continues his father's fight, stamps out the epidemic, and is rewarded with a silver loving cup. He experiences what moralists used to call a change of heart, gives up his wild ways, and becomes engaged to one of Alma's pupils. When he and Alma meet again, it is only to part because there exists between them a subtle alienation, an inability to understand each other, based on an incompatibility of temperaments. As Alma puts it: "I came to tell you that being a gentleman doesn't seem so important to me any more, and you're telling me I've got to remain a lady." The last we see of Alma, she is being escorted by a traveling salesman to Moon Lake Casino.

Mr. Williams seems to be trying to tell us that each individual is compounded of good and bad impulses; he is arguing for the multiple personality, the vagaries of the mind, the inconsistencies of conduct, and the inner contradictions that plague us all. He has made both Alma and John divided in their natures, and such a division, which can be described, analyzed and explained by the novelist, is difficult for the playwright to present, because his reliance is solely on the spoken word. Mr. Williams could not make his dialogue behave—it stumbles and lags and repeats itself to the point of dullness—and to cover this deficiency he introduces a symbolism so simplified and overemphasized as to verge on the ludicrous. In the center of the single stage setting is a fountain topped by a kneeling angel; this is flanked by two "interior" sets, the rectory parlor at the left and at the right the doctor's office adorned with a life-size anatomical chart such as doctors do not have on display. Lights are cast upon the angel at appropriate moments, and John uses the chart in a lecture to Alma about the three hungers which men endure.

The allegory could not be posited more plainly, and the pity is that Mr. Williams was not able to make the two protagonists emerge from it as individuals who might in real life have compromised their differences and found happiness. That is the chief defect in a play that is overpopulated with minor characters who are virtually supernumeraries, and marred by a malicious ridicule of such small-town activities as a literary club.

"Every play is a charade," said Paul Valery. If the spectator expects to guess the meaning, he must identify himself with someone who is on the stage. This cannot be done unless the playwright presents clearly defined individuals with whom identification is possible through sympathy. This focus Mr. Williams successfully fixed upon Laura Wingfield in *The Glass Menagerie*, a play so fragile and translucent in its symbolism that the very situation was charged with sympathy for the central figure. He failed again in *A Streetcar Named Desire*, where Blanche Du Bois does not arouse sympathy, for all her envolvement in a sordid nexus of deceit. The long run of *Streetcar* may be partly accounted for by the amount of good, old-fashioned melodrama mixed into it.

Many as his technical ineptitudes are and numerous his errors in estimation of his material, one follows and applauds Mr. Williams for the courage of his convictions. There are in his plays flashes of beauty, glimpses of insight, and moments when the poet in him becomes a magician with a transforming touch. He has not yet learned how to prolong those moments and enchant the spectator with lasting illusion, but what he has done in his apprenticeship makes one hopeful for his progress in skill.

The maker of plays, like the composer of music, is hampered in his contacts with the public by the fact that the projection of his work is fleeting, and that its meaning must be caught on the wing. Reading the manuscript of a play or the score of a symphony is quite a different experience from the one gained during a performance, because so much depends on the astuteness and finesse of the interpreters. Those who saw *The Glass Menagerie* on the stage were largely in agreement that Julie Haydon's interpretation of Laura's role was the decisive factor; while the consensus seems to be that neither Margaret Phillips nor Tod Andrews could cope triumphantly with the bafflements peculiar to *Summer and Smoke.*—RAY C. B. BROWN, "Tennessee Williams: The Poetry of Stagecraft," *Voices*, Summer 1949, pp. 4–8

Question: Can we talk frankly?

Answer: There's no other way we can talk.

Q: Perhaps you know that when your first successful play, *The Glass Menagerie*, was revived early this season, a majority of the reviewers felt that it was still the best play you have written, although it is now twelve years old?

A: Yes, I read all my play notices and criticisms, even those that say that I write for money and that my primary appeal is to brutal and ugly instincts.

Q: Where there is so much smoke—!

A: A fire smokes the most when you start pouring water on it.

Q: But surely you'll admit that there's been a disturbing note of harshness and coldness and violence and anger in your more recent works?

A: I think, without planning to do so, I have followed the developing tension and anger and violence of the world and time that I live in through my own steadily increasing tension as a writer and person.

Q: Then you admit that this "developing tension," as you call it, is a reflection of a condition in yourself?

A: Yes.

Q: A morbid condition?

A: Yes.

Q: Perhaps verging on the psychotic?

A: I guess my work has always been a kind of psychotherapy for me.

Q: But how can you expect audiences to be impressed by plays and other writings that are created as a release for the tensions of a possible or incipient madman?

A: It releases their own.

Q: Their own what?

A: Increasing tensions, verging on the psychotic.

Q: You think the world's going mad?

A: Going? I'd say nearly gone! As the Gypsy said in *Camino Real,* the world is a funny paper read backwards. And that way it isn't so funny.

Q: How far do you think you can go with this tortured view of the world?

A: As far as the world can go in its tortured condition, maybe that far, but no further.

Q: You don't expect audiences and critics to go along with you, do you?

A: No.

Q: Then why do you push and pull them that way?

A: I go that way. I don't push or pull anyone with me.

Q: Yes, but you hope to continue to have people listen to you, don't you?

A: Naturally I hope to.

Q: Even if you throw them off by the violence and horror of your works?

A: Haven't you noticed that people are dropping all around you, like moths out of season, as the result of the present plague of violence and horror in this world and time that we live in?

Q: But you're an entertainer, with artistic pretensions, and people are not entertained any more by cats on hot tin roofs and Baby Dolls and passengers on crazy streetcars!

A: Then let them go to the musicals and the comedies. I'm not going to change my ways. It's hard enough for me to write what I want to write without me trying to write what you say they want me to write which I don't want to write.

Q: Do you have any positive message, in your opinion?

A: Indeed I do think that I do.

Q: Such as what?

A: The crying, almost screaming, need of a great world-wide human effort to know ourselves and each other a great deal better, well enough to concede that no man has a monopoly on right or virtue any more than any man has a corner on duplicity and evil and so forth. If people, and races and nations, would start with that self-manifest truth, then I think that the world could sidestep the sort of corruption which I have involuntarily chosen as the basic, allegorical theme of my plays as a whole.

Q: You sound as if you felt quite detached and superior to this process of corruption in society.

A: I have never written about any kind of vice which I can't observe in myself.

Q: But you accuse society, as a whole, of succumbing to a deliberate mendacity, and you appear to find yourself separate from it as a writer.

A: As a writer, yes, but not as a person.

Q: Do you think this is a peculiar virtue of yours as a writer?

A: I'm not sentimental about writers. But I'm inclined to think that most writers, and most other artists, too, are primarily motivated in their desperate vocation by a desire to find and to separate truth from the complex of lies and evasions they live in, and I think that this impulse is what makes their work not so much a profession as a vocation, a true "calling."

Q: Why don't you write about nice people? Haven't you ever known any nice people in your life?

A: My theory about nice people is so simple that I am embarrassed to say it.

Q: Please say it!

A: Well, I've never met one that I couldn't love if I completely knew him and understood him, and in my work I have at least tried to arrive at knowledge and understanding.

I don't believe in "original sin." I don't believe in "guilt." I don't believe in villains or heroes—only right or wrong ways that individuals have taken, not by choice but by necessity or by certain still-uncomprehended influences in themselves, their circumstances, and their antecedents.

This is so simple I'm ashamed to say it, but I'm sure it's true. In fact, I would bet my life on it! And that's why I don't understand why our propaganda machines are always trying to teach us, to persuade us, to hate and fear other people on the same little world that we live in.

Why don't we meet these people and get to know them as I try to meet and know people in my plays? This sounds terribly vain and egotistical.

I don't want to end on such a note. Then what shall I say? That I know that I am a minor artist who has happened to write one or two major works? I can't even say which they are. It doesn't matter. I have said my say. I may still say it again, or I may shut up now. It doesn't depend on you, it depends entirely on me, and the operation of chance or Providence in my life.—TENNESSEE WILLIAMS, "The World I Live In: Tennessee Williams Interviews Himself" (1957), *Where I Live,* eds. Christine R. Day, Bob Woods, 1978, pp. 88–92

In *The Night of the Iguana,* Tennessee Williams has composed a little nocturnal mood music for muted strings, beautifully performed by some superb instrumentalists, but much too aimless, leisurely, and formless to satisfy the attentive ear. I should add that I prefer these Lydian measures to the unmelodious banalities of *Period of Adjustment* or the strident masochistic dissonances of *Sweet Bird of Youth,* for his new materials are handled with relative sincerity, the dialogue has a wistful, graceful, humorous warmth, the characters are almost recognizable as human beings, and the atmosphere is lush and fruity without being outrageously unreal (no Venus flytraps snapping at your fingers). With this play, Williams has returned once again to the primeval jungle, where—around a ramshackle resort hotel near Acapulco—the steaming tropical underbrush is meant to evoke the terrors of existence. But he has explored this territory too many times before—the play seems tired, unadventurous, and self-derivative. Furthermore, the author's compulsion to express himself on the subjects of fleshly corruption, time and old age, the malevolence of God, and the maiming of the sensitive by life has now become so strong that he no longer bothers to provide a substructure of action to support his vision. *The Night of the Iguana* enjoys no organizing principle whatsoever; and except for some perfunctory gestures toward the end, it is very short on plot, pattern, or theme.

One trouble is that while Williams has fully imagined his personae, he has not sufficiently conceived them in relation to one another, so that the movement of the work is backward toward revelation of character rather than forward toward significant conflict. "The going to pieces of T. Lawrence Shannon," a phrase from the play, might be a more appropriate title, for it focuses mainly on the degradation and breakdown of its central character—a crapulous and slightly psychotic Episcopalian minister, very similar to the alcoholic Consul in Malcolm Lowry's *Under the Volcano*. Thrown out of his church for "fornication and heresy"—after having been seduced by a teenage parishioner, he refused to offer prayers to a "senile delinquent"—Shannon now conducts guided tours in Mexico, sleeping with underage girls, coping with hysterical female Baptists, and finding evidence of God in thunder, in the vivisection of dogs, and in starving children, scrabbling among dungheaps in their search for food. Other characters brush by this broken heretic, but they hardly connect with him, except to uncover his psycho-sexual history and to expose their own: the Patrona of the hotel, a hearty lecherous widow with two Mexican consorts, out of *Sweet Bird of Youth;* Hannah Jelkes, a virgin spinster with a compassionate nature, out of *Summer and Smoke;* and Nonno, her father, a ninety-seven-year-old poet—deaf, cackling, and comatose—out of *Krapp's Last Tape*. The substance of the play is the exchange, by Hannah and Shannon, of mutual confidences about their sexual failures, while the Patrona shoots him hot glances and the poet labors to complete his last poem. When Shannon goes berserk, and is tied down in a hammock and harassed by some German tourists, the iguana is hastily introduced to give this action some larger symbolic relevance: the lizard has been tied under the house, to be fattened, eaten, and to have its eyes poked out by native boys. Persuaded by Hannah to be kinder than God, Shannon eventually frees the iguana, tying its rope around his own neck when he goes off, another Chance Wayne, to become one of the Patrona's lovers. But though Shannon is captured, Nonno is freed. Having completed his poem about "the earth's obscene corrupting love," he has finally found release from such corruptions in death.

The materials, while resolved without sensationalism or sentiment, are all perfectly familiar: the defeated perverse central character, punished for his perversity; the Strindbergian identification of the human body with excrement and defilement; the obsessively sexual determination of every character. But by keeping his usual excesses to a minimum, Williams has provided the occasion for some striking performances. Margaret Leighton, especially, has endowed the stainless Hannah with extraordinary sensibility and tenderness, plumbing depths which Williams himself has been unable to reach since his earliest work. Bette Davis, playing the Patrona in flaming red hair and blue jeans, bats her pendulous lids in her laugh lines and is always on the surface of her part, but she is still a strongly felt personality; Alan Webb's Nonno is humorously senescent; and Patrick O'Neal plays Shannon with suppressed hysteria and a nagging, relentless drive which sometimes remind one of Fredric March. Always on hand to produce rain on the stage, Oliver Smith has forcibly stifled his passion for opulence in the setting, within which this gifted ensemble seems to find its way without directorial eyes (Frank Corsaro's name is still on the program, but I can detect his influence only in a couple of Method Mexican extras).

For all its virtues, though, the play is decidedly a minor opus. A rich atmosphere, a series of languid scenes, and some interesting character sketches are more than Williams has offered us in some time, but they are still not enough to sustain our interest through a full evening. Perhaps Williams, identifying with Nonno, has decided to think of himself as only "a minor league poet with a major league spirit," and there is enough fatigue in the play to suggest that, again like Nonno, he feels like "the oldest living and practicing poet in the world." But even a minor poet fashions his work with more care and coherence than this; even an aged eagle occasionally spreads its wings. I am inclined to persist in my heresy that there is at least one more genuine work of art left in Williams, which will emerge when he has finally been able to objectify his personal problems and to shape them into a suitable myth. Meanwhile, let us put down *The Night of the Iguana* as another of his innumerable exercises in marking time. —ROBERT BRUSTEIN, "A Little Night Music" (1962), *Seasons of Discontent*, 1965, pp. 126–29

JOHN GASSNER

"Tennessee Williams: Dramatist of Frustration"

College English, October 1948, pp. 1–7

In an addendum written in March, 1944, for the published text of *Battle of Angels*, Tennessee Williams affirmed his allegiance to the plastic medium of the theater. "I have never for a moment doubted that there are people—millions!—to say things to," he concluded. "We come to each other, gradually, but with love. It is the short reach of my arms that hinders, not the length and multiplicity of theirs. With love and with honesty, the embrace is inevitable,"[1] When *The Glass Menagerie* reached Broadway one year later, on March 31, 1945, the embrace was consummated. The thirty-one-year-old southern playwright met and won his audience, and the planet's most formidable band of critics awarded him the New York Drama Critics' Circle prize for the best American play of the 1944–45 season. If in the fall of 1945 a second occasion for an embrace, his earlier-written dramatization of a D. H. Lawrence story under the title *You Touched Me,*[2] proved less ardent, it was still an encounter with a well-disposed public that patronized the play for several months. Two years later, moreover, *A Streetcar Named Desire* quickly took its place after the Broadway *première* on December 3, 1947, as the outstanding American drama of several seasons, holding its own even against so strong a rival as *Mister Roberts* and winning a second Drama Critics' Circle award as well as the Pulitzer Prize. By common consent its author is the foremost new playwright to have appeared on the American scene in a decade, and our theater capital is at present eagerly awaiting *Summer and Smoke*, concerning which reports have been glowing ever since Margo Jones produced it in Dallas in the summer of 1947.

I

All was not well when Tennessee Williams predicted an inevitable embrace between himself and the theater, and a less resolute young man might hastily have retreated from the battlefield of the stage. After having written four unsatisfactory and unproduced full-length plays by 1940, he had seemed to be riding on the crest of the wave when *Battle of Angels* was put into production by the Theatre Guild in the fall of that year. A group of his one-acters, aptly entitled *American Blues*, since their scene was the depression period, had won a small cash award from the Group Theatre in 1939. He had received a Rockefeller Foundation fellowship and had been given a scholarship to an advanced playwrights' seminar at the New School for Social Research in February, 1940, by Theresa Helburn and John Gassner. Since both instructors were associates of the Theatre Guild, they submitted their student's play to the Guild when he showed them a draft of *Battle of Angels* at the end of the semester. The play went into rehearsal under excellent auspices, with Margaret Webster as director and Miriam Hopkins as the leading lady. But the results were catastrophic when the play opened in Boston. The play concluded melodramatically with a conflagration, which the stage manager, previously warned that he was weakening the effect by his chary use of the smokepots, decided to make thoroughly realistic. An audience already outraged by examples of repressed sexuality in a southern community was virtually smoked out of the theater, and Miss Hopkins had to brush away waves of smoke from her face in order to respond to the trickle of polite applause that greeted the fall of the curtain. The reviewers were lukewarm at best, and soon Boston's Watch and Ward Society began to make itself heard. The Theatre Guild withdrew the play after the Boston tryout and sent a hasty apology to its subscribers. The author, who had lost an unusual opportunity to make his mark in the theater, became once more, as he put it, that "most common American phenomenon, the rootless wandering writer," who ekes out a living by doing odd jobs. He was ushering in a movie theater for a weekly wage of seventeen dollars when Metro-Goldwyn-Mayer took him out to Culver City along with other young hopefuls. The studio promptly forgot about him after his submission of an outline for a screenplay that contained the germ of *The Glass Menagerie*, wrote him off as just another bad penny in Hollywood's expensive slot-machine, and dismissed him at the end of his six months' term.

If his prospects seemed bleak in the early months of 1944, Tennessee Williams nevertheless had reasons for self-confidence. He had been sufficiently inured to straitened circumstances during his youth, especially while pursuing his studies at the University of Missouri, Washington University, and the University of Iowa. His education had even been interrupted by two years of depressing employment as a clerk for a shoe company. His later apprenticeship to the writing profession had included desultory work as a bellhop in a New Orleans hotel, as a typist for engineers in Jacksonville, Florida, and as a waiter and reciter of verses in a Greenwich Village night club. He also knew the direction he was taking and had, in fact, already covered some of the road, having absorbed considerable experience and poured out a good deal of it in the remarkable one-act plays later collected under the title of *27 Wagons Full of Cotton*.[3] He was developing a precise naturalism, compounded of compassion and sharp observation and filled with some of those unsavory details that Boston had found offensive but that Williams considered a necessary part of the truth to which he had dedicated himself. He was certain that, although he had written poetry[4] and short stories, his métier was the theater because he found himself continually thinking in terms of sound, color, and movement and had grasped the fact that the theater was something more than written language: "The turbulent business of my nerves demanded something more animate than written language could be."[5] He was also moving toward a fusion of the most stringent realism with symbolism and poetic language wherever such writing seemed dramatically appropriate.

Above all, Williams was ready to carve out plays that would be as singular as their author. Although one may surmise that he was much affected by Chekhov and D. H. Lawrence and possibly by Faulkner, he drew too much upon his own observation to be actually imitative. Nor did he fall neatly into the category of social and polemical dramatists who dominated the theater of the 1930's, even if his experience of the depression inclined him toward the political left. His interest was primarily in individuals rather than in social conditions. His background alone would have distinguished him from urban playwrights like Odets, Arthur Miller, and Lillian Hellman, who were attuned to political analysis and regarded personal problems under the aspect of social conditioning. By comparison with his radical contemporaries, this Mississippi-born descendant of Tennessee pioneers (he was born in Columbus on March 26, 1914) was insular and had been conventionally reared and educated. His father, formerly a salesman in the delta region, was the sales manager of a shoe company in St. Louis, and his maternal grandfather was an Episcopalian clergyman. Cities appalled Williams. He disliked St. Louis, where he spent his boyhood, and he never felt acclimated to New York. His inclinations, once he felt free to wander, took him to Florida, Taos, Mexico, or the Latin Quarter of New Orleans, where he still maintains an apartment. The pattern of his behavior established itself early in his life, and it was marked by a tendency to isolate himself, to keep his individuality inviolate, and to resort to flight whenever he felt hard-pressed.

II

The one-act plays which first drew attention to Williams foreshadow his later work both thematically and stylistically. The first to be published, *Moony's Kid Don't Cry*,[6] presents a factory worker who longs to swing an ax in the Canadian woods, a carefree youth who doesn't hesitate to buy his month-old baby a ten-dollar hobbyhorse when he still owes money to the maternity hospital. Moony, whose effort to escape is effectively scotched by his practical wife, is a prototype of the restive young heroes of *Battle of Angels* and *The Glass Menagerie*. The sturdy one-acter *27 Wagons Full of Cotton* gives a foretaste of the rowdy humor that was to prove troublesome in *Battle of Angels* and was to establish a fateful environment for the heroine of *A Streetcar Named Desire*. The pungent naturalism of Erskine Caldwell and William Faulkner is very much in evidence in this extravaganza about a cotton-gin owner who loses his wife to the man whose cotton gin he burned down in order to acquire his business. *The Purification*, a little tragedy of incest and Spanish "honor," reveals Williams' poetic power and theatrical imagination, and *The Long Goodbye* anticipates *The Glass Menagerie* with its retrospective technique.

Most noteworthy, however, are those evidences of compassion for life's waifs which transfigure crude reality in the one-acters. Pity glows with almost unbearable intensity in the red-light district atmosphere of *Hello from Bertha*, in which an ailing harlot loses her mind. Pity assumes a quiet persuasiveness in the vignette, *Lord Byron's Love Letter*, in which two women's pathetic poverty is revealed by their effort to subsist on donations from Mardi Gras tourists to whom they display a letter from Byron; and Williams is particularly affecting in his treatment of battered characters who try to retain shreds of their former respectability in a gusty world. Self-delusion, he realizes, is the last refuge of the hopelessly defeated, and he studies its manifestations in *The Portrait of a Madonna* with such clinical precision that this one-acter would be appalling if it were less beautifully written. Its desiccated heroine, who imagines herself being violated by an invisible former admirer and who plays the southern belle of her girlhood by bandying charming talk with imaginary beaux, is almost as memorable a character as Blanche Du Bois in *A Streetcar Named Desire*. Williams would like to grant these unfortunates the shelter of illusions, and it pains him to know that the world is less tender. Mrs. Hardwick-Moore of *The Lady of Larkspur Lotion* is the butt of her landlady, who jibes at the poor woman's social pretensions and at her invention of a Brazilian rubber plantation, from which her income is incomprehensibly delayed. Only a fellow-boarder, a writer nearly as impoverished as Mrs. Hardwick-Moore, is charitable enough to realize that "there are no lies but the lies that are stuffed in the mouth by the hard-knuckled hand of need" and to indulge her increasingly reckless fabrication as she locates the plantation only a short distance from the Mediterranean but near enough to the Channel for her to distinguish the cliffs of Dover on a clear morning.

It is quite apparent that Williams was nearly fully formed in these short plays as a painter of a segment of the American scene, a dramatist of desire and frustration, and a poet of the human compensatory mechanism. It is a curious fact about American playwriting that, like O'Neill, Paul Green, Odets, and Irwin Shaw, Williams should have unfolded his talent in the one-act form.

III

When the young author wrote *Battle of Angels*, the first of the full-length plays to attract a Broadway management, he was on less securely charted territory. He did not yet know his way through the maze of a plot sustained for an entire evening. He was so poorly guided in the revisions he made for the Theatre Guild that the play as produced was inferior to the script that had been accepted, and he also appears to have been fixed on D. H. Lawrence somewhat too strongly at this stage to be able to master the play's problems. *Battle of Angels* is unsatisfactory even in the revision published in 1945, which differs in several respects from the play that failed in Boston, for it lacks the Wagnerian conflagration climax, stresses the note of social protest in one scene, and employs a prologue and epilogue as makeshift devices. He had plainly tried to throw together too many of the elements he had dramatized separately in his best one-acters. He brought his vagabond hero, Val Xavier, into a decayed town, involved him with a frenzied aristocratic girl, grouped an assorted number of repressed matrons and unsympathetic townsmen around him, and made him fall in love with the frustrated wife of a storekeeper dying of cancer. He not only made the mistake of multiplying dramatic elements instead of fusing them but piled up fortuitous situations, such as the arrival of an avenging fury in the shape of a woman from whom he had escaped and the killing of the wife, Myra, by the jealous storekeeper—a murder for which Val is innocently lynched. Williams, moreover, made the mistake of offering an ill-defined cross between a provincial vagrant and a D. H. Lawrence primitive as an example of purity of spirit. A somewhat ill-digested romanticism would have vitiated the play even if its dramaturgy had been firmer.

Battle of Angels, nevertheless, contained some of his most imaginative dialogue and memorable character-drawing. Myra is a rounded portrait, and Williams has yet to improve upon his secondary character, Vee Talbot. Vee painted the Twelve Apostles as she saw them in visions, only to have them identified as "some men around Two River County," and paints the figure of Christ, only to discover that she has drawn Val Xavier. If Williams had been able to exercise restraint, he could have made his mark in 1940 instead of having to wait five years.

He did achieve simplification with his next work, *You Touched Me*, a comedy in which a Canadian soldier liberates a girl from her musty British environment and the mummifying influence of a spinster. But here he was working with another writer's material, paying an over-due debt to D. H. Lawrence. The lack of personal observation was apparent in this competent dramatization; the play did not bear his own special signature of anguish. Even simplification had to become a highly personal achievement in Williams' case. Only when this transpired in *The Glass Menagerie* was there no longer any doubt that the theater had acquired a new dramatist.

IV

The plays that thrust Tennessee Williams into the limelight have much in common besides their clear focus and economical construction. Both *The Glass Menagerie* and *A Streetcar Named Desire* transmute the base metal of reality into theatrical and, not infrequently, verbal poetry, and both supplement the action with symbolic elements of mood and music. A major theme is southern womanhood helpless in the grip of the presently constituted world, while its old world of social position and financial security is a Paradise Lost. But differences of emphasis and style make the two dramas distinct.

The Glass Menagerie is a memory play evoked in the comments of a narrator, the poet Tom, who is now in the merchant marine, and in crucial episodes from his family life. The form departs from the "fourth wall" convention of realistic dramaturgy and suggests Japanese Noh-drama, in which story consists mostly of remembered fragments of experience. If Williams had had his way with the Broadway production, *The Glass Menagerie* would have struck its public as even more unconventional, since his text calls for the use of a screen on which pictures and legends are to be projected. Disregarded by the producer-director Eddie Dowling, these stage directions nevertheless appear in the published play. They strike the writer of this article as redundant and rather precious; the young playwright was straining for effect without realizing that his simple tale, so hauntingly self-sufficient, needs no adornment.

As plainly stated by Tom, the background is a crisis in society, for the depression decade is teetering on the brink of the second World War. His tale belongs to a time "when the huge middle-class of America was matriculating in a school for the blind," when "their eyes had failed them, or they had failed their eyes, and so they were having their fingers pressed forcibly down on the fiery Braille alphabet of a dissolving economy," while in Spain there was Guernica. But his memory invokes his home life and the provocations that finally sent him to sea. In episodes softened by the patina of time and distance he recalls the painful shyness of his lovable crippled sister, Laura, and the tragicomic efforts of his mother, Amanda, to marry her off, as well as his own desperation as an underpaid shoe-company clerk. The climax comes when, nagged by the desperate mother, Tom brings Laura a "gentleman caller" who turns out to be engaged to another girl.

Without much more story than this, Williams achieved a remarkable synthesis of sympathy and objectivity by making three-dimensional characters out of Tom's family and the gangling beau, who is trying to pull himself out of the rut of a routine position and recover his self-esteem as a schoolboy success. The carping mother could have easily become a caricature, especially when she remembers herself as a southern belle instead of a woman deserted by her husband, a telephone man who "fell in love with long distances" but who probably found an incitement in his wife's pretensions. She is redeemed for humanity by her solicitude for her children, her laughable but touching effort to sell a magazine subscription over the telephone at dawn, and her admission that the unworldly Laura must get a husband if she is to escape the fate of the "little birdlike women without any nest" Amanda has known in the South. And Laura, too shy even to take a course in typewriting after the first lesson, acquits herself with sweet dignity and becoming stoicism when let down by her first and only gentleman caller; she is an unforgettable bit of Marie Laurencin painting. At the same time, however, Williams knows that pity for the halt and blind must not exclude a sense of reality, that Tom's going out into the world was a necessary and wholesome measure of self-preservation; it is one of humanity's inalienable traits and obligations to try to save itself as best it can. Although Tom will never forget Laura and the candles she blew out, he is now part of the larger world that must find a common salvation in action, "for nowadays the world is lit by lightning."

In *A Streetcar Named Desire*, too, health and disease are at odds with each other, but here the dialectical situation flares up into relentless conflict. The lines are sharply drawn in this more naturalistic drama, whose story, unlike that of *The Glass Menagerie*, is no longer revealed impressionistically through the merciful mist of memory. Nothing is circuitous in *A Streetcar*, and the dramatic action drives directly to its fateful conclusion as plebeian and patrician confront each other. Like other southern heroines of Williams, who invariably suggest Picasso's dehydrated "Demoiselles d'Avignon," Blanche Du Bois is not only a recognizable human being but an abstraction—the abstraction of decadent aristocracy as the painter's inner eye sees it. It is her final tragedy that the life she encounters in a married sister's home cannot spare her precisely when she requires the most commiseration. Her plantation lost, the teaching profession closed to her, her reputation gone, her nerves stretched to the snapping-point, Blanche has come to Stella in the French Quarter to find her married to a lusty ex-sergeant of Polish extraction. She is delivered into his untender hands when he discovers her lurid past and, although he may be momentarily touched by her fate on learning of the unhappy marriage that drove her to moral turpitude, his standards do not call for charity. With her superior airs and queasiness she has interfered with Stanley's married happiness, and she must go. Loyal to his friend, who served in the same military outfit with him, he must forewarn Mitch, who is about to propose to her, that the southern lady has been a harlot, thus destroying her last hope. Having sensed a challenge to his robust manhood from the moment he met Blanche, he must even violate her. It is his terrible health, which is of earth and will defend itself at any cost, that destroys Blanche, and sister Stella herself must send the hapless woman to a state institution if she is to protect her marriage and preserve her faith in Stanley.

As in *The Glass Menagerie* and in the one-acters, the private drama is pyramided on a social base. Blanche is the last descendant to cling to the family plantation of Belle Reve, sold acre by acre by improvident male relatives "for their epic fornications, to put it plainly," as she says. Her simple-hearted sister declassed herself easily by an earthy marriage to Stanley Kowalski and saved herself. Blanche tried to stand firm on quicksand and was declassed right into a house of ill-fame. The substructure of the story has some resemblance to *The Cherry Orchard*, whose aristocrats were also unable to adjust to reality and were crushed by it. Nevertheless, Williams subordinated his oblation to reality, his realization that Stanley and the denizens of the New Orleans slum street called Elysian Fields represent health and survival, to a poet's pity for Blanche. For him she is not only an individual whose case must be treated individually but a symbol of the many shorn lambs for whom no wind is ever tempered except by the godhead in men's hearts and the understanding of artists like Williams himself. It is surely for this reason that the author called his play a "tragedy of incomprehension" and "entered," in the words of his quotation from Hart Crane, "the broken world to trace the visionary company of love, its voice an instant in the wind (I know not whither hurled)." It is in the light of this compassion that the pulse of the play becomes a succession of musical notes and the naturalism of the writing flares into memorable lines, as when Blanche, finding herself loved by Mitch, sobs out, "Sometimes there's God so quickly."

As his plays multiply, it will be possible to measure him against dramatists whom his writing so often recalls—against Chekhov, Gorki, O'Neill, and Lorca. That such comparisons can be even remotely envisioned for an American playwright under thirty-five is in itself an indication of the magic of his pen; and it will soon be seen whether this magic works in *Summer and Smoke*, another, but more complicated, southern drama which carries a woman's soul to Tartarus. The test may prove a severe one, since the new play is episodic enough to be considered a chronicle. Further testing will also gauge the range of his faculties. Williams has himself detected a limitation in the sameness of theme and background in his work. He is turning toward new horizons with two uncompleted plays; one of them is set in Mexico, the other in Renaissance Italy. In time we shall also discover whether he overcomes noticeable inclinations toward a preciosity that could have vitiated *The Glass Menagerie* and toward a melodramatic sensationalism which appears in the rape scene of *A Streetcar Named Desire* and in the addition of wedlock with a homosexual to Blanche's tribulations. All that is beyond question at the present time is that Tennessee Williams is already a considerable artist in a medium in which there are many craftsmen but few artists.

Notes

1. *Pharos*, Spring 1945, p. 121.
2. In making this dramatization Tennessee Williams had collaborated with a friend, Donald Windham.
3. New Directions, 1945.
4. *Five Young American Poets* (New Directions, 1939). A collection of Williams' short stories, *One Arm and Other Stories*, is scheduled for publication in 1948.
5. *Pharos*, Spring 1945, p. 110.
6. *The Best One-Act Plays of 1940*, ed. Margaret Mayorga (Dodd, Mead & Co., 1941).

WALTER KERR
From "Playwrights"
Pieces at Eight
1957, pp. 125–34

The failures of Tennessee Williams are worth talking about. Mr. Williams, it seems to me, is the finest playwright now working in the American theater; every failure he has represents a real loss not only to himself but to all the rest of us. When so substantial and exhilarating a talent appears, the hope must be for the largest possible body of durable work.

Almost alone among his contemporaries, and without

wholly shaking off the realistic tradition that is ours, Williams sees and writes as an artist and a poet. He makes plays out of images, catching a turn of life while it is still fluid, still immediate, before it has been sterilized by reflection. Arthur Miller may sometimes build a better play, but he builds it out of bricks; Williams is all flesh and blood. He writes with his eyes and his ears where other men are content to pick their brains—poetry with them is an overlay of thought, not a direct experience—and his best plays emerge in the theater full-bodied, undissected, so kinetic you can touch them.

The curious thing about Williams' lapses is that they seem to represent a conscious straining away from the virtues that are most naturally his, a rebellion against self that takes the form of wanting to shatter—or escape from—the mirror he has taken such pains to perfect. Life is his for the patient echoing; he occasionally seems to want, wantonly, to silence the echo.

The least of his vices, but one that has been with him from the beginning, is his inability—or refusal—to conclude anything, to find endings for his narratives that will embrace, take account of, and face up to the materials out of which he has begun them. *The Glass Menagerie* simply stops; the play has been so accurate and so touching that we do not really mind. *A Streetcar Named Desire* escapes into the heroine's insanity; the play remains thrilling, but this is to wash out the struggle rather than resolve it. *The Rose Tattoo*—here the matter becomes serious—winds up by junking a character complexity that has fascinated us all evening in favor of a simple sexual gesture, a gesture that is totally inadequate to the needs of the play.

The Rose Tattoo has two exhilarating acts. The first is concerned with the emotional paralysis that overtakes a volatile Sicilian woman living in the Gulf country near Mobile when the husband in whom she takes fierce pride is killed. The second is concerned with her reluctant reawakening at the hands of a man who, compared to her own idea of her first husband, is little more than a clown. While these events are taking place the theater swims in vitality and rich good humor.

In the third act, as Williams casts about for a resolution, both the action and the characterization begin to fray. The heroine has been presented to us as a quicksilver compound of physical passion, intense idealism, and hysterical religiosity. That a single sexual act should reduce these qualities to a happy harmony is implausible; it tends to suggest that there was no real conflict in the first place. At this point we begin to feel that we know the woman better than Williams does—sexual gratification would hold her down for about an hour—and the bland surrender with which Williams waves away her personal torment destroys, rather than absorbs, the complexity that has made her interesting.

It further brings into focus a certain sentimentality about sex that runs through Williams' earlier work, a kind of humorless dedication which leads his characters into locutions like "getting them colored lights going" and earnest apostrophes to "the glory" of it. Where Williams is earthily realistic about everything else, he is somewhat romantic about sex, and his wide-eyed wonder at it all goads him into occasional disproportions bordering on parody—as in a third-act scene during which an avid ingénue tries to break down an agonized but rigidly responsible young sailor. There is some assumption behind these plays that the psychological aberrations of the universe can be quickly settled on one big bed; it is one of the few failures of honest observation in Williams' work.

Both *The Glass Menagerie* and *A Streetcar Named Desire* are vigorous enough in other ways—in many other ways—to make us accept their escape-hatch endings. But the collapse of character in *The Rose Tattoo*, the hasty flight toward an unrealistic panacea, is a more disturbing matter: what was formerly a small structural blight now eats dangerously into the heart of the play, diminishing its human validity. Because the play as a whole fails in this final swift substitution of sentimentality for complexity, we are forced to write off some glorious portraiture.

A similar flight from the concrete to the symbolic, from the hardrock particular to the hazily general, also began to be troublesome in *The Rose Tattoo*. There had been, it is true, an incidental toying with symbols in *The Glass Menagerie*. Crippled Laura's menagerie of figurines is in itself a symbol; but a shelf of small crystal animals is also possible, probable in the circumstances, and concrete. Less concrete in its use was the photograph of a father who had earlier run out on this unhappy household. In the stage directions for the play Mr. Williams had asked that the absent father's portrait be lighted up arbitrarily—that is to say, without realistic motivation—at certain key points in the dramatic action. In production, this slight gesture toward the abstract was somewhat played down. Its presence, however, suggested a dramatist who rather liked to intrude on the life he had so painstakingly caught, a dramatist whose hand—poking into the world he had created and pointing a finger at certain of its objects—might one day prove as meddlesome as his eye was meticulous.

In *The Rose Tattoo* the hand became much more obtrusive: it went in for tattooing. To serve as a crucial moment in the play's emotional development we were given the sudden, symbolic appearance on the hero's chest of a meaningful "rose." At this vital point the characters were inexplicably robbed of the power to act for themselves; they stood passive and inert while the playwright scrawled significant designs upon them. What is wrong here is that a growing relationship is not permitted to fulfill itself out of the characters' temperaments, though those temperaments are—as we have seen—wonderfully capable. At the very moment of crisis, of the final "coming together" of two thoroughly alive people, something cuts across life and, in effect, denies it. That something is the playwright, impatient now with life, appearing in person.

With his next theater piece, *Camino Real*, the playwright was alone on the stage, playing with puppets. Here life was rejected on two counts: in the content of the play, which seemed to hold that the world is a desert of vice deserving only of abandonment; and in the method of the play, which discarded the three-dimensional universe altogether and replaced it with symbolic placards that could be juggled into various kaleidoscopic patterns at will.

In reading over *Camino Real*, it is possible to discover what Mr. Williams is after, in method at least. He has—quite often—been called a poet; in the sense that a poet works primarily with images rather than with syllogistically reasoned ideas, he has quite often been one.

He has also, along the way, noticed that a good poetic image has very little of logic in it. Words that have no literal relationship to one another are thrown into unlikely juxtaposition, rubbed back to back in odd and apparently irrational fashion. When T. S. Eliot writes that "the evening is spread out against the sky like a patient etherized upon a table," there is no common-sense connection between a sky and a man who is about to be operated upon. When Stephen Crane writes that a mother's "heart hung humble as a button on the bright splendid shroud of her son," there is no realistic relationship between the idea of a heart and the idea of a button. A heart doesn't look like a button, act like a button, or ever—in the ordinary course of affairs—seem like a button. Yet, out of this highly implausible combination a third thing magically emerges: a clear feeling about a mother's emotion.

Mr. Williams, it seems to me, is here plainly after this third thing: the fleeting, stunning intake of breath that sometimes comes from such nonliteral, nonrealistic mismatches. To get it he has constructed a play of calculated *non sequiturs*.

In a courtyard that looks vaguely Mexican but is never identified, a man who is never identified stumbles down a flight of stone steps. An ominous policeman, uniformed but otherwise unidentified, steps out of the shadows and shoots him. The man is suspended for a moment—long enough to talk about a pony he once owned—before he falls. Falling, he is collected by two trash men who cart him off in a two-wheeled container.

Kilroy enters, looking for a "normal American." The first "normal American" he greets turns out to be a French homosexual. The second turns out to be Casanova. Casanova, now a mangy "old hawk," is having a twilight affair with the consumptive Camille. But Camille deceives him with a younger man and, as streams of confetti rain down from the heavens, Casanova is crowned "king of the cuckolds."

Figures in death masks lurk on the stairways. A surly, gravel-voiced man growls popular song titles from a balcony window. Camille attempts to board an outgoing plane, the "Fugitivo," but has lost her passport. Kilroy, an ex-fighter with a heart as big as the head of a baby, barters his Golden Gloves for a chance to lift the veil from the face of a gypsy's daughter. Kilroy's heart is removed by white-jacketed surgeons and turned in at the nearest pawnshop. Byron limps forward to anguish over the ashes of Shelley. Don Quixote comes in for a drink of water. A narrator wanders about asking "Where are we, what does it all mean, what is real?"

These are some of the strangers—the realistically unrelated figures—who brush shoulders in the play in the hope of setting off sparks, of evoking unexpected but nevertheless revealing relationships. Once in a while—as when Kilroy comforts Casanova with a Tin Pan Alley tune, or when the same Kilroy swings his fists wildly against nothing at all—there is a faint whisper of interior vitality, of ironic meaningfulness.

But ninety-nine per cent of the time that sought-after third thing—that fresh, clear picture, that stabbingly felt emotion—never emerges. The odd contrasts are made; but they seem merely odd. The consciously unlike elements refuse to mate; no new reality is born of their union.

Why? I think there are, roughly, three reasons for so thundering a mishap. One is that the business of constructing an intelligible narrative for the stage is not at all like the business of constructing a single image to be placed in a lyric poem. The theater does use poetry; but it climbs to poetry through the development of a coherent narrative and three-dimensional characters; language comes last and reveals these earlier concrete values. The effort to put the methods of language into the topmost position and to treat story and characters as fragmentary tools which can be bandied about in the interests of such methodology—the effort to treat root and branch as though they were the result, rather than the cause, of the flower—is probably a theatrical dead end.

Another reason, no doubt, lies in the author's own imaginative equipment. In the sense in which the term is understood nowadays, Mr. Williams may be called a dramatic poet. But that is, again, not the same thing as being a lyric poet. So long as Williams is working outward from a lifelike stage situation, he hits upon wonderful streaks of earthy imagery; there are dozens of lines in *The Glass Menagerie* and *Summer and Smoke* and *A Streetcar Named Desire* that have the stamp of poetry upon them.

But when, as in *Camino Real*, he turns to the poetic for its own sake, he produces a sort of song-writer's jargon ("There's a cold wind blowing out of the mountains and over the desert and into my heart") and the mildly embarrassed humor of a sophomore who knows he is too ambitious for his own good ("I don't see nothin' but nothin'—and then some more nothin'," a construction which is echoed more seriously in the "nobody ever gets to know nobody" of the later *Orpheus Descending*).

Lastly, and most importantly, Mr. Williams has reversed the poet's intention. The poet is primarily in search of reality; if he permits himself a certain license along the way, an intuitive reaching out for normally unlikely combinations, it is in order to speed up and intensify the search. Momentary unreason ends in a more vivid actuality. Mr. Williams has made the unreason an end in itself, has exalted method above substance, has permitted method—rather than the face of life itself—to determine the shape and degree of everything else in the work. In *Camino Real* there is a strong hint not simply of disgust with reality but of disbelief in it; the mathematics of image-making become more important than the matter out of which images are made. We are on the threshold of a world that distrusts the world and places its faith in some place or thing beyond the mountains: in craft detached from the coarseness of life, in man detached from men.

The drift toward Olympian detachment is given sharp crystallization two plays later, in the thorough and considered revision of the earlier *Battle of Angels* now called *Orpheus Descending*. Here a virtuous young guitar player who has descended into the hell of a small Southern town looks about him in horror. He sees corruption everywhere: in the storekeeper who is a prisoner of her bigot husband; in a once idealistic child who has bitterly sold her soul to the jukeboxes; in the frustrated and hysterical wives of the men of the community; and in the men themselves, swift to dispense "justice" with switchblade knives.

He extends a gentle, gingerly hand to several of the local Eurydices, feeling as he does so that he is touching "corruption," that he is apt to be drawn into the inferno himself. And he is drawn into it. His reluctant surrender to the forlorn and passionate storekeeper involves him hopelessly in the crude and possessive maneuverings of "animals sniffin' around each other" (sex is losing its position as panacea, becoming part of the tainted world). His gesture of kindness to an elderly religious fanatic brings down on him the wrath of a lynch-minded mob. In the end, like the Orpheus of legend, he is torn to pieces by a pack of dogs (Men).

Mr. Williams' theatrical sense is such that his juxtaposition of innocence and depravity sometimes takes on the sharp terror of a blood-drained face staring helplessly up at an uncontrollable fire, a fire that is burning down everything in sight. When the storekeeper stands in ashen disbelief while her husband taunts her with the information that he has helped kill her father, the sting of gratuitous cruelty is keen as a whiplash. When the boy twists his face into simultaneous desire and loathing for the sexual snare that is being drawn about him, the sense of disastrous involvement is painfully clear. When, at last, a trigger-happy sadist puts a bullet through the pregnant heroine's back, the shock is powerful indeed.

Yet behind this succession of shattering crises there lurks an echo of emptiness that will not be quieted. Whatever seems fiercely true in the heat of the immediate moment reverberates hollowly in the larger pattern of the play as a whole, as though an exciting sound had been produced that had no real source in nature. An increasing insistence on pattern—on an arbitrary arrangement of the shape of the world—is evident. A philosophical commitment, begun in *Camino Real,* seems to be hardening.

The hero of *Camino Real* was a wide-eyed innocent with a "heart as big as the head of a baby"; this innocent was subjected to every temptation and torment a nightmare universe could devise; he ended by leaving the universe, in the company of Don Quixote.

The hero of the play that followed, *Cat on a Hot Tin Roof,* was a married innocent, symbolically crippled; he was subjected to the demands of a wife that he enter a venal bed and the demands of a family that he join it in a life of "mendacity"; if his struggle—on Broadway—ended in compromise, it was not because Williams had written the play that way.

The hero of *Orpheus Descending* is a maker of music who has been in the world, been corrupted by it, and risen above his corruption by refusing all entanglements; the moment he has any fresh traffic with flesh and blood he is freshly tainted, ripe for outright destruction.

The special crystallization of Mr. Williams' attitude toward these obviously parallel figures comes when, midway in the third play, our music-maker pauses to define himself.

There is, he tells us, a species of bird that has no legs, no means of touching the earth; it spends all of its time in the air, sleeping—when it sleeps—on the wind; it has a protective coloration that makes it resemble the pure blue sky and keeps it safe from hawks; it can never be corrupted because it never lights anywhere until it is dead. "God has made one perfect creature," this Orpheus concludes. While it is always dangerous to read an author's symbols too literally, it is difficult to escape the inference now: that this young man, like those other young men in *Cat on a Hot Tin Roof* and *Camino Real,* is potentially just such a perfect creature, kept from his destiny by the ineradicable vice of all who walk the earth.

The steady movement of Mr. Williams' later vision seems to me, then, to be toward the unqualified rejection of that perverse complexity—that mercurial combination of good and evil—that we call human. Whatever is explicitly human, whatever actually puts foot to the earth, is unequivocally bad: greedy, treacherous, gross and unsalvageable. The only escape is total escape: the shedding of legs, of the delusion of love, of all companionship except that of Don Quixote. The world is divided into the wholly pure and the wholly impure (or, as *Orpheus Descending* has it, into "the buyers and those who are bought") and is then declared unfit for the wholly pure.

On the one hand we are confronted by angels, virgins, birds; on the other by beasts alone. The middle ground—the ground we walk and stub our toes on—disappears.

For a time there were no endings; for a time there was sex; now there is strategic withdrawal, the substitution of imaginary blacks and whites for plausible grays, of fantasy for flesh.

The brilliance of Williams' best work lies precisely in its admission of complexity—in Blanche du Bois tying a noose around her own white throat, in Alma Winemuller defeating her purposes with every pitiful word she utters—and in the humble acceptance of complexity as the root condition of all our lives. The danger in the growing angel-devil commitment is that we may continue to admire Mr. Williams' passion but fail to recognize his people.

ARTHUR MILLER

From "The Shadow of the Gods" (1958)
The Theater Essays of Arthur Miller
ed. Robert A. Martin
1978, pp. 189–94

Williams has a long reach and a genuinely dramatic imagination. To me, however, his greatest value, his aesthetic valor, so to speak, lies in his very evident determination to unveil and engage the widest range of causation conceivable to him. He is constantly pressing his own limit. He creates shows, as all of us must, but he possesses the restless inconsolability with his solutions which is inevitable in a genuine writer. In my opinion, he is properly discontented with the total image some of his plays have created. And it is better that way, for when the image is complete and self-contained it is usually arbitrary and false.

It is no profound thing to say that a genuine work of art creates not completion, but a sustained image of things in tentative balance. What I say now is not to describe that balance as a false or illusory one, but one whose weighing containers, so to speak, are larger and greater than what has been put into them. I think, in fact, that in *Cat on a Hot Tin Roof,* Williams in one vital respect made an assault upon his own viewpoint in an attempt to break it up and reform it on a wider circumference.

Essentially it is a play seen from the viewpoint of Brick, the son. He is a lonely young man sensitized to injustice. Around him is a world whose human figures partake in various ways of grossness, Philistinism, greed, money-lust, power-lust. And—with his mean-spirited brother as an example—it is a world senselessly reproducing itself through ugly children conceived without the grace of genuine affection, and delivered not so much as children but as inheritors of great wealth and power, the new perpetuators of inequity.

In contrast, Brick conceives of his friendship with his dead friend as an idealistic, even gallant and valorous and somehow morally elevated one, a relationship in which nothing was demanded, but what was given was given unasked, beyond the realm of price, of value, even of materiality. He clings to this image as to a banner of purity to flaunt against the world, and more precisely, against the decree of nature to reproduce himself, to become in turn the father, the master of the earth, the administrator of the tainted and impure world. It is a world in whose relations—especially between the sexes—there is always the element of the transaction, of materiality.

If the play confined itself to the psychiatry of impotence, it could be admired or dismissed as such. Williams' plays are never really that, but here in addition, unlike his other plays, there is a father. Not only is he the head of a family, but the very image of power, of materiality, of authority. And the problem this father is given is how he can infuse his own personality into the prostrated spirit of his son so that a hand as strong as his own will guide his fortune when he is gone—more particularly, so that his own immortality, his civilization will be carried on.

As the play was produced, without the surface realism of living-room, bedroom, walls, conventional light—in an atmosphere, instead, of poetic conflict, in a world that is eternal and not merely this world—it provided more evidence that Williams' preoccupation extends beyond the surface realities of the relationships, and beyond the psychiatric connotations of homosexuality and impotence. In every conceivable fashion there was established a goal beyond sheer behavior. We were made to see, I believe, an ulterior pantheon of forces and a play of symbols as well as of characters.

It is well known that there was difficulty in ending this play, and I am certainly of no mind to try it. I believe I am not alone in saying that the resolutions wherein Brick finally regains potency was not understandable on the stage. But my feeling is that even if this were more comprehensively motivated so that the psychiatric development of the hero were persuasively completed, it in itself could not embrace the other questions raised in the play.

We are persuaded as we watch this play that the world around Brick is in fact an unworthy collection of unworthy motives and greedy actions. Brick refuses to participate in this world, but he cannot destroy it either or reform it and he turns against himself. The question here, it seems to me, the ultimate question is the right of society to renew itself when it is, in fact, unworthy. There is, after all, a highly articulated struggle for material power going on here. There is literally and symbolically a world to win or a world to forsake and damn. A viewpoint is necessary, if one is to raise such a tremendous issue, a viewpoint capable of encompassing it. This is not a study in cynicism where the writer merely exposes the paradoxes of all sides and is content to end with a joke. Nor, again, is it mere psychiatry, aiming to show us how a young man reclaims his sexuality. There is a moral judgment hanging over this play which never quite comes down. A tempting analogy would be that of a Hamlet who takes up his sword and neither fights nor refuses to fight but marries an Ophelia who does not die.

Brick, despite his resignation from the race, has thrown a challenge to it which informs the whole play, a challenge which the father and the play both recognize and ignore. But if it is the central challenge of the play—as the play seems to me to emphasize—then the world must either prove its worthiness to survive, or its unworthiness must lie dramatically proved, to justify Brick's refusal to renew it—or, like a Hamlet who will neither do battle nor put down his sword, it must condemn Brick to inaction and perhaps indifference to its fate.

Because of Williams' marvelous ability, I for one would be willing to listen—and perhaps to him alone—even as he pronounced ultimate doom upon the race—a race exemplified in his play by the meanest of motives. This is a foundation grand enough, deep enough, and worthy of being examined remorselessly and perhaps even shaken and smashed. Again, as with *The Diary of Anne Frank*, had the implicit challenge ripened, we should no longer be held by our curiosity or our pity for someone else, but by that terror which comes when we must in truth justify our most basic assumptions. The father in this play, I think, must be forced to the wall in justification of his world, and Brick must be forced to his wall in justification of his condemning that world to the ultimate biological degree. The question of society's right to insist upon its renewal when it is unworthy is a question of tragic grandeur, and those who have asked this question of the world know full well the lash of its retaliation.

Quite simply, what I am asking is that the play pursue the ultimate development of the very question it asks. But for such a pursuit, the viewpoint of the adolescent is not enough. The father, with the best will in the world, *is* faced with the problem of a son he loves best refusing to accept him and his spirit. Worse yet, it is to the least worthy son that that spirit must be handed if all else fails. Above the father's and the son's individual viewpoints the third must emerge, the viewpoint, in fact, of the audience, the society, and the race. It is a viewpoint that must weigh, as I have said, the question of its own right to biological survival—and one thing more, the question of the fate of the sensitive and the just in an impure world of power. After all, ultimately someone must take charge; this is the tragic dilemma, but it is beyond the viewpoint of adolescence. Someone must administer inequity or himself destroy that world by refusing to renew it, or by doing battle against its injustice, or by declaring his indifference or his cynicism. The terms upon which Brick's potency returns are left waiting to be defined and the play is thus torn from its climax.

Again, I am not criticizing this play, but attempting to mark the outlines of its viewpoint—which is an extension of our theater's viewpoint to its present limits. Nor is this an entirely new and unheralded idea. Be it Tolstoy, Dostoevsky, Hemingway, you, or I, we are formed in this world when we are sons and daughters and the first truths we know throw us into conflict with our fathers and mothers. The struggle for mastery—for the freedom of manhood or womanhood as opposed to the servility of childhood—is the struggle not only to overthrow authority but to reconstitute it anew. The viewpoint of the adolescent is precious because it is revolutionary and insists upon justice. But in truth the parent, powerful as he appears, is not the source of injustice but its deputy.

A drama which refuses or is unable to reach beyond this façade is denying itself its inherited chance for greatness. The best of our theater is standing tiptoe, striving to see over the shoulders of father and mother. The worst is exploiting and wallowing in the self-pity of adolescence and obsessive keyhole sexuality. The way out, as the poet has said, is always *through*. We will not find it by huddling closer to the center of the charmed circle, by developing more and more naturalism in our dialogue and our acting, that "slice-of-life" reportage which is to life what an overheard rumor is to truth; nor by setting up an artificial poetic style, nor by once again shocking the householders with yet other unveilings of domestic relations and their hypocrisies. Nor will we break out by writing problem plays. There is an organic aesthetic, a tracking of impulse and causation from the individual to the world and back again which must be reconstituted. We are exhausting the realm of affects, which is the world of adolescence taken pure.

The shadow of a cornstalk on the ground is lovely, but it is no denial of its loveliness to see as one looks on it that it is telling the time of the day, the position of the earth and the sun, the size of our planet and its shape, and perhaps even the length of its life and ours among the stars. A viewpoint bounded by affects cannot engage the wider balance of our fates where the great climaxes are found.

In my opinion, if our stage does not come to pierce through affects to an evaluation of the world it will contract to a lesser psychiatry and an inexpert one at that. We shall be confined to writing an *Oedipus* without the pestilence, an *Oedipus* whose catastrophe is private and unrelated to the survival of his people, an *Oedipus* who cannot tear out his eyes because there will be no standard by which he can judge himself; an *Oedipus*, in a word, who on learning of his incestuous marriage, instead of tearing out his eyes, will merely wipe away his tears thus to declare his loneliness. Again, where a drama will not engage its relevancy for the race, it will halt at pathos, that tempting shield against ultimate dramatic effect, that counterfeit of meaning.

Symbolically, as though sensing that we are confined, we have removed the doors and walls and ceilings from our sets. But the knowing eye still sees them there. They may truly disappear and the stage will open to that symbolic stature, that realm where the father is after all not the final authority, that area where he is the son too, that area where religions are made and the giants live, only when we see beyond parents, who are, after all, but the shadows of the gods.

A great drama is a great jurisprudence. Balance is all. It will evade us until we can once again see man as whole, until sensitivity and power, justice and necessity are utterly face to face, until authority's justifications and rebellion's too are tracked even to those heights where the breath fails, where—because the largest point of view as well as the smaller has spoken—truly the rest is silence.

SIGNI FALK

"The Profitable World of Tennessee Williams"

Modern Drama, December 1958, pp. 172–80

Tennessee Williams has been called "an artist to the fingertips," "a master of sensitive characterization," a writer with "hypnotic qualities," of "exquisite tastes," and "the foremost new playwright to have appeared on the American scene in a decade." And yet, the fact that many critics, after having ridiculed a particular play unmercifully, have given the highest praise to the acting and the production, raises the question whether the quality of the playwright's work has not been obscured by brilliant productions. A partial list of performers is impressive: the late Laurette Taylor as Amanda in *The Glass Menagerie* and in the film version, the late Gertrude Lawrence; Kim Hunter, Marlon Brando, and Jessica Tandy in *A Streetcar Named Desire*; Margaret Phillips and Tod Andrews in *Summer and Smoke*; Maureen Stapleton in *The Rose Tattoo*; Barbara Bel Geddes and Burl Ives in *Cat on a Hot Tin Roof*. And above all, a dramatist, most of whose work has been interpreted by so distinguished a director as Elia Kazan, must indeed call himself fortunate.

Tennessee Williams is frequently credited with returning poetry to the theater. He has been compared with Eugene O'Neill whose work is significant for poetic overtones. Both dramatists are concerned with sensitive spirits trying to find their niche in a mammon-worshipping society. Both are interested in describing decadent aristocratic families as well as tramps from the fringe areas; in portraying the corroding effect of empire-building; in deploring the homelessness in America of sensitive, creative souls; and in praising uninhibited expressions of physical love as superior to a socially imposed restraint upon passions. But the differences outnumber the similarities. O'Neill leaves the impression of a writer who has hacked away at the pseudo-religious crustations that dwarf men's lives and has attempted to find a more honest relationship between man and his God. O'Neill described the soul-destroying quality of New England puritanism, which does not make people happy though it makes them successful business men and pillars of society. It is the hypocritical pretense to goodness that O'Neill hates and against which his poet-heroes struggle. In so doing he may have resorted to all the stage tricks, played every chord for emotional effect, exaggerated his symbols to the point of the grotesque to make his point, but he was always a man of ideas. He was, in the parlance of recent criticism, a dramatist as thinker.

One of the most frequently repeated jibes thrust at Williams is that he feels but does not think, or "only thinks that he feels." He has uttered a number of elaborate pronouncements about the significance of his own plays which have little to do with the plays themselves. In the preface to *The Rose Tattoo*, a lusty "comedy" about two sex-starved females portrayed against a chorus of "man-crazy women" keeping up a cacophony of urgency throughout the play, he says that he is interested in ideas about the "arrest of time," and "that special condition of a *world without time*," and the nobility of Greek tragedies. Since *The Rose Tattoo* is an amusing paean to sexual indulgence, his sententiousness makes him sound like a high school orator on a binge: "The great and only possible dignity of man lies in his power deliberately to choose certain moral values by which to live as steadfastly as if he, too, like a character in a play, were immured against the corrupting rush of time." He prefaces another play, *Camino Real*, with the lines from a Shaw character: "I believe in Michelangelo, Velasquez, and Rembrandt; in the might of design, the mystery of color," a rather conceited statement from the author of that confused "phantasmagoria of decadence." In the preface to *Cat on a Hot Tin Roof*, he says, "I thought of myself as having a highly personal, even intimate relationship with people who go to see plays. . . . I still don't want to talk only about the surface aspect of their lives, the sort of things that acquaintances laugh and chatter about on ordinary social occasions." The correlation between this noble statement and the conversation in the play is remote, to say the least. One dramatic critic wonders if even in the world of Tennessee Williams people really *do* ask one another, as they do in this play, "How good is he in bed?"

In actual playwriting Williams tends to give to a character a kind of punch line of philosophical comment which might, perhaps, be considered a thesis statement of the play. It usually sounds, however, like the concluding argument to a very different subject. Its relationship to the characters and the action is usually peripheral. For instance, the bedroom farce of Serafina and Alfaro of *The Rose Tattoo* is to be dignified, it seems, by the line, "Love and affection! in a world that is lonely and cold." And again, after more noisy pursuits than a class-B movie would allow, *Camino Real* closes with the line, "The violets in the mountains have broken the rocks." And still again, to the cynical and alcoholic Brick, who drinks his way through *Cat on a Hot Tin Roof*, his frustrated wife, Margaret, speaks the final lines: "Oh, you weak, beautiful people who give up with such grace. What you need is someone to take hold of you—gently, with love and hand back your life to you, like something gold you let go of."

After seeing the plays, one is left with the feeling that Williams is basically a sentimentalist who fluctuates like a thermometer in uncertain weather between bathos and poetic rhetoric, between the precious and the bawdy, and between adolescent admirations and histrionic displays of violence. He sobs over failures, the aimless, weak, frustrated seekers; envies vicariously his own characters, male and female, radiantly happy in their physical love; idolizes those men who inherited the virility of a prize bull; and lacerates those human beings, mostly women, driven by an unsatisfied sexual hunger. Perhaps he *is* a dramatist who feels rather than thinks, because he seems to be more interested in emotional crises involving a few character types than in developing an idea, or character, or action, as is habitual with the Greeks he professes to admire. Like so many modern writers who are afraid that they will be uttering the obvious, he indulges in the kind of obvious symbolism that has been called "ladies' club mystifications," in fancy names and fancy settings, in mood music, in tableaus— affected Madonna poses and settings in della Robbia blues. There is so much posturing in the plays, so much of the same thing over and over again, one has the feeling that Williams writes like a man who has spent hours before the mirror, playing a limited number of roles in a variety of exotic costumes.

This Pulitzer prize-winning dramatist has confessed, "The more I go on, the more difficult it becomes not to repeat myself," perhaps one of the truest statements he has made to date about his work. If one considers the types that keep reappearing in his plays, and what they represent, he will find that the world of Tennessee Williams is a very limited one, where people are characters created by a writer who is sometimes perceptive and honest, sometimes sentimental and cruel, and sometimes merely vulgar. The fact that this dramatist has been able to provide for gifted actors and actresses a kind of shorthand script for characterization that has enabled them to add to their own prestige suggests that the *commedia dell' arte* technique has not been relegated to the history books. It is also obvious that Williams has been able to endow his few stock types with such an effective emotional coloring that he not only obscures their basic similarities but also what they really have to say for themselves.

The rebel-dreamer-failure type is a favorite with the dramatist. The Tom Wingfields almost seem like autobiographical figures who might have existed before their creator found the golden key to the box office. Tom, the unwilling breadwinner in *The Glass Menagerie,* trapped by his mediocre warehouse job and the "hawklike attentions" of his mother, writes poetry on the boss's time and escapes to the movies at night where he dreams of far-away places like his father, "a telephone man who fell in love with long distance" and left for good. Tom's situation is pitiable but his vague longings, his inarticulate hopes, and his shiftlessness are so much romanticized that it seems as if the writer were making virtues out of weaknesses.

A variation more sentimental than Tom is Kilroy of *Camino Real,* a twenty-seven-year-old American boy with a heart in his body "as big as the head of a baby," one-time boxing champ now looking for a woman not "afraid of a big hard kiss." Like Tom he is vaguely rebelling against something in America that might be identified as the crass American dollar; since there is no escape from this grim valley of greenbacks, the unlucky boy can only indulge himself in self-pity and lovemaking. A third example, Brick in *Cat on a Hot Tin Roof,* an ex-football player with a sick conscience over his friend's death—the relationship between these two men is left in murky doubt—holds the stage record for self-pitying drinkers. His big howl against American life is "mendacity" which includes his greedy brother, the church, the luncheon clubs, and his wife's craving to have a baby. A typical Williams blubberer, the inheritance he faces is a dreary prospect: "twenty-eight thousand acres of the richest land this side of the Valley Nile." It is just the kind of thing to drive a young American to drink.

Williams' most passionately lyrical tribute is bestowed on a type of male animal, a figure worthy of citation at an international stock show. Stan Kowalsky of *A Streetcar Named Desire* has not been spoiled by the American Way of Life: "Animal joy in his being is implicit in all his movements and attitudes. Since early childhood the center of his life has been pleasure with women, the giving and taking of it, not with weak indulgence, dependently, but with power and pride of a richly feathered male bird among hens. . . . He sizes up women with a glance, with sexual satisfactions, crude images flashing into his mind and determining the way he smiles at them." He belongs to Williams' concept of the Elysian Fields, the heaven of poker players, "men at the peak of their physical manhood, as coarse and direct and powerful as primary colors." When Stan, a drunken primitive with a single idea about women, takes the deranged Blanche DuBois, a sentimental prostitute, off to the bedroom and speaks the line, "We've had this date from the beginning!" Williams has arrived theatrically. It is reported that waves of titillated laughter swept over the audience. It was the effect, no doubt, that Williams sought. But it bears no resemblance to the Greek tragedy with which he identifies himself.

Williams' amusing eulogy of Stan is repeated in *The Rose Tattoo* about Serafina's second mate, the Italian truckdriver, Alvaro ⟨Mangiacavallo⟩, Eat-a-Horse. Radiantly virile with "massively sculptured torso and bluish-black curls," but so inarticulate that "he frequently seems surprised at his own speeches and actions," he never leaves any doubt about his sexual prowess. A third representative appears as a young doctor in *Summer and Smoke.* John Buchanan, a clumsy dramatic symbol not only of the Body but also of the Soul, is supposed to retain his nobility in spite of dissipating his Promethean energy in liquor and sex. With considerable posturing and self-pity this virile American escapes a stagnant society and "a doctor's life [that] is walled in by sickness and misery and death."

Williams' best virile male character to date is Big Daddy in *Cat on a Hot Tin Roof,* sixty-five and woman-hungry, a cancer-ridden plantation owner who built up an estate which he inherited from two homosexual bachelors. He is a contradiction to the Williams tradition because, although he seems to have made a lot of money, prosperity has not spoiled his character. Virile, lusty in speech, disappointed in, but still loving his alcoholic son Brick, with whom he seeks a kind of communication and understanding, he is a considerable character when he is free to talk. But Williams was obviously stymied. It is a curious deviation from dramatic laws that the playwright would drop Big Daddy from the last act of the play only to bring him back at the request of his director, Elia Kazan, very briefly, and for an antiquated and a vulgar story that had to be deleted for the sake of public taste. If there ever was a truism made in the theater, it can be said of Big Daddy: he is a character in search of an author.

A third type of male character, the gentleman caller, seems to represent the average American who more or less conforms to the mores of contemporary society. Jim O'Connor of *The Glass Menagerie* is unimaginative and ambitious, but not slated for distinction. He is not a radiant male, only an ex-football player. His self-esteem is momentarily restored by the crippled Laura who has been secretly infatuated with him since high school days. Complacent in his renewed euphoria, unaware of the depth of her love, this blunderbuss dances with her—the music "The Golondrina," one of Williams' favorite records—and clumsily breaks the unicorn as he breaks her heart. About to leave for his date, he moralizes: "The power of love is pretty tremendous! Love is something that—changes the world—Laura!" The author has assigned to this young extrovert some of his favorite philosophy but it sounds like words of lip service from a man studying how to get on in the world.

Another gentleman caller is Mitch, Blanche DuBois' last hope in *A Streetcar Named Desire,* a blundering, aging mama's boy. Shocked by his fiancée's past, he throws apron-string ideals out the window and makes a comically ineffective pass at his streetwalker sweetheart. A third example, Rosa's sailor in *The Rose Tattoo,* is another good boy, a shellback with three equator crossings to his credit but his mother's teachings still in his heart. He is one of Williams' more slightly developed characters, but one of his best, and proof that when he is willing to deliver straightforward, honest writing, rather than indulge in phony symbolism and posturing, he can write with power. A fourth example of the gentleman caller is Roger Doremus in *Summer and Smoke*, more securely mother-attached than either Tom Wingfield or Mitch, a dull young man who drinks lemonade with Alma and waxes enthusiastic about the meeting of his mother and father: "returning from India with dysentery they met on the boat."

Among the women characters Laura of *The Glass Menagerie* epitomizes Williams' fragile, pathetic Southern women. "Like a piece of her own glass collection, too exquisitely fragile to move from the shelf," she has retreated into her world of "little glass ornaments and phonograph records." In the characterization there are almost too many tears. Not only shy but neurotic, and saddled with a clanking brace, she is also harrassed by a determined and unimaginative mother. She meets her dream lover under the most trying circumstances, lives a whole lifetime of romance in a few minutes, only to be sickened by his pity. He breaks her unicorn as he breaks her heart, but she forgives. So many cards are stacked against the girl that the writer seems to have grown maudlin over his portrait of failure and pathos.

An escapist like her daughter, Amanda also lives unhappily in her cocoon of dreams. A Southern belle grown middle-aged and garrulous, she "flounces girlishly" whenever there is a man around. In her pathetic refusal to be realistic, she clings to such delusions as a certainty that she could have married any of her now wealthy gentlemen callers if she had not fallen in love with the man in the soldier suit, or her conviction that her children are exceptional. Distressingly prim, she grows furious over her son's declaration that "Man is by instinct a lover, a hunter, a fighter," forbidding him to use the word, instinct, when speaking of "Christian adults." It is a caustic picture that Williams paints of an over-refined, silly, oldish belle, who gains "dignity and tragic beauty" only when her chatter cannot be heard. In spite of the playwright's insistence that his play is not realistic, the better scenes in *The Glass Menagerie* involve this shrill hysterical woman trying to keep her daughter from being one of those barely tolerated spinsters . . . stuck away in some little mouse-trap of a room . . . little bird-like women without any nest."

Another escapist, Blanche DuBois, unable to face family deaths and the decay of the estate to a "mere twenty acres and a graveyard," turns prostitute in her efforts to find kindness. She is married at sixteen to a young poet, sentimentally described: "Something different about the boy, a nervousness, a softness and a tenderness which wasn't like a man's, although he wasn't effeminate looking." She is widowed shortly afterwards because she discovers this shy boy's relations with an older man. She later becomes an English teacher with rather unusual extracurricular activities: "After the death of Allan—intimacies with strangers was all I seemed able to fill my empty heart with. . . . I think it was panic, just panic that drove me from one to another, hunting for some protection—here and there, in the most unlikely places—even, at last, in a seventeen-year-old boy." Strangely enough, she seems surprised that her superintendent should find her "morally unfit for her position." But this may be only Williams' idea of callow American society, too insensitive to understand the exotic and the delicate.

This glamorized neurotic is another of Williams' tragic heroines of the South. Homeless, she descends upon her sister and behaves like an injured grand duchess. She lies about her age, lies about taking liquor, although she has emptied Stan's bottle, lies about her strict ideas of purity though she has been run out of town, turns sexy and exhibitionist before Stan's poker-playing friends, and goes on an emotional drunk with saccharine love songs. She, like her author, insists that she doesn't want realism, but magic. Her condition is deplorable. But the question arises whether she isn't basically another self-centered, dishonest woman, perhaps a nymphomaniac, and whether the writer is not guilty of trying to bewitch his audience with a sentimental portrait of a fraud.

Another pathetic misfit, Alma in *Summer and Smoke*, is an intellectual and spinsterish snob who gilds the lily in her Southern parish. For this bluestocking the Gothic cathedral symbolizes "the secret, the principle back of existence—the everlasting struggle and aspiration for more than our human limits have placed within our reach." But, according to Williams, this sensitive girl, rejected by her man who finds her incapable of "intimate relations," takes up with a traveling salesman, the first, presumably, of a series of bedroom adventures. The plight of the single woman, hag-ridden by family or other responsibilities, is a common story, and a rich subject for the theater, but obviously stage prostitutes are more easily described, and much more attractive at the box office.

If one of Williams' theories is that a better than average IQ makes a woman prissy and either sexually incompetent or sexually insatiable, then the opposite theory naturally obtains: woman is a mating animal who can find happiness only in sex. Blanche's younger sister, Stella, symbolizes the idea of fulfillment. Not only that, she is a Madonna figure whose "eyes have that almost narcotized tranquility that is on the faces of Eastern idols." It is startling to have the girl, a Madonna symbol, mated with a representative of Capricorn the Goat. Stan Kowalsky's treatment of his pregnant wife ranges violently and rapidly from drunken beating, breaking the furniture, to maudlin crying, "I want my baby," whenever the girl runs for cover. Stella tells her sister that she is so much in love with Stan that their intimacies make up for all the violence of his drunken orgies. It almost seems as if the writer has a theory that American girls are fed up with civilized lovers and would give their all to be beaten black and blue by alcoholically odoriferous Neanderthal men.

Williams plays with the great mother symbol in a minor character, Nellie, in *Summer and Smoke;* she is an adolescent with the enthusiasm of a bobby-soxer and the aggressiveness of an aging streetwalker. Another is the voluptuous, uncomfortably corseted, love-lonesome Seraphina who quite candidly asserts that "the big bed was beautiful like a religion," and brags to her less amorous friends that she "*knows* what lovemaking was." Her happiest memory, she says, was knowing that she "conceived on the very night of conception." Her daughter, overendowed with her mother's glandular talents, but a "sweet, refined" girl according to her creator, propositions her sailor boy friend: "You don't need to be very old to understand how it works out. One time, one time, only once, it could be! God! to remember." Helpless before such importunate pleas, the able seaman risks discovery and "a ten-year stretch in the brig." The great mother symbol takes a different slant with Margaret, the cat on the hot tin roof, roused to anger because her husband no longer wants to sleep with her. A mercenary wench, she is also terrified that Big Daddy will cut them out of his will. Like her sisters-in-the-flesh she waxes lyrical about her man's one-time lovemaking: "with absolute confidence and perfect calm, more like opening a door for a lady, or seating her at a table, than giving expression to any longing for her."

These are the character types which keep reappearing in the world of Tennessee Williams. Most of them, according to discriminating critics, have been more deeply affected by the theater than by life. It is generally recognized that this writer has a talent for penetrating human character, for describing frustrations and various forms of escapism, as well as for catching the spirit of joyous living. However, when he obscures this special insight by indulging in theatrical lies, and creates scenes dripping with sentiment or relying on shock and violence for effect, then he deserves the ridicule he has received.

It is obvious that Mr. Williams takes himself very seriously, but that fact need not be the cue for others. He has not the range nor wisdom of a Gorky, nor the mordant sense of humor of a Chekhov, Russians with whom he has been compared. The Greeks to whom he himself so glibly refers often concerned themselves with passion, incest, and adultery, rather than biology. They described the effect of irrational indulgence, of love and ambition, or anger and revenge, of the illusion of happiness, of man's great possibilities and his follies, factors conducive to a good life or a tragic one. Greek drama was a part of a generally accepted moral order in which man, because he was a rational being, was partly responsible for the pattern of his life.

Mary McCarthy's caustic comment about *Streetcar*, overstating the point that "his talent is rooted in pay dirt," carries an element of truth: "His work reeks of literary ambition . . . it is impossible to witness one of Mr. Williams' plays without being aware of the pervading smell of careerism. . . . Whatever happens to the characters, Mr. Williams will come out rich and famous, and the play merely another episode in Mr. Williams' 'career'."

Even though his plays leave much to be desired, the actors, directors, and the producers have been able to make of his scripts exciting evenings in the theater. It is a curious comment on the mid-twentieth century that the success of Tennessee Williams rests, to a large degree, on his repudiation of values and attitudes which most intelligent and genuinely sensitive Americans care about. It is, indeed, a very curious comment on the times that his tawdry success has been accompanied, in so many quarters, by so much respect.

HAROLD CLURMAN

From "Tennessee Williams" (1959/1962)

The Naked Image

1966, pp. 123–28

Sweet Bird of Youth, *1959*

Tennessee Williams' *Sweet Bird of Youth* interested me more as a phenomenon than as a play. Its place in the author's development and its fascination for the audience strike me as more significant than its value as drama.

Williams is a romantic; one of the characteristics of the romantic is a pressing need to reveal himself. Though the play's narrative is realistic, the characters are frequently called upon to address the audience directly. Both in its content and its form one senses the author's urgent impulse to say everything he feels right out. Here I am, he seems to be telling us, naked and unabashed, and I am going to speak my piece. At the end of the play the central character turns to us and says, "I do not ask for your pity or even your understanding. I ask you only to recognize me in yourselves."

What is it we are asked to recognize in ourselves? That we are corrupted by our appetite for the flash and clamor of success, that we are driven to live debased existences by the constrictions and brutality which surround us, that the sound instincts of our youth are thus frustrated and turned to gall, and that we have an inordinate fear of age, for the passing of time makes us old before we mature.

There may be truth in this. More important is the manner in which this truth is conveyed. Chance Wayne is an average smalltown boy born and reared somewhere on the Gulf Coast. At the age of seventeen he has an idyllic affair with a girl of fifteen. But because he is poor, the girl's father—political boss of the town—calls an abrupt halt to the romance. The boy goes to New York in the hope of becoming enough of a big shot as an actor to impress the folks back home. Because he has good looks but very little training, he gets nothing but jobs in the chorus of musicals. He also gives unbounded satisfaction to numerous women.

He is drafted for the Korean War and he suffers the awful fear that his splendid youth will be cut off by mutilation and his ambition thwarted by death. After his release from the Navy one of his jobs is that of masseur at a Florida beach resort. He earns money on the side as a gigolo. One of the women he encounters is a fading movie star in flight from impending failure. Her terror makes her take refuge in drugs and promiscuity. Chance Wayne brings her back to his home town. He clings to this woman—whose whore he becomes—because he plans to make her the key to a Hollywood career for himself. To make sure that she will live up to her end of the agreement, he uses a dictaphone to blackmail her—she has confessed to having smuggled the hashish they both smoke. In the meantime, he uses her Cadillac and takes her money to spend conspicuously so that his former girl, her father and the boyhood friends will be awed by his "position."

At some point before these latter events, Chance had resumed his affair with the girl who is his true love. Sometime during his career as a gigolo he had contracted a veneral disease and had unknowingly infected his beloved. Her father has her undergo an operation which renders her sterile. The girl bids the boy—still ignorant of what has happened—to leave town for good lest her father have him killed.

There are many more details portraying the girl's despair, the vile hypocrisy of her father, the maniacal vindictiveness of her brother, the savagery of the town's political gang. In the end the movie star, who for a moment had shown signs of compassion for the boy, abandons him because she has made a Hollywood comeback and can think of nobody but herself. By remaining in town after he has been repeatedly warned to get out, the boy virtually invites the castration with which he has been threatened.

I have no categorical objection to this heap of horrors. I can believe that they occur in life, indeed that they have occurred. But the telling of this story is very close to lurid melodrama. What saves it from being just that is the fluently euphonious idiom and vivid grace of Williams' writing. Even more telling is Williams' ache and what might be called his ideology.

Is there any virtue at all in Chance Wayne? Williams names it. Chance has given *great pleasure*. He is consummately male, a wonderful lover. When he hears that a Negro in his town has been castrated for assaulting a white woman, Chance cries out, "I know what that is: it's sex envy"—which is surely the author's comment rather than the character speaking. Sex potency is held forth as a special order of merit bestowing amnesty for every misdeed.

Williams does not ask us to admire the boy, but the whole play suggests that he is sufficiently typical to induce us to share some kinship with him. A nonentity can be made central to a modern tragedy as is Clyde Griffith in Dreiser's book, but the novelist did this by weaving a web of environmental circumstance so complete in each detail that we are objectively convinced. Taken literally, Chance Wayne is an atrocity. He is not a real person but a figment of Williams' commanding sentiment.

The simplification and distortion which mark the portrait of Chance are evident in the play's other characters as well—schematic types whose bareness is covered only by Williams' colorful verbiage. The movie actress is the best of them, for there is a grotesque humor about her—a kind of wry pity not far removed from contempt. The most crudely drawn figure is that of Boss Finley, a caricature of a Dixiecrat, a dirty dog beyond compare, more bogey than man. Indeed, there is something about all the people in the play which seems calculated to scare us to death.

Much of what Williams has attempted to say here has been implied in some of his earlier plays, but they had more texture in characterization and reality. What we suspect in *Sweet Bird of Youth* is that Williams has become immobilized in his ideology; that it has not been refreshed either by any new experience or by mature thought. He has only become much bolder. The result is that we feel in this play an inverted sentimentality and a willful stress which produce more ugliness than lyricism or credence.

We know that a great part of what Williams feels about American life is valid; many novels and sociological studies in the past thirty-five years or more have helped us recognize its validity. So it is perhaps useful for Williams to alarm theatre audiences still largely protected from the rumor of the real world. Scandal on Broadway may be beneficent. But I observe that the audience at *Sweet Bird* is entertained rather than stirred, piqued rather than sobered. It does not truly believe what it sees; it is simply enjoying a show with a kick in it. And this lack of shock may be attributed to something specious in the stage proceedings. 〈. . .〉

The Night of the Iguana, *1962*

Some years ago, defending a novel by a famous writer which had been thoroughly roasted in all the reviews, Tennessee Williams said that he liked the book because the novelist had succeeded in thoroughly exposing his inner being. That is a romantic view of the function of art, but since all works of art do in fact reveal the men who made them—though I doubt that it is their main purpose or value—I am not prepared to contest Williams' defense.

While Tennessee Williams' latest play, *The Night of the Iguana*, is certainly not strict autobiography, it does give us an idea of how Williams sees and judges himself. At the moment, this seems to me the most rewarding aspect of the play, though not the only one. Indeed, it is easy to assert that it is the best American play of the season—since there is nothing else to stand beside it.

There is sentimentality in all of Williams' work, but in *The Night of the Iguana* he is not trying to show himself in a favorable light. The reverse may be closer to the truth. If there is pardon in the play, it results from confession and self-castigation—which is one of the forms a puritanic romanticism takes.

The central character is the still young Lawrence Shannon, an Episcopal minister who has shocked his congregation by denouncing its God and substituted for Him a pantheistic deity, or to put it more plainly, a god as amoral as the forces of nature themselves. Shannon's church is closed to him and he has become a tourist guide in Mexico. He takes pleasure in showing his (American) clients the shady or seamy side of the places they visit, not only because that is what attracts him but also because it fascinates them. He is given to promiscuous fornication—usually with young persons, even minors.

The personal association is clear, is it not? A man of religious disposition desires to spread the Word, but the old God of vengeance is too narrow and shallow for him. Since he cannot renounce instructing and preaching, he must bring to everyone's attention the secret and foul byways of man's experience. Unless these are disclosed life cannot be wholly known or accepted. (This too is what *audiences* hunger to have displayed in a repressed and morally worried community such as ours.) To dedicate oneself to such instruction may have its reprehensible side, but there is a grave mission in it as well.

There is very little indulgence in the portrait of Reverend Shannon. He meets a beautiful and very spiritual New England spinster who travels about with her grandfather, once a well-known minor poet. To support themselves in their extensive peregrinations she paints watercolors and he recites his verse in hostelries, restaurants, holiday resorts. The girl is chaste without strain, pure without vanity. She understands all, forgives all. She is the image of what the outcast preacher considers almost sacred. He knows he cannot corrupt, break or defile her. She has her own strength. Nor can he ever measure up to what she embodies. So he reconciles himself to becoming the companion in waywardness of the lewd and gusty lady whose hotel is the scene of the play. Smiling ruefully, Williams must be content (like his poet) to set himself down as "frightened me."

If one does not perceive the drift of *Iguana* in its relation to its author's legend, the play may seem meaningless, shapeless, a little unreal. Every character is more conceptual than specifically true. (I must allow, but find it especially difficult to believe, that Shannon was ever an ordained minister.) Yet such is Williams' talent that the play breathes with its own artistic life.

The writing, to begin with, is lambent, fluid, malleable and colloquially melodious. It bathes everything in glamour. Colored lights seem to illuminate all the play's people, lending them an odd dimension. I do not care for the hinted psychoanalytic explanation given of Shannon's behavior, but one cannot resist Williams' intuitive invention. For example, cavorting through the seedy Mexican hotel is a chorus of comic maenads in the shape of German (Nazi) tourists—so many fat grubs infesting the place with a sick-making health.

These and the terrifyingly funny secondary characters—the hysterical girl Shannon has seduced (it is interesting to note that he maintains the girls have seduced him), the righteously indignant American schoolteacher infuriated by Shannon—all form part of a picture that not only lends the play credibility but an extraordinary vividness.

ARTHUR GANZ

"The Desperate Morality of the Plays of Tennessee Williams"

American Scholar, Spring 1962, pp. 278–94

"Moralist," desperate or not, may seem a perverse appellation for a playwright whose works concern rape, castration, cannibalism and other bizarre activities, but in examining the work of Tennessee Williams it is exactly this point—that he is a moralist, not a psychologist—that should be borne in mind. Williams' powers of characterization are real, but they are not his central gifts: witness *Cat on a Hot Tin Roof* which contains Big Daddy, one of Williams' most striking characterizations, but which fails none the less because in this play Williams' moral vision becomes blurred, and it is in the clarity and force of that moral vision that his strength as a playwright lies.

Admittedly, Williams' morality is not the morality of most men, but it is a consistent ethic, giving him a point of view from which he can judge the actions of people. Yet to say that Williams rewards those who, by his standards, are virtuous and punishes those who are evil is to oversimplify, for in the world of Williams' plays, good often has a curious affinity with evil. Beneath the skin of the Christlike martyr destroyed by the cruel forces of death and sterility lies the disease, the sin that has made his creator destroy him. The character who is most fiercely condemned may at the same time be the one for whom pardon is most passionately demanded. From the self-lacerating desire simultaneously to praise and to punish stems the violence that disfigures so many of Williams' plays.

To understand this violence in Williams' work we must first look at his gentlest plays, those in which the virtuous are rewarded, for here is most directly revealed the morality by which the guilty are later so terribly condemned. Surprisingly, one of Williams' most significant plays is an indifferent and undramatic one-acter about the death of D. H. Lawrence, only slightly redeemed by the audacious and successful title, *I Rise in Flame, Cried the Phoenix*. The play is significant because it gives us the central fact we must have to understand Williams' work, the nature of his literary parentage. In art, a son must seek out a father who will give him what he needs. Williams needed a rationale for the sexual obsessions that dominate his work, and it was this that Lawrence seemed to give him. In the Preface to *I Rise in Flame* Williams wrote, "Lawrence felt the mystery and power of sex, as the primal life urge, and was the lifelong adversary of those who wanted to keep the subject locked away in the cellars of prudery," and in the play he makes Frieda exclaim, "You just don't know. The meaning of Lawrence escapes you. In all of his work he celebrates the body."

Whether or not Williams assesses Lawrence correctly is, for an understanding of Williams' own work, irrelevant. The important thing is that from a very early point in his career (*I Rise in Flame* dates from 1941) Williams saw Lawrence as the great writer who "celebrates the body" and apparently saw himself as that writer's disciple. Like many disciples, however, Williams introduced his own variations on the master's doctrine. Williams betrayed Lawrence primarily by extending the approval of Lawrentian doctrine to areas of sexual experience beyond the normal, but first he did so by basing a very bad play on one of Lawrence's short stories.

The play, called *You Touched Me* from Lawrence's story of that title, is an early work, copyrighted in 1942. Although it shows little of the doctrinal variation on which Williams' later work is based, the distortions that were introduced as the story was transformed into a play are highly revealing. In addition, *You Touched Me* is important for establishing the structural pattern of two of Williams' most attractive plays, *The Glass Menagerie* and *The Rose Tattoo*.

Lawrence's story concerns the marriage between Matilda, the daughter of a retired pottery manufacturer, and his adopted son, Hadrian. Although the marriage is brought about by the father's threatening to leave his daughters penniless, it is a good marriage that rescues Matilda from her empty life and eases the spirit of the old man who, at the end of the story, asks the newlyweds to kiss and murmurs as they do so, "That's right! That's right!"

Williams' play, which he wrote in collaboration with Donald Windham, is a stunning vulgarization of Lawrence's story. The younger sister, Emmie, is changed into a frigid maiden aunt who represents, in Williams' words, "aggressive sterility." Matilda herself, a thin, large-nosed woman of thirty-two, turns into a pale girl of twenty, the cliché of the frail, sheltered maiden. Hadrian, in the story a neat, scheming little soldier with a common-looking mustache, is transformed into "a clean-cut, muscular young man in the dress uniform of a lieutenant in the Royal Canadian Air Force," much given to speeches about faith, the glories of the future, and the conquering of new countries of the mind. And the elderly pottery manufacturer is turned into a spry, if alcoholic, old sea captain, portrayed on the stage by Edmund Gwenn, everyone's lovable old grandfather. Given this set of popular-magazine characters, the play has no trouble reaching its predictable conclusion as the captain helps the handsome airman defeat the aunt and win the shy Matilda.

What is important here is not that, working with unfamiliar material at this early stage in his career, Williams should write a poor play, but that, while retaining the essential Lawrentian theme, he should so alter Lawrence's material as to produce an unmistakable Tennessee Williams play. The light but subtle characterizations around which Lawrence built his story are in the play coarsened to the point where the characters are as obviously broken down into the bad guys and the good guys as those in any television western; Hadrian, Matilda and the captain are in favor of sexuality while the frigid Emmie and her suitor, an impotent clergyman, are opposed to it. Williams is not a psychologist, and he "understands" his characters very little; rather, he is a moralist, although a very special one, and he judges them.

Although Williams has distorted Lawrence's work by sentimentalizing it and by introducing into it caricatures of frigidity and impotence, he is genuinely sympathetic to its real theme, the awakening of life, and particularly sexual life, in one who had previously been dead to it. In both the play and the story, Hadrian (the conquering emperor from the warm South) defeats the forces of sterility and rouses Matilda to new life. It was this action, which Williams sees as profoundly good, that he developed in this early play and then made the center of two of his most pleasing works.

Both *The Glass Menagerie* and *The Rose Tattoo* are variations on the material first used in *You Touched Me*. In each play the central character, a woman who has retired from life, lives in a closed world that excludes sexuality, "the primal life urge." Into this world comes a man, like Hadrian the sexual force designed to release the woman from her bondage. But although he succeeds in one case, in the other he fails. The reasons for this difference are worth noting.

The figure of Laura in *The Glass Menagerie* has clearly been developed from that of Matilda of *You Touched Me*, who is described by Williams as having "the delicate, almost transparent quality of glass." Both are shy, fragile creatures, remote from the life around them. But where Hadrian awakens Matilda and brings her back to life, Laura's gentleman caller gives her only a momentary glimpse of normal life before she drifts back into the fantasy world of glass animals. In Williams' moral system the rejection of life is the greatest crime, and those guilty of it are visited by the kind of punishment that falls upon Blanche DuBois in *Streetcar* and Sebastian Venable in *Suddenly Last Summer*. Laura, however, is innocent; she does not reject but rather is rejected, not because of her limp, which does not exist in "Portrait of a Girl in Glass," Williams' own short story upon which he based his play, but because she is the sensitive, misunderstood exile, a recurrent character in Williams' work, one of the fugitive kind, who are too fragile to live in a malignant world.

The vigorous Serafina Delle Rose of *The Rose Tattoo*, however, openly rejects life after the death of her husband. She lives an existence as solitary and sterile as that of Laura among the glass animals. Only when the truck driver Alvaro Mangiacavallo, who has the face of a clown but the body of her husband, appears does she disclaim her rejection and return to the world of life and sexuality. Again it was to this favorite theme that Williams turned when he converted his one-acter *27 Wagons Full of Cotton* into the script for the film *Baby Doll*. The vengeful sadist Vicarro becomes in the film the Lawrentian lover Vacarro who awakens the virginal heroine to sexual life.

Period of Adjustment, perhaps Williams' worst play, seems to belong to this group of gentle plays, for at its conclusion the two couples achieve sexual harmony as the phallically named community of High Point sinks further into the cavern beneath it. But before the playwright allows this to happen, each of the two men who are its central figures is humiliated and forced to admit his weakness. They have been great fighters and war heroes, but one has abased himself to marry for money, and before he can be forgiven he must be bullied by his father-in-law and forced to accept his unattractive wife. The other has rejected his homosexual nature, or at least pretended to a virility he does not possess. He must publicly admit his weakness before he is bedded down, blissfully it is assumed, with his hysterical bride. The play falls apart because Williams cannot decide whether his central figures are to be forgiven or to be punished.

When Williams does not doubt that a character who has transgressed his moral code must be punished, his work is at its most powerful. Of all the crimes in this code the greatest is that from which Matilda and Serafina are preserved, the rejection of life. This theme of punishment for an act of rejection is at the center of a group of Williams' plays very different from that already examined, but it is expressed most explicitly in a short story, "Desire and the Black Masseur," from the volume *One Arm and Other Stories*. The central character, Walter Burns, a man who has yielded completely to the loveless, conventional life surrounding him, is haunted by a nameless, unfulfilled desire which is finally satisfied by a giant Negro masseur in a Turkish bath. Under the manipulations of the masseur, Burns discovers that his desire has been masochistic, and gradually the masseur, the instrument of his destiny, beats him almost to death. As the story veers toward fantasy, they go to the masseur's room where he kills Burns and proceeds to eat him in the atmosphere of a sacred ritual.

Although this story is bizarre and perhaps a little ridiculous, it says a great deal that is revealing of the cast of mind of its author. To him, Walter Burns is not an individual but a broad symbol of human guilt, for Williams believes that the sins of the world "are really only its partialities, its incompletions, and these are what sufferings must atone for." He sees these sufferings as ritual, a device for removing guilt. This is the function of "the principle of atonement, the surrender of the self to violent treatment by others with the idea of thereby clearing one's self of his guilt." For all its macabre elements, in the mind of its author, as the end of the story shows, "Desire and the Black Masseur" is an example of a wider vision comprehending the world and the place of suffering in it. "And meantime," Williams concludes, "slowly, with barely a thought of so doing, the earth's whole population twisted and writhed beneath the manipulation of night's black fingers, the white ones of day with skeletons splintered and flesh reduced to pulp, as out of this unlikely problem, the answer, perfection, was slowly evolved through torture."

We need not believe that anything like perfection could be evolved from the process described in "Desire and the Black Masseur" to see its significance in relation to Williams' major work. The story concerns an elaborate, ritual punishment of one who has rejected life, and, more specifically, rejected sexuality. A whole group of Williams' plays including some of his most remarkable—*A Streetcar Named Desire, Summer and Smoke, Cat on a Hot Tin Roof* and *Suddenly Last Summer*—is centered on this idea of the terrible punishment that is visited on one because of an act of sexual rejection.

The stage action of *A Streetcar Named Desire*, still Williams' finest play, consists almost entirely of the punishment that its heroine, Blanche DuBois, endures as atonement for her act of rejection, her sin in terms of Williams' morality. Since Williams begins the action of his play at a late point in his story, the act itself is not played out on stage but only referred to. Not realizing that she is describing the crime that condemns her, Blanche tells Mitch of her discovery that her adored young husband was a homosexual and of the consequences of her disgust and revulsion:

> *Blanche*: . . . He'd stuck the revolver into his mouth, and fired—so that the back of his head had been—blown away! (She sways and covers her face.) It was because—on the dance floor—unable to stop myself—I'd suddenly said—"I saw! I know! You disgust me . . ." And then the searchlight which had been turned on the world was turned off again and never for one moment since has there been any light that's stronger than this—kitchen—candle . . .

While Blanche delivers this speech and the ones surrounding it, the polka to which she and her husband had danced, the Varsouviana, sounds in the background. At the end of the play, when Blanche sees the doctor who is to lead her off to the asylum, her punishment is complete and the Varsouviana sounds again, linking her crime to its retribution. As Blanche flees from the doctor, "the Varsouviana is filtered into a weird distortion accompanied by the cries and noises of the jungle." These symbolize simultaneously Blanche's chaotic state and the instrument of her destruction, Stanley Kowalski, the complete sensual animal, the equivalent in function to the black masseur.

Although Kowalski's primary function, to destroy Blanche, is clear, there are certain ambiguities evoked by his role. By becoming Blanche's destroyer, Kowalski also becomes the avenger of her homosexual husband. Although he is Williams' melodramatic exaggeration of the Lawrentian lover, the embodiment of admired male sexuality, it is appropriate from Williams' point of view that Kowalski should to some degree be identified with the lonely homosexual who had been driven to suicide, for Williams saw Lawrence not only as the propagandist of sexual vitality but as the symbol of the solitary, rejected exile. (See the poem called "Cried the Fox" from Williams' collection, *In The Winter of Cities*. In it Lawrence is symbolized as the fox pursued by the cruel hounds.) By implication, then, Williams has extended Lawrentian approval to the rejected homosexual (an act that probably set Lawrence spinning in his grave). Yet this approval is never whole-hearted; for the exile homosexual, as he appears in Williams' work, is always tormented and often despairing. He cannot, after all, be a martyr until Williams has had him crucified.

Those who crucify, however, can never be guiltless.

Kowalski, although an avenger, is as guilty of crucifying Blanche as she is of crucifying her husband. For Blanche, who has lost the plantation Belle Reve, the beautiful dream of a life of gracious gentility, is an exile like the homosexual; her tormentor, the apelike Kowalski, from one point of view the representative of Lawrentian vitality, is from another the brutal, male torturer of a lonely spirit. But however compassionately Blanche is viewed, she remains a woman who, in effect, has killed her husband by her cruelty, and her attempts to turn away from death to its opposite—"the opposite is desire," as Blanche herself says—are fruitless. Even as she tells Mitch about her promiscuity, a Mexican woman stands at one side of the stage selling flowers for the dead. *"Flores para los muertos,"* she calls, *"flores—flores."*

A variant on the act of rejection is performed in Scene Six of *Summer and Smoke.* The characters are similar to those already encountered: the frail, spinsterish Southern girl with her sensuality repressed by a puritanical background; the man who is seeking spiritual relief through a sexual union. Like many of Williams' characters he needs love as relief from solitude. At one point, while giving Alma an ironic anatomy lecture, he shouts, "This part down here is the sex—which is hungry for love because it is sometimes lonesome." At the crucial moment she rejects his advances and rushes off. Although Alma, like Blanche, has sinned and must atone, she has not sinned out of cruelty nor has she caused the death of her lover. After he has passed through his spiritual crisis and found a wife and a place in the world, Alma realizes what she had done. Like Blanche she is condemned to be tormented by the urges she had turned away from, and like Blanche she turns to promiscuity, but because her sin has been somewhat mitigated by her realization of it there is a suggestion at the end of the play that the traveling salesman she has picked up may lead her to salvation rather than destruction.

Williams' most recent play, *The Night of the Iguana* (a reworking of his short story of the same title), has, like *Summer and Smoke,* affinities with both the severity of *Streetcar* and the gentleness of *The Glass Menagerie.* Its heroine, Hannah Jelkes, a New England spinster artist, is placed in a position that closely parallels that of Blanche DuBois. But unlike Blanche, when confronted by an appeal for help from one with abnormal sexual inclinations (a homosexual in the original story, but converted for stage purposes to an unfrocked minister with a taste for pubescent girls), instead of driving him to suicide, she offers him what help she can. That help, however, is limited. When he asks to be allowed to travel with her, she cannot accept him. Because like Laura and Alma she is too delicate and too repressed to take on a full emotional relationship, Shannon's rescue is finally left to the sexually vital hotel proprietor, while Hannah must continue in loveless solitude. By her sympathy for Shannon and for the pathetic fetishist she had previously aided, she has earned, however, a fate far gentler than the breakdown meted out to Blanche and to her own predecessor in the original story.

In *Cat on a Hot Tin Roof,* however, Williams produces something much nearer the pattern of *Streetcar.* In fact, from one point of view *Cat* is simply a reworking of the materials of the earlier play, but with a crucial change that made it almost impossible for Williams to bring his play to a reasonable conclusion. Again we are presented with a work in which the motivating figure does not appear, and again that figure is the rejected homosexual. But now because the rejector, the sinner who must atone, in not a woman but a man, certain problems arise. The audience, although it sympathizes with Blanche, can accept her as guilty. She is a woman, and had she been able to giver her husband love instead of contempt, she might have led him back to normal life. Brick, however, confronted with Skipper's telephoned confession of a homosexual attachment, is hardly in a position to do the same—short of admitting a similar inclination. Yet Williams, although he is ambiguous about several points in this play, is not ambiguous about Brick's guilt. Big Daddy himself, who despises mendacity, condemns his son. "You! dug the grave of your friend," he cries, "and kicked him in it!—before you'd face the truth with him!" But it is beyond Big Daddy's power to explain how Brick was to do so.

Yet in a play designed for the modern professional theater, Williams cannot openly punish Brick for failing to be an honest homosexual. When he showed *Cat* to the representative of that theater, Elia Kazan, and Kazan suggested certain changes, Williams accepted his advice. As a result, the comparatively optimistic third act performed on Broadway contains the shift in Brick's character that leads to the suggestion that his castration, symbolized obviously enough by his broken ankle, will not be permanent. In the published version of the play, in which the Broadway third act is printed as a kind of addendum to the original, Williams claimed that he had agreed to Kazan's suggestions to retain his interest. There is no reason to disbelieve this statement, but it is worth noting that by mitigating Brick's punishment, Williams was relieved of the necessity of asking his audience to agree that Brick deserved to be castrated for an act which most members of that audience would not consider to be a crime.

Although the tentativeness of Williams' condemnation of Brick makes it difficult to know whether Brick was so condemned for rejecting his homosexual friend or for rejecting his own homosexual nature, in *Cat,* at least, homosexuality itself carries no stigma. In contrast to the castrated Brick, who has rejected, stands Big Daddy, who has accepted. Although he is a man of almost ostentatious virility, as well as the most powerful and sympathetic figure in the play, he had served and respected the two idyllically conceived homosexuals, Straw and Ochello, and received his land from them as a kind of benediction. Yet in *Suddenly Last Summer,* the last play to date of what may be called the "punishment" group, Williams has produced a work in which the homosexual—so often for him the symbol of the lonely, rejected exile—becomes the rejector, the sinner who must be punished.

But neither this shift in Williams' usual pattern nor the *bizarrerie* of the play's atmosphere should conceal the fact that *Suddenly Last Summer* follows closely the structure of the other plays in this group. Once more the pivotal figure, the exile homosexual, has met a violent death before the opening of the play. As the sterile Brick is contrasted with Big Daddy, the life-giving father of *Cat,* so the cruel Sebastian is played off against the loving and merciful Catharine who gives herself not, it seems, out of desire but as an act of rescue. "We walked through the wet grass to the great misty oaks," she says, "as if somebody was calling us for help there." If we remember that this act of rescue is exactly what Blanche, Alma and Brick failed to perform, we realize that Williams means us to accept Catharine as entirely good. Although Sebastian is, as we expect him to be, the loveless rejector who is punished for his sins, there is a surprising similarity between his vision of a world dominated by remorseless cruelty—as expressed in the description of the Encantadas, the Galápagos Islands, where baby sea turtles are killed and devoured by canivorous birds of prey —and the vision of a world undergoing perpetual punishment expressed in "Desire and the Black Masseur." However, in punishing Sebastian, Williams is not disclaiming this vision. Sebastian's sin lay not in perceiving the world as, for Williams, it is, but in his believing, with a pride bordering on *hubris*, that he could exalt himself above his kind, that he could feed upon people like one of the devouring birds of the Encantadas. As always in Williams, the punishment monstrously fits the crime. As Sebastian had cruelly watched the turtles being eaten, as he had fed the fruit flies to the devouring plant, so he is fed to the band of children whom he has perverted and is devoured by them.

Sebastian's crime then is the very one committed by Blanche, Alma and Brick. He has turned away from his suffering fellow creatures and, instead of offering love, has offered hate. He has not understood, as Catharine has, that although all men may be on a stricken ship sinking into the sea, "that's no reason for everyone drowning for hating everyone drowning." And yet there is a difficulty for the spectator in accepting the nature of Sebastian's punishment, however fierce he knows Williams' morality to be. It is not merely that Sebastians' fate is so violently grotesque but that, unlike Blanche and Brick, he has not performed a specific act that brings his punishment upon him; he is punished for what he is rather than for what he does. He is not only a rejector but also a homosexual, always in Williams' work an object simultaneously of sympathy and of revulsion. The ambiguity already noted in *Streetcar* appears in all Williams plays that touch on homosexuality. There is an intimate connection between the guilty rejector and the martyred homosexual; the punishment visited on the former regularly echoes the fate of the latter, so that the two characters are not always distinguishable. In *Streetcar* the rejector and the homosexual victim were separate, but both met desperate ends. In the ambiguous Brick these figures began to converge, and in *Suddenly Last Summer* they have completely coalesced. The pain felt by the cruel rejector is also felt by the sterile and guilty homosexual; neither can escape corruption and despair.

Here lies the source of that vision of universal corruption that pervades so much of Williams' work and that makes it at once so violent and so pathetic. In a world dominated by cruelty, Williams maintains, the innocent are not only destroyed; eventually they too are corrupted. Williams has produced three plays centered on this theme and on the figure that embodies it, the wandering innocent. *Camino Real*, *Orpheus Descending* and *Sweet Bird of Youth* all tell the story of a wanderer who is or has been innocent, who comes into the world of universal corruption and who is thereupon destroyed by it.

Williams has said flatly that the sinister fantasy world of the Camino Real "is nothing more nor less than my conception of the time and world that I live in." It is a time in which greed and brutality are the ruling forces and a world in which those pathetic souls who attempt to show some affection for their fellow creatures are remorselessly crushed and then thrown into a barrel and carted away by the street cleaners. Although this is admittedly a nightmare world, it does not differ in any essential way from the American South as it appears in *Orpheus Descending* and *Sweet Bird of Youth*. This too is a nightmare world where greed, brutality and sterility rule and where those who love are castrated or burned alive. In these last two plays, Williams has attempted to give this world some resemblance to a recognizable social reality, but this reality is always closer to the mysterious country of the Camino Real than to anything in the southern United States. As an epigraph to *Camino Real* Williams has selected the opening lines of Dante's *Inferno;* the setting of that play is the place to which Orpheus descended, hell.

As we would expect, the ruler of hell is Death; more specifically, he is the god of sterility. In *Camino Real*, Gutman, the proprietor of the Siete Mares hotel, is cruel and sinister enough, but he always remains a little remote from the action. Had Williams personified the evil of the place in a single powerful figure, he might have been less able to end the play with its suggestion (however unconvincing) of optimism. Like Gutman, Jabe Torrance, the proprietor of the mercantile store in *Orpheus Descending*, takes little direct part in the action, but he is a far more heavily drawn figure and a far more violent antagonist. The evil creature who destroys life wherever he can find it is, as Williams describes him in a stage direction, "death's self and malignancy." He is not only "death's self," but the personification of sterility and impotence. Nurse Porter, who seems to have supernatural perception, can tell at a glance that Lady is pregnant and that Jabe is not the father. As he had burned the wine garden of Lady's father where the fig tree blossomed and true lovers met, so he calls upon the fires of the hell of impotence to burn her and her lover. (It should be noted that while Williams' work has changed in tone from the gentleness of *You Touched Me*, where the impotent clergyman was a figure of fun, it has not shifted in point of view.) Even more heavily than Jabe, however, Boss Finley of *Sweet Bird of Youth* is drawn as the symbol of malignant impotence. Miss Lucy, his mistress, has scrawled in lipstick across the ladies' room mirror, "Boss Finley is too old to cut the mustard." By implication, at least, he had presided over the castration of an innocent Negro and, as the play ends, is about to preside over that of its hero, Chance Wayne. (The anti-Negro social elements, like the Nazis of *The Night of the Iguana* who are also irrelevant to the drama, are no more than a ploy, a device to win for the hero the sympathy of a liberal New York audience.) The best description of Boss Finley is not in the play but in a poem called "Old Men with Sticks" found in *In the Winter of Cities*. In the poem, senile old men with sticks (lifeless phalli) clump about on "the iron earth of winter."

> Drawn from the pouch that hangs
> Like a withered testicle at the belted waist,
> pearles without luster are passed without passion
>   amongst them;
> the dim but enduring stones of hatred
> are trafficked amongst them by stealth.

As a result, "youth from his lover/draws apart in shame," and frost covers the land.

When Boss Finley's impotence is contrasted with Chance's attitude toward the emasculation of the Negro, the natures of the opposing forces in the play become clear. "You know what that is, don't you?" Chance cries. "Sex-envy is what that is, and the revenge for sex-envy which is a widespread disease that I have run into personally too often for me to doubt its existence or any manifestation." Boss Finley, Chance says, "was just called down from the hills to preach hate. I was born here to make love." Each of the three wanderers, Kilroy, Val and Chance, had been born to make love, but each has been wounded by a hostile world. Kilroy's heart condition prevents him from continuing as a prizefighter or from staying with his "real true woman." Of the three he is the only true innocent and, significantly, the only one who is alone. Val and Chance both speak of the corrupt lives they have lived and of the waning of their youths, but in reality they are bound not by time or by their past lives but by their relationships with an older woman.

Williams developed this relationship most elaborately in his novella, *The Roman Spring of Mrs. Stone*. In that book a once beautiful actress, who had married lovelessly "to escape copulation," finds herself an aging widow at the end of her career and is reduced to buying sexuality from the lowest and most sinister of gigolos. What is most striking here is not the recognizable punishment-for-rejection pattern but the fact that Mrs. Stone's real inclinations are toward lesbianism. Her most vivid sexual experience had been an abortive moment with a schoolgirl friend. In addition, during a brief affair with a young actor, she had enveloped him in an embrace "in a manner that was more like a man's with a girl, and to which he submitted in a way that also suggested a reversal of gender."

If the suggestion of homosexuality that underlies the relationship between the older woman and the younger man in *The Roman Spring of Mrs. Stone* is extended to *Orpheus* and *Sweet Bird* (in each case the ostensible woman is an older person having a forbidden affair with a beautiful young man), these works fit very easily into the pattern of ambiguity we have observed in the "punishment" group. From one point of view we have the wandering love-giver—Val, whose phallic guitar is an obvious symbol, and Chance, who has a speech about his vocation as a love-maker for the middle-aged, the ugly, the sad and the "eccentric"—who enters the nightmare world of Hades in *Orpheus* and of what the Princess in *Sweet Bird* calls "the ogre's country at the top of the beanstalk, the country of the flesh-hungry, blood-thirsty ogre." There he attempts to rescue a lover, and in the attempt he is brutally destroyed by the giant.

From another point of view, however, the wanderer is not innocent but corrupt. Beneath the apparent heterosexual relationship lies one that is homosexual, and from it spreads an aura of corruption that pervades the plays. Chance calculates his age by the level of rot in him, and Val, who has been "on a party" in the bars of New Orleans since he was fifteen, is trying vainly to flee from his past. In his poem called "Orpheus Descending," Williams writes, "Now Orpheus, crawl, O shamefaced fugitive, crawl back under the crumbling broken wall of yourself." As before, the seeming-innocent is himself guilty and must be hideously punished. Once his moral sense has been appeased, however, Williams can allow himself the luxury of a sentimental apotheosis. *Orpheus* and *Sweet Bird* take place at Easter, and in both plays there is a suggestion that the dead wanderer should be viewed as a martyred Christ figure whose spirit is resurrected in Carol Cutrere and the Princess. (However, where the suggestion of resurrection is not incredible in *Orpheus*, the idea that the pathetic gigolo of *Sweet Bird* could be a Christlike martyr is merely bizarre.) It is the wanderer's sin that brings him to destruction and only after he has been punished and destroyed can he be revered.

It is from this conflict between the need to condemn and the desire to pardon that the weakness of Williams' work stems, for it is ironically the strength of his moral temper that forces him to censure what he wishes to exalt. Williams is passionately committed to the great Romantic dictum inherent in his neo-Lawrentian point of view, that the natural equals the good, that the great natural instincts that well up out of the subconscious depths of men—and particularly the sexual instinct, whatever form it may take—are to be trusted absolutely. But Williams is too strong a moralist, far too permeated with a sense of sin, to be able to accept such an idea with equanimity. However pathetic he may make the martyred homosexual, however seemingly innocent the wandering love-giver, the moral strength that led Williams to punish the guilty Blanche impels him to condemn Brick and Chance. But because he is condemning what he most desires to pardon, he must sometimes, in order to condemn at all, do so with ferocious violence.

When the conflicts among Williams' sympathies are at a minimum, when his morality is clearly focused and has some recognizable relation to one that most men find intelligible, as in *Streetcar*, he is at his best. When, however, his mind is confused, when we cannot tell whether the central figures of his plays are innocent or guilty, as in *Cat*, or when we are asked to believe that the obviously guilty have in some mysterious way retained their innocence, as in *Sweet Bird*, our credulity is strained, and the desperation of the most powerful moral playwright of our time becomes painfully visible.

ESTHER MERLE JACKSON

"Williams and the Lyric Moment"

The Broken World of Tennessee Williams

1965, pp. 26–42

And so it was I entered the broken world
To trace the visionary company of love, its voice
An instant in the wind (I know not whither hurled)
But not for long to hold each desperate choice. [1]

This quotation from the American poet Hart Crane is the epigraph with which Tennessee Williams introduces the play often judged as his masterwork. In these lines, which are inscribed on the frontispiece of *A Streetcar Named Desire*, Williams provides an appropriate point of departure for a discussion of his idea of form. For the words embody a concept of artistic imitation, an appropriate definition of his form. Williams, like Crane, is concerned with the reality of a "broken world."[2] Form in his drama is the imitation of the individual search for a way of redeeming a shattered universe. [3]

Thus Williams may not properly be described as a realist. Both his concept of reality and his mode of imitation reject certain fundamental realist principles. There is greater justification for regarding him as a romantic, for a study of his work shows that his indebtedness to romantic sources—to Shakespeare, Goethe, Wagner, and the symbolist poets of the late nineteenth and early twentieth centuries—is considerable. Moreover, much of Williams' pattern of figuration is romantic in quality, especially in its preoccupation with hallucinatory levels of experience: with gargoyles, monsters, and the dark-in-light patterns which Victor Hugo described as *grotesque*. Williams, who often describes himself as a romantic, is concerned with poetic paradox—with light in dark, good within evil, body against soul, God and Satan. His dramatic form, like that discussed by Hegel, represents the struggle of man to transcend his humanity, to provide for himself a mode of reconciliation with divine purpose. [4] But Williams' form is also of expressionistic lineage. Like the objective expressionists—notably Wassily Kandinsky—the playwright is concerned with the objectification of subjective vision, with its transformation into concrete symbols. [5] Indeed, one of the most important aspects of Williams' dramaturgy derives from this motive. Like the objective expressionists, the playwright regards art as one of the great life forms, as an instrument of reconciliation no less important than religion, philosophy, politics, or human love.

The search for a concrete expressive form—a shape congruent with poetic vision—is a motif that appears throughout the work of Williams. It is the central theme of *The Glass Menagerie*. Similarly, it is an important aspect of dramatic development in the middle works: *A Streetcar Named Desire*, *Summer and Smoke*, *Cat on a Hot Tin Roof*, *Camino Real*, and *Orpheus Descending*. It is a more obscure element of action in *The Rose Tattoo* and *Sweet Bird of Youth.* In *The Night of the Iguana*, Williams emphasizes again this lyric theme: his search for truth and meaning within the moment of poetic vision. In this late drama he gives expression to the complete cycle of poetic search. He states this theme, shows its development, and arrives at a resolution in the poem which his "Tiresias" finishes, appropriately, at the moment of death. The poem, recited in its entirety at the climax of the play, is here quoted in full:

> How calmly does the orange branch
> Observe the sky begin to blanch
> Without a cry, without a prayer,
> With no betrayal of despair.
>
> Sometime while night obscures the tree
> The zenith of its life will be
> Gone past forever, and from thence
> A second history will commence.
>
> A chronicle no longer gold,
> A bargaining with mist and mould,
> And finally the broken stem
> The plummeting to earth; and then
>
> An intercourse not well designed
> For beings of a golden kind
> Whose native green must arch above
> The earth's obscene, corrupting love.
>
> And still the ripe fruit and the branch
> Observe the sky begin to blanch
> Without a cry, without a prayer,
> With no betrayal of despair.
>
> O Courage, could you not as well
> Select a second place to dwell,
> Not only in that golden tree
> But in the frightened heart of me?[6]

Williams describes his elemental form as "personal lyricism." In an essay called "Person to Person," he defines personal lyricism as "The outcry of prisoner to prisoner from the cell in solitary where each is confined for the duration of his life."[7] The dramatist describes the human condition as a state of metaphysical loneliness. He writes of life,

> It is a lonely idea, a lonely condition, so terrifying to think of that we usually don't. And so we talk to each other, write and wire each other, call each other short and long distance across land and sea, clasp hands with each other at meeting and at parting, fight each other and even destroy each other because of this always somewhat thwarted effort to break through walls to each other. As a character in a play once said, "We're all of us sentenced to solitary confinement inside our own skins." (Preface to *Cat on a Hot Tin Roof*, p. vi)

Like other contemporaries, Williams perceives in the human condition a constant threat of diminution. He speaks of this corrosive influence in the introduction to *The Rose Tattoo:*

> It is this continual rush of time, so violent that it appears to be screaming, that deprives our actual lives of so much dignity and meaning, and it is, perhaps more than anything else, the *arrest of time* which has taken place in a completed work of art that gives to certain plays their feeling of depth and significance. . . . Contemplation is something that exists outside of time, and so is the tragic sense. . . . If the world of a play did not offer us this occasion to view its characters under that special condition of a *world without time*, then, indeed, the characters and occurrences of drama would become equally pointless, equally trivial, as corresponding meetings and happenings in life.[8]

It is clear here, as in other instances in the dramatist's critical analyses, that Williams hopes to extract from art a truth greater than that ordinarily apprehensible in life. The central problem of his anti-realist dramaturgy is how to reconstitute felt experience in such a manner as to reveal—or to create—absolute truth.

This problem is explored in the short verse drama, *The Purification.* Here the playwright dramatizes the conflict which the poet experiences as he struggles to give concrete form to vision. In the following lines, the Son, the poet-figure, speaks of his frustration, of the insufficiency of his technique:

> The truth?
> Why ask me for that?
> Ask it of him, the player—
> for truth is something alluded to in music.
> But words are too loosely woven to catch it in . . .
> A bird can be snared as it rises
> or torn to earth by the falcon.
> His song, which is truth,
> is not to be captured ever.
> It is an image, a dream,
> it is the link to the mother,
> the belly's rope that dropped our bodies from God
> a longer time ago than we remember![9]

But the problem of the lyric form, as defined by Williams, is not merely one of technique. In *Camino Real* he draws a portrait of a poet who has "sold" his art and in consequence lost his power of vision. The decadent "Lord Byron" speaks of the cessation of "celestial music":

> —That was my vocation once upon a time, before it was obscured by vulgar plaudits!—Little by little it was lost among gondolas and palazzos!— . . .
>
> . . . Oh, I wrote many cantos in Venice and Constantinople and in Ravenna and Rome, on all of those Latin and Levantine excursions that my twisted foot led me into—but I wonder about them a little. They seem to improve as the wine in the bottle—dwindles . . . *There is a passion for declivity in this world!*
>
> And lately I've found myself listening to hired musicians behind a row of artificial palm trees—instead of the single—pure-stringed instrument of my heart . . .
>
> Well, then, it's time to leave here!— . . .
>
> —There is a time for departure even when there's no certain place to go!
>
> I'm going to look for one, now. I'm sailing to Athens. At least I can look up at the Acropolis, I can stand at the foot of it and look up at broken columns on the crest of a hill—if not purity, at least its recollection . . .
>
> I can sit quietly looking for a long, long time in absolute silence, and possibly, yes, *still* possibly—The old pure music will come to me again. . . .[10]

In his concept of form, then, Williams recapitulates certain ideas drawn from the romantic tradition. Particularly, he follows the romantics in ascribing to art the ability to mediate between dark drives and luminous truth, between body and soul.[11] Like the romantics, he assigns the function of revelation—the disclosure of absolute knowledge—to the artist. This aspect of his theory of form finds perhaps its most illuminating discussion in the writings of Henri Bergson. Bergson wrote in his famous essay *Laughter:*

> What is the object of art? Could reality come into direct contact with sense and consciousness, could we enter into immediate communion with things and with ourselves, probably art would be useless, or rather we should all be artists. . . . So art, whether it be painting or sculpture, poetry or music, has no other object than to brush aside the utilitarian symbols, the conventional and socially accepted generalities, in short, everything that veils reality from us, in order to bring us face to face with reality itself.[12]
>
> Hence it follows that art always aims at what is *individual.* What the artist fixes on his canvas is something he has seen at a certain spot, on a certain day, at a certain hour, with a coloring that will never be seen again. What the poet sings of is a certain mood which was his, and his alone, and which will never return. What the dramatist unfolds before us is the life-history of a soul, a living tissue of feelings and events—something, in short, which has once happened and can never be repeated. We may, indeed, give general names to these feelings, but they cannot be the same thing in another soul. They are *individualized.* Thereby, and thereby only, do they belong to art.[13]

Williams conceives drama in such individualized terms. Each of his plays takes the shape of a vision proceeding from the consciousness of the protagonist. In *The Glass Menagerie,* the play represents the memory of the hero, while in *A Streetcar Named Desire* the spectator observes the "Elysian Fields" as it appears to the troubled mind of Blanche. *Cat on a Hot Tin Roof* is approached from the angle of vision belonging to Brick; *Summer and Smoke* through the eyes of Alma; and *Camino Real* through the dreams of Don Quixote. Williams employs varied rationales to account for the angle of distortion in these visions. His interpretative devices—memory, insanity, intoxication, dreams, and death—do not, however, invalidate the acute perception of the protagonist. For, like Shakespeare, Williams seeks to provide a way through which the spectator may be alienated from the "false" world of appearances and induced to share the discovery—or creation—of a world of eternal truth. In the prologue to *The Glass Menagerie,* the poet-figure explains to the spectator: "Yes, I have tricks in my pocket, I have things up my sleeve. But I am the opposite of a stage magician. He gives you illusion that has the appearance of truth. I give you truth in the pleasant disguise of illusion."[14] Through the playwright's intermediaries, the "fevered visions" of life pass before the spectator and metamorphose into images embodying a greater meaning than does the experience which they are intended to interpret.

If Williams is indebted to the romantic and postromantic traditions for some aspects of his personal lyricism, there are other factors which differentiate his work from that of earlier dramatists. For he is specifically concerned with the interpretation of those crises—inner and outer—which attend the human condition in the world of today. His basic perspective at this point shows fundamental correspondences to those of other contemporaries. Jean-Paul Sartre, in an essay on the theatre in France, has written that it is the responsibility of the drama to help modern man to discern the ultimate significance of his own life. Sartre contends that it is the specific function of the theatre to provide an appropriate structure for moral exploration, to create a form in which the human dilemma—in its present dimensions—may be given vivid exposition:

> For them [the playwrights] man is not to be defined as a "reasoning animal," or a "social" one, but as a free being, entirely indeterminate, who must choose his own being when confronted with certain necessities, such as being already committed in a world full of both threatening and favorable factors among other men who have made their choices before him, who have decided in advance the meaning of those factors. He is faced with the necessity of having to work and die, of being hurled into a life already complete which yet is his own enterprise and in which he can never have a second chance; where he must play his cards and take risks no matter what the cost. That is why we feel the urge to put on the stage certain situations which throw light on the main aspects of the condition of man and to have the spectator participate in the free choice which man makes in these situations.[15]

Williams' comment on this question, though more poetic in its language, nevertheless contains much of the same content:

> The great and only possible dignity of man lies in his power deliberately to choose certain moral values by which to live as steadfastly as if he, too, like a character in a play, were immured against the corrupting rush of time. Snatching the eternal out of the desperately fleeting is the great magic trick of human existence. As far as we know, as far as there exists any kind of empiric evidence, there is no way to beat the game of *being* against *non-being,* in which non-being is the predestined victor on realistic levels. (Preface to *The Rose Tattoo,* p. ix)

Williams and Sartre reflect, in this instance, much the same point of view, a fact which may be traced to the presence of similarities in perspective among all dramatists in the contemporary group. For both the philosophically oriented European drama and the poetically biased American kind share a concept of form as the imitation of a moment of critical insight, a moment alienated from human time. While Sartre presumes the explication and indeed the perception of such a moment to be primarily rational in nature, O'Neill, Saroyan, Miller, and Williams interpret this instant of knowing in more poetic terms. Williams describes the lyric moment, the subject of his poetic vision, in these terms: "In a play, time is arrested in the sense of being confined. By a sort of legerdemain, events are made to remain *events,* rather than being reduced so quickly to mere *occurrences.* The audience can sit back in a comforting dusk to watch a world which is flooded with light and in which emotion and action have a dimension and dignity that they would likewise have in real existence, if only the shattering intrusion of time could be locked out."[16] It is clear that the reality which Williams seeks to imitate does not, in its entirety, correspond to that which appears in the drama of the nineteenth-century romantics. For the drama of Williams is concerned with a far more ambiguous truth.[17]

The romantics, despite their predilection toward revolt, posited an ideal universe which rested on an unmoved power—a power Hegel called "God." Goethe threatened Faust with damnation for his envy of divine power and knowledge. The celebration of a revolutionary individualism in *Sturm und Drang* did not displace the romantic belief in a pre-existent order in the universe. Even Wagner, in his discussion of form, identifies in reality fixed entities such as religion, state, individual, and nature; he defines human experience in terms of ideals such as passion, imagination, and hate.[18] The romantics did not, then, even in their recognition of a dynamic element in experience, deny the presence of an essentially static order in the moral universe. Of the romantics, apparently only Nietzsche could conceive of a truly unsystematized existence. Indeed, Nietzsche, filled with Faustian envy of the Creator, sought to conceive a kind of art which should usurp divine power and create new universes superior to existent forms.

Williams, like Nietzsche, is inclined to challenge the pre-established reality of romantic description. He rejects, moreover, many of the fundamental principles which underlie the romantic theory of image-making. Rather, he is concerned with the creation of an art which is superior to and often in contradiction to known reality. Like the expressionists, Williams regards form as abstraction, as a dynamic structure suspended in metaphysical time and space. He writes of such a form in the preface to *Camino Real:*

> The color, the grace and levitation, the structural pattern in motion, the quick interplay of live beings, suspended like fitful lightning in a cloud, these things are the play, not words on paper, nor thought and ideas of an author. . . . (Afterword, p. xii)
>
> A convention of the play is existence outside of time in a place of no specific locality. . . . (Foreword, p. viii)
>
> My desire was to give these audiences my own sense of something wild and unrestricted that ran like water in the mountains, or clouds changing shape in a gale, or the continually dissolving and transforming images of a dream. This sort of freedom is not chaos nor anarchy. On the contrary, it is the result of painstaking design, and in this work I have given more conscious attention to form and construction than I have in any work before. . . . (Foreword, p. ix)

This idea of image-making poses a difficult question which must also be raised in regard to the claims of the expressionists: Can form actually be created? Must not form correspond to some aspect of experience, or to the poet's faculties of knowing? Certainly it would seem logical to suggest that Williams, even in *Camino Real*, has drawn from some phase of experience. The solution to this critical dilemma seems to rest in the playwright's poetic intent. For the images created by Williams are not conceived as copies of any known reality. If there is a nature, a state, an individual, a reality, a truth, or a God in the universe of Williams, it has been derealized. For Williams, reality itself lies shattered. In the fragmentary world of his theatre, new images are pieced together from partialities: they are composed from splinters of broken truths.

The playwright describes this fragmented world imperfectly reflected in his "dark mirror":

> For the sins of the world are really only its partialities, its incompletions. . . . A wall that has been omitted from a house because the stones were exhausted . . . —these sorts of incompletions are usually covered up or glossed over by some kind of make-shift arrangements. The nature of man is full of such make-shift arrangements, devised by himself to cover his incompletion. He feels a part of himself to be like a missing wall or a room left unfurnished and he tries as well as he can to make up for it.[19]

Clearly, then, the images which appear in the theatre of Williams are not records of events; nor are they symbols drawn intact from the stream of consciousness. For the playwright has subjected his lyric moment to process. In his theatre, the instant of vision has been re-created: its image has been enlarged and enhanced.

Williams uses, as the symbolic instrumentation of his imagemaking, the "eye" of the motion picture camera.[20] His images are composed as by montage; that is, they are made up, after the manner of cinematic technique, by the superimposition of figures one upon the other. This technique, introduced into contemporary literature by James Joyce, appears also in the work of other American dramatists, notably in that of Eugene O'Neill and Thornton Wilder. It has, in addition, been employed by a number of French dramatists, including Apollinaire, Jean Giraudoux, and Paul Claudel, as well as by Picasso, Cocteau, and their friends, in that delightful charade *Parade.*[21] Like these dramatists, Williams uses his camera eye sensitively. With it he is able to arrest time, to focus upon the details of his vision, to emphasize elements of its structural composition, to vary his point of view, and to draw a wide variety of parallels.

An example of this camera technique may be seen in an early play, *This Property Is Condemned*, a cinematographic essay on the life of a deprived child. In this work Williams follows his conventional pattern of articulating a key image. He gives sensible form to the poetic universe of the play:

> SCENE: *A railroad embankment on the outskirts of a small Mississippi town on one of those milky white winter mornings peculiar to that part of the country. The air is moist and chill. Behind the low embankment of the tracks is a large yellow frame house which has a look of tragic vacancy. Some of the upper windows are boarded, a portion of the roof has fallen away. The land is utterly flat. In the left background is a billboard that says "GIN WITH JAKE" and there are some telephone poles and a few bare winter trees. The sky is a great milky whiteness: crows occasionally make a sound of roughly torn cloth. (In* 27 Wagons Full of Cotton, *p. 197)*

Here Williams has created an image after the manner of the surrealist painters. In this dream-world, with its death symbols, he places a grotesque figure, the child Willie. He describes her in these words:

> *The girl Willie is advancing precariously along the railroad track, balancing herself with both arms outstretched, one clutching a banana, the other an extraordinarily dilapidated doll with a frowsy blond wig.*
>
> *She is a remarkable apparition—thin as a beanpole and dressed in outrageous cast-off finery. She wears a long blue velvet party dress with a filthy cream lace collar and sparkling rhinestone beads. On her feet are battered silver kid slippers with large ornamental buckles. Her wrists and her fingers are resplendent with dimestore jewelry. She has applied rouge to her childish face in artless crimson daubs and her lips are made up in a preposterous Cupid's bow. She is about thirteen and there is something ineluctably childlike and innocent in her appearance despite the makeup. She laughs frequently and wildly and with a sort of precocious, tragic abandon.* (Page 197)

It is clear that this world of the play is a carefully devised reconstruction of poetic vision. The playwright is concerned with the evocation of a single image. In the twenty minutes or so which make up the playing time, only one other character appears. When the child departs from the stage, no event has taken place, no changes have been made in her life, no information has been given which was not evident upon her appearance. The play exists only to reveal to the spectator a vision of the distorted world in which the child lives. Each element in the scene has been chosen for its symbolic value. The railroad embankment, with its bare trees and singing crows, is as bereft of humanity as the child—a dilapidated doll. Her attempts to clothe her nakedness with baubles remind us of Shakespeare's Lear.

The dramatist follows this same general pattern of image-making in his longer works. Each of the plays represents an attempt to give exposition to poetic vision. Each play is composed like a poem: the dramatist spins out symbolic figures which are its lyric components. *A Streetcar Named Desire* is composed of eleven theatrical images. *Summer and Smoke* has a like number. *Camino Real* is divided into sixteen scenes. *Orpheus Descending* has nine. Some plays, such as *The Rose Tattoo, Cat on a Hot Tin Roof, Suddenly Last Summer,* and *Sweet Bird of Youth,* do not appear at first glance to be composed of such poetic components. Beneath the apparently continuous flow of action, however, a similar structural design may be found. For Williams, the play is an ordered progression of concrete images, images which together give sensible shape to the lyric moment.

The effectiveness of this technique of explication may be measured by the revisions which the playwright was to make in an early work, *Battle of Angels.* This work, which failed in a professional tryout in 1940, was returned to the stage in 1957 as *Orpheus Descending.* A study of the structural alterations made by Williams is enlightening. The playwright seems to have revised the work by adapting its themes to the more complex method of image-making which he had, by 1945, fully developed. *Orpheus Descending* explores the same themes as did *Battle of Angels.* Moreover, it retains most of the same characters. It does not, however, represent the same quality of imitation. For in *Orpheus Descending* Williams gains dramatic power by allowing his symbols to connote many of the contents to which he gave extended explanation in the earlier work. In this way, many of his observations about the depravity and bestiality of life are absorbed into the text at more tolerable levels of apprehension.

Williams plotted his later version to parallel the legendary account of Orpheus' descent into Hell. He describes the death of his Eurydice—Lady Torrance—in a grotesque fertility ritual, a dance of death in life:

> *[In a sort of delirium she thrusts the conical gilt paper hat on her head and runs to the foot of the stairs with the paper horn. She blows the horn over and over, grotesquely mounting the stairs, as* VAL *tries to stop her. She breaks away from him and runs up to the landing, blowing the paper horn and crying out:]* I've won, I've won, Mr. Death, I'm going to bear! *[Then suddenly she falters, catches her breath in a shocked gasp and awkwardly retreats to the stairs. Then turns screaming and runs back down them, her cries dying out as she arrives at the floor level. She retreats haltingly as a blind person, a hand stretched out to* VAL, *as slow, clumping footsteps and hoarse breathing are heard on the stairs. She moans:]*—Oh, God, oh—God. . . .[22]

One of the most effective illustrations of Williams' concept of "personal lyricism" is *The Glass Menagerie.* This play, still a favorite of American audiences, players, and critics alike, shows Williams' lyric technique in a lighter tone than does *A Streetcar Named Desire.* Although these plays show differences in textural quality—and in coloration—the architectonic pattern in both is much the same. In *The Glass Menagerie,* as in the later work, Williams has ordered his vision in a clear and highly schematic design. In the opening moments of the play, Tom—the poet-figure—speaks to the audience of the conventions which will be observed as the phantoms of his memory are projected before the spectator:

> (MUSIC)
> The play is memory.
> Being a memory play, it is dimly lighted, it is sentimental, it is not realistic.
> In memory everything seems to happen to music. That explains the fiddle in the wings.
> I am the narrator of the play, and also a character in it.
> The other characters are my mother, Amanda, my sister, Laura, and a gentleman caller who appears in the final scenes.
> He is the most realistic character in the play, being an emissary from a world of reality that we were somehow set apart from.
> But since I have a poet's weakness for symbols, I am using this character also as a symbol; he is the long delayed but always expected something that we live for. (Scene I, p. 5)

Clearly this play is not a factual record of memory; that is, *The Glass Menagerie* is not "automatic writing." Nor is it a psychological account, the clinical record of days. On the contrary, it is a synthetic image, a vision carefully composed by montage. It is an illusion projected by an imaginary camera eye, turned inward upon the self and backward upon the memory. Like Proust, Williams pieces together his images of the past from the fragments of shattered consciousness. The image which he composes in *The Glass Menagerie* is a figure made of diverse perspectives.[23] In essence, this play represents a recapitulation of the poetic journey. The poet-figure Tom invites the spectator to share with him the task of finding meaning in past experience. His final speech in the play summarizes his grasp of universal truth. As Laura blows out her candle, the poet speaks:

> I didn't go to the moon, I went much further—for time is the longest distance between two places—
> Not long after that I was fired for writing a poem on the lid of a shoe-box.
> I left Saint Louis. I descended the steps of this fire-escape for a last time and followed, from then on, in my father's footsteps, attempting to find in motion what was lost in space—
> I traveled around a great deal. The cities swept about me like dead leaves, leaves that were brightly colored but torn away from the branches.
> I would have stopped, but I was pursued by something.
> It always came upon me unawares, taking me altogether by surprise. Perhaps it was a familiar bit of music. Perhaps it was only a piece of transparent glass—
> Perhaps I am walking along a street at night, in some strange city, before I have found companions. I pass the lighted window of a shop where perfume is sold. The window is filled with pieces of colored glass, tiny transparent bottles in delicate colors, like bits of a shattered rainbow.
> Then all at once my sister touches my shoulder. I turn around and look into her eyes . . .
> Oh, Laura, Laura, I tried to leave you behind me, but I am more faithful than I intended to be!
> I reach for a cigarette, I cross the street, I run into the movies or a bar, I buy a drink, I speak to the

nearest stranger—anything that can blow your candles out!
(LAURA *bends over the candles.)*
—for nowadays the world is lit by lightning! Blow out your candles, Laura—and so good-bye. . . .
(She blows the candles out.)
THE SCENE DISSOLVES
(Curtain Speech, pp. 123–24)

In *The Glass Menagerie*, then, there is little if any action in the Aristotelian sense; that is, there is in this vision no strict pattern of causal development, from beginning to end. For in the lyric moment, action is aesthetic; it is the growth of understanding. Through his poet-figure, the dramatist invites the spectator to share his fragmentary vision, to re-create his incomplete understanding, and to reflect upon a partial truth about the nature of all human experience. Throughout the fabric of his subsequent work, Williams retains this basic form. At some point in his writing, however, he decided that this drama of "personal lyricism" was too limited an expressive form.[24] The major development of the period immediately following the appearance of *The Glass Menagerie* was the emergence of a second level of dramatic exposition. Above the level of his lyric form, Williams erected an interpretative "scaffold." The plays written after 1945 increasingly show the presence of a kind of superstructure; a rational schema designed to interpret the moment of vision in the language of reason.

Notes

1. The quotation is from a poem by Hart Crane, "The Broken Tower," which appears in *The Collected Poems of Hart Crane* (New York, 1933), pp. 135–36.
2. In his preface to *Miss Julie* (in *Six Plays of Strindberg*, trans. Elizabeth Sprigge [Garden City, NY, 1955], p. 65), Strindberg gave a similar definition. He wrote: "My souls (characters) are conglomerations of past and present stages of civilization, bits from books and newspapers, scraps of humanity, rags and tatters of fine clothing, patched together as is the human soul."
3. The later expressionists, of course, attempted to create such a symbol from shattered images. Herbert Read describes their synthetic image as "constructive." See his discussion of image-making in *The Philosophy of Modern Art* (New York, 1952), pp. 47–48.
4. Certain elements of Williams' theory parallel those of the romantic aestheticians. See Georg W. F. Hegel, *"Lectures on Aesthetics"* in *The Philosophy of Hegel*, trans. Bernard Bosanquet and William Bryant (New York, 1953). A particularly pertinent passage reads as follows (p. 358):

   Thus, spiritual reconciliation is to be conceived and represented only as an activity, a movement of the spirit—as a process in the course of which there arises a struggle, a conflict; and the pain, the death, the agony of nothingness, the torment of the spirit and of materiality *(Leiblichkeit)* make their appearance as essential moments or elements. For as, in the next place, God separates or distinguishes *(ausscheidet)* finite actuality from Himself, so also finite man, who begins with himself as outside the divine kingdom, assumes the task of elevating himself to God, of freeing himself from the finite, of doing away with nugatoriness, and of becoming, through this sacrifice *(Ertödten)* of his immediate actuality, that which God, in His appearance as man, has made objective as true actuality.
5. See, for example, the discussion of this principle in the theory of Paul Klee (*The Inward Vision: Watercolors, Drawings, Writings*, trans. Norbert Guterman [New York, 1958]), pp. 6–10.
6. *The Night of the Iguana* (New York, 1962), Act III, pp. 123–24.
7. Preface to *Cat on a Hot Tin Roof* (New York, 1955), p. vi.
8. Preface to *The Rose Tattoo* (New York, 1951), pp. vi–vii.
9. 27 *Wagons Full of Cotton* (Norfolk, CT, 1946), p. 40.
10. *Camino Real* (Norfolk, CT, 1953), Block VIII, pp. 77–78.
11. See Nietzsche, *The Birth of Tragedy* and *The Genealogy of Morals*, trans. Francis Golffing (Garden City, New York, 1956). Williams, like Nietzsche, sees in experience a conflict between the claims of the life force and the impulse toward abstract knowledge.
12. Henri Bergson, *Laughter* trans. Cloudesley Brereton and Fred Rothwell (New York, 1911), pp. 150–57.
13. Ibid., p. 161.
14. *The Glass Menagerie* (New York, 1945), Scene I, pp. 4–5.
15. Jean-Paul Sartre, "Forgers of Myth," *Theatre Arts*, XXV (June, 1946), 325; reprinted by permission of *Theatre Arts* Magazine.
16. Preface to *The Rose Tattoo*, pp. viii–ix.
17. The playwright articulates some tenets of his system of image-building in the Preface to *Camino Real*.
18. See Richard Wagner, *Opera and Drama*, trans. Edwin Evans (London, 1913), I, 317–96.
19. "Desire and the Black Masseur," in *One Arm and Other Stories* (Norfolk, CT, 1948), p. 85.
20. Many artists, including Hart Crane, have been convinced that there is, operating in contemporary symbol-making, a "machine aesthetic." Williams, like Joyce, Eliot, and Pound—and like plastic artists such as Léger—seems to create such "synthetic" symbols: to invent shapes and forms out of the fusion of organic elements. The great film artist Sergei Eisenstein discussed this technique in modern art. He claimed, for example, that Joyce was aware of using the cinematic technique of montage. See Sergei Eisenstein, *The Film Sense*, trans. Jay Leyda (New York, 1947), p. 17. Arthur Miller also discusses the use of the camera eye in his Introduction to *Collected Plays* (New York, 1957), pp. 23–26.
21. *Parade*, produced in 1917 by Picasso, Cocteau, and Erik Satie, was intended as an example of theatrical montage.
22. *Orpheus Descending* (New York, 1958) Scene III, p. 114.
23. *The Glass Menagerie*, Production Notes, pp. ix–xii.
24. Preface to *Cat on a Hot Tin Roof*, p. vi.

RUBY COHN
From "The Garrulous Grotesques of Tennessee Williams"
Dialogue in American Drama
1971, pp. 97–102, 121–29

The last plays of Eugene O'Neill were produced after World War II; the first plays of Arthur Miller and Tennessee Williams were produced after World War II. Though Miller and Williams, strain, like O'Neill, toward tragedy, each of them early settled into his own idiom, little tempted by O'Neill's restless experimentation. Since Miller and Williams dominated a decade of American theater, their names have often been coupled, if only for contrast. The British critic Kenneth Tynan wrote of them: "Miller's plays are hard, 'patrist,' athletic, concerned mostly with men. Williams's are soft, 'matrist,' sickly, concerned mostly with women. What links them is their love for the bruised individual soul and its life of 'quiet desperation.'"[1] What also links them is the dramaturgy whereby those souls are bruised; not at all quiet in their desperation, these victim-souls indulge in language to evoke our pity. The most effective dialogue of Miller often relies on his Jewish background, whereas that of Williams leans on his Southern background.

Always expansive, Williams has written many more plays than Miller, but they do not all deserve close attention. Williams often reuses the same materials—phrase, theme, scene, or character. Williams himself acknowledged: "My longer plays emerge out of earlier one-acters or short stories I may have written years before. I work over them again and again."[2] Consistently, Williams reworks by expansion, and comparison of the short works with the longer plays illuminates his focus on dialogue of pathos.

The Glass Menagerie, Williams' first popular play, emerged in several stages from a fifteen-page short story, written in the early 1940's but not published until 1948.[3] In dramatizing the story, Williams wrote four, perhaps five, versions. A one-act play may have preceded a movie scenario called *The Gentleman Caller*, which was submitted to MGM in 1943. Subsequently, Williams wrote a five-scene, sixty-page play, twenty-one pages of which were incorporated into a seven-scene, hundred-and-five page typescript (now in the University of Virginia library). This last manuscript became the so-called "reading version" of *The Glass Menagerie*, and it is better known than the final eight-scene revision, first staged in 1944.

The original short story, "Portrait of a Girl in Glass," contains four characters—the narrator Tom, his nameless mother, his sister Laura, and a red-headed Irishman named Jim Delaney. The first half of the story is largely expository, but the second half is the kernel of the Gentleman Caller scenes of the dramatic versions. In the story, Laura is not lame, but she has withdrawn so deeply into her private world that she is not quite sane. In the story, Laura and Jim share no high school past, but, because he has freckles, she equates him with the freckled, one-armed orphan in a novel by Gene Stratton Porter—as real to her as her St. Louis apartment. In "Portrait of a Girl in Glass," Laura "covered the walls with shelves of little glass articles," but the articles have no particular shape. As in Williams' subsequent dramas, Tom brings Jim to dinner, but Laura does not show him her glass collection. As in the dramatic versions, Laura and Jim dance after dinner, but they scarcely converse; Laura's entire dialogue is: "Oh—you have freckles! . . . Freckles? . . . What?"

The most sustained dialogue of the short story begins with the interruption of Laura's mother:

> "Good heavens! Laura? Dancing?"
>
> Her look was absurdly grateful as well as startled.
>
> "But isn't she stepping all over you, Mr. Delaney?"
>
> "What if she does?" said Jim, with bearish gallantry. "I'm not made of eggs!"
>
> "Well, well, well!" said Mother, senselessly beaming.
>
> "She's light as a feather!" said Jim. "With a little more practice she'd dance as good as Betty!"
>
> There was a little pause of silence.
>
> "Betty?" said Mother.
>
> "The girl I go out with!" said Jim.
>
> "Oh!" said Mother.
>
> She set the pitcher of lemonade carefully down and with her back to the caller and her eyes on me, she asked him just how often he and the lucky young lady went out together.
>
> "Steady!" said Jim.
>
> Mother's look, remaining on my face, turned into a glare of fury.
>
> "Tom didn't mention that you went out with a girl!"
>
> "Nope," said Jim. "I didn't mean to let the cat out of the bag. The boys at the warehouse'll kid me to death when Slim gives the news away."
>
> He laughed heartily but his laughter dropped heavily and awkwardly away as even his dull senses were gradually penetrated by the unpleasant sensation the news of Betty had made.
>
> "Are you thinking of getting married?" said Mother.
>
> "First of next month!" he told her.
>
> It took several moments to pull herself together. Then she said in a dismal tone, "How nice! If Tom had only told us we could have asked you *both!*"

The story's climactic revelation is softened in the play—Jim first reveals his engagement to Laura, and then, separately, to Amanda, so that we watch the effect on each of them. Laura is almost wordless as she gives Jim the broken glass unicorn—"A—souvenir." But Amanda nags Tom so vociferously that he leaves the family shortly afterwards. Williams has expanded the story to evoke our compassion for all four characters.

As Williams developed the Gentleman Caller incident from story to short play, and then again to full-length play, he had room to intensify the pathos. Except for a residual "Freckles" in the reading version, Laura no longer identifies Jim with the Gene Stratton Porter character; she no longer reads to escape from reality. No longer "foolish" as in the story, Laura appeals to us by her fragility—lameness, pleurosis, and pathological shyness. Though Amanda refuses to use the word "crippled," Laura faces that reality about herself. She talks to Jim about "clumping up the aisle with everyone watching" even as we have watched her clump around the stage. Because she is lame, the dancing scene is poignant. But Williams also bends her few sentences to evoke our pity, and he emphasizes the glass menagerie—both verbally and theatrically—to show Laura's pathos.

As far back as high school, sensitive Laura was attracted to worldly Jim. Neither a gentleman nor a caller on Laura, the "gentleman caller" mouths clichés of practicality and progress, but his actual career has been a constant retrogression from its high school pinnacle. At the warehouse, Jim evidently uses Tom to recall his high school glory, and in the apartment Jim audibly uses Laura to bolster his sagging self-confidence. Reduced to stale jokes, sports reports, and makeshift psychology, Jim boasts: "I'm not made of glass." (as opposed to the story's less pointed: "I'm not made of eggs!"). However, we can read his fragility through his veneer of psychology, electrodynamics, and public speaking. While dancing with Laura, Jim bumps into a table, breaking the horn of Laura's glass unicorn. As even Jim knows, unicorns are "extinct in the modern world." In the remainder of the scene, Jim virtually breaks Laura, a girl in glass, who lives on imagination and is therefore almost extinct in the modern world. After Jim pays attention to Laura with well-worn clichés—"I'm glad to see that you have a sense of humor." "Did anybody ever tell you that you were pretty?" "I'm talking to you sincerely."—after he kisses her, he reveals that he will not call again because he is engaged to Betty. By the time Amanda intrudes upon the intimacy of Laura and Jim, the brief romance is over. Vulnerable as Jim is in the wider world, he has been injurious to the world of the glass menagerie. The Gentleman Caller of the old South has been replaced by a pathetic shipping clerk of industrial St. Louis, and even he has other allegiances.

More complex than either Jim or Laura, Tom evolves considerably from the narrator of the short story. Designated as a poet in the final version of the play, Tom carries Williams' lyric flights, his verbal creation of atmosphere, and his ironic commentary upon the action. Unlike Wilder's State Manager, Tom remains a character in his own right—fond of his sister, ambiguous about his mother, and eager to follow in his father's escapist footsteps. As Laura is symbolized by her glass unicorn, Tom is symbolized by his movies, which we know only through dialogue. He explains movies to his mother as sublimated adventure, but by the time Jim comes to the house, Tom is tired of vicarious adventures: "People go to the *movies* instead of *moving*. . . . I'm tired of the movies and I'm about to move!" Tom's final speech tells us how far he had moved, and yet he has been unable to escape Proustian recollections of his sister, which are inevitably triggered by colored glass or music.

Though Narrator Tom closes *The Glass Menagerie* on our view of Laura blowing out her candles in a world lit by lightning, the stage viability of the play has always rested upon the character of Amanda. No longer the mere martinet of the short story, she possesses as many qualities "to love and pity . . . as to laugh at."[4] She speaks the most distinctive as well as the most extensive dialogue of the play. It is Amanda who names Laura's collection a "glass menagerie," in which animal drives are frozen into esthetic objects, and it is she who longs for gentleman callers in an ungentle world. At once nostalgic about her genteel past and minimally practical about the sordid present, she puncuates her drawling elegance with sharp questions and terse commands. She recalls every detail of the balls of her youth, and she goes into absurd physiological detail about the daily lives, and especially meals, of her children. In the final version of the play, Williams heightens the Southern quality of her speech, increases her use of "honey" to Laura, her nagging of Tom, and her repetitions. The cumulative effect of these final revisions (particularly the added opening lines about her rejection at church) is to endear her to us, and to evoke pity for the garrulous mother, as for the timid daughter.

After the Gentleman Caller leaves, near the end of the play, Amanda accuses Tom: "You live in a dream; you manufacture illusions!" But the play's pathos arises from the illusions manufactured by *all* the characters. Though the glass menagerie is most directly relevant to Laura, all four characters have sublimated their animal drives into esthetics. Laura has her glass animals, Tom his movies and poems, Amanda her jonquil-filled memories distorted into hopes, and Jim his baritone clichés of progress.

The Glass Menagerie has often been called Chekhovian in its atmospheric rendition of a dying aristocracy. As the last scene opens, a blackout pointedly occurs while Jim and Amanda toast the Old South. What dies into darkness, however, is not a class but a frail feminine household, and we do not feel, as in Chekhov's plays, that the household represents a class. In subsequent plays, however, Williams dramatizes various aspects of the disintegration of the Old South. The cumulative effect embraces a dying civilization, which makes its impact through rhythm and imagery.[5] ⟨. . .⟩

Though Williams is often called a poetic playwright, all the plays examined (and most of those not examined) accept the realist convention of psychologically and sociologically coherent characters, grotesque though they may be. These grotesque characters are exceptionally verbal, given to a degree of imagery that is unusual in American realistic drama. In a few of his plays, Williams combines verbal with theatrical imagery to insist upon a symbolic resonance beyond the realistic surface—*Glass Menagerie, Streetcar Named Desire, The Rose Tattoo, The Night of the Iguana.* There is also a more candidly symbolic strain in his playwriting, bordering on allegory. His first excursion into this domain was the short *Ten Blocks on the Camino Real,* revised and expanded in 1953. With modification, Williams continued the non-realistic form in *The Milktrain Doesn't Stop Here Any More* and his two "Slapstick Tragedies." In contrast to their experimental, often expressionistic form, these plays use crisp, colloquial dialogue.

Though five years separate *Ten Blocks on the Camino Real* from the first Broadway production of *Camino Real,* no substantive change occurs. The earlier play is subtitled "A fantasy," and the fantastic elements are increased in the full-length play. The hero in each play is Kilroy, whose name derives from the ubiquitous American soldier of World War II; in Williams' plays, however, he is not a soldier, but an ex-Golden Gloves winner. He speaks in American slang of the 1940's, which contrasts with the more literary locutions of such characters as Marguerite Gautier, Jacques Casanova, Baron de Charlus, a gypsy daughter Esmeralda, Don Quixote, and a sinister Mr. Gutman. In the shorter play, Kilroy appears on seven of the ten blocks; in the longer one, he is present on eleven of the sixteen blocks, his importance steadily increasing as the play progresses. Moreover, a prologue suggests that the entire play is a dream of Don Quixote, and Williams' Expressionistic technique is thus indebted to Strindberg's *Dream Play,* often considered the first Expressionist drama.

A quest play like *The Dream Play, Camino Real* mirrors Kilroy's quest by the separate quests of Jacques Casanova, Proust's Baron de Charlus, Lord Byron, and the arch-dreamer Don Quixote. Trapped in sixteen blocks of no man's land, all these dreamers are rejected from the Royal Way, so that they are compelled to stray on the Real Road—as Williams puns on the Spanish and English meanings of "real." There are three possible exits from this country of fantasy: escape in an airplane appropriately named Fugitivo; bold egress into the desert of the Terra Incognita; death and degradation at the hands of the sinister Streetcleaners who deliver corpses to a medical laboratory. In the diffusion of scenes, action centers on the Camino Real; none of the major characters reaches the Fugitivo, Lord Byron sets out for Terra Incognita, Baron de Charlus falls to the Streetcleaners, and, in his fidelity to Marguerite Gautier, Jacques Casanova will spend eternity shuttling back and forth from Royal Way to Real Road. But Kilroy, ex-champ and ex-Patsy, pure-hearted lover of an ever-renewed Virgin, becomes garbage for the Streetcleaners, guinea pig for the medical students, to be resurrected as the companion to Don Quixote in his venture into Terra Incognita.

Williams summarized the play's theme: "*Camino Real* doesn't say anything that hasn't been said before, but is merely a picture of the state of the romantic non-conformist in modern society. It stresses honor and man's sense of inner dignity which the Bohemian must re-achieve after each period of degradation he is bound to run into. The romantic should have the spirit of anarchy and not let the world drag him down to its level."[6] In the play itself, Esmeralda, the gypsy's daughter, who is a prostitute and always a virgin, utters much the same sentiment in more determinedly colorful idiom: "God bless all con men and hustlers and pitch-men who hawk their hearts on the street, all two-time losers who're likely to lose once more, the courtesan who made the mistake of love, the greatest of lovers crowned with the longest horns, the poet who wandered far from his heart's green country and possibly will and possibly won't be able to find his way back, look down with a smile tonight on the last cavaliers, the ones with the rusty armor and soiled white plumes, and visit with understanding and something that's almost tender those fading legends that come and go in this plaza like songs not clearly remembered, oh, sometime and somewhere, let there by something to mean the word *honor* again!" Not only does the prayer embrace the literary characters of the play, but it uses the clichés of romantic literature—heart, love, green country, armor, plumes, legends, songs, honor. Camille accuses Casanova: "Your vocabulary is almost as out-of-date as your cape and your cane." And the charge can be made against much of Williams' dialogue.

What distinguishes Kilroy, however, is his colloquial innocence in this literary company. Announced as "the Eternal Punchinella," Kilroy arrives with his concrete idiom: "I just got off a boat. Lousiest frigging tub I ever shipped on, one continual hell it was, all the way up from Rio. And me sick, too. I picked up one of those tropical fevers. No sick-bay on that tub, no doctor, no medicine or nothing, not even one quinine pill, and I was burning up with Christ knows how much fever. I couldn't make them understand I was sick. I got a bad heart, too. I had to retire from the prize ring because of my heart. I was the light heavy-weight champion of the West Coast, won these gloves!—before my ticker went bad." More than two decades after the original version of the play, when its staging no longer seems inventive, the play's spine lies in Kilroy's idiom. His slang has dated with his legend, so that Williams' wandering American is a pathetic anachronism, who talks too much, but who endears himself to us because all that talk is a whistling in the dark at the human condition.

Other than Kilroy, only the Gypsy speaks vigorously in the cynical language of commercial enterprise, which has dated less than Kilroy's slang. Before the farcical scene in which the Chosen Hero Kilroy courts the Prostitute Virgin Esmeralda, the Gypsy summarizes the action: "There's nobody left to uphold the old traditions! You raise a girl. She watches television. Plays be-bop. Reads *Screen Secrets*. Comes the Big Fiesta. The moonrise makes her a virgin—which is the neatest trick of the week! And what does she do? Chooses a Fugitive Patsy for the Chosen Hero! Well, show him in! Admit the joker and get the virgin ready!"

As the concreteness of Stanley overwhelms Blanche's esthetic abstractions and clichés, the commercial vigor of the Gypsy and the visual menace of the Streetcleaners overwhelm the ethical abstractions and clichés of the literary characters on Camino Real. But with determined optimism, Williams gives the final inspiring words to Don Quixote, in whose shadow walks Kilroy. Earlier, on Block X, faithful Jacques Casanova had attempted to convince faithless Marguerite Gautier: "The violets in the mountains can break the rocks if you believe in them and allow them to grow!" Though there is no evidence of belief on Marguerite's part, we last see her rising from the bed of her young lover to invite Jacques from Skid Row to her sumptuous hotel. As they embrace, Don Quixote raises his lance to proclaim: *"The violets in the mountains have broken the rocks!"* The old idealist *"goes through the arch with Kilroy."* Clearly, Williams intends triumph for the grotesque Bohemians, in spite of stale slang and stale literary phrases.

As in his more realistic dramas, Williams plays upon a theatrical symbol—the heart. Kilroy's heart is as large as a baby's head, and Kilroy himself calls it a "ticker" in this land where time is running out. Lord Byron describes how Trelawney "snatched the heart of Shelley out of the blistering corpse!" Byron disapproves of Trelawney's action, asking: "What can one man do with another man's heart?" Jacques Casanova responds with passion; speaking for himself and all lovers, he takes a loaf of bread and accompanies his words with actions—twisting, tearing, crushing, and kicking the heart-loaf. By Block XV, Esmeralda has done all this to Kilroy's heart, and he lies dead on a dissecting table. When his heart is removed, it is seen to be the size of a baby's head, and it is made of solid gold. Kilroy rises from the operating table, grabs his heart, and escapes from the laboratory to the loan shark, where he pawns his heart for gifts for Esmeralda—romantic to the last. When she rejects him and the gypsy ejects him, Kilroy joins Don Quixote on Skid Row, with words that summarize the action more truly than the violets in the mountains: "Had for a button! Stewed, screwed and tattooed on the Camino Real! Baptized, finally, with the contents of a slop-jar!—Did anybody say the deal was rugged?!"

Comparable colloquialism is rare in Williams' more realistic plays, but in his most recent work—a combination of realism and fantasy—he has sought a popular idiom, with a minimum of the pretentious images that spring so readily to the lips of his garrulous grotesques. *The Milktrain Doesn't Stop Here Any More* (1963) is based on Williams' short story with a pidgin English title, "Man Bring This Up Road." Though much of the dialogue (as well as the name Sissy Goforth) is transferred intact from story to play, Williams invents tough talk for Sissy, the ex-stripper, even while he underlines the symbolic meaning of the whole. Williams' foreword declares that the play has been "rightly described as an allegory and as a 'sophisticated fairy tale.'" One may quibble at the word "sophisticated," but the allegorical quality is instantly conveyed in the names of the two main characters. The seventy-two-year-old millionairess, Sissy Goforth, is a sissy about going forth from this world, and she herself dwells on the pun of her name: "Sissy Goforth's not ready to go forth yet and won't go forth till she's ready. . . ."

The erstwhile poet, present maker of mobiles, is named Chris Flanders (as opposed to Jimmy Dobyne of the short story). Flanders Field is an obvious association with death in battle, and Chris suggests both Christ and St. Christopher, the patron saint of travelers. Influenced perhaps by the Angel of Death in Albee's *Sandbox*, Williams calls Chris the Angel of Death because he is present at the death of rich dowagers. In spite of these same central characters, however, the play changes the focus of the story. In the latter, Sissy drives the poet out to the oubliette while she plans a big party; in the later work, Chris becomes a kind of ministering angel at the death of Sissy Goforth.

Much more than in the story, the two opposing characters are distinguished by their dialogue; the rebellious cynicism of Sissy is opposed to the calm formality of Chris. Blackie, Sissy's secretary not present in the story, calls Mrs. Goforth a "dying monster," but for all her egotism, Sissy is the most attractive character in the play, because of her determined spit and fire: "Hell, I was born between a swamp and the wrong side of the tracks in One Street, Georgia, but not even that could stop me in my tracks, wrong side or right side, or no side."

Though Chris claims that Sissy and he have reached "the point of no more pretenses," his rhetoric is still pretentious as he affirms that he has ceased to believe in reality, and only human communication can restore that belief. Sissy, on the other hand, does not pretend, admitting candidly that she wants a last love, impecunious though he is, Chris is too proud to perform this office: "I wouldn't have come here unless I thought I was able to serve some purpose or other, in return for a temporary refuge, a place to rest and work in, where I could get back that sense of reality I've been losing lately." A few minutes later, however, Chris admits that he came because, as Sissy phrases it: "You've been tipped off that old Flora Goforth is about to go forth this summer." In a passionate monologue, Sissy denies that she is dying, but she clings to Chris as she dies. Chris assures Sissy's secretary that the end was peaceful.

Between story and play, Williams has shifted sympathy from the young man to the dying dowager. Avoiding the pathetic helplessness of such earlier characters as Laura, Blanche, or even Kilroy, Williams summons our admiring pity for a tough spirit. An older version of Maggie the Cat, and in more desperate straits, Sissy Goforth is imbued with "fierce life." But her life—with the many repetitions of her reluctance to "go forth"—cannot carry the play, whose conflict is diluted by a movie gangster, stage Italian servants, and Kabuki stagehands, none of them bearing any relation to the basic form. In his realistic plays, moreover, Williams' imagery was unusual and sometimes arresting; in such a determinedly experimental play, however, Sissy's tough talk is overwhelmed by Chris' airy platitudes and the visual business on stage. In spite of a striking scene or two—Sissy greeting the Capri Witch, Sissy on the point of death—the various gothic elements are never integrated into a whole.

In his preface to *Slapstick Tragedy*, Williams associates *Glass Menagerie*, *Camino Real*, and these short plays of 1965 as "diversions" which share "experimentation in content and in style, particularly in style." *Glass Menagerie* uses narrator and flashback; *Camino Real* is a fantasy of legendary characters; *Slapstick Tragedy* is composed of two separate short plays, a miracle and a saint's legend. The kind of experimentation changes with the years.

The Mutilated, a miracle play, contains a feud between Celeste Delacroix Griffin, shoplifter and prostitute (that her name belies), and Trinket Dugan, whose breast was amputated. Comic dialogue is heavily based on their need for alcohol, love, and friendship on Christmas Eve. Like the verbal thrusts of the Capri Witch and Sissy Goforth in *The Milktrain*, these two denizens of tawdry Hotel Wonder fling insults at each other. Given Trinket's mutilation, breasts echo through their dialogue. Celeste, proud of her firm symmetry, picks up a scornful metaphor of Sissy Goforth, proud of her own firm symmetry:

> *Sissy:* Some women my age, or younger, 've got breasts that look like a couple of mules hangin' their heads over the top rail of a fence.
>
> *Celeste:* . . . many women past forty or even thirty have boobs like a couple of mules hanging their heads over the top rail of a fence.

By Christmas Day, Trinket Dugan, having felt a lump and pain in her single breast, emerges from being "dug in," and offers hospitality to a destitute Celeste. As the two women, differently mutilated, drink cheap wine, they feel the presence of the Virgin. Suddenly, Trinket loses lump and ache, and the two women kneel in praise, sharing the ecstasy over the miracle, as Christmas Carolers enter singing. From Rotrou to Claudel, playwrights have found that miracles are untractable on stage. In this faithless age, it is hard to share the ecstasy of Williams' mutilated women.

Gnädiges Fräulein is German for the Blessed Virgin, but in Williams' second slapstick tragedy, the name belongs to a grotesque creature who, to gain the attention of a seal-trainer, caught in her mouth fish intended for a trained seal. Gradually, Gnädiges Fräulein has had to catch her fish (traditional symbol for Christ) before less and less distinguished audiences, until she performs on the southernmost Florida Key, in rivalry with the dangerous cocalooney birds. For a change in Williams' work, the play's grotesque protagonist is almost speechless, and we learn about the Gnädiges Fräulein from Molly, the boarding-house keeper, and Polly, a society page columnist. While cocalooney birds and a blonde "erotic dream" of an Indian strut picturesquely on the stage, the two old crones rock our their spiteful gibes. As in *Milktrain*, the religious symbolism is imposed upon a vigorous idiom, but the dialogue lacks development and tension. Like Sissy Goforth, Molly recalls a Dixie Doxie, and like Chris Flanders, the Gnädiges Fräulein loses her sense of reality. This time, however, death does not arrive to restore reality. In the final scene, Molly and Polly have stolen the fish from the blinded Fräulein, and Indian Joe has deserted her to share the fish with the old crones. As the three sinners partake of the fish, the indomitable Fräulein hears the whistle of the fishing-boat, and she *"starts a wild, blind dash for the fish docks."*

Hardly the "wildly idiomatic sort of tragedy" that Williams claims it is, the play does abound in malicious colloquial comedy against which we see the pathos of his most grotesque character, the Gnädiges Fräulein. More than *The Mutilated*, this play uses the slapstick of farce. But the word "tragedy" is wrong for these slight pieces in which grace is granted.

In spite of his prolific output, Tennessee Williams is narrow in range. Most of his plays are set in Southern United States, which he contrives to give an exotic hue. Most of his plays focus on protagonist-victims who manage to combine humor with deformity. Unlike the monosyllabic characters of many American realistic plays, Williams' grotesques are luxuriously loquacious—with incantatory repetitions and self-conscious images. Williams uses set, music, light, rhythm, image to impose symbolic meaning upon his realistic surfaces; the more blatant the symbolism, the more frail the play. Like Tom in *Glass Menagerie*, Williams has "a poet's weakness for symbols." The emphasis should be placed on the word "weakness." Insistence on symbols weakens the dramatic drive of several Williams' plays—*Summer and Smoke*, *The Rose Tattoo*, *Suddenly Last Summer*, *Cat on a Hot Tin Roof*, *Night of the Iguana*, *The Milktrain Doesn't Stop Here Any More*, *Slapstick Tragedy*, and *Kingdom of Earth*. Williams' symbolic imagery is most effective when its weakness is built into the fabric of the drama—the stale nostalgia of Amanda in *Glass Menagerie*, the cultural yearning of Blanche in *Streetcar*, the dated slang of Kilroy in *Camino Real*. In these plays, the inadequacies of Williams' lyricism function thematically and theatrically, to evoke our sympathy for his garrulous grotesques.

As Miller moves a limited step beyond O'Neill in his use of colloquial rhythms and idiom, Williams reacts against O'Neill in his profuse images and relatively complicated syntax. Pithy or lyrical as suits the character, Williams' dialogue endowed the American stage with a new vocabulary and rhythm. Though his lines lack the taut coherence of Southern poets like Ransom or Tate, and though his plots lack the human complexity of Southern novelists like Faulkner, Welty, or O'Connor, Williams gave Southern grotesques dignity on the Broadway stage. Even the farcical *Rose Tattoo* is peopled with giants by comparison with *Tobacco Road*. Though shocking sexuality rather than human warmth may account for his Broadway success, Williams has managed to combine shocking sexuality with human warmth, sometimes in the same play. His major instrument in this combination is distinctive dialogue that embraces nostalgia, frustration, sadness, gaiety, cruelty, and compassion. Like O'Neill and Miller, Williams wrote few organically flawless dramas. He does not often hammer like O'Neill, he does not often preach like Miller, but he too often indulges in gratuitous violence and irrelevant symbol. At his best, however—*Menagerie*, *Streetcar*, first version of *Cat*, *Iguana* and even *Camino Real*—Williams expands American stage dialogue in vocabulary, image, rhythm, and range.

Notes

1. Kenneth Tynan, *Tynan on Theatre* (Baltimore, 1961), 141.
2. "Talk with the Playwright," *Newsweek* (March 23, 1959), 75.
3. Lester A. Beaurline, "*The Glass Menagerie*: From Story to Play," *Modern Drama* (September, 1965), 142–149. Mr. Beaurline kindly allowed me to examine his xerox of the Williams manuscript in the University of Virginia Library.
4. Williams' Introduction to New Directions edition, vii.
5. Cf. Thomas E. Porter, "The Passing of the Old South," in *Myth and Modern American Drama* (Detroit, 1969).
6. Program for the Los Angeles Mark Taper Forum Theater production of *El Camino Real*, n.p.

JAMES HAFLEY

"Abstraction and Order in the Language of Tennessee Williams"

Tennessee Williams: A Tribute, ed. Jac Thorpe

1977, pp. 753–62

The American theater—the theater of the United States, at least—has impressive traditions of stagecraft and even of acting, but has next to no literary tradition whatsoever: it has no Sophocles or Webster, no Racine or Yeats; and lacking even solitary poets, it is of course lacking in anything like a community of theme. In a drama in which *The Cocktail Party* is looked upon as theatrical literature by critical and careless alike, one need not hope to find any established sense of language itself taken seriously as art, as dramatic art. Indeed, the worst thing a drama critic can say of a play is that this or that in it is "literary"; and "theatrical" is a corresponding insult whenever an English professor uses it.

It is perhaps for this reason that so much depends upon, but so little comes of, our continual references to the "poetic style" of Tennessee Williams: the one style, the only sustained style, in our theater that clearly isn't "prosy" and that is hence a sort of vindication for literary and theater people alike; but nonetheless a style whose poeticism is generally illustrated (never demonstrated) by instances of trope or local usage, for all the world as though nothing else *could* be meant by "poetic style." Thus, we expect Williams somehow alone to absolve our theater of the sin of language intensely boring in itself (yes—the language of O'Neill off stage, which sags till propped up by a production), and at the same time we neglect to investigate beyond our most superficial sense of the singular importance of his language not just to his own art but to that of our entire theater, which Williams' style is expected to fructify like a linguistic TVA. We ask almost everything, and yet we make scant effort to understand how very much he gives us.

It seems to me that Williams' style—by which I mean no more nor less than his care for our language—is precisely not a natural resource but a burgeoning in the desert that makes it perhaps the chief single technical glory of our theater to date. If I cannot begin to explore that thesis in the scope of one brief essay, that is all right; what I want to do is only suggest a way or so in which it can be justified by anyone interested in literary excellence. And it is because so often, too often, Williams' "poetic" quality is located in concretes—in simile and metaphor, in symbol—that I choose to point out some instances of how even the mere vocabulary of abstraction he employs can be studied to rich advantage. I do not think I shall call upon a single regionalism of word or syntax here, and I shall cite concretes only in their relation to abstractions. Further, though I can't resist some generalization about the language, I don't want to emphasize how it works in the plays (a subject for at least a book) but mostly to cite examples from the poems. Yet everything I say should be applicable most valuably to the plays, and apprehensible at its most complex there. When O'Neill wants "poetry" at the end of *Long Day's Journey* he injects extended passages from Swinburne into his text; when Williams wants such intense effects he doesn't have to import them. The last speech of Blanche is generated out of the play's own poetic matrix.

II

Williams' abstractions invariably relate to absolutes, about which he is disarmingly ambivalent: he at once celebrates and shies from transcendence. Thus, the white blackbird and black blackbird of his epigraph to *Moise* exist in a Neoplatonic pattern which is familiar enough; but a tension between conventional longing for the absolute (named by a world of abstract nouns) and individual preference for the spatial/temporal even at its most perilously transitory—this is what is characteristic of Williams. In Williams is neither a sacrificing of real for ideal, nor (as in some Keats or Whitman, say) a total discovery of the ideal in the real; there is dualism and the pull of spirit against flesh, abstraction against concretion, but at the same time a grudge against the very idea of the absolute. His is a world longing for otherness and yet sad or spiteful that such a concept even exists to disturb location in the self; yet self-consciousness defines but also damns by delimitation the identity that it defines.

This ambivalent attitude towards the idea of the ideal is everywhere apparent in Williams' language, where it is dramatized at least as thoroughly as in event. A title like *A Streetcar Named Desire* is apt demonstration. The abstraction "desire"—ranging in its meanings from longing for the absolute to a contradictory lust—is evoked only to be ridiculed as naming a mechanical contrivance, a vulgar corruption of some such conveyance as the ship of life. At the same time, in double irony, the vehicle seems poignantly in need of a magnitude beyond it, like a mailman trying to perform one of the labors of Hercules, or a tenement child named for a king. But the ultimate revelation is of Desire itself as merely a place name, no more in stature or consolation than the streetcar that literally goes there. In the play, Blanche says desire is the opposite of death: it is her conviction prompted by her encounter with the Mexican woman offering flowers for the dead. But she is wrong, and these two grand abstractions, "death" and "desire" ("desire" in Blanche's sense of longing for transcendence) are the same; Stanley's "desire," lust, is the true opponent of death, and the life he gives, like the home he gives, is both pitifully sordid and absolutely necessary to sanity. In this play about homes, Blanche's sublimation of earthy desire that has been denied her leads her from a lost Paradise to a rest home: from innocence to innocence. Stanley's desire and Stella's keep them soundly, vitally located in the experience of time present, in the slum that is the very nutrient of life lived. The situation is not unlike that in Shelley's *Alastor:* humankind can be grateful to the poet, to Blanche, for reaching out to saving ideals; but though the ideal is a model for the salvation of humankind, it is just as surely an illusive alternate to the reality of experienced life. Shelley's speaker, at the end of his account of the idealist poet, cries "O, that the dream . . . were the true law / Of this so lovely world!" In Williams' play, Stella, pulled between the unreal beauty of Blanche's "home" and "desire" and the naked realities of Stanley's, opts for the latter, for law instead of dream—indeed for the legal kinship of her bond to him rather than for her past familial kindness to Blanche. Blanche must rely upon strangers in seeking her kind: sisterhood is a kindness far too real to sustain her elevated sense of home and family, impossibly ideal, impossibly lost. Williams' epigraph from Hart Crane's "The Broken Tower" points to this theme, to "the visionary company" that is a "kindness of strangers," versus the civic family that is a cruelty of kin. *Desire, lost, home*—these words recur tellingly among the play's abstractions. Belle Reve is prelapsarian; the real Elysian Fields is to be found between the L & N tracks and the river.

But major throughout the play are words of relationship (familiarity): *species, type, attachment, kind*, and *kindness, companionship*, developing up to Blanche's last speech and giving it its astonishing poetic power and control. In the battle between love and sex, desire and desire, Stanley's crude but real strength, relying on kidneys and not souls, is like the gross earth that alone can nourish belief, imagination, the reaching for the moon which the play defines as "lunacy" in the literal sense of the term. Life is redeemed only by lunatic aspiration, yet it must violate the ideal if only to sustain its desperate knowledge that the L & N tracks are after all not the woodland of Weir. Blanche's name may mean *white*, but her legal name, her married name, is Grey. And all the wonderfully exciting conflicts of this play are first and last conflicts among words, just as the network of conflict I have noticed here is one of battle between concrete and abstract words handled with full awareness of their self-defeating contradictions.

III

Williams' favorite abstracts seem to be *light* (regularly "fading" or "dimming"), *love, reverence, blue* and the constantly recurring *youth*. *Light* is most often related to imagery of glass, from Laura's animals to a profusion of mirrors to the ice of *Moise*. Glass exhibits the favored ambivalence: it can reveal, or seem to, what is beyond, or it can reflect what is only before it; it can tell truth, but is the most fragile of substances; like smoke it hovers as image between the concrete and the abstract: next to invisible, yet with a visibility that must ultimately damn it into mortality. For in Williams' world knowledge has only negative value when pitted against the lunatic falsehood of justifying fancy. The light as it dims, as it fades, proves the glass to be literal glass only.

Light can be either a concrete or an abstract noun; even more so *youth*, which as word and image (object) is central in this art. *Youth* is at once the most attractive abstract and the most transitory concrete: what's soonest lost but most needs finding, soonest faded but most deserves perduration. The poem "Testa Dell' Effebo"—"Testa" both real and simulated—is a convenient example of the paradox of youth as both lost and saved: as real in life but ideal in art. The sculpture of that poem is analogous to the word *youth* (art) as opposed to the condition of youth (life). The sculpture, the word, are at once involved with life and safe from it: art is a solution infinitely preferable to lunacy. Art allows comedy as lunacy demands tragedy (here mortality). In this poem the language dramatizes the word become Word (compare Hart Crane's *Voyages*). The real youth after his youth has ended, dimmed, must have become lunatic; the youth in art remains youth to time present—"this" time—and indeed prompts the language of life in this speech of praise. He has progressed from Flora to copper, but the speech reenacts his past most comfortably, and the copper cast exhibits, eternalizes, the "luster" and "repose" (the only two abstract words in the poem), hence realizing the ideal as it idealizes the real in a turning of change to permanence. Indeed, the last line suggests both that the sculpture has immortalized the youth and that he has shed his mortality, cast it off in pure ideality. The ancillary imagery here of eyes, glasses, birds, typically marks the youth's turning from seeming to genuine permanence. Like the marvelous children of "In Jack-O-Lantern's Weather" he exists "north of time": located beyond location.

But art itself is subject to decay, as the mere thought of *The Glass Menagerie* insists. If a zoo of Kowalskis can be tamed into glass, its fixity is transparent in both senses. And if the obligingly mediating glass can not only idealize the real but also realize the ideal, the unicorn, that realization is almost certainly a betrayal into the merely ordinary, the horse. Glass is for Williams a grand correlative for abstraction as ideal: a meeting ground where the miracle occurs but, occurring, subjects itself to time and hence to destruction. As the copper of "Testa" permitted the comic ars longa (art endures), so, and much oftener, the glass announces vita brevis ars brevisque (both life and art soon perish). Like Laura's unicorn the abstractions of *Menagerie* are shattered by the concretes, just as time present in that play is mere illusion, and time past (the same thing) only a memory.

However, despite his distrust of airy realms (or suspicious admiration of them)—which is of course rendered provocative because of a concomitant disdain for the essential earthy—Williams effects relationships between abstract and concrete in many satisfying ways other than by invoking the fusing miracle of art. And his verbal strategies remind me of none more than of Wordsworth's when he affirms the possibility of a peace or at least a truce between real and ideal.

"Mornings on Bourbon Street" is in its modest way Williams' "Tintern Abbey." In Wordsworth's poem language again and again not only describes but enacts, dramatizes, the union of real and ideal. One instance will suffice to illustrate that: "these steep and lofty cliffs,/That on a wild secluded scene impress/Thoughts of more deep seclusion; and connect/The landscape with the quiet of the sky." I am interested here not so much in how cliffs impress thoughts, or in how a secluded scene is productive of seclusion itself, as in how cliffs connect landscape with quiet—concrete cliffs impress abstract thoughts and thereby connect concretion (landscape) and abstraction (quiet). It is purely a verbal maneuver and as such it is stunning: a painter might pictorialize cliffs connecting landscape and sky, but never landscape and quiet: that is a relationship possible only as language.

Now the situation in "Mornings on Bourbon Street" is amazingly similar to that in "Tintern Abbey": will time present and future vindicate a conviction of time past? Williams' poem does not answer the question but only shows how truly it is a question; Wordsworth's poem may seem to answer, but in fact concludes in such tentativeness of diction and syntax as to provide no more than the wishful thinking of Williams. (Aside: Surely it is not a question we want answered: reassurance is a cheap commodity.) But more remarkable than the similarity of situation is that of language between these two poems, as if Williams has, not remembered Wordsworth, but worked out the same linguistic solution to the same psychic problem. The vocabulary of epistemology and of abstraction doesn't require underscoring. Nor does the conflict between knowing and believing, saying and believing (because saying is not believing, any more than seeing is). What does demand attention is the relationship between concretion and abstraction, absorbed together into a texture of affirmation that both justifies the speaker's problem and suggests the salvific importance of a positive answer to his question. A line like "faint mumble of benediction with faint surprise" demonstrates this perfectly: the concrete (or sensuous) "mumble" joined through syntactical balancing with the abstract (or metaphysical) "surprise," each qualified with the emotive "faint" and each given new meaning through the spiritual "benediction." The amalgam of sensuous/emotive/conceptual/spiritual here is every bit as impressive as in Wordsworth; this is indeed poetic style dependent upon effects that are achieved only through a most rigorous technique, a most intense concentration of and upon language, for the line that I have isolated is characteristic of a linguistic enactment continuous in the whole poem and in Williams' art almost everywhere.

Incidentally, if this poem is Williams' "Tintern Abbey," surely "Heavenly Grass" is his little "Immortality Ode." Can anyone have failed to notice that? And the title itself plays upon the same tragicomic paradox so dear to Williams. The impulse to ballad everywhere in Williams' verse is surely related to the motive to drama; enactment, whether as language or event, is his passion, and *Moise* can be read as not least a dramatization of the act of writing itself. At the end of "In Jack-O'-Lantern's Weather" there are "geometry problems whose Q.E.D./is surely speechless wonder," and *Moise* more than any other work by Williams inverts that to translate speechless wonder into Q.E.D.

"A Separate Poem," the last of *In the Winter of Cities*, most clearly of all the poems handles concretes and abstracts to dramatize what I might call Williams' stoic hedonism—the two birds in the bush undeniably better than one in the hand, but after all not to be hoped for whereas the one is surely someday to be despaired of. This poem more or less glosses that strange utterance from "The Dangerous Painters," "It was not good, it was God,/and I could not endure it. I had to go away." There is the center of Williams' Angst. God is better than good, but good is as much as one can endure in a condition of mutability that seems positively unalterable save in death and in that version of art which is also beyond the framework of life lived. "A Separate Poem" settles for the tarnished image that lasts awhile, rather than reaching for the sweet bird already on the wing. It predicates an end of error, but that is clearly less satisfying than an ending truth: "lies die, but truth doesn't live except in the truth of our island/which is a truth that wanders." And the last three lines of the poem find out that transience even in art, even of the intransigent, had better be accepted ruefully than let go of for any suprahuman stability. One is reminded, as so often, of the great looking-glass scene in *Sweet Bird*, and Alexandra's victory over Chance. For however close to the Romantics Williams may approach, he can't, even for the moon, let go of his earthly wisdom, the world of reason.

IV

I have been trying to think what are my expectations as I sit in a theater waiting for a Tennessee Williams play, new or in new production—new to me or known from its first production and on through many others. What exactly am I expecting, and how is it special, how is it different from my expectation before a performance of, say, O'Neill or Albee? What would, in a new play, most surprise me were it not there? What missing item would I wait for and grow restless at not having?

These are difficult questions for me. Easiest to start with O'Neill. I expect information. In some instances—*A Touch of the Poet*—I am overwhelmed by so much more than I expected that I want to complain there won't be time to do anything with so much. But in other instances—*Long Day's Journey*—I see that a long speech of information (about the speaker now, the speech as act, as well as about what he tells of, to be sure) is beginning and I lean forward to the excitement of it; then there is reaction (my own but most significantly that of the other players), and that builds toward another moment of information: the Monumental Informative. I think that in O'Neill almost every other thing—revelation or concealment—comes as information.

And in Albee I expect surprise. Well, that is what one expects always from every play, I suppose: anticipated surprise, the paradox of art. But in Albee I expect the unanticipated more than elsewhere. Surprise in stage properties (*Tiny Alice* so filled with phrenological specimen and caged cardinal and dollhouse-Hell that one could enjoy the empty stage a long while for all of its surprises) and in talking fish and in Agnes' complex, unfinished sentence in *A Delicate Balance* that is surprisingly and simply finished much later on. Surprise in the absurdly pleasant surprises of *The American Dream* and horrible ones of *Zoo Story*, and in even the unsurprising as surprising: the announcement at the end of *All Over* that it's all over.

In Tennessee Williams I may receive both information and surprise (but there is very little of either, if you compare), but what I expect, what I am awaiting is the excitement of speech itself. This may be called poetic style, or language as gesture, or drama as literature, or—more properly—literature as theater, but it is speech itself. I listen and the language builds and develops itself into structures that both are and lead to the gloriously inevitable. With Williams, the more I know the more my expectation is rewarded. I have cited Blanche's last speech to suggest how this phenomenon occurs, how her last line is great because it depends on the kindness of all the language that has preceded it. I can cite Amanda's last line in *Glass Menagerie* just as well, as another particularly evident example of the thousands in these plays. She will say "Go, then! Then go to the moon—you selfish dreamer!" The language of the play has made this last speech, these particular last words, of hers all but inevitable, just as Tom's smashing the glass on the floor right afterwards is all but inevitable in the directions. (Yet a production is perfectly sensible without that event; it would be unthinkable without Amanda's line.) Her speech puts all but the last few pieces into an almost completed pattern of enacted language.

And it is this inevitability of speech itself that makes each production of a known play brand new to me. I have heard descriptions of how the legendary Laurette Taylor said that line, and I can try to imagine it and wish I'd been able to hear it, to remember it myself; I can remember how many Amandas said it (most thrillingly for me Helen Hayes as if using up the very last breath of her life to get it said), and at a recent new production I could hear the superb Maureen Stapleton say it. I have not a central memory of Amandas in appearance, gesture, "personality"—in fact Katharine Hepburn's tremor distracted me precisely by making me think how appropriate it was—but of Amandas in speech, and of course in all of their speeches, and of all the plays as speech itself enacting and enacted. I understand through Williams alone in American theater the joy Racine's audiences can have comparing versions of his great central speeches. The same joy I have in opera thinking of Albanese's Violetta or Pons's or Sutherland's. And the comparison with opera is perhaps most suiting of any: the theater of Williams is a drama of language itself as art, as fine art.

William Carlos Williams

1883–1963

William Carlos Williams was born on September 17, 1883, in Rutherford, New Jersey, to William George and Raquel Helene (née Hoheb) Williams. He was educated at the University of Pennsylvania (M.D. 1906) and the University of Leipzig. In 1912 he married Florence Herman; they had two children. Williams was a practicing physician in Rutherford from 1910 until his retirement in 1951. He edited *Contact* from 1920 to 1923 (with Robert McAlmon) and in 1932 (with Nathanael West). In 1948 he was a visiting professor at the University of Washington. He was appointed Consultant in Poetry to the Library of Congress in 1952, but did not serve.

Williams dedicated his literary life to the exploration of the American idiom. His first book, *Poems*, was published privately in 1909; his next several books were either printed privately or subsidized by friends. For years Williams's work went largely unnoticed, although he was a respected figure among new American poets such as H.D., Marianne Moore, and his friend Ezra Pound. Though he was briefly active as an Imagist, Williams was from the beginning an individual voice, fascinated with the rhythms of colloquial speech and determined to explore the possibilities of a new American tradition firmly rooted in the concrete and owing little to traditional English poetry.

Eventually Williams's accumulated output began to receive considerable attention, thanks partially to the relentless promotion of Ezra Pound. Williams's reputation solidified when New Directions started to publish his work, beginning with *The Complete Poems of William Carlos Williams 1906–1938* (1938). The five-volume poem *Paterson* (collected in its entirety in 1963), Williams's most ambitious work, received lavish praise for its subtle evocation of small-town America and its metaphoric identification of man with his city, and criticism for its haphazard structure and occasional diffuseness. His late poetry, especially *The Desert Music and Other Poems* (1954) and *Pictures from Breughel and Other Poems* (1962), is generally considered among his most accomplished and was nearly universally praised.

Williams also published several novels and collections of short stories, all written in his colloquial American style; especially notable are the trilogy *White Mule* (1937), *In the Money* (1940), and *The Build-up* (1952), and a number of works of criticism and social history, notably *In the American Grain* (1925). Williams is now considered one of the great American poets of the twentieth century; his work is frequently cited as a primary inspiration for modern poets as diverse as Robert Lowell, Charles Olson, Allen Ginsberg, and Denise Levertov. Williams was awarded the National Book Award in 1950 for his *Selected Poems* (1949) and *Paterson: Book Three* (1949), the Bollingen Prize in poetry in 1952, and the Pulitzer Prize in poetry in 1963 for *Pictures from Breughel*. He died on March 4, 1963.

MARIANNE MOORE

"'Things Others Never Notice'"

Poetry, May 1934, pp. 103–6

Struggle, like the compression which propels the steam-engine, is a main force in William Carlos Williams. He "looks a bit like that grand old plaster cast, Lessing's Laocoon," Wallace Stevens says in the introduction to ⟨*Collected Poems, 1921–1931*⟩. And the breathless budding of thought from thought is one of the results and charms of the pressure configured. With an abandon born of inner security, Dr. Williams somewhere nicknames the chain of incontrovertibly logical apparent non-sequiturs, rigmarole; and a consciousness of life and intrepidity is characteristically present in "Stop: Go"—

> a green truck
> dragging a concrete mixer
> passes
> in the street—
> the clatter and true sound
> of verse—

Disliking the tawdriness of unnecessary explanation, the detracting compulsory connective, stock speech of any kind, he sets the words down, "each note secure in its own posture—singularly woven." "The senseless unarrangement of wild things" which he imitates makes some kinds of correct writing look rather foolish; and as illustrating that combination of energy and composure which is the expertness of the artist, he has never drawn a clearer self-portrait than "Birds and Flowers," part 2:

> What have I done
> to drive you away? It is
> winter, true enough, but
> this day I love you.
>
> This day
> there is no time at all
> more than in under
> my ribs where anatomists
> say the heart is—
>
> And just today you
> will not have me. Well,
> tomorrow it may be snowing—
>
> I'll keep after you. Your
> repulse of me is no more
> than a rebuff to the weather—

If we make a desert of
ourselves—we make
a desert . . .

William Carlos Williams objects to urbanity—to sleek and natty effects—and this is a good sign if not always a good thing. Yet usually nothing could better the dashing shrewdness of the pattern as he develops it and cuts it off at the acutely right point.

With the bee's sense of polarity he searches for a flower and that flower is representation. Likenesses here are not reminders of the object, they are likenesses:

And there's the river with thin ice upon it
fanning out half over the black
water, the free middlewater racing under its
ripples that move crosswise on the stream.

He is drugged with romance—"O unlit candle with the soft white plume"—but like the bee, is neither a waif nor a fool. Argus-eyed, energetic, insatiate, compassionate, undeceived, he says in "Immortal" (in *The Tempers*), "Yes, there is one thing braver than all flowers, . . . And thy name, lovely One, is Ignorance." Wide-eyed resignation of this kind helps some to be cynical but it makes Dr. Williams considerate; sorry for the tethered bull, the circus sea-elephant, for the organgrinder "sourfaced," for the dead man "needing a shave—"

the dog won't have to
sleep on his potatoes
any more to keep them
from freezing—

He ponders "the justice of poverty its shame its dirt" and pities the artist's prohibited energy as it patiently does for the common weal what it ought to do, and the poem read by critics who have no inkling of what it's about. But the pathos is incidental. The "ability to be drunk with a sudden realization of value in things others never notice" can metamorphose our detestable reasonableness and offset a whole planetary system of deadness. "The burning liquor of the moonlight" makes provable things mild by comparison. Art, that is to say, has its effect on the artist and also on the patron; and in Dr. Williams we have an example of art that disregards crochets and specifications. The poem often is about nothing that we wish to give our attention to, but if it is something he wishes our attention for, what is urgent for him becomes urgent for us. His uncompromising conscientiousness sometimes seems misplaced; he is at times almost insultingly unevasive, but there is in him—and this must be our consolation—that dissatisfied expanding energy, the emotion, the cock-spur of the medieval dialectician, the "therefore" that is the distinguishing mark of the artist.

Various poems that are not here, again suggest the bee—the plausibility of keeping bees and preëmpting the disposition of the honey.

Dr. Williams does not compromise, and Wallace Stevens is another resister whose way of saying is as important as what is said. Mr. Stevens' presentation of the book refreshes a grievance—the scarcity of prose about verse from one of the few persons who should have something to say. But poetry in America has not died, so long as these two "young sycamores" are able to stand the winters that we have, and the inhabitants.

RANDALL JARRELL

From "The Poet and His Public"

Partisan Review, September–October 1946, pp. 493–98

Paterson (Book I) seems to me the best thing William Carlos Williams has ever written; I read it seven or eight times, and ended up lost in delight. It seems a shame to write a little review of it, instead of going over it page by page, explaining and admiring. And one hates to quote much, since the beauty, delicacy, and intelligence of the best parts depend so much upon their organization in the whole; quoting from it is like humming a theme and expecting the hearer to guess from that its effect upon its third repetition in a movement. I have used this simile deliberately, because—over and above the organization of argument or exposition—the organization of *Paterson* is musical to an almost unprecedented degree: Mr. Williams introduces a theme that stands for an idea, repeats it over and over in varied forms, develops it side by side with two or three more themes that are being developed, recurs to it time and time again throughout the poem, and echoes it for ironic or grotesque effects in thoroughly incongruous contexts. Sometimes this is done with the greatest complication and delicacy; he wants to introduce a red-bird whose call will stand for the clear speech of nature, in the midst of all the confusion and ugliness in which men could not exist except for "imagined beauty where there is none": so he says in disgust, "Stale as a whale's breath: breath!/Breath!" and ten lines later (during which three themes have been repeated and two of them joined at last in a "silent, uncommunicative," and satisfying resolution) he says that he has

Only of late, late! begun to know, to
know clearly (as through clear ice) whence
I draw my breath or how to employ it
clearly—if not well:
Clearly!
speaks the red-breast his behest. Clearly!
clearly!

These double exclamations have so prepared for the bird's call that it strikes you, when you are reading the poem, like the blow which dissolves an enchantment. And really the preparation has been even more complicated: two pages before there was the line "divorce! divorce!" and half a page before the birds and weeds by the river were introduced by

. . . white, in
the shadows among the blue-flowered
Pickerel-weed, in summer, summer! if it should
ever come . . .

If you want to write a long poem which doesn't stick to one subject, but which unifies a dozen, you can learn a great deal from *Paterson*. But I do not know how important these details of structure will seem to an age which regards as a triumph of organization that throwing-out-of-blocks-upon-the-nursery-floor which concludes *The Waste Land*, and which explains its admiration by the humorless literalness of believing that a poet represents fragments by eliminating metre, connectives, and logic from the verses which describe the fragments.

The subject of *Paterson* is: How can you tell the truth about things?—that is, how can you find a language so close to the world that the world can be represented and understood in it?

Paterson lies in the valley under the Passaic Falls
its spent waters forming the outline of his back. He
lies on his right side, head near the thunder

of the water filling his dreams! Eternally asleep,
his dreams walk about the city where he persists
incognito. Butterflies settle on his stone ear.

How can he—this city that is man—find the language for what he dreams and sees and is, the language without which true knowledge is impossible? He starts with the particulars ("Say it, no ideas but in things") which stream to him like the river, "rolling up out of chaos, / a nine months' wonder"; with the interpenetration of everything with everything, "the drunk the sober; the illustrious / the gross; one":

It is the ignorant sun
rising in the slot of
hollow suns risen, so that never in this
world will a man live well in his body
save dying—and not know himself
dying . . .

The water falls and then rises in "floating mists, to be rained down and / regathered into a river that flows / and encircles"; the water, in its time, is "combed into straight lines / from that rafter of a rock's / lip," and attains clarity; but the people are like flowers that the bee misses, they fail and die and "Life is sweet, they say"—but their speech has failed them, "they do not know the words / or have not / the courage to use them," and they hear only "a false language pouring—a / language (misunderstood) pouring (misinterpreted) without / dignity, without minister, crashing upon a stone ear." And the language available to them, the language of scholarship and science and the universities, is

a bud forever green
tight-curled, upon the pavement, perfect
in justice and substance but divorced, divorced
from its fellows, fallen low—
Divorce is
the sign of knowledge in our time,
divorce! divorce!

Girls walk by the river at Easter and one, bearing a willow twig in her hand as Artemis bore the moon's crescent bow,

holds it, the gathered spray,
upright in the air, the pouring air,
strokes the soft fur—
Ain't they beautiful!

(How could words show better than these last three the touching half-success, half-failure of their language?) And Sam Patch, the drunken frontier hero who jumped over the Falls with his pet bear, could *say* only: "Some things can be done as well as others"; and Mrs. Cumming, the minister's wife, shrieked unheard and fell unseen from the brink; and the two were only

a body found next spring
frozen in an ice-cake; or a body
fished next day from the muddy swirl—
both silent, uncommunicative.

The speech of sexual understanding, of natural love, is represented by three beautifully developed themes: a photograph of the nine wives of a Negro chief; a tree standing on the brink of the waterfall; and two lovers talking by the river:

We sit and talk and the
silence speaks of the giants
who have died in the past and have
returned to those scenes unsatisfied
and who is not unsatisfied, the
silent, Singac the rock-shoulder
emerging from the rocks—and the giants
live again in your silence and
unacknowledged desire . . .

But now the air by the river "brings in the rumors of separate worlds," and the poem is dragged from its highest point in the natural world, from the early, fresh, and green years of the city, into the slums of Paterson, into the collapse of this natural language, into "a delirium of solutions," into the back streets of that "great belly / that no longer laughs but mourns / with its expressionless black navel love's / deceit." Here is the whole failure of Paterson's ideas and speech, and he is forced to begin all over; Part II of the poem ends with the ominous "No ideas but/in the facts."

Part III opens with this beautiful and unexpected passage:

How strange you are, you idiot!
So you think because the rose
is red that you shall have the mastery?
The rose is green and will bloom,
overtopping you, green, livid
green when you shall no more speak, or
taste, or even be. My whole life
has hung too long upon a partial victory.

The underlying green of the facts always cancels out the red in which we had found our partial, temporary, aesthetic victory; and the poem now introduces the livid green of the obstinate and compensating lives, the lifeless perversions of the industrial city: here are the slums and the adjoining estate with its acre hothouse and weedlike orchids and French maid whose sole duty is to "groom / the pet Pomeranians—who sleep"; here is the university with its clerks

spitted on fixed concepts like
roasting hogs, sputtering, their drip sizzling
in the fire
Something else, something else the same.

Then (in one of the fine prose quotations—much altered by the poet, surely—with which the verse is interspersed) people drain the lake there, all day and all night long kill the eels and fish with sticks, carry them away in baskets; there is nothing left but the mud. The sleeping Paterson, "moveless," envies the men who could run off "toward the peripheries—to other centers, direct" for some "loveliness and / authority in the world," who could leap like Sam Patch and be found "the following spring, frozen in / an ice cake." But he goes on thinking to the very bitter end, reproduces all the ignorance and brutality of the city; and he understands its pathos and horror:

And silk spins from the hot drums to a music
of pathetic souvenirs, a comb and nail-file
in an imitation leather case—to
remind him, to remind him! and
a photograph-holder with pictures of himself
between the two children, all returned
weeping, weeping—in the back room
of the widow who married again, a vile tongue
but laborious ways, driving a drunken
husband . . .

Yet he contrasts his own real mystery, the mystery of people's actual lives, with the mystery that "the convent of the Little Sisters of / St. Ann pretends"; and he understands the people "wiping the nose on sleeves, come here / to dream"; he understands that

Things, things unmentionable
the sink with the waste farina in it and
lumps of rancid meat, milk-bottle-tops: have
here a still tranquillity and loveliness . . .

Then Paterson "shifts his change," and an earthquake and a "remarkable rumbling noise" frighten but do not damage the city—this is told in the prose of an old newspaper account; and, at the end of the poem, he stands in the flickering green of the cavern under the waterfall (the dark, skulled world of consciousness), hedged in by the pouring torrent whose thunder drowns out any language; "the myth / that holds up the rock, / that holds up the water thrives there— / in that cavern, that profound cleft"; and the readers of the poem are shown, in the last words of the poem,

> standing, shrouded there, in that din,
> Earth, the chatterer, father of all
> speech. . . .

It takes several readings to work out the poem's argument (it is a poem that *must* be read over and over), and it seemed to me that I could do most for its readers by roughly summarizing that argument. There are hundreds of things in the poem that deserve specific mention. The poem is weakest in the middle of Part III—I'd give page numbers if good old New Directions had remembered to put in any—but this is understandable and almost inevitable. Everything in the poem is interwoven with everything else, just as the strands of the Falls interlace: how wonderful and unlikely that this extraordinary mixture of the most delicate lyricism of perception and feeling with the hardest and homeliest actuality should ever have come into being! There has never been a poem more American (though the only influence one sees in it is that of the river scene from *Finnegans Wake*); if the next three books are as good as this one, which introduces "the elemental character of the place," the whole poem will be far and away the best long poem any American has written. I should like to write a whole article about it; I leave it unwillingly.

LESLIE A. FIEDLER

From "Some Uses and Failures of Feeling"

Partisan Review, August 1948, pp. 927–31

Williams has long been testifying to the uses of sentimentality. He is, in a sense, the Dashiell Hammett of American poetry; there exists in his work the precise mixture of realism and sentimentality, the masculine soupiness under the hardboiled surfaces ("The Reaper from Passenack" defines in a short lyric all that James M. Cain was ever after) of the boys in the back room. "Noble," he says someplace in praise of another poet, "has become No Bull!" And that's Bill all over.

⟨. . .⟩ his reputation has flourished among those who have despised manifestations of the same complex of feeling in prose fiction—and Williams has in the meantime attained the status of a Grand Old Man, a survivor, who saw the young Ezra plain, who dates back to the almost unimaginable heyday of Imagism, and who has persisted (unlike the Hammetts, to be sure), uncommercialized, doggedly outliving the little reviews that have continued to print him. That modernist poetry has already survived long enough to have produced Old Men, is a fact that in itself constantly astounds us, and we fail perhaps to evaluate them precisely, carried away by our adulation of them as original Witnesses.

But it is with Williams' unswerving sentimentality, his role of the hard-shelled doctor with the secret sympathetic heart, that we must begin: his sentimentalization of the working-class, bulls, the New Jersey landscape—and the balancing crustiness: the crabbed forms, the use of anti-poetic detail, the guttural grunts, the constant self-mockery, in short, the attributes of realism.

That we have had only this one respectable realistic poet in twentieth-century America confuses us; we are always lumping Williams with the wrong people, for it seems utterly improbable that one highly admired by, say, Wallace Stevens, could have radically less in common with him than with the obsolescent Carl Sandburg—and, of course, there is the bent and coloration given once and for all to the realism of Williams by the Imagist movement and the Japanese short poem as they imperfectly understood it. "Imagism"—the word comes up out of that darkness in which we store a handy vocabulary for discussing (if improbably pushed to it) what no longer interests us—and clinging to it the dead and the mad and the honest: Amy Lowell, Ezra Pound and W. C. Williams. Well, we like to think of Pound; madness has been at least optional among poets for a long time—but Amy Lowell!

Yet we cannot reject what Williams' astonishing persistence evokes—the questionable ghost of *vers libre*, the tyranny of the eye. The realist is ultimately the *voyeur*—for seeing is the most literal of the senses, the remotest from abstract or symbolic thought ("No ideas but in things," Williams intones at the beginning of *Paterson*, his lifelong credo), and it is the happiest of coincidences that the Hammett hero is the Private Eye, precisely as in the center of Williams' long poem the watcher whose vision makes the body of his world: the Shamus, the Private Eye, unnoticed epiphanies imbedded in our speech.

What the exploitation of that single sense, plus an unmitigated honesty, can do, Williams has done all right, and the simple devotion to seeing gives to some of his poems a magnificent, a manic vividness. But how far can you go on *one* sense! This is not quite fair, perhaps; though the visual obsesses Williams, sounds occasionally touch him: the noise of water, the mythic pissing of his Falls, grunts, the thick voices of his wise wops talking, but there is no song in him. His entirely visual concept of poetic form inhibits what incipient melody comes (a few honorable exceptions, noticeably some stanzas from the center of the Beautiful Thing sequence in *Paterson II*, come to mind); he pursues absolutely the seen poem: speech that rejects the illusion of being heard; lines broken on the page regardless of cadence to make the eye's pattern or emulate plastic form; at last, the absurd periods set off by chaste white space . , as if they were the poem ultimately reduced and framed by a respectful silence.

It was, I suppose, Pound who started it all, or rather through him Ernest Fenellosa with his Sinologist's myth of the Ideograph: the presumed unity in Oriental verse of the drawn shape of the characters and the poem as sound, as sense. But proposed in our world where not the brush, intimate with the hand, but a remote machine composes the poem on the page, there is an inevitable air of nostalgia, or even parody about the attempt to unify the seen and heard forms of the poem—and in the end what is involved is a kind of betrayal, a surrender to typography of music and resonance:

THIS IS JUST TO SAY

> I have eaten
> the plums
> that were in
> the icebox
> and which
> you were probably
> saving
> for breakfast

Which is a parody of Williams, to be sure, but oddly enough, written by Williams himself in his pursuit of the ultimate, the utopian Skinny Poem; beyond this there is only

* * *
* S *
* O *
* D *
* A *
* * *

whose obvious aspiration toward the phallic (think of it up or down, tumescence or detumescence) perhaps defines an ulterior meaning of Williams' form.

What on the face of it seems more incredible than that the supreme practitioner of the reduced poem among us should be tempted toward the Long Poem; what seems less probable than his success, especially when he proposes, who has fled all but the sentimental-ironic picture, a dissertation on the mythic city and the definition of man—tempted toward philosophy as well as discursiveness. And yet here in hand is the second volume of *Paterson*, already substantially realized, in the most literal sense—a wonder! To be sure, there was a form ready to solve the dilemma of the short breath and the long intent without teaching an old dog new tricks of substantial structure; the pattern had long been set for what I suppose we might as well call the Ezra-istic poem: the collage of fragments whose architecture is a continuing irony of disjunction, set once and for all when Pound revised for Eliot *The Waste Land*, confirmed in Pound's own *Cantos* and in *The Bridge* of Hart Crane. It has been a long time since any serious poet among us has attempted any other strategy for the long poem—and we recognize the convention in Williams, adhered to with a basic conservatism that gives his poem a classic, an expected air. Here are the rapid shifts in point of view, the urban subject, the intruded quotations, the counterpoint of a formal diction and the overheard brutalities of common speech; here are the harsh distorted forms and the Greek allusion to justify the fallacy of imitative form (sufficient unto the day is the incoherence thereof) that prompts them.

It is so far a work with real virtues, above all a kind of unflagging candor, a freshness of vision from which Williams astonishingly does not wither, and all the charm of a personality that at his age he can afford to inflict upon us with a lucid self-confidence unavailable to the young. He is, as we say, a self-made man. There is a certain appeal too in his conjunction of a radical vagueness of ideas and a sensual precision, real charm in his respect for language, his ironic and tender regionalism. But the poem's faults are even now apparent, disturbing: the lack of a felt necessity in its transitions and conjunctions, and a pervading wilfulness, a self-indulgence most usually discreet, but occasionally blatant as in its injection into the work's progress of some old letter given at needless length, or even an impassioned irrelevance about Lilienthal and the "guilty bastards" in our Senate completely out of the poem's time, assailing its fictive integrity. It is doubtful if in the end the total credibility of the poem can survive such lapses; if we think even for a moment, "Padding!"—all is imperilled. Besides, the old faults persist: the polar failures of flatness and sentimentality, the philosophical weakness, the impulse to subsume everything into sight.

Of one thing I am sure: that there is no point in being as extravagantly kind to Williams as the reviewers apparently were to the first volume of *Paterson*. A muddled sort of sentiment seems to me to blur any possibility of definition in the page-full of excerpts from critics New Directions sends along with this volume to bully us by creating an atmosphere in which any dissent from absolute enthusiasm appears an impiety. To be sure, we owe something to the conscientious practitioner who has survived our own vagaries of taste through half a dozen minor aesthetic revolutions, but what we owe him is, I suspect, a devotion equal to his own, but in our case turned to the difficult and sometimes impious business of discrimination.

RANDALL JARRELL
From "A View of Three Poets"

Partisan Review, November–December 1951, pp. 698–700

Paterson (Book I) seemed to me a wonderful poem; I should not have supposed beforehand that William Carlos Williams could do the organizing and criticizing and selecting that a work of this length requires. Of course, Book I is not organized quite so well as a long poem *ought* to be, but this is almost a defining characteristic of long poems—and I do not see how anyone could do better using only those rather mosaic organizational techniques that Dr. Williams employs, and neglecting as much as he does narrative, drama, logic, and sustained movement, the primary organizers of long poems. I waited for the next three books of *Paterson* more or less as you wait for someone who has gone to break the bank at Monte Carlo for the second, third, and fourth times; I was afraid that I knew what was going to happen, but I kept wishing as hard as I could that it wouldn't.

Now that Book IV has been printed, one can come to some conclusions about *Paterson* as a whole. My first conclusion is this: it doesn't seem to *be* a whole; my second: *Paterson* has been getting rather steadily worse. Most of Book IV is much worse than II and III, and neither of them even begins to compare with Book I. Book IV is so disappointing that I do not want to write about it at any length: it would not satisfactorily conclude even a quite mediocre poem. Both form and content often seem a parody of those of the "real" *Paterson;* many sections have a scrappy inconsequence, an arbitrary irrelevance, that is extraordinary; poetry of the quality of that in Book I is almost completely lacking—though the forty lines about a new Odysseus coming in from the sea are particularly good, and there are other fits and starts of excellence. There are in Part III long sections of a measure that sounds exactly like the stuff you produce when you are demonstrating to a class that any prose whatsoever can be converted into four-stress accentual verse simply by inserting line-endings every four stresses. These sections *look* like blank verse, but are flatter than the flattest blank verse I have ever read—for instance: "Branching trees and ample gardens gave / the village streets a delightful charm and / the narrow old-fashioned brick walls added / a dignity to the shading trees. It was a fair / resort for summer sojourners on their way / to the Falls, the main object of interest." This passage suggests that the guidebook of today is the epic of tomorrow; and a more awing possibility, the telephone book put into accentual verse, weighs upon one's spirit.

Books II and III are much better than this, of course: Book II is decidedly what people call "a solid piece of work," but most of the magic is gone. And one begins to be very doubtful about the organization: should there be so much of the evangelist and his sermon? Should so much of this book consist of what are—the reader is forced to conclude—real letters from a real woman? One reads these letters with involved, embarrassed pity, quite as if she had walked into the room and handed them to one. What has been done to them to make it possible for us to respond to them as art and not as raw reality? to make them part of the poem *Paterson?* I can think of no answer except: *They have been copied out on the typewriter.* Anyone can object, *But the context makes them part of the poem;* and anyone can reply to this objection, *It takes a lot of context to make somebody else's eight-page letter the conclusion to a book of a poem.*

Book II introduces—how one's heart sinks!—Credit and Usury, those enemies of man, God, and contemporary long poems. Dr. Williams has always put up a sturdy resistance to Pound when Pound has recommended to him St. Sophia or the Parthenon, rhyme or metre, European things like that; yet he takes Credit and Usury over from Pound and gives them a good home and maintains them in practically the style to which they have been accustomed—his motto seems to be, *I'll adopt your child if only he's ugly enough.* It is interesting to see how much some later parts of *Paterson* resemble in their structure some middle and later parts of the *Cantos:* the Organization of Irrelevance (or, perhaps, the Irrelevance of Organization) suggests itself as a name for this category of structure. Such organization is *ex post facto* organization: if something is somewhere, one can always find Some Good Reason for its being there, but if it had not been there would one reader have missed it? if it had been put somewhere else, would one reader have guessed where it should have "really" gone? Sometimes these anecdotes, political remarks, random comments seem to be where they are for one reason: because Dr. Williams chose—happened to choose—for them to be there. One is reminded of that other world in which Milton found Chance "sole arbiter."

Book III is helped very much by the inclusion of "Beautiful Thing," that long, extremely effective lyric that was always intended for *Paterson;* and Book III, though neither so homogeneous nor so close to Book I, is in some respects superior to Book II. But all three later books are worse organized, more eccentric and idiosyncratic, more self-indulgent, than the first. And yet that is not the point, the real point: the *poetry,* the lyric rightness, the queer wit, the improbable and dazzling perfection of so much of Book I have disappeared—or at least, reappear only fitfully. Early in Book IV, while talking to his son, Dr. Williams quotes this to him: "What I miss, said your mother, is the poetry, the pure poem of the first parts." She is right.

I have written (sometimes in *Partisan Review*) a good deal about Dr. Williams' unusual virtues, so I will take it for granted that I don't need to try to demonstrate, all over again, that he is one of the best poets alive. He was the last of the good poets of his generation to become properly appreciated; and some of his appeciators, in the blush of conversion, rather overvalue him now. When one reads that no "living American poet has written anything better and more ambitious" than *Paterson,* and that Dr. Williams is a poet who gives us "just about everything," one feels that the writer has in some sense missed the whole point of William Carlos Williams. He is a *very* good but *very* limited poet, particularly in vertical range. He is a notably unreasoning, intuitive writer—is not, of course, an intellectual at all, in either the best or the worst sense of the word; and he has further limited himself by volunteering for and organizing a long dreary imaginary war in which America and the Present are fighting against Europe and the Past. But go a few hundred years back inside the most American American and it is Europe: Dr. Williams is just as much Darkest Europe as any of us, way down there in the middle of his past.

In his long one-sided war with Eliot Dr. Williams seems to me to come off surprising badly—particularly so when we compare the whole of *Paterson* with the *Four Quartets.* When we read the *Four Quartets* we are reading the long poem of a poet so temperamentally isolated that he does not even put another character, another human being treated at length, into the whole poem; and yet the poem (probably the best since the *Duino Elegies*) impresses us not with its limitations but with its range and elevation, with how much it knows not simply about men but about Man—not simply about one city or one country but about the West, that West of which America is no more than the last part.

HAYDEN CARRUTH

"William Carlos Williams as One of Us"

New Republic, April 13, 1963, pp. 30–32

The death of William Carlos Williams on March 4 was expected and even longed for, in the pitiable way that human beings must adopt when they are touched and concerned, by those who knew him. He had been ill for a long, long time. We can be grateful, on his account and our own, that even during the last tortured years he was able to write some of the time. The work of the final decade contains some of his most beautiful writing, as full of life as ever. And that—his undeviating dedication to life and all it implied—was the key to everything he wrote, everything he did. It gave him, one fervently hopes, the satisfaction he deserved. Certainly it will continue to satisfy us and those who come after us, if there are any, as we turn to it again and again in his poems.

In paying tribute to Williams, I should like to quote a poem of his which has never appeared in any of his books. It was found last summer by Mrs. Williams when she was rummaging among family papers; somehow it had got mislaid. It is called "Child and Vegetables," and was published in the magazine *This Quarter* (Vol. II, No. 4, dated April–May–June 1930); probably it was written about a year earlier. Here it is:

The fire of the seed is in her pose
upon the clipped lawn, alone

before the old white house
framed in by great elms planted there

symmetrically. Exactly in the center
of this gently sloping scene,

behind her table of squash and green
corn in a pile, facing the road

she sits with feet one by the other
straight and closely pressed

and knees held close, her hands
decorously folded in her lap. Precise

and mild before the vegetables,
the mouth poised in an even smile

of invitation—to come and buy,
the eyes alone appear—half wakened.

These are the lines of a flower-bud's
tight petals, thoughtfully

designed, the vegetables, offerings
in a rite. Mutely the smooth globes

of the squash, the cornucopias
of the corn, fresh green, so still

so aptly made, the whole so full
of peace and symmetry . . .

resting contours of eagerness
and unrest—

No doubt the most famous statement Dr. Williams ever uttered is the theme recurrent in his poems, especially *Paterson*, that there are "no ideas but in things." And no doubt it is also the least understood by his disciples and admirers (who today are many), even though Williams took trouble to amplify his meaning.

When they set aside everything in *Paterson* beyond the statement that there are "no ideas but in things," when they say that the statement is literally true, when they claim it as a sanction for their anti-intellectual attitudes, and finally when they use it as a warrant for attempting to write poems without ideas, poems which (in their terms) will have the "purity" of "self-existent objects," then they are doing Williams, themselves, and all poetry, a grave disservice.

On the face of it, the statement is literally not true. Williams, who was a physician as well as a poet and by all accounts a good one, did not believe it to be literally true; without sophistry, he couldn't do so. Take an idea of the order of "a stitch in time saves nine." It is a simplistic idea, coated with layers of sanctimony and unction. Nevertheless, it can be stripped of its offensive qualities and revealed at the center as a true idea, what is called a "self-evident" idea. But it is not self-evident because it occurs objectively; on the contrary, no objects combined in nature could ever express it; it did not exist until a mind made it, and it could not exist now if there were no mind to recover it.

For a long time people have been trying to invent a truth of art which could supersede the truth of objective reality. At some rather indeterminate point in the history of culture it was seen that the work of art is a dynamic structure, and that like all dynamic structures it possesses a certain self-existent quality, or what we call autonomy. Then about a hundred years ago the concept was seized upon as a means of turning art into an anti-reality which would have its own laws and hence would be more interesting, beautiful, and durable than the whole objective world. At first the effort issued merely in art-for-art's-sake dilettantism, soon discredited. But through the refinements of the symbolists, expressionists, futurists, surrealists, neo-metaphysicals, etc., the notion has gained wide currency among artists and intellectuals, and even among certain branches of philosophy. In essence it holds that language, through the "revolution of the word," has constituted itself a new reality with its own self-revealing authority, different from and fundamentally opposed to the old-fashioned reality, whatever that may have been. At the same time, however, the poem, being a structure of language, possesses its own solely objective validity.

Meanwhile, other people, including some artists and intellectuals, were being consumed in furnaces, intoxicated in gas chambers, afflicted by rapists and tortures, disinfected by brainwashers—all reality's old merry pranks.

Clearly, neither things nor ideas (nor poems, of course) have the kind of irrelative self-completeness (which the autonomists desire), and such self-completeness is only the dream-product of a deeply divisive mania. The truth is that things and ideas and poems are realities among many realities, conformable to the general laws, not opposable in any useful sense.

But reality (whatever it is) is intractable, and usually ugly and boring as well, with the result that some people will always try to escape it by one means or another. You can't blame the poets more than the rest. Beyond this, reality consists of Right and Wrong; and since Wrong is by nature ascendant, Right is continually tempted into sanctimony and unction (to say nothing of bigotry), and the effort to resist these temptations is difficult and tedious—another reason for escaping. It is all a misfortune, the whole business; so grave a misfortune indeed that people lately have taken to calling it an absurdity. But no degree of absurdity can extricate man from reality, or relieve him, so long as he is alive, from the necessity of thinking about it.

What does Williams say? "When a man makes a poem, makes it, mind you, he takes words as he finds them interrelated about him and composes them—without distortion which would mar their exact significance—into an intense expression of his perceptions and ardors that they may constitute a revelation in the speech that he uses." I was tempted to cut this statement in order to make it more readable, but I didn't; here it is in all its ambiguity and inclusiveness. Williams' fine instinct for style always deserts him when he comes face-to-face with an ultimate question of principle. Here his emphasis on *words*, *speech*, *expression*, etc., seems to put him squarely in the anti-realist camp, alongside Valéry and Gottfried Benn. But we know from his whole work that Williams devoted himself, perhaps more fervently than any other modern poet, to life as it is lived. He was drawn two ways at once, a deep ambivalence that runs through all his writing.

He speaks also of a *revelation* without saying what is revealed, though elsewhere he seems to imply that it is beauty in the Keatsian sense. Is it equal to truth, to morality? One can't possibly tell, because like other poetic radicals of his generation Williams distrusts these terms and seldom uses them except in disparagement. Nor can we learn much from observing that Williams connects *revelation* to *perceptions* and *ardors*, two imprecise terms which are interesting here chiefly because they denote the subjectivity of poetic materials. But if we go back to the verb in Williams' statement—*composes*—I think we can get at the active part of his view of poetry, and we can see how it works by looking once more at the rediscovered "Child and Vegetables."

It isn't a great poem, but it is good enough and quite characteristic. Here are a number of objects—a child, a house, trees, a table, some vegetables, a road. With the great skill which was always his, Williams presents them in all their immediacy and self-proclaiming presence. Very good. But did these objects occur this way in reality? The answer is no. Can things collected objectively possess symmetry or any other mode of arrangement? No again. The arrangement was made by the poet. If you like, it was *seen* by the poet; to me the distinction is academic. The point is that another poet might have seen these objects quite differently; haphazardly or even brutally.

The arrangement, the composition, the disposition—it is everything and it is an idea; it is an idea in the mind, not in things. And can anyone doubt that it is also an idea which entails an act of judgment, *an act of morality?* Even if the whole force and tone of the poem did not assure this, Williams himself made it explicit by his use of such loaded words as *peace* and *symmetry*. This is as close as he ever came to sanctimony, but it is close enough; the poem might be better if these words were removed (though it is interesting to see that *symmetrically* in the fifth line appears without distortion and hence is properly poetical). The poem is an idea, it is a specifically moral idea, and it lives because this is so.

On a far broader scale and in a far more complex condition of control, *Paterson* also is a moral idea. In its substance it is, like all fine poems, a life-affirming idea. It is a defense of the Right without sanctimony. It is an acknowledgment of reality, and a confrontation as well, with no feelings spared. It is, incidentally, an explicit avowal that the poet's mind in all its faculties is an indigenous component of reality;

that is what is meant by "no ideas but in things." Finally, it is not an escape into any kind of anti-reality, linguistic or other, but an assertion of ultimate human dignity; that is to say, an assertion of the efficacy of ideas (especially the procedural ideas of love and justice) in the face of whatever is brought to bear against us.

Certainly it is time now to say these things loudly and lovingly. William Carlos Williams was one of us; committed to our life, our reality, our enigma. He was a man of courage who required neither escape nor mystification. His poems will be our bulwark, I think, long after the anti-realists have followed their inadequate doctrines into the history books.

NEIL MYERS

"William Carlos Williams' *Spring and All*"

Modern Language Quarterly, June 1965, pp. 285–301

Spring and All, published in 1922, is William Carlos Williams' first major achievement and "one of the most important volumes of modern poetry" of the twenties, "a veritable 'books of examples' of the principles (implicit and explicit) that governed the making of it. . . ." The book is an intensely stylized set of exercises in reduction, often intentionally confusing and difficult; in it Williams perfected a technique of ordering objects into "a still life of a special kind . . . in which progress is clearly seen either in spatial and temporal movement or in symbolic pattern."[1] But to call this poetry "still life," even "of a special kind," is misleading; it is anything but still. It consists of consciously formal, almost geometrical arrangements of hard-edged things, but it is also full of powerful inward tension, of strongly contrasting elements put together in coherent, graceful patterns under great stress. It suggests energy meeting forms which remain facile and elegant while being barely able to hold their content.

The basic importance of *Spring and All* is that it is Williams' first major study of the relation of formal art to the various forms of human and natural energy that he would explore for the rest of his career. The book makes particularly explicit Williams' fascination with forms of violence—age, inarticulate pain, frustration, exploitation, urban disintegration, death—that the pastoral mood of earlier poems half concealed. The real change is that what Williams now poses against violence is no longer largely a matter of reported images—the grace of "Wu Kee; young, agile, clear-eyed / And clean-limbed, his muscles ripple / Under the thin blue shirt" ("The Young Laundryman")—or of outright ecstatic pronouncements of "Joy! Joy!" ("Complaint").[2] Williams still draws on the vitality of commonplace men and things, but they are made almost elemental by his strenuous forms. The lines of a rose, a piece of jazz, the order and disorder of a downtown wilderness are all isolated from their full natural background, cut through and viewed in heightened sections, so that bits of words, phrases, objects, and complex scenes are drawn into a bewildering but dynamic whole. In large part, Williams' effort is to fight stock response by the cubist technique of exploding things into hard, fascinating, independently viable pieces, and rearranging them into "spatial and temporal" patterns whose first recognizable quality is an utterly new rhythm and coherence. The end, even in the most despairing poems of the book, "To an Old Jaundiced Woman" and "To Elsie," is a mood of exuberance, of sudden enthusiastic delight over the imagination's ability to master violence.

Throughout *Spring and All*, Williams is interested in the kinds of violence that work on his immediate world. Violence can mean "J.P.M." (in "At the Faucet of June"), raping a native Persephone with his quick robber-baron solutions, his alien art, "A Veronese or / perhaps a Rubens—" and his "cars . . . about / the finest on / the market today—."[3] It can mean failing to see things as they are, and so not coping with actual fragmentation and destruction—the "Black winds" that

> from the north
> enter black hearts. Barred from
> seclusion in lilies they strike
> to destroy—

the stock response that is dangerous in any form because it cannot handle the real source of energy, the "strident voices, heat / quickened, built of waves / Drunk with goats or pavements" ("The Black Winds," p. 245). It can mean a surrealistic moonlit world horribly resembling the world of daylight but sucked of "juice / and pulp . . . where peaches hang / recalling death's / long-promised symphony" ("Rigamarole," pp. 278–79). It can mean the chaos implicit wherever "energy *in vacuo*" occurs, especially in cities—in the anarchic subway-poster collages of "Rapid Transit":

> Somebody dies every four minutes
> in New York State—

behind them the innate violence of nature, the threat of absurdity:

> To hell with you and your poetry—
> You will rot and be blown
> through the next solar system
> with the rest of the gases—
> . . .
> AXIOMS
> Don't get killed
> Careful Crossings Campaign
> Cross Crossings Cautiously
> (p. 282)

It can mean normal death ("To an Old Jaundiced Woman") which, in one stark, terrible vision of natural process, is at the center of the book:

> I can't die
> —moaned the old
> jaundiced woman
> rolling her
> saffron eyeballs
> I can't die
> I can't die
> (p. 268)

Everywhere in *Spring and All* Williams assumes that "destruction and creation / are simultaneous." The fundamental material of all life is always unpredictable and dangerous, like "the crowd . . . alive, venomous," the "dynamic mob" for whom movies, ball games, anti-Semitism, "the Inquisition, the / Revolution" alike are art ("Light Becomes Darkness," pp. 266–67, and "At the Ball Game," pp. 284–85). Human fertility can appear in pagan "drivers for grocers or taxi-drivers" who become satyrs in the spring, "horned lilac blossoms / in their caps—or over one ear / . . . Dirty . . . / vulgarity raised to the last power," destructive,

> They have stolen them
> broken the bushes apart
> with a curse for the owner—

sneering and delightful:

> adorned with blossoms
> Out of their sweet heads

dark kisses—rough faces
("Horned Purple," pp. 273–74)

Or, without control (in "To Elsie"), it can become barren, grotesque, a "numbed terror / under some hedge of chokecherry / or viburnum," part of a social collapse that leaves only a nameless sexual idiocy, a woman "expressing with broken / brain the truth about us / . . . as if the earth under our feet / were / an excrement of some sky"; so that imagination, art, the ability to respond to nature are meaningless. There is "something / . . . only in isolate flecks" and an industrialized insanity—

Somehow
it seems to destroy us
. . .
No one
to witness
and adjust, no one to drive the car
(pp. 270–72)

Even the introductory "Spring and All" centers around a birth that is only deceptively limited to the small things of a "dazed spring," "lifeless . . . sluggish" and trivial in a world of "waste," of "broad, muddy fields / brown with dried weeds" (p. 241). Williams always finds birth awesome and irresistible; later, in "Catastrophic Birth" (*The Wedge*, 1944), he equates it with the eruption of Mount Pelée. In the context of the whole book, spring's "stark dignity of entrance," the rooting and awakening that quietly impinge on the observer, setting off the static, deadly "contagious hospital" and creating constant "clarity, outline of leaf" (pp. 241–42), implies a power that anyone interested in unity and grace must both follow and resist. "Spring and All" is a carefully chosen title; it means energy that demands an equivalent human response. "The Farmer" must cope with it by becoming an "artist figure / . . . composing / —antagonist," a dramatic hero "pacing through the rain / among his blank fields . . . / in his head / the harvest already planted," imposing order when the dynamic world around him is ready for it:

On all sides
the world rolls coldly away:
black orchards
darkened by the March clouds—
leaving room for thought.
(p. 243)

The problem is to establish control, to find things, to order them and one's reaction to them, to resist "the old mode" and "cling firmly to the advance" ("The Black Winds," p. 246). Like the farmer "artist . . . antagonist," one must come up against the truth which is always present, always new, the bare "dashes of cold rain," and thereby *plan*.

The critical danger is stock response, which *Spring and All* attacks by attempting to formalize the energy of things wherever it occurs. Imagist, objectivist, cubist, whatever one calls his techniques, Williams sees them as essential to recognize and deal with the energy we live in and represent. We can choose between "writing," "clean" art, or stock response and death:

Wrigley's, appendicitis, John Marin:
skyscraper soup—
Either that or a bullet!
("Young Love," p. 253)

Thus in every poem here, the ordered vitality which means art is made to appear where normal dulled response would take something for granted as trivial or static. A line beginning at a rose petal penetrates "the Milky Way" ("The Rose," p. 250); the ordinary skyline of the city becomes

a crown for her head with
castles upon it, skyscrapers
filled with nut-chocolates
dovetame winds—
stars of tinsel
("Flight to the City," p. 244)

and a casual "nameless spectacle" on a nameless road takes on "supreme importance" ("The Right of Way," p. 258). This is the real source of the internal event that marks Williams' best poetry. In the famous, extremely reduced "Red Wheelbarrow," an inconspicuous scene is brought to expression by focusing on relationships: on the barrow "glazed with rain / water," asserting itself at the heart of the scene and pulling everything together; and on an outright introductory statement of significance, "so much depends," which, in view of the trivial objects, barrow and chickens, seems firmly impertinent (p. 277). The process is clearest in the later "Between Walls" (*Collected Poems 1934*), in which "the broken / pieces of a green / bottle" are brought to life by a central verb, made to "shine" amid conventional death, the cinders of

the back wings
of the
hospital where
nothing
will grow. . . .
(p. 343)

In such reduced poetry the image, centered clearly in precise architectural arrangements of objects, means self-expression which reveals real order; like the "bridge stanchions" of "The Agonized Spires," it can finally "knit peace" and bring meaning and "rest" to an "untamed" world (pp. 262–63). To isolate centers of life in words and things is to restore their original force, despite the conventionality that threatens to make them meaningless. Similarly, later in his short stories, Williams' point would be the assertion of life against the most grotesque conditions of slum life, in a tough, starved, six-month-old infant or in an adolescent "Girl with the Pimply Face." In the last poems it would be the expression of the artist's own vitality in the face of death.

The best poems of *Spring and All* attack stock response through sharply dramatic internal movement. In "Death the Barber" the process literally means a momentary defeat of death. Most of the poem summarizes death in a way that makes it inhuman and macabre. Death is like a barber, a barber tells Williams, "cutting my / life with / sleep to trim / my hair"; it's "just / a moment"; we "die / every night," when we are apart from our usual selves; death means second childhood, baldness, "old men / with third / sets of teeth," etc. But the unpredictable reality suddenly appears as Williams is talking,

to the cue
of an old man
who said
at the door—
Sunshine today!
for which
death shaves
him twice
a week
(pp. 264–65)

Typically, the brief quiet scene and the strongest of the terse two-beat lines—"Sunshine today!"—turn the poem upside down. The old man approaching death is a reality, not a distant curiosity; he carries "Joy!" as certain as the gold needle of the sun which the ministering doctor sees against the winter "misery" and "vomiting" of the earlier "Complaint" (p. 199). The *fact* of the old man's delight humanizes everything by forcing attention on concrete life; it makes the barber himself seem a sentimentalist, genuinely like "death." The last stanza is openly ironic: death remains strange and frightening, but it is no longer a game for complacent metaphor-makers.

"To Have Done Nothing" suggests the basis of Williams' attempt to subvert stock response in *Spring and All.* The poem is an elegant, formalized wordplay which changes the value of ordinary words; like the 1915 "Portrait of a Lady," it describes *not* doing something, in this case directly doing "nothing." At most, doing "nothing" means death; at least, the lack of commitment to ordinary virtues. Williams makes it a tangible, precisely ordered, rhythmic act. His images are sentence parts, fragmented over the lines, so that each part takes on a weight far beyond its normal stress:

> No that is not it
> nothing that I have done
> nothing
> I have done
>
> is made up of
> nothing
> and the diphthong
>
> ae
>
> together with
> the first person
> singular
> indicative
>
> of the auxiliary
> verb
> to have
>
> everything
> I have done
> is the same. . . .

The poem begins with a sudden outright denial and goes on to talk about its lack of content; but content lies in the actual concentration of negatives. The basic words and phrases become meaningful by isolation, by continued, almost hypnotic rhythmic stress and repetition: with the title, "nothing" occurs four times in seven brief lines, and "I have done" twice in four lines; at every repetition, context and color of word and phrase shift, emphasis becomes stronger. The "ae," at once a phonetic sign and a cry, rises both naturally and unexpectedly out of the sentence rhythm and syntax; because it occupies a whole stanza, it adds emotional stress to the general feeling of undefined but powerful intention. Gradually, the word "nothing" becomes as substantial as any visual image; against it, a conventional definition of "everything," which is "the same" and from the beginning "not it,"

> involving the
> moral
> physical
> and religious
>
> codes

seems slack, stock, and banal. What Williams wants is not to define a word but, like Gertrude Stein, to make it hard, colored, particular, and expressive in its literal, grammatical context, by means of ordered rhythmic play—like a fragment of a sign, a newspaper, or the hands of a clock, on a Braque canvas. Forms which fail to do this, to give things their concreteness, to make them alive—even seemingly abstract units of ordinary sentences—forms which remain just "codes," lead to chaos:

> for everything
> and nothing
> are synonymous
> when
>
> energy *in vacuo*
> has the power
> of confusion

while to ignore "everything," "to / have done nothing" in the face of official pressures, simply to avoid stock response—to respond to sunshine, watch a wheelbarrow, or play with language—is a crucial step away from "confusion" and toward art:

> which only to
> have done nothing
> can make
> perfect
> (pp. 247–48)

In "The Right of Way," Williams develops an experience of idleness, of the delight of doing nothing. Nothing literally happens; Williams drives along "passing with my mind / on nothing in the world / but the right of way / I enjoy on the road by / virtue of the law." But the "law" means not restriction but the right to exploit rather than suffer normal experience. Williams sees a brief "nameless spectacle":

> an elderly man who
> smiled and looked away
>
> to the north past a house—
> a woman in blue
>
> who was laughing and
> leaning forward to look up
>
> into the man's half
> averted face
>
> and a boy of eight who was
> looking at the middle of
>
> the man's belly
> at a watchchain—

Like "The Red Wheelbarrow," the poem ties together seemingly disparate objects; it has a similar enigmatic ascription of "supreme importance," and a similar sense of a luminous event reduced to essentials, incomplete but final and expressive. The point is partly the freedom to observe, to draw art and order from the most basic, seemingly trivial and capricious fragments. Partly it is the discovery of relationships, of nameless, almost unindividual people stripped to the essence of a common concrete act, committed to each other, concentrating, "laughing" in a perfect moment of delight. When the whole process is repeated at the end, it becomes a response to a conventional problem of value:

> Why bother where I went?
> for I went spinning on the
>
> four wheels of my car
> along the wet road until
>
> I saw a girl with one leg
> over the rail of a balcony
> (pp. 258–59)

Like a period, the still watching girl balances and ends the poet's movement. The "supreme importance" of the whole "nameless spectacle" is that, if approached without preconception and with an eye for their full assertion, things fit into an equilibrium that absorbs the chaos of life and constitutes the basis of art.

Meaning resides in equilibrium; it can be established even where the material is most fragmented, conventionally hopeless. Several poems of *Spring and All* study a world emphatically broken up; they suggest a strenuous conflict between the artist-antagonist and equally antagonistic materials. In "The Eyeglasses" it is simply a matter of visual garbage strewn about, "the candy / with melon flowers that open / about the edge of refuse / proclaiming without accent / the quality of the farmer's / shoulders and his daughter's / accidental skin. . . ." Against it are "eyeglasses" that can interpret with a "favorable / distortion . . . / that see everything and remain / related to mathematics." Artificial and commonplace, "in the most practical frame of / brown celluloid made to / represent tortoiseshell," they discover the means of art:

A letter from the man who
wants to start a magazine
made of linen

They lie amid a repose of ordinary forms ready for organization, emblems of quiet depth, of potentiality for compelling violence, "tranquilly Titicaca" (pp. 256–57).

In other poems, the process is less tranquil. In "The Agonized Spires" it is a problem of painfully making sense out of an urban explosion in which everything is tormented and flowing, caught in "thrusts of the sea / Waves of steel / from swarming backstreets." The poem alternates images of roughly textured disorder with equally violent images of insane urban conglomeration, like a neon sign flashing on and off:

Lights
speckle
El Greco
lakes
in renaissance
twilight
with triphammers
which pulverize
nitrogen
of old pastures
to dodge
motorcars
with arms and legs—

The order that rises out of this chaos is, like the rest of the poem, harsh and linear, a strong vertical thrust upward out of the "aggregate / . . . untamed." The "but / of agonized spires" suddenly appears pitted against and channeling the "encapsulating / irritants" below, and, in the masculine, forward movement of the poem, "knits peace"

where bridge stanchions
rest
certainly
piercing
left ventricles
with long
sunburnt fingers
(pp. 262–63)

The imagery still describes pain and tension, but the "stanchions" hold the collage together as they hold a suspension bridge, at once at "rest" and under enormous tension, enigmatically pointing somewhere else, in difficult dynamic repose.

The difficulty of forging such equilibrium, of bringing living things under formal rhythmic control that preserves their full liveliness, is the real problem of *Spring and All.* The artist is an "antagonist" basically because he is caught in a struggle both to keep from being overwhelmed by natural energy, and to keep art from deadening it: hence Williams' constant references to the traditional materials of art and to artists, from El Greco, Veronese, Rubens, Juan Gris, John Marin, Tolstoi, Pound's "Song of the Bowmen of Shu," to movie houses, passion plays, and "the cave of / *Les Trois Frères*" ("The Avenue of Poplars," p. 281). The artist's most explicit appearance is as the jazz musician of "Shoot it Jimmy!"—a poem put immediately after "To an Old Jaundiced Woman" like an alternative, his enthusiastic vitality opposed to her lust for death. The poem is an assertion of eagerness, of the sheer joy of self-expression; it rejects any stock response, any "sheet stuff," and moves constantly forward with intense syncopated rhythms and a slang sense that catches up all clichés in easy metaphorical language of its own:

Our orchestra
is the cat's nuts—
Banjo jazz
with a nickelplated
amplifier to
soothe
the savage beast—

Here, in the center of the book, chaos is given speech, measure, caught unobtrusively and fully up in the momentum of language. To "Get the rhythm" is to "soothe / the savage beast." The jazzman has the artist's natural equilibrium: his talk is that of violence contained. Like the farmer, he is riding the flow of energy that threatens to overwhelm other poems:

Man
gimme the key
and lemme loose—
I make 'em crazy
with my harmonies—
Shoot it Jimmy

Through the ability of art to use "nothing," to put fragments together and improvise on them, to "imitate" and control chaos, the jazzman emerges as unique, individual, and *found:*

Nobody
Nobody else
but me—
They can't copy it
(p. 269)

Equally suggestive of an explicit conception of art are the flower poems that appear in the book. Like the collage poems "Composition" and "The Eyeglasses," they are clearly painterly, especially the abstract, meditative "The Rose," written in imitation of a Juan Gris etching—an anticipation of the great 1930 "Crimson Cyclamen," a memorial to Charles Demuth. The poem studies a rose petal's natural lines, clean and dynamic enough to restrain and order violence. It begins with a statement about stock response, like an apparent surrender: "The rose is obsolete"; it ends as

The fragility of the flower
unbruised
penetrates space

and calmly masters the absurd "solar system" into which, in "Rapid Transit," poet and poetry will "be blown . . . / with the rest of the gases." The flower's "edge" is like an artifact which "cuts without cutting," and Williams immediately relates it to human artifacts, its "double facet / cementing the grooved / columns of air" like a classical design. It "renews / itself in metal or porcelain"; as it becomes "Sharper, neater, more cutting," it is "figured in majolica— / the broken plate / glazed with a rose"; then it suggests "copper roses / steel roses," like the product of an effortless craftsman:

Crisp, worked to defeat
laboredness—fragile
plucked, moist, half-raised
cold, precise, touching

Like a mathematical design, the poem moves continually forward, neatly cutting, circling, and doubling on itself. Stanza form and language emphasize constant stopping, self-questioning; the line ends abruptly "somewhere," then quietly reappears, always firmer and wider in scope. "The edge / . . . renews"

itself in metal or porcelain—
whither? It ends—
But if it ends
the start is begun
so that to engage roses
becomes a geometry—
. . .
Somewhere the sense
makes copper roses
steel roses—
. . .
What
The place between the petal's
edge and the
From the petal's edge a line starts
that being of steel
infinitely fine, infinitely
rigid penetrates
the Milky Way
without contact—lifting
from it—neither hanging
nor pushing

This forward, comprehensive movement is part of an attempt to identify the nature of the power of art, at once a craftsman's principle of "geometry," the "favorable / distortion of eye-glasses / that see everything and remain / related to mathematics" (pp. 256–57), and "love," which appears suddenly at the center of the poem, an expression of a final harmonious "end," of controlled, ordered strength which brings everything relevant together:

The rose carried weight of love
but love is at an end—of roses
It is at the edge of the
petal that love waits
("The Rose," pp. 249–50)

Even in the slight final poem of the book, "The Wildflower," the theme is implicitly the same: the "Black eyed susan / rich orange / round the purple core" is more powerful than the "Crowds" of white daisies because it expresses violence turned by natural art into harmony and strength. Typically, Williams' imagery is at once social, sexual, and a description of art: "the white daisy / is not enough":

Crowds are white
as farmers
who live poorly
But you
are rich
in savagery—
Arab
Indian
dark woman.
(p. 287)

Many of the poems of *Spring and All* are slight, and in many ways they seem to come close to the dehumanization frequently ascribed to Williams.[4] The artist as active, subjective, personal presence does not dominate the book, but the *creating* artist certainly does, sometimes explicitly, always implicitly. *Spring and All* may be impersonal, but it is not dehumanized; it is simply neither romantic nor expressionistic. The point about a poem like "To an Old Jaundiced Woman" is not that it is lacking in pity, but that it evokes ordered art out of a commonplace scene which, if left to stock response, would be genuinely oppressive. To hear "I can't die" or "Shoot it Jimmy!" is to face, through Williams' stylization, strong feelings of horror or delight before a human reality.

Williams' intention in *Spring and All* is to develop an art that can draw not just "meaning" but "Joy!" from the energy of commonplace events. This is why he attempts to imitate rigorously the effort of cubist painters to break up old patterns and reorder them—something prefigured by Sterne but never accomplished successfully before this by a poet writing in English. This is the reason *Spring and All* is Williams' most stylized, reduced work; never again would he be so intent on reproducing the structure of painting throughout a single book, although he would continue to use painterly themes. After *Spring and All*, Williams moves toward both maintaining the clear rhythmic externality he had achieved here and developing "measured" looseness and flow of structure and intense emotionality of theme—in long, expansive poems like "An Elegy for D. H. Lawrence," "Two Pendants: for the Ears," "The Desert Music"; or in sudden brief visions of life, reduced to essentials and deeply inward, like the beautiful "Young Woman at a Window" of *Adam and Eve and the City* or "The Wood-thrush" of *Pictures from Brueghel*. *Spring and All* establishes the central themes for most of this poetry. It does away with the vague sentimentality of the earlier books and establishes the identity of art, love, and the dance and their struggle with universal violence. The struggle is brought to a climax in *Paterson*, where Faitoute dies without "the language," the ability to

Burst it asunder
break through to the fifty words
necessary—
("Flight to the City," p. 244)

and where, in the great last *Paterson* V, "the Jew / in the pit / among his fellows / when the indifferent chap / with the machine gun / was spraying the heap" can use "necessary" words as an expression of consummate love, a final defiance of chaos:

he had not yet been hit
but smiled
comforting his companions.[5]

His act is treated as a full expression of the dance of art, of the cubist effort to "shatter" the "tyranny of the image" and build new "designs." *Spring and All* is Williams' first full description of those designs, forty years earlier, and it is full of sunlight.

Notes

1. Frederick J. Hoffman, "Williams and His Muse," *Poetry*, LXXXIV (1954), 23–24.
2. *Sour Grapes*, in *Collected Earlier Poems of William Carlos Williams* (New York, 1951). pp. 204, 199. Page references in the text are to this edition.
3. *Spring and All*, pp. 251–52. All further references are to *Spring and All* unless otherwise noted.
4. See William Van O'Connor, *Sense and Sensibility in Modern Poetry* (New York, 1963), p. 64.
5. *Paterson (Book Five)* (New York, 1958).

THOM GUNN
"William Carlos Williams"
Encounter, July 1965, pp. 67–74

At one time it must have seemed as if T. S. Eliot and William Carlos Williams had divided between them the gifts of their friend Ezra Pound—Eliot taking the polish of *Mauberley*, the emphasis on a constantly shifting and mysterious tone, the sense of dislocated internal drama, and Williams taking the wistful sentiment of *Cathay*, the emphasis on the image, and the concern for clear delineation of the external world. Though this would be an over-simplification, it is true that they did originally share a common meeting-place in Pound, the potentiality of each being strengthened by this man who, both in his own poetry and in that of his friends, was the originator of what we uncomfortably call Modernism.

Yet because the gifts they took were so different they developed in decisively different directions. Williams, in fact, soon came to see Eliot as the Enemy. In his *Autobiography* he speaks of *The Waste Land* as "the great catastrophe to our letters," and elsewhere he says of *Prufrock*: "I had a violent feeling that Eliot had betrayed what I believed in. He was looking backward; I was looking forward . . . I felt he had rejected America."

Williams had his mystique of what is American and what isn't, but as a gloss we may take his prose book of 1925, *In the American Grain*. American is here seen as a New World in spirit as well as in fact: most of the colonists made the great mistake of attempting to understand it and even remould it only in terms of the Old, America being "a living flame" compared to the "dead ash" of England. But there were some who had the ability to see what was there: Daniel Boone, for instance, who found in the wilderness a "power to strengthen every form of energy that would be voluptuous, passionate, possessive in that place which he opened"; or the Père Rasles, for whom "nothing shall be ignored. All shall be included." Such attitudes Williams considers necessary to the American poet, and he sees Eliot as denying them by the very completeness of his achievement. Eliot is the American poet who has acquired an "English" detachment, turning to the dry ash of European subject matter, ignoring the new terms that even now must be found for the interpretation and continuation of a New World, and rejecting what Williams came to call the American idiom. Williams was apt to restate his thesis so hastily that it sometimes becomes mere anti-intellectualism, but in its most careful definition it was not so: it embodied a desire that the unknown and unexpressed should not be treated in terms of the already known and expressed.

The desire takes form in Williams' work not as a programme, but as something more important, an exploration. It is true that he was, early on, an Imagist, and he presumably subscribed to Pound's somewhat fuzzily expressed programme for Imagism. But Imagism merely overlapped with the inclinations of Williams himself. He was in love with the bare fact of the external world, its thinginess; and the love mastered him for a lifetime.

In his early poem, "Tract," he rejected the rituals of the past, and he came more and more to realise that his subject matter lay in the present, and had to be defined without the help of other than what it is. And as much of it had to be defined as possible. "Nothing shall be ignored. All shall be included." His love for the external world led him to search for ways of incorporating more and more of it into his poetry. This search is the preoccupation of any good writer, particularly when he is starting to write, and moreover it is fully in accord with an American literary tradition; but for Williams it was the central fact of his poetry, accounting for his greatest successes and worst failures. He was delighted by what he saw at the Armory Show of 1913:

> I went to it and gaped along with the rest at a "picture" in which an electric bulb kept going on and off; at Duchamp's sculpture (by "Mott and Co."), a magnificent cast iron urinal, glistening in its white enamel.

In much the same way he was later to include in poems such unmodified "objects" as the label of a poison-bottle, with skull and crossbones, or a line of Keats. He was to find perfectly proper subject matter in the wallpaper of a room or in a "lovely ad." More important, he became increasingly concerned with the attempt to reproduce and recreate the rhythms and language of speech—something we can see he succeeded in doing better than any other poet of the century, if we compare the style of "The Raper from Passenack" with Pound's curious dialects or the embarrassing pub scene from *The Waste Land*. By so incorporating the things of the New World you can realise a new world of poetry: you become like Boone or Rasles among the Indians of wild Kentucky or Maine.

Such was the emphasis he made, as a writer. We, as readers, may consider that we do not need to make such an emphasis—the acts of exploration and incorporation are made once they are made, and what should continue to interest us is the recorded manner in which they are performed. But we would be missing something important if we merely noted how quickly he eliminated the exclamatory romanticism of his earliest style, and did not also note the romanticism of feeling that remained once that elimination had been made (a feeling Wallace Stevens characterised as "sentimental"—in a favourable sense), and that derived from his love, a romantic love, for the subject of his poem.

In such a poem as "The Red Wheelbarrow," for example, the whole point is in the fact that he has written it, that he has bothered to record with fidelity and economy a phenomenon of the external world. Of the sixteen words in the poem, only the first four, "So much depends/upon," are suggestive of explanation. And so we have to look into the impulse behind the writing of the poem if we wish to speak about its meaning. Indeed, what "depends" on such a perception if not everything, man's power to perceive the world? But Williams was not content with writing only this kind of poem. This, and the perhaps even finer "Poem" of ten years later, describing how a cat jumps over a jam-closet, are legitimate extensions of a particular mode, and perhaps they are more purely Imagist than any of the original works of the Imagists. But as a mode it is limited by the very wideness of its implication, and Williams was aiming at other things as well, in which the technique of description is combined with direct or indirect comment.

"The Red Wheelbarrow" appears in *Spring and All*, a sequence of twenty-eight poems originally mixed with prose when it was published in 1923. In it Williams has reached a full and confident maturity, and a few of the poems must rank among the best in the language. The sureness of direction and the grasp of subject matter seem to result from his decision about the role of the poet, which is defined in the third poem with a firmness in strong contrast to the slight whimsicality of such earlier poems touching the subject as "Sub Terra" or "To a Solitary Disciple" or to the later uneasiness of *Paterson*. Here the farmer walking through the rainswept fields in March, meditating on "the harvest already planted," is seen explicitly as the artist composing. He is also called an "antagonist," (a word to be taken in both senses, I think, since he is both the antagonist in his work of art and the antagonist to disorder). The poet organises, plants, and meditates on what he has planted, "in deep thought." In spite of a hint at the organicism of art, a hint that is undeveloped, the poet could as well be from the seventeenth century as from the twentieth.

It is the greater certainty about his role that accounts for the success of Williams' structural experimentation in this sequence. One of his main concerns seems to be with the ways in which you can go beyond Imagism without abandoning its virtues. How do you not only incorporate things on their own terms (as he does with the red wheelbarrow) but also convey what you conceive to be their value? How, in fact, should meaning enter the poem? On the one hand there is Imagism, where (I have suggested) meaning is to be found in the impulse that causes the poem to be written rather than in the words themselves; and on the other there is general statement, where the poet explicitly *tells* us what value the images have for him. Williams was not, as we might expect, opposed to statement: in spite of the Imagist training he was never to forget completely, he was not afraid of reproducing the content as well as the shape of experience, and the reproduction of content usually takes the form of statement. Between image and statement there is, of course, metaphor: he had indeed earlier experimented with the possibilities of the poem as extended metaphor in "To Waken an Old Lady" and the more complex "The Widow's Lament in Springtime," but though these are successful, if rather fragile poems, he had now come to see such direct metaphor as an evasion of the bareness of reality, which is merely itself, without recourse to comparisons.

The most successful resolution to his problem is the title poem, "Spring and All," which looks at first sight like description and only that, and certainly lacks any element of direct discourse. It is about the appearance of leaves at the beginning of spring. Williams was much preoccupied with the image of buds or leaves on a branch. They grow with that peculiar combination of un-self-aware vitality and vulnerability that he values so much; in many of his poems there are sexual connotations to his descriptions of them, when he speaks of their "thrust," or the buds "erect with desire against the sky," or of the leafless beech-tree that "seems to glow/of itself/with a soft stript light/of love." But in this poem the associations are not sexual. Indeed at first sight there seem to be no associations at all: the things in it are subtly and accurately and decisively *there*, and the poem seems to be about them and them only.

> They enter the new world naked,
> cold, uncertain of all
> save that they enter. All about them
> the cold, familiar wind—
> Now the grass, tomorrow
> the stiff curl of wildcarrot leaf

Yet because of the feeling behind the poem, which is far deeper and more complex than that behind "The Red Wheelbarrow," and which is here the sum of numerous hints at feeling in the words themselves, one is moved by the appearance of the leaves: any generalisations about the act of self-definition, of entrance into a cold world, are made by oneself after finishing the poem, but one inevitably makes them. A perfect accuracy of description, by means of which the world is both mastered and lived in, becomes thus a moral perception.

Elsewhere in the sequence are poems in which moral perception is explicit, as general statement—in "At the Ball Game," where it is as frank as in a poem by Matthew Arnold, in "Horned Purple," where it is overcome and superseded by the images, and in "To Elsie," where it is used in correlation with the images. The three poems together constitute a fresh incorporation of material for Williams, sociological in kind, each being about a class of people rather than an individual. "To Elsie" is the most ambitious. It consists of two very long sentences followed by three short ones.

In the first, generalisation moves into more and more limited generalisation—almost like a camera panning in from all America to New Jersey, to particular types of people in New Jersey, and finally to one type, the "young slatterns" who are seduced,

> . . . succumbing without
> emotion
> saved numbed terror
> under some hedge of choke-cherry
> or viburnum—
> which they cannot express

At this momentary point of rest there is both an implicit comparison between the girls and the hedge-plants, which "cannot express" either, and an implicit contrast, for the hedge-plants have no terror to express. The second sentence starts with a continued limitation of the generalisation until we are shown a particular girl, Elsie, the help in Williams' house; but the instance is not to be a culmination of the process, as it at first appears: it is used as the basis for the largest statement of all, for Elsie embodies a truth about the rest of us:

> as if the earth under our feet
> were
> an excrement of some sky
> and we degraded prisoners
> destined
> to hunger until we eat filth
> while the imagination strains
> after deer
> going by fields of goldenrod in
> the stifling heat of September.

The deer and the goldenrod are related to the choke-cherry and viburnum, those things that are complete from lacking consciousness and the needs imposed by even the inarticulate consciousness of an Elsie. Elsie is merely the extreme example of our helplessness in a state where there is "no one to drive the car," where we are left at the side of the highway at the mercy of ourselves. It is a poem that might have been no more than an exercise in sentimental pessimism, but the generality of feeling that dominates it is securely held down to the ground by guy-ropes of precise statement, which in turn are pegged there by precise images.

After *Spring and All*, Williams published no poetry in book form for some years, but when he did so again in the early 1930s he continued to write poems clearly springing from the same image of the poet as source of control. In "The Sea Elephant," "The Bull," "New England," "View of a Lake," "The Raper from Passenack," and "Fine Work with Pitch and Copper," the only new tendency to be discerned is that he attempts more often to exploit the rhythms of direct speech. In technique these poems and those from *Spring and All* have little to do with the post-Symbolist tradition as developed by Yeats, Stevens, Crane, Eliot, or Pound. They make use, as Yvor Winters has pointed out in his discussion of "Spring and All," of traditional methods alternating with or strengthened by an Imagist discipline. Their distinction is not only in the excellence of the writing, but in the feeling served by such methods, a feeling "possessive in that place" which Williams opens.

It is later that a change becomes apparent. In spite of its title, the *Collected Later Poems* is chronologically the second of the four collections of Williams' poetry published (the *Earlier* is not yet available in England), and includes his shorter work of the 1940s. Considering it covers only ten years' work, it is surprisingly long; it is also surprisingly dull. The book contains a small number of fairly good poems, and numerous echoes of earlier successes, but many of them are spoiled by the presence of moralising personal assertions, and the tone is often rather tired and hurried, possibly because during this period the best of Williams was going into *Paterson*.

Paterson is the long poem on which he started work in the 1930s. It was planned as four books: the fourth was published in 1951, but a fifth—something of an afterthought—came out in 1958. Each Book is divided into three sections. Paterson is a town in New Jersey, but the poem is also about a man called Paterson—the town is to be seen in terms of a man, the man in terms of a town—and it becomes clearer and clearer as it progresses that the man is Williams himself. The intention was that each Book of the poem should treat of a stage in the course of the river that runs through Paterson, and at the same time of the interrelated aspects of life and poetry suggested to Williams by the activity of the river. The ideas were to emerge from the physical things themselves: the repeated slogan of the poem is "no ideas but in things," and the first lines make a modest enough announcement of what sounds like inductive method:

> To make a start
> out of particulars
> and make them general, rolling
> up the sum, by defective means—

But in the result ideas tend less to exist in or emerge from things than to alternate with them. There is symbolic and even allegorical writing, there is exact description; there are sustained passages of verse, there are isolated half-lines; there are pieces of prose by Williams, and there are extracts (many of them quite long) from old newspapers, documents, and private letters addressed to Williams. In using material from the past, Williams does not repeat the triumph of *In the American Grain*, where he was prepared to take the past on what he saw as its own terms, living through its style so intensely that it becomes for the time being another kind of present. Instead, he has here turned, surprisingly and disappointingly, to the Poundian technique of fragmentary juxtaposition, particularly between the past and the present. The direct influence of the *Cantos* on *Paterson* is very clear, not only in the structure but even at times in the ideas (talk of credit, etc.) and in the style (the passage starting "without invention" appears to be a very successful imitation of Pound's "with usura," for example). And, since the structure is largely thematic, with little assistance from narrative or logical methods, it is as apparent as in the *Cantos* that there is going to be a good deal of waste involved, and that what satisfaction we get will be local rather than from the work as a whole. Williams did print some of the best passages separately before their inclusion in *Paterson*, and reprinted others after, and so in fact we may feel a certain justification in making our own anthology of extracts, as we do with the *Cantos*.

In the early Books, the Falls of the river are established as a symbol of primitive energy. Williams finds the present lacking, and it is so specifically because language has undergone a "divorce" from that energy. The poem is an attempt to examine the ways in which we are divorced and the ways in which we are still "married" to it.

Most readers agree that the quality of the writing declines during the course of the poem, and the common assumption is that it does so after Book II, but I find the good poetry in greatest concentration in the second section of Book III. The Book as a whole is entitled "The Library," and its subject is the relation between books and life. From the start of the first section there is an intermittent evocation of "Beautiful thing," first seen as a blossoming locust tree, and then merging into a girl in a white lace dress, possibly a bride, and certainly the victim of assault. We may be helped in identifying her by bearing in mind the prose sentences at the beginning of Book I: "Rigour of beauty is the quest. But how will you find beauty when it is locked in the mind past all remonstrance?" She is like the budded branch, or the "blameless beasts," and she has the

> dazzled half sleepy eyes
> Beautiful thing
> of some trusting animal.

She is the most important aspect of the new world, she is the subject-matter and the language of poetry that are for Williams poetry itself if they can be allowed to live free on their own terms—not locked in, and not raped.

The first twelve pages of the second section are about the workings of Fire. The image is associated with the process of writing:

> They have
> manoeuvred it so that to write
> is a fire and not only of the blood.

Fire is destructive. There is an account of an Indian fire-rite, in "a place hidden from/affection, women and offspring," where, "in the tobacco hush," the Indians lie "huddled (a huddle of books)," books being further interpreted as "men in hell,/their reign over the living ended." There follow prose accounts of fires in towns. Fire destroys even Sappho's poems. But fire also transforms:

> An old bottle, mauled by the fire
> gets a new glaze, the glass warped
> to a new distinction, reclaiming the
> undefined.

The fire as it advances, consuming, takes on a power which recalls that of the imagination. It becomes like the Falls of the river, but "a cataract reversed." And at times, Beautiful thing is glimpsed through the fire, but it is difficult to know at this point whether she is apart from the flames or of the flames—though she is seen once "intertwined" with them, suggesting the subject of poetry intertwined with the process of writing, and we are finally told that she is "the flame's lover."

Most of the description of the fire's advance is very vivid, but the explanation supplied by the discursive elements is often unclear; partly, I think, because Williams is no longer content with the image of the poet as farmer, and has become genuinely uncertain about the value of his writing, as we can tell from the following rather clumsy lines:

> nothing is so unclear, between man and
> his writing, as to which is the man and
> which the thing and of them both which
> is the more to be valued.

Books are valueless, he goes on to say, if they contain "nothing of you," "you" being the writer. But the admonition is so loose that it tells us very little. Finally the fire dies down and we are left among the ruins and the dead, which are apparently the books.

There follows a letter to a woman beginning *"Hi Kid"* and signed *"DJB."* It is barely literate, but has the charm of directness. It could be used to exemplify either the poverty of language after its rape or the virtues of the unliterary American idiom. Williams probably intends it to do the latter, but we cannot be certain, because its relationship with what comes before and after is merely that of juxtaposition.

The remaining four pages or so of the section take us from the process of writing to the subject itself. A doctor is visiting Beautiful thing in the basement smelling of "furnace odour" where she lies, her "long/body stretched out negligently on the dirty sheet." The movement of the verse, gentle and hesitant, carries much of the feeling:

—for I was overcome
by amazement and could do nothing but admire
and lean to care for you in your quietness—
who looked at me, smiling, and we remained
thus looking, each at the other . in silence .
You lethargic, waiting upon me, waiting for
the fire and I
attendant upon you, shaken by your beauty

She is still in life, not yet intertwined with the fire she is awaiting that will make her into poetry. She is Elsie-like, vulnerable yet strangely powerful in her lack of developed consciousness. There follow images of the tapestry hunt of the unicorn, images which Williams is to resume in Book V, and then the fine passage ("But you!/in your white lace dress") part of which had been printed separately in the 1930s, which shows how Beautiful thing has been misused: she has been given a "busted nose," and "maled and femaled . . . jealously."

And how is he, after all, to bring her into his poetry without destroying her? He must preserve the thing she is by preserving the precarious mixture of reverence and tenderness that he feels for her: and if writing is like a fire then the fire he brings to brighten her corner must be different from the other, it must be neither destructive nor transforming, it must be "a dark flame."

The whole four pages are as good as anything in *Paterson*, and go far to redeem the frequent messiness of the poem elsewhere. Williams is more unsure than he was in *Spring and All* about the relation between life and its transformation (or destruction) in writing, and his unsureness shows at times in the unclear connections between the description of the fire and the meanings attributed to it, in spite of the power of much of that description. But in this last part it is his very unsureness that is the subject of his writing, while his style takes on assurance. The tenative formation of relationship between doctor and patient, or between lover and lover, becomes the relationship between writer and subject in the process of realisation; and the contrasting passage that follows, about the savaging of Beautiful thing, in its account of the denial of that process, is equally moving and equally assured.

It was Eliot who dominated poetry until the early 1950s, and such is literary fashion that apparently Williams could not but suffer—being misunderstood or, more commonly, disregarded under such dominance. By all the critics who followed Eliot's lead (that is, by most critics), Williams was regarded, when he was remembered, as a kind of Menshevik, without importance. His work was unpublished and thus largely unread in England until after his death, and less than ten years ago an influential English critic could still sum it up as "William Carlos Williams' poetry of red brick houses, suburban wives, cheerful standardised interiors." America is larger than England, and thus has a little more room for variety, but there too literary opinion is centralised, and in that huge landscape Williams often went undiscerned in the 1930s and 1940s.

What must be stressed, at this late date, is that he offers a valid alternative of style and attitude to the others available. It is offered not in his theory, which is fragmentary, sometimes inconsistent, and often poorly expressed, but in his poetry, which is among the best of our time. He is somebody from whom it is time we started taking lessons. Although he insisted on the American idiom, we must remember why: writing "thoroughly local in origin has some chance of being universal in application"; that idiom is part of a widely-used language, his enrichment of which has a bearing on all of us who read it and write it.

The first book of his to be published over here was his most recently written, *Pictures from Breughel*, which contains his last three collections of poems. There is a bareness about it that I can imagine was at first disconcerting to readers unfamiliar with Williams. But the bareness is not a sign of tiredness, rather it is the translation into language of a new ease in his relationship with the external world. A result of the ease is seen in the much greater emphasis on the personal that we find in this volume. In "Dog Injured in the Street" and "The Drunk and the Sailor," for example, poems which twenty years before would merely have implied Williams as onlooker, the subject is Williams himself so much involved in what he witnesses that he as good as participates in it. Another result of the ease is in the style, which is transparent to his intentions as never before. Statement emerges from Williams as both subject and author of the poem, not from him merely as author.

It is, however, from *Paterson* that Williams consciously dates his final development in style. The passage from Book II that he here reprints as a separate poem entitled "The Descent" contains many lines divided into three parts, which he called "variable feet." I do not find the name very clear: as Alan Stephens has pointed out in a review, a variable foot is as meaningless a term as an elastic inch; but if calling it so helped Williams to write this last volume, then it is sufficiently justified. Specifically, it gave him a rationale for the short lines grouped in threes that he wanted to use, of which the rhythms are as flexible and varied as in the best of his earlier poetry. This poem is about old age and is expressed largely in abstract terms; in tone, even in sound, it bears an astonishing—though we may hardly assume derivative—resemblance to some of the best passages of the *Four Quartets:* it advances with a halting, exploratory movement which is itself much of the poem's meaning. He is speaking of the recreation achieved by memory:

No defeat is made up entirely of defeat—since
the world it opens is always a place
formerly
unsuspected. A
world lost,
a world unsuspected,
beckons to new places
and no whiteness (lost) is so white as the memory
of whiteness .

Memory is a means of renewal, and for Williams anything that renews is an instrument for the exploration and definition of the new world, which he labours both to "possess" and be part of. For possession of the details is achieved not through the recording of them, but through the record's adherence to his feeling for them. The process is not of accumulation but of self-renewal.

The roar of the present, a speech
is, of necessity, my sole concern

he has said, in *Paterson*, but he is agent for the present only through the fidelity of his love for it.

The nature of the process is defined in this book with a renewed confidence, also. If in *Spring and All* the poet is seen as the firm antagonist to disorder and in *Paterson* as helplessly involved with that disorder, he is seen in "The Sparrow" finally as in a world where perhaps the words order and disorder are irrelevant. The sparrow is to a certain degree helpless, but he can "flutter his wings/in the dust" and "cry out lustily." In this poem the poet and his subject-matter share in the same activity, the essence of which is the expression of delight at one's own vigour. Vigour and delight inform the style itself, relating anecdote, description and statement smoothly and easily. "It is the poem/of his existence/that triumphed/finally," he says of the sparrow, and in saying so might have been writing his own epitaph, for poem and existence are seen here to be expressed in similar terms.

There is more than self-expression involved; and, clearly, if we wish to learn from Williams' achievement, we should mark the clarity of evocation, the sensitivity of movement, and the purity of language in his efforts to realise spontaneity. But at the same time we should remember that these qualities, easy as they are to localise, cannot be learned from him in isolation. They, and the self-discipline controlling them, derive from a habitual sympathy, by which he recognises his own energy in that of the young housewife, the boys at the street corner, the half-wit girl who helps in the house, the sparrow, or the buds alternating down a bough. His stylistic qualities are governed, moreover, by a tenderness and generosity of feeling which makes them fully humane. For it is a humane action to attempt the rendering of a thing, person, or experience in the exact terms of its existence.

LOUIS L. MARTZ

From *The Poem of the Mind*

1966, pp. 125–61

VII. *William Carlos Williams: On the Road to Paterson*

During the years 1946–51 we had the privilege of watching one of the most exhilarating sights in recent literature. A writer over sixty, whose work for nearly forty years had seemed only a series of new starts, burst into a fury of creation that suddenly lifted him to a major place among American writers. This, of course, was not surprising to Dr. Williams: he had always planned to do it as soon as his other essential occupation—his medical practice—would permit. He once explained to a friend, "You see, as a writer I haven't even begun to do anything yet. All I've been able to achieve so far has been survival. . . . I made up my mind that I'd have to live to be very old, like Titian or the Jap whose name I have forgotten, before I should be able to get into that peaceful country where I could sit down to the difficult task of composition."[1] Well, that peaceful country (need we say?) was hard to find. Parents continued to break up his vacation in New England by calling from Denver to ask about a sick child; and in 1950 we still find him interrupting a note with this apology: "23 hours later—15 minutes to myself—one of them used up now: the violence of my life at least serves to break up some overly devoted moods and give me a fresh start."[2]

Nevertheless, as these remarks indicate, Williams faced the facts of his and our existence with acceptance and toleration—and better still, with amusement and a wry enthusiasm for so live a chaos, He sat down to do what he could, as best he could; and the result, in that short, uneasy wait between wars, was astounding. The year 1950 saw the publication of his collected stories, *Make Light of It*, and his *Collected Later Poems;* the first of these contained twenty-one stories that had not hitherto appeared in any of his books, thirteen of them here printed for the first time; while the second presented a rich and varied collection of about two hundred poems written during the decade of the 1940's. In addition to these we had, at intervals, the four books of his long poem, *Paterson* (1946, 1948, 1949, 1951)—the complete poem, according to Williams' original plan. Also in 1951 came the *Autobiography*, along with a massive reminder of his previous achievement, the *Collected Earlier Poems*, which included his poetry up through 1939. Beyond these demonstrations of power, old and new, we had the play, *A Dream of Love* (1948) and the excellent *Selected Poems* (1949), to say nothing of essays, notes, reviews, and a chapter from the third part of his trilogy of novels.

Through all this apparent welter of production there is an order, a reason, a firm and central purpose to be discerned. An effort to discover this unity might very well begin with the *Selected Poems*, using some of the insights suggested by Randall Jarrell in his witty introduction. For in this volume, certainly, we have a fair sampling of the best among Williams' shorter poems, from his early echoes of Pound, Kreymborg, and Imagism, through the terse lyrics of his middle years, to the more ambitious, often sprawling efforts of his later years. The whole volume produces, I think, exactly the effect created by reading the *Collected Later Poems* in the light of Williams' earlier poetry—a sense that, somehow, the poems "lack culmination," as R. P. Blackmur has said.[3] About a quarter of the way through this selection, in the poems from *Spring and All* (1923), we have the sense of a settled achievement, a new form in the short lyric, mastered. The poems that follow do not very often succeed in extending this style: concrete details, presented with spare, terse commentary, in short lines, brief stanzas, clipped, rigorously designed:

> The pure products of America
> go crazy—
> mountain folk from Kentucky
> or the ribbed north end of
> Jersey
> with its isolate lakes
> . . .
> No one
> to witness
> and adjust, no one to drive the car.
> (*Spring and All*, poem XVIII)

Here, essentially, is the mode of such later successes as "It Is a Living Coral," "Perpetuum Mobile," or "Burning the Christmas Greens"—and of forty or fifty brief and brilliant pieces in the volume of *Collected Later Poems*.

It is clear, though, that during the 1940's Williams found this style inadequate; he began to reach out for a wider range of reference, a more inclusive and flexible style. "The Clouds" and "The Pink Church" represent violent attempts to break the mould, through abstractions, learned reference, the hieratic voice; but the seed here dies on what for Williams is barren ground. There is, however, another style in these later poems that, often diffuse, shows a new and fertile direction—a style of easy, rippling, colloquial rumination, very close to prose, but pitched just one tone higher:

> When with my mother I was coming down
> from the country the day of the hurricane,

trees were across the road and small branches
kept rattling on the roof of the car
There was ten feet or more of water
making the parkways impassible with wind
bringing more rain in sheets. Brown torrents
gushed up through new sluices in the
valley floor . . .
("The Forgotten City")

That style, we feel, may lead somewhere—but the end is not achieved among these shorter poems; the style of *Spring and All* still dominates.

A review of Williams' earlier volumes of poetry, as they appeared, would, I think, reinforce the impression that this volume of 1923 represents the fulfillment of one cycle in Williams' career. The poems of *Spring and All* come indeed almost with the effect Williams suggests in the spoofing, bombastic prose that introduces them: "Now at last that process of miraculous verisimilitude, that . . . copying which evolution has followed, repeating move for move every move that it made in the past—is approaching the end. Suddenly it is at an end. THE WORLD IS NEW." And the opening poem is, significantly, that old anthology-exhibit, "By the road to the contagious hospital." In many ways this whole volume bears the marks of a new certainty, as compared with the "casual character," the "miscellany" of his five earlier volumes. It was one of these—*Al Que Quiere!* (1917)—that evoked this description of its contents from Wallace Stevens, along with his warning that "to fidget with points of view leads always to new beginnings and incessant new beginnings lead to sterility."[4] But *Spring and All* quiets such misgivings.

The twenty-eight poems of the volume are imbedded in passages of prose criticism that show Williams' theory of poetry—and his view of his own poetry—fully formulated. "I think often of my earlier work and what it has cost me not to have been clear. I acknowledge I have moved chaotically about refusing or rejecting most things." But now, he continues, "I have come to a different condition. I find that the values there discovered can be extended . . . I find that there is work to be done in the creation of new forms, new names for experience and that 'beauty' is related not to 'loveliness' but to a state in which reality plays a part." Reading the original volume, one can feel the honesty and rigor of the critical thinking out of which these poems have grown, while the poems themselves prove the soundness of the theory. Sometimes they seem to sprout directly from the commentary, as with the two poems, "The rose is obsolete" and "The sunlight in a yellow plaque," which are placed in the middle of a discussion—literally in the middle of a sentence—about a picture by Juan Gris. As the prose swirls around these poems we see how both cunningly represent the methods of contemporary painting applied to poetry: "One thing laps over on the other, the cloud laps over on the shutter, the bunch of grapes is part of the handle of the guitar . . . All drawn with admirable simplicity and excellent design—all a unity—" That judgment is true for "The rose is obsolete," but not for the other poem here, which is only a witty exercise, showing the kind of materials that might, theoretically, be set together in this "new form":

The sunlight in a
yellow plaque upon the
varnished floor

is full of a song
inflated to
fifty pounds pressure

at the faucet of
June that rings
the triangle of the air

pulling at the
anemonies in
Persephone's cow pasture—

This is the sort of thing that often happens in Williams' poetry—experiments too obviously set to try a theory. But more than half the poems here are certainly successful, though many of them will not appear to full advantage unless the poems are read in their original, numbered sequence. One will note then that the first three poems form a tight triad of spring-songs. First the tenacity of life, human and vegetable, amid the atmosphere of death and disease: the plants are reborn like convalescents emerging from the contagious hospital: both like infants facing the first light:

They enter the new world naked,
cold, uncertain of all
save that they enter. All about them
the cold, familiar wind—

Now the grass, tomorrow
the stiff curl of wildcarrot leaf

One by one objects are defined—
It quickens: clarity, outline of leaf

But now the stark dignity of
entrance—

With Poem II we move indoors to find the potted plant in flower, waiting to be set outdoors. And in III we return to the landscape of Poem I, now completed by the figure of a dominant human creator:

Down past the brushwood
bristling by
the rainsluiced wagonroad
looms the artist figure of
the farmer—composing
—antagonist

Most of the other poems are not by any means so tightly related as the first three; nevertheless, they cling together, through similarity in form, through certain strands of imagery and theme, and through the total pressure of the personality that gives the view,

in the most practical frame of
brown celluloid made to
represent tortoiseshell—
(Poem X)

One mode, then, has been mastered, but others lie ahead. This, perhaps, is the meaning of the long section at the end of *Spring and All*, where the commentary attempts in many different ways to define the difference between prose and poetry:

> prose: statement of facts concerning emotions, intellectual states, data of all sorts—technical expositions, jargon, of all sorts—fictional and other—
>
> poetry: new form dealt with as a reality in itself.
>
> The form of prose is the accuracy of its subject matter—how best to expose the multiform phases of its material
>
> the form of poetry is related to the movements of the imagination revealed in words—or whatever it may be—
>
> the cleavage is complete

In any case, the year 1923 marks such a cleavage in Williams' work, for in this year also appeared his first book of prose-fiction, *The Great American Novel.* From then until 1940, Williams' work in prose almost overwhelmed his output of poetry: three thick novels,[5] a novelette, two volumes of short stories, and his excursion into history, *In the American Grain.*

It is tempting to take the volume of collected stories as an index to Williams' achievement in the realm of prose. But of course it will not work out this way. For the range of the successful stories here is severely limited: the volume, uncannily, produces much the same impression that we had in reading the *Selected Poems.* First, experiments, then mature mastery of a narrow range continued in the best of the later stories. The volume falls into three sections: the stories first collected in *The Knife of the Times* (1932), those that appeared in the larger volume, *Life along the Passaic River* (1938), and a final section presenting the twenty-one stories not previously collected.[6] The lack of culmination, however, is felt more acutely in this book, for the last section is clearly the least successful of the three. There is no story here that can match the half-dozen perfect stories of *Life along the Passaic River,* or the best story of the earliest volume, "Old Doc Rivers." The finest stories—and they rank with the best of our time—are all presented in the guise of a doctor's reminiscences, packed with clear and often clinical detail; there is a bareness, a frankness in the language that reveals the narrator's sympathies, starkly, as if by incision: "Jean Beicke," "A Face of Stone," "The Girl with a Pimply Face," "The Use of Force." When all is said, these stories look like by-products of the novels, which in turn lack the development that one would expect to see in a major achievement.

More and more, as the books of *Paterson* appeared, all Williams' writings began to look like by-products, preliminary steps, the results of "practicing" (as Wallace Stevens has suggested)[7] for the central work of his career. The title, *Life along the Passaic River,* is enough to point the way. And now, as one looks back over his shorter poems, anticipations of *Paterson* appear everywhere, even in the early volumes. Thus in *Al Que Quiere!* (1917) we have the long poem, "The Wanderer," containing a section entitled "Paterson—the Strike," from which Williams took four lines almost verbatim to place near the opening of *Paterson II:*

> . . the ugly legs of the young girls,
> pistons too powerful for delicacy! .
> the men's arms, red, used to heat and cold,
> to toss quartered beeves and .

The same poem ends with the speaker's dedication of his talents to "The Passaic, that filthy river":

> Then the river began to enter my heart,
> Eddying back cool and limpid
> Into the crystal beginning of its days.
> But with the rebound it leaped forward:
> Muddy, then black and shrunken . . .

Here, thirty years before, Williams had found his central symbol: the river that courses through and unifies his major poem. In the *Collected Poems* of 1938 we find several excerpts headed "At the Bar: from 'Paterson,'" "Paterson: Episode 17," and so on; most of which later appeared, modified and scattered through the first three books of *Paterson.* And in the *Collected Later Poems* we find the first poem announcing the theme that rings throughout *Paterson I:* "no ideas but in things"; we find a poem called "Paterson: the Falls," which presents the whole plan of *Paterson* along with numerous phrases echoed in the long poem; and there are other parallels of phrase and theme. It is fair, I think, to see the whole relation of the *Later Poems* to *Paterson* in the light of one significant fact: nine of the poems, here presented independently, appeared in a numbered sequence of *The Broken Span* (1941) under the general title, "For the poem, *Paterson.*"

Thus, in his short poems and prose-fiction (and in his plays also, though these are less important) Williams had been discovering his materials, perfecting his technique, waiting for the day when this mastery of prose and poetry could be fused into one major work. But the central principle, the furious heat that makes this fusion ("culmination") possible, cannot be found until we turn to that unique and most significant work of Williams' early career: *In the American Grain* (1925). It is a book that defies classification; but one thing seems certain: these sketches of figures and events in the development of the New World are not to be regarded primarily as "history." Considered historically, the portrait of Columbus may be "true," as the portrait of Aaron Burr is probably "false"; but the work cannot ultimately be judged on such grounds, any more than Shakespeare's *Henry IV* can be so judged. Through the medium of these materials, *In the American Grain* explores the nature of man's fate, presents an attitude toward life, conveys, through historical symbols, the ethical and aesthetic ideals from which Williams' life and work have grown.

The problems are presented in American terms: as problems that confront American writers—and all Americans—in the present. Yet the fundamental problem is universal: how to blend the Old World with the New, how to pass from old ways of thought to new, how to deal with achieved and dying forms amid the active flux of the new and unachieved. *In the American Grain* presents two opposite ways of meeting the problem. One is symbolized in Williams' presentation of the Puritan: the way of those who, being "afraid to touch," set up a "resistance to the wilderness," "Having in themselves nothing of curiosity, no wonder, for the New World—that is nothing official—they knew only to keep their eyes blinded, their tongues in orderly manner between their teeth, their ears stopped by the monotony of their hymns and their flesh covered in straight habits. . . . All that they saw they lived by but denied."[8] Against this creed, with "its rigid clarity," Williams sets another view, represented in a rich array of heroes—men who are aroused by the "wonder" of the new life about them. Columbus, who wrote of his New World as if it were another Eden; De Soto, whose wonder at the new could not be satisfied till he was blended with the mud of the Mississippi's bottom; Raleigh, "seer who failed, planter who never planted," but who knew "shoal water where we smelt so sweet and so strong a smell, as if we had been in the midst of some delicate garden." Or, in a chapter placed between two searing chapters on the Puritans, Champlain: "a man after my own heart," says Williams, "the perfection of what we lack, here," a man whom he describes in words that seem a manifesto of his own ideals: "To me there is a world of pleasure in watching just that Frenchman, just Champlain, like no one else about him, watching, keeping the thing whole within him with almost a woman's tenderness—but such an energy for detail—a love of the exact detail—."

In such heroes we have a sense of wonder quite unlike Cotton Mather's "Wonders of the Invisible World," from which Williams gives us large extracts to set against his accounts of the great explorers. For in Mather's "Wonders" we have a world of perverted detail: observations grotesquely warped to serve a narrow creed: humanity destroyed by false witness. We turn with a shock from these records of the witchcraft trials to the chapter headed "Père Sebastian Rasles;" and here, exactly in the middle of the book, its themes and purposes become explicit. Suddenly we are in the Paris of the 'twenties, with Picasso, Braque, and Joyce, with Gertrude, Ezra, and a dozen other expatriates; and Williams is talking at length with Valery Larbaud about the problems facing American writers. Williams is vehement, evangelical: in this ancient scene, where his friends are finding comfort in their exile, Williams (encouraged only by the subtle Frenchman) proclaims a view that looks toward home.

"There is a source *in America* for everything we think or do," he cries. "What has been morally, aesthetically worth while in America has rested upon peculiar and discoverable ground." Then he outlines this "ground" in terms of "two flaming doctrines" that have acted "as contrasting influences in shaping the aesthetic and the moral fiber of the growing race": the Puritan, and its opposite, here represented by Rasles, the French Jesuit who lived among the Indians for thirty-four years, "*touching* them every day." In Rasles, as in his other heroes, Williams finds a spirit "rich, blossoming, generous, able to give and to receive, full of taste, a nose, a tongue, a laugh." This, he declares, is "a moral source not reckoned with, peculiarly sensitive and daring in its close embrace of native things." We can see what it all means, in this Parisian setting: these exiles—are they not the true descendants of the Puritans? "There was no ground to build on, with a ground all blossoming about them—under their noses."

The point is driven home in the next chapter, where, treating "The Discovery of Kentucky," Williams summarizes the issues:

> For the problem of the New World was, as every new comer soon found out, an awkward one, on all sides the same: how to replace from the wild land that which, at home, they had scarcely known the Old World meant to them; through difficulty and even brutal hardship to find a ground to take the place of England. . . .
>
> Boone's genius was to recognize the difficulty as neither material nor political but one purely moral and aesthetic. Filled with the wild beauty of the New World to overbrimming so long as he had what he desired, to bathe in, to explore always more deeply, to see, to feel, to touch—his instincts were contented.

To be sure, the "orchidean beauty" which Cortez saw in Montezuma's city is gone—destroyed by the attempt to use and dominate, and not simply to feel the new and wonder at its texture. The result, in *Paterson*, is symbolized in the devastated landscape of northern New Jersey, with its "thrashing, breeding, debased city," its incredible mixture of races, its welter of factories mingling with the remnants of aboriginal green: all strewn along the polluted waters of the Passaic. But it is still a new world to be discovered after the manner of Poe, who appears in *In the American Grain* as "a new DeSoto," a writer whose greatness lies in the fact that he "faced inland, to originality, with the identical gesture of a Boone."

> He was the first to realize that the hard, sardonic, truculent mass of the New World, hot, angry—was, in fact, not a thing to paint over, to smear, to destroy—for it *would* not be destroyed, it was too powerful,—it smiled! That it is *not* a thing to be slighted by men. Difficult, its very difficulty was their strength. It was in the generous bulk of its animal crudity that their every fineness would be found safely imbedded.

There is the task of *Paterson:* to search out this fineness, this goodness, this "Beautiful Thing," and display it imbedded in all its crudity and truculence.

It was in fact about this time (1925) that plans for *Paterson* began to take shape. Vivienne Koch has found among Williams' manuscripts of this period a significant passage that enables us to see *Paterson* as the product of a plan matured through twenty years of rigorous preparation:

> Note! The conception of a lyric or tragic drama demands lyrics! Studies in language should precede that, the spontaneous . . . as it is heard. Attempt to feel and then transcribe these lyrical languages in *Paterson*. The drama, the lyric drama (Lope de Vega) should be one expanded metaphor. Poetry demands a different material than prose. It uses another facet of the same fact; . . . Fact, but just before and just after the incident which prose (journalism) would select and by that, miss the significance poetry catches aslant![9]

"Studies in language . . . as it is heard"—an appropriate description of Williams' stories, and parts of his novels as well. For many of the stories sound like pages from a writer's (doctor's) journal: conversations, brief anecdotes, whose impact lies in their record of the ring of speech: the Italian, the Negro, the teen-ager, the garage attendant, the steel-worker, the housewife, held tight in the mind, their speech pressing against the language of the doctor-narrator:

> I'll see you in a couple of days, I said to them all.
>
> Doctor! the old woman was still after me. You come back. I pay you. But all a time short. Always tomorrow come milk man. Must pay rent, must pay coal. And no got money. Too much work. Too much wash. Too much cook. Nobody help. I don't know what's a matter. This door, doctor, this door. This house make sick. Make sick.
>
> Do the best I can, I said as I was leaving. ("The Girl with a Pimply Face")

It all follows from the glimpse of Williams' methods that we have in a passage of *In the American Grain,* where he quotes a Negro's vivid speech, and comments, "It is water from a spring to talk with him—it is a quality. I wish I might write a book of his improvisations in slang. I wish I might write a play in collaboration with him." And then he adds, "His old man is a different sort: I once made several pages of notes upon his conversation—" (see the chapter, "Advent of the Slaves"). Only one of the short stories is called "Verbal Transcription," but that title, we suspect, would hold for many more.

Remembering the manuscript passage, quoted above, and giving it just a bit more weight than it will bear, may we not say something like this: that in the prose-fiction Williams was "attempting to feel" the speech for *Paterson,* while in the short poems he was practicing how to "transcribe these lyrical languages"? At any rate, *Paterson* consists of intermingled prose and poetry: prose of exactly the two kinds that Williams had trained himself to master. One is the prose of *In the American Grain,* where the flavor of old documents is frequently retained by generous quotation or by subtle imitation; thus the prose of Columbus, of Franklin, of John Paul Jones, of Cotton Mather, all cut their figure in the grain. Just so in *Paterson,* on a local scale, we have quotations from, or subtly archaized imitations of, old records, chiefly newspaper accounts, dealing with events that figure in the grain of northern New Jersey. And along with these, to form a montage of past and present, we have anecdotes and letters representing every level of modern speech, from the almost illiterate ("I know you just about to shot me")—to the intricate letters of the female poet whose appeals to "Dr. P." bulk so large in *Paterson II.* This prose—one "facet of the fact"—is imbedded in and held together by a matrix of poetry that "catches aslant" the significance which "prose (journalism)" misses.

The correlation between prose and poetry is very sharply pointed up in many places. Early in Book I a turgid, archaic piece of prose relates a strange event in 1812, when a minister's wife, viewing the Passaic Falls, somehow plunged to her death in the waters below. Immediately the poetry makes of this a symbol that recurs, a symbol of the death that awaits humanity unless the poet (in us all) can release a redeeming language:

> A false language. A true. A false language pouring—
> a language (misunderstood) pouring (misinterpreted)
> without dignity, without minister, crashing upon a
> stone ear.
>
> (Book I)

> and leaped (or fell) without a
> language, tongue-tied
> the language worn out
>
> (Book II)

> —at the magic sound of the stream
> she threw herself upon the bed—
> a pitiful gesture! lost among the words:
>
> (Book II)

> They plunged, they fell in a swoon .
> or by intention, to make an end—
>
> (Book III)

Or the relationship may be one of ironical contrast, as in the central section of Book II, where the poetical sermon of the Evangelist against riches is interlarded with prose-passages telling of Alexander Hamilton's financial schemes for the young republic and of his plans for a "National Manufactory" powered by the Passaic Falls.

The method is made explicit in Book III, where the poet, reading in the city library, finds his symbols growing as he reads:

> Old newspapers files,
> to find—a child burned in a field,
> no language.
> And there rises
> a counterpart, of reading, slowly, overwhelming
> the mind; anchors him in his chair.

Thus in the middle section the central symbol of the book gradually emerges, as the poet reads of a fire that once swept over Paterson, attended by cyclone and flood: these catastrophes become signs of the forces against which man's creative energies fight their stubborn actions, defensive, defeated, or triumphant.

Not all the prose passages are so closely related to the verse as these; yet all serve their function in terms of the big, encompassing symbol of the poem: the roar of the Passaic Falls, representing the reverberations of the daily world (including hints of the past) in the cavernous brain of Paterson, city, man, and poet, as he "lies on his right side, head near the thunder / of the waters filling his dreams!" (Book I)

> Caught (in mind)
> beside the water he looks down, listens!
> But discovers, still, no syllable in the confused
> uproar: missing the sense (though he tries)
> untaught but listening, shakes with the intensity
> of his listening .
>
> (Book II)

> Clearly, it is the new, uninterpreted, that
> remoulds the old, pouring down .
>
> (Book II)

It is the roar of life in the mind, "the whole din of fracturing thought," "pouring down"—the last phrase a dozen times repeated and coming to a climax in the lyric that ends Book III:

> The past above, the future below
> and the present pouring down: the roar,
> the roar of the present, a speech—
> is, of necessity, my sole concern .
> I must
> find my meaning and lay it, white,
> beside the sliding water: myself—
> comb out the language—or succumb

For there is, as he has suggested at the opening of Book I, a "common language" to be "combed into straight lines / from that rafter of a rock's / lip": a meaning, a poem, "the highest falls," thus presented in a lyric of Book I which implies the whole process of poetic creation:

> Jostled as are the waters approaching
> the brink, his thoughts
> interlace, repel and cut under,
> rise rock-thwarted and turn aside
> but forever strain forward—
> they coalesce now
> glass-smooth with their swiftness,
> quiet or seem to quiet as at the close
> they leap to the conclusion and
> fall, fall in air!

So, amid the tales of murdered Indians, feats of diving, witchcraft, a hideous dwarf, industrial power, a dog, a poetess, fire, flood, pearls, and red sandstone—out of it all, yet tight within its texture of reality, flowers the "Beautiful Thing." The meaning of that phrase, the refrain of Book III, can never be abstractly defined: but we grasp its import through concrete scenes ("no ideas but in things"). The old Evangelist of Book II, preaching "in shirtsleeves" to his sparse and listless audience in the park, "calling to the birds and trees," a faded St. Francis. Or, nearby, the man in tweeds, combing the hair of a "new-washed Collie bitch . . . until it lies as he designs, like ripples in white sand giving off its clean-dog odor." In Book III we may find it in the middle of disaster: "Beautiful thing—intertwined with the fire." The Library "aflame"; "An old bottle, mauled by the fire . . . The glass splotched with concentric rainbows";

> the awesome sight of a tin roof (1880)
> entire, half a block long, lifted like a
> skirt, held by the fire—

Or, clearest scene of all, the "Beautiful Thing" that is the woman in the basement (Book III):

> —flat on your back, in a low bed (waiting)
> under the mud plashed windows among the scabrous
> dirt of the holy sheets .
>
> You showed me your legs, scarred (as a child)
> by the whip .

It is, in short, the human spirit, tenacious of its dreams, refusing to submit to squalor or disaster, finding pleasure in the strength of its own perceptions, in its sympathies, its loves, its ability to mold a world in which

> Things, things unmentionable,
> the sink with the waste farina in it and
> lumps of rancid meat, milk-bottle-tops: have
> here a still tranquility and loveliness
> Have here (in his thoughts)
> a complement tranquil and chaste.
>
> (Book I)

Here, then, in this fabric of local associations, is the "reply to Greek and Latin with the bare hands" which Williams promised in the epigraph to *Paterson:* his answer to Pound and Eliot and others who in Williams' view could not see the "ground all blossoming about them," and instead went abroad to seek other modes of redemption. Indeed the wry echo of Eliot's "East Coker" at the very opening of *Paterson*—

For the beginning is assuredly
the end—since we know nothing, pure
and simple, beyond
our own complexities—

suggests that the four books of *Paterson* may be considered a deliberate counterpart of Eliot's *Quartets:* the eternal Pelagian's answer to the doctrine of original sin. At least, a general comparison with both Pound and Eliot is certainly demanded in these lines toward the end of Book I:

Moveless
he envies the men that ran
and could run off
toward the peripheries—
to other centers, direct—
for clarity (if
they found it)
          loveliness and
authority in the world—
a sort of springtime
toward which their minds aspired
but which he saw,
within himself—ice bound

Williams knew very well what Eliot had been doing; he (quite grudgingly) respected Eliot as poet and sized him up carefully, as one estimates a strong opponent in the ring. That early tirade in *Improvisations* (1920) was, as Miss Koch has pointed out,[10] an attack not so much on Eliot as on the British critic who had held up Prufrock as a "New World type," and had called "La Figlia" the "very fine flower of the finest spirit of the United States." Williams read these poems with great insight: "Prufrock, the nibbler at sophistication, endemic in every capital . . . I cannot question Eliot's observation. Prufrock is a masterly portrait . . . but the type is universal." As for the New World, Williams added, it is "Montezuma or since he was stoned to death in a parley, Guatemozin who had the city of Mexico levelled over him before he was taken." The point is that, for Williams, this was not American poetry—it did not present a way that American writers should follow. A page or so later he says pretty much the same thing about his friend Ezra Pound: "E. P. is the best enemy United States verse has. . . . He does not, however, know everything, not by more than half. The accordances of which Americans have the parts and the colors but not the completions before them pass beyond the attempts of his thought." We can understand, then, the tartness of the tone with which in 1950 he answered a British questionnaire about American poetry: "Eliot's work stopped the development of American poetry for over twenty years by the tremendous popular success of its mannerisms. His influence here today is paltry though there is no one in America who does not acknowledge his skill or in fact who does not take pleasure in his successes. We have learned, however, not to be thrown off our gait by him."[11]

Williams fairly analysed this whole issue in his "Letter to an Australian Editor,"[12] one of his best critical pieces, perceptive, tentative, ramifying, in the way of Eliot's better essays. It is mainly an attempt to explain, Williams says, "how diametrically I am opposed (in my work) to such a writer as Ezra Pound—whom I love and deeply admire." Williams here sets up two kinds of poets. The first consists of those who "think in terms of the direct descent of great minds," who feel a "mind to mind fertilization" arising from their massive reading in past writers; these men tend to compose "in the forms of the past and even when they deviate from the fixed classic forms it is nevertheless precisely the established and accepted work of the masters from which they consciously deviate, by which they are asserting their greatest originality." (Note the parallel with Eliot's "Tradition and the Individual Talent.") But there is also another kind of poet, "another literary source continuing the greatness of the past which does not develop androgynetically from the past itself mind to mind but from the present," a poet for whom both the fertility and the forms of his art "arise from the society about him of which he is (if he is to be fed) a part—the fecundating men and women about him who have given him birth."

It is a helpful distinction to recall as we read and re-read the *Quartets*, the *Cantos*, and *Paterson*. For Williams' achievement, in its own way, deserved the tribute of this company.

VIII. *William Carlos Williams: Inventions for the Loom*

and as for the solidity of the white oxen in all this
perhaps only Dr Williams (Bill Carlos)
will understand its importance,
its benediction. He wd / have put in the cart.
(Pound, Canto 78)

Throughout the books of *Paterson* the presence of Ezra Pound has become more and more significant, more and more explicit. After the hints of a difference in aim in Book I, we find that difference subtly suggested in a passage of Book II, where Williams seems to echo wryly one of the most famous passages of Pound, Canto 45, on usury, where Pound adopts the manner of a medieval or a renaissance preacher:

With usura hath no man a house of good stone
each block cut smooth and well fitting
that design might cover their face,
with usura
hath no man a painted paradise on his church wall
harpes et luthes
. . .
with usura the line grows thick
with usura is no clear demarcation
and no man can find site for his dwelling.
Stone cutter is kept from his stone
weaver is kept from his loom
. . .
Came not by usura Angelico; came not Ambrogio
    Praedis,
Came no church of cut stone signed: *Adamo me fecit*
. . .
Usura rusteth the chisel
It rusteth the craft and the craftsman
It gnaweth the thread in the loom
None learneth to weave gold in her pattern . . .

And now this from *Paterson:*

Without invention nothing is well spaced,
unless the mind change, unless
the stars are new measured, according
to their relative positions, the
line will not change
. . .
          without invention
nothing lies under the witch-hazel
bush, the alder does not grow from among

the hummocks margining the all
but spent channel of the old swale,
the small foot-prints
of the mice under the overhanging
tufts of the bunch-grass will not
appear: without invention the line
will never again take on its ancient
divisions when the word, a supple word,
lived in it, crumbled now to chalk.

What does this contrast say of these two poets at their best? Williams' own critical acuteness gives us the answer in one of his letters of 1932:

> So far I believe that Pound's line in his *Cantos*—there is something *like* what we shall achieve. Pound in his mould, a medieval inspiration, patterned on a substitution of medieval simulacra for a possible, not yet extant modern and living material, has made a pre-composition for us. Something which when later (perhaps) packed and realized in living, breathing stuff will (in its changed form) by the thing. [13]

It is a summary of Williams' achievement in *Paterson:* the mold is Pound's, combining verse and prose; the line is Pound's, with its flexible cadences, breaking the pentameter; but everything is altered through Williams' invention, his conviction that bold exploration of the local will result in the discovery of a new world blossoming all about him. Pound's mind lives at its best among the splendors of ancient human artifacts, and when these splendors seem threatened, Pound seeks a social answer. He seeks to make art possible by reforming the economic basis of society. It is a difference between the two friends that Pound has acutely described in his essay on Williams (1928), as he contrasts their two temperaments: "If he wants to 'do' anything about what he sees, this desire for action does not rise until he has meditated in full and at leisure. Where I see scoundrels and vandals, he sees a spectacle or an ineluctable process of nature. Where I want to kill at once, he ruminates."[14]

At the same time, in his ruminative way, Williams gradually implies some degree of sympathy with Pound's economic views. Among the prose passages of the second book of *Paterson*, we find attacks on the Federal Reserve System; we find, too, implied attacks on Alexander Hamilton's plans for federal financing and for creating a great "National Manufactory." These prose excerpts on financial matters are interwoven with the poetical sermon of the evangelist who, in the second book of *Paterson*, delivers his sermon against money to the birds and trees of the park. But this financial theme, thus introduced, is tightly contained within the section: it lies there dormant, recessive, exerting a tacit pressure on the landscape, until, in the center of Book IV, it bursts out again in a highly Poundian diatribe beginning "Money: Joke." Here is a section composed in something like Pound's broken multi-cultural style, with expressions in Hebrew, Spanish, and German, along with very crude American slang; and including too some allusions to the Parthenon, Phidias, and Pallas Athene—all this ending with an overt echo of Pound's unmistakable epistolary style:

IN
venshun.
O.KAY
In venshun

(It sounds like Pound nodding his head to the passage on invention that I have just quoted.)

and seeinz az how yu hv/started. Will you consider
a remedy of a lot:
I.E. LOCAL control of local purchasing
power .
? ?
Difference between squalor of spreading slums
and splendor of renaissance cities.

It is a tribute to Pound, yes; but it is not for Williams to conclude his own poem in this foreign vein, it is not for Williams to excoriate the present and celebrate the "splendor of renaissance cities." This is the kind of invitation that Williams has already refused to accept in the third book of *Paterson*, entitled "The Library," where we find the poet attempting to discover a "sanctuary to our fears" amid the "cool of books":

A cool of books
will sometimes lead the mind to libraries
of a hot afternoon, if books can be found
cool to the sense to lead the mind away.

He is attempting to escape from the roar of the Falls, for that roar in his mind, "pouring down," has left him exhausted.

. . . a falls unseen
tumbles and rights itself
and refalls—and does not cease, falling
and refalling with a roar, a reverberation
not of the falls but of its rumor
unabated

Here, the mysterious evocative symbol of the great Falls of the Passaic comes as close to clarity as we shall ever find it. It seems to represent the roar of language coming down from the past, mingling with the present, and now bursting downward over the brain of "Paterson," who seeks to find somehow, in that fall of speech, the beautiful thing that is the ground of his desire. "What do I do? I listen, to the water falling. . . . This is my entire occupation." But now he is

Spent from wandering the useless
streets these months, faces folded against
him like clover at nightfall,

and he feels that somehow

Books will give rest sometimes against
the uproar of water falling
and righting itself to refall filling
the mind with its reverberation.

But it is not so. As he sits there reading old annals of Paterson, he finds the roar there, too: stories of fire, cyclone, and flood that now beset the poet until his mind "reels, starts back amazed from the reading," until the very poem threatens to break apart upon the page. [15] Where to turn? What to do? In ironical answer, Williams brings in certain excerpts from a letter headed "S.Liz," that is, from St. Elizabeth's Hospital:

re read *all* the Gk tragedies in
Loeb.—plus Frobenius, plus Gesell.
plus Brooks Adams
ef you ain't read him all.—
Then Golding's Ovid is in
Everyman's lib.

& nif you want a readin
list ask papa—but don't
go rushin to *read* a book
just cause it is mentioned
eng passang—is fraugs.

"That's French." Williams' answer to Pound's ribbing is sly. On the next page, he prints an excerpt from some record evidently found in the Paterson Library concerning the drillings taken at the artesian well of the Passaic Rolling Mill, Paterson. As the results of this local rock-drill run down the page, the excerpt concludes with this significant suggestion: "The fact that the rock salt of England, and of some of the other salt mines in Europe, is found in rocks of the same age as this, raises the question whether it may not also be found here."

"Whether it may not also be found here." For Williams, it may and it will be found here, as he proves by giving in the final section of Book IV a recovery of the source: the pastoral Paterson of early days at peace with the Falls.

> In a deep-set valley between hills, almost hid
> by dense foliage lay the little village.
> Dominated by the Falls the surrounding country
> was a beautiful wilderness where mountain pink
> and wood violet throve: a place inhabited only
> by straggling trappers and wandering Indians.
>
> . . .
>
> Just off Gun Mill yard, on the gully
> was a long rustic winding stairs leading
> to a cliff on the opposite side of the river.
> At the top was Fyfield's tavern—watching
> the birds flutter and bathe in the little
> pools in the rocks formed by the falling
> mist—of the Falls . . .

Here is our home, says the poet, inland by the Falls and not in the outgoing sea, as Williams concludes in the rousing finale of Book IV:

> I warn you, the sea is *not* our home.
> the sea is not our home

Here the sea appears to symbolize something more than simple death, national or personal annihilation. For this is also a sea where "float words, snaring the seeds":

> the nostalgic sea
> sopped with our cries
> Thalassa! Thalassa!
> calling us home .
> I say to you, Put wax rather in your
> ears against the hungry sea
> it is not our home!
> . draws us in to drown, of losses
> and regrets .

The sea appears to represent the pull of longing toward a lost culture, a pull outward from the source, as he goes on to indicate by an overwrought cry that seems to parody the longing of a Pound or an Eliot:

> Oh that the rocks of the Areopagus had
> kept their sounds, the voices of the law!
> Or that the great theatre of Dionysius
> could be aroused by some modern magic
> . . .
> Thalassa! Thalassa!
> Drink of it, be drunk!
> Thalassa
> immaculata: our home, our nostalgic
> mother in whom the dead, enwombed again
> cry out to us to return .

". . . not our home!" cries the poet again in violent protest, "It is NOT our home." And suddenly at the very close of this fourth book, the scene shifts, the tone shifts, to a common seashore with a man bathing in the sea, and his dog waiting for him on the beach.

> When he came out, lifting his knees
> through the waves she went to him frisking
> her rump awkwardly .
> Wiping his face with his hand he turned
> to look back to the waves, then
> knocking at his ears, walked up
> to stretch out flat on his back in
> the hot sand .

And finally after a brief nap and a quick dressing, the man

> turned again
> to the water's steady roar, as of a distant
> waterfall . Climbing the
> bank, after a few tries, he picked
> some beach plums from a low bush and
> sampled one of them, spitting the seed out,
> then headed inland, followed by the dog

"Headed inland"—here at the very close, Williams echoes his prose preparation for this poem, *In the American Grain,* for in the closing pages of that earlier book, he had used similar phrasing to describe the achievement of Edgar Allan Poe. "His greatness," Williams there declared, "is in that he turned his back" upon everything represented by a Longfellow and "faced inland, to originality." And indeed Williams' account here of Poe's method in his tales is perhaps the best account of *Paterson* that we have yet received:

> the significance and the secret is: authentic particles, a thousand of which spring to the mind for quotation, taken apart and reknit with a view to emphasize, enforce and make evident, the *method.* Their quality of skill in observation, their heat, local verity, being *overshadowed* only by the detached, the abstract, the cold philosophy of their joining together; a method springing so freshly from the local conditions which determine it, by their emphasis of firm crudity and lack of coordinated structure, as to be worthy of most painstaking study.

II

Steadily, tenaciously, amid the demands of a medical career, the books of *Paterson* appeared, and in 1951 the promised four books thus stood complete, fulfilling the early dedication of "The Wanderer," and carrying out exactly the four-part invention announced in the first edition of Book I:

> This is the first part of a long poem in four parts—that man in himself is a city beginning, seeking, achieving and concluding his life in ways which the various aspects of a city may embody—if imaginatively conceived—any city, all the details of which may be made to voice his most intimate convictions. Part One introduces the elemental character of the place. The Second Part will comprise the modern replicas. Three will seek a language to make them vocal, and Four, the river below the falls, will be reminiscent of episodes—all that any one man may achieve in a lifetime.

No wonder, then, that some admirers of *Paterson* were struck with consternation and dismay, a few years later, at the news that a *fifth* book of *Paterson* was in progress! That four-part design, so carefully announced and explained on several occasions—was it to be discarded now? To say the least, the whole procedure showed little consideration for those critics who had published explanations of the poem's symmetry, and indeed gave encouragement to those who had felt that Book IV did not fulfill the poem's brilliant beginning. But when, in 1958, the threatened Book V at last appeared, it seemed rather like an epilogue or coda, for it was much shorter than the other books, and it was written in a highly reminiscent mode that served to recapitulate and bind together all the foregoing poem. As Williams says in a letter cited on the dust jacket of Book V: "I have come to understand not only that many changes have occurred in me and the world, but I have been forced to recognize that there can be no end to such a story I have envisioned with the terms which I had laid down for myself. I had to take the world of Paterson into a new dimension if I wanted to give it imaginative validity. Yet I wanted to keep it whole, as it is to me." The wholeness of which he speaks is highly personal, in the manner of *Leaves of Grass*, *Don Juan*, or *The Prelude*: the "epic" of the Romantic self that knows no formal ending, no classical symmetry. At his death, in 1963, Williams was at work on a sixth book of *Paterson*.

Yet as it stands now the poem has a wholeness of the kind that Williams implies and illustrates in Book V. The chief symbol of that wholeness is one that may at first seem incongruous with Williams' lifetime dedication to the local, his persistent refusal to adopt or approve the learned, foreign allusions of Ezra Pound or T. S. Eliot: in Book V the organizing symbol is the series of matchless tapestries in The Cloisters representing "The Hunt of the Unicorn." True, Williams had dealt briefly with these tapestries in the third book of *Paterson*.

A tapestry hound
with his thread teeth drawing crimson from
the throat of the unicorn

But there the allusion to the world of traditional art seemed ironically overwhelmed by the surrounding scenes of basement ugliness and the fighting between "the guys from Paterson" and "the guys from Newark." Literally, it is only a short drive from Paterson to The Cloisters—yet the gap of nearly five hundred years, the distance from France to the Passaic—these are dimensions strange to Williams, however familiar they may be to Pound or Eliot. But an afternoon spent with the great tapestries will show once more the canniness and subtlety of Williams' poetical strategies in *Paterson*.

Williams is defending and explaining his own technique by suggesting an analogy with the mode of the tapestries; and however unlikely any similarity may at first appear, the essential kinship is truly there. For these tapestries, like *Paterson*, achieve their success through a peculiar combination of the local and the mythical. We have the one hundred and one trees, shrubs, herbs, and flowers so realistically woven that eighty-five of them have been identified by botanists and praised for the exactitude of their reproduction; the "mille-fleurs background" is not composed of merely symbolical designs, but the colors burst forth from the actual, recognizable violet, cornflower, daisy, calendula, or dandelion. Yet all this actuality serves to border and center the mythical beast of oriental legend, serves to enfold and surround the human figures, the dogs, birds, and wild beasts, the castles and streams, the spears and hunting horns that crowd the scenes with a happy disregard of perspective—even to the point where the sixth tapestry superimposes the wounding of the unicorn upon an upper corner of the larger scene where the mythical beast is presented dead before the King and Queen. Meanwhile, amid the brilliant distortions of art and the splendor of color in flowers and costume, we find the brutal faces of certain varlets, the dog gutted by the unicorn's horn, the dog biting the unicorn's back, the vicious spears stabbing the "mild-white beast," the slanting, provocative, betraying eyes of the female attendant upon the virgin.

. cyclamen, columbine, if the art
with which these flowers have been
put down is to be trusted—and
again oak leaves and twigs
that brush the deer's antlers . .
    the brutish eyes of the deer
    not to be confused
    with the eyes of the Queen
    are glazed with death .

. . .

    a tapestry
silk and wool shot with silver threads
    a milk white one horned beast
        I, Paterson, the King-self
saw the lady
    through the rough woods
        outside the palace walls
among the stench of sweating horses
    and gored hounds
        yelping with pain
the heavy breathing pack
    to see the dead beast
        brought in at last
across the saddle bow
    among the oak trees.

The placing of that line, "I, Paterson, the King-self," implies a parallel between "Paterson," the poet, man, self, and city of the poem, and the Unicorn. The mythical beast is the spirit of the imagination, the immortal presence of art:

    The Unicorn
has no match
    or mate . the artist
    has no peer .
So through art alone, male and female, a field of
flowers, a tapestry, spring flowers unequaled
in loveliness.
    through this hole
    at the bottom of the cavern
    of death, the imagination
    escapes intact
he bears a collar round his neck
    hid in the bristling hair.

Thus in the last of the series, the most famous of the tapestries, the Unicorn appears in peaceful resurrection. So "Paterson" now writes "In old age"—the opening line of Book V—and knows the threat of mortality as well as the reassurance promised by everything that the Unicorn represents—as we learn from the long closing passage dominated by the tapestries:

—the aging body
    with the deformed great-toe nail
makes itself known
  coming
        to search me out—with a
        rare smile
among the thronging flowers of that field
    where the Unicorn
        is penned by a low
wooden fence
    in April!

. . .

the cranky violet
    like a knight in chess,
        the cinque-foil,
yellow faced—
    this is a French
        or Flemish tapestry—
the sweetsmelling primrose
    growing close to the ground, that poets

have made famous in England,
I cannot tell it all:

. . .

Yellow centers, crimson petals
and the reverse,
dandelion, love-in-a-mist,
corn flowers,
thistle and others
the names and perfumes I do not know.
The woods are filled with holly
(I have told you, this
is a fiction, pay attention),
the yellow flag of the French fields is
here
and a congeries of other flowers
as well: daffodils
and gentian, the daisy, columbine
petals
myrtle, dark and light
and calendulas.

Anyone who reads the excellent pamphlet on the flora of the tapestries provided by the museum[16] will see at once that most of the flowers here included by Williams are clearly recognizable and listed under these names; but the poet is recreating the act of personal, immediate, imaginative apprehension. Thus at times the poet gives his own familiar names, draws his own conclusions, imagines likenesses. The "myrtle, dark and light," for instance, must be the "periwinkle (*Vinca*)" which "appears only in the two normal colors of white and blue." And the "cinque-foil,/yellow faced" is not mentioned in the museum's account, but it is hard to find it suggested by certain flowers. Most important, the familiar, intimate quality of the poet's account reminds us that many of these flowers have appeared in the dozens of flower-poems and the hundreds of flower-images scattered throughout the poetry of William Carlos Williams, from his early tributes to the daisy, the primrose, and the "yellow cinquefoil," down through the great tribute to Demuth, "The Crimson Cyclamen," and on into the long flower-tribute to his wife, "Asphodel, That Greeny Flower," where the poet recalls his boyhood collection of "pressed flowers." Williams is one of the great poets of flowers and foliage, which he observes and represents with a loving and a scientific accuracy akin to that of the Unicorn tapestries. In a passage typical of *Paterson*'s mode of organization, this fifth book itself reminds us from the outset of the poet's love of flowers by including on its fourth page a personal letter to "Dear Bill":

> I wish you and F. could have come. It was a grand day and we missed you two, one and all missed you. Forgetmenot, wild columbine, white and purple violets, white narcissus, wild anemonies and yards and yards of delicate wild windflowers along the brook showed up at their best. . . .
>
> How lovely to read your memories of the place; a place is made of them as well as the world around it. Most of the flowers were put in many years ago and thrive each spring, the wild ones in some new spot that is exciting to see. Hepaticas and bloodroot are now all over the place, and the trees that were infants are now tall creatures filled this season with orioles, some rare warbler like the Myrtle and magnolia warblers and a wren has the best nest in the garage. . . .

So Book V suggests that we might regard *Paterson* as a kind of tapestry, woven out of memories and observations, composed by one man's imagination, but written in part by his friends, whose letters are scattered throughout, by his patients, whose words are remembered throughout, and by all the milling populace of Paterson, past and present, including that unicorn in the center of the field: the King-self, within whose mind these thoughts assemble like

A flight of birds, all together,
seeking their nests in the season
. . .
The
colors of their plumage are undecipherable
in the sun's glare against the sky
but the old man's mind is stirred
by the white, the yellow, the black
as if he could see them there.

Their presence in the air again
calms him. Though he is approaching
death he is possessed by many poems.

Notes

1. *Briarcliff Quarterly*, 3 (1946), 163–4.
2. *Modern American Poetry*, ed. B. Rajan (London, Dennis Dobson, 1950), p. 188.
3. Blackmur, *The Expense of Greatness* (New York, Arrow Editions, 1940), p. 233.
4. See Williams, "Prologue" to *Kora in Hell: Improvisations* (Boston, Four Seas, 1920), pp. 17–18; reprinted in Williams' *Selected Essays* (New York, Random House, 1954).
5. *A Voyage to Pagany* (1928), and the first two novels of his trilogy, *White Mule* (1937) and *In the Money* (1940); the third novel of the trilogy, *The Build-Up*, appeared in 1952.
6. The collection has been republished, with one additional story, under the title *The Farmers' Daughters* (Norfolk, Conn., New Directions, 1961); the long new story, which gives the volume its title, helps to focus the whole volume.
7. See Wallace Stevens' perceptive note, "Rubbings of Reality," in *Briarcliff Quarterly*, 3 (1946), 201–2; included in Stevens' *Opus Posthumous* (New York, Alfred A. Knopf, 1957), pp. 257–9.
8. See the chapter "Père Sebastian Rasles."
9. Koch, *William Carlos Williams* (Norfolk, Conn., New Directions, 1950), p. 152.
10. Koch, pp. 30–31; see "Prologue" to *Kora in Hell*, pp. 25–8.
11. *Modern American Poetry*, ed. Rajan, p. 189.
12. *Briarcliff Quarterly*, 3 (1946), 205–8.
13. *The Selected Letters of William Carlos Williams*, ed. John C. Thirlwall (New York, McDowell, Obolensky, 1957), p. 135.
14. *Literary Essays of Ezra Pound*, ed. T. S. Eliot (London, Faber & Faber, 1954), p. 392.
15. See *Paterson* (New York, New Directions, 1963), p. 164.
16. E. J. Alexander and Carol H. Woodward, *The Flora of the Unicorn Tapestries*, 2nd edn. (The New York Botanical Garden, 1947).

HUGH KENNER

From "Something to Say"
A Homemade World

1975, pp. 85–90

Practicing medicine, ⟨William Carlos Williams⟩ spent much of each day of his life with people who had a desperate need to tell him something. His ear for compelled speech was nearly absolute:

Will you please rush down and see
ma baby. You know, the one I talked
to you about last night

What was that?
Is this the baby specialist?
Yes, but perhaps you mean my son,
can't you wait until . ?
I, I, I don't think it's brEAthin'

A fieldwork note; and when he writes prose dialogue it rings as if transcribed; Williams was not, like Dickens or like Faulkner, an *impersonator*. But the habit of listening to voices extended to his own voice, so that he could write down the way he heard himself phrasing things:

THE POEM

It's all in
the sound. A song.
Seldom a song. It should
be a song—made of
particulars, wasps,
a gentian—something
immediate, open
scissors, a lady's
eyes—waking
centrifugal, centripetal

You hear the staccato phrasing of a taut voice. You also hear things speech wouldn't know how to clarify: the auditory relationships in

sound. A song.
Seldom a song. It should
be a song—

with the white space prolonging the tension after "should"; and "open" floating between "immediate," which it clarifies, and "scissors," which it specifies (the delay of the white space again withholding "scissors" till we've had time to take "open" with "immediate"). "A lady's," similarly, seems to go with "scissors" till round the corner of the line we encounter "eyes," and the last two words—"centrifugal, centripetal"—seem to tell us how the lady's wakened attention turns outward then inward, until we remember the title and think to include "centrifugal, centripetal" among the specifications for "The Poem." It's not "oral," it's too quirky and tricky for orality, but one of its qualifications for anatomizing its theme is that it knows what a voice sounds like.

It's not only not "oral," this poem, it's not fully present, not even quite intelligible, in being read aloud, nor yet in being looked at on the page. It's an audio-visual counterpoint, and "the Imagination" Williams talked about is as good a name as any for the region where the complete poem can be said to exist.

This ability to move close to quite simple words, both hearing them spoken—not quite the same thing as hearing their sounds—and seeing them interact on a typewritten page, gave Williams the sense of constant discovery that saved him from feeling constantly responsible for weighty problems. He liked a poem he could spin round on one corner, and it freed him not to be encumbered with pronouncements. He typed and retyped sequences of a few dozen words, changing a word or two, or shifting the point in a phrase at which the eye must turn back round a line's end. "No ideas but in things" meant that the energy moving from word to word would be like that of the eye moving from thing to thing, and not like that of the predicating faculty with its opinions:

—through metaphor to reconcile
the people and the stones.
Compose. (No ideas
but in things) Invent!
Saxifrage is my flower that splits
the rocks.

The same poem tells us that the writing is to be of words; he never supposed that "things" got onto the page. And "Saxifrage is my flower": though he did not need the convention that Nature was speaking, he was untroubled by any sense of its remote exteriority because he sensed his own biological kinship with processes of struggle and growth. A way to be part of the world is to consider that through the world as through yourself moves the energy of a cellular dance: not much of an "idea" as ideas go, but true enough to get many poems out of.

. . . The petals!
the petals undone
loosen all five and
swing up
The flower
flows to release—
Fast within a ring
where the compact
agencies
of conception
lie mathematically
ranged
round the
hair-like sting—
From such a pit
the color flows
over
a purple rim
upward to
the light! the light!
all around— . . .

Helped out by experiences Wordsworth couldn't have—time-lapse films of opening flowers, and a biology of dynamics, not of classifications—this kind of writing about natural process belongs to a new phase in the history of poetry. To a reader of professional books on nutrition and mitosis, "Nature" meant something both intimate and thrusting.

Process: growth and emergence: these were his themes: the effort of the new organism to define itself. They were comprised in what he meant by spring, by flowers and buds, by the "American idiom" (something *new*), by the effort at communal self-definition he discovered and re-enacted *In the American Grain*. Birth, for the obstetrician-poet, was the triumphant moment, not an instant beginning but the culmination of something nine months or nine millennia prepared. "She entered, as Venus from the sea, dripping": so he began a novel. "The air enclosed her, she felt it all over her, touching, waking her. If Venus did not cry aloud after release from the pressures of that sea-womb, feeling the new and lighter flood springing in her chest, flinging out her arms—this one did. Screwing up her tiny smeared face, she let out three convulsive yells—and lay still."

The struggle to get born, that was always Williams' plot; flowers fascinated him because they achieved it visibly, effortlessly. And then—the other half of his plot—the closure of the prison-house, as in Wordsworth and Blake, round the newborn potentiality. That prison-house—he is closer to Blake than to Wordsworth—is a communal failure, the lapsed Imagination. How do men think so little of themselves that they put up with what they put up with?

She stirs, distraught,
against him—wounded (drunk), moves
against him (a lump) desiring,

against him, bored .
flagrantly bored and sleeping, a
beer-bottle still grasped spear-like
in his hand .
while the small, sleepless boys, who
have climbed the columnar rocks
overhanging the pair (where they lie
overt upon the grass, besieged—
careless in their narrow cell under
the crowd's feet) stare down,
from history!
at them, puzzled and in the sexless
light (of childhood) bored equally,
go charging off .

All these people once entered "as Venus from the sea, dripping," the boys more recently, and as for the boys, if they now look down "from history," they perhaps will be looked down upon in turn when their present sexlessness has become desire. Is that all anybody can imagine? Citizen of a country that can remember its beginnings, he looked (like his classmate Pound) for a point of failure in history: no metaphysical wound (for the flowers with which we share life are not wounded) but a failure of vision, a lapsing of the Imagination. Hence his interest in the past of Paterson (which was never anything but a company town), and his singling out of the moment when "they saw birds with rusty breasts and called them robins."

> Thus, from the start, an America of which they could have had no inkling drove the first settlers upon their past. . . . For what they saw were not robins. They were thrushes only vaguely resembling the rosy, daintier English bird. . . .
>
> The example is slight but enough properly to incline the understanding. Strange and difficult, the new continent induced a torsion in the spirits of the first settlers, tearing them between the old and the new. And at once a split occurred in that impetus which should have carried them forward as one into the dangerous realities of the future. . . .

That is his myth of history, a birth rejected out of fear. His long career means that a poet needs no more ideas than that. (It is not made of ideas, said Mallarmé of poetry; it is made of words.) Chiefly a poet needs a passionate interest in the language, in the words people use, and the words they might use but do not. (And why do they not? Why is "torsion" not a word we hear spoken? It would fill one air-pocket.) What people say, what they do not say but might: that, related to a myth of history, was Williams' field of preoccupation. And the myth—remembering settlers who did not guess how much depended on what they should call the bird they chose to call "robin"—is written invisibly down the margins of his least pretentious poems, which affirm, again and again, no more than "how much depends": depends upon the act of finding a few dozen words, and upon their array once a poet has found them.

. . . Look at
what passes for the new.
You will not find it there but in
despised poems.
It is difficult
to get the news from poems
yet men die miserably every day
for lack
of what is found there.

LOUIS SIMPSON

"Modernity"

Three on the Tower: The Lives and Works of Ezra Pound, T. S. Eliot and William Carlos Williams

1975, pp. 242–59

How shall I be a mirror to this modernity?
("The Wanderer")

He did not like what he saw of the Germans—they were not gifted with inspiration. He condemned their militarism: they feared France and England and hoped to overcome their fear not by faith in the brotherhood of man but by an army to crush and kill. [1]

That year he went over to London and saw Ezra in his habitat—Church Walk, Kensington. Ezra introduced him to Mrs. Shakespear and her daughter. One evening they went to hear Yeats reading poems by candlelight. When they entered he was reading, of all things, Dowson's "Cynara." In a beautiful voice . . . but it wasn't Williams' dish. After a while he and Pound started to leave, but Yeats called out, "Was that Ezra Pound who was here?" He had something to say to Pound, so Ezra returned "and remained a few additional moments with the great man while we waited." This may have been, says Williams, the first time Pound met Yeats. [2]

The word "great" as he uses it is ironic. He is not taken in by the posturing of men such as Pound and Yeats.

He went with Pound to a lecture Yeats gave with Sir Edmund Gosse presiding. Yeats spoke of the young men of the nineties, Lionel Johnson among them, who had been denied an audience in England. What else was left for them but "drunkenness, lechery or immorality of whatever other sort?" At this point Sir Edmund banged his palm down on the bell beside him. Yeats tried to continue—the bell rang again. Pound and Williams failed to speak up in support of Yeats. "What a chance it had been for me," Williams says, "but I wasn't up to it . . . and so I sank back once more into anonymity." [3]

He didn't shine in public, couldn't think on his feet. He wasn't cut out for the occasions that were Ezra's meat and drink. Ezra didn't shine either, but he wasn't embarrassed—he behaved in a manner he had got out of books, unconscious of the effect this might be having on others.

There was the time that Ezra stared at the woman in the National Gallery. She was a tall, wan creature, a "curious, detached figure." Ezra postured, leaning back on his cane (did he have a cane? perhaps not), his legs apart, his pointed beard atilt, and stared at her. She was conscious of it and "began to move her thighs and pelvis in such a way that it became very apparent that she was greatly moved and excited." Then there came a snigger from the ceiling—some workmen had been watching the scene. Ezra stopped staring at the woman and stepped back and stared at them until they stopped sniggering. By this time the woman had vanished. She may well, Williams speculates, have served as the model for the one in *Mauberley* whom Pound compares to a skein of silk blown against the railing. [4]

She would like some one to speak to her,
And is almost afraid that I
will commit that indiscretion.

The poem he is thinking of is Pound's "The Garden," in *Lustra*. [5]

During his year abroad Williams traveled to Paris and Italy, where his brother Ed showed him around. He gazed at buildings, statues, and pictures. Then he went to Spain. One evening in Toledo he drank wine with some shepherds and listened to a man play the guitar. "That's another place," he thinks, "in which I might have stayed forever without loss." But the thought is followed by another: "They might have robbed me, stuck me with a knife and thrown the body over the cliff and no one the wiser for it."[6]

So back to Rutherford . . . "Home and the practice of medicine had begun."[7]

In 1911 he bought his first Ford. It was a beauty with brass rods in front holding up the windshield, and acetylene lamps, but no starter. Sometimes on a winter day he would crank the car for twenty minutes until he got it going, then, in dripping sweat, go in and take a quick bath and change his clothes, before setting out on his calls.[8]

He saw Floss every day. "Happy days and nights—if lovers are ever happy!"

They waited three years to be married. Three years was too long—he "wore the streets out between the two houses"—yet when he looked back he thought that the long period of breaking in was all that had made their later marriage bearable. He had to do a lot of readjusting to come out softened down for marriage. "My mind was always rebellious and uneasy. This was to be my wife-to-be, excluding all the rest. How could one stand or understand it? And yet, there was Flossie, no Venus de Milo, surely—Flossie, in some ways hard as nails, thank heaven. She had to be."[9]

They were married in December 1912 and went to Bermuda for their honeymoon. They bought a house at Number 9 Ridge Road. Then Floss was pregnant.

One day he was digging a trench for rhododendrons in front of the house when a young woman he knew came walking down the street.

"Happy?" she said.

"Sure," he said, "why not?"

She laughed and kept on walking. What was biting her, he wondered. Then he thought about the question. Was he happy? Who could tell?[10]

He had begun by imitating Keats. Now he imitated Pound, who himself was writing imitations of Renaissance poetry, pre-Raphaelite poetry, and Robert Browning.

In these prewar years Pound was in the ascendant. He published book after book. He knew Yeats and other famous authors. He was beginning to have a reputation in London. In comparison with Pound, Williams was a nonentity.

Therefore he took Pound as his mentor and heeded his advice. He observed the laws Pound handed down. These were the years in which Pound led the Imagist movement—Williams became an Imagist, more deeply committed to the principles than Pound himself. Williams was a slow reader—he lingered behind, still considering, while Pound went leaping ahead, changing from one thing to another. Williams believed . . . he believed in Ezra Pound. He took to heart the Imagist principles that writing must be based in sensory experience, and that poetry does not declaim or explain, it presents.[11] He held to these principles all his life.

Pound was his master. This is evident in Williams' fascination with Pound's theatrical behavior and his way of approaching women. There was a good deal of the woman in Williams, he liked to explain. He accepted Weininger's division of male and female psychology. Writing to Viola Baxter Jordan he said, "Men disgust me and if I must say it fill me with awe and admiration. I am too much a woman."[12] He liked theatricals himself, but had subdued that part of his character in order to be a doctor and family man. He remained fascinated, however, with people who dared to act their dreams.

He submitted to Pound's authority. And Pound was two years younger! He swallowed his pride and submitted. It was hard, for he had a pride of his own—prided himself on being ordinary. Like Whitman he contained multitudes.

For the time being he set himself to imitating Pound. He wrote Renaissance poems in Ezra's English:

> Lady of dusk-wood fastnesses,
> Thou art my Lady.
> I have known the crisp, splintering leaf-
> tread with thee on before,
> White, slender through green saplings . . .[13]

He wrote a rhyming imitation of Pound's imitations of Browning's dramatic monologues. He began with a Poundian exclamation:

> It is useless, good woman, useless: the spark fails me.
> God! yet when the might of it all assails me . . .[14]

He wrote an imitation of the spirit, if not the technique, of H.D.'s pseudo-Greek poems:

> So art thou broken in upon me, Apollo,
> Through a splendor of purple garments
> Held by the yellow-haired Clymene . . .
>
> . . .
>
> This is strange to me, here in the modern twilight.[15]

It was not just strange, it was alien to Williams, for unlike H.D. he wanted to be modern. In the year following the publication of these poems he wrote, "How shall I be a mirror to this modernity?"[16]

Pound undertook to help Williams as, within a short time, he would be helping Eliot. He saw to it that seven of Williams' poems were published as a group in *The Poetry Review*, London, "With Introductory Note by Ezra Pound." This was Williams' first appearance in a magazine. Pound arranged for Williams' second book, *The Tempers*, to be published by Elkin Mathews, his own publisher. The book appeared in September 1913. Pound reviewed it himself in *The New Freewoman*. He praised the vigor of the poems. The emotions expressed were original and this gave hope for Williams' future work.[17]

Pound recommended the publication of four of Williams' poems in *Poetry*, Chicago, Harriet Monroe's magazine.[18] But Williams and Harriet did not see eye to eye. She found fault with some of his lines and he assumed the role of an iconoclast: "The poet comes forward assailing the trite and established while the editor is to shear off all roughness and extravagance."[19] Williams means: "while the editor thinks that he must shear off. . . ." He did not have time to spare—when he wrote prose he was content to approximate a meaning.

His tone in their subsequent correspondence became downright insulting: "I wish you well in your work but I heartily object to your old-fashioned and therefore vicious methods."[20]

Williams now thought of himself as a modern poet "assailing outworn conventions." In March 1913 his wife gave him a copy of Whitman's poems. Though he seems to have gotten very little from Whitman—only the idea of writing free verse—Whitman's emphasis on contemporaneity appealed to him. The air was full of new ideas, *l'esprit nouveau* as they called it in France. Modern art began in the prewar years—it seems to have been stimulated by the approaching cataclysm. In 1913 the Armory Show in New York introduced works by Cézanne, Gauguin, Renoir, Matisse, Picasso, Braque, Picabia, Gleizes and Duchamp, the most sensational being

Duchamp's "Nude Descending a Staircase." There were innovations in the dance, led by Isadora Duncan and Ruth St. Denis. Among poets there was talk of Futurists and Imagists.

Williams frequented artistic circles in New York. He found that he could have his cake and eat it too—being Doctor Williams in Rutherford and William Carlos Williams, poet, in Manhattan. He took Floss to parties, then he started leaving her home.[21] She didn't seem to enjoy the company of artists and writers as much as he did, and besides it was inconvenient—there was the trouble of getting someone to stay with the child. They agreed, however, that for the sake of his writing he should keep in touch with what was going on. He would try not to stay out late—he couldn't afford to anyway, seeing that he had to be up early in the morning. He cranked the Ford and headed for New York.

The party might be at the "sumptuous studio" of Walter Arensberg.[22] Arensberg edited *The Glebe*. Ten numbers appeared, one being Pound's Imagist anthology, *Des Imagistes*. "Arensberg could afford to spread a really ample feed with drinks to match. You always saw Marcel Duchamp there. His paintings on glass, half-finished, stood at one side. . . ."[23] Man Ray might be there or Charles Sheeler. Or Charlie Demuth, Williams' old friend from student days. Isadora Duncan was there.

In 1914 Williams began meeting poets associated with *Others*, Alfred Kreymborg's magazine. "There was . . . wild enthusiasm among free verse writers. . . . Good verse was coming in from San Francisco, from Louisville, Kentucky, from Chicago, from 63rd street. . . ."[24] On Sunday afternoons the *Others* crowd would congregate at the Kreymborgs' house in Grantwood, New Jersey. "On every possible occasion," says Williams, "I went madly in my flivver to help with the magazine which had saved my life as a writer. Twenty-five dollars a month kept it going. . . ."[25]

He came to know Wallace Stevens and Marianne Moore, poets like himself, and Kenneth Burke, the poet and critic who became a lifelong friend. He knew Maxwell Bodenheim and Malcolm Cowley. He went to literary gatherings in the Village. Amy Lowell was there, smoking a cigar.

Amy was involved in Imagism. In face, she had taken it over and Pound had dropped it. Just as well . . . she had heard that he was being dropped himself by everyone in London. Pound was impossible, an egotist. On the other hand, truly great poets had sympathy. As Keats said, "If a sparrow come before my window, I take part in its existence and pick about the gravel."

Williams had had enough of Keats. He went over and talked to Charlie Demuth. He loved Charlie's attitude to life—sophisticated, sharp-witted, irreverent. It corresponded to his own appetite for "something new . . . Something to enliven our lives by its invention, some breadth of understanding, some lightness of touch."[26] Charlie didn't like the taste of liquor but found that the effect on his mind was delightful. Li Po has written his best poetry while being supported in the arms of the Emperor's attendants and with a dancing girl to hold the tablet.[27]

Were there any dancing girls present? One or two, said Charlie, one or two.

In March 1914 Williams' "The Wanderer" appeared in *The Egoist*, London. The poem of three hundred lines announced his intention to be modern. It was in free verse and the theme was new: the Wanderer immersed himself in the stream of life, symbolized by the Passaic River. The river was filthy, but he bathed in it. In this manner he was reborn—he became the river and knew everything it knew.

Keats says that beauty is truth. Williams was taking a different view: "We have discarded beauty; at its best it seems truth incompletely realized."[28] The new poetry would include:

Faces all knotted up like burls on oaks,
Grasping, fox-snouted, thick-lipped,
Sagging breasts and protruding stomachs . . .[29]

The Wanderer is taken by his muse to the city. For this purpose she has transformed herself:

Ominous, old, painted—
With bright lips, and lewd Jew's eyes . . .[30]

She shows him Broadway, a breadline, and a strike. Then she leads him through the meadows of New Jersey to the Passaic. She dabbles her hands in the filthy water and bathes both their foreheads. She tells him to enter the river: "Enter, youth, into this bulk," and tells the river, "Enter . . . into this young man." He enters the river and, he says, "I knew all—it became me."[31]

This is Whitmanesque—the sense of absorbing everything, becoming it.

The Wanderer is transformed and sees the last of his old self being borne off by the water. "I could have shouted out in my agony / At the sight of myself departing." But there is some happiness left: "deep foliage, the thickest beeches . . . / Tallest oaks and yellow birches." There are birds. The place, "For miles around, hallowed by a stench," shall be the temple of poetry.[32]

As with much that Williams wrote, "The Wanderer" echoes Keats. Here the echoes are of Keats' "Ode to Psyche":

Yes, I will be thy priest, and build a fane
In some untrodden region of my mind . . .

At this time the Imagist movement was flourishing. The typical Imagist poem was brief and restricted to presentation of sensory details. Then the concept of Imagism degenerated—anything written in free verse was thought to be Imagist. The unsure taste of Amy Lowell and Harriet Monroe was responsible for this, Pound having left the movement.

For a while Williams considered himself an Imagist. "The immediate image, which was impressionistic, sure enough, fascinated us all. We had followed Pound's instructions, his famous 'Don'ts,' eschewing inversions of the phrase, the putting down of what to our senses was tautological and so, uncalled for, merely to fill out a standard form. Literary allusions, save in very attenuated form, were unknown to us. Few had the necessary reading."

The public thought that the Imagists had definite ideas, but the Imagists themselves were not so sure. "No one knew consistently enough to formulate a 'movement.' We were restless and constrained, closely allied with the painters. Impressionism, dadaism, surrealism applied to both painting and the poem. What a battle we made of it merely getting rid of capitals at the beginning of every line!"[33] It was the line that really concerned them, "the poetic line and our hopes for its recovery from stodginess."[34] That, and the structure of the poem . . . "Imagism was not structural: that was the reason for its disappearance."[35] The mere presentation of an image was not enough.

Williams worked at his writing like a painter or sculptor, struggling with the material. He was having trouble with his lines—"The Wanderer" moved in jerks and gasps. He was not happy with the freedom of free verse. As for structure, the poem had none; it was episodic, like the discarded poem modeled on *Endymion*.

The air was full of theories. Poetry must cleave to the senses—but it was also true that poetry was nothing without imagination. "The thing that stands eternally in the way of really good writing is always one: the virtual impossibility of lifting to the imagination those things which lie under the direct scrutiny of the senses."[36] Were these ideas contradictory? It didn't matter. Ideas were like tubes of paint—they were not what you looked at. The poem was an object—a shape and a sound.

He did not hold theories—he had them, which is a different thing entirely. He echoed Weininger's views of psychology. Then he discovered Kandinsky's ideas about art. There are, said Kandinsky, three modes of expression, and he listed them in an ascending order of importance:

> 1. A direct impression of nature, expressed in purely pictorial form. This I call an 'Impression'.
> 2. A largely unconscious, spontaneous expression of inner character, non-material in nature. This I call an 'Improvisation'.
> 3. An expression of slowly formed inner feeling, tested and worked over repeatedly and almost pedantically. This I call 'Composition'. Reason, consciousness, purpose, play an overwhelming part. But of calculation nothing appears: only feeling.[37]

Kandinsky's treatise *On the Spiritual in Art* was well known among writers and artists. Marsden Hartley met Kandinsky in Germany in 1912 and 1913, and extracts from the treatise were printed in Alfred Stieglitz's *Camera Work*. The third idea stated above sounds like a description of Williams' poetry: "An expression of slowly formed inner feeling, tested and worked over repeatedly and almost pedantically . . . But of calculation nothing appears: only feeling."

There were other ideas in Kandinsky that agreed with ideas Williams had been developing out of the circumstances of his life. An artist must express his personality. He must express what is characteristic of his epoch—this is the element of style, "composed of the speech of the epoch, and the speech of the nation." And he must express what is particular to all art everywhere—elements that are not bound by time or space. If the first two principles are observed, the third will follow of its own accord. But—and this is important—if the third element, the "eternal qualities," are emphasized, the work of art will not reach a contemporary audience. This last idea, says Mike Weaver, helped Williams to develop the idea of "locality" with which he belabored Pound and Eliot.[38]

Between 1913 and 1916 Williams wrote poems that fitted Kandinsky's description of an "impression." "If one were to turn for an analogy in painting for the poems in the collection *Al Que Quiere!*, it would be to the Ashcan school of realism, in which the dignity of human life was rendered by impressionistic means."[39]

> the old man who goes about
> gathering dog-lime
> walks in the gutter
> without looking up
> and his tread
> is more majestic than
> that of the Episcopal minister
> approaching the pulpit
> of a Sunday.[40]

Apart from the realism of the subject, the most noticeable change is in the use of words and the shaping of lines as units. The lines are tight and short, and they seem to break with a purpose. There is a clear reason, for instance, why one line, "And his tread," has only three syllables which must be uttered slowly. The syllables in their ponderousness and sound represent the walk of the lime-gatherer.

This is like a poem written a hundred years before—Wordsworth's poem about an old man gathering leeches. Whether or not Williams is conscious of the resemblance, in his attempt to dignify the ordinary he resembles Wordsworth. Moreover, his insistence on the use of the American idiom is like Wordsworth's argument, in *Lyrical Ballads*, for "a selection of language really used by men." "I have wished," says Wordsworth, "to keep the Reader in the company of flesh and blood."[41] It is equally true of Williams.

Most of the poems in *Al Que Quiere!* are written in short lines because, Williams says, his writing reproduces the pace of his speech. "I didn't go in for long lines because of my nervous nature. I couldn't. The rhythmic pace was the pace of speech, an excited pace because I was excited when I wrote."[42] The idea that poetry should reproduce the rhythms of speech or feeling has now become so common that it passes unnoticed. But when Williams started writing this was a new idea. Traditionally poems had been written in meter—the rhythm of the line was determined not by the feelings of the poet but by literary conventions.

The poems in *Al Que Quiere!* look carved—a block of lines counterpoised by another block. Not the traditional division of the poem in stanzas mechanically repeated. Williams works in blocks of rhythm as a sculptor works in marble or a painter in colors. A Williams poem is irregular—but not free verse, "the senseless / unarrangement of wild things."[43] There is an organic relationship between one part and another. Therefore it is as difficult to represent Williams' poetry with quotations as it would be to represent a statue by a finger or a painting by a few inches of the canvas. "My liking," he says, "is for an unimpeded thrust right through a poem from the beginning to the end, without regard to formal arrangements."[44]

The poetry is concentrated. This he has learned from the Imagist movement. A poem may be only a few lines.

> It's a strange courage
> you give me ancient star:
> Shine alone in the sunrise
> toward which you lend no part![45]

The writing is vivacious; it conveys a sense of enjoyment. This is not common—in Chinese or Japanese poems perhaps, but not in our traditions. The English or American poem traditionally has set out to do something, to make a statement or move the reader. But in many of Williams' poems the aim is enjoyment, nothing more.

> if I in my north room
> dance naked, grotesquely
> before my mirror
> waving my shirt round my head
> and singing softly to myself:
> "I am lonely, lonely.
> I was born to be lonely,
> I am best so!" . . .[46]

This is original, and when poetry speaks of "Old men who have studied / every leg show / in the city . . ." we are hearing a language that has not been in American poetry since Whitman. It has what Williams calls "the inclusive sweep of the great tradition."[47]

Al Que Quiere! has been said to mark the start of Williams' metric experiments.[48] But it was more than a beginning—after *Al Que Quiere!* though he varied he did not radically change his style.

At this point, when he achieved a kind of mastery, began the trouble of his life.

There is nothing in literary history quite like the feelings William Carlos Williams had when he thought about T. S. Eliot. Byron said of Keats, who had apparently been killed by bad reviews of his poems, "'Tis strange the mind, that very fiery particle, / Should let itself be snuff'd out by an article." Stranger still for one writer to dislike another to the point that, like King Charles' head, he sees him everywhere. In the middle of an essay on Marianne Moore, Williams interjects, "It is a talent which diminishes the tom-toming on the hollow men of a wasteland to an irrelevant pitter-patter."[49] In an essay on Karl Shapiro, "Well, you don't get far with women by quoting Eliot to them."[50]

He wishes that Eliot were dead. "Let us once and for all understand," Williams writes to Kay Boyle in 1932, "that Eliot is finally and definitely dead."[51]

There are reasonable explanations for his dislike of Eliot. It was natural for him to oppose Eliot's Anglophilia, believing as he did in the value of locality. Then Eliot was converted to Anglo-Catholicism, and Williams thought it was eyewash: "Every little cleric who happens to bleat and consider himself an artist because of his association with the Church has no title whatever to consider himself so for that reason."[52] And Eliot was no lover of democracy—nor was Williams in certain moods, but he did have an affection for ordinary people.

But the difference in their ideas does not account for Williams' virulent hatred of Eliot. Nor did it begin, as is commonly thought, in 1922 with the publication of Eliot's *Waste Land*. It began years before, when Pound discovered the American poet he had been hoping for and it was not Williams. "Here is the Eliot poem," Pound wrote to Harriet Monroe in 1914. "The most interesting contribution I've had from an American."[53] From then on it was clear that with Pound it was Eliot who came first. He continued to be interested in Williams, but did not expect great things of him, nothing to what might be expected of Eliot.

Williams had followed Pound, even unto the Renaissance. He had been loyal to Ezra. "There are people," he wrote Harriet Monroe in 1915, "who find E. P. chiefly notable as a target—and yet they cannot perceive his greatness."[54]

Now he felt betrayed. And with Eliot's success he felt even worse. The publication in 1917 of Eliot's *Prufrock and Other Observations* cast him into the shade. There was, for example, an English critic who said that American poets were no good, with the exception of Eliot. The critic's name was Jepson and it seems that he lived in Kensington—like Pound, though Williams did not say so. Williams said, "There is always some everlasting Polonius of Kensington forever to rate highly his eternal Eliot. It is because Eliot is a subtle conformist. It tickles the palate of this archbishop of procurers to a lecherous antiquity to hold up Prufrock as a New World type. Prufrock, the nibbler at sophistication, endemic in every capital, the not quite (because he refuses to turn his back), is 'the soul of that modern land,' the United States!"

Jepson had praised Eliot's "La Figlia Que [sic] Piange," the delicate rhythm, et cetera. "IT CONFORMS," Williams shouts, that's why Jepson likes it. He admits that there is "a highly refined distillation" in the poem, a "conscious simplicity." The line "Simple and faithless as a smile and shake of the hand" is perfect. But the last stanza is made almost unintelligible by straining after a rhyme, "the very cleverness with which this straining is covered being a sinister token in itself." He sees Eliot's rhyming as sinister—it conceals some deeper, evil purpose.[55]

He was so hurt by Pound's preference for Eliot over himself that he never forgave Eliot and for a while he had harsh things to say about Pound. "E. P.," he said, "is the best enemy United States verse has."[56] He visualized an international congress of poets—Remy de Gourmont had called for one. "I do believe," Williams wrote, "that when they meet Paris will be more than slightly abashed to find parodies of the middle ages, Dante and *langue d'oc* foisted upon it as the best in United States poetry."[57]

He was no longer willing to accept Pound's tutelage from the other side of the Atlantic. "Criticism must originate in the environment that it is intended for."[58]

But he did not long direct his fire against the one who had actually hurt him. He did not hate Pound. It was the favorite he hated, Eliot with his coat of many colors. And to this day Williams' admirers have carried on the vendetta against Eliot. They would like his works to be erased from the memory of men. As this cannot be arranged, the next best thing is to misread them. "'The Waste Land,'" says James Breslin, "is a kind of anti-epic, a poem in which the quest for meaning is entirely thwarted and we are left, at the end, waiting for the collapse of western civilization."[59]

Paterson, on the other hand, is a "pre-epic, showing that the process of disintegration releases forces that can build a new world."[60] It seems that for Williams to be a great poet, it must be proved at any cost that Eliot is not.

But Williams was not so different from Eliot as he has been made to seem, and at this time he was feeling a bit like Prufrock himself, anticipating middle age: "In middle age the mind passes to a variegated October. This is the time youth in its faulty aspirations has set for the achievement of great summits. But having attained the mountain top one is not snatched into a cloud but the descent proffers its blandishments quite as a matter of course. At this the fellow is cast into a great confusion and rather plaintively looks about to see if any has fared better than he."[61]

He wondered if he had made the right choice. Pound was in London doing what he liked, writing, while he had to practice medicine. There was something ludicrous about his position, for an artist. "I have defeated myself purposely," he said, "in almost everything I do because I don't want to be thought an artist. I much prefer to be an ordinary fellow. I never wanted to be separated from my fellow mortals by acting like an artist."[62] But the price of being an ordinary fellow came high. "He would want to be quiet, want to relax, and had to go on without respite. To hell with home, his kids, herself, everything . . . if he could only get out and away—anywhere."[63]

The suburbs were getting him down. He was becoming dull. So he turned to women for excitement—"the quiver of the flesh under the smooth fabric."[64]

"I have discovered," Williams says in the Prologue to *Kora in Hell*, "that the thrill of first love passes!" This was written when he had been married six years. He goes on to say, "I have been reasonably frank about my erotics with my wife. I have never or seldom said, my dear I love you, when I would rather say: My dear, I wish you were in Tierra del Fuego."

Once more, Williams' prose is a little "off." His saying that he has been frank about his erotics with his wife is not followed, as we expect, by his saying that his wife knows about his affairs. It is followed by something quite different. The confusion comes of his setting out to say something, then thinking better of it and saying something else that shows him in a better light. But he does not rewrite the first part of his thought.

He goes on to say, "I have discovered by scrupulous attention to this detail and by certain allied experiments that we can continue from time to time to elaborate relationships quite equal in quality, if not greatly superior to that surrounding our wedding."

As Williams' wedding was delayed three years, this is nothing to brag of.

He concludes the glimpse into his marriage with the statement that the best times have followed the worst. "Periods of barrenness have intervened . . . our formal relations have teetered on the edge of a debacle to be followed, as our imaginations have permitted, by a new growth of passionate attachment. . . ."[65]

He was the straying husband who knows that he will be forgiven. This is shown in the following dialogue from his play, *A Dream of Love*. The play is autobiographical, so much so that the poem Doc reads to Myra, "Love Song," which he wrote when they were first married, is included in Williams' collected poems.[66]

> *Myra:* . . . what would you do without all your women, darling?
> *Doc:* I'd find one up a tree somewhere.
> *Myra:* You sure would. And drag her down by the hair—if she didn't drop on you first from a low branch. I don't care—so long as I have my garden.
> . . .
> *Myra:* . . . you went to a hotel with that woman.
> *Doc:* Sure. Anything you can do you must do. I'm not proud. If it comes my way I do it.[67]

It was a common enough way of looking at sex. Williams seems to have suspected that it was too common, for he tried to describe it as romantic: the other women were visionary, or his wife was all women, subsuming the rest. In "The Basis of Faith in Art" he has this conversation with his brother:

> Did it ever occur to you that a marriage might be invigorated by deliberately breaking the vows?
> That is impossible.
> Nothing is impossible to the imagination.[68]

Nevertheless, he was feeling disillusioned. There was no letup in his work as a doctor. His affairs provided only temporary relief. He was past thirty and he was not famous—it seemed unlikely that he would ever be, living in Rutherford. It was one of the low points of his life. It compelled him to think—to think things through and see where he stood and why. It was not the kind of thinking philosophers do—it came of a way of life, not out of books. Kandinsky was not as convincing as "The odor of the poor farmer's fried supper . . . mixing with the smell of the hemlocks, mist . . . in the valley."[69]

"The local is the universal."[70] And "There is no universal except in the local."[71]

Believing this enabled him to make a new start. And developing the belief he found others who held it too. John Dewey said, "The local is the only universal, upon that all art builds."[72] Keyserling said the same thing in different words. Williams had discovered it for himself, by living in Rutherford. He had to believe it. But it wasn't just a matter of necessity—he had chosen to live where he did. He might have lived in Toledo—"That's another place in which I might have lived forever." Or in London, like Pound and Eliot. But he had chosen to live here—so it was a matter of conviction, not mere necessity. Other men dreamed, but he had vision—he saw life as it was.

Keyserling said, "Every autochthonous culture in the world began as a local culture. Culture is always a daughter of spirit, married to earth. A man who is not yet the native son of a soil can conquer matter spiritually only on a small scale."[73] Williams believed this. From this time forward he strove to emphasize the "universality of the local. From me where I stand to them where they stand in their lives here and now. . . ."[74]

The word "local" may be misleading. It doesn't mean Rutherford, nor even America—it means experience, of which sensory experience is primary—"a local definition of effort."[75] This is how locality comes in, but the emphasis isn't on the locality; it is on the experience. As the point is so important we had better have it in his own words: "We have said simply and as frequently as possible and with as many apt illustrations as we could muster that contact with experience is essential to good writing or, let us say, literature. We have said this in the conviction that contact always implies a local definition of effort with a consequent taking on of certain colors from the locality by the experience, and these colors or sensual values of whatever sort are the only realities in writing or, as may be said, the essential quality in literature. We have even given what seem to be definite exceptions to the rule: unattached intelligence (the Jewish sphere), virtuosity (Russian violinists)."[76]

The corollary is opposition to those who do not show "local definition of effort." In his opinion, Pound and Eliot do not show it. "Being inclined to run off to London and Paris, it is inexplicable that in every case they have forgotten or not known that the experience of native local contacts which they take with them, is the only thing that can give that differentiated quality of presentation to their work which at first enriches their new sphere and later alone might carry them far as creative artists in the continental hurly-burly. Pound ran to Europe in a hurry. It is understandable. But he had not sufficient ground to stand on for more than perhaps two years. He stayed fifteen. Rereading his first book of poems it is easy to see why he was so successful. It was the naive warmth of the wilderness—no matter how presented. But in the end they played Wilson with him.

"Unfortunately for the arts here, intelligence and training have nearly always forced a man out of the country. Cut off from the dominant of their early established sensory backgrounds these expatriates go a typical and but slightly variable course thereafter."

It is not surprising that Williams has been called provincial.[77] He seems to think that American writers should stay in America and write about local subjects. In the 1920's expatriatism was an issue, with writers such as Pound, Eliot, Hemingway and Fitzgerald preferring to live in Europe and others arguing for America. "I remember," says Fitzgerald, "a fellow expatriate opening a letter from a mutual friend of ours, urging him to come home and be revitalized by the hardy, bracing qualities of the native soil. It was a strong letter and it affected us both deeply, until we noticed that it was headed from a nerve sanitarium in Pennsylvania."[78]

Williams tried to remove the impression that by "locality" he meant simply place. In a letter to Pound—"For the luv of God snap out of it! I'm no more sentimental about 'murika' than Li Po was about China or Shakespeare about Yingland or any damned Frog about Paris. I know as well as you do that there's nothing sacred about any land. But I also know (as you do also) that there's no taboo effective against any land, and where I live is no more a 'province' than I make it."[79]

The argument against expatriatism is not chauvinistic—it is a matter of aesthetics: "He who does not know his own world, in whatever confused form it may be, must either stupidly fail to learn from foreign work or stupidly swallow it without knowing how to judge of its essential value."[80]

Therefore it appears that when Williams argues for the local he means the artist's sensory experience rooted in place—not merely staying in one place. Locality is "the sense of being attached with integrity to actual experience."[81] Yet Williams was so attached to one place that the meaning has been taken to be this. The place for him was Number 9 Ridge Road. He persuaded himself that it was, making a virtue of necessity. Believing this enabled him to believe in the importance of what he was writing, even if it were only a few lines dashed off about something he had seen that day. Living in Rutherford was as significant as living in London or Paris. No one, not even Eliot, could know what he knew—no one else could be William Carlos Williams.

Notes

1. William Carlos Williams to Edgar I. Williams, 11 August 1909, *The Selected Letters of William Carlos Williams*, John C. Thirlwall, ed., New York: McDowell, Obolensky, 1957, p. 18. Hereafter cited as *Letters*.
2. Williams, *Autobiography*, New York: New Directions, 1951, p. 114.
3. Ibid., pp. 115–16.
4. Ibid., pp. 117.
5. Ezra Pound, *Personae*, New York: New Directions, 1926, p. 83.
6. Williams, *Autobiography*, p. 123.
7. Ibid., p. 127.
8. Ibid.
9. Ibid., pp. 127–30.
10. Ibid., pp. 132–33.
11. Williams, "A Note on Poetry," *Oxford Anthology of American Literature*, ed. by William Rose Benét and Norman Holmes Pearson (1938), p. 1313.
12. William Carlos Williams to Viola Baxter Jordan, 6 January 1911, cited in *William Carlos Williams: The American Background* by Mike Weaver, Cambridge University Press, 1971, p. 22.
13. Williams, "First Praise," *Collected Earlier Poems*, New York: New Directions, 1951, p. 17. Hereafter cited as *C.E.P.*
14. Williams, "The Death of Franco of Cologne: His Prophecy of Beethoven," *C.E.P.*, p. 25.
15. Williams, "An After Song," *C.E.P.*, p. 22.
16. Williams, "The Wanderer," *C.E.P.*, p. 22.
17. Emily Mitchell Wallace, *A Bibliography of William Carlos Williams*, Middletown, Conn.: Wesleyan University Press, 1968, p. 10.
18. Ezra Pound to Harriet Monroe, March 1913, *Selected Letters of Ezra Pound 1907–1941*, D. D. Paige, ed., New York: New Directions, 1950, p. 14.
19. William Carlos Williams to Harriet Monroe, 5 March 1913, *Letters*, p. 23.
20. William Carlos Williams to Harriet Monroe, 26 October 1916, *Letters*, p. 39.
21. Williams, *Autobiography*, p. 157.
22. Williams, "Prologue to *Kora in Hell*" [1918], *Selected Essays of William Carlos Williams*, New York: New Directions, 1954, p. 5. Hereafter cited as *Essays*.
23. Williams, *Autobiography*, p. 136.
24. William Carlos Williams to the Editor of *The Egoist*, 1915, *Letters*, p. 31.
25. Williams, *Autobiography*, p. 135.
26. James Guimond, *The Art of William Carlos Williams*, Urbana: University of Illinois Press, 1968, p. 43.
27. Williams, "Prologue to *Kora in Hell*," *Essays*, pp. 25–26.
28. Williams, "The Wanderer," *C.E.P.*, pp. 3–12.
29. Ibid., p. 7.
30. Ibid., p. 5.
31. Ibid., pp. 11–12.
32. Ibid., p. 12.
33. Williams, *Autobiography*, p. 148.
34. Ibid.
35. Williams, "The Poem as a Field of Action" [1948], *Essays*, p. 283.
36. Williams, "Prologue to *Kora in Hell*," *Essays*, pp. 11–12.
37. W. Kandinsky, "Concerning the Spiritual in Art," ed. Robert Motherwell (1947), p. 77, cited by Weaver, p. 39.
38. Weaver, pp. 37–39.
39. Ibid., p. 39.
40. Williams, "Pastoral," *C.E.P.*, p. 124.
41. William Wordsworth, "Preface," *Lyrical Ballads* (1800).
42. Williams, *I Wanted to Write a Poem*, Boston: Beacon Press, 1958, p. 15.
43. Williams, "This Florida: 1924," *C.E.P.*, p. 330.
44. William Carlos Williams to Alva N. Turner, 27 February 1921, *Letters*, p. 50.
45. Williams, "El Hombre," *C.E.P.*, p. 140.
46. Williams, "Danse Russe," *C.E.P.*, p. 148.
47. Williams, "Against the Weather" [1939], *Essays*, p. 215.
48. J. Hillis Miller, ed., *William Carlos Williams: A Collection of Critical Essays*, Englewood Cliffs, New Jersey: Prentice-Hall, 1966, p. 175.
49. Williams, *Essays*, p. 292.
50. Ibid., p. 259.
51. William Carlos Williams to Kay Boyle, 1932, *Letters*, p. 129.
52. Williams, "Against the Weather" [1939], *Essays*, p. 215.
53. Ezra Pound to Harriet Monroe, October 1914, *Selected Letters of Ezra Pound 1907–1941*, p. 41.
54. William Carlos Williams to Harriet Monroe, 8 May 1915, *Letters*, p. 29.
55. Williams, "Prologue to *Kora in Hell*," *Essays*, pp. 21–23.
56. Ibid., p. 24.
57. Ibid., pp. 23–24.
58. William Carlos Williams to Kenneth Burke, 26 January 1921, *Letters*, p. 48.
59. James E. Breslin, *William Carlos Williams: An American Artist*, New York: Oxford University Press, 1970, p. 202.
60. Ibid.
61. William Carlos Williams, *Kora in Hell: Improvisations*, Boston: Four Seas Co., 1920, p. 25.
62. "William Carlos Williams in conversation with John C. Thirlwall," "Introduction," *Letters*, p. xvii.
63. Williams, "Hands Across the Sea," *The Farmers' Daughters*, Norfolk, Conn.: New Directions, 1961, p. 17.
64. Williams, *Kora in Hell*, p. 42.
65. Williams, *Essays*, p. 19.
66. Williams, *Many Loves*, Norfolk, Conn.: New Directions, 1961, pp. 125–26; "Love Song," *C.E.P.*, p. 174.
67. Williams, *Many Loves*, pp. 117–206.
68. Williams, "The Basis of Faith in Art" [1937], *Essays*, p. 188.
69. Williams, *Kora in Hell*, p. 30.
70. Williams, "Introduction," *Essays*, p. 233.
71. William Carlos Williams to Horace Gregory, 5 May 1944, *Letters*, p. 224.
72. Willliams, *Autobiography*, p. 391. Williams is referring to Dewey's article, "Americanism and Localism," *The Dial* LXVIII [1920], pp. 687–88. "We are discovering that the locality is the only universal."
73. Herman Keyserling, *America Set Free* (1929), p. 48, cited by Weaver, pp. 34–36.
74. Williams, "Against the Weather," *Essays*, p. 198.
75. Williams, "Yours, O Youth" [1922], *Essays*, p. 32.
76. Ibid., p. 35.
77. By Eliot among others. "For me, without one word of civil greeting (a sign of his really bad breeding, which all so-called scholars show—protectively), he reserves the slogan 'of local interest perhaps,'" Williams to T.C. Wilson, 12 July 1933, *Letters*, p. 141.
78. F. Scott Fitzgerald, "Echoes of the Jazz Age."
79. William Carlos Williams to Ezra Pound, 23 March 1933, *Letters*, p. 139–40.
80. Williams, "Comment I" [1921], *Essays*, p. 28.
81. Williams, "The Work of Gertrude Stein," *A Novelette and Other Prose*, Toulon: Imprimerie F. Cabasson, 1932, pp. 108–09.

ALLEN GINSBERG
"Williams in a World of Objects" (1976[1])
William Carlos Williams: Man and Poet
ed. Carroll F. Terrell
1983, pp. 33–39

Accuracy. Williams' accuracy. The phrase "clamp your mind down on objects" is his. The phrase "no ideas but in things" is his. Does everybody understand what that means? . . . It means, "no *general* ideas in your poetry," Don't put out any abstract ideas about things, but present the things themselves that gave you the ideas. Let's try and understand what Williams is trying to say and then we'll propose a different theory. [Here are three lines from "Dance Russe"]:

> And the sun is a flame-white disc
> in silken mists
> above shining trees,—

Now he is being very fair there. He is just telling you what you can see. He's not laying a trip on you about the sun in general. Here he puts your eyes on the sun in one specific kind of day so that you can see it with your own eyes. He is saying "just put down the details of the things you see in front of you." If you can't begin there, what good are any ideas. Begin with what the sense offers. If you can't do that, you'll have to go to astronomy. But astronomy is based on observations of some kind.

Suppose a dying man! If you can't *see* the dying man in front of you, you can't see what is wrong with your behavior toward him. Here is not a *change* of ideas; it's a change of *directive stance*. Once understood, Williams' phrase becomes a basic building block: for a system maybe, or a reference point; for a complete system in itself or usable with other systems. But until the phrase [no ideas but in things] is understood in itself, there is no common ground to begin with. In the lines from the poem, what's the one common ground we begin with? We've got the sun, an orange ball going down over the maple tree, or the sun just as we see it. How artfully can we describe what we see, so that it is common ground, where everybody is in the same place, so that one can use it like a reference point. It may be fictional but it is the common ground. If we don't have any reference point in the physical world, then what have we got? Here's one common reference point at least: everybody's breathing. That's where Buddhism starts—at that one place and moves from there. Starts at one place that everybody can locate: the tip of the nose where everybody is breathing in and out. Start close to the nose. That is a reality where everybody is or can be: we must begin where we are.

Williams got into this because *reality* had become so confusing in the twentieth century, and poetry had got so freaked out that it was strange: he didn't know what poetry was! He didn't know what anything was! But he knew where his nose was and could begin there. He gave up all ideas [meaning abstractions] and started with things themselves. Naturally everybody sees things differently: The word is not The Thing. The word "word", a concept in itself, is an abstraction, an idea. The entire world is fictional. "Words themselves are ideas!": There is a little double-dealing in that phrase. But, everybody can come down to the same place and begin there: the one place where *everybody* can be. There is only one place where everybody can be.

STUDENT: Isn't it weird that he started with something that is so susceptible to change—and not being what it seems to be? Actions like jumping?

RESPONSE: Jumping is more abstract. The question is, Where are we going to begin? [The answer is] let's begin with what we can see in front of us. Williams was looking for a place where everybody could begin together in poetry because everything was new; a new continent, newly discovered, newly invaded with European ideas plastered all over it. He was trying to clean up the slate and start all over again. That's why he wrote a book called *In the American Grain*, trying to reach American history, to see what fresh planet we'd come upon. "The natural object is always the adequate symbol": That's Pound's way of saying the same thing: "Don't bother with abstractions." In other words, no poetry but in "for instances," no ideas but in things. He would say you could include feelings, but you'd have to deal with them as observed things and not get lost. It is very similar to the process of meditation: paying attention to the breaths, wandering off into a daydream, and then becoming unconscious of the mind moving into the daydream, of the breaths, and then you could describe the thought you had but you no longer are obsessed by it or lost in it. Don't lose perspective. There is always the home base to touch back on. He's saying let's fill with *our* attention the things that other people can see and fill with *their* attention. Then we can both check our consciousness, one against another, and see where we are, like triangulating the stars.

Here's two short poems:

GOODNIGHT

> In brilliant gas light
> I turn the kitchen spigot
> and watch the water plash
> into the clean white sink.
> On the grooved drain-board
> to one side is
> a glass filled with parsley—
> crisped green.
>   Waiting
> for the water to freshen—
> I glance at the spotless floor—:
> a pair of rubber sandals
> lie side by side
> under the wall-table
> all is in order for the night.
>
> Waiting, with a glass in my hand
> —three girls in crimson satin
> pass close before me on
> the murmurous background of
> the crowded opera—
>   it is
> memory playing the clown—
> three vague, meaningless girls
> full of smells and
> the rustling sounds of
> cloth rubbing on cloth and
> little slippers on carpet—
> high-school French
> spoken in a loud voice!
>
> Parsley in a glass
> still and shining
> brings me back.
> I take a drink and
> yawn deliciously.
> I am ready for bed.

He brings us through the whole process.

The mundaneness is interesting, to me, because it sees so clearly that it becomes crisp in meaning, still and shining. The water glass suddenly is a totemic object. It becomes a symbol of itself, of his investment in his attention in that object: *it* becomes a symbol of itself also.

Because he sees it so clearly, he notices what about the object that shines, what's particular about the object that could be written down in a word—he sees the object without association. That's characteristic of visionary moments: you get supernatural visions by giving up supernatural visions; just looking at what is in front of you. You are not superimposing another idea or another image on the image that's already there.

The poem, "Thursday," shows that he really is a Buddhist:

I have had my dream—like others—
and it has come to nothing, so that
I remain now carelessly
with feet planted on the ground
and look up at the sky—
feeling my clothes about me,
the weight of my body in my shoes,
the rim of my hat, air passing in and out
at my nose—and decide to dream no more.

When I discovered this poem, I realized its thematic Buddhism: the practice we were doing and the pragmatic practice had intersected and there was a common ground. Williams had arrived at the same place that everybody else was studying and got there early and on his own: it reconfirmed my feelings that he was some kind of a saint of perception.

This is a beginning: to understand his basic principle and then extend it as we have to. Well, you can be mindful of generalizations if you are mindful of the particulars out of which you draw: *No ideas but in facts!*

II

Williams is the clearest and simplest and most direct when trying to tie the mind down, to bring the imagination down to earth again and put all of his intensity and all of his energy into seeing what is actually there, what anybody can see in the light of day: no imagination except what he's conscious of as daydreams while looking directly at people, cars, horses, bushes, maple trees, or Rutherford, New Jersey. He's a doctor. Let's start with a couple of his early sketches:

LATE FOR SUMMER WEATHER

He has on
an old light grey fedora
She a black beret

He a dirty sweater
She an old blue coat
that fits her tight

Grey flapping pants
Red skirt and
broken down black pumps

Fat Lost Ambling
nowhere through
the upper town they kick

their way through
heaps of
fallen maple leaves

still green—and
crisp as dollar bills
Nothing to do. Hot cha!

PROLETARIAN PORTRAIT

A big young bareheaded woman
in an apron

Her hair slicked back standing
on the street

One stockinged foot toeing
the sidewalk

Her shoe in her hand. Looking
intently into it

She pulls out the paper insole
to find the nail

That has been hurting her

Williams was a friend of Reznikoff's. They were practicing the same poetics together trying to get it to boil down to the direct presentation of the object that they were writing about with no excess words. They composed their poems out of the elements of natural speech, their own speech, as heard on the porch or in talk over the kitchen table. Poetry that would be identical to spoken conversation that you could actually hear as regular conversation and not recognize it as poetry at all unless you suddenly dug that there was something going on, curiously sharp and fresh that was smart people talking.

Here's the doctor, maybe out on a call:

THE YOUNG HOUSEWIFE

At ten a.m. the young housewife
moves about in negligee behind
the wooden walls of her husband's house.
I pass solitary in my car.

Then again she comes to the curb
to call the ice-man, fish-man, and stands
shy, uncorseted, tucking in
stray ends of hair, and I compare her
to a fallen leaf.

The noiseless wheels of my car
rush with a crackling sound over
dried leaves as I bow and pass smiling.

So, what's the use of being so flat and prosaic? Or, what's the purpose of trying to make poetry out of the objects seen under the aspect of ordinary minds? Generally we don't see ordinary objects at all. We are filled with daydream fantasy so that we don't see what is in front of us. We are not aware of what is close to the nose, and we don't even appreciate what everyday tables and chairs have to offer in terms of service for food or a place to sit; in terms of the centuries of maturing that it took to give us a place for the food. Zeroing in on actuality with the ordinary mind and abandoning any thought of heaven, illumination; giving up any attempt to manipulate the universe to make it better than it is; but, instead, coming down to earth and being willing to relate to what is actually here without trying to change the universe or alter it from the one which we can see, smell, taste, touch, hear and think about. Williams' work as a poet is very similar to Zen Buddhist mindfulness practice, because it clamps the mind down on objects and brings the practitioner into direct relations with whatever he can find in front of him without making a big deal about it; without satisfying some ego ambition to have something more princely or less painful than what already *is*.

Williams was good friends with extraordinary people: Pound, H.D., Marianne Moore. They all knew each other at the University of Pennsylvania I believe. But Williams was a square. He always thought Pound was a little cranky and crazy. Williams was kind of naive; square but inside he was such a humane man. Since he learned to deal with what was around him he learned to sympathize, empathize. His growth was totally self-made, totally natural. He had the idea of going in that direction very early and just kept working at it. He had the ideal [about poetry] and thought about working on it, like going through medical school. Going through poetry and developing his focus was just like going through medical school. He deliberately stayed in Rutherford, New Jersey, and wrote poetry about the local landscape, using local language. He wanted to be a provincial from the point of view of really being there where he was; really knowing his ground. He wanted to know his roots, know who the iceman and fishman were; know the housewife; he wanted to know his town—his whole body in a sense. A strange idea; he might have got it from some literary sources like Guy de Maupassant; Keats might have given him some hints.

He was dealing with actual birth rather than literary birth, actual eyes, hair, etc. He was somebody no different from ourselves, actually, somebody you don't have to worry about pulling a fast metaphysical trick on you and declaring another universe. That's the whole point; dealing with *this* universe. And that was a fantastic discovery: that you can actually make poetry by dealing with this universe instead of creating another one.

Notes

1. In the fall of 1976, Ginsberg was teaching a course about 20th century poets in which Williams became the central topic a number of times. The sessions were recorded on the old-fashioned reel-to-reel tapes. Allen provided me with several of the tapes where Williams and Pound were central to his talks and discussions. These pages are excerpted from them with only slight editorial interventions: the kind that fills in what voice and gesture would make clear. Interpolated phrases are put in brackets. The first was made on November 16th and the second, November 25th. When he reads the same poem in the second class, a cross reference has been made. I contrived the title "Williams in a World of Objects" as being inclusive of what's said and to provide for various indexing needs.—C.F.T.

CHARLES DOYLE

"Conclusion"

William Carlos Williams and the American Poem

1982, pp. 169–78

For criticism, the important question is: what criteria are we to apply in judging Williams's poems? Many American poets, of the past two decades in particular, have signified their approval of his work either by imitating it or advancing it. Critical difficulty is encountered not so much in characterizing his discoveries concerning 'the poem' as in deciding which among his typical poems are successful, and good, poems, and why this is so.

At the beginning of his career, and by now the point has been made often enough, Williams's poems were highly literary, modelled on approved masters in the English tradition, both in diction and measure. When he broke away from this stale sense of poetry, it was first through the influence of Pound and Imagism. As he suggests in the Preface to *Kora in Hell*, Williams, at this period, escaped from a common mental attitude of the literary poet—considering, or thinking about, one thing in terms of another. Simile, analogy and metaphor he rejected as inappropriate to his sense of 'the poem', preferring to assert the necessity of keeping one's eye on the object, recognizing the 'true value', 'that peculiarity which gives an object a character by itself' (*SE*, 11), discovering 'in things those inimitable particles of dissimilarity to all other things which are the peculiar perfections of the thing in question' (*SE*, 16). Such insistence on the specific individuality of the object, as opposed to its likeness and relation to other objects, is distinctly American, as is the aim for 'vividness' rather than propriety.

Seeing clearly was, for him, the great virtue, as it was for his painter friends Demuth and Sheeler. Throughout Williams's career we encounter the isolation of the moment of clear perception or experience as if it were hard won from the ever-encroaching flux. In a constant state of alertness the artist makes his discoveries, but he is also active, and morally so, a selector, who 'must keep his eye without fault on those things he values, to which officials refuse to give the proper names' (*SE*, 231). Genuine contact is made through concentration on the object with great intensity, to 'lift it' to the imagination. An object lifted to the imagination yields up its 'radiant gist'. Sometimes this is simply discovered, while at others (given that the field of energy does not stop at the skin or outer envelope of the human being), the process is completed by the poet by means of invention or structuring. In poems such as 'The Red Wheelbarrow', Williams draws our attention simultaneously to the world out there and to our relationship with it, which must be fresh, now. Here is one significance of his assertion that 'Nothing is good save the new' (*SE*, 21), which is far from claiming that a thing is inevitably good *merely because* it is new.

'Nothing is good save the new' because what is important is here and now, our immediate experience. In the face of centuries of traditional poetic form, which had run into the nineteenth-century mire of 'moral homily' (seeing the poem as aiming for perfection in long-established verse-forms along with the expression of edifying or uplifting material), Williams had the insight to see that the significance of the poem is not in its subject-matter (which is nearly always 'phantasy' or 'dream'), but, as he asserts over and over again in many different ways, in its form.[1] Given his deep convictions on the need for contact and that 'the local is the only universal' it is natural that he should have rejected traditional forms and measure, since these are not local, nor have Americans direct access to their sources. Where to look, then, for new form?

Seen in this way, Williams's position is both perceptive and sensible. A poem is made with words and possesses whatever reality it may have through 'the shapes of men's lives in places'. What more natural than to use the language of those men? When, in his 1948 essay 'The Poem as a Field of Action', Williams, looking back, observed that 'Imagism was not structural: that was the reason for its disappearance' (*SE*, 283), he meant that it did not derive purely from the speech-patterns of its day. Having recognized the vital link between poetry and speech, he then had to work for most of a lifetime before achieving a sound technical base (the variable foot), which could incorporate the American idiom on all occasions without strain. Even while he was working towards this there appears to have been a subsidiary approach to measure in his work, related to syllable-counting, some Pythagorean musical conception (for which there is only slight occasional evidence, but enough to confuse a tracking of the main line of development).

Only the tradition-bound will by now find it hard to accept Williams's innovations in the line. From *Al Que Quiere!* on, he largely escaped the tyranny of quantitative measure, employing instead a measure based on phrasing. A difficulty in making categorical assertions about Williams's measure (and therefore codifying it) is that his practice varies somewhat. Occasionally it is purely 'musical'. In this early, Imagist period it depended considerably on the syntax and phrasing of written statement. Very often, at its strongest throughout his career, it related to speech. Sometimes (as in

'Struggle of Wings', for example) it can be criticized as too long, or heavy; but even length is no sure criterion, as witness some writing in 'The Clouds' (*CLP*, 124). Generally, however, it can be said that the longer line is most successful when deployed to create a forward verbal flow. Much of the work in *Collected Later Poems* ('The Mind's Games', for example, or 'Aigeltinger') is not easy to classify in terms of the line. Almost all of it is natural in flow, which saves it from the charge of being 'chopped-up prose', but a great deal of it is not far removed from prose. Sometimes (as in 'Aigeltinger') one suspects a deliberate tinkering with quantitative measure. Ultimately our bases for judging Williams's line must be broad ones: its energy in the specific instance, its 'naturalness' (which, almost inevitably, depends on the spoken word).

Naturalness as a criterion may remind us of another statement in the Prologue to *Kora in Hell*: 'By the brokenness of his composition the poet makes himself master of a certain weapon which he could possess himself of in no other way. The speed of the emotions is sometimes such that thrashing about in a thin exaltation or despair many matters are touched but not held, more often broken by the contact' (*SE*, 14). We may think of poems as various as "Della Primavera Trasportata al Morale' (*CEP*, 57) and "Perpetuum Mobile: the City' (*CEP*, 384), which have this quality, but they are held together by a definite relation to speech rhythms. For Williams, 'brokenness' and naturalness are of a piece. Where he fails, according to his own aims, is in such a poem as "The Yachts', close as it obviously is to quantitative measure, even to the extent that its closing lines depend on a regularly established rhythm for making their 'dying fall' effect.

Traditional prosody is fixed, while for Williams measure in the poem is always relative. He never insisted on establishing a new set of rules, beyond observing the (for him) undeniable relationship between American measure and American speech. 'The only reality we can know is MEASURE' (*SE*, 283), but different worlds call for different measures, each consonant with its own time and place. Any critic would seem to be in the position of recognizing and adumbrating the prosodic rules established by Williams, but there are (ultimately) no rules, except in the most general sense. Having limited ourselves to observing that Williams is in the American (as opposed to the English) tradition, we must note the further restriction that each man's 'line' is, implicitly, his own (hence Williams's explanation of his own short line: 'I didn't go in for long lines because of my nervous nature. I couldn't. The rhythmic pace was the pace of speech . . .' —*IWWP*, 15).

Williams's basic short line was established in *Al Que Quiere!* Poem after poem in that volume, some quiet some less so, shows surprising tautness and strength of line. Much depends on the energy in the specific line, used with great range and subtlety:

When I was younger
it was plain to me
I must make something of myself.
Older now. . . .

Here, and in numerous other instances, the line disposition entirely suits the action of the poem (an obvious example here is the muting of line 4). Beyond this everything depends on the articulation of lines throughout. Hence, the poem is 'a field of action', and hence Williams's recognition of the rightness of Olson's theory of composition by field, rather than through accumulating well-turned lines.

Part of the outcome of this new sense of measure as 'relative'[2] is a new respect for the individual word, accepting it freshly not as a label but as an alternative reality, an object in its own right. The word is a 'thing-in-itself', but it derives energy (usually in the form of 'meaning') through contact with other words. Much can be understood concerning Williams's use of the line if we recognize the range of his sentence structures. Vividness is gained very often by employment of the present tense, but he can (through syntactical arrangement) create a sense of immediacy without it:

Then I raised my head
and stared out over
the blue February waste
to the blue bank of hill
with stars on it
in strings and festoons—
but above that:
one opaque
stone of a cloud
('Winter Sunset', *CEP*, 127)

Frequently Williams's poems begin with a question or an exclamation or exhortation, all indicating his eagerness, wonder, curiosity, and usually transmuting his excitement into the energy of the poem. Typically, throughout his career his language is simple and, despite subtle sentence variation, clearly and directly organized. In much of his verse of the late 1930s, early 1940s, which makes *Collected Later Poems* disappointing compared with *Collected Earlier Poems*, he allows himself discursive sentence structures, employing pause, parenthesis and qualification to a greater extent than he had earlier. Seen in the perspective of his whole development, it may be that much of the work of that period is preparatory for *Paterson*, an effort to extend his means deliberately in the direction of discursiveness, which bore fruit not so much in *Paterson* as in the assured, relaxed statement of many poems in *The Desert Music* and *Journey to Love*. Meantime, to the extent that he forgot Pound's dictum that the good writer 'uses the smallest possible number of words',[3] Williams's work of that period lost distinction.

To summarize thus far, the attributes of the true poem, according to Williams, are that: it recognizes the *uniqueness* of each thing or object in experience; the poet's task is to perceive this uniqueness with as great a clarity as possible and to render it as a poem with as much 'vividness' as he can command; to pursue this task he must be in deeply attentive contact with his immediate environment and he must have the imaginative insight to recognize the object or detail which will be key to the universal in the local; 'what actually impinges on the senses must be rendered as it appears' (*SE*, 119), but the poet gives it structure without in any way interfering with its essential nature, so it is simultaneously a discovery (in itself) and an invention (by his relating it to all else, through rendering it in words). The true poem must be 'new' because our experience is always new, even though it is always in danger of being dominated by the past. As each age has its own brand of experience, so also it will have a typical prosody and a characteristic type of poem, but inside that each individual makes his own poems, never by an outdated means or measure, according to his own imagination and internal rhythms, but inevitably influenced by the 'weather' and speech of his environment.

Technically, each poem will create its own shape, having the general characteristics of simplicity, clarity and naturalness, succeeding according to the strength and/or appropriateness of energy discharge over its whole field.

Like Pound, Williams employs the technique of juxtaposition, but where Pound juxtaposes literary or cultural 'echoes' or apparent correspondences, Williams (until *Paterson*) tends to place together things-in-themselves. Even his juxtapositions in *Paterson* are treated so, not intended to suggest analogies, but to present the quality of American experience direct and without interference. Sometimes his juxtaposed objects possess 'one-thousandth part of a quality in common', but often they deliberately (or carelessly) clash. Therefore, in some sense, juxtaposition is 'suggestive', but the reader is not necessarily led through a thought process, almost certainly to a flash of recognition which is an energy-discharge linking the juxtaposed items. Not that Williams is against activity of the intelligence. Traditional metaphor means the positive presence of the writer, in the text, directing his reader, contrary to Williams's belief that the artist should be 'remote from the field' and that art is created through 'concrete indirections' (*SL*, 24).

Not the artist's autobiography, but the quality of his experience is important. To prevent his experience from being trammelled by convention it must be 'open' and not preconceived. A sense of form must be allied to a willingness to descend to the "formless ground'. Williams's advice to 'write carelessly' is not really at odds with his insistence on accuracy of observation and rendering. What must be avoided is 'thought about' the object or experience, and (again from Williams's point of view) before *Paterson* evidence of deliberate thought in the *details* of a poem (like over-attention to 'subject-matter') would constitute a weakness in that poem. Perception and the imaginative disposition of perceptions, these are primary to the poem. Verbal and causal connectives, any verbal arrangement which is based on the structure of thought, these adulterate the poem, diminishing its purity and effectiveness. Apart from escaping the tyranny of quantitative measure, this must have been Williams's pre-eminent consideration in his search for, and development of, the variable foot.

All these criteria, and others, are positive and reasonable. Nothing can bridge the hiatus between Williams's intentions and those critics who cannot accept his major requirement—the rejection of quantitative measure for contemporary American poetry. However, almost everywhere the variable foot and composition by field have been accepted at least as legitimate, valuable extensions of the poetic means. Given this, Williams's own requirements for the poem offer adequate tools by which to assess his work, up to the mid-1940s.

Paterson poses fresh problems for the critic. What are to be his evaluative criteria for it? One is the valuable notion of the metamorphic poem implicit in the work, put forward by Sister M. Bernetta Quinn.[4] Williams's own 'theory' of 'interpenetration' accords well with the metamorphic technique. His use of 'raw material' in the form of a variety of prose passages is of a piece both with his rejection of the 'anti-poetic' and his belief in the thing-in-itself.

To consider Williams's poetic development progressively is to wonder, at times, if he was sidetracked by Imagism and Objectivism. Although 'not structural', Imagism certainly persuaded him of the value of intense concentration upon the object. Objectivism may have intensified this in two ways: by emphasis on the removal of self from the poem and by (consequently) drawing the attention to the speech or music in which the objective experiences presented themselves (such an influence is evident today in fine poet craftsmen, from Lorine Niedecker—an associate of the original Objectivists, whose work is too little known—to Paul Blackburn and many of the contributors to Cid Corman's *Origin*).

Both Imagism and Objectivism are in the same theoretical line as Poe's insistence on the poem as a striving for a single effect. In its very name each of these 'movements' suggests a concentration on noun or thing as opposed to 'an easy lateral sliding' through a statement of abstractions easily divorced from reality. His insistence on the value of the thing-in-itself is important in Williams, but even more important is his sense of process. More than many of his associates he was conscious of the antithesis between, so to speak, Heraclitus and Parmenides. As we have seen, there are the tight 'imagist' poems and the poems which flow 'carelessly'. Perhaps the crucial clue in the *Paterson* headnotes is 'by multiplication a reduction to one' (*P*, 10). Implying, as it does, movement, activity, this categorically shifts the emphasis of Williams's poem from thing to process, a passing through. His central means is in the metamorphoses of Paterson himself/itself. How are we to judge the value or success of this means? If the nature of Paterson, the man-city, becomes very clear at any one point in the poem, would not this be distracting? Would it not limit the range of possible response? Quest, perpetual change, fluidity, instability—these are characteristic of *Paterson*, giving it vitality. All objects in the poem are instantaneously there and are instantly gone. They are *here and now*. *Paterson I–IV* is a search for order. As originally conceived, the poem is search only, process only, and the failure of Paterson, the man-city, is comparable with that of, say, Père Sebastian Rasles in *In the American Grain*, a failure which has its own kind of success, in recognizing that '*La Vertue est toute dans l'effort*'. Notably, *Paterson* V, which concerns itself with the tapestry, the relationship of art to life and Williams's lifelong Kora–Venus preoccupation, has a greater immediate clarity, concentration upon the object, and a more obviously discursive point.

The earlier books of *Paterson* are sustained, paradoxically, as much by the fragments of 'experience' or 'thing' as they are by the necessarily fluid central metaphor. Curiously, metamorphosis *invites* discourse, while the 'gathering up' of its own weight has, at times, an effect opposite to the 'taking up of slack'. If one has any reservation about *Paterson* V, it is that the appeal to art, to imagination, is obvious rather than new, or penetrating, or decisive. Yet as a 'resolution', it confirms the tendency of Williams's whole career and is very much of a piece with all the work of his last phase.

Williams's late concentration on the imagination, his alignment of imagination and love, his self-searching, these are not narcissism. Rather his belief in the imagination is similar to his lifelong sense of the local. Emphasis is not on *his* locality, or imagination, because they are *his*. Imagination works from material in one's own experience (whoever one may happen to be). That experience differs from one phase to another, so constant reference to it is simply carrying devotion to 'the new' to its ultimate conclusion.

From his Objectivist period onward all Williams's work implies a sense of the self other than the merely autobiographical or egotistical. In 1947 he observed: 'The objective in writing is to reveal. . . . The difference between the revealer and others is that he reveals HIMSELF, not you' (*SE*, 269). Again, this stems from a realization that, just as the place a person can truly know is his own locality, so the only self he can truly know is his own. Avoidance of falsification, pretence, is at back of this and of the finally developed sense of imagination. In the long run, love is the important emotion in human experience. What keeps man alive (or kills him, for that matter) is his own imagination and how it relates to the world. Imagination has the power of transforming or maintaining the world, and is the chief metamorphic agent:

But love and the imagination
are of a piece,
swift as the light
to avoid destruction.
(*PB*, 179)

Williams's latest work is generally discursive in comparison with his pre-*Paterson* poems. Interestingly, this is due at least in part to his metrical experimentation. The stepping of the three-tiered line, which he had used first in 'The descent beckons' *(Paterson II)*, has the effect of casting aside the static, fixed-object presentation of many earlier poems. To suggest that Williams was never discursive in his earlier work would be inaccurate. Even though expressed negatively ('No ideas but in things!'), Williams's awareness of the 'idea' in poetry is about as long as his career. His late development of 'the variable foot' allowed him to be discursive without abandoning the cadence and rapidity of natural speech. The order of speech, of prose statement, has replaced a repetitive, metronomic pattern, as the *expected* element in Williams's line. By and large, the line units are dictated by speech, but they have a flexibility and offer a range of possible discovery far exceeding those of traditional meter. Looking for criteria to judge 'the variable foot' we may suggest: (a) is it natural, true to speech? (b) are the variations vital and interesting? For Williams the anti-poetic would be aping of traditional literary forms of copying the speech and/or measure of others.

As an innovator, Williams shared many of his positions with Pound, but he may in the long run prove to be more influential. Pound to a much greater degree applied himself to, and found his material in, art and literature. Williams, likewise interested in simultaneity and interaction rather than causality, suggests his own far different sense of experience in chapter 54 of the *Autobiography*. He refers to the exciting secrets of the 'underground stream' of human experience itself, unselected. Attending closely to it, 'there is no better way to get an intimation of what is going on in the world' (*Autob.*, 360). His whole objective, as it ultimately became clear to him, is to lift the 'inarticulate' up to imagination. A sense of the common people as prime source of life, shared in the early years with Eliot, seems never to have left Williams, despite a discouragement made plain at least as late as *Paterson II*.

A 'lifetime of careful listening' to the speech arising from his daily tasks and contacts, convinced him that poem and life, also, are one—and that each person is trying to communicate to the world the poem of himself. In many works, but particularly in *Kora in Hell, In the American Grain, Collected Earlier Poems, Paterson* and the late poems, he demonstrated the informing need for imagination, having realized early that 'The imagination transcends the thing itself' (*KH*, 24). An explorer and discoverer, always conscious of the handful of men who had contributed positively to the shaping of the American spirit, he takes his place alongside them.

Notes

The following abbreviations are employed in the text: *Autob.*, for *The Autobiography of William Carlos Williams* (New York: Random House, 1951); *CEP*, for *The Collected Earlier Poems of William Carlos Williams* (Norfolk, Conn.: New Directions, 1951); *CLP*, for *The Collected Later Poems of William Carlos Williams* (Norfolk, Conn.: New Directions, 1950, rev. 1963); *IWWP*, for *I Wanted to Write a Poem*, ed. Edith Heal (Boston, Mass.: Beacon Press, 1958); *KH*, for *Kora in Hell: Improvisations* (San Francisco: City Lights Books, 1957; also included in *Imaginations*, ed. Webster Schott, New York: New Directions, 1971); *P*, for *Paterson I–V* (New York: New Directions, 1963); *PB*, for *Pictures from Brueghel and Other Poems* (New York: New Directions, 1962); *SE*, for *Selected Essays* (New York: Random House, 1954); and *SL*, for *The Selected Letters of William Carlos Williams* ed. John C. Thirlwall (New York: McDowell, Obolensky, 1957).

1. 'The So-Called So-Called,' *Patroon*, vol, I, no. 1 (May 1937), p. 1.
2. ' . . . prosodic values should rightly be seen as only relatively true . . .', *Poetry*, vol. XLIV, no. 4 (July 1934), pp. 221–2.
3. Pound, *Literary Essays* (London: Faber & Faber, 1954), p. 50.
4. Sister M. Bernetta Quinn, *The Metamorphic Tradition in Modern Poetry* (New Brunswick, N.J.: Rutgers University Press, 1955), Introduction.

DENISE LEVERTOV
"The Ideas in the Things"
William Carlos Williams: Man and Poet
ed. Carroll F. Terrell
1983, pp. 141–51

There are many more 'ideas' in William Carlos Williams' 'things' than he is commonly credited with even today; and this is true not only of Paterson and the post-Patersonian, clearly meditative poems in triadic lines, but also of a great deal of his earlier work. Because he did write numerous poems that are exercises in the notation of speech or in the taking of verbal Polaroid snapshots, it is assumed that many other short or medium-length poems of his are likewise essays in the non-metaphorical, the wholly objective. And because he said, 'Let the metaphysical take care of itself, the arts have nothing to do with it,' it is forgotten that he immediately followed those words with these: 'They will concern themselves with it if they please.' It is not noticed that he himself frequently *did* so please. Williams, for much of his life, did take on, it is true, the task of providing for himself and others a context of objective, anti-metaphysical, aesthetic intent in order to free poetry from the entanglement of that sentimental intellectualism which only recognizes the incorporal term of an analogy and scorns its literal, sensuous term. This view denies the equipoise of thing and idea, acknowledging only a utilitarian role for the literal (as if it were brought into existence expressly, and merely, to articulate the all-important abstract term), rather than perceiving concrete images as the very *incarnation* of thought. This view insults the imagination, for the imagination does not reject its own sensory origins but illuminates them, and connects them with intellectual and intuitive experience. Williams, working against that insult to imagination, needed to assert and re-establish a confidence in the actuality and value of observable phenomena and a recognition of the necessity of sensory data to the life and health of poetry. But by so doing he incurred much misunderstanding from his admirers (not to speak of his detractors) and, I suspect, endured a good deal of (mainly unacknowledged) inner conflict; for he was frequently obliged to betray his stated principles in favour of the irresistible impulsion towards metaphor which is at the heart of *poeisis*.

I find it interesting to sort out, in the *Collected Early Poems*, those poems which are indeed snapshots, descriptive vignettes, notations of idiom and emphasis (as are some of the very late shorter poems also), from those which have unobtrusively the resonance of metaphor and symbol.

The mystery and richness of *further significance* which such poems of his possess is akin to what R. H. Blyth delineated for us in his commentaries on Japanese haiku. The allusive nature of the Zen art, possible only in a culture alert to the ubiquity of correspondences and familiar with an elaborate symbology, has of course no exact parallel in 20th century America; yet Blyth could have been evoking the art of W. C. W. when he quoted this haiku by Kyoroku,

> Even to the saucepan
> where potatoes are boiling—
> a moonlit night.

and commented, 'It is only when we realize that the moon is in the saucepan with the potatoes that we know the grandeur of the moon in the highest heaven. It is only when we see a part that we know the whole.'

Readers who come to Williams' pre-*Paterson*ian or pre-*Desert Music* poems with the expectation of simple depictive Imagism of a classic, ascetically single-visioned objectivity (which was not in fact the stated aim of the objectivists, incidentally) miss these resonances, that sense of discovering, in a vivid part, the adumbration of an unnamed but intensely intuited whole; they forego the experience of becoming aware precisely through the physical p*resentness* of what is *de*noted, of the other presentness—invisible but palpable—of what is *con*noted. They come to the poems solely for the Things, but inherent in the Things are the Ideas.

I'd like to present two examples, and a running commentary on what I believe is to be found beneath their surfaces:

'The Farmer,' the third poem from *Spring and All* (a series detached, in CEP, from its prose context), is not a depiction of a farmer which compares him to an artist, but vice versa. Read thus, as a portrait of the artist, each of its images has a double meaning. The literal *is there*, vivid in every detail. But climate, landscape, everything, takes on *along with* (not instead of) its denotative significance a symbolic one. The poet is a *farmer*, one who tends the land of language and imagination and its creatures, who makes things grow, poem-things, story-things, not out of nowhere but out of the ground on which he walks. At present the rain is falling, the climate is cold and wet, as was the critical climate of the time for Williams the poet; he is exposed to that wet and cold, and his fields—the fields of his art—are apparently empty. But he's trudging around *in* that climate and *in* the fields of language, calmly, hands in his pockets, intent on imagining the future poems; and the rain prepares the soil and the seeds. 'On all sides / the world rolls coldly away'—he's left quite alone with his imagination. The orchard trees are black with the rain—but it is spring (the preceding prose has announced, 'Meanwhile, SPRING, which has been approaching for several pages, is at last here'—and the poem states that it is March). Soon those trees (the deeprooted anatomy of what grows from his terrain) will be white with blossom: there are implied poems in this superficially unpromising landscape; and the very isolation in which the poet is left by the world gives him 'room for thought.' His dirt road (his own road among his fields) is sluiced (and thus deepened) by the rain that will help the seeds to sprout. He's not a small, lost figure in nature, this artist farmer—he 'looms' as he moves along past the scratchy brushwood that, trimmed and dried, will make good tinder. The poet is *composing* as he goes—just as a farmer, pacing his fields on a Sunday at the end of winter, composes in his mind's eye a picture of spring growth and summer harvest. He is an *antagonist*—to what? To the hostility of the environment, which, however, contains the elements that will nourish his crops. And in what sense? In the sense of the struggle, *to* compose, not to *im*pose order but to *com*pose the passive elements into a harvest, to grow not tares but wheat.

A poem I'm very fond of and which, besides being full of implication and resonances, has many of the qualities of a short story, (indeed, as well as being *set* in Russia, it has a flavour or tone quite Chekhovian), is 'A Morning Imagination of Russia,' a part of *The Descent of Winter.* Webster Schott's selection from Williams' prose and poetry, *Imaginations,* restored the full context of that series, as well as of 'Spring and All'; and Schott, unlike some of Williams' critics, doesn't treat him as wholly lacking in thought. Nevertheless, intent upon an enthusiastic, but careless, reading of this poem, which sees it as speaking figuratively of Williams' own situation *vis-à-vis* American poetry, he misses the clear drama of its narrative. He quite unjustifiably claims that it depicts *Williams himself on an imaginary visit* to Russia after the revolution, whereas (however much he may be a projection of the poet's sensibility) it seems to me quite clear that the protagonist is not intended as a persona in the sense of a mere mask for the self, but is a more fully projected fictive personage, a member of the intelligentsia who is casting his lot with the masses. The time is very early in the revolution. Nothing has yet settled down. No new repressive bureaucracy has yet replaced the old oppression—the whole atmosphere is like that of a convalescent's first walk in pale sunshine after a time when bitter storms in the world outside paralleled his inner storm of fever and life-and-death struggle.

> The earth and the sky were very close
> When the sun rose it rose in his heart,

it begins. The dawn is, equally, an actual one and the dawn of an era. And he feels one with it.

> It bathed the red cold world of
> the dawn so that the chill was his own.

The red is the red of sunrise *and* of revolution.

> The mists were sleep and sleep began
> to fade from his eyes . . .

The mists are both morning mists and the mists of the past, or prerevolutionary sleep. His consciousness is changing.

> below him in the
> garden a few flowers were lying forward
> on the intense green grass where
> in the opalescent shadows oak leaves
> were pressed hard down upon it in patches
> by the night rain . . .

The beauty of flowers and grass, opalescent shadows, patches of rain-soaked dead oak leaves, is vividly evoked. It can all be read with validity as pure, precise description. But it too has a doubleness; the whole scene has been through a night of storm, the flowers are bowed forward by it, the grass is more vividly green than it would have been without it, but parts of the grass are hidden and half-smothered by the fallen brown leaves. All this is the counterpart of his own experience and of events in the historical moment. The flowers and common grass of his own life, after the storm, are more vivid and yet almost broken—and some of his life is gone, is fallen, like the leaves, gone with the lives and the ways of living fallen in war and revolution.

> . . . There were no cities
> between him and his desires,
> his hatreds and his loves were without walls
> without rooms, without elevators
> without files, delays of veiled murderers
> muffled thieves, the tailings of
> tedious, dead pavements, the walls
> against desire save only for him who can pay
> high, there were no cities—he was
> without money—

Cities had faded richly
into foreign countries, stolen from Russia—
the richness of her cities.—

Here, deep in rural Russia, deep into the attempt to construct a new society, he is not impeded by the complexities of urban, Westernized Russia. His nature—with its desires, hatreds, loves—is out in the open; and the 'city' here clearly stands for more than an architectural and demographic agglomeration, but for the money values of capitalism. He has no money—but here and now he doesn't need it. All the desirable contents of Russia's cities have been stolen away, gone West with the emigrés.

Scattered wealth was close to his heart
he felt it uncertainly beating at
that moment in his wrists, scattered
wealth—but there was not much at hand.

The 'scattered wealth' he feels (scattered like money and jewels dropped by fleeing thieves) is his own and Russia's—it has not been, and cannot be, wholly robbed, absconded with. He feels that, feels it close. But also he feels a tickling wave of nostalgia:

Cities are full of light, fine clothes
delicacies for the table, variety,
novelty—fashion: all spent for *this*.
Never to be like that again:
the frame that was. It tickled his
imagination. But it passed in a rising calm.

He feels a nostalgia for all which (for now, anyway—and perhaps forever) must be given up for the sake of the new thing yet to be defined. The old context, the frame, gone. But now '*this*': the 'few flowers,' the vividness he will know.

But it passes (that wave of nostalgia) in a *rising* calm—not the sinking calm of resignation, but a lift of the spirits.

Tan dar a dei; Tan dar a dei!
He was singing. Two miserable peasants
very lazy and foolish
seemed to have walked out from his own
feet and were walking away with wooden rakes
under the six nearly bare poplars, up the hill.
There go my feet.

Singing with lifted spirits, (singing, one notices—and there is an irony in this—that medieval refrain we associate with spring, love and courtesy, ancient forests, knights errant and troubadours) he feels as much one with the peasants he watches from his window as he had with the chill red dawn. He sees them as lazy and foolish, as well as miserable, just as he might have done from the viewpoint of prerevolutionary class privilege: he does not idealize them; but the difference is that now he identifies with them, lazy and foolish as they are, and with their task—to rake away rubbish, perhaps dead leaves—to which they must go *up hill*. 'There go my feet.'

He stood still in the window forgetting
to shave—
The very old past was refound
redirected. It had wandered into himself
The world was himself, these were
his own eyes that were seeing, his own mind
that was straining to comprehend, his own
hands that would be touching other hands
They were his own!
His own, feeble, uncertain . . .

In this new world—around him and within him—he finds ancient roots, not the immediate past which has been razed but the '*very old past*,' taking new directions. Identified with what is happening historically, he feels himself a microcosm; the proposition invites reversal—it is not only that he is intimately and intensely involved but that, just as his mind strains to comprehend, so the mind of the peasants, the mind of all Russia collectively, strains to see, to comprehend. His hands, reaching out to touch others, are feeble and uncertain, though; and so are the hands of the multitude.

. . . He would go
out to pick herbs, he graduate of
the old university. He would go out
and ask that old woman, in the little
village by the lake, to show him wild
ginger. He himself would not know the plant.

He will go humbly, as pupil of the old peasant, the ancient root wisdom—not as teacher of others.

A horse was stepping up the dirt road
under his window

—a live thing moving on unpaved earth: not merely a descriptive detail but a metaphor.

He decided not to shave. Like those two [the two
peasants]
that he knew now, as he had never
known them formerly. A city, fashion
had been between—
Nothing between now.

He would go to the Soviet unshaven. This
was the day—and listen. Listen. That
was all he did, listen to them, weigh
for them. He was turning into
a pair of scales, the scales in the
zodiac.

This is evidently the day of the regular meeting of the local Soviet, which he is attending not for the first time, as one can gather from the syntax,—but it is also the day of a new access of consciousness and resolve, a *first* day in some sense. He puts his university education at the service of the community. Perhaps he weighs physical supplies—grain, fertilizer, medicines—bringing specific professional skills into play: that's not specified. But there's more to weighing than that. He not only feels, with a mixture of humility and amusement, that he becomes his function, becomes a pair of scales, but that they are the zodiacal scales, charged with moral, mythic, psychological symbolism.

But closer, he was himself
the scales . . .

That is, not only did his work of weighing transform him into a function, but he was anyway, intrinsically, an evaluator, he realizes.

The local soviet. They could
weigh . . .

That is, in his new sense of identification with his fellows, others too are intrinsically, as humans, evaluators.

. . . If it was not too late.

That is, if too much damage had not already been done, too much for the revolution to have a future after all, too much for that human ability to measure for themselves, to evaluate justly, to manifest itself among the many.

. . . He felt
uncertain on many days. But all were uncertain
together and he must weigh for them out
of himself.

His 'weighing' is a service he performs as an intellectual, contributing his ability to listen closely, which has been trained by education; but his judgements must be made out of a commitment, a centre in himself, and not merely abstractly, which would be perfunctory. It is 'out of himself,' his very substance, he must act.

He took a small pair of scissors
from the shelf and clipped his nails
carefully. He himself served the fire.

He reasserts his education, maintains his standards of hygiene and decent appearance. But to attend to the fire in his hearth himself—this is new for him. To use his hands, with their clean, clipped nails. And that fire: it is literal, and it is the fire of life, hope, revolution. Now he soliloquizes:

We have cut out the cancer but
who knows! perhaps the patient will die

He reiterates his own realistic uncertainty. Then he proceeds to define the 'patient,' which is not solely Russia, a country in the throes of total reorganization:

The patient is anybody, anything
worthless that I desire, my hands
to have it—
. . . anybody, anything

lines which I would gloss thus: . . . anybody, anything, *albeit considered* 'worthless,' that I desire, my hands *desiring* to have it—that's to say, the 'patient' is the sum of things that, though the world think them tawdry, assigning them no value, Williams consistently saw as having the glitter of life, cats' eyes in the dark. Beautiful Thing. 'Melon flowers that open / about the edge of refuse' / . . . 'the small / yellow cinquefoil in the / parched places.' Or those starlings in the wind's teeth. And, too, the 'patient' whose survival is in question is desire itself, the desire to touch that aliveness with bare hands,

—instead of the feeling [he goes on]
that there is a piece of glazed paper
between me and the paper—invisible
but tough running through the legal
processes of possession—

That glazed top sheet, a transparent obstacle to touch, covers the surface even of the documents that proclaim possession of what is desired; and thus cancels out the *experience* of possession.

—a city that
we could possess—

that is, *my hands desire to have a city that we could possess.* (The syntax is clearer here if instead of dashes before the word 'instead' and after the word 'possession' we enclose those lines in parentheses.) A city, then, that—unlike the cities that have 'faded richly / into foreign countries' and were only to be enjoyed by those who 'can pay high'—would embody an accessible life.

It's in art, it's in
the French school.
What we lacked was
everything. It is the middle of
everything. Not to have.

Here both 'it's' refer back to the 'patient' in the aforementioned sense of that embodiment of the quality of immediacy which, in the prose passage immediately preceding 'A Morning Imagination of Russia' in the *Descent of Winter* sequence, and dated only one day before it, Williams had said was the very goal of poetry: 'poetry should strive for nothing else, this vividness alone, *per se*, for itself'—and further, 'The vividness *which is* poetry.' So, *'It's* in art, in the French school,'—here he draws on his own educated knowledge and experience, on all that makes him different from those two 'miserable, lazy, and foolish' peasants—and also *'It* is the middle of everything'—*it* is not *only* in art but in all kinds of things, common experience, and here he reasserts his sense of brotherhood. But 'What we lacked was everything . . . *Not to have,*' was what, till now, we experienced. I am reminded here of Wallace Stevens' lines

'That's what misery is,
Nothing to have at heart':

Both the intellectual, because of his sense of that invisible wall of glazed paper between him and life, and the oppressed and ignorant people, have hitherto been cut off from the 'everything' in the middle of which are found the sparks of vivid beauty; instead they have experienced only *not having*, absence.

We have little now but
we have that. [The 'it,' the sparks, the poetry.]
We are convalescents. Very
feeble. Our hands shake. We need a
transfusion. No one will give it to us,
they are afraid of infection. I do not
blame them. We have paid heavily. But we
have gotten—touch. The eyes and the ears
down on it. Close.

The whole people is convalescent from the convulsions of revolution. The transfusion they need is not forthcoming—seen historically, such a 'transfusion' would have meant international support for their experiment, instead of an economic and psychological blockade. But other nations, other governments, were scared. The protagonist, like a true Chekhovian character, says he can't blame them; he sees what scares them, and why—he is not doctrinaire. And he recognizes that a great price has been paid, and will perhaps be further exacted. But what has been gained is precisely what he has desired: touch itself. Williams the doctor knew how the touch of hands could diagnose, cure, bring to birth; his fictive Russian knows the imagination as an intimate form of touch—without which all is dull, hopeless, ashen. What he celebrates—here, at the end of the poem, returning to its opening, when earth and sky are close, known, touched with the imagination—is the sun rising in his heart.

The prose which immediately follows the poem and is dated four days later, begins with the words, 'Russia is every country, here he must live. . . .' And a few pages further on Williams breaks off from diverse topics to return to the protagonist of the poem, in these sentences, 'He feels the richness, but a distressing feeling of loss is close upon it. He knows he must co-ordinate the villages for effectiveness in a flood, a famine.' I see two ways of reading that, and they are complimentary, not conflicting. If, as I've been doing, one reads the poem without disregard for its narrative reality, the truth of its fiction, and thus the universality of the poem's Russia—'every country; here he must live'—then the richness that 'he,' the protagonist, feels is the richness of new beginnings, the reassertion of the 'very old' past, and also the democratic 'everything' of human experience; while the 'distressing feeling of loss' that comes close upon it concerns the equally real subtleties, nuances, desirable complexities, that 'scattered wealth' he earlier felt 'beating at his wrists,' which as yet we have not figured out how to attain in any social system without sacrifice of justice and mercy. But one can also read 'A Morning Imagination of Russia' somewhat as Webster Schott chose to do, that is, as a parable of Williams' poetic struggle in the twenties (it was written in 1927). According to the first reading, the hero's recognition of the need to 'co-ordinate the villages for effectiveness in a flood, a famine,' reminds one of Chekhov's letters in the early 1890s when he was an unpaid local medical inspector during the cholera epidemic. If one looks beyond the Russian scene (set just a few years before the writing of *The Descent of Winter*) to an analogy in Williams' own struggles to establish a new sense of poetry and the imagination in the American 20s, we may see in those words about co-ordinating the villages an almost Poundian missionary spirit, for then one takes the 'villages' to be outposts of intelligent poetry, and the flood or famine as aspects of the hostile or uncomprehending world of readers, critics, other poets, the public at large. Webster Schott, reintroducing *The Descent of Winter* in 1970, saw it as *entirely* a struggle 'to verbalize a theory of contemporary poetry' and 'to realize a clear conception of himself as an artist.' That is partially true; but when Williams wrote the words 'We have paid heavily. But we / have gotten—touch' he was not speaking in a vacuum, as if from an airtight aesthetic island in which the political images with which, in *A Morning Imagination*, he had chosen to work, had no meaning *except* as metaphor, as figurative ways to speak about literature. Those images work as Chekhovian narrative description; they work as implications of political ideas; *and* they work as analogies for the poet's need to act in society, humbly and with an understanding that in trying to serve the commonweal he will serve also his own need for intimate experience of the living mystery. Ideas without Things are vaporous, mere irritants of the detached and insensate intellect; but Things abound, and are choc-a-bloc with the Ideas that dance and stumble, groan or sing, calling and beckoning to one another, throughout the decades of his poetry.

CARL RAPP

"Williams' Version of the Myth of the Fall and the Problem of Symbols"

William Carlos Williams and Romantic Idealism

1984, pp. 31–51

> A fall of some sort or other—the creation, as it were, of the non-absolute—is the fundamental postulate of the moral history of man. Without this hypothesis, man is unintelligible; with it, every phenomenon is explicable. The mystery itself is too profound for human insight. (Coleridge, *Table Talk*, 1 May 1830)

For all their significance, neither "Vortex" nor "The Wanderer" is the most revealing of Williams' early texts. That distinction belongs, I would argue, to the fourth essay in a group of *Five Philosophical Essays* written by Williams sometime between 1910 and 1915. Although he never published any of these essays, the fourth, entitled "Love and Service," happens to be the clearest and most comprehensive explanation Williams ever wrote of what his work as a whole is all about. Reading it, we learn how deeply committed he was to a certain conception of the fall and how much that conception influenced his adoption of the epistemology and aesthetics of idealism. As a result, the rationale behind Williams' poetry, so often misconstrued in the past, becomes finally clear.

The essay begins boldly with the assertion that perception, and perception alone, constitutes the whole duty of man. We start with perception and end with perception, though, as we shall see presently, both our starting point and our end point are curiously elusive. By comparison to what Williams regards as the most important activity of man, which is to admire everything that exists, the activities whereby we acquire formal knowledge, like the more practical activities of "routine life" whereby we insure our material existence, are trivial and irrelevant:

> AS FAR as any ultimate problem of the universe is concerned man on earth must forever be totally ignorant. For him all simply exists. He cannot know anything; he cannot even begin to know; he can merely appreciate; his sole possible activity can be but of two orders: to behold and to behold more. The why is unthinkable and action and will are merely corollaries of sight, not separate. Man is to thrill as the great horses of existence prance by him, he being one of them also, and to keep from being stepped on by knowing where the hoof will fall next. His only actions are to prance to cheer and to point, all of which are but one thing: praise. (*EK*, 178)

"Thus," says Williams, "we live and eat merely to go about in the face of wonder in the fullest glory of our senses only differing from infants in a breadth of accomplishment and expression" (*EK*, 180–81). The act of pure appreciation can be called a starting point because, according to Williams, it is especially characteristic of the consciousness of children ("infants") and primitives. At the same time, however, it must also be called an end point or a goal, because it represents the "consummation" of life's "essential spirit" (*EK*, 180). Even for the most sophisticated adult, the whole meaning of life remains concentrated in "moments of intense feeling" that are occasioned by perceptions and devoted entirely to praise and appreciation.

The trouble is that we have left our starting point behind; we *have* become sophisticated. When the activity of pure appreciation is eclipsed by other activities, as it surely is both in the life of the individual and in the life of the race, a fall occurs. As soon as he eats of the tree of knowledge, man starts building the edifices of science and philosophy, and simultaneously he begins to lose his capacity for wonder. Instead of devoting himself naïvely and directly to the mystery of existence, he starts to explain the mystery and thence becomes distracted by his own explanations. The result is a form of sophisticated idolatry so abhorrent to Williams that he launches into a passionate defense of what he takes to be its opposite, namely, the unsophisticated worship of primitives:

> That native was no fool who first praised the sun and the moon. We too shall have moon and sun feasts; we shall come to realize much that we now do not understand. Call this native an idolater, call him what you will. What is the moon to him? It is a light, a sign. He doesn't even know it is round. To him it is merely wonder, the unknown that is beautiful; to him it is an unconscious symbol which he used for praise. His, until perversion sets in through ignorance, is true expression, but you, you can see nothing but a dead sphere of clay which is not even true vision but half superstitious fancy, but the native sees beauty, wonder! You are the fool, not he. Or else what do you do that is better if you will not be called a fool? You have no beauty your own nor even a symbol of beauty except dead words, though there are many live ones, dead words which are symbols of symbols, twice removed from vitality—on a string like dried apples or Swedish bread. You are the idolaters, not the native. Oh you hypocrites, you shall yet kneel to the sun and moon and be cleaned. (*EK*, 181)

The difference between the native and ourselves is this: whereas the native uses that which he sees as a symbol, we mistake our symbols for that which we see. The native is not an idolater (not, that is, "until perversion sets in through ignorance") because he does not worship the sun and moon in and for themselves. Rather he expresses, by means of his praise of the sun and the moon, what Williams regards as a properly worshipful attitude toward that which transcends all symbols, namely, "the unknown" or "the mystery about which nothing can be said" (*EK*, 182). Since this alone is the real object of his praise, his use of the sun and moon as vehicles of praise constitutes "true expression," not idolatry. We, on the other hand, *are* idolaters, though not because we use symbols. We are idolaters because the symbols we use do not point directly to the mystery. Instead, they point to other symbols. As Williams puts it, they are "symbols of symbols." What he means by this, I think, is that we no longer apprehend the world of the senses as a symbol of the unknown—instead we apprehend it as an object of knowledge. Accordingly, we have developed increasingly complex systems of explanation that refer to the world as though it were a thing in itself, the terminus of all explanation. As these systems grow in complexity, they eventually interfere with our awareness of the things they are supposed to explain, so that, if we are not careful, we find ourselves attending exclusively to representations of things that are themselves representations of the unknown, or "symbols of symbols." Instead of remaining awed by the ineffable mystery of existence, we substitute in the most complacent and idolatrous fashion our own conceptions for that which is ultimately inconceivable. This is what Williams means by the fall.

But the fall is more than just an accidental by-product of personal or cultural development. It is the inevitable consequence of every act of expression that attends every act of perception. No matter how pure it is in its origin, every attempt to give shape or form to one's admiration of the mystery of existence involves the use of symbols, and when these symbols are confused with the reality they stand for, the fall occurs. In a way, then, the fall is as much the result of a misapprehension of works of art as it is the result of science and philosophy. Even the native's "true expression" is potentially idolatrous, as Williams admits when he refers to the apparently inevitable moment "when perversion sets in through ignorance." The fall, therefore, is not to be interpreted as an event that occurs once and for all in the history of a culture or in the history of an individual. It is, so to speak, an eternal event, an ongoing event, constantly repeated, whose necessity springs, oddly enough, from the very mystery that excites our admiration and compels our praise.

We may say, in fact, that the fall occurs because, as Williams describes it, the act of perception leads naturally and inevitably to expression, and the act of expression is always, in some sense, a misrepresentation. What happens during one of those moments of pure appreciation when no distraction separates a man from his sense of the mystery? Williams tells us:

> He finds no use for any formality he practices by habit, all he knows how to do is mechanically rejected by his mind until at last he is totally powerless in speech and limb, his whole being given to sight, to appreciation. Then comes a miracle, he has no satisfaction in his learned activities so at once he invents something new. He tries to sing, he tries to dance, to speak praises in accordance with that which he sees but, of course, fails. The point however is that he tried to do a thing which had he been able he would have done and that thing was to perform some act which would symbolize the beauty he sees, reflect it and this is expression, the outgrowth of sight, an act of appreciation, praise. One wishes to be a poet, a painter, a something instinctively known to be supreme, a something of which the essence is sight in the broad sense, to include hearing, but the reality he would express is silence. (*EK*, 180)

Being "outgrowths" of sight, all forms of expression can be said to have as their ultimate ground those acts of pure perception that constitute the fruit of our immediate contact with the world. Nevertheless, since the real object of our perceptions is the unknown "about which nothing can be said," every attempt to express this real object must fail. Since the reality we would express is "silence," every speaking is necessarily not in accordance with that which prompts us to speak. And yet, Williams insists, "we must seek for forms by which to express, for we cannot, except in silence, praise direct, it must take a form and that form is beauty" (*EK*, 181).

The artist, it seems, no less than the philosopher or the scientist, creates misrepresentations of reality. Even his work is the symbol of a symbol in the sense that the beauty he makes is merely a symbol of the beauty he sees and that beauty, in turn, is a symbol of that which is formless and ineffable. On the other hand, he cannot be silent without, in a way, betraying his perception, for it is the perception itself that impels him to speak. Another, more pressing reason for not remaining silent has to do with the fact that previous expressions of all sorts are constantly interfering with new acts of appreciation and must, therefore, be destroyed. In order to liberate himself and others from the powerful charm exerted by these distractions, the artist must make a positive gesture to cancel or negate them. Finding himself surrounded by symbols and knowing the difference between symbols and the reality beyond symbols, he must demonstrate the difference and abolish idolatry by using symbols in such a way as to reveal that they are just that—mere symbols. Furthermore, he must do this not only with the symbols of his art, with paint or words or tones, but also with the "natural" symbols of his experience, with the things he encounters in daily life:

> But two things we must avoid. We must not forget that we praise the unknown, the mystery about which nothing can be said; and second, that we praise in silence, the rest being but perishable signs. Then lest we mistake our signs for the reality let them be ever new, forever new for only by forever changing the sign can we learn to separate from it its meaning, the expression from the term, and so cease to be idolaters.
>
> For I could live forever in a hut in a valley and if I were born there I would mistake the valley for peace, the hut for comfort, my dog for love, one flower for beauty and myself for king of creation just as has been done many times in the past. Therefore I travel. Manners that differ, customs, worships that differ show that no language, no custom, no worship is the truth but the truth is a formless thing which lies in them as within a suit of clothes, in part. Then I see that I must be forever new lest I become an idolater in my valley, but I would be the biggest fool imaginable if I took my valley to express nothing. (*EK*, 182)

These remarks make it plain beyond a doubt that Williams' notorious iconoclasm is, above all, conservative.[1] It seeks to conserve, not to destroy, what it takes to be an original intuition of the ultimate ground of our existence—the formless truth. When the icon is smashed, when the symbol is allowed to perish, then that which stands above icons and symbols may be apprehended as utterly transcendent. Or, to use Willliams' terms, "when the form is destroyed the permanent shines out for the first time clearly" (*EK*, 185). Here we see a corroboration of Emerson's paradoxical observation that "the spiritualist finds himself driven to express his faith by a series of skepticisms" (*CE*, IV, 181).

In "Love and Service," however, Williams does not hesitate, as he does almost everywhere else, to express his faith openly and directly. With prophetic fervor he declares that "men shall come to the great altar of the Unknown with pomp and singing and processions" (*EK*, 181), thereby cancelling the idolatry into which they have fallen. When this happens, we shall have come in one sense full circle, for we shall have regained that original apprehension of the unknown which Williams supposes to have flourished prior to the perversions of sophistication. In the beginning, apparently, this apprehension was facilitated by the use of "unconscious symbols." In the end, it will be facilitated by the highly conscious process of using symbols to displace symbols. Thus, in another sense, we shall have risen from a lower plane to a higher. Starting with a naïve affirmation of particular symbols (the valley standing for peace, the hut for comfort, the dog for love, etc.), we end by rejecting such symbols as inadequate manifestations of the formless truth.

But what, after all, is this truth? What is this mystery about which nothing can be said except that it is "the Unknown"? The title of Williams' essay, "Love and Service," comes as near as possible to providing an answer, because love and service as Williams describes them constitute the most significant expressions in human experience of what the mystery means. Indeed, the relationship that exists between love in its essence, or love in itself, and a pair of human lovers is exactly the same as the relationship that exists between the formless truth and the perishable forms. "Love," therefore, is one of the primary names Williams gives to the unknown, without intending thereby to diminish its ineffability, for the effect of using such a name is not so much to clarify the mystery as it is to make love itself, as we normally understand it, even more mysterious.[2] When two human beings love each other, says Williams, their experience of love is "a mere repetition" of one of those "moments of intense feeling" that are devoted to praise and appreciation. For this reason, they are caught up in the same dialectic that governs experience in general. As time passes, they must learn that physical passion is merely an expression or form of love, so that "as passion is less and less useful, love shines more and more out" (*EK*, 183). Then they must learn that even they themselves as individuals are merely symbols to each other of a mystery that includes them but also goes beyond them. As the drama unfolds, the lovers have the opportunity to become more and more conscious both of themselves and their relation to the mystery:

> Each becomes an unconscious symbol in the other's eyes, a symbol of love which is beautiful, but mistaking the symbol for the reality they overlook deformity and misery or else at last through ignorance become cynics. This is the commonest phenomenon of all. From the beginning of time, or of history at least, one has seen love, but trying to describe it, describes the symbol and in that love is so much greater than its terms finds it impossible not to magnify, impossible not to think that here, in the symbol, is the greatest beauty of all. But often this symbol is suddenly destroyed when we see at last that love is not anything mortal, that it flows over the forms of the world like water that comes and withdraws. Yet as the objects of life are all we can know love by, this coming and going discloses us to be involved in a destiny more than we can imagine, which must be very marvelous. (*EK*, 184)

"Love," then, being one of the primary names of the nameless truth, Williams concludes his essay by declaring that "it goes beyond life, where no knowledge goes and is the most daring of all the mysteries and the most wonderful, which is a sufficient pretext for the presence here of man" (*EK*, 185).

What then of service? "Service" is the term Williams uses to designate the highest expression of love of which man is capable, for it refers not to fidelity with respect to the beloved but rather to fidelity with respect to the mystery. The ordinary kinds of service that have a practical application in everyday life are to be admired, but more admirable still is the desire to communicate to others our own sense of the ultimate reality. Thus "our only service" of any real consequence is "to give praise, to put into form what we see" (*EK*, 185). In this way, not only what we see but, more importantly we ourselves in our own persons come to symbolize the mystery we praise. In bearing witness to the mystery, we deliberately become its chief vehicle, its chief form of expression. In fact, it is not so much that we express the mystery as it is that the mystery expresses itself in us and through us. It is in this sense that "service" may be defined as fidelity to the mystery: it is "to believe proudly in love as a law and to stand for this clear intellectual belief permanently, so that a form be given to the reality in your own person, than which there is no greater praise, which it solely is" (*EK*, 185). If in the beginning there is only the "I" facing the Unknown, consumed by wonder to such a degree that everything else becomes subordinate to our act of admiration, in the end there is only the "I" representing the Unknown, the "I" as the ultimate image of the imageless truth. The whole world and everything it contains offers itself as material for effecting or demonstrating this higher revelation.

The argument of "Love and Service," while not explicitly idealistic in a philosophical sense, is nevertheless compatible with the idealism of Williams' other writings, for it makes the drama of consciousness the thing of main importance. The absolute foundation of all that concerns us is an act of mind, an act of apprehension, wherein the phenomenal world is used as a means to an end. Indeed, the phenomenal world from the very beginning is radically symbolic, referring simultaneously to the "I" and to the unknown mystery. The sun and the moon in Williams' analysis are never mere objects in their own right. They are one thing to the native who uses them as instruments of praise, something else to the scientist who explains them, but always one thing or another according to the nature of the mind that perceives them. The fall occurs when the phenomenal world assumes (for the mind of a fool, as Blake would say) the character of a thing in itself, a finality, a fixity, independent of the mind that perceives it. No longer functioning as a symbol or as a set of symbols, it becomes that "solid apparition" Williams decries so eloquently in the "Prologue" to *Kora in Hell*. It becomes the "natural or scientific array," "the walking devil of modern life" (*I*, 14). The fall, then, is really an abnegation of self, a denial of consciousness as the essential component of that which is experienced. Indeed, from Williams' point of view, the superstructures of science and philosophy represent a massive exercise in self-alienation wherein the mind constructs, in opposition to itself, an infinitely complex "reality" to which it then fancies itself inferior and subordinate. It is precisely to combat this illusion that Williams takes upon himself the task of being a poet. Against the "solid apparition" of an independent reality he sets himself—a free, autonomous spirit—the very picture of Emersonian self-reliance. By establishing his own freedom and his own autonomy with respect to the so-called real world (which he does by using whatever parts of that world he chooses in whatever way he pleases for the purposes of his art), he also establishes the autonomy and freedom of the formless truth with respect to its own manifestations. *His* freedom and independence, which are exercised by "forever changing the sign," become the superlative image of *its* freedom and independence, so that by making all things a vehicle for himself he becomes a vehicle for it.

It cannot be emphasized too strongly that whatever Williams says in "Love and Service" about the formless truth or the unknown applies equally to the self—not to the finite, empirical self but to the transcendental self, the ego. At the deepest level, this self and the unknown are identical, as Williams makes clearer in some of his later pronouncements. The mystery about which nothing can be said except that it "is not anything mortal" and that it "flows over the forms of the world like water that comes and withdraws," is not finally distinguishable from the "rare element" that Williams in his *Autobiography* claims to have been pursuing all his life, the "rare presence" that "will not use the same appearance for any new materialization" (A, 362). After thirty-five years, he still calls it "the thing I cannot quite name," "the thing . . . of which I am in chase" (A, 288). Its true location, despite the fact that its appearances are shifting and fleeting, is "in the self," in the "secret gardens of the self" (A, 288). It is "our very life," it is "we ourselves" (A, 362). "Within us," as Williams says in his "Advice to the Young Poet," "lies imprisoned the infinitely multiplex quarry . . . a nascent thing, a variety, living and firm."[3] That is why he can claim of the work of art that it "makes the unknown a form which eyes, ears, nose, mouth, and fingers can experience" while at the same time, and for that very reason, it allows man "to say, *I am*, in concrete terms" (*ARI*, 212). "I am" equals "the Unknown."

One of the most important consequences of the myth of the fall as it is presented in "Love and Service" is that it enables Williams to remain perpetually dissatisfied with all current expressions of the formless truth, including his own. On the one hand, he can look back with nostalgia to a hypothetical past when a relatively pure, unsophisticated consciousness prevailed and expression was "true." On the other hand, he can also look forward to an equally hypothetical future when the effects of our apostasy shall be completely reversed and "men shall come to the great altar of the Unknown with pomp and singing and processions" (*EK*, 181). Such a prospect gives him the opportunity to denigrate the present moment and to find the conditions of art and experience inadequate as they now exist. Indeed, the myth of the fall is more than just a pseudo-historical explanation of the loss and recovery of the autonomy of consciousness vis-à-vis the world. It is also an instrument of criticism, a pretext for passing negative judgments on contemporary culture—something Williams has to be able to do in order to avoid idolatry. He has to be in a position to reject every manifestation of the "rare presence" in order to affirm his own spiritual autonomy and to affirm the fact that "the infinitely multiplex quarry" transcends its own finite embodiments.

Most readers have supposed that Williams was a keen admirer of all things here and now and that, consequently, he must have looked approvingly on the contemporary American scene and on modern art in general. Nothing could be further from the truth. The evidence indicates that while Williams certainly countenanced every attempt to escape from the present by dashing headlong toward the beckoning future, he took a very dim view of his own immediate culture and regarded the modern period, especially with respect to art, as a sort of Dark Age with only occasional flashes of promise. In *Paterson*, he looks back to an earlier time when "the word" lived in the ancient divisions of the poetic line, hoping it will live there again in a new measure. In our own time, however, "poetry is in an age of darkness" (*EK*, 129). Indeed, if we look carefully at what Williams has to say about his contemporaries, we find the myth of the fall almost everywhere implicit in his judgments, even when they are seemingly most generous.

In praising Joyce's work, for example, which he was not always prone to do, Williams calls attention to the way Joyce appears to *restore* the original qualities of words in his work after *Ulysses:*

> Joyce maims words. Why? Because meanings have been dulled, then lost, then perverted by their connotations (which have grown over them) until their effect on the mind is no longer what it was when they were fresh, but grows rotten as *poi*—though we may get to like *poi*.
>
> Meanings are perverted by time and chance—but kept perverted by academic observance and intention. At worst they are inactive and get only the static value of anything, which retains its shape but is dead. All words, all sense of being gone out of them. Or trained into them by the dull of the deadly minded. Joyce is restoring them. (*SE*, 89–90)

Joyce's work, then, is fundamentally conservative since he makes it possible for words "to be understood again in an original, a fresh, delightful sense" (*SE*, 90). In doing so, he resembles the surrealists, who, as Williams remarks on another occasion, "have invented the living defense of literature" by similarly emphasizing "the elusive reality of words": "It appears to be to them to knock off every accretion from the stones of composition. To them it is a way to realize the classical excellence of language, so that it becomes writing again" (*SE*, 96–97).

Williams himself tries to do something similar in his essays on American history, which he describes at the beginning of his book *In the American Grain* as essays in restoration or reconstruction. The truth about America lies dormant, unavailable, in history's "original records." Only the most vigorous efforts of interpretation can ferret it out and state it again, so that it becomes fresh once more: "In letters, in journals, reports of happenings I have recognized new contours suggested by old words so that new names were constituted" (*IAG*, v). In surmounting the obstacles imposed by "borrowed titles" and "misappellations," Williams hopes to deliver the spirit from the letter, "the strange phosphorus of the life" from the fossil records, by going back to a truth that precedes even the original documents, a truth that must be regarded as the source of all his sources. Indeed, his own activity as a historian may be compared to the pioneering activities of the men and women he writes about, those who left the old world of Europe to make a new beginning in America. They too, like him, may be thought of as voyagers into the past, leaving behind them the "modern" culture of Europe and sailing to a primitive, almost mythic, land of origins. In a sense, the New World was really the old world restored, a kind of golden age all over again. More than a place, it was "a beloved condition . . . in which all lived together" (*IAG*, 138), "in its every expression, the land of heart's desire" (*IAG*, 139). Always it seems, with the passage of time, this condition is lost, and so we must be continually returning to it: "However hopeless it may seem, we have no other choice: we must go back to the beginning; it must all be done over" (*IAG*, 215). That is what the Europeans were doing, and that is what we must do ourselves if we want to recover the original potential of the New World condition.

In the American Grain is, finally, a work of prophecy in which Williams urges us to repent by recalling us to the promise of the past. The question he poses again and again in these essays is this: to what extent does America today reflect the "beloved condition" of America as it used to be? The answer is that it reflects it hardly at all. Just as the "true character" of American history has been lost in a "chaos of borrowed titles," so the very essence of the New World spirit has been lost in the growth of American culture. America today is simply a wasteland of decay and ignorance. (Williams was writing this, it will be remembered, during the effervescent, sophisticated twenties.)

> We believe that life in America is compact of violence and the shock of immediacy. This is not so. Were it so, there would be a corresponding beauty of the spirit—to bear it witness; a great flowering, simple and ungovernable as the configuration of a rose—that should stand with the gifts of the spirit of other times and other nations as a standard to humanity. There is none. (*IAG*, 174)

As Williams analyzes it, the rot set in almost from the very beginning so that only a few heroes like Père Sebastian Rasles, Daniel Boone, or Edgar Allan Poe, appear to have recognized what the New World could mean. For the most part, a vast cultural inertia has manifested itself all along in terms of a collective failure of consciousness, in "the niggardliness of our history, our stupidity, sluggishness of spirit, the falseness of our historical notes, the complete missing of the point." "In the confusion," it seems, "almost nothing remains of the great American New World but a memory of the Indian" (*IAG*, 157). Such despair is not totally unmitigated. Williams' own heroic attempt to revive the past by writing a book about it is meant to suggest the possibility at least of a more general revival in American life. The odds, however, are mostly against it. If the availability (to Williams) of historical truth implies the potential availability of the New World spirit to all the rest of us, still Williams will not allow us to forget that the most serious misconceptions are likely to prevail, their effects being as real and as terrible as Cortez's destruction of Tenochtitlan. Like the Puritans before us who had "nothing of curiosity, no wonder, for the New World" (*IAG*, 112), we are so degraded by our ignorance that it is doubtful whether we can ever make anything of our neglected opportunities:

> The primitive destiny of the land is obscure, but it has been obscured further by a field of unrelated culture stuccoed upon it that has made that destiny more difficult than ever to determine. To this latter nearly all the aesthetic adhesions of the present day occur. Through that stratum of obscurity the acute but frail genius of the place must penetrate. The seed is tough but the chances are entirely against a growth. It is possible for every vestige of virtue from the New World to be lost, like the wood pigeon. (*IAG*, 212)

Skeptical as he was about the quality of contemporary culture as a whole, Williams was even more skeptical about the quality of modern art, especially the art of poetry. It is true he endorsed the experiments of the avant-garde, but he did so primarily because he regarded such experiments as protests against the prevailing spirit of the times. The arts, he believed, had fallen into a state of ill health, and drastic remedies alone promised to revive them. Here too it was a question of going back to the beginning, of dismissing the traditions that constituted his immediate heritage and returning to principles that lay far back in the past. In the preface to his *Selected Essays*, he reconsidered his long career and reached the conclusion that all along he had been trying to reestablish the validity of "ancient rules":

> Meanwhile I went on writing my poems. I had better say, constructing my poems. For I soon discovered that there were certain rules, certain new rules, that I became enmeshed in before I had gone far, which I had to master. These were ancient rules, profoundly true but long since all but forgotten. They were overgrown with weeds like ruined masonry. Present teaching had very little to do with them, but that they existed I had no doubts; it remained only for me to rediscover them. (*SE*, Preface, [ix–x])

Did he, in fact, rediscover them and apply them successfully in his own poetry? Did his contemporaries rediscover them? It is tempting to think so and even more tempting to suppose that Williams thought so. In reality, however, he was perpetually haunted by a sense of failure, not only with respect to his own work but also with respect to the whole modernist endeavor. Even at the end, when for a time he thought he had found a philosopher's stone in the variable foot, the cloud of skepticism did not lift. Even then, it seemed to him that poets were still just on the verge of writing really splendid poetry, just on the verge of pinpointing the new measure that would magically restore our lives and usher in the millennium.

In 1921, he announced his hopes for American art in an editorial for his new magazine *Contact:*

> We want to give all our energy to the setting up of new vigors of artistic perception, invention and expression in the United States. Only by slow growth, consciously fostered to the point of enthusiasm, will American work of the quality of Marianne Moore's best poetry come to the fore of intelligent attention and the ignorance which has made America an artistic desert be somewhat dissipated. (*SE*, 29)

This editorial set the stage for a series of complaints that can be found scattered throughout Williams' writing during the 1920s. In *The Great American Novel*, he observes that we have "no art," "no words": "I touch the words and they baffle me. I turn them over in my mind and look at them but they mean little that is clean. They are plastered with muck out of the cities" (*I*, 175). In *Spring and All* he writes in the same vein, noting that "the greatest characteristic of the present age is that it is stale—stale as literature" (*I*, 134). Indeed, the situation is dire, since "the most of all writing has not even begun in the province from which alone it can draw sustenance" (*I*, 129). Six years after *Spring and All*, Williams saw no reason to change his opinion. He writes in 1929, "There is very little light in literature today."[4] Despite the fact that poetry is "just at the brink of its modern development,"[5] for the moment, at least, "language is in its January" (*SE*, 96), having been "enslaved, forced, raped, made a whore by the idea venders" (*SE*, 96).

If much of this sounds like a polemic aimed at modernism's reactionary enemies, there can be no mistake about Williams' intentions in an important letter written to Kay Boyle in 1932. Here his criticisms are aimed squarely at the modernists themselves. In passing, he mentions ten writers, without most of whom the modernist movement would be inconceivable—Walt Whitman, Robinson Jeffers, E. A. Robinson, Robert Frost, Yvor Winters, Wallace Stevens, Gertrude Stein, James Joyce, T. S. Eliot, and Ezra Pound. Incredibly, not one of these writers can be said to provide a good model of what the modern poet ought to be doing. Thus, Williams concludes, "there is no clear perception of poetic form operative today," nor can there be any "until the poem itself appears as the rule in fact" (*SL*, 133). Since "the present moment," as far as poetry is concerned, is merely "a formless interim," since the term "modern poem" is virtually an oxymoron, the most satisfactory way of referring to the modern period would be to call it "the pre-masterly period":

> It is a period without mastery, that is all. It is a period in which the form has not yet been found. It is a formative time whose duty it is to bare the essentials, to shuck away the hulls, to lay open at least the problems with open eyes. (*SL*, 133)

Ironically, the writers who have done their best to shuck away the hulls, such as Joyce and Stein, are also the ones who have most inhibited the positive development of new form. Joyce and Stein have been paramount, claims Williams, "in knocking the props from under a new technique in the past ten years and enforcing it. They have specifically gone out of their way to draw down the attention on words, so that the line has become pulverous instead of metallic—or at least ductile" (*SL*, 129). Whatever their virtues, their influence has been pernicious:

> Some of the young men seem to me to be too much influenced by the disintegrationists, the users of words for their individual forms and meanings. They are after meanings (Joyce) and their objectivity as things (Stein). Well, as far as poetry is concerned, what of it? (*SL*, 131)

Although he looks forward to a definite departure from these influences in the direction of "a metrical coherence of some sort" (*SL*, 129), Williams as yet cannot see how to proceed. All he knows is that "the modern line must have an internal tension which is now nowhere" (*SL*, 135). The only poet who even comes close to what Williams is looking for is Pound, and his work too is merely a preparation for good things to come:

> So far I believe that Pound's line in his *Cantos*—there is something *like* what we shall achieve. Pound in his mould, a medieval inspiration, patterned on a substitution of medieval simulacra for a possible, not yet extant modern and living material, has made a pre-composition for us. Something which when later (perhaps) packed and realized in living, breathing stuff will (in its changed form) be the thing. (*SL*, 135)

For his own part, Williams claims to have achieved very little—just "a few patches of metrical coherence which I don't as yet see how to use" (*SL*, 130). Such is the situation as of 1932: a few patches of metrical coherence, in the *Cantos* possibly a pre-composition, but nowhere as yet "the poem itself." At their best, the modernists are to be regarded as indispensable prophets crying in the literary wilderness, preparing the way with their relentless experiments, "long before the final summative artist arrives" (*SE*, 103).

In the 1940s, Williams' quest for form became increasingly urgent. Still in pursuit of what he liked to call "the new measure," he made it clear in his essay "An Approach to the Poem" that considerable effort lay ahead:

> do not believe, I keep repeating, that the form of the age will spontaneously appear; that is, that the great age will just accidentally find the unique representation of itself. . . . Nothing could be more fatuous. It is the work, the exhausting work of the artist who . . . will MAKE the world today.[6]

To Parker Tyler he related the following anecdote, which reveals how seriously he took his own, personal efforts to discover the principles of the modern poem. The anecdote concerns an incident that had occurred after one of Williams' public readings:

> Someone in the audience . . . asked me if I thought I had given any evidence of the "new way of measuring" in anything I had read that night or in anything that I myself had written at any time. It was a fair question but one I shall have to postpone answering indefinitely. I always think of Mendelejeff's table of atomic weights in this connection. Years before an element was discovered, the element helium, for instance, its presence had been predicted by a blank in the table of atomic weights.
>
> It may be that I am no genius in the use of the new measure I find inevitable; it may be that as a poet I have not had the genius to do the things I set up as essential if our verse is to blossom. I know, however, the innovation I predict must come to be. Someone, some infant now, will have to find the way we miss. Meanwhile I shall go on talking.
>
> For one thing: what I see, the necessity which presents itself to me has already motivated and colored my critical opinions. I see many past writers in an entirely new light when I set them against the scale by which I am coming more and more to measure. And for myself, if I can write three lines—the day before I die, three lines inspired by the true principle by which I work—everything else, good or bad, in my life will have been justified.
>
> Next time I'm going to speak of my own work only. As far as I am able I'm going to tear it apart in the light of my newer concepts. Either what I have done in the past has helped to clarify that or it has not. If it has not then it must be rejected and the reason for rejecting it shown lucidly. (*SL*, 243)

In the austerity of his requirements, if nothing else, Williams sounds like a latter-day Matthew Arnold. In 1947, he observed to Kenneth Burke: "For myself I reject all poetry as at present written, including my own. I see tendencies, nodes of activity, here and there but no clear synthesis" (*SL*, 257).

In the early 1950s, the long-awaited breakthrough seemed at hand. The new measure appeared to beckon to Williams in one of his own poems, the second book of *Paterson*, which provided an example of the triadic line, and Williams at last thought he was on the right track. To Martha Baird, he described himself as a man "who has been searching for a solid footing": "But at last I am just beginning to know, to know firmly what the present day mind is seeking. I finally have caught a glimmer of the basic place which we, today, must occupy."[7] In the *Autobiography* as well, there is a feeling of relief that comes with the suspicion that Eliot's influence is finally on the wane: "Only now, as I predicted, have we begun to catch hold again and restarted to make the line over" (*A*, 174–75).

But, despite these glimmerings of hope, Williams went right on talking as though the new measure were still to come, as though even his own efforts to use it were but crude approximations. Almost a year after the publication of *The Desert Music and Other Poems,* he was still lamenting that "the measure by which the poem is to be recognized has at present been lost" (*SL,* 331). The verse he approved of was still a verse he could only "envisage" (*SL,* 332). In his statement on measure for Cid Corman, Williams refers to the poems included in *The Desert Music* as "a few experiments," not to be taken as final: "There will be other experiments but all will be directed toward the discovery of a new measure" (*SE,* 340). In the same breath he admits "there is no one among us who is consciously aware of what he is doing." In 1958, the new meaure is "beyond our thoughts."[8] In 1961, it is "what we must get to in the modern world."[9] No wonder, then, when Williams was contemplating the end of his career, he seriously considered grouping all his poems together under a singularly appropriate title—not the *Complete Poems* or the *Collected Poems* but *The Complete Collected Exercises toward a Possible Poem.*[10]

The reason Williams' critical judgments are generally so negative, despite his (usually temporary) enthusiasms for the particular achievements of particular artists, is that he needs to be able to say at any given moment that a work of art or even whole schools of art are unsatisfactory, inadequate. He needs to be able to say that they are merely "perishable signs," which point beyond themselves to the formless truth. In saying so, Williams himself comes forward in his own person as the true representative of that which is formless; for it is not the work that matters so much as the power that calls it into being. That Williams understood the higher necessity of not finding the form he claimed to be seeking seems clear enough from his letter to John Riordan of 13 October 1926. There he explains that it is precisely his desire to "encircle" everything that makes it impossible for him to work inside determinate patterns:

> But my failure to work inside a pattern—a positive sin—is the cause of my virtues. I cannot work inside a pattern because I can't find a pattern that will have me. My whole effort . . . is to find a pattern, large enough, modern enough, flexible enough to include my desires. And if I should find it I'd wither and die.[11]

Here Williams explicitly formulates the paradox of Hegel's romantic artist who seeks and uses determinate, sensuous forms but only in order to designate the freedom and indeterminacy (i.e., the absolute inwardness) of his own spiritual subjectivity. Perhaps a closer analogue to Williams' letter can be found in Emerson's "Circles," for Emerson was equally familiar with the romantic dilemma. In "Circles," he refers to himself as "an endless seeker," having learned that every pattern, or every circle, is less than the power from which it emanates:

> Whilst the eternal generation of circles proceeds, the eternal generator abides. That central life is somewhat superior to creation, superior to knowledge and thought, and contains all its circles. Forever it labors to create a life and thought as large and excellent as itself, suggesting to our thought a certain development, as if that which is made, instructs how to make a better. (CW, II, 188)

Like Williams nearly a century later, Emerson was deeply concerned with the paradoxical relationship between self and world, between the formless truth and the perishable sign, which seems at once to require both the affirmation and the negation of the particular work of art. It is to Emerson, then, that we must apply ourselves if we would understand the American roots of Williams' American brand of idealism.

Notes

In the preceding, quotations from the works of Ralph Waldo Emerson have been taken from *The Centenary Edition of the Complete Works of Ralph Waldo Emerson,* ed. Edward Waldo Emerson, 12 vols. (Boston: Houghton, Mifflin, 1903–04), and are identified by parenthetical references to the abbreviation *CE* followed by the appropriate volume and page numbers. Also cited has been *The Collected Works of Ralph Waldo Emerson,* II, eds. Joseph Slater, Alfred R. Ferguson, and Jean Ferguson Carr (Cambridge: Harvard Univ. Press, 1979), abbreviated CW.

Texts of William Carlos Williams' work have been quoted by using the following abbreviations: *ARI* for *A Recognizable Image: William Carlos Williams on Art and Artists,* ed. Bram Dijkstra (New York: New Directions, 1978); *A* for *The Autobiography of William Carlos Williams* (New York: New Directions, 1967); *EK* for *The Embodiment of Knowledge,* ed. Ron Loewinsohn (New York: New Directions, 1974); *I* for *Imaginations: Kora in Hell, Spring and All, The Great American Novel, The Descent of Winter, A Novelette and Other Prose,* ed. Webster Schott (New York: New Directions, 1970); *IAG* for *In the American Grain* (New York: New Directions, 1956); *SE* for *Selected Essays of William Carlos Williams* (New York: New Directions, 1969), and *SL* for *The Selected Letters of William Carlos Williams,* ed. John C. Thirlwall (New York: McDowell, Obolensky, 1957).

1. They also make it plain that Williams was influenced more by Herbert Spencer than perhaps he remembered or cared to admit. In *Yes, Mrs. Williams* (New York: McDowell, Obolensky, 1959), he mentions that, as a boy, he read the philosophy of Spencer but was more impressed by Spencer's "habit of dictating to an amanuensis while in the act of rowing a boat" (p. 8) than by the content of Spencer's text. However, a comparison of "Love and Service" with Spencer's *First Principles* (New York: Appleton and Co., 1900) reveals that Williams' concept of the Unknown has much in common with Spencer's concept of the Unknowable, which is developed at length in Part One of *First Principles.* In fact, Williams' crucial emphasis on the importance of "forever changing the sign" so as not to confuse any particular sign with the mystery to which it refers is hardly distinguishable from Spencer's emphasis in the following passage from *First Principles:*

   > Very likely there will ever remain a need to give shape to that indefinite sense of an Ultimate Existence, which forms the basis of our intelligence. We shall always be under the necessity of contemplating it as *some* mode of being; that is—of representing it to ourselves in *some* form of thought, however vague. And we shall not err in doing this so long as we treat every notion we thus frame as merely a symbol. Perhaps the constant formation of such symbols and constant rejection of them as inadequate, may be hereafter, as it has hitherto been, a means of discipline. Perpetually to construct ideas requiring the utmost stretch of our faculties, and perpetually to find that such ideas must be abandoned as futile imaginations, may realize to us more fully than any other course, the greatness of that which we vainly strive to grasp. By continually seeking to know and being continually thrown back with a deepened conviction of the impossibility of knowing, we may keep alive the consciousness that it is alike our highest wisdom and our highest duty to regard that through which all things exist as The Unknowable. (pp. 96–97)

   That Williams, having enunciated his own "first principles," turns his attention to the more practical problems of manipulating signs may be compared to the fact that Spencer, following his discussion of the Unknowable, proceeds in the rest of his philosophy to describe the dynamics of that which can be known.
2. Williams has so many names for the mystery about which nothing can be said that he often reminds one of the paradoxical theology of Pseudo-Dionysius, who declares in his treatise *On the Divine Names,* trans. C. E. Rolt (New York: Macmillan, 1940), that "the

Universal and Transcendent Cause must be both nameless and also possess the names of all things" (p. 62). In an effort to speak in some fashion about the Unknown, Williams calls it, among other things, the secret spring of all our lives, the strange phosphorus of the life, this rare presence, the radiant gist, the face of wonder, silence, the light, spirit, mind, force, imagination, a living flame, beauty, the intangibles, music, reality, truth, the thing we are. Moreover, the names we give to the ordinary things we encounter in our daily lives are necessarily, for Williams, secondary names for the Unknown. Since, as Pseudo-Dionysius says, "the Supra-Vital an Primal Life is the Cause of all Life," it follows that "we must draw from all life the attributes we apply to It when we consider how It teems with all living things, and how under manifold forms It is beheld and praised in all Life" (p. 146).

3. "Advice to the Young Poet," *View*, 2, No. 3 (1942), 23.
4. "A Note on the Art of Poetry," *Blues*, 1, No. 4 (1929), 78.
5. Williams, "For a New Magazine," *Blues*, I, No. 2 (1929), 31.
6. "An Approach to the Poem," in *English Institute Essays, 1947* (New York: Columbia Univ. Press, 1948), p. 61.
7. "To Martha Baird," 3 November 1951, *The Williams-Siegel Documentary*, eds. Martha Baird and Ellen Reiss (New York: Definition Press, 1970), p. 9.
8. "A Note on the Turn of the View Toward Poetic Technique," *The Hanover Forum*, 5, No. 1 (1958–59), 62.
9. See Williams' Introduction to Mimi Goldberg's *The Lover and Other Poems* (Philadelphia: Kraft Printing Co., 1961), pp. iv–vi.
10. Reported in Emily Mitchell Wallace, *A Bibliography of William Carlos Williams* (Middletown, Conn.: Wesleyan Univ. Press, 1968), p. xix.
11. Cited in Mike Weaver, *William Carlos Williams: The American Background* (Cambridge: Cambridge Univ. Press, 1971), p. 164.

Edmund Wilson

1895–1972

Edmund Wilson was born on May 8, 1895, in Red Bank, New Jersey, to Edmund and Helen Mather (née Kimball) Wilson. He was educated at Princeton University (A.B. 1916). From 1917 to 1919 he served in the army intelligence corps. He married four times: to Mary Blair (1923), Margaret Candy (1930), writer and critic Mary McCarthy (1938), and Elena Thornton (1946); he had three children, one each by his first, third, and fourth marriages. He worked as a reporter for the *New York Evening Sun* from 1916 to 1917, and was then managing editor at *Vanity Fair* (1922–23), associate editor (1923–24) and contributing editor (1925–31) for the *New Republic*, and as a book reviewer for the *New Yorker* (1944–48).

Wilson was one of America's most thoughtful and versatile men of letters. While his eight books of verse, two novels (*I Thought of Daisy*, 1929, and *Galahad*, 1967), and several plays were all praised and continue to be appreciated (particularly admired is his short-story cycle *Memoirs of Hecate County*, 1946), it is as a literary and social critic that Wilson made his reputation. His first book of criticism, *Axel's Castle: A Study in the Imaginative Literature of 1870–1930* (1931), attracted immediate attention and is still considered one of his strongest works. It explores the French Symbolist movement and its influence on major writers of the period (Yeats, Stein, Eliot, Valéry, Proust, Joyce). In *Axel's Castle* Wilson introduced his critical approach, dealing with works of art within their historical and cultural contexts in order to understand not only the works themselves but the circumstances surrounding them. Later books continued to develop Wilson's emphasis on what criticism reveals in the artist rather than the art itself, especially in the controversial *The Wound and the Bow: Seven Studies in Literature* (1941), in which Wilson proposed his theory that artistic ability grew out of compensation for a psychological wound. *Patriotic Gore: Studies in the Literature of the American Civil War* (1962) is an impressive work of both social and literary criticism, though some critics thought it too polemical. *To the Finland Station: A Study in the Writing and Acting of History* (1940), an examination and explication of Marxist thought and the Russian Revolution, has proven to be Wilson's most enduring work of social criticism. Also significant in this area are *Red, Black, Blond, and Olive: Studies in Four Civilizations: Zuni, Haiti, Soviet Russia, Israel* (1956), *Apologies to the Iroquois* (1960), and *O Canada: An American's Notes on Canadian Culture* (1965). Many of Wilson's articles and reviews were gathered in *The Shores of Light: A Literary Chronicle of the Twenties and Thirties* (1952), *Classics and Commercials: A Literary Chronicle of the Forties* (1950), and *The Bit between My Teeth: A Literary Chronicle of 1950–1965* (1965). His notebooks, which he had begun to prepare for publication before his death, were edited posthumously by Leon Edel as *The Twenties* (1975), *The Thirties* (1980), *The Forties* (1983), and *The Fifties* (1985). Wilson's *Letters on Literature and Politics 1912–1972* were published in 1977, and *The Nabokov-Wilson Letters 1940–1971* in 1979.

Wilson's wide-ranging intelligence and easygoing didacticism made him one of literature's most valued resources. He was a recipient of the Presidential Medal of Freedom in 1963 and the National Institute of Arts and Letters Gold Medal for nonfiction in 1955, among other awards. He died on June 12, 1972.

JOHN UPDIKE

"Wilson's Fiction: A Personal Account" (1976)
Edmund Wilson: The Man and His Work
ed. John Wain
1978, pp. 163–73

Memoirs of Hecate County came out in 1946; I read a copy borrowed from the Reading, Pennsylvania, public library, where it sat placidly on the open shelves while the book was being banned in New York State. Mere reading must have seemed a mild sin in the Reading of those years; it was a notoriously permissive town, famous for its rackets, its whores and its acquitting juries. In 1946 I was 14. What that slightly sinister volume, a milky green in the original Doubleday edition, with the epigraph from Gogol in Russian and a sepia photograph of a three-faced Hecate opposite the title page, meant to me, I can reconstruct imperfectly. Certainly I skipped the pages of French that the curious Mr. Blackburn spouts toward the end, and probably I skimmed the inside-the-book-business ax-grinding of 'The Milhollands and their Damned Soul'. But the long, central story, 'The Princess with the Golden Hair', the heart and scandal of this collection of six 'memoirs', I read, as they say, avidly, my first and to this day most vivid glimpse of sex through the window of fiction.

All of my life I have remembered how Anna, 'as a gesture of affection and respect', held the hero's penis in her hand as they drifted off to sleep; and how Imogen in coitus halted her lover and 'did something special and gentle' that caused her to have her climax first; and how one of the women (I had forgotten which) gazes at the narrator, and through him at the amazed young reader, over the curve of her naked hip. This last image, redolent of the casual intimacy and exposure that adults presumably enjoyed, affected me so powerfully I was surprised, rereading, to discover how brief it is:

> . . . once, when I came back into the room, I found her curled up on the bed and was pleased by her eyes, very cunning and round—at once agate like marbles and soft like burrs—looking at me over her hips.

It is Anna, of course, and the emphasis—typical of Wilson's erotic art—is all on her eyes. The mechanically and psychologically complicated business of Imogen's backbrace touched me less memorably, but like the images above it smelled of the real, it showed sex as a human transaction that did honestly take place, not in the infinitely elastic wonderland of pornography but on actual worn furniture, in moods of doubt and hangover, in a muddle of disillusion and balked comfort: the hero does not omit to let us know that he found Anna's fond trick of penis-holding 'in the long run . . . uncomfortable'. There was something dogged and humorless and pungent about Wilson's rendition of love: the adjective 'meaty' recurs, spoiling pleasant contexts, and the simile everyone remembers from *I Thought of Daisy* tells of the heroine's held feet, 'in pale stockings . . . like two little moist cream cheeses encased in covers of cloth'. Pungent, and savage: I was blinded by the journal entry, in 'Princess', that begins '——ing in the afternoon, with the shades down and all her clothes on—different from anything else—rank satisfactory smell like the salt marine tides we come out of . . .'. And a very naked moment comes in the last story, at the Blackburns' party, when the hero throws Jo, the third of his willing fornicatrices, onto the bed full of guests' wraps:

> She put one arm up over her eyes; her legs dangled, like a child's, from her knees . . . 'Move forward', I said, and put her legs up. Her white thighs and her lower buttocks were brutally laid bare; her feet, in silver openwork sandals, were pointing in opposite directions.

Of course I could have got this sort of thing, in 1946, from Erskine Caldwell or John O'Hara, indeed *did* get it from the Southern California detective fiction of James Cain and Raymond Chandler; but the sex in these writers was not fortified by Wilson's conscious intention of bringing European sexual realism into American fiction at last. The publication of Wilson's notebooks, *The Twenties*, from which the Anna sections of *Hecate County* are taken almost verbatim, show his sexual scorecards mingled as if naively with landscape descriptions and intellectual ruminations and the anecdotes of his rather silly upper-class friends. The original jacket of *Hecate County* describes it as 'the adventures of an egoist among the bedeviled'. America seemed incorrigibly alien to Wilson, though fascinating, and intrinsic to his destiny. Like Dante, he is a tourist *engagé*. The lonely bookish child stares with a frown from the shadows of the Red Bank mansion, where the mother was deaf and the father nervously fragile; the America he perceives seems grim and claustrophobic, though hectic. There is a true whiff of Hell in Hecate County, less in the specific touches of supernatural diabolism with which this utter rationalist quaintly adorned his tales, but in the low ceilings and cheap underwear of the sex idyll, the clothes and neuroses of the copulators. America has always tolerated sex as a joke, as a night's prank in the burlesque theater or fairground tent; but not as a solemn item in life's work inventory. It was Wilson's deadly earnest, his unwinking naturalistic refusal to release us into farce, that made *Hecate County* in all its dignity and high intent the target of a (successful!) prosecution for obscenity. Earnest, but not Ernest Hemingway, who never in his fictional personae shows himself compromised, as this sweating, fumbling hero of Wilson's so often is; Hemingway's heroes make love without baring their bottoms, and the women as well as the men are falsified by a romantic severity, an exemption from the odors and awkwardness that Wilson, with the dogged selfless honesty of a bookworm, presses his own nose, and ours, into with such solemn satisfaction.

Rereading, now, in this liberated age, and in the light of the notebooks, one expects to find the sex tame. And so, in a sense, it is. '——ing' turns out to be, in the unexpurgated journals, merely 'Fucking', rather than the more exotic activity I tried to imagine, and the tender journal accounts of cunnilingus and fellatio [1] and Anna's 'monthlies' did not find their way into even the revised edition of 1959.

In the fiction, Wilson sets down no sexual detail in simple celebration, to please and excite himself, but always to illuminate the social or psychological condition of the two women. The Anna of 'Princess', compared to the confusing love-object of the journals, is admirably coherent, as the product of certain cultural and economic conditions in Brooklyn; how telling, for instance, is her reluctance to be seen naked, as if nudity—to the upper classes an aesthetic proclamation, a refutation of shame—evokes inhibitions having nothing to do with sexual acts, which she performs freely. And how plausibly, if ploddingly, are the clothes of the two women described and made to symbolize their social presences. Such details—seized, we sometimes feel, by a sensibility that doubts its own grasp on the 'real'—lend the factual sexual descriptions a weight, a heat, far from tame.

It is Imogen (her original may be waiting exposure in the

unpublished journals of the thirties; married for sixteen years, she seems too old for the narrator at the age he assigns himself, 'on the verge of thirty') who occasions Wilson's subtlest, harshest instances of sexual realism. After two years of yearning, the hero greets their tryst in a mood of nervous lassitude. The very perfection of her body distances her—'I found that I was expressing admiration of her points as if she were some kind of museum piece'—and her eager lubricity, 'making things easy for the entrant with a honey-sweet sleek profusion', dulls his triumph: 'She became, in fact, so smooth and open that after a moment I could hardly feel her . . . I went on and had a certain disappointment, for, with the brimming of female fluid, I felt even less sensation; but—gently enough—I came, too.' Gently enough, the failure of an overprepared, ideal love to connect is masterfully anatomized, and movingly contrasted with his tawdry, harried affair with Anna, that involves him with criminal types and gives him gonorrhea. One's breath is snatched to see, in the journals, the patrician, pontifical Wilson led by sex to the edge of the abyss of poverty, its diseases, its tangled familial furies, its hopeless anonymity. He did not fall in. The last story of *Hecate County*, surreal and troubled, prefigures the hero's marriage to Jo Gates, a well-off, cheerful 'Western girl' like Margaret Canby, whom Wilson married in 1930, closing out the decade, and clamping down on 'a feeling that, fond though I was of Margaret and well though we got along, we did not have enough in common'.

The journals make clear more abundantly than the novella how much Wilson had loved Anna, how fully she satisfied him and gave him his deferred manhood. 'The Princess with the Golden Hair' is a love-poem to her and one of the best of his writing generation's obligatory love-poems to the lower classes.

> Yet for them the depression was always going on like a flood that swept away their houses . . . and the attitudes, I knew, that I assumed to myself and in my conversations with others meant nothing in that bare room in Brooklyn where Anna and her garment-worker cousin were so sober and anxious and pale.

Like Thornton Wilder's *Heaven's My Destination*, 'Princess' is a generous aberration, a visit to the underworld by a member of the last predominantly Wasp generation of writers, the last that conceived of itself as an aristocracy. Wilson's portrait of this one slum-child lives by her light, the 'something so strong and instinctive that it could outlive the hurts and infections, the defilements, among which we lived'. The fiction she inhabits, as its true princess, overtops the flanking Gothic vignettes (though 'Ellen Terhune' has its authenticity, and the last story a wrenched pain) and makes plausible Wilson's insistence that *Memoirs of Hecate County* was his favorite among his many books. His fiction, generally cluttered, savoring of the worked-up, of collected details moved by *force majeure* of the writer's mind, here finds a theme that moves *him*. Sex was his one way *in*, into the America to which his response, however much he wished it otherwise, was to reach for anaesthesia, whether found in books or bottles. Imogen, in this respect, is a better metaphor for America than Anna; her flamboyant costumes and greedy orgasms serve the same narcissism, reflect the same blank passion to succeed; in her richly, ironically particularized and overfurnished setting, she ends as a comic vision, empty but not unlovable, a gaudy suburban witch, in a land where, after 1946, Hecate Counties would spread and multiply and set the new cultural tone. Freud more than Marx would bias our lives; the suburban home would replace the city street as the theatre of hopes; private fulfillment and not public justice would set the pace of the pursuit of happiness. Until the mid-sixties this remained true, and Wilson, writing out of notebooks kept in the twenties, foretold it, casting his fiction in the coming mode, of sexual candor, dark sardonic fantasy, and confessional fragment.

I read *I Thought of Daisy* years later, and there is some inverse progression in this, for it is the more rounded novel, more thoroughly intended and unified than the six disparate 'memoirs', though in the earlier book too Wilson has composed his narrative in a series of—in this case, five—discrete panels. Here too is the first-person narrator given to essayistic asides and hopeful of unriddling America through the person of a female native less intellectual and well-born than himself. Again, the book is liveliest in its landscapes and erotic scenes, and relatively leaden in its sociological disquisitions; the presentation, for instance, of Hugo Bamman as the type of twenties radical seems 'blocked in' with large shadows and thick lines, and lifts free into specificity only in the mad moment when Hugo apparently embarks on a boat to Afghanistan straight from a taxi containing the hero and Daisy. The hero tells us that he is under Hugo's sway, but in fact seems, as narrator-analyst, on top of him from the start. In his introduction to the revised edition of 1953 Wilson confesses how 'schematic' *Daisy* is, and claims to be 'rather appalled by the rigor with which I sacrificed to my plan of five symphonic movements what would normally have been the line of the story'. The character of Rita, based upon that of Edna St. Vincent Millay, especially resisted his scheme, dominating sections where she was meant to be subordinate, and yet remaining more mysterious, in her involvement with the narrator, than she should have been.

Yet for all Wilson's strictures upon himself the book has much that is lovely about it, beginning with the title. The phrase, 'I thought of Daisy', occurs in each section but the last, and here, oddly, in the excursion to Coney Island that is closely derived from an account in the journals of such a trip with 'Florence', Wilson fails to transcribe a note of what may be the original inspiration:

> postcards: American flag with silver tinsel inscription—'I thought of you at Coney Island'.

The twenties journals throw considerable light upon the genesis of this novel. Wilson began it in 1926 or '27, and rewrote it drastically in a beach house in California, near the home of Margaret Canby, late in 1928. He confided to Maxwell Perkins that *Axel's Castle*, which he was carrying forward simultaneously, 'being literary criticism, is easier to do, and in the nature of a relief, from *Daisy*'. To John Peale Bishop he wrote that 'it was to be a pattern of ideas and all to take place, as to a great extent it does, on the plane of intelligence—and when I came to write the actual story, this had the effect of involving me in a certain amount of falsified psychology'. He got the book off to Perkins early in 1929, and in the midst of his near-breakdown later that winter, within the sanitorium at Clifton Springs, New York, he went over the page proofs. The period of crisis in which he completed this novel is also the time of his romance with Anna, and in his journals he was writing, without knowing it, his one other extended fiction. After 1929 a certain abdication and consolidation took place; he got a divorce and remarried, forsook Anna, and settled on criticism as his métier. As a critic, he has said all that need be said against his own first novel. What needs to be added is how good, if ungainly, *Daisy* is, how charmingly and intelligently she tells of the speakeasy days of a Greenwich Village as red and cozy as a valentine, of lamplit islands where love and ambition and drunkenness[2] bloomed all at once. The fiction writer in Wilson was real, and his displacement a real loss.

In 1953 he stated that *Daisy* was 'written much under the influence of Proust and Joyce'. Though the novel constitutes a kind of portrait of the artist as a young man, and gives New York a little of the street-guide specificity Joyce gave Dublin, the influence of Proust is far more conspicuous. The *longueurs*, the central notion of changing perspectives and 'intermittences of the heart', the importance of party scenes, the contraction of some intervals of time (e.g. the hero's European trip) into mere summary while other moments are expansively and repeatedly treated, the search for 'laws' of behavior and perception, the mock-scientific rigor with which aesthetic and subjective impressions are examined, the musical, wide-ranging speculativeness—all this is Proustian. Wilson, indeed, was one of the few Americans intellectually energetic enough to put Proust's example to work. This example fused surface and thought, commonplace reality with a 'symphonic' prose of inexhaustible refinement. Wilson had Proust's love for whatever could be assimilated to his mind. Daisy, with her cream-cheese feet and her way of saying 'um' for 'them', is not as floral an apparition as Odette, nor do Wilson's glimpses of our hard seaboard resonate like the steeples at Martinville; but there is that same rapt reception of the glimpse as a symbol:

> Then suddenly I had almost caught my breath—I had been curiously moved by the sight of a single, solitary street lamp on the Staten Island shore. It had merely shed a loose and whitish radiance over a few feet of the baldish road of some dark, thinly settled suburb. Above it, there had loomed an abundant and disorderly tree. But there was America, I had felt with emotion—there under that lonely suburban street lamp, there in that raw and livid light!

The young hero, coming out onto Professor Grosbeake's glassed-in porch at Princeton after an evening spent in intoxicating, idealistic conversation, feels the winter chill mix with his mentor's abstract theology:

> . . . and as I took leave of Grosbeake—gazing out through the glass at the pavement lightly dappled with leaves and the dark grass glittering with wet—my mind bemused with a vision of God as a vast crystal fixing its symmetry from a liquified universe—I felt a delicious delicacy of iciness, glossy fall-leaf slivers and black rain-glinting glass.

Such interpenetration of mind and matter is surely a great theme, and few Americans were better qualified to dramatize it than Wilson, with his polymathic curiosity and his pungent earthiness, his autocratic intellect and initially quite benign and humble willingness to sniff out the grubbiest lessons that mysterious America could set for him.

In its final printing in his uniform edition, *Daisy* is bound with a short story, 'Galahad', composed by Wilson in the early twenties. Its adolescent hero, Hart Foster, about to assume leadership of his prep-school Young Men's Christian Association, is nearly seduced by the sister of a friend, who takes off her clothes and gets into bed with him.

> As she bent over him for a moment, Hart had a glimpse of her firm round breasts; he was surprised to find them so big; he had always supposed that girls' breasts were little low dotted things.

The ingenuously confessed surprise is Wilsonian, as is the genuine ethical struggle of the boy upon his return to the school. He does not lightly dismiss the Puritan morality, nor the opposed morality that follows the revelation that 'this was the real Barbara, this solid living body!—not merely the face at the top of a dress that one knew in ordinary life'. He plays truant from the school to visit her, and faced with her again becomes 'a helpless child' before 'the terrible prestige of her sexual experience'. She advises him to return, and he does. The story commands considerable suspense, as it presents in open conflict, near the outset of their long conjoined career, the polarities of Wilson's self-education: the conscientious humanist and the anarchic concupiscent. Especially vivid for me, in 'Galahad', was the train ride down from New England toward New York, a ride I often took in my own student days, gazing like Hart Foster through the gliding windows 'with a kind of morbid relish for every dry winter meadow mottled with melting snow, for every long flat factory building, for every black ice-glazed stream, for every hard square-angled town with its hollow-looking boxlike houses . . .'. Wilson is peculiarly a poet of this wintry, skeletal, Northeastern landscape, and his journals of the twenties end with a glorious display of Connecticut snowbound as the thirties begin.

Why did the author of 'Galahad' produce so little else in the way of short fiction? Why did the author of *Daisy* not go on to become the American Proust? Why, for that matter, did the best-selling memoirist of *Hecate County* not follow this most favorite of his books with something similar? One answer, no doubt, is drably practical: no one much encouraged him to write fiction. A negative practical consequence of *Hecate County*'s *succès de scandale* was Wilson's later run-in with the federal government over unpaid taxes, and the truculent anti-Americanism of *The Cold War and the Income Tax*. He was as astonished to discover that America's laws applied to him as Hart Foster was to discover that breasts were big; and took the fact less kindly. Another answer may lie in the nature of his great intelligence: he could extrapolate from facts but not much budge them. An immensely mobile gatherer of information, he wrote no fiction without a solidly planted autobiographical base, and his fantasy, when it intervenes, as in the side-pieces of *Hecate County*, seems clumsy and harsh. He drew on journal notations and didn't much trust his memory, that great sifter of significance; forgetfulness, the subconscious shaper of many a fiction, had no place in his equipment. And a third answer, of course, is that the fiction-writer went underground and greatly enriched the reporter, lent the critic his bracing directness and energy, co-authored the plays and vivacious self-interviews of Wilson's antic moods, and lay behind the flamboyance of those feats of reading and startling acquisitions of expertise that kept lengthening the shelf of his squat, handy volumes. He worked up subjects like the Dead Sea scrolls and the Iroquois Indians much as popular novelists like Irving Stone and James Michener appropriate Hawaii or Michelangelo, to turn them into books. The comparison is well-meant: Wilson wrote in the marketplace; he aimed to become a writer in a professional sense unimaginable to most serious young men now; the scholar and drudge within him served a poet of reality.

Notes

1. '. . . the cool moisture of her lips when she has bent lower for fellatio, so delightful, so curiously different from the warm and mucilaginous moisture of ordinary intercourse—the incredible-feeling caress, gently up and down, until the delightful brimming swelling of pleasure seems to make it flow really in waves which fill her darling woman's mouth.' The passage, so lyrical, goes on however to observe 'the man a little embarrassed, feels a little bit differently about her mouth, but affectionately kisses her'.

2. There is quite a lot of drunkenness in Wilson's scant fiction. The third chapter of *Daisy* and the last of *Hecate County* both show the gradual derangement of the narrator within 'That enchanted country of drink that was the world one had been young in, in the twenties!' The funniest and most harrowing bibulous episode occupies the 1934 sketch, 'What to Do Till the Doctor Comes (From the Diary of a Drinker-Out)', reprinted in *The American Earthquake*, with three other pieces of reportorial 'fiction'.

CLIVE JAMES
"The Poetry of Edmund Wilson"
New Review, November 1977, pp. 39–42

Apart from *Poets, Farewell!*, which was published in 1929 and has been unobtainable for most of the time since, the two main collections of Edmund Wilson's verse are *Note-Books of Night* and *Night Thoughts*. Of these, *Note-Books of Night* was published in America in 1942, took three years to cross the Atlantic (Secker & Warburg brought it out in May, 1945) and has since become fairly unobtainable itself, although it is sometimes to be found going cheap in the kind of second-hand book shop that doesn't know much about the modern side. *Night Thoughts*, published in America in 1961 and in Britain a year later, is still the current collection. It regroups most of the work in *Note-Books of Night* into two sections, interspersing a good deal of extra matter, ranging from lyrics written in youth to technical feats performed in age. The final effect is to leave you convinced that although *Night Thoughts* is good to have, *Note-Books of Night* remains the definitive collection of Wilson's verse. Less inclusive, it is more complete.

Being that, it would be an interesting book even if Wilson's verse were negligible—interesting for the sidelight it threw on the mind of a great critic. But in fact Wilson's verse is far from negligible. Just because Wilson's critical work is so creative doesn't mean that his nominally creative work is a waste of time. Even without *Memoirs of Hecate County* and *I Thought of Daisy*, the mere existence of *Note-Books of Night* would be sufficient evidence that Wilson had original things to say as a writer. It is a deceptively substantial little book which looks like a slim volume only by accident. There are more than seventy pages of solid text, with something memorable on nearly every page. Thirty pages are given to prose fragments and the rest to poetry. It isn't major poetry, but some of it is very good minor poetry.

Wilson was no shrinking violet, but he knew his limitations. He knew that his touch with language wasn't particularly suggestive so he went for precision instead. He possessed a lot of information to be precise with. Where his verse is excessive, it is the excess of the seed catalogue—a superfluity of facts. He never usurps the lyrical genius's prerogative of saying more than he knows. Nor did he ever consider himself talented enough to be formless—his formal decorum always reminds us that he stems from the early 20th-century America which in retrospect seems more confident than Europe itself about transmitting the European tradition. The work is all very schooled, neat, strict and assured. And finally there is his gift for parody, which sometimes led him beyond mere accomplishment and into the realm of inspiration. In 'The Omelet of A. MacLeish', for example, the talent of his verse is reinforced by the genius of his criticism, with results more devastating critically than his essays on the same subject, and more vivid poetically than his usual poems.

In *Note-Books of Night* the poems are arranged in no chronological scheme. From the re-arrangement in *Night Thoughts* it is easier to puzzle out when he wrote what, but even then it is sometimes hard to be sure. Eventually there will be scholarly research to settle the matter, but I doubt if much of interest will be revealed touching Wilson's development as a writer of verse. After an early period devoted to plangent lyricism of the kind which can be called sophomoric as long as we remember that he was a Princeton sophomore and an exceptionally able one into the bargain, Wilson quickly entered into his characteristic ways of seeing the world. Like other minor artists he matured early and never really changed. Indeed he was writing verse in the Thirties which forecast the mood of the prose he published in the early Seventies at the end of his life. The desolate yearning for the irretrievably lost America which makes *Upstate* so sad a book is already there in *Note-Books of Night*, providing the authentic force behind the somewhat contrived Arnoldian tone of poems like 'A House of the Eighties'. Wilson's poetry of the Thirties frequently deals with houses going to rack and ruin. The houses are in the same condition that we find them in forty years later, in *Upstate*. They are in the same places: Talcottville, Provincetown, Wilson's ancestral lands. Houses pointing to the solid old New England civilisation which once found its space between the sea and the Adirondacks and was already being overtaken by progress when the poet was young. In his essays of the Thirties (notably 'The Old Stone House' collected in *The American Earthquake*) Wilson wrote optimistically about an America 'forever on the move'. But if his essays were true to his then-radical intellect, his poetry was true to his conservative feelings. His dead houses are metaphors for a disappearing way of life.

And when they found the house was bare
The windows shuttered to the sun
They woke the panthers with a stare
To finish what they had begun.

The poem is called 'Nightmare'. As we know from his great essay of 1937, 'In Honour of Pushkin' (collected in *The Triple Thinkers* and rightly called by John Bayley the best short introduction to Pushkin—a decisive tribute, considering that Bayley has written the best long one), Wilson was particularly struck by the supreme poetic moment in *Evgeny Onegin* when Lensky is killed in a duel and his soulless body is compared to an empty house, with whitewashed windows. The image is one of the climactic points in all poetry—it is like Hector's address to Andromache, or Eurydice holding out her useless hands, or Paolo kissing Francesca's trembling mouth—so it is no wonder that Wilson should have been impressed by it. But you also can't help feeling that the image was congenial to his personal psychology. Although in books like *Europe without Baedecker* Wilson did his best to secede from the weight of the European heritage, the fact always remained that by his education—by his magnificent education—and by his temperament he was inextricably committed to an American past which owed much of its civilised force to the European memory. This was the America which was dying all the time as he grew older. One of the several continuous mental struggles in Wilson is between his industrious loyalty to the creative impulse of the new America and his despairing sense—which made itself manifest in his poetry much earlier than in his prose—that chaos could in no wise be staved off. The decaying houses of his last books, with their cherished windows broken and highways built close by, are all presaged in the poetry of his early maturity.

But in some respects maturity came *too* early. Coleridge, perhaps because he had trouble growing up, favoured a slow ripening of the faculties. There was always something unsettling about the precocity of Wilson's mimetic technique: his gift as a parodist was irrepressibly at work even when he wanted it not to be, with the result that his formally precise early lyrics tend towards pastiche—they are throwbacks to the end of the century and beyond. The tinge of Arnold in 'A House of the Eighties'—the pale echo of his melancholy, long withdrawing roar—is compounded even there, it seems to me, by memories of Browning. At other times you can hear Kipling in the background. Wilson's attempts at plangent threnody call up the voices of other men.

Wilson's elegiac lyrics are never less than technically adroit: their high finish reminds us forcibly not only of the standards which were imposed by Christian Gauss's Princeton (standards which we can see otherwise in the poetry of John Peale Bishop) but of a whole generation of American poets, now not much thought about, who had complete command of their expressive means, even if they did not always have that much to express. Edna St Vincent Millay and Elinor Wylie have by now retreated into the limbo of the semi-read—Eleanor Farjeon and Ruth Pitter might be two comparable examples from this side of the water—but when you look at the work of Elinor Wylie, in particular, it is astonishing how accomplished she was. Wilson's criticism helped American writing grow out of its self-satisfaction at mere accomplishment, but he knew about the certain losses as well as the possible gains. In his poetry he committed himself to the past by synthesising its cherishable tones, but he paid the penalty of mimetic homage in not sounding enough like himself. In 'Disloyal Lines to an Alumnus' he satirised the poetry of Beauty—

> And Beauty, Beauty, oozing everywhere
> Like maple-sap from maples! Dreaming there,
> I have sometimes stepped in Beauty on the street
> And slipped, sustaining bruises blue but sweet . . .

but his own lyric beauty was not different enough from the Beauty he was satirising. These lines from 'Riverton' take some swallowing now and would have needed excuses even then.

> —O elms! O river! aid me at this turn—
> Their passing makes my late imperative:
> They flicker now who frightfully did burn,
> And I must tell their beauty while I live.
> Changing their grade as water in its flight,
> And gone like water; give me then the art,
> Firm as night-frozen ice found silver-bright,
> That holds the splendor though the days depart.

Give me then the art, indeed. He had the artifice, but the art was mainly that of a pasticheur. When consumed by Yeats's business of articulating sweet sounds together, Wilson was the master of every poetic aspect except originality. Listen to the judiciously balanced vowel-modulations in 'Poured full of thin gold sun':

> But now all this—
> Peace, brightness, the browned page, the crickets in the grass—
> Is but a crust that stretches thin and taut by which I pass
> Above the loud abyss.

A virtuoso is only ever fully serious when he forgets himself. Wilson is in no danger of forgetting himself here. In his later stages, which produced the technical games collected in *Night Thoughts,* his urge to jump through hoops clearly detached itself from the impulse to register feeling; but it should also be noted that even early on the division existed. His penchant for sound effects, like his ear for imitation, usually led him away from pure expression. On occasions, however, when consciously schooled euphuistic bravura was lavished on a sufficiently concrete subject, Wilson got away from tricksy pastoralism and achieved a personal tone—urban, sardonic, tongue-in-cheek, astringent. The consonant-packed lines of 'Night in May'—'Pineapple-pronged four-poster of a Utica great-great'—were a portent of what Wilson was able to do best. Such a line is the harbinger of an entire, superb poem: 'On Editing Scott Fitzgerald's Papers', which first appeared in the preliminary pages of *The Crack-Up* and stands out in *Note-Books of Night* as a full, if regrettably isolated, realisation of the qualities Wilson had to offer as a poet.

Speaking personally for a moment, I can only say that it was this poem, along with certain passages in Roy Campbell's bloody-minded satires, which first convinced me that the rhyming couplet of iambic pentameter was still alive as a form—that in certain respects it was *the* form for an extended poem. Wilson, like Campbell, by accepting the couplet's heritage of grandeur was able somehow to overcome its obsolescence: once the inevitable effect of archaic pastiche was accepted, there was room for any amount of modern freedom. In fact it was the fierce rigour of the discipline which made the freedom possible. And Wilson was more magnanimous than Campbell: his grandeur really *was* grandeur, not grandiloquence: 'Scott, your last fragments I arrange tonight . . . '

The heroic tone is there from the first line. (It is instructive, by the way, that only the tone is heroic: the couplets themselves are not Heroic but Romance—i.e., open rather than closed.) It would have been a noble theme whatever form Wilson had chosen, because Wilson's lifelong paternal guardianship of Fitzgerald's talent is a noble story. Fitzgerald was the Princeton alumnus who *didn't* benefit from the education on offer. From Wilson's and Fitzgerald's letters to Christian Gauss we can easily see who was the star student and who the ineducable enthusiast. But Wilson, like Gauss, knew that Fitzgerald was destined to make his own way according to a different and more creative law. Wilson called *This Side of Paradise* a compendium of malapropisms but knew that it had not failed to live. When the masterpieces arrived he saw them clearly for what they were. Much of his rage against Hollywood was on Fitzgerald's behalf: he could see how the film world's sinister strength was diabolically attuned to Fitzgerald's fatal weakness. He understood and sympathised with Fitzgerald even in his most abject decline and guarded his memory beyond the grave.

Such a story would be thrilling however it was told. But the couplets are ideal for it: the elegiac and narrative strains match perfectly, while the meretricious, Condé Nast glamour of the imagery is entirely appropriate to Fitzgerald's debilitating regard for the high life—the well-heeled goings-on to which, as Wilson well knew, Fitzgerald sacrificed his soul but which he superseded with his talent. Hence Wilson evokes the memory of Fitzgerald's eyes in terms of a *Vogue* advertisement. Passing their image on to what they mint, they

> . . . leave us, to turn over, iris-fired,
> Not the great Ritz-sized diamond you desired
> But jewels in a handful, lying loose:
> flawed amethysts; the moonstone's milky blues;
> Chill blues of pale transparent tourmaline;
> Opals of shifty yellow, chartreuse green,
> Wherein a vein vermilion flees and flickers—
> Tight phials of the spirit's light mixed liquors;
> Some tinsel zircons, common turquoise; but
> Two emeralds, green and lucid, one half-cut,

One cut consummately—both take their place
In Letters' most expensive Cartier case.

The consummately cut emerald is obviously *The Great Gatsby;* the half-cut emerald is probably *Tender Is the Night;* and we suppose that the tinsel zircons are the hack stories Fitzgerald turned out in order to pay his bills. But apart from the admittedly preponderant biographical element, what strikes you is the assured compression of the technique. In lines like 'Tight phials of the spirit's light mixed liquors' Wilson was forging a clear, vital utterance: that he was to take it no further is a matter for regret. In this poem his complicated games with language are confined within the deceptively simple form and serve the purpose. Here is the public voice which Wilson so admired (and by implication adumbrated for our own time) in the artistry of Pushkin. In 'On Editing Scott Fitzgerald's Papers' his playfulness, his seriousness, his severe humour and his sympathetic *gravitas* are all in balance. The proof of Wilson's mainly fragmentary achievement as a poet is the conspicuous force he attained on the few occasions when his gifts were unified. The artist who is all artist—the artist who, even when he is also a good critic, is nevertheless an artist first of all—can recognise this moment of unity within himself and lives for nothing else but to repeat it. Wilson had too many other interests: which, of course, it would be quixotic to begrudge him.

There are other narrative poems by Wilson but they lack the transforming discipline of the couplet. Similarly he has other strong subjects—especially sex—but as with most revelations their interest has become with time more historical than aesthetic. Yet other poems are full of named things, but the names deafen the vision. Three different kinds of deficiency, all of them interesting.

The first deficiency is mainly one of form. Wilson's narrative poems are an attempt at public verse which certainly comes off better than comparable efforts by more recognised American poets. Nobody now could wade through Robinson Jeffers's *Roan Stallion*, for example. Wilson's 'The Good Neighbour' is the story of Mr and Mrs Pritchard, who become obsessed with defending their house against invaders. Wilson guards against portentousness by casting the tale in hudibrastics, but the results, though very readable, are less popular than cute. The technique is too intrusive. Another narrative, 'The Woman, the War Veteran and the Bear', is an outrageous tale of a legless trapeze artist and a girl who married beneath her. It is full of interesting social detail but goes on too long: a glorified burlesque number that should have been a burlesque number. The stanzas are really ballad stanzas, but the poem wants to be more than a ballad. 'Lesbia in Hell' is better, but again the hudibrastics are the wrong form: they hurry you on too fast for thought and leave you feeling that the action has been skimped. Doubly a pity, because the theme of Satan falling in love with Lesbia involves Wilson in one of his most deeply felt subjects—sexual passion.

It still strikes the historically minded reader that *Note-Books of Night* is a remarkably sexy little book for its time. Wilson, we should remember, had a share in pioneering the sexual frankness of our epoch. *Memoirs of Hecate County* was a banned book in Australia when I was young. Wilson lived long enough to deplore pornographic licence but never went back on his liberal determination to speak of things as they were. Poems like 'Home to Town: Two Highballs' convey something of the same clinical realism about sex which made Wilson's prose fiction extraordinary and which still gives it better than documentary importance. In *Memoirs of Hecate County* Wilson drew a lasting distinction between the high society lady, who appealed to the narrator's imagination but left his body cold, and the low-born taxi-dancer who got on his nerves but fulfilled him sexually. The chippie seems to be there again in 'Two Highballs'.

And all the city love, intense and faint like you—
The little drooping breasts, the cigarettes,
The little cunning shadow between the narrow
thighs . . .

Paul Dehn, mentioning this passage when the poem was reprinted in *Night Thoughts*, found it ridiculous, but I don't see why we should agree. Wilson's attempts at a bitter urban poetry—

And the El that accelerates, grates, shrieks, diminishes, swishing, with such pain—
To talk the city tongue!

are at least as memorable, and certainly as frank about experience, as the contorted flights of Hart Crane. Of Crane, when I search my memory, I remember the seal's wide spindrift gaze towards Paradise and the bottles wearing him in crescents on their bellies. There were things Crane could do that Wilson couldn't—the wine talons, the sublime notion of travelling in a tear—but on the whole, Wilson did at least as good a job of reporting the city. And in matters of sex he was more adventurous than anybody—ahead of his time, in fact.

But if you are ahead of your time only in your subject, then eventually you will fall behind the times, overtaken by the very changes in taste you helped engender. So it is with Wilson's sexual poetry: all the creativity goes into the act of bringing the subject up, with no powers of invention left over for the task of transforming it into the permanence of something imagined. Ideally, Wilson's sexual themes should have been a natural part of a larger poetic fiction. But as we see in 'Cooper and White' (not present in *Note-Books of Night*, but *Nights Thoughts* usefully adds it to the canon) what they tended to blend with was greenery-yallery *fin de siècle* lyricism.

I knew that passionate mouth in that pale skin
Would spread with such a moisture, let me in
To such a bareness of possessive flesh!—
I knew that fairest skin with city pallor faded,
With cigarettes and late electric light,
Would shield the fire to lash
The tired unblushing cheeks to burn as they did—
That mouth that musing seemed so thin,
Those cheeks that tired seemed so white!

It is as if Ernest Dowson and Lionel Johnson had been asked to versify Edith Wharton's discovery of passion as revealed in her secret manuscript *Beatrice Palmato.* The very tones of out-of-dateness. But the informing idea—of loneliness in love—is still alive. It should have been the poem's field of exploration, but Wilson was content to arrive at the point where his admired Proust began. Wilson was protective about his selfhood, as major artists never can be.

As to the naming of names—well, he overdid it. Great poetry is always full of things, but finally the complexity of detail is subordinated to a controlling simplicity. Wilson wrote some excellent nature poetry but nature poetry it remains: all the flowers are named but the point is seldom reached when it ceases to matter so much what kind of flowers they are. In 'At Laurelwood', one of the prose pieces in *Note-Books of Night,* he talks of how his grandfather and grandmother helped teach him the names of everyday objects. His range of knowledge is one of the many marvellous things about Wilson. In poems like 'Princetown, 1936' he piled on the detail to good effect:

Mussels with broken hinges, sea crabs lopped
Of legs, black razor-clams split double, dried
Sea-dollars, limpets chivied loose and dropped
Like stranded dories rolling on their side:

But in the long run not even concrete facts were a sufficient antidote to the poetry of Beauty. Humour was a better safeguard. On the whole, it is the satirical verse which holds up best among Wilson's work. Quite apart from the classic 'The Omelet of A. MacLeish', there are 'The Extrovert of Walden Pond' (with its *trouvé* catch-phrase 'Thoreau was a neuro') and 'The Playwright in Paradise', a minatory ode to the writers of his generation which borrows lines from 'Adonais' to remind them that in Beverly Hills their talents will die young. In these poems Wilson's critical intelligence was at work. If he had possessed comic invention to match his scornful parodic ear, he might have equalled even E. E. Cummings. But 'American Masterpieces' (which makes its only appearance in *Night Thoughts*) shows what Cummings had that Wilson hadn't: in knocking the clichés of Madison Avenue, Wilson can win your allegiance, but Cummings can make you laugh. At the last, Wilson's jokes are not quite funny enough in themselves—they don't take off into the self-sustaining Empyrean of things you can't help reciting. His humour, like his frankness, ought ideally to have been part of a larger fiction.

Useless to carp. A minor artist Wilson remains. But it ought to be more generally realised that he was a very good minor artist, especially in his poetry. Of course, *Night Thoughts* didn't help. Inflated with juvenilia and senescent academic graffiti even duller than Auden's, the book blurred the outlines of Wilson's achievement—although even here it should be noted that its closing poem, 'The White Sand', is one of Wilson's most affecting things, a despairing celebration of late love so deeply felt that it almost overcomes the sense of strain generated by the internally-rhymed elegiacs in which it is cast.

What has worked most damagingly against Wilson's reputation as a poet, however, is his reputation as a critic. It is hard to see how things could be otherwise. As a critical mind, Wilson is so great that we have not yet taken his full measure. He is still so prominent as to be invisible: people think they can know what he said without having to read him. When he is read again, it will soon be found that he saw both sides of most of the arguments which continue to rage about what literature is or ought to be. Among these arguments is the one about modern poetry and its audience. Nobody was more sympathetic than Wilson to the emergence of a difficult, hermetic poetry or better-equipped to understand its origins. But equally he was able to keep the issue in perspective. First of all, his standards were traditional in the deepest sense: knowing why Homer, Virgil, Dante, Shakespeare and Pushkin were permanently modern, he knew why most of modern poetry was without the value it claimed for itself. Secondly, he had an unconquerable impulse towards community. All his writings are an expression of it, including his verse. He would have liked to read fully intelligible works while living in an ordered society. As things turned out, the works he admired were not always fully intelligible and the society he lived in was not ordered. But at least in his own creative writings, such as they were, he could try to be clear. So his poems are as they are, and the best of them last well.

GORE VIDAL

"Edmund Wilson: This Critic and This Gin and These Shoes" (1980)

The Second American Revolution

1982, pp. 26–35

On February 2, 1821, gin-drinker Lord Byron wrote in his Ravenna Journal: "I have been considering what can be the reason why I always wake at a certain hour in the morning, and always in very bad spirits—I may say, in actual despair and despondency, in all respects—even of that which pleased me overnight. . . . In England, five years ago, I had the same kind of hypochondria, but accompanied with so violent a thirst that I have drank as many as fifteen bottles of soda-water in one night, after going to bed, and been still thirsty. . . . What is it?—liver?"

In Edmund Wilson's journal, published as *Upstate*, he wrote, in 1955: "One evening (August 13, Saturday) I drank a whole bottle of champagne and what was left of a bottle of Old Grand-Dad and started on a bottle of red wine—I was eating Limburger cheese and gingersnaps. This began about five in the afternoon—I fell asleep in my chair, but woke up when Beverly came, thinking it was the next morning. I decided to skip supper; and felt queasy for the next twenty-four hours." The sixty-year-old Wilson does not ask, what is it? as Byron did. Wilson knows. "This kind of life," he writes, rather demurely, "in the long run, does, however, get rather unhealthy."

About the time that Wilson was munching on those gingersnaps and Limburger cheese, washed down with fiery waters, I received a letter from Upton Sinclair (whom I had never met), asking me about something. Then, obsessively, from left field, as it were, Sinclair denounced John Barleycorn. In the course of a long life, practically every writer Sinclair had known had died of drink, starting with his friend Jack London. Needless to say, this was not the sort of unsolicited letter that one likes to read while starting on one's fifteenth bottle of soda water, or to be precise and up-to-date, Coca-Cola, Georgia's sole gift to a nation whose first century was recently described in a book titled, eponymously, *The Alcoholic Republic* . . . of letters, I remember adding to myself when I first saw the book.

In this century, it would be safe to say that a significant percent of American writers are to a greater or lesser degree alcoholics and why this should be the case I leave to the medicine men. Alcoholism ended the careers of Hemingway, Fitzgerald, and Faulkner, to name three fashionable novelists of our mid-century. Out of charity toward the descendants and keepers of the still flickering flames of once glorious literary figures, I shall name no other names. Heavy drinking stopped Hemingway from writing anything of value in his later years; killed Fitzgerald at forty-four; turned the William Faulkner of *As I Lay Dying* into a fable.

Meanwhile, the contemporary of these three blasted stars, Edmund Wilson, outlived and outworked them all; he also outdrank them. Well into his seventies, Wilson would totter into the Princeton Club and order a half dozen martinis, to be prepared not sequentially but simultaneously—six shining glasses in a bright row, down which Wilson would work, all the while talking and thinking at a rapid pace. To the end of a long life, he kept on making the only thing he thought worth making: sense, a quality almost entirely lacking in American literature where stupidity—if sufficiently sincere and authentic—is deeply revered, and easily achieved. Although this *was* a rather unhealthy life in the long run, Wilson had a very long run indeed. But then, he was perfect proof of the proposition that the more the mind is used and fed the less apt it is to devour itself. When he died, at seventy-seven, he was busy stuffing his head with irregular Hungarian verbs. Plainly, he had a brain to match his liver.

Edmund Wilson was the last of a leisurely educated generation who were not obliged, if they were intellectually minded, to join the hicks and hacks of Academe. Wilson supported himself almost entirely by literary journalism, something not possible today if only because, for all practical purposes, literary journalism of the sort that he practiced no longer exists. Instead, book-chat is now dominated either by academic bureaucrats, crudely pursuing bureaucratic careers, or by journalists whose "leprous jealousy" (Flaubert's pretty phrase) has made mephitic the air of our alcoholic literary republic. But then, Flaubert thought that "critics write criticism because they are unable to be artists, just as a man unfit to bear arms becomes a police spy." Wilson would have challenged this romantic notion. Certainly, he would have made the point that to write essays is as much an aspect of the literary artist's temperament as the ability to evoke an alien sensibility on a page while sweating to avoid a double genitive. In any case, Wilson himself wrote stories, plays, novels. He knew how such things were made even if he was not entirely a master of any of these forms.

Of what, then, was Edmund Wilson a master? That is a question in need of an answer, or answers; and there are clues in the book at hand, *The Thirties: From Notebooks and Diaries of the Period*. At the time of Wilson's death, eight years ago, he was editing the notebooks that dealt with the Twenties. He had already finished *Upstate*, a chronicle of his works and days from the early Fifties to 1970. *Upstate* is a highly satisfactory Wilsonian book, filled with sharp personal details, long scholarly asides on those things or people or notions (like New York religions) that had caught his fancy. Although he had planned to rework his earlier records, he soon realized that he might not live long enough to complete them. He then designated, in his will, that Professor Leon Edel edit the remains, with the injunction that the text be published the way he wrote it, except for straightening out "misspellings and faulty punctuations" (but not, apparently, faulty grammar: Wilson often "feels badly"—it *is* liver). With *The Thirties*, Professor Edel had his work cut out for him because, he writes, "It is clear from the condition of the typescript that [Wilson] intended to do much more work on this book." That is understatement.

At the beginning of the Thirties, Wilson completed *Axel's Castle*; at the end, he had finished *To the Finland Station*. He wrote for *The New Republic*, supported, briefly, the American Communist party, visited the Soviet Union, Detroit, Appalachia, Scotsboro, and tried a season of teaching at the University of Chicago. The decade, in a sense, was the making of him as critic and triple thinker. Emotionally, it was shattering: in 1930 he married Margaret Canby; in 1932 she died. He also conducted a wide range of affairs, many on the raunchy side.

Professor Edel rather flinches at Wilson's "record of his own copulations" in general and the notes about his marriage in particular (so unlike the home life of our own dear Master): "some readers may be startled by this intimate candid record of a marriage." But Professor Edel is quick to remind us that this is all part of "the notebooks of a chronicler, a way of tidying the mind for his craft of criticism. . . . He tries, rather, to be a camera, for this is what he finds most comfortable." Well, yes and no.

In 1930 Edmund Wilson was thirty-five. He was a member of the minor Eastern gentry, a Princeton graduate, a World War I overseas noncombatant. In the Twenties, he had lived the life of the roaring boy but unlike the other lads that light-footed it over the greensward, he never stopped reading and writing and thinking. Thanks, in large part, to the Christers who had managed to prohibit the legal sale of spirits, alcohol was as much a curse to that generation as Gin Lane had been to the poor of eighteenth-century London. I suspect that a great deal of the grimness of this volume is a result of hangover and its concomitant despairs. At the same time, it is the record of an astonishing constitution: Wilson would write while he was drinking—something I should not have thought possible for anyone, even his doomed friend Scott Fitzgerald.

From thirty-five to forty-five men go from relative youth to middle age. The transit is often rocky. As a man's life settles into a rut, in mindless rut the man is apt to go. Certainly, this was true of Wilson, as readers of *Memoirs of Hecate County* might have suspected and as readers of *The Thirties* will now know for certain. During the so-called "ignoble" decade, despite constant drinking, Wilson was sexually very active. He enjoyed trade in the form of the Slavic Anna, a working-class woman whose proletarian ways fascinated him. He had sex with a number of those women who used to hang about writers, as well as with ladies at the edge of the great world. He bedded no Oriane but he knew at least one Guermantes *before* her translation to the aristocracy.

Although Wilson's bedmates are sometimes masked by initials, he enjoys writing detailed descriptions of what Professor Edel calls his "copulations." These descriptions are mechanistic, to say the least. Since they are not connected with character, they are about as erotic as a *Popular Mechanics* blueprint of the sort that is said to appeal to the growing boy. I am not sure just why Wilson felt that he should write so much about cock and cunt except that in those days it was a very daring thing to do, as Henry Miller had discovered when his books were burned and as Wilson was to discover when his own novel, *Memoirs of Hecate County*, was banned.

In literature, sexual revelation is a matter of tact and occasion. Whether or not such candor is of interest to a reader depends a good deal on the revealer's attitude. James Boswell is enchanting to read on sex because he is by self, as well as by sex, enchanted and possessed. The author of *My Secret Life* (if for real) is engaging because he is only interested in getting laid as often as possible in as many different ways and combinations. We also don't know what he looks like—an important aid to masturbation. Frank Harris (not for real) has the exuberance of a natural liar and so moves the reader toward fiction.

The list now starts to get short. The recently published (in English) letters of Flaubert are interesting because he has interesting things to say about what he sees and does in the brothels and baths of North Africa. Also, tactfully, mercifully, he never tells us what he feels or Feels. The sex that Flaubert has with women and men, with boys and girls, is fascinating to read about (even though we know exactly how *he* looks). This is due, partly, to the fact that his experiences are, literally, exotic as well as erotic and, partly, to that famous tone of voice. Today one is never quite certain why memoirists are so eager to tell us what they do in bed. Unless the autobiographer has a case to be argued, I suspect that future readers will skip those sexual details that our writers have so generously shared with us in order to get to the gossip and the jokes.

In Wilson's notebooks, he liked to describe sex in the same way that he liked "doing" landscapes. "It is certainly very hard," he concedes, "to write about sex in English without making it unattractive. *Come* is a horrible word to apply to something ecstatic." Finally, he did neither sex scenes or landscapes very well. But in sexual matters, he has no real case to make, unlike, let us say, the committed homosexualist who thinks, incorrectly, that candor will so rend the veil that light will be shed upon what the society considers an abominable act and in a blaze of clarity and charity all will be forgiven. This is naïve, as Wilson himself demonstrates in these pages. He was very much an American of his time and class and the notebooks are filled with innumerable references to "fairies" that range from derisive to nervous; yet Wilson also admits to occasional homosexual reveries which he thought "were a way of living in the grip of the vise, getting away into a different world where those values that pressed me did not function."

Nevertheless, it is disquieting to find Wilson, in the Thirties (having admired Proust and Gide), quite unable to accept the fact that a fairy could be a major artist. In *Axel's Castle,* he has great trouble admitting, or not admitting, the sexual source of Proust's jealousy.

On the other hand, he made a curious and admirable exception in the case of Thornton Wilder.

During the Twenties and Thirties, Wilder was one of the most celebrated and successful American novelists. He was also one of the few first-rate writers the United States has produced. Fortunately for Wilder's early reputation, he was able to keep his private life relatively secret. As a result, he was very much a hero in book-chat land. In *The Twenties* Wilson describes a meeting with Wilder. He was startled to find Wilder "a person of such positive and even peppery opinions." Wilson had not read any of Wilder's novels because he thought that "they must be rather on the fragile and precious side" (what else can a fairy write?). As it turned out, each had been reading the new installment of Proust's novel and Wilson was delighted to find that Wilder thought Saint-Loup's homosexuality unjustified. Over the years, Wilson was to review Wilder seriously and well. When Wilder was the victim of a celebrated Marxist attack, Wilson came to Wilder's defense—not to mention literature's. But the word was out and Thornton Wilder's reputation never recovered; to this day, he is a literary nonperson. Nevertheless, it is to Wilson's credit that he was able to overcome his horror of fairydom in order to do justice to a remarkable contemporary.

Of a certain Victorian Englishman it was said that no lady's shoe, unescorted, was safe in his company. It could be said of Edmund Wilson that, like Cecil B. De Mille, "he never met a woman's foot he didn't like." Is there any reader of Wilson's novel *I Thought of Daisy* who does not recall Wilson's description of a girl's feet as being like "moist cream cheeses"? But Wilson's podophilia did not stop there: he could have made a fortune in women's footwear. From *The Thirties:* ". . . shoes, blue with silver straps, that arched her insteps very high . . .," "Katy's little green socks and untied gray moccasins . . .," "young Scotch girl M.P. [with] large feet bulging out of black shoes . . .," ". . . silver open-work shoes that disclosed her reddened toenails, such a combination as only she could wear. . . ." In *The Thirties,* I counted twenty-four references to shoes and feet; each, let me quickly say, belonging to a woman. When it came to shoes, Wilson was sternly heterosexual—not for him the stud's boot or the little lad's Ked. But, to be absolutely precise, there is one very odd reference. Wilson is struck by the number of Chicago men who wear spats. Reverie: "Excuse me, sir. But a hook is loose on your left spat. As chance would have it, I have with me a spats-hook. If you'll allow me, sir. . . ." Whenever Wilson strikes the Florsheim note, he is in rut.

As a lover, Wilson is proud of his "large pink prong." (Surely, Anaïs Nin said it was "short and puce"—or was that Henry Miller's thumb?) In action, "My penis went in and out so beautifully sensitively, caressing (me) each time so sweet-smoothly (silkily). . . ." Yet he refers, clinically, to his "all too fat and debauched face" not to mention belly. He was a stubby little man who drank a lot. But his sexual energy matched his intellectual energy; so much for Freud's theory of sublimation.

The section called "The Death of Margaret" is fascinating, and quite unlike anything else he was ever to write. He started scribbling in a notebook aboard an airliner in 1932, en route to California where his wife of two years had just died of a fall. A compulsive writer, Wilson felt, instinctively, that by a close running description of what he saw from the plane window and in the air terminals he could get control of the fact of death and loss, or at least neutralize the shock in the act of recreation. He writes a good many impressionistic pages of the trip before he gets to Margaret. Some very odd items: "—touching fellow passenger's thigh, moving over to keep away from it, did he move, too?—shutting eyes and homosexual fantasies, losing in vivid reality from Provincetown, gray, abstract, unreal sexual stimulus—also thought about coming back with Jean Gorman on train as situation that promises possibilities; but couldn't stomach it—young man too big, not my type—" Then impressions of his time together with Margaret: "I felt for the first time how she'd given me all my self-confidence, the courage that I hadn't had before to say what I thought. . . ."

In Santa Barbara, he stays with her family. "At Mrs. Waterman's house [Margaret's mother], when I began to cry, she said, I've never broken down. . . ." "Second night: homosexual wet dream, figures still rather dim, a boy. Third night: nightmare—the trolls were in the dark part of the cellar. . . ." Finally, the inevitable epitaph; "After she was dead, I loved her." That is the story of every life—and death. For the next decade, Wilson dreams of Margaret and writes down the dreams. In these dreams he usually knows that she is dead but, somehow, they can overcome this obstacle. They don't; even in dreams. Eurydice always stays put: It is the blight man was born for.

During the Thirties, Wilson's interests were more political than literary. The Depression, the New Deal, the Soviet experiment absorbed him. Wilson is at his most attractive and, I should think, characteristic when he describes going to Russia. He wanted to think well of communism, and, to a point, he was enthralled by the "classless" society and by the way that one man, Lenin, "has stamped his thought and his language on a whole people." This is not the treason but the very nature of the true clerk: the word as absolute can be motor to behavior and to governance. Gradually, Wilson is disillusioned about Stalin and the state he was making.

But what is fascinating to read today is not Wilson's account of what he saw and did but the way that he goes about taking on a subject, a language, a world. This is what sets him apart from all other American critics. He has to get to the root of things. He will learn Hebrew to unravel the Dead Sea scrolls. Read a thousand windy texts to figure out the Civil War. Learn Russian to get past the barrier of Constance Garnett's prose. He was the perfect autodidact. He wanted to know it all. Or, as he wrote, after he had a nervous breakdown in the Thirties, "I usually know exactly what I want to do, and it has only been when I could not make up my mind that I have really gone to pieces."

Early in *The Thirties*, Wilson is a fellow traveler of the American communists' *faute de mieux*. He can see no other way out of the Depression than an overthrow of the form of capitalism that had caused it. Before the election of 1932, he wrote: "Hoover stands frankly for the interests of the class who live on profits as against the wage-earning classes. Franklin Roosevelt, though he speaks as a Democrat in the name of the small businessmen and farmers and is likely to be elected by them in the expectation that he can do something for them, can hardly be imagined effecting any very drastic changes in the system which has allowed him to get into office. Whatever amiable gestures he may make, he will be largely controlled by the profit-squeezing class just as Hoover is." This is prescient. Apropos the fireside chats: "Roosevelt's unsatisfactory way of emphasizing his sentences, fairyish, or as if there weren't real conviction behind him—in spite of his clearness and neatness—but regular radio announcers, I noticed later, did the same thing. (The remoteness of the speaker from his audience.)" It is a pity that Wilson, who was on the fringes of the New Deal, never got to know the president. "Roosevelt is reported to have answered when someone had said to him that he would either be the best president the country had ever had or the most hated: No—that he would either be the most popular or the last."

Wilson often traveled to Washington in the Thirties and he had a sense of the place (derived from Henry Adams?) that makes him sound like one of us cliff-dwellers: "Washington is really a hollow shell which holds the liberalism of the New Deal as easily as the crooks and thugs of the Harding Administration—no trouble to clean it out every night and put something else in the past Administration's place."

Wilson goes to see one Martha Blair—"a rather appealing mouth and slim arms, though pale thyroid eyes: pink flowered print dress, with sleeves that gave a glimpse of her upper arms . . . she complained of the small town character of Washington—if you said you had another engagement, people asked you what it was—when she had said she was going to Virginia for the weekend they had asked her where in Virginia." It is odd to see this old formidable "socialite" of my childhood (she was then in her early thirties) as viewed from a totally different angle. Martha Blair kept company in those days with Arthur Krock of *The New York Times*. They were known as Martha'n'Artha. Wilson thinks they were married in 1934. I don't. At about that time, I remember there was a great row between my mother and her husband over whether or not the unmarried couple Martha and Arthur could stay overnight at our house in Virginia—where she was so often headed. My mother won that round. They were often at Merrywood, and Arthur Krock was the first Jew that I ever met. Anti-Semitism was in full boisterous American flower in the Thirties, and Wilson's record of conversations and attitudes haunt a survivor in much the same way that the background of a Thirties movie will reverse time, making it possible to see again a *People's Drug* store (golden lettering), straw hats, squared-off cars, and the actual light that encompassed one as a child, the very same light that all those who are now dead saw then.

Wilson notes, rather perfunctorily, friends and contemporaries. Scott Fitzgerald makes his usual appearances, and in his usual state. Once again we get the Hemingway-Wilson-Fitzgerald evening. "When Scott was lying in the corner on the floor, Hemingway said, Scott thinks that his penis is too small. (John Bishop had told me this and said that Scott was in the habit of making this assertion to anybody he met—to the lady who sat next to him at dinner and who might be meeting him for the first time.) I explained to him, Hemingway continued, that it only seemed to him small because he looked at it from above. You have to look at it in the mirror. (I did not understand this.)" I have never understood what Hemingway meant either. For one thing, Fitzgerald had obviously studied his diminutive part in a mirror. Even so, he would still be looking down at it unless, like a boy that I went to school with, he could so bend himself as to have an eye to eye, as it were, exchange with the Great American (Male) Obsession.

"Scott Fitzgerald at this time [1934] had the habit of insulting people, and then saying, if the victim came back at him: 'Can't take it, huh?' (I learned years later from Morley Callaghan that this was a habit of Hemingway's, from whom Scott had undoubtedly acquired it.)" There is altogether too little about Wilson's friend Dawn Powell, one of the wittiest of our novelists, and the most resolutely overlooked. But then American society, literary or lay, tends to be humorless. What other culture could have produced someone like Hemingway and *not* seen the joke?

Wilson's glimpses of people are always to the point. But they are brief. He is far more interested in writing descriptions of landscapes. I cannot think where the terrible habit began. Since Fitzgerald did the same thing in his notebooks, I suppose someone at Princeton (Professor Gauss? Project for a scholar-squirrel) must have told them that a writer must constantly describe things as a form of finger-exercise. The result is not unlike those watercolors Victorian girls were encouraged to turn out. Just as Wilson is about to tell us something quite interesting about e. e. cummings, he feels that he must devote a page or two to the deeply boring waterfront at Provincetown. A backdrop with no action in front of it is to no point at all.

There were trolls in the cellar of Wilson's psyche, and they tended to come upstairs "When I was suffering from the bad nerves of a hangover. . . ." There is also an echo of Mrs. Dalloway's vastation in the following passage: "Getting out of an elevator in some office building—I must have been nervously exhausted—I saw a man in a darkened hall—he was in his shirt sleeves with open neck, had evidently been working around the building—his eyes were wide open, and there seemed to be no expression on his face: he looked, not like an ape, but like some kind of primitive man—and his staring face, as I stared at him, appalled me: humanity was still an animal, still glaring out of its dark caves, not yet having mastered the world, not even comprehending what he saw. I was frightened—at him, at us all. *The horrible look of the human race.*"

As a critic, Wilson was not always at his best when it came to the design or pattern of a text—what used to be called aesthetics. He liked data, language. He did not have much sympathy for the New Critics with their emphasis on text *qua* text. After all, nothing human exists in limbo; nothing human is without connection. Wilson's particular genius lay in his ability to make rather more connections than any other critic of his time. As Diderot said of Voltaire: "He knows a great deal and our young poets are ignorant. The work of Voltaire is full of things; their works are empty."

But Wilson was quite aware that "things" in themselves are not enough. Professor Edel quotes from Wilson's Princeton lecture: "no matter how thoroughly and searchingly we may have scrutinized works of literature from the historical and biographical point of view . . . we must be able to tell the good from the bad, the first-rate from the second-rate. We shall not otherwise write literary criticism at all."

We do not, of course, write literary criticism at all now. Academe has won the battle in which Wilson fought so fiercely on the other side. Ambitious English teachers (sic!) now invent systems that have nothing to do with literature or life but everything to do with those games that must be played in order for them to rise in the academic bureaucracy. Their works are empty indeed. But then, their works are not meant to be full. They are to be taught, not read. The long dialogue has broken down. Fortunately, as Flaubert pointed out, the worst thing about the present is the future. One day there will be no. . . . But I have been asked not to give the game away. Meanwhile, I shall drop a single hint: Only construct!

YVOR WINTERS

1900–1968

Arthur Yvor Winters was born on October 17, 1900, in Chicago, Illinois. He was educated at the University of Chicago, the University of Colorado (B.A., M.A. 1925), and Stanford University (Ph.D. 1935). In 1926 he married writer Janet Lewis; they had two children. He taught at the University of Idaho from 1925 to 1927, and at Stanford University from 1927 to 1966. In 1929 he founded the *Gyroscope*, and he was regional editor for the *Hound and Horn* from 1932 to 1934. From 1948 to 1950 he was a Fellow at Kenyon College.

Winters was prominent as both a poet and a critic. His early poetry (collected in *The Immobile Wind*, 1921, *The Magpie's Shadow*, 1922, and *The Bare Hills: A Book of Poems*, 1927) was heavily influenced by the Imagists and William Carlos Williams, utilizing free verse and actively avoiding abstract ideas. Later Winters began to use more conventional meters and rhyme structures, and while his poetry remained firmly grounded in images, he began to utilize them to explore abstractions. *Before Disaster* (1934) is usually seen as the beginning of Winters's mature period; it is rational and formal, and explores its subjects with an eye toward moral judgment, an approach that is antithetical to Imagist methods.

Though Winters was an important poet (his revised *Collected Poems*, published in 1960, won the Bollingen Prize), he is probably best remembered for his criticism, which, though frequently insightful and penetrating, is often iconoclastic and eccentric. Winters considered romanticism to be a regressive influence on modern literature, and he was sharply at variance with the New Critics, who were the primary influence upon criticism during the period of Winters's peak activity. Winters's examination of the relationship between form and content in poetry and his exploration of the function of literature remain important influences upon modern American criticism, though he gained notoriety for his outright dismissal of figures generally considered major, such as Yeats, Pound, and Gerard Manley Hopkins, while elevating to improbable importance such writers as Robert Bridges, T. Sturge Moore, and Elizabeth Daryush. Ultimately, his criticism is usually thought valuable for its theoretical insight rather than its specific evaluations. He died on January 25, 1968.

(I) *Mont St. Michel and Chartres* and *The Education of Henry Adams* represent the radical disintegration of a mind that had produced, in the *History of the United States during the Administrations of Thomas Jefferson and James Madison*, the second-greatest historical work in English. (2) In Wallace Stevens's "Sunday Morning," one of the greatest contemplative poems of the English language, we first encounter the ennui which is to obsess the later work of the poet and ultimately to wreck his talent. (3) The theory of T. S. Eliot's criticism and the influence of his poetry have grown upon our time with all the benumbing energy of a bad habit, till any attempt to analyze the defects of modern poetry in the light of civilized standards is accepted merely as evidence that the critic is not of the elect. (4) According to John Crowe Ransom, poetry is an obscure form of self-indulgence, in which we proceed from a limited and unsatisfactory rational understanding of our subject to as complete a confusion as we are able to achieve.

These four patched-together sentences convey, as fairly (I hope) as single sentences can, the burden of the four essays that compose the body of Yvor Winters' latest book of criticism ⟨*The Anatomy of Nonsense*⟩. In addition to its body, the book has a head-piece, to set forth Winters' principles theoretically, and a tail-piece, whose bright feathers include an encomium of modern universities and little-known writers such as Adelaide Crapsey—"who is certainly an immortal poet."

If this is an irritable-sounding description of *The Anatomy of Nonsense*, it was not Winters' critical principles that provoked the irritation. His definition of what makes a good poem, besides being both coherent and appealing, is in general accord with the theory latent in the practice of other serious present-day critics, like Brooks and Warren; but it takes heroic patience not to want to scrap the principles when their author grimly hands down such paradoxes as that "Gather Ye Rosebuds" is a better poem than "To His Coy Mistress," Sturge Moore is a better poet than Yeats, Tate is anti-intellectual, and "Eliot suffers from the delusion that he is judging [the modern chaos] when he is merely exhibiting it." With his compelling insistence upon the rôle of reason in poetry and his attacks on critical relativism, Winters is a good person to have around at a time when the opposite views are demanding, and getting, *Lebensraum*; but are his intellect and his absolute values obliged to lead him into a kind of neo-classical isolationism? He can be as perverse as Doctor Johnson is when the Doctor discloses that one passage in Congreve surpasses anything in Shakespeare. Winters is a great amateur of geniuses: in fact there have not been so many rescued from base neglect since people were pinching themselves after a glance through *The Oxford Book of Modern Verse*.—ROBERT DANIEL, "The Discontent of Our Winters," *SwR*, Oct.–Dec. 1943, pp. 602–3

Yvor Winters is a very considerable poet indeed, with a most curious career. Out of all his generation he was the one who read the modern European poetry in the original languages and for pleasure, and furthermore with understanding and assimilation. Poets slightly younger than himself eagerly read everything he published, from the earliest poems by "Arthur Winters" or "A. Y. Winters" in *The Double Dealer* and *The Little Review* to his fully developed first style in *Broom*, and they looked on him as an explorer and leader for their generation.

Reading the Imagist Manifesto one might think that the resulting poetry would be something like Pierre Reverdy. With the Imagists it was not, but it was with Yvor Winters. He pushed the intense sensitivity of H.D. to the breaking point, and he did it with a more radically dissociated and reconstructed verse, with a new prosodic power, and with, to put it simply, more content. Winters' early poems are overtly erotic or philosophical; besides being more "abstract" (a foolish word to apply to the art of words) they are more concrete and communicative than those of any of his predecessors. He was incomparably the best poet to have developed in the post-war Chicago school centered in the University, which included Glenway Wescott, Elizabeth Madox Roberts, Mark Turbyfill, Samuel Putnam, Maureen Smith, and Janet Lewis, later Mrs. Winters.

When most of his friends and most of his literary generation went to Paris and met the great, Winters discovered he had fairly advanced tuberculosis and was forced to live the rest of his life in a dry climate. He taught school for a while in an ugly mining town, Raton, New Mexico, and then college in Moscow, Idaho, and finally in the late Twenties he came to Stanford, where he remained for the rest of his life. He was the true exile, the true *aliené*. Years must have gone by where nobody knew what he was talking about except his wife, or his echoing students. He became cranky and cantankerous and is responsible for some of the most wrong-headed and eccentric criticism ever written.

He changed the style of his verse to a stark neo-classicism of his own invention, which he always insisted owed much to, of all people, the late Tudor writer of doggerel, Barnaby Googe. Actually he is more like Walter Savage Landor, whom he admired, or A. E. Housman, whom he did not. His great admiration was Paul Valéry, and his poems are somewhat like a highly simplified Paul Valéry, an eccentric divagation from Valéry. The unconscious motive was probably épatéism, *pour épater les avant-gardistes.* Winters' Barnaby Googe is to Eugene Jolas as Marcel Duchamp's urinal labelled "Mutt" is to George Babbitt. Winters stood Dadaism on its head, as Marx did Hegel, and his critical ideas cannot be appreciated unless this is understood. They were designed to give Eugene Jolas running and barking fits.

At Stanford Winters built a highly disciplined little school of poets in almost no time at all. They were taught to write according to specific rules and with a single strictness, far greater than anything in any neo-classic tradition, something perhaps like the *skalds* and *filidhs* in ancient Scandinavia and Ireland. It didn't seem to do them any harm. A generation later, after Winters was dead, they were still amongst some of the best poets around, notably J. V. Cunningham and Ann Stanford, and as a group there had never been anything like them in the history of American poetry.

Years later, past middle age, Winters tried to organize another circle, a second generation of his "poets of the Pacific." Some of them, Scott Momaday, Alan Stevens, Thom Gunn, Edgar Bowers, deserve to be better known. But none of these people made the impression the earlier group had. He is an example of what a great teacher, however wrong-headed, can do. After all, the first group were just people who liked to write poems who happened to be going to Stanford. Horace Gregory once called him, paraphrasing Hokusai, "an old man mad about poetry"—when he was still less than forty years old.—KENNETH REXROTH, *American Poetry in the Twentieth Century*, 1971, pp. 92–94

Yvor Winters, Jarrell pointed out in a rare moment of impatience, indulged in a 'willed and scrupulously limited talking down . . . a kind of moral baby-talk'. Most of Winters's essays collected in *Uncollected Essays* (the book's title seems to be a variation of the paradox in which the Cretan insists that all Cretans are liars) were written about contemporary poetry—mainly American—as it was published from the early Twenties on. This is how the Sage of Stanford sounded when he was still a critic. He was a pretty good one: if the ability to sort wheat from chaff in current poetry is the true test of critical intelligence, then Winters passed it. But even in the earliest pieces you can watch emerging the strange precepts which were eventually to establish him as an obscurantist.

Winters was always a theoretician, yet his early theories were so complicated that anything good could gain acceptance. Lyric poetry was the only kind of poetry you could have. There were, however, five different kinds of lyric, and each kind could have an 'essential unit' composed of either an 'image' or an 'anti-image', which really made, by my calculations, at least ten kinds altogether. There was no hope of applying this scheme with any rigour, and responsiveness was unfettered as a result—everything he admired could be accommodated in it somewhere. He admired extravagantly, but there are worse faults in a young critic, and anyway his heroes and heroines included Marianne Moore and Hart Crane, about both of whom he said some acute things. In Marianne Moore, he wrote, 'the humorous attains that which it is supposed to be unable to attain, a maximum of poetic beauty'. A good point to make, which he would be unable to make later on. He called Hart Crane's tone 'heroic'—it was—and numbered him as one of the five or six greatest poets then writing in English, which he was apt to say about anyone who took his fancy; but the sin was venial and anyway in Crane's case he was right.

It was a considerable gymnastic feat on Winters's part to transform this impressionable but energetic flexibility into the dogmatic torpor he evinced in the Thirties, when Robert Bridges became 'the most valuable model of poetic style to appear since Dryden', and the drear T. Sturge Moore was presented as outsoaring Yeats. Formal versatility and purity of diction: those were the new watchwords. That Bridges's diction abounded with nays, thro's, 'neaths, 'tises and yeas, and that Moore's diction was choc-a-bloc with fains, quaffings, e'ens and dosts, and that the 'formal versatility' of either bard was the most abject pattern-making, Winters didn't mind or even mention. His suicidal tendencies were as fully developed as Rickword's, with the difference that he didn't need Marxism to help him go ga-ga.—CLIVE JAMES, "The Four Just Men," *NS*, Feb. 21, 1975, pp. 243–46

It is ironic that a man committed to a vision of the classical, to what is central and constant in the human experience of the world, should have found himself so much at odds with the poetic practice and critical theory of his own day. In *Maule's*

Curse, published in 1938, he ridiculed Poe's "process of systematic exclusion, in the course of which he eliminates from the field of English poetry nearly all of the greatest acknowledged masters, reserving the field very largely to Coleridge, Tennyson, Thomas Moore, himself and R. H. Horne." At the time this was written his own judgments had a breadth of sympathy and understanding that made Poe's ad hoc tradition seem absurdly exclusive and eccentric: and yet there are moments in Winters's last book, *Forms of Discovery*, where he appears to have painted himself into a similarly lonely corner. The concern with the classical vision gradually gave place to a related concern with those few who, Winters believed, could discern this vision: in the work of poets as various as Gascoigne, Churchill, Very, and Robinson, it was as much their stoic sense of being disregarded by fortune and men's eyes as the actual vision they recorded that moved Winters's interest. In a similar way, though Winters's version of the poet (after 1929) was always of a man embattled with reality, the metaphysical battles of the criticism of his thirties—with time, death and the "invasion of the impersonal"—were often replaced, as he became more concerned with ethical and social issues, by battles with the "dead living." Yet his achievement remains, when all is said and done, major. The best of his early verse has a freshness and limpidity, and a sensitivity to rhythm, unequaled save in the best work of William Carlos Williams. What he considered to be his major important poetry—that written after 1929—has been unjustly neglected, largely I suspect because of his reputation as a pugnaciously antimodernist critic, rather than for reasons intrinsic to the verse itself. To live with these poems is to be aware of a mind intensely sensitive to the reality of both the life of the intellect, and the nature of the physical world in which that intellect must live. The consciousness that informs the poetry is perpetually attuned to the claims of both spirit and world; it works toward balance, toward a just vision, toward a true and clear understanding of the nature of our life. The "massive calm" of these poems is intensely moving to one who has experienced the reality of their premises and who can sympathize with Winters's temperamental need to define the limits of our understanding with lapidary certainty. His best poems, "Apollo and Daphne," "The Slow Pacific Swell," "The Marriage," "On a View of Pasadena from the Hills," "John Sutter," "The California Oaks," "Sir Gawaine and the Green Knight," present us with sensory experience—a sense of the mind drenched in the physical reality of the world—and, simultaneously, an intellectual passion for understanding rarely equaled in the poetry of this century.

The significance of his criticism was, for Winters, as I have attempted to demonstrate, intimately bound up with his notions of what was wrong with modern literature, in particular modern poetry. He read literature as a poet, looking for warnings, models, pitfalls. Again his ideal was one of balance, and his dislike of so much modern literature was largely a regret for what it had sacrificed rather than disdain for what it had achieved. He welcomed the increase in sensitivity that he discerned in the work of the late romantics, he merely regretted that this increase had been gained at the expense of logical form, of denotative meaning. His ideal was a combination of such sensitivity with rigorous and verifiable logical structure; he claimed to have found such a combination in the best work of Valéry and Wallace Stevens. Yet to a reader more interested in Winters's ostensible subjects than in his own poetic preoccupations, his writings—especially on sixteenth-century poetry and nineteenth-century American literature—are among the clearest and most useful available. It is time he was accorded his true place, as one of the major figures of twentieth-century American literature.

As we have seen (from his remarks, for example, on the poetry of Frost and Yeats) Winters became more and more concerned, as he grew older, with the social and ethical implications of poetry. He characterized himself as a "reactionary," and it has even been suggested that his concern with order and form was somehow indicative of an incipient fascism. The charge was somewhat nebulously made by Robert Gorham Davis in the Winter 1949–50 issue of the *American Scholar*. In the April issue Winters wrote an angry and pained reply, setting out his theoretical opposition to fascist beliefs and listing his (impeccably liberal) practical political activities and affiliations. His answer, in part, is as follows:

> I believe in the reality of absolute truth; and since I am not a Platonist, I accept the theistic explanation of this reality offered by Averroes, Avicenna and Aquinas—namely that true judgement and true knowledge reside in God, that it is the duty of every man to approximate them as closely as his particular talents permit. Now is this is actually or potentially a fascistic notion, then every believing Christian and Jew is a fascist, to say nothing of many others. Actually this belief is immovably anti-fascist, for it places the responsibility for his own development (and perhaps salvation) solidly on the individual, and it indicates that any arbitrary interference with his assuming the responsibility is evil. The fascist, (or any totalitarian) state, however, indicates that true knowledge and judgement reside in the Leader, and that it is the duty of the citizen to accept his verdicts without question. There is no conceivable reconciliation of these points of view. [P. 299]

In fact, Winters's concern with individual ethical responsibility, with his view of poetry as a process of moral evaluation whose chief end is the modification of the reader's sensibility so that he understands more clearly and fully the nature of human existence in the world, both point to a moral sensitivity hardly compatible with either the glorification of violence or the demand that the individual merge his being in that of a greater whole, be it state or race, endemic in fascism. Further, as we have seen from his own poetry, his ideals of human existence in the world were deeply imbued with notions of self-restraint, dignity and moral decorum. He viewed all suggestions of violation, spoliation, and trespass beyond natural and abiding limits with horror.—DICK DAVIS, "Conclusion," *Wisdom and Wilderness: The Achievement of Yvor Winters*, 1983, pp. 233–35

A. ALVAREZ

"Yvor Winters" (1960)

Beyond All This Fiddle: Essays 1955–1967

1969, pp. 255–59

There are two kinds of critic: the professional and the amateur. Of course, I am using both words in their literal, not their derogatory senses. The amateurs are those who love literature for its own sake. The printed word and the effort of writing inspire in them a devotion which is very close to awe. For them criticism is a matter of selection and arrangement, like floral decoration or stage lighting, to show off the work to its best advantage. They will find something good to be said for every work, no matter how trivial. Now these amateurs may seem professional; they may be sunk in writing up to their ears—as dons with the most rigorous standards of scholarship or as literary journalists haunted by the weekly need to be lively on the subject of dead books—but by their judgement shall ye know them; or by their lack of it.

The professionals, on the other hand, are those who are vowed to the job by a kind of act of faith. They make their living out of literature in the true sense, which is not a question of cash but of moral habit. In short, they use literature to build up for themselves a world of values. Inevitably, they don't like much, for in all viable moralities the elect are, of necessity, few. So their work is devoted to keeping up the standards, always with an intellectual passion, sometimes with a certain savagery. Like old-fashioned doctors, they believe that blood must at times be let to preserve the health of the system. In England, the foremost professional critic is in this sense F. R. Leavis; in America, he is Yvor Winters.

In Defense of Reason has taken a long time to reach us. It is made up of three independent but related books: *Primitivism and Decadence*, an analysis of modern American poetry, was first published in 1937; *Maule's Curse*, on the classical American novel and its intellectual tradition, appeared in 1938; *The Anatomy of Nonsense*, on American critical theory, came out in 1943; the complete collection, with an additional essay on Hart Crane, was published in the States in 1947. It is a pity that the book has been so long on the way, for original ideas spread their light before them; a number of Winters's suggestions have become fashions and he has not been given credit for them. He was, for instance, the first man to debunk Eliot's claims to classicism by showing how his theories descend straight from the late Romantics; he attacked the vagaries of neo-Symbolism and the craze for Laforguian irony (which he blandly equated with 'careless writing'); he praised Melville, James and, with reservations, Stevens, Crane and Hawthorne, long before any of them had become cult-figures. All this he had writ large in the thirties and early forties. We are just catching up with him.

But Winters would wish to base his ultimate reputation less on his originality or on the profundity of his insights than on his ability to produce a system that works. He has a rage for order and is fierce in proportion to an author's lack of it. He calls himself an absolutist, which means he demands nothing less than everything:

> It will be seen that what I desire of a poem is a clear understanding of motive, and a just evaluation of feeling; the justice of the evaluation persisting even into the sound of the least important syllable. Such a poem is a perfect and complete act of the spirit; it calls upon the full life of the spirit; it is difficult of attainment, but I am aware of no good reason to be contented with less.

Stated briefly, with such massive and ironic Johnsonian certainty, there is no arguing with Winters. But principles, particularly when they concern the enormous complexity of artistic and moral judgement, are better left brief or implicit than explained. The critic creates his audience and his context more by his intellectual tone than by spelling things out. Leavis, when challenged to define one of his terms, would, I imagine, prefer to point to a work of art than to launch into abstractions. Winters, on the other hand, is determined to have everything down in black and white. The results are often less flexible and profound than his practice:

> The artistic process is one of moral evaluation of human experience, by means of a technique which renders possible an evaluation more precise than any other. *The poet tries to understand his experience in rational terms, to state his understanding, and simultaneously to state, by means of the feelings which we attach to words, the kind and degree of emotion that should properly be motivated by this understanding*. . . . The 'intensity' of the work of art, which is different from the intensity of crude experience, lies in this: that what we call intensity in a work of art is a combination of the importance of the original subject and the precision of the judgement; whereas that which we call intensity in life is most often *the confused and therefore frightening emotion* resulting from a situation which we have not yet had time to meet and understand. . . . [My italics]

The business of the poet is to know himself: by his art he makes clearings of sanity in the encroaching jungle of experience; and because of his skill, these clearings are more lucid, more precise, more generally meaningful than those of other people. His method, for Winters as for Wordsworth, is that of 'emotion recollected in tranquillity'.

So far, so good—or almost so good. The flaw is in the first sentence I italicized. Winters makes it sound as though the *rational* understanding always came before the poem rather than during the process of writing, or even after it; as though each poem were accreted round a separate pearl of wisdom. He also implies that there are rules for the degree of emotion proper to each subject. It sounds more like a Renaissance than a modern theory. What he is describing, I suggest, is less the act of poetry than the act of criticism.

It is easy to see why. Like Winters, I too dislike obscurantism and the cant of blind inspiration. I am all for poets knowing what they mean. But knowing is not a clear-cut business. In the twentieth century, to be intelligent does not mean simply to be rational. It means the ability to make one's reason supple and subtle enough to include the irrational without being overwhelmed by it. The physicists have long worked with this element of irrationality, which they call entropy, the measure of chance or probability. In other terms, the whole of Freud's work was devoted to showing how irrational desires and fears run deep and compulsively below the most rational motives. The irrational, in short, is a vital element in modern reason.

When Winters, however, calls his book *In Defense of Reason* he really means it. He is not only Johnsonian in style; like the Doctor, he believes absolutely in the power of rational common sense. Because he is a peculiarly fine critic, his logic is always instinct with feeling, but he seeks to reduce everything to its terms. It doesn't always work. Eliot's importance, for example, has nothing to do with his Symbolist tricks and obscurity: instead it is in the way he worked out for our time a language in which great formal intelligence combines with great psychological depth, in which the rational and irrational meet and illuminate each other. But Winters will have none of him. He opts instead for the totally rational. And that means Robert Bridges, Adelaide Crapsey and Elizabeth Daryush, 'the finest British poet since T. Sturge Moore'—'that sheep', Yeats called him, 'in sheep's clothing'.

It is perhaps the least distinguished 'great tradition' any important critic has produced. Yet although Winters has deliberately set his face against American modernism, his choice is not dictated by mere perversity. Like Zeno with his arrow, he is in a logical quandary: Winters admires above all sureness and clarity of moral choice; therefore he is against the experimental because it attempts to cope more or less directly with 'the confused and therefore frightening emotion' of unregulated experience; therefore he makes a virtue out of the traditional which 'endeavours to utilize the greatest possible amount of the knowledge and wisdom, both technical and moral . . . to be found in precedent poetry. It assumes the ideal existence of a normal quality of feeling'; therefore he chooses Bridges & Co. The flying arrow does not move; the great poets are the consolidators, not the transformers of art. For all his originality, Winters is, by force of logic, profoundly reactionary.

Yet this taste for clear logic and moral certainty is also the strength of his criticism. His method is to combine literary insight with the history of ideas. Lucidly, stringently, he builds up the world of ideas and beliefs in which his authors wrote. He then goes through their works showing how the ideas were transformed and coloured by the writers' sensibilities. It is a kind of paraphrase done from the inside, so that at the moment of defining what a work of art says, Winters is defining how it feels:

> [*The Awkward Age*] is a tragedy of manners, in which no genuine moral issue is involved, but in which vague depths of moral ugliness, especially in Vanderbank, are elusively but unforgettably suggested. Vanderbank is a creature through whose tranquil and pellucid character there arises at the slightest disturbance of his surface a fine cloud of silt, of ugly feeling far too subtle to be called suspicion, but darkening his entire nature and determining his action.

It takes a major critic to combine that degree of aesthetic understanding with so firm and pervasive a judgement.

So, in the end, his tight, restrictive moral system seems not only justified but necessary. He is a man of acute moral instincts with no strong moral system to which he can instinctively adhere. Although he deeply understands the New England tradition, he is not part of it. He belongs, apparently, to no organized church. So he is left with his belief in literature, his logic and his considerable ability as a writer (he is also a distinguished poet). From these he has erected, by Johnsonian reasonableness, a moral and literary tradition of his own. One may not agree with it, but it is impossible not to admire his skill, his courage and the superb criticism it has enabled him to write.

JAMES DICKEY
"Yvor Winters" (1962)
Babel to Byzantium
1968, pp. 182–86

Regardless of what else may be said of him, Yvor Winters is the best example our time has to show of the poet who writes by *rules*, knows just what he wants to do when he begins to write a poem, and considers himself compelled to stick to his propositions in everything he sets down. He tells us in a note that he regards this book ⟨*Collected Poems* by Yvor Winters (Denver, Alan Swallow, 1962)⟩ as "a kind of definition by example of the style I have been trying to achieve for a matter of thirty years." Since his early poems are notably different from his later ones, this must mean, not that the style he mentions is in all the poems, but that the poems are arranged to show how and through what routes the style has been reached. These early peoms which Winters has seen fit to supersede are very much influenced by those of William Carlos Williams, but they seem to me better than any poems Williams has ever written. They not only show great spontaneity and imagination—an imagination really working with and in and *through* its subjects—but also a high degree of intuitive linguistic perceptiveness; above all, they are wonderfully free of the will, that Medusa-face that turns hearts and poems to stone. They are very much the poems of a man who, though not quite sure of what he is doing, is yet seeing and experiencing newly, freshly, in each poem as if for the first time, his world and the words by which it may be explored and lived. I believe this Winters entirely when he says, "Adventurer in / living fact, the poet / mounts into the spring, / upon his tongue the taste of / air becoming body." Among certain reviewers in the past it has been a commonplace to denigrate Winters's later poems by praising his earlier ones, but these first poems exist, and there are always going to be people like myself who prefer them. Their most surprising characteristic is their wonderful feeling for motion—one somehow thinks of Winters as inert—their feeling for color and light, set down with young uncertainty and eagerness. There are twenty-three of these early poems, arranged in what I take to be chronological order, and a group of excellent translations, before the later style makes its appearance, appropriately enough in a poem called "The Moralists." It begins, "You would extend the mind beyond the act, / Furious, bending, suffering in thin / And unpoetic dicta; you have been / Forced by hypothesis to fiercer fact." Here in full force is the kind of writing by which Winters wishes to be remembered: the strict metrics, the hard, obvious rhymes, the hard-jawed assurance, the familiar humorless badgering tone, the tendency to logic-chop and moralize *about* instead of presenting, the iron-willed determination to come up with conclusions, to "understand" and pass definitive judgments no matter what. As one reads, it gets more and more difficult to believe that a man's *life* is supposed to be contained in these pages, with the warmth, joy and sorrow, the disappointments and revelations that must surely have been parts of it. One can't help being struck by the poverty of Winters's emotional makeup; there are only a few things which seem to have made much of an impression on him. The principal one of these is what he conceives to be the function of the university intellectual, the teacher, whose role it is to instill "precision" in the students' minds. He believes, apparently, that in the arena of the university, the arena that opens out into the world of action, the essential battles of the mind are fought, and its heroes are those who teach "well," discern "the truth" (rather than *a* truth), pass it on, and so condition "the mind" of students to take care of itself, know good from evil, false coin from good, in any circumstances thereafter. In these matters, the teacher must first *know*, and as a result of what he knows, others may come to know, too. These are worthy enough themes, though one is inclined to question whether a teacher of literature, even one like Winters, can really have such a profound influence as all that. Though his thesis is grave and perhaps important, the poems in which he sets it forth are unfortunately Winters's worst, full of his tiresome truculence, his mien of sage and defender of the faith, his dogmatic, hectoring manner, his rhymed belaboring of concepts and abstractions, and in general all the rarification, stiffness, and peculiar dusty dryness of the style he has been "trying to achieve for a matter of thirty years." It seems to me that it is this being "hot for certainties" and the uncompromising insistence that he has got them that has ossified Winters as a poet, cut him off from the early exploratory "accessibility to experience" that promised so much, and actually deprived him of any important or even very interesting subject matter. The tightness and concision of his writing are bought at altogether too high a price: that of deliberately stifling the *élan* and going-beyond that first-rate poets count on blindly and rightly. This results in calcified and unlikely poems, academic and "correct" according to the set of rules one has arrived at, and doubtless from this standpoint capable of being defended logically and/or eloquently, but only in arguments which are, in view of what they come to in the poems themselves, simply beside the point. It is evident that this kind of poem is principally an exercise of the logical faculties, a display of what one has come to deem proper as to method and statement. Even this might be all right if the qualities Winters has chosen were not so drastically limiting, or if his means of embodying them were other than they are. The kind of thinking and writing that Winters fosters is good enough for small poets, and doubtless enables them to concentrate and consolidate their modest gifts in a way which is as good as any they may hope for. But for a big talent, which must go its own way, it is and probably has been ruinous, and I am haunted by the vision of a Yeats or Dylan Thomas or W. S. Graham laboring diligently to get into the same Stanford Parnassus with J. V. Cunningham, Donald Drummond, Howard Baker, and Clayton Stafford. The trouble with verse of this sort is, quite simply, that it is all but dead, not only to the power of giving something of the mystery and fortuitous meaningfulness and immediacy of life to the reader, but dead also, and from conception, to the possibilities of receiving these upon itself.

This is not quite, however, the whole story on Winters's later verse. From poems like "To the Holy Spirit" and "Moonlight Alert," one comes to see that Winters's most enduring and characteristic theme is not really the teacher's part, but Nothingness, and the perhaps illusory stand of the mind against it. The pessimism and stoicism and honesty of his poems about himself, not as laying down the law in the William Dinsmore Briggs Room, but as a solitary night-watching man, are utterly convincing. Though they are not free of the moralizing tendency that ruins so many of the later poems, the occasions for this and his other familiar qualities seem more nearly right, and for that reason, and because of Winters's awesome unflinchingness in the face of approaching old age, they are good poems, and compare favorably with the best of the early ones. Maybe these few pieces are worth all the enforced sterility; I suppose it can be argued that good poems are worth whatever price must be paid, even this one. Yet I am immensely saddened by most of Winters's work, and find the touch of it lifeless and life-destroying. But more than that, I cannot imagine anyone sincerely loving his poems or being changed, illuminated, helped, or even significantly instructed by them. And there it is.

KENNETH FIELDS

From "The Free Verse of Yvor Winters and William Carlos Williams"

Southern Review, July 1967, pp. 767–74

The Early Poems of Yvor Winters 1920–28 contains some of his uncollected early poetry as well as his first three volumes of poems (the third written in free verse) and all of the free verse that appeared in his fourth volume. The earliest poems were written when Winters was nineteen years of age, the latest when he was twenty-seven; most of these poems are now made available for the first time in more than forty years. The book offers a wide variety of forms, including two short plays and three prose poems. And the author's brief autobiographical introduction is extremely interesting.

The book should be of great value to the serious student of the experimental poetry of the tens and twenties, for Winters' free verse is more vigorous and much more varied than that of any other writer of the form. More successfully even than Williams he introduces complexities of feeling into his poems by way of rhythmical devices. Most of the poems of the first book, *The Immobile Wind* (1921), are written in standard meter, as for example, "Death Goes Before Me," or "The Wizard"; but several of them, though in standard meter, employ a short line that frequently runs over, the effect being a rapidity resembling his later free verse, as in the following poem, "The Morning":

The dragonfly
Is deaf and blind
That burns across
The morning.

And silence dinned
Is but a scream
Of fear until
One turns in dream.

I see my kind
That try to turn:
I see one thin
Man running.

Like others from *The Immobile Wind*, the poem is dominated by the obscure feeling of the inability to get beyond one's own private and hallucinatory perceptions, and the rapid movement serves to intensify the feeling. It is helpful to compare the feeling and movement of the poem with a much slower one written only slightly later—"Hill Burial," from *The Bare Hills* (1927):

Goatherds inevitable as stones
And rare
As stones observed.

Jesus Leal
Who aimed at solitude,
The only mean,
Was borne by men.

Wet air,
The air of stone.

He sank to God.

The poem is written in slow free verse, and the feeling is much calmer than that of "The Morning." The association of stoniness with the non-living may be found in other poems; the quiet association, in two lines, of water, stone, and air gives a sense of finality to the last line in which the lowered corpse sinks like a drowned man. The sequence of poems that follows is in part seasonal, and the finality of "Hill Burial," the first poem in the book, is necessary for the irony of the spring poems wherein significant renewal is denied; it is "spring, the sleep of the dead." Much later, in the *Fire Sequence* (1927) Winters reintroduces the theme in "Tragic Love" which is in part a denial of resurrection or incarnation after death, pantheistical or other. The only renewal, as one sees in another spring poem, "Quod Tegit Omnia," is to be found by the individual poet encountering and transforming new experience.

"The Morning" and "Hill Burial" are both minor poems,

the second much more successful than the first and beautifully written, but they illustrate something of the rhythmic variety to be found in the collection. *The Bare Hills*, the best of the individual books, is written in free verse: in part I the movement of the poems is predominantly slow; in part II it is predominantly fast; part III contains two prose poems. The poems of the *Fire Sequence* together with those from *The Proof* (1930), wherein the subjects have become increasingly more violent, are mostly written in very rapid rhythms; for especially successful examples of this rhythm one should examine "November" and "Primavera."

But from the very beginning Winters also sought complexities of other kinds, even in the simplest of his poems, the one-line, six-syllable poems of *The Magpie's Shadow* (1922). As Winters himself has written, the primary influences on these poems were certain translations from the American Indian poetry. One gets, in the best of *The Magpie's Shadow*, instantaneous perceptions of arrested movement, such as "The Walker": "In dream my feet are still." But the less obvious device is the association of two perceptions in a single line, the perceptions sometimes related, as in "Still Morning": "Snow air—my fingers curl." Or sometimes unrelated, as in "Sunrise": "Pale bees! O whither now?" But the poems also show the influence of the Imagists and their theories. The image, according to Pound, was "an intellectual and emotional complex in an instant of time," and the poet was instructed to "use no superfluous word." As for the association of perceptions, the chief preoccupation of Fenollosa was with "words highly charged" by juxtaposition and by "interaction." And Pound was fond of citing Aristotle's definition of metaphor as the "swift perception of relations." *The Magpie's Shadow*, simple but deceptive, seems to achieve the aims of the Imagists better than they themselves were usually able to do; the best features of the Japanese translations are there without the sentimentality, and Winters' poems are far more concise. Moreover, the complexity of feeling does not rely on the artificial and, I gather, inaccurate description of the Chinese character given by Fenollosa to account for "Moon rays like pure snow" which, rendered in English, cannot escape flatness. And the best of these small poems are certainly much finer than Pound's celebrated "In a Station of the Metro." A close study of this book seems to me an excellent way in which to understand some of the subtle methods of the Imagists, methods that Winters clearly had learned.

I shall leave the reader with a final example, adding that the procedure of complex associations continues throughout the rest of Winters' work. In the poem that follows, the image is one of arrested motion, for it fixes the transitory moment of noon, but it is a perception of rapid movement as well, the instantaneous report of noon traveling along the road with the speed of the sun. "God of Roads": "I, peregrine of noon."

But of course *The Magpie's Shadow*, though beautiful, is a simple book with obvious limitations. However, in the later and more important poems the complexity, frequently amounting to obscurity, does not come from the method only, but from many of the particular ideas that Winters held; in these poems one finds natural description just as sharp as that of Williams at his best and frequently sharper, but there is none of the simplemindedness of "The Red Wheelbarrow." The details are sharp partially, I think, owing to the assumption, found also in the Imagists, of the virtue of the unique perception; but such perceptions for Winters are often attended by a curious feeling that the unique perception seems somehow unreal—in spite of the accurate description. Much of the hallucinatory feeling in the first stanza of "José's Country," for example, proceeds from the separation of the visual perception, which is lovely, from the audible:

A pale horse,
Mane of flowery dust,
Runs too far
For a sound
To cross the river.

Sometimes, owing perhaps to Winters' early interest in protozoology and biology and to certain discoveries about the nature of matter by modern physicists, the feeling comes from an intense magnification of natural events which are normally unseen, as for example in "Primavera": "Atoms seethe into / the sun . . ." and "the / chlorophyl booms." The physical universe that Winters seems to be confronting in isolation, especially in the later of the experimental poems, is very close to the universe of atomic physics of the twenties as described by Whitehead and others. It is marked by relativity of time and space which renders relationships arbitrary; hence, perhaps, something of the method of disparate associations. It is marked by the interchangeability of matter and energy in a kind of Heraclitean flux, in which apparently solid matter is divisible into atoms in constant motion. From "The Vigil" *(The Proof)*:

The floor burns underfoot, atomic
flickering to feigned rigidity: God's
fierce derision.

And from "The Streets":

the wilderness, inveterate and
slow, a vastness one has
never seen, stings to the tongue and
ear. The terror in the taste
and sound of the unseen has
overwhelmed me; I am on the
mythical and smoky soil at last—

The comfort implied by *at last* is ironic and is rejected later in the poem. Little comfort is to be had in a world where immobility is death (as in "Hill Burial," above) and where change is terrifying confusion; often related to these ideas are the metaphoric uses of stones, and of bees and flame, and the recurrence of words such as *crumbling*. In this world of real deprivation and violence, the observer is alone, the only constant feature being his own identity.

Moreover, the existence of the identity itself is tenuous in these poems, insofar as the observer is a participant in the flux. Robert Jungk, in *Brighter Than a Thousand Suns: the story of the men who made the bomb* (1958), provides a useful summary of the relevant scientific theories of the time (for instance, the marvelous quotation of the physicist, James Franck: "The only way I can tell that a new idea is really important is the feeling of terror that seizes me"); Jungk writes, "in the act of observing submicroscopic processes it was no longer possible to draw any clear distinction between the subject (that which observed) and the object (that which was observed). . . ." This lack of distinction between subject and object is regarded with horror by the poet; thus in many of the poems one finds the beautiful and violent world of sensation impinging upon the identity, threatening to overtake it, as in the line from the early poem, "Alone": "My brain is a thousand bees." It is important to point out the danger of exaggerating the scientific or any other theories, especially in the very early poems; the theories furnish terms for describing states of mind which Winters seems to have developed quite early from a close and intense consideration of the immediate natural world and the relationship of his perceptions to it. But the plight of the identity confronting the atomic "feigned rigidity" of the material world, as seen, for instance in "Snow-Ghost," is a theme which often recurs in the poems. The plight is stated with precision in "The Longe Nightes When Every Creature . . .":

> I lie alone an eddy
> fixed, alive with
> change that is not I:
> slow torture
> this to lie and hold
> to mind against the stream
> with nought
> to seize on.

As in the other poems, no solution is offered save endurance; here, there are no answers—only the evocations of desperate situations. The conclusion of the poem leaves the poet without the slightest sentimental or romantic consolation for his "slow torture," in lines which are nevertheless nostalgic:

> The humming tongue
> burrows the nightwind
> of the nightingale
> that comes no more.

As I have remarked above, the rhythms of the later poems are most often rapid and thus more or less appropriate to their subjects, appropriate to the nervous energy of despair.

One solution, however, suggested many times in the poems is the preservation of the identity by the act of writing; that is to say, the poet becomes more alive as his perceptions are more unique, more specifically his own; thus style assumes great personal importance. As I have shown, the basis of *The Magpie's Shadow* is the unique perception. The poem is to have its own integrity, generally a rhythmic coherence in which intense perceptions are linked together by some kind of association. The danger, as Winters himself has written elsewhere, is that the poem may become "a kind of verbal hallucination," its relationship to experience threatening to become private and almost entirely linguistic. On the one hand, one has the terror of the unrelieved and immediate universe, and on the other, the arbitrariness of poetry, the private vision,

> this
> oblivion, this
> inert labyrinth
> of sentences that
> dare not end.
> ("The Cold")

"Genesis," from *The Bare Hills,* seems to be about the poet who is locked within his own perceptions, the perceptions being intense states of mind evoked by common objects. The complete poem:

> The door became a species of mystery.
> It opened inward or stood closed.
> It was the twofaced god that was able to learn
> nothing, save its own reversible path.

The predicament may owe something initially to Stevens, but, as one gets it in the poems, it seems more real than Stevens' problems concerning reality and the imagination. For the most moving and most comprehensive poem on the subject, one should read "The Bitter Moon." The poem is difficult to discuss out of its context in the *Fire Sequence,* so I shall not attempt it here, except briefly to point out the association of the poetic vision with the insubstantial light of the moon and, elsewhere, with electricity, the constant element in the interchange of matter and energy. The title depends upon the preceding poem where the vision is seen as

> this
> crystallized electric hatred
> bitter with no sense
> it is a dream.

More than ten years later Winters was to write about his Imagistic days:

> Where is the meaning that I found?
> Or was it but a state of mind,
> Some old penumbra of the ground,
> In which to be but not to find?
> ("A Summer Commentary")

Throughout *The Early Poems* the themes of hallucination and madness are to be taken as real threats; this explains some of the curious feelings evoked by the poems. Winters' insistence on examining these states of mind, while taking his ideas and methods seriously, is both honest and courageous. The best of the later traditional poetry is greater than anything in *The Early Poems,* and it is well-known that he abandoned many of the early ideas and methods. However, it is also true that certain aspects of the ideas and something of the methods remain in the later poems; but that is another matter. The early poems, as they are, have their own independent virtue.

HOWARD KAYE

From "The Post-Symbolist Poetry of Yvor Winters"

Southern Review, Winter 1971, pp. 176–97

Yvor Winters' reputation as an important, if eccentric, critic is well established, but his poems are another matter. They seldom appear in anthologies. In discussions of modern poetry, he is usually omitted; or if he appears, it is in a monitory reference to the dangers of academic formalism. His poetry is not taught in college literature courses, except by a few of his former students. He is so little known as a poet that one can scarcely speak of a standard view of his poetry, but as far as such a view exists, it is expressed by Stanley Edgar Hyman: "Much of it is occasional or dedicatory in nature, all of it is restrained, and it simply depends on one's personal preference whether it seems graceful and quietly moving or academic and deadly dull." The faults most often imputed to Winters' poetry are summarized by James Dickey, who speaks of "the strict metrics, the hard, obvious rhymes, the hard-jawed assurance, the familiar humorless badgering tone, the tendency to logic-chop and moralize about instead of presenting."

If most readers of poetry today think of Winters' poems at all, it is in these terms. Yet among certain men, Winters enjoys an entirely different reputation as a neglected poet of major proportions. Most of those holding this view have been his friends and students, but that is far from the whole story.

> Yvor Winters is, I now strongly suspect, our great unacknowledged contemporary poet. (Frederick Morgan)
>
> Yvor Winters' *Collected Poems* contains at least a half-dozen lyrics that are, though unassuming, the equal of anything written in the United States since the death of Emily Dickinson. (Hayden Carruth)
>
> Among American poets who appeared soon after the first war he is, Crane being dead, the master. (Allen Tate)
>
> Surely, Yvor Winters is an immortal poet, a poet of great kindness and stamina. (Robert Lowell)

> I believe he must be acknowledged the greatest living poet of the English language. (Alan Swallow, Winters' publisher)

Though his admirers are far-flung, Winters is still largely a coterie poet. It is not that he wrote only for the delectation of a select group, but most critics and readers have never discerned his intentions and recognized his accomplishments. It is easy enough to attack him on the basis of his weakest poems, some of which justify Dickey's objections. There are poems, however, which have nothing to do with Dickey's description, and these are poems that his detractors ignore. Most of his best poems are written according to a method or style which he called post-Symbolist. This is, briefly, a way of charging sensory details with abstract meaning: a particular variety of metaphoric language. The post-Symbolist method repairs deficiencies in each of the two other principal methods Winters used at various times to relate the concrete and the abstract: the style of his free verse and his later abstract style.

In the twenties Winters was writing experimental free verse which was rapid in movement, spare, and frequently violent. He was influenced by Williams, by the Imagist movement and its offshoots, by translations of American Indian poetry. His early poetry aimed at intensity of individual images and lines; rational content was not a primary concern. He described his early poems later as "material cohering by virtue of feeling and rhythmic structure, and very little by virtue of intelligible theme." Some of the poems confine themselves to description, or description for the sake of mood, and make no attempt to deal with ideas.

> the small boys
> shriek amid white rocks,
> run at the river;
> and the sky has
> risen in red dust
> and stricken
> villages with distance
> till the brown feet quiver
> on the rock like
> fallen eyelids and the
> goat's hoof, tiny,
> jet, is like a twig about
> to burst in flame.

In some of the early poems Winters deals with intellectual themes, but never straightforwardly. For a brief time in the twenties he favored the term "anti-image" to describe an idea in a poem. An idea was only poetic if it fused with sensory images and sound patterns, or other, apparently unrelated, ideas, to become an anti-image. The single idea, directly expressed, had no place in his system. "Even perspicuous generalities do not constitute poetry." Intellectual statements sometimes appear in the early poetry, but they never have an easily definable relation to each other, and to the other elements of the poem. If the ideas were obscure, Winters believed, this might facilitate the real work of the poem. This is a section of "Quod Tegit Omnia":

> When
> Plato temporizes on the nature
> of the plumage of the soul the
> wind hums in the feathers as
> across a cord impeccable in
> tautness but of no mind.

"Quod Tegit Omnia" can be explicated; it is about the poem as something that exists both within time and beyond time. But the meaning is fugitive, associative; and to recall the *Phaedrus* with its analogy of the soul to a charioteer driving two winged steeds is only to come within conjecturing distance of the sense of the passage I have quoted.

When Winters switched abruptly from free verse to regular meters in 1928, he began to make increasing use of undisguised abstraction in his poetry. He was no longer opposed to perspicuous generalities. Most of his poems still depended primarily on sensory detail, but by the time of *Before Disaster* (1934) he had developed an almost purely abstract style, and he wrote in this style intermittently throughout the rest of his career.

> Passion is hard of speech,
> Wisdom exact of reach;
> Poets have studied verse;
> And wit is terse.

The influence of the plain-style poets of the Renaissance, especially Ben Jonson, is perceptible in some of these poems. One frequently expressed view of his poetry as a whole is that it slavishly imitates Renaissance models; Winters is a warmed-over George Gascoigne. This is true to a degree of those poems in the abstract style, though there are other influences, and though some of the poems are vigorous and memorable whatever their affinities; but his abstract style is only a minor part of his mature poetic work. It always exasperated Winters to be taxed with rewriting Renaissance poetry; he knew that his most characteristic and important poems were based on post-Symbolist methods which had nothing to do with the plain style of the sixteenth century.

Winters' abstract style tends to be heavy-handed. It is frequently severe and portentous, inflexible in its solemn tone. Its heavy gravity is sometimes in excess of a fairly simple or obvious theme.

> He who learns may feed on lies:
> He who understands is wise.

It often seems to hover on the verge of wit and incisiveness, but to fall short.

> The prince or statesman who would rise to power
> Must rise through shallow trickery, and speak
> The tongue of knavery, deceive the hour,
> Use the corrupt, and still corrupt the weak.

The notion is very likely true, but the statement seems oversimplified. He did not find the abstract style a completely satisfactory medium in which to deal with ideas. He needed a method which would convey the ideas while retaining from the imagistic free verse the sensory vividness and sensitivity to sound which made him one of the great experimental poets. This method was the post-Symbolist one.

In post-Symbolist poetry, as Winters uses the term, sensory details are presented in language which also conveys philosophical ideas. The method depends on a heightened sensory awareness which he attributes to the Symbolist poets. Instead, however, of the Symbolist effort to isolate sensory vividness from rational meaning, the post-Symbolist poet gives us "the sharp sensory detail contained in a poem or passage of such a nature that the detail is charged with meaning without our being told of the meaning explicitly, or is described in language indicating such meaning indirectly but clearly." Abstract statement may be used to point up the meaning which the language of the sensory details reveals. "We have a theme of some intellectual scope with enough abstract statement to support the theme; theme and abstract statement charge the imagery with meaning, with the result that the imagery has the force of abstract statement." The poems Winters first used to illustrate the method, and which he considered the classical examples of it, were Valéry's "Le Cimitière marin" and "L'Ébauche d'un serpent" and Stevens' "Sunday Morning."

His use of the post-Symbolist method can be seen in "Sir Gawaine and the Green Knight." The poem, on the narrative and descriptive level, follows the medieval story; on the level of ideas, it deals with the relationship of the rational to the unconscious mind, of man to nature, and of the artist to his experience. The imagery treats these intellectual questions at the same time it recounts Gawaine's adventures. I quote the first and the fifth stanzas:

> Reptilian green the wrinkled throat,
> Green as a bough of yew the beard;
> He bent his head, and so I smote;
> Then for a thought my vision cleared.
> . . .
> He beat the woods to bring me meat.
> His lady, like a forest vine,
> Grew in my arms; the growth was sweet;
> And yet what thoughtless force was mine!

The adjectives "reptilian" and "wrinkled" imply the alien qualities of the knight, who with his lady represents the alluring forces of blind nature and the unconscious mind: a kind of death. This suggestion is reinforced by the funereal yew. Sir Gawaine must resist the urge toward descent into the unconscious by asserting his own rational identity; and this theme is introduced by "thought" in the last line of the first stanza. In the fifth stanza, "thoughtless" similarly indicates the direction of the poem's abstract meaning. Beginning to merge with the lady, pure sense, Sir Gawaine feels an access of power; but this, we see, is the growth of mindlessness, the power of the brute. The stanzas can be read purely as description, but in the context of the poem they take on a more specific and abstract meaning.

In Winters' view this type of poetry works in a discernibly different way than other methods of combining concrete detail and abstract meaning. In Symbolist poetry meaning is inseparable from sensory detail, but it is not meaning in his sense. The Symbolist poet emphasizes the connotative rather than the denotative aspects of his language. He works with the feeling or the tone of meaning rather than with an actual paraphrasable rational meaning. In post-Symbolist poetry on the other hand, according to Winters, "we have the tone which convinces us that the details have meaning; but we also have the meaning, and the meaning is of quite as fine a quality as the rest."

The Renaissance poem generally uses imagery in the form of explicit and fully developed similes or metaphors. The theme is stated, and then a figure is provided to illustrate it; and the figure is merely decoration. "The vehicles are more interesting than the tenor: therefore they are ornaments, and the tenor—the essential theme—suffers." Ideally, in the post-Symbolist poem, "sense-perception and concept are simultaneous; there is neither ornament nor explanation, and neither is needed." The distinction between these types of imagery seems to be quantitative; the Renaissance vehicles Winters calls ornamental are not devoid of thematic significance, but may be less closely involved with the articulation of the poem's abstract ideas than is the case with a few poems which fulfill his ideals. Winters finds Donne's compasses in "A Valediction Forbidding Mourning" ornamental, though there is obviously a continuous parallel between compasses and lovers. I think Winters overstates his case, but there does seem to be at least a quantitatively different use of imagery between Donne's poem and Herbert's "Church Monuments," a poem which Winters describes as verging on the post-Symbolist method. "The thought is wholly and clearly embodied in the figures, phrase by phrase, and it could not have been so well expressed in any other way."

An abstract style on the one hand, without sensory details, and the metaphoric-ornamental and Symbolist methods on the other, where sensory vehicles eclipse the abstract meaning, bracket the sort of post-Symbolist imagery Winters praised in his criticism and used in his poetry. His fullest treatment of post-Symbolism is in his last book of criticism, *Forms of Discovery* (1968). He approaches the method not as an historical movement, or an influence transmitted from one poet to another, but as a type of reaction peculiar to a few poets in a romantic or post-romantic period. Under the rubric of post-Symbolism, he discusses F. G. Tuckerman, Emily Dickinson, Wallace Stevens, Louise Bogan, Edgar Bowers, and N. Scott Momaday. "These poets have in common with each other and with Valéry the modes of writing which I have discussed . . . but otherwise there is no marked resemblance among them." Other poets use the sort of imagery Winters has in mind, for example Robert Frost. Probably none of the poets who have written this way, with the exception of Winters and his students, thought he was using a distinct method, doing something special. It is a method that develops in one direction out of ordinary descriptive poetry, and in the other out of ordinary figurative language which conveys abstractions; at a point where the descriptive language is sufficiently charged with ideas, or the abstractions take on sufficiently concrete embodiment, we have what we can call post-Symbolist poetry. It is a useful way of describing the way some poems are put together, including Winters' own.

A poem like "A Spring Serpent," for example, is hard to approach except through the notion of a sensory vehicle with an implicit abstract tenor.

> The little snake now grieves
> With whispering pause, and slow,
> Uncertain where to go
> Among the glassy leaves,
> Pale angel that deceives.
>
> With tongue too finely drawn,
> Too pure, too tentative,
> He needs but move to live,
> Yet where he was is gone;
> He loves the quiet lawn.
>
> Kin to the petal, cool,
> Translucent, veinëd, firm,
> The fundamental worm,
> The undefinëd fool,
> Dips to the icy pool.

The poem seems to describe a snake in a garden, a rather peculiar garter snake. However, the pattern of his peculiar behavior—his wavering movement, grief, deception, purity, foolishness, and so on—is intended to alert the reader to a generalized meaning for the serpent. Winters' own explanation of the poem is fortunately available:

> The grief and uncertainty (for their own sake) are romantic traits, and so is the hedonistic sensuousness throughout the poem; the snake is a deceiver, and this is always true of the indefinable and shifting perception; his tongue is too pure, and pure poetry, the extreme form of romantic poetry, is poetry as free as possible from concept, from definition; lines eight and nine describe the snake but also summarize the romantic doctrine to the effect that true being can be found only in the moment of change . . . the last stanza continues with these ideas, but its first two

> lines emphasize the remoteness of the snake from all human concerns or intelligence, and the remoteness is proper to both vehicle and tenor.

The serpent represents, in fact, the Symbolist image.

The tenor is never explicit; nothing in the poem states that it is about Symbolist poetry. One problem the poem presents is how we know what the tenor is. It may be true, as Winters avers, that the ideas in the poem "are as well known among scholars as the dates of the civil war," yet to move from the poem's statements about a spring serpent to generalizations about romantic poetry is a path which may not suggest itself inevitably to every reader. It was this difficulty of *context* which, I think, prompted Alan Stephens to call the poem "cultish." Winters took the epithet to imply that the subject of the poem was trivial and of interest only to a small group, but I believe what Stephens meant was that the key to the tenor was available only to a small group. It is possible to read the poem and to believe it is about a snake. The poem requires some knowledge of Winters' ideas and attitudes, but certainly no greater amount of background study than is necessary to read Yeats, Eliot, or Pound.

In the post-Symbolist method, the tenor more often than not reveals itself through loaded words and phrases, words bearing more than their share of the abstract weight of the argument. The "tongue too pure" is an example. While the phrase could be glossed in descriptive terms—and it is striking as description—it really belongs more to the tenor than the vehicle. It is difficult to visualize. Sandwiched between two other adjectives, "finely-drawn" and "tentative," which can be visualized, it acquires by association more sensory specificity than it would enjoy by itself. While it works for the purposes of the vehicle, it is a word which, in the context of Winters' ideas, alerts the reader to the import of the poem.

The same function is served by the theological or Satanic references. "Pale angel that deceives" invokes the traditional association of the serpent with Satan, a deceiver and a fallen angel who lost his brightness. This is, momentarily, a different vehicle. If the whole poem is an elaborated implied metaphor—the spring serpent is a Symbolist image—then this line implies the metaphor: Satan is a Symbolist image. But the serpent, like the fallen angel, is pale, and the serpent still comprises part of the vehicle. Winters maintains the convention he has set up, the double stream of meaning; but he extends the implications of his characterization of the Symbolist aesthetic to more general terms of moral evil.

The last line of the poem sounds like pure description, but in context has considerable abstract significance. It suggests something more specific than a sense of strangeness or death. The icy pool is associated with the remoteness from human concerns which is a property of the Symbolist image, with the unimaginable world where Mallarmé's swans float, and with the fatal effect on the human intelligence of following an aesthetic like Mallarmé's. For the reader who has acquired a minimal familiarity with Winters' work these ideas are in the poem, and they are there by virtue of the post-Symbolist construction. ⟨. . .⟩

One of the most difficult of Winters' mature poems is "Midas," and I think the difficulty can be described as stemming from the unique variation of the post-Symbolist method which he employs in the poem.

> Where he wandered, dream-enwound,
> Brightness took the place of sound.
> Shining plane and mass before:
> Everywhere the sealëd door.
> Children's unplacated grace
> Met him with an empty face.
> Mineral his limbs were grown:
> Weight of being, not his own.
> Ere he knew that he must die,
> Ore had veinëd lip and eye:
> Caught him scarcely looking back,
> Startled at his golden track,
> Immortalized the quickened shade
> Of meaning by a moment made.

The tenor involves the consequences of the Symbolist aesthetic, and the vehicle is the story of Midas. (Winters viewed the romantic mystique as self-destructive, and therefore made Midas himself turn to gold, destroyed by the power he coveted.) The strangeness of this poem lies mainly in the fact that the vehicle, which in Winters' poems is usually concrete and sensory, is here often abstract or metaphoric. For example, the second line: "Brightness took the place of sound." On the level of the vehicle, this means that when Midas changed things to gold, they could no longer move or speak. But, expressed in generalized nouns, the idea becomes mysterious and elusive. This may be an imitation of the emotional effects of the Symbolist poem itself: a bending of style to imitate within limits the feeling of the poetry on which Winters is commenting. The tenor in "Midas" is established by the metaphoric connotations of the language of the vehicle, already abstract or metaphoric. "Brightness" suggests the self-contained aestheticism of the Symbolist poem, and "sound" its opposite in his system, the moral and rational view of human experience. In the case of "sound," vehicle and tenor are connected by a pun.

Consider another line: "Everywhere the sealëd door." The vehicle is metaphoric, with the sealëd door suggesting the world of substances which is sealed off from Midas by a barrier of gold which he creates. The tenor further generalizes the sealëd door, into the aesthetic barrier which the Symbolist poet creates between himself and the realm of moral understanding. (Compare Winters' characterization of Hawthorne seeking significance: "his groping was met wherever he moved by the smooth and impassive surface of the intense inane.")

"Children's unplacated grace" suggests the world of moral values from which the Symbolist poet has exiled himself. There can be no commerce between that world and his own, and the face, the concept of good, is empty to him. In the framework of the Midas story, the children, changed to golden statues at Midas' touch, stare blankly back at him. He is unable to establish any human relation with them now; he cannot "placate" their "grace," their humanity. As a narrative vehicle, the references to Midas are hardly straightforward, yet there is a pattern of meaning throughout the poem which relates to Midas, and simultaneously a pattern of meaning which relates to the Symbolist poet, and the relation between those two patterns is that of vehicle and tenor.

Like "Orpheus," "Midas" ends on an image more closely allied to tenor than vehicle.

> Immortalized the quickened shade
> Of meaning by a moment made.

This is hard to gloss in terms of Midas. It may mean that Midas, turned to gold in a moment, became meaning in the sense of an example to passersby. But "meaning" refers primarily to the meaning of the Symbolist poem, which exists only within the terms of the poem, in the conjunction of sounds and images and feelings. It is momentary and non-transferable, "an intellectual and emotional complex in an instant of time," as Pound defined the Image. "Immortalized the quickened shade" suggests something suddenly frozen, caught in the act. The transitory balance of emotions is crystallized into the immortality of the poem. The poet's gold is an image of the living mind.

It is the fine "shade of meaning," the nuance, that is caught by the poem. But "shade" may also mean the ghost of meaning, the lesser sort of meaning that is "by a moment made" and not "true" independent of the poem. Winters is aware that the "truth" of a poem depends on the momentary shades of meaning by which it is expressed. Still, he would draw a distinction between the kinds of "meaning" or the relation to general human experience in a poem by Mallarmé and one by Baudelaire. He would hold that Baudelaire lays claim to a dimension of meaning, a rational statement about human experience, which Mallarmé disdains. "Meaning by a moment made," then, while in one sense applicable to any poem, in another sense refers specifically to the "pure" aesthetic self-containment of the Symbolist poem. The phrase includes both an acknowledgment of the delicate magic of Symbolist poetry and a judgment of its limitations.

Winters' post-Symbolist poems are the most characteristic and important of his mature work. They belie the common view of Winters as primarily a poet of abstractions; and if he is didactic and moralistic, these qualities inhere in poems displaying a surface texture of intense sensuousness. In discussing these poems I have concentrated on their abstract significance, in order to show something of the way his method works. This sort of analysis is one-sided, and it makes the poems sound mechanical. The poems I have discussed are extraordinarily perceptive in respect to the external world they describe and in respect to language; the precise yet evocative language is, in his own phrase, a form of discovery. The lines are living lines.

Winters is, I think, a major poet, a poet of no less stature than Williams, Pound, Eliot, Crane, or Frost. If this is true, then the low state of his reputation may seem to require some explanation. One problem is that to many readers his poems have seemed old-fashioned, having nothing to say to them, not "modern." His restrained tone, his emphasis on rationality and control of the emotions, his sometimes explicit moralism, are partly the basis of this feeling, along with the regularity of his metrical and stanzaic forms. Even poets like Frost or the early Robert Lowell, who use regular meters, are rougher in their rhythms, closer to speech. Neither Winters' ideas, his tone, nor his forms provide for many readers anything they can identify as modern, and it seems reasonable to them to conclude that he is irrelevant to the course of poetry in this century.

Winters himself considered his poetry modern in essential respects. "From first to last," he said, "most of my favorite poets have been relatively modern, and my matter and my methods have been modern." The methods he meant, in his mature poems, were those of post-Symbolism, which depends upon a willingness to base the poem on sensory detail, vividly delineated in itself; this is a development of the late nineteenth and the twentieth centuries. Winters' matter is modern in that it builds upon the romantic and Symbolist traditions in opposing them. As a "counter-romantic," he was on the same track as Yeats and Crane, though he was going the other way. J. V. Cunningham, who called him a "congenital romantic" despite Winters' notorious repudiation of romanticism, recognized that Winters' concern with self-control arises out of a specifically romantic context. The temptations which the poet of "The Slow Pacific Swell" must resist are the temptations which Wordsworth and Crane invited. "A Spring Serpent" and "Midas" are replies to Mallarmé, rather than abstract speculations about poetic pitfalls. But the last word on Winters' modernist credentials belongs to Stanley Kunitz:

> There is no definition of modernity that covers the wide range of poetic activity in our time. There are fashions in modernity as in everything else. For my money, any contemporary whose words stick in one's craw is modern enough to stand up and be counted among us. Winters' collection will be treasured long after most of his flashier colleagues have retreated into oblivion.

The fact is, though, that Winters' words have not stuck in most craws. The majority of reviewers have taken his poems in the abstract style as typical of his later verse; they have not been aware of how the post-Symbolist poems work, or what they are about. There is also a tendency to regard his poems as versified footnotes to his criticism, which has attacked virtually every well-known literary figure since the eighteenth century and earned Winters the reputation of a crank. Winters' best post-Symbolist poems, though their paraphrasable content is consistent with his critical essays, are less assertive and dogmatic. His ideas, in the adventure with form that produces poetry, are complicated and qualified; but critics have used his more immediately accessible poems in the abstract style to attack his "banality and oversimplification." The effect of Winters' criticism is to imply a position of exclusiveness: if you admire Robert Bridges, you cannot admire T. S. Eliot. His detractors have taken him at his word, and admiring the poets he denigrates, they have brushed aside his own poetry. Scornful of his claims for Elizabeth Daryush or T. Sturge Moore, they have assumed that Winters' poems must be more of the same.

Winters' poetry commends patience, fortitude, thoughtfulness, and self-control. He does not commend passion, perhaps the cardinal virtue to the modern mind, and this has led many readers to suppose that his poems must be passionless. For them, the self-discipline which restrains the forces of the irrational is the only visible element in the poems. It is as if a party of the gods were to yawn at the tableau in Venus' boudoir; were, unconscious of the activity caught beneath the remorseless fibers, to find the workmanship of Vulcan's net empty formalism.

The two phases of Winters' career are not entirely disjunct, and the later poems should be read in the light of the earlier ones. His early free verse is often violent, even to the point of hysteria. For example, "Song of the Trees," the last poem he wrote in free verse.

> Belief is blind! Bees scream!
> Gongs! Thronged with light!

The hysteria in these lines has gone about as far as it can, and though he complained that the speaker in the poem is the trees, the same quality of feeling is evident in poems written in Winters' own voice.

> Atoms seethe into
> the sun it is
> the solid
> whirling of the
> sun itself the
> chlorophyl booms.

When young, Winters was obsessed with what he called "the metaphysical horror of modern thought," and this was an immediate fear, almost a physical fear. The state of mind in the poems verges on madness, and the poet, the voice speaking, knows this. After 1928, the horror, the violence, the madness are restrained, but their effect on the poetry is as important as before; they are the impetus behind his adamant faith in reason. Irrationality, spontaneous impulse, "spiritual extroversion" seemed to him the first step to madness; and the annihilation of the mind was associated with physical dissolution. "Ruin has touched familiar air," he wrote of a garden, and ruin was always imminent. This is the central theme of his mature poetry; it is the theme even of so apparently "literary" a poem as "Midas." There is a stanza he added to "Sir Gawaine and the Green Knight" after it first appeared in the *New Republic*, apparently to make the abstract significance of the poem more explicit:

> By practice and conviction formed,
> With ancient stubbornness ingrained,
> Although her body clung and swarmed,
> My own identity remained.

The idea in paraphrase is that the sensual and instinctual self must be subdued by the rational self or destruction ensues—a paean to reason, one might say. But so much of the poem is devoted to the attractions of the lithe lady, the fatal allure of the irrational. Even the didactic stanza above, as Allen Tate observed, builds steadily to the climactic sensual third line. The poem is about a terrible struggle, not about an academic retreat from feeling.

> Her beauty, lithe, unholy, pure,
> Took shapes that I had never known;
> And had I once been insecure,
> Had grafted laurel in my bone.

To see Winters' later poetry as cold and emotionless is to miss half the point.

There is a hardness, a "cold certitude," an immobility in Winters' poems, but this is the result of the spiritual discipline which formed the man and the poems, not the result of congenital stolidity. He achieved the stasis of his poetry only at great cost, and the cost is evident in the poetry. In the last poem in his *Collected Poems*, Winters summarizes his career: his struggle to live his principles and to write truly, the derision of his critics. He takes for himself the metaphor of an immobile tree, and his critics would find this admission damningly apt. But Winters knew the implications of everything he wrote. "Bare to core, but living still!" he insists, in a line which implies a lifetime of renunciation. Let me end my essay, as Winters did his book, with "A Dream Vision."

> What was all the talk about?
> This was something to decide.
> It was not that I had died.
> Though my plans were new, no doubt,
> There was nothing to deride.
>
> I had grown away from youth,
> Shedding error where I could;
> I was now essential wood,
> Concentrating into truth;
> What I did was small but good.
>
> Orchard tree beside the road,
> Bare to core, but living still!
> Moving little was my skill.
> I could hear the farting toad
> Shifting to observe the kill,
>
> Spotted sparrow, spawn of dung,
> Mumbling on a horse's turd,
> Bullfinch, wren, or mockingbird
> Screaming with a pointed tongue
> Objurgation without word.

Gene Wolfe

1931–

Gene Rodman Wolfe was born on May 7, 1931, in Brooklyn, New York, to Roy Emerson and Mary Olivia Ayres Wolfe. He was educated at Texas A & M University, the University of Houston (B.S. 1956), and the University of Miami. From 1952 to 1954 he served in the army, and fought in Korea. He married Rosemary Frances Dietsch in 1956; they have four children. From 1956 to 1972 he worked as a project engineer for Procter & Gamble, where he invented the machine that manufactures Pringle's potato chips. He was an editor of the trade magazine *Plant Engineering* from 1972 to 1984, when he quit to write full-time.

Wolfe entered the science fiction field quietly with a series of eccentric short stories, largely published in Damon Knight's innovative *Orbit* original anthology series in the late 1960s. His first novel, *Operation ARES* (1970), was inconsequential, but his next, the novella cycle *The Fifth Head of Cerberus* (1972), raised him to major status in the field. It is Wolfe's first attempt at presenting an intricate and mysterious society through the accumulation of small details, with little overtly explained. Though some critics thought it unnecessarily obscure, most thought it revolutionary in concept and execution. Subsequent works have borne out the early promise. *Peace* (1975) is an ambitious rendering of the internal process of aging and the accumulation of memory (a recurring theme in Wolfe's fiction). *The Book of the New Sun*, a tetralogy (*The Shadow of the Torturer*, 1980; *The Claw of the Conciliator*, 1981; *The Sword of the Lictor*, 1982; *The Citadel of the Autarch*, 1983), is already considered one of science fiction's classic works. Wolfe received considerable praise for his stunning evocation of a far-future, decaying, once-great culture, narrated by an exile from the torturer's guild who forgets nothing. Wolfe's most recent novels are *Free Live Free* (1984) and *Soldier of the Mist* (1986). The latter is the first in a forthcoming series of books set in ancient Greece, narrated by a soldier who forgets everything on a daily basis, neatly inverting an earlier Wolfe motif.

Wolfe is also a prolific short-story writer, and has published two collections: *The Island of Doctor Death and Other Stories and Other Stories* (1980) and *Gene Wolfe's Book of Days* (1981). The former contains several of Wolfe's novellas, a length at which he excels. Especially notable are "The Death of Doctor Island," "The Eyeflash Miracles," and "Seven American Nights." Wolfe has won the World Fantasy Award for Best Novel (for *The Shadow of the Torturer*) and twice won the Nebula award. He is firmly established as one of science fiction's most engaging thinkers and careful stylists.

The Claw of the Conciliator is the second volume of a tetralogy-in-progress, *The Book of the New Sun*, which already seems assured of classic status within the subgenre of science fantasy. This alone would be faint praise, for science fantasy is a doubtful sort of hybrid in which the more decorative elements of science fiction proper—*Star Wars* hardware, dinosaurs, apemen, etc.—cohabit with the traditional chimeras of myth and legend. Characteristically, writers of science fantasy set wind-up heroes in quest of some grail across a bedragoned landscape quite as though Cervantes had not long since laughed picaresque romance off the literary map. Even when practiced by writers I ordinarily admire—Ursula Le Guin, Michael Moorcock, Brian Aldiss—science fantasy strikes me as inauthentic, coy, and trivial—circus costumery and paste diamonds, the lot of it.

Insofar as it is possible to judge any tetralogy by its first two volumes, *The Book of the New Sun* is a vast exception to that rule. Gene Wolfe has managed to do what no science fantasy author has done heretofore—he's produced a work of art that can satisfy adult appetites and in which even the most fantastical elements register as poetry rather than as penny-whistle whimsy. Furthermore, he's done this without in any way sacrificing the showmanship and splashy colors that augur a popular success. Quite a balancing act, as Wolfe notes himself in passing, when, toward the end of the first novel of the series, *The Shadow of the Torturer*, the narrator Severian, an apprentice in the guild of torturers, relates a tale he was told in his school days, "of a certain Master Werenfrid of our guild who in olden times, being in grave need, accepted remuneration from the enemies of the condemned and from his friends as well; and who by stationing one party on the right of the block and the other on the left, by his great skill made it appear to each that the result was entirely satisfactory. In just this way, the contending parties of tradition pull at the writers of histories. . . . One desires ease; the other, richness of experience in the execution . . . of the writing."

One could not ask for a tidier summing up of Wolfe's own achievement as an author—so long as one places the emphasis on "experience" rather than "richness" in that last phrase. Richness of imaginary detail is all too easily come by in a universe of unicorns and dragons: no sooner is one peril surmounted than Fancy, like the Hydra, supplies a pair in its stead. But experience—in the sense of relevance to a real life intensely lived—is precisely what escapist fantasies are escaping *from*. In allegorical fantasies (and science fantasy is, in its nature, allegorical) it is only possible to achieve intensity and depth if each of the individual elements of the fantasy—the swords, ogres, magic jewels—bears a weight of meditated meaning that intensifies and deepens as the tale progresses. (In the manner, say, of Wagner's *Ring* cycle.) In most hands these props are deployed with the artless caprice of children trimming a tree with their family's heritage of Christmas ornaments. Wolfe, however, is a Wagnerian, not a tree trimmer; his allegory actually has something to say, and it is said with art, acuity, wisdom and wit.

At the risk of compressing it into extinction, I would submit that Wolfe's central theme is the nature of political authority and the use of terror as a necessary means to secure social stability in any society (but especially ours). "Here the master and I do our business still," says Severian, as he pantomimes his trade as torturer in a masque performed at the Autarch's court. "We do it still, and that's why the Commonwealth stands." This cannot be said to be his last word on the subject; rather, the first—the subject up for debate. Here at the center of the labyrinth it is impossible to second-guess the outcome of that debate, but that it will be satisfying can scarcely be doubted.

This is not to say that the web is flawless. I doubt that any tetralogy has ever been written in which the second volume didn't come off as second-best. There are chapters in *The Claw of the Conciliator* that venture perilously close to pulp magazine hugger-mugger, and other chapters—one long interpolated masque, in particular—that are too archly Significant, after the manner of Thornton Wilder's *The Skin of Our Teeth*. (Wilder is a writer whom Wolfe resembles in other, and happier, respects.)

The acclaim and attention that *The Book of the New Sun* is winning among both critics and readers should further consolidate the reputation Gene Wolfe has won as a writer of short fiction. Eighteen of his stories are assembled in *Gene Wolfe's Book of Days*, a collection that aspires to unity by the doubtful device of matching the separate tales to national holidays: for Lincoln's birthday a story about the reintroduction of slavery as a solution to the problem of over-crowded prisons; for Valentine's Day a whimsy about computer matchmaking; and so on through the calendar. Actually, the stories suit their occasions fairly well, but sometimes I suspected that Wolfe was dipping toward the bottom of his barrel in order to accommodate his format. Even so, there are many first-rate stories, most notably the selection for Labor Day, "Forlesen," a novella in which all the morose absurdities of a life devoted to middle management job dissatisfactions are compressed into one day of high-speed, low-keyed nightmare.

A parting word concerning these books as items of commerce. Timescape Books has seen fit to wrap *The Claw of the Conciliator* in a cover so lurid that only confirmed fans who have passed beyond shame would dare to be seen taking it from a bookshelf. The book itself is handsomely produced. By contrast, Doubleday (all too typically) disdains the decorums and amenities of book publishing so arrogantly that they might more honestly dispense with typesetting and binding altogether and simply market Xerox copies of their author's manuscript. Gene Wolfe deserves better, and so does anyone who pays $10 for a book.—THOMAS M. DISCH, "A Wizard of the Fabulous," *WPBW*, March 22, 1981, p. 11

As a piece of literature, ⟨*The Book of the New Sun*⟩ is simply overwhelming. Severian is a character realized in a depth and to a breadth we have never seen in SF before; of all unlikely things, a detailed, likeable portrait of the skilled artisan as a young man is emerging here; courageous, professional—distasteful of the slavering onlookers as he breaks his victims' thighs deftly—rather wise but certainly unsophisticated, he is still being led around by his private parts. But that will change.

As a piece of craftsmanship, the work so far is so good that some of Wolfe's moves cannot be analyzed. All writing, fiction more than the rest, is organized illusion. We who are also in that guild each have a working knowledge of how illusion is generated, sustained, and brought to a climax. When we read the work of others, we can invariably detect how they do it, even when they don't do it the way we would. Or so I have always thought.

No more. I am in the presence of a practitioner whose moves I cannot follow; I see only the same illusions that are seen by those outside the guild. I know the cards are up the sleeve somewhere, but there are clearly extra arms to this person. I know the rabbit has been in the hat all along, but an instant ago the man had no hat. And though I saw him slip a rabbit at the last instant into a compartment that could hold only a rabbit, a gyrfalcon has come out.—ALGIS BUDRYS, *F & SF*, June 1981, p. 49

I have given up reading most "fantasy" epics; the horses in them are disguised cars and the women are inflatable; everybody speaks a mixture of Arthurian and Elizabethan, and the authors have never seen a wilderness except from inside a shell of ripstop Nylon, those who have seen one at all. Quick—ask any one of them to tell you the difference between a necromancer and a thaumaturgist. A castle and a keep. A baron and an earl. Still too hard? A mangonel and a ballista? Dzeus Piter save it, most of them even think Gene Wolfe *invents* his terms!

Gene Wolfe. Gene Wolfe writes speculative fiction. Technically, his *Book of the New Sun* tetralogy is science fiction, since all of the "fantasy" elements in it are located in a Terrestrial culture a million years hence, and are explicable as advanced science under Clarke's Dictum. ("A sufficiently advanced science is indistinguishable from magic," or words to that effect from Arthur C. Clarke, who may be right if we slop what we mean by "distinguishable.") Furthermore, Pocket/Timescape's press release on *The Sword of the Lictor* claims firmly that the tetralogy is science fiction and goes into an incoherent synopsis to prove it. But I wonder. I wonder if anybody would regard this book in any different way if it were set on some planet entirely unconnected to our Earth, and if the "magic" were magic *per se*.

No immediate matter. No *immediate* matter. The fact is that every would-be writer of fantasy epics ought to read this book, the two preceding volumes, and the fourth volume when it comes out some months hence. The effect may be to drive many of them right into some other field where elegance has not yet set standards; so much the better.

But matters catch up with us. For one thing, *The Shadow of the Torturer* has won the "Howard" Award of the International *Fantasy* Convention as the best novel of 1980, so my point, and Clarke's, are even further underscored while, for Timescape's blurb writers, here is a dilemma they will, of course, ignore. One thing over-rides marketing categories: a marketable gimmick, which is how they will regard it without reference to the sincere compliment intended by the convention or the gratification due an author who has earned it.

For another matter, I spoke of "this book" meaning *The Book of the New Sun*, which will surely stand as one of the most ambitious, most thoroughgoingly created, most highly individualized works of speculative fiction in the twentieth century. (Whether it will be one of the "best," or widely known outside our community, are matters which are still partially in the hands of the author and in the laps of the gods as well.) These qualities will continue to be evident no matter how the work is categorized, and, at this point, no matter how it ends. (My money says it will end very well; that is, the wordage of the concluding fourth will so deftly interdepend with the preceding wordage that the reader will perceive a major work of craft and art.)

These are all qualities, however, which stem from the author's energy, ingenuity and talent; the bent of mind that leads a man to put in a full work-week at a job (with whatever satisfactions and felicities it entails), and then, in the daily hours of early morning and late night, pursue the creation of a masterpiece where almost all his peers in a similar situation are content with yardgoods. Pretty good yardgoods, in some cases, with hundreds of thousands of satisfied readers. But things written to please, with a nice balance between the ideal and the attainable-under-the-circumstances. What Wolfe is doing for the community of writers, as distinguished from the community of readers, is to set a standard before which, as noted, even many full-time sorcerers' apprentices must quail. But what of *The Sword of the Lictor*, specifically?

For one thing, it enormously expands the landscape of its world. Severian the torturer in this volume undertakes an epic flight, away from a wrathful potentate and also from his own conception of himself. The sheer physical vistas this journey reveals are eye-popping. As he has done before, Wolfe casually adds post-factum revelations that stop you cold. You knew, for instance, that his world had mountains; they have been mentioned many times. In *Sword* we are shown, in this purposefully offhand manner, that they have all at some time been carved into the busts of now-forgotten monarchs. Hey, presto! the entire panorama stored in our minds has been transmogrified, and yet we don't for an instant feel that this is an instance of an author covering up an earlier lapse with an afterthought. No, the mountains have been that way all along, as Dorcas has been what she was, all along.—ALGIS BUDRYS, *F & SF*, April 1982, pp. 26–28

With *The Citadel of the Autarch*, we have the fourth and final volume of Gene Wolfe's superb long science fiction novel, *The Book of the New Sun*. Maybe now we can forget *The Shadow of the Torturer* and *The Claw of the Conciliator* and *The Sword of the Lictor* ⟨. . .⟩ and forget this title, which is confusingly interchangeable with those that misrepresent its three predecessors, and from now on think only of the novel as a whole, under the continuing subtitle which defines it as such. For *The Book of the New Sun*, all 400,000 grave and polished words of it, is far greater than the sum of its parts. So let us call it *The Book* for short, and spend some time in praise of the new Dante.

Well, not quite, perhaps. *The Book* isn't quite *The Divine Comedy* in four bumper parts instead of only three. It doesn't quite have the stature, though Wolfe does have something of Dante's appalling assurance; nor does *The Book* quite manage to shape reality so that an entire culture can apprehend something of the Word of God as He writes It out, layer after layer. But if Gene Wolfe is to be taken seriously—and however thrilling or pleasing *The Book* may seem, there is simply no point at all in thinking of its author as a creator of mere speculative entertainment—then he must be taken as attempting something analogous to Dante's supreme effort. With great urgency, layer after layer, he has created a world radiant with meaning, a novel that makes sense in the end only if it is read as an attempt to represent the Word of God. How intimate—how dizzyingly remote—how comforting or alienating that Word can be, each reader will of course discover.

We are on Urth, millennia upon millennia hence. So densely impacted with millions of years of human life is this world that even commercial mines, dug however deep into the ransacked planet, produce only bone and brick and artifact and icon, layer upon layer of human meaning, most of it indecipherable at first or second glance (just like certain passages of *The Book*). So the very earth radiates significance, as do its inhabitants, who live awash in ancientness, but who seem to glow with the fabulousness of their environment, strangely youthful, strangely assured. They have the deep polish of the citizens of the legends of childhood. But Urth is dying. The sun is red; stars are visible in the dark sky of midday. The starships of earlier epochs have become the dwelling places and headquarters of guilds themselves ancient. The mountains of Urth have been carved into giant sculptures of Autarchs, themselves fossils unearthed from deep mines.

Through this world—for three volumes—we have followed the adventures of young Severian, journeyman Torturer in exile for allowing a "client" to kill herself. It may be the case that for some readers Severian's earlier experiences may have seemed picaresque, somewhat random in nature, though colorful enough. But inexorably it becomes more and more clear that nothing in Severian's narrative—he tells the whole tale himself some time after he has become Autarch of the land of his birth—is accidental. Everything in his life becomes substance, and the reader can feel at times a kind of sweet cold terror as the true shape of that life begins to come clear. Much that happens to Severian has been lived before (in a manner which the fourth volume reveals) and is therefore twice-told, a code reverently to be broken. But much has not happened before, and represents something new on Urth. New on Urth is the Severian who will redeem humanity by becoming the New Sun/Apollo, or the New Son/Christ.

A miracle is required. The miracle (as T. H. White, quoting Malory, once said of Lancelot) is that Severian is allowed to perform a miracle. Early in volume one, he has—it seems inadvertently—acquired from a passel of traveling nuns their most treasured relic, the Claw of the Conciliator. The Conciliator is a Redeemer of a past age who may come again. At first the Claw seems to be a kind of weapon, but slowly we come to realize that—in direct contradiction of all the habits of science fantasy—it does nothing but heal. And the land blossoms where Severian sleeps. Only in the fourth volume do we see that the Claw is not the miracle, that it merely releases in Severian his true nature. He returns the Claw to its keepers. He becomes Autarch, in a scene terrible with desire and hints of the burdens to come. Animate projections from his childhood tell him something of what he must face—it is one of the hoariest of all science fiction clichés that he will soon be pitting his wits against, but Wolfe somehow manages to transform it (as he transforms so much else) into something moving, and rich and strange. And Severian goes to the Ocean, and stands upon the beach, where he realizes that:

"The thorn was a sacred Claw because all thorns were sacred Claws; the sand in my boots was sacred sand because it came from a beach of sacred sand. The cenobites treasured up the relics of the sannyasins because the sannyasins had approached the Pancreator. But everything had approached and even touched the Pancreator, because everything had dropped from his hand. Everything was a relic. All the world was a relic. I drew off my boots, that had traveled with me so far, and threw them into the waves that I might not walk shod on holy ground."

He then ascends the Throne.

Like Funes the Memorious in Borges' story, Severian cannot forget anything, so that *The Book* which tells his life is like a Theater of Memory, where everything stands for something else, where everything is a relic. Severian's life is a performance which he cannot help but memorize for any future occasion. He needs no prompting; he writes *The Book of the New Sun* to prompt us.

Volume four of this gift is harrowing, but is full of pleasures as well. There are four new-minted fables set into the text. There is Master Ash, who roots Yggdrasil-like back through time to observe Severian's Urth. There is time travel, space travel, teleportation; there are laser duels and gentle Mammoths; and delirium and dreams and the tying-up of loose threads. *The Book* is a feast and a eucharist; layer after layer, we have just begun to know it.—JOHN CLUTE, "The Urth and All Its Glory," *WPBW*, Jan. 30, 1983, pp. 1–11

Rarely has there been a work of genre fiction in which the import of the story is so elusive, to say nothing of the bare facts. Such was its appeal to the literary detective in me that halfway through this last volume I could resist no longer and phoned up my old friend and fellow Wolfe-enthusiast, John Clute, to suggest that we not wait the dozen or so years that even a masterpiece is supposed to age in the cask but set about at once to edit a volume of interpretive essays, supplemented with a glossary and other suitable rites of scholarship. John said, "Good idea," and immediately began to jot down some questions that remained moot after his first reading of the four volumes, but still seemed answerable. As a sample of the fascination of *The Book of the New Sun*, I can't resist quoting (with his permission) from John's list of conundrums:

"—Who is the woman lying bleeding beneath the Matachin Tower whom Severian almost forgets?

"—Just how is an Autarch actually chosen? And who is Paeon?

"—Are all the khaibits in the novel identified as such? And just how do exultants prolong their lives?

"—Is Cyriaca S's mother?" (After more reflection, John concluded that Cyriaca was not Severian's mother, and he developed an ingenious theory of who, amazingly, his mother might be, which I'm sworn not to hint at here, as John's entitled to dibs for his discovery.)

Do you begin to sense what very odd books these must be that they can leave such questions in the air and still generate such applause and loyalty? Of the four volumes *Citadel* is surely the oddest, for it is almost perversely anticlimactic in its denial of those pleasures usually associated with finishing a long epic narrative; there are no confrontation scenes between Severian and the many major characters from the earlier volumes (no accounting, indeed, for many of them), no poetic justice for the villains, no coronal ceremonies for the triumphant hero. The last eight chapters, which show Severian as Autarch, are one long dying fall, as though no music would suit the rites of passage to ethical maturity (for this is what the allegory is allegorizing; that much at least is clear) save the muffled drumbeats of a funeral march.

I realize this is not the stuff that blurb-writers' dreams are made of, but most sf readers by now will already have begun to read *The Book of the New Sun* and will know their own taste in the matter. Nor can I imagine that any reader of the first three volumes could be *prevented* from continuing to the end. At this moment the whole tetralogy seems simply too large for ordinary critical epithets to apply; one might as well scrawl "pretty damned big!" on the Great Pyramid.—THOMAS M. DISCH, *TZ*, May–June 1983, p. 9

ROZ KAVENEY

Foundation, February 1981, pp. 79–83

In a characteristically counsel-darkening exaggeration, Barry Malzberg has claimed (in his introduction to his collection *Out of Ganymede*) that it is science fiction which keeps alive the short story as a form in which quality and significance are possible in our time. A possibly more accurate formulation is that sf is a field in which it is what happens in a short story which gives that story its significance and in which that significance extends to things beyond the story itself. This is not the only recipe for quality in the form; it is however one recipe. This collection of Gene Wolfe's stories ⟨*The Island of Doctor Death and Other Stories and Other Stories*⟩—containing most of his major work over the last decade or so and a reasonable selection of minor work as well—contains a number of tales which are largely unchallengeable as artifacts in which little could usefully, or other than destructively, be altered or rearranged. They are witty and wise and all those other standard complimentary adjectives; a part of their efficient craft is the way in which they convince the reader, at least for the duration of a reading of the story in question, that something eternally valid and sensible is being said through this specific instance, some great humane and innocent truth.

Wolfe is of course quite unscrupulous in the means he uses to produce this effect in his reader, using transparently simple devices to condition our sympathy from the beginning of a story. Our attention is clearly focused on a protagonist who is usually largely solitary save for our attention, and is in some way deeply innocent whether by virtue of being a child or by dint of foreignness, amnesia or mental incapacity; the standard Wolfe protagonist is getting a rough deal under which he bears up admirably. In all of this Wolfe falls in with and usually transcends the models of sf as wish-fulfilment literature for alienated male adolescents. His other major concession to the standard behaviour of science fiction writers is the way that all his characters talk in quotations, in phrases or sentences clearly designed to be memorable outside their immediate narrative context—but as is rarely the case with Heinlein or even with Sturgeon, when a Wolfe character says something intended to be wise or touching or witty, it usually is those things while remaining something that that character might actually say. Wolfe is both artist and craftsman in a way which puts the alleged craftsmanship of sf's anti-art brigade to shame.

To descend to cases; Wolfe has produced a lot of slight and quirky shorts, many of them for anthologies like *Orbit*, and this collection presents a number of pleasant but forgettable very short stories as well as his two short masterpieces. Of the minor pieces, "Cues" is a squib which makes efficient points about the price of developing a talent, but ends in a pun—intended to clinch the matter—which makes the story misfire as the meaningful statement it was possibly meant to be. "Three Fingers" is an exercise in paranoid dread which proves that with a few simple tricks—having your protagonist eternally watchful and surprisingly knowledgeable—you can prepare the reader for a revelation about his antagonists which will be believed in dread, no matter how silly it is; in this particular instance it turns out to be the Disney Organization that the hero is running away from. "Feather Tigers" is an eco-Vietnam story in which aliens resurrect, unwisely, the fauna of Earth; "The Toy Theatre" is an exercise in the what-is-art, what-is-identity, which-is-the-mask-and-which-the-face mode, with an odd sexual twist at the end. Both of these stories are efficient, both are a little pseud; "The Toy Theatre" is memorable for a useful statement of Wolfe's methods:

> The Japanese puppet theatre. The operators stand in full view of the audience but the audience pretends not to see them.

In some ways the slightest but possibly still the best of these minor pieces is "La Befana", Wolfe's story of Christmas on a pauper colony with an unwelcome and xenophobic grandmother, an exercise in Little-Nellery which affected this reader more than anything since Edward Woodward reduced the Oxford Playhouse to liquid sobs with "Christmas Day in the Workhouse", a piece which "La Befana" somewhat resembles. Wolfe is always concerned with the effect of his story on the reader; these short pieces are his laboratory for trying new ways of achieving his designs on us and it is not wholly surprising that in some of them these designs are misjudged or mishandled.

Two of the short stories in this collection are precisely judged machines for putting the reader through a gruelling emotional experience and for making us *feel* that we are wiser and better for that experience. "The Hero as Werewolf" shows us the underside of Utopia, the left-over human beings who were judged unsuitable for inclusion in the programme of massive genetic improvement and who of necessity live on the hyper-intelligent but passive majority. Paul is competent but doomed; Wolfe knows his audience well enough not to try and make us empathize with a cannibal who actually gets away with it. This story also crystallizes a tendency which occurs from time to time in Wolfe's work—viz. a slight sentimentality about the small rural freeholdings doomed in an efficient but not necessarily just society. The father of Paul's retarded bride talks in terms—"There wasn't no more seed but what was saved . . . then one day just before Christmas these here machines started tearing up our fields"—which are paralleled in "The Eyeflash Miracles" by the self-justifications of Tib's murderous father—"Look what we been. Moving from place to place, working construction, working the land . . . Pretty soon now there won't be any call at all for people to do that. We've got to join them before it's too late", it is only fair that an author so adroit at manipulating sentiment should have an area in which he feels strongly enough to slip out of his usual fine verbal control into the American equivalent of Mummerset . . .

The title story is the definitive non-sf short story about the sf readership; it takes the observation that the Golden Age of Science Fiction is about twelve and turns it into a story about the agonies and pains from which adolescents escape into pulp literature. Or does it? Some critics have complained of the sorrows of young Tackman, his separated parents, the isolated big house, the drug addicted mother and her sexually equivocal companions, that all of this mechanism is impossibly melodramatic and phony, as of course it is, which is why the story is called "The Island of Doctor Death and Other Stories". Little Tackie's is one of those other stories; at the end of it the charmingly sinister Doctor Death rises from both death and the pages of a magazine and can say to him: "But if you start the book again we'll all be back . . . You're too young to realize it yet but it's the same with you". Wolfe uses alienation of both the artistic and the literal kind in order to represent that which he is saying purely and clearly; he gets to have his cake and eat it, as he does also with his fine artistic sensibility and love of trash by including wonderfully dreadful fragments of pulp embedded in the main text.

Wolfe's fondness for genre is also the driving force behind the less interesting (comparatively) of the longer stories in this book. In "Tracking Song" an amnesiac, probably a marooned explorer, finds himself among the semihuman cannibalistic primitives of a snowbound land and sets off in pursuit of the "Great Sleigh" which abandoned him. Wolfe makes aphasia and amnesia reinvigorate the tired old quest with its cyborg monsters, touchingly loyal semi-human girl and lost city; they seem new and memorable because the narrator is seeing these things and coping with these concepts for the first time. "Alien Stones" is a gray competent piece about the totally alien and different human ways of looking at things; "Hour of Trust" is a dated and dotty political piece in which the hero sides with the big corporations against the revolt of the hippies through a mixture of self-interest, and romantic pseudo-existentialism. He comes to a predictably grisly and deserved end in a way which points up an odd contrast in Wolfe's work between a theoretical anti-sexism and a tendency to portray women as bringers of doom. This tendency has a major outbreak at the end of "Seven American Nights" spoiling with emotional extremism a moving tale of cultural relativism and similarly cerebral concepts. The tale—in which a young Persian a century hence visits a financially, agriculturally and genetically bankrupt America—deals with the dangers of knowledge. America has poisoned itself with preservatives because it thought it knew how to use them; Nadan is destroyed by his quest for understanding of what the old America was like. The denouement reverses the sexual roles in the story of Cupid and Psyche—often taken as an allegory of the soul's quest for divine love—so that Nadan sees in sudden light that his beloved Ellen is in some way revoltingly mutated (possibly he only thinks he sees this, under the influence of a drug which he may or may not have taken). This descent into melodrama obscures the real core of the story, agnosticism about the human capacity to understand the other, and is less effective than quiet scenes like that in which the crippled actor Barry quotes Fitzgerald's paraphrase of Omar Khayman to Nadan and the Persian has no idea what he is on about. Wolfe seems in this story keen on the idea that there are limits to what we can or should seek to know and that those limits are never closer than when we are making a real effort to know.

This mysticism and other types of confusion predominate in the patchily brilliant "Eyeflash Miracles" in which a blind child wanders through an over-mechanized and inhumanly bureaucratized America spreading sweetness, light, hallucination and healing. This story is deliberately and genuinely heartwarming, if often mawkish in incidentals when Wolfe simply tries too hard. A characteristically embarrassing if partially effective moment comes when little Tib is talking to his father, who has been sent by the Government to kill him as a threat to public order, about the genetic project through which his powers were discovered:

> "The brains and spinal cords of the boys and girls involved would be turned over to the biologists for examination."
>
> "Oh, I know this story", Little Tib said. "The three wise men come and warn Mary and Joseph and they take Baby Jesus to the Land of Egypt."
>
> "No, this isn't that story at all . . ."

A difficulty with this story for English readers is the heavy reliance of its imagery on the Oz books; Little Tib is not only Christ and Krishna but also Tip, protagonist of some of the later of these. Appearances by Dorothy, the Scarecrow and the Tin Woodman are at least partially comprehensible to an audience which knows the MGM film but Wolfe should have foreseen the possibility that the story would have its effect spoiled for audiences, of which this critic is an example, for whom the final transformation of Tib's Negro sidekick Nitty into the Shaggy Man has no childhood reference. This miscalculation diminishes the story, though not sufficiently to deny it considerable power; Tib is far more convincingly a small child than most of the infant Messiahs with which sf has been plagued, and the implied society through which he joyously moves is, with economy, made utterly loathsome.

Probably the least successful of the stories in this volume, though one of the more ambitious, is "The Doctor of Death Island" which has, unlike "The Death of Doctor Island", the air of having been written to fit its title, and is, in spite of certain felicities, rather diffuse and perfunctory. Alvard, inventor of a type of talking book, has got life for pushing his partner out of a window, has been cryogenically preserved until a cure for his cancer could be found, and wakes into a society which will give him immortality but not freedom. It has been decided that murderers must be kept imprisoned forever, when a dangerous criminal on the streets might cost someone all of eternity. Alvard, with a few traditional twists of an improvised screwdriver, sets in motion an adaptation of his invention which will punish society for stealing his invention and force it to set him free to deal with it. He has not allowed—or perhaps he has—for the complexities of his emotional life and the hallucinations of the doctor who froze him. Wolfe is just playing games with stock themes here and for once the game means little beyond its own movements. In spite of boosting as an example of the moral superiority of the hick ("Farm people don't steal . . . but they'll kill you if they get mad enough") Alvard is one of Wolfe's least sympathetic protagonists and both author and reader are in consequence fatally uninvolved with his fate.

An unbearably deep involvement is on the other hand the artistic effect of "The Death of Doctor Island". Inasmuch as the title is a play on its predecessor, the title story, it is a cruel jest appropriate to the callous society implied in the story—here death is literal, irrevocable, and cruelly engineered. The title plays both on the destruction which at the climax the disturbed adolescent hero plots for his robot psychiatrist, and on the surcease which the machine is designed to provide for a majority of its clients in the interests of those whom society is more interested in curing. Part of the terror of the story comes from the way these psychiatric policies are made to seem rational and truly kind save at moments when we see them, as society avoids seeing them, in terms of abused dead flesh, and when it is revealed in passing how carelessly the bureaucracy decides its human priorities. If there is a weakness in the story it is that the conflict between Nicholas and the homicidal genius Ignacio is less interesting than the ultimate conflict with Doctor Island, less because of building to a climax than because Ignacio is imperfectly realized, consisting of a few mannerisms of speech and a few locally coloured confessions about boyhood in Brazil. The doomed Diana is a little thinly done as well; a charitable view would say that this is to make her fate less than intolerably painful, rather than because of Wolfe's difficulty with female characters. The story also rebukes a lot of the sf of the seven years since it was published by being set inside a big dumb complicated unlikely artefact which works both as metaphor for a cruel society and as a way of provoking a gasp of surprise from the reader.

Wolfe is not a prolific writer; this collection makes his work readily available and makes clear that he is one of the names most to be reckoned with, for all my passing cavils, in the literate science fiction of today. His efficiency puts to shame sloppier writers; his humanity more cold-blooded ones;

his usual rationality more muddleheaded ones. In his best work he utilizes or casts aside what faults he possesses, and so far has not begun to repeat himself in serious ways. This admirable collection could by itself almost justify the sf short story in its generation.

COLIN GREENLAND

Foundation, February 1982, pp. 82–85

What do you get if you cross Dr Susan Calvin with Conan of Cimmeria?

What is the connection between science fiction and sword and sorcery anyway? Peter Nicholls says, "It is an accident of publishing history . . . both have roots in 1930s pulp fiction, and they are often written by the same people." And read by the same people, to quite a large extent; which suggests that they fulfill comparable functions, though it doesn't seem to get us any nearer to understanding what those functions are. A hundred thousand readers effortlessly cross the gap that trips the critic up. Gene Wolfe's Book of the New Sun, of which these two volumes ⟨*The Shadow of the Torturer* and *The Claw of the Conciliator*⟩ make up the first half, portrays in detail the sort of feudal society of lictors and portreeves that is a prerequisite of sword and sorcery. There is a sword in it, the Torturer Severian's sword, which has, as is only proper, a name, *Terminus Est*. There also seems to be sorcery, but here Wolfe blurs the definition because, like Vance, Moorcock, and Harrison, he sets his feudal society in the remote future, after the rise and fall of a "high and gleaming culture." Relics (ray-guns, rockets, troglodyte mutants) indicate that we ourselves are still on the way up, and that the cultural acme will be pretty much your science fiction standard, technologically anyway. There will even be trading with other planets, so any apparently sorcerous doings in Severian's later epoch may actually have a basis in future or alien science. Clarke's Third Law (all together now): any sufficiently advanced technology is indistinguishable from magic. The apparent distinction between science fiction and sword and sorcery that the one works by logic and the other by magic, is only a difference of emphasis. Science and sorcery are culture-specific terms. As Merryn the acolyte says in *The Claw of the Conciliator*, "There is no magic. There is only knowledge, more or less hidden."

The next question is hidden by whom? indistinguishable to whom? To the characters, the readers, or both? One common spice in the future-feudal novel is a sprinkling of relics of forgotten science, things we can identify but the characters cannot: circuit diagrams in *A Canticle for Leibowitz*, nuclear fission in *Riddley Walker*. They reinterpret the science as religion, in accordance with the rationalist argument that faith in the irrational is only a temporary substitute for science. When knowledge is hidden, it is necessary to invent God; ironically, Wolfe calls Him "the Increate". The Book of the New Sun is named after a lost and possibly fabulous apocalyptic scripture which tells of the messianic Conciliator, who will come again as the New Sun to remake Heaven and Urth. Is the myth a fabrication on behalf of the Autarch, the absolute ruler, affirming his own quasi-divinity and pacifying the populace now that the old sun is cooling? Or is it really a divine prophecy? Science, in the scheme of eternity, may be only a temporary substitute for faith. Wolfe is a Catholic, as was Walter Miller.

Properly hidden, knowledge is power. Wolfe makes full use of the divisive structure of feudalism to show Urth as a world of class distinctions, conspiracies, underground citadels, and secret passages. Myths are propagated here. The apprentice Severian learns that torture and execution are a science, a "mystery", just as Shakespeare's Abhorson claimed. Even the Witches have their own guild. The story is also full of mysteries in the narrative sense. Some, like the mystery of the flying palace, receive explanations later in the text. Some, like the mysterious identity of Jolenta, you can work out for yourself first from evidence planted by the author. Some, like the mystery of the Botanic Gardens, which seem to distort time, space, and memory, are unexplained, and seems like divagations into the supernatural. When Severian steps backwards and finds himself inside a picture on the wall, unable to see the corridor where he had been standing a moment before, the sense of sorcery is the same, but a mechanistic explanation is provided immediately. Though not very convincing, the explanation alters the status of the incident and its relation to the phenomenological system, the universe of possibility, of the book. It makes (or should make) us adjust our perception of the incident, and therefore of the whole text. Perhaps similar rationalizations will be forthcoming for the Botanic Gardens in the next two volumes, *The Sword of the Lictor* and *The Citadel of the Autarch*. Other "mysteries" are like the Leibowitz circuit diagrams, mysteries only to the characters, not to us. What is this ancient painting of a warrior in full armour, standing in the desert with his strange, stiff banner? As Severian watches the old curator sponge away the grime, he sees that the figure's gold visor shows no eyes, only a reflection of more desert; and "there's your blue Urth coming over his shoulder . . ."

Puzzles like this are fun. Functionally they remind us that the society is really a future one, however antiquated its cultural forms. They put the science fiction in the sword and sorcery. The same thing happens, more subtly and inventively, at the semantic level of the text. The language generally refers to a conventional pseudo-mediaeval technology: length is measured in cubits; things happen "before the candle had burned a finger's width." Badelaires and vascula are only two of the many archaisms Wolfe has cunningly revived to supply the restored antiquity of the "posthistoric" world. "Wrong" words intermittently show us the true perspective of the restoration. In the dormitory of the apprentice torturers "Master Malrubius . . . was waking us by drumming on the bulkhead with a spoon." That bulkhead goes with other clues to reveal that the guild's Matachin Tower is a converted rocket.

Other writers who have recently provided science fiction contexts for fantasy stories have been content to blend the two genres smoothly, to entertain both audiences. The black hole and the biological engineering in Joan Vinge's *The Snow Queen* give a scientific imprimatur to the possibly unfashionable metaphors of Hans Andersen and Robert Graves. Wolfe's mixture works the other way round. There is an incipient black hole in the Book of the New Sun too, but it is the metaphor, for death both personal and cosmic, and the stimulus for people's preoccupation with eschatology. When science fiction constructions interrupt the discourse of fantasy Wolfe makes us think about them and work out their implications. One of Severian's companions, of uncertain history, recalls the time he used to spend aboard ship, reading. He says, "I asked the ship and she gave me another book." That a ship can be referred to by a feminine personal pronoun is a sentimental convention obsolescent in our own time. That a ship can be a female agent who responds to verbal requests takes us out of history into the domain of the impossible, territory of fiction. Severian's friend has just been wounded and is babbling of getting air to the compressors. The "wrong" word, referring to a vanished technology, directs us away from supposing that the female ship is some elfin barque, a product of sorcery. She must therefore be a product of a sufficiently advanced science, or at least of science fiction: readers of Anne McCaffrey will recognize a cyborg spaceship. The enigmatic sentence is even more complex than that. Since it is spoken in delirium, and the man ostensibly cannot be old enough to remember an age of spaceflight, what we have just identified as a science fiction trope also functions as a different sort of fantasy, the fantasy of delusion. Yet delirium is a state in which people, especially characters in fiction, offer unconscious revelations about themselves. The man has begun to talk a science fiction language we understand and Severian does not; we will be inclined to accept what he says. Just to tie the final knot, his mention of the female ship also suggests a clue, discernible only by hindsight, to his own identity. That's the kind of density Wolfe achieves in his writing, which is why it needs to be read over and over, and yields more on every reading.

Having thus switched the signs on us once, in the next chapter, four pages on, Wolfe does it again. The chapter is a tale within the tale: Severian tells us a folk story called "The Tale of the Student and His Son." In the tale, which has clear Greek and Arabian antecedents, the student's son, himself an artificial creature "fleshed from dreams", has to fight an ogre in the form of a naviscaput—a being half humanoid, half ship. On inspection, a mystery (which may seem to belong to magic and the irrational mode of fantasy) turns out to be science fiction; which on closer inspection turns out to be just another species of fantasy. Of an incident in his boyhood Severian says:

> It was in this instant of confusion that I realized for the first time that I am in some degree insane . . . Now I could no longer be sure my own mind was not lying to me; all my falsehoods were recoiling on me, and I who remembered everything could not be certain those memories were more than my own dreams.

Yet he continues to make so many claims for the infallibility of his memory that we start to disbelieve him. After one such protestation at the very beginning of the second volume he recalls an incident from the very beginning of the first, giving us a chance to compare—and yes, there is a slight disparity between the accounts. It is another mark of Wolfe's mastery that he manages to keep things shifting so subtly in a story of such overwhelming substance; for it is substantial, I have hardly touched upon a tenth of it, on the richness of detail and fertility of invention, on the humour and excitement and the resourcefulness of plot and sub-plot, the interleaving of scenes that fold out of each other in a way that makes you happy to lose track and bemused how he got them in there in the first place. The style is elegant and inventive. Even the archaisms are set so carefully that you can read it perfectly well without turning to the dictionary every few minutes. The characters are curiosities, every one. There is an error towards sympathy, a certain lack of malice: evil seems to reside, implacable, in the world itself, in the landscape, in the gaps between basically quite nice people. But we can put that down to the vague determinism of the whole scheme, and to a lingering naïveté in Severian himself. There is also (apart from the unionization of the Witches) a dull and fairly durable sexism throughout; but we can put that down as a necessary constituent of any pseudo-mediaeval society. I hope. It would be depressing if one of sf's newest and best writers were guilty of one of its oldest and worst crimes.

The story so far is of the gradual and partly accidental politicization of a slightly arrogant, rather ignorant, very likeable young man, rather like Perian in Aldiss's *The Malacia Tapestry*. Severian is more or less working for Vodalus, the radical, the outlaw. And yet we know full well from the very first chapter that by the time of writing his memoir Severian has become the new Autarch. Other than his unknown parentage and a few wild omens of election, there is absolutely no indication of this eventuality in the first half of his story. Lots of time to go, as Bamber Gascoigne would say, anything can happen yet. People are already talking of the Book of the New Sun as the next classic sf sequence, on a par with *Earthsea*, the Titus Groan books or even (ah!) the *Foundation* trilogy. It will be surprising if Wolfe doesn't earn—and achieve—that crown. It will be very surprising if, even with that conclusion foregone, he doesn't continue to startle, baffle, delight and enrich us all along the road.

C. N. MANLOVE

"Terminus Non Est: Gene Wolfe's *The Book of the New Sun"*

Kansas Quarterly, Summer 1984, pp. 7–20

The Book of the New Sun, which is made up of four titles—*The Shadow of the Torturer* (1980), *The Claw of the Conciliator* (1981), *The Sword of the Lictor* (1982) and *The Citadel of the Autarch* (1983) [1]—has been hailed by numbers of science fiction writers and critics as being the event of the 1980s for the genre. Certainly it is a highly wrought, intelligent, perceptive work, full of amazing bursts of imaginative creation. It is reminiscent of Peake and Borges in its richness of creation, its inwardness, and its questioning of reality. Its hero Severian the torturer, with his coolness of intellect, recalls Peake's much more evil Steerpike, or Borges's narrators with their methodical rationality. Whether the tetralogy is strictly science fiction or fantasy is long in doubt, apart from the fact that it deals with our earth a long way into the future when, as in Aldiss's *Hothouse*, the sun is dying, though here by its growing colder and feebler; the society described is largely of an antique or medieval character, with rituals, guilds, myths and religions, and few machines. Reference is made occasionally to a previous, aeons-past technological age of interplanetary travel, but that is all. The work is most evidently science fiction in its preoccupation with the workings of mind and its sense of the plasticity of identity. [2]

The story—and the word must be used advisedly in more than one sense—centres on one Severian, brought up in the Guild of Torturers in the citadel of the city of Nessus somewhere in the southern hemisphere of "Urth." He, like his fellow guild-members, has no known parents, but he has perfect recall of his life from an early age, and he tells us much of his apprenticeship, episodes during it, and the various stages of his elevation to journeyman torturer. One night in the cemetery about the citadel he helps Vodalus, enemy of the ruling Autarch, escape, and thereafter dedicates himself to Vodalus's cause. The Chatelaine Thecla, formerly of the inner circle of the Autarch's court, is sent to the torturers, perhaps (though later the Autarch is to give a different reason (CA, 204)) to be used as a bargaining counter with Vodalus, to whom Thecla's sister Thea has fled from the court. Severian befriends her and learns from her something of the Autarch and his House Absolute to the north of Nessus. When the order for Thecla's torture eventually comes through and her first "excruciation" has taken place, Severian gives her a knife in her cell: from the trickle of blood that subsequently comes under the door he concludes that she is dead, tells his masters, and is exiled, being sent as a carnifex or executioner to the "City of the Windowless Rooms," Thrax, far to the north. His journey to and beyond Thrax and eventually back again occupies the remainder of the series, during which he gains and later loses the miraculously potent gem, the Claw of the Conciliator, passes through the House Absolute, reaches Thrax and soon quits it and his office, travels further north into the mountains and fights in armies both for and against the Autarch and finally returns to Nessus as Autarch himself. During his journey he is intermittently accompanied by a variety of companions, including the treacherous female Agia, the enigmatic Jonas and a troop of travelling players under the direction of one Dr. Talos; a more constant friend is the devoted young woman Dorcas, resurrected by the power of the Claw. By the last book, however, he is on his own.

More than almost any other work of science fiction this book refuses us a context. We learn but little and late what process of human development has led to the strange society portrayed on Urth: for most of the tetralogy no one seems to know of the past any more. There are occasional "contextual" moments in the third and fourth books, but these provide no more than glancing and sometimes mutually inconsistent hints.[3] The House Absolute remains as mysterious as the House of Silence in W. H. Hodgson's *The Night Land* (which is set on an Earth after the sun has gone dead). What made the Autarch, quite what relations Urth now has with other worlds, what made the guilds, what god if any is behind the doings of life, are matters never fully clear. Mervyn Peake refuses much of the history of his Gormenghast in the same way; but for him it has always been as it is, and that is the ground of its being. Though Peake does not describe the early growth of Ritual or how the Groans became rulers, he is quite prepared to explain how the observance of the Ritual has become over time purely mechanical. In Wolfe's book we know that the torturers are used as a means of punishment for criminals and enemies of the Autarch, but why they should be tortured, since usually no information of value is to be gained, is left quite obscure. As for the nearby Guild of Witches, we know nothing at all of their function, only of their rickety residence. We know for what purpose, however limited, the Hall of Bright Carvings in Gormenghast was created: it exists to house the carvings of the Outer Dwellers of the castle that have won the annual contest for the finest and most beautiful, the others having been consigned to a ceremonial fire. We do not know, however, the full purpose of the Botanical Gardens in Nessus, with their many different gardens "Of Delectation," "Of Sleep," "Of Pantomime," "Of Antiquities," "The Jungle Garden," "The Sand Garden" and so forth: each is of course a different bioscape for the delight of tourists, yet each contains experiences that are far more than botanical.

Wolfe's method is in contrast to that of most works of science fiction. In Frank Herbert's *Dune* we have an overview of the situation: we know, sooner or later, what is going on, even down to the discovery at the end that the Guild of Steersmen depends on the drug melange from the planet Arrakis to pilot its way through hyperspace. We know the significance of Dune to the Harkonnens and the Emperor, we know what motivates the native Fremen and Paul Atreides. Similarly in P.J. Farmer's Riverworld series the whole object of the books is for the protagonists to gain a full understanding of what beings are behind the construction of a planet on which the whole of humanity has been resurrected, and this they do. Each stage reached has been cleared away by the machete of reason: almost always the hero finds that there is an explanation for what has happened, that everything makes sense. Even where the mystery is not plumbed, as in Arthur C. Clarke's *Rendezvous with Rama*, where the nature, existence, and source of the Ramans are never discovered, one is to feel that somewhere there is an explanation. Indeed, knowing and finding out could be said to be central to "science" fiction. Wolfe, however, suggests that the world is not subject to explanation, that rational enquiry is inadequate to comprehend it, is indeed almost out of court. Severian is not till late concerned at all with finding out about Urth. Nor does Wolfe offer us much in the way of an overview of Urth and its situation. His emphasis is much more on the locality of knowledge. He himself in the appendices to the books claims ignorance, pleading himself at the mercy of such information only as Severian's books leave him, insisting that language itself can only render an often inaccurate account of the speech, customs, and indeed beings of the world of Urth. Severian his protagonist frequently says he has perfect recall, but his recall covers only the limited sphere of his own life. Everywhere information and knowledge are local and hypothetical, and they remain so, though more hints are gathered. Among the more certain facts we have are the book's own literary ancestry—not to be dismissed as mere irrelevance, though, in a work so concerned with its own fictiveness: this ancestry includes Jack Vance's *The Dying Earth*, Silverberg's *Nightwings* for the guilds, the ruined earth, the lack of technology and the star dwellers; Peake and Robert Graves (of *I, Claudius*) for the narrator Severian; Hodgson, David Lindsay, Peake, Borges.

The book also often refuses us a continuously gripping story line. There are two "exciting" and suspenseful events in *The Shadow of the Torturer*: one concerns the approaching excruciation or official torture of the Chatelaine Thecla; the other the duel Severian is to fight with the supposed Hipparch who has challenged him. The Chatelaine's suffering is long postponed, even to the point where the reader can feel it may not actually take place, and in the interim Severian's developing relationship with her is far more central. The challenge is separated by seventy pages from the duel that takes place on the same day: during that space Severian is shown some of the sights of Nessus by a woman shopkeeper Agia, has a chariot race through the streets, arrives at the strange cathedral of the nun-like Pelerines, visits the Botanic Gardens on an island in the River Gyoll, and on the way to the duelling ground has a lengthy sojourn at an inn—all these episodes being filled with material and speculations which have nothing to do with the approaching duel. Despite Severian's posting to Thrax it takes him almost two rambling volumes to get there; and then it is soon to reject his office and leave. Between consecutive volumes there is a narrative gap. At the end of *The Shadow of the Torturer* Severian is still in the gateway of Nessus, having just met a seeming man called Jonas; at the beginning of *The Claw of the Conciliator* he is in a village somewhere, by now established as a carnifex and about to exercise his office on certain people we have not met but of whose character he speaks familiarly; and he and Jonas (who is to turn out to be actually a damaged robot star-dweller) are now companions. At the end of *The Claw* he is still far from Thrax, trying to get to Lake Diuturna via a strange moving stone village; at the beginning of *The Sword of the Lictor* he is already in Thrax with a long history unseen by us, as a travelling carnifex. *The Sword* closes with Severian at the castle of Baldanders; *The Citadel of the Autarch* opens with him in the midst of the war on the Autarch's northern frontiers. And *The Citadel* ends with his stellar mission as Autarch still to be performed.

Unlike many modern fantasy or science fiction epics of travel, *The Book of the New Sun* provides us with no maps: the location of places is uncertain, and one may be near and far at once. It is true that *The Sword of the Lictor* contains much more of a steady narrative thrust; equally it could be argued that *The Claw* and *The Citadel of the Autarch* are at an opposite extreme of refusing forward or directional movement; with the more celebrated *The Shadow* providing a fine fusion of the two impulses. Considered overall, however, narrative excitement is deliberately dulled—as, incidentally, are any merely sensationalist thrills. Severian tells us, "as one mind to another," "I have recounted the execution of Agia's twin brother Agilus because of its importance to my story, and that of Morwenna because of the unusual circumstances surrounding it. I will not recount others unless they hold some special interest. If you delight in another's pain and death you will gain little satisfaction from me" (CC, 39). If we pass over the possible pruriences of narrative interest, what remains is the fact that we are denied a consistently exciting story of the kind that is present in *Foundation* or *Dune*, where a fixed quest is constantly in view. And the same might be said even of psychological development in the novel: Severian, despite being the not unattractive psyche through whom events are related, is in his relatively steady coolness not a fascinating focus to the book: it cannot be said that the reader is meant to be seized by eagerness to find out how he develops. It *can* be said almost that the author refuses a centre to the work. Severian admits as much, telling us that like an executioner the author is concerned not only with the act itself but with the act as rite and as meaning, and with its connection to other acts (*ST*, 280–1). Thus it is that Severian describes in detail minor events and places from his early history which have no direct causal relation to the story, or he will digress from present events to describe others in the past.

The imagination behind the series, particularly in *The Shadow of the Torturer*, is formidable, coming near to the prodigality of a David Lindsay, and yet always controlled and integrated. Most science fiction writers settle for one or two images or worlds about which their books revolve. The landscape of the desert planet Dune remains single and consistent: we simply find out more about how people live in it. P. J. Farmer's Riverworld series starts with amazing power in an image of universal resurrection in a void; and follows that with a strange riverbank landscape which is to remain a constant throughout the work. Even Mervyn Peake provides just one central image, that of Gormenghast, and his attempts to create other worlds are relative failures. Only Brian Aldiss in *Hothouse* has something of the prolific creativity of Wolfe (a proliferation which is in keeping with a prolific vegetable world), but his creations are all of them set within the one context. Wolfe creates one medium after another, each world for the time isolated from others, all of them visited on Severian's strange journey. There is Nessus, the city of vast and uncertain extent, threaded by the sluggish and foetid Gyoll and surrounded by a cloud-high wall of metal. Within that there is the walled necropolis, the dead of which have to be guarded against those who would use them for dark purposes. Within that is the Citadel, and further, in that, the Matachin Tower of the Torturers, with its medieval existence, its rigidities of conduct, its bureaucratic approach to the administration of formalised pain to "clients," its atmosphere in some ways that of a police barracks, a boarding school, and a family rolled together.

Outside the Citadel Severian comes to the cathedral of the Pelerine order. It is worth dwelling on this to show how finely the author's imagination works to bring places to life. Severian has been in a chariot race through Nessus, and he and his companion Agia, attempting a short cut, have found their way barred by an immense building, the walls of which give before them "like the fabric of a dream," whereupon they rush through a cavernous space and crash into an altar "as large as a cottage and dotted with blue lights" (*ST*, 165). Severian, knocked unconscious, eventually wakes:

> We seemed to be near the centre of the building, which was as big around as the Great Keep and yet completely empty: without interior walls, stairs, or furniture of any kind. Through the golden, dusty air I could see crooked pillars that seemed of painted wood. Lamps, mere points of light, hung a chain or more overhead. Far above them, a many-coloured roof rippled and snapped in a wind I could not feel.
>
> I stood on straw, and straw was spread everywhere in an endless yellow carpet, like the field of a titan after harvest. All about me were the battens of which the altar had been constructed: fragments of thin wood braved with gold leaf and set with turquoises and violet amethysts. (*ST*, 166)

By now we can tell, as Severian, brought up amid rectangles of stone and metal, cannot, that he is in a tent the size of a big top, and that the unexpected blockage of the short cut across the common was caused by the tent's recent pitching. By this means the cathedral is created for and by us as we read, and thus gains heightened vividness. But the account is also given vigour by the precision of observation of the pieces of the altar, by the slightly strange juxtaposition with our usual sense of an altar as a solid and heavy structure of the fact that it is composed of thin wood only, and by the mixing of matchwood and precious stones. If the strangeness of the cathedral becomes the familiarity of a tent, it then gains further imaginative potency by once more becoming strange: the straw which spreads everywhere begins to burn towards Agia and Severian, and as they run they suddenly come upon a group of scarlet-clad people carrying scimitars and led by a tall hooded woman who has Severian's sword.

The author creates his images with such apparent effortlessness that they seem to have been come upon, to have been always there, rather than to have been invented. Every stage of Severian's journey is accompanied by a startling new image or landscape: the brown lake in the Garden of Endless Sleep in the Botanic Gardens, wherein are sunk thousands of shot-filled bodies for burial; the evening fight with giant flowers called averns between Severian and Agia's brother Agilus in the communal dwelling grounds near the wall of Nessus; the forest feast with Vodalus where Severian is served with Thecla's cooked body, after dining on which he finds her identity joined to his; the mysteries of the House Absolute, most of which is underground and covered with pleasure-gardens; the huge white undine that, failing to coax Severian into the water of a stream, surges upward from the water on weak legs with blood running from her nostrils only to fall back; the prisoners in Thrax, chained in rows on either side of a rock shaft driven into the cliff within the city; the mountain that is the image of a living autarch; the giant Baldanders suddenly seen falling slowly from the sky upon Severian; the vast five-armed war-machines that rush revolving through the air in the war with the Ascians (CA, 166–7).

For many another writer the creation of these and numerous other images of clarity and power, with all the assurance that the author has, might be enough. But with

Wolfe the images are not meant only to surprise; though clearly there is much plain delight in such elastic creativity. Rather they all appear as though inevitable and called for. Severian fighting Agilus with averns is not the same as Alice playing croquet with flamingoes. The avern is a killer plant about the size of a sapling: the idea is to hold it aloft in one hand by its stem and detach its heavy, razor-edged poisonous leaves with the other, to send them skimming at one's opponent. More than this, however, to fight with flowers is to conduct war with an image of peace, and such reversal fits with one of the themes of the work. The Pelerines' tent becomes perfectly explicable at the level of the evangels who go about our own world wooing thousands under canvas: but again, as an interior, it fits into a motif concerning interiors and rooms—indeed of a journey into the interior, upriver (as in *Heart of Darkness*) to Thrax, the City of Windowless Rooms—that recurs throughout. It is always clear that concerns other than those of the image alone are also present. We are directed to pay careful attention to the way the protagonist views such sights; the sights themselves are often as much metaphysical as physical, or else may be illusions, like the apparently long room behind the picture in the House Absolute, which is in fact a trapezoid with converging sides that meet only a few feet back, or the mushroom-shaped tower of Baldanders that is actually a tower surmounted by a space ship.

In the gardens of the House Absolute Severian approaches a "white shape" which he then opens a new chapter to describe:

> There are beings—and artifacts—against which we batter our intelligence raw, and in the end make peace with reality only by saying, 'It was an apparition, a thing of beauty and horror.'
>
> Somewhere among the swirling worlds I am so soon to explore, there lives a race like and yet unlike the human. They are no taller than we. Their bodies are like ours save that they are perfect, and that the standard to which they adhere is wholly alien to us. Like us they have eyes, a nose, a mouth; but they use these features (which are, as I have said, perfect) to express emotions we have never felt, so that for us to see their faces is to look upon some ancient and terrible alphabet of feeling, at once supremely important and utterly unintelligible.
>
> Such a race exists, yet I did not encounter it there at the edge of the gardens of the House Absolute. What I had seen moving among the trees, and what I now—until at last I saw it clearly—flung myself toward, was rather the giant image of such a being kindled to life. Its flesh was of white stone, and its eyes had the smoothly rounded blindness (like sections cut from eggshells) we see in our own statues. It moved slowly, like one drugged or sleeping, yet not unsteadily. It seemed sightless, yet it gave the impression of awareness, however slow.
>
> I have just paused to reread what I have written of it, and I see that I have failed utterly to convey the essence of the thing. Its spirit was that of sculpture. If some fallen angel had overheard my conversation with the green man, he might have contrived such an enigma to mock me. In its every movement it carried the serenity and permanency of art and stone; I felt that each gesture, each position of the head and limbs and torso, might be the last. Or that each might be repeated interminably. . . .
>
> My initial terror, after the white statue's strangeness had washed away my will towards death, was the instinctive one that it would do me hurt.
>
> My second was that it would not attempt to. To be as frightened of something as I was of that silent, inhuman figure, and then to discover that it meant no harm, would have been unbearably humiliating. (*CC*, 116–7)

The concern here is not only with the object, but with the effect of the object on the beholder. We do not even know that the shape is a statue till the third paragraph, and even then that identification is in doubt. The first paragraph tells us it cannot be described adequately; the second speaks at length of a race on another planet, of which race the third then tells us the object was not a member; then there is an attempt at direct description, after which Severian interrupts his own account to tell us that what we have been reading is quite inadequate. The experience is made metaphysical: we are to sense the otherness of the phenomenon through the relative failure of attempts to capture it. Its movements are slow as though it is drugged or sleeping, yet it is not unsteady; it seems sightless, yet aware. Severian apprehends it in conceptual as much as physical terms. Looking at it he feels that every move it makes has definition and finality; yet at the same time he feels each move could be repeated indefinitely. He tells us of the philosophic impact of the statue before mentioning his fear of it. And even when he comes to his fear he does not say "I was terrified," but analyses his fear in two parts, giving moral terror far greater place then merely physical fright.

Once Severian tells Dorcas that, in a brown book he brought Thecla from the library beneath the Citadel, he read that one of the keys to the universe "was that everything, whatever happens, has three meanings" (*ST*, 272). The first meaning is the literal one, the level of empirical fact, of real cows eating real grass. Paradoxically this is said to be hardest to grasp: it is reality in all its resistant "thisness." This may explain the recurrent preoccupation of the book with rendering experience in painstaking detail, and the frequent admissions of failure to describe adequately. "The second [meaning] is the reflection of the world about it. Every object is in contact with all others, and thus the wise can learn of the others by observing the first." This implication occurs throughout the series, where we are frequently turned from the physical datum alone to others which it is like or recalls. So it is at the beginning and end of each book, where the author draws our attention to the fact that he began and finished the first with a gate through which Severian went, the second book with a village, the third with a fortress, and that he ended the fourth with another gate. And all things are at once themselves and interconnected. Severian at one point wonders whether he, without family though he is, may not somehow be related to the little boy with his own name whom he meets in the mountains beyond Thrax, "or for that matter to anyone I met" (*SL*, 137–8). Every present moment too is shared with the past and the future. Gazing at the lake in the Garden of Endless Sleep Severian comments, "Mist was rising from the water, reminding me first of the swirling motes of straw in the insubstantial cathedral of the Pelerines, then of steam from the soup kettle when Brother Cook carried it into the refectory on a winter afternoon" (*ST*, 211). Severian is the torturers' apprentice, he is Death, he is the Autarch; the Autarch is the androgynous brothel-keeper in Nessus, and in himself he is "Legion," the vessel of the distilled identities of a multitude of individuals (CA, 209–10).

And the third meaning of every object? "The third is the transubstantial meaning. Since all objects have their ultimate origin in the Pancreator, and all were set in motion by him, so all must express his will—which is the higher reality" (*ST*,

272). This is one of the few references to a deity in *The Book of the New Sun:* yet it is one of the skills of the author that everything in the work seems shot through with the numinous. The stone, the Claw of the Conciliator, which Severian comes by in the Pelerines' cathedral has—if intermittently—the power to perform miracles of healing (an ironic power to be in the possession of an executioner). We do not know whether the Autarch is fully mortal, just as we do not know whether the "cacogens" are simply beings from other stars or the agents of a supernatural force. What the birth of the New Sun can mean in any but a mystical sense is not clear.[4] Clearly some Christian reference is behind the Conciliator who has come to Urth before; and the feast at which Thecla's body is eaten (CC, ch. XI) and the later offer of the world to Severian by the mountain-autarch Typhon (*SL*, ch. XXVI) have strong overtones of the Eucharist and of the Temptation in the Wilderness. With these hints of cosmic significance the mystery prevading events and objects becomes imbued with spiritual resonance.

One of the bases of the book is reversal. Forward movement is partly illusion. Severian writes as Autarch already: he tells us that he "backed into the throne." Continually we experience reversal as we read, by taking Severian's account as though written by the dispossessed character that we see, only to be told that he is ruler of all. His very motives seem "back to front." He gives us no history of libertarian sentiments or any suggestion of prior knowledge of Vodalus to explain his apparently sudden commitment to the cause of a man who robs graves. Rather he proposes that the coin Vodalus gives him as a keepsake for saving his life may have made him a Vodalarian, though he announced himself as such to Vodalus before: "We believe that we invent symbols. The truth is that they invent us; we are their creatures, shaped by their hard, defining edges" (*ST*, 17). To desire nothing and to have nothing may be the way to have all things. Severian has no parents, and through his helping of Thecla, no home. He is happy that the dog Triskele, which he saved from death, should choose another master. He is not concerned that he should lose his life in the duel with Agilus. He wishes to give back the Claw, and uses it to help others. His very wandering, his placelessness, like that of the Pelerines, suggests his readiness to go dispossessed. Others he meets desire what he has or seek power—Agia, Agilus, Baldanders, Typhon. Yet the Claw comes to him; and the throne also, in a temporal collapse typical of the book. And about him, a mere exile, many "great" events come to revolve. Thus "no-thing" becomes "all things."

In *The Citadel of the Autarch,* in a reversal designed perhaps to show that it has been his objective all along and that he has never left it, Severian returns to the Citadel from which he set forth. In Nessus, Severian at one point feels that he may be already in Thrax, the City of Windowless Rooms (*ST*, 260). For him it may be, as George Macdonald's Mr Raven puts it in his *Lilith*, that "The more doors you go out of, the farther you get in!"[5] The world of Urth is the world of the remote future, yet that future has many of the aspects of our pre-technological past, with Roman names and behaviour, medieval-seeming guilds and soldiers, castles and feudal autocrats. The author thus upends time from the first chapter of *The Shadow*, with its title "Resurrection and Death"; and also by starting the first chapter with "It is possible I already had some presentiment of my future," and the second with "Memory oppresses me." In a dream he sees his fight with Baldanders long before it takes place (*ST*, 141–2). The face on the funeral bronze that has fascinated Severian in boyhood later comes to life (CC, 293). The coin that Vodalus gives Severian has on its obverse the very flying ship that, found on a bronze device in a mausoleum, he has for long adopted as part of an imaginary coat of arms.

Throughout, Severian insists that his past is so vivid to him that it becomes almost more real than the present. When he emerges from a tunnel beneath the Citadel, through which he has searched for the lost dog Triskele, he finds himself in a wintry courtyard on the leaning face of a huge dial containing many clocks, all showing different times. He is told by a girl Valeria whom he meets there that the place, which is called the Atrium of Time, did not receive its name from the dials, but the dials were put there because of the name (*ST*, 44). During his conversation with the librarian Ultan in the stacks, Severian observes, with seeming irrelevance: "We were already walking back in the direction we had come. Since the aisle was too narrow for us to pass one another, I now carried the candelabrum before him, and a stranger, seeing us, would surely have thought I lighted his way." (*ST*, 66) The librarian, however, is blind. Severian recounts stories to learn from them (*ST*, 183). Several times during the narrative death is reversed and life restored (for Dorcas in *The Shadow*, the uhlan in *The Claw*, Jader's sister in *The Sword*, the soldier in *The Citadel*).

Expectations, too, are reversed. We suppose that to be a torturer is to be committed to violence, but actually torturing proves a tightly controlled discipline, a craft, in which the pain inflicted is merely functional, and small pleasure taken in its administration; commitment to the guild involves a dedication bordering on idealism (it is said that women, who were cruel, were banished from the guild [*ST*, 20]). A torturer has to know as much medicine as a doctor, but he is a doctor in reverse: he uses his knowledge of the body not to reconstruct it but to dismantle it; apprentice torturers take the morning round of "clients" like housemen following a consultant and having the various operative techniques used pointed out to them (*ST*, 29–30). In the midst of organized horror they are bidden to take their hands out of their pockets when spoken to (*ST*, 30). The whole book can be said to be founded on the notion of taking away our certainty as to what a thing is. To go north here is to go to warmer lands, for the book is set in the southern hemisphere: Severian thinks of the northern hemisphere as the world upside down (*ST*, 210). Throughout we do not know whether the New Sun, which the series purports to be about, has come, is coming, or is about to come; perhaps all three, as in Christian prayer. In the shape—whatever that is—of the Conciliator, we learn that it has come before; insofar as Severian for the time wields the Claw he may be the Conciliator returned; insofar as the old sun is dying, some new sun of futurity must be man's only hope. More widely, so far as the sun as solar body is concerned, this *Book of the New Sun* takes place in the senility of the old one.[6]

In a book which denies us a grand design, a pattern, an overview, or even, often, a mere narrative, to stand still may be to go forward and to advance may be to return to where one is. Hence, perhaps, the circularities of the books. In such a context the moment may contain more than the sequence of moments that makes the history, and the part may be able to contain the whole. During his conversation with Ultan, Severian mentions the belief that by eating the flesh of a dead person one could take that person's identity, and asks Ultan whether by eating only a part of the person, were it only the tip of a little finger, that identity might still be transmitted. Ultan says yes, and when Severian voices his sense of the disproportion in this, asks him, "How big is a man's life?" To which Severian can only reply, "I have no way of knowing, but isn't it larger than that?" Ultan's answer is typical of the depth of intelligence that has gone into this book, while being entirely in character: "You see it from the beginning, and anticipate much. I, recollecting it from its termination, know how little there has been." (*ST*, 66) Size thus depends on the perceiver. And the identity of a thing is not fixed: it depends on a multitude of perspectives and observations. Ultan's use of the word "termination" reminds us that the name of Severian's sword "Terminus Est" may be translated in more than one way. Ultan (a name meaning *last*) then chooses an analogy from the reverse of death to explain how identity may be conveyed through a part: family resemblances can endure through generations, "Yet the seed of them all was contained in a drachm of sticky fluid."

An instance of this "microcosmic" mode can be seen in Severian's visit with the theatrical producer Dr Talos and his supposed assistant Baldanders to a cafe in Nessus where they are served by a girl who tells them that her master pays her nothing and she depends on tips to survive: "If you don't give me anything, I will have served you for nothing" (*ST*, 148). To whom Dr Talos replies, in typical reversal, "Quite so, quite so! But what about this? What if we attempt to render you a rich gift, and you refuse it?": takings are replaced by givings, and their possible refusals by hers; at which Severian proceeds to freeze the moment in a deepening reflection:

> Dr Talos leaned toward her as he said this, and it struck me that his face was not only that of a fox (a comparison that was perhaps too easy to make because his bristling reddish eyebrows and sharp nose suggested it at once) but that of a stuffed fox. I have heard those who dig for their livelihood say there is no land anywhere in which they can trench without turning up the shards of the past. No matter where the spade turns the soil, it uncovers broken pavements and corroding metal; and scholars write that the kind of sand that artists call polychrome (because flecks of every colour are mixed with its whiteness) is actually not sand at all, but the glass of the past, now pounded to powder by aeons of tumbling in the clamorous sea. If there are layers of reality beneath the reality we see, even as there are layers of history beneath the ground we walk upon, then in one of those more profound realities, Dr Talos's face was a fox's mask on a wall, and I marveled to see it turn and bend now toward the woman, achieving by those motions, which made expression and thought appear to play across it with the shadows of the nose and brows, an amazing and realistic appearance of vivacity. "Would you refuse it?" he asked again, and I shook myself as though waking. (*ST*, 148)

The conversation and narrative are suspended during this lengthy reflection: it is as though Dr Talos and the girl wait for Severian to have it before continuing, with Dr Talos repeating his question; as though Severian's thoughts occupied the same reality as their words. Such is the character of *The Book of the New Sun*, in which "intellectual" speculation alternates continually with accounts of an "external" world, and mental constructs have no less reality than supposedly physical events—Severian's dream which comes true, Dr Talos's play at the House Absolute which in some way furthers the action at a spiritual level. Here Severian is concerned not only to recount a conversation, but the quality of the experience: he is as interested in the nature of the moment itself, indeed every aspect of it, as in what it leads to. As he looks at Dr Talos he sees him as a fox, but then at once not only as a fox, so that his identity shifts all the time. When he speaks of the fox's mask we are reminded of other masks that occur in the series: the mask Severian wears as torturer and as carnifex, the mask Agilus wears to disguise himself as Hipparch, the masks of the other-worlders, the cacogens, masks by which one identity is hidden and another revealed. When he speaks of the fox looking more like a stuffed fox, we are perhaps reminded of the features of the funeral bronze that find flesh, or the huge statue of terrible beauty which is like the far-off star dwellers—but there the dead come to life, whereas here the live being becomes the image of a dead animal.

Characteristically, when Severian turns to talk of what seems some quite unrelated matter—e.g., the omnipresence of the past beneath the dry skin of the planet—we are given a fragment of information about the larger history of Urth only in a casual aside: yet what seems to be separated is in fact closely linked to the subject, just as are other separations in the book, such as between one identity and another, the past and the future, one place and another infinitely far off. For the mention of Urth's past is used to give Severian's vision the status of fact. If there are layers and layers of history below us, then there may be layers and layers of reality, and on one of these levels Dr Talos is a fox. Curiously the way Severian puts this transforms it as we watch from hypothesis to actuality—not a hypothetical "If," but a logical deduction from an "If" to a "then": it is a clever trick, like the strange mirrors of Father Inire in the House Absolute, through which a reflection can become a reality (*ST*, 185–6), or like the reflection of a woman's face seen in the water when no woman is present, in the story of the fisherman told in the Jungle Garden in the Botanic Gardens (*ST*, 189). By this point Dr Talos's face *is* a fox's mask on a wall, and from within that reality Severian now wonders at the fact that it moves and seems to imitate the processes of thought and feeling: he has entered his own vision and made it truth. Thus we see how any instant within the book, any identity, is connected to others, deepening our understanding not only of the figure or event before us, but of other events and figures in the book till they swirl about it. Take any part of the book and it has this power to animate the whole, just as Dr Talos is "animated" here.

What then is the book about? There is no answer, but the lack of one is not from its absence so much as from the sense that it is just over one's shoulder or that it is too many things to pin into one. As we have said, the book has no centre as such, apart from Severian: it explores many things. And each thing may mean multitudes, as the author at one point tells us: Severian recounts a story of the Autarch and the many interpretations it has been given; he feels sure that the story remains as mysterious as his own, yet the attempt to understand it will be made (*ST*, 158–9). The Autarch literally contains multitudes, in having within him the living identities of a thousand individuals.[7] One of the themes—or perhaps motifs, rather—of *The Book of the New Sun* is that nothing finally has boundaries or limits: just as one thing may mean all things, so it may be them. During Dr Talos's play at the House Absolute, the audience is continually involved, so that the distinction between fiction and reality is worn down. Dreams, such as that of Severian concerning Baldanders, become realities. Images come to life, such as the bronze face or the flying ship. The dead come alive in Dorcas, and in another way in Thecla. Devoured by the terrible beast, the alzabo, the members of a family retain their idientities within it (*SL*, ch. XVI). The living can be dead, as the ebullient Dr Talos turns out to be a homunculus manufactured by the cacogens. The metal hand of Jonas does not indicate that he is a human with an artificial limb; rather the "human" part of him, the organic and fleshly, has been grafted onto what is a robot, who crashed to earth from space and lost several parts of his body. Typhon survives by grafting himself onto the body of Piaton. Thecla, eaten by Severian, becomes a part of him and he shares in her thoughts and memories. Dorcas is—in one way—Cas, the dead wife sought by the fisherman in the Garden of Endless Sleep; and perhaps there is a piece of her, like her name, in Cadroe of the Seventeen Stones at the duelling ground, and in Casdoe, mother of little Severian (*SL*, 112–14). Dr. Talos seems in charge of the giant Baldanders; then, to Dorcas, the roles seem reversed, so that Baldanders is a slow father and Dr Talos his brilliant son (*CC*, 201).

Severian, for all that he is burdened by the solidity of his past, is as a torturer a myth, a creature of fiction to anyone beyond the Citadel (*ST*, 133). To Dr Talos and the fearful man he encounters in the Jungle Garden, he is Death, though Dorcas says such a name is mere metaphor (CC, 200–1). The man in the Jungle Garden can see Severian, but his wife and the native with her cannot. Several of the characters become allegorized (there is even a chapter entitled "Personifications"): Agia is the Lady, Dorcas Innocence, Jolenta Desire. Jolenta is a serving maid metamorphosed to the archetype of human sexual beauty. Severian meets a child with his own name. The ramifications of the passages beneath the Citadel may be great enough to merge into those of the House Absolute; and as to the latter Severian has no idea where it ends, if it ever ends (CC, 241). And as we have seen, the present, the past, and the future often come together, just as do one place and another supposedly distant from it; and one person may appear in many guises in the work. Even in genre the book melts down identity, being a fusion of fantasy, science fiction, and horror story. Other works that mix genres in this way tend to come down on one side or the other, as C. S. Lewis's science fictional romance *Out of the Silent Planet* ends as pure supernatural fantasy; or Clifford Simak's supernatural-seeming *Enchanted Pilgrimage* is engulfed in a science-fictional action and explanation. Wolfe maintains the ambiguity, the uncertainty of boundaries, and thus heightens the mystery.

Perhaps the central point to be made about Wolfe's work is its inclusiveness. Severian's mind is obsessed to madness by his total recall of the past. We cover every experience possible, and that is why the work contains not one but many images; why, too, each image itself contains multitudes. Given the motif of plasticity in the book, it is only fitting that the work should have no single fixed or identifiable meaning. We can if we like read into it serious themes concerning alienation of the self or man's distance from reality (imaged perhaps in the torturers, for whom the infliction of pain has nothing to do with emotion), but to do so is to limit that which refuses limits.

In one sense the book asks us what it is to be meaningful. We ourselves may feel that most "significance" resides in such episodes as the disquisition on Father Inire's mirrors and their relation to reality (*ST*, ch. XX), or in the allegorical play produced by Dr Talos on a new Paradise and the Last Things (*CC*, ch. XXIV); but, by virtue of the equal attention to apparently "physical" acts the book asks us how much less significance, however unidentifiable, is contained in them:

> I examined the block. Those used outside the immediate supervision of the guild are notoriously bad: 'Wide as a stool, dense as a fool, and dished, as a rule.' This one fulfilled the first two specifications in the proverbial description only too well, but by the mercy of Holy Katherine it was actually slightly convex, and though the idiotically hard wood would be sure to dull the male side of my blade, I was in the fortunate position of having before me one subject of either sex, so that I could use a fresh edge on each. (*CC*, 33)

Is this intractable block less meaningful because identifiably so than, say: "The past cannot be found in the future where it is not—not until the metaphysical world, which is so much larger and so much slower than the physical world, completes its revolution and the New Sun comes" (*SL*, 55)? The book would have us wonder, just as it presents us with what is and is not a narrative, and with experiences that are at once real and dreams. The whole work is a mixture of adventures, experiences recorded in as much loving detail as snapshots, speculative psychological perceptions, all acutely rendered. Perhaps a meaning, or many meanings, might on the level of the perfect star beings' intelligence (*CC*, 116), be found to inform all the phenomena; but each phenomenon and apprehension may on its own contain an autonomous world of significance both like and unlike any other. It is part of science fiction's dialectic with the alien that it presents us with powerful images which at once invite and refuse interpretation, at once virginal and elusive like the Pelerines, and suggestive of universal availability like the desirable Jolenta. It is an art brought to perfection by Wolfe. It is there in the civilization of old Urth, which is and is not the earth, which is so suggestive of Roman and medieval society and yet, as C.S. Lewis observed of near-identity, the more totally unlike for the approximation: "A few days before I had been given a set of paper figures. They were soubrettes, columbines, coryphees, harlequines, figurantes, and so on—the usual thing' (*ST*, 182).[8]

Notes

1. References are to the Arrow Books (Sidgwick and Jackson, London) paper editions of 1981, 1982, 1983, and 1983, respectively; cited hereafter as *ST*, *CC*, *SL* and *CA*.
2. On whether the book is "sword and sorcery" or "science fiction" see the review by Colin Greenland of *ST* and *CC* in *Foundation*, 24 (Feb. 1982):82–5.
3. Compare the history of the human race given in *SL*, 51–5, with the sheerly different one in *CA*, 278–80.
4. See also T.D. Clareson, "'The Book of Gold': Gene Wolfe's *Book of the New Sun*," *Extrapolation*, 23.3 (Fall, 1982): 271.
5. George Macdonald, *Lilith* (London, 1895), 13.
6. Wolfe's fondness for reversal can be seen elsewhere in his fiction, most notably in his three short stories "The Death of Doctor Island," "The Island of Doctor Death," and "The Doctor of Death Island."
7. A notion Wolfe may well have derived from the multitudinous identities of Leto II and Alia in Frank Herbert's *Children of Dune* (1976).
8. C. S. Lewis, *Perelandra* (London, 1943), 236; *Surprised by Joy: The Shape of My Early Life* (London, 1955), 170.

JOHN CLUTE

From "The Mother of the Autarch" (1986)

Strokes: Essays and Reviews 1966–1986

1987

In ⟨the⟩ material I've put together to make up this sequence of responses to Gene Wolfe's high crafty art, there is surely—I can taste it while correcting and transcribing these pieces—a kind of decorous and perhaps not over-courageous effect of wallowing, in the interpretations put on display here. Of course no one wants to look a fool, though in a moment I'm going to demonstrate how easy it is to look a fool about Gene Wolfe, and there is a natural impulse to avoid coming to a hard reading of a Wolfe story in case one has entirely missed the point of it. At the same time, one should really do him the initial courtesy of assuming that he wishes to be understood (though in fact he may have no such wish). Specifically, one should begin (it will be a bare beginning) to try to make some sense of his major work to date, *The Book of the New Sun*.

Making sense of Gene Wolfe, it seems to me, is initially a job of decipherment. Interpretation of the text must follow its decipherment, must subtend some consensus about the raw configurations of the story itself. Most readers of *The Book* will have undertaken for themselves something of this task, will have made a large number of "hard readings" of points in the text. They will have understood how an apparent work of loose fantasy cashes out in fact as the firmest of SF texts—how, for instance, the Matachin Tower, which seems initially to be some sort of donjon, can turn out on being hard-read to be one of a group of long-disused spaceships. This turn—this translation—most readers will have taken as a model for more serious turns in which the seemingly vague or ambivalent or fantastic or merely colouristic focuses into a hard datum, as though one's eyes had been washed: and the world shines forth in its true array. Using this model of *turning*, readers will have been able to understand the true sanctity—as opposed to the jiggery-pokery sword-and-sorcery magic "power"—of the Claw of the Conciliator, which is "merely" the thorn of a rose. And most readers of the tetralogy will have been forced—forced indeed by Gene Wolfe himself, as he makes it clear that there is *some* mystery to be solved—into making some kinds of speculation about the nature of Severian's secret family, though perhaps not everyone will share my conviction that decipherment can have a stop, and the fuller task of interpretation begin, only when some sense of the identity of that family has been established.

Is there a sister in the text? A father? A mother?

We are told that *Severian* is a name usually given to one of a pair of twins. If there is a sister, she will have been raised in the Witches' Keep in the Citadel, and she may well make some sort of appearance. I have myself gotten nowhere in identifying her, or in tracing any significance that might attach to her presence in *The Book*, though if she does appear I suspect it is on the road to Thrax.

In his essay on *The Book* ⟨. . .⟩ C. N. Manlove urges the need for a fervency of interpretation, but seems at times to shy from making firm statements about the raw shape of *The Book* or the identity of its cast. His reading of Dorcas is particularly reticent; while recognizing that she is important to the text, he goes no further than to suggest that she *seems* to have been resurrected (Acts IX:39 provides Biblical sanction, by the way, for both her resurrection and her subsequent occupation), and fails to make any comment on her family connection to Severian. Many readers will have found little real difficulty in identifying Severian's father as Ouen, the waiter in the tree restaurant at the end of the first volume who runs away when he recognizes in Dorcas his mother reborn (after 40 years); and their recognition of Dorcas as Severian's paternal grandmother will have sharpened their response to his affair with her, as well as to much else in the text. Professor Manlove's failure to establish this profound linkage vitiates his reading of Dorcas, and in general leaves him standing outside a book he correctly identifies as requiring copious exegetical work. And in so far as he fails to make this relatively simple identification available to his own readers, he fails to bring *The Book of the New Sun* into focus.

Dorcas and Ouen (we will see that his name is also significant) are fairly straightforward figures to place, and the reader will have been richly rewarded for doing the work of placing them. It is by no means as simple a task to identify Severian's mother, or even to be more than intuitively certain that she inhabits the text, subcutaneously informing Severian's grasp of the world. There is nothing apodictic about the signs of her presence, and I for one feel a kind of vertigo—as though my interpretive faculties had become unglued at the task, had overheated, become feverish—at the thought of trying to pin her down. Nor am I by any means certain of the richness of the reward for making a fix that seems inherently contestable—for the miracle of most of Wolfe's conundrums is that, once solved, they seem perfectly obvious, and enrich one's reading. All the same, the text does seem to ask one to look for a mother, though ultimately it may make mock of one's efforts. At the time of writing ⟨my⟩ review of *The Citadel of the Autarch* ⟨in *The Washington Post Book World*, Jan. 30, 1983⟩, I did in fact arrive at a tentative identification of Severian's mother, one which seemed to fit the basic criterion of enriching my reading of the text, but one about which I could feel no security, nor do I now. If I therefore present some speculations about her, it is less because I expect I am correct than it is to demonstrate the kind of deciphering tactics *The Book of the New Sun* seems to demand of readers who become engaged in its conundrums.

Every woman in *The Book of the New Sun*, except Dorcas, is of course a candidate. *In some fashion* she will need to have been in a position to have slept with Ouen about 20 years previously; she will have called herself Catherine; she will have had some relationship to an order of monials, but not necessarily that of postulant; and because of some trouble she is in she will have been picked up by the law when pregnant and given birth to Severian while inside the Matachin Tower. Beyond those criteria, she could be anyone. Some candidates, perhaps wrongly, got short shrift. I spent no time on Agia, for instance, nor on the head of the Pelerine order of monials, nor on Thecla's sister, nor on Jolanta, nor on the mother of the boy-Severian on the road from Thrax. Tom Disch—one of several friends and colleagues to whom I mentioned the problem and my sense of its significance—passed swiftly over some plausible names and settled on Morwenna, the woman Severian executes at the beginning of *The Claw of the Conciliator*, on the basis that her name sort of rhymed with Ouen's, but he was joking. After this, only four obvious candidates remained.

Cyriaca seemed plausible enough, up there in windowless Thrax. She was about the right age, she had been involved with monials in her youth and had escaped them, she had been travelling at the right time, and she even makes a motherly reference to Severian. But I did not like the choice, nor do I now. It was, and is, a *boring* choice, nor would making it much help to explain Severian's seemingly elaborate masking of his mother's identity—an objection which does not apply to my final choice; Cyriaca was simply too lightweight to bear the burden of the secrecy that surrounds the mystery. (In a personal letter, Gene Wolfe also—*I think*—rejected her, while at the same time he refused to make any positive statement on the issue.)

Thecla seemed much more likely, and Greg Benford has said he'd assumed she was Severian's mother long ago, on reading *The Shadow of the Torturer* when it first came out. The blood seeping under the door of her cell (he thought) was an analogue of birth blood; and something about her behaviour and appearance also triggered him. Thecla is of course ostensibly much too young, but we *are* told that exultants—in a fashion connected to the clone/khaibits who impersonate them—enjoy extended lifespans, so that she might be much older than she looks. She is very tall. Her reaction on first seeing Severian *may* relate as much to seeing her son (who, we are told, bears an extraordinary resemblance to his father) as to seeing her torturer. But he *is* nearly identical to Ouen, and her reaction, all considered, does seem to fall short of what one might expect (as does Cyriaca's when she first sees him under similarly heightened circumstances). There is no hint that she is in fact older than she seems, nor that she has ever called herself Catherine, nor that she has ever had any connection with an order of monials, nor that she has ever been imprisoned before. And, most significantly, her central role in the text as a sort of co-protagonist and deep sister is neatly exemplified—and exhausted—by Severian's ingestion of her.

Valeria too would seem simply too young—and too unsurprised—though the language Gene Wolfe uses to describe her and the Atrium of Time which fronts her residence, plus the undeveloped but intensely felt significance of the fact that Severian goes to her at the close of the tetralogy, all does lead to some sense of hushed heightened *burden*. There is something pregnantly odd about Valeria ("I am all the sisters we breed. And all the sons.") and the Atrium of Time which, we remember, is not named after the sundials that cluster within it: they have been placed there because it is the Atrium of Time. We also remember that in volume one Severian arrives for the first time at the Atrium from underground—is reborn into it—after having followed the dog Triskele's three-legged paw-marks into the mazes under the Citadel. Seeing the light of the sun, he climbs up into the Atrium, a high narrow courtyard into which indeed the sun—the sun is always significant in this text—is shining. It is as though the sun is always shining into the Atrium: as though Time were held in its palm. Severian then meets Valeria, who bears the name of a Roman family famous for having served Emperors over the span of a millennium, and is deeply struck by her. A thousand pages later, when as Autarch he wants to find her again, he cannot, with all the devices at his command, locate the Atrium of Time at all. Only when he once again traces Triskele's path, only by following the *exact route* he had once followed, the marks of Triskele's paws and his own feet still visible in the deep passages of the Citadel, can he come once again into the sunlit Atrium. This experience exactly replicates an experience earlier in the same volume, when Severian can only reach the house of Master Ash, who is a traveler in the Corridors of Time, by following the precise route laid down for him. Once within the holy confines of the rose-choked Atrium of Time, Severian then speaks Autarchal words of power, which Valeria's habitation clamorously recognizes, and the novel ends. All in all, Valeria sounds more like a wife-to-be than a mother.

So we have a shallow aunt, a deep sister, and a wife-to-be. We do not yet have a mother. We come to the woman who serves in the ceremony at the Matachin Tower in which Severian becomes a journeyman torturer. As far as Severian claims to know, this woman appears only once a year, when it comes time to perform the ceremony of induction, and has been doing so as long as he—who forgets nothing—can remember. In the ceremony, she takes on the role of Saint Katharine, patroness of the order of torturers; before she can be strapped to the Wheel to be tortured (as was the original Saint Catherine of Alexandria), the Wheel breaks forth in roses; after she is bound to it, it dissolves. Her age is not easy to fix; as far as Severian can judge, she has never changed (one thinks of the masked hierodules). She is intimate with the Matachin Tower, and may once have been an inmate there. She will certainly have seen Severian frequently enough, over the years of his childhood and adolescence, not to be surprised at his startling resemblance to a possible former lover. Severian's reaction to her is extraordinary, and is couched by Gene Wolfe with that deceiving air of intense lucidity he shifts into only at moments of high significance, when through layers of crystalline syntax the reader can fall for ever. She is tall, slender, "dark of complexion, dark of eye, raven of hair. Hers was such a face as I have never seen elsewhere, like a pool of pure water found in the midst of a wood." Severian then performs the ceremony, cutting off her head, which indeed is only wax, made in her semblance. Something inchoate here reaches for expression. This Katharine/Catherine represents a pattern of associations of a very strong order, and I for one am disinclined to challenge it. But if we are to grant that this woman is Severian's mother, who then is this woman?

We come to one of the most difficult passages in *The Book*. ⟨. . .⟩ We enter the Borgesian house of mirrors of the Corridors of Time, where semblance meets semblance, significances multiply. After the ceremony, having drunk too much, Severian is taken to his bunk, where he has what seems to be a dream like others he has recounted. Only later are we told that these "dreams" are not dreams at all but genuine experiences in the Corridors. In his "dream," a semblance of Catherine is succeeded by a whiff of Thecla's perfume as used by her khaibit in the House Azure, which is itself a house of mirrors; Severian then becomes the risen Christ. We must now enter dangerous territory; Catherine may be no one but herself, her absences from the Matachin Tower explainable by her presence in the Corridors of Time. Perhaps later—in the fifth volume, perhaps—Severian will meet her again, and she will be as she has ever been, with her haunting eyes, her face (her mask) like a shadowed pool; and they will speak together. But this seems—almost literally—an escapist reading of the text; *The Book* in our hands (it seems to me) needs to *contain* Catherine. Let us return to the khaibit, who is not seen but smelled: only Catherine is seen. Any reference to the khaibit evokes her doyen, as does any reference to the House Azure. The reader will remember that when he first meets this figure, earlier in the same first volume of *The Book*, Severian is greatly affected by the encounter. The doyen speaks with the voice of a contralto, his eyes seem like windows through which it is possible to see "a sky of summer drought." On remembering that the sky of Urth is dark even at midday, the reader will understand that Severian's image is one of translucent darkness, "like a pool of pure water found in the midst of a wood," it may be. In any case, Severian's response to the doyen strikingly resembles his response to Catherine. They are intrinsicate. As we discover only in volume two, however, the doyen of the House Azure, who first introduces Severian to the khaibit Thecla, and who is now evoked in the person of his mother, is in fact the Autarch. As though a semblance had been discarded, we never see the "young woman" of the ceremony again.

But how can we be persuaded that an unfantastical reading of *The Book of the New Sun* could lead to the conclusion that Severian's mother is the Autarch? Is the maid not sufficient in herself? Perhaps we can put the question of sex to one side for a moment, and ask if it is at all plausible to think that the Autarch can play the role of Catherine? If it is simply a question of disguises, we know the answer to be in the affirmative. When we first meet "him," the Autarch is, after all, playing a role in the House Azure, which itself parodies the

House Absolute, and throughout the tetralogy there are hints that "he" may well haunt the text in a variety of semblances, gathering information, haunting the Corridors of Time. We do know, not at all incidentally, that "he" has long had a privy source of information in the Matachin Tower itself. Much later, of course, in *The Citadel of the Autarch*, we find out that the Autarch is in fact *legion*, having ingested the memories of all previous Autarchs (including the first Severian's) as part of the assumption of Autarchy that Severian himself undergoes. It is intrinsicate with the condition of Autarchy (remember that Severian, having at first ingested only Thecla, is more than once mistaken for her) that the Autarch wear many faces.

The text does offer a series of widely separated cues. The Autarch, as we know, is an androgyne, having been de-sexed by the heirodules for failing to bring in the New Sun. There is, of course, no reason to insist that this mysterious de-sexing process could not transform a woman as well as a man. Throughout the text, whenever Severian sees the Autarch's profile on a coin of the realm, he first assumes that the profile is female. Early in the first volume, it is recorded that the apprentices in the Matachin Tower have speculated that the Autarch may be a woman dressed as a man; it can be assumed that they know of the consequences of failing to bring in the New Sun, and that their speculations must be rooted in something more than the mere fact of androgyny. With regard to the de-sexing, it is of couse understood that it took place some time after the Autarch ascended the throne; by definition some time after the birth of Severian. (A further exploration, only profitably to be entered upon on the surety that the current speculation fits the text, might seek to fix the date of the Autarch's ascent, whether before or after Severian's conception: if the former, then Severian would be, of course, in a sense, his own mother.) In any case, in the intimate dialogue that precedes the Autarch's death in volume four, he/she records to Severian having been involved about twenty years previously in vaguely criminal activities—just as Ouen had been, and at about the same time: which gives opportunity. It is possible to deduce from utterances the Autarch has made that at the same time he/she was taken off by the authorities. In conversation, Gregory Feeley has noted the unusual way in which Gene Wolfe has couched the Autarch's utterances at this point. When the Autarch says to Severian of his/her activities at that time, ". . . that would be in about the year you were born, I suppose . . ." for the only time in the tetralogy a phrase is marked off by ellipses. In a writer of the acute consciousness of style Gene Wolfe everywhere displays, this pair of ellipses is a marker of considerable significance; it is, once again, a syntax through which the reader can fall for ever. It might be mentioned at this point that the Autarch more than once addresses Severian (and no one else) as "My son." This may be a standard form of Autarchal address, but if that were the case one might expect Severian to use the same locution when he becomes Autarch himself; and he does not.

Finally there is the name Ouen. We know that throughout the tetralogy names, from Dorcas to Triskele, have offered significant analogies from our own world. The Ouen who most appositely supplies a sense of fitting analogy is that Owen Tudor (d. 1461) who comes from Wales to the English court and sleeps with a woman named Catherine. She is the queen-mother. As Henry VII, their grandson ascends the throne and brings to an end the Wars of the Roses. England enters a new age, which will culminate in the reign of Elizabeth, who is often figured as Astraea. Hermetic images of the rule of a new sun constantly infiltrate the language of those who would do honour to the Tudors, whose badge—like Severian's—is a Rose.

So.

There remains the problem of Severian's concealing the nature of his secret family. This may be explained in part—for he is, after all, only a creature of fiction—as simply reflecting Gene Wolfe's almost invariable refusal to make clear expository statements about the deep realities that govern the shape of his best work. All the same, Severian is a clear example of the typical SF protagonist who, by remembering the *truth* about himself and the universe, becomes the saviour of that universe. The entire narrative of *The Book of the New Sun* is ostentatiously an act of what in rhetoric is known as *anamnesis*. ("In anamnesis, the person acknowledges who he is, who his father and mother really are . . . even when such knowledge is horrible as with Oedipus. In anamnesis we 'remember who we are' and the memory is placed in a definite social context; on the contrary, in moments of nostalgia we admit that we are lost."—D. E. Richardson in *The Sewanee Review*, Winter 1981, p. 136.) Like Oedipus at the end, Severian knows who he is, which involves knowing who his parents are; but, unlike Oedipus, he is a liar, if only by omission. The reason for this may be—I'm half-convinced that it must be—related to the function of the text he gives us. Although it is couched as a confession, *The Book of the New Sun* is in fact a political document (whose full import will presumably unfold in the sequel Gene Wolfe is now reportedly completing); it is a position paper for redemption. Under these circumstances, it is perhaps unsurprising that Severian, self-declared advocate of Vodalus's opposition to the very concept of Autarchy, should seek to obscure his blasphemous and bastard connection to the very heart of a world whose Autarchs (it will be remembered) are forbidden to found dynasties.

As far as a case can be made (by me) out of this interminable vertigo of hints for decipherment, a case for deriving conclusions from a particular style of reading Gene Wolfe has been made. There is one further point to suggest about the Autarch, however, one which may seem frivolous, but which all the same goes to the heart of how I conceive Gene Wolfe to work. Readers may have noted that, of all characters of any importance in *The Book of the New Sun*, the Autarch is the only one who goes unnamed. Previous Autarchs not only have names but are (I think always) given soubriquets as well. Even Severian, as Autarch, is known as Severian the Lame. So what then is the Autarch's name? If there is a secret name embedded in the text, can it be anything but Catherine? But does she have a nickname as well, if only as a releasing device in Gene Wolfe's mind? At this point a digression is called for. In ⟨a⟩ 1983 SF class I ⟨taught⟩, Gene Wolfe talked for a while about the first of the tales within the text of *The Book*, "The Tale of the Student and his Son." Central to his shaping of the tale (he told us) were two plays on words, one fairly obvious, the other—the more important one—both obscure and maybe frivolous-seeming. The easier wordplay involved the ironclad "ship"/monster that the Son—the man fleshed from dreams—finds at the heart of the watery labyrinth into which he has sailed; this monster is called the Monitor, after the ironclad warship from the American Civil War, but as the man shaped from dreams is clearly a version of Theseus, then the monster is clearly a version of the Minotaur. Many readers will have registered this pun; fewer, I suspect, will have registered the more important (though indeed only subtextual) one, the one that offers so clear an illustration of the workings of Gene Wolfe's mind. For the Student in the city of pale towers, fleshing *Theseus* out of dreams is just the same as writing a *thesis* out of the primordial Word. In the beginning (in the Library of the Autarch) is the Word. Theseus (or Severian, for the story is clearly a parable) is the Word (or *The Book of the New Sun*) made flesh. *Theseus/thesis:* that is how, in the procreative secrecy of his art, Gene Wolfe works. We return to the Autarch. I spoke to Greg Feeley on the telephone about some of these conundrums. I mentioned to him the fact that the Autarch had no name.

—Right (he said), and no soubriquet either, unlike the other Autarchs. I wonder (he added) what the Autarch's name actually is?

—Catherine the Wheel (I said).

—But how do you spell Wheel? (he said).

—W-e-a-l (I said).

A weal is a welt, of course, and could stand for the scar inflicted on Catherine by the hierodules when they desexed her. But far more importantly, weal (I take *Webster's New World Dictionary* as likely to give a commonly accepted definition) is a substantive meaning "a sound or prosperous state; well-being, welfare; *the body politic.*" (My italics.) So. The Autarch, who is legion, who is the body politic of the state, who is the mother of the New Sun, is Catherine the Weal.

Thomas Wolfe

1900–1938

Thomas Clayton Wolfe was born on October 3, 1900, in Asheville, North Carolina, to William Oliver Wolfe and Julia Elizabeth Westall. He was educated at the University of North Carolina (B.A. 1920) and Harvard University (M.A. 1922). He taught at New York University from 1924 to 1930, after which he became a full-time writer.

Wolfe considered himself a playwright for the first several years of his career, but few of his plays were produced during his lifetime, and only two were eventually published: *The Return of Buck Gavin* (1924) and *The Third Night* (1938), both of which were originally produced in 1919. Two more plays were published posthumously: *Gentlemen of the Press* (1942) and *Mannerhouse* (1948).

Wolfe's reputation rests almost entirely upon four novels published within the space of eleven years. They are linked thematically, and to some degree narratively, and are extremely autobiographical. The first, *Look Homeward, Angel: A Story of the Buried Life* (1929), was bought and published by Maxwell Perkins at Scribner's, and was enthusiastically received. Wolfe continued to develop his personal vision of life as dark, lonely, and transient in his subsequent novels (*Of Time and the River: A Legend of Man's Hunger in His Youth*, 1935; *The Web and the Rock*, 1939, edited by Edward C. Aswell; *You Can't Go Home Again*, 1940, edited by Edward C. Aswell) which he considered aspects of a continuing work. Though many critics remained enthusiastic, others felt that Wolfe had plumbed the depths of his own soul perhaps a bit too thoroughly, to the detriment of his social comment. Nevertheless, Wolfe's evocation of the need for curiosity and achievement in the face of inevitable isolation and alienation has continued to strike a powerful chord with readers and critics since his death, and he is felt by many to be one of the most important and prototypical American writers in the line of Sandburg, Thoreau, and Emerson.

In addition to novels and plays, two collections of stories by Wolfe were published: *From Death to Morning* (1935) and *The Hills Beyond* (1941, edited by Edward C. Aswell). A book of verse (*A Stone, a Leaf, a Door: Poems*, edited by John S. Barnes) was published in 1945, and *The Short Novels*, edited by C. Hugh Holman, appeared in 1961. Various collections of his letters and journals have been published as well, and Wolfe's description of his collaborative work with Maxwell Perkins on Wolfe's early novels was published as *The Story of a Novel* in 1936. Wolfe died of pneumonia on September 15, 1938.

BERNARD DE VOTO
"Genius Is Not Enough"
Forays and Rebuttals
1936, pp. 324–33

Some months ago *The Saturday Review* serialized Mr. Thomas Wolfe's account of the conception, gestation and as yet uncompleted delivery of his Novel, and Scribners' are now publishing the three articles as a book. It is one of the most appealing books of our time. No one who reads it can doubt Mr. Wolfe's complete dedication to his job or regard with anything but respect his attempt to describe the dark and nameless fury of the million-footed life swarming in his dark and unknown soul. So honest or so exhaustive an effort at self-analysis in the interest of esthetics has seldom been made in the history of American literature, and *The Story of a Novel* is likely to have a long life as a source-book for students of literature and for psychologists as well. But also it brings into the public domain material that has been hitherto outside the privilege of criticism. Our first essay must be to examine it in relation to Mr. Wolfe's novels, to see what continuities and determinants it may reveal, and to inquire into their bearing on the art of fiction.

Let us begin with one of many aspects of Mr. Wolfe's novels that impress the reader, the frequent recurrence of material to which one must apply the adjective placental. (The birth metaphors are imposed by Mr. Wolfe himself. In *The*

Story of a Novel he finds himself big with first a thunder-cloud and then a river. The symbolism of waters is obviously important to him, and the title of his latest novel is to be that of the series as a whole.) A great part of *Look Homeward, Angel* was just the routine first-novel of the period which many novelists had published and many others had suppressed, the story of a sensitive and rebellious adolescent who was headed toward the writing of novels. The rest of it was not so easily catalogued. Parts of it showed intuition, understanding and ecstasy, and an ability to realize all three in character and scene, whose equal it would have been hard to point out anywhere in the fiction of time. These looked like great talent, and in such passages as the lunchroom scene in the dawn that Mr. Wolfe called nacreous some fifty times, they seemed to exist on both a higher and a deeper level of realization than any of Mr. Wolfe's contemporaries had attained. But also there were parts that looked very dubious indeed—long, whirling discharges of words, unabsorbed in the novel, unrelated to the proper business of fiction, badly if not altogether unacceptably written, raw gobs of emotion, aimless and quite meaningless jabber, claptrap, belches, grunts and Tarzan-like screams. Their rawness, their unshaped quality must be insisted upon: it was as if the birth of the novel had been accompanied by a lot of the material that had nourished its gestation. The material which nature and most novelists discard when its use has been served. It looked like one of two things, there was no telling which. It looked like the self-consciously literary posturing of a novelist too young and too naïve to have learned his trade. Or, from another point of view, it looked like a document in psychic disintegration. And one of the most important questions in contemporary literature was: would the proportion of fiction to placenta increase or decrease in Mr. Wolfe's next book?

It decreased. If fiction of the quality of that lunchroom scene made up about one-fifth of *Look Homeward, Angel*, it constituted, in *Of Time and the River*, hardly more than a tenth. The placental material had enormously grown and, what was even more ominous, it now had a rationalization. It was as unshaped as before, but it had now been retroactively associated with the dark and nameless heaving of the voiceless and unknown womb of Time, and with the unknown and voiceless fury of the dark and lovely and lost America. There were still passages where Mr. Wolfe was a novelist not only better than most of his contemporaries but altogether out of their class. But they were pushed farther apart and even diluted when they occurred by this dark substance which may have been nameless but was certainly far from voiceless.

Certain other aspects of the new book seemed revealing. For one thing, there was a shocking contempt of the medium. Some passages were not completely translated from the "I" in which they had apparently been written to the "he" of Eugene Gant. Other passages alluded to incidents which had probably appeared in an earlier draft but could not be found in the final one. Others contradictorily reported scenes which had already appeared, and at least once a passage that had seen service already was reënlisted for a second hitch in a quite different context, apparently with no recollection that it had been used before.

Again, a state of mind that had been appropriate to the puberty of Eugene seemed inappropriate as the boy grew older, and might therefore be significant. I mean the giantism of the characters. Eugene himself, in *Of Time and the River*, was clearly a borderline manic-depressive: he exhibited the classic cycle in his alternation between "fury" and "despair" and the classic accompaniment of obsessional neurosis in the compulsions he was under to read all the books in the world, see all the people in Boston, observe all the lives of the man-swarm and list all the names and places in America. That was simple enough, but practically every other character in the book also suffered from fury and compulsions, and, what was more suggestive, they were all twenty feet tall, spoke with the voice of trumpets and the thunder, ate like Pantagruel, wept like Niobe, laughed like Falstaff and bellowed like the bulls of Bashan. The significant thing was that we were seeing them all through Eugene's eyes. To a child all adults are giants: their voices are thunderous, their actions are portentous and grotesquely magnified, and all their exhibited emotions are seismic. It looked as if part of Eugene's condition was an infantile regression.

This appearance was reinforced by what seemed to be another stigma of infantilism: that all the experiences in *Of Time and the River* were on the same level and had the same value. When Mr. Gant died (of enough cancer to have exterminated an army corps), the reader accepted the accompanying frenzy as proper to the death of a man's father—which is one of the most important event's in anyone's life. But when the same frenzy accompanied nearly everything else in the book—a ride on a railroad train, a literary tea-fight, a midnight lunch in the kitchen, a quarrel between friends, a walk at night, the rejection of a play, an automobile trip, a seduction that misfired, the discovery of Eugene's true love—one could only decide that something was dreadfully wrong. If the death of a father comes out even with a ham-on-rye, then the art of fiction is cockeyed.

Well, *The Story of a Novel* puts an end to speculation and supplies some unexpected but very welcome light. To think of these matters as contempt of the medium, regression and infantilism is to be too complex and subtle. The truth shows up in two much simpler facts: that Mr. Wolfe is still astonishingly immature, and that he has mastered neither the psychic material out of which a novel is made nor the technique of writing fiction. He does not seem aware of the first fact, but he acknowledges the second with a frankness and an understanding that are the finest promise to date for his future books. How far either defect is reparable it is idle to speculate. But at least Mr. Wolfe realizes that he is, as yet, by no means a complete novelist.

The most flagrant evidence of his incompleteness is the fact that, so far, one indispensable part of the artist has existed not in Mr. Wolfe but in Maxwell Perkins. Such organizing faculty and such critical intelligence as have been applied to the book have come not from inside the artist, not from the artist's feeling for form and esthetic integrity, but from the office of Charles Scribner's Sons. For five years the artist pours out words "like burning lava from a volcano"—with little or no idea what their purpose is, which book they belong in, what the relation of part to part is, what is organic and what irrelevant, or what emphasis or coloration in the completed work of art is being served by the job at hand. Then Mr. Perkins decides these questions—from without, and by a process to which rumor applies the word "assembly." But works of art cannot be assembled like a carburetor—they must be grown like a plant, or in Mr. Wolfe's favorite simile like an embryo. The artist writes a hundred thousand words about a train: Mr. Perkins decides that the train is worth only five thousand words. But such a decision as this is properly not within Mr. Perkins's power; it must be made by the highly conscious self-criticism of the artist in relation to the pulse of the book itself. Worse still, the artist goes on writing till Mr. Perkins tells him that the novel is finished. But the end of a novel is, properly, dictated by the internal pressure, osmosis, metabolism—what you will—of the novel itself, of which only the novelist can have a first-hand knowledge. There comes a point where the necessities of the book are satisfied, where its organic processes have reached completion. It is hard to see how awareness of that point can manifest itself at an editor's desk—and harder still to trust the integrity of a work of art in which not the artist but the publisher has determined where the true ends and the false begins.

All this is made more ominous by Mr. Wolfe's almost incredibly youthful attitude toward revision. No novel is written till it is revised—the process is organic, it is one of the processes of art. It is, furthermore, the process above all others that requires objectivity, a feeling for form, a knowledge of what the necessities of the book are, a determination that those necessities shall outweigh and dominate everything else. It is, if not the highest functioning of the artistic intelligence, at least a fundamental and culminating one. But the process appears to Mr. Wolfe not one which will free his book from falsity, irrelevance and its private encumbrances, not one which will justify and so exalt the artist—but one that makes his spirit quiver "at the bloody execution" and his soul recoil "from the carnage of so many lovely things." But superfluous and mistaken things are lovely to only a very young writer, and the excision of them is bloody carnage only if the artist has not learned to subdue his ego in favor of his book. And the same juvenility makes him prowl "the streets of Paris like a maddened animal" because—for God's sake!—the reviewers may not like the job.

The placental passages are now explained. They consist of psychic material which the novelist has proved unable to shape into fiction. The failure may be due either to immature understanding or to insufficient technical skill: probably both causes operate here and cannot be separated. The principle is very simple. When Mr. Wolfe gives us his doctors, undertakers and newspapermen talking in a lunchroom at dawn, he does his job—magnificently. There they are, and the reader revels in the dynamic presentation of human beings, and in something else as well that should have the greatest possible significance for Mr. Wolfe. For while the doctors and undertakers are chaffing one another, the reader gets that feeling of the glamour and mystery of American life which Mr. Wolfe elsewhere unsuccessfully labors to evoke in thousands of rhapsodic words. The novelist makes his point in the lives of his characters, not in tidal surges of rhetoric.

Is America lost, lonely, nameless and unknown? Maybe, and maybe not. But if it is, the conditions of the novelist's medium require him to make it lost and lonely in the lives of his characters, not in blank verse bombast and apocalyptic delirium. You cannot represent America by hurling adjectives at it. Do "the rats of death and age and dark oblivion feed forever at the roots of sleep"? It sounds like a high school valedictory, but if in fact they do, then the novelist is constrained to show them feeding so by means of what his characters do and say and feel in relation to one another, and not by chasing the ghosts of Whitman and Ezekiel through fifty pages of disembodied emotion. Such emotion is certainly the material that fiction works with, but until it is embodied in character and scene it is not fiction—it is only logorrhea. A poem should not mean but be, Mr. MacLeish tells us, and poetry is always proving that fundamental. In a homelier aphorism Mr. Cohan has expressed the same imperative of the drama: "Don't tell 'em, show 'em." In the art of fiction the *thing* is not only an imperative, it is a primary condition. A novel *is*—it cannot be asserted, ranted or even detonated. A novelist represents life. When he does anything else, no matter how beautiful or furious or ecstatic the way in which he does it, he is not writing fiction. Mr. Wolfe can write fiction—has written some of the finest fiction of our day. But a great part of what he writes is not fiction at all; it is only material with which the novelist has struggled but which has defeated him. The most important question in American fiction to-day, probably, is whether he can win that encounter in his next book. It may be that *The October Fair* and *The Hills beyond Pentland* will show him winning it, but one remembers the dilution from *Look Homeward, Angel* to *Of Time and the River* and is apprehensive. If he does win it, he must do so inside himself; Mr. Perkins and the assembly-line at Scribners' can do nothing to help him.

That struggle also has another aspect. A novelist utilizes the mechanism of fantasy for the creation of a novel, and there are three kinds of fantasy with which he works. One of them is unconscious fantasy, about which Dr. Kubie was writing in these columns something over a year ago. A novelist is wholly subject to its emphases and can do nothing whatever about them—though when Mr. Wolfe says that the center of all living is reconciliation with one's father he comes close to revealing its pattern in him. There remain two kinds of fantasy which every novelist employs—but which everyone employs in a different ratio. Call them identification and projection, call them automatic and directed, call them proliferating and objectified—the names do not matter. The novelist surrenders himself to the first kind, but dominates and directs the second kind. In the first kind he says "I am Napoleon" and examines himself to see how he feels. In the second kind, he wonders how Napoleon feels, and instead of identifying himself with him, he tries to discover Napoleon's necessities. If he is excessively endowed with the first kind of fantasy, he is likely to be a genius. But if he learns to utilize the second kind in the manifold interrelationships of a novel he is certain to be an artist. Whatever Mr. Wolfe's future in the wider and looser interest of Literature, his future in the far more rigorous interest of fiction just about comes down to the question of whether he can increase his facility at the second kind of fantasy. People would stop idiotically calling him autobiographical, if he gave us less identification and more understanding. And we could do with a lot less genius, if we got a little more artist.

For the truth is that Mr. Wolfe is presented to us, and to himself, as a genius. There is no more dissent from that judgment in his thinking about himself than in Scribners' publicity. And, what is more, a genius of the good old-fashioned romantic kind—possessed by a demon, driven by the gales of his own fury, helpless before the lava-flood of his own passion, selected and set apart for greatness, his lips touched by a live coal, consequently unable to exercise any control over what he does and in fact likely to be damaged or diminished by any effort at control. Chaos is everything, if you have enough of it in you to make a world. Yes, but what if you don't make a world—what if you just make a noise? There was chaos in Stephen Dedalus's soul, but he thought of that soul not as sufficient in itself but merely as a smithy wherein he might forge his novel. And listen to Mr. Thomas Mann: "When I think of the masterpiece of the twentieth century, I have an idea of something that differs essentially and, in my opinion, with profit from the Wagnerian masterpiece—something exceptionally logical, clear, and well developed in form, something at once austere and serene, with no less intensity of will than his, but of cooler, nobler, even healthier spirituality, something that seeks its greatness not in the colossal, the baroque, and its beauty not in intoxication." Something, in other words, with inescapable form, something which exists as the imposition of order on chaos, something that *is,* not is merely asserted.

One can only respect Mr. Wolfe for his determination to realize himself on the highest level and to be satisfied with nothing short of greatness. But, however useful genius may be in the writing of novels, it is not enough in itself—it never has been enough, in any art, and it never will be. At the very least it must be supported by an ability to impart shape to material, simple competence in the use of tools. Until Mr. Wolfe develops more craftsmanship, he will not be the important novelist he is now widely accepted as being. In order to be a great novelist he must also mature his emotions till he can see more profoundly into character than he now does, and he must learn to put a corset on his prose. Once more: his own smithy is the only possible place for these developments—they cannot occur in the office of any editor whom he will ever know.

JOHN PEALE BISHOP
"The Sorrows of Thomas Wolfe" (1939)
The Collected Essays of John Peale Bishop
ed. Edmund Wilson
1948, pp. 129–37

I

Thomas Wolfe is dead. And that big work which he was prepared to write, which was to have gone to six long volumes and covered in the course of its narrative the years between 1781 and 1933, with a cast of characters whose numbers would have run into the hundreds, will never be finished. The title which he had chosen for it, *Of Time and the River,* had already been allowed to appear on the second volume. There its application is not altogether clear; how appropriate it would have been to the work as a whole we can only conjecture. No work of such magnitude has been projected by another of his generation in America; Wolfe's imagination, it appears, could conceive on no smaller scale. He was, he confesses, devoted to chance; he had no constant control over his faculties; but his fecundity was nothing less than prodigious. He had, moreover, a tenacity which must, but for his dying, have carried him through to the end.

Dying, he left behind him a mass of manuscript; how much of it can be published there is now no knowing. Wolfe was the most wasteful of writers.

His aim was to set down America as far as it can belong to the experience of one man. Wolfe came early on what was for him the one available truth about this continent—that it was contained in himself. There was no America which could not be made out—mountains, rivers, trains, cities, people—in the memory of an American. If the contours were misty, then they must be made clear. It was in flight from a certain experience of America, as unhappy as it had been apparently sterile—it was in Paris, in an alien land, that Wolfe first understood with hate and with love the horror and the wonder of his native country. He had crossed the seas from West to East only to come upon the North Carolina hills where he had been born. "I found out," he says, "during those years that the way to discover one's own country was to leave it; that the way to find America was to find it in one's own heart, one's memory and one's spirit, and in a foreign land. I think I may say that I discovered America during those years abroad out of my very need of her."

This is not an uncommon experience, but what made it rewarding in Wolfe's case was that his memory was anything but common. He could—and it is the source of what is most authentic in his talents—displace the present so completely by the past that its sights and sounds all but destroyed surrounding circumstance. He then lost the sense of time. For Wolfe, sitting at a table on a terrace in Paris, contained within himself not only the America he had known; he also held, within his body, both his parents. They were there, not only in his memory, but more portentously in the make-up of his mind. They loomed so enormous to him that their shadows fell across the Atlantic, their shade was on the café table under which he stretched his long American legs.

"The quality of my memory," he said in his little book, *The Story of a Novel,* "is characterized, I believe, in a more than ordinary degree by the intensity of its sense impressions, its power to evoke and bring back the odors, sounds, colors, shapes and feel of things with concrete vividness." That is true. But readers of Wolfe will remember that the mother of Eugene Gant was afflicted with what is known as total recall. Her interminable narratives were the despair of her family. Wolfe could no more than Eliza Gant suppress any detail, no matter how irrelevant; indeed, it was impossible for him to feel that any detail was irrelevant to his purpose. The readers of *Look Homeward, Angel* will also remember that Eugene's father had a gift, unrivalled among his associates, of vigorous utterance. Nobody, they said, can tie a knot in the tail of the English language like old W. O. But the elder Gant's speech, for all that it can on occasion sputter into fiery intensity, more often than not runs off into a homespun rhetoric. It sounds strong, but it has very little connection with any outer reality and is meaningless, except in so far as it serves to convey his rage and frustration. We cannot avoid supposing that Wolfe drew these two characters after his own parents. At the time he began writing *Look Homeward, Angel,* he stood far enough apart from them to use the endlessness of Eliza's unheard discourses, the exaggerated violence of old Gant's objurgations, for comic effect. He makes father and mother into something at once larger and less than human. But in his own case, he could not, at least so long as he was at his writing, restrain either the course of his recollections or their outcome in words. He wrote as a man possessed. Whatever was in his memory must be set down—not merely because he was Eliza's son, but because the secret end of all his writing was expiation—and it must be set down in words to which he constantly seems to be attaching more meaning than they can properly own. It was as though he were aware that his novel would have no meaning that could not be found in the words. The meaning of a novel should be in its structure. But in Wolfe's novel, as far as it has gone, it is impossible to discover any structure at all.

II

It is impossible to say what Wolfe's position in American letters would have been had he lived to bring his work to completion. At the moment he stands very high in the estimation both of the critics and of the common reader. From the time of *Look Homeward, Angel,* he was regarded, and rightly, as a young man of incomparable promise. *Of Time and the River* seemed to many to have borne out that promise and, since its faults were taken as due merely to an excess of fecundity, it was met with praise as though it were the consummation of all Wolfe's talents. Yet the faults are fundamental. The force of Wolfe's talents is indubitable; yet he did not find for that novel, nor do I believe he could ever have found, a structure of form which would have been capable of giving shape and meaning to his emotional experience. He was not without intelligence; but he could not trust his intelligence, since for him to do so would have been to succumb to conscience. And it was conscience, with its convictions of guilt, that he was continually trying to elude.

His position as an artist is very like that of Hart Crane. Crane was born in 1899, Wolfe in 1900, so that they were almost of an age. Both had what we must call genius; both conceived that genius had been given them that they might celebrate, the one in poetry, the other in prose, the greatness of their country. But Wolfe no more than Crane was able to give any coherence to his work than that which comes from the personal quality of his writing. And he found, as Crane did before him, that the America he longed to celebrate did not exist. He could record, and none better, its sights, its sounds and its odors, as they can be caught in a moment of time; he could try, as the poet of *The Bridge* did, to absorb that moment and endow it with the permanence of a myth. But he could not create a continuous America. He could not, for all that he was prepared to cover one hundred and fifty of its years, conceive its history. He can record what comes to his sensibility, but he cannot give us the continuity of experience. Everything for Wolfe is in the moment; he can so try to impress us with the immensity of the moment that it will take on some sort of transcendental meaning. But what that meaning is, escapes him, as it does us. And once it has passed from his mind, he can do nothing but recall another moment, which as it descends into his memory seems always about to deliver itself, by a miracle, of some tremendous import.

Both Crane and Wolfe belonged to a world that is indeed living from moment to moment. And it is because they voice its breakdown in the consciousness of continuity that they have significance for it.

Of the two, Wolfe, I should say, was the more aware of his plight. He was, he tells us, while writing *Of Time and the River*, tormented by a dream in which the sense of guilt was associated with the forgetting of time. "I was unable to sleep, unable to subdue the tumult of these creative energies, and, as a result of this condition, for three years I prowled the streets, explored the swarming web of the million-footed city and came to know it as I had never done before. . . . Moreover, in this endless quest and prowling of the night through the great web and jungle of the city, I saw, lived, felt and experienced the full weight of that horrible human calamity. [The time was that of the bottom of the depression, when Wolfe was living in Brooklyn.] And from it all has come, as a final deposit, a burning memory, a certain evidence of the fortitude of man, his ability to suffer and somehow survive. And it is for this reason now that I think I shall always remember this black period with a kind of joy that I could not at that time have believed possible, for it was during this time that I lived my life through to a first completion, and through the suffering and labor of my own life came to share those qualities in the lives of the people around me."

This passage is one of extreme interest, not only for what it tells us of Wolfe at this time, but for the promise it contains of an emotional maturity. For as far as Wolfe had carried the history of Eugene Gant, he was dealing with a young man whose isolation from his fellow men was almost complete. Eugene, and we must suppose the young Wolfe, was incarcerated in his own sensibility. Locked in his cell, he awaits the coming of every moment, as though it would bring the turning of a releasing key. He waits like Ugolino, when he woke uncertain because of his dream and heard not the opening but the closing of the lock. There is no release. And the place of Wolfe's confinement, no less than that of Ugolino, deserves to be called Famine.

It can be said of Wolfe, as Allen Tate has said of Hart Crane, that he was playing a game in which any move was possible, because none was compulsory. There is no idea which would serve as discipline to the event. For what Wolfe tells us was the idea that furiously pursued him during the composition of *Of Time and the River*, the search for a father, can scarcely be said to appear in the novel, or else it is so incidentally that it seems to no purpose. It does not certainly, as the same search on the part of Stephen Dedalus does in *Ulysses*, prepare a point toward which the whole narrative moves. There was nothing indeed in Wolfe's upbringing to make discipline acceptable to him. He acts always as though his own capacity for feeling, for anguished hope and continual frustration, was what made him superior, as no doubt, along with his romantic propensity for expression, it was. But he was wrong in assuming that those who accept any form of discipline are therefore lacking in vigor. He apparently did not understand that there are those who might say with Yeats, "I could recover if I shrieked my heart's agony," and yet like him are dumb "from human dignity." And his failure to understand was due to no fault of the intelligence, but to lack of love. The Gant family always strikes us, with its howls of rage, its loud hah-hahs of hate and derision, as something less than human. And Eugene is a Gant. While in his case we are ready to admit that genius is a law unto itself, we have every right to demand that it discover its own law.

Again like Crane, Wolfe failed to see that at the present time so extreme a manifestation of individualism could not but be morbid. Both came too late into a world too mechanic; they lacked a wilderness and constantly tried to create one as wild as their hearts. It was all very well for them, since both were in the way of being poets, to start out to proclaim the grandeur of America. Such a task seemed superb. But both were led at last, on proud romantic feet, to Brooklyn. And what they found there they abhorred.

They represent, each in his way, a culmination of the romantic spirit in America. There was in both a tremendous desire to impose the will on experience. Wolfe had no uncommon will. And Crane's was strong enough to lead him deliberately to death by drowning. For Wolfe the rewards of experience were always such that he was turned back upon himself. Isolated in his sensations, there was no way out. He continually sought for a door, and there was really none, or only one, the door of death.

III

The intellectual labor of the artist is properly confined to the perception of relations. The conscience of the craftsman must see that these relations are so presented that, in spite of all complications, they are ultimately clear. It is one of the conditions of art that they cannot be abstractly stated, but must be presented to the senses.

What we have at the center of all Wolfe's writing is a single character, and it was certainly the aim of that writing to present this character in all his manifold contacts with the world of our time. Eugene has, we are told, the craving of a Faust to know all experience, to be able to record all the races and all the social classes which may be said to exist in America. Actually, Eugene's experience is not confined to America.

But when we actually come to consider Eugene closely, we see that, once he is beyond the overwhelming presence of his family, his contacts with other people are all casual. The perfect experience for Eugene is to see someone in the throes of an emotion which he can imagine, but in which he has no responsible part. From one train, he sees people passing in another train, which is moving at a faster speed than his own.

"And they looked at one another for a moment, they passed and vanished and were gone forever, yet it seemed to him that he had known these people, that he knew them far better than the people in his own train, and that, having met them for an instant under immense and timeless skies, as they were hurled across the continent to a thousand destinations, they had met, passed, vanished, yet would remember this forever. And he thought the people in the two trains felt this, also: slowly they passed each other now, and their mouths smiled and their eyes grew friendly, but he thought there was some sorrow and regret in what they felt. For having lived together as strangers in the immense and swarming city, they had now met upon the everlasting earth, hurled past each other for a moment between two points of time upon the shining rails; never to meet, to speak, to know each other any more, and the briefness of their days, the destiny of man, was in that instant greeting and farewell."

He sees from a train a boy trying to decide to go after a girl; wandering the streets of New York, he sees death come to four men; through one of his students at the university, he comes in contact with an old Jewess wailing a son dead for a year. Each of these moments is completely done; most of them, indeed, overwrought. From the country seen from a train he derives "a wild and solemn joy—the sense of nameless hope, impossible desire, and man's tragic brevity." He reacts to most circumstances, it must seem to us, excessively. But to men and women he does not really answer. The old Jewess's grief fills him "with horror, anger, a sense of cruelty, disgust, and pity." The passion aroused returns to himself. And it is precisely because his passions cannot attain their object, and in one person know peace,that he turns in rage and desire toward the millions. There is in Eugene every emotion you wish but one; there is no love.

The most striking passages in Wolfe's novels always represent these moments of comprehension. For a moment, but a moment only, there is a sudden release of compassion, when some aspect of suffering and bewildered humanity is seized, when the other's emotion is in a timeless completion known. Then the moment passes, and compassion fails. For Eugene Gant, the only satisfactory relationship with another human creature is one which can have no continuity. For the boy at the street corner, seen in the indecision of youthful lust, he has only understanding and pity; the train from which he looks moves on and nothing more is required of Eugene. But if he should approach that same boy on the street, if he should come close enough to overhear him, he would hear only the defilement of language, words which would awaken in him only hate and disgust. He would himself become lonely, strange and cruel. For emotions such as these, unless they can be used with the responsibility of the artist, must remain a torment to the man.

The only human relationship which endures is that of the child to his family. And that is inescapable: once having been, it cannot cease to be. His father is still his father, though dying; and his brother Ben, though dead, remains his brother. He loves and he hates and knows why no more than the poet he quotes. What he does know is that love has been forbidden him.

The only contemporary literary influence on Wolfe which was at all strong was that of Joyce. I shall consider it here only to note that while we know that Joyce could only have created Stephen Dedalus out of the conflicts of his own youth, we never think of Stephen simply as the young Joyce, any more than we think of Hamlet as Shakespeare. He is a creation. But in Wolfe's novels it is impossible to feel that the central figure has any existence apart from the author. He is called Eugene Gant, but that does not deceive any one for a moment; he is, beyond all doubt, Thomas Wolfe. There is, however, one important distinction to be made between them, and one which we should not allow ourselves to forget: Eugene Gant is always younger, by at least ten years, than Thomas Wolfe.

Wolfe described *Of Time and the River* as being devoted to "the period of wandering and hunger in a man's youth." And in it we are meant to take Eugene as every young man. The following volume would, Wolfe said, declare "a period of greater certitude, which would be dominated by a single passion." That, however, still remains to be seen. So far, Eugene has shown no capacity as a lover, except in casual contact with whores. When for a moment he convinces himself that he is in love with Ann, who is a nice simple conventional girl from Boston, he can only shriek at her and call her a bitch and a whore, which she certainly is not. The one contact which lasts for any time—leaving aside the blood ties which bind him to the Pentlands, his mother's people, and the Gants—is that with Starwick. Starwick is the only friend he makes in his two years at Harvard, and in Paris, some years later, he still regards his friendship with Starwick as the most valuable he has ever known.

It ends when he discovers that Starwick is a homosexual. And it has usually been assumed that the violence and bitterness with which it ends are due to disillusionment; the sudden turn in Eugene's affectons for the young man may well be taken as a natural reaction to his learning, first that Ann is in love with Starwick, and only a little later how hopelessly deep is Starwick's infatuation with the young tough he has picked up, by apparent chance, one night in a Paris bar. But that is, I think, to take too simple a view of the affair. There is more to it than that. What we have been told about Starwick from his first appearance in the book is that, despite a certain affectation and oddity of manner, he is, as Eugene is not, a person capable of loving and being loved. What is suddenly revealed in Paris is that for him, too, love is a thing the world has forbidden. In Starwick's face Eugene sees his own fate. Just as in his brother Ben's complaint at his neglect, he had looked back through another's sight at his own neglected childhood and in his brother's death foremourned his own, so now, when he beats Starwick's head against the wall, he is but raging against his own frustration and despair.

In his father's yard, among the tombstones, has stood for years a marble angel. Old Gant curses it, all hope he thinks lost that he will ever get his money back for it. It stands a magnificent reminder of the time when as a boy, with winged ambition, he had wanted to be not merely a stonecutter but a sculptor. Then, unexpectedly a customer comes for it. The one symbol of the divine in the workshop is sold to adorn the grave of a prostitute; what the boy might have been the man lets go for such a purpose. It cannot be said that Thomas Wolfe ever sold his angel. But the faults of the artist are all of them traceable to the failures of the man. He achieved probably the utmost intensity of which incoherent writing is capable; he proved that an art founded solely on the individual, however strong his will, however vivid his sensations, cannot be sound, or whole, or even passionate, in a world such as ours, in which "the integrity of the individual consciousness has been broken down." How far it has broken down, I do not believe he ever knew, yet all that he did is made of its fragments.

BETTY THOMPSON
"Thomas Wolfe: Two Decades of Criticism"
South Atlantic Quarterly, July 1950, pp. 378–92

The tenth anniversary of the death of Thomas Wolfe on September 15, 1948, was unmarked by critical fanfare in erudite journals which observe historical events in connection with their favorites. The interest in the North Carolina writer, who was one of the most controversial literary figures of the thirties, was no less vigorous in the forties, but the pattern of the argument had not changed significantly. As early as 1929, when *Look Homeward, Angel* appeared, the outline for the long critical debate was apparent; after 1935, when Wolfe published *Of Time and the River*, a continuation of the story of the protagonist of the first novel, and *From Death to Morning*, a volume of short stories, both attack and defense were monotonously predictable. Bernard DeVoto, the most vociferous of the dissenters, published his "Genius Is Not Enough" article in 1936 as a belligerent review of Wolfe's *The Story of a Novel*, a slender volume concerning his methods of writing. At the time of Wolfe's death a decade ago in the Johns Hopkins Hospital in Baltimore, his implacable enemies had their manifesto, and his equally fanatic admirers had been told that he resembled everyone from Melville to Proust.

With every new account we read of the "depressingly familiar" legend of Thomas Wolfe. It is almost impossible for a biographer or critic to begin without reviewing it. Despite Wolfe's lack of attention from the "new critics" and space in their journals, two book-length critical estimates have been published. Herbert Muller, whose *Thomas Wolfe* surprisingly turned up in 1947 in a New Direction series featuring more esoteric and fashionable modern writers, plunged into the legend in the first paragraph to get rid of it. *Hungry Gulliver*, the "English critical appraisal" issued in 1948, is British novelist Pamela Hansford Johnson's summary of the myth in a two-word title and less than two-hundred pages of discussion. Even those most weary of the legend, Maxwell Geismar, who wrote the Introduction for the *Portable Wolfe*, and James K. Hutsell, who told the story of Thomas Wolfe and Asheville in the *Southern Packet* for April, 1948, had to repeat in order to refute.

According to Mr. Hutsell's version:

> Here was a man too big for ordinary beds. Here was a man so outsize that, in an alien basement flat in the Assyrian quarter of South Brooklyn, he wrote standing up—with the top of a refrigerator for a desk—and literally tossed millions of words (pencil-scrawled on yellow paper) into a packingbox in the middle of the floor. Here was life's hungry man, insatiable in his hunger for food and drink and more insatiable still with a hunger to know all places, all hearts and all of fury and chaos.
>
> All these things about Thomas Wolfe are true. But they are a portion of the truth. . . . Gargantuan has become a favorite adjective for him in the dozens of Wolfe clubs that dot American campuses. It is almost time that somebody should object.
>
> It is true that Wolfe by his own gusto, his own turmoil, his own undisciplined flow of words has been partially responsible for this twisted view of him. He was full of raptures and incontinences. His real weakness was not perhaps that he dramatized his life, but that Wolfe the writer dramatized it more than Wolfe the man.

After the Wolfe legend must come the comparison of Thomas Wolfe and his heroes, Eugene Gant and George Webber. Although Wolfe denied from the start that he was merely a diary keeper, in the preface to his first novel he said he had no answer for the charge that his book was autobiographical, as were all works of fiction. He spoke of turning over half the people of a town to make a single figure in a novel. That he turned over considerably less than half became painfully obvious when the citizens of Asheville recognized not only Tom Wolfe and his family but themselves and each other. Their reactions have been described by Wolfe in *The Story of a Novel* and in the portions of *You Can't Go Home Again* (his fourth and last novel, published posthumously in 1940) that deal with the reception accorded by the people of "Libya Hill" to "George Webber's" book, *Home to Our Mountains*. It is now evident that Wolfe's incessant war against the term *autobiographical* was not merely resentment at the accusation that he wrote "unconsciously boring catalogues of details and meaningless autobiographical reminiscences." He was concerned over the outraged reaction of Asheville people against his work and over the pain his frank portraits caused his friends and family.

Eugene Gant was the son of a lusty, rhetorical stonecutter and a driving, acquisitive mother, who kept a boarding house, Dixieland. Like William Oliver Gant, W. O. Wolfe, Tom's father, was a monument shop proprietor, who was born in Pennsylvania and who liked to quote Shakespeare and Gray's *Elegy*. Julia Elizabeth Westall Wolfe is hardly distinguishable from Eliza Pentland Gant by those who know both or who have read either Hayden Norwood's conversational biography *The Marble Man's Wife* or *Thomas Wolfe's Letters to His Mother*, edited by his friend and biographer, John Skally Terry. Visitors to Asheville flock to the Old Kentucky Home, which Mrs. Wolfe kept as a boarding house until her death in 1945. This house at 48 Spruce Street has become a memorial to the writer according to the plans of the Thomas Wolfe Memorial Association headed by Don Shoemaker, editor of the Asheville *Citizen*. Little is heard these days from the individuals who thought that Wolfe should be tarred and feathered. Sight-seers are directed to places described in Wolfe's novels, and the outrage of twenty years ago is less important than the fame Wolfe has brought to North Carolina.

The Thomas Wolfe issue of the *Southern Packet* is demonstration enough that Thomas and Eugene were one. The excellent photographs of buildings and people described in *Look Homeward, Angel* are accompanied by fragments of descriptions from the novel as captions. His teachers at the North State Finishing School are without question the Leonards of the novel; letters from Wolfe to his teacher and friend, Mrs. J. M. Roberts, which were published three years ago in the *Atlantic Monthly*, increase the certainty. The reminiscences of his friends mention persons and events we have read about in the chapters of his first two novels that deal with Eugene at "Pulpit Hill" and Harvard.

Eugene Gant and Thomas Wolfe were born on October 3, 1900. Their parents have been described; Eugene's hill-rimmed city was Altamont, Tom's Asheville. Eugene had twin brothers named Benjamin Harrison and Grover Cleveland. So did Tom. Their brothers and sisters correspond in personalities and ages. Youth in Asheville and Altamont was lost and lonely. The years at the state university were anguished but successful. As a bridge between these biographical facts and the treatment of Wolfe by the critics, it is convenient to use one of the many anecdotes.

In 1916 a gangling, overgrown boy not quite sixteen

years old left his Asheville home to go to the University of North Carolina at Chapel Hill. The boy was filled with the wild, furious energy of genius and a lust for knowledge and experience which by its intensity set him apart from his fellow students as decisively as his wild looks and excessive tallness separated him from them physically. He felt that he was different, and that feeling made him lonely and unhappy. He felt that his difference was due to his superiority, and he exulted in his variation. By his own admission, he performed brilliantly in those things which touched his interest and dully, or not well at all, in those subjects which did not.

Being a genius, he knew before Mr. DeVoto told him, was not enough. He longed to be accepted by the smooth, confident fraternity men whom he envied. By spring of his junior year, this story goes, one of the most exclusive fraternities had been forced by urgent financial difficulties into admitting boys who were not hereditary Greek-letter material. One day a brother brought in a possible pledge who was a trifle too unkempt, the gangling youth from Asheville. Just as he was about to be blackballed it was reported that a visiting celebrity had commented that the strange youth was "probably genius." The chance was worth taking, the brethren decided, and Thomas Wolfe was elected to membership.

The story, like most of the Wolfe legend, is a mixture of fact and fiction, drawn from what he has written and what others have related about him. It could as easily be false as true, but the significant thing is that the attitude of the critics was much like that of the typical or mythical fraternity brothers. At the time of the publication of *Look Homeward, Angel*, there was much about his prodigious volume they did not like. Few, however, could deny his genius, so he was elected to the ranks of "great American novelists." The vote lacked unanimity, for there were those who distinguished between a genius's novel and a novel of genius.

The appearance of *Look Homeward, Angel* has been called the nearest thing to a literary thunderbolt in the twentieth century. Leo Gurko makes this exaggerated claim in the *Angry Decade*, his social and literary interpretation of the ten-year period 1929–1939. Since the selected reading list printed with this book includes such "criticism" as that of J. Donald Adams, Bernard DeVoto, and Granville Hicks, it is not hard to decide whether the social or the literary determines Gurko's judgment. His extravagant statement looks silly in the light of such real literary "thunderbolts" as James Joyce's *Ulysses* or T. S. Eliot's *The Waste Land*. Wolfe's millions of lyrical, undisciplined words, his power to create great living characters, and his vivid exploration of middle-class American life caused him to be labeled original. His talent was marvelous, but he was not a creator of new forms or new modes of expression. In fact, *Look Homeward, Angel* was less startling to the general public than *A Farewell to Arms* and *All Quiet on the Western Front*, both published in 1929. William Faulkner's *The Sound and the Fury* was also first issued that year, and critics who have long since washed their hands of the mighty Wolfe are still pondering the mysteries of his fellow Southerner. Alfred Kazin in *On Native Grounds* considers Faulkner and Wolfe together as exponents of "the rhetoric and the agony." If we are to trust the editor of the Penguin book edition of Wolfe's stories, Faulkner himself is a great admirer of Wolfe.

The first chapter of the Gant saga did receive appreciative reviews: John Chamberlain in the *Bookman*, Basil Davenport in the *Saturday Review of Literature*, and Geoffrey Hellman in the *New Republic*. In his speech of acceptance for the Nobel Prize in 1930, Sinclair Lewis cited Wolfe as one of the most promising of the younger writers and said that his novel was worthy of comparison with the best literature America had produced. But his defects did not go unnoticed. From the first there were critics for whom Wolfe was chaotic, exhausting, overemotional, and revolting.

None of Wolfe's books was ever praised more exorbitantly or criticized more unmercifully than *Of Time and the River*, which was published six years after his first. Mr. Muller in his balanced (too balanced for some who feel that he builds up Wolfe's defense only to tear it down himself) study finds the second novel something more than another slice of the life of Tom and Eugene. The difference, this diligent and thoughtful student of Wolfe thinks, is intellectual and moral rather than technical, because Eugene gets away from the unity given his first book as a description of the process of growing up and gets out into the world beyond his own state. *Of Time and the River* lacks plot but has greater depth and variety. The framework is still that of Wolfe's life: graduate study at Harvard, life in New York as a university instructor, travel in Europe. To Muller it is more than tales of wandering and Faustian hunger. He documents his claims for greater maturity by explaining the transition from the personal legend to the American legend through Wolfe's realization of community in loneliness.

In the midst of the critical storm, Wolfe was compared to Whitman, Dostoevski, Dickens, the Bible, De Quincey, Homer, and Jack London! Robert Penn Warren reminded the melancholy Tar Heel that Shakespeare "merely wrote Hamlet, he was not Hamlet." DeVoto, obsessed by the psychological jargon of the period, found in Wolfe examples of manic-depression, infantile regression, and compulsion neurosis. The problem which Wolfe had to solve before most serious critics would put any final evaluation upon his work was stated by John Donald Wade in an essay entitled "Prodigal" and published in the July, 1935, issue of the *Southern Review:*

> So far his work has been the record of his passage through the world. Whether he can transfer his peculiar virtues to books in which he is not himself the protagonist, is something that the performance only can indicate.

The critical obituaries which appeared in 1938 judged Wolfe on the strength and weakness of his first two novels and the book of short stories published during his lifetime. The general conclusion was that Wolfe suffered from some very American complaints. He was endowed with a profusion of remarkable talents and extraordinary vitality, but he was, for all his energy and genius, a classic American failure. Waste and immaturity, indigenous faults, cancel out the virtues in the final equation. Many reviews of Muller's appraisal called Wolfe's reputation declining. Actually, critical opinion of Wolfe has not changed very much in the decade since his death. Not enough, Muller believes, since the books about George Webber, *The Web and the Rock*, 1939, and *You Can't Go Home Again*, 1940, attained the greater objectivity Wolfe had promised in *The Story of a Novel*. The unfinished historical novel, *The Hills Beyond*, differed in style and was chronologically impossible of autobiography. The performance, it must be admitted, did not demonstrate the transfer of the "peculiar virtues."

If critics have failed to take into account the change in Wolfe's attitude toward society and himself as set forth in the posthumous novels, the judgments of his work generally have been more temperate, if somewhat arrogantly regretful of his shortcomings. There have always been, and there will continue to be naïve, hysterical idolators proclaiming his tremendous powers at one end of the pole, while niggardly, unsympathetic critics expose his excesses at the other. Hamilton Basso, once among Wolfe's staunchest defenders, expressed in a *New Yorker* review of the *Portable Wolfe* his reluctance to enter the controversy, as though it were something of recent origin, and referred to Wolfe as the darling of one cult and the villain of another.

Both Mr. Muller and Mrs. Johnson believe that Wolfe's writing made for hyperbolic criticism. Says Muller:

> His elemental powers are remarkable but they are also obvious; so are his elementary faults. He offers critics plenty of opportunity to exercise their eloquence in celebrating his powers, or their wits in ridiculing his faults; he offers little opportunity for acute analysis, subtle appreciation, or the knowing kind of criticism that distinguishes this age. Nor is the reader's judgment of his work likely to be affected much by criticism. Whether one is most impressed by his splendid gifts or by his shocking sins as an artist is chiefly a matter of temperament. One may have to learn to like caviar; one does not cultivate a taste for roast beef.

Of Wolfe's works generally, Mrs. Johnson says:

> It is difficult to write with moderation, for the grandiose epithets persistently reiterated—"huge," "vast," "enormous," "fine," "rare"—tend to transfer themselves to relevant criticism. They are his words, expressive of his own height, his own thought, his own conception of America.

"Rooted in Adolescence" is Caroline Gordon's title for her review of these two books, which compares them only indirectly. Writing in the New York *Times Book Review*, Miss Gordon discounts Wolfe's myth-making powers as expounded by Mr. Muller in his "interesting" and "uncritical" study. As for Mrs. Johnson, she remarks that "Wolfe's characters seem to be accepted as typically American by those persons whose history and affections are not deeply rooted in America."

Miss Gordon's comments on Wolfe himself are of more interest, since she and her friends are among the chief practitioners of that "acute analysis, subtle appreciation, or the knowing kind of criticism."

> Wolfe's intention was praiseworthy, but there was a lack of artistic intelligence. Webber's repudiation of Foxhall Edwards seems not so much a denial of the friend and father as a repudiation of the man's vision of life and art. The "testament" concludes with the words: "The wind is rising and the rivers flow," but the wind, one fears, is only the rustle of rhetoric, and a critic contemplating Wolfe's controlling image in *Of Time and the River* is reminded of Henry James's figure of the artist who, cultivating his instinct rather than his awareness, sits finally in a stale and shrinking puddle.

A critic contemplating Miss Gordon's remark is reminded that this knowing criticism can rarely get through even such a short article as that just quoted without reference to Henry James. It is by the standards of James that Wolfe is such a monstrous artistic failure. Certainly, his "point of view" fails to interest students of the Jamesian method. A further revealing insight is offered when Miss Gordon suggests that John Peale Bishop's article in the first issue of the *Kenyon Review* in 1939 probably remains the best thing written about his work. That article, "The Sorrows of Thomas Wolfe," is indeed a lucid and fascinating piece of criticism, comparing Wolfe and Hart Crane. Bishop, according to Miss Gordon, paid Wolfe the compliment his admirers rarely do, of measuring his intention against his execution. The Bishop article is mentioned by Muller as one of the critical obituaries unable to take into account the unpublished novels. Miss Gordon's belief that Wolfe's later work made no difference is reflected both in her choice of Bishop's interpretation and her comments on Wolfe's credo.

In an attempt to be objective Mr. Muller fills his book with references to critics almost wholly unsympathetic to Wolfe. To prove that Wolfe was more than a regionalist and nothing of the provincial, he chooses Allen Tate's distinction between regionalism and provincialism. Mr. Tate has said in the classroom and perhaps in print that Thomas Wolfe not only did harm to the art of the novel, but moral damage to his readers. Wolfe, for Mr. Muller, becomes a myth-maker through Mark Schorer's definition of myth as a "large controlling image . . . which gives philosophical meaning to the facts of ordinary life, that is to say, which has organizing value for experience." Mr. Schorer in his recent article on "Technique as Discovery" gives a detailed demolition of Wolfe as artist:

> The books of Thomas Wolfe, were, of course, journals, and the primary role of his publisher in transforming these journals into the semblance of novels is notorious. For the crucial act of the artist, the unique act which is composition, a sympathetic blue pencil and scissors were substituted. The result has excited many people, especially the young, and the ostensibly critical have observed the prodigal talent with a wish that it might have been controlled . . . for until the talent is controlled, the material organized, the contest achieved, there is simply the man and his life.

The title of Wolfe's second book is for Schorer simply a euphemism for *Of Man and His Ego.* Had Wolfe had adequate respect for and been able to pursue technique, he continues, he might have been able to write a great novel on his true subject, the dilemma of romantic genius. "Like Emily Brontë, Wolfe needed a point of view beyond his own which would separate his material and its effect." Rather than as a great myth-maker, Wolfe appears to Schorer as a subjectivist, whose record of the bewilderment of the age is no more valuable to us than our own diaries and letters.

The sympathetic editor whose blue pencil and scissors are notorious was the late Maxwell Perkins of Scribner's, to whom Wolfe dedicated *Of Time and the River* and to whom many other writers, including Miss Gordon, have dedicated their books in appreciation for his services as editor and friend. Undeniably, Perkins, who is the Foxhall Edwards of the last Webber novel, helped Wolfe tremendously in preparing his manuscripts for publication, but the part of the Wolfe legend which deals with his methods of creation is the most enormously magnified of all. Edward Aswell, the editor who worked with Wolfe after he transferred to Harper's, refers to the belief "that when Tom was in the throes of composition all he had to do was to open the sluice gates and the words tumbled forth in an irresistible torrent like the surge of pent-up waters suddenly released." The popular conception of Wolfe's methods of writing was described by Wolfe in an amusing and touching letter to F. Scott Fitzgerald. Schorer is not alone in believing Wolfe to be a cut-and-paste artist who took his fictional diaries to Mr. Perkins to be made with infinite patience into publishable books. When this "collaboration" was discovered, Wolfe sought to disguise his methods by changing his hero's name to Webber and taking packing cases filled with thousands of sheets of paper over to Harper's where a new tailor would attempt similar miracles.

In an article on which he was working at the time of his death, which was published in the *Harvard Library Bulletin*, Autumn, 1947, as an introduction to the William B. Wisdom Collection of Thomas Wolfe, Perkins explained his literary relationship to Wolfe. The editor expressed his conviction that Wolfe made a horrible mistake in changing his hero from Gant to the presumably objective Webber. Perkins says that when he first read Wolfe's manuscript he felt that it was autobiographical in the sense in which *David Copperfield* or *War and Peace* is, but that he realized as he worked with Wolfe that it was often almost literally autobiographical. The amount of cutting was far less than has been supposed. The work was really a matter of reorganization. But neither Wolfe's denials nor those of his editors have been able to destroy the notions some critics have concerning his total dependence on his editors. John Terry found it necessary to state again in a recent article that Perkins never rewrote a single word of Wolfe's and that most of the cutting was done by the author himself on the editor's advice.

Perkins in his exposition of their co-operative working methods tells of an instance in which Wolfe ignored his advice and turned out to be right. Working on the principle that Wolfe's unity and form in *Of Time and the River* came through the senses of Eugene, Perkins tried to persuade Wolfe that the episode of his father's death was outside the perception and knowledge of the general character, who was at Harvard at the time. Wolfe agreed but wrote on as he planned, creating the magnificent death of stoneman Gant. Perkins realized that it was he who was wrong, even if right in theory: "What he was doing was too good to let any rule of form impede him."

The schism between George Webber and Foxhall Edwards had, in addition to the philosophical undertones revealed by Webber, a very practical reason. He wanted to prove to his detractors and perhaps to himself that he could write an objective book without the aid of his friend. His editors have written truthfully of his constant rewriting, of the many versions before he was satisfied that a single episode was ready for print. Maxwell Geismar submits as proof that Wolfe was not purely a quantitative writer the three years he spent in writing his first novel, the complete abandonment of his next book, *K-19*, a novel about a train and its passengers, and the years of work on *Of Time and the River*. That he learned at least enough discipline to have plays he wrote as a result of three years of drama study under Professor George Pierce Baker of Harvard considered for Broadway production is for Muller an indication that he was capable of restraint. However, *Mannerhouse*, the recently published (1948) Wolfe play, contains most of his excesses of romantic feeling and rhetoric.

Regardless of what misconceptions they might hold concerning his methods of writing, the critics primarily interested in standards measured Wolfe by their criteria and found him a megalomaniac without form or real style. The strength of the opposition of the best critics is shown in the parenthetical remarks of their historian and critic, Stanley Edgar Hyman, in *The Armed Vision*. The critic of critics says of Van Wyck Brooks, "He is probably the most repetitious writer since Thomas Wolfe died." Of R. P. Blackmur's concept of the fallacy of expressive form he says that it has been employed consistently "to demolish writers like Thomas Wolfe and Carl Sandburg, as well as bigger game." He criticizes Harry Slochower by stating that "windy bores like Wolfe are treated as comparable to Kafka and Rilke." In the reviews found in most of the better quarterlies Thomas Wolfe is equated with artless raving.

Critical detestation of Wolfe was not limited to the aesthetic group. The other principal school of the thirties, the social critics who judged all literature by Marxist standards, found Wolfe equally abhorrent for different reasons. Edwin Berry Burgum called *Of Time and the River* an example of the third and worst of his categories of bourgeois novels. The rise of fascism was reflected in this type, which presented a distortion of contemporary society through the optimism of an idealistic or Nietzschean interpretation. It is interesting to contrast this utterance with Burgum's "Thomas Wolfe Discovers America" in the *Virginia Quarterly Review*, Summer, 1946. Rather than a sinister precursor of fascism, Wolfe is the voice of average American youth of the postwar period, "better than Hemingway (who represented the minority of the sophisticated), better than Dos Passos (who only described the appearance of things)." This reversal is perhaps less a sign that criticism takes a more tolerant view of Wolfe than a symptom of the widespread modifications and retractions of the social critics in the forties.

With accuracy Gurko has remarked that the width of Wolfe's scope and the abundance of his energy make him fuel for almost any thesis. Bella Kussey, writing in the *Sewanee Review* in 1942, found in Wolfe a sensual primitivism, a kinship with Whitman, Nietzsche, and the Nazis. Franz Schoenberner's article "Wolfe's Genius Seen Afresh" appearing on the front page of the New York *Times Book Review*, August 4, 1946, was a German intellectual's affirmation of the belief that Wolfe alone among the most famous of contemporary writers was endowed "with the prophetic Ethos and the poetic Pathos of the true genius." The article praised Wolfe for discerning the terror of Nazism before it was fashionable to do so and for giving in the comparatively brief account of George Webber's visit to Germany a better insight into the problems of those days than the combined cables and reports of the correspondents there.

This eloquent defense by the editor of *Simplicisimuss* and the author of *Confessions of a German Intellectual* was countered by the late Russell Maloney, who described himself as "Spokesman for a small number of cads who believe that Thomas Wolfe was only a part-time genius." His letter attacked Wolfe, whose place among Germans as the American Homer was traced to anti-Semitism and other provincial prejudices. "Our theory is that he did not like the Third Reich only because he didn't properly understand it."

More than intellectual and temperamental differences in the readers cause Wolfe to appear a spiritual Nazi to one and a vigorous anti-Fascist to another. The explanation lies in the opposing emotions and thoughts which co-exist in Wolfe and his heroes. Diverse students of Wolfe realize these incongruities as a major key to his writing and to his unique personality. Gurko calls the constant alternation "the immutable counterpoint" and "this tormented interplay of opposites." As a sociologist, he is interested in the anti-Semitism, which is balanced by Gant's affection for his Jewish student, Abe Jones, in *Of Time and the River* and his anguished love for his Jewish mistress, Esther Jack, of the Webber novels, whom he both adores and despises for her Hebraic richness. Wolfe's slighting references to Negroes are matched by his bitterness at the cruel stupidity of lynchers. Paranoia and naïve egocentricity have their counterparts in common sense and humility.

As literary critic, Mr. Muller finds in Wolfe's handling of typical incongruities abounding in his work something like "the melancholy, ironic detachment" of Joseph Conrad. To Mr. Muller the constant stress upon incongruity is the peculiar quality of Wolfe's fiction, and in the death of Ben Gant in *Look Homeward, Angel* he finds a scene unsurpassed in contemporary literature for resolution of complex disharmonies. In her analysis of Wolfe's style, Mrs. Johnson is also aware of the incongruities. When the two critics arrive at similar conclusions, however, it is seldom by the same methods. Mrs. Johnson's book may be regarded as the one some critics, displeased with the emphasis Muller placed on Wolfe's failings, would have had him write. The adverse criticism in Muller deals legitimately with Wolfe's artistic failures, while his praise is directed more to his intellectual and moral development. On the other hand, Mrs. Johnson finds Wolfe acceptable as an artist, while she deplores the philosophy and middle-class prejudices she feels his environment bred. His saving force, she believes, was his natural optimism and his belief in the grandeur of mankind. She finds the purest expression of his optimism in Eugene Gant; of his conflict, in George Webber.

Growth is for Muller the theme of all Wolfe's work, and he is convinced that it is the explicit theme of *You Can't Go Home Again*. In the conclusion to this book he discovers the culmination of organic growth in the faith Wolfe has in the promise of America and in the dignity of man, which was implicit in his earliest work. But while the English critic calls the ending "one of the most flawless conclusions to any novel in the English language," the American considers the whole farewell to Edwards a personal postscript of more interest to the biographer than the novel reader, not "an artistically logical or effective ending."

The constant references to the new critics in Muller's book are not merely to impress the reader with his superior knowledge of them. Simply because he is a contributor to their journals and an admirer of their excellent work, Muller is much concerned with their values. He mentions William Empson on Proust, Cleanth Brooks on metaphysical poetry, T. S. Eliot on tradition, Constance Rourke on the American character. Although his discussions often seem farfetched, the superiority of his method over the rhapsodic approach of Mrs. Johnson stands out in their very different final chapters. "Wolfe and the Tradition," Muller's conclusion, is a brilliant survey of American literature, measuring Wolfe against Hawthorne, Melville, Whitman, Emerson, and James as well as the Agrarians, Dos Passos, Sinclair Lewis, and other contemporaries. Mrs. Johnson, in a much briefer and more limited survey, finds Wolfe's comparative importance unassessed. "Beside him Faulkner appears neurotic and obscure, Hemingway oversophisticated and Steinbeck, a novelist of power and solidity, to have a certain recessive quality." Her further comments on these writers reveals a lack of understanding of them; all of them, she says, might easily have been Europeans. She follows Kazin in his belief that Wolfe was a perpetual boy. Mrs. Johnson's style itself is overblown, given to such extravagances as:

> The words strike response from the heart as the sun strikes arrows of bronze from the shield. In their clangour, their grasping weight of effort, they force the imagination to the realization of Wolfe's whole being and desire, as narrowly, as nearly, as the battering ram breaches the walls which will not yield.

William B. Wisdom, whose vision and industry kept together the practically complete assembly of Wolfe's letters, manuscripts, publications, library, and other possessions of interest to the scholar, has donated his remarkable collection to the Harvard College library. It is said to constitute a concentration of research material unsurpassed for a major literary figure. Here all the subliterary questions on this intensely personal author can eventually be solved. Mr. Muller observes that personal taste and fashion, not eternal principles of prose, dictate verdicts.

> Here in contemporary America is our first and last concern; for the immediate world is the only world we have. And here is the final significance of Wolfe for contemporaries; he made himself at home in this world.

Whether Wolfe's faults are the flaws of greatness or of a magnitude to preclude greatness is a decision the individual reader along with the conscious literary critic must make. He is out of the literary fashion; he fails by the standards of some of the finest critics of the age. But his significance for his contemporaries is that he did create with marvelous words and powerful emotions a world in which they also could be at home. And we can wonder how declining the Wolfe reputation is when David McDowell's sympathetic review of French translations appears among a group of articles devoted to the celebration of new critic John Crowe Ransom's birthday and when the income from the sale of his books is three times what it was in 1938.

C. HUGH HOLMAN

"Rhetorical Hope and Dramatic Despair"

The Loneliness at the Core: Studies in Thomas Wolfe

1975, pp. 86–106

Thomas Wolfe was the master of two distinct modes of writing—although there are unkind critics, such as Bernard De Voto, who would say that he was mastered by them. One of these modes is that of rhetoric; the other is that of dramatic rendering. By rhetoric I mean the direct statement of ideas and emotions in language designed to persuade the reader. In fiction it is the substitution of the description of emotion for the evocation of emotion. On the other hand, dramatic rendering presents characters and actions and makes its appeal through the feelings they evoke. This distinction was in Henry James's mind when he defined the "sign of the born novelist" as being "a respect unconditioned for the freedom and vitality, the absoluteness when summoned, of the creatures he invokes," and contrasted it to "the strange and second-rate policy of explaining or presenting them by reprobation or apology—of taking the short cuts and anticipating the emotions and judgments about them that should be left, at the best, to the perhaps not most intelligent reader."[1]

The two are often fundamentally incompatible, but when they are used to reinforce each other they can function with great strength. Contrast, for example, these two selections from *Of Time and the River*. In the first the dying W. O. Gant is talking with his wife:

> "Eliza,"—he said—and at the sound of that unaccustomed word, a name he had spoken only twice in forty years—her white face and her worn brown eyes turned toward him with the quick and startled look of an animal—"Eliza," he said quietly, "you have had a hard life with me, a hard time. I want to tell you that I'm sorry."
>
> And before she could move from her white stillness of shocked surprise, he lifted his great right hand and put it gently down across her own.[2]

The second selection is a meditation on Gant's death as it affects his son Eugene. Although it runs on for several pages, the opening is typical:

> October had come again, and that year it was sharp and soon: frost was early, burning the thick green on the mountain sides to massed brilliant hues of blazing colors, painting the air with sharpness, sorrow and delight—and with October. Sometimes, and often, there was warmth by day, an ancient drowsy light, a golden warmth and pollenated [*sic*] haze in afternoon, but over all the earth there was the premonitory breath of frost, an exultancy for all the men who were returning, a haunting sorrow for the buried men, and for all those who were gone and would not come again.
>
> His father was dead, and now it seemed to him that he had never found him. His father was dead, and yet he sought him everywhere, and could not believe that he was dead, and was sure that he would find him. It was October and that year, after years of absence and of wandering, he had come home again.[3]

In these passages Wolfe writes of the same fundamental situation—and one of his major themes—death. In the first he writes as a novelist and in the second as a prose poet. But this mixed style bothers us relatively little, for the rhetorical passage extends and universalizes the particular incident that is presented with objective force in the first selection. The notebooks contain ample evidence that such prose poems—and this one in particular—were sketched out independent of their later use.[4] But this fact is ultimately of little significance, for however he came to write them first, in his early books Wolfe usually wedded these rhetorical passages effectively to their final dramatic context.

At the opening of Book VII of *Of Time and the River*, there is a much less certain union of scene and rhapsody. This is the section that begins: "Play us a tune on an unbroken spinet. . . . Waken the turmoil of forgotten streets, let us hear their sounds again unmuted, and unchanged by time, throw the light of Wednesday morning on the Third Crusade, and let us see Athens on an average day."[5] This famous passage is an attempt to impose the themes of time and the quest for the father on material in which they are not necessarily apparent. In other words, here rhetoric is not reinforcing dramatic scene but is being used as a substitute for it. And the problem is further complicated by the fact that in the passage on October and death, the brooding rhetoric is Eugene's and thus has a kind of dramatic propriety, while in the passage on the unbroken spinet the rhetoric seems to be the expression of some undefined auctorial persona who differs from Eugene, and who is, in fact, commenting on the protagonist's experience. The temptation is strong to say that Wolfe as recorder of the conversation of Gant and Eliza is working as a novelist, and that Wolfe evoking music from the unbroken spinet is indulging in direct self-expression.

That Wolfe should have felt no compulsion to synthesize these elements is not surprising, for he seems to define reality in terms of negations, to deal in oppositions, to be unable to bring forth any idea without setting against it a contradiction. And he seems, too, to have a confident faith that the synthesis of these opposites is a consistent function of reality itself, that it inevitably happens and does not need his guiding hand. Thus he can shift from scene to exhortation, from action to explanation, from immediacy to nostalgic perspective without sensing that he is doing primary violence to his view of the world.[6] The result is that his books consist of segments written in different styles and contrasting modes. Thus he produces works which, if judged in the terms of Northrop Frye's definitions of genres,[7] are mixtures of two or three fictional modes, or, in Mr. Kennedy's term, are fictional thesauruses.[8]

The tendency for these modes to be separate rather than reinforcing increases very much in the posthumous novels, despite the fact that Edward Aswell assembled them from manuscript material and in so doing exercised great freedom in excision, rearrangement, and even rewriting on occasion. Of course, acting against Aswell's attempt to achieve unity through editing was the circumstance of his having to work with a vast and very fragmentary and incomplete manuscript.

You Can't Go Home Again, the book in which I wish to examine Wolfe's use of these two modes, is a fictional record of the conflict of the American dream with a capitalistic society and the descent of that dream into nightmare. Early in the book, its protagonist, George Webber, says that "we are all savage, foolish, violent, and mistaken; that, full of our fear and confusion, we walk in ignorance upon the living and beautiful earth, breathing young, vital air and bathing in the light of morning, seeing it not because of the murder in our hearts."[9] Wolfe has expressed here in miniature a controlling theme and a shaping opposition that governs the book. For almost as clearly as John Steinbeck did, he contrasts the dream and promise represented by the natural world with the nightmare that man makes for himself within it. The dream is basically simple and rural; its betrayal is the achievement of complex urban and industrial forces.

You Can't Go Home Again cannot accurately be called a novel. It lacks a formal plot; it is a collection of incidents that happened to or are observed by the protagonist but in which that protagonist frequently plays only a minor part. It was left in a fragmentary form at Wolfe's death and was assembled by his new editor Aswell, working from an outline and having to choose among versions, write links, change names, and give the appearance of a unified work of fiction to a mass of manuscript of an incomplete novel. Yet the work has special merits that none of Wolfe's other works possess, and although it is an anthology of parts, the parts themselves are often magnificently realized. It stands at the opposite end of the spectrum from Wolfe's first novel, *Look Homeward, Angel*. That book was the lyric cry of a self-centered and introspective boy, a record of the adventures of his spirit in "the meadows of sensation." *You Can't Go Home Again* is the social testament of a maturing—if not fully mature—man.

In *Look Homeward, Angel*, the self-discovery of the artist was the focus, but by the time of *You Can't Go Home Again* Wolfe had come to believe that such a focus was wrong. He has George Webber say of his first novel—which was transparently also Wolfe's—"The young genius business . . . the wounded faun business . . . twists the vision. The vision may be shrewd, subtle, piercing, within a thousand special frames accurate and Joycean—but within the larger one, false, mannered, and untrue."[10] In the later book the focus has shifted to the outer world, and he attempts to make the central personality function in a manner he described once in a letter: "The protagonist becomes significant not as the tragic victim of circumstances, the romantic hero in conflict and revolt against his environment, but as a kind of polar instrument round which the events of life are grouped, by means of which they are touched, explained, and apprehended, by means of which they are seen and ordered."[11]

In this respect *You Can't Go Home Again* is markedly similar to the work of Herman Melville—a writer to whom

Wolfe's debts have not been fully acknowledged. In fact, structurally there are remarkable parallels between the works of the two men. Melville's protagonists are usually minor actors in his works, and the dramatic action is centered on other characters whom the protagonist observes. The weight of interpretation rests upon this almost passive but observing narrator and is more a function of style and metaphysical conceit than of action. This characteristic is obvious in *Moby-Dick*, where from time to time Ishmael almost becomes Emerson's "transparent eyeball," through whom we view Captain Ahab and his quest. Yet Ishmael comes from the voyage of the *Pequod* having learned not Ahab's course but the error of it. A similar role is played by Redburn, by White-Jacket, and by Taji in *Mardi* (although Melville apparently gives the final answer to Babbalanja in that work). When Melville, in *Pierre*, shifts from the first-person discursive narrator to the third person many of the difficulties which we also encounter in Wolfe appear, including the great problem of distinguishing between the attitudes held by Pierre Glendenning and those held by the author. The result is that *Pierre* is often called autobiographical in a derogatory sense. Wolfe's effort to use a first-person narrator in *Of Time and the River*—an effort defeated by his publishers—would have resolved the similar problem in this work to a substantial extent. *You Can't Go Home Again* would also have benefited very much from first-person narration; indeed, the last section shifts to the first person, but so late that the reader has the mistaken impression that it is Wolfe speaking directly rather than George Webber.

The essential vision of this personality is that of the provincial, middle-class American. Wolfe had grown up in a small southern mountain town, close to the towering hills and responding intensely to the natural forms of beauty around him. He had absorbed from the sociopolitical Populism which was still strong in North Carolina during his childhood and youth a democratic liberalism, and he brought to bear upon his people a criticism—very much like that of Sinclair Lewis—both mocking and loving. This attitude is shown in the satire of *Look Homeward, Angel*, where the young artist simply rejects the ugliness and materialism of the environment in which he lives, dreaming of shining cities, distant people, and inevitable triumphs.

The structure of *Look Homeward, Angel* and the maturing of the protagonist are consonant; between the outer view of society and the inner seeking of the soul there is a shared and constant dream, the aspiring dream of every middle-class provincial American boy who has turned his back upon home to seek triumphs in the citadels of culture and power. *Look Homeward, Angel* is structurally the most satisfying of Wolfe's novels not only because the *Bildungsroman* has a built-in pattern and wholeness but also because the American boy's dream is at its center—a dream not yet torn by fundamental doubts; its realization is not only possible, it seems almost within the outstretched, grasping fingers.

But Gant-Webber moves from the hill-encircled world of his childhood into a series of persistent disillusionments. He greets the enfabled rock of Manhattan with a joyous cry, only to discover that it harbors cruelty, falseness, and betrayal. He seeks friendship with a limber-wristed aesthete, Francis Starwick, and only when the fact is driven home with a force so great that it can no longer be resisted does he acknowledge that Starwick is a homosexual. He visits Europe, but everywhere the promised order is denied him. He goes to Hitler's Germany and finds himself the darling of the great capital city; it takes him a while to recognize beneath the orderliness, the beauty, the symmetry, the green faerie world of the Tiergarten and the efficiency of the city trams, that there is the calamity of man's injustice and hatred, the bitter desire to emasculate and to destroy, and so he must bid farewell to "the other part of his heart's home." But it is America caught in the bitter struggle of the Depression that put his dream to its most severe test and converted it into a nightmare of poverty and suffering.

Like Whitman, whom he resembles more than he does any other American writer, Wolfe celebrates the beauty and glory of his native land, the wonder and grandeur of its towering mountains and its rolling plains. Like Whitman he makes music from the names of places and people, streams and towns. Like Whitman he sees himself as a representative American. But like the Whitman of *Democratic Vistas*, Wolfe, too, sees the cancerous growth that gnaws away at the body politic. Wherever he turns he finds hungry men, mistreated men, men weighed down by injustice. How to reconcile the two—the glorious promise of America and the injustice, cruelty, and oppression of America—becomes for him both a personal problem and an artistic dilemma.

You Can't Go Home Again is the record of the ultimate failure of that effort at reconciliation. When Wolfe moves from the focus on the individual to a focus on society, he needs something other than the coexistence of these attitudes. Either they must be reconciled or one must triumph over the other. Or if they are to be held in balance, they must be treated with equal force and dramatic conviction. It is not enough to have one dramatized and the other rhetorically expressed.

Wolfe's view of the American nightmare, pretty clearly grounded in his attitude toward the economic system, is the middle-class Agrarian view opposed to industrial capitalism. George Webber says at one place in *You Can't Go Home Again*: "Sometimes it seems to me . . . that America went off the track somewhere—back around the time of the Civil War, or pretty soon afterwards. Instead of going ahead and developing along the line in which the country started out, it got shunted off in another direction—and now we look around and see we've gone places we didn't mean to go. Suddenly we realize that America has turned into something ugly—and vicious—and corroded at the heart of its power with easy wealth and graft and special privilege."[12] *You Can't Go Home Again* is a record of that wrong track, told in the form of almost disjointed episodes of disillusionment and failure.

You Can't Go Home Again consists in large part of materials originally written as self-contained units—"Boom Town," "The World That Jack Built," and " 'I Have a Thing to Tell You.' " As a result sections like Books III and IV and the conclusion, where the hortatory and rhetorical voice of the author, either thinly disguised as George Webber or in several cases not disguised at all, are more different in mode from the dramatic than such passages had been in the earlier novels. One is inclined to say that in fact in their present form such passages are not representative of their author's intentions—as indeed Hamilton Basso declared upon the publication of the book[13] and many others, including Richard S. Kennedy,[14] have noted since. But I fear they are letting Wolfe off a little more easily than they are justified in doing. There are, in fact, two thematic elements in the novel—thematic elements that are not truly congenial—and each is expressed in a distinctly different stylistic mode, so that we can with some justice say that *You Can't Go Home Again* is a mixture of rhetorical hope and dramatic despair. The rhetorical passages and the dramatic scenes in *You Can't Go Home Again* differ from the earlier books also in subject matter. In this novel what Webber does and thinks matters less than what he sees: hence there is a much stronger social content in the action of the book. And the rhetorical sections, which in the earlier books had elaborated upon the emotions surrounding events as the "timeless valley" section at the end of Chapter 30 does in *Look Homeward, Angel,* tend here to express more abstract attitudes about the social world, as the famous "Credo" that closes the novel does.

The increasing presence of these disparate elements largely resulted, I think, from Wolfe's growing concern with the outer world and its problems, a concern that led him frequently to use a kind of incident that appears only occasionally in the earlier works. The life which had impressed itself hauntingly upon his mind during the years of his maturity, it must be remembered, was the life of Depression-stricken America. He knew it through the suffering of his own family in Asheville, a suffering which he portrayed in the last five chapters of the first book and in Chapters 25 and 26 of *You Can't Go Home Again;* and he knew it through direct observation in Brooklyn and Manhattan. In *The Story of a Novel* he is very explicit about what he saw in New York during the Depression:

> Everywhere around me . . . I saw the evidence of an incalculable ruin and suffering. My own people, the members of my own family had been ruined, had lost all the material wealth and accumulation of a lifetime. . . . And that universal calamity had somehow struck the life of almost everyone I knew. Moreover, in this endless quest and prowling of the night through the great web and jungle of the city, I saw, lived, felt, and experienced the full weight of that horrible human calamity.
>
> I saw a man whose life had subsided into a mass of shapeless and filthy rags, devoured by vermin; wretches huddled together for a little warmth in freezing cold squatting in doorless closets upon the foul seat of a public latrine within the very shadow, the cold shelter of palatial and stupendous monuments of wealth. I saw acts of sickening violence and cruelty, the menace of brute privilege, a cruel and corrupt authority trampling ruthlessly below its feet the lives of the poor, the weak, the wretched, and the defenseless of the earth. [15]

You Can't Go Home Again tells of George Webber's life in Brooklyn; of the real-estate boom and collapse in his hometown, Libya Hill; in a complex and carefully wrought short novel, of the world of the very rich in contrast to that of the laboring classes that serve it; of the disillusionment that follows Webber's success as a novelist; of his journey to England and of a meeting with a famous novelist, Lloyd McHarg—Sinclair Lewis under very thin disguise—who shows him the emptiness of fame; in a tightly constructed short novel, of his love for Germany and his sense of its evil, and finally—in a letter to his editor—a statement of what he feels his credo to be. It is loaded with dramatic pictures of the nightmare world which Wolfe believes America in the Depression to be. And, as he usually does, Wolfe makes his statements through representative characters, through typical actions, through descriptive passages that become vignettes that express his meaning, and most emphatically through direct rhetorical assertion. To a startling degree the dream in *You Can't Go Home Again* is expressed through rhetorical assertion, and the nightmare through dramatic presentation. The nightmare makes the more powerful impact, although the dream may be more quotable.

Wolfe seems to see a common—and simplistic—basis for the darkness that engulfs the American dream, and an examination of a few of the dramatic modes in the novel points to it. Four characters, each indicative of the failure of the promise, show a distorted way of life. Judge Rumford Bland, the syphilitic blind man, who embodies much of the best tradition of the South of his boyhood and yet is totally corrupt, appears only briefly in the novel, when Webber meets him on the train to Libya Hill. His background has to be dragged in as remembrance, yet he is certainly a powerful representative of his culture. He makes his living through the most cruel and usurious lending to Negroes. He has an office as an attorney in a disreputable building within thirty yards of the city hall, and he is a creature of the night. Though he was an able man, there was, Wolfe wrote, "something genuinely old and corrupt at the sources of his life and spirit." But he added, "At the very moment that [people] met him, and felt the force of death and evil working in him, they also felt—oh, call it the phantom, the radiance, the lost soul, of an enormous virtue. And with the recognition of that quality came the sudden stab of overwhelming regret." [16]

Another figure of this nightmare evil is Adolf Hitler, "the dark messiah." Webber—and Wolfe—had felt at first in Germany that "it was no foreign land to him," and there he had tasted the intoxication of great acclaim. It was not easy for him finally to see in *Der Führer,* who had brought such great material order to Germany, the "shipwreck of a great spirit." He wrote of Webber's experience: "The poisonous emanations of suppression, persecution, and fear permeated the air like miasmic and pestilential vapors, tainting, sickening, and blighting the lives of everyone he met. It was a plague of the spirit—invisible, but as unmistakable as death." [17]

Another is Mr. Merrit, the representative of the Federal Weight, Scales, and Computing Company, who was all Rotarian smiles and good fellowship but who, when overheard tongue-lashing Webber's friend Randy Shepperton, gave George the feeling that he was "in some awful nightmare when he visions someone he knows doing some perverse and abominable act." When later Randy tries to explain that Merrit has to do these things because "he—he's with the Company," Webber remembers a picture he had seen

> . . . portraying a long line of men stretching from the Great Pyramid to the very portals of great Pharaoh's house, and great Pharaoh stood with a thonged whip in his hand and applied it unmercifully to the bare back and shoulders of the man in front of him, who was great Pharaoh's chief overseer, and in the hand of the overseer was a whip of many tails which he unstintedly applied to the quivering back of the wretch before him, who was the chief overseer's chief lieutenant, and in the lieutenant's hand a whip of rawhide which he laid vigorously on the quailing body of his head sergeant, and in the sergeant's hand a wicked flail with which he belabored a whole company of groaning corporals, and in the hands of every corporal a knotted lash with which to whack a whole regiment of slaves. [18]

Still another is Mr. Frederick Jack, Wall Street financier, living in great luxury and playing with stocks and dollars in a vast and amusing gamble. Speaking of such speculators, Wolfe said, "They bought, sold, and traded in an atmosphere fraught with frantic madness. . . . it was one of the qualities of this time that men should see and feel the madness all around them and never mention it—never admit it even to themselves." At the other end of this mad gamble of speculation is a figure absurd enough to be in contemporary black comedy, Libya Hill's town sot, old Tim Wagner—"diseased and broken . . . his wits were always addled now with alcohol," but the word had gotten around among real-estate speculators that he had a mysterious power of financial intuition, so the men of the town "used him as men once used divining rods," and he rode in a magnificent car with a liveried chauffeur, and moved with "princely indolence."[19]

All these men are exploiters, but Wolfe has too a large gallery of the exploited. They include Randy Shepperton, a kind and generous man; the anonymous citizens of Libya Hill who are swept under in the collapse; the servants at Jack's upon whom the success of his personal life depends; Mr. C. Green, who commits suicide by leaping from the Admiral Drake Hotel and only in that violent moment elicits attention to the gray cipher which his life has been; Lloyd McHarg, Nobel Prize novelist for whom world fame is not enough and who constantly tastes bitter ashes on his tongue.

The two finest sections of the book were originally written as short novels—"The World That Jack Built" and "'I Have a Thing to Tell You.'" "The World That Jack Built"—the title is a pun—is a 175-page account of a great party given by Mr. and Mrs. Frederick Jack just a week before the stock market collapse which precipitated the Depression. This novella is Wolfe's best and most objective piece of sustained narrative. It is rich in social satire, in portraits of people from all classes, and in interlinked symbols that carry a heavy freight of meaning. The party ends in a fire which drives the guests and apartment house residents into a courtyard where for a moment they feel a sense of community; the fire also takes the lives of two gentle, kindly elevator operators, one old and one young, but both of whom believe in the economic system. Wolfe was here attempting to imprison a view of a society in a single complex social act, modeling his effort on Proust's *Sodom et Gomorrah*.[20] At the conclusion he comes to a direct judgment of the people of this world. He sees them as gifted and personally honorable, but he condemns "their complaisance about themselves and about their life, their loss of faith in anything better." Webber is at what he realizes to be the apex of one aspect of his dream—the highest point of success and acceptance by the world's great—yet he is dismayed rather than delighted: "Now to have the selfless grandeur turn to dust, and to see great night itself a reptile coiled and waiting at the heart of life! . . . To find man's faith betrayed and his betrayers throned in honor, themselves the idols of his bartered faith."[21]

But there is another aspect of Wolfe's work which can best be understood if we contrast him with John Dos Passos, a writer with whom social historians often link him, as a novelist of the 1930s deeply concerned with the quality of experience in that anguished decade. Such a comparison is apt, for both writers attempted to imprison a record of American life in long, ambitious works with many formal oddities, works that can be called novels only if the term is loosely used. Henry Steele Commager has said that "Dos Passos was the most social minded of the major novelists" between the two world wars and that "Thomas Wolfe's quarrel with his society remained . . . personal and . . . artistic."[22] But the differences go deeper than this. Dos Passos belonged, as Alfred Kazin has noted, to "those American writers from the upper class, born on the eve of our century . . . [who] were brought up in . . . the last stable period in American history"[23] and whose dreams of an admirable order were betrayed by the First World War, so that they left its battlefields, where they had been ambulance drivers and Red Cross workers, with a profound sense of disillusionment. Wolfe, on the other hand, was born into a middle-middle-class family in which his personal security seemed threatened by intense domestic schisms, with the result that, despite an overly possessive mother, he appeared always to have seen himself as alone and defenseless.[24] Furthermore, he grew up in a small southern provincial city, imbibed from his closest companions—the books he read—most of the ideals of a standard middle-class world, was educated in a state university which he regarded as a wilderness outpost of "great Rome," and was too young to participate in the war, which—like many young middle-class sixteen- and seventeen-year-olds of the time—he romanticized as the last chivalric crusade.[25]

Furthermore, the long years of introspection which culminated in the lyrical *Look Homeward, Angel* pretty effectively shut him off—except for the fairly superficial satire of the Sinclair Lewis type—from a critical examination of the postulates of middle-class America. He vigorously declared himself not to be of the "Lost Generation," and could, on occasion, in letters and elsewhere, attack the critics of American life with all the pride of a Rotarian and the unquestioning energy of the provincial.[26] When, in the loneliness of Europe, he discovered that America was his subject, the America he discovered was still tied for him in powerful ways to the nineteenth-century dream which had gone up in the holocaust of the world war for writers like John Dos Passos, Ernest Hemingway, E. E. Cummings, and Edmund Wilson.

Hence, to the end, Wolfe held firmly to a belief in America that was of a different dimension and quality from that of his contemporaries, while he portrayed in telling detail in his pictures of the life around him many of the assumptions and despairs of the Depression world he inhabited. Expressed another way, Wolfe moved physically and artistically out into the great world of Boston, New York, and Europe, but he remained a sojourner rather than a native, a spectator rather than a participant, an observer rather than a true believer in the postulates of this larger world he inhabited for most of his adult life. Hence he brought the childlike vision of experience continuingly to bear on a steadily widening world, and therein lay one of his greatest powers; but he also brought to bear on the complexities of commitment in that larger world the simpler and uninstructed faith of the Populist democracy in which his social and political being had been nurtured. What he saw and what he believed came into increasingly tormented conflict, and he neither felt the need nor had the time in which to reconcile them. But he did have two methods of writing which allowed him in the late years to do a kind of justice to both vision and belief. That they rent the ideological fabric of his work would, I think, have bothered him relatively little.

Again the contrast with John Dos Passos is illuminating. In *U.S.A.* Dos Passos attempted to make the dynamics of history in his time the fundamental structure of his work, and he brought to it fresh and complex techniques—the Newsreels, the case histories of fictional representative Americans, and the biographical sketches of real persons who embodied common beliefs or attitudes. Along with these objective treatments Dos Passos included another mode of statement, "the Camera Eye," which gives us a lyrical and intense expression of the author's attitudes and emotions at the time of the action of the story. The Camera Eye sections are not fixed in some later time; they record the growing disillusionment of the author, as he encounters a world of widening experience. He moves from the child's view in "The Camera Eye (7)" which ends: "we clean young American Rover Boys handy with tools Deerslayers played hockey Boy Scouts and cut figure eights on the ice Achilles Ajax Agamemnon I couldn't learn to skate and kept falling down"[27] to the despair of "The Camera Eye (50)" which begins "they have clubbed us off the streets they are stronger they are rich" and reaches the ultimate expression of rejection in:

> all right we are two nations
> America our nation has been beaten by strangers who have bought the laws and fenced off the meadows and cut down the woods for pulp and turned our pleasant cities into slums and sweated the wealth out of our people.[28]

Wolfe presented dramatic pictures of that same world, pictures which portrayed it in terms not significantly different from those of Dos Passos. But Wolfe's are drawn not objectively by experimental methods but directly as the experience of his increasingly faceless protagonist. When the author Wolfe wishes to speak, he does so directly, and from time to time we are confused as to whether he intends his remarks to be comments on the protagonist's experience or comments by the protagonist. These rhetorical comments reflect Wolfe's relatively static view and are seemingly fixed in the present rather than the time of action of the book. In Dos Passos' metaphor, the lens setting of Wolfe's camera eye undergoes surprisingly little adjustment as the book progresses.

I suppose this is what Robert Penn Warren was talking about when he made his famous wisecrack about Wolfe: "It may be well to recollect that Shakespeare merely wrote *Hamlet*; he was *not* Hamlet."[29] But that remark is actually more scintillating than sensible; for the genres in which the two writers worked are radically dissimilar. Wolfe *did* choose both to play Hamlet and to write it, for his great subject was the impact of the world on a protagonist frankly quite like himself. In Shakespeare's play there is action and there is rhetoric; the action is Shakespeare's presentation of Hamlet's world; the rhetoric is Hamlet's (and others') interpretation of that world. I suppose what bothers us about *You Can't Go Home Again* is that what George Webber sees and what happens to him is very much like Hamlet's description of the world as

> an unweeded garden,
> That grows to seed; things rank and gross in nature
> Possess it merely.[30]

Yet many of his remarks about it, his rhetorical flourishes, smack a little too much of Polonius—or, to be fairer, of Walt Whitman evoking the spirit of America and its promise.

It is significant, I think, that when Wolfe, in *The Story of a Novel*, describes the growth of the impulse that led him to see America as his proper subject, that launched him on an artistic effort that has marked similarities to that of the epic poet, he assigns the motive force to loneliness and a haunting sense of loss. This occurred in Europe, and Wolfe says, "I discovered America during these years abroad out of my very need of her. The huge gain of this discovery seemed to come directly from my sense of loss." And he adds a little later, "Now my memory was at work night and day, in a way that I could at first neither check nor control and that swarmed unbidden in a stream of blazing pageantry across my mind, with the million forms and substances of the life that I had left, which was my own, America."[31] In a sense, then, the substance of Wolfe's work was America recollected in nostalgia. Even *You Can't Go Home Again* primarily describes events that occurred in 1929 and 1930 (the German episode is later but it is unique in this respect), but he views them from the vantage point of a later time. Indeed, Wolfe's whole concept of time in the novel required that a sense of the past and the present commingle against an awareness of eternity: thus he shares with Dos Passos a great interest in time and history, but in his case it is history viewed more philosophically than socially.

In *You Can't Go Home Again* Wolfe skillfully uses the novelist's basic tool, character, to portray his world and its corruption. Judge Rumford Bland, whom everyone instinctively knew to be evil, is a microcosmic representation of the town of Libya Hill. Randy Shepperton is the average American caught in the Depression, and Wolfe is very explicit about it. He says, "Behind Randy's tragedy George thought he could see a personal devil in the form of a very bright and plausible young man, oozing confidence and crying 'Faith!' when there was no faith. . . . And it seemed to George that Randy's tragedy was the essential tragedy of America." Mr. Jack epitomizes the capitalistic system, and again Wolfe is explicit: Mr. Jack enjoyed, he says, "the privilege of men selected from the common run because of some mysterious intuition they were supposed to have." And he adds, "It seemed to Mr. Jack . . . not only entirely reasonable but even natural that the whole structure of society from top to bottom should be honeycombed with privilege and dishonesty." Amy Carleton, rich millionairess of many marriages and of total moral collapse, symbolizes the decay of high society. Wolfe writes, "It seemed, therefore, that her wealth and power and feverish energy could get her anything she wanted . . . [But] The end could only be destruction, and the mark of destruction was already apparent upon her." And C. Green is a type of all the nameless, faceless people who are the victims of an inhuman system in an unseeing city. Of him Wolfe declares: "He was life's little man, life's nameless cipher, life's manswarm atom, life's American—and now he lies dejected and exploded on a street in Brooklyn! He was a dweller in mean streets . . . a man-mote in the jungle of the city, a resident of grimy steel and stone, a mole who burrowed in rusty brick." And the indictment does not stop with people, but extends to descriptions of scenes and actions. Of a hill in Libya Hill he writes: "It had been one of the pleasantest places in the town, but now it was gone. An army of men and shovels had advanced upon this beautiful green hill and had leveled it down to an ugly flat of clay, and had paved it with a desolate horror of white concrete, and had built stores and office buildings and parking spaces—all raw and new."[32]

In a vignette that defines his position well he writes of Libya Hill, effectively embodying in a series of images what seems to have been a fundamental position for him:

> The air brooded with a lazy, drowsy warmth. There was the last evening cry of robins, and the thrumming bullet noises in undergrowth and leaf, and broken sounds from far away—a voice in the wind, a boy's shout, the barking of a dog, the tinkle of a cow bell. There was the fragrance of intoxicating odors—the resinous smell of pine, and the smells of grass and warm sweet clover. All this was just as it had always been. But the town of his childhood, with its quiet streets and old houses which had been almost obscured below the leafy spread of trees, was changed past recognition, scarred now with hard patches of bright concrete and raw clumps of new construction. It looked like a battlefield, cratered and shell-torn with savage explosions of brick, cement, and harsh new stucco. And in the interspaces only the embowered remnants of the old and pleasant town remained—timid, retreating, overwhelmed—to remind one of the liquid leather shuffle in the quiet streets at noon when the men came home to lunch, and of laughter and low voices in the leafy rustle of the night. For this was lost![33]

Nazi Germany, with its old dark evil, comes finally to symbolize for him the end of the path on which America also is traveling. "It was," he says, "a picture of the Dark Ages come again—shocking beyond belief, but true as the hell that man forever creates for himself." And he adds, "I realized fully, for the first time, how sick America was, and saw, too, that the ailment was akin to Germany's—a dread world-sickness of the soul." This condition of sickness strikes George Webber with a sense of profound disillusionment. Wolfe declares: "To find man's faith betrayed and his betrayers throned in honor, themselves the idols of his bartered faith! To find truth false and falsehood truth, good evil, evil good, and the whole web of life so changing, so mercurial! It was so different from the way he had once thought it would be—and suddenly, convulsively, forgetful of his surroundings, he threw out his arms in an instinctive gesture of agony and loss." This despair comes to one who, Wolfe says, knew "that if he was ever to succeed in writing the books he felt were in him, he must turn about and lift his face up to some nobler height." For Wolfe the writers of his time were people each of whom "had accepted part of life for the whole . . . some little personal interest for the large and all-embracing interest of mankind." And Webber asked himself, "If that happened to him, how, then, could he sing America?"[34]

Yet sing America Wolfe did. In spite of all he saw about him, he remained more totally committed to the nineteenth-century American dream of an egalitarian society than any other major American novelist of this century, and at place after place in his novels he employed his great gift for poetic language to create ringing assertions of hope for the success of that democracy. A part of that faith was a still unshaken belief in man himself. In a long section, "The Locusts Have No King," he writes:

> This is man: for the most part a foul, wretched, abominable . . . hater of his kind, a cheater, a scorner, a mocker, a reviler, a thing that kills and murders in a mob or in the dark. . . .
>
> [But] Behold his works:
>
> He needed speech to ask for bread—and he had Christ! He needed songs to sing in battle—and he had Homer! . . . He needed walls and a roof to shelter him—so he made Blois! . . . It is impossible to scorn this creature. For out of his strong belief in life, this puny man made love. At his best, he *is* love. Without him there can be no love, no hunger, no desire.[35]

And he extends this faith to America in one of his two or three best known passages, one that is written in a very Whitmanesque context, that of being seated at night on the hackles of the Rocky Mountains and looking to East and West and thus gaining a vast continental vision. He concludes: "So, then, to every man his chance—to every man, regardless of his birth, his shining, golden opportunity—to every man the right to live, to work, to be himself and to become whatever thing his manhood and his vision can combine to make him—this, seeker, is the promise of America." Even in these ecstatic moments, he is not blind or forgetful of the dark canker at the heart of his native land, but this evil is an enemy whose triumph is unthinkable to Wolfe: "I think," he says, "the enemy is here before us, too. But I think we know the forms and faces of the enemy, and in the knowledge that we know him, and shall meet him, and eventually must conquer him is also our living hope."[36] His final judgment of America is one that Whitman would have applauded:

> I believe that we are lost here in America, but I believe we shall be found. And this belief, which mounts now to the catharsis of knowledge and conviction, is for me—and I think for all of us—not only our own hope but America's everlasting, living dream. . . . America and the people in it are deathless, undiscovered, and immortal, and must live.
>
> I think the true discovery of America is before us. . . . I think the true discovery of our own democracy is still before us. And I think that all these things are certain as the morning, as inevitable as noon.[37]

These are magnificent words and they express a confidence in man, a faith in democracy, and an allegiance to America and its old dream which it is heartening to hear. Who else of all our writers since Whitman has celebrated man and America with a nobler rhetoric and a more inspiriting assurance? But, as I have already suggested, these sentiments—and I think that Wolfe meant them from the bottom of his heart—are asserted in rhetorical passages rather than exemplified in the episodes of the novel. They come in sections of hortatory prose and are appropriately poetic rather than dramatic in rhythm and in content. The separation between action and idea, which we observed beginning in passages such as the "Unbroken Spinet" rhapsody, is here almost complete. The novelist portrays a dispiriting and despairing world, but the poet-seer lifts his voice to chant the ideal and the promise of America.

Few of us would want to dispense with the dramatic scenes that make *You Can't Go Home Again* a book of truly splendid fragments. And few of us would want to give up the firm assertion of the American dream and possibility which this provincial man kept somehow unsullied through all his contacts with the Depression world. I also suspect that few of us would seriously question that *You Can't Go Home Again* would have been a different and a far better work had Thomas Wolfe lived to find a way of putting the visionary dream and the disillusioning view of man into some harmonious relationship to each other.

Max Lerner has declared that Wolfe's prevailing mood is "the sense of being ravaged and lost, yet finding some . . . assertion of life's meaning."[38] And J. B. Priestley, writing admiringly of Wolfe's position in the great tradition of western literature, declared, "No matter how piercing and appalling his insights, the desolation creeping over his outer world, the lurid lights and shadows of his inner world, the writer must live with hope, work in faith."[39] Though imperfectly, Wolfe shored up hope against the ultimate despair, and fixed our eyes for the moment on distant goals and noble aspirations.

Notes

1. Henry James, "Ivan Turgénieff," *Library of the World's Best Literature* (1897), reprinted in M. D. Zabel (ed.), *The Portable Henry James* (New York, 1968), 457.
2. *Of Time and the River* (New York, 1935), 265.
3. Ibid., 327.
4. Richard S. Kennedy and Paschal Reeves (eds.), *The Notebooks of Thomas Wolfe* (2 vols.; Chapel Hill, N.C., 1970).
5. *Of Time and the River*, 853.
6. I have discussed this aspect of Wolfe's work at length in my essay, "Thomas Wolfe" in William Van O'Connor (ed.), *Seven Modern American Novelists* (Minneapolis, 1964), 189–225. The essay is reprinted in modified form as Chapter I in this volume.
7. Northrop Frye, *Anatomy of Criticism* (Princeton, 1957).
8. Richard Kennedy, "Thomas Wolfe's Fiction: The Question of Genre," in Paschal Reeves (ed.), *Thomas Wolfe and the Glass of Time* (Athens, Ga., 1971), 1–44.
9. *You Can't Go Home Again* (New York, 1940), 14.
10. Ibid., 385.
11. Elizabeth Nowell (ed.), *The Letters of Thomas Wolfe* (New York, 1956), 714.

12. *You Can't Go Home Again*, 393.
13. Hamilton Basso, review of *You Can't Go Home Again*, *New Republic*, September 23, 1940, pp. 422–23.
14. Richard S. Kennedy, *The Window of Memory: The Literary Career of Thomas Wolfe* (Chapel Hill, N.C., 1962), 403–11.
15. *The Story of a Novel* (New York, 1936), 59–60.
16. *You Can't Go Home Again*, 77.
17. Ibid., 633.
18. Ibid., 139.
19. Ibid., 195, 118.
20. Marcel Proust, *Sodome et Gomorrhe I* (1921) and *Sodome et Gomorrhe II* (1922), translated together as *Cities of the Plain*, trans. C. K. Scott Moncrieff (New York, 1927).
21. *You Can't Go Home Again*, 260, 263.
22. Henry Steele Commager, *The American Mind* (New Haven, Conn., 1951), 267–69.
23. Alfred Kazin, "John Dos Passos: Inventor in Isolation," *Saturday Review*, March 15, 1969, p. 17.
24. See, for example, Nowell (ed.), *Letters*, 370–71.
25. See William Braswell and Leslie A. Field (eds.), *Thomas Wolfe's Purdue Speech: "Writing and Living"* (West Lafayette, Ind., 1964), 36–37.
26. See C. Hugh Holman and Sue F. Ross (eds.), *The Letters of Thomas Wolfe to His Mother* (Chapel Hill, N.C., 1968), 94.
27. John Dos Passos, *The 42nd Parallel* (New York, 1937), 81.
28. John Dos Passos, *The Big Money* (New York, 1937), 461–63.
29. Robert Penn Warren, "The Hamlet of Thomas Wolfe," in Richard Walser (ed.), *The Enigma of Thomas Wolfe* (Cambridge, Mass., 1953), 132.
30. *Hamlet*, I, ii, 135–37.
31. *The Story of a Novel*, 30–31, 31–32.
32. *You Can't Go Home Again*, 395–96, 189, 249, 467–68, 111.
33. Ibid., 145–46.
34. Ibid., 728, 279–30, 263, 321, 262–63.
35. Ibid., 434–36.
36. Ibid., 508, 741.
37. Ibid., 741.
38. Max Lerner, *America as a Civilization* (New York, 1957), 791.
39. J. B. Priestley, *Literature and Western Man* (New York, 1960), 440.

LOUIS D. RUBIN, JR.

"Thomas Wolfe and the Place He Came From"

A Gallery of Southerners

1982, pp. 67–84

Thomas Wolfe and the South was the subject of the first essay on southern literature I published, almost a quarter-century ago. In that essay I went about demonstrating, or attempting to demonstrate, that Wolfe was indubitably a southern writer, as if that were of itself a kind of badge of literary honor; and to prove it I drew up a list of characteristics customarily ascribed to southern writers and tried to show how each applied to Wolfe's writing. These included such things as the fondness for rhetoric, the sense of place, the storytelling quality and the sense of family that is supposed to go along with it, the consciousness of the past and of time, the sense of evil, and so forth. I came to dislike that essay very much, and the next time I had occasion to revise and augment the set of essays on contemporary southern literature in which it appeared, I scrapped it and got my friend and Chapel Hill colleague C. Hugh Holman to write one instead. He did so, and more to my satisfaction. My early essay, however, remains available; every so often somebody discovers it, and I am always embarrassed to see it quoted. I have not wavered at all in my conviction that Wolfe is a southern writer, but I don't think that lining up a set of the official characteristics of southern literature and then trying to show that Wolfe fits them and so is eligible for the prized blue ribbon—or should I say blue-and-gray ribbon—is very helpful in understanding either Wolfe or southern literature. It is something like trying to prove that a great batter like Ted Williams was a good baseball player because he knew how to play line drives off the left field wall in Fenway Park.

Wolfe isn't a southern writer because he sometimes wrote like William Faulkner or Robert Penn Warren, but because most of the time he wrote like Thomas Wolfe. And if a writer as good as Wolfe was at his best doesn't fit the official list of characteristics of southern writing, then what should be suspect is not Wolfe but the list. What I tried to do, I am afraid, both in that earlier essay and in part in the book I published on Wolfe several years later, was to make Wolfe into an honorary member of the Nashville Agrarians, which strikes me now as a pretty gratuitous enterprise. Wolfe did what he had to do, and they did what they had to do, and what is nice is that we have both.

On the other hand, it is instructive to recall why it seemed a good idea to try to show, back in 1953, that Thomas Wolfe was beyond question a southern writer. This was the time when the Southern Literary Renascence that began after the First World War was just beginning to be identified as an important phenomenon in American literary history—until then it had been thought of primarily as a fortuitous assortment of good books. The book for which my essay was written was the first full-fledged examination of the overall achievement of modern southern literature. William Faulkner, after years of toiling in something resembling critical obscurity, was only just beginning to be recognized as perhaps the premier writer of fiction of our century, and the excitement of this discovery was widespread. On the other hand, the southern poet-critics—Ransom, Tate, Warren, Brooks—were at the height of their authority, and what they said was so about literature meant a great deal (and still does to me).

We had recently been through a depression, a new deal, and a world war. Each of these phenomena had involved a great deal of ideological paraphernalia, and as is always the way, literature had been placed in their service. In the 1930s it was the Marxist, proletarian novel. In the 1940s it was the novel of involvement. We had gone through a long period of trying to make out that books such as *The Grapes of Wrath*, *U.S.A.*, *For Whom the Bell Tolls*, *A Bell for Adano*, *Studs Lonigan*, *Strange Fruit*, and so on were the principal achievements of modern American literature.

We were a little tired of it; we wanted to learn how to read fiction and poetry again *as* fiction and poetry, for their formal literary excellence, and not as ideological documents. So the novelists such as Faulkner and Warren and Porter and other southerners, and the poets such as Tate, Ransom, and Warren, who had never lost sight of that fact and had generally refused to take part as novelists and poets in the various popular causes, were now being discovered or rediscovered with delight. These were, as a scholar-friend of mine once wrote, the southern years, and the traditional southern literary virtues of formal excellence and moral relevance, having been revitalized and given great imaginative energy as the literary South had moved into the modern world, now seemed very attractive indeed. There was also the additional advantage that the literary marketplace in New York had run out of ideological gimmicks, now that literary proletarianism and literary patriotism had run their course, so it couldn't put up much of a fight against literature as literature, however unsalable and superficially unexciting mere literary excellence might be. So until the civil rights movement got going in the late 1950s and New York had a good excuse for dealing with literature (some of it very good literature indeed) as ideology once again, the rich formal achievement of the best southern literature was permitted to be read and admired, as generally it wasn't before and hasn't been since.

For these reasons and others, then, the period of the late 1940s and early 1950s was a time when merely being a good southern writer seemed to be a gesture in the direction of literary distinction, and there was widespread and deserved appreciation of the best southern writing of our time.

The trouble was, however, that with any such consensus of taste, no matter how good, there always goes along a kind of orthodoxy. Virtues are soon codified; the approaches and techniques that are, for good writers, the creative means for the act of discovery that is literature are made into the ends themselves. Because some southern authors (e.g., Faulkner and Tate) went at the art of literature in certain creative ways, and because those ways had clearly worked and filled certain genuine artistic needs, it followed that that was the southern way to do it, and any writer who didn't do it that way was inferior and not a true southern literary man. Thus, because Wolfe didn't write fiction the way Faulkner wrote fiction, Wolfe was neither as important nor as "southern" a novelist as Faulkner.

Now I happen to believe that Wolfe *isn't* as important a writer as Faulkner, but the reason he isn't is not that he didn't write his books the way that Faulkner wrote his; it's because Faulkner wrote a different kind of novel better than Wolfe wrote his kind. And conversely, if Wolfe *is* an important novelist, as I certainly believe he is, the reasons why he is might well have nothing to do with resembling Faulkner.

Perhaps that seems obvious—certainly it is trite enough to be obvious—but it isn't the way literary movements and schools and groups tend to approach things. We tend to erect our characteristic methods, techniques, and attitudes into orthodoxies. We make the highly creative techniques of some writers into legalisms that impede our own imaginative response to other writers. One writer's method is another's impoverishment; one writer's need is another's inhibition.

Well and good. But what if one is so struck with the imaginative achievement of one group of writers and finds so much that is good and stimulating in the way they approach their craft and at the same time one is also powerfully drawn to another and different kind of writer, whom those writers and many critics generally don't like (and also don't always understand)? What does one do? I expect that one attempts to do what I think I tried to do with Thomas Wolfe: to take the insights and apparatus and attitudes that fit the one group and try to demonstrate—both to oneself and to others whom one likes and admires—that the writer in question has been misread and really isn't so different and is a good writer *because* at bottom he is really doing the same things that the others are. Thus Thomas Wolfe is an important southern writer, not because of Thomas Wolfe's own unique version of the human experience in southern guise, but because he resembles other important southern writers. Which is a pretty silly business.

Now the American South is a large and complex region, with some vastly different subregions within it, and the literature it has produced partakes of these divisions—Hugh Holman has identified these as the Tidewater, the Piedmont, and the Deep South. He has selected Ellen Glasgow as exemplar of the Tidewater sensibility in literature, Wolfe for the Piedmont, and Faulkner for the Deep South. But if you are not careful, you tend to think of the South exclusively in terms of one of these subregions and to say that the writing characteristic of the particular subregion is southern literature and anything else isn't southern literature.

It is also true that the sense of community was so strong throughout the South, and still in many ways remains so, that to say one is a southerner is not merely a description but an act of community identification. "In Dixie Land I'll take my stand." To be a southerner has meant to *belong* to a club, as it were, or perhaps a fraternity, a cult, a society, with some social prestige attached to the membership. In William Faulkner's novel *Absalom, Absalom!*, when Quentin Compson is told by a Canadian that he can't understand why southerners feel the way they do, Quentin tells him, "You can't understand it. You would have to be born there." I have seen that remark excoriated by some critics as snobbish, undemocratic, pretentious—but none of the critics who object to it is a southerner. Well, there *is* a certain amount of cliquishness attached to it; to an extent it is not just Quentin explaining, but his creator bragging a bit. Whether he had any right to feel privileged or whether anyone has such a right, because of being a southerner, is another matter; the fact is that many have felt that way, and still do, and that among them have been William Faulkner and also Thomas Wolfe.

Yet in certain ways Wolfe didn't appear to belong to the club. For part of this self-conscious identification as a southerner had, perhaps even still has, a certain amount of social overtone, as well as literary and critical assumptions, and in a kind of complex but not clearly defined way there was a relationship between the two. Most of the important southern writers of the 1920s, 1930s, and 1940s were of the gentry, or perhaps the upper middle class would be a better way of describing it; in any event, "of good family" as the expression went (which as I think Ellen Glasgow once pointed out was to say something very different from they were "of good people"—i.e., of the rural working or lower middle class, the so-called "yeomanry."). The southern writers weren't aristocrats, mind you, and none grew up in stately Tidewater mansions. But the "Big House" and the southern gentlemen were involved in the southern ideal, and almost every one of the twentieth-century southern writers has at one point in his or her work (often at frequent points) presented, with more than a little approval, characters who look down disdainfully upon the "trash" and the "riff-raff" without "family"—i.e., without approved social connections.

But Thomas Wolfe made a *point* of his working-class lineage. He wrote an autobiographical novel about growing up in a boarding-house. He was actively hostile to and critical of southern aristocratic pretense, and he liked to boast that his background was working class, yeomanry. Now it would have been all right if he had simply accepted the fact; but to boast of it, and furthermore to suggest, as he sometimes did, that because of his origins *he* was honest and open and democratic and genuine, while those who weren't from similar origins were snobbish and defensive and aristocratic and full of pretense, was another matter entirely.

This was not merely a matter of subject matter or of authorial biography. It also, and more importantly perhaps, involved ideas about literary technique and attitude. The literary virtues of the best southern writing—formal elegance, a reverence for tradition, restraint, self-sufficiency—were, in an important way I believe, those customarily ascribed to the aristocracy. And the two tended to get all involved with each other, in a fashion that was not logical perhaps but was nonetheless pervasive.

Let me offer two quotations from the critical writings of Allen Tate (the man whom, I might add, I happen to admire most among all twentieth-century authors). In one, dated 1931, Tate was writing about poetry: "A mind without moral philosophy is incapable of understanding poetry. For poetry, of all the arts, demands a serenity of view and a settled temper of the mind, and most of all the power to detach one's own needs from the experience set forth in the poem. A moral sense so organized sets limits to human nature, and is content to observe them." In the other, dated 1936, Tate was writing about the Old South: "Antebellum man, insofar as he achieved a unity between his moral nature and his livelihood, was a traditional man. He dominated the means of life; he was not dominated by it. I think that the distinguishing feature of a traditional society is simply that. In order to make a livelihood men do not have to put aside their moral natures." The terms in the two passages are almost interchangeable; the same sense of restraint, of classical wholeness, of unified personality that characterizes the gentleman of the Old South is used to characterize the writing of poetry. Tate, to be sure, wasn't confusing the two realms, but many people did.

Such terms clearly didn't fit the work of Thomas Wolfe. His was no serenity of view, and his temper of mind was not settled but highly volatile and excitable. The idea of a harmonious unity of personality, dominating every facet of its experience, acting unconsciously and classically out of a completely traditional and accepted set of responses to experience, was the last way one might think to describe how Wolfe went about either living his life or writing his books. He was highly and voraciously romantic; he wanted to storm the gates of Heaven, and never mind the consequences. Restraint? Why, he poured the language on at all times, held back not at all. And as for detaching his own needs from the experience set forth in his books, it is obvious that no more literally autobiographical and nakedly personal a writer than Thomas Wolfe ever lived.

What I am suggesting is that those literary characteristics which were most valued by most of the southern writers of the 1920s and 1930s, and which in many ways exemplify the best features of much of their art, were also seen as socially characteristic of an aristocratic ideal—and there was the implication, though nobody ever came right out and said it, that the creator of Eugene Gant, though born in a state of the former Confederacy, was from the wrong side of the tracks and wrote like it. Mind you, the best of the other southern writers didn't think of it that way at all, as far as I know; but a good many lesser authorities who wrote about southern letters suggested as much.

I recall, for example, approaching an American literature scholar of some reputation, who liked very much to think of himself as a southern gentleman, and asking him to direct a dissertation I wanted to write on Thomas Wolfe as a southern writer. His response was that he didn't think of Wolfe as being a southern writer; he thought that in spirit Wolfe belonged among the midwestern writers. So I had to look elsewhere (and finally found a Frenchman who was willing to help me). Ostensibly the man was making a literary distinction—i.e., that Wolfe's work could be best understood when viewed alongside such writers as Dreiser, Lewis, Anderson, Sandburg, and so forth, rather than alongside Faulkner and Warren and the other southerners. But he was also expressing, conscious of it or not, a social judgment; he was telling me that as a writer Wolfe was not a gentleman.

For like many other readers, this scholar had formed his notion of what a southern author should be from the local color and genteel literature of the late nineteenth and early twentieth centuries, and when the newer writers came along, once the shock of their being different was blunted, he had somehow managed to fit them into the same social milieu. The perspective from which the literature was ostensibly to be viewed and supposedly had been written was that of the gentleman. Since Thomas Wolfe wasn't a southern gentleman and had few of the virtues, either literary or social, customarily ascribed to southern gentlemen, it was quite clear that Wolfe wasn't a southern writer!

Consider another illustration of the same kind of bias, this time from, of all persons, Herbert Marshall McLuhan. (Few people recall that back in the old days, before Marshall McLuhan discovered mediums and messages, he was a mere literary critic.) Here are several sentences from his essay on "The Southern Quality": "The impersonal formal code which permits a formal expression of inward emotion makes it pointless for people to interpret one another constantly, as they do in most 'realistic' novels. There is thus in the Southern novel a vacuum where we might expect introspection. (It is quite pronounced even in *Huck Finn.*) The stress falls entirely on slight human gestures, external events which are obliquely slanted to flash light or shade on character."

The image—and McLuhan was quite aware of it—is of the gentleman, reserved, formal, punctilious, who is never so vulgar as to attempt to penetrate beyond the formal, arm's-length social ambience. McLuhan then goes on to point out that Thomas Wolfe partook of this impulse, too, but in his case the result was to leave him "locked up in his own passionate solitude." Wolfe, he continues, "has all the passion without any of the formal means of constraint and communication which make it tolerable. He was a Southerner by attitude but not by tradition."

The implied social judgment is obvious. Wolfe was not a gentleman, so didn't know the inherited rules of gentlemanly conduct, but since he was a southerner by birth, he couldn't help but have absorbed the proper attitude from his betters! Now what bosh and balderdash, as they say. The idea of the southern novel not permitting characters to interpret each other leaves out such episodes as Thomas Sutpen talking to General Compson and Miss Rosa Coldfield talking to Quentin Compson and Quentin Compson talking to Shreve McCannon in Faulkner's *Absalom, Absalom!* It leaves out Lacy Buchan's whole method of narration in Tate's *The Fathers.* It leaves out Jack Burden on the subject of Willie Stark in *All The King's Men.* It leaves out Eudora Welty's *The Optimist's Daughter.* It leaves out—but a better way to get at the appropriateness of that particular pronouncement might be to say what it includes. It includes, so far as I can tell, Stark Young and Thomas Nelson Page, and not a great deal else.

Why such a pronouncement from a critic with as much intelligence as Marshall McLuhan? It was simply that McLuhan confused the subject matter of some southern fiction with its techniques—captivated with what Allen Tate, John Ransom, and others have written, often admiringly, *about* the southern gentleman, he moved insensibly to assuming that Tate, for example, wrote *as* a southern gentleman, which is precisely what Tate often went to demonstrate was quite impossible to do if one was a modern writer with anything important to say. That, Tate said, was why Poe had once been more or less driven out of Richmond, and why the good writers of his own generation had extreme difficulty in making a living while resident in the South. But such is the thematic pervasiveness of the gentlemanly ideal that it also hooked Marshall McLuhan into making numerous absurd statements, such as: "Even the characters of Erskine Caldwell are free at least from self-pity." And that statement is made about *Jeeter Lester!*

But I digress. What I have been attempting to do is to show what some of the problems are in discussing the question of Thomas Wolfe and the South. We all have our Souths, to which in varying degree we are drawn. We also have the example of some very powerful and very persuasive authors and critics who had definite ideas of what the South was and should be, and who can have a very formative and even controlling influence upon our own ways of thinking about the South and its writers, and some of their ideas are very much intertwined with their social attitudes. Yet no matter how much we may admire and value such insights, we must finally judge for ourselves in matters that concern us.

Very well, what of Thomas Wolfe and the South? *Is* Wolfe a southern writer, or merely a writer born in the South but not of it, so far as his imagination and way of writing go?

I want now to quote a fairly well-known passage from *Look Homeward, Angel*, describing Eugene Gant in his eleventh or twelfth year.

> His feeling for the South was not so much historic as it was of the core and desire of dark romanticism—that unlimited and inexplicable drunkenness, the magnetism of some men's blood that takes them into the heart of the heat, and beyond that, into the polar and emerald cold of the South as swiftly as it took the heart of the incomparable romanticist who wrote *The Rime of the Ancient Mariner*, beyond which there is nothing. And this desire of his was unquestionably enhanced by all he had read and visioned, by the romantic halo that his school history cast over the section, by the whole fantastic distortion of that period where people were said to live in "mansions," and slavery was a benevolent institution, conducted to a constant banjo-strumming, the strewn largesses of the colonel and the shuffle-dance of his happy dependents, where all women were pure, gentle, and beautiful, all men chivalrous and brave, and the Rebel horde a company of swaggering, death-mocking cavaliers. Years later, when he could no longer think of the barren spiritual wilderness, the hostile and murderous intrenchment against all new life—when their cheap mythology, their legend of the charm of their manner, the aristocratic culture of their lives, the quaint sweetness of their drawl, made him writhe—when he could think of no return to their life and its swarming superstition without weariness and horror, so great was his fear of the legend, his fear of their antagonism, that he still pretended the most fanatic devotion to them, excusing his Northern residence on grounds of necessity rather than desire.
>
> Finally, it occurred to him that these people had given him nothing, that neither their love nor their hatred could injure him, that he owed them nothing, and he determined that he would say so, and repay their insolence with a curse. And he did.

This passage has been cited to illustrate Wolfe's lack of relationship to the South. It is certainly a passage of repudiation. It rejects southern history, southern aristocratic pretense, southern manners, southern speech, southern womanhood, southern clannishness, southern notions of chivalry, southern culture; it describes southern life as a "barren spiritual wilderness," and it asserts that Eugene Gant eventually learned to recognize his superiority to what he had been taught to revere as southern, so that he had vowed to "repay their insolence with a curse," which, of course, was not only the passage itself but *Look Homeward, Angel* as a whole. The passage thus makes the direct autobiographical association between Thomas Wolfe's protagonist and the author himself, and is clearly intended to so do.

Now there is a passage somewhat reminiscent of that in William Faulkner's *Absalom, Absalom!* After Quentin Compson and Shreve McCannon have unraveled the long story of Thomas Sutpen and his descendants, Shreve asks Quentin why he hates the South, and Quentin replies, "at once, immediately" that he doesn't hate it, repeating the statement a half-dozen times or so. Beyond doubt we are meant to see that Quentin does hate the South, and also loves it, and that love-hate relationship *is* the South for him—*is* Quentin.

But in Eugene Gant's instance there is no equivocation. He does hate it, all of it, and he wants to make it perfectly clear. He hates it because of what it did to him, and because of the hold it had for so long kept on him, and now he has told it off for good, repaid its "insolence with a curse."

Well, *is* that what he did? Not if *Look Homeward, Angel* is any indication. Along with considerable satire and savaging, there is also tremendous affection and admiration, passages of great delight with the people and places he knew in Asheville and elsewhere, passionate affirmations of its beauty, episode after episode infused with the creative joy of recollected memory, recreated experience. If one were to take all of the passages in the Wolfe fiction which attack the South and put them against all the passages which portray it, and his relation to it, in generally admiring fashion, I think they would just about balance out. In other words, there is every bit as much a love-hate relationship involved with Eugene Gant and Thomas Wolfe as with Quentin Compson and William Faulkner.

Wolfe in the passage quoted castigates the distortion of the southern plantation myth, the phony glamour of the legend of the Confederacy. He also wrote the story entitled "Chickamauga," however, and those descriptions of Lee's army en route to Gettysburg; and more importantly, he took his own particular family's history, the Westalls and Pattons who settled in the mountains of North Carolina, and the history of his father's people as well, and he did what almost every southern author of his generation did: portrayed his protagonists as the inheritors of a specific and tangible history, deeply marked and shaped by the past, and very much the creatures of the forces that placed them where they were and at the time in which they found themselves living.

Not only does the author of that passage concern himself with history and take it seriously enough to want to rectify it, but there is an important sense in which that passage *is* southern history. For what it exemplifies is the process of dislodgment, of the breaking up of the old closely knit southern premodern community before the forces of change. Wolfe describes Eugene Gant as having been born into and still very much molded by the older community, with its own history and mythology and its clearly defined social stratifications. He points out that even after he left it, he was for a long while so influenced by its pieties and its imaginative hold upon him that he pretended to a continuing allegiance. Then he says that finally he realized he was free, no longer bound and obligated, and his response was "to repay their insolence with a curse." Obviously he isn't nearly as free as he imagines, for if he were, there would be no need for so impassioned a denunciation. Wolfe is really in the position, as that paragraph amply demonstrates, of the two Quentin Compsons in *Absalom, Absalom!*—the Quentin who would live in the twentieth century and the Quentin who because he was of his time and place was still bound to the old ghost times, as Faulkner puts it. And just as Miss Rosa Coldfield suggested that Quentin might someday want to do, Wolfe has written a book about it. Surely this is precisely the cultural situation of the twentieth-century southern writer as elucidated by Allen Tate and many others: "With the war of 1914–1918, the South reentered the world—but gave a backward glance as it stepped over the border; that backward glance gave us the Southern renascence, a literature conscious of the past in the present."

But there is something more basically southern involved in the passage, even. To see it fully, we must put the episode in context. It occurs as Wolfe is describing Eliza Gant's yearly winter journeys into the South, to such places as Florida and Arkansas, for reasons of health and business. Wolfe tells how Eliza went South because of her innate suspicion of northerners—a feeling, he says, involving "fear, distrust, alienation"—and how Eugene was always taken along, "into the South, the South that burned like Dark Helen in Eugene's blood." He then proceeds to inform us of the "core and desire of dark romanticism—that unlimited and inexplicable drunkenness, the magnetism of some men's blood" that characterizes his feeling for the South.

Does this feeling evaporate when he grows older and learns to regard its mythology and its society as cheap, tawdry, oppressive? I would say that it does not, and not merely because of the evidence of so much of his work, but also because of the quality of the passage of explanation and repudiation itself. For clearly Wolfe is not describing merely a geographical section, or a set of objective environmental factors. When he depicts the South as "burning" like "Dark Helen" in his protagonist's blood, he is talking about a state of consciousness, a passionate emotional response, an entity of the spirit not to be discussed merely as quantity or as economic or sociological data. He portrays it in feminine terms, and though the South may not be "the proud Lady with the heart of fire" described in John Ransom's poem, she is a prideful woman even so; and if he has ultimately fallen out of love with her as he says, she still makes his blood run hot and he feels it necessary to tell her off in quite passionate terms. "And he did." To me, that dimension alone is enough to counter any arguments about the alleged absence of a "southern" relationship in Wolfe's work.

I recall something that Robert Penn Warren wrote in connection with Faulkner. "It is clear that Faulkner, though he gives a scrupulously faithful report of the real world, is 'mythic' . . . he is dramatizing clashes of value in a root way." Wolfe's South—more importantly, Wolfe's relationship to it—may involve a great deal of realistic description, but the affair goes beyond reportage or realistic experience, because it is powerfully caught up in feeling and emotion and in values of truth and goodness. When Auden wrote of Yeats that "mad Ireland hurt you into poetry," he was saying something that could as readily be declared of Wolfe and, for that matter, of all his southern contemporaries. And like that of his contemporaries, Wolfe's response was not only to a set of specific acts and topical problems; it was to a moral entity, one that had to be dealt with accordingly. Not only was there no room for neutrality, but the involvement involved the constant and often agonizing need to define his own moral identity in terms of the relationship to the time and place. Wolfe saw places as suffused with moral qualities, and he saw his South, above all other regions, in terms of place. "And suddenly Eugene was back in space and color and in Time," he writes in describing his own return to North Carolina, "the weather of his youth was round him, he was home again." This is not only a description of his feelings about reality; it is an accurate judgment of his fiction, which most often is surest, most firm, most vivid and least empty and forced, when it is grounded in "the South that burned like Dark Helen" in Eugene Gant's blood. It is exemplary of what Eudora Welty has written, that "it seems plain that the art that speaks most clearly, explicitly, directly, and passionately from its place of origin will remain the longest understood. It is through place that we put our roots, wherever birth, chance, fate, or our traveling selves set us down." And that place, for Wolfe, was his South—North Carolina, not merely as locale but as passionate realm of moral decision.

It is such imaginative dimensions as these and not the little descriptive motifs that I once used to "prove" a point that, presented in that way, was not worth proving, that constitute Wolfe's southern sensibility. Of course he has the addiction to rhetoric, and he uses time thematically, and he has the famous regional storytelling sense, and he is concerned with evil, and he has much to say about death, and he has the passion for detail and not much skill at abstraction. But these are only the trappings of his art, and do not of themselves help account for its distinctiveness; they would apply equally well to the fiction of, say, Edna Ferber or the late Harry Stillwell Edwards. It is the passionate moral involvement in a time and place that lies beneath these, and gives them character and form, that constitutes Thomas Wolfe's relationship with the South.

We confront the fact, however, that there does exist an important element in Wolfe's fiction which is notably different from almost every other southern author of Wolfe's day. The passage from Eugene Gant and the South certainly exemplifies it. In that passage, Wolfe is not simply telling about a character named Eugene Gant and how his feelings toward the South changed; he *is* Eugene Gant, or more properly Eugene is Thomas Wolfe, and he wants the reader to know it. In that passage he comes very close to telling us that Eugene wrote the book we are reading, and what was at least part of his motivation for so doing. This is "autobiographical fiction"—which is a way of saying that not only does the material come pretty closely and directly out of the author's experience, but that we are compelled to read it that way, and, if it is done well, cannot otherwise properly appreciate the story.

This is a kind of storytelling that we do not often find in southern fiction. Faulkner, for example, uses a great deal of his own personal experience in his fiction, but nobody reads, say, "The Bear" with the feeling that the author is asking us to watch him in the woods as a boy. It isn't told that way. Faulkner the writer usually keeps out of his fiction, in the sense of requiring us to keep in mind at all times a personal relationship between what is being described and the biographical author writing the description.

Wolfe, by contrast, wants us to do just that, and he tells his story so that we will do so. There is thus little or no "objectivity," and the deliberate and intense assertion of the writer's personality, with a view toward making us think and feel emotion about him and what he has done and thought, is very uncharacteristic of other southern authors. It is this, I think, that more than any other aspect of Wolfe's art accounts for the dislike that many good southern critics have felt toward him. Robert Penn Warren (who later became quite friendly with Wolfe) declared of *Of Time and the River* that it "illustrates once more the limitations, perhaps the necessary limitations, of an attempt to exploit directly and naively the personal experience and the self-defined personality in art."

And he ended by pointing out that Shakespeare "merely wrote *Hamlet;* he was *not* Hamlet."

I rather doubt that the Warren who wrote the poetry he has been writing for the past two decades would have put the matter quite in that fashion if he were reviewing Wolfe's novel today. But the point is well taken, and I think it is an objective way of recording a reaction that was—perhaps not for Warren so much as for some of his contemporaries—not merely literary but personal. They didn't *like* Wolfe's personality; they were less than charmed by his continual assertions of uniqueness and sensibility, and thought him more than a little boorish and egotistical. The professional writer, they felt (and with considerable justification), didn't place himself on exhibition as a person, but let his art speak for him. Furthermore, that person on exhibition was hugely and passionately romantic and fascinated by the intensity of his own emotional responses. As Warren wrote, "The hero [of *Of Time and the River*] is really that nameless fury that drives Eugene. The book is an effort to name that fury, and perhaps by naming it, to tame it. But the fury goes unnamed and untamed." Warren and his contemporaries had no objection to the presence of fury in fiction. But they felt emphatically that the fury should take the form of fiction, not the author's feelings about himself and his personal experience.

I once attempted to account for the presence of this subjective, autobiographical assertion of personality in the Wolfe novels by noting the difference between Wolfe's background and early life and that of almost all his southern contemporaries. He came from a family that, as he portrays them, had little sympathy with intellectual interests and a tradition of literary sensibilities. The result was that he was led to turn his deepest feelings inward, to erect a barrier between the outside world and himself, and to develop a stern defensiveness about his literary and intellectual interests. With no public outlet for his feelings, the result was pent-up emotions and a fierce self-preoccupation that ultimately erupted in an intense fictional assertion of his own uniqueness and of the justification for it. If I may quote myself, "When the qualities of mind that made Thomas Wolfe into a novelist instead of a stone mason or a real estate salesman did come fully into light, there was not surprisingly an explosive force to their emergence, a furious emotional subjectivity that could be disciplined only with great difficulty and always imperfectly."

I still believe there is considerable logic to that, so far as it goes, but upon reflection it seems too simple and too literal. The nature of artistic creativity, and the forms that it takes, are too complex and intricate to be ascribed to any such easy social formulation. I suspect that if there is an explanation of why Wolfe's artistic sensibilities sought the kind of expression they did, it would involve as much depth psychology as social studies, but the few attempts that have been made along that line have seemed less than impressive to me. Genius, Bernard DeVoto declared of Thomas Wolfe, is not enough, which may be true, but without it there would be no such interest as now exists in the novels and the man who wrote them, and because the genius was present, there are limits to logical explanation.

So perhaps it is best simply to accept, with considerable gratitude, that the man wrote as he did, and to note that there is little warrant for contending that the particular form that Wolfe's art took, with its passionate and direct assertion of personality, is somehow alien to his southern background. For while it is quite true that his southern literary contemporaries do not exhibit it, but on the contrary share with each other a marked formal objectivity, it is equally true that in other fields of activity there has been plenty of personal assertion on the southern scene. No one has ever suggested, for example, that Ellen Glasgow and James Branch Cabell were backward in writing quite personally and openly about themselves in their nonfictional writing, yet there is hardly much in the way of working-class experience in the background of those two Virginia patricians. Or consider more recent works such as James Agee's *Let Us Now Praise Famous Men,* or Willie Morris' *North towards Home,* or such nineteenth-century productions as Mrs. Chestnut's *Diary,* first edited for publication by that lady herself, or the spate of memoirs of the Civil War period, some of them quite choleric, that were published during the late years of the last century and the early years of this. My point is not that they are comparable to Wolfe's writings, and still less that they are all equally works of art, but only that they are evidence that it has been by no means without precedent for a southerner to write directly and assertively about his own experience. Where Wolfe differs is that he did it in the form of autobiographical fiction—an important difference, but hardly a justification for considering him and his work as somehow not an outgrowth of southern experience.

I think it is wise, in considering the problem of Thomas Wolfe, and the South, to adopt Hugh Holman's insight: that Wolfe's subject is "the American self," that "this pattern of development is grounded in the South, but it is grounded in a South which is steadily expanding outward," that Wolfe's "fiction was determined by the Piedmont middle-class world which he knew," and that "when he moved from it, he moved outward to embrace the nation and to attempt to realize the promise of America." This is an old southern custom, you know: it began at least as early as Thomas Jefferson, and among its distinguished literary practitioners have been Mark Twain and the author of *Look Homeward, Angel.* So all in all, we would probably do well to take Thomas Wolfe as he comes; and the place he came from is Asheville, North Carolina.

JOHN HAGAN

"Thomas Wolfe's *Of Time and the River:* The Quest for Transcendence" (1982)

Thomas Wolfe: A Harvard Perspective

ed. Richard S. Kennedy

1983, pp. 3–20

"In a system where things forever pass and decay, what is there fixed, real, eternal? I search for an answer . . ." (Letter to Horace Williams, September 9, 1921)

Criticism today has left *Of Time and the River* largely ignored, Thomas Wolfe's reputation—such as it is—resting almost exclusively on *Look Homeward, Angel.* There are several reasons for this unfortunate situation. In part, of course, it is simply the result of current taste and academic fashion. But paramount among its deeper causes is the fact that ever since its publication in 1935 Wolfe's second novel has been almost unanimously assailed for its "formlessness." Some critics have even gone so far as to deny that it is a novel at all. The latter view is obviously arbitrary and extreme, but the first is so plausible that any attempt to question it might seem to be perverse revisionism. Nevertheless, it may be that our detailed knowledge of the extremely disorderly way in which the book was written and of the facts of Wolfe's life on which it is heavily based has predisposed us to read *Of Time and the River* in an inadequate way—to see it too much as raw, undisciplined autobiography rather than as self-contained fiction. Because it is a mixture of radically different rhetorical modes, we must be careful not to assume that it lacks unity of theme or action. Above all, because it is not a tightly constructed Flaubertian or Jamesian novel, we must not jump to the conclusion that it is therefore chaotic. Between chaos and strict order there is a very broad spectrum of possibilities, ranging from those "loose, baggy monsters" like Thackeray's *The Newcomes* and Tolstoy's *War and Peace* that James stigmatized but that have turned out on subsequent analysis to be more satisfactorily structured than he realized, to novels like some by Scott and Cooper in which the coherent design is less perfectly achieved, but is nonetheless discernible and significant. It is in the latter category, I believe, that *Of Time and the River* belongs, and it is an outline of that kind of design that I should like to sketch in the present paper. Flawed Wolfe's book certainly is, but it can still offer the sympathetic reader a uniquely compelling, deeply moving experience. Essential to its appreciation, as I hope my discussion will suggest, is a recognition that although it is undeniably "realistic" in its overall method, there runs very deep in it a strain of the mythical, the parabolic, and the visionary.

I

As many commentators have noted, a basic constituent of *Of Time and the River* (as of all Wolfe's novels, for that matter) is the Quest. On whatever level we examine the work—its language, its action, its authorial commentary, or the psychology of its protagonist, Eugene Gant—the motif of questing is everywhere. But what are the objects of Eugene's quests? What is he looking for? The answer to this question lies in his obsession with time. In few major American novels of this century is time a more pervasive presence than in *Of Time and the River*; dramatic evocations of it appear on almost every page. Eugene's preoccupation with time, however, has little in common with the technical, abstract, and specialized interest of the professional metaphysicians. His concern is emotional rather than intellectual, and pertains to those familiar aspects of time that each of us immediately experiences in his ordinary, everyday life—in particular, loss of various kinds and especially the dreadful reality of death. Time is a source of some of Eugene's deepest anguish because, having been profoundly affected by the unforgettably poignant deaths of his brother Ben and his father, he habitually regards it as a threat, an enemy, which destroys not only everything we value, but ultimately our very existence itself. Innumerable passages record his horror or extinction, his vision of "the bitter briefness of our days," of all things being swept up by time into the huge graveyard of the past. The theme of transiency is also richly developed by several recurring metaphors and symbols, such as smoke, dreams, the river, the sea, trains, a face glimpsed for a moment in passing and never seen again, and various places, especially Dixieland, Mrs. Gant's old boardinghouse, which for Eugene is almost literally haunted by the ghosts of all "the lost, the vanished people," including himself as a child, who have ever lived there.[1] In fact, it is just at Eugene's age, Wolfe asserts, that "the knowledge of man's brevity first comes to us" and that "we first understand . . . that the moment of beauty carries in it the seeds of its own instant death, that love is gone almost before we have it, that youth is gone before we know it, and that, like every other man, we must grow old and die" (p. 701. Cf. pp. 138–139, 454, 869).

In the light of this theme, the incentives and objects of Eugene's quests become clear. For time, Eugene's preoccupation with it, and the profound anxiety it instills in him are not merely incidental features of the main action of the novel; they are its essential impetus. Between Eugene's sense of time and his quests there is a vital causal connection, in that the core of all his longing is his desire to transcend the limits of mortality, his tireless will to believe that "he could never die," after all (pp. 95, 159, 160, 281, 282, 673, 685), or, as Wolfe succinctly put it in one of his notebooks, his yearning to "escape into life . . . that has no death in it."[2] The epigraph of the novel (from *Ecclesiastes*, 3:21) points both to "the spirit of the beast that goeth downward to the earth," which in this context is a metaphor of various kinds of death, and to "the spirit of man that goeth upward," which serves as a metaphor of resurrection (cf. p. 141). Death and resurrection are also juxtaposed in the prose poem that precedes Chapter 1: after "wandering forever," there comes "the earth again"—that is, the grave; but from the grave emerge "the big flowers, the rich flowers, the strange unknown flowers" of "immortal love," to which "we cried" and which will rescue us "from our loneliness" (Cf. pp. 413–414). Moreover, the river and the sea, which, as I have just remarked, symbolize on one level the ephemerality of all things, can inspire the traveler with hope too, as in the magnificent passage at the end of the novel where the ship that Eugene boards both connotes man's tragic journey toward death (p. 909), and is "alive with the supreme ecstasy of the modern world, which is the voyage to America" (p. 906. Cf. p. 500). Another, more traditional way in which Wolfe depicts death and resurrection is by the cycle of the seasons. The month of October, in particular, is a microcosm of this cycle, because it is the season of both endings and beginnings, departures and returns, "sorrow and delight" (p. 327), "huge prophecies of death and life" (p. 333), the "sense of something lost and vanished, gone forever," and the "still impending prescience of something grand and wild to come" (p. 392. Cf. pp. 329–332, 367, 421). If his trip in October, 1920, takes Eugene to the dying Gant in Baltimore, it also takes him to what he believes will be a thrilling new life in the North; and if, after his return to Altamont in October, 1923, he laments the death of his father and the rejection of his play by a Broadway producer, he also hears the voice of a spirit that is both "a demon and a friend" assuring him that Ben and all the other dead young men will "walk and move again tonight . . . speaking to you their messages of flight, of triumph, and the all-exultant darkness, telling you that all will be again as it was once" (pp. 328–329).

Such thematic patterns indicate that, although Eugene has no formal religion or even any discernible belief in God, his quests for some kind of deliverance from death spring essentially—albeit unconsciously and in a broad, elementary sense—from a powerful religious instinct, a desperate craving for a secular equivalent of transcendent religious faith. What Wolfe said in a letter about one of these quests definitively illuminates them all: "it comes, I think, from the deepest need in life, and all religiousness is in it."[3] Eugene is an image of "modern man caught in the Faustian serpent-toils of modern life" (p. 661), who is always searching for a way back to Eden, a return to the lost Earthly Paradise, a "door" (one of the novel's key terms) through which he can pass from the harsh reality of pain and death into an idyllic realm of beatitude like that celebrated by Mignon's famous lyric in *Wilhelm Meister*, "Kennst du das Land," which prefaces *Of Time and the River*, Book I. He is seeking a "shining," "elfin," "glorious," and "fabulous" region of "enchantment" and "magic," where he can find "strength" and "love," "triumph" and "splendor," "exultancy" and "ecstasy." He is looking, in short, for a fusion of Actuality and Romance in a world so intense, vital, and magnificent that it is larger than life, ideal, "more true than truth, more real than . . . reality" (p. 883. Cf. pp. 389, 748). The imagery of the novel is consistently polarized between this kind of paradisaical vision, on the one hand, and various kinds of Wasteland or Hell, on the other.

Above all, the "religious" or "mythic" character of Eugene's quest for an Earthly Paradise is apparent in his hunger for permanence. Eugene is very much like one of Wolfe's favorite poets, Keats, in that, although he takes a lusty delight in all the pleasures of the senses, he also yearns for the changeless and eternal, as in the following typical passage, which describes the earliest and best phase of his relationship with Starwick:

> Now, with Starwick, and for the first time, he felt this magic constantly—this realization of a life forever good, forever warm and beautiful, forever flashing with the fires of passion, poetry, and joy, forever filled with the swelling and triumphant confidence of youth, its belief in new lands, morning, and a shining city, its hope of voyages, its conviction of a fortunate, good, and happy life—an imperishable happiness and joy—that was impending, that would be here at any moment (p. 274).

Both contributing to and reflecting this insatiable desire for an immutable Earthly Paradise, and setting up an insistent counter-current to his sense of flux, are numerous important occasions scattered throughout the book when Eugene experiences a certain radiant and visionary sensation of timelessness suggestive of "the calm and silence of eternity" (p. 417). These experiences are of several kinds. Again and again, he is aware, for example, that time, although it is the enemy that brings change and death, is itself changeless and deathless, in the sense that it is a feature of reality inherent in Being itself (p. 497). Similarly, he repeatedly perceives the earth and the cosmos as a whole as "everlasting" and "eternal," in contrast to the fleeting lives of individual men. But Eugene's most significant experiences of timelessness are those that result from his recurring sense that the "lost" past is not really lost at all—that it survives somehow, somewhere, in defiance of death, and can be recaptured, made to "blaze instantly with all the warmth and radiance of life again" (p. 805). Such Proustian moments or Wordsworthian "spots of time" appear everywhere in the novel, especially in connection with Eugene's experiences of *déjà vu*—that strange, dream-like sensation that something which has happened before, or seems to have happened before, is repeating itself. Thus, as Eugene makes his first visit to the estate of his friend, Joel Pierce, in Rhinekill on the Hudson, the whole scene seems "hauntingly familiar" to him (p. 526), and he encounters it "without surprise, as one who for the first time comes into his father's country, finding it the same as he had always known it would be, and knowing always that it would be there" (p. 569. Cf. pp. 580, 582, 882–883). Other equally memorable experiences occur, as we might expect, on trains, which, when used as a symbol of time, powerfully heighten the *déjà vu* effect by contrast, as in the marvelously luminous passage on the town of Troy in upstate New York, which Eugene's train passes through in the middle of the night, and which, as he glimpses it through the window, seems to him "as familiar as a dream" and "like something he had known forever" (pp. 471, 475).

The most important means by which Eugene experiences the illusion of recapturing the past, however, is his phenomenal memory—a "memory that will not die" (p. 865)—which enables him to recall with extraordinary intensity not only major happenings and persons, but "the 'little' things of life—a face seen one time at a window, a voice that passed in darkness and was gone, the twisting of a leaf upon a bough . . ." (p. 803. Cf. pp. 155, 160, 200). This power of almost total recall, this enormous retentiveness, is both a liability and an asset: a liability, because it makes Eugene agonizingly aware of time and death in the first place; but an asset too, because it permits him to transcend those limits by restoring the lost world to life again—making it "living, whole, and magic" (p. 200)—and thereby imparting to it a kind of immortality.

All these various, quasi-mystical experiences, then, help to develop in Eugene an unusually strong sense of timelessness, which in turn nourishes and mirrors his "religious" longing for an Earthly Paradise. But the principal roots of that longing pre-date all of these experiences and lie deep in Eugene's childhood. It was then that he heard "the sound of something lost and elfin and half-dreamed" (p. 139), and glimpsed a "half-captured vision of some magic country he has known . . . which haunts his days with strangeness and the sense of imminent, glorious re-discovery" (p. 622)—wonderful phrases that suggest those recollections of a Platonic and Wordsworthian pre-natal "heaven" that played an even more conspicuous part in *Look Homeward, Angel*. Furthermore, partly because of these recollections, partly because of the reading of fairy-tales and romantic literature that stimulated his boyhood's imagination (pp. 570, 598, 820, 894, 898), and partly because of the rich, colorful life once provided him by the great life-force figure of his father, Eugene now, looking nostalgically back, sees his childhood itself as a Paradise (pp. 29, 58, 271, 328, 333), the loss of which as a result of both his father's death and the disappearance of small-town America in general, he always regards "with an intolerable sense of pain" (p. 200. Cf. pp. 327, 329, 592–595, 898–899). Paradoxically, therefore, his quests to transcend the limits of mortality, no matter how far and wide they lead him, are always at the deepest level expressive of a desire to recapture what he perceives as the lost pastoral idyll of his childhood by discovering an equivalent Paradise in the present.

II

These quests for transcendence are mainly of four overlapping kinds. One is a quest for *adventure*—for plenitude of experience—which is motivated by a "Faustian" desire to race against death, a voracious passion to conquer time by seeing and doing as much as possible in the brief span of days that life allows: Eugene "was driven by a hunger so literal, cruel and physical that it wanted to devour the earth and all the things and people in it" (p. 91. Cf. pp. 150, 443, 660).

A second kind of quest on which he embarks is for *knowledge* (pp. 175, 458), especially that "recorded knowledge" that is to be obtained by " 'reading all the books that were ever printed' " (p. 709. Cf. p. 150). Through such knowledge Eugene hopes to reach beyond time and death by discovering the ultimate meaning—by plumbing "the source, the well, the spring from which all men and words and actions, and every design upon this earth proceeds" (p. 92); by finding some definitive "answer to the riddle of this vast and swarming earth" (p. 137); by acquiring " 'an everlasting and triumphal wisdom' " (p. 587).

A third quest is for *security*—or, as Wolfe designated it in *The Story of a Novel*, for "a father . . . the image of a strength and wisdom external to . . . [a man's] need and superior to his hunger, to which the belief and power of his own life could be united."[4] In his horror of oblivion, Eugene is yearning for that simple, elemental kind of physical and emotional stability and happiness that the words "father" and "home" connote literally, and that he identifies with the "silence, peace, and certitude" (p. 30) he enjoyed in that lost paradise of his childhood where the foundations of all his other quests were laid as well. The very first episode in the novel—Eugene's journey to Harvard—results not only from his desire for adventure and knowledge, but from his desire to travel to the North, which, because W. O. Gant had been born and raised in Pennsylvania, he envisages as "his heart's hope and his father's country, the lost but unforgotten half of his own soul" (p. 24. Cf. pp. 58, 569, 680, 898). After Gant's death, his search intensifies, and reaches a brilliant climax in one of the novel's most moving passages, the eloquent prayer that constitutes the penultimate paragraph of Chapter 39:

> Come to us, Father, in the watches of the night, come to us as you always came, bringing to us the invincible sustenance of your strength, the limitless treasure of your bounty, the tremendous structure of your life that will shape all lost and broken things on earth again into a golden pattern of exultancy and joy . . . For we are ruined, lost, and broken if you do not come, and our lives, like rotten chips, are whirled about us onward in darkness to the sea (p. 333. Cf. pp. 327–328).

Finally, and most important, there is a fourth way by which Eugene attempts to transcend time and death: this is his quest for *art*, his desire to become a writer. For he not only dreams of art as a means of winning fame and fortune (pp. 93, 334, 353, 590), but, lacking the religious faith he unconsciously craves but cannot attain, ultimately comes to believe that art alone can triumph over flux, and, acting on that belief, begins the process of transforming his life itself into the Earthly Paradise by recapturing the otherwise irretrievable past in memory and rendering it immortal in artistic form. Although he certainly does not think of it in such terms, art becomes, in effect, his surrogate religion.

Before Eugene can appreciate the full significance of art or begin authentically creating it, however, he must first learn that the ideal life he is seeking is unattainable in any other way; he must discover the vanity of all his other quests. The stages of this discovery add up to most of the novel's main action, and are deeply ironic. The basic structural pattern of Eugene's experiences is a series of cycles, each of which (almost like the mood swings of a manic-depressive) consists of some great expectation followed by frustration and disillusionment, some youthful dream shattered by its denial. No matter how often his hopes fail to materialize, they revive, but only inevitably to be dashed again. Nothing ever turns out as he has imagined it would; fantasy and reality always collide; the satisfactions for which he struggles prove unattainable. As in the cycles of futile striving and eternal recurrence described in one of Wolfe's favorite texts, *Ecclesiastes*, each of the attempts Eugene makes to escape some kind of death only brings him back to death in another form. The pattern of Book I, in which the euphoria that he enjoys while traveling northward on the train gives way to "a feeling of horror" when he stops in Baltimore to see his dying father (p. 86), thus encapsulates the plot of the novel as a whole: five major cycles are climaxed by his disenchantments with Professor Hatcher's play-writing course at Harvard in Book II; with the Broadway producer who rejects his play in Book III; with New York City, his teaching job, and the Pierce family in Book IV; with Starwick in Book V; and with Europe in Books VI and VII. Within these main cycles there are also several smaller ones. In short, although Eugene's hunger is like that of Faustus, his fate is like that of Tantalus, the victim of "a thousand shapes of impossible desire" (p. 469. Cf. pp. 28, 90–92, 207, 431, 455, 601, 883–886).

Reinforcing the irony produced by this cyclical pattern is Wolfe's use of another device: the alter ego. Eugene's experiences of hope and disillusionment are paralleled throughout the novel by those of various other characters who have also sought and failed. The most important of these characters fall into two groups. One consists of the young, like Eugene's brothers Ben and Luke, his sister Helen, and his friends, Robert Weaver and Frank Starwick—characters of or close to Eugene's own age, whose hopes and disillusionments are more or less contemporaneous with his own (or, in the case of Ben, would have been contemporaneous, if Ben had lived). The other group consists of the old, like Uncle Bascom Pentland, Dr. Hugh McGuire, and, most important of all, W. O. Gant, Eugene's father—characters much farther along in life than Eugene, whose hopes and disillusionments have for the most part taken place a long time in the past or have extended over a great many years, and who now have nothing left to confront but despair and death. Both of these groups of characters function not only to exemplify the kinds of "death-in-life" from which Eugene is confident he can escape, but to comment ironically, as a kind of chorus, on the naivete of that confidence by foreshadowing or playing variations on his inevitable frustrations and defeats. Each is a *memento mori*—a death's head at the feast of life—whose presence in the novel is a constant reminder of that vanity of human wishes that Eugene is trying so hard not to face, but that his own disappointments sooner or later force him to acknowledge. The unromantic reality his alter egos experience and symbolize is very different from his romantic conceptions, but one that he must eventually confront.

Yet the final effect of *Of Time and the River* is far from despairing or cynical. On the contrary, like that of all Wolfe's books, it is profoundly affirmative, for not all of Eugene's quests for an Earthly Paradise that is immune to death end ironically in defeat; his solitary and painful pilgrimage through the darkness leads him ultimately to the light. What distinguishes Eugene from his alter egos and makes possible his transcendence of the trap of mortality and futility in which they are caught is his possession of artistic talent. If *Of Time and the River* is a specimen of the *Bildungsroman*, it is also an example of its subgenre, the *Künstlerroman*, because, as I have noted, along with the bitter story of the disillusionments and frustrations resulting from Eugene's quests for adventure, knowledge, and security, and in counterpoint to that story, there has been running throughout the novel another one, less conspicuous, perhaps, but essential to the denouement—namely, that of his successful growth as a writer. This development consists of several clearly marked stages, results in three vital discoveries about the nature of art and the artistic process, and culminates in a feverish act of authentic and redemptive creation.

III

In Book I, which begins where *Look Homeward, Angel* left off, Eugene sets out for graduate study at Harvard, dreaming naively "that he would write a book or play every year or so, which would be a great success, and yield him fifteen or twenty thousand dollars at a crack" (p. 93). He soon discovers, however, that the creation of art is not so easy. For, although in Book II he enrolls in Professor Hatcher's "celebrated course for dramatists" (p. 94) and there writes a play that we later learn he submits to a Broadway producer, he is plagued by self-doubts (pp. 301–304) that are only too emphatically confirmed in Book III when his work is rejected (pp. 360–361). His next effort, a play called *Mannerhouse*, which he writes in Book IV while teaching in New York City, is presumably somewhat better; at any rate, the praise he receives from his friend Joel Pierce and Joel's sister, Rosalind, to whom he reads it does much to restore his confidence (pp. 549–553). But again self-doubts emerge when he contemplates the great Pierce library, and reflects on the power of wealth to reduce "all the glory, genius, and magic of a poet's life . . . [to] six rich bindings, forgotten, purchased and unread" (p. 591). Seeking to regain his inspiration, he travels in Book V to Europe, where he manages to fill "a great stack of . . . ledgers" (p. 646), and at last begins to recognize that the artist's life consists of "the sweat and anguish of hard labor . . ." (p. 657). Two crises, however, soon develop. The first results from his lack of any coherent artistic purpose: driven by an insane, "Faustian" desire to cram all human experience into "one final, perfect, all-inclusive work," he succeeds only in filling his notebooks with a "mad mélange" of "splintered jottings" (pp. 660, 661. Cf. pp. 661–680, 858). The second crisis arises when his old friend from Harvard, Starwick, suddenly appears in Paris with two women from Boston who are in love with him. Eugene becomes infected for a time with Starwick's growing apathy, and consequently falls into a life of idleness and dissipation that brings his writing to a halt and nearly overwhelms him with feelings of shame and guilt. Even after he has broken off with Starwick and the women, he continues in Book VI merely to drift from place to place, accomplishing little or nothing. Nevertheless, he finally recovers and begins writing again, more earnestly than ever before, after his arrival in Tours in the opening two chapters (96–97) of Book VII. Indeed, not only are these chapters among Wolfe's finest lyrical passages, but they carry Eugene's development as an artist as far as the novel will take it, and thus bring *Of Time and the River* as a whole to its climax and resolution.

To understand what happens in these key chapters and makes them possible we first have to examine three crucial discoveries about art that Eugene has made earlier. One of these concerns the process of creation itself and where it can be performed. Influenced by his desire for an Earthly Paradise in general, Eugene has long hoped to find a place where he can write under the most ideal and romantic conditions. In Orleans, however, he realizes the folly of such a dream; making a giant leap from romanticism to realism, he concludes that, as a condition for the creation of art, an Earthly Paradise of any literal, physical, geographical sort is wholly unnecessary: ". . . he knew now . . . 'the place to write' was Brooklyn, Boston, Hammersmith, or Kansas—anywhere on earth, so long as the heart, the power, the faith, the desperation . . . were there inside him all the time" (p. 835).

A second major discovery, analogous to this, concerns the subject-matter of art: just as the artist must look for some never-never land of fantasy and romance in which to create, so he must not try to depict such a place in his work itself, but, drawing heavily upon memory, must faithfully represent the reality of life as he has come to know it. Eugene begins to make this discovery in Book III, after he and some companions are arrested and jailed in Blackstone, South Carolina, for drunken driving. The extreme humiliation he suffers on this occasion leads Eugene to feel "a more earthly, common, and familiar union with the lives of other men than he had ever known," and thus ultimately results in his rejecting Shelley's poetry "of aerial flight and escape into some magic and unvisited domain" in favor of Homer, the poets of the Bible, Chaucer, the Elizabethans, and others, "who wrote not of the air but of . . . the golden glory of the earth, which is the only earth that is . . . the only one that will never die" (pp. 389–390). Another step toward realism and an art based on memory occurs when Eugene writes the play that he reads to Joel and Rosalind Pierce at their estate in Rhinekill. Although this work is uneven in quality, and, as was his earlier one, is still in many respects imitative of stale theatrical conventions, he has begun to use in it "some of the materials of his own life and experience," and to depict "some of the real grandeur, beauty, terror, and unuttered loneliness of America" (p. 549. Cf. p. 545). Finally, to complete his realization that his art is now moving in the right direction there is the town of Rhinekill itself. For this privileged, sheltered world of the Hudson Valley rich is merely the counterpart of the dream worlds created by the Harvard esthetes and Shelley. However painful it is, therefore, to return to the ugliness of New York City, Eugene now knows that upon doing so depends his artistic salvation (pp. 570–571).

The third and last discovery that leads to the climax of his development as an artist and to the resolution of the novel as a whole occurs during the reading of his play to Joel and Rosalind, when he suddenly realizes, "in one blaze of light" (p. 550), that, of all man's works, art and art alone can achieve timelessness. The passage that describes this epiphany is, in fact, the fullest and most memorable statement of the theme in all Wolfe:

> This is the reason that the artist lives and works and has his being: that . . . he may distill the beauty of an everlasting form . . . cast his spell across the generations, beat death down upon his knees, kill death utterly, and fix eternity with the grappling-hooks of his own art. His life is soul-hydroptic with . . . the intolerable desire to fix eternally in the patterns of an indestructible form a single moment of man's living, a single moment of life's beauty, passion, and unutterable eloquence, that passes, flames, and goes, slipping forever through our fingers with time's sanded drop, flowing forever from our desperate grasp even as a river flows and never can be held (pp. 550–551. Cf. pp. 389–390, 425, 587–589).

In these three major discoveries about art, then, lies the key to Eugene's coming-of-age as a writer and hence to the achievement of his quests for transcendence and the resolution of the entire novel. The Earthly Paradise immune to death that he has so futilely sought in his quests for adventure, knowledge, and security, will turn out to be his life as he has already lived it (including, presumably, his quests themselves, with all their cycles of hope and disappointment) when that life has been recaptured by memory and embodied in art. He will be able to confer transcendence upon his own earlier self and experiences by means of the immortalizing and apotheosizing power of the creative process itself. All that remains to complete the design of *Of Time and the River*, therefore, is for such a process to begin, and this is precisely what happens in the two great opening chapters (96–97) of Book VII. The catalyst is an unbearable feeling of homesickness that has been building up in Eugene for months and now becomes profounder and more intense than ever before.

Arriving by chance in the old French town of Tours, and there finding peace and quiet for the first time after months of hectic travel, Eugene falls almost immediately into a rapt, mesmeric, trance-like state that lasts for several weeks, during which he feels himself transported into the very realm of timelessness that he has apprehended so often before (pp. 856–857, 870). His surroundings virtually disappear from his conscious awareness, and are replaced by preternaturally vivid memories of "home" and teeming impressions of America that from the beginning of the novel have been embedding themselves "in every atom of his flesh and tissue . . ." (p. 859. Cf. pp. 860–869). He knows now that, although he has been "wandering forever," he must return to "the earth [i.e., America] again" (p. 866).

The consequence of all this is not only his literal return a few chapters later (pp. 903–912), but, far more crucially, his return by means of art. For in Tours all his memories bred of homesickness finally trigger a furious burst of creativity, the object of which is to get every scrap of his remembered experience down on paper, to disgorge all of his life into language:

> . . . he began to write now like a madman . . . all ordered plans, designs, coherent projects for the work he had set out to do went by the board, were burned up in the flame of a quenchless passion, like a handful of dry straw . . . he wrote ceaselessly from dawn to dark, sometimes from darkness on to dawn again . . .
>
> And in those words was packed the whole image of his bitter homelessness, his intolerable desire, his maddened longing for return . . .
>
> They were all there—without coherence, scheme, or reason—flung down upon paper like figures blasted by the spirit's lightning stroke, and in them was the huge chronicle of the billion forms, the million names, the huge, single, and incomparable substance of America (pp. 858–859).

This episode is the point toward which Eugene's development as an artist has been implicitly tending from the beginning, and, as such, it constitutes the novel's climax and resolution. If only in a half-conscious way, Eugene has now begun the process of dealing more compulsively and completely than ever before with what must henceforth be the central subject of his art—America and the life he has already lived there. It is true that his frenzied burst of creativity is very brief; it is both the first and the last of its kind in the novel. But we are not allowed to imagine that such a crucial event will have no long-range consequences, for Eugene's memory, now more powerfully and purposefully activated than ever before, continues to operate strongly even after he leaves Tours (pp. 880–881, 882, 891–892, 894–896, 898–899), and thus provides a source of inspiration to which his creative impulse will surely return many times in the future. In short, Eugene has embarked upon the task of producing an authentic autobiographical art that will rescue his past from the maw of time, confer upon it "the beauty of an everlasting form" (p. 550), and thereby impart to it a radiant immortality. In doing so, he is at last on the verge of attaining the goal of all his quests—the transcendence of death.

This account of the novel's closure is, of course, incomplete. After Chapters 96–97, for instance, Eugene's futile, romantic quests for transcendent adventure, knowledge, and security continue anticlimactically for five more chapters, which culminate in his shipboard meeting with the woman who, in *The Web and the Rock* and *You Can't Go Home Again*, is to be known as Esther Jack, and to become the mistress of Wolfe's next protagonist, George Webber. Distracted, perhaps, by the mere "chronicle" aspect of what he was writing, Wolfe clearly did not know when to stop, and for this, as well as other reasons, *Of Time and the River* is far from being a perfect book. So much I conceded at the outset. Nevertheless, it is also far from being "formless." Considered in its broadest outline, indeed, the form turns out to be nothing less than a late avatar of that age-old, fundamentally religious one so brilliantly described by M. H. Abrams in his distinguished study of Romanticism, *Natural Supernaturalism*. This is the design (originating in pagan and Christian Neo-Platonism, modified by the nineteenth-century Romantics, and passed on to a number of moderns) of the "circuitous journey" or "the great circle," which expresses a vision, in Abrams's words, of "the course of all things" as "a circuit whose end is its beginning, of which the movement is from unity out to the increasingly many and back to unity, and in which this movement into and out of division is identified with the falling away from good to evil and a return to good."[5] In the terms implicitly proposed by *Of Time and the River*, this circle consists of four phases related to the key concepts of "home" or "paradise": paradise itself, paradise lost, paradise sought, and paradise regained. Paradise corresponds to the recollections of pre-existence and the romantic dreams that Eugene enjoyed in childhood and even to his childhood itself when in later years he nostalgically recalls it; paradise lost corresponds to the anguished awareness of time and death that comes to him in his youth; paradise sought corresponds to his many (also cyclical) quests for adventure, knowledge, and security; and paradise regained corresponds to the beginning of authentic artistic creation whereby he will finally be able to transcend time and death by making of all the transitory and tormented moments of his life itself a thing of timeless beauty.

Notes

1. *Of Time and the River* (New York: Scribner's, 1935), p. 404. Henceforth page references to this novel will be to this edition, and will be given parenthetically in the text.
2. Richard S. Kennedy and Paschal Reeves, eds., *The Notebooks of Thomas Wolfe* (Chapel Hill: The University of North Carolina Press, 1970), II. 624.
3. Elizabeth Nowell, ed., *The Letters of Thomas Wolfe* (New York: Scribner's 1956), p. 656. Cf. Andrew Turnbull's remarks in *Thomas Wolfe* (New York: Scribner's, 1967): Wolfe "had once described himself to Perkins as 'a religious and believing person'—not, of course, in the orthodox sense. Like many romantics, he belonged to a race of lost believers wandering the earth, the yearning and mysticism in their work being to some extent a religious residue. Wolfe lived in what could be called the area of the absence of God, acutely feeling the lack" (p. 308).
4. *The Story of a Novel* (New York: Scribner's, 1936), p. 39. Cf. in *Of Time and the River*, paragraph 2 of the prose poem prefacing Book I, and pp. 159, 855–856, 865, 869–870.
5. (New York: Norton, 1971), p. 150 and Parts 3–5 passim.

TOM WOLFE

1931–

Thomas Kennerly Wolfe, Jr., was born on March 2, 1931, in Richmond, Virginia, to Thomas Kennerly and Helen (née Hughes) Wolfe. He was educated at Washington and Lee University (B.A. 1951, *cum laude*) and Yale University (Ph.D. 1957). In 1978 he married Sheila Berger; they have one child. Throughout his career he has worked as a journalist for a variety of newspapers and magazines, including the *Washington Post*, the *New York Herald Tribune*, *New York* magazine, *Esquire*, and *Harper's*. He is also an artist, and frequently illustrates his own writing; in addition, he exhibited drawings in one-man shows at Maynard Walker Gallery (1965) and the Tunnel Gallery (1974).

Tom Wolfe is primarily known as a leading figure in the "New Journalism," a movement that also includes such writers as Hunter S. Thompson, Gay Talese, and Jimmy Breslin. Wolfe's journalism is notable for his use of prose techniques usually confined to fiction, employing pyrotechnic language and an extremely subjective viewpoint. His first book, *The Kandy-Kolored Tangerine-Flake Streamline Baby* (1965), was a collection of his early essays, and attracted considerable notice; some saw Wolfe as a welcome shot in the arm for journalism, while others believed his techniques reduced journalism to mere opinion. His next several books increased both the attention and the controversy: *The Electric Kool-Aid Acid Test* (1968) was an influential study of Ken Kesey and the psychedelic "Merry Pranksters"; and *Radical Chic and Mau Mauing the Flak Catchers* (1970) lost Wolfe some of his previous staunch defenders with its uncompromising attack upon wealthy white liberals.

In recent years Wolfe's style has become more conventional, and his observations have become less controversial as his methods have been accepted and absorbed by mainstream American journalism. *The Painted Word* (1975) and *From Bauhaus to Our House* (1981) are studies in the cultures of American modern art and modern architecture, respectively; while Wolfe continued to be praised for his often penetrating insights into the mechanisms of American culture and art, many critics thought the books demonstrated an unfortunate conservative streak and an automatic suspicion of the new or different. *The Right Stuff* (1979), a history of the development of the American space program, was Wolfe's least controversial and most popular book, and was made into a critically praised film.

Wolfe's later essays have been collected in *The Pump House Gang* (1968), *Mauve Gloves and Madmen, Clutter & Vine, and Other Short Stories* (1976), *In Our Time* (1980), and *The Purple Decades: A Reader* (1982). With E. W. Johnson he edited *The New Journalism* (1973). He has been awarded the Society of Magazine Writers Award for Excellence, the Columbia Journalism Award, and the 1980 American Book Award and National Book Critics' Circle Award for *The Right Stuff*. He lives in New York City.

No crueler writer ever lived. If he were a lepidopterist (and he is, in his way) he wouldn't find his pleasure in the chase, out there in the fields with his net and his handbook, creeping up on a butterfly as it rested on a twig, its beautiful wings breathing in and out. He'd like that well enough—the wonderful moment when you know you're going to get it—but the real pleasure would come later, as he shook it gently into his chloroform bottle, careful not to disturb the dust on its gorgeous wings, and later still, back in his study, when he took a plain steel pin, the kind tailors use, and skewered the plump little dead body to the mat board in his display case. A perfect specimen of its type. *Nailed.*

Tom Wolfe is not a generous writer. He's gifted in almost heroic proportion, not only with the writer's ear for irresistible words (a common enough talent, in truth), but with independence of mind, an amiable manner which persuades people to tell him things, and a genius for effortless self-promotion. He's not just good at what he does; he's a figure as well, somebody in particular, a presence, unique. People instinctively see his work as a whole; each new article enlarges our perception of who he is. It's hard to say what he'll add up to in the end, but he has certainly burst the cocoon of anonymity, and his ability gives him a fair shot at being the sort of writer people call great. But no one ever called Tom Wolfe generous.

His peculiar gift is for satire, but it is satire of an odd sort. He is not like Juvenal, angry and excoriating, animated by fierce passion. Far from it. His portraits are pitiless enough, but he seems to speak from a great distance, as if none of this mattered very greatly to him. Occasionally he speaks of himself as "the man in the white suit," amused and remote, a visitor at the carnival taking in the sideshows. His targets are ordinary humbug, inflated self-esteem, cant, childish preoccupation with style, confused and timid sensibilities. His world is a pampered place, filled with the rich, sometimes pugnacious follies of the over-protected. But Wolfe is not trying to reform us; the silliness amuses him, just as it would have amused him at the court of Louis XIV. He might have written a fine piece about the Duc de Saint Simon, who would strut and preen for a month in the afterglow of an amiable remark by the King. Unlike Juvenal, Wolfe does not long for a braver age. There is no Puritan or Republican fire in him. He is amused in the manner of a man convinced that human nature is immutable, and it is his strength to see that our age is as sunk in vanity and folly as all the rest.—THOMAS POWERS, "The Lives of Writers," *Com*, March 3, 1978, pp. 142–43

PETER MICHELSON
From "Tom Wolfe Overboard"

New Republic, December 19, 1970, pp. 17–19

Although Wolfe may genuinely be trying to illuminate a native American culture, he himself is harnessed into the same Anglo-European, eastern establishment liberal pretensions of which he is so contemptuous. For instance, though he clearly admires ⟨George⟩ Barris, his admiration is tainted with condescension. For Barris, an American primitive bagged by Wolfe on one of his safaris through the American veld, is apparently, unlike ⟨Ed⟩ Roth, not bright enough to get out of the ethos.

Wolfe has a strange love-hate game going with that ethos, and one has the feeling that he hunts down trophies with a vengeance, to show his former professors at Yale how far they are from knowing what America is. Wolfe knows who he is talking to. Not the American primitives, who are merely grist for his mill, but those professors, the Anglo-European culturati. And he is by god going to rub their noses in the real thing. Yet there is no question but that Wolfe is larger than his vendetta. When, as in *The Electric Kool-Aid Acid Test*, he breaks out of the confines of journalism and gets more or less clear from bludgeoning the dead horse Culturatus, he is at his best. *The Acid Test* is a good book because it not only documents the episodes and personalities crucial to the development of acid culture but it also provides a point of view that no first-person account could. It is at once sympathetic and disengaged. Wolfe's gamesmanship is minimal. He really does tell the story of Kesey's bus, the story of the Big Trip so symbolically central to understanding current goings-on.

So what happened in his new book, *Radical Chic & Mau Mauing the Flak Catchers?* Perhaps the most important thing is that the condescension smoldering through the earlier work has burst into the full flame of contempt in the "Radical Chic" half of this book (it consists of two long essays, "Radical Chic" and "Mau-Mauing the Flak Catchers"). Both pieces have Wolfe's characteristic strengths—wit, incisiveness, and cultural savvy. But in "Radical Chic" they go berserk and have, their nicety notwithstanding, the effect of a rather pointlessly ruptured spleen, all over Leonard Bernstein and his Radical Chic friends. The invention of Leonard Bernstein as a symbolic comfort for the well-upholstered and high-toned in their time of trouble must have come to Wolfe like the soft underbelly of a lamb.

No summary or description can show how thoroughly Wolfe thrashes chic society's sentimentalities, gamesmanship, guilt, and moral confusion, their "tried and true *nostalgie de la boue*"; but, does one really need a two-ton wrecking ball to swat a vestigial winged fruit fly? So the chic sorts in New York society take a Panther home to dinner, so they are caught in the act, so they are ridiculous, so *what?* And what kind of kick is there in ridiculing a man who, in the face of being at the clean end of a dirty stick, is no more ludicrous, no more confused, and neither more nor less guilty than anyone else, including Wolfe? Somehow—maybe it's the ad hominem effect of an attack on Bernstein, maybe it's Wolfe's cool superiority to it all—but somehow, laughable as it is, there isn't even much humor in Wolfe's account. Just more smugness. Neither is there the sense of ethical alternative that might make the story satirical. Anyway, why bother to satirize a "class" of people—the New York chic set—who are socially and politically inconsequential? To parody vacuousness, as Wolfe has done in "Radical Chic," is to come up after all with just that, a vacuous parody.

"Mau-Mauing the Flak Catchers," because it has at least some ethical sense and because it does have genuine humor, is much closer to Wolfe's good work. Here he dismounts his hobby horse and tracks substantive prey. The first paragraph beautifully articulates a very real problem, how a profoundly ignorant bureaucracy reduces the administration of the poverty program to a ridiculously degrading game:

> Going downtown to mau-mau the bureaucrats got to be the routine practice in San Francisco. The poverty program *encouraged* you to go in for mau-mauing. They wouldn't have known what to do without it. The bureaucrats at City Hall and in the Office of Economic Opportunity talked "ghetto" all the time, but they didn't know any more about what was going on in the Western Addition, Hunters Point, Potrero Hill, the Mission, Chinatown, or south of Market Street than they did about Zanzibar. They didn't know where to look. They didn't even know who to ask. So what could they do? Well . . . they used *the Ethnic Catering Service* . . . right . . . They sat back and waited for you to come rolling in with your certified angry militants, your guaranteed frustrated ghetto youth, looking like a bunch of wild men. Then you had your test confrontation. If you were outrageous enough, if you could shake up the bureaucrats so bad that their eyes froze into iceballs and their mouths twisted up into smiles of sheer physical panic, into shit-eating grins, so to speak—then they knew you were the real goods. They knew you were the right studs to give the poverty grants and community organizing jobs to. Otherwise they wouldn't know.

The consequences of *this* game being so lethal, and the players of the game being so crucial to understanding our national malaise, Wolfe's portrayal of it performs a difficult and important cultural service—pinpointing the causes both of the poverty program's ineffectuality and the too frequent dissipation of black power energies into theatricality and other symbolic diversions. Unlike Radical Chic, mau-mauing and flak catching are not trivial. Their choreography, as Wolfe so perceptively and brilliantly illuminates, is a principal cause of the paralysis of social justice in this country. For the noncommunication between the impoverished and the bureaucracy of the poverty program has become a theatrical event rehearsed each night on our television screens—ADC mothers, migrant workers, fair employment, fair housing, regularly the same story: the Invisible Man talking to Monopolated Edison.

Wolfe locates the key to the trouble in the yea-saying, know-nothing bureaucrat whose job it is to sympathize with complaints, absorb the hostility of the plaintiff, and return him to the block hopefully purged of his impotent fury: " 'Now I'm here to try to answer any questions I can,' he says, 'but you have to understand that I'm only speaking as an individual, and so naturally none of my comments are binding, but I'll answer any questions I can, and . . .,' "

> And then it dawns on you, and you wonder why it took so long for you to realize it. This man is the flak catcher. His job is to catch the flak for the No. 1 man. He's like the professional mourners you can

> hire in Chinatown. They have certified wailers, professional mourners, in Chinatown, and when your loved one dies, you can hire the professional mourners to wail at the funeral and show what a great loss to the community the departed is. In the same way this lifer is ready to catch whatever flak you're sending up. It doesn't matter what bureau they put him in. It's all the same.

That's the Flak Catcher, the man who, naturally, can't answer any questions but whose job it is to answer any questions he can. Wolfe observes that, when the Mau-Maus come into an OEO office and meet the Flak Catcher rather than the Man, "Everybody knows the scene is a shuck, but you can't just walk out and leave. You can't get it on and bring thirty-five people walking all the way from the Mission to 100 McAllister and then just turn around and go back. So . . . might as well get into the number . . ." The number is that the Mau-Maus ask the Flak Catcher the questions he can't answer, which he proceeds not to answer at some length, until they mau-mau him (a simulated terrorizing played out by both parties), demanding he deliver their complaints to the Man direct, which he promises to do—mañana. But, as Wolfe notes, tomorrow never comes. Mau-mauing, like all good theater, is purgative. After the show your passion is spent. If you're lucky your act taps you into an auxiliary line and you get a few kilowatts. And the beat goes on. A few Mau-Maus get a little bread, and things change the same.

There is a comic dimension to all this that Wolfe reveals. Such as the story of Earl Williams and his New Society. Under the name of Jomo Yarumba, dressed in a dashiki, and surrounded by an army of sixty black children armed with "the greatest grandest sweetest creamiest runniest and most luscious mess of All-American pop drinks, sweets and fried food ever brought together in one place," Williams invaded San Francisco's much gilded City Hall, announcing, when told the mayor was completely tied up all day, that, "We ain't budging, man. We're here to tend to business." Whereupon his army sets to "filling the very air with a hurricane of malted milk, an orange blizzard of crushed ice from the Slurpees, with acid red horrors like the red from the taffy apples and the jelly from the jelly doughnuts, with globs of ice cream in purple sheets of root beer," etc. "And Earl Williams orchestrated the madness in his whirling dashiki." Soon enough the mayor is untied and Earl Williams' New Society Dashiki Factory is set up for business. So goes social progress in these States.

Wolfe's new book is saved by "Mau-Mauing the Flak Catchers." Unlike "Radical Chic," it not only exposes and spanks social absurdities but also suggests ethical alternatives to bureaucratic paralysis. Quite simply, it tells the Man to show himself, and then to talk straight as well to himself as to those who need his services. Further it tells us, those of us who are willy-nilly agents of the Man, how profoundly out of touch we are with both our own governmental structures and the realities of the poverty that flourishes in the midst of our plenty. Finally, and perhaps most surprisingly important, it tells the black man how vulnerable he is to gamesmanship.

The authority and persuasiveness of the documentary narrative form that Wolfe works in, along with such others as Norman Mailer, Truman Capote, and John Hersey, depend on the quality inherent in the events documented as much as the writer's ability to represent them. The importance of the right event can be seen in the failure of "Radical Chic" and the success of "Mau-Mauing the Flak Catchers." Both of them get the Wolfe treatment, but Radical Chic doesn't survive either Wolfe's journalistic jive or his personal contempt for his subject. And it reveals what had not surfaced so blatantly in Wolfe's work before, an unresolved three-way tug of war between the demands of his trademark journalistic style, the demands of his personal condescension and superiority, and the demands of a documentary form.

When one compares Wolfe's new book with John Hersey's recent *Letter to the Alumni*—both of which treat roughly the same subject, the interaction of black militancy and white liberalism and the establishment power structure—one gets a sense of what's missing in Wolfe. Hersey's book is altogether unhip, but it very carefully and very sympathetically—sympathetically for conservative and liberal and radical alike, treating them with understanding and respect for their humanity, regardless of whatever moral and intellectual failures they exhibit—lays out the components, dynamics, potential, and meaning of Yale's Mayday crisis last spring. It is that care and human sympathy that seem lacking in Wolfe, his unwillingness to subordinate himself to his subject, to see not only its dazzling surfaces but also its human depths. That is why he cannot penetrate to where we hurt most, at the core of hate, fear, impotence, and degradation that festers beneath the American game of life.

ALAN TRACHTENBERG
"What's New?"

Partisan Review, 1974, pp. 296–302

The New Journalism heralds an epos. Fiction is dead. The novel is out as "literature's main event." Long live New Journalism. Twenty-three "examples of the genre" make up Part Two; two of them are by Tom Wolfe, who also takes up all the space in Part One. It is really Wolfe's book throughout: his blurbs present each selection, calling roll like an announcer at the fights. "Hunter Thompson's career as a 'Gonzo Journalist' began after he wrote his first book, *Hell's Angels, a Strange and Terrible Saga*. Infuriated because *Playboy* wouldn't run a story they had commissioned . . ." The blurbs tell the story of the story. And they point out the thing to notice. "The up-shot was a manic, high-adrenal first-personal style in which Thompson's own emotions continually dominate the story." Or they thrust bits of know-how at the reader, making sure he doesn't miss such fine points of the new genre as "any time a nonfiction writer uses an autobiographical approach, he is turning himself into a character in the story." This shrewd observation gets us into Mailer's contribution, *Armies of the Night*—"quite a charming book," considering that the author is normally a "very shy reporter, reluctant to abandon the safety of the Literary Gentlemen of the Grandstand."

Your true New Journalist has long since abandoned the safe grandstand. Only a decade or so back you joined a newspaper to see the world, thinking all the while that the job was "a motel you checked into overnight on the road to the final triumph. The idea was to get a job on a newspaper, keep body and soul together, pay the rent, get to know 'the world,' accumulate 'experience,' perhaps work some of the fat off your style—then at some point, quit cold, say goodbye to journalism, move into a shack somewhere, work night and day for six months, and light up the sky with the final triumph. The final triumph was known as The Novel." Then sometime in the sixties the tables turned. Mysteriously the novel drifted from its path, turned its back on "experience," on how people really live, and became "Neo-Fabulism"—"a puzzling sort of fiction . . . in which characters have no background, no personal history." Meanwhile, feature writers for mass-circulation newspapers and their Sunday supplements were making an extraordinary discovery: "It just might be possible to write journalism that would . . . read like a novel." For Wolfe himself the moment came in 1963, unexpectedly, serendipitously. "A great many pieces of punctuation and typography [were] lying around dormant when I came along. . . . [my ellipses] I found that things like exclamation points, italics, abrupt shifts (dashes) and syncopations (dots) helped give the illusion not only of a person talking but of a person thinking." But the main discovery came when he "started playing around with the device of point-of-view." This led him on, and soon he realized that all "this extraordinary power" of social realism comes from "just four devices." No. 1 is "scene-by-scene construction"; No. 2 is dialogue—the best thing going for involving the reader; No. 3 is "third-person point of view," getting inside your character, showing each scene through someone's eyes. The whole game could come a cropper on this device, for how can a journalist claim to be inside characters he didn't invent but only just met? "The answer proved to be marvelously simple: interview about his thoughts and emotions, along with everything else." And No. 4, the device gleaned from Balzac of recording minute details of gesture, habit, furniture, clothing, food, decor, all the symbols of "status life": "the entire pattern of behavior and possessions through which people express their position in the world or what they think it is or what they hope it to be."

As for the rest, "from character to moral consciousness (whatever that may be)," that depends on what you have in the way of "genius." The argument is only that "the genius of any writer—again, in fiction or nonfiction—will be severely handicapped if he cannot master, or if he abandons the techniques of realism." All the power of "Dickens, Dostoyevsky, Joyce, Mann, Faulkner, is made possible by the fact that they first wired their work into the main circuit, which is realism."

So much for technical explanations. There is a social explanation as well, an explanation from history. Wolfe is describing a revolution in aesthetics, in culture: a take-over by the sans-culottes of the world of letters. New Journalists are the *lumpenproles*, the Low Rent crowd, "ignoring class lines," and they have had "the whole crazed obscene uproarious Mammon-faced drug-soaked mau-mau lust-oozing Sixties in America all to themselves." *The New York Times Book Review* and the *New York Review of Books* disapprove. They are trying to protect the old class structure which has the novelist at the top and the Grub Streeters below.

Waxing prophetic Wolfe foresees "a tremendous future for a sort of novel that will be called the journalistic novel or perhaps the documentary novel." And it will not be an isolated event. In Wolfe's world revolution from below has been the main event in American society since World War II, and New Journalism is part of the uproarious scene. Wolfe wants to align the new kind of writing with all the mad energies bursting the old social styles at the seams.

Behind all this is a coherent vision. It came to Wolfe while he was trying to write up a California "Teen Fair." He found in California an "incredible combination of form plus money" taking place among teen-agers and altering history. "Practically every style recorded in art history is the result of the same thing—a lot of attention to form, plus the money to make monuments to it." But always "it has been something the aristocracy has been responsible for." Think of Inigo Jones's designs. Versailles, Palladian classicism: "These were the kinds of forms, styles, symbols . . . that influence a whole society." Now, it comes from below, where least expected. "Suddenly classes of people whose styles of life had been practically invisible (even to themselves?) had the money to build monuments to their own styles. Among teen-agers, this took the form of custom cars, the twist, the jerk, the monkey, the shake, rock music generally, stretch pants, decal eyes—and all these things, these teen-age styles of life, like Inigo Jones' classicism, have started having an influence on the life of the whole country." Not only teen-agers; it is happening all over. For example, racing has replaced baseball, and "this shift from a fixed land sport, modeled on cricket, to this wild car sport (a water, air, or fire sport?) . . . [my ellipses] this symbolizes a radical change in the people as a whole."

Radical changes in "the people as a whole" is what Wolfe is after, where his subject lies. Because nobody else seems to notice. A "built-in class bias" gets in the way. "Nobody will even take a look at our incredible new pastimes, things like stock car racing, drag racing, demolition derbies, sports that attract five to ten million more spectators than football, baseball and basketball each year." Presumably all those people themselves noticed, but "nobody" means "the educated classes in this country," those who "control the visual and printed communications media," and who are still "plugged into what is, when one gets down to it, an ancient, aristocratic aesthetic." But the truth is that Las Vegas is our Versailles, the neon skyline "the new landmarks of America, the new guideposts, the new way Americans get their bearings." The sixties were a time, Wolfe teaches us in another book fleshing out his sociohistorical vision, of "a . . . Happiness Explosion." Our "serious thinkers," our "intellectuals and politicians" resist this "scary" notion, that the proles are swimming in affluence, are learning "sheer ego extension," against all the ancient rules—the workers are learning to be happy.

Without New Journalism we might not know all this. Without New Journalism we might go on thinking that the sixties were another decade of war and political assassination, of activism and reaction, instead of "the decade when manners and morals, styles of living, attitudes toward the world changed the country more crucially than political events." The recent "revivals" of the thirties and forties should set us straight: movies, pop songs, makeup, hair styles—these were the true changes, not unions, fascism, world war. It is style that matters, not politics; pleasure, not power; status, not class; the illusion of thinking, not thought. New Journalism is the noticing of the new way.

What about the twenty-three examples of "the first new direction in American literature in the last fifty years?" Let it be said on behalf of most of the contributors, the claim is Wolfe's, not theirs. It is a mixed group, some of it journalism only in the loosest construction. Capote's *In Cold Blood* appeared several years after the events, had no relation to what we normally call news, and belongs to an older practice of picking up stories in the press and *imagining* them into novel form. It is the kind of novel of which *An American Tragedy* is the most distinguished example; Henry James's notebooks show him fascinated with similar sources. Capote and Mailer are smuggled into the book. *Armies of the Night* is a sustained reflection on events and their meanings, and reflection is one kind of thinking, or the illusion of such, notably scarce elsewhere in the book. Some of the pieces grow out of news-making events, such as Vietnam; others are examples of what we can still call political reporting, interviews with celebrities, "in-depth" stories of specific social types (the detective, the Hollywood producer), "human interest" accounts of murderers and their backgrounds. Some are fine jobs of reporting, written with insight, sympathy, conviction, and a desire to communicate a point of view. The Vietnam stories (especially Michael Herr's), Garry Wills's "Martin Luther King Is Still on the Case," James Mills's "The Detective," and Joan Didion's "Some Dreamers of the Golden Dream" are the best. Judged as writing, journalism new or old, fiction or nonfiction, these are good, worthwhile pieces of work.

In fact there is nothing new in writing narratives of firsthand experiences in contemporary society with dialogue, scene, dramatization. Edmund Wilson did it better than anyone in the book in his trial coverages in the twenties and in "American Jitters." Wolfe has a section in his pseudoscholarly appendix called "Is the New Journalism Really New," and lists earlier "Not Half-Bad Candidates." He mentions some obvious names: Mark Twain in *Innocents Abroad*, Stephen Crane, John Reed, Orwell. (Agee is dismissed earlier as "a great disappointment." True, "he showed enterprise enough, going to the mountain and moving in briefly with a mountain family." But "reading between the lines I would say that his problem was extreme personal diffidence. His account abounds in 'poetic' descriptions and is very short on dialogue.") But Wolfe misses the point of the examples. They exist because the phenomenon is as old as the newspaper. Moreover, since the late nineteenth century it has been associated with a zest for enlarging the social experience of readers, often with reform as a plain motive. See Jacob Riis, *How the Other Half Lives*. Or Jack London, *People of the Abyss*. Or the muckrakers. Or the reportage of the 1930s (Wolfe might start with William Stott's recent book, *Documentary Expression and Thirties America*, where he will learn just where Agee went and lived). Many of the selections in *The New Journalism* fit a familiar, well-tried mold.

If not a "new thing," there is still something special, something that needs pointing out, in the composition of the collection. It lies in the relation of the ensemble to its presumptive subject, America in the 1960s. Although there are exceptions, the dominant social voice in *The New Journalism* is degrees cooler than was true in past reportage, less outrage, more understatement, juxtaposition, irony. There is less undisguised social purpose, less passion for exposure, for change. And less concern simply for "the facts." Wolfe writes: "When one moves from newspaper reporting to this new form of journalism, as I and many others did, one discovers that the basic reporting unit is no longer the datum, the piece of information, but the scene, *since most of the sophisticated strategies of prose depend upon scenes*" [my italics]. The motive revealed here might clear up a puzzling point that appeared earlier. Why should Wolfe worry about whether literary intellectuals and other class-biased souls take notice of the wave of new styles that occupy so many millions of people? Because the cutting edge of his kind of writing is the claim that he is seeing what others, the rulers of taste, the intellectual elite, refuse to see. The assumption behind this kind of writing is that until somebody notices an event, it is not real. But the somebody has to be somebody other than the people in the event, somebody who by noticing thereby gives the event what it needs to become real: status, prestige. The same thing is true about the writing itself; it asks to be noticed, to have conferred upon it the status of "style," and now of "art."

In Wolfe's works, including his present claims to a new kind of writing, the mechanisms of a middlebrow mass culture are transparent. In *Electric Kool-Aid Acid Test*, his book about Ken Kesey, the Merry Pranksters, and the California LSD scene, Wolfe writes: "I have tried not only to tell what the Pranksters did but to recreate the mental atmosphere or subjective reality of it. I don't think their adventure can be understood without that." Unquestionably a clever mimic, a shrewd observer, and sometimes pretty funny, Wolfe performs neat jobs of ventriloquism with his "downstage" voices. The gimmick is that all the words are authentic, taken from observation, correspondence, interviews, publications. They are ingeniously reassembled and appear as if they are the spontaneous generation of the narrated action itself. This way Wolfe seems to merge with his subjects, to be speaking their thoughts, feelings, words. Wolfe is at pains to authenticate his sources, but the claim matters little except as a device to keep the reader from noticing that the true facts of the genesis of the work—the interviews, research, listening to tapes, even being on the scene—are kept hidden. Unlike Terry Southern and Hunter Thompson, Wolfe does not dramatize his own participation. He is almost not there. This means that along with the actual apparatus of journalism, anything like a substantive perspective is impossible to locate. The corrugated verbal surface, the hyped-up prose, its tachycardiac speed, its fevered illusion of thinking and feeling, all disguise the *reporter*. That is why the direct quotations from a letter by a woman recounting her first experience with LSD come with such relief: at last, a real voice. The rest is illusion of a group subjectivity, only and sheerly verbal, never complete, never completing itself in the reader's imagination, except as display, as spectacle.

What Wolfe gains by his pyrotechnics is an easy experience for the reader: just lean back and let it happen to you. But it is a deceit: by disguising itself and its procedures, by mystifying the presence of the author as a merely neutral recorder when he is in fact the only active producer of the product, Wolfe's work is a revealing instance of mass culture. The appearance of spontaneity is the product of the most arch manipulation and manufacture. By pretending to render the world always as someone's experience, from the inside, Wolfe may seem to be revitalizing the craft of journalism and preventing the loss of experience that comes with hardened journalistic formulae. But just the opposite results. He converts experience into spectacle, fixes it, reifies it as a reader's vicarious experience. He cheats us with illusions of deeper penetrations into segregated realities but the illusion is a calculated product that disguises what it is we are actually reading.

Wolfe's genre is a cool flaneur's version of the comic journalism practiced by Mark Twain and his brethren. He dons the guise of the Low Rent rebel, speaking on behalf of those who have been deprived of their status by the literary, intellectual, and political elite. His devices include a bogus erudition and intellectuality, an OED vocabulary of technical terms, outrageous but "learned" neologisms, and catalogue after catalogue of the names and things that fill the days and hours of American popular life, all presented without punctuation, as a kind of synchonistic pop mandala. He panders to both a hatred and an envy of intellectuals. His *lumpenprole* revolution is no more than a botched theft of what he thinks is the prize jewel of the intellectuals, the label of "art." Far from revolutionary it is a conformist writing, whose message at a low frequency is that you have never had it so good. Wolfe cannot see beyond the "chic" in middle-class radicalism, nor beyond the gamesmanship in confrontation (made into slick theater in "Mau-Mauing the Flak-Catchers"). Hardly a vision to disturb the sleep of the proprietors and managers. In many ways it is also their vision. Wolfe's revolution changes nothing, inverts nothing, in fact is *after* nothing but status. It is full of half-baked versions of ideas in currency. The best that might be said for it is that it is a put-on. But I doubt it. I think he is dead serious.

HUGH KENNER

"All the Angels Have Big Feet"

National Review, February 18, 1983, pp. 193–94

Wheeeeeeeeeeeeee! went the Sixties, and Tom Wolfe was *there*, on the scene, in the scene, in Sulka four-in-hand and four-piece suit—make that *five*-piece?—yellow piping running round the grey like lemon neon, the lime weskit deep-lapeled and double-breasted; the Sixties, back when there was still a Walter Winchell, and Truman Capote was oooh, *big*;

and Thuddathud-*kerbump!* went the Seventies like Paul Volcker falling downstairs, and *Life* itself folded, and Drew Pearson had departed earth's scenes un-whoreshipped, watch it, unhorsewhipped, and there was Tom Wolfe still, still as tall and just a tad greyer, still the nonchalant master of the neon-piped sentence,

and Gassssp, wheeeeze, go the Eighties, and, ta da! Heeeeere's . . . Tom!!!, the smile still tight, the amused candid eyes unblinking, with a *Reader*, no less (pages that won't stay open bound in hideous purple cloth that wrinkles up the spine because that is what book manufacture has come to in the Eighties, even at $17.50 and Farrar, Straus & Giroux should be ashamed), to show us in his mocking mirrors what we've all been through.

How intact we've survived it all is disputable, but Tom Wolfe has been there to help, not least by devising a style the range of which can get so much of it together. He is famous for his paratactic syntax hand in hand with typographic hi-jinx—

> . . . and boy, they run out like ants and pull those barrels and boards and sawhorses out of the way, and then—Ggghhzzzzzzzhhhhhhgggggzzzzzzeeeeeong! —gawdam! there he goes again, it was him, Junior Johnson! with a gawdam agent's si-reen and a red light in his grille!

That's Junior Johnson running a revenooers' roadblock in a car he's disguised as a revenooer's by nothing more than a siren and a red light. That's also Tom Wolfe, in temporary disguise as a good ol' boy, letting you hear Junior's story the way the boys tell it in No'th Ca'lina where by damn they're *talking* not for gawd's sakes writing.

Such is his trick: disguise: sink into the woodwork: become the very *voice* of the woodwork. It's been misunderstood; when "The Pump-House Gang" (1966) voiced the very throb of adrenalin that drove mindless voyeurs through the Watts riots ("Watts was a blast"), *Partisan Review* did not fail to call the brilliant paragraph "a virtual endorsement of the attitudes it mimics." But literati always tend to think that mimicry betokens admiration (else why the trouble? They take trouble only over measured Presbyterian judiciousness). Literati also worry when horrid alienations aren't allowed to evanesce but get fixed in print: some reader might *acquire* them!

Literati, there's the problem. We're all literati, else we'd not be fixed on this page. We look to print for information and opinion, and most of America has more sense (though, alas, it looks to TV). Tom Wolfe writes (for literati—for page-turners) about people who seldom turn pages: stock-car drivers, a self-made "art collector" whose fiscal base was a taxi fleet, hangers-out with surfboards, cunning intimidators of bureaucrats, "The Girl of the Year" (whose name, if you've forgotten from '64, was Baby Jane Holzer), astronauts, Vietnam pilots. . . . Literati find such types strange, unless the *New York Times* reporter makes them talk like a *Times* editorial, as he normally does.

Wolfe's only recourse is to make them seem stranger than strange: either so purple their purpleness turns neutral and we get a fix on their world—that's what distressed the *Partisan Review* man—or so one-foot-after-the-other reasonable that we follow hypnotized the decisions of, say Chuck Yeager, who led mankind through the sound barrier after a night so wild he'd broken two ribs, and in sober daylight had to hide his condition from the higher-ups, then whang the X-1's door shut with his only operative hand, his left, abetted by a nine-inch piece of broomstick.

Wolfe's prose tends to swerve toward list-dominated or else verb-dominated passages. These reflect, respectively, people defined by what they *have* and by what they *do*. The list is the oldest of all written forms. (Writing had to be invented to preserve lists; stories you can remember.) And lists gratify imaginations fixated by *things*. When Linear-B was an undeciphered script, scholars hoped for hexameter uplift. But once cracked, its inscriptions proved to be storehouse inventories.

Linear-B was the tool of Minoan bureaucrats. Bureaucrats always need to know your inventory of wine jars or dark oxen or flush toilets. They flourish among thing-centered people, who likewise live amid lists, as Flaubert and Joyce knew, and Wolfe knows. Leopold Bloom's thousand-word beatific vision of 1904 was confected by his creator from hardware-store catalogues:

> . . . watercloset on mezzanine provided with opaque singlepane oblong window, tipup seat, bracket lamp, brass tiered brace, armrests, footstool, and artistic oleograph on inner face of door . . .

Here is a Tom Wolfe equivalent, 1981:

> . . . The couch would be a mattress on top of a flush door supported by bricks and covered with a piece of monk's cloth. There would be more monk's cloth used as curtains and on the floor would be a sisal rug that left corduroy ribs on the bottoms of your feet in the morning. The place would be lit by clamp-on heat lamps with half-globe aluminum reflectors and ordinary bulbs replacing the heat bulbs. At one end of the rug, there it would be . . . *the Barcelona chair*. . . . When you saw that holy [i.e., $550] object on the sisal rug, you knew you were in a household where the fledgling architect and his young wife had sacrificed everything to bring the symbol of the godly mission into their home.

Another, 1965:

> Out front there are two gasoline pumps under an overhanging roof. Inside there are a lot of things like a soda-pop cooler filled with ice, Coca-Colas, Nehi drinks, Dr. Pepper, Double Cola, and a gumball machine, a lot of racks of Red Man chewing tobacco, Price's potato chips, Okay peanuts, cloth hats for working outdoors in, dried sausages, cigarettes, canned goods, a little bit of meat and flour, fly swatters and I don't know what all.

Another, 1966:

> . . . apartments where the lobby and the doorman look so great you feel you have to dress up to step on the sidewalk or you're letting down the building, esoteric New York day schools for the younger children and boarding schools for the older ones, lunches at La Grenouille where expensive matrons in Chanel suits have two bloody Marys and smile—

teeth!—at tailored young men with names like
Freddy, Ferdi, and Tug . . .

Things have no social existence save as they are valued. These are lists of *choices*, of acts of precious attention. Their contours yield the fever-charts of subcultures. (And your UHF circuitry picks up Wolfe's preference for the store with the gumball machines, the choices it offers being less pressured by mere chic.)

At the bottom of a *thing* subculture is appetite, which is static: when you have the Chanel suit or the gumball, you have it. (Though appetite soon gets bored, and wishes it had something else.) Against his cultures of lists, which encompass parts of America no other literatus has visited, Wolfe plays the cultures of *deeds*, which are normally relegated to the Huntin' Shootin' Stock Car magazines and to Action Comics. For twenty years he has been fascinated by this polarization. His book on art as a collectible (*The Painted Word*, 1975) derives from the earliest piece in the present *Reader*, "Bob & Spike," 1966. His fascination with the test pilots and astronauts of *The Right Stuff* (1979) is continuous with his interest in stock-car racer Junior Johnson, "The Last American Hero" (1965).

Certain moral discriminations do not waver. Bob & Spike Scull's drive to collect "art" is untouched by timeless contemplation: they are magnetized by the money and the status it brings. Of Junior Johnson and Chuck Yeager on the contrary we cannot define something that they want to accomplish. Hemingway talked of a Code, and Wolfe gets little further. They exemplify the Right Stuff.

As a satirist, therefore, Wolfe can complete his arc; as a laudator, he remains a stiff-lipped romantic. We're not yet past Hemingway in that domain. "The Truest Sport," a day with two naval pilots and as fulfilling a piece of writing as came out of the Vietnam mess, finally tells us only that such pilots lock themselves into a stoical myth of their own survival.

And Tom Wolfe? No, unlike Hemingway he's not locked into a myth. His mobile viewpoint still saves him, and his self-mockery. Despite appearances, he has no self-dramatization. The double-breasted weskits, the ivory-handled rolled umbrellas, these are not him, nor even his values, but appurtenances to speak for him.

They say, "Absurd. I am no part of identifiable society; in New York a transplanted Southern Gentleman perhaps, though in the South an anachronism. No, I am a *writer:* as absurd as that. I cannot help it if chic readers condescend to my subjects. On the side, I amuse myself with the resources of the printing-press, the ultimate resources a writer has. They permit me to write down strings like 'Gggghhzzzzzzzhhhhhhg-gggggzzzzzzzeeeeeong!,' and if you think that absurd, or me absurd, or (heaven help you) Junior Johnson absurd, then your mirror is clouded indeed."

ALEXANDER WOOLLCOTT

1887–1943

Alexander Humphreys Woollcott was born on January 19, 1887, at Phalanx, New Jersey, to Walter and Frances Bucklin Woollcott. His grandfather, John Bucklin, had founded the Phalanx, a Fourierist cooperative group that occupied an eighty-five-room house. An attack of mumps at age thirteen left him obese and impotent for the rest of his life. He attended Hamilton College, where he edited the literary magazine and founded, acted in, and directed the drama club. He began his career in journalism as a reporter for the *New York Times*. When the regular drama critic of the *Times* resigned in 1914, Woollcott took over and soon displayed an exceptional talent for the job. His first book, *Mrs Fiske—Her Views of Acting, Actors, and the Problems of the Stage*, was published in 1917. That year he joined the staff of the military newspaper *Stars and Stripes*, and wrote articles from the front that were later collected in his second book, *The Command Is Forward* (1919).

In 1922 Woollcott became the drama critic of the New York *Herald*, and as such brought the first true criticism to American theatre; previously, shilling for the promoters had been the norm. His was an immensely influential voice, and his opinion could frequently make or break a show. In later years he contributed a theatre column to the *New Yorker*, and in addition wrote pieces for such magazines as *McCall's*, *Vanity Fair*, *Collier's*, and *Cosmopolitan*. He founded and hosted the Algonquin Round Table, the illustrious literary circle of the period that included such wits as Dorothy Parker, George S. Kaufman, Robert Benchley, Harpo Marx, and Harold Ross.

During the thirties, in his position with CBS radio as "The Town Crier" and "The Early Bookworm," he became an important book critic and a national celebrity. A collection of his articles and reviews, *While Rome Burns* (1934), was applauded by the critics and was a bestseller.

Woollcott wrote two popular plays with George S. Kaufman, *The Channel Road* (performed in 1929) and *The Dark Tower* (performed in 1933, published in 1934), which received mixed notices. His greatest stage triumph was his appearance toward the end of his life in the role of the waspish Sheridan Whiteside, a character closely modeled on himself, in the Kaufman and Hart play, *The Man Who Came to Dinner.* Woollcott died of a heart attack during a radio broadcast on January 23, 1943. Better known as a personality than as a writer at the time of his death, Woollcott has in recent years declined in significance as a literary figure, largely because of the ephemeral nature of much of his work. However, his horror story "Moonlight Sonata" continues to be one of the most frequently reprinted works of its kind.

The urge to act is even more common than the one to write for the theatre. There are those who have also the urge to produce a play themselves. There are many who achieve a hero worship for the idols of the stage. Charles Dickens, however, was all of these things. The theatre fascinated him, and to it he brought the infectious spirit of the supreme amateur. *Mr. Dickens Goes to the Play* by Alexander Woollcott, the dramatic critic, is a delectable potpourri. Mr. Woollcott's own essays in the book are informative and altogether pleasing, and his selection of Dickens anecdote and quotation is skilful. Of Dickens's letters to the actor Macready, enough cannot be said. ⟨. . .⟩ Whether *Mr. Dickens* or *Shouts and Murmurs* is Mr. Woollcott's first book, I don't know. Probably he would prefer to be hailed for the latter, since it is all his own. This is right and proper; for *Shouts and Murmurs*, a collection of essays around and about the theatre, is fresh, original, and informed. It is more readable than most books about the stage; it is current, humorous, and wise, though opinionated. After all, what is a critic if not an opinion? "That mountain might be brown", said the man, "or it might be blue", and there was no arguing the matter, so I proclaimed it black, and we fought unto the death. Alexander Woollcott is a man with whom it is well worth fighting; but timid souls should not enter the lists.—J. F., "A Critic's First Two Books," *Bkm*, Nov. 22, 1922, p. 339

Nero had only a fiddle. Mr. Woollcott knows more ways to be entertaining than that. He weaves his runes with a difference. He gives us the impression ⟨in *While Rome Burns*⟩ of having thriftily amassed a great collection of phonograph records that preserve the japes and witticisms of his friends. These he plays over and transposes into the pastel rhythms of his hand-painted-china style. The melodies are sometimes beguiling, often a little too roguish. They serve to amuse his parishioners while Rome burns.

So, inescapably, there is in this pasticcio of his recent magazine pieces not only a profile of Dorothy Parker. There is also a fine assortment of epithetical scars inflicted by what might be called the Parker House rowels. And a daisy chain of brief and pointed commentaries like this: "That woman speaks eighteen languages and she can't say No in any of them." Some of these Algonquinades are of rosy antiquity. Those that used to be told about Dorothy Parker's Hollywood rustication have been given New York settings. Possibly they wanted to come back East to die. Who knows? The gilt has long since tarnished on the one about what she had lettered on the door. On the other hand, there is the tale of what she said to the man who blamed her gentle dachshund in a fracas with his burly Scotty. "I have no doubt," she told him with some bitterness, "that he was also carrying a revolver."

It was Dorothy Parker herself who remembered Howard Dietz's critical analysis. That consisted entirely in calling her doting biographer "Louisa M. Woollcott." No one mentions the radio-age child who was hearing a morsel of Dickens. "Did Mr. Woollcott make that up himself?" he asked. "Not yet, little Oscar. He will."

Woollcott devotees who imagine they have already seen everything in this book by reading periodicals are crazy. He has revised his ruminations on Russian travel, phony economists, ladies and gentlemen of the stage, authors of all categories, the Orient, celebrated crimes and antic criminals, A Century of Progress, books that send his cap right over the Eighth Avenue subway, mildly stuffy overindulgences in the manner of Charles Lamb's "Dream Children," and all the rest, here and there. He has given them parsley-sprig paragraphs of introduction. He has introduced new characters who up to now had taken no part whatever in the conversation. He has strewn lavish footnotes that convey stop-press commentaries and such information as Robert E. Sherwood's disenchanted observation at Monte Carlo: "Only the brave *chemin de fer*."

It is in the course of a good deal of puffing and grunting about how hard it is to get Charles MacArthur's mercurial character on paper that we learn about Mr. MacArthur's return to Chicago after service on the Mexican border. It seems that he broke cover when the troops were parading down Michigan Avenue "with two women dressed up as Mexican prisoners in chains beside him" in an old Ford car. The car led the parade.

Shaw's postcard to Mrs. Patrick Campbell when Mrs. Campbell was furiously demanding his permission to publish the unvegetarian letters he had written her, read, Mr. Woollcott discloses in the course of his noble tribute to her, something like this: "No, Stella, I will not play horse to your Lady Godiva."

Nearly all these gossipy trophies of a thousand table-cloth sessions are written in Mr. Woollcott's own system of Basic English. All his idolaters know the test. It is simple. The mere matter of looking for the clue words and phrases settles it. Any piece that does not contain one or (a great many) more of these—"waggish," "blandly," "elfin," "a dark suspicion," "faintly surprised," "shoon" and so forth—may be thrown out as a clumsy forgery. Offhand we should say the potpourri in *While Rome Burns* stood the test with flying choler. ⟨. . .⟩

Mr. Woollcott discloses that his disinclination to read the papers much these days is rooted in a conviction. This, he says, is that "by faithfully absorbing the wisdom of the two Walters (Lippmann and Winchell)," he can learn all he wants to know about what goes on. As something of a Winchellectual himself, he acquires diverting gossip enough, we should think, to make him consider giving even his own journalistic Rosencranz and Guildenstern a holiday while he retires to brood upon and embellish for publication his lore, in that Elsinore of his own, "Wit's End." Then, in case this our Rome proves temporarily fireproof, he can bring out a sequel to be called, possibly, *False Alarm*.—C. G. Poore, "Mr. Woollcott Runs On and On," *NYTBR*, March 4, 1934, p. 2

A posthumous collection of Woollcott leavings, called by the publishers, for no easily discernible reason, *Long, Long Ago*, is out and ready to delight the hearts and mist the eyes of friends and admirers of the incomparable Woollcott. Here are stories about all sorts of people, from Miss Cornell to the homespun paragrapher, Robert Quillen, whom Woollcott knew or tracked down. Here are his so-so reconstructions of some famous murder trials, with an account of one case—that of the English schoolboy, Archer-Shee—that is truly rewarding. Here are miscellaneous pieces and anecdotes and radio broadcasts and legends of the *déjà vu* and literary enthusiasms and shouts of delight about plays—all *echt* Woollcott, all the product of a completely unified personality. For Woollcott was ever himself, always coherent, marked with a single style. Those who thought him a poseur were, I think, wrong. He never played any part but himself, but of course he was a theatrical personality.

So are these carefully written oddments, in no invidious sense, theatrical—filled with a feeling for audience values, for the laws of timing, for the requisites of a good curtain. Like certain kinds of good theatre, they handle sentimentality to perfection, always stopping short of bathos, always safely within the terrain of perfect taste.—Clifton Fadiman, *NY*, Nov. 13, 1943, pp. 105–6

When Woollcott retired as a drama critic something of the

theatre died with him. There were no halfway measures with him; he either liked something or he didn't like it, and there was no equivocation. His friend Charles Brackett, writing of a fictitious character obviously inspired by Woollcott, said "his criticisms were either unadulterated treacle or pure black bile." His idols—an odd assortment ranging from Minnie Maddern Fiske to Harpo Marx—could do no wrong, and his unbridled enthusiasms on one occasion inspired his fellow critic, George Jean Nathan, to dub him "the seidlitz powder of Times Square." By the same token, what he fancied to describe as "a bit of urchin pebble-shying" became, in his hands, a brick heaved through a plate glass window. His honest and frankly hostile comments on some of the Shuberts' shoddier presentations resulted in his being barred from their theatres, the result of which, paradoxically, was to give him his first by-line and make him famous.

"Drama criticisms," Woollcott once remarked to me, "have degenerated to a trickle of disparagement. Nobody ever gives anything a good sock, or a rave notice." An opinion which, I feel, can be applied to drama criticism today.

Whatever Woollcott's merit as a drama critic, there can be no doubt that as a littérateur he was and is in a class by himself. Many of the short pieces he did for *The New Yorker* magazine under the heading "Shouts and Murmurs" are minor masterpieces. As one commentator noted, "the descriptive adjectives stick up in his writings like cloves in a Virginia ham." Yet who but Woollcott could so briefly and graphically sum up Calvin Coolidge and his native State of Vermont as "small, lean and crabbed; frugal and addicted to old ways," or could find in the silent screen art of Lillian Gish, "the pathos of little bronze dancing boots come upon suddenly in an old trunk"?

Like Joseph Conrad, Alexander Woollcott was a "wordist." And, like Conrad, Woollcott and his words will survive. —DANTON WALKER, "The Man Who Came to Dinner," *TA*, Jan. 1951, p. 96

SAMUEL HOPKINS ADAMS
"The World of A. Woollcott"

Reader's Digest, May 1943, pp. 9–13

To Mr. Pickwick's rotundity add a pinch of Sheridan Whiteside's waspish temper and a dash of Bernard Shaw's diabolic wit. Lace plentifully with the milk of human kindness, add a cupful of treacle—and you have the recipe for Alec Woollcott. Not that these ingredients are likely to combine again, now that our beloved and effervescent friend is gone. For when the "Times Square Seidlitz Powder" (as George Jean Nathan called him) ceased to bubble, something unique and sparkling faded from the American scene.

When Alec Woollcott was a little boy in New Jersey he always wanted to be kidnaped like Charley Ross; he would sit by the roadside for hours patiently waiting for the smiling man with the bag of candy. Later the lonely child grew into a famous raconteur and critic, but the need for self-dramatization persisted. Tirelessly, eloquently, he devoted himself to the portrayal of a character known as Alec Woollcott, and succeeded in charming an entire generation with his vagaries, japes and enthusiasms.

Nature was a cruel stepmother to Alec Woollcott. He was a puny, nearsighted child; an attack of mumps at 13 transformed him into an obese, waddling youth. The oddity of his appearance was emphasized by the bizarre costumes he favored. At Hamilton College he wore a red fez, owlish glasses and a turtle-neck sweater of a loathsome, putty hue. This garb, coupled with his flamboyant vocabulary, made him the natural butt of campus horseplay, to which he responded with dogged and ineffectual belligerency. "He never shirked a fight and never won one," reports Alex Osborn, a classmate. Later, as a member of the AEF, he showed the same fearlessness under fire. During one particularly heavy bombardment at Thiaucourt, he lay in a shell crater volubly explaining to a top sergeant the subtle differences between the Camilles of Duse and Bernhardt.

It was as dramatic critic on *The New York Times* that Woollcott won his reputation as "the most insulting and insulted man on Broadway." His reviews were salty and ruthless; players and producers feared his lash. It was said that if he were mysteriously murdered, the police could hold at least 2000 New Yorkers on suspicion. Once when he was dieting, one victim of his criticism said to another: "I see where Woollcott has dropped 100 pounds." Asked the other: "On whom?"

Yet Woollcott's tongue and pen were not always barbed. The night he saw Thornton Wilder's moving play, *Our Town*, the producers found him seated on a fire escape in the theater alley sobbing. "Pardon me, Mr. Woollcott," one of them said. "Will you endorse the play?"

Woollcott rose to his feet. "Certainly not!" he blubbered. "It doesn't need it. I'd as soon think of endorsing the Twenty-Third Psalm!"

Woollcott had a gargantuan appetite for friendship. Edna Ferber once remarked that he had 800 intimate friends. A brilliant company of artists, writers and actors thronged his apartment, which Dorothy Parker dubbed "Wit's End," there to take fearful and affectionate lashings from their host, lolling day-long in gaudy pajamas. "Hello, Repulsive," was his favorite greeting; "Get the hell out of here, you bore me," his fond farewell. Not everyone could take it. Edna Ferber, her first passion having cooled, stated that she was "getting damned sick of this New Jersey Nero who mistook his pinafore for a toga." Another bosom friend, surfeited perhaps with Woollcott's monologues, called him "an exploding gravy-bomb." Yet they all clung to him, magnetized by the mad waggeries that went on at Wit's End, with "Big Nemo" as ringmaster.

Woollcott dearly loved to gamble; high-stake games of cribbage, poker and anagrams nine letters long were his favorite relaxations. He suffered acutely while losing, and would warn his companions: "My doctor forbids me to play unless I win." At a meeting of the Thanatopsis Literary and Inside Straight Club—a gang of poker bandits which included Heywood Broun, Herbert Bayard Swope and Franklin P. Adams—Woollcott once lost $3000 and flew into a tantrum of heroic proportions. Yet he could drop $200,000 in the stock market and remark with equanimity: "A broker is a man who runs your fortune into a shoestring."

This overgrown Figaro took a prankish delight in embarrassing his friends. Dorothy Parker's husband, Alan Campbell, once gave Woollcott's name as a reference when opening a charge account at Wanamaker's. Woollcott obliged with the following: "Gentlemen: Mr. Alan Campbell, the present husband of Dorothy Parker, has given my name as a reference in his attempt to open an account at your store. I hope that you will extend this credit to him. Surely Dorothy Parker's position in American letters is such as to make shameful the petty refusals which she and Alan have encountered at many hotels, restaurants and department stores. What if you never get paid? Why shouldn't you stand your share of the expense?"

In self-defense, perhaps, Woollcott cultivated a deliberate

rudeness toward importunate hero-worshippers. Once after a lecture in Utica a member of the audience rose to recall: "When we were kids I used to ride on your sled." Woollcott glared at the man. "I never owned a sled—and if I did, you couldn't *buy* a ride."

A women's club group presented a citation to Woollcott, who accepted it silently and bowed. "Only a bow?" chided the chairman. "Won't you say just one word?" Woollcott nodded, fixed the group with a cold stare, and uttered one word: "Coo."

This acerbity gave way to sympathy and understanding when Alec sat down for a heart-to-heart talk with a friend. Then all exhibitionism dropped from him. As he once confided to me: "Sam, I never pose except in public."

Conversely, he never performed a kindness except in private. Almost secretively he sent three young men through college, and he was constantly handing out cash to actors and writers who had seen better days. Nor would he accept repayment. "Pass it along to someone else who needs it," he would grunt. Once he received $1000 for an hour's talk, and promptly gave half of it to The Seeing Eye, his favorite philanthropy; the remainder he donated to a local school of which he knew nothing except that some good people were struggling to support it. Dorothy Parker, by no means given to saccharine sentiment, said of Woollcott: "He has done more secret good than anyone I know."

Like Horace, Woollcott had a kind of Sabine farm—an island on Lake Bomoseen, Vermont, to which he retreated for contemplation and rest. But he could not bear to be alone for more than half an hour, so he would dispatch letters and telegrams summoning his friends with such tempting calls as: "The autumn colors can't last, and neither can I. Come." In response to such an invitation, Harpo Marx once arrived at Woollcott's place in an aged and decrepit jalopy. Woollcott stared at it. "What's this?" he asked. Harpo said: "That's my town car." Alec nodded. "The town, I take it, was Pompeii."

At Bomoseen the chief outdoor sport was croquet. The host wielded a mean mallet and took a perverse delight in transforming this spinsterish sport into a greensward Monte Carlo. The stakes ran high, and the losers—frequently Moss Hart and George Kaufman—would sit on the sidelines audibly saying mean things about their host. But when the game was over they would tenderly lift his boneless 230-pound carcass into a rickshaw and drag him coolie-fashion around the island.

Woollcott, a gallant trencherman and lover of rich pastries, limited his exercise to a morning dip in the lake. Once, viewing a ski meet at Sun Valley, he took out a memo-pad and wrote: "Remind self never to go skiing."

The man was terrifically sentimental, especially about birthdays and Christmas. He sent telegrams or letters to many of his friends on their birthdays, and was deeply hurt unless he received similar remembrances in return. To insure a good haul, he sometimes sent out the following letter to 20 selected friends: "Another milestone in American literature is approaching. January 19th is my birthday, in case a sudden flood of sentiment should seek expression in gifts or cash or certified checks."

The so-called proprieties bothered Woollcott not at all. The Gotham Hotel in New York, where he lived during the last few years, had a rule barring dogs. One day his friend Ina Claire came to call, and the desk clerk announced her. "Send her up," said Woollcott. "I can't," said the unhappy clerk, "she has a dog." "Either Miss Claire's dog comes up," said Woollcott, "or I'm coming down. And I'm in my pajamas." The dog came up.

Even at the White House, where he was a frequent visitor, Woollcott's manners where uninhibited. Mrs. Roosevelt referred to him as her "most interesting guest," but the President sometimes showed annoyance at Woollcott's brashness. "Did you get that last batch of mystery stories I sent you?" bellowed Alec across the room at the President. "No," said FDR shortly, quietly adding to his secretary: "I did, but I'm not going to give him the satisfaction of letting him know it."

Mrs. Roosevelt once said to him quite seriously: "Alec, I don't understand how you find the time and energy to do all the things you do, and get around to so many places."

"My Days!" murmured Woollcott, suppressing a chuckle.

His influence on public taste was enormous; a blurb from Woollcott could "make" a book or play. James Hilton's *Good-bye, Mr. Chips* was kicking around the remnant counter when Woollcott discovered it; an enthusiastic radio puff lifted it to the top of the best-seller list. Woollcott's own anthologies, *The Woollcott Reader* and *While Rome Burns*, were tremendously successful; the latter sold over 250,000 copies. Other critics, envious no doubt, pointed out that Mr. Woollcott's taste sometimes ran to fudge. The most envious among them, hearing the Town Crier read touchingly from *Little Women*, referred to him as "Louisa M. Woollcott."

Often condemned as a sentimentalist, Woollcott was in reality the enemy of exaggerated whimsy; in *Shouts and Murmurs* he broke many a lance against overcuteness, especially in advertising copy. He blenched at such coy nomenclature as "Dry-Dees" (a comfy diaper, invented oddly enough by a Mrs. Allsop) and "No-Tum-Suk" (a preparation to discourage babies from sucking their thumbs). But his special hate was reserved for "Bekkus Puddy" (a breakfast food) and a chain of grocery stores called "Heepie Cheepie." Yes, the age can be grateful to this man who dared give simpering advertisers a kicksy-wicksy in the pantsy-wantsy.

In 1932, when he was 45, Woollcott made his stage debut in *Brief Moment*—and stole the show. Next season he got a larger part in *Wine of Choice*. The play wasn't doing so well, so the cast agreed to take a pay cut. That is, all but Woollcott, who, judging correctly that the customers came to see him, demanded a *raise* in salary. He got it, too—a feat which caused Harpo Marx to observe: "Alec is a dreamer with a fine sense of double-entry bookkeeping."

His greatest role in the theater was that of Sheridan Whiteside in the West Coast production of *The Man Who Came to Dinner*. Moss Hart and George Kaufman, the authors, endowed the central character with the more poisonous aspects of Woollcott's personality. It delighted Alec to portray himself nightly to packed houses, and to read reviews describing him as "despot" and "sadist." Once, however, while making a curtain speech, he said: "It's not true that the role of the obnoxious Sheridan Whiteside was patterned after me. Whiteside is merely a composite of the *better* qualities of the play's two authors."

Burdened with ills of the flesh, Woollcott made a comedy of them and refused to abate the tempo or intensity of his life. Until the last he was his own infuriating, affected, brilliant, generous self. Advised by his doctor that coffee and conversation were bad for his heart, he continued to drink 40 cups a day and talk with undiminished unction half the night. When his friends protested this recklessness, Woollcott said that he could see no profit in a life spent in cotton wool. The end came, last February, much as he would have wished it; almost in the very act and excitement of his favorite occupation—talking. Only the day before, he had made arrangements for a new series of broadcasts in which he was to celebrate obscure acts of heroism and courage in everyday life.

Alexander Woollcott's importance is not as a radio commentator, actor or critic. His secret—though he made no mystery of it; indeed, he spent his days trying to convey it to the world at large—was his extraordinary rapture with life. He was forever seeking new adjectives and new means to describe life's incomparable sparkle, so that everybody to whom he talked might at least partially live it with him. He insisted upon making every hour an adventure in friendship and originality.

BENNETT CERF
"Woollcott: A Minority Report"
American Mercury, August 1944, pp. 173–79

I

The temptation to forget a man's faults after his death, and to overemphasize his deeds and contributions, is understandable enough. "Do not speak ill of the dead" is a maxim to which almost everybody subscribes. In the case of Alexander Woollcott, however, this glorifying process, it seems to me, is assuming the proportions of deification. His letters have been collected by loving friends (who took good care to leave out the more waspish and vitriolic ones), members of his family are composing elegies for sundry magazines, and now Samuel Hopkins Adams, his old fellow alumnus and sponsor from Hamilton, is writing a biography which may be expected to give the great Woollcott myth another shot in the arm.

Not even Woollcott's worst enemies—a goodly assemblage with representatives in every city and hamlet that the Master hit in the course of his wanderings—will deny that he was an extraordinary man who made a genuine contribution to the gaiety of the nation. He was a superb story teller, although he often padded his tales with whimsy-whamsy of the most appalling variety. He fought with no holds barred for the things he believed in, although he could become as much aroused in a defense of Minnie Madden Fiske as for an all-out campaign against fascism. He truly loved the theatre, and his unbounded enthusiasm helped some really good plays to catch on with the public. He turned several books into best-sellers single-handed, although a summary of the titles reveals all too clearly a taste that was most erratic, if not downright over-sentimental and second-rate. (A few of his more violent enthusiasms: *Beside the Bonnie Briar Bush, The Chicken Wagon Family, Lost Horizon, Goodbye Mr. Chips.*)

One of the prerequisites for his idea of a masterpiece was its discovery by himself. A new play or book that was recommended by somebody else was usually doomed in advance. When he raved about something and the whole world did not echo his sentiment, Woollcott became truly convinced he had discovered a classic and embarked upon a crusade that stopped at nothing. George Macy had the temerity to appoint him a co-judge for the Readers Club with Sinclair Lewis, Clifton Fadiman and Carl Van Doren. He never agreed with them on anything; the oftener they rejected some of his weird proposals, the harder he would thump for them at the next meeting. Because of him, they finally changed the whole procedure governing selections.

Woollcott's manners, atrocious to begin with, became progressively worse when he discovered how much people were willing to take from a great celebrity. *The Man Who Came to Dinner* crystallized and enhanced the Woollcott myth a hundred fold; it turned his insults into high comedy, and undoubtedly prevented his being socked in the jaw at least twice a week. His closest friends forgave him his rudeness, his bad sportsmanship, his failure to understand the very fundamentals of fair play. True, Harpo Marx dubbed him "just a big dreamer with a remarkable sense of double-entry bookkeeping." Noël Coward addressed him as "Little Nell of Old Dreary." Robert Benchley called him "Louisa M. Woollcott." To George Jean Nathan he was the "Seidlitz Powder of Times Square." Charlie Brackett swore that he wouldn't even talk to a man who wouldn't make a good magazine article; Heywood Broun added that an exception might be made for sycophantic souls who would play ghost to his Hamlet—and *never* step out of character. Edna Ferber averred that he was just "a New Jersey Nero who mistook his pinafore for a toga."

These, mind you, were Woollcott's friends. What some of the myriad of people he had insulted in one way or another called him may be left to the reader's imagination. Woollcott rather liked being called bad names by his friends; common salutations among the little set he bullied and bellwethered were, "Oh it's you, you fawn's behind," or "Who is this harpy standing here like the kiss of death," or "Get out, repulsive. You are beginning to disgust me." Such shenanigans he considered the height of humor. Let somebody outside the charmed circle take a swipe at him, however, and Woollcott reacted like so many other people who specialize in lampooning and mocking others. When his old friend Harold Ross, editor of the *New Yorker*, ran a profile of him by Wolcott Gibbs that told a few unpleasant truths, Woollcott went into a monumental rage, and didn't speak to him again for years.

II

Alexander Woollcott was born in 1887, in Phalanx, New Jersey, in a settlement that had once been dedicated to community, or cooperative living. The experiment hadn't worked, and Woollcott's grandfather had taken over the property. In 1889, the Woollcotts moved to Kansas City, where, according to Gibbs, little Alec developed such a knack for bellowing when he was hurt that a group of bullies formed a syndicate to exploit his talent. When they saw an adult approaching, they would throw Alec off the veranda of his home onto his head. He bawled so hard that the passerby frequently gave him a nickel as hush money. The gang then took the nickel. Woollcott swore that this story was a malicious lie.

In 1897 the Woollcotts moved to Philadelphia, and Alec attended Central High School there. Classmates were Ed Wynn and Harry Scherman, the guiding genius of the Book-of-the-Month Club. The three lads had little in common. Woollcott chose Hamilton College, in Clinton, New York, as his alma mater because he had been impressed by the worldly manner of a graduate of that institution. He had a fine time there, and Hamilton, along with the Seeing Eye, Mrs. Fiske, the Marx Brothers, Laura Richards, Ruth Gordon, Rebecca West, Sibyl Colfax, Dr. Eckstein and a few assorted articulate murderers and yegg-men became the greatest enthusiasms of his declining years.

As an undergraduate, he edited the college magazine, and starred in female rôles in the dramatic club productions. To a snowbound group in his dormitory he introduced the game of choosing for each person on the campus the one adjective which fitted him more perfectly than any other. He pointed out that, if the proper selections were made, everybody could be identified from the list of adjectives. For himself he selected "noble," but admitted later that "this was voted down in favor of another which reduced the whole episode in his memoirs to the proportions of a disagreeable incident." When he graduated, Sam Adams gave him a letter of introduction to Carr Van

Anda of the New York *Times*, where, after vain efforts to attune his expanding bulk and personality to the requirements of news reporting, he was given a whack at drama reviewing as a last resort. That was in 1914. It was the beginning of Woollcott's period of glory. A new despot came into his own.

Following a brief interlude as reporter for *Stars and Stripes* in France in 1918, where he wrote stories in the manner of Ernie Pyle with an overlarding of Elsie Dinsmore, Mr. W. settled down for an indefinite run as the country's most respected drama critic, most relentless and feared gossip, and infinitely most accomplished raconteur. All three qualities made a radio career inevitable, and as "the Town Crier" Woollcott became famous, wealthy and more ruthless and domineering than ever.

His social life was unbelievably complicated. He summoned whomever he willed to his home on East Fifty-second Street (named "Wit's End" by Dorothy Parker); surprisingly few refused. He spent weeks at the White House, and told the Roosevelts whom to have in to dine with him. He spoke at department store book fairs, autographing copies of his own anthologies, and insulting his audience and other authors who appeared with him. He bought an island in Vermont, charged his guests hotel rates, and banished them when they wouldn't play croquet, cribbage, or hearts according to his own special rules. He installed a big double bed in the ground-floor guest room of this island retreat. It was comfortable but creaky, letting out a tell-tale groan when anybody moved in it. Woollcott called it the "informative double." His opinions became more and more didactic, his prose style more lush and untrammeled.

The Man Who Came to Dinner was the direct result of a typical Woollcottian sojourn at Moss Hart's new Bucks County estate. He bullied the servants, condemned the food, invited friends of his own from Philadelphia to Sunday dinner, and wrote in Hart's guest book, "This is to certify that on my first visit to Moss Hart's house I had one of the most unpleasant times I ever spent." He also suggested that Moss write a play in which he could star. The next day Hart was describing Woollcott's behavior to George Kaufman. "Wouldn't it have been horrible," he ruminated, "if he had broken a leg or something and been on my hands the rest of the summer!" The collaborators looked at each other with dawning delight on their faces and took the cover off the typewriter.

Some months later, Woollcott fulfilled a lecture date in Newark, and wheedled Hart into driving him over and back. "I'll do it on one condition," proposed Hart. "I once clerked in a bookstore in Newark and I'd like to show them that I'm a big shot now. I want you to let me sit on the platform with you, and be introduced to the audience." When they entered the hall there was a single folding chair, sure enough, to the left of the speaker's table. Hart sat down, and began crossing and uncrossing his legs, while Woollcott delivered his lecture without making the slightest reference to him. At its conclusion, he said, "I usually have a question period at this time but tonight we'll dispense with it. I'm sure you'd all want to know the same thing: who is this foolish looking man seated here on the platform with me?" With this he retired, leaving Hart to get out of the hall as best he might!

Woollcott's last years were devoted principally to playing himself in a road company of *The Man Who Came to Dinner*. The rigors of the trip, coupled with the heart strain induced by a strenuous diet that lopped off over fifty pounds, weakened him to such an extent that he was prey to the slightest ailment. When he felt death approaching, the spluttering vindictiveness went out of his writing; he began to make peace with the world, and to write conciliatory notes to long-time enemies. He even made up with Harold Ross. This lent weight to the contention of his friends that at heart he never was quite the irascible, ill-mannered tyrant he pretended to be. He was stricken in the midst of a broadcast in New York; his last words were a bitter denunciation of weak-minded sentimentalists who were willing to make a soft peace with Germany.

III

Woollcott was a confirmed bachelor, whose only known romances were of a literary variety, or the plain hero-worship he bestowed on great ladies of the stage. Edna Ferber, departing for Europe one summer, declared, "I want to be alone on this trip. I don't expect to talk to a man or woman—just Alec Woollcott." Rebecca West wrote in a copy of one of her books that she sent him, "I append my married name to remind us both to keep our passion in bounds;" she was only joking, of course. The paucity of his own love life did not prevent his superintending the amours of his little circle, plotting the career of a protegé named Frode Jensen, or suggesting the steps to be taken in the bringing up of his four nieces. When one of them, Nancy, was twelve, her friends whipped up a magazine and rejected her every prose and poetry contribution promptly and firmly. Alec was as indignant as Nancy. He heartily approved when she inserted a paid advertisement (cost: six cents cash) which read as follows:

MISS NANCY B. WOOLLCOTT
THE MOST CHARMING WOMAN
IN THE WORLD
CALL BETWEEN 2:30 AND 3

When Nancy and her sisters visited their uncle, his grand manner and famous friends awed them completely. They reported to their horrified mother that he had a portrait of himself reading on the toilet set right into the tiles of his bathroom, entitled "Laxation and Relaxation." They also were present when Ross, who has a lamentable gap between his front teeth, asked Woollcott's man for some dental floss. "Never mind floss," said Woollcott airily, "Bring him a hawser!" Woollcott was very proud of these nieces until they began to criticize him. One winter he sent his friends one of his slushy, raving notes—not about a book, play, or favorite charity this time, but a brand of whiskey. He was paid handsomely for the effort. The Lord knows what he would have said had any of his friends stooped to such commercial prostitution. The nieces sent him a note reading: "Buy stocks on margin if you must, but don't trail the family name in the dust!" In a sharp note to their father, Mr. W. remarked that if he could discover which of the nieces had dared perpetrate such sacrilege, he "would break her goddam neck!"

Woollcott accompanied Edna Ferber to an auction one afternoon. Suddenly she spied her mother, and made the mistake of hailing her by an uplifted hand. There was a crash of the auctioneer's hammer, and Miss Ferber discovered that she had become the owner of a particularly hideous grandfather's clock. Every time Woollcott told the story, the price of the clock was a little higher. On the George Kaufmans' fifth wedding anniversary (in 1922) he wrote them, "I have been looking around for an appropriate wooden gift, and am pleased hereby to present you with Elsie Ferguson's performance in her new play." When Gertrude Stein visited New York in 1933, she dared to dispute a statement of the great Mr. W. "I will forgive you this once," he said grandly. "You have not been here long enough yet to know that *nobody* disputes me!" "Woollcott," said Miss Stein with a hearty laugh, "You are a colossal fool!" The host, who happened to be myself, rolled off his chair with delight.

One evening I brought to a dinner party a lovely young lady whose aunt and uncle are both well-known California novelists. Woollcott was playing cribbage with Alice Duer Miller, and couldn't be bothered with rising from his seat. He inspected her coolly, however, and deigned to remark, "I know your aunt and uncle, of course. Your aunt is a splendid woman. Your uncle is an obscenity." (I borrow here a Hemingway device to indicate a four letter word that is not used in family magazines.) The young lady won my heart by replying, "My definition of that word, Mr. Woollcott, is a man who uses it to a lady he is meeting for the first time!" I'll say for Woollcott that he threw back his head and roared with approving laughter.

My own relations with him were severed by the Random House edition of Marcel Proust. C. K. Scott-Moncrieff, the translator of the first six parts, died before he could complete his task. After long deliberation and consultation, we selected Frederick A. Blossom to translate the seventh and last of the Proust novels. Every critic approved of his work but Woollcott, who launched into a tirade in the *New Yorker*, and made statements that enabled us to prove publicly that he didn't know what he was talking about. This was the sort of thing Woollcott couldn't forgive. One thing led to another, and finally I struck his name from the Random House review list. I made a perfect picture of a man cutting his nose to spite his face—because Woollcott's enthusiasms could make a book a bestseller more surely than anything else. I think it only fair to tell this story here, to indicate that this report is not exactly impartial, and that my recollections of Mr. Woollcott are not set down with what might be termed Olympian detachment.

While George Kaufman and Moss Hart were working on *The Man Who Came to Dinner*, Hart went to stay with Woollcott to study him once more at first hand. Hart has an insatiable curiosity for reading messages not intended for his eyes, an idiosyncrasy that did not escape Woollcott's attention. One morning Hart was busy devouring several of Mr. W's missives, not yet stamped and addressed, when he found one that read, "I'll ask you up here just as soon as I can get rid of that nauseating Moss Hart, who hangs on here like a leech, although he knows how I detest him." Hart was beginning to quiver with rage when he came to the postscript which read, "Moss, my puss: I trust this will cure you of the habit of reading other people's mail!"

In the early thirties, Woollcott visited Russia, where he created a great commotion because of his striking resemblance to the bloated capitalist invariably depicted in Soviet cartoons. He weighed over two hundred pounds at the time; Soviet citizens had seen nothing like him since the fall of the Czars. Their hoots of laughter did not increase his love for the Russian experiment. ("Hoot" is used advisedly; one Moscow journalist declared that Woollcott looked exactly like an owl!) In England, Woollcott attended a small dinner given in honor of Edward, then Prince of Wales. He was deeply flattered when the Prince called him into private consultation after the ladies had left the room, but his elation vanished when the reason became apparent. "Woollcott," said the Prince, "you've got something to do with that blasted *New Yorker* magazine, haven't you? Well, why the devil do my copies reach me so irregularly?"

Later Woollcott visited Japan, where he was made so much of that he came back home with an overflowing heart. He raved about their "neatness and love of flowers—the sweet hum of their voices and the occasional deep boom of a vast gong at a temple on a hill." He then ventured an opinion on our "future war with Japan," of which "he heard nothing from the Japanese—but in the bar of the Pekin Club, or in the veranda café of a Pacific liner, or among our own Army and Navy officers who are stationed in the Far East and have a lot of time on their hands." "I only hope," he concluded, "that if there ever is such a war and we win it, we shall remember that we won it because we are larger, richer, and more numerous, and not feel too proud about it. For I have seen just enough of Japan and the Japanese to suspect that such a victory might be only another of history's insensitive triumphs of quantity over quality!"

Well, more profound folk than the ingenuous Mr. Woollcott were taken in by the wily little Japs, and maybe it isn't quite fair to bring the matter up. At least, Woollcott lived to learn how wrong he had been.

All of his life, Alec Woollcott raged because people insisted on confusing his beloved Hamilton College, at Clinton, with Colgate University, at Hamilton, New York, not many miles away. When he died, he stipulated that his ashes be deposited in the Hamilton cemetery. David Beetle, editor of the *Hamilton Alumni Magazine*, reports that, by the irony of fate, they were shipped first to Colgate, and had to be readdressed.

HERMAN WOUK

1915–

Herman Wouk was born on May 27, 1915, in New York City, to Abraham Isaac and Esther (née Levine) Wouk. He was educated at Columbia University (A.B. 1934). From 1942 to 1946 he served in the naval reserve, achieving the rank of lieutenant. He married Betty Sarah Brown in 1945; they have three children (one deceased). He worked as a gag writer for radio comedians during 1934 and 1935, and as a scriptwriter for Fred Allen from 1936 to 1941. During 1941 he also wrote and produced plays for the U.S. Treasury Department to help promote War Bond sales. He taught at Yeshiva University in New York from 1951 to 1958, and from 1961 to 1969 was a trustee at the College of the Virgin Islands. Wouk was a scholar-in-residence at the Aspen Institute in Colorado from 1973 to 1974. He was a member of the board of directors of the Washington National Symphony from 1969 to 1971, and of Kennedy Center Productions in 1974 and 1975.

Wouk published his first novel, *Aurora Dawn*, in 1947; it was, however, his third novel, *The Caine Mutiny* (1951; Pulitzer Prize), that first attracted significant attention. It is a gripping narrative of the events surrounding a World War II mutiny and the subsequent court-martial and acquittal of the mutineers. Wouk, although a competent prose stylist and craftsman and a sometimes fascinating narrator, is stylistically and socially conservative. His later novels have consistently been bestsellers but have been subject to critical attack as well. Prominent among them is *Marjorie Morningstar* (1955), in which a young Jewish woman pursues freedom and individuality but ultimately concludes that the old ways of motherhood and servitude are best. His best-known recent works, *The Winds of War* (1971) and *War and Remembrance* (1978), concern a navy admiral and his family through World War II and the breakup of his marriage. Although some consider Wouk one of America's most articulate voices of social conservatism, others think he is at his best when avoiding serious issues altogether, as in the comic novel *Don't Stop the Carnival* (1965). Wouk has also written several plays and short stories, and two books of nonfiction.

HENRY SWADOS

From "Popular Taste and *The Caine Mutiny*"

Partisan Review, March–April 1953, pp. 252–56

It must be noted that Mr. Wouk is an exceptionally good storyteller. Willie Keith's adventures, travails and loves ⟨in *The Caine Mutiny*⟩ are handled with a directness and a swiftness that bear the mark of the practiced professional writer. But this is true of a good many other novels, even novels dealing with the Second World War, that have not had a tenth the success of this book. What we must consider is the special quality that has made *The Caine Mutiny* seem important to so many people.

It is a quality not to be found in many best-sellers that depended for their popularity simply on romance, sword-play, décolletages and civil wars. For those books, despite obvious attractions, cannot possible involve the modern middle-class reader's deepest feelings about sex, war and society, in a way that flatters him into the belief that he is participating in a thoughtful intellectual experience.

Let us turn to Willie's love affair. It is one of the novel's main themes and also serves technically both as counterpoint and relief. When Willie first meets Marie Minotti they fall in love, but are kept from intimacy by the bittersweet realization that their social backgrounds are worlds apart, for he is still under his mother's domination and she is only the daughter of a Bronx immigrant. So far their relation has a certain comfortable familiarity—tragedies have been written on just this theme and innumerable soap operas, too. There is, to be sure, a certain flavor of the archaic in tracing the difficulties of a love affair between two young people who come from utterly different milieux; when J. P. Marquand treats it, as he does so often, he removes the love affair a generation or two from current reality, presenting it as part of the recollections of an aging man. Furthermore, the liberal-minded middle-class reader is well aware of the impediments that have been removed from the path of true love by the withering away of the uppermost and nethermost classes in American society and the consequent expansion of the middle sector. Nevertheless he is also reminded by his parents and by columnists, whose sensible advice to the lovelorn is increasingly spiced with modern psychiatric lingo, of the dangers inherent in romance between young people whose family backgrounds are "incompatible."

In any case, Willie cannot bring himself to break off with Marie, and when he returns to the West Coast from his first Pacific cruise, he impetuously goes to bed with her. Here the reader is brought from the world of impossible romance into a world that he knows perfectly well exists. The author makes it quite clear that the couple have transgressed, although they are young, healthy and heedless; thus the reader has the double advantage of feeling that the love affair is realistic while protecting his moral sense. Marie, however, refuses to repeat the experience with Willie, who appreciates her new-found reserve, but begins to wonder if he can possibly love a girl who has given herself to him so easily, even if only once.

Although the reader knows that Willie is still rationalizing his snobbishness, Willie goes on torturing himself until his naval experiences bring him maturity and the need for permanent companionship. When he returns to New York in command of the *Caine* at the end of the war, he finds Marie singing for a prominent dance-band leader, and apparently living with him too. But now Willie is no longer a boy. He stands his ground and announces to Marie that he is going to take her away from the bandleader and marry her; she, fearing that Willie is simply feeling sorry for her, reveals that she has not *really* been sleeping with the bandleader, although everyone thinks so. At the close of the book it seems fairly certain that Willie will win the girl.

Here I think is an almost perfect correspondence between current sexual morality and the realities of the American experience. For a reading public caught between Sunday School training and exposure to the *Kinsey Report*, the dilemma of Willie Keith, although it can add no new dimension to their lives or depth to their experience, must seem completely "true to life" and overwhelmingly poignant. Even the falsity of his hard-won "maturity," which enables him to assert his love by suddenly disregarding the profound social differences between himself and Marie, is accepted by an audience eager for a description of love more meaningful than moonlight and roses but which still does not deprive them of the consolation of a happy ending. Virtue must still be rewarded; it is only that the rules defining virtue have been modified by the economic necessity for delayed marriages and by the back seats of forty million automobiles. Willie's virtue in loving Marie despite her affair with the bandleader is rewarded with the revelation that she has not *really* slept with the man. It is as though Mr. Wouk were subconsciously attuned to the precise degree of sexual liberation which the popular mind is ready to grant to American youth, as well as to the exact amount of traditional romance with which the depiction of the liberation must be leavened.

Indeed, any analysis of the most successful components of popular culture would compel us to refer to the ability of men like Mr. Wouk to let us have our cake and eat it, to stimulate us without unduly provoking us, to make us feel that we are thinking without really forcing us to think.

Just as Willie's virtue is rewarded with the revelation of his girl's purity, so are his heroism and his steadfast support of Maryk rewarded with a medal, a command, and a hero's return. Keefer, on the other hand, is punished for his sophistry, irresponsibility and cowardice, not by official action, but—what is worse for him—by the consciousness of his ineradicable inadequacy despite his literary success. And Maryk, in what is perhaps the neatest touch of all, is formally acquitted of the "mutiny," thanks to the brilliant defense of

Greenwald, but suffers for his presumption in deposing Queeg by being deprived forever of the possibility of realizing his life's ambition—a career as an officer in the regular navy. Thus, the lives of all the principals are composed in accordance with their just deserts, i.e., with accepted standards of reward and retribution.

What the new middle class wanted—and found in *The Caine Mutiny*—was an assurance that its years of discomfort and hardship in the Second World War were not in vain, and that its sacrifices in a permanent war economy and its gradual accommodation to the emergence of the military as a dominant element in civil life have been not only necessary but praiseworthy. More than this, it requires such assurance in a sophisticated form, allowing it to feel that alternatives have been thoughtfully considered before being rejected: in *The Caine Mutiny* ample space is given over to consideration of "psychoanalytic" motivations in Queeg and in Keefer too, and even the Cain-Abel analogy is mentioned as evidence that the title is not an unmotivated slip of the pen.

The taste of the middle-class reading public is conditioned by an increasing prosperousness in a military economy, tending to reinforce conservative moral concepts and to strengthen a traditional envy and distrust of intellectuals and dissidents. But its taste is modified by an indebtedness to its European forebears, New Deal heritage, and continuously higher level of education. Thus it is inclined toward a sophisticated and hospitable acceptance of those entertainments of the vanished European aristocracy which have flowed into the mainstream of Western liberal culture through the channels of mass production. Witness the phenomenal increase of ballet audiences and the number of people buying "classical" records. Writers like Herman Wouk will inevitably arise directly from this class to verbalize its inchoate and often contradictory attitudes. Indeed Mr. Wouk's background—he has combined a faithful adherence to Orthodox Judaism and a career as a radio gag writer with no apparent discomfort—has prepared him admirably for his task as a practitioner of popular culture.

LESLIE A. FIEDLER
From "*Clarissa* in America: Toward Marjorie Morningstar"
Love and Death in the American Novel
1960, pp. 248–53

Herman Wouk, profiting by the collapse of hyper-genteel taboos in the bourgeoisie itself, has managed to attain (middlebrow popularity). The struggle of writers like Dreiser, ironically enough, made it possible to write in 1955 the pure bourgeois novel of seduction as originally created by the female Richardsonians. Only one fundamental revision has been made in the mythos of seduction between *Charlotte Temple* and *Marjorie Morningstar* (their very titles indicate their kinship): the newer genteel Sentimentalism will not let the fallen woman die. That Marjorie in losing her virginity has been permanently maimed, incapacitated for the full enjoyment of marriage, Mr. Wouk does not doubt; yet he insists on marrying her off into a bitter-sweet happy ending. The twentieth-century Clarissa no longer is condemned to end her life by suicide or a broken heart, when her honor is lost; she is granted the partial redemption of marriage to an athletic lawyer, ends not in the wretched hovel where Charlotte came to die, but in the split-level house beautiful of exurban New York. Perhaps this is why she can no longer save anyone but herself, though she is still capable of damning the man who devirginates her. Something of the old mythic power still clings to her, some last trace of the aura of Clarissa, that secular savior, whose piety and sexuality were felt, for all their absurdly conventional dress, as real and terrible. But Marjorie has followed the downward path of travesty already foreshadowed in Charlotte, seems finally only a silly girl who turns into a dull suburban lady, the ghost (dead she would have been more alive) of the Protestant virgin, oddly turned Jew.

Between Richardson and Wouk, falls the shadow of Flaubert, who has taught Wouk (he is not, like the earliest lady Sentimentalists, sub-literate) what middle-class life has become, what dreams and frustrations the daughters of Clarissa have inherited since the bourgeois revolution has been converted into business-as-usual. Clarissa has become Madame Bovary—as even Dreiser's portrait of Sister Carrie manages to convey; though he, too, refuses his heroine either the Richardsonian benediction or the Flaubertian chastisement of death. Wouk, however, will not confess this truth, which even the facts of his own fable substantiate, but attempts to exorcise it by editorial comment and implicit moralizing, trying to lift our hearts high above such earthbound reflections. The voice which, despite his censorship, keeps whispering to him and his readers alike, "Clarissa is Bovary, Marjorie is Bovary, you are Bovary," he identifies with the voice of the Seducer, against whose wiles it is his function to warn the bourgeois American world.

Who is the Seducer in Wouk's novel, the modern counterpart of the irresistible Lovelace, whose struggle with the immovable Clarissa all Europe once followed through a million words? He is called Noel Airman, which is to say, *Luftmensch*, the impractical schemer who never touches the ground, though he was born Ehrman, which is to say, man of honor. Denying his Jewish birthright, Wouk apparently means to tell us, by denying his Jewish name, Noel also denies virtue; and we are not surprised to discover that he is not only an actor, pianist, and playwright, but also a value-less bohemian and, especially, Don Giovanni once more! His long love-combat with Marjorie (it takes him nearly four hundred pages to achieve her deflowering) is fought for the Richardsonian prize, that female virginity which symbolizes the salvation of both contesting parties. As in Richardson, the sexual contest represents not only a clash of persons but of classes—in the older book, of course, a struggle between the spokesman for middle-class piety and the mouthpiece of aristocratic cynicism, a real class war though one played out in boudoir and brothel.

Airman, like Lovelace before him, is both seducer and freethinker, besides being possessed of a grace alongside of which bourgeois manners and morality seem grubbily and unpleasantly safe and sane. Lovelace, however, was an aristocrat, survivor of the class just then blending (as Richardson shows by the possibility of his wooing Clarissa) into the mercantile bourgeoisie; Airman is not sure where he belongs. He is intended to be a member of a self-appointed aristocracy of culture, a highbrow (miserable imitation of Noel Coward that he actually is): the equivalent to the middlebrow imagination of the Dandy and the *poète maudit*. And this finally is the true subject of Wouk's book, its underground theme. The bourgeoisie has won its fight against the old nobility, the last item on its agenda having been the Freedom from Seduction. But suddenly, from among its own sons, a new enemy appears to cry that there is no seduction, that all is permitted, that the values for which their fathers fought against the old nobility are lies.

There is some justification, after all, for recasting Lovelace as Airman, since, as we have seen, it was on the model of the former that Rousseau created his Saint-Preux, on whom in turn Goethe modeled Werther; and from Werther have stemmed all the portraits of the artist as a young seducer down to our own time. Conversely, in the vulgarized bourgeois sentimental novel of the early nineteenth century and after, the artist-free-thinker had been used as a villain, thus projecting the anti-intellectualism of its readers. It is Wouk's unique contribution to American letters to have identified this bugaboo of middle-class ladies with the "Jewish intellectual," trading on a stereotype of such highbrows as cynical, bohemian, neurotic, negative, much given to idle talk about obscure books and Sigmund Freud. To the fear of the Jewish intellectual as seducer, which troubles the sleep of lower-middlebrow Anglo-Saxon maidens, he has finally given genteel literary expression (Ben Hecht had played with it ironically in *A Jew in Love*). But beside his bad Jew, Wouk is careful to set good ones: soft-hearted, handball-playing professional men; kindly, old, ridiculous uncles; warm, expansive mamas—but especially Marjorie herself, out of Susanna Rowson by Molly Goldberg!

From the earliest moment, Jewish heroines have been viable in American novels; the rich widow, Mrs. Achsa Fielding, whom Arthur Mervyn marries in Brockden Brown's romance, is a Jewess, as is Hawthorne's Miriam in *The Marble Faun*. They soon become, however, forbidden exotics—dark, alien types whom the hero, after Brown, is not permitted to marry—for lurking behind and beside them is the Jewish villain, the Smiler with a Knife. In the deepest American imagination, the Jewish male (high priest and Father Abraham) is an embodiment of evil, a threat: his lineage extends from the Gabriel Von Gelt of Lippard's *Quaker City* to the Wolfsheim of Scott Fitzgerald's *The Great Gatsby*; but the female (Mary, Mother of Jesus, Rachel weeping for her children) is postulated as desirable, in some sense good. Shylock and Jessica, Isaac and Rowena: these are the prototypical pairs reflected in such American works as Melville's *Clarel* and *Mrs. Peixada* by "Sidney Luska." The Jew as ultimate Father and Mother is the uneasy dream which stirs behind such literary representations, though the Jewess is typically represented as the daughter; such a demotion mitigates a little the guilt involved, but it cannot dissipate it completely. Ivanhoe gives up Rebecca, Clarel loses Ruth—there is the blight of a profound taboo on the relationship; to marry the Jew's daughter does not cease to be a sin even if she is converted, though Shakespeare may once have believed it did. In *The Yoke of the Torah*, "Sidney Luska" de-mythicizes the Jew's daughter at last, portrays her as a dull, bourgeois girl whose marriage to the sensitive hero of the novel means his spiritual and moral death.

Marjorie is the end-product of this de-mythicizing process, by which Scott's Rebecca becomes Luska's Tillie ("'Oh my daughter, she works like a horse. . . . And such a *good* girl. Only nineteen years old and earns more than a hundred dollars a month. . . . She's grand. She's an angel'"), but she is Tillie mythicized again, Tillie as Clarissa—out of the fire into the frying pan! However, there is a further, an essential difference. Marjorie is, first of all, detached from the melodrama of the encounter with the gentile, allowed to choose only between the Jewish intellectual and the Jewish bourgeois. The effect of putting her into so totally Jewish a context is to make her seem scarcely Jewish at all (though much is made of her difficulties with religion), hardly distinguishable from the Sweetheart of Sigma Chi. In another sense, Wouk's novel represents the entry of the newest shibboleth of sentimental liberalism into the sentimental novel of seduction, the assimilation of anti-anti-Semitism into the kind of book which had already assimilated abolitionism, Christian socialism, woman's rights, temperance, etc., etc.

Marjorie Morningstar is, in this respect, the first fictional celebration of the mid-twentieth-century *détente* between the Jews and middle-class America; and the movie which has followed, the *Time* story and the *Time* cover picture are, in effect, public acknowledgments of that fact. Among the enlightened minority audience of the arts, the transformation of the Jew from bugaboo to culture hero is as old as Kafka and James Joyce. In the high literature of Europe and, more slowly, in that of the United States, gentile and Jew have joined forces to portray the Jewish character as a figure representing man's fate in the modern, urbanized world. In general, the point of such portrayals is to suggest that we live in an age of rootlessness, alienation, and terror, in which the exiled condition so long thought peculiar to the Jew comes to seem the common human lot. This is neither a cheery nor a reassuring view; and it is therefore incumbent on the lower-middlebrow novelist, Wouk, to suggest a counter-view: the contention that the Jew was never (or is, at least, no longer) the rootless dissenter, the stranger which legend has made him, but rather the very paragon of the happy citizen at home, loyal, chaste, thrifty, pious, and moderately successful—in short, not Noel Airman but Marjorie Morningstar!

In a struggle where so much is symbolically at stake—not only the peace of mind of the bourgeois community, but the status of the Jew within it—there can be only one outcome. The temporary victory of the enemy (Marjorie is deflowered and converted into the actress Morningstar) is turned into his final defeat (Airman proposes marriage, which Marjorie rejects to become the true Morgenstern again). The artist-seducer-villain is brought down to humiliation and defeat, stands at Marjorie's wedding to her bourgeois second choice with a "baffled, vacant" stare, his "eyes wet." He is not even capable of scorn at the vulgarity of the $6500 catered spectacle which crowns Marjorie's return to virtue and bourgeois accommodation. After such tears and loss of faith in his own cynicism, there is nothing for Airman but a further fall to the status of a third-rate television actor, married to a woman who is probably a Nazi! It is the final bourgeois indignity—to be not even a success. To such an end Hurstwood and Carrie have come; for the sake of this philo-Semitic fable, Dreiser (even more virulently anti-Semitic than his contemporaries Hemingway, Anderson, and Fitzgerald) fought the good fight against the Jews of New York and Hollywood. It is all an American comedy, whose secret star is the girl who will not die (though alone among fictional characters she has been provided with an actual grave), Charlotte Temple.

GRANVILLE HICKS

New York Times Book Review, November 14, 1971, pp. 4–5, 52

Herman Wouk has written a long, mildly interesting, moderately informative novel ⟨*The Winds of War*⟩ about the beginnings of World War II, from the signing of the Soviet-Nazi act in August, 1939, to the Japanese attack on Pearl Harbor. The central figure is a Navy man, Victor Henry, usually called "Pug," a shore-bound commander when the novel opens, a four-striper waiting for sea duty when it ends.

He and his wife, Rhoda, have two sons, Warren and Byron, and a daughter, Madeline. Warren has followed Pug to Annapolis and has chosen naval aviation. Byron has revolted—against the naval tradition *and* his father—although, after the adoption of the draft in the fall of 1940, he enlists as a submariner. Madeline leaves college, against Pug's wishes, to serve as the secretary of a popular broadcaster.

From the outset, *The Winds of War* brings Upton Sinclair's Lanny Budd series to the mind of anyone old enough to have read it. Like Lanny, Pug becomes a kind of secret Presidential agent. In this role, he turns up at most of the places where history is being made, starting as naval attaché in Berlin. What he misses some member of his family takes in. Sinclair, it may be remembered, surveyed a longer period of time—from 1913 to about 1948—but he ran to several volumes.

It is not merely in subject matter and method that Wouk reminds me of Sinclair. There is the same indifference to quality, the same reliance on clichés and broad casual strokes. When, for example, Byron Henry is falling in love with Natalie Jastrow, Wouk writes: "She gave him a playful smile, clutching the green and yellow ticket to her bosom." In his account of the wedding of Warren Henry and Janice Lacouture, we read: "As the bride paced down the aisle on the congressman's arm, moving like a big beautiful cat, Rhoda started to cry."

Wouk must have been taught at some time that it is of supreme importance to tell how characters *look*, and he has a formula that serves his purpose well. For example: "Beryl Jastrow had a broad nose, heavy eyebrows, and surprisingly blue deep-set eyes with an almost Tartar slant." Or: "Despite the big Lacouture nose, a mark of French ancestry, and rather irregular front teeth, Janice was one of the belles of Pensacola. Her mouth, skin, and hazel eyes were lovely; her figure was so striking that all men automatically stared at her as at a fire."

Historical characters are treated in the same mechanical fashion. Here is Franklin Delano Roosevelt: "Pug had not seen him, except in newsreels and photographs, in more than twenty years. His high coloring was unchanged, and he was the same towering man, gone gray-headed, much older and very much heavier; and though he had the unmistakable lordly look of a person in great office, a trace remained in the upthrust big jaw of the youthful conceit that had made the ensigns on the Davey snicker. His eyes were sunken, but very bright and keen." Almost everybody, it appears, has eyes, a nose, a mouth, and so on. All the writer has to worry about is variety in the adjectives.

I would not make so much of the commonplaces, the awkward phrases, and the cookie-cutter descriptions if they were not symptomatic of a greater weakness: the failures of Wouk's style betray the failures of his imagination. Like Sinclair, he writes journalese, and he never rises far above that level. His characters, even Pug Henry, are never living human beings. Although he tries to give these men and women some semblance of reality by involving them in more or less complicated love affairs, they remain essentially observers and reporters.

Despite its faults, of course, this king-size book will sell. Wouk has the trick—or, if you prefer, the gift—of compelling narrative; he tells a story so that the reader stays with him to learn what happens next. Although some pages are sluggish, his flat, undemanding style permits one to skip without missing much.

The book's second asset is the vast amount of information it contains. Many lazy people like to read biography and history in novel form, as painless education. From *The Winds of War* anyone under 35 can learn a lot about an important crisis in the history of America and of the world. No authority on the period, I am inclined to guess that Wouk is accurate in all essential matters—though he does not provide a bibliography, as Sinclair did.

Pug Henry sees at close range Hitler, Churchill, Stalin and Roosevelt, to say nothing of Mrs. Roosevelt and Fala. (If you don't know who Fala was, you are one of the millions for whom this book was written.) Byron Henry is in Warsaw when the Nazis bomb it. Janice Henry sees the raid on Pearl Harbor. Palmer Kirby (Rhoda Henry's lover) works on the A-bomb. Pug, on top-secret missions, flies as an observer on the first R.A.F. air strike at Berlin. Aboard the last Clipper from the Far East to Hawaii, he's just in time to witness the Japanese air strike at Wake Island. As if all this weren't enough, Wouk also presents extracts from a fictitious treatise, *World Empire Lost*, by a fictitious German general, Armin von Roon—who holds that Hitler was a master politician but a poor strategist. He also holds that Roosevelt was as opportunistic, ruthless, and mendacious as Hitler, but smarter and luckier.

In size and scope, this is Wouk's most ambitious novel. His first success, *The Caine Mutiny*, also concerned World War II, but dealt with a small dramatic episode: to my mind, it is the best of his books. I have always been troubled, however, by his sudden shift in position in the climactic chapter. Actually, there are two climaxes. The first comes at the court-martial, when the defense counsel, Lieutenant Greenwald, with standard legal expertise, wins the acquittal of the executive officer responsible for the "mutiny" that put the paranoid Captain Queeg off his bridge during a typhoon. The second occurs at the officers' victory dinner, when Greenwald turns against Keefer (the real instigator of the mutiny), denounces him as a coward and a traitor, and praises Queeg. Wouk, who has already amply persuaded the reader to sympathize with the rebels, now brings that same reader back to his right mind—as I am sure Wouk himself sees it—by waving Old Glory.

There is a comparable reversal in Wouk's second success, *Marjorie Morningstar*—which, in any case, was too formless and too long-drawn-out for my taste. Once again, an intellectual turns out to be the villain, whereas the hero is a solid, conventional, middle-class suburbanite—as good as gold and, as Marjorie has felt all along, pretty dull. It is this virtuous, self-righteous young man with whom we are ultimately supposed to sympathize. Not with poor, wayward Marjorie, and certainly not with the Bohemian poseur who has seduced her.

The Winds of War has no such tricky reversal of roles—and, in fact, no sharply-defined climax. Pearl Harbor is a beginning, not an end, for the characters, as well as for the American people in general. In a prologue, the author quotes from Julien Benda: "Peace, if it ever exists, will not be based on the fear of war, but on the love of peace. It will not be abstaining from an act, but the coming of a state of mind. In this sense the most insignificant writer can serve peace."

Whether Wouk believes his novel will contribute to the development of the desired state of mind is not clear. Pug Henry (certainly a man of good will) knows a lot about Roosevelt's machinations but accepts them as necessary to American survival. He is not exactly an optimist: "Maybe the vicious circle would end with this first real world war. Maybe it would end with Christ's second coming. Maybe it would never end."

The author has already said that a sequel is in the works—and one cannot help wondering if there may be a whole series. Sinclair took 10 volumes to tell *his* story—then, by popular demand, added an 11th, *The Return of Lanny Budd*. If Wouk should proceed at his present pace, he will need more than 1,500 pages overall before he even reaches Hiroshima. He will not carry me with him. But I do wonder what his climax may be—if he ever reaches it.

PAUL FUSSELL

New Republic, October 14, 1978, pp. 32–33

This novel ⟨*War and Remembrance*⟩, a continuation of Wouk's 885-page *The Winds of War* (1971), is, as *Publisher's Weekly* would put it, the big one for fall, and its 1,042 pages will engage the book-club customers well into spring. The whole two-volume work constitutes a very good popular history of the Second World War and the Holocaust in the guise of a very bad novel. Actually Wouk is only dubiously a novelist, presumably enticed to that genre by the emoluments now attaching to it and its residuals. He is really something else, and when he functions as something else his work is often interesting and occasionally admirable.

But when he is merely novelizing he is embarrassing. The characters and plot of *War and Remembrance* are purely early 1950s Metro-Goldwyn-Mayer. Victor ("Pug") Henry (to be played by Spencer Tracy) is a mature naval officer married to the martini-loving Rhoda (Tallulah Bankhead). One of their sons, Byron (Anthony Perkins), is a brave and successful submarine officer. Another, Warren (Van Johnson), is a brave and successful naval aviator, killed at Midway. Their daughter Madeline (Ava Gardner) cohabits for a while with the USO entertainer Hugh Cleveland (Jack Carson), but finally comes to her senses and dumps him in favor of a chap working on the bomb in Los Alamos. Byron is married to Natalie (Claire Bloom), the niece of Aaron Jastrow (Sam Jaffe), said to be an impressive Jewish philosopher. Commander (later Captain and finally Rear Admiral) Victor Henry is away a lot, commanding the heavy cruiser *Northampton* until it's sunk near Guadalcanal, and then running high-powered errands all over the world for Roosevelt—expediting Lend-Lease operations in Persia, clearing up bottlenecks in landing craft production in England and the States. While he's away, Rhoda falls for the atomic scientist Palmer Kirby (Robert Young). At the same time, Pug finds himself beloved by Pamela Tudsbury (Vivien Leigh), the toothsome daughter of famed British broadcaster Alistair ("Talky") Tudsbury (Robert Morley). Aaron Jastrow and Natalie and her infant Louis are trapped in Siena, where they are beguiled by the plausible but cunning German diplomat Dr. Werner Beck (Hume Cronyn). After Aaron bravely resists Beck's pressures to deliver treasonous broadcasts, he and Natalie and her child find themselves delivered to the detention and transport mechanisms of the Final Solution, and Aaron ends in the gas chamber at Auschwitz. When the war is over, Natalie and Louis are found to have survived and are reunited with Byron. Admiral Henry's marriage with Rhoda having come apart, he finds happiness with Pamela and is appointed naval aide to President Truman. Choral music. House lights up.

The character of Victor Henry, the Lanny Budd of these proceedings, abundantly indicates what's wrong with *War and Remembrance* as fiction. He is not to be believed. As Madeline tells her brother Byron, "You and I have an incredible father." Too true. With his "awkward smile" and habit of being always right, he charms the world's leaders, who never tire of complimenting him. "You have insight, Pug," Roosevelt tells him, "and a knack for putting things clearly." He is a master of every subject—not just naval and military strategy and engineering, but wine and food, tanks, atomic fission, the history of philosophy, international politics, art history, and the history of Europe since 1870. He speaks languages and reads "Shakespeare" and "the Bible." He drinks but doesn't get drunk. His bravery is legendary. His personal mail is likely to include chatty letters on "creamy" White House stationery. He is gifted at literary composition, and he translates and edits like a scholar. He is one of those rare creatures whose obtuse superiority makes him "popular" instead of hated. ("Popular fella, aren't you?" Harry Hopkins says to him once.) Powerful fantasy seems to be at work in Wouk's creation of Pug, and unkind readers may suspect autobiographical projection. Although Pug is actually a prig for all seasons, Wouk imagines that the reader will admire him without reservation. Pug's world is equally unreal: the telephones always work, people keep appointments, binoculars and toilet paper are always at hand, soldiers and sailors obey orders, and eyewitness accounts are to be relied on.

One stylistic symptom of Wouk's primitive conception of character and his rationalist view of the world is Elegant Variation. Thus Pug is "the naval officer," W. Somerset Maugham (who makes a brief guest appearance) "the British novelist," Stalin "the Communist dictator," Hitler "the Austrian adventurer," and FDR "the masterful old cripple" residing in "the executive mansion." Without typecasting everybody and everything Wouk would be lost in a world more complicated than he and his readers can tolerate. Unable to conceive an original character or to equip anyone with feelings above the commonplace, he must resort to wholly external classifications. His people are devoid of inner life. Their professional identity is their whole reality and they are entirely what they seem: stick-figures whose only function is to take their places in Wouk's retrograde middle-class allegory of success.

Although Wouk imputes sadism and unreason to the Nazis, he has eliminated the irrational from the behavior of the Allies, with the result that the war fought by the Henrys, unlike Heller's war, or Vonnegut's or Pynchon's, lacks the crucial dimension of the lunatic, the cruel, and the self-destructive. As an antidote to Wouk's simple, patriotic dramatization of the justness of war it is useful to remember Dwight MacDonald on General Patton: "Far from the justness of the war excusing Patton's barbarism, Patton's barbarism calls into question the justness of war. There is something suspect about an end which calls for such means." A mere 20 years after the heroic sacrifices Wouk celebrates, infantrymen were fragging their officers. From *War and Remembrance* it would be impossible to guess why. It is depressing to discover finally that a novel whose size, scope and method remind us of *War and Peace* and whose theme is bound to remind us of Mann's *Doctor Faustus* has for its real hero the United States Navy.

Thus the soap-opera part of *War and Remembrance*: trash, essentially, fabricated by the Wouk who's going to flog the whole thing to the movies. But there's another part, never satisfactorily joined to the MGM part, written by what I take to be more authentic Wouk, the learned descriptive and analytic essayist, and it is surprisingly fine. Much of it consists of powerfully imagined strategic theory and military history from the pen of the fictive German general Armin von Roon, whose book *Land, Sea and Air Operations of World War II*, written while its author is imprisoned for war crimes, is translated by Victor Henry, who annotates the text and sets the author straight on numerous points. The quality of the military reasoning in this document—the whole comprises 122 pages—is impressive, and so is Wouk's scholarship (that really is the correct word) in contemporary history. Impressive too is the strategic and tactical understanding in Wouk's accounts of naval battles like Midway and Leyte Gulf. Indeed, in his narration of Leyte Gulf he seems to recognize how much more interested he is in the history of naval operations than in the behavior of One Man's Family, whom he forgets for pages while he goes on, admirably, in the role of naval historian. As a historian of naval warfare Wouk is as good as Samuel Eliot Morison, while as an analytic narrator of land battles, particularly Soviet here, he invites comparison with someone like B. H. Liddell Hart. If the idea of "the novel" had not been his fatal Cleopatra, he could have distinguished himself as a contemporary historian. As it is, his failure to achieve a masterpiece can be seen as a generic miscarriage.

When he turns from people to significant public environments and "things," Wouk is also wonderful. A modern image hard to forget is the immense floating bottom of a destroyer capsized during the typhoon in *The Caine Mutiny* (1951). Seen from the *Caine*, it is a bizarre shiny red island with no life on it. "Waves were breaking over it in showers of foam," and the observers are properly awestruck by the sight and the silence. Wouk is as good presenting what we might see at a farcical Second Front Now rally at Hollywood Bowl or what Himmler sees when he inspects the extermination and cremation facilities at Auschwitz. Perhaps Wouk's triumph in this line is his depiction of Theresienstadt, the "Paradise Ghetto" in Czechoslovakia, while it is being prettied up late in the war to deceive a delegation from the Danish Red Cross. Aaron and Natalie are confined there together with thousands of "specials" and *prominente*, and the Great Beautification goes on all around them to their astonishment and anxiety. Flowers are set out, bandstands erected and painted, cafes established (with Jews rehearsed to play happy boulevardiers), a soccer field is laid out and "teams" drilled to play on it, fake shops are opened and "shoppers" rehearsed. The Danish delegation believes it all, and a few days later the residents of Theresienstadt are all shipped East. Wouk does even the inside of the cattle cars superbly: give him an environment of any kind—the Kremlin, Hitler's Wolfsschanze in the East Prussian forest, the president's private quarters in the White House, a gas chamber posing as a mass shower-bath, the flag-plot room on a battleship, an atomic pile, the interior of a submarine or a bomber—and he renders it persuasively. There's hardly a contemporary writer so good at depicting locales authentically, places as varied as Honolulu, Bern, Lisbon, Leningrad, Columbia University, and London. They are perfect. I find it also to Wouk's credit that he is serious about the Second World War and conceives that interpreting it is the most pressing modern intellectual and moral problem. I respect the elegiac impulse that prompts him to interrupt his narrative of the Battle of Midway to display on three pages the names of the actual dead naval aviators from *Yorktown*, *Enterprise*, and *Hornet*. It is only with living people that he fails.

He has wanted to register the facts of the Holocaust so that they will never be forgotten. It is sad that the vulgarity of his romance of the Henrys compromises this admirable end, and by proximity demeans his skillful historiography.

CHARLES WRIGHT

1935–

Charles Penzel Wright, Jr., was born on August 25, 1935, in Pickwick Dam, Tennessee. He was educated at Davidson College (B.A. 1957), the University of Iowa (M.F.A. 1963), and the University of Rome. From 1957 to 1961 he served in the army intelligence corps, achieving the rank of captain. He married Holly McIntire in 1969; they have one child. From 1966 to 1983 he taught at the University of California at Irvine; since 1983 he has been a Professor of English at the University of Virginia. In addition, he has been a visiting lecturer at the University of Padua, the University of Iowa, Princeton University, and Columbia University.

Wright published his first book of poems, *The Voyage*, in 1963. Since then he has gradually become recognized as one of America's most distinctive and complex new voices in poetry. He cites Ezra Pound and Eugenio Montale as primary influences upon his work; his poetry, like theirs, is often embedded with several layers of meaning that must be closely analyzed to be fully appreciated. Unlike Pound, however, Wright's work is primarily personal. He has been praised for his sense of sound and rhythm and his perceptive imagery. Notable volumes include *The Dream Animal* (1968), *The Grave of the Right Hand* (1970), *Hard Freight* (1973), *Bloodlines* (1975), and his most praised and perhaps best-known book, *China Trace* (1977). Wright won the American Book Award in 1983, and has also published two books of translations: *The Storm and Other Poems* by Eugenio Montale (1978) and *Orphic Songs* (1984).

KATHLEEN AGENA
"The Mad Sense of Language"
Partisan Review, 1976, pp. 625–30

When Charles Wright's poems work, which is most of the time, the poetic energies seem to break the membrane of syntax, exploding the surface, reverberating in multiple directions simultaneously. It is not a linear progression one finds but rather a ricocheting, as if, at the impact of a single cue, all the words bounced into their pockets, rearranged, and displaced themselves in different directions all over again. And it seems to happen almost by accident, as if Wright simply sets the words in motion and they, playing a game according to their own rules, write the poem. Certainly Wright is aware of this strange power of words; all three of his books contain poems which, strictly speaking, refer only to words and their maneuverings. Here is one from *The Grave in the Right Hand:*

BLACK SONNET

0. Psittacosis
1. Cuckoopint
2. Reliquary
3. Pysidium
4. Entelechy
5. Wyvern
6. White bryony
7. Zymotic
8. Contrapposto
9. Typolysis
10. Syzygy
11. Anti-matter
12. X
13. Carthago delenda est

Whereas "Black Sonnet" is raunchy and humorous, a sort of burlesque in which the words parade themselves like Las Vegas showgirls, "Tattoos 12," another poem about words, from *Bloodlines*, displays a different kind of word eroticism which operates between the words themselves. It is an eroticism which some might deem perverse in that the words seem to be attracted to each other through a dynamic which appears to defy not only syntax but semantic "sense":

Oval, oval oval oval push pull push pull . . .
Words unroll from our fingers.
A splash of leaves through the windowpanes,
A smell of tar from the streets:
Apple, arrival, the railroad, shoe.

The words, like bees in a sweet ink, cluster and drone
indifferent, indelible,
A hum and a hum:
Back stairsteps to God, ropes to the glass eye:
Vineyard, informer, the chair, the throne.

Mojo and numberless, breaths
From the wet mountains and green mouths, rust-
lings,
Sure sleights of hand,
The news that arrives from nowhere:
Angel, omega, silence, silence . . .

("Tattoos 12")

One reads a poem like "Tattoos 12" and the first response is "that felt good!"; and only later . . . "what happened?" Of course, Wright's poems are not without "sense," not without conceptual-symbolic dimensions, but it is the sense of primal consciousness, the sense of paradox and multiplicity that binds these words and their meanings. Or, to use Lacan's terminology, it is "the letter in the unconscious," which, though it may oppose conscious purpose, is never arbitrary. So in the afterglow of the initial reading one can go back and, unwinding the words from their embrace, realize, for example, that the reason "oval oval oval oval" works so well with "push, pull" is that an oval is a circle which has been squeezed, "pushed," or elongated, "pulled," at two points, that oval is the transcendent ease of the perfect equilibrium of the circle being subjected to pressure. The oval is also an egg, birth, the push and pull of form coming into existence. And what do "apple, arrival, the railroad, shoe" have to do with each other? Is this just perverse eroticism at work again? No, there is meaning in the apparent madness. All the words are related to movement—the "apple" to the movement toward knowledge, the expulsion from grace, the fall into the limits of temporal existence and guilt. With "apple" in the first slot and "arrival, the railroad, shoe" functioning as substitutions thereafter, the series together carries meanings of movement-knowledge-guilt-limit with a progressive emphasis on limitation: "apple" signifying a transcendental causal function; "arrival," because it is used nonspecifically, signifying an abstract goal of movement; "railroad" reducing the abstract movement to a finite vehicle of movement; and "shoe" further restricting movement and the vehicle of movement. The limit-restriction element is both a reverberation back to and an amplification of the first line—that is, it amplifies the sense of stress of "oval" and "push, pull" and it extends the notion of imperfectness implied there. The movement-knowledge-guilt-limit motif is also evident in the second, third, and fourth lines: "windowpanes," suggesting consciousness itself which receives the knowledge, immediately becomes contaminated with the "smell of tar," black, sticky, clinging guilt. Further, all of these motifs get connected with the "meaning" of words: after the first line, which simply establishes a process, comes the first subject in the poem ("words") and all the subsequent subjects which follow must be seen as substitutions, replacements, which serve to multiply the significations connected with that first subject. So, the first stanza as well as the entire poem is about words, about the way they come to carry meaning, the dynamic that exists between words as signifiers and the things they signify, the guilt of words as opposed to the purity of silence.

Anyway, after making meaning sense of these things, after justifying the words, one feels almost that the explanation is a rationalization of sorts. The simple truth is that one is hooked on the words and that Wright's power as a poet lies in just this ability to hook us, to intoxicate us with a language that radiates paradox—that is, the realm of symbol. To accomplish this demands, I think, a kind of surrender on the part of the poet, a loosening of intent, a trusting in the mad sense of language. And, in fact, Wright's poetry fails when he refuses to surrender enough, when he holds the reins on the words too tightly, when he seems too intent upon getting an idea across and, ironically, ends up writing poems less rich in meaning. But when the right balance between abandon and control is achieved, the nature of the tension is erotic:

Carafe, compotier, sea shell, vase:
Blank spaces, white objects;
Luminous knots along the black rope.

The clouds, great piles of oblivion, cruise
Over the world, the wind at their backs
Forever. They darken whomever they please.

("White")

The connective threads, the concepts, that run through Wright's poems and make his collection read, as James Tate puts it, "like a book not a miscellany," have to do with Wright's insistence that the human is but one system, one way of ordering, one center exerting its force while simultaneously being permeated by the force of other systems, that progress in terms of any single system is an illusion; the center is always shifting. There is simply process, displacement, the perpetual turning of transformation:

You thought you climbed, and all the while you
descended
Go up and go down, what other work is there
For you to do, what other work in this world?
The seasons back off. The hills
Debase themselves, and keep on growing. Over the
land,
Your feet touch down like feathers,
A brushstroke here, a gouge there, lacking a print
Always, and always without direction.
Or so it seems. But what, for one meandering man,

Is all that, who looks for the willow's change,
The drift and slip of smoke through the poplar
leaves.
The cliff's dance and wind's shift,
Alone with the owl and the night crawler
Where all is a true turning, and all is growth.
("Skins 19")

In each of his books, Wright has moved closer and closer to this radical level: in his latest book, he situates himself, metaphorically, in the flux itself. It is the numen of the blood that Wright explores in *Bloodlines*. In "Virgo Descending," the first poem in the collection, Wright draws us directly into a transformative dissolution and leads us to an archetypal image of the blood, the high priestess of the irrational, chthonic forces—the Great Mother:

Through the viridian (and black of the burnt match)
Through ox-blood and ochre, the ham-colored clay,
Through plate after plate, down
Where the worm and the mole will not go,
Through ore-seam and fire-seam,
My grandmother, senile and 89, crimpbacked,
stands
Like a door ajar on her soft bed.
("Virgo Descending")

Significantly, in "Virgo Descending" there is no directive agent, no subject which initiates the action. Instead, there is simply process itself and various stages in this process; the grandmother image does not signify an end stage of the process but rather its final opening-out. The grand-Great-mother is crimpbacked and senile. There is something monstrous about her and her senility implies the irrationality of her nature. At the same time, she embodies an awful receptivity to those elements which are outside reason; she is openness, the "door ajar," and even "the worm and the mole will not go" there. Yet this is precisely where Wright takes us, into a place where there are no stable subjects, only momentary foci or centers of action, where the "I" itself is a "something else" that is, subjectively, nothing because it is perpetually subject to change:

Now I am something else, smooth,
Unrooted, with no veins and no hair, washed
In the waters of nothingness
Anticoronal, released . . .
("Tattoos 5")

The release from stable identity to process brings with it a "release" from security. It is a willingness to accept a subjectless play of forces similar to the Oriental concept of Tao and Wright's insight is that as long as one yearns for a permanently fixed center, an arbitrary pattern not found within the flux, within the blood (blood lines) there will, ironically, be only emptiness:

Trust in the fingernail, the eyelash,
The bark that channels the bone.
What opens will close, what hungers is what goes
half-full.
("Easter, 1974")

HELEN VENDLER

"Charles Wright: The Transcendent 'I'" (1979)

Part of Nature, Part of Us

1980, pp. 277–88

I was born on the 25th of August in 1935 . . . in Hardin County, Tennessee, in a place called Pickwick Dam . . . My father worked for the TVA at the time as a civil engineer . . . In the tenth grade I was sent to a school that had eight students . . . My last two years of high school were at an Episcopal boarding school with the unlikely name of Christ School, in Arden, N.C.

This summary of the early career of the poet Charles Wright comes from an interview during a visit to Oberlin, transcribed and published in *Field* (Fall 1977). Wright went on to Davidson College ("four years of amnesia, as much my fault as theirs"), then spent four years in the Army (three of them in Italy) and two years at the University of Iowa. As he said to his audience, this represents "pretty much the biography of almost everyone here . . . We all went through more or less the same things." The connections between that life lived in Tennessee and North Carolina and the poems that have issued from it—*The Grave of the Right Hand* (1970); *Hard Freight* (1973); *Bloodlines* (1975); *China Trace* (1977)—are intermittently evident, but the effort of the poetry is to render them tenuous, often invisible. Because Wright's poems, on the whole, are unanchored to incident, they resist description; because they are not narrative, they defy exposition. They cluster, aggregate, radiate, add layers like pearls. Often they stop in the middle, with a mixed yearning and premonition, instead of taking a resolute direction backward or forward. It may be from the Italian poet Eugenio Montale (1896–) that Wright learned this pause which looks before and after; Wright recently issued his translation, done in the sixties, of Montale's powerful 1956 volume entitled *La Bufera e altro (The Storm and Other Poems)*.

The translation offers an occasion for a glance at both Montale and Wright; the conjunction helps to define what sort of poet Wright has become. Montale wrote *La Bufera* during the postwar years, and his pauses in the midst of event come as often as not in the midst of nightmare: "The Prisoner's Dream" shows a speaker imprisoned in a time of political purges, tempted, like everyone else, to "give in and sign," but instead waiting out the interminable trial, addressing from prison his fixed point of reference—a dreamed-of woman who represents beauty, justice, truth:

And the blows go on, over and over . . . and the
footsteps;
and still I don't know, when the banquet is finally
served,
if I shall be the eater or the eaten. The wait is long;
my dream of you is not yet over.

This poetry, though it implies a better past and an uncertain future, incorporates them in the burning-glass of the present. It renounces, as forms of articulation, narrative, the succession of events, the sequence of action and reaction. The spatial form, one of many in Montale, is for Wright the most natural. It can be seen in "Spider Crystal Ascension," his poem about the rise of the Milky Way at night. The galaxy, full of energy, resembling a cosmic and eternal spider-web made of crystal, is watched, as death might be watched, by the temporary inhabitants of an earthly lake:

The spider, juiced crystal and Milky Way, drifts on
his web through the night sky

AP/WIDE WORLD PHOTOS

THOMAS WOLFE

TOM WOLFE

UPI/BETTMANN NEWSPHOTOS

ALEXANDER WOOLLCOTT

AP/WIDE WORLD PHOTOS

YVOR WINTERS

PATTI PERRET

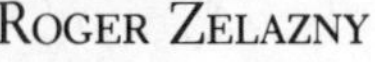

ROGER ZELAZNY

UPI/BETTMANN NEWSPHOTOS

HERMAN WOUK

UPI/BETTMANN NEWSPHOTOS

RICHARD WRIGHT

AP/WIDE WORLD PHOTOS

JAMES WRIGHT

And looks down, waiting for us to ascend . . .
At dawn he is still there, invisible, short of breath,
mending his net.
All morning we look for the white face to rise from
the lake like a tiny star.
And when it does, we lie back in our watery hair and
rock.

The spider looks, we look, he drifts through the sky, we rock in the lake, his net is patient, we will be caught from our lake one day and ascend with him, he is crystal, we are flesh, he can electrocute, we are mortal, the end is foreseen but not yet accomplished. This arrested motion, this taking thought, though it is congenial to Wright, requires nevertheless certain sacrifices.

The first sacrifice is autobiography. The autobiographical sequence "Tattoos," which appeared in *Bloodlines*, solved the problem of reference by appending, at the end of twenty poems, a single note on each one: a sample note reads "Automobile wreck; hospital; Baltimore, Maryland." Instead of a first-person narrative of the crash and its surgical aftermath, Wright produces a montage of sensations:

So that was it, the rush and the take-off,
The oily glide of the cells
Bringing it up—ripsurge, refraction,
The inner spin
Trailing into the cracked lights of oblivion.

In *Bloodlines* these verses are encountered with no title, no explanation; the note is to be read later, and then the poem reread, from the crash to the hospital:

Re-entry is something else, blank, hard:
Black stretcher straps; the peck, peck
And click of a scalpel; glass shards
Eased one by one from the flesh;
Recisions; the long bite of the veins.

It is easy to see how interminable, predictable, and boring a plain narrative might appear after this "jump-cut" (Wright's words) monitoring of sensation. The problem of affixing closure to sensation and perception (since of themselves they have no closure but unconsciousness) has bothered Wright a good deal. The automobile wreck finds closure in sententious question-and-answer, with echoes of Williams and Berryman:

And what do we do with this,
Rechuted, reworked into our same lives, no one
To answer to, no one to glimpse and sing,
The cracked light flashing our names?
We stand fast, friend, we stand fast.

The danger of this three-stanza form, as Wright realized, is that it is unduly "comfortable":

> Three stanzas is good because you can present something in the first, work around with it a bit in the second and then release it, refute it, untie it, set fire to it, whatever you want to, in the third. And that's its main problem for me. I felt I'd explored enough of what could be done, so I changed it for the next [long] poem.

The words Wright uses for the functions of that third stanza are all in some way linear, logical, causal: the problem can be "released," "refuted," "untied," torched. In any case, the problem goes away. The premise is that of syllogism in the realm of mind, action in the realm of morals. The premise, by extension, implies a world of meaning ranging from solutions to revolutions. The interesting thing about Wright's development is that he found he could no longer work within such a frame.

His next experiment, in the second sequence in *Bloodlines* (a wonderful poem called "Skins"), was to abandon the three equal pieces—presentation, complication, and conclusion—of "Tattoos" for a set of seamless meditations, each fourteen lines long. Though these have of course affinities with sonnets, they are sonnets that go nowhere, or end where they began: either the second half of the poem repeats the first, or the last line reenters the universe where the first line left it. Even the poems which seem to evolve in a linear way show only a moment in a life-cycle itself endlessly repeated; they are therefore more fated than free, as in the case of the sixth and most beautiful meditation, about the metamorphosis of a mayfly:

Then
Emergence: leaf drift and detritus; skin split,
The image forced from the self.
And rests, wings drying, eyes compressed,
Legs compressed, constricted
Between the dun and the watershine—
Incipient spinner, set for the take-off . . .
And does, in clean tear: imago rising out of herself
For the last time, slate-winged and many-eyed.
And joins, and drops to her destiny,
Flesh to the surface, wings flush on the slate film.

This is almost too ravishing in sound and sight, in its mimetic instability between the grotesque and the exquisite, to be thought about. The mind of the reader is delayed by the felicities of the slate wings on the slate water-film, by the dun detritus of chrysalis played off against the watershine, by the flesh flush on the surface, by the conjugation of drift and force, compression and incipience, and by the brief cycle of wings drying, rising, dropping. This sensual music precludes thought, almost; but the subject of metamorphosis is so old and so noble, the flesh as chrysalis so perennial a metaphor, that the conceptual words—image, self, imago, destiny—work their own subsidiary charm in the long run. In spite of the ephemeral nature of the cycle, Wright rescues by his vocabulary a form of transcendence. ("The nitty-gritty of my wishes . . . would be to be saved, but there's no such thing.")

Wright has talked about the "sparring match I had for about ten years with the Episcopal Church, in which I was raised, in which I was tremendously involved for a short amount of time and from which I fled and out of which I remain. But it had a huge effect on me":

> It's a very strange thing about being raised in a religious atmosphere. It alters you completely, one way or the other. It's made me what I am and I think it's okay. I can argue against it, but it has given me a sense of spirituality which I prize.

There are other names for this "sense of spirituality": it might just as well be named a sense of euphony, a sense for the Platonic or the seraphic. It is no doubt what attracted Wright to Montale. Montale preserved an exacerbated but inflexible fidelity to a principle itself exigent, even aggressive, in its purity and fierceness. This principle is figured in his absent "Clizia," named after the nymph who so loved the sun that she was metamorphosed into the sunflower forever faithful to radiance no matter how distant its path. Clizia burns through *The Storm* as a presence, even in absence, not to be put by, no less a Fury than an angel, sometimes rainbow, sometimes lightning-bolt, sometimes in tatters, sometimes in flames. The world is more often than not at odds with her: sometimes the ambience is vicious, sometimes simply obstructive. In "Hitler Spring," as Mussolini and Hitler appear together, Clizia must exist in the midst of "the sirens, the tolling bells / that call to the monsters in the twilight / of their Pandemonium." In "The Eel," Clizia is sister to those ambitious swimmers into unpromising landscapes:

> The eel, whiplash, twisting torch,
> love's arrow on earth, which only
> our gullies and dried-out, burned-out streams
> can lead to the paradises of fecundity;
> green spirit that hunts for life
> only there, where drought and desolation gnaw,
> a spark that says everything starts
> where everything is charred, stumps buried.

The eel's world, full of momentum, is the paradoxical one of inception in extinction. The mystery of such motion defies linearity, and consequently allies itself with those Christian paradoxes of the dying grain and the lost life saved, antithetical to the prudential and the providential alike, since foresight and backward glances have nothing to do with illumination, conversion, metamorphosis.

Wright's aim in translating Montale has been to be idiomatic, within his own idiom as well as within Montale's. Robert Lowell's "imitation" of "The Eel" is more fluent and more condensed:

> The eel, a whipstock, a Roman candle,
> love's arrow on earth, which only
> reaches the paradise of fecundity
> through our gullies and fiery, charred streams;
> a green spirit, potent only
> where desolation and arson burn;
> a spark that says everything
> begins where everything is clinker.

Wright attempts greater fidelity, at the cost of some loss of naturalness (and, I have been told, of accuracy). Surely both Lowell and Wright, with their Italianate "paradise of fecundity," are themselves bettered by John Frederick Nims, who substitutes "edens of fertility." Montale—compressed, allusive, oblique, full of echoing sound—is relatively untranslatable; his poems swell awkwardly as they take on English under anyone's hands, and his infinitely manipulable Italian syntax begins to hobble, hampered by stiff English clauses. Wright's translations, as he says, taught him things:

> I feel I did learn . . . how to move a line, how to move an image from one stage to the next. How to create imaginary bridges between images and stanzas and then to cross them, making them real, image to image, block to block.

These are not—though they may appear to be—idle concerns. If conclusions are not the way to get from A to B, if discursiveness itself is a false mode of consciousness, if free-association in a surrealist mode (to offer the opposite extreme) seems as irresponsible as the solemn demonstrations of the discursive, what form of presentation can recreate the iconic form of the mind's invention? It is really this question that Wright takes up in *China Trace* and subsequent poems. Chinese poetry, as it entered twentieth-century literature through Waley and Pound, came to stand for an alien but immensely attractive combination of sensation and ethics, both refined from crudeness by their mutual interpenetration. Suggestion and juxtaposition seemed adequate to replace statement, as Pound's petal-faces on the Métro-bough would claim. Wright's trace—*vestigium*—of China is in part a homage to Pound, but it also pursues, yet once more, the problem of the potential complacency of stanzas, especially of repeated stanzas. Who is to say that today's poem, like yesterday's, should have three stanzas? or one stanza of fourteen lines? And yet to insist that every form is a nonce form—good for only one use and then to be discarded—is to falsify what we know of recurrences and rhythms in the mind's life.

For *China Trace*, says Wright,

> I decided, rather arbitrarily, that no poem was going to be longer than twelve lines. In the first section I wanted to have an example of each length of poem from one to twelve lines but I *couldn't* write a four line poem. It was the hardest thing. They always came out sounding like a stanza that needed another stanza, or two more stanzas.

This problem is less superficial than it may seem. Aside from light verse, gnomes, or riddles, poems in English often have either two or three stanzas, chiefly because thought and feeling often proceed either by comparison or antithesis (resulting in two stanzas) or by statement, complication or amplification, and resolution (yielding three stanzas or divisions). Perception, unsupported by reflection, tends to seem truncated, unfinished, uncommented upon. That analytic restlessness which causes the second, and even the third, stanzas to be written is absent in the Chinese lyrics—compact, single, coherent—favored by Waley, and hovering over *China Trace*. But in spite of Wright's deliberate variety of form, a principle of repetition has its way in the design of the book: each of its halves is prefaced by the same citation from Calvino's *Invisible Cities*, envisaging the day when, knowing all the emblems, one becomes an emblem among emblems. This Yeatsian notion stands side by side with a Chinese epigraph, about the ambition "to travel in ether by becoming a void," or, failing that, to make use of a landscape to calm the spirit and delight the heart. In these epigraphs Wright reveals his own disembodied ethereality in coexistence with his pure visual sense.

The poems in *China Trace* are frosty, clear, descriptive, seemingly dispassionate, wintry even in spring. Even in April,

> [I] know I want less—
> Divested of everything,
> A downfall of light in the pine woods, motes in the rush,
> Gold leaf through the undergrowth, and come back
> As another name, water
> Pooled in the black leaves and holding me there, to be
> Released as a glint, as a flash, as a spark . . .

Throughout the volume Wright persistently imagines himself dead, dispersed, re-elemented into the natural order. ("And I am not talking about reincarnation at all. At all. At all.") In focusing on earth, in saying that "salvation doesn't exist except through the natural world," Wright approaches Cézanne's reverence for natural forms, geometrical and substantial ones alike. *China Trace* is meant to have "a journal-like, everyday quality," but its aphorisms resemble *pensées* more than diary jottings, just as its painters and poets (Morandi, Munch, Trakl, Nerval) represent the arrested, the composed, the final, rather than the provisional, the blurred, or the impressionistic. *China Trace* is in fact one long poem working its desolation by accretion; it suffers in excerpts. Its mourning echoes need to be heard like the complaint of doves—endless, reiterative, familiar, a twilight sound:

> There is no light for us at the end of the light.
> No one redeems the grass our shadows lie on.
> Each night, in its handful of sleep, the mimosa blooms.

Each night the future forgives.
Inside us, albino roots are starting to take hold.

The entire life-cycle—light, dark, blooming, sleep, guilt, forgiveness, pallor, growth—takes place each night, and no phase is inextricable from its opposite. In a linear view, by inexorable necessity, the "first minute, after noon, is night" (Donne's version). Wright, in opposition, urges in "Noon" the extension of life, altered, into our perception of death:

Extension that one day will ease me on
In my slow rise through the dark toward the sweet wrists of the rose.

The "me" here defined is a biological, not a spiritual, entity:

The dirt is a comforting, and the night drafts from the sucker vines.
The grass is a warm thing, and the hollyhocks, and the bright bursts from the weeds.
But best of all is the noon, and its tiny horns,
When shadows imprint, and start
their gradual exhalation of the past.

Wright is not innocent of influence; one recognizes Whitman, Pound, and Stevens, as well as Berryman and Williams, among his predecessors. On the other hand, he is obsessed with sound rather more than they were. Sound adds to his poems that conclusiveness which logic and causality confer on the poetry of others: "Mostly I like the sound of words. The sound, the feel, the paint, the color of them. I like to hear what they can do with each other. I'm still trying to do whatever I can with sound." The tendency of sound to despotism does not go unrecognized. "Sometimes I think [Hopkins'] sound patterns are so strong that you miss what he is saying." Wright's poems would be endangered if they were constructed on a more casual base, but he seems to work with infrastructures which are powerfully organized; the one for "Skins," in all its twenty items, is spelled out in the interview in *Field*. These sub-scaffoldings may in the long run drop away, but they keep the poems from being at the mercy of whims of sound.

If *China Trace* can be criticized for an unrelenting elegiac fixity, nonetheless its consistency gives it incremental power. Its deliberateness, its care in motion, its slow placing of stone on stone, dictate our reading it as construction rather than as speech. It is not surprising that as a model Wright has chosen Cézanne, that most architectural of painters:

> I like layers of paint on the canvas. I also know after I'm tired of lots of layers on the canvas, I'm going to want just one layer of paint and some of the canvas showing through . . . I've been trying to write poems . . . the way a painter might paint a picture . . . using stanzas in the way a painter will build up blocks of color, each disparate and often discrete, to make an overall representation that, taken in its pieces and slashes and dabs seems to have no coherence, but seen in its totality, when it's finished, turns out to be a very recognizable landscape, or whatever. Cézanne is someone who does this, in his later work, to an almost magical perfection.

Wright's eight-poem sequence, "Homage to Cézanne" builds up, line by line, a sense of the omnipresent dead. Wright's unit here is the line rather than the stanza, and the resulting poem sounds rather like the antiphonal chanting of psalms: one can imagine faint opposing choruses singing the melismatic lines:

The dead fall around us like rain.
They come down from the last clouds in the late night for the last time
And slip through the sod.
They lean uphill and face north.
Like grass,
They bend toward the sea, they break toward the setting sun.

Wright does this poetry of the declarative sentence very well, but many poets have learned this studied simplicity, even this poetry of the common noun. What is unusual in Wright is his oddity of imagery within the almost too-familiar conventions of quiet, depth, and profundity. As he layers on his elemental squares and blocks of color, the surprising shadow or interrupting boulder emerge as they might in a Cézanne:

High in the night sky the mirror is hauled up and unsheeted.
In it we twist like stars.

To Wright, death is as often ascent as burial; we become stars, like Romeo, after death, as often as roses. The modern unsheeted mirror reveals the Tennysonian twist of the constellations round the polestar, in this Shakespearean image of the posthumous—or so we might say if we look at Wright for his inheritances as well as for his originality.

Wright claims, like all poets, a return to original nature: the refusal to particularize his individual existence implies his utterance of universal experience, predicable of everyone. Everyone's dead are ubiquitous: we all "sit out on the earth and stretch our limbs, / Hoarding the little mounds of sorrow laid up in our hearts." On the other hand, the oracular mode sacrifices the conversational, and Wright evanesces under the touch in his wish to be dead (or saved), to enlarge the one inch of snowy rectitude in his living heart into the infinite ice of the tomb. In "Virginia Reel" he stands among family graves, in "the dirt their lives were made of, the dirt the world is, / Immeasurable emptiness of all things," and sees himself as a "bright bud on the branch of nothing's tree." A hand out of the air, like one of Montale's spirit-talons from an angel, touches his shoulder, and

I want to fall to my knees, and keep on falling, here,
Laid down by the articles that bear my names,
The limestone and marble and locust wood.

The hunger for the purity of the dead grows, in these poems, almost to a lust. So far, as a poem quoting Dickinson's gravestone says, he has been "Called Back" by the bird songs and flowers of the world; but the ice-edged and starless cloak of night outshines his bougainvillea and apple blossoms. The eternal and elemental world is largely unrelieved, in *China Trace* and after, by the local, the social, the temporary, the accidental, the contingent. Some very good poetry has incorporated riotous, and occasionally ungovernable, irruptions of particularity; the "purer" voice of finely ascetic lyric has a genuine transmitter in Wright. His synoptic and panoramic vision, radiating out from a compositional center to a filled canvas, opposes itself to the anthropocentric, and consequently autobiographical or narrative, impetus of lyrics with a linear base. If there is nowhere to go but up from making the unsupported line your unit, the dead your measure of verity, and the blank canvas meticulously layered with single cubes of color your creative metaphor, Wright's poetry is bound to change. As it stands, it is engaged in a refutation of the seductions of logic, of religion, and of social roles. By its visionary language it assumes the priority of insight, solitude, and abstraction, while remaining beset by a mysterious loss of something that can be absorbed and reconstituted only in death.

The spiritual yearning in Wright is nowhere regarded, as it sometimes is in Montale, by a certain faith in an absolute—damaged no doubt, elusive surely, disagreeable often, but always unquestioned and recoverable. The difference in part may be historical. Montale, who fought in World War I and saw the shambles of post-war Italy give rise to Mussolini, faced pressing social evils that demanded a choice of sides; he refused to join the Fascist party and lost his job in consequence. Virtue made visible by its denunciation of the evils of Pandemonium can appear emblematic, allegorical, winged, embattled. Without a historical convulsion, tones of poetry subside into perplexity, sadness, elegy. Wright's debt to Montale, attested to by original poems as well as by these early translations, is more than stylistic: the disciple exhibits that desire and hopelessness we associate with Montale at his most characteristic. Montale's description (in *Auto da Fé*, 1952) of the solitude of the artist can stand as a program for Wright:

> Man, insofar as he is an individual being, an empirical individual, is fatally alone. Social life is an addition, an aggregate, not a unity of individuals. The man who communicates is the transcendent "I" who is hidden in us and who recognizes himself in others. But the transcendent "I" is a lamp which lights up only the briefest strip of space before us, a light that bears us toward a condition which is not individual and consequently not human . . . The attempt to fix the ephemeral, to make the phenomenon non-phenomenal, the attempt to make the individual "I" articulate, as he is not by definition, the revolt, in brief, against the human condition (a revolt dictated by an impassioned *amor vitae*) is at the base of the artistic and philosophic pursuits of our era.

Wright's verse is the poetry of the transcendent "I" in revolt against the too easily articulate "I" of social engagement and social roles. Whether one "I" can address his word to other, hidden "I's" across the abyss of daily life without using the personal, transient, and social language of that life is the question Wright poses. Remembering Montale's eel venturing into the rocks and gullies of a scorched earth, I would hope to see in Wright's future poetry a more vivid sense of the social and familial landscape in which the soul struggles. "Life itself," Montale wrote, "seems like a monstrous work of art forever being destroyed and forever renewed." While Montale foresaw a popular art—utilitarian and almost playful—for the masses, he also predicted (and incarnated) a "true and proper art, not very different from the art of the past, and not easily reduced to cliché." The creators of this art—and for Montale, who translated Eliot, Eliot would be a case in point—though they may seem hermetic, isolated, and inaccessible, are not really such:

> It is these great isolated personalities who give a meaning to an era, and their isolation is more illusory than real . . . In this sense, only the isolated speak, only the isolated communicate; the rest—the mass-communication men—repeat, give off echoes, vulgarize the poets' words.

In making Montale better known, Wright makes his own aims better understood, and his remote and severe writing more accessible.

JAMES WRIGHT

1927–1980

James Arlington Wright was born on December 13, 1927, in Martins Ferry, Ohio. He was educated at Kenyon College (B.A. 1952) and the University of Washington (M.A. 1954, Ph.D. 1959). He was married twice, the second time to Edith Anne Runk; they had two children from a previous marriage. He taught at the University of Minnesota from 1957 to 1964, at Macalester College from 1963 to 1965, and at Hunter College from 1966 to 1980.

Wright was an experimental poet who was rarely satisfied with repeating past successes. His first two books, *The Green Wall* (1957) and *Saint Judas* (1959), are largely formal in structure and language, and are suffused with pain, human suffering, and loss, themes that would remain primary concerns throughout Wright's career. *The Branch Will Not Break* (1963) is much looser in form, and heavily dependent upon direct language and stark imagery. The poems focus upon human emotion and experience, and mark a shift in Wright's poetry from the objective to the subjective. Later poems continue that shift, and are increasingly despairing and hopeless. *Shall We Gather at the River* (1968) is particularly dark, and received some criticism for unevenness of execution. Subsequent volumes (notably *Two Citizens*, 1973; *To a Blossoming Pear Tree*, 1977; *This Journey*, 1982) combine an increasing looseness of structure with an occasional return to formal rhyme and meter; while suffering and pain surface again as themes, the hopelessness has largely been replaced by thoughtful contemplation. Many critics find his late poetry the most accomplished. Throughout his career Wright was noted for his lucid imagery; he was associated for a time with such "deep image" poets as Louis Simpson, Robert Bly, and William Stafford. His *Collected Poems* (1971) won the Pulitzer Prize. He died on March 25, 1980.

GEORGE S. LENSING AND RONALD MORAN
From "James Wright"
Four Poets and the Emotive Imagination
1976, pp. 87–106

Both James Wright and Louis Simpson markedly alter their methods of composition at the end of the 1950s and beginning of the 1960s. To understand the extent to which these changes represent new departures, it is necessary to pay attention to the earlier poems, which comprise two fine canons written almost within the conventions of rhyme, meter, and stanza divisions.

In the prefatory remarks to his first volume, *The Green Wall* (1957), a Yale Series of Younger Poets selection, James Wright comments that he wanted to emulate the manner of Edwin Arlington Robinson and Robert Frost, and further, that he "wanted to make the poems say something humanly important instead of just showing off with language." To a limited extent, these poems suggest Frost's manner of calm, direct statement; but more important, the poems in *The Green Wall* and to a greater extent those in his second volume, *Saint Judas* (1959), do indeed have sources both in subject matter and in method in the work of Robinson. Although the "showing off with language" that Wright eschews is ironically a charge leveled at *The Green Wall* in Bly's "The Work of James Wright," Ralph J. Mills, Jr., in a 1964 essay first published in the *Chicago Review*, describes the success Wright has had in attaining the objectives he shares with Frost and Robinson:

> In that initial book, and in his second one, *Saint Judas* (1959), the poet sets himself to this task through poems that are meditations on his own experience, observations of other lives, dramatic situations; his speech is direct, his sympathy and judgment are undisguised. The world called up by his imagination in poetry is unmistakably the one we know, in which people are born, endure pain, discover love, encounter success or defeat in their efforts, and go down to death. It is not a symbolic world or a self-contained poetic cosmos, but a reality composed of men and women, of animals and birds, of stones, and trees, and is usually located in the American Midwest, in Ohio and Minnesota where Wright has spent so much time.[1]

Certainly the subject of death—except for *The Branch Will Not Break* (1963), Wright's most important volume—has been a constant one for Wright; in fact, one is correct in saying that of all American poets (Edgar Lee Masters excepted), past or present, there is no one obsessed with death to the degree evident in the poetry of Wright. Frankly, there are too many poems that in one way or another treat death to permit individual discussion. It will suffice to provide a selective listing of titles taken from *The Green Wall* alone: "On the Skeleton of a Hound," "Three Steps to the Graveyard," "Father," "Elegy in a Firelit Room," "Arrangements with Earth for Three Dead Friends," "A Poem about George Doty in the Death House," "To a Fugitive," "A Gesture by a Lady with an Assumed Name," "The Angel," and "The Assignation."

Several of these poems merit brief attention for the death motif; others will be discussed later in different contexts. "Three Steps to the Graveyard" is about the speaker's father and is structured metaphorically, each stanza concerning different perspectives distanced by time and seasonal change. "Father" is a moving, surrealistic treatment of the relationship of a father and son. The speaker, the son, is talking as if he were dead in "paradise," as he tells us in the first line of the poem. "Father" ends simply, but the emotion conveyed is genuine: "He drew me from the boat. I was asleep. / And we went home together." Both "The Angel" and "The Assignation" employ the same technique as that of "Father": the speaker is a ghost who returns to earth, in each instance to see what happened after the speaker's death. And both poems work with the subject of love and the theme of betrayal.

With *The Branch Will Not Break* and *Two Citizens* (1973) as exceptions, Wright's poetry deals extensively with characters on the fringe or outside of what most people define as "normal" society. Prostitutes, drunkards, bums, and criminals abound in his poetry, as well as what we might call ordinary human beings who are lonely and alienated in large measure from the rest of society. As Stephen Stepanchev says in *American Poetry since 1945*: "[In *The Green Wall*] he writes about people, about simple, desperate, unhappy people like those who populate the poems of Edwin Arlington Robinson and Robert Frost."[2] And Mills notices that Wright's characters' actions "have transgressed the conventions of the community" and, as a result, they "are converted into scapegoats of society." Mills comments further: "With other modern poets as dissimilar as E. E. Cummings and Stanley Kunitz, Wright takes the side of the alienated individual, the hunted and persecuted, and opposes the impersonal majority or the monolithic state."[3]

In 1952/53, Wright had a Fulbright grant to study in Vienna. Crunk[4] writes that during this time the poet was introduced to the poetry of Georg Trakl, an introduction that, in some measure, was instrumental in prompting Wright's later abandonment of the conventions in favor of a looser, more colloquially based style that relied on the efficacy of images and on the exciting use of tropes. At any rate, Crunk comments that when Wright compared the poems he had been writing to those by Trakl, "he came to the conclusion that his own work was not actually poetry; it had not helped anyone else to solitude, and had not helped him toward solitude."[5] Wright's own concern with poetry's "helping" is not unlike that expressed by Robinson in two letters dated respectively May 13, 1896, and February 3, 1897, to Harry de Forest Smith. Here are the pertinent excerpts:

> If printed lines are good for anything, they are bound to be picked up some time; and then, if some poor devil of a man or woman feels any better or any stronger for anything that I have said, I shall have no fault to find with the scheme or anything in it.
>
> I also make free to say that many of my verses [were] written with a conscious hope that they might make some despairing devil a little stronger and a little better satisfied with things—not as they are, but as they are to be.[6]

Indeed, Wright may well have been drawn to his primary character types by those Robinson chose, since his admiration for the older poet is great and his imitation of Robinson's method is apparent in certain of his poems, particularly those from *Saint Judas*.

The concluding lines to "The Fishermen," a poem in which the speaker, accompanied by a friend, is walking along a seacoast, describe effectively the physical characteristics and the psychic conditions of the old fishermen, for whom the speaker has understanding and compassion, two qualities everywhere apparent in the poetry of Robinson:

Saurian faces still as layered lime,
The nostrils ferned in smoke behind their pipes,
The eyes resting in whorls like shells on driftwood,
The hands relaxing, letting out the ropes;
And they, whispering together,
The beaten age, the dead, the blood gone dumb.

Although the fishermen are not excluded, as such, from conventional society, other characters in *The Green Wall* for whom Wright expresses unabashed sympathy are clearly beyond the definitive boundaries: George Doty, the rapist and murderer, in "A Poem about George Doty in the Death House"; the protagonist identified as Maguire in "To a Fugitive"; the lesbian who had an affair with a married woman and who was scorned by her neighbors in "Sappho"; and the prostitutes in "A Gesture by a Lady with an Assumed Name" and in "Morning Hymn to a Dark Girl."

The last two poems belong in a loosely defined sequence of love poems; both will be discussed later in this chapter: "Morning Hymn to a Dark Girl," an excellent poem, as illustrative of Wright's use of the richly rhetorical; and "Sappho" as a pre-Emotive Imagination poem. The other poems in the love sequence—"Eleutheria," "Autumnal," "The Shadow and the Real," "Witches Waken the Natural World in Spring," and "The Quail"—are descriptive lyrics in which the women are treated in images of the natural world. One senses that the women in these poems are "inserted" in order to permit the poet to write descriptively about nature. These women are only vaguely realized; the dramatic action seems to reside in the descriptive element. The closing stanza of "Witches Waken the Natural World in Spring" documents this vagueness and the image-creating nature of the poem:

Except that spring was coming on
Or might have come already while
We lay beside a smooth-veined stone;
Except an owl sang half a mile
Away; except a starling's feather
Softened my face beside a root:
But how should I remember whether
She was the one who spoke, or not?

"The Quail," another in which the woman does not possess a distinct character but rather is blended into the natural setting, does not do much more than celebrate one aspect of a relationship in a rather superficial manner, though the poem is technically impressive.

Indeed, the poems in *The Green Wall* represent high technical achievement, and Wright demonstrates more than competence in a variety of meters, in complex rhyme and near-rhyme patterns, and in stanzas in which he deftly manipulates both length and sense. Most of the poems in the volume do adhere rather strictly to the technical conventions, though Wright is not bound to them so strictly that he compromises the integrity of the poem as poem. "The Seasonless," the second poem in the book, is typical of an early Wright lyric, consisting of four stanzas of ten iambic tetrameter lines rhymed somewhat irregularly but essentially following an *a b a b c d e e c d* pattern. Concerned with the correspondence of winter to the sense of emptiness a man experiences, "The Seasonless" is rhythmically insistent, as are a number of Wright's early lyrics. He achieves this insistence through a fine command of metrics and an equally fine use of parallel structure, the latter evident in the following excerpts taken from the first and second stanzas:

The blistered trellis seems to move
The memory toward root and rose,
The empty fountain fills the air
With spray that spangled women's hair.
. . .
How painlessly a man recalls
The stain of green on crooked walls,
The summer never known before,
The garden heaped to bloom and fade.

Insistent rhythms gained through parallel structure in the opening lines of "A Girl in a Window"—a poem about the pleasure her outlined figure at twilight provides for men walking by—establish the sensuous force the poem intends:

Now she will lean away to fold
The window blind and curtain back,
The yellow arms, the hips of gold,
The supple outline fading black,
Bosom availing nothing now,
And rounded shadow of long thighs.

Crunk objects to Wright's "elaborate syntax" and to what he labels Wright's "mushiness," the product of his commitments to the conventions of syntax, in *The Green Wall* and to a lesser extent in *Saint Judas*. These impede, according to Crunk, the "two energies [that] have been trying to get free in James Wright's work: the first is natural American speech, the second images." He continues: "What prevented the natural speech [of Wright in *The Green Wall*] from coming free was a nest of syntax in which the speech became hopelessly entangled." Wright, he concludes, "has had a heavy struggle with syntax."[7] Certainly there are poems in *The Green Wall* in which Wright is enamored of the lushly rhetorical, but this alone is not what Crunk finds objectionable: "Despite all the voices to the contrary, the iambic meter is not suited to the English language. The language may fall naturally into tum de tum, as conservatives repeat at every beaufest, but in order to maintain iambic meter, an elaborate syntax is necessary. It is the elaborate syntax which is unnatural in English."[8]

"Morning Hymn to a Dark Girl" contains as many instances of "elaborate syntax" and "mushiness" as any other poem in *The Green Wall;* yet in part because of its very lushness, which is perfectly appropriate to the subject, this lyric to a black prostitute named Betty is a remarkably successful poem. In iambic pentameter and structured by a series of contrasts, the poem begins by the speaker's negative observations of the setting in which he finds himself:

Summoned to desolation by the dawn,
I climbed the bridge over the water, see
The Negro mount the driver's cabin and wave
Goodbye to the glum cop across the canal,
Goodbye to the flat face and empty eyes
Made human one more time. That uniform
Shivers and dulls against the pier, is stone.

At dawn the city is a dull, aseptic sight, with buses drifting over the bridge, which is ironically called the "upper world" in contrast to the lower, archetypal world symbolized in the dream world of Africa. "Over the lake," the speaker continues, "The windows of the rich waken and yawn"; this is a particularly apt personification.

After the speaker concludes his descriptive treatment of the pale town and its morning inhabitants, he turns his attention to Betty, whom he celebrates in the seventeenth line of this forty-four-line poem:

I celebrate you, Betty, flank and breast
Rich to the yellow silk of bed and floors;
Now half awake, your body blossoming trees;
One arm beneath your neck, your legs uprisen,
You blow dark thighs back, back into the dark.

The "dark" to which the speaker alludes is Betty's dream world, which is replete with images of her ancestry in the jungles of Africa, the dark continent that in her mind she has never left and that in her dream takes on the proportions of a mythic paradise. The pale, lifeless world of day in the American city is thus contrasted unfavorably with the lush land of her background, which in a dream allows her to escape from the "snickers" in the whorehouse where she works.

The language employed in describing Betty's dream world is rightly lush and elaborate, sensuously recreating the rich primitive life inherent in Betty, who must necessarily sleep during the daytime. The images, rhythms, and tone of these lines help to establish the clear superiority of Betty's imagined life over the real lives most of us lead. Though the following quotation is lengthy, it illustrates the exceptional quality of Wright's "elaborate syntax" properly used:

> Your shivering ankles skate the scented air;
> Betty, burgeoning your golden skin, you poise
> Tracing gazelles and tigers on your breasts,
> Deep in the jungle of your bed you drowse;
> Fine muscles of the rippling panthers move
> And snuggle at your calves; under your arms
> Mangoes and melons yearn; and glittering slowly,
> Quick parakeets trill in your heavy trees,
> O everywhere, Betty, between your boughs.
>
> Pity the rising dead who fear the dark.
> Soft Betty, locked from snickers in a dark
> Brothel, dream on; scatter the yellow corn
> Into the wilderness, and sleep all day.
> For the leopards leap into the open grass,
> Bananas, lemons fling air, fling odor, fall.
> And, gracing darkly the dark light, you flow
> Out of the grove to laugh at dreamy boys,
> You greet the river with a song so low
> No lover on a boat can hear, you slide
> Silkily to the water; where you rinse
> Your fluted body, fearless; though alive
> Orangutans sway from the leaves and gaze,
> Crocodiles doze along the oozy shore.

"Morning Hymn to a Dark Girl" proceeds by tropes, one of which is personification. In fact, Wright's use of personification has never been notably absent from his work, though its frequency increases dramatically in his poems of the Emotive Imagination in *The Branch Will Not Break*. Since Bly, Wright, Stafford, and to a lesser degree Simpson work regularly with personification, it is not surprising that the poems of the Emotive Imagination are highly metaphorical, because personifications are tropes and thus metaphoric in nature. Several examples from "Eleutheria" suffice to demonstrate Wright's use of the personification method early in his career.

> The pale cloud walking home to winter. . . .
>
> The stripping twilight plundered trees of boughs. . . .
>
> The dark began to climb the empty hill. . . .
>
> She glides lightly; the pale year follows her. . . .
>
> The moments ride away. . . .

Of the poems included in *The Green Wall*, "Sappho" is the closest in technique to the later Wright poems in the manner of the Emotive Imagination. Despite the rhythmic insistence in certain passages, the language is more colloquial than other poems in the collection, the line lengths are irregular at times, and, most important, the poem relies on metaphor more than others in *The Green Wall*. For example, the woman with whom the lesbian-speaker is having an affair is referred to as both a "blue blossom" and an apple; and the speaker at one point states directly, "Love is a cliff." Toward the end of "Sappho," the speaker discusses her situation of martyrdom and exclusion from society through the metaphoric use of fire imagery:

> I am given to burn on the dark fire they make
> With their sly voices.
>
> But I have burned already down to bone.
> There is a fire that burns beyond the names
> Of sludge and filth of which this world is made.
> Agony sears the dark flesh of the body,
> And lifts me higher than the smoke, to rise
> Above the earth, above the sacrifice;
> Until my soul flares outward like a blue
> Blossom of gas fire dancing in mid-air:
> Free of the body's work of twisted iron.

There are some, but not many, indications in the poems of *Saint Judas*, published two years after *The Green Wall*, that Wright's poetry is moving in the direction of the Emotive Imagination. Several poems—notably "All the Beautiful are Blameless," "The Revelation," "A Prayer in My Sickness," and perhaps "At the Executed Murderer's Grave"—suggest that the poet's work is loosening up somewhat. Even though "All the Beautiful Are Blameless," in which the speaker meditates on the drowning of a woman, contains some occasional rhyming, its language is in part colloquial and conversational as these lines illustrate: "Only another drunk would say she heard / A natural voice / Luring the flesh across the water." In this poem the reader senses Wright's need for some semblance of external forms on which to fix the poem and his conflicting desire to break into a more open manner. Crunk argues that in this volume the "voices are stronger, though the syntax is often still literary," by which he means that Wright's commitment to meter impedes his natural voice from coming out freely as it does in *The Branch Will Not Break*. Crunk observes, and rightly so, that as "he writes more, Wright's poems depend less and less and less on elaborate syntax to give the illusion of form, and as the syntax retreats, hearable voices come forward."[9]

The concluding stanza of "The Revelation," an essentially iambic tetrameter, rhymed, and stanzaic poem about his father, reveals an interesting combination of formal elements and the imaginative use of metaphor:

> And weeping in the nakedness
> Of moonlight and of agony,
> His blue eyes lost their barrenness
> And bore a blossom out to me.
> And as I ran to give it back,
> The apple branches, dripping black,
> Trembled across the lunar air
> And dropped white petals on his hair.

Even more emotive is "A Prayer in My Sickness," a ten-line poem that, apart from the sameness of line length, could easily have been extracted from *The Branch Will Not Break*. Perhaps Wright felt that the speaker's delirium provided justification for the intense subjectivity of the poem. In any event, the poem is significant enough as a forerunner of the later poems to permit its reproduction here:

> You hear the long roll of the plunging ground,
> The whistle of stones, the quail's cry in the grass.
> I stammer like a bird, I rasp like stone,
> I mutter, with gray hands upon my face.
> The earth blurs, beyond me, into dark.
> Spinning in such bewildered sleep, I need
> To know you, whirring above me, when I wake.
> Come down, come down. I lie afraid.

I have lain alien in my self so long,
How can I understand love's angry tongue?

More so than in *The Green Wall* and therefore an indication that Wright's poetry, if not changing as such, is preparing to change, is his increased use of the personification method in *Saint Judas*. Three poems—"Sparrows in a Hillside Drift," "Dog in a Cornfield," and "The Cold Divinities"—employ at least two personifications each, and the personifications, unlike those in *The Green Wall*, are grounded firmly in the natural world, to which the following from "Dog in a Cornfield" testify: "The lazy maples wailed beyond the crust / Of earth and artificial man. / Here lay one death the autumn understands."

Yet, despite these excursions away from the manner characterizing the poems of *The Green Wall*, most of the selections in *Saint Judas* owe allegiance to prosodic conventions. "Complaint," the opening poem of the collection, is written in heroic couplets, and "Saint Judas," the closing one, is a qualified Italian sonnet. In between, Wright remains with his most comfortable thematic considerations, such as a preoccupation with death and with those alienated in contemporary society: "*Saint Judas* continues most of the interests of Wright's first book, but a more penetrating insight into the poet's own person is apparent in many of these poems. The injurious and tragic aspects of existence are examined freely, and the quality of Wright's poetic speech becomes even more direct and terse as he attempts relentlessly to locate and state the human truths that matter to him."[10] And Crunk observes that in the poems of *Saint Judas* "one can see his determination to keep the modest syntax of Robinson, at least, and still bring in the living voice."[11]

Nearly half the poems in the volume deal with the subject of death in one way or another. Perhaps the Robinson influence is in part responsible for Wright's obsessive concern with the subject. Despite Wright's own comments concerning Robinson in his prefatory statement to *The Green Wall*, the Robinson manner of writing—unadorned, lean, spare poems in which characterization is infinitely more important than description—is more evident in *Saint Judas* than in the initial book. "Paul," for example, owes a debt to Robinson's "The House on the Hill" for some of the phraseology, while the rhythms and situation of the poem bear general resemblances to those of Robinson. "Old Man Drunk" works with a sad, lonely man like Robinson's Eben Flood and Bewick Finzer, and the use of the word *futile* at the close of the poem seems to be borrowed from the conclusion of "Bewick Finzer":

Face by face
He grins to entertain, he fills my glass,
Cold to the gestures of my vague *alas*,
Gay as a futile god who cannot die
Till daylight, when the barkeep says goodbye.
("Old Man Drunk")

He comes unfailing for the loan
We give and then forget;
He comes, and probably for years
Will he be coming yet,—
Familiar as an old mistake,
And futile as regret.
("Bewick Finzer")

"The Refusal," in its direct, unadorned narrative set at a funeral and told from the collective "we" point of view, is similar in situation to any number of Robinson poems in which, as the case is in "The Refusal," the individual or individuals are condemned by others for not conforming to a specific behavioral pattern.

Saint Judas continues the studies of the outcasts and lonely begun in *The Green Wall*. For example, "A Note Left in Jimmy Leonard's Shack" concerns two old bums. But his poems of this ilk that deserve the most attention are those dealing with criminals. Crunk sees Wright in *Saint Judas* as possessed of two convictions: one, an awareness "that he is in some sense a criminal," and the other, "that he is somehow a man of goodwill."[12] It is the former that engages our interest here, as does a remark Crunk makes in the early portion of his essay: "[Wright] has more respect for those who break laws than those who keep them."[13] There are three poems in the collection that focus on the criminal: "Saint Judas," the title poem, "American Twilights, 1957," dedicated to Caryl Chessman, and "At the Executed Murderer's Grave." In these poems, as Mills notes, Wright is obsessed with "themes of guilt and innocence, justice and punishment, moral right and hypocrisy."[14]

"At the Executed Murderer's Grave" is divided into seven parts and, according to both Mills and Friedman, anticipates the manner Wright adopts in *The Branch Will Not Break*; they cite the subjectivity of the poem, the colloquial language and rhythms, the directness, and the regionalism as evidence.[15] Granting the above—the poem begins, "My name is James A. Wright, and I was born / Twenty-five miles from this infected grave, / In Martins Ferry, Ohio."—we are not convinced that the poem evidences enough of the qualities of the later poems to say unreservedly that it is a forerunner of the Emotive Imagination. Rather, the poem is more of a subjective confession of feelings Wright owns, and, at the same time, a self-indictment: He admits that he lies, that he croons his "tears at fifty cents per line," that he pities not the dead but the dying, that he pities himself, that he is an "unskilled criminal," and that he does not want to die.

In a 1962 anthology of British and American literature designed as a composition reader, James Wright is represented by two poems, one of which is "To the Ghost of a Kite," a poem that Wright has never published in any of his collections. Yet the poem is a brilliant accomplishment and represents one of his finest poems written strictly within the conventions. "To the Ghost of a Kite" consists of four stanzas of eight iambic pentameter lines rhymed *a b b a c d c d*. Traditional as the form of the poem assuredly is, the internal structuring is highly imaginative in the use of metaphor and symbol. The anthology, *Literature for Writing*, gives the poem's first publication as 1957, which means that "To the Ghost of a Kite" was available for publication in any of Wright's volumes. Several years ago the poet was asked why this poem, which we and other colleagues admire greatly, was not reprinted in any of his volumes. Surprised that the poem was held in such repute, Wright replied, "I didn't think it was any good," and said that he would consider including it in *Collected Poems*, which was then in the making. To the volume's loss, he did not. Perhaps he held to his original estimation; perhaps the personal nature of the subject was too painful; perhaps echoes of "To the Ghost of a Kite" in his other already published poems were too clear. (There are similarities of phraseology and technique between the poem and "The Seasonless" and "The Horse" from *The Green Wall*, and "The Assignation" and "Evening" from *Saint Judas*.) Whatever his reasons, we are nonetheless convinced that "To the Ghost of a Kite" deserves serious attention and thus reproduce it below:

Winter has wrecked the legend of your wings
And thrown you down beside the cold garage.
The silken gold that caught the air at large
Wrinkles and fades among some rusted springs.
There was a wind that sang below your breast,

Astonished air blown seaward on your breath.
That summer sound, lifted away and lost,
Mutters around the corners of the earth.

The season wrecks the legend of my child
And blows his image of the summer down.
He found the relic of your feathers blown
To common birds, depleted and defiled.
He was the child who ran below your flight,
The dark hair flopping leaf-like over eyes,
Who saw you leave your ballast for the light
And shouted your escape across the skies.

Back to the winter like a root he goes
To nurture some great blossoms of your fire,
To bring the year back and the pure desire
For silken wings that never touch the grass.
Winter has wrecked the legend of all wings.
The sparrows scatter as I reach to hold
One remnant of those proud, uncommon things:
A warping stick turned yellow in the cold.

Ghost of a dragon, tell me how to charm
The spirit back to fill the body now.
You vanished to the wind one year ago
And left a broken string across my arm.
Tell me the rune, the ballad, or the song
To fling a rag upon a wand and build
Some high magnificence to last as long
As the clear vision of the summer child.

The speaker is a father who has lost his son; the title, imagery, and context suggest that the son died. The setting is delineated in the first two lines; the speaker sees the remnants of a kite next to a garage. This leads him to remember the soaring of a kite in summer, establishing early the contrast of winter to summer, the former standing for despair, loss, and death, and the latter for fullness of life, exhilaration, and joy. In addition, the opening stanza establishes the downward movement in imagery that is carried through the third stanza. The positive and exultant lines of the first stanza ("The silken gold that caught the air at large" and "There was a wind that sang below your breast, / Astonished air blown seaward on your breath") are tonally qualified by the negative lines immediately following in which loss and destruction are set forth. The use of the words *breast* and *breath* appear to serve as personification; but the speaker does use the kite throughout the poem on two elemental levels—as a manmade device and as a bird of the hawk family, a powerful predator. He also uses the kite and its ghost on several metaphoric levels, as well, as the poem progresses. Clearly, "To the Ghost of a Kite" is rich in what John Crowe Ransom calls "texture." The word *legend* in the first line, which is repeated in lines nine and twenty-one, introduces the concept of ritual on which the concluding stanza is predicated. The opening stanza, then, indicates the loss and suggests death, though the reader is unaware of the latter at this point in the poem.

The son is introduced in the opening line of the second stanza where the speaker recounts his son's delight in kite flying in the summer and his son's excitement as the kite string snapped. In addition, the fusion of kite as a device representative of adventure and kite as uncommon bird occurs in lines eleven and twelve. Just as death has wrecked the legend of the kite, so too has death ("The season") wrecked the legend of his child to the speaker-father, the first concrete indication in the poem that the boy died. The use of the words *image* and *relic* prepare us for the ritual ending of the poem.

Part of the thematic statement of the poem is contained in the opening four lines of the third stanza. Now winter assumes a different symbolic role: not death, but the state of dormancy necessary for rebirth. In this case, the speaker is not asking, nor does he ever ask in the poem, that the impossible be done, that his son be returned to life. Instead, he acknowledges that it is now time for him to bury deep in his mind the thoughts and memories he holds of his son so that there they may act as roots to provide some future growth for the father, in this instance to provide the father with the same fullness of life he experienced while his son was alive: "To bring the year back and the pure desire / For silken wings that never touch the grass." Thus the kite serves here the symbolic function of summer—fullness of life. But this act of consciously forgetting in the hope that renewal will occur is no easy task, as the father indicates when the reality of death strikes him: "Winter has wrecked the legend of all wings." Sparrows, the common birds contrasted to the hawk, scatter as the speaker-father reaches "to hold / One remnant of those proud, uncommon things," which, in the reality of winter's starkness, is only "A warping stick turned yellow in the cold." The stanza then ends with his having gone from the dream of hope to the desolation death exacts.

The final stanza is in the form of an invocation to the ghost of a kite, which was emblazoned with a dragon, to supply the spirit with something to replace the emptiness. The invocation itself, coupled with words like *rune* and *wand*, suggests some form of ancient magic, some ritualistic pattern that has existed since man first knew the need for spiritual replenishment. Interestingly, "Tell me the rune, the ballad, or the song" is, in fact, an historical survey of lyric poetry. The word *rune* has several meanings applicable to poetry: (1) rhymes or poetry in general; (2) Old Norse poetic lore; and (3) any poem that is mystic in nature. *Ballad* is self-explanatory, and *song*, of course, refers to a lyric poem. Now the main thematic thrust of "To the Ghost of a Kite" gains a clear perspective: the speaker-father wants to write a poem ("Some high magnificence") that not only will help to mitigate the loss he feels but will achieve a form of immortality and therefore will not be subject to death. It will be an immortality similar to "the clear vision of the summer child." In the poem proper, the speaker needs some form of magic to assist in the writing of the poem ("To fling a rag upon a wand"); this magic describes, as well, the construction of a kite, the kite then standing symbolically for "Some high magnificence." "To the Ghost of a Kite" is just that poem.

James Wright has built a remarkable poem of emotional depth, metaphoric and symbolic complexity and subtlety, and of structural and technical excellence. The death of a child is an emotional event that can be unparalleled in the life of a parent. Yet in this poem Wright's speaker-father does not use emotionally charged diction to convey his feelings; he lets metaphor, symbol, and the right rhythms carry the weight of the subject and attitude. To those like Crunk who fault Wright for his reliance on iambic pentameter, which Crunk believes needs "elaborate syntax" to sustain it and which necessarily hampers the natural voice, we offer "To the Ghost of a Kite" as self-sufficient evidence to the contrary. The poem is also exemplary of Wright's early work. It treats the subject of death; its protagonist is lonely and alienated (from himself); and it works exclusively within the conventions of rhyme, meter, and stanzas.

Notes

1. Ralph J. Mills, Jr., *Contemporary American Poetry* (New York: Random House, 1965), 198.
2. Stephen Stepanchev, *American Poetry since 1945* (New York: Harper & Row, 1965), 182.
3. Mills, *Contemporary American Poetry*, 200–201.

4. A pseudonym used by the poet Robert Bly.
5. Crunk, "The Work of James Wright," *Sixties*, IV (Fall, 1960), 59.
6. Denham Sutcliffe (ed.), *Untriangulated Stars: Letters of Edwin Arlington Robinson to Harry de Forest Smith 1890–1905* (Cambridge, Mass: Harvard University Press, 1947), 247 and 273.
7. Crunk, "The Works of James Wright," 70–72.
8. Ibid., 72.
9. Ibid., 70–71.
10. Mills, *Contemporary American Poetry*, 204.
11. Crunk, "The Work of James Wright," 72.
12. Ibid., 57.
13. Ibid., 54.
14. Mills, *Contemporary American Poetry*, 206.
15. Ibid., 208; and Norman Friedman, "The Wesleyan Poets—III," *Chicago Review*, XIX (1967), 70.

STEPHEN YENSER
"Open Secrets" (1978)
The Pure Clear Word: Essays on the Poetry of James Wright
ed. Dave Smith
1982, pp. 136–58

"It is a ridiculous demand which England and America make, that you shall speak so that they can understand you. Neither men nor toadstools grow so. . . . I fear chiefly lest my expression may not be *extravagant* enough, may not wander far enough beyond the narrow limits of my daily experience, so as to be adequate to the truth of which I have been convinced." (Thoreau, *Walden*)

I

At least since *The Branch Will Not Break* [1963] James Wright's poetry has been pulled in two directions—or in one uncertain direction by two sometimes opposing wishes. We might as well make these wishes horses, especially since, as he reaffirms in *Moments of the Italian Summer*, Wright considers horses perhaps "the most beautiful of God's creatures." One of them we could call David, after Robert Bly's swaybacked palomino who has appeared in several of Wright's poems. He is the older, the more reliable, the more steadily paced of the two—the likelier wheelhorse. He wants to keep the vehicle, if not in the ruts, at least on the road and headed toward home. On the other side there is Dewfall, also known as Nightrise and Basilica, all three of whose names, according to a riddling poem in *To a Blossoming Pear Tree*, were stolen by Napoleon from Spanish horses and later given to some heavenly swans. She is high-spirited and erratic. It is she who always sees something fascinating off to the side of the road and takes Wright out of his way. Sometimes she gets the bit between her teeth and tears off, and then neither David nor the driver can do much but go along until she winds herself.

Every writer knows some version of the situation, the tension between the impulses to give rein to "the imagination, that mysterious and frightening thing," as Wright has called it in an interview, and to keep the work in hand, moving constantly to some end that will seem appointed.[1] Wright sets them in historical perspective in "The Pretty Redhead," from the French of Apollinaire, where, addressing himself to the "long quarrel between tradition and imagination / Between order and adventure," he sides with adventure:

You whose mouth is made in the image of God's
  mouth
Mouth which is order itself
Judge kindly when you compare us
With those who were the very perfection of order
We who are seeking everywhere for adventure.[2]

The poem overlooks in the interest of polemic the fact that the two impulses are complexly interdependent for the individual poet, but its insistence on the "quarrel" suits a poetry distinguished by an obvious restlessness, a sometimes dramatic movement, whether among poems or within a given poem, back and forth between modes.

Wright's adventurousness, his extravagance, in the root sense resurrected by Thoreau, often declares itself in the "deep image" and in what some have understandably called surrealism. In "The Pretty Redhead" his party searches for "vast strange domains / Where mystery flowers into any hands that long for it" and where there are "A thousand fantasies difficult to make sense out of." This search yields much that is whimsical, cryptic, uncanny, or weirdly beautiful. It is not always possible to decide which. To it we owe, for instance, this sudden detour in a love poem in *Two Citizens*. Wright has been recalling a walk with his wife in the Yugoslavian countryside:

The one thing that I most longed for to meet in the
  wildness
Here was a spider. I already know
My friends the spiders. They are mountains.
Every spider in America is the shadow
Of a beautiful woman.[3]

Making "here" instead of the expected "there" his occasion, and slipping into the present tense, he swerves in a new direction, so that the "wildness" is no longer the natural setting for the walk but the very nature of the poem. We come around the bend of that first line into a strange domain indeed, as though Wright meant to show us how close to the neat, grammatical path the imagination, "that mysterious and frightening thing," is. For whatever dark purpose, the impulse to adventure asserts itself here in a characteristic manner.

Its steadier counterpart cannot be simply equated with Wright's "craft," or "the active employment of the intelligence," which he pairs with "imagination." The preceding lines have their own craftiness; the long first line that suspends and intensifies the longing itself, the shrewd positioning of "Here," the accentuation of the new, wry tone by the iambic meter in lines two and three, and the light rhyme, for example, testify to certain "patient pains," as Yeats called his complement to "passionate impulse." Carefully made as they are, however, those lines plunge off into inscrutability. The element in Wright's temperament that I have in mind not only resists such tangents but also urges him to speak as straightforwardly and plainly as possible. In addition to some dull or commonplace verse it fosters much taut, dramatic, moving poetry. (My examples would include "Autumn Begins in Martins Ferry, Ohio," "Two Hangovers," and "A Blessing" in *The Branch Will Not Break;* "Speak," "The Mourners," "Poems to a Brown Cricket," and "To the Muse" in *Shall We Gather at the River;* "A Mad Fight Song for William S. Carpenter, 1966," "Small Frogs Killed on the Highway," and "Northern Pike" in "New Poems" in *Collected Poems.*) When it exerts its influence in *Two Citizens* we get stanzas like these, which conclude "The Last Drunk":

I sired a bitter son.
I have no daughter.
When I at last get done
I will die by water.

She, what she might have been,
Her shoulder's secret gold,
Thin as her mother is thin.
I could have grown old!

Anyone who has read much Wright might sense the tug of adventure in the second line of the last stanza, but that would be partly because the word *secret* so often signals a veering into mystery in his work—and partly because the passage as a whole is so direct.

This is the side of Wright that demands clarity, immediacy, even simplicity, that convinces him that "To speak in a flat voice / Is all that I can do" ("Speak"), and that drives him to deny the applicability of the term "surrealism" to his work on the grounds that it is used to label passages in which his "attempt to be clear has failed."[4] If it is precisely his extravagance that comes to mind when he contrasts the practice of some other poets with his own object in "Many of Our Waters: Variations on a Poem by a Black Child" ("New Poems"), the well-known stanza itself avoids the incongruity:

The kind of poetry I want to write is
  The poetry of a grown man.
The young poets of New York come to me with
Their mangled figures of speech,
But they have little pity
For the pure clear word.

In effect, this stanza reprimands the speaker in "The Pretty Redhead," with his enthusiasm for the enigmatic and the *outré;* it might even remind us of a poet whose work Wright surely considers more ordered than adventurous. T. S. Eliot is glossing a remark in one of D. H. Lawrence's letters about the necessity of "stark directness" in modern poetry:

> This speaks to me of that at which I have long aimed, in writing poetry; to write poetry which should be essentially poetry, with nothing poetic about it, poetry standing naked in its bare bones, or poetry so transparent . . . that in reading it we are intent on what the poem *points at*. . . . To get *beyond poetry*, as Beethoven, in his later works, strove to get *beyond music*.[5]

Wright surprises himself with his own stark directness in "Inscription for the Tank" *(Shall We Gather at the River)*: "My life was never so precious / To me as now. / I gape unbelieving at those two lines / Of my words, caught and frisked naked." By the time of "Many of Our Waters" the abashed surprise has become a rather defensive pride:

This is not a poem.
This is not an apology to the Muse.
This is the cold-blooded plea of a homesick vampire
To his brother and friend.

If you do not care one way or another about
The preceding lines,
Please do not go on listening
On any account of mine.

Of course Wright's specificity also reveals the difference between his aim and Eliot's. Eliot wants the poem to be a means of clarification whose art effaces itself. In the discursive sections of *Four Quartets* his transparency comes largely from delicate distinction, exactness of diction, an exquisite circumspection—all those virtues of discretion defined and exemplified at the beginning of "Little Gidding, V." Wright's clarity is closer to that of Catullus, whose ghost haunts *Moments of the Italian Summer* and *To a Blossoming Pear Tree*, the two most recent volumes. We begin to characterize it in terms of bluntness, idiomatic language, overstatement, reckless intensity. He wants the poem to be an emphatic statement whose passion seems to override its art.[6]

Its clarity notwithstanding, however, the preceding passage consorts oddly with "The poetry of a grown man." Simple clarity is not, after all, maturity, and the petulance of Wright's lines—whether gratuitous or strategic seems beside the point—embarrasses his explicit desire. Nor is "the pure clear word" the same as an unalloyed emotion, although Wright seems to identify those two as well. If his extravagance sometimes leads him into obscurity, his clarity courts sentimentality and simplism. Here is the conclusion of "Ohio Valley Swains" *(Two Citizens)*, where he recalls some unspecified assault by a teenager on a girl he knew when he was a child:

You thought that was funny, didn't you, to mock a
  girl?
I loved her only in my dreams,
But my dreams meant something
And so did she,
You son of a bitch,
And if I ever see you again, so help me in the sight
  of God,
I'll kill you.

Even if we can overlook its disconcerting egocentrism ("And so did she"), this stanza tries the patience. Either we must believe that the same James Wright who abhors capital punishment would kill a man who molested a girl some forty years ago, regardless of what has happened to him since; or we must suppose that the poem works up the simplest emotion for the sake of immediacy.

We might try to write these lines off as ironic bluster—in the vein of Wright's vow that *Two Citizens* was his last book: "God damn me if I ever write another."[7] But that seems as desperate a resort as wringing a pun from the first word of the title of "Lying in a Hammock at William Duffy's Farm in Pine Island, Minnesota" *(The Branch Will Not Break)* to justify that poem's famous conclusion: "I have wasted my life." That line, too, has always made me want to reverse Proust and say, *il est trop sincère d'être honnête*. What distinguishes it from the last sentence of Rilke's "*Archïscher Torso Apollos*," surely Wright's model, is precisely its passionate oversimplification. Rilke's "*Du musst dein Leben ändern*" summarizes the effect of the radiant sculptural fragment, which, like some transfiguring mirror, lets the poet see himself as though from a god's point of view and inspires in him an unspecific, perhaps undischargeable, but undeniable obligation: "You must change your life." Wright's poem fails as it were to gain the vantage of his floating hawk, collapses back into the deep well of the self, pronounces a melodramatic because impossibly harsh judgment, and therefore invites sympathetic correction. But that's not so, one wants to say—as indeed it was not. Rilke's poem crystallizes an insight while Wright's fans a flickering feeling.

Wright commits such excesses in the name of "the pure clear word"; they measure his desire for transparency, not to say confrontation. It is all the more remarkable, then, that he has so cherished his extravagance. A few lines after scorning those callow, "mangled figures of speech" he can say of the "grown man" that "The long body of his dream is the beginning of a dark / Hair under an illiterate / Girl's ear." One tries to imagine the expression on the face of the illiterate girl to whom these lines might be slowly read (with appropriate attention to *rejet*). Perhaps they demonstrate ironically the foregoing admission that he is "not yet a grown man"—but in context the metaphor looks less rueful than solemn. "The one tongue I can write in / Is my Ohioan," he proclaims in *Two Citizens*, yet the volume is fraught with exotic locutions like this: "Somewhere in me there is a crystal that I cannot find / Alone, the wing that I used to think was a poor / Blindness I had to live with with the dead." Evidently he means to have it both ways.

II

In *Moments of the Italian Summer* he does.[8] This is a splendid little book, a chain of "brilliants," to borrow one of Wright's charmed words. Its fourteen prose poems, introduced by a poem by Annie Wright, are as transparent as anything he has written, though they are shot through with whimsy. In fact, in the best of them, extravagance provides coherence and sophistication alike.

A note by Annie Wright, published earlier with some of these pieces in Michael Benedikt's anthology, *The Prose Poem*, confirms what one immediately suspects: they grew out of daily journal entries.[9] Reading through this book, surely everyone will recall certain inspired jottings—written in the diary while the setting sun turned ochre the old house across from the pensione or scrawled on a paper napkin stained with cappuccino while the promenaders streamed by—jottings that somehow never came to anything more. Wright's version of the prose poem, with its evident tolerance for loose ends, its appetite for digression, its fugitive unity, seems exactly the form to contain without warping them. But to think that mere acquaintance with this sequence would make the difference is of course an illusion. One might as well depend upon a visit to Athens to produce a maid to write about. These prose poems are no less personal and earned than Wright's best verse, their beguiling capriciousness and clarity no more inherent in the genre than Brunello di Montalcino is in the grape.

They often begin like postcards, with a designation of setting that flaunts its artlessness. "I am sitting contented and alone in a little park near the Palazzo Scaligere in Verona," Wright announces, or "It is a fresh morning of late August in Padova," or "I am sitting in an outdoor cafe across the street from the Colosseum." Then the warming up turns into something serious and exciting, as imagination and memory (if they are not the same thing) take over and the prose carries us on and on. A prose poem called "Young Don't Want to Be Born" in *To a Blossoming Pear Tree* puts into parable form what happens to the poet when "that mysterious and frightening thing" sweeps him away. The "you" is knocked off his feet by the riptide and comes up clinging to the tail of a giant stingray headed out to sea and destinations unknown. Something of that sort often occurs in these pieces, although the force that takes us out beyond our depth is gently suasive rather than overpowering. This passage, at the heart of "The City of Evenings," might serve as a model:

> Streamers, motorboats, trash-scows are moving past in large numbers, and gondolas are going home. In a little while we too will meet the twilight and move through it on a vaporetto toward the Lido, the seaward island with its long beach and its immense hotel, its memories of Aschenbach and his harrowing vision of perfection, of Byron on horseback in the moonlight, and the muted shadows of old Venetians drifting as silently as possible in flight from the barbarians, drifting as far away as the island of Torcello, taking refuge as Ruskin said like the Israelites of old, a refuge from the sword in the paths of the sea.

One thing leads to another as the reader drifts on in the current of association, sensing but hardly noticing that, as easily as the historical flows into the fictional, the Giudecca Canal merges with another body of water and that one is moving among shades other than those of evening. Wright does it all "as silently as possible"; as the elegiac overtones dissolve back into the tourist's language you are even sure you heard them—though the concluding reference to passing time probably suggests that the poet has: "Maybe Torcello was nothing much for the princes of the sea to find, but the old Venetians discovered the true shape of evening, and now it is almost evening." This piece almost describes itself, for Wright too, drawn out of his way (or so it seems), thereby discovers his real subject and its own "true shape."

Progression by means of digression, toward a transformation of the present "moment," structures most of these prose poems. In some cases the movement seems more desultory than in others, and one feels that the process is not a matter, as for Herrick's Julia, of contriving an alluring disorder, but rather of teasing a welter of material into a tenuous form. "A Lament for the Martyrs," set near the Colosseum, meanders from Mussolini to God, thence to Horace and President Nixon, the barbarians and the Barberinis, the crooked politicians of the Ohio River Valley during Prohibition, a childhood essay on Howells, and so on, to conclude with reflections on the Christian martyrs. It seems at first an example of the journal entry insufficiently chastened. But then it appears that the archaeologist's work ("a careful revelation" of subterranean passages thronged with shadows and ghosts) corresponds to Wright's disclosure of his past ("the antiquities of my childhood: the beautiful river, that black ditch of horror"), itself linked with the political history of the United States, and to his rediscovery of Roman history. If the "starved people" and the "hungry" lions blur together in the shadows along with beauty and atrocity, so do Roman and American, distance and recent history. For all its apparent waywardness, the prose poem digs its own "intricate and intelligent series of ditches" that parallel and intersect one another, and by its end it has become a compassionate indictment of history's "hateful grandeur," the inextricable "greatness and horror" that fascinated Lowell in his treatment of Rome and the United States in *Near the Ocean*.

The modus operandi is not new in Wright's work. In 1967 he remarked that "if any principle of structure can be disentangled from the poems that I have written in free verse, it is, I suppose, the principle of parallelism, a term which of course need not be limited to a strictly grammatical application." Eight years later he was thinking about the same method when he said that Georg Trakl had influenced him as much as anyone. Trakl, he said, "writes in parallelisms, only he leaves out the intermediary, rationalistic explanations of the relation between one image and another."[10] Like "A Lament for the Martyrs," "The Legions of Caesar" might be viewed as a domestication of Trakl's mode. While he watches some men fish for piccolini, Wright muses on the cessation of bombing in Cambodia, Catullus, Caesar's invasions of Britain, and the poet and composer William Barnes. These elements recur in new combinations, like filaments of sunlight in the shallows weaving themselves anew each moment. At the conclusion some boys are chasing a piccolino that has wriggled out of the bag:

> They are serious, hurrying, before the little fish stops struggling back towards the water and turns to stone. I don't know what time it is in Cambodia. I wonder if there is ever any silence there. Where is it, hiding from the invaders? The sunlight once glinted off William Barnes's coffin. From a hill so far away it seemed the other side of the earth, his friend Thomas

> Hardy wrote down the sunlight as a signal. He knew
> his friend was opening a hand, saying goodbye.

The importance of the piccolini becomes apparent—perhaps too apparent—when he calls the boys invaders; otherwise the conclusion leaves us to draw our own.[11] Curiosity perhaps takes us back to Hardy's tough, touching poem, "The Last Signal." Before the lines that Wright's last two sentences paraphrase, Hardy wrote that he "knew what it meant— / The sudden shine sent from the livid east scene; / It meant the west mirrored by the coffin of my friend there." One does not need to compare the two pieces to gather that Wright means the more recent "livid east scene" in Cambodia to parallel the Roman invasions, but Hardy's provokes us to contemplate a different twilight in the west, and its elegaic nature makes Wright's more resonant. It is interesting that Hardy says nothing of his hill's being "so far away it seemed the other side of the earth." Wright invents that detail both to coax out a parallel between himself and Hardy and to acknowledge the irrevocable distance between himself and the Cambodian victims (in preparation for the subtle daring of the implied friendship between them). Maybe we also hear echoes, because Catullus has come up earlier, of the elegy ending *"ave atque vale,"* especially since the brother for whom he wrote it died in the east. In any case, the loose connections that make the surface so casual also allow Wright to shape a response to a political situation that defies frontal assaults. How different this quietly moving piece is from "Ohio Valley Swains."

In his wonderfully evocative "The Lambs on the Boulder" Wright begins by comparing Giotto, "the master of angels," with Mantegna, whose "dead Christ looks exactly like a skidroad bum fished by the cops out of the Mississippi," and then goes on to meditate on the story ("which so intensely ought to be real that it is real") of Cimabue's discovery of Giotto, a shepherd boy, patiently sketching his lambs on a boulder with a sharp rock. At the end Wright recalls a painting by Giotto in which, far back in "a huge choir of his unutterably beautiful angels . . . singing out of pure happiness the praises of God," one smaller angel has turned from the light and hidden his face. "I don't know why he is weeping," Wright says, "but I love him best." He concludes with a sentence whose last clause lifts this embroidered story into parable:

> I think he must be wondering how long it will take Giotto to remember him, give him a drink of water, and take him back home to the fold before it gets dark and shepherd and sheep alike lose their way in the darkness of the countryside.

The young Giotto and his frightened lamb, the mature Giotto and his weeping angel, Cimabue and the shepherd boy, the poet and the "befuddled drunkards" he has known, Mantegna and the dead Christ: by subtly commenting on one another, these parallels—or variations on the shepherd and the lost sheep—keep the prose poem from losing its way even as they enlarge and complicate its vision. In the end it tells us something about the survival of the artist's early feelings in his later work, the mingling in that work of joy and sorrow, fear and hope, and losses and gains and the memory and discipline that mediate between them.

As these pieces range out from the moments at their centers they tend also to forsake the literal. They are imaginative flights, forms of trancendence. The ascent is actual in the last part of "A Letter to Franz Wright," where the poet tells us how he and his companions "drove up, and up, and around, and up, and around, and up again" until they arrived late one evening at San Gimignano, where the next morning they incredulously found themselves "poised hundreds of feet in the air" and "felt . . . strange in that presence, that city glistening there in the lucid Tuscan morning, like a perfectly cut little brilliant sparkling on the pinnacle of a stalagmite." "Saying Dante Aloud," the central and shortest piece, takes such an uplifting of spirit as its subject. This is the whole of it, round as Giotto's O: "You can feel the muscles and veins rippling in widening and rising circles, like a bird in flight under your tongue." One can feel the imagination itself moving in widening and rising circles in "Under the Canals," in which an old man carrying a ladder and a net, probably a chimney sweep, becomes richer and stranger as Wright muses on the odd figure he cuts. First he notices "the green moon-slime on his shoes" and half believes that he has "just climbed up some of those odd stairs out of a nearby narrow canal"; and later the old man becomes a "sweeper of sea-stairs" who has left behind him "a chimney, swept free, till this hour passes, of all the webs they weave so stoutly down there, the dark green spiders under the water who have more than all the time they need." In "The Silent Angel," a man with something in his hand, standing in "the vast petals of rose shadows" cast by the arena in Verona, becomes first a musician with a baton and then an ambiguous angel: "The wings of the smiling musician are folded. . . . my musician, who meant me no harm and only wanted to wave me away as gently as possible out of the beautiful space he guarded. . . . He may be fallen, as I am. But from a greater height, unless I miss my guess."

What happens in such pieces is that the bud of the actual blossoms into the extravagant flower of vision. What is seen is seen through, and we are made aware of the uniqueness and power, the potential centrality of any given moment. "The service of philosophy . . . toward the human spirit, is to rouse, to startle it to a life of constant and eager observation. Every moment some form grows perfect . . . for that moment only. Not the fruit of experience, but the experience itself is the end." Would Wright have been rereading *The Renaissance* during this stay in Italy? "But I care more now for the poetry of the present moment," he admits in "Piccolini"; he entitles another piece "The Language of the Present Moment"; and in the concluding prose poem he celebrates not "the enduring fruits of five hundred years," the paintings in an exhibit in Padua, but "The Fruits of the Season." Pater exhorted us to "be present always at the focus where the greatest number of vital forces unite in their purest energy"—and here is the last paragraph of "A Small Grove," which begins with a description of the poet's wife standing in some trees:

> She stands among them in her flowered green clothes. Her skin is darker gold than the olives in the morning sun. Two hours ago we got up and bathed in the lake. It was like swimming in a vein. Everything that can blossom is blossoming around her now. She is the eye of the grove, the eye of mimosa and willow. The cypress behind her catches fire.

In her "flowered green clothes" Annie Wright is, for the moment, the focus, the absolute and radiant center of those vital forces. At that center, as the inspired choice of "eye" tells us, subject and object, sight and sight are one. Slight as it is, this piece, to my mind, would better bear comparison with Rilke's sonnet than "Lying in a Hammock. . . ."[12]

"A Small Grove" might be described either as a dilation of its central moment or as a penetration of it. The same is true of "The Secret of Light," which focuses on the possibility of bringing to light the secret of the perceived object and the closely related possibility of bringing to the surface the beauty, the hidden light of the loved one. I take the following delicately skewed sentence to be central. Wright sees a woman sitting on a park bench in front of him:

> Her hair is as black as the inmost secret of light in a perfectly cut diamond, a perilous black, a secret light that must have been studied for many years before the anxious and disciplined craftsman could achieve the necessary balance between courage and skill to stroke the strange stone and take the one chance he would ever have to bring that secret to light.

"Secret of light . . . a secret light . . . that secret to light": even as Wright turns his subject around to study it first from one angle and then from another (the whole prose poem repeats certain words like some prose canzone), he strikes the blow he imagines. Unlike this "anxious and disciplined craftsman," the poet never has only "one chance"—except in the sense that Pater stresses and that Wright mentions later in this piece, that he has "only one life"—but like him Wright has found in these prose poems "a necessary balance." A balance, that is, between the courage to be extravagant and the skill to make that extravagance disclose the moment's essence. Moving out from each moment, Wright moves in on it in order to make it and himself (as he says of the Adige and himself) "both an open secret." The phrase applies not only because the prose poems seem to expose the operations of "that mysterious and frightening thing" but also because the craft that makes them transparent itself remains virtually hidden.

III

Seven of these prose poems also appear in *To a Blossoming Pear Tree*, where some of them are considerably and wisely pruned. Like several of the prose poems, some of the poems rely upon our intuition of unexplained parallelisms. Take "Redwings," the subject of which is the redwing blackbirds whose increase has made them pests. ("It turns out / You can kill them," Wright begins; "It turns out / You can make the earth absolutely clean.") Like so many of his poems, this one understands the world to be divided into two camps. On our side, tenuously connected with one another, are those who are on nature's: the redwings, nameless "solitaries," a "skinny girl" the poet once loved who now has five children (the prolific birds too "used to be willowy and thin"), a kindly derelict who slept by the river (either Wright has known more saintly bums than Kerouac or he has multiplied a few experiences like loaves), and of course the poet himself. On the other side, equally loosely associated, are the scientists who have figured out how to exterminate the redwings, the strip miner the skinny girl married (or at least his bosses), and those reponsible for "the dead gorges / Of highway construction." (Wright long ago consigned earth gougers to one of the lower circles in Hell.) He manages all this unobtrusively enough, but the poem arrives in its next to last stanza when he impulsively identifies himself (and all of us—the scientists are in an airplane) with the birds:

> Together among the dead gorges
> Of highway construction, we flare
> Across highways and drive
> Motorists crazy, we fly
> Down home to the river.

The transitions into and from this stanza are also first-rate, but this is the crucial passage, with its simultaneous description and incorporation of the birds' startling movement and its equation of the dangerous with the threatened species—which gently implies that our wars on nature are wars on ourselves. Here again extravagance is directness. At this surprising juncture, the whole poem comes together.

Or almost the whole poem. Earlier, describing the Kokosing River from an airplane, Wright says it looks

> Secret, it looks like the open
> Scar turning gray on the small
> Of your spine.
> Can you hear me?

This is another sort of flaring across the highway, as the question seems to acknowledge. Whose spine is involved? Anyone's, as it were? But why then the particular specificity in "the small"? And what is an "open / Scar"—since a scar is a closed wound? Almost the only thing we can ascertain is that this passage is more "secret" than "open." I am concerned with it not because it especially damages a fine poem (it does not—it is at worst a small scar), but rather because it represents a return, after the pervasive inventions in the prose poems, to that peculiar local kinkiness of the earlier work. Curiously, such passages often incorporate the word "secret." Thus in "Neruda" Wright tells us puzzlingly that "The leaves of the little / Secret trees are fallen" after he has discovered "The little leaves / That are trees in secret." "One Last Look at the Adige: Verona in the Rain" begins and ends beautifully, but halfway through we find the poet

> Alive in the friendly city
> Of my body, my secret Verona,
> Milky and green,
> My moving jewel, the last
> Pure vein left to me.

Perhaps I misunderstand these mysterious lines if I take them to convey a loneliness so extreme that it dotes on itself—but I do not see how else they might be taken.[13]

Sometimes it is as though the impulse to adventure had been suppressed and were revenging itself—or as though Wright were determined to invoke certain enigmas as evidence of a rarefied sensibility. He seems to need to insinuate that a part of his experience is ineffable, that the best he can do is drop his depth charges into the reader's subconscious and hope that they jar loose something similar. He has put the case for the subjective correlative, to adapt a term used by James Merrill, explicitly and persuasively in "A Letter to Franz Wright," where he sends to his son "these fragments of words I picked up on the hither side of my limits. I am sending them to you, because you will love them. Consequently, you will know to piece them together into a vision of your own design. Your imagination is not mine. How could it be? Who would want it to be? I wouldn't. You wouldn't. But I love both, so I trust yours. Here are some fragments of my hammer that broke against a wall of jewels." Given the fact of publication, the "you" graciously extends itself, at least in part, to include any sympathetic reader. And what reader, in view of such trust and in the face of such a generous supposition of his uniqueness and sensitivity, could fail to reciprocate—to grant Wright his license? Wouldn't to do so be to confess one's own shallowness? But I do not want to quarrel with this passage. It says quite eloquently what we have all felt when confronted with something "so appallingly beyond accounting for" as San Gimignano was for Wright, and in any case he later evokes the beauty of the place in terms that are faceted rather than fragmented. In short, his warning serves not to justify his account but to put it in perspective. I suspect, however, that a form of the intense subjectivity embraced here at least justifies and perhaps necessitates the arcana that ornament his poems.

"What Does the Bobwhite Mean?" insists nearly belligerently on the essential secrecy of significant experience. "I don't know / Yet," the poem answers the question, which was evidently put by the man to whom it is dedicated: "Only you know."

As for me, as for mine,
We have held each other's hands alone, each alone,
And felt the green dew turn dark gold, brilliants
In the darkness outside.
A town called Fiesole.
What can the name of Fiesole mean to you?
What does the bobwhite mean?

And so on: "What will your loneliness mean to me? / What does the bobwhite mean?" Perhaps unintentionally, the recurrent question comes to seem a mocking refrain, and the poem ends with a curt dismissal: "You know. / Go, listen"—as though to say that we are all poets and therefore have nothing to say to one another. We are "each alone," like the "solitary armadillos" that appear at one point. Wright's telling sympathy for shelled creatures reappears in "With the Shell of a Hermit Crab." Composed of tetrameter quatrains, each self-contained and fragile as the shell itself, it belongs to the tradition that began with Catullus's poem on the death of Lesbia's sparrow, whose opening line gives Wright his epigraph. But instead of Catullus's outcry against all-devouring death and his attention to Lesbia we have Wright's lament for the crab's former "loneliness" and a nearly reproachful allusion to his own (for the "you" must refer to an absent person):

Today, you happen to be gone,
I sit here in the raging hell,
The city of the dead, alone,
Holding a little empty shell.

The relationship between the two hermits can hardly be ignored. Even in this mournful poem, however, one feels an undercurrent of grim satisfaction in the isolation. As he sits contemplating the empty shell the poet recalls some cinquecento St. Jerome, alone by choice in the desert, gazing into the eye sockets of a death's-head.

As for the purportedly lonely crab, during his brief life he moved "How delicately no one knows." That is his secret. And since no one knows, any degree of delicacy can be ascribed. Just as we know nothing of the crab's delicacy, so we are ignorant of "The snail's secret" in "By the Ruins of a Gun Emplacement: Saint-Benoît" (which alludes to "The Snail's Road" in *Two Citizens*):

I met a snail on a stone at Fleury,
Where, now, Max Jacob walks happily among the
candles
Of his brothers, but I still do not know
The snail's secret.
I do not even know
What we shall do if the round moon comes down
The river and strolls up
Out of the Loire
To take once more your startling face up
Among his drowsed swans.

I do not even know for sure what the round moon might portend, although I suspect from its earlier appearances, the setting of the poem, and the allusion to Jacob (who was arrested at Saint-Benoît and died in a concentration camp at Drancy) that it is meant to be at once ominous and seductive, a softly luminous skull with which (the diction and rhythms suggest) the poet is half in love. But then I wonder, since Wright's imagination is not mine, whether I have not placed the eerily beautiful fragments together into a vision of my own design. I wonder too whether the mystery is not the essence of the poem, whether that is not the point of the lines on the snail, whether I am not being invited to go look at the moon and be sensitive myself.

Another poem that I want very much to admire goes out of its way to create a secret. "On a Phrase from Southern Ohio" recalls a childhood incident and reads for the most part like a sarcastic response to "Fern Hill": "it is not / Maiden and morning on the way up that cliff. / Not where I come from." Here the hill is a foothill, across the Ohio River from Steubenville, whose side has been jackhammered away and covered with concrete. Instead of princes of the apple towns, Wright and his friends are punks who steal a skiff to get over to that "Smooth dead / Face" so that they can climb it. Once on top they find instead of an idyllic orchard "a garden of bloodroots, tangled there, a vicious secret / Of trilliums" and two black boys, whom they beat up and chase off. Instead of Adam in Eden this is Cain in Nod, and it is all done with a marvelous sense of the rawness and the sourness and the savagery of the summer life of boys growing up to become strip miners and jackhammer operators in a spoiled mid-American town. Then the poem ends:

And still in my dreams I sway like one fainting strand
Of spiderweb, glittering and vanishing and frail
Above the river.
What were those purple shadows doing
Under the ear
Of the woman who was weeping along the Ohio
River the woman?
Damned if you know;
I don't.

The first sentence suggests memories of a light-headedness after the incident, but it is too portentous for that to be its sole purpose. In addition to his own "A Dream of Burial" *(The Branch Will Not Break)*, Wright might want us to call up "A Noiseless Patient Spider" with its "gossamer thread" unanchored, so these lines might say something of his hopeless isolation. But the elegantly swaying sentence itself floats free of the poem and retains its mystery. Along with the odd personification and the superfluous question, it seems intended to bemuse, while the last sentence, which pugnaciously recasts the slang phrase in the second person, flatly dares us to make sense of any of this. One has the feeling that to do so would be somehow to demean the poem, to rob Wright of its experience. And then one remembers "The Jewel," back in *The Branch Will Not Break*, with its bristling, defensive warning:

There is this cave
In the air behind my body
That nobody is going to touch:
A cloister, a silence
Closing around a blossom of fire.

Why, precisely: Wright's poems seem to embody, in respect to "the pure clear word," what the psychologists call an approach-avoidance conflict—he wants to be open and direct, yet he seems to fear that in doing so he will snuff out that "blossom of fire," lose his singular vision. Hence perhaps the withdrawals into shell, caves, and secrecy. The fainting strand of spiderweb, the moving jewel of the body, and so on—these images both prove his isolation and validate it.

Is it true that in the absence of such vagaries Wright's poems can be breathtakingly plain. "What Does the King of the Jungle Truly Do?" is a prose poem in praise of leonine purity that ends "Small wonder Jesus wept at a human city," and one longs for the sentiment to be even thinly disguised. "Simon," which comes perilously close to "plain American which cats and dogs can read," is little more than a schmaltzy tribute to Robert Bly's "huge gross" Airedale ("We slobber all over each other's faces"). Yet how nicely the simplicity of this poem sets off the tiny gem of adjectival wit, which in turn dignifies the sentiment, in the poem's last stanza. One has only to know that Simon was always picking up cockleburs in his long coat:

Simon,
Where are you gone?
Some shaggy burdocks in Minnesota
Owe their lives to you,
Somewhere.

The sensuous directness of "The First Days," to continue moving up the scale, leads up to a sudden, inspired allusion to Virgil. Wright remembers a morning in Italy when he saw "a huge golden bee ploughing / His burly right shoulder into the belly / Of a sleek yellow pear." The pear fell to the ground with the bee inside, and he knelt

And sliced the pear gently
A little more open.
The bee shuddered, and returned.
Maybe I should have left him alone there,
Drowning in his own delight.
The best days are the first
To flee.

The last clause translates the poem's epigraph, *"Optima dies prima fugit,"* an abridged version of the *Georgics*, III, 66–67. Wright lends Virgil's words an ironic depth by virtue of his preceding, nearly obstetrical image, and at the same time he uses them to throw into relief his conclusion, with its glance at the utterly changed landscape:

The best days are the first
To flee, sang the lovely
Musician born in this town
So like my own.
I let the bee go
Among the gasworks at the edge of Mantua. [14]

By making his last line turn Virgil's lament for lost youth so discreetly into prophecy, Wright elegizes the world that produced the *Georgics* and yet avoids sentimental cliché. Such touches are small but perfect, and no less inventive than the fainting strand of spiderweb.

In "Hook" and "To a Blossoming Pear Tree," both of which seem to owe something to "In Terror of Hospital Bills" *(Shall We Gather at the River)*, Wright comes as close to "the bare bones of poetry" as anyone would want. "Hook" conveys a desolate scene in language so stark that it spurns even realism as frivolous embellishment. It has the economy of dream. The poem recounts a meeting years past on a street corner in Minneapolis with a Sioux man. The young poet is "in trouble / With a woman," alone in the snow with hours to wait for a bus, when the Sioux looms out of the night. "What did they do / To your hand?" the poet asks when he sees the prosthetic hook—and it turns out that the Sioux also "had a bad time with a woman." Then he puts sixty-five cents into Wright's "freezing hand" (which, like the "they" who do not need to be identified, also implies a mutual predicament) and the poem ends: "I took it. / It wasn't the money I needed. / But I took it." Surely what he needed was a sign of understanding or of the possibility of coming through; and the coins are a sort of viaticum, an irreducible symbol of both the bond between the two men and their unalterable loneliness. Cavafy could hardly have done it more cleanly.

The counterpart of this incident occurs in the title poem, where Wright remembers an old man who appeared out of another snowy night in Minneapolis. The man, "willing to take / Any love he could get," rather like Wright in "Hook" (which must be the point of the juxtaposition of the poems), made an advance that the poet rejected. The conclusion makes what amends it can, as it addresses in its richest language the self-sufficient pear tree, as aloof from such humbling experiences as Keats's "Cold pastoral," and affirms the necessity of *humanitas:*

Young tree, unburdened
By anything but your beautiful natural blossoms
And dew, the dark
Blood in my body drags me
Down with my brother.

This testimony is everywhere borne out: by the increasing burden of the consonants, by the downward pull of the enjambment and the delayed verb, by the disposition of stresses in the last lines. Still, and in spite of the sharp division precisely at the middle of the central line between the natural and the human, this sentence has something of the simple, effortless beauty of the tree itself—and that is one reason that Wright is finally at least as proud as he is envious or wistful. Dragged down though he must be, because he must be dragged down, he has made a poem that will stand—and keep that tree standing so gracefully. "Perfect, beyond my reach," he says earlier of the blossoming tree, a "Little mist of fallen starlight." Yet it is even truer to say, as the last stanza does, that human imperfection is beyond the tree's reach. Absolutely clear and nonetheless as mature in attitude as in technique, this stanza seems to me as round an example as we could wish of "The poetry of a grown man."

But to talk so much about these lines is to fog with one's breath the glass we should just see through. The very directness of such a poem might be thought extravagant. And Wright's extravagance, whatever its sources and however it shows itself, makes him one of the most original and exciting poets we have. But that last is no secret at all.

Notes

1. Peter Stitt (Interview with James Wright), "The Art of Poetry, XIX," *Paris Review*, no. 62 (Summer 1975), 58. Robert Hass, in "James Wright," *Ironwood 10* (1977), 74–96, has a good deal to say about Wright's "lean, clear, plain language" and especially about his "mere sensitivity" or "will to be beautiful." I read Hass's stimulating, far-ranging essay in the course of writing an earlier version of this one and, looking back at his piece now, I realize how much it helped me shape my thoughts.
2. In "New Poems" in *Collected Poems* (Middletown, Conn.: Wesleyan University Press, 1971), p. 178. Quotations from Wright's other volumes before *Two Citizens* also come from *Collected Poems*.
3. "Afternoon and Evening at Ohrid," *Two Citizens* (New York: Farrar, Straus and Giroux, 1973), p. 12.
4. "Art of Poetry," p. 51.
5. Unpublished lecture delivered in 1933, quoted in F. O. Matthiessen, *The Achievement of T. S. Eliot*, 3rd ed. (New York: Oxford University Press, 1959), pp. 89–90.
6. One might also compare Wright's lines with Ortega's comments on aesthetic transparency. "By art," Ortega says, most people "understand a means through which they are brought into contact with interesting human affairs": "Take a garden seen through a window. . . . The purer the glass, the less we see it. But we can also deliberately disregard the garden and, withdrawing the ray of vision, detain it at the window. We then lose sight of the garden; what we still behold of it is a confused mass of color. . . . But not many people are capable of adjusting their perceptive apparatus to the pane and the transparency that is a work of art. Instead they look right through it and revel in the human reality with which the work deals." (José Ortega y Gasset, *The Dehumanization of Art*,

trans. Willard A. Trask [Garden City, N.Y.: Doubleday, Anchor, 1956], pp. 9–10.) Wright sometimes seems less interested in cleaning the window than in kicking it out. That the attempt quoted above fails on the face of it, and perhaps ends in smudging the glass, alters nothing. (Nabokov treats transparency in terms remarkably similar to Ortega's, by the way, in Chapter One of his novel titled after *Roget's* category, *Transparent Things*.)
7. "Art of Poetry," p. 56.
8. *Moments of the Italian Summer* (Washington, D.C.: Dryad Press, 1976). Several of the prose poems have appeared in different versions. In addition to *Moments* and *To a Blossoming Pear Tree* (New York: Farrar, Straus and Giroux, 1977), see *American Poets in 1976*, ed. William Heyen (Indianapolis: Bobbs-Merrill, 1976); *The Prose Poem*, ed. Michael Benedikt (New York: Dell, 1976); and *The New Naked Poetry*, ed. Stephen Berg and Robert Mezey (Indianapolis: Bobbs-Merrill, 1976).
9. *Prose Poem*, p. 605.
10. *Naked Poetry*, ed. Stephen Berg and Robert Mezey (Indianapolis: Bobbs-Merrill, 1969), p. 287; and "Art of Poetry," p. 48.
11. The apparently earlier version in *American Poets in 1976* lacks the reference to the boys as "invaders" and simply notes that the little fish is "like so much else."
12. The version in *American Poets in 1976* does not have the now indispensable last sentence.
13. If I understand his point, this is the sort of passage that Robert Hass explains as evidence of both "Calvinist and solipsistic doctrine" and "decadence" in Wright's work. In Hass's view, Wright's urge to utter merely "beautiful things" from the sanctuary of his "isolated inner world" derives from an alienated and further alienating rejection of the "degraded social world."
14. "Mantova," the earlier version of this poem published in *New Naked Poetry*, ends with the translation from Virgil. Because of the absence of the "gasworks" and its implications, "Mantova" is a thinner poem.

Richard Wright

1908–1960

Richard Nathaniel Wright was born on September 4, 1908, near Natchez, Mississippi, to a schoolteacher mother and an illiterate sharecropper father. His father abandoned the family when Wright was very young, and he was raised by his maternal grandmother. He dropped out of school after ninth grade and moved to Memphis, then to Chicago and New York. He educated himself, and was particularly interested in literature, sociology, and psychology. In 1932 he joined the Communist Party, and his literary career was encouraged by the Communist-affiliated John Reed Club. Much of his early writing appeared in leftist publications. He worked for the Federal Negro Theatre Project and the Federal Writers Project; while associated with these organizations he published *12 Million Black Voices* (1941), a Marxist analysis of the American class struggle. He was Harlem editor for the *Daily Worker* in New York. In 1938 he married Rose Dhima Meadman; they were later divorced, and Wright married Ellen Poplar, with whom he had two children. From 1947 to his death he lived in Paris.

Wright first came to the attention of the American reading public with the publication of *Uncle Tom's Children: Four Novellas* in 1938; the stories concern the struggles to maturity of oppressed black women and men. Wright's second book, *Native Son* (1940), was Wright's major critical and popular breakthrough, and remains one of the most influential American novels of the twentieth century. It concerns the life and destruction of Bigger Thomas, a poor black youth from the slums of Chicago. Wright's evocative portrayal of a life of fear and enslavement struck a powerful chord with his readership, despite some critics' complaints that the latter third of the book is expository and slow-moving.

Though none of Wright's subsequent books had the immediate impact of *Native Son*, he was admired as a solid stylist and spokesman for the poor and oppressed. Probably his most important later novel is *The Long Dream* (1958); his sociological studies, including the autobiographical *Black Boy: A Record of Childhood and Youth* (1945), *Black Power: A Record of Reactions in a Land of Pathos* (1954), *The Color Curtain: A Report on the Bandung Conference* (1956; originally published in French in 1955), *Pagan Spain* (1956), and *White Man, Listen!* (1957), were also widely read and admired. Wright died on November 28, 1960. His autobiography, *American Hunger*, was published in 1977; *The Richard Wright Reader*, edited by Ellen Wright and Michael Fabre, was published in 1978.

RALPH ELLISON
"Richard Wright's Blues" (1945)
Shadow and Act
1953, pp. 77–94

If anybody ask you
who sing this song,
Say it was ole [Black Boy]
done been here and gone.[1]

As a writer, Richard Wright has outlined for himself a dual role: to discover and depict the meaning of Negro experience; and to reveal to both Negroes and whites those problems of a psychological and emotional nature which arise between them when they strive for mutual understanding.

Now, in *Black Boy*, he has used his own life to probe what qualities of will, imagination and intellect are required of a Southern Negro in order to possess the meaning of his life in the United States. Wright is an important writer, perhaps the most articulate Negro American, and what he has to say is highly perceptive. Imagine Bigger Thomas projecting his own life in lucid prose, guided, say, by the insights of Marx and Freud, and you have an idea of this autobiography.

Published at a time when any sharply critical approach to Negro life has been dropped as a wartime expendable, it should do much to redefine the problem of the Negro and American Democracy. Its power can be observed in the shrill manner with which some professional "friends of the Negro people" have attempted to strangle the work in a noose of newsprint.

What in the tradition of literary autobiography is it like, this work described as a "great American autobiography"? As a non-white intellectual's statement of his relationship to Western culture, *Black Boy* recalls the conflicting pattern of identification and rejection found in Nehru's *Toward Freedom*. In its use of fictional techniques, its concern with criminality (sin) and the artistic sensibility, and in its author's judgment and rejection of the narrow world of his origin, it recalls Joyce's rejection of Dublin in *A Portrait of the Artist*. And as a psychological document of life under oppressive conditions, it recalls *The House of the Dead*, Dostoievsky's profound study of the humanity of Russian criminals.

Such works were perhaps Wright's literary guides, aiding him to endow his life's incidents with communicable significance; providing him with ways of seeing, feeling and describing his environment. These influences, however, were encountered only after these first years of Wright's life were past and were not part of the immediate folk culture into which he was born. In that culture the specific folk-art form which helped shape the writer's attitude toward his life and which embodied the impulse that contributes much to the quality and tone of his autobiography was the Negro blues. This would bear a word of explanation:

The blues is an impulse to keep the painful details and episodes of a brutal experience alive in one's aching consciousness, to finger its jagged grain, and to transcend it, not by the consolation of philosophy but by squeezing from it a near-tragic, near-comic lyricism. As a form, the blues is an autobiographical chronicle of personal catastrophe expressed lyrically. And certainly Wright's early childhood was crammed with catastrophic incidents. In a few short years his father deserted his mother, he knew intense hunger, he became a drunkard begging drinks from black stevedores in Memphis saloons; he had to flee Arkansas, where an uncle was lynched; he was forced to live with a fanatically religious grandmother in an atmosphere of constant bickering; he was lodged in an orphan asylum; he observed the suffering of his mother, who became a permanent invalid, while fighting off the blows of the poverty-stricken relatives with whom he had to live; he was cheated, beaten and kicked off jobs by white employees who disliked his eagerness to learn a trade; and to these objective circumstances must be added the subjective fact that Wright, with his sensitivity, extreme shyness and intelligence, was a problem child who rejected his family and was by them rejected.

Thus along with the themes, equivalent descriptions of milieu and the perspectives to be found in Joyce, Nehru, Dostoievsky, George Moore and Rousseau, *Black Boy* is filled with blues-tempered echoes of railroad trains, the names of Southern towns and cities, estrangements, fights and flights, deaths and disappointments, charged with physical and spiritual hungers and pain. And like a blues sung by such an artist as Bessie Smith, its lyrical prose evokes the paradoxical, almost surreal image of a black boy singing lustily as he probes his own grievous wound.

In *Black Boy*, two worlds have fused, two cultures merged, two impulses of Western man become coalesced. By discussing some of its cultural sources I hope to answer those critics who would make of the book a miracle and of its author a mystery. And while making no attempt to probe the mystery of the artist (who Hemingway says is "forged in injustice as a sword is forged"), I do hold that basically the prerequisites to the writing of *Black Boy* were, on the one hand, the microscopic degree of cultural freedom which Wright found in the South's stony injustice, and, on the other, the existence of a personality agitated to a state of almost manic restlessness. There were, of course, other factors, chiefly ideological; but these came later.

Wright speaks of his journey north as

> . . . taking a part of the South to transplant in alien soil, to see if it could grow differently, if it could drink of new and cool rains, bend in strange winds, respond to the warmth of other suns, and perhaps, to bloom. . . .

And just as Wright, the man, represents the blooming of the delinquent child of the autobiography, just so does *Black Boy* represent the flowering—cross-fertilized by pollen blown by the winds of strange cultures—of the humble blues lyric. There is, as in all acts of creation, a world of mystery in this, but there is also enough that is comprehensible for Americans to create the social atmosphere in which other black boys might freely bloom.

For certainly, in the historical sense, Wright is no exception. Born on a Mississippi plantation, he was subjected to all those blasting pressures which in a scant eighty years have sent the Negro people hurtling, without clearly defined trajectory, from slavery to emancipation, from log cabin to city tenement, from the white folks' fields and kitchens to factory assembly lines; and which, between two wars, have shattered the wholeness of its folk consciousness into a thousand writhing pieces.

Black Boy describes this process in the personal terms of *one* Negro childhood. Nevertheless, several critics have complained that it does not "explain" Richard Wright. Which, aside from the notion of art involved, serves to remind us that the prevailing mood of American criticism has so thoroughly excluded the Negro that it fails to recognize some of the most basic tenets of Western democratic thought when encountering them in a black skin. They forget that human life possesses an innate dignity and mankind an innate sense of nobility; that all men possess the tendency to dream and the compulsion to make their dreams reality; that the need to be ever dissatisfied and the urge ever to seek satisfaction is implicit in the human organism; and that all men are the victims and the beneficiaries of the goading, tormenting, commanding and informing activity of that imperious process known as the Mind—the Mind, as Valéry describes it, "armed with its inexhaustible questions."

Perhaps all this (in which lies the very essence of the human, and which Wright takes for granted) has been forgotten because the critics recognize neither Negro humanity nor the full extent to which the Southern community renders the fulfillment of human destiny impossible. And while it is true that *Black Boy* presents an almost unrelieved picture of a personality corrupted by brutal environment, it also presents those fresh, human responses brought to its world by the sensitive child:

> There was the *wonder* I felt when I first saw a brace of mountainlike, spotted, black-and-white horses clopping down a dusty road . . . the *delight* I caught

> in seeing long straight rows of red and green vegetables stretching away in the sun . . . the faint, cool kiss of *sensuality* when dew came on to my cheeks . . . the vague *sense of the infinite* as I looked down upon the yellow, dreaming waters of the Mississippi . . . the echoes of *nostalgia* I heard in the crying strings of wild geese . . . the *love* I had for the mute regality of tall, moss-clad oaks . . . the hint of *cosmic cruelty* that I *felt* when I saw the curved timbers of a wooden shack that had been warped in the summer sun . . . and there was the *quiet terror* that suffused my senses when vast hazes of gold washed earthward from star-heavy skies on silent nights. . . .[2]

And a bit later, his reactions to religion:

> Many of the religious symbols appealed to my sensibilities and I responded to the dramatic vision of life held by the church, feeling that to live day by day with death as one's sole thought was to be so compassionately sensitive toward all life as to view all men as slowly dying, and the trembling sense of fate that welled up, sweet and melancholy, from the hymns blended with the sense of fate that I had already caught from life.

There was also the influence of his mother—so closely linked to his hysteria and sense of suffering—who (though he only implies it here) taught him, in the words of the dedication prefacing *Native Son,* "to revere the fanciful and the imaginative." There were also those white men—the one who allowed Wright to use his library privileges and the other who advised him to leave the South, and still others whose offers of friendship he was too frightened to accept.

Wright assumed that the nucleus of plastic sensibility is a human heritage: the right and the opportunity to dilate, deepen and enrich sensibility—democracy. Thus the drama of *Black Boy* lies in its depiction of what occurs when Negro sensibility attempts to fulfill itself in the undemocratic South. Here it is not the individual that is the immediate focus, as in Joyce's *Stephen Hero,* but that upon which his sensibility was nourished.

Those critics who complain that Wright has omitted the development of his own sensibility hold that the work thus fails as art. Others, because it presents too little of what they consider attractive in Negro life, charge that it distorts reality. Both groups miss a very obvious point: That whatever else the environment contained, it had as little chance of prevailing against the overwhelming weight of the child's unpleasant experiences as Beethoven's Quartets would have of destroying the stench of a Nazi prison.

We come, then, to the question of art. The function, the psychology, of artistic selectivity is to eliminate from art form all those elements of experience which contain no compelling significance. Life is as the sea, art a ship in which man conquers life's crushing formlessness, reducing it to a course, a series of swells, tides and wind currents inscribed on a chart. Though drawn from the world, "the organized significance of art," writes Malraux, "is stronger than all the multiplicity of the world; . . . that significance alone enables man to conquer chaos and to master destiny."

Wright saw his destiny—that combination of forces before which man feels powerless—in terms of a quick and casual violence inflicted upon him by both family and community. His response was likewise violent, and it has been his need to give that violence significance which has shaped his writings.

What were the ways by which other Negroes confronted their destiny?

In the South of Wright's childhood there were three general ways: They could accept the role created for them by the whites and perpetually resolve the resulting conflicts through the hope and emotional cartharsis of Negro religion; they could repress their dislike of Jim Crow social relations while striving for a middle way of respectability, becoming—consciously or unconsciously—the accomplices of the whites in oppressing their brothers; or they could reject the situation, adopt a criminal attitude and carry on an unceasing psychological scrimmage with the whites, which often flared forth into physical violence.

Wright's attitude was nearest the last. Yet in it there was an all-important qualitative difference: it represented a groping for *individual* values, in a black community whose values were what the young Negro critic, Edward Bland, has defined as "pre-individual." And herein lay the setting for the extreme conflict set off, both within his family and in the community, by Wright's assertion of individuality. The clash was sharpest on the psychological level, for, to quote Bland:

> In the pre-individualistic thinking of the Negro the stress is on the group. Instead of seeing in terms of the individual, the Negro sees in terms of "races," masses of peoples separated from other masses according to color. Hence, an act rarely bears intent against him as a Negro individual. He is singled out not as a person but as a specimen of an ostracized group. He knows that he never exists in his own right but only to the extent that others hope to make the race suffer vicariously through him.

This pre-individual state is induced artificially—like the regression to primitive states noted among cultured inmates of Nazi prisons. The primary technique in its enforcement is to impress the Negro child with the omniscience and omnipotence of the whites to the point that whites appear as ahuman as Jehovah, and as relentless as a Mississippi flood. Socially it is effected through an elaborate scheme of taboos supported by a ruthless physical violence, which strikes not only the offender but the entire black community. To wander from the paths of behavior laid down for the group is to become the agent of communal disaster.

In such a society the development of individuality depends upon a series of accidents, which often arise, as in Wright's case, from conditions within the Negro family. In Wright's life there was the accident that as a small child he could not distinguish between his fair-skinned grandmother and the white women of the town, thus developing skepticism as to their special status. To this was linked the accident of his having no close contacts with whites until after the child's normal formative period.

But these objective accidents not only link forward to these qualities of rebellion, criminality and intellectual questioning expressed in Wright's work today. They also link backward into the shadow of infancy where environment and consciousness are so darkly intertwined as to require the skill of a psychoanalyst to define their point of juncture. Nevertheless, at the age of four, Wright set the house afire and was beaten near to death by his frightened mother. This beating, followed soon by his father's desertion of the family, seems to be the initial psychological motivation of his quest for a new identification. While delirious from this beating Wright was haunted "by huge wobbly white bags like the full udders of a cow, suspended from the ceiling above me [and] I was gripped by the fear that they were going to fall and drench me with some horrible liquid . . ."

It was as though the mother's milk had turned acid, and

with it the whole pattern of life that had produced the ignorance, cruelty and fear that had fused with mother-love and exploded in the beating. It is significant that the bags were of the hostile color white, and the female symbol that of the cow, the most stupid (and, to the small child, the most frightening) of domestic animals. Here in dream symbolism is expressed an attitude worthy of an Orestes. And the significance of the crisis is increased by virtue of the historical fact that the lower-class Negro family is matriarchal; the child turns not to the father to compensate if he feels mother-rejection, but to the grandmother, or to an aunt—and Wright rejected both of these. Such rejection leaves the child open to psychological insecurity, distrust and all of those hostile environmental forces from which the family functions to protect it.

One of the Southern Negro family's methods of protecting the child is the severe beating—a homeopathic dose of the violence generated by black and white relationships. Such beatings as Wright's were administered for the child's own good; a good which the child resisted, thus giving family relationships an undercurrent of fear and hostility, which differs qualitatively from that found in patriarchal middle-class families, because here the severe beating is administered by the mother, leaving the child no parental sanctuary. He must ever embrace violence along with maternal tenderness, or else reject, in his helpless way, the mother.

The division between the Negro parents of Wright's mother's generation, whose sensibilities were often bound by their proximity to the slave experience, and their children, who historically and through the rapidity of American change stand emotionally and psychologically much farther away, is quite deep. Indeed, sometimes as deep as the cultural distance between Yeats' *Autobiographies* and a Bessie Smith blues. This is the historical background to those incidents of family strife in *Black Boy* which have caused reviewers to question Wright's judgment of Negro emotional relationships.

We have here a problem in the sociology of sensibility that is obscured by certain psychological attitudes brought to Negro life by whites.

The first is the attitude which compels whites to impute to Negroes sentiments, attitudes and insights which, as a group living under certain definite social conditions, Negroes could not humanly possess. It is the identical mechanism which William Empson identifies in literature as "pastoral." It implies that since Negroes possess the richly human virtues credited to them, then their social position is advantageous and should not be bettered; and, continuing syllogistically, the white individual need feel no guilt over his participation in Negro oppression.

The second attitude is that which leads whites to misjudge Negro passion, looking upon it as they do, out of the turgidity of their own frustrated yearning for emotional warmth, their capacity for sensation having been constricted by the impersonal mechanized relationships typical of bourgeois society. The Negro is idealized into a symbol of sensation, of unhampered social and sexual relationships. And when *Black Boy* questions their illusion they are thwarted much in the manner of the occidental who, after observing the erotic character of a primitive dance, "shacks up" with a native woman—only to discover that far from possessing the hair-trigger sexual responses of a Stork Club "babe," she is relatively phlegmatic.

The point is not that American Negroes are primitives, but that as a group their social situation does not provide for the type of emotional relationships attributed them. For how could the South, recognized as a major part of the backward third of the nation, nurture in the black, most brutalized section of its population, those forms of human relationships achievable only in the most highly developed areas of civilization?

Champions of this "Aren't-Negroes-Wonderful?" school of thinking often bring Paul Robeson and Marian Anderson forward as examples of highly developed sensibility, but actually they are only its *promise.* Both received their development from an extensive personal contact with European culture, free from the influences which shape Southern Negro personality. In the United States, Wright, who is the only Negro literary artist of equal caliber, had to wait years and escape to another environment before discovering the moral and ideological equivalents of his childhood attitudes.

Man cannot express that which does not exist—either in the form of dreams, ideas or realities—in his environment. Neither his thoughts nor his feelings, his sensibility nor his intellect are fixed, innate qualities. They are processes which arise out of the interpenetration of human instinct with environment, through the process called experience; each changing and being changed by the other. Negroes cannot possess many of the sentiments attributed to them because the same changes in environment which, through experience, enlarge man's intellect (and thus his capacity for still greater change) also modify his feelings; which in turn increase his sensibility, i.e., his sensitivity, to refinements of impression and subtleties of emotion. The extent of these changes depends upon the quality of political and cultural freedom in the environment.

Intelligence tests have measured the quick rise in intellect which takes place in Southern Negroes after moving north, but little attention has been paid to the mutations effected in their sensibilities. However, the two go hand in hand. Intellectual complexity is accompanied by emotional complexity; refinement of thought, by refinement of feeling. The movement north affects more than the Negro's wage scale, it affects his entire psychosomatic structure.

The rapidity of Negro intellectual growth in the North is due partially to objective factors present in the environment, to influences of the industrial city and to a greater political freedom. But there are also changes within the "inner world." In the North energies are released and given *intellectual* channelization—energies which in most Negroes in the South have been forced to take either a *physical* form or, as with potentially intellectual types like Wright, to be expressed as nervous tension, anxiety and hysteria. Which is nothing mysterious. The human organism responds to environmental stimuli by converting them into either physical and/or intellectual energy. And what is called hysteria is suppressed intellectual energy expressed physically.

The "physical" character of their expression makes for much of the difficulty in understanding American Negroes. Negro music and dances are frenziedly erotic; Negro religious ceremonies violently ecstatic; Negro speech strongly rhythmical and weighted with image and gesture. But there is more in this sensuousness than the unrestraint and insensitivity found in primitive cultures; nor is it simply the relatively spontaneous and undifferentiated responses of a people living in close contact with the soil. For despite Jim Crow, Negro life does not exist in a vacuum, but in the seething vortex of those tensions generated by the most highly industrialized of Western nations. The welfare of the most humble black Mississippi sharecropper is affected less by the flow of the seasons and the rhythm of natural events than by the fluctuations of the stock market; even though, as Wright states of his father, the sharecropper's memories, actions and emotions are shaped by his immediate contact with nature and the crude social relations of the South.

All of this makes the American Negro far different from the "simple" specimen for which he is taken. And the "physical" quality offered as evidence of his primitive simplicity is actually the form of his complexity. The American Negro is a Western type whose social condition creates a state which is almost the reverse of the cataleptic trance: Instead of his consciousness being lucid to the reality around it while the body is rigid, here it is the body which is alert, reacting to pressures which the constricting forces of Jim Crow block off from the transforming, concept-creating activity of the brain. The "eroticism" of Negro expression springs from much the same conflict as that displayed in the violent gesturing of a man who attempts to express a complicated concept with a limited vocabulary; thwarted ideational energy is converted into unsatisfactory pantomime, and his words are burdened with meanings they cannot convey. Here lies the source of the basic ambiguity of *Native Son*, wherein in order to translate Bigger's complicated feelings into universal ideas, Wright had to force into Bigger's consciousness concepts and ideas which his intellect could not formulate. Between Wright's skill and knowledge and the potentials of Bigger's mute feelings lay a thousand years of conscious culture.

In the South the sensibilities of both blacks and whites are inhibited by the rigidly defined environment. For the Negro there is relative safety as long as the impulse toward individuality is suppressed. (Lynchings have occurred because Negroes painted their homes.) And it is the task of the Negro family to adjust the child to the Southern milieu; through it the currents, tensions and impulses generated within the human organism by the flux and flow of events are given their distribution. This also gives the group its distinctive character. Which, because of Negroes' suppressed minority position, is very much in the nature of an elaborate but limited defense mechanism. Its function is dual: to protect the Negro from whirling away from the undifferentiated mass of his people into the unknown, symbolized in its most abstract form by insanity, and most concretely by lynching; and to protect him from those unknown forces *within himself* which might urge him to reach out for that social and human equality which the white South says he cannot have. Rather than throw himself against the charged wires of his prison he annihilates the impulses within him.

The pre-individualistic black community discourages individuality out of self-defense. Having learned through experience that the whole group is punished for the actions of the single member, it has worked out efficient techniques of behavior control. For in many Southern communities everyone knows everyone else and is vulnerable to his opinions. In some communities everyone is "related" regardless of bloodties. The regard shown by the group for its members, its general communal character and its cohesion are often mentioned. For by comparison with the coldly impersonal relationships of the urban industrial community, its relationships are personal and warm.

Black Boy, however, illustrates that this personal quality, shaped by outer violence and inner fear, is ambivalent. Personal warmth is accompanied by an equally personal coldness, kindliness by cruelty, regard by malice. And these opposites are as quickly set off against the member who gestures toward individuality as a lynch mob forms at the cry of rape. Negro leaders have often been exasperated by this phenomenon, and Booker T. Washington (who demanded far less of Negro humanity than Richard Wright) described the Negro community as a basket of crabs, wherein should one attempt to climb out, the others immediately pull him back.

The member who breaks away is apt to be more impressed by its negative than by its positive character. He becomes a stranger even to his relatives and he interprets gestures of protection as blows of oppression—from which there is no hiding place, because every area of Negro life is affected. Even parental love is given a qualitative balance akin to "sadism." And the extent of beatings and psychological maimings meted out by Southern Negro parents rivals those described by the nineteenth-century Russian writers as characteristic of peasant life under the Czars. The horrible thing is that the cruelty is also an expression of concern, of love.

In discussing the inadequacies for democratic living typical of the education provided Negroes by the South, a Negro educator has coined the term *mis-education*. Within the ambit of the black family this takes the form of training the child away from curiosity and adventure, against reaching out for those activities lying beyond the borders of the black community. And when the child resists, the parent discourages him; first with the formula, "That there's for white folks. Colored can't have it," and finally with a beating.

It is not, then, the family and communal violence described by *Black Boy* that is unusual, but that Wright *recognized* and made no peace with its essential cruelty—even when, like a babe freshly emerged from the womb, he could not discern where his own personality ended and it began. Ordinarily both parent and child are protected against this cruelty—seeing it as love and finding subjective sanction for it in the spiritual authority of the Fifth Commandment, and on the secular level in the legal and extralegal structure of the Jim Crow system. The child who did not rebel, or who was unsuccessful in his rebellion, learned a masochistic submissiveness and a denial of the impulse toward Western culture when it stirred within him.

Why then have Southern whites, who claim to "know" the Negro, missed all this? Simply because they, too, are armored against the horror and the cruelty. Either they deny the Negro's humanity and feel no cause to measure his actions against civilized norms; or they protect themselves from their guilt in the Negro's condition and from their fear that their cooks might poison them, or that their nursemaids might strangle their infant charges, or that their field hands might do them violence, by attributing to them a superhuman capacity for love, kindliness and forgiveness. Nor does this in any way contradict their stereotyped conviction that all Negroes (meaning those with whom they have no contact) are given to the most animal behavior.

It is only when the individual, whether white or black, *rejects* the pattern that he awakens to the nightmare of his life. Perhaps much of the South's regressive character springs from the fact that many, jarred by some casual crisis into wakefulness, flee hysterically into the sleep of violence or the coma of apathy again. For the penalty of wakefulness is to encounter ever more violence and horror than the sensibilities can sustain unless translated into some form of social action. Perhaps the impassioned character so noticeable among those white Southern liberals so active in the Negro's cause is due to their sense of accumulated horror; their passion—like the violence in Faulkner's novels—is evidence of a profound spiritual vomiting.

This compulsion is even more active in Wright and the increasing number of Negroes who have said an irrevocable "no" to the Southern pattern. Wright learned that it is not enough merely to reject the white South, but that he had also to reject that part of the South which lay within. As a rebel he formulated that rejection negatively, because it was the negative face of the Negro community upon which he looked most often as a child. It is this he is contemplating when he writes:

> Whenever I thought of the essential bleakness of black life in America, I knew that Negroes had never been allowed to catch the full spirit of Western civilization, that they lived somehow in it but not of it. And when I brooded upon the cultural barrenness of black life, I wondered if clean, positive tenderness, love, honor, loyalty and the capacity to remember were native to man. I asked myself if these human qualities were not fostered, won, struggled and suffered for, preserved in ritual from one generation to another.

But far from implying that Negroes have no capacity for culture, as one critic interprets it, this is the strongest affirmation that they have. Wright is pointing out what should be obvious (especially to his Marxist critics) that Negro sensibility is socially and historically conditioned; that Western culture must be won, confronted like the animal in a Spanish bullfight, dominated by the red shawl of codified experience and brought heaving to its knees.

Wright knows perfectly well that Negro life is a by-product of Western civilization, and that in it, if only one possesses the humanity and humility to see, are to be discovered all those impulses, tendencies, life and cultural forms to be found elsewhere in Western society.

The problem arises because the special condition of Negroes in the United States, including the defensive character of Negro life itself (the "will toward organization" noted in the Western capitalist appears in the Negro as a will to camouflage, to dissimulate), so distorts these forms as to render their recognition as difficult as finding a wounded quail against the brown and yellow leaves of a Mississippi thicket—even the spilled blood blends with the background. Having himself been in the position of the quail—to expand the metaphor—Wright's wounds have told him both the question and the answer which every successful hunter must discover for himself: "Where would I hide if *I* were a wounded quail?" But perhaps that requires more sympathy with one's quarry than most hunters possess. Certainly it requires such a sensitivity to the shifting guises of humanity under pressure as to allow them to identify themselves with the human content, whatever its outer form; and even with those Southern Negroes to whom Paul Robeson's name is only a rolling sound in the fear-charged air.

Let us close with one final word about the blues: Their attraction lies in this, that they at once express both the agony of life and the possibility of conquering it through sheer toughness of spirit. They fall short of tragedy only in that they provide no solution, offer no scapegoat but the self. Nowhere in America today is there social or political action based upon the solid realities of Negro life depicted in *Black Boy;* perhaps that is why, with its refusal to offer solutions, it is like the blues. Yet in it thousands of Negroes will for the first time see their destiny in public print. Freed here of fear and the threat of violence, their lives have at last been organized, scaled down to possessable proportions. And in this lies Wright's most important achievement: He has converted the American Negro impulse toward self-annihilation and "going-under-ground" into a will to confront the world, to evaluate his experience honestly and throw his findings unashamedly into the guilty conscience of America.

Notes

1. Signature formula used by blues singers at conclusion of song.
2. Italics mine.

JAMES BALDWIN
From "Many Thousands Gone"
Notes of a Native Son
1955, pp. 30–45

The most powerful and celebrated statement we have yet had of what it means to be a Negro in America is unquestionably Richard Wright's *Native Son.* The feeling which prevailed at the time of its publication was that such a novel, bitter, uncompromising, shocking, gave proof, by its very existence, of what strides might be taken in a free democracy; and its indisputable success, proof that Americans were now able to look full in the face without flinching the dreadful facts. Americans, unhappily, have the most remarkable ability to alchemize all bitter truths into an innocuous but piquant confection and to transform their moral contradictions, or public discussion of such contradictions, into a proud decoration, such as are given for heroism on the field of battle. Such a book, we felt with pride, could never have been written before—which was true. Nor could it be written today. It bears already the aspect of a landmark; for Bigger and his brothers have undergone yet another metamorphosis; they have been accepted in baseball leagues and by colleges hitherto exclusive; and they have made a most favorable appearance on the national screen. We have yet to encounter, nevertheless, a report so indisputably authentic, or one that can begin to challenge this most significant novel.

It is, in a certain American tradition, the story of an unremarkable youth in battle with the force of circumstance; that force of circumstance which plays and which has played so important a part in the national fables of success or failure. In this case the force of circumstance is not poverty merely but color, a circumstance which cannot be overcome, against which the protagonist battles for his life and loses. It is, on the surface, remarkable that this book should have enjoyed among Americans the favor it did enjoy; no more remarkable, however, than that it should have been compared, exuberantly, to Dostoevsky, though placed a shade below Dos Passos, Dreiser, and Steinbeck; and when the book is examined, its impact does not seem remarkable at all, but becomes, on the contrary, perfectly logical and inevitable.

We cannot, to begin with, divorce this book from the specific social climate of that time: it was one of the last of those angry productions, encountered in the late twenties and all through the thirties, dealing with the inequities of the social structure of America. It was published one year before our entry into the last world war—which is to say, very few years after the dissolution of the WPA and the end of the New Deal and at a time when bread lines and soup kitchens and bloody industrial battles were bright in everyone's memory. The rigors of that unexpected time filled us not only with a genuinely bewildered and despairing idealism—so that, because there at least was *something* to fight for, young men went off to die in Spain—but also with a genuinely bewildered self-consciousness. The Negro, who had been during the magnificent twenties a passionate and delightful primitive, now became, as one of the things we were most self-conscious about, our most oppressed minority. In the thirties, swallowing Marx whole, we discovered the Worker and realized—I should think with some relief—that the aims of the Worker and the aims of the Negro were one. This theorem—to which we shall return—seems now to leave rather too much out of account; it became, nevertheless, one of the slogans of the "class struggle" and the gospel of the New Negro.

As for this New Negro, it was Wright who became his most eloquent spokesman; and his work, from its beginning, is most clearly committed to the social struggle. Leaving aside the considerable question of what relationship precisely the artist bears to the revolutionary, the reality of man as a social being is not his only reality and that artist is strangled who is forced to deal with human beings solely in social terms; and who has, moreover, as Wright had, the necessity thrust on him of being the representative of some thirteen million people. It is a false responsibility (since writers are not congressmen) and impossible, by its nature, of fulfillment. The unlucky shepherd soon finds that, so far from being able to feed the hungry sheep, he has lost the wherewithal for his own nourishment: having not been allowed—so fearful was his burden, so present his audience!—to recreate his own experience. Further, the militant men and women of the thirties were not, upon examination, significantly emancipated from their antecedents, however bitterly they might consider themselves estranged or however gallantly they struggled to build a better world. However they might extol Russia, their concept of a better world was quite helplessly American and betrayed a certain thinness of imagination, a suspect reliance on suspect and badly digested formulae, and a positively fretful romantic haste. Finally, the relationship of the Negro to the Worker cannot be summed up, nor even greatly illuminated, by saying that their aims are one. It is true only insofar as they both desire better working conditions and useful only insofar as they unite their strength as workers to achieve these ends. Further than this we cannot in honesty go.

In this climate Wright's voice first was heard and the struggle which promised for a time to shape his work and give it purpose also fixed it in an ever more unrewarding rage. Recording his days of anger he has also nevertheless recorded, as no Negro before him had ever done, that fantasy Americans hold in their minds when they speak of the Negro: that fantastic and fearful image which we have lived with since the first slave fell beneath the lash. This is the significance of *Native Son* and also, unhappily, its overwhelming limitation.

Native Son begins with the *Brring!* of an alarm clock in the squalid Chicago tenement where Bigger and his family live. Rats live there too, feeding off the garbage, and we first encounter Bigger in the act of killing one. One may consider that the entire book, from that harsh *Brring!* to Bigger's weak "Good-by" as the lawyer, Max, leaves him in the death cell, is an extension, with the roles inverted, of this chilling metaphor. Bigger's situation and Bigger himself exert on the mind the same sort of fascination. The premise of the book is, as I take it, clearly conveyed in these first pages: we are confronting a monster created by the American republic and we are, through being made to share his experience, to receive illumination as regards the manner of his life and to feel both pity and horror at his awful and inevitable doom. This is an arresting and potentially rich idea and we would be discussing a very different novel if Wright's execution had been more perceptive and if he had not attempted to redeem a symbolical monster in social terms.

One may object that it was precisely Wright's intention to create in Bigger a social symbol, revelatory of social disease and prophetic of disaster. I think, however, that it is this assumption which we ought to examine more carefully. Bigger has no discernible relationship to himself, to his own life, to his own people, nor to any other people—in this respect, perhaps, he is most American—and his force comes, not from his significance as a social (or anti-social) unit, but from his significance as the incarnation of a myth. It is remarkable that, though we follow him step by step from the tenement room to the death cell, we know as little about him when this journey is ended as we did when it began; and, what is even more remarkable, we know almost as little about the social dynamic which we are to believe created him. Despite the details of slum life which we are given, I doubt that anyone who has thought about it, disengaging himself from sentimentality, can accept this most essential premise of the novel for a moment. Those Negroes who surround him, on the other hand, his hard-working mother, his ambitious sister, his poolroom cronies, Bessie, might be considered as far richer and far more subtle and accurate illustrations of the ways in which Negroes are controlled in our society and the complex techniques they have evolved for their survival. We are limited, however, to Bigger's view of them, part of a deliberate plan which might not have been disastrous if we were not also limited to Bigger's perceptions. What this means for the novel is that a necessary dimension has been cut away; this dimension being the relationship that Negroes bear to one another, that depth of involvement and unspoken recognition of shared experience which creates a way of life. What the novel reflects—and at no point interprets—is the isolation of the Negro within his own group and the resulting fury of impatient scorn. It is this which creates its climate of anarchy and unmotivated and unapprehended disaster; and it is this climate, common to most Negro protest novels, which has led us all to believe that in Negro life there exists no tradition, no field of manners, no possibility of ritual or intercourse, such as may, for example, sustain the Jew even after he has left his father's house. But the fact is not that the Negro has no tradition but that there has as yet arrived no sensibility sufficiently profound and tough to make this tradition articulate. For a tradition expresses, after all, nothing more than the long and painful experience of a people; it comes out of the battle waged to maintain their integrity or, to put it more simply, out of their struggle to survive. When we speak of the Jewish tradition we are speaking of centuries of exile and persecution, of the strength which endured and the sensibility which discovered in it the high possibility of the moral victory.

This sense of how Negroes live and how they have so long endured is hidden from us in part by the very speed of the Negro's public progress, a progress so heavy with complexity, so bewildering and kaleidoscopic, that he dare not pause to conjecture on the darkness which lies behind him; and by the nature of the American psychology which, in order to apprehend or be made able to accept it, must undergo a metamorphosis so profound as to be literally unthinkable and which there is no doubt we will resist until we are compelled to achieve our own identity by the rigors of a time that has yet to come. Bigger, in the meanwhile, and all his furious kin, serve only to whet the notorious national taste for the sensational and to reinforce all that we now find it necessary to believe. It is not Bigger whom we fear, since his appearance among us makes our victory certain. It is the others, who smile, who go to church, who give no cause for complaint, whom we sometimes consider with amusement, with pity, even with affection—and in whose faces we sometimes surprise the merest arrogant hint of hatred, the faintest, withdrawn, speculative shadow of contempt—who make us uneasy; whom we cajole, threaten, flatter, fear; who to us remain unknown, though we are not (we feel with both relief and hostility and with bottomless confusion) unknown to them. It is out of our reaction to these hewers of wood and drawers of water that our image of Bigger was created.

It is this image, living yet, which we perpetually seek to evade with good works; and this image which makes of all our good works an intolerable mockery. The "nigger," black, benighted, brutal, consumed with hatred as we are consumed with guilt, cannot be thus blotted out. He stands at our shoulders when we give our maid her wages, it is his hand which we fear we are taking when struggling to communicate with the current "intelligent" Negro, his stench, as it were, which fills our mouths with salt as the monument is unveiled in honor of the latest Negro leader. Each generation has shouted behind him, *Nigger!* as he walked our streets; it is he whom we would rather our sisters did not marry; he is banished into the vast and wailing outer darkness whenever we speak of the "purity" of our women, of the "sanctity" of our homes, of "American" ideals. What is more, he knows it. He is indeed the "native son": he is the "nigger." Let us refrain from inquiring at the moment whether or not he actually exists; for we *believe* that he exists. Whenever we encounter him amongst us in the flesh, our faith is made perfect and his necessary and bloody end is executed with a mystical ferocity of joy.

But there is a complementary faith among the damned which involves their gathering of the stones with which those who walk in the light shall stone them; or there exists among the intolerably degraded the perverse and powerful desire to force into the arena of the actual those fantastic crimes of which they have been accused, achieving their vengeance and their own destruction through making the nightmare real. The American image of the Negro lives also in the Negro's heart; and when he has surrendered to this image life has no other possible reality. Then he, like the white enemy with whom he will be locked one day in mortal struggle, has no means save this of asserting his identity. This is why Bigger's murder of Mary can be referred to as an "act of creation" and why, once this murder has been committed, he can feel for the first time that he is living fully and deeply as a man was meant to live. And there is, I should think, no Negro living in America who has not felt, briefly or for long periods, with anguish sharp or dull, in varying degrees and to varying effect, simple, naked and unanswerable hatred; who has not wanted to smash any white face he may encounter in a day, to violate, out of motives of the cruelest vengeance, their women, to break the bodies of all white people and bring them low, as low as that dust into which he himself has been and is being trampled; no Negro, finally, who has not had to make his own precarious adjustment to the "nigger" who surrounds him and to the "nigger" in himself.

Yet the adjustment must be made—rather, it must be attempted, the tension perpetually sustained—for without this he has surrendered his birthright as a man no less than his birthright as a black man. The entire universe is then peopled only with his enemies, who are not only white men armed with rope and rifle, but his own far-flung and contemptible kinsmen. Their blackness is his degradation and it is their stupid and passive endurance which makes his end inevitable.

Bigger dreams of some black man who will weld all blacks together into a mighty fist, and feels, in relation to his family, that perhaps they had to live as they did precisely because none of them had ever done anything, right or wrong, which mattered very much. It is only he who, by an act of murder, has burst the dungeon cell. He has made it manifest that *he* lives and that his despised blood nourishes the passions of a man. He has forced his oppressors to see the fruit of that oppression: and he feels, when his family and his friends come to visit him in the death cell, that they should not be weeping or frightened, that they should be happy, *proud* that he has dared, through murder and now through his own imminent destruction, to redeem their anger and humiliation, that he has hurled into the spiritless obscurity of their lives the lamp of his passionate life and death. Henceforth, they may remember Bigger—who has died, as we may conclude, for them. But they do not feel this; they only know that he has murdered two women and precipitated a reign of terror; and that now he is to die in the electric chair. They therefore weep and are honestly frightened—for which Bigger despises them and wishes to "blot" them out. What is missing in his situation and in the representation of his psychology—which makes his situation false and his psychology incapable of development—is any revelatory apprehension of Bigger as one of the Negro's realities or as one of the Negro's roles. This failure is part of the previously noted failure to convey any sense of Negro life as a continuing and complex group reality. Bigger, who cannot function therefore as a reflection of the social illness, having, as it were, no society to reflect, likewise refuses to function on the loftier level of the Christ-symbol. His kinsmen are quite right to weep and be frightened, even to be appalled: for it is not his love for them or for himself which causes him to die, but his hatred and his self-hatred; he does not redeem the pains of a despised people, but reveals, on the contrary, nothing more than his own fierce bitterness at having been born one of them. In this also he is the "native son," his progress determinable by the speed with which the distance increases between himself and the auction-block and all that the auction-block implies. To have penetrated this phenomenon, this inward contention of love and hatred, blackness and whiteness, would have given him a stature more nearly human and an end more nearly tragic; and would have given us a document more profoundly and genuinely bitter and less harsh with an anger which is, on the one hand, exhibited and, on the other hand, denied.

Native Son finds itself at length so trapped by the American image of Negro life and by the American necessity to find the ray of hope that it cannot pursue its own implications. This is why Bigger must be at the last redeemed, to be received, if only by rhetoric, into that community of phantoms which is our tenaciously held ideal of the happy social life. It is the socially conscious whites who receive him—the Negroes being capable of no such objectivity—and we have, by way of illustration, that lamentable scene in which Jan, Mary's lover, forgives him for her murder; and, carrying the explicit burden of the novel, Max's long speech to the jury. This speech, which really ends the book, is one of the most desperate performances in American fiction. It is the question of Bigger's humanity which is at stake, the relationship in which he stands to all other Americans—and, by implication, to all people—and it is precisely this question which it cannot clarify, with which it cannot, in fact, come to any coherent terms. He is the monster created by the American republic, the present awful sum of generations of oppression; but to say that he is a monster is to fall into the trap of making him subhuman and he must, therefore, be made representative of a way of life which is real and human in precise ratio to the degree to which it seems to us monstrous and strange. It seems to me that this idea carries, implicitly, a most remarkable confession: that is, that Negro life is in fact as debased and impoverished as our theology claims; and, further, that the use to which Wright puts this idea can only proceed from the assumption—not entirely unsound—that Americans, who evade, so far as possible, all genuine experience, have therefore no way of assessing the experience of others and no way of establishing themselves in relation to any way of life which is not their own. The privacy or obscurity of Negro life makes that life capable, in our imaginations, of producing anything at all; and thus the idea of Bigger's monstrosity can be presented without fear of contradiction, since no American has the knowledge or authority to contest it and no Negro has the voice. It is an idea, which, in the framework of the novel, is dignified by the possibility it promptly affords of presenting Bigger as the herald of disaster, the danger signal of a more bitter time to come when not Bigger alone but all his kindred will rise, in the name of the many thousands who have perished in fire and flood and by rope and torture, to demand their rightful vengeance.

But it is not quite fair, it seems to me, to exploit the national innocence in this way. The idea of Bigger as a warning boomerangs not only because it is quite beyond the limit of probability that Negroes in America will ever achieve the means of wreaking vengeance upon the state but also because it cannot be said that they have any desire to do so. *Native Son* does not convey the altogether savage paradox of the American Negro's situation, of which the social reality which we prefer with such hopeful superficiality to study is but, as it were, the shadow. It is not simply the relationship of oppressed to oppressor, of master to slave, nor is it motivated merely by hatred; it is also, literally and morally, a *blood* relationship, perhaps the most profound reality of the American experience, and we cannot begin to unlock it until we accept how very much it contains of the force and anguish and terror of love.

Negroes are Americans and their destiny is the country's destiny. They have no other experience besides their experience on this continent and it is an experience which cannot be rejected, which yet remains to be embraced. If, as I believe, no American Negro exists who does not have his private Bigger Thomas living in the skull, then what most significantly fails to be illuminated here is the paradoxical adjustment which is perpetually made, the Negro being compelled to accept the fact that this dark and dangerous and unloved stranger is part of himself forever. Only this recognition sets him in any wise free and it is this, this necessary ability to contain and even, in the most honorable sense of the word, to *exploit* the "nigger," which lends to Negro life its high element of the ironic and which causes the most well-meaning of their American critics to make such exhilarating errors when attempting to understand them. To present Bigger as a warning is simply to reinforce the American guilt and fear concerning him, it is most forcefully to limit him to that previously mentioned social arena in which he has no human validity, it is simply to condemn him to death. For he has always been a warning, he represents the evil, the sin and suffering which we are compelled to reject. It is useless to say to the courtroom in which this heathen sits on trial that he is their responsibility, their creation, and his crimes are theirs; and that they ought, therefore, to allow him to live, to make articulate to himself behind the walls of prison the meaning of his existence. The meaning of his existence has already been most adequately expressed, nor does anyone wish, particularly not in the name of democracy, to think of it any more; as for the possibility of articulation, it is this possibility which above all others we most dread. Moreover, the courtroom, judge, jury, witnesses and spectators, recognize immediately that Bigger is their creation and they recognize this not only with hatred and fear and guilt and the resulting fury of self-righteousness but also with that morbid fullness of pride mixed with horror with which one regards the extent and power of one's wickedness. They know that death is his portion, that he runs to death; coming from darkness and dwelling in darkness, he must be, as often as he rises, banished, lest the entire planet be engulfed. And they know, finally, that they do not wish to forgive him and that he does not wish to be forgiven; that he dies, hating them, scorning that appeal which they cannot make to that irrecoverable humanity of his which cannot hear it; and that he *wants* to die because he glories in his hatred and prefers, like Lucifer, rather to rule in hell than serve in heaven.

For, bearing in mind the premise on which the life of such a man is based, i.e., that black is the color of damnation, this is his only possible end. It is the only death which will allow him a kind of dignity or even, however horribly, a kind of beauty. To tell this story, no more than a single aspect of the story of the "nigger," is inevitably and richly to become involved with the force of life and legend, how each perpetually assumes the guise of the other, creating that dense, many-sided and shifting reality which is the world we live in and the world we make. To tell his story is to begin to liberate us from his image and it is, for the first time, to clothe this phantom with flesh and blood, to deepen, by our understanding of him and his relationship to us, our understanding of ourselves and of all men. But this is not the story which *Native Son* tells, for we find here merely, repeated in anger, the story which we have told in pride. Nor, since the implications of this anger are evaded, are we ever confronted with the actual or potential significance of our pride; which is why we fall, with such a positive glow of recognition, upon Max's long and bitter summing up. It is addressed to those among us of good will and it seems to say that, though there are whites and blacks among us who hate each other, we will not; there are those who are betrayed by greed, by guilt, by bloodlust, but not we; we will set our faces against them and join hands and walk together into that dazzling future when there will be no white or black. This is the dream of all liberal men, a dream not at all dishonorable, but, nevertheless, a dream. For, let us join hands on this mountain as we may, the battle is elsewhere. It proceeds far from us in the heat and horror and pain of life itself where all men are betrayed by greed and guilt and bloodlust and where no one's hands are clean. Our good will, from which we yet expect such power to transform us, is thin, passionless, strident: its roots, examined, lead us back to our forebears, whose assumption it was that the black man, to become truly human and acceptable, must first become like us. This assumption once accepted, the Negro in America can only acquiesce in the obliteration of his own personality, the distortion and debasement of his own experience, surrendering to those forces which reduce the person to anonymity and which make themselves manifest daily all over the darkening world.

MICHEL FABRE

From "Introduction"

The Richard Wright Reader

eds. Ellen Wright and Michel Fabre

1978, pp. vii–xxiv

The literary reputation of Richard Wright has been secure since the 1940s, when he became famous with the publication of *Native Son* and *Black Boy*. Most Americans know these books by title, yet few people under forty have actually read them, and students are often inclined to consider Wright as a forefather, whose outspokenness was indispensable to the blossoming of Ralph Ellison and James Baldwin, but whose aesthetic achievement has been somewhat overshadowed and superseded by these writers. To some degree, the revival of interest in black literature that began in the sixties has led the public to reconsider its view of this special body of American writing and to reassess its central figures. Among other things, the uniqueness of the Afro-American perspective and its relationship to Western culture have been gauged anew, and Wright's historical importance is more widely recognized. The complexity and scope of his works, however, remain largely unsuspected for a number of reasons. First, Wright's style is widely regarded as visceral and inspired, but at the same time too simple and too naturalistic to be truly literary. It has been held that such writing cannot rival the supposedly more sophisticated and universal achievement of, say, Ellison's *Invisible Man*. Second, it has been alleged that Wright's exile in France, where he lived from 1946 to his death in 1960, dealt a death blow to his creative imagination by estranging him from the situation of the blacks at home. A third line of criticism, mostly espoused by black nationalist critics, contends that Wright's vision of black life in the United States was too white-oriented and too generally bleak to allow him to relate to the more vital aspects of Afro-American culture. ⟨. . .⟩

The depiction of the black struggle under adverse social and racial conditions often explicitly constitutes the subject of Wright's writing, but because of his sometimes conflicting attitudes towards black life in the United States the coherence of his purpose is not always apparent. It does not appear, either, that his major purpose was to demonstrate the universality of the black struggle as a reflection and example of the condition of modern man (although certainly much can be made, as will be seen, of Wright's contention that "the Negro is America's metaphor"). Wright's enduring concern was, in fact, more personal and more basic: it amounted to nothing less than the interchange and conflict between the individual and society.

Rooted as it is in an existential sense of freedom, Wright's blossoming into print should be construed as an act of defiance, an assertion of the equation between literature and rebellion, an avatar of the myth of Prometheus who stole fire and knowledge from the Gods for the benefit of all men. In Wright's case, the gap between life and literature is so narrow that the awakening and development of his avocation closely follow the expanding circles of his self-awareness and his intellectual growth.

It is largely through—books even more than through experience—that Wright progressively emerged from the destitution of his lower-class Southern childhood, from the restrictive definition imposed upon blacks by racism, from the anti-intellectual climate of post-war America, and finally from a self-complacent definition of Western humanism. By the time he put together, in *White Man, Listen*, the lectures that constitute his ideological testament, he saw himself as one of those men "who carry on their frail but indefatigable shoulders the best of two worlds—and who, amidst confusion and stagnation, seek desperately for a home which, if found, could be a home for the hearts of all men." His individual growth thus went along with his affirmation of human solidarity and of the writer's special duty.

Such an affirmation was already foreshadowed in the opening chapters of *Black Boy* and Wright's later, humanistic commitment can appear as a rationalization and acceptance of what was originally a compulsive need for self-assertion in the face of a crushing environment. To put it another way, Wright always wanted to recreate himself, and others, against the definition imposed by society.

From whatever source his sense of freedom may have sprung, if we consider him as the product of the sharecropping South, his conviction of his innate worth and dignity constitutes the cornerstone of his personality. Conversely, such childhood traumas as his father's desertion of the family, his mother's strict enforcement of obedience, finally the necessity for him to depend on the support of relatives, all these rooted Wright's outlook in precariousness, thus increasing his tendency to self-protective rebellion. In *Black Boy*, he describes himself as emotionally deprived, and he projects upon the community in which he lived an unexpected lack of warmth. Before Wright could confront white racism, he had to assert himself against a black familial environment where Seventh Day Adventism seemed oppressive because it served to justify frugality and the banning of secular entertainments.

From his feelings of deprivation Wright sought refuge in fantasy. Books became for him a vicarious means of establishing meaningful relationships with others. But his use of literature as a means of self-fulfillment also alienated him further from his community which perceived it as a deviant practice. Wright's originality was considered, in fact, a possible source of trouble since it challenged the whites' desire to have Negroes conform to the stereotype. Wright therefore seldom saw his black environment as a sustaining community, but rather as a network of constraints aimed at securing subservient behavior.

Wright's conception of individual freedom was thus forged in opposition to the discipline imposed by the family and religion. His attempt to reconcile freedom and a definition of himself not only made him flee the repressive racial order of the Deep South but it partly alienated him from the restrictive (black) way of life he had known; it increased his emotional kinship with the sort of liberal or social writing to which he had access, starting with H. L. Mencken and the American naturalists.

Reaching Chicago at the outset of the Depression enabled Wright to further conceptualize his problem of relating to society. Daily experiences at the relief stations convinced him that his plight was by no means exceptional. Also, racism, which had loomed so large in the South, now appeared as only one aspect of capitalist oppression. Although Wright had to bear the special onus of being black in America, there were, in fact, millions of people in the country who were alienated by displacement, urbanization and the societal changes inherent in industrialization.

Wright joined the Communist party in 1932 largely in order to reconcile his desire for a sustaining society and his need for freedom. In this broader circle, his rebellion was not directed only against the subservience inculcated by racial oppression but against the American capitalist system. In moving terms, which come out lyrically in his revolutionary poetry, he dreamed of building a world of brotherhood. More important still, he joined the Party in order to continue his association with the Chicago John Reed Club, a left-wing artists' and writers' group in which he had found for the first time an acceptable and rewarding peer-group.

It was unavoidable that, when confronted with Party demands tending to limit the freedom of the intellectual or with conciliatory tactics disregarding black protest in the era of the United Front, Wright should have reasserted his emotional, moral and racial individualism. One may even wonder why he continued Party activities until as late as 1942. His novellas of black militancy, like "Fire and Cloud" or "Bright and Morning Star" definitely sprang out of his revolutionary convictions but, in order better to understand what has been called Bigger Thomas' political confusion, one must reflect that *Native Son*, far from being a one-sided propaganda novel, also reflected Wright's belief that Communism did not represent a totally satisfactory approach to the racial question.

Ever and again in his public utterances at that time ⟨. . .⟩ Wright asserted the writer's duty to proclaim his personal vision against the pressures of political expediency. When he ended his relationship with Communist intellectuals, Wright lost, however, an emotionally satisfying community and, at the apex of success, he found loneliness again, although he was not without sustenance. "The best American Negro novelist," he wielded some power, although the title conferred upon him by critics and audiences tended to impose subtle limits to the recognition thus granted him. His sense of being a "representative Negro," a spokesman denouncing the outrages suffered by his race, accordingly prompted him further to assert his solidarity with them. *Twelve Million Black Voices* and *Black Boy* partly came out of this sense of racial responsibility. At the time, Wright also launched several projects in order to fight segregation and discrimination. His choice probably amounted more to intellectual adhesion than to instinctive, emotional kinship. This did not detract from its validity and sincerity but it helps explain why Wright kept looking for answers to social problems beyond the scope of racial, and even political, commitment.

An agnostic, opposing the repression of institutionalized religion, Wright was still by no means indifferent to the manifestations of the spiritual. His sense of waging a somewhat solitary fight and his growing alienation from American society, now that he had measured what it could offer him, drove him again to explore, this time in philosophical terms, the conflict that he was experiencing between the self and society. Out of his quest grew "The Man Who Lived Underground," completed as early as 1942, and *The Outsider* which was published in 1953 at the close of a seven-year period of self-examination and doubts.

Far from being initiated by the French existentialists, whom Wright befriended only after he went to Paris in 1946, this philosophical interest stemmed from his early existential experiences as well as from the sense of being both inside and outside American culture, which he considered typical of the Afro-American and which he had already explored in "The Man Who Lived Underground." Indeed, anguish, dread and alienation were to be found in *Native Son* as forceful, emotional components before appearing as governing concepts in *The Outsider*, in which the influence of Heidegger and Kierkegaard is more perceptible than that of Camus and Sartre.

Despite its structural and stylistic flaws, *The Outsider* is a novel whose ideological importance rivals that of *Native Son*. *Native Son* mostly attempted to explore the psychological effects of racism and the ambiguous potentialities, be they fascistic or revolutionary, underlying Bigger Thomas' deviant act of self assertion. *The Outsider* analyzed and repudiated both Fascism and Communism as models for society, and it probed the source of alienation lying at the heart of modern man, not as an effect of oppression but as a manifestation of his destiny. It carried individual freedom to its ultimate limit only to conclude on the necessity of the social bond: "Alone, man is nothing."

It may be argued that Bigger Thomas has potentially more in him of the black nationalist than of the left-wing revolutionary but it is difficult to claim him for a metaphysical rebel. In "The Man Who Lived Underground," Fred Daniels went beyond Bigger in terms of transcending everyday conditions of socialized behavior: in his territory under and beyond, on the reverse side of reality, he experienced the alienation that plagues the human condition. Cross Damon, the protagonist in *The Outsider*, provides even more speculative rationalization for his acts. Only accidentally due to his race, his alienation is that of a present-day intellectual whose philosophical beliefs remove him from the rules of society. Liberated by chance from the snare of economic and familial dependence, he undertakes to remold his destiny according to individual choice and shuns conventional morality. Like Wright, Damon is a product of secularization and he is driven, emotionally and intellectually, to extol the subjective in himself and thereby affirm the value of his individual personality against the collective discipline that reduces people to fragments in the social whole. It should be emphasized that Damon is not defeated because of the intransigence or single-handedness of his attempt but because of the violent methods he is compelled to use. Violence contaminates him and breaks his bond with others. The woman he loves commits suicide out of horror at what he has become: a murderer playing God to other men. Wright thus clearly stresses the necessity for emotional attachment, compassion and solidarity.

Completed at the end of a long transitional period, *The Outsider* constitutes Wright's spiritual autobiography for those years, a dramatization of his dilemma in his quest for balance between individual freedom and the necessity for social order.

Wright's attraction towards existentialism was, however, more than a search for philosophical illumination. The end of World War II had brought about a new surge of consumerism and materialism in the United States, which Henry Miller was describing as "the air-conditioned nightmare," and it was possible to believe, at the time, that humanism could only be restored through an infusion of the traditional European values of the Enlightenment and the Age of Revolution. Western Europe was then struggling to recover an identity independent of both Soviet Russia and the United States. Among others, the French existentialists embodied a type of humanism which appeared as a bulwark against the dislocations attending urbanization and industrialization. Like Wright, they were dissatisfied with American materialism and with Stalinist totalitarianism, although, like him, they strove for action along Marxist lines. What has sometimes been described as "Wright's roll in the hay with existentialism" should therefore be seen as more than a fad or an experiment on his part. It was a sincere attempt at recreating the sustaining and purposeful community he had once known in the John Reed Club. And, this time, he started from ideological premises which were more sophisticated and more likely than Communism to guarantee individual freedom. Also, whereas in the 1930s he had embraced Communism as he would a religion, Wright now explored the ontological implications of existentialism with a critical eye.

To the degree that Wright projected in *Black Boy* his development as representative of black Southern youth, one is tempted to read the insecurity and alienation of Cross Damon as a projection of existential conditions or personality features construed in order to make the American Negro a representative of modern man. However, although he linked Damon's psychological make-up with his lack of social values and to the utter desacralization of his universe, Wright did not project Negro alienation as typical of modern (or Western) man. Contrary to what existentialism might have led him to do, he stopped short of using the Negro as a choice metaphor for the alienation of modern man because he gradually came to see existentialism as a philosophy born of "the decline of the West" and to believe that Afro-American history was more than a part of Western history, because it not only reflected the disruptions brought about by the passing of the Third World from feudalism to the modern age but also foreshadowed the renewal of civilization to come.

Wright thus found himself grappling with problems not only of racial definition or struggle against oppression but of the shape modern society was to take if the humanity in man were to be preserved. In the thirties and forties he had considered that his role as a black writer forced him first to destroy the stereotypes of the "noble savage" and Uncle Tom and then to expose the definition of "the Negro" given by America. Already in *Twelve Million Black Voices* he had viewed the history of Africans in America as a parable for the transition from agrarianism to industrialism, but by 1946 he claimed that American Negroes were the symbol of modern man's transition to an industrial way of life now starting *on a global scale*. In a July 1946 letter published in the French magazine *Les Nouvelles Epitres*, he clearly defined the scope of his metaphoric reference:

> By social definition, I am an American Negro and what I'll have to say deals with Negro life in the U.S., not because I think that life or its problems are of supreme importance, but because Negro life in the U.S. dramatically symbolizes the struggle of a people whose forefathers lived in a warm, simple culture and who are now trying to live the new way of life that dominates our time: machine-civilization and all the consequences flowing from it.
>
> It must be understood that when I talk of the American Negroes, I am talking about everybody . . .

In the next paragraph, Wright describes the plight of Afro-Americans as that of an "internal colony" (a concept often used by Black Power theoreticians in the 1960s) and he sets up two conflicting cultural choices:

> The Negro is intrinsically a colonial subject, but one who lives not in China, India, or Africa but next door to his conquerors, attending their schools, fighting their wars, and laboring in their factories. The American Negro problem, therefore, is but a facet of the global problem that splits the world in two: Handicraft vs. Mass production; Family vs. the Individual; Tradition vs. Progress; Personality vs. Collectivity; the East (the colonial peoples) vs. the West (exploiters of the world).
>
> Nowhere on earth have these extremes met and clashed with such prolonged violence as in America between Negro and white, and this fact alone endows the American Negro problem with a vital importance, for what happens between whites and blacks in America foreshadows what will happen between the colored billions of Asia and Africa and the industrial whites of the West. Indeed, the world's fate is symbolically prefigured today in race relations in America.

One may remark that neither paradigm corresponded to Wright's personal preferences: although he might sentimentally cling to "handicraft" and "the East" and he definitely preferred "personality" to "collectivity," he undoubtedly chose "the individual" rather than "family" and "tradition," as can be seen in his strategies for the modernization of Africa.

In 1946, however, Wright was more interested in the plight of the *individual* subjected to the jump from tradition to modernization than in political systems. He stated in the same letter that he was "merely a man who is curious about the tissue and texture of human experience," and he exclaimed:

> Imagine people stolen from the warm nest of their ancient living, stripped of their culture, defined in economic terms, worked for 300 years and suddenly freed! . . . How did these people fare? What happened inside of them? What personality traits did they acquire as a result of such an experience? What kinds of cultural manifestations did they express?

In this perspective, the Afro-American's psychological pattern appears clearly to be the result of social change and industrialization rather than a primarily racial component setup. Speaking for all comparable peoples and groups, Wright thus took the Afro-American experience as a unique instance of the most advanced step taken from traditional society to modern society, not as an instance of metaphysical alienation.

Partly due to the influence of his friend George Padmore, one of the major proponents of Pan-Africanism, Wright's ideological preoccupations shifted from his metaphysical concerns. His opposition to Americanism and Stalinism in the name of European humanism soon became opposition to Western colonialism for the sake of Third World liberation. He turned away from a community of Western intellectuals bent upon preserving the freedom of man in Europe and toward the "lonely outsiders," the colored elites attempting to restore freedom in Africa and Asia.

Most of his later work, including his fiction, should be evaluated in that light. To many critics, *The Long Dream* seemed at the time to be merely a return to the roots of Wright's inspiration, that is, the closed Mississippi society he had known as a child, yet the novel was conceived as only the first step in a trilogy. In the initial volume, Wright examined the psychological survival and forced alienation of Fishbelly in a racist (colonial) context. He then, in a second novel, the still unpublished "Island of Hallucinations," proceeded to analyze the sequels of this conditioning in the freer (post-colonialization) atmosphere of Paris. The third volume, which was sketched but never written, would have taken the protagonist to Africa, where he would have discovered new allegiances and overcome his lingering intellectual oppression before returning to the American soil.

Of course, there is a good deal of wishful thinking in such an ending. But Wright's interest lay in that direction. In a different, often more humorous vein found in later short stories like "Big Black Good Man" and "Man, God Ain't Like That," he explored white fears of black power and the psychological havoc inflicted by missionaries trying to impose Christianity upon paganism. Practically all of Wright's nonfiction in the fifties was concerned, directly or indirectly, with the Third World.

Often opposed to Leopold Sengor's "*négritude*," the strategies that Wright considered fit for the liberation of Africa would deserve separate treatment. In "Tradition and Industrialization," a paper given at the First Conference of Black Artists and Writers in September 1956, Wright, who had often regretted the lack of traditions in the United States, advocated the destruction of stifling African beliefs in unambiguous terms:

> The white Western world, until relatively recently the most secular and free part of the earth . . . labored unconsciously and tenaciously for five hundred years to make Asia and Africa (that is, the elite in those areas) more secular-minded than the West! . . . I do say "Bravo!" to the consequences of Western plundering, a plundering that created the conditions

> for the possible rise of rational societies for the greater majority of mankind. . . . That part of the heritage of the West which I value—man stripped of the past and free for the future—has now been established as lonely bridgeheads in Asia and Africa. . . . It means that the spirit of the Enlightenment, of the Reformation, which made Europe great now has a chance to be extended to all mankind! (*White Man, Listen!*)

Wright clearly fell back on his own childhood experience to advocate the moves that had liberated him: breaking the shackles of religion and any world-view making for human stagnation. He distrusted the mystical tenets of "*négritude*," like the concept of "the sensitive African" opposed to "the rational European," not because he was unable to perceive the mystical components of African life, but because such conceptions defeated colonial independence by fettering the individual in communal cultures ill-equipped to confront the technological and cultural domination of the West. Wright's attitude towards institutionalized religion was the same as his unrelenting opposition to the oppressive, self-denying beliefs once prevalent in his grandmother's house. Especially after he witnessed the role played by race and religion at the Bandung Conference, he held the religious world-view of Asia and Africa largely responsible for the deprivation and immobility of millions whose emotional satisfaction he could only construe as a dream. He had personally experienced the stresses inflicted by desacralization and industrialization in America, yet he claimed that the Third World should go the way of the West in order not only to confront the West but to establish a freer sort of society:

> My decalogue of beliefs does not imply that I've turned my back in scorn upon the past of mankind. . . . Men who can slough off the beautiful mythologies, the enthralling configurations of external ceremonies, manners, and codes of the past, are not necessarily unacquainted with, or unappreciative of, them; they have interiorized them, have reduced them to mental traits, psychological problems. . . . It is my profound conviction that emotional independence is a clear and distinct human advance, a gain for all mankind. (*White Man Listen*)

It has been said that Wright had finally settled into the role of a detached observer of Third World nations, a black man of the West, an outsider on the margins of two cultures. Such a view does not, however, take into account his continuing conflict and spiritual questioning. The more he appeared to trust rationality as a means towards political freedom and social development, the more concerned he seemed with the emotional and irrational dimensions of spirituality. As an artist, it had always been his inclination to "revere the fanciful and the imaginative," which, in his eyes, made for the powerful creativity of folk life. His visceral reactions to the impact of African beliefs during his visit to the Gold Coast show that he had grown ever more aware of the spiritual dimension of life, to the point of reconsidering some of his assumptions, or at least of wondering about the dangers of modernization:

> The pathos of Africa would be doubled if, out of her dark past, her people were plunged into a dark future, a future that smacked of Chicago or Detroit . . . What would be the gain if these benighted fetish-worshippers were snatched from their mud-huts and their ancestor idolatry, and catapulted into the vast steel and stone jungles of cities, tied to monotonous jobs, condemned to cheap movies, made dependent upon alcohol? Would an African, a hundred years from now, after he had been trapped into the labyrinths of industrialization, be able to say when he is dying, when he is on the verge of going to meet his long-dead ancestors, those traditional mysterious words:
>
> I'm dying
> I'm dying
> Something big is happening to me . . . ?
>
> (*Black Power*)

Considered as a mode of living rather than as an institution, religion was not condemned by Wright. On the contrary, closer contact with African beliefs prompted him further to explore the religious foundations of the human personality. He did so in Freudian terms in *Savage Holiday*, his nonracial psychoanalytical novel. He did so, again, in the broader sociological context of *Pagan Spain*, in which he described the heathen substratum of the most Christian, and the least European, country in the West. At the end of his life, his delight in recreating the spiritual moods of Japanese haiku poetry denoted a similar falling back on intuition, on feeling, very possibly because the models of rational societies thus far propounded to man threatened to turn into well-organized nightmares.

In evaluating Wright's conception of individual freedom and fulfillment in relation to organized society, one must make allowances for the changes that occurred between the 1930s and the 1960s, as even quasi-feudal Mississippi grew into an industrial society, with some attending racial liberation. Also, Wright's major theme and lifelong concern, the issue that, in his eyes, made the plight of the Afro-American symbolic of the modern world, was a question no single man could answer. In a review of Michel Del Castillo's novel, *The Disinherited*, which he wrote shortly before his death, Wright expressed his doubts that the rational society he envisioned might be able to answer man's deepest needs:

> May it not develop that man's sense of being disinherited is not mainly political at all, that politics serve it as a temporary vessel, that Marxist ideology in particular is but a transitory makeshift pending a more accurate diagnosis, that Communism may be a painful compromise containing a definition of man by sheer default?

As a result of this unreconciled striving for a balance between rational organization and imaginative creativity, Wright's works reflect more than a critical commitment to his race and his country, far more than a passionate fight for social justice. His intellect craved progress and modernity, his feelings could not be content with such. The poet in him always hankered after wholeness of vision, after an organic view of existence which the thinker could not achieve. Speaking of pre-colonial Africa, he remarked in *Black Power* that social change might destroy the organic vision that made "people want to live on this earth and derive from that living a sweet even if sad meaning."

The nostalgic note evoked by that phrase is indeed present in Wright's own writings, in his early fiction and haiku poetry alike, as an essential though subdued counterpart to his more naturalistic approach. Only through the exclusion of such imaginative, organic moods and quasi-pastoral metaphors can Wright's style be restrictively defined as stark realism, lacking in symbolic quality.

This quality is most obvious in the almost surrealistic pattern of imagery and situations that helps make "The Man Who Lived Underground" a masterpiece. It is also evident in a number of novellas where it serves the function of balancing Wright's often bleak picture of black life couched in naturalistic terms. It must be borne in mind that, while evoking the deprivation inherent in the poverty and oppression characteristic of *Native Son* and *Black Boy*, Wright also suggested, in *Uncle Tom's Children* and *Twelve Million Black Voices*, the communal and sustaining qualities black life could take in the South. In the early novellas of *Uncle Tom's Children* the organic world-view of the black peasant is often evoked in lyrical terms even though white violence is ever present. This nearly pastoral approach stands in dramatic contrast to the social realism prevalent in *Native Son*. Without taking it into account one cannot do justice to Wright's non-naturalistic style of writing or to his portrayal of the positive qualities of black life. He does indeed set up believable figures of proud, militant blacks like Preacher Taylor in "Fire and Cloud." Far from being content with terse "realistic" prose, he turns to Biblical imagery, patterns of color, and poetic indirection, all of which make "Down by the Riverside" a success in symbolism through the metaphorical value of the flood as immediate source of, and image for, the trials and confusion of Brother Mann.

Even if one discounts the positive, at times heroic, quality of characters ranging from Tyree Tucker in *The Long Dream* to Aunt Sue in "Black and Morning Star," the most cursory appreciation of *Lawd Today*, not to mention later humorous stories like "Man of All Works" and "Big Black Good Man," reveals that Wright's preference for realism did not prevent him from creating funny and congenial figures and situations. Nor indeed from incorporating into his writing many elements characteristic of black folk culture. Although in *Lawd Today* Wright does not turn to Southern pastoralism but to what rural folkways have become after a generation in Northern ghettos, he recreates in passing the whole context of verbal creativity which explodes in songs, jokes, the dozens, toasts and bombast. When contrasted with the uptight utterances of the whites, this makes for a warm image of black life even if it is also pathetic in the light of the facts of economic oppression. As he expressed it at the time, Wright's interest lay in exposing the system which imposed a "cheap" quality of life upon lower-class blacks, but his desire for authenticity made him emphasize those cultural rituals and interchanges that ensured cohesion and solidarity in the day-to-day struggle of ghetto existence.

Wright's style appears at times as visceral, inspired and naturalistic as it is supposed to be, yet he is by no means the innocent and interesting neo-Dreiserian primitive some critics have contrasted with Ralph Ellison's virtuosity and technical flexibility. The unequalled emotional power Wright attains in his best stories stems just as much from an extremely skilled *poetic* realism, in which intense suffering is achieved through symbolic connotation, as from the climaxing of comparatively short and self-contained dramatic episodes. This poetic, even prophetic, dimension should not be overlooked. In many ways, Wright's art was vision just as his writing was force, meaning and direction. His quest was largely and ultimately an attempt to establish a political and cultural context for the birth of the (black) man in world-wide terms. His vision rested both upon his confidence in the individual self and upon his belief in the power of writing. Was this not the message he expressed when he wrote in *White Man, Listen:*

> I am convinced that the humble, fragile dignity of man, buttressed by a tough-souled pragmatism, implemented by methods of trial and error, can sufficiently sustain and nourish human life, can endow it with ample and durable meaning . . . I believe that art has its own autonomy, a self-sufficiency that extends beyond, and independent of, the spheres of political or priestly power or sanction.

Was it not Wright's way of saying that the real struggle is humanism against totalitarianism, imagination against fear? A way of saying that art is soul?

JERRY H. BRYANT

From "The Violence of *Native Son*"

Southern Review, Spring 1981, pp. 307–19

Bigger is a modern paradox. Born of our civilization, he is a major threat to it. The type he represents is described by Jose Ortega y Gasset in *The Revolt of the Masses* (1929). Bigger is like Ortega's "mass-man," aching for sensation, ignorant of the complex elements of the new world, godless, valueless. He has been estranged, says Wright of Bigger, not only from the "folk," but from the past and from himself. Without work or faith or tradition to sustain him, Bigger and the "mass-man" find no soil to hold their roots or give them nourishment. They live a pale vicarious life watching others do the things they want to do. Bigger exhausts himself, says Wright, trying "to react to and answer the call of the dominant civilization whose glitter came to him through the newspapers, magazines, radios, movies, and the mere imposing sight and sound of daily American life." This is a dangerous man to society. The resentment he feels over "the balked longing for some kind of fulfillment and exultation," Max warns the judge hearing Bigger's case, "makes our future seem a looming image of violence."

Part of the meaning of Bigger's violence is not only that he is a black man striking out against the boundaries of racism, but that he is a man living a key modern experience. In his conviction that at the bottom of that experience is violence, Wright stands very close to two other American writers of the 1930s, James T. Farrell and Nathanael West. That Wright knew Farrell and absorbed some of his naturalistic techniques has been frequently demonstrated. Wright probably did not know West's work, but the two are alike in their reading of the modern spirit. In *The Day of the Locust* (1939), West gives us a picture of that spirit.

Tod Hackett, West's narrator, is working on a painting he calls "The Burning of Los Angeles." Hackett takes great pains to render precisely the "torchbearers" that lead the mob in its destructive frenzy. Bored by their jobs, by their leisure, by their social life, these are people who have come to Hollywood from all over America to seek fulfillment in the illusions of the movies and the lives of the false gods and goddesses the movie industry has invented. Like Bigger, they are separated from real life fulfillment by their fantasies, which they strive to actualize in the celluloid images of film and in the newspaper headlines that exaggerate every human misfortune into an exciting epic catastrophe. But they cannot stimulate their jaded senses into life with the false-front, movie-set world they reside in. So they engineer the ultimate excitement—the destruction of Los Angeles. Their demeanor is murderous but without passion or hate. Tod has an awed respect for them, and believes that, as Wright does of Bigger, "they had it in them to destroy civilization."

The similarly starved sensibilities that lead to such mindless sensation-seeking produce the Armistice Day frenzy in *The Young Manhood of Studs Lonigan* (1934). Like Bigger, Studs and his friends live lives of trivial fantasies and stunted goals, and have an appetite for violence. At the 1918 Armistice Day celebration in Chicago, the bored urban youths behave like West's torchbearers, flowing about in aimless crowds, craning for a view of something real—sex, blood, violence—and behaving with impersonal brutality. Like cattle, they move from one atrocity to the next: gangs of Marines walking over the beaten, bleeding body of a drunk; a girl getting her dress torn off; a man falling through a plate glass window and nearly being decapitated.

Violence, these writers suggest, grows out of a stultifying American culture and a developing totalitarianism in Europe and Asia. Confronted by a sense of growing isolation, an increasing loss of self and respect for individual life, and an alienation of people from themselves, their work, and each other, the mass-man pursues violence in order to feel alive. However humanly intense Bigger's agitation is as he commits the crimes upon Mary and Bessie, it is a self-absorbed one. Like the mobs of Farrell and West, Bigger does not identify with the living person of his victims. Mary is "not real" to him, "not a human being." This estrangement from life is the foundation of the fascist character. Bigger likes "to hear of how Japan was conquering China; of how Hitler was running the Jews to the ground; of how Mussolini was invading Spain." He thinks dimly of a dictatorship in which a black man "would whip the black people into a tight band . . . make all those black people act together, rule them, tell them what to do, and make them do it."

This is perhaps the most disturbing thing of all for Wright—the use of violence for national and self-fulfillment. Ruling black people, forcing them into a fighting instrument, would be, for Bigger, "one way to end fear and shame." Bigger's motive here is not the simple and heroic one that makes him want to go down fighting, the brave black of Claude McKay's "If We Must Die." Bigger gets satisfaction from the power over others his violence gives him. It is on this basis that the dictatorships of Japan, Germany, and Italy appeal to him.

Today we speak of the "holocaust," and try to explain it. And we are still puzzling over the Moscow trials of the 1930s. Wright, without the full evidence of the ovens at Auschwitz and Buchenwald and probably unwilling to examine too closely what little news leaked out about the Communist purges, sensed something in the air of his time. He tried to combine the unformed image of some horror stalking the modern world with the well-defined image of the ghetto black man, seeing in them a dangerous similarity. Bigger was for Wright much more than a "bad nigger," or even a black revolutionary. He was a creature of the new world.

II

The mass-man is also something of an "existentialist," and so is Bigger. I use the word here not to define a technical philosophical position but to evoke the ideas behind the European movement of the late 1930s led by Jean-Paul Sartre and Albert Camus. Wright, so far as anyone knows, had not read anything by either Frenchman when he wrote *Native Son*. Camus's *The Stranger* and *The Myth of Sisyphus* appeared in 1942 and were not translated and published in America until 1946 and 1955, respectively. Sartre's *Nausea* came out in 1938, but he did not become known in America until after World War II. The point to be made here is that Wright's understanding of the new world's tilt toward violence and totalitarian force and his experience as a black man in America lead him to explore some of the same problems and advance some of the same answers as do Sartre and Camus, but independently.

The common ground upon which these writers meet is the sense of a "contingent" world which is implacably *there*, "in the way" (*de trop*, as Sartre puts it), and fraught with injustice. Alone in this world, the human being is faced with the question of how he, as a free and undetermined individual, can deal with pain and evil, without recourse to the supernatural or worldly assistance beyond his grasp. In *Native Son*, Wright has whites appear as a natural force in the world. America for Bigger is not a country of human beings who treat each other with mutual respect. "To Bigger and his kind white people were not really people; they were a sort of great natural force, like a stormy sky looming overhead, or like a deep swirling river stretching suddenly at one's feet in the dark." Bigger does not face people who have feelings, but a dangerous world of "mountains, floods, seas," like the existential universe, indifferent to his individual fate. White people make up an environment that is inimical to black life, one that is chaotic, blind, like the plague in Camus's later novel, or the German occupation of France which some say the plague symbolizes.

Wright had already made forays into this theme in *Uncle Tom's Children* (1938), in which the natural and social details of his black characters' lives dramatize their helplessness against the white plague. Circumstances created by a racist social order, natural occurrences, and chance put the characters into an intolerable position that forces them to do something violent, final, self-destructive. Yet, their violent gesture, though it bring death to them, seems to be preferable to abject submission, spiritual enslavement, moral paralysis, denial of self—in the same way, perhaps, joining the Resistance against the Germans as preferable to passive survival, or fighting a hopeless battle against a baffling disease was better than expecting help from an unknown and hidden God. In these terms, Bigger's murder of Mary Dalton under the pressure of the intimidation he feels from Mrs. Dalton becomes an expression of rebellion against the ultimate encroachment upon the self of (in a human sense) an immoral world, one that says with Camus's rebel, "This far and no farther."

The similarities in the way Wright and his two French contemporaries respond to their experience produce similarities in their work as well. All of their protagonists grope for what is rudimentary to human existence: a sense of being someone, of existing, the need for a certainty that the self can verify. They seek to break through the assumptions and presuppositions that fix people in roles and stereotypes. When Roquentin, the protagonist of *Nausea*, does just that, he experiences a "nausea," an anxiety at being cast up on a strange shore without any way of accounting for it. His whole world takes on a disturbing unfamiliarity, for he discovers that all the old ways of making life intelligible and coherent are illusions. They prevent one from directly experiencing existence.

What seeps into Roquentin's world explodes into Bigger's. When he kills Mary Dalton, he blasts through the racial and social categories through which he has always experienced his life. He moves toward the self lying beneath the masks he has been forced to wear, finding it in a strange world bounded by new and different limits. Bigger does not experience nausea or anxiety, but excitement and impatience to get on with it. To be free of the old categories elates him; he feels for the first time that he is in control of his own life, that he can plan for what he might be.

Bigger is now the "stranger" in a way he never was as a black accepting his white limits. He has been to the abyss, done and seen things that shock and terrify those still blinded by the expected and the familiar. Indeed, blindness, as many have pointed out, has an important symbolic value for Wright. Most obviously, Mrs. Dalton's blindness is the blindness of all whites toward the humanity of blacks. But it is also the blindness in the explanations invented to comfort those who need to be assured that life is safely understandable. Wright says that this particular kind of blindness is not restricted to whites. Musing upon his own family after he has killed two people, Bigger thinks that they live

> without thinking, making for peace and habit, making for a hope that blinded. He felt that they wanted and yearned to see life in a certain way; they needed a certain picture of the world; there was one way of living they preferred above all others; and they were blind to what did not fit.

Native Son and *The Stranger* resemble each other even more strongly. Both novels make the point that "insiders" maintain a deliberate blindness toward the truth of the real world around them. Both novels proceed from a crime committed by their protagonist to the protagonist's imprisonment, followed by a trial and a period of contemplation, and ending in the protagonist's being left in his cell to face death alone. Both protagonists experience a deep change in their feelings about themselves and life. And in both novels, the protagonist is, for the middle-class majority, more than a murderer; he is a monstrous and grotesque outsider. Bigger is an animalistic brute; Meursault is a man who does not love his mother.

Both novelists focus their attention on violent acts by their protagonists. In their trials, Bigger and Meursault face judgment by the caretakers of middle-class morality—an Algerian jury and a white judge. Both are prosecuted by attorneys who play upon their judges' prejudices. Meursault's prosecutor tries him not for the murder of the Arab for which he is technically on trial, but for outraging conventional sentiment by not showing adequate grief at his mother's funeral. When it becomes known that a parricide will come up for judgment the next day, the prosecutor links Meursault's crime with that of the parricide, contending that Meursault "set a precedent" and therefore "is also guilty of the murder to be tried tomorrow in this court." State's Attorney Buckley makes Bigger's crime "rape," which has much greater shock value for white sensibility than mere murder. And at the coroner's inquest, the Deputy Coroner, inquiring into Bigger's guilt of Mary Dalton's murder, brings in the body of Bessie Mears to prove his murder of Mary.

Both novelists suggest that those who look at the world out of the eyes of convention only impose a connection upon otherwise disconnected events, avoiding an understanding of the real world and maintaining the illusion of a coherent and just world that serves their interests. The outsider, having seen the truth, knows those connections exist nowhere but in the controlled imagination of the insider. Out of their need to make their world familiar and unthreatening, insiders must brand the outsider with the mark of Cain, inherent guilt. Thus, the crowds that gather around the courtroom view both Bigger and Meursault with a loathing born of fear. The fact that they have killed is less important than that they are different. They have had the temerity to do what the crowd has not dared to do: to damn themselves.

But the existential protagonist refuses to be damned by the conventional morality. As Camus says of the "absurd" man, all he feels is "his irreparable innocence." Sartre gives this guilt-innocence discussion an illuminating form. In his version of the Orestes-Clytemnestra myth, *The Flies*, Sartre says that guilt is what the "gods" want humans to feel in order to retain control of them, not only of their actions but of their image of themselves. Zeus's means of making Electra feel guilty are the Furies, which come to attack her after she has helped Orestes murder Clytemnestra, as the Dalton cat stares at Bigger after he has killed Mary. Accepting the moral conventions that declare her guilty, she repents. Because she submits, Zeus "saves" her. Orestes refuses to feel any guilt, though he is the principal in the act of violence. He insists upon his freedom from Zeus and refuses to bow to the Furies. He takes responsibility for the murder of his mother.

Bigger assumes a similar responsibility. To become a whole man, he must deny the white world the power to judge him guilty for having a black skin. The gravity binding him to the awesome planet of white judgment is so strong that he must commit an extreme act to break free of it into his own space. He must do what Orestes does—affirm his natural act. When Bigger's friends and family crowd into his tiny jail cell, it becomes clear they consider him guilty—on all counts. Even his mother had constantly accused him of being "the most no-countest man I ever seen in all my life!" Now everyone feels sorry for him. His mother weeps. But as he witnesses this performance from his transformed world, he reacts like Orestes:

> Bigger felt a wild and outlandish conviction surge in him: *They ought to be glad!* It was a strange but strong feeling, springing from the very depths of his life. Had he not taken fully upon himself the crime of being black? Had he not done the thing which they dreaded above all others? Then they ought not stand there and pity him, cry over him; but look at him and go home, contented, feeling that their shame was washed away.

Referring to his killing of Clytemnestra and his violating the law of Zeus, Orestes speaks to the jeering crowd in similar language:

> You see me, men of Argos, you understand my crime is wholly mine; I claim it as my own, for all to know; it is my glory, my life's work, and you can neither punish me nor pity me. . . . As for your sins and your remorse, your night-fears, and the crime Aegisthus committed—all are mine, I take them all upon me.

Bigger lacks Orestes' regal confidence. In fact, there is something of the boasting juvenile in his words. But he declares his integrity as no black fictional character has done before him.

For both Wright and his European contemporaries, conventional religion would rob every person of that integrity. Religion preaches a pernicious hope that one might be exempted from the limits and the debts of the contingent world, if only one puts oneself into the hands of God. Both Wright and Camus bring a priest of God into the death cell of their protagonists. The priest urges surrender to the conventional morality and the admission of sin. But both Meursault and Bigger erupt in anger at the smugness of the priest and grow violent with him. Through their rejection of the priest's appeal, both achieve a "hopelessness" that gives them an exhilarating certainty. Both learn to take responsibility for their own acts. "Whatever he thought or did from now on," concludes Bigger, "would have to come from him alone, or not at all."

This conclusion lays the ground for the final stage of Bigger's development, in which he learns his true relationship with the world and his own meaning. Most students of *Native Son* have been so taken up with Max's long defense of Bigger and its ideological preachiness that they tend to pass over what happens to Bigger in the third book. He is forced by his incarceration from action to unaccustomed reflection. After the frantic movement of Books I and II, Book III is contemplative, but not peacefully so. Mentally, Bigger is as changeable as he always was. He swings back and forth from an existential "dream of nothingness" after he first gets caught, to hope when Mr. Max shows a genuine interest in him at their first interview. He struggles for self-control, for meaning and understanding, then succumbs to a sense "that it was all foolish, useless, vain."

These oscillations are different, though, from the wild changes he undergoes in the early part of the novel. In Book III, Bigger experiences the absurd opposition between the human need for unity and coherence, and the human realization that that need can never be filled by this world. For Camus, the absurd is largely a philosophical and epistemological problem. For Bigger, it is part of the grain of his life. He has tasted the freedom of self- awareness, but he cannot finally fill the gap between his desire for meaning and his fear that his life is meaningless. He seeks completeness in Mr. Max, that final answer to the puzzle of his new existence. True to what seems to be an instinct for the absurd, Wright has Bigger's final discovery, in one of its aspects, become something other than what he seeks. He searches for completeness, ultimate meaning. He gets a knowledge of emptiness.

When Mr. Max visits Bigger in his cell after an appeal to the Governor has failed, Bigger is more eager for some explanation of life than for saving his own. But the attorney does not understand what Bigger wants when the young black man begins putting odd, elliptical questions to him. Bigger wants to communicate. Max, too, however, has been conditioned by American racism and cannot fathom the depth or the nature of Bigger's need. But the distance between Bigger and Max is not simply the conventional one between black and white; it is the one between all human beings. Bigger must learn that we are all isolated, and the point makes the last book of the novel the climax to the evolution of Bigger's consciousness. Bigger has moved along two tracks during the novel. One has led him into himself, his own individual, concrete, immediate being. The other has led him to some outside assistance, a sort of Marxist Christ: "If only someone had gone before and lived or suffered or died—made it so that it could be understood!" But his own violence, his trial, and the final failure of Max to guess at what Bigger needs demonstrate the nature of the human condition—a lonely passage through a meaningless world in which the only salvation lies in the discovery and acceptance of one's own self.

In his last hours, shaped by his experience with the priest and Mr. Max, Bigger finds that *his* meaning does not come from others but from himself. His existence is the only thing he can rely upon, the one thing he knows for certain. That is the wellspring of his violence, and when he learns that, he undergoes a subtle but distinct change, and the reader comes to a new understanding. The murders of Mary Dalton and Bessie Mears bring to him the truth about himself and his world, and they affirm his own identity. "They wouldn't let me live and I killed," he tells Max in their final meeting. "Maybe it ain't fair to kill, and I reckon I really didn't want to kill. But when I think of why all the killing was, I begin to feel what I wanted, what I am." The essence of human life is not the heartbeat, but self-awareness, the sense of owning oneself, of being intensely in the world, making choices according to one's own integrity. As a human being and as a black man in America, Bigger feels this need with double volume.

But if there is illumination in this for Wright, there is also the horror that Bigger had to kill to learn this, the horror in discovering how far humans will go, when pushed, to save themselves. It is this horror that links the mass-man in Bigger with the existentialist and that is the foundation of Wright's critique of American racism and his analysis of the modern experience.

Our last glimpse of Bigger finds him alone in his cell, the doors closing behind the departing Max and echoing through Bigger's isolation. His jail cell and death sentence have forced upon him a knowledge of ineluctable reality. He cannot escape the death that is coming in the electric chair. He can accept it as the debt he must pay, and in doing so create his own meaning in a world that has no inherent meaning discoverable by humans. The result is an acuity of consciousness that leaves Bigger, not in the state of cleansed joy that ends *The Stranger*, but slightly sorry and a little bitter that the world could have been something else, but was not. But this is a condition far preferable to the false hope of the black preacher and Bigger's family. Bigger's knowledge of his own truth and his strength in facing it show his worth as a moral being.

III

"In all my life," says Wright, describing his arrival in Chicago in 1927, "though surrounded by many people—I had not had a single satisfying, sustained relationship with another human being and, not having had any, I did not miss it." Loneliness is a Wright trait. Almost all of his major protagonists are isolated in some way, reflecting Wright's own feeling of being alienated from his family and friends when he was a child and from other blacks when he became a man. It is not a temporary feeling either. Just a few years before his death in 1960, he described himself in *White Man, Listen!* as a "rootless man" who did not "need as many emotional attachments, sustaining roots, or idealistic allegiances as most people." He even cherished "the state of abandonment, of aloneness," as the "natural, inevitable condition of man." It was this temperament, perhaps, that drew Wright toward the existential viewpoint before he was quite sure there was such a viewpoint, and that made it easy for him to feel more or less at home in the French intellectual world when he went to Paris after World War II. It was also this temperament that led him to weave into the character of Bigger Thomas a reflective quality that modifies the mindless violence of the mass-man.

A third side of Bigger also springs from Wright's temperament. Writing in *American Hunger*, the sequel to his autobiography *Black Boy*, Wright describes his inability to carry on a conversation with a young black woman with whom he was having an affair. He speaks of how angry he was "sitting beside a human being to whom I could not talk, angry with myself for coming to her, hating my wild and restless loneliness." It may be that Wright believed in the natural loneliness of the human condition. But the complement to that belief was Wright's need to get close to people, to form warm, gratifying ties. One of the more moving passages in *American Hunger* emphasizes the importance of such ties:

> The problem of human unity was more important than bread, more important than physical living itself; for I felt that without a common bond uniting men, without a continuous current of shared thought and feeling circulating through the body, there could be no living worthy of being called human.

This comes from the Wright that sought out the American Communist Party in the early 1930s both for its promise of sustained personal relationships and its offer of "the possibility of uniting scattered but kindred peoples into a whole." Along with the sensation-seeking mass-man and the existential solitary, the Marxist humanist takes its place in Bigger, who seeks membership in the collective even while he learns about isolation. But it is a Marxist humanism given Wright's very personal twist. Wright's main interest is neither class warfare nor the inevitable triumph of the working class, but rather how society can be organized and people motivated in order to promote the human harmony that preoccupied many of his non-Marxist contemporaries.

Bigger's need to become part of the human group drives him to question Max in the final hours of his life. In his pre-trial interrogations of Bigger, Max has opened some lines of communication unprecedented in Bigger's life. Both Max and Jan strive to convince Bigger that they care about him as a human being, and Max attempts to explain to Bigger that he, too, is a member of the human race because he acts and feels like others. But Max, the Communist intellectual, fails. He reacts in horror to Bigger's final affirmation of the crime that brought him new self-consciousness. He thinks Bigger wants comfort for the death he is about to face, not understanding that Bigger's real need is not only the self-understanding mentioned in the previous section but the satisfaction of being questioned about himself. It is now the reverse of the usual black-white relationship. It is Mr. Max who fails to make his way into Bigger's world. Bigger is physically imprisoned and isolated at the end, but he is psychologically free in a way that even Max is not, and he is ready to enter into the true human community. Max walks out of the literal prison back into the figurative prison of American society. Max's failure suggests that the Communist Party, like Mrs. Dalton, like Bigger's family, is blind, too.

Wright does not try to wring propaganda out of Bigger's new potential for human ties. He wants Bigger to remain unresolved as a character, one whose unity is, like Engels' dialectical organism, composed of irreconcilable forces. Therefore, he only fleetingly hints at the new Bigger in the last few paragraphs of the novel. As David Bakish has pointed out in *Richard Wright*, Max remains "Mr." to Bigger; but through Max, Bigger sends a message—a communication—to Jan Erlone, whose name suggests that he, too, is alone. It may be that aesthetically Jan is a cardboard character who displays virtually no sorrow or shock over the murder and mutilation of Mary Dalton, his sweetheart. It may be that he shows a superhuman capacity for forgiving the man who violated his loved one. We see from Bigger's point of view, and all Bigger sees is that Jan, too, has suffered, which qualifies him to become the first real communicant with Bigger's new world. The solidarity between them, established with such difficulty and over such tragedy, emerges when, as Bakish has noted, Bigger drops the "Mr." and uses the familiar "Jan." It is consolidated when Bigger says "goodbye" to Mr. Max, but asks Max to say "hello" to Jan. The climax of Bigger's life comes not when someone leads or pushes him into unity with others, but when he achieves the consciousness that permits him to forge his own bonds, and this possibility becomes a more powerful stimulant than violence.

Bigger's sudden grasp of what Jan means to him is strictly personal, and it suggests one of the main conclusions to be drawn from the novel. Personal sympathy is the basis of human community, not impersonal organizations. Violence, personal or organizational, destroys the bonds between people. But in *Native Son*, Wright shows a world in which people are placed in situations in which they have to kill if, paradoxically, they are to remain human. Given the nature of the human being—his thirst for understanding, for personal worth, for identity, for sensation—and the kind of world he lives in, killing becomes nearly inevitable. To say this is not necessarily to agree with Wright's view of the world or to accept it as a law of human life. Yet one suspects that no other view could have come out of Wright's own experience in America or the knowledge he had of the contemporary world. The pathos lies in his willingness to face the truth as he saw it, even while he craved the gentler way. He holds the pessimism of a man who sees no appeal from the conditions of the given world, and the hope of one who believes in the power of the self to take up ties with others, or at least dream of it. Bigger Thomas, in his own way, comes to a deep certainty of human limitations and a vivid sense of what might have been.

When we emerge from the violent world of *Native Son*, we have a sense of having traveled through the emotional climate of the 1930s, and not just the American racial climate, either. Wright, with his remarkable but undisciplined mind, tries to understand that climate. He is influenced by a tangled variety of ideas, which are not always smoothly or compatibly meshed. At the center of the 1930s milieu is an act of violence, which we come to understand in the several terms that Wright learned to think and feel in. The three taken up here do not exhaust the possibilities. But they display the rich intellectual and emotional density of the novel. *Native Son* evokes not so much the images of the era, or its sights and sounds, as the submerged stresses in the lives of real people and the historical events that carry them toward their uncertain futures.

ELINOR WYLIE

1885–1928

Elinor Hoyt Wylie was born on September 7, 1885, in Somerville, New Jersey, to Anne McMichael and Henry Martyn Hoyt. She was raised in Rosemont, Pennsylvania, and Washington, D.C., and attended private schools in those areas. In 1905 she married Philip Hichborn; she left him in 1910 and he died a year later. She married Horace Wylie in 1916; they were divorced in 1923, and she married the poet William Rose Benét later that year. She had one child by her first marriage. From 1923 to 1925 she was the poetry editor for *Vanity Fair*, and an editor for the Literary Guild in New York from 1926 to 1928.

Both as a poet and as a writer of fiction, Wylie was an exact and fastidious stylist, concerned largely with the beauty of objects and images in and of themselves. "Delicate," "vivid," and "austere" are adjectives typically employed to describe her work. She was primarily concerned with the realm of the intellect rather than that of the emotions; consequently, some critics find her work cold, though others consider it accomplished and highly individual. She published her first book of poetry, *Incidental Numbers*, privately in 1912. Her first commercially published book of poems was *Nets to Catch the Wind* (1921); it was praised by Edmund Wilson among others, and was her first work to receive substantial attention, though her intelligence and charm had already made her a prominent member of American literary circles. The last seven years of her life saw the publication of four more books of poetry and four Victorian-influenced novels, including *Jennifer Lorn: A Sedate Extravaganza* (1923) and *The Venetian Glass Nephew* (1925). She was extremely popular during her lifetime; almost inevitably, her reputation has declined since her death. Though she was not an innovator, writing rhymed stanzas during a time of great literary experimentation, she remains appreciated for her skill and clarity. She died of a stroke on December 16, 1928.

⟨. . .⟩ A poem by Elinor Wylie is the quick notation of a guess, a situation, a metaphor; it contains a bit of drama, rarely a narrative, often a character drawn briefly, but not hastily. Her metre is like Eliot's; her images have a similar air of being jumbled together, with deliberation; her vocabulary, though not the same, is parallel and includes strange words, words out of history and science, words used for their own sake, but exactly, with a parade of erudition which is justified in the fact. Alarums rhymes with bar-rooms and sentient with bent; Apeneck Sweeney nods his maculate head in approval.

But the resemblance to Eliot is more on the surface than beneath, and when Miss Wylie uses the same dictionary and the same metrics she uses them to her own purpose. She has a personality which is in many ways his opposite. He is afraid of intimate emotions, hides them politely, holds them at arm's length when he wishes to describe them; she is both emotional and intimate, as if her subject were a penny world to eat with Pippit behind the screen.

She writes in a medium which Eliot never attempted: magazine verse. Literature takes curious forms and magazine verse is one of them. It is bound by conventions as rigid, perhaps, as those of Racinian tragedy or the Noh drama; the perspective of a century will be needed to appreciate how they are narrow. Magazine verse must fill the bottom of a page, agreeably. It is limited to certain subjects treated with a certain degree of lyricism; to emotions neither too personal nor impersonal and to a few stanzas in a minor tradition. Apparently these conventions should prevent the writing of even passable verse, but talent thrives on conventions. Miss Wylie is talented.

She writes genuine poetry while observing even the minor conventions of her medium. For example it is the general consent that human bodies are composed of breast, hands, head. *Black Armour* is in five sections to cover them: breastplate, gauntlet, helmet, beaver (Beaver Up!) and plumes. The legs are left unprotected through delicacy, or they are lacking. And nevertheless *Black Armour* gives no sense of being incomplete; within limitations it is unexcelled. The verse is hard and bright as a piece of machinery; there are no loose screws about it; metres are varied with astonishing skill. Miss Wylie is a craftsman who cannot be praised too highly, but her real achievement is to write magazine verse which is not repulsive to the intelligence. I doubt whether any one else has done as much.

Only, you form such a high opinion of her talents that you expect too much of them, saying to yourself: The last poem was agreeable, but the next will be a masterpiece . . . or surely the one after. At the end of the book you are left still unsatisfied, still expecting another something which will come, perhaps, in a future volume. The feeling is not disagreeable. Sometimes you wish she would write in other conventions, more ambitious, complete anatomically, giving more scope to her notations of character and her dramatic power. As it is, she never lacks charm and only at her worst is she cute.

Apparently her greatest virtue should be the fact that she combines, in wise proportions, intellect with emotion. It is a defect instead, perhaps her gravest, for although she combines them in a book she has fused them perfectly in no single poem. She has emotion and fantasy by turns. She thinks in one poem and thinks well; feels in one poem and feels strongly; allows thought and feeling to be separate. She is the Owl and the lyric Nightingale at sea in a beautiful pea-green boat; during the honeymoon they write verses dedicated to each other, but obviously by two authors.

It is the Owl who is more modern. . . . There is a group of phenomena in contemporary letters, which, if taken together, are the elements of a movement perhaps important enough to be compared with the classicism of the seventeenth century or the romanticism of the nineteenth. Different aspects of the movement have been referred to as cubist, neo-classical, abstract, fantastic, but the one term which includes all its tendencies is Intellectualism. The decade, perhaps the century will be intellectualist. . . . Miss Wylie, with her double personality, is half in the movement and half outside of it. In a way this is a judgement, for although it is no virtue to be modern, none to be conservative, there is a difficult virtue in extremes.—MALCOLM COWLEY, "The Owl and the Nightingale," *Dial*, June 1923, pp. 625–26

JAMES BRANCH CABELL
From "Sanctuary in Porcelain: A Note as to Elinor Wylie"

Virginia Quarterly Review, July 1930, pp. 338–41

These two books, *Jennifer Lorn* and *The Venetian Glass Nephew*, I regard, I admit, as something very like masterpieces in their own sharply limited romantic field. That field is not large nor is it especially lofty. Yet it now and then repays the thorny toil of bemused gardeners very prettily, with frail blossoms.

For there are, to my finding, two kinds of romance. They differ in their causes, in their materials, and in their purposes: they agree but as to the desirability of embellishing the course of human life as men actually do live it. There is that major romance which gilds actuality with the gold of a highly superior sun, as opposed to that minor romance over which one is tempted to say the moon presides, to ensorcel all with a wizardry of amiably prevaricating shadows and with vivid patterns of silver. I must here mix metaphors by admitting that sometimes this is only German silver, of no great intrinsic worth: but the patterns are very often exquisite.

There is, I mean, the normal, the wholesome, the really childlike kind of romance in which the writer joyously accepts this world and the broad flowering ways of human life, but enlivens each with more propitious and with more picturesque happenings than occur in the ratio he depicts. Thus Scott worked, as Dumas did after him, in a pleased quest of the improbable. These titans we may reasonably acclaim the supreme masters in this kind of romance writing. And they embellished human life because they loved it. They adorned it with superb adventures in precisely that frame of mind in which the favored lover brings jewels to his mistress. They wrote, in short, as happy persons alone may write in a complacent glow of prosperity. Both of them performed their great labors in days of semi-fabulous success and material well-being, when the masters of Abbotsford and of the Château de Monte Cristo held each his princely court, in entire financial stability, and went with critical fanfares among applauding underlings. Yet a little later, in the more prosaic presence of bankruptcy, that necromancy which had summoned up Rob Roy could evoke but Count Robert of Paris, and across the forsaken battle fields of the three musketeers the Whites and the Blues wavered like paralytic phantoms. When once life had proved unlovable, and misfortune had touched these mages heavily, it would seem that their magic failed. When Walter Scott and Alexandre Dumas could no longer love life with complete confidence, and with a boisterous optimism as to all life's orderings, then they could write of life but haltingly. One is tempted to infer that the major romance is a tropic growth which does not thrive in the inclement zones of fortune. It is a branch of literature to which, in any case, do not belong *Jennifer Lorn* and *The Venetian Glass Nephew*.

For there is, to the other side, that quite different kind of romance which embellishes life because the writer has found life to be unendurably ugly. It embellishes life very much as one might cover the face of a leper. The origin of all such romance writing is thus appreciably removed from being love, in that if it be not entirely hate it is, at mildest, aversion. It demands, with Baudelaire, the inaccessible places and strange adorers: with Flaubert it seeks for new perfumes, for vaster flowers, and for pleasures not ever before attained. Its goals are not of this world. It does not hunt the improbable: it evokes in desperation that which it over well knows to be impossible.

We call this—dully enough—"the literature of escape." Brisk gentlemen rather more enamored of a striking phrase than of strict veracity have even been known to commend it as the literature of something like blasphemy. For it is, say these tremendous fellows, a literature composed by persons almost equally tremendous who have found the globe they inhabit and the unappreciative mammals about them to be the productions of a most inferior and ill inspired Author. Its poetry is thus in exact truth a criticism of life, a criticism of the stout old slashing *Edinburgh Review* school, which begins with the time-hallowed formula "This will never do!" It is a poetry—a "making"—which thereafter goes on to set a better example (for the instruction of a no doubt properly impressed Providence) by creating a really acceptable sort of world exhilarated by congenial inhabitants. Thus say these godlings, where we calmer communicants incline to rather less of a pother, in the light of our private knowledge that books after all are only books, even if the Trinity have much time for reading.

We may grant, nevertheless, that this kind of romance writing is a poetry—a "making"—to which the unhappy contribute. They contribute so widely and so very variously that where a wastrel like Marlowe from out of his pot-house squalor may augment this branch of literature with a *Hero and Leander*, a restrained schoolmaster like Charles L. Dodgson, from out of the forlorn stuffiness of that atmosphere which is thought most suitably to develop the minds of the young, will bring forth an *Alice in Wonderland*. We may grant also that this is a branch of literature to which, through plain enough reasons, do belong *Jennifer Lorn* and *The Venetian Glass Nephew*.

I must here of necessity approach to matters which as yet stay delicate. It suffices to remark that the corporal life of Elinor Wylie was but too often at odds with her circumstances. The nature of this very beautiful and tragic woman was not ever in all adapted to that makeshift world in which perforce moved her superb body. She had found, after marrying several of them, that this world was over full of disappointments. She, who possessed the needed ability and an urgent need to use it, created therefore quite another sort of world, building amid desolation a baroque pagoda to be the sanctuary of wounded dreams and unfed desires. She created, in brief, a retreat wherein the rebuffed might encounter no more inglorious fiascos of the spirit and of the affections.

Into this quaint and brittle sanctuary of Elinor Wylie's creation neither the spirit nor the affections, or any other human plague, may enter, for the reason that there is in this sparkling place no human heart. For not only Rosalba and Virginio, but all the other inhabitants likewise, I take to be handsome porcelain figures animated by a pure and hurtless white magic. They have been shaped and colored with a pleasingly faded elegance. They have been given life: but there is no more blood in them than there is grossness. They enact their well-bred comedy, which includes a toy misery or so. It touches now and then the exaltedly tragic as if with a caress. A few of them may even pretend to die, with unruffled decorum. Their little porcelain tongues lend to their speaking a light stiffness whensoever these fine manikins converse. They converse too in their own idiom, for the vernacular of this point-device land is an ever-courteous blending of ironic epigram and neat periods and apt literary allusions. Yet a discerning audience will watch all with the connoisseur's calm approval. For this, we know, is but a make-believe land of animated figurines, wherein not lust nor death, not poverty nor bankrupt love, but the cool joys of virtuosity, and of finesse, and of each tiny triumph in phrase-making, are the sole serious matters.

For one, I still delight in the wistful humors and the fine prose of this little land: I commend to you, as I said at outset, the color and the legerity and the glitter of this sanctuary against the rude real. Yet I am far from declaring that oncoming ages will forever treasure these books. For tastes change: and in art also, we incline to forget our benefactors. It is on the cards that very few, and perhaps none, of our descendants may care to travel with Jennifer Lorn all the exotic long way of her journeying (even from the spring sunlight of Devonshire to the crimson pillows of the unvirtuous Banou's bed) or to advance happily with Rosalba Berni from the classical summer-house at Altachieri into the fires of the smelting furnace at Sèvres. Posterity, I admit, may forget both of these books. But I add that posterity will thus acquire a quite valid claim on our pity.

MORTON DAUWEN ZABEL
From "The Pattern of the Atmosphere"
Poetry, August 1932, pp. 276–82

Mrs. Elinor Wylie was a poet of late development but of enviable successes. By the testimony of every acquaintance, the graces exhibited in her verse are corroborated in her actual life. An agile wit was the factor which propelled her from charm to charm in her choice of materials: from historic themes of the most ingenious fragility and inaccessibility, to familiar encounters rendered desirable by the humor and elegance of imagination she brought to them. Thus seventeenth-century Venice had no riches to strike envy in the heart of a pioneer farmer on the Chesapeake: for each of them she conjured an experience of equal splendor. There was a prodigality in her verbal invention which certainly stemmed from something deeper than museum catalogues or encyclopedias; if we are to praise phonetic dexterity in Byron and Browning, we must praise it in her. The pictorial and impressionistic efforts of the 'nineties wilt feebly in comparison with the brittle imagery of her designs. In the tradition of *Emaux et Camées* she is, on first acquaintance at least, an austere and distinguished disciple. Of that style in contemporary art which shifts from tenet to tenet under the name of "classicism," she is undoubtedly a notable exemplar, and students of modern poetry will be grateful to Mr. Benét for issuing her *Collected Poems*, with many hitherto inaccessible additions (but a somewhat unfortunate "Foreword"), and in a distinguished format. To anyone acquainted with her work since its first appearance, however, and who re-reads poems now quite familiar, this gratitude is tempered by two inescapable convictions: that throughout her work Mrs. Wylie never crossed the line that separates her from poets of her own admiration, like Donne, Waller, and Landor, or from Emily Brontë and Miss Dickinson; and that from the beginning she mistook virtuosity for convictions, and that it betrayed her in the end.

It is a principle of any usage that the energy of forms is exhaustible, and that overuse depletes it. Mrs. Wylie aimed at concreteness. She did not favor the practice of certain of her more philosophic contemporaries who have brought to the humiliation of parody the terms of their favorite themes: *time, mind, despair, change, heart, silence.* Like Miss Sitwell's, her mind operated best under the spur of allegory, and thus her pages spill with meteors, moonstones, goblins, knights, fairy goldsmiths, mandrakes, blackamoors, and saints; with filigree, mistletoe, snowflakes, wasp-nests, stalactites, bronze, goldfish, silver, moonbeams, *marbre, onyx,* and *émail* upon which a labor no longer rebellious was required for fashioning and shaping. Tray after tray of choice images is heaped before the enchanted banquet, a banquet at all events enchanted when this connoisseurship in exquisite miracles and jewels followed a decade of gusty eloquence in various national and partisan literary causes. For her American contemporaries Mrs. Wylie's service resembled that of Rossetti for his generation, of Gautier for his coterie, of the first (but latterly impoverished) imagists for their pioneer readers. Mrs. Wylie has had her imitators, for whom she cannot be held responsible. Yet among them must be counted herself, if we are to count as imitation a duplication of effects which is unjustified by something new to say. There is never, in her work, the slightest difficulty in understanding her meaning—when a meaning is present. In "Address to My Soul" there is perhaps material for a quatrain; it has been expanded into eight:

> Fear not, pathetic flame;
> Your sustenance is doubt:
> Glassed in translucent dream
> They cannot snuff you out.
>
> Wear water, or a mask
> Of unapparent cloud;
> Be brave and never ask
> A more defunctive shroud.
>
> The universal points
> Are shrunk into a flower;
> Between its delicate joints
> Chaos keeps no power.

Of ear-pleasure there is a share here, but it requires little inquiry into the content of these statements, or into the mere possibility of a single entity's being capable of sustaining these sleight-of-hand changes in identification *(flame—water—cloud—shroud—flower—chaos)*, to reveal the almost complete emptiness of the entire performance.

Excess of verbal symbols is, however, a sin that requires indulgence in Spenser, Shelley, and Swinburne. In itself it is not the worst offense against a creative endowment. But inevitably it endangers the judgment itself, and the reserves of honesty and authority over which the judgment discriminates. Mrs. Wylie celebrated the value of life at its richest, and for her the Puritan instinct disclosed richness in fundamental aspects of simple experience which, however she may have lived apart from them, won her envy and praise. The integrity of human faculties was her single clue to the accessibility of this rich and final experience. Her poems progressively enlarge upon this theme: "Wild Peaches," "Velvet Shoes," "True Vine," "Innocent Landscape," "Havre de Grace," "One Person," "Hymn to Earth," "This Corruptible," "Nonsense Rhyme," "Indentured." These are her most ambitious poems; her actual successes lie among the fanciful morsels of her own delight, but there the success was easy. It is in the effort toward philosophy that she invites greater sympathy. Like too many of her contemporaries, however, her praise of integrity is not accompanied by a sufficient respect for it. This could be traced in several details; one of them is her exploitation of the erotic. Mr. Tate has recently referred (*The Symposium*, April, 1932) to the subtle interfusion of the erotic in Emily Dickinson, its unsuspected but essential reinforcement of her symbols, and its relevance to the emotional capacities of a mind which required no mysterious lover for realization. Instinct with a sense of realism, her images at once shock and survive in the mind, and the motivation of them seldom errs through sensational emphasis. Miss Dickinson did not write, in a traditional sense, love poetry, whereas Mrs. Wylie did. Here the amatory element is forthright, and thus open to the dangers of having its mysterious and esthetic energy immediately reduced. In "One Person" the philosophic theme is involved in a great deal of traditional literary rhetoric; in only three sonnets it merges with the available symbolism—particularly in *VIII;* in most of the others a species of rhetorical forcing is applied, with the result that an exhaustion sets into the lines, reduces their ability to communicate, and finally escapes by the slightest subterfuge from rendering the intended poignance of the conclusion banal. What distresses one here, as in *Fatal Interview,* is that a strenuously urgent and heroic enthusiasm has been reduced to a perilous relationship with the spurious by reason of over-lavish *pastiche* and by redundant ornamentation, although Mrs. Wylie has been wise enough to curb her design to eighteen sonnets. And there remains the conviction that the celebrated clairvoyance of modern love poetry does not discredit the finest achievements in this line among the Victorians—the ten or twelve masterpieces among *The Sonnets from the Portuguese,* or the extraordinary power of that singular and almost unrivalled poem, *Modern Love.*

Pastiche was, indeed, the threat that dogged Mrs. Wylie, like a number of her conspicuous contemporaries, from the beginning. In the sense that one ascribes a grasp of the past to Bridges, Pound, and Eliot, she hardly knew the past at all. Her imitative phrases soon took on the hollow quality of mere baroque excresence, and resulted in the dispiriting fables which she tolerated in most of her ballads. Folklore was the past she tried to transfix; she also toyed with late Renaissance romances, with artificial epochs such as furnished her with material for her novels, and with the seventeenth-century metaphysical mysteries. With none did she stay long enough to make them her own, although where so much purely meretricious writing succeeds in the market, it is doubtless reprehensible to charge with defection from seriousness the author of *The Venetian Glass Nephew, Jennifer Lorn,* and her various narrative poems. The point is that Mrs. Wylie earnestly sued for an exceptional dignity in her work, and even gave frequent promise of it. Superficially she was a master of her technique: she brought it to yield all that she exacted of it. She did not, however, exact the purposes we look for in significant poetry. She hardly surpassed Miss Lowell in what she had to say, although from the start she was removed by mere fastidious choice from the technical chaos and mental dissipation into which Miss Lowell steadily drifted. Of verbal exercises Mrs. Wylie, in "Minotaur," confessed her fatigue. Of the trumpery of specious feeling and faith, she wrote a malediction in "Innocent Landscape." For her art she hoped more than a "pattern of the atmosphere." She did not achieve it, but she lived to provide a volume of divertissements among which are the half-dozen poems that confess a consciousness of esthetic responsibility and ambition which she did not live to fulfil. They do not place her among the exceptional talents of her time, but it is to them, and not to personal testimonials, that the reader of poetry must go for her quality. With any understanding of the genuine sources of modern creative authority he will discern her shortcomings without wishing to sacrifice the pleasure, which, at their best, her wit and dexterity provide.

JUDITH FARR
"Afterword"
The Life and Art of Elinor Wylie
1983, pp. 207–12

Elinor Wylie's sudden death in her forty-third year occurred at the height of her fame and at a turning point in her life. Had she lived, she intended to leave America and to settle permanently in England, thus numbering herself in a company of expatriate American artists with whom she shared various insights: Henry James, James NcNeill Whistler, Edith Wharton, T. S. Eliot, the young H.D., and Ezra Pound. Her desire was in one way personal. She fantasized a romantic return to the English countryside where she had once been happy with Horace Wylie. In another, it was strictly professional. She wished to escape Manhattan and to conduct a more ascetic life in which her art could develop.

Wylie was, as she knew and said, a distinctly American writer "down to the Puritan marrow of [her] bones" *(Collected Poems* [New York, 1932], p. 12). Her poetry described the landscape of Maine, Maryland, Virginia, Delaware, and Pennsylvania as well as the streets of New York City. In *The Orphan Angel* she "recreated" most of the United States. She was proud of what she thought a johnnycake side. Yet, like Edith Wharton's, her personal elegance, breeding, and assumptions were those of an American upper class that had read widely, traveled much, and felt at home in great houses. Like Wharton, Eliot, and James, she was cosmopolitan, often setting her scenes in a Europe as familiar to her as her own country. With the great James, in fact, she shared more than this urbane or patrician taste. A few of her themes recall his own—conflict between art and life, the dangers of overrefinement, especially the antagonism between sophistication and innocence expressed in the dominion of a worldly man over a naïve girl. Still, her devotion to foreign places, especially England, never drove out her passion for a wilder land. Perhaps more than James or Eliot, who became British subjects and were, like Wylie, snubbed as Americans by the Woolf circle, she regarded her roots as inalienably Yankee. Proclaiming herself "an American in England," she qualified her sympathetic allegiance to the land of her forebears yet confessed her keen need at last of the comfort it offered: "Let the divided heart come home" (297). Wylie's contemporary, Ezra Pound, who never wholly forswore the Aestheticism she shared, sought English shores to escape Idaho and American provincialism. Wylie had settled first in England to escape moral censure. Yet, like Pound's, her English sojourn in the early 1900s put her in close touch with a literature she could learn from and react against. Like H.D.'s, a few of whose Greek poems she imitated in *Black Armour,* [1] her career was partially formed by English influences.

Well-traveled in France and Italy, Elinor Wylie was nonetheless anglophile in her serious tastes; for her the Continent was primarily a setting for fiction. Hating what she thought the white neon glare of Paris, she separated herself from the large group of Americans from Whistler and Wharton to Williams and Gertrude Stein who sought nourishment there. Still, as I have suggested elsewhere, the relation between her art and Whistler's is succinct. His wistful romanticization of English scenes, particularly in the *Nocturnes*, finds its analogues in her own, especially in *Mr. Hodge and Mr. Hazard*. England was not wholly kind to Whistler as an artist but it was for him as for Wylie a challenge, a test, made by an older yet related civilization, of his creative powers.

Had she lived to become what she planned, an expatriate in England, Wylie might have joined those Americans whose imaginative careers resembled her own. Yet her life and art pose challenges to a settled view of her. At her death Wylie was planning to live near Henley-on-Thames and to write a novel about the witches of Salem, one of whom was her ancestress. Her interest in magic, like her devotion to fairy tales, had always been pronounced and became clear in *The Venetian Glass Nephew*. Had she lived, she planned to combine it with a typically Aesthetic fascination with curious religious practices in a novel about witch-burnings. Thus England would be her home; early America, her subject.

Much has been said in this book about her debt to English writers because it is evident and immediate. Yet a consideration of Wylie's themes shows her bond with such earlier American writers as Nathaniel Hawthorne and Edgar Allan Poe. Hawthorne's Puritan suspicion that art provides undue, perhaps dangerous, satisfactions was not shared by Wylie to whom great art was holy. Nevertheless, in stories like "The Artist of the Beautiful" or "The Prophetic Pictures" and especially in *The Marble Faun* Hawthorne concerned himself with what he considered the generative antipathy between brute fact and imagination and with a reconciling theme of metamorphosis. For him as for Wylie, life and art were opposed but could have mutually nutritive and affective powers. Hawthorne's "artist of the beautiful" who attempts to "spiritualize machinery"[2] prefers delicate small objects as do the subjects of Wylie's poems. That preference both exalts and ruins him as it does the usual Wylie protagonist. Strikingly, Hawthorne provides in *The Blithedale Romance* the vision of Zenobia, a gorgeously seductive woman, who is, at one point, in one view, "transformed . . . into a work of art." That she becomes so horrifies yet pleases Hawthorne's narrator, Miles Coverdale, even as Rosalba's transformation is appalling yet ultimately acceptable to those who love her. Hawthorne's interest in female sexuality—indeed, in women's rights in *Blithedale*—expresses itself in emblematic transformation, as does Wylie's in the poems and the *Nephew*. He, too, was attracted like the Wylie of *Jennifer Lorn* to the theme of "the miraculous power of one human being over the will and passions of another."[3] Furthermore, Hawthorne clearly imagines that art has mysterious occult powers, a vision embodied in the Wildean story of the "Prophetic Pictures," a story whose interest in cosmetic transformations provides a true analogue to Wylie's story of Virginio and Rosalba.

The "American" art of Elinor Wylie may be related to Poe as well. His preoccupation with lovely, enervated women and his delineation of the antagonism between life and art recall her own. In his "Oval Portrait," for instance, the struggle between the power of life, represented by the painter's radiant young wife, and the genius of art, symbolized by the painter himself, calls to mind *The Venetian Glass Nephew*. Poe's painter must nullify his wife's vitality in order to achieve the exuberance of the painting; as she starves and dies, the painting comes to life. This terrible exchange, accepted so docilely by the female model, is what Wylie describes in her novel. It testifies to a preoccupation with the problem of art that transcends time and country but was as American as it was European.

In a sense Wylie had two careers, one as a fabulist, the other as a poet. How and what would she have written had she lived beyond her forty-third year? Her unfinished manuscripts in the Wylie Archive—the *April, April*, fragments about Shelley, a romance about Henry VIII's sister Mary, a symbolic tale about the "Moon" and "Starr" sisters of Philadelphia—suggest that in fiction she would have continued to write fantasies. She looked forward to beginning her "witch" novel with an enthusiasm bred, I think, of a precise understanding of her own powers. Her passion for history, her fascination with magic, the surreal, and the occult (a fascination shared by her hero Shelley and her admirer and supporter Yeats) would doubtless have resulted in tales that were more and more austere philosophically and increasingly shrewd in nuance and invention. Her last poems, *Angels and Earthly Creatures*, might suggest that her poetic style had taken new directions. Yet though she said she liked, in her last days, to "enjoy with Donne a metaphysical frolic" and spoke of Thomas Browne as her "brother," I do not think she would ever have become a true "Daughter of Donne"[4] (276, 302). Her interest in metaphysical and Elizabethan verse was timely, wrought not of Eliot's fashionable prescriptions but of her love for Woodhouse, who admired it, and of her suspicion of the advent of death. Good scholar that she was, she associated last ends and fatal loves with that school of poetry which had most richly expressed them. *Angels and Earthly Creatures* was on the whole a "nonce" volume, struck out with a special purpose. Her real vision was Aesthetic and comprehended the nature and problems of Aestheticism. Her two great subjects—art and her personal deficiencies—were related to the tensions between the pure Romanticism of Shelley and the Neo-Romanticism of the Aesthetes.

That she had evolved a highly personal style as a poet in the seven years of her professional career became apparent in the parodies of that style written most effectively by Edmund Wilson in poems such as "Nocturne: To Elinor."[5]

> The foxes wink their onyx eyes;
> The tranced witches twitch their wigs;
> The pixies snap, like startled pies,
> Their frozen filigree of twigs.
>
> Ice-sheeted crofts, close-hedged with thorn,
> Confront Diana's dinted shield;
> The watch-dog's bellowing, forlorn,
> Chills sharper sharp-chilled stream and field
>
> Then come! in some deep-sunken hole
> Below the drifts you shall be kis't;
> Or, crouching in some hollow bole
> Snow-cushioned for the hidden tryst.
>
> Cold bone shall ring against cold bone;
> The skeleton like flint shall spark;
> A high thin thrilling javelin tone
> Shall glance like ice-beams on the dark . . .

Had Wylie lived, she would not, I think, have been able to abandon this personal style. On the other hand, that quest for grander utterance especially in spiritual matters that appears in her later poems would no doubt have grown. A considerable number of the poems in her last two volumes concern the Christian mysteries. The "Birthday Sonnet" chosen by William Rose Benét to conclude the volume of her *Collected Poems*, which first appeared in 1932 and is still the standard edition of her verse, poignantly reveals her old sense of personal delinquency. It speaks of her pride as an artist, a role she clearly felt might ransom her spiritual faults. Deeply confessional, it rehearses the stages and attitudes of her life: her need to be protected from the "secular danger" that sometimes overtook her; her awareness that she was inadequate as a woman; her desire to "preserve Thy gift," her creative powers. It begins with language reminiscent of the Book of Common Prayer she read in childhood, "Take home Thy prodigal child, O Lord of Hosts!" and ends with a phrase that some who knew her ill could not have imagined her using: "Defend Thy prodigal" (311). This sonnet with its alternate conviction of guilt in life and salvation through art is almost classically Aesthetic. Its extreme intensity as well as the increased number of religious poems in Wylie's last books lead me to speculate that had she lived she might have turned her attention not only to the problem of art and the self but to the problem of God and the self. Had that happened, she would once again have behaved like an American artist: like T. S. Eliot or Wallace Stevens, the first of whom perplexed her and the second—so like her in taste—whom she never knew.

But Elinor Wylie did not live beyond 1928. She has left to us a surprisingly large body of poetry and prose as well as the myth of her translation from a woman limited by social position into an artist, independent and self-aware. Both have lasting attraction. Her determination to achieve a life of meaning in a cosmos of trivial appearances resulted in her concern with the problem of art, a concern that was characteristically modern yet typically American. That concern produced her fables, her experiments in lyrical form—elegies, ballads, dialogues, epistles, couplets, sonnets—and the respect for literary tradition that enabled her mimetic exploits in verse and fiction. True Aesthete, she never wholly suppressed an idiosyncratic spirit as Eliot would command poets to do. But, rewardingly, her spirit commended the language of art above every other good.

Notes

1. See the last poems in that volume, for example, "To Aphrodite, with a Talisman," "On a Singing Girl" ("Musa of the sea-blue eyes,/Silver nightingale . . ."), and "To Claudia Homonoea" (Elinor Wylie, *Collected Poems* [New York, 1932], 100, 102, 103).
2. Nathaniel Hawthorne, *Mosses from an Old Manse*, "The Artist of the Beautiful," in William Charvat, Roy Harvey Pearce, and Claude M. Simpson (eds.), *The Centenary Edition of the Works of Nathaniel Hawthorne* (14 vols.; Columbus, Ohio, 1962–80), X, 465.
3. Hawthorne, *The Blithedale Romance*, ibid., III, 164.
4. For a different view see Herbert S. Gorman, "Daughter of Donne," *North American Review*, no. 169 (May, 1924), 679–86. Allan Tate in his *Collected Essays* (Denver, 1951), 329, declared that there was "as little evidence of the influence of Donne" in Wylie's poetry "as one might derive from Tennyson." The metaphysical attribution is widely made, however: George Dillon called her imagination "metaphysical . . . in the rare, true sense" (Tate, "A light never on land or sea," *Poetry*, June 29, 232); Louis Untermeyer spoke of her "metaphysical" imagination (*Modern American Poetry* [New York, 1950], 295); and Dayton Kohler compared her to Donne ("Elinor Wylie: Heroic Mask," *South Atlantic Quarterly* XXXVI [1937]).
5. Ms. 207 in the Wylie Archive ⟨Yale University, New Haven, CT⟩.

Richard Yates

1926–

Richard Yates was born on February 3, 1926, in Yonkers, New York, to Vincent M. and Ruth (née Maurer) Yates. He was educated at the Avon School in Connecticut. From 1944 to 1946 he served in the army. He married Sheila Bryant in 1948; they had two children before their divorce in 1959. He then married Martha Speer in 1968, and they had one child before their divorce in 1974. He worked as a financial reporter and rewriter for the United Press Association from 1946 to 1948, as a publicity writer for Remington Rand, Inc., from 1948 to 1950, and as a freelance public relations writer from 1953 to 1960. He has taught at the New School for Social Research and at Columbia University; since 1964 he has taught at the University of Iowa. In addition, he has worked as a screenwriter for United Artists and Columbia Pictures and was a speech writer for Robert Kennedy. During 1971 and 1972 he was a writer-in-residence at Wichita State University.

Yates published his first novel, *Revolutionary Road*, in 1961, and his first collection of short stories, *Eleven Kinds of Loneliness*, the next year. Yates writes of a dull, hopeless world in which even the bright and imaginative can experience only moments of happiness. His protagonists are ordinary people who at best achieve a kind of nobility through acceptance of the world in all its unpleasantness and hypocrisy, often even embracing failure and collapse. His solid prose style and sympathy for his lost characters remind some critics of J. D. Salinger. Among his most admired novels are *Disturbing the Peace* (1975), *A Good School* (1978), and *Young Hearts Crying* (1984); Yates's later short stories are collected in *Liars in Love* (1981). Though he is a conventional writer mining traditional themes and motifs, Yates is praised for his unusual clarity and an honesty that rarely descends to the puerile. He lives in Boston.

Disturbing the Peace is as good as its title, beginning with the hero, John Wilder, committed to the alcoholic ward of Bellevue just at the onset of the long Labor Day weekend. Wilder, back from a business trip to Chicago (he works for a distilling company) and a week of insomnia and heavy drinking, suddenly finds himself in deep trouble and is persuaded by a mutual friend of his and his wife's to enter the hospital. You expect lost-weekend nightmares and sadistic keepers, but the stay in Bellevue is brilliantly managed, funny and horrible by turns, complexities of caring and despair seen from the inside. Any one who has read Richard Yates's first novel, *Revolutionary Road* (1961)—and if you have it's time to read it again—knows him to be a master at dramatizing how things go wrong in American marriages, how with the best of intentions people, particularly men, destroy what they've built, extending themselves through fantasies of liquor and sex into crazy versions of people for whom things go wrong and wronger. Yates's writing, so close to the banal, is in fact rivetting in the extreme, to the extent where you ask yourself whether anything this compulsively readable mustn't be slick rather than art.

Maybe it's both. In the excellent young literary magazine *Ploughshares* (vol. I, no. 3) Yates admitted, in a good interview, that his first drafts read like soap operas and that he revises and revises in order to "Get deep enough into it to bring it off." But the soap-opera base is still there, providing a firm one on which to proceed and perhaps accounting for Yates's spellbinding. One could open the book just about anywhere and find description and dialogue wholly authentic in rhythm and diction; here is the beginning of chapter 3 when after getting out of hospital Wilder, Janice and son Tommy head for a few days in the country:

> What the Wilders called "the country" was a clapboard bungalow on half an acre of ground, fifty miles up the west bank of the Hudson. It would have been exposed to a great many other bungalows except for the dense shrubbery and trees shielding it on three sides and a high rustic fence along the fourth—that gave it the seclusion they prized, and there was a small lake for swimming close by.
>
> But the best and most bracing part of the country was getting there: The trip across the George Washington Bridge and the long pastoral ride up the divided highway. As with certain other family pleasures, expectation topped fulfillment.
>
> ". . . I think this is my favorite time of year," Janice was saying, "when it's just beginning to get fresh and cool again. Oh, I suppose it'll be even nicer in a few more weeks when the leaves really turn—all those lovely yellows and oranges and reds and browns—but even so, this is marvelous."
>
> "Mm," he said. She had done a great deal of talking since he came home from Bellevue yesterday—most of it serving no purpose except to fill silence—and he knew that was because he'd said so little himself: he had mostly drunk bourbon and looked out of windows, or sat blinking in bewilderment along the shelves upon shelves of tightly packed books. "Well," he said now, doing his best, "it'll sure feel great just to lie on a blanket in the grass."

Sure enough it doesn't. Even a game of catch with his son quickly goes sour:."Well over half of Tommy's throws were wild and sent his father racing breathlessly over the grass or down on all fours under the bushes, where twigs whipped his face and mud soaked the knees of his clean chino pants. Once a pine needle stabbed him in the eye." Little he sees in nature or in the family that is his; next day he cuts out, back to New York and trouble. Even if one feels Yates has a problem about how to end a disaster-chronicle like this one, the achievement, the writing page-by-page, is high enough to make it not matter much. One hopes we will begin to be more grateful for American writers like him: if you can't be Pynchon why try to be second best? Richard Yates works superbly within the limits of his strength.—WILLIAM H. PRITCHARD, "Novel Auguries," *HdR*, Spring 1976, pp. 151–52

The journey from innocence to experience, from illusion to reality, has long been a traditional undertaking of the novel. *Easter Parade*, the fifth novel of Richard Yates, plays with this tradition as he describes a journey from innocence to renewed innocence, from illusion to fresh illusion.

Easter Parade explores the lives of a woman and her two daughters; it is a sad tale of marriage and divorce, and a still sadder one of sexual liberation. Pookie, the mother, walks out of a marriage in which she feels "stifled" when Sarah is 9 years old and Emily 5. The girls spend their childhood moving from place to place, as their mother tries to launch a career in suburban real estate and pursues a certain style of life she calls "flair," found more often among the rich than the middle class.

The mother's life follows an oblique course between extremes: never the dependent wife, yet never truly in control of her life. The daughters find no reason to emulate her; instead, each embraces a path of no compromise. The life choices of the three women make a striking diagram, like a vector analyzed backwards into its original coordinates. Sarah quickly settles into a commonplace marriage and refuses to leave it, in spite of its increasingly destructive course, while Emily makes her independent way swiftly in and out of marriage, and through countless affairs. It is Emily who grips the reader's attention throughout. Seemingly hard-headed—"the original liberated woman"—but secretly vulnerable, she moves from man to man in an apparently limitless capacity for self-deception.

Emily's sexual career began inauspiciously enough. It was during the summer doldrums the year she graduated from high school, a season of loneliness and self-doubt. One night she met a soldier in the park, whose name she didn't quite catch. "She didn't say yes, but she certainly didn't say no. . . . She was helpless and he was helping her."

Emily's recovery from this encounter was remorseless and swift. College began, and she was to be the first member of her family to have a college education. Emily soon decided that she was an intellectual. "An intellectual might lose her virginity to a soldier in the park, but . . . could learn to look back on it with wry, amused detachment."

Consistent with Emily's new self-image was her choice of Andrew Crawford, a graduate assistant in philosophy. When Andrew went into psychotherapy to clear up some technical difficulties in their lovemaking, Emily was on her own again. But not for long—a young merchant seaman, both worldly and intellectual, introduced her to life in Hell's Kitchen.

After the seaman there was a temporary respite. "There would be no more sex, she promised herself . . . until she was absolutely sure of what she was doing. . . . She broke her promise in November with a haggard law student who said he was a Communist, and broke it again in February with a witty boy who played the drums in a jazz combo. The law student stopped calling her because he said she was 'ideologically impure,' and it turned out that the drummer had three other girls."

The marriage that followed these adventures was briefer than many another affair, and there were "a good many men" in the aftermath of the marriage. "In the space of two years she had two abortions. The first would have been the child of a man she didn't like very much, and the central problem with the second was that she couldn't be sure whose child it would have been."

Emily was in her early thirties when Jack Flanders entered her life. For a while, he provided love and companionship. The trouble was that Jack was a Yale Younger Poet grown older, a fading talent mired in self-pity. It became necessary to leave him. "She would go back to New York . . . she would embark on a new and better life, and she would be free."

Free—only to wake up in a strange bed with a man she did not recognize. There was broken glass on the floor. "The word 'sordid' came into her mind; this was sordid."

"Ted Banks lasted only a few months. . . . Things were on a much more intelligent footing with Michael Hogan. . . . The best thing about him was that he made almost no emotional demands upon her." On the other hand, the executive Howard Dunninger seemed to offer permanence and safety; he was large, sturdy, middle-aged. She wanted "to curl up and ride in his pocket like a kitten." She was encouraged when he decided to use her apartment for their meetings rather than his own. It seemed, on first thought, to imply a greater commitment. "Or did it? . . . When he was the visitor he could always get up and go away. . . . He was shy at first about moving his things in."

When Howard announced that he was moving out to rejoin his wife, Emily could think of nothing else to say than the "weak, meek little phrase she had hated herself for using since childhood: 'I see.'" This is her lifelong response to uncomprehended pain, and the irony is that there is very little that she ever does see, only a parade of figures, posturing, passing, each brightly decked out in whatever seems to be the momentary answer to her needs.

Emily's condition is far from unique and certainly not limited to women. It seems to be a peculiarly contemporary American confusion: the pinning of diverse, even incompatible, needs for community, creativity, self-definition and transcendence upon a frail and transitory sexual bond.

Easter Parade is a spare, yet wrenching tale. Yates enters completely and effortlessly into the lives of his characters. There are no calligraphic embellishments of any kind, no stunts, nothing flashy. The author is wholly absorbed in his story; his prose is very close to the rhythms of actual speech.

Yates is capable of speaking eloquently on the death of the family with a casual, deft question. When Emily visits her sister in the state hospital where both Sarah and Pookie are confined, she asks Sarah how to reach her mother's building. "And Emily instantly realized what a foolish question that was. How could Sarah know the location of any other building when she was locked into this one?"

The image of mother and daughter locked into separate stone buildings in some vast impersonal construction is never underlined by the author; it is nothing spectacular, but its strength is considerable and cumulative, and, when compounded with others like it, takes on the solidity of brick upon brick.

Pookie, Sarah and Emily are a sad threesome, inextricably related yet locked in separateness, unable to connect, unable to learn from their own lives or from one another. Emily, the most gifted, is the most disappointing of the three, since our hopes for her are greater. Taking upon himself a seemingly thankless task, Yates writes powerfully of exasperating people, of people who refuse to shape up, of experience that never ripens into wisdom, of reality persistently shunned, but never evaded for long.—A. G. MOJTABAI, *NYTBR*, Sept. 19, 1976, p. 4

THEODORE SOLOTAROFF

"The Wages of 'Maturity'"

Commentary, July 1961, pp. 89–92

Judging from all one reads and hears, there seem to be as many writers tramping around the suburbs these days as there are postmen: for every man carrying in the news, another is sending it out. Since *Revolutionary Road* is one of the more interesting American novels that has appeared in some time, one might expect it to contain some arresting inversions of its material. But the truth is that its major figure, Frank Wheeler, is still another bright young man who has lost the way and ended up in a New York corporation, where, limp with boredom, he pushes sales correspondence around on his desk. He spends his weekends attempting to build a stone walk or trying to hold his troubled marriage together or lapsing into a mild alcoholic haze. His wife April is still another handsome but frustrated woman—an ex-drama student who is beginning to lose her hold. Their two young children are equally familiar; so are almost all of the minor characters, the nondescript house in Connecticut, the office tedium, the suburban anomie. The dust-jacket tells us that Richard Yates spent five years working on this, his first, novel, and since he is a writer of intelligence and imagination, I suspect that he spent a good part of the time asking himself if he could really bring off a book burdened by so much banal typicality. That he has been able to do so is a tribute not only to his talent but to his feeling for the material, to his power—at times, almost obsessive—of identifying with the world of Frank Wheeler. The result is a book that carries the reader along by the very fact of its being so literal and intimate and intensely American. I have a number of quarrels with *Revolutionary Road*, but have only admiration for the way its author has turned flat, worked-over material into an arrestingly relevant novel.

What makes the book as good as it is, is mainly Yate's ability to tell the truth—both about the little, summary moments of work and marriage today and—though less clearly—about the larger social issues which the behavior and fate of the Wheelers represent. Passage after passage has the simple, unmistakable ring of authenticity: Frank's sinking feeling as he returns to his desk on Monday morning, his writhing with self-irony as he nods deferentially at an important executive's vulgarities, his different poses in order to look masculine or "interesting." Yates has the novelist's natural instinct for the nuances by which people give themselves away; he can render Frank's glib denunciations of the illusions and the sentimentalities of American life as unerringly as he catches Frank demonstrating them. The fights between Frank and April, the long earnest "talks" in which nothing of their real feelings gets communicated, the network of dependency and egotism, guilt and self-righteousness, supportiveness and betrayal, in which the young couple is trapped—all of this Yates catches with remarkable aptness.

The broader ramifications have much the same immediate truth. Early in the novel, the Wheelers are driving home from an amateur theatrical in which April, along with the rest of the cast, has flopped dismally. Frank consoles himself with the thought: "It simply wasn't worth feeling bad about. Intelligent, thinking people could take things like this in their stride, just as they took the larger absurdities of deadly dull jobs in the city and deadly dull homes in the suburbs . . . the important thing was to keep from being contaminated. The important thing, always, was to remember who you were."

Much of the story that follows is patient documentation of the contradiction here that Frank tries to live by—one of his characteristics that makes him representative. A nagging concern with one's "identity" lands most of the young "thinking" people today in the same boat, just as it has become one of the leading themes of postwar fiction: the critical need to locate a self that is independent of one's daily circumstances. But once one subtracts the effects on the personality of an unsatisfying job and home life—subtracts, that is, all but a few hours of life out of each week—the identity that remains becomes painfully abstract and problematic. So Frank and April both learn—and with disastrous consequences. Frank is also typical of many members of his generation in having to go back seven years to his student days at Columbia to remember who he is, for it was there that he had his last, as well as his first, chance to develop.

The leading fact about Frank is, in a sense, his typicality, for he is made of the promising but unstable human stuff that the culture shapes according to its dominant values. At Columbia he rebels against his middle-class family; he is the World War II veteran, still wound up from his experience, alertly stalking ideas and girls in the streets of Greenwich Village. However, all the while, he is merely enacting the vague tribute the educated middle class pays to intellect and independence; for all real purposes, his rebellion is over by the time he is twenty-three. After graduation, he has married and his wife has gotten pregnant; now bent on behaving "maturely," so that she will carry the baby, he takes a job at Knox Business Machines. The important thing about the job is that it is dull and undemanding; in that way, he can preserve his "own identity" until he has enough money to go to Europe. But under the familiar banner of "maturity," the process has now begun by which the Village rebel will turn into a solid consumer and the uncommitted student of the humanities will eventually become a committed salesman of the new computers.

Seven years later he is still with Knox, still doing "the mature thing" by owning a home in the suburbs, and still trying to preserve his identity as one of the thinking, intelligent people. But there is "a faint chronic fever of bewilderment in his eyes," his "thinking" is confined largely to self-projections about the sickness and emptiness of American life, and his intelligence is employed mainly in analyzing and manipulating his wife. Now and then he looks sadly at his impressive collection of books "which were supposed to have made all the difference but hadn't." When his wife offers him the chance to "find himself" while she supports them in Europe, he is more threatened than pleased; the years at Knox have taken their toll and he sees himself in Paris "hunched in an egg-stained bathrobe, on an unmade bed, picking his nose." What he has really come to want is the more prestigious job that is offered at Knox.

Over the whole novel broods this sense of incompleteness and attrition, of landscape that has become commercialized without losing its rawness, of young couples whose best possibilities are already years behind them, who have had to rely too much on their marriages, who work at life—as April sees in her moment of truth near the very end—in a way that is "earnest and sloppy and full of pretension and all wrong." "Maturity," "love," "morality," "self-identity"—these are the catchwords of the Wheelers, and, as has been pointed out in recent years, of their World War II generation. But as the novel argues convincingly, these words stand less for viable values than they do for excuses and evasions of failure. With each of these words as a justification, Frank manipulates April to give up the idea of Europe and carry their third child, and then uses the same slogans to detach himself from her predicament in order to concentrate on his new role as a rising young executive. Eventually he makes it to shore as a successful, if completely hollowed-out, huckster of the Madison Avenue vintage. Meanwhile April has given up, has tried too late to abort the baby, and died.

Who is to blame—Frank? April? the failure of both their parents to raise them adequately? the *Zeitgeist?* modern American life? All of these are implicated in the disaster of the Wheelers, and there is at first glance a satisfying complexity in the moral vision with which Yates distributes the blame. However, it is just here that the novel betrays a certain equivocation and patness of conception that blurs its meaning and dissipates its power. The commentary on the times, both implicitly and explicitly, tries to go beyond the Wheelers' smug criticism of America's "drugged and dying culture." Every so often the son of the competent and awful Mrs. Givings emerges from the state mental hospital to tell the truth about everyone and everything; but his comments on the "hopeless emptiness" of the times are hardly more substantial or illuminating than what we have been hearing from Frank. Most of the explicit social criticism explains too much or too little: its indictment is amorphous and merely irritable, and compromises the powerful commentary implicit in the details.

At the same time, the psychology of the novel has a way of letting the air out of whatever large social protest is being made. Embedded in the narrative are a number of flashbacks that explain why Frank and April behave as they do—why he has problems with masculinity and why she is crippled as a wife and mother. The stress on their supposedly determinative childhoods undercuts the other issues being raised, for in making his tragedy neatly probable, Yates is saying in effect that the Wheelers probably would have failed under the best of circumstances. To write a more meaningful novel about the deadening effects of modern work and marriage, Yates needed characters who could have put up considerably more resistance. As is, Frank and April retain their social significance only to the extent that their early deprivations are typical. And the larger cultural point is obscured: the white-collar man today has a tough time with the problem of masculinity whether or not his father was as overbearingly virile as Frank Wheeler's; nor do the April Wheelers need to grow up without their parents in order to have serious trouble relating their lives to the demands of their husbands and children. Further, the neat consistency with which the Wheelers' behavior is shown to betray their emotional problems, the ease with which they are seen through, weakens considerably the impact of their tragedy. Psychology, as Raskolnikov discovered, is a two-edged knife: depended upon too schematically in a novel, it leads the reader to begin to play the same game as the novelist, and it is easy to end up thinking—if only April had found a good psychiatrist in time.

In the end, *Revolutionary Road* is too obsessive and portentous a novel, too laden with personal meanings of all sorts placed on the frame of a slender and overly simplified story. But it is also an extremely *conscious* book, and Yates's ability to see so much in his material, to bring out so much of the truth that lies behind the clichés about suburbia and the organization man is more important finally than his partial failure to dramatize his characters and ideas effectively. One of his ideas seems particularly interesting. Frank Wheeler is a son of sturdy, hard-working middle-class stock; for all his joking about it, he follows his father's example of working for Knox and eventually becomes a highly attenuated and slick version of him. April is a daughter of the reckless "golden people" of the 1920's, cherishing the memory of their glamour and freedom and, in her way, she becomes a coarsened, joyless version of the former aristocracy. In other words, the attrition that marks their life together lies along a greater curve of decline in American life—a thinning out of class vitalities from generation to generation, an ever-diminishing legacy from the national dream of combining hardiness and grace. The revolution invoked by the title has several possible references, but the main point is that its spirit in America is nearing the end of the road.

MARK TAYLOR

"Modern Tragedies"

Commonweal, September 24, 1976, pp. 631–34

I

At the beginning of an early short story about an infantry platoon going through basic training toward the close of the second World War, Richard Yates's narrator describes the platoon's drill instructor, Sergeant Reece, as "typical—almost a prototype—of the men who had drifted into the Regular Army in the thirties and stayed to form the cadres of the great wartime training centers. . . ." Out of context this sentence looks unremarkable, but I happened to read the story in which it occurs before I had read any of Yates's novels, and then when I did come to the novels, these few words about Sergeant Reece and his confreres kept returning to mind, unsought. It is the first verb, "drifted," I think, that has given the sentence such emblematic significance for me, because almost all of Yates's characters appear to have arrived wherever they have arrived by some species of drifting, of motiveless and ineffective participation in their own lives, of only token interference with the dread forces that shape and direct them. These people are not necessarily without announced purposes: some of them, like Frank Wheeler in *Revolutionary Road*, are veritable demons of self-improvement, at moments, anyway, and in their conscious intentions, but seen with the ironical and uncompromising vision that Yates shares with his readers, they seem somehow not to know the rules of the deadly game they play. And yet it is the only game and, paradoxically in the face of the characters' apparent drifting, its rules are unalterable.

The story about Sergeant Reece is "Jody Rolled the Bones"; it was reprinted in 1962 in a collection of Yates's stories, *Eleven Kinds of Loneliness*. For years that volume equaled nearly one third of Yates's production; there were also two novels, *Revolutionary Road* (1961) and *A Special Providence* (1969), plus a handful of other short stories not reprinted in book form. It appeared self-evident that Yates, who is now fifty, was not, and would not become, a prolific writer, and then, suddenly, two more novels in two years, *Disturbing the Peace* last fall and *The Easter Parade* now. The fact is all the more remarkable when one considers the kind of writer Yates is: careful, scrupulous, exact, faultless, every inch a purveyor of *le mot juste*, the antithesis of someone like, say, Thomas Wolfe. His pages must have been reworked many times, but it is impossible, seeing them in print, to imagine them in any other, earlier state.

And the creative outburst is more remarkable still when one considers the consuming desolation of Yates's world, perfectly uniform in its misery throughout the five books. Loneliness is part of it, what Yates has himself called "the spectre of personal isolation that haunts everyone." His characters need, as Forster wrote in *Howards End*, "only connect," and yet they almost never can. In one story a woman dutifully visits her husband, dying in a tuberculosis ward; she would rather be elsewhere, and he would rather have her elsewhere. After a few perfunctory words, he starts reading the magazines she has brought along. In another story, a class of endlessly forgiving school children ask simply that their teacher open herself to the love they have to give her; she can't. Profound human inadequacy is part of Yates's world, and so, more superficially, are alcohol and hospitals. *Disturbing the Peace*, which chronicles the descent of John Wilder through alcohol into madness, belongs to a literary sub-genre that treats of that particular form of self-destruction, books including Lowry's *Under the Volcano*, Exley's *A Fan's Notes*, and Berryman's *Recovery*. But even where excessive drinking is not Yates's nominal subject, it is still a pervasive condition of the lives of all his adult characters. And so are hospitals: public and private institutions, VA hospitals, tuberculosis wards, state hospitals for the insane and the neglected, Bellevue, Camarillo, Islip. They lurk at the end of every road, or even before the end. For all Yates's supreme mastery over his materials, it sometimes seems a wonder he can go on. It may be, however, that now he has arrived somewhere we have every reason to hope for and no reason to expect.

The Easter Parade tells the story of two sisters, Sarah and Emily Grimes, from childhood into early middle age. Actually, the book belongs to Emily much more than to her older sister; it is through her eyes that we watch the action unfold, it is her continuing disasters that we experience first-hand, it is her friends and lovers whom we come to know, and it is her final gesture in the book that suggests something very new in Yates's fiction. Emily is a bright and articulate girl; an English major at Barnard, and the darling of academic cocktail parties during her undergraduate years ("I could've sworn you were a grad student. You have a very—I don't know. You seem very sure of yourself," one boyfriend tells her), she goes on to a succession of never-quite-literary jobs like trade journals and ad agencies, which frustrate the talent she never wholly defines. For Emily, and Sarah, too, is a writer *manquée:* she starts numerous stories and books that come to nothing. (Indeed, it may well be part of Yates's achievement, here and elsewhere, to posit something about the reaction of the artist to the stresses of the modern world.) And, of course, Emily drifts along through the lives of men, and men through her life: the soldier who takes her virginity in Central Park; an impotent philosophy student; a bisexual sailor; a no longer luminescent poet who teaches in the Writers' Workshop at the State University of Iowa (where Yates himself has taught); a lawyer still in love with his estranged wife; these, and others, all of whom come wonderfully alive in a few or many pages.

But the direction of Emily's drifting is always, if often imperceptibly, downward. She gets older, less able to hold her liquor, less attractive to desirable men, less able to attend to the tedious details of her job. And then, when she seems about ready for the state hospital into which have drifted most of her family, an astonishing thing happens. She goes to visit her nephew Peter, the only one of Sarah's three boys to have made something of himself, and to Peter she admits the confusion of her whole life, and in so doing defines it to herself and offers some promise, in the book's last ambiguous pages, of finding personal renewal. It is an act of total surrender, which may signal an upward turn. This is astonishing, because only once before, by my calculation, has a fiction of Richard Yates's had anything approximating a happy ending; that was *A Special Providence*, whose ending is nevertheless equivocal: good for Robert Prentice, bad for his mother Alice.

The conclusion of *The Easter Parade* is astonishing, furthermore, because if it is happy, it is partly so in Christian terms. Peter is an Episcopalian priest, and the language in which the normally mildly-spoken Emily addresses him, however profane, has an implied frame of reference absent from her earlier discourse: "Jesus, Peter, I hope you do better than *that* in your sermons"; "Christ, what a cop-out"; "What's *that*, for God's sake?"; "Lord God—talk about fantasies coming to life." It is as if these words and the patience and love of her gentle nephew release something within Emily and allow a connection that none of her innumerable liaisons made possible. Since Emily's redemption is couched, in this way, in theological terms, it may be permissible to see her fundamental sin as sloth (is this the besetting sin of all Yates's drifters?), what people in the Middle Ages knew as *acedia:* the paralysis of the will, the inability to direct oneself toward the good.

The book's title refers to *an* Easter Parade in which Sarah Grimes, at 20, enjoyed probably the grandest moments of her life. Emily often recalls that time. The title also suggests, naturally, Irving Berlin's song, a verse of which is sung in an early Yates story, "The Best of Everything." It is to be wondered whether Yates has now recovered some sacred significance from this most secular of celebrations. This is one large question with which a reader will await his next work.

II

I am aware that my summary of *The Easter Parade* does an insufficient job of showing what is new and different about the novel—different not only from Yates's own earlier books but also from other tales of poor victimized girls who somehow manage to straighten themselves out at the end. It is a perceptible fact about Yates's fiction that any paraphrase or abridgment of it trivializes it and flattens it out almost beyond recognition; in outline, it does not leave a reader marveling over inventiveness and originality as, for instance, *Gravity's Rainbow* and *JR* do, even in outline. Why this should be so may be demonstrated by two very brave things Yates does in *Disturbing the Peace.*

Toward the end of that novel John Wilder and his girlfriend Pamela have gone to Hollywood to try to peddle the story of Wilder's life—his business success, extreme drunkenness, family problems, breakdown, confinement in Bellevue, partial recovery, release, still uncertain future—to the men who make movies. They have some letters of introduction, and at first things go well: contacts are made, a production company is formed, and a preliminary conference of Wilder, Pamela, the director Munchin, and a writer, Jack Haines, gets under way. Haines begins by describing the character he is envisioning for the film: "He's unhappily married and he's got kids he can't relate to and he feels trapped. He's solidly middle class. I don't know what he does for a living, but let's say it's something well paid and essentially meaningless, like advertising. When he gets out of Bellevue he's scared and lost but he doesn't know where to turn." Haines goes on a while longer in this vein, and what he is doing, of course, is offering an abstract but perfectly accurate sketch of John Wilder as he has developed to this point, about fifty pages from the end of the book. But then Munchin interrupts him: "I can see you've given this a lot of thought, but I can't help feeling there's a quality of cliché about everything you've said so far. Unhappy advertising man, gray flannel suit and all that." This is daring; Yates is throwing down the gauntlet. He is inviting the reader to see the proximity of his character to cliché, and yet implicitly insisting that he nevertheless transcends any cliché. It is the sort of thing, as novelists say, that other novelists can appreciate.

Such an invitation, however, entails the obvious and considerable risk of getting one hoist by his own petard; an author shouldn't perhaps, alert critics to those spots in his work that bear even a specious semblance of weakness. Still, Yates gets away with it, and partly because it is their hovering nearness to cliché that enables many great fictional creations to become enduring cultural types. Reduce books to plot outlines, deny characters the full context they inhabit, above all, take away the author's *language,* and how much literature becomes soap opera or grotesquerie; the classic exhibit here is Tolstoy's rendition of *King Lear.* It is easy to make even the greatest literature sound banal and silly. Jack Haines's summary of Wilder—a cliché in the way that almost anyone put in five or six sentences becomes a cliché—is in a sense a brief for the integrity of a text, an arguing of the inviolable association of plot and characters. Yates has justified the abiding affection for an early short story, "A Really Good Jazz Piano," that led to his letting it represent him in a recent anthology (*Writer's Choice,* ed. Rust Hills, New York: David McKay, 1974): "To use a standard writers' word whose elusive meaning often seems clear only to editors and critics, I think [the story] 'works.' It seems to grow out of its characters rather than being imposed on them; the scenes and narrative sections fit into each other without much transitional fooling around; the pace may not be fast but does seem to gather momentum at just about the necessary speed."

Most of Yates's fiction "works" for exactly those reasons, especially the first: the incidents that constitute the plot seem always to grow out of the characters and never to be arbitrary. Thus, in *Disturbing the Peace* Haines projects the future of the movie character: "He systematically destroys everything that's still bright and promising in his life, including the girl's love, and he sinks into a depression so deep as to be irrevocable. He winds up in an asylum that makes Bellevue look like nothing." This is the other brave thing Yates does, for the forecast corresponds precisely to the way the rest of Wilder's life will unfold. Yates can tell us in advance because he knows that the character he has drawn can behave no other way, and we know it, too. It is in the inevitability with which his characters' lives proceed that Yates shows that tragic art is still possible.

A recent essay by Gore Vidal in the *New York Review of Books* got a friend and me to talking about some of the limitations of contemporary fiction. Generally agreeing with Vidal's severe critique of several of our most prominent writers, my friend said that the problem with our fiction—he meant American novels since World War II—was its dearth of characters who were convincing and, more, memorable as characters, who led the reader to be genuinely concerned with them as with complicated, sympathetic, real, and yet individualized human beings. We tried to name exceptions to this generalization, characters who inspired the happy fallacy of having one regard them as people independent of the books where they live (as one can regard Jake Barnes and Jay Gatsby), and didn't get very far: Holden Caulfield, Sebastian Dangerfield, a few of Bellow's creations. This list can surely be extended, though I doubt very far, but it will imperatively include a dozen or more characters in the work of Richard Yates, not only his protagonists but also slighter figures like John Givings in *Revolutionary Road* and Charlie and Dr. Spivack in *Disturbing the Peace.* There is no more certain sign of Yates's importance among our witers.

Roger Zelazny

1937–

Roger Joseph Zelazny was born on May 13, 1937, in Cleveland, Ohio. He was educated at Western Reserve University (B.A. 1959) and Columbia University (M.A. 1962). From 1960 to 1963 he served in the Ohio National Guard, and from 1963 to 1966 in the army reserve. In 1964 he married Sharon Steberl; they were divorced in 1966. He married Judith Callahan in 1966; they have two children. After working for several years as a claims specialist for the Social Security Administration, he quit in 1969 to write full-time.

Zelazny sold his first story, "Passion Play," to *Amazing Stories* in 1962, and quickly established himself with such stories as "A Rose for Ecclesiastes" and "For a Breath I Tarry" as one of the new generation of American science fiction writers—among them such figures as Thomas M. Disch, Joanna Russ, and Ursula K. Le Guin—who were more concerned with prose than plot. Zelazny's first novel, *This Immortal* (1966), won the Hugo award for best science fiction novel of the year. His next three novels, *The Dream Master* (1966; expanded from award-winning novella *He Who Shapes*), *Lord of Light* (1967; Hugo award for best novel), and *Isle of the Dead* (1969), were all praised, sometimes extravagantly, for Zelazny's inventive use of myth and pyrotechnic prose. *Lord of Light*, concerning the overturning of a society run by corrupt near-gods, is usually considered his strongest novel. Zelazny's early short stories, considered by some critics to be his work of most enduring value, are collected in *Four for Tomorrow* (1967) and *The Doors of His Face, the Lamps of His Mouth and Other Stories* (1971).

Most critics feel that the quality of Zelazny's fiction dropped around 1970, as his prose became more workmanlike and his plots more straightforward. Still, some feel that the best of his more recent work, especially the Amber series (*Nine Princes in Amber*, 1970; *The Guns of Avalon*, 1972; *Sign of the Unicorn*, 1975; *The Hand of Oberon*, 1976; *The Courts of Chaos*, 1978), *Doorways in the Sand* (1976), and *Eye of Cat* (1982), stands up to the best of his earlier fiction.

Zelazny is one of science fiction's most honored authors, having won the Nebula award three times and the Hugo award five times. He lives near Santa Fe, New Mexico.

SAMUEL R. DELANY
From "Faust and Archimedes" (1968)
The Jewel-Hinged Jaw
1977, pp. 191–205

Zelazny?

A few months before I first went to Europe, a young woman music student came knocking on my door, waving a copy of *The Magazine of Fantasy and Science Fiction* with an absolutely obsessed expression: "Have you read this, Chip? Have you *read* this? Who is he? Do you know anything about him? What has he written before?"

The Doors of His Face, the Lamps of His Mouth was headed by one of *F&SF*'s less informative blurbs. I read it; that copy of the magazine went with me to Europe. I gave it to half a dozen people to read; meanwhile, here in the U.S. the tale took one of those twelve-pound blocks of lucite with the beautiful things inside—a Nebula award. And almost a year later I was to hear, on the same day that I actually met Zelazny in person at the World Science Convention in Cleveland, one of the most intelligent and sensitive readers in the s-f community say, "I can't see why everybody is so excited about a short story that's just a watered down version of *Moby-Dick*." 〈. . .〉

To date the body of Zelazny's writings consist of: the novelettes and novellas, "A Rose for Ecclesiastes"; "King Solomon's Ring"; "The Doors of His Face, the Lamps of His Mouth"; "The Graveyard Heart"; "The Furies"; *He Who Shapes*; "The Keys to December"; "For a Breath I Tarry"; "This Moment of the Storm"; "This Mortal Mountain"; *Damnation Alley*; the full length novels, . . . *And Call Me Conrad* (1965); *Lord of Light* (1967); *Creatures of Light and Darkness* (1969); and the material added to *He Who Shapes* that completes the novel *The Dream Master* (1966).

The whole *oeuvre* tends to mesh into one gorgeous fabric. Here and there evening lights pick out a scene—is it a desert on the Mars of "A Rose for Ecclesiastes," or is it the Egypt of *Conrad?*—perhaps a storm—does it take place on the Venus of "Doors / Lamps," or is it on the farther world described in "This Moment of the Storm"? The themes merge as well.

Immortality appears in one form or another in almost all his works; when it doesn't, there is suicide: faces of one coin. The clearest example is in the moving tale "The Keys to December," in which the point is made that once immortality is achieved, to relinquish it *is* suicide.

Zelazny's basic premise about immortality is quietly revolutionary. The classical supposition—what makes Ahasuerus' fate a curse—is that given all eternity to live, life becomes gray, meaningless, and one must be crushed by the ennui of experience upon experience, repetition upon repetition. Implicit in Zelazny's treatment is the opposite premise: Given all eternity to live, each experience becomes a jewel in the jewel-clutter of life; each moment becomes infinitely fascinating because there is so much more to relate it to; each event will take on new harmonies as it is struck by the overtones of history and like experiences before. The most dour and colorless happening will be illuminated by the light of the ages. This is the *raison* behind the hallucinated, intensively symbolic language. Zelazny's gallery of immortals, Conrad Nomikos and Leota Mathilde Mason, Moore, Ungerer, Sam, Frost, and M'Cwyie (as well as the suicides like Charles Render and Jarry Dark), are burdened with the apprehension of "terrible beauty." Faust's desire to be totally involved experiencing life is the fate of Zelazny's heroes. The theme is Faustian; again, as with Disch, the treatment is Archimedean.

There is no other writer who, dealing with the struggle between life and death on such a fantastically rarified level, can evoke so much hunger for the stuff of living itself. In "A Rose for Ecclesiastes," where the immortality almost fades into the russet desert of Mars, the battle is waged most movingly in the heart of the hero, Gallinger. He is a poet who has come on this early Martian expedition because of his phenomenal linguistic abilities. But although his poetry is brilliant, there is an implication that his soul is dead, partially through the stifling influence of his deceased minister father. The Martians, a race now almost entirely composed of longevous women, have resigned themselves to the sterility of their men and extinction. But when the dancer Braxa is gotten with child by Gallinger, he is compelled to return the sense of life the Martians have given him.

"Life is a disease of inorganic matter; love is a disease in organic matter."

This is the pessimism of the Martians Gallinger must overcome. To it, he holds up a rose.

"The final flower turns a burning head . . ."

And the flame sheds light on all that vivid, arid land "where the sun is a tarnished penny, the wind is a whip, where two moons play at hot-rod games, and a hell of sand gives you the incendiary itches every time you look at it."

Banks Mebane in his analysis of Zelazny's prose has pointed out its kinship with the metaphysical poets. But it is highly colloquial as well. The wonder of the prose is that it manages to keep such intensely compressed images alive and riding on the rhythms of contemporary American.

Though Gallinger is victorious in "Rose," the victory is pyrrhic. His coming and triumph have been predicted; Braxa's pregnancy turns out to have been contrived; and she does not love him. The "immortality" of the Martians is not real immortality . . . they do die eventually. And Gallinger's suicide attempt fails. The mitigation of the usual Zelazny parameters makes "Rose" a more immediate work than, say, *Lord of Light*, where they exist as absolutes. The mitigation also probably explains its popularity.

There are several of his tales that I prefer to it, however: "Doors / Lamps," "For a Breath I Tarry," and "The Graveyard Heart," for example.

But in the numerous lists of Zelazny stories ranged by preference, it is indicative of the man's breadth of appeal that there is such a variety of heading titles.

Zelazny's tale most openly related to the Faust theme is his novella *He Who Shapes*. Charles Render, psychiatrist extraordinaire, victim of his own death wish and the medieval phantasies of a beautiful, blind and wholly contemporary Lady of Shalott (herself a psychiatrist), is as much a modern Faust as Louis Sacchetti. Render not only has knowledge of the human mind, but a technological power that makes him master of a special effects gallery to rival Pal and Kubrick. He can shape the minds of his patients through controlled dreams.

The rendering of Render, his movements real and fantastic, has a sophistication that Disch, with all his intellectual bravura, misses. Zelazny makes Doctor Render a man with a domestic past and present, and delineates his fall within the limits of an exquisitely evoked profession. Perhaps the simple bid for reality adds the touch of density missing from poet Sacchetti.

Within its perfectly open framework, *He Who Shapes* is a difficult tale. Once the difficulties have been broken through, it is a disturbing one.

The execution of the original novella was superb; it won Zelazny his second Nebula in 1965.

About a year later, he added some ten thousand words to the story, filling out the length of a standard novel, published by Ace as *The Dream Master*.

But let me backtrack some.

The original title of the novella was *The Ides of Octember*. The phrase comes from the opening fantasia on the steps of the Senate where Antony is being murdered while Caesar begs to be assassinated:

> "Have you an ill omen for me this day?"
> "Beware!" jeered Render.
> "Yes! Yes!" cried Caesar. "'Beware!' That is good! Beware what?"
> "The ides—"
> "Yes? The ides—?"
> "—of Octember."
> "What is that you say? What is Octember?"
> "A month."
> "You lie! There is no month of Octember!"
> "And that is the date noble Caesar need fear—the non-existent time, the never-to-be-calendared occasion." . . .
> "Wait! Come back! . . . You mock me," Caesar wept . . . "I want to be assassinated too!" he sobbed. "It isn't fair."

The scene ends, and we learn that Render is a psychiatrist and Caesar is his patient, a Representative Erikson, who has erected a paranoid anxiety syndrome (not quite a delusional system) in which people are trying to assassinate him. Render terminates the therapy, successfully, by making the politician realize that the general depersonalizing forces of modern society, coupled with Erikson's tendency to suppress completely his own individualism in pursuit of his political ends, has forced his ego to rebel by erecting these anxieties in an attempt to prove to himself that he is important enough to assassinate. Erikson's desire for assassination is one side of a double-faced mirror; one surface reflects the malady of the future time Zelazny writes of, the other shows us something terribly familiar. To catch the resonance with the real world, consider Zelazny's tale in light of the assassination of Kennedy that had taken places less than a year before he wrote the story; or the assassination of Martin Luther King, which took place within a week of this writing. Zelazny has picked images that vibrate sympathetically with the times.

Because *He Who Shapes* is so much a story built on the mechanics of a contemporary predicament, and because it shows so much insight into their workings, internal hindrances that mute the impact, or impede the evaluation of those insights, are terribly frustrating. One cannot simply dismiss the new material added to make *The Dream Master:* Scene for scene, it is beautifully done, and amplifies both major and minor themes. My uneasiness is with placement, pacing and emphasis, which destroy the original dramatic unity of the whole; and because of the real excellences in the new material, the frustration is doubled.

The resonances of this tale of Faust-as-psychiatrist and his blind Helen are multiple. The man who makes fantasies real is an analogue for any artist or scientist; the death wish, the temptation to let fantasies completely cut one off from the real world, is a pertinent problem in today's blueprints.

I think the best way to approach *He Who Shapes* is to read the novella version first, and then turn to the new material in the novel (contained between pages 54 and 109 of *The Dream Master* in the Ace edition) as a commentary and amplification.

This is the only way I can think of to get the benefits of both versions and avoid the distraction of the novel's structural weakness.

Faust risks destruction before the intensity of his own vision: and in this tale, the one thing left unambiguous in both versions, he is destroyed.

SIDNEY COLEMAN

Fantasy and Science Fiction, August 1974, pp. 51–55

Maybe the Joe Blotz test will help.

The test is used by honest editors considering stories by famous writers: "What would I think of this if it were a story by somebody I had never heard of, by Joe Blotz?" I think I would give *To Die in Italbar* by Joe Blotz an ecstatic review. "Blotz writes well; he can describe fast action and strong emotions with equal skill; he has a fertile imagination and creates colorful characters. Joe Blotz is clearly one of the most promising new writers to appear in a long time. Perhaps he is too much influenced by Roger Zelazny, but . . ."

No, it doesn't help. There is no avoiding the shadow; it is impossible to write about late Roger Zelazny without comparing it to early Roger Zelazny.

In 1963 Roger Zelazny published "A Rose for Ecclesiastes"; in 1968 *Lord of Light* won the Hugo. These dates define Zelazny's prime; *sans peur et sans reproche*, he was the darling of science fiction. I remember asserting publicly in 1967 that there was more real science in a page of Zelazny than in the collected works of George O. Smith; at about the same time, Harlan Ellison wrote that Zelazny was the reincarnation of Geoffrey Chaucer. I quote these statements as evidence of the spirit of the age rather than of critical acumen; either of them could be translated as "Wow!" with negligible loss of content.

But we were wowing with good reason. In an important sense Zelazny really was without fear and without blame; he would try the most daring tricks, and bring them off. Zelazny's famous skill as a culture-magpie is an outstanding instance: He would cast a computer as both Faust and Adam, mix grail legend with electric psychotherapy, work a line from the *Cantos* into a story whose basic plot was the old pulp chestnut about the white hunter and Miss Richbitch. ("For a Breath I Tarry", *He Who Shapes*, "The Doors of His Face, the Lamps of His Mouth".) Any fool could have tried these things, and, maddened by Zelazny's example[1], many did; for a time we had myths like some people have mice. But Zelazny was not his epigones; he made it work.

How did he do it? We can get a clue by looking at one of Zelazny's favorite devices, a rapid shift of viewpoint, or, better yet, shift of values. In the simplest case, this is a shift from a noble view of high heroism to a comic one. An example: in *Lord of Light*, a band of heroes is planning an assault on Heaven. One of them, Tak, has been incarnated for much of the book in the body of an ape. Great deeds are being plotted, and the conversation is in Zelazny's best high-mimetic tone, full of noble vows and Homeric epithets. ("I have always wanted to go to battle at the side of the Binder.") After the strategy meeting, refreshments are served. Tak requests a banana. Blackout. Another: In . . . *And Call Me Conrad*, the Black Beast of Thessaly is about to annihilate Conrad when it is annihilated itself by a bolt from stage left. The bolt has been fired by Conrad's wife Cassandra, whom he had believed to be dead until this moment. His first words to her are, "Uh—hi, Cassandra. How've you been?" (The editor of the book version (*This Immortal*) changed this line to "Cassandra!" He felt the original text was inappropriate. Indeed it was; that was the point.)

This is an old device. It is a form of internalized comic relief—not the porter in *Macbeth*, but Hamlet in *Hamlet*. It is even an old device in our world; Fritz Leiber has used it systematically since the beginning of his career; *Adept's Gambit* is permeated with it. It is sometimes called irony, but this is not quite the right word, for the comic vision does not undercut the heroic one, but underlines it. Wit is a better word, if we remember that it is the root of both witty and witting. The double vision is richer than the sum of its parts, because each part illuminates the other.

This method of multiple vision, of playing one aspect of a thing against another, is characteristic of much of the best work of Zelazny's high period. It occurs in more complicated forms than the one I have described. For example, any moderately well-trained English major could write pages on the way Frost is played against Faust in "For a Breath I Tarry." Parts of the story are direct parody; Frost makes Faust funny. This leads to an implicit comparison between Faust's sophistication and Frost's naivete; Faust makes Frost funny. The endings of the stories illuminate each other; Frost succeeds where Faust fails because it is better to seek humanity than divinity. Etc.

Another approach to the same statement: There are worlds in science fiction that stick in your mind; they are solid. Hal Clement's Mesklin, Frank Herbert's Dune, Ursula Le Guin's Winter are very different places in most respects, but they do have this in common. They extend beyond the books that contain them; one feels that there is more to be said. Typically, Zelazny's worlds are not like this. They have no physics, no ecology, no sociology. They are intricately patterned and brightly colored, but they are flat, stage-sets, cartoons. But they do not need to be solid; for Zelazny's purposes, a solid world would be as useless an object as a solid violin. The function of the thing is to resonate.

This is one great advantage of working with multiple visions, of being both witty and witting. It enables the writer to assimilate material that would be too thin, too inappropriate, or simply too silly to handle in any other way. Consider the problem of the Hero. Science Fiction deals frequently with large actions; large actions are done by Heroes, people larger than life, and most readers over the age of fourteen find such mighty doers of great deeds ludicrous. The problem is to keep the man who saves the world from being preposterous. One solution is to humanize him, show him as being sometimes afraid, confused, tired, and wrong-headed. This is the solution favored by a writer like Ursula Le Guin (*The Lathe of Heaven*).

Another solution is to root him firmly in an imagined world, so his heroism is seen as a natural outgrowth of his social and psychological background. This is the solution favored by a writer like Samuel Delany (*Nova*).[2] Zelazny's solution was not to eliminate the preposterousness, but to exploit it. Conrad Nomikos is an immortal man who experiences high adventures and ends up owning Earth. You find this hard to take seriously? So did Zelazny. It's one of the things he plays against in . . . *And Call Me Conrad*, and this play is not only interesting in itself, it makes the heroism more acceptable. Conrad the admirable real hero and Conrad the preposterous comic-book hero define two surfaces; in the space they enclose Zelazny creates his resonances.

(I except from most of this *He Who Shapes* (*The Dream*

Master). This marvelous short novel is in many ways a direct contradiction of the main themes and method of Zelazny's early work. A sign: *He Who Shapes* is as full of myth as any Zelazny story of the period, but the myth is here explicitly identified with psychopathology. It occurs to me that this may be meta-wit: Zelazny playing against Zelazny.)

Of course, this is a paradigmatic Zelazny I have been describing, triple-distilled essence of Zelazny, Zelazny as Zelazny-hero, if you want. The real Zelazny was more complicated and requires a lengthier analysis with many more qualifying phrases. Nevertheless, I think I have the essential outlines right; this is how he did it, how he made it work. But this makes what happened in the late sixties very strange. For, about this time, Zelazny abandoned his method but retrained the material that made sense only when coupled with the method. *To Die in Italbar* has flat backgrounds: Italbar itself has the social and economic structure of an American town, for all that it is set on an alien planet and has a few pieces of futuristic machinery and a pet lizard or two stuck here and there in the foreground. It has gigantically larger-than-life protagonists: Two of the main characters have literally god-like powers, another is a highly-successful one-man commando army, fighting an interstellar state from his private fortress, another is a paranoid prostitute redeemed by love, another is a living dead man. You find this hard to take seriously? So do I, but Zelazny has no qualms: everything in *To Die in Italbar* is viewed straight on, with a single vision, as dead serious as ⟨E. E. Smith's⟩ *Children of the Lens*.

I do not know why Zelazny began this process of reverse alchemy five years ago, why he put away his magician's tricks and turned his gold into lead. Maybe he simply ran out of steam; it happens often enough in literary careers; being a genius is a profession for the young. Or it might have been the pressures of the market. Zelazny began free-lancing full time about five years ago, and the economics of sf writing are not such as to allow time for tinkering with the elaborate and delicate machineries of wit. I don't know why; all I know is that we once had something unique and wonderful, and it is gone, and what we have in its place is only a superior writer of preposterous adventures.

Still, I enjoy reading preposterous adventures as much as anyone, and I enjoyed reading *To Die in Italbar*, for it is a superior specimen of the type. It is well written; fast action and strong emotion are described with equal skill; the author has a fertile imagination and creates colorful characters. Pity it wasn't written by Joe Blotz.

Notes

1. And those of Samuel R. Delany and Cordwainer Smith, who were mining some of the same veins, though with different tools.
2. In this sense, Delany (another darling of the sixties, and also with good reason) was Zelazny's opposite. Typically, Delany would strive to maintain a single vision, work for solidity, carefully develop detailed scientific, cultural, and psychological background. Even Delany's deliberate homage to Zelazny, "We, in Some Strange Power's Employ, Move on a Rigorous Line," shows the difference; nothing could be less like Zelazny than the meticulous anatomy of Delany's imagined global power network.

THOMAS F. MONTELEONE
From "Introduction"
Isle of the Dead
1976, pp. v–xii

What makes *Isle of the Dead* such an important work of science fiction, above all other things, is that Zelazny created a unique mythology which adds dimension to his alien Pei'an culture. The novel is the culmination of Zelazny's fascination with the function of myth in man's psyche—a theme which runs through many of his short stories and early novels. There has always been a need in literature for the mythic character, the hero of larger-than-life proportions through which ordinary men could pattern their own lives. Modern literature, Zelazny feels, has somehow lost its grip upon the mythic figure and has consequently suffered for it. To make up for this loss, Zelazny consciously attempted to create a science fiction mythos, a model from which new forms of the genre might arise. In public appearances and private conversation Zelazny has explained his views on this subject by paraphrasing the noted literary critic, Northrop Frye, who sees all literature being classified into four basic "modes." The highest, or "Mythic Mode," concerns characters greater than men, greater than the natural forces of the universe—in effect, gods. Next is the "High Mimetic Mode," in which the characters are more powerful than ordinary men—such as kings, rulers, men of influence or wealth—who are capable of controlling the fate of other men. (The character of Francis Sandow of *Isle of the Dead* falls somewhere in between these two modes: a character of the High Mimetic aspiring to, or perhaps unconsciously gravitating towards, the Mythic.) The third classification is the "Low Mimetic Mode," filled with common men combatting natural forces in totally realistic or naturalistic ways—like the characters of Jack London or Frank Norris. Lastly is the "Ironic Mode," in which the characters are inferior to ordinary men, unable to cope with the obstacles of the world—such as those found in the works of Franz Kafka, Eugene Ionesco, or Kurt Vonnegut.

Using the above conception of literary characters as his model, Zelazny was able to add a new and exciting dimension to science fiction. *Isle of the Dead* contains all the elements of a true future-epic: a larger-than-life hero, a pantheon of ancient gods, a mystical quest, transcendence, and the transfiguration of the hero. The book sparkles with a freshness of language and an exhilarating rush of symbol and metaphor which further enhances the mythic flavor of the narrative.

There are many elements in *Isle of the Dead* which contribute to the book's overall effect, but before examining them in detail, perhaps it would be beneficial to discuss the development of Roger Zelazny as a science fiction writer so that one might better appreciate what this novel represents.

Zelazny's first science fiction story appeared in the August, 1962 issue of *Amazing Stories*. A scant five years later, he was science fiction's newest superstar, having won the Hugo Award twice in the novel category, and the Nebula Award twice for best novella and best novellette.

⟨. . .⟩ In 1965, his first novel appeared as a serial in *The Magazine of Fantasy and Science Fiction* under the title ". . . And Call Me Conrad" and was published the following year in paperback (Ace Books, 1966) as *This Immortal*. The book was one of those rare first novels that met with almost universal acclaim, winning the Hugo Award for best novel at the 1967 World Science Fiction Convention. *This Immortal* was an important book for Zelazny, especially since it was his first novel-length statement on the themes of immortality and the power of myth—ideas that would continue to influence his later work and culminate in *Isle of the Dead*.

Also in 1965, his brilliant novella, *He Who Shapes*, was published in the January and February issues of *Amazing*; and the Science Fiction Writers of America recognized the story as the best novella of the year in 1966—the same year that an expanded book-length version of the tale appeared under the title *The Dream Master* (Ace Books, 1966; Gregg Press, 1976). The story is a superb blend of modern science fiction and classical tragedy, employing elements of medieval legend, Greek and Norse mythology, and modern psychology. Through the use of magical imagery and an impressionistic style, Zelazny created a satisfying novel of symbology and power.

Zelazny's third novel, *Lord of Light* (Doubleday, 1967), was also a stunning success, winning the Hugo Award for best novel of the year. It represented another evolutionary step in the author's attempt to define the High Mimetic and Mythic Modes in terms of modern science fiction. It is the tale of the Prometheus-like figure who struggles against overwhelming odds to achieve his personal dreams. Using the Hindu mythos as his model, Zelazny explored the function of myth and the power of religion in society. Stylistically, he was able to capture a certain essence of Eastern narrative, embodying the images and metaphors of a cosmology that is basically unfamiliar to most readers. In many ways, the novel is the end-point, the realization of Zelazny's desire to shape science fiction and existing myth into a single entity—a feat that he felt, perhaps, that he must accomplish before trying to create an entirely *new* myth-system as he does in *Isle of the Dead*. ⟨. . .⟩

Written in the first person, *Isle of the Dead* has a sense of immediacy and power that is conveyed through the personality of its protagonist, Francis Sandow. In fact, Sandow's characterization is one of the novel's strongest assets. Zelazny heroes are marked by many recurring traits: formidable intellect, a position of power, a sense of the poetic combined with great perceptive abilities, long-life (sometimes immortality), and perhaps best of all a wry sense of humor. Sandow possesses all these attributes, plus one thing more—enormous wealth; he is a pan-galactic Howard Hughes. Sandow is wise through the benefit of his long life, but he is also intelligent and innately moral. This does not mean, however, that he is averse to violence, retribution, or even revenge if he believes it necessary. As mentioned before, Sandow is a carefully-fashioned character in Frye's "High Mimetic Mode," and it is through the action of *Isle of the Dead* that Sandow toys with the role of Pei'an godhood, ultimately discovering a new, yet fundamental, truth about himself. Joseph Sanders notes this aspect of characters like Sandow when he says that "Zelazny's stories thus involve a character going through a process of growth, leading not so much to certainty about what he *is* as to a realization that, since he is so much more than ever known or admitted before, he can go on growing."[1] This is an illustration of one of Zelazny's recurring themes: man's unlimited potential for change and ultimate growth.

Taken in this light, *Isle of the Dead* can be read as a quest tale on several levels. There is the basic element of plot which makes it a mystery/detection story until the true identity and motivation of Green-Green are discovered. In addition there is the slow unfolding of Sandow's relationship with Shimbo of Darktree, Shrugger of Thunders, and how Sandow learns more about who he actually is. In keeping with the traditions of the novel of detection, Zelazny has altered his style to fit the occasion in a manner that is reminiscent of John D. MacDonald. The personal asides, the great use of flashbacks, and the introduction of characters in these episodes are familiar techniques found in MacDonald's narratives. Even Sandow's tough yet sophisticated manner is slightly evocative of MacDonald's Travis McGee.[2]

But *Isle of the Dead* is more than a quest for enlightenment. It is also a marvelous vehicle through which Zelazny can continue to explore his fascination with mythology. The entire concept of Sandow returning to a place of the dead (regardless of the figurative/literal meanings employed here) strongly suggests the Orpheus myth, with Kathy playing Eurydice through the miracle of some highly-advanced biological engineering. It is important to note, however, that the Orpheus motif is merely suggested, alluded to, rather than slavishly followed and merely dressed in science-fictional garb. The really fresh and fascinating mythological aspects of the novel are found in Zelazny's finely detailed and logically structured pantheon of *alien* gods. When Sandow visits his Pei'an mentor, Marling, or when he enters the mysterious Pei'an temples, Zelazny shows the reader something entirely new: a pantheon of deities that are wholly removed from anything familiar. What is even more inventive is the way Zelazny has married Sandow's "profession" of reshaping whole worlds with the theosophy and religion of the ancient Pei'an culture. That aspect of the novel is suggestive of several oriental philosophies, such as Zen, which require that a man's work in the world be coordinated with beliefs and perceptions about the nature of the universe. This new mythology adds an exotic element to *Isle of the Dead*, and provides Zelazny with a new and exciting vehicle in which to manipulate his High Mimetic and Mythic characters.

The result of this is, through Sandow/Shimbo of Darktree, science fiction received a new kind of archetype. Zelazny's creation of a new myth-system is without a doubt based on his belief that the old myths—the tales and lessons by which early civilized man learned to survive in a world of unknowns—have lost their power to enchant modern cultures. The images have lost their familiarity, the symbols have lost their power and demand to be replaced. Through the indirection of his fiction, Zelazny is asking two important questions: what shape is modern man's mythology going to assume? and could that shape possibly be the science fiction as speculation that is represented by *Isle of the Dead?* As man's technology continues to expand at a geometric rate, a pace which far outstrips the rates of cultural and social change, the border's of known territory are being pushed further outward. But somewhere in the depths of man's psyche, Zelazny believes, there is still a need to replace the computer and the nuclear weapon with more *human* symbols. Myth functions at the margins of man's understanding—a watcher at the gates to the darkness beyond—and through the creation of new myths man can more fully understand his true nature. Novels in the tradition of *Lord of Light* and *Isle of the Dead* can be seen, then, as one possible way of fulfilling the need for new legends in the technological age.

Notes

1. Joseph Sanders, in an article tentatively entitled "Zelazny: Unfinished Business," to be published in *Voices for the Future*, Vol. 2, edited by Thomas D. Clareson, Bowling Green Popular Press, 1976.
2. Ted White, "Review of *Isle of the Dead*," *Fantastic*, August, 1969, p. 131.

ORMOND SEAVEY
From "Introduction"
The Dream Master
1976, pp. v–xii

Roger Zelazny has written recently that science fiction exhibits a characteristic and basic ambivalence regarding the transformations of physical reality that are its subject. The tension he describes is between Pygmalion and Frankenstein—"an internal and perhaps eternal debate as to whether man's creations will destroy him or live happily with him forever after."[1] It is an intriguing contrast. Ovid's Pygmalion brings Galatea to life through his art and his devotion to the goddess of love. Mary Shelley's Frankenstein employs science to bring his repellent monster to life. In Shelley's world the defiance of the distinction between life and death takes on the quality of a violated sacrament, since physical reality is the only possible source of value. In Ovid's world, life and death are merely phases. Zelazny's distinction between these two impulses also underlies his novel *The Dream Master*. The story appears to be about a Pygmalion figure, a life-giving artist. It proves in the end to be about a self-deluded scientist, a Frankenstein.

The protagonist is named Render. "Render" resembles what Freud called a primal word—that is, a word whose meanings are directly opposite to each other. Just as dreams often include elements whose significance is directly opposite to their apparent meanings, the opposing meanings of primal words point to a pre-linguistic state of consciousness where all opposites have a hidden kinship. "To render" means to depict, to illustrate; it also means to boil down or melt down. And a "render" is one who rends, who tears violently asunder. Charles Render is a neuroparticipant therapist, commonly known as a "shaper." By means of an Omnichannel Neural Transmission and Receiver unit, he can manipulate the dreams of his patients to alter their deepest fantasies. He is "Render the Shaper—one of the two hundred or so special analysts whose own psychic makeup permitted them to enter into neurotic patterns without carrying away more than an esthetic gratification from the mimesis of aberrance—a Sane Hatter."[2] Render can create in dreams the assassination of Julius Caesar (although he changes it to the assassination of Mark Antony) or the sinking of the lost continent of Atlantis. He is not, however, in perfect control of his medium. As a participant, he shares control of the dream with the patient, whose disturbed sense of reality contests with his for dominance. By rendering these dreams, he boils down and destroys the neuroses of his patients.

His Galatea is a beautiful blind woman named Eileen Shallot. Tennyson wrote of the Lady of Shalott, who lives exiled on her river island watching the people on the nearby road to Camelot. She must die if she ever looks back toward Camelot, which she does when distracted by the sight of Sir Launcelot. The poem is a Victorian confection of nostalgia for a lost chivalric idyll. Eileen Shallot is a psychiatrist who wishes to become a shaper. She arranges to meet Render at dinner and convinces him to take her on as his student. To learn the dreaming wisdom that is Render's, she must descend naked into the egg-shaped compartment called the ro-womb, where Render can create for her the world of vision she has been deprived of from birth.

She is accompanied by her dog Sigmund (as in Sigmund Freud, a typical instance of Zelazny's saucy allusiveness). Sigmund is a "mutie," a dog with a rudimentary capacity to speak and reason. He has the behavior and loyalty of a dog; his human traits are a surgically induced deformity. Sigmund reminds Render of the Fenris wolf, a frightening mythological creature who appears sometimes in Render's own dreams. According to the *Voluspa Edda*, the Fenris wolf has been confined for a time, but in the twilight of the gods it will break its bonds and devour Odin in the final cataclysm.

Myth is a central subject of *The Dream Master*. Sessions of the Act a Myth Club form a counterpoint to the narrative; at the club meetings participants act out myths like a variation of charades. The story of Tristan and Isolde in particular lies behind the final dream sequences—with the essential difference that the cup of everlasting and beautiful love which Tristan drinks becomes for Render an emblem of suicidal illusions.[3] In expanding *The Dream Master* from its original published version as a novella, Zelazny added particularly to the emphasis on myth. In a speech he is writing, Render muses over the interest in traditional myths at the end of the twentieth century, his own present. "An intense study of mental illness," he intones into his lapel microphone, "is often quite revealing as to the nature of the stresses in the society where the illness was made. If anxiety-patterns fall into special groups and classes, then something of the discontent of society can be learned from them. Karl Jung pointed out that when consciousness is repeatedly frustrated in a quest for values it will turn its search to the unconscious; failing there, it will proceed to quarry its way into the hypothetical collective unconscious. . . . There are historical periods when the group tendency for the mind to turn in upon itself, to turn back, is greater than at other times. We are living in such a period of Quixotism in the original sense of the term." (pp. 49–50) Traditional myths served to explain an otherwise terrifying and meaningless world. The sources of physical and psychic anxieties are nearly eliminated by Render's time, but the urge to regress to a mythic past grows even stronger.

Another effect of the novel's imagined technology is the blurring of a whole series of distinctions. Man and machine, man and beast, God and man, illusion and reality—all seem to be not opposing states but merely alternative modes of perception. Render and his girl friend Jill deVille go to a dance program performed by robots programmed with eerily human mannerisms; the machines seem interchangeable with men. The existence of Sigmund disrupts the distinction between man and beast. There is also the cautionary tale of Pierre, a philosophy student at the University of Paris doing a dissertation on the evolution of consciousness. He entered the dream machine with an ape, the ape became frightened, and Pierre's mind was transformed into that of a frightened ape. Render becomes both God and Adam in the dreams he shares with Eileen Shallot. Together they wander through the world he has prepared. Render uses Walt Whitman's *Song of Myself* as a kind of guidebook to sensations. In all these mixtures of fantasy and reality, fantasy exercises an irresistible force. The way out of illusions is harder than the way into them.

⟨. . .⟩ Render is not a swashbuckling interplanetary Errol Flynn, but he has the self-confidence of later Zelazny heroes. And what he confronts is finally the fatal dangers inherent in the confident manipulations he must perform professionally. He is a smooth operator; the world seems perfectly accessible to his plastic powers. The fault lies in himself. He has compared himself to God, as a Shaper and creator of dream universes. Trying to give sight to the blind, he is blind himself—to the needs of his son and his mistress, to the dangers of violating another consciousness, to his own human vulnerability.

Blindness is one of the subjects of *The Dream Master*. The windows of buildings and vehicles can be made instantaneously transparent or opaque. "Blindspin" is a favorite diversion, in which the automatically directed automobiles are programmed to drive in an arbitrary and unknown direction. "Flashing across the country in the sure hands of an invisible chauffeur, windows all opaque, night dark, sky high, tires assailing the road below like phantom buzzsaws—and starting from scratch and ending in the same place, and never knowing where you are going or where you have been—it is possible, for a moment, to kindle some feeling of individuality in the coldest brainpan, to produce a momentary awareness of self by virtue of an apartness from all but a sense of motion." (p. 23) Blindspin produces the illusion of self-awareness, but only because the traveller feels the reassuring total helplessness of the womb.

Eileen Shallot seems also to be driven by the sure hands of an invisible chauffer in her neuroparticipant analysis, but the chauffeur is mortal. Mortals make mistakes while driving. A few years earlier, before cars were automatically controlled, Render's wife and his daughter Miranda drove off an embankment and were killed. Eileen Shallot, however, has blind confidence in Render's control. Like the Lady of Shalott, she imagines Render in a suit of armor when she sees him in their dreams. Armor is a psychoanalytic metaphor for all the modes of self-possession and self-control. Armoring, Freud recognized, is a necessary protection for the self against the demands of others and against the self's most basic drives. Only Sigmund (the dog, not the psychoanalyst) recognizes that Render's armor is vulnerable. He can smell that Render is afraid.

The Dream Master is about myth and blindness. It is also about manipulation. Both the artist and the con man are manipulators; what distinguishes them is not merely their motives but also their concern for their materials. Render sees himself as an artist, manipulating myth in order to cure and to teach. He proves in the end to be an unwitting con man, overcome by the very myths which he thought he could control. Render pretends to himself that he is Pygmalion, the life-giver, when he has never been more than Frankenstein, assembling discordant elements into a grotesque similitude of life. Like the participants in the Act a Myth Club, Render is only a creator of little parlor entertainments on classical subjects, however elaborate his machinery might be.

Notes

1. Roger Zelazny, "Some Science Fiction Parameters: A Biased View," *Galaxy* 36 (July 1975), p. 8.
2. Roger Zelazny, *The Dream Master* (New York: Ace Books, 1966; Boston, Gregg Press/G. K. Hall, 1976), p. 14. Further page citations will be given in the text; page numbers refer to both editions.
3. Thomas Monteleone, "Science Fiction as Literature: Selected Stories and Novels of Roger Zelazny," unpublished master's essay, University of Maryland, 1973, p. 84.

Louis Zukofsky

1904–1978

Louis Zukofsky was born on January 23, 1904, in New York City, to Russian Jewish immigrants; his first language was Yiddish, and neither of his parents spoke English. He was educated at Columbia University (M.A. 1924). In 1939 he married Celia Thaew; they had one child. He taught at various institutions, including the University of Wisconsin, Colgate University, Polytechnic Institute of Brooklyn, San Francisco State College, and the University of Connecticut.

Zukofsky's initial interests were sociological and historical; he was particularly interested in the theories of Karl Marx and Henry Adams, who would remain influences upon his later work. He became interested in poetry in his teens, and was associated with the Objectivist school of poets, a group whose practice was abstracted from the theories of Ezra Pound and especially William Carlos Williams, and which included such poets as Charles Reznikoff, George Oppen, and Lorine Niedecker. Pound and Williams were friends of Zukofsky, and were supportive of him throughout his career.

Zukofsky dedicated most of his literary life to the composition of the long poem "A," written in twenty-four parts and completed in 1978, shortly before his death. It was published in its entirety in 1979. Zukofsky was especially fascinated with language as music, and much of his poetry is written to be read on a number of levels, with little or no "absolute" meaning. He delighted in rhythm and sound, and in exploring the varieties of formal structure. "A" was intended to explore life in its many varieties as it presented itself to Zukofsky in the course of the poem's composition; the essentially random collection of themes and motifs that resulted was strongly tempered by Zukofsky's firm sense of structure and music.

Though Zukofsky remains largely unknown to the general public, his work has been a significant influence on modern poets such as Robert Creeley and Robert Duncan, and figures as influential as Hugh Kenner and Kenneth Rexroth have considered him one of the overlooked American geniuses of his generation. In addition to "A," Zukofsky published much short poetry; most of it, including the much-admired "Poem Beginning 'The,'" is collected in *All: The Collected Short Poems 1923–1964* (1971). Zukofsky also published a play, *Arise, Arise* (1973), three books of fiction, considerable criticism (collected in *Prepositions: The Collected Critical Essays, 1967*), and his *Autobiography* (1970). He died on May 12, 1978.

Zukofsky is an American who has been writing for forty-five years. There are so many American poets now on the scene that it is difficult for many English readers to decide for themselves which are important and which are less so. Zukofsky is important. He represents, for all his modernistic technical experiments, the middle way of American poetry during the past thirty or so years. His poetic godfather is William Carlos Williams, but his vision is entirely his own. He is really an impressionist who is able to capture an atmosphere or seal an idea within remarkably small compass. He possesses a sensitive eye and an individual way of communicating thoughts and feelings. Nothing seems to escape him. He is as much at home with natural phenomena as with everything else in the contemporary American scene, though he does not dwell for long on fashionable politics. In his way he is a satirist not unlike our own Stevie Smith. But although his bite is sharp, he does not leave behind lasting wounds. He may, perhaps, have written too much about the same things and in the same way, but he is a satisfying writer whose poems on the page give as much pleasure to the eye as they do to the ear. —LEONARD CLARK, "Motions of the Heart," *PoR*, Summer 1968, p. 109

We respect Zukofsky for his honesty more than for anything else. He isn't a very skillful writer or even a very careful one, but in everything he does we have the sense of a man trying in all simplicity to express the nuances of a subtle understanding. His technique is sufficient only to let the intention be perceived, not to fulfill it; he seems never to have realized that subtlety cannot be expressed without subtlety.

The new volume *Ferdinand* ⟨London, 1969⟩ comprises in its ninety-four pages, along with a bibliography and a biographical note, two stories—"Ferdinand" and "It Was"—from the earlier volume *It Was* (Tokyo, 1961), which included in addition two other stories, "A Keystone Comedy" and "Thanks to the Dictionary." The two that are now reprinted are unmistakably better than the two that are not; they represent Zukofsky at his best as a writer of fiction; but they are distressingly flimsy in the details of construction, like summer houses personally hand-made by an architect who is a good architect but not a good carpenter. Here are a few weak joints spotted at random among many others. "Hard knocks in the past seemed responsible for many of his violent resentments and unexplained recurrent breaches short of sportsmanship." Why the "short"? Can Zukofsky have been unable to make up his mind between "breaches of sportsmanship" and "fallings short of sportsmanship"? Or was he playing one of his coy etymological games and expecting us to read "breaches" as "breakings"? Or didn't he know what he was saying? We can't dismiss the last possibility, for the very next sentence reads, "He was yawning excessively when he stepped into bed." "Got," yes; "sank," yes; "fell," possibly; "stepped," absolutely no. Ferdinand sees some Indians in Arizona who subsist by making "clay pots and baskets," meaning "baskets and clay pots." An Indian woman seems to him to exist like a hidden petal of a vine in the grass: "Though, with respect to her, the sky, whose blue resembled the petals that are seen and glared over the empty road in the sun, might be hidden instead of her." Reading this sentence the way we naturally read English, we read "the petals that are seen and glared" and wonder what it means. Then we stop and reread and get "resembled the [visible] petals and glared." That's better, but the sentence still doesn't make sense: "Though, with respect to her, the sky might be hidden instead of her." God damn it, Zukofsky, what the hell are you trying to say? On almost every page we have to do the writer's work for him:

> Ferdinand's thought drifted back to the embassy. He wondered if the youngster who had replaced him there had made good, if anyone still could make good in a bankrupt country.
>
> All his family, father, uncles, distant cousins on both sides had been either farmers or gardeners, he heard the man say to his uncle.

After the "he" and the "him" in the first paragraph, we naturally assume that the "his" in the second refers to Ferdinand, and discover once again that Zukofsky has unintentionally misled us. And what bankrupt country?

But his rickety prose is worth repairing as we go along, which is more than can be said for most rickety prose—that is to say, for most of the prose now being written. "Ferdinand" is the story of a French foreign minister's son who, as a little boy whose parents had no time for him, had fallen deeply and permanently in love with the little daughter of a kindly Italian gardener who was like a father to him; since the gardener hoped to marry his daughter to an independent vineyardist, the boy dreamed of becoming one; of course he didn't, but went away to a lycée and the University of Paris and began to have casual mistresses and became an attaché of the embassy in Washington; several years later, still unmarried, still romantically wishing he could be a vineyardist, etc., he resigned because France had been taken by the Nazis, started driving across the United States on a vacation with his exiled aunt and uncle, and deliberately smashed up the car and killed them all, re-enacting a childhood accident with a toy car. The End. Thus robbed of detail, the plot seems as corny as that of any nineteenth-century opera or twentieth-century movie. The car is an all too obvious symbol of his parents' way of life and the values they thought he shared; the aunt and uncle, who in fact had brought him up away from home, are all too obvious substitutes for his parents. And nevertheless the story is lyrical and true. It is a good story in spite of almost everything.

"It Was" is even more improbably true. It deals with a writer's long effort, conscious and unconscious, to write a perfect simple sentence that will put the only possible words in the only possible order; suddenly the sentence comes to him, and Zukofsky ends the story with it. Since the story is only four pages long, it should have been and doubtless was intended to be a little miracle of enclosure, a work of art whose subject is itself; but Zukofsky's prose, though better here than in "Ferdinand," is far from miraculous: his narrator's sentence, for example, in the absence of its imaginary context is not impressive. And even so, this story comes through, as most of Zukofsky's poetry comes through, largely on the strength of its good intentions. Our abjectly commercial writers, however skillful at their business, don't have good intentions. That was a difficulty Aristotle didn't have to consider when he said the intention was nothing and the performance all.—J. MITCHELL MORSE, "Brand Names and Others," *HdR*, Summer 1969, pp. 318–20

All literatures have a Zukofsky—a Lu Chi, a Lichtenberg, a Bashô, a Mallarmé. He is the patient craftsman who applies discipline to what everyone else has done in a hurry. He works with the diamond-cutter's precision, placing technical demands upon the act of composition so incredibly difficult that one wonders how he has written anything at all.

Imagine, for example, the great speech of God in The Book of Job when He speaks from the whirlwind translated so that the Hebrew vowels and consonants remain pretty much where they are in the original, and the rhythms are kept so closely that the English when read aloud sounds like the

Hebrew. This Zukofsky does in his long poem "A". Now imagine the same process applied to the poems of Catullus, all 116 of them. This Zukofsky has also done. Reading them aloud, one's tongue helplessly reproduces the Latin original while one's eye reads English.

Now imagine the same process complicated a few more turns—a translation from Italian this time, a long, rich *canzone* of the late Middle Ages. The rhyme scheme is one of the most musical in all literature, but Zukofsky has set himself the task of translating only with phrases from the Everyman translation of Marx's *Das Kapital*. Moreover, as Hugh Kenner points out in a recent issue of *Poetry*, the n's and r's of this already rather busy text are distributed according to the formula for plotting conic sections. Music is used to such intricate patterning, and poetry was, too, once upon a time. Dante, for instance, would not have batted an eye at Zukofsky's invisible under-structures, and a medieval Japanese poet would have been delighted with them. 〈. . .〉

Most of these works have been around for years. "Ferdinand," a short novel, was published eight years ago in Tokyo, in an edition of 250 copies, presumably the author's experienced estimate of the number of literate people who might be interested to read it. Who would? Well, anyone who has responded to Kafka or Walser or Borges or Donald Barthelme will recognize a similar breath-taking deftness of narration, and feel something of their remoteness from the interchangeable themes and styles of the large part of current fiction.

"Ferdinand"—like all of Zukofsky's writing—has an air about it of having been written in another century and only now discovered and found to be eerily pertinent to our times. Zukofsky's sense of place and time is inward and subjective. As in Kafka, the emotional intensity of his vision excludes that comforting realism which fiction feeds us as so much pabulum. "Ferdinand" is set in Italy, France, and the United States, none of which is identified for us.

The protagonist enacts a tragedy of a dark and disturbing nature indeed, but this is left for us to discover after we have closed the book. The action unfolds as in a dream, or a movie in a foreign language which we know a few words of; we see intuitively that the story has weight and significance, and realize that senses which we rarely use are being called into use. This is not a major work; it is rather a finely turned story from a sensibility of extraordinary range and skill.

It is characteristic of Zukofsky that he abandons a form after satisfying himself with his mastery over it. *One* cycle of lyrics, *one* long poem, *one* book of essays. A few years ago the Kentucky poet Wendell Berry told him about an Appalachian craftsman who could not be programed into the current Federal project for alleviating unemployment. The craftsman in question was a magnificent wood-worker. The Government figured that a batch of rocking-chairs like the one in the shop would sell very well. But the craftsman replied that he made only one of everything he did; and he had already made a rocking-chair. Zukofsky promptly sent a request to know more about this fellow artist.—GUY DAVENPORT, *NYTBR*, June 15, 1969, pp. 5, 31

No use asking me to explain it, I've no idea how an explanation would start: unless by taking note of the awesome, hermetic self-discipline that has now finished, in 1975, a long poem in 24 parts planned and begun in 1927. (The poet, at 71, now has plans for a new project; the plans entail its completion date.)

Part of the poem is its own publication history, including the fact that "A" 24, the finale, was published three years ago, and concludes with a quotation from "A" 20, where it was a quotation from verses the poet's son wrote at not-quite-nine. So when "A" goes into a collected volume its last words will be "What is it, I wonder that makes thee so loved"; but its last *published* words will be the final line of "A" 23: "z-sited paths are but us."

"Z-sited" not only incorporates the poet's initial, it remembers the first line of "A" 1, which is simply "A": A

Round of fiddles playing Bach.

That "A" is not only the indefinite article but the "A" musicians tune by, hence the sound that was in the concert hall before the playing began. Analogously, "A" 23 ends with an alphabet, which is also "A living calendar, names inwreath'd," so living that its final syllables, "are but us," name the arbutus.

All of which would be a frigid pedantic game but for Zukofsky's ineluctable passion to order a half-century's public and domestic experience: living from one's twenties into one's seventies, teaching and writing, undergoing the Depression, the war, assassinations and kindred insults; watching a son elude the family circle; traveling, assimilating the human past and within it the Jewish heritage; never having to cope with fame. He can catch, it seems, the essence of any transient phenomenon: a screening of Robert Flaherty's "Man of Aran" for instance:

. . . the social burden
Of the Aran Islanders . . .
The burden of the horizon
Can be as heavy as any,
Its burden filmed thru the
Eyes of a child
Wailing, let me go!

That's from "A" 12, a quarter-century ago. The sonorities of "A" 4 (1928) include:

And to the Sun I bow
On the gray mountains,
Where multiply
The stars of crags, my prayer
Will follow you, still Heir—
Bestower—
Of man and tree and sand,
When your face upon the land
Flames in last redness, allow me of your light—

—the sounds woven together, by Zukofsky's later standards, nearly an assault on the ear.

Like Picasso, he has left behind a manifest facility in doing what laggard taste admires. Yet though the semantic thread grows nearly untraceable, the auditory skill is still audible in "A" 22 under such sequences as

Too full for talk, 4
tones of black glisten, healall
of black night, dark, light,
no more than a sound
can be painted, or wind
in the hollow of hand—

Our problem, we grow to understand, is that we are muscle-bound, that we cannot readily emulate those leaps. We are also grossly ignorant of the English language, which Zukofsky understands with the passion of a rabbinical boy who learned it word by word, having first encountered *Hiawatha* in Yiddish translation. ("Healall" is in the dictionary: a plant.)

Mallarmé, his orienting predecessor, learned English in order to read the great Poe. Zukofsky learned it to survive in New York, and also to read its riches. One result was "A", the most hermetic poem in English, which they will still be elucidating in the 22nd century. At present its best explicator is an Englishman, Kenneth Cox, and the three volumes prior to the present one are in print only in England. One day Americans will be awestruck by what's been given them: the dialect of the Hudson Basin tribe, purified, counted, measured, subdued to unimaginable rules and made to give back to sufficiently curious minds the lore of our age (we lived it all without knowing) that a pharoah's tomb gives Egyptologists. Whatever went into them, tombs, when they are opened, contain no trivia.—HUGH KENNER, *NYTBR*, March 14, 1976, pp. 15–16

I think that what makes good poetry is always the same, the use of words in such a way that "the thing is in the word." Empty words are empty, whether they are arranged according to modernist or traditional tenets. The defence of modernist technique is the vitality of the work it produces. In the work of Louis Zukofsky there is considerable vitality. The publication of Zukofsky's "A" is completed with these two new sections ("A" 22 & 23, 1976) (the musical conclusion, "A" 24, was published three years ago). The poem that began with "A Round of fiddles playing Bach . . ." reaches here a kind of musical speaking in which sound verges on a total displacement of meaning. But it is not that simple. A language reduced to sound would be no language at all. Zukofsky does something else; he uses words in ways that make their meaning appear tenuous, a momentary crystallizing of the flow of sound. The effect is one of discovery and surprise, of *initial speaking*. And that seems to be the burden of the opening, stanzaic section of "A" 22: "sweet treble hold lovely—initial." The middle section is an undivided passage (it runs for twenty-two small pages) constructed on a principle stated this way at the start: "word time a voice bridled / as order, what is eternal / is living. . . ." It is a history of a sort, but Zukofsky says, "History's best emptied of names' / impertinence. . . ." It is geological history, or a history embedded in geology. The asides that point to that understanding are only asides; the main thing is in the words moving in rhythm that represent historical growth-as-presence. Part of that process is the growth of language, and the rising of thought out of language, through methods of recording, like knots in the rope that the Incas used for communication: "new knots renewed ink anew." Midway through, Zukofsky begins to give his Book of Proverbs—lines and fragments from the Presocratic philosophers, the Hellenistic commentators, Epicurus, the Buddha, some of them charmingly translated: "Man featherless two-legs." Charm must be the frailest of poetic qualities. Much of the poetry here, and all through "A" depends on it: "little horse can you speak / won't know till it speaks." But it holds its place in the poem, as its signum. Interspersed with fragments from the philosophers are passages that mouth the original words, the way his *Catullus* mouths the Latin, and, in keeping with his principle, none of them is named in other than punning ways: "Pith or gore has 4 / seasons. . . ." What his thinkers thought is not important to the poem; that is, it is not *thought* in the poem. What was once recorded is unearthed here, caught still in the substance of human speech. Language is to thought as the earth is to history: the "anachronous stone" is there in your hand. That is the nature of Zukofsky's historical materialism, which he sets in opposition to the historicism of the "scribes" who "conceive history as tho / sky, sun, men never were."

"A" 22 ends with another stanzaic section, which seems to be a kind of botanical lament, thematically pointed in the line: "the comedy's divine, tragic a Thought." "A" 23 continues the impulse of the previous section, its opening stanzas ending in a clear statement:

> words earth—the saving history
> not to deny the gifts
> of time where those who
> never met together may hear
> this other time sound *one*.

The long concluding section begins with a Zukofskian rendering of the Gilgamesh story and leads into speakings of Greek, Latin, fragments of the *Bacchae* and other mythical bits, Provençal, Anglo-Saxon (the opening of *Beowulf*), some passages of sixteenth-century English (Shakespeare and others), all performed with great mastery of word-sense and verse movement. It is an enactment of Zukofsky's vision of "this other time" in a fit of glossolalia: an inhabited cosmos speaking all at once. The charm of his writing imparts a human warmth, a lived-in quality to the whole of "A", which, for all its length, remains a small poem, enclosed, a household. To place it alongside the *Cantos*, as some readers have done (speaking rather indiscriminately of "the long poem"), is to realize that the two are opposites, that "A" is the anti-epic *par excellence*, that the epic is the poem of unhoused mankind but that this poem has always been what it becomes here: a spiritual canticle of human habitation, "beginning ardent; to end blest."—RICHARD PEVEAR, "Poetry and Worldlessness," *HdR*, Summer 1976, pp. 315–16

WILLIAM HARMON

"*Eiron* Eyes"

Parnassus: Poetry in Review, Spring–Summer 1979, pp. 5–23

If the Hindus are right and the destiny of every creature in the universe is governed by an inescapably just Karma that dictates the types and durations of an indefinite succession of reincarnations inflexibly delivering rewards and punishments that match what one has done in previous existences, then Harriet Monroe (1860–1936), founder of *Poetry* magazine, will by now have undergone any number of rebirths, via the wombs of a crawling insect (for her pedestrian imagination), flying insect (capriciousness and inability to sit still), jellyfish (occasional spinelessness and tendency to sting the innocent), tortoise (taking too much time with some important chores), jay (hysteria plus silly litigiousness), third-world churchmouse (to compensate for excessive wealth), and chairpersoness of the Greater Teaneck Arts Council and Begonia Guild (on general principles plus two counts of suffering Morton Dauwen Zabel gladly).

Any schoolchild today can look back at Ms. Monroe's errors in just the single year of 1915 and think, "Jesus! How could she have been such a ninny? She sat on 'Prufrock' for eight months before burying it in the back pages, all the while showcasing Arthur Davison Ficke and similar jive-turkeys. Deaf to the essential integrity of the original eight-stanza 'Sunday Morning,' she made Stevens omit three stanzas, so that he felt constrained to rearrange the remaining five. She was a poet of zero talent herself, and she so overrated Masters, Sandburg, and Robinson that she had insufficient I.Q. left when the time came to give Hart Crane the appreciation and sympathy that he frantically needed."

We—you and I—can be sure, can't we, that *we* would never be guilty of such mistakes; we'd have "Prufrock" right up there in the front of the magazine with no eight-month delay (if, that is, we have ever mustered the courage and resources to get a magazine going); we'd keep "Sunday Morning" intact all along without putting Stevens and his obviously brilliant poem through what must have been a humiliating and emasculating experience; if we had been calling the shots, Hart Crane would probably still be alive, surrounded by sycophants gaily helping to celebrate his eightieth birthday with a cake in the shape of a big Life Saver; and . . . and, well, and *everything.*

You bet.

My point is that, if the Hindus are right, Ms. Monroe ought to be about due for some release from her punishing passage through all those mortifying wombs, some recognition for the things she managed to do at least half-right. Death's first minister and chief of data processing, old Citragupta, will be on hand to recite evidence from his scrupulous printout that Ms. Monroe *did,* after all, found the magazine and run it vigorously for many years; she paid her contributors; she *did,* after all, print Eliot and Stevens and dozens of other first-rate poets; she *did* have the perspicacity to accept the advice of Ezra Pound when he was twenty-six (exactly half her age), even before he got so buddy-buddy with Yeats. And she *did,* early in 1924, publish a sonnet that had been written by a teenage prodigy in New York City:

"Spare us of dying beauty," cries out Youth,
"Of marble gods that moulder into dust—
Wide-eyed and pensive with an ancient truth
That even gods will go as old things must."
Where fading splendor grays to powdered earth,
And time's slow movement darkens quiet skies,
Youth weeps the old, yet gives her beauty birth
And molds again, though the old beauty dies.
Time plays an ancient dirge amid old places
Where ruins are a sign of passing strength,
As in the weariness of aged faces
A token of a beauty gone at length.
Yet youth will always come self-willed and gay—
A sun-god in a temple of decay.
("Of Dying Beauty")

You guessed it: Louis Zukofsky (1904–1978). And your verdict is correct: not bad—for a kid (he turned twenty in January 1924 but the poem was written earlier) not bad at all. He may have absorbed too much Santayana, he may have affected the dark-fantastic too much, but he was no damned ego-freak (no "I" mars the poem) and he knew how to write a good dignified sonnet.

Scarcely seven years later, Ms. Monroe turned her magazine over to the same prodigy for a special number (February 1931) devoted to "Objectivist" poetry along with some modest polemics that provoked from her in the next issue a few condescending but indulgent remarks about the arrogance of youth (she was seventy, her guest-editor twenty-seven). But she *did* let Zukofsky edit a whole issue, even though nobody had any very prismatic idea of what an "Objectivist" poem may be (years later Kenneth Rexroth summarized the contributors as "anybody who would say yes and didn't write sonnets," but some of Zukofsky's own offerings were sonnets; and the point was in no way cleared up by the publication of Zukofsky's *An "Objectivists" Anthology* in 1932). Here is a poem from the special issue of *Poetry:*

The moving masses of clouds, and the standing
Freights on the siding in the sun, alike induce in us
That despair which we, brother, know there is no
withstanding. . . .

The note on the contributor of those lines says, by the way: "Whittaker Chambers, of Lynbrook, N.Y., was born in 1901. He has appeared in *The Nation, The New Masses,* and is a translator of note." Small world.

Zukofsky's own contribution to these "Objectivist" enterprises was a part of a long poem called "A" of which seven movements were finished by 1930. To approach a discussion of the whole poem, I want to start by looking at the original opening of the second movement:

The clear music—
Zoo-zoo-kaw-kaw-of-the-sky,
Not mentioning names, says Kay,
Poetry is not made of such things,
Old music, itch according to its wonts,
Snapped old cat-guts from Johann Sebastian,
Society, traduction twice over.

The version, called "A" 2 in the eventual book form, shows some interesting adjustments:

—Clear music—
Not calling you names, says Kay,
Poetry is not made of such things,
Music, itch according to its wonts,
Snapped old catguts of Johann Sebastian,
Society, traduction twice over.

I want first to note that the poet had put his own name into the poem but in a mangled form, like the cries of beasts and birds: "Zoo-zoo-kaw-kaw-of-the-sky"; later he eliminated the name entirely, here and in other passages. Such a distortion of one's name followed by effacement of it impresses me as the gesture of a particular sort of personage, the *eiron* of antiquity who was both an ethical and a theatrical type.

Aristotle (*Nicomachean Ethics* 4) described the *eiron* and other such types so as to outfit a kind of Central Casting for life and literature. Zukofsky's generation, *Epigonoi* coming after a generation of giants like Stevens, Williams, Pound, and Eliot, may seem particularly rich in pure types: Charles Olson a *philosophus gloriosus et maximus,* Beckett a tragic clown, Rexroth a lordly pedant of incredible erudition in sixty-seven languages, and Zukofsky himself, in person and in print, the classic *eiron* described in Northrop Frye's *Anatomy of Criticism:* self-deprecating, seldom vulnerable, artful, given to understatement, modest or mock-modest, indirect, objective, dispassionate, unassertive, sophisticated, and maybe foreign (all of these terms apply to the *eiron* both as author and as character). The derivation of *eiron* from a Greek word meaning "to say" (and kin to "word," "verb," "verve," "rhematic," and "rhetor") suggests that irony is chiefly a kind of speech and that the *eiron* is recognized chiefly by a manner or habit of speaking. He—whether Socrates, Swift, or Art Carney in the role of Ed Norton—says less than he means; now and then he says the reverse. He may be Prufrock, crying, "It is impossible to say just what I mean!" or Polonius, knowing how we "With windlasses and with assays of bias, / By indirections find directions out."

Now, from an objective or Objectivist point of view, epic contains history along with one or another measure of myth. The greater the measure of myth, the higher the status of the epic poet himself, so that Moses, Homer, and Vyāsa (who was said to have compiled the *Mahābhārata*) are themselves legendary, as, in modern times, such poets as Milton, Whitman, and Pound have become. So grand is the epic enterprise, indeed, that the author thereof threatens to turn into a boastful *alazon,* ordering the Muses around and organizing gods and devils in overweening patterns. Besides, these poets make up among themselves a kind of hermetic society of trade secrets and inside dope, a tradition of precursors, guides, and counsellors, each one becoming "*mio Virgilio*" for the next one, who becomes "*il miglior fabbro*" for his associate, and so on. Since 1700, we have seen a succession of secularized or individualized epics or mock-epics, all of them more or less inconsistent and turbulent (if they are not outright flops), and they test the possibility of a sustained poem without a sustaining body of supernatural lore. The question seems to have been: What, other than a system of myth-dignified ideological conflicts and resolutions, can keep a long poem going?

The obvious answer from the *eiron*'s viewpoint: *Nothing.* A somewhat less obvious addendum from the viewpoint of the modern *eiron* would be: *But it doesn't make any difference.* There persists an article of faith that supposes that we have somehow lost a paradise, that Homer or Dante or Milton could write tremendous poems because the poet and his audience *in illo tempore,* in that spell of magic and an organic oral tradition, shared a whole complex of beliefs capable of organizing and running an epic poem. That's a crock. If Homer, Dante, and Milton have anything in common, it is that they seem, fitfully, to have entertained beliefs that nobody could share. A cursory look at the debates among their audiences and successors will show very quickly that their appeal was not based on any shared system of beliefs, opinions, or even historical data. Their appeal was and still is based on their extremely powerful presentation of artworks so compelling that they overwhelm our disbelief with enchantment, and we—if we believe anything short of suicidal nihilism—assent.

Nothing is lost, but things can change and centers can shift around among comedy, tragedy, romance, and irony. It looks as though the general drift since 1700 has been toward irony, maybe because of the rise of science and the spread of middle-class commerce. In any event, we have been privileged witnesses to a prolonged flowering of ironies, some very amusing and some very touching. The general environment is a diachronic matrix, so to speak, in which mythic meanings have fled from literature to music, and a modernist-ironist like Zukofsky can best orient his own most ambitious literary work by going back two centuries—from 1928 to 1729—pick up a moment of metamorphosis ("traduction twice over," which means the two ironically contrasted meanings of "traduction"—from Old and New Testament to German to English—along with the transferral of energy from score to performance to repeated performance) and to chase that moment or movement as a fugue:

A
Round of fiddles playing Bach.
Come, ye daughters, share my anguish—
Bare arms, black dresses,
See Him! Whom?
Bediamond the passion of our Lord,
See Him! How?

. . .
The Passion According to Matthew,
Composed seventeen twenty-nine,
Rendered at Carnegie Hall,
Nineteen twenty-eight,
Thursday evening, the fifth of April.
The autos parked, honking.

These lines of condensed polyphonic counterpoint enact the marriage of music and irony. For whatever reason (and reasons are legion), the *eiron*'s art—irony—amounts to saying two or more things at one time, so that an auditor with 20 / 20 ears ought to hear an ironic utterance as a chord of sorts, one that displays its own meaning in its own sound as harmonies among *cord* and *chord, accord* and *a chord,* even *choral* and *coral.* (In the case of Zukofsky's introductory "Round," we are dealing with a fact. In 1928, Seder was Wednesday, 4 April, and Passover began the next day, which was also Maundy Thursday for Christians, and on that evening in Carnegie Hall there was a performance of Bach's St. Matthew Passion by the Detroit Symphony Orchestra and Choir, conducted by Ossip Gabrilowitsch. Olin Downes's enthusiastic review the next day noted that the conductor "had requested plain dark dress and a silent reception of the masterpiece.")

At times, the drawing together of many meanings in one word amounts to an ecstatic joining of ostensible opposites, as when Hopkins, in "The Windhover," uses "buckle" to mean, simultaneously, both "fall apart" and "come together." Freud, in a note based on some pretty unruly speculations of the linguist Karl Abel, explored the possible psychic meaning of the "antithetical sense of primal words," such as the English "let," "fast," and "still" (or those contrasting twin daughters of a single mother, "queen" and "quean"). The presence of such Siamese chords permits the approach of monophonic language to polyphonic music. Oddly, "fugue" itself is fugal, because it means both "a polyphonic musical style or form" and "a pathological amnesiac condition" (both meanings derive from the concept of "chase" or "flight"). Whether perfidious or merely economical, the capacity in language for such halvings and doublings will give a high rhetorical valence to such figures as zeugma and syllepsis (which don't mean *quite* the same thing) and such devices as parallel plots and contrast-rhymes ("hire"-"fire," "town"-"gown," "womb"-"tomb," and so forth).

What the solo modern prose voice at the beginning of "A" accomplishes is, then, to suggest both irony and fugue complexly: by talking about a piece of vocal-instrumental polyphony and by doing so in ways that are themselves fugal or quasi-fugal:

A
Round of fiddles playing Bach.

"A" equals air *(aria)* with different values in ancient and modern English, or in English and other European languages, or in English itself variable according to stress. Prefixed in this way or that, it means "with" and it means "without." It means "one" and "he" and "they" and "of." Here, right off the baton, it plays "around" against "a round," which is iridescent with musical, poetic, geometric, and mundane meanings. The part-for-whole figure of "fiddles" (for "fiddlers") plays against the whole-for-part figure of "Bach" (for "a work by Bach"), and "playing," as I have been leaking none too subtly, means everything that both "work" and "play" can mean, including the ideas of performance and impersonation and contest. (At about the same time, Yeats was scrutinizing near-by ranges of meaning in "play" and "labor" in another poem that has to do with time, memory, age, youth, and music: "Among School Children," which moves from an ironic "I walk" to an ecstatic "dance?").

Then, hundreds of pages later, in an interpolation in "A" 21 (p. 474), Zukofsky resumes the theme of roundness by means of a related word, "rote":

there cannot be too much
music R—O—T—E
rote, fiddle
like noise of surf . . .

Let me confess that I went for most of my life with only one meaning for "rote," one phrase ("learn by rote"), and one circumscribed connotation (bad). I took that verbal poverty with me to a study of Eliot's "The Dry Salvages" and appraised the line "The distant rote in the granite teeth" as a very effective figure of speech that rendered the sound of water against a rock as a lesson mechanically repeated (*rota:* circle). In fact, English "rote" has three meanings, of which Eliot, writing in 1942, used two and Zukofsky, in 1967, used all three. It also means "a medieval stringed instrument" and "the sound of surf breaking on the shore" *(American Heritage Dictionary)*. (It could appear in the name of an enterprise called POTH, if that name be Greek.) The verbal chord may be tabulated:

rote	rote 1	routine	ME from Lat. *rota*, wheel	IE *ret*—to run, roll
	rote 2	surf	ON *rauta*, to roar	IE *reu*—to bellow
	rote 3	instrument	OF from Gmc.	IE *krut*—instrument

Such an etymological history of three words converging in a single sound—*rote*—may be seen as a model of Zukofsky's main themes and techniques in "A." No modern ironic poem of any length could possibly be self-standing, and Zukofsky's resembles those by Williams, Pound, and Eliot in including precursors and companions. A shrewd programmer should design a map that would show Pound appearing in Eliot's and Williams' poems (and, later, in Lowell's and Berryman's), Eliot and Williams in Pound's (and Lowell's and Berryman's), and so on, in a serial *agon* that is at the same time an old-boy network. As is noted in "A" 1, Zukofsky's poem gets going not long after the death of Thomas Hardy in January 1928. Some unconscious ironist says of the most conscious ironist of modern letters, "Poor Thomas Hardy he had to go so soon" (which is ironic because he had been born in 1840). But that note is enough to suggest that the long poem at hand will carry on the work of *The Dynasts*, Hardy's immense epic drama that could be called "The Convergence of the Twain," because it traces, in a somewhat fugal staggered form, the fate of two men born in 1769, Napoleon and Wellington, whose paths finally cross, or collide, at Waterloo. As Hardy is dying, the successors maintain the ironic dynasty, and Zukofsky launches his long poem by assimilating the techniques of Pound, Eliot, Williams, and Hardy. With Zukofsky, the focus is on technique and the fabric of the language itself, but the notion of tellingly ironic convergence remains as it had been in Hardy's poems.

Zukofsky begins his poem on a particular April evening in 1928, and for him—as for Whitman, Yeats, and Eliot before him—this paschal time of Passover and Passion, converging in the syncretism of Eos-East-Easter with its terrible beauty, furnishes an ideal prism for seeing the world clearly and for intelligently hearing its ironies and harmonies. (Of "When Lilacs Last in the Dooryard Bloom'd," "Easter 1916," *The Waste Land*, *Ulysses*, and *The Sound and the Fury* alike, one could say that the typical modern literary work begins and centers on a particular day in spring. Oddly, for both Faulkner and Zukofsky, the focus happens to be the same few days in April 1928.) Given this matrix of ideal convergences, the *eiron*'s eyes and ears can subject language to a detailed inquisition, though it hardly takes the full third degree to remove hide and hair from verbal surfaces. In a sixty-year career, Zukofsky experimented with every species of rhematic and thematic irony as ways of saying more than one thing at a time, and he devoted an inordinate amount of his genius to the transfiguration into English of various foreign texts. Since Zukofsky tried to preserve sound and sense alike—which is impossible—"translation" is not quite the correct word for this process. Pound's "creative translations" showed the path here, especially in versions of Old English and Latin (to which I shall come back in a few moments), but Pound is only one member of a large modern club that has trafficked in the Englishing and modernizing of many sorts of foreign and ancient texts. Some years ago, for instance, there was a black film version of "Carmen" called "Carmen Jones," in which Escamillo became "Husky Miller." Any number of modern characters, in their names if not otherwise, show this sort of metempsychosis: Shaw's John Tanner out of Don Juan Tenorio, O'Neill's Ezra Mannon out of Agamemnon, Eliot's Harcourt-Reilly out of Heracles, Faulkner's Joe Christmas out of Jesus Christ, Updike's Caldwell out of Chiron. Zukofsky's refinement, which may echo certain Talmudic or Cabalistic techniques of interpretation, has been to apply this principle of nomenclature to whole texts, typically ironic or comic-lyric, and to produce a complete *Catullus* by this method, as well as a version (appearing as "A" 21) of Plautus' *Rudens*, which is evidently a reworking of a lost Greek play by Diphilus.

One of those shipwreck-and-lost-daughter comedies, *Rudens* (i.e., *The Rope*) resembles Shakespeare's *Pericles* (although it is not, strictly speaking, the source of *Pericles*, as one critic has stated). At any rate, we may note here that Volume II of Zukofsky's *Bottom: On Shakespeare* is a musical setting for *Pericles* by Zukofsky's wife, Celia. One may regard all of *Bottom* as a long poem that works as an appendix to "A." It is typically ironic of Zukofsky to see all of Shakespeare through the eyes of Nick Bottom, big-mouthed weaver and man of the theatre (not to mention part-time ass and boyfriend of the fairy queen).

Zukofsky's novel handling of Latin and other foreign languages has been duly admired by some, but I have to say that I think his Catullus and Plautus are dull distortions. Their purpose may be to breathe (literally) new breath through their consonants and vowels, but the result is a high-handed botch.

I am not qualified to discuss the fine points of this complicated problem of translation. It's just that sound and sense cannot be transferred from one language to another, and it may also be true that not even sense by itself can be moved. Now and then, as in the acoustic and semantic nearness of Hebrew *pāsah*, Latin *passiō*, and English *pass*, there seems to be a linguistic kinship that resembles the connection among *Pesach*, *Passion*, and Passover; but such harmonies are rare. More commonly, even "cognates" from closely related languages may not be good translations for one another, especially in the realm of abstractions. *Stupor Mundi* just isn't "stupor of the world."

Consider these two lines from *Rudens*, in which Charmides (a *senex*) is needling his friend, the pimp Labrax, about a shipwreck:

> *Pol minime miror, navis si fractast tibi,*
> *scelus te et sceleste parta quae vexit bona.*

"Pol" is a faint oath that abridges something like "by Pollux." "Minime" is an adverb meaning "least" (or "not at all"). "Miror" (as some may recall from their high-school Latin version of "Twinkle, Twinkle, Little Star") is the present first-person singular declarative of a deponent verb (hence the passive form) meaning "I wonder." "Well, by God, I'm not a bit surprised," as you might say. The Loeb translation by Paul Nixon captures all of these meanings: "Gad! I don't wonder at all that your ship was wrecked, with a rascal like you and your rascally gains aboard." Zukofsky:

> Pole! minimal mirror! the ship
> fractured from your ill-begot goods.

Well: "Pole! minimal mirror!" does preserve the general sound pattern of "Pol minime miror," and it may preserve some of the sense (if calling one "Pole" and "minimal mirror" suggests that he doesn't do much reflecting). But at what price? This: the subordination of sense to sound, which is exactly what

Imagists and Objectivists complain about in the verse of sonneteers and what Olson complained about in Pound's later Chinese translations. And this: the sacrifice of the character's personal style. Kept up doggedly for seventy pages, Zukofsky's Plautus' Diphilus' *Rudens* is the most tiresome part of "A."

The next most tiresome part is "A" 24, which is another fugal experiment. "A" 21 amounts to a superposed transmogrification of the folk theme of the recovered daughter with Greco-Roman voices joined by synthetic English (a tricky sort of technique that Pound was intelligent enough, in Canto I, to limit to seventy-six lines and to carbonate, ad lib, with matter, rhythms, and "cross-lights" from sources other than his Greek-Latin-English triad). "A" 24, which was composed by Celia Zukofsky (with help from the Zukofsky's brilliant son, Paul) before Louis Zukofsky wrote "A" 22 and "A" 23, is not so much the real conclusion of "A" as a kind of addendum called *L. Z. Masque*, "a five-part score—music, thought, drama, story, poem." The score is presented contrapuntally with music in two staves (treble and bass) above four verbal lines in type of varying sizes. The music is Handel's, the words from Zukofsky's *Prepositions* (thought), *Arise, Arise* (drama), *It was* (story), and "A" itself (poem). The two acts are divided into nine scenes named for characters and musical forms (Cousin: Lesson, Nurse: Prelude & Allegro, Father: Suite, Girl: Fantasia, Attendants: Chaconne, Mother: Sonata, Doctor: Capriccio, Aunt: Passacaille, and Son: Fugues). The text is about 240 pages, with an indicated duration of about 70 minutes. Presumably, a harpsichord plays while four voices speak the words ("The words are NEVER SUNG to the music. . . . Each voice should come through clearly"). I have taken some pains to describe "A" 24, because I don't want to be judged indifferent or careless when I say that the thing is unreadable. I have done my best, line-by-line and also measure-by-measure, and in my cranial studio I get only the effect of five non-profit educational stations going at one time. I'll keep at it, but for the present I can't find anything to admire. In both "A" 21 and "A" 24 the fugue fails.

That failure is more than disappointing. It is heartbreaking. As the ironic poem progresses through its early and middle phases, its moments of greatest tenderness and beauty coincide with the moments of most concentrated attention on Zukofsky's marriage to Celia Thaew in 1939 and the birth, on 22 October 1943, of their son, the *Wunderkind* violinist Paul Zukofsky, whose childhood experiences contributed to Louis Zukofsky's novel called *Little. Baker's Biographical Dictionary of Musicians*, edited by Nicolas Slonimsky, praises Paul Zukofsky's sympathy for contemporary music and the "maximal celerity, dexterity, and alacrity" of his playing. Even so, the Plautus translation, which was probably done as the Catullus was—by Louis and Celia Zukofsky together—and the five-part happening of "A" 24, in which all three Zukofskys had a part, subtract from the overall integrity and intensity of "A."

The remaining twenty-two sections add up to about five hundred pages of poetry that takes the initial fugal subjects and styles through a forty-five-year development, conditioned by external historical and personal events but never, I think, completely irrelevant to the promises potently implicit in

> A
> Round of fiddles playing Bach.

Earlier I suggested a number of the possible meanings, but I did not mention the chance that the fiddles are playing B A C H, which, in a peculiar German style of notation used at one time before the seven-note nomenclature was adopted, would sound as B-flat, A, C, B-natural. J. S. and C. P. E. Bach used this sequence as a musical subject, as did Schumann, Liszt, Rimsky-Korsakov, and a score (ha) of other composers. Zukofsky's use of this musical acrostic to organize the very long (135 pages) "A" 12—

> Blest
> Ardent
> Celia
> unhurt and
> Happy—

brings us back to the alphabet and its gifts and challenges to the ironic poet.

Bach's adding his "signature" to a piece of music is an uncommon but not a unique phenomenon. It is recorded that Bach, who may have written a four-note "cruciform" motif for the Crucifixion in the *St. Matthew Passion*, once sketched out a canon formula for a friend named Schmidt. Translating *Schmidt* into the Latin *faber*, Bach then canonized his friend in the form of F A B E Repetatur, then signed the formula with the tribute, *Bonae Artis Cultorem Habeas*. It is said that the *paytanim*, composers of Hebrew liturgical poetry, "signed" their works by placing their names or anagrams thereof as an acrostic at the beginning of each line. It is also said that certain Jewish names may have been formed as acronyms drawn from devotional formulae, as "Atlas" from *akh tov leyisrael selah* ("Truly God is good to Israel") and not from the Greek name of the world-bearing Titan or the German word for "satin." That may belong in the same uncertain category as the oddity of the King James version of Psalm 46, written when Shakespeare was 46 years old: the forty-sixth word from the beginning is "shake," the forty-sixth from the end "spear." It is certain, however, that writers now and then have used their own names or initials to "sign" their works internally, as it were, as well as on the title page. Shakespeare and Donne used "will" and "done" in poems as puns on their own first or last names. Robert Browning used his initials for *The Ring and the Book*, and T. S. Eliot may have had a variation of the same policy in mind when he titled a play *The Elder Statesman*. J. D. Salinger once named a character Jean de Daumier-Smith, and Martin Gardner's fascinating column in *Scientific American* is called "Mathematical Games."[1] In modern prose's grandest ironic epic, Mann's *Doktor Faustus*, the composer Leverkühn repeatedly uses certain notes, Bach-fashion, to trace non-musical meanings over musical themes; and at the end of the book, in the *Nachschrift*, the author's own names rises touchingly through the prose of his rather foolish narrator, "Dr. phil. Serenus Zeitblom": "*Es ist getan*," he says. He now writes as "*ein alter Mann, gebeugt. . . .*" Pound reversed the process once, in Canto IV, when he alluded to Whitman's "Beat! beat! . . . whirr and pound" but changed the wording to "Beat, beat, whirr, thud." Later, though, he made up for this avoidance of his own names by putting three archaic Chinese characters on the title page of *Thrones: pao en tê*, pronounced, more or less, "Pound."

So what? So the work of art inherently resists being used for autobiography or any other kind of direct representation. Only by certain tricks can an artist register his own presence in a self-willed medium, especially if he is an *eiron* approaching that medium and its social environment from below or outside. The *eiron*'s infra-structural position resembles the alien's extra-structural condition, so that if one has to be both—a talented son, say, of Yiddish-speaking immigrants—then one's ears will, with luck, be attuned to speech as a foreign entity and, particularly, to American English as the native property of others. "Abcedminded," then, as it says in *Finnegans Wake*, verbal comedy leads ironic outsiders of various sorts to write *The Comedian as the Letter C* and an uproarious novel called V. and a long poem called "A" (just as Stephen Dedalus contemplated calling his novels by letters of the alphabet). This is elevated comedy, a plane of discourse where linguistic perspicuity and literally broken English are joined in rapturous wedlock. Here Gandhi, mindful of the gentry's "plus fours," will describe his loincloth as "minus fours," and Vladimir Nabokov will notice how, on more than one level, "therapist" may equal "the rapist." The fine ear of Zukofsky's Wisconsin friend Lorine Niedecker will pick up and decoct the miraculous fission of language when it is forced through the double warp of music and translation:

> O Tannenbaum
> the children sing
> round and round
> one child sings out:
> atomic bomb

(This is, incidentally, part of a garland, *For Paul*, written for Zukofsky's son.) Poetry tests the language as language tests the world.

An ironic epic, accordingly, is going to be partly an ordeal for words themselves, starting, conventionally enough, with the virtually pure air of the first letter and first vowel, *a*. The purpose of the ordeal, from the viewpoint of ironic skepticism, will be to follow the contours of language without undue distortion, so that most of Zukofsky's prosody is a natural-seeming measure of syllables-per-line or words-per-line with no twisting, chipping, or padding to fit an imposed meter that may depend on an arbitrary Morse of qualitative or quantitative dots and dashes given further shape by a rhyme scheme. Once the measure by syllable-unit or word-unit is established along with a modest devotion to short lines, however, the purest music of consonant and vowel, stress and pitch, fancy and plain can come through with an effect, usually, of delicacy, eloquence, accuracy, and fidelity.

Such an idiom works best with its inherent data of ambiguity, inquisition, and multiple irony. These data are most lucidly presented in fairly short poems (like Zukofsky's, and like those of Cid Corman and Robert Creeley, both of whom owe much to Zukofsky's example) in which the courtesy and modesty can balance the potentially injurious clarity of perception and memory. The idiom does not work so well in longer flights, in which it tends to become otiose or academic. ("A" comes equipped with an index, but it quirkily omits some important items. Lorine Niedecker seems to be in the poem—pp. 165 and 214–15, for example—but is not in the index; neither is "A friend, a Z the 3rd letter of his (the first of my) last name"—p. 193—who I think must be Charles Reznikoff.) Yet another difficulty with this idiom is the way it refreshingly insists on seeing everything anew, with unprejudiced eyes; but that means the propagandist for the idiom, whether in lyric or in critical writing, had better be sure he is original. Often, however, Zukofsky seems merely derivative. His *A Test of Poetry*, for instance, promises to chuck out academic biases but winds up as little more than a replay of Pound's "How to Read" and *A B C of Reading*, even to the extent of repeating Pound's dogmatic concentration on Book XI of the *Odyssey*. A teacher can get a funny feeling when a bold student merely repeats the once-original gestures of Creeley, say, and justifies them on principles that really are "academic" in the worst sense: "I do this because Creeley does, because Olson and Zukofsky told him, because they got it from Pound, because Pound thought Fenollosa was right," etc. I am not sure that originality is very important. I am not even sure it is quite possible. But if you make a fuss about it, then you ought to be able to do some other thing than imitate, echo, and repeat.

At his best, Zukofsky dissolves illusion and punches sham to pieces. He breaks things up into particles and articles: under his testing, for example, the ambiguity-loaded *anathema* is analyzed into "*an, a, the*—" (p. 397). Once the alphabet has been taken apart, though, the problem is how to put it back together with honest energies and designs. Zukofsky's life must have confirmed some of his early ironic suspicions; after twenty years at a technical school, he retired as an associate professor, and for a long time he "was not well." The one time I met him, in June 1975, he was frowning through the sickliest-looking yellow-green complexion I think I have ever seen; but his voice was very youthful, his wit intact. On the whole, though, I think he found himself on the receiving end of an enjoyable destiny. He was brilliant, he loved his noble father, he found the perfect wife, his son appeared with the New Haven Symphony at the age of eight, and his work tended after all in the direction suggested by the title of a late poem: "Finally a valentine."

As "A" 24 is arranged, the whole book ends on a nicely cadenced C-minor chord in the harpsichord, the drama voice saying, "New gloves, mother?" and the poem voice repeating the end of "A" 20, "What is it, I wonder, that makes thee so loved." Finally, with "love" sounding simultaneously in "gloves" and "loved," a valentine, indeed.

Well, I must be churlish. I prefer consigning "A" 24 to the status of appendix or addendum, because I think the poem itself (if not the life of the poet) finds a more authentic and convincing conclusion in the end of "A" 23, which was the last part written by Zukofsky. It does not end, *Heldenleben*-style, with a survey and synthesis of the artist's life-in-work, but with a return to the alphabetical keynote that started "A" 1. What we have is a scrupulously measured twenty-six-line alphabet-stretto:

> A living calendar, names inwreath'd
> Bach's innocence longing Handel's untouched.
> Cue in new-old quantities—'Don't
> bother me'—Bach quieted bothered;
> since Eden gardens labor, For
> series distributes harmonies, attraction Governs
> destinies. Histories dye the streets:
> intimate whispers magnanimity flourishes: doubts'
> passionate Judgment, passion the task.
> *Kalenderes enlumined* 21–2–3, *nigher. . fire*—
> Land or—sea, air—gathered.
> Most art, object-the-mentor, donn'd one—
> smiles ray *immaterial Nimbus. . Oes*
> sun-pinned to red threads—thrice-urged
> *posato* (poised) support from the
> source'—horn-note out of a
> string (Quest returns answer—'to
> rethink the Caprices') *sawhorses silver*
> *all these fruit-tree tops:* consonances
> and dissonances only of degree, never-
> Unfinished hairlike water of notes
> vital free as Itself—impossible's
> sort-of think-cramp work x: moonwort:
> music, thought, drama, story, poem
> parks' sunburst—animals, grace notes—
> z-sited path are but us.

This garland names names (Bach, Handel) and suggests others without quite pronouncing them outright (Landor, Mozart, maybe Anaximander, John Donne inwreathed, as is fitting, with Don Juan). It covers instruments, voices, plants, animals (including a goat inside "Caprices" and an A-shaped sawhorse that is a Wooden Horse too: a running theme through the poem, so to speak). I don't know what all is included in "z-sited," aside from the author's and alphabet's final monogram, but I suspect it may include a reminder that the early Semitic and Greek character for *zayin-zeta* looked like this: I, which may be pronounced "eye" or "I," which is roughly what the Hebrew *zayin* still looks like—hence "eyesight." "Are but us" looks and sounds like a re-vision of "arbutus" with an adumbration of widespread (if not universal) identity, community, and harmony.

That hermetic hint is, I think, a more satisfying conclusion than an adventitious pun on "love." We have come too far through too many agonies and mazes at too much intellectual and emotional expense to accept at the end the weakly established assertion that love matters or some similar Hallmark sentiment. It's like the Calvin Coolidge whom one can imagine in Purgatory taking a look at Pound's sweet little Canto CXX. "What's it about, Cal?" "Forgiveness." "What's he say?" "He's for it."

One of these days a scholarly critic with time on his hands is going to discover or invent a tabular schema. In "A" 12 there is evidence that Zukofsky had the twenty-four-book plan in mind by 1950 and possibly somewhat earlier. There too (p. 258) there is a recognition that both of Homer's epics have been divided into twenty-four books by scholars, and it would not surprise me to learn that Zukofsky knew that Bach's *St. Matthew Passion* can be divided into twenty-four scenes: Schweitzer calculated it as "twelve smaller ones, indicated by chorales, and twelve larger ones, marked by arias." But Zukofsky's general design does not gracefully fall into twenty-four shapely parts. With or without the marginal "A" *21 (Rudens)* and "A" 24 *(L. Z. Masque)*, the shape of the whole is asymmetrical. The contour may match that of a diary or revery, but there is no essential literary progression. Such development as may emerge is more along the lines of an experimental fugue and variations, with room along the way for one poem 135 pages long ("A" 12) and another four words long ("A" 16). "A" 6 asks

> *Can*
> The design
> Of the fugue
> Be transferred
> To poetry?

When the "plot" has to include a piece of history—such as the death of Williams or the assassination of President Kennedy—then the writing slackens, and the grief seems perfunctory. In other stretches, the author's vigor and sincerity seem to thin out and his wordplay ("Pith or gore has" for "Pythagoras") nosedives towards the asymptote of crossword puzzles and tricks like Henny Youngman's superseding "diamond pin" with "dime and pin."

The scholiasts have their work cut out for them. For all I know, the audience for poems like Zukofsky's may be nothing but scholiasts. I hate to think that world poetry today amounts to nothing more than a hundred people writing something for an audience of a hundred (probably the same hundred). The dismal situation would be no less dismal if that figure were a thousand or even a million, because the proportion is so small up against the whole human race. Maybe the University of California Press ought to keep a few copies of the full "A" available for specialists, and they may be wise to market it in an ugly Clearasil-pink dust jacket, to keep amateurs at arm's length. But maybe the publisher should also issue a 250-page volume of selections. I would suggest that 1–7, 9–11, 15–18, and 20 could be kept as wholes, 21 and 24 done without, and the rest given in generous selections. That sort of book would reach more people with a more concentrated representation of a fine poet's best work. Whatever is planned in the way of new editions, the Index should be re-done to provide a better key to main themes, motifs, and characters (including those in any number of alphabets).

Notes

1. Two further examples: The Boy Scouts chose a motto with initials to match those of their founder, Lord Baden-Powell; and in the graphic arts, Al Hirschfeld always weaves the name of his daughter Nina into his caricatures, hidden there among wrinkles or ruffles or extravagant coiffures.

ADDITIONAL READING

ROBERT STONE

Gold, Ivan. "Apocalypse in New Orleans." *New York Times Book Review*, 24 September 1967, p. 4.

Karaguezian, Maureen. "Interview with Robert Stone." *TriQuarterly* 53 (1982): 248–58.

McConnell, Frank. "Transfiguration of Despair." *Commonweal*, 12 March 1982, pp. 153–55.

Ottaway, Robert. "Whisky Academic." *Listener*, 19 November 1981, p. 618.

Towers, Robert. "Navigating through Reefs." *Atlantic* 248, November 1981, pp. 86–88.

REX STOUT

Anderson, David R. *Rex Stout*. New York: Ungar, 1984.

De Voto, Bernard. "Alias Nero Wolfe." *Harper's* 209 (July 1954): 8–9, 12–15.

McAleer, John. *Royal Decree: Conversations with Rex Stout*. Ashton, MD: Pontes Press, 1983.

Rauber, D. F. "Sherlock Holmes and Nero Wolfe: The Role of the 'Great Detective' in Intellectual History." *Journal of Popular Culture* 6 (1972–73): 483–95.

MARK STRAND

Bedient, Calvin. "Poetry Comfortable and Uncomfortable." *Sewanee Review* 87 (1979): 8–9.

Crenner, James. Review of *Darker*. *Seneca Review* 2 (April 1971): 84–89.

Howard, Richard. "Mark Strand: 'The Mirror Was Nothing without You.'" In Alone with America. New York: Atheneum, 1980.

Lieberman, Laurence. "New Poetry in Review." *Yale Review* 58 (1968): 147–49.

Shaw, Robert B. "Quartet." *Poetry* 139 (1981–82): 175–77.

Young, Vernon. "Poetry Chronicle: The Light in Dark Enough." *Hudson Review* 34 (1981): 147–48.

JESSE STUART

LeMaster, J. R., ed. *Jesse Stuart: Selected Criticism*. St. Petersburg, FL: Valkyrie Press, 1978.

———. *Jesse Stuart: Kentucky's Chronicler-Poet*. Memphis: Memphis State University Press, 1978.

Pennington, Lee. *The Dark Hills of Jesse Stuart*. Cincinnati: Harvest Press, 1967.

Perry, Dick. *Reflections of Jesse Stuart*. New York: McGraw-Hill, 1971.

Richardson, H. Edward. *Jesse: The Biography of an American Writer Jesse Hilton Stuart*. New York: McGraw-Hill, 1984.

THEODORE STURGEON

Friend, Beverly. "The Sturgeon Connection." In *Voices for the Future: Essays on Major Science Fiction Writers*, ed. Thomas P. Clareson. Bowling Green, OH: Bowling Green University Popular Press, 1976, pp. 153–66.

Sackmary, Regina. "An Ideal of Three: The Art of Theodore Sturgeon." In *Critical Encounters: Writers and Themes in Science Fiction*, ed. Dick Riley. New York: Ungar, 1978, pp. 132–43.

Williams, Paul. "Introduction" to *Venus Plus X* by Theodore Sturgeon. Boston: Gregg Press, 1976, pp. v-xxi.

WILLIAM STYRON

Baumbach, Jonathan. "Paradise Lost: The Novels of William Styron." *South Atlantic Quarterly* 63 (1964): 207–17.

Canzoneri, Robert, and Page Stegner. "An Interview with William Styron." *Per/Se* 1 (Summer 1966): 37–44.

Clarke, John Henrik, ed. *William Styron's* Nat Turner: *Ten Black Writers Respond*. Boston: Beacon Press, 1967.

Crane, John Kenny. *The Root of All Evil: The Thematic Unity of William Styron's Fiction*. Columbia: University of South Carolina Press, 1984.

Fenton, Charles A. "William Styron and the Age of the Slob." *South Atlantic Quarterly* 59 (1960): 469–76.

Galloway, David. "The Absurd Man as Tragic Hero." In *The Absurd Hero in American Fiction*. Austin: University of Texas Press, 1981.

Geismar, Maxwell. "William Styron: The End of Innocence." In *American Moderns: From Rebellion to Conformity*. New York: Hill & Wang, 1958.

Klotz, Marvin. "The Triumph over Time: Narrative Form in William Faulkner and William Styron." *Mississippi Quarterly* 16 (Fall 1963): 9–20.

Lang, John. "God's Averted Face: Styron's *Sophie's Choice*." *American Literature* 55 (1983): 215–32.

Lawson, John Howard. "Styron: Darkness and Fire in the Modern Novel." *Mainstream* 13 (October 1960): 9–18.

O'Connell, Shaun. "Expense of Spirit: The Vision of William Styron." *Critique* 8 (Winter 1965–66): 20–33.

Rubin, Louis D., Jr. "William Styron and Human Bondage: *The Confessions of Nat Turner*." *Hollins Critic* 4 (December 1967): 1–12.

Shepherd, Allen. "The Psychopath as Moral Agent in William Styron's *Sophie's Choice*." *Modern Fiction Studies* 28 (1982–83): 604–11.

MAY SWENSON

Howard, Richard. "May Swenson." *Tri-Quarterly* 7 (1966): 119–31.

Stepanchev, Stephen. "Other Recent Poets: May Swenson." In *American Poetry since 1945*. New York: Harper & Row, 1965, pp. 202–4.

Swenson, May. Interview with Karla Hammond. *Parnassus: Poetry in Review* 7 (1978): 60–75.

BOOTH TARKINGTON

Crowley, Richard. "Booth Tarkington: Time for Revival." *America*, 13 February 1954, pp. 508–10.

Fennimore, Keith J. *Booth Tarkington*. New York: Twayne, 1974.

LeGates, Charlotte. "The Family in Booth Tarkington's *Growth* Trilogy." *Midamerica* 6 (1979): 88–99.

Russo, Dorothy Ritter, and Thelma L. Sullivan. *A Bibliography of Booth Tarkington 1869–1946*. Indianapolis: Indiana Historical Society, 1949.

Wertenbaker, Charles. "Booth Tarkington." *Life*, 4 September 1939, pp. 55–60.

Woodress, James. *Booth Tarkington: Gentleman from Indiana*. Philadelphia: Lippincott, 1955.

Wyatt, Edith Franklin. "Booth Tarkington: The Seven Ages of Man." *North American Review* 216 (1922): 499–512.

ALLEN TATE

Beatty, Richmond C. "Allen Tate as Man of Letters." *South Atlantic Quarterly* 47 (1948): 226–41.

Blackmur, R. P. "San Giovanni in Venere: Allen Tate as Man of Letters." *Sewanee Review* 67 (1959): 614–31.

Dupree, Robert S. *Allen Tate and the Augustinian Imagina-*

tion. Baton Rouge: Louisiana State University Press, 1983.

Johnson, Carol Holmes. "The Heroism of the Rational: The Poetry of Allen Tate." *Renascence* 17 (Winter 1964): 89–96.

Kermode, Frank. "Old Orders Changing (Tate and Lampedusa)." In *Puzzles and Epiphanies*. New York: Chilmark Press, 1962, pp. 131–39.

Lowell, Robert. "Visiting the Tates." *Sewanee Review* 67 (1959): 557–59.

Nemerov, Howard. "The Current of the Frozen Stream: An Essay on the Poetry of Allen Tate." *Furioso* 3 (February 1948): 50–61.

Ransom, John Crowe. "In Amicitia." *Sewanee Review* 67 (1959): 528–39.

Squires, Radcliffe. *Allen Tate: A Literary Biography*. New York: Pegasus, 1971.

PETER TAYLOR

Blum, Morgan. "Peter Taylor: Self-Limitation in Fiction." *Sewanee Review* 70 (1962): 559–78.

Brown, Ashley. "The Early Fiction of Peter Taylor." *Sewanee Review* 70 (1962): 588–602.

Farrelly, John. "Transition." *New Republic*, 8 March 1948, pp. 25–26.

Peden, William. "Metropolis, Village, and Suburbia: The Short Fiction of Manners." In *The American Short Story: Continuity and Change 1940–1975*. Boston: Houghton Mifflin, 1975, pp. 39–44.

Robinson, Marilynne. "The Family Game Was Revenge." *New York Times Book Review*, 19 October 1986, pp. 1, 52.

Warren, Robert Penn. "Introduction" to *A Long Fourth and Other Stories* by Peter Taylor. New York: Harcourt, Brace, 1948.

SARA TEASDALE

Brenner, Rica. "Sara Teasdale." In *Poets of Our Time*. New York: Harcourt, Brace, 1941, pp. 205–42.

Carpenter, Margaret Haley. *Sara Teasdale: A Biography*. Norfolk, VA: Pentelic Press, 1977.

Deutsch, Babette. "Indian Summer." *New Republic*, 1 December 1926, pp. 48–49.

Drake, William. *Sara Teasdale: Woman and Poet*. San Francisco: Harper & Row, 1979.

Munroe, Harriet. "A Farewell." *Poetry* 43 (1933–34): 96–98.

Rittenhouse, Jessie B. "Sara Teasdale." *Bookman* (New York) 65 (1927): 290–94.

PAUL THEROUX

Beatty, Jack. Review of *The Mosquito Coast*. *New Republic*, 24 February 1982, p. 40.

Busch, Frederick. "Dr. Faustus in the Jungle." *Washington Post Book World*, 14 February 1982, pp. 1–2.

Cunningham, Valentine. "Mixed Urbs." *New Statesman*, 26 March 1976, p. 410.

Tyler, Anne. "The Artist as an Old Photographer." *New York Times Book Review*, 18 June 1978, pp. 10, 25.

HUNTER S. THOMPSON

Booth, Wayne C. "Loathing and Ignorance on the Campaign Trail: 1972." *Columbia Journalism Review* 12 (November-December 1973): 7–12.

Raban, Jonathan. "The New Mongrel." *London Magazine* 12 (June-July 1973): 96–105.

Vonnegut, Kurt. "A Political Disease." In *Wampeters Foma & Granfalloons*. New York: Delacorte Press, 1974, pp. 231–35.

Wills, Garry. "Hunter S. Thompson: Rollercoasting through the '60s and '70s." *Washington Post Book World*, 19 August 1979, pp. 1, 5.

Woods, Crawford. Review of *Fear and Loathing in Las Vegas*. *New York Times Book Review*, 23 July 1972, pp. 17–18.

JAMES THURBER

Black, Stephen A. *James Thurber: His Masquerades*. The Hague: Mouton, 1970.

Holmes, Charles S. *The Clocks of Columbus: The Literary Career of James Thurber*. New York: Atheneum, 1972.

Mann, Ann Ferguson. "Taking Care of Walter Mitty." *Studies in Short Fiction* 19 (1982): 351–57.

May, Charles E. "Christian Parody in Thurber's 'You Could Look It Up.'" *Studies in Short Fiction* 15 (1978): 453–54.

Stonier, G. W. Review of *Fables for Our Time*. *New Statesman*, 14 December 1940, p. 632.

Sundell, Carl. "The Architecture of Walter Mitty's Secret Life." *English Journal* 56 (1967): 1284–87.

Tobias, Richard C. *The Art of James Thurber*. Athens: Ohio University Press, 1969.

Weales, Gerald. "The World in Thurber's Fables." *Commonweal*, 18 January 1957, pp. 409–11.

Unsigned. "James Thurber." *New Yorker*, 11 November 1961, p. 247.

JEAN TOOMER

Cooke, Michael G. "Tragic and Ironic Denials of Intimacy: Jean Toomer, James Baldwin and Ishmael Reed." In *Afro-American Literature in the Twentieth Century*. New Haven: Yale University Press, 1984, pp. 177–99.

McKay, Nellie Y. *Jean Toomer, Artist: A Study of His Literary Life and Work, 1894–1936*. Chapel Hill: University of North Carolina Press, 1984.

Scruggs, Charles W. "The Mark of Cain and the Redemption of Art: A Study of Theme and Structure of Jean Toomer's *Cane*." *American Literature* 44 (1972): 190–215.

DALTON TRUMBO

Cook, Bruce. *Dalton Trumbo*. New York: Scribner's, 1977.

Nathan, George Jean. *"The Biggest Thief in Town."* In *The Theatre Book of the Year 1948–1949*. New York: Knopf, 1949, pp. 333–35.

Rapf, Maurice. "The Unfriendly Witness." *Nation*, 7 May 1977, pp. 566–70.

ANNE TYLER

Gibson, Mary Ellis. "Family as Fate: The Novels of Anne Tyler." *Southern Literary Journal* 15, No. 3 (1983): 47–58.

Updike, John. *Hugging the Shore*. New York: Knopf, 1983, pp. 273–99.

JOHN UPDIKE

Burchard, Rachael C. *John Updike: Yea Sayings*. Carbondale: Southern Illinois University Press, 1971.

Crews, Frederick. "Mr. Updike's Planet." *New York Review of Books*, 4 December 1986, pp. 7–14.

Detweiler, Robert. "John Updike and the Indictment of Culture—Protestantism." In *Four Spiritual Crises in Mid-Century American Fiction*. Gainesville: University of Florida Press, 1963, pp. 14–24.

Greiner, Donald J. *The Other John Updike: Poems, Short Stories, Prose, Play*. Athens: Ohio University Press, 1981.

Hamilton, Alice, and Kenneth Hamilton. *The Elements of*

John Updike. Grand Rapids, MI: William B. Eerdmans, 1970.

Harper, Howard M., Jr. "John Updike—The Intrinsic Problem of Human Existence." In *Desperate Faith*. Chapel Hill: University of North Carolina Press, 1967.

Hendin, Josephine. "The Victim Is a Hero." In *Vulnerable People: A View of American Fiction since 1945*. New York: Oxford University Press, 1978, pp. 88–99.

Hunt, George W. *John Updike and the Three Great Secret Things: Sex, Religion, and Art*. Grand Rapids: William B. Eerdmans, 1980.

La Course, Guerin. "The Innocence of John Updike." *Commonweal*, 8 February 1963, pp. 512–14.

Markle, Joyce B. *Fighters and Lovers: Theme in the Novels of John Updike*. New York: New York University Press, 1973.

Mellard, James M. "The Novel as Lyric Elegy: The Mode of Updike's *The Centaur*." *Texas Studies in Literature and Language* 21 (1979): 112–27.

Mizener, Arthur. "The American Hero as High School Boy: Peter Caldwell." In *The Sense of Life in the Modern Novel*. Boston: Houghton Mifflin, 1964, pp. 247–66.

Oates, Joyce Carol. "Updike's American Comedies." *Modern Fiction Studies* 21 (1975): 459–72.

Podhoretz, Norman. "A Dissent on Updike." In *Doings and Undoings*. New York: Farrar, Straus, 1964, pp. 251–57.

Rupp, Richard. "John Updike: Style in Search of a Centre." *Sewanee Review* 75 (1967): 693–709.

Samuels, Charles Thomas. *John Updike*. Minneapolis: University of Minnesota Press, 1969.

Tanner, Tony. "A Compromised Environment." In *City of Words: American Fiction 1950–1970*. New York: Harper & Row, 1971.

Taylor, Larry E. *Pastoral and Anti-Pastoral Patterns in John Updike's Fiction*. Carbondale: Southern Illinois University Press, 1971.

Vargo, Edward P. *Rainstorms and Fire: Ritual in the Novels of John Updike*. Port Washington, NY: Kennikat Press, 1973.

Waxman, Robert E. "Invitations to Dread: John Updike's Metaphysical Quest." *Renascence* 29 (1977): 201–10.

Zylstra, S. A. "John Updike and the Parabolic Nature of the World." *Soundings* 56 (1973): 323–37.

MARK VAN DOREN

Claire, William. "Introduction" to *The Essays of Mark Van Doren*. Westport, CT: Greenwood Press, 1980, pp. xiii–xxv.

Lindeman, Jack. Review of *Morning Worship*. *Poetry* 97 (1960): 109–13.

Tate, Allen. "Center of the Language." *Nation*, 15 March 1935, pp. 339–40.

———. "Very Much at Ease in Formal Attire." *New York Herald Tribune Book Week*, 29 September 1963, p. 4.

CARL VAN VECHTEN

Clark, Emily. "Carl Van Vechten." In *Innocence Abroad*. New York: Knopf, 1931, pp. 129–45.

Gloster, Hugh M. "The Carl Van Vechten Vogue." In *Negro Voices in American Fiction*. Chapel Hill: University of North Carolina Press, 1948, pp. 157–63.

Kellner, Bruce. *A Bibliography of the Works of Carl Van Vechten*. Westport, CT: Greenwood Press, 1980.

Lueders, Edward. *Carl Van Vechten*. New York: Twayne, 1965.

———. *Carl Van Vechten and the Twenties*. Albuquerque: University of New Mexico Press, 1955.

Wilson, Edmund. "Late Violets from the Nineties." In *The Shores of Light*. New York: Farrar, Straus & Young, 1952, pp. 68–72.

GORE VIDAL

Ackroyd, Peter. "Blood, Thunder and Gore." *Spectator*, 27 March 1976, p. 20.

Aldridge, John W. "Gore Vidal: The Search for a King." In *After the Lost Generation*. New York: McGraw-Hill, 1951, pp. 170–83.

Berryman, Charles. "Satire in Gore Vidal's *Kalki*." *Critique* 22, No. 2 (1980): 88–94.

Boyette, Purvis E. "*Myra Breckinridge* and Imitative Form." *Modern Fiction Studies* 17 (1971): 229–38.

Buckley, William F., Jr. "On Experiencing Gore Vidal." *Esquire*, August 1969, pp. 108–13, 122–32.

Clarke, Gerald. "Petronius Americanus: The Ways of Gore Vidal." *Atlantic* 229 (March 1972): 44–51.

Dick, Bernard F. *The Apostate Angel: A Critical Study of Gore Vidal*. New York: Random House, 1974.

Edwards, Owen Dudley. "On an Earlier President." *Encounter* 64 (January 1985): 33–38.

Gilder, Joshua. "Gore Vidal's Last Escapade." *Saturday Review*, May 1982, pp. 20–26.

Goodfriend, Arthur. "The Cognoscenti Abroad—Gore Vidal's Rome." *Saturday Review*, 25 January 1969, pp. 36–39.

Renault, Mary. "The Wise Lord and the Lie." *New York Review of Books*, 14 May 1981, pp. 29–30.

Walter, Eugene. "Conversations with Gore Vidal." *Transatlantic Review* No. 4 (Summer 1960): 5–17.

White, Ray Lewis. *Gore Vidal*. New York: Twayne, 1968.

KURT VONNEGUT

Cargas, Harry James. "Are There Things a Novelist Shouldn't Joke About?: An Interview with Kurt Vonnegut, Jr." *Christian Century*, 24 November 1976, pp. 1048–50.

Giannone, Richard. *Vonnegut: A Preface to His Novels*. Port Washington, NY: Kennikat Press, 1977.

Greiner, Donald J. "Vonnegut's *Slaughterhouse-Five* and the Fiction of Atrocity." *Critique* 14, No. 3 (1973): 38–51.

Hume, Kathryn. "The Heraclitean Cosmos of Kurt Vonnegut." *Papers on Language and Literature* 18 (1982): 208–24.

———. "Kurt Vonnegut and the Myths and Symbols of Meaning." *Texas Studies in Literature and Language* 24 (1982): 429–47.

———. "Vonnegut's Self-Projections: Symbolic Characters and Symbolic Fiction." *Journal of Narrative Technique* 12 (1982): 177–90.

Klinkowitz, Jerome, and John Somer, eds. *The Vonnegut Statement*. New York: Delacorte/Seymour Lawrence, 1973.

Leff, Leonard J. "Utopia Reconstructed: Alienation in Vonnegut's *God Bless You, Mr. Rosewater*." *Critique* 12, No. 3 (1971): 29–37.

Nadeau, Robert L. "Physics and Metaphysics in the Novels of Kurt Vonnegut, Jr." *Mosaic* 13 (Winter 1980): 37–47.

Olderman, Raymond M. "Out of the Waste Land and into the Fire: Cataclysm or the Cosmic Cool." In *Beyond the Waste Land: A Study of the American Novel in the Nineteen-Sixties*. New Haven: Yale University Press, 1972.

O'Sullivan, Maurice J., Jr. "*Slaughterhouse-Five*: Kurt Vonnegut's Anti-Memoirs." *Essays in Literature* 3 (1976): 244–50.

Scholes, Robert. "'Mithridates, He Died Old': Black Humor and Kurt Vonnegut, Jr." *Hollins Critic* 3 (October 1966): 1–12.

Tanner, Tony. "The Uncertain Messenger: A Study of the Novels of Kurt Vonnegut, Jr." *Critical Quarterly* 11 (1969): 297–315.

Vanderbilt, Kermit. "Kurt Vonnegut's American Nightmares and Utopicas." In *The Utopian Vision: Seven Essays on the Quincentennial of Sir Thomas More*, ed. E.D.S. Sullivan. San Diego: San Diego State University Press, 1983.

MIRIAM WADDINGTON

Pearce, Jon. "Bridging the Inner and Outer: Miriam Waddington." In *Twelve Voices: Interviews with Canadian Poets*. Ottawa: Borealis Press, 1980, pp. 177–87.

Ricou, L. R. "Into My Green World: The Poetry of Miriam Waddington." *Essays on Canadian Writing* 12 (Fall 1978): 144–61.

DIANE WAKOSKI

Gerber, Philip L., and Robert J. Gemmett, eds. *A Terrible War: A Conversation with Diane Wakoski*. Winnipeg: University of Manitoba Press, 1970.

Gilbert, Sandra M. "A Platoon of Poets." *Poetry* 128 (1976): 294–96.

Meinke, Peter. "On Poetry." *New Republic*, 14 June 1975, pp. 25–26.

ALICE WALKER

Christian, Barbara. "The Country Black Women of Alice Walker: A Study of Female Protagonists in *In Love and Trouble*." *Black Scholar* 12 (1981): 21–30, 70–71.

Ensslen, Klaus. "Collective Experience and Individual Responsibility: Alice Walker's *The Third Life of Grace Copeland*." In *The Afro-American Novel since 1960*, eds. Peter Bruck and Wolfgang Karrer. Amsterdam: Gruner, 1982, pp. 189–218.

Parker-Smith, Bettye J. "Alice Walker's Women: In Search of Some Peace of Mind." In *Black Women Writers, 1950–1980*, ed. Mari Evans. Garden City, NY: Doubleday, 1984, pp. 478–93.

Towers, Robert. "Good Men Are Hard to Find." *New York Review of Books*. 12 August 1982, pp. 35–36.

Smith, Dinitia. "'Celie, You a Tree.'" *Nation*, 4 September 1982, pp. 181–83.

ROBERT PENN WARREN

Anderson, Charles R. "Violence and Order in the Novels of Robert Penn Warren." *Hopkins Review* 6 (1953): 88–105.

Bentley, Eric. "The Meaning of Robert Penn Warren's Novels." *Kenyon Review* 10 (Summer 1948): 407–24.

Bohner, Charles H. *Robert Penn Warren*. New York: Twayne, 1964.

Callander, Marilyn Berg. "Robert Penn Warren's *Chief Joseph of the Nez Pierce*: A Story of Deep Delight." *Southern Literary Journal* 16 (1982): 24–33.

Fiedler, Leslie A. "Three Notes on Robert Penn Warren." In *No! In Thunder: Essays on Myth and Literature*. Boston: Beacon Press, 1960, pp. 119–33.

Grimshaw, James A., Jr. *Robert Penn Warren: A Descriptive Bibliography 1917–1978*. Charlottesville: University Press of Virginia, 1982.

Guttenberg, Barnett. *Web of Being: The Novels of Robert Penn Warren*. Nashville: Vanderbilt University Press, 1975.

Justus, James H. *The Achievement of Robert Penn Warren*. Baton Rouge: Louisiana State University Press, 1981.

Létargez, J. "Robert Penn Warren's View of History." *Revue des Langues Vivantes* 22 (1956): 533–43.

Longley, John L., Jr., ed. *Robert Penn Warren: A Collection of Critical Essays*. New York: New York University Press, 1965.

Moore, L. Hugh, Jr. *Robert Penn Warren and History: The "Big Myth We Live."* The Hague: Mouton, 1970.

Rubin, Louis D., Jr. "All the King's Meanings." *Georgia Review* 8 (1954): 422–34.

Spiegelman, Willard. "The Poetic Achievement of Robert Penn Warren." *Southwest Review* 62 (1977): 411–15.

Stewart, John T. "The Achievement of Robert Penn Warren." *South Atlantic Quarterly* 47 (1948): 562–79.

Strandberg, Victor. *The Poetic Vision of Robert Penn Warren*. Lexington: University of Kentucky, 1977.

Tjanos, William. "The Poetry of Robert Penn Warren: The Art to Transfigure." *Southern Literary Journal* 9 (1976): 3–12.

Walker, Marshall. *Robert Penn Warren: A Vision Earned*. Glasgow: Robert MacLehose, 1979.

THEODORE WEISS

Gibbons, Reginald. "The Cure: Theodore Weiss's Poetry." *Modern Poetry Studies* 9 (1978): 18–33.

Weiss, Theodore. "Toward a Classical Modernity and a Modern Classicism." In *Poets on Poetry*, ed. Howard Nemerov. New York: Basic Books, 1966, pp. 212–24.

EUDORA WELTY

Appel, Alfred, Jr. *A Season of Dreams: The Fiction of Eudora Welty*. Baton Rouge: Louisiana State University Press, 1965.

Bishop, John Peale. "The Violent Country." *New Republic*, 16 November 1942, pp. 646–47.

Bowen, Elizabeth. Review of *The Golden Apples*. In *Seven Winters and Afterthoughts*. New York: Knopf, 1962, pp. 215–18.

Desmond, John F., ed. *A Still Moment: Essays on the Art of Eudora Welty*. Metuchen, NJ: Scarecrow Press, 1978.

Devlin, Albert J. *Eudora Welty's Chronicle: A Story of Mississippi Life*. Jackson: University Press of Mississippi, 1983.

Hicks, Granville. "Eudora Welty." *College English* 14 (1952): 69–76.

Howard, Zelma Turner. *The Rhetoric of Eudora Welty's Short Stories*. Jackson: University and College Press of Mississippi, 1973.

Kreyling, Michael. *Eudora Welty's Achievement of Order*. Baton Rouge: Louisiana State University Press, 1980.

Manz-Kunz, Marie-Antoinette. *Eudora Welty: Aspects of Reality in Her Short Fiction*. Bern: Francke Verlag, 1971.

Porter, Katherine Anne. "Eudora Welty and *A Curtain of Green*." In *The Days Before*. New York: Harcourt, Brace, 1952, pp. 101–8.

Prenshaw, Peggy Whitman, ed., *Conversations with Eudora Welty*. Jackson: University Press of Mississippi, 1979.

Randisi, Jennifer Lynn. *A Tissue of Lies: Eudora Welty and the Southern Romance*. Washington, DC: University Press of America, 1982.

Ransom, John Crowe. "Delta Fiction." *Kenyon Review* 8 (1946): 503–7.

Thomson, Victor H. *Eudora Welty: A Reference Guide*. Boston: G. K. Hall, 1976.

Vande Kieft, Ruth M. *Eudora Welty*. New York: Twayne, 1962.

GLENWAY WESCOTT

Johnson, Ira. *Glenway Wescott: The Paradox of Voice*. Port Washington, NY: Kennikat Press, 1971.
Kahn, Sy Myron. "Glenway Wescott: A Bibliography." *Bulletin of Bibliography* 22 (1956–59): 156–60.
Kohler, Dayton. "Glenway Wescott: Legend Maker." *Bookman* 73 (1931): 142–45.
Quinn, Patrick R. "The Case History of Glenway Wescott." *Frontier and Midland* 19 (Autumn 1938): 11–16.
Rueckert, William H. *Glenway Wescott*. New York: Twayne, 1965.

NATHANAEL WEST

Abrahams, Roger D. "Androgynes Bound: Nathanael West's *Miss Lonelyhearts*." In *Seven Contemporary Authors*, ed. Thomas B. Whitbread. Austin: University of Texas Press, 1966, pp. 51–72.
Comerchero, Victor. *Nathaenael West: The Ironic Prophet*. Syracuse: Syracuse University Press, 1964.
Hyman, Stanley Edgar. *Nathanael West*. Minneapolis: University of Minnesota Press, 1962.
Klein, Marcus. "Nathan Weinstein and Nathanael West." In *Foreigners: The Making of American Literature 1900–1940*. Chicago: University of Chicago Press, 1981, pp. 249–69.
Light, James F. *Nathanael West: An Interpretative Study*. Evanston, IL: Northwestern University Press, 1971.
Long, Robert Emmet. *Nathanael West*. New York: Frederick Ungar, 1985.
Madden, David, ed. *Nathanael West: The Cheaters and the Cheated*. De Land, FL: Everett/Edwards, 1973.
Malin, Irving. *Nathanael West's Novels*. Carbondale: Southern Illinois University Press, 1972.
Martin, Jay. *Nathanael West: The Art of His Life*. New York: Farrar, Straus & Giroux, 1970.
Murray, Edward. "Nathanael West—The Pictorial Eye in Locust-Land." In *The Cinematic Imagination*. New York: Ungar, 1972, pp. 206–16.
Perelman, S. J. "My Brother-in-Law." *Esquire* 95 (June 1981): 93–99.
Reid, Randall. *The Fiction of Nathanael West: No Redeemer, No Promised Land*. Chicago: University of Chicago Press, 1967.
Schulz, Max F. "Nathanael West's 'Desperate Detachment.'" In *Radical Sophistication: Studies in Contemporary Jewish-American Novelists*. Athens: Ohio University Press, 1969, pp. 36–55.
White, William. *Nathanael West: A Comprehensive Bibliography*. Kent, OH: Kent State University Press, 1975.
Widmer, Kingsley. *Nathanael West*. Boston: Twayne, 1982.

PHILIP WHALEN

Jaffe, Dan. "Voice of the Poet" Oracular, Eerie, Daring." *Saturday Review*, 6 September 1969, p. 62.
Knight, Arthur Winfield. Review of *Heavy Breathing*. *Western American Literature* 17 (1984): 238–39.
Reed, John R. "Magicians and Others." *Poetry* 122 (1973): 51–52.
Rexroth, Kenneth. "A Hope for Poetry." *Holiday* 39 (March 1966): 147–51.
———. Review of *On Bear's Head*. *New York Times Book Review*, 31 August 1969, p. 8.

EDITH WHARTON

Auchincloss, Louis. "Edith Wharton and Her New Yorks." In *Reflections of a Jacobite*. Boston: Houghton Mifflin, 1961, pp. 11–28.
Bazin, Nancy Toppings. "The Destruction of Lily Bart: Capitalism, Christianity, and Male Chauvinism." *Denver Quarterly* 17 (1982): 97–108.
Brooks, Van Wyck. "Edith Wharton." In *The Confident Years: 1885–1915*. New York: Dutton, 1952, pp. 283–300.
Gargamo, James W. "*The House of Mirth:* Social Futility and Faith." *American Literature* 44 (1972): 137–43.
Gimbel, Wendy. *Edith Wharton: Orphancy and Survival*. New York: Praeger, 1984.
Lewis, R. W. B. *Edith Wharton: A Biography*. New York: Harper & Row, 1975.
McDowell, Margaret B. "Viewing the Custom of Her Country: Edith Wharton's Feminism." *Contemporary Literature* 15 (1974): 521–38.
Saunders, Judith P. "Becoming the Mask: Edith Wharton's Ingenues." *Massachusetts Studies in English* 8, No. 4 (1982): 33–9.
Smith, Allan Gardner. "Edith Wharton and the Ghost Story." *Women and Literature* 1 (1980): 149–59.
Springer, Marlene. *Edith Wharton and Kate Chopin: A Reference Guide*. Boston: G. K. Hall, 1976.
Walton, Geoffrey. *Edith Wharton: A Critical Interpretation*. 2nd rev. ed. Rutherford, NJ: Fairleigh Dickinson University Press, 1982.
Wegelin, Christof. "Edith Wharton and the Twilight of the International Novel." *Southern Review* 5 (1969): 398–418.
Wharton, Edith, *A Backward Glance*. New York: Appleton-Century, 1934.
Wolff, Cynthia Griffin. *A Feast of Words: The Triumph of Edith Wharton*. New York: Oxford University Press, 1977.

JOHN HALL WHEELOCK

Bedient, Calvin. "Poetry Comfortable and Uncomfortable." *Sewanee Review* 87 (1979): 7–8.
Cotter, James Finn. "Familiar Poetry." *Hudson Review* 32 (1979): 121–22.
Taylor, Henry. "Letting the Darkness In: The Poetic Achievement of John Hall Wheelock." *Hollins Critic* 7 (December 1970): 1–15.
Unsigned. Review of *Dust and Light*. *Outlook*, 10 December 1919, p. 469.
Untermeyer, Louis. "John Hall Wheelock." In *The New Era in American Poetry*. New York: Henry Holt, 1919, pp. 215–30.

E. B. WHITE

Core, George. "The Eloquence of Fact." *Virginia Quarterly Review* 54 (1978): 733–36.
Muggeridge, Malcolm. "The Complete New Yorker." *Harper's* 254 (March 1977): 94–99.
Neumeyer, Peter. "What Makes a Good Children's Book? The Texture of *Charlotte's Web*." *South Atlantic Bulletin* 44 (1979): 66–75.
Schott, Webster. "E. B. White Forever." *New Republic*, 24 November 1962, pp. 23–24.
Sheed, Wilfrid. Review of *Letters of E. B. White*. *New York Times Book Review*, 21 November, 1976, pp. 1, 26, 28.
Solheim, Helene. "Magic in the Web: Time, Pigs, and E. B. White." *South Atlantic Quarterly* 80 (1981): 391–405.

Steinhoff, William R. "*The Door*: 'The Professor,' 'My Friend the Poet (Deceased),' 'The Washable House,' and 'The Man out in Jersey.'" *College English* 23 (1961): 229–32.

Thurber, James. "E.B.W." *Saturday Review*, 15 October 1938, pp. 8–9.

Unsigned. "E. B. White." *New Yorker*, 14 October 1985, pp. 31–33.

REED WHITTEMORE

Fussell, Paul. "William Carlos Williams and His Problems." *Virginia Quarterly Review* 52 (1976): 509–15.

Logan, John. "Wit and Wisdom." *Saturday Review*, 28 July 1956, p. 10.

Lowe, Robert Liddell. "Comic Mask." *Poetry* 71 (1947–48): 97–101.

Moynahan, Julian. "The Professional Amateur." *New York Times Book Review*, 2 June 1963, p. 19.

Parisi, Joseph. "Personae, Personalities." *Poetry* 126 (1975): 222–25.

RUDY WIEBE

Keith, W. J., ed. *Epic Fiction: The Art of Rudy Wiebe*. Edmonton: NeWest Press, 1981.

———. *A Voice in the Land: Essays by and about Rudy Wiebe*. Edmonton: Alberta University Press, 1981.

Lecker, Robert. "Trusting the Quintuplet Senses: Time and Form in *The Temptations of Big Bear*." *English Studies in Canada* 8 (1982): 333–48.

Meeter, Glenn. "Rudy Wiebe: Spatial Form and Christianity in *The Blue Mountains of China* and *The Temptations of Big Bear*." *Essays on Canadian Writing* 22 (1981): 42–61.

RICHARD WILBUR

Dwyer, Dorothy Kurre. "'Achievements of Place': The Poetry of Richard Wilbur." Ph.D. diss.: Washington University, 1982.

Field, John P. *Richard Wilbur: A Bibliographical Checklist*. Kent, OH: Kent State University Press, 1971.

Hill, Donald L. *Richard Wilbur*. New York: Twayne, 1967.

Jensen, Ejner J. "Encounters with Experience: The Poems of Richard Wilbur." *New England Review* 2 (1979–80): 594–613.

McGuinness, Arthur E. "A Question of Consciousness: Richard Wilbur's *Things of This World*." *Arizona Quarterly* 23 (1967): 313–26.

Oliver, Raymond. "Verse Translation and Richard Wilbur." *Southern Review* 11 (1975): 318–30.

Reibetanz, John. "What Love Sees: Poetry and Vision in Richard Wilbur." *Modern Poetry Studies* 11 (1982): 60–85.

Stitt, Peter. "The Sacramental Vision of Richard Wilbur." In *The World's Hieroglyphic Beauty*. Athens: University of Georgia Press, 1985, pp. 9–38.

Thurley, Geoffrey. "Benign Diaspora: The Landscape of Richard Wilbur." In *The American Moment*. New York: St. Martin's Press, 1977, pp. 35–50.

Wilbur, Richard. "The Art of Poetry" (interview). *Paris Review* No. 72 (1977): 68–105.

THORNTON WILDER

Brunauer, Dalma H. "Creative Faith in Wilder's *The Eighth Day*." *Renascence* 25 (1972): 46–56.

Cowley, Malcolm. "Introduction" to *A Thornton Wilder Trio*. New York: Criterion Books, 1956.

DeMott, Benjamin. "Old-Fashioned Innovator." *New York Times Book Review*, 2 April 1967, pp. 1, 51–52.

Ericson, Edward, Jr. "Kierkegaard in Wilder's *Eighth Day*." *Renascence* 25 (1972): 123–38.

Fergusson, Francis. "Three Allegorists: Brecht, Wilder, and Eliot." *Sewanee Review* 64 (1956): 544–73.

Goldstein, Malcolm. *The Art of Thornton Wilder*. Lincoln: University of Nebraska Press, 1965.

Greene, George. "An Ethics for Wagon Trains: Thornton Wilder's *The Eighth Day*." *Queen's Quarterly* 88 (1981): 325–35.

Haberman, Donald. *The Plays of Thornton Wilder: A Critical Study*. Middletown, CT: Wesleyan University Press, 1967.

Hewitt, Barnard. "Thornton Wilder Says 'Yes.'" *Tulane Drama Review* 4 (December 1959): 110–20.

Hicks, Granville. Review of *Theophilus North*. *New York Times Book Review*, 21 October 1973, pp. 1, 16.

Kronenberger, Louis. "Book Notes from Limbo." *Atlantic Monthly* 222 (November 1969): 117–20.

Scott, Winfield Townley. "Our Town and the Golden Veil." *Virginia Quarterly Review* (1953): 103–17.

Sprague, Marshall. "Remembering Mr. Wilder." *New York Times Book Review*, 27 January 1974, p. 31.

TENNESSEE WILLIAMS

Alvarez, A. "Hurry on Down." *New Statesman*, 23 May 1959, pp. 721–22.

Hilfer, Anthony C., and R. Vance Ramsey. "*Baby Doll*: A Study in Comedy and Critical Awareness." *Ohio University Review* 11 (1969): 75–88.

Hurt, James R. "*Suddenly Last Summer*: Williams and Melville." *Modern Drama* 3 (1961): 396–400.

McCann, John S. *The Critical Reputation of Tennessee Williams*. Boston: G. K. Hall, 1983.

Nardin, James T. "What Tennessee Williams Didn't Write." In *Essays in Honor of Esmond Linworth Marilla*, eds. Thomas A. Kirby and William J. Olive. Baton Rouge: Louisiana State University Press, 1970, pp. 331–41.

Nelson, Benjamin. *Tennessee Williams: The Man and His Work*. New York: Oblensky, 1961.

Peden, William H. "Mad Pilgrimage: The Short Stories of Tennessee Williams." *Studies in Short Fiction* 1 (1964): 243–50.

Riddel, Joseph N. "*A Streetcar Named Desire*: Nietzsche Descending." *Modern Drama* 5 (1963): 421–30.

Spoto, Donald. *The Kindness of Strangers: The Life of Tennessee Williams*. Boston: Little, Brown, 1985.

Starnes, Leland. "The Grotesque Children of *The Rose Tattoo*." *Modern Drama* 12 (1970): 357–69.

Tischler, Nancy Marie. "The Distorted Mirror: Tennessee Williams's Self-Portraits." *Mississippi Quarterly* 25 (1972): 389–403.

———. *Tennessee Williams: Rebellious Puritan*. New York: Citadel Press, 1961.

Williams, Tennessee. Interview by Cecil Brown. *Partisan Review* 45 (1978): 276–305.

WILLIAM CARLOS WILLIAMS

Breslin, James E. *William Carlos Williams: An American Artist*. New York: Oxford University Press, 1970.

Burke, Kenneth. "The Methods of William Carlos Williams." *Dial* 82 (February 1927): 94–98.

Coles, Robert. *William Carlos Williams: The Knack of Survival in America*. New Brunswick, NJ: Rutgers University Press, 1975.

Creeley, Robert. Review of *Selected Essays. Black Mountain Review* 1 (Winter 1954): 53–58.

Dijkstra, Bram. *The Hieroglyphics of a New Speech: Cubism, Stieglitz and the Early Poetry of Williams Carlos Williams.* Princeton: Princeton University Press, 1969.

Gonarroe, Joel. *William Carlos Williams'* Paterson: *Language and Landscape.* Philadelphia: University of Pennsylvania Press, 1970.

Guimond, James. *The Art of William Carlos Williams: A Discovery and Possession of America.* Urbana: University of Illinois Press, 1968.

Kenner, Hugh. "With the Bare Hands." *Poetry* 80 (1952): 276–90.

Mariani, Paul. *William Carlos Williams: A New World Naked.* New York: McGraw-Hill, 1981.

Mazzaro, Jerome. *William Carlos Williams: The Later Poems.* Ithaca, NY: Cornell University Press, 1973.

Miller, J. Hillis. "Williams' *Spring and All* and the Progress of Poetry." *Daedelus* 99 (1970): 405–34.

Nelson, Cary. "Suffused-Encircling Shapes of Mind: Inhabited Space in Williams." *Journal of Modern Literature* 1 (1971): 549–64.

Ostrom, Alan. *The Poetic World of William Carlos Williams.* Carbondale: Southern Illinois University Press, 1966.

Paul, Sherman. *The Music of Survival: A Biography of a Poem by William Carlos Williams.* Urbana: University of Illinois Press, 1968.

Quinn, Sister Bernetta, O.S.F. "*Paterson:* Listening to Landscape." In *Modern American Poetry: Essays in Criticism,* ed. Jerome Mazzaro. New York: David McKay, 1970, pp. 116–82.

Riddel, Joseph N. *The Inverted Bell: Modernism and the Counterpoetics of William Carlos Williams.* Baton Rouge: Louisiana State University Press, 1974.

Thirlwall, John C. "William Carlos Williams' *Paterson:* The Search for a Redeeming Language—A Personal Epic in Five Parts." *New Directions* 17 (1961): 252–310.

Townley, Rod. *The Early Poetry of William Carlos Williams.* Ithaca, NY: Cornell University Press, 1975.

Wagner, Linda Welshimer. *The Poems of William Carlos Williams: A Critical Study.* Middletown, CT: Wesleyan University Press, 1964.

———. *The Prose of William Carlos Williams.* Middletown, CT: Wesleyan University Press, 1970.

———, ed. *Interviews with William Carlos Williams: "Speaking Straight Ahead."* New York: New Directions, 1976.

———, ed. *William Carlos Williams: A Reference Guide.* Boston: G. K. Hall, 1978.

Weaver, Mike. *William Carlos Williams: The American Background.* Cambridge: The University Press, 1971.

Winters, Yvor. "Poetry of Feeling." *Kenyon Review* 1 (1939): 104–7.

Zukofsky, Louis. "William Carlos Williams." In *Prepositions.* London: Rapp & Carroll, 1967, pp. 39–47.

EDMUND WILSON

Aaron, Daniel. "Introduction" to *Letters on Literature and Politics 1912–1972* by Edmund Wilson, ed. Elena Wilson. New York: Farrar, Straus & Giroux, 1977, pp. xv–xxix.

Castronovo, David. *Edmund Wilson.* New York: Ungar, 1984.

Costa, Richard Hauer. *Edmund Wilson: Our Neighbor from Talcotville.* Syracuse: Syracuse University Press, 1980.

Douglas, George H. *Edmund Wilson's America.* Lexington: University Press of Kentucky, 1983.

Epstein, Joseph. "Never Wise—but Oh, How Smart." *New York Times Book Review,* 31 August 1986, pp. 3, 16.

Frank, Charles P. *Edmund Wilson.* New York: Twayne, 1970.

Howe, Irving. "Edmund Wilson and the Sea Slugs." In *A World More Attractive.* New York: Horizon Press, 1963, pp. 300–307.

Paul, Sherman. *Edmund Wilson: A Study of Literary Vocation in Our Time.* Urbana: University of Illinois Press, 1965.

Schwartz, Delmore. "The Writing of Edmund Wilson." *Accent* 2 (1942): 177–86.

YVOR WINTERS

Barrett, William. "Temptations of St. Yvor." *Kenyon Review* 9 (1947): 532–51.

Fraser, John. "Winters' *Summa.*" *Southern Review* 5 (1969): 184–202.

Isaacs, Elizabeth. *An Introduction to the Poetry of Yvor Winters.* Athens: Swallow Press/University of Ohio Press, 1981.

Lohf, Kenneth A., and Eugene P. Sheehy. *Yvor Winters: A Bibliography.* Denver: Alan Swallow, 1959.

Powell, Grosvenor. *Language as Being in the Poetry of Yvor Winters.* Baton Rouge: Louisiana State University Press, 1980.

Ransom, John Crowe. "Yvor Winters: The Logical Critic." In *The New Criticism.* Norfolk, CT: New Directions, 1941, pp. 211–75.

Sexton, Richard J. *The Complex of Yvor Winters' Criticism.* The Hague: Mouton, 1973.

Tate, Allen. "Yvor Winters." In *The Poetry Reviews of Allen Tate, 1924–1944,* eds. Ashley Brown and Frances Neel Cheney. Baton Rouge: Louisiana State University Press, 1983, pp. 66–68.

Van Deusen, Marshall. "In Defense of Yvor Winters." *Thought* 32 (1957): 409–36.

Weiss, Theodore. "The Nonsense of Winters' *Anatomy.*" *Quarterly Review of Literature* 1 (1944): 212–34; 300–318.

GENE WOLFE

Bishop, Michael. "Gene Wolfe as Hero." *Thrust* No. 16 (Fall 1980): 10–13.

Gordon, Joan. *Gene Wolfe.* Mercer Island, WA: Starmont, 1986.

Greenland, Colin. Review of *The Citadel of the Autarch. Foundation* No. 28 (July 1983): 89–91.

Malzberg, Barry. "An Imaginary Interview on Gene Wolfe's 'Cues.'" *Algol* No. 22 (May 1974): 29–31.

Pollack, Rachel. Review of *Free Live Free. Foundation* No. 35 (Winter 1985–86): 99–102.

Swanson, Elliott. "Gene Wolfe: Interview." *Interzone* No. 17 (Fall 1986): 38–40.

Wolfe, Gene. *The Castle of the Otter: A Book about* The Book of the New Sun. Willimantic, CT: Ziesing Brothers, 1982.

THOMAS WOLFE

Austin, Neal F. *A Biography of Thomas Wolfe.* Austin, TX: Roger Beacham, 1968.

Field, Leslie A., ed. *Thomas Wolfe: Three Decades of Criticism.* New York: New York University Press, 1968.

Gurko, Leo. *Thomas Wolfe: Beyond the Romantic Ego.* New York: Crowell, 1975.

Holman, C. Hugh, ed. *The World of Thomas Wolfe.* New York: Scribner's, 1962.

Idol, John J., Jr. "The Plays of Thomas Wolfe and Their Links with His Novels." *Mississippi Quarterly* 22 (1969): 95–112.

Johnson, Pamela Hansford. *Thomas Wolfe: A Critical Study.* London: Heinemann, 1947.

Kennedy, Richard S. *The Window of Memory: The Literary Career of Thomas Wolfe.* Chapel Hill: University of North Carolina Press, 1962.

Muller, Herbert J. *Thomas Wolfe.* Norfolk, CT: New Directions, 1947.

Phillipson, John S. *Thomas Wolfe: A Reference Guide.* Boston: G. K. Hall, 1977.

Reeves, Paschal, ed. *Thomas Wolfe and the Glass of Time.* Athens: University of Georgia Press, 1971.

Rubin, Louis D., Jr. *Thomas Wolfe: The Weather of His Youth.* Baton Rouge: Louisiana State University Press, 1955.

Snyder, William U. *Thomas Wolfe: Ulysses and Narcissus.* Athens: Ohio University Press, 1971.

Walser, Richard, ed. *The Enigma of Thomas Wolfe: Biographical and Critical Selections.* Cambridge, MA: Harvard University Press, 1953.

Wank, Martin. "Thomas Wolfe: Two More Decades of Criticism." *South Atlantic Quarterly* 69 (1970): 244–56.

TOM WOLFE

Dickstein, Morris. "The Working Press, Literary Culture, New Journalism." In *Gates of Eden: American Culture in the Sixties.* New York: Basic Books, 1977, pp. 139–43.

Dunne, John Gregory. "Hog Heaven." *New York Review of Books,* 8 November 1979, pp. 9–11.

Epstein, Joseph. "Rococo and Roll." *New Republic,* 24 July 1965, pp. 27–29.

ALEXANDER WOOLLCOTT

Adams, Samuel Hopkins. A. *Woollcott: His Life and His World.* New York: Reynal & Hitchcock, 1945.

Brown, John Mason. "Introduction" to *The Portable Woollcott,* ed. Joseph Hennessy. New York: Viking Press, 1946, pp. xi–xxviii.

Gibbs, Woollcott. "Big Nemo." In *More in Sorrow.* New York: Holt, 1958, pp. 79–125.

Hoyt, Edwin Palmer. *Alexander Woollcott: The Man Who Came to Dinner.* New York: Abelard-Schuman, 1968.

Nathan, George Jean. "Alexander Woollcott: The Seidlitz Powder in Times Square." In *The Magic Mirror,* ed. Thomas Quinn Curtis. New York: Knopf, 1960, pp. 64–74.

Tarkington, Booth. "Ave Atque Vale." *Atlantic* 171 (June 1943): 64.

Wilson, Edmund. "Alexander Woollcott of the Phalanx." In *Classics and Commercials.* New York: Farrar, Straus, 1950, pp. 87–93.

HERMAN WOUK

Beichman, Arnold. *Herman Wouk: The Novelist as Social Historian.* New Brunswick, NJ: Transaction Books, 1984.

Jones, Peter G. "The Literature of Command." In *War and the Novelist.* Columbia: University of Missouri Press, pp. 73–79.

Podhoretz, Norman. "The Jew as Bourgeois." *Commentary* 21 (February 1956): 186–88.

CHARLES WRIGHT

Stewart, Pamela. "In All Places at Once." *Ironwood* No. 19 (1982): 162–66.

Wright, Charles. "Charles Wright at Oberlin." *Field* 17 (1977): 46–85.

JAMES WRIGHT

Dougherty, David C. "The Sceptical Poetry of James Wright." *Contemporary Poetry* 2, No. 2 (1977): 4–10.

Kalaidjian, Walter. "'Many of Our Waters': The Poetry of James Wright." *Boundary 2* 9 (1981): 101–21.

Smith, Dave, ed. *The Pure Clear Word: Essays on the Poetry of James Wright.* Urbana: University of Illinois Press, 1982.

RICHARD WRIGHT

Fabre, Michel. *The Unfinished Quest of Richard Wright.* Tr. Isabel Barzun. New York: William Morrow, 1973.

Hakutani, Yoshinobu, ed. *Critical Essays on Richard Wright.* Boston: G. K. Hall, 1982.

Kinnamon, Kenneth. *The Emergence of Richard Wright.* Urbana: University of Illinois Press, 1972.

Margolies, Edward. *The Art of Richard Wright.* Carbondale: Southern Illinois University Press, 1969.

Pudaloff, Ross. "Celebrity as Identity: Richard Wright, *Native Son,* and Mass Culture." *Studies in American Fiction* 11 (1983): 3–18.

Wright, Richard. *American Hunger.* New York: Harper & Row, 1977.

———. *Black Boy.* New York: Harper & Row, 1945.

ELINOR WYLIE

Gray, Thomas Alexander. *Elinor Wylie.* New York: Twayne, 1969.

Olson, Stanley. *Elinor Wylie: A Life Apart.* New York: Dial Press, 1979.

Pizer, Donald. "'Symbolic Resonances of the Mind': The Novels of Elinor Wylie." *Centennial Review* 24 (1980): 284–301.

Tate, Allen. "Elinor Wylie's Poetry." *New Republic,* 7 September 1932, p. 107.

Wright, Celeste Turner. "Elinor Wylie: The Glass Chimaera and the Minotaur." *Twentieth Century Literature* 12 (1966): 15–26.

RICHARD YATES

Atlas, James. "A Sure Narrative Voice." *Atlantic* 248 (November 1981): 84–86.

Buitenhuis, Peter. "Windows Opened on Experience." *New York Times Book Review,* 25 March 1962, pp. 4, 45.

Chappell, Fred. "Richard Yates's *Revolutionary Road.*" In *Rediscoveries,* ed. David Madden. New York: Crown, 1971, pp. 245–55.

Oates, Joyce Carol. "Dreams without Substance." *Nation,* 10 November 1969, pp. 512–13.

Penner, Jonathan. "The Novelists." *New Republic,* 4 November 1978, pp. 42–45.

ROGER ZELAZNY

Ikin, Van. "Flashes and Imagining." *Science Fiction Commentary* No. 57 (November 1979): 9.

Krulik, Theodore. *Roger Zelazny.* New York: Ungar, 1986.

Monteleone, Thomas. "Fire and Ice—On Roger Zelazny's Short Fiction." *Algol* 13 (Summer 1976): 9–14.

Panshin, Alexei and Cory. Review of the *Amber* series. *Fantasy and Science Fiction* 49 (August 1975): 52–53, 162.

Sanders, Joseph L. *Roger Zelazny: A Primary and Secondary Bibliography.* Boston: G. K. Hall, 1981.

———. "Zelazny: Unfinished Business." In *Voices for the Future: Volume Two,* ed. Thomas D. Clareson. Bowling Green, OH: Bowling Green University Popular Press, 1979, pp. 180–96.

Shippey, T. A. "Obsequious in Soace." *Times Literary Supplement*, 20 February 1976, p. 187.
Wood, Michael. "Coffee Break for Sisyphus." *New York Review of Books*, 2 October 1975, pp. 3–7.
Yoke, Carl B. "Personality Metamorphosis in Roger Zelazny's 'The Doors of His Face, The Lamps of His Mouth.'" *Extrapolation* 21 (Summer 1980): 106–21.
———. *Roger Zelazny*. West Linn, OR: Starmont House, 1979.

LOUIS ZUKOFSKY

Cary, Joseph. "Poems of a Lifetime." *Nation*, 19 May 1979, pp. 573–74.
Charters, Samuel. "Essay Beginning 'All.'" *Modern Poetry Studies* 3 (1973): 241–50.
Dembo, L. S. "Louis Zukofsky: Objectivist Poetics and the Quest for Form." *American Literature* 42 (1972): 74–96.
Duddy, Thomas A. "The Measure of Louis Zukofsky." *Modern Poetry Studies* 3 (1973): 250–56.

ACKNOWLEDGMENTS

Samuel Hopkins Adams. "The World of A. Woollcott," *Reader's Digest*, May 1943, copyright © 1943 by Reader's Digest, Inc. Reprinted with permission of Brandt & Brandt Literary Agents, Inc.

Kathleen Agena. "The Mad Sense of Language," *Partisan Review*, 1976, copyright © 1976 by Partisan Review, Inc.

Brian Aldiss. "Sturgeon: Mercury Plus X," *Cheap Truth*, copyright © 1985 by Brian Aldiss. Reprinted with permission of Robin Straus Agency.

John W. Aldridge. "The Private Vice of John Updike," *Time to Murder and Create*, copyright © 1966 by John Aldridge. Reprinted with permission of the author. "Three Tempted Him," *New York Times Book Review*, March 9, 1952, copyright © 1952 by New York Times Co., Inc. Reprinted with permission of the publisher.

Bruce Allen. "Three Master," *Sewanee Review*, Summer 1982, copyright © 1982 by University of the South. Reprinted with permission of the publisher.

Mary Allen. "John Updike's Love of 'Dull Bovine Beauty,'" *The Necessary Blankness: Women in Major American Fiction of the Sixties*, copyright © 1976 by Board of Trustees of the University of Illinois. Reprinted with permission of University of Illinois Press.

A. Alvarez. "Yvor Winters," *Beyond All This Fiddle: Essays 1955–1967*, copyright © 1969 by A. Alvarez. Reprinted with permission of Aitken & Stone, Ltd.

Elizabeth Ammons. "The Business of Marriage," *Edith Wharton's Argument with America*, copyright © 1980 by University of Georgia Press. Reprinted with permission of the publisher.

James Baldwin. "Many Thousands Gone," *Notes of a Native Son*, copyright © 1955, 1983 by James Baldwin. Reprinted with permission of Beacon Press and Pluto Press.

Jane Barnes. "John Updike: A Literary Spider," *Virginia Quarterly Review*, Winter 1981, copyright © 1981 by *Virginia Quarterly Review*. Reprinted with permission of the publisher.

Elizabeth Barthelme. "Victory over Bitterness," *Commonweal*, Feb. 11, 1983, copyright © 1983 by Commonweal Foundation. Reprinted with permission of the publisher.

Joseph Warren Beach. "The Peacock's Tail," *The Outlook for American Prose*, copyright © 1926 by University of Chicago Press. Reprinted with permission of the publisher.

Warren Beck. "E. B. White," *College English*, April 1946, copyright © 1946 by National Council of Teachers of English. Reprinted with permission of the publisher.

Millicent Bell. "Tobacco Road Updated," *New York Times Book Review*, Nov. 21, 1965, copyright © 1965 by New York Times Co., Inc. Reprinted with permission of the publisher.

Vereen Bell. "A Study in Frustration," *Shenandoah*, Summer 1963, copyright © 1963 by *Shenandoah*. Reprinted with permission of the publisher.

Michael Benedikt. "Listening and Not Listening," *Poetry*, June 1968, copyright © 1968 by Modern Poetry Association.

Charles Berryman. "After the Fall: Kurt Vonnegut," *Critique*, Winter 1985, copyright © 1985 by Helen Dwight Reid Educational Foundation. Reprinted with permission.

John Peale Bishop. "The Poetry of Mark Van Doren," "The Sorrows of Thomas Wolfe," *The Collected Essays of John Peale Bishop*, ed. Edmund Wilson, copyright © 1948 by Charles Scribner's Sons.

Everetta Love Blair. "Conclusion," *Jesse Stuart: His Life and Works*, copyright © 1967 by Everetta Love Blair. Reprinted with permission of University of South Carolina Press.

Harold Bloom. "The Central Man," *New York Review of Books*, July 19, 1984, copyright © 1984 by *New York Review of Books*. Reprinted with permission of the publisher. "Dark and Radiant Peripheries: Mark Strand and A. R. Ammons," *Southern Review*, Jan. 1972, copyright © 1972 by The Louisiana State University.

Charles A. Brady. "Our Man in the Moon: What Thurber Saw," *Commonweal*, Dec. 8, 1961, copyright © 1961 by Commonweal Foundation. Reprinted with permission of the publisher.

John M. Brinnin. "Views of the Favorite Mythologies," *Poetry*, Dec. 1944, copyright © 1944 by Modern Poetry Association. Reprinted with permission of the author and publisher.

Cleanth Brooks. "Allen Tate," *Poetry*, Sept. 1945, copyright © 1945 by Modern Poetry Association. "Eudora Welty and the Southern Idiom," *Eudora Welty: A Form of Thanks*, eds. Louis Dollarhide and Ann J. Abadie, copyright © 1979 by University Press of Mississippi. Reprinted with permission of the publisher. "The Past Reexamined: The Optimist's Daughter," *Mississippi Quarterly*, Fall 1973, copyright © 1973 by *Mississippi Quarterly*. Reprinted with permission of the publisher.

Rosellen Brown. "Plentitude and Dearth," *Parnassus: Poetry in Review*, Spring–Summer 1973, copyright © 1973 by Poetry in Review Foundation. Reprinted with permission of the publisher.

Spencer Brown. "The Odor of Durability," *Sewanee Review*, Winter 1978, copyright © 1978 by University of the South. Reprinted with permission of the publisher.

Robert Brustein. "A Little Night Music," *Seasons of Discontents*, copyright © 1965 by Robert Brustein. Reprinted with permission of Simon & Schuster.

C. D. B. Bryan. "Kurt Vonnegut, Head Bokonist," *New York Times Book Review*, April 6, 1969, copyright © 1969 by New York Times Co., Inc. Reprinted with permission of the publisher.

Jerry H. Bryant. "The Hopeful Stoicism of William Styron," *South Atlantic Quarterly*, Autumn 1963, copyright © 1963 by Duke University Press. Reprinted with permission of the publisher. "The Violence of *Native Son*," *Southern Review*, Summer 1981, copyright © 1981 by Louisiana State University. Reprinted with permission of the author and publisher.

Anthony Burgess. "Honest Abe's Obsession," *Times Literary Supplement*, Sept. 28, 1984, copyright © 1984 by Times Newspapers Ltd.

James Branch Cabell. "Sanctuary in Porcelain: A Note as to Elinor Wylie," *Virginia Quarterly Review*, July 1930, copyright © 1930 by University of Virginia. Reprinted with permission of the publisher.

William Cahill and Molly McKaughan. "John Hall Wheelock: The Art of Poetry XXI," *Paris Review*, Fall 1976, copyright © 1976 by *Paris Review*, Reprinted with permission of the publisher.

Paul Carroll. "Laureate of the Day after the Seven Days of Creation," *Poetry*, Feb. 1971, copyright © 1971 by Modern Poetry Association. Reprinted with permission of the author and publisher.

Hayden Carruth. "The Cycle of Sensibility," *Nation*, Jan. 4, 1971, copyright © 1971 by Nation, Inc. Reprinted with permission of the publisher. "William Carlos Williams as One of Us," *New Republic*, April 13, 1963, copyright © 1963 by Harrison-Blaine, Inc.

Everett Carter. "The 'Little Myth' of Robert Penn Warren," *Modern Fiction Studies*, Spring 1960, copyright © 1960 by Purdue Research Foundation.

Leonard Casper. "The Running Gamble," *Robert Penn Warren: The Dark and Bloody Ground*, copyright © 1960 by University of Washington Press. Reprinted with permission of the publisher.

Harold Clurman. "Tennessee Williams," *The Naked Image: Observa-*

tions on the Modern Theater, copyright © 1966 by Harold Clurman. Reprinted with permission of Macmillan Publishers.

John Clute. "The Mother of the Autarch" (1986), *Strokes: Essays and Reviews 1966–1986*, copyright © 1986, 1987 by John Clute. "The Urth and All Its Glory," *Washington Post Book World*, January 30, 1983, copyright © 1983 by Washington Post Co. Reprinted with permission of the publisher.

Samuel Coale. "Styron's Disguises: A Provisional Rebel in Christian Masquerade," *Critique*, Winter 1985, copyright © 1985 by the Helen Dwight Reid Education Foundation. Reprinted with permission.

Ruby Cohn. "The Garrulous Grotesques of Tennessee Williams," *Dialogue in American Drama*," copyright © 1971 by Indiana University Press.

Peter Conrad. "Re-inventing America," *Times Literary Supplement*, March 26, 1976, copyright © 1976 by Times Newspapers Ltd.

Philip Corwin. "Oh, What the Hex," *Commonweal*, June 1, 1984, copyright © 1984 by Commonweal Foundation. Reprinted with permission of the publisher.

Alexander Cowie. "The Bridge of Thorton Wilder," *Essays on American Literature in Honor of Jay B. Hubbell* ed. Clarence Gohdes, copyright © 1967 by Duke University Press. Reprinted with permission of the publisher.

Robert Daniel. "The Discontent of Our Winters," *Sewanee Review*, Oct.–Dec. 1943, copyright © 1943 by University of the South. Reprinted with permission of the publisher.

Guy Davenport. "Review of *Ferdinand*, *New York Times Book Review*, June 15, 1969, copyright © 1969 by New York Times Co., Inc. Reprinted with permission of the publisher.

Ann Morrissett Davidon. "Doing Well by Doing Wrong," *Nation*, April 17, 1976, copyright © 1976 by Nation, Inc. Reprinted with permission of the publisher.

Dick Davis. "Conclusion," *Wisdom and Wilderness: The Achievement of Yvor Winters*, copyright © 1983 by University of Georgia Press. Reprinted with permission of the publisher.

Samuel R. Delany. "Faust and Archinaedes," *The Jewel-Hinged Jaw*, copyright © 1977 by Samuel R. Delany. "Sturgeon," *Starboard Wine*, copyright © 1984 by Samuel R. Delany.

Benjamin DeMott. "Funny, Wise and True," *New York Times Book Review*, March 14, 1982, copyright © 1982 by New York Times Co., Inc. Reprinted with permission of the publisher.

Babette Deutsch. "The Solitary Ironist," *Poetry*, Dec. 1937, copyright © 1937 by W. S. Monroe and E. S. Fletcher. Reprinted with permission of the author's estate and publisher.

James Dickey. "The Death and Keys of the Censor," *Sewanee Review*, Spring 1961, copyright © 1961 by University of the South. Reprinted with permission of the author. "Five Poets," *Poetry*, November 1956, copyright © 1956 by Modern Poetry Association. Reprinted with permission of the author and publisher. "Yvor Winters," *Babel to Byzantium*, copyright © 1962, 1969 by Farrar, Straus & Giroux, Inc. Reprinted with permission of Farrar, Straus & Giroux, Inc., and Raines & Raines.

William Dickey. "A Time of Common Speech," *Hudson Review*, Summer 1970, copyright © 1970 by The Hudson Review, Inc.

George Dillon. "Style and Many-Headed Beast," *Poetry*, Aug. 1955, copyright © 1955 by Modern Poetry Association.

Thomas M. Disch. "A Wizard of the Fabulous," *Washington Post Book World*, March 22, 1981, copyright © 1981 by Washington Post Co. Reprinted with permission of the publisher.

Denis Donoghue. Review of *The Swimmers and Other Selected Poems* and *Essays of Four Decades*, *Spectator*, Jan. 16, 1971, copyright © 1971 by The Spectator Ltd.

Charles Doyle. "Conclusion," *William Carlos Williams and the American Poem*, copyright © 1982 by St. Martin's Press. Reprinted with permission of the publisher.

Jeffrey L. Duncan. "The Problem of Language in *Miss Lonelyhearts*," *Iowa Review*, Winter 1977, copyright © 1977 by The University of Iowa.

Carolyn A. Durham. "William Styron's *Sophie's Choice*: The Structure of Oppression," *Twentieth Century Literature*, Winter 1984, copyright © 1985 by Hofstra University Press. Reprinted with permission of the publisher.

Gerald Early. "*The Color Purple* as Everybody's Protest Art," *Antioch Review*, Summer 1986, copyright © 1986 by Antioch Review, Inc.

Leon Edel. "The Nature of Psychological Evidence," *Stuff of Sleep and Dreams: Experiments in Literary Psychology*, copyright © 1982 by Leon Edel.

David Eggenschwiler. "The Ordered Disorder of *Ethan Frome*," *Studies in the Novel*, Fall 1977, copyright © 1977. Reprinted with permission of the publisher.

Ralph Ellison. "Richard Wright's Blues," *Shadow and Act*, copyright © 1953 by Ralph Ellison. Reprinted with permission of Alfred A. Knopf and William Morris Agency.

Michel Fabre. "Introduction" to *Richard Wright Reader*, eds. Ellen Wright and Michel Fabre, copyright © 1978 by Ellen Wright and Michel Fabre.

Signi Falk. "The Profitable World of Tennessee Williams," *Modern Drama*, Dec. 1958, copyright © 1958 by A. C. Edwards. Reprinted with permission of *Modern Drama*, University of Toronto.

Judith Farr. "Afterword," to *The Life and Art of Elinor Wylie*, copyright © 1983 by Louisiana State University Press. Reprinted with permission of the publisher.

Lillian Feder. "Allen Tate's Use of Classical Literature," *Centennial Review*, Winter 1960, copyright © 1960 by *Centennial Review*. Reprinted with permission of the author and publisher.

Leslie Fiedler. "*Clarissa* in America: Toward *Marjorie Morningstar*," *Love and Death in the American Novel*, copyright © 1960 by Leslie Fiedler. Reprinted with permission of Stein & Day Publishers. "Some Uses and Failures of Feeling," *Partisan Review*, Aug. 1948, copyright © 1948 by *Partisan Review*. Reprinted with permission of the author and publisher.

Kenneth Fields. "The Free Verse of Yvor Winters and William Carlos Williams," *Southern Review*, July 1967, copyright © 1967 by The Louisiana State University Press.

O. W. Firkins. "Singers New and Old," *Nation*, Jan. 6, 1916, copyright © 1916. Reprinted with permission of the publisher.

R. W. Flint. "Something New," *New Republic*, Nov. 16, 1963, copyright © 1963 by New Republic.

Marilyn French. "The Emergence of Edith Wharton," *New Republic*, June 13, 1981, copyright © 1981 by Marilyn French.

Edmund Fuller. "Thorton Wilder: The Notation of the Heart," *American Scholar*, Spring 1959, copyright © 1959 by United Chapters of Phi Beta Kappa. Reprinted with permission of the author and publisher.

Paul Fussell. "On the Go Again," *New York Times Book Review*, Aug. 26, 1979, copyright © 1979 by New York Times Co., Inc. Reprinted with permission of the publisher. Review of *War and Remembrance*, *New Republic*, Oct. 14, 1978, copyright © 1978 by New Republic.

Edward L. Gallingan. "The Comic Art of Rex Sout," *Sewanee Review*, Spring 1981, copyright © 1981 by University of the South. Reprinted with permission of the publisher.

David Galloway. "The Absurd Man as Saint," *The Absurd Hero in American Fiction*, copyright © 1966, 1970, 1981 by David D. Galloway.

Arthur Ganz. "The Desperate Morality of the Plays of Tennessee Williams," *American Scholar*, Spring 1962, copyright © 1961 by

United Chapters of Phi Beta Kappa. Reprinted with permission of the publisher.

John Gassner. "Tennessee Williams: Dramatist of Frustration," *College English*, Oct. 1948, copyright © 1948 by National Council of Teachers of English. Reprinted with permission of the publisher.

William Gilmore. "A Few Ghosts," *Poetry*, Dec. 1937, copyright © 1937 by Modern Poetry Association.

Robert S. Gingher. "Has John Updike Anything to Say?," *Modern Fiction Studies*, Spring 1974, copyright © 1974 by Purdue Research Foundation. Reprinted with permission of the publisher.

Allen Ginsberg. "Williams in a World of Object," *William Carlos Williams: Man and Poet*, ed. Carroll F. Terrell, copyright © 1983 by National Poetry Foundation, University of Maine. Reprinted with permission of the publisher.

Marion Glastonbury, "E. B. White's Unexpected Items of Enchantment," *Children's Literature in Education*, May 1973, copyright © 1973 by APS Publications, Inc.

Frank Graziano. "The Matter Itself: Warren's *Audubon: A Vision*," *Homage to Robert Penn Warren*, copyright © 1981 by Logbridge-Rhodes, Inc. Reprinted with permission of the publisher.

Peter Green. "Resuscitated Emperor," *New Republic*, June 13, 1964, copyright © 1964 by Harrison-Blaine, Inc.

Colin Greenland. Review of *The Shadow of the Torturer* and *The Claw of the Conciliator*, *Foundation*, Feb. 1982, copyright © 1981 by Science Fiction Foundation. Reprinted with permission of the publisher.

Edward Grossman. "Vonnegut and His Audience," *Commentary*, July 1974, copyright © 1974 by American Jewish Committee. Reprinted with permission of the author and publisher.

Doris Grumbach. "Edith Wharton," *New Republic*, April 21, 1973, copyright © 1973 by New Republic.

Thomas Gunn. "William Carlos Williams," *Encounter*, July 1965, copyright © 1965 by *Encounter*. Reprinted with permission of Faber & Faber, Ltd.

James Hafley. "Abstraction and Order in the Language of Tennessee Williams," *Tennessee Williams: A Tribute*, ed. Jac Thorpe, copyright © 1977 by University Press of Mississippi. Reprinted with permission of the publisher.

John Hagan. "Thomas Wolfe's *Of Time and the River*: The Quest for Transcendence," *Thomas Wolfe: A Harvard Perspective*, ed. Richard S. Kennedy, copyright © 1983 by Croissant & Co.

William Harmon. "*Eiron* Eyes," *Parnassus: Poetry in Review*, Spring–Summer 1979, copyright © 1979 by Poetry in Review Foundation. Reprinted with permission of the publisher.

Trudier Harris. "Violence in *The Third Life of Grange Copeland*," *CLA Journal*, copyright © 1975 by College Language Association. Reprinted with permission of the publisher.

Richard Harvard. Review of *Black and White*, *Nation*, March 15, 1965, copyright © 1965 by Nation, Inc. Reprinted with permission of the publisher.

Louis Hasley. "James Thurber: Artist in Humor," *South Atlantic Quarterly*, Autumn 1974, copyright © 1974 by Duke University. Reprinted with permission of the publisher.

S. I. Hayakawa. "The Allusive Trap," *Poetry*, June 1939, copyright © 1939 by Modern Poetry Association.

Richard Hayes. "The Ministers without Portfolio," *Commonweal*, April 29, 1960, copyright © 1960 by Commonweal Foundation. Reprinted with permission of the publisher.

John Hellmann. "Corporate Fiction, Private Fable and Hunter S. Thompson's *Fear and Loathing: On the Campaign Trail '72*," *Critique*, 1979, copyright © 1979 by James Dean Young. Reprinted with permission of the Helen Dwight Reid Educational Foundation.

Granville Hicks. "John Updike," *Literary Horizons: A Quarter Century of American Fiction*, copyright © 1970 by New York University. Review of *The Winds of War*, *New York Times Book Review*, Nov. 14, 1971, copyright © 1971 by New York Times Co., Inc. Reprinted with permission of the publisher.

Edward Hirsch. "To Hell with Holy Relics," *American Poetry Review*, May–June 1976, copyright © 1976 by *American Poetry Review*. Reprinted with permission of the author and publisher.

C. Hugh Holman. "Original Sin on the Dark and Bloody Ground," *Robert Penn Warren's A Brother to Dragons: A Discussion*, ed. James A. Grimshaw, copyright © 1983 by The Louisiana State University Press. Reprinted with permission of the publisher. "Rhetorical Hope and Dramatic Despair," *The Loneliness at the Core: Studies in Thomas Wolfe*, copyright © 1975 by The Louisiana State University Press. Reprinted with permission of the publisher.

Richard Howard. "Gary Snyder: 'To Hold Both History and Wilderness in Mind,'" *Alone with America*, copyright © 1969, 1980 by Richard Howard.

Michael Hulse. "The Poetry of Richard Wilbur," *Quadrant*, Oct. 1981, copyright © 1981. Reprinted with permission of the author and publisher.

Esther Merle Jackson. "Williams and the Lyric Movement," *The Broken World of Tennessee Williams*, copyright © 1965 by Esther Merle Jackson. Reprinted with permission of University of Wisconsin Press.

Josephine Jacobsen. "Political Poet," *New Republic*, Oct. 12, 1974, copyright © 1974 by New Republic, Inc.

Clive James. "The Four Just Men," *New Statesman*, Feb. 21, 1975, copyright © 1975 by New Statesman and Nation. "The Left-Handed Gun," *New Statesman*, Aug. 19, 1977, copyright © 1977 by Statesman and Nation Publishing Co., Ltd. "The Poetry of Edmund Wilson," *New Review*, Nov. 1977, copyright © 1977 by TNR Publications.

Henry James. Letter to Edith Wharton (Dec. 9, 1912), *Henry James Letters*, Vol. 4, ed. Leon Edel, copyright © 1984 by Alexander R. James. Reprinted with permission of Harvard University Press and Macmillan Ltd.

Randall Jarrell. "The Poet and His Public," *Partisan Review*, Sept.–Oct. 1946, copyright © 1946 by Partisan Review, Inc. Reprinted with permission of the author's estate and publisher.

A. Norman Jeffares. "Poetic Deliberation," *Journal of Commonwealth Literature*, June 1971, copyright © 1971 by Oxford University Press. Reprinted with permission of the publisher.

Diane Johnson. "Southern Comfort," *New York Review of Books*, Nov. 7, 1985, copyright © 1985 by *New York Review of Books*. Reprinted with permission of the publisher.

James H. Justus. "The Mariner and Robert Penn Warren," *Texas Studies in Literature and Language*, Spring 1966, copyright © 1966 by University of Texas Press.

Howard Kaye. "The Post-Symbolist Poetry of Yvor Winters," *Southern Review*, Winter 1971, copyright © 1971 by Louisiana State University.

Alfred Kazin. "The Educations: Edith Wharton and Theodore Dreiser," "The Exquisites," *On Native Grounds*, copyright © 1942 by Alfred Kazin. Reprinted with permission of Little, Brown & Co. "Professional Observers: Cozzens to Updike," *Bright Book of Life*, copyright © 1971, 1973 by Alfred Kazin. Reprinted with permission of Little, Brown & Co.

X. J. Kennedy. "Reed Whittemore's Mock Epic," *Poetry*, Feb. 1963, copyright © 1963 by Modern Poetry Association. Reprinted with permission of the author and publisher.

Hugh Kenner. "All the Angels Have Big Feet," *National Review*, Feb. 18, 1983, copyright © 1983 by The National Review. "Something to Say," *A Homemade World*, copyright © 1975 by Hugh Kenner. Reprinted with permission of Alfred A. Knopf, Inc. Review of "A 22 & 23," *New York Times Book Review*, March 14, 1976, copyright © 1976 by New York Times Co., Inc. Reprinted with permission of the publisher.

Alvin B. Kernan. "The Mob Tendency: *The Day of the Locust,*" *The Plot of Satire,* copyright © 1965 by Yale University. Reprinted with permission of the publisher.

Walter Kerr. "Playwrights," *Pieces of Eight,* copyright © 1952, 1957 by Walter Kerr. Reprinted with permission of the author and Brandt & Brandt.

Ruth M. Vande Kieft. "The Vision of Eudora Welty," *Mississippi Quarterly,* Fall 1973, copyright © 1973 by Mississippi State University. Reprinted with permission of the publisher.

Robert Kirsch. "Introduction" to *Night of the Aurochs* by Dalton Trumbo, copyright © 1979 by Cleo Trumbo. Reprinted with permission of Viking Penguin Inc.

Jerome Klinkowitz. "Hunter S. Thompson," *The Life of Fiction,* copyright © 1977 by Board of Trustees of the University of Illinois. Reprinted with permission of the publisher. "The Literary Career of Kurt Vonnegut, Jr.," *Modern Fiction Studies,* Spring 1973, copyright © 1973 by Purdue Research Foundation. Reprinted with permission of the publisher.

Vivienne Koch. "The Poetry of Allen Tate," *Kenyon Review,* Summer 1949, copyright © 1949 by Kenyon College. Reprinted with permission of the publisher.

Leonard Kriegel. "Dalton Trumbo's *Johnny Got His Gun,*" *Proletarian Writers of the Thirties,* ed. David Madden, copyright © 1968 by Southern Illinois University Press.

Joseph Wood Krutch. "Crowned by the Boosters Club," *Nation,* March 19, 1924, copyright © 1924. Reprinted with permission of the publisher.

Charles R. Larson, "*Cane* by Jean Toomer," *New Republic,* June 19, 1976, copyright © 1976 by New Republic, Inc.

Q. D. Leavis. "Henry James's Heiress: The Importance of Edith Wharton," *Scrutiny,* Dec. 1938, copyright © 1938 by Cambridge University Press.

Christopher Lehmann-Haupt. "Books of the Times," *New York Times Book Review,* March 13, 1986, copyright © 1986 by New York Times Co., Inc. Reprinted with permission of the publisher.

George S. Lensing and Ronald Moran. "James Wright," *Four Poets and Emotive Imagination: Robert Bly, James Wright, Louis Simpson, William Stafford,* copyright © 1976 by The Louisiana State University Press. Reprinted with permission of the publisher.

John Leonard. "Vidal: Another Opinion," *New York Times Book Review,* Oct. 28, 1973, copyright © 1973 by New York Times Co., Inc. Reprinted with permission of the publisher.

Denise Levertov. "The Ideas in the Things," *William Carlos Williams: Man and Poet,* ed. Carroll F. Terrell, copyright © 1983 by National Poetry Foundation, University of Maine. Reprinted with permission of the publisher.

R. W. B. Lewis. "Days of Wrath and Laughter," *Trials of the Word,* copyright © 1965 by R. W. B. Lewis. Reprinted with permission of the publisher.

Laurence Lieberman. "The Expansional Poet: A Return to Reality," *Yale Review,* Winter 1968, copyright © 1967 by Yale University.

Gary H. Lindberg. "The Emergence of Society: Manners in Narrative," *Edith Wharton and the Novel of Manners,* copyright © 1975 by University Press of Virginia. Reprinted with permission of the publisher.

Carl M. Lindner. "Thurber's Walter Mitty—the Underground American Hero," *Georgia Review,* Summer 1974, copyright © 1974 by University of Georgia. Reprinted with permission of the publisher.

David Lodge. "Chasing after God and Sex," *New York Times Book Review,* Aug. 31, 1986, copyright © 1986 by New York Times Co., Inc. Reprinted with permission of the publisher.

Thomas M. Lorch. "The Inverted Structure of *Balso Snell,*" *Studies in Short Fiction,* Fall 1966, copyright © 1966 by Newberry College. Reprinted with permission of the publisher.

Robert Lowell. "Prose Genius in Verse," *Kenyon Review,* Autumn 1953, copyright © 1953 by Kenyon College. Reprinted with permission of the publisher.

F. L. Lucas. "Two Poetesses," *New Statesman,* November 29, 1924, copyright © 1924.

Mabel Dodge Luhan. "At 23 Fifth Avenue," *Initimate Memories,* Vol. 3 *(Movers & Shakers),* copyright © 1936 by Harcourt Brace Jovanovich. Reprinted with permission of the publisher.

Eugene Lyons. "John Updike: The Beginning and the End," *Critique,* 1972, copyright © 1972 by *Critique.* Reprinted with permission of the Helen Dwight Reid Educational Foundation.

Deborah E. McDowell. "The Self in Bloom: Alice Walker's *Meridian,*" *CLA Journal,* March 1981, copyright © 1981 by College Language Association. Reprinted with permission of the publisher.

Norman Mailer. "The Argument Reinvigorated," *Cannibals and Christians,* copyright © 1966 by Norman Mailer. Reprinted with permission of Scott Meredith Literary Agency.

C. N. Manlove. "Terminus Non Est: Gene Wolfe's *The Book of the New Sun,*" *Kansas Quarterly,* Summer 1984, copyright © 1984 by *Kansas Quarterly.* Reprinted with permission of the publisher.

Katherine Mansfield. Review of *The Age of Innocence* (1920), *Novels and Novelists,* ed. John Middleton Murry, copyright © 1930 by Alfred A. Knopf, Inc.

J. P. Marquand. "Tarkington and Social Significances," *Saturday Review,* March 1, 1941, copyright © 1941. Reprinted with permission of the publisher.

Louis L. Martz. "William Carlos Williams: On the Road to Paterson," "William Carlos Williams: Inventions for the Loom," *The Poem of the Mind,* copyright © 1966 by Louis L. Martz.

Susanah Mayberry. *My Amiable Uncle: Recollections about Booth Tarkington,* copyright © 1983 by Purdue Research Foundation. Reprinted with permission of Purdue University Press.

Robert Merrill. "Vonnegut's *Breakfast of Champions:* The Conversion of Heliogabalus," *Critique,* 1977, copyright © 1977 by James Dean Young. Reprinted with permission of the Helen Dwight Reid Educational Foundation.

Bruce F. Michelson. "Richard Wilbur: The Quarrel with Poe," *Southern Review,* April 1978, copyright © 1978 by Bruce Michelson. Reprinted with permission of the author and publisher.

Peter Michelson. "Tom Wolfe Overboard," *New Republic,* Dec. 19, 1970, copyright © 1970 by Harrison-Blaine, Inc.

Arthur Miller. "The Shadow of the Gods," *The Theater Essays of Arthur Miller,* ed. Robert A. Martin, copyright © 1978 by Arthur Miller and Viking Penguin Inc. Reprinted with permission of Viking Penguin Inc.

Thomas F. Monteleone. "Introduction" to *Isle of the Dead,* copyright © 1976 by Thomas F. Monteleone.

L. Hugh Moore. "The Undersea World of Robert Stone," *Critique,* 1969, copyright © 1969 by *Critique.* Reprinted with permission of the Helen Dwight Reid Educational Foundation.

Marianne Moore. "Things Others Never Notice," *Poetry,* May 1934, copyright © 1934 by Modern Poetry Association.

J. Mitchell Morse. "Brand Names and Others," *Hudson Review,* Summer 1969, copyright © 1969 by The Hudson Review, Inc.

Eric Mottram. "The Limits of Self-Regard," *Parnassus: Poetry in Review,* Fall–Winter 1972, copyright © 1972 by Poetry in Review Foundation. Reprinted with permission of the publisher.

Julian Moynahan. "No Nonsense," *New Statesman,* Dec. 14, 1962, copyright © 1962 by New Statesman and Nation.

Neil Myers. "William Carlos Williams' *Spring and All,*" *Modern*

Language Quarterly, Spring 1965, copyright © 1965 by University of Washington. Reprinted with permission of the publisher.

Gerald B. Nelson. "Lonelyhearts," *Ten Versions of America*, copyright © 1972 by Gerald B. Nelson. Reprinted with permission of Alfred A. Knopf, Inc.

Blake Nevius. "Toward the Novel of Manners," *Edith Wharton: A Study of the Fiction*, copyright © 1953 by The Regents of the University of California. Reprinted with permission of the publisher.

Patrick and Teresa Nielsen Hayden. *A Study Guide for* One Writer's Beginnings, copyright © 1986 by Warner Books, Inc.

Anaïs Nin. Diary Entry for Dec. 1945, *The Diary of Anaïs Nin 1945–1947*, copyright © 1971 by Anaïs Nin. Reprinted with permission of Harcourt Brace Jovanovich and Peter Owen: London.

Joyce Carol Oates. "The Art of Eudora Welty," *Shenandoah*, Spring 1969, copyright © 1969 by *Shenandoah*. Reprinted with permission of the publisher.

Shawn O'Connell. "Styron's Nat Turner . . .," *Nation*, Oct. 16, 1967, copyright © 1967 by Nation, Inc. Reprinted with permission of the publisher.

J. D. O'Hara. "The Winds of Vidal," *Nation*, March 21, 1981, copyright © 1981 by Nation, Inc. Reprinted with permission of the publisher.

Donald Pizer. "The Novels of Carl Van Vechten and the Spirit of the Age," *Toward a New American Literary History: Essays in Honor of Arlin Turner*, copyright © 1980 by Duke University Press. Reprinted with permission of the publisher.

Katha Pollitt. Review of *Searching for Caleb*, *New York Times Book Review*, Jan. 18, 1976, copyright © 1976 by New York Times Co., Inc. Reprinted with permission of the publisher.

C. G. Poore. "Mr. Woollcott Runs On and On," *New York Times Book Review*, March 4, 1934, copyright © 1934 by New York Times Book Co., Inc. Reprinted with permission of the publisher.

J. F. Powers. "Books," *Commonweal*, June 25, 1948, copyright © 1948 by Commonweal Foundation. Reprinted with permission of the publisher.

Peggy W. Prenshaw. "Woman's World, Man's Place: The Fiction of Eudora Welty," *Eudora Welty: A Form of Thanks*, copyright © 1979 by University Press of Mississippi. Reprinted with permission of the publisher.

William H. Pritchard. "Novel Auguries," *Hudson Review*, Spring 1976, copyright © 1976 by The Hudson Review, Inc. "Novel Sex and Violence," *Hudson Review*, Spring 1975, copyright © 1975 by The Hudson Review, Inc. "Telling Stories," *Hudson Review*, Autumn 1978, copyright © 1978 by The Hudson Review, Inc. "Poet of the Academy," *Southern Review*, Oct. 1979, copyright © 1979 by The Louisiana State University. Reprinted with permission of the author and publisher.

V. S. Pritchett. "On the Tracks," *New Statesman*, Oct. 17, 1975, copyright © 1975 by New Statesman.

Jonathan Raban. "A Subject of Commodities: The Novels of Nathanael West," *The American Novel and the Nineteen Twenties*, copyright © 1971 by Edward Arnold, Ltd. Reprinted with permission of the publisher. "Theroux's Wonderful, Bottomless Novel," *Saturday Review*, Feb. 1982, copyright © 1982 by Saturday Review Magazine Corp. Reprinted with permission of the publisher.

Carl Rapp. "Williams' Version of the Myth and Fall and the Problem of Symbols," *William Carlos Williams and Romantic Idealism*, copyright © 1984 by Brown University. Reprinted with permission of the author and University Press of New England.

Barbara Raskin. "Southern-Fried," *New Republic*, Oct. 18, 1969, copyright © 1969 by Harrison-Blaine, Inc.

Ben Ray Redman. "In the Midst of Death," *Saturday Review*, Sept. 9, 1939, copyright © 1939. Reprinted with permission of the publisher.

Kenneth Rexroth. *American Poetry in the Twentieth Century*, copyright © 1971 by Herder & Herder, Inc.

H. Edward Richardson. "Stuart Country: The Man-Artist and the Myth," *Jesse Stuart: Essays on His Work*, copyright © 1977 by University Press of Kentucky. Reprinted with permission of the publisher.

Jack Richardson. "Easy Writer," *New York Review of Books*, July 2, 1970, copyright © 1970 by *New York Review of Books*. Reprinted with permission of the publisher.

Paul Rosenfeld. "Jean Toomer," *Men Seen: Twenty-four Modern Authors*, copyright © 1925 by Dial Press, Inc.

M. L. Rosenthal. "'Poor Innocent': The Poetry of A. J. M. Smith," *Modern Poetry Studies*, Spring 1977, copyright © 1977 by Jerome Mazzaro. Reprinted with permission of the author and publisher.

Louis D. Rubin. "Robert Penn Warren: Critic," *A Southern Renascence Man: Views of Robert Penn Warren*, ed. Walter B. Edgar, copyright © 1984 by The Louisiana State University Press. Reprinted with permission of the publisher. "Thomas Wolfe and the Place He Came From," *A Gallery of Southerners*, copyright © 1982 by Louisiana State University. Reprinted with permission of the publisher.

Josh Rubins. "Balancing Act," *New York Review of Books*, Dec. 18, 1980, copyright © 1980 by *New York Review of Books*. Reprinted with permission of the publisher.

Roger Sale. Review of *Homage to Daniel Shays*, *New York Times Book Review*, Dec. 31, 1972, copyright © 1972 by New York Times Co., Inc. Reprinted with permission of the publisher.

Charles Thomas Samuels. "John Updike: The Art of Fiction XLIII," *Paris Review*, Winter 1968, copyright © 1968 by *Paris Review* and Viking Penguin Inc. Reprinted with permission of the publisher.

C. E. Schorer. "The Maturing of Glenway Wescott," *College English*, March 1957, copyright © 1957 by National Council of Teachers of English. Reprinted with permission of the publisher.

Winfield T. Scott. "A Late Flowering," *New York Times Book Review*, Oct. 22, 1961, copyright © 1961 by New York Times Co., Inc. Reprinted with permission of the publisher. "Tarkington and the 1920's," *American Scholar*, Spring 1957, copyright © 1957 by United Chapters of Phi Beta Kappa. Reprinted with permission of the publisher.

Ormond Seavey. "Introduction" to *The Dream Master*, copyright © 1976 by G. K. Hall & Co.

Wilfrid Sheed. "Affairs of State," *Commentary*, Sept. 1967, copyright © 1967 by American Jewish Committee. Reprinted with permission of the author and publisher.

John Simon. "Dapper Gore," *Commonweal*, April 5, 1968, copyright © 1968 by Commonweal Foundation. Reprinted with permission of the publisher. "Vishnu as Double Agent," *Saturday Review*, April 29, 1978, copyright © 1978 by Saturday Review Corp. Reprinted with permission of the publisher.

Louis Simpson. "Modernity," *Three on the Tower: The Lives and Works of Ezra Pound, T. S. Eliot and William Carlos Williams*, copyright © 1975 by Louis Simpson. Reprinted with permission of William Morrow & Co. "The Poet as Journalist," *New York Times Book Review*, July 25, 1976, copyright © 1976 by New York Times Co., Inc. Reprinted with permission of the publisher.

Theodore Solotaroff. "The Wages of 'Maturity,'" *Commentary*, July 1961, copyright © 1961 by American Jewish Committee. Reprinted with permission of the author.

Ian Souton. "The Lyric Craft of Miriam Waddington," *Dalhousie Review*, Summer 1959, copyright © 1959 by *Dalhousie Review*. Reprinted with permission of the publisher.

Stephen Spender. "Private Eye," *New York Review of Books*, March

22, 1973, copyright © 1973 by *New York Review of Books*. Reprinted with permission of the publisher.

Ann Stanford. "Mary Swenson: The Art of Perceiving," *Southern Review*, Winter 1969, copyright © 1969 by Louisiana State University. Reprinted with permission of the author and publisher.

W. J. Stuckey. "The Fortunes of War," *The Pulitzer Prize Novels: A Critical Backward Look*, copyright © 1981 by University of Oklahoma Press. Reprinted with permission of the publisher.

Henry Swados. "Popular Taste and *The Caine Mutiny*," *Partisan Review*, March–April 1953, copyright © 1953 by Partisan Review, Inc.

Robert S. Sward. Review of *Riprap*, *Poetry*, July 1960, copyright © 1960 by Modern Poetry Association. Reprinted with permission of the author and publisher.

May Swenson. "The Experience of Poetry in a Scientific Age," *Poets on Poetry*, ed. Howard Nemerov, copyright © 1966 by Howard Nemerov. "Perpetual Worlds Taking Place," *Poetry*, Feb. 1980, copyright © 1980 by Modern Poetry Association. Reprinted with permission of the author and publisher.

Henry Taylor. "The Collected Poems of John Hall Wheelock," *Sewanee Review*, Summer 1971, copyright © 1971 by University of the South. Reprinted with permission of the publisher.

Mark Taylor. "Modern Tragedies," *Commonweal*, Sept. 24, 1976, copyright © 1976 by Commonweal Foundation. Reprinted with permission of the publisher.

Wayne A. Tefs. "Rudy Wiebe: Mystery and Reality," *Mosaic*, Summer 1978, copyright © 1978 by *Mosaic*. Reprinted with permission of the publisher.

Betty Thompson. "Thomas Wolfe: Two Decades of Criticism," *South Atlantic Quarterly*, July 1950, copyright © 1950, 1977 by Duke University Press. Reprinted with permission of the publisher.

Larry E. Thompson. "Jean Toomer: As Modern Man," *The Harlem Renaissance Remembered*, ed. Arna Bontemps, copyright © 1972 by Arna Bontemps.

David Thorburn. "A Fearful and Mindless Violence," *Nation*, April 1, 1968, copyright © 1968 by Nation, Inc. Reprinted with permission of the publisher.

Claire Tomalin. "Out of Africa," *New Statesman*, Oct. 4, 1974, copyright © 1974 by New Statesman, Inc.

Alan Trachtenberg. "What's New?," *Partisan Review*, 1974, copyright © 1974 by Partisan Review, Inc.

John Updike. "All's Well in Skyscraper National Park," "Loosened Roots," "The Shining Note," *Hugging the Shore*, copyright © 1983 by John Updike. Reprinted with permission of Alfred A. Knopf, Inc. "Indignations of a Senior Citizen," *New York Times Book Review*, Nov. 25, 1962, copyright © 1962 by New York Times Co., Inc. "Summonses, Indictments, Extenuating Circumstances," *New Yorker*, Nov. 3, 1986, copyright © 1986 by John Updike. Reprinted with permission of *The New Yorker*. "Wilson's Fiction: A Personal Account," *Edmund Wilson: The Man and His Work*, ed. John Wain, copyright © 1976 by Phaidon Press, Ltd. Reprinted with permission of the publisher.

Helen Vendler. "Charles Wright: The Transcendent 'I,'" *Part of Nature, Part of Us: Modern American Poets*, copyright © 1980 by The President and Fellows of Harvard College. "Fugal Requiems," *On Extended Wings*, copyright © 1969 by The President and Fellows of Harvard College.

Gore Vidal. "Edmund Wilson: This Critic and This Gin and These Shoes," *The Second American Revolution*, copyright © 1980, 1982 by Gore Vidal. Reprinted with permission of Random House and William Morris Agency. "Introduction" to *The Edith Wharton Omnibus*, copyright © 1978 by Gore Vidal.

Robert Penn Warren. "*All the King's Men:* The Matrix of Experience," *Yale Review*, Winter 1964, copyright © 1964 by Robert Penn Warren. Reprinted with permission of William Morris Agency. "The Love and the Separateness in Miss Welty," *Kenyon Review*, Spring 1944, copyright © 1944 by Kenyon College. Reprinted with permission of the publisher.

A. K. Weatherhead. "Richard Wilbur: The Poetry of Things," *ELH*, Dec. 1968, copyright © 1968 by Johns Hopkins University. Reprinted with permission of the publisher.

Paul West. *Robert Penn Warren*, copyright © 1964 by University of Minnesota Press. Reprinted with permission of the publisher.

Marguerite Wilkinson. "Death as a Poet Sees It," *New York Times Book Review*, Oct. 31, 1920, copyright © 1920 by New York Times Co., Inc. Reprinted with permission of the publisher.

Tennessee Williams. "The World I Live In," *Where I Live*, eds. Christine R. Day and Bob Woods, copyright © 1957 by Tennessee Williams.

Alan Williamson. "The Future of Personal Poetry," *Introspection and Contemporary Poetry*, copyright © 1984 by The President and Fellows of Harvard College.

Edmund Wilson. "The Boys in the Back Room," "Why Do People Read Detective Stories?," *Classics and Commercials*, copyright © 1950 by Edmund Wilson. Reprinted with permission of Farrar, Straus & Giroux, Inc. "Connolly's *Unquiet Grave;* Thurber's *White Deer*," *New Yorker*, Oct. 27, 1945, copyright © 1945 by Edmund Wilson. Reprinted with permission of Farrar, Straus & Giroux, Inc. "Justice to Edith Wharton," *The Wound and the Bow*, copyright © 1947 by Edmund Wilson. Reprinted with permission of Farrar, Straus & Giroux, Inc.

Yvor Winters. "Wallace Stevens or the Hedonist's Progress," *On Modern Poets*, copyright © 1943 by New Directions, copyright © 1947, 1957 by Yvor Winters.

P. G. Wodehouse. "Foreword" to *Rex Stout: A Biography* by John McAleer, copyright © 1977 by John McAleer. Reprinted with permission of Little, Brown & Co.

Gene Wolfe. Review of *The Island of Doctor Death and Other Stories*, *Foundation*, Feb. 1981, copyright © 1981 by Science Fiction Foundation. Reprinted with permission of the publisher.

C. Vann Woodward. "Southerner with Her Own Accent," *New York Times Book Review*, Feb. 19, 1984, copyright © 1984 by New York Times Co., Inc. Reprinted with permission of the publisher.

James Wright. "The Stiff Smile of Mr. Warren," *Kenyon Review*, Autumn 1958, copyright © 1958 by Kenyon College. Reprinted with permission of the publisher.

Francis Wyndham. "Hooray for Hollywood," *Times Literary Supplement*, April 11, 1975, copyright © 1975 by Times Newspapers Ltd.

Richard Yates. Review of *The Easter Parade*, *New York Times Book Review*, Sept. 19, 1976, copyright © 1976 by New York Times Co., Inc. Reprinted with permission of the publisher.

Stephen Yenser. "Open Secrets," *Parnassus: Poetry in Review*, Spring–Summer 1978, copyright © 1978 by Poetry in Review Foundation. Reprinted with permission of the publisher.

Morton Dauwen Zabel. "The Pattern of the Atmosphere," *Poetry*, Aug. 1932, copyright © 1932 by Modern Poetry Association. Reprinted with permission of the author and publisher.

Unsigned. "A Conversation with Mark Strand," *Ohio Review*, Winter 1972, copyright © 1972 by Ohio University. "Fables for Our Time," *Times Literary Supplement*, Nov. 27, 1959, copyright © 1959 by Times Newspapers Ltd.